Officers who died in the Service of British, Indian and East African Regiments and Corps 1914 – 1919

S.D. & D.B. Jarvis

Dedicated to Jenny and Ruth

Copyright (C) 1993 by Roberts Medals Ltd, P.O. Box 1, Brimpton, Reading
RG7 4RJ, England

ISBN 1873058 26 8

INTRODUCTION

To compile a three volume set of the Officers who died in the Great War and who served in the British, Commonwealth and Colonial Regiments and Corps in alphabetical listing, is by any standard a monumental task. Every Commonwealth War Graves Register known to exist was carefully searched and the information extracted. With great patience the compilers checked the information given against other publications, many out of date, to enable readers to follow up further leads where appropriate. Discrepancies of a major nature are shown.

The conflict was so great, the number of deaths so enormous, that no reference book on the subject of the Great War can be perfect. The information given at the time was prone to mis-spelling and of course to mis-recording. The compilers could not judge what was right or wrong and have faithfully recorded what they read and what was written down. They have of course discovered many Officers not previously listed and great differences in units, rank and dates. The reader will need to do his own research into why these discrepancies occurred. An intriguing and hopefully rewarding task.

In their search to be as accurate as possible, the compilers checked names against town registers, national magazines and memorial books; the public school registers were particularly helpful. These are too numerous to list individually. For those who wish to research further, two main first opportunities exist - The Commonwealth War Graves Registers (the appropriate number is shown in the text), give in addition to what is listed some information on the next of kin and address. The British and Commonwealth War Graves Commission are based at 2 Marlow Road, Maidenhead, Berks SL6 7DX. In seeking further information from them it is strongly suggested a donation to their general fund would be welcomed. Secondly, the excellent information contained in the original HMSO Publication 'Officers Died' is now re-printed and available with additional sections from J.B. Hayward & Son, The Old Rectory, Polstead, Sussex C06 5AE. The information is given in regimental order and is therefore extremely helpful. The appropriate page number, if known, is shown in the text.

One further point concerns the Royal Flying Corps, as the Air Arm existed prior to the 1st April 1918 as a Corp, Volume 1 of this series contains the British Officers, Volume 3 the Commonwealth and Colonial. Volume 2 covers the Royal Naval Air Service and Royal Air Force.

Messrs S.D. and J.B. Jarvis are to be congratulated for what amounts to ten years diligent research. They will, in the process of their work, have laid low a number of "ghosts" and no doubt thrown up a great number of challenging questions.

Trevor J Davies March 1993

How to Interpret the Information Given

ABBATI, William Reginald, Lt ded 9.8.16, 3ESS p.264, CR Hamps 216, 2Lt. 7.8.16

SURNAME:	ABBATI
FIRST NAMES:	William Reginald
RANK:	Lieutenant
DECORATIONS:	None identified
CAUSE OF DEATH:	Died
DATE:	9.8.1916
UNIT:	3rd Battalion The Essex Regiment
OTHER REFERENCE:	Seen in Officers Died p.264
REGISTER:	CR Hampshire 216 (see Appendix 1)
INFORMATION FROM ALTERNATIVE SOURCES:	2nd Lieutenant Died 7.8.1916

ABRAHAM, Geoffrey William Pepperall, Capt dow 19.11.17, Glam Yeo p.203 CR Egypt 7, Pepperell, 24 Welch R.

SURNAME:	ABRAHAM
FIRST NAMES:	Geoffrey William Pepperall
RANK:	Captain
DECORATIONS:	None
CAUSE OF DEATH:	Died of Wounds
DATE:	19.11.1917
UNIT:	Glamorgan Yeomanry
OTHER REFERENCE:	Seen in Officers Died p.203
REGISTER:	CR Egypt 7 (see Appendix 1)
INFORMATION TAKEN FROM ALTERNATIVE SOURCES:	Possible spelling 'PEPPERELL' CR Unit '24 Welch R'

ACKROYD, Harold, V.C., M.C., TCapt Kia 11.8.17, RAMC att. 6Berks, p.145, CR Belgium 113

SURNAME:	ACKROYD
FIRST NAMES:	Harold
RANK:	Temporary Captain
DECORATIONS:	Victoria Cross, Military Cross
CAUSE OF DEATH:	Killed in action
DATE:	11.8.1917
UNIT:	Royal Army Medical Corp attached to 6th Battalion Royal Berks
OTHER REFERENCE:	Seen in Officers Died p.146
REGISTER:	CR Belgium 113 (see Appendix 1)

A

ABADIE,Eustace Henry Egremont,DSO.Maj kia 30-11-15 9Lancers p22 MR29,30-10-14

ABADIE,Richard Nevile.DSO.LtCol kia 10-7-17 KRRC p148 MR31

ABBATI,William Reginald Lt ded 9-8-16 3Ess p264 CR Hamps216,2Lt 7-8-16

ABBAY,Marmaduke John Norman Capt dow 10-5-15 IA 87Punjabis att47Sikhs p273 CR Suff106

ABBEY,G.Lt 7-9-20 RDC CR Shrop138

ABBEY,Noel Roland Lt kia 12-4-18 4GrenGds p49 MR32

ABBIS,Reginald Donaldson 2Lt dow 2-12-17 3att2YLI p142 CR Belgium18

ABBISS,John Lee Lt ded 25-7-18 1ESurr att7LightArmBtyMGC Motors p111&181 CR Iraq8

ABBOTT,Alfred 2Lt dow 26-4-18 EYorks att9YLI p83 MR30

ABBOTT,Clifford Hewson T2Lt dow 7-5-17 2Lincs p74 CR France1468

ABBOTT,Duncan William Sydney Elphinstone TCapt kia 26-9-15 10Y&L p158 MR19

ABBOTT,Edward John White Lt kia 17-5-15 2RIrFus p170 MR29

ABBOTT,Eric Goward 2Lt kia 14-3-17 1/5NStaffs p238 CR France281 dow

ABBOTT,Ernest Henry Fortescue.MC.Lt kia 9-7-18 4att2N&D p133 MR30 Capt

ABBOTT,Geoffrey Dyett Lt kia 2-11-14 1ConnRgrs p172 CR France706

ABBOTT,George Lt kia 23-8-18 Herts p252 CR France798

ABBOTT,George Shrubb 2Lt kia 19-7-16 2/4RBerks p234 CR France1887

ABBOTT,John Gurney 2Lt kia 21-9-17 6RB att57TMB p177 MR30

ABBOTT,Joseph Octavius 2Lt kia 28-7-17 RGA 179SB p37 CR Belgium29 J.D.

ABBOTT,Lionel Pilkington TLt kia 14-7-16 7Leic p87 CR France453

ABBOTT,Sidney Herbert 2Lt kia 4-11-18 2Beds p85 CR France521

ABBOTT,Thomas Aveling Capt&Adjt kia 24-5-15 2WRidRFA p24 CR France347

ABBOTT,Thomas Walker 2Lt kia 18-8-17 GL &11RFC p4 MR20

ABBOTT,Victor Stephen Henry 2Lt kld 15-9-16 SR &RFC p2 CR Wilts116

ABBOTT,W.F.Maj 28-2-21 RAMC CR Glouc9

ABBOTT,William David Rev ded 3-12-18 RAChDept p199 CR France 377

ABBOT-ANDERSON,Francis Wyatt LtCol ded 1-1-16 RLancs p58 CR Egypt9,2-1-16 Cmdg6Bn

ABBS,Bertie Edward T2Lt kia 26-3-18 7Suff p77 MR27

ABE,Frank E.T2Lt kia 23-7-18 8WYorks p80 CR France 1689

A'BEAR,Hedley John.MM.T2LtACapt kia 10-7-17 7RWSurr p55 CR Belgium15

ABECASIS,Arthur Philip T2Lt kia 9-4-17.3SomLI p79 CR France532 5Bn

ABEL,Frederick T2Lt drd 30-12-17 3Norf p73 CR Egypt6

ABEL,George Fowtrell.MM.2Lt ded 20-6-18 GL p189 Iraq6

ABEL,James Edgar.MC.T2Lt dow 22-12-17 PoW 6RWKent p140 CR France660

ABEL,John Duncan T2Lt kia 26-3-18 7SfthH p164 MR27

ABELL,Albert Reginald T2Lt ded 10-6-17 PoW 1Dev p76

ABELL,John Lloyd Williams Howard Capt kia 3-7-16 11Ches p95 MR21,William

ABELL,William Henry Maj kia 23-8-14 4Mddx p145 CR Belgium 242

ABERCROMBIE,Alexander Ralph,DSO.MC.Capt ded 31-12-18.1RWSurr p55 CR Surrey118

ABERCROMBIE,Alexander William LtCol ded PoW 5-11-15 2ConnRgrs p172 CR Germany4

ABERCROMBIE,Robert Henry Chester 2Lt kia 3-5-15 1/8Mddx p236 CR Belgium151

ABERCROMBY,John Stevenson T2Lt dow 29-4-17 17Mddx p145 CR France95

ABERDEEN,Louis Frederick 2Lt kia 10-9-16 3att12Lond p245 MR21,9-9-16

ABINGER,Bernard Russell.MC.2Lt kia 25-9-15 2RBerks MR32 served as RUSSELL

ABBISS,Frederick Thomas Lee Lt dow 27-10-17 76RFA p24 CR France64,ded

ABLETT,Arthur 2Lt dow 22-4-18 4MGC p181 CR France248

ABLETT Frank Ellis 2Lt kia 20-9-17 Suff att1/8Lpool p77 MR30

ABLETT,Leslie Wallace T2Lt kia 15-10-17 NumbF att11Bn Res p59 MR30

ABRAHAM,Arthur Thomas,MC.2LtACapt kia 22-10-17 23Manch p153 MR30

ABRAHAM,Frederick Henry T2Lt kia 2-10-18 16LancF p91 CR France237 Henri

ABRAHAM,Geoffrey William Pepperall Capt dow 19-11-17 GlamYeo p203 CR Egypt7 Pepperell 24WelchR

ABRAHAMS,Arthur Charles Lionel Lt kia 13-4-18 3CldGds p50 MR32

ABRAHAMS,Montague TMaj kia 3-9-16 16RB p177 MR21

ABRAHAMS,Robert Bernard 2Lt kia 14-9-16 4Yorks p220 MR21

ABRAM,Robert 2LtACapt kia 26-10-17 3 att2BordR p116 MR30

ABRAMS,Lawrence Golding TLt ded 3-11-18 RASC p192 CR France85

ABRAMS,Reginald Arthur Lt kia 4-3-17 8N&D p233 CR France281

ABREY,Charles Gordon 2Lt kia 21-7-16 O&BLI BucksBn p231 CR France832

ACHESON,Joseph T2Lt dow 7-6-18.2SLancs p125 CR France1778

ACHESON,Percival Havelock Maj kld 29-4-16 RASC p192 CREire70

ACHESON,Vincent Andrews TCapt kia 10-9-16 6 att7RInniskF p104 CR Greece3

ACHURCH,William Henry T2Lt dow 6-12-17 2/5RWar p64 CR France398

ACKERLEY,Peter Roger TLt kia 7-8-18 8ESurr p111 CR France116

ACKERLEY,Ronald Hermann Lt kia 16-5-15 3att1RWelshF p97 CR France705

ACKLAND-ALLEN,Hugh Thomas Lt kia 23-10-14 1RWFus p97 MR29

ACKLOM,Spencer,DSO&Bar.MC.MajTLtCol kia 21-3-18 HLI att22NumbF p162 MR20

ACKROYD,Harold,VC.MC.TCapt kia 11-8-17 RAMC att6RBerks p194 CR Belgium113

ACKROYD,Thomas 2Lt kia 23-4-17 1 att9Beds p85 MR20

ACLAND,John Henry Dyke TCapt kia 12-7-16 RAMC att1SomLI p194 CR France643

ACLAND TROYTE,Heyl Leonard LtCol kia 17-4-18 5Lincs p269 CR France498,Hugh 4Dev attXI CpsHQ

ACOMB,Horace T2Lt kia 21-8-16.2Yorks att2Dev p89 CR France423,11Bn

ACTON,Armar Edward Rev Chap4Cl MID dow 4-11-17 RAChDept att2BordR p199 CR France64

ACTON,Charles Annesley TMaj kia 25-9-15 9RWelshF p97 MR19

ACTON,Norman Frederick T2Lt kia 23-4-17 4Worc p107 MR20

ACTON,Reginald 2Lt dow 9-5-15 5SLancs p230 CR France284

ACWORTH,Douglas Harry.MC.Maj ded 6-2-19 IA 55Rif p273 CR Egypt7

ACWORTH,Gordon William 2Lt dow 7-6-17 15Lond p249 CR Belgium11

ACWORTH,John Arden 2Lt dow 13-10-17 1/7Worc p225 CR Belgium16

ADAIR,Angus McPherson TLt kia 21-11-17 48MGC Inf p181 CR France1489

ADAIR,John Thomas TLt dow 22-8-15 10Beds att1BordR p85 MR4

ADAIR,William Finlay Capt kia 30-10-14 IA 129Baluchis p273 MR29

ADAM,Alan Gordon Acheson.MID Capt kia 21/22-1-16 5EKent p212 CR Iraq5

ADAM,Alexander Russell Lt kia 3-7-17 6SfthH attRFC p17&241 CR France481

ADAM,Allan Lt kia 1-10-18 7A&SH att2MGC Inf p186&243 CR France1483

ADAM,Arthur Innes Lt kia 16-9-16 1Camb p244 CR France518 Capt dow

ADAM,Arthur de Bels TCapt kia 1-7-16 18Lpool p71 MR21

ADAM,Douglas Walter TLt dow 4-4-18 LancF att18MGC p181 MR27

ADAM,Frank Dalziel Lt dow 16-7-18 6RB p177 CR France161 3Bn

ADAM,George 2Lt kia 22-10-17 att16RScots p53

ADAM,Gerald Wallace.MID 2Lt ded 10-8-19 Leic p263 MR70 &CR Europe180 att13Yorks

ADAM,James Robert T2Lt kia 18-8-16 13Mddx p145 MR21

ADAM,John Isabel TLt kia 10-5-18 A307RFA p24 CR France1106

ADAM,John Stewart 2Lt kia 11-8-18 D11RFA p208 CR Belgium11

ADAM,Matthew.MC.Lt kia 7-8-18 5RScotF attRAF p222&258

ADAM,Norman Macleod.MC.CaptAMaj kia 28-8-18 19RFA p24 CR Scot756

ADAM,Peter.MC.2Lt kia 31-7-17 3RB p177 MR29

ADAM,Ronald William.MC.2Lt ded 11-9-17 13/56RFA p24 CR Iraq8

ADAM,Walter Capt ded 3-11-18 EKentYeo attMGC Inf p186&204 CR Kent259 Lt

ADAM,Walter William TCapt kld 14-12-15 6RScotF p94 CR Belgium4 12-12-15

ADAM,William Frederick 2Lt kia 25-8-16 7 att5ScotRif p224 CR France453

ADAMS,Arthur Charles Henry 2Lt kia 21-3-18 1/2att2/8Worc p107 MR27

ADAMS,Arthur Joseph LtTCapt kia 30-8-18 3RWar p64 CR France421 1Bn

ADAMS,Arthur Marston.MC.2Lt dow 20-9-17 1/9Lpool p216 CR Belgium8

ADAMS,Auriol Charles Andrew T2Lt kia 16/18-8-16 10RLancs p58 CR France294 Aurial

ADAMS,Bernard Pye TLt dow 27-2-17 11RWelshF p97

ADAMS,Briggs Kilburn T2Lt kia 14-3-18 18RFC p15 CR France134,Kilburn Lt

ADAMS,C.E.DCM.Lt 21-3-21 1RFus CR Notts112

ADAMS,Charles John Norman 2Lt dow 14-11-18 2GrenGds p49 CR France146

ADAMS,Dudley ACapt kia 21-3-18 RGA 130HB p37 MR27

ADAMS,Edward Carrington 2Lt kia 25-9-15 20Lond p231 CR France550 Carrington

ADAMS,Ernest Frederick T2Lt kia 22-6-17 26RFus p66 CR Belgium154

ADAMS,Ernest Geoffrey T2Lt dow 26-6-18 8Norf p73 CR France84 7Bn

ADAMS,Frederick 2Lt kld 12-5-17 GL &53RFC p4 CR Belgium152

ADAMS,Frederick.MC.Lt selfInflictWound 29-11-20 IARO att45Sikhs p273 CR Iraq8

ADAMS,Frederick Leslie 2Lt kia 15-9-18 RGA 232SB p37 CR France841

ADAMS,Geoffrey Julian Balcombe 2Lt dow 27-9-18 1/5Lond p246 CR France113

ADAMS,Geoffrey Henry Cadwallader 2Lt kia 1-11-16 4Suff p217 MR21

ADAMS,George Allsop 2Lt kia 9-4-17 3 att7ESurr p111 CR France531

ADAMS,George Garnet Price Domel Lt 21-2-20 IARO CR EAfrica19

ADAMS,George Gordon Crymole Lt ded 9-3-18 RAMC p194 CR EAfrica11 &CR Tanzania 1,Crymoll

ADAMS,George Norman Capt ded 20-10-18 6SStaffs p255 CR Staffs78

ADAMS,George Stopford Maj kia 11-5-15 1LancF p91 CR Galipoli1

ADAMS,Harold Towns Lt 28-3-18 GL &43RFC MR20

ADAMS,Henry Frederick Reginald Lt dow 20-10-17 A159RFA p24 CR Belgium13

ADAMS,Henry Gordon 2Lt kia 5-10-17 RFA SthMidBde p208 CR Belgium12

ADAMS,Hugh Irving TLt kia 1-7-16 1Hamps p120 CR France643

ADAMS,James Andrew T2Lt kia 17-4-18 11Mddx p145 CR France324

ADAMS,James Allison Wilson 2Lt kia 9-4-17 9RScots p212 CR France184 Alison

ADAMS,James Scovell T2Lt dow 8-8-18 7RWSurr p55 CR France69

ADAMS,John Bernard Pye TLt dow 27-2-17 1RWFus p97 CR France204

ADAMS,John Gould Capt kia 5-5-15 Leinst p174 MR29

ADAMS,John Hanna 2Lt kia 18-11-16 8NStaffs p156 CR France384

ADAMS,John Henry Capt ded 25-2-19 ArmyPayDept p268 CR Kent85

ADAMS,John Percy Fitzherbert Lt kia 14-10-17 4DLI att20RFC p4&160 CR Belgium11

ADAMS,John Wood Maj kia 3-9-17 6RScots p211 CR France8

ADAMS,Joseph 2Lt kia 23-7-16 3 att2RSuss p118 MR21

ADAMS,Lawrence Kingston Lt kia 16-5-15 7Lpool p215 CR France279 Laurence

ADAMS,Lestock Hanley TLt kia 22-4-18 1RB p177 CR France411 Handley

ADAMS,Ord T2Lt kia 20-3-16 RFA p24 CR Belgium73

ADAMS,Percy Ernest Capt kia 4-4-17 5N&D p232 CR France725

ADAMS,Percy Horace 2Lt kia 3-10-18 4 att1N&D p133 CR France184 Lt

ADAMS,Percy Lionel Lt dow 3-10-18 18Lond attMGC Inf p185&250 CR France194

ADAMS,Philip Rockley T2Lt kia 27-5-18 6SomLI att2Dev p79 MR18

ADAMS,Ralph.MC&Bar.Lt kia 1-7-16 1/8RWar p215 CR France742

ADAMS,Ralph Newton.MC.Capt kia 10-10-16 7RFus att23RFC p2&66 MR20

ADAMS,Reinhold Meitzen Maj dow 22-4-17 IA 51Sikhs p273 MR38

ADAMS,Robert 2Lt kia 12-8-15 5Norf p216 MR4

ADAMS,Robert Sefton LtACapt kia 5-10-17 12/35RFA p24 CR Belgium116

ADAMS,Robert Leonard Powys Lt kia 17-5-19 IA 1/35Sikhs p273 MR43

ADAMS,S.H.T.2Lt kia 28-3-18 GL & RFC p261&266

ADAMS,Stanley T2Lt dow 9-9-17 9NumbF p59 CR France1494

ADAMS,Theodore Dawson Capt kia 7-11-15 LancsRFA attRFC p17&207 CR France604,Dowson

ADAMS,Thompson 2Lt kia 7-10-16 4YLI att36MGC p186&235 MR21

ADAMS,Valentine Harold 2Lt dow 5-5-17 78RFC p4 CR France1032

ADAMS,Wilfred Evan 2Lt kia 14-5-17 212MGC p181 MR20

ADAMS,William John 2Lt drd 30-12-17 Norf p73 MR41

ADAMS-POSNER,Robert Cecil T2Lt kia 18-9-18 1KSLI p144 MR16

ADAMSON,Alexander Hutton 2Lt kia 9-4-17 5SfthH p241 CR France96,7Bn

ADAMSON,Alan John 2LtACapt kia 20-9-17 RGA 69SB p38 CR Belgium24

ADAMSON,Charles John Henry TCapt kia 22-9-17 NumbF att11Bn p59 MR30 20-9-17

ADAMSON,Charles Young TCapt&QM kia 17-9-18 8RScotF p94 CR Greece6

ADAMSON,Daniel Lt ded 7-6-19 RE att2S&M p43 MR43

ADAMSON,Duncan Francis Charles 2Lt kia 12-9-18 20att9Lond p251 MR16

ADAMSON,Francis Douglas Lt kia 16-11-15 2BordR p116 CR France279

ADAMSON,George T2Lt kia 15-9-15 12HLI p162 MR19,25-9-15

ADAMSON,George Addis T2Lt kia 12-10-17 6KOSB p101 MR30

ADAMSON,Gilbert Edgar Lt kia 25-8-18 7Mddx p235 CRFrance504,24-8-18

ADAMSON,Harry 2Lt kia 15-4-18 RGA 6SB p38 MR30

ADAMSON,Henry Bardell TCapt dow 30-10-16 21WYorks p80 CR France145

ADAMSON,James LtACapt kia 5-5-17 C242RFA p207 CR France68

ADAMSON,John Conway Lt kia 4-10-17 NumbF att1Lincs p59 MR30

ADAMSON,John Thomas Graves Maj ded 25-10-18 IA 119Inf p273 MR65

ADAMSON,Maurice Leslie 2Lt kia 1-7-16 RScotF att10IrRif p94 MR21

ADAMSON,Peter,MC.T2Lt kia 27-2-18 att1/4LNLancs p135 CR France765

ADAMSON,Robert Thorburn Adamson TLt kia 23-4-17 13RScots p53 MR20

ADAMSON,Robert William 2Lt kia 26-5-15 7DLI p239 MR29

ADAMSON,Travers Farrant T2Lt kia 1-7-16 9Dev p76 CR France330

ADAMSON,William TCapt kia 24-4-16 6LNLancs p135 MR38

ADAMSON,William Campbell TCapt kia 5-9-16 6RFC p1 CR Belgium140,kld

ADCOCK,Harold Meredyth TCapt kia 5-7-16 10LancF p91 MR21

ADCOCK,Harold Norman T2Lt kia 8-10-18 1EKent p57 CR France445

ADCOCK,Keith White Lt ded 30-10-18 RE p210 CR Herts81

ADCOCK,St.John Maj kia 9-5-15 3Leinst att1RLancs p174 MR29

ADDAMS-WILLIAMS,Donald Arthur T2Lt kia 13-8-15 4SWBord p99&257 CR Gallipoli17

ADDENBROOK,John Homfrey T2Lt kia 23-11-16 NStaffs att11Manch p156 CR France701,ADDENBROOKE Homfray

ADDENBROOKE,Arthur.MID TCapt dow 5-10-16 14War p64 CR Herefd &Worc144

ADDENBROOKE,Guy Besley 2Lt kia 7-5-15 YLI p142 MR27

ADDERLY,Douglas Herbert T2Lt kia 16-6-17 7Nhampt p137 MR29

ADDERLEY,William Harris 2Lt dow 27-10-18 9WRid & 59RAF p115 CR France398

ADDEY,George T2Lt kia 2-9-18 att7EYorks Res p83 MR16

ADDEY-JIBB,Arthur Harwood.MID Lt&QM dow 12-4-18 RAMC att94FA p194 CR France860

ADDIE,Robert Leatham 2Lt kia 20-11-17 2/5LancF p221 MR21

ADDINGTON,Cyril John Flinton T2Lt kia 2-7-16 16 att24Mddx p145 CR France35,Flintan dow

ADDINGTON,Geoffrey William 2Lt kia 1-12-17 2DLI p160 CR France711

ADDINGTON,William Leonard Maj ded 15-12-19 ExRWSurr p262 CR Devon72

ADDIS,David Malcolm 2Lt dow 9-6-17 26RFus p66 MR29

ADDIS,Henry Dansey T2Lt kld 24-1-17 GL & 43RFC p4&189 CR Oxford74

ADDIS,Ronald Forrester LtACapt kia 3-9-16 2KOSB att181MGC Inf p101&18 CR France402

ADDIS,Thomas Henry Liddon Lt kia 21-3-18 4RDubF p176 CR France212

ADDISON,Alfred Charles Capt kia 25-4-15 2Hamps p120 CR Gallipoli15

ADDISON,Arthur Joseph Berkeley TLtCol kia 1-7-16 9Y&L p158 CR France515

ADDISON,Frank T2Lt ded 22-3-16 8RSuss p118 CR France22

ADDISON,George Mellsome 2Lt dow 9-8-18 5SStaffs p229 CR Italy4

ADDISON,Noel Goodricke.MC.Lt kia 9-4-18 1KEdwsHorse p24 MR19

ADDY,James Carlton.MC.Capt kia 3-5-17 10EYorks p83 MR20

ADDY,Kenneth James Balguy T2Lt kia 13-10-15 1KRRC p148 CRFrance423 Balgay 3-10-15

ADDYMAN,Oscar James Lt kia 4-2-15 1EYorks p83 MR29

ADEANE,Henry Robert Augustus Capt kia 2-11-14 1CldGds p50 MR29

ADENEY,Robert Edward 2Lt ded 11-4-17 PoW 3RWSurr &48RFC p55&4 CR France1276,dow

ADEY,William Thomas Henworth 2Lt drd 10-10-18 W'mlnd&CumbYeo p206 CR Eire14

ADIE,Arthur A.DCM.2Lt kia 3-5-18 1/5RLancs p58 CR France106

ADIE,Harry Morton Ellis T2Lt kia 1-5-16 RFC p2 CR France62,Lt

ADIE,George Carl T2Lt kia 22-8-17 10DLI p160 CR Belgium116

ADIE,Robert Roland 2Lt kia 21-4-17 2DLI p160 CR France115

ADKIN,Arthur Wellesley 2Lt kia 3-6-17 20Lond p251 CR Belgium56

ADKIN,Frederick Edward.MM.T2Lt kia 24-9-18 RSuss att2Bn p118 CR France1700

ADLER,Henry George Vergettini 2LtAMaj kia 21-6-17 RGA 184SB p38 CR Belgium10,Vergottini

ADLERCRON,G.R.L.DSO.Capt 16-3-20 8Hrs MR65

ADLINGTON,Ernest Mason T2Lt kia 14-9-16 13 att9WYorks p80 CR France164

ADNEY,George Henry.MC.TLt kia 2-9-18 7TankCps p188 CR France1484

ADRIAN,William Kearns 2Lt kia 24-8-16 5RIrReg att1RIrRif p88 CR France423,ADRAIN

ADSETTS,William Henry 2Lt dow 1-10-15 3Y&L p158 CR France98 1Bn

ADSHEAD,Sydney Douglas T2Lt kia 23-4-17 18Manch p153 MR20

ADYE,Walter.CB.Col ded 3-9-15 GSO WarOfficeStaff p1 CR Lond4

AERTS,Francis Robert.MC.2Lt ded 26-12-19 13WelshR p264 CR Kent83

AGANOOR,Aganoor John 2Lt kia 15-9-16 17Lond p250 CR France432

AGAR,Richard Paterson 2Lt kia 14-10-16 2SfthH p164 CR France374

AGAR,Richard St.George Tracy Lt kia 29-9-18 RHA 16HQ p24 CR France725

AGAR-ROBARTES,Thomas Charles Reginald.Hon.MP.MID TLtACapt dow 30-9-15 1CldGds p50 CR France88

AGATE,Harold Capt kia 14-4-17 16Lond p249 MR20

AGATE,Norman Stanford 2Lt dow 23-3-18 18Lond p250 CR France177

AGATE,Sydney Herbert 2Lt kia 13-11-16 3 att4Beds p85 CR France220

AGELASTO,August.MC.MID Lt kia 8-11-16 1 att4Dors p123 CR France374 1 att6Bn

AGERUP,Harold Lt acckld 5-6-18 SL att222MGC &195RAF p201 CR Egypt8,GL

AGG,Arthur William TLt ded 2-4-16 SL p201 CR Glouc133

AGIUS,Richard Victor Joseph Roy Capt kia 26-10-17 2/3Lond p245 MR30

AGLIONBY,Arthur Hugh.MC.Maj dow 7-11-18 219RGA p209 CR France276

AGNEW,Andrew Eric Hamilton Capt ded 3-11-18 RDubF p176

AGNEW,Graham TCapt kia 26-9-15 13NumbF p59 MR19

AGNEW,James Watson 2Lt kia 21-5-15 1HLI p162 MR22

A'HERNE,David Joseph 2Lt 27-5-18 RGA 116SB MR18

AHERN,Patrick Joseph Lt&QM kia 9-9-16 7Leinst p174 MR21

AIKEN,James Douglas 2Lt ded 9-11-16 RFA attY14TMB p24 CR France1182 dow

AIKINS,Joseph Russell 2Lt mbk 26-3-18 59RFC p256 CR France1483

AIKMAN,William Hudson Lt dow 27-9-17 1/6HLI p240 CR France34,29-9-18

AIKMAN,William Saunders T2Lt kia 23-4-17 9NumbF p59 MR20,22-4-17

AIMER,George Edmond Vernon 2Lt kld 20-6-16 RFC p2 CR Mddx34

AINGER,Herbert Cecil Lt kia 4-10-17 3RScots &19RFC p4&53 MR20

AINGER,Thomas Edward 2Lt kia 21-8-15 BerksYeo p203 CR Galipoli5

AINLEY,Frederick William Rev Chap4Cl ded 5-12-18 RAChDept p199 CR France34

AINLEY,Hefford William Ernest Lt ded 4-2-17 D168RFA p24 CR France74

AINLEY,John Hirst 2Lt kia 21-6-18 1RB p177 CR France411

AINLEY,Kendrick Edward Denison 2Lt kia 9-6-15 RE p210 CR Gallipoli14

AINSCOUGH,Cyril LtACapt kia 7-8-15 5Manch p236 MR4

AINSCOUGH,Henry 2Lt kia 11-4-18 1BordR p116 MR32 13-4-18

AINSCOUGH,Thomas 2Lt kia 25-1-18 RGA 303SB p38 CR France711

AINSLEY,Archie Robson Lt kia 12-10-18 RGA 91SB p209 CR France1392

AINSLIE,Archibald 2Lt kia 19-4-17 4KOSB p224 MR34

AINSLIE,Denys Alfred Lafone Lt kia 24-10-14 1Dev p76 MR22,Lafore

AINSLIE,George.MC.TCapt dow 21-8-18 6KOSB p101

AINSLIE,Henry Percival LtCol ded 6-7-19 IA 1/63PalamcottahLI p273 CR Pakistan50A

AINSLIE,John 2Lt dow 11-4-17 9RScots p212 CR France95,9 att11Bn

AINSLIE,John Archibald Capt kia 19-5-17 KOSB p101 CR France184

AINSLIE,John Elliott T2Lt kia 28-9-15 12RScots p53 MR19,Elliot

AINSLIE,Montague Forwood TLt dow 17-5-16 12Lpool p71 CR Belgium11,17-4-16

AINSLIE,Walter Gordon 2Lt kia 10-11-16 RFA attX33TMB p24 MR21

AINSWORTH,Harry Lawrence Capt drd 30-12-15 IA 1/10GurkhaRif p273 MR41

AINSWORTH,Herbert Green 2Lt kia 9-10-17 9Manch p237 MR30

AINSWORTH,John Stirling Lt kia 14-10-14 11Huss p22 CR France324

AINSWORTH,William Maj kia 16-4-17 5LNLancs p234 CR France525

AIR,Charles Alexander Capt kia 25-9-15 4BlkW p230

AIRD,Allan Muir T2Lt kia 21-10-18 17 att18KRRC p148 CR Belgium140

AIRD,Archibald Thomas 2Lt kia 30-11-17 18Lond p250 MR17

AIRD,James Gilbert T2Lt kia 1-7-16 15LancF p91 MR21

AIREY,Henry William Sachs 2Lt kia 11-1-17 5WYorks p217 CR France505

AIREY,John Barker 2Lt ded 3-12-18 3DLI p265 CR Numb43,acckld

AIREY,Norman George 2Lt kia 22-11-17 2/W5Yorks p218 MR17

AIRTH,Rennie Alexander TLt kia 29-7-18 8Beds att7RFC p4&85 CR Belgium16

AIRY,Arthur Langton Lt kia 11-1-15 3 att1Nhampt p137 MR22

AIRY,James Oswald Capt 21-7-20 1Manch CR Eire77 &CR Eire14

AITCHESON,Thomas Charles 2Lt kia 19-10-16 2Hamps p120 MR21

AITCHISON,Andrew Leslie 2Lt dow 3-11-16 1KOSB p101 CR France833

AITCHISON,Douglas James Lt ded 17-4-18 RFA attRAF p269 CR Lond3 dow

AITCHISON,John T2Lt died 23-10-18 LabCps p266

AITCHISON,John Brebner 2Lt kld 10-5-15 5RScots p211 MR4

AITCHISON,Peter 2Lt kia 8-5-18 Yorks p254 MR30

AITCHISON,Ronald Andrew Colquhoun Lt dow 14-12-14 1RLancs p58 CR Belgium451

AITCHISON,Scott McDiamid TLt kia 22-3-18 5 att1RInniskF p104 MR27

AITCHISON,Thomas Andrew Jamieson T2Lt dow 9-6-16 14 att12HLI p162 CR France423

AITCHISON,Thomas Donald 2Lt kia 28-6-15 4RScots p211 MR4

AITCHISON,Walter Maj kia 12-7-17 ScotHorse p205 CR Belgium6,attRGA HB

AITCHISON,William John.MID T2Lt kia 23-10-15 12HLI p162 CR France423

AITKEN,Alexander 2Lt dow 15-5-17 4GordH p241 CR France52

AITKEN,Andrew Danskine Lt kia 4-8-16 RE 2/2FC p210 CR Egypt2

AITKEN,Andrew Ramsey T2Lt acckld 2-3-18 RFC p15 CR Scot757,Ramsay

AITKEN,Archibald Bruce.MC.AMaj kld 4-8-19 RE att2S&M p254 CR Iraq8

AITKEN,Frank Thompson 2Lt kia 20-11-17 6SfthH p241 CR France1498

AITKEN,James 2Lt dow 3-5-17 5CamH p167 CR France1182

AITKEN,James Maj ded 29-7-17 RAMC p269 CR Scot761

AITKEN,James T2Lt kia 3-10-18 1GarBnWorc att11SomLI p107 CR France255

AITKEN,James Hunter 2Lt dedacd 2-6-16 7TrBnBlkW p231 CR Bucks60

AITKEN,John Christie.MC.Capt kia 25-9-15 2A&SH p172 CR France114

AITKEN,John Francis T2Lt kia 7-9-17 GL & 1/6LancF p189 CR Belgium8,6-9-17

AITKEN,John Malcolm T2Lt dow 12-10-18 D82RFA p24 CR France398

AITKEN,Robert Capt ded 17-1-19 RAMC SR p194 CR Iraq8

AITKENS,Albert Reginald Knight 2Lt dow 31-5-15 7Lond p247 CR France64

AITKENS,Cyril Arthur Charles Lt dow 10-7-16 RE p210 CR France397

AITON,Alexander Hamilton Capt kia 28-9-18 5HLI p240 CR Belgium84

AITON,William 2Lt kia 21-3-18 5 att3RB p177 MR27

AIZLEWOOD,Leslie Peach,MC.Maj kia 29-9-18 5Y&L &RAF p255

AKAM,James Rhodes Lt kia 1-7-16 18WYorks p80 MR21

AKED,George Lt kia 5-3-15 5Leic p220 CR Belgium33

AKED,Robert Basil Cautley.MC.Lt kia 21-3-18 2/5NStaffs p237 MR20

AKERMAN,Alexander Grant T2Lt kia 17-9-18 11Ess p131 CR France835

AKERMAN,Charles Savidge Annand Maj ded 26-9-15 RE HQ5SigCoy p43 CR France64

AKERMAN,Ralph Portland 2Lt dow 3-10-15 11Lond p248 CR Hamps64

AKHURST,Norman Walter TLt dow 8-6-18 35MGC p181 CR France63

AKRILL-JONES,Edward Trevor Lt kld 18-3-18 4N&D attRFC p15 CR Derby51

AKRILL-JONES,Robert Rowland 2Lt kia 9-4-17 2YLI CR France591

ALABASTER,Frederic Clifford 2Lt dow 25-8-16 5RWar p214 CR War3,Frederick

ALBAN,Clifton Frederick Lt 6-4-17 7Lond & 59RFC MR20 served as BAILEY.C.F.

ALBAN,Harry Chayton Lt kia 9-2-15 1Leinst p174 CR Belgium80

ALBERTSON,Armand Howard T2Lt kia 9-8-18 2TankCps p188 CR France649

ALBINSON,William Arthur 2Lt kia 26-4-18 3 att7RWSurr p55 CR France489

ALBRECHT,Charles Esmond Redlin Lt kia 24-8-14 2SLancs p125 MR15

ALBRECHT,John Ernest North 2Lt kia 1-8-17 33RFA p24 CR Belgium10 2-8-17 55RFA

ALBRIGHT,Martin Chicheley Maj dow 8-11-17 1/1WorcYeo p206 CR Palestine 8

ALBURY,Norman Howard T2Lt dow 15-9-17 GL &24RFC p4 CR France251

ALCOCK,Alfred 2Lt kia 21-8-16 18 att1Glouc p106 MR21

ALCOCK,Empson Lt kia 21-8-17 RFA 2NthMidBde p207 CR France1495

ALCOCK,Frank Lt ded 3-9-17 RhodR att3/2KAR p202 CR Tanzania1

ALCOCK,Randal Arthur T2Lt kia 1-9-18 7EYorks p83 CR France307

ALCOCK,Richard Evans Capt ded 1-3-17 RGA 99CoyMaltaGarr p38 CR Europe1

ALDANA,Juan Manuel TLt kia 21-4-17 12Worc p107 CR France531

ALDER,Thomas Gordon Edgecombe 2Lt kld 28-7-18 5ELancs &RAF p226&255 CR Glouc86

ALDERMAN,William.MC.Capt&QM kia 28-8-16 1Dors p123 CR France1472,31-8-18

ALDERMAN,William John.DSO.CaptALtCol kia 20-11-17 6RWKent p140 CR France379

ALDERSEY,Hugh Capt kia 10-3-18 ChesYeo p203 CR Palestine3,10ShropLI

ALDERSEY,Mark 2Lt kia 1-11-17 1Ches p95 MR30

ALDERSON,Albert Evelyn LtACapt drd 11-3-18 3RWSurr att1YLI p55 CR Greece3

ALDERSON,Alex George Jermyn 2Lt kia 19-10-16 5DCLI attMGC p186&227 CR Dors &C/146

ALDERSON,Arthur Roy TLt kia 22-3-16 RE 87FC p43 CR France423

ALDERSON,Bernard Henry Maj ded 2-9-17 IA 34PoonaHorse p273 CR France787

ALDERSON,Reginald.MC.ACapt dow 25-3-18 1/8LancF p221 CR France103

ALDERTON,Charles John Woodward 2Lt kia 20-11-17 7GordH p242 CR France662

ALDERTON,Colin Frederick T2Lt kia 7-7-16 12Manch p154 CR France667

ALDERWICK,Ernest Ewart Gladstone T2Lt kia 26-8-17 11Suff p77 CR France1462

ALDIN,Dudley Cecil 2Lt kia 15-5-16 RE 105FC p43 CR France68

ALDIS,Chas 2Lt ded 1-5-16 IARO att67Pujabis p273 CR Iraq1

ALDIS,Ralph Harry Lt kia 31-10-17 2/21Lond p251 CR Israel1

ALDOUS,Alan Edward T2Lt kia 3-7-16 8BordR p116 CR France393

ALDOUS,Stewart John Capt kia 26-3-16 5N&D p232 CR France68,Steuart 25-3-16

ALDRICH,Arnold 2Lt ded 1-5-16 1 att1/8Worc p107 CR Italy4,2-5-18

ALDRICH,Francis Pelham 2Lt kia 6-7-17 1/6NumbF p214 CR France421

ALDRICH,George Richard 2Lt kia 4-12-17 21Lond p251 MR17,1/23Lond

ALDRICK,Charles Pelham Gardner 2Lt kia 7-10-16 26RFus p66 CR France744

ALDRIDGE,Archie Horace.MC.2Lt dow 8-11-18 4RWSurr p212 CR France146

ALDRIDGE,Evelyn,OBE.MajALtCol ded 30-3-19 RGA p38 CR Hamps64

ALDRIDGE,Joseph George Rev 8-10-18 YMCA attSAfrBde CR France844

ALDRIDGE,Reginald John Petty Devenish Capt kia 7-10-14 2RSuss p118 CR France1329

ALDRIDGE,Reginald Percy T2Lt kld 26-3-18 39MGC p181 MR27

ALDWINKLE,Bernard Lt dow 3-11-18 RFA 421HB p24 MR70 &CR Europe179

ALDWINKLE,Ralph 2Lt kia 15-11-16 11RLancs att10LNLancs p58 CR France533

ALDWORTH,Douglas Gilbert Hayward 2Lt drd 10-10-18 att3RBerks p138 CR Eire14

ALDWORTH,Thomas Rupert Capt kia 11-3-18 2RBerks p138 CR France709

ALEXANDER,Alan Mansell 2Lt kia 8-12-17 2/16Lond p250 CR Palestine3

ALEXANDER,Alexander John 2Lt kia 27-11-17 5 att2/6WRid p227 MR17

ALEXANDER,Alfred Herbert 2Lt kia 3-12-17 6 att2Hamps p229 MR17

ALEXANDER,Alister Ralph Spiers Capt dow 9-2-16 IMS att2/7Gurkhas p273 CR Iraq1

ALEXANDER,Archibald Charles Edward Lt kia 11-3-15 3 att2RScotF p94 MR22

ALEXANDER,Charles.VD.Maj 15-11-16 2HighBde RFA CR Scot386

ALEXANDER,Edward Mayne LtCol ded 11-8-16 SfthH p265

ALEXANDER,Frank Esmond T2Lt ded 25-7-16 98MGC Inf p181 CR France145,dow 27-7-16

ALEXANDER,Frank Wilson 2Lt kia 14-4-17 4 att16HLI p162 MR21

ALEXANDER,George Luard CaptTMaj kia 5-8-17 8Lond p247 CR France255

ALEXANDER,George Thomson Dickson T2Lt kia 11-4-17 2SfthH p164 CR France604

ALEXANDER,Gordon Reuben T2Lt kia 24-4-17 RSuss att2Bn p118 CR France379

ALEXANDER,Harold John 2Lt kia 25-7-18 7Lond p247 MR27

ALEXANDER,Harold Percy Maj kia 26-3-17 6Ess p232 MR34

ALEXANDER,Harry 2Lt kia 17-10-15 1GrenGds SR p49 CR France1059

ALEXANDER,Henry Talbot T2Lt kia 1-7-16 1Hamps p120 CR France1492

ALEXANDER,James.MID 2Lt kia 7-7-16 11NumbF p59 MR21

ALEXANDER,James Capt kia 2-12-17 16HLI p162 MR30

ALEXANDER,James Edward 2Lt kia 19-9-17 RFA 277ArmyBde p24 CR France285

ALEXANDER,James Kidd 2Lt kia 20-9-17 4 att9RScots p211 MR30

ALEXANDER,John T2Lt kia 15-7-16 8Leic p87 MR21

ALEXANDER,John Alexander Elliot TLt kia 16-8-15 12HLI p162 CR France149,15-8-15

ALEXANDER,John Petrie T2Lt ded 14-5-17 GL &4RFC p4 CR Scot244

ALEXANDER,John Rees 2Lt dow 4-9-18 6Lond p246 CR France833

ALEXANDER,John William Ewart 2Lt ded 14-4-16 BordR Ex10Norf p73&264 CR Norf301

ALEXANDER,Noel Legard T2Lt kia 1-7-16 9YLI p142 CR France267

ALEXANDER,Peter James.MC.Capt kia 12-10-17 7BlkW p231 CR Belgium125

ALEXANDER,Philip Mansell T2Lt dow 30-7-16 11 att5GordH p165 CR France833

ALEXANDER,Reginald LtCol dow 29-12-14 3RB p177 CR France284

ALEXANDER,Robert Lt dow 3-11-17 26RFA p24 CR Belgium3,117RFA

ALEXANDER,Samuel Aubrey Lt ded 15-11-18 5Mddx p269 CR Mddx40

ALEXANDER,Sydney Dawson Moray Maj 14-1-17 IOD MR66

ALEXANDER,Thomas Loudon 2Lt kia 8-5-17 10BlkW p128 MR37

ALEXANDER,Thomas Mitchell Lt kia 12-7-15 4KOSB p223 MR4

ALEXANDER,Thomas Wedderspoon.MID Maj kia 21-3-18 RGA att255RFA p209 MR20

ALEXANDER,Walter Lorenzo LtCol kia 14-5-15 2Yorks p89 CR France727

ALEXANDER,William LtCol ded 9-3-19 RAMC p269 CR Ches193

ALEXANDER,William Ewart 2Lt ded 14-4-16 10Norf p73 See ALEXANDER,John William Ewart

ALEXANDER,William Fairlie Lt kia 12-10-18 9HLI p240 CR France230

ALEXANDER,William Gemmell 2Lt kia 15-5-15 7Lpool p215 MR22

ALEXANDER,William Henderson Capt&QM ded 25-6-19 RE p262 CR Kent62

ALEXANDER,William Mercer T2Lt kia 1-7-16 17HLI p162 MR21

ALFORD,Allen Charles George 2Lt kia 3-9-16 10Glouc att3Worc p106 MR21,Allan

ALFORD,Edward Nicholas Capt ded 11-1-19 7Ess p232 MR43,2GarBnBeds

ALGAR,Arthur Patrick LtACapt kia 26-3-18 IARO att24Punjabis p273 CR Iraq8

ALGAR,Horace 2Lt ded 12-4-17 RE p269 CR Numb60

ALGEO,Norman Capt dow 30-11-17 3Leinst p174 CR France446

ALGEO,William Bensley Capt kia 17-5-16 1Dors p123 CR France1504

ALGER,George Crosbie T2Lt kld 7-6-17 GL &RFC p4 CR Scot398

ALINGTON,Geoffrey Hugh 2Lt kia 9-8-16 5RSuss p228 CR France296

ALINGTON,George Henry 2Lt kia 24-2-17 IARO att2/9GurkhaRif p273 MR38,23/24-2-17

ALISON,George Newdegate.MID Capt kia 1-7-16 SfthH &MGC Inf p181&164 CR France643

ALISON,Laughton Hassard 2Lt kia 15-5-15 1RBerks p138 MR22

ALLAM,Percy John 2Lt dow 22-5-18 PoW RLancs attTMB p58 CR Germany2

ALLAN,Alfred T2Lt kia 31-7-16 2HLI p162 see Allen,Alfred

ALLAN,Alwyn Munton.MC.Capt dow 21-4-18 1RWSurr p55 CR France40

ALLAN,Archibald.MC.Capt dow 17-6-18 4 O&BLI p231 CR Italy11

ALLAN,Arthur Gordon 2Lt dow 8-12-18 108RFA p24 CR France34,B106RFA

ALLAN,Charles Frederick Lt kia 28-6-15 4RScots p211 MR4

ALLAN,Frank Cecil T2Lt dow 29-9-16 21 att13DLI p160 CR France145

ALLAN,George 2Lt kld 14-3-16 19Lond p250 CR Scot531

ALLAN,George A.T2Lt kia 16-1-16 RGA p38 CR Belgium101

ALLAN,George McLachlan 2Lt dow 14-7-15 RE p210 MR4,Maclachan

ALLAN,Henry Somerset 2Lt dow 2-10-16 6Lond p246 CR France40

ALLAN,Hubert Gordon Rev 7-4-15 YMCA CR France1

ALLAN,Hugh Drummond Lt kia 24-4-17 3A&SH p172 CR France434,2Bn

ALLAN,James Grant TLt kia 25-9-15 9GordH p165 MR19

ALLAN,James Stanley 2Lt dow 22-10-16 3A&SH p172 CR France177

ALLAN,John 2Lt dow 4-11-16 GL &11RFC p2&189 CR France46

ALLAN,John.MC.T2LtACapt dow 9-6-17 6MGC HB p181 CR France285

ALLAN,John Love Strathearn T2Lt kia 25-9-15 7KOSB p101 MR19

ALLAN,John Steele T2Lt kia 12-10-16 9 att2RScotF p94 CR France744

ALLAN,JohnWilliam Anderson.MC. 2Lt dow 10-4-18 8BordR p116 see ALLEN,J.W.A.

ALLAN,Lawson Ellis Lt kia 26-4-17 W'morland&CumbYeo attRFC p17&206 MR20

ALLAN,Lewis Davidson TLt kia 27-9-18 8RScotF p94 CR France530

ALLAN,Marshall Thomson TLt kia 26/29-9-15 6RScotF p94 MR19

ALLAN,Noel James Capt ded 18-10-18 RAMC p253 CR Iraq6

ALLAN,Peter 2Lt dow 19-7-18 3 att5CamH p167 CR France134,kia

ALLAN,Ramsay 2Lt kld 22-4-18 GL &2RAF p189 CR France179

ALLAN,Robert 2Lt kia 23-4-17 8ScotRif att16KRRC p225 MR20

ALLAN,Robert Beausire Lt ded 5-4-18 4RScots p211 CR France64

ALLAN,Robert Gregor 2Lt kia 9-4-17 2KOSB p101 CR France550,Grigor

ALLAN,Wallace Capt ded 29-6-16 1GarrBnLincs p74 CR Egypt15,Ex7RScotF

ALLAN,William AssCommsyHonLt ded 28-11-16 IA S&TCps p273 CR Iraq6

ALLAN,William Alexander 2Lt kia 7-6-17 4 att11RScots p211 MR20 &CR France1896

ALLAN,William Halliday T2Lt kia 31-7-17 7/8KOSB p101 MR29

ALLAN,William Lewis Campbell HonMaj kia 12-10-14 3KOSB p101 CR France260,14-10-14 2Bn

ALLAN,William Stanley Lt kia 17-5-15 7Lpool p215 MR22

ALLAN-HAY,Edward James 2Lt ded 5-9-18 IA p273

ALLANSON,Henry Peter 2Lt kia 20-7-16 1 att2Suff p77 MR21

ALLARD,Philip Hayward LtACapt kia 23-6-17 3/45RFA p24 CR Belgium113,dow

ALLARDICE,Colin McDiarmid Lt kia 26-4-15 IA 14 att47Sikhs p273 CR Belgium101

ALLARDICE,Harry LtCol kia 1-7-16 IA 36JacobsHorse att13NumbF p273 CR France188

ALLASON,Lionel Theopilus Capt kia 7-10-14 1LNLancs p135 MR15

ALLATT,Henry Thomas Ward Col ded 8-5-16 SL &DCLI p201 CR Hamps1

ALLAWAY,Trevor Rhys.MC.Capt dow 29-6-16 3SWBord attWelshR p99 CR Egypt9,acckld

ALLBON,Bernard Charles Jeaves TCapt ded 3-2-19 3 att6Dors p123&257

ALLBERRY,Cecil Charles TCapt kia 25-9-16 10 att9Leic p87 MR21

ALLCHIN,Sidney Milton T2Lt kia 13-12-17 3RWKent p140 CR Belgium106,dow

ALLCHIN,Walter John T2Lt kia 26-10-17 14War p64 MR30

ALLCHORN,Edward Walter.MM.T2Lt dow 5-11-17 1 att4EYorks p83 CR France64

ALLCOCK,Christian 2Lt dow 30-3-18 49MGC p181 CR Belgium3

ALLCOCK,Joseph 2Lt kia 16-10-17 54RGA attRE Sigs p38 CR France190

ALLCOCK,William Thomas Lloyd Capt kia 5-6-17 40RFC p4 MR20

ALLDAY,Stanley Owen Lt kia 13-10-15 1/5SStaffs p229 MR19

ALLDEN,Joseph Henry 2Lt kia 28-4-17 2/4 O&BLI p231 MR21

ALLEN,Albert Alexander 2Lt kia 11-10-17 GL &46RFC p4 CR France568

ALLEN,Alfred T2Lt kia 31-7-16 2HLI p162 MR21,ALLAN

ALLEN,Alfred James Benedict T2Lt kia 3-3-16 17RWelshF p97 CR France727

ALLEN,Archibald Stafford TLt kia 3-10-15 8RFus p66 CR France115

ALLEN,Arthur Haviland T2Lt kia 4-10-17 11 att1RDubF p176 MR30

ALLEN,Charles Arthur 2Lt kld 12-3-19 5NumbF &RAF p213

ALLEN,Charles Rayle.MC.Capt kia 27-9-18 6Manch p236 CR France712,Royle 7Bn

ALLEN,Charles St.Vincent 2Lt ded 16-2-17 3EKent attMGC Inf p57&181 CR Herts12

ALLEN,Cuthbert George Llewellin T2Lt dow 3-11-15 RE 175FC p43 CR Belgium11

ALLEN,Cyrus 2Lt kia 13-3-18 GL &RFC p15 CR France403

ALLEN,D.G.A. Capt kld 8-10-18 4DLI &RAF p160

ALLEN,Francis Edward Lt kia 11-4-18 1/5Y&L p238 MR30

ALLEN,Frederick John T2Lt kia 25-9-15 9Dev p76 CR France88,dow 27-9-15

ALLEN,Geoffrey Austin 2Lt kia 1-7-16 2Ess p131 MR21

ALLEN,Geoffrey Charles TLt dow 5-4-18 6EKent p57 CR France62

ALLEN,Geoffrey May 2Lt kia 2-9-16 GL &RFC p2&189 CR France233

ALLEN,Geoffrey Peake 2Lt kld 21-12-15 4RWSurr p212 CR Surrey6

ALLEN,George James T2Lt dow 12-10-17 att7RWKent p140 CR Belgium18

ALLEN,Harry TCapt dow 16-1-18 8Glouc p106 CR France398

ALLEN,Henry Edward TLt drd 24-4-17 GL attGambiaCoy WAFF p201 MR40

ALLEN,Herbert 2Lt kia 1-7-16 1/5SStaffs p229 MR21

ALLEN,Herbert Thomas TCapt kia 25-9-15 9SfthH p164 CR France114

ALLEN,Hugh Charles.DCM.2Lt kia 25-4-17 1/7BlkW p231 CR France604,23-4-17

ALLEN,Humphrey Decius TLt kia 1-7-16 10WYorks p80 CR France373

ALLEN,J.Capt&QM 15-9-20 10YLI CR Yorks547

ALLEN,James Lt&AssCommsy ded 22-10-18 IMS p273 MR65

ALLEN,John 2Lt ded 29-11-19 LabCps p266 CR Wales1

ALLEN,John Edric Russell.MIDx2 Lt dow 8-4-18 16Lancers p22 CR France145,Capt

ALLEN,John Francis Capt dow 4-11-14 LNLancs p135 CR Belgium57,5-11-14

ALLEN,John Hugh Lt kia 13-6-15 13Worc p107 CR Gallipoli6

ALLEN,John Stanley.MC.TMaj kia 11-4-18 9NumbF p59 MR32

ALLEN,John Thomas.MID Lt ded 18-2-16 RFA p24 CR Dorset &C/133,Capt

ALLEN,John William Anderson.MC.2Lt dow 10-4-18 8BordR p116 MR32,ALLAN

ALLEN,Kenneth Harris TLt dow 11-10-18 13 att9Manch p154 CR France446

ALLEN,Lawrence John Maynard T2Lt kia 2-7-16 6Wilts p152 MR21

ALLEN,Leslie John Spencer Capt dow 15-2-17 7Hamps p229 CR Iraq5

ALLEN,Lionel Raymund Whateley Lt kia 27-3-18 9SWBord attMGC12Div p99&181 MR27

ALLEN,Mary Ann SNurse ded 5-1-20 QAIMNS CR Lancs483

ALLEN,Maurice Reginald T2Lt kia 13-9-16 2N&D p133 MR21

ALLEN,Melville Richard Howell Agnew Lt ded 21-3-17 RFC p4 CR Beds&Hunts23

ALLEN,Merwyn Richard William T2Lt kia 2-8-17 7 att2/5Norf p73 CR France154,Mervyn

ALLEN,Norman TCapt kia 14-4-18 2 posted14RWar p64 CR France346

ALLEN,Owen Augustus Ellis TLt kld 3-11-17 GL &RFC p4 CR Camb1,O.E.A.

ALLEN,Percivall Knight TCapt kia 23-4-17 10WYorks p80 CR France531

ALLEN,Percy 2Lt kia 4-10-17 59RFA SR p24 MR30

ALLEN,Percy Hampson 2Lt kia 20-4-16 3Y&L p158 MR29

ALLEN,Percy Herman Charles Lt kia 9-5-15 3 att2ELancs p110 CR France566

ALLEN,Raymond Francis 2Lt kia 18-11-18 1/6RWar attRAF p258 CR Ches182,kld

ALLEN,Richard Gerrard Ross,2LtACapt kia 16-11-15 5WYorks attRFC p17&218 CR France742,2Lt

ALLEN,Richard Lancelot Baugh Lt ded 27-12-18 67RFA p261 CR Egypt9

ALLEN,Stephen Dexter T2Lt kia 27-8-18 Beds att4Bn p85 MR16,att7RFus

ALLEN,Stephen Henry Hammans Lt kia 27-3-18 3/5Dev att6NumbF p217 MR27

ALLEN,Sydney Raymond T2Lt kia 12-7-16 16Manch p154 MR21

ALLEN,Thomas 2Lt kia 25-2-15 1IrGds SR p52 CR France720,26-2-15

ALLEN,Thomas Gordon Lt kia 26-8-18 5EYorks p219 CR France432

ALLEN,Valentine Francis T2Lt kia 17-11-17 RB att16Bn p177 MR30

ALLEN,Walter Smith 2Lt kia 21-3-18 2/5N&D p232 MR20

ALLEN,Wellesley Roe Capt ded 11-3-19 RAMC att2Ech p194 CR Egypt9,GHQ 3Ech

ALLEN,William Lt ded 12-10-18 6Hamps p228 CR Asia82,1/4Bn

ALLEN,William Frederick 2Lt kia 9-10-17 3 att2/4ELancs p110 CR Belgium125

ALLEN,William Henry T2Lt kia 12-4-18 31MGC Inf p181 MR32

ALLEN,William Lynn.DSO.Maj kld 28-10-14 2BordR p116 MR29

ALLEN,William Maxey TLt kia 26-9-15 13NumbF p59 MR19

ALLEN,William Sproston Lt kia 14-3-18 1RFA attRGA252SB p207 CR Belgium19

ALLEN,W.J.Lt 20-1-17 EAUL attIntelDept CR EAfrica39

ALLENBY,Augustus Heathcote LtCol kia 7-8-15 IA att7RScotF p94&273 CR France222,H.A.

ALLENBY,Horace Michael Hynman.MC. Lt dow 29-7-17 14RHA p24 CR Belgium24

ALLENDER,George Frederick LtCol ded 29-9-16 5Lpool Res p269 CR Ches190,Col 2-10-16

ALLENDER,John Harold 2Lt ded 7-10-16 1Lond p245 MR21

ALLFREY,Frederick de Vere Bruce Lt kia 6-9-14 9Lancers p22 CR France1432,7-9-14

ALLFREY,Hugh Lionel Capt kia 19-9-18 10EKent p204 CR France212,18-9-18

ALLGOOD,Bertram Capt kia 6-12-14 1RIrRif p168 CR France768

ALLGOOD,George T2Lt kia 15-4-17 10RDubF p176 MR20

ALLIBAN,William Beaumont.MID Lt kia 5-5-17 2/5N&D p232 MR21

ALLIES,Alfric Evan Lt kia 16-8-15 8RWelshF p97 MR4,Ewan 15-8-15

ALLIN,Harold Arthur T2Lt kia 23-10-17 17LancF p91 MR30

ALLIN,Harold Wyse TLt dow 13-12-17 6KSLI p144 CR Egypt2

ALLINSON,Athelstan John William Ward.MID Lt kia 9-4-18 A121RFA p24 CR France1140

ALLINSON,Cyril Hugh 2Lt kia 13-11-16 3 att2Suff p77 MR21

ALLINSON,David.DCM.Lt kia 29-3-18 7ScotRif att12KRRC p224 MR27

ALLINSON,Fred.MC.T2Lt ded 27-3-17 GL 8RWSurr &70RFC p4 CR France1349

ALLISON,Charles Anderson TLt kia 12-3-15 2ELancs p110 CR France924

ALLISON,Gordon Lt kia 8-6-19 IA 3/1GurkhaRif p273 MR43

ALLISON,Harry Lt kia 27-8-18 3 att13RWelshF p97 CR France402

ALLISON,Henry James Noel Palmer Lt ded 4-2-19 3GordH CR Durham25

ALLISON,Hazlett Samuel.MID Maj kia 9-8-17 7RIrRif p168 MR29

ALLISON,James 2Lt kia 20-9-17 8RScots p211 MR30

ALLISON,James Stewart Lt ded 18-9-17 6BlkW att11GreekLabBn p231 CR Greece9

ALLISON,John Lt kia 24-11-17 9A&SH p244 CR France256

ALLISON,John T2Lt kia 21-3-18 14A&SH p172 MR20

ALLISON,Robert Stafford 2Lt kia 16-6-17 1DenbighYeo p203 CR Palestine8,dow

ALLISON,Thomas Capt kia 18-5-15 4CamH p242 MR22

ALLISON,Thomas McGregor TMaj kia 30-5-18 12Glouc p106 CR France1689

ALLISON,William Frederick 2Lt kia 23-4-17 7GordH p242 CR France604

ALLNUTT,Albert Edwin T2Lt kia 27-9-18 KSLI att7BnRes p144 CR France.357

ALLOM,Charles Cedric Gordon Lt dow 20-10-17 C1NMidRFA p207 CR France145

ALLOTT,Thomas Richard T2Lt dow 4-11-18 1YLI p142 CRFrance206

ALLOWAY,Howard George 2Lt kia 30-11-17 4Leic p220 MR19

ALLPASS,Esmond Theodore T2Lt kia 21-8-15 9N&D p133 MR4

ALLPASS,Henry Blythe King 2Lt kia 16-9-16 4Ess att1Camb p232 MR21

ALLPASS,Samuel Rosslee TCapt dow 21-1-17 185MGC Inf p181 MR38

ALLPORT,Harrison Kingsley 2Lt kia 21-8-16 4A&SH p172 CR France453

ALLPORT,Ivor Merlin 2Lt kia 9-1-17 7Nhampt p137 CR France149

ALLPORT,Morton 2Lt ded 10-11-16 70RFC p2 MR20

ALLPORT,Thomas Coote Capt kia 1-8-15 5Y&L p238 CR Belgium85

ALLSOPP,Jerome Boileau.DSO.MIDx3 MajALtCol kia 27-5-18 SLancs p125 MR18

ALLTREE,Charles Derek TLt dow PoW 27-3-18 RWelshF att9Bn p97 CR France1277

ALLURED,Will T2Lt kia 14-9-16 6BordR p116 CR France251

ALMACK,Alfred Christopher Turnour 2Lt kia 27-9-16 MGC att3Nhampt p181

ALMACK,Edward Poulton Capt kia 25-1-16 RHA att85RFA p24 CR France430

ALMON,Harold Pryor 2Lt kia 31-7-17 3 att11LancF p91 CR Belgium34

ALMOND,Charles Percy Lt ded 5-4-17 RE BaseDepot p262 CR France145

ALMOND,George Hely-Hutchinson TCapt kia 9-8-18 RAMC 3CavFA p194 CR France652

ALMOND,Henry Tristram 2Lt kia 31-3-16 MGC att3GordH p181 CR France513 3GordH attMGC

ALMOND,Owen Edmund 2Lt kia 29-9-15 2LNLancs p135 CR EAfrica58

ALMOND,Rowland Latimer Lt kia 28-10-14 RE att21Coy3S&M p43 CR France98

ALNACK,A.C.T.3Nhampt attMGC p137 MR21,See ALMACK,A.C.T

ALSTON,Claude McCaul 2Lt kia 25-10-14 2RScotF p94 MR29,24-10-14

ALSTON,Ernest Alfred Brooke.MIDx3 MajTLtCol kia 10/11-8-17 2Nhampt att10DCLI p137 CR Belgium173,11-8-17

ALSTON,Garwood Kencingdale 2Lt kia 12-8-15 5Suff p217 MR4,Keningale

ALSTON,James 2Lt kia 28-9-18 5HLI p240 CR Belgium111

ALSTON,James William.MID MajTLtCol kia 15-4-15 2RIrRif p168 CR Belgium28

ALSTON,James William Hamilton TMaj ded 3-1-17 11A&SH p172 CR France430

ALSTON,John Capt kia 16-10-17 RAMC 103FA p194 CR Belgium12

ALSTON,John Douglas Lt kia 10-3-15 3 att2ScotRif p103 CR France260

ALSTON,Robert Charles Wallace Capt dow 18-8-15 1HLI p162 CR France924,kia

ALSTON,Rowland Evelyn 2Lt kia 17-8-16 B52RFA p24 CR France924

ALT,George Earl Capt kia 18-4-15 3YLI p142 CR Belgium152

ALTOFT,George Herbert 2Lt kia 17-7-17 4WYorks p80 CR Belgium132,G.A.

ALTY,Daniel 2Lt kia 9-9-18 9Lpool att2SStaffs p216 MR16,5-9-18

ALTY,Henry.DCM.2Lt dow 30-9-18 9Lpool p216 CR France256

ALVES,Alexander TLt kia 26-5-18 RASC att7RFus p192 CR France233

ALVES,John William Jerome Maj ded 29-10-18 IA 93BurmaInf p273 CR India48

AMBLER,Edward T2Lt kia 26-4-18 1/5Y&L p158 CR Belgium103

AMBLER,Edward Sharp Lt kia 8-5-18 2ScotsGds p51 CR France120

AMBLER,George Lt dow 3-8-17 6WYorks p218 CR Yorks410

AMBLER,Percy Capt dedacc 28-9-19 2/5Lpool CR Ches182

AMBLER,R.2Lt 24-11-18 13Lpool CR Lancs491

AMBRIDGE,William T2Lt kia 7-4-18 8 att6Beds p85 CR France798

AMBROSE,Donald 2Lt kia 21-3-18 23Lond p252 MR20

AMBROSE,Gerald Leslie 2Lt dow 28-5-19 IA 1/22Punjabis p273 MR43,27-5-19

AMERY,Harold Francis Saphir.MID Maj dow 24-11-15 1BlkW p128&263,ded CR Lond8

AMERY-PARKES,Douglas John.MC&Bar.LtAMaj dow 30-4-18 2Mddx att119MGC p145 181&258 CR France102

AMES,Ivan Wilson 2Lt ded 6-9-19.9RWKent p265 CR SAfrica42,Wilton

AMES,Peter Ashman Lt kld 21-11-20 GL &1GrenGds CR Lond9

AMES,Robert Henry TCapt kia 6-1-16 2Leic p87 MR38

AMES,William Kerr Lt dow 16-9-14 RWKent p140 CR France1227

AMESBURY,Frank Cholmondely Dering Maj ded 7-2-18 9WRid p115&268 CR Sussex111 ExIA WarwickRecs SL

AMESBURY,Hugh Frederick Raleigh 2Lt kia 20-11-17 5 att8Beds p219 CR France711

AMESS,Frederick Thomas 2Lt dow 22-7-17 3KOSB p101 CR Glouc11,3Beds

AMEY,Harold 2Lt kia 27-9-18 7KSLI p144 CR France437

AMIES,Arthur George T2Lt kia 9-10-17 1/5Y&L p158 CR Belgium125

AMIES,Kenneth Francis T2Lt kia 23-9-17 2/6NStaffs p156 CR Belgium10

AMOR,Ernest John T2Lt kia 15-5-16 14Mddx attRFC p2&145 CR France95,12-5-16

AMOROSO,Michele TLt kia 3-7-16 D96RFA p24 CR France189

AMOS,A.J.Lt 30-4-20 RE IWT CR Essex83

AMOS,Charles Edward 2Lt kia 22-3-18 40MGC p181 MR20

AMOS,Frank Edward T2Lt kia 20-9-18 A230RFA p24 CR France1495

AMOS,Gilbert Stratton 2Lt kia 14-9-14 2KOSB p101 CR France864

AMOS,John Vince Lt ded 13-2-17 RFA 37DAC p24 CR France345

AMOS,William Hope T2Lt kia 14-10-16 7EKent p57 CR France744

AMPHLETT,Richard Ferrand 2Lt kia 5-4-17 8Worc p226 CR France1495

AMPHLETT,Edward Maylie Capt kia 4-6-15 12Worc attRFus p107 CR Gallipoli6,Baylie

AMPHLETT MORTON,James Fairfax.MID 2Lt kia 10-1-15 KRRC p148 CR France260

AMPT,Norman Crosland T2Lt dow 22-8-15 1BordR p116 MR4

AMY,Adolphe Barbier 2Lt kia 19-9-16 9RIrRif p168 MR29,Barber

AMYATT-BURNEY,Horace A.Maj ded 8-3-19 RDC p253 CR Yorks38

ANCILL,S.J.Capt 4-7-20 GL DentalSurg CR Iraq9

ANCRUM,J.A.2LtACapt kia 16-7-18 8HLI p240 see below

ANCRUM,James Alexander,MC.Capt dow 17-7-18 9HLI p240 CR Belgium18

ANDERSEN,Peter Johansen See ANDERSON,P J

ANDERSON,A.John MajTCol ded 11-8-18 RASC p192 CR Greece9,10-8-18 DDST

ANDERSON,Abdy Fellowes Capt kia 23-4-15 3ScotRif attKOSB p103 MR29

ANDERSON,Alan James Ramsay 2Lt kia 20-10-14 3 att2RIrReg p88 MR22

ANDERSON,Albert Stewart T2Lt ded 1-2-17 9RInnisF p104 CR France285

ANDERSON,Alec David 2Lt kia 6-11-18 1GrenGds p49 CR France948

ANDERSON,Alexander Campbell Capt kia 20-4-15 RAVC p198 CR Belgium84

ANDERSON,Alexander Clairmonte Capt dow 23-11-14 IA 6Jats p273 CR France80,dedacc

ANDERSON,Alexander Douglas Lt kia 17-7-16 4Glouc p225

ANDERSON,Alexander John MajTCol ded 11-8-18 RASC p192

ANDERSON,Alexander Ronald 2Lt dow 8-10-15 3 att1HLI p162 CR France924

ANDERSON,Andrew 2Lt ded 29-10-19 RFA p261 CR Scot766,Lt

ANDERSON,Andrew Douglas McArthur Lt kia 8-5-15 9A&SH p244 MR29,MacArthur

ANDERSON,Andrew Stewart Maj kia 16-6-15 10Lpool p216 MR29

ANDERSON,Archibald John Scott 2Lt kia 27-8-16 3 att11Ches p95 CR France246

ANDERSON,Archibald Joseph TCapt kia 1-7-16 10WYorks p80 CR France373

ANDERSON,Arthur T2Lt kia 29-3-17 9RWar p64 MR38

ANDERSON,Arthur Ferneaux Dalgairno 2Lt kia 1-7-16 4 att1LancF p91 CR France221,Furneaux Dalgairns

ANDERSON,Basil Arthur.MC.TCapt kia 21-3-18 5 O&BLI p129 CR France1061

ANDERSON,Bernard Gordon.MC.TLt dow 8-8-16 10Lincs p74 CR Yorks323.Gordan

ANDERSON,Brian Hallam T2Lt kld 8-9-17 GL &RFC p4 see ANDERSON,F.B.H.

ANDERSON,Charles Alexander Kenneth 2Lt kia 10-11-14 1KRRC p148 MR29,12-11-14 att1RSFus

ANDERSON,Charles Alfred Walker TLtCol kia 18-9-16 1NStaffs att1/5RLancs p156 CR France374

ANDERSON,Charles Edward Capt kia 20-7-16 GordH att8Bn p165 CR France176,2Bn

ANDERSON,Charles Henry 2Lt ded 25-8-15.13HLI p265 CR Scot142

ANDERSON,Charles Hamilton Capt kia 19-12-14 HLI p162 MR22

ANDERSON,Charles Ogilvy Lt dow 2-10-15 2 att3RScots p53 CR France40,3 att2Bn

ANDERSON,Clifford William Lt kia 24-10-18 B190RFA p207 CR Belgium143

ANDERSON,Colin Knox Lt kia 23-8-14 3RWKent p140 CR Belgium201

ANDERSON,Duncan.MM.TLt ded 4-5-18 RASC p192 CR Surrey1

ANDERSON,David,MC.T2LtACapt kia 23-4-17 7CamH att44TMB p167 CR France1182

ANDERSON,David Lt kia 23-4-17 4GordH p241 CR France1194

ANDERSON,David TLt ded 13-9-17 RAMC 37MAC att4SH p194 CR France134

ANDERSON,David Alexander 2Lt kia 17-8-16 10/11HLI p162 MR21

ANDERSON,David Horace T2Lt kia 22-4-16 11 att2BlkW p128 MR38

ANDERSON,David William.MC&Bar.Capt kia 8-8-18 6Lond p246 CR France1170,Wilson

ANDERSON,Denis Vipont Friend Capt kia 25-4-15 F Coy 1RDubF p176 CR Gallipoli15

ANDERSON,Donald Fraser Lt kia 27-4-18 4RWKent p234 CR Belgium188

ANDERSON,Donald Knox.MC.TLtCol kia 3-12-17 MGC att61EKentDiv p57&181,TLt MR17

ANDERSON,Edward Darnley.DSO.TMaj ded 13-11-17 1NStaffs p156 CR France201

ANDERSON,Edward Kerr Capt kld 16-3-18 5HLI attRFC p17&240 CR Scot87

ANDERSON,Edwin Frederick Spurrier Lt dow 1-11-18 4NStaffs att35MGC Infp156 CR Belgium143,2-11-18

ANDERSON,Eric James Capt kia 13-11-16 6SfthH p241 CR France131

ANDERSON,Ernest Lionel Lane.MID 2Lt kia 10-11-14 1RSFus p94 MR29

ANDERSON,Francis TLt kia 18-11-16 7SLancs p125 MR21

ANDERSON,Francis Maj dow 28-1-17 2 att12RScots p53 CR France95

ANDERSON,Francis Brian Hallam T2Lt kld 8-9-17 GL &RFC p4 CR Norf151 see ANDERSON,B.H.

ANDERSON,Francis Sainthill.MC.CaptAMaj kia 25-8-18 A15RFA p24 CR France514

ANDERSON,Frank Gordon Donald TCapt kia 11-10-18 6Y&L p158 CR France405,9Bn

ANDERSON,Frederick Henry.MC.2Lt ded 15-5-18 50RFA p24 CR France1359

ANDERSON,Frederick Kinloch 2Lt kia 25-9-15 1/4BlkW p230 CR France705

ANDERSON,Fredk William Capt kia 29-3-18 RE 416FC p209 CR France184

ANDERSON,George Alexander Lt ded 27-2-19 4BlkW p269 CR Scot677,acckld 27-1-19

ANDERSON,George Grantham TCaptAMaj ded 3-11-18 RAMC att51GH p194 CR France40

ANDERSON,George John T2Lt kia 22-4-16 2BlkW p128 CR Iraq5

ANDERSON,George Ogilvie.DCM.2Lt kia 26-10-17 2GordH p165 MR30

ANDERSON,George Rutherford T2Lt kia 18-8-16 73MGC Inf p181 CR France400

ANDERSON,George Whitfield HonMaj&QM ded 31-8-15 SfthH attEgyptArmy p164 CR Egypt9,Whitefield

ANDERSON,Gerard Rupert Laurie 2Lt kia 9-11-14 3 att1Ches p95 MR29

ANDERSON,Goldie Fraser.MC.Lt kia 19-7-16 RE 90FC p43 CR France34,19-7-18

ANDERSON,Gordon Wright TCapt ded 20-11-18 RASC p192 CR Kent96

ANDERSON,Harry Frederick Cortlandt 2Lt dow 14-2-17 IA 102Grens p273

ANDERSON,Harry John 2Lt kia 10-4-18 3Wilts p152 CR Palestine9

ANDERSON,Henry Angus 2Lt kia 21-7-18 4GordH p241 CR France34

ANDERSON,Henry Lawrence LtCol dow 29-10-14 IA 9BhopalInf p273 CR France705

ANDERSON,Henry McDonald Lt kia 30-5-18 5NumbF att63MGC p186&213,McDonnell CR France84,dow

ANDERSON,Herbert Norman Scott T2Lt kld 24-12-17 GL &RFC p4 CR Scot151

ANDERSON,James TLt kia 20-8-16 SL &87TMB 26/10RFA p201 MR29

ANDERSON,James 2Lt kia 20-8-16 16ScotRif att87/2TMB p254 CR Belgium101

ANDERSON,James T2LtACapt kia 25-9-16 2KOSB p101 MR21

ANDERSON,James Capt dow 5-7-17 8HLI att5YLI p240 CR France8

ANDERSON,James Alexander T2Lt kia 19-10-16 11 att8BlkW p128 MR21

ANDERSON,James Kirkwood Capt dow 24-11-17 1/7ScotRif p224 CR Palestine3

ANDERSON,James Lennox 2Lt dow 25-5-17 1/7BlkW p231 CR France97

ANDERSON,James Morton 2Lt kia 1-5-17 C70RFA p24 CR France1182

ANDERSON,James Parker 2Lt ded 26-12-18 4SfthH p269 CR Scot199

ANDERSON,James Richard Haig Lt kia 11-5-15 2CamH p167 MR29

ANDERSON,James Skelton T2Lt dow 10-10-16 21KRRC p148 CR France833

ANDERSON,J.L.K. 2Lt kia about31-5-18 SL &RAF p201

ANDERSON,J.P Lt 9-6-20 IndDefForce 37Bn CR India97A

ANDERSON,John Capt ded 17-5-18 RAMC p253 MR43

ANDERSON,John Alexander 2Lt kia 21-3-18 2/4ELancs p226 MR27

ANDERSON,John Frederick Capt&Adjt kld 14-7-15 2 att10HLI p162 CR France727

ANDERSON,John Gavin Lt kia 3-5-17 212MGC Inf p181 CR France644

ANDERSON,John George.MC.MID Capt kia 21-3-18 RAMC att1/6BlkW p255 MR20

ANDERSON,John Macnabb Lt kia 17-6-15 3 att2RScots p53 MR29

ANDERSON,John Turnbull 2Lt kia 5-10-17 20MGC Inf p181 MR30

ANDERSON,John Victor Cortlandt Capt kia 8-6-18 IA CpsofGuides p273 CR Palestine9

ANDERSON,John William T2Lt kia 17-8-16 7CamH p167 MR21

ANDERSON,Jonas William.MC.Maj dow 26-3-18 RAMC 3FA p253 CR France103

ANDERSON,Joseph Henry 2Lt kia 9-12-17 21Lond p251 CR Palestine3,2/22Bn

ANDERSON,Lawrence 2Lt kia 11-10-15 4Lincs p217 MR19

ANDERSON,Leigh Maxwell Lt ded 3-2-15 9RInniskF p264 see below

ANDERSON,Leigh Maxwell TLt ded 1-9-15 9RIrFus p170&p264 CR Ireland71

ANDERSON,Macclesfield Heptinstall Maj kia 29-4-15 IA 33Cavalry p273 MR61

ANDERSON,Martin Alan.MC.Capt dow 9-5-17 RE 211FC p43 CR France113,Maj

ANDERSON,Mathew Capt kia 22-8-16 9HLI p240 CR France402

ANDERSON,Matthew T2Lt kia 11-6-17 6KOSB p101 CR France604

ANDERSON,Max Edward Alwyn TCapt dow 13-9-16 14Lpool p71 CR Greece6

ANDERSON,Mervyn Kebble T2Lt dow 11-5-15 2RIrReg p88 CR France102

ANDERSON,Norman Ruthven Maj kld By Sepoy 20-11-14 IA 130Baluchis p273 MR65

ANDERSON,Patrick Alexander T2Lt kld 19-10-17 GL &RFC p4 CR Scot235

ANDERSON,Percival Robert T2Lt kia 12-10-15 13WYorks p80 CR Gallipoli27

ANDERSON,Percy Hume Aufrey Capt kia 5-9-15 21Lancers p23 MR43,Allfrey

ANDERSON,Peter Johnson Lt kia 19-4-17 1/11Lond p248 CR Palestine8,ANDERSEN P Johansen

ANDERSON,P.G.Rodney LtCol 14-6-16 76Punjabis MR65

ANDERSON,Philip Maurice Ramsey.MID 2Lt dow 24-2-15 3RIrReg p88 CR France284

ANDERSON,Reginald D'Arcy Maj ded 14-8-17 RGA AOrdDept 384SB p38 MR38

ANDERSON,Reginald Dudley Bawawen 2Lt kia 1-7-16 15Y&L p158 CR France1492,Bawdwen

ANDERSON,Richard William Laurence T2Lt ded 12-6-17 GL &1RFC p4 Cr Belgium115,FltLt

ANDERSON,Robert 2Lt dow 23-3-18 2RScots p53 CR France103

ANDERSON,Robert Lt drd 29-5-18 SL &RE IWT p201 MR38

ANDERSON,Robert Ballantine Lt kia 19-4-17 1/4KOSB p223 CR Palestine8

ANDERSON,Robert Brown Lt ded 15-2-19 5RScotF p269 CR Kent129

ANDERSON,Robert Coventry 2Lt dow 4-11-17 282RFA p24 CR Belgium16

ANDERSON,Robert Cunningham Capt dow 27-9-15 1BlkW p128 CR France178,kia 26-9-15

ANDERSON,Robert Graham Lt kia 12-11-17 1/1GloucYeo p203 CR Palestine8

ANDERSON,Robert Lionel Lt drd 7-11-18 406RASC p192 CR France34

ANDERSON,Robertson Topping.MC.Lt kia 24-10-18 9HLI p240 CR France230

ANDERSON,Samuel Stephen 2Lt kia 30-12-15 5RScotF p222 CR Gallipoli6

ANDERSON,Thomas Binnie T2Lt dow 22-11-16 1BlkW p128 CR France397

ANDERSON,Vincent Tollemach T2Lt dow 13-4-18 1MGC p181 CR France88

ANDERSON,William.MC.2Lt kld 21-9-18 RGA114HB att7RAF p38 CR Belgium18

ANDERSON,Walter Kinloch LtACapt kia 22-7-18 5BlkW p230 CR France1695

ANDERSON,Wilfred Cruttenden Lt kia 30-10-14 2Beds p85 MR29

ANDERSON,William TLt kia 25-9-15 10ScotRif p103 MR19

ANDERSON,William T2Lt dow 23-4-17 11 att9BlkW p128 CR France113

ANDERSON,William 2Lt kia 4-6-17 1LovatScts p204 CR France1182

ANDERSON,William TLt dow 27-3-18 217RE p43 CR France185

ANDERSON,William TCapt ded 25-7-18 1LancF p91 CR Hamps57

ANDERSON,William TLt kia 20-10-18 15RIrRif p168 CR Belgium140,20Bn

ANDERSON,William Angus 2Lt ded 8-12-18 5A&SH p172 CR France1858 see below

ANDERSON,William Arthur 2Lt ded 8-12-18 6A&SH &RAF p255

ANDERSON,William Bruce.MC.2Lt kia 7-3-17 1/5GordH p242 CR France15,7-4-17

ANDERSON,William Christian Col ded 28-6-17 79RFA p261 CR Scot774

ANDERSON,William Francis Capt dow 10-12-15 3RFus p66 CR Belgium59,15-2-15

ANDERSON,William Francis Outram 2Lt kia 23-4-17 4GordH p242 CR France604

ANDERSON,William Harold 2Lt kia 13-6-17 5BordR p228 CR Belgium168

ANDERSON,William Henry Lt ded 4-12-18 RGA p38 CR Kent61

ANDERSON,William Herbert.VC.TMajALtCol kia 26-3-18 12HLI p162 CR France630,25-3-18

ANDERSON,William James Maj kia 19-10-15 WRidHQstaff 9ArmyCps p115 CR Gallipoli6

ANDERSON,William K.Lt ded 7-1-18 RFC CR Canada1430

ANDERSON,William Trevor Lt ded 8-4-17 6SfthH attRFC p269 CR Scot874,12-4-17

ANDERSON,William Wallace 2Lt kia 10-11-16 15RFA 526HB p24 CR France462

ANDERSON,W.J.Capt 26-8-17 EAMS CR EAfrica58

ANDERSON-MORSHEAD,Rupert Henry.DSO.MIDx3 CaptALtCol kia 27-5-18 Dev p76 MR18

ANDERTON,Albert.MC&2Bars.LtAMaj dow 5-4-18 110RFA p24 CR France5,kia

ANDERTON,Edwards Lt ded 30-11-18 EAfrCensorDept CR EAfrica19

ANDERTON,Frank Westall 2Lt kia 1-7-16 3 att1LancF p91 CR France1492

ANDERTON,George Eric Asquith.MID Lt kia 22-3-18 LancF att119MGC p91&181 MR20

ANDERTON,James Devereux T2Lt kia 13-11-16 10Suff p77 CR France802

ANDERTON,William Frederick T2Lt kia 31-3-17 A15RFA p24 CR France68,Frederic

ANDERTON,William Lyon 2Lt kia 21-8-15 4WRid p227 MR29

ANDRE,Frederick William 2Lt kia 16-8-17 8Mddx p236 MR30

ANDREW,Arthur 2Lt kia 23-11-17 1Lond p245 MR17

ANDREW,Ellen ARRC Sister kia 21-3-18 TFNS att 58CCS CR France ?

ANDREW,Ernest John Lt kia 23-3-18 10 att1EYorks p83 MR27

ANDREW,Frank 2Lt kia 23-4-17 7BordR p116 MR20

ANDREW,Frank Douglas 2Lt dow 31-3-18 PoW 7Manch p237 CRFrance441,Lt

ANDREW,Frederick 2LtTLt kia 27-2-15 EYorks attWAfrR p83&200 CR WAfrica28,2Lt

ANDREW,Harold Lt kia 14-7-16 24Manch p154 MR21

ANDREW,Harry Townsend T2Lt kia 25-6-16 RE 96FC p43 CR Belgium6

ANDREW,Herbert Leslie 2Lt ded 14-10-18 6RWar att137PoWCoyLabCps p214 CR France146

ANDREW,James Lionel 2Lt kld 13-12-17 RFC SR p4 CR Herts87

ANDREW,John 2Lt kia 1-7-16 3 att10YLI p142 CR France267

ANDREW,John James T2Lt dow 29-4-17 20NumbF p60 CR France40

ANDREW,Malcolm TLt kia 4-11-18 LancF att104TMB p91 CR France206

ANDREW,Robert Lt kia 8-5-17 12A&SH p172 MR37

ANDREW,William Dickie 2Lt kia 22-3-18 10 att15RScots p212 MR20

ANDREW-MARSHALL,Joseph Lt kia 20-11-17 6Lond att B'TankCps p246 MR17

ANDREWES,Charles Nesfield T2Lt ded 29-11-18 8LabCps p266 CR Kent154,ANDREWS

ANDREWES,George Lancelot LtCol ded 17-9-16 5Suff p269 CR Suff225,Col

ANDREWS,Alan Charles Findlay 2Lt kia 29-6-15 16RFus p66 MR4

ANDREWS,Alfred George T2Lt dow 14-10-18 4Mddx p145 CR France146

ANDREWS,Archibald TLtACapt dow 30-5-17 RFA 23DAC p24 CR Belgium11,29-5-17

ANDREWS,Arthur Alfred Capt ded 16-10-18 11Hamps p120 CR Hamps1

ANDREWS,Bertram John William T2Lt dow 31-7-17 13RSuss p118 CR Belgium16

ANDREWS,Charles Capt ded 21-7-18 RAOC p198 CR Essex118

ANDREWS,Charles Edward Maj kia 25-10-16 11HLI p162 CR France151

ANDREWS,Charles George Williams Capt kia 28-10-14 2BordR p116 MR29

ANDREWS,Charles Nesfield see ANDREWES,C.N.

ANDREWS,Charles Neville 2Lt kia 24-3-15 3LNLancs p135 CR France632

ANDREWS,Charles Raymond Capt kia 24-5-15 2Ches p95 MR29

ANDREWS,Charles William T2Lt kia 13-4-17 10WYorks p80 MR20

ANDREWS,E.C.H.MBE.Lt 17-5-20 RGA CR Lond29

ANDREWS,Eric Bernard 2Lt kia 16-9-18 RFA &RAF p208&258 CR France1252

ANDREWS,Edward Norman 2Lt dow 22-8-18 3EKent p57 CR France119,23-8-18

ANDREWS,Edwin Charles T2Lt ded 12-8-18 8RWKent p140 CR Hamps186

ANDREWS,Ellen Sister TFNS kia 21-3-18 p254 see ANDREW,E.

ANDREWS,Eric Cauty T2Lt kia 12-10-16 RE 9FC p43 MR21

ANDREWS,Francis Nicholas T2Lt dow 11-10-15 15RIrRif p168 CR France34,Lt

ANDREWS,Frank Henry.MC.2Lt kia 11-8-18 3 att1Glouc p106 MR19

ANDREWS,Frederick Charles 2Lt kia 16-3-15 3Leinst p174 CR France1141,2Bn

ANDREWS,Frederick Dudley.MC.Lt kia 14-8-17 1/4Glouc p225 CR Belgium27

ANDREWS,Frederick George Lt kia 21-10-14 4Lpool att2SLancs p71 MR22

ANDREWS,Frederick Seymour T2Lt dow 29-4-17 GL &13RFC p4 CR France40

ANDREWS,Geoffrey Fleetwood T2Lt dow 16-9-18 RGA 499SB p38 CR France526

ANDREWS,George Leonard TCapt kia 3-5-18 RGA 76SB p38 CR France41

ANDREWS,Glyndwr Levi TCapt kia 21-8-18 19 att16RWelshF p97 CR France432

ANDREWS,Hector George Robert Frank Lt kia 28-6-15 14WYorks p80 MR4

ANDREWS,Henry George 2Lt kia 25-3-18 1/7LancF p221 MR20

ANDREWS,Henry John.VC.MBE.TCapt kia 22-10-19 IMS p273 MR43

ANDREWS,Herbert George TLt kia 19-4-17 16Mddx p145 CR France418

ANDREWS,Horace Gibson TCapt kia 7-6-17 8Y&L p158 CR Belgium167

ANDREWS,James Alfrey Capt kia 1-7-16 2Dev p76 CR France1890,Allfrey

ANDREWS,John Alfred Raymond 2Lt kld 14-4-18 6Lincs attRAF p74 CR France31,kia

ANDREWS,John Leonard.MM.T2Lt dow 19-5-18 10RFus p66 CR France145,Lt

ANDREWS,Joseph Hamilton Millar 2Lt dow 16-8-17 11RIrRif p168 CR Belgium84

ANDREWS,Leigh Courtney T2Lt kia 3-7-16 9Lincs p74 MR21

ANDREWS,Leslie Ernest.MC.TCaptAMaj kia 20-9-17 10RWSurr p55 MR30

ANDREWS,Maynard Percy.MID Capt kia 15-8-15 4WRid p227 CR Belgium67

ANDREWS,Percy Heath Lt dow 28-3-18 RE 151 reposted73FC p43 CR France113,kia

ANDREWS,Reginald Lt kia 31-7-17 7LancF p221 MR29

ANDREWS,Reginald Hugo Catchpole 2Lt kia 8-5-17 12A&SH p172 MR37

ANDREWS,Robert Freeman T2Lt kia 15-11-16 10LNLancs p135 CR France533,Lt

ANDREWS,Robert Hutchinson T2Lt kia 25-9-15 1RIrRif p168 CR France684

ANDREWS,Sidney Mottram Capt 8-10-18 RAOC p198 CR France85

ANDREWS,Walter Capt kia 14-4-15 IA 95Inf att120Inf p273 CR Iraq6

ANDREWS,William 2Lt kia 25-4-15 1RDubF p176 CR Gallipoli15,26-4-15

ANDREWS,William Ernest LtTCapt kia 2-8-15 RIrRif p168 CR Belgium101

ANDREWS,William James Morrison T2Lt kld 4-6-17 GL &RFC p4 CR Ireland229

ANDREWS,William Thomas 2Lt kia 11-1-17 IARO 87Punjabis att2/124Baluchis p273 CR Iraq5

ANGAS,Lionel George T2Lt kia 3-5-17 3 att7Beds p85 MR20

ANGELL,Benjamin Eyre Lt kia 20-2-17 1KAR p202 CR EAfrica40

ANGELL,Geoffrey 2Lt kia 13-5-15 IA 1/8 att2/8GurkhaRif CR France631 p273

ANGLES,Robert.MC.T2Lt dow 13-11-17 Y&L p158 CR Durham182

ANGLISS,Henry James.DCM.Lt kld 21-11-20 RInniskF CR Lond1

ANGOOD,Percival George 2Lt kld 12-9-17 RFC p4 CR Camb84,11-9-17

ANGUS,H.C.2Lt 6-6-21 MGC Motors CR Scot235

ANGUS,James Robert ALtCol drd 17-9-17 16WelshR att11SWBord p126 CR France275

ANGUS,Leonard John Lt&QM drd 20-8-15 9Mddx p269 CR Herts30

ANGUS,Norman John 2Lt dow 18-9-17 4 att9GordH p242 CR France40

ANGUS,Raymond Brocklehurst 2Lt kia 22-9-15 RE p210 CR Gallipoli3

ANGUS,Robert Edward Lt kia 20-11-17 AyrYeo attRFC p17&203 MR20

ANGUS,Stewart 2Lt kia 2-7-16 RE 1FC p210 MR21,1-7-16

ANGUS,William John T2Lt kia 29-10-16 RScotF att1ScotRif p94 MR21,31-10-16

ANKER,Albert George Lt ded 8-8-19 8Lincs p263 CR Germany1

ANKETELL,Charles Edward.MM.2Lt kld 11-5-18 RFus att206RAF p66 CR France134

ANKETELL-JONES,John Hobart Capt ded 16-11-19 5Lancers attEgyptArmy RoO p261 CR EAfrica116

ANNAHEIM,George Herbert.MID TLt kia 4-10-18 1RMunstF p175 CR France256

ANNAND,Allan Young T2Lt kia 11-1-17 1HLI p162 MR38

ANNANDALE,F.W.Lt 29-3-20 3SStaffs CR Scot269

ANNE,Crathorn Edward Isham Charlton TMaj drd 15-4-17 GL &RFC p4 MR35

ANNELY,Ernest George 2Lt kia 4-5-17 5WYorks p218 MR20,3-5-17

ANNESLEY,Albemarle Cator.DSO.LtCol dow 8-7-16 8RFus p66 CR France44,7-7-16

ANNESLEY,Hon.Arthur Capt kia 15-11-14 10Huss p22 CR Belgium57,16-11-14

ANNESLEY,James Ferguson St.John TCapt ded 20-5-17 RAMC p267 CR Suff173,19-5-17

ANNESLEY,James Howard Adolphus.CMG.DSO.LtCol ded 22-4-19 1DragGds Ret p261 CR Surrey160

ANNESLEY,William Richard Norton.DSO.Maj 29-11-14 RWKent CR Scot142

ANNETT,Hugh Clarkson 2Lt kia 15-9-16 6DLI p239 CR France387

ANNS,Frederick 2Lt kia 6-11-15 4 att2Beds p85 CR France279

ANSCOMBE,Gilbert Allen Henry 2Lt kia 1-2-17 IARO att36Sikhs p273 CR Iraq5

ANSELL,Arthur George T2Lt dow 25-4-18 RE 1FdSurvCo p43 CR France102

ANSELL,George Kirkpatrick LtCol kia 1-9-14 5DragGds p21 CR France1230

ANSELL,Harry Clements 2Lt 9-5-20 RASC MT CR War134

ANSELL,Thomas ACapt kia 23-10-16 2ScotRif p103 MR21

ANSON,Arthur Lt kia 8-10-15 3GrenGds p49 CR France1726,11-10-15

ANSON,George Lechmere Capt kia 20-10-14 2N&D p133 MR32

ANSON,Harris Hartis 2Lt kia 30-8-18 5WRid p227 CR France421,Hortas

ANSON,Henry Percy Richmond Capt&Adjt kia 25-5-15 1 att8Mddx p145 CR Belgium46

ANSON,Nigel Frederick Edward.MC.2Lt kia 10-7-17 5 att2KRRC p148 MR31

ANSON,Stanley Edmund T2Lt kia 4-6-16 1EYorks p83 CR France189

ANSON,Walter Frank Vernon 2Lt kia 8-11-17 1/6RWelshF p223 CR Israel1

ANSTEE,Joseph 2Lt kia 1-7-16 2Lincs p74 MR21

ANSTEY,Alexander Burgess T2Lt kld 22-2-18 RFC p15 CR Oxford74

ANSTEY,George Alexander Capt kia 24-6-15 1Dev att2Ches p76 CR Belgium37

ANSTEY,Henry T2Lt kia 11-4-17 7RB p177 CR France532

ANSTICE,John Spencer Ruscombe.MID Lt kia 2-5-15 2RFus p66 CR Gallipoli2

ANSTIE,Edward Basil 2Lt kia 23-3-18 6 att2RB p177 MR27

ANSTRUTHER,John Arnold St.C.Lt kia 26-12-14 6DragGds att2LifeGds p21 MR29,30-10-14

ANSTRUTHER,R.E.MC.Capt 22-7-21 BlkW CR Scot92

ANTHONY,Albert Frederick T2Lt dow 10-4-18 18WelshR p126 CR France1094

ANTHONY,Clarence Case TCapt dow 15-12-15 13RFus p66 CR France1016

ANTHONY,Charles Stanley 2Lt kia 19-9-18 1/4Nhampt p234 CR Palestine9

ANTHONY,George Adam Moriarty Lt kia 24-1-16 9RWSurr attNigR p55&201 CR WAfrica56

ANTHONY,Henry Leonard Capt kia 2-5-17 RAVC 1/1LancsMobileSect p254 CR France1182

ANTHONY,John Richard Capt dow 25-5-17 6RWelshF att1RFC p17&223 CR Belgium18

ANTHONY,Percy TMaj kia 10-7-16 15WelshR p126 MR21

ANTHONY,Thomas Vaughan 2Lt kia 10-8-15 4Ches p222 MR4

ANTON,Edwin Vincent 2Lt kia 17-5-17 6 att5GordH p242 MR20,16-5-17

ANTROBUS,Cecil Hugh TCapt kia 26-9-15 6CamH p167 MR19

ANTROBUS,Charles Alexander Capt kia 25-4-15 KOSB p101 CR Gallipoli6

ANTROBUS,Edmund Lt kia 24-10-14 1GrenGds p49 MR29

ANTROBUS,Norman Briggs TCapt kia 1-10-15 4SLancs p229 CR Belgium28,2-10-15

APERGIS,Tassi Scott See ARERGIS,T.S

APLIN,Elphinstone D'Oyly Lt dow 13-5-15 2Glouc p106 CR France284

APLIN,Eric Scott LtACapt dow 11-3-18 2Worc p107 CR Belgium3

APLIN,Kenneth Sharland 2Lt kia 1-11-14 2RInniskF att2Bn p104 MR32,Shorland

APPELBEE,Thomas T2Lt kia 20-8-16 15WYorks p80 CR France727

APPERLEY,Basil Lang Marling T2Lt dow 19-4-17 8RWKent p140 CR France40,APPERLY 6Bn

APPERLEY,Charles Milton 2Lt kia 24-3-18 51MGC Inf p181 CR France924,28-3-18

APPERLY,B.L.M. see above

APPERLY,Arthur Lancelot 2Lt kia 27-8-16 5Glouc p225 MR21

APPLEBY,Eric 2Lt dow 28-10-16 48/2RFA p24 CR France105

APPLEBY,John Gill TLt kia 14-7-16 8SLancs p125 MR21

APPLEBY,Robert Charles Alfred Lt dow 28-6-16 1 att13RScots p53 CR France423

APPLEBY,Sidney Derrick 2Lt kia 18-7-17 11 att8LNLancs p135 MR29

APPLEGARTH,Thomas Forster 2Lt kia 5-11-16 6DLI p239 CR France385

APPLEGARTH,Thomas William T2Lt dow 20-3-18 PoW 11DLI p160 CR France652,ded 8-4-18

APPLETON,Aaron 2Lt kia 17-3-17 RFA &RFC p208 MR20

APPLETON,Francis Martin.VD.Maj ded 6-12-14 4SLancs p269 CR Kent267

APPLETON,Henry Metcalfe Capt ded 26-1-18 1DragGds &4RRofCav p261 CR Hamps1

APPLETON,Percy Robert Agnew 2Lt kia 3-5-17 4WRid p227 MR20

APPLETON,Richard Aidan Lt kia 21-3-18 2DLI p160 MR20

APPLEYARD,Benjamin Sydney T2Lt kia 29-9-18 6 att2Yorks p89 CR France273

APPLEYARD,Harry Elston T2Lt kia 14-7-16 12WYorks p80 CR France453

APPLEYARD,James Eric.MC.Capt kia 20-7-18 8WYorks p219 CR France622

APPLEYARD,John Ernest.MC.Lt kia 26-4-18 RE 222FC p43 CR France180

APPLEYARD,Richard TLt kia 4-8-16 14 att10N&D p133 CR France151,11Bn

APPLEYARD,William TLt kia 22-8-15 6Yorks p89 MR4

APPLIN,Geoffrey Walter Henry T2Lt kia 1-7-16 1Lincs p74 MR21

APPLIN,Richard 2Lt kia 29-4-17 GL &19RFC p4 MR20

APPS,Jack Harry Mason T2Lt kia 20-11-17 1NumbF p60 CR France1489,1/5Bn

APPS,Reginald Denman 2Lt kia 17-5-15 1RBerks p138 MR22

APSIMON,Arthur Injwerm TLt dow 4-8-17 14RWelshF p97 CR Belgium23,Tryweryn

APTED,Eardley Lt kia 1-8-17 9 att11RWSurr p55 MR29,Capt

ARBER,Archibald Guy T2Lt kia 21-10-15 BordR att1/7HLI p116 CR Gallipoli3

ARBERY,Ernest Edward T2Lt kia 6-6-17 GL &RFC p4 CR Belgium171

ARBERY,Frederick James TCapt dow 9-10-17 1DCLI p113 CR France139

ARBUCKLE,Hubert Hugh T2Lt kia 2-9-18 2RIrReg p88 CR France646

ARBUTHNOT,Aliser Dare Staveley Capt kia 8-3-16 RE att20S&M p43 MR38

ARBUTHNOT,Ashley Herbert Capt dow 15-5-15 12Lond p248 CR France1

ARBUTHNOT,Gavin Campbell 2Lt dow 6-8-15 7NStaffs p156 MR4

ARBUTHNOT,Gerald Archibald Lt kia 25-9-16 2GrenGds SR p49 CRFrance394

ARBUTHNOT,Hugh Hamilton 2Lt dow 28-12-15 IA 67Punjabis p273 CR Iraq1

ARBUTHNOT,John TLt dow 18-9-16 2GrenGds p49 CR France329,16-9-16

ARBUTHNOT,Kenneth Wyndham Maj kia 25-4-15 2SfthH p164 CR Belgium129,Windham

ARBUTHNOT,Lenox Stanley Capt kld 1-11-18 SL &RAF p201

ARBUTHNOT,Maurice Armitage.MC.LtTCapt ded 14-10-18 16Lancers p22 CR Surrey72

ARBUTHNOT,Ronald George Urquart Lt kld 3-12-18 16Lancers attRAF p22 CR Herts10

ARBUTHNOT,William John Capt 9-1-17 IARO att5Sikhs MR38

ARCH,Arthur James T2Lt dow 27-5-18 2RB p177 CR France1107

ARCHBOLD,John 2Lt kia 19-6-17 232RFA p208 CR Belgium34

ARCHBOLD,William Heslehurst T2Lt dow 21-10-18 RE 228FC p43 CR Belgium11

ARCHBUTT,William Henry Maj ded 8-2-15 9Manch p237 CR Egypt9

ARCHDALE,Charles William Capt kia 20-11-17 5 att7Norf p216 MR17

ARCHDALE,Dominick Mervyn TLt kia 13-11-16 1KAR attNyasaVolRes p202 CR EAfrica40

ARCHDALE,George Mervyn 2Lt dow 30-4-17 3 att1Berks p138 CR France95

ARCHDALE,Theodore Montgomery.DSO.LtCol drd 10-10-18 RHA p24 CR Eire3

ARCHDALE-PORTER,John Grey.DSO.CaptAMaj dow 22-11-17 9Lancers p22 CR France439

ARCHDALL,Nicholas James Mervyn Maj kia 25-9-15 3 att5CamH p167 MR19

ARCHER,Albert Erskine Carson 2Lt kia 9-2-16 EKent att242RFC p2&57 CR France134

ARCHER,Eli Townend 2Lt kia 23-7-16 1/4YLI p235 MR21

ARCHER,Harry.DSO.MID LtAMaj kia 25-11-17 2Dev p76 MR30

ARCHER,Henry Charles 2Lt kia 8-10-18 1Mon p244 CR France1710

ARCHER,John William Butts Lt dow 16-2-15 2EKent p57 MR29

ARCHER,Ronald Hedley T2Lt dow 27-12-17 1NumbF p60 CR France512

ARCHER,Thomas Lt kia 25-4-18 6KOSB p101 CR Belgium393

ARCHER,Walter Dunlop 2Lt kia 25-4-18 6WYorks p218 MR30

ARCHER-SHEE,George Lt kia 31-10-14 3 att2SStaffs p121 MR29

ARCHIBALD,James Duncan TLt dow 20-7-16 10Ess p131 CR France66

ARCHIBALD,John.MC&Bar.Capt dow 31-3-18 6GordH p242 CR France40

ARCHIBALD,Max Stanfield Eaton.MC.MID 2Lt dow 12-5-18 RE att18RAF p43 CR France95,kia

ARCHIBALD,William Maj dow 18-6-15 RE p209 CR Gallipoli6

ARDEN,Humphrey Warwick 2Lt dow 6-6-17 RGA 156HB p38 CR.France285

ARDEN,John Henry Morris.DSO.MID LtCol ded 22-7-18 25NumbF attRAF 2 att3CadetWing RoO p60 CR Egypt1

ARDEN,Reginald Douglas 2Lt kia 8-10-18 1/1Lond p245 MR21

ARDILL,Ivan Roy 2Lt kia 25-9-15 8KOSB p101 MR19

AREND,Ronald Sydney 2Lt kia 23-3-18 12RScots p53 MR27

ARERGIS,Tasso Scott 2Lt kia 10-9-18 10 att16Lond p248 MR21,APERGIS Tassi 10-9-16

ARGYLE,Percival Edgar T2Lt kia 9-4-17 1ELancs p110 CR France452

ARIS,Thomas Arthur TLt kia 16-4-17 23RFus p66 CR France1191

ARKCOLL,Frederick Thomas T2Lt kia 30-6-16 10 att7RSuss p118 MR19 12Bn

ARKLE,Norman Armitage T2Lt kia 1-7-16 20NumbF p60 MR21

ARKLESS,John William T2Lt kia 30-12-15 17 att15DLI p160 CR France1140

ARKWRIGHT,Frederick George Alleyne Capt kld 14-10-15 11Huss &RFC p22 CR Derby122,Frederic

ARMATAGE,Robert T2Lt dow 6-6-17 21NumbF p60 CR France95

ARMER,Arthur T2Lt kia 5-9-17 BordR att11Bn p116 CR Belgium24

ARMES,Raymond Linay TCapt kia 9-4-16 7NStaffs p156 MR38

ARMES,William Morriss.TD.LtCol kia 12-8-15 5Suff p217 MR4

ARMFIELD,Archie Seaward 2Lt kia 31-7-17 2IrGds p52 CR Belgium12

ARMISTEAD,Tom Elsworth.MC.2Lt kia 3-5-17 6WYorks p218 MR20

ARMIT,Napier.MC.Capt kia 4-8-16 16RScots p53 MR21

ARMITAGE,Alfred Cecil 2Lt kld 21-7-15 1RWSurr p55 CR France571

ARMITAGE,Arthur William Capt kia 1-10-16 8YLI p142 CR France239

ARMITAGE,Douglas William 2Lt kia 25-9-15 9RSuss p118 MR19

ARMITAGE,Eric 2Lt dow 4-10-17 46RFC p4 CR France49

ARMITAGE,Edward Stoney 2Lt kia 29-8-18 76RFA p24 CR France927

ARMITAGE,Ernest George T2Lt kia 14-7-18 RE 4SpecCo p43 CR France547

ARMITAGE,Francis Arthur William.DSO.MajALtCol kia 22-4-18 1WYorks att1Hamps p80 CR France250

ARMITAGE,Frank Rhodes.DSO.Capt kia 30-7-17 RAMC att232RFA p253 CR Belgium7

ARMITAGE,Geoffrey Ambler TCapt kia 27-2-17 16WYorks p80 CR France580

ARMITAGE,George T2Lt kia 16-9-16 6DCLI p113 MR21

ARMITAGE,George Duncan T2Lt kia 6-8-15 11ESurr att2Hamps p111 MR4

ARMITAGE,George Jones 2Lt kia 17-6-17 GL &4RFC p4 CR Belgium10

ARMITAGE,J.A.R.Capt 19-7-19 15WYorks p52 CR Sussex178

ARMITAGE,John Basil Capt kia 17-5-17 5Ches p222 CR France581

ARMITAGE,Laurie Ritchie.MC.T2Lt dow 25-11-16 9WRid p115 CR Yorks447,Lt

ARMITAGE,Noel Lt kia 25-4-18 2/3ScotHorse att12Glouc p205 CR France18

ARMITAGE,Sidney Robert Lt kia 11-5-17 RASC NMidDivTrn p253 CR France223

ARMITAGE,William Harold TLt kia 22-5-16 9Yorks p89 CR France559

ARMOUR,Robert Stanley.MID TCapt ded 1-12-18 RAMC p194 CR EAfrica36,Maj

ARMSTRONG,Allan.DSO.LtCol dow 19-9-18 1/4Wilts p152 CR Palestine9

ARMSTRONG,Arthur Keith Capt dow 15-9-14 RAMC p194 MR15

ARMSTRONG,Arthur Sutcliffe Capt dow 31-5-17 1/1Camb p244 CR Belgium11

ARMSTRONG,Cecil 2Lt kia 21-9-16 12DLI p160 CR France703

ARMSTRONG,Charles Arthur MajTLtCol kia 1-10-15 2NumbF p60 CR France423

ARMSTRONG,Charles MacDonald 2Lt kia 25-9-16 10YLI p142 MR21,McDonald

ARMSTRONG,Charles Martin T2Lt kia 8-2-17 10RDubF p176 CR France339

ARMSTRONG,Christopher 2Lt kia 9-4-16 14RFus att6NLancs p66 CR Iraq5

ARMSTRONG,Denys Lt dow 3-10-16 5NumbF p213 CR France385,kia

ARMSTRONG,Edward Randolph Maj ded 25-2-21 IMS p273 MR43

ARMSTRONG,Edward William 2Lt dow 11-7-15 6 att3RB p177 CR Belgium11

ARMSTRONG,Ellen.MID Sister 20-3-19 QAIMNS CR France146

ARMSTRONG,Foster Moore Maj kia 25-9-17 251Numb RFA CR France592

ARMSTRONG,Frederick Edmund John Lt ded 27-10-19 IARO att1/69Punjabis p273 MR43

ARMSTRONG,George Canning Staples Lt kia 3-5-17 3RIrFus p170 CR France604

ARMSTRONG,George Pierce Lt kia 2-7-15 IA 34Sikhs p273 CR France768

ARMSTRONG,Gwin Henry TLt ded 28-10-18 Norf att4NigR p73&202 CR WAfrica40

ARMSTRONG,Guy Spearman 2Lt kia 28-9-15 ScotGds att1Bn p51 MR19,27-9-15

ARMSTRONG,George Carlyon 2Lt kia 25-1-15 CldGds att1Bn p50 MR22

ARMSTRONG,Harold 2Lt kia 14-11-16 21NumbF p60 MR21,28 att1/5Bn

ARMSTRONG,Harry William Thomas 2Lt dow 14-7-15 7ESurr p111 CR France922

ARMSTRONG,Helen Sister ded 20-3-19 QAIMNS p200

ARMSTRONG,Henry Leslie Lt kia 25-4-18 4 at6KOSB p223 MR30

ARMSTRONG,Henry Louis Winthrop T2Lt kia 29-11-15 7SomLI p79 CR France525

ARMSTRONG,Hilliard Mark T2Lt acckld 14-11-17 RFC p4 CR Scot235

ARMSTRONG,James Lt kia 28-3-17 RIM attRE IWT p273 MR64

ARMSTRONG,James Noble TLt kia 22-8-15 RAMC att2DLI p194 CR Belgium2

ARMSTRONG,John T2Lt kld 27-3-18 RFC p15 CR Ches28

ARMSTRONG,John Lewis Pasteur 2Lt kia 22-6-16 RASC att25RFC p17&253 CR France924,FltLt

ARMSTRONG,John Nicholas Fraser TMaj kia 5-7-16 RE 128FC p43 CR France372

ARMSTRONG,John Norman TLt dow 16-1-17 15 att8NumbF p60 CR France74,Capt

ARMSTRONG,John Owen 2Lt kia 15-7-16 10RFus p66 MR21

ARMSTRONG,John White T2Lt kia 21-10-18 20DLI p160 CR Belgium11

ARMSTRONG,Joseph Lt kia 5-5-17 2/4WelshRFA p207 CR France558

ARMSTRONG,Leonard William 2Lt kia 19-5-17 3 att1BordR p116 MR20

ARMSTRONG,Michael Richard Leader T2Lt kia 22-4-16 RE 150FC p43 CR France702

ARMSTRONG,R.V 2Lt 17-3-17 ImpCamCps Egypt CR Egypt2

ARMSTRONG,Sarah Jane Miss ded 12-12-18 VAD p200 CR Egypt9

ARMSTRONG,Sydney 2Lt kia 17-2-18 RFA attRFC p15&24 CR Essex211

ARMSTRONG,Sydney John 2Lt kia 26-9-15 12NumbF p60 MR19

ARMSTRONG,Thomas Herbert TLtACapt ded 15-5-17 13NumbF p60 CR France40,2Lt

ARMSTRONG,Walter Seymour TCapt ded 31-5-16 RAMC attMhowIndCavFA p194 CR France1,dow

ARMSTRONG,William Arthur 2Lt dow 26-10-18 3RInniskF p104 CR Ireland239

ARMSTRONG,William David 2Lt kia 12-10-18 1/4SfthH p241 CR France241

ARMSTRONG,William Kings Capt kia 11-4-18 4SLancs p229 MR19

ARMSTRONG,William Maurice(Pat).MC.MID Capt kia 23-5-17 10Huss att86BdeHQ p22 CR France1182

ARMSTRONG,William Wilberforce 2Lt kia 27-12-17 7BlkW p231 CR Palestine3

ARMSTRONG-DASH,Arthur Lt kia 22-4-18 12Lancf p91 CR Europe50/57A,dow 1-5-18

ARMSTRONG-LUSHINGTON-TULLOCK,Graham de Montmorency Lt kia 5-10-14 1ConnRgrs p172 CR France1157,Montmorencey 5-11-14

ARNAUD,Frederick Cooper T2Lt kia 1-7-16 GL 16NumbF attTMB p189 CR France293,Lt

ARNELL,Douglas Carstairs Capt kia 13-7-16 2Hamps p120 MR21

ARNELL,Reginald Brandt T2Lt kia 30-7-15 7KRRC p148 MR29

ARNEY,Frank Stanley 2Lt kia 18-4-18 RFA 1MedTMB p208 CR Greece5

ARNHOLTZ,Ronald Henry Preuss Lt kia 23-8-18 1Herts att1Beds p252 CR France239

ARNISON,Edward Burra 2Lt dow 18-8-18 14RGA 11SB p38 CR France526

ARNOLD,Alban Charles Phidias T2Lt kia 7-7-16 18 att6RFus p66 MR21

ARNOLD,Alfred Huntriss Capt dow 30-12-16 2WYorks p80 CR Surrey2

ARNOLD,Alfred Lewis 2Lt kia 15-8-17 22Lond p251 CR Belgium115,24Bn

ARNOLD,Arthur Douglas T2Lt kia 9-4-16 10 att9RWar p64 CR Iraq5

ARNOLD,Arthur Edward.MC.2Lt kia 13-10-18 RE 416FC p210 CR France429,Ernest MM

ARNOLD,Barnard Marcus 2Lt dow 6-2-16 7KRRC p265&181 CR France102

ARNOLD,Bernard Marcus T2Lt dow 6-2-16 MGC p181

ARNOLD,Bernard William LtACapt kia 21-3-18 87/2RFA p24 MR20

ARNOLD,Edward Gladwin.MID Lt kia 21-3-18 RFA 232ArmyBde p24 MR27

ARNOLD,Frank William 2Lt kia 30-11-17 1RGLI p200 MR17

ARNOLD,Frederick Arthur T2Lt dow 13-10-18 RWKent att6Bn p140 CR France106

ARNOLD,Frederick Marshall Lt kia 27-3-18 1/5 att9RWelshF p223 MR20

ARNOLD,Geoffrey Francis Capt kia 8-3-16 5SomLI p218 MR38

ARNOLD,Hedley Graham 2Lt kia 11-4-18 2SWBord p99 CR France297

ARNOLD,Henry 2Lt dow 10-10-18 Dev att9Bn p76 CR France52

ARNOLD,Herbert Edward 2Lt ded 26-12-16 GL &5RFC p2&189 CRFrance1484

ARNOLD,Hugh TLt kia 11-8-15 8NumbF p60 MR4

ARNOLD,Hugo Cholmondeley 2Lt dow 12-6-17 4EKent p212 CR France40

ARNOLD,Joseph T2Lt kia 2-9-18 18 att1/5Manch p154 CR France308

ARNOLD,Joseph V Lt 3-9-18 4RWFus attRAF CR Yorks33

ARNOLD,Karl Ferdinand Franck William Capt kia 23-4-15 1Suff p77 CR Belgium167

ARNOLD,Leonard Frank Cecil.MC.Lt dow 21-12-19 3Lond att82Punjabis p269&273 MR43

ARNOLD,Margaret Trevener Miss ded 12-3-16 VAD p200 CR France1

ARNOLD,Oliver Vaughan 2Lt dow 11-8-16 6 att2Worc p107 CR War135,Vaughton

ARNOLD,Peter Forrester Capt ded 8-8-18 8LancF &RAF p221 CR Egypt1

ARNOLD,Thomas Sorrell 2Lt dow 11-10-17 3ESurr att2/7LancF p111 CR Belgium3

ARNOLD,Thomas Wilson TLt dow 15-9-16 8Beds attGoldCoastR p201 CR EAfrica39

ARNOLD,Victor Capt kia 15-1-17 1/4EKent p212 MR38

ARNOT,Arthur Alison McDonald 2Lt kia 12-4-18 GL &3RAF p189 CR France220,Lt

ARNOT,Colin T2Lt kia 22-3-18 1Glouc p106 MR30

ARNOT,L.A.D. see ARNOTT,L.A.D.

ARNOTT,David William Lt kia 3-9-16 2RWar p64 MR19 &CR France1890

ARNOTT,Evan Edward 2Lt dow 23-9-16 2WelshR p126 CR France385,Euan

ARNOTT,Frederick 2Lt kia 29-3-18 11DLI p160 MR27

ARNOTT,John(Punch).MC.Capt kia 30-3-18 15Huss p22 CR France1172

ARNOTT,Kenneth Hugh Lowden.DSO.MC.CaptTLtCol kia 30-5-18 2ELancs att7KSLI p110 CR France33

ARNOTT,Laurian Anthony Deane T2Lt kia 25-9-15 2GordH p165 MR19,ARNOT

ARNOTT,Robert Louis Irving 2Lt kia 19-9-18 IA 3CofGs 1CpsofGuidesInf p273 MR34

ARNOTT,Thomas Henry.MM.Lt 18-3-21 5BordR CR C'land&W'land6

ARNOTT,Thomas John 2Lt kia 26-10-17 2GordH p165 MR30

ARNOTT,W.Lt 15-8-20 2ScotRif CR Scot241

ARNOULD,Derek Clement Lt ded 7-5-18 4RFus attRTE p66 CR France40

ARNSTRONG,Forster Moore Maj kia 25-9-17 RH&FA p206 see ARMSTRONG,F.M.

ARON,Frederick Adolphus TLt kia 23-8-18 2SLancs p125 MR30

ARROW,George William Lt ded 25-1-19 GL p189

ARTAUD,Gerald Frank Deveniere TLt kia 26-9-17 7KSLI p144 MR30

ARTHUR,Alexander.MC.MM.T2Lt dow 1-10-18 25NumbF att1/7Lpool p60 CR France214

ARTHUR,David.MC.Capt ded PoW 31-7-17 IMS p273 CR Iraq8

ARTHUR,George Stuart 2Lt kia 1-7-16 5Ches p222 MR21

ARTHUR,Henry Bartle Compton Maj kia 10-8-16 5RFA p24 CR France267

ARTHUR,Hugh.MC.Capt kia 29-5-18 LabCps att48ChineseLabCps p189 CR France88

ARTHUR,John T2Lt kia 26-9-15 8GordH p165 MR19,25-9-15

ARTHUR,John Richard Capt 9-2-17 S&T Cps MR43

ARTHUR,William Herbert T2Lt kld 13-12-17 GL &RFC p4 CR Hamps4

ARTHURS,Thomas Andrew TLt ded 6-12-18 GL &134ChineseLabCps p189 CRFrance85 T.A.A.Capt

ARUNDEL-SMITH,Harold Edward 2Lt kia 23-7-16 13Lpool p71 MR21,Ex9Lancers

ARUNDELL,Reinfred Tatton Capt kia 3-2-15 IA 2Rajputs p273 CR Egypt8

ASCROFT,Robert Geoffrey Lees 2Lt kia 4-6-15 10Manch p237 MR4

ASH,Alfred William 2Lt kia 13-6-18 KRRC att12Bn p148 MR20

ASH,Basil Claudius Lt kia 20-9-14 2N&D p133 MR15 &CR France1893

ASH,Edwin Alexander Rays TLt dow 26-4-18 11 att10LancF p91 CR Belgium38

ASH,Gilbert Stanley 2Lt kia 3-9-16 14Hamps p120 MR21

ASH,John Rev Chap4Cl 7-9-17 RAChDept att48DAC RFA p199 CR Belgium10

ASH,John Cuxton TLt kia 2-7-18 8 att2Beds p85 CR France44,Luxton 3-7-18

ASH,Wilfred John Lt kia 16-2-15 3Mddx p145 MR29

ASH,William Behne TCapt kia 16-8-17 8NumbF p60 MR30

ASH,William Claudius Casson.DSO.TLtCol dow 29-9-16 23Mddx p145&258 CR France40

ASHBURNER,Daniel T2Lt kia 10-12-16 13Lpool p71 CR France5

ASHBURNHAM,Cromer Maj ded 11-9-19 KRRC p265 CR Sussex177

ASHBY,Donald Jesse 2Lt kia 17-7-16 4EYorks p219 CR Belgium60

ASHBY,George William Capt kia 25-9-15 6Lond p246 CR France149

ASHBY,Henry Herbert T2Lt kia 28-9-15 att3Mddx p145 MR19

ASHBY,Howard Dudley.MC.Maj ded 7-4-19 RGA A/A Bty p38 CR Germany1

ASHBY,Leslie T2Lt kia 20-10-18 LancF att2/5Bn p91 CR Belgium420

ASHBY,Samuel Lt&QM ded 13-2-16 10BordR p116 CR Sussex200

ASHBY,Thomas Philip T2Lt kia 5-9-18 7RSuss p118 CR France511

ASHBY-BROWN,Kenneth Capt kia 14-4-17 5ScotRif p224

ASHCROFT,Edward Davey Capt dow 30-11-17 RE 7FC p43 CR Palestine9

ASHCROFT,Edward Stanley TLt dow 12-5-18 PoW 17Lpool p71 CR Belgium140

ASHCROFT,Ernest TLt kia 25-9-15 8Dev p76 MR19

ASHCROFT,Frederick T2Lt kia 9-4-17 Lpool att18Bn p71 CR France595

ASHCROFT,George 2Lt kia 3-7-17 5LNLancs p234 MR29,Lt 31-7-17

ASHCROFT,John T2Lt kia 2-10-18 1/2 att16LancF p91 CR France237

ASHCROFT,John Robson.MC.LtTCapt kia 23-3-18 4 att9ScotRif p103 CR France1893

ASHCROFT,William TLt kia 22-3-18 19Lpool p71 CR France672

ASHCROFT,William Worsley.MID TLtAMaj kia 11-4-18 25MGC Inf p181 MR32

ASHE,Edward Neville.MC.Capt kia 21-3-18 8 att16Manch p237 MR27

ASHER,Albert T2Lt kia 24-9-18 1/2 att1/5Leic p87 CR France699

ASHER,Kenneth John Penrith T2Lt kia 1-7-16 10YLI p142 CR France189

ASHER,Ronald Stuart 2Lt kia 21-9-17 GL &46RFC p4 CR France924

ASHFORD,Isaac Dobson T2Lt dow 26-1-18 199MGC Inf 41Div p181 CR Italy74,kia

ASHFORTH,Dudley Sutton T2Lt kia 15-9-16 8RB p177 MR21

ASHFORTH,Isaac John 2Lt dow 27-4-16 IARO att15Lancers p273

ASHINGTON,Henry Sherard Osborn TLtACapt dow 31-1-17 7EYorks p83 CR France785

ASHLEY,Claude T2Lt kia 1-7-16.15 att2NumbF p60 MR21,att22Bn

ASHLEY,James 2Lt kia 2-5-18 RLancs p58 MR19

ASHLEY,Maurice 2Lt kia 23-11-17 1RIrFus p170 MR17

ASHMAN,Sidney John.MC.T2Lt kia 10-10-18 13Mddx p145 CR France916

ASHMAN,Stanley TLt kia 3-5-17 5 O&BLI p129 MR20

ASHMEAD-BARTLETT,Francis George Coningsby Capt kia 13-11-16 4Beds p85 CR France220

ASHMORE,Geoffrey William Paley Lt drd 4-5-17 RE WesternSigCoy p210 CR Italy13

ASHTON,Alexander Leslie T2Lt kia 1-7-18 6RWSurr p55 CR France61,Lt

ASHTON,Cyril James TLtACapt dow 12-3-18 6RWKent p140 CR France345

ASHTON,Edward Deakin T2Lt kia 1-7-16 9 att19LancF p91 CR France251

ASHTON,Edward Kitton Venning Lt ded 4-12-18 IA 29Lancers p273 CR Egypt1,Kittow 55Rif

ASHTON,Frederick James T2Lt kia 21-3-18 1/2 att11Leic p87 MR20

ASHTON,Frederick William Rev ded 18-11-18 RAChDept p254

ASHTON,George Francis TLt kia 20-10-18 42MGC p181 CR France270

ASHTON,G.G. 2Lt kia 23-7-18 5WRid attRAF p227

ASHTON,Hardric Grey Lt dow 11-3-18 2/11Lond att25RFC p17&248 CR France88,Capt

ASHTON,Henry Oswald Lt kia 29-8-18 5Suff p217 CR France614

ASHTON,Herbert 2Lt kia 27-11-17 Y&L att2/5Bn p254 MR17

ASHTON,James Ormrod 2Lt 5-7-16 ACycCps att13Worc p181 MR21

ASHTON,John Richard Wilmot 2Lt dow 6-11-17 1/4ELancs p226 CR France1361

ASHTON,Robert Mark.DCM.T2Lt kia 7-11-17 1/12LNLancs att2/19Lond p135 CR Israel1

ASHTON,Roger Hay 2Lt kia 30-7-16 2RScotF p94 MR21

ASHWELL,Alfred T2Lt kia 4-4-17 1 att10KRRC p148 CR France415

ASHWIN,Guy John Hamilton Lt kia 7-11-16 5DLI p238 CR France385

ASHWORTH,Brian Wilding T2Lt dow 4-8-17 11RWKent p140 CR France139

ASHWORTH,Edgar 2Lt kia 22-9-17 4 att6Ches p222 CR Belgium112

ASHWORTH,Edward Rose T2Lt kia 28-3-18 5MGC Inf p181 CR France777

ASHWORTH,Frank 2Lt dow 29-7-18 YLI att1/4Bn p142 MR30

ASHWORTH,Fred T2Lt dow 10-4-17 23NumbF p60 CRFrance53

ASHWORTH,Frederick Giles T2Lt kia 16-8-17 25MGC Inf p181 MR30

ASHWORTH,George T2Lt kia 2-10-16 19N&D att8LNLancs p135 MR21

ASHWORTH,George Bertram dow 10-8-16 3 att7Suff p77 CR France66

ASHWORTH,Hugh Stirling LtCol kia 26-3-17 4RSuss p228 MR34

ASHWORTH,James Francis Gordon 2Lt dow 25-6-16 9DLI p239 CR Belgium21

ASHWORTH,John Percival Curtis.MC.TLt kia 28-4-17 7Suff p78 MR20

ASHWORTH,Leonard 2Lt dow 12-4-18 13Y&L p158 MR32

ASHWORTH,L.T.LtCol ded 22-3-18 RFA p24 CR Nhampt161

ASHWORTH,Roger William Lt ded 26-4-18 8Hamps &15TrSqnRAF p229&258 CR Lond14,2Lt kld

ASKER,Arthur Howard 2Lt ded 30-1-17 6Ess p232 CR Staffs109

ASKEW,Cyril Horace 2Lt kia 9-4-17 1/8Mddx p236 CR France1185

ASKEW,Geoffrey.MC.2Lt dow 25-3-18 10TankCps p188 MR20

ASKEW,Henry Adam Capt kia 19-12-14 2BordR p116 MR32

ASKEY,Cecil Henry Leonard 2Lt dow 5-4-18 3 att8Lincs p74 CR France169,Lt

ASKHAM,Sydney Thomas T2Lt kia 21/22-8-16 9Suff p78 MR21

ASKHAM,William Capt kia 11-4-18 ACycCps p181 MR32

ASKWITH,Thomas Nowelle 2Lt kia 24-10-17 250RFA p24 CR Belgium13,Nowell

ASLACHSEN,Hector Shields T2Lt kia 23-4-17 4Lpool p71 CR France591

ASPDEN,Ernest Harold T2Lt kia 9-4-17 6RWSurr p55 CR France54

ASPDEN,Frank Hartley TLt dow 20-9-18 6RWSurr p55 CR France511

ASPDEN,Fred.MC.T2Lt kia 14-10-18 17LancF p91 CR Belgium157

ASPDEN,Ronald William.MM.2Lt dow 8-8-17 5RFus p66 CR Belgium16 2Bn

ASPINALL,Francis Clifford(Frank)2Lt kia 17-9-18 70RFA p24 CR France224

ASPINALL,Frank Toole T2Lt kia 1-8-16 16RWar p64 CR France397

ASPINALL,J.V.Capt 15-5-18 GL &11RAF CR France63

ASPINALL,Robert Lowndes.DSO.TLtCol kia 3-7-16 11Ches p95 CR France296

ASPLAND,Stanley Richard 2Lt kia 3-10-18 61MGC p181 CR France1887

ASPREY,Bernard Noel Lt kia 24-2-15 1WYorks p80 CR France1140

ASPREY,Maurice Capt kia 12-8-16 3EKent attTMB p57 CR France164

ASQUITH,Arnold Senior 2Lt dow 2-10-18 9RScots p212 CR Belgium11,17Bn

ASQUITH,Ernest T2Lt kia 17-9-16 1EYorks att9YLI p142 MR21

ASQUITH,Gordon William 2Lt kia 2-12-17 3YLI p142 MR30

ASQUITH,Raymond Lt dow 15-9-16 3GrenGds SR p49 CR France294

ASSER,Harold Edward T2Lt kia 1-7-16 Mddx att16Bn p145 MR21

ASSER,Leslie Ernest T2Lt kia 10-8-18 5TankCps p188 CR France360

ASSHETON-SMITH,Thomas Capt ded 3-5-19 IARO attVetCps p273

ASSINDER,William Alfred 2Lt kia 16-6-18 6RWar p214 CR Italy3

ASTBURY,Thomas Leslie Capt kia 21-3-18 6SStaffs p229 MR20

ASTE,Norman Henry 2Lt dow 5-8-16 RGA 23HB p38 CR France430,4-8-16

ASTELL,Frances Ethel Sister ded 17-2-17 TFNS p254 CR Greece9

ASTELL,Somerset Charles Godfrey Fairfax.DSO.Capt ded 24-3-17 8NStaffs att37RFus p156 CR Numb4

ASTILL,Ernest William Dearle 2Lt kia 30-3-18 9Lond p248 MR27

ASTINGTON,Thomas Jeffery T2Lt kia 28-2-17 8ESurr p112 MR21

ASTLE,Albert George TLtACapt kia 3-5-17 8Leic p87 MR20

ASTLEY,Alexander Gifford Ludford Capt kia 5-3-17 14Huss p22 MR38

ASTLEY,Aston Giffard.MC.TMaj kia 1-10-16 2RFus att61MGC p66&181 CR France397

ASTLEY,Christopher Basil Lt dow 27-7-18 10Lpool att1/6SfthH p216 CR France145

ASTLEY,Edward Dugdale D'Oyley.MID LtACapt kia 1-6-18 3 att1RBerks p138 CR France120

ASTON,Frederick Marriner TCapt kia 30-7-15 6DCLI p113 CR Belgium453,Frederic

ASTON,Henry Norman 2Lt ded 6-11-18 3Y&L p158 CR Yorks643,Capt

ASTON,Herbert Selwyn.MC.CaptTMaj dow 13-7-18 4HLI att9MGC p162&181 CR France27,kia

ASTON,Leonard Hugh T2Lt kld 6-9-17 GL &RFC CenFlySch p4 CR Surrey148

ASTON,Ronald Moseley Lt kia 14-3-15 2DCLI p113 MR29

ASTON,Walter Douglas Capt dow 2-11-17 1/1Camb p244 CR Belgium11

ASTWOOD,Edward Leicester Stuart T2Lt dow 20-9-16 26RFus p66 CR France145

ATACK,Percy T2Lt kia 4-7-18 6RROfCav attTankCps p23&188 CR France1170

ATCHISON,Charles Ernest.DSO.MajALtCol kia 24-8-17 KSLI p144 CR Belgium72,Cmdg6YLI

ATCHISON,George M HonCapt 15-4-18 GL CRCanada1245

ATCHISON,Harold Vivian 2Lt dow 26-8-18 RGA 19SB p38 CR France370

ATCHISON,John Osborne 2Lt kia 13-7-15 5YLI p235 CR Belgium85

ATHA,Leonard Edward T2Lt kia 5-3-18 GL &2RFC p15 CR France1203

ATHERLEY,Christopher Ernest Lt dow 17-6-15 11YLI att1RDubF p142 CR Gallipoli1

ATHERSTONE,George Henry Capt ded 21-2-18 RFA p24 MR65

ATHERTON,Edward.MC.TLt ded 18-2-19 MGC &6Manch p266 CR Lancs176

ATHERTON,Francis Wright Lt kld 15-5-18 RFA att30RAF p24 MR38

ATHERTON,Walter Lt kia 30-12-17 4KSLI p235 CR France379

ATHOL,Charles Colbourne TLt kia 26-8-18 att21MGC p181 MR16

ATKEY,Freeman Archibald Haynes TCapt kia 5-7-16 9Yorks p89 CR France515

ATKIN,Charles Percy.MC.LtAMaj kia 23-11-17 B70RFA 70ArmyBde p24 CR France415

ATKIN,George Dawson Hope 2Lt dow 16-7-16 4Lpool p71 CR France66

ATKIN,Jesse Marson Lt kia 7-11-14 N&D att3Worc p133 MR32

ATKIN,Keyser Capt dow 6-6-18 RAMC 1/1N.FA p253 CR France622

ATKIN,Richard Walter Lt kia 14-8-17 92RFA p24 CR Belgium86

ATKINS,Arthur Charles 2Lt kia 9-9-16 3 att1/12Lond p245 MR21

ATKINS,Basil Elmo.MID T2LtACapt kia 25-2-17 7NStaffs p156 MR38

ATKINS,Herbert de Carteret TLt dow 10-10-15 15DLI p160 CR France1

ATKINS,Herbert Lonsdale 2Lt kia 30-7-16 8RScotF p94 MR21

ATKINS,Kenneth Croydon 2Lt dow 30-5-18 6 att10Worc p107 MR18

ATKINS,Leslie Gordon 2Lt kia 25-5-18 1Lond p245 CR France177,24-5-18

ATKINSON,Ambrose TLt ded 7-7-17 RAMC att3Suff p194 CR Suff55

ATKINSON,Arnold Francis Crossley Lt ded 22-1-19 RE 75TC attS&M p262 MR43

ATKINSON,Arthur Wilfrid T2Lt kia 1-7-16 19Manch p154 MR21

ATKINSON,Bernard Stewart Capt kia 30-11-17 6SStaffs p229 CR France1498

ATKINSON,Charles Lt ded 4-7-19 171LabCps attChineseLabCps p266 CR France146

ATKINSON,Charles Mason TLt kia 9-8-17 RAMC 14FA TC att1Norf p194 CR France184

ATKINSON,Charles Richard 2Lt kia 16-10-15 2Y&L p158 MR29

ATKINSON,Edward William.DSO.MBE Maj 22-7-20 1RInniskF MR67

ATKINSON,Elwyn Lt dow 18-5-17 D291RFA p207 CR France518

ATKINSON,Fred T2Lt kia 23-4-17 13KRRC p148 MR20

ATKINSON,Fred.MC.TCapt kia 27/30-9-18 1 att9Lpool p71 CR France256

ATKINSON,Frederick Batty 2Lt kia 25-9-18 87RFA p24 CR France727

ATKINSON,Frederick St.John Maj kia 30-11-17 IA 9HodsonsHorse CR France364

ATKINSON,Geoffrey Howard.MID Lt dow 1-2-17 IA 45Sikhs p273 MR38

ATKINSON,Geoffrey J.Buddle Lt kia19-6-15 5Worc p107 CR Gallipoli6

ATKINSON,Geoffrey William Lt kia 19-7-16 O&BLI BucksBn p231 MR19

ATKINSON,George Louis TCapt drd 20/21-3-17 RAMC p194 CR Devon1

ATKINSON,Gilbert Lt dow 4-10-18 8DLI p239 CR Belgium38

ATKINSON,Guy Cheselden Renell T2Lt dow 30-10-16 12 att2ELancs p110 CR France105,Reuell

ATKINSON,Harry 2Lt kia 28-9-17 RGA 155SB p38 CR Belgium79

ATKINSON,Harry John T2Lt kia 17-8-16 9YLI p142 CR France402

ATKINSON,Hon.Hector John Capt ded 26-5-17 RIrFus p170 CR Eire5

ATKINSON,Henry Noel.DSO.MID 2Lt mbk 22-10-14 1/2Ches p256 CR France924,3 att1Bn

ATKINSON,Hugh.MID T2Lt kia 22-11-17 10RIrRif p168 MR17

11

ATKINSON,James.MC.T2Lt kia 2-9-18 1RScotF p94 CR France646

ATKINSON,John T2Lt kia 24-3-18 2SStaffs p121 MR20

ATKINSON,John Broadwood TLt ded 24-12-15 5RIrFus p170 CR Egypt6,Capt

ATKINSON,John Cyril Lt kia 19-12-14 IA 59Rif p273 MR28

ATKINSON,John Ismay TLt kia 29-6-16 13NumbF p60 MR21

ATKINSON,Lawrence Evans TCapt kia 20-4-16 2Y&L p158 CR Belgium73,Laurence

ATKINSON,Lewis de Burgh.MID TLtACapt kia 16-8-16 2RSuss p118 MR21

ATKINSON,Lionel Edward Mapletoft Lt kia 9-5-15 3 att2RBerks p138 MR32

ATKINSON,Miles Linzee T2Lt kia 20-11-17 E'TankCps p188 CR France711

ATKINSON,Noel Mitford Henson T2Lt acckld 27-12-16 3ELancs &RFC p2&110 CR Glouc5,Milford

ATKINSON,Owen Dayott.MC.CaptAMaj dow 27-10-18 RE 200FC p43 CR France276,Dayot

ATKINSON,Richard Dermott 2Lt kia 16-7-16 16KRRC p148 MR21

ATKINSON,Rollo Edward Lt kia 20-2-16 9DLI p239 CR Belgium127

ATKINSON,Surtees.MC.CaptAMaj ded 7-2-18 RFA p24 CR Yorks38

ATKINSON,Thomas Joyce TMaj kia 1-7-16 9RIrFus p170 CR France339

ATKINSON,Victor Rupert 2Lt kia 23-11-17 1/6WRid p227 CR Belgium88

ATKINSON,William.MC.Lt dow 18-7-17 RFA 25DAC p24 CR Belgium11

ATKINSON,William Edward Capt kia 6-8-15 9DCLI p113 MR4

ATKINSON,William Ernest T2Lt kia 12-4-18 TankCps p188 MR32

ATKINSON,William Henry Jepson St.Leger Capt kia 12-5-15 1Drags p21 CR Belgium2,13-5-15

ATKINSON,William Noel Capt kia 29-6-15 IA 2/10GurkhaRif p273 CR Gallipoli6

ATKINSON-JOWETT James TLt kia 16-9-16 11 att6YLI p142 MR21

ATLAY,Hugh Wordsworth.DSO.Maj kia 11-4-15 52RFA p24 CR Belgium58

ATOCK,Arthur George.MC.T2Lt kia 13-9-18 RE 155FC p43 CR France106,Lt

ATTENBOROUGH,John Haddon T2Lt kia 1-7-16 8Norf p73 MR21

ATTER,Christopher Francis Lt kia 21-3-18 1Leic p87 MR20

ATTERBURY,Lewis John Rowley 2Lt kia 7-10-16 4Lond p246 MR21

ATTFIELD,Sidney Hunrich Lt kia 19-4-17 9RWSurr attHamps p55 CR Palestine8

ATTREE,Francis William Wakeford Town Capt kia 10-5-15 1Suff p78 MR29,8-5-15

ATTRIDE,Raymond George.MID Capt kia 14-8-16 1/4RBerks p234 MR21

ATTWATER,Ernest T2Lt kia 22-3-18 58MGC Inf p181 CR France1473

ATTWATER,Humphrey St.John TCapt kia 26-6-16 1Nhampt p137 CR France149

ATTWATER,Reginald Henry 2Lt kia 9-4-17 1/8Mddx p236 CR France1185

ATTWELL,Ernest T2Lt kia 15-6-18 Worc att1/7Bn p107 CR Italy3

ATTWOOD,Algernon Foulkes Capt kia 8-10-14 4RFus p66 MR15,14-9-14

ATTWOOD,Langley Latton 2Lt kia 12-8-17 RGA 333SB p38 CR Belgium10

ATTWOOD,Stanley Albert Lt kia 3-10-18 15Lond p249 CR France82

ATWELL,Robert Erskine Lt kia 2-9-18 4ConnRgrs p172 CR Belgium89

AUBER,Charles St.Lo Lt kia 29-10-16 4RFA p207 CR France15,2Lt

AUBERTIN,William Aldworth Maj ded 20-2-19 13RWFus attOCB Egypt p97&257 CR Egypt9

AUBIN,Alfred Charles Capt kia 30-8-14 ELancs att2NigR p110 CR WAfrica57

AUBIN,John Fosbrooke Gerrard.DSO.MC&Bar.MID Capt kia 9-4-18 6DLI p239 MR32,Jehu

AUCHINLECH,Armar Leslie Capt kia 17-9-16 ScotRif 4SR att123MGC p181&254 MR21

AUCHINLECK,Daniel George Harold Capt kia 20-10-14 2RInniskF p104 CR Belgium451,21-10-14

AUCKLAND,Ernest T2Lt dow 30-10-16 24 att1Mddx p145 CR France105

AUCUTT,Donald.MID 2LtACapt kia 9-10-17 2RWar p64 MR30

AUDAER,Ernest Clifford 2Lt kia 1-7-16 13LancF p91 MR21,15 Ex13Bn

AUERBACH,Albert Arthur.MC.Lt kia 1-9-18 1 att3Lond p245 CR France216

AULTON-SMITH,Montague W. T2Lt kia 4-11-15 80RFA p24 CR Belgium35

AURET,Ben TCapt kia 21-9-16 112RFA p24 CR France430

AUSLIN,Percy Edward 2Lt dow 24-10-18 3SomLI p79 CR France612, AUSTIN 1Bn

AUST,Henry Ernest Lt kia 18-9-18 1/4Yorks p220 MR16

AUSTEN,Arthur Neville.MC.CaptAMaj dow 28-3-18 A51RFA p24 CR France62

AUSTEN,Edward John Lt kia 21/23-3-18 3Lond p245 MR27,22-3-18

AUSTEN,Ernest.DCM.2Lt ded 25-8-16 14Huss p22 MR69

AUSTEN,George Alan 2Lt kia 26-10-17 9Dev p76 CR Belgium143

AUSTEN,William Henry Ambrose T2Lt kia 13-11-16 27 att17Mddx p145 CR France742

AUSTEN-CARTMELL,Arthur James Lt kia 1-6-16 1KRRC p148 CR France924

AUSTEN-CARTMELL,Geoffrie Hugh LtACapt kia 13-11-16 2HLI p162 MR21

AUSTEN-LEIGH,Arthur Alexander Capt kia 11-5-18 2/4RBerks p234 MR27

AUSTER,Norman Conway H. 2Lt kia 16-7-18 SWBord att27RAF p263 CR France1410,L.

AUSTIN,Arthur Hyndman Piercy Capt kia 4-8-16 13DLI p160 MR21

AUSTIN,Cyril Frederic 2Lt kia 10-3-15 2RWSurr p55 CR France706

AUSTIN,Cyril John T2Lt kia 16-5-18 1RLancs p58 CR France412

AUSTIN,Edgar William T2Lt kia 23-7-18 1Ches att4RSuss p95 CR France524

AUSTIN,Edward Gerrard T2Lt kia 18-9-18 Ches att2/24Lond p95 CR France369

AUSTIN,Frederick Hubert 2Lt ded 12-11-18 IA p273 CR France1848,1Ess

AUSTIN,Frederick William.OBE.Maj&QM ded 28-11-19 BordR p264 CR C'land&W'land17

AUSTIN,George Elliott Lt kia 27-8-17 6RWar p214 MR30

AUSTIN,George Frederick T2Lt kia 19-7-16 15Ches p95 MR21

AUSTIN,George Frederick T2Lt kia 11-10-17 RBerks att6Bn p138 CR Belgium23,Fredrick

AUSTIN,Harold Lunn Ferrier T2Lt kia 6-1-16 12 att9Worc p107 CR Gallipoli6

AUSTIN,Hubert Morell T2Lt kia 13-8-16 12HLI p162 CR France239,Morrell

AUSTIN,James T2Lt dow 21-6-17 13Manch p154 CR Greece7

AUSTIN,John Carson Lt kia 29-12-15 5RScotF p222 CR Gallipoli6,2Lt 30-12-15

AUSTIN,John Henry Edward Col ded 26-4-17 RAMC p194 CR Mddx16

AUSTIN,Oliver 2Lt kia 9-5-15 2RSuss p118 MR22

AUSTIN,P.E. see AUSLIN,P.E.

AUSTIN,Robert George T2Lt kia 26-10-18 257MGC Inf p181 MR38

AUSTIN,Stephen Phillip TLt dow 27-9-18 RASC att7LancF p192 CR France712,Philip kia

AUSTIN,Thomas Carnelly MacDonald TCapt kia 9-4-16 4SWBord p99 CR Iraq5

AUSTIN,Vernon James Lt kia 26-1-15 RFA p24 CR Kent177

AUSTIN,William Girvan Lt dow 23-8-17 5RScotF p222 CR Scot520

AUTERAC,Robert Sames T2Lt kia 18-10-16 28MGC p181 MR21

AVELING,Lancelot Neville Lt dow 29-4-15 ConnRgrs p172 CR France200

AVENT,E.Rev 25-8-20 Chap2Cl CR Yorks38

AVERDIECK,George Gerald TLt dow 14-9-16 10RB p177 CR Yorks292

AVERDIECK,Godfrey Harold T2Lt kia 11-3-16 16KRRC p148 CR France114

AVERILL,Thomas Hanson T2Lt kia 30-8-17 17Lpool p71 CR Belgium97

AVERY,Clare Havill LtACapt dow 11-4-17 2Ess att12TMB p131 CR France95

AVERY,Edward John 2Lt ded 1-2-15 4DCLI p227 MR43,Lt

AVERY,Frederick Graeme.MC.Capt kia 13-4-18 RE DivSigCoy att101InfBde p43 CR Belgium11

AVERY,Henry Norris T2Lt kia 5-6-18 6 att1RBerks p138 CR France120,Morris

AVERY,Joseph Francis T2Lt kia 31-7-17 10WelshR p126 CR Belgium65

AVERY,Thomas 2LtTCapt kia 16-6-15 5KSLI p144 CR Belgium58

AVERY,Sir William Eric Thomas Bart.MC.Maj ded 20-11-18 RASC attGdsDivMTCoy p192 CR France146

AVERY,William Ernest 2Lt kia 1-7-16 16NumbF p60 MR21

AWBERY,Charles Luker.MC.Capt kia 31-7-17 4Ess p232 MR29

AWDRY,Carol Edward Vere 2Lt kia 27-8-14 2RMunstF p175 CR France1751

AWDRY,Charles Selwyn.DSO.Maj kia 24-3-18 WiltsYeo p206 MR27

AWDRY,William Walter Lt dow 16-4-18 1 att6Wilts p152 MR30

AXTENS,Harold Surridge Lt kia 6-4-18 4 att7RWFus p223 CR France232

AYER,Leonard Stuart TCapt dow 15-7-16 13RWFus p97 CR France833

AYERS,George Mansfield Lt kia 31-7-17 38RFA p24 MR29

AYLES,Francis Powell Lt ded 1-6-18 GrenGds &RAF 5TrSqd p49 CR Dors&C/1111

AYLETT-BRANFILL,Capel Capt ded 11-5-16 GlamYeo p203 see BRANFILL,C.L.A.

AYLING,Arthur Henry T2Lt kia 28-4-17 25NumbF p60 MR20

AYLMER,Gerald Hans Hendrick Lt kia 16-4-17 2 att1RInniskF p104 MR20

AYLMORE,Alick Guyer Aylmer 2Lt kia 23-3-18 15Lond p249 MR20

AYMER,Alfred Ireland Lt dow 25-9-18 IARO att1/152Punjabis p273 CR Palestine9

AYNSLEY,Ronald Walker 2Lt dow 15-6-15 5NStaffs p238 CR France285

AYRE,Bernard Pitts TCapt kia 1-7-16 8Norf p73 CR France513

AYRE,Stanley Fawcett 2Lt kia 30-11-17 RFA 170ArmyBde p24 MR17

AYRES,Clement 2Lt kia 20-9-17 12RB p177 MR30

AYRES,Giles Frederick 2Lt kia 9-5-15 3Dors attLincs p123 MR32

AYRES,Stanley Frank TCapt kia 20-11-17 7ESurr p112 MR17

AYRES,Victor Albert 2Lt kia 1-9-18 4RFus p66 CR France568

AYRIS,Norman Lt kia 31-12-15 RE 98FC p43 CR France682

AYRTON,Frank Frederick Joseph Capt kia 28-6-15 16RFus p66 MR4

AYRTON,John 2Lt dow 29-4-17 1WYorks p80 CR France80

AYSCOUGH,Walter Guy.MC.Capt kia 25-9-17 7Rajputs attBharatpurInf p273 CR EAfrica11 &CR Tanznia1,Maj

AYTOUN,Robert Merlin Graham Lt dow 27-8-14 2A&SH p172 CR France717

B

BABB,Royland Nettleton T2Lt ded 15-10-18 1/2WRid p115 CR France40,Roland Lt 9Bn

BABBAGE,John Colston 2Lt kia 18-11-16 2Manch p154 MR21

BABINGTON,Ralph Vivian 2Lt kia 9-10-17 3CldGds p50 CR Belgium87

BABINGTON,Thomas Zachary Dodson Lt died 16-10-18 IARO att49Bengalis p273 MR43

BACCHUS,William Hubert Ogden Capt dow 13-9-15 2Y&L p158 CR Belgium11

BACHE,Harold Godfrey T2Lt kia 15-2-16 10LancF p91 MR29,16-2-16

BACK,Courteny Douglas SubLt ded 16-6-16 RIM p273 CR Iraq6

BACK,Horace Aubrey 2Lt kia 22-9-16 3 att1Glouc p196 CR France453

BACK,Louis William Alexander T2Lt kia 23-4-17 4Lpool p71 CR France591

BACKHOUSE,Gerald Lovell 2Lt kld 2-8-16 Norf &RFC p2&73 CR Eire411

BACKHOUSE,Herbert Franklin T2Lt kia 25-8-18 4Mddx p145

BACKHOUSE,Henry.TD.LtCol drd 30-12-15 7Ches p222 MR41

BACKHOUSE,Horace Heptonstall.MC.TLt kia 23-8-18 8RLancs p58 CR France927

BACKHOUSE,Hubert Edmund ACapt kia 15-10-16 N&D att2Bn p133 MR21

BACKHOUSE,John William Capt kia 10-2-16 BucksBn O&BLI p231 CR France1327

BACKHOUSE,St.John Salmon 2Lt kia 3-4-18 10ELancs attRAF p110 CR Europe20,CamH

BACKHOUSE,William Henry T2Lt kia 13-3-18 1/6WYorks p80 CR Belgium72

BACKLAKE,Brian Ashber TLt kia 3-5-17 8RFus p66 MR20,Ashbee

BACKLAKE,Denis Ives T2Lt kia 19-10-16 1SomLI p79 MR21

BACKLER,Alfred Milne 2Lt ded 25-5-18 4Lond &RAF p246&258

BACKUS,Arthur Ronald.MC.TCapt ded 23-9-17 1 att8RB p177 CR Belgium90

BACKUS,Charles Howard Capt ded 28-12-19 RAMC 7FA p267 CR Germany1

BACKWELL,Charles William T2Lt kia 22-6-17 20LancF attX35TMB p91 CR France212

BACON,Allan Harvey Lt kia 6/7-8-15 7Manch p237 MR4,6-7-15

BACON,Arthur Robert Dick Lt kia 25-4-17 1RBerks p138 CR France184

BACON,Basil Kenrick Wing Maj kia 13-12-14 1Worc p107 MR22

BACON,Charles Vallance TLt ded 4-11-18 RE p43 CR Kent61

BACON,Douglas Haviland Lt kia 16-11-16 60RFC p2 MR20

BACON,Dudley Francis Cecil 2Lt dow 1-11-15 4DLI attNumbF p168 CR Hamps182

BACON,Edward Sivewright Lt kia 31-8-17 RFA att66RFC p17&207 MR20

BACON,Frank William Capt ded 4-12-18 5Ess p232

BACON,John Lionel Rev ded 1-12-18 YMCA CRFrance85

BADCOCK,Arthur Lawrence T2Lt kia 13 10 15 6YLI p142 CR Belgium105,Lt

BADCOCK,Benjamin Morley 2Lt kia 9-7-18 5N&D p232 CR France109,1/6Bn

BADCOCK,Edmund Downes TLt kia 22-7-16 1Nhampt p137 MR21

BADCOCK,Harold John 2Lt kia 18-10-16 4Norf p216 CR France307

BADCOCK,Minden Francis.MC.Capt kia 26-3-18 2/5Glouc p225 MR27,27-3-18

BADCOCK,Stanley Edgar CaptTMaj kia 26-4-15 6DLI p239 MR29

BADDELEY,Alfred James Lt kia 23-10-18 RSuss att2TMB p118 MR16

BADDELEY,Edward Lawrence.TD.Maj kia 6-6-15 1/8LancF p221 CR Gallipoli1

BADDELEY,John Frederick T2Lt kia 1-7-16 7EKent p57 CR France397

BADDELEY,Kenneth T2Lt kia 15-9-16 15Hamps p120 CR France277

BADDELEY,Percy Kynnersley T2Lt kia 29-6-16 RFA p24 CR France394

BADDOCK,Thomas Agnew TLt dow 3-12-17 8RB p177 MR30

BADDON,Wallace TCapt kia 3-9-16 147MGC p181 MR21

BADELOW,John George 2Lt dow 27-12-15 63RFA 6DAC p24 CR Iraq1

BADEN,Reginald T2Lt kia 26-6-16 7Beds p85 CR France513

BADENOCH,Ian Forbes Clark T2Lt ded 19-3-17 20RFus p66 CR France67

BADGLEY,James Chester T2Lt kia 7-6-17 1Wilts att58TMB p152 CR Belgium102,6Bn

BADHAM, Leslie Charles.MC.Capt 30-12-20 1ConnRgrs MR67

BADMAN,Raymond Clarence T2Lt kia 21-10-18 2SLancs p125 CR Belgium443

BADSWELL,Frank George 2Lt drd 4-5-17 Glouc p106

BAGGS,Harold Frank TLt dow 28-1-17 8WelshR p126 CR Iraq5

BAGGS,Henry Ernest 2Lt dow PoW 30-6-18 43MGC p181 CR Germany3, Lt 29-6-18

BAGGULEY,James Lionel TLt kldacc 6-12-17 13DLI p160 CR Belgium192

BAGLEY,Arthur Bracton.MC.Capt dow 29-10-18 2 att8RDubF p176 CR France13

BAGLEY,Frank Adams.MID Capt dow 2-10-15 2SLancs p125 CR Belgium11

BAGLEY,Thomas William Ashton.MID TMaj ded 14-11-15 RASC p192 CR Greece8

BAGNALL,George Barry Lt kia 23-4-17 6 att13RB p177 MR20

BAGNALL,John Angus 2Lt kia 15-9-16 4NumbF p213 CR France239

BAGNALL,Philip Walter Jowett 2Lt kia 10-8-15 6RWelshF p223 MR4

BAGNALL,Richard Gordon 2Lt kia 1-7-16 RGA 114HB p38 CR France296

BAGOT,Alan Desmond.Sir Lt ded 11-1-20 RHGds CR C'land&W'land92

BAGOT,Edward Luke Henry 2Lt kia 10-9-16 WelshGds p53 CR France374

BAGOT-CHESTER,Greville John Massey Capt&BtMaj kia 28-11-17 2ScotsGds p51 CR France1498

BAGOT-CHESTER,Walter Grevile.MC.Capt dow 28-3-18 IA 2/3 att3/3GurkhaRif p273 CR Palestine9,Greville kia

BAGOT-De-La-BERE,Cyril John Lt 18-8-16 10Glouc MR21

BAGSHAW,Arthur Samuel T2Lt kia 22-8-16 7Wilts p152 CR Greece6

BAGSHAW,Frank Vivian Maj ded 29-11-18 RGA p269

BAGSHAW,Henry Kenyon TLt kia 13-4-18 197RASC att1/7WRid p192 MR30

BAGSHAWE,Edward George Clarkson Capt kia 20-7-16 5Yorks p220 CR Belgium60

BAGSHAWE,Geoffrey Hamilton 2Lt kia 13-5-15 5RRofCav att1DragGds p23 MR29,1Drags

BAGSHAWE,Leonard Vale Capt kia 16-6-15 3KOSB att1NumbF p101 MR29

BAILDON,Christopher Nevile T2Lt kia 3-5-17 21 att15DLI p160 MR20

BAILE,George Frederick Cecil TLt dow 9-11-17 RE p43 CR Lond8

BAILE,George William Rev Chap4Cl ded 27-1-18 RAChDept att64CCS p199 CR France40

BAILE,Robert Carlyle T2Lt kia 16-10-15 RE 76FC p43 CR France423

BAILES,John Thomas 2Lt dow 9-5-17 6DLI p239 CR Durham27,9Bn

BAILEY,Alfred John T2Lt kia 3-9-16 17KRRC p149 CR France701

BAILEY,Allan Richard 2Lt dow 15-6-17 A88RFA p24 CR Belgium102

BAILEY,Anthony Drummond 2Lt kia 16-12-16 8N&D att12RB p233 MR21

BAILEY,Anthony Yorke 2Lt kia 27-7-16 5 att1KRRC p149 MR21

BAILEY,Arnold T2Lt kia 24-3-18 8RLancs p58 CR France174

BAILEY,Arthur MacDougall Lt kia 22-8-18 7 att9Ess p232 CR France370

BAILEY,Arthur William Lt kia 4-6-15 9 OBLI p129 CR Gallipoli6

BAILEY,Cecil Arthur Lt kia 5-5-15 4WYorks att2WRid p80 MR29

BAILEY,Charles Lt ded 20-2-19 RGA p254 CR Ches44

BAILEY,Charles Frederick T2Lt kia 9-5-16 GL 8DubF attTMB p189 CR France223

BAILEY,Clifton Frederick Lt kia 6-4-17 7Lond att59RFC p17&247 MR20 See ALBAN,C.F.true name

BAILEY,Clive Maxwell T2Lt kia 3-8-17 GL &RFC p4 CR Surrey29

BAILEY,Dermot Harvey 2Lt kia 24-5-17 1/8RScots 211 CR France97,23-5-17

BAILEY,Donald William T2Lt kia 4-10-17 1 att12Glouc p106 CR Belgium125

BAILEY,Douglas Ingram Lt ded 16-11-18 12Lond att1GarBnRWar p248 CR Egypt15

BAILEY,Ernest T2Lt kia 28-10-16 21Lpool p71 CR France374

BAILEY,Felix Charles T2Lt dow 28-3-18 46RFC p15 CR France95,kld

BAILEY,Frank Lt kia 6-9-17 8LancF p221 MR30

BAILEY,George Haddon T2Lt dow 6-4-17 145MGC Inf p181 CR France363

BAILEY,Gerald Hinton T2Lt dow 20-10-15 13DLI p160 CR France285,Lt

BAILEY,Gerald Sergison.Hon 2Lt kia 10-8-15 2GrenGds att1BnSpecRes p49 CR France279

BAILEY,Gilbert Maj kia 22-11-15 IA 104Rif p273 MR38

BAILEY,Guy Frederick.MC.Capt kia 7-7-17 2Y&L p158 CR France115

BAILEY,Guy Horsman.MC.LtAMaj kia 28-2-17 15RH&FA p24

BAILEY,Herbert Lt ded 24-5-15 RFA 2AC p24 MR43 &CR Pakistan50A

BAILEY,Herbert Packer.MC.2Lt kia 31-7-17 12ESurr p112 MR29

BAILEY,Hubert Percy Andrew T2Lt kia 24-11-17 17WelshR p126 MR17

BAILEY,Hugh Gardner Lt ded 31-1-19 8 att1/4SomLI p79 MR66

BAILEY,J.A.SenAssSurg 22-11-14 IMS MR66

BAILEY,James Connor Maxwell.OBE.MID Lt ded 13-4-19 RAMC p267 CR EAfrica35 &Tanzania1,Capt Conor

BAILEY,John Bodley 2Lt kia 20-9-17 1EYorks att7RFC p4&83 CR Belgium18

BAILEY,John Lancelot.Hon Capt ded 26-10-18 SWBord BrecknockBn p223 MR65

BAILEY,John William 2Lt drd 30-12-17 3Ches p95 MR41

BAILEY,John Winckworth 2Lt kld 31-3-16 RFC p2 CR Mddx34

BAILEY,Louis John T2Lt kia 17-6-17 GL &41RFC p4 CR Belgium11

BAILEY,Philip Gerald TCaptAMaj kia 26-4-17 36RFA p24 CR France265

BAILEY,Richard Percival Lt&QM ded 30-5-15 YorksHuss p206 CR Yorks34

BAILEY,Robert Humphrey David Lt kia 3-5-17 8SomLI p79 MR20

BAILEY,Robert Neale Menteith Lt dow 1-12-17 ERidYeo p206 CR Egypt9

BAILEY,Roland Henry Lt ded 4-1-19 C251RFA p24 CR France457

BAILEY,Tom Edmond Geoffrey.MC.Capt kia 2-4-19 6Beds att6Yorks p85&89 MR70 &CR Europe179

BAILEY,W.Nurse 23-9-18 VAD 38SH CR Italy12 see BAILY,W.

BAILEY,Walter Arthur Francis 2Lt kia 23-3-18 2 O&BLI p129 MR20,24-3-18

BAILEY,Walter George William TCapt kia 15-9-16 15Hamps p120 CR France1890

BAILEY,Wilson Rhodes T2Lt kld 19-1-18 RFC p15 CR Lancs157,Willie

BAILIE,Thomas Manbourg Douglas Maj kia 15-9-16 1IrGds p52 CR France394

BAILLIE,Alan La Touche TCapt kia 29-10-15 10ScotRif p103 CR France423

BAILLIE,Duncan Lt kia 2-11-14 IA 2/9GurkhaRif att1/9 p273 CR France924

BAILLIE,Evan Henry TCapt kia 25-9-15 10ScotRif p103 MR19

BAILLIE,Gawaine George Stuart.Bart 2Lt kia 7-9-14 2Drags p21 CR Scot728

BAILLIE,George Maj kia 18-11-14 RFA p24 MR29

BAILLIE,George T2Lt kia 5-6-17 21NumbF p60 MR20

BAILLIE,George Richard Lancelot Lt kia 3-10-18 6RInniskF p104 CR France234

BAILLIE,Hugh Montgomery Capt kia 21-3-18 16RIrRif p168 MR27

BAILLIE,Humphry John Lt kia 2-3-16 2Dors p123 CR Iraq1,Humphrey

BAILLIE,Ian Henry Capt dow 22-5-15 4CamH p242 CR France145

BAILLIE,John Henry 2Lt kia 3-5-17 15DLI p160 MR20

BAILLIE-HAMILTOM,Arthur Buchanan Capt kia 9-5-15 1SfthH p164 CR France721,BUCHANAN-BAILLIE-HAMILTON

BAILLON,Gerald Wolstan T2Lt kia 25-9-15 15Lpool p71 CR France163,1Bn

BAILWARD,Theodore Lt kia 29-4-15 IA 26Cav att7Lancers p273 MR38

BAILY,Arthur Alexander Russell 2Lt kia 4-11-18 RFA att17TMB p24 CR France737

BAILY,Denis Joseph.MC.TLt kia 21-2-17 9RMunstF p175 CR Belgium100

BAILY,Wilhelmina Miss ded 23-9-18 VAD StJAB 38SH p200 CR Italy12 see BAILEY,W.

BAIN,Alec Magnus Harold 2Lt kia 22-3-18 1/4Lincs p217 MR20

BAIN,Alexander Neill T2Lt kia 19-5-16 10GordH &7CamH p166&265 CR France423

BAIN,Andrew Lusk.MID Lt kia 4-11-18 1IrGds p52 CR France985

BAIN,Annie Watson Sister.MID kia 1-6-18 VAD StJAB p200 CR France40

BAIN,David McLaren Capt kia 3-6-15 3 att2GordH p166 CR France260

BAIN,John Meikle T2Lt kia 14-7-16 12 att9ScotRif p103 CR France513

BAIN,Nicol T2Lt kia 16-10-18 RWKent att8Bn p140 CR France206

BAINBRIDGE,Carlyle T2Lt kia 13-10-15 6EKent p57 CR France423

BAINBRIDGE,Eric Lt kia 5-9-16 GL &32RFC p2&189,ded MR20

BAINBRIDGE,James Scott Capt kia 22-3-18 4Yorks p220 MR27

BAINBRIDGE,John Stuart TLt kia 26-9-17 14Hamps p120 MR30

BAINBRIDGE,Thomas Emery T2Lt kia 9-4-17 29 att21NumbF p60 CR France265

BAINBRIDGE,Thomas Lindsay kia 29-4-15 5NumbF p213 CR Belgium113

BAINBRIDGE,Wilfred Hudson Lt dow 15-3-16 6NumbF p213 CR France40

BAINBRIGGE,Philip Gillespie 2Lt kia 18-9-18 5LancF p221 CR France906

BAINES,Arthur Edward Carrow Lt kia 9-4-16 Lincs attRWelshF p74 MR38,Capt

BAINES,Athelstan Basil TCapt kia 3-4-17 6 O&BLI p129 CR France568

BAINES,Cecil Talbot Maj dow 26-4-17 RASC p253 CR Greece7

BAINES,Ellis Eylon TCapt ded 7-8-18 RAVC p198 CR France145,Eyton RAOC

BAINES,Frederick Athelstan Fanshawe 2Lt kia 25-5-15 4KRRC p149 MR29

BAINES,George T2Lt dow 3-6-17 GL 23Mddx att48RFC &48RFC p4 CR France40

BAINES,Henry Burgess 2Lt dow 4-6-17 C240(SM)RFA p208 CR France512

BAINES,Henry Parkyns Bridge T2Lt kia 3-2-17 15 att7Glouc p106 MR38

BAINES,Herbert 2Lt 14-1-17 RE CR Lancs255

BAINES,Hubert.MC.MID Capt dow 22-10-18 IA 75CarnaticInf p273 CR Asia62

BAINES,Jack Gordon Barrymore 2Lt kia 25-2-17 2RWar att2/3RFC p4&64 CR France167,kld

BAINES,John Hugh T2Lt kia 3-7-16 10Lincs p74 MR21

BAINES,Joseph TCapt kia 29-7-16 20Mddx p146 CR France115

BAINES,Kenneth James Mackenzie 2Lt kia 2-1-16 3Lpool p71 MR32

BAINES,Thomas Leo Rev Chap4Cl dow 31-5-18 RAChDept att152RFA p199 CR France31,kia

BAINTON,Herbert Sidney 2Lt dow 16-2-18 28Mddx p146 CR Kent175

BAIRD,Andrew Augustus Dering 2Lt kia 8-7-15 1Worc p107 CR France924,Arthur Lt

BAIRD,Barrington Hope Capt kia 21-12-14 1HLI p162 MR22

BAIRD,Charles Arthur Lt kia 12-10-18 9HLI p240 CR France230

BAIRD,Charles Edward Capt kia 1-7-16 SfthH p164 CR France1890

BAIRD,David Capt ded 22-12-17 WRid p264 CR France102

BAIRD,Joseph Franklin Montague Capt ded 10-9-17 9A&SH p269 CR Scot77

BAIRD,George Henderson Capt ded 9-11-19 RAMC p267 CR Ireland5

BAIRD,Gilbert Campbell T2Lt kia 28-7-17 Worc att229MGC p107&181 CR Palestine8

BAIRD,James Chap4Cl ded 13-2-19 RAChDept p199&258 CR France134

BAIRD,Leonard Barron.MC.Capt kia 20-4-17 RAMC att1/10Manch p253 CR France446

BAIRD,Louis Latham TLt dow 11-4-16 66RFA p24 CR Iraq5

BAIRD,Percy Thomas Charles Maj kia 15-2-15 CamH p167 CR Belgium80

BAIRD,William T2Lt kia 15-9-18 1Lpool p71 CR France530

BAIRD,William Frank Gardiner Capt dow 5-11-14 4Beds attLincs p85 CR France102

BAKE,Arthur Trevithick Tyack Lt kia 14-2-20 IA 126Baluchis p273 MR38

BAKE,Noel 2Lt kia 10-4-18 GL att1/6BlkW p189 MR19,ExMddx

BAKEL,Frank T2Lt kia 20-5-17 14Y&L p158 CR France644

BAKER,Albert Parkes 2Lt kia 22-8-17 3HLI att10DLI p162 CR Belgium125

BAKER,Alfred Parkes TLt dow 1-12-15 11RScots p53 CR France102

BAKER,Arnold Rennie 2Lt kia 16-8-17 GL att27RFC p4 CR France1032

BAKER,Arthur Brimfield 2Lt dow 26-9-16 3SStaffs att3MGC p181&254 CR France177

BAKER,Arthur Forbes LtTCapt kia 11-4-17 3DCLI att52RFC p4&113 CR France415,FltCmdr

BAKER,Arthur Leslie 2Lt kia 9-10-17 8WYorks p219 MR30

BAKER,Arthur William 2Lt kia 28-7-16 1/5YLI p235 MR21

BAKER,Aubrey Halliwell Capt kia 8-3-16 4SomLI p218 MR38

BAKER,Aveling John Wing 2Lt kia 23-3-18 4 att7A&SH p172 MR20

BAKER,Basil Howard Lt kia 22-5-18 2 att13RB p177 CR France81

BAKER,Bertram Reginald T2Lt kia 3-5-16 17RFus p66 CR France559

BAKER,Cecil Douglas Lt kia 29-7-17 1GrenGds SR p49 CR Belgium20,Capt

BAKER,Charles 2Lt kia 22-10-17 RGA 27SB p38 CR Belgium23

BAKER,Charles Hammond AssCommsy HonLt ded 14-7-17 IndMiscList attIMS p273 CR Iraq8

BAKER,Charles Tanqueray Capt kia 15-8-15 5Beds p219 CR Gallipoli4

BAKER,Colin Claude T2Lt dow 12-5-17 10N&D p133 CR France40,Claud

BAKER,Cyril Percival Lt dow 8-5-17 7O&BLI p129 MR37

BAKER,Douglas James T2Lt kia 28-4-17 24NumbF p60 CR France604

BAKER,Douglas Stanley Lt dow 23-7-16 RE 87FC p43 CR France74

BAKER,Edward Benjamin.MID Lt kia 26-10-14 3 att1Lpool p71 MR29

BAKER,Edward Carleton Capt dow 19-9-16 RE 228FC p43 CR France40

BAKER,Eric Trezier 2Lt kia 19-1-18 65RFC p15 MR20,Trezise

BAKER,Frank Alexander.MM.2Lt kia 1-10-18 14Lond p249 CR France647

BAKER,Frank Bernard T2Lt dow 17-9-16 EKent attRWSurr p57 CR France400

BAKER,Frank Vincent T2Lt kia 22-3-18 21 att7KRRC p149 MR27

BAKER,Frederick Gerald T2Lt kia 17-4-18 18WYorks p80 CR Belgium191

BAKER,Frederick Herbert 2Lt kia 24-3-18 58MGC p181 MR27,Harbert

BAKER,Frederick William Stewart Capt kia 20-9-17 4LNLancs p233 CR Belgium96,Stuart

BAKER,George Arthur 2Lt kia 29-11-17 RGA 342SB p38 CR Belgium176

BAKER,George Lionel John 2Lt kia 23-4-17 1Mddx p146 CR France434

BAKER,George Stanley Charles 2Lt kld 23-9-16 2DCLI p114 CR Glouc9,dedacc

BAKER,George William Capt dow 5-12-17 1/19Lond p250 CR France145

BAKER,Gordon Lennox ACapt kia 11-8-18 3Dors p123 CR France360

BAKER,Guy Talbot Lt kia 7-1-16 1/5EKent D'Coy p213 CR Iraq5

BAKER,Harold Carl 2Lt kld 8-10-16 49RFC p2 CR Kent7,dedacc

BAKER,Harold Glasspool.MC&Bar.TCapt dow 5-4-18 8SomLI p79 CR France62

BAKER,Harry Leslie.MC.TLt kia 8-11-18 18Lpool p71 CR France930

BAKER,Herbert Norman Lt ded 30-8-17 Herts attigR p252 CR EAfrica39,Ex 28Lond

BAKER,Herbert Shorey.MIDx2 TCapt kia 4/5-4-16 9RWar p64 CR Iraq5

BAKER,Hubert George 2Lt kia 17-8-16 1/4Glouc p225 MR21

BAKER,James TLt&QM ded 4-6-17 SL p201 CR France145 Ex RFA

BAKER,James Henry T2Lt kia 1-7-16 8Y&L p158 CR France293

BAKER,John Bartrup Harwood T2Lt kia 1-9-17 8RFus p66 CR France1182

BAKER,John Francis Lt kia 28-8-18 13Lond p249 CR France568

BAKER,John Kildour TCapt kia 9-10-18 1ScotRif p103 CR France230,Kilgour

BAKER,Joseph T2Lt kia 29-6-17 NStaffs Res att6Bn p156 MR20

BAKER,Joseph Franklin 2Lt dow 16-11-18 79RGA 185SB p38 CR Nhampt76,Lt

BAKER,Joseph Leffler 2Lt dow 14-12-15 C76RFA p24 CR France345

BAKER,Kingsley.MC.Lt dow 30-3-18 A51RFA p24 CR France52

BAKER,Lawrence Edgar T2Lt kld 1-5-17 GL attRFC p4 CR Numb99

BAKER,Lionel Charles Edwin.MC.2LtACapt kia 1-10-18 11RWSurr p55 CR Belgium112

BAKER,Micheal Granville Lloyd Capt kia 23-4-16 GloucYeo p203

BAKER,Neville Ernest TLt dow 31-7-17 RE attTankCps p43&188 CR Belgium124

BAKER,Osbert Clinton LtCol kia 9-5-15 1RIrRif p168 MR32

BAKER,Percy Gordon T2Lt dow 9-6-18 RE 81FC p43 MR34 moved fromCR France1693

BAKER,Reginald Cecil Capt ded 14-2-20 19TankCps CR Canada31

BAKER,Reginald Lawrence Capt kia 12-5-15 3Mon p244 CR Belgium126

BAKER,Richard Stanley Maj ded 13-11-18 IARO attS&TCps p273

BAKER,Robert Cunynhame Slade.MC.Lt kia 9-8-17 1RBerks p138

BAKER,Robert Geoffrey.DSO.Maj kia 24-2-17 IA 82Punjabis p273 MR38,23-2-17

BAKER,Roger Dyke Maj dow 13-8-15 ELancs Staff 38InfBde p110 CR Greece10

BAKER,St.John Vashon Capt ded 2-12-15 11Lancers CR India48

BAKER,Sidney TCapt dow 28-5-17 8SomLI p79 CR Mddx39

BAKER,Silvanus Wilfred T2Lt kia 26-9-15 8SomLI p79 MR19

BAKER,Sydney Harold TMaj kia 23-3-18 1Glouc att12Entrenching Bn p106 MR27

BAKER,Tom TCapt kia 1-7-16 10Lincs p74 CR France150

BAKER,Thomas LtACapt kia 28-7-17 RGA 203SB p38 CR Belgium24

BAKER,Thomas Sydney 2Lt kia 14-4-17 16Lond p250 MR20,Sidney

BAKER,Waldeman John 2Lt kia 25-10-17 83RFA p24 CR Belgium23

BAKER,Walter.MC.LtACapt dow 23-10-17 3 att14Glouc p106 CR Belgium16

BAKER,Walter George 2Lt kia 14-11-16 5RSuss p228 CR France392

BAKER,Walter Henry T2Lt dow 20-10-18 3GMGC Inf p181 CR Belgium140

BAKER,Walter Percy 2Lt kia 14-7-16 3Dors att7RWar p123 MR21

BAKER,Ward T2Lt dow 21-9-17 11WYorks p80 CR Belgium11

BAKER,Wilfred Harry T2Lt kia 2-7-16 8SomLI p79 CR France74,3-7-16

BAKER,William Frank T2Lt kia 15-5-16 12 att11LancF p91 CR France68

BAKEWELL,George John T2Lt dow 16-11-17 GL 6BordR att21RFC p4 CR Belgium16

BALAAM,Augustus Orlando Lt kia 24-10-17 5Suff attRFC p17&217 CR France95,4Bn

BALBIRNIE,John Victor Elphinstone T2Lt kia 7-9-18 23RFus p66 MR19

BALBOUR,Frank Douglas.MC.Capt kia 23-3-18 NCycBn att15Lond p253 MR20,BALFOUR

BALCH,Percy Frederick Lt 26-2-19 RFC CR Lincs156

BALCHIN,John Richard Aubrey.MC.TLt dow 14-11-16 152MGC p181 CR France131,kia

BALCOMBE,Charles Percy Lionel.MC&Bar.TCaptAMaj dow 29-10-18 RE 11FC p43 CR France332

BALCOMBE-BROWN,William Edward 2Lt kia 29-6-15 68RFA p24 CR Belgium94

BALD,Alan Henry Capt kia 15-10-15 IA 2/3GurkhaRif p273

BALDERS,Arthur William Capt kia 27-11-15 Norf att1NigR p73&201 CR WAfrica58,26-11-15

BALDERSON,Eric Francis Richard 2Lt kia 28-3-16 C158RFA p24 CR France705

BALDERSON,Henry Leslie Paxton T2Lt kia 23-7-16 Dev attGlouc p76 CR France832

BALDERSTON,Chester Thomas 2Lt ded 26-6-17 C58RFA p24 CR France285,dow

BALDIE,John Boyd Lt kia 6-11-18 Fife&ForfarYeo &RAF p203&258

BALDING,Reginald Norman TLt kia 30-3-17 5Beds attMGC Inf p186&219 MR38

BALDOCK,Charley Blair LtCol ded 19-10-15 IA 108Inf p273 CR Asia63

BALDOCK,John William 2Lt dow 21-7-18 4YLI p235 CR France1415

BALDOCK,Thomas Agnew Lt dow 3-12-17 8RB CR Belgium84

BALDOCK,W.P.Capt mbk 22-8-15 6Y&L p256 MR4

BALDRY,Arthur T2Lt kia 4-12-16 14Y&L p158 CR France342

BALDRY,Edgar George Lt 12-12-18 APD CR Norf162

BALDRY,Edwin James 2Lt kia 24-3-18 1NStaffs p156 MR27

BALDRY,William George Forsyth T2Lt dow 7-11-17 14 att11Ess p131 CR Iraq8

BALDWIN,Alan Aquilla Lt kia 26-4-18 5LNLancs p234 MR30

BALDWIN,Anthony Hugh ColTBrigGen kia 10-8-15 HQ Staff Cmdg38InfBde p1 MR4

BALDWIN,Austin Provost T2Lt kia 27-9-18 2Suff p78 CR France357

BALDWIN,David Aitken TLt ded 31-8-15 8Leic p87 CR France1017

BALDWIN,Herbert Donald TLt dow 18-7-16 156RFA p24 CR France833

BALDWIN,Frederick Charles 2Lt dow 11-5-18 2Beds p85 CR France142

BALDWIN,Harold John Taylor 2Lt kia 23-10-16 16Mddx p146 MR21

BALDWIN,Harry Sandford T2Lt kia 23-7-16 1DCLI p114 MR21

BALDWIN,Hugh Laurents Chenevix Capt kia 23-11-14 IA 58Rif p273 CR France80

BALDWIN,Hugh Reginald Lt kia 27-8-18 1IrGds p52 CR Frnce614

BALDWIN,J.Engr 17-7-18 BRCS CR Iraq8

BALDWIN,Lancelot Hugh Maj 6-11-14 1/8GurkhaRif CR India97A

BALDWIN,Norman Edward 2Lt kia 8-10-16 5Lond p246 CR France432

BALDWIN,Osborne George de Courcy TCapt kia 26-1-16 8RMunstF p175 CR France222

BALDWIN,Terence Kennett James Lt kia 20-3-18 5RLancs p213 CR France1092,Kennet

BALDWIN,William Everton 2Lt dow 25-8-18 8Manch att18RAF p237 CR France41

BALDWIN,William Frederick.MC.TLtAMaj kia 27-5-18 RE 7FC p43

BALE,Thomas Henry Thriscutt Lt kia 24-4-18 3 att2Yorks p89 CR Belgium11,25-4-17

BALE,Thomas William 2Lt dow 10-8-18 13TankCps p188 MR16

BALES,Keith 2Lt kia 16-5-15 2BordR p116 MR22

BALES,Theodore Alfred Herbert T2Lt dow 13-10-18 6RR ofCav att7DragGds p23 CR France146

BALFOUR,Adrian Clive 2Lt kia 8-10-16 21Lond p251 CR France385

BALFOUR,Alan Scott 2Lt kia 13-1-18 RFA &RFC p15&24 CR France446

BALFOUR,Bernard Lt kia 16-4-18 1Lond &65RAF p245&255,21Bn MR20

BALFOUR,Evan Murray Macgregor.MC.2Lt kia 24-8-18 2ScotsGds p51 CR France502

BALFOUR,Frank Douglas.MC.Capt 23-3-18 NCycBn att15Lond MR20 see BALBOUR,F.D.

BALFOUR,George James 2Lt kia 15-9-16 6HLI p240 CR France402

BALFOUR,Guy Edward Capt ded 5-9-17 IA 98Inf MR67 p273

BALFOUR,Isaac Bayley Lt kia 28-6-15 14RScots p53 CR Gallipoli6

BALFOUR,James Alfred CaptAMaj kia 11-1-17 1HLI p162 CR Iraq5

BALFOUR,John.MC.Capt kia 21-3-18 2ScotsGds attDivSigCo p51 CR France1182

BALFOUR,John Melville.MC.CaptAMaj kia 6-10-17 91RH&FA p24 CR Belgium12

BALFOUR,Percy.DSO.MajTLtCol kia 12-12-17 3Beds &HLI att2/7Worc p85 CR France439

BALFOUR,Robert 2Lt kia 20-5-18 4LNLancs p234 CR France204

BALFOUR,Robert Frederick Capt kia 28-10-14 1ScotsGds p51 MR29 &CR Belgium453

BALFOUR,Robert Wilson Maj ded 6-1-18 RGA 95SB p209 CR France512

BALFOUR,Thomas Henry.MC.Maj ded 16-3-20 RAMC MR43

BALFOUR-MELVILLE,James Elliot 2Lt kia 25-9-15 3 att2BlkW p128 MR19

BALKWILL,Albert Thomas James 2Lt kia 17-10-16 8BlkW p128 CR France385

BALKWILL,Charles Vince 2Lt kia 1-7-16 1/5Lond p246 MR21

BALKWILL,John 2Lt kia 1-7-16 6RWar p214 CR France605

BALKWILL,William Horniman 2Lt kia 9-4-17 2Wilts p152 CR France214

BALL,Albert.VC.DSO&2Bars.MC.Capt kia 7-5-18 7N&D att58RFC p17 CR France1279,7-5-17

BALL,Alec Radford 2Lt dow 17-8-17 3 att5Dors p123 CR Belgium18

BALL,Arnold Harding Lt kia 9-4-18 5RSuss p228 CR France163

BALL,Arthur 2Lt kld 19-2-17 3RLancs &57RFC p4&58 CR Egypt8

BALL,Arthur T2Lt kld 17-3-18 RFC p15 CR Scot252

BALL,Arthur Hugh.MC.2LtACapt dow 30-10-17 RGA 186SB p38 CR Belgium3,29-10-17

BALL,Arthur Sherley,MC.Lt kia 16-8-17 A186RH&FA p24 MR30,Shirley 2Lt C186

BALL,Benedict Hanly 2Lt kia 3-9-16 13 att14Hamps p120 MR21,Hanley

BALL,Catherine Sister drd 31-12-17 VAD p200 CR Egypt1

BALL,Charles Bent,Bart LtCol ded 17-3-16 RAMC p194 CR Ireland24

BALL,Charles Herbert Lt dow 3-4-18 WiltsYeo att5MGC Cav p186&206 CR France145

BALL,Frank Granville 2Lt kia 16-8-16 3 att9ESurr p112 MR21

BALL,George 2Lt kia 21-3-18 7N&D p233 MR20

BALL,George Frederick 2Lt ded 6-12-18 ACycCps 2/1HighCycBn p244 p269 CR Numb96,Lt

BALL,George William 2Lt kia 25-3-15 2Mddx p146 CR France1472

BALL,Gerald Harman.MC.T2Lt kia 12-4-18 31MGC Inf p181 MR32

BALL,Gerald Wheatley Lt kia 19-5-17 RE 445WRidFC p210 CR France1182

BALL,Henry Lt kia 13-1-16 3EYorks attRE 180TC p83 CR France279

BALL,Howell Thomas 2Lt kia 26-4-17 36RFA p24 CR France265

BALL,James.MC.Capt ded 23-1-18 1DCLI p114&257 CR Surrey1

BALL,John Joseph Barry Lt kia 27-6-16 2LondRFA p207 CR France1327

BALL,John Harry 2Lt dow 1-9-18 2/4LNLancs p234 CR France103,Lt

BALL,Joseph T2Lt kia 8-8-18 4TankCps p188 CR France487

BALL,Leslie Alfred Capt kia 4-10-17 10Mddx p236 MR30

BALL,Malcolm Edward Lt dow 10-4-16 RAMC att9Worc p194 MR38

BALL,Mark Christopher Lt dow 9-4-18 RE 231FC p43 CR France1094

BALL,Oliver Herbert T2Lt kia 28-9-16 10Yorks p89 CR France374

BALL,Oswald Frederic Grevatte T2Lt kia 5-4-17 GL RSuss att13RFC p4 CRFrance

BALL,Richard Anthony Lt kia 10-7-16 1/7Dev att1/8Worc p217 CR France1887

BALL,Robert Gordon TCapt ded 3-2-20 RAMC p267 CR Ireland24

BALL,Samuel George 2Lt kia 20-3-18 RWelshF p97 CR France646

BALL,Theodore Thomas Hollyman T2Lt kld 21-1-17 GL attVI Cps IntelDept p189 CR France46,dedacc

BALL,Thomas Henry Lt ded 22-1-18 RFA 25DAC p24&257 CR Lond28

BALL,Walter William T2Lt kia 24-11-15 10Yorks p89 CR France1140

BALL,William Charles 2Lt kia 27-9-18 2Manch p154 MR16

BALL,William Linnington 2Lt kia 5-11-18 NumbF att1RFus p60 CR France521

BALL,William Ormsby Wyndham Lt kia 25-9-14 RAMC p194 MR15,26-9-14

BALL-ACTON,Reginald Thomas Annesley Capt kia 22-5-16 7YLl p142 CR Belgium101.Maj

BALLAMY,Harold William Lt kia 15-8-17 B231RFA p207 CR France570

BALLANCE,Leslie Arthur Capt kia 28-9-16 4 att2KRRC p149 CR France277

BALLANTYNE,Allen James T2Lt dow 10-11-17 GL att46RFC p4 CR France49 see BALLANTYRE

BALLANLYNE,James Allan T2Lt kia 1-8-17 20DLI p160 MR29,Alan Lt

BALLANTYNE,Philip Hugh Lt kia 28-10-18 4SfthH p241 MR16

BALLANTYNE,William T2Lt kia 13-10-15 1BlkW p128 MR19

BALLANTYNE,W.C.AssSurg3rdCl 9-11-17 ISMD MR69

BALLANTYRE,Allen James T2Lt dow 10-11-17 GL att46RFC p4 CR France49,BALLANTYNE kld

BALLARD,Charles Naesmyth Bruere LtCol died 11-2-15 15RFA p24 CR France102

BALLARD,Charles Edward Penfold 2Lt kia 10-3-18 1WelshGds p53 CR France545

BALLARD,Charles William.MC.TCapt kia 25-11-17 7RSuss p118 MR17,Willard

BALLARD,Dennis Arthur.MID Capt kia 12-12-17 3RLancs p58 CR France155,1Bn

BALLARD,Ernest Fryer Capt ded 23-10-18 RAMC CR Sussex111

BALLARD,Frank Watson 2Lt kia 11-10-18 3 att1Nhampt p137 MR16

BALLARD,Godfrey Adolphus 2Lt kia 27-9-15 1/23Lond p252 MR19

BALLARD,Maurice Arnold 2Lt dow 29-5-15 23Lond p252 CR France473, Lt 30-5-15

BALLARD,Oliver Charles.MID 2Lt dow 17-10-18 21/2RFA p24 CR France1266,kia

BALLARD,Robert Francis Cooper T2Lt kia 30-7-16 2Beds p85 MR21

BALLEINE,Cuthbert Francis Capt kia 2-7-15 8RB p177 CR Belgium165

BALLINGER,Francis Allen 2Lt kia 22-5-15 4Lpool p71 MR22,Allan

BALLINGER,Henry John 2Lt kia 13-10-15 1Mon p244 MR19

BALLINTINE,Joseph Capt kia 1-7-16 11RInniskF p104 CR France383

BALLOCH,Humphrey Colquhoun 2Lt ded 2-6-15 3GordH p166 CR Scot280

BALLS,Frank William Lt ded 1-7-18 3Suff attRAF p78 CR Egypt1

BALMAIN,Roy Frederick.MC.TLtACapt dow 1-10-18 51RFA p24 CR Belgium157

BALMAIN,Walter.MM.2Lt kia 18-4-18 1BlkW p128 CR France279

BALME,Edward Nettleton.MC.Lt dow 22-4-18 3 att11Ess p131 CR Belgium18

BALMER,Pringle 2Lt kia 27-5-18 5DLI p239 MR18

BALMFORTH,Alfred Capt kia 31-7-17 8Manch p237 MR29

BALSHAW,Newton Kesteven Capt kia 13-4-18 16KRRC p149 MR32

BALSHAW,Walter 2Lt kia 20-10-14 2Manch p154 MR22

BALSOM,Ernest Henry TLt kia 30-8-18 14WelshR p126 CR France217

BALY,Cyril James Price Tyson Sugar Lt kia 15-9-16 1EKent p57 MR21

BAM,Cyril Turpin T2Lt kia 14-7-16 7Leic p87 MR21

BAMBER,Claude Charles Capt s/InflictedWound 26-1-19 IA RWar att3/9GurkhaRif p273 MR43

BAMBER,John Walton TLt kia 1-7-16 10YLI p142 CR France267

BAMBERGER,Cecil David Woodburn Capt kia 20-12-17 RE p43 CR France80,19-12-14

BAMBERGER,William Ewart Woodburn 2Lt kia 16-8-17 Glouc att1/5Bn p106 MR30

BAMBOROUGH,Thomas Clarence T2Lt dow 25-9-17 20DLI p160 CR France139

BAMBRIDGE,Bertram Stacpoole T2Lt kia 19-11-16 7EKent p57 CR France314,18-11-16

BAMBRIDGE,Harry Liddall.MC.2Lt kia 31-3-18 7EYorks p83 MR20

BAMBRIDGE,Rupert Charles.DSO.MC&Bar.MM.TCapt dow 23-5-18 10RFus p66 CR France145

BAMBRIDGE,William Herbert TLtACapt kia 19-8-17 24RFus p66

BAMFORD,Edwin Scott Capt dow 24-4-15 1Y&L p158 CR Belgium151,23-4-15

BAMFORD,Harold Walley 2Lt dow 26-11-15 1KSLI p144 CR France40

BAMFORD,Joseph Lamont.MIDx2 T2Lt kia 20-8-17 GL RScotsF &17RFC p4&94 CR Greece7

BAMFORD,Oswald Joseph Capt kia 13-10-15 6NStaffs p238 MR19

BAMKIN,Carl Jocelyn T2Lt kia 19-8-18 Dors att12Norf p123 CRFrance19

BAMKIN,Harold Picton 2Lt kia 19-7-15 7Suff p78 CR Belgium33

BAMPTON,James Henry TCapt dow 25-8-17 RAMC att70RFA p194 CR Belgium8

BANBURY,Charles William Capt kia 16-9-14 3CldGds p50 CR France1112,dow

BANBURY,Ralph Frontenac T2Lt died 8-1-16 9EYorks p83

BANBURY,William Michael Victor Capt kia 17-8-17 16RB p177 CRBelgium124

BANCE,Robert Arman T2Lt kia 9-8-16 9 att5RBerks p138 CR France150

BANCROFT,Stanley Fleming TLt kia 19-8-16 12 att10WelshF p97 MR21

BAND,George Laidman TCapt&Adjt kia 20-6-17 10NumbF p60 CR Belgium29

BAND,Lawrence T2Lt kia 28-4-17 17Lpool p71 CR France540

BANDEY,George Henry 2Lt ded 6-11-18 PoW 59MGC Inf p181 CR Europe149

BANES WALKER,Frederick Cecil 2Lt 9-5-15 2Dev CR France566 see WALKER,F.C.B.

BANES WALKER,Gerald Capt 22-11-17 1/5SomLI CR Palestine3

BANFIELD,Cyril Barnet 2Lt kia 21-3-18 RFC p15 MR20

BANHAM,Ernest T2Lt kia 29-9-18 13Y&L att10EYorks p158 CR Belgium49

BANHAM,Joseph John.MID TMaj kia 27-3-18 9RSuss p118 MR27

BANHAM,William Henry.MC.2Lt dow 8-9-18 A119RFA p24 CR France25

BANISTER,Charles Wilfred 2Lt kia 16-6-15 RFus p66 MR29

BANISTER,Maurice James TLt. dow 17-2-16 7LNLancs p135 CR France727

BANKES,Edward Nugent Capt kia 26-4-15 3RDubF p176 MR29

BANKS,Arthur Byers.MID Lt ded 6-3-19 RGA p38&257 CR France85

BANKS,Arthur Chaplin 2Lt kia 22-6-16 2RWelshF p97

BANKS,Bertie Charlton 2Lt kia 5-11-16 8DLI p239 MR21,Charleton

BANKS,Charles Hunter Donaldson 2Lt dow 1-7-15 3Worc p107 CR Camb16

BANKS,Cyril D'Albini Sykes.MC.CaptAMaj ded 4-11-18 RGA 226SB p38

BANKS,Edward Francis 2Lt kia 28-2-17 2RFus p66 MR21

BANKS,Frederick 2Lt ded 2-6-18 1/2Ess &RAF p131 CR Lond12,3Bn

BANKS,Henry 2Lt kia 27-8-18 4Yorks p220 MR16

BANKS,Henry Crawford 2Lt kia 30-6-18 4RScots p211 CR France25,Harry

BANKS,John Cook.MC.TCapt kia 1-5-17 20KRRC p149 CR France581,2-5-17

BANKS,John Howard TLt dow 15-8-17 176MGC p181 CR Belgium12

BANKS,Leon Thomas Victor,MC.Maj dow 29-6-18 5RWar p214

BANKS,Percy Abbott,MC.T2Lt ded 22-2-19 RWKent &RAF p140

BANKS,Percy D'Aguilar.MID Capt kia 26-4-15 IA CpsofGuides att57Rif p273 MR29

BANKS,Randolph TCapt dow 5-7-17 161MGC p181 CR Palestine2

BANKS,Raymond D'Albini Sykes Capt kia 21-4-17 IA 9BhopalInf p273 MR38

BANKS,Thomas George Lt kia 26-4-18 RE p210 CR France880

BANKS,William T2Lt dow 6-4-18 PoW 11DLI p160 CR France987

BANKS,William John.MC.MID TCapt kia 30-7-16 15RFA p24 CR France397

BANKS,William Sykes Maj ded 19-2-16 Dors RoO p123

BANNATYNE,Douglas Alexander Lt kia 1-8-18 1/9RScots p212 CR France524

BANNATYNE,Edgar James.DSO.LtTMaj kld 11-9-17 19Huss &RFC p4&23 CR Glouc60

BANNATYNE,Ian McNiven 2Lt kia 18-11-16 9HLI p240 MR21

BANNATYNE,James Fitzgerald TMaj dow 14-5-16 11Huss att23Manch p22 CR France345

BANNATYNE,John Miller T2Lt dow 2-8-17 HLI att12Bn p162 CR Belgium7

BANNATYNE,Ninian John.MID Capt mbk 3-5-17 1Lpool p256 MR20

BANNATYNE,William Sterling LtCol kia 24-10-14 1Lpool p71 MR29

BANNEHR,Harold James Thomas Lt kia 5-11-15 7DLI p239 MR21,5-11-16

BANNELL,Leonard Henry 2Lt kia 3-12-17 2/6Glouc p225 see BANWELL,L.H.

BANNER,Frederick William T2Lt kia 12-5-17 7Yorks p89 MR20

BANNERMAN,Eric 2Lt kia 20-11-17 8A&SH p243 CR France712

BANNERMAN,G.G.Lt kld 8-6-19 RE attRAF p43

BANNERMAN,Oriel William Erskine Capt dow 3-2-15 IA 15Lancers p273 CR France102

BANNERMAN,Robert Gilroy TLt kia 25-7-16 157RFA p24 CR France399

BANNERMAN,Stanley Cyril Forster LtTCapt dow 7-11-17 RASC attRGA 375SB p192 CR Belgium23

BANNESTER,John 2Lt kia 4-10-18 16Lond p250 CR France567

BANNING,Percy Stuart Lt kia 4-11-14 2RMunstF p175 CR Belgium57

BANNISTER,Henry William T2Lt kia 14-6-17 10Lincs p74 CR France644

BANNISTER,Samuel Capt dow 15-4-17 4Worc p107 CR France113

BANNISTER,William George Lt kia 28-3-18 RGA 405SB p38 CR France1182

BANTICK,Reginald Arthur Jay Lt kia 19-5-15 19Lond p250 CR France279

BANTOCK,Arthur Thomas T2Lt dow 23-11-15 13RFus p66 CR Gallipoli27

BANTOFT,Edward Spencer 2LtTLt dow 10-9-16 5Lond p246 CR France23,11-9-16

BANWELL,L.H.MR17 See BANNELL,L.H.

BANYARD,James Hirst 2Lt kia 3-9-16 3 att1Beds p85 MR21

BARBE,Adrien Espinasson Lt ded 27-5-18 5HLI &RAF p240 MR41,drd

BARBER,Bradley King Bell 2LtTCapt kia 4-9-17 1NumbF att9RFC p4&60 MR20

BARBER,Frank William Lt kia 30-6-15 RGA 26HB p38 CR France571,2Lt

BARBER,Geoffrey Carew Capt kia 25-4-15 5Yorks p220 MR29

BARBER,George T2Lt kia 3-10-16 16 att18RFus p66 CR France374

BARBER,George Edward 2Lt kia 24-8-18 1GrenGds p49 CR France1489

BARBER,George Ernest 2Lt kia 7-7-16 10LancF p91 MR21

BARBER,Gordon TCapt kia 22-7-16 1CamH p167 CR France515

BARBER,Gordon Henderson.MC.2Lt ded 20-10-18 8Worc p226 CR France146

BARBER,Graham Brooke TLt kia 25-8-18 13KRRC p149 CR France578

BARBER,Harry Mason T2Lt kia 8-8-18 8ESurr p112 CR France247

BARBER,Henry Cecil T2Lt drd 9-11-17 14Glouc &WAFF p106 MR40,Lt

BARBER,Herbert Graham.MC.Capt kia 7-7-16 4Y&L p238 CR France702

BARBER,Herbert Sydney T2Lt dow 15-5-18 18 att10Mddx p146 CR France100

BARBER,John Lt kia 27-9-17 4Ess p232 CR France1361,Ex28Lond

BARBER,John Christian 2Lt kia 16-6-15 10Lpool p216 MR29

BARBER,Leonard Harry 2Lt kia 5-6-15 6Manch p236 MR4

BARBER,Maurice Capt.MID kia 25-11-17 2/4Y&L p238 MR17,26-11-17

BARBER,Walter Edward 2Lt ded 9-11-16 RGA CR Kent83

BARBER,Wilfred 2Lt kia 27-11-17 Y&L p158 MR17

BARBER,Willard T2Lt kld 5-1-18 2Yorks p89 CR Belgium127

BARBER,William Geoffrey Wright 2Lt kia 1-7-16 1/5N&D p232 MR21

BARBER-STARKEY,William Henry Joseph Capt dow PoW 11-9-15 RFA p24 CR France717,11-9-14

BARBOR,Robert Christopher Lt ded 25-5-15 54RFA p24 CR Surrey 150

BARBOUR,Hastings Duncan 2Lt kia 21-10-17 GL &10RFC p4 CR Belgium383,Lt

BARCLAY,Allen 2Lt kia 24-4-15 RE p43 MR22

BARCLAY,David Frederick Lt kia 1-4-18 2DragGds A'Sqn p20 CR France1170,2-4-18

BARCLAY,David Stuart Lt dow 24-4-17 1ScotsGds p51 CR Norf137

BARCLAY,Edward Wilfred Howard 2Lt kia 27-1-18 2 O&BLI p129 CR France439

BARCLAY,Eric Callender.MID TLt kia 25-9-15 MGC Mtrs att3MGCS RFA p181 MR29,Ex12Ches

BARCLAY,F.Lt ded 1-11-18 RDC &RAF p253

BARCLAY,Geoffrey William.MC.MID TMaj kia 28-7-16 1RB p177&258 CR Belgium73

BARCLAY,George Eric.MID Capt kia 24-1-17 RLancs att4Nig p58&201 CR EAfrica39

BARCLAY,George Reinhold TLt kia 30-10-18 GL Intelligence p189 CR Belgium393,Capt Ex7Suff

BARCLAY,Henry 2Lt kia 15-10-16 DLI att2Bn p160 CR France307,Harry

BARCLAY,James George Lt ded 23-7-17 6A&SH p243 CR Iraq8

BARCLAY,Marshall Stuart.MID TLt kia 28-3-18 17RScots p53 MR27

BARCLAY,Peter T2Lt kia 15-11-18 RE 180Co p43 CR France1495

BARCLAY,Rafe Hedworth Myddleton 2Lt kia 14-9-14 2KRRC p149 MR15

BARCLAY,Robert Stephen 2Lt kia 21-3-18 3 att16RScots p53 MR20

BARCLAY,Samuel Dugald 2Lt drd 10-10-18 5ScotRif p224 CR Ireland14

BARCLAY,Thomas Hubert Maj drd 4-5-17 1/1SurrYeo p205 CR Italy13

BARCLAY,William Kirk Lt dow 20-6-15 1/7BlkW p231 CR Scot105

BARCLAY-SMITH,J. AMatron ded 28-4-16 QAIMNS p200

BARDER,Sam Gerald T2Lt kia 30-9-16 8ESurr p112 MR21

BARDSWELL,Hamilton Ainsworth 2Lt kia 30-11-17 1/10Lpool p216 MR17

BARE,Arnold Edwin.MVO.Capt kia 30-10-17 28Lond p252 MR30

BARFIELD,John Claude Horsey 2Lt kld 29-6-15 3RFC p1 CR France200

BARFOOT,George Allan 2Lt kld 20-6-15 3Worc p107 CR Belgium112,20-6-18

BARFORD,Kenneth Purnell 2Lt mbk 27-3-18 2RFC p256 MR20

BARGH,George 2Lt kia 10-5-15 Lpool att1Suff p71 MR29

BARHAM,Wilfred Saxby TCapt dow 10-10-15 3 att1EKent p57 CR Belgium5,Wilfrid

BARING,Cecil Christopher T2Lt dow 21-3-18 8RWKent p140 CR France987,kia

BARING,Guy Victor.Hon.MIDx2 TLtCol kia 15-9-16 1CldGds p50 CR France394

BARK,Norman Lt kia 1-10-18 6KOSB &RAF p101 CR Belgium157

BARK,Robert Charles T2Lt kld 28-3-18 RFC p15 CR Essex1,R.T.

BARKAS,John Charles Pearson Lt kia 15-9-16 DLI att10Bn p160 MR21

BARKBY,Hartley 2Lt kia 1-8-16 13/277WLancsRFA p208 CR France630,2-8-16

BARKER,Albion Mitchell 2LtTLt dow 19-7-17 20 att2/5LancF p91 CR Belgium11

BARKER,Arnold Septimus 2Lt died 29-5-17 7DLI CR Asia45

BARKER,Arthur 2Lt kia 9-10-17 6WYorks p218 MR30

BARKER,Arthur 2Lt ded 20-12-18 RGA 150HB p38 CR Germany1

BARKER,Arthur Edward James Col ded 8-4-16 RAMC p233 CR Greece7

BARKER,Cecil Massey Arbuthnot T2Lt kia 17-8-15 6RIrF p170 MR4

BARKER,Cecil Noel T2Lt kia 19-11-16 1Dors p123 MR21

BARKER,Charles Haydn 2Lt dow 8-10-18 1Lond p245 CR France146

BARKER,Charles Ivor T2Lt dow 17-3-16 6RWKent p140 CR France80,Ivo

BARKER,Charles William Tone.MC.Capt dow 24-3-18 15DLI p160 MR27

BARKER,Christopher James.MID TLtACapt dow 12-4-18 RE attHQ 30Div p43 CR Belgium20

BARKER,Clarence Moores Childe Capt kia 22-2-17 IA 126Baluchis att53Sikhs p273 MR38

BARKER,Edith Frances Miss ded 3-4-18 VAD 90Detachment p200 CR France134

BARKER,Edward CaptTMaj ded 2-1-16 Mddx attEss p146

BARKER,Edward Bannister Maj 2-1-16 Mddx attEss CR Gallipoli1

BARKER,Edward Walter Chap4Cl dow 18-3-18 RAChDept att176TMB p199 CR France518

BARKER,Frank Edward Lt ded 13-1-19 W'moreld&CumbldYeo &RAF p206&258

BARKER,Frederick Ernest T2Lt kia 13-10-17 10WYorks p80 MR30

BARKER,Geoffrey Capt kia 22-11-17 2/6WYorks p218 MR17

BARKER,George Frederick T2Lt kia 12-5-17 2Ess p131 CR France97

BARKER,Godfrey Maj 29-4-15 RM DrakeBn RNDiv CR Gallipoli6

BARKER,Gordon T2Lt dow 23-10-18 7EYorks p83 CR France332

BARKER,Harold Frederick.MID Maj kia 29-3-18 29RGA att126RFA p209 MR27,Frederic

BARKER,Harold William TLt dow 1-7-16 16Mddx p146 MR21

BARKER,Harry T2Lt kia 4-9-18 1LancF p91 CR France297

BARKER,Henry Arthur Eric T2Lt kia 20-11-17 YLI att2/4Bn p142 CR France530

BARKER,Henry Watson 2Lt kia 17-4-18 4Lincs p217 CR France285

BARKER,Herbert Leslie 2Lt kia 22-3-18 N&D att12Bn p133 MR27

BARKER,Holroyd Birkett Lt ded 15-8-17 RGA 134SB p38

BARKER,Hubert Joseph T2Lt dow 28-3-18 Mddx att1/8Bn p146 CR France266

BARKER,Hugh Edwin 2Lt ded 31-1-18 6RFus p66 CR Ireland33

BARKER,John Edward 2Lt kia 13-10-15 4Leic p220 MR19

BARKER,John Hawksworth Jackson Lt kia 7-8-15 5ELancs p226 CR Gallipoli2

BARKER,Nello Lt ded 14-3-17 6RScots p211 CR Lancs464

BARKER,Osmund Vincent T2Lt kia 28-11-17 97MGC Inf p181 MR30

BARKER,Paul Studholme.MC.TLtACapt kia 26-10-17 78RFA p24 CR Belgium25

BARKER,Percy T2Lt kia 13-4-18 33MGC Inf p181 CR France324

BARKER,Randle Barnett.DSO&Bar.TBrigGen kia 24-3-18 RWelshF Maj RoO p97 CR France430,99InfBde Ex RWFus

BARKER,Richard Raymond.MC.Maj kia 20-4-18 NumbF &3RAF p262 MR20

BARKER,Richard Vincent Capt kia 31-10-14 1RWelshF p97 MR29

BARKER,Robert Arnold.MC.TLtACapt dow 13-10-18 10N&D p133 CR France1393

BARKER,Sydney Clare Lt kia 21-3-18 4 att9Norf p216 MR20

BARKER,Theodore T2Lt kia 13-5-17 22Manch p154 MR20

BARKER,Thomas Chesman 2Lt kia 3-11-18 RE 218FC p43 CR France940,4-11-18

BARKER,William CaptTMaj dow 15-8-18 9Worc p107 MR4

BARKER,William Gordon Steiglitz Capt ded 1-12-16 ConnRgrs p172 CR Surrey128,2-12-16

BARKER,William Harold Capt dow 5-11-15 RGA HQ 24SB p38 CR Gallipoli29,Harald

BARKER,W.J.2Lt kld 27-4-18 GL &RAF p189

BARKER-MILL,William Claude Frederick Vaudrey TCapt kia 15-9-16 8RB p177

BARKLEY,Martin Bell 2Lt kia 2-9-18 4RScotF p222 CR France646

BARKWORTH,H.A.S.Maj 28-1-17 BordR CR Mddx26

BARKWORTH,Humphrey Robertson Capt dow 3-7-16 2NumbF p60 CR France44

BARLING,Harold T2Lt kia 15-6-16 8Leic p87 CR France283

BARLING,William Bingham 2Lt kia 12-3-15 6 att3Worc p107 MR29

BARLOW,Cecil George 2Lt dow 18-5-17 B156RFA p24 CR France113

BARLOW,Charles Alfred T2Lt dow 17-8-17 11RSuss att4RFC p4&118 CR Belgium11

BARLOW,Charles Leslie.DSO.BtLtCol kia 5-8-18 WYorks att1/5A&SH p80 CR France866

BARLOW,Cuthbert Charles Lambert Maj kia 1-11-14 1Lincs p74 MR29

BARLOW,Geoffrey Petrie.MC.2Lt kia 2-9-17 6N&D p233 CR France115

BARLOW,Harold Carver TLt kia 18-6-17 20LancF &9RFC p4&92 MR20

BARLOW,Harry Archibald T2Lt kia 10-7-17 16LancF p91 CR Belgium174

BARLOW,Harry Loftus TLt kld 18-3-18 RE &RFC p15&43 CR Hereford &Worc186

BARLOW,J.E.DSO.MC.Maj 3-6-20 2Yorks CR Iraq8

BARLOW,John Lancashire.MID T2Lt kia 23-9-17 GL &40RFC p4 CR France32

BARLOW,Leonard Monteagle.MC&2Bars LtTCapt kld 5-2-18 RFC SR p15 CR Surrey6

BARLOW,Lovel Hardwick T2Lt kia 16-8-16 13Lpool p71 MR21

BARLOW,Osborn.MC.TCapt dow 14-4-18 8SStaffs p122 CR Belgium183

BARLOW,Percy T2Lt kia 15-11-17 19Lpool p71 CR Belgium84

BARLOW,R.T.Capt kia 30-7-18 SL &RAF p201

BARLOW,Theodore Kenneth TLt dow 15-7-16 1SStaffs p122 CR France833,8Bn

BARLOW,William Howard 2Lt kia 2-5-17 GL &RAOC p266

BARLTROP,Eric Arthur Lt kia 23-4-17 RE(EAnglia) att22RFC p17&210 CR France366

BARNABY,William Gordon.MID TCapt kia 23-8-16 7YLI p142 MR21

BARNARD,Albert T2Lt kia 1-10-18 2Suff p78 CR France359

BARNARD,Arthur Wilson T2Lt dow 29-3-18 12Suff p78 CR France40

BARNARD,Dudley Henry Lionel 2Lt ded 10-2-15 130RFA p24 CR France64

BARNARD,Edward Armstrong 2Lt kia 29-9-17 RFA att10RFC p4&24 CR France98

BARNARD,Ernest Yorke TCapt ded 5-3-18 GL &RFC p201&266 CR Lond8

BARNARD,Humphrey Denzil 2Lt kia 21-8-16 6 att3RB p177 MR21

BARNARD,Laurence Claude TMaj ded 12-1-18 RASC p192 CR France377

BARNARD,Lawrence Reginald 2Lt kia 1-10-16 17Lond p250 MR21

BARNARD,Lewis Harold TLt kia 25-8-16 GL attTMB p189 CR France294

BARNARD,Norman Arthur Southard T2Lt kia 8-7-16 18Lpool p71 CR France630

BARNARD,Robert Cyril TLt dow 5-9-17 RASC 58DivTrHQ p192 CR Belgium18

BARNARD-SMITH,William Woodthorpe Barnard T2Lt kia 21-10-16 38RFA p24 CR Frnce513

BARNARDISTON,Nathaniel Walter MajGen ded 18-8-19 Staff p261 CR Essex95

BARNE,M.DSO.TMaj ded 17-9-17 ScotsGds &1SuffYeo p205&51,17-8-17 CR Belgium18

BARNE,Seymour.MC.Capt kia 23-4-17 20Huss att35RFC p4&23 CR France95

BARNES,Arthur Randall 2Lt kia 4-10-17 3SomLI p79 MR30

BARNES,Arthur William TLt kia 11-4-18 9Ches p95 MR30,Capt

BARNES,Aubrey T2Lt kia 22-3-18 17Lpool p71 MR27

BARNES,Basil Goodall Lt dow 19-8-18 4 att10N&D p133 CR France13

BARNES,Benjamin King T2Lt ded 28-6-18 3NumbF att9RFus p60 CR France122

BARNES,Bertram Morris Lt kia 26-4-17 9 att12Manch p237 MR20

BARNES,David John T2Lt kld 25-4-17 GL &RFC p4 CR Kent7,24-4-17

BARNES,Edmund T2Lt kld 27-1-18 GL &RFC p15 CR Lincs61

BARNES,Edmund Lyndon.MID TCapt&Adjt kia 3-4-16 8RLancs p58 MR29

BARNES,Edward James 2Lt dow 4-5-18 5 att2RFus p66 CR France180,Lt

BARNES,Edward William 2Lt dow 10-7-17 5 att2KRRC p149 MR31

BARNES,Eric 2Lt kia 1-11-14 1Lincs p74 MR29

BARNES,Eric 2Lt kia 16-11-18 18Lond p250 CR Belgium195,6-11-18

BARNES,Eric Earle Capt kia 7-11-17 RE &102RFC p5&43 CR France1029

BARNES,Francis(Frank) T2Lt dow 1-7-16 22Lpool p71 CR France397,kia

BARNES,Frank 2Lt kia 28-10-17 20Lond p251 CR France646

BARNES,George Gaylor Lt kia 16-7-16 6 att3Worc p107 MR21

BARNES,George West LtCol 5-2-19 APD CR France40

BARNES,Harry Scott TLt kia 9-4-17 1NumbF p60 CR France581

BARNES,Henry T2Lt kia 25-9-15 11 att2GordH p166 CR France219

BARNES,Herbert Charles T2Lt kia 22-12-17 162MGC Inf p181 CR Palestine9

BARNES,Herbert George T2Lt kia 16-9-16 9 att7DCLI p114 MR21

BARNES,Herbert George T2Lt ded 31-8-17 KRRC att7Bn p149 CR Belgium8

BARNES,Hugh Cecil.MC.Lt kia 21-7-18 RSuss att2TMB p118 MR19,Cyril Capt

BARNES,James 2Lt dow 28-12-18 7N&D p233 CR France120,28-12-16

BARNES,John Backham 2Lt kia 9-5-17 87RFA p24 CR Belgium5,Buckham

BARNES,John Christopher Craven TCapt kia 29-5-16 8BordR p116 CR France68

BARNES,John Edward Templeman T2LtACapt kia 3-2-17 7Glouc p106 MR38

BARNES,John Robert Evans 2Lt dow 18-4-16 9 att6KSLI p144 CR France40

BARNES,Lawrence Fairbank T2Lt kia 24-7-17 YLI att10Bn p142 CR Frnce1186

BARNES,Leon Thomas Victor.MC.Maj 29-6-18 7KSLI CR France33

BARNES,Ralph George 2Lt kia 30-10-17 2/8Lond p247 MR30

BARNES,Vincent Kendall 2Lt kia 29-4-17 24RFus p66 MR20

BARNES,Walter Lt&QM ded 30-3-16 18Lond p269 CR Mddx53,30-6-16

BARNES,Wilfred Oliver T2Lt kia 18-11-16 10RFus p66 CR France701

BARNES,Will 2Lt kia 2-11-18 A26RFA p208 CR France1257

BARNES,William Sibson TLt kia 5-6-16 11BordR p116 CR France702

BARNET,D.G.Lt ded 31-10-18 RH&FA &11RAF p24 CR France512

BARNET,Henry Morton T2Lt dow 23-4-18 PoW 1KRRC p149 CR Germany3

BARNET,James Howieson 2Lt kia 1-8-18 4BlkW p230 CR France524

BARNET,James Knox TLt ded 2-11-18 RASC MT p192 CR Egypt9

BARNET,Walter 2Lt dow 22-11-18 6Dev p217 CR France146,BARNETT

BARNETT,Alan Gerrard Lt kia 22-8-17 7Lpool attTankCps p189&215 MR30

BARNETT,Bertram Leeds Thomas Capt ded 18-4-15 RASC p192 CR Hamps1

BARNETT,Bret Hercules 2Lt kia 10-8-17 11RFus p66 MR29

BARNETT,Carew Maj kia 12-8-15 6DCLI p114 CR Belgium84

BARNETT,Charles Edward TCapt dow 1-10-15 9ESurr p112 CR France1276

BARNETT,Charles Frederick Robert 2Lt kia 20-4-15 5Glouc p225 CR Belgium70,19-4-15

BARNETT,Denis Oliver TLt dow 16-8-15 2Leinst p174 CR Belgium5

BARNETT,Edwin Bertram Capt kia 30-10-17 8Lond attMGC Inf p186&247 MR30

BARNETT,Edwin James Lt kia 7-8-17 RE p210 CR Belgium29

BARNETT,Gerald 2Lt kia 3-11-15 3RScots p53 CR France423,13Bn

BARNETT,Gilbert Mortimer 2Lt kia 28-9-18 6WRid p227 CR France358

BARNETT,Guy 2Lt kia 11-3-15.5 att1Worc p107 MR22

BARNETT,Harold Thornton 2LtTLt dow 21-10-15 9ESurr p112 CR Belgium11,20-10-15

BARNETT,Harold Walter 2Lt kia 30-12-17 5SLancs p230 MR30

BARNETT,Harry Mortimer Stacey 2Lt kia 6-4-16 23RFA p24 CR Belgium28,107

BARNETT,Herbert William T2Lt kia 20-9-17 26RFus p66 CR Belgium112

BARNETT,Herbert William Capt kia 9-5-15 13Lond p249 MR32,Walter

BARNETT,James 2Lt kia 12-7-15 4RScotF p222&269 MR4

BARNETT,Lascelles De Barry TCapt kia 3-7-16 6RWKent p140 CR France1890

BARNETT,Lionel TLt ded 6-2-17 6Yorks p89 CR Glouc27

BARNETT,Phillip 2Lt kia 2-7-16 4Mddx p146 CR France267

BARNETT,Ralph Edward Fulton Lt kia 6-9-17 8LancF att125MGC Inf p221&186 CR Belgium125

BARNETT,Ralph Thurlby 2Lt kia 12-10-16 3 att2LancF p92 MR21

BARNETT,Reginald Walter.MC&Bar LtTMaj kia 12-8-18 KRRC attStaffDivHQ p149 CR Belgium40

BARNETT,R.T.F.Capt 12-2-20 RAMC CR Wales564

BARNETT,T.E.TD.Maj 5-12-18 6SStaffs CR Staffs57

BARNETT,Thomas William 2Lt ded 17-1-19 EYorks &RAF p83 CR Yorks244

BARNETT,Victor Baron TLt kia 25/27-9-15 12NumbF p60 MR19

BARNETT,Wilford Mainwaring Cornish 2Lt 13-9-15 IARO attS&T Cps MR43

BARNETT,William Augustus T2Lt dow 15-11-17 21RFC p5 CR Belgium20

BARNETT,William Raymond T2Lt kia 29-4-18 8 att1/5SStaffs p122 CR France572

BARNETT-BARKER,R.see BARKER,R.B.

BARNEWALL,Reginald Nicholas Francis Mary.Hon Lt dow 24-3-18 5 att2Leinst p174 CR France329,Capt

BARNEY,Montagu Mydelton T2Lt kia 27-4-16 RE 253TC p43 CR France423,Middleton

BARNI,Noel Henry Louis TLt dow PoW 29-3-18 47MGC p181 CR France660

BARNICOT,Arthur William Capt 22-11-16 3/2MtdDivSigsRF CRSurrey57

BARNICOT,John Livingston 2Lt kia 22-12-16 3Lincs p74 CR France423,1Bn

BARNIDGE,John 2Lt dow 26-10-17 Manch att21Bn p154 MR30

BARNS,A.Lt 20-4-17 RFC CRHamps4

BARNS,Charles Stanley Capt ded 22-7-18 17Lond attMGC p186&250,22-8-18 CR Essex40

BARNSLEY,Alan Capt kia 25/27-10-14 4LancF attNumbF p92 MR22

BARNSLEY,Thomas Kenneth Capt kia 31-7-17 1CldGds p50 CR Belgium12

BARNWELL,George Woodruffe T2Lt kia 13-4-18 RLancs att1/4YLI p58 MR30

BARON,Margaret Alice Nurse 22-10-18 VAD ELancs CR Lancs222

BARON,Stephen Timmis 2Lt kia 8-12-16 6Glouc p225 CR France251

BARON,Sydney Percival 2Lt kia 5-7-16 1N&D p133 MR21

BARON,William 2Lt dow 19-10-17 RGA 203SB p38 CR France1361

BARR,David Buik.MC.Capt dow 13-7-19 3ELancs p110 MR70 &CR Europe179

BARR,George Fleet TCapt ded 23-3-16 RAMC att42FA p194 CR France1182,Flett

BARR,Henry Keith Maj ?? 25-10-16 IA 38CenIndHorse p273

BARR,Herbert Carrick T2Lt kia 11-12-16 GL &RFC p2&189

BARR,Hugh TCapt ded 21-2-17 RAMC att42AmbTongaTrain p194 CR Greece7

BARR,Hugh T2Lt dow 30-9-18 35MGC Inf p181 MR30

BARR,James Lt dow 16-10-18 D121RFA p207 CR France398

BARR,James Hamilton TLt kia 1-9-18 11RIrRif att7/8RInniskF p168 CR Belgium89

BARR,John Lyle T2Lt dow 26-7-16 D159RFA p24 CR France51,Lt C157

BARR,John William T2Lt kld 14-11-17 GL &49RFC p5 CR Durham26

BARR,John William 2Lt kia 24-3-18 5 att8BlkW p231 MR27

BARR,John Young Lt kia 26-4-15 7A&SH p243 MR29,25-4-15

BARR,Ninian Horrell 2Lt kia 3-9-16 RFA p208 CR France233

BARR,Percival Fowler.MC.T2Lt kia 2-3-17 20Mddx p146

BARR,Samuel Tudor TLt kia 23-2-15 3Huss p21 CR Belgium112

BARR,William T2Lt kia 11/18-7-16 13NumbF p60 CR France188

BARR,William Arthur 2Lt kia 27-8-18 RGA 328SB p38 CR France1489,Ex 4SfthH

BARR,William Speirs TCapt dow 23-5-17 18HLI p162 CR France439

BARRACLOUGH,G.W.MC.2Lt 29-9-18 6WRid CR France358 see BARRMCLOUGH,G.W.

BARRACLOUGH,William 2Lt kia 28-9-16 5WYorks p218 CR France383

BARRAN,Alfred Rawson T2Lt dow 31-3-18 9WRid p115 CR France62,kia

BARRAN,Roland Noel Lt ded 19-3-19 2LifeGds p20 CR Berks84,Capt

BARRAND,Sidney TLt kia 14-8-18 1KRRC p149 CR France1014,Sydney

BARRAS,William.MM.2Lt dow 25-3-18 7A&SH p243 CR France300

BARRAT,William Topley T2Lt dow 25-4-17 26 att13Manch p154 CR Greece6

BARRATT,Ernest Bird Maj dow 7-5-16 IA 128Pioneers p273 CR Iraq8

BARRATT,Geoffrey Ravenscroft 2Lt kia 7-7-16 10LancF p92 MR21

BARRATT,George Herbert 2Lt kia 9-10-17 9Manch p237 MR30,Lt

BARRATT,Harold Charles Edward T2Lt dow 18-5-17 9Glouc p106 CR Greece7

BARRATT,John Leslie T2Lt kia 27-9-17 13Lpool p71 MR30

BARRATT,John Roland Lt ded 24-1-19 23GHQ Res MT 1144RASC p192 CR France40

BARRATT,Kenneth Franklin Lt kia 1-7-16 3Ess attMGC p131&181 MR21

BARRE,Gerald Benedict 2Lt kld 9-8-18 11RDubF &6RAF p176 MR20

BARRELL,Philip James 2Lt kia 1-5-15 Ess p131 MR29

BARRELL,Victor Henry T2Lt kia 22-8-18 11RFus p66 CR France177

BARRETT,Adrian Hamilton Silverton T2Lt kia 10-7-16 RWelshF att14Bn p97 MR21

BARRETT,Alec Roland TLt kia 4-10-17 10YLI p142 MR30

BARRETT,Arthur Edward T2Lt kia 22-8-17 KRRC att8Bn p149 MR30

BARRETT,Arthur Lennard 2Lt kia 1-10-17 1/2 att8Leic p87 MR30

BARRETT,Bernard Thomas T2Lt kia 12-4-18 15RWar p64 MR32

BARRETT,Cecil Roy.MC.2Lt dow 25-6-17 C113RH&FA p25 CR Belgium15

BARRETT,Charles John Chard Capt kia 13-11-14 RScotsF p94 MR29

BARRETT,Colin Frederick,MC.LtTCapt dow 23-9-18 8 att11YLI p142 CR Italy5

BARRETT,David Ernest SenAssSurg2Cl ded 8-10-18 IMS MR52

BARRETT,Edgar Bradley 2Lt ded 11-7-17 RE p269 CR Hamps4

BARRETT,Ernest William TCapt kia 29-5-16 29RFC p2 CR Belgium11,FltCmdr

BARRETT,Frederick Alan T2Lt kld 22-4-16 9Leinst att8Ches p174 MR38,8Ches att9Leic

BARRETT,George TLt kia 6-8-15 12RWar att2Hamps p64 MR4

BARRETT,Gerald Herbert Johnson Capt kia 24-4-16 IA 93BurmaInf p273 MR38

BARRETT,H.G.MM.2Lt 16-8-17 1Newfndland MR30

BARRETT,Hebron TLt dow 27-3-18 10RDubF p176 CR France185

BARRETT,Herbert Victor.MC.2Lt dow 22-4-18 D110RFA p25 CR France100

BARRETT,Hugh Treherne Lt ded 6-11-17 SL NyassalandFldForce p201 CR EAfrica40

BARRETT,Jack Ainslake 2Lt kia 28-4-17 13Ess p131 MR20,John Aislabie

BARRETT,Jack Harper Phillip Lt ded 1-11-18 1Lincs &RAF p74 CR Lond12,Capt

BARRETT,John Ambrose T2Lt kia 31-7-17 16RB p177 CR Belgium96

BARRETT,Joseph Gordon.MC.T2Lt kia 10-4-18 9LNLancs D'Coy p135 MR32

BARRETT,Keith Joy.MID TLt dow 16-4-17 2RFus p66 CR France40,Capt

BARRETT,Knox Gordon 2LtALt kia 20-9-17 RFA attZ20TMB p25 CR Belgium12

BARRETT,Lindsay Alfred.MC.TMaj kia 17-3-16 1NumbF att1/4Yorks p60 CR Belgium5

BARRETT,L.K.W.2Lt kld 24-4-18 GL &RAF p189

BARRETT,Noel Bertram T2Lt kia 29-4-18 Ess att2Bn p131 CR France250

BARRETT,Norman Kenyon 2Lt kia 18-9-18 4Yorks att1EYorks p220 MR16

BARRETT,Philip Godfrey Capt kia 27-8-14 2RMunF p175 CR France1751

BARRETT,Reginald T2Lt kia 15-5-16 11LancF p92 CR France68

BARRETT,Reginald Albert Baber Lt kia 7-11-17 2/23Lond p252 CR Palestine1

BARRETT,Reginald James Lt kia 21-8-18 6Lpool p215 CR France619

BARRETT,Sophia Violet Nurse drd 10-10-18 VAD p200 MR40

BARRETT,Thomas Cyril T2Lt dow 4-7-16 Lincs p74 CR France207

BARRETT,Walter Ralph Lt kia 2-11-17 7Ess p232 MR34

BARRETT,Wilfred Varnish 2Lt dow 28-9-18 8RWar p215 CR France512

BARRETT,William T2Lt kia 11-8-16 11ELancs p110 CR France631

BARRICK,George Oliver James 2Lt kia 6-11-17 C168RFA p208 CR Belgium23

BARRIE,David Capt&QM ded 8-12-17 SL HLI p201 CR Surrey15

BARRIE,Walter 2Lt kia 7-6-17 3KOSB att6BordR p101 CR Belgium155

BARRIE,William Cowan Ogilvy Lt kia 14-10-16 5BlkW p231 MR21

BARRINGTON,Allan Leslie T2Lt kldacc 29-7-16 120MGC Inf p181 CR France550

BARRINGTON,Noel Scott Lt kia 10-3-15 1RIrRif p168 CR France706

BARRINGTON-KENNETT,Aubrey Hampden 2Lt dow 20-9-14 O&BLI p129 CR France1107

BARRINGTON KENNETT,Basil Herbert BtMaj kld 18-5-15 GrenGds attRFC p1&49 CR France727

BARRINGTON-KENNETT,Victor Annesley TMaj kia 13-3-16 RFC p2 CR France1504

BARRMCLOUGH,George William.MC.2Lt kia 29-9-18 6WRid p227 CR France358,BARRACLOUGH

BARRON,Francis Harry Lt ded 20-7-20 IARO attS&TCps p273 MR67

BARRON,James TMaj dow 27-9-15 7CamH p167 CR France924

BARRON,John George T2Lt kld 25-6-17 GL &RFC p5 CR Lond33

BARRON,Louis TLt kia 19-7-16 10BordR att2/6RWar p116 MR19

BARRON,Sydney William James Lt ded 25-7-18 IARO att53Sikhs p273 CR Egypt1

BARRON,Vincent 2Lt dow 4-11-18 4Nhampt p234 CR France146

BARROW,Alexander Egan Lt kia 4-10-17 3/4RWSurr B'Coy p212 MR30

BARROW,Alfred James.MC.Capt dow 24-6-18 PoW 10LancF p92 CR Germany3

BARROW,Edmund Sprotson Knapp 2Lt kia 8-5-17 4 att14RWar p64

BARROW,Ernest Isaac TLt kia 23-10-16 3SLancs att2ELancs p125 MR21

BARROW,Federick William 2Lt kia 3-9-16 14 att13RSuss p118 CR France339

BARROW,Geoffrey Selwyn.OBE.LtTCapt ded 26-12-18 RFA att8DivCycCps p25 CR France1856

BARROW,Hector Henry 2Lt kia 20-10-15 8RFus p66 MR19

BARROW,Howard Cyril TLt kia 20-9-17 MGC p181 MR30

BARROW,James HonTLt&QM dow 1-6-16 8RBerks p138 CR France178

BARROW,Lawrence Alfred Howard T2Lt kia 1-9-16 10 att11RSuss p118 CR France1013,31-8-16

BARROW,Spencer Ellwood Lt dow 16-11-15 5RLanc p213 CR Lancs77

BARROW,Wynford Capt 1-3-20 20DeccanHorse CR France1571

BARROWCLIFF,Cyril Herbert Ford T2Lt kia 27-10-17 1/2Leic p87 MR30,6Bn

BARROWS,John Cecil Russell SubCdr ded 18-11-18 IA IOD p273

BARROWS,Maxwell Dalton 2Lt kia 3-10-18 1/5N&D p232 CR France375,Dalston

BARRS,Noel Coghlan 2Lt kia 15-9-16 11RWKent p140 MR21

BARRY,Cecil Lt kia 21-8-17 17RIrR &57RFC p5&88 CR Belgium125

BARRY,Francis Renton Capt kia 4-9-18 5ESurr p226 CR Belgium111

BARRY,Frederick Fitzgerald Lt 6-1-19 5WYorks CR Ches3

BARRY,James Lawrence.CMG.LtCol 12-6-20 1DragGds CR Lond12

BARRY,Nathaniel James Merriman Capt kia 20-10-17 SL EATrnptCps p268 CR Tanzania1,21-10-17

BARRY,R.2Lt 28-6-15 6Ess CR Essex5

BARRY,Robert Cooke Capt kia 18-7-16 17RScots p53 MR21

BARRY,Sheil Ronald 2Lt kia 7-10-16 11 att1/12Lond p248 MR21

BARRY,William Patrick T2Lt kia 25-8-18 9WRid p115 CR France239,28-8-18

BARRY-ROBERTS,Frederick Leslie Lt kia 22-12-17 IA 2 att7Rajputs p273 CR Asia62,2Lt

BARRY-WALSH,Stephen Michael Lt dow 8-9-15 RAMC 1CavFA CRFrance8

BARSTOW,Edmund Leonard James Lt kia 1-2-17 IA 35 att36Sikhs p273 CR Iraq5,2Lt

BARSTOW,John Eric Jackson Capt kld 27-1-19 NSomYeo &RAF p205&258

BARSTOW,John Baillie Maj kia 31-8-14 RE p43 CR France1063

BARSTOW,Michael William 2Lt kia 3-6-17 RGA 203SB p38 CR Belgium17

BARTELT,F.W.Capt ded 11-9-16 2/4SomLI p218 CR Somerset101

BARTEN,Donald.MM.2Lt kia 30-11-17 8RFus p66 MR17

BARTHOLOMEW,Benjamin James 2Lt kia 18-11-16 4CamH p243 CR France515

BARTHOLOMEW,Claude.MC.TCapt kia 15-9-16 1ScotsGds att&MGC Inf p52&181&258 CR France400

BARTHOLOMEW,George Hugh Freeland.MID TLtACapt dow 2-10-17 14A&SH p172 CR France398

BARTHOLOMEW,George Leo Walter 2Lt ded 6-4-19 RFus CR Essex1

BARTHOLOMEW,Guy Wollaston TCapt kia 25-8-16 7KRRC p149 CR France513

BARTHOLOMEW,William George 2LtTLt ded 26-4-15 BordR p116 CR Gallipoli3

BARTHORP,Arthur Herbert LtCol ded 18-6-18 Nhampt p265 CR Suff126

BARTHORP,Michael Arthur Raymond Lt kia 20-7-16 1Nhampt p137 MR21

BARTHORPE,Alec Scott Lt kia 25-4-18 14Lond p249 CR France54

BARTHROPP,Sidney Alfred Nathaniel Shafto 2Lt kia 29-1-15 RSuss att2Bn p118 CR France720

BARTLE,George T2Lt kia 2-11-16 18 att9RWelshF p97 MR21

BARTLEET,Henry Booth 2Lt kia 10-9-18 5Lond p246 CR France369

BARTLEMAN,Thomas Edward 2Lt kia 6-9-17 5SfthH p241 CR Belgium126

BARTLETT,Allan Owen T2Lt kld 16-10-18 RASC p192 CR Palestine3,kia 15-10-18

BARTLETT,Arthur 2Lt dow 12-4-18 PoW 4RWelshF p223 CR France706

BARTLETT,Cedric Drummond 2Lt ded 1-12-15 3KOSB p101 CR Scot237

BARTLETT,Cyril.MC.TMaj dow 14-11-17 13RSuss p118 CR France193

BARTLETT,Cyril Ward.MC.TCapt kia 9-10-18 11N&D p133 MR16

BARTLETT,Ernest Jack T2Lt kia 16-4-17 1WYorks p80 CR France115

BARTLETT,Herbert Claude.MC.MID TCapt kia 15-9-16 11Ess p131 MR21

BARTLETT,Howard John.MID TCapt ded 1-12-18 RASC p192 CR Italy6

BARTLETT James 2Lt ded 6-5-18 GL RE IWT p189 CR Iraq6

BARTLETT,Leonard TLt kia 1-10-18 2 O&BLI p129 CR France256

BARTLETT,Leonard Percival T2Lt kia 9-4-17 5RBerks p138 CR France1182

BARTLETT,Lionel Arthur Capt dow 14-10-15 RE p43

BARTLETT,Lionel Arthur Lt kia 22-7-16 1RWKent p140

BARTLETT,Robert Nigel Oldfield TCapt dow 6-4-16 6ELancs p110 CR Iraq5

BARTLETT,Tom Brensley T2Lt kia 19-9-18 Dors att1/8Hamps p123 CR Palestine9

BARTLETT,William Bertram 2Lt kia 18-8-15 8Hamps p229 MR4

BARTLETT,William Herbert Lionel T2Lt kia 13-5-17 11Mddx p146 MR20

BARTLEY,Edward Hall LtACapt kia 31-7-17 2WYorks p80 MR29

BARTLEY,Frederick John Lt kia 26-3-17 1/5Ess p232 CR Palestine8,2Lt

BARTLEY,John.MC.T2Lt kia 31-10-18 14RWelshF p97 CR France1478

BARTLEY,Stanhope Cole Capt kia 12-3-16 RGA attD176RFA p38 CR France275

BARTOM,William Sidney 2Lt dow 26-4-18 Ess att10Bn p131 MR27,BARTON

BARTON,Albert Ernest.MID LtTCapt dow 24-5-17 6Dors p123 CR France1182,Maj

BARTON,Albert Thomas Lionel 2Lt kia 7-11-14 2RInnisF p104 MR32

BARTON,Arthur Everard Hale TLt kia 25-9-15 D20RFA p25 CR France114,2Lt

BARTON,Bernard TMaj kia 11-8-18 1/2Worc p107 CR France21,LtCol 1 att2/8Bn

BARTON,Charles Erskine Capt dow 23-8-18 4 att2RIrRif p168 CR France34

BARTON,Charles Geoffrey.MC.TCapt kia 17-10-18 6RInnisF p104 CR France660

BARTON,Charles John Lt kia 7-4-17 2/4 O&BLI p231 MR21

BARTON,Clarence Harry T2Lt kia 26-10-17 GL &6RFC p5 CR Belgium116

BARTON,Conwell Paris 2Lt kia 27-8-16 6ESurr att1/8RWar p226 MR21

BARTON,Edwin William 2Lt ded 27-4-17 2/5LancF p221 CR Lancs19

BARTON,Eric Percy Mervyn 2Lt kia 3-9-16 1Wilts p152 MR21

BARTON,Ernest Lt ded 1-4-19 RFA p269 CR Surrey148

BARTON,Francis Hewson Capt kia 2-11-14 IA 2/2GurkhaRif p273 CR Frnce706

BARTON,Frank Hubert T2Lt kia 5-11-18 1RFus att17LtTMB p66 CR France521

BARTON,Frederick Pembroke 2Lt dow 18-10-18 5Lincs p220 CR France725

BARTON,Frederick St.John Capt kia 24-7-15 1/4Hamps p120 CR Iraq6

BARTON,George Frank T2Lt kia 10-4-17 7Norf p73 CR France1182

BARTON,George Rawson Capt kia 9-4-18 11Ches p95 MR32,Rawdon 10-4-18

BARTON,Harold William Ferguson 2Lt kia 18-10-14 1RScotsF p94 MR22

BARTON,Harry 2Lt kia 22-3-18 3Lond p245 MR27

BARTON,Hugh Fabian T2Lt kia 12-2-16 9Norf p73 CR Belgium101

BARTON James.MC.2Lt kia 17-8-18 RGA 11SB p38 CR France526,Capt

BARTON,Kenneth Cyril T2Lt kia 7-10-16 9RFus p66 MR21

BARTON,L.F.2Lt kld 17-5-18 GL &RAF p189

BARTON,Reginald Frederick Lt kia 17-6-17 2Suff p78 MR20

BARTON,Robert 2Lt kia 12-1-16 RFC p2 CR France1887

BARTON,Stanley Ernest 2Lt kia 31-7-17 1RFus p66 CRBelgium96

BARTON,Thomas Eyre 2Lt kia 16-7-16 14 att2RIrRif p168 CR France393

BARTON,Vivian Alfred 2Lt kia 22-9-17 C162RFA p25 CR Belgium15

BARTON,William Bernard T2Lt kia 28-4-17 103MGC Inf p181 MR20,Barton

BARTON,William Edgar 2Lt kia 22-3-18 9RInnisF p104 MR27

BARTON,William Ewart 2Lt dow 25-8-18 1Lond p245 CR France119

BARTON,William Sidney 2Lt 26-4-18 10Ess MR27 see BARTOM,W.S.

BARTRAM,Alan 2Lt kia 14-8-16 4RBerks p234 CR France293

BARTRAM,Arthur Allan T2Lt kia 30-9-16 8ESurr p112 MR21

BARTRAM,Harold Franc 2Lt kia 24-4-17 7Wilts p152 MR37

BARTRAM,Harry Brocklesby Capt ded 16-9-14 RHA p25 CR Kent8

BARTRAM,William Elliot Lt dow 1-5-17 1Lincs p74 CR France214

BARTRAM,Howard Laidlaw TCapt ded 8-7-18 7Yorks D'Coy p89 CR Yorks176,BARTRUM

BARTRUM,H.L. see BARTRAM,H.L.

BARTTELOT,Walter Balfour.Bart.DSO.MID MajBTLtCol kld 23-10-18 CldGds p50 CR Asia82

BARWELL,Edward Egerton Maj kia 29-10/2-11-14 1A 57Rif MR29,W.E.

BARWELL,Frederick Leycester Capt kia 29-4-17 16Lond p249 CR France1310

BARWELL,Humphrey Eames T2Lt kia 3-2-18 41RFC p15 CR France62

BARWELL,Hugh William Eames.MC.Capt kia 25-3-18 RFC p15 MR20

BASCOMB HARRISON,Arthur Montague Mattison 2LtTLt dow 27-10-15 RE 96FC p43 CR France345

BASCOMBE,Cecil Reginald T2Lt kld 10-10-17 RFC p5 CR Suff176

BASDELL,Frank George 2Lt drd 4-5-17 Glouc p106 CR Italy14

BASDEN,Maurice Duncan 2Lt kia 20-5-16 16Lond attRFC p17&250 CR France276

BASEDEN,Eric Lt kia 26-10-16 3 att2RBerks p138 CR France307

BASELEY,Albert Lawrence.MID kia 11-8-17 2/6LancF p221 CR Belgium24

BASELOW,Henry Frank T2Lt kia 5-10-17 220MGC Inf p181 CR Belgium308

BASFORD,Bromley Alfred 2Lt kia 4-10-17 5N&D p232 CR Belgium165,6Leic

BASHFORD,Charles 2Lt kia 20-9-17 KRRC att21Bn p149 MR30

BASHFORD,Radcliffe James Lindsay.OBE.MIDx3 Maj ded 20-8-21 DADOS RAOC CR Wilts12

BASHFORTH,John Francis Cuthbert T2Lt kia 15-9-16 9Norf p73 MR21

BASING,George Limbery,CB.Lord HonBrigGen ded 8-4-19 1RDrags p261 CR Hamps122,Limbrey

BASKER,Reginald Hugh T2Lt kia 26-9-15 8SomLI p79 MR19

BASKERVILLE,Ralph Hopton Capt kia 9-4-18 GlamYeo att18WelchR p203 MR32,Ex 1Drags

BASKETT,Edmund Graham TCapt ded 27-10-18 GL 9 O&BLI attNigR p189&201 CR WAfrica45

BASKETT,Roger Mortimer T2Lt dow 14-11-16 14 att16Ches p95 CR France1182

BASKOTT,James Edward.MM.2Lt dow 11-12-17 RGA 193SB p38 CR Belgium18

BASON,Theodore Creceas T2Lt dow 29-4-18 Manch att1Worc p154 CR France29,Crescens Lt

BASS,Charles Brodie 2Lt kia 25-9-15 10Yorks p89 MR19

BASS,Charles Harold Capt kia 27-8-14 3 att2LancF p92 CR France611,26-8-14

BASS,Harold.MC.TCapt kia 24-4-18 10Yorks att2WYorks p89 MR27

BASS,Phillip Burnett Lt kia 1-7-16 5Ches p222 MR21,Philip Burnet

BASSANO,Edward Arthur T2Lt kia 1-10-16 13 att11N&D p133 MR21

BASSETT,Geoffrey Edward Lt kia 21-3-19 RASC p192

BASSETT,George Sidney T2Lt dow 6-7-17 Res att10LancF p92 CR France113

BASSETT,Robert John TLt drd 10-12-18 RAMC p194 CR Eire78,10-10-18

BASSETT,William Frederick.MC.TLt kia 27-10-18 10BlkW att2RScots p128 MR70 &CR Europe180

BASSETT,William George Lt ded 17-12-15 5RScots p211 CR Ches3

BASSETT-SMITH,Thurstan Francis T2Lt ded 23-11-16 RFC p2 CR Cornwall123

BASSHAM,Reginald Owen 2Lt kia 31-5-17 5RB p177 CR France581

BASTARD,William Lt kia 27-10-14 Beds p85 MR29

BASTIAN,Stanley 2Lt kia 9-5-15 4SfthH p241 MR22

BASTIN,Eric Charles T2Lt kia 4-10-17 RWar att1/8Bn p64 MR30

BASTOW,Frank Capt kia 27-5-18 3WYorks p80 MR18

BASTOW,Norman Lt kia 23-10-16 3WYorks att23TMB p80 MR21

BASTOW,William Henry T2Lt ded 26-11-15 C66RFA attRNAS p25 CR Gallipoli1

BASWITZ,Albert.MC.MID Capt kia 16-9-16 1/22Lond p251 CR France453

BATCHELAR,Robert Thomas 2Lt kia 23-3-18 7RWSurr p55 MR27

BATCHELOR,Edward 2Lt kia 26-9-17 24Lond p252

BATCHELOR,Frederick Arthur.MC.Capt 29-11-17 2/2KAR CR WAfrica30

BATCHELOR,Henry Washington TCapt kia 24-3-18 RAMC att43FA p104 CR France1063

BATCHELOR,Percival Horace T2Lt dow PoW 10-4-18 RWar att2/6NStaffs p64 CR Belgium241

BATCHELOR,T.A.Capt dow 29-11-17 2/2KAR p201

BATE,Alan Charles Lorraine Capt ded 25-10-18 RGA CR Herford &Worc154

BATE,Alfred Francis Lt kia 14-3-15 4RDubF att2Leinst p176 CR France1141

BATE,Eric Raoul Hender 2Lt kia 25-9-15.9ESurr p112 MR19,26-9-15

BATE,Frederick Over ALt kia 25-9-17 9MGC p181 CR Belgium8

BATE,George Beaumont T2Lt kia 29-4-17 18LNLancs &RFC p5&135 CR France646,9LNLancs att18RFC

BATE,Harold Lt kia 17-7-16 13 att12Manch p154 MR21,7-7-16

BATE,Maurice Charles Thornton 2Lt kia 13-8-17 2/9Lond p248 MR29

BATE,Thomas Lt kia 26-5-17 5RWelshF p223 MR34,26-3-17

BATEMAN,Arthur Cyril.MC.Capt kia 28-3-18 RAMC att7CamH p194 MR27

BATEMAN,Bernard Montague Basil.MC.Lt dow 24-7-15 113/21RFA p25 CR Mddx26

BATEMAN,Hubert Harry T2Lt kia 23-4-17 14 att4Worc p108 CR France155

BATES,Alfred Neville 2Lt kia 1-7-16 5N&D p232 CR France281

BATES,Allan Harold 2Lt kia 13-4-17 SR 25RFC p5 CR France1314

BATES,Archibald Claude.MC.Lt dow 20-10-17 6Nhampt p137 CR Belgium18

BATES,Arthur James Edmund T2Lt dow 30-7-17 RE 90FC p43 CR Herts29

BATES,Arthur William 2Lt kia 30-3-16 1Norf p73 CR France1182

BATES,Ernest Harold T2Lt kia 13-5-16 13Ches p95 CR France68,15-5-16

BATES,Eric George Henry Lt kia 23-8-16 BucksBn O&BLI p231 CR France393

BATES,Frances Mary SpProb ded 9-4-16 QAIMNS p200 CR Surrey41

BATES,Harold Christopher 2LtTLt kia 18-8-15 RE SR p43 CR France354

BATES,Harry Cecil TMaj kia 7-8-15 11Manch p154 MR4

BATES,John Hayes 2Lt kia 31-8-16 4YLI p235 CR France293

BATES,Leonard John.MC.TLtACapt ded 9-11-17 TankCps p188 CR Ireland14,10-11-17

BATES,Lewis George T2Lt dow 24-5-17 RWar att6ELancs p64 CR Iraq8,24-5-16

BATES,Madeline Elsie dow 22-12-17 VAD BRCS CR Essex29

BATES,Percy Joseph T2Lt kia 28-3-17 RE 179Coy p43 CR France1182

BATES,Reginald Plumtre Lt kia 10-3-15 2Dev p76 CR France706,Raymond Plumtre

BATES,Stanes Geoffrey Capt kia 13-5-15 7Huss p22 MR29,Ex Adjt NSomYeo

BATES,Stanley Knight Lt kia 9-5-15 1/5RLancs p213 CR Belgium88

BATES,Thomas Oates Halliday 2Lt dow 12-4-16 IARO att89Punjabis p273 MR38,Holliday

BATES,Thomas William TLtACapt dow 12-10-18 49MGC Inf p181 CR France214

BATES,William T2Lt dow 13-5-18 101LabCps p189 CR Frnce145 Ex DLI

BATES,William George Henry Capt kia 26-4-15 1Leinst p174 MR29

BATESON,John.MC.Lt kia 14-10-18 A28RFA p25 CR Belgium157

BATH,Edgar Norman 2Lt kia 18-4-15 IARO att1/8Rajputs MR43

BATH,John Euel Witherden TCapt kia 22-12-15 5RBerks p138 CR France279

BATH,Reginald Fred 2Lt kia 7-10-16 10Lond p248 CR France374

BATHO,Arnold Capel 2Lt kia 15-9-16 8Mddx p236

BATHO,John.MID Lt dow 30-9-15 RE 54FC p43 CR France98

BATLEY,Arthur George 2Lt kia 27-9-18 4 att11Manch p154 CR France272

BATSON,Alfred William Lt kia 14-3-15 2DCLI p114 CR Belgium74

BATSON,Henry Thomas T2Lt kia 11-9-17 10RWSurr &48RFC p5&55 CR Belgium137

BATSON,Leonard Henry T2Lt kia 3-7-16 EKent p57 CR France393

BATSON,Robert Evelyn T2Lt kia 11-10-16 10LancF att7TMB p92 CR France293

BATT,Francis Joseph TLt kia 13-3-18 RFC p15 CR France699

BATTE,Sydney 2Lt dow 20-1-18 19Lond p250 CR France398

BATTEN,John Hardman T2Lt kld 18-2-18 RFC p15 CR Lancs179

BATTEN,John Henry Strode Capt kia 25-10-14 1Lpool p71 MR29

BATTEN,Joseph Keith Capt kia 27-9-18 5Beds p219 CR France1496,4Bn

BATTENBURG,Maurice Victor Donald.KCVO.Prince.Lt kia 27-10-14 KRRC p149 CR Belgium57

BATTERSBY,Augustus Wolfe Lt ded 8-6-15 4ConnRgrs att2NigR p172 CR WAfrica61

BATTERSBY,Caryl Lionel Morse 2Lt kia 18-11-16 3YLI p142 CR France742

BATTERSBY,Charles Fremoult Preston Capt kia 4-11-14 113/25RFA p25 CR Belgium57

BATTERSBY,Eric May Capt kia 28-10-14 3 att1RWKent p140 MR22

BATTERSBY,Ernest Joseph 2Lt dow 13-6-17 18Lond att2/7Manch p250 CR France201

BATTERSBY,George Lefroy Maj ded 29-10-19 2/6RWFus p269 CR Ireland24

BATTERSBY,Henry Lewis Col ded 12-2-20 RAMC p267 CR Surrey159

BATTERSBY,J.C.LtCol 8-4-19 RAMC CR Ireland231

BATTERSBY,James Wilfred.MC.Capt kia 24-10-16 38RFA p25 CR France744,53/2RFA

BATTESBY,Philip Worsley Lt kia 7-7-17 WSomYeo attRFC p17&205 MR20

BATTISON,William.MC.Lt dow 13-10-18 7A&SH p243 CR Scot226

BATTLE,Arthur Newsum T2Lt kia 10-11-15 9Lincs att6Lancs p74 CR Gallipoli5

BATTLE,Edward Charles Vulliamy 2Lt kia 21-10-14 3Worc p108 MR22

BATTLEY,Frederick Walter T2Lt kia 21-4-16 11RSuss p118 CR France279

BATTOCK,Thomas William Lt kia 21-3-18 2/5ELancs p226 MR27

BATTY,Charles Frederick T2Lt kia 19-1-16 10DLI p160 CR Belgium73

BATTY,Geoffrey George Horn TCapt dow 27-9-16 6Nhampt p137 MR21

BATTY,William Liley Capt kia 25-10-16 4Yorks p220 MR21

BATTY-SMITH,Francis Clive TLt kia 4-6-16 13RFus p66 CR France505

BATTYE,Charles 2Lt kia 13-8-18 4WRid att1/8LancF p227 CR France5

BATTYE,Clinton Wynyard.DSO.MajALtCol kia 24-11-17KSLI att14HLI p144 CR France1496

BATTYE,Cyril Wynyard Lt kld 13-3-16 RBerks &RFC p138&2,Wynard CR Berks84

BATTYE,Harry 2Lt kia 21-3-18 8RWar p215 MR27,31-3-18

BATTYE,Hedley Morton Maj kia 4-6-15 IA 1/5GurkhaRif p273 MR4

BATTYE,Ivan Quinton Richmond 2Lt ded 19-5-21 IAUL att2RWar MR43

BATTYE,John 2Lt kia 25-3-18 5Yorks p221 MR27

BATTYE,Reginald T2Lt kia 23-10-18 LancF att1/7Manch p92 CR France287, 25-10-18

BATY,Bertie Cecil TCapt kia 16-9-16 23DLI p160 MR21

BAUGH,Bertram Percival 2Lt kia 16-6-18 RGA p38 CR France116

BAUGH,Charles T2Lt dow 5-4-18 9RFus p66 CR France62

BAUGH,James Thomas 2Lt dow 3-11-18 6Manch p236 CR France1266

BAUMANN,Maximillian Otto 2Lt kia 13-7-17 GL &70RFC p5 MR20

BAUMER,Derek Edward Lewis Venn Lt dow 21-10-17 32RFA p25 CR Belgium25

BAUSOR,Thomas Paul T2Lt kia 6-4-16 9KSLI &TMB p144 MR29

BAVA,Camille Bernard Colin 2Lt kia 26-9-15 14NumbF p60 CR France423

BAVIN,Geoffrey Wynne 2Lt kldacc 1-4-16 Lincs attRFC p2&74 CR Herts31

BAVIN,Nigel Benjamin Lt kia 23-5-15 3 att2Ess p131 CR Belgium96

BAVIN,William T2Lt kia 29-9-18 N&D att6Bn p133 MR16,1Bn

BAWDEN,Leslie John T2Lt dow 1-10-16 9 att6DCLI p114 CR France121

BAX,George Thomas T2Lt dow 8-9-16 15MGC Mtrs p181 CR France390,7-9-16

BAXENDALE,John Thompson 2Lt kia 18-7-17 RFA 30DAC att149Bde p25 CR Belgium15,17-7-17

BAXENDINE,John Young T2Lt kia 1-7-16 1BordR att5RScots p116 CR France1501

BAXTER,Alexander Carnegie.MC.Lt kia 17-4-17 6ScotRif att154MGC p186&224 CR France97

BAXTER,Andrew 2Lt kia 22-10-17 3 att16RScots p53 MR30,3 att17Bn

BAXTER,Angus Cameron 2Lt kia 31-7-17 4CamH p243 MR29

BAXTER,Arthur Sunderland T2Lt dow 2-1-16 18Mddx p146

BAXTER,Cecil Hubert 2Lt kia 1-2-17 A55RFA p25 MR38

BAXTER,Charles Arthur T2Lt dow 8-10-17 RWar att15Bn p64 CR Belgium112.kia

BAXTER,Edward Felix.VC.Lt kia 18-4-16 1/8Lpool p215 CR France1512,mbk

BAXTER,Frederick Cumber 2Lt kia 16-4-18 1/7WYorks p254 MR30

BAXTER,Fred Oscar.MC.Lt kia 17-3-17 IARO 33Punjabis att21RFC p273 CR France134,kld

BAXTER,Fredrick Bowden 2Lt ded 26-11-19 2WelchGds SR p262 CR W'land &C'Land85

BAXTER,Gavin Hector.MC.TLt dow 23-3-18 RE 157FC p43 CR France987

BAXTER,George William TLt kia 14-4-17 13 att2Hamps p120 MR20

BAXTER,Gerald William 2Lt kia 9-10-17 10Manch p237 MR30

BAXTER,Gordon Eyre T2Lt kia 8-10-18 2Dev p76 CR France97

BAXTER,Ian Alexander.MC.TCapt kia 30-5-18 9RWelshF p97 CR France1689

BAXTER,John Lt kia 10-11-17 1/5A&SH p243 CR Palestine8

BAXTER,John Denham 2Lt kia 7-11-18 18Lond p250 CR France1058

BAXTER,Leonard Arthur 2Lt kia 8-3-17 107RFA 23ArmyBde p25 CR France430

BAXTER,Leonard Josiah 2Lt dow 12-11-18 4EKent p212 CR France146

BAXTER,Leslie William Lt kia 28-5-18 95RFA p25 MR18

BAXTER,Paul Robert Elmhirst Lt kia 8-3-16 1Manch p154 MR38

BAXTER,Ralph Frederick 2Lt kia 25-9-15 2RSuss p118 CR France219

BAXTER,Rowland Percival 2Lt kia 16-9-16 5BordR p228 MR21

BAXTER,Walter Herbert LtCol ded 18-5-17 4Dors p229 MR66

BAXTER,William T2Lt kia 22-3-18 11Leic p87 MR20

BAXTER,William Hedley Bruce Capt kia 27-8-17 6RWar p214 CR Belgium125,5Bn

BAYARD,Reginald Aubrey Richard Lt kia 17-5-16 1EKent p57 CR Belgium73

BAYER,Henry Michael Capt ded 8-12-14 RAMC p269 CR Wales629

BAYETTO,Tone Hippolyte Capt 28-7-18 GL &RFC CR Mddx34

BAYFIELD,Herbert Lockington Lt dow 15-3-15 2Leic p87 CR France727

BAYFIELD,John Stanley Lucas 2Lt kia 29-8-18 14Lond p249 MR16

BAYLAY,George Frederick Lt kia 23-3-18 RE 1CavFdSqd p43 CR France605

BAYLEY,Albert Clarence 2Lt dow 13-12-17 14Lond p249 CR France145

BAYLEY,Charles Humphrey TCapt dow 7-8-17 9SLancs p125 CR France193

BAYLEY,Daniel James Capt kia 21-3-18 7GordH p242 MR20

BAYLEY,Edward Vincent 2Lt kld 24-2-17 6SStaffs attRFC p17&229 CR France1844

BAYLEY,George Baird.MID 2Lt kia 26-10-14 KOSB p101 MR29

BAYLEY,John Philip Lt dow 13-1-20 IA 1/34 att3/34SikhPnrs p273 MR43

BAYLEY,Norman David.MC.2Lt ded 20-10-18 3 att2RBerks p138 CR Hamps10

BAYLEY,Peter Ferguson 2Lt kia 23-3-18 9RB p177 MR27,Ex9HLI

BAYLEY,Reginald John 2Lt kia 29-4-17 13RFus p66 MR20

BAYLEY,Richard Joseph Capt ded 8-9-19 LabCps att40ChineseLabCps CR France375,acckld

BAYLEY,William Kercheval Maj kia 13-10-15 5RBerks p138 MR19

BAYLIS,Alfred Keppel T2Lt dow 24-4-18 2Suff p78 CR France40

BAYLIS,Charles John 2Lt ded 6-6-17 GL &42RFC p5 MR20

BAYLIS,Joseph Anno Jones TCapt kia 13-6-17 8SLancs p125 CR Belgium42

BAYLIS,Thomas Forbes 2Lt kia 14-7-17 20Lond p251 CR Belgium24

BAYLISS,John Edwin.MC.TLtAMaj dow 29-9-17 RFA A76ArmyBde p25 CR Belgium16

BAYLISS,Percival Baron.MID TLtACapt kia 3-10-18 TankCps p188 MR16

BAYLISS,Percy James 2Lt kia 27-9-18 RLancs p58

BAYLISS,Reginald Blencowe 2Lt dow 18-11-16 2Manch p154 MR21

BAYLY,Brian Brock.MC.TLtACapt dow 30-10-17 RE 254TC p43 CR Belgium3

BAYLY,Charles George Gordon Lt kia 20-8-14 RE 56FC att5RFC p1&43 CR Belgium406,22-8-14

BAYLY,Charles Ramsay TLt kia 29-3-18 29RH&FA p25 CR France266

BAYLY,Erskine Cochrane 2Lt kia 1-7-16 6RBerks p138 CR France513

BAYLY,Harry Ayrton T2Lt kia 14-6-17 12RFus p66 MR29

BAYLY,John.TD.Maj ded 26-2-18 RNDevYeo p203 CR Devon233

BAYLY,Launcelot Myles.MC.LtACapt dow 22-10-18 3RIrRif p168 CR Belgium20,5Bn

BAYLY,Noel Douglas Lt kia 27-11-17 2IrGds p52 CRFrance256

BAYLY,Vere Talbot T2Lt kia 8-5-16 7 att1Dors p123 CR France702

BAYNE,Edward Gordon TLt kia 4-10-17 2 att1ESurr p112 MR30

BAYNES,Denman Lambert Henry.MC.MID ACapt kia 14-10-18 RGA 115SB p38 CR Belgium112

BAYNES,Nigel William Francis Maj ded 19-3-15 3 att1Glouc p106 CR Bucks82, 20-3-15

BAYNES,Richard Henry Beindge Lt kia 14-7-16 1RWelshF p97 MR21

BAYNES,William Henry.MM.2Lt ded 12-10-18 1RWSurr p55&257 CR Kent175

BAYS,Albert William 2Lt kia 10-10-17 6 att4Mddx p146 CR Belgium56

BAYSPOOLE,Bernard Capt kia 9-4-16 6SLancs p125 MR38

BAYZAND,Alec T2Lt kia 10-10-16 19 att16N&D p133 MR21

BAZALGETTE,William Thomas Arnold 2Lt kia 9-5-17 1Dev p76 MR29

BAZELEY,Roland Arthur T2Lt kia 28-1-16 10 att9RSuss p118 MR29

BAZETT,Arthur Hugh Capt kia 10-8-15 4Ches p222 CR Gallipoli5

BAZIN,Geoffry Martyn Lt kia 19-9-15 1/2HAC p206 CR Belgium6

BAZLEY,Ernest Edward 2Lt kia 4-10-17 A298RH&FA p25 CR Belgium10

BAZLEY,Walter Neville Capt dow 23-5-15 1/6Manch p236 CR Gallipoli1

BEACALL,Arthur T2Lt kia 1-7-16 10 att11ELancs p110 CR France156

BEACALL,Hugh Lt&Adjt dow 14-5-15 2KSLI p144 CR France102

BEACH,John William Victor 2Lt ded 7-3-19 18TankCps CR Devon200

BEACH,Joseph Norman 2Lt kia 31-7-17 5SLancs p230 MR29

BEACH,Lionel H adwen F letcher.DSO.Capt ded 28-11-18 2/4RWSurr p212 CR Surrey6 F.H

BEACHAM,Cecil James 2Lt kia 9-10-17 8Worc D'Coy p226 MR30

BEACHCROFT,Cyril Shakespear TLt kia 12-10-17 HouseholdBn p20 CR Belgium126

BEACHCROFT,Gerald William 2Lt kia 31-7-17 RLancs p58 MR29

BEACHCROFT,W.F.Lt ded 21-7-18 RH&FA &RAF p25 CR Berks39

BEADELL,Alfred George 2Lt kia 13-4-17 4Glouc p225 CR France212

BEADLE,George Whitmore.MC.Lt ded 8-3-19 501RASC p253 CR Germany1

BEADON,Basil Herbert Edwards Capt kia 10 -8-15 7RWelshF p223 MR4,1-8-15

BEADON,William LtCol kia 13-1-16 IA 51Sikhs CR Iraq5

BEAFORD,Thomas Arthur 2Lt mbk 5-11-18 9WYorks p256

BEAGLEY,Frederick Parkman.MC.2Lt kia 26-8-18 4EKent p212 CR France177

BEAHAN,Arthur T2Lt kia 15-6-18 11NumbF Res p60 CR Italy4

BEAK,Basil Charles T2Lt ded 4-11-18 7MGC p181 CR Italy7

BEAK,Frank Leslie TLt kia 9-4-18 RH&FA att3CoSpecBde RE p25 MR32

BEAL,Arnold James 2Lt kia 1-7-16 12Y&L p158

BEAL,Edward Gerald TLt dow 6-11-18 1 att 8 N&D p133 CR France985,11Bn

BEAL,Ernest Frederick.VC.T2Lt kia 22-3-18 13Yorks p89 MR20

BEAL,Henry Benjamin Lt ded 23-6-19 RFA p25 CR Iraq1

BEALE,Alfred Percy Gordon Lt dow 28-3- 17 D158RFA p207 CR France1182,Capt 28-3-18

BEALE,Cecil Charles T2Lt dow 29-1-17 16RB p177 CR Belgium6

BEALE,Clifford William TLt kia 3-3-16 7RSuss att36TMB p118 MR19

BEALE,Edmund Lansdowne LtACapt kia 22-3-18 1Camb p244 MR27

BEALE,Ernest Frederick T2Lt kia 28-4-17 17RFus p66 MR20

BEALE,Norman Stuart Charles Gascoigne T2Lt kia 18-8-16 7Nhampt p137 MR21

BEALE,Oscar Child T2Lt kia 4-10-16 12 att10RInniskF p104 CR Belgium100

BEALE,Robert Anthony 2Lt kia 15-3-17 1Glouc p106 CR France1472

BEALES,Frederick Charles Lt kia 4-11-18 4Lincs p217 CR France733

BEALES,George Ninian 2Lt kia 21-3-18 3 att22NumbF p60 MR20

BEALES,Henry T2Lt kia 9-5-17 1 att14Y&L p158 MR20

BEALEY,A.C.Capt 22-11-17 2/4SomLI CR Palestine3

BEALEY,Frederick Arthur Harold Capt ded 17-11-18 PoW 2/6LancF p221 CR Germany3

BEALL,Albert Ernest Lt kia 29-9-17 1/5YLI p235 CR France1361

BEALL,Roy Dixon Lt kia 4-6-15 7RFA p25 CR France631

BEALL,Stephen Spencer ACapt kia 18-9-18 5EKent p213 CR France511,6Bn

BEAMAN,E.R.H.Capt ded 17-12-18 RE &RAF p209

BEAMAN,William Archie.MC.Lt kia 10-4-18 7Worc p225 MR30

BEAMER,Archie Mainland T2Lt kia 4-2-18 22RFC p15 CR France31

BEAMISH,John Spread Hamilton Lt ded 2-11-15 KSLI p144 CR Surrey160

BEAN,Arthur Charles Stanley 2Lt dow PoW 14-10-18 24Lond p252 CRFrance567

BEAN,Bevis Heppel Lt kia 18-6-17 6RWelshF attRFC p17&223 MR20 &CR Belgium451

BEAN,Charles Reginald Chamberlayne 2Lt kia 26-10-15 1SStaffs p122 MR29,Chamberlin Lt 26-10-14

BEAN,Ernest Edward T2Lt ded 11-11-18 Norf p263 CR Norf209

BEAN,C.A.Maj 30-5-18 7Lpool CR Ches192

BEAN,Humphrey LtACapt kia 19-9-18 1SfthH p164 CR Palestine9

BEAN,Kenneth Foster Lt dow 12-4-18 7RScots p211 CR France139

BEAN,Maurice Gordon Capt drd 30-12-15 IA 81Pnrs p273 MR41

BEAN,William Stuart Lt kia 21-1-18 RE att30RFC p17&210 CR Iraq8

BEANLAND,George Edward 2Lt kia 30-4-17 2N&D p133 CR France551

BEANLAND,John Everard 2Lt kia 26-5-18 161RFA attX32TMB p25 CR France924,initial E.only

BEANLAND,Joseph Wilfred TCapt kia 14-8-15 7RWelshF p223 MR4

BEANLANDS,Bernard Paul Gascoyne.MC.Capt ded 8-5-19 Hamps &RAF p120 CR Kent154,Gascoigne

BEAR,John.Hon. Lt&QM ded 18-12-17 NStaffs 258InfBn p156 CR Staffs109

BEAR,Sydney James 2Lt dow 31-7-17 4Mddx p146 MR29

BEARBLOCK,C.H. see BEARDLOCK,C.H.

BEARD,Edwin Cyril Lt kia 26-3-17 5Ess p232 MR34

BEARD,Frederick Gerald Vesey TLt kia 4-7-16 9 att4Worc p108 MR21

BEARD,Frederic Whiteley T2Lt kia 10-10-16 2WRid p115 MR21

BEARD,Harold Clifford 2LtTLt kia 8-10-16 1/5Lond p246 MR21

BEARD,Lewis Digby Mansergh T2Lt kld 19-10-16 MGC Inf p181 CR Ireland14

BEARD,Philip Lee TLt dow 9-9-16 15RWar p64 CR France51,Leo kia

BEARD,Valentine Edward 2Lt dow 24-11-17 RLancs p58 CR Greece6

BEARDLOCK,Charles Henry TLt dow 20-10-15 9Ess p131 CR France423,BEARBLOCK

BEARDMORE,Sydney Alfred 2Lt dow 1-9-18 1/14Lond p249 CR France103

BEARDSELL,Richard Ernest 2Lt kia 22-4-18 12LancF p92 MR37

BEARDSHAW,Reginald Dudley T2Lt dow 21-10-16 2SWBord p99 CR France277,Lt

BEARDSWORTH,James Lt ded 29-6-19 87RGA p262 CR Asia33

BEARMAN,Cecil Laurence T2Lt kia 23-8-18 7RWSurr p55 CR France515

BEARMAN,Frank TLt ded 5-8-17 7ELancs p110 CR Numb4,3Bn

BEARN,Octavius Leslie TLt kia 23-4-17 9BlkW p128 CR France924

BEARN,Percy Dare 2Lt kia 3-9-16 13 att14Hamps p120 MR21

BEART,Errol George Montague T2Lt kia 31-7-17 RASC attRGA 228SB p192 CR Belgium124

BEART,Vere Leopold Dunstan 2Lt kia 17-9-16 4 att13DLI p160 MR21

BEASLEY,Albert William.MM.2Lt kia 14-8-16 1/4RBerks p234 MR21

BEASLEY,James Joyce T2Lt kia 9-8-15 6RIrF p170 MR4

BEATER,Louis Nie Bohr 2Lt ded 13-3-15 3ConnRgrs p172 CR Ireland14 &CR Eire77,Niebuhr

BEATH,William Alexander 2Lt s/InflictWound 7-5-18 IARO att117Mahrattas p273 MR43

BEATON,Grover Cleveland.MC.2Lt dow 30-9-18 RGA 143SB p38 CR France146

BEATON,William James T2Lt kia 24-9-17 174MGC Inf p181 MR30

BEATSON,Beaumont Crowther Oswald 2Lt kia 23-4-17 7BlkW p231 CR France604

BEATSON,Charles Ellis Stewart.MC.CaptAMaj dow 3-10-17 105/22RFA p25 CR Belgium11,Elles Stuart

BEATSON,Roger Stewart Montresor TLt kia 1-7-16 6 att10YLI p142 CR France267,2-7-16

BEATSON,Walter William Gordon 2Lt kld 18-7-16 RFC p2 CR Beds23

BEATTIE,Charles TLt kia 20-7-18 GordH att1/7Bn p166 MR18,Capt

BEATTIE,G.A.Capt 17-2-21 IraqRlys CR Iraq1

BEATTIE,George.MC.T2Lt kia 23-4-17 11A&SH p172 MR20

BEATTIE,James Walker TCapt ded 23-7-18 RAMC p194 CR Durham28

BEATTIE,Malcolm Bartlett TLt dow 16-10-17 5RBerks p138 CR France113

BEATTIE,Maurice Alexander.DSO.Maj 13-2-20 RGA Cmdg54SB CR Kent261

BEATTIE,Thomas Lt kia 27-10-18 11WRid p115 CR Italy8

BEATTIE,William 2Lt kia 15-4-17 7ScotRif p224 CR France672

BEATTIE,William Francis.MC.Lt dow 3-10-18 73/5RFA p25 CR France446,Frances Maj

BEATTIE,William Lindsey 2Lt kia 27-1-17 1BordR p116 CR France399,Lindsay

BEATTIE,William Marshall 2Lt kia 13-4-18 9HLI p240 MR32

BEATTIE-BROWN,William TCapt kia 9-1-17 25NumbF p60 MR20

BEATTIE-CROZIER,P.Capt 19-5-15 IA 4Rajputs att15Sikhs CR France924

BEATTY,Arthur Harry Wolseley TLt kia 31-7-17 Manch att19Bn p154 MR29,2Lt

BEATTY,Benjamin George 2Lt kia 28-7-17 GL &45RFC p5 MR20

BEATTY,Carl John T2Lt kia 15-9-16 7RFC p2 CR France526

BEATTY,Charles Harold Longfield.DSO.TMaj dow 17-5-17 SL RWar ADC CanCpsHQ p201 CR War37

BEATTY,Charles St.John Lt dow 16-9-16 4 att1RMunstF p175 CR France66

BEATTY,Desmond Henry 2Lt dow 21-2-15 4ESurr p112 CR France102,2Bn

BEATTY,Eric Edge TLt kia 29-4-16 6ConnRgrs p172 CR France178

BEATTY,Eric Leslie Finch T2Lt kia 23-6-16 GL 12N&D attTMB p189 CR Belgium17

BEATTY,Hugh Hogg TCapt kia 31-3-18 13RIrRif p168 MR27

BEATTY,Richard George Capt 9-6-15 IA 1Lancers MR67

BEATTY,William John.OBE.Maj ded 10-2-19 RASC p192 CR Belgium330

BEATY-POWNALL,George Ernest.DSO.MajALtCol dow 10-10-18 2BordR att1KOSB p116 CR Belgium11

BEATY-POWNALL,Thomas Trelawny 2LtACapt kia 24-3-17 3 att2BordR p116 CR France616

BEAUCHAMP,Edward Archibald 2Lt dow 22-12-14 1CldGds p50 CR France201

BEAUCHAMP,Eric Westgate 2Lt dow 23-11-17 2/4Dors att2/4Hamps CR Palestine3

BEAUCHAMP,Leslie Heron T2Lt kld 6-10-15 8SLancs p125 CR Belgium70

BEAUCHAMP,Penrith Sutton T2Lt kia 25-1-17 10Worc p108 CR Iraq5

BEAUCLERK,Aubrey Nelthorpe Maj died 22-4-16 2NStaffs p156 MR67

BEAUCLERK,Nevill Alfred de Vere Lt kia 20-6-15 12 att2Ess p131 MR4,17-6-15

BEAUFORT,Francis Hugh Capt kia 16-5-15 2 O&BLI p129 MR22

BEAUFORT,Ostcliffe Harold 2Lt kia 13-10-15 6NStaffs p238 MR19

BEAUFOY,Clive Marston T2Lt kia 25-9-18 10RWar p64 CR France1106

BEAUFOY,Katy A/Matron drd 26-2-18 QAIMNS p200 MR40

BEAUMONT,Charles Leslie T2Lt kld 20-5-17 GL &RFC p5 CR Suff173

BEAUMONT,D.J.Lt ded 24-11-18 11Glouc CR Surrey160

BEAUMONT,Eric Paton.MC.T Lt dow 2-4-18 17Lpool p71 CR France145,Capt

BEAUMONT,George.MC.Capt kia 9-4-18 6 att13ESurr p226 MR32

BEAUMONT,George Joseph TLt ded 18 -1-17 11ELancs p110 CR France41,24-1-17

BEAUMONT,James Hutchings Lt ded 24-6-17 2/7WRid p227 CR France102

BEAUMONT,John Barrie T2Lt kia 20-10-18 1Dev p76 CR France1388

BEAUMONT,Leslie T2Lt kia 17-8-16 12WYorks p80 MR21

BEAUMONT,Phillip Fairclough T2Lt kia 9-10-17 YLI att4Bn p142 MR30

BEAUMONT,Samuel George TCapt kia 25-9-15 5KSLI p144 MR29

BEAUMONT,Seymour James Gordon Maj ded 18-5-20 IA 101Grenadiers p273 CR Norf101,S.J.B.

BEAUMONT,Sydney.MC.T2Lt dow 28-3-18 ELancs att2/4Bn p110 CR France52

BEAUMONT,Thomas Somerville Capt kia 24-9-17 2/8Manch p237 CR Belgium173

BEAUMONT,Wilfrid Newton 2Lt kia 25-9-15 2BordR p116 MR19,Newlon

BEAUMONT-CHECKLAND,Montmorency Beaumont Lt kia 17-8-17 2/1WSomYeo MR30

BEAUMONT-EDMONDS,William George Beaumont 2Lt kia 17-9-16 22Lond p251 MR21

BEAUMONT-NESBITT,Wilfrid Henry.MC.LtACapt kia 27-11-17 2GrenGds p49 MR17

BEAUSIRE,Charles Edward 2Lt kia 14-2-15 12Lond p248 MR29

BEAUSIRE,Herbert Arthur William 2Lt kia 6-3-15 RFus p66 CR France683,15-3-15

BEAVEN,Charles Simeon 2Lt kia 14-4-18 7TankCps p188 MR32

BEAVER,John Denistoun Campbell 2Lt dow 15-5-18 KRRC att13Bn p149 CR Bucks12,17-5-18

BEAVER,Leslie Arnold T2Lt kia 21-9-18 7Lincs p74 CR France415,20-9-18

BEAVON,Donald James 2Lt kia 27-8-17 4Glouc p225 MR30

BEAVON,John Leonard 2Lt kia 1-7-16 26NumbF p60 MR21

BEAZER,Archibald Harold 2Lt dow 21-4-19 7Worc p225 CR Hereford & Worc189

BEBEE,Alexander Denman T2Lt kia 30-9-16 6RBerks p138 CR France246

BECHER,Edward Richard Fane T2Lt dow 19-7-16 8RMunstF p175 CR France223,Lt

BECHER,Harry Owen Dabridgecourt Capt kia 13-3-15 ScotRif p103 CR France83,Henry Da Bridgecourt

BECHER,Henry Sullivan Maj kia 2-11-14 IA 2/2GurkhaRif att34SikhPnrs p273 MR28

BECHER,John Pickard.DSO.Maj dow 1-1-16 8N&D p233 CR France51

BECHER,Maurice Andrew Noel Capt kia 26-4-15 1KOSB p101 MR4

BECK,Albert Edward Alexander.MC.Lt kia 12-8-15 5Norf p216 MR4

BECK,Arthur Evelyn.MC.Capt kia 19-4-17 1/5Norf p216 CR Palestine8

BECK,Aubrey Moore 2Lt kia 15-5-17 HAC p206 MR20

BECK,Bernard TCapt kia 18-8-16 3Lpool p71 CR France453

BECK,Charles Broughton Harrop 2Lt dow 15-8-15 7Ches p223 CR Greece10

BECK,Donald Coker Lt kld 21-9-16 RFA attRFC p17&207 CR Bucks120

BECK,Edmund Wallis TLt dow 9-1-16 8Beds p85 CR France102

BECK,Frank Reginald Capt kia 12-8-15 5Norf p216 MR4

BECK,Frederick Charles 2Lt kia 14-9-17 17Lond p250 MR29

BECK,Herbert Charles T2Lt dow 19-10-18 A152RFA p25 CR France34

BECK,Herbert Musgrove T2Lt kia 22-1-18 3 att6RFC p15 CR France300

BECK,J.A.Lt 26-1-20 RFA CR Iraq8

BECK,James Fenn T2Lt kia 28-4-17 5MGC Inf p181 MR20

BECK,John Stanley.MC.Capt kia 16-8-17 4Norf att17KRRC p216 CR Belgium124

BECK,Percy Latham 2Lt kia 6-3-15 RE &RMon SR p43 CR Belgium59

BECK,Philip Henry Harcourt Capt kia 2-4-17 2/6Glouc p225 CR France840

BECK,Theodore David Vodden 2Lt kia 16-9-16 6SomLI p79 MR21,Ex HAC

BECK,Thomas Mc.Lt kia 1-10-18 2HLI &48RAF MR20 p265

BECK,William Lt&QM ded 18-4-18 1KRRC p149 CR Yorks408

BECK,William.DCM.2Lt kia 26-4-18 6Y&L p158 MR19

BECK,William Crabbe.MID Maj kia 28-3-18 C301R&FA p206 CR Palestine3

BECKER,Charlie Hereward LtTCapt kld 8-8-18 3ESurr attRFus p112 CR USA187

BECKER,John Edward Lt ded 21-9-18 RE CR EAfrica36,20/21-9-18

BECKER,Jonathan Otto Gustavus Lt kia 12-3-15 2ESurr p112 CR Belgium168

BECKERLEG,Stephen Trevor Lt kia 15-10-15 3 att2DCLI p114 CR France526

BECKETT,Ernest Whitton 2Lt kia 22-3-18 1/4Leic p220 MR20

BECKETT,Frank Shaw T2Lt kia 31-5-18 RE 2SpCo p43 CR France25

BECKETT,Hubert Edge 2Lt kia 23-7-17 1/4Y&L p238 CR Belgium173

BECKETT,James Ranald T2Lt dow 4-7-16 17HLI p162 CR France74

BECKETT,John 2Lt kia 28-6-15 2BordR p116 CR France260

BECKETT,John Douglas Mortimer.DSO.MajTLtCol kld 9-2-18 10Hamps p120 CR Greece9,Douglass

BECKETT,Philip Arthur 2Lt kia 14-2-17 3 att7RWKent p140 MR21

BECKETT,Victor Louis Sydney TMaj dow 19-7-16 9Yorks p89 CR France833

BECKH,Robert Harold T2Lt dow 15-8-16 12EYorks p83 CR France924

BECKHAM,Arthur Thomas Grafton Capt kia 26-4-15 IA 32 att34SikhPnrs p273 CR Belgium58

BECKHUSON,Donald Frederic T2Lt kia 2-3-16 9WRid p115 CR Belgium167,Frederick

BECKINGSALE,Beauclerc Leigh TLt kia 21-3-18 RIrF att1Bn p170 MR27

BECKINGSALE,John Elgar T2Lt kia 23-8-17 6DCLI p114 MR30

BECKLEY,Eric White T2Lt dow 9-6-18 3DLI att36NumbF p160 CR France10

BECKTON,James Robson Lt kia 18-2-18 RE p210 CR France446

BECKTON,William Lt kld 23-3-18 5RWelshF &RFC p17&223 CR Egypt15

BECKWITH,William John.OBE.HonCapt ded 21-12-18 RAOC p198 CR Belgium316

BECTON,H.Lt 23-9-19 RFA CR Essex176

BEDALE,Charles Lt ded 20-2-19 RGA p262

BEDALE,Charles Lees Rev Chap4Cl ded 8-3-19 RAChDept p254,H. CR Camb1

BEDBROOK,Ernest Arthur St.George T2LtAMaj ded 1-5-18 SWBord p99&263 CR USA169

BEDDOES,Henry Roscoe LtCol drd 15-1-19 4 att9RDubF p176 MR40

BEDDON,John Frederick Heber Capt kia 3-11-17 1/4Ess p232 CR Palestine8,BEDDOW

BEDDOW,Cecil Victor T2Lt kia 1-7-16 2Dev p76 CR France1890

BEDDOW,J.F.H. see BEDDON,J.F.H.

BEDDY,E.Col 8-5-19 29Punjabis CR Hamps64

BEDDY,Keith Charles Lt kia 6-2-18 RFC &5Hamps P261&269,kld CR Wilts1

BEDDY,Rafe Langdon Lt dow 4-6-15 IA 1/5GurkhaRif p273 CR Gallipoli3

BEDELL,E.A.Capt 5-2-17 ISMD MR69

BEDELL,F.SenAssSurg 22-10-18 ISMD MR66

BEDELL,H.J.AssSurg 18-10-18 IMS MR43

BEDELLS,Cecil Arthur 2Lt kia 26-9-15 11Ess p131

BEDFIELD,James Stewart EngrSubLt 24-4-19 RIM attRE IWT MR65

BEDFORD,Alan William T2Lt kia 20-11-17 WYorks att2/6Bn p80 CR France530

BEDFORD,Cecil Clarke T2Lt kia 8-3-16 1Manch p154 MR38

BEDFORD,Edward Terence Bertyn LtACapt kia 28-5-17 RGA 34SB 1AnzacCpsTroops p38 CR France518

BEDFORD,Kenneth Savile.MID Capt kia 12-10-16 Y&L att3Bn p158 MR37

BEDFORD,Robert Harold.MID Capt kia 25-3-18 6Manch p236 MR27

BEDFORD,Rowland.MC&Bar.TLt kia 13-9-18 9Dev p76 CR

France357,Roland

BEDFORD,Seaton Hall T2Lt kia 1-7-16 2RBerks p138 MR21

BEDFORD,Yhomas Arthur 2Lt kia 4-11-18 9WYorks CR France953

BEDFORD-PIM,Edward Woodley Lt ded 5-7-18 RH&FA p207 CR Kent91,RGA

BEDINGHAM,Albert T2Lt kia 25-2-17 Mddx att23Bn p146 CR Belgium28

BEDSON,Eric Hamilton Capt kia 7-8-17 8LancF att9RFC p221 CR Belgium20

BEDWELL,Charles Theodore Lt kia 12-4-18 1Y&L p158 MR30

BEDWELL,Victor Leopold Stevens 2Lt kia 18-8-16 4Suff p217 MR21

BEE,William Lt dow 24-9-17 RD94FA p207 CR Belgium11

BEEBY,Charles Stuart Lt kia 27-5-18 4Leic p219 MR18

BEEBY,William Sorley Marden Capt kia 3-5-17 4Y&L p238 MR20,Sorby Mardon

BEECH,John TLtACapt kia 12-5-18 RE 4FdSurCo p43 CR Belgium36,Ex 10SStaffs

BEECH,John Robert.CMG.DSO.LtCol ded 6-11-15 ScotHorse p205 CR Scot180

BEECH,Leonard 2Lt 11-12-20 2/5SStaffs CR Staffs60

BEECH,Norman William.DCM.2Lt kia 9-10-17 5WYorks p218 MR30

BEECH,Robert Clyde Capt kia 18-10-16 1RB p177 MR21

BEECH,Rowland Auriol James Lt kia 21-2-15 16Lancers p23 CR Belgium57

BEECH,Rowland John LtCol ded 30-8-19 WarYeo p269 CR Staff93

BEECHENO,James Herbert T2Lt dow 25-10-18 KRRC att13Bn p149 CR France332

BEECHER,Frank Alfred 2lt dow 16-9-16 6Lond p246 CR France188

BEECHEY,Frank Collett Reeves T2Lt dow 14-11-16 13EYorks p83 CR France120,Reeve

BEECHING,Geoffrey Charles Lt kia 12-9-18 12Lond p248 MR16

BEECROFT,William Henry 2Lt kia 22-7-18 6Glouc p225 CR France5

BEEDLE,Frank Symons Bussel.MC.2Lt kia 11-4-18 4 att7GordH p242 MR19

BEEMAN,Arthur Cecil Capt kia 26-10-14 1RWKent p140 MR22

BEEMAN,John Neville.MC.Lt kia 29-9-18 Mddx att1Bn p146 CR France407

BEER,Arthur Henry.MC.Lt dow 21-4-18 275RFA p207 CR France88

BEER,Edward Albert 2Lt kia 22-9-17 RGA 298SB p38 CR Belgium124

BEER,Harold Herbert T2Lt kia 23-4-17 14 att11Manch p154 MR20

BEER,Henry Oliver T2Lt kia 26-9-15 8RWKent p140 MR19

BEER,John Henry MajTLtCol kia 19-7-16 8RWar p214 MR32 &CRFrance1887,2/4Berks

BEER,Lewis Charles 2Lt kia 28-3-18 5DCLI p227 MR27

BEER,Robert Alexander T2Lt kia 5-10-17 12Glouc p106 MR30,4-10-17

BEER,Robert Gerald 2Lt kia 30-11-17 4 att6EKent p212 MR17

BEER,William John T2Lt kia 21-2-18 14RFC p15 CR Palestine3

BEERBOHM,Clarence Evelyn LtAMaj kia 26-9-17 12Lancers att162RFA p22 CR Belgium19

BEESLEY,Edwin.MC.T2LtACapt kia 27-9-18 1Lpool p71 CR France1483

BEESON,Ralph 2Lt drd 15-2-18 IARO 1S&M p273 MR66

BEESTON,Harold Lewis Lt ded 24-10-18 5RWKent p269 CR Kent95

BEETON,Arthur Charles Lt kia 23-8-15 1/6Ess p232 MR4

BEETON,Robert Henry T2Lt kld 1-2-18 RFC p15 CR Norfl11

BEEVER,Jonathan Holt Lt kia 25-3-18 17RFA p25 MR27

BEEVER,William Henry Capt kia 1-7-16 1RB p177 MR21

BEEVOR,Felix Victor 2Lt kia 1-7-16 att51Mddx p146 MR19

BEEVOR,Vernon Saville,MC.T2Lt kia 10-3-17 14 att10Ess p131 CR France239,Savile

BEGARD,Michael T2Lt kia 22-3-18 TankCps p188 MR27

BEGBIE,Alfred Vincent T2Lt dow 11-4-17 6CamH p167 MR20

BEGBIE,Sydney Claude Hamilton Lt ded 22-4-18 3ESurr attRAF p112 CR France1027,kia

BEGG,Arthur 2LtACapt ded 21-3-18 4Norf att2/5Lincs p216

BEGG,Alexander James.MC.TLt dow 10-7-16 17HLI p162 CR France51

BEGG,Alexander James Bartlett.MC.TLt kia 21-3-18 22NumbF p60 MR20,Bartlet

BEGG,Andrew Currie LtTCapt&Adjt kia 30-7-16 1/7BlkW p231 CR France1890

BEGG,Henry Capt kia 14-11-16 RAMC 2/1Highland FA p253 CR France3

BEGG,Henry Berners 2Lt kia 23-11-16 24RFC p2 MR20

BEGG,John Henderson Capt kia 23-7-16 8GordH p166

BEGG,Patrick Hunter Capt MurderedByHisBearer 24-8-21 IA 2/96Inf p273 CR Iraq8

BEGG,Robert Henderson Capt kia 24-12-15 RGA attStaff 6Div HQ p38 CR Iraq1,RA

BEGG,William 2Lt kia 13-11-16 5BlkW p231 CR France221

BEGG,William Pollock TCapt kia 9-4-18 RGA 157SB p38 MR32

BEGGS,Henry Parker Lt kia 1-7-16 8RIrRif p168 MR21,Capt

BEGGS,James T2Lt kia 9-4-18 21Mddx p146 MR32

BEHRENS,Robert Philip Lt dow 26-4-15 2SWBord p99 MR4,25-4-15

BEHRENS,Walter Louis 2Lt kia 9-7-17 C122RFA p208 CR Belgium23,10-7-17

BEILBY,Julius Henry Capt kia 23-4-16 RAMC p253 MR34

BEIT,Rupert Owen ACapt dow 29-7-17 RE p209 CR Belgium15,28-7-17 9ArmyTrpCoy

BEIT,Theodore Hamilton 2Lt ded 26-1-17 1Drags p21 CR Herts60

-BELAS,George Henry TCapt kia 3-6-17 RFA 4DAC p25 CR France96

BELAS,Reginald Charles William T2Lt kia 21-3-18 8RDubF p176 CR France212

BELCHAMBER,Ernest Henry T2Lt kia 23-4-17 7BordR p116 MR20

BELCHEM,Howard Matthew 2Lt dow 19-3-15 1/5NumbF p60 CR Belgium59,Lt kia

BELCHER,Austin Charles Sandham Capt&Adjt kia 10-8-15 5Wilts p152 MR4,Austen

BELCHER,Basil Henry 2Lt kia 1-7-16 2RBerks p138 CR France1890

BELCHER,Francis Terence Julian Lt kia 4-2-17 25Lond att1/6War p252 CR France1472

BELCHER,Frederick Percy TCaptAMaj dow 5-8-18 C92RFA p25 CR France34

BELCHER,Gordon.MC.Capt kia 15/17-5-15 3 att2RBerks p138&258 CR France632

BELCHER,Harold Thomas.DSO.LtCol kia 8-7-17 52RFA p25 CR Belgium29

BELCHER,Humphrey Gilbert TLt dow 7-8-15 5Wilts p152 MR4

BELCHER,Raymond Douglas.MC.DSO.TCaptAMaj dow 7-12-17 C63RFA p25 CR France13

BELCHER,Robert Henry Chap4Cl ded 25-10-16 25Lond CR Sussex185

BELCHER,Wilfrid Frank Lt dow 17-12-17 2/5NStaffs p237 CR France398

BELCHIER,Frank Elliot.MC.Capt kia 20-5-15 1ELancs p110 CR Belgium96

BELDING,Clare 2Lt kia 11-3-15 1Nhampt p137 MR22

BELEMORE,R.A.see BELLEMORE,R.A.

BELFIELD,Eric Capt mbk 31-7-17 4Mddx p256 MR29

BELFIELD,James Steward EngLt ded 21-4-19 RIM p273

BELFORD,Charles Roberts 2Lt kia 2-9-18 9BlkW p128 CR France1723

BELGRAVE,James Dacre.MC&Bar.Capt kia 13-6-18 1/2 2 O&BLI att60RAF p129 CR France105,Dacres

BELK,Charles Maj ded 16-12-17 RDC p253 CR Devon207

BELL,Adam Dickson Maj ded 8-4-18 4Huss p21

BELL,Albert T2Lt kia 27-3-18 att118ELancs p110 MR20

BELL,Alexander 2Lt ded 27-2-19 1A&SH p266 CR Yorks2,27-1-19

BELL,Alexander Murray MacGregor Capt dow 28-4-15 RScotF p94 CR Lond8

BELL,Alfred Gordon.MC.2Lt dow 18-4-17 10DLI SR p160 CR France40

BELL,Alfred Herbert Capt kia 25-9-15 11RScots p53 MR19

BELL,Alfred Joseph TLt kia 13-5-17 2SStaffs p122 MR20

BELL,Alfred Roy Lancaster 2Lt dow 17-5-15 5RDubF p176

BELL,Arthur McLean TLt kia 20-5-18 BlkW att1GordH p128 CR France33

BELL,Arthur Walton 2Lt kia 28-3-18 1/9DLI p239 MR20

BELL,Aveling Francis T2Lt kia 12-8-15 4SWBord p99 MR4

BELL,Cecil Charles 2Lt kia 28-11-17 16LancF p92 CR Belgium63

BELL,Charles Henry.MC.Chap4Cl kia 23-8-18 RAChDept att1RBerks p199 CR France927

BELL,Charles Ockley 2Lt kia 12-10-14 Beds p85 MR29

BELL,Clifford Thiselton Capt ded 2-2-19 RAMC p253 CR Scot280

BELL,Colin T2Lt kia 29-10-17 N&D att15Bn p133 MR30,30-10-17

BELL,Cuthbert Patrick TLt dow 23-2-18 9Dev p76 CR Italy7

BELL,David 2Lt kia 6-10-18 13BlkW p205 MR16,7-10-18

BELL,Donald Simpson.VC.T2Lt kia 10-7-16 9Yorks p89 CR France267

BELL,Edward Augustine T/HonCapt drd 11-7-16 RAMC att5BRCHosp p194 CR France64

BELL,Edward Inkerman Jordan.MC&Bar.Capt kia 24-3-18 GL 17Mddx att Staff 99Inf Bde p189&258 CR France430

BELL,Edward Nevinson Lt ded 16-2-18 IARO att1/70BurmaRif p273 MR66

BELL,Edward William 2LtTLt kia 8-12-17 209MGC p181 CR Palestine3

BELL,Elvis Albert T2Lt kia 22-9-17 GL &22RFC p5 CR Belgium17

BELL,Eric Norman Frankland.VC.TCapt kia 1-7-16 GL 9InniskF att109LightTMB p189 MR21

BELL,Eric Victor T2Lt dow 14-8-15 11Manch p154 MR4

BELL,Francis de Beauvoir Maj dow 24-4-15 2Norf p73 CR Iraq6

BELL,Francis Richard Lowry T2Lt kia 22-2-16 10 att2BordR p116 CR France189

BELL,Gawain Murdoch.DSO.Maj kia 31-7-17 11Hamps p120 CR Belgium6

BELL,George Henry LtCol ded 3-9-16 IA 9BhopalInf p273 MR67,27Punjabis

BELL,George Russell.MC.2Lt dow 4-12-18 C124RFA p25 CR France146

BELL,G.F Capt&QM 11-6-20 RASC CR Cornwall40

BELL,Guy Bayford Lt kia 28-4-17 5LancF att35MGC Inf p186&221 MR20

BELL,Harold 2Lt kia 13-11-16 13EYorks p83 CR France1890

BELL,Harold Stormont 2Lt mbk 2-12-17 att2/8Worc p256 MR17,dow

BELL,Henry 2Lt dow 17-10-17 8Yorks p89 see BELL,T.H.A.

BELL,Henry Capt dow 25-1-17 5BordR p228 CR France177

BELL,Henry Hogarth TCapt kia 5-9-16 4NumbF p213 CR France432,15-9-16

BELL,Henry Oswin.VD.TMaj ded 30-11-18 RASC p192 CR Yorks38

BELL,Hugh Randolph Ryan Lt dow 29-8-17 8Worc p226

BELL,Hugh Reginald.MID TCaptAMaj kia 3-9-18 11TankCps p188 CR France924

BELL,Jack Whateley TLtTCapt kia 26-3-17 1 att4Ess p131 CR Palestine8,Whateley

BELL,James T2Lt kia 11-1-17 11RScots p53 CR France1182

BELL,James T2Lt kia 22-4-18 19DLI p160 CR France296

BELL,James Clifford Aveling Lt dow 30-5-18 175RFA p25 MR27,kld

BELL,James Donald Allen 2Lt kia 21/23-3-18 6LancF p221 CR France1494,21-3-18

BELL,James Ernest Kirkham TLt dow 5-8-16 8BordR p116 MR21

BELL,James Rogerson 2Lt dow 1-4-18 10RScots p212 CR France40

BELL,James William.MC.TCapt kia 7-11-18 21Manch p154 CR France951

BELL,John Capt dow 27-12-17 68RFC p5

BELL,John T2Lt kia 27-5-18 BordR att8Bn p116 MR18

BELL,John Cunningham TLt ded 22-11-15 RAMC att7RScots p194 CR Egypt3

BELL,John Dobree Lt ded 30-10-18 RFA 19CpsHQ attIntell p25 CR France34

BELL,John James Maj ded 2-3-15 AyrYeo p203 CR Scot547

BELL,John Mercer Grimshaw Lt dow 11-10-18 RFA att7RAF p25 CR France34

BELL,John Murray TCapt kia 27-9-15 9BlkW p128 CR France219,25-9-15

BELL,John Murray T2Lt kia 24-4-17 10HLI p162 MR20

BELL,John Scott 2Lt kia 1-8-17 RE 15FC p43 CR Belgium112

BELL,John Wilson 2Lt ded 18-2-17 RE p210 CRScot235

BELL,Joseph 2Lt kia 17-4-17 5WYorks p218 MR19

BELL,Kenneth Frederick Hamilton 2Lt kia 25-9-15 1Lond p245 MR32

BELL,Lee T2Lt kia 17-10-18 7RDubF p176 CR France716

BELL,Leonard TLt dow 22-5-18 3RB p177 CR France81

BELL,Leslie Harrison 2Lt ded 26-9-18 10Glouc att58RAF p106 CR France134,kld

BELL,Malcolm Arthur Russell Capt kia 20-12-14 IA 54Sikhs p273 CR France727

BELL,Norman 2Lt kia 18-8-17 10Ches att57RFC p5&95 CR Belgium140

BELL,Norman Henderson 2Lt kia 1-7-16 3 att1Hamps p120 MR21

BELL,Philip Lawrence Lt kia 10-8-15 10Hamps p120 MR4

BELL,Quentin David 2Lt kia 31-10-15 2GordH p166 MR29,31-10-14

BELL,Richard Logsdaile.MC.2Lt kia 9-4-18 1 att2/5Hamps p120 CR Palestine9

BELL,Robert de Houghan Mark.MID TLt kia 3-9-16 10KRRC p149 CR France39,Hougham

BELL,Robert James 2Lt kia 2-11-18 3 att1/4Nhampt p137 CR Palestine8,2-11-17

BELL,Robert Norman 2Lt kia 14-4-17 9DLI p239 CR France420

BELL,Robert Stephen T2Lt dow 17-4-18 10Ches p95 CR France40

BELL,Robert William Popham Capt kia 5-7-16 3 att2RIrReg p88 MR21

BELL,Samuel Edward.MC.TLtACapt dow 19-11-16 7SLancs p125 CR France40

BELL,Sydney James 2Lt dow 13-10-16 7Lpool p215 CR Lancs381

BELL,Sydney Parker Capt kia 26-9-15D106 RFA p25 MR19

BELL,Thomas 2Lt kia 26-5-18 5RScotF p222 CR France268

BELL,Thomas Ernest 2Lt dow 1-4-18 5BordR p228 CR France145

BELL,Thomas Hector T2Lt kia 9-2-16 11 att9BlkW p128 CR France423

BELL,Tomas Henry Andrew 2Lt 17-10-17 8Yorks CR France145

BELL,Thomas Henry Stanley Capt kia 1-10-15 RAMC 36FA SR p194 CR France423,2-10-15

BELL,Walter Albert 2Lt kia 13-4-18 1DCLI p114 MR32

BELL,Walter Ernest 2Lt kia 25-4-18 8LancF p221 MR30 Ex19Bn

BELL,Walter Stanley 2Lt kia 16-4-18 12/13NumbF p60 MR30

BELL,William 2Lt dow 3-7-16 18DLI p160 CR France167

BELL,William Lt kia 10-4-17 7A&SH p243 MR20

BELL,William T2Lt dow 26-7-16 RE 252FC p43 CR France5

BELL,William 2Lt kia 3-5-17 5 att8BlkW p231 MR20

BELL,William Arundel T2Lt kia 14-6-17 BordR att8Bn p116 CR Belgium168

BELL,William Henry Dillon TCapt kia 31-7-17 1KEdwHorse p24 MR29

BELL,William James Knox.MC.2Lt kia 5-4-18 RGA 9SB p38 CR France5

BELL,William Robert T2Lt kia 12-10-17 11NumbF p60 MR30

BELL,Wilson Capt kia 5-3-17 2/4YLI p235 MR21,15-3-17

BELL-BATHURST,Basil Woodd Bambridge CaptAMaj dow 23-4-17 RHA p206 CR France512

BELL-HUGHES,John Otto T2Lt kia 28-9-17 Mddx att2/5LancF p146 MR30,20-9-17

BELL-IRVING,William 2Lt kld 28-10-15 10RScots attRFC p17&212 CR Scot617,Lt 27-10-15

BELL-IRVING,Kenneth Capt dow 22-10-17 8ESurr p112 CR Belgium16

BELL-IRVING,William Ogle.MC.Capt kia 29-11-17 11Huss p22 CR Palestine9

BELLAMY,Alfred Wraith 2Lt dow 22-10-17 Manch att23Bn p154 MR30

BELLAMY,Charles Henry TCapt dow 23-7-16 10Lincs p74 CR France145

BELLAMY,David Humphrey TLtACapt kia 2-4-17 10 att9Dev p76 CRFrance568

BELLAMY,Frank William T2Lt dow 8-10-18 6 att4Beds p85 CR France914

BELLAMY,Geoffrey GeorgeCapt dow 1-9-18 7Dev att4MGC p156&217 CR France14,Maj

BELLAMY,Harold Edward Lt kld 28-7-18 19Mddx &RAF CR Ches158

BELLAMY,Howard Claxson.MID TLt kia 2-1-17 11RScots p53 CR France1182,3-1-17

BELLAMY,James Thomas Reynell 2Lt ded 14-11-18 RE 272RlyCoy p43 CR Syria2

BELLAMY,John Holland T2Lt dow 4-10-16 13 att11N&D p133 CR France177

BELLAMY,John James 2Lt kia 24-4-17 B116RFA p25 MR37

BELLAMY,Osmund Lt kia 21-3-18 315RFA p207 MR27

BELLAMY,Thomas Bilbous T2Lt dow 13-5-17 6RLancs p58 CR Iraq8,Billows

BELLASIS,Philip Joseph TCapt kia 24-8-16 5KSLI p144 MR21

BELLEMORE,Raymond Alfred Capt dow 8-6-17 4ConnRgrs p172 CR France285,BELEMORE

BELLEW,Alexander 2Lt kia 23-10-16 2ScotRif p103 MR21

BELLEW,Richard Courtenay 2Lt dow 21-8-17 2IrGds p52 CR Belgium16

BELLINGHAM,Alan 2Lt kia 26-10-17 4LNLancs p234 MR30

BELLINGHAM,Robert Charles Noel.MID Capt ded 4-3-15 RFA p25 CR Belgium80 &CR Belgium187

BELLIS,Cecil Magnus 2Lt dow 9-7-16 3 att13Ches p95 CR France23,3Bn

BELLOC,Louis 2Lt kia 26-8-18 RE &209RAF p254&257 MR20

BELLOT,Byson Lt ded 27-3-18 1/1NSomYeo p205 CRFrance52,Bryson

BELLWOOD,Frank TCapt kia 14-7-16 8Dev p76 CR France513

BELSCHNER,William Frederick T2Lt kia 8-10-18 25MGC Inf p181 CR France844

BEMAND,George Edward Kingsley T2Lt kia 26-12-16 RFA attY5TMB p25 CR France727

BEMROSE,Karl 2Lt kia 1-7-16 1/5N&D p232 MR21

BEMROSE,Roderick Henry.MC.Lt ded 7-11-18 C285RFA p207 CR France34

BENBOW,Edwin Louis.MC.Capt kld 3-5-18 RFA att85RAF p25 CR Belgium20,kia 30-5-18

BENBOW,Sidney T2Lt kia 29-9-18 10 att2Worc p108 CR France665

BENBOW,Walter Harold.MM.T2Lt kia 23-8-18 7KSLI p144

BENCE-TROWER,Alfred 2Lt kia 29-5-18 1ScotsGds CR France1014

BENCE-TROWER,Edward.MC.Maj kia 30-5-18 5SWBord p99 MR18

BENCH,James George 2Lt kia 24-4-17 10Hamps p120 MR37

BENCHER,Gilbert Alfred Lt dow 9-12-17 2/19Lond p250 CR Palestine3

BENDER,Alfred Courteney TLt kia 20-9-17 15Hamps p120 MR30

BENDING,Edward Owen 2Lt ded 24-1-19 KRRC CR Somerset40,Lt

BENEDICT,Albert Edward Julius Wilbraham Scott.DSO.Lt ded 16-12-15 RBucksYeo p269 CR Norf151

BENETT,Rita Mary Miss ded 3-11-18 VAD p268

BENETT-DAMPIER,J.T. see BENNETT-DAMPIER,J.T.

BENFORD,Charles George T2Lt kld 5-1-18 7DCLI p114 CR Belgium127

BENGER,Alfred Horace TMaj dow 17-4-17 11Leic p87 CR France223

BENGOUGH,Charles William 2Lt kia 21-3-18 RGA 277SB p38 CR France381

BENGOUGH,John Crosbie.MID TCapt kia 26-2-16 GloucYeo attDorsYeo p203 CR Egypt6

BENGOUGH,L.MC.Maj 7-2-21 Ches CR Germany1

BENHAM,Charles Henry TMaj ded 8-11-16 RAMC p253 CR Europe1

BENHAM,Frank Benham Capt dow 23-8-16 C81RFA p25 CR Staffs134

BENHAM,John Russell 2Lt dow 4-5-15 100RFA p25 CR France285

BENHAM,Malcolm Erick 2Lt kia 29-9-15 3Mddx p146 MR19,Erik

BENHAM,Ralph George T2Lt kia 11-9-18 6SomLI p79 CR France258

BENHAM,Walter Edward 2Lt ded 3-11-18 A245RFA p25 CR France146

BENINGFIELD,John Philip 2Lt dow 27-4-15 59RFA p25 CR Belgium35,Lt

BENINGFIELD,Maurice Victor 2Lt kia 10-3-15 1Worc p108 MR22

BENISON,Eric William 2Lt ded 13-8-15 RGA p209 CR Dorset/CI135

BENISON,Robert Burton 2Lt kia 20-9-14 2ConnRgrs p172 CR France1329

BENJAMIN,Herbert Seymour Capt kia 9-10-17 1/8Worc p226 CR Belgium126

BENJAMIN,John Alfred TCapt kia 5-7-16 9WRid p115 CR France267

BENN,Alfred Maurice Lt kia 27-9-16 9WYorks p80 MR21

BENN,Bertie William T2Lt kia 19-7-16 8Norf p73 MR21

BENN,Joseph Reginald Tankard TCapt kia 2-9-15 RFA 11WRidHB p207 CR Belgium85,1-9-15

BENN,Oliver Williams Capt kia 6-6-15 9SomLI att1Ess p79 MR4

BENN,Walter Horace T2Lt kia 2-8-17 7Norf p73 CR France154

BENNALLACK,William Frederick 2Lt kia 17-10-18 RE 446FC p210 CR France1386

BENNELL,Donald Bruce Lt kia 16-4-17 315RFA p25 CR France265

BENNER,Walter TLt kia 2-9-18 16N&D att101TMB p133 MR30

BENNET,C.H. see BENNETT,C.H.

BENNET,G.Lt 21-11-20 SL &RASC CR Lond9

BENNET,Helena Stewart SNurse ded 18-10-18 QAIMNS p200 CR Scot381

BENNET,James Hampton.MC.2Lt kia 22-9-16 4 att2RMunstF p175 MR21

BENNET,Trevor Moutray.MC.TLt kia 10-11-16 10RIrRif &RFC p169 see BENNETT,T.M.

BENNETT,Albert Henry 2Lt dow 6-11-16 6N&D p233 CR France134,6Leic

BENNETT,Alfred Charles.DSO.LtCol ded 16-1-15 WYorks p80 CR Essex268

BENNETT,Alfred John 2Lt kia 9-8-17 2Ess p131 MR20

BENNETT,Arnold John.MC.Chap4Cl ded 26-1-18 RAChDept attRAMC 230FA p199 CR Egypt2

BENNETT,Arthur Hugh T2Lt kia 18-8-16 6DCLI p114 MR21

BENNETT,Arthur Shirley TLt kia 14-7-16 9Leic p87 MR21

BENNETT,C.W.Lt ded 13-10-18 DCLI attRGA CR Italy19 see BENNETT,V.C.W.

BENNETT,Charles Henry.MC.Lt drd 27-5-18 BucksYeo p203 MR41

BENNETT,Charles Hosken Lt died 25-2-19 RFA p261 BENNET

BENNETT,Charles Tudor.MID Capt kia 22-7-16 3 att1RWKent p140 MR21

BENNETT,Claude Denman Capt dow 18-7-17 2/6WRid p227 CR France518

BENNETT,F Lt 12-8-17 N&D CR Lond10

BENNETT,Edwin Herman T2Lt kia 5-5-18 29MGC p181 CR France24

BENNETT,Eric Fairfax.MC.TLtACapt kia 18-9-18 7RWSurr p55 CR France365

BENNETT,Ernest TLt ded 12-8-17 8LNLancs p135 MR29

BENNETT,Ernest Edward Sebastian Maj ded 26-3-19 IA 66Punjabis p273 CR India48

BENNETT,Francis Evans T2Lt kia 8-8-15 7RMunstF p175 MR4

BENNETT,Frank Dann Capt kia 21-3-18 5NStaffs p237 MR20,Dunn

BENNETT,Frederick Barberry Maj dow 22-10-18 C84RFA p206 CR France329

BENNETT,Frederick Martin 2Lt kia 10-9-18 20 att2/2Lond p251 MR16

BENNETT,Geoffrey Ernest Layton T2Lt kia 1-7-16 2Yorks p89

BENNETT,George Arthur T2Lt kia 3-12-17 RWar att2/6Bn p64 MR17

BENNETT,George Robert T2Lt kia 21-8-15 5ConnRgrs p172 MR4

BENNETT,George William 2Lt kia 3-12-17 W'land&C'landYeo p206 CR Palestine3

BENNETT,George William.MC.TLtACapt ded 29-11-18 Y&L att5Bn p158&258 CR Greece2,1Bn

BENNETT,Harold Capt mbk 14-11-14 IA 2/3GurkhaRif MR28

BENNETT,Harold Percy Lt kia 21-3-18 2Lond p245 CR france1893

BENNETT,Harold Presdee T2Lt kia 15-11-16 10LNLancs p135 MR21

BENNETT,Harold Stanley 2Lt kld 25-4-15 RGA p38 CR Glouc159

BENNETT,Henry Richard Lt ded 4-1-18 RHA 3CavDiv p25 CR France446

BENNETT,Henry Ryan TCapt kia 23-3-18 11Lpool p71 MR27

BENNETT,Herbert T2Lt kia 22-4-18 16RWelshF p97 MR27

BENNETT,Herbert Sydney TLt dow 18-10-18 1 att9SWBord p99 CR France1266

BENNETT,Ivan Provis Wentworth TCapt kia 14-7-16 7RWSurr p55 MR21 CR France1891,13-7-16

BENNETT,J.A.2Lt 5-2-20 RB CR War9

BENNETT,James T2Lt kia 28-11-16 RE 129FC p43 CR France149

BENNETT,John Alick T2Lt kia 22-8-18 9Ess p131 CR France370

BENNETT,John Benson T2Lt kia 28-3-18 3RB p177 MR27

BENNETT,John Blake T2Lt kia 21-3-18 GL &1Aircraft Supply Depot RFC p15 CR France102

BENNETT,John Edgar Capt kia 3-9-16 1 att2RIrReg p88 MR21

BENNETT,John Edwin Francis Theodore.MM.2Lt kia 24-7-16 8RWar att143MGC p186&215 CR France150

BENNETT,John Francis 2Lt kia 26-8-18 9Hamps p229 CR France614

BENNETT,John Nicoll 2Lt kia 19-5-17 RGA 121SB p38 CR France729

BENNETT,John William Lt kia 13-10-15 3RMunstF p175 CR France219

BENNETT,Lawrence Ernest T2Lt kia 24-8-16 9 att1RWSurr p55 MR21

BENNETT,Leslie Punsfer 2Lt dow 16-2-17 4RWSurr p212 CR France164

BENNETT,Maurice Porter 2Lt dow 6-10-17 2RWSurr p55 CR France139

BENNETT,Philip Dennis Capt ded 24-2-19 5RWar p269 CR War102

BENNETT,Ralph T2Lt kia 4-9-18 10Worc att1Hereford p108 MR30

BENNETT,Reginald 2Lt kia 3-9-16 13Glouc p106 MR21

BENNETT,Reginald George 2Lt kia 26-10-17 5RLancs p213 MR30

BENNETT,Robert Davis T2Lt kia 7-12-17 GL 1ArmySupplyDepot RFC p5 CRFrance31

BENNETT,Robert Granville T2Lt kia 4-10-17 YLI att9Bn p142 MR30

BENNETT,Robertis Charles Rudolph Busby.MC.Lt kia 24-8-18 20Lond p251 MR16,Robertio

BENNETT,Sydney Garnet 2Lt kia 20-7-16 2Suff p78 MR21

BENNETT,Theodore John Lt kia 7-9-18 1/5Worc att17IndInf p273&108 MR52 CR Palestine3

BENNETT,Trevor Mountray.MC.TLt kia 10-11-16 RFC &10RIrRif p2 CR France530

BENNETT,Vere Raymond Lt kia 10-4-17 3N&D att64MGC Inf p133&181 CR France591

BENNETT,Victor Cyril Wentworth Lt ded 13-10-18 DCLI attRGAp114 CR Italy19,C.W.

BENNETT,Vivian Wilfred Lt kia 21-10-17 RE 209FC p43 CR Belgium23,208FC

BENNETT,Walter James T2Lt kia 4-7-16 14 att12RScots p53 CR France399

BENNETT,William Frank T2Lt kia 23-4-17 1Lpool p71 MR20

BENNETT,William Harris Capt ded 16-1-20 Mddx attHQ RAF MR53

BENNETT,William Henry 2Lt kia 11-4-17 8N&D p233 CR France616

BENNETT,William Henry Pope.MC.TLtACapt kia 3-3-18 13RSuss p118 MR21

BENNETT,William Munro Lt dow 18-6-16 8A&SH p243 CR France15

BENNETT,William Pyt Maj kia 15-7-16 RGA att162RFA p38 CR France188

BENNETT,Wilmer Annie Miss ded 21-11-18 VAD CR Surrey156

BENNETT-DAMPIER,John Tudor 2Lt kia 2-3-15 2Ches attN&D p95 CR Belgium89,BENETT

BENNETT-GOLDNEY,Francis TCaptAMaj ded 26-7-18 SL & Staff p201 CR France477

BENNIE,Andrew T2Lt kia 30-9-18 17RScots p53 CR Belgium116

BENNIE,Hugh Osbourne Lt 31-7-17 5HLI attMGC p186&240 MR29

BENNIE,Robert Smith 2Lt kld 5-6-17 SR 45RFC p5 MR20

BENNIE,William Lt ded 10-10-17 RDC p269 CR Scot212

BENNIE,William Robertson 2Lt kia 2-12-17 7 att16HLI p240 MR30

BENNING,Murray Stuart Lt dow 1-11-14 3ESurr p112 CR France102

BENNISON,Miles 2Lt kia 1-10-17 9Yorks p89 MR30

BENNITT,Harry Pynson Capt dow 7-10-15 7SfthH p164 CR France40

BENNS,Arthur Lionel 2Lt kia 1-7-16 1/5Lond p246 MR21

BENSON,Alfred Hugh Maj ded 24-9-16 RAMC CR Yorks192

BENSON,Cyril Samuel T2Lt kia 24-4-17 6 O&BLI p129 CR France904

BENSON,Eric William TLtCol kia 15-9-16 9KRRC p149 MR21

BENSON,Frederick William.Sir.KCB.MajGen ded 19-8-16 RoO RemountSer p1 CR Canada1531,21Lancers

BENSON,George Agar Trevor.MC.2Lt kia 28-10-16 1Mddx p146 MR21

BENSON,Henry Lawrence.MID 2Lt kia 11-4-16 6NumbF p214 CR Belgium17,Laurence

BENSON,Hugh Cecil Lt kia 22-6-15 9RB p177 MR29

BENSON,Isaac TLtACapt kia 2-12-17 11BordR p116 MR30

BENSON,John Martin ACapt kia 27-5-18 4NumbF att149TMB p213 MR18

BENSON,John Peurice Capt kia 23-8-14 1ESurr p112 CR Belgium201

BENSON,Richard Erle LtCol dow 27-9-14 1EYorks p83 CR Wales54

BENSON,Thomas Brooke Lt kia 13-3-15 2RScotF p94 MR22

BENSON,Thomas Washington 2Lt kia 22-8-17 4RScots p211 CR Belgium92

BENSON,William Arthur 2Lt kia 21-3-18 6LancF p221 MR27

BENSON,William Roy Gwyn 2Lt kia 2-7-16 2SStaffs p122 CR France924

BENSTEAD,Harry Edwin 2Lt kia 14-4-17 7 att5Lond p247 CR France162

BENT,Percy Temple 2Lt kia 1-7-16 1KOSB p101 MR21,12Bn

BENT,Philip Eric.VC.DSO.TLtCol kia 1-10-17 9Leic p87 MR30

BENTALL,Ernest Hammond 2Lt kia 3-10-15 1KRRC p149 CR France423

BENTALL,William Douglas 2Lt kia 16-9-16 3 att6YLI p142 MR21

BENTHAM,George Andrew 2Lt kia 3-11-16 7ESurr &RFC p2&112,ded MR20

BENTHAM,Harley T2Lt dow 16-9-18 9WRid p115 CR France1184

BENTHAM,Richard Capt kld 8-11-16 7Manch attRFC p17&237 CR Lancs216

BENTHAM,Thomas TLt ded 12-3-19 SL RAMC p268 CR Surrey15

BENTINCK,Henry Duncan BtMaj dow 2-10-16 2CldGds p50 CR France145

BENTLEY,Arthur Fletcher T2Lt dow 11-3-16 13 att10N&D p133 CR France40

BENTLEY,Arthur Webb Butler T2Lt ded 2-12-18 3Yorks p89 CR Somerset157

BENTLEY,Basil T2Lt kia 11-9-17 2/5Y&L p158 CR France563

BENTLEY,Charles Arthur Campbell Capt kia 23-10-14 1RWar p64 CR France922

BENTLEY,Clarence Leslie 2Lt kia 28-10-14 2Manch p154 MR22

BENTLEY,Claud Louis T2Lt kld 23-12-16 15HLI p162

BENTLEY,Frank Mercer.MC.Capt kia 13-10-18 1/5LancF p221 CR France1266

BENTLEY,Frederick Donald.DCM.2Lt kia 30-11-17 GrenGds att1GdsMGC p49 CR FRance415

BENTLEY,Freeland Martell Lt kia 18-6-15 3 att2GordH p166 MR22

BENTLEY,Geoffrey Malcolm Capt dow 29-10-14 1Nhampt p137 CR Belgium57

BENTLEY,George Greenwood Lt dow 17-9-16 GL 13War att32RFC p2&189 CR France167,2Lt

BENTLEY,George Warwick T2Lt ded 13-1-17 GL RFus &3RFC p5 CR France927

BENTLEY,Gerald Wilson Capt kia 12-10-14 4Mddx p146 CR France1106

BENTLEY,Harry 2Lt drd 10-10-18 NumbF p60 MR40

BENTLEY,Howard Lidyard T2Lt kia 28-2-17 2RFus p66 MR21

BENTLEY,Joseph Elgey 2Lt kia 11-10-18 4WRid p227 CR France612

BENTLEY,Leonard Holt T2Lt ded 30-5-18 RASC p192 MR40

BENTLEY,Tom Capt dow 4-5-17 2/5WRid p227 CR France518

BENTLEY,Tom 2Lt dow 31-7-18 5YLI p235 CR France1358

BENTON,Frank T2Lt kia 15/17-9-16 15 att21KRRC p149 MR21,15-9-16

BENTON,John Walford 2Lt kia 28-9-16 19 att11N&D p133 MR21

BENTON,Ronald Mackenzie 2Lt kia 7-6-16 DLI attIAUL 53Sikhs p160&273 CR Iraq5

BENTON,Sydney T2Lt kia 27-10-17 1Norf p73 MR30

BENTON,William Manstead TCapt dow 17-8-16 12Manch p154 CR France833

BENZECRY,Solomon Lt kia 30-11-17 10Lond att17RFus p248 MR17

BENZIE,William Gardner 2Lt dow 10-4-17 8ScotRif p225 CR France113,9-4-17

BERESFORD,Charles Zaragoza de La Poer Lt kia 9-5-15 Nhampt p137 MR32

BERESFORD,Harold.MC.Lt dow 24-5-18 RFA p207 CR France180

BERESFORD,Percy William.DSO.MIDx2 LtCol dow 26-10-17 2/3Lond p245 CR Belgium36

BERESFORD,Rebecca Rose SNurse drd 26-2-18 QAIMNS p200 MR40

BERESFORD,Spencer Charles T2Lt kia 5-6-18 1RBerks p138 CR France120

BERESFORD,William TLt ded 30-3-17 RE IWT p43 CR Kent7

BERESFORD,William Maj ded 9-10-17 RDC p269 CR Somerset197

BERESFORD-POER,Hubert Piers.MID Maj kia 24-4-18 A91RFA CR France889

BEREY,Charles Eric Capt ded 10-12-19 IARO 9GurkhaRif attPoliticalDept p273 CR Iraq8

BERKELEY,Alfred Fitzhardinge Murray T2Lt kia 7-6-17 74MGC p181 CR Belgium43

BERKELEY,Christopher Lt kld 30-1-19 2CldGds &30TDS RAF p50 CR Mddx34,2Lt

BERKELEY,Maurice Henry Fitzhardinge Maj 1-1-18 RASC 27AmmPk CR Kent83

BERKELEY,Philip Charles Oswald TLtAMaj kia 29-9-18 123MGC Inf p181 CR France530

BERKELEY,Thomas Berkeley Hartman Lt ded 7-11-18 3Suff att7MGC p78&181 CR Italy9,Hardtman 9-11-18

BERKELEY,Thomas Mowbray Martin BtLtCol kia 20-5-16 BlkW CampCmdt 10Cps Staff DAQMG p1 CR France43

BERKLEY,John Humphrey Capt dow 8-4-16 10WYorks p80 CR France285

BERLAID,E.H.AssSurg 31-3-19 ISMD MR67

BERLEIN,Charles Maurice Lt kia 16-6-15 5 O&BLI p129 CR Belgium10

BERLEIN,Leslie Herman TLt kia 25-10-15 8RBerks p138 CR France219,Hermann

BERNARD,Arthur Basil LtACapt dow 4-5-17 PoW 5 att16KRRC p149 CR Germany1

BERNARD,Bernard Frederick Paul 2Lt kia 21-12-14 RWar p64 MR32

BERNARD,Frederick Joseph AssSurg2ndCl 22-10-14 ISMD CRFrance1841

BERNARD,George Robert.MC.T2Lt kia 8-4-17 RE 254Co p43 CR France80

BERNARD,Henry Claude T2Lt kia 3-9-16 7Glouc p106 MR21,att3Worc

BERNARD,Herbert Clifford Col kia 1-7-16 IARO att10RIrRif p265&273 CR France232

BERNARD,Lawrence Arthur Lt kia 20-9-14 2N&D p133 MR15 &CR France1893

BERNARD,Robert Lt kia 25-4-15 1RDubF p176 CR Gallipoli15,26-4-15

BERNERS,Hamilton Hughs Capt kia 14-9-14 1IrGds p52 CR France1112,Hugh

BERNEY,George Norman.MID Capt kia 6-11-17 1/1Hereford p252 CR Palestine1

BERNSTEIN,Maurice Leon.MC.T2Lt kia 10-4-18 11LancF p92 CR France1092

BERRIDGE,Jesse Dell.MC.TLt kia 24-5-18 RE JspecCo p43 CR France103

BERRIDGE,Victor Arnold T2Lt kia 6-3-17 Beds &34RFC p4&85 CR France424

BERRIDGE,William Alfred.MC.MM.2Lt ded 15-2-19 4Leic p269 CR Leic120,5Bn

BERIDGE,William Eric T2Lt dow 20-8-16 6SomLI p79 CR France833

BERRIE,Charlotte Sister ded 8-1-19 QAIMNS p200 CR Palestine3

BERRILL,Bernard Francis Gotch Lt kia 7-3-15 6RFus p66 MR29

BERRILL,Frank Gale Lt ded 28-9-18 57/43RFA p25 CR France113,dow

BERRIMAN,George WO ded 17-7-16 IA RIM p273

BERRINGTON,Caradoc Trevor Davies Capt kia 10-3-16 IA 15Lancers attC86RFA p273 CR France354

BERRY,Algernon Lawrence 2Lt kia 7-7-16 14 att8RFus p66 MR21

BERRY,Alexander James T2Lt kia 22-8-16 19 att20LancF p92 CR France630

BERRY,Andrew Reginald.CB.LtCol ded 24-3-17 2/9Lond p247 CR France120

BERRY,Bernard Lt kia 6-6-18 6Ches p222 CR France1689

BERRY,Claude Vincent Cameron 2Lt kia 27-7-17 112RFA p25 CR Belgium72

BERRY,David Douglas Anderson ACapt kia 26-9-17 2RScots p53 MR30

BERRY,Edward Fleetwood.MC.Capt kia 17-4-16 IA 2/9 att1/9GurkhaRif p273 MR38

BERRY,Edward James 2Lt kia 28-11-17 Manch att19Bn p154 CR Belgium112

BERRY,Eustace Carlton 2Lt kld 5-7-16 RFA attRFC p2&25 CR Numb4

BERRY,George Herbert 2Lt dow 9-10-17 D315RFA p25 CR Belgium11

BERRY,George Wilfred 2Lt kia 25-8-17 5DLI p239 CR France363,19Bn

BERRY,Harry T2Lt kia 1-11-18 WYorks p80 CR France1254

BERRY,James Frederick Williamson TLt ded 22-11-18 17 att1/5Lpool p71 CR France34,Wilkinson

BERRY,John Anthony T2Lt kia 25-9-15 2GordH p166 MR19

BERRY,John Granville,MC.2Lt mbk 16-8-17 2WYorks p256 MR30

BERRY,John Leslie TLt kia 4-7-18 13TankCps p188 CR France1170

BERRY,John Leslie 2Lt kia 12-10-18 7WRid p227 CR France718

BERRY,Oswald William 2Lt kia 8-4-17 9KOSB &48RFC p5&101 CR France924

BERRY,Percy Haycraft Lt drd 10-3-16 RAMC attBerksYeo p194 CR Egypt1

BERRY,Reginald 2Lt kia 30-5-16 4 att2SStaffs p122 CR France1896

BERRY,Reginald Douglas.MID TLt kia 12-5-17 12Y&L p158 CR France1191

BERRY,Samuel George TLt kia 22/23-3-18 7SomLI p79 CR France1061

BERRY,Tom Cecil Hayn Capt kia 30-8-18 5WelshR p230 CR France217,Haydn

BERRY,William T2Lt ded 4-7-17 56RASC DivTrain p192 CR Norf209

BERRY,William Herbert Stuart Lt kia 24-5-15 4RInniskF att2RIrReg p104 CR France285

BERRYMAN,John William T2Lt dow 27-11-17 15Yorks att2/4YLI p89 MR17

BERTHON,Leonard Tinne.MID TCapt kia 25-1-17 9RWar p64 CR Iraq5

BERTIE,Claude Peregrine Capt kia 19-3-17 6LondRFA att59RFC p17&207 CR France614

BERTIE,Ninian Mark Kerr 2Lt kia 8-5-15 KRRC p149 MR29,att4Bn

BERTIE,Richard Frederick Norreys Lt kia 20-11-17 BerksYeo p203 CR Palestine3

BERTINI,Umberto Michael Chap4Cl ded 30-9-18 RAChDept p268 CR Hamps144

BERTLIN,Hugh Anthony T2Lt kld 12-7-15 RE p43 CR Beds78

BERTRAM,Cyril Robertson 2Lt kld 18-6-16 1KEdwHorse &RFC p2&24 CR EAfrica7 &CR Tanzania1

BERTRAM,William Maj ded 18-2-15 11Manch p154 CR Scot789

BERTRAM WEARE,Albert James Capt ded 18-4-18 DLI 20Div CR War7

BERWICK,Robert George T2Lt kld 7-7-17 GL &RFC p5

BERWICK,William.TD.Lt&QM kia 11-9-18 5BordR p228 CR France511

BESCOBY,Edgar Laurence T2Lt dow 18-6-17 12RFus p66 CR Belgium11

BESLEY,Howard Napier 2Lt kia 29-6-17 1Lond p245 CR France581

BESLY,Barton Hope.MID Capt kia 25-10-14 1Dev p76 MR22

BESSELL,Mowbray TCapt kia 15/17-9-16 10RWSurr p55 MR21

BEST,Arthur Horris 2Lt dow 25-3-18 165RH&FA p25

BEST,Arthur Stephen Middleton TLt kia 23-2-17 RE 71FC p43 CR Iraq5

BEST,Douglas Kenneth Lt kia 16-8-17 6Ess att22RFC p17&232 CR France31

BEST,Edgar Harold T2Lt dow 18-9-18 2KRRC p149

BEST,Francis Behrens Lt kia 29-7-17 RASC attRFC p17&253 MR20

BEST,Frank Harrington Lt kia 13-2-17 SWBord BrecknockBn p223 MR38

BEST,Frank Robson Lt kia 2-1-16 4LNLancs p234 CR France702

BEST,Henry Reginald Lt ded 13-8-21 RASC CR Europe51

BEST,Jack TLt kia 15-5-18 34MGC p181 CR France59,Capt

BEST,James Henry T2Lt kia 25-6-16 RE 96FC p43 CR Belgium6,25-7-16

BEST,Norrys Aubrey 2Lt kia 19-7-17 3RFA p208 CR Belgium10

BEST,Stephen Wriothesley Lt kia 30-4-17 SWBord BrecknockBn p223 MR38

BEST,Thomas Andrew Dunlop.DSO&Bar.MajTLtCol kia 20-11-17 1/2RInniskF p104 CR France755

BEST,Thomas Edward Lt kia 9-8-15 8WRid p115 MR4

BEST,Wilfred Robert T2Lt dow 27-8-18 WRid p115

BEST-DUNKLEY,Bertram.VC.CaptTLtCol dow 5-8-17 Cmdg2/5LancF p92 CR Belgium18

BESTALL,Edward Douglas Lt kia 3-7-16 9Ess p131 MR21

BESTER,R.A.Capt 16-3-21 GL &RlyTransOff attDADRT CR Germany1

BESWICK,John Charles 2Lt ded 22-4-17 PoW 11RLancs p58 CR France403

BETHELL,Charles Francis Ithel 2Lt kia 22-2-16 RE 70FC p43 CR France423,Ithell

BETHELL,Christopher.MID TCapt kia 20-2-16 10YLI p142 CR France922

BETHELL,Edward Walter Capt kia 21-9-18 1RWSurr p55 CR France369

BETHELL,Frank Harry 2Lt kia 25-9-15 3ConnRgrs p172 MR29,Lt

BETHELL,Richard Carrington T2Lt dow 22-5-16 11 att9Yorks p89 CR France570

BETHELL,Thomas Henry Capt kia 19-7-16 7RWar p214 MR32

BETHUNE,Henry Ewart.MC.LtTCapt kia 30-9-18 12HLI p162 CR Belgium116

BETHUNE,John Lt dow 29-10-17 A24RFA p207 CR Belgium3,28-10-17

BETLEY,Eric 2Lt kia 28-3-18 82RFC &RGA p261&262 MR20,Lt

BETTELEY,William Lawrence.MC.T2Lt kia 25-6-17 7SomLI p79 CR France1488

BETTERIDGE,James Harper 2Lt kia 14-4-17 5BordR att16Lond p228 MR20

BETTESWORTH,Tom T2Lt dow 3-11-15 12RFus attRE 172FC p66 CR France40

BETTISON,Mark Hedley Capt kia 18-4-16 9DLI p239 CR Belgium37

BETTLES,Joseph T2Lt kia 7-11-18 5Leic p87 CR France1766

BETTRIDGE,R.F.Lt 19-6-21 RFA CR Devon266

BETTS,Henry Lee T2Lt kia 20-9-17 26RFus p66 CR Belgium112,Lt

BETTS,John Hamilton TCapt kia 7-7-16 12Manch p154 CR France267

BETTS,John William 2Lt kia 9-5-15 2WelshR p126 MR22

BETTS,Thomas Walter T2Lt kia 31-7-17 17N&D p133 MR29

BETTY,Alfred William HonLt&QM ded 23-3-17 13RB p266 CR Somerset157

BEUTTLER,Charles Brereton Oakley 2Lt dow 24-12-16 A94RFA p25 CR France80

BEVAN,Alan Harry Reynolds Capt 30-12-20 9BhopalInf attPoliticDept CR Egypt7

BEVAN,Clement Beckford ACapt kia 20-7-16 3 att2Suff p78 MR21

BEVAN,Francis Harry Vaughan TCapt kia 19-4-17 GL &14RFC p5 MR34

BEVAN,Oliver Lewen 2Lt dow 25-10-18 RFA 25ArmyBde p25 CR France146

BEVAN,Percival Johnstone Lt kia 10-3-15 1KRRC p149 MR22

BEVAN,Thomas William TLtACapt ded 22-10-18 RE p43 CR France1359

BEVAN,Wilfrid 2Lt kia 3-12-17 GL &20RFC p5 MR20

BEVEN,Thomas T2Lt kia 3-7-16 9 att2SLancs p125 MR21

BEVERIDGE,Alan Primrose.MC&Bar.LtAMaj kia 16-9-18 RGA 35HB p38 CR France841

BEVERIDGE,Bernard Gordon.MC.Capt dow 21-3-18 RAMC 2/1HighlandFA p253 CR France307,kia

BEVERIDGE,David Alexander T2Lt ded 14-9-15 RFA HQ 54Bde p25 CR Europe1,13-9-15

BEVERIDGE,Douglas Lionel Lt ded 7-11-18 IA 1/94RussellsInf p273 MR65,2Lt

BEVERIDGE,Edmund Waller St.Clair Capt ded 24-11-19 IARO attLabCps p273 MR66

BEVERIDGE,James O'Shaughnessey Capt dow 22-11-17 RAMC att137FA p194 CR France245,Shaughnessy

BEVERIDGE,John Baxter TLt kia 22-10-16 14HLI p162 CR France115

BEVERIDGE,Walter Joseph Paterson TLtACapt kia 23-10-18 8GordH p166 CR France206,Patterson 1Bn

BEVERLAND,Charles Ferris T2Lt kia 4-12-16 2RInniskF p104 CR France568

BEVERS,Isaac Gwilym T2Lt dow 2-8-17 16RWelshF p97 CR Belgium16

BEVES,Trevor Howard.MC.Capt kia 1-7-16 1BordR p116 CR France35

BEVILLE,Alfred Geoffrey 2Lt kia 8-4-17 16Lond p250 CR France420

BEVINGTON,William Joseph ACapt kia 5-11-16 39RFA p25 MR21

BEVIR,Cyril Edward Francis Lt kia 29-10-15 76RFA p25 CR France1106

BEVIR,Raymond T2Lt kia 15-7-16 10RFus p66 MR21

BEVIS,Charles Thomas Capt ded 18-2-19 RE p255 CR Wales491

BEVON,William Victor Lt ded 29-11-17 RFC p261 CR Staffs78,17-11-17

BEWES,Reginald Charles Hope Lt kia 23-5-15 Lpool &RFC p1&71 CR France350

BEWICK,Norman 2Lt kia 22-1-18 157RFA p25 CR Belgium64

BEWICKE,Calverley George Lt kia 26-7-16 1WelshR p126 MR21

BEWICKE,Ralph Nathaniel 2Lt kia 29-9-16 8DLI p239 MR21,BEWICK

BEWICKE-COPLEY,Redvers Lionel Calverly Capt kia 21-12-16 CldGds p50

BEWLAY,Thomas Henry 2LtACapt dow 21-5-17 RGA 36SB p38 CR France1186

BEWLEY,Edward Capt ded 19-8-18 19RB p244 CR Egypt1

BEWLEY,Edward Neville 2Lt kia 26-6-17 2/6N&D p233 CR France662

BEWLEY,Frederick Norman T2Lt kia 20-9-17 N&D att16Bn p133 MR30

BEWLEY,Isaac Capt kia 10-10-18 7DLI p239 MR16,att13Bn

BEWSHER,Francis Alexander Lt dow 18-4-18 C255RFA p25 CR France134

BEYNON,Ernest John Wilson T2Lt kia 9-10-17 4Y&L p158 CR Belgium125

BEYNON,Ian William Arthur 2Lt dow 27-9-18 RGA 27SB p38 CR France433

BEYNON,William Charles 2Lt dow 3-5-17 4RWFus att2SWBord p223 CR France113,4-5-17

BEYTS,Julian Falvey.DSO.TLtCol kia 5-10-17 15DLI p160

BEZUIDENHOUT,Pieter Hendrick Schalk.MC.2Lt kia 24-12-16 A94RFA SR p25 CR France423

BHARGAVA,M.P.Capt 6-10-19 IMS MR43

BHAT,K.H.Lt drd 31-12-17 IMS MR41

BIANCHI,Edward Almachilde Lt kia 21-3-18 4 O&BLI att184TMB p231 MR27

BIBBS,Philip Henry Samuel Lt ded 25-10-19 RE p269

BIBBY,David Houghton TCapt kia 13-4-18 22NumbF p60 MR32

BIBBY,Francis Stephen 2Lt kia 20-7-16 3 att1ScotRif p103 MR21

BIBBY,Gerald Maurice Gosset T2Lt kia 6-3-17 GL 16RFC p5 CR France12

BIBBY,Henry Leigh Maj kia 4-5-17 LancsYeo p204 CR Italy14

BIBBY,John Patrick TLt kia 10-3-15 2ScotRif p103 CR France260

BIBBY,John Pengelly Lt 12-10-17 1GrenGds CR Belgium106 see BIDDY,J.P.

BIBBY,Joseph Morton 2Lt kia 3-5-17 8EYorks p83 MR20

BIBLE,Geoffrey Roskell T2Lt kia 1-7-16 101MGC Inf p181 MR21

BICE,William Francis T2Lt kia 4-9-16 10Norf p73 MR21,1Bn

BICK,Percy Arthur 2Lt kia 3-9-16 3 att2RIrReg p88 CR France402

BICKERDIKE,Robert.MC.Capt kia 20-11-17 6WYorks p218 CR France274

BICKERSTETH,Stanley Morris TLt kia 1-7-16 15WYorks p81

BICKERTON,William T2Lt kia 20-9-17 56MGC p181 CR Belgium22

BICKFORD,Arthur Louis Maj dow 9-3-16 IA CIE 56Rif p273 MR38

BICKHAM,Arthur Rushton.MID TLt ded 15-2-19 RGA 155HB p262 CR Ches183,Capt Ex RE

BICKLEY,George Howard TLtACapt kia 4-10-17 237MGC Inf p181 MR30

BICKMORE,Bertram George 2Lt kia 21-3-18 A232RFA p25 CR France672

BICKMORE,David Francis.DSO.LtALtCol kia 19-7-18 Norf att4GordH p73 MR18

BICKNELL,Herman Bysshe Bagshaw 2Lt kia 28-5-18 1Yorks p89 MR18

BICKNELL,Herman Kentigern TCapt ded 24-7-17 1 O&BLI p129 CR Iraq8

BIDDLE-COPE,Anthony Cyprian Prosper 2Lt kia 25-4-15 KSLI att2Bn p144 MR29

BIDDULPH,Leonard Shrapnell Capt dow 29-12-16 RFA attNigR p25&201 CR EAfrica38 &CR Tanzania1

BIDDULPH,Michael.OBE.LtCol 8-4-20 RAPayDept CR Asia51

BIDDULPH,Percival Vincent T2Lt kia 19-7-17 GL &1/3KAR p201 CR EAfrica38 &CR Tanzania1,Lt

BIDDULPH,Robert Assheton 2Lt ded 19-11-16 2DragGds p20 CR Eire487

BIDDULPH,Victor Roundell George 2Lt kia 15-9-16 5 att8RB p177 MR21

BIDDULPH,William 2Lt kia 3-9-18 4Ches p222 CR Belgium74

BIDDY,John Pengelly Lt kia 12-10-17 1GrenGds p49 CR Belgium106

BIDEN,Lawrance Trouse Gregory Vernon Lt dow 10-10-17 2RWar p64 CR Sussex112

BIDGOOD,Frank 2Lt kia 10-9-18 16Lond p250 CR France369

BIDGOOD,Thomas Aylmer Tattnall Lt dow 28-10-17 96RGA 91HB p38 CR Egypt2

BIDIE,George Maxwell Vereker Lt kld 8-7-16 RFC &RScots p2&53 CR Scot82,2Lt

BIDLAKE,Herbert Cooper Keith T2LtACapt kia 25-2-17 9Worc p108 MR38

BIDMEAD,Charles Hugh T2Lt kia 10-11-16 GL &25RFC p2&189 CR France88,Lt

BIDWELL,Claude Arthur Stephen T2Lt kia 21-9-15 10LNLancs p135

BIEDERMAN,Harry Charles Ernest 2Lt kia 10-8-17 OxfYeo att57RFC p17&205 MR20,BIEDERMANN

BIGELOW,Braxton.MID Capt kia 23-7-17 RE 170TC p43 CR France924

BIGG,Albert Charles T2Lt kia 31-7-17 18Lpool p71 MR29

BIGG,Walter Lt kia 27-5-18 8DLI p239 CR France1753

BIGGAME,Francis Joseph.MID TLt kia 16-8-17 8RMunstF att48TMB p175 MR30

BIGGAR,Kenneth T2Lt kia 26-9-15 6CamH p167 MR19,25-9-15

BIGGAR,William Francis Wilson 2Lt ded 20-10-18 10WYorks p81 p263 CR Scot621

BIGGE,John Neville.Hon Capt kia 15-5-15 1KRRC p149 MR22

BIGGER,John Alfred Whittard 2Lt kia 8-5-17 4 att1ESurr p112 MR20

BIGGERTON-EVANS,Arthur Basil George Lt ded 17-12-19 3SWBord p263 CR Europe17,Capt

BIGGS,Arthur Ridley T2Lt kia 2-7-16 6Wilts p152 CR France393

BIGGS,Bernard George Dawson Maj ded 1-12-16 5DLI p238 CR Durham88

BIGGS,George Henry WO ded 29-6-16 RIM p273 CR Iraq6

BIGGS,John Geoffrey.MC&Bar.Lt dow 1-9-17 NSomYeo att53MGC p186&205 CR France52

BIGGS,Seward T2Lt ded 26-11-18 332RASC attRWFus p192 CR France658

BIGHAM,William T2Lt ded 19-9-15 13NumbF p60 CR Staffs156,6-9-15

BIGLAND,George Braddyll 2Lt kia 15-6-15 5RLancs p213 MR22,1/4Bn

BIGNELL,Claude Arthur Capt ded PoW 21-11-16 IA 4Rajputs att24Punjabis p273 CR Iraq8

BIGNELL,Gurth Capt kia 15-7-16 6Beds p85

BIGSBY,Edgar Arthur 2Lt kia 25-9-15 8RWKent p140 MR19

BILBY,Eustace John 2Lt kia 16-8-17 Mddx att2Bn p146 MR30

BILL,J.H.LtCol 2-11-19 IndCivilServ CR Iraq8

BILL,John Alexander Patterson 2Lt kia 16-8-17 18 att12RIrRif p169 MR30

BILL,John Francis Capt dow 29-3-15 SWBord p99 CR France924,kia

BILL,Rodney Edward 2Lt kia 26-8-18 RGA 38HB p38 CR France924,27-8-18

BILLING,John T2Lt kia 2-9-18 EYorks att5YLI p83 CR France1484

BILLINGER,Hector Fussell T2Lt kia 23-11-16 8ELancs p110 MR21

BILLINGS,David Kitto 2Lt kld 15-9-17 RFC p5 CR War65,14-9-17

BILLINGS,Herbert T2Lt kia 6-4-16 9 att6Leic p87 MR38

BILLINGS,Hugh Bradish T2Lt ded 9-8-17 SR 29RFC p5 MR20,Braddish

BILLINGSLEY,Harold Hinton T2Lt kia 30-4-17 RWar att6ELancs p64 MR38

BILLINGTON,Frank Norman Lt kld 30-9-18 RAOC &RAF p198 CR France1483

BILLINGTON,Leslie Charles 2Lt 9-7-15 4 att2LancF p92 MR29,7-7-15

BILLINGTON,Whitworth Leonard T2Lt kia 17-5-17 RE Z'SpCo p43 CR France438

BILLMAN,Walter Melville Lt dow 5-11-16 6 att1Mddx p146 CR France105

BILSLAND,James.MC.T2Lt kia 9-6-16 11 att10ScotRif p103 CR France423

BILTON,E.B.MID ACapt kia 14-3-17 1/1HighCycBn att2/5YLI p253 CR France239,15-3-17

BILTON,Harold Charles Lt died 4-3-19 24Lond p269 CR Surrey152

BILTON,Lewis Edward Albert Samuel T2Lt kia 23-4-17 1EKent p57 CR France551,L.A.E.S.

BIMROSE,Charles 2Lt kia 3-10-18 1/6N&D p233 CR France375

BINDLOSS,Edward Alexander Morgan Maj kia 15-6-18 5RWar p214 CR Italy3

BINER,Benjamin Clive 2Lt ded PoW 21-7-18 18RIrRif att4EYorks p169 CR Germany1

BINER,Frank Amsden T2Lt kia 3-12-17 GL &22RFC p5 CR France31

BING,Eric Coppin Lt 15-8-18 2/3RFA CR Kent177

BINGEN,Carl Adolf Max Lt kia 11-2-16 5RSuss p228 CR France1327,Charles 10-2-16

BINGHAM,Arthur Doyle Lt ded 3-10-17 IARO RFC &RAVC p273 CR Lond2

BINGHAM,Bentinck Agliomby 2Lt kia 12-5-17 3 att10LancF p92 MR20

BINGHAM,David Cecil Lt kia 14-9-14 3CldGds p50 MR15

BINGHAM,Frank Miller Capt kia 22-5-15 5RLancs p213 MR29

BINGHAM,Frank Oldfield T2Lt dow 14-9-18 8 att9RFus p66 CR France145,Lt

BINGHAM,Harold 2Lt kia 15-9-18 C78RFA p25 CR France398

BINGHAM,John Warnock Capt ded 10-3-19 RAMC p194 CR Belgium241,10FA

BINGHAM,Montague Hearfield Lt kia 13-4-18 5YLI p235 MR32

BINGHAM,William Henry.OBE.LtCol S/InflictWound 18-3-20 IA 69Punjabis p273 CR Asia81

BINGHAM-DAY,Thomas Hulkes LtCol ded 11-4-17 4Dev p273 CR Wilts157,5Bn

BINGLEY,Arthur Noel T2Lt kia 14-6-16 110MGC p181 CR France283

BINKS,Basil Henry T2Lt kia 23-10-16 1RLancs p58 MR21

BINLEY,Percy Augustine.MC.T2Lt kia 23-8-18 10Ess p131 CR France430

BINNEY,Edward Hibbert 2LtALt&Adjt ded 11-10-17 N&D p133 CR Ches111,Capt

BINNEY,Leslie Wingfold 2Lt kia 15-4-18 126RFA p208 CR France149,Lt

BINNEY,Robert Humphrey.MC.ACapt dow 23-3-18 10Ess p131 CR France1893

BINNIE,David Willis 2LtTLt kia 27-5-17 5HLI p240 CR France1489,2Lt 9Bn

BINNIE,Philip 2Lt kia 26-9-17 5ScotRif p224 CR Belgium112

BINNIE,William Harold Lt kia 22-7-18 7RScots att206RAF p211,224&258 CR FRance134

BINNING,Albert Huteson T2Lt kia 13-11-16 13EYorks p83 MR21

BINNING,George Baillie Hamilton.Lord.CB.MVO.BrigGen ded 12-1-17 RHGds 1stMtdBde p20,204&261 CR Scot644

BINNING,Robert Inglis Capt ded 16-8-16 IA IMS p274 CR Iraq6

BINNING,William Barclay T2Lt dow 24-4-16 28MGC p181 CR France285

BINNS,Christopher 2Lt kia 26-9-17 RGA 154SB p38 CR Belgium19

BINNS,Clement Stanley T2Lt kia 1-7-16 20NumbF p60 MR21

BINNS,Eric Douglas 2Lt kia 7-10-16 7 att4Mddx p235 MR20

BINNS,George Alfred T2Lt kia 8-4-18 6Beds p85

BINNS,John Eric 2Lt kia 9-4-16 3 att5Wilts p152 MR38

BINNS,John Houghton T2Lt ded 4-9-17 GL &29RFC p5 CR Belgium125,Lt

BINNS,Raymond Louis T2Lt kia 10-7-16 8Yorks p89 CR France515,Raymund

BINNS,William Adam Ferrer 2Lt ded 18-5-20 6 att18KRRC CR Norf101

BINNY,Steuart Scott.DSO TLtCol kia 3-3-16 10RWelshF p97 CR Belgium131,BINNY Ex 19Huss MR29,BINNEY

BINSTEAD,Gerald Charles.MC.CaptTMaj kia 8-4-15 2Ess p131 CR Belgium33,BINSTEED

BION,Kenneth Norman,MC.MIDx2 LtACapt kia 21-3-18 1 att2N&D p133 MR20

BION,Rupert Euston Lt kia 9-4-18 20Huss &40RAF p23 MR20

BIRBECK,Sidney Walker 2Lt kia 9-10-17 5WYorks p218 MR30

BIRCH,Arthur T2Lt dow 17-2-17 6RBerks p138 CR France246

BIRCH,Charles Richard Eli Lt&QM ded 12-8-17 9ESurr p112 CR France40

BIRCH,Edward Cecil Lt ded 26-1-19 3RWSurr &RAF p55 CR Surrey153

BIRCH,Eric Wykeman.MC.Lt dow 17-1-17 4WRid attMGC p186&227 CR France62,Wykeham

BIRCH,Francis Wykeham Wallace 2Lt kia 23-1-20 IA 2/2 att2/9GurkhaRif p274 MR43

BIRCH,Frederick William Maj kia 17-4-16 4SWBord p99&274,IA Ret MR38,dow

BIRCH,George Owen Lt kia 14-9-14 WelshR p126 MR15,3 att2Bn CR France390

BIRCH,Gilbert Wilson Fitzroy TLtACapt kia 24-8-17 11YLI p142 MR30

BIRCH,Harold 2Lt dow 21-4-16 IARO att128Pnrs p274 CR Iraq6

BIRCH,Howard T2Lt kia 9-4-16 12 att8RWelshF p97 MR38

BIRCH,John 2Lt kia 5-7-15 13Worc p108 CR Gallipoli6

BIRCH,Leonard Capt kia 23-4-17 7BordR p116 MR20

BIRCH,Percy Hall 2Lt mbk 21-3-18 RGA 199SB p256 MR20

BIRCH,S.C.Capt ded 1-8-17 NumbF p60

BIRCH,W.MBE.Capt 3-3-20 RHA CR Lond29

BIRCH,Walter Robert.MID TCapt kia 7-10-16 6 O&BLI p129 MR21

BIRCH,William Claud Kennedy.MC.CaptAMaj kld 5-1-18 2Yorks p89 CR Belgium127

BIRCH,William Elric Hawthorn T2Lt kia 31-7-15 6DCLI p114 CR Belgium453,Lt

BIRCH-REYNARDSON,Edward Vere Lt kia 25-12-15 3 att1ESurr p112

BIRCHALL,Arthur Percival Dearman CaptTLtCol kia 24-4-15 RFus attCanInf p66 MR29

BIRCHALL,Edward Vivian Dearman.DSO.Capt dow 10-8-16 O&BLI BucksBn p231 CR France40

BIRCHALL,Wilfred Arthur Lt kia 28-11-17 NottsYeo p205 CR Palestine3,SherRgrs

BIRCHAM,Humphrey Francis William.DSO.TLtCol dow 23-7-16 2KRRC p149 CR France23

BIRD,E.A.Lt 29-8-20 CentIndRlyBn MR65

BIRD,Arthur Leonard 2Lt kia 6-9-17 2/5RWar p214 CR Belgium125

BIRD,Basil William.MC&Bar.MID TCapt dow 24-11-18 11N&D p133 CR France146

BIRD,Clement Eustace T2Lt dow 28-6-17 9RFus p66 CR France154,kia

BIRD,Charles Lt ded 6-8-18 RFA p261 CR Essex81

BIRD,Charles Edwin 2Lt kia 17-2-17 5Ess p232 CR France314

BIRD,Dudley Joseph de Anguld Lt kia 27-6-17 RFA attRFC p17&207 CR France421,Angulo

BIRD,Edward Kenelm Capt ded 27-9-19 IA 29 att20Punjabis p274 CR Egypt9

BIRD,Edwy Harold TCapt kia 24-2-17 10RWSurr p55 CR Belgium21

BIRD,Eric Hinckes Lt dow 27-6-16 1RFus att25RFC p266 CR France88.kia

BIRD,Eric James T2Lt dow 25-4-17 4Worc p108 CR France113

BIRD,Eric Stephen 2Lt kia 12-8-17 3 att8RIrF p170 CR Belgium125,6 att8Bn

BIRD,Ernest Walter Capt dow 27-7-16 1/6Glouc p225 CR France169

BIRD,Francis Clifford 2Lt kia 2-3-15 3KSLI p144 CR Belgium111

BIRD,George Brown.MC&Bar.TCapt kia 30-7-16 10RWar p64 MR21

BIRD,Henry Lt ded 12-4-19 1GrenGds att1/5KAR p49,201&257 CR EAfrica59

BIRD,Henry Tattersall 2Lt kia 27-3-18 160RFA p25 MR20

BIRD,John Greville Hobart Lt kiaAbout 25-10-14 RWSurr p55 MR29

BIRD,John Woodall T2Lt kia 21-12-17 RHGds HouseholdBn p20 CR France1182

BIRD,Laurie Edna SNurse ded 19-8-19 QAIMNS CR Surrey160

BIRD,Percy Charles Hilton T2Lt kia 5-4-16 10Norf att6LNLancs p73 MR38

BIRD,Raymond 2Lt kia 16-8-16 4Glouc p225

BIRD,Rex William T2Lt kia 24-8-16 1Wilts att7MGC Inf p181 MR21

BIRD,Robert.MVO.LtCol ded 30-3-18 IA CIE IMS p274 MR66

BIRD,Stanley Treadgold T2Lt dow 20-8-16 7KRRC p149 CR France177

BIRD,Walter Cyril TLt kia 4-3-17 8 att2Nhampt p137 MR21

BIRD,Wilfrid Stanley Lt kia 9-5-15 5 att2KRRC p149 MR22

BIRD,William Edmund T2Lt dow 28-4-17 RSuss p118 CR France102,2RFus

BIRD,William Gustave Capt ded 7-2-20 RASC CR Hamps1

BIRD,William Henry T2Lt kia 12-10-16 10 att2Beds p85 MR21

BIRD,William Ryder T2Lt kia 8-10-15 6 att8KRRC p149 MR29

BIRD,William Thornton Maj kia 12-7-15 7ScotRif p224 MR4

BIRDSEYE,Arthur Thomas T2Lt dow 25-4-18 2MGC p181 CR France62,Lt

BIRDSEYE,Douglas Martin T2Lt dow 10-2-17 8SStaffs p122

BIRDWOOD,C.B.2Lt 18-7-18 CldGds CR Surrey4

BIRDWOOD,Christopher William Brodrick Capt dow 7-6-15 IA 1/6GurkhaRif p274 CR Gallipoli3

BIRDWOOD,Gordon Alic Brodrick 2Lt kia 19-9-14 SLancs p125 CR France1107,Alick 20-9-14

BIRDWOOD,Herbert Frederick Lt kia 2-3-16 20Lond attRFC p17&251 CR France1308

BIRDWOOD,Richard Lockington Capt kia 17-11-14 IA PoliticDept p274 CR Iraq6

BIRKBECK,Edward Lt kia 7-8-15 IA 128Pnrs att1/5GurkhaRif p274 MR4

BIRKBECK,George Lt ded 19-2-15 NorfYeo p204 CR Norf128

BIRKBECK,Gervase William Capt kia 19-4-17 5Norf p216 MR34,20-4-17

BIRKBECK,Morris Lt kia 14-7-15 IA 24Punjabis p274 CR Iraq6,14/15-7-15

BIRKBY,Henry Alexander T2Lt dow 20-4-16 9 att5RBerks p138 CR France80

BIRKETT-BARKER,Holroyd Lt ded 15-8-17 RGA 134SB CR Greece9

BIRKIN,Thomas Richard Chetwynd 2Lt kia 12-6-17 7DragGds att25RFC p5&21 CR France88,Lt

BIRKS,Alfred Owen T2Lt dow 13-3-18 1Dors p123 CR Belgium38

BIRLEY,Hugh Kennedy TCapt kia 23-7-16 19Manch p154 MR21

BIRLEY,Joseph Hornby TCapt kia 2-9-18 19Manch p154 CR France744

BIRMINGHAM,William Arthur T2Lt kia 9-8-15 6RIrF p170 MR4

BIRNEY,John Gordon Lt kia 11-1-17 1HLI p162 MR38

BIRNIE,Edward D'Arcy.DSO.MC.TLtACapt dow 22-3-18 8BordR p116 CR France177

BIRNIE,Edward John Wilfrid 2Lt kia 14-2-15 2ESurr SR p112 MR29,Wilfred

BIRNIE,Gerald Lt dow 4-11-18 46/39RFA p25 CR France146

BIRNIE,William 2Lt kia 24-10-16 RE 2/2HighlandFC p210 CR France131

BIRNIE,William John Gordon Lt kia 23-11-17 8GordH att B'TankCps p166&188 MR17

BIRRELL,Andrew Smith T2Lt kia 9-4-17 6KOSB p101 CRFrance581

BIRRELL,George Henry Gordon 2Lt kia 12-5-15 9A&SH p244 MR29,10-5-15

BIRRELL,Stuart Erskin TCapt dow 11-7-16 6SomLI p79 MR20

BIRRELL,Thomas Yates TLt kia 17-2-16 8SStaffs p122 CR Belgium120,15-2-16

BIRRELL,William George.MIDx2 MajGen ded 23-8-18 RAMC p194 CR Scot275

BIRRELL,William Henry 2Lt dow 20-9-18 8 att11ScotRif p225 CR Greece6

BIRRELL-ANTHONY,Henry Anthony 2Lt kia 8-5-15 1Mon p244 MR29

BIRT,Lascelles William TCapt dow 1-10-17 O&BLI att1/4Bn p129 CR Belgium18

BIRT,Lightly Harold.DSO.Capt kia 5-1-15 1RBerks p138 CR France727

BIRT,Wilfrid Beckett Capt ded 18-4-16 PoW 9ESurr p112 CR Germany1,Wilfred

BIRTLES,Leonard 2Lt kia 16-9-16 2DLI p160 MR21

BIRTLES,Roland Powell TLtACapt kia 4-3-17 1Worc p108 CR France439

BIRTWISTLE,Norman.MC.Lt kia 8-10-18 19Huss p23 CR France341

BISCOE,Archibald Fairhead Lt ded 22-2-19 RASC p192 CR Germany1,attIICps

BISCOE,Arthur John Capt dow 12-3-15 1RIrRif p169 CR France102

BISCOE,Frederick Crozier Frazer Capt dow 19-5-15 2Worc p108 CR France80

BISHOP,Alfred Wedderburn T2Lt kia 12-5-17 1Hamps p120 MR20

BISHOP,Arthur Walter 2Lt kia 21-3-18 4 att9RSuss p228 CR France528,22-3-18

BISHOP,Basil Frederic.MC.MajALtCol kia 18-9-18 9SLancs p125 MR37

BISHOP,Bernard Bennett 2Lt kia 9-9-17 5DCLI attRFC p17&227 CR France1361

BISHOP,Charles Dudley 2LtACapt kia 17-4-18 2Worc p108 MR32

BISHOP,Charles Frederick T2Lt kia 4-4-18 13RFus p66 MR20

BISHOP,Charles Gamble.DSO.MC.Maj kia 30-10-17 RE p209 CR Belgium23

BISHOP,Charles Harold.MC.T2Lt dow 23-10-18 13DLI p160 CR France441

BISHOP,Charles Trevor T2Lt kia 29-3-17 5Wilts p152 MR38

BISHOP,Colville Jones Lt ded 22-4-18 RASC attRGA p192 CR France134,James

BISHOP,Edwin Maurice Lt kia 18-10-14 3Dors attYLI p123 MR22

BISHOP,Ernest Eldred 2LtALt kia 14-3-17 RGA attY6TMB p38 CR Frnce149

BISHOP,Frank Ernest T2Lt kia 12-7-17 GL &57RFC p5 CR Belgium10

BISHOP,Frederick Capt ded 21-2-19 5Ches p269 CR Hamps202

BISHOP,George Bernard Hamilton Chap4Cl kia 27-5-18 RAChDept att6NumbF p199 MR18

BISHOP,Gerald Clement William T2Lt kia 11-8-17 Mddx att16Bn p146 MR29

BISHOP,John Edmund TCapt kia 18/19-4-16 10 att6ELancs p110 MR38

BISHOP,John Ellis 2Lt kia 21-9-17 7Lond p247 MR29

BISHOP,Keith Ford 2Lt kia 8-8-16 RGA 23HB p38 CR France430

BISHOP,Nigel Fyfe Watson 2Lt kia 13-10-15 1/5NStaffs p238 MR19

BISHOP,Parkyn Sydney 2Lt kia 30-11-17 8Lond p247 MR17

BISHOP,Ralph Murdock T2Lt dow 15-4-18 PoW 34MGC Inf p181 CR Belgium451

BISHOP,Rowland Bridgeman.MID LtACapt kia 19-4-17 1/4Nhampt p234 CR Palestine8,Bridgman

BISHOP,Samuel James Webb 2Lt kia 3-5-17 6Ess att7Mddx p232 MR20

BISHOP,Wilfrid T2Lt dow 6-7-17 BordR att11Bn p116 CR Belgium173

BISHOP,William Reason 2Lt kia 2-10-17 GL SStaffs att55RFC p5 CR Belgium140

BISPHAM,David Charles T2Lt kld 4-11-17 GL &RFC p5 CR Lond9

BISSEKER,Arthur Vanderkists Lt kia 4-10-17 6RWar p214 CR Belgium128,Vanderkiste

BISSEKER,John Wallis 2Lt kia 1-4-17 6RWar p214 CR France369

BISSET,J.L.Lt 26-3-21 RE CR Scot267

BISSETT,Edgar George William 2Lt dow 7-1-17 5GordH attRFC p17&242,BISSET CR Belgium18

BISSETT,Fenton Capt 16-4-18 4SomLI CR France88

BISSETT,George.DSO.MC&Bar.LtAMaj dow 18-10-18 1RScotF p94 CR France512,LtCol 10-10-18

BISSICKS,Francis Ronald T2Lt kld 2-1-17 GL &48RFC p5&189 CR glouc9

BISSLEY,William Howe T2Lt kia 18-8-16 8RBerks p138 MR21

BITTLES,G.H.HonMaj ded 21-9-16 RAOC p267 CR Ireland181,IOD

BLACK,Allan Capt kia 27-5-18 RE 490FC p209 MR18

BLACK,Allan Maclean T2Lt kia 18-7-16 5CamH p167 CR France402

BLACK,Charles Morrison T2Lt ded 9-7-17 RIrRif attRInniskF p265 CR Ireland137,RIrFus

BLACK,Cyril Herbert Charles Pakenham T2Lt kia 18-8-16 13Mddx p146 MR21

BLACK,David T2Lt kld 3-10-17 GL &RFC p5 CR Scot591

BLACK,David Hammond 2Lt kia 8-5-18 20 att17Lpool p71 MR30,Hammond Dudley

BLACK,David Smith.MC.2LtTCapt kia 27-3-18 3 att7Suff p78 MR27

BLACK,Donald MacGregor Capt kia 6-8-15 1Ess p131 CR Gallipoli6

BLACK,Donald Walter Bryce T2Lt kld 3-1-18 RFC p15 CR Hamps57

BLACK,Eleanor Eileen Miss drd 4-6-18 VAD BRCS p200 MR40

BLACK,Eric Osborne Lt kia 9-5-15 2Lincs p74 MR32

BLACK,Ernest Charteris T2Lt kia 22-11-15 9 att7RScotF p94 CR France423

BLACK,Francis Henry LtTCapt kia 25-4-15 4 att1RWar p64 CR France705

BLACK,George Balfour.MC.LtTCapt dow 23-8-18 17Lancers att13TankCps p23&188 CR France1170

BLACK,George Bennett T2Lt kia 7-10-17 11A&SH p172 MR20

BLACK,George Dudley Austin TLt kia 21-6-16 22RFus p66 CR France924

BLACK,Hammond Dudley 2Lt 8-5-18 20 att17Lpool MR30 see BLACK,David Hammond

BLACK,J.LtCol 5-2-20 WarYeo CR Europe23

BLACK,James T2Lt dow 19-8-17 7/8KOSB p101 CR Belgium8

BLACK,James Ashton 2Lt kia 21-3-18 3DLI p160 CR France1484

BLACK,James Elliot,MC Capt kia 19-4-17 RAMC att8Beds p194 CR France115

BLACK,James Dykes.MC.Maj ded 5-7-18 5HLI p269 CR Scot756

BLACK,James George HonMaj ded 18-2-18 RLancs p262 CR Mddx29

BLACK,James Muir 2Lt kia 1-8-18 1/9RScots p212 CR France524

BLACK,James Somerville T2Lt kia 29-4-17 GL &16RFC p5 CR France134

BLACK,John Capt ded 26-9-17 RLancs p58 CR France145

BLACK,John TLt dow 23-8-18 6TankCps p188 CR France103

BLACK,John Montgomery T2Lt kld 5-2-18 RFC p15 CR Scot775

BLACK,John Neill.MID TCaptAMaj kia 9-4-17 6SomLI p79 CR France532

BLACK,Maurice Adam Maj kia 11-2-17 5DragGds &RFC p5&21 CR Europe58

BLACK,Maurice Charles Osborne Lt kia 24-8-16 GL 7BordR attTMB p189 CR France397,25-8-16

BLACK,Norman Annandale TCapt kia 23-5-16 A105RFA p25 CR France558

BLACK,Robert Robin 2Lt dow 22-10-18 1/5A&SH p243 CR Belgium11

BLACK,Robert Alaister McGregor TLtACapt kia 27-7-18 1/8GordH p166 CR France524

BLACK,Thomas Lloyd T2Lt kia 2-6-15 RE 171FC p43 CR Belgium4

BLACK,Thomas Porteous TCapt kia 9-8-15 9N&D p133 MR4

BLACK,Tom T2Lt kia 18-9-16 19 att17N&D p133 MR21

BLACK,W.N.2Lt 19-8-20 4KOSB CR Scot696

BLACK,William Rev Chap4Cl ded 10-7-18 RAChDept p199 CR France34

BLACK,William Duncan Thomson Rev kia 22-8-17 RAChDept att7CamH p199 CR Belgium8

BLACK,William McMillan Capt kia 31-10-14 IA 58Rif p274 CR France80

BLACK,William Thomas Lt kia 24-9-17 4Ess attRE p232 CR Belgium124

BLACK-HAWKINS,Claude Cranstoon Ridout Capt kia 10-8-15 2 att10Hamps p120 MR4,Cranstoun

BLACKABY,Arthur 2Lt kia 17-5-15 Ches p95 MR29

BLACKALL,Charles Walter.MIDx2 Capt kia 24-3-18 3EKent att4SStaffs p57 MR20,LtCol

BLACKALL-SIMONDS,George Prescott Lt kia 26-9-14 1SWBord p99 MR15

BLACKBOURN,Edgar Singleton T2Lt dow 29-9-16 7KRRC p149 CR France40

BLACKBURN,Charles James Critchley LtACapt kia 25-4-18 5WYorks D'Coy p218 MR30

BLACKBURN,Edward 2Lt kia 9-8-16 1/5LNLancs p234 MR21

BLACKBURN,Edward 2Lt kia 21-3-18 3 att2/7Manch p154 MR27

BLACKBURN,Ernest Lt kia 9-8-16 1/5LNLancs p234 MR21

BLACKBURN,Frank 2Lt kia 24-10-17 5ELancs attMGC p226&186 MR30

BLACKBURN,Geoffrey Gaskell TCapt kia 1-7-16 10WYorks p81 CR France373

BLACKBURN,George Stanley 2Lt dow 30-10-18 4BordR p228 CR Cumb'd&W'more'd40

BLACKBURN,Gideon 2Lt ded 18-2-19 1/7WYorks p269 CR Yorks344

BLACKBURN,Harry Clement T2Lt kld 23-3-18 1 att1/7WYorks p81 CR Belgium72

BLACKBURN,Harry Dudley Lt kia 5-4-17 1RBerks &43RFC p5&138 CR France924

BLACKBURN,John Herbert Lt ded 7-2-17 4YLI p235 CR Belgium11,8-2-17 9Bn

BLACKBURN,Norman Henry Gershorn.MC.T2Lt kia 23-10-18 RBerks att8Bn p138 CR France190

BLACKBURN,Reginald Herbert 2Lt ded 5-11-18 Beds p85&263,Lt

BLACKBURN,Stanley West T2Lt kia 9-10-17 Y&L p158 MR30

BLACKBURNE,Charles Harold.DSO.Capt&BtLtCol drd 10-10-18 5DragGds p21 CR Ireland27

BLACKBURNE,Harry Devereux Lt kia 27-9-17 9Lond p247 MR30

BLACKBURNE,John George.MID TMaj kia 22-8-15 9N&D Lt RoO p133 CR Gallipoli5

BLACKDEN,Arthur Worsley 2Lt kia 28-9-16 189RFA p25 MR21

BLACKDEN,Wilfred Worsley CaptTMaj ded 10-1-16 11NumbF p60 CR France40,Wilfrid

BLACKEBY,Joseph Edward T2Lt kia 21-2-18 RFC p15 CR Belgium13

BLACKER,Cecil Francis Lt dow 6-9-14 2ConnRgrs p172 CR Eire336

BLACKER,George Frederick Lt kia 9-5-15 3 att2Nhampt p137 MR32

BLACKER,John Robin 2Lt kia 28-9-15 1CldGds p51 MR19

BLACKER-DOUGLASS,Robert St.John.MC.Lt kia 1-2-15 1IrGds p52 CR France720

BLACKETT,Charles Robert 2Lt kia 25-4-15 KSLI p144 MR29

BLACKETT,William Stewart Burdett Lt dow 25-11-14 LeicYeo p204 CR Belgium150,Capt 24-11-14

BLACKIE,Albert Ferguson TCapt dow 17-4-17 16HLI p162 CR France583

BLACKIE,Frank Herndon Lt kia 11-4-18 8ScotRif att1KAR p225 MR52,Ex9HLI

BLACKIE,John.MC.Lt kia 22-10-18 8 att11RScots p211 CR Belgium143

BLACKIE,John Stewart Lt kia 18-10-16 5 att1RB p177 MR21

BLACKLAWS,Alec Stuart.MC.2Lt kia 7-1-18 D161RFA p25 CR Belgium20

BLACKLEDGE,Ewan John 2Lt mbk 23-11-17 1Lpool &11RFC p256

MR20,Lt

BLACKLOCK,Algernon Haden 2Lt kia 21-10-14 2A&SH p172 CR France566

BLACKLOCK,Alice May Sister ded 13-8-16 TFNS p254 CR Iraq6

BLACKLOCK,William T2Lt ded 12-9-16 11BlkW p128 CR Europe1

BLACKMAN,George Hugh Willoughby TLt kia 30-7-16 2RScotF p94 MR21

BLACKMAN,Wilfred Ernest Arthur.MID T2Lt ded 14-10-18 MGC p181 CR Kent83,Capt

BLACKMAN,William.DCM.2LtACapt kia 8-5-17 1ESurr p112 MR20

BLACKMORE,Edwin 2Lt kia 16-8-16 1/5DCLI att9MGC Inf p186&227 MR21

BLACKSTOCK,John T2Lt kia 6-10-18 RASC att12NStaffs p192 CR France1140

BLACKWELL,Aubrey Francis.MC.Lt kia 2-6-17 6LondRFA p207 CR Belgium5

BLACKWELL,Basil Bernard 2Lt kia 3-9-16 3 att8EKent p57 CR France1890

BLACKWELL,Charles 2Lt kia 20-7-15 4RFus p66 CR Belgium37

BLACKWELL,Cyril T2Lt kia 1-7-16 16RFus p66 MR21

BLACKWELL,George John Rowland T2Lt kia 30-3-18 Manch att2/6Bn p154 MR27

BLACKWELL,Gerald Davis Lt kia 7-6-17 6NumbF att47MGC p186&213 CR Belgium60,Davies

BLACKWELL,Julian Victor T2Lt kia 11-4-18 11LancF p92 MR32

BLACKWELL,Samuel Frederick Baker.DSO.TCapt kia 20-11-17 TankCps p188 CR France711

BLACKWELL,Thomas T2Lt kia 27-3-18 7Suff p78 MR27

BLACKWELL,Walter TLt dow 28-9-18 11RDubF p176 CR Belgium38

BLACKWELL,William Gordon TLt kia 5-10-16 8RFus p66 MR21

BLACKWOOD,Henry Stear Lt dow 1-5-17 9Lond p248 CR War84

BLACKWOOD,John Angus 2Lt ded 10-9-16 3BlkW p128 p264 CR Scot760

BLACKWOOD,Miles Harry 2Lt kia 1-7-16 2SfthH p164 CR France643

BLACKWOOD,Walter Lennox TLt kia 31-7-17 RScotF attMGC Tanks p94 CR Belgium112

BLAD,Kenneth Sven T2Lt ded 26-11-18 RE &4TankCps p43&188 CR France1512,Lt

BLADEN,Eustace Clement T2Lt dow 4-11-15 11 att8WRid p115 CR Gallipoli27

BLADES,Laurence Turner 2Lt ?? 5-7-15 6 att1RB p177 CR Belgium85,Lawrence

BLADES,William Henry 2Lt kia 3-5-17 8RB p177 MR20

BLADON,Henry James 2Lt dow 1-9-18 4WelshR p230 CR France217,kia

BLADWELL,Leonard Joseph T2Lt kia 14-10-18 RE 237FC p43 CR Belgium157

BLAGBROUGH,George Stanley TMaj kia 11-12-16 EYorks att16WYorks p83 CRFrance203

BLAGDEN,Maurice Bernard 2Lt kia 21-9-18 1RWSurr p55 CR France369

BLAGDEN,Robert T2Lt dow15-5-16 10 att7Norf p73 CR France8,12-5-16

BLAGG,Sidney.MID T2Lt kia 29-7-18 N&D att1/4Suss p133 MR18

BLAGROVE,Richard Coore Lt&Adjt kia 12-8-15 DCLI att6Bn p114 CR Belgium84

BLAIN,Charles Victor 2Lt kia 3-9-16 1Ches p95 CR France453

BLAIN,Mary Maude Miss ded 15-3-19 WLA CR Ches131

BLAIR,Alexander McPherson TCapt kia 3-7-16 2SLancs p125 CR France293,Macpherson

BLAIR,Alexander Neville Lt ded 13-3-17 5BlkW p231 MR65

BLAIR,Claud Leslie.MC.TLt kia 16-6-17 RE 106FC p43 CR Belgium97

BLAIR,Duncan James Nugent Capt ded 10-1-17 5Lancers RoO attRFA p21

BLAIR,Edward James.MC.Capt kia 11-4-17 RAMC p253 CR France15

BLAIR,G.L.Maj 7-8-19 36Sikhs CR Lond14

BLAIR,George Young 12Lt dow 24-7-15 DC3RFA p25 CR France263 kia

BLAIR,Herbert Samuel Penny 2Lt dow 31-10-16 3DCLI p114 CR Europe1

BLAIR,James Mcdonald T2Lt dow 9-4-18 35MGC p181 CR France116

BLAIR,John 2Lt dow 16-6-18 8 att10ScotRif p225 CR France14

BLAIR,John Lt dow 12-10-18 8DLI p239 CR Belgium38

BLAIR,Patrick Alexander.MC.Capt kia 23-4-17 9RScots p212 CR France545

BLAIR,Patrick Charles Bentley 2Lt kia 6-7-15 5RB p177 CR Belgium85

BLAIR,Patrick Edward Adam 2Lt kia 29-10-14 1BlkW p128 MR29

BLAIR,Richard Curwen Richmond.DSO.Capt kia 21-6-16 5BordR p228 CRBelgium97,Robert 21-7-16

BLAIR,Robert Hannay 2Lt kia 21-3-18 B79RFA p25 CR France568

BLAIR,Sidney Barclay 2Lt kia 16-5-15 3 att1RWar p64 CR France727,3 att2Bn

BLAIR,Thomas.MC&Bar.2Lt dow 21-11-18 6HLI p240 CR France34

BLAIR,William T2Lt kia 23-4-17 8SfthH p164 CR France536

BLAIR,William Alexander 2Lt dedacc 8-12-18 3 att2HLI p162 CR France289

BLAIR,William Kenneth Playfair Maj dow 14-5-15 96RFA p25 CR France102

BLAIR CUNYNGHAME,Ronald Ogilvy Capt dow 5-5-15 2GordH p166 CR France284

BLAIR-OLIPHANT,Philip Lawrence Kington.DSO.LtCol dow 8-4-1811/13RIrRif CRFrance145

BLAKE,A.R.2Lt 14-2-16 IARO MR65

-BLAKE,Alfred Joseph William.MID TLt kia 21-8-15 5ConnRgrs p172 MR4

BLAKE,Bernard Cecil Lt dow 9-4-18 A275RFA p207 CR France98

BLAKE,Cecil TLt ded 30-10-18 RAMC p194 p267 CR Staffs114

BLAKE,Cecil Francis John 2Lt kia 7-10-18 Mddx att2Bn p146 CR France545,Charles

BLAKE,Cecil Rodolph TCapt kia 4-4-17 10KRRC p149 MR21

BLAKE,Charles Edwin Norman.MC.LtAMaj kia 30-7-18 70RFA p25 CR France865

BLAKE,Charles Stanley TCapt kia 7-8-15 10SLancs p125 MR4

BLAKE,Christopher 2Lt kia 4-9-16 3 att1Beds p85 MR21

BLAKE,Edith S/Nurse drd 26-2-18 QAIMNS p200 MR40

BLAKE,Edward Algernon Cleader Maj kia 20-10-14 2DLI p160 MR32

BLAKE,Edward William Richmond 2Lt 31-7-17 4 att18SomLI MR29

BLAKE,Francis Seymour TCapt kia 1-7-16 15Lpool att2SWBord p71 MR21

BLAKE,Francis William.MC.T2Lt kia 31-10-18 19DLI p160 CR Belgium143

BLAKE,Geoffrey Stuart Lt kia 5-9-17 RE 203FC p43 CR France364

BLAKE,George Cyril TLt ded 5-11-17 GL 1/4WelchR attRecruitStaff p189 CR Yorks34

BLAKE,George Morley 2Lt kia 21-3-18 2/4ELancs p226 MR27

BLAKE,George Penderell TCapt kia 20-7-16 10RWelshF p97 CR France744

BLAKE,George Victor T2Lt kia 3-12-17 1KSLI p144 CR France911

BLAKE,Harold Frederick Capt kia 7-10-16 Wilts att13DLI p152 CR France385,Frederic

BLAKE,Harold Martin Joseph Lt dow 20-11-17 1RMunstF p175 CR France689

BLAKE,James Alexander Jeffrey Lt kia 18-8-16 RFA 47DAC p207 CR France1890,Jeffery

BLAKE,James Edward 2Lt kia 6-4-17 RE &45RFC p5&43 CR Belgium406

BLAKE,James Robert.MIDx2Capt kia 25-3-18 8 att14Worc p226 MR20

BLAKE,Jerrold Edward Capt kia 23-7-16 4 O&BLI p231

BLAKE,John Morgan 2Lt kia 4-10-17 1Dev p76 MR30

BLAKE,Maurice Frederic Lt kia 14-9-14 2KRRC p149 MR15

BLAKE,Norman Pilkington TCapt kia 14-7-16 8EYorks p83 CR France399

BLAKE,Reginald Joseph Albert TLt kia 13-4-18 1 att11ELancs p110 MR32

BLAKE,Reginald Howard T2Lt kia 1-6-18 2/8Lpool p71 CR France204

BLAKE,St.John Lucius O'Brien Acheson French.MC.TMaj kia 19-4-17 21Lancers attWorcYeo p23

BLAKE,Valentine Charles Joseph Capt kia 28-1-16 1IrGds SR p52 CR France1157

BLAKE,William Henry Maj ded 19-5-16 1RGA p209 CR Numb99

BLAKE,William Lovewell 2Lt dow 27-3-18 4Norf p216 CR France62

BLAKELEY,Frank Roland 2Lt kia 22-2-17 IA 53Sikhs p274 CR Iraq5

BLAKELEY,George Finney Maj ded 15-12-19 2/5RWar p269 CR Yorks588,dow

BLAKELY,John Douglas T2Lt kia 9-4-17 9GordH p166 CR France924

BLAKEMAN,Albert Victor T2Lt kia 7-10-18 SStaffs att1KSLI p122 CR France375

BLAKEMORE,John Edward.MC.TCaptAMaj dow 5-10-17 42/24RFA p25 CR France98

BLAKENEY,Edward Charles William Lt ded 20-1-19 IARO 36JacobsHorse&44Cav p274 MR67

BLAKENEY,Leslie St.Leger Lt drd 28-3-15 2LancF &GoldCoastR p92&201 MR40

BLAKESTON,Bernard Moore 2Lt kia 25-3-17 IARO 1/1GurkhaRif p274 MR38

BLAKEWAY,James Maj ded 4-12-18 RAVC DADVS p254 CR France457

BLAKEWAY,Noel Carleton 2Lt kia 27-3-16 3 att1Dors p123 CR France392

BLAKEWAY,Philip John Thomas Chap1Cl ded 16-6-15 1MddxYe0 p204&268 CR Egypt8

BLAKEY,George 2Lt kia 16-9-16 9YLI p142 MR21

BLANCHARD,Frederick John.MID Capt kia 1-6-18 1/5DCLI p227 CR France31

BLANCHARD,Frederick Wilson Capt dow 26-1-18 PoW 1/2DCLI att2/5RWar p114 CR Germany3

BLANCHARD,John Balsillie 2Lt kia 13-10-15 6NStaffs p238 MR19,Baldsillie

BLANCHARD,Neville 2Lt ded 26-7-17 3 att2Dors p123 CR Iraq5

BLANCHARD,William Hutchison Capt ded 8-10-17 RAVC att155AFA p198

BLANCHETTE,Charles Matthew Lt ded 22-3-18 RAMC p267 CR War19

BLAND,Alfred Edward TCapt kia 1-7-16 22Manch p154 CR France397

BLAND,Braithwaite T2Lt dow 31-8-16 8RLancs p58 CR France201,Capt

BLAND,Bridgman Elsey Capt ded 26-10-17 5Lond p146 CR Essex208

BLAND,Cecil Francis Ramsden.MC.Lt kia 7-7-19 3RBerks att1SlavBritLegion p138&257 MR70 &CR Europe179

BLAND,Charles Edward TCapt kia 9-9-16 11Hamps p120 MR21

BLAND,Charles Ernest William.DSO.Capt kia 23-4-15 3 att2KOSB p101 MR29,3-4-15

BLAND,J.Capt ded 28-1-18 WYorks p263 CR Yorks408

BLAND,John George 2Lt dow 9-7-16 2RIrRif p169 CR France40,9-7-16

BLAND,Malcolm Gordon 2Lt kia 23-3-18 1KRRC p254 MR20

BLAND,Percy Richard Capt kia 3-5-17 3 att1Lpool p71 MR20

BLAND,Thomas Russell 2Lt kia 20-7-17 5NStaffs p238 MR19

BLAND-HUNT,Ernest Sydney de Vere Maj kia 4-9-15 RGA 6SB p38 CR Belgium84,Sidney De

BLANDE,Arthur Frederick William Lt kia 20-9-17 8Lond p247 MR29

BLANDY,Claude Milberne TCapt ded 8-4-16 110AC RFA p25 CR France145

BLANDY,Claude Reginald Bowe 2Lt ded 19-4-18 5SLancs p269

BLANDY Francis Dawson.MC.LtCol kia 14-8-17 RAMC 24FA p253 CR Belgium15

BLANDY,Gerald Castleton 2LtACapt kia 9-10-17 4 att2RWar p64 MR30

BLANDY,Gurth Swinnerton.MC.TCapt dow 24-4-17 RAMC attRE 29Div p194 CR France40

BLANE,Hugh Seymour Capt dow 1-11-14 IA 19Lancers att5DragGds p274 CR Belgium170,31-10-14

BLANE,James Pitcairn TCapt dow 23-11-15 8KRRC p149 CR Belgium11

BLANE,Malcolm Gilbert Stewart Lt kia 25-9-15 3 att5CamH p167 MR19

BLANE,Sidney Taylor 2Lt kia 16-8-17 3 att11Manch p154 MR30

BLANFORD,Charles Edward Maj dow 11-7-15 RGA 30MountainBty p25 CR Iraq6

BLANFORD,Frank Burrell Capt ded 25-4-17 2RGLI p200 CR Dorset/CI139,Lt

BLATCHLY,Walter John Atherton T2Lt kia 12-5-15 1Leinst p174 MR29

BLATHERWICK,Robert Hugh 2Lt kia 1-7-16 10WYorks p81 CR France373

BLATHWAYT,Gerald Wynter Capt kia 14-9-14 56/44RFA p25 CR France1329

BLATHWAYT,Henry Wynter Maj dow 30-11-17 A74RFA p25 CR France1498

BLAXALL,Harold Gurney 2Lt kia 8-10-17 7Mddx p235 MR20

BLAXLAND,John Bruce Capt kia 24-1-17 4SWBord p99 CR Iraq5

BLAXLEY,Stewart Lenton 2Lt kia 23-4-17 4RWelshF p223 CR France162

BLAZEY,John William Victor 2Lt kia 26-9-15 1RBerks p138 MR19,RegNo.2492

BLEADEN,Lionel TLt kia 6/9-7-16 13RFus p66

BLEASE,Harvey TCapt kia 7-8-15 15Lpool att7LancF p71 MR4

BLEASE,Richard Morris Stanley TCapt kia 3-5-17 15WYorks p81

BLEAZARD,Fred.DCM.2Lt kia 21-3-18 RFA 169ArmyBde p25 CR France1074

BLECH,Evelyn Lewis T2Lt kia 18-8-16 73MGC p181 CR France294, BLECK,17-8-16

BLECKLY,Henry Lt ded 25-5-21 2/1ChesYeo CR Ches11

BLEEZE,Frank James T2Lt kia 29-7-18 O&BLI att1/4RSuss p129 CR France524

BLENCH,Alfred Chapman T2Lt dow 6-7-16 20Manch p154 CR France300

BLENCOWE,Charles Edward T2Lt kia 3-5-18 RSuss att1Wilts p118 MR30

BLENCOWE,Ernest Cecil Blencowe TCapt kia 16-12-16 6Dors p123 MR29,16-2-16

BLENCOWE,Lawrence Cave 2Lt kia 29-6-17 2/10Lpool p216 MR32

BLENCOWE,Mabel Edith Sister ded 10-3-17 TFNS p254 CR France134

BLENCOWE,Oswald Charles T2Lt kia 7-10-16 6 O&BLI p129 MR21

BLENKINSOP,Edward Winnington 2Lt dow 26-9-15 3 att2War p64 CR France98

BLENKINSOP,Frank T2Lt kia 5-5-17 15DLI p160 MR20,6-5-17

BLENKINSOP,William Millford TLt dow 7-11-18 12DLI p160 CR Italy7

BLEST,Malcolm Alexander Capt ded 30-12-15 8Mddx p235 CR Surrey94

BLEW,Kynnersley 2Lt kia 12-4-18 3 att7RWKent p140 MR27

BLEWCHAMP,Ernest John T2Lt kia 14-7-16 7RWSurr p55 MR21

BLEWITT,Arthur TLtCol dow 4-9-17 5LabCps Ex KRRC p189 CR France134,Col KRRC att5LabCps

BLEWITT,Baker Arthur Rawson Capt kia 8-3-16 IA 1/9GurkhaRif p274 MR38

BLEWITT,John Henry.MID Lt dow 22-4-17 IA 54Sikhs att53 p274MR38,53 att54

BLIGH,Eric Lt kia 9-5-17 3 att2ELancs p110 CR France566

BLIGH,Frederick Arthur TMaj ded 15-11-15 8/154RH&FA p25 CR Hamps85

BLIGH,Jack Frederick.MC.AMaj 1-7-17 D121RFA p25 CR Belgium1

BLIGHT,Ernest James T2Lt kia 11-3-17 27NumbF p60 CR France1182

BLIGHT,Horace Vincent.MC.TLt kia 15-6-18 RASC att4RFus p192 CR France33

BLINCH,Wilfrid Joseph Hastings 2Lt kia 16-8-16 13Lpool p71 MR21

BLISS,Arthur Joseph 2Lt kia 9-9-16 4 att7Leinst p174 MR21,ExRAMC

BLISS,Charles.CIE.Maj dow 22-12-14 IA 1/1GurkhaRif p274 CR France201

BLISS,Francis Kennard T2Lt kia 28-9-16 59RFA 459HB p25 CR France251

BLISS,James.MC&Bar.Capt kia 31-7-17 1/6SfthH p241 CR Belgium36

BLISS,Thomas 2Lt dow 23-12-16 6SfthH p241 CR France251

BLISS,Wilfrid Marryat LtCol kia 10-3-15 2ScotRif p103 CR France260

BLISSETT,Percy Cecil 2Lt kia 9-10-17 HAC p206 MR30

BLOCK,F.J.Maj 22-9-18 3Glouc Ex RWar CR Sussex183

BLOCK,Maurice William Palmer Col ded 5-3-19 RH&FA p25 CR France1788

BLOFELD,Dudley.MC.2Lt kia 8-10-16 1/22Lond p251 MR20

BLOFELD,Robert Alban 2Lt dow PoW 20-4-17 8Hamps p229 MR34

BLOFIELD,Frank D'Arcy 2Lt kia 13-5-15 2LifeGds p20 MR29,BLOFELD 12-5-15

BLOGG,Edward Basil.DSO.Maj dow 15-3-16 RE 4LondFC p209 CR France80,kia 16-3-16

BLOIS,Dudley George.DSO.LtCol dow 14-7-16 84RFA p25&258 CR France141

BLOIS-JOHNSON,Thomas Gordon.CMG.CIE.LtCol 5-11-18 IA 2/67Punjabis p274 MR67

BLOMFIELD,Arthur Eustace Lt ded 28-10-17 RFA 23DAC p207 CR Italy7,28-10-18

BLOMFIELD,Charles George Massie Maj kia 9-6-15 1RWar p64 CR Belgium85

BLONFIELD,William Henry T2Lt dow 26-10-17 RASC p192 see BONFIELD,W.H.

BLOOD,Bindon Capt kld 29-7-15 4Huss attRFC p1&21 CR Surrey162

BLOOM,Bertram T2Lt ded 30-6-18 3Lpool p71 CR Eire84

BLOOM,Henry TLt kia 14-2-17 12Yorks p89

BLOOMER,Arnold Grayson Lt dow 3-8-17 3 att2Lincs p74 CR Belgium7

BLOOMER,Guy Howard Walmesley T2Lt kia 5-9-18 2Lincs p74 CR France245

BLOOMFIELD,Arthur Herbert 2Lt kia 9-7-17 8Glouc p106 MR29

BLOOMFIELD,Gerald Arthur T2Lt kld 13-2-18 RFC p15 CR Berks37

BLOOR,Guy Hegan Lt ded 20-11-18 3RFA p207 CR Italy7

BLOOR,Ronald Terence 2Lt kia 23-1-18 5SStaffs p229 CR France115,1/6Bn

BLOOR,Vincent Uzielli 2Lt ded 25-8-14 2DLI p265 CR Staffs134

BLOOR,William Henry TLt.ACapt kia3-1-18 149RFA p25 CR Belgium15

BLOORE,Ronald Henry TLt.ACapt kia 28-4-18 14 att17Lpool p71 CR Belgium111

BLOSSE,Francis Lynch Capt ded 17-2-15 WIndReg p267

BLOTT,Thomas Watkin TLt.ACapt kia 9-4-17 24NumbF p60 CR France184

BLOUNT,Greville Hubert Robins Capt dow 23-9-14 RFA p25 CR France1839

BLOUNT,J.H.2Lt ded 6-7-18 1/2 O&BLI &RAF p129 CR Suff55

BLOWERS,Charles Paxton 2Lt dow 2-10-18 4Suff p217 CR France512,2Bn

BLOWS,Cyril Sydney George 2Lt kia 9-9-16 1/4Lond p246 MR21

BLOY,Laurence Henry Capt kia 29-6-16 5LancF p221 CR France1512

BLUE,Dougall Capt dow 11-5-15 ScotRif att2Bn p103 CR France345

BLUMER,John T2Lt dow 26-9-16 283RFA p25 CR France329

BLUMFELD,Hubert Winterbotham Lt kia 23-2-17 9Mddx attMGC p186&236 MR38

BLUMFIELD,William George 2Lt dow 21-3-18 RGA 186SB p38 CR Belgium85

BLUNDELL,William Kennedy TCapt ded 13-12-18 12Beds p254 CR Somerset25

BLUNDEN,Lewis 2Lt kia 22-7-16 5RSuss p228 CR France296

BLUNDEN,Oswald TCapt kia 4-7-16 16RB p177 CR France727

BLUNT,Charles George T2Lt kia 21-3-18 3RB p178 CR France725

BLUNT,Duncan Hamilton.DSO.MIDx2 MajTLtCol kia 3-10-17 1Dev p76 MR30

BLUNT,Ernest Lindsay LtACapt kia 2-11-18 RGA 24SB p38 CR France231

BLUNT,Francis Clifford 2Lt dow 14-10-15 1/4Leic p220 CR France98

BLUNT,Harold Ernest.MC.Capt ded 16-2-19 SussYeo p205 CR Belgium396

BLUNT,John 2Lt dow 15-10-15 5Lincs p220 CR France98

BLURTON,Cyril Evers 2Lt kia 22-10-17 1 att15N&D Z'Coy p133 MR30

BLY,Harold Alfred Edwin 2Lt ded 17-11-18 RGA p209 CR Essex274

BLYTH,Alick Frederick Lt kia 22-8-17 NCycBn att2/5Gloucp253 MR30,23-8-17

BLYTH,Benjamin Hall LtCol ded 13-5-17 RE

BLYTH,Dennis Carleton T2Lt kia 28-8-15 RE 93FC p43 CR Belgium28

BLYTH,Edward John 2Lt kia 26-3-18 RFC p15 MR20

BLYTH,Herbert Russel MajTLtCol ded 17-1-18 Ess 2GarrBn p131 MR65

BLYTH,James Charles 2Lt kia 13-4-17 5 att1KRRC p149 CR France728

BLYTH,James Reginald T2Lt kia 10-7-16 11RB p178 MR29

BLYTH,Reginald Crommelin Popham Capt kia 4-6-15 Glouc attRFus p106 MR4

BLYTH,Robert Paterson 2Lt kia 10-7-17 6CamH p167 CR Belgium58

BLYTH,Stuart Wynter Lt ded 13-11-15 5RWKent Res p269 CR Kent122

BLYTH,William TLt dow 7-11-18 46MGC Inf p181 CR France441

BLYTHE,Alan Lancelot Capt ded 27-11-18 1RFA CR Lancs196

BLYTHE,Harold T2Lt ded 10-2-17 GL &32RFC p5 CR France1489

BLYTHE,Norman Harry T2Lt kia 4-8-16 12Manch p154 MR21

BLYTHE,Percy Alfred.MID Capt kia 30-7-16 18Manch p154 CR France402

BLYTON,Arthur Allister 2Lt kia 5-9-18 A70RFA p208 CR France421

-BOADEN,William Freeman T2Lt kia 16-4-18 49MGC Inf p181 MR30

BOAG,Alfred 2Lt kld 29-4-16 7Lond attRFC p17&247 CR Mddx34,Lt

BOAG,Archibald Fullarton 2Lt kia 23-3-16 4A&SH p172 CR France114

BOAG,Herbert Edward T2Lt kia 31-7-17 MGC att B'BnTankCps p181 MR29

BOAL,James Spence 2Lt dow 29-1-17 RGA 109SB p38 CR France177

BOAL,John Kirk LtACapt kia 3-5-17 3 att1RIrF p170 MR20

BOAL,William Wainhouse T2Lt dow 10-10-18 7Nhampt p137 MR16,kia

BOARD,George William Lt kia 30-11-17 7ESurr p112 MR17,Ex RFC

BOARD,Richard Frank Lt dow 30-10-18 RE 479FC p210 CR France739,Capt kia

BOARD,William John 2Lt dow 22-9-18 130RFA att31Bde p25 CR Greece1

BOARDLEY,Harold TLt kia 26-9-17 8KSLI p144 MR30

BOARDMAN,Alfred 2Lt kia 21-9-18 RSuss att16Bn p118 MR16,Arthur

BOARDMAN,John Hopwood CaptTMaj dow 25-4-18 PoW 2 O&BLI att9RB p130 CR Germany3

BOARDMAN,Thomas Henry.DSO.TLtCol dow 5-8-17 8InniskF p104 CR Belgium7

BOARDMAN,William.DCM.2Lt kia 28-10-18 4SfthH p241 CR France1254

BOAS,Ernest George 2Lt kia 1-7-16 5 att13RIrRif p169 MR21

BOASE,Edgar Leslie Capt kia 30-7-16 1/4 att1/7BlkW p230 CR France1890

BOAST,Frederick 2Lt kld 28-12-19 23Lancs CR Ireland14

BOAST,John S.MC.Capt kia 22-3-18 2SLancs p125 CR France438

BOAST,Thomas Townshend.MID 2Lt kld 29-9-18 3Norf p73 CR France905

BOBBY,Arthur Lawrence T2Lt kia 20-11-17 att16Mddx p146 MR17,Laurence

BOBBY,Sidney Fitzgerald T2Lt kia 1-7-16 GL 18DLI att93TMB p189 MR21

BOCKETT,Harold Arthur Palmer 2Lt kia 3-5-17 2HAC p206 MR20

BOCKING,Bernard.MC.T2Lt kia 21-8-18 12Yorks att11EYorks p89 CR France193

BOCKING,John Webb 2Lt kia 24-4-18 3YLI att2/4Lond p142 MR27

BODDAM-WHETHAM,Cecil Capt kia 14-12-14 3BlkW attGordH p128 MR29

BODDAM-WHETHAM,A.C.DSO.LtCol kld 22-6-19 4A&SH attRAF p172

BODDINGTON,Cecil Herbert TCapt kia 11-4-17 HouseholdBn p20 MR20,BODINGTON

BODDINGTON,Guy Livingstone Capt kia 19-12-16 6RWar p214 MR21,Livingston

BODDINGTON,Myles.MC.TCapt kia 1-7-16 6KSLI p144 CR Belgium4

BODDINGTON,Oswald William Lt kia 13-10-15 5NStaffs p238 CR France423

BODDINGTON,Ralph Thomas 2Lt kia 2-11-17 25Lond p252 CR Palestine8, 1/10Bn

BODDINGTON,Vincent Coke Chap4Cl ded 13-3-17 RAChDept att35GenHosp p199 CR Berks125

BODDY,G.G.D.T2Lt kia 27-3-16 9RFus p66 MR29,4Bn

BODEL,Frederick Ernest.MC.Capt kia 31-7-17 8Lpool p215 MR29,Frederic

BODEN,Anthony Drummond Maj kia 24-9-14 3RB p178 MR15

BODEN,Hugh Charles Wollaston TCapt kia 11-10-15 12N&D p133 CR Belgium111

BODEN,Samuel Standidge T2Lt kia 15-10-16 14DLI att14MGC Inf p160&181 MR21,15-10-16

BODENHAM,Charles James Lt kia 9-8-18 HampsYeo p203 MR30

BODENHAM,Henry Edward Charles Hyacinth Lt kia 7-9-16 49MGC Inf p181 CR France630

BODENHAM,S.W.2Lt ded 25-10-18 RGA 117HB p38 CR Glouc9,Lt

BODEY,Alan Ralph Lt kia 28-6-16 7Lpool p215 MR20

BODGER,Robert Hendry Lt ded 15-7-18 IARO att1/32SikhPnrs p274 MR67,Capt

BODKER,John George TLt kia 20-11-17 Y&L att2/6WRid p158 CR France755,2/5Bn

BODKIN,Leo Francis.DSO.Maj ded 30-8-19 IA 113Inf p274 MR65,112Inf

BODLE,A Maj 3-3-15 RE CR Hamps179

BODMAN,Charles Walter T2Lt kia 24-8-18 15DLI p160 MR16

BODVEL-ROBERTS,Harold Owen,MC 2Lt dow 18-11-15 7Lond CR France1

BODY,Edward Upton.MC.TCaptAMaj kia 4-11-18 130/40RFA p25&258 CR France1081

BODY,Frank Lydford TCapt dow 18-6-17 8Beds p85 CR France80

BODY,Grant Trenavin Capt kia 14-9-14 1LNLancs p135 MR15

BODYCOMB,George Thomas T2Lt kld 18-2-18 RFC p15 CR Kent124

BOGLE,Albert T2Lt kia 10-8-17 12 att10RInniskF p104 MR29

BOGLE,Andrew Blyth McCulloch T2Lt kia 14-7-16 11RScots p53 CR France399

BOGLE,David Morrow 2Lt dow 1-9-18 2RInniskF p104 CR France100

BOGLE,George Stafford T2Lt dow 15-10-15 RE 68Coy p43 MR4

BOGLE,John.MC.Capt kia 20-9-17 5ScotRif p224 MR30

BOGUE,Patrick Yule T2Lt kia 23-7-17 9ESurr p112 CR Belgium29,24-7-17

BOGUE,Robert Alexander,MC.Lt dow 26-9-17 A Coy 16HLI CR Scot85

BOILEAU,Edmund Kenyvett LtACapt kia 18-10-17 RE p43 CR EAfrica11 &CR Tanzania1

BOILEAU,Edward Bulmer Whicher Lt kia 3-10-18 1Dors p123 CR France699

BOILEAU,Frank Ridley Farrer Col dow 26-8-14 RE Cmd &Staff 3Div p43 CR France34 &1202,28-8-14

BOIS,Dudley Gillespy Lt ded 4-10-15 RGA 6HB p38 MR4

BOLAND,Michael Thomas T2Lt kia 26-2-18 2RMunstF p175 CR France364

BOLAY,A.R.2Lt kld 27-5-18 GL &65RAF p189 CR France71

BOLES,Hastings Fortescue 2Lt dow 24-5-15 17Lancers &RFC p1&23 CR France285,Lt

BOLES,Noel Henry Lt kia 11-1-16 2Dors attRNAS p123 CR Gallipoli1

BOLES,Robert Stephen T2Lt dow 6-5-18 1RDubF p176 CR France180,Lt kia

BOLGER,Katie SNurse ded 5-3-16 QAIMNS CR Wilts167

BOLITHO,Geoffrey Richard 2Lt ded 25-10-16 4RFC p2 CR France514 Ex DevR

BOLITHO,Victor Ayling T2Lt dow 9-4-17 HouseholdBn p20 CR France730

BOLITHO,William Edward Thomas.DSO.LtCol ded 21-2-19 1DevYeo CR Cornwall172

BOLITHO,William Torquill Macleod Lt kia 24-5-15 19Huss p23 MR29

BOLLAND,Frederick William Henry 2Lt kia 7-6-17 7RFus p66 MR29

BOLLAND,Theodore Julian Maj kia 9-5-15 9Lpool p216 MR22

BOLLOM,Johnson 2Lt kia 24-9-16 12DLI p160 CR France703

BOLLOND,John Wulstan Charles T2Lt kia 9-4-17 10Norf p73 CR France1182,BOLLAND

BOLSTER,C.Hawkes Capt 8-12-14 9KRRC CR Eire143

BOLSTER,Francis Julian LtACapt dow 4-4-17 RGA 31SB p38 CR France96

BOLSTER,George Emil Maj dow 23-10-14 RFA p25 CR Belgium57

BOLSTER,Richard.MC.CaptAMaj kia 4-6-17 124/28RFA p25 CR France68,5-6-17

BOLT,Bertram Leslie T2Lt dow 13-5-16 7KSLI p144 CR France285

BOLTER,Charles Albert T2Lt kia 12-4-18 29MGC Inf p181 CR France298

BOLTON,Cecil Rawley TCapt kia 22-2-17 22Lpool p71 CR France420,19Bn

BOLTON,Edward Trevor.MID TLt kia 10-4-18 11Suff p78 CR France685

BOLTON,Geoffrey Charles 2Lt kia 1-8-16 17N&D p133

BOLTON,Gilbert Benson T2Lt kia 18-11-16 8NStaffs p156 CR France215

BOLTON,Gordon Wallace Capt kia 24-4-18 1EYorks p83 MR30

BOLTON,H.S.Lt 22-3-21 RFA CR Scot533

BOLTON,Harry Hargreaves Capt dow 23-5-15 5ELancs p226 MR4,24-5-15

BOLTON,Henry Albert TCapt kia 1-7-16 23NumbF p60 MR21

BOLTON,Herbert Frederick TLt dow 3-5-17 10SLancs att103MGC p125&181 CR France95

BOLTON,John Lt dow 4-6-15 5ELancs p226,2Lt&Lt 2entries CR Gallipoli6

BOLTON,John Ritso Nelson.MID Lt dow 27-9-15 104/22RFA p25 CR France109,25-9-15

BOLTON,Maurice Baldwin.MC.Capt kia 21-3-18 5ELancs p226 CR France716,dow PoW 26-3-18

BOLTON,Percy James T2Lt dow 5-11-18 RWKent att7Bn p140 CR France341

BOLTON,Reginald Lightbown Capt drd 3-8-18 7Manch p237

BOLTON,Robert Frederick T2Lt dow 10-6-17 11NumbF p60 CR Belgium11

BOLTON,Stuart Lt kia 17-3-18 4RLancs p213

BOLTON,William Curtis.MC.TLt kia 1-7-16 8Y&L p158 MR21

BOLUS,Dorothy Kathleen Mary Miss drd 4-6-18 VAD p200 CR Devon2,Dorothea

BOMBER,Jeffrey Allan TLt kia 14-4-18 3Worc p108 MR32

BONATHAN,Frank Stanley.MC.2Lt kia 28-4-17 17Mddx p146 MR20

BONCKER,Barry Robert 2Lt kia 1-7-16 1EYorks p83 MR21

BOND,Alfred Dalton 2Lt ded 22-5-16 5Y&L p238 CR Yorks574,Lt

BOND,Bernard TLt dow 2-8-16 19 att11N&D p133 CR France44

BOND,Cecil William Capt kia 2-8-17 RAMC att97FA p194 MR29

BOND,Charles Edward TMaj kia 10-7-16 13WelshR p126 MR21,9-7-16

BOND,Charles Gordon Capt kia 25-11-15 2Wilts p152 CR France279

BOND,Charles Nesbit Lt dow 30-6-16 3SomLI att1/4Lincs p79 CR Frane281,Nesbitt kia

BOND,Charles Reginald 2Lt kia 26-9-17 2Suff p78 MR30

BOND,E.M.Sister 3-11-18 QAIMNS CR Lincs156

BOND,Edmund Lt kia 1-10-18 5WRid att32MGC p186&227 CR France237

BOND,Ernest Frederick T2Lt kia 26-9-18 RBerks att5Bn p138 CR France369

BOND,Frank Bertram T2Lt kia 24-10-18 31/35RFA p25 CR Italy7

BOND,Frederick Hamilton Bligh 2Lt dow 13-5-15 122RFA p25 CR Belgium101

BOND,Gustave Samuel 2Lt kia 9-4-18 B276RFA p25 CR France260

BOND,H.H.DSO.BrCol 10-11-19 RFA CR Eire71

BOND,Hubert Samuel Emery Lt kld 17-6-17 7WelshR attRFC p17&230 CR Wales17,2Lt

BOND,Reginald Edwin Maj kia 3-3-15 IA 4Rajputs p274 MR61

BOND,Robert Harold Lt kia 14-9-14 2KRRC p149 CR France1329,dow

BOND,Thomas Morgan T2Lt kia 3-5-15 11RIrRif p169 MR32

BOND,William Arthur.MC&Bar.TLtTCapt kia 22-7-17 YLI &40RFC p5&142 MR20

BOND,William Henry Hugh T2Lt kia 22-6-17 26RFus p66 CR Belgium154

BONE,Albert Edward Capt dow 3-11-18 B242RFA p25 CR France40,ded

BONE,Charles John T2Lt kia 9-8-18 14TankCps p188 CR France649,dow

BONE,George Drummond 2Lt kia 9-5-15 1/1BlkW p128 MR22

BONE,Harry Whittenburg 2Lt kia 25-9-15 1SStaffs p122 MR19,Whittenbury

BONE,John Craigie 2Lt kia 28-4-17 8RScots p212 CR France581

BONE,John Hugh 2Lt kia 22-7-16 6ESurr att1/5N&D p226 CR France504

BONE,Quintin TCapt kia 19-9-18 RLancs p58 CR Greece6

BONE,Ronald Walter 2Lt kia 12-10-17 5EKent p213 MR30

BONE,Thomas William TLtACapt ded 6-8-18 SomLI 1GarBn p79 MR43 &CR Pakistan50A

BONE,Victor Arnold TCapt kia 18-9-18 11RWelshF p97 CR Greece5

BONES,A.M.TLt kia 1916 KAR p202

BONEY,A.H.Lt 10-2-19 KRRC CR Lond14

BONFIELD,William Henry 2Lt kia 26-10-17 RASC CR Belgium172 seeBLONFIELD,W.H.

BONHAM,Denis Pierpont 2Lt dow 16-11-16 1HAC p206 CR France40

BONHAM,William Daniel T2Lt kia 14-10-17 7Norf p73 MR20

BONHAM-CARTER,Arthur Thomas Capt kia 1-7-16 3 att1Hamps p120 CR France1890

BONHAM-CARTER,Guy Capt dow 15-5-15 19Huss attOxfYeo p23 CR Belgium4

BONHAM-CARTER,Norman T2Lt kia 3-5-17 HouseholdBn p20 CR France546

BONNAR,James Crawford Lt kld 22-5-15 9A&SH p244 CR Scot82

BONNER,Augustine T2Lt kia 30-4-17 GL &13RFC p5 CR France1188

BONNER,Singleton.DSO.Maj dow 1-5-17 1SStaffs att10RFus p122 CR France40,LtCol

BONNER,William 2Lt kld 19-6-18 RLancs attRAF p58 CR France84

BONNEY,James Patterson 2Lt kia 6-10-17 RGA 351SB p38 CR Belgium20

BONNEY,Sydney Richard T2Lt kia 26-9-16 12 att10Ess p131 MR21

BONNIN,Ronald Homfray(Tom).MID Lt kia 24-8-18 1/2KOSB att47Inf p101 CR France210

BONNYMAN,Edward William.DSO.MC.TCapt dow 11-8-18 10A&SH p173 CR France29,BONNEYMAN

BONSER,Geoffrey Alwyn Gershom Capt kia 29-9-18 RAMC att12Norf p253 CR Belgium451

BONSER,Winfield Joice TCapt kia 25-9-15 12RB p178 MR32

BONSEY,Edwin Kenneth 2Lt dow 2-7-18 RGA 99SB p38 CR France31

BONSEY,Francis Henry William 2Lt ded 20-12-18 IARO p274 MR65

BONAHOR,John 2Lt dow PoW 26-7-18 2/6SStaffs p229 CR Germany4

BONSOR,Malcom Cosmo Capt kia 10-3-18 NorfYeo p204 CR Palestine3,Malcolm

BONVALOT,Edward St.Laurent 2Lt dow 9-10-15 RoO att2CldGds att2Bn p51 CR France80

BONYUN,Frank Vernon T2Lt kia 2-1-18 32RFC p15 CR Belgium18

BOOCOCK,Herbert Jennings 2Lt kia 6-11-17 7Worc att17Suff p226 CR Palestine1

BOOCOCK,William Narey 2Lt ded 3-3-19 RWar p263 CR War101

BOOKER,Stanley Charles.MC.Lt kia 10-10-16 2/7Worc p225 CR France631

BOOKLESS,James Donald 2Lt dow 24-5-15 4 CamH p243 CR France102

BOOMER,Walter Charter.MC.TCapt dow 1-10-18 12RIrRif p169 CR Belgium157

BOON,Arthur 2Lt kld 29-3-17 7Manch attRFC p17&237 CR War50

BOONE,Charles Frederick de Bohun Capt dow 23-9-14 2Ess p131 CR France462

BOONE,Henry Griffith.DSO.Maj dow 5-9-17 94RFA p25 CR Belgium18,6-9-17

BOONE,William Ernest 2Lt kia 20-4-15 YLI p142 MR29

BOONHAM,W.H.2Lt dow 10-8-20 3LancF CR Lancs102

BOOR,Alaric Pinder TLt dow 31-10-17 GL 7 O&BLI att13RFC p5 CR Palestine1

BOORNE,George Howard T2Lt kld 28-3-17 37RFC p5 CR Lancs103

BOOSEY,Frederick Cecil Lt kia 22-11-15 7Norf p73 MR38

BOOSEY,Noel Charles Lt dow 22-7-15 22Lond p251 CR France98,Capt

BOOSEY,Rupert George 2Lt kia 22-5-15 4DragGds p21 CR Belgium57,24-5-15

BOOTE,Charles Edward.TD.LtCol kia 1-7-16 5NStaffs p237 CR France576,Edmund

BOOTE,Charles William TCapt kia 4/5-4-16 8Ches p95 MR38

BOOTH,Ainslie TLt dow 30-4-16 RAMC att7KOSB p194 CR France423,kia

BOOTH,Arthur Wilfred T2Lt kia 22-3-18 19Lpool p71 MR27

BOOTH,Baron Brooke 2lt kia 15-9-16 7NumbF p214 MR21

BOOTH,Cecil Richard T2Lt dow 21-3-16 1GordH p166 CR France40

BOOTH,Cyril Talbot 2Lt kia 10-6-17 17Lond p250 MR29

BOOTH,Edward Arthur Lt mbk 23-9-19 GL NR p256 MR70 &CR Europe180

BOOTH,Francis Hardinge Follett ACapt kia 26-9-17 6 att1Worc p108 MR30,6 att2Bn

BOOTH,Fred T2Lt dow 24-4-18 56MGC p181 CR France95

BOOTH,Frederick Arthur.DCM.T2Lt kia 11-10-18 WYorks att1/7WRid p81 CR France612

BOOTH,Frederick Atkins T2Lt kia 27-9-15 2EKent p57 MR19

BOOTH,Harold Stanley T2Lt kia 1-7-16 11 att8Y&L p158 MR21

BOOTH,Herbert T2Lt dow 3-5-17 12WYorks p81 CR France1182

BOOTH,James,MC TLt kia 6-11-18 56MGC Inf p181 CR Belgium195

BOOTH,John 2Lt kia 7-10-16 6RFus p66 MR21,att8Bn

BOOTH,John Charles Lt ded 30-9-16 att281LondRFA p207 CR France145

BOOTH,John George 2Lt kia 22-11-17 2/6WYorks p218 MR17

BOOTH,John Lyon.MC.TLtACapt kia 18-4-18 2SfthH p164 CR France98

BOOTH,John Thomas T2Lt dow 19-11-17 GL &2AircraftSupplyDepot RFC p5 CR France40

BOOTH,Joseph William 2Lt dow 8-10-18 B93RFA p25 CR France256

BOOTH,Lawrence Elliot.MC&Bar.CaptAMaj kia 13-4-18 38RFA p25 CR Belgium89,Lawrence

BOOTH,Major William T2Lt kia 1-7-16 15WYorks p81 CR France74,Lt

BOOTH,Patrick Dick.DSO.MC.TCapt dow 2-12-17 26RFA DivTM Officer p25 MR17

BOOTH,Percival Edward Owen 2Lt kia 1-7-16 14Mddx &93MGC p181 CR France156

BOOTH,Philip Eustace 2Lt dow 4-12-17 11Mddx p146 CR France145

BOOTH,Philip John Lt ded 2-3-20 2RScotF p263 CR Asia51

BOOTH,Robert Hutchinson Capt ded 1-1-16 RASC 42ELancsFA p253 CR Europe1

BOOTH,William T2Lt dow 28-12-17 1RB &17RFC p5&178,28-2-17 &78RFC CR Belgium18,att7RFC

BOOTH,William Albert T2Lt kia 23-11-17 GL &8RFC p5 CR France403

BOOTH,William Leslie Capt dow 28-5-15 6Lond p246 CR France102

BOOTH,William Stanley 2Lt kia 8-7-16 4WRid p227 CR France252

BOOTHBY,Charles Geoffrey T2Lt kia 28-4-16 RE 177TC p43 CR Belgium114

BOOTHBY Ernest Brooke T2Lt kia 10-7-16 13RB p178 MR29

BOOTHBY,John Henry Lt kia 23-7-16 U'RHA p25 CR France188

BOOTHROYD,Edwin 2Lt dow 21-3-18 PoW 4 att26N&D p133 CR Germany1,17-4-18

BOOTY,William George Stanbury T2Lt kia 30-10-16 GL &1KARif p201 CR EAfrica40

BOQUC,Robert Alexander.MC.TLt dow 26-9-17 16HLI p162

BORAIN,Harold Goldsmith 2Lt dow 5-11-17 22RH&FA p25 CR France40,27/32

BOREHAM,Harry Pendry T2Lt kia 16-4-18 18Mddx p146 MR32,Lt

BORLAND,George McPhearson 2Lt kia 14-4-18 3 att9NumbF p60 MR32,McPherson

BORLAND,Sydney Douglas 2Lt ded 6-11-18 IARO attS&TCps p274 MR43,Lt

BORMAN,George Wilson TLt dow 2-1-16 12N&D p133

BOROUGH,Alaric Charles Henry Lt kia 1-12-17 1WelshGds p53 CR France415

BOROUGH,George Herbert TCapt ded 7-11-16 RASC 578HT AuxCo att2Ind C Div p192 CR France40,8-11-16

BORRELL,Lancelot T2Lt dow 10-7-16 12NumbF p60 CR Numb19

BORRER,John Maximilian 2Lt ded 9-9-17 4RSuss p228 CR Egypt1,Lt

BORRETT,Alfred Frank Cyril LtACapt kia 24-11-17 11RGLI p200 MR17

BORRETT,Arthur Henry 2Lt kia 17-2-17 IA 2/8 att1/8GurkhaRif p274 CR Iraq5

BORRETT,M.A.Lt 24-6-21 IA 16Cav MR67

BORROUGH,Horace William ACapt dow 18-8-16 3 att1Dors p123 CR France114

BORROW,Cyril Ernest Lt ded PoW 24-3-19 Nhampt p265 CR Leic97

BORROW,Frederick Guy Lomer Lt dow 22-8-17 1/4Nhampt p234 CR Egypt1

BORST,Charles Louis 2Lt kia 24-11-17 4 att6RWSurr p212 MR17

BORTHISTLE,William John 2Lt kia 29-1-18 RMunstF &RFC p15&175 CR France1061

BORTHWICK,Arthur Pollock Sym T2Lt dow 15-4-18 58MGC p181 CR Frqnce145,Pollok

BORTHWICK,Donald Walker 2Lt kia 28-12-16 4RWSurr attMGC Inf p186&212 MR37

BORTHWICK,George Williamson T2Lt kia 28-6-16 6CamH p167 MR19

BORTON,Cyprian Edward Maj kia 2-8-17 IA 129Baluchis att&MalayStGdes p274 CR Asia62

BOSANQUET,Armytage Percy.MC.Capt kia 25-1-17 3DCLI att5Wilts p114 CR Iraq5

BOSANQUET,Graham Bromhead.MC.Maj kia 1-7-16 1Glouc p106 CR France267

BOSANQUET,Lionel Arthur TLtCol kia 22-8-15 9N&D p133 MR4

BOSANQUET,Sidney Courthorpe 2Lt dow 17-12-14 SR att1Mddx p146 CR France1140,Courthope kia

BOSCAWEN,Vere Douglas.Hon.2Lt kia 29-10-14 1CldGds p51 MR29

BOSCOWEN,George Edward.Hon.DSO.Maj dow 7-6-18 RFA 116SB p25 CR France1753

BOSHELL,Frederick Stephen T2Lt kia 23-7-18 5RBerks p138 CR France1014,1Bn

BOSHELL,Hugh Thomas Barron Capt kia 22-3-18 4 att10/11HLI p162 MR20

BOSHER,Alfred Henry Bruce 2Lt kia 16-8-17 45RFA p25 CR Belgium140

BOSTOCK,Alexander Gordon 2Lt ded 12-1-19 RGA p209 CR Suff83,Lt

BOSTOCK,Alfred Sidney 2Lt mbk 27-5-18 8DLI p257 MR18,D.S.

BOSTOCK,Archibald Thomas TCapt dow 30-9-15 14NumbF p60 CR France40

BOSTOCK,Clifford 2LtTLt kia 20-9-17 10RWar p64 MR30

BOSTOCK,Edward Lyon 2Lt dow 5-4-17 4RSuss p228 CR France164

BOSTOCK,Eric Norman.MC.2Lt mbk 27-5-18 4Nhampt p257 MR18,2Bn

BOSTOCK,Guy Edwin TCapt kia 30-1-16 8RMunstF p175 CR France222

BOSTOCK,Hugh William 2Lt kia 12-6-15 6SStaffs p229 CR Belgium43

BOSTOCK,Joseph 2Lt kia 21-3-18 C'Coy10Ches p95 CR France1484,24-3-18

BOSTOCK,Neville Stanley 2Lt kia 22-4-17 B162RFA p25 CR France1182

BOSTOCK,Robert Ashton TCapt ded 17-8-17 RAMC p267

BOSTOCK-SMITH,Claude Lt kia 5-10-18 RE p210 CR Belgium44,attRFA

BOSTON,Lawrence TLt accded 6-5-16 9WYorks p81 CR Hamps1

BOSTON,Thomas TLt ded 25-12-18 10MGC Inf p181 CR Egypt9

BOSWALL,James Donaldson Capt kia 13-6-15 10SfthH att1Ess p164 MR4,6-6-15

BOSWELL,Claude Oliver Lt kia 9-10-17 5ELancs p226 MR30

BOSWELL,Denis St.George Knox.MIDx2 CaptTMaj ded 28-9-18 DCLI att82MGC p114&181 CR Greece2

BOSWELL,James Baxendale Maj&QM ded 23-3-16 RAMC 2/2FA p253 CR Yorks362

BOSWELL,Paul Victor 2Lt ded 29-6-19 D175RFA p261 CR Staffs52

BOSWELL,Percy George T2Lt kia 1-7-16 8YLI p142 MR21

BOSWELL,William Gerald Knox Capt dow 28-7-16 5 att2RB p178 CRFrance51

BOSWORTH,Arthur Wright 2Lt kia 26-9-15 8Lincs p74 MR19

BOSWORTH,Philip Charles Worthington Lt kia 26-9-15 8Lincs p74 MR19

BOSWORTHICK,William Howard 2Lt kia 7-11-18 1/5Dev p217 CR France924

BOTHAM,Arthur Frederick.MID 2Lt dow 18-6-17 D106RH&FA p25 CR Belgium11

BOTHAMLEY,Richard Arnold T2Lt kia 9-4-18 40MGC Inf p181 MR32 &CR France1896 ExWKentYeo

BOTHAMLEY,William Broughton 2Lt kia 25-9-16 4/10Mddx p236 CR France397

BOTHWELL,Alec.MC.TLtACapt kia 26-4-17 1GordH p166 CR France531,Alexander

BOTT,Charles Stuart 2Lt kia 17-4-17 Lincs p74 CR France1188,Lt

BOTT,Francis George Lt dow 20-8-20 IA 35ScindeHorse p274 CR Iraq6

BOTT,George 2Lt kia 9-2-17 6 att1RB p178 CR France115,3Bn

BOTT,George Gerald Randell.MC.Lt kia 13-4-18 3SLancs att8BordR p125&258 CR Belgium168

BOTT,John Arden TCapt ded 5-8-17 17RFus p263 CR Wales535

BOTT,John George 2Lt 18-9-18 1EYorks CR France666 See BUTT

BOTT,William Ernest TCapt kia 18-9-18 9RFus p66 CR France369

BOTTING,William Rolph 2Lt kia 25-9-17 3 att11RSuss p118 MR30

BOTTOMLEY,Edwin Rhodes 2Lt kia 2-6-17 RFA WRidDAC attRFC p17&208 CR France839,Lt

BOTTOMLEY,Eric William Capt kia 15-6-17 2/4Lond p246 MR20

BOTTOMLEY Frederick T2Lt drd 4-5-17 3RWelshF p97 CR Italy14

BOTTOMLEY,Frederick T2Lt kia 2-9-18 YLI att5Bn p142 CR France617

BOTTOMLEY,Harry Roderick LtCol dow 18-5-15 2RWSurr p55 CR France80

BOTTOMLEY,John Cecil 2Lt kia 3-9-16 8WYorks p219 MR21

BOTTOMLEY,Thomas Reginald Lt kia 23-9-14 1EYorks p83 MR15

BOTWOOD,Edward Keightley Rev 28-7-16 RAChDept CR Devon11

BOUCH,John Lt ded 23-11-18 1/4ELancs att130RFA p207 CR Surrey1

BOUCHER,Alan Estcourt TCapt dow 25-7-16 9Leic p87 CR France145

BOUCHER,Albert Adolph T2Lt dow 16-10-16 7KSLI att8TMB p144 CR France203,Adolphe

BOUCHER,Alec Edward.MC.TLt kia 18-11-16 11RWar p64 CR France339

BOUCHER,Arthur Guy 2Lt kia10-7-17 6 att2KRRC p149 MR31

BOUCHER,Basil Edward Cresswell.MID Lt ded 10-5-19 1/2RWFus p263 CR Staffs91,Bazil

BOUCHER,Charles Bailey Lt kia 9-8-15 Y&L p158 MR29

BOUCHER,Henry Mason.MC.LtTCapt kia 23-4-18 3 att1SomLI p79 CR France98

BOUCHER,William Moore Lt kia 20-11-17 6RWKent p140 CR France379

BOUCHIER,Charles Arthur T2Lt kia 4-11-18 1/2 att9WRid p115 CR France206,Claude

BOUCK-STANDEN,Percy Edward Capt ded 31-10-18 3Hamps MinOfMuns p264 CR Glouc9

BOUGHEY,Anchital Edward Fletcher TLt drd 10-10-18 8RB p178 CR Ireland14,Anchitel

BOUGHEY,Stanley Henry Parry.VC.2Lt dow 4-12-17 1/4RScotF p222 CR Palestine8

BOUIE,Jean Auguste Andre T2Lt kld 24-3-17 GL &RFC p5 CR EAfrica66,BOUIC

BOULLY,Frederick Courtnay 2Lt kia 10-7-17 attRFA p208 MR31

BOULNOIS,Edmund TCapt kia 23-10-16 21WYorks p81 MR21

BOULT,Reginald Herbert Swinton 2Lt kia 8-8-16 6Lpool p215 MR21

BOULTBEE,Arthur Elsdale Lt kia 17-3-17 Nhants &25RFC p5&137 MR20 &CR France1896

BOULTER,George William Capt DC ded 4-7-18 IA MilWorksServ p274

BOULTER,Jack Edward Hewitt.MC.2Lt dow 15-10-18 2RDubF p176 CR France528

BOULTER,Sidney Frederick 2Lt dow 18-2-17 25Lond p252 CR France177

BOULTIMG,Stanley Ernest 2Lt kld 14-4-17 4Suff attMGC p217 CR France1366,118TMB

BOULTON,Alec Gordon T2Lt ded 19-2-16 SL Intpr to 129Baluchis &APM HQ 3Army p201 CR France167

BOULTON,Arthur Vane 2Lt dow 25-2-17 1&2 att8Glouc p106 CR France40

BOULTON,Charles Valentine T2Lt kia 9-11-17 RE 314RdConstrCo p43 CR Belgium34

BOULTON,Christian Harold Ernest TLt kia 12-10-17 5CamH Staff p167 MR30

BOULTON,Clifford John.MC.TCapt kia 30-8-18 13WelshR p126 CR France217

BOULTON,Frederick Charles William T2Lt kia 30-7-17 8NStaffs p156 CR Belgium60,Lt

BOULTON,Harold Webster T2Lt kia 26-9-15 15DLI p160 MR19

BOULTON,James Babington 2Lt kia 17-2-17 3 att6Nhampt p137 CR France314

BOULTON,Wallace Dawson T2Lt kia 20-4-16 11 att7Glouc p106 MR38

BOUNDY,Frank Everard.MC.TLt dow 30-7-16 17Lpool p71&258 CR France294,kia

BOURCHIER,Arthur George 2Lt kia 9-5-15 2Berks p138 MR32

BOURDILLON,James Imbert Fulton Lt kia 15-7-16 RE 222FC p43 CR France432

BOURDILLON,Paul Aime 2Lt ded 20-3-19 RE

BOURDILLON,Tom Louis.MC.TMaj kia 24-8-17 KRRC att8Bn p149 CR Belgium125

BOURKE,Albert William 2Lt kia 9-5-15 3RIrF att2RIrRif p171 CR France566

BOURKE,Bertram Walter Capt kia 9-5-15 5 att2RDubF p176 MR29

BOURKE,Eustace George Walter Capt kia 16-6-15 KRRC att9Bn p149 CR Belgium165

BOURKE,James Gay Shute T2Lt kia 15-4-18 Lpool att1RWar p71 MR32

BOURKE,Patrick Miller 2Lt kia 25-7-16 28RFA 65HB p25 CR France397

BOURN,John 2LtTLt kia 31-7-17 8NStaffs p156 MR29,1Bn

BOURNE,Austin Spencer 2Lt dow 23-4-17 8SStaffs p122 MR20

BOURNE,Cecil Alfred.MC.CaptAMaj ded 11-12-18 RFA 411/126ArmyBde p25 CR France1142

BOURNE,Cyprian T2Lt dow 11-4-17 6RWSurr p55 CR France113

BOURNE,Gerald Hugh Temple T2Lt kia 18-3-17 KRRC &4RFC p5&149 CR France614

BOURNE,James Matthew 2Lt 17-6-18 2MadrasSMRRifs MR66

BOURNE,John Callander 2Lt kia 18-7-15 9Worc p108 MR4,Callender

BOURNE,Leonard Cecil.MC.T2Lt dow 14-8-17 2RFus p66 CR Belgium16

BOURNE,Ralph 2Lt kia 10-9-17 158RFA p25 CR Belgium24

BOURNE,Rowland Hurst 2Lt kia 24-10-18 RASC att7Suss p192 CR France1142

BOURNE,Stanley Mackenzie TLt kia 4/5-4-16 8RFus att8RWFus p66 MR38,4SWBord

BOURNER,Rowland Moody Nicholson T2Lt dow 28-3-18 3MGC p181 CR France64,Rowley Lt

BOURNS,Charles Lt kia 25-5-15 6 att4RB p178 MR29

BOUSFIELD,A.S.TLt ded 28-6-18 RASC p192 CR Wilts3

BOUSFIELD,Edmund Emerson LtCol dow 25-9-15 IA 123Rif att1/1GurkhaRif p274 CR France631

BOUSFIELD,Mary Cawston.ARRC.MID Miss ded 24-2-19 VAD 8GH p200 CR France146

BOUSKILL,Edward T2Lt kia 4-10-17 21Manch p154 CR Belgium308,Lt

BOUSTEAD,Harry Atheling Russell Lt dow 5-4-17 8Mddx attRFC p17&236 CR France832

BOUSTEAD,Lawrence Clive.MID Lt kia 28-6-15 1RDubF W'Coy p176 CR Gallipoli6,29-6-15

BOVE-BLANDY,C.R.2Lt 18-4-16 5SLancs CR Lancs380

BOVE-BLANDY,S.R.Sister 13-1-19 QAIMNS CR Lancs380

BOVET,William MajTLtCol dow 5-7-18 RE CRE 12Div p43 CR France84

BOVEY,William Bernard 2Lt dow 15-11-16 19Lond p250 CR Belgium11

BOVILL,Charles Harry Lt dow 24-3-18 1CldGds p51 CR France113

BOVILL,Edward Henry 2Lt kia 1-7-16 1/16Lond p250 MR21

BOVILL,John Eric 2Lt kia 23-1-16 6DragGds p21 CR France423

BOW,George Clark 2Lt kia 25-3-17 7A&SH attMGC Inf p186&243 MR38

BOW,Herbert Christie 2Lt kia 23-3-18 7 att9ScotRif p224 MR27

BOWATER,George William 2Lt ded 20-2-17 RGA p38 CR War5

BOWDEN,Alfred John Hamilton.DSO.LtCol kia 2-3-17 2Mon p244

BOWDEN,Edward Ratcliffe Lt dow 29-4-15 6NumbF p213 CR France51,28-4-15

BOWDEN,Eric Gordon.MC.MID TMaj kia 22-7-18 11RWSurr p55 CR France924,LtCol

BOWDEN,Horace George Cecil T2Lt kia 11-3-17 45RFC 9Wing p5 CR Belgium11

BOWDEN,James T2Lt kia 30-3-18 66MGC Inf p181 MR27

BOWDEN,Norman 2Lt kia 25-4-18 8N&D attRAF p233&258 CR France1170

BOWDEN,Percival John 2Lt kia 15-4-18 1RWar p64 MR32

BOWDEN,Reginald Charles T2Lt dow 3-3-16 8RLancs p58 CR Belgium11

BOWDEN,Richard Thomas T2Lt kia 16-8-17 4Worc p108 MR30

BOWDEN,Walter Horace T2Lt kia 12-4-18 16Mddx p146 MR32,15-4-18

BOWDEN-SMITH,Ernest Baldwin Lt 26-6-16 RIM CR Iraq6

BOWDEN-SMITH,Walter Ardrian Carnagie Capt dow 28-8-14 RFus p66 CR Belgium244,Adrian Carnegie

BOWE,Eric Arthur T2Lt kia 27-5-18 DLI p160 MR18

BOWE,Stanley Gordon TLt dow 15-5-18 18 att2/5LancF p92 CR France10

BOWELL,Archibald Gordon Edward T2Lt kia 15-7-16 8Leic p87 MR21,14-7-16 Ex9Bn

BOWELL,Ernest Philip 2Lt kia 20-11-17 7 att2/5LancF p221 MR21

BOWELS,James Arthur Lt kia 26-8-14 RH&FA p25 see BOWLES,J.A.

BOWEN,Alan T2Lt kia 7-8-15 8Manch p237 MR4

BOWEN,Alfred John Hamilton.DSO&Bar.MID LtCol kia 2-3-17 22Mon CR France786

BOWEN,Cuthbert Edward Latimer Lt 1-12-14 EAfrPolice CR EAfrica44

BOWEN,Eynon George Arthur Lt ded PoW 8-9-16 RGA &RFC p2&38 MR20

BOWEN,Francis Moull Storer TLt kia 1-7-16 9RWKent att1InniskF p140 CR France339

BOWEN,Geoffrey Grenside.MC.LtTCapt kia 2-9-18 2LancF p92 CR France155

BOWEN,George Eustace Summers.MC.Capt dow 26-7-17 A83RFA p25 CR Belgium11

BOWEN,Henry Lt&QM kia 21-5-17 1/8ScotRif p225 CR Palestine8

BOWEN,Ivor Lt ded 25-2-17 RE 207FC p43 CR France95

BOWEN,Joseph Jones,MC Lt kia 9-4-18 18WelshR p126 CR France348,9-6-18

BOWEN,Leslie Harold Lt kia 22-12-15 3Lincs p74 CR France924,1Bn

BOWEN,Martin.MC.Capt dow 9-10-17 O&BLI 1/1BucksBn p231 CR France64

BOWEN,Roger Frederick Lt dow PoW 1-9-18 9RWar p64 MR61

BOWEN,Rowland George Breece Lt kia 9-5-15 1Lond p245 CR France348,11Bn

BOWEN,Thomas Henry T2Lt kia 2-8-16 6Leinst att11InniskF p174 CR Belgium339

BOWEN,William 2Lt dow 30-8-18 3 att15WelshR p126 CR France805

BOWEN,William Lloyd.MC.Lt dow 1-9-18 3 att6Mon p244 CR France924

BOWEN-COLTHURST,Robert MacGregor Capt kia 15-3-15 1Leinst p174 MR29

BOWER,A.E.Lt ded 4-7-19 RASC p267

BOWER,Alfred Percy T2Lt kia 1-11-18 1SomLI p79 CR France1079

BOWER,Charles Francis TLtACapt kia 13-9-17 16N&D p133 CR Belgium21

BOWER,Donald Robert T2Lt kia 20-9-18 CamH Res att1SfthH p167 CR Palestine9

BOWER,Edwin Harland Lt kia 21-3-18 2Y&L p158 MR20

BOWER,Frank.MID 2Lt dow 31-3-17 NumbF &60RFC p5&60 CR France164

BOWER,Frederic William TCapt kia 8-3-18 20RFus p66 CR Belgium112

BOWER,Gerard Rimington 2Lt kia 15-7-16 1RWSurr p55 MR21

BOWER,Henry Raymond Syndercombe Lt kld 18/19-12-14 5SStaffs p122 MR32,1Bn

BOWER,Maurice Syndercombe Lt ded 13-1-19 RASC MT p192&257 CR Europe20

BOWER,Thomas Geoffrey T2Lt kia 3-5-17 RHGds HouseholdBn p20 CR France1194

BOWER,William Carroll 2Lt ded 9-8-16 1RLancs p58 CR Belgium11

BOWER,William Charles Ernest TLt kia 19-10-16 RAMC att1NewfndlandR p194 CR France374

BOWER-SMITH,Cedric Gray Capt kia 4-11-15 Glouc &WAFF p201&106

BOWERMAN,Arthur James Lt kia 9-9-16 8SomLI &RFC p2 CR France882

BOWERS,Arthur Hugh Mansell Capt kia 9-8-15 2DLI p160 MR29

BOWERS,Frank Ewart 2Lt dow 31-3-18 5 att10RWSurr p212 CR France64

BOWERS,Frederick Henry Capt kld 29-5-17 RE p209 CR Lincs61

BOWERS,Thomas 2Lt ded 31-8-19 ACycCps p266 CR Norf179

BOWERS,Thomas James Lt kia 7-11-16 3N&D att7LNLancs p133 MR21

BOWERS,William Aubrey Lt dow 3-7-16 5NStaffs p238 CR France120,2-7-16

BOWERS-TAYLOR,Archibald Capt kia 7-6-17 1/6Manch p236 MR29

BOWES,Cyril Hulme T2Lt kia 1-7-16 2WRid p115 CR France1890

BOWES,Ellis Arthur 2Lt kia 12-3-18 4Leic p220 CR France369

BOWES,Roy.MC.TLtACapt dow 5-8-17 15RWelshF p97 CR Belgium16

BOWES,Stanley Ward 2Lt kia 29-9-15 3Dors attRFus p123 MR19

BOWES-LYON,Charles Lindsay Claude Lt kia 23-10-14 3 att1BlkW p128 CR Belgium96

BOWES-LYON,Fergus.Hon.TCapt kia 27-9-15 8BlkW p128 MR19

BOWES-LYON,Gavin Patrick Lt kia 27-11-17 3GrenGds p49 MR17

BOWES-SCOTT,Harry George Rodney Lt kia 21-3-16 IARO att29Punjabis p274

BOWES-WILSON,George Hutton Capt kia 17-6-15 24Yorks p220

BOWES-WILSON,John Hutton LtCol 7-6-17 1WRid att9Y&L CR Belgium127

BOWHAY,Eustace Gilbert Capt kia 8-3-16 6Dev p217 MR38

BOWIE,Allan Stuart Hunter 2Lt dow 8-5-18 RGA 23SB p38 CR Belgium38

BOWIE,David Drummond.MM.MID TCapt dow 31-5-18 7KSLI p144 CR France33,MC

BOWIE,George T2Lt kia 12-10-17 RScots att11Bn p53MR30

BOWIE,Henry Lt kia 28-7-18 3 att6BlkW p128 CR France622

BOWIE,Ralph Archibald 2Lt kia 26-9-17 5Leic p220 MR30

BOWKER,Francis Jearrad LtCol kia 21-1-16 1/4Hamps p228 CR Iraq5

BOWKER,Robert Bucknall Maj 5-9-17 RE CR War14

BOWKER,Tom.MID T2Lt kia 9-4-18 244MGC Inf p181 CR France525

BOWLAND,Conrad Cloutman 2Lt dow 26-10-18 6Glouc p225 CR France332

BOWLBY,Geoffrey Vaux Salvin Capt kia 13-5-15 RHGds p20 MR29

BOWLBY,George Elliott Lowe TCapt kia 15-3-16 8Lincs p74 CR France922,Lowes

BOWLBY,Lionel Henry Salvin Lt dow 5-6-16 2Drags p21 CR Belgium167,kia 4-6-15

BOWLBY,Thomas Rupert Capt kia 17-9-14 1Norf p73 MR15

BOWLER,Alfred Arthur 2Lt kia 27-5-18 5NStaffs p238 CR France1755

BOWLER,Sydney 2Lt kia 21-10-17 RGA 237SB p38 CR Belgium36

BOWLER,Thomas Chester 2Lt dow 3-10-18 3 att1/4LNLancs p135 CR France88,Chesters

BOWLER,Thomas George 2Lt kia 30-6-17 RGA 6SB p38 CR Belgium339

BOWLER,William T2Lt kia 9-8-17 74MGC Inf p181 MR29

BOWLES,Alan John.MID TCapt kia 10-4-16 1RBerks p138 CR France515,2Bn

BOWLES,Bernard Geoffrey T2Lt kia 3-9-16 EKent p57 CR France402

BOWLES,Edgar Branson 2Lt kia 31-3-18 108RFA 23ArmyBde p25 MR20,21-3-18

BOWLES,James Arthur Lt kia 26-8-14 28RFA p25 CR France716

BOWLES,John Campbell.MIDx2 Capt kia 19-2-15 RE 3FC p43 MR29

BOWLES,John George T2Lt kia 1-11-16 7SLancs p125 CR France384

BOWLES,Percy William.MC.2Lt kia 10-9-18 C219 RFA p25 CR France308

BOWLES,Reginald Julian Albany Lt dow 20-7-16 3RWelshF p97 CR France66,2Bn

BOWLES,Wilfred Spencer 2Lt kia 10-7-16 5Ess attMGC Inf p186&232 CR France397

BOWLEY,Thomas Henry 2Lt kia 26-10-14 1Leic p87 MR32

BOWLING,Arthur Henry 2Lt ded 29-9-18 RGA 160SB p38 CR Mddx59

BOWLING,Edwyn Randolph T2Lt kia 4-6-16 9 att8RWKent p140 CR Belgium97

BOWLING,Victor Macdonald 2Lt kia 4-3-17 SR 29RFC p5 CR France158,acckld 12RFC

BOWLY,Reginald Walter TLt kia 29-5-18 22 att20Manch p154 CR France21,20Manch att1Ches

BOWMAN,Alexander White 2Lt kia 25-9-16 EYorks attMGC p83&181

BOWMAN,Anthony Harvey 2Lt dow 20-5-16 37RFA p25 CR France158

BOWMAN,Claude Herbert 2Lt kia 16-8-17 4 O&BLI p231 MR30

BOWMAN,Clive Septimus Lt kia 18-9-17 3 att11NumbF p60 MR30

BOWMAN,Edward Oliver T2Lt kia 31-10-18 NumbF att9Bn p60 CR France206

BOWMAN,Henry Arthur 2Lt kia 28-3-18 13Lpool p71 MR20

BOWMAN,Hugh James T2Lt kia 10-1-16 16Mddx p146 CR France163

BOWMAN,John T2Lt dow 23-11-15 5 O&BLI p130 CR Belgium140

BOWMAN,Leslie Spencer Lt kia 25-6-17 4Lancs att52RFC p17&213 MR20

BOWMAN,Robert Moore T2Lt kia 5-8-16 81RFA p25 CR France513

BOWMAN,William Powell Lt kia 17-10-16 19WYorks att11RFC p2&81 CR France568

BOWMER,Vernon.MC.Lt ded 9-10-19 16N&D p264 CR Derby32

BOWN,Cecil Bertini Watkin TLt ded 20-3-17 4Aux(Petrol)RASC p192 CR France145

BOWN,Cyril Walter Lt dow 1-12-17 WSomYeo attH'TankCps p189&205 MR17

BOWN,Edward Elms T2Lt kia 2-11-17 GL att1/4Nhants p189 CR Palestine8

BOWN,William George 2Lt kia 31-7-17 44MGC Inf p181 MR29

BOWRAN,Robert Orton 2Lt kia 9-10-17 1/8WYorks p81 MR30

BOWRING,Arthur Hantague LtCol ded 14-9-19 RFA p261 CR Essex146

BOWRING,Francis Stephen Capt kia 22-11-15 IA 22Punjabis MR38

BOWRING,Frank Harvey TMaj kia 28-8-18 Lpool att9Bn p71 CR France592

BOWRON,Keith Stuart.DCM.MID Capt kia 8-8-18 14 att2/10Lond p249 CR France116

BOWSER,Ida Thekla Sister 11-1-19 VAD StJ CR Sussex178

BOWSHER,William Henry.MC.TLtACapt dow 25-10-18 20Manch p154 CR France231

BOWYER,Douglas Michael 2Lt kia 23-8-16 1BordR p116 CR Belgium101

BOWYER,Edgar George 2Lt kia 15-10-16 1Camb p245 MR21 Ex MonR

BOWYER,Edgar Raymond 2Lt kia 1-10-18 4Y&L p238 CR France406

BOWYER,Fritz 2Lt kia 25-7-16 GL &RFC p2&189,ded MR20

BOWYER,George Henry T2Lt kia 1-7-16 2SWBord p99 MR21

BOWYER,John Lt ded 10-7-21 RAOC CR Iraq6

BOWYER,John William TCapt kia 10-4-17 13RB p178 CR France154

BOWYER,Joseph.MC.HonLt&QM kia 9-6-17 11LancF p92

BOWYER-BOWER,Eldred Wolferstan Capt kia 19-3-17 3ESurr &59RFC p5&112 CR France614

BOWYER-SMITH,Cedric Gray Capt kia 4-11-15 Glouc att3NigR p201&106 CR WAfrica55

BOX,G.H.Lt kld 25-8-18 SL &RAF p201

BOX,Harold Francis Lt kia 29-10-18 5Ess attRE p232 CR France290

BOX,Philip John Murray TLt kia 7-8-15 Lincs p74 MR4

BOX,Raymond TLt dow 11-7-17 12Manch p154 CR France52

BOX,Reginald George 2Lt kia 30-11-17 7Ess p232 MR17

BOX,Roy Leslie 2Lt kia 9-10-16 RE 2/2WRidFC p210 CR France294,10-10-16

BOXALL,Alfred.MC.T2Lt dow 25-10-17 RE 262RlyCoy p43 CR Belgium165

BOXALL,Carze Lermithe Capt dow 4-5-15 2Hamps p120 MR4,Caryl Lermitte 27-4-15

BOXALL,William Gratbatch 2Lt dow 15-4-18 22Lond p251 CR France226,Greatbatch

BOXER,Hugh Edward Richardson.DSO.Maj kia 16-6-15 Cmdg 1Lincs p74 MR29,LtCol

BOYCE,Arthur Cecil Lt ded 10-8-17 RE p269

BOYCE,Charles Wallace 2Lt kia 24-10-18 4Glouc attMGC p186&255 CR France290

BOYCE,Perceval Capt kldRegMutiny 17-2-15 IA 5LightInf p274 CR Asia45,kia 15-2-15

BOYCOTT,Harold Charlton Lt dow 21-3-18 2CldGds p51 CR France1182

BOYD,Alexander Charles T2Lt kia 4-6-16 12RSuss p118 CR France114,5-6-16

BOYD,Brian.MM.T2Lt dow 7-6-17 14RIrRif p169 CR France285

BOYD,Cecil Vincent T2Lt kia 23-11-17 8RIrRif p169 MR17

BOYD,Charles Gordon 2Lt kia 3-5-17 7N&D att9Leic p233 CR Frnce434

BOYD,David Thomas 2Lt kia 3-5-17 6ScotRif p224 CR France40

BOYD,Edward Fenwick.MID Lt kia 19-9-14 1NumbF p60 CR France1107,20-9-14

BOYD,Frederick Ennis 2Lt kia 20-5-17 5RDubF p176 CR France1191

BOYD,Gavin T2Lt kia 13-7-16 4SpBde RE p43 CR France503

BOYD,Gavin Haddow T2Lt kia 2-12-17 KRRC att16Bn p149 CR Belgium125

BOYD,George Francis Edward TLt ded 19-10-16 10SfthH attY51TMB p164 CR France64

BOYD,George Pratt 2Lt dow 3-9-17 1IrGds p52 CR Belgium13

BOYD,George Vallance McKinlay TCapt kia 1-7-16 17HLI p162 MR21

BOYD,Harold Alexander 2Lt kia 19-9-14 2RInniskF p104 CR France1435,7-9-14

BOYD,Henry Ormsby T2Lt kia 9-5-16 6SLancs p125 MR38

BOYD,Herbert Cust Lt ded 17-2-18 RASC p267 CR Canada1380,attYLI

BOYD,Hugh Lennox Fleming Capt kia 18-11-17 1BlkW p128 CR Belgium126

BOYD,James Duncan.MC.Lt kia 25-9-18 27RFA p25 CR France518,25-8-18,119RFA

BOYD,James Peter LtTCapt kia 25-9-15 2GordH p166 CR France115

BOYD,James Stanley Newtown LtCol 1-2-16 RAMC CR Mddx16

BOYD,James Wilson Brack TCapt dow 16-7-16 3 att2Y&L attTMB p158 CR Belgium6,kia

BOYD,John 2Lt kia 29-10-16 6 att1ScotRif p224 MR21

BOYD,John T2Lt kia 12-4-18 2RScotF p94 MR32

BOYD,John Lt ded 24-9-18 4CamH att2/1LovatScts p269 CR Scot455

BOYD,John Bain 2Lt kia 22-3-18 1/7GordH p242 MR20

BOYD,John Brodie Capt ded 8-7-19 RAMC p267 CR Scot204

BOYD,Nigel John Lawson 2Lt dow 12-10-14 1BlkW p128 CR Scot237

BOYD,Philip Bentinck 2Lt kia 13-4-17 GordH &59RFC p5&166 MR20

BOYD,Reginald Russell T2Lt dow 4-5-17 12ScotRif p103

BOYD,R.H.2Lt kld 12-4-18 GL &5RAF p189 CR France95,Lt

BOYD,Robert Colin LtTCapt kia 14-7-16 8Dev p76 CR France453

BOYD,Robert Mitchell Stewart Lt kia 12-7-15 6HLI p240 MR4

BOYD,Stanley LtCol ded 1-2-16 RAMC p269

BOYD,Stuart Lt dow 7-10-16 N&D at1LNLancs p133 CR France177

BOYD,Thomas Cecil Lt dow 21-7-16 1 att7CamH p167 CR France64,Capt

BOYD,Thomas Moffatt TLt ded 25-10-18 RAMC p194 CR EAfrica90

BOYD,William Lt kia 5-11-16 8DLI p239 MR21

BOYD,William.MC.Lt kia 24-3-18 RFA att252RE p207 CR France512,25-3-18

BOYD,William Gaston(Tony)T2Lt dow 13-10-16 9RInniskF p104 CR France285

BOYD,William Graham TLt kia 16-8-17 9RIrF p171 MR30

BOYD,William Hatchell 2Lt kia 9-9-16 9RDubF p176 MR21

BOYD,William Noel Lawson 2Lt kia 23-4-15 2SfthH p164 MR29,25-4-15

BOYD CARPENTER,Victor Charles Douglas TLt kia 29-8-16 RE 89FC p43 CR France402

BOYD-MOSS,Ernest William.DSO.Maj kia 10-8-15 9Worc p108 CR Gallipoli13

BOYDELL,William Vernon 2Lt dow 8-6-15 8LancF p221 CR Gallipoli1

BOYDEN,Arnold Kingsley Maj ded 14-2-19 RASC GHQ p192&257 CR France40

BOYER,Charles Cyril Roslington Lt ded 23-11-19 RASC p267 CR Lincs25

BOYER,Ernest Alexander 2Lt kia 5-4-18 7 att1/22Lond p247 MR20

BOYER,Sydney James T2Lt kia 12-10-16 1RIrF p171 MR21,Lt

BOYERS,Edwin Capt ded 25-10-18 RAMC p194&267 CR Eire401

BOYES,James Ferguson 2Lt dow 25-8-18 15Lond p249 CR France100,Fergusson

BOYHAN,Thomas Francis 2Lt dow 12-9-16 3 att7RIrRif p169 CR France66

BOYLE,Charles Capes 2Lt kia 23-4-17 4EYorks p219 CR France162

BOYLE,David Erskine Lt kia 26-8-14 2LancF p92 MR15

BOYLE,Ernest Charles Patrick.DSO.LtCol kia 7-2-17 1HAC p206 CR France701

BOYLE,Godfrey Henry Patrick Maj ded 16-10-19 SfthH attRE Sigs p265 CR Surrey160,Col

BOYLE,James.Hon.Capt kia 18-10-14 1RScotF p94 MR22

BOYLE,John Antonio Saochey 2Lt kia 30-11-17 RGA 2/1LancsHB p38 MR17,Scochey

BOYLE,John Kennedy.MC.MIDx2 Lt ded PoW 21-10-18 7RDubF p176 CR Germany1,Kemmy 2RIrRif

BOYLE,Montgomerie Maj ded 27-3-19 RASC p253 CR Somerset172

BOYLE,Thomas Houston 2Lt kia 12-10-16 7 att2RScotF p94 MR21

BOYLE,William 2Lt kia 26-10-17 4LNLancs p234 MR30

BOYLE,William Scott TLt kia 4-1-17 11ScotRif p103 CR Greece6,4/5-1-17

BOYNE,Harry Horace 2Lt dow 21-7-16 4Suff attMGC Inf p186&217 CR France833,kia

BOYS,Edward Percival T2Lt kia 22-3-18 RE 5ArmySigCo p43 MR27,21-3-18

BOYS,Richard Harvey TLt kia 13-11-16 2 att4Beds p85 CR France220

BOYS,Sydney Charles TLt kia 23-6-18 RSuss att7Bn p118 CR FRance61,22-6-18

BOYS-STONES,George Lawden.MC.Capt dow 30-3-17 7Lancers att6CavBde CR Iraq8

BOYSON,Frank 2Lt kia 26-3-18 22DLI p160 MR27

BOYTON,Bertram Alfred Lt dow 9-11-17 A301RFA p207 CR Egypt2

BOYTON,Victor Henry Thompson 2Lt kia 31-5-17 RGA 289SB p38 CR Belgium4

BOYTON,Henry James Lt kia 14-12-16 4GrenGds p49 CR France785

BRABAZON,Alan.MIDx3 TCapt dow 8-3-18 6Leinst p174 CR Palestine3

BRABAZON,Hon.Ernest William Maitland Molyneux.DSO.Capt kia 17-6-15 CldGds p51 CR France114

BRABAZON,Terence Anthony Chaworth Lt dow 3-8-16 1Ess p131 CR Wilts179,Capt

BRABOURNE,W.W. see BRADBOURNE,W.W.

BRACE,F.E.SNurse ded 21-9-16 QAIMNS p200 CR Europe1

BRACELIN,Daniel Aloysius.MID T2Lt kia 20-7-18 BlkW att1/7Bn p128 CR France1695

BRACEWELL,Harry T2Lt dow 21-9-17 17N&D p133 CR Belgium15

BRACEY,Ernest Clifford 2Lt kia 28-9-18 SStaffs att5Bn p122 MR16

BRACEY,Frederick Sidney TLt kia 13-11-16 24RFus p66 CR France1491

BRACEY,Victor Charles Edelsten T2Lt kld 23-9-17 RFC p5 CR Somerset19

BRACHER,Frank Vivian TMaj kia 1-6-18 16 att9WelshR p126 MR19

BRACHER,Guy 2Lt kia 3-7-16 EKent p57 CR France251

BRADBEER,Alfred Harold 2Lt kia 21-10-16 3Manch att11LancF p154 MR21

BRADBEER,Francis Henry T2Lt kia 21-3-18 11Ess p131 MR20

BRADBEER,W.J.2Lt 8-8-20 RGA CR Somerset43

BRADBOURNE,Wyndham Wentworth.Lord.Capt kia 11-3-15 1GrenGds SR p49 MR22,BRABOURNE

BRADBROOK,Edward John Lt kia 20-4-18 18Lond att8RAF p250&258 CR France40

BRADBURY,Austen.MC.TLtACapt kia 8-8-18 5TankCps p188 MR16

BRADBURY,Dennis John Freeland T2Lt dow 15-11-16 RLancs att10LNLancs p58 CR France131

BRADBURY,Edward Kinder.VC.Capt kia 1-9-14 RFA L'Btyp25 CR France1231

BRADBURY,Ernest Alfred 2Lt ded 2-5-17 3 att12Glouc p106 CR France12,dow 2-4-17

BRADBURY,George Hartley Lt 18-2-21 5Y&L CR Scot313

BRADBURY,Harry TLt ded 3-12-18 RE p43 CR Egypt1,DGO 53DivHQ

BRADBURY,Harry Claude T2Lt kia 16-4-18 18Mddx p146 MR32

BRADBURY,John Cregean Lt dow 6-10-18 2/7Lpool p215 CR France40,Cregeen

BRADBURY,Thomas Piers Lt kia 26-4-18 7WRid p227 MR30

BRADBURY,William Rowland T2Lt kia 7-9-18 WYorks att10EYorks p81 CR France297

BRADBY,Daniel Edward TCapt kia 9-4-17 9RB p178 CR France581

BRADDELL,Edward Terrence Lt dow 27-3-17 RE 484FC p210 CR Palestine8,Terence

BRADDYLL,Edward Clarence Lt kia 5-9-16 IA 10Lancers attRFC p274 CR Belgium140,5-9-15

BRADFIELD,James Thomas Capt kia 13-8-20 1/4SomLI CR Iraq8

BRADFORD,Alfred Royal Lt kia 14-10-16 1Camb p244 CR France293

BRADFORD,Cecil Aubrey Capt drd 24-4-17 Yorks attNigeria p89&201 MR40

BRADFORD,Evelyn Ridley,Bart LtCol kia 14-9-14 SforthH p164 CR France867

BRADFORD,Frederick Reith Campbell 2Lt kia 1-7-16 1/4Lond p246 MR21

BRADFORD,George William Bathurst 2Lt kia 4-2-17 GL &15RFC p5

BRADFORD,James Barker.MC.T2Lt dow 14-5-17 18DLI p160 CR France113

BRADFORD,Roland Boys.VC.MC.BrigGen kia 30-11-17 2DLI &Staff 186InfBdeHQ p160 CR France529

BRADLEY,Arthur.MM.2Lt kia 24-8-17 YLI att6Bn p142 MR30

BRADLEY,Arthur Newsome Capt ded 6-11-18 RHA(WRid) p207 CR France403

BRADLEY,Augustus James Hector 2Lt kia 23-4-18 RGA 129HB p38 CR France62,dow

BRADLEY,Cyril Montague Lt kia 2-4-17 HQ 296RFA p207 CR France446

BRADLEY,Frank Gilbert Lt drd 3-1-21 1/8RWar CR Herefor&Worc208

BRADLEY,Frederick Hoysted.DSO.CaptALtCol kia 22-9-18 RAMC att15FA p194 CR France562

BRADLEY,Geoffrey Montagu.MID Lt kia 22-12-14 6RB attWelshR p178 MR22,2Bn

BRADLEY,George Joseph TCapt ded 17-2-19 LabCps 211EmpCoy p189 CR France40 Ex 2/2Lond

BRADLEY,George Page 2Lt kia 27-10-17 GL &43RFC p5 CR France924

BRADLEY,Gordon 2Lt kia 24-8-16 5 O&BLI p130 MR21

BRADLEY,Harry Thomas Lt&QM ded 2-4-17 MGC Inf p266 CR Notts68

BRADLEY,Horace Walter 2Lt kia 10-2-17 5RWFus p223 CR France631

BRADLEY,Hubert Mark 2Lt kld 27-5-18 21Lond p251 CR France44,kia 26-5-18

BRADLEY,James 2Lt kia 21-7-16 2Suff p78 MR21

BRADLEY,James T2Lt dow 26-10-18 RSuss att7Bn p118 CR France113

BRADLEY,John TCapt ded 17-2-19 RAVC att296RFA p198 CR France106

BRADLEY,John McDonald TLt dow 30-9-18 11RDubF p176 CR France512,17Bn

BRADLEY,Leslie 2Lt ded 11-7-16 IARO 56Rif MR65,Lt

BRADLEY,Philip Warden Lt kia 23-4-15 3 att1RWKent p140 MR29

BRADLEY,Reginald Ernest T2Lt dow 25-12-16 RE p43 CR France251

BRADLEY,Richard Lt kia 31-7-17 4RLancs p213 MR29

BRADLEY,R.J.LtCol 10-12-19 IMS CR Egypt2

BRADLEY,Robert Hubert Francis.MID T2Lt kia 25-1-17 9NStaffs p156 CR Iraq5

BRADLEY,Shephin Lt kia 25-5-15 Suff p78 MR29

BRADLEY,William Allan.OBE.MC.Capt ded 23-12-19 7DLI p269 CR Lond1

BRADLEY,Walter Robinson Lt ded 29-6-18 1N&D &RAF p133 CR Greece7

BRADLY,John Frank Lt dow 2-7-15 3 att1SWBord p99 CR Europe1

BRADNEY,Philip Edwin TCapt kia 31-7-15 6SomLI p79 CR Belgium58

BRADNEY,Walter 2Lt kia 24-3-18 1TankCps p188 MR27

BRADON,Harry 2Lt kia 16-11-16 1Suff p78 CR Greece3

BRADSHAW,Arthur Edwin Capt kia 13-10-14 IA 14Lancers att 15Huss p274 CR France1106

BRADSHAW,Arthur William Archibald 2Lt kia 25-9-15 1RWSurr p55 MR19

BRADSHAW,Bartle 2Lt kia 11-6-15 3BordR p116 CR Gallipoli6

BRADSHAW,Ernest Edwin TLt kia 30-9-17 D48RFA p25 CR Belgium17

BRADSHAW,Frank Seymour Capt kia 19-12-14 1SomLI p79 CR Belgium70

BRADSHAW,Harold James T2Lt dow PoW 18-5-17 1Norf p73 CR Palestine11,17-5-17,1/4Bn

BRADSHAW,Henry Herbert T2Lt kia 22-7-17 RE 74FC p43 CR Belgium6

BRADSHAW,Huyshe Arthur 2Lt BombAccident 19-8-16 IARO 112Inf p274 CR Iraq5

BRADSHAW,Percival Challon T2Lt kia 1-5-16 9 att6KOSB p101 CR Belgium137,Chalton

BRADSHAW,Peter Dennison T2Lt dow 14-7-16 15 att13NumbF p60 CR France176,kia

BRADSHAW,Richard Edward Kynaston Lt kia 1-7-16 1/12Lond p248 MR21

BRADSHAW,William Douglas 2Lt kia 31-10-16 88RFA p25 CR France251

BRADSHAW,William Robert T2Lt kia 19-2-17 5ConnRgrs p172 CR Belgium17,6Bn

BRADSTREET,Gerald Edmund.MIDx2 2LtTLt kia 7-12-15 RE 72FC SR p43 CR Gallipoli4

BRADSTREET,Lionel Arthur T2Lt kia 1-6-16 17Mddx p146 CR France924

BRADY,Charles TLt ded 15-8-15 RScots SL p53 p268 CR Scot279

BRADY,James TLt kia 26-8-18 15DLI p160 MR16

BRADY,Sydney Vincent.MC.2Lt ded 5-7-19 2Manch p265 CR Hamps119

BRAGG,Arthur Spencer T2Lt ded 28-3-19 10Ess p264 CR Essex43,Albert Lt

BRAGG,D.Lt 1-9-18 GL att1WAfrServBde CR WAfrica41

BRAGG,Frederick John T2Lt dow 25-9-17 Dev att1/9Lpool p76 CR Belgium3

BRAGG,Robert Charles T2Lt dow 2-9-15 58RFA p25 MR4

BRAGG,William Robyns Lt kia 3-12-17 1DevYeo p203 CR Palestine3

BRAGGINS,Albert Edwin 2Lt kia 29-4-18 7Worc p226 CR Belgium21

BRAIDE,G.F.W.LtCol 30-12-15 IMS MR67

BRAIDFORD,Percy.MC.2Lt kia 21-9-17 3DLI p160 MR30

BRAIDFORD,William T2Lt kia 24-7-16 19DLI p160 MR21

BRAIDWOOD,Robert Simpson,DCM.T2Lt kia 31-10-18 1/2 att1/8ScotRRif p103 CR Belgium140

BRAIN,Francis Sydney.MID TLt kia 3-10-18 RBerks att1Dors p138 CR France699,Capt

BRAIN,William Henry Oliver 2Lt kia 10-6-17 RGA 90HB p38 CR Belgium48,Lt

BRAINE,William Thomas Coker 2Lt kia 9-10-16 3 att2WRid p115 CR France374

BRAITHEWAITE,Michael Lloyd Lt kld 17-5-15 RFC p1 CR France473,BRAITHWAITE

BRAITHWAITE,Arthur 2Lt kld 11-3-18 5DLI p239 CR Durham164

BRAITHWAITE,Ernest 2Lt kia 22-7-16 14RWar p64 CR France432

BRAITHWAITE,Francis Joseph Maj kia 4-11-14 2LNLancs p135 MR47

BRAITHWAITE,Humphrey Layland T2Lt kia 10-7-16 RE p43 CR Belgium54

BRAITHWAITE,James Leslie 2Lt kia 22-7-16 Q'RFA attU'RHA p25 CR France188

BRAITHWAITE,Matthew Woodhouse Maj ded 9-11-18 7Ess p232 CR Essex10

BRAITHWAITE,M.D.Miss ded 3-3-19 VAD p200

BRAITHWAITE,M.L.see BRAITHEWAITE,M.L.

BRAITHWAITE,Philip Pipon.MID Capt kia 23-9-18 IARO att36Horse p274 CR Palestine11

BRAITHWAITE,Richard Wilfred TCapt kia 31-7-15 10DLI p160 MR29

BRAITHWAITE,Sydney Lt ded 4-12-16 SL p201

BRAITHWAITE,Valentine Ashworth.MC.2Lt kia 2-7-16 1SomLI p79 MR21

BRAITHWAITE,W.VD.Maj 18-2-17 7WYorks CR Yorks372

BRAKE,Frederick Carlton James T2Lt kia 21-3-18 10Worc p108 MR20

BRAKENBERRY,William Horace.MM.T2Lt dow 23-10-18 13KRRC p149 CR France1266

BRAKES,Bertram.DCM.Lt ded 5-1-18 2Leic att210MGC p87&181 CR Egypt2

BRAKSPEAR,Ronald William TMaj dow 2-10-15 8RBerks p138 CR France40

BRAKSPEAR,William Rae LtCol mbk 25-9-15 1A 2/3GurkhaRif p274 MR28

BRAMALD,John 2Lt kia 9-10-17 4YLI p235 MR30

BRAMBLE,George Henry Joseph 2Lt kia 1-7-16 3 att1Hamps p120 MR21,Gerald

BRAMELD,John Neville T2Lt dow 19-9-15 1KOSB p101 CR Gallipoli4

BRAMLEY,Arthur Henry 2Lt kia 8-6-18 1/2 att23Manch p154 CR France924

BRAMLEY,Cyril Richard Capt kia 20-2-17 2/5YLI p235 CR France339

BRAMLEY,Harold 2Lt kia 13-5-15 5YLI p269 MR29

BRAMLEY,Harry Brian T2Lt dow 15-7-18 13Lpool p71 CR France10

BRAMLEY,Samuel Leslie John 2Lt kia 23-9-17 SR 57RFC p5 CR Belgium140

BRAMPTON,Harry Lee T2Lt kia 7-6-17 3Worc p108 CR Belgium89

BRAMWELL,Charles Guy.MID Capt&Adjt kia 28-6-15 8ScotRif p103 MR4

BRAMWELL,Norman 2Lt kia 30-3-18 2/7LancF p221 MR27,Ex3/5Bn

BRAMWELL,William Dargue.Agent ded 1-12-18 EAIntelDept CR EAfrica36 Ex BowkersHorse

BRANCH,Albert 2Lt kia 1-7-16 4Mddx p146 CR France267

BRANCKER,James Donaldson Dulany.DSO.Maj kia 1-5-17 RGA 116SB p38 CR France581

BRAND,David Halyburton.MC.LtACapt kia 29-3-18 1ScotGds p52 CR France214

BRAND,Douglas William McLeod Capt dow 23-11-17 9Lond p247 CR France245,24-11-17

BRAND,Eric Jermyn T2Lt kia 23-8-18 1Ess p131 CR France578

BRAND,Ernest Stanley Capt kia 8-10-14 RFus attKAR p66&201 CR WAfrica28

BRAND,Geoffrey Jermyn T2Lt kia 1-7-16 GL att101TMB p189 MR21

BRAND,George Ellard Maj(Commsy) ded 6-8-18 IA MilWorksServ p274 CR India164

BRAND,Percy Alfred Easterling T2Lt kia 28-9-17 12RB A'Coy p178 MR30,20-9-17

BRAND,Robert.MC.T2Lt kia 8-5-18 RE 406RenfrewFC p43 CR France250

BRAND,Stanley Oliver TLtACapt kia 14-6-17 6Y&L p158 CR Belgium75

BRAND,W.J.H.Maj 20-1-20 LondScot CR Surrey47

BRANDER,Alfred Ernest 2Lt kia 13-11-16 8A&SH p243 CR France131

BRANDER,Bruce MacDonald Capt ded 30-11-18 RAMC attWaterTankCoy RASC p253 CR France1142,McDonald

BRANDER.J.Lt 19-7-19 RASC CR Scot287

BRANDER,Robert Brander 2Lt ded 27-9-17 RE p43 CR Cheshire31,Lt

BRANFILL,Capel Lisle Aylett Capt ded 11-5-16 GlamYeo p203 CR Egypt9 see AYLETT-BRANFILL,C.

BRANDON,Arthur Chester Capt&Adjt kia 21-1-16 4Hamps p228 MR38

BRANDON,Brian Lloyd T2Lt kia 4-9-18 KSLI att1/7Ches p144 CR Belgium100

BRANDON,Edgar Thomas Colin Lt kia 3-4-17 11RFC p5 MR20

BRANDON,William George T2Lt ded 13-7-18 7DCLI p114 CR Eire286

BRANDRAM,Christopher 2Lt dow 1-9-18 9 att2/4Lond p248 CR France833

BRANDRETH,Charles Reginald 2Lt kia 21-3-18 7 att2/8N&D p233 MR20

BRANDRETH,Lyall Maj Kia 4-6-15 2RFus p66 MR4,6-6-15

BRANDT,Douglas Robert Lt dow 6-7-15 RB p178 MR29,Druce

BRANFOOT,Clayton T2Lt kia 25-8-17 Lincs p74 CR France1462

BRANSURY,John Eric Cecil 2Lt ded 1-4-16 RGA 16HB p38 CR France15

BRANKER,Walter Robert.MC.T2Lt kia 5-10-18 KRRC att11N&D p149 CR France234

BRANNIGAN,Ernest Edward 2Lt kia 3-9-16 1/7WYorks p218 MR21

BRANSBURY,Vernon Dudley Bramsdon Lt kia 25-10-14 3Lincs p74 MR22

BRANTOM,William Harper.DCM.2Lt kia 3-7-16 15Lond p249 CR France558,4-7-16

BRASH,Edmund 2Lt dow 2-9-18 5 att13RWFus p223 CR France41

BRASH,James.DSO.MC.LtACapt dow 9-11-18 3 att7SfthH p164 CR France34

BRASH,John T2Lt kia 25-8-18 8 att1/5ELancs p110 CR France643

BRASH,Wilfred 2Lt kia 9-3-17 1/5RLancs p213 CR Belgium4

BRASIER,James Charles Capt&QM ded 26-12-16 1YLI p142 CR Greece7

BRASINGTON,Frederick Thomas T2Lt kia 9-10-17 GL &9RFC p5 MR20

BRASNETT,Thomas John Grose Jack T2Lt kia 13-10-15 7ESurr p112 MR19

BRASS,Ewart Stanley 2Lt kia 31-3-17 HAC p206 CR France568,1-4-17

BRASS,James Robson Lt dow 26/27-4-15 8DLI p239 CR Belgium44

BRASS,John.DCM.T2Lt accded 28-7-18 RASC 16ArmyAux HT Cps p102 CR France13

BRASSEY,Gerard Charles 2Lt kia 27-8-18 2CldGds p51 CR France615

BRASSEY,Harold Ernest TLtCol kia 15-7-16 RHGds att8SLancs p20 CR France296

BRASSINGTON,William Henry.MM.TLt kia 23-8-18 7TankCps p188 CR France518,25-8-18

BRASTED,Frederick Elliott Lt accded 18-8-17 7Ess p232 CR France113

BRATT,Alfred Charles LtACapt kia 4-10-17 1/5RWar p214 CR Belgium125

BRAUN,Charles Lema TCapt ded 19-6-17 Ess 2GarrBn p131 MR65

BRAWN,Mark.DCM.Lt&QM kia 1-9-18 4Beds p85 CR France592

BRAY,Aubrey Mellish.MC.TLt dow 8-8-18 8RBerks p138 CR France71,Capt

BRAY,Francis Patrick Maj kia 23-3-18 RE 518FC p209 MR20

BRAY,Frank Hugh 2Lt kld 28-5-18 3 att9RSuss p118 CR France149,kia

BRAY,George Thomas T2Lt dow 26-10-17 32RFus p66 CR France145

BRAY,George William Reginald TLt dow 16-8-16 7RBerks p138 CR Greece6

BRAY,Gerald Theodore 2Lt kia 9-8-15 2/5RWSurr p212 MR4

BRAY,Reginald Boydon T2Lt kia 23-10-18 9Norf p73 CR France190

BRAY,Sidney Herbert T2Lt kia 20-7-18 WYorks att8Bn p81 CR France622

BRAYBROOKS,Sidney T2Lt ded 3-2-19 LabCps att17RSuss p189 CR France134

BRAYDEN,Kevin 2Lt kia 23-12-17 18Lond p250 CR Palestine3

BRAYSHAW,Percy St.Quentin 2Lt ded 14-1-18 RFA p25 CR Belgium18

BRAYSHAY,William Stead Capt kia 6-4-17 RASC attRFC p18&253 CR Belgium406

BRAZIER,Albert Edward T2Lt kia 20-9-17 RWar att10Bn p64 MR30

BRAZIER,Anthony David Cecil T2Lt kia 10-3-17 3 att1RBerks p138 CR France393

BRAZIER,Charles Henry Lt ded 17-2-16 RGA p38 CR Essex81

BREARLEY,Arthur Joseph Capt kia 20-6-16 1/7Dev attRE N'Coy p217 CR Belgium15,20-6-17

BREARLEY,Norman Blackburn T2Lt kia 17/19-4-16 12 attRWar p64 MR38

BRECHIN,Robert Hood 2Lt kia 30-9-16 5SfthH att1A&SH p241 CR Greece3

BRECKELL,Edward Ryder Lt ded 8-2-18 3SLancs p215 CR Lancs2

BRECKELL,Ralph Leicester 2Lt kia 9-7-15 3SLancs att2LancF p125 MR29

BREE,Edward Russell Stapylton Lt kia 18-9-18 8DCLI p114 MR37

BREED,John Bennington 2Lt kia 31-7-17 RGA 236SB p38 CR Belgium102

BREEN,Thomas Francis Pennefather CaptAMaj kia 18-9-18 RAMC att142FA p194 CR France437

BREENE,Thomas Frederick TLt kia 1-7-16 1RWar attMGC p64&181 MR21

BREESE,William Laurence 2Lt kld 14-3-15 RHGds p20 CR France134

BREGAZZI,Edward 2Lt ded 9-11-18 1/5N&D p232 CR France65,8-11-18

BREINGAN,Samuel Karr 2Lt kia 26-5-17 3Y&L p158 CR Belgium127

BREMMER,George.DSO.MC.TCaptAMaj kia 23-3-18 RE 80FC p43 CR France1893

BREMNER,David T2Lt dow 9-7-16 10 att1BordR p116 CR France62

BREMNER,James TLt dow 24-6-17 1RScots p53 CR Belgium11,1/8Bn

BREMNER,John TCapt&QM ded 28-11-18 KAR p200 CR WAfrica30

BREN,Henry Alfred Hogarth Lt kia 9-9-16 4 att7Leinst p174 MR21

BRENAN,Byron Edward 2Lt kia 18-4-15 3Glouc p106 CR Belgium58,Lt 2Bn

BRENCHLEY,John,MC 2Lt kia 12-10-17 4CldGds p51 CR Belgium87

BRENDEL,John Daniel George T2Lt kld 27-1-18 RFC p15

BRENNAN,Jeremiah Lt kld 8-8-18 LancHussYeo att1IntelCps p204 CR France226

BRENNAN,John Henry Capt kia 19-10-14 3RWelshF p97 MR29

BRENNAN,Lester Luke T2Lt kld 25-2-18 99RFC p15 CR Wilts129

BRERETON,Charles MacLeod T2Lt kia 25-9-15 5CamH p167 MR19

BRERETON,Herbert TLt kia 21-12-16 GL att15RFC p2&189 CR France41

BRERETON,Leonard Leader 2Lt dow 29-4-17 1/5Beds p219 CR Egypt9

BRERETON-BARRY,William Roche 2Lt kia 16-8-17 10RDubF p176 MR30

BRESLAW,Geoffrey Reynell 2Lt kia 7-10-16 15Hamps p120 CR France385

BRESLIN,John 2Lt ded 11-7-17 1HLI p162 CR Iraq5

BRESSEY,Denys John 2Lt kia 14-10-17 12/35RFA p25 CR Belgium19

BRESSEY,Sydney Herbert.MM.T2Lt kia 21-9-18 RE 74DivSigCo p43 CR France1494

BRETHERTON,Walter Kington Lt ded 13-5-16 IARO attS&TCps p274 MR65

BRETON,Walter Guy Nicholas.DSO.MIDx2 Maj kia 14-9-17 RGA 2/1NMidHB p209 CR Belgium101

BRETT,Charles Arthur Hugh.DSO.MID LtCol kia 26-8-14 2Suff p78 MR15

BRETT,Ernest Edward 2Lt kia 23-4-17 BordR att7Bn p116 MR20

BRETT,Ernest Hugh William T2Lt dow 2-8-16 9 att1/5DCLI p114 CR France1887,kia

BRETT,Francis Joseph T2Lt kia 30-7-16 25Manch p154 CR France744

BRETT,Hugh Corthorn TCapt kia 29-7-16 7DCLI p114 CR France344

BRETT,Nora Veronica SNurse 20-5-15 TFNS CR War7

BRETT,W.G.A Capt 14-3-16 76Punjabis CR Devon72

BRETT,William Frank 2Lt dow 15-10-17 RGA 24SB p38 CR Belgium132,kia

BRETTELL,Sidney Walter TLt kia 10-7-16 10 att8SStaffs p122 MR21

BREUL,Oswald George Frank Justies T2Lt ded 16-10-17 RE 5CpsHQ p43 CR France134,Justus AR CableSect

BREW,Cyril Huleatt Lt dow 12-10-16 2IrGds SR p52 CR France145,Hulcatt

BREW,John George Maj dow 6-4-18 PoW 9RIrF p171 CR France987

BREWER,Cecil Harold 2Lt kia 4-10-17 4 att7LancF p92 CR Belgium83

BREWER,Edmund 2Lt dow 12-1-18 GlamYeo att12SWBordp203 CR France518

BREWER,John Angus.MID TCapt dow 18-9-18 9SLancs p125 CR Greece6,James

BREWER,John Giblett Lt ded 2-11-18 IARO attSap&Min p274 CR Lancs7,Giblette

BREWER,John Patrick Lt ded 20-7-19 1DragGds attMotor MGC p261 CR Hamps64

BREWER,Reginald England T2Lt kia 10-10-16 43/24RFA p25 CR France513

BREWER,Wilfred Aubrey TLt kia 21-11-17 1N&D p133 CR Belgium126

BREWERTON,Augustine T2Lt kia 26-9-16 12Mddx p146 MR21

BREWERTON,Robert Henry Lt kia 30-4-18 8 att19Lpool p215 MR30,Roland

BREWIN,Harold Rowland Nelson 2Lt kia 19-7-16 2Wilts p152 CR France1887,Roland 2/1 O&BLI

BREWIN,Harry Hedley T2Lt kia 12-8-18 15 att2Hamps p120 CR France28

BREWIS,Alfred Percy.MID LtTCapt dow 1-6-17 1NumbF att1/5ELancs p60 CR France905

BREWIS,H.W.MC.TCapt ded 4-6-18 10Glouc p264 CR Glouc27

BREWIS,John Arthur Gardner Lt kia 29-4-17 40RFC p5 MR20

BREWIS,Robert Henry Watkin MajTLtCol kia 18-12-14 2RWar p64 CR France253

BREWITT,James Leonard Lt dow 1-12-17 1/1StaffsYeo p205 CR Palestine9

BREWITT,William Sydney T2Lt kia 29-6-16 RFA p25 CR France394

BREWITT-TAYLOR,Raymond.MC.Capt kia 22-8-18 RAMC 7FA CR France504 see TAYLOR,R.B.

BREWSTER,Basil Stockbridge Lt kia 3-5-17 6Norf att2/5YLI p217 MR20

BREWSTER,Harold Staples Lt ded 6-12-16 RFC CR Canada1464

BREWSTER,Hugh Percival 2Lt kia 9-9-16 49MGC Inf p181 CR France785

BREWSTER,Richard Gardiner 2Lt kia 21-3-18 SlrHorse att7RIrReg p24 MR27

BRIAN,Arthur Gerald.MID TLt dow 16-10-17 10DCLI p114 CR Belgium3,Capt

BRIAN,Herbert Cecil 2Lt kia 9-5-15 RGA 59SB p38 CR France348

BRIANT,Thomas TSubCdr ded 10-11-17 IA CpsofMilStaffClerks p274

BRIARD,Ernest Felix Victor Capt kia 24-8-14 1Norf p73 CR Belgium198

BRIARD,John Fortescue 2Lt ded 15-10-19 IA 1/35Sikhs p274 MR43

BRICE,Ernest Maj ded 5-4-16 RAMC p269 CR Wales168

BRICE,Harry Copeland Lt dow 11-6-15 1/4Leic p219 MR29,Henry &CR France285

BRICE-SMITH,John Kenneth T2Lt dow 11-9-15 7Lincs p74 CR Belgium11

BRICKELL,Frederick William Lt kia 20-6-18 5DLI attMGC p186&238 MR30

BRICKLAND,Charles Hampton 2Lt kia 25-3-15 2RFus p66 MR4

BRICKMAN,Frederick William TLt kia 26-10-17 149MGC Inf p181 MR30

BRICKMANN,Hugh Morton Gairn TLt dow 1-10-16 GL 12ScotRif attTMB p189 CR France40,BRICKMAN

BRICKMANN,Noel.MID TCapt kia 29-10-16 3 att1ScotRif p103 MR21

BRICKNELL,Ernest Thomas Samuel T2Lt dow 20-10-16 9 att2SWBord p99 CR France401

BRICKWOOD,Arthur Cyril 2Lt ded 15-4-15 1Y&L p158 CR Hamps83

BRIDCUTT,John Henry.DSO.CaptALtCol kia 1-10-18 2RIrRif p169 CR Belgium157

BRIDDON,Charles Clark TCapt dow 30-9-17 177LabCps p189 CR Belgium16,Ex 17Y&L

BRIDGE,Donald Gerald Clive 2Lt dow 23-5-15 2RBerks p138 CR Lond2

BRIDGE,F.TLt ded 24-10-18 LabCps p266 CR Yorks575,2Lt

BRIDGE,George Francis Reginald 2Lt dow 15-4-18 7Worc p226 CR France31,2/8Bn

BRIDGE,John Kelly Capt ded 31-1-19 1/5LancF p221 CR Egypt9

BRIDGEMAN,Humphrey Herbert Orlando Lt kia 11-5-17 HouseholdBn p20 MR20

BRIDGER,Arthur Kynaston 2Lt kia 19-7-16 4Y&L p238 MR31

BRIDGER,Francis Albert Lt 77108 10-9-18 RFusPostal 2/2Lond

BRIDGER,Herbert John 2Lt kia 1-11-18 307RFA p25 CR France739

BRIDGES,Fitz-Stephen Henry Maj ded 24-9-16 IA 2/5GurkhaRif attKashmirLancers p274 MR67

BRIDGES,Fleming Hardy 2Lt kia 10-4-18 3 att8Glouc p106 MR30

BRIDGES,Roland Harley.DSO.MID MajALtCol ded 22-8-18 RAMC p194 CR Palestine9,drd

BRIDGES,Walter.MIDx2 Capt ded 25-1-19 RASC 1034MT Coy p192&257 CR Italy15,25-1-18

BRIDGES,William Robert 2Lt dow 23-4-17 3 att4Beds p85 CR France95,kia

BRIDGEWATER,Arthur Sidney.MC.T2Lt kia 8-10-18 9Dev p76 CR France234

BRIDGEWATER,Clement Joseph Bentley Capt kia 1-12-17 6Drags p22 CR France407

BRIDGEWATER,Samuel Ernest T2Lt kia 29-3-16 15N&D p133 CR France706,BRIDGWATER 30-3-16

BRIDGFORD,Stanley Lyon Capt dow 8-4-18 6Manch p236 CR Belgium353

BRIDGLAND,Neville Linton Lt kia 22-10-14 ESurr att1Bn p112 CR France705

BRIDGMAN,William Louis 2Lt dow 20-9-17 6RFus p66 MR30

26

BRIDGWATER,S.E. see BRIDGEWATER,S.E.

BRIDGWOOD,Dudley Edward 2Lt dow 10-10-17 1/5NStaffs p238 CR Staffs152

BRIDLE,C.Lt 11-3-19 Dors CR Dorset/Cl148

BRIDLE,Robert Reginald 2Lt kia 26-9-17 20Lond p251 MR30

BRIDSON,Charles Edward Ridgway.MID Capt dow 4-4-16 3 att8RLancs p58 CR Belgium15

BRIDSON,John Paul Ridgway 2Lt kia 25-9-15 8Dev p76 MR19

BRIEN,Charles 2Lt kia 27-8-16 5Glouc p225 CR France383

BRIEN,Desmond Cecil Bagge 2Lt kia 2-10-15 3 att2Ches p95 MR19

BRIEN,Frederick George TLt kia 30-4-18 RFA attY45TMB p25 CR France21,dow 20-4-18

BRIERCLIFFE,Louis Bernard Lt kia 31-3-17 3ELancsRFA p207 CR France53

BRIERLEY,Charles Leonard Maj dow 16-9-15 2LancF p92 CR Lancs413

BRIERLEY,George Raworth 2Lt dow 9-5-17 4YLI p235 CR France120,1-5-17

BRIERLEY,Harold Holland 2Lt kia 27-7-16 MGC Inf p181 MR21

BRIERLEY,Horace James TLt kia 7-8-15 9LancF p92 CR Gallipoli27

BRIERLEY,Hugh Colley Capt kia 23-6-17 6Manch p236 CR France755

BRIERLEY,Roger Christian Lt kia 14-7-17 5Ches p222 CR Belgium6,6Bn

BRIERLEY,Vincent.MC.T2Lt dow 28-5-18 8RLancs p58 CR France84,23-8-18

BRIERLEY,William Hunstone Capt kia 26-9-17 6N&D p233 CR Belgium96

BRIGGS,Arthur Desmond TCapt kia 25-9-15 9ScotRif p103 MR19

BRIGGS,Eric Mackie 2Lt kia 3-5-17 6LancF p221 CR France452

BRIGGS,Frederick Cecil Currer.DSO.Maj ded 22-11-19 2Lpool p263 MR43

BRIGGS,Frederick Clifton BtCol ded 30-12-16 3BordR p116 CR Lancs40

BRIGGS,Geoffrey Featherstone Lt kia 11-7-16 2/6Glouc p225 CR France1887

BRIGGS,George Clark.MID Capt kia 15/16-10-14 1RScotF p94 CR France1107,14-9-14

BRIGGS,Harley Knollys 2Lt kia 26-7-16 B166RFA p25 CR France188

BRIGGS,John Mackay TCapt&Adjt ded 2-10-16 18RIrRif p169 CR Ireland138,Mackey

BRIGGS,Orriell LtACapt kia 4-11-18 8SomLI p79 CR France206,Orrie

BRIGGS,Oswald Kershaw Lt ded 22-4-20 2RFA p269 CR Yorks425,Capt

BRIGGS,Richard Stanley Lt kia 29-7-15 7WYorks p218 CR Belgium73

BRIGGS,Thomas.MC.2Lt kia 18-10-18 6LancF p221 CR France319

BRIGGS,William Lake LtTCapt kia 21-7-16 6LancF p221&269,Blake MR29,31-7-17 2/7 att2/5Bn

BRIGGS,William Lonsdale T2Lt dow 14-9-17 1RLancs att1/5LancF p58 CR France40

BRIGGS-GOODERHAM,Ernest John Robinson 2Lt kia 13-12-16 36MGC Inf p181 CR France420

BRIGHT,Archibald Viccars Lt kia 7-6-17 3 att11N&D p133 CR Belgium127

BRIGHT,Cecil Desborough 2Lt kia 21-3-16 IARO 93BurmaInf p274 MR38

BRIGHT,Francis John 2Lt kia 20-9-17 32RFus p66 MR30

BRIGHT,Frank Arnold 2Lt kia 13-10-15 7N&D p233 CR France115

BRIGHT,Frederick George T2Lt kia 23-8-18 56MGC Inf p181 CR France927

BRIGHT,Harold Viccars 2Lt kia 21-9-18 4N&D p133 CR France835,2Bn

BRIGHT,John Leslie T2Lt kia 25-9-15 2RSuss p118 MR19

BRIGHT,Kenneth Coldwell 2Lt kia 18-8-16 2 att9RSuss p118 MR21

BRIGHTEN,Ralph Dalton Jarvis 2Lt kia 15-8-15 5Beds p219 CR Gallipoli4

BRIGHTMAN,Sidney Charles 2Lt kia 22-3-18 RE p210 MR34

BRIGINSHAW,Herbert William Oswald TLt ded 30-11-18 RASC p192 CR Ireland14,Henry

BRIGSTOCKE,Hugh Fraser TLtACapt kia 9-1-17 7/8KOSB p101 CR France151

BRIMFIELD,Ernest Gaskarth 2Lt kia 2-11-17 7Lond p247 CR Palestine8

BRIMS,James Sutherland.MID TLt kia 8-11-16 D79RFA p25 CR France430

BRINCKMAN,Denys Lt kia 10-6-15 1RIrF p171 CR Belgium4

BRIND,Ralph Montacute.MC.Capt kia 13-1-16 IA 37Dogras p274 CR Iraq5,2-2-16

BRINDAL,Gladstone 2Lt dow 24-3-16 6Glouc p225 CR France85

BRINDLE,John James 2Lt 6-3-20 5Lpool CR Lancs278

BRINDLE,John Laurence Capt ded 13-3-18 4LNLancs p233 CR Lancs346

BRINDLEY,Charles Stuart T2Lt kia 23-4-16 1/8 att1/4RScotF p94 CR Egypt2

BRINDLEY,Frank Ewart 2Lt dow 4-10-18 6NStaffs p238 CR France446

BRINE,Everard Lindesay Lt ded 24-9-18 1/4Hamps p228 CR Asia82

BRINK,Albert Drury 2Lt kia 20-9-17 6LancF p221 CR Belgium125

BRINK,Johannes Hieronymus Lt dow 11-4-17 RFA &14RFC p5&25 CR France564

BRINKWORTH,Arthur Robert 2Lt dow 7-9-16 14RWar p64 CR France630,kia

BRINKWORTH,Edwin John T2Lt dow 9-9-18 15DLI p160 CR France398

BRINKWORTH,Wilfred Henry Lt kld 4-8-18 RFus &215RAF p263 MR20,2Lt

BRINSLEY-RICHARDS,Roland Herbert Wyndham 2Lt kia 30-7-16 10WRid p115 MR21

BRINTON,M.G.SNurse 30-10-18 TFMS CR Durham1

BRISCO,Richard Brown.MC.TCapt kia 9-4-17 RE 172TC p43 CR France68

BRISCOE,Edward Villiers.MIDx2 Lt dow 27-8-16 1 att10RWar p64 MR29,Capt 26/27-8-16

BRISCOE,Frederick John Lt kia 11-5-15 3Y&L p158 CR Belgium58,10-5-15,1Bn

BRISCOE,Henry Whitby T2Lt ded 15-4-17 RIrF 3GarrBn p171 MR35,drd

BRISCOE,Mervyn Whitby TLt kia 23-7-17 RFA &6RFC p5&25 MR20

BRISTOL,Harold James TLtACapt dow 4-5-18 4SStaffs att10Ches p122 CR France100

BRISTOLL,Clarence T2Lt ded 9-11-18 ACycCps p181 CR France146

BRISTOW,Cuthbert George 2Lt kia 17-7-17 1 att3RWKent p140 MR20

BRISTOW,Percy Henry 2Lt kia 23-3-18 2/9Lond p248 MR27

BRISTOWE,Robert Owen.MID Lt kia 10-3-15 2Dev p76 CR France706

BRITT,Eric John Robert 2Lt kia 30-3-18 22Lond p251 CR Syria2

BRITTAIN,Edward Harold.MC.LtTCapt kia 15-6-18 2 att11N&D p133 CR Italy4

BRITTAIN,Frank Morris Engr ded 2-7-16 BRCS CR Iraq5

BRITTEN,Arthur Herbert.MC.TLt kia 14-4-18 8Glouc p106 MR30

BRITTEN,Charles Edward TLt dow 20-7-16 RFA 5DAC p25 CR France51,2Lt 29-7-16 2DAC

BRITTEN,Charles Wells.MID TLtAMaj kia 26-4-17 RFA DTMO p25 CR Belgium167

BRITTEN,Edward William Capt kia 10-8-15 10Mddx p236 MR4

BRITTEN,Richard Spencer TMaj ded 18-8-18 RBucksHuss 5ArmyHQ p24 CR France31

BRITTEN,Thomas Xavier.MID LtCol dow 14-4-15 IA 110Mahrattas p274 CR Iraq6,15-4-15

BRITTIN,Edward Whicker T2Lt kia 31-7-17 20DLI p160 MR29,BRITTON 1-8-17

BRITTON,Arthur John Allan 2Lt kia 10-8-15 5WelshR p230 MR4

BRITTON,Herbert Edward 2Lt dow 15-10-16 62RFA p25 CR France188

BRITTON,William Kerr Magill 2Lt kld 23-5-17 1RMunstF &29RFC p5&175 CR Ireland248

BRITTS,Charles William Gordon 2Lt kld 6-11-15 4 att9ESurr p112 CR France1369,5-11-15

BROAD,Alfred Evans.MC.TLt dow 2-3-16 6Dors p123 CR France40

BROAD,Arthur Maurice TLt kia 12-7-16 15RFus attMGC Inf p66&181 CR France630

BROAD,Clifford Newman T2Lt dow 9-4-16 2RSuss p118 CR France178

BROAD,Francis Boase.MC.LtACapt kia 24-10-18 1Mddx p146 CR France230

BROAD,Frank Cuthbert 2Lt kia 22-9-18 10Lond p248 CR France665

BROAD,Hubert Frederick Lt ded 25-10-18 3Leinst p174

BROAD,John Eric Lt kia 23-3-18 Herts p252 MR27

BROAD,Malcolm Percy Eyre 2Lt kia 9-10-17 5Y&L p238 MR30

BROAD,Reginald Leigh Maj ded 18-9-17 SL RE attIWT p268 CRGlouc5 Ex WelchR

BROAD,Richard Blunson.MID LtAMaj ded 6-11-18 U'RFA p25 CR France85,Blunsom

BROAD,Walter Victor Mantach Lt kia 22-3-18 15Lond p249 MR20,23-3-18

BROAD,William George.MM.T2Lt dow 28-3-18 19DLI p160 CR France44

BROADBENT,Cecil Hoyle 2Lt dedacc 1-3-16 4YLI p235 CR France43

BROADBENT,Edgar Richards.MC.Maj ded 31-10-18 8Huss p22 CR Mddx39

BROADBENT,George Carvel 2Lt kia 21-5-18 1/5SStaffs p229 CR France109

BROADBENT,Hermann TLtACapt&Adjt kia 15-2-17 Y&L att10Bn p158 CR France115

BROADBENT,Sidney TCapt kia 18-2-18 RFC p15 CR France765,Sydney

BROADBENT,Wilfred Stuart Stidston Lt kia 19-4-17 153MGC p181 CR Frnce451

BROADFOOT,William Allison 2Lt kia 13-7-15 6HLI p240 MR4

BROADHURST,Cecil Howard 2Lt dow 1-12-17 3Lpool p71 CR France518

BROADHURST,Gerald Henry Lt ded 8-5-15 52RFA p25 MR29

BROADHURST,Thomas Clifford 2Lt kld 28-9-17 GL &RFC p5 CR Lancs478

BROADLEY,Harry TCapt kia 6-8-17 2RInniskF p104 CR Belgium45

BROADRICK,Frederick Benjamin Dumaresq Maj ded 19-4-18 RFA p25 CR France85

BROADRICK,George Fletcher.MID LtCol kia 22-8-15 6BordR p116 MR4

BROADWAY,Hugh Alexander.MID 2Lt dow 30-3-15 RE 5FC p43 CR France102,Lt

BROADWAY,Neville Harris Lt kia 1-12-17 IA 2Lancers p274 MR28

BROADWOOD,Maximilian Francis 2Lt kia 24-8-14 1RWKent p140 CR Belgium20

BROADWOOD,Robert George.CB.LtGen dow 21-6-17 12Lancers Staff GOC 57Divn p1 CR France255

BROADWOOD,W.A.Capt 2-5-21 6LNLancs CR Lond1

BROCK,Alfred Herbert TCapt ded 3-11-19 RGA p269 CR Durham97,3-1-19 RE

BROCK,Alfred Lawrence Capt kia 14-4-17 6DLI p239 CR France162

BROCK,Algernon Bertram 2Lt dow 26-10-17 9Dev p76 MR30

BROCK,Cecil Howard TLt dow 4-11-18 8 att9Dev p76 CR France231,kia

BROCK,Edgar Nathaniel Loftus Capt kia 21-5-15 5 att3Worc p108 CR Belgium28,20-5-15

BROCK,Eric George.MC.LtACapt kia 31-7-17 7Lpool p215 MR29

BROCK,George Selby Capt ded 7-10-18 IA IMS p274 CR Pakistan50A &MR43

BROCK,Herbert Leslie TLt kia 10-4-18 29MGC Inf p181 MR32

BROCK,Percy Douglas 2Lt kia 29-5-18 1Lincs D'Coy p74 CR France1332

BROCK,Sydney Edward.MC.Capt dow 11-11-18 10RScots p212 CR Scot725

BROCK-HOLLINSHEAD,Laurence Maj kia 26-9-15 8RWKent p140 MR19

BROCKBANK,Charles Norman TCapt kia 1-7-16 18Lpool p71 CR France397

BROCKBANK,Herbert T2Lt kia 28-4-17 27NumbF p60 MR20

BROCKIE,J.Capt 28-10-18 RFA CR Scot142

BROCKINGTON,Conrad Clive Lt kia 8-9-16 2WelshR p126 MR21

BROCKLEBANK,Bertram Vincent Lt kia 1-8-17 2CldGds p51 CR Belgium106

BROCKLEBANK,Lawrence Seymour 2Lt kia 26-8-14 3 ATT1RLancs p58 CR France611,BROCKELBANK

BROCKLEBANK,Ralph Royds 2Lt dow 16-5-17 1RWelshF p97 CR France518

BROCKLEBANK,Ralph Eric Royds Maj ded 13-2-21 5Lpool p216 CR Ches193

BROCKLEBANK,Thomas Geoffrey Capt kia 5-8-16 277RFA p207 CR France141,dow

BROCKLEHURST,Archibald Henry Capt dow 29-7-16 1KRRC p149 CR France23

BROCKLEHURST,Edward Henry Capt kia 5-5-15 6Lpool p215 MR29

BROCKLEHURST,John Sidney T2Lt kld 1-11-15 14 att11Manch p154 CR Gallipoli27

BROCKLEHURST,Thomas Pownall TCapt kia 1-7-16 2RWSurr p55 CR France397

BROCKLEHURST,Wilfrid Stanley Maj 15-5-20 RWFus CR Wales537 Ex DerbyYeo

BROCKLESBY,Horace Markham 2Lt kia 1-7-17 113RFA p208 CR Belgium173

BROCKMAN,Albert John 2Lt kia 8-8-16 4RLancs p213 MR21

BROCKS,Archibald William T2Lt dow 10-3-18 PoW 3Ches att10Dev p95 CR Iraq8

BRODBECK,Edwin Charles 2Lt kia 26-7-18 7N&D p233 MR19

BRODBELT,Arthur Dell Lt dow 18-4-18 RGA 264SB p38 CR France98

BRODBELT,Guy Lt kia 14-4-16 9Lpool p216 CR France927

BRODHURST,Bernard Maynard Lucas Maj kia 27-4-15 IA 1/4GurkhaRif p274 CR Belgium92

BRODERICK,Herbert Thomas Lt dow 29-12-17 2/24Lond p252 CR Palestine3

BRODERICK,Thomas Joseph TLt kia 15-4-16 6RIrReg p88 CR France178

BRODIE,Allan TLt dow 27-7-16 13 att15HLI p162 CR France88

BRODIE,Charles Gordon Lt kia 23-5-17 5Lond att6RFC p18&246 CR Belgium11

BRODIE,Colin James 2Lt kia 9-9-16 1/4Lond p246 MR21

BRODIE,Douglas Edward TCapt kia 17-8-16 3 att1CamH p167 CR France432

BRODIE,Douglas Fontaine.MC.Lt kia 12-10-18 9HLI p240 CR France718

BRODIE,Duncan Smith T2Lt kia 15-6-18 8Y&L p158 CR Italy1

BRODIE,Ewen James Capt kia 12-11-14 1CamH p167 MR29

BRODIE,George T2Lt dow 2-8-17 8SfthH p164 CR Belgium8

BRODIE,Hugh Gordon Capt ded PoW 26-4-17 IA 103Mahrattas p274 CR Asia51

BRODIE,Hugh William TCapt kld 13-10-15 6EKent p57 MR19

BRODIE,John Capt dow 26-9-15 6RScotF p94 MR19

BRODIE,John 2Lt kia 13-11-16 4Beds p85 CR France220,Lt

BRODIE,John Miller T2Lt kia 15-5-18 Mddx att8Bn p146 CR France54

BRODIE,Mark Moyle T2Lt kia 7-1-16 10 att1SfthH p164 MR38

BRODIE,Mitchell Miller.MC.TLt dow 14-7-17 12NumbF p60 CR France145

BRODIE,Peter Bellinger Lt ded 12-8-16 4RWSurr att51ImpCamCps p212 CR Egypt9

BRODIE,Philip Wyndham Lt ded 18-11-18 1SfthH &RAF p164 CR Italy6,Capt

BRODIE,Sidney Edward T2Lt dow 17-4-17 17RFus p66 MR20

BRODIE,Walter Hamilton T2Lt kia 9-4-18 15RScots p53 CR France644

BRODIE,Walter Lorrain.VC.MC.ALtCol kia 23-8-18 2HLI p162 CR France745

BRODIE,William Alan 2Lt dow 13-5-18 3 att16RWelshF p97 CR France145

BRODIE,William Eastdale Lt kia 29-3-18 6ScotRif p224 CR Belgium8,1Bn

BRODIE-INNES,Ian Stuart.MID 2Lt mbk 25-9-15 8SomLI p256 MR19

BRODIGAN,Francis John Capt kld 9-5-15 1Glouc p106 MR22

BRODRIBB,William Carr Capt kld 26-8-14 3Manch p154 CR France716

BRODRICK,Edward TLt kia 31-7-17 13Manch p154 MR29,Capt

BRODRICK,Eric William 2Lt ded 22/23-7-16 PoW 5Yorks p221 CR Belgium132,dow

BROGDEN,Frederick Newman 2Lt kia 3-5-17 9EYorks att8TMB p83 MR20,8Bn

BROGDEN,Ingram Richard Rhodes TLt drd 15-4-17 RAMC p194 MR35

BROMBY,William Girdlestone Lt ded 29-5-21 10EYorks CR Yorks97

BROMET,John Neville Lt kia 30-11-17 63RFA p25 MR17,mbk

BROMFIELD,Harry Hickman.DSO.Maj kia 10-9-16 1WelshGds p53 MR21

BROMFIELD,William Henry 2Lt dow 31-10-18 RGA 278SB p38 CR France146

BROMHALL,John Coventry,MC&Bar.TLtAMaj kia 7-8-18 19MGC p181 CR France33

BROMHAM,Charles Adolphus Row Lt kia 17-10-18 5Dev attYLI p217 CR France190,2Lt

BROMILOW,John Nisbet Maj kia 1-7-16 Cmdg1RLancs p58 CR France742,2-7-16

BROMILY,James T2Lt kld 28-6-18 RASC MT RGA att391SB Amm Col p192 CR France770

BROMLEY,Cuthbert.VC.Tmaj drd 13-8-15 1LancF p92 MR4

BROMLEY,Hugh Frederic T2Lt kia 25-9-15 2RSuss p118 MR19

BROMLEY,John Edouard Marsden.DSO.TCaptAMaj kia 7-6-18 17/41RFA p25 CR France266

BROMLEY,John Ledger Lt ded 29-9-18 RASC MT &11RAF p192 MR20,kld Flying

BROMLEY-SMITH,H.R.2Lt ded 1-1-16 S p268

BROOK,Alexander.VD.LtCol dow 19-5-15 8RScots p211 CR France80,14-5-15

BROOK,Arthur Charles 2Lt kia 4-6-15 5Manch p236 CR Gallipoli2

BROOK,Cecil Frederick T2Lt ded 5-4-16 9 att8EYorks p83 CR Belgium11

BROOK,Charles William 2Lt kld 26-3-18 3WRid &RFC p15&115 CR Yorks644

BROOK,George William 2Lt ded 12-11-18 4WRid p269

BROOKE,Arthur Goulbourn T2Lt kld 10-12-16 RFC p2 CR Camb21

BROOKE,Cecil Berjew.DSO.2Lt kia 1-7-16 Yorks p90 CR France630,Charles Lt Ex Suff SR &1RWSurr

BROOKE,Cecil Rupert T2Lt kia 24-4-17 8GordH p166 MR20

BROOKE,Charles Pearson Joseph Lt kia 3-9-16 1Wilts p152 MR21

BROOKE,Clarence T2Lt kia 31-3-18 13EYorks p83 MR20

BROOKE,Cyril Thomthwaite 2LtACapt kia 22-8-17 3Dors att6SomLI p123 MR30

BROOKE,Frederick Arthur John Robertson TCapt kia 27-5-18 RAMC att1Wilts p194 MR18

BROOKE,George Lt dow 2-10-14 1IrGds SR p52 CR France1112,7-10-14

BROOKE,George Cecil.MID Maj kia 28-4-15 1BordR p116 CR Gallipoli3

BROOKE,George Miller Lt kia 25-4-18 1/7WYorks p218 CR Belgium104

BROOKE,George Townshend Capt kia 6-5-15 RE 1NMidFC p210 CR Belgium101,5-5-15

BROOKE,Gerald Douglas Capt kia 3-7-16 7Suff p78 MR21

BROOKE,Harold William TCapt kia 24-4-17 7EYorks p83 MR20

BROOKE,Henry Brian Capt dow 24-7-16 2GordH p166 CR Scot287

BROOKE,Henry Hastings Maj dow 19-2-20 4ConnRgrs CR Hamps220

BROOKE,Henry John 2Lt 27-2-20 Berks CR Ches51

BROOKE,Herbert Leonard 2Lt kia 12-4-18 7 att10Ess p232 MR27

BROOKE,James Anson Otho.VC.Capt kia 29-10-14 2GordH p166 CR Belgium116

BROOKE,John Josselyn 2Lt kia 4-10-17 2/6Suff att3/4RWSurr p218 MR30

BROOKE,Leonard.MC.2Lt kia 9-4-18 4LNLancs p234 CR France1106

BROOKE,Percy TLt.ACapt kia 28-3-18 WYorks att9TMB p81 CR France1185

BROOKE,Richard Reginald Maude.MID Capt kia 31-5-15 1 O&BLI p130 MR38

BROOKE,Thomas Wickham.MC.Capt dow 30-11-17 6Lond p246 CR France530

BROOKE,Victor Reginald.CIE.DSO.Maj ded 29-8-14 IA 9Lancers p22 CR France1236

BROOKE,William Alfred Cotterill 2Lt kia 14-6-15 8Lond p247 CR France554

BROOKE,William John Capt dow 9-4-18 3KSLI att21Mddx p144 MR32,Maj

BROOKE-MURRAY,Kenneth Algernon TCapt dow 23-9-16 RASC att15RFC p2 CR France102

BROOKE-TAYLOR,Arthur Cuthbert Lt 4-6-15 6Manch MR4

BROOKER,James T2Lt kia 2-12-17 2RB p178 MR30

BROOKES,Ben 2Lt kia 21-3-18 att1NStaffs p156 MR27

BROOKES,Eric Guy.DFC.Capt kia 8-8-18 Worc &65RAF CR France526

BROOKES,Gordon Byron TCapt kia 16-9-16 9 att6DCLI p114 MR21

BROOKES,Harry T2Lt dow 12-4-18 17LancF p92 CR France64

BROOKES,Henry Richard Lt kia 4-11-14 IA 101Grenadiers MR47 p274

BROOKES,Percy 2Lt kia 22-11-17 6Ches p222 CR Belgium112

BROOKES,Ronald Baines 2Lt kia 13-3-18 RFC p15 CR France1643

BROOKFIELD,Sydney Freeman TCapt kia 3-9-16 17N&D p133 MR21

BROOKING,Hugh Cyril Arthur Capt ded 31-5-18 NSomYeo p155 CR Somerset96

BROOKING,Walter Arthur 2Lt kia 19-1-16 RHA attRFC p2&25 CR France1050,Lt

BROOKS,Archibald Buckley Capt kia 7-10-17 2/6Manch p236 CR Belgium84

BROOKS,Bazil Benjamin Burgoyne Capt kia 23-7-16 4 O&BLI p231 CR France832

BROOKS,Charles Alfred Capt kia 8-7-17 Wilts attRFC p5 MR34

BROOKS,Colin Robert Percy.MC.Lt dow 2-4-18 3Huss att4MGC Cav p2&182 CR France880

BROOKS,Ernest William TLtACapt kia 20-9-17 6 O&BLI p130 CR Belgium83

BROOKS,Francis Cyril 2Lt kld 17-8-17 RFA &47RFC p5&25 CR Surrey160

BROOKS,Frank Smith T2Lt kia 1-7-16 20Manch p154 CR France397

BROOKS,Frederick Jacob 2Lt kia 13/15-11-16 4 att2SStaffs p122 CR France156,Fredrick Lt 13-11-16

BROOKS,George Thomas 2Lt kia 30-11-17 1/13Lond p249 MR17

BROOKS,George William T2Lt kia 29-5-18 20KRRC p149 CR France98

BROOKS,Horace William.MC.T2Lt kia 4-11-18 8SomLI p79 CR France521

BROOKS,John Lt&Adjt ded 28-10-17 RDC p253 CR Lancs256

BROOKS,Leonard Samuel TLt kia 9-5-18 A50RFA p25 CR Belgium11

BROOKS,Leonard William 2Lt kia 6-7-17 8Hamps attRFC p18&229 CR France161,4Bn

BROOKS,Leslie Lt kia 25-9-15 4WYorks attLincs p81 MR32

BROOKS,Reginald St.George T2Lt kia 26-9-15 97RFA p25 CR France219

BROOKS,Rowland Causer 2Lt kia 4-6-15 6Manch p236 MR4

BROOKS,Thomas Edward Lt kia 13-5-15 LeicYeo p204 MR29 &CR Belgium152

BROOKSBANK,Hugh Freeth Gilbert T2Lt kia 8-7-16 1Worc p108 MR21,7-7-16

BROOKSBANK,Hugh Geoffrey.MID 2Lt dow 16-12-14 Yorks p90 CR Yorks308,Godfrey

BROOKSBANK,Stamp Lt kia 26-9-15 3Yorks p90 MR19,Capt

BROOKSMITH,John Douglas.MC.Capt mbk 21-3-18 47RFA p256 MR20

BROOM,Cyril Thomas 2Lt ded 15-7-15 10HLI p162 CR France525

BROOM,Frederick John Maurice 2Lt kia 7-6-17 8Mddx p236 CR Belgium29

BROOM,Frederick Jordan T2Lt kia 1-7-16 2SfthH p164 CR France643

BROOM,Lewis John.MBE.Capt 12-4-18 4WelchR attKAR CR EAfrica92

BROOMAN,Edward James.MC.T2LtALt kia 1-4-17 16LancF p92 CR France672

BROOMAN-WHITE,Ronald George 2Lt dow 15-5-15 4RInniskF attRIrF p104 CR Belgium4

BROOME,Louis George 2Lt dow 5-6-15 2RScots p53 CR France102

BROOME,R.C.CIE.MajGen 26-8-15 Army Remount Dept India CR Asia9

BROOMFIELD,James Taylor T2Lt kia 3-12-16 12 att1Ess p131 CR France374

BROOMHALL,Harry 2Lt kia 22-3-18 8Worc att2RBerks p226 MR27

BROOMHALL,Oscar Arthur 2Lt dow 18-4-18 5Lpool att4RAF p255 CR France180,Lt

BROPHY,Ernest Gordon T2Lt kia 1-7-16 2WYorks p81 CR France296

BROPHY,John Bernard.MID 2Lt kld 24-12-16 2RFC p2 CR Lincs136,Lt

BROPHY,Thomas Joseph T2Lt kia 22-3-18 att2Leinst p174 MR27

BROSTER,Harold Broughton T2Lt kia 30-11-17 11KRRC p149 MR17

BROSTER,Robert Buck ACapt kia 11-10-18 4WRid p227 CR France612

BROTHERHOOD,Frank Ridgway T2Lt kia 15-9-17 GL &55RFC p5 CR France134

BROTHERS,Arthur Stanley TCapt kia 2-7-16 RE 178TC p43 CR France189

BROTHERS,Malam Capt kia 28-5-17 2/4ELancs p226 CR France163

BROTHERTON,Vincent T2Lt dow 14-10-16 1WYorks p81 CR France105

BROUGH,Alexander T2Lt kia 18-11-15 12ScotRif att6Y&L p103 CR Gallipoli27

BROUGH,James Lindsay T2Lt kia 1-7-16 15RScots p53 MR21

BROUGH,John.CMG.MVO.LtCol ded 29-7-17 RH&FA GSO HQ61Div p26 CR France134,dow

BROUGH,John William.MIDx2 Lt&QM ded 20-10-18 1/1StaffsYeo p205 CR Lebanon1

BROUGHTON,Coote Edgar Capt kia 6-10-19 IA 34Horse attBhopalLancers p274 MR43

BROUGHTON,Ernest Chamier LtCol ded 17-12-14 3Y&L p158 CR Mddx16

BROUGHTON,Gerald Filose Capt kia 11-7-17 IA 17Inf p274 CR EAfrica40

BROUGHTON,Hugo Delves TCapt kia 4/5-4-16 8Ches p95 MR38 Ex 1Bn

BROUGHTON,Norman Walford.DSO.MID TCapt kia 9-9-16 RAMC att73RFA p194 CR France397,10-9-16

BROUGHTON,Thomas Dugdale T2Lt dow 10-4-17 7YLI p142 CR France164

BROUGHTON-ADDERLEY,Peter Handcock.MC.2LtACapt dow 16-10-18 1ScotsGds p52 CR France380

BROUN,Ernest Scott Capt kia 30-10-14 Yorks p90 MR29,Scot

BROUN,Richard Clive McBryde TLt kia 6-12-15 6RDubF p176 MR37

BROUNGER,William Henry Prescott T2Lt kia 9-4-17 22NumbF p60 CR France265

BROUNSWORTH,Edmund Arthur 2Lt dow 27-5-16 1Leic p87

BROWETT,Archibald T2Lt kia 20-11-17 37MGC Inf p182 MR17,Ex 9Lond

BROWETT,Arnold Leslie Thackall Capt kia 5-7-16 2/7RWar p214 CR France705

BROWETT,Reginald 2Lt kia 26-9-17 2/9Lond p248 MR30

BROWETT,Thomas Norman Lt ded 30-10-18 5Ess att1/7KAR p232&268 CR EAfrica36

BROWN,Aitken Capt dow 21-4-18 5BlkW p230 CR France40,1/6Bn

BROWN,Alan Francis Donald T2Lt kia 8-9-16 1Glouc p106 MR21

BROWN,Alan Moray Capt.MC.kia 13-3-15 IA 47Sikhs p274 CR France279,12-3-15

BROWN,Albert Edward T2Lt kia 9-10-18 1Leic p87 CR France235

BROWN,Alexander T2Lt kia 28-4-17 16RScots p53 MR20

BROWN,Alexander Henry T2Lt kia 9-8-18 6RWKent attRE 87FC p140 CR France636

BROWN,Alexander Johnstone TLt dow 11-4-18 1/5SfthH p164 CR France40,Capt

BROWN,Alexander Russell.MID TCapt kia 18-8-16 7KOSB p101 CR France432,17-8-16

BROWN,Algernon James T2Lt dow 1-12-16 2RB p178 CR France145

BROWN,Allan George TLt kia 27-10-18 10NumbF p60 CR Italy7,Alan

BROWN,Allison T2Lt kia 26-10-17 GordH att2Bn p166 CR Belgium112

BROWN,Andrew Cranstoun see BROWNE,A.N.

BROWN,Andrew Norman.MC.Lt kia 27-5-18 6DLI p239 MR18,Capt

BROWN,Angus Graham Capt kia 1-9-18 20Lond p251 CR France439

BROWN,Anthony William Scudamore Lt kia 18-8-16 6 att3RB p178 CR France402

BROWN,Archibald.MC.T2Lt kia 20-4-18 14A&SH p173 CR France113

BROWN,Archibald Campbell Lt kia 27-5-18 A95RFA p207 CR France1332

BROWN,Archibald Dimock Montagu TCapt kia 23-10-16 3 att1RLancs p58 MR21

BROWN,Archibald Gibson Capt kia 25-5-15 9A&SH p243 CR Belgium113

BROWN,Archie Maynard 2Lt kia 6-4-18 RGA 126HB p38 CR France343

BROWN,Arnold Nimmo ACapt ded 8-9-19 RGA 13SB p262 CR Germany1

BROWN,Arthur T2Lt dow 5-10-17 1Lincs p74 CR France139,kia

BROWN,Arthur Anthony.MC.LtACapt ded 4-3-18 271RFA p207 CR Palestine9

BROWN,Arthur George Maj 20-3-21 IMD CR India97A

BROWN,Arthur Horace Mortimer 2Lt kia 10-7-16 27Manch p154 CR France393

BROWN,Arthur Lyster T2Lt kia 25-9-15 2RWSurr p55 MR19

BROWN,Arthur Roberts 2Lt kia 6-4-17 RFA &2RFC p5&26 MR20

BROWN,Austin Hanbury.DSO.MC.Maj kia 27-3-18 RE 2FC p43 MR20

BROWN,Benjamin Albert TLt dow 4-10-17 RE 253FC p43 CR Belgium16,TC

BROWN,Benjamin Ewart ACapt kia 9-9-16 Lincs att1RMunstF p74 MR21

BROWN,Bernard Loftus.MC.Lt kld 1-11-20 RGA 26HB MR40

BROWN,Bertram TCapt kia 3-9-16 16RB p178 MR21

BROWN,Cecil Abraham Lt kia 23-4-17 6N&D p233 CR France58,Arthur

BROWN,C.F.Lt kia 25-7-18 1/2DLI attRAF p160

BROWN,Charles.MM.2LtACapt kia 25-4-18 RGA 242SB p38 CR Belgium11

BROWN,Charles Arthur 2Lt kia 5-7-17 4YLI p235 CR Belgium173

BROWN,Charles James Wilkins 2Lt dow 22-4-18 RGA 73SB p38 CR France88,Lt

BROWN,Charles King Valentine Maj ded 25-10-18 IA 102Grenadiers p274 MR65

BROWN,Charles Lawrie 2Lt dow 18-6-16 9RScots p212 CR France85

BROWN,Charles Roydon.MC.MID Capt kia 14-4-17 13Ess p131 CR France604,1Bn late9&13Bn

BROWN,Charles Tolme 2Lt kia 17-3-17 5A&SH p243 CR France728

BROWN,Charles William T2Lt dow 23-5-17 6KOSB D'Coy p101 CR Scot713

BROWN,Christopher 2Lt ded 24-10-18 8Worc p226 CR France146

BROWN,Christopher Wilkinson Capt kia 1-5-16 3 att1RScotF p94 CR Belgium28

BROWN,Claude Algernon Felix TLt kia 26-12-16 GL &RFC p2&190

BROWN,Claude Fitzgerad Sedley 2Lt kia 19-10-16 9LNLancs p135 CR France446,Fitzgerald

BROWN,Claude Joseph John Lt ded 18-11-18 3Nhampt att1/2KAR p137&201 CR EAfrica52

BROWN,Clive Andrews Capt ded 7-11-18 RE p210 CR Surrey6

BROWN,Colin Selwyn Capt kia 1-7-16 11BordR p116 CR France293

BROWN,Daniel T2Lt kia 25-9-15 12HLI p162 MR19,Ex 9Bn

BROWN,David Lt ded 23-9-15 8HLI att7RScots p240 MR4

BROWN,David Douglas T2Lt kld 27-9-15 13RScots p53 MR19

BROWN,David Hepburn TCapt kia 25-9-15 6KOSB p101 CR France219

BROWN,David Westcott Capt kia 17-7-16 6Leic p87 MR21,14-7-16

BROWN,Denis Sidney Lt SelfInflictWound 11-10-19 IA 1/39GarhwalRif p274

BROWN,Donald Andrew 2Lt ded 22/23-7-16 PoW 9DLI p239 CR France705

BROWN,Donald Morton TLt kia 17-10-18 CamH att1Bn p167 CR France1268

BROWN,Douglas Crow Lt dow 13-9-17 3RScots attMGC Inf p53&182 CR France1361,2Bn

BROWN,Douglas Knox.MC.Lt kia 30-11-17 9HLI att217MGC Inf p186&240 MR17

BROWN,Douglas Paton McRae 2Lt kia 24-11-16 22Lond p251 CR Belgium167

BROWN,E.C.Lt kia 18-10-18 RWKent &RAF p140 CR France341

BROWN,Edgar Archer 2Lt kia 23-8-18 2BucksBn O&BLI p231 CR France745

BROWN,Edward TLt kia 7-8-17 18 att2RIrRif p169 CR Belgium19

BROWN,Edward Dell T2Lt kia 16-8-17 KRRC A'Coy att12Bn p149 MR30

BROWN,Edward Frederick Montagu Lt dow 8-1-18 1/1Herts p252 CR Belgium20

BROWN,Edward James 2Lt ded 14-11-18 IARO attCentLaboratoryBaghdad p274 CR Iraq8

BROWN,Edward John 2Lt kia 17-8-17 45RFC p5 CR Belgium11

BROWN,Edwin Charles 2Lt dow 10-8-18 RWKent att7Bn p140 CR France69

BROWN,Edwin Percival Wildman Lt kia 4-9-16 1Norf p73 CR France402

BROWN,E.L Sister 19-2-19 QAIMNS CR Sussex111

BROWN,Eric Francis TLtACapt dow 1-4-17 5Wilts p152 MR38

BROWN,Eric Howard TLt kia 22-10-17 10Ess p131 CR Belgium126

BROWN,Eric Landon.MC.MID Capt kia 18-8-15 4SuffYeo p205&217,4SuffR CR France924,4SuffR

BROWN,Eric Metcalfe TLt kia 29-9-17 MGC A'HB p182 CR Belgium112 A'TankCps

BROWN,Eric Russell Wilkie 2Lt ded 19-11-18 IA 2/30Punjabis p274 CR Egypt9

BROWN,Eric William 2Lt kia 3-5-15 5SLancs p230 MR29

BROWN,Ernest LtACapt kia 20-11-17 2N&D p133 CR France379

BROWN,Ernest Albert Lt ded 23-11-18 RGA 188SB p38 CR France403

BROWN,Ernest Edward Lt kia 8-5-16 1Wilts p152 CR France68

BROWN,Ernest James 2Lt kia 31-7-17 4RWelshF p223 MR29

BROWN,Ewart Cudemore Lt dedacc 14-8-17 RFC CR Lincs181 Ex PPCLI

BROWN,Foss Hunter 2Lt kia 31-7-17 RE 76FC p43 CR Belgium20

BROWN,Francis.MC.T2Lt kia 5-4-18 Lincs att63TMB p74 MR27

BROWN,Francis Alfred Joseph T2Lt kia 9-9-16 6Leinst att8RMunstF p174 MR21

BROWN,Francis Arthur Noel 2Lt kia 21-7-16 1/7Worc p226 MR21

BROWN,Francis Clement.MID Lt kia 8-12-17 16Lond p249 CR Palestine3

BROWN,Francis Wrentmore TLt dow 16-9-16 23Mddx p146 CR France105

BROWN,Frank Frederick.MC.Lt ded 21-2-19 32RGA 35SB p38 CR France63

BROWN,Fred 2Lt kia 11-12-15 1 O&BLI p130 CR Iraq1

BROWN,Frederick Anderson Lt kia 26-10-17 7NumbF p214 CR Belgium126

BROWN,Frederick Arthur T2Lt kia 13-11-16 7RFus p66 CR France339

BROWN,Frederick Charles 2Lt mbk 7-8-15 9N&D p256 MR4

BROWN,Frederick David 2Lt kia 8-3-17 13EYorks p83 MR21

BROWN,Frederick Francis T2Lt ded 28-9-18 4MGC p182 CR France84

BROWN,Frederick George Capt kia 4-11-14 IA 101Grenadiers MR47 p274

BROWN,Frederick Henry 2Lt kia 29-5-18 6 att1RB p178 CR France250

BROWN,Frederick Peter T2Lt dow 24-5-18 3 att10RWKent p140 CR France142

BROWN,Frederick Seddon Capt kia 26-5-15 5Manch p236 CR Gallipoli1

BROWN,Frederick Vincent Capt 35376 kia 1-9-18 NZFA p274 CR France745

BROWN,Frederick William Archer T2Lt kia 25-4-18 1Lincs p74 CR Belgium185

BROWN,G.B.DSO.LtCol 6-1-19 RFA CR Yorks501

BROWN,Geoffrey Hubert Lt kia 23-10-18 3 att2WelshR p126 CR France190

BROWN,George Capt kia 16/18-6-15 8Lpool p215 MR22

BROWN,George Alexander Capt ded 6-6-16 RE p43 CR Mddx77

BROWN,George Congdon T2Lt dow 8-5-17 11Worc p108 CR Greece7

BROWN,George Easter 2Lt drd 20-4-17 HAC p206 MR20

BROWN,George James Rankine T2Lt dow 21-5-17 2BlkW p128 CR Iraq5

BROWN,George Lothian TLt dow 15-11-17 LNLancs att1Bn p135 CR Belgium11

BROWN,George Miller.MC.Lt kia 28-11-17 12Lancers p22 MR17

BROWN,George Russell TLt kia 11-2-18 18NumbF p60 CRFrance592

BROWN,George Sydney Robert Johnston 2Lt dow 22-5-15 3 att1RScotF p94 CR France102

BROWN,George Trevor Lt kld 12-2-17 6WelshR &RFC p18&230 CR Wales171

BROWN,George West Lt ded 23-2-18 Lincs 1GarrBn p74 CR Asia60,William 24-2-18

BROWN,Gerald Brindley Lt ded 21-4-18 5Manch p236 MR34

BROWN,Gerald Dick.MC.LtAMaj kia 14-4-18 3Wilts p152 MR32,1Bn

BROWN,Gerald Knapton Lt kia 3-5-17 2/6WYorks p218 CR France568

BROWN,Gilfrid Elliott T2Lt kia 18-11-16 11BordR p116 CR France803

BROWN,Gordon Hargreaves Capt kia 29-10-14 1CldGds p51 MR29

BROWN,Granville Albert Lt ded 18-2-19 RAOC 69XCD p198 CR Belgium11

BROWN,G.Selwyn 2Lt ded 25-7-19 RGA p262

BROWN,Guy Frank Courtney 2Lt dow 11-5-17 2/22HAC p206 CR France40

BROWN,H.W.S.Maj 19-1-17 Mddx CR Lond8

BROWN,Harold.DSO.MC.Maj kia 23-3-18 5Yorks p220 MR27

BROWN,Harold Atherton 2Lt kia 15-5-15 2Leic p87 MR22

BROWN,Harold Halstead 2Lt kia 18-7-16 3 att1GordH p166 MR21

BROWN,Harold James.MC.Capt dow 10-1-20 12SWBord CR Wales17

BROWN,Harold Masters.MC.T2Lt dow 9-7-16 5RBerks p138&258 CR France40

BROWN,Harold Montague 2Lt kia 9-4-16 3ELancs C'Coy p110 MR38

BROWN,Harold Vernon T2Lt kia 3-5-17 8 att11ESurr p112 MR20

BROWN,Herbert 2Lt ded 6-6-19 IARO att1/30Punjabis p274 MR65

BROWN,Herbert James Lt kia 6-11-17 1/7RWelshF p223 CR Palestine1

BROWN,Horace Leslie 2Lt dow 11-3-18 4EKent p212 CR France345

BROWN,Horace Manton.MC.Lt dow 14-4-18 4Suff p217 CR Belgium18

BROWN,Hubert William Lt dow 19-9-14 RIrReg att2NigR p88 CR WAfrica57

BROWN,Hugh T2Lt kia 31-7-17 6RIrRif p169 MR29

BROWN,Hugh Alexander T2Lt kia 14-7-16 9ScotRif p103 CR France399

BROWN,Ian Macdonald TCapt kia 15-11-16 RAMC att190RFA p194

BROWN,Ian Macgregor Knox 2Lt kia 25-9-15 11RScots p53 MR19

BROWN,James Capt kia 15-6-15 6ScotRif p224 CR France549

BROWN,James Alfred 2Lt kia 25-7-16 RFC SR p2 MR20

BROWN,James Cartmell Dennison 2Lt dow 28-4-15 5DLI p239 CR France200,27-4-15

BROWN,James Cavet 2Lt mbk 24-3-18 5A&SH p257

BROWN,James Ferguson T2Lt kia 24-4-17 14 att1/6Glouc p106 MR21

BROWN,James Hardie,MC Capt dow 7-6-18 1/6A&SH p243 CR France31

BROWN,James Herbert T2Lt dow 8-10-17 Yorks Res att2Bn p90 CR Belgium138,2WYorks

BROWN,James Leonard 2Lt kld 29-3-18 RFC p15 see BROWNE,James Lawrence

BROWN,James McDonald T2Lt kia 21-3-18 10RB p178 MR27

BROWN,James Macpherson Gordon Lt kia 6-5-15 3 att2KOSB p101 MR29

BROWN,James Stanley Lt kld 20-10-18 5ELancs &RAF p255&226

BROWN,James Sutherland TLt kia 30-9-17 SL att3NigR p201 MR52

BROWN,James Sydney T2Lt kia 20-10-18 12Manch att15Ches p154 CR Belgium402

BROWN,James Tod 2Lt dow 27-4-18 4BlkW p230 CR France100

BROWN,James Turner TLt drd 4-5-17 RAMC p194 CR Italy13

BROWN,James Westhall Lt kia 14-5-17 RFA 2/3HighlandHB attRFC p261&269 CR France418

BROWN,James William 2Lt dow 2-11-14 26RFA p26 MR29

BROWN,James William,MC Capt kia 21-3-17 11RScots p53 MR20

BROWN,John.MID T2Lt dow 11-8-16 RFA&RFC p2&26 CR Egypt2

BROWN,John T2Lt drd 4-5-17 3RWelshF GarrBn p97 CR Italy14

BROWN,John.MC&Bar.Capt kia 21-3-18 17RIrRif p169 MR27,8 att1Bn

BROWN,John.MC.Capt kia 21-3-18 2/7Manch p237 MR27

BROWN,John T2Lt dow 26-3-18 12HLI p162 CR France232,Lt

BROWN,John Lt kia 11-4-18 6SfthH p241 CR Belgium111

BROWN,John Capt kia 20-7-18 1/4GordH p241 CR Frnce622

BROWN,John Lt ded 27-6-19 4RScots p269 CR Scot262BROWN,John Albert Hunter ACapt kia 18-8-16 3 att1GordH p166 MR21

BROWN,John Alexander TLtACapt dow 22-10-18 9 att13RB p178 CR France287

BROWN,John Ambrose T2Lt kia 12-3-17 7YLI p142 CR France513

BROWN,John Arbuckle T2Lt dow 3-7-16 16HLI p162 CR France296

BROWN,John Carolan.MC.LtACapt kia 8-8-18 4ConnRgrs &1TankCps p172&188 CR France589

BROWN,John Cuthbert Backhouse TLt kia 29-9-18 Mddx att1Bn p146 CR France407

BROWN,John Dunlop 2Lt dow 3-12-17 6HLI p240 CR Belgium18

BROWN,John Edward LtACapt kia 14-9-18 D113RFA p26 CR Belgium188

BROWN,John Edward Guy Capt kia 22-2-15 2 att1RWKent attRBerks p140 CR Belgium133

BROWN,John Gordon Lt dow 5-2-17 SuffYeo p205 CR France624

BROWN,John Gordon.MC.Capt kia 5-10-18 RFus attRFA 47DivArtyHQ p66 CR France82

BROWN,John Rankine Capt dow 23-4-17 7HLI p240 CR Palestine2

BROWN,John Ritchie TLt dow 7-11-16 RAMC p194

BROWN,John Samuel 2Lt kia 18-5-17 RGA 61SB p38 CR France581

BROWN,John William.MC.T2Lt dow 1-8-17 Yorks Res att2Bn p90 CR Belgium18

BROWN,John William 2Lt kia 16-8-17 1/9 att1/5Lond p248 MR29

BROWN,John William 2Lt kia 16-10-17 7Yorks p90 MR30

BROWN,John William.MM.2Lt dow 11-4-18 10 att5Yorks p90 CR France1092

BROWN,Joseph Jackson TLt kia 5-8-18 2RScotF p94 CR France25

BROWN,J.W.Lt 10-11-14 RFA CR Belgium58

BROWN,Keith Andrews LtTCapt dow 22-9-18 1RWSurr A'Coy p55 CR France906

BROWN,Kenneth Ashby Capt 14-4-17 5ScotRif CR France434

BROWN,Kenneth Edward.MC&Bar.Capt dow 12-4-18 PoW 2/4 O&BLI p231 CR France934,13-4-18

BROWN,Kenneth Wallace 2Lt ded 24-8-17 6RWar p269 CR Numb39

BROWN,Laurence Clerke Lt kia 11-10-15 3 att1Glouc p106 MR19

BROWN,Lawrence Crawford T2Lt kia 16-8-17 8RInniskF p104 MR30,Laurence

BROWN,Lawrence Smith Blanche.MC.T2Lt kia 28-11-17 97MGC p182 CR Belgium63,Laurence 27-11-17

BROWN,Leonard James 2Lt kia 19-8-18 1ESurr att2RFus p112 MR32

BROWN,Lionel George Henry 2Lt ded 8-12-17 GL &52RFC p5 MR20

BROWN,Louis Foster TLt dow 15-5-18 115MGC p182 CR France13,14-5-18 38MGC

BROWN,Macdonald Warriner TCapt kia 12-10-16 17Manch p154 MR21

BROWN,Miles Wheelton Lt kia 25-9-15 2Leic p87 CR France1157

BROWN,Norman Algernon 2Lt ded 1-3-19 4Lond p246 CR Beds65,28-2-19

BROWN,Norman Watson 2LtTLt dow 1-5-17 3ELancs att103MGC p110&182 CR France113

BROWN,Osbert Harold.DSO.MC.TCapt kia 1-11-16 11Suff p78 CR France83

BROWN,Oscar Lt kia 24-4-15 IA 7Lancers att4DragGds p274 CR Belgium20

BROWN,Osmond Pickard 2Lt dow 31-7-17 3 att11RWKent p140 CR Belgium118,kia

BROWN,Oswald Stanley 2Lt kia 22-12-15 3 att1BlkW p128 MR19

BROWN,P.W.SubCdr 16-4-20 IndiaP&T Dept MR43

BROWN,Philip Anthony TLt kia 4-11-15 13DLI p160 CR France82

BROWN,Phillip Kentish 2Lt kia 13-10-15 9 att5Lincs p74 MR19

BROWN,Ralph Adair 2Lt kia 1-7-16 1/14Lond A'Coy p149 MR21

BROWN,Reginald Charles T2Lt kia 21-2-18 80RFC p15 CR France255

BROWN,Reginald Roy.MC.LtAMaj ded 31-10-18 RHA 14ArmyBde p26 CR France332

BROWN,Richard Clerke T2Lt kia 20-8-16 RE 103FC p43

BROWN,Richard Gavin Lt ded 14-2-16 RAMC p267 CR Hamps10

BROWN,Richard Stanley 2Lt ded 9-2-16 14Ches p95 CR Lancs7

BROWN,Richard Walker 2LtACapt kia 9-4-17 3 att2Wilts p152 CR France162,Walter

BROWN,Robert Lt ded 6-2-19 1/7HLI p254&265 CR Scot674

BROWN,Robert Lt ded 13-6-21 DCLI attS&T Cps MR43

BROWN,Robert Alexander 2Lt kia 16-9-18 14Lond p249 CR Belgium192,17-9-18

BROWN,Robert Cunningham 2Lt dow 11-4-17 9RScots p212 CR France95

BROWN,Robert Henry 2Lt dow 16-1-17 1/5WRid p227 CR France120

BROWN,Robert Laurie 2Lt kia 19-7-18 BlkW att8Bn p128 CR France324

BROWN,Robert Stanley 2Lt kia 1-7-16 16HLI p162 CR France293

BROWN,Robin Lewis Campbell T2LtALt dow 8-6-17 GL RFA attX8TMB p190 CR Belgium11

BROWN,Roland 2Lt kia 13-7-18 4Yorks p220 CR Belgium115

BROWN,Samuel T2Lt dow 27-9-18 CamH Res att11Bn p167 CR France25

BROWN,Sidney Frederick 2Lt ded 21-7-17 SR 21RFC p5 CR Belgium125,Capt

BROWN,Sidney Frederick 2Lt kia 15-5-18 RGA 239SB p209 CR France1182

BROWN,Sidney Wilfred 2Lt mbk 5-9-18 11ELancs p256 MR32BROWN,Stanley Newman T2Lt kia 27-8-18 RBerks att8Bn p138 CR France401

BROWN,Stewart Patrick T2Lt dow 31-12-17 RE 248FC p43 CR France398

BROWN,S.V.2Lt ded 9-11-18 3LancF p92 CR Staffs109

BROWN,Sylvester Samuel.MC.Lt kia 25-4-18 9Lond att&MGC p186&248 MR27

BROWN,Theodore Anthony.MC.2Lt kia 15-4-17 3 att1EKent p57 MR19,Capt

BROWN,Thomas 2Lt kia 4-9-16 1Norf p73 CR France402

BROWN,Thomas Campbell TLt ded 17-12-17 RASC p192 CR Surrey55

BROWN,Thomas Elliot Thorburn Lt dow 20-9-18 3KOSB p101

BROWN,Thomas Fletcher 2Lt kia 30-5-15 7Manch p237 CR Gallipoli2

BROWN,Thomas Muirhead TLt dow 16-4-18 RE 9 ObsGrp 1FdSurvCo p43 CR France102

BROWN,Tom T2Lt kia 13-11-16 10 att7ELancs p110 CR France384

BROWN,Valentine Oakley Lt kia 9-10-18 3DragGds p21

BROWN,Walter T2Lt kia 18-8-16 2A&SH p173 CR France432

BROWN,Walter Hugh SubCdr ded 23-2-19 IA S&TCps p274 CR Iraq6

BROWN,Walter Ravenhill.MC.Lt kia 21-11-17 7WYorks p218 CR France905

BROWN,Walter Sidney LtCol kia 6-7-16 Wilts p152 CR France246

BROWN,Wilfred Stephenson Capt ded 27-3-19 RAMC 19CCS p194 CR France85

BROWN,William 2Lt kia 5-10-17 1/4 att6BlkW p230 CR France592

BROWN,William T2Lt kia 1-3-18 3RMunstF att2RinniskF p175 CR Frnce1061

BROWN,William Lt kia 11-8-18 6RScots p211CR France360

BROWN,William Chap4Cl ded 10-3-19 RAChDept p268 CR Hamps1

BROWN,William Archibald Ross T2Lt kia 22-11-17 H'TankCps p188 MR17

BROWN,William Charles Lt ded 7-11-18 RGA 387SB p38 CR Kent267

BROWN,William Clark 2Lt kia 21-5-17 4RScots p211 CR France522,21-5-18

BROWN,William Douglas Capt dow 29-12-17 LanarkYeo p204 MR34

BROWN,William Elmer TLt dow 18-5-18 RAMC att10FA p194 CR France10,att2WRid

BROWN,William George Charteris LtCol ded 26-5-19 RE p43 CR Sussex178

BROWN,William Gordon 2Lt kld 7-5-18 GL &19RAF p190 CR France95,kia

BROWN,William Herbert 2Lt dow 19-7-18 18DLI p160 MR32

BROWN,William Joseph Lt kld 21-2-18 1Cty of LondYeo &RAF p18&204 CR Egypt9

BROWN,William Leonard 2Lt kia 25-9-15 6N&D p233 CR Belgium82

BROWN,William Noel Sneade Lt ded 1-8-19 4SomLI p269 CR Berks71

BROWN,William Robertson T2Lt dow 30-9-17 1RScotF p94 CR Belgium16

BROWN,William Sandilands LtACapt kia 14-10-18 3NStaffs p156 CR Belgium112

BROWN,William Wallace Lt kia 28-6-15 7ScotRif B'Coy p224 CR Gallipoli6

BROWN,Winifred Maud Miss drd 31-12-17 VAD p200 CR Egypt1

BROWN,Wynyard Keith.MID Capt kia 4-6-15 IA 1/5GurkhaRif att9WYorks p274 MR4

BROWN,W.J.H.Capt kia 4-9-16 3 att15Norf p73 MR21

BROWN-CONSTABLE,John Cecil Lt kia 1-7-16 14Lond p249 CR France798

BROWNBRIDGE,Herbert Edward T2Lt ded 7-12-18 47MGC p182 CR France34

BROWNE,Alfred James Haslip 2Lt dow 23-4-17 8SStaffs p122 MR20

BROWNE,Andrew Cranstoun T2Lt kia 2-7-16 8SStaffs p122 CR France397,BROWN

BROWNE,Archibald Trevor TCapt kia 29-9-18 20DLI p160 CR Belgioum111

BROWNE,Arthur Davies Lang 2Lt kia 11-9-17 3 att1ConnRgrs p172 MR38

BROWNE,Arthur George 2Lt kia 20-10-14 N&D p133 MR32

BROWNE,Arthur Richard Howe Lt kld 5-12-15 RFC p1 CR France518

BROWNE,Bernard Score.MC.TCapt kia 15-4-18 RAMC att2Ches p194 MR37

BROWNE,Charles Eric Wyndham 2Lt dow 24-10-16 2Ess p131 CR France105

BROWNE,Charles Nicholas Foster 2Lt kia 13-5-15 1Drags p21 CR Belgium2

BROWNE,Charles Pierson Capt dow 11-4-15 IA CpsofGuides att15Lancers p274 CR France924

BROWNE,Dominick Augustus Capt&Adjt kia 1-7-16 1RIrRif p169 MR21

BROWNE,Frank Douglas Maj dow 17-1-16 IA 56Rif p274 CR Iraq5

BROWNE,Frederick MacDonnell,DSO Maj dow 1-10-15 RE 38FC p43 CR France98,Macdonell

BROWNE,Geoffrey Dennis.MID Maj kia 19-9-16 C240RFA p206 CR France251

BROWNE,George Brownlie T2Lt kia 7-2-16 10 att9BlkW p128 CR France423

BROWNE,George Buckston.DSO.LtCol ded 6-1-19 RH&FA p261&269,Maj

BROWNE,George Edwin TLt dow 21-1-18 RFC p15 CR France446

BROWNE,Gordon Stewart Lt dow 27-11-14 1Wilts p152 CR Kent63

BROWNE,Harold Vernon Capt dow 7-9-15 DorsYeo p203 CR Gallipoli27

BROWNE,Henry Arthur T2Lt kia 26-10-18 Ess att2Bn p131 CR France1266

BROWNE,Herbert Maxwell T2LtALt kia 26-3-17 1/5Ess p131 CR Palestine8B

ROWNE,James Lawrence 2Lt kld 29-3-18 11ELancs attRFC p254&15,Leonard CR Lancs474

BROWNE,John Hazell T2Lt kia 20-4-16 12 att9RWar p64 MR38,18-4-16

BROWNE,Langford Kyffin T2Lt kia 9-4-17 32 att25NumbF p60 CR France265

BROWNE,Lionel Charles 2Lt kia 29-6-17 1/7N&D p233 CR France570,Lt 30-6-17

BROWNE,Lord Alfred Eden.DSO.ALtCol kia 27-8-18 HQ 186RFA p26 CR France54

BROWNE,Maurice.MID Capt kia 19-9-18 IARO att92Punjabis p274 CR Palestine9

BROWNE,Maurice Henry Dermot.Hon.MID Lt kia 29-9-15 1CldGds p51 CR France423

BROWNE,Maximilian Herbert.MC.TLtACapt kld 21-6-18 RIrRif att108TMB p169 CR France142,Maximillian

BROWNE,Montague Bernard 2Lt dow 30-4-16 8N&D p233 CR Ireland5

BROWNE,Percival Leathley Capt kia 9-8-15 6Lincs p74 CR Gallipoli5

BROWNE,Peter 2Lt kia 1-10-18 4 att6ConnRgrs p172 CR Belgium157,Lt

BROWNE,Robert Geoffrey.DSO.Maj ded 1-11-18 Manch p154 CR France1858

BROWNE,W.L.LtCol 6-2-20 RGA CR Lond28

BROWNE,William Angus TLt kia 21-9-17 8RInniskF &53RFC p5&104 CR France705

BROWNE,William Lindsay T2Lt dow 5-7-16 8YLI p142 CR France74

BROWNFIELD,Reginald John(Roy).MID Capt kia 18-12-14 2RWar p64 MR32

BROWNING,Charles Hunter Capt kia 26-8-14 124/28RFA p26 CR France716

BROWNING,Charles Stuart Capt kia 10-12-16 IA 129Baluchis p274 CR EAfrica38 &CR Tanzania1

BROWNING,Edwin Ormonde T2Lt kia 20-4-16 11 att7Glouc p106 MR38

BROWNING,Ernest George 2Lt dow 19-7-17 14Lond p249 CR France512

BROWNING,George Howard T2Lt kia 13-3-18 7 att1ELancs p110 CR France616

BROWNING,George Stanier TCapt ded 25-2-16 SL p201&257 CR Eire163,Stamer

BROWNING,James Alexander.MID Maj kia 31-10-14 2DragGds p20 CR Belgium89

BROWNING,Oakley Alsop 2Lt kld 11-8-17 GL &RFC p5 CR Yorks178

BROWNING,Reginald Arthur.MC.T2Lt dow 10-4-17 20NumbF p60 CR France53

BROWNING,Reginald Gordon Snell Capt kia 2-10-15 6WelshR p230 MR19

BROWNING,Stanley Forrester TCapt kia 3-5-17 GL &41RFC p5 CR Belgium125

BROWNING-PATERSON,Norman Alexander Capt kia 21-7-16 RFA &RFC p2&26 MR20

BROWNLEE,Wilfred Methven 2Lt ded 12-10-14 3Dors p123 CR Glouc5

BROWNLESS,John Wilson Lt dow 16-6-15 RAVC p198 CR Gallipoli3

BROWNLIE,John Reid T2Lt kia 29-6-16 11 att1ScotRif p103 CR France765

BROWNLIE,William.MC.TCapt kia 25-3-18 RAMC att13Yorks p194 CR France434

BROWNLOW,Charles Henry.GCB.Sir.FldMar ded 5-4-16 Commdg20Punjabis CR Berks47

BROWNLOW,Wilfred Herbert Cecil Capt kia 28-5-18 NumbF 2att12/13Bn p60 CR France1331

BROWNLOW,William Lionel 2Lt kia 9-5-15 NumbF att2BlkW p60 CR France631

BROWNRIGG,John Huleath Lt kia 14-4-15 2Norf p73 CR Iraq6

BROWNRIGG-JAY,George Harvey TLt kia 21-9-18 124MGC p182 CR France364

BROWNSON,Alfred Reginald TLt kia 18-9-18 11WelshR p126 CR Greece5

BROWNSON,Roger Dawson Duffield Capt ded 21-10-18 RASC p192 MR43,RAMC

BROWNSWORD,Douglas Anderson Capt dow 25-12-17 RASC p253 CR Greece22

BROWNSWORTH,E.A.2Lt dow 27-5-16 1Leic CR Belgium11

BROWSE,Reginald T2Lt kia 25-4-18 9ScotRif p103 MR30

BROXUP,John William T2Lt dow 24-4-17 10RWelshF p97 CR Lancs427

BRUCE,Alexander Angus 2Lt kia 24-6-18 B156RFA p26 CR Belgium36

BRUCE,Alexander Charles Arbuthnot.MID Capt kia 23-4-16 RASC p253 CR Egypt2

BRUCE,Andrew Moffat 2Lt kia 29-9-18 9HLI p240 CR France663

BRUCE,Bethune Duncan TCapt kia 27-9-15 13RScots p53 MR19

BRUCE,Charles James 2Lt dow 20-5-17 ACycCps 52Div p244 CR Egypt9

BRUCE,Charles William Capt kld 22-11-17 GordH &RFC p5&166 CR Essex86

BRUCE,Christopher Yule T2Lt kia 28-3-18 RE 176TC p43 CR France68

BRUCE,Colin TLt dow 5-9-18 14HLI p162 CR France52,6Bn

BRUCE,Douglas Fraser T2Lt kia 10-7-16 13RB p178 CR France832

BRUCE,Edward Tyrrell T2Lt dow 9-6-18 8MGC Inf p182 CR France622

BRUCE,Eric T2Lt ded 17-11-16 11 att2BlkW p128 CR Iraq5

BRUCE,Ernest John Webster.MC.Capt ded 17-4-19 94RFA p261 CR Lond8

BRUCE,George James.DSO.MC.TCapt kia 2-10-18 GL 109InfBde 36Div p190 CR Belgium157,BdeMaj Ex 13RIrRif

BRUCE,George McDonald Lt ded 18-2-19 4A&SH attCamH p173 CR Belgium316,MacDonald

BRUCE,Harry Kendal Walpole.MC.Maj kia 1-2-17 IA 1/2GurkhaRif p274 CR Iraq5

BRUCE,Henry Lyndhurst.Hon.Capt kia 14-12-14 3 att2RScots p53 MR29

BRUCE,Herbert William T2Lt kia 17-2-17 2BlkW p128 CR Iraq5

BRUCE,Jack Curtis 2Lt kia 25-3-18 2/4Leic p254 MR20

BRUCE,James 2LtACapt kia 25-7-17 256RFA p26 CR Belgium5

BRUCE,James Anderson Lt ded 6-1-19 AyrYeo &RAF p203&258

BRUCE,Jasper.MID Lt ded 17-2-19 2Remounts RASC attChes p95 CR France85

BRUCE,John Elliot Lidderdale Maj kia 29-5-15 26RGA p38 CR Gallipoli30

BRUCE,John Fryer 2Lt dow 28-2-18 2A&SH p173 CR Belgium3

BRUCE,John Gardiner Lt kia 14-4-18 ScotHorse att1ScotRif p205 MR32

BRUCE,John Russel TMaj kia 1-7-16 15RScots p53 Mr21

BRUCE,Jonathan Maxwell Maj kia 24-11-14 IA 107Pnrs p274 CR France80

BRUCE,Malcolm Ronald 2Lt kia 22-8-17 14Lond p249 CR Belgium125

BRUCE,Norman Martin TLt kia 7-8-15 6Yorks p90 MR4

BRUCE,Oliver T2Lt dow 9-6-18 PoW 2RB p178 CR France34

BRUCE,Philip Thomson Lt ded 30-5-18 10Lpool &43RAF p216,269&258,P.John MR20 Ex 87Sqn

BRUCE,Philip Thomerson 2Lt kia 31-5-18 10Lpool &RAF See Above

BRUCE,Robert.Hon.Capt kia 26-8-14 2A&SH p173 CR France716

BRUCE,Robert Lt dow 25-9-15 16LondRFA p207 CR France219

BRUCE,Robert 2Lt ded 7-7-16 IARO att14S&TCps p274 CR Iraq5,Lt

BRUCE,Robert James 2Lt kia 2-2-18 6SStaffs p229 CR France1483

BRUCE,Robert Lloyd TLt kia 19-11-16 11ScotRif p103 CR Greece6

BRUCE,Robert Stuart Malcolm T2Lt kld 17-8-17 GL att111RFC p5 CR Palestine2

BRUCE,Stanley Malcolm Maj kia 25-5-18 IA 37 att15Lancers

BRUCE,Thomas Robert Capt ded 8-2-17 14Huss p22 CR Iraq5

BRUCE,Vincent Connell Lt kia 26-3-16 5GordH p242 MR20,Ex 13RScots

BRUCE,Wallace Edward Lt kia 31-7-17 1RFus p67 MR29

BRUCE,William.MC.2Lt kia 3-12-18 RE 206FC p210 CR Belgium337,dedacc

BRUCE,William Arthur McCrae.VC.Lt kia 19-12-14 IA 59Rif p274 MR28

BRUCE,William George Lt kia 25-4-18 RE att156RFA p210 MR30

BRUCE-CLARK,William Robert.MBE.Capt ded 1-12-18 14Lond &RAF p255 CR Camb16

BRUCE-LOCKHART,Norman Douglas Stewart Lt kia 25-9-15 7SfthH p164 MR19

BRUDENELL-BRUCE,James Ernest John Lt dow 11-4-17 1NhamptYeo p204 CR France113

BRUFTON,Howard Charles 2Lt kia 9-7-17 20RB &47RFC p18&244 CR Greece1,8-7-17

BRUFTON,Wilfred Eustace 2Lt dow 3-9-18 119/27RFA p26 CR France156,5-9-18

BRUMAN,Albert Victor T2Lt dow 31-5-18 19MGC Inf p182 CR France1693 &34

BRUMBLEY,Walter James Joshua.MC.2Lt kia 27-3-18 3 att7Norf p73 MR27

BRUNDLE,Henry Carlton Bulman LtTCapt kia 9-10-17 12LancF p92 MR37

BRUNDRETT,George Frederick 2Lt dow 24-8-18 5Ches att7KSLI p222 CR France145

BRUNGER,Robert.DSO.Capt kia 8-10-18 9Norf p73 CR France375

BRUNNER,Cecil Heywood Capt dow 25-10-17 RFA p207 CR Belgium16

BRUNNER,Francis Wilfred Maj kia 11-8-15 RE 67FC p43 CR Gallipoli5

BRUNO,Carlo TLt kia 29-4-16 RFC p2,261kld&268,CaptEAUL SL CR EAfrica13

BRUNSDEN,Edward James T2Lt dow 25-4-17 45MGC Inf p182 CR France113

BRUNSDON,Henry George 2Lt dow 24-4-17 1/9RScots p212 CR France53

BRUNSKILL,James Harold Capt kia 29-9-17 RASC NCycBatt p253 2entries CR France1361,ACycCps

BRUNSKILL,John Jesmond T2Lt kia 23-4-17 4Worc p108 MR20 &CR France1896,44Bn

BRUNSTROM,Waldemar.MC.2Lt kia 19-8-18 C223RFA p208 CR France1016,18-8-18

BRUNT,Henry John Francis Lt kia 25-9-15 3 att1RWelshF p97 MR19

BRUNT,John Jarvis 2Lt kia 24-3-18 12 att10RInniskF p104 CR France1170

BRUNT,William Edward T2Lt kia 1-7-16 22Manch p154 CR France397

BRUNTON,Douglas Capt kia 9-10-17 HAC p206 MR30

BRUNTON,Edward Benjamin Durnford 2Lt kia 13-11-16 17Mddx p146 MR21

BRUNTON,Edward Henry Pollock TLt kia 8-10-15 RAMC att4GrenGds p194 CR France423

BRUNTON,George Lt dow 11-4-18 4 att8RScots p211 CR France88

BRUNTON,Hereward T2Lt kia 1-7-16 17HLI p162 MR21

BRUNTON,James McLeod 2Lt kia 1-8-17 6RScots p211 MR34

BRUNTON,Theodore Stuart Lt ded 3-6-19 IARO attS&M p274 MR65,13-6-19

BRUNWIN-HALES,Greville Oxley Capt kia 24-3-17 8Ess att13RFC p18&232 CR France95

BRUNWIN-HALES,Henry Tooke 2Lt kia 13-10-15 1/4Lincs p217 CR France423

BRUTON,Basil Vassar Capt kia 15-6-18 1/5Glouc p225 CR Italy2,dow

BRUTON,Thomas A.MM.2Lt kia 1-9-18 6 att4Worc p108 CR France285

BRUTTON,Eric West.MC.Lt kia 14-4-18 3Dev D'Coy attMGC p76&182 MR32

BRUTTON,Robert Hall.TD.Maj ded 15-1-16 1/5SomLI p218 MR65

BRUTY,Edward Douglas T2Lt kia 15-10-17 11NumbF p60 MR30,4Bn

BRYAN,Alfred.MC.Lt kia 23-8-18 3 att2HLI p162 CR France745

BRYAN,Cecil Clive.DSO.Maj kia 11-8-17 RE 490FC p209 CR Belgium15

BRYAN,Frederick Stawell.MC.TCapt kia 23-11-17 15 att21Mddx p146 MR17

BRYAN,Sterry James ACapt kia 8-2-17 1HAC p206 CR France339

BRYAN,Sydney Arthur T2Lt kia 1-7-16 9Y&L p158 MR21

BRYANS,John Lt dow 28-10-17 2/5LNLancs p234 CR Belgium16

BRYANT,Alan,DSO MajTLtCol kia 17-10-17 1Glouc p106 CR Belgium85

BRYANT,Alfred Francis Maj dow 26-11-17 RA attAyrshireRHA p26 CR Palestine9 ,kia

BRYANT,Frederick James Mansell 2Lt kia 26-3-17 4WelshR p230 MR34

BRYANT,Frederick Vivian James 2Lt ded 28-3-19 RGA p262 CR Herts12

BRYANT,George Herbert.OBE.MID HonMaj kia 1-8-18 RE p43 CR France34

BRYANT,Harvey.MC.2Lt kia 12-9-18 Hamps att2/4Bn p120 CR France530

BRYANT,Henry Grenville.DSO.Capt dow 1-5-15 2KSLI p144 CR Belgium383

BRYANT,John Evelyn TCapt kia 4-8-16 6 O&BLI p130 CR France643

BRYANT,Oliver Mackensie Beadon Lt kld 11-12-16 2/2KAR p201 CR EAfrica38 &CR Tanzania1

BRYANT,Reginald Eyre T2LtACapt kia 20-1-17 14DLI p160 CR France114

BRYANT,Richard Leslie Algernon 2Lt dow 23-5-17 7Suff attRGA 35TMB p78 CR France40,Lt ded

BRYANT,Thomas Capt kia 11-4-17 5Lincs p220 CR France366

BRYCE,David Grieg Maj ded 24-2-16 IA 76Punjabis p274

BRYCE,James TLt kia 27-5-18 17RIrRif p169 MR18

BRYCE,Samuel 2Lt kia 21-12-14 7DragGds p21 MR22

BRYCE,William Hulton T2Lt kia 2-3-16 14 att12RScots p53 CR Belgium53,Hutton

BRYCE-SMITH,Norgrave Ingram TLt kia 25-4-18 3 att6KOSB p101 MR30

BRYDEN,Richard Joseph.VD.Maj ded 16-1-15 RAMC p269 CR Kent129

BRYDON,Alec Whitworth Lt kia 31-8-15 4RWSurr p212 CR Gallipoli5 Ex 2/6Ches

BRYDON,John Earnsclinch Capt dow 27-6-17 RAMC p253 CR France592,Earnscleugh

BRYDON,Thomas Edward T2Lt dow 1-2-17 RE 88FC p43 CR Iraq5

BRYETT,Lewis Henry Frederick 2Lt dow 25-10-18 A307RFA p26 CR France380

BRYSON,Alexander 2Lt dow 25-6-17 5KOSB p224 CR Belgium11,7/8Bn

BRYSON,Andrew T2Lt dow 19-11-18 HLI att1/5Bn p162 CR France646,19-9-18

BRYSON,James Harvey T2Lt kia 20-10-18 RFA &X24TMB p26 CR France403,Y24

BRYSON,John T2Lt dow 14-10-17 NumbF att21Bn p60 CR Belgium25

BRYSON,Joseph 2Lt kia 6-10-18 1 att9RIrF p171 MR30

BRYSON,Lauder W.TCapt kia 30-7-16 14RWar p64 MR21,George Lander Unite

BRYSON,Thomas Harold 2Lt ded 27-2-19 GL 6/7RScotsF att207PoWCoy LabCps p190&266,TLt LabCps CR France134,Lt 28Bn

BRYSON,Thomas Lees Capt ded 16-4-19 LabCps attChineseLabCps p266 CR Asia45

BRYSON,William Miller 2Lt kia 1-9-18 1/1ERidYeo p206 CR France1484

BUBB,Harry Wilfred LtACapt dow 1-1-17 NStaffs attTMB p156 CR Staffs84

BUCH,Charles Justus T2Lt kia 14-9-16 9 att8Beds p85 MR21,13-9-16

BUCHAN,Alastair Ebenezar TLt dow 9-4-17 6RScotF p94 CR France113,Ebenezer

BUCHAN,Charles Rev T2Lt dow 2-12-17 1 att15LancF p92 CR Belgium84

BUCHAN,David,TLt kia 9-4-17 1GordH p166 MR20

32

BUCHAN,Ernest Norman.DSO.Capt kia 25-9-15 1Manch p154 MR19

BUCHAN,Francis Hall T2Lt dow 7-8-18 11RB p178 CR France547

BUCHAN,James 2Lt kia 22-3-18 LNLancs att15Bn p135 MR27

BUCHAN,James Wilson T2Lt kia 23-4-17 3ScotRif att5BordR p103 CR France1185

BUCHAN,John Crawford.VC.2Lt mbk 22-3-18 7 att8A&SH p257 CR France528

BUCHAN,Leslie Alexander T2Lt dow 30-7-16 6/40RFA p26 CR France51

BUCHAN,Roy Eric Victor T2Lt kia 27-3-16 40RFA p26 CR Belgium35

BUCHAN,William Erskine T2Lt kld 9-3-18 RFC p15 CR Hamps192

BUCHAN,William George T2Lt kia 12-10-16 7SfthH p164 MR21

BUCHANAN,Adam Heaton T2Lt kia 5-10-18 GordH att5Bn p166 CR France115

BUCHANAN,Andrew MacFarlane ALt dow 13-6-17 GL RFA &90TMB p190 CR Belgium11

BUCHANAN,Archibald Ure T2Lt dow 28-9-15 1GordH p166 CR Belgium11,27-9-15

BUCHANAN,Arthur Sanderson ACapt ded 15-2-19 RE p26CR Scot237

BUCHANAN,Claude Gray Capt kia 4-11-14 IA 53Sikhs att2/8GurkhaRif p274 MR28

BUCHANAN,David T2Lt kia 1-7-16 2SfthH p164 CR France643

BUCHANAN,David Neil Griffiths 2Lt kia 21-1-16 IARO att37Dogras p274 CR Iraq5

BUCHANAN,Edward Lawrie Capt kia 15-8-20 RFA &RAF CR Iraq8

BUCHANAN,Fraser Campbell 2Lt kia 9-4-17 13RScots p53 CR France924

BUCHANAN,Harold Cyril Dudley TLt dow 12-11-16 1Mddx p146 CR France40

BUCHANAN,James Herbert Lt kia 16-3-15 7RIrF attLeinst p171 CR Belgium28,4IrF 15-3-15

BUCHANAN,James MacKenzie TLt ded 18-2-18 RE 180FC p262 CR Scot674

BUCHANAN,James Robert TLt dow 1-4-18 13RIrRif p169 CR France145

BUCHANAN,Richard Brendan 2Lt dow 20-6-15 1/5RScotF p222 CR Gallipoli1

BUCHANAN,William Archibald Lt ded 2-6-16 1ConnRgrs &RFC p2 CR Wilts115,7-6-16

BUCHANAN,William Arthur Irvine Capt dow 24-7-17 RAVC 50MobileTrps p198 CR Belgium5,kia sect39Div

BUCHANAN,William Learmouth Capt dow 20-11-17 5HLI p240 CR Palestine9,Learmonth

BUCHANAN-BAILLIE-HAMILTON,Arthur.MID Capt 9-5-15 1SfthH CR France721 see BAILLIE-HAMILTON,A.B.

BUCHANAN-DUNLOP,Colin Napier.DSO.Maj kia 14-10-15 F'RHA p26 CR France423

BUCHANNAN,Alexander 2Lt kia 21-7-17 6 att16WYorks p218 CR France268

BUCK,Archibald Charles Watson 2Lt kia 9-8-16 10Lpool p216 MR21

BUCK,Arthur TLt kld 9-9-18 RE att67RGA p43 CR France570

BUCK,Bertram Forster TLt kia 3-9-16 17N&D p133 MR21

BUCK,Charles ACapt kia 15-5-18 1/4RBerks p234 CR Italy2,15-6-18

BUCK,Charles Melvill Lt mbk 24-1-17 IARO att53RFC p274 CR Belgium152

BUCK,Cyril Alfred Spencer.MM.2Lt kia 26-10-17 18 att2/3Lond p250 MR30

BUCK,Cyril Bernard Wilson.MC.Rev kia 29-9-18 RAChDept att5Leic p199&258

BUCK,Geoffrey Sebastian.MC.DFC.Capt kia 3-9-18 1Lond &RAF p245&258

BUCK,Robert Stanley Maj ded 11-3-19 GL LancF p263 CR Surrey6

BUCK,William Pallister T2Lt dow 24-10-18 NumbF att4RFus p60 CR France332

BUCKELL,Christopher James Allardyce 2Lt kia 19-4-17 3Norf p73 CR Palestine8

BUCKELL,Francis William Ashton Lt kia 21-3-18 4 att8RWSurr p212 MR27

BUCKELL,Harold Claude.MC.2LtTCapt kia 21-9-17 13DLI p160 MR30

BUCKERIDGE,Guy Dennis TLt kld 21-8-17 GL &RFC p5 CR Norf254,22-8-17

BUCKHAM,Norman Langley TLtACapt ded 30-10-18 RAOC GHQ p198 CR France65

BUCKINGHAM,Aubrey Webster Maj kia 17-11-14 3 att1GordH p166 CR Belgium84,1/5Bn

BUCKINGHAM,Henry Lt&QM ded 20-12-17 4Hamps p220 CR Iraq8

BUCKINGHAM,Maude Amy Matron 4-12-15 QAIMNS CR Lond8

BUCKINGHAM,P.E.MC.2Lt kld 8-11-18 1/2RWKent att7RAF p140 CR Belgium159,Lt

BUCKINGHAM,Thomas Nock Lt kia 26-10-17 6 att8Dev p217 MR30,Noel

BUCKINGHAM,William Albert T2Lt dow 3-10-18 Res att5Berks p138 CR France146

BUCKLAND,Cecil John 2Lt ded 19-8-18 1/4RFus &RAF p67 CR Wilts18,5Bn kld flying

BUCKLAND,Ernest Blas TLt kia 5-10-16 13ESurr p112 CR France115

BUCKLAND,John 2Lt kia 16-6-17 Y&L att12Bn p158 CR France644

BUCKLAND,John Arnold 2Lt kia 1-3-17 7SomLI p79 CR France744

BUCKLAND,Thomas Adrian TLt kia 18-10-15 7Norf p73 MR19,19-10-15

BUCKLE,Archie Stewart BrigGen ded 18-8-16 RA 17Div p26 CR France833

BUCKLE,Arthur Charles LtCol ded 21-12-18 Nhampt p137 CR Staffs125

BUCKLE,Christopher Galbraith.DSO.MC.ALtCol kia 27-5-18 2Nhampt p137 CR France1753

BUCKLE,Cuthbert Charles Corbett 2Lt kia 3-7-16 8RWKent p140 CR France1890,6Bn A'Coy

BUCKLE,Dudley Francis de Crespigny AMaj ded 24-4-19 3NumbF p254 CR Numb11A

BUCKLE,Harry Capt dow 4-10-14 PoW RFA p26 CR Germany1

BUCKLE,Matthew Perceval.DSO.Maj kia 27-10-14 1WKent p140 CR France924

BUCKLE,William T2Lt dow 7-6-17 8Yorks p90 CR Belgium11

BUCKLER,Annie Elinor SNurse ded 17-10-18 QAIMNS CR Hamps56

BUCKLER,Eric Wilson.MIDx2 Capt kia 16-6-15 6 att3Worc p108 MR29

BUCKLEY,Arthur Dashwood Bulkeley.CB.Col ded 3-4-15 Hamps p120 CR Wilts86

BUCKLEY,Edmund Cecil Gladstone Capt dow 5-8-16 6Lpool p215 CR France513

BUCKLEY,Edmund Maurice 2Lt dow 12-8-15 7RWFus p223 CR Gallipoli1

BUCKLEY,Edward Capt kia 30-9-17 3 att2Y&L p158 CR France550

BUCKLEY,Felix George.MC.TCapt dow 17-8-17 8NumbF p60 CR Belgium96

BUCKLEY,George William T2Lt kia 27-8-18 RBerks att8Bn p138 CR France515

BUCKLEY,Godfrey Lt kld 15-8-17 3 att9ELancs p110 CR Greece1

BUCKLEY,Hubert Hyde Lt kia 14-4-17 3 att1KSLI p144 CR France115

BUCKLEY,Humphry Paul Stenneth Capt dow 29-7-17 7EYorks p83 MR20

BUCKLEY,John F.Lt 23-2-19 3LancF p263 CR Ches72,Capt 3-3-19

BUCKLEY,John Herbert Wellington.MID Lt ded 5-3-19 RGA p262 CR Hamps240,Capt

BUCKLEY,Joseph Michael.MC.TCapt kia 23-12-17 9RB p178 CR Belgium101

BUCKLEY,Robert 2Lt dow 9-1-17 4Manch p154 CR France41

BUCKLEY,Sidney James 2Lt kia 24-3-18 5 att2SStaffs p229 MR20

BUCKMAN,James Leslie TCapt kia 15-9-16 12ESurr p112 MR21

BUCKMASTER,Charles Oliver Brook TLt ded 16-3-19 7DCLI p254 CR Hamps221

BUCKMASTER,Henry Augustine 2Lt kia 28-9-18 2/4LNLancs p234 CR France256

BUCKMASTER,Ralph Nevill Lendon.MID Capt kia 30-11-17 1/4LNLancs p233 MR17

BUCKNALL,Marc Antony 2Lt dow 6-3-17 3 att10DCLI p114 CR France177

BUCKNALL,Walter Harry Corfield Lt kia 3-5-17 2 att1NumbF p60 MR20,Capt

BUCKNELL,Harry Hill 2Lt kia 22-7-17 6WelshR p230 CR Belgium73

BUCKNELL,William Wentworth.MID Lt kia 10-8-17 103RH&FA p26 CR Belgium29

BUCKNILL,John Charles.MC.MIDx2 Lt kia 21-1-16 1/4Hamps p228 MR38

BUCKNILL,Llewllyn Morris.MID Maj dow 18-5-15 105RFA p26 CR France80

BUCKOKE,Oswald Lee T2Lt kia 8-7-17 11Suff p78 CR France366

BUCKTON,Arthur Scott TLtACapt dow 9-4-17 RGA 100SB p38 CR France1182

BUCKWORTH,Alan Benjamin 2Lt kia 16-8-17 3RInniskF p104 CR Belgium125

BUCKWORTH,Charles Raymond Lt kia 1-7-16 2SfthH attMGC Inf p164&182 CR France1890

BUCKWORTH,Wallace Alfred 2Lt kia 8-5-15 RInniskF p104 MR4

BUCKWORTH,William TLt kia 14-8-17 10RB p178 MR29 &CR Belgium152

BUDD,Edward.MC&2Bars.LtACapt kia 8-5-18 1IrGds p52 CR France925

BUDD,Eric Frank Corydon TLt kia 11-9-17 RE &52RFC p5&43 CR Belgium173

BUDD,Frederick George.MC.T2Lt dow 15-10-18 16KRRC p149 CR France398,MM

BUDD,Wrinch Joseph Charles Lt kia 28-6-15 9 att2SWBord p99 MR4

BUDDEN,Harold William T2Lt kia 14-9-16 12LancF p92 MR34

BUDDEN,Henry Richard 2LtTLt kia 25-9-15 3Dors att2Lincs p123 CR France349

BUDDEN,Ronald Anderson 2Lt kia 31-7-17 1Worc p108 MR29

BUDDICOM,Walter Digby Lt dedacc 6-6-18 4Huss p21 CR France40

BUDDS,Charles Walter 2Lt kia 8-9-18 5YLI p235 CR France415

BUDDS,Percy Harold Lt ded 29-10-18 6EKent att12RAF p57 CR France40

BUDENBURG,Donald Harlow 2LtACapt kia 25-4-18 4 att17Manch p154 CR Belgium115,BUDENBERG

BUDGE,Hubert Lionel TLtCol dow 13-7-16 12RScots p53 CR France513

BUDGE,John Henry Capt dow 14-3-15 4SfthH p241 CR Scot968

BUDGE,Philip Prideaux.DSO.BtLtCol dow 11-9-18 323RFA p26 CR France103,232RFA

BUDGE,Preston Frederick TLt kia 8/9-5-17 12RWSurr attRBerks p55 MR37

BUDGEN,Sidney Norman Lt kia 4-10-17 A291RFA p207 CR Belgium20

BUDIBENT,Cecil T2Lt kia 25-9-15 2Lincs p74 MR32,Cedil

BUDIBENT,George Maj ded 2-10-18 RASC p254 CR Surrey3

BUDWORTH,Charles Edward Dutton.CB.CMG.MVO.MIDx10 MajGen 5-7-21 RA MR65

BUFTON,Edward Evan T2Lt ded 20-11-18 13Y&L p158 CR Wales429

BUGDEN,Robert Gordon TLt kia 24-8-15 5KSLI p144 CR Belgium165

BUGG,Herbert 2Lt kia 19-7-18 D106RFA p26 CR France570

BUGG,William Arthur Lt ded 9-6-20 IA TC att37Dogras p274 MR65,9-6-17

BUGLASS,Cyril T2Lt dow 23-3-18 12NumbF p60 CR France987

BUGLER,Leonard Herbert 2Lt 2-4-18 C'Coy 2/5Glouc CR Glouc15

BUIK,Henry Douglas 2Lt kia 9-4-17 5RScotF p222 CR France418,Lt 1Bn

BUIST,Charles Edward.MC.Capt dow 21-10-17 RGA 67SB p209 MR30

BUIST,George Bruce TLt kia 25-9-16 20Mddx p146 CR France115

BUIST,Kenneth Lt kia 25-1-15 1BlkW p128 CR France720

BILBECK,Henry Edmund TLt kia 6-11-16 16 att20RFus p67 MR21

BULKELEY,Charles Ivor Rivers Capt kia 16-5-15 2ScotsGds p52,C.S.R. MR22

BULKELEY,Edmund Burke Mabbot Capt ded 13-11-16 2Lpool p71 MR43

BULKELEY,Llewllyn Alfred Henry TCapt kia 10-4-18 RAMC att15Ches p194 CR France41

BULKELEY,Thomas Henry Rivers.CMG.MVO.Capt kia 22-10-14 2ScotsGds p52 MR29

BULKELEY-HUGHES,George Montagu Warren TLtACapt kia 27-2-17 6 att12KRRC p149 CR France374,Montague

BULKELEY-JOHNSON,Charles Bulkeley ADC BrigGen kia 11-4-17 2Drags Cmdg8CavBde p1 CR France104

BULKLEY,Howel Stephen Capt kia 19-7-17 IA 33Punjabis p274 CR EAfrica38 &CR Tanzania1

BULL,Alfred George 2Lt kia 6-8-18 5 att8KRRC p149 MR20

BULL,Arthur Henry 2Lt ded 14-12-18 2Dors p123 CR Egypt9

BULL,Benjamin Allen Capt kia 16-9-17 RAMC p253 CR Belgium23

BULL,Bernard George Sheen 2Lt kia 4-4-15 RE 1HomeCountiesFC p210 CR France924

BULL,Frederick John 2Lt kia 27-1-16 6Lond p246 CR France149

BULL,George.DSO.TBrigGen dow 11-12-16 RIrF Comdg8InfBde p171&258 CR France41

BULL,Geoffrey Spencer.MC.Capt S/InflictWound 25-3-16 IA 58Rif p274 CR Egypt3

BULL,Godfrey John Oswald Lt kia 8-7-15 RE 2ELancsFC p210 CR Gallipoli3

BULL,Henry Spencer.DSO.TMaj ded 30-7-18 6ELancs p110 CR Iraq6

BULL,John Edward 2Lt kia 29-9-15 3Dors attRFus p123 MR19

BULL,John Lionel Robin 2Lt kia 30-11-17 10KRRC p149 MR17 Ex 1Bn

BULL,Joseph William T2Lt dow 1-10-16 RE 98FC p43 CR France145

BULL,Lovelace Rowat TLt dow 3-5-17 MGC Inf p182 CR France1182

BULL,Percival John 2Lt kia 7-10-16 6 att9RFus p67 MR21

BULL,Robert Edward Bristow TLt kia 16-5-15 O&BLI p130 MR22

BULL,Ronald John Howard Capt kld 13-7-17 16Lond attRE p249 CR Belgium12

BULL,Ronald Page 2Lt kia 30-10-18 4Nhampt p234 CR France190

BULL,Wilfred Herbert TCapt kia 3-5-17 7Beds p85 CR France700

BULLARD,Ernest Gilbert Lt kia 1-8-15 IA IndPostalServs p274 CR France345

BULLEN,Henry Stanley Tempest Lt kia 14-4-17 D251RFA p207 CR France418

BULLEN,Roy Evans 2Lt dow 29-4-17 2KRRC p149 CR France149,Capt

BULLEN,William Francis 2Lt mbk 16-6-15 10Lpool p257 MR29

BULLER,Arthur Edward Adderley Capt ded 21-9-18 Inns of Court OTC att1/5Norf p252 CR Palestine9

BULLER,Herbert Cecil.DSO.LtCol kia 3-6-16 RB &PPCLI p178 CR Belgium111,2-6-16

BULLER,Lesley Montagu Lt kia 24-8-14 1Lincs p74 CR Belgium202

BULLER,Richard Francis Montague Capt kia 24-8-18 7 att8Mddx p235 MR16,Maj

BULLIVANT,Alfred James T2Lt dow 21-7-17 17N&D p133 CR France80

BULLIVANT,Eric Claud 2Lt kia 24-3-18 18KRRC p149 MR20,Claude

BULLIVANT,Ritchie Pelham Capt kia 24-9-18 1Coy of LondYeo p204 MR34

BULLIVANT,Robert Walker 2Lt dow 1-5-17 SomLI att8Bn p79 CR France64,Roland Walter

BULLMAN,Haddon Robert Horsley 2Lt kia 30-11-17 3RWKent att71MGC Inf p140&182 CR France439

BULLOCK,Alan Marlowe 2Lt kia 4-11-18 15 att1/4Lond p249 CR France1142

BULLOCK,Albert Edward T2Lt kia 26-10-18 2Worc p108 CR France1478

BULLOCK,Arthur Ernest TCapt kia 26-9-15 RAMC att4Mddx p194 CR Belgium6

BULLOCK,Charles Sidney 2Lt dow 6-9-18 1/4Ches p222 CR Belgium15

BULLOCK,Geoffrey Ernest Lt kia 16-7-18 5NStaffs att148RAF p238&255 CR France10

BULLOCK,Gervas Frederick 2Lt kia 31-7-18 11SWBord p99 MR29

BULLOCK,Henry Acton Linton 2Lt kia 14-7-16 7RWar p214 MR21

BULLOCK,Robert TLt kia 20-9-17 26RFus p67 MR30,BULLOCH 2nd entry as BULLOCK

BULLOCK,Robert Poe Story.OBE.Lt ded 17-2-20 IA 89Punjabis p274 CR Ireland165,Capt H.

BULLOCK,Robert Stanley Capt kia 17-4-16 IA 27Punjabis MR38 p274

BULLOCK,Thomas Eben Grainger 2Lt mbk 24-4-17 1EKent p256 MR19,22-4-17

BULLOCK,Thomas William MajALtCol kia 11-4-18 1Dors p123 CR France745

BULLOCK,William 2Lt dow 12-5-18 3Yorks p90 CR France65,6Bn

BULLOCK,William Acton 2Lt ded 25-10-18 RFus att2/17Lond p67 CR France34

BULLOUGH,Charles Berthold.DSO.Maj kia 25-4-18 RGA 117HB p38 CR France285

BULLOUGH,Frederick William 2Lt kia 8-11-17 RGA 152SB p38 CR Belgium106

BULLOUGH,John Leodius Lt kia 25-9-15 2A&SH p173 MR19

BULLOUGH,Thomas Horrolin Stanley T2Lt kia 7-7-16 11 att9LNLancs p135 MR21,Horrobin

BULMAN,Andrew Lt kia 12-7-15 4KOSB p223 MR4

BULMER,Charles Forsyth Lt kia 12-3-18 10Mddx p255 MR34,Ex WKentYeo

BULMER,Frank Stedman 2Lt kia 1-10-16 20Lond p251 MR21

BULMER,Geoffrey Percival.MC.Lt ded 15-2-18 GL &RFC p261&266 CR Hereford/Worc18

BULMER,John Legge 2Lt kia 3-5-17 4att5 O&BLI p231 MR20

BULTEAL,Sam Dominic CaptAMaj kia 5-4-17 45RFA p26 CR France511,BULTEEL

BULTEEL,Thomas Edward Lt kld 24-2-18 RFA &RFC p15&26 CR Wilts4

BUMPUS,Bernard Ebenezer.MID T2Lt kia 3-7-16 12NumbF p60 MR21

BUNBURY,Godfrey Hugh St.Pierre Capt kia 1-2-17 IA 15 att36Sikhs p274 CR Iraq5

BUNBURY,Hugh St.Pierre T2Lt dow 25-8-16 B70RH&FA p26 CR France40,90RFA

BUNBURY,Patrick Stanney St.Pierre 2Lt kia 19-12-16 2Suff p78 CR France133

BUNBURY,Thomas St.Pierre Capt kia 31-8-18 RFA &64RAF p26 CR France421

BUNBURY,Wilfred Joseph Capt kia 15-4-17 4NumbF p213 CR France162

BUNCE,George Owen 2Lt kia 12-5-15 2SWBord p99 MR4,9-5-15

BUNCE,Hugh Pollock T2Lt ded 5-10-16 8NStaffs p156 CR France200

BUNCH,Charles Walter 2Lt kia 13-11-16 RGA 128SB p38 CR France745,Lt

BUNCLE,Ronald 2Lt ded 16-10-15 RFA p208 CR Scot239

BUNDEY,Albert Arthur T2Lt kia 21-3-18 MGC p182 CR France307

BUNDLE,Harry Norman 2Lt kia 20-9-17 13Lond p249 CR Belgium125

BUNGARD,Eric George 2Lt mbk 30-11-17 3 att6EKent p256 MR17

BUNGEY,Gerald Edwards T2Lt kia 4-8-16 9RFus p67 MR21,Edward

BUNKER,Harold John T2Lt kia 28-9-17 9Yorks p90 MR30

BUNN,Ernest Walton 2Lt ded 11-6-18 5Suff p217 CR Suff176,kldacc

BUNN,Jack Coulson T2Lt kia 13-5-18 1/5SStaffs p122 CR France109

BUNT,Harry 2Lt kia 17-5-19 IARO att1/15Sikhs p274 MR43

BUNTINE,Robert T2Lt dow 31-3-18 GordH att8/10Bn p166 CR France64

BUNTINE,Walter Horace Carlyle.MC.2Lt kld 19-6-17 4N&D &RFC p5&133,Carlisle CR Scot520

BUNTING,Henry.MC.TLtTCapt ded 5-2-18 1BordR p116 CR C'land&W'land68

BUNTING,Robert Russell TLt kia 6-8-15 12 att1Ess p131 CR Gallipoli6

BUNTING,Thomas Edward 2Lt kia 24-8-18 RIrF p171 CR France855

BUNTING,William.MC.TCapt kia 11-8-17 8Norf p73 CR Belgium19

BURBAGE,Edwin Joseph 2Lt dow 1-4-17 2/10Mddx p236 CR Egypt2

BURBIDGE,Howard Churchill T2Lt dow 13-9-16 13EYorks p83 CR France98

BURBRIDGE,Frederick T2Lt dow 28-8-18 15WYorks p81 CR France34,BURBIDGE

BURBURY,Francis William LtCol ded 11-9-1 3RWKent att24RB p265 MR67

BURBURY,John Francis 2Lt dow 23-2-15 RWKent p140 CR Belgium165,kia

BURCH,Charles Leonard 2Lt kia 18-8-16 6 att13Mddx p146 MR21

BURCH,Herbert Percival T2Lt ded 20-10-16 15MGC Motor p182 CR France188

BURCH,R.S.2Lt kia 28-6-18 Res &RAF p254

BURCH,Sydney Gasking Lt kia 13-11-16 SNottsHuss p205 CR France293

BURCHELL,Lawrence,MC 2Lt ded 31-12-18 RGA 153SB p38 CR Germany1

BURCHILL,Vivian TLt kia 2-6-16 22Manch p154 CR France329

BURD,Frederick Braham 2Lt kia 20-9-17 1/13Lond p249 MR20

BURDALL,Albert HonLt ded 3-1-16 RAOC p198 CR Kent7

BURDEKIN,Geoffrey Eric 2Lt kia 26-1-15 N&D attNLancs p133 CR France557

BURDEKIN,Sydney 2Lt kia 28-9-15 RFA p26 MR19,att10TMB

BURDESS,Matthew Forster Rev Chap4Cl kia 18-4-17 RAChDept att1/6Glouc p199 CR France363

BURDETT,Charles Plantagenet Balfour T2Lt kia 7-7-16 15 att9RFus p67 CR France393

BURDETT,Edward Jerome Capt kia 25-6-15 IA 11Rajputs att89Punjabis p274 CR France708

BURDETT,Glanville 2Lt kia 4-10-17 1ESurr p112 MR30

BURDETT,H.SubCdr 17-10-18 S&T Cps CR Iraq8

BURDETT,Halford Gay Capt ded 3-3-16 2Coy of LondYeo p204 CR Kent267

BURDETT,Thomas George Deane.MC.Capt kia 6-11-17 1/7RWelshF p223 CR Palestine1

BURDETT,William Allen.MC.ACapt kia 31-7-17 1RFus p67 MR29

BURDETT,William Edward Capt kia 29-8-18 5RLancs p213 CR France646,Edwards

BURDGE,Reginald John 2Lt dow 9-10-17 C58RFA p26 MR21

BURDICK,Frederick William.MC.TCapt kia 29-8-18 20Lond att4RAF p251 CR France352,16-6-18

BURDIN,Frank Amesbury Lt kia 16-5-15 2RWar p64 CR France727

BURDITT,Stanley Wilbraham TLtACapt dow 1-10-17 RASC p192 CR France193,Sanley

BURDON,John Lt kia 8-3-16 1Manch p154 MR38

BURDON,Rowland TCapt kld 10-1-17 GL &RFC p5 CR Durham108

BURDON-SANDERSON,Guy Askew James 2Lt dow 21-2-17 3 att9NumbF p60 CR France145

BURFOOT,W.M.2Lt kld 22-5-18 3Dors &RAF p123

BURFORD,Francis Emery 2Lt kia 4-6-18 1Leic p87 CR Belgium3

BURFORD,Richard Ellis T2Lt dow 8-10-18 Ess att9Norf p131 CR France446

BURGE,Montague TMaj kia 1-7-16 23NumbF p60 MR21

BURGE,P.S.TCapt kia 12-7-18 SL attRAF p201

BURGES,Eric Laurence Arthur Hart 2Lt kia 23-10-14 3 att2Wilts p152 MR29,Lawrence

BURGES,George Herbert LtCol ded 6-8-19 3Glouc p264CR Berks47,Col

BURGES,James Alexander Stewart TLt dow 23-4-17 RAMC att49FA p194 CR France95

BURGES,Walter Travers 2Lt kia 8-5-17 3 att12Glouc p106 MR20

BURGES,William Armstrong Lt kia 10-3-18 1RIrRif p169 CR France706,10-3-15

BURGESS,Alexander James HonCapt ded 3-5-19 RAOC IA p267 CR Scot438

BURGESS,Charles Capt kia 11-10-18 RFA p207 CR France256

BURGESS,Eric Archibald 2Lt kia 17-2-17 6 att22RFus p67 MR21

BURGESS,Frank Harold Lt DCM kia 10-6-20 IA 2/102Grenadiers p274 MR43

BURGESS,Harold T2Lt kia 27-10-18 10NumbF p60 CR Italy9

BURGESS,Harold Torrence 2Lt kia 2-4-17 3Lond p245 CR France420,Torrance

BURGESS,Leonard George 2Lt kia 17-2-17 IARO att20Inf p274 CR Iraq5

BURGESS,Matthew Wylie TLt kia 23-7-18 2MGC Inf p182 CR France745

BURGESS,Philip Gulson T2Lt dow 14-10-15 8RWSurr p55 CR France1276,13-10-15

BURGESS,Reginald TLt ded 7-7-16 PoW ACycCps &22RFC p2&181,dow CR France927

BURGESS,Reginald Charles 2Lt kia 3-5-17 23RFus p67 MR20

BURGESS,Robert Balderston TCapt dow 10-12-15 RE p43 CR France285,9-12-15

BURGESS,Wallis Edward Lt&QM ded 30-9-16 ACycCps p266 CR Mddx44

BURGESS,Walter Capt kia 13-10-15 2RSuss p118 MR19

BURGESS,Wilfred Charles 2Lt kia 22-8-17 4SomLI p218 CR Belgium112,Wilfrid

BURGESS,William Frederick 2Lt kia 18-8-16 2Suff p78 MR21,Frederic

BURGESS,William Henry Langdon.MID Capt kia 20-7-16 3 att1ScotRif p103 CR France432

BURGESS,William Vernon T2Lt kia 19-7-16 RBerks att6Bn p138 MR21

BURGH,Edward Henry.MC.Lt dow 4-1-18 B223RFA p207 CR France755

BURGHOPE,Gerald Harry Vernon 2Lt kia 23-4-17 1RWSurr p55 MR20

BURGIS,Edward 2Lt kia 16-10-17 3 att18Manch p154 MR30

BURGOYNE,John Heywood 2Lt kia 31-10-16 88RFA p26 CR France251

BURGOYNE-JOHNSON,Luther Vincent Capt 26-4-15 8DLI MR29

BURGOYNE-WALLACE,Douglas Burgoyne Lt kia 3-3-15 IA 7Rajputs p274 MR61

BURKE,Charles James.DSO.MajALtCol kia 9-4-17 1RIrReg attELancs p88 CR France452,2Bn

BURKE,Edward Terrence Lt&QM kia 25-4-18 Nhampt att9MGC p137&182 CR Belgium11,Terence

BURKE,Edward William 2Lt kia 14-9-16 6RFus att70RFC p2 CR France169

BURKE,Gordon William 2Lt ded 29-7-18 15RWFus p263 CR Lond7

BURKE,Henry Joseph Lt kia 25-9-15 1SStaffs p122 MR19

BURKE,J.Lt&QM 2-4-18 1/4LNLancs CR Lancs102

BURKE,John Capt ded 21-12-18 RAMC p194 CR Iraq8

BURKE,John Bernard Mary.MC.Capt dow 1-12-17 4GrenGds p49 CR France415

BURKE,John Errol T2Lt kia 21-8-15 5ConnRgrs p172 MR4

BURKE,John Laurence 2Lt kia 30-4-16 RGA Z25TMB p38 CR France68,29-4-16 2TMB

BURKE,Martin 2Lt kia 18-9-16 1WYorks p81 MR21

BURKE,Michael Arthur 2Lt kia 6-11-17 5BordR p228 CR Belgium13

BURKE Osborne Samuel T2LtACapt kia 25-9-16 C77RFA p26 CR France630

BURKE,Robert Alfred T2Lt kia 21-7-17 ConnRgrs att2Leinst p172 CR Belgium19,31-7-17

BURKE,Roland Edmund 2Lt dow 17-11-18 5Ess p232 CR France341

BURKE,Sydney Slaven 2Lt kia 22-12-17 2/18Lond p250 CR Palestine3

BURKE,Thomas Campbell Capt kia 19-12-14 IA 1/1GurkhaRif MR28

BURKE,Thomas Edward 2LtTCapt dow 14-4-17 1 att5KSLI p144 CR France120,11-4-17

BURKETT,Francis Edgar T2Lt kia 26-9-18 14DLI p160 MR19,26-9-15

BURKETT,Harold TCapt dow 5-6-17 10KSLI p144 CR France1186,10YLI

BURKETT,Harry William Bradly Lt kia 14-4-18 4Wilts p236 CR France285,Capt 1Bn

BURKETT,William Peter 2Lt kld 23-4-18 2Yorks p90 CR France180

BURKINSHAW,Francis William TCapt dow 30-3-16 9/19RFA p26 MR38

BURKINSHAW,Herbert Thornton 2Lt dow 20-9-18 LNLancs att5Y&L p135 MR16

BURLEIGH,Bennett Lt dow 15-7-15 7LancF p221 CR Gallipoli1

BURLEIGH,Finlay Swan Lt dow 2-10-18 1/4RScotF p222 CR France1184

BURLEIGH,James Emil.MC.T2Lt kia 12-10-17 12A&SH p173 MR30,Lt

BURLEIGH,Robert Lt kia 29-8-16 RE att15RFC p18&210 CR France220

BURLES,Thomas John 2Lt kia 24-6-17 RGA 21SB p38 CR Belgium1

BURLEY,Charles Frederick 2Lt kia 18-11-16 4 att10RWar p64 MR21

BURLEY,Cyril Percival T2Lt kia 9-8-18 7RSuss p118 CR France247,8-8-18

BURLEY,Ernest Sidney T2Lt ded 15-2-19 LabCps att112ChinLabCoy p189&257 CR France65

BURLEY,Robert James 2Lt dedacc 19-3-18 RFC 80CentTrStn CR Canada1688

BURLTON,,Arthur Vivian Capt kld 30-8-17 RASC attRFC p5 CR Yorks178

BURLTON,George Philip.MC.Lt kia 5-6-16 1Norf p73&258 MR20

BURLTON,Ralph Harry Lt kia 2-2-16 IA 34Horse att33Cav p274 MR38,1-2-16

BURLURAUX,John Rene Cornelius T2Lt kia 1-7-16 27NumbF p60 CR France393,Lt

BURMANN,Robert Moyle.DSO.MC.MIDx6 Capt kia 27-10-18 ELancs attHQ 7InfBde p110 CR France231

BURMESTER,Charles Mansel TCapt dow 8-10-18 3SWBord p99 CR France375

BURMESTER,Maurice George TLt dow 25-8-15 Ess att1Bn p131 MR4

BURN,Arthur George McCausland Capt kia 29-10-14 2ESurr p112 MR29

BURN,Arthur Herbert Rosdew 2Lt kia 29-10-14 1Drags p21 MR29,Posden

BURN,Arthur Morton Stanley 2Lt ded 7-6-16 IARO attS&M p274 MR65,BURNE Lt

BURN,Arthur Roland T2Lt kia 26-3-18 14 att6DLI p160 MR27

BURN,Arthur Sidney Pelham.MID 2Lt kia 2-5-17 6GordH p242 CR France768,Lt

BURN,Charles Scott Lt kia 3-11-17 1SfthH p164 MR38

BURN,Cuthbert John Lt kia 1-10-17 9Leic p87 MR30 Ex 3Bn

BURN,Hugh Henry.MC.TCapt dow 16-9-16 2CldGds p51 CR France105

BURN James T2Lt kia 17-10-17 NumbF att23Bn p60 CR Belgium83

BURN,Maurice Edward Pelham TLt kia 9-4-17 BlkW att8Bn p128 CR France924

BURN,William Gladstone Lt kia 9-5-15 13Lond p249 MR32

BURN-MURDOCH,Colin Thomas Capt kia 30-5-19 IA 20Inf attSWaziristanMil p274 MR43

BURNABY,Eustace Hotham Capt kia 5-8-15 7Glouc p106 MR4

BURNABY,Geoffrey Lt dow 23-10-16 1Lond p245 CR France40

BURNABY,Hugo Beaumont.DSO.LtCol kia 8-9-16 11RWSurr p55 CR France397

BURNAND,Cyril Francis 2Lt kia 11-3-15 1GrenGds SR p49 MR22

BURNAND,Geoffrey Chasmore Lt kia 7-4-17 SR 48RFC p5 CR France120,Chasemore 2Lt

BURNE,A.M.S.see BURN,A.M.S.

BURNE,Edward Robert.DSO.LtCol kia 1-10-18 15RFA p26 CR Belgium84

BURNE,Newdigate Owen Lt dow 27-10-17 IA 40Pathans p274 CR EAfrica38 &CR Tanzania1

BURNE,Thomas Oldbury 2Lt kia 25-3-18 2RBerks p138 MR27

BURNELL,Arthur Lt kia 20-7-18 5YLI p235 CR France1689

BURNELL,Arthur Coke Capt kia 18-3-16 2RB p178 CR France348

BURNELL,George Cuthbertson 2Lt dow 24-6-15 10Lpool p216 CR France102

BURNESS,Alfred Richard Lt dow 25-4-15 2SfthH p164 CR Belgium129

BURNET,Francis Alexander Lt kia 11-4-18 8RScots p211 MR32

BURNET,Robert LtCol dedacc 28-1-15 RAMC 2FA p253 CR Lancs346

BURNET,Stanley Lt 3-5-18 5Beds att17RAF CR Beds75

BURNETT,Charles Guy Arobiun Lt kia 30-6-16 7NumbF p214 CR Belgium60,Arbouin

BURNETT,Ian Alistair Kendale Capt kia 31-5-17 3 att8ELancs p110 MR20

BURNETT,John T2Lt dow 15-9-16 1Leic p87 MR21

BURNETT,John David Napier 2Lt kia 25-2-16 3 att6RWSurr p55 CR France423

BURNETT,Leslie Cecil James 2Lt kia 14-3-18 RFA p26 CR Belgium21

BURNETT,Maurice.MID Lt kia 14-4-15 RAMC p194 CR Iraq6,Capt

BURNETT,Noel Compton TLt kia 14-7-16 7Leic p87 MR21

BURNETT,Robert Capt ded 9-11-16 9Lpool p269 CR Lancs2

BURNETT,William.DSO.LtCol dow 3-7-16 5NStaffs p237CR France120

BURNEY,Geoffry Asteley Capt kia 7-7-16 ScotHorse att4RFC p18&205 CR France44

BURNEY,Gilbert Edward.MID TLt dow 28-9-15 GL 8GordH &Staff p190 CR France98,27-9-15

BURNHAM,Andrew William T2Lt kia 13-11-16 15RFus p67 MR21,att24Bn

BURNHAM,Albert Frederick James T2Lt kia 28-6-16 7Nhampt p137 CR Belgium17

BURNIE,Donald 2Lt kia 1-10-15 6WelshR p230 MR19,2-10-15

BURNIER,Richard Lt dow 21-2-18 att9RSuss p118 CR France446

BURNINGHAM,Ralph Horace T2Lt kia 22-3-18 10RWar p64 MR20

BURNLEY,Ernest Sidney T2Lt kia 5-11-18 9WYorks p81 CR France1142

BURNLEY-CAMPBELL,Colin William 2Lt kia 26-6-15 3A&SH p173 CR France681,27-6-15 1Bn

BURNS,David Chalmers 2Lt kia 30-9-18 BlkW att8Bn p128 CR Belgium163

BURNS,Digby TCapt drd 10-10-18 RAMC p194 CR Ireland14

BURNS,Francis.MC.T2Lt kia 31-7-17 SfthH att8Bn p164 MR29

BURNS,George William 2Lt dow 22-7-15 4NumbF CR France102

BURNS,Islay Ferrier T2Lt kia 10-7-17 97MGC Inf p182 MR31

BURNS,James Rattray.MC.Lt 10-6-18 ScotRif att193RAF CR Egypt1

BURNS,Joseph Dobson Rev Chap4Cldow 7-6-18 RAChDept attRGA p199 CR France180

BURNS,Percival Fossey-Thackaberry.MID T2Lt dow 21-3-17 13Lpool p71 CR France158,Fossy

BURNS,Robert Henry T2Lt kia 1-11-18 8RDubF p176 CR France1079

BURNS,Russell Johnstone T2Lt kia 16-9-16 10HLI p162 MR21

BURNS,Walter Bell Lt kia 9-10-17 3KSLI att1/4Glouc p144 MR30

BURNS,Walter Scot Lt dow 1-7-15 RE p210 MR4

BURNS,William Lt kia 21-3-18 StaffsYeo att2N&D p205 MR20

BURNS,William Beaumont 2Lt kia 8-7-16 1Worc p108 MR21

BURNS-BEGG,Robert Col ded 9-1-18 SL Staff p201&268 CR Scot152

BURNSIDE,Edward Edmund T2Lt kia 21-3-18 16RIrRif p169 CR France1061

BURNSIDE,Eustace Bruce Caldecott TCapt&Adjt kia 12-10-17 7EKent p57 CR Belgium83

BURNYEAT,Hugh Ponsonby MajALtCol kia 30-10-18 RFA 65ArmyBde p26 CR France1482

BURNYEAT,Norman Quayle Maj dow 6-8-17 4RFA p206 CR Belgium24

BURR,Clifford John Frederick Lt 6-5-15 5RWKent MR66

BURR,Frederick Bonham 2Lt kia 12-3-15 3Worc ResOffList p108 CR Belgium17

BURR,Frederick Godfrey TCapt kia 26-9-15 7RScotF p94 CR France219

BURR,G HonLt&QM Acckld 6-6-17 Dev CR Hamps58

BURRELL,Arthur David Claypham TLt kia 15-8-17 MGC p182 MR29

BURRELL,Frederick George 2Lt kia 4-5-17 2RWar p64 MR20

BURRELL,John Stamp Garthorne 2Lt kia 10-8-15 4Ches p222 MR4,9-8-15

BURRELL,Percy Edmund 2Lt kia 21-8-15 3 att2SWBord p99 MR4

BURRELL,Raymond Francis Topham 2Lt kia 26-9-15 8RWKent p140 MR19

BURRELL,Stanley Walter TLt ded 22-7-16 RAMC p194 CR France833

BURRELL,Sydney 2Lt dow 20-7-16 1 att5Mddx p146 CR France833,Sidney

BURRETT,Mervyn Alan Lt ded 24-6-21 IA 16Cav p274

BURRIDGE,Guy Biddulph.MC.Lt 4-5-18 45/42RFA p26 CR France33

BURRIDGE,Henry Gardiner Lt 17-11-14 IA 107Pnrs p274 CR France80,dow 16-11-14

BURRIDGE,Richard Arthur Lt kia 29-12-21 IA 25Cav attIraqLevies p274

BURROUGH,Francis Thomas TCapt kia 1-7-16 6KSLI p144 CR Belgium4

BURROUGHES,Bernard Hollis Lt ded 11-12-19 RE p262 CR Suff83

BURROUGHES,Randall 2Lt kia 12-8-15 5Norf p216 MR4

BURROUGHES,Stephen 2Lt kia 4-11-18 KRRC att2Bn p149 CR France190

BURROUGHS,Bernard Prendergast 2Lt dow 16-3-17 1RDubF p176 CR France145

BURROW,Edward Lt dow 31-5-16 1ConnRgrs p172 CR France354

BURROW,Reginald Lt ded 15-2-19 1/8Lpool p269 CR Ches8

BURROWES,Guy Walter TLt kia 16-8-15 6RMunstF p175 MR4

BURROWS,Arnold Hayes TCapt kia 13-3-16 6Nhampt p137 CR France513

BURROWS,Arthur Cecil T2Lt dow 5-6-16 14 att8Ches p95 MR43

BURROWS,C.N.SubCdr dow 28-7-16 IndiaP&TDept CR Iraq5

BURROWS,Charles Selss.MC.TCapt kia 28-5-18 14NumbF p60 MR18

BURROWS,David T2Lt dow 3-7-16 MGC p182 CR France5

BURROWS,Donald TCaptAMaj ded 7-11-18 RAMC p194 CR Ches28

BURROWS,Edward William Montague Lt kia 26-8-16 42/2RFA p26 CR France630,Edmund Montagu

BURROWS,George William Cruttwell TLt kia 25-8-18 DCLI att7Leic p114 CR France385

BURROWS,James Cooke ACapt kia 14-4-18 4YLI p235 MR30

BURROWS,Leonard Righton T2Lt kia 2-10-15 9NumbF p60 CR Belgium132

BURROWS,Leonard Victor 2Lt kia 2-9-18 1/6N&D p233 CR France109,1-9-18

BURROWS,Percival Ernest.MC.Lt kia 19-9-18 3N&D att2/3GurkhaRif IA p133&274 CR Palestine9,Capt

BURROWS,Stanley Eric T2Lt kia 30-12-15 9 att5 O&BLI p130 CR Belgium20,dow 31-12-15

BURROWS,William Arthur 2Lt kia 15-9-16 3Lond p245 MR21

BURROWS,William George Ritson 2Lt kia 3-5-17 27MGC Inf p182 MR20

BURSTALL,Arthur 2Lt kia 24-9-18 4EYorks att1WYorks p219 CR France1701

BURSTALL,John.MID Capt ded 12-4-19 RASC p192 CR France34,dow

BURT,Andrew Lt kia 18-12-14 8RScots p211 MR32

BURT,Arthur George LtCol kia 23-4-15 1Y&L p158 CR Belgium96

BURT,Charles Herbert 2Lt ded 27-10-18 3Coy of Lond Yeo p204 CR Surrey75

BURT,Frank Eliot Lt kia 3-10-18 1/6NStaffs p238 CR France341

BURT,Frank William 2Lt kia 5-7-16 1N&D p133 CR France390

BURT,Frederick Stanley TLt dow 21-2-17 16Lpool att6NLancs p71 CR Iraq5,Capt

BURT,James 2Lt kia 19-7-18 3 att8BlkW p128 CR France324

BURT,Lewis H.2Lt kld 31-10-17 RE Reinf att Works directorship Basra p43 MR38

BURT,Mary de Burgh Sister 7-4-16 ScotWomensHosp attSerbianArmy CR Greece7

BURT,Owen Lyndon TLt kia 23-7-17 GL &6RFC p5 MR21

BURT,Roger Frederick 2Lt kia 27-3-16 7NumbF p214 CR Belgium127

BURT,Theodore Charles Arthur TLt kia 15-7-16 12/35RFA p26 CR France399

BURT,William James Lt kia 18-8-16 6 att13Mddx p146 MR21

BURT-MARSHALL,William Marshall Capt dow 17-11-14 PoW 2A&SH p173 CR France1159

BURTON,Alexander Brown.MC.Capt kia 9-4-18 14HLI att13ESurr p162 MR32

BURTON,Alfred Lt kia 11-1-16 1RWSurr p55 CR France163

BURTON,Alfred Henry Wellesley Capt kia 23-10-16 7 att2Lincs p74 CR France1891

BURTON,Arthur Richard Capt kia 31-1-16 RFA p26 CR France745

BURTON,Arthur Robert LtCol ded 24-1-18 IA Cmdg94Inf att93 p274 CR Iraq6

BURTON,B.CB.CMG.MajGen 6-8-21 RA CR Cornwall40

BURTON,Charles Arthur T2Lt kia 23-3-18 14 att12Glouc p106 MR27

BURTON,Charles William Gordon 2Lt kia 22-11-17 6 att2RFus p67 MR17

BURTON,Cyril Henry 2Lt kia 1-7-16 1/7N&D p233 MR21

BURTON,Francis Charles Deane Maj ded 3-2-15 RFA p26&261,Capt CR Yorks396

BURTON,Francis Hugh T2Lt kia 14-10-18 15N&D p133 MR30

BURTON,Frank T2Lt dow 3-3-18 11RSuss p118 MR27,30-3-18

BURTON,Frederick Raymond Capt ded 16-4-19 LabCps 176PofW.Co p266 CR Kent38

BURTON,Geoffrey Bunnell Lt dow 3-8-17 1/6Lpool p215 CR Belgium11

BURTON,Geoffrey Walter Melvin Lt kia 3-7-16 EKent p57 CR France393

BURTON,George 2Lt kia 24-8-17 Mddx att13Bn p146 CR Belgium125

BURTON,George Ethelbert Earnshaw Lt dow 16-7-16 4Suff p217 CR France833,2Lt

BURTON,Gerard William.DSO.Maj kia 12-10-15 IA 2/39GarhwalRif p274 CR France765

BURTON,Henry Patrick Claude LtACapt kia 27-7-16 1Beds p85 MR21

BURTON,Henry Reginald 2Lt kia 11-9-18 3 att10DCLI p114 CR France1499

BURTON,Howard 2Lt dow 14-10-17 3SStaffs att1/7RWar p122 CR Belgium16

BURTON,Hubert T2Lt kia 9-10-17 1/5Y&L p158 MR30,Herbert

BURTON,James Wilson.MID Capt ded 5-7-19 RAMC att18GH p267 MR43 &CR Pakistan50A

BURTON,John Lees T2Lt kia 24-4-17 9BlkW att1GarrBnHLI p128 MR20,27-4-17 1BlkW att9HLI

BURTON,John Stanley 2Lt kia 16-5-16 GrenGds att2BnSR p49 CR Belgium84

BURTON,Kenrick Hammond Lt kia 16-6-18 6Lpool p215 MR30

BURTON,Louis LtAMaj dedacc 9-6-17 D70RFA p26 CR France225

BURTON,Percy Charles 2Lt kia 5-4-16 4EYorks p219 CR Belgium79

BURTON,Percy Herbert Capt kia 12-5-17 RAMC p253 MR20,att2/4Lond

BURTON,Reginald Cooksey 2Lt dow 9-4-16 IARO att125Rif MR38 p274

BURTON,Reginald John 2Lt dow 15-4-18 PoW 8Worc p226 CR Belgium393

BURTON,Richard Lt dow 24-6-15 1N&D p133 CR France354,kia

BURTON,Richard TCapt ded 9-3-19 RASC p267 CR Kent268

BURTON,Robert Cecil Capt dow 16-3-15 2RB p178 CR Sussex176

BURTON,Sidney Rex T2Lt kld 11-9-17 GL &78RFC p5 CR Derby99

BURTON,Stephen John Maj kia 28-7-17 1CldGds p51 CR Belgium12,20-7-17

BURTON,Thomas John Lt dow 27-3-18 6DLI p239 CR France185

BURTONWOOD,Ernest T2Lt kia 1-9-18 13WelshR p126 CR France217

BURTT,Edward TLt drd 13-8-15 RASC att8LabCoy p192 MR4

BURTT,William John 2Lt dow 23-3-18 RGA 286SB p38 CR France102

BURY,Edmond William TCapt kia 5-12-15 11KRRC p149 CR France525

BURY,Eric Lindsay.MC.T2LtTCapt ded 9-11-18 RE attRFA HQ2Cps p43 CR Glouc9

BURY,Harold Sterndale Entwisle 2Lt kia 25-1-15 1GrenGds SR p49 MR22

BURY,John Lt kia 5-7-15 ELancsRFA p207 MR4

BUSBY,Frederick William Merewether 2Lt dow 11-2-17 165RFA p26 CR France251

BUSBY,Harry Eldred T2Lt kld 11-9-17 GL &RFC p5 CR Mddx59

BUSBY,Reginald George Camden T2Lt kia 16-12-16 18DLI p160 CR France342

BUSBY,V.Capt ded 8-6-18 RE &RAF p43

BUSBY,William Baldwin T2Lt kia 15-2-17 12 att9Worc p108 CR Iraq5

BUSBY,William Walter.MC.Lt kia 13-11-16 D'Coy 13Ess p131 CR France1890,Capt

BUSE,Philip 2Lt kia 23-4-18 4 att1SomLI p218 CR France98

BUSH,Alfred John T2Lt kia 31-7-17 2Lincs p74 MR29

BUSH,Charles Gerald.DSO.TMaj ded 26-11-18 RASC 19DivTrn p192 CR France332,25-11-18 19

BUSH,Frederick Charles 2Lt dow 9-5-17 1Dev p76 MR20

BUSH,Hugh Godfrey de Lisle.MC.Lt dow 17-1-17 3Glouc p106 CR Glouc203

BUSH,James Cromwell.MC.Lt kia 7-10-17 Dors att22RFC p5&254 CR France1050

BUSH,John Stewart de Lisle Capt ded 25-8-17 PoW 3SomLI att41RFC p5&79 CR France660

BUSH,John Wheler T2Lt kia 25-9-15 RScotF p94 MR19,25/28-9-15

BUSH,Victor George Anderson TCapt kld 8-2-18 GL &RFC p15 CR Scot245

BUSH,Walter Donald Capt kia 4-6-15 4Worc p108 MR4

BUSHBY,Joseph Bryan 2Lt dow 9-10-18 6SStaffs p229 CR France446,1/5Bn

BUSHBY,Thomas Maj ded 1-1-16 RAMC p269 CR War84

BUSHE,Gervase Gray T2Lt dow 4-6-16 11Ches p95 CR France145

BUSHELL,Christopher.VC.DSO.CaptTLtCol kia 8-8-18 7RWSurr p55 CR France116

BUSHELL,Horace TLtACapt kia 6-9-18 57MGC Inf p182 CR France309

BUSHELL,R.H.C.2Lt kia 27-7-16 7RFus p67 MR20

BUSHELL,Roland 2Lt dow 26-9-17 A282RFA p208 CR Belgium36

BUSHER,Charles Joseph TLt dow 30-1-16 11WYorks p81 CR France285

BUSHER,Denis John Bryan T2Lt kia 24-4-17 8Lincs p74 MR20

BUSK,Edward Teshmaker 2Lt ded 5-11-14 RE attRFC p18&210 CR Hamps1,Lt

BUSK,George Laurence 2Lt ded 19-5-17 2RFA p208 CR Hamps13BUSS,Benjamin Capt dow 4-11-18 5EKent p213 CR Kent282

BUSS,Hilary Thomas T2Lt kld 21-1-18 RFC p15 CR Lincs100

BUSS,Percy Charles 2Lt kia 24-6-17 5 att1EKent p213 MR19

BUSS,Thomas Weston 2Lt kia 9-4-17 5 att6EKent p213 MR20

BUSSELL. Lt 11-6-15 NigR attS&TCps CR WAfrica58

BUSSELL,F.J.Lt 15-12-17 GL &NigR CR EAfrica35 &CRTanzania1

BUSSELL,Henry Richard 2Lt dow 17-8-17 5 att7SomLI p218 MR30

BUSSELL,John Garrett Capt kia 28-6-15 7RSuss p118 CR Belgium137

BUSSEY,Frank TCapt dow 15-8-17 1RE p43 CR Kent83

BUSSEY,Harry Martin 2Lt kia 3-5-17 3 att1RIrF p171 CR France604,Marslen

BUSSY,Cyril T2Lt kia 3-1-16 10 att8SStaffs p122 CR Belgium72

BUSSY,Julian T2Lt kia 29-9-16 7SStaffs p122 MR21

BUSWELL,Thomas Hubert 2Lt mbk 26-3-18 52RFC p256 MR20

BUSZARD,Stanley George Lt kia 8-12-17 NorfYeo p204 CR Palestine3

BUTCHARD,Robert Archibald TLt kia 5-11-16 31RFus p67 CR France374

BUTCHER,Arthur Algernon Lionel Hastings T2Lt kia 4-3-17 7RBerks p138 CR France1182

BUTCHER,Arthur James Basil 2Lt kia 3-9-16 17KRRC p149 CR France339

BUTCHER,Charles Geoffrey Lt kld 2-5-15 Dors p123 CR Belgium81

BUTCHER,Charles Leslie TCapt kia 24-7-16 2/7Worc p225 CR France1887

BUTCHER,Clarence Edward 2Lt kia 3-5-17 4Lond att8KRRC p246 MR20

BUTCHER,Cyril Arthur Mecrate T2LtACapt kia 6-7-17 GL 10Yorks att62TMB p190 CR France593

BUTCHER,Eugene Andrew Lt ded 23-11-19 IA TC att1/48Pnrs p274 MR66

BUTCHER,Francis Percival Herbert 2Lt kia 30-8-16 3 att1ELancs p110 CR Belgium127

BUTCHER,Frederick AMaj kia 22-5-18 A92RFA p26 CR France547

BUTCHER,Gilbert Thomas 2Lt kia 11-6-17 4NStaffs p156 CR Belgium127

BUTCHER,Harold Thomas T2Lt kia 17-2-16 11RB p178 CR Belgium73,18-2-16

BUTCHER,Henry Townsend BtCol kia 20-9-15 RFA p26 CR France219

BUTCHER,John Philip Henry 2Lt kia 22-5-16 18Lond p250 MR20

BUTCHER,Norris de Gruchy Lt&QM dow 23-5-18 13KRRC p149 CR France63

BUTCHER,Percival Drew Pitts Capt ded 3/4-11-18 RE 607Coy p255 CR Devon1,Lt 3-11-18

BUTCHER,Ralph Wycombe 2Lt kia 14-3-17 4 att22Manch p154 CR France576

BUTCHER,Richard Norman T2Lt dow 5-8-16 20Lpool p71 CR France66

BUTCHER,Vivian Haweis Lt dow 27-3-17 4Ess p232 CR Palestine8

BUTCHER,William Guy Deane Capt kia 16-8-17 1/5Lond p246 MR29

BUTLAND,George TLt kia 21-5-18 2Y&L p158 CR Belgium3

BUTLAND,William Henry T2Lt dow 31-1-16 10DLI p160 CR Belgium11

BUTLER,Archibald Stanley 2Lt kia 16-8-16 RFA 2/4SMid HB att25RFC p18&208 CRFrance88

BUTLER,Armar Somerset TLt kia 16-10-17 SLancs att7Wilts p125 CR Greece1,attRFC

BUTLER,Aubrey Edward Walter 2Lt kia 3-7-16 9 attRBerks p138 MR21

BUTLER,Bernard Arnold Barrington.DSO&Bar.LtCol dow 23-10-18 156RFA p26 CR France1478

BUTLER,Brian Danvers.Hon.TLt kia 18-8-16 13 att7KRRC p149 MR21

BUTLER,Charles Capt kld 27-8-17 RE attRFC p18&210,ded CR Yorks345

BUTLER,Charles Kingstone Capt&Adjt kia 1-7-16 10YLI p142 MR21

BUTLER,Charles Reginald Lt ded 28-11-18 19Lond p250 CR France1027

BUTLER,Clifford Hicks 2Lt kia 23-4-17 5BlkW p231 CR France604

BUTLER,Cyril Frank 2Lt dow 8-6-18 112RFA p26 CR France622

BUTLER,Desmond George Lt kld 17-3-18 Leinst &RFC p15&174 CR Mddx35,Capt 21-3-18

BUTLER,Edmund William.MC.TLtTMaj dow 18-4-18 2LifeGds att8Glouc p20 CR France40

BUTLER,Eric 2Lt kia 25-8-16 1Wilts p152 MR21

BUTLER,Eric Busvine 2Lt kia 30-9-17 D211RFA p208 MR30

BUTLER,Francis Mourilyan LtACapt kia 8-10-17 RFA 93ArmyBde p26 Belgium12

BUTLER,Frederick Harold 2Lt kia 1-1-16 1/6Lond p246 MR19

BUTLER,Geoffrey Lewis Lt kia 15-5-17 4 att11LancF p92 CR Belgium43

BUTLER,George Victor TLt kia 23-3-18 2/5Lincs p74 CR France927

BUTLER,Gordon Kerr Montague Lt ded 17-7-16 2ScotHorse attMGC p186&205 CR Egypt2,Montagu

BUTLER,Harold T2Lt kia 22-2-18 28RFC p15 CR Italy9

BUTLER,Harry 2Lt kia 25-3-18 70RFC p5 CR France245,Lt

BUTLER,James William 2Lt kia 3-5-17 3 att7EKent p57 MR20

BUTLER,John Fitzhardinge Paul.VC.DSO.Capt dow 5-9-16 2KRRC attGoldCoastR p149 CR EAfrica39

BUTLER,John Goodwin 2Lt dow 29-3-17 1/6WRid p227 CR France631

BUTLER,John Henry Rippon 2Lt dow 16-9-16 2CldGds p51 CR France105

BUTLER,John Leslie.MC.Capt dow 17-5-19 RFA Staff p26 MR43

BUTLER,John Ormond 2Lt ded PoW 11-4-18 GL 23RAF p15 CR Belgium241

BUTLER,Leonard Gray Capt kia 21-8-16 6 att3RB p178 MR21

BUTLER,Leonard William 2Lt kia 20-11-17 4 att7RIrF p171 CR France1489

BUTLER,Noel 2Lt kia 15-9-16 SR att1IrGds p52 CR France402

BUTLER,Owen James T2Lt kia 16-10-18 7Norf p73 CR France1284

BUTLER,R.A.Lt ded 20-7-18 RE &RAF p43

BUTLER,Richard Jefferson.MBE.Capt ded 1-7-19 YLI att8RWFus p265 MR43,kia att2SomLI

BUTLER,S.E.Sister ded 14-4-16 QAIMNS p200 CR Egypt3

BUTLER,Sidney Capt ded 22-1-19 16Lond p249 CR France65

BUTLER,Stanley Reginald.MM.2Lt kia 27-3-18 7SomLI p79 MR27

BUTLER,W.H.Capt&QM 21-8-21 RAMC CR Lond7

BUTLER,William T2Lt kia 22-3-18 7Leinst p174 MR27

BUTLER,William Andsley 2Lt kia 16-11-16 3SStaffs att1/8RWar p122 CR France239

BUTLER,William Martin CaptAMaj ded 5-3-19 RE 1MonSB p209 CR France1142

BUTLER-BOWDEN,Basil Joseph Bernard 2Lt kia 28-3-18 2LancF p92 MR20,BOWDON Lt

BUTLER-STONEY,Thomas Lt dow 1-10-17 1IrGds p52 CR Eire194,30-9-17

BUTLIN,Sir Henry Guy Trentham.MID Capt&Adjt kia 16-9-16 1/1Camb p244 MR21

BUTT,Alfred 2Lt kia 4-1-18 5Beds attRFC p15&85 CR Palestine3

BUTT,Charles Edward 2Lt kia 4-4-18 10Glouc p106 CR France1170

BUTT.F.W.2Lt kld 26-5-18 GL &RAF p190 see BUTT,W.F.R.

BUTT,George Lt&QM(Hon) ded 6-6-17 Dev p76

BUTT,Harry Alfred TCapt kia 8-6-16 14Glouc p106 CR France705

BUTT,AssSurg 26-10-18 ISMD MR65

BUTT,John George T2Lt dow 18-9-18 1EYorks p83 CR France666 SeeBOTT

BUTT,John Gillis Lt kia 29-10-14 RAMC att1GrenGds p194 MR29

BUTT,Lewis John Dalgleish T2Lt kia 4-7-16 16RB p178 CR France727

BUTT,Robert Acton T2Lt kia 9-1-16 9 att5KSLI p144 CR Belgium188

BUTT,William Frederick Reginald 2Lt dow 29-5-18 RGA 202SB p38 CR France29

BUTTANSHAW,Edward Henry Underwood Lt kia 27-4-15 EKent p57 CR Belgium84,dow 25-4-15

BUTTENSHAW,Leonard Horace Lt kia 27-6-18 4 att9WYorks p81 CR France223

BUTTER,Henry John TCapt kia 15-7-16 8BlkW p128 MR21,14-7-16

BUTTERFIELD,Charles Williams 2Lt kia 11-5-17 5NStaffs p238 MR19

BUTTERS,Henry Augustus T2Lt kia 31-8-16 B109RFA p26 CR France370,Harry

BUTTERWORTH,Benjamin 2Lt dow 25-3-17 3Manch p154 MR38

BUTTERWORTH,Edward Cyril T2Lt dow 21-11-17 9RFus p67 CR France446

BUTTERWORTH,F.2Lt kld 14-9-18 1/2WYorks attRAF p81 CR Belgium192

BUTTERWORTH,George Sainton Kaye.MC.Lt 5-8-16 13DLI MR21 See KAYE-BUTTERWORTH

BUTTERWORTH,Hugh Montagu TCapt kia 25-9-15 9RB p178 MR29

BUTTERWORTH,Harold.MC.Lt kia 20-9-18 RFA AA Bty p207 CR France327

BUTTERWORTH,Harold Winstone 2Lt kld 15-7-16 RFC p2 CR France924

BUTTERWORTH,Norman 2Lt kia 9-5-17 5Manch attRFC p18&236 CR France164,kld

BUTTERWORTH,Stanley Woodall Lt ded 16-1-18 7Ess p232 CR Suff55

BUTTERWORTH,Walter Cecil 2Lt kia 21-7-16 3 att1RWSurr p55 MR21

BUTTERY,Charles Henry 2Lt dow 1-10-16 6Lpool p215 CR France833

BUTTERY,Henry George 2Lt kia 27-9-18 5RWar p214 CR France415

BUTTERY,Robert Arthur T2Lt kia 15-6-18 1 att4 O&BLI p130 CR Italy2

BUTTERY,Walter 2Lt kia 20-8-18 5EYorks p219 CR France193

BUTTLE,Albert Edward TLt dow 2-10-18 17 att2RIrRif p169 CR Belgium38

BUTTLE,Bertram Haward T2Lt dow 1-10-17 RE att5Army HQ Z'SpCo p43 CR Belgium16,Howard

BUTTON,Charles Augustus 2Lt kia 27-5-18 45RFA p26 MR18

BUTTON,Norman Frederick TLt kia 4-11-17 1SomLI att11TMB p79 CR France154

BUXTON,Andrew Richard Lt kia 7-6-17 6RB p178 CR Belgium152,3Bn

BUXTON,Bertie Reginald 2Lt kia 1-7-16 1/2Lond p245 MR21

BUXTON,Hon.Denis Bertram Sydney 2Lt kia 9-10-17 2CldGds p51 MR30

BUXTON,George Barclay 2Lt kia 28-7-17 5Norf attRFC p18&216 MR20

BUXTON,Gurney White Capt ded 9-9-15 RAMC 2MtdBdeFA p253 MR4

BUXTON,Hugh Forster Lt dow 2-11-16 SR 5 att2RB p178 CR France105,3-11-16

BUXTON,Jocelyn Murray Victor 2Lt kia 1-7-16 6RB att25MGC Inf p178 MR21

BUXTON,Richard Percy ACapt kia 15-6-18 4 O&BLI p231 CR Italy2

BUY,Kenric Ellis Godson 2Lt dow 1-10-18 4BordR p228 CR France375,kia Ex NumbHuss

BYARD,Hubert 2Lt kia 6-11-17 1DCLI p114 MR30

BYATT,Harry Vivian Byatt Capt kia 14-3-15 RAMC att2RB p194 CR France768

BYERS,Henry Elliott 2Lt kld 12-11-16 3DCLI &RFC p2&114 CR Ireland14

BYERS,Henry Stagg TLt ded 3-2-16 RAMC p267 CR Europe1

BYERS,Richard Knight TCapt kia 20-7-16 8Glouc p106 MR21

BYFIELD,Arthur Thomas Stoneman Lt ded 24-3-15 3 att2DCLI p114 CR France64,2Lt

BYLES,Arthur Benzeville 2LtACapt dow 11-12-17 4 att2N&D p133 CR France446,Beuzeville

BYNG,Arthur Maitland Capt kia 14-9-14 RFus p67 MR15

BYNG,Francis Dacre TCapt kia 3-9-16 10RB p178 CR France294,Dacres

BYNG,Harry Gustave 2Lt dow 18-5-15 2BordR p116 CR France80,Gustav

BYNG,Leonard Gustave.MC.Lt dow 24-8-18 1GrenGds p49 CR France214,Gustav

BYNG,Percy Howard 2Lt ded 25-9-16 RFA 44Bty p26 CR Iraq5

BYRES,James Hope T2Lt kia 27-8-17 13RScots p53 MR30

BYRNE,Brennan Claude Sydney ObsOff 3-9-20 RE &47RAF CR Egypt9

BYRNE,Edward 2Lt kia 12-3-17 4GordH attRFC p18&242 CR France924

BYRNE,Edward T2Lt kia 23-8-17 6DCLI p114 MR30

BYRNE,Edward Aloysius T2Lt kia 24-4-17 11 att1RDubF p176 MR20

BYRNE,Edward James Widdrington Capt kia 29-4-16 3 att2SWBord p99 MR21,Edmund

BYRNE,Gerald William 2Lt ded 11-8-19 KSLI p265 CR Mddx53

BYRNE,Hubert Corbett 2Lt kia 2-9-18 5RSuss p228 CR Belgium111

BYRNE,Hugh Vyvian Edward.MC.TCapt kia 15-4-18 8 att9Norf p73 MR30

BYRNE,John Cahill Lt ded 11-10-18 IARO attOrdnanceDept p274 MR66

BYRNE,John Gilbert Lt kia 21-1-16 IA 37Dogras p274 CR Iraq5

BYRNE,Leo Francis T2Lt kia 21-8-16 6RIrReg p88 CR France178

BYRNE,Leslie Noel Lt ded 8-11-18 8Ess p232 CR Essex146

BYRNE,Louis Frederick T2Lt kia 1-7-16 24NumbF p60 CR France267

BYRNE,Patrick Anthony Laugan.DSO.MID 2Lt ded 17-10-16 129/30RFA &24RFC p2&26 MR20

BYRNE,Ralph Eugéne.MM&Bar.2Lt kia 4-4-18 C180RFA p26 CR France144

BYRNE,Samuel Hubert TCapt kia 13-9-16 9Suff p78 MR21

BYRNE,Thomas Edmond 2Lt kia 9-3-18 1WelshGds p53 CR France545

BYRNE,Vincent Cornel 2Lt kia 31-7-17 3 att1RIrRif p169 MR29,Connel

BYRNE,Walter T2Lt kia 30-9-18 LNLancs att1/4Bn p135 CR France572

BYRNE,William T2Lt dow 26-9-16 27NumbF p60 CR France285

BYRNE-JOHNSON,John Vivian.MID Capt kia 22-8-16 2RB p178 CR France423

BYRON,Clement John 2Lt kia 10-1-17 2HAC p206 CR France221

BYRON,Harry 2Lt kia 2-9-18 10Manch p237 CR France308

BYRON,Henry 2Lt dow 8-9-16 1/5SLancs p230 CR France188

BYTHEWAY,Gertrude Miss ded 31-12-17 VAD BRCS p200 CR Egypt1

C

CABLE,George Pickersgill 2Lt kia 9-5-15 5 att2RB p178 MR32

CABLE,Gordon Porter Capt ded 2-1-18 IARO attImpServTroops p274 CR Iraq8,attJaipurTransCps

CABLE,James Sydney Lt ded 5-9-18 RGA 46SB p38 CR France95,kldacc

CADDICK,Alfred Armstrong.MID TMaj kia 1-7-16 8RWar p214 MR21

CADDY,W.L.Capt 14-1-21 5Lancs CR Lancs71

CADE,Arthur Gordon.DSO.MC&Bar.MID CaptALtCol kia 26-4-18 2Mddx p146 MR30

CADE,Francis Thomas Darrel TCapt kia 6-9-16 11Hamps p120 MR21

CADE,Reginald Henry Maj kia 27-9-18 1/7LancF p221 CR France758,Harry

CADELL,Assheton Biddulph 2Lt dow 19-12-16 Dev att8RWKent p140 CR Belgium11,19-2-16

CADELL,Richard Lewis 2Lt dow PoW 28-5-18 RE 98FC p43 CR France1331

CADENHEAD,George 2Lt kia 10-5-15 3CamH p167 MR29

CADGE,Francis Edward Lt kia 30-4-15 1Ess p131 MR4

CADGE,William TLt kia 26-9-15 9Norf p73 MR19

CADIC,Bernard Francis Capt ded 20-8-16 RGA p209 CR Kent129

CADIC,Lawrence William Ludovic.MC.Capt dow 10-10-17 2Ess p131 CR Belgium83

CADMAN,Charles Joseph.MC.TLt kia 26-1-17 RE 150InfBdeSigs p43 CR France453

CADMAN,Edward Cadman LtCol kia 27-5-18 5RLancs p213 MR18

CADMAN,Philip Smelter Cadman Maj ded 31-3-19 ERidYeo p269 CR Yorks328

CADOGAN,Henry Osbert Samuel LtCol kia 30-10-14 1RWelshF p97 Belgium112

CADOGAN,William George Sidney.Hon.MVO.Maj kia 14-11-14 10Huss & Staff p22 CR Belgium57,12-11-14

CADZOW,Robert T2Lt kld 22-1-18 RFC p15 CR Scot783

CAESAR,Charles Patrick Lt 14-7-16 7KSLI MR21 see CEASAR,C.P.

CAESAR,George Theodore Lt dow 2-5-18 MGC &1ESurr attTankCps p112&182 CR France1170

CAFFRFEY,Charles James TCapt ded 1-7-16 RASC p192 CR Lond29

CAFFYN,Chalenor McCrae Humphrey Mannington 2LtTLt kia 28-3-17 ESurr att60RFC p5&112 CR France46,Chaloner

CAFFYN,Harold Hunt Capt kia 22-3-15 3 att1NStaffs p156 MR32

CAHILL,Alfred Gilbert 2Lt kia 8-10-16 3Lond p245 CR France374

CAHILL,John Archibald.MC.TCapt kia 16-8-17 RBerks p138 MR30

CAHILL,John Nugent Capt kia 16-8-17 13RIrRif p169 MR30

CAHILL,Patrick Leopold Lt kia 21-3-18 4RMunstF p175 CR France369

CAHILL,Thomas Laurence.MM.T2Lt kia 26-3-18 8 att1RDubF p176 MR27

CAIE,Robert George Hyndman TCapt ded 10-2-19 GL RFus p266 CR Surrey57,11-2-19

CAIGER,Frederick Howard Stewart 2Lt kia 11-11-16 92/17RFA p26 CR France432

CAIN,Alan Victor 2Lt kia 19-10-16 3 att2Hamps p120 MR21,18-10-16

CAIN,Edward 2Lt kia 2-12-17 2YLI p142 MR30

CAIN,Ernest William 2Lt kia 31-7-17 3Wilts p152 MR29

CAIN,Frank Backwell T2Lt dow 13-4-18 15HLI p162 CR France169

CAIN,Walter Frank Capt dow 3-5-17 17Lond p250 CR France113

CAIRD,Ernest Thomson T2Lt kia 24-3-18 11RScots p53 MR27

CAIRD,Frank Clagget 2Lt dow 22-11-16 3 att2InniskF p104 CR France74

CAIRD,John Roberts Capt kia 23-4-15 3att2KOSB p101 MR29,James Robert

CAIRN-DUFF,Norman 2Lt kia 25-4-18 RGA 242SB p38 CR Belgium11

CAIRNES,Alfred Bellingham TMaj kia 9-9-16 7RIrRif p169 CR France374

CAIRNES,Charles Beresford 2Lt kia 22-4-17 C146RFA p26 CR France616,148RFA

CAIRNES,William Jameson Capt kia 1-6-18 1Leinst &74RAF MR20

CAIRNIE,David Dandie.MC.2Lt kia 21-3-18 5SfthH p241 MR20

CAIRNS,George Morton 2Lt kia 13-11-16 6BlkW p231 CR France35

CAIRNS,George Ritchie 2Lt dow 4-1-16 RFA 52DAC p208 CR Gallipoli1

CAIRNS,George Thomas Lt kia 30-7-18 1/8ScotRif p225 CR France524,Thomson

CAIRNS,Herbert T2Lt kia 4-10-17 13KRRC p149 MR30

CAIRNS,James Lt kia 23-3-19 RASC p253 MR27,att2/4Lond

CAIRNS,John Anderson Gibson 2Lt kia 29-12-15 4KOSB p224 CR Gallipoli5

CAIRNS,Stanley Ewart.MC.Lt kia 30-9-18 7N&D p233 CR France1704

CAIRNS,William Anderson TLt kia 30-9-18 15 att17RScots p53 CRBelgium116

CAIRNS,William Jameson Capt kia 1-6-18 1Leinst &74RAF MR20

CALCOTT,Charles David TLt kia 23-4-17 15Lpool p71 CR France541

CALCUTT,Albert Birch 2Lt kia 30-3-18 13Glouc p106 MR27

CALDECOTT,John Leslie Lt kia 9-9-14 RGA p38 CR EAfrica80

CALDER,Alexander Lt kia 10-8-17 8 O&BLI &57RFC p5&130 MR20

CALDER,Alexander Frazer.MC.2Lt kia 19-7-16 3 att2A&SH p173 MR21

CALDER,Alexander Scott T2Lt kia 25-9-16 8 att10NumbF p60 MR21

CALDER,George MacBeth T2Lt kia 25-9-15 8SfthH p164 CR France219

CALDER,Harold Joseph.MID 2Lt kia 17-9-16 14Lond p249 CR France294,18-9-16

CALDER,John Kellick Lt kia 22-3-18 4SfthH p241 MR20

CALDER,John Stewart.MC&Bar.Capt kia 28-3-18 5Lond p246 MR20

CALDER,Kenneth William T2Lt dow 21-12-15 66RFA p26 CR Gallipoli1

CALDER,William Herbenton Lt dow 22-8-17 3/4KAR p202 CR EAfrica10 &CR Tanzania1

CALDER,William Menzies Grant T2Lt kia 15-9-16 13 att15Hamps p120 MR21

CALDER,William Paul T2Lt kia 14-6-17 18KRRC p149 MR29

CALDER-SMITH,Raymond Alexander 2Lt 1-7-16 3Lond MR21

CALDERON,George Lt kia 4-6-15 9 O&BLI att1KOSB p130 MR4

CALDERWOOD,Alex Taylor T2Lt kia 21-8-15 10Hamps p120 MR4

CALDERWOOD,William Sewell 2Lt kia 31-7-17 8ScotRif p225 MR29

CALDICOTT,Alan TCapt kia 7-12-16 GL 10LNLancs att1/2KAR p202 CR EAfrica38 &CR Tanzania1

CALDWELL,Anthony Steel T2Lt kldacc 4-5-17 GL &RFC p5 CR Yorks500

CALDWELL,Gavin Ralston Mure Lt kia 9-10-18 2CldGds p51 CR France1355

CALDWELL,James Robert McDonald T2Lt kia 26-10-18 RFA 403HB p26 MR38

CALDWELL,John Hay Lt kia 24-1-18 CamH attRFC p15&167,ded CR Iraq8

CALDWELL,Lindsay Roy Lt ded 6-1-20 IA 2/24BaluchistanInf p274 CR Palestine9,2/124Bn

CALDWELL,Robert Col 4-4-19 RAMC CR Devon258

CALDWELL,Robert Seddon T2Lt kia 11-6-18 8ACycCps p181 CR France1693

CALDWELL,Thomas.MM.T2Lt kia 3-10-18 1/2 att1/4KOSB p101 CR France242

CALE,Sidney 2Lt dow 29-8-17 5 att4Worc p108 CR Belgium16

CALEB,Clement Daryl Nicoll T2Lt kia 2-4-17 8Dev p76 CR France568

CALEY,Hugh William Capt ded 16-9-18 RASC p192 CR Berks84

CALEY,Pelham Russell 2Lt dow 14-8-17 9Lond p248 CR Belgium18,kia

CALEY,Vernon Christopher Russell.MC.ACapt kia 22-8-17 7RWar p214 MR30

CALIANDER,W.R.C.Lt 7-2-18 IARO MR66 see CALLANDER,W.R.C.

CALKIN,Brian Penry Bernard Lt kia 10-7-18 3 att8RWSurr p55 CR France161

CALKIN,John Ernest T2Lt kia 9-4-17 22NumbF p60 CR France265

CALLAGHAN,Arthur Nickson.MID TLt kia 30-8-17 14Lpool p71 CR Greece6

CALLAGHAN,Eugene Cruess 2Lt kia 27-8-16 19RFC p2 MR20

CALLAGHAN,J.C.MC.TMaj kld 2-7-18 1/2RMunstF att87RAF p175 CR France59,7Bn

CALLAGHAN,Joseph Patrick Aloysious 2Lt kia 1-7-16 64MGC p182 MR21

CALLAGHAN,Leslie Wilfred Capt kia 9-10-17 8WYorks p219 MR30

CALLAGHAN,Stanislaus Cruess LtTCapt kld 28-6-17 GL &RFC p5

CALLAN-MACARDLE,Kenneth 2Lt kia 10-7-16 17Manch p154 MR21,9-7-16

CALLANAN,Michael T2Lt kia 20-12-16 2RMunstF p175 CR France744

CALLANDER,William Ramsay Corson Lt ded 7-2-18 IARO p274 see CALIANDER,W.R.C.

CALLARD,Malcolm Ernest 2Lt dow 26-1-15 LNLancs p135 CR France80,25-1-15

CALLARD,Stanley Edwin 2Lt kia 23-4-15 2EYorks p83 CR Belgium96,Edwyn

CALLARD,William Kingsley 2Lt kia 1-7-16 5Leic p220 CR France281

CALLAWAY,Gilbert Charles 2Lt 28-4-17 2 O&BLI MR20 see CALLOWAY,G.C.

CALLAWAY,Robert Furley 2Lt kia 13-9-16 2N&D p133 CR France294

CALLEAR,Herbert TCapt kia 16-8-17 9RDubF B'Coy p176 MR30

CALLENDER,George Wilfred.MID TLtACapt kia 25-1-17 9Worc p108 CR Iraq

CALLENDER,Gerald Claude Lt kia 26-4-18 3RScots p53 MR30

CALLENDER,John Clement Lt kia 21-8-17 4 O&BLI p231 MR30

CALLENDER,Reginald Henry T2Lt kld 5-10-15 17DLI p160 CR France922

CALLEY,Oliver John Lt kia 12-3-15 1Wilts p152 CR Belgium60

CALLIER,E.F.M.Sister 22-6-19 QAIMNS CR Lond29

CALLINAN,Thomas William 2Lt kia 25-4-15 8DLI p239 MR29

CALLINGHAM,Frank Reginald T2Lt ded 26-2-19 N&D att10Bn p133 CR Lond12,25-2-19

CALLINGHAM,Stanley Breach Lt ded 18-1-19 6Norf p217 CR Essex137,5Bn

CALLISON,Robert William Lt kia 24-3-18 1/2 att8Leic p87 MR27

CALLOW,Donald 2Lt kia 2-7-16 1/5N&D p232 MR21,1-7-16

CALLOWAY,Gilbert Charles T2Lt kia 28-4-17 2 O&BLI p130 MR20,CALLAWAY

CALROW,William Robert Launcelot 2Lt kia 7-10-14 LNLancs p135 MR15

CALTHROP,Alfred Gordon.MID 2Lt kia 10-8-17 11RFus p67 MR29

CALTHROP,Calthrop Guy Spencer.Bart.LtCol ded 23-2-19 RE p269 CR Herts84

CALTHROP,Everard Ferguson MajTLtCol kia 19-12-15 38RFA p26 CR Belgium84

CALVERLEY,Geoffrey Walter.DSO.Lt kld 7-1-18 RIrRif attRFC p15&169 CR Wilts116

CALVERT,Cecilius Frederick Holcombe 2Lt kia 14-9-15 3SStaffs att2ELancs p122 CR France430,Cecil attRE 179Co

CALVERT,Eric Ruegg T2Lt kia 8-8-17 8RSuss p118 CR Belgium29

CALVERT,Francis 2Lt dow 19-9-17 2/4YLI p235 CR France512

CALVERT,Geoffrey Clifford TLt ded 15-1-19 16YLI p142 CR France1211

CALVERT,George Maj 25-8-20 RFA CR Devon50

CALVERT,James Howard T2Lt kld 24-4-16 6RIrRif p169 CR Ireland79

CALVERT,John Dutton Lt kia 14-2-15 RB p178 CR Belgium80,15-2-15

CALVERT,Lionel T2Lt kia 30-1-17 RE 175TC p44 CR France251

CALVERT,Reginald Cullen Capt dow 15-7-17 7WYorks p218 CR France74

CALVERT,Robert Mayson T2Lt kia 9-7-16 17Manch p154 CR France1890

CALWELL,Theophilus Legate.MC.TLt kia 7-10-16 9RFus p67 MR21

CALWELL,Walter Henry Lt dow 27-8-18 5 att2RIrRif p169 CR France100

CAM,Alan Noel T2Lt kia 16-8-17 RE 150FC p44 MR30

CAMBLE,Edward Maurice Baldwin TLt kia 1-7-16 8YLI p142 MR21,CAMBIE

CAMBLE,Graham Douglas Maj kia 25-9-15 40Pathans att10A&SH MR28

CAMBRIDGE,Thomas 2Lt kia 3-11-17 2/44RWKent p234 CR Palestine1,CAMBIDGE

CAMBRIDGE,William Kenneth 2Lt kia 26-3-18 331RFA p26 MR27

CAMBROOK,Horace.MC.T2Lt dow 17-10-18 8RWKent p140 CR France106

CAME,Harold Charles T2Lt kia 20-9-17 RWKent att11Bn p140 MR30

CAMERON,Alexander Leckie Capt kia 21-3-18 6 att8A&SH p243 MR27

CAMERON,Allan George Capt kia 25-9-14 1CamH p167 CR France1339

CAMERON,Archibald Capt kia 3-5-17 3 att5CamH p167 MR20

CAMERON,Archie.MM.2Lt kia 11-4-18 8BordR p116 MR32

CAMERON,Arthur Ian Douglas 2Lt dow 25-4-15 2SfthH p164 CR Belgium129

CAMERON,Charles Munnis T2Lt kia 12-6-16 RE 173TC p44 CR France178

CAMERON,Charles Peter Gwydyr.MC.Capt dow 30-4-18 RGA HvyArt attStaff 9CpsHQ p38 CR France100

CAMERON,Charles Tolmie 2Lt kia 21-3-18 4SfthH p241 MR20

CAMERON,Charles Wilson T2Lt kia 18-12-17 GL &21RFC p5 CR Belgium16

CAMERON,Colin Mackenzie Capt&Adjt kia 12-4-18 4SfthH p241 CR France194,11-4-18

CAMERON,Colin Neil Capt kia 10-8-15 7Ches p222 MR4

CAMERON,Cyril Henry 2Lt kia 12-3-15 N'RHA p26 CR France710

CAMERON,David.MIDx2 Capt&QM 1-1-20 1CamH CR Pakistan50A MR43

CAMERON,Donald T2Lt kia 25-3-18 3RFC p15 MR20

CAMERON,Donald Ronald Colin TLt kia 13-9-15 11HLI p162 CR France114

CAMERON,Douglas Robert Lt kia 31-7-17 3A&SH p173 CR Belgium46,dow

CAMERON,Duncan Lt ded 5-12-18 9A&SH attBaseDepotCarriers MGC p186&244 CR France40

CAMERON,Duncan Alexander.MC.Capt kia 1-12-17 IA CpsofGuides att38CentIndHorse p274 CR France446

CAMERON,Evan Stuart 2Lt kia 11-4-17 4 att6CamH p243 MR20

CAMERON,Ewen Arthur Lt kia 16-12-15 49RFA p26 MR29

CAMERON,Ewen Henry Lt ded 27-8-15 RDubF p266 CR Ireland24

CAMERON,Francis Blake TLt dow 19-8-16 7CamH p167 CR France74

CAMERON,Frederick Lt kia 23-4-17 7A&SH p243 CR France545

CAMERON,George Brown.MC.Lt dow 26-8-18 RASC p253 CR France832

CAMERON,George Grant 2Lt kld 16-10-17 4GordH attRFC p18&242 CR Scot280

CAMERON,Hector William Lovett 2Lt kia 14-9-14 1CamH p167 MR15

CAMERON,Henry Robley TLt ded 6-6-17 RFA 1stB ResBde p26 CR Sussex159

CAMERON,Hugh Alexander 2Lt dow 21-11-17 5Hamps p228 CR Palestine9,Lt

CAMERON,Hume Smith Capt kia 4-9-16 3Norf p73 CR France402

CAMERON,James Alistair Gordon 2Lt kia 18-11-16 3CamH p167 CR France515

CAMERON,James Callum 2Lt kia 23-4-17 4RScotF p222 CR France539

CAMERON,James Hunter Lt kia 25-9-15 9BlkW p128 MR19

CAMERON,James Macdonald 2Lt kia 10-5-15 368RFA p26 MR4

CAMERON,James Ritchie Capt kia 21-3-18 6LancF p221 MR27

CAMERON,John Capt ded 18-2-19 RAMC p267 CR Scot674

CAMERON,John Charles Schreiber Lt ded 28-5-18 SL(Censor) p268

CAMERON,John Gilmour 2Lt kia 9-11-16 CamH &RFC p2&167 CR France518,Ian

CAMERON,John Hunter.MID Lt ded 14-3-18 IARO att5MahrattaLI p274 MR66

CAMERON,John McAlister 2Lt ded 11-11-19 UL p269 CR Berks43

CAMERON,Kenneth.MC.CaptTMaj kia 26-9-18 2CamH p167 CR Belgium36,5Bn

CAMERON,Macdonald 2Lt kia 2-12-17 6HLI p240 MR30,Lt

CAMERON,Napier Charles Gordon Capt kia 26-9-14 1CamH p167 CR France1339

CAMERON,Nathaniel 2Lt dow 17-12-17 6SfthH p241 CR France52

CAMERON,Neil Kennedy Capt kia 25-9-15 5CamH p167 MR19

CAMERON,Percy Grant Lt kia 14-8-17 RGA &10RFC p5&38 MR20

CAMERON,Robert T2Lt dow 4-6-17 GL 7ScotRif att16RFC p5 CR France81

CAMERON,Robert Barton TLt kia 7-1-18 9RFC p15 CR Belgium18

CAMERON,Robert Campbell 2Lt dow 2-4-17 GL &8RFC p5 CR France120

CAMERON,Roy Douglas TLt kia 26-10-15 6CamH p167 MR19

CAMERON,Thomas Wright T2Lt kia 17-10-16 5CamH p167 MR21,18-10-16

CAMERON,Tom Finlayson Lt dow 30-4-18 2/14Lond p249 CR Palestine3

CAMERON,Waldo Hastie T2Lt kia 11-4-17 6CamH p167 CR France154

CAMERON,William Lt dow 27-10-15 1CamH p167 CR Scot447

CAMERON,William T2Lt kia 17-6-18 5CamH p167 CR France25

CAMERON,William George T2Lt kia 4-9-18 1/2WRid att1/5LancF p115 CR France239

CAMERON,William Henry Veitch Capt kia 20-12-14 1HLI p162 MR22

CAMERON,William McAdam T2Lt kia 14-7-16 8BlkW p128 MR21

CAMIES,Ernest Arthur T2Lt kia 15-7-16 2RWFus p97 CR France701

CAMM,Bertram Cunliffe.MC.ACapt kld 7-1-18 2Yorks p90 CR Belgium127

CAMM,Percy 2Lt ded 10-11-18 4ELancs &RAF p226&258,kld 20-10-18

CAMMACK,Edith Mary SNurse ded 1-3-18 TFNS 4SthGH &GH Salonika p254 CR War100

CAMPBELL,Alexander Boswell Lt dow 13-9-17 SussYeo p205 CR Belgium20,Capt

CAMPBELL,Alexander Charles Penn TLt kia 26-9-15 9ESurr p112 MR19

CAMPBELL,Alexander Findlay T2Lt kld 22-9-17 GL &RFC p5 CR Scot395

CAMPBELL,Alexander John.MIDx2 Capt kia 29-7-18 1/5A&SH p243 CR France866

CAMPBELL,Alexander Mather T2Lt kia 22-3-18 8SfthH A'Coy p164 CR France1182

CAMPBELL,Allan William George Lt dow 20-9-14 CldGds p51 CR France1329

CAMPBELL,Angus Hamilton.MC.Lt ded 12-3-19 RE p262 CR Lond13,13-3-19

CAMPBELL,Archibald Augustus Ava.Bart.TLt kia 9-5-16 6CamH p167 CR France423

CAMPBELL,Archibald Douglas Lerago TCapt kia 18-11-15 15DLI p160 CR France1140

CAMPBELL,Archibald Thomsom TCapt ded 22-2-16 RAMC p194 CR Scot764

CAMPBELL,Archibald Wright TCapt dow 13-12-17 RAVC 6MtdBde p198 CR Egypt2

CAMPBELL,Aubone Charles.DSO.CaptTMaj dow 3-4-18 1KOSB att11RScots p101 CR France62,2Bn

CAMPBELL,Brabazon 2Lt kia 18-12-14 4RWar p64 MR32

CAMPBELL,Bruce Hutchinson TLt kia 19-9-18 12A&SH p173 CR Greece5

CAMPBELL,C.C.K.Capt kia 28-9-15 3CamH attACycCps p167 MR19

CAMPBELL,Cecil Awdry Lt drd 4-10-18 RE 250FC p44 MR40,TC

CAMPBELL,Charles T2Lt dow 10-1-18 13KRRC p149 CR Belgium124

CAMPBELL,Charles T2Lt dow 20-4-18 11RFus p67 CR France300

CAMPBELL,Charles Arthur Lt kia 24-8-14 1Ches p95 CR Belgium197

CAMPBELL,Charles Bruce T2Lt ded 29-11-17 GL &49RFC p5 CR France403,48Sqn

CAMPBELL,Charles Duncan Mile.MBE.Maj ded 9-3-18 RFC p15 CR Kent83,Miles

CAMPBELL,Charles Frederick.MC.CaptAMaj kia 18-9-18 402/14RFA p26 CR France835

CAMPBELL,Charles Lionel Kirwan.CB.CMG.BtLtColTBrigGen ded 31-3-18 16Lancers5CavBde2CavDiv p23 CR Scot237

CAMPBELL,Charles Montage Gordon Capt ded 19-10-18 RAMC p194 CR France1858

CAMPBELL,Clarence Victor 2Lt kia 26-10-17 1/7N&D p233 CR France115

CAMPBELL,Claude Henry.DSO.TLtCol kia 14-3-16 1CamH att12WYorks p167 CR France157,Cmdg1/4SfthH

CAMPBELL,Colin Archibald Heron Maj kia 29-9-17 C296RFA p26 CR Belgium84

CAMPBELL,Colin Boyd 2Lt kia 28-7-16 6MGC p182 MR21

CAMPBELL,Colin Frederick Fitzroy Capt kia 29-10-14 1ScotsGds p52 MR29

CAMPBELL,Colin Gernon Palmer.MC.2Lt dow 10-10-17 94RFA p26&258 CR France139

CAMPBELL,Colin Richmond 2Lt kia 11-1-17 3HLI p162 CR Iraq5

CAMPBELL,Colin St.George 2Lt kia 6-4-17 SR 45RFC p5 CR Belgium406

CAMPBELL,David Wylie T2Lt dow 28-9-18 2Suff p78 CR France278

CAMPBELL,Donald Lt kia 17-2-15 RAMC att2EYorks p194 MR29

CAMPBELL,Donald Lt kia 19-7-16 CldGds p51 CR Belgium73

CAMPBELL,Donald George TCapt kia 13-8-16 12HLI p162 CR France453

CAMPBELL,Donald William Auchinbolck Capt kia 23-11-14 4SStaffs attN&D p122 MR22

CAMPBELL,Duncan Capt kia 18-5-15 2BlkW p128 CR France924

CAMPBELL,Duncan 2Lt ded 27-11-18 RGA att4ArmyGunPark p38 CR France146

CAMPBELL,Duncan Donald Heron.MC.MID Capt kia 7-6-17 RGA att112RFA p38 CR Belgium43

CAMPBELL,Duncan Frederick.DSO.MID LtCol ded 4-9-16 3BlkW Cmdg2/7WRid p227&264,Capt 9-9-16 CR Scot525,dow

CAMPBELL,Edward Lt kia 18-11-16 NStaffs att3rd p156 CR France384

CAMPBELL,Eric Octavius.Hon.DSO&Bar.TLtCol ded 4-6-18 8SfthH Staff p164 CR Wales416

CAMPBELL,Ernest Valentine Capt kia 26-9-15 4BlkW p230 MR19

CAMPBELL,Evan McDonald.MID T2Lt kia 5-10-17 RB att13Bn p178 CR Belgium112

CAMPBELL,Francis James Brook LtCol 1-7-18 IA MR65

CAMPBELL,Frederick Arthur 2Lt kia 22-3-18 2TankCps p188 MR27

CAMPBELL,Frederick Charles T2Lt kia 24-3-18 17RFus p67 MR20

CAMPBELL,Frederick William 2Lt ded 12-12-18 IARO att105LabCps p274 MR43,11-12-18

CAMPBELL,Geoffrey Arthur.MID Lt kia 29-10-14 1CldGds p51 MR29

CAMPBELL,George Edward Forman Lt kia 7-8-15 IA 2/10GurkhaRif p274 MR4

CAMPBELL,George Wands T2Lt kia 18-11-16 16HLI p162 CR France533

CAMPBELL,Graham Douglas Capt kia 26-9-15 IA 40Pathans attA&SH p274

CAMPBELL,Guy.MC.MID TCapt ded 26-5-17 4MGC Motors p182 CR Lincs61

CAMPBELL,Harry La Trobe.DSO.TD.LtCol ded 19-2-19 RE p269 CR Glouc9

CAMPBELL,Henry Bethune 2Lt kia 23-2-15 A&SH p173

CAMPBELL,Henry Wallace 2Lt kia 22-6-16 6RWar p214 CR France1157

CAMPBELL,Hugh TLt kia 22-8-15 11Manch p154 CR Gallipoli5

CAMPBELL,Ian Dermid 2Lt kia 30-11-17 GL &24RFC p5 MR20

CAMPBELL,Ian Patrick 2Lt kia 9-5-17 1CamH p167 CR France279

CAMPBELL,Ian Stuart T2Lt kia 30-6-16 23NumbF p60 MR21

CAMPBELL,Islay McKinnon Lt dow 4-4-18 SussYeo att11RScots p205 CR France145,Mackinnon

CAMPBELL,Ivan 2Lt dow 8-1-16 3A&SH attSfthH p173 MR38

CAMPBELL,Ivan.Hon.Capt ded 16-3-17 SL AssCensor p268

CAMPBELL,James 2Lt dow 23-7-18 8ScotRif p225 CR France865

CAMPBELL,James Archibald Lochnell Capt dow 19-3-15 1A&SH p173 CR Scot22 Ex 6GordH

CAMPBELL,James Henderson.MC.T2Lt kia 24-4-17 10/11HLI p162 MR20

CAMPBELL,John.MID.Capt kia 17-5-15 4CamH p242 MR22

CAMPBELL,John TCapt ded 19-2-19 RAMC p254 CR Lancs368

CAMPBELL,John Argentine TLt dow 2-12-17 6Drags p22 CR France660

CAMPBELL,John Beresford.Hon.DSO.Capt kia 25-1-15 CldGds p51 MR22

CAMPBELL,John Davies Lt 1-9-14 L'RFA p26 CR France1231

CAMPBELL,John Dundas T2Lt kia 24-8-16 9RWSurr p55 CR France432,1Bn

CAMPBELL,John Fyshe 2Lt dow 10-4-17 9A&SH p244 CR France95,8Bn

CAMPBELL,John Greenbank 2Lt kia 8-5-18 2Yorks p90 MR30

CAMPBELL,John Guy 2Lt dow 30-4-17 RGA 125SB p38 CR France1188,J.C.

CAMPBELL,John Kennedy T2Lt kia 28-7-17 GL &29RFC p5 MR20

CAMPBELL,John King T2Lt kia 21-4-16 RE 253Coy p44 CR France423

CAMPBELL,John Santiago Capt kia 28-9-17 9A&SH attRFC p18&243 CR France705

CAMPBELL,John W.DCM.2Lt dow 20-4-18 2SforthH p164 CR France10

CAMPBELL,John William Ronald.MC.Lt kia 14-4-18 3Worc p108 MR32

CAMPBELL,J.V.TLt ded 14-10-17 5CamH p167

CAMPBELL,Kenneth Gordon TLt kia 25-9-15 12HLI p162 CR France219

CAMPBELL,Kenneth James 2Lt kia 12-5-15 9A&SH p244 MR29

CAMPBELL,K.T.2Lt kia 17-6-18 GL &RAF p190

CAMPBELL,Lawford Bwine TLt kia 1-7-16 2RIrRif p169 MR21,Burne 12Bn

CAMPBELL,Montagu Irving Mitchell.MC.Maj dow 4-9-16 3ConnRgrs att2WelshR p172 CR France141

CAMPBELL,Neill Diarmid LtCol kia 12-4-18 8A&SH p243 MR32

CAMPBELL,Neil Leslie T2Lt kia 8-8-15 1/5RScots p53 CR Gallipoli6

CAMPBELL,Norman Phillips TLtACapt kia 3-5-17 RE 189Coy SpecBdeO SpCo p44 MR20

CAMPBELL,Oscar William 2Lt dow 24-6-17 RE 228FC p210 CR Belgium11

CAMPBELL,Quentin Hewes ACapt kia 19-7-17 5YLI p235 CR Belgium173

CAMPBELL,Robert Alexander Rankine 2Lt kia 1-7-16 2WYorks p81 MR21

CAMPBELL,Robert Gillies Capt ded 1-2-15 10SfthH p164 CR Scot926,Maj

CAMPBELL,Robert Burns Lt kia 3-5-17 5KOSB p224 MR20

CAMPBELL,Robert Charles Cowburn Capt dow 19-5-17 1KOSB p101 CR Lond4

CAMPBELL,Robert Colin 2Lt ded 28-11-18 1/1Lothian&BorderHorseYeo p204 CR Greece3

CAMPBELL,Robert William Procter Maj kia 15-11-15 RGA 2SB p38 CR France423

CAMPBELL,Ronald Walter Francis TCapt dow 11-8-16 10RFus p67 CR Scot22

CAMPBELL,Samuel MacDonnell TLt kia 1-7-16 GL 13LancF att86TMB p190 CR France221,2Lt

CAMPBELL,Stanley Frederick John 2Lt kia 27-8-18 1/6Lond p246 CR France214

40

CAMPBELL,Thomas Capt dow 3-8-16 RGA 19SB p38 CR France51

CAMPBELL,Thomas Callender TLt dow 8-10-15 RE 86Coy p44 MR4

CAMPBELL,Thomas Henderson Capt kia 4-5-16 6ScotRif p224 CR France114

CAMPBELL,Thomas Steel 2Lt kia 23-4-17 5RScotF p222 MR34

CAMPBELL,Tom Catto Pirie,MC Lt kia 28-3-18 4GordH p241 MR20,Calto

CAMPBELL,Torquil Lorne 2Lt kia 1-3-17 8 att1A&SH p243 CR France511

CAMPBELL,Victor Robert Wilkie T2Lt kia 7-9-18 RWelshF 3GarrBn att23Ches p97 CR France263,6-9-18

CAMPBELL,Walter Stanley.MC.Lt kia 7-10-16 1Lond p245 MR21

CAMPBELL,W.C.2Lt kia 23-4-17 7BordR p116 MR20

CAMPBELL,William.MC.TCapt dow 5-9-16 RAMC att7RFA p194 CR France188

CAMPBELL,William Lt kia 6-7-17 RFA &2RFC p5&26 CR France161

CAMPBELL,William.MC.2Lt kia 31-7-17 9RScots p212 CR Belgium73

CAMPBELL,William T2Lt kia 20-9-17 Mddx att23Bn p146 MR30

CAMPBELL,William Archibald Lt dow 21-9-17 1/7WYorks att10RFC p18&218 CR France98

CAMPBELL,William Barton Rev2Lt kia 19-4-17 5KOSB p224 MR34

CAMPBELL,William Kenneth Hamilton Maj ded 19-5-18 IA 12Pioneers p274 CR Devon237,9-5-18

CAMPBELL,William Mackenzie T2Lt kia 1-7-16 9RIrRif p169 MR21

CAMPBELL,William John 2Lt ded 25-5-15 RGA p38 CR Asia45

CAMPBELL,William Percy 2Lt kia 24-10-14 3 att2Wilts p152 MR29

CAMPBELL,William Robinson.DSO.Maj kia 13-5-15 14Huss p22 MR29

CAMPBELL,William Ulick Middleton Capt kia 14-3-15 1HLI p162 CR France279

CAMPBELL,William Watson 2Lt kia 9-1-17 7Manch p237 CR France701

CAMPBELL,Willie T2Lt kia 4-11-18 2/4Y&L p158 CR France1081

CAMPBELL,W.K.Lt 7-9-16 2DAC attRFC CR Canada 1203

CAMPBELL-IRONS,Arthur Capt kia 8-3-16 3HLI p162 MR38

CAMPBELL-JOHNSON,Patrick Seymour Campbell.MC.Lt dow 30-8-19 RFA p254 CR Essex29

CAMPBELL-MACGREGOR,John Rev dow 4-11-16 Chap4Cl attCamH CR France377

CAMPBELL-MURDOCH,Louis Forde 2Lt dow 19-9-16 2ScotsGds CR France300

CAMPBELL-ORDE,John Vernon TLt ded 14-10-17 5CamH p167&265,7Bn CR Scot44,kldacc

CAMPION,Edward MajTLtCol ded 25-2-16 2SfthH p164 CR Sussex136

CAMPION,Raoul Rene TLt kia 17-2-17 RGA att73 SR SBHvy p38 CR France314

CAMPION,William Ernest Maj kia 28-10-14 1EYorks p83 CR France82

CAMPKIN,Reginald Ernest 2Lt kia 28-3-18 4Lond p246 MR20

CAMPLIN,Ernest.MM.T2Lt kia 29-9-18 1 att6RWKent p140 CR France369

CANBY,Ronald Leslie Lt kia 8-5-17 6NStaffs p238 MR20

CANCELLOR,Desmond Bertram.MC.Lt kia 1-11-18 3 att1Hamps p120 CR France1252

CANDY,Douglas Bowhill 2Lt dow 25-9-16 4 att1Beds p85 CR France329

CANE,Leonard Dobbie TCapt&Adjt kia 24-1-16 20RFus p67 CR France114

CANE,Lionel Alfred Francis Capt kia 7-11-14 1ELancs p110 CR Belgium68

CANE,Maurice T2Lt kia 4-8-17 1/153RFA p26 CR Belgium96

CANE,Reginald Shapland T2Lt kia 1-7-16 1Hamps p120 MR21

CANEY,Charles.MC.2Lt dow 29-8-18 6EKent p57 CR France119

CANFOR,Arthur Reginald T2Lt kia 23-3-18 8ESurr p112

CANN,Leonard 2Lt kia 13-3-18 RFC p15 CR France34

CANN,P.R.2Lt dow 2-4-18 GL &RAF p190

CANNAN,Horatius James.DSO.TCapt dow 2-11-16 B78RFA p26 CR France145

CANNELL,Hugh Featherstone Cameron Lt dow 31-10-18 IA 1Lancers att72RAF p274 MR38

CANNING,Edward 2Lt kia 6-7-16 6KOSB p101 MR21

CANNING,Ernest Harold.DFC.2Lt kld 5-10-18 1Glouc &102RAF p106 CR France404

CANNON,Richard Lt kia 5-4-16 8Wilts p152 MR38

CANNON,Sidney Leslie 2Lt ded 14-9-18 KSLI attRAF p144 CR Egypt1,Lt

CANSDALE,Lionel.MIDx22Lt kia 29-3-18 1Dors p123 MR16,29-3-18

CANSFIELD,Victor Morton T2Lt kia 24-2-16 95RFA p26 CR France922

CANSINO,Joshua T2Lt kia 2-6-17 22Manch p154 MR21

CANTAN,Henry Thomas.CMG.LtCol kia 16-4-16 1DCLI p114 CR France1182

CANTLE,Leonard Heath Lt kia 8-4-17 SurrYeo attRFC p18&205 MR20

CANTON,Herbert Westrup LtTCapt kia 13-5-15 ELancs p110 MR29

CANTY,Frederick William T2Lt dow 29-6-18 3EYorks Res att2Y&L p83 CR France142

CAPE,George Augustus Stewart.CMG.TLtColTBrigGen kia 18-3-18 RFA 39DivArty p26

CAPEL CURE,B.A Capt dow 1-10-16 2Glouc CR Greece4 see CURE,B.A.C.

CAPELL,Arthur Edward T2Lt kia 13-11-16 10RWelshF p97 MR21

CAPELL,Arthur George Coningsby Capt kia 12-3-15 1Nhampt p137 MR21

CAPELL,Bruce Lorence.MC.2Lt kia 7-6-18 RGA 2/1NorthMidHvyBty p38 CR France504

CAPERN,Henry James T2Lt kia 22-3-18 10KRRC att59TMB p149 MR27,11Bn

CAPPELL,James Leitch Rev ded 23-1-8 RAChDept att1/9RScots p199 CR France85

CAPPER,Adam Clarke T2Lt kia 9-9-16 20 att7RIrRif p169 CR France402

CAPPER,Bass Durant TCapt kld 6-12-17 RFC p5 CR Ireland33

CAPPER,Charles Arthur TLt ded 11-3-19 ArmyPayDept p200 CR France134

CAPPER,Edward Walter Lt kia 14-4-17 MontgomeryYeo attRFC p18&204 MR20

CAPPER,Ernest Raphael.MC.TCapt dow 24-12-17 9Ess p131 CR Germany9

CAPPER,George William Maj ded 7-1-19 1EYorks GarrBn p83 MR66

CAPPER,John Beausire Copeland.MC.2Lt kia 26-9-16 A70RH&FA p26 CR France453

CAPPER,Thompson.Sir.KCMG.CB.DSO.MajGen dow 27-9-15 Staff ELancs GOC7Div p1 CR France201

CAPRON,Thomas Harvey Overbury TLt kia 26-3-17 1 att1/5Ess p131 CR Palestine8

CARBERY,Miles Bertie Cunningham Capt kia 18-10-14 1RIrF C'Coy p171 CR France1140,Cunninghame 17-10-14

CARBINES,Henry 2Lt mbk 27-3-18 8Lpool &RFC p257 MR20

CARBONELL,William Charles 2Lt dow 1-9-16 3 att1SStaffs p122 CR France66

CARD,Arthur Henry.MC.2Lt kia 26-9-16 12Mddx p146 MR21

CARD,John Victor.MC.Lt kia 25-3-19 3ESurr p112 MR70 &CR Europe179,Capt

CARD,Stormont Hays 2Lt kia 10-4-17 1SomLI p79 MR20

CARDELL,Edmund Powne.MC.Maj kia 21-3-18 46RFA p26 MR27

CARDEN,Derrick Alfred LtCol dow 25-5-15 SfthH att7A&SH p164 CR France200

CARDEN,Henry Charles.DSO.Maj kia 25-9-15 8Dev p76 MR19

CARDEN,John.CMG.LtCol kia 10-8-15 5Wilts p152 MR4 &MR22

CARDEN,John Rutter Maj dow 30-4-15 IA 15Sikhs p274 CR France102

CARDEN,Ronald Hugh 2Lt kia 14-3-15 SL attWilts p201 MR22

CARDEN,Ronald James Walter TLtCol kia 8-7-16 17Lancers att16RWelshF p23 CR France513,10-7-16

CARDEW,Edward Bellasis Capt kia 26-9-15 RE 7FC p44 MR19

CARDEW,George Eric.MC.Capt kia 9-4-18 4Dev att6DLI p220 MR32

CARDEW,John Haydon.MC.LtACapt dow 5-10-17 73RFA 5ArmyBde p26 CR Belgium16

CARDEW,Richard Cornelius Arthur 2Lt kia 24-4-18 3 att2Dev p76 CR France144

CARDWELL,Hugh Brodie Lt dow 9-8-18 B256RFA p207 CR France145

CARE,Graham Bristowe 2Lt kia 19-4-17 1/4RScots p211 CR Palestine8

CAREFULL,John Holt TCapt kia 21-3-18 12Lpool p71 MR27

CAREW,Coventry George Warrington TCapt dow 20-11-16 7 att1Dors p123 MR21

CAREW,Cyril Joseph Theodore 2Lt dow 29-4-15 2EYorks p83 CR France1

CAREW,Francis Ludovis 2Lt kia 30-10-14 20Huss p23 MR29,Ludovic

CAREW,Jasper 2Lt kia 14-10-14 WYorks p81 CR France276

CAREW,Robert Thomas Col ded 11-2-17 Leinst p266 CR Eire238

CAREW HUNT,Aubrey Noel Capt kia 5-6-16 3 att2 O&BLI p130 CR France68

CAREY,Allan Stewart T2Lt kld 27-5-17 GL &45RFC p5 CR Belgium140

CAREY,Arthur John Edward 2Lt kia 22-8-17 3 att8/10GordH p166 MR30,Lt

CAREY,Arthur Stanley Lt kia 15-9-16 1/8Mddx p236 CR France785

CAREY,Bertram Chepmell.MC.LtACapt dow 22-9-18 1Nhampt p137 CR France673

CAREY,Francis Ambrose 2Lt kia 15-9-16 32RFus p67 MR21

CAREY,Frederick Capt ded 22-1-16 RGA attAOD India p26 MR43 &CR Pakistan50A,Maj

CAREY,Henry Pattison TLt kia 7/11-8-15 9N&D p133 MR4

CAREY,Leicester William le Marchant Capt kia 17-10-14 RFus p67 MR22,19-10-14

CAREY,Leonard Arthur T2Lt kia 1-7-16 2Dev p76 MR21

CAREY,Loyd Carleton T2Lt kia 4-9-16 13 att1ESurr p112 MR21

CAREY,Mansell Ernest.MC.2Lt kia 30-11-17 1/4RWKent p234 MR17,Mansel

CAREY,M.J.MC.Lt&QM 16-11-20 GL &12RB CR Hamps202

CAREY,Richard Cyril T2Lt dow 8-7-16 12Suff p78 MR20,3-7-16

CAREY,Timothy S.J.Rev Chap4Cl ded 27-2-19 RAChDept p199 CR France1374

CAREY,Thomas Augustus 2Lt kia 5-12-17 1IrGds p52 MR17

CAREY,William Alexander Lt kia 29-12-17 2/19Lond p250 CR Palestine3

CARFRAE,Charles Francis Kirkpatrick Capt kia 25-9-15 O&BLI att5Bn p130 MR29

CARGILL,Duncan Campbell.MC.T2Lt kia 2-11-18 2SfthH p164 CR France1266,20-11-18

CARGILL,John Capt dow 24-4-17 7BlkW p231 CR France95

CARGIN,Norman J.A.T2Lt dow 1-5-16 7 att10NStaffs p156 CR Iraq6

CARLESS,Albert William Buchan Lt dow 27-9-15 5 att1Mddx p146 CR France98

CARLESS,Hugh Dobbie 2Lt dow 24-4-17 3GordH p166 CR France113

41

CARLESS,Wilfred Townsend Maj kia 12-8-15 1Hereford p252 MR4,Wilfrid Townshend

CARLESS,William Stanley Capt ded 18-12-18 RAVC p269 CR Hereford208

CARLEY,B.AssMatron 26-4-20 TFNS CR Suff68

CARLEY,Henry Victor T2Lt dow 14-10-15 7Norf p73 CR France98,Harry Lt

CARLEY,Samuel Newman T2Lt kia 25-9-17 207MGC Inf p182 CR Belgium125

CARLEY,Thomas Morgan T2Lt kia 27-9-18 Manch att2/9Bn p154 CR France712

CARLILE,Edward Hildred Hanbury Capt kia 22-3-18 HertsYeo p204 MR20

CARLILE,Thomas T2Lt kia 16-8-17 11RInniskF p104 MR30

CARLINE,Norman John 2Lt kia 22-3-18 LNLancs att10Bn p135 CR France366

CARLINE,Thomas T2Lt kia 30-9-18 18Lpool att15LancF p71 CR France376

CARLISLE,Arthur Lewis Capt kia 29-8-18 4RASC 8DivTrain p192 CR France184,2Berks

CARLISLE,Francis Bruce Maj ded 31-12-14 4RWKent p234 MR65

CARLISLE,Frederick Albert 2Lt kia 15-9-17 2/4Lond p246 CR Belgium10

CARLISLE,John Edward Gordon Capt dow 11-5-15 IA 107Pnrs p274 CR France80

CARLISLE,Reginald TLtACapt kia 3-5-17 10EYorks p83 MR20

CARLISLE-CROWE,William Maynard Capt 11-11-14 RWar att1Nhampt MR29 see CROWE,W.M.C.

CARLOS,Ernest Stafford 2Lt kia 14-6-17 4EKent p212 CR Belgium56,Lt 8Bn

CARLTON,Claude Gray 2Lt kia 26-10-17 Dev att9Bn p76 MR30

CARLTON,Roy Septimus 2Lt ded 30-5-17 RFC p261 CR Kent83,Lt 8SLancs

CARLTON,William Fergus 2Lt kia 17-6-16 4EYorks p219 CR Belgium79

CARLYLE,George Pasley 2Lt kia 14-10-18 14Lond att9MGC Inf p249 CR Belgium157

CARLYLE,Robert 2Lt kia 12-7-17 1/5KOSB p224 CR Gallipoli2

CARLYLE,Thomas Johnstone Lt kia 5-10-17 5KOSB p224 CR Belgium84

CARLYLE,William Mackay 2Lt kia 26-10-16 60RFC p2 MR20

CARLYON,Lionel George T2Lt kia 3-5-17 9ScotRif p103 CR France604,W.G.

CARLYON,Thomas Tonkin 2Lt dow 28-6-18 RGA 99SB p209 CR France31

CARMAN,Leslie Guy.MID 2Lt kia 4-10-16 3EKent p57 CR France1890,7Bn

CARMICHAEL,Andrew T2Lt kia 12-10-17 6KOSB p101 MR30

CARMICHAEL,Andrew Gemmell T2Lt kia 11-4-17 6CamH p167 CR France311

CARMICHAEL,Archibald 2Lt dow 22-5-18 C108RFA p26 CR France71,D108

CARMICHAEL,Chalmers 2Lt kia 15-7-16 1/8N&D p233 MR21

CARMICHAEL,David Arthur Lt kia 17-4-18 3RFus att25MGC Inf p67&182 MR30,9Bn

CARMICHAEL,Douglas TCapt kia 25-9-15 9RB p178 MR29

CARMICHAEL,George Clement 2Lt kia 18-8-16 2A&SH p173 MR21 CR France393

CARMICHAEL,George Gordon Lt kia 1-8-18 4KOSB p223 CR France524,1/5Bn

CARMICHAEL,Gilbert 2Lt kia 21-3-18 10 att2/6Manch p237 MR27

CARMICHAEL,John T2Lt dow 25-3-18 20DLI p160 CR France62

CARMICHAEL,Robert Henry Morris Lt kia 12-7-15 5A&SH p243 MR4

CARMICHAEL,Thomas Sydney T2Lt dow 18-5-16 1LNLancs p135 CR France80

CARNAGHAN,James T2Lt kia 23-10-16 12ScotRif p103 MR21

CARNALL,Ronald Gundry TLt dow 29-11-16 143MGC p182 CR France177

CARNDUFF,Kenneth McLeod.MIDx2 Capt dow 11-1-16 RE 2FC p44 CR France423,12-1-16

CARNE,John Reeves T2Lt dow 25-7-17 12RSuss p118 CR Belgium11

CARNE,Maxwell Halford T2Lt dow 23-12-16 2DCLI p114 CR Europe1

CARNECY,James Maj kia 3-7-16 NStaffs att8Bn p156 MR21,CARNEGY

CARNEGIE,David Alexander 2Lt kia 2-4-17 B122RH&FA p26 CR Belgium1

CARNEGIE,Theodore Arthur Lt kia 16-8-17 12KRRC p149 MR30

CARNEGY,Frederick Alexander TLt kia 13-10-15 10Glouc p106 MR19

CARNEGY,Richard Lloyd Maj kia 10-8-15 RLancs IA 9GurkhaRif p58 CR Gallipoli17

CARNELL,Frederick Harry Wright.MC.TCapt kia 9-6-18 9WYorks p81&258 CR France223,9-5-18

CARNELLEY,Joseph Arthur TLt dow 16-6-16 RE 173TC p44 CR France285

CARNES,William Jameson Capt kia 1-6-18 Leinst &RAF p266

CARNLEY,Ronald Lt kia 27-5-18 5Leic p220 MR18

CARO,Jacob Pisa 2Lt kia 2-5-18 17Lond p250 MR27

CARPENDALE,Maxwell Montagu.MC.Maj ded 14-10-18 IA 36Horse p274 CR Syria2

CARPENTER,Bernard Melville 2Lt dow 3-4-18 6 att19Mddx p146 CR France40

CARPENTER,Cedric Theodore Arundel Lt dow 6-11-18 7Ches p223 CR France332

CARPENTER,Charles McElroy T2Lt kld 21-3-18 RFC p15 CR Shrop130

CARPENTER,Clarence T2Lt kia 17-2-17 23RFus p67 CR France314

CARPENTER,Ernest Lt kia 30-10-18 Worc &24RAF p264 MR20,3-10-18

CARPENTER,Henry Alfred Stanley T2Lt kia 2-9-16 130MGC p182 CR France151

CARPENTER,Herbert Montagu Soame TCapt kia 5-7-16 10WRid p115 CR France515

CARPENTER,Hubert Granville 2Lt dow 25-2-16 ACycCps 2LondDiv p244 CR France134,26-3-15

CARPENTER,John Neilson.MC.T2Lt kia 1-7-16 17HLI p162 MR21

CARPENTER,John Philip Morton TLt kia 15-9-16 RFA p26 CR France277,16-9-16

CARPENTER,Robert Leslie Lt kia 26-10-15 1/17Lond p250 CR France219

CARPENTER,Ronald Percy Victor TLt kia 6-9-18 57MGC Inf p182 CR France309

CARPENTER-GARNIER,John Trefusis Maj kia 14-9-14 1ScotsGds p52 CR France1328,15-9-14

CARPENTER-TURNER,Eric Walter Lt dow 9-8-16 2Hamps p120

CARR,Alexander Gunning Capt ded 14-2-19 RGA CR Lond2,dow

CARR,Alfred Rothwell 2Lt kia 9-4-17 9Lpool p216 CR France596

CARR,Arthur Clunes Hooper Lt dow 15-2-15 RE p44 MR29

CARR,A.W.2Lt ded 6-7-18 RIrF &22RAF p171 CR Egypt1,ConnRgrs

CARR,Basil Alderson 2Lt kia 25-7-17 RGA SR p38 CR Belgium24

CARR,Charles Frederick 2Lt dow 20-2-17 17 att4N&D p133 CR France64

CARR,Cyril(Dick).MC.TLt kia 11-4-18 RE 224FC p44 CR France193

CARR,Donald Neville.MC.LtTCapt ded 26-11-18 4BordR attSPersiaRif p116 MR61

CARR,Dudley Reed Lt kia 23-2-17 2Norf p73 MR38

CARR,Edgar Joseph Austin Lt dow 18-5-15 5RLancs p213 CR Lond9,Augustin

CARR,Eric Marcus T2Lt kia 1-7-16 12Y&L p158 MR21

CARR,Frank Clifford T2Lt dow 24-4-17 TurkPoW MGC p182 MR34,19-4-17

CARR,Frank Henry T2Lt dow 23-3-18 7Leic p87 CR France987

CARR,Frederick Wysses MajTLtCol ded 10-11-17 RAVC attEgyptianArmy p198 CR Yorks436,Ulysses

CARR,Hugh T2Lt dow 23-1-16 RE 172Coy p44 CR Belgium11

CARR,James 2Lt kia 21-3-18 296RFA p26 MR20

CARR,James Walter,MC.DCM.MID Lt ded 16-11-18 23RFus att99TMB p67 CR Surrey1

CARR,John Cory Capt&QM kia 21-10-18 Lpool att2/5Bn p71 CR Belgium 406,20-10-18 2/6Bn

CARR,John Stanley Lt kia 31-7-17 5LNLancs p234 MR29

CARR,Leslie George.MC&Bar.Capt dow 27-4-18 1Lond att4SStaffs p245 CR France102

CARR,Martin Raymond Capt kia 18-9-14 2Worc p108 CR France1329

CARR,Robert Meredith TLt kia 29-5-18 10Lincs p74 CR France1332

CARR,Stanley Theodore TLt kia 27-9-16 11Manch p154 MR21

CARR,Victor Francis LtACapt kia 21-5-18 RGA 108HB p38 CR France106

CARR,William Parsons Lt kia 13-12-17 2/21Lond p251 CR Palestine3

CARR-ELLISON,Oswald Fenwicke-Clennall.MID Lt kia 5-10-18 2NumbF p60 CR France234,Clennell

CARR-HARRIS,Ernest Dale Capt kia 3-11-14 RE p44 MR47

CARR-WEST,Herbert St.John Maj dow 27-10-18 12DLI CR Italy7

CARRALL,John Edwin 2Lt kia 3-5-17 12EYorks p83 MR20

CARRE,Edward Mervyn TLt kia 16-10-16 8Lincs attRFC p74&2 CR France1327

CARRE,Gilbert Trenchard TLt kia 20-11-17 9 att6RWKent p140 CR France379

CARRETTE,Albert Ernest T2Lt kia 27-4-16 9RDubF p176 CR France423

CARRICK,James Douglas 2Lt kia 11-9-18 RFA attX42TMB p26 CR France568

CARRICK,John.MID TLt kia 31-7-17 6CamH p167 CR Belgium7

CARRICK,Richard Hamilton T2Lt kia 2-4-17 9Dev p76 CR France568

CARRIDEN,William Scott T2Lt ded 12-2-19 RASC p254&267 CR Scot754

CARRIE,Fred George Lt kia 26-10-17 5LNLancs p234 MR30

CARRIER,John Russell 2Lt kia 8-10-16 5Lond p246 MR21

CARRIGAN,Colin Herbert.MC&Bar.Capt kia 2-9-18 1RMunstF p175 CR France592

CARRINGTON,Charles Harold Lt kia 9-4-18 5DLI p238 MR32

CARRINGTON,Edmund Alfred 2Lt kia 18-10-15 2Wilts p152 MR19

CARRINGTON,Edward Worrell.MC.TCapt kia 27-9-15 RAMC att2Worc p194 CR France423

CARRINGTON,Harold Edward TCapt kia 15-9-16 15Hamps p120 MR21

CARRITT,Harry William TCapt kia 8-7-16 2Nhampt p137 MR21

CARROLL,Frederick Stanley T2Lt kia 21-11-16 7RInniskF p104 CR France432

CARROLL,Henry Arthur TLtCol ded 31-10-18 RMunstF p266 CR Hamps64

CARROLL,James Charles Lt dow 26-3-18 RGA att1TankCps p38 CR France300

CARROLL,James Francis Joseph R.Capt ded 24-3-19 RDubF p266 CR Ireland12

CARROLL,Patrick T2Lt kia 8-2-17 10RDubF p176 CR France339

CARROLL,William.MC.ACapt kia 3-5-17 12EYorks p83 CR France1191

CARROLL-LEAHY,Nöel Edward Joseph Lt kia 9-8-18 O/5RFA CR France1170

CARROTHERS,John Samuel 2Lt kia 16-8-17 8RInniskF p104 MR30

CARRS,Stuart TLt dow 28-7-16 RE 212FC p44 CR France51

CARRUTH,John TLt dow 10-10-18 6RDubF attRIrRif p176 CR France446

CARRUTH,Matthew 2Lt kia 9-9-16 6RIrReg att6ConnRgrs p88 MR21,4Bn

CARRUTHERS,Cameron Roy Capt kia 31-7-17 4CamH p242 MR29

CARRUTHERS,E.S.Maj ded 16-5-17 RE p44 CR Kent153

CARRUTHERS,George MacLellan T2Lt kia 10-8-17 11LancF p92 MR29

CARRUTHERS,Gordon T2Lt dow 27-11-18 1 att5WRid p115 CR France146

CARRUTHERS,James Mein Austin TCapt dow 26-4-17 16Mddx p146 CR France40

CARRUTHERS,William 2Lt kia 24-4-17 RE 154FC p44 Ex 3RIrRif France452,Lt

CARRUTHERS,William Alexander.MC.TLt dow 3-9-18 NumbF att1RScots p60 CR Greece6

CARRUTHERS,William Keith 2Lt kia 3-4-17 BucksBn O&BLI att2/4Lincs p231 MR21

CARRYER,Charles Ivan 2Lt kld 18-8-16 RFC p2,263&261,18-3-16 EYorks CR Leic63,13-8-16

CARSE,Robert Mercer 2Lt kia 12-4-18 174RFA p208 CR France881

CARSE,William Kenric T2Lt kia 13-2-17 GL &3RFC p5 CR France833

CARSLAW,John Howie Lt dow 26-11-17 A262RFA p207 CR Palestine3

CARSON,Charles Graham.MC.TCapt dow 28-11-16 13Ess C'Coy p131&258 CR France145,19-11-16

CARSON,Frederick Glover 2Lt kia 30-11-17 1KOSB p101 MR17

CARSON,Herbert William.DSO.CaptAMaj ded 12-10-18 RAMC p194 CR Syria2

CARSON,James Arthur Balfour Capt ded 9-8-18 GL RAMC attRAF p194&266 CR Egypt9

CARSON,Lindsay Hubert TCapt dow 31-10-18 10Ess p131 CR France1392

CARSON,Murray TCapt ded 20-4-17 RASC p192

CARSON,Richard Hartley 2Lt dow 4-9-17 1GrenGds p49 CR Belgium16

CARSON,Robert Maj dow 21-8-16 RGA 71HB p38 CR France232,24-8-16 139HB

CARSON,Samuel Murray Capt 20-4-17 RASC CR Kent175

CARSON,Sidney Thomas T2Lt kia 2-9-18 2RIrReg att1RMunstF p88 MR16

CARSON,Thomas Long 2Lt kia 31-7-17 GL 4RFC p5 MR20

CARSON,Thomas Wright 2Lt kia 27-12-15 6WRid p227 MR29 &CR Belgium453

CARSON,William John White 2Lt mbk 1-7-16 14RIrRif p256 MR21

CARSON-PACKER,Gaythorne Raymond Robertson T2Lt dow 5-10-15 C47RFA p26 CR Belgium11

CARSS,Herbert Crosley T2Lt dow 8-10-17 14NumbF p60 CR France134

CARSWELL,Henry Bradshaw Capt kia 6-10-18 7Ches p222 CR Belgium115

CARSWELL,John Dingwall TCapt kia 14-7-16 8BlkW p128 MR21

CARSWELL,John Jamieson T2Lt kia 25-9-15 10ScotRif p103 MR19

CARSWELL,Malcolm Shanks TLt kia 17-9-17 RBerks att2Bn p138 CR Belgium52

CARSWELL,Robert Nevin 2Lt kia 26-10-14 3 att2YLI p142 MR22

CARSWELL,William Alexander.MC.Capt dow 21-3-18 10 att1/7BlkW p128 MR20

CARSWELL-HUNT,William David.MC.Maj ded 5-4-17 7 att6DLI p239 CR France787

CART De LAFONTAINE,Alfred Edwin Cecil.MC.Capt kia 9-7-16 EYorks attHQ Staff 76InfBde3Div p83 CR France513,Edweard

CARTE,Alan Simpson 2Lt dow 9-6-17 12Lond p248 CR France512

CARTER,Albert 2Lt kia 12-4-17 RSuss att9Bn p118 MR20

CARTER,Alfred Cecil Capt ded 15-1-19 RASC p192 CR Europe42

CARTER,Alfred Henry LtCol ded 3-7-17 RAMC p267 CR Berks1,4-4-18

CARTER,Alfred John T2Lt kia 13-5-17 7Dev p76 CR France214

CARTER,Archibald Wren 2Lt kia 13-5-17 5Mddx p146 CR France427

CARTER,Arthur Donald Dundas Lt BombAcc 20-7-15 IA 2/4 att1/4GurkhaRif p274 CR France345

CARTER,Aubrey John.DSO.Maj kia 4-11-14 1LNLancs p135 MR29

CARTER,Audsley Ralph Maj dow 28-8-18 RGA attRAF 1Wing p38 CR France95

CARTER,Basil Ernest Arnold Lt ded 14-2-21 IARO 17Inf TC p274 MR66

CARTER,Bernard Robert Hadow T2Lt kld 7-11-17 GL &RFC p5 CR Glouc72

CARTER,Bertram 2Lt kia 18-9-18 1Camb p245 CR France369,Lt

CARTER,Cecil Edward.MID 2Lt kia 20-9-17 2/1Lond p245 CR Belgium10

CARTER,Charles Arthur.MC.T2Lt kia 14-10-18 29DLI p160 CR Belgium42

CARTER,Charles Oscar Percival T2Lt kia 26-4-18 Ess att10Bn p131 CR France125

CARTER,Cleary George Molyneux Capt kia 23-10-14 2Wilts p152 MR29

CARTER,Desmond Patrick Webb Lt ded 12-12-16 RE 1FldSigCo p44 CR France177

CARTER,Edward 2Lt kld 25-9-15 107RFA p26 MR29

CARTER,Edward Maurice Capt kia 11-8-20 IA 11Lancers p274 CR Iraq8

CARTER,Ernest 2Lt kia 15-6-18 C240RFA p26 CR Italy3

CARTER,Ernest Lionel.MM.2Lt kia 24-10-18 13RFus p67 CR France1480

CARTER,Frank Leslie Lt kia 22-4-17 ESurr &3RFC p5&112 CR France530,2Lt

CARTER,Geoffrey Herbert TLt dow 12-11-16 2RBerks p138 CR France513

CARTER,George Augustine T2Lt kia 5-12-17 GL &13RFC p5 CR France113

CARTER,George Herbert 2Lt ded 18-11-15 2/4RFA p269 CR Durham26

CARTER,George Sidney.MC.2Lt dow 28-11-17 9ESurr A'Coy p112 CR France145

CARTER,George Thomas T2Lt kia 10-3-16 10Norf p73 MR38

CARTER,Gerald Francis T2Lt dow 30-7-15 7KRRC p149 MR29

CARTER,Gerald Mark FlOff 17-1-20 RWar &RFC CR Hamps53

CARTER,Harold Major T2Lt dow 28-8-18 3Gar RWFus att13ELancs p110 CR France28,kia

CARTER,Harvey Gerald Carminow.MC.Capt kia 8-10-18 8Worc C'Coy p226 CR France1462

CARTER,Henry 2Lt kia 16-6-15 1NumbF p60 MR29

CARTER,Henry T2Lt kia 28-2-18 111LabCps p189 CR Belgium20

CARTER,Henry Gordon T2Lt kia 19-8-15 8NumbF p60 MR4

CARTER,Henry John 2Lt kia 22-10-18 1/7LancF p221 CR France287

CARTER,Henry William Whittard T2Lt kia 2-7-17 SL 59RFC p5 CR France446,Harry

CARTER,Herbert Augustine Maj.VC.ded 13-1-16 IA 101Grndrs att40Pathans p274 CR Cornwall177

CARTER,Herbert Francis George.MC.CaptBtMajTLtCol ded 28-2-19 YLI p142 MR70 &CR Europe193

CARTER,Hugh Harry Lt kia 8-10-18 1EKent p57 CR France445

CARTER,J.2Lt kld 30-10-18 RH&FA &RAF p26

CARTER,James Shuckburgh LtACapt kia 27-9-18 1GrenGds p49 CR France1497

CARTER,John 2Lt kia 29-5-18 15DLI p160 CR France1332

CARTER,John Allen TLt ded PoW 2-4-17 6DCLI p114 MR20,Alan

CARTER,John Lovelace.MC.2LtACapt ded 18-4-18 RASC 37DivTrain p192 CR Devon73

CARTER,John Robert Blackhall Graham LtCol ded 14-1-19 IA SuppList p274

CARTER,John Taylor 2Lt kia 9-10-17 7WYorks p218 MR30

CARTER,John Wilfred T2Lt kia 7-8-15 8WRid p115 MR4

CARTER,Malcolm Russell LtACapt kia 23-3-18 1 att8ESurr p112 MR27

CARTER,Norman Cecil T2Lt dow 23-7-16 13 att14RSuss p118 CR France80

CARTER,Percy Lt kia 9-4-18 4SLancs p230 CR France80

CARTER,Richard Ivens T2Lt dow 12-11-15 RE 68FC p44 CR Gallipoli27

CARTER,Richard Thellusson.MC.CaptAMaj dow 18-8-18 RGA 11SB 14Bde p38 CR France526

CARTER,Ronald John Frederick 2Lt kia 26-4-18 22Lond p251 MR27

CARTER,Seton Rodney T2Lt kia 14-4-17 17LancF att52RFC p5&92 CR France662

CARTER,Stephen Charles T2Lt kia 18-11-16 7RWKent p140 MR21

CARTER,Sydney Chatterton T2Lt dow 3-7-16 11N&D p133 CR France23

CARTER,Sydney Robert Eric 2Lt dow 8-7-16 4YLI p235 MR21

CARTER,Walter James T2Lt dow 29-8-18 1/7Worc p108 CR Italy5

CARTER,Walter James Coe T2Lt kia 14-7-16 8Dev p76 CR France453

CARTER,W.E.Lt 22-3-18 LdStrathconasHorse &RFC CR Wilts28

CARTER,Wilfred Arthur Douglas 2Lt kld 23-5-17 3Dors &RFC p5&123,Wilfrid CR Wilts28

CARTER,William Arthur Roise Capt kia 23-4-15 1/5RLancs p213 CR Belgium88

CARTER,William Henry Seaman TLt kia 14-7-16 13Lpool p71 MR21

CARTER,William James T2Lt kia 21-9-18 10Ess p131 CR France212

CARTER,William Leonard TLt ded 4-7-17 RE 40Coy p44 CR Asia33

CARTER,William Thomas Capt kia 12-10-16 7SfthH p164 MR21

CARTER-WOOD,Joseph Alan Lt kia 1-2-15 2CldGds p51 CR France720,Allan

CARTHEW,Sydney George 2Lt kia 26-3-18 2Dev p76 MR27

CARTLAND,Arthur Edward T2Lt kld 25-2-18 RFC p15 CR Sussex95

CARTLAND,Guy Trevor.MID Capt&Adjt kia 1-7-16 1RB p178 CR France1890,George

CARTLAND,James Bertram Falkner CaptAMaj kia 27-5-18 1Worc p108 MR18

CARTLEDGE,Charles Ashforth T2Lt kia 30-7-16 5Nhampt p137 CR France251

CARTMAN,James Victor 2Lt kia 19-6-18 5 att13Lpool p215 CR France33

CARTMELL,Thomas T2Lt dow 8-5-16 19LancF p92 CR France43

CARTTER,Arthur Edward Lt ded 4-4-19 3Lond CR Surrey152

CARTWRIGHT,Alfred Grahame Maj ded 5-8-17 7Yorks p263 CR Numb74,Col

CARTWRIGHT,Arthur 2Lt kia 30-9-10 7A&SH p213 CR France236

CARTWRIGHT,Charles T2Lt kia 19-4-16 8Beds p85 MR29

CARTWRIGHT,Donald Read TLtACapt dow 5-10-18 C153RFA p26 CR Belgium44

CARTWRIGHT,Eric Percival St.George 2Lt kia 12-8-16 4Leinst att45MGC p174&182 CR France515,13-8-16

CARTWRIGHT,Ernest 2Lt kia 1-11-18 5WRid p227 CR France1256

CARTWRIGHT,Ernest Mills T2Lt kia 14-4-18 11TankCps p188 CR France98

CARTWRIGHT,Frank 2Lt kia 22-3-18 19Manch p154 CR France1061

CARTWRIGHT,George Arthur T2Lt dow 28-11-17 WRid att2/7Bn p115 CR France398

CARTWRIGHT,George Crellin Capt kia 25-9-15 4 att2RWar p64 CR France423

CARTWRIGHT,John Digby 2Lt kia 9-8-15 DLI p160 MR29

CARTWRIGHT,Joseph Harry T2Lt dow 2-6-18 11 att20LancF p92 CR France84

CARTWRIGHT,Nigel Walter Henry 2Lt kia 21-9-17 20DLI p160 MR30

CARTWRIGHT,Pybus 2Lt kia 4-11-18 YLI &RAF p265

CARTWRIGHT,Ronald William St.George T2Lt kia 26-2-18 GL &16RFC p15 CR France95

CARTWRIGHT,Samuel Francis Lt dow 5-11-18 3 att6Y&L p158 CR France938,Capt

CARTWRIGHT,Stanley TLt kia 17-8-16 8Nhampt attMGC p137&182 CR EAfrica39

CARTY,Bertram Samuel T2Lt kia 21-8-16 12N&D p133 CR France400

CARTY,William George T2Lt kia 25-3-16 13 att10RWar p64 CR France1157

CARUS-WILSON,Trevor.DSO.TD.LtCol dow 27-3-18 1/5DCLI p227 CR France145

CARUTH,James Gordon 2Lt kia 25-9-15 5 att2RIrR p88 MR29

CARUTHERS-LITTLE,Arthur William Palling Capt kia 7/11-8-15 5Dors p123 MR4,7-8-15

CARVER,Basil Armitage 2Lt kia 21-8-16 6Drags p22 CR France68,kld

CARVER,Christian Creswell Lt dow 23-7-17 A83RH&FA p26 CR Belgium11

CARVER,Frank Maitland TLt kia 25-9-15 8Dev p76 MR19

CARVER,George Sholto Douglas 2Lt kia 1-7-16 2Dev p76 MR21

CARVER,Harold Quinan TLt kia 30-7-16 19Lpool p71 CR France294

CARVER,Lionel Henry Liptrah 2Lt kia 26-5-18 1IrGds p52 CR France925

CARVER,Oswald Armitage Capt dow 7-6-15 1/2RE p210 CR Gallipoli1

CARVER,Walter Lionel Capt kia 6-11-17 1/1Hereford p252 CR Palestine1

CARY,Launcelot Sulyarde Robert T2Lt kia 20-7-16 9Dev p76 MR21

CARY,Richard Harry 2Lt kia 1-7-16 9Lond p248 MR21

CARY-ELWES,Douglas George Lt kia 25-11-17 A262RFA p26 CR Belgium10,Dudley

CARY-ELWES,Wilfred Gervase Lt kia 27-11-17 2IrGds p52 MR17

CASE,Albert Robert.MC.TLtACapt kia 26-8-18 1EYorks p83 CR France385

CASE,Charles Henry 2Lt ded 29-9-18 12Manch &RAF p154 CR France376,11Bn

CASE,Elliott Dryden Lt kia 27-7-15 RE att2FC p44&210,kld CR France922

CASE,Frederick Marcus Beck T2Lt kia 10-8-16 7Norf p73 CR France150

CASE,Geoffrey Lt kia 22-3-18 2SLancs p125 MR27

CASE,George Robert Ashburner 2Lt kia 25-9-15 3 att2SLancs p125 MR29

CASE,Harry Ernest 2Lt kia 14-8-15 RE 1FC p210 CR France922

CASE,Harold John Turner.MID Lt ded 17-4-20 46RE CR Egypt9

CASE,John Wyatt T2Lt kia 21-10-16 8Norf p73 MR21

CASE,Joseph A.Lt dow 15-11-18 5 att1RFus p67 CR France146

CASE,Lionel Trevor Elliott TCapt kia 30-11-17 7ESurr p112 MR17

CASEBOURNE,Rowland Telford Lt kia 2-7-16 3Yorks att5WYorks p90 MR21

CASEBY,William Robert Brown.MC.T2Lt kia 25-4-17 RScots att1LancF p53 MR20

CASEMENT,Roger LtCol ded 21-12-17 58RFA p261 CR Eire539

CASEY.E.H.Capt 2-12-19 RIM WRid CR Asia20

CASEY,James Lt kia 30-10-14 1KRRC p149 MR29

CASEY.J.P.N.Capt ded 13-12-18 RAMC attRAF p253 CR Glouc9

CASEY,Michael Francis TCapt kia 19-7-16 9RMunstF p175 CR France223,18-7-16

CASH,Ernest Alfred T2Lt dow 17-6-17 14DLI p160 CR France178

CASH,Geoffrey Edwin Lt kia 27-8-16 6 att8LNLancs p135 CR France744

CASHIN,James T2Lt kia 13-10-17 102RFA p26 CR Belgium19

CASHMORE,Charles 2Lt 2-11-19 MGC Inf CR Lond14

CASHMORE,Edwin 2Lt dow 4-10-18 1/4Leic p220 CR France327

CASLEY,Hugh de Chastelai Lt kia 7-8-15 6Yorks p90 MR4

CASLON,Thomas White 2Lt kia 25-11-15 97RFA p26 CR France922

CASS,Hugh Launcelot 2Lt kia 19-6-15 3SWBord p99 CR Gallipoli6,2Bn

CASS,Leonard Francis TCapt kia 13-12-15 7RSuss p118 CR France260

CASS,William Edward T2Lt kld 4-6-17 GL &RFC p5 Kent269

CASSELL,Frank Lt 1-3-21 3RWar CR Surrey55

CASSELLS,Robert Wilson TCapt kia 1-7-16 17HLI p162 CR France293

CASSELS,Frank Lionel TLt kia 20-7-16 RE 222FC p44 CR France453

CASSELS,Hugh Kennedy TCapt kia 25-9-15 8RBerks p138 CR France552

CASSELS,Hugh Lindsay T2Lt kia 8-8-18 1TankCps p188 CR France360

CASSELS,Wilfrid Gardiner.MID TCapt kia 13-7-16 8BordR p116 CR France296

CASSERLY,William Alphonse 2Lt kia 1-3-17 5RMunstF att1RInniskF p175 MR21

CASSIDY,Bernard Matthew.VC.T2Lt kia 28-3-18 2LancF p92 MR20

CASSIDY,Cyril Martin 2Lt dow 17-5-15 1KRRC p149 CR France80

CASSIDY,Michael Bernard 2Lt kia 13-4-18 2IrGds p52 MR32

CASSIE,Leith 2Lt dow 11-12-17 3A&SH p173 CR Belgium11,2Bn

CASSON,Randal Alexander 2Lt kia 26-9-17 2RWelshF p97 CR Belgium126

CASSON,Thomas.MC.2Lt ded 17-5-17 6Ches p222 CR Ches160

CASSON,William.TD.TMaj kia 25-9-15 7Lond p247 CR France550

CASSWELL,Colin Garth Charles William Langlois TMaj kia 14-1-16 8Y&L p158 CR France525

CASSWELL,Eric Denison Seymour Capt kia 7-11-17 6RB att102RFC p5&178 CR France1029

CASSWELL,Frederick Charles T2Lt drd 13-8-15 10Beds att1Ess p85 MR4

CASTBERG,Francis Albert Harboe Capt dow 13-3-15 2Mddx p146 CR France345,Arthur

CASTELLI,Ernest Charles 2Lt kia 9-5-15 13Lond p249 MR32

CASTLE,Cecil Wells Lt kia 3-8-17 2SLancs p125 CR Belgium58,4-8-17

CASTLE,Cottam Harry Hunt Capt ded 30-10-18 6Glouc p225 CR Glouc19

CASTLE,Edward William 2Lt dow 25-8-18 RGA 126SB p38 CR France1170

CASTLE,Errington Edward TLt kld 12-8-17 GL &RFC p5 CR Yorks178

CASTLE,Sidney Batho Lt ded 4-1-16 6Mddx p146 CR France134

CASTLE,Tudor Ralph T2Lt kia 31-8-16 6RWSurr p55 CR France397

CASTLE,Vernon William Blyth Lt kld 15-2-18 RFC 43Wing p15 CR USA169

CASTOR,Richard Henderson.MID LtCol 30-12-20 IMS CR Lond14

CATCHPOLE,Charles Edward.MM.T2Lt kia 12-10-16 7Suff p78 MR21

CATCHPOLE,Thomas John Capt dow 3-11-17 1/5Suff p217 CR Palestine2

CATER,John White Capt kia 9-7-17 9Mddx p236 CR Germany3,dow

CATER,Walter Henry.MC.T2Lt ded 16-8-18 8RSuss p118 CR France145,dow

CATES,Geoffrey T2Lt kia 21-3-18 10 att2DLI p160 MR20

CATES,George Edward.VC.2Lt ded 9-3-17 2RB p178 CR France624

CATFORD,Cyril Herbert Barclay Lt dow 5-10-17 1DLI p160 CR France177

CATHCART,Augustus Ernest Capt kia 14-9-14 KRRC p149 CR France1342

CATHCART,David Andrew 2Lt kia 13-7-16 7RWKent p140 CR France630

CATHCART,Francis John T2Lt kia 3-6-18 A55RFA p26 MR38

CATHCART,Richard Robert 2Lt kia 16-8-17 1RInniskF p104 MR30

CATHER,Geoffrey St.George Shillington.VC.TLt&Adjt kia 2-7-16 9RIrF p171 MR21

CATHERALL,William Cecil 2Lt kia 2-11-17 Nhampt att1/5Norf p137 MR34

CATHIE,Archibald James T2Lt kld 11-7-17 GL &RFC p5 CR Glouc67

CATHIE,H.W.Lt 9-12-15 GL att3NigR CR WAfrica55

CATHRO,James Grant T2Lt kia 24-10-18 1ScotRif p103 CR France 230

CATLEY,James Thatcher Capt kia 12-9-17 HAC attRFA p206 CR Belgium102,Maj

CATLING,Bernard.MC.LtACapt dow 20-10-18 52/15RFA p26 CR France560

CATMUR,Graham Gunn Capt kia 30-6-18 RASC att6RWKent p192 CR France61

CATMUR,Harry Albert Frederick Valentine.MID Lt kia 1-7-16 3RSuss attMGC p118&182 MR21

CATNACH,Thomas Burnett T2Lt dow 19-4-17 26NumbF p60 CR France40,Burney

CATO,Geoffrey Maidens Walter Gaven T2Lt kia 6-11-17 GL &6RFC p5 CR Belgium11

CATON,Florence Missouri Sister 15-7-17 ScotWomensHosp attSerbianArmy CR Greece7

CATON,Frederic William T2Lt kia 28-6-16 RE p44 CR France559

CATON,Norman Newton.MC.Lt kia 21-4-18 C124RFA p26 CR France204

CATOR,Edward Philip Douglas LtACapt kia 11-4-18 RE 69FC p44 MR27

CATT,Archibald William.MC.2LtTLt ded 9-3-18 RWKent att3NigR p140&201 CR EAfrica35 &CR Tanzania1

CATTANACH,John TLt dow 27-7-15 RAMC att9RWar p194 MR4

CATTARNS,Glanvill Richards.MC.TCapt kia 12-2-17 6SLancs p125 MR38

CATTELL,Frank Douglas Bernard T2Lt kld 22-10-17 GL &RFC p5 CR Nhampt74

CATTERALL,Albert Lt kia 21-3-18 7N&D p233 CR France646

CATTERSON-SMITH,Thomas Mervyn Osborne.DSO.Capt dow 10-2-20 IA 1/12Pnrs att3/34Sikhs p274 MR43 &CR Pakistan50A

CATTLE,Eustace Shipstone.MC.2Lt kia 7-7-16 1/5Y&L p238 MR21

CATTLE,James Henry Nightingale Capt dow 1-5-17 D230RFA p207 CR France161

CATTLEY,Cyril Francis.MC.TMaj kia 30-11-17 1 att6EKent p57 MR17

CATTLEY,William.MC.2LtACapt kia 3-5-17 12EYorks p83

CATTO,Robert Kilgour Thom Capt kia 4-11-16 4GordH p241 CR France131

CATTO,Thomas Lt kia 22-8-18 4HLI C'Coy p162 CR France745,23-8-18

CATTO,William Basil T2Lt kia 11-9-16 23NumbF p60 CR France275

CAUDLE,Cedric 2Lt kia 3-5-17 HAC p206 MR20

CAUDWELL,Thord ACapt kia 30-11-17 16Lond p249 CR France1496

CAULFIELD,Algernon Montgomerie.DSO.Maj kia 7-8-15 6BordR p116 MR4,CAULFEILD DCM 9-8-15

CAULFIELD,Gordon 2Lt kia 30-11-17 3 att7SomLI p79 MR17

CAULFIELD,James Crosbie Lt kia 18-11-14 2Manch p154 CR Belgium42

CAULFIELD,St.George Robert Sanderson LtCol ded 29-4-16 RE p262 CR Suff55

CAULFIELD,Toby St.George 2Lt kia 16-6-17 45RFC p5 MR20

CAUNTER,John Charles Ashford Capt kia 28-10-17 1WelshR &60RFC p5&126 MR20

CAUNTER,Robert Lawrence Luscombe T2Lt dow 18-12-16 7Glouc p106 CR Iraq5

CAUSLEY,Frederick George.DCM.2LtACapt kia 31-7-17 7/8KOSB p101 MR29

CAUSTON,Jervoise Purefoy Capt kia 22-4-18 6Hamps p228 CR France250,1Bn

CAUTHERLY,Charles Stewart Lt kia 26-4-18 Herts p252 MR30

CAUTLEY,William Oxenham.DSO.Maj kia 9-5-15 3Suff p78 MR22

CAVANAGH,Bryan George.MIDx2 Capt&QM kld 24-5-19 GL attNigR p254 CR WAfrica54

CAVANAGH,Frank.MC.CaptAMaj dow 26-9-18 88/14RFA p26 CR France327

CAVANAGH,John 2Lt drd 26-2-18 GL RE IWT p190 MR38

CAVANAGH,Patrick Felix Lt kia 12-7-18 6RScots p211 CR France26

CAVAYE,George Ross LtCol 6-9-17 Staff CR Scot237 Ex CamH

CAVE,Arthur Douglas Lt ded 10-11-18 1/2DLI &RAF p160 CR Sussex111

CAVE,Edward Charles.MC.Lt dow 29-8-18 17Lond att56MGC p186&250 CR France84

CAVE,Eric Arthur 2Lt kia 13-2-16 24RFC p2 CR France34

CAVE,Frank 2Lt kia 17-2-17 4 att2SStaffs p122 MR21

CAVE,Joseph T2Lt dow 21-9-17 11WYorks p81&257 CR Belgium11

CAVE,Walter Henry Charles 2Lt kia 16-3-15 3 att1Dors p123 CR Belgium59,Lt 15-3-15

CAVE-PENNY,Evelyn Anthony Lt kia 8-6-18 IA CpsofGuides Inf p274 CR Palestine9

CAVELL,Hubert John TLt dow 22-4-17 11N&D p133 CR Somerset126

CAVENDISH,Hugh Crawford Maj kia 1-8-16 B87RFA p26 CR France453

CAVENDISH,Godfrey Lionel John Capt dow 22-12-14 IA 97Inf att1/9BhopalInf p274 CR France201

CAVENDISH,Lord John Spencer.DSO.Maj kia 20-10-14 1LifeGds p20 CR France924

CAWLEY,Harold Thomas Capt kia 23-9-15 6Manch p236 CR Gallipoli1 seeCR France1231

CAWLEY,John Stephen.MID Maj kia 1-9-14 20Huss 1CavBde p23 CR France1231

CAWLEY,Oswald Capt kia 22-8-18 10KSLI p205 CR France1231

CAWLEY,Robert Lt&QM ded 30-6-18 8RWFus p97 MR66

CAWOOD,William Benjamin Crane Capt ded 24-5-15 RFA p207 MR65

CAWS,Ronald Newton.MC.TCapt&Adjt dow 31-7-17 10Glouc p106 CR France1357

CAWS,Stanley Winther Lt kia 21-9-15 10RFC p1 MR20

CAWSON,George Adrian T2Lt kia 30-11-17 GL &56RFC p5 MR20

CAWSTON,George 2Lt ded 29-10-18 2RWSurr attRAF p55 CR Surrey83

CAY,Albert Jaffray Lt kia 23-4-16 WorcYeo p206 MR34

CAYFORD,George Everett T2Lt kld 16-7-17 GL &RFC p5 CR Essex1

CAYLEY,Francis Digby Edward T2Lt kia 29-9-15 8 att1KRRC p149 CR France423

CAYLEY,Sir George Everard Arthur Capt ded 15-11-17 RDC p253 CR Yorks186 Ex 3RWFus

CAZALET,Edward 2Lt kia 10-9-16 WelshGds p53 CR France394

CAZALET,Ronald de Bode.MC.TCapt ded 8-1-20 GL &TankCps p266 CR Asia81

CEASAR,Charles Patrick TLt kia 14-7-16 7KSLI p144 MR21,CAESAR

CECIL,Charles 2Lt kia 16-7-16 2/4RBerks p234 CR France1887

CECIL,George Edward 2Lt kia 13-9-14 4GrenGds 4Coy p49 CR France1108,1-9-14

CECIL,Rotherham Bagshawe 2lt kia 1-7-16 1/5N&D p232 MR21

CECIL,Rupert Edward Gascoyne 2LtTLt kia 11-7-15 4 att1Beds p85

CECIL,William Amherst.Hon.Capt kia 16-9-14 2GrenGds p49 CR France1112

CEMERY,Arthur Frank.MID Capt kia 19-7-17 1EYorks p83 CR France591

CENTENO,Leon 2Lt ded 6-7-16 4Suff p217 CR Suff55

CESARI,Sydney Fraser McAlpine Capt kia 3-10-15 RAMC att6FA p194 CR France80 3-9-15

CHADDOCK,John Glover 2Lt kia 30-3-18 RFA att86ArmyBdeSigSect RE p26 MR20

CHADS,Herbert Charles Lt dow 6-1-17 1NStaffs p156 CR France681

CHADWICK,Arthur Clarkson Capt&Adjt kia 29-10-15 1/4YLI p235 CR Belgium23

CHADWICK,Douglas Gordon Lt dow 20-7-16 O&BLI 2/1BucksBn p231 CR France345

CHADWICK,Edward Neale 2Lt kia 4-10-17 3SfthH p164 MR30

CHADWICK,Francis Joseph 12Lt kia 12-10-16 2Beds p85 MR21

CHADWICK,Frederick James.MID Capt dow 13-4-15 IA 104Rif p274 CR Iraq6

CHADWICK,James Henry.DSO.TLtCol kia 4-5-17 24Manch p154 CR France614

CHADWICK,John 2Lt kia 2-11-18 8LancF p221 CR France933

CHADWICK,John Collinge 2Lt kia 25-3-17 1/8WYorks p219 CR France1887

CHADWICK,Norman Stuart T2Lt kia 6-11-17 5SLancs att12SomLI p125 CR Palestine1,dow

CHADWICK,Percival Miller Lt kia 22-9-18 RE 459FC p210 CR France835

CHADWICK,Richard Markham Lt dow 12-5-15 RGA 11SB p38 CR France80,2Lt kia 13-5-15

CHADWICK,R.M.Lt ded 17-3-16 2KAR attRhodesiaR p268

CHADWICK,W.E.A.VenArchdeacon 30-9-17 EAChapDept CR EAfrica38& CRTanzania1

CHAFFEY,Charles Russell T2Lt dow 10-3-17 23Manch p154 CR France692

CHAFFEY,Henry Percival 2Lt kia 10-8-17 HAC p206 MR29

CHAIZE,Jean Edward Gabriel T2Lt dow 18-8-17 RSuss att13Bn p118 CR France102

CHALAND,Maurice Leslie.MC.TLt dow 1-12-17 7Norf p73 CR France398

CHALCRAFT,George Arthur Lt dow 7-5-15 4WYorks att2WRid p81 CR Belgium35,5-5-15

CHALK,Theodore Wilson 2Lt kia 3-7-16 3 att7Suff p78 MR21

CHALKER,Eric.MID Lt kia 19-7-16 46/39RFA p26 MR21

CHALKLEY,Francis Henry.MBE.Maj ded 17-8-18 RAOC p267

CHALKLEY,Thomas Henry T2Lt kia 29-8-18 56MGC Inf p182 CR France593

CHALLEN,Christopher Frank.MID Capt dow 13-11-18 1/7Mddx p235 CR Lond14

CHALLENER,Arthur Cecil Lt kia 25-9-16 9Lpool p216 CR France277

CHALLENER,Percival Crawley T2Lt kia 12-12-17 13Lpool p71 CR France563

CHALLENOR,Norman Bowen Capt kia 31-7-15 3 att2RBerks p138 CR France349

CHALLINER,William Henry 2Lt dow 13-8-16 1/9Lpool p216 CR France141

CHALLINOR,Elizabeth Annie SNurse ded 26-10-18 QAIMNS CR Surrey118

CHALLINOR,Frederick William 2Lt kia 22-5-17 156RGA p38 CR France1186

CHALLIS,Alfred Edward HonLt ded 9-3-19 MGC Inf p266 CR Essex1

CHALLIS,Arthur Bracebridge.TD.Maj kia 21-9-18 RGA 133SB p209 CR France687

CHALLIS,Ivor James 2Lt kia 14-4-18 1/2 att11LancF p92 CR France298

CHALLIS,Thomas Archie.MC.2Lt ded 3-11-18 13TankCps p188

CHALLIS,Thomas Holt 2Lt dow 28-4-17 RGA 256SB p38 CR France113,27-4-17

CHALLIS,William Guy Fawcett TLt kia 13-7-16 3 att15Hamps p120 CR Belgium54,2Lt

CHALLONER,Alan Crawhall 2Lt kia 30-7-15 6DCLI p114 CR Belgium453

CHALLONER,Thomas Bennet Capt 3-11-15 RASC CR Lond29

CHALLONER,Thomas Rex.MC.Lt dow 25-7-16 RE 1FC p210 CR France102

CHALMERS,Archibald Douglas TLt ded 9-12-18 1A&SH p173 CR Greece9

CHALMERS,Arthur Lakes 2Lt kia 23-9-16 7Lpool p215 CR France401,Jakes

CHALMERS,David TLtACapt kia 18-9-18 GL 6Nhampt p137 CR France511

CHALMERS,Francis 2Lt kia 25-9-16 3 att1EYorks p83 MR21

CHALMERS,Henry Stewart LtACapt dow 29-9-17 C295RFA p207 CR Belgium11

CHALMERS,James.MC.DCM.TCaptAMaj kia 23-3-18 5RScots attMGC p187&211 MR27

CHALMERS,James Stewart T2Lt dow 7-10-16 12A&SH att1CamH p173 CR Scot387

CHALMERS,John Alexander T2Lt ded 21-10-18 LabCps 1032Coy p254 CR Syria2

CHALMERS,John Binny 2Lt ded 8-10-14 RFA p269 CR Wilts2 &CR Devon207

CHALMERS,John Cyril.MM.T2Lt kia 15-10-16 20NumbF p60 CR France275

CHALMERS,John Hunter.MID Capt&Adjt dow 25-3-18 5 att7A&SH p243 CR France300

CHALMERS,John James 2Lt ded 20-11-18 PoW 5GordH p242 CR Germany3,Lt

CHALMERS,John Leslie.MC.LtACapt kia 27-3-18 5RIrF p171 MR27

CHALMERS,John Robert Thornburn T2Lt kia 1-7-16 8SomLI p79 MR21

CHALMERS,John Stuart Maj kia 17-4-18 9HLI p240 MR32

CHALMERS,Ralph Capt kia 10-5-15 2Suff p78 MR29,8-5-15

CHALMERS,Robert Lt dow 25-5-15 15Lond p249 CR France98,26-5-15

CHALMERS,William Hamish 2Lt kia 13-4-16 IARO att19Punjabis p274 MR61

CHALONER,Richard Godolphin Hume Capt ded 3-4-17 3Wilts p152 CR France8

CHAMBERLAIN,Arthur 2Lt ded 11-2-19 5NStaffs p238

CHAMBERLAIN,Cyril John TLt kia 6-10-17 1RB p178 MR30,7-10-17

CHAMBERLAIN,Eric Dunstan 2Lt kia 30-11-17 att1/5LNLancs p135 MR17

CHAMBERLAIN,George Herbert T2Lt kia 4-10-16 14Ches p95 CR France1182,3-10-16

CHAMBERLAIN,James Russell Lt kld 2-6-16 RFC p2 CR Canada1688,Chamberlin

CHAMBERLAIN,John.MC.Capt kia 13-5-17 3SWBord att1WelshR p99 CR Belgium1,14-5-17 att14

CHAMBERLAIN,John Harold 2Lt dow 21-11-15 1Lond p245 CR France285

CHAMBERLAIN,John Robert William 2Lt kia 13-9-18 20 att2/10Lond p251 CR France511,CHAMBERLIN Capt

CHAMBERLAIN,Norman Gwynne Lt kia 1-12-17 1GrenGds p49 CR France439

CHAMBERLAIN,Rupert Maurice 2Lt dow 20-5-18 2ScotGds p52 CR France120

CHAMBERLAYNE,Arthur 2Lt dow 10-4-17 16LancF p92

CHAMBERLAYNE,Athelstone LtCol kia 14-1-20 IA 1Lancers Cmdg2/76Punjabis p274 MR43

CHAMBERLAYNE,Thomas Edmund Onslow TLt kia 18-8-16 73RFA p26 CR France397

CHAMBERLIN,Eric Valentine George 2Lt kia 31-12-17 RH&FA179ArmyBde p26 CR France905

CHAMBERLIN,Hugh Frederick Whitmore 2Lt kia 15-10-16 2DLI p160 MR21,CHAMBERLAIN

CHAMBERLIN,J.R.W. see CHAMBERLAIN,J.R.W.

CHAMBERS,Alfred Ernest.MC.TLt dow 29-10-18 26RFus p67 CR Belgium158

CHAMBERS,Anthony Gerald 2Lt kia 1-7-16 4Mddx p146 CR France267

CHAMBERS,Arthur Joseph Ferguson 2Lt dow 11-8-16 1/1WarYeo p205 CR Egypt2

CHAMBERS,B.K.ChEngr 19-6-17 RIM CR Iraq5

CHAMBERS,Charles Colhoun.MC.Capt kia 10-7-16 RGA 12SB p38 CR France399

CHAMBERS,Cleveland Hugh 2Lt kia 3-9-16 8RBerks p138 MR21 &CR France390

CHAMBERS,C.P.E 2Lt 26-3-17 EgyptLabCps CR Egypt1

CHAMBERS,David Macdonald TCapt kia 20-2-17 12DLI p160 CR Belgium127

CHAMBERS,Edward Chandos Elliot T2Lt kia 1-7-16 19LancF A'Coy p92 CR France296

CHAMBERS,George Alfred 2Lt kia 22-8-17 1 att6SomLI p79 MR30

CHAMBERS,Henry 2Lt dow 11-8-18 1/1Camb p245 CR France69

CHAMBERS,James Edward 2Lt dow 1-10-16 4 att1WessexRFA p208 CR France177

CHAMBERS,John Paul 2Lt dow 4-4-17 4Ess p232 CR France80

CHAMBERS,L.E.AssSurg 26-8-21 IMD MR65

CHAMBERS,Norman Archibald 2Lt dow 17-8-16 3 att1Nhampt p137 CR France74

CHAMBERS,Percival Arthur T2Lt dow 10-4-16 10 att9RWar p64 CR Iraq5,6-4-16 11 att9

CHAMBERS,Percy Wilmot TCapt dow PoW 13-8-17 GL &22RFC p6 CR France1276

CHAMBERS,Philip Carlisle 2Lt kia 22-3-18 2TankCps p188 MR27

CHAMBERS,Robert SubCdr ded 23-7-22 IA IndOrdDept p274

CHAMBERS,Robert Avalon Montagu 2Lt dow 15-10-15 3Hamps att1Glouc p120 CR France88

CHAMBERS,Robert Seymour Bennet TLtACapt kia 24-12-17 8KRRC p149 CR Belgium126

CHAMBERS,Stanley Walter Graham Capt kia 24-11-17 11RWar p64 CR Belgium111

CHAMBERS,Stewart Capt kld 15-11-20 Lpool MR40

CHAMBERS,Wilfrid John TLt kia 18-8-16 11 att13ESurr p112 CR France550

CHAMBERS,William Trant.MID Maj dow 2-6-15 RFA 1DivHQ p26 CR France98

CHAMBERS,William Geoffrey Capt kia 15-5-18 1/2Lincs &49RAF p74 MR20

CHAMBERS-HUNTER,Charles Allardyce Jopp 2Lt kia 1-4-16 3 att1GordH p166 MR29

CHAMEN,Harold Ashcombe Lt dow 1-8-16 2Beds p85 CR France23

CHAMIER,Cyril Kinnaird Lt kia 23-4-15 Y&L p158 MR29

CHAMP,Leonard Lt ded 19-3-18 7Ess p232

CHAMPION,Eric Osbourne T2Lt kia 10-6-17 11SLancs C'Coy p125 CR Belgium165,11-6-17

CHAMPION,Leonard John Lt dow 4-10-18 NRhodPolice CR Tanzania1

CHAMPION,Reginald James Lt dow 18-7-17 1ScotGds attTMB p52 CR Belgium12,kia

CHAMPION,Rowland Laughton 2Lt kia 17-3-17 20Lond p251 CR Belgium167,Roland

CHAMPION,Sydney George TLt dow PoW 17-3-17 5RFus att2KAR p67&268 MR52

CHAMPION DE CRESPIGNY,Claude Norman Lt kia 1-9-14 2DragGds p20 CR Essex106

CHAMNEY,Harold D'Arcy 2Lt dow PoW 29-4-18 12Yorks p90 CR Germany3

CHAMPNEYS John Dalrymple Lt dow 22-11-15 6Leic p87 CR France283

CHANCE,Albert Henry 2Lt kia 22-3-18 2/7RWar p214 MR27

CHANCE,Andrew Ferguson Capt kia 3-10-15 B85RFA p26 CR France727

CHANCE,Edward Seton CaptBtMaj kia 29-5-18 2DragGds att6Leic p20 MR18

CHANCE,Eric Godwin T2Lt kia 19-1-18 28RFC p15 CR Italy48

CHANCE,Eustace George St.Clair 2Lt kia 27-9-18 2CldGds p51 CR France1497

CHANCE,Frank Meryon 2Lt kia 25/26-5-15 24Lond p252 MR22

CHANCE,Guy Ogden de Peyster Lt kia 19-10-14 1RWelshF p97 MR29

CHANCELLOR,Geoffrey Ellis 2Lt kia 9-7-16 3RWSurr attRFC p2&55 CR France134,Lt

CHANCELLOR,Richard Albert Beresford TCapt dow 24-12-16 7RBerks p138 CR Greece1

CHANDLER,Cecil William.MC.TCapt dow 30-3-18 8RMunstF p175 CR France401

CHANDLER,Charles Robert T2Lt kia 29-9-15 2ESurr p112 CR France423

CHANDLER,Clive 2Lt kia 17-11-14 1Wilts p152 MR29

CHANDLER,Dorothy Maud Sister 15-11-17 QAIMNS CR Surrey91

CHANDLER,Edwin Spencer T2Lt kia 14-2-16 10N&D p133 MR29

CHANDLER,Eric Oatey 2Lt kia 11-4-18 RE 510FC p210 MR32

CHANDLER,Henry Leonard T2Lt kld 30-10-17 RFC p6 Lond14

CHANDLER,J.W.Lt 3-5-20 1Dev CR Devon1

CHANDLER,James Cook T2Lt kia 11-7-16 17 att11Ches p95 CR France296,12-7-16

CHANDLER,John.MC.2Lt kia 2-10-16 19Lond p250 MR21

CHANEY,Henry Edward.OBE.MIDx2 TMaj ded 27-2-19 LancF &RAF p263 CR Surrey150

CHANING-PEARCE,Wilfred Thomas.MC.TCapt kia 1-10-17 RAMC att18Lpool p194 CR Belgium75

CHANT,Thomas Roy Lt ded 7-11-18 13Lond p269 CR Herts110

CHANTRILL,Reginald Percy TLt kia 26-10-17 78RFA p26 CR Belgium25

CHAPLIN,Arthur Hugh Bates Maj dow 21-5-17 1/1Camb p244 CR Camb39,Capt

CHAPLIN,Aubrey Fletcher Lt kia 10-4-17 NhamtYeo p204 CR France418

CHAPLIN,Charles Montague 2Lt kia 26-9-17 1Camb p245 MR30

CHAPLIN,Charles Slingsby LtCol kia 30-7-15 9KRRC p149 MR29

CHAPLIN,Frederick Hardress Maj ded 27-5-16 RGA 154HB p38&209 Belgium6

CHAPLIN,Herbert 2Lt kia 19-10-17 4Suff &RFC p217 MR20

CHAPLIN,Humphrey Marmaduke Lt kia 11-5-15 3 att1Ches p95 MR29,Henry

CHAPLIN,Rowland Edward Ernest T2Lt kia 22-4-17 RE 7FC p44 CR France1185

CHAPLIN,Sydney Stranger Lt kia 21-3-18 2/5Manch p236 MR27

CHAPLYN,Cyril Edward T2Lt kia 26-4-18 10Ess p131 MR27

CHAPMAN,Albert Charles TCapt kia 20-8-16 RFA 29TrMortSchl p26 CR France701

CHAPMAN,Alfred John T2Lt ded 18-9-17 GL &41RFC p6 CR France660,kia

CHAPMAN,Alfred Reginald T2Lt kia 2-12-17 6MGC Inf p182 CR France529

CHAPMAN,Alfred Reginald Beeves Lt kia 6-6-16 1/5LNLancs p234 CR France504,Bewes

CHAPMAN,Alister Hillyar Darby Capt kia 27-9-15 1Drags p21 CR France178

CHAPMAN,Arthur Allsop Lt kia 25-4-17 7 att9WRid p227 CR France531

CHAPMAN,Arthur Donald 2Lt kia 1-7-16 1/5NStaffs p238 MR21

CHAPMAN,Arthur Frederick 2Lt kia 25-9-16 2ScotGds p52 CR France513

CHAPMAN,Arthur Gerald TLt ded 5-5-17 29Mddx p146 CR Essex81 Ex 5Lancs

CHAPMAN,Arthur Thomas Capt kia 26-4-15 3ESurr att1Hamps p112 CR Belgium152

CHAPMAN,Ben Fletcher T2Lt kia 19-4-17 RGA 1MtnBty Singapore p38 CR Palestine8

CHAPMAN,Bertie Robert Wyand 2Lt dow 13-6-18 1/4SLancs p230 CR France40

CHAPMAN,Charles Dudley T2Lt kld 19-1-18 RFC p15

CHAPMAN,Charles George.MID TLt dow 17-4-16 RE p44 MR38

CHAPMAN,Charles Lancelot.MC.Maj dow 22-8-17 D173RFA p206 CR Belgium11

CHAPMAN,Charles Meredith Bouverie.MC.LtTMaj dow 1-10-17 EKent att29RFC p6&57 CR Belgium18

CHAPMAN,Claude Bertram T2Lt kia 18-9-18 2Y&L p158 CR France1701

CHAPMAN,David Archibald James 2Lt kia 15-9-16 2ScotGds p52 MR21

CHAPMAN,David Markwell TLt kia 25-3-18 3RB p178 MR27

CHAPMAN,Donald John Stuart T2Lt dow 13-7-16 8RFus p67 CR France51

CHAPMAN,Douglas Collier Lt kia 20-10-18 RE 429FC p210 CR France1387

CHAPMAN,Edward Henry TLtCol kia 7-8-15 6Yorks p90 CR Gallipoli4

CHAPMAN,Edward Wynne Lt kia 17-11-14 3DragGds p21 CR Belgium57

CHAPMAN,Ernest Herbert Stuart Maj died 1-11-18 IA 31Lancers p275,Earnest CR Asia82

CHAPMAN,Frank Edward SubCdr ded 30-3-19 IA MilWorksServ CR Surrey1

CHAPMAN,Frank Reginald 2Lt dow 25-9-15 18Lond p250 CR France178,Lt

CHAPMAN,Fred 2Lt kia 22-8-18 1/23Lond p245 CR France396

CHAPMAN,Frederick Alan TLt dow 29-5-18 13Manch att1Worc p154 CR France1693 &CR France34

CHAPMAN,Fred Tarlington Lt dow 18-12-17 C173RFA p207 CR France518

CHAPMAN,Geoffrey Arthur T2Lt kia 28-3-16 11RScots p53 CR Belgium71

CHAPMAN,George Edwin 2Lt dow 27-9-16 5Yorks attMGC p187&221 CR France105

CHAPMAN,George Martin Lt kia 13-5-15 RAMC p194 CR Belgium45,Capt

CHAPMAN,Gordon Humphrey Capt kia 9-3-16 IA 53Sikhs p275 CR Iraq5,dow

CHAPMAN,H.F.2Lt 30-5-17 Leic CR Leics64

CHAPMAN,Henry Ernest.MC.Capt dow 22-3-18 G/17RHA p26 MR27

CHAPMAN,Henry James.MC.T2Lt kia 8-8-18 7RWKent p140 CR France247

CHAPMAN,Henry Randal 2Lt kia or dow 9-10-17 10Manch p237 MR30,Randall

CHAPMAN,Henry Reynolds Maj kia 27-6-15 10DLI p160 MR29,Harry

CHAPMAN,Herbert Foster.DCM.2LtTLt dow 29-5-15 1RWFus p97 CR France134

CHAPMAN,John Capt dow 30-5-15 5Leic p220

CHAPMAN,John TCapt kia 16-7-16 21Manch p154 CR France397,14-7-16

CHAPMAN,John Percy Lt kia 21-7-16 O&BLI 1/1BucksBn p231 MR21

CHAPMAN,Joseph Robert T2Lt kia 8-4-17 5KSLI p144 CR France581,9-4-17

CHAPMAN,Lawrence Vaughan TLt kia 25-9-15 2RB p178 MR32

CHAPMAN,Laurence Oxley 2Lt kia 31-7-17 5 att3RB p178 MR29

CHAPMAN,Leonard T2Lt dow 2-9-18 5RBerks p138 CR France145

CHAPMAN,Lewis Carlton T2Lt ded 16-4-17 GL &60RFC p6 MR20

CHAPMAN,Marion Dorothy Miss ded 10-8-18 VAD att17GH p200 CR Egypt1

CHAPMAN,Michael.MC.Lt kia 12-4-18 4GrenGds p49 MR32

CHAPMAN,Montague Gerald Herbert T2Lt kia 14-8-17 10RB p178 CR Belgium83,Lt

CHAPMAN,Perceval Christian Capt dow 1-5-15 IA RFA 26MtnBty p26 CR Egypt6

CHAPMAN,Raleigh George Aubrey Lt ded 1-3-19 RASC 7DivTrain p192 CR Italy59

CHAPMAN,Samuel Eric 2Lt kia 25-9-15 7CamH p167 MR19

CHAPMAN,Sidney George 2Lt dow 28-9-16 8 att7SStaffs p122 CR France74

CHAPMAN,Sydney Victor T2Lt kia 11-6-17 8NumbF p60 CR Belgium168

CHAPMAN,Theodore Victor.MC.LtACapt kia 12-5-17 2RWSurr p55 MR20

CHAPMAN,Wilfred Hubert TCapt kia 7-8-15 6Yorks p90 CR Gallipoli4

CHAPMAN,William Henry T2Lt kia 20-9-17 1/2 att11RB p178 MR30

CHAPMAN,William James 2Lt kia 26-3-18 1Camb p245 MR27

CHAPMAN,William Wetheral Lt kia 7-10-17 EKent attRFC p6&57 CR France1050

CHAPPEL,William Elden Lt kld 4-4-17 2/4DCLI attRFC p226 CR Egypt15

CHAPPELL,Edwin Francis T2Lt kia 3-2-16 RE 3FC p44 CR France423

CHAPPELL,Ernest Roland 2Lt dow 30-9-18 RGA C BtyAA p38 CR France106,Lt

CHAPPELL,Francis Harold T2Lt kia 3-9-16 16N&D p133 MR21

CHAPPELL,George Henry Lt ded 20-12-19 RASC p267 CR Mddx39

CHAPPELL,Stanley Lt kld 2-3-18 RFC p15

CHAPPLE,James Walter 2Lt dow 31-7-17 1GrenGds p49 CR Belgium12

CHAPPLE,Reginald Charles 2Lt kia 12-4-18 4DCLI p227 MR32

CHAPPY,Athol Isdale 2Lt kia 24-9-18 3 att11Ess p131 CR France835

CHARD,Robert Alexander Farmer TCapt kia 8-7-16 8RFus p67 MR21

CHARD,Thomas Norman T2Lt kia 23-4-17 1DCLI p114 MR20

CHARLES,Albert 2Lt kia 1-7-16 1/7N&D p233 MR21

CHARLES,Angus Alan Macgregor.MID Capt kia 20-12-14 73RFA p26 CR France571

CHARLES,B.S.2Lt ded 7-12-18 GL &RAF p190

CHARLES,Cecil Arthur 2Lt dow 22-9-18 12Lond p248 CR France194

CHARLES,George Harold 2Lt kia 31-10-18 14RWFus p97 CR France1478

CHARLES,James Arthur Merriman 2Lt dow 10-2-15 KSLI p144 CR Nhampt164

CHARLES,John James Percival.MC.TCapt ded 6-10-17 RAMC att1/1Herts p194 CR France 102

CHARLES,Leslie Stafford Capt ded 30-7-16 6Worc &60RFC p2&108 CR France528

CHARLESTON,Ebenezer T2Lt kia 20-9-17 KRRC att11Bn p149 MR30

CHARLESTON,Frederick 2LtTLt dow 7-7-15 2LancF p92 CR Belgium1

CHARLESWORTH,Alick Thomas Bentall T2Lt kld 30-5-17 GL &RFC p6 CR Lincs67,dedacc

CHARLESWORTH,Frederick T2Lt ded 1-2-19 2WRid p264 CR Yorks635,Lt

CHARLESWORTH,Frederick Raymond Capt dow 19-9-18 25RWFus p204 CR France194

CHARLESWORTH,George Lt kia 3-5-17 6WYorks p218 MR20

CHARLESWORTH,George Vernon 2Lt kia 28-9-18 6WRid p227 CR France358

CHARLESWORTH,Herbert T2Lt kia 26-10-17 91MGC Inf p182 CR Belgium112

CHARLESWORTH,John Stobart Maj 10-11-18 12YLI CR Yorks274

CHARLESWORTH,Reginald.MC.Capt dow 9-4-18 7Mddx p235 CR France185

CHARLESWORTH,Thomas Stephens T2Lt dow 10-7-16 25NumbF p60 CR France267

CHARLESWORTH,Walter Alexander T2Lt kia 7-2-17 3 att1Leic p87 CR France423

CHARLESWORTH,William Henry TMaj kia 15-9-16 6YLI p142 CR France402

CHARLEWOOD,William Henry TCapt dow 22-7-16 6NumbF p213 CR France285

CHARLTON,Arthur Nesbit.MC.LtTCapt kia 30-11-17 7Norf p73 MR17

CHARLTON,Bernard Hedley.MC.LtCol kia 22-3-18 4Yorks p220 CR France528

CHARLTON,Brian Lt kia 27-10-18 TankCps att82RAF p188 CR Belgium159

CHARLTON,Douglas Ferrier Lt kia 24-3-18 6DLI p239 CR France446,23-3-18

CHARLTON,Ernest Henry 2Lt ltia 31 3 18 1/4LYorks p219 MR27

CHARLTON,Frank Tysor 2Lt dow 3-10-18 3SLancs attY55TMB p125 CR France98,Tysoe 1/5Bn

CHARLTON,George Fenwick Hedley.MID Capt kia 6-10-16 10SWBord p99 CR Belgium167

CHARLTON,Hugh Vaughan Lt kia 24-6-16 7NumbF p214 CR Belgium60

CHARLTON,John 2Lt kia 2-9-18 3 att1RScotF A'Coy p94 CR France433,Lt

CHARLTON,John Lawther T2Lt dow 15-9-18 18MGC p182 CR France145

CHARLTON,John Macfarlan TCapt kia 1-7-16 21NumbF p60 MR21

CHARLTON,Norman Ewart T2Lt kia 15-6-18 11NumbF p60 CR Italy3

CHARLTON,Ralph Turnbull T2Lt kia 20-9-17 20DLI p160 MR30,21-9-17 Ex 6NumbF

CHARLTON,Robert.MC.TCapt dow 5-10-17 11 att7SStaffs p122 CR Belgium16

CHARLTON,Robert Arthur Lt kia 21-3-18 3 att1WYorks p81 MR20

CHARLTON,St.John Alan Lt kia 26-10-14 4 att1Beds p85 CR France924

CHARLTON,William 2Lt kia 25-3-18 4 att2/5ELancs p226 MR27

CHARLTON,William Ferrier 2Lt kia 18-9-16 6DLI p239 CR France239

CHARLTON,William Godfrey TLt kia 26-8-18 15DLI p160 CR France385

CHARLWOOD,William Roger T2Lt kia 18-7-17 1RWSurr p55 CR France421,6Bn

CHARMAN,Arthur Leonard Charles Lt 15-2-21 KentCycBn CR War7

CHARMAN,John Ewart 2Lt dow 25-9-17 1/4RSuss p228 CR Belgium140

CHARRIER,Paul Alfred Maj kia 27-8-14 2RMunstF p175 France1751

CHARRINGTON,Arthur Craven Capt dow 21-10-14 1Drags p21 CR Belgium57,20-10-14

CHARRINGTON,Edwin Milward Capt kia 13-11-16 3 att13Ess p131 MR21

CHARSLEY,Reginald Burton TMaj kia 30-11-17 12Lpool p71 MR17

CHART,Eric Nye Lt kia 25-9-16 1WYorks p81 MR21 CR France390

CHARTERIS,Ivo Alan.Hon.2Lt kia 17-10-15 GrenGds att1Bn SR p49 CR France257,Yeo

CHARTERIS,Thomas TCapt kia 27-9-15 10Yorks p90 MR19,26-9-15

CHASE,Archiblad Alderman.DSO.Capt&BtMaj dow 11-3-17 RE attRSuss p44 CR France251

CHASE,Harold Charles 2Lt kia 8-6-17 4Lincs p217 MR20

CHASE,Philip Hugh.MID T2Lt dow 1-7-16 12Mddx p146 CR France66

CHATHAM,George Henry 2Lt kia 23-11-16 10RFus p67 MR21

CHATTAWAY,Philip Spencer 2Lt kia 14-10-16 6Ches p222 CR France293

CHATTERIS,Tom Brodie TCapt kia 9-8-15 N&D att2Bn p133 MR29

CHATTERLEY,D.R.Capt ded 7-9-14 RAVC p269

CHATTERTON,Alfred Henry Goodbarne Lt ded 21-7-17 215RFA p207 CR Iraq8

CHATTERTON,Arthur Measures T2Lt kld 30-7-17 GL &RFC p6 CR Wilts28

CHATTERTON,Harold Montagu Newnham T2Lt dow 18-6-16 9RWSurr p55 CR France285

CHATTERTON,Roden Latham Capt kia 28-3-18 Leinst attRFC p15&174 CR Kent205,kldacc 29-3-18

CHATTOCK,Reginald Harvey 2Lt kia 13-3-16 4Glouc p225 CR France643

CHAUDHURY,S.R.Capt 22-3-20 IMS MR43

CHAVASSE,Aidan Lt kia 4-7-17 17Lpool p71 MR29

CHAVASSE,Arthur Ryland TCapt ded 12-3-16 RAMC p194 CR France85

CHAVASSE,Noel Godfrey.VC&Bar.DSO.MC.Capt dow 4-8-17 RAMC att10Lpool p253 CR Belgium7

CHAVASSE,Percy Lt kia 8-10-18 IARO &59RAF p275 MR20

CHAVE,John Haydon TLt dow 15-4-18 19MGC p182 CR Belgium21

CHAVENTRE,Alfred 2Lt kia 1-9-18 126A HAC p26 CR France421,2A/126RFA

CHAWNER,Alain Percy Mark.MID 2Lt kia 20-10-16 13Ess p131 CR France400,Lt 21-10-16 3 att1Bn

CHAWNER,Meredith Andre Capt kia 21-5-17 2Ess p131 CR France311

CHAWORTH-MUSTERS,Patricius George Lt dow 12-1-15 1KRRC p149CR France80,11-1-15

CHAWORTH-MUSTERS,Philip Mundy.MC.LtTCapt kia 18-7-17 25RFA p26 CR Belgium5

CHAWORTH-MUSTERS,Robert.MC.Capt ded 10-10-18 12KRRC att3MuskCamp p149 CR Notts2

CHAWORTH-MUSTERS,Roger Michael 2Lt kia 7-5-17 Leic &56RFC p6&87 MR20

CHAYTOR,Alban Kingsford 2Lt dow 26-5-15 6 att3Worc p108 CR Belgium21

CHAYTOR,Hugh Cleivaux Capt kia 31-10-14 IA 26Cav att11Huss p275

CHEAPE,John de Caerick TLt kia 3-9-16 8 att13RSuss p118 CR France701,Carrich

CHEAPE,Leslie St.Clair Capt&adjt kia 23-4-16 1DragGds attWorcYeo p20 MR34

CHEATLE,Charles Chesterfield 2Lt kia 5-5-17 GL &23RFC p6 MR20

CHEATLE,Walter John North Lt kia 25-4-15 1KOSB p101 CR Gallipoli6,26-4-15

CHECKLAND,Montmorency Beaumont Lt kia 16-8-17 WSomYeo p205

CHEERS,Donald Heriot Anson 2Lt kldacc 17-4-18 3ESurr attRAF p112 CR Scot235

CHEERS,Ronald Anson Vlascow 2Lt kia 27-9-15 3 att4SLancs p125 CR Belgium28,Vlassow 25-9-15

CHEESBROUGH,Harold T2Lt kia 4-9-18 WYorks att10EYorks p81 CR France262

CHEESE,Ernest Velmont TLt ded 30-7-16 ArmyPayDept p200 CR France145

CHEESE,William Gerard Chap4Cl ded 7-11-18 RAChDept att8Lincs p199 CR France146

CHEESEMAN,Anthony Alfred TLt kia 5-5-17 7EKent p57 MR20

CHEESMAN,Arthur Edwin Capt ded 26-9-16 1/5EKent p213 CR Iraq5

CHEESMAN,George Leonard TLt kia 10-8-15 10Hamps p170 MR4

CHEESMAN,John Frederick 2Lt kld 25-1-18 RFC p15 CR Suff83

CHEETHAM,Alan Humphrey Lt kia 16-12-16 2WRid p115 MR21

CHEETHAM,Charles Joseph LtCol ded 9-12-16 63RegDistRectgOff CR Lancs416

CHEETHAM,Frederick George Charles Beresford Lt ded 27-12-19 RH&FA p261

CHEETHAM,Herbert Lt kia 9-10-17 8WYorks att146TMB p219 CR Belgium125,1/6Bn

CHEETHAM,William Lt ded 6-2-20 RE p269 CR Lancs43

CHELL,Harold TLt dow 10-8-15 8RFus p67 CR France285

CHELLEW,John Maurice 2Lt dow 26-5-17 RGA 26SB p38 CR France512

CHENE,Charles Leslie 2Lt dow 21-4-18 5RScots p211 CR Germany4,11Bn

CHENE,Henry Maj kia 10-7-17 189RFA p206 CR Belgium29,Harry

CHENEVIX-TRENCH,Francis Maxwell Maj kia 31-10-14 RFA p26 CR Belgium58 2DivStaff

CHEPMELL,John Dobree Lt kia 10-4-18 2 att14RWar p64 MR32

CHEPMELL,William Dobree TLt kia 12-4-17 10RSuss attTMB p118 CR France480,9Bn

CHERRY,Alfred Douglas TLtACapt kia 4-4-17 Dors attSomLI p123 CR France162

CHESHIRE,Edgar Murray T2Lt kld 6-3-18 RFC p15 CR Surrey15

CHESHIRE,Eric Corveroy Lt kia 3-5-17 4RFus p67 MR20

CHESHIRE,Raymond Russell T2Lt kia 4-10-17 1/8RWar p64 MR30

CHESHIRE,William Robert T2Lt kia 1-7-16 1Ess p131 CR France220

CHESNEY,Charles Cornwallis Lt kia 24-11-15 IARO att117Mahrattas p275 MR38,22-11-15

CHESNEY,H.F.CMG.Col 21-3-20 RE CR Devon73

CHESTER,Greville Arthur Bagot 2Lt kia 13-10-14 3NStaffs p156 CR France193

CHESTER,Harry Keppel Capt dow 28-3-17 1/5Ess p232 CR Palestine2

CHESTER,James Leslie TLt kld 6-7-15 1/9Lpool p216 CR France114

CHESTER,Lewis Charles Bagot T2Lt kia 4-4-18 15LancF p92 MR20

CHESTER-MASTER,Richard Chester.DSO&Bar.BtMajTLtCol kia 30-8-17 13KRRC p149 CR Belgium183

CHESTERS,John Richards TLt kia 15-9-16 12ESurr p112 MR21

CHESTERTON,Frank Sidney 2Lt dow 11-11-16 C92RFA p26 CR France105

CHESTNUT,John Albon Lt dow 20-12-15 RFA 6DAC p26 CR France40,2t

CHETHAM-STRODE,Edward Randall Capt kia 1-10-17 3 att2BordR p116 MR30

CHETTLE,Ernest Frederick Lt dow 5-4-18 7Mddx att4RWFus p235 CR France102

CHETWOOD,Ernest Stanley.MID Capt kia 30-10-17 1/28Lond C'Coy p252 MR30

CHETWYND STAPYLTON,G.J.Maj kia 25-8-14 30/107RFA CR France206

CHETWYND-STAPYLTON,Henry Miles Capt kia 14-11-15 107RFA p26 CR Belgium15,dow

CHEVERS,Herbert Longmore Grant Maj ded 10-8-19 RAMC p267 CR Hamps218

CHEVERTON,Stanley Campbell Lt kia 27-1-17 1BordR p116 CR France399

CHEVERTON,Thomas Bird Maj kia 24-3-18 RFA p206 MR27

CHEVREAU,Louis Raymond de Montlehu T2Lt kia 22-3-18 16 att1/4NumbF p60 MR27

CHEW,George Douglas.MC.Capt 15-11-16 3NStaffs att11LNLancs p156 MR21

CHEYNE,Charles George 2Lt kia 14-4-18 6ScotRif p224 CR France324

CHIBNALL,George William Russell 2LtTLt kia 26-8-18 3DragGds att9WRid p21 MR16

CHIBNALL,Ronald Stanley TLt kia 31-7-17 8Suff p78 MR29

CHICHESTER,Edmund Basil Capt dow 7-11-14 3 att1EKent p57 CR France102

CHICHESTER,Henry Arthur Capt kia 20-10-14 3Dev p76 MR22

CHICHESTER,Robert Guy Incledon Capt kia 13-11-14 2HLI p162 MR29

CHICHESTER,William George Cubitt Lt kia 15-9-16 1Lond p245 CR France432,Capt

CHICK,Francis William Lt mbk 4-10-17 7 att1Dev p257 MR30

CHIDGEY,Percy Harold T2Lt dow 12-4-18 RE 200FC p44 CR Belgium38

CHIDSON,Laurence Drury.MC.TLtACapt kia 24-4-17 13KRRC p149 MR20,23-4-17

CHIGNELL,Hugh 2Lt kia 26-4-18 3Worc p108 MR30

CHILCOTT,Gilbert George Cardew 2Lt kia 18-4-17 1DCLI p114 MR20

CHILD,David Leslie Lt dow 11-9-16 2Lond p245 CR France329,2Lt

CHILD,Edward T2Lt kia 24-8-18 Mddx att1/8Bn p146 CR France927

CHILD,Gerald Julius Lt kia 18-4-15 YLI p142 MR29

CHILD,Gilbert Richard Gregory 2Lt kia 9-5-15 RSuss p118 MR22

CHILD,Henry Russell Capt kia 27-3-18 GL &11RFC p154&257 MR20

CHILD,James Martin.MC.Capt kld 23-8-18 1/2Manch &RAF p154 CR Essex40

CHILD,Joseph Alfred 2Lt kia 7-6-17 9Yorks att69TMB p90 CR Belgium167

CHILD,Philip Herbert T2Lt kia 23-8-18 16 att16RWar p64 MR16

CHILDE,Charles Murray TCapt dow 21-3-16 8Glouc p106 CR France345

CHILDE,Derrick Francis 2Lt kia 19-12-15 1/5Y&L p238 CR Belgium23

CHILDE-FREEMAN,John Arthur.MC.Capt kia 25-9-15 2RWFus p97 CR France114

CHILDE-PEMBERTON,Edward William Baldwin T2Lt dow 13-4-17 18 att11Huss p23 CR France12,Edmund Baldwyn

CHILDERHOUSE,Francis James T2Lt kia 23-9-16 9Lincs att2EYorks p74 MR37

CHILDS,George Willmot 2Lt kia 22-1-18 4Beds p85 CR France398

CHILDS,Robert Edward TLt dow 26-9-18 7RBerks p138 CR Greece6

CHILDS,Royden James 2Lt kia 27-7-16 3 att1RBerks p138 MR21

CHILES-EVANS,David Brynmor.DSO.LtCol kia 23-4-17 RAMC 3WelshFA p253 CR France80

CHILL,John Metcalfe 2Lt kia 8-11-16 att7EKent p57 MR21,18-11-16

CHILTON,F.Lt kia 20-6-15 13A&SH p173 MR4,4-6-15

CHILTON,Henry Lt ded 18-9-20 GL &RE IWT CR Iraq1

CHILTON,Hubert C.T2Lt kia 23-4-18 2LancF p92 CR France412,24-4-18

CHILVERS,Reginald Cuthbert T2Lt kia 19-4-17 10Norf p73 MR34

CHILVERS,Roland Clifford 2Lt kia 29-7-17 15Lond p249 CR France662

CHILWELL,Eric Robert T2Lt kia 16-9-16 7DCLI p114 MR21

CHINN,Lilian Ella Nurse 24-6-17 VAD attDevonportHosp CR Somerset49

CHINNERY,Esme Fairfax Capt kld 18-1-15 CldGds &RFC p1&51 CR Surrey86

CHINNERY,Harry Broderick TLt kia 28-5-16 13KRRC p149 CR France501

CHINNERY,Reginald Charles 2Lt kia 31-7-17 7Lpool p215 MR29

CHIPLIN,William Henry Capt kia 1-7-16 15RIrRif p169 MR21

CHIPMAN,John Douglas TLt kia 17-2-17 2SStaffs p122 MR21

CHIPPENDALE,Frank Dean 2Lt kia 10-4-18 4WRid p227 MR30

CHIPPERFIELD,Arnold Henry T2Lt kia 24-4-18 12Mddx att2/2Lond p146 MR27

CHIPPINDALL,Bertrand Thorold 2Lt kia 16-11-16 3SomLI p79 CR France339

CHIPPINGTON,Horace Leonard T2Lt dow 23-8-18 12Suff att16War p78 CR France84,24-8-18

CHIRSTIE,James Hugh CaptTMaj kia 24-5-15 4RIrReg p88 MR29,CHRISTIE,2Bn

CHISENHALE-MARSH,Harold Atherton Capt kia 28-9-18 9Lancers attSattf34DivHQ p22 CR Belgium11

CHISHOLM,Alasair Edward Lt kia 25-9-15 3RScots attRScotF p53 MR29

CHISHOLM,Alexander Lt kia 14-10-17 4 att7CamH p242 MR20

CHISHOLM,Edward Alexander.MC&2Bars.TMaj kia 7-11-18 C161RFA p26 CR France943,Ex 16CanadaFA

CHISHOLM,John Oliver TLt dow 23-7-18 RScots att1/8Bn p53 CR France1693 &CR France34

CHISHOLM,Kenneth James TLt dow 18-8-16 5Nhampt p137 CR France74

CHISHOLM,William Dempster T2Lt dow 23-3-18 5BordR p116 CR France987

CHISHOLM,William Malcolm Lt dow 27-8-14 1ELancs p110 CR France1349

CHISHOLM,William Turner 2Lt dow 1-9-16 2/23Lond p252 CR France95

CHISHOLM-BATTEN,James Forbes LtCol ded 17-3-15 ArmyPayDept p268

CHISHOLM-BATTEN,James Utermarck 2Lt kia 29-9-15 3Dors att3RFus p123 MR19

CHISHOLM BATTEN,John de Haviland CaptAMaj kia 7-8-17 RFA p26 CR Belgium89,Havilland

CHISLETT,Angus Robert Joseph Capt kia 24-4-17 8 att12HLI p240 MR20

CHISNALL,George Henry Lt dow 24-10-14 RAMC p194

CHISSELL,George Edwin.MC.TCapt dow 29-10-17 RAMC att1RWFus p194 CR Belgium11

CHISWELL,Henry Pettit.MC.Lt kia 25-3-18 RE 490FC p210 MR27

CHITTENDEN,Arthur George 2Lt kia 21-8-17 RFA p26 CR France255

CHITTENDEN,Arthur Grant Bourne 2Lt dow 9-9-14 Manch p154

CHITTY,Ernest Richard Inglis LtCol mbk 25-3-17 IA 105Mahrattas p275 MR38

CHITTY,James Malcolm 2Lt kia 1-12-17 4GrenGds p49 MR17

CHIVERS,Herbert T2Lt dedacc 18-6-18 RASC attRGA 153SB p192 CR France69

CHIVERS,Wreford 2Lt kia 17-8-17 GL &32RFC p6 MR20

CHOLMELEY,Eric Randolph Lt kia 1-7-16 2WYorks p81 MR21

CHOLMELEY,Harry Lenin Lt kia 1-7-16 3 att1BordR p116 MR21,Lewin

CHOLMELEY,Hugh Ralph 2Lt dow 14-6-15 45/42RFA p26 CR France285

CHOLMELEY,Hugh Valentine 2Lt kia 7-4-16 1GrenGds SR p49 CR Belgium84

CHOLMELEY,Montague Aubrey Rowley.Bart.Capt kia 24-12-14 2GrenGds RoO p49 MR22

CHOLMELEY,Roger James.MC.Capt drd 16-8-19 Ches p254 MR70 &CR Europe180

CHOLMONDELEY,Charles Almeric John Capt kia 28-10-14 2BordR p116 MR29

CHOLMONDELEY,Reginald Capt kld 12-3-15 RB att3RFC p1&178 CR France98

CHORLEY,Arthur Reginald Capt dow 28-4-18 1/4YLI p235 CR France102

CHORLEY,Charles Leonard.MC.T2Lt kia 26-4-18 1/2 att2/5LancF p92 MR19

CHORLTON,Herbert Bichonall 2Lt kia 26-3-18 2 att4ELancs p110 MR27

CHOVEAUX,Nigel Lt kia 14-3-17 1/5SStaffs p229 CR France281,Capt

CHOWN,Francis Jack T2Lt kia 20-9-17 GL att1RFC p6 CR Belgium112

CHOWN,William Leonard 2Lt kia 30-7-16 3Dors att2 O&BLI p123 MR21

CHOWNE,Gerard Henry Tilson TCapt dow 2-5-17 9ELancs p110 CR Greece6

CHOWNS,William Pharoah.MIDx2 Capt kld 5-1-21 IARO attS&TCps p275 CR Iraq8,Maj dow

CHREE,George William Johnstone.MC.TCapt&Adjt kia 14-7-16 1 att2RScots p53 CR France164,dow

CHRISTAIN,Albert T2Lt kia 27-9-18 TankCps p188 CR France662

CHRISTIAN,Aviet Thadeus Lt ded 6-11-18 IARO attWorksDirectorate p275 CR Iraq6

CHRISTIAN,Edward.MC.Capt dow 19-10-16 B235RFA p207 CR France40

CHRISTIAN,Edward Charles TCapt kia 11-9-16 7SStaffs p122 CR France251

CHRISTIE,Albert William Ernest 2Lt kld 27-9-15 2Worc p108 CR France281,27-9-16

CHRISTIE,Cedric Pasche T2Lt dow 16-12-15 11Lpool p71 CR France102

CHRISTIE,Denis Halstead T2Lt kia 21-9-18 11 att1RSuss p118 MR16

CHRISTIE,Dugald Roderick 2Lt kia 24-2-16 66RFA p26 MR38

CHRISTIE,Harold Reginald Morris 2Lt kia 16-7-16 4 att1ScotRif p103 MR21

CHRISTIE,Henry Robert Stark.DSO.OBE.LtCol ded 24-11-19 RE p262 CR Scot237

CHRISTIE,Herbert Bertram TLt ded 9-12-16 RemountService RASC p24 CR Lond14

CHRISTIE,James Allan T2Lt dow 6-11-17 6RWSurr p55

CHRISTIE,James Hugh Maj 24-5-15 2RIrReg MR29 see CHIRSTIE,J.H.

CHRISTIE,John 2Lt kia 22-7-18 4SfthH p241 CR France1228

CHRISTIE,Lawrence William Lt ded 7-5-17 RIM attRE IWT p275 CR Iraq6

CHRISTIE,Lindsay Bruce Stark Maj ded 30-9-15 RA CR Scot237

CHRISTIE,Murray Inglis.DSO.T2Lt.ACapt dow 24-3-18 32RFus A'Coy p67 CR France745

CHRISTIE,Paul Norman Jones 2Lt kia 9-10-17 1/2Beds C'Coy p85 MR30

CHRISTIE,Richard Colin Lt dow 15-12-15 RE 80FC p44 CR France22

CHRISTIE,Robert Francis Sanderson T2Lt kld 15-10-17 GL &RFC p6 CR War7

CHRISTIE,Robert Main Maj dow 15-5-18 10LabCps p189 CR France145

CHRISTIE,Ronald.MC.LtACapt dow 12-4-18 RASC attRGA p192 CR France1107

CHRISTIE,William Lt&QM ded 8-11-17 3GordH p166 CR Scot330

CHRISTIE,William Charles.MIDx2 Maj kia 13-10-14 1RWar D'Coy p64 CR France324

CHRISTIE,William Edward Tolfrey.CMG.OBE.DSO.MajTCol ded 22-10-18 RASC p192 CR SAfrica171

CHRISTIE-MURRAY,Maurice.MC.TLt dow 9-9-16 112RFA p26 CR France430

CHRISTISON,Frederick John TLt dow 4-12-15 10A&SH p173 CR Belgium4

CHRISTISON,Robert Colin Lt kia 25-9-17 10GordH p166 MR19

CHRISTMAS,Bernard Lovell Capt dow 11-5-16 1/3Lond p245 CR France,19-5-16

CHRISTMAS,Dudley Vivian LtStaffCapt kld 23-10-15 5Suff p217

CHRISTMAS,Edwin Cecil Russell T2Lt dow 7-10-16 18KRRC p149 MR21

CHRISTMAS,Leslie Frederick T2Lt kia 3-11-16 17 att14Mddx p146 CR France742,13-11-16

CHRISTOPHER,John Hosken 2Lt kia 22-2-17 IARO att92Punjabis p275 CR Iraq5

CHRISTOPHER,Leonard de Lona Capt kia 26-4-15 IA att40Pathans p275

CHRISTOPHER,Richard TLt kia 29-9-18 16TankCps p188 CR France212

CHRISTY,Basil Robert Francis 2Lt dow 3-10-16 1CldGds p51 CR France105

CHRISTY,John George T2Lt kia 3-10-18 1/2 att1/5Leic p87

CHRISTY,Philip Archibald Lt kia 10-2-15 2Ess SR p131 CR Belgium33

CHRISTY,Stephen Henry.DSO.Capt kia 27-8-14 20Huss SR p23 CR France1445,3-9-14

CHRISTY,Stephen Edmund Fell Lt kia 12-7-16 1IrGds p52 CR Belgium84

CHRISTY,Thomas Hill 2Lt kia 12-4-18 EssYeo att10Ess p203 MR27,Hills

CHRONNELL,Hubert.MC.2LtACapt kia 31-7-17 1/5LNLancs p135 CR Belgium10

CHRYSTAL,George Gordon Lt kia 25-5-15 9A&SH p244 MR29

CHRYSTAL,Ian Campbell 2Lt kia 1-5-17 3 att9SfthH p164 CR France452

CHRYSTIE,James Alexander 2Lt kia 30-11-14 3 att2RScotF p94 MR29

CHRYSTIE,John Maj kia 17-11-14 RGA 1SB p38 CR Belgium57

CHUBB,Alan Travers 2Lt kia 9-9-16 11Hamps p120 MR21

CHUBB,Francis John MacLardie 2Lt kia 18-4-15 3 att2YLI p142 MR29

CHUBB,Geoffrey Capt kia 12-7-15 6RWSurr p55 CR Belgium137

CHUBB,Theodore 2Lt kia 17-2-17 10Lond attRFus p248 CR France314

CHURCH,Arthur.MC.Lt ded 14-2-18 EAfrIntelDept CR EAfrica11& CR Tanzania1

CHURCH,Arthur Gilbert Walsh Capt kia 20-7-18 1/5Dev p217 CR France622

CHURCH,Frederick James.DCM.2Lt kia 10-5-15 2RDubF p176 MR29

CHURCH,Geoffrey William.MC.2Lt kia 3-5-17 7EKent p57 MR20

CHURCH,Harold Capt kia 19-7-16 O&BLI 2/1BucksBn p231 CR France1887

CHURCH,Horace Major Scrimshire 2Lt dow 10-2-18 7LancF p221 CR France98

CHURCH,John Victor Lt kia 10-12-17 3 att6KSLI p144 CR Egypt1,2Lt

CHURCH,John William Lt dow 30-3-18 Herts p252 MR27

CHURCH,W.A.Maj 17-6-20 DCLI CR Devon1

CHURCH,Walter Harry 2Lt kia 23-7-16 3 att1DCLI attTMB p114 MR21

CHURCH,William Campbell Capt kia 28-6-15 8ScotRif p224 MR4

CHURCHER,Bryan Thomas LtCol ded 31-12-18 RWSurr p55 CR Berks124

CHURCHER,Edgar TLt kia 14-7-17 3RB &32RFC p6&178 CR Belgium11

CHURCHFIELD,Sidney Percival T2Lt kia 1-7-16 4Mddx p146 CR France267

CHURCHILL,Arthur Lindsay Maury Capt ded 24-6-17 RAMC att18Lond p253 CR Egypt8

CHURCHILL,Charles Henry Matthew Capt kia 17-2-17 IA att20Inf p275 CR Iraq5

CHURCHILL,Clarence Harold 2Lt kia 15-12-17 RGA p38 CR Belgium101

CHURCHILL,George Ross Deas.DSO.LtCol kia 20-12-19 IA Cmdg2/19Punjabis p275 MR43

CHURCHILL,Herbert Payn T2Lt ded 20-10-15 RE p44 CR Europe1

CHURCHMAN,Charles Harvey Lt kia 3-5-17 6Suff att2/5WYorks p218 MR20

CHURCHWARD,Hubert Alan 2Lt kia 16-8-17 2Coy of LondYeo attRFC p18&204 MR20

CHURCHYARD,Arthur Stewart TCapt ded 28-1-17 6RB att1DubF p178 CR Mddx5

CHUTE,Challoner Francis Trevor Lt kia 27-8-14 2RMunstF p175 CR France1751

CHUTER,Harry Athelstan Lt kia 25-3-17 2RFus &70RFC p6&67 CR France234

CHUTTER,George Philip Lt kia 15-6-18 1/5Glouc p225 CR Italy2

CINNAMOND,Francis T2Lt ded PoW 13-11-18 10 att2RInniskF p104 CR Europe149

CITY,S.G.E.2Lt 30-5-17 IARO att1RGA MR67

CLACHAN,William James Capt kia 6-1-18 2Mddx att1KAR p146&202 CR EAfrica77

CLAGUE,George.MC.2Lt kia 14-3-15 1HLI p162 CR France279

CLAIRMONTE,George Egerton 2Lt kia 25/26-9-15 1Glouc p106 CR France550

CLAKE,see CLARKE,A.C.

CLANCEY John Austin.MC.Maj ded 22-7-18 RIrF &MGC p171&182 CR Berks84

CLANCEY,Trevor John 2Lt kia 28-10-14 2BordR p116 MR29,24-10-14

CLANCY,George David Louis 2Lt drd 4-5-17 4RIrRif att1Leinst p169 CR Italy14

CLANCY,William John 2Lt ded 16-10-18 RASC p192 CR Lond29,Joseph

CLAPHAM,Alan Charles 2Lt kld 3-1-16 4EYorks p219 CR Belgium127

CLAPHAM,Barnard Aubrey Lt dow 27-3-17 4Ess p232 CR Palestine8

CLAPHAM,Christopher Albon T2Lt kia 10-2-16 8Y&L p158 CR France347,Christofer

CLAPHAM,Edgar Lt dow 5-11-18 6WRid p227 CR France332

CLAPHAM,Graham Windyer 2Lt dow 10-5-17 71RFA p26 CR France113

CLAPHAM,Robert Sydney T2Lt dow 28-9-17 12WYorks p81 CR Belgium16

CLAPP,Alfred Henry Lt ded 15-5-16 RAVC p198 CR France207

CLAPP,Leonard Bishop T2Lt dow 2-10-17 BordR att1Bn p116 CR Belgium16

CLAPP,William Gilbert Elphinstone 2Lt dow 29-4-17 NorfYeo att7Norf p204 CR France113

CLAPPEN,Wilfred Joseph 2Lt dow 22-9-16 10DLI p160 CR France833

CLAPPERTON,James Hugh Maj dow 7-5-17 B317RFA p206 CR France40

CLAPTON,Arthur 2Lt kia 5-9-16 32RFus p67 MR21,15-9-16

CLARE,Arthur Vernon 2Lt kia 15-9-16 21Lond p251 CR France385

CLARE,Horace Townshend.MID LtAMaj kia 29-4-18 A245RFA p26 CR Belgium8

CLAREMONT,Frederick Victor Leszynski 2Lt kia 14-8-17 RGA 184SB p38 CR Belgium23

CLARK,Algernon Basil.MC.MIDx2 Capt kia 3-10-18 3BlkW att2RAF p128 CR France223

CLARK,Alan Glover 2Lt kia 21-9-18 3 att1ScotRif p103 CR France666

CLARK,Albert Victor.MC.2Lt dow 2-1-18 5Beds p219 CR France398

CLARK,Alexander.MC.Lt&QM dow 13-4-18 9SforthH p164 CR Belgium38

CLARK,Alfred Matthews Lt kia 20-11-17 1/4RLancs p213 MR21,Mathew

CLARK,Alick Morton 2Lt kia 27-1-17 1BordR p116 CR France374

CLARK,Allan La Barte Capt kia 18-9-18 RAMC att12Ches p194 MR37

CLARK,Andrew Scott Duncan T2Lt dow 22-4-17 9RScotF att1/4Bn p94 CR Egypt2

CLARK,Anthony Dalzell TCapt dow 4-12-17 N&D p133 CR Egypt2

CLARK,Archibald Strachan T2Lt kia 8-10-18 13Lpool p71 CR France338

CLARK,Arthur Lt 26-1-20 RASC CR Egypt6

CLARK,Arthur Henry T2Lt dow 3-5-18 PoW 49MGC Inf D'Coy p182 CR France1029

CLARK,Arthur James Richard Lt dow 9-10-16 8RFus p67 CR France833,kia

CLARK,Arthur Vivian T2Lt kia 20-4-16 GL att7Glouc p190

CLARK,Basil Vyse Lt kia 24-7-18 121RFA p26 CR France4

CLARK,Bruce Lt kia 9-11-16 1/4Glouc p225 MR21

CLARK,C.B.Capt kia 3-11-16 SL att1KAR p202 MR50

CLARK,Charles 2Lt kia 24-3-18 19Lond p250 CR France216

CLARK,Charles.MC.MID LtAMaj kia 25-4-18 295RFA p26 CR France745

CLARK,Charles Augustus 2Lt kia 1-7-16 5 att1RB p178 MR21

CLARK,Charles Douglas.TD.LtCol ded 22-1-20 5RWKent p269 CR Kent95

CLARK,Charles Inglis Capt ded 6-3-18 RASC 976MT p192 CR Iraq8

CLARK,Charles William T2Lt kia 20-11-17 RWKent att6Bn p140 CR France379

CLARK,Charlie T2Lt kia 9-4-18 2 att5LancF p92 CR France1106

CLARK,Claude Frederick 2Lt dow 1-10-18 4Nhampt p234 CR France34,6Bn

CLARK,Clifford Stanley Lt ded 30-5-19 465/65RFA p26 CR Germany1

CLARK,Colbert Walter 2Lt kia 26-4-18 13RB p178 MR27

CLARK,David Ian Graham 2Lt kia 20-9-17 4SfthH p241 CR Belgium83

CLARK,Donald Gordon.DSO.MC.Capt dow 13-4-18 1/6GordH p292 CR France40

CLARK,Douglas Maj dow 29-6-15 8HLI p240 MR4

CLARK,Douglas Scott Dalrymple Capt kia 15-9-16 18KRRC attTMB p149 MR21 &CR France1890

CLARK,Egbert Douglas Lt dow 15-2-17 2Ches p95 CR Iraq5

CLARK,Ellis 2Lt kia 1-5-15 1LancF p92 CR Gallipoli1,25-4-15

CLARK,Eric Alan 2Lt kld 20-3-18 5RFC p15 CR Lancs386

CLARK,Eric Foster TLt kia 1-1-17 EKent &RFC p6&57 CR France833

CLARK,Eric Groby 2Lt kia 23-4-17 6 att1Mddx p146 MR20

CLARK,Eric Henry Lloyd 2Lt kia 1-7-16 5/3RFA p208 MR21

CLARK,Ernest Vaughan 2Lt kia 29-11-17 RFus &20RFC p6 MR20

CLARK,Frank Adams Maj dow 20-11-17 1/5Dev p217 CR Palestine9

CLARK,Frank Nelham 2Lt kld 29-4-17 GL &RFC p6

CLARK,Fred Sumner 2Lt kia 14-10-18 10Lpool att1/4SfthH p216 CR France611

CLARK,Frederick Percy Capt&QM 8-10-18 3Huss CR Kent180

CLARK,George 2Lt kia 3-11-17 RGA 189HB p38 CR Palestine8

CLARK,George Ernest Cecil TCapt kia 9-1-16 8LNLancs p135 CR Belgium70

CLARK,George Mackay Lt kia 12-11-17 4RScots p211 MR34

CLARK,George Milburn T2Lt kia 14-7-18 12Yorks att1WYorks p90 CR Belgium3

CLARK,George Reginald Heylin.MID Lt kia 26-8-18 7NStaffs p156 MR38

CLARK,Gerald Maitland TMaj kia 14-7-16 9Nhampt p137 MR21,6Bn

CLARK,Harold Conquest.MC.Lt dow 7-2-18 3 att2Wilts p152 CR France1063,Capt

CLARK,Henry Featherstone T2LtTLt kia 3-5-17 11Dev att2/6Glouc p76 CR France1701

CLARK,Henry Robert Ernest see CLARKE,H.R.E.

CLARK,Herbert George Lt ded 16-4-18 IARO attStaffBombay p275 MR65

CLARK,Horace Arthur Capt kia 14-9-16 24Lond p252 CR France387

CLARK,Hugh Reginald Stanley T2Lt kia 18-8-16 11GordH p166 MR21

CLARK,James.CB.LtCol kia 10-5-15 9A&SH p243 CR Belgium6

CLARK,James Smith 2Lt kia 3-5-17 6GordH att5CamH p242 MR20

CLARK,James Tony 2Lt kia 9-9-16 2Suss p118 MR21

CLARK,Jasper Lt kia 2-10-18 6A&SH p243 CR France236

CLARK,John T2Lt kld 6-8-17 GL &RFC p6 CR Scot122

CLARK,John Dormet 2Lt kia 27-5-17 6 att1ScotRif p224 MR20,Dormer

CLARK,John Frederick 2Lt ded 10-9-18 6Mddx &RAF p265

CLARK,John Harold.MID 2Lt kia 25-9-15 3 att2Wilts p152 MR19

CLARK,John Ladyman TCapt ded 16-12-18 RAVC attIndVetHosp p198 CR Egypt9

CLARK,John MacTaggart Capt ded 18-11-18 8RWSurr attDLI p55 CR Essex146

CLARK,John Ryder 2Lt kia 20-10-17 RGA 196SB p38 CR Belgium87,dow

CLARK,Laurence Fraser T2Lt dow 7-12-17 1EKent p57 CR France446

CLARK,Lyonel Latimer 2Lt kia 2-8-16 LeicRFA attRFC p208 CR France837

CLARK,Marcus Broadfoot TLt kia 25-9-17 2A&SH p173 CR Belgium112

CLARK,Neville Arthur Lt dow 28-11-17 1CldGds p51 CR France398

CLARK,Noel T2LtACapt dow 1-4-18 2Nhampt p137 CR France145

CLARK,Norman Lt kia 18-3-18 RFA att54RFC p18&207 CR France333,FlLt

CLARK,Norman Henry 2Lt dow 25-11-17 BedsYeo p203 CR France298,Harry

CLARK,Norman Pickslay T2Lt kia 24-8-16 7 att2RMunstR p175 MR21

CLARK,Oscar William T2Lt kia 22-7-16 1ESurr p112 MR21,23-7-16

CLARK,R.A.Ronaldson Lt ded 19-10-18 RH&FA &RAF p26

CLARK,Reginald Burton 2Lt dow 1-5-17 60RFC p6 CR France13,CLARKE

CLARK,Reginald William T2Lt kia 19-8-17 3 att17N&D p133 CR Belgium120

CLARK,Richard T2Lt kia 15-5-15 8 att7KOSB p101 CR France423,14-5-16

CLARK,Robert TCapt dow 7-11-18 RAMC att20Huss p194 CR France943

CLARK,Roland Hope T2Lt dow 24-3-18 16RB p178 CR France300

CLARK,Samuel Clarkson Lt dow 17-9-18 1GordH p166 CR Scot798

CLARK,Sidney George 2Lt kia 4-4-18 15Lond p249 CR France296

CLARK,Stanley Lowndes TLt kia 13-4-18 ACycCps att13Lpool p181 CR France88

CLARK,Stewart T2Lt kia 21-3-18 7RB p178 MR27

CLARK,Sydney Capt kia 2-10-16 RAMC 5LondFA p253 CR France397

CLARK,Thomas James Maj&QM ded 10-9-16 RE p269 CR Kent46

CLARK,W.R.LtCol 4-2-19 IMS CR Lancs401

CLARK,Walter Llewellyn T2LtTCapt kia 23-5-17 GL &6RFC p6 CR Belgium11

CLARK,William T2Lt kia 27-3-17 16Manch p154 CR France214

CLARK,William 2Lt kia 23-4-17 5A&SH p243 CR France434

CLARK,William Brown TCapt kia 12-3-17 RAMC att2ScotsGds p194 CR France329

CLARK,William Campbell 2Lt dow 27-10-18 7A&SH p243 CR France13

CLARK,William Frederick Hunter 2Lt dow 23-2-16 3RScotF p94 CR Greece7,CLARKE

CLARK,William Henry 2lt kia 6-7-17 8Mddx attRFC p18&236 MR20

CLARK,William Muir T2Lt kia 20-11-17 BlkW att1/7Bn p128 CR France398

CLARK,William Sowerby.MC.TCapt kld 10-7-17 10EYorks p83 CR France68,dedacc

CLARK,William Spenceley TCapt kia 1-7-16 12Y&L A'Coy p158 CR France1890,dow

CLARK-KENNEDY,Alexander Kenelm Capt kia 19-4-17 1/5KOSB p224 CR Palestine8

CLARK-KENNEDY,Archibald Douglas Hewitt.MID Capt dow 18-9-18 5RScotF p222 CR France646,kia

CLARKE,Albert Edward T2Lt kia 20-4-16 2Y&L p158 CR Belgium33

CLARKE,Albert Edward 2Lt dow 9-7-16 6RWar p214 CR Germany1

CLARKE,Alexander Maj ded 2-8-18 SL 7Hrs RecruitOff p268 CR Essex80

CLARKE,Alexander Norwall 2Lt kia 24-8-18 7A/317RFA p26 CR France577

CLARKE,Alfred Lord 2Lt kia 27-3-18 3 att2/6LancF p92 MR27

CLARKE,Algernon Percy 2Lt dow 24-7-15 23Lond p252 CR France98

CLARKE,Ambrose Childs 2Lt kia 10-5-15 1/4Leic p220 CR Belgium99

CLARKE,Arthur 2Lt ded 17-11-18 1Worc p264 CR Staffs61

CLARKE,Arthur Aubrey.MC.Lt kia 1-10-17 7Leic p87 CR Belgium112,Capt

CLARKE,Arthur Cecil Grafton T2Lt kia 28-5-18 2/6RWar p64 CR France1161

CLARKE,Arthur Cyril T2Lt kia 9-4-17 2Wilts p152 CR France214,CLARKE

CLARKE,Arthur Henry Gilbert 2Lt kia 9-9-16 Nhampt p137 CR France432

CLARKE,Arundel Geoffrey 2Lt kia 1-7-16 5RB p178 CR France744

CLARKE,Austin Basil.MC.Capt kia 23-11-17 RAMC att1/9Lond p194 CR France245

CLARKE,Booth Frederick 2Lt kia 26-1-17 2ESurr p112 MR37

CLARKE,Brian Lloyd Lt dow 19-4-15 IA 23Cav &RFC p275 CR France200

CLARKE,Cecil Andrews.MM.MIDx2 2Lt kia 23-4-17 1/7Mddx p235 CR France15,24-4-17

CLARKE,Charles Basil 2Lt kia 21-4-16 66RFA p26 MR38

CLARKE,Charles Edward 2Lt 27-9-18 WYorks att20RAF CR France1061

CLARKE,Charles Henry Geoffrey Mansfield Maj ded 27-7-19 RB p266 CR Bucks91

CLARKE,Charles Louis TLt kia 8-10-16 7Nhampt p137 CR France81

CLARKE,Charles St.Aubyn 2Lt ded 30-7-18 IA 74Punjabis p275 MR66

CLARKE,Claud Fitzroy Maj ded 30-6-18 20DeccanHorse CR Surrey37

CLARKE,Claude Hamilton Law 2Lt ded 22-3-18 RFC p15 CR Mddx39

CLARKE,Cyril T2Lt dow 16-6-16 11 att8ESurr p112 CR France23,kia

CLARKE,Cyril George TLt dow 26-9-15 8EYorks p83 CR France178

CLARKE,Cyril John Digby Lt dow 15-9-17 RASC p253 CR Belgium10

CLARKE,David T2Lt kia 22-3-18 11Ches p95 MR20

CLARKE,Donald T2Lt kia 26-8-16 GL &7RFC p2&190 CR France44

CLARKE,Edward George.MID LtTCapt kia 13-11-16 7RFus p67 CR France220

CLARKE,Edward Rupert 2Lt kia 9-4-17 4Lond p246 MR20 CR France581,9KRRC

CLARKE,Edwin Alfred 2Lt dow 1-10-16 2/20Lond p251 CR France95

CLARKE,Edwin Charles Kaye.MC.Capt kia 31-8-18 Inns of Court OTC p252 MR16

CLARKE,Eric Fitzgerald Capt kia 9-4-17 3Lond p245&204,3Co of LondYeo CR France419

CLARKE,Eric Groby T2Lt kia 23-4-17 7BordR p116

CLARKE,Ernest George 2Lt 23-4-17 7BordR MR20

CLARKE,Francis Arthur T2Lt kia 31-7-16 1Norf p73 CR France402

CLARKE,Francis Charles Erlin Lt dow 11-10-17 3Worc &5RFC p6&108 CR France113

CLARKE,Francis Herbert.MC.2Lt kia 1-11-18 RFA 28ArmyBde p26 CR Belgium140,124RFA

CLARKE,Frederick John Noel 2Lt kia 29-6-15 6 att3Worc p108 MR29 &CR Belgium453

CLARKE,Frederick Thomas Phillip 2Lt kia 19-4-17 11Lond p248 MR34

CLARKE,Geoffrey d'Almaine Campbell TLt kia 11-1-16 RFA att92TMB p26 CR France515

CLARKE,George Alexander T2Lt kia 21-3-18 8RDubF p176 CR France660,Lt

CLARKE,George Edward 2Lt kia 23-7-16 10RWar p64 MR21

CLARKE,George Henry 2Lt kia 22-4-18 3 att1Norf p73 CR France21,21-4-18

CLARKE,George Thomas TLt dow 18-9-18 C/114RFA p26 CR Greece1

CLARKE,Gerald Foulkes T2Lt dow 6-10-17 8 att1DCLI p114 CR Belgium11

CLARKE,Gilbert Roderick Bernard 2Lt dow 13-6-18 7ScotRif p224 CR France102

CLARKE,Gordon Elstone.MC.T2Lt kia 28-8-16 6DCLI p114 MR21

CLARKE,Hamlet John 2Lt kia 21-5-18 1Dors p123 CR France502

CLARKE,Harold Frank TLt kia 25-9-15 5 O&BLI p130 MR29

CLARKE,Harold Joyce Lt kia 17-5-15 3 att1RBerks p138 MR22,16-5-15

CLARKE,Harold Martin Lt kia 26-9-15 1/17Lond p250 CR France550

CLARKE,Harold Percival Lt dow 9-5-15 6 att2RB p178 MR32,kia

CLARKE,Harry Charles TLt kia 6-7-17 48RFC p6 CR France403

CLARKE,Harry Herbert TLt ded 14-7-18 4RRofCav p261

CLARKE,Henry Colin TCapt ded 25-5-16 170RASC p192 CR France80,Harry

CLARKE,Henry Hugh Franklin T2Lt kia 24-9-17 87RFA p26 CR France179

CLARKE,Henry Robert Ernest 2Lt dow 3-6-16 15Lond p249 CR France98,CLARK 3-6-15

CLARKE,Hilary Calvert TLt dow 31-8-18 31MGC Inf p182 CR France324

CLARKE,Horace Yelverton Chatfield 2Lt kia 23-4-17 2SWBord p99 MR20

CLARKE,Hugh Robert 2Lt ?-8-21 RMunstF CR Eire408

CLARKE,H.W.2Lt dow 2-9-18 28Lond &RAF p255

CLARKE,Ian Alexander TCapt kia 16-11-16 RAMC att1Dors p194 CR France131

CLARKE,Ian Hay Steuart Lt mbk 2-11-14 IA 57Rif p275

CLARKE,James Burford 2Lt kia 2-9-18 4SLancs p230 CR France511

CLARKE,James Henry Fisher T2Lt kia 1-7-16 7Yorks p90 CR France397

CLARKE,James Leonard Courtney Lt kia 5-1-17 IARO att47Sikhs p275 MR38,5-11-17

CLARKE,John Edward Langton.MC.Lt kia 14-9-14 50RFA p26 CR France1329

CLARKE,J.Gay TCapt kia 27-9-15 9RSuss p118 MR19

CLARKE,Job Lt 16-10-15 S&TCps MR65

CLARKE,John Capt kia 9-9-15 RAMC 1FA p253 CR Gallipoli27

CLARKE,John 2Lt kia 18-9-18 5SLancs &35RAF p230 MR20

CLARKE,John Lt ded 24-10-18 16Manch p154 CR Germany1

CLARKE,John Granshields Lt 26-3-16 RIndMarine CR India97A

CLARKE,John James Gordon ACapt kia 28-4-17 6Ess p232 MR21,13Ess att1 O&BLI

CLARKE,John Kingham 2Lt kld 22-7-18 3ConnRgrs &RAF p172

CLARKE,John Michell LtCol ded 21-4-18 RAMC p253 CR Glouc9

CLARKE,John Percy Dalzell 2Lt ded 21-2-15 Worc p264 CR Surrey160

CLARKE,John Seymour Denison TLt kia 10-11-17 13A&SH p173 CR Palestine18

CLARKE,Joseph.MC.Lt kld 1-10-19 Worc &99RAF p264 MR65

CLARKE,Kenneth Herbert 2Lt kia 30-9-17 1/6A&SH p243 CR Belgium127,Lt

CLARKE,Leonard Lt dow 4-10-17 4 att7KSLI p235 CR Belgium16

CLARKE,Leonard William T2Lt dow 14-11-16.11ELancs p110 CR France2

CLARKE,Montagu Christian Cuthbert Lt kia 10-5-15 1A&SH p173 MR29,8-5-15

CLARKE,Mordaunt Edward Leonard Hannam Lt kia 26/27-8-14 3Worc p108 CR France657,26-8-14

CLARKE,Nathaniel Fuhrmann T2lt kld 1-6-17 GL &RFC p6 CR War135

CLARKE,Neville Dutton 2Lt ded 18-4-16 5RIrRif p171&265 CR Ireland33,10-4-16

CLARKE,Nicholas Vincent T2Lt kldacc 19-6-17 GL &57RFC p6 CR Egypt8

CLARKE,Percy Thomas T2Lt kia 19-8-18 3 att1/5Suff p78 CR Palestine9

CLARKE,Peter TLt dow 30-7-16 GL Wilts Cmdg13LgtTMB p190 CR France51,Capt

CLARKE,Reginald Burton see CLARK,R.B.

CLARKE,Richard John Capt kia 10-3-15 IA 8Rajputs att1/39GarhwalRif p275 CR France355 &CR France1887

CLARKE,Richard Stanley.MC.T2Lt kia 4-10-18 47MGC Inf p182 CR France1106

CLARKE,Robert George 2Lt kia 9-9-18 72RFA p26 CR France439

CLARKE,Robert Shuttleworth TCapt kia 25-9-15 5KSLI p144 MR29

CLARKE,Robert William Capt ded 10-8-16 RAVC p254 CR Egypt9,19-8-16

CLARKE,Roland Harry 2Lt ded 23-5-18 3 att1RWKent p140 CR France65,Lt

CLARKE,Roland Harwood TLt drd 21-2-17 20RFA p26 MR35

CLARKE,Russell Frank 2Lt kia 21-5-17 15Lond p249 MR20

CLARKE,S.S.S.Maj 11-5-18 CamH CR Scot45

CLARKE,Samuel Frank 2Lt kia 7-8-17 6Hamps p229 CR Belgium10

CLARKE,St.A.2Lt 30-7-18 74Punjabis MR66 see CLARKE,C.St.A.

CLARKE,Sidney Herbert.MC&Bar.LtTCapt kia 2-9-17 3Wilts att1AircraftDepotRFC p6&152 CR France134

CLARKE,Stanley Vingoe Lt kia 6-5-17 5Dev p217 CR France407,2Bn

CLARKE,Stephen Rev Chap4Cl kia 4-10-17 RAChDept att7LancF p199 MR30

CLARKE,Thomas Henry 2Lt kia 28-9-18 4ELancs p226 CR Belgium50

CLARKE,Thomas Purcell Lt kia 30-9-16 6Y&L p150 MR21

CLARKE,Thomas Veitch Lt accdrd 30-9-20 IA 9Horse att41Dogras p275 CR Palestine9

CLARKE,Vincent Charles T2Lt dow 12-10-16 10DLI p160 CR France158,Capt dedacc

CLARKE,W.A.Col 18-4-15 9Y&L CR Hamps1

CLARKE,Walter Stanley Arnold 2Lt kia 10-7-16 6Dors p123 MR21

CLARKE,Walter Sidney 2Lt kia 25-6-16 5 att2RMunstF p175 MR20,Sydney

CLARKE,Wilfred John 2Lt dow 9-9-16 5 att8RDubF p176 MR21

CLARKE,Wilfrid Randall TLt kld 4-2-18 RFA &RFC p15&26 CR Lincs61

CLARKE,William Frederick Hunter see CLARK,W.F.H.

CLARKE,William Hamilton 2Lt kia 12-3-15 5Worc p108 CR Belgium17,3Bn

CLARKE,William Mitchell 2Lt kia 12-11-16 RE 1/1FC p210 CR France392

CLARKEN,George Capt ded 3-1-19 RFA p254 CR Yorks294,Maj

CLARKSON,Amos.MC.TLt dow 24-10-18 WYorks att8Bn p81 CR France380

CLARKSON,Charles Capt ded 12-2-17 2/4WRid p227 CR France169

CLARKSON,Donald James 2Lt kia 9-8-18 1/6N&D att6Bn p133 CR France109

CLARKSON,Harold 2Lt kia 11-4-17 MGC D'HB attD'TankCps p182 MR20

CLARKSON,John James TLt kia 30-12-17 10A&SH p173 CR France439

CLARKSON,John Osborne Price 2Lt kia 10-3-17 13Huss p22 MR38

CLARKSON,Leslie Cecil Bentinck Capt ded 31-3-17 RASC p192 CR France102

CLARKSON,Thomas T2Lt kia 22-3-18 23Manch p154 MR20

CLARKSON,Wilfred Bamforth T2Lt ded 20-6-18 2Y&L p158 CR France142,Wilford

CLATWORTHY,Thomas Eland 2Lt kia 7-1-16 IARO att37Dogras p275 MR38,6-1-16

CLAUGHTON,Ian Drummond TLt kia 2-3-16 11Suff p78 CR France83

CLAUGHTON,John Harold 2Lt kia 30-11-17 35MGC p182 MR17

CLAUGHTON,Wilfred Maj ded 24-3-18 25LabCps p189 CR France102,Wilfrid

CLAXTON,Eric Abley 2Lt dow 31-7-17 KRRC att18Bn p149 MR29

CLAY,Arthur Joseph CaptTMaj ded 18-2-15 2/6NStaffs p238&255 CR Staffs180

CLAY,Henry George Walter 2Lt kia 29-7-16 1ESurr p112 MR21

CLAY,Lionel Pillean Capt kia 18-2-18 YorksDrag p206 CR France446,Pilleau

CLAY,Louis John 2Lt kia 5-4-18 6LancF p221 CR France745

CLAY,Vernon Harcourt.MC.T2Lt dow 26-10-16 10LancF p92 CR Yorks738

CLAY,Vivian Hastings Capt kia 18-10-16 2Wilts p152 MR21

CLAYDON,Archer William Ridge Lt ded 31-5-18 3KAR p202 CR EAfrica47,SL att1/6KAR

CLAYE,Charles Geoffrey Lt kia 5-7-18 5N&D &RAF p232&258,6-5-18

CLAYE,Geoffrey Woolley Lt dow 29-3-17 1/7Ches p223 CR Egypt2

CLAYHILLS,George.DSO.Capt kia 2-11-14 1ELancs p110 CR Belgium68

CLAYPHAN,George Alfred T2Lt kia 4-12-17 GL &12RFC p6 CR France214

CLAYTON,Albert James.MC.2Lt dow 24-8-18 2Lond p245 CR France100

CLAYTON,Arthur Oliver.MID Capt kia 21-3-18 3 att2Wilts p152 MR27

CLAYTON,Benjamin Chipchase.MC.T2LtACapt kia 16-8-17 2WYorks p81 MR30

CLAYTON,Charles Cam Thackwell 2Lt dow 19-7-17 1Glouc p106 CR Belgium24

CLAYTON,George 2Lt kia 17-10-16 1WYorks att11RFC p2 CR France568,Lt

CLAYTON,George 2Lt dow 24-10-16 1WYorks &11RFC p81

CLAYTON,Harold Robert Capt kia 4-6-15 1LancF C'Coy p92 CR Gallipoli6

CLAYTON,J.A.Capt 20-3-20 CentIndRlyBn MR65

CLAYTON,James Edward.MC.LtAMaj kia 24-6-18 B155RFA p26 CR France924

CLAYTON,James Gardner TCapt kia 20-8-16 Dors att1Nhampt p123 CR France387

CLAYTON,John Alfred 2Lt ded 5-3-19 8N&D p269 CR Notts85

CLAYTON,John Arnold.MID 2Lt kia 26-3-17 7Ches p223 MR34

CLAYTON,Keith Herbert Lt kia 22-8-18 1/1Camb p244 CR France196

CLAYTON,Norman 2Lt kia 23-8-16 1/4RBerks p234 MR21,23-7-16

CLAYTON,Norman Lt dow 13-4-18 RFA attPortugueseCps p26 CR France134

CLAYTON,Norman 2Lt kia 14-10-18 1/4YLI p235 CR France1196

CLAYTON,Richard Stopford Lt ded 26-1-16 4HLI CR Scot241

CLAYTON,William Ernest Albert T2Lt dow 22-4-16 9Ches p95 CR France345

CLAYTON-SMITH,Albert Butler Henkersfeldt Lt kia 19-12-15 1/5YLI p235 CR Belgium23,Heukensfeldt

CLAYTON-SMITH,Horace Edward Henkersfeldt.MC.Lt kia 23-7-17 1/5YLI p235 CR Belgium173,Capt

CLEAL,Harry.MC.T2Lt kia 10-12-17 11Ess B'Coy p131 CR France711

CLEALL,Ernest Harry TCapt drd 4-5-17 92RGA p38 CR Italy13

CLEALL,Percy Cawdell Lt dow 26-8-18 6 att10Ess p232 CR France481

CLEARY,Michael Hugh 2Lt kia 28-3-18 GL &62RFC p261&266 MR20

CLEARY,Robert Ernest T2Lt kld 18-12-17 GL &RFC p6 CR Shrop52

CLEASBY-TAYLOR,Ian 2Lt kia 4-12-17 8RScots CR France307

CLEAVE,Norman 2Lt kia 8-11-18 6RWar p214 CR France965,10Bn

CLEAVER,Claude Rex Capt dow 19-7-15 IA 29Punjabis p275 CR EAfrica13

CLEAVER,Digby Crunden 2Lt kia 29-12-15 RFC p1 CR France200

CLEAVER,Eric Arnold TLt dow 3-7-17 GL &RFC p6 CR France219 ExEYorks

CLEAVER,Frank T2Lt dow 3-10-18 RE ROD SurveyCoy p44 CR France113

CLEAVER,Frederick Canning Rev Chap4Cl 17-6-17 CR Iraq6

CLEAVER,Herbert Leonard HonLt&QM ded 11-11-14 2/5SLancs p269 CR Lancs164

CLEAVER,Horace Gregory T2Lt kld 17-3-18 RFC p15 CR Oxford74

CLEE,Thomas Howard 2Lt ded 7-11-18 10Worc att23LancF p108 CR France1028

CLEEF,Henry Victor T2Lt kia 6-12-17 8RWSurr p55 CR France366

CLEEVE,Frederick John Stewart BtCol ded 13-10-16 RFA 10DAC p26 CR Greece7

CLEEVE-EDWARDS,Cecil T2Lt kia 16-10-18 RE 2FC p44 CR France777

51

CLEGG,Albert SubCdr ded 13-7-19 IA S&TCps p275
CLEGG,Alexander 2Lt kia 1-7-16 13LancF p92 MR21
CLEGG,Alfred Victor Capt kia 7-8-15 6LancF p221 CR Gallipoli1
CLEGG,Frank Cecil TCapt kia 22-8-15 6BordR p116 MR4
CLEGG,James Lt dow 25-5-15 10Manch p237 MR4
CLEGG,John Hamer Capt dow 4-6-15 10Manch p237 MR4
CLEGG,Joseph TCapt kia 16-9-16 6YLI p142 MR21
CLEGG,Lionel TLt kia 22-8-18 7TankCps p188 CR France798
CLEGG,Percy T2Lt kia 1-7-16 1Lancs p58 CR France643
CLEGG,Richard Bagnall Lt kia 18-7-16 RE 15FC p44 CR France144
CLEGG,Robert Burton 2Lt kia 17-2-17 C250RFA p208 CR France1472
CLEGG,Robert Leslie Lt kia 3-9-17 4LancF att45RFC p6&92 CR France285
CLEGG-HILL,Arthur Reginald.Hon.DSO.TLtCol kia 18-9-18 12Ches p95 MR37
CLEGHORN,Allan James T2Lt ded 7-9-16 11 att1GordH p166 CR France201
CLEGHORN,Herbert Stuart Capt kia 2-9-17 RE att1AircraftDepotRFC p18&210 CR France134
CLELAND,Frank Lee TCapt dow 5-7-16 RAMC att2Ess p194 CR France145,4-7-16
CLELAND-HOLLAMBY,Douglas MacDonald T2Lt kld 22-8-17 RWKent &RFC p6&140
CLELLAND,Robert Marshall 2Lt ded 22-12-18 IARO attSap&Min p275 MR66
CLEMENT,Carleton Main.MC.Capt kia 19-8-17 GL &22RFC p6 MR20
CLEMENT,Herbert TLtACapt kia 10-10-17 3 att14RWar p64 MR30
CLEMENT,Hubert Arnold 2Lt kia 3-5-17 att83BlkW p128 MR20
CLEMENT,Walter Albert 2Lt kia 21-3-18 59MGC p182 MR20
CLEMENT,William Honeycott Lt ded 27-6-19 18Lond p255 CR Palestine11,CLEMENTS
CLEMENTS,Claude Casburn 2Lt kia 9-10-18 4RBerks p234 CR France916
CLEMENTS,F.C.Lt kia 6-9-15 3SStaffs A'Coy p122 CR France163,dow
CLEMENTS,Francis Carey 2Lt dow 11-1-17 RE BO CableSect attF'CpsSigCo p44 CR France158
CLEMENTS,F.W.R.Col 2-3-15 RE CR Hamps34
CLEMENTS,George William Valentine Capt&QM 3-3-16 Drags CR Norf209
CLEMENTS,Louis Walter ACapt kia 9-10-17 3Norf p73 MR30
CLEMENTS,Reginald Francis.MC.TLt kia 14-8-18 7RSuss p118 CR France633
CLEMENTS,Robert Cooper 2Lt kia 7-8-18 4NumbF p213 CR France193,8-8-18
CLEMENTS,Thomas Lipton T2Lt kia 23-3-18 11 att9RInniskF p104 MR27
CLEMENTS,W.G.LtCol 16-1-20 RAMC CR Hamps13
CLEMENTS,William Hunter.MSM.2Lt kia 16-8-17 11RInniskF p104 CR Belgium96
CLEMENTS,William Vincent Lt ded 28-2-19 RASC MT att58SBAmmCol p192 CR Belgium267,2Lt 20-2-19
CLEMENTZ,Denis Murray T2Lt kia 6-3-18 24RFC p15 CR France1203
CLEMES,Percival Henry 2Lt kia 2-12-17 IA 6Cav p275 CR France415
CLEMETSON,David Louis Lt kia 21-9-18 PembrokeYeo p205 CR France212
CLEMINSON,Robert 2Lt kia 25-9-16 3 att1EYorks p83 MR21
CLEMSON,John Oliver LtTCapt dow 9-12-15 RNDevYeo p203 CR Gallipoli26
CLENCH,Gordon McDakin.TD.Maj ded 26-7-18 3RFA CR Scot381
CLENDINNING,T.H. See GLENDINNING
CLENT,James Tom HonCapt ded 20-4-17 ArmyPayDept p200 CR Mddx66
CLEPHAN,William Richmond.MC.2Lt kia 7-7-17 6NumbF p214 MR20
CLERK,Beauchamp Capt kia 11-3-15 IA 82Punjabis att59Rif p275 CR France727
CLERK,Robert Vere Capt&Adjt kia 28-6-15 ScotRif p103 MR4
CLERK,Ronald Malcolm Capt kia 9-4-17 RLancs att6RWSurr p58 CR France1182
CLERKE,Francis William Talbot Lt kia 21/26-9-16 2CldGds p51 CR France218,26-9-16 &CR France374
CLERKE-BROWN,Richard 2Lt kia 20-8-16 RE 103FC CR France402
CLERY,Carleton Lumley St.Clair 2Lt kia 12-3-15 ULIA att4Lpool p71&275 CR France1106
CLERY,Daniel Richard Lt kia 10-8-15 6RDubF p176 MR4
CLERY,James Albert.CB.SurgGen 10-2-20 AMS CR Lond29
CLERY,John Cosney Lewis 2Lt kia 1-5-17 78RH&FA p26 CR France418
CLERY,John Francis Capt kia 16-8-17 RMunstF att1RIrRif p175 MR30
CLERY,Noel Cairns.MC.TCapt kia 24-7-16 RFA DivHQ p26 CR France399
CLESHAM,Thomas Henry T2Lt kia 1-7-16 17Manch p154 MR21
CLEVELAND,Alfred Sherwood 2Lt kia 16-10-16 2N&D p133 MR21
CLEVELAND,Ernest Herbert 2Lt kia 31-7-16 13N&D att8Y&L p133 CR France515
CLEVELAND,Frederick Walter.MC.MID Chap4Cl dow 11-10-18 RAChDept att1/6NStaffs p199 CR France146
CLEWS,Robert.MC.TLt dow 28-4-18 RE 235ArmyTroopCoy p44 CR France102
CLIBBORN,Cecil Hamilton Capt dow 7-4-16 IA 92Punjabis p275 MR38
CLIBBORN,Cuthbert John Hamilton.MID Capt kia 14-12-15 D'RFA p26 CR France275

CLIDERO,Herbert T2Lt kia 1-9-18 1Yorks att8WYorks p90 CR France1484,2Bn
CLIEVE,James Francis Maj&QM ded 7-2-17 RWFus p263 CR Wales,6-2-19
CLIFF,Cecil Robson Lt ded 3-10-18 161RFA p27 CR Yorks323
CLIFF,Frank Pearce TLt kia 4-10-17 10Yorks p90 MR30
CLIFF,Grosvenor Talbot Maj dedacc 10-2-18 3DragGds p21 CR France446
CLIFF,Harold Martin.MID LtCol ded 1-2-17 RDubF p176 CR Lond8
CLIFF,Herbert Theodore Maj kia 13-10-14 3WYorks p81 CR France193
CLIFF,Percy Jack 2Lt dow 16-6-17 4 att5NStaffs p156 CR France178,John
CLIFF,Reginald Bertram Talbot Capt dow 23-9-15 1RFA p207 CR Belgium11
CLIFF-McCULOCH,Walter Alexander TLt kia 27-2-18 7RIrRif p169 CR France423,McCULLOCHN 27-2-16
CLIFFORD,Anthony Clifford 2Lt kia 2-6-15 3DragGds RoO p21 CR Belgium4
CLIFFORD,G.K Lt 1-7-18 13Lond CR Devon107
CLIFFORD,Henry Francis Maj kia 9-1-17 1/1GloucYeo p203 CR Egypt2
CLIFFORD,Henry Frederick Hugh.DSO.TBrigGen kia 11-9-16 2Suff attStaff Cmdg149InfBde p78&258 CR France430
CLIFFORD,Herbert Edward Capt dow 19-7-16 2SAfrInf CR France145
CLIFFORD,Herbert James TLtACapt kia 20-9-17 11KRRC p149 MR30
CLIFFORD,Hugh Gilbert Francis Lt kia 1-7-16 Lincs p74 CR France393
CLIFFORD,Leonard Price 2Lt kia 7-6-17 23Lond p252
CLIFFORD,Norman Charles T2Lt ded 13-2-19 ExMGC p266 CR Hamps 138
CLIFFORD,Ralph Montague Lewis TCapt kia 15-10-16 GL 11Ess attTMB p190 MR21
CLIFFORD,Walter Francis Joseph 2Lt kia 27-9-15 IrGds SR att2Bn p52 MR19
CLIFFORD,Watling Wallis T2Lt dow 12-10-17 8RFus p67
CLIFFORD,Wigan.DSO.MajTLtCol 20-6-17 1 att10NumbF p60 CR Belgium29,Wigram
CLIFFORD,William James 2Lt kia 25-4-17 GL &48RFC p6 MR20
CLIFT,Marcus Henry T2Lt kia 8-11-17 11EYorks p83 MR20
CLIFT,Maurice Richard 2Lt dow 4-8-16 3Dors att9Dev p123 CR France40
CLIFTON,George Leake Cecil Lt ded 22-7-17 RFC 2AircraftDepot p6 CR France62
CLIFTON,Harold Norton 2Lt dow PoW 1-2-15 1CldGds p51 CR France924
CLIFTON,Hubert Arthur T2Lt dow 6-4-16 10ELancs p110 CR Iraq6,8-4-16
CLIFTON,Hubert Everard.MC.2Lt dow 4-10-16 1Dev p76 CR Devon258
CLIFTON,Percy James.DSO.MID Maj dow 26-8-18 A232RFA p206 CR France119,kia
CLIFTON,Ralph 2Lt dow 22-5-17 RFA att14DivHQ p27 CR France 102
CLIFTON,William Gerard Talbot 2Lt kia 31-3-17 3 O&BLI att11RFC p6&130 CR France1311
CLIMIE,Agnes Murdoch SNurse kia 1-10-17 TFNS 58GH p254 CR France134,30-9-17
CLIMO,Verschoyle Crawford Maj ded 19-2-19 Manch MinOfPensions p265 CR Hamps159
CLINTON,Walter Lawrence Capt ded 22-11-18 KRRC p149 CR Europe56
CLISSOLD,Harry.DSO.Maj kia 28-9-17 RE 474FC p209 CR Belgium20,Henry
CLIVE,Percy Archer.DSO.TLtCol kia 5-4-18 1GrenGds Cmdg1/5LancF p49 MR20
CLIVE,Percy Robert H.Viscount Capt dow 31-10-16 1WelshGds p53 CR Wales358
CLIVE-SMITH,Colin Metcalfe T2Lt kia 24-3-18 12RB p178 CR France987
CLIVELY,John Harold 2Lt kia or dow 3-5-17 4Y&L p238 MR20
CLIXBY,Edward Denis 2Lt kia 13-10-15 4Lincs p217 MR19
CLODE-BAKER,George Edmund Lt kia 1-7-16 5Lond p246 CR France798
CLOETE,Harry Durie.MC.Maj gunwound 29-2-20 IA 92Punjabis att2AssamRif p275 MR66
CLOETE,Lawrence Balfour.MC.LtCol 25-1-20 41Dogras MR65
CLOSE,Barry Samuel Lt kia 27-9-18 1IrGds p52 CR France1497
CLOSE,Charles Paul T2Lt dow 14-11-16 10RDubF p176 CR France74
CLOSE,Frederick Mackdonald.MIDx2 Col dow 30-3-19 RA CR Suff98
CLOSE,Henry Burke Lt ded 1-11-18 RDubF att1/2Bn p176&257 CR Ireland12
CLOSE,Max Arthur 2Lt kia 14-3-15 1HLI p162 CR France279
CLOSE,Robert William Mills Lt kia 27-5-18 4Yorks p220 MR18
CLOSE,William Collins 2Lt kia 20-3-17 3 att6Nhampt p137 MR20
CLOSE-BROOKS,Arthur Brooks.MC.Capt dow 10-1-17 3Manch p154 CR Iraq5
CLOSEBROOKS,John Charles Lt kia 30-10-14 1LifeGds p20 MR29
CLOTHIER,John Keith Capt kia 7-12-14 1WYorks p81 CR France82
CLOTHIER,Robert Frank Capt kia 3-11-14 IA 13Rajputs p275 MR47
CLOUDESLEY,Hugh TLt kia 1-7-16 7RWSurr p55 CR France397
CLOUGH,Alan TCapt kia 1-7-16 16WYorks p81 MR21
CLOUGH,Charles Eric Maj ded 12-3-15 RASC 28DivTrn p253 CR France134
CLOUGH,Edgar T2Lt ded 14-10-18 RE 97FC p44 CR France123
CLOUGH,Ernest Rowan Butler 2Lt dow 27-6-16 Dev att11DLI p76 CR Belgium6

CLOUGH,Gilbert Seymour T2Lt dow 27-3-18 65MGC p182 CR France40,Lt 55Bn

CLOUGH,Harry Collier T2Lt kia 30-7-16 14 att18Manch p154 MR21

CLOUGH,Hugh Francis Lt kia 14-3-17 4RWKent p234 MR38

CLOUGH,Mary SNurse ded 12-10-16 QAIMNS p200 CR Europe1

CLOUGH,Morris Capt kia 25-4-18 18WYorks p81 MR30

CLOUGH,Thomas Capt mbk 2-2-19 IARO att1/72Pujabis p275 MR34

CLOUGH,Walter George 2Lt kia 18-9-18 1Lincs p74 CR France415

CLOUTMAN,Thomas Henry T2Lt dow 7-3-17 16Mddx p146 CR France145

CLOUTMAN,Wolfred Reeve.MIDx2 TLt kia 22-8-15 RE 178Coy p44 CR France189,21-8-15

CLOVER,Harwood Linay TLt ded 25-12-16 7RDubF C'Coy attRFC p2&176 CR Suff225,23-12-16

CLOW,David James.DCM.2Lt kia 24-8-18 4BordR att15DLI p228 MR16

CLOW,George Robert T2Lt kia 17-3-16 9BlkW p128 MR19

CLOW,Oswald William 2Lt kia 25-4-18 156RFA p27 MR30

CLOWES,Charles George Edric Lt dow 18-2-15 1 att3KRRC p149 CR France284

CLOWES,Henry Arthur LtCol ded 8-3-16 1StaffsYeo p205 CR Egypt9

CLOWES,Warren Peter Lt kia 30-3-18 8Huss p22 CR France1172

CLUBB,Howard William Lt kia 27-3-17 6Ess p232 MR34

CLUE,Henry May T2Lt kia 30-7-16 10 att7RLancs p58 MR21

CLULOW,Frederick Reginald 2Lt dow 24-4-18 3 att1N&D p133 CR France29,25-4-18

CLUNIE,William Halkerston 2Lt kia 26-4-18 9RScots p212 CR Belgium185,6-4-18

CLUNIES ROSS,H.E.Capt 27-9-18 KAR CR Sussex 30 See ROSS,H.E.Clunies

CLUTTERBUCK,Arthur Stanley 2Lt kia 14-7-16 8Worc p226 CR France643

CLUTTERBUCK,Arthur Vincent Maj ded 31-10-16 1 att3Ess p131 CR Suff54,LtCol

CLUTTERBUCK,Bernard Valentine 2Lt kia 13-7-17 RFA attZ29TMB p27 CR Belgium12,14-7-17

CLUTTERBUCK,David TLt dow 6-5-17 126/28RFA p27 CR France95

CLUTTERBUCK,Henry Capt kia 31-8/2-9-14 RLancs p58 CR France1350,26-8-14

CLUTTERBUCK,Hugh Guy Daniel 2Lt mbk 19-4-16 IARO att1/7GurkhaRif p275 MR38,17-4-16

CLUTTERBUCK,Norman Eckstein Lt kia 24-4-17 8Worc p226 CR France1495

CLUTTERBUCK Peter Lt kia 20-10-14 1EYorks p83 MR32

CLYDESDALE,Robert Alexander Crawford 2Lt ded 27-2-19 Fife&ForfarYeo p255 CR Scot97

CLYNE,Daniel Miller Lt kia 23-7-18 1/5SfthH p241 CR France1697

COADE,William Henry Lt dow 5-11-18 3Leinst p174 CR Surrey1

COADY,John 2Lt 21-8-18 ConnRgrs att2RIrReg MR16

COAKLEY,Charles Stewart T2Lt kia 30-10-17 KSLI att1/4Bn p144 MR30

COAKLEY,G.H.Cdr 28/29-9-19 IndMiscList attMilWks MR43

COAKLEY,Joseph Lynch Capt ded 19-10-17 LabCps p189&266,RoO RB CR Eire86 Ex RB

COALES,Stephen James T2Lt dow 18-9-16 6RWKent p140 CR France158

COAPE-ARNOLD,R.de N.Lt ded 28-6-18 5SStaffs &RAF p229

COAR,Edward Roland T2Lt dow 8-1-18 2ELancs p110 CR Belgium11

COATE,Alfred Melbourne T2Lt kia 28-8-18 36RFA p27 CR France927

COATE,William Henry TLtACapt kia 25-10-17 16ACycCps p181 MR37

COATES,Alan David Lt kia 27/28-4-15 4Lond p246 CR Belgium101,28-4-15

COATES,Arthur 2Lt kia 27-10-16 4Yorks p220 MR21

COATES,Basil Montgomery T2Lt kia 7-9-15 10RB p178 MR32

COATES,Cecil Evelyn Maj kia 23-7-16 6Glouc p225 CR France832

COATES,Clifford Marsh 2Lt kia 3-5-17 RGA 174SB p38 MR20,Marsden 146SB

COATES,Donald Newton 2Lt kia 21-3-18 25NumbF p60 MR20

COATES,Frederick Noel T2Lt dow 4-4-17 22NumbF p60 CR France1182

COATES,George Henry Capt ded 25-12-15 2/9DLI p239 CR Durham88

COATES,George Washington Tate.MID 2Lt kia 10-3-15 33RFA p27 MR22

COATES,Harold Capt kia 25-9-15 Lincs p74 MR19

COATES,Harold Brearley T2Lt kia 1-7-16 7Yorks p90 CR France397

COATES,Harold Edward TMaj kia 3-5-17 13Lpool p71 MR20

COATES,James Ernest 2Lt dow 22-8-18 RGA 336SB p38 CR France103

COATES,John 2Lt kia 15-8-18 ERid of YorksYeo att11EYorks p206 CR France19

COATES,Percy T2Lt kia 15-4-16 RE 180Co p44 CR France423

COATES,Stanley Harvey 2Lt kia 7-6-17 4EKent p212 CR Belgium131

COATES,Sydney T2Lt kia 27-5-17 GL att52RFC p6 CR France1468

COATES,W.F.Capt dow 30-4-15 6 att1RFus p67 CR France683

COATH,Leonard Charles 2Lt kia 4-9-16 10 att1Norf p73 MR21

COATS,Eric Robert Lt kia 17-5-18 1ScotsGds p52 CR France927

COATS,J.LtCol 11-5-19 RAMC CR Scot503

COATS,John Alexander Hamilton 2Lt kia 8-8-16 10RScots att164TMB p255 MR21

COATS,Lawrence Armstrong T2Lt kia 28-10-15 15 att8NumbF p60 CR Gallipoli4

COATS,Thomas T2Lt kia 30-9-18 5CamH p167 CR Belgium157

COATS,William Evans T2Lt dow 4-11-17 17RScots p53 CR France145

COATSWORTH,Alfred Henry T2Lt dow 8-9-16 1RWar att10MGC p64 CR France1,9-9-16

COBB,Francis Walker 2Lt ded 28-3-18 42RFC p15 CR Mddx48,Walter

COBB,Frederick Charles TCapt kia 25-9-15 6KOSB p101 CR France114

COBB,James Cassels Lt kia 23-8-18 5RWKent p235 CR France177

COBB,John Elbridge 2LtTLt dow 14-8-17 RASC att21RFC p6&192 CR Belgium16

COBB,Kenneth Rhodes Capt kia 1-7-15 15KRRC p149 CR Gallipoli6

COBB,Reginald T2Lt kia 13-10-16 5RBerks A'Coy p138 CR France277

COBB,Reginald John Preston 2Lt kia 11-10-17 WRid &56RFC p6&115 MR20

COBB,Sydney James T2Lt dow 20-7-16 8RMunstF p175 CR France64,Sidney

COBB,T.W.2Lt 15-12-20 EgyptLabCps CR Hamps18

COBB,William Ralph.MC.LtACapt dow 5-10-17 RWKent p140 MR30

COBBETT,Arthur Irvin Brooke 2Lt dow 23-8-18 1DCLI p114 MR16

COBBETT,Charles Newberry Capt ded 7-10-19 RAMC p267 CR Dorset52

COBBOLD,Charles Augustus TCapt kia 13-10-15 7Suff p78 MR19

COBBOLD,Charles Townsend 2Lt kia 3-10-16 32RFA p27 MR21

COBBOLD,Edgar Francis Wanklyn Lt kia 12-1-16 7Ches attRFC p18&223 CR France924

COBBOLD,Robert Henry Wanklyn Lt kia 9-9-15 6 att2RB p178 CR France276

COBBOLD,Robert Towshend T2Lt kia 25-9-15 6RFA p27 CR Belgium6,Rowland

COBDEN,Frank Pargeter Lt kia 7-7-18 MGC att104RAF p182 CR Germany3

COBHAM,Elijah Rev Chap4Cl dow 19-9-17 RAChDept attKAR p199 CR EAfrica8 CR Tanzania1,kia

COBHAM,Frederick George Brian Lt kia 8-8-18 1Camb p244 CR France196

COBON,Harold Gardiner.MC.2Lt dow 24-1-18 NorfYeo p204 CR Egypt9

COBURN,Charles 2Lt kia 31-7-17 KRRC att18Bn p149 MR29

COBURN,Frederick Isaac.MID TLt ded 4-10-17 1RASC SupplyCoy p192 CR France85

COCHRAN,Frances Alexander 2Lt kia 25-9-15 1GordH p166 CR Belgium112,Francis

COCHRAN,Herbert Philip Gordon.DSO.LtCol kia 24-3-18 Mddx att15Ches p146 CR France402

COCHRAN,Lionel Francis Abingdon Capt kia 4-2-15 IA 72Pujabis att92 p275

COCHRANE,Cyril Lt kia 25-9-15 1GordH p166 MR29

COCHRANE,Donald James Capt kia 8-5-15 65RFA p27 MR29

COCHRANE,Edwin Arthur Lt dow 4-8-18 4 att2/6NStaffs p156 CR France10,1/6Bn

COCHRANE,George T2Lt kia 19-9-17 att7RB p178 CR Belgium42,18-9-17

COCHRANE,George King Hicks T2Lt kia 25-3-17 1HLI att 1/1Gurkhas IA p162&275 MR38

COCHRANE,Hugh Paterson Maj kia 20-9-17 8 att2/5LancF p221 MR30

COCHRANE,Reginald.MID 2Lt kia 18-8-17 B282RFA p27 CR Belgium36

COCHRANE,Walter Francis Capt kia 19-4-17 1/4KOSB p223 CR Palestine8

COCHRANE,William T2Lt kia 26-9-17 1RScotF p94 CR Belgium125

COCK,Hubert Charles Langslow Maj kia 22/24-11-15 17RGA attStaff p38 MR38

COCK,John Herbert 2Lt kia 14-4-17 GL &60RFC p6 CR France1310

COCKADAY,Aubrey George.MID 2Lt dow 31-10-18 10/147RFA p27 CR France241

COCKAYNE,Arthur Edward 2Lt kia 1-7-17 5NStaffs p238 MR19

COCKBURN,Charles James Lt.MC.kia 7-1-16 IA 6Jats p275 MR38

COCKBURN,George Percival Lt kia 23-3-18 6Suff att7RWSurr p218 MR27

COCKBURN,Henry Howard 2Lt kia 1-4-17 4RIrReg att2RInniskF p88 CR France675

COCKBURN,James 2Lt kia 12-10-16 4A&SH att90MGC p173&182 MR21

COCKBURN,John 2Lt kia 25-4-15 RWar p64 MR29

COCKBURN,Robert Bowes TCapt ded 27-9-18 RAVC att130RFA p198 CR Greece18

COCKBURN,Robert Claude Radcliffe Lt ded 25-11-18 IA 36Sikhs p275

COCKCROFT,Arthur Clarence T2Lt kia 1-7-16 11 att10YLI p142 CR France267

COCKE,Robert Sturgeon Capt ded 16-11-18 RAMC p267 CR Lond14,20-11-18

COCKER,Arthur Wilfred Kingsley 2Lt kia 30-11-17 17RFus p67 MR17

COCKER,Thomas Edge LtACapt kia 21-3-18 A/153RFA attY36TMB p27

COCKERELL,Andrew Pepys 2Lt kia 15-8-16 2KRRC p149 CR France397

COCKERELL,Donald Chessum 2Lt kia 6-11-18 5Lond p246 CR Belgium195

COCKERELL,Samuel Pepys 2Lt ded 20-3-15 RFC p1 CR Egypt8,Lt

COCKERILL,George Edward LtTCapt dow 3-7-16 PoW 16Lond B'Coy p249 CR France1484

COCKETT,Edward Allan T2Lt dow 9-9-16 1Glouc p106 CR France833

COCKETT,William Arthur 2Lt mbk 26-10-17 3 att2GordH p256 CR Belgium112

COCKEY,John Edmund Percival 2Lt kia 30-7-16 20Lpool p71 MR21

COCKFIELD,Charles Francis 2Lt kia 27-8-16 RGA 142SB p38 CR France630

COCKING,Charles Oscar John 2Lt kia 11-4-17 5SLancs p230 CR France705

COCKING,Frank Kenneth Lt kia 23-7-16 3DCLI p114 MR21,Stennett

COCKLE,Clarence Tapscott Lt kia 10-9-18 5Suff p217 MR30

COCKRELL,William Archer Lt ded 11-11-17 RemountService RASC p24 CR Berks113

COCKRILL,Alick Charles 2Lt kia 23-4-17 4Norf p216 MR20

COCKRILL,Charles Whalley Lt kia 2-2-18 C180RFA p207 CR France364

COCKS,Edward James Trist.MID 2Lt kia 5-8-18 5Worc p108 CR France28,4Bn

COCKS,Edward Louis 2Lt kia 8-8-16 17Mddx p146 MR21

COCKS,John Stanley Capt ded 29-1-19 RAMC att1EguptDetHosp p194 CR Lebanon1,Maj

COCKS,Percy Frank Anderson Lt ded 25-5-16 5RWSurr p212 MR38

COCKS,Willard Fleetwood TLt dow 9-4-17 3Lincs p74 MR20

COCKSEDGE,Robert James 2Lt kia 25-9-18 1Norf p73 CR France905

CODD,Herbert Charles Capt ded 6-11-18 IARO attLabCps p275 MR69,19-3-20

CODD,Stephen Arthur Herbert T2Lt kia 9-9-16 11 att10Glouc p106 MR21

CODDINGTON,Charles Ernest 2Lt kia 4-12-17 10Lpool attRFC p17&216 CR France120

CODDINGTON,Hubert John Capt kia 7-7-15 DLI p160 CR Belgium92

CODE,Harold T2Lt kia 25-8-18 Manch p154 CR France239

CODNER,Christopher Cardew 2LtACapt kia 3-5-17 1SomLI p79 CR France1194

CODRINGTON,Ernest LtCol ded 20-4-16 IA 120Inf p275 CR Iraq1

CODY,John 2Lt kia 21-8-18 ConnRgrs att2RIrReg p172

CODY,Samuel Franklyn T2Lt kia 23-1-17 GL &41RFC p6 CR Belgium115

COE,Frederick Hermann Lt ded 28-4-17 6LancF p269 CR Lancs475

COE,George T2Lt kia 1-7-16 1 att11BordR p116 MR21

COE,Herbert James T2Lt kia 8-8-18 2TankCps p188 CR France526

COE,James George Lt dow 1-10-18 4SfthH p241 CR Belgium157

COE,Joseph William Maj ded 21-10-17 RAVC att59Div p254 CR France145

COE,Sydney Urie Charles T2Lt kia 30-11-17 16KRRC p149 CR Belgium125

COFFEE,Francis Warren 2Lt kia 16-8-17 5 att14RIrRif p169 MR30

COFFEY,Charles Reay Lt kld 27-5-18 GL &RAF p190 MR20

COFFIN,Sebright Edward 2Lt dow 20-12-15 3 att2RScots p53 CR Belgium11

COGAN,Lionel Gatrell Lt ded 7-10-18 IA 1/153Inf p275 MR65,1/153Punjabis

COGGIN,Algernon Oswald TLt kia 27-10-16 20RFus p67 CR France374

COGGINS,Wilfred George 2Lt dow 15-12-16 4RWKent att16RB p234 CR France145

COGHILL,Hugh Bernard Mackay Capt kia 25-9-15 4HLI p162 MR19,2Bn

COGHILL,Norman Harry Lt dow 28-3-18 ScotsGds attMGC p52 CR France62,attGds MGR

COGHILL,Sinclair Baxter T2Lt kia 9-9-16 5 att8RInniskF p104 MR21

COGHLAN,Clifford Edward Leslie Lt kia 27-8-17 SStaffs att9Bn p122 MR30

COGHLAN,Joseph Patrick.MC.Lt kia 20-9-17 RE 228FC p44 CR Belgium124

COGHLAN,Thomas Reginald 2Lt dow 24-10-18 3RIrF p171 CR Belgium358

COGHLAN,William Humphrey 2Lt kia 26-8-14 11/15RFA p27 CR France716

COHAN,E.M.2Lt 5-8-14 RFA CR Lancs181

COHEN,Aaron Simeon Lt kia 25-9-15 RAMC att8SomLI p194 MR19

COHEN,Adolph Broadfield TLt dow 22-7-17 17WYorks p81 CR France145

COHEN,Benjamin TLt dow 3-7-17 RAMC att122RFA p195 CR Belgium18,kia

COHEN,Cecil Hope Lt ded 18-11-18 RGA Sig p38 CR Mddx40

COHEN,Dudley Trevor 2Lt dow 20-11-17 4 att7RSuss p228 MR17

COHEN,Edward.MC.T2Lt kia 31-7-17 12RFus p67 MR29

COHEN,George Herbert Lt kia 16-5-17 5Lpool p215 CR France279

COHEN,Harold T2Lt ded 18-7-15 9RBerks p138 CR Mddx27,8Bn

COHEN,John Icely TCapt dow 11-8-17 Dev p76 CR Belgium16,3ELancs

COHEN,Moss.MM.LtACapt kia 24-9-18 2DLI p160 CR France835

COHEN,Moss 2Lt kia 15-9-16 21Lond p251 CR France385

COHEN,Simon Capt ded 23-11-19 LabCps p266 CR Egypt9,dow 22-11-19 EgyptLabCps

COHEN,Solomon Maurice Lt kia 9-9-16 12Lond p248 MR21

COILL,Caesar Alfred Capt ded 11-11-18 RGA p269

COKE,Arthur George.Hon.2Lt kia 21-5-15 2Coy of LondYeo p204 MR29

COKE,Langton Sacheverell Lt kia 31-10-14 1IrGds RoO p52 MR29

COKE,Leigh Rigby Capt kia 2-11-17 8Hamps p229 CR Palestine8

COKER,Cadwallader John Lt kia 22-6-15 1WelshR p126 CR Belgium37

COKER,John Cadwallader.MID Lt dow 26-9-14 1SWBord p99 CR France1329

COLBECK,Leonard George 2Lt ded 3-1-18 C59RFA p27&261 MR40

COLBORN,Albert George Lt ded 10-10-18 RH&FA p27 CR Oxford73

COLBORNE,Reginald Elgar 2Lt ded 6-11-18 IARO p275 MR65

COLBORNE,Richard Arthur Pell Rev Chap4Cl kia 28-5-18 RAChDept att1/1Lond p199 CR France54

COLBOURNE,Eric Krabbe.MC.2Lt dow 27-6-15 3 att1RBerks p139&258 CR France98

COLBOURNE,Frederick William Lt ded 25-2-19 RAOC 3rdArmy p198 CR France

COLBY,Laurence Robert Vaughan.MID Maj kia 24-10-14 1GrenGds p4 MR29

COLCHESTER,Bernard Valentine T2Lt kia 25-4-17 6Beds p85 MR20

COLCOTT,Ernest Harry 2Lt kia 11-9-16 1/8Mddx p236 CR France164,COLLCOTT

COLCUTT,Thomas Mills.MID T2Lt kia 9-9-18 8Glouc p106 CR France1106

COLDHAM,George Herbert TLt dow 17-9-16 64MGC p182 CR France188

COLDICOTT,Arden Cotterell.MC.Capt kia 16-8-18 15RWar p64 CR Germany1,dow14-8-18

COLDICOTT,Hubert Eric 2Lt kia 21-5-17 15 att2/6Lond p249 MR20

COLDRICK,Thomas 2Lt kia 21-3-18 7 att10Worc p226 MR20

COLDWELL,Edward Smith 2Lt 15-2-19 RE CR Lond12

COLDWELL,Herbert David T2Lt kld 11-3-18 RFC p15 CR Wilts116

COLDWELL,Norman Goodman.MC.T2Lt dow 16-5-18 2WRid p115 CR France40

COLDWELL,Vincent Capt ded 18-4-16 IA 4Cav p275 CR Iraq6

COLDWELLS,Charles Albert T2Lt kia 28-9-15 108RFA p27 CR France219

COLDWELLS,Francis Baker 2Lt kia 1-7-16 2Dev p76 MR21

COLE,Arthur Willoughby George Lowry.CB.DSO.ColTBrigGen dow 9-5-15 Staff 25InfBde p1

COLE,Cecil Clark 2Lt dow 13-10-17 RGA 149Bde p38 CR Belgium16

COLE,Charles Henry 2Lt kia 4-10-16 11Lond p248 MR21

COLE,Clarence Claridge T2Lt kia 8-5-18 2Y&L p158 CR Belgium3

COLE,Clifford Spearing Lt kia 19-6-16 2/5Glouc p225 CR France706

COLE,Cyril Charles 2Lt ded 14-11-18 13Ess &RAF p131

COLE,Cyril Lawson Capt ded 14-3-19 2/5Glouc p225 CR France40

COLE,David T2Lt kia 3-7-16 16RIrRif p169 CR France252

COLE,Dorothy Helen Sister ded 24-10-18 TFNS CR Surrey180

COLE,Emily Helena Sister 21-2-15 QAIMNS CR France64

COLE,Ernest T2Lt dow 8-8-16 14 att8Yorks p90 CR France44

COLE,Ernest Lockett 2Lt kia 27-9-16 8Nhampt p137 MR21

COLE,Frederick John Lt kia 19-4-17 4Norf p216 MR34

COLE,Fred Creighton 2Lt kia 23-4-17 3 att1Norf p73 CR France58,Lt

COLE,Gerald Arthur Capt ded 6-2-19 RDC &RFus p253 CR Lond1

COLE,Henry Munroe Capt ded 4-12-18 4Dev att1/4Wilts p220 CR Egypt2,Maj

COLE,Herbert William 2Lt kia 14-4-18 3 att1ScotRif p103 MR32

COLE,Humfrey Theodore Shuldham 2Lt dow 12-2-17 19Lond p250 CR France41

COLE,Humphrey Porteus T2Lt dow 3-4-16 9Dev p76 CR France22

COLE,Kenneth Leonard Lt kia 29-9-15 3Y&L p158 MR19

COLE,Leonard Baker TCapt ded 9-5-18 RAVC p268 CR France119

COLE,Leslie Stewart 2Lt kia 3-10-15 3 att2Ches p95 MR19

COLE,Maxwell Gerard T2Lt kia 18-5-17 GL &1RFC p6 CR Belgium152,Lt

COLE,Mowbray Lyster Stanley Owen Capt ded 14-9-14 4RFus p67 MR15

COLE,Nigel Edwin Fitz Roy 2LtTLt kia 5-10-17 6EKent C'Coy p57 CR France154

COLE,Percival James Lt dow 22-9-16 WessexRFA p207 CR France105

COLE,Reginald Price 2Lt kia 20-5-17 7HLI p240 MR20

COLE,Richard Harry 2Lt kia 25-7-16 1SWBord p99 MR21

COLE,William Maurice.MC.2Lt dow 29-6-18 1/5Leic p220 CR France10

COLE,William Norman 2Lt kia 5-2-17 7SLancs p125 MR21

COLE,Wilfred Samuel TLt ded 11-5-16 25RFus p67 CR EAfrica52,Wilfrid

COLE,William Thomas 2Lt kia 29-7-18 4Yorks p220 CR France1689

COLE-HAMILTON,Arthur Richards TLtCol dow 10-8-15 6ELancs p110 CR Gallipoli17

COLE-HAMILTON,Con William Eric Capt kld 2-7-17 2RScots att20RFC p6&53 CR Herts87

COLEBROOK,Geoffrey Bathurst 2Lt kia 27-7-15 1RWSurr p55 CR France721,26-7-15

COLEBROOK,Leslie Charles T2Lt kia 1-2-17 14Hamps p120 CR Belgium4

COLEMAN,Arthur T2Lt kia 1-7-16 20NumbF p60 MR21

COLEMAN,Edward Charles Lt kia 2-4-17 114RFA attA'TMB p207 CR Greece5

COLEMAN,Eric 2Lt kia 31-7-17 3Norf attMGC p73&182 MR29

COLEMAN,Ernest Harold 2Lt kia 15-2-15 2RIrF p171 MR29

COLEMAN,Frederick Charles T2Lt kia 25-9-15 6Wilts p152 MR19

COLEMAN,Fred Creighton 2Lt kia 23-4-17 3 att1Norf p73 CR France58,Lt

COLEMAN,Gerald Arthur Capt ded 6-2-19 RDC &RFus p253 CR Lond1

COLEMAN,Herbert Edward Evatt 2Lt kia 9-9-16 2RSuss p118 MR21

COLEMAN,John Albert David 2Lt kia 3-5-17 9Mddx p236 MR20,10 att12Bn

COLEMAN,John Roberts T2Lt ded 26-11-18 RE SpecBde p44 CR France1029

COLEMAN,Sydney Capt dow 14-10-18 1Lond p245 CR France214

COLEMAN,Walter William 2Lt ded 12-3-19 6MGC Inf p266 CR Kent301,Lt

COLERIDGE,Luke Frederick Rennell 2Lt kia 22-12-14 1CldGds p51 MR22

COLES,Albert Edward 2Lt mbk 4-10-17 1SomLI att11TMB p256 MR30

COLES,Arthur Norman TLt kia 24-8-18 8RB p178 CR France400

COLES,Crewe 2Lt kia 4-6-15 4ELancs p226 MR4

COLES,Daisy Kathleen Mary Miss kia 30-9-17 VAD BRCS 58GH p200 CR France134

COLES,Donald Mackintosh Lt kia 25/27-10-14 3 att1NumbF p60 CR France567,27-10-14

COLES,Edgar Ralph Capt kia 12-5-15 3DragGds p21 MR29

COLES,Frederick George.MC.2Lt kia 25-9-17 RFA attY16TMB p27 CR France616

COLES,Henry James Capt kia 30-6-17 5N&D p232 MR20

COLES,Herbert 2Lt kia 18-11-17 2RB A'Coy p178 MR30

COLES,Herbert Stonehouse Capt kia 16-5-15 RWFus p97 MR22

COLES,James Hugh.DSO.CaptALtCol kia 24-4-18 1EYorks p83 MR30

COLES,Lionel George TCapt kia 1-7-16 16RScots p53 CR France267

COLES,Reginald Walter T2Lt kia 12-10-17 RWKent att7Bn p140 MR30

COLES,Rowland Humphrey Lt kia 9-5-17 WSomYeo attRFC p18&205 CR France415

COLES,Sidney Harcourt Lt kia 12-10-14 4Mddx p146 CR France1106

COLES,Thomas Wallace Lt dow 1-5-16 A184RFA p27 CR France80

COLES,William Henry Lt kia 27-12-17 5Yorks p220 CR Belgium125

COLES,William Price Vivian.MM.2Lt kia 7-10-16 7Lond C'Coy p247 CR France385

COLEY,Allen Cowen TLt kld 6-3-18 RFC p15 CR Hamps4

COLEY,Joseph Alfred 2LtACapt kia 22-3-18 5 att4RFus p67 MR20

COLEY,William John 2Lt kia 15-7-16 1Dors p124 CR France296,Lt

COLFER,James Richard TLt ded 26-2-17 9RMunstF p175 CR France64

COLFOX,Thomas David 2Lt kia 14-6-18 42RFA p27 CR France33,41RFA

COLGATE,Roger Edward.MM.2Lt kia 18-11-16 3 att8Glouc p106 MR21

COLGATE,Roy TCapt dow 12-7-16 114MGC p182 CR France66,Robert 13-7-16

COLIN,Felix Augustus 2Lt kia 3-5-17 1 att7ESurr p112 MR20

COLLCOTT,Ernest Harry see COLCOTT,E.H.

COLLCUTT,Philip Martin Blake TLt kia 12-5-17 7EYorks p83 MR20

COLLEDGE,Arthur Vincent Lt kia 10-8-19 4Worc att45RFus p254 MR70 &CR Europe180

COLLEN,John 2Lt mbk 25-10-16 7RInniskF &7RFC p256 MR20

COLLEN,Norman Owen T2Lt kia 25-9-16 EYorks p83 CR France385

COLLEN,William Stewart T2Lt kia 7/10-8-15 6RInniskF p104 CR Gallipoli5,Lt 7-8-15

COLLENS,Edwin Theobald Lt dow 3-9-18 1Lond p245 CR France103,2Lt

COLLER,Bernard Tarrant Lt kia 26-9-16 GL &RFC p2&190,ded MR20

COLLER,Charles Mervyn Capt kia 21-3-18 4 att9Norf p216 MR20

COLLES,Arthur Grove Capt kia 12-3-15 RDubF att1RIrRif p176 MR22

COLLETT,Arthur Leigh T2Lt dow 18-11-16 8Glouc p106 CR France384,Lt

COLLETT,Clive Franklyn.MC.LtTCapt kld 23-12-17 70RFC p6&258 CR Scot235

COLLETT,Thomas Theodore 2Lt dow 15-2-17 7Yorks p90 CR France105

COLLEY,Archibald 2Lt kia 14-3-15 2DCLI p114 MR29

COLLEY,Douglas James 2Lt kia 29-11-16 6Lpool p215 MR29

COLLEY,Ernest Vincent 2Lt dow 23-8-17 B'TankCps p88 MR30

COLLEY,Harold 2Lt kia 1-7-16 18WYorks p81 MR21

COLLEY,Harry Leonard.MC.2Lt kia 4-11-18 WYorks att2YLI p81 CR France933

COLLEY,Philip Wellesley 2Lt ded 31-10-18 A156RFA p27 CR Hamps1,21-10-18

COLLEY,Robert Archibald Lt kia 22-3-18 8DLI att25MGC p187&239 MR20

COLLEY,William Arthur TCapt kia 1-7-16 12Y&L p158 MR21

COLLIE,M.A.T.LtCol 3-12-18 IMS CR Lancs40

COLLIER,Bertram T.2Lt dow 5-11-16 31 att25NumbF p60 CR France297

COLLIER,Ernest Stebbing 2Lt dow 2-4-18 9RGA p38 CR France1071

COLLIER,Frederick 2Lt dow 11-5-17 2/8Manch p237 CR France134

COLLIER,Frederick Herbert Mark TLt kia 23-4-17 15N&D p133 MR20

COLLIER,George T2Lt dow 9-8-18 8MGC p182 CR France95

COLLIER,Guy Cecil Lt kia 23-7-18 3 att10ScotRif p103 CR France865

COLLIER,Harry Ronald.MC.LtACapt kia 17-4-18 1KOSB p101 CR France324

COLLIER,Hubert Charles de Zoete 2Lt dow 4-4-17 21Manch att91TMB p154 CR France156

COLLIER,John Thomas T2Lt kia 2-11-17 3RWar att1/4Norf p64 CR Palestine8

COLLIER,Reginald Charles 2Lt ded 17-11-18 RGA 196SB p38 CR France85

COLLIER,Reginald John T2Lt kld 12-2-18 RFC p15 CR Ireland107

COLLIER,Samuel Francis Capt kia 22-3-18 6Manch p236 MR27

COLLIER,Samuel Robert T2Lt kia 20-7-16 6RBerks p139 MR21

COLLIER,Sidney.MC.Lt kia 28-3-18 6Manch attRFC p18&236 CR France58

COLLIER,Simon.MC.Lt kia 14-9-18 2Wilts p206 CR France80 Ex WiltsYeo

COLLIN,Joseph Henry.VC.2Lt kia 9-4-18 4RLancs p213 CR France1106

COLLIN,Kenneth Glenfield T2Lt kia 12-10-16 12Lpool p71 CR France385

COLLINGE,John Chisholm 2Lt dow 25-10-17 PoW 8LancF p221 CR Germany2

COLLINGE,Wharton Rye Lt dow 7-8-17 2/6Lpool p215 CR France345

COLLINGS,Eric D'Auvergne 2Lt kia 23-8-16 1RWSurr p55 CR France399

COLLINGS,Frank Reginald 2Lt kia 3-12-17 16NumbF p60 MR30

COLLINGS,Harry Colston 2Lt kia 19-9-18 RGA 284SB p38 CR France673

COLLINGS,L.L.2Lt ded 3-10-18 2DLI &RAF p160

COLLINGS,Sydney Walter T2Lt kia 20-4-18 11RFus p67 CR France300,Sidney

COLLINGS,Walter.MC.Lt kia 10-4-18 1/3Mon p244 CR France19,11-4-18

COLLINGS,William Norman TLt kia 6-10-18 2NumbF p60 CR France234

COLLINGS-WELLS,John Stanhope.VC.DSO CaptALtCol kia 27-3-18 4Beds p85 CR France516

COLLINGWOOD,Carlton Capt dow 8-8-16 4SLancs p229 CR France141

COLLINGWOOD,George Albert T2Lt kia 10-8-15 6BordR p116 CR Gallipoli5,COLLINWOOD

COLLINGWOOD,Gordon Francis TLt dow 28-3-18 RGA 405SB p38 CR France113

COLLINGWOOD-THOMPSON,Edward James Vibart 2Lt dow 10-9-14 2RWFus CR France1445

COLLINS,Albert Shepherd 2Lt dow 25-9-17 5ScotRif p224 MR30,10Bn

COLLINS,Alexander Kilpatrick T2Lt kia 29-5-18 12/13NumbF p60 MR18

COLLINS,Alfred John 2Lt kia 29-9-18 1DCLI p114 CR France245

COLLINS,Arthur Duppa T2Lt dow 1-4-17 GL &52RFC p6 CR France105

COLLINS,Arthur Edward Jeune.MID Capt kia 11-11-14 RE 5FC p44 MR29

COLLINS,Arthur Michael Austen Lt ded 28-10-18 IA 38Dogras att1/1Brahmans p275 MR66

COLLINS,Charles.MID Lt dow 28-7-16 1KRRC p149 MR21

COLLINS,Charles Bury.CMG.DSO.LtColTCol ded 1-3-17 RE p44 CR EAfrica39

COLLINS,Charles Edwin Lt kia 21-3-18 24RFA p27 MR20

COLLINS,Claude Henry James T2Lt dow 16-4-18 18NumbF p60 MR30

COLLINS,Ernest Stanley 2Lt kia 31-7-17 1Worc p108 MR29

COLLINS,Francis John Lt accdrd 25-3-17 RIM attRE IWT p275 CR Iraq6

COLLINS,Frank Basil 2Lt kia 22-8-17 1RFA p208 CR Belgium10

COLLINS,Frederick William T2Lt ded 29-4-16 1LifeGds p20 CR France134

COLLINS,George Edwin T2Lt kia 11-1-18 2RB p178 CR Belgium22

COLLINS,Harold George TLt kia 9-4-17 RASC &48RFC p6&192 CR France120

COLLINS,Harold Stafford T2LtACapt ded 17-11-17 GL EgyptLabCps p190 CR Egypt1

COLLINS,H.B.Maj ded 12-9-18 RAMC p269 CR Hamps246

COLLINS,Henry Herbert John Chap4Cl kia 9-4-17 RAChDept att9BlkW p199 CR France924

COLLINS,Herbert Charles TLt died 11-2-17 24Manch p154 CR France40

COLLINS,Horace Alexander TLt kia 18-9-17 SStaffs att246RFA attRE49SigCo p122 CR Belgium17

COLLINS,James Henry William.MC.T2Lt dow 6-5-17 6LNLancs p135 CR Iraq8

COLLINS,John Ferdinando T2Lt kia 28-3-18 56MGC Inf 182 CR France184

COLLINS,John Gerrard TMaj kia 27-9-15 8BlkW p128 MR19

COLLINS,John Stratford Lt kia 5-4-18 RSuss att12Bn p118 CR France516

COLLINS,L.E.2Lt kld 5-4-18 GL &100RAF p190 CR France1404

COLLINS,Lionel Drummond Kyrle 2Lt kia 11-5-16 3 att13RScots p53 CR France423

COLLINS,Maurice Lt kia 11-9-18 RGA 305SB p38 CR France1484

COLLINS,Neville Lancelot 2Lt kia 15-8-16 3 att2RSuss p118 CR France432

COLLINS,Newton Henry T2Lt kia 27-4-16 5RInniskF p104 CR France115,7Bn

COLLINS,Norman Cecil 2Lt kia 9-8-16 3 att7Suff p78 MR21

COLLINS,Percival George TLt kia 18-8-16 6DCLI p114 MR21

COLLINS,Percy Hugh Campbell.MC.Capt 11-8-20 1Y&L CR Wilts115

COLLINS,Percy Robert Murdoch.DSO.CaptAMaj dow 25-6-17 RGA 13SB p38 CR Belgium29,kia

COLLINS,Philip Capt kia 30-7-15 7RB p178 CR Belgium116

COLLINS,Reginald Thomas.DSO.MajTLtCol kia 18-9-18 RAMC att17FA p195 CR France835

COLLINS,Robert Hayes Maj kia 20-5-17 6Lond p246 CR France614

COLLINS,Robert Simpson T2Lt kia 9-3-18 2RFC p15 CR France98

COLLINS,Samuel William 2Lt kia 21-3-18 2/7N&D p233 MR20

COLLINS,Stanley Thomas Lt dow 29-4-17 5LancF p221 CR France80,2Lt

COLLINS,Thomas TLtACapt ded 23-2-19 RAOC p198 CR France403

COLLINS,Vincent Henry 2Lt kia 12-2-17 IARO att102Grenadiers p275 CR Iraq5

COLLINS,Vivian Donald Berry Lt kia 9-5-15 13N&D attGurkhaRif p133 MR22

55

COLLINS,Valentine St.Barbe Lt kia 2-9-18 SL &RAF p268 MR20

COLLINS,William 2Lt kia 30-7-16 3 att8Glouc p106 MR21

COLLINS,William Geoffrey Lt dow PoW 21-1-18 7Norf p73 CR Germany2

COLLINS,William Henry Lt kld 7-3-18 YorksHussYeo attRFC p206&18 CR Wilts3

COLLINSON,Arthur Amery Capt kia 25-9-15 9ESurr p112 MR19

COLLINSON,Frank Graham.VD.HonCol ded 3-3-19 6Lond p269 CR Italy15,LtCol

COLLINSON,George Edward Cleather Lt kld 13-4-17 CamH &RFC p6&167 CR Devon230

COLLINSON,Jeffreys Lewis William 2Lt kia 15-7-16 3 att2SLancs p125 CR France393

COLLINSON,John Harold 2Lt kia 21-3-18 18MGC p182 MR27

COLLINSON,William Holmes 2Lt kia 5-1-16 6NumbF p214 CR Belgium127

COLLIS,Bert Humphrey Lt dow 20-12-15 3 att9Suff p78 CR Belgium11

COLLIS,Frank Reginald Maj kia 27-9-16 2NthMidRFA p206 CR France630

COLLIS,Hugh Humphrey 2Lt dow 12-4-17 5Suff p217 CR France113

COLLIS,Percy Harold 2Lt dow 31-7-17 4Hamps p228 CR Belgium36,12Bn

COLLIS,William Henry TCapt kia 9-5-17 7RInniskF p104 CR Belgium60

COLLIS-BROWNE,Alfred Ulick.MID Lt kia 13-4-15 1YLI p142 MR29

COLLIS-SANDES,Maurice James.MID Capt kia 17-2-17 11RFus B'Coy p67 CR France314

COLLISON,Edgar Henry 2Lt ded 26-6-16 4Norf p216 CR Norf184

COLLISON-MORLEY,Harold Duke.MID MajTLtCol kia 25-9-15 EKent Cmdg19Lond p57 CR France219

COLLISSON,Edwin Read CaptAMaj kia 13-10-15 1/6SStaffs p229 MR19

COLLISSON,Evelyn Ernest Arnold T2Lt kia 23-2-16 2Beds A'Coyp85 CR France699

COLLOT,Thomas Alexander 2Lt kia 1-7-16 6RBerks p139 CR France513

COLLYER,Arthur Alan.OBE.LtCol ded 11-12-19 RAPC p268 CR Scot204 Ex Beds

COLLYER,Arthur Hamilton 2Lt dow 23-4-17 5GordH p242 CR France451

COLLYER,William James T2Lt kia 31-7-17 RSuss att13Bn p118 MR29

COLLYMORE,Hubert Aubrey Lt kia 17-4-18 9Beds att25MGC p85&182 MR30

COLLYNS,Robert Henry.MC.TLt dow 1-6-18RE97FC p44 CR France1693 &CR France34,Maj

COLMER,Arthur Cecil 2Lt kia 1-7-16 A96RFA p27 CR France188

COLNETT,Richard Daunteshey Capt mbk 13-8-18 8Ess p257&275,IA 3/151Punjabis MR34,2entries

COLOMB,George Lushington.DCM.Lt kia 22-11-16 4Lond &RFC p246 CR France169

COLOMB,Mervyn William 2Lt dow 11-5-15 4Lond attRFC p18&246 CR Hamps1

COLQUHOUN,A.S.2Lt kld 20-4-18 GL &RAF p190

COLQUHOUN,Ernest Forbes Campbell 2Lt kia 26-9-17 3 att2RWFus p97 CR Belgium126

COLQUHOUN,Ivor Kenneth T2Lt ded 9-9-15 14WelchR p126 CR Wales165

COLQUHOUN,Phillip Hugh Leslie Campbell.MC.Capt kia 19-9-18 3 att1BlkW p128 CR France835,Lumsden

COLQUHOUN,Robert Clark T2Lt dow 3-7-16 9RScotF att2ScotRif p94 CR France40

COLQUHOUN,Robert Fletcher TLtACapt kia 16-11-16 13 att15HLI p162 MR21

COLQUHOUN,William Wallace TCapt kia 25-9-15 11HLI p162 MR19

COLSON,Anthony Francis Douglas.MC.Lt kia 10-11-17 RFA p207 CR Belgium10

COLSON,Cecil.MC.CaptAMaj kia 14-12-16 RGA 21SB p38 CR Belgium4

COLSON,Douglas Fairley.DSO.Maj ded 3-2-19 RE 521FC p209 CR Syria2

COLSON,Edward.MID Maj dow 20-1-16 IA 41Dogras p275 CR Iraq5

COLSTON,Harold Kelway Maj kia 23-4-15 1Y&L p158 MR29

COLTHART,Robert Herd Capt dow 2-11-18 14BlkW p203 CR France1033

COLTHURST,Arthur Beadon TCapt kia 25-10-16 14Glouc p106 CR France1182

COLTMAN,Richard Lester 2Lt kia 27-11-17 CldGds att2GdsMGCps p254 MR17

COLTMAN,Walter Joseph 2Lt dow 2-6-17 2/6Lond p246 CR France518

COLTON,Stanley Edmonds.MC.2Lt kia 28-3-18 1NumbF p60 MR20

COLVER,Edward Watkin.MID Lt kia 28-6-15 RE 455FC p210 MR4

COLVER,Henry Capt kia 19-12-15 1/5Y&L p238 CR Belgium23,dow

COLVILL,George Chaignian Capt kia 30-11-17 SIrHorse att7RIrReg p24 CR France1489,Chaigneau

COLVILL-JONES,Robert.MC.Capt 4-11-18 13RB &RAF CR France733

COLVILLE,Harold Linklater T2Lt dow 6-7-16 9SomLI p79 CR France145

COLVILLE,Henry George Coulson Capt kia 22-9-15 1KSLI attHQ16InfBde p144 CR Belgium92

COLVIN,Kenneth Colquhoun T2Lt ded 6-9-15 RASC att348Co p192 CR Wilts2

COLVIN,Robert Alexander Capt&Adjt kia 10-3-15 2WYorks p81 CR France279

COLVIN,Russell Alexander TCapt kia 1-5-17 10A&SH p173 CR France451

COLWELL,Albert Edward 2Lt kld 23-2-18 RFC p15 CR Mddx66

COLYER,Wilfred Victor T2Lt kia 22-10-18 Hamps att15Bn p120 CR Belgium408

COLYER-FERGUSSON,Thomas Riversdale.VC.2LtACapt dow 31-7-17 Nhampt p137 CR Belgium72

COMBE,Boyce Anthony Lt kia 11-11-14 6RFus att4Bn p67 MR29

COMBE,George Henry Richard TLt kia 15-9-16 7RB p178 MR21

COMBE,Samuel Barbour Lt 1-10-14 NIrHorse MR22

COMBE,Stanley Greatrex Lt ded 11-10-18 3Co of LondYeo p204 CR Egypt8,attImpCamCps

COMBE-CEATON Frank T2Lt kia 14-10-18 ESurr att12Bn p112 CR Belgium157

COMBER,Andrew Pater Capt ded 29-6-15 7Dev p269 CR Lond8

COMBER,Turner.MC&Bar.T2LtACapt kia 19-9-18 9Ess p131 CR France369

COMBER-TAYLOR,Eric Horace Capt kld 16-6-18 GL &10RAF p190 CR France142

COMBRIDGE,Leslie Ernest T2Lt kia 22-8-18 6EKent p57 CR France370

COMLEY,Edgar Cyril.MC.Lt kld 27-9-18 4RMunsF p175 CR France686

COMMINS,Arthur Edward 2Lt kia 23-4-17 150MGC p182 MR20

COMMON,Henry Alder 2Lt dow 4-10-18 1/2 att1/4KOSB p101 MR16

COMPSTON,John Milton T2Lt kia 8-10-18 WYorks p81 CR France375

COMPTON,Cyril Henry 2Lt kia 23-7-16 3RWKent att19Manch p140 MR21

COMPTON,Florence D'Oyly Sister ded 15-1-18 QAIMNS att65GH p200 CR Iraq6,drd

COMPTON,Guy T2Lt kia 27-7-17 RSuss att9Bn p118 MR29

COMPTON,Harold William TLtCol dow 7-7-17 12RFus p67 CR France40

COMPTON,Neville George T2Lt kia 20-4-16 9Worc p108 MR38

COMPTON,Rex Lt kia 12-8-17 5Ess p232 MR29

COMPTON,Lord Spencer Douglas Lt kia 13-5-15 RHGds p20 MR29

COMPTON,William Henry Capt ded 6-12-18 RAMC p195 CR Sussex183

COMPTON,William Horace Gordon 2Lt dow 17-6-17 B186RFA p27 CR Belgium5,kia

COMPTON,William Walter 2Lt kia 25-4-18 RH&FA p27 CR France139

COMPTON-SMITH,Geoffrey Lee.DSO.Maj kld 30-4-21 2RWFus CR Eire95

COMPTON-SMITH,Roger Noel 2Lt dow 27-5-15 6Manch p236 CR Gallipoli2

COMPTON-THORNHILL,Richard Anthony Lt kia 16-9-14 1ScotsGds p52 MR15,14-9-14

COMRIE,Alexander T2Lt ded 15-8-16 RE 257Coy p44 CR France98,kldacc

COMRIE,William Ritchie 2Lt dow 27-11-17 HLI att16Bn p162 CR Belgium18

COMYN,David Charles Edward Ffrench Maj kia 12-5-17 10LancF p92 MR20

CONAN-DAVIES,Brynmor Ivan HonLt ded 23-11-18 7Y&L p158 CR Lond14

CONCANNON,James Aloysius 2Lt kia 3-5-17 2LancF p92 MR20

CONDER,Philip Capt ded 15-7-17 IA 24 att19Punjabis p275 CR Iraq8

CONDI,Allen George 2Lt kia 1-10-16 4BordR p228 CR France239,5Bn

CONDIE,George Rev Chap4Cl ded 30-6-18 RAChDept p199 CR Scot674

CONDON,David Lt ded PoW 23-7-17 1NumbF p60 CR Germany2

CONDON,Thomas 2Lt kld 28-5-16 A108RFA p27 CR Belgium97

CONDUITT,Robert Bruce 2Lt kia 16-4-15 1SfthH p164 CR France924 Ex 14Lond

CONEN,James Henry T2Lt kia 25-7-18 12Manch p154 MR27

CONEYBEARE,Herbert William T2Lt dow 24-10-16 2Lincs p74 MR21

CONGLETON,Henry Bligh Fortescue Parnell.Lord.MID Lt kia 10-11-14 GrenGds p49 CR Belgium134

CONGREVE,William La Touche.VC.DSO.MC.Capt&BtMaj kia 20-7-16 RB p178 CR France23

CONHEENY,Gerald,MC T2Lt kld 5-12-18 1/5RLancs p58 CR Germany4,Lt

CONIBEAR,Arthur Edward 2Lt dow 14-10-16 1/6Lpool p215 CR France40,Lt

CONLAN,Arthur Underhill 2Lt kia 22-5-16 18Lond p250 MR20

CONLEY,William Cockayne.MC.TLt kia 26-10-17 1SStaffs att91TMB p122 MR30

CONLIN,Bernard Francis 2Lt dow 9-10-16 28RFA p27 CR France833

CONMEE,John Alphonsus Lt kia 3-5-17 4Y&L p238 MR20

CONN,James Fullerton Caldwell Capt dow 1-5-17 7A&SH p243 CR France64,Fullarton

CONNAL,Alexander Campbell 2Lt kia 9-4-18 RGA 99SB p39 CR France572

CONNAL,Arthur William Campbell Lt kia 24-10-16 53/38RFA p27 MR21

CONNELL,Alfred Hamilton CaptTMaj kia 28-9-15 2RScotF p94 CR France257

CONNELL,Harry Bertram LtCol dow 16-11-16 RAMC p195 CR France74

CONNELL,John Capt ded 18-5-20 RAMC p267 CR Berks112

CONNELL,Sydney Dennis Lt kia 28-11-14 Manch p154 MR22

CONNELL,Victor John Alexander BtMaj ded 7-7-20 IA 13Lancers attGuidesCav p275 MR43

CONNELL,William Patrick.MID LtACapt kld 24-11-18 55RFA p27 CR Iraq8

CONNELLAN,Peter Martin Maj kia 20-10-14 Hamps p120

CONNELLY,Montagu Edward Lt ded 14-1-18 RFC p15 CR USA228,2Lt

CONNER,Frederick Attenborrow T2Lt kia 1-7-16 2SfthH p164 MR21,Frederic

CONNER,Richard Maj dow 7-9-15 Glouc p106 CR Surrey160

CONNERY,Michael Henry.MC.LtCol ded 25-4-21 1/9Manch CR Lancs416

CONNING,Thomas Rothsay.MC.Lt kia 27-5-17 2RWFus p97 CR France1489

CONNOCHIE,Robert Hope see CONOCHIE,R.H.

CONNOLLY,Hugh Aloysius 2Lt kia 27-8-18 IrGds att4GdsMGReg p52 CR France568

CONNOLLY,James Harris TCapt ded 23-10-18 RAMC p195

CONNOLLY,John Henry T2Lt dow 1-9-16 6RMunstF att11RIrRif p175 CR France285

CONNOLLY,Matthew G Capt 4-9-19 RAVC CR Canada1087

CONNOR,Albermarle Dare Maj ded 9-7-20 IA 1/42Deolali p275 MR65

CONNOR,Amos Lloyd 2Lt dow 30-6-17 2N&D p133 CR France178

CONNOR,Cleveland Alexander TLt kia 23-10-18 ChinLabCps att1/8Worc p189 CR France231

CONNOR,Isaac Joscelyn Maj kia 25-7-16 RE 101FC p44 CR France372

CONNOR,James Patrick.MC.2Lt kia 7-6-17 B119ArmyBde RH&FA p27 CR Belgium165

CONNOR,Samuel Maurice 2Lt kia 10-8-17 5Beds p219 MR29

CONOCHIE,Robert Hope 2Lt kia 31-7-17 4KOSB p224 MR29,CONNOCHIE

CONOCHIE,Robert Pollock 2Lt kia 19-5-18 8ScotRif p225 CR France547,18-5-18

CONOLLY,B.D.Capt&QM 6-2-21 RAMC CR Kent7

CONRAN,Owen Mostyn Maj kia 29-7-17 RLancs att10RFC p6&58 CR France98,28-7-17

CONRAN,Percy Wogan Drysdale Capt dow 12-4-18 1LancF p92 CR France352

CONRATH,Percy Thorpe T2Lt kia 4-9-18 20DLI p160 MR32

CONROY,Bernard 2Lt kia 5-7-15 2RDubF p176 CR Belgium23,6-7-15

CONROY,Hugh Tracey T2Lt ded 28-10-18 LabCps att85IndLabCoy p189 CR France52

CONSIDINE,Christopher Daniel 2Lt kia 24-5-15 2RDubF p176 MR29

CONSIDINE,Heffernan James.MC.Capt kia 27-10-16 4 att2RIrReg p88 CR Belgium17

CONSIDINE,John William Capt kia 25-9-15 2RMunstF p175 CR France219,Maj

CONSIDINE,Patrick Francis Lt dow 12-7-15 4RScots p211 CR Europe4

CONSTABLE,Archibald Thomas Wynne CaptTMaj dow 16-10-15 9Ess p131 CR France98

CONSTABLE,Arthur Leslie 2Lt kia 17-3-17 43RFC p6 CR France924

CONSTABLE,Basil John Leslie Clymping Capt kia 9-8-15 1/4RSuss p228 CR Gallipoli5

CONSTABLE,Douglas Oliaphant Lt kia 25-9-16 4GrenGds SR p49 CR France374

CONSTABLE,Ralph TCapt kia 25-9-16 10NumbF p60

CONSTANCE,William Ernest 2Lt kia 9-8-18 7 att8Lond p247 CR France247

CONSTANTINE,Frank Iveson T2Lt dow 20-8-18 22NumbF att2Lincs p60 CR France84,Francis Ivison kia

CONSTANTINE,Hebden Stringer 2Lt dow 13-5-17 2/7Worc C'Coy p226 CR France610

CONSTANTINE,Herbert Norman.MC.Capt kia 27-5-18 4Yorks p220 CR France1753

CONSTANTINE,Robert Baxandall Capt ded 4-3-19 2/6WYorks p218 CR Yorks408

CONSTANTINE,William.MC.TLt kia 18-9-18 7BordR p116 MR16

CONSTERDINE,Arthur Edward TCapt kia 26-12-16 WYorks att9Bn p81 CR France701

CONSTERDINE,Henry Stanley Lt ded 11-6-18 RE IWT p262 CR Scot241

CONSTERDINE,V.C.SNurse 6-11-18 QAIMNS CR Notts84

CONSTERDINE-CHADWICK,Robert Thompson Consterdine TLtACapt kia 4-10-18 17 att3RFus p67 CR France234

CONVERY,J.A.Lt 11-3-18 RFA CR France1277

CONWAY,Arthur Septimus.DSO.Maj kia 17-6-17 1NStaffs p156 CR Belgium127

CONWAY,Brian Wiseman TLtACapt kia 4-10-17 22Manch p154 MR30

CONWAY,Edgar Philip Maj kia 10-8-15 6RMunstF p175 CR Gallipoli27

CONWAY,Guy T2Lt kia 29-9-18 11RWSurr p55 MR30

CONWAY,Joseph Michael T2Lt kia 7-7-16 7RLancs p58 MR21,8-7-16

CONYERS,Charles MajTLtCol dow 12-5-15 RIrF p171

CONYERS,Harold Cater T2Lt kia 22-9-18 2 att8Glouc p106 CR France1106

CONYERS,Walter Neville T2Lt kia 13-8-16 8RBerks p139 MR21,19-8-16

CONYBEARE,Edward Bruce.MC.MIDx2 Capt kia 5-4-16 1 att9Worc p108 MR38

CONYBEARE,Maynard Henry Crawford Lt ded 14-1-15 114Mahrattas&7Yorks CR Devon238

CONYNGHAM,Cecil Allan Taylor Capt kia 4-11-14 RAMC p195 MR47

CONYNGHAM,Victor George Henry Francis Lt ded 9-11-18 7RIrReg p24 CR Eire459

COOBAN,Adrian Deighton TMaj kia 16-7-16 16KRRC p149 CR France432

COOCH,Charles Rollo Lt kia 17-12-14 BordR B'Coy p116 CR France525

COOCH,T.A.Capt 17-9-19 Worc &2RAF CR France457

COOIL,Caesar Alfred Capt 11-11-18 RGA CR Wales491

COOIL,Henry Stuart T2Lt kia 9-9-18 YLI att9Bn p142 CR France415

COOK,Albert Edward T2Lt kia 20-2-18 ESurr att2/22Lond p112 MR34

COOK,Alexander James Lt kia 28-4-17 4Lincs p217 CR France1495

COOK,Alfred Burton TCapt kia 20-11-17 GL att57RFC p6 CR France134

COOK,Alfred John Lt ded 8-6-19 RE att1S&M p44 MR43

COOK,Arthur Basil Kemball T2Lt kia 7-7-16 9RFus p67 MR21

COOK,Arthur Clifford T2Lt kia 16-8-16 16 att4Lpool p71 CR France453

COOK,Arthur Thomas 2Lt dow 9-8-16 3 att8Glouc p106 CR France833

COOK,B.E.2Lt ded 7-11-18 RE p44 CR Wilts56

COOK,Bernard 2Lt kia 6-9-16 7Lpool p215 MR21

COOK,Cecil Haddon T2Lt kia 22-10-17 23Manch p154 MR30

COOK,Charles Adam T2Lt kia 11-3-16 1Beds p85 CR France924,Adams

COOK,Charles Reynolds T2Lt kia 29-5-18 2Hamps p120 CR France24

COOK,Charles Stanley Blannin 2Lt kia 15-9-16 3/5SomLI att1/8Lond p218 CR France252

COOK,Cyril Annesley TCapt kia 25/26-9-15 8RWSurr p55 MR19

COOK,Cyril Edward Lt dow 8-7-16 2RSuss p118 CR France98

COOK,Cyril Frank T2Lt kia 5-8-17 32RFus p67 CR Belgium116

COOK,Cyril Mountfort 2Lt kia 27-8-17 7Worc p226 CR Belgium125

COOK,Cyril Ramsay 2Lt kia 9-6-17 4N&D att9Bn p133 MR29

COOK,E.J.SubCdr 9-10-14 S&T Cps MR43

COOK,E.K.SNurse 8-9-17 QAIMNS CR Egypt1

COOK,Earl Allen T2Lt kld 22-3-18 RFC p15 CR Bucks96

COOK,Edwin Archibald Douglas Lt ded 11-1-20 2CamH p265 CR Canada423

COOK,Edwin Berkeley.MVO.LtCol dow 4-11-14 1LifeGds p20 CR Kent252

COOK,Ernest Arnold Lovell.MC.Maj mbk 1-11-18 122RFA p256 MR16

COOK,F.W.Lt&QM 1-1-18 EYorks CR Yorks2

COOK,Francis Richardson TLt kld 22-2-18 EYorks &RFC p15 CR Egypt15

COOK,Frank Ecaden.MC.Lt kia 20-10-18 1/10Manch p237 CR France287,Eaden

COOK,Frederick Charles Lt dow 9-10-19 Beds attRAF CR Beds75

COOK,Frederick James T2LtTCapt dow 30-11-15 10BordR att1/4RScots p116 CR Gallipoli3

COOK,Geoffrey Bruce TLt kia 1-10-18 RE IWT att1/5LNLancs p44 CR France256

COOK,George Albert 2Lt kia 10-3-15 2Mddx p146 CR France706

COOK,George Trevor-Roper.CMG.DSO.MIDx2 LtCol kia26-3-18 20Huss p23 MR27

COOK,Gerald Haslam Capt dow 25-7-15 IA 101Grenadiers p275 CR EAfrica6 &CR Tanzania1

COOK,Godfrey Burton Lt dow 29-3-18 PoW 19Huss p23 CR France1266,23-3-18 20Bn

COOK,Harold Joseph Bede Lt dow 28-5-18 B46RFA p27 CR France33,Capt kia

COOK,Henry 2Lt kia 23-4-17 4RScots p211 CR France545

COOK,Henry James T2Lt dow 6-10-15 8YLI p142 CR France40

COOK,Henry Rodham T2Lt kia 7-9-17 12Manch p154 CR France1190

COOK,Henry Vincent 2Lt kia 21-3-18 7 att11Ess p232 MR20

COOK,Horace Herbert T2Lt kia 25-3-18 RE 438FC p44 MR27

COOK,Horace Montague 2Lt kia 21-3-18 7Lond p247 CR France1893

COOK,Howard Mortimer TLt kia 9-8-18 12MGC p182 CR France59

COOK,Humphrey Noel Felix T2Lt kia 26-6-17 11RWSurr p55 CR Belgium29

COOK,James Robert Capt kia 26-4-15 IA 21Punjabis att47Sikhs p275 CR Belgium96

COOK,John T2Lt kia 23-10-16 22DLI p160 CR France400

COOK,John Blair.DSO.MC.LtCol kia 24-11-17 1/5RScotF p222 CR Palestine3

COOK,John Duncan Howe Capt kia 28-9-17 IA 1/5GurkhaRif p275 CR Iraq8,Home

COOK,Kenneth Richmond T2Lt dow 30-7-16 8BlkW attTMB p128 CR Surrey152

COOK,Leonard Nield.MC.2Lt kia 7-7-17 3RLancs p58 CR France379

COOK,Norman George 2Lt kia 29-6-17 4 att6NStaffs p156 CR France550,28-6-17

COOK,Percy Mellows T2Lt kia 4-10-16 18KRRC p149 MR21

COOK,Philip Harry 2Lt kia 19-7-17 8Lond p147 CR Belgium118

COOK,Philip John Cecil 2Lt kia 14-10-18 7WelshR p230 CR France258

COOK,Randolph 2Lt kia 9-4-17 7ScotRif att9KRRC p224 CR France581

COOK,Reginald Cyril T2Lt dow 11-7-18 RB att8Bn p178 CR France84,13Bn

COOK,Reginald William.MC.2Lt kia 1-9-18 3Dev p76

COOK,Richard Edward T2Lt dow 13-4-18 11Suff p78 CR Belgium18

COOK,Robert Alexander T2Lt kia 30-6-16 2KOSB p101 MR20

COOK,Robert Guy T2Lt kia 9-2-17 3Worc p108 CR Belgium138,Lt

COOK,Robert Leslie 2Lt kia 7-8-15 6Lincs p74 MR4

COOK,Taylor 2Lt ded 21-3-17 7A&SH p243 CR France15

COOK,Thomas 2Lt kia 2-10-15 12Ess att6Lincs p131 MR4

COOK,John Valentina see COOKE,J.V.

COOK,Walter 2Lt kia 16-4-18 5N&D p232 CR Belgium183

COOK,William Edward 2Lt kia 12-3-17 2YLI p142 CR France649

COOK,William Edwin T2Lt dow 27-4-18 1/2 att4Yorks p90 CR France1142

COOKE,Alan Welldon Hands Capt kia 24-3-18 22DLI p160

COOKE,Archibald Ernest 2Lt dow 1-5-18 1Leic p87 CR France142

COOKE,Arthur 2Lt ded 22-8-17 2/6N&D p233 CR France699

COOKE,Arthur Francis.MID 2Lt kia 4-3-17 29RFA p27 CR France626

COOKE,Cecil Pybus T2Lt kia 22-8-17 KSLI att5Bn p144 MR30

COOKE,Charles Earsham.MC.Lt dow 24-5-17 1/9Manch p237 CR France145

COOKE,Charles Ernest.MID 2Lt kia 25-5-15 3 att1RIrF p171 MR29

COOKE,Charles Herbert T2Lt kia 21-9-17 2RB p178 CR Belgium52

COOKE,Charles Taylor Capt kia 10-8-15 7Ches p222 MR4

COOKE,Charles Reginald 2Lt ded 12-2-19 7LNLancs p274 CR Lancs481

COOKE,Denys Capt kia 18-4-18 3 att1BlkW p128 CR France279

COOKE,E.K.SNurse ded 8-9-17 QAIMNS p200

COOKE,Ernest Richard TCapt kia 25-4-16 8RIrF p171 CR France423,26-4-16

COOKE,George Frederick Lt ded 22-10-19 5Mddx p265 CR Ches197

COOKE,George Josiah 2Lt kia 23-11-17 2/2Lond attRFC p18&245 CR France1361,kldacc

COOKE,Hans Hendrick Anthony Capt kia 24-1-17 ConnRgrs att3NigR p172&201 MR50

COOKE,Harold Esmond.MC.Capt kia 30-11-17 12Lpool p71&258 MR17

COOKE,Henry Frederick.MID 2Lt kia 4-8-16 7RSuss p118 MR21

COOKE,Hugh William Fothergill Maj kia 14-5-15 IA 24Punjabis CR Iraq6

COOKE,I.A.E.Lt kia 19-7-17 SL attTMB p201

COOKE,J.K.Maj 29-7-15 Ches CR Ches186

COOKE,James Gore Capt kia 8-10-16 16N&D p133 MR21

COOKE,John T2Lt ded 20-6-16 DLI &RFC p2&160 CR France518

COOKE,John Howard TLt ded 9-10-18 RASC MT attRGA p192 CR France123

COOKE,John Irwin Lt dow 3-9-17 RE 4LROD p44 CR Belgium15,33LROC

COOKE,John Valentina.MC.TLtACapt kia 1-10-18 11RWSurr attTMB p55 CR Belgium116,COOK Valentine

COOKE,Leslie Frederick T2Lt kia 26-9-16 12 att10Ess p131 CR France396

COOKE,Reginald Charles.MC.T2Lt kia 7-7-16 9WelshR p126 MR21

COOKE,Samuel Arthur LtCol ded 26-3-18 IA 38CentIndHorse p275 CR Hamps7

COOKE,Sydney Philip 2Lt ded 4-11-18 8Norf p73&263 CR Norf209,Sidney

COOKE,Thomas Lt ded 30-5-17 RGA att18HAC p39 CR France113

COOKE,Vincent Joseph.MC.Lt dow 1-3-21 7Mddx CR Scot359

COOKE,William Harry Coleman TCapt kia 1-9-18 1YLI GarrBn att2/6DLI p142 CR France496

COOKE,William Henry 2Lt kia 9-8-15 2N&D p133 MR29

COOKE,William Wesley T2Lt kia 25-4-18 9MGC Inf p182 MR30

COOKSEY,Joseph Arnold 2Lt kia 1-5-17 RGA 116SB p39 CR France581

COOKSEY,Kenneth Bassano 2Lt kia 8-4-17 3RWKent &RFC p6&140 CR France924

COOKSEY,Maurice Wilfrid T2Lt dow 13-4-17 RE B SpCo p44 CR France12,Wilfred M.

COOKSON,Alan Capt kia 27-6-17 10Lpool p216 CR France275

COOKSON,Bernard T2Lt kia 10-4-17 EYorks Res att1Bn p83 CR France162

COOKSON,Mostyn Eden Maj kia 14-9-14 2RSuss p118 MR15

COOLE,Arthur Evans 2Lt ded 14-5-19 IA 1/32SikhPnrs p275 CR Sussex24

COOMBE,Leslie Clarence T2Lt kia 25-3-18 1 att1/5DCLI p114 MR27

COOMBE,Samuel Barbour Lt ded 1-10-14 NIrHorse p24

COOMBE,William John TLt kia 1-10-16 7DCLI p114 MR21

COOMBE,William Robert Lt kia 27-5-18 NottsYeo p205 MR41,drd

COOMBER,Harry Alan.MC.Lt dow 29-4-18 RGA 138HB p209 CR France145

COOMBER,Horace Bertram Capt kia 12-10-17 8Manch attRFC p18&237 CR Belgium157

COOMBES George 2Lt kia 16-8-17 RIrF att7/8Bn p171 CR Belgium128

COOMBES,George Wilson T2Lt kia 3-5-17 1RLancs p58 CR France604

COOMBES,Herbert Victor 2Lt kia 28-3-18 21Lond p251 MR20

COOMBES,John Edwin Henshaw Lt dow 1-4-18 5BordR p228 CR France145

COOMBS,Claude Stuart T2Lt dow 6-7-16 6RWKent p140 CR France102

COOMBS,Debenham Stuard Lt ded 31-10-18 7Ess Res p269 CR Hereford208

COOMBS,Henry Whitaker TLt dow 2-7-16 18NumbF p60 CR France23

COOMBS,James Roy 2Lt kia 24-3-18 RFA 93ArmyBde p27 MR20

COOMBS,Percy Douglas 2Lt kia 14-4-17 7 att1Ess p232 MR20

COONEY,Albert George Lt kia 12-5-17 291RFA p27 MR20

COONEY,Charles Robert T2Lt kia 9-10-16 7RDubF att2RIrRif p176 MR21,Richard

COONEY,Edmund Luke T2Lt kia 4-6-17 9RDubF p176 CR Belgium182

COONEY,Patrick Augustine T2Lt kld 22-2-18 LabCps attEgyptLabCps p189 CR Egypt2

COOPER,Anne.MID Sister ded 17-11-19 QAIMNS p268 CR Lancs30

COOPER,Albert Frederick T2Lt dow 9-5-18 11Mddx p146 CR France142,1Bn

COOPER,Alexander Stewart Capt dow 25-4-15 1KOSB p101 MR4,26-4-15

COOPER,Alfred Lynn 2Lt kia 15-9-16 19Lond p250 CR France390

COOPER,Arthur T2Lt dow 10-7-16 14Manch p154 CR France119

COOPER,Arthur Charles Capt kia 16-5-15 1/4Leic p219 CR Belgium99

COOPER,Arthur Herbert Augustus Lt kia 4-10-17 4RWSurr p212 MR30

COOPER,Arthur Miles Gilpin 2Lt ded 23-10-16 12RBerks p265

COOPER,Astley de Borde T2Lt dow 7-7-15 RE 1SigCo p44 CR France80

COOPER,Cecil Bernard 2Lt kia 9-8-17 A38RH&FA p27 CR Belgium7

COOPER,Cecil Davey T2Lt dow 29-1-18 3ResReg of Cav att6Wilts p23 CR France905

COOPER,Cecil Fletcher Maj ded 5-9-16 D121RFA p27 CR France64

COOPER,Charles Morris Lt kia 20-10-17 7Manch p237 CR France287

COOPER,Clarence Edwards Nooth Lt kia 16-9-16 3Lincs attRFC p2&74 CR France105 dedacc 2Bn

COOPER,Clarence Percy TLt dow 2-4-17 Ess att1/4 p131 CR Egypt2

COOPER,Claude Huntley.MM.T2Lt drd 17-1-18 9Yorks p90 CR Italy7

COOPER,Clifford T2Lt kia 22-4-18 18Mddx p146 CR France490

COOPER,Clifford Edward Gordon T2Lt kldacc 26-11-17 GL &62RFC p6 CR Kent7

COOPER,Corin Henry Benedict TLt dow 20-11-16 RE 178FC p44 CR France40,TC

COOPER,Cyril Ashley T2Lt kld 29-6-17 GL &RFC p6 CR Scot520

COOPER,Cyril Henry 2Lt kia 6-4-16 RGA 132HB p39 CR Belgium4

COOPER,David Cameron Lt kia 23-7-18 6GordH p242 CR France622,Donald

COOPER,Donald Keith T2Lt kia 9-9-16 1Nhampt p137 CR France432

COOPER,E.S.Maj 27-11-20 11RWFus CR Norf231

COOPER,Edward George Capt kia 4-8-16 3Lpool att1KAR p71&268 CR EAfrica40

COOPER,Ernest Walter T2Lt dow 13-10-18 9Ess p131 CR France106

COOPER,Francis Nicholas Nooth Lt kia 21-11-17 RASC &SWBord p192 CR France911

COOPER,Frank Douglas Towers 2Lt kia 22-7-16 2RScots p53 MR21,23-7-16

COOPER,Frank Penley 2Lt kia 26-9-16 17 att16RWar p64 MR21

COOPER,Frederick Edmund TLt dow 18-12-18 26RFus p67 CR Dorset20

COOPER,Frederick John T2Lt kia 27-5-18 SLancs p125 MR18

COOPER,Frederick William.MC.TLt kia 17-4-18 RE 105FC p44&258 MR30

COOPER,Frederick William Harvey.MM.T2Lt kia 9-3-18 10EKent p57 CR Palestine3

COOPER,G.C.M.ACapt ded 23-11-18 RE attRAnglesey p44 CR Surrey2

COOPER,Geoffrey Rowsell 2Lt ded 8-11-16 3RBerks p139

COOPER,George Frederick T2Lt kia 24-2-17 RASC p192 CR France749

COOPER,George Spencer T2Lt kia 17-2-17 6Nhampt p137 MR21

COOPER,George Stanley Capt ded 28-6-15 5RWKent p235 MR66

COOPER,Harold Leslie T2Lt kia 31-3-18 7EYorks p84 MR20

COOPER,Henry Mark Hugh Lt dow 29-7-15 1KEdwardsHorse p24 CR Lond2

COOPER,Henry Weatherley Frank T2Lt dow 28-4-17 7RFus p67 CR France113,29-4-17

COOPER,Herbert Ambrose TCapt kia 21-6-16 11RFC p2 CR France95

COOPER,Herbert Leonard 2Lt kia 16-9-16 7Mddx p235 CR France785

COOPER,Horace Burnaby 2Lt kia 23-10-18 4 att1Wilts p236 CR France1477

COOPER,Horace Charles Henry T2Lt kld 15-4-17 GL &RFC p6 CR Wilts116

COOPER,Howard Frank Byrne 2Lt kia 1-7-16 1KOSB A'Coy p101 CR France339

COOPER,Hubert T2Lt dow 30-3-18 16RB p178 CR France52

COOPER,Jack Oliver TCapt kia 23-7-16 att21RFC p2 MR20

COOPER,James 2Lt ded 5-11-18 TankCps p266 CR Lancs14

COOPER,James Alfred 2Lt kldacc 17-5-16 7N&D p233 CR France747,2Bn

COOPER,John Bruce Capt ded 21-11-15 RASC p192&253

COOPER,John Stephen TLt kia 25-3-17 GL &70RFC p6 CR France568

COOPER,Joseph T2Lt kia 26-9-16 14 att11Manch p154 MR21

COOPER,Leonard Gosse T2Lt kia 9-8-15 4SWBord p99 MR4

COOPER,Leonard Russell T2Lt drd 23-10-15 RFA 29DAC p27 MR35

COOPER,Maurice Stanley Charles T2Lt dow 10-8-16 9 att6Beds p85 CR France197,9-8-16

COOPER,Nowell Edwin Lt dow 16-10-18 1HuntsCycBn att2Suff p253 CR France560

COOPER,Oliver Henry Donald Lt kia 8-5-17 6HLI p240 MR37

COOPER,Percy TLt kia 22-3-18 18MGC p182 MR27,23-3-18

COOPER,Percy Newbery TLt dow 6-7-16 1N&D p133 CR France23

COOPER,Percy Valentine T2LtACapt kia 8-8-18 7RWSurr p55 CR France247

COOPER,R 2Lt 8-11-16 RBerks CR Surrey148

COOPER,Richard 2Lt kia 8-6-17 1 att10RWar p64 MR29

COOPER,Robert Charles TLt dow 12-4-18 18WelshR att119TMB p126 CR France25

COOPER,Ronald 2Lt dow 16-6-17 119RFA p27 CR Belgium127

COOPER,Spencer Bruce T2Lt dow 24-4-18 Wilts p152 CR France119,Lt

COOPER,Sydney Gordon 2Lt dow 17-9-15 4 att1RWar p64 CR France344

COOPER,Thomas Gill T2Lt ded 25-3-18 49MGC p182 CR France145

COOPER,Victor Travers T2Lt kia 22-6-17 1/8RWar p64 CR France381

COOPER,William 2Lt kia 25-9-15 1SStaffs p122 MR19

COOPER,William Campion Lt mbk 13-12-15 IA 53Sikhs att59Rif p275 MR41,drd 30-12-15

COOPER,William Dermot.MID Capt kia 30-8-17 AyrYeo p203 CR Palestine8

COOPER,William F.T2Lt kia 31-7-17 12RFus p67 CR Belgium112

COOPER,William Ferguson 2Lt dow 28-6-18 2KOSB p101 CR France21

COOPER,William Marsden 2Lt kia 17-2-17 2Worc p108 CR France511

COOPER,William Randolph 2Lt kia 13-5-18 4LNLancs p234 CR France261

COOPER,Willie.OBE.VD.LtCol 18-12-20 5WRid CR Yorks643

COOPER-BROWN,Arthur Neville 2LtACapt dow 27-10-18 3 att2Ess C'Coy p131 CR France613

COOPER-KING,Reginald Garret Maj dow 20-12-14 2WYorks p81 CR France768,21-12-14

COOPER-MARSDIN,Arthur Cooper Rev ded 16-8-18 RAChDept Ret p268

COOPER-SMITH,Reginald Burston 2Lt kia 10-3-17 5Ess p232 CR France624

COOTE,Arthur Eyre 2Lt kia 1-7-16 8RIrRif p169 MR21,1/2-7-16

COOTE,Charles Gartside Eyre Lt kia 22-3-18 11Huss p22 MR27

COOTE,George Bertrand Lt kia 27-5-18 RWKent att50MGC p182&140,Bernard MR18

COOTE,Philip Edward 2Lt kia 15-9-16 8Lond p247 CR France390

COOTE,Richard Markham TCapt kia 13-10-15 8RBerks p139 MR19

COPE,Edward Moseley Lt ded 3-6-19 NStaffs att52Leic p254 CR Germany1

COPE,George Eric TLt kia 1-7-16 20NumbF p60 MR21

COPE,Gerald Quin 2Lt dow 24-5-17 2/9Manch p237 CR France134

COPE,W.G.Capt 6-9-18 Yorks CR Mddx16

COPELAND,Douglas Chatterton Bruce.MC.Capt dow 21-6-18 12Lond p248 CR Essex75

COPELAND,Eric Neville Van de Ben TLt kia 26-3-18 63MGC p182

COPELAND,Frederick.MID Maj kia 6-6-15 IA 69Punjabis p275 CR France924

COPELAND,John Stuart T2Lt dow 20-2-17 2YLI p142 CR France62,Lt

COPELAND,Rupert Ramsay.DSO.MC.MIDx2 LtCol kld 24-7-20 39RFA MR38

COPELAND,William Alan 2Lt kia 25-4-15 1RScots p53 CR Belgium4

COPEMAN,Ernest Hugh 2Lt kia 18-3-16 6RWKent att37MGC p140&182 MR19

COPEMAN,Herbert Guy Hele 2Lt kia 3-9-16 6 O&BLI p130 CR France294

COPEMAN,Robert George Henry T2Lt dow 12-1-16 9Ess p131 CR France80

COPINGER,John Patrick 2Lt kia 10-9-17 4 O&BLI p231 CR Belgium96

COPLAND,Dudley Charles James 2Lt kia 9-5-15 1N&D p133 CR France566

COPLAND,George Harold T2Lt kia 31-7-17 18Lpool p71 MR29

COPLAND,Reginald Wallace ACapt kia 16-7-19 IA 3/1GurkhaRif p275

COPLEY,Alan T2Lt kia 2-4-17 19Manch p154 CR France596,Allan

COPLEY,Alfred Beresford T2Lt kia 26-8-17 101MGC Inf p182 CR France1461

COPNER,Arthur Bruce Lt kia 25-9-15 Dev p76 MR19

COPPACK,Charles Richard Stewart 2Lt dow 24-3-18 22 att24RFus p67 MR20,25-3-18 24 att22Bn

COPPARD,Stuart Benjamin Hayes T2Lt kia 20-11-17 GL att57RFC p6 CR France134

COPPARD,William John T2Lt dow 23-3-18 24RFus p67 MR20

COPPEN,William Joseph Lt kia 2-11-17 2Lond p245 MR34

COPPIN,Richard Alfred TCapt kia 11-4-17 6RWSurr B'Coy p55 CR France531,12-4-17

COPPING,Arthur Milton.MM.2Lt kia 18-9-16 6Lond p247 MR21

COPPOCK,Hugh Searle MID TLt kia 10-4-10 0 att23Lancs p125 MR32

CORAH,Leslie Capt kia 13-10-15 4Leic p219 MR19

CORAH,Sydney Lt kia 3-10-18 5Leic p220

CORBALLY,Lewis Capt dow 6-5-15 RFA p27 CR France284

CORBAN,Joseph 2LtTLt kia 17-7-17 10Y&L p158 CR Belgium100

CORBAN-LUCAS,Percival Laurence TCapt dow 15-12-16 1RSuss att9Worc p118 MR38

CORBEN,Victor Leslie 2Lt ded 22-7-18 26RFus p67

CORBET,George Frederick Francis 2Lt dow 25-1-16 WelshR p126 CR Surrey160

CORBET,John Hugh T2Lt kia 13-1-18 KSLI &RFC p15&144 CR France1276

CORBET,Reginald Vincent Campbell Lt kia 25-4-15 1RDubF p176 MR4

CORBET,Roland James.Bart.Lt kia 15-4-15 3CldGds p51 CR France279

CORBETT,Alfred Edward TCapt kia 1-7-16 11BordR p116 MR21

CORBETT,Charles Crauston TCapt ded 31-1/3-2-18 RAVC p268 CR Belgium18,Cranston 3-2-18

CORBETT,Charles Harold Maj kia 13-5-15 18Huss p23 CR Belgium126

CORBETT,Cyril Dudley Hely LtCol 4-12-18 RAMC &RAF CR Mddx26

CORBETT,David Bertram T2Lt kia 3-7-16 17RIrRif p169 CR France232

CORBETT,Frank Harvey.MC.TCaptAMaj kia 5-5-18 B75RFA p27 CR France745

CORBETT,Frederick St.John Chap3Cl ded 14-3-19 3Lond p269 CR Mddx34

CORBETT,Harry 2Lt kia 23-7-16 1Dev att1/6Glouc p76 MR21

CORBETT,Herbert Vincent Capt kia 17-10-18 1Camb att11Ess p244 CR France441

CORBETT,John Whitworth 2Lt kia 14-7-17 8N&D p233 CR France1489

CORBETT,Reginald David de la Cour Maj ded 25-12-17 IA 48Pnrs attRFC p275 CR Iraq8

CORBETT-WILSON,Denys Lt kia 10-5-15 RFC p1 CR France924

CORBIN,Charles Robert Peel TLt dow 21-10-16 11Worc p108 CR Greece7

CORBIN,Christopher Lt kia 5-6-17 RGA 141HB p39 CR Belgium2

CORBISHLEY,Ronald Heathcote 2Lt kia 28-7-17 8Dev &57RFC p6&76 CR Belgium149

CORBITT,John Frederick Lt ded 1-1-17 RDC p253 CR Numb3

CORBOLD,Henry Maurice Lt ded 26-8-16 19RFC p2 CR France528

CORBRIDGE,Arthur.MC.T2Lt kia 20-5-17 4Lpool p71 CR France434

CORBYN,Edwin Christian LtCol kia 1-12-17 IA 18Lancers p275 CR France417

CORCORAN,Alban Thomas 2Lt dow 2-12-17 3 att2YLI p142 CR Belgium20

CORCORAN,William James Maj dow 25-10-14 5Mddx p146 CR France80

CORDER,Hugh Gerald Annerley Lt kia 9-5-15 WelshR p126 MR22

CORDER,Terence Spence Lt 13-4-21 RFA CR Iraq6

CORDES,Hugh de Bary.MC.2Lt kia 27-9-18 1ScotsGds p52 CR France1497

CORDEUX,Edward Henry Noble Lt kia 1-10-15 7N&D p233 CR Belgium122

CORDINER,Roy Grote.MC.TCapt kia 4-10-17 8Lincs p74 MR30

CORDNER,James,MC TLt kia 16-4-18 17RIrRif p169 CR Belgium64

CORDNER,James Henry TLt dow 8-8-18 15TankCps p188 CR France699

CORDON,Henry James 2Lt dow 17-10-16 2Wilts att21TMB p152 CR Hamps1

CORE,Charles Gooch 2Lt kia 10-8-17 11RFus p67 MR29

COREN,Edward Walker 2Lt dow 15-6-15 RFA p27 CR Belgiumn165

CORFIELD,A.B Sister 2-2-16 QAIMNS CR Egypt3

CORFIELD,Egerton Anson Frederick T2Lt dow 17-6-17 153RFA p27 CR France200

CORFIELD,Frederick.J.A.Lt 19-10-20 1/1 O&BLI CR Ches56

CORFIELD,Herbert Roy Lt dow 5-11-17 266RFA p207 CR Palestine1,Hubert Ray 2Lt

CORFIELD,Hubert Vernon Auchitel T2Lt kia 6-7-16 7ELancs p110 MR21,Anchitel,7-7-16

CORISH,Thomas Power T2Lt kia 16-9-16 12Lpool p71 MR21

CORKE,Frederick William 2Lt kia 10-4-18 10Lincs p74 MR32

CORKE,Guy Harold T2Lt kia 17-9-16 15 att22NumbF p60 CR France402,15 att12Bn

CORKE,Hubert William T2Lt kia 19-4-16 10Glouc C'Coy p106 CR France149

CORKER,Francis Llewelyn Lt kia 4-6-16 14WelshR p126 MR19,5/6-6-16

CORKILL,Ernest 2Lt kia 28-2-17 4LancF p92 CR France390

CORKRAN,Reginald Seymour 2Lt dow 15-6-15 2GrenGds SR p49 CR Surrey45,11-6-15

CORLESS,John Stanley T2Lt kia 17/19-9-18 2N&D p133 MR16

CORLETT,Douglas Lt ded 9-10-16 RIM p275 CR Iraq6

CORLETT,Douglas Stephen TLtACapt dow 12-11-18 3RFus p67 CR France146

CORLEY,Edward Cecil T2Lt kia 23-2-17 7RWKent p140 MR21

CORLEY,Frederick Charles 2Lt kia 12-4-18 BordR att8Bn p116 MR32

CORLEY,William Raymond.MID T2Lt kia 27-3-18 9ESurr p112 MR27

CORMAC-WALSHE,Edward Joseph Capt dow 5-11-14 2Leinst p174 CR France102

CORMAC-WALSHE,Henry Capt dow 7-11-17 125/29RH&FA p27 CR Belgium16,Harry

CORMACK,Reginald Ormiston 12Lt kia 1-7-16 15DLI p160 MR21

CORMACK,Sidney.MC.2Lt dow 19-11-17 D15RFA p27 CR France146,19-11-18

CORN,Frederick T2Lt kia 29-4-18 2Ess p131 CR France250

CORNABY,George Ernest.MCABar.TCapt dow 23-9-18 11RFus p67 CR France34

CORNABY,Hubert Arthur T2Lt kia 15-7-16 10Yorks p90 MR21

CORNELIUS,Cecil Victor Powell Lt kia10-11-14 3WelshR p126 MR29

CORNELIUS,Frank Stuart.MC.T2Lt kia 3-10-17 8Dev p76 CR Belgium112

CORNELIUS,Herbert Walter T2Lt kia 20-7-18 1Beds p85 MR32

CORNELL,Arthur George T2Lt kia 7-7-16 9NumbF p60 MR21

CORNER,Cecil Gerald Sedgeley Lt,ded 29-12-20 IA 1MS p275 CR Egypt6,Sedgerley

CORNER,Edward Franklin T2Lt kia 25-9-15 8RKent p57 MR19

CORNER,Herbert Edward TLt ded 30-10-17 GL attGoldCoastR p201 CR Hamps13

CORNES,Henry Percy Griffiths T2Lt kia 27-9-17 23RFus att99TMB p67 CR France163

CORNFOOT,David Henry Harman Capt ded 2-5-16 9Lond p247 CR Lond8

CORNFORD,Ross Lt kia 17-8-17 GL 7RSuss att22RFC p6 CR Belgium132

CORNFORD,William Day 2Lt kia 22-7-16 1RWKent p140 MR21

CORNFORTH,Norman Leslie T2Lt kia 18-1-18 2RFC p15 CR France98

CORNISH,Charles Lawson Lt kia 13-11-14 2HLI p162 MR29

CORNISH,William Oliver T2Lt kia 20-9-17 GL &32RFC p6 MR20

CORNOCK-TAYLOR,Gerald Oldroyd.OBE ALtCol ded 14-2-19 SL p201 CR France1512,CBE GL

CORNWALLIS,Fiennes Wykeham Mann Capt kld 15-5-21 17Lancers CR Kent239

CORNWELL,Joseph T2Lt dow 29-5-16 13RSuss p118 CR France80

CORP,Benjamin.MC.Capt kia 18-9-16 1WYorks p81&258 MR21

CORRALL,Arthur 2Lt dow 24-12-15 2Dors p124 CR Iraq1

CORRIDON,Vesey Richard T2Lt dow 8-10-16 55MGC p182 CR France74,3-10-16

CORRIDON,W.J.Capt 19-11-17 IMS MR43

CORRIE,William Ronald 2Lt dow 23-4-17 1 att8EYorks p84 CR France40

CORRIGALL,John.MID LtACapt dow 8-5-18 5SfthH p241 CR Scot871

CORRIGAN,Francis Stanislaus TLt kia 31-8-18 13Lpool p71 France433 Ex Lancs

CORRIS,William Henry 2LtACapt dow 31-8-18 1RB p178 CR France14

CORRY,Armar Valentine Lowry.MC.Lt kia 12-9-16 1GrenGds p49

CORRY,E.J.Lt 18-3-20 WYorks CR Yorks447

CORRY,Frank Moring 2Lt dow 13-12-17 8N&D att65RFC p18&233,7Bn CR Belgium11,12-12-17

CORRY,John Beaumont.DSO.Maj kia 5-11-14 RE p44 CR France706

CORRY-SMITH,A.C.Lt 30-12-20 Mon CR War7

CORSCADDEN,Francis Theodore George T2Lt dow 18-6-16 14RIrRif p169 CR France44

CORSCADEN,James Noel 2Lt kia 17-10-18 4 att6InniskF p104 CR France190

CORSE-SCOTT,Alexander Capt ded 13-3-19 RScots p254 CR Scot711

CORTIS,John Halsted 2Lt kia 15-6-15 3 att2Wilts p152 MR22

CORTLANDT-ANDERSON,Harry Frederick Lt dow 14-2-17 102Grndrs CR Iraq5

CORY,Charles Willoughby 2Lt kia 12-8-15 5Suff p217 MR4,Woolnough

CORY,Cyril Noel Capt kia 31-10-16 RFA attTMB p27 CR France394

CORY,E.Q.2Lt ded 9-8-18 3RRofCav CR Beds8

COSENS,Harold Stanley Frederick Lt kia 27-10-14 1EYorks p84 CR France82

COSGROVE,Albert Bruce T2Lt dow 31-5-16 22NumbF p60 CR France208,acckld

COSGROVE,Gordon Sallnow T2Lt kld 4-11-17 GL &RFC p6 CR Lond14

COSSAR,James 2Lt dow 16-8-16 3 att12HLI p162 CR France145

COSSAR,Norman Thomson T2Lt kia 15-5-17 7RB p178 CR France594

COSSER,George Alfred Lt ded 15-5-16 6Hamps p229 MR38

COSTA,Luigi Gausche T2Lt kld 19-3-18 RFC p15

COSTEKER,John Henry Diver,DSO BtMaj kia 25-4-15 RWar 88InfBde 29Div p64 CR Gallipoli15,Dives

COSTELLO,Archibald Gordon 2Lt kia 15-9-16 17Lond p250 CR France432

COSTELLO,Edward William Lt kia 1-7-16 3RInniskF att87MGC Inf p104&182 MR21

COSTELLO,Gabriel Patrick T2Lt kia 16-8-15 5RIrReg p88 MR4

COSTER,Cecil Vincent.MC.TLt kia 24-9-18 17MGC Cav p182&258 CR Palestine11 Ex WKentYeo

COSTER,Ernest.MC.T2LtACapt kia 26-9-17 1/2RWFus p97 MR30

COSTER-EDWARDS,John Francis Capt dow 11-11-18 3 att24RWFus p34 CR France34

COSTIN,Bruce Duffus LtTCapt dow 24-10-14 1WYorks p81 CR France102

COSTIN,Henry William 2Lt kia 1-8-17 10RWKent p140 MR29

COSTLEY,Horace George Thompson Maj kia 7-2-16 IA 44Inf p275 MR38,Thomson

COTCHIN,Joseph 2Lt kia 9-10-17 1Beds p85 MR30

COTES,Digby Charles Bathe TCapt dow 15-10-18 7NStaffs p157 CR Belgium20

COTGRAVE,Christopher Russell Farmar Capt ded 29-12-17 Worc att100TMB p108

COTHILL,William Henry Thomas T2Lt kia 23-10-18 1Beds p85 CR France1476

COTMAN,R.A.TLt kia 26-3-18 4RFC p15 CR France98,2Lt

COTSWORTH,John Henry 2Lt kia 28-9-18 4Ches p222 CR France364

COTTAM,Clement John T2Lt kia 18-12-15 4Mddx p146 CR France682,19-12-15

COTTAM,Horace Charles Bowman.MC.Capt kia 30-9-18 7Hamps p229 CR France357

COTTAM,Hubert Frank 2Lt kia 23-3-18 3 att7Y&L p158 MR20,28-3-18

COTTEN,Leonard John Lionel.MC.Lt ded 13-6-20 Hamps CR Hamps10

COTTER,George Edmund Sackville Capt ded 19-4-17 RGA p262 CR Norf101,RA

COTTER,George Herbert 2Lt kia 12-4-15 5Lond p246 CR Belgium71

COTTER,Harold Cecil 2Lt kia 10-4-18 1/2 att11LancF p92 MR32

COTTER,Harry John.CIE.DSO.BrigGen ded 28-6-21 Late RA MR40

COTTERELL,Basil William 2Lt kia 30-10-18 3N&D attRAF p133 CR Belgium241

COTTERELL,Frederick Hampson Lt dow 16-12-16 5SStaffs p229 CR France300,acckld

COTTERELL,Robert Victor 2Lt kia 23-4-17 5 att8SStaffs p229 MR20

COTTERILL,Arthur Capt kia 21-3-18 5NStaffs p237 MR20

COTTERILL,Denis TCapt ded 2-12-18 RAMC att20CCS p195 CR France441,50CCS

COTTERILL,Frank T2Lt dow 11-11-18 Y&L p158 CR France289

COTTERILL,Harold Gordon Knight Lt ded 6-6-17 RFA att35RFC p6&27,dow CR France234

COTTERILL,John Henry 2Lt dow 15-3-17 3 att2BlkW p128 MR38

COTTIER,Walter Kaneen 2Lt dedacc 23-8-18 1/8 att1/6Lpool p215 CR France34

COTTLE,Frank Lt ded 9-2-19 RASC p267 CR Ches182 Ex RE

COTTLE,Sidney Joseph TLt kia 31-7-17 Dev attMGC p76 CR Belgium113

COTTLE,Walter Edward Worsdale Lt kia 31-7-17 GrenGds att1GdsBde MGR p49&53 MR29

COTTON,Arthur Edward 2Lt kia 7-7-16 13Ches p95 MR21

COTTON,Aubrey Nightingale TCapt kia 30-6-16 12RSuss p118 CR France631

COTTON,Brian Gordon Hamilton Capt dow 8-11-17 2/17Lond p250 CR Palestine1

COTTON,Harold Temple.DSO.LtCol kia 3-9-16 2SLancs p125 MR21

COTTON,Herbert Joseph Maj ded 23-5-16 IA 99Inf att76Punjabis p275 CR Iraq8

COTTON,John T2Lt dow 1-7-16 150RFA p27 CR France141

COTTON,Montague Arthur Finch Capt kia 18-5-15 6Lond p246 CR France260

COTTON,Ralph Charles Fairbairn.MID Lt dow 28-3-18 1/1HampsYeo attMGC p187&203 CR France1799

COTTON,Robert Douglas.MC.2Lt ded 5-4-19 14Lond p249 CR Hereford110

COTTON,Robert Hugh Alban T2Lt ded 12-10-18 RASC p192 CR Italy6

COTTON,William John Stanley T2Lt dow 23-8-17 Suff p78 CR Belgium172,Norf att1/4Bn

COTTON,William Martin Vernon 2Lt kia 21-12-16 GL &RFC p2&190 MR20

COTTON,Willoughby Lynch Capt ded 6-1-18 SL KSLI p201 CR Shrop19

COTTRELL,George Frederick 2Lt kia 11-5-15 RGA 108HB p39 CR Belgium135

COTTRELL,Harold William 2Lt kia 30-9-16 2SLancs p125 CR France832

COTTRELL,John Prince T2Lt dow 24-8-18 1RWKent att7RFus p140 CR France84

COTTRELL,Leonard Samuel Joscelyn TLt kia 13-4-18 9ACycCps p181 MR32

COTTRELL,Percy Bagliatto.MC.MID TLt dow 27-9-18 GL p190 CR Greece1,Baglietto

COTTRELL-DORMER,Charles Melville.DSO.Lt dow 8-2-15 3CldGds p51 CR France80

COTTRELL-DORMER,Clement Lt kia 27-10-14 2ScotsGds p52 MR29,26-10-14

COUCHE,Henry John.MC.Lt kia 9-1-20 MGC p266 CR Asia81

COUCHER,George Walter 2Lt kia 15-4-18 4 O&BLI p231 CR France248,16-4-18

COUCHMAN,Cyril Seymour 2Lt kia 8-5-17 2/6NStaffs p238 MR21

COUGHLAN,Julius Edward.MC.DCM.ACapt kia 25-10-16 1Mddx p146 MR21

COULDREY,Douglas John 2Lt dow 31-10-17 24 att2/22Lond p252 CR Palestine1

COULDRIDGE,Jack Oswald Lt kia 6-11-16 12 att2Worc p108 MR21

COULES,Eric Allan Gifford 2Lt kia 28-10-17 RE 129FC p44 CR France527

COULL,Andrew Mearns T2Lt kia 3-7-17 RE 178TC p44 CR France439

COULL,John Frederick TLt kia 30-9-18 RFus att23Bn p67 CR France914

COULL,James Christie Lt ded 13-2-19 RFA p269 CR Numb96

COULSON,Arthur.MM.2Lt kia 27-3-18 NumbF att1/5Bn p60 CR France526

COULSON,Coulson Tregarthen.MC.Capt dow 8-9-18 RGA 546SB p209 CR France100

COULSON,Jack Baxter 2Lt dow 20-6-16 5Lincs p220 CR France1

COULSON-MAYNE,Eric William Lt dow 25-4-17 5DLI D'Coy p238 CR France120

COULTAS,Thomas Bestwick TLt kia 26-9-18 6EYorks p84 CR France251

COULTER,Sidney T2Lt kia 25-8-18 12Manch p154 CR France402

COULTER,Thomas 2Lt ded 25-11-19 RASC p267 CR Egypt9,Lt

COULTER,Walter McFarlane.MC.Capt kia 20-5-17 6 att8HLI p240 MR20

COULTER,William Hugh Lt kia 22-2-15 5Lancers p21 CR Belgium57

COULTARD,Ernest TLt ded 12-11-18 RASC attCanadaForestryCps p192 CR France1798

COULTARD,Eustace Frank T2Lt kia 6-4-16 9 att1 O&BLI p130 MR38

COULTHWAITE,James 2Lt kia 5-8-17 5BordR p228 CR France614

COULTHURST,Temple Capt kia 11-10-18 6WRid p227 CR France612

COULTON,Aubrey Ewan Capt kia 20-7-16 6Norf att6RWar p217 MR32,19-7-16

COUNSELL,Christopher Herbert 2Lt dow 6-7-16 3 att2Hamps p120 CR France169

COUNSELL,Henry Cecil 2Lt kia 27-5-18 45RFA p27 MR18

COUNSELLOR,Thomas Bell Small.MM.2Lt ded 8-12-18 7NumbF p214 CR Belgium330

COUNT,William Charles LtACapt kia 5-7-17 63/14RFA p27 CR France570

COUPAR,Sydney Bell Nicoll.MID Capt ded 30-12-18 7A&SH p243 CR France512

COUPE,Albert Capt kia 9-4-17 9Lpool p216 MR20

COUPE,Thomas Harold Lt ded 26-7-17 4ELancs attRFC p18&226 CR Lancs199,kld

COUPER,Charles Miller Capt dow PoW 28-9-15 4BlkW D'Coy p230 CR France347

COUPER,James Mudie Lt dow PoW 4-4-18 B256RFA p207 CR France1252

COUPER,John Ralph TLtACapt kia 15-11-16 10LNLancs p135 MR21

COUPLAND,Henry Lt dow 24-4-15 5RLancs p213 CR France284

COUPLAND,John Charles Gerald Lt kia 6-5-17 RFA &2RFC p6 MR20

COUPLAND-SMITH,Frederick Vyvyan TLt kia 2-7-17 173RFA p27 CR Belgium62

COURAGE,Godfrey Michell.MID T2Lt kia 1-7-16 6RBerks p139 CR France513

COURT,Eric McClintock Wathen TCapt kia 6-8-16 13 att4Worc p108 MR4

COURT,Gordon Frederick 2Lt kia 16-9-16 MGC HvyBrch p182 MR21

COURT,Reginald Walter Southwood 2Lt kia 26-3-17 1Hereford p252 MR34

COURT,Richard T2Lt kia 9-4-18 RLancs p58 MR19

COURT,Robert Ambrey TCapt kia 26-4-17 9WYorks att8WRid p81 CR France529

COURT,William Hubert Roylance Capt kia 24-5-15 9Lancers p22

COURTENAY,Arthur Patrick 2Lt dow 28-6-15 IARO att8Cav p275 MR66,Lt

COURTENAY,Hugh.DSO.MC.BtMajALtCol dow 23-8-18 1Beds p85 CR France84

COURTENAY,K.S. see COURTNAY,K.S.

COURTENAY,Michael Hudson LtCol dow 4-1-16 RGA Cmdg1HB p39 CR Iraq1

COURTHOPE,William George Lt ded 21-10-18 4Beds &RAF p85 CR France1858

COURTHOPE-MUNROE,John Wilfrid T2Lt ded 24-1-16 RASC 597MTCoy p192 CR Egypt3,Wilfred

COURTICE,G.R.A.Rev 3-6-17 IndEcclesDept MR65

COURTICE,Reginald Leyster T2Lt kia 2-7-16 8Lincs p74 MR21

COURTIS,John Harold.MIDx2 Capt kia 22-11-15 1 O&BLI p130 MR38

COURTNAY,Kilcoursie Sigismond Lt kia 11-8-18 3Dors p124 CR France360,COURTENAY Sigismund

COURTNEY,Edward Derek Lt ded 9-8-18 55RASC MT'Coy GHQ TrpSplyCol 192 CR France40

COURTNEY,F.Capt 17-7-20 LabCps CR Wales613 Ex RWFus

COUSANS,Guy Newson 2Lt kia 9-9-16 3InnisF att70RFC p2&264,Newsome CR France23

COUSENS,George Edward T2Lt kia 24-8-18 Mddx att1/8Bn p146 CR France214

COUSIN,Arthur Norman TCapt kia 7-12-17 12Y&L p158 CR France184

COUSIN,John Denholm Lt kia 9-4-18 4HLI p162 MR32

COUSINS,Charles Hope 2Lt dow 27-4-15 1Ess p131 MR4

COUSINS,Donald Threlkeld 2Lt kia 10-4-17 4EKent p212 CR France420

COUSINS,Eric Cyril 2Lt kia 21-3-18 13 att2N&D p133 MR20

COUSINS,Leonard T2Lt kia 14-4-17 1Ess p131 MR20

COUTTS,Norman Vawdrey 2Lt dow 26-9-15 9ESurr p112 MR19

COUTTS,Paul Campbell T2Lt kia 23-8-18 MGC p182 CR France239

COUTTS,Robert Disher Lt kia 25/27-9-15 4GordH p241 MR29

COUTTS,Walter Gordon T2Lt kld 2-12-17 GL &RFC p6

COUTTS,William Ernest Capt kia 22-3-18 6BlkW p231 CR France245,dow

COVELL,Howard Charles T2Lt ded 26-6-16 C69RFA p27 CR Iraq6

COVENEY,William Robert 2Lt ded 23-7-19 RE 303RdConst p262 CR Kent179

COVENTRY,Edgar Ernest Capt kia 1-11-14 1ELancs p110 CR Belgium68

COVENTRY,Eric T2Lt kia 20-7-16 20RFus p67 MR21 See ZEEDERBERG real name

COVENTRY,Leslie Corbett Capt kia 27-5-18 NottsYeo p205 MR41,drd

COVENTRY,William St.John.MID Lt kia 22-10-14 Beds p85 MR22

COVENTRY,Wyndham John Capt dow 1-1-16 IA 7Lancers p275 CR Iraq5

COVENTRY-DAVIES,Charles Capt ded 7-8-19 GL &11RWFus p266 CR France1775

COVINGTON,Edwin Thornton 2Lt kia 9-3-17 4ESurr att6NLancs p112 MR38

COWAN,Albert Arthur 2Lt ded 16-7-18 RFA &RAF p27 CR Egypt9

COWAN,Adam TLt kia 18-11-16 RE 82FC p44 CR France215

COWAN,Andrew Galbraith Maj murdered 1-6-15 IA 74Punjabis att53Sikhs p275 CR Egypt15

COWAN,Basil Terence Reilly Lt kia 6-8-15 Lincs attManch p75 MR4

COWAN,Charles John Alexander Capt dow 25-3-18 3RScots p53 CR France699

COWAN,Dennis Walker Lt ded 2-11-18 RFA p269 CR Lancs14

COWAN,Douglas Henderson 2Lt kia 26-8-14 1Hamps p120 MR15

COWAN,Eric Hamilton Lt ded 28-2-16 RGA p209 CR Lancs14

COWAN,George Deas.MID Maj kia 23-4-18 9RScots p212 CR France248

COWAN,Henry Vivian.CB.CVO.Col ded 24-1-18 RA p27 CR Devon37

COWAN,James.MM.2Lt ded 25-10-18 ScotHorse p205 CR Scot212

COWAN,John Grave Capt kia 16-8-15 4Ess p232 MR4

COWAN,John Orr Craig Capt kia 14-7-16 3RScots p53 CR France399

COWAN,Philip Chalmers Capt kia 8-11-17 8Manch attRFC p18&237 MR20

COWAN,Reginald Percival T2Lt ded 16-8-15 6BordR p116 MR4

COWAN,Robert Craig 2Lt kia 24-10-14 3RScots p53 MR22

COWAN,Ronald 2LtTLt kia 13-7-15 6HLI p240 CR Gallipoli1,dow

COWAN,Sidney Edward.MC&2Bars.TCapt kia 17-11-16 29RFC p2 CR France647

COWAN,William Wilson Lt kia 14-4-17 8RScots attRFC p211 CR Scot239,6-6-19 &CR France583,14-4-17

COWARD,Henry TLt dow 20-4-17 1BordR p116 CR France120

COWARD,John Bayman 2Lt kld 26-3-18 RFC p15 CR France300

COWARD,Leslie Graham Capt kia 25-9-15 5 att1Mddx p146 CR France114

COWD,Arthur Martin Chap4Cl ded 22-12-18 RAChDept att81FA p199 CR France1571

COWDELL,Charles Joseph Morton T2Lt kia 12-9-17 RE 212FC p44 CR Belgium37

COWDEROY,Horace 2Lt kia 15-9-16 20Lond p251 CR France432

COWDY,Harold Evans T2Lt kia 16-8-17 9RIrF p171 MR30

COWE,Archibald TCapt kia 2-12-17 RAMC att2Lincs p195 MR30

COWELL,Albert Victor John Capt ded 29-1-15 6RB p178 CR Yorks106

COWELL,Charles Stanley TLt ded 13-4-17 GL &RFC p190 CR Durham28

COWELL,George Edmund Maurice Maj kia 30-12-17 RFA p206 CR France398

COWELL,Henry Pulleine John Maj dow 9-8-15 RFA p27 MR4

COWELL,Jocelyn Gore 2Lt kld 28-1-18 RFus attRFC p15&67 CR Dorset70

COWELL,John Edward 2Lt kia 29-11-17 NStaffs att2/6Bn p157 MR17

COWEN,Henry Walter 2Lt kia 29-9-18 RGA 6SB p39 CR France528

COWHERD,John.MC.T2Lt kia 29-9-18 5 att4Worc p108 CR Belgium112

COWIE,Alexander Gordon Capt dow 6-4-16 SfthH p164 CR Iraq5

COWIE,Arthur William Spring T2Lt kia 8-7-16 7Lincs p75 CR France397

COWIE,Daniel MacDougall TCapt dow 17-9-16 10/11HLI p162 CR France197

COWIE,George 2Lt kia 22-10-17 GL &54RFC p6 CR Belgium125

COWIE,Gerald James Hardwicke.MC.T2Lt kia 23-4-17 10RFus p67&258 MR20

COWIE,Henry Benedict T2Lt kia 10-7-16 10WelshR p126 CR France297

COWIE,Hugh Norman Ramsay.CMG.DSO.Maj dow 20-5-15 1Dors p124 WestWoodhayChurchyard Berks

COWIE,John George Capt ded 26-2-19 6GordH p269 CR Scot838

COWIE,Lionel Jack Hardwicke T2Lt kia 24-4-17 2RFus p67 MR20

COWIE,William T2Lt dow 28-9-16 13RScots p53 CR France40

COWIE,William Anderson.MC.LtACapt kia 30-5-18 9RWFus p97 MR18

COWIN,Henry Hampton T2Lt kia 1-7-16 21Manch p154 CR France397

COWING,Ralph Henry 2Lt dow 15-7-15 3Y&L p158 CR France285

COWL,John Douglas 2Lt kia 23-4-17 4EYorks p219 MR20

COWLAND,Herbert Samuel 2Lt kia 15-4-17 291RFA p27&208 CR France568

COWLEY,Alexander 2Lt kia 1-7-17 8N&D p233 MR19

COWLEY,Charles Selwyn Lt kia 9-5-15 1Nhampt p137 MR22

COWLEY,Francis Llewellyn ACapt ded 18-3-19 RE p262 CR Kent46

COWLEY,Frank Wheatley.MC.TLt dow 9-8-18 11EYorks att92LightTMB p84 CR France134

COWLEY,Frederick John Bodenham T2Lt kia 11-8-18 Glouc att1Dors p106 CR France360,Bodnum

COWLEY,George Evelyn.MID TMaj dow PoW 18-6-18 8RDubF p176 CR France716

COWLEY,Victor Travers TLt kia 23-7-18 7/8KOSB C'Coy p101 CR France865

COWLING,Alexander 2Lt kia 26-4-18 1Camb p245 MR30

COWLING,Frederick Watkin 2Lt dow 20-10-18 5DLI p239 CR France337

COWMAN,Frederick Gregory.DCM.2Lt kia 28-9-18 6Lpool p215 CR France914

COWPE,George Bleazard Lt kia 31-7-17 6Ches p222 MR29

COWPER,Frank Neville 2Lt kia 12-10-16 7Suff p78 MR21

COWPER,Geoffrey Moore.MID TCapt dow 3-10-18 RAMC attDors p195 CR France113

COWPER,Gordon Capt ded 2-2-19 9GordH p166 CR Belgium321

COWPER,Leonard Harris T2Lt dow 7-11-16 32 att20NumbF p60 CR France297

COWPER,Ronald Macphail T2Lt kia 27-4-16 14HLI p162 CR France423

COWPER-COLES,S.W.Capt kld 14-10-18 RASC &RAF p192 CR Belgium18

COWTAN,Francis Scott Capt kia 24/25-4-17 WiltsYeo att7Wilts p206 CR Greece5

COX,Albert Henry 2Lt kia 24-7-16 RGA 109SB p39 CR France397

COX,Arthur George T2Lt kia 15-12-17 GL &42RFC p6 CR Italy7

COX,Arthur Johnson T2Lt kia 3-5-17 8EYorks p84 CR France924

COX,Cecil Arthur TCapt dow 16-10-16 26RFus p67 CR France121

COX,Cecil John 2Lt dow 24-4-18 RGA 331SB p39 CR France37,Lt

COX,Charles Frederick Lt kia 31-3-18 3N&D p133 CR France988

COX,Clarence Frederick Stuart.MC.TLt kia 29-10-17 10N&D p133 CR Belgium87

COX,Clarence Rupert TCapt dow 13-4-17 12RSuss &RFC att5Wing p6&118 CR Egypt2

COX,Derek Percy 2Lt kia 21-8-17 GL &27RFC p6 CR France924

COX,Douglas Weld 2Lt dow 17-5-15 3Suff p78 CR Belgium383,Lt

COX,Edgar William.DSO.MajABrigGen drd 26-8-18 RE StaffGHQ 1stEch p44 CR France40

COX,Ernest 2Lt dow 8-12-17 3 att7SomLI A'Coy p79 CR France319

COX,Eustace Richard Alan Calthrop.MC.Capt ded 18-3-17 3Dev p76 CR Berks19

COX,Francis Henry 2Lt kia 23-10-16 1RWar p64 MR21

COX,Frederick Percy 2LtTCapt kia 3-5-17 3 att9Leic p87 MR20

COX,George Beckett 2Lt kia 16-8-17 7Lond p247 MR29

COX,George Cyril Addison.MC.Capt 2-6-21 1BordR MR43

COX,George Henry Lt kia 30-10-14 3 att2KOSB p101 MR22

COX,George Pottinger Capt kia 24-12-15 1Ess p131 CR Gallipoli1

COX,George Walker Capt kia 3-5-17 1RWar att1Ess p64 MR20,Maj

COX,Harleigh Capt kia 3-7-16 8Glouc Res p106 MR21

COX,Harold 2Lt dow 16-4-18 12Lond attMGC Inf p187&248 CR Belgium168

COX,Harold Edward Leys Capt kia 1-7-16 9Lond p247 MR21

COX,Henry Bowerie TCapt kia 8-8-16 1/5Lpool p215 MR21,Harry

COX,Henry George 2Lt kia 3-7-16 EKent p57 CR France251

COX,Henry Hayr 2Lt kld 16-5-17 A64RFA attRFC p208 CR France98

COX,Henry Jack TCapt kia 31-7-17 12RFus p67 CR Belgium112

COX,Hugh Bertram Hamilton 2Lt kld 29-1-17 RFA &RFC p6&27 CR Lancs403,Lt

COX,John Alonzo.DSO.Maj kia 29-9-18 1HighCycBn att12HLI p253 CR Belgium88

COX,John James 2Lt dow 29-5-15 2Leic p87 CR France345,Lt

COX,John Lennox Lt kia 19-9-18 4 att11ScotRif p103 CR Greece5

COX,John Ramsay Capt kia 11-3-15 6Worc p108 MR22

COX,Joseph Henry Silvanus 2LtTLt kia 30-9-17 93LabCps p189 MR30

COX,Leonard Albert T2Lt kia 10-6-18 KSLI p144 CR France547

COX,Lupton James T2Lt kia 18-4-18 1Glouc p106 CR France765

COX,Margaret Annie SNurse 7-2-19 TFNS CR Eire492

COX,Norman John TLt kia 23-8-15 7RSuss p118 CR France1140

COX,Percival Elliot Capt dow 23-5-17 4NumbF p213 CR France1184

COX,Percy Cyril 2Lt kia 28-4-17 25NumbF p60 MR20

COX,Reginald John Ponsonby Maj kia 27-9-15 A&SH att8GordH p173 MR19

COX,Richard 2Lt kld 24-8-18 2/7Mddx p235 CR France504,kia

COX,Robert Ernest 2Lt kia 11-3-15 HLI p162 MR22

COX,Robert William Talbot.MID T2Lt kia 15-2-16 6Dors p124 CR Belgium131

COX,Theodore Russell 2Lt kia 27-9-15 14DLI p160 MR19

COX,Thomas Henry 2Lt kia 21-6-17 4ScotRif p103 CR Belgium115

COX,Walter Ewart 2Lt kia 18-5-17 4Glouc Z'Coy p225 CR France1701

COX,William Charles LtCol ded 21-4-19 1/4SomLI p218 CR Egypt15

COX,William George T2Lt ded 22-9-18 RE p44 CR Iraq8

COX,William Joseph LtTCapt kia 16-5-15 1RBerks p139 CR France632

COXE,Arthur Nelson 2Lt dow 3-11-14 105RFA p27 CR Belgium135

COXE,Cecil Henry 2Lt kia 1-7-16 6RFC p2 CR France452

COXE,Eric Noel T2Lt dow 9-6-17 SStaffs att7Bn B'Coy p122 CR France285

COXHEAD,Maurice Edward CaptTMaj kia 3-5-17 9RFus p67 CR France1182

COXON,Herbert Archibald 2Lt kia 1-7-16 14Lond p249 MR21

COXON,Percy Hunter.MC.TCapt kia 13-4-18 8BordR p116 CR Belgium168

COXON,William Basil 2Lt kia 11-4-18 NumbF p60 CR France297

COXON,William Hugh 2Lt kia 11-3-15 3N&D p133 MR22

COXSON,Lawrence Frederick 2Lt kia 17-10-16 12RSuss p118 CR France383

COXWELL,W.S.G.Lt dow 18-10-17 RhodR att2KAR p202 CR Tanzania1,att1Bn

COY,Alfred Reginald 2Lt kia 2-7-16 7WYorks p218 MR21

COY,John Christopher Capt kia 27-9-18 12/13NumbF GarrBn p60 CR France415

COYLE,Clement William Lt ded 19-2-19 GL Cmd &Staff p190 CR France1028

COYLE,Leonard Joseph T2Lt kia 23-11-16 10KRRC p149 MR21

COYNE,Cecil Thomas TCapt dow 27-8-17 9WYorks p81 CR Belgium83

COYNE,John Joseph Aloysius T2Lt kia 10-8-17 9RDubF p176 MR29

COZENS,Leslie Capt dow 14-10-15 5SStaffs p229 CR France98

COZENS-BROOKE,John Gilbert Somerset Lt kia 18-10-14 3 att1RScots p94 MR29

COZENS-HARDY,Raven 2Lt kia 9-10-17 4Norf p216 MR30

CRABB,Leonard George Bruce 2Lt kia 12-3-15 2ESurr p112 CR Belgium168

CRABB,Thomas Henry,MC 2Lt dow 18-3-16 4RFus p67 CR Belgium11

CRABBE,Campbell Tempest Eyre Lt kia 27-9-15 3GrenGds p49 MR19

CRABBE,Hubert Lyon Bingham 2Lt kia 15-5-18 3Huss &RAF p21 CR France513

CRABBE,John T2Lt dow 6-5-16 13RScots p53 CR France257

CRABTREE,Fred Walmseley TLt kia 15-8-15 7Yorks p90 CR Belgium111

CRABTREE,John Hebron 2Lt kia 26-9-17 4KSLI p235 MR30

CRABTREE,Lawrence C.T2Lt kia 24-4-18 WYorks p81 CR France424

CRABTREE,Stephen Mark Lt kia 28-6-16 18EYorks p84 CR France744

CRABTREE,Walker.MM.T2Lt kia 21-8-18 1SomLI p79 CR France250,Walter

CRABTREE,William 2Lt ded 10-2-15 8Lincs p75 CR Yorks500

CRACKNELL,Charles George Raphael Lt dow 29-12-17 1 att2/24Lond p252 CR Palestine3

CRACROFT,Robert Brian Lt kia 10-7-16 3EYorks p84 CR France453,7Bn

CRACROFT-WILSON,Clive Winthorpe TLt ded 12-11-18 4SWBord p99 MR65

CRADDOCK,Percy Frederick Capt kia 25-2-17 6RWFus p223 CR Belgium23

CRADDOCK,Reginald 2Lt kia 21-3-18 5NStaffs p238 MR20

CRADDOCK,Victor 2Lt dow 11-10-18 5SStaffs p229 CR France375

CRADOCK WATSON,Arthur Vivian See WATSON,A.V.C.

CRAFTER,James.MC.Lt ded 7-7-17 PoW 20Lond attRFC p18&251 MR20

CRAGG,John Francis T2Lt kia 1/3-7-16 8Lincs p75 MR21,1-7-16

CRAGG,Sydney Bolton T2Lt kia 9-11-17 GL &25RFC p6 CR France1553

CRAGGS,John James 2Lt kia 17-2-17 6 att1KRRC p149 CR France251

CRAGGS,Mabel Olive Nurse 20-1-15 BRCS CR France461

CRAGGS,Percival 2Lt kia 30-9-18 13Y&L p158 CR Belgium451

CRAIG,Archibald.MC.LtACapt kia 23-3-18 3GordH att267TMB p166 MR27

CRAIG,Arthur Francis Capt dow 4-10-18 1/4RWKent att30MGC p187&234 CR France25

CRAIG,Charles Frederick T2Lt kia 3-7-16 17RIrRif p169 CR France232,10Bn

CRAIG,Donald Leslie Langford.MC.Lt kia 31-7-17 RFA p207 MR29

CRAIG,Edmund Robert T2Lt dow 1-6-16 17RScots p53 CR France80

CRAIG,Eric Ericksen T2Lt kia 30-8-16 20 att10RIrRif p169 CR Belgium43,Erichsen

CRAIG,George Barton 2Lt kia 21-2-17 60RFC p15 CR Belgium158,Lt

CRAIG,George Robert.MC.Lt kld 19-8-17 ELancs &RFC p6&110,19-7-17 CR Lancs277

CRAIG,Gordon Robert T2Lt dow 3-4-18 7Beds p85 CR France185

CRAIG,Hedley William T2Lt kia 15-4-17 RE &RFC p6&44 CR Iraq8

CRAIG,Henry David Cook.MC.MID Maj ded 13-2-20 2HLI p265 MR70

CRAIG,Isaac Murray ACapt kia 22-8-18 RE 66FC p44 CR Palestine9

CRAIG,J.2Lt kld 11-4-18 GL &RAF p190

CRAIG,James Glen.MC.2Lt kia 23-4-18 3 att2RScots p53 CR France88

CRAIG,James Young TLt dow 24-10-17 3A&SH att1/2KAR p173&202 CR EAfrica35 &CR Tanzania1

CRAIG,John Arnott Taylor T2Lt kia 1-7-16 11RInniskF D'Coy p104 CR France215

CRAIG,John Beverley 2Lt kia 3-6-17 RH&FA p208

CRAIG,John MacAdam Lt dow 1-11-14 IA 57Rif att58 p275 CR France80,McAdam

CRAIG,John William Archibald Capt dow 26-8-16 1BerksRHA attB300RFA p207 CR France53,J.W.J.26-7-16

CRAIG,Robert Clark Capt kia 22-7-17 RGA p209 CR Belgium10,215SB

CRAIG,Robert Hunter T2Lt kia 21-3-18 9NumbF p60 CR France1489

CRAIG,Robert William.MC.T2Lt kia 17-4-18 34MGC Inf p182 MR32

CRAIG,R.Stewart 2Lt kld 22-4-18 GL &RAF p190 CR France103

CRAIG,Thomas Forrest TCapt ded 2-2-18 RAMC p195 MR41,dow

CRAIG,Thomas Patrick TLt kia 22-3-18 7Leinst p174 MR27

CRAIG,Walter George 2Lt ded PoW 5-11-18 11DLI p160 CR Europe149

CRAIG,William 2Lt kia 8-5-18 5ScotRif p224 CR Belgium111

CRAIG,William Colston T2Lt dow 20-1-17 10 att6SLancs p125 CR Iraq5,Willie

CRAIG,William Tait TLtACapt kia 21-9-18 1ScotRif p103 CR France666

CRAIG,William Younger Lt kia 20-9-17 5Lpool p215 MR30

CRAIGE,George 2Lt ded 28-10-18 10Lpool p216 CR Lancs149

CRAIGHEAD,John Marr T2Lt kld 25-9-17 EKent p57 CR Belgium21

CRAIGMILE,Alexander Murray.MC.Capt kia 29-3-18 6RB p178 CR France544

CRAIK,John Beverley 2Lt 3-6-17 2(Lond)RFA CR France96

CRAIKE-PICKERING,M.S.C.MC.TLt ded 14-4-18 MGC p182 CR Sussex 110

CRAM,Hubert Arthur T2Lt dow 16-4-18 16KRRC p149 CR Belgium102

CRAM,John Edwin.MC.2Lt kia 30-9-18 4Yorks att2/4WRid p220 CR France358

CRAMB,Wilfrid Brown 2Lt kia 14-4-17 4A&SH &9RFC p6&173 CR France913,Lt

CRAMER,George L'Estrange Lt dow 16-7-15 4RMunstF p175 CR France80,kia 2Bn

CRAMER-ROBERTS,Edward Herbert 2Lt kia 10-8-15 3EKent p57 CR Belgium97,2Bn

CRAMER-ROBERTS,Walter Evelyn BtLtCol ded 12-3-19 2Norf p263 CR Lond4

CRAMP,George Herbert 2Lt dow 18-11-18 RGA 301SB p39 CR France34,233SB

CRAMPTON,Edgar Walter 2Lt kia 9-10-17 5 att2RFus p67 MR30

CRAMPTON,William.MC.Lt ded 17-2-19 A94RFA p27,2Entries CR France40

CRAMSIE,Arthur Butler Lt kia 8-5-15 2 att5NumbF p60 MR29

CRANE,Charles Edward 2Lt dow 18-9-14 1DCLI p114 CR France1107

CRANE,Herbert Donovon T2Lt kia 22-3-18 10LNLancs B'Coy p135 CR France366

CRANE,John Robert Capt ded 8-5-18 RAVC p269 CR Notts84

CRANE,Lancelot 2Lt ded 15-3-18 RGA 159HB p39 CR France40

CRANE,Lucius Francis T2Lt kia 8-10-18 14Worc p108 CR France530

CRANE,Reginald Hooper T2Lt kia 4-10-17 1EYorks p84 MR30

CRANE,William Henry Lt ded 13-3-18 GL p266 CR Norf77

CRANK,Harry T2Lt kia 22-10-17 1/2 att17LancF p92 MR30

CRANMER,Guy Paterson 2Lt kia 9-10-17 5YLI p235 MR30

CRANMORE,George William Lt kia 19-7-18 10Lond p248 CR France886

CRANSTON,Archibald Lindsay 2Lt dow 16-8-18 5KOSB p224 CR France28,1Bn

CRANSTON,John Tennent 2Lt kia 15-7-16 9HLI p240 CR France402

CRANSTON,William Weir TLt kia 18-12-17 RE 173TC p44 CR Belgium12

CRANSWICK,George Alec 2Lt kia 18-11-17 Y&L &23RFC p6&158 MR20

CRANSWICK,Gilbert 2Lt kia 26-10-16 4EYorks p219 CR France387

CRANWILL,Valentine Arthur Butler.MC.LtACapt kia 24-4-18 2ELancs p110 CR France304

CRAPP,Cyril Frederick T2Lt ?? 22-5-17 GL &78RFC p6 CR Sussex182

CRAPPER,Charles.MM.2Lt dow 26-4-18 3 att5Yorks p90 CR Yorks740

CRASTON,Frank Marshall Lt kia 28-8-17 5ELancs att13Manch p226 CR Greece5

CRASTON,John 2Lt dow 19-4-15 3 att1RWKent p140 CR Belgium165

CRATHORNE,Frederick TLt kia 14-1-16 GL attRE 252TC p190 CR France76

CRAUFURD,John Gordon Capt kia 22-11-15 IA 37Dogras att12DivSigCo p275 MR38

CRAVEN,Asa T2Lt kia 19-10-16 8 att11BlkW p128 CR France385

CRAVEN,Austen James Arthur TLt ded 27-8-18 SL &RA p201 CR Lond9,Austin

CRAVEN,Brian Thornthwaite T2Lt kia 1-7-16 RFA p27 CR France513

CRAVEN,Frank 2Lt kia 28-3-18 2WYorks p81 MR27

CRAVEN,George Alfred Senior Lt dow 15-9-17 RFA p207 CR France592

CRAVEN,George Edward Rev ded 7-12-18 RAChDept p199 CR Greece9

CRAVEN,Leo Lt ded 31-10-20 IA TC attRGA 6MtnBty p275 MR66

CRAVOS,Cyril Stephen T2Lt kia 2-3-17 GL &5RFC p6 CR Greece927

CRAWFORD,Alexander Basil TCapt kia 10-5-16 17WYorks p81 CR France631

CRAWFORD Cecil James 2Lt kia 23-10-17 7 att12Mddx D'Coy p235 MR30

CRAWFORD,Charles Noel 2Lt kia 8-4-16 1Nhampt p137 CR France551

CRAWFORD,Daniel David Dunlop Lt ded 10-12-17 RE att25RlwyCps S&M p44 CR EAfrica10 &CR Tanzania1

CRAWFORD,David Lt ded 10-12-17 IARO attS&M p275

CRAWFORD,Donald T2Lt kia 27-7-16 9MGC 99Coy p182 MR21

CRAWFORD,Edward Lt dow 27-5-15 3 att2RInniskF p104 CR France64

CRAWFORD,George Rainier.CB.Col ded 22-8-15 10WRid IA Retd p115 CR Glouc31

CRAWFORD,Gerald Shakespear Maj dow 10-8-17 6SWBord p99 CR Belgium11

CRAWFORD,James T2Lt dow 19-7-16 7CamH p167 CR France80

CRAWFORD,James Carpenter 2Lt kia 1-10-16 20Lond p251 CR France385

CRAWFORD,John Cane 2Lt kia 31-8-16 F14RHA p27 CR France397

CRAWFORD,John Russell 2Lt dow 27-9-16 13 att9N&D p133 CR France246,kia

CRAWFORD,John Stirrit 2Lt ded 5-3-19 5RScotF p269 CR Scot514

CRAWFORD,Kelvin Capt kia 11-4-18 MGC &60RAF p266 MR20

CRAWFORD,Kenneth Clark 2Lt kia 2-9-18 4RScotF p222 MR16,1 att14Bn

CRAWFORD,Reginald Waring Lindsay 2Lt dow 13-7-16 C63RFA p27 CR France51

CRAWFORD,Robert T2Lt died 15-11-18 12HLI p162 CR Scot679

CRAWFORD,Robert McLarg T2Lt kia 14-8-16 8RFus att10HLI p162 MR21,McLay

CRAWFORD,Robert Stobo 2Lt kia 17-5-15 2RScotF RoO p94 CR France279

CRAWFORD,Sydney George 2Lt drd 10-10-18 1RDubF p176 CR Scot660,Lt 3Bn

CRAWFORD,William Charlton T2Lt kia 17-11-16 GL &RFC p2&190 MR20

CRAWFORD,William Montgomery T2Lt dow 5-9-16 12HLI p162 CR Scot685

CRAWFORD,William Scott 2Lt kia 15-4-17 14Lond p249 CR France162

CRAWFORD-KEHRMANN,Jessel Lt kia 24-1-15 3RB attSStaffs p178 CR France681

CRAWFORD-LESLIE,Reginald William Henry Maj ded 3-4-16 ScotHorse Res p269 CR Scot310

CRAWFORD-WOOD,Guy Lt kia 1-7-16 1WelshGds p53 CR Belgium6,2Lt

CRAWHALL,Fritz Portmore 2Lt kia 10-3-15 KRRC p149 MR22

CRAWHALL,Neil Grant Lt kia 7-7-16 Manch att2ELancs p154 MR21

CRAWLEY,Albert T2Lt dow 9-5-17 7Lincs p75 CR France40,Lt

CRAWLEY,Eric TLt ded 26-2-17 10RInniskF p104 CR France285

CRAWLEY,Eustace Maj kia 2-11-14 12Lancers p22 MR29

CRAWLEY,Henry Thomas 2Lt dow 6-5-18 4Worc p108 CR France24

CRAWLEY,Thomas Henry Ouseley Capt kia 6-5-15 Worc p108 MR4

CRAWLEY-BOWEY,Thomas Russell TCapt dow 30-8-16 14Glouc p106 CR France66,BOEVEY

CRAWLEY-BOEVEY,Edward Martin Capt kia 24-12-14 1RSuss attRFus p118 CR Belgium17

CRAWSHAW,Charles Neville.MC.Capt&Adjt kia 19-9-18 8RScotF p94 MR37

CRAWSHAW,T.H.Lt 5-9-20 1/5Y&L CR Yorks575

CRAWSHAY,Mervyn Capt kia 31-10-14 5DragGds p21 MR29

CRAYMER,Douglas Charles 2Lt kia 15-9-18 RGA 232SB p39 CR France841

CREAGH,Aubrey Osborne Capt kia 14-4-15 IA 120Inf p275 CR Iraq6

CREAGH,Henry James Perceval.MC.MID TLtACapt dow 23-11-18 11Suff p78 CR France13

CREAGH,Leo Capt kia 20-12-14 1Manch p154 MR22

CREAGH,O'Moor Charles Lt kia 23-4-18 RFA 108ArmyBde p27 MR20,O'Moore 23-3-18

CREAGH,Reginald Simon Macnamara TLt ded 5-12-17 14RB p178 CR Lond9

CREAGH,William Nagle 2Lt dow 7-3-17 3Leinst p174 CR Belgium100

CREAN John Fitzgerald Capt ded 17-10-18 LancHuss p269 CR Lancs10

CREAN,Theodore Capt kld 26-10-14 Nhampt &RFC p1&137 MR20

CREAR,Malcolm Charlton 2Lt ded 3-8-17 RH&FA &RFC p27 see CRERAR,M.C.

CREASEY,Arthur Andrew 2Lt kia 14-7-17 1Beds att22RFC p6&85 CR France95

CREASY,Francis Symons T2Lt kia 23-4-17 8SStaffs p122 MR20

CREASY,Harry William Hay TCapt kia 13-6-16 11Ess p131 CR Belgium73

CREASY,Robert Leonard.MC.LtAMaj dow 22-10-18 D190RFA p27 CR Belgium392

CREBBIN,William Arthur.MC.TCapt kia 4-4-18 8RB p178 MR27

CREE,Adrian Victor T2Lt kia 17-2-16 10RWFus p97 MR29

CREE,Arthur Thomas Crawford Lt kia 12-5-15 7DLI p239 CR Belgium165

CREE,Charles Edward Victor Lt kia 20-7-16 6N&D p233 CR France504

CREE,James Fleming 2Lt kia 3-9-18 3 att22NumbF p60 CR France258

CREE,Robert Scott Capt dow 14-11-17 1/8ScotRif p225 CR palestine2

CREE,William Cecil Holt Capt ded 24-10-14 RFA p27 CR Cornwall40

CREED,Charles Odell 2Lt dow 2-6-15 2GrenGds SR p49 CR France145

CREERY,Ronald Hulbert.MC.2Lt dow 23-4-17 RGA 121SB p39 CR France113

CREES,William 2Lt kia 1-7-16 2RWSurr p55 CR France630

CREEY,Cuthbert John 2Lt kia 20-10-16 21RFC p2 CR France833,CREERY

CREIGHTON,Oswin Chap4Cl kia 15-4-18 RAChDept att42RFA p199 CR France98

CRELLIN,Douglas Mark T2Lt ded 25-12-18 RE p262 CR Lancs156,Lt Worc

CRELLIN,William Anderson Watson.DSO&Bar.CaptTLtCol dow 8-10-18 15N&D p133 CR Belgium11

CREMEN,Leonard Francis Lt kia 4-6-15 IA 14Sikhs p275 CR Gallipoli3

CREMETTI,Max Arthur Eugene T2Lt kld 14-8-17 GL &RFC p6 CR Mddx17

CREMIN,Bernard Felix Ambrose 2Lt kia 11-10-16 10A&SH att26TMB p173 MR21

CREMONINI,James Henry T2Lt kia 18-10-17 66RFC p6 CR France31

CRERAR,Donald Campbell Lt kia 24-4-18 4RFA attRE 254TC p207 CR France144

CRERAR,John Lt kia 31-7-17 5A&SH p243 CR Belgium96

CRERAR,Malcolm Charlton 2Lt kld 3-8-17 RFA &RFC 5Wing p6&27 seeCREAR,M.C.CR Palestine2

CRESSEY,George Ernest Lister Lt kia 26-9-15 2Yorks p90 MR19

CRESSWELL,Alfred Sackville Capt kia 13-3-15 2EKent p57 CR Belgium17

CRESSWELL,Clarendon Hyde Capt ded 29-10-18 LancsYeo p269 CR Scot239,CRESWELL

CRESSWELL,Edward Arthur Capt kia 13-10-15 6SStaffs p229 MR19

CRESSWELL,Francis Joseph Capt kia 24-8-14 1Norf p73 CR France1196

CRESSWELL,Frank T2Lt kia 18-5-16 9Leic p87 CR France283

CRESSWELL,H.O.TCapt ded 7-6-18 SL p268 CR Surrey80,H.C.

CRESWELL,Leonard Curtis Lt dow 13-10-16 3Y&L p158 CR Greece4

CRESWELL,Ronald Arthur 2Lt kia 13-1-16 2 O&BLI p130 CR France152,13-11-16

CRESWICK,Wilfred Bertram Capt kia 10-4-16 4YLI attRE 179FC p235 MR21

CRESSY,Charles Howard T2Lt kia 25-9-15 8RWSurr p55 MR19

CREW,Denis Meirville Lt kia 5-7-17 7Ches p223 MR29 &CR Belgium310,Dennis

CREWDSON,Dorothy Mary Lynerette.MM.Sister ded 13-3-19 VAD p200 CR France40,Dorothea Lynette 12-3-19

CREWDSON,Theodore Wright TCapt dow 6-11-16 20Manch p154 CR France102

CREWE,Clifford Whatley T2Lt kld 13-8-17 GL &RFC p6 CR Mddx66

CREYKE,Edmund Ralph Capt kia 5-7-16 5YLI p235 CR France702

CRICHTON,Alexander Godfrey T2Lt kia 16-8-15 7RDubF p176 MR4

CRICHTON,Arthur James.MC.T2Lt kia 15-7-16 1RWSurr p55 MR21

CRICHTON,Cyril William Alfred 2Lt kia 10-3-15 3Lond p245 CR France727,C.A.W.

CRICHTON,Henry Richmond Lt dow 22-2-17 IA 54Sikhs att51 p275 CR Iraq5

CRICHTON,Henry William.MVO.DSO.Viscount.MajBtLtCol kia 31-10-14 RHGds p20 CR Belgium116

CRICHTON,Herbert Clowe T2Lt dow 7-10-16 18Manch p154 CR France188

CRICHTON,Hubert Francis Maj kia 1-9-14 1IrGds p52 CR France1113

CRICHTON,John Arthur Maj 6-2-17 6Hamps attRE 1WT CR Iraq6

CRICHTON,John Drummond TCapt kia 22-3-18 9LNLancs p135 MR20

CRICHTON,McVeag Maj kia 19-12-20 IA 1/103Mahrattas p275 MR43,McVeagh

CRICHTON,Norman 2Lt kia 16-11-16 4SforthH p241 MR21

CRICHTON,Robert Renfrew 2Lt kia 20-11-17 6GordH p166 CR France1498

CRICHTON,Ronald 2Lt kia 22-8-17 5RWar p214 CR Belgium126

CRICHTON-BROWNE,Cecil Harold Verdin.MC.CaptAMaj ded 13-12-18 3KOSB p101 CR Belgium241

CRICHTON-STUART,Lord Ninian Edward LtCol kia 2-10-15 6WelshR p230 CR France80

CRICK,Cyril George Lt kia 27-8-17 HuntsCycBn att2/8Worc p253 MR30

CRICK,Walter Haliburton Routledge ACapt kia 9-4-18 4Dors p229 CR Palestine9

CRICK,William Edward T2Lt dow 9-4-17 9YLI p142 CR France214

CRIGHTON,Harold Reginald 2Lt kia 10-4-18 10Lpool p216 MR19

CRIGHTON,John TLt kia 27-9-15 8BlkW p128 CR France219,25-9-15 9Bn

CRIGHTON,John Arthur Maj ded 6-2-17 5Hamps p228

CRICHTON,John Fairweather TLt kia 18-7-16 8BlkW p128 MR21,CRICHTON

CRIMMIN,Florence Lt kia 24-4-17 RNDevYeo p203 MR37

CRIPPEN,George Oliver Lt kia 14-5-15 5SLancs p230 MR29

CRIPPIN,Harry William.MC.Capt kia 8-9-16 RFA 56DivHQ p27 CR France

CRIPPS,Henry Reginald HonCapt ded 6-1-15 lateRE p262

CRIPPS,Reginald Edward T2Lt kia 5-11-17 RBerks att6Bn p139 MR30

CRISP,Cyril Bright Lt kia 16-8-17 5SomLI p218 CR Belgium106

CRISP,Ernest Geoffrey T2Lt dow 16-12-15 15RWar p64 CR France625,kia

CRISP,Francis Edward Fitzjohn 2Lt kia 5-1-15 1GrenGds p49 CR France566

CRISP,Frederick George T2Lt kia 9-10-17 16RWar Res p64 MR30

CRISP,Harold Dudley 2Lt kia 6-11-17 RFC p6 MR40

CRISP,Reginald 2Lt kia 29-3-18 att74EKent p212 MR27

CRISP,Stanley Searle AMaj dow 8-12-17 RFA 63A/ASec Bty p27 CR Italy7

CRISPIN,Hugh Trevor LtCol kia 30-10-14 2RSuss p118 MR29

CRITCHLEY,Frank T2Lt dow 10-4-18 SLancs att1/4Bn p125 CR France98

CRITCHLEY,John T2Lt kia 11-7-16 11RWar p64 MR21

CRITCHLOW,Charles T2Lt kia 26-10-17 21Manch p154 MR30

CRITTENDEN,Frederick 2Lt ded 7-9-17 RGA 170SB p39 CR Surrey15

CROAGER,Norman Eustace Sassoon T2Lt kld 8-11-17 GL &RFC p6 CR War98

CROAGER,Lawrence William 2Lt kia 3-5-17 2Ess p131 MR20

CROAL,Kenneth McFarlane T2Lt kia 19-10-18 6RFus att2/10RScots p67 MR70 &CR Europe179

CROALL,John James Capt kia 4-10-17 5RScotF p222 MR30

CROCKER,Edward TCapt kia 24-4-17 13ESurr p112 CR France379

CROCKER,Francis George T2Lt kia 14-7-16 8EYorks p84 MR21

CROCKER,Joseph Lt kia 19-9-17 5WRid p227 MR30

CROCKER,Percival James Wilberforce TLt ded 16-11-18 2 att1/5RWKent p140 CR Iraq8

CROCKET,John Lt kia 25-9-14 RAMC att1CamH p195 CR France1339

CROCKETT,Charles Love T2Lt kia 28-4-16 12RInniskF p104 CR Ireland196

CROCKETT,Clifden James Lt kia 18-8-16 4Nhampt att6War p234 CR France832

CROCKETT,Laurence Charles Capt ded 17-10-18 RAMC attSL DentalSurg p195 CR Nhampt78,Lawrence

CROCKETT,R.B.Lt&QM 8-4-21 GL CR Glouc168

CROFT,Benjamin Capt kia 10-11-18 28 att10Lond p252 CR Belgium256

CROFT,Cyril Talbot Burnley 2Lt kld 8-12-15 SomLI &RFC p1&79,Burney CR Somerset222

CROFT,Eric.MC.MID LtACapt ded 17-1-18 106/22RFA p27&261 CR Lond29,kldacc

CROFT,George Wheeler TLt kia 16-2-18 Lincs &48RFC p15&75 CR France1203,kld

CROFT,Herbert Archer.Bart.Capt kia 11-8-15 1Hereford p252 MR4

CROFT,Herbert Arthur 2Lt kia 14-2-17 GL &2RFC p6 CR France924

CROFT,John Arthur Christopher 2Lt kia 18-4-18 4RWar att2WRid p64 MR29

CROFT,Leslie Robert 2Lt kia 30-10-14 RSuss p118 MR29

CROFT,Randal William Shuckburgh TCapt kia 12-5-17 7Yorks p90 MR20

CROFT,Robert John 2Lt kia 21-3-15 2Glouc p106 CR Belgium28

CROFT-SMITH,Edwin Spencer 2Lt kia 8-5-15 1KRRC p149 MR29,10-5-15

CROFTON,Charles Woodward Maj kia 10-8-15 9Worc RoO NStaffs p108 CR Gallipoli13

CROFTON,Edward Vivian Morgan Lt kia 14-7-17 RE 61FC p44 CR Belgium102

CROFTON,Hugh Lefroy Capt kia 22-5-15 RInniskF p104 CR Gallipoli6

CROFTON,Thomas Horsfall.MC.Capt kia 21-3-18 3 att6ConnRgrs p172 MR27

CROFTS,Charles Howard.MC.T2Lt kia 20-7-18 RLancs attYLI p58 MR18

CROFTS,Edmund Cyril Iveson 2Lt dow PoW 28-4-18 1KOSB p101 CR Germany3

CROFTS,Frederick Wilkinson.MC.Capt dow 15-9-16 17Lond p250 CR France188

CROFTS,George Robert Murray Lt kia 9-5-15 3 att2WelshR p126 MR22

CROFTS,R.DSO.Maj 16-2-16 RAMC CR Eire138

CROFTS,William Lt kia 5-12-17 6LancF att2/7RWar p221 MR17

CROGER,Nathaniel William 2Lt dow 25-9-18 RGA 434SB p39 CR France13

CROGGAN,Josiah Fenwick Sibree TCapt ded 18-11-18 14 att10N&D p133 CR France52,CROGGON

CROKER,Frederick Reginald 2Lt kia 27-4-17 6LancF &RFC p221 MR20

CROLE,David Clement TCapt kia 23-3-18 RAMC att19Huss p195 MR27 &CR France1890

CROLEY,Frank William Capt dow 14-8-16 IARO RE 178TC attS&M p275 CR France197

CROLL-JONES,Eustace Alvanley 2Lt kia 15-4-18 RFA 9/38ArmyBde p27 MR30

CROMARTY,Donald Everard Capt 7-3-20 RGA CR Mddx25

CROMB,David Rankin T2Lt kia 23-4-17 3 att13RScots p53 CR France421

CROMBIE,Ian Osborne TCapt kia 28-7-16 11Mddx p146 CR France296

CROMBIE,James 2Lt dow 24-6-18 7HLI p240 CR France169

CROMBIE,James McHattie 2Lt dow 2-7-17 3 att10RWKent p140 CR Belgium11

CROMBIE,John Eugene Capt dow 23-4-17 4GordH p241 CR France113

CROMBIE,Stewart Phyn Lt kia 4-12-18 1/5KOSB p224 CR Palestine8

CROMBIE,William Edgar.MC.Lt kia 31-8-18 7RWar attRAF p214&258

CROMBIE,William Lauder 2Lt kia 1-7-16 3RScots p53 MR21

CROMBIE,William Maurice Lt ded 17-2-19 IA IMS p275 CR Kent157,Capt

CROMIE,Henry Julian TCapt kia 23-10-16 3 att1Hamps p120 MR21

CROMIE,Maurice Francis Lt 4-6-15 3 att2Hamps MR4

CROMIE,Samuel Osborne Lt dow 17-11-16 2CldGds p51 CR France105,2Lt

CROMPTON,Arthur Harold T2Lt kia 3-7-16 7BordR p116 CR France397

CROMPTON,Cyril T2Lt ded 17-9-15 11YLI p142 CR Lancs267

CROMPTON,Henry Dent 2Lt kia 4-12-16 WLancsRFA att4RFC p18&208 CR France59,Harry

CROMPTON,Nigel George.MID TLt kia 5-11-15 RE 1-1FCp44 CR France275

CROMPTON,Thomas Lt kia 13-4-18 1RWSurr p55 MR32

CRONE,Bertram John Fenwick T2Lt dow 13-9-16 7Lancs p58 CR France922

CRONE,Percy Alexander 2Lt kia 8-9-16 4 att7RMunstF p175 MR37

CRONEEN,Laurence 2Lt kia 28-4-17 6RScots p211 MR20

CRONEY,Reginald Harry Talbot 2Lt kia 9-8-18 1 att8NStaffs p157 CR France33

CRONHELM,Arthur Geoffrey Lt kld 6-9-17 2/22Lond att23RFC p18&251 CR Egypt1

CRONIN,Harold William Lt dow 2-12-17 5Beds p219 CR Palestine8

CRONIN,John Francis 2Lt ded 10-3-17 14DLI p160 CR Europe51

CRONK,William Guy 2Lt kia 26-10-14 3EKent attKRRC p57 MR29

CRONSHAW,Thomas Edgar T2Lt dow 8-3-17 11ELancs p110 CR France339

CRONUN,William Benn TCapt ded 1-2-18 RAVC p198 CR France85,CRONYN

CROOK,Ernest Richard T2Lt dow 13-10-16 D59RFA p27 CR France59

CROOK,Harry 2Lt dow 20-4-18 17Lpool p71 MR30

CROOK,Leslie Arthur,MC TLtACaptAAdjt kia 25-9-17 1RWSurr p55 MR30

CROOK,Philip Joseph Lt kia 9-11-17 D of LancsYeo p204 CR Palestine8

CROOK,William George T2Lt kia 9-3-18 10RFus p67 CR Belgium113

CROOKE,Charles Croydon TLt ded 22-11-18 LabCps p266 CR War66

CROOKE,Elliot Hampden TCapt kia 3-7-16 8Glouc p106 MR21

CROOKE,Hugh Neville 2Lt kia 10-12-16 RE 67FC p44 CR France701

CROOKE,Walter T2Lt kld 12-11-17 GL &40RFC p6 CR Surrey6

CROOKES,Ronald Orme T2Lt kia 4-6-18 24RFus p67 CR France549

CROOCKEWIT,Alexander Edward 2Lt dow 26-10-17 3 att1Beds p85 CR Belgium11

CROOKHAM,Hugh Antony Rupert TLt dow 3-8-15 1Camb p244 CR France1

CROOKS,Edward Neilson 2Lt kia 22-3-18 12KRRC p149 CR France1204

CROOKSHANK,Wilfred Plassy Capt kia 8-3-16 IA 1/1GurkhaRif att123Rifs p275 MR38

CROOKSTON,William John 2Lt kia 12-4-18 4ScotRif att8BordR p103 MR32

CROOM,William Charles 2Lt kia 7-6-17 10Lond p248 MR29

CROOM-JOHNSON,Brian Lt kia 9-5-15 4RWFus p223 MR22

CROOME,William Hardman Capt kia 30-11-17 8Ess p232 MR17

CROPLEY,Reginald John T2Lt dow 22-9-18 1Beds p85 CR France512

CROPLEY,William 2Lt kia 21-9-18 4Suff p217 CR France212

CROPPER,Alexander 2Lt dow 22-10-16 Wilts att22RFC p2&152 CR France59

CROPPER,Edward Percival.MC.Lt kia 25-3-18 2WYorks p81 MR27

CROPPER,John TLt drd 21-11-16 RAMC p195 MR35

CROPPER,Thomas Andrew Lt dow 19-4-18 D75RFA p27 CR France84,2Lt

CROPPER,William 2Lt kia 22-8-18 6 att19Lond p247 MR16

CROSBIE,John Colin Lt dow 7-9-17 RGA att70RFC p6&39 CR France31

CROSBIE,Thomas Edward Chapman.MC&Bar.T2LtACapt dow 15-4-18 9RIrF p171 MR30

CROSBIE,Walter Robert Lt kia 12-4-18 4 att1/7BlkW p230 MR19

CROSBY,Arthur Barnard Lifford 2Lt dow 24-4-17 5DLI p239 CR France120

CROSBY,Frederick Howard 2Lt kia 7-3-18 2/17Lond p250 CR Palestine3

CROSBY,John Claude Parry T2Lt dow 21-1-18 1Lpool p71 CR France769,kia

CROSBY,Timothy Hugh Stowell Lt kia 3-2-18 5DLI att1AircraftDepotRFC p238 CR France134,kld

CROSFIELD,Guy Henry Goad Lt kia 26-1-18 5 att1RB p178 CR France154

CROSHAW,Oswald Moseley.DSO.LtCol dow 26-9-18 QOGlasgowYeo att53AustInf p203 CR Belgium165,26-9-17

CROSHER,William John 2Lt dow 20-5-17 RGA 239SB p39 CR France40

CROSIER,Vernon Swann 2Lt dow 6-4-18 7Lond p247 CR France62

CROSLAND,G.W.K.DSO.Maj 31-12-19 WRid CR Yorks643

CROSLAND,John Herbert Lt ded 13-4-19 3RWFus att6KAR p97,202&266,GL MR46

CROSLAND,Trevor Allington 2Lt kia 22-6-16 2RWFus p97 CR France924

CROSLAND,William Philip T2Lt kia 16-8-17 2WYorks p81 MR21

CROSLEY,Cecil.MID 2Lt kia 16-8-15 RIrFus att5Bn p171 MR4

CROSS,Alfred 2Lt kia 13-11-16 1Lpool p71 CR France131

CROSS,C.E.P.Lt 4-10-18 3RFus CR France234 see CROST,C.E.P.

CROSS,David Ronald.MC.MID Lt kia 21-2-15 16Lancers p23 MR29

CROSS,Dennis Patrick.MC.LtACapt kia 24-8-18 2Beds p85 CR France177

CROSS,Ernest 2Lt kia 24-4-18 5 att2Mddx p146 CR France144

CROSS,Frank Alan T2Lt kia 25-2-17 7Glouc p106 MR38 Ex 1RFus

CROSS,Fred Capt ded 5-5-18 IARO att15CarnaticInf p275 CR India164

CROSS,George Herbert TCapt kia 30-9-18 RASC att9RIrFus p192 CR Belgium157

CROSS,Henry Hazelock Graham T2Lt kia 13-11-16 10RDubF p176 CR France220,Havelock

CROSS,Howard 2Lt dow 27-9-18 5Lond p246 CR France113

CROSS,James Lt dow 3-9-17 RFA 41DAC 10Cps p27 CR France139

CROSS,James Capt ded 9-11-19 RAMC p267 CR Lancs171

CROSS,John TCapt ded 21-7-18 RAMC p195 MR66

CROSS,Leslie Lt dow 30-9-15 44RFA p27 CR France345

CROSS,Maurice Assheton Capt kia 18-8-16 1LNLancs D'Coy p135 CR France402

CROSS,Philip Frank 2Lt kia 22-7-16 1RWKent p140 MR21

CROSS,Philip Frederick Lt kia 9-9-17 4 att6RIrReg p88 MR21

CROSS,Reginald Carlton Lt kia 7-6-18 DorsYeo attSLancs p203 CR France204

CROSS,Robert Singlehurst Lt ded 2-1-20 10Lpool p269 CR Lancs1

CROSS,Ronald Sydney TCapt kia 27-7-16 18WYorks p81 CR France631

CROSS,Russell W.Lt kld 24-7-19 RFC CR Canada116

CROSS,Samuel Allison 2Lt kia 14-1-18 KRRC att2Bn p149 MR30

CROSS,Sidney William T2Lt dow 23-10-18 RWKent att10Bn p140 CR Belgium143

CROSS,Solomon TCapt kia 22-3-18 RAMC att11Suff p195 MR20

CROSS,Thomas Edward Kynaston Capt kia 13-7-17 B70RFA p27 CR Belgium6

CROSS,Wilfrid 2Lt kia 22-7-16 4Leic p220 CR France745

CROSSE,Edward Arthur Willson 2Lt kia 27-9-18 1CldGds p51 CR France1497

CROSSE,Ewins Charles Marlborough Lt dow 16-5-15 Leic p87 MR22

CROSSE,M.E.B.2Lt kia 13-3-15 2Yorks p90 CR France279

CROSSE,Robert Grant TLt dow 14-7-16 7RWKent p140 CR France630

CROSSE,Thomas Latymer TCapt kia 3-7-16 7BordR p116 CR France397

CROSSLAND,Albert Lt ded 7-8-19 5YLI p269 CR Yorks323

CROSSLE,Howard Maj ded 26-11-19 IMS p275 MR43

CROSSLEY,Allen Hastings Lt dow 10-5-17 1/1Hereford p252 CR Egypt9,Alan

CROSSLEY,Arthur Reginald Gordon TLt ded 10-3-19 WYorks p263 CR Yorks468,Capt

CROSSLEY,Brian.MID Lt kia 17-5-15 3 att2HLI p162 MR22

CROSSLEY,Cyril 2Lt kia 1-7-16 15LancF p92 MR21

CROSSMAN,Guy Danvers Mainwaring T2Lt kia 10-7-16 13WelshR p126 CR France453

CROSSMAN,Lionel Gordon Capt ded 11-12-17 RAMC p253 CR Iraq6

CROSSMAN,Richard Douglas.MC.LtACapt kia 27-9-18 3RScots p53 CR France437

CROSSMAN,William Ronald Morley 2Lt kia 2-11-14 2KRRC p149 MR29

CROST,Christopher Edric Percy Lt kia 4-10-18 3RFus p67 CR France234,CROSS

CROUCH,Alan T2Lt kia 25-8-16 RB att42TMB p178 CR France402

CROUCH,Augustus Barton T2Lt kia 27-4-17 10Lincs p75 MR20

CROUCH,Clarence Cecil.MC.2Lt dow 22-10-17 A50RFA p27 CR France40

CROUCH,Frederick Charles.MID LtAMaj dow 2-11-17 RGA 113HB p39 CR Belgium165

CROUCH,Foster Brooke TLt kia 23-3-18 10DCLI p114 MR20

CROUCH,George Percy T2Lt dow 4-10-17 1DCLI p114 CR Belgium72

CROUCH,Lionel William Capt kia 21-7-16 O&BLI BucksBn p231 CR France832

CROUCH,William Ballard 2Lt kia 13-4-17 RGA 270SB p39 CR France924

CROUCHER,Cecil 2Lt ded 26-2-17 6N&D p233 CR France120

CROUCHER,Frederick William 2Lt kia 27-4-15 1RWKent p140 CR Belgium96

CROUGH,Francis Harris.MC.Capt kia 21-3-18 5 att2LancF p221 MR27,CROUCH Harrie

CROUSAZ,Cecil Francis Lt kia 31-11-14 1SStaffs p122 MR29,31-10-14

CROW,Arthur Arnold Pte kia 10-10-17 Ess Ex LNLancs CR Belgium83 Resigned Capt re-enlisted as Pte

CROW,Charles Maurice 2Lt kia 23-4-17 16RFC p6 CR France32

CROW,Henry Paterson Capt ded 9-11-18 RAMC p195 MR66

CROW,Norman Howard 2Lt kia 14-9-17 GL &56RFC p6 CR Belgium140

CROWDER,Harry 2Lt kia 14-3-17 1Lpool p71 MR21

CROWDY,James Dunscomb.DSO.Maj kia 14-1-20 IA 2/5GurkhaRif p275 MR43

CROWE,Cecil Alexander T2Lt kia 9-9-16 7RInniskF D'Coy p104 CR France402

CROWE,Harold Archer 2Lt dow 1-6-15 1Lond p245 CR France345

CROWE,Hugh Barby Lt drd 28-10-15 RFus p67 MR4

CROWE,William Herbert SubCdr 2561/33233 ded 24-6-20 IA IndOrdDept p275 CR Iraq8

CROWE,William Maynard Carlisle Capt kia 11-11-14 RWar attNhampt p64 MR29,CARLISLE-CROWE

CROWLEY,Cedric Hugh Lt kia 25-4-15 4 att2RWar p64 MR29,att1Bn

CROWLEY,Cyril Raymond 2Lt kia 4-10-17 1Dev p254 CR Belgium125

CROWLEY,Daniel Joseph Lt ded 27-9-19 RAMC p267 MR65

CROWLEY,Frederick Augustus T2Lt kld 26-2-18 SL &RFC p15 CR Essex211

CROWLEY,John Cyril Capt kia 11-9-16 4RWSurr p212 CR Iraq6

CROWLEY,Philip TLt kia 7-7-17 RLancs p58 CR France379

CROWTHER,Eric Stuart 2Lt dow 21-11-16 7GordH p242 CR France40,Lt

CROWTHER,Ernest T2Lt kia 25-10-18 RE 92FC p44 CR France716

CROWTHER,George 2Lt kia 28-6-17 1/4WRid p227 CR France258

CROWTHER,Leslie Oakes TCapt kia 6-12-16 GL &12RFC p2&190 CR France46

CROWTHER,Leslie Taylor 2Lt kia 15-6-15 5WRid p227 CR France347,16-6-15

CROWTHER,Norman 2Lt kia 14-10-18 3Ches att15Suff p95 CR France567

CROWTHER,Percy TCapt ded 14-9-16 RASC p192 CR Hamps205

CROWTHER,Philip Townsend TLt kia 5-5-17 RE 211FC p44 CR France1191

CROWTHER,Stanley Lorne 2Lt kia 20-9-17 29RFC p6 CR Belgium123

CROWTHER,William Osborne T2Lt kia 24-11-16 3 att9N&D p133 CR France701

CROXSON,Sidney T2Lt ded 16-9-16 8Dev p76 CR France145

CROYDON-FOWLER,Hilgrove TLt kia 12-10-18 2Worc 1stGarrBn p108 MR16,Hillgrove

CROYSDALE,Marjorie Sister ded 2-3-19 QAIMNS p200 CR France40

CROZIER,Gerald Irvine Lt ded 28-6-20 6Leinst CR Asia53

CROZIER,James Cyril Baptist 2Lt kia 27-8-14 2RMunstF B'Coy p175 CR France1751

CROZIER,Percy Beattie Capt kia 19-5-15 IA 4Rajputs att15Sikhs p275

CROZIER,Thomas Alexander.MC.TLt kia 23-3-18 11RWSurr p55 CR France307

CROZIER,William Magee Lt kia 1-7-16 9RInniskF p104 MR21

CRUDDAS,Hugh Wilson.DSO.LtCol dow 20-1-16 IA 41Dogras att1/4Suff p275 CR France178,kia

CRUDDAS,Sandwith George Peter T2Lt kia 20-9-15 6DCLI p114 CR Belgium84,21-9-15

CRUESS-CALLAGHAN,Stanislaus Capt ded 27-6-17 44RFC CR Canada1601

CRUICKSHANK,Alexander Douglas.MC.T2Lt kia 23-10-18 50MGC Inf p182 CR France1386

CRUICKSHANK,Andrew John Tuke 2Lt kia 7-7-16 RGA att70RFC p2&39 CR France134

CRUIKSHANK,Arthur Henry Prinsep Capt dow 28-4-15 IA 32SikhPnrs att34 p275 CR France200

CRUICKSHANK,Donald Edward 2Lt kia 9-4-16 10BordR att5Wilts p116 MR38

CRUICKSHANK,Eric TCaptAMaj dow 26-9-18 D87RFA p27 CR France88

CRUICKSHANK,Ernest Alec Watson Lt kia 21-8-18 48/36RFA p27 CR France1014

CRUICKSHANK,Guy Lindsay.DSO.MC.Capt kia 15-9-16 RFC p2 CR France1465

CRUICKSHANK,Harold Arthur Lt dow 28-9-15 3 att2RScotF p94 CR France80

CRUICKSHANK,Harold Thomas Capt kia 25-9-15 1 att8KOSB p101 MR19

CRUICKSHANK,Isabella Sister drd 10-4-17 QAIMNS p200 CR France85

CRUICKSHANK,James 2Lt dow 3-8-16 7ScotRif p224 CR France145

CRUICKSHANK,Kenneth George 2Lt ded 12-7-17 GL &32RFC p6 MR20

CRUICKSHANK,Philip TCapt kia 1-7-16 RInniskF p104 MR21

CRUICKSHANK,Raymond Alfred 2Lt kia 23-4-17 3Mon p244 CR France427,2Bn

CRUICKSHANKS,Ernest TCapt kia 17-10-15 14 att9KRRC p149 See WESTON J.true name

CRUIKSHANK,Eric Onslow Lt kia 19-9-14 3Wilts p152 CR France864

CRUISE,Henry B.Capt ded 23-4-17 SL NyasalandFF p268 CR EAfrica78,Richard 22-4-17

CRUM,Stewart Alexander 2Lt kia 1-7-16 2SfthH p164 CR France1890

CRUM-EWING,Alexander.MID 2Lt kia 22-12-14 3SfthH att1CamH p164 MR22

CRUMPTON,Thomas 2Lt kia 17-4-18 RGA 6SB p39 MR32

CRUNDWELL,Alan Lt kia 23-3-18 11Lpool p71 MR27

CRUTTWELL,Hugh Lockwood 2Lt kia 12-10-17 RGA 118SB p39 CR Belgium19

CRYER,Bernard Noel 2Lt kia 15-9-17 7Lond p247 MR29

CRYER,Harold James T2Lt kld 13-10-17 GL &RFC p6

CRYMBLE,Cecil Reginald Lt kia 20-11-14 3 att1RIrF p171 MR32

CRYMBLE,John Gordon T2Lt dow 28-12-16 9RIrF p171 CR France285

CRYMBLE,William Capt ded 12-10-16 RAMC p195 CR Egypt15

CUBBON,Francis Richard.MC.Capt mbk 9-6-17 IA 72Punjabis attRFC p275 MR20

CUBEY,Joseph Berkeley TCapt kia 1-7-16 23NumbF p60 CR France393

CUBIE,Adam 2Lt kia 30-7-18 119/27RFA p208 CR France21

CUBITT,Alick George.Hon.Lt kia 24-11-17 15Huss p22 MR17

CUBITT,Bryan Barton TLt kia 26-9-15 8EYorks p84 MR19

CUBITT,Edward Randall Capt kia 12-8-15 5Norf p216 MR4

CUBITT,Eustace Henry Capt kia 19-4-17 1/5Norf p216 CR Palestine8

CUBITT,Henry Archibald Capt kia 15-9-16 3CldGds p51 CR France513

CUBITT,Terence Algernon Kilbee.MC.Capt kia 22-8-18 4Norf p216 CR France281,1Bn

CUBITT,Victor Murray TLt kia 12-8-15 5Norf p216 MR4

CUBITT,William Hugh.Hon.Lt dow 24-3-18 1Drags p21 CR France1063

CUBITT-IRELAND,Leslie Woodhouse 2Lt kia 12-2-17 12Manch CR France786

CUDMORE,Milo Massey.MC.TLt kia 27-3-16 RFA 31THBty p27 MR29

CUFFEY,Maurice O'Connor Lt kia 20-5-15 att2RDubF p176 MR29

CUFFLEY,Joseph Ison.MC.T2Lt dow PoW 31-3-18 61MGC Inf p182 CR France1061,Lt

CULL,Arthur Tulloch Capt kia 11-5-17 1SfthH &48RFC p6&164 MR20

CULL,Leslie TLt kia 8-11-17 21MGC Cav p182 CR Palestine1

CULL,Percival Stuart.MIDx2 2Lt kia 14-4-18 3 att1NumbF p60 CR France1896

CULLEN,C.F Lt 1-4-20 1/4Y&L CR Germany1

CULLEN,Gerald Somerville Yeats 2Lt kia 11-4-17 1RIrF p171 CR France604

CULLEN,Harry William 2Lt 21-8-20 7LancF CR Staffs6

CULLEN,James.MC.2Lt dow 3-10-18 1RIrF p171 CR Belgium38

CULLEN,John T2Lt kia 15-9-16 13A&SH p173 CR France239

CULLEN,Ralph Neville 2Lt kia 6-12-15 6RIrF p171 MR37

CULLEN,Thomas T2Lt dow 22-9-18 33MGC Inf p182 CR France906

CULLEN,William Barbour Alexander Kennedy Maj ded 29-3-21 IA p275 MR69

CULLEN,William Geoffrey Langley 2Lt ded 30-3-15 8RScots p212 CR Scot237,9Bn

CULLEN,William Harold T2Lt kia 11-7-16 113MGC p182 MR21

CULLERNE,Alan Baird.MC.T2Lt kia 23-10-18 7RWKent p140 CR France717

CULLEY,Geoffrey Matthew George TCapt kia 15-9-16 11RWKent p140 CR France277

CULLEY,Walter Duncan T2Lt dow 12-7-17 Hamps att1Bn p120 CR France10,12-7-18

CULLIMORE,H Capt 15-2-15 JohoreForces CR Asia45

CULLIMORE,John.MIDx2 TLt dow 16-4-18 8Ches p95 CR Iraq5

CULLIMORE,Joseph Albert T2Lt kia 23-5-16 8RIrF p171 CR France423

CULLIMORE,Smart TCapt kia 20-2-16 11SWBord p99 CR France727

CULLINAN,Robert Hornidge TCapt kia 8-8-15 7RMunstF p175 MR4

CULLING,Harold William T2Lt kia 7-7-16 9WRid p115 MR21

CULLIS,Edmund Herbert 2Lt ded 19-8-17 RE p269 CR Glouc102

CULLIS,Henry Thoreau T2Lt kia 10-12-15 15 att12RB p178 CR France276

CULLY,Leslie T2Lt dow 27-10-17 91MGC p182 CR Belgium11

CULME-SEYMOUR,George.MID Capt kia 7-5-15 KRRC p149 MR29

CULPEPER,A.G.Lt 9-5-20 IMD MR65

CULPIN,Charles Henry T2Lt dow 15-5-17 1 att10Glouc p106 CR France88,Lt

CULSHAW,Ronald Henry 2Lt kia 14-7-18 3WYorks p81 CR Belgium3,1Bn

CUMBERLAND,Andrew John T2Lt kld 3-1-18 RFC p15 CR Shrop52

CUMBERLAND,Brian Clark Capt kia 15-8-15 5Beds A'Coy p219 CR Gallipoli4

CUMBLEY,Reginald T2Lt kia 19-9-18 RBerks att8Bn p139 CR France212

CUMING,Arthur Eric MacMorrough.MC.LtACapt dow 26-10-18 1RIrF p171 CR France34

CUMING,William Edward T2Lt kia 31-7-17 5ConnRgrs attRInniskF p172 CR Belgium106

CUMMING,Adam Smith 2Lt dow 20-4-17 5A&SH p243 CR Palestine8

CUMMING,Alex Bryant Lt kia 22-4-16 3BlkW p128 CR Iraq5

CUMMING,Alfred Lionel T2Lt kia 7-6-17 GL att15RFC p6 CR France41

CUMMING,Andrew Alexander 2Lt ded 6-2-18 4RScots p211 CR Scot742

CUMMING,Anthony Dyson Lt kia 6-3-17 4LNLancs attMGC p187&234 CR France624

CUMMING,Colin Edward Lt dow 25-2-15 103RFA p27 CR Belgium151

CUMMING,Edward John Capt ded 15-11-18 IA 102Inf p275

CUMMING,Frederick Kenneth 2Lt kia 23-10-18 3 att14BlkW p128 CR Belgium428

CUMMING,George T2Lt kia 9-7-16 8SLancs p125 MR21

CUMMING,Gilmour 2Lt kia 21-3-18 5 att1/7BlkW p231 MR20

CUMMING,H.R.DSO.BrigGen 5-3-21 Staff CR Mddx26 Ex DLI

CUMMING,James Leslie T2Lt kldacc 24-3-18 64RFC p15 CR Scot380

CUMMING,Lewis Robertson 2Lt kia 28-9-14 1BlkW p128 MR15

CUMMING,Lionel George T2Lt kia 9-5-17 8Dev p76 MR20

CUMMING,Robert John Alfred 2Lt kia 27-8-18 7 att1/6HLI p240 CR France162,Lt

CUMMING,Robert Scott.MC.Capt 14-3-21 RAMC CR Iraq6

CUMMINGS,Eric.MID Capt ded 26-4-16 IA 93Inf p275 CR Iraq5

CUMMINGS,Ralph Michael 2Lt kld 15-1-18 RFC p15 CR USA77,16-1-18

CUMMINGS,Thomas Horsfield 2Lt ded 15-7-18 5DLI p239 CR Durham39

CUMMINGS,William Capt kia 18-5-17 RAMC p253 CR France614

CUMMINGS,William Allen Wesley 2Lt kia 13-4-18 MGC p182 CR France193,Lt

CUMMINS,Archibald Wilfred.MID SubAssSurgCl3 17-7-15 IMS CR France354

CUMMINS,Fenton King.MC.LtACapt kia 21-3-18 6ConnRgrs p172 CR France365,Lt

CUMMINS,Harry Jackson.MID Lt kia 21-8-15 IA 1/5GurkhaRif p275 MR4

CUMMINS,Herbert Charles Bruce TCapt dow 7-5-17 9SfthH p164 CR France264

CUMMINS,Herbert Waller Lt kia 24/25-5-15 4Yorks p220 MR29,24-5-15

CUMMINS,Ian Ashley Marsham Maj ded 20-7-18 RGA p39 MR21 &CR Ireland14

CUMMINS,Leslie T2Lt kia 1-7-16 10Lincs p75 MR21

CUMMINS,Thomas Coote 2Lt kia 25-3-18 3Y&L p158 CR France385,7Bn

CUMMINS,Thomas Morris 2Lt ded 7-11-18 3Lond p269 CR Mddx40,Lt 8-11-18

CUMNER,Cyril William 2Lt kia 24-4-18 1Lond p269 CR France144

CUMPSTON,Basil Lancelot T2Lt dow 10-5-17 2BordR p116 CR France518

CUNDALL,Cecil.MC.LtACapt kia 30-11-17 2RInniskF p104 MR30

CUNDALL,Hubert Walter 2Lt kia 1-7-16 1Lond p245 MR21

CUNDALL,John Ernest 2Lt kia 3-5-17 5YLI p235 CR France1186

CUNDALL,Stanley T2Lt kia 21-4-18 9YLI p142 CR Belgium102,20-4-18

CUNDLE,Thomas William 2LtTLt kia 27-9-17 GL att2KAR p202 CR EAfrica38 &CR Tanzania1

CUNINGHAM,Charles Arthur Capt kia 10-8-15 6BordR p116 MR4

CUNINGHAM,George Edmund Maj ded 6-12-18 IARO attASC p275 CR Asia82,CUNNINGHAM

CUNINGHAM James Campbell see CUNNINGHAM,J.C.

CUNINGHAME,Alfred Keith Smith.MID TCapt kia 25-9-16 2GrenGds D'Coy p49 CR France394

CUNINGHAME,Boyd Alexander Maj ded 16-3-17 5A&SH attNRhodRif CR WAfrica8

CUNINGHAME,William John see CUNNINGHAME,W.J.

CUNLIFFE,Clement Wallwork 2Lt kia 24-9-17 6Manch p236 CR Belgium173

CUNLIFFE,Edward Gilbert TLt kia 25-3-18 37MGC p182 CR Belgium19

CUNLIFFE,Ernest Nicholson Maj ded 31-3-19 RAMC p255 CR C'land&W'land108

CUNLIFFE,Foster Hugh Egerton.Bart.TMaj kia 10-7-16 13RB p178 CR France150,dow

CUNLIFFE,G.Capt 23-2-20 HertYeo CR Kent281

CUNLIFFE James Grimshaw.MC.TCapt dow 1-8-17 18Manch p154 CR Belgium11

CUNLIFFE,John Brooke Maj dow 20-4-17 NhamptYeo p204 CR Shrop63

CUNLIFFE,John Leonard TCapt kia 4-9-16 21Manch p154 MR21

CUNLIFFE,Robert Ellis T2Lt kia 9-5-15 SL att2RBerks p201&254 MR22 &MR32

CUNLIFFE,Thomas Hathorn LtCol ded 25-5-15 9Manch p237 CR Lancs472,Hethorn

CUNLIFFE,Thomas Henry Withers Capt kia 4-6-15 1LancF p92 CR Gallipoli1

CUNNACK,George James.MC.TLtACapt dow 17-10-18 RE 180TC p44 CR France846

CUNNELL,Donald Charles Capt kia 12-7-17 5Hamps &RFC p228 CR France285

CUNNINGHAM,Alexander Campbell T2Lt kia 21-8-15 RMunstF p175 MR4

CUNNINGHAM,Alexander Pinman.MM.T2Lt dow 19-9-18 2KRRC p149 CR France327

CUNNINGHAM,Archibald John Lt kia 24-3-18 A110RFA p27 MR20

CUNNINGHAM,Arthur Joseph.DCM.2Lt kia 15-9-16 18Lond p250 CR France432

CUNNINGHAM,Bernard Camelis Josh TCapt kia 21-3-18 7RDubF p176 CR France212

CUNNINGHAM Charles Albert Glentworth Capt kia 6-6-15 12ScotRif att1KOSB p103 MR4

CUNNINGHAM,Charles Clement Francis Capt dow 19-8-16 2A&SH p173 CR France176

CUNNINGHAM,Charles Stewart 2Lt kia 1-2-17 IARO att36Sikhs p275 CR Iraq5

CUNNINGHAM,David T2Lt ded 27-10-17 2Yorks p90&263 CR France285

CUNNINGHAM,Douglas Murray 2Lt dow 11-6-18 3 att4/5BlkW p128 CR France113

CUNNINGHAM,Edward 2Lt kia 28-1-18 11RFC p15 MR20

CUNNINGHAM,Edward Hamilton T2Lt kia 11-8-18 Hamps att1Dors p120 CR France360

CUNNINGHAM,Edward Malcolm.MC.LtTCapt kia 4-8-17 2 att9WRid p115&258 CR France97,5-8-17

CUNNINGHAM,George Edmund see CUNINGHAM,G.E.

CUNNINGHAM,Harold John.MC.TCapt dow 4-10-17 6Beds p85 CR Belgium132

CUNNINGHAM,Hugh Rose 2Lt kia 26-4-18 12RScots p53 MR30

CUNNINGHAM,James T2Lt kia 1-7-16 9 att7Beds p85 MR21

CUNNINGHAM,James Campbell 2Lt kia 14-3-16 15RFC p2 CR France518,CUNINGHAM

CUNNINGHAM,James Michael TLtACapt dow 28-3-18 7Suff p78 CR France169

CUNNINGHAM,James Nelson TLt dow 19-10-17 GL &56RFC p6 CR France297

CUNNINGHAM,Joseph Francis Crowley T2Lt kld 28-11-17 GL &RFC p6 CR Mddx68

CUNNINGHAM,Kenneth Edward Capt dow PoW 3-5-17 2WRid p115 MR20

CUNNINGHAM,Lyman Holden 2Lt kld 14-1-18 RFC p15 CR Wilts121

CUNNINGHAM,Peter Nesbit 2Lt kia 2-12-17 HLI att17Bn p162 MR30

CUNNINGHAM,Robert William Capt kia 1-7-16 9Lond p247 MR21

CUNNINGHAM,Samuel Andrew Capt kia 12-7-15 5RScotF p222 MR4

CUNNINGHAM,Stuart Gordon 2Lt kia 22-10-17 12/35RFA p27 CR Belgium19

CUNNINGHAM,William 2Lt kia 1-10-18 4 att1RIrF p171 MR30

CUNNINGHAM,William John Lt&QM ded 18-5-15 ShropYeo p205

CUNNINGHAM REID,Duncan Flower 2Lt kia 19-12-15 IARO 17Lancers attRFC p275 CR Belgium379

CUNNINGHAME,William John Maj ded 19-3-19 NottsYeo (SNottsHuss) p205 CR Germany1,CUNINGHAME

CUNNINGTON,Cecil Henry Lt ded 24-10-17 215MGC Inf p266 CR Lond12,26-10-17

CUNNINGTON,Edward Charles TCapt kia 23-3-18 RAMC att95FA p195 CR France924

CUNNINGTON,Joseph Herbert 2Lt ded 19-10-18 Ex RE p262 CR Devon107

CUNNISON,Alan Watson 2Lt kia 29-10-16 3 att1ScotRif p103 MR21 &CR France34

CUPPLES,William Capt kia 25-9-15 3RInniskF p104 MR29

CURE,Basil Alfred Capel Capt dow 1-10-16 2Glouc p106 CR Greece4,CAPEL CURE

CURETON,Edward Robert Maj ded 18-5-16 KOSB attHamps p120 CR Hamps202

CURGENVEN,William Charles Capt kia 21-10-14 SWBord p99 CR Belgium115

CURLE,William Sydney Noel.MC.Maj dow PoW 23-3-18 B107RFA p27 CR France441

CURLETT,Patrick Alexander Lt kia 3-7-15 3Lpool p71 CR France163

CURLEY,Alfred T2Lt kld 5-3-18 11RFC p15 CR Lancs18

CURLEY,Francis Lt kia 25-9-15 AngleseyRE p44 MR19

CURLING,Edward Charles James Lt&QM ded 2-5-17 RAMC att133FA p195 CR France102

CURLING,Edward Thomas Lt kld 15-2-18 22Lond att93RFC p18&251 CR Hamps192

CURLING,Frank Trevor ACapt kia 31-8-18 18Lond p250 CR France218

CURNOCK,George Ashwin Lt kia 14-8-17 6 att10RB p178 MR29

CURPHEY,William George Sellar.MC.TCapt ded 15-5-17 GL &32RFC p6 CR France924

CURR,Thomas 2Lt kia 4-10-16 4 att18HLI p162 CR France1182

CURRALL,Norman Frank 2Lt kia 18-10-16 1ELancs p110 MR21

CURRAN,Henry 2Lt kia 25-4-17 10RWelshF p97 CR France531

CURRAN,Nevil William.MC.MID Lt kia 4-10-16 2 att3RIrReg p89 MR32

CURRER,Thomas Russell 2Lt kia 26-9-17 1RScotF p94 MR30

CURREY,Donald Saunders Capt kia 24-4-17 1Mon att7RBerks p244 MR37

CURREY,George Capt ded 15-11-19 RAVC p268 CR C'land&W'land17

CURREY,George Grafton TCapt kia 22-8-15 6Yorks p90 MR4

CURREY,Vere Fortrey Maj kia 13-10-15 7Suff p78 MR19

CURRIE,Adam TCapt kia 28-3-18 17RScots p54 MR27

CURRIE,Clarence Algernon TLt dow 19-12-15 RE p44 CR France285

CURRIE,Claud George Ironside Maj ded 3-12-16 Dors p264 CR Lond8

CURRIE,Frederic Rivers Lt kia 8-8-15 3 att1KSLI p144 MR29 &CR Belgium453,Frederick

CURRIE,Gilbert Heron.DCM.2Lt kia 12-10-16 3 att10A&SH p173 CR France924

CURRIE,Harold Maxwell T2Lt kia 1-8-17 1/2 att10ScotRif p103

CURRIE,Horatio Charles Lt ded 24-4-18 KAR &SL p268 CR EAfrica92

CURRIE,James Alexander Vance 2Lt kia 13-3-17 10Lond p248 CR France175

CURRIE,James Hamilton Lt kia 25-8-18 3Hamps p120 CR France28,2Bn

CURRIE,John Eugene Havelock T2Lt kia 11-9-15 8 att1RScotF p94 MR22

CURRIE,R.A.M.CMG.DSO.MIDx4 BrigGen 30-3-20 SomLI &GenStaff CR Europe150A

CURRIE,William George.MC.2Lt kia 22-3-18 1Lincs p75 CR France364,28-3-18

CURRIE,William Thomson Capt dow 31-7-18 3 att1/5GordH p166 CR France1225

CURROR,William Edwin Forrest 2Lt kia 1-7-16 14Lond p249 CR France798

CURRY,Ralph.MID Capt dow 9-4-18 8DLI p239 CR France193

CURRY,Vernon Edward T2Lt kia 23-4-17 1Beds p85 MR20

CURRY,William Gordon T2Lt kia 7-6-17 12 att13Ches p95 CR Belgium89

CURRY,William Horace.DSO.2LtACapt kia 25-10-17 3 att1SStaffs p122 MR30

CURRY,William Leonard TCapt dow 9-11-16 RGA 87SB p39 CR France74

CURSHAM,Francis George Maj ded 31-8-18 8N&D p269

CURSHAM,Geoffrey Lt kia 12-10-17 1RLancs p58 MR30

CURTEIS,Lancelot 2Lt kia 4-7-16 8BordR p116 MR21,3-7-16

CURTEIS,R.Nurse 14-11-18 VAD CR Hamps1

CURTICE,Frederick Russell Lt dow 17-11-16 C79RFA p27 CR France74

CURTIES,Dudley Thomas Lees Lt ded 24-10-18 2HAC p206 CR Italy12,25-10-18

CURTIES,Lionel Charles Alfred TCapt kia 25-10-15 GL attMGC p190 MR29

CURTIS,Arthur.MC.Capt kia 27-8-18 3Lond p245 MR16

CURTIS,Eric Calvin 2Lt kia 28-7-18 5SfthH p241 CR France865

CURTIS,Ernest John 2Lt dow 22-1-18 5 att7RWKent p235 CR Belgium106,kia

CURTIS,Evelyn St.George 2Lt kia 3-5-17 7 att12Mddx p235 MR20

CURTIS,Frank Warren 2Lt kia 14-8-17 9RFC p6 CR Belgium18

CURTIS,Frank William TLt kia 4-11-16 6Leic A'Coy attKSLI p87 MR30

CURTIS,Harry Reginald TMaj kia 18-9-18 11RWFus p97 CR Greece5

CURTIS,Henry Edward 2Lt drd 21-2-17 RE 117ConstnCoyRlwy p44 MR35

CURTIS,Henry Neville T2Lt kia 25-7-17 GL &45RFC p6 CR France1049

CURTIS,Henry Thomas 2Lt dow 12-2-17 24Lond p252 CR France41

CURTIS,Hubert James Lt kia 4-11-18 SL att87RAF p201 MR20

CURTIS,Horace Lt kia 7-8-15 9WYorks p81 MR4

CURTIS,Jocelyn Stewart 2Lt kia 21-3-18 3RB p178 MR27

CURTIS,John Handel 2Lt kia 24-11-17 4 att18WelshR p230 MR17

CURTIS,Keith Saxby T2Lt kia 26-10-17 14RWar Res p64 MR30

CURTIS,Ralph Luxmore T2Lt ded PoW 21-9-17 GL &48RFC p6 CR Belgium140

CURTIS,Robert Henry T2Lt kia 20-9-17 10RWSurr p55 MR30

CURTIS,Thomas Britt T2Lt dow 25-10-17 11Ches p95 CR France80,kia

CURTIS,William 2Lt kia 14-3-15 1Manch p154 CR France706,Lt 12-3-15

CURTIS,William Charles T2Lt kia 3-10-18 5TankCps p188 MR16

CURTIS,William Edward 2Lt kia 18-8-16 5RWar p214 MR21

CURTIS,William Michael.Bart.Capt ded 19-1-16 RDC p253 CR Shrop74

CURTIS-BEALS,Harold T2Lt kld 15-3-18 GL &38RFC p15 CR Egypt9,Harry

CURTIS-RALEIGH,H.T.R.Capt 27-9-14 2Berks MR65

CURTLER,Frederick Gwatkin Oldham Lt kia 21-10-14 5 att2Worc p108 MR29

CURWEN,Cecil Neil TLt kia 15-9-16 18KRRC p149 MR21,Niel

CURWEN,Gilbert Christopher 2Lt kia 3-6-18 16Lond p250 CR France887

CURWEN,Henry Stanley T2Lt kia 13-10-15 7Norf p73 MR19

CURWEN,Wilfred John Hutton Capt kia 9-5-15 6 att3RFus p67 MR29

CURWEN,William Lynedoch.MC&Bar.TLt dow 30-10-17 RGA att27MtBty SR p39 CR EAfrica10 &CR Tanzania1

CURZON,Fitzroy Edmund Penn LtCol kia 9-9-16 6RIrReg p89 CR France513

CUSACK,Reginald Ernest 2Lt ded 15-4-15 4RDubF p176 CR Kent71,Lt

CUSACK,Thomas William Stanley 2Lt ded 25-6-19 18Lond p269 CR Staffs114

CUSHEN,Aylett Cameron 2Lt kia 30-6-16 11RSuss p118 MR19

CUSHING,Geoffry Edgar 2Lt kld 29-12-17 RFC p6 CR Suff83,Lt

CUSHING,Robertson Macaulay 2Lt dow 30-4-18 RGA 190SB p39 CR Belgium3

CUSHNY,Donald Lt kia 14-4-15 Dors p124 CR Iraq6

CUSSELL,Stanley James T2Lt kia 29-5-18 RASC p192 MR18

CUST,Bertram Mitford T2Lt kia 9-11-15 10Yorks p90 CR France1140

CUTBILL,Bernard TCapt ded PoW 24-3-18 8Norf p73 CR France481

CUTBUSH,Douglas.MC.2LtACapt kia 10-4-17 5 att4Mddx p146 CR France545

CUTCLIFFE,John TLt kia 26-9-18 1EYorks att9WRid p104 CR France383,2Bn

CUTHBERT,Charles Louttit T2Lt dow 18-8-16 9ESurr p112 CR France141

CUTHBERT,David TCapt kia 7-10-16 29 att8RFus p67 MR21

CUTHBERT,David Wilson Harper T2Lt dow 9-4-17 9BlkW p128 CR France113

CUTHBERT,Gordon Capt kia 27-4-15 8Mddx p235 MR29

CUTHBERT,James Harold.DSO.Capt dow 27-9-15 1ScotsGds p52 MR19

CUTHBERT,John George Gunn TLt dow 19-10-16 28MGC p182 CR France177

CUTHBERT,J.Stewart Ross Lt dedacc 28-12-17 RFC CR USA228

CUTHBERT,Leonard Arthur.MC.Capt kia 20-12-19 IA 2/19Punjabis p275 MR43

CUTHBERT,Olaf Ranson TCapt kia 1-7-16 8Y&L p158 CR France246

CUTHBERT,Reginald Vaux T2Lt dow 28-4-17 8SfthH p164 CR France113

CUTHBERTSON,Edward Hadley Lt ded 24-7-17 RWar p64 CR Iraq5,Hedley

CUTHBERTSON,Eric Ian 2Lt kia 23-10-17 RGA 327SB p39 CR Belgium85

CUTHBERTSON,George Chapman.MC.Capt dow 8-4-18 GL &54RAF 22Wing CR France145

67

CUTHBERTSON,Hugh 2Lt kia 14-4-18 B275RFA p27 CR France109

CUTHBERTSON,Norman William Maj ded 12-2-15 1BlkW CR Mddx16

CUTHELL,Algernon Hubert.MID TMaj kia 22-8-15 9WYorks p81 MR4

CUTLER,Edward Trevor 2Lt kia 9-8-17 7 att2Ess p232 MR20

CUTLER,Frank 2Lt kia 18-9-16 14DLI p160 CR France744

CUTLER,Harold Arthur Lt kia 23-3-18 39MGC p182 MR27

CUTLER,Herbert Cecil Lt kia 10-5-17 2/1WorcYeo attRFC p18&206 CR France1495

CUTLER,Leslie Durban 2Lt ded 8-10-18 13Lond p269 CR Kent99,2-10-18

CUTLER,Stuart le Geyt LtTCapt kia 9-8-17 RASC &21RFC p6&192,Staurt Le Guyt CR Belgium16

CUTLER,William Reynolds T2Lt kia 18-11-17 GL &70RFC p6 CR France40

CUTTLE,Geoffrey 2Lt kia 14-3-15 2Yorks p90 MR22

CUTTLE,George Robin 2Lt ded 9-5-18 RFA &RAF p27 MR20

CUTTLE,George William 2Lt kia 4-6-17 8EYorks p84 CR France154,5-6-17

CUTTING,Edward James 2Lt kia 9-10-18 4RBerks att7Nhampt p234 CR France270

CUTTS,Leonard Edwin TLt ded 11-10-18 RE 256TC p44 CR France1063

CUTTS,Thomas Bernard TCapt kia 20-7-16 15N&D p133 CR France294

CUXSON,Basil Pryce 2Lt kia 14-7-15 2RScots p54 CR Belgium167

CUZEN,Richard 2Lt kia 5-4-18 6Nhampt p137 CR France587

D

Da COSTA,Oscar Michael John LtCol ded 11-10-18 IA 35ScindeHorse p275 MR65

DACRE,Brian TCapt kia 12-10-18 9WRid p115 CR France230

DACRE,John Kenneth.MC.Lt dow 30-9-16 71RFA p27 CR France197

DACRES,Leonard Seymour Lambert Capt ded 20-4-19 IARO attPoliticalDept p275 CR Iraq8,att21Cav

DADD,Edmund Halton.MC.TCapt kia 3-9-16 1RWFus p97p258 MR21,Hilton

DADD,Ivor Llewellyn T2Lt ded 17-7-17 RE IWT p44 CR Iraq6,DADDS

DADD,Reginald John T2Lt kia 5-4-18 7RFus p67 MR20

DADSWELL,Clifford Irwin 2Lt kia 7-7-16 3 att7RSuss p118 CR France1890

DAFFEN,Harold Charles Lt kld 26-4-16 2/8N&D p233 CR Ireland14,kia

DAFFURN,Oswald.MC.2Lt kia 1-4-18 1BordR p116 MR32

DAFT,Harry 2Lt kia 13-4-17 17Lond p250 CR France184

DAGGE,Albert Lima 2Lt kia 1-7-16 B168RFA p27 CR France215

DAGGETT,Cedric Hunton.MC.Capt kia 11-2-17 23NumbF p60 MR32

DAGLISH,John William 2Lt 10-12-19 DLI CR Durham23

DAIN,Sidney Edward T2Lt ded 7-12-18 RE PostalSect p44 CR France52

DAINES,Allan Edward 2Lt kia 30-12-17 7RFus p67 MR21

DAINES,Roland Lewis T2Lt kia 3-8-17 32RFus p67 MR29

DAINES,Sidney T2Lt kia 16-5-18 1Hamps p120 MR19

DAINTITH,James T2Lt kia 13-8-17 RE 150FC p44 CR Belgium101

DAINTON,Howard Hillier T2Lt dow 5-4-18 14Glouc att7RWKent p106 CR France37,1Bn

DAKERS,John 2Lt kia 12-5-17 14Lond p249 MR20

DAKIN,Albert Edward T2Lt dow 16-9-18 Wilts att2Bn p152 CR France88

D'ALBERTANSON,Ronald.MC.2Lt dow 8-8-16 3ESurr att6Dors p112 CR France176

DALBIAC,Charles James Shelley 2Lt kia 16-6-15 1NumbF p60 MR29

DALBY,Herbert Charles T2Lt kia 1-7-16 11Y&L p158 MR21

DALBY,Herbert Ernest Maj ded 14-10-17 RAMC p195 CR Iraq6

DALE,Alfred Parks T2Lt kld 15-3-18 57RFC p15 CR Egypt8

DALE,Alwyn Percy.OBE.Maj kia 1-3-17 5WYorks p218 CR France514,Alwyne

DALE,Andrew Murray Capt ded 1-5-19 Ex YLI p265

DALE,Arthur 2Lt dow 12-3-15 1NStaffs p157 CR France681

DALE,Arthur 2Lt kia 25-9-16 Dev p76 MR21

DALE,Arthur William 2Lt kia 1-7-16 7NumbF p214 CR Belgium60

DALE,Charles Lt ded 16-10-18 337RFA p207 CR Iraq8

DALE,Frank Cottrell 2Lt dow 26-5-18 4Ches p222 CR Ches84

DALE,Harry T2Lt kia 24-4-18 TankCps p188 CR France424

DALE,James Ritchie TLt ded 14-1-19 RE 96FC p262 CR Surrey1

DALE,John Ernest T2Lt dow 14-9-17 Ess att9Bn p131 CR France113

DALE,Rayner William Maj ded 25-8-16 RFA p27 CR Scot253,RGA

DALE,Robert Clunie 2Lt kia 18-8-16 B109RFA p27 CR France370

DALE,Robert Jacomb Norris Lt kia 31-1-18 9Manch BallSect &RFC p237 CR Italy7

DALE,Robert Percy.MC.LtTCapt kia 25-10-18 4 att9ScotRif p103 CR Belgium140

DALEY,Alexis T2Lt dow 14-4-17 1/2NStaffs att2Y&L p157 CR France8

DALEY,Richard T2Lt kia 25-10-18 LancF att2/5Bn p92 CR Belgium406,dow

DALGLEISH,George Walter.MID LtCol ded 17-2-19 RFA 2DAC p27 CR Germany1

DALGLEISH,William.MC.Lt kia 12-11-17 4RScots p211 MR34,DALGLIESH

DALGLISH,Charles Antoine de Guerry Capt dow 9-9-14 BlkW p128 CR France1451,8-9-14

DALGLISH,James Wilson 2Lt kia 14-2-16 3 att4Yorks p90 CR Belgium5

DALGOUTTE,George Cork T2Lt kia 3-5-17 8RB p178 MR20

DALL,John T2LtTCapt ded 12-10-18 1HLI p162 MR66

DALLAS,A.S.MC.Lt 30-1-21 RA MR66

DALLAS,George Barnes Lt kia 1-9-19 SomLI att8MGC Inf p254 MR70 &CR Europe179

DALLAS,John Sweetland Capt dow 12-9-15 IA 1/6GurkhaRif p275 CR Egypt3

DALLAS,Raymond Vivian Leslie.MC.TCapt kia 13-4-18 9NumbF p60 MR19

DALLAS,William Frederick Lt kia 9-4-16 WelchR att6ELancs p126 MR38

DALLAS,William Loraine Seymour Chap4Cl kia 20-9-17 RAChDept att5Lpool p199 MR30

DALLAS,William Reid 2Lt kld 24-12-18 RASC MT att215RAF CR France134

DALLEY,John Pomeroy Lt mbk 15-10-17 IARO att20RFC p275 MR20,14-10-17

DALLOW,William Ewart 2Lt kia 9-4-17 7KSLI p144 CR France581,Ewart W.

DALMAHOY,John Francis Cecil Capt kia 26-4-15 IA 40Pathans p275 CR Belgium96

DALRYMPLE,Hew T2Lt kia 1-7-16 8SomLI p79 MR21

DALRYMPLE,Ian Douglas Capt kia 5-5-15 2HLI att2KOSB p162 MR29

DALRYMPLE-CLARK,Douglas Scott.MC.Capt 15-9-16 18KRRC attTMB CR France1890

DALRYMPLE-WILLES,Patrick Lt ded 29-9-18 RLancs &RAF p58

DALTON,Charles LtCol dow 18-9-14 RAMC p195 CR France1139

DALTON,George Henry 2Lt dow 14-8-16 3RIrReg att4 O&BLI p89 CR France354

DALTON,Horace Montague T2Lt kia 3-5-17 8EYorks p84 MR20

DALTON,J.G.2D/147Sister 20-3-16 QAIMNS CR Scot26

D'ALTON,James George 2Lt 27-10-17 162RFA p27 MR30

DALTON,Richard Gregory T2Lt kia 31-8-17 18WYorks p81 CR France268

D'ALTON,Thomas Joseph 2Lt dow 9-6-17 4RIrReg att7InniskF p89 CR France40,DALTON

DALY,Alexis 2Lt dow 14-4-17 1/2NStaffs attY&L CR France8 see DALEY,A.

DALY,Arthur Charles de Burgh 2Lt kia 9-9-16 5RDubF p176 CR France402

DALY,Cyril Francis St.Felix T2Lt kia 14-10-17 7RWSurr p55 MR20 6Bn

DALY,Darby T2Lt kia 4-10-18 ConnRgrs p172 CR France1495,2MunstF

DALY,Donald Lynott Lt ded 12-4-15 SL &3NigR CR WAfrica46

DALY,Thomas.CMG.Col ded 15-4-17 RAMC p195 MR35,drd

DALY,Valentine Maurice 2Lt dow 20-4-18 30MGC p182 CR France64

DALY,William Cecil Thomas 2Lt kia 18-8-16 3RB p178 CR France400

DALZELL,Thomas Frost 2Lt kia 21-3-18 18MGC p182 MR27

DALZELL-WALTON,Hubert Pulteney.MID TLtCol kia 9-9-16 8RInniskF p104 CR France329

DALZIEL,Charles Sutherland 2Lt kia 8-1-17 7DLI p239 CR France453

DALZIEL,John Morrison T2Lt kia 14-11-18 RScots att2/10Bn p54 MR70 &CR Europe179

DAMAN,Geoffrey Windeath 2Lt kia 24-5-15 4SfthH p241 CR France924,Windeatt Lt

DAME,John William Malvern 2Lt kia 27-11-17 2IrGds p52 MR17

DAMER,Wilfred Percy T2Lt kia 18-11-16 7RWSurr p55 CR France535

DAMES,William Stanley 2Lt ded 17-7-19 RE p262 CR Lincs179

DAMIAND,Walter Henry Alexander 2Lt dow 2-7-16 2RDubF p176 CR France167,DAMIANO

DAMPIER,Glenny William 2Lt kia 11-12-16 10RFC p2 CR France765

DANAHER,Mary SNurse ded 12-10-18 QAIMNS p200 CR Palestine8

DANBRIDGE,William Leslie Lt dow 5-10-18 RAMC att103FA p195 DANDRIDGE

DANBY,Charles David.MC.Capt 18-7-18 RE &RAF p210 CR Durham182,kld

DANBY,Francis Geoffrey Lt kia 27-12-17 5Yorks p220 CR Belgium125,28-12-17

DANCE,Charles Edward LtCol ded 23-7-18 RE p44 CR Lond4

DANCER,Alfred Christopher.MC.TLtACapt kia 4-10-17 5Dors p124 MR30

DANCKWERTS,Richard William Lt kia 21-12-14 1Glouc p106 CR France260,2Lt 22-12-14

DANCY,George.MC.Lt&QM ded 2-6-19 1 O&BLI p130 MR70 &CR Europe179

DANDRIDGE,George Sidney T2Lt kia 1-7-16 7RWSurr p55 CR France397

DANE,Victor Lewis Yate Capt kia 22-11-15 IA 22Punjabis p275 MR38

DANE,Wilfred Spencer T2Lt kia 18-11-16 12 att10Worc p108 MR21

DANES,Thomas T2Lt ded 13-11-18 RASC p192 CR Glouc9

DANGAR,Clive Colingwood.MC.MID TMaj ded 4-7-18 GL HQ AIF p190 CR Australia112,Collingwood

DANGERFIELD,William Cecil Hay.MID TLt&Adjt kld 26-12-16 11ScotRif p103 CR Greece6

DANIEL,Archibald Morris T2Lt kia 4-10-17 1RWKent p140 CR Belgium125

DANIEL,Ernest Lt kia 21-10-18 4 att1RIrRif p169 CR Belgium140

DANIEL,Fleetwood Earnscliffe T2Lt kld 20-12-17 GL &RFC p6 CR Wilts115

DANIEL,Ralph Picton TCapt kia 31-7-17 17RWelshF p97 CR Belgium106

DANIEL,Thomas George TLt kia 23-11-17 22 att19RWelshF p97 MR17

DANIELL,Archibald Steuart Lindsey.MID 2Lt kia 19-12-14 1RB p178 CR Belgium71

DANIELL,Edward Henry Edwin.DSO.TMajLtCol kia 20-10-14 RIrReg p89 MR22

DANIELL,Francis Edward Lloyd.DSO.TLtCol dow 4-3-16 SfthH GenStaff 21Div p164 CR France922,kia

DANIELL,George Francis Blackburne 2Lt kia 24-4-17 6 att2RFus p67 MR20

DANIELL,Hubert John Capt ded PoW 19-8-16 IA 20Punjabis p275 CR Iraq8

DANIELL,Neville Reay.DSO.CaptTLtCol kia 4-10-17 DCLI Cmdg9YLI p114 MR30

DANIELL,William Raymond Maj dow 1-12-17 IA 1/123Rif p275 CR Egypt2

DANIELS,Cecil William T2Lt ded 4-11-18 1N&D p133&257

DANIELS,Edwin Ambrose TLtACapt kia 21-10-16 8SLancs p125 MR21

DANIELS,Fred.MC.2Lt kia 3-12-17 2/5RWar p214 MR17

DANIELS,George 2Lt kia 20-11-17 1/8Lpool p215 MR21

DANIELS,James T2Lt kia 28-9-18 1Ches p95 CR France415

DANIELS,James Alfred TLtACapt dow 21-9-17 Hamps att15Bn p120 CR Belgium11

DANIELS,Russell John Lt ded 29-8-18 2ScotsGds p52 CR Lond10

DANIELS,Thomas Harold Rayner 2Lt kia 9-4-16 RLancs p58 MR38

DANN,Ernest T2Lt dow 22-11-15 6Beds p85 CR France1016

DANN,Henry Norman Groves T2Lt kia 15-9-17 GL &55RFC p6 CR France134

DANN,Tom Vincent 2Lt kia 13-10-15 5SStaffs p229 MR19

DANN,Wilfred 2Lt dow 30-10-17 3 att12Glouc p106 CR Belgium11

DANN,Wilfred Stephen 2Lt kld 16-5-18 3EKent att70RAF p57 CR France63,dow

DANNAHY,William T2Lt kia 25-10-16 92RFA p27 CR France513

DANNE,Arthur William Brian Lt kia 30-3-18 3 att13Glouc p106 MR27

DANSEY,Felix Ramon Arthur 2Lt kia 25-7-18 7Lond p247 CR France62

DANSON,Francis Rudolf Lt 10-8-15 4Ches MR4

DANVERS,Charles 2Lt kia 9-4-17 15RWar p64 MR20

DANVERS,Robert William Ford 2Lt kia 26-8-17 3Suff p78 CR France1462

DANZIG,Morris William TLt drd 15-4-17 RAMC p195 MR35

DANZIGER,Charles William Jack 2Lt dow 15-5-17 9Manch p237 CR France518

DARBISHIRE,Arthur Dunkinfield 2Lt ded 26-12-15 RGA p39

DARBY,Ernest 2Lt ded 4-6-15 10SWBord p99 CR Wales571,Lt 3-6-15

DARBY,Frederick.MID 2Lt kia 29-11-14 1Worc p108 MR22

DARBY,John Sprake Capt kia 28-3-18 4RBerks p234 CR France1170

DARBY,Joseph Capt 27-6-16 IndMilWksServ CR War6

DARBY,Maurice Alfred Alexander.MID Lt kia 11-3-15 1GrenGds p49 CR Shrop60

DARBY,Norman Leslie 2Lt kia 16-8-17 5Manch p236 CR Belgium96,Lt

DARBY,William Edward Cleve Augustus Lt kia 11/13-10-15 1Mon p244 MR19,Clere

DARBY-GRIFFITH,Octavius Sidney.MC.TCaptAMaj kia 27-5-18 11 att9LNLancs p135 MR18

DARBYSHIRE,Graham Hirtzell Capt kia 7-10-17 RFA p207 CR Belgium10,8-10-17

DARBYSHIRE,Percy Capt ded 30-5-18 Res p269 CR Lancs256

DARCH,Stanley Percival T2Lt kia 22-4-16 10Glouc p106 CR France149

D'ARCY,Lionel George 2Lt kia 20-12-17 ConnRgrs &RFC p2 MR20

D'ARCY-IRVINE,Charles William Capt kia 6/12-8-15 6Leinst p174 MR4

DARDIER,Leonard Henry T2Lt dow 4-10-15 RHA 30Bty p27 CR France423

DARGIE,Arnold Maj kia 18-9-17 RGA 137HB p209 CR France161

DARKE,Hugh Cubt Maj ded 12-7-16 220RFA p269 MR67,Cuff

DARKER,Ernest Naismith 2Lt dow 10-9-17 RGA 262SB p39 CR Belgium16

DARKER,Neil Campbell 2Lt kia 3-5-17 2RScots p54 MR20

DARKER,Richard Owen 2Lt kia 12-4-18 2RFus p67 MR32

DARLEY,Desmond John 2Lt kia 1-7-16 11Suff p78 MR21

DARLEY,John Evelyn Carmichael.MID LtCol kia 31-3-18 4Huss p21 CR France988

DARLEY,William Hastings La Touche.OBE.Maj ded 11-10-18 IA 12Pnrs attStaff DAAG GHQ 3Ech p275 CR France146

DARLING,Alan Heppell T2Lt kia 10-7-16 8Yorks p90 CR France515

DARLING,Claude Henry Whish 2Lt kia 12-12-15 3 att2RIrRif p169 CR Belgium137

DARLING,Jack.MC.2Lt dow 26-10-18 4RIrF p171 CR Belgium159,John

DARLING,Robert.MC.Lt kia 16-9-18 9Lpool p216 CR France433

DARLING,James William Kingsley Capt kia 11-8-18 5RScots p211 CR France360

DARLING,William Oliver Fortesque Lt kia 16-10-15 3 att1RIrRif p169 CR France276

DARLINGTON,Tom.MC.MM.Lt kia 1-10-18 11RWSurr p55 MR30

DARLINGTON,William Charles 2Lt kia 4-11-17 2/4RWKent p234 CR Palestine1

DARLOW,John William Edward.MC.TLt kia 29-8-18 1RWKent att16RWar p140 CR France1484

DARNELL,Charles Verdon 2Lt kia 25-4-17 ConnRgrs &25RFC p6&rp172 MR20

DARNEY,Clarence Edwin 2Lt kia 2-9-18 7BlkW p231 CR France511

DARNEY,Henry Whiting Lt ded 8-9-19 IARO attMilPolice p275

DARRAGH,James Robinson Lt dow 5-7-17 1/6WRid p227 CR France98

DARRAGH,Matthew Sloan 2Lt kia 20-3-17 6WRid p227 MR19

DARREL,Richard Frederick William T2Lt ded 26-2-19 TankCps p188 CR Essex5

DARRELL,Albert 2Lt kia 25-12-15 1ESurr p112 MR21

DARRICOTTE,Gilbert Haley 2Lt kia 6-9-18 1HuntsCycBatt p253 CR France511

DARRINGTON,Clarence Philip Lt dow 27-11-18 1/5Lond p246 CR France40

DARRINGTON,Harold Edgar Lt dow 20-11-17 9Mddx att27RFC p18&rp236 CR France88 Ex 5Lond

DARSIE,George Lt dow 31-7-18 Fife&ForfarYeo p203 CR France1225

DART,Hugh TCapt dow 2-7-16 13Y&L p158 CR France5,1-7-16

DARTNALL,Albert John T2Lt kia 20-11-17 RLancs att1/4Bn p58 MR21

DARTNELL,Wilbur.VC.TLt kia 3-9-15 25RFus p67 CR EAfrica58,William Thomas

DARTON,Edward John 2Lt ded 30-4-15 RE 80FC p44 CR Essex146

DARTS,William 2Lt kia 8-3-17 RFA 66Bde p27 CR Iraq8

DARVELL,Frederick William.MC.2Lt kia 27-5-18 BordR att8Bn p117 MR18

DARVELL,George William 2Lt kia 8-5-18 6RWar p214 MR19

DARWALL,Gordon Cecil Capt ded 31-3-17 3SomLI attACycCps p79&263 CR Lond8

DARWELL,Claude Randall T2Lt kia 10-8-15 6BordR p117 CR Gallipoli5

DARWELL,Thomas Walter 2Lt kia 18-9-18 RWelshF att14Bn p97 CR France415

DARWIN,Erasmus 2Lt kia 25-4-15 4Yorks p220 MR29

DARWIN,John Henry Bradshaw Lt dow 5-12-17 8Manch p237 CR France660

DASHWOOD,Claude Burrand Lewes TMaj dow 26-4-16 9NumbF p60 CR France285

DASHWOOD,Ernest George Capt kia 12-5-15 1/4 O&BLI p231 CR Belgium71

DASHWOOD,Lionel Albert T2Lt kia 16-5-15 O&BLI p130 MR22

DASHWOOD,Robin Henry Lyndsay LtACapt kia 27-5-18 2WYorks p81 MR18,Robert Lindsay

DASHWOOD,Ronald Phillimore T2Lt kia 7-10-16 15 att12RB p178 CR France307

DASHWOOD,Wilfred James Lt dow 2-8-17 1GrenGds p49 CR Belgium16

DAUBENEY,George Henry James Lt kia 26-9-15 6 att2Worc p108 CR France423

DAUBENEY,Giles Robert 2Lt kia 23-4-15 3 att1RWKent p140 MR29

DAUBENY,Charles John Odinel LtACapt dow 16-6-17 3 att1SomLI p79 CR France95

DAUBER,John Henry LtCol drd 13-8-15 RAMC p253 MR4

DAUKES,Archibald Henry MajTLtCol kia 7/11-8-15 7SStaffs p122 MR4

DAUN,Edward Charles Lt kia 14-9-14 RSuss p118 MR15

DAUNT,Barry 2Lt kia 22-9-18 RSuss att7Bn p118 CR France369

DAUNT,Conrad O'Neill 2Lt kld 29-9-18 8SLancs &RAF p125 CR France329,Lt

DAUNT,Giles Wellacott 2Lt kia 9-4-16 10 att6SLancs p125 MR38,Vellacott

D'AUVERGNE,Francis Arthur Payne Lt kia 12-4-18 1RGLI p200 CR France297

DAVALL,Cecil George T2Lt kia 23-8-18 2Suff p78 CR France927

DAVENPORT,Allen Arthur Orme.MC.Lt dow 24-3-18 1/2 att4ELancs p110&258 CR France650

DAVENPORT,Arthur Lt kia 23-8-18 6RB p178&266,11MGC CR France927

DAVENPORT,Barnabas Tom Wilcox 2Lt kia 15-12-17 RWar att1/4Norf p64 CR Palestine9

DAVENPORT,Cyril Francis T2Lt dow 2-8-16 14Hamps A'Coy p120 CR France80

DAVENPORT,Edmund Sharrington T2Lt ded PoW 3-1-18 RFC p15 MR20

DAVENPORT,Francis Edward Alexander 2Lt kia 21-3-18 1KSLI p144 MR20

DAVENPORT,Frank Maturin Capt kia 22-11-15 O&BLI p130 MR38

DAVENPORT,Fred.DSO.MC.Maj kia 25-9-17 A296RFA p206 CR Belgium84

DAVENPORT,Harold 2Lt kia 21-3-18 RGA 122SB p39 MR27

DAVENPORT,Hughes Nares.MC.Maj kia 26-3-18 2/4 O&BLI p231 CR France1203,24-3-18

DAVENPORT,Leonard Merriott 2Lt dow 6-9-16 3 att7RIrFus p171 CR France66

DAVENPORT,Robert 2Lt kia 3-5-17 2LancF p92 MR20

DAVENPORT,Robert 2Lt dow 20-10-18 1/5ELancs p226 CR France270

DAVENPORT,Thomas Lowe 2Lt kia 27-4-17 4RFA A'Coy p208 CR France581

DAVENPORT,Vyvyan Hope Lancelot 2Lt kia 14-7-16 8Leic p87 MR21

DAVEY,Archibald Henry Pingston TMaj kia 14-10-17 1RGLI p200 CR Belgium83

DAVEY,Albert Victor Patrick 2Lt kld 2-6-18 RFA &82RAF p27 CR France1564,Lt

DAVEY,Charles Leonard TLt kia 17-10-18 18MGC Inf p182 CR France660

DAVEY,Charles Richard.MC.MM.T2LtACapt dow 30-10-18 7Lincs B'Coy p75 CR France40

DAVEY,Ernest Charles 2Lt ded 1-11-18 RGA 210SB 98Bde p39 CR France146

DAVEY,Herbert 2Lt kia 18-4-17 3 att6ELancs p110 MR38

DAVEY,Hubert Burgoyne Lt 5-12-18 SWBord CR Hereford208

DAVEY,John Burneford Lt ded 2-3-19 EX RFA p261 CR Somerset201

DAVEY,John Stanley Lt kia 17-11-14 NSomYeo p205 CR Belgium57

DAVEY,Reginald Lt kia 5-5-18 6RSuss att1KAR p228&268 MR52

DAVEY,Reginald Hubert Lt ded 28-11-19 1RGLI p268 CR France34

DAVEY,Roland Alfred T2Lt kld 8-8-17 GL att14RFC p6 CR Palestine2

DAVEY,Sydney Guy LtAMaj kia 25-3-18 4Norf att40MGC p187&216,ded MR20

DAVEY,Thomas Kerrison 2Lt dow 31-3-18 6 att1RB p178 CR France40

DAVEY,Wilfrid Charles TLt dow 21-11-17 RASC att15RFC p6&192,Wilfred CR France398

DAVEY,William Aubrey Carthew T2Lt kia 21-8-18 9Ches p96 CR France33

DAVEY,William Hamilton.OBE.Maj ded 29-8-20 27NumbF B'Coy CR Ireland40

DAVEY,William Henry.MC.2Lt kia 9-9-16 4Lond p246 MR21

DAVEY,William Roy 2Lt kia 1-7-16 12Lond p248 CR France798

DAVID,Arthur Walter 2Lt kia 14-9-18 1SWBord p99 CR France725

DAVID,Edward Harold T2Lt kia 5-11-18 1Ches p96 CR France521

DAVID,Frederick John Louis T2Lt dow 18-9-18 SWBord att15WelshR p99 CR France415

DAVID,Lionel Adolf David T2Lt kia 1-7-16 7Yorks A'Coy p90 CR France397

DAVID,Thomas William Capt kia 27-7-17 5WelshR p230 CR Belgium23,4Bn

DAVID,William Jenkin 2Lt kia 27-5-18 NumbF Res att6Bn p60 MR18

DAVIDSON,Alexander Bonn 2Lt kld 26-9-16 RFC SR p2 CR Kent160

DAVIDSON,Alexander James 2Lt kia 8-4-17 4SfthH p241 CR France728

DAVIDSON,Alexander Ritchie Lt kia 21-4-16 3SfthH p164 MR38

DAVIDSON,Andrew Pearson T2Lt kia 5-9-16 11 att2GordH p166 MR21

DAVIDSON,Archibald Randall Capt kia 15-6-17 1GordH p166 MR20,14-6-17

DAVIDSON,Arthur Gerrard 2Lt kia 9-9-17 4GordH attRFC p18&241,Lt CR France1361

DAVIDSON,Charles 2Lt kia 26-10-17 GordH p166 MR30

DAVIDSON,Charles Lingard 2Lt kia 6-8-15 13N&D p133 MR4

DAVIDSON,Christopher Edmund Grant Capt kia 13-10-15 1 att6EKent p57&257 CR France423

DAVIDSON,David Adams 2Lt kld 28-7-17 RGA 179SB p39 CR Belgium29

DAVIDSON,Donald Alastair Leslie.MC.MID Capt kia 30-4-17 9RFC p6 MR20

DAVIDSON,Donald Frederick Cluney Cdr ded 30-4-18 IA att9Div S&TCps p275 CR Iraq8

DAVIDSON,Douglas Byers Capt mbk 30-10-14 IA 2/8GurkhaRif p275 MR28

DAVIDSON,Duncan Hemelin Capt kia 9-5-15 SforthH p164 MR22

DAVIDSON,Edward Gordon.MC.Capt dow 2-4-18 19Huss p23 CR France145

DAVIDSON,Farquhar Biggam 2Lt dow 10-9-15 1/6HLI p240 CR Gallipoli3

DAVIDSON,Francis Charteris Capt kia 10-5-17 IARO attSWaziristanMil p275 MR43

DAVIDSON,George Leslie Capt kia 2-12-17 4 att16HLI p162 MR30

DAVIDSON,George William Smyttan 2Lt kia 25-9-16 1CamH p167 CR France453

DAVIDSON,George Wilson T2Lt dow 27-12-17 15WYorks p81 CR France184

DAVIDSON,Gerald Louis.MC.TLt dow 11-7-16 6Dors p124 CR France833

DAVIDSON,Gordon Parsons 2Lt kia 3-5-17 1RScotF p94 MR20

DAVIDSON,Henry Hutcheon ACapt ded 27-1-21 IARO att15LabCps p275 MR43

DAVIDSON,Henry Steele Lt kia 17-5-15 3 att1HLI p162 MR22

DAVIDSON,Hugh Douglas T2Lt kia 28-8-16 6YLI p142 CR France402

DAVIDSON,Ian Sprot 2Lt kia 11-11-14 A&SH p173 CR Belgium96

DAVIDSON,James.MID Capt kia 30-11-17 RAMC attKRRC p195 MR17

DAVIDSON,James T2Lt dow 27-5-18 NumbF att15DLI p60 MR18

DAVIDSON,James Eadie.DSO.TCaptAMaj dow 16-10-18 RGA 19SB p39 CR France528

DAVIDSON,James Samuel TCapt kia 1-7-16 13RIrRif att108MGC Inf p169&182 CR France1890

DAVIDSON,John HonLt&QM ded 19-12-15 13HLI p162 CR Scot671

DAVIDSON,John T2Lt dow 15-10-17 BordR att8Bn p117 CR France1180

DAVIDSON,John Philip 2Lt kia 9-8-16 1/10Lpool p216 MR21

DAVIDSON,John Whitworth Lt dow 5-3-17 4 att10N&D p133 CR France164

DAVIDSON,Norman Randell.DSO&Bar.MajBTLtCol dow 5-10-17 RHA HQ4Div p27 CR Belgium16

DAVIDSON,Ralph Ivan Meynell Lt dow 24-11-14 Manch p154 CR France705

DAVIDSON,Robert Henry Walter T2Lt kia 1-7-16 8Dev p76 CR France330

DAVIDSON,Robert William TLt kia 12-10-17 10A&SH p173 MR30

DAVIDSON,Roland Cooper TLt kia 1-7-16 20NumbF p60 MR21

DAVIDSON,Ronald Riach TCapt kia 27-3-16 12RScots p54 CR Belgium15

DAVIDSON,Sydney 2Lt kia 21-5-18 GL &RAF p190 CR Belgium24

DAVIDSON,Thomas Andrew 2Lt dow 9-4-18 RGA 12SB p39 CR France31

DAVIDSON,W.H.2Lt 6-9-17 32SikhPnrs MR67 see DAVISON,W.H.

DAVIDSON,William 2Lt kia 31-10-17 GL &10RFC p6 MR20

DAVIDSON,William 2Lt kia 23-3-18 7 att9ScotRif p224 MR27

DAVIDSON,William Adrian 2Lt dow 2-7-16 2GordH p166 CR France633

DAVIDSON,William Leslie.CB.Col ded 3-8-15 RFA 4GenBaseDepot p27 CR France145

DAVIDSON,William Mason Lt dow 29-3-18 5GordH p242 CR France103,26-3-18

DAVIDSON,William Thomas Chorley Capt kia 13-10-14 Dors p124 MR22

DAVIDSON-HOUSTON,Charles Elrington LtCol mbk 25-9-15 IA 58Rif p275 MR28

DAVIDSON-SMITH,Adam 2Lt 2-10-18 4RScots CR France699

DAVIE,Archibald Charles T2Lt kia 19-9-18 1Wilts p152 CR France1106

DAVIE,Frank.MM.2Lt dow 2-6-17 4EYorks p219 CR Yorks2,11Bn

DAVIE,Fred TLt kia 1-4-17 1 att1/7HLI p162 CR Palestine8

DAVIE,Henry William Wilson VetSurgeon drd 23-11-15 RAVC p198 CR USA234A

DAVIE,John.MC.T2LtACapt kia 11-5-18 GL &13RScots p190 CR France113

DAVIE,Robert Chapman Capt ded 4-2-19 RAMC p253 CR Scot530

DAVIE,Sidney John 2Lt kia 10-10-17 1/8Manch p237 CR Belgium24

DAVIES,A.C.R.2Lt ded 27-10-15 5NStaffs p238 CR Mon19

DAVIES,Alun Edwards 2Lt kia 28-5-18 12/13NumbF p60 MR18

DAVIES,Alan Wilmot Lt kld 23-4-16 45RFA attRFC p2&p27 CR Lond28

DAVIES,Albert T2Lt kld 19-6-17 GL &55RFC p6 CR Essex1

DAVIES,Albert Gordon 2Lt dow 1-8-17 7RWelshF p223 CR France285

DAVIES,Aldborough Henry 2Lt dow 18-4-16 RFA p27 MR38

DAVIES,Arthur 2Lt ded 19-10-18 IA(TC) attMtnArt RGA p275 CR Pakistan50A

DAVIES,Arthur Charles Capt kia 10-8-15 6RWelshF p223 MR4

DAVIES,Arthur Cyril Richard 2Lt ded 27-10-15 5NStaffs &RFC p261&269

DAVIES,Arthur Peter T2Lt kld 22-3-18 RFC p15 CR Ches182

DAVIES,Arthur Trevor Capt kia 7-6-17 5WelshR p230 MR29

DAVIES,Bengiman Evan Stedman TCapt kia 31-7-17 11SWBord p99 MR29

DAVIES,Benjamen Jones Capt kia 19-5-17 3SWBord p99 MR20

DAVIES,Benjamin Daniel Rowland T2Lt kld 11-3-18 RFC p15 CR Wales163,D.D.R.

DAVIES,Brinley Owen Lt kia 22-4-18 WelshR att16RWFus p126 MR27

DAVIES,Cecil James Lt died 25-11-18 RFA p207 CR Egypt9

DAVIES,Cecil Lloyd T2Lt dow 25-11-16 28Mddx att2RBerks p146 CR France105

DAVIES,Charles Albert 2Lt kia 22-9-18 7SWBord p99 MR37

DAVIES,Charles Bernard Lt kia 9-6-16 3RDubF p176 CR France514

DAVIES,Charles Hugh T2Lt kia 17-1-16 9WelshR p126 CR France727

DAVIES,Clifford Thomas 2Lt kia 7-6-17 10RWKent p140 MR29

DAVIES,Cyril Nutcombe Lt ded 1-3-19 RE p254&262,ACapt CR Surrey29

DAVIES,Cyril Thomas Morris Capt kia 1-7-16 6RWar p214 MR21

DAVIES,D.O.Capt 22-5-17 7RWFus CR Wales693

DAVIES,Dan TCapt dow 10-9-17 10WelshR p126 CR Belgium23

DAVIES,David T2Lt kia 13-11-16 10RWFus p97 MR21

DAVIES,David Benyon Lt kia 11-8-17 GL &52RFC p6 CR Belgium173

DAVIES,David Claude Graham 2Lt dow 15-5-15 RGA 1SB p39 CR France80,Claud Lt

DAVIES,David Daniel 2Lt dow 26-8-18 235RFA p208 CR France209,kia

DAVIES,David Ethelstone TLt kia 18-6-17 10WelshF p97 CR France531

DAVIES,David Evan 2Lt kia 29-4-17 GL att12RFC p6 MR20

DAVIES,David Guy.MC.TCapt kia 4-4-17 10KRRC p149 CR France415

DAVIES,David Harold T2Lt dow 18-11-18 PoW Wilts att1Bn p152 CR Germany3

DAVIES,David James 2Lt kia 31-7-17 MGC HB C'Bn p182 MR29

DAVIES,Donald Frederick.MID T2Lt kia 15-4-18 22 att23RFus B'Coy p67 CR France103

DAVIES,Edward Stanley TCapt kia 10-9-18 NStaffs att8Bn p157 CR France80

DAVIES,Edward Thomas 2Lt kia 13-10-18 RGA 140SB p39 CR France147

DAVIES,Edwin Alfred Capt ded 25-1-15 8Lpool p215 2entries CR Lancs2

DAVIES,Ellerton Osborne 2Lt kld 2-4-15 1/2Mon p244 CR Belgium33

DAVIES,Emlyn H.Rev 18-3-18 YMCA attIndLabCps CR France699

DAVIES,Ernest Frank T2Lt kia 24-8-16 7DCLI p114 CR France400,25-8-16

DAVIES,Ernest Glyn TCapt kia 5-7-16 19WelshF p97 CR France550

DAVIES,Ernest Owen 2Lt kia 9-9-18 5NStaffs p238 CR France80

DAVIES,Evan TMaj kia 27-7-17 15WelshF p97 CR Belgium86,28-7-17

DAVIES,Evan James 2Lt kia 28-3-18 1WelshGds p53 MR20

DAVIES,Evan Walter T2Lt kia 26-3-17 GL 1/7RWFus p190 CR Palestine8

DAVIES,Fairfax Llewelyn Lt kia 8-7-17 6Norf p217 CR France646

DAVIES,Francis Hugh Lt kia 10-12-17 3 att1Dors p124 CR Belgium22,9-12-17

DAVIES,Frank Arnold 2Lt kia 1-7-16 5Ches p222 CR France798

DAVIES,Frederick 2Lt kia 12-9-18 5NStaffs p238 CR France662,9Bn

DAVIES,Frederick Anscombe T2Lt kia 14-5-17 12Y&L p158 MR20,13-5-17

DAVIES,Frederick Charles TCapt kia 17-10-17 RAMC att9NumbF p195 CR Belgium85

DAVIES,Frederick George T2Lt kia 6-2-16 9RB p178 CR Belgium85

DAVIES,Geoffrey Boisselier TCapt kia 26-9-15 11Ess p131 MR19

DAVIES,Geoffrey David TLt dow 28-11-17 18WelshR att119TMB p126 CR France398

DAVIES,George Herbert Lt kia 9-8-15 3 att1KSLI p144 MR29

DAVIES,George Llewelyn 2Lt kia 15-3-15 6KRRC att4RB p149 CR Belgium111

DAVIES,George Price T2Lt kia 29-9-15 2SWBord p99 CR Belgium116

DAVIES,George Stewart Berrington Lt ded 26-10-19 RB p266 CR Wales214

DAVIES,Geraint.MC.Capt dow 14-4-18 4NumbF p213 CR Belgium183,9Bn

DAVIES,Gilbert Vere Faithfull TLt kia 23-4-17 13RScots p54 MR20

DAVIES,Glyn Lloyd T2Lt kia 15-2-17 4SWBord p99 MR38

DAVIES,Graham TLt dow 27-7-17 A121RFA p27 CR Belgium12

DAVIES,Griffith 2Lt dow 1-5-15 24Lond p252 CR France80,Lt

DAVIES,Griffith 2Lt kia 2-10-15 1WelshR 126 MR19

DAVIES,Gwynonfryn Albert Hayden 2Lt kia 7-6-17 3Mon attRFC p18&244 MR20,Haydn

DAVIES,Harold Bellamy T2Lt kia 3-11-17 7RWar attEss p64 CR Palestine8

DAVIES,Harold Blakeney 2Lt kia 23-4-16 1WYorks p81 CR Belgium73

DAVIES,Harold Casamajor Capt kia 26-9-14 2WelchR p126 CR France1328

DAVIES,Harold Percival 2Lt kia 11-4-17 MGC D'Bn p182 MR20

DAVIES,Harry T2Lt dow 10-4-16 2RBerks p139 CR France515,kia

DAVIES,Harry Harding 2Lt kia 10-11-17 3 att1SWBord p99 MR30

DAVIES,Harry Llanover.MID Lt dow 25-10-14 RHA p27 MR29

DAVIES,Harry Noel T2Lt kia 1-7-16 10 att11ELancs p110 MR21

DAVIES,Henry T2Lt kia 13-11-16 6 att2 O&BLI p130 CR France1491

DAVIES,Henry Robert Griffith Lt kia 13-10-15 5NStaffs p238 MR19

DAVIES,Herbert Howard Capt kia 24-8-17 10DLI D'Coy p160 MR30

DAVIES,Hugh Frederick.MID 2Lt kia 3-7-15 1/5Ches p222 CR Belgium28,Frederic

DAVIES,Hugh Mercer.DCM.2Lt kia 12-10-18 RE 430FC p210 CR France1392

DAVIES,Idris Powell 2Lt dow 21-8-18 7Ches att7KSLI p223 CR France745

DAVIES,Ivor Garfield T2Lt kia 8-8-18 Wilts att2Bn p152 CR France411,Ifor

DAVIES,Ivor Theophilus 2Lt kia 22-6-15 5 O&BLI p130 MR29

DAVIES,James Gordon TCapt dow 9-2-16 10WelshR D'Coy p126 CR France727

DAVIES,James Gordon 2Lt kia 1-6-17 1KSLI p144 MR19

DAVIES,James Parton T2Lt kia 26-10-18 KSLI att7Ches p144 CR Belgium406,25-10-18

DAVIES,James Thomas TLt dow 14-4-18 1SomLI p79 CR France88

DAVIES,John 2Lt kia 30-3-18 RWar att1Bn p64 MR20

DAVIES,John Charles T2Lt dow 12-4-17 18RWelshF p97

DAVIES,John Hickman T2Lt kia 9-10-17 2RWar p64 CR Belgium308

DAVIES,John Howard 2Lt kia 4-7-17 4 att2RWelshF p223 CR Belgium23

DAVIES,John James 2Lt dow 29-9-17 3 att9WelshR p126 CR France193

DAVIES,John Llewelyn TMaj kia 25-9-15 11Ess p131 MR19

DAVIES,John Morris T2Lt kia 8-10-18 16RWelshF p97 MR16

DAVIES,John Rhys 2Lt dow 28-11-17 23Lond p252 CR Palestine3

DAVIES,John Wesley TLt kia 26-3-16 16RWelshF p97 CR France727

DAVIES,Joseph Charles Gladstone Lt drd 6-1-18 RFA p207 MR34

DAVIES,Joseph Ithel Jehu T2Lt dow 3-9-16 8 Cmdg1RWFus p97 CR France402,Lt kia

DAVIES,Kenneth Lt ded 5-11-18 6SStaffs p255 CR Staffs78

DAVIES,Kenneth George TLt kia 19-5-17 RE H CableSect p44 CR France68

DAVIES,L.C.MC.Lt ded 16-3-18 5ScotRif &54TrgDepotStn RFC p224 CR Hamps98

DAVIES,Leonard TLtACapt kia 3-6-17 5 att9RB p178 CR France1185

DAVIES,Leslie Capt kia 15-9-16 15Lond p249 CR France432

DAVIES,Leslie Frederick St.John.MC.MID TCaptAMaj ded 10-11-18 20MGC p182 CR Lebanon1

DAVIES,Lindsay Ramsay T2Lt dow 5-7-16 18Lpool p71 CR France66

DAVIES,Llewelyn Crighton.MC.2Lt kld 16-3-18 3ScotRif attRFC p18&224,Llewellyn ded 5Bn

DAVIES,Maurice Albert Mervyn T2Lt kia 25-9-15 Dev p76 MR19

DAVIES,Noel John T2Lt kia 27-4-16 8RDubF p176 CR France178

DAVIES,Norman Stollard Lt kia 2-9-18 7Ess p232 CR France427

DAVIES,Owen Griffith 2Lt kia 15-11-16 6A&SH p243 CR France533

DAVIES,Percy Hier LtTCapt kia 16-8-17 17 att15WelchR p126 MR30

DAVIES,Ralph Howell TLt kia 9-4-16 9RWar p64 MR38

DAVIES,Reginald Charles T2Lt kia 1-6-16 19NumbF p60 CR France1106

DAVIES,Reginald Charles Spurgeon 2Lt kia 21-3-18 17Lond p250 MR20

DAVIES,Rhys Beynon 2Lt kia 1-5-17 4NumbF attRFC p18&213 CR France1744

DAVIES,Richard Cecil.VD.Maj ded 17-5-17 RE p44 CR Ches28

DAVIES,Richard Harry Seymour TLt dow 29-7-16 C88RFA p27 CR France145

DAVIES,Richard Hutton.CB.MajGen ded 9-5-18 Staff p1 CR Lond4

DAVIES,Robert Finden Capt kia 9-9-16 9Lond p247 MR21

DAVIES,Robert Glynne TCapt kia 14-8-16 4Lpool p71 CR France432

DAVIES,Robert Humphrey T2Lt kia 23-8-18 13RWelshF p97 CR France516

DAVIES,Robert Lloyd TLt kia 12-4-17 RE 129FC p44 CR France480

DAVIES,Robert Thomas T2Lt dow 2-4-17 21Manch p154 CR France620

DAVIES,Robert William Marengwyn T2Lt kia 6-4-17 22NumbF &52RFC p6&60,59Sqn CR France1321,Maengwyn

DAVIES,Roland Arthur Llewellyn TLt kia 4-10-18 3RFus p67 CR France1495

DAVIES,Rudolph Ellis Lt dow 11-8-17 1/7WRid p227 CR Belgium172

DAVIES,Sydney Bruce 2Lt kia 26-3-18 5ESurr p226 MR27,ESurr att9Bn

DAVIES,Sydney Francis T2Lt dow 15-11-17 11RSuss p118 CR Belgium112

DAVIES,Sydney George T2Lt kia 31-7-17 9RWelshF p97 MR29,Sidney

DAVIES,T.H.TLt ded 26-10-18 RE p44 CR Shrop97

DAVIES,Thomas Lt ded 20-9-18 RE p262 CR Wales1

DAVIES,Thomas Howell Capt 6-10-19 11SWBord CR Wales199

DAVIES,Thomas John Carlyle 2Lt kia 2-10-15 1WelshR p126 MR19

DAVIES,Thomas Llewelyn.MC.Maj kldacc 16-9-18 RFA attRAF p27 CR Wales167

DAVIES,Tom Llewelyn 2Lt kia 26-5-17 RE IWT p44 MR38

DAVIES,Trevor Arthur Manning Lt kia 1-7-16 RFA NMidDAC p207 CR France798

DAVIES,T.W.E.LtACapt ded 20-5-18 RFA No1depot RFA p27 CR Kent100

DAVIES,Valentine Clements.MC.TCapt dow 10-7-16 6/40RFA p27 CR France141

DAVIES,Wallis Rowland Henry Rochfort 2Lt ded 8-3-16 3SomLI p79

DAVIES,Walter T2Lt kia 18-9-18 9RLancs p58 CR Greece5,19-9-18

DAVIES,Walter Ambler 2Lt 15-6-15 4LNLancs MR22 See DAVIS

DAVIES,Walter Bomford 2Lt ded 3-11-18 SomLI p263 MR65

DAVIES,Walter LLewelyn T2Lt dow 15-7-16 7KSLI p144 CR France66

DAVIES,Walter Owen 2Lt kia 27-11-17 2/5WRid p227 MR17

DAVIES,Wilfred John Lt kia 5-11-16 70RFA p27 CR France385

DAVIES,William T2Lt kia 10-4-17 13RFus p67 CR France154

DAVIES,William Capt kia 11-4-18 2SWBord p99 MR32

DAVIES,William Bryan 2Lt ded 18-9-16 6N&D p269 CR France46

DAVIES,William Edward 2Lt dow 29-1-17 1/5Ches p222 CR France639

DAVIES,William John Lt dow 14-10-18 RGA 140SB p39 CR France214,1/4SB

DAVIES,William Lloyd T2Lt kia 31-7-17 13RWFus C'Coy p97 CR Belgium86

DAVIES,William Robert TLt kia 1-11-18 19NumbF p60 CR Belgium143

DAVIES,William Thomas Lt dow 13-4-18 6SWBord p99 CR Belgium183

DAVIS,Alistair Ingram 2Lt kia 11-4-18 4A&SH p173 MR32

DAVIS,Anthony Hugh 2Lt kia 6-4-16 10 O&BLI p130 MR38,1Bn

DAVIS,Arthur George 2Lt kia 16-8-17 11Lond p245 MR29

DAVIS,Basil Raymond Lt dow 20-9-17 RFus &45RFC p6 CR Belgium157

DAVIS,Bernard Samuel 2Lt kia9-4-17 5BordR p228 CR France214,Capt

DAVIS,Brian Charles 2Lt dow 22-8-18 7 att1/22Lond p247 CR France119

DAVIS,C.H.G.Lt 23-3-21 IAUL att2RWSurr MR43

DAVIS,Cecil Capt dow 27-3-17 5WelshR p230 MR34

DAVIS,Charles 2Lt kia 4-10-17 RGA 210SB p39 CR Belgium23

DAVIS,Charles Edwin T2Lt drd 15-9-18 14RWar Res p64 CR France13

DAVIS,Charles Henry 2Lt kia 24-5-15 2 att5BordR p117 CR Belgium101

DAVIS,Charles Stewart 2Lt kia 1-7-16 5 att2Mddx p146 CR France393

DAVIS,Clement John Burton Capt dow 29-9-17 RE 470Coy p210 CR Belgium3

DAVIS,Cyril Arthur Ernest T2Lt kia 31-7-17 A108RFA p27 CR Belgium7

DAVIS,Cyril York TCapt kia 15-9-16 12ESurr p112 MR21

DAVIS,Douglas Stalman Lt ded 27-1-19 HAC p206 CR Italy15

DAVIS,Edward Bernard T2Lt kia 31-7-17 225MGC Inf p182 CR Belgium112

DAVIS,Edward Thomas Lt kia 27-12-17 24Lond attMGC p187&252,Edwin CR Palestine3

DAVIS,Eugene T2Lt kia 28-3-18 2Dev p76 MR27

DAVIS,Francis Edward T2Lt kia 9-10-17 9 att1/5YLI p142 MR30

DAVIS,Fredk John Stockham Maj ded 4-11-18 5Dev p217 CR Devon69

DAVIS,George Edward Lt kia 11/13-10-15 RE p210 MR19

DAVIS,George Frederick.MID Maj mbk 15-8-15 11Lond p257 MR4

DAVIS,George Leith Blakeman 2Lt kia 27-9-18 23RFus p67 CR France714

DAVIS,Gronow John.DSO.LtCol ded 20-6-19 IA 22Punjabis att9KRR p275 CR Mddx26

DAVIS,Guy Clifton Lt ded 11-5-18 1/7NumbF p214 CR France1525

DAVIS,H.R.2Lt 22-12-17 RFC CR Norf261

DAVIS,Harold Charles 2Lt kia 4-4-17 4Lond p246 CR France662,att11KRRC

DAVIS,Harold Charles 2Lt kia 26-6-18 9Ess att104RAF p131 CR France1632

DAVIS,Harry.MM.2Lt 20-5-19 3RWar att59RAF CR Germany1

DAVIS,Henry Carlisle Monsell Lt kia 7-4-20 IA 2/3GurkhaRifatt2/5 p275 MR43

DAVIS,Henry Christopher 2Lt kia 2-7-16 16KRRC p149 MR19

DAVIS,Henry Ouseley Capt kia 27-10-14 5 att2RIrRif p169 MR22

DAVIS,Henry William Warren Lt kia 18-4-15 1WelshR p126 CR Belgium167

DAVIS,Herbert Gough Lt kia 14-2-15 3Norf p73 CR Belgium98

DAVIS,Herbert Nathaniel Lt dow 22-2-15 RE 3FC p210 CR Belgium58

DAVIS,Herbert Pinder T2Lt dow 29-7-16 13Ess p131 CR France141

DAVIS,Horace John 2Lt kia 6-2-17 3Lincs att15RFC p6&p75 CR France41

DAVIS,Hugh Courtenay 2Lt kia 5-8-16 3RBerks attRFC p2&p139 CR France31

DAVIS,Hugh Courtney T2Lt kia 25-7-16 20LancF p92 MR21

DAVIS,James Walden Fortune McNaught Lt kia 17-1-15 SWBord p99

DAVIS,John Charles Reginald Lt kia 13-5-15 3 att2Ess p131 MR29

DAVIS,John Henry TCapt ded 21-6-16 RAMC p267 CR Ireland33

DAVIS,Joseph T2Lt kld 20-1-18 RFC p15

DAVIS,Joseph Frederick.MC.Lt ded 19-3-19 RE p269 CR Hamps1

DAVIS,Lawrence Alan T2Lt kia 23-6-17 GL &4RFC p6 CR Belgium11

DAVIS,Leigh Jacob Capt kia 15-9-16 19Lond p250 CR France390

DAVIS,Leo Edwin 2Lt kia 7-8-15 5Manch p236 MR4

DAVIS,Leslie James George 2Lt kia 5-4-18 4EKent p212 CR France196

DAVIS,Leslie Sansome Lt kia 30-9-18 RH&FA &RAF p261

DAVIS,Maurice Oliver Arthur 2Lt dow 1-3-18 13 att18Lond p249 CR France398

DAVIS,Mellville Allen Duff.MC.T2Lt ded 29-5-18 KRRC att9Bn p149 CR Lancs43

DAVIS,Norman K.2Lt kia 4-10-17 YLI att9Bn p142 MR30

DAVIS,Oswyn St.Leger LtCol dow 5-4-18 6Manch Cmdg8LancF p236 CR France745,DAVIES

DAVIS,Owen Mazzinghi T2Lt kia 27-6-16 9EYorks p84 CR France643

DAVIS,Philip Henry Halton 2Lt dow 9-11-18 3Manch p154 CR France341

DAVIS,Percy Hill T2Lt dow 26-10-17 14RWar Res p64 CR Belgium165,kia

DAVIS,Percy Warren Theodore 2Lt kia 30-3-17 1EKent p57 MR19

DAVIS,Ralph Salway T2Lt kia 16-9-16 7Dors att6SomLI p124 MR21

DAVIS,Reginald 2Lt kia 20-10-16 GL &RFC p2&p190 CR France833

DAVIS,Reginald Noël.MID TCapt kia 12-10-16 3 att2WRid p115 CR France374

DAVIS,Reginald Percy 2Lt dow 5-10-15 4RWelshF p223 CR France259,DAVIES

DAVIS,Richard Christopher 2Lt kia 8-3-16 3 att1Manch p154 MR38

DAVIS,Richard Samuel Lt kia 22-3-18 2/5Leic p220 MR20

DAVIS,Robert 2Lt dow 11-1-17 IA 59Rif p275 CR Iraq5,10-1-17

DAVIS,Sidney Alfred 2Lt kia 22-8-17 5Glouc p225 MR30 Ex 1/4Bn

DAVIS,Sidney John 2Lt dow 28-3-18 5SStaffs p229 CR France40,4Bn

DAVIS,Thomas Edward George T2Lt kia 27-5-17 2RWelshF p97 CR France644

DAVIS,Thomas William 2Lt ded 14-11-18 5Beds att43TMB p269 CR Norf209

DAVIS,Uriah Philip 2Lt kia 16-4-17 10Lond att20RFus p248 MR20

DAVIS,Vivian Alfred T2Lt kia 4-9-18 9RIrFus p171 CR Belgium89

DAVIS,Wallace Howard 2Lt kia 1-7-17 4 att2N&D p133 MR19

DAVIS,Walter Ambler 2Lt kia 15-6-15 4LNLancs p234 MR22,DAVIES

DAVIS,Walter Arthur T2Lt kia 1-7-16 11N&D p133 CR France246

DAVIS,Wilfred Allen 2Lt kia 21-4-15 4 att1ESurr p112 MR29,Wilfrid

DAVIS,Wilfred Jervis Lt kia 30-6-16 7NumbF p214 CR Belgium60,Wilfrid

DAVIS,William T2Lt kia 18-10-16 12 att9Ess p131 MR21

DAVIS,William.MID Lt 28-5-21 2NumbF CR India97A

DAVIS,William Jeffery Capt&Adjt kia 30-7-15 8KRRC p149 MR29,T.

DAVIS,William Rhys Lancelot TLtACapt kia 23-4-17 10N&D p133 MR20

DAVIS,William Richard TCapt kia 28-9-15 2EKent p57 MR19

DAVIS,William Stanley Lt kia 22-3-18 5 att4Beds p219 MR20

DAVIS,William Thomas Hadley 2Lt kia 21-3-18 2DLI p160 MR20

DAVISON,Charles Montague 2Lt dow 10-4-18 4NumbF p213 CR France1094

DAVISON,Charles William Joseph T2Lt kia 14-9-16 9WYorks p81 MR21

DAVISON,Edmund 2Lt kia 24-9-17 3 att11RSuss p118 MR30

DAVISON,Frederick William 2Lt kia 17-4-18 Y&L p158 MR30

DAVISON,Guy Middleton TCapt ded 30-11-18 RE IW&DconstructSect p44 CR Kent25

DAVISON,Henry James Goddard T2Lt kia 4-6-15 13WYorks att3LancF p81 MR4

DAVISON,Joseph Jonathan 2Lt dow 23-6-17 2DLI p160 CR France178

DAVISON,Ralph Lt kia 9-5-15 3 att1Nhampt p137 MR22

DAVISON,Robert.MC.Lt dow 8-10-16 12Lpool p71 CR France105

DAVISON,Robert Charles 2Lt dow 19-5-17 5 att4RFus p67 CR France40

DAVISON,Rosnell Montague Rasnell TCapt dow 27-1-19 3NStaffs att8Leic p157 CR Surrey148,Rashell Rashell

DAVISON,Rutherford Willoughby 2Lt dow 10-10-16 3Lond p245 CR France105

DAVISON,Stuart 2Lt kia 14-9-14 2KRRC p149 CR France1329

DAVISON,William Hope 2Lt ded 6-9-17 IARO att2/32Pnrs p275 MR67,DAVIDSON

DAVISSON,Bertram 2Lt ded 22-2-19 RE p262 CR Lancs34,Lt RGA

DAVITT,Felix William T2Lt kia 12-4-18 12GordH p166 MR32

DAVOREN,Ambrose Joseph Stanislaus Lt kia 18-7-17 RFA Z25TMB p207 CR Belgium5

D'AVREY,William Septimus 2Lt kia 22-11-15 IARO att48Pnrs p275 MR38

DAVSON,Thomas Gordon Lt kia 13-5-15 RHGds p20 MR29

DAVY,Howard Samuel 2Lt kia 15-2-15 2RIrRif p169 CR Belgium17

DAVY,John Alfred Lt kld 8-11-16 GL &RFC 19ResSqd p2&p190 CR Surrey160

DAVY,John Evelyn.DSO.Maj ded 9-12-18 266RFA p206 CR Italy6

DAVY,Philip Francis.MC.T2LtACapt kia 4-11-18 13RB p178 CR France733

DAVY,Reginald 2Lt kia 21-10-18 3ESurr p112 CR France1388,20-10-18 1Bn

DAVY,William Edward TCapt&Adjt kia 7-7-16 18Ches p96 MR21,13Bn

DAVY,William James 2Lt kia 7-7-16 6SomLI p79 MR21,18-8-16

DAVY,William Reginald Capt kia 21-8-18 7Ess att10TankCps p189&232 MR16

DAW,Frederick Pole LtACapt kia 18-10-16 4Worc p108 CR France307

DAW,Reginald Samuel TCapt dow 25-9-16 9KRRC B'Coy p149 CR France177,25-8-16

DAW,T.Maj&QM 10-1-20 1Mddx CR Mddx46

DAW,Thomas Herbert TCapt kia 9-5-15 2ELancs p110 CR France706

DAW,William Westaway T2Lt ded 12-11-18 RE 171TC p44 CR France34

DAWE,Alfred Henry T2Lt kia 11-4-17 13KRRC p149 MR20

DAWE,James Jeffery Lt on or since7-6-18 GL &24RFC p2 CR France649

DAWE,Richard Henry O'Neill 2Lt kia 13-9-16 1Dev p76 CR France785

DAWE,Sydney Charles.MC.Capt kld 13-2-18 5Lincs p220 CR France439

DAWES,A.E.Sister 23-10-18 QAIMNS CR Beds23

DAWES,Arthur Irwin TCapt ded 22-6-17 9SomLI att10Gurkhas p79 CR Asia51

DAWES,Charles Edmund 2Lt dow 28-1-15 1LNLancs p135 CR France721

DAWES,George Hugh TLt&A/Adjt kia 16-9-16 5BordR p228 CR France432

DAWES,Hubert.MM.James 2Lt kia 8-5-18 3Suff att2Yorks p78 CR Belgium102

DAWES,Morris 2Lt kia 26-4-18 Ess att10Bn p131 MR27

DAWES,Oswald Stephen Bernard 2Lt kia 8-5-17 5NStaffs att14Y&L p238 MR20

DAWES,Roy Samuel 2Lt kia 9-9-16 13Lond p249 MR21

DAWES,Sidney Francis 2Lt kia 9-10-18 RGA 236SB p39 CR France341

DAWES,Walter Richard Aston Capt kia 23-8-14 1Wilts p152 CR Belgium261

DAWES,William Henry George T2Lt kia 29-9-18 8TankCps p188 CR France1495

DAWKINS,Charles John Randle T2Lt kia 25-9-15 9WelshR p126 CR France260

DAWKINS,Charles Tyrwhitt.KCMG.CB.MajGen ded 4-10-19 Commd &Staff p261

DAWKINS,Frank Lt ded 11-10-18 RE &RAF p44

DAWKINS,Frederick Clifton.MC.2Lt dow 2-9-17 A86RFA p27 CR Belgium11

DAWKINS,Guy Stacey T2Lt dow 25-9-15 ScotsGds att2Bn p52 CR France66

DAWKINS,Norman Leslie T2Lt kia 14-4-18 Y&L att1/5Bn p158 MR30,13-4-18

DAWN,Arthur Lt&QM drd 8-2-19 IARO att1/70BurmaRif p275 MR66

DAWN,Harold Frederick 2Lt mbk 22-1-17 IARO att6Jats p275 MR38,22-1-16

DAWNEY,Hugh.Hon.DSO.Maj kia 6-11-14 2LifeGds p20 CR Belgium140,DAWNAY

DAWS,Edwin 2LtTLt kia 2-11-17 16 att1/4RScots p54 CR Palestine8

DAWS,Harold T2Lt kld 26-12-16 10DLI p160 CR France1182

DAWSON,Albert George CaptALtCol kia 22-4-17 4Mddx p146 CR France604,23-4-17

DAWSON,Alfred.MC.Maj kia 20-5-17 88/14RFA p27 CR France570

DAWSON,Allan T2Lt kia 3-9-16 22MGC p182 CR France402

DAWSON,Anthony Lt kia 13-7-16 5 att2RB p178 CR France423

DAWSON,Arthur T2Lt kld 21-1-18 RFC p15 CR Scot396

DAWSON,C.C.Lt ded 23-9-16 3KAR p202 MR46, see DAWSON Mc.

DAWSON,Cecil Hubert Thrower Lt&QM mbk 24-3-18 10RIrRif p256 CR France1216,23-4-18

DAWSON,Dan Magill TLt dow 8-9-16 24NumbF A'Coy p60 CR France145

DAWSON,David Stewart 2Lt ded 20-10-17 3GordH p265 CR Scot280,Lt

DAWSON,Douglas James Septimus 2Lt ded 26-1-15 4Ess p269 CR Essex16

DAWSON,Eveline Maud Matron drd 10-4-17 QAIMNS p200 CR France40

DAWSON,Francis Rudolf Lt kia 10-8-15 4Ches p222

DAWSON,Frank Maitland Fraser 2Lt kia 20-9-17 4GordH p242 MR30

DAWSON,Frederick Albert.MC.T2Lt kia 7-8-18 8ESurr p112 MR27

DAWSON,Frederick Charles Blakeman T2Lt kia 3-5-17 11RFus attHAC p67 MR20

DAWSON,Frederick William 2Lt kia 8-9-16 5SLancs p230 CR France400

DAWSON,Gerald Moore TLt kia 1-7-16 18Lpool p71 MR21

DAWSON,Harold 2Lt kldacc 14-7-17 7Lond p247 CR France662

DAWSON,Harold Percy T2Lt kld 9-3-18 RFC p15 CR Mddx1

DAWSON,Harold William T2Lt kia 4-10-17 GL &19RFC p6 CR France285

DAWSON,Herbert Edward Capt kia 14-9-14 1Lincs p75 MR15

DAWSON,Herbert George T2Lt ded 29-5-18 12Manch attRE 86FC p154 CR France106,11Bn

DAWSON,Herbert Henry Mawson T2Lt kia 19-7-16 148RFA p27 CR France400

DAWSON,James 2Lt ded 2-4-17 3 att2BlkW p128 CR Scot625

DAWSON,James 2Lt kia 29-5-18 BordR att15DLI p254 MR18,28-5-18

DAWSON,John T2Lt kia 25-9-15 11 att4GordH p166 MR19

DAWSON,John T2Lt dow 22-7-16 9DLI p160 CR France1415

DAWSON,John Douglas Maj kia 28-6-15 7RScots p211 MR4

DAWSON,John Leonard T2Lt ded 6-5-16 10 att1/5Beds p85 CR Egypt15

DAWSON,John Stewart Lt ded 14-8-18 IARO att2S&M p275 MR65

DAWSON,Leonard T2Lt kia 4-6-15 13 att1WYorks attLancF p81 MR4

DAWSON,Leonard Leslie TLt kia 27-5-18 1N&D p133 CR France1332

DAWSON,M.C.Lt 23-9-16 3KAR MR46 see DAWSON,C.C.

DAWSON,Norman Currey TLt kia 28-3-18 13Lpool p71 MR20

DAWSON,Niel Creaton T2Lt dow 12-7-16 16N&D attTMB p133 CR France80,kia

DAWSON,Phillip Lt kia 26-3-18 RE 283ArmyTroopCoy p210 CR France526

DAWSON,Reginald Todd 2Lt kia 13-11-16 3 att2RScots p54 CR France742

DAWSON,Richard Long Capt kia 20-11-14 CldGds p51 CR Belgium134

DAWSON,Roger Graham 2Lt kia 18-9-15 3 att6Nhampt p137 CR France511,18-9-18

DAWSON,Sydney TLt&Adjt kia 1-7-16 8Y&L p158

DAWSON,Thomas Reginald 2Lt dow 4-2-16 19Lond p250 MR20

DAWSON,Walter Henry Mountiford Westropp 2Lt kia 24-5-15 2Ches p96

DAWSON,Wilfred Leedham 2Lt kia 3-12-17 2/6RWar p214 MR17

DAWSON,William T2Lt kia 11-4-17 SfthH p164 CR France604

DAWSON,William Arthur TLt kia 23-7-16 7 att11LNLancs p135 CR France432

DAWSON,William Ernest Capt ded 16-9-18 RFA &RAF p207&258 CR Mon81

DAWSON,William Healey 2Lt kia 20-7-18 7WYorks p218 CR France622,2/8Bn

DAWSON,William Ordford Charles Maj drd 22-1-17 IA IndCivVetDept p275,MR41,30-12-15 O'C.

DAWSON,William Robert Augrue.DSO&3Bars.CaptTLtCol dow 3-12-15 6RWKent p140 CR France40,Aufrere,3-12-18

DAWSON-DAMER,George Seymour.Hon.2Lt dow 12-4-17 10Huss p22 CR France104,13-4-17

DAWSON-GREENE,Charles John 2Lt dow 23-4-18 4GrenGds p49 CR France40

DAWSON-SCOTT,John Kearsley Capt kia 29-11-14 RE 5FC p44 MR29,29-10-14

DAWSON-SMITH,Charles Frank Lt ded 11-1-20 4 O&BLI att5KAR p269 CR EAfrica59

DAWSWELL,George Alec 2Lt kia 20-3-16 19Lond p250 CR France924

DAY,Charles Norris 2Lt kia 1-5-18 RGA 298SB p39 CR France139

DAY,Charles Spencer 2Lt dow 25-4-18 D59RFA p27 CR France106

DAY,Dennis Ivor T2Lt dow 7-10-15 106RFA p27 CR Hunts104

DAY,Douglas Knowles T2Lt dow 19-11-15 10 att6ELancs p110 CR Gallipoli27

DAY,Francis Innes Maj kia 21-12-14 2RMunstF p174 MR22,22-12-14

DAY,Francis Thomas Pressland TCapt dow 25-3-18 15WYorks p81 CR France103

DAY,Frederick Charles Capt kia 31-7-17 RFus att12Bn p67 MR29

DAY,Geoffrey Reynolds Lt kia 27-8-16 5Beds att1/8RWar p219 MR21

DAY,George Francis Hermitage 2Lt kia 11-9-16 125RFA attRGA 42SBp27 MR21,10-9-16

DAY,George Samuel Lt kia 1-10-18 12Lond &RAF p250&258&248

DAY,Gerald Harlow 2Lt kia 24-4-17 12Worc att7RBerks p108 MR37

DAY,Gerald Philip Lt dow 26-9-16 2Lincs p75 CR France105

DAY,Harry Montague TLt kia 15-4-18 59MGC Inf p182 MR32

DAY,Henry Brodie 2Lt kia 4-2-18 1Camb C'Coy p245 CR France439,3-2-18

DAY,Henry James 2Lt kia 7-7-17 71RFA p27 CR Belgium72

DAY,Henry Julian Dunlop TLt ded 3-12-18 MGC Inf p182 CR Norf132

DAY,Herbert T2Lt kia 10-7-16 8LNLancs p135 CR France832

DAY,Herbert James 2Lt dow 8-8-17 Glouc &11RFC p6&106 CR France214

DAY,Horace Frederick T2Lt kia 5-9-16 8NStaffs p157 CR Belgium89

DAY,Hubert Francis T2Lt kia 10-8-17 11RFus p67 MR29

DAY,Hubert Victor T2Lt kia 9-4-17 13RFus p67 MR20

DAY,James Arthur Percival SubCdr ded PoW 29-4-16/11-2-17 IA S&TCps p275 MR38

DAY,John Charles 2Lt kia 9-5-17 3RSuss &52RFC p7&p118 CR France415

DAY,John Edward TCapt dow 6-4-17 6RIrReg A'Coy p89 CR France285

DAY,Leslie Terrett TLt kia 1-7-16 RFA attTMB p27 MR21

DAY,Maurice 2Lt kia 9-5-15 RBerks p139 MR32

DAY,Maurice Charles 2Lt kia 3-11-14 IA 13Rajputs p275 MR47

DAY,Norman Leslie T2Lt kia 14-9-16 14Lpool p71 MR37

DAY,Oliver 2Lt dow 3-9-17 17WYorks p81 CR France658

DAY,Owen Heathcote Lacy Capt kia 6-8-15 2Hamps p120 CR Gallipoli6

DAY,Percy Oliver James T2Lt kia 19-7-16 17KRRC p149 CR France727

DAY,Reginald Harry TLt kia 4/5-4-16 12 att9RWar p64 CR Iraq5

DAY,Richard.MC.Maj dow 23-2-18 RFA p206 CR Belgium10

DAY,Samuel Albert 2Lt kia 10-11-16 3 att15WYorks p81 CR France342

DAY,Shirley Cuthbert.MC.TLtACapt kia 12-10-17 10N&D p133 MR30

DAY,Sidney 2Lt kia 11-8-16 5Y&L p238 CR France293

DAY,Walter Evan Capt kia 5-6-16 RE p44 CR Belgium137

DAY,William Leonard Lt kia 6-4-17 BordR &59RFC p7&117 MR20

DAYSH,Maurice T2Lt kia 23-4-18 12WYorks p81 CR France2,10Bn

D'CRUZ,Peter Clement AssSurg 2-2-16 ISMD MR59 &CR EAfrica61,2-2-17

DEACON,Charles.MC.MID LtAMaj dow 14-5-18 113RFA p27 CR France102

DEACON,Ernest Cecil Watson 2Lt kld 22-4-18 YLI att27RAF p143 CR France140,kia

DEACON,Edmund LtCol kia 13-5-15 EssYeo p203 MR29

DEACON,Raymond Eric 2Lt kia 7-8-15 10NStaffs att8LancF p157 MR4

DEACON,Stanley Alfred T2Lt kia 28-2-17 10Glouc p106 CR France1472

DEACON,William Warren.MC.Lt kia 22-8-18 1/5RLancs p213 CR France106,23-8-18

DEAKIN,Cedric Guy 2Lt kia 20-5-16 14Huss p22 MR38

DEAKIN,Cedric Kenworthy Lt kia 21-3-18 2/8Manch p237 MR27

DEAKIN,Charles Joseph John King T2Lt dow 2-7-16 16Mddx p146 CR France62

DEAKIN,George Welsley TCapt ded ?-2-16 RE IWT p262 CR Ches8,Welsby,21-3-16

DEAKIN,Robert Hartley 2Lt kia 22-7-17 IA 10Jats att45RFC p275 MR20

DEAKIN,William Ewart T2Lt kia 4-3-17 1Worc p108 MR21,Wilfrid

DEALTRY,Herbert Arthur Berkeley Capt kia 26-9-15 9ESurr p112 MR19

DEAN,Albert.MC.T2Lt dow 15-10-18 29DLI p160 CR France25

DEAN,Arthur T2Lt kia 8-11-16 21 att10LancF p92 CR France307

DEAN,Arthur Lt selfInflictGunshot 22-3-21 IA 80CarnaticInf att2/154Inf p275

DEAN,Arthur LeRoy 2Lt kld 9-8-17 RFC p7 CR Norf58

DEAN,Arthur Reginald.DCM.2Lt kia 4-7-17 4EYorks p219 CR France1489,3-7-17

DEAN,Cyril Edward Brietycke.MID 2Lt kia 15-9-16 RGA 121HB p39 MR21,Brietzcke

DEAN,Frank.MID 2Lt kia 31-10-14 KRRC p149 MR29

DEAN,George Frederick 2Lt kia 16-10-17 162RFA p27 MR30

DEAN,George Murray Lt kia 13-9-18 5GordH p27 p242 CR France115

DEAN,Harold.MC.T2LtACapt kld 5-1-18 2Yorks p90 CR Belgium127

DEAN,Harry T2Lt kia 11-4-18 EYorks p84 CR Belgium19,2Y&L

DEAN,Hedley T2Lt kia 21-3-18 10WYorks p81 MR20

DEAN,Henry James Lt ded 27-8-18 RE p262 CR Norf101,Capt

DEAN,John Henry Ellis.MC&Bar.TCapt kia 27-5-15 13 att10Ches p96 MR18

DEAN,Josiah Stanley Capt dow 27-5-15 7Lpool p215 CR France102

DEAN,Langley 2Lt ded 19-6-19 IARO 10EKent att2/28Punjabis p275 CR India48

DEAN,Leonard Lawson 2Lt kia 3-10-18 1LNLancs p135 CR France1710

DEAN,Reginald Evan 2Lt kia 7-6-17 10 att21Lond p248 CR Belgium60

DEAN,Rosser Fellowes Marriott 2Lt kia 1-7-16 4RWar att93MGC p64&p182 CR France156

DEAN,Thomas Albert Wray 2lt dow 8-5-18 20Lpool p71 MR30

DEAN,Thomas Walton T2Lt kia 7-6-17 9Yorks p90 MR29

DEAN,William 2Lt kia 1-7-16 3 att10RIrRif p169 MR21

DEAN,William Homer 2Lt kia 11-10-15 7N&D p233 MR19

DEAN-PITT,D.C.Maj 5-2-17 AssSec BRCS CR France461

DEANE,A.Lt 23-3-21 IA 2/154Inf MR65

DEANE,Arthur Denman T2Lt kia 14-7-17 1 att2RIrReg p89 MR21

DEANE,Arthur Francis T2Lt kia 16-8-17 167MGC Inf p182 CR Belgium167

DEANE,Arthur Reginald Lt dow 14-11-17 5RSuss p228

DEANE,Denis 2Lt kia 23-10-14 2RWar p64 MR29

DEANE,Ernest Cotton.MC.Capt kia 25-9-18 RAMC att2Leic p195 CR France1157

DEANE,George Frederic T2Lt kia 22-4-17 11Ess att18TMB p131 CR France115

DEANE,George Frederick 2Lt ded 29-11-17 RE p269 CR Berks85

DEANE,Gordon Alexander Capt dow 11-4-18 PoW 1RIrFus p171 CR France928

DEANE,John Henry Maj kia 30-4-15 Hamps p120 MR4

DEANE,Lancelot Colin William.DSO.MC.MIDx2 TMajALtCol kia 29-5-18 6SWBord p99 CR France 1689

DEANE,Richard John 2Lt kld 18-7-17 117/26RFA p27 CR Belgium29

DEANE,Wellesley Venables.MID 2Lt kia 24-9-17 D95RFA p208 CR Belgium19

DEANE,William.MC.Lt kia 20-3-20 4Norf &20RAF p269 MR43

DEANE-OLIVER,Richard Edward TLt kia 8-9-16 RE 75FC p44 CR France515,7-9-16 74FC

DEANE-SPREAD,Frederick Bradshaw Lt kia 25-9-15 IARO att58Rif p275 MR28

DEANS,Albert Victor 2Lt mbk 11-4-18 7 att12Yorks p256 CR France1092

DEANS,Geoffrey Chase Capt kia 6-5-15 4Worc p108 CR Gallipoli6

DEANS,Harold Mackenzie Capt kia 17-9-18 3 att7/8KOSB p101 CR France115

DEANS,William Wilkie TCapt dow 4-1-16 RAMC att54RFA p195 CR Gallipoli1

DEAR,Roy Evers T2Lt kia 30-4-17 RWar att6ELancs p64 MR38

DEARE,F.A.LtCol ded 24-1-15 RBerks p139 CR Berks121

DEARDEN,James Ferrand.DSO.MC&2Bars.Capt ded 6-10-19 RFus p263 CR Glouc31

DEARDEN,Walter Lt kia 19-12-16 NStaffs p157 MR38

DEARNALEY,Irvine 2LtTCapt kia 23-11-15 9Manch p237 CR Gallipoli6

DEAS,John Cairns Lt ded 31-12-19 3BlkW p264 CR Mddx26,30-12-19

DEAS,William Darling TLt dow 30-9-15 11A&SH p173 CR France1142

DEASE,Maurice James.VC.Lt kia 23-8-14 4RFus p67 CR Belgium242

DEASE,Trevor Herbert Llewellyn 2Lt kia 12-10-16 4 att1RIrFus p171 CR France1890

De BECK,George Clifford T2Lt kia 18-2-17 23RFus p67 MR21

DeBEER,Bendix Hallenstein 2Lt kia 10-7-17 RGA 94SB p39 CR Belgium173

DEBELL,Francis 2Lt kia 9-10-17 4Y&L C'Coy p238 CR Belgium125

DEBENHAM,Herbert.MID TLt kia 9-8-15 6ELancs p110 MR4

DEBENHAM,Herbert Austin 2Lt kia 1-11-18 4RWKent p234 MR16

DEBENHAM,Keith Lt dow 4-12-16 3HLI p162 CR Lond4

DEBERIGNY,Charles Etienne 2Lt dow 29-4-17 43RFC p7 CR France32,kia 45Sqn

De BLABY,Reginald Swithun Capt dow 9-8-16 3 att4LNLancs p135 CR France23

DeBLAQUIERE,John.Hon.Lt kia 10-3-15 2ScotRif p103 CR France260

DeBRUYN,Douglas Bayly 2Lt kld 27-5-16 RLancs &RFC p2&58,ded CR Camb16

DeBURGH,Francis Vavasour Cdr 7-12-18 RIM MR65

DeBURGH,Thomas.MID Lt mbk 17-9-14 IA 13Lancers att5 p275 MR28

DeBURIATTE,John Philip 2Lt kia 12-3-15 2ESurr p112 CR Belgium168

DeBURIATTE,Warwick Huxley Lt ded 19-10-18 RGA 92SB p262 CR Bucks69

De BUSSY,Walter 2Lt kia 14-10-16 6Y&L att82RFC p265 CR Belgium157,DeBUSSEY 14-10-18 RAF

DeCANDOLE,Alec Corry Vully Lt kia 3-9-18 4Wilts attMGC p187&236,4-9-18 CR France95

De CANN,Harold John T2Lt kia 29-7-16 9 att2Lincs p75 CR France423

De CASTRO,James Vivian Reynell Capt kia 1-10-15 3Suff p78 CR Belgium167

DeCAUX,Harry T2Lt kia 15-10-18 29DLI p160 CR Belgium42

De CAUX,William TCapt kia 15-9-16 9Norf p73 MR21

De CHAZAL,Robert Lt kia 9-4-16 11LNLancs p135 MR38

DECK,Richard Frank T2Lt kia 30-9-15 2Suff p78 CR Belgium115,Richmond

DeCONWAY,John Lt mbk 15-6-17 LovatScouts &RFC p257 MR20

DeCOUNDOUROFF,George 2Lt mbk 25-7-19 SL p256 CR Asia81

DeCOURCY,Henry Joseph.MID 2Lt kia 18-1-17 3Leinst att6RIrReg p174 CR France149

DeDENNIE,Thomas Geoffrey 2Lt kia 4-10-17 4Dev p220 MR30

DEDMAN,William Albert Lt ded 4-2-18 1/8WYorks p219 CR France200

DEEDES,Arthur Gordon Rev ded 29-11-16 RAChDept p199 CR Surrey160

DEEDES,Herbert Philip TCapt kia 16-7-16 16KRRC p149 MR21

DEEKS,Edward Charles Lt ded 4-8-19 RFA 31DAC p261 MR65,3DAC

DEEKS,Frederick William 2Lt dow 13-9-15 RH&FA 69Bty28Div 31Bde p27 CR France40

DEEMING,Frank Tetlow TLtACapt kia 21-3-18 12NumbF p60 MR27

De FALLOT,Carl Clare Capt dow 15-6-15 6LNLancs p135 CR Gallipoli3,15-7-15

De FAYE,Edward Francis T2Lt kia 1-12-17 TankCps p188 MR17

DeFERRANTI,Basil Ziani.MC.Maj dow 12-7-17 RGA 21SB CR France64

DeFONTAINE,Edward Harold Lt dow 17-11-15 19Lond p250 CR France1

DeFRECE,Cyril T2Lt kld 10-8-16 RFC p2 CR Mddx41

De FREYNE,Arthur Reginald French.Lord.Capt kia 9-5-15 3 att1SWBord p99 CR France924

DEFIES,Frederick.MID Lt kia 6-4-18 5 attMddx p146 MR37

DeGEX,Francis John.CB.CMG BrigGen ded 2-4-17 Staff BaseCommdt Rouen p1 CR France145

DeGUNZBERG,Baron Alexis George 2Lt kia 6-11-14 11Huss attRHGds p22 CR Belgium134,RHG att11Huss

DEHN,Thomas George Rudolph 2Lt dow 19-4-17 3Wilts attBerks p152 CR Lancs30

De HOUGHTON,Vere Capt kia 11/13-10-15 Lincs p75 MR19

DEIGHTON,Bartholomew James LtTCapt kia 25-9-15 1Mddx p146 MR19

DEIGHTON,Frederick Hamilton Lt dow 18-6-15 1KOSB p101 CR Europe1

DEIGHTON,Gerald William.MC.MID Capt kia 3-7-16 7Suff p78 MR21

DEIGHTON,John Capt dow 20-9-16 RAMC att1/5RLancs p195 CR France833,19-9-16

DeJASTRZEBSKI,Hubert Stephen Slepowron 2Lt dow 5-4-17 24Lond p252 CR France164

DeKNOOP,John Julius Jersey Capt kia 7-8-16 1/1ChesYeo att611ImpCamelCps p203 CR Egypt2

DeLaBERE,Charles Edward 2LtACapt&Adjt kia 10-9-18 66RGA p39 CR France433

DeLaBERE,Cyril John Baghot TLt kia 18-8-16 10Glouc p106

De LACEY,John Matthew 2Lt kia 23-9-17 18WYorks &57RFC p7&p81 CR Belgium140

DeLACOUR,Herbert Hedges Hyde Lt dow 3-12-19 RNDevYeo p269 CR Surrey37

De LACY-WHITE,Cyril T2Lt ded 27-6-18 13WelshR p126 CR France145,Capt

De La FONTAINE,Henry Victor Mottet.DSO.MajTLtCol kia 5-8-17 9ESurr p112 CR Belgium15,dow

DeLaHAYE,Cyril T2Lt dow 23-5-18 RE N SpecCo p44 CR France41

DELAHUNT,Peter Godfrey 2Lt dow 28-8-18 4 att1/7BlkW p230 CR France14

DELAINE,Frederick John TCapt ded 21-3-18 RAVC att119RFA p198 CR Canada1691

DeLALOUBERE,John Louis Claude Alfred Lt ded 24-9-17 RDC p253 CR Camb16

DELAMAIN,Frank Gun 2Lt kia 21-9-16 104RFA p27 CR France453

DELAMAIN,Henry Cresswell 2Lt ded 17-4-15 3Dors p124 CR Hamps28

DELAMERE,Percy Herbert TCapt ded 23-2-18 RAMC p195 CR Hamps7

DELAMOTTE,Hubert Thomas.MC.MID Capt dow 30-10-18 IA 29Punjabis CR Surrey160

DeLANDRE-GROGAN,Leon Victor St.Patrick.MC.TLt kia 13-10-18 Y&L p158 MR32

DELANEY,James Alfred Leo T2Lt kia 10-6-17 7RLancs attTMB p58 CR Belgium102

DELANEY,Michael Capt 29-3-19 16GpHQ RAF &Yorks CR Yorks557

DELAP,John Follansbee Bredin 2Lt kia 18-10-16 1Yorks p90 CR France744

DeLaPASTURE,Charles Edward Capt kia 29-10-14 1ScotsGds p52 MR29

DeLARUE,Francis T2Lt dow 23-7-18 10ScotRif p103 MR18

DeLaRUE,Thomas Capt ded 28-7-17 RLancs p58 CR Lancs77

DELAVOYE,F.B.Capt 11-8-16 RASC CR Surrey158

DELEPINE,Helenus George Sheridan 2Lt kia 17-4-15 1DCLI p114 CR Belgium165

DeLISLE,Alexander Charles Nicholas March Phillipps TLt kia 20-11-17 GL 9Leic &21RFC p7 CR Belgium165

DeLISLE,Richard de Beauvoir 2Lt mbk 21-1-16 IA 97Inf p275 MR38

DeLISLE-SMITH,Frank 2Lt ded 31-10-18 RH&FA p27

DeLUSIGNAN,Raymond Lt kia 25-4-15 RDubF p176 CR Gallipoli15,26-4-15

DELL,Louis Michael T2Lt kia 14-7-16 7KSLI p144 MR21

DELL,Reginald TLt dow PoW 8-5-18 20MGC Inf p182 CR France928

DELL,Stephen Arthur Hayton 2Lt dow 5-10-17 RGA 15SB p39 CR France446

DELLER,Harold James 2Lt kia 30-7-17 104RFA p27 CR Belgium29

DELLOW,Richard 2Lt ded 8-7-19 19NumbF p262 CR Durham8

DELMAR-WILLIAMSON,George Frederick Lt kld 12-7-18 1/2BlkW &RAF p128 CR Glouc31

DELMEGE,Eyre Bolton Massy.MC.MID Capt kia 23-10-16 2ELancs p110 CR France307,dow

DELMEGE,James O'Grady 2LtTLt ded 27-5-15 4DragGds p21 CR France285,dow

DeMATTOS,Gerald Comber Capt dow 11-8-19 9ELancs p254 MR70 &CR Europe179,Maj

DE MAYO,J. ? RE PMR attROD CR Egypt2

DEMETRIADI,L.P.LtCol 26-10-18 RAMC CR Yorks645

DeMEZA,Jacob.MC.MID Capt kia 22-8-18 19Lond p250 CR France210,Jack 23-8-18

DeMOUBRAY,Leslie St.John Capt ded 6-9-19 5RBerks p254&265 CR Kent230,Leslye

DEMPSTER,David Burns.MC.LtACapt kia 26-10-17 3KOSB att2BordR p101 MR30

DEMPSTER,Francis Erskine 2Lt kia 23-7-16 3 att1CamH p167 MR21

DEMPSTER,George Henry Capt kia 20-12-14 IA 35Sikhs att1/9Inf p276 MR28

DEMPSTER,Ian MacKay 2Lt kia 24-2-18 52RFC p15 CR France1266,25-2-18

DEMPSTER,James Lionel Cathcart.MID Lt dow 24-11-15 IA 66Punjabis p76 MR38

DENBY,Isaac Cecil 2Lt kia 27-6-17 6 att1/4WRid p227 CR France258

DENDRINO,Stephen 2Lt ded 27-9-16 RFC p2 CR France1185

DENDY,Ralph.MC.TCapt kia 15-10-18 RASC HT att2SWBord p192 CR Belgium157

DENEUFVILLE,Eustace Charles.DSO.Maj mbk 21-3-18 RGA 262SB p256 MR20

DENHAM,Aubrey Crawshaw Lt ded 1-4-15 6Beds att10Bn p85 CR Yorks643

DENHAM,Francis Bardon Lt kia 7-7-16 5 att1Worc p108 MR21

DENHAM,George Parsons TCapt dow 14-4-17 10A&SH A'Coy p173 CR France40

DENHAM,Reginald Grainger Lt kia 30-5-18 Wilts att11TMB p152 CR France1689

DENHAM,W.A.Lt 27-5-18 RFA att50DAC MR19

DENHAM,Wm.Malcolm 2Lt kld 3-1-18 RFC p15 CR Beds23

DENHAM-COOKES,Arthur Brownlow Capt ded 5-11-18 24Lond CR Essex176

DENHOLM,Thomas Stobie T2Lt dow 5-4-18 PoW 7CamH p167 CR France1276

DENIS-MARKLEW,Leslie Ernest 2Lt dow 12-10-17 7Lincs p75 MR30

DENISON,Archibald Campbell.MID Capt kia 25-9-15 2BlkW p128 MR19

DENISON,Bertram Noel Capt dow 15-9-14 2YLI p143 CR France717

DENISON,Gerald Evelyn Henry T2Lt kia 25-9-15 12RB p178 CR France768

DENISON,Harry.DSO.Maj dow 28-8-17 RHA p27 CR Belgium16

DENISON,John William.MC.Lt kia 18-9-18 6WRid p227 CR France415

DENISON,Robert Charles TCapt kia 27-8-16 8RWar p214 CR France383

DENISON,William Frank Evelyn T2Lt dow 22/28-3-18 15N&D p133 CR France300,26-3-18

DENLEY,Herbert Owen T2Lt kia 30-3-18 1Worc attCamelCps p27 MR34

DENMAN,Frank Christopher 2Lt kia 17-8-17 84/11RFA p27 CR Belgium13

DENMAN,Percy Darrell 2Lt kia 1-7-16 2Yorks p90 CR France630

DENMAN,Richard Charles Lt kia 1-12-17 4GrenGds p49 CR France662,2-12-17

DENMAN-JUBB,Cyril Oswald Capt kia 24-8-14 2WRid p115 CR Belgium201

DENNE,Vincent Alured T2Lt ded 5-1-17 10 att7RLancs p58 CR France169

DENNE,William Henry.DSO.Maj dow 21-2-17 Beds p85 CR Glouc51

DENNEHY,W.C.Capt ded 22-7-17 IA IndPostalDept p276 CR Iraq6

DENNES,Wilfred.MC.TCaptAMaj kia 21-3-18 82RFA p27 MR27

DENNETT,Stephen Hepworth T2Lt kld 11-5-17 8KSLI &23RFC p7&p144 CR Egypt1

DENNETT,Thomas,Frank Preston Thwaites 2Lt dow 5-8-17 4RWSurr att52RFC p18&p212 CR Belgium24,4-8-17

DENNETT,William Charles 2Lt kia 27-3-18 3RFC p15 MR20

DENNING,John Edward Newdigate Poyntry 2LtACapt dow 26-10-16 1Lincs p75 CR France833,Poyntz

DENNIS,Albert Claude.MID TCapt dow 27-7-16 7RWKent att12Mddx p146 CR France145

DENNIS,Charles Cowley 2Lt kia 25-9-18 1/19Lond attRFC p18&p250 CR France120

DENNIS,Edward 2Lt kia 22-3-18 7N&D attRFC p18&p233 MR20

DENNIS,Frederick Claude T2Lt kia 1-8-16 17N&D p133 CR France765

DENNIS,George Stanley Lt ded 1-7-19 11DLI p265 CR Germany1

DENNIS,James Owen Cuninghame Lt kia 24-10-14 12/35RFA p27 MR29

DENNIS,John Edmund William Lt kia 23-8-14 DCLI p114 MR15,Edward

DENNIS,John Neville.MC.TLt dow 15-10-17 11NStaffs att41MGC p157&p182 CR France139

DENNIS,L.V.TLt kia 31-7-18 SL attRAF p201

DENNIS,Michael Frederick Beauchamp.DSO.MajTLtCol kia 19-5-18 7/8KOSB p101 CR France68

DENNIS,Richard Thomas T2Lt ded 19-12-18 17RlrRif p169 CR France34

DENNIS,W.Lt 7-2-16 EAfrIntelDept CR EAfrica56

DENNISON,Harry Glanville 2Lt ded 24-2-19 RGA p254&262 CR Mddx77

DENNISON,James 2Lt kia 9-9-18 RGA 101SB p39 CR France298

DENNISON,Ralph Edward McKie 2Lt kia 9-5-15 5RSuss p228 MR22

DENNISS,Charles Sherwood LtCol 8-12-17 RE CR War6

DENNISS,Kenneth George T2Lt kia 15-7-16 16KRRC p149 MR21

DENNISS,Thomas Vivian Bartley.MID Capt dow 28-8-18 RBerks p139 CR Mddx83,LtCol

DENNISTON,Jack Evelyn T2Lt dow 20-9-16 10 att1BlkW p128 CR France453,21-9-16

DENNISTOUN,James Robert Lt dow PoW 9-8-16 NIrHorse &RFC p2&p24 CR Germany3

DENNY,Barry Maynard Rynd 2Lt dow 26-10-14 Lpool p71

DENNY,Ernest 2Lt dow 4-8-17 15Lond att17KRRC p249 CR Belgium16

DENNY,James T2Lt kia 23-10-18 1RlrFus p171 CR Belgium140

DENNY,Leonard George 2Lt ded 21-4-17 133RFA p27 CR Mddx26,dow

DENNY,Leon Serena Capt kia 13-5-15 1DragGds RoO att5DragGds p21 MR29

DENNY,Thomas David William.MM.2Lt ded 6-3-19 3Glouc p264 CR Kent234,Lt

DENNYS,Cecil Hector Massy Capt kia 9-2-17 IA 4GurkhaRif p276 MR65,25-4-20

DENNYS,Edward Massy Capt kia 9-2-17 IA 2/4GurkhaRif p276 CR Iraq5

DENNYS,Kenneth Rose 2Lt kia 9-5-15 RMunstF p174 CR France924

DENNYS,Richard Molesworth TCapt dow 24-7-16 10LNLancs A'Coy p135 CR France145,Molesworth

DENOVAN,Allan McNab 2Lt kia 26-3-18 1RFC p15 MR20,Macnab

DENROCHE-SMITH,Archibald John Lt kia 13-9-14 18Huss p23 MR15

DENSHAM,Walter Henry.MC.Lt dow 5-4-18 ELancsRFA p207 CR France62

DENT,Arthur Evelyn.MID LtACapt kia 9-4-17 1 att9KRRC p149 CR France581

DENT,Cornelius Costall 2Lt kia 20-5-16 10HLI p162 CR France423,21-5-16

DENT,Edgar Dent Capt kia 12-4-18 2IrGds p52 CR France346

DENT,Joseph Leslie.DSO.MC.Capt&BtMaj kia 11-4-17 2SStaffs p122 CR France182

DENT,Reginald Teesdale 2Lt kia 24-3-18 6 att2RB p178 MR27

DENT,Wilfred Harry TMaj kia 27-9-15 10Yorks p90 CR France924,26-9-15

DENTON,Arthur Capt kia 16-8-15 5Ess p232 MR4

DENTON,Arthur 2Lt kia 16-6-17 20 att2Lond p251 MR20

DENTON,Brian Maurice TLt kia 19-8-16 6SomLI p79 CR France402

DENTON,George Clarke.MIDx3 Maj kia 9-10-16 IA 12Pnrs attJindInf p276 CR EAfrica36

DENTON,Philip Sydney 2Lt kia 13-8-17 A&SH att10CamH p173 MR21

DENTON,Reginald 2Lt 30-1-19 9Lpool CR Ches175

DENTON-CARDEW,Warnell de Montigny T2Lt kia 30-11-17 KRRC att12Bn p150 MR17

DENWOOD,Thomas William 2Lt ded 22-10-18 3RLancs att2/6Suss p58 MR67,2/6Lancs

DENYER,Augustus Andrew.MC.T2Lt kia 7-6-17 9Y&L p158 MR21

DENYER,Horace Frederick.MID TLt kia 13-7-17 12Ches p96 CR Greece6

De PARAVICINI,John Marcus Maj kia 30-11-17 KRRC att11Bn p150 MR17

De PASS,Crispin Asabel 2Lt kia 22-3-18 2TankCps p188 MR27,Asahel

De PASS,Frank Alexander.VC.Lt kia 25-11-14 IA 34 PoonaHorse p276 CR France80

DePASS,William Hugh David Lt kia 25-3-18 6 att13Mddx p146 CR France692

DePENNINGTON,Alan Lt kia 4-9-17 4ELancs p226 CR Belgium113

DEPENTHENEY-O'KELLY,Henry Arundel Capt dow 19-5-15 18Huss RoO p23

DePENTHENY-0'KELLY,Edmund Capt ded 14-2-19 LancF p263 CR Lond9

De PIERRES,Eric Noel 2Lt dow 16-9-17 C190RFA p27 CR Belgium15

De PLEDGE,Edward Karl TCapt kia 3-6-17 15WYorks p81 CR France5

De POMEROY,Norman 2Lt kia 20-10-16 GL &RFC CR France647

DEPREZ,Austin Edward Capt kia 12-11-17 C62RFA p27 CR France423

DEPUIS,Alfred 2Lt dow 8-8-16 1Lincs p75

DERBYSHIRE,Albert 2Lt kia 30-4-17 9Ess p131 MR20

D'ERF Wheeler,Geoffrey Noel Popham 2Lt kia 26-9-16 7 att5Dors p124 MR21

D'ERF Wheeler,Percival Francis Crommelin Capt kld 24-7-17 3Dors &RFC p7&p124

DERING,Rupert Cholmeley Yea Capt dow 19-4-15 2KOSB p101 CR Belgium151

De RITTER,Victor Frank T2Lt dow 9-8-16 1SomLI p79 CR Belgium11,kia

DeROCHIE,Curtis Matthew 2Lt kia 14-7-17 27RFC p7 CR Belgium175

DeROSS,Adam Gower Sutherland T2Lt kia 14-2-17 GL &3RFC p7 MR20

DeROSSE,Joseph Albert.MC.Lt ded 2-12-18 IARO att2S&M p276 CR Egypt9,Capt

DeROTHSCHILD,Evelyn Achille.MID Maj dow 17-11-17 BucksYeo p203 CR Palestine14

DeROUGEMONT,Maurice Henry 2Lt kia 16-5-15 2RWSurr p55 CR France279,dow

DERRICK,Alan James 2Lt kia 15-11-16 7NumbF p214 MR21

DERRICK,John Leslie TCapt kia 27-8-17 6Yorks p90 MR30

DERRICK,Leslie James 2Lt kld 3-5-18 3EKent att15RAF p57 CR France116

DERRIMAN,Gerard Lysley Capt dow 7-8-15 4GrenGds RoO p49 CR France1

DERRY,Daniel 2Lt ded 18-4-18 5NStaffs p238 CR Belgium18

DERRY,Douglas Alfred Laurie TLt dow 9-10-16 2Y&L p158 CR France374

DERRY,Richard Courtnay Powell T2Lt kia 6-8-15 2Hamps p120 CR Gallipoli6,Lt

DeRUTZEN,Alan Frederick James Lt kia 7-8-16 1/1Pembroke Yeo att61ImpCamelCps p205 CR Egypt2

DERWENT,Robert Ivor T2Lt kia 1-7-16 18WYorks p81 CR France156

DESAGES,Owen Loftus 2Lt kia 27-5-18 Wilts p152 MR18

DESAGES,Wilfrid Roland Capt kia 21-3-18 24Lond p252 MR20,Wilfred

DESAI,F.C.Capt 7-11-17 IMS MR43

DeSALIS,George Roldolph 2Lt kia 21-6-17 8Mddx p236 CR France594

DeSALIS,Jerome Joseph Fane 2Lt dow 3-10-15 8Mddx p236 CR Mddx62,Lt 3Bn

DeSALIS,Peter Fabin Fane 2Lt kia 22-1-17 3 att2SfthH p164 CR France511

DeSATGE,Frederick Gordon Capt kia 15-9-16 1 att7KRRC p150 MR21

DeSAUMAREZ-BROCK,Ranulf Steinthal TLt kia 24-5-17 RFA Y23TMB p27 CR Belgium6

DESBOROUGH,Laurence Vernon Lt kia 30-11-17 RFA att15RFC p18&207 MR20

De SEGUNDO,Robert Charles Edward Stewart 2Lt kia 17-2-17 1Lpool p71 CR France239

DESLANDES,Denis George T2Lt kia 27-11-16 7ESurr p112 CR France175

DESPARD,Charles Beauclerk.DSO.MC.TCapt kia 18-4-18 InniskDrags att9RlrFus p171 MR30

DESPARD,Ernest Richard T2Lt dow 26-9-17 E'TankCps p188 CR Belgium16

DESPARD,Marcus Carden 2Lt kia 19-7-17 3InniskF p104 CR Belgium85,1Bn

DESPICHT,Leonard Terry.MC.MID Lt&Adjt kia 11-2-17 4Beds p85 CR France220

DESPREZ,Warwick Haynes T2Lt kia 24-8-18 3Glouc att7RWKent p141 CR France177

DeSTACPOOLE,Robert Andrew 2Lt kia 20-9-14 2ConnRgrs p172 MR15

DeSTACPOOLE,Roderick Algernon Antony.MID 2Lt kia 11-3-15 RFA 1Bty p27 CR France705,Anthony

De St CROIX,Aubrey.MIDx2 Capt kia 3-2-17 IA 2/119Inf p276 MR38

De Ste CROIX,Wilfred Hungerford T2Lt ded 24-7-17 RASC p192 CR Iraq8

DeSt.PAER,Louis Emile.MC.Maj dow 8-5-18 B246RFA p206 CR Belgium8

DES-VOEUX,Frederick William Lt kia 14-9-14 2GrenGds p49 CR France1112

DES VOEUX,Harold Charles 2Lt dow 11-6-15 1AUL attRMunstF p276 CR Gallipoli1,Lt

DES VOEUX,Seymour Capt dow 1-2-17 IA 36Sikhs p276 CR Iraq5

DeTEISSIER,Aubrey T2Lt kld 12-10-17 GL &RFC p7 CR Essex45,2-10-17

DeTRAFFORD,Henry Joseph Capt kia 25-9-15 3 att1SStaffs p122 MR19

De TRAFFORD,Ralph Edric Galfrid Antony Lt kia 25-4-15 2RFus p67 MR4,Eric Galrid

DeTRAFFORD,Reginald Francis Lt dow 9-5-15 3RLancs attGlouc p58 CR France727

De TRAFFORD,Thomas Cecil Capt kia 10-11-14 RFus p67 MR29

De TUYLL,Maurice Arthur Capt kia 13-5-15 10Huss p22 CR Belgium45

DEUCHAR,Alic Guthrie Capt kld 22-11-17 NCycBn attRFC p269 CR Numb4

DEUCHAR,Robert 2Lt ded 27-5-16 3/2ScotHorse p269 CR Numb75

DEVAS,Arthur Edward Lt ded 15-2-15 Ess p131 CR Somerest139,1-2-15

DEVAS,Bertrand Ward TLt kia 13-11-16 2Suff p78 CR France801

DEVENISH,Arthur Henry Noel Maj ded 5-10-16 RFA p27 CR Surrey160

DEVENISH,Donald Henry TLt ded 17-1-16 14WelshR p126 CR France80,17-1-15

DEVENISH,George Weston Lt kia 6-6-17 RFA &35RFC p7&p27 MR20

DeVERE,Roger TLtTCapt ded 1-12-18 RE 99FC attStaff GHQ p44 CR Italy11

DEVERELL,Richard Seddon T2Lt ded 4-11-16 14 att15WYorks p81 CR Lond2

DEVEREUX,Frederick Herbert T2Lt kia 31-7-17 23Mddx p146 MR29

DEVEREUX,Humphrey William Lt kia 26-6-16 5SStaffs p229 CR France747

DeVILLE,Charles Arthur 2Lt kia 20-7-18 2/5WYorks p218 CR France622

DeVINE,Hatton Bertram St.John Rev kia 27-4-16 RAChDept att10GordH p199 CR France423

DEVINE,Henry 2Lt ded 17-2-19 10RIrrF p265 CR Ireland14,RIrRif

DEVINE,John Ross.MC.Lt kia 26-8-17 15RScots p54 MR21

DEVIS,Francis 2Lt kia 11-4-17 4 att2RWar p64 CR France604

DEVITT,Guy Francis Ormond T2Lt kia 30-7-15 7RB p178 MR29,Ormand

DEVITT,Herbert John 2Lt kia 12-9-18 16 att13KRRC p150 CR France245

DEVLIN,Henry Little Lt kia 19-9-17 5A&SH att9RFC p18&243,Harry CR Belgium18

DEVONSHIRE,Feray Vullramy Lt 20-7-19 7Huss &RAF MR43

DeVRIES,Harry Kumbring 2Lt kia 20-11-17 3 att5RBerks p139 MR17

DEW,Albert William John 2Lt kia 10-4-17 7 att26NumbF p214 MR20

DEW,Frederick Thomas T2Lt kia 24-8-17 10DLI A'Coy p160 MR30

DeWAEL,Cecil Hubert Lt dow 6-4-18 LondRFA p207 CR France64

DEWAR,Alan Douglas 2Lt ded 22-6-19 RE p262 CR Lond14

DEWAR,Alexander.MID Lt dow 21-12-14 RE 15FC p44 CR France768

DEWAR,David(Sonnie).MID TLt kia 22-3-18 14MGC Inf p182 CR France1061

DEWAR,George TLt kia 3-2-16 RAMC att48FA p195 CR France747

DEWAR,Harold Ernest.MC.T2Lt dow 12-7-16 11Ches p96&258 CR France833,11-7-16

DEWAR,Ian Dalrymple TCapt kia 16-3-16 5CamH p167 CR Belgium53,17-3-16

DEWAR,James Evan 2Lt kia 8-10-16 5Lond p246 MR21

DEWAR,James Melville TLt kia 16-10-18 1/7BlkW p128 CR France760

DEWAR,James Tyrie T2Lt kia 14-2-17 13RIrRif p169 CR Belgium43

DEWAR,Margaret Smith SNurse kia 12-3-17 QAIMNS p200 CR Greece9

DEWAR,Robert T2Lt kia 18-11-16 17HLI p162 CR France534

DEWAR,Robert Johnman.DCM.2Lt dow 3-10-18 153RFA p27 CR Belgium44,5-10-18

DEWAR,William Capt kia 22-3-18 9ScotRif p103 MR27

DEWARBURG,Hermann Vivian T2Lt kia 7-10-16 122MGC p182 CR France744

DEWDNEY,Clifford Mostyn French Capt kia 4-4-18 14Glouc att7RWKent p106 MR27

DEWE,William Horsley LtCol ded 31-3-18 RDC p253 CR Sussex 128

DeWEND,Douglas Fenton Lt kia 11-11-14 2WRid p115 MR29

DEWES,Bryan Osmond T2Lt kia 30-7-15 1Mddx p146 CR France707

DEWHIRST,Alfred Guy T2Lt kld 10-8-18 RASC MechTransport p192 CR France145

DEWHURST,George Charnley Littleton TLt kia 1-7-16 1RB p178 CR France1890

DEWHURST,Joseph Mullineaux Lt dow 7-11-17 1/4ELancs p226 CR France1361

DEWHURST,Robert William Millington.MID TLt dow 26-4-16 5Wilts p153 CR Iraq5

DeWIND,Edmund.VC.2Lt kia 21-3-18 15RIrRif p169 MR27

DEWING,Robert Edward.DSO.CaptALtCol kia 4-4-18 RE att8RBerks p44 MR27

DeWINTON,Walter Frederick 2Lt kia 6-9-14 3CldGds p51 CR France1402 &CR France1895

DeWOLF,George Le Blanch TLt kia 14-2-16 3 att9RSuss p118 CR Belgium72

DEXTER,E.I.Lt ded 4-5-18 9NumbF attRAF p60

DEY,Herman Francis 2Lt kia 31-7-17 5Lpool p215 MR29

DIACK,William 2Lt kia 20-9-17 4GordH C'Coy p213&242 MR30

DIAMOND,Julius.MC.Lt kia 8-10-17 KOSB &7RFC p7&p101 MR20

DIBB,William Reginald.MC.Lt dow 27-5-18 RFA X37TMB p27 CR France745

DIBBEN,Harold William 2Lt kia 30-9-17 4KSLI p235 CR France1182

DIBBS,Thomas Graythwaite Burton T2Lt kia 27-8-15 7Y&L p158 CR Belgium111

DICK,Alexander Young T2Lt dow 1-10-16 13 att15HLI p162 CR France134

DICK,Andrew Campbell T2Lt dow 23-10-18 2KRRC p150 CR France146,24-10-18

DICK,Andrew Robertson T2Lt kia 18-7-18 1BordR p117 MR32

DICK,Arthur James Seaber Lt kia 22-3-18 1RInnskF p104 MR27

DICK,Charles William Lt ded 9-11-18 RAF CR Scot237

DICK,George Frederick Graeme 2Lt kia 9-5-15 N&D p133 CR France566

DICK,James.MM.2Lt dow 28-10-17 9DLI p239 CR Belgium18

DICK,John Campbell Capt kia 9-5-15 RMunstF p175 MR22

DICK,John Young Farquhar T2Lt dow 14-11-16 HLI p162 CR France1492

DICK,Norman Brabazon 2Lt kia 28-4-17 6 att17Mddx p146 MR20

DICK,Robert Henry.MIDx3 Lt 15-3-21 4RFus CR Iraq6

DICK,Thomas Aitken Maj ded 27-1-19 RFA p254 CR Surrey1

DICK,Watson Tullock.MC.Capt&Adjt kia 18-9-18 7SWBord p99 CR Greece5

DICK,William LtCol 12-11-17 RAMC CR Mddx53

DICKASON,Reginald Percy 2Lt kia 14-2-17 6 att1Mddx p146 CR France511

DICKENS,Cedric Charles Maj kia 10-9-16 13Lond p249 MR21 &CR France218,9-9-16

DICKENS,Guy TCapt dow 17-7-16 13KRRC p150 CR France300,DICKINS

DICKENS,Maurice Wilfred Lt kia 27-2-25 25RFC p15 CR France40

DICKENS,William Castle.MID T2Lt kia 13-10-18 1 att10LancF p92 CR France315

DICKENSON,Aubrey Greville Newton TLt dow 1-7-16 2KRRC p150 CR France80,2Lt

DICKENSON,Lawrence Aubrey Fiennes Wingfield Lt dow 10-5-15 4Beds attRIrRif p85 CR France345

DICKERSON,Charles Henry T2Lt kia 14-7-16 11A&SH p173 MR19

DICKERSON,Jersey Horrex T2Lt kia 22-4-18 15N&D p133 MR27

DICKETTS,George Humphrey Lt dow 21-7-18 3/24RFA p27 CR Belgium11,111/24RFA

DICKEY,Robert George Alexander Capt ded 14-11-18 5Manch C'Coy p236 CR Lancs210

DICKIE,Cecil Barron Lt kia 18-7-18 BlkW &107RAF p264 MR20

DICKIE,Edward Gordon TLt kia 30-11-17 GL &84 att54RFC p7 CR France1472,2Lt

DICKIE,Herbert 2Lt kia 2-10-16 8SLancs p125 CR France535,21-10-16 3Bn

DICKIE,Robert Bruce 2Lt kia 1-6-18 7 att1GordH p242 CR France33

DICKIE,William 2Lt kia 1-7-16 6BordR att9KOSB p117 MR21

DICKIN,Albert Edward T2Lt kia 21-10-16 13Ches p96 CR France314

DICKINS,Albert Light Moody.MC.Capt kia 21-3-18 7N&D p233 MR20

DICKINS,G. see DICKENS,G.

DICKINS,Wyndham Harold TCapt dow 28-9-15 12N&D p133 CR France51,Maj

DICKINSON,Alan Piele.MC.Capt dow 1-6-18 10Lpool p216 CR France106,Peile kia

DICKINSON,Arthur Frowde TLt kia 22-3-18 14NumbF p60 MR27

DICKINSON,Arthur Thomas Searle.MIDx3 Maj kia 24-11-15 IA 51Sikhs attHQ Staff30Bde p276 MR38,22-11-15

DICKINSON,Bruce Norman T2Lt kia 29-6-16 10RWKent p141 CR Belgium30

DICKINSON,Colin James Henry T2Lt kia 28-7-16 15Ches p96 CR France453

DICKINSON,Digby Cecil Cales 2Lt kia 18-8-18 2SWBord p99 CR France28

DICKINSON,Edward Capt kia 28-6-15 11Yorks p90 MR4

DICKINSON,Francis Arthur Maj dow 11-4-15 DCLI p114 CR Somerset118

DICKINSON,Francis John Twysden LtTCapt kia 17-9-18 2att7SWBord p99 CR Greece5

DICKINSON,Frederick William 2Lt kia 17-3-18 7Leic p87 MR21

DICKINSON,Geoffrey Garbutt 2Lt kia 2-10-17 B255RFA p208 CR Belgium10

DICKINSON,George Bairnsfather Lt kia 3-5-15 3ELancs p110 MR29

DICKINSON,George Sidney TCapt kia 2-7-16 7Lincs p75 CR France630

DICKINSON,Harry Chap4Cl kia 30-10-17 RAChDept att1/28Lond p199 CR Belgium123

DICKINSON,Henry Waite Lt dow 9-8-18 PoW 12/13NumbF p60 CR Germany3

DICKINSON,Herbert.MC.LtACapt kia 27-5-18 10Glouc att2Mddx p106 MR18

DICKINSON,Hubert John 2Lt kia 20-9-17 2Lincs p75 CR France452

DICKINSON,Hugh Carey CaptTLtCol ded 18-12-18 1SomLI att2/3KAR p202&79 CR EAfrica36,att3/3KAR

DICKINSON,Humphrey Neville 2Lt dow 13-10-16 3 att6RWKent p141 CR France145

DICKINSON,John.MC.Lt kia 9-4-17 72RFA p207 CR France68,8-4-17

DICKINSON,John 2Lt kia 28-8-17 3RScots p54 CR Belgium88

DICKINSON,John Archibald Lt kia 13-4-18 4 att1RWSurr p212 MR32

DICKINSON,John Malcolm Lt dow 12-6-18 2RSuss CR France10 see DICKISON,J.M.

DICKINSON,Leonard T2Lt kia 11-4-18 12Y&L p158 MR32

DICKINSON,Leslie Alfred T2Lt dow 17-11-17 1Norf p73 CR Herts30

DICKINSON,Lewis George 2Lt kia 1-10-15 6N&D C'Coy p233 CR Belgium131,30-9-15

DICKINSON,Lionel St.Clair 2Lt kia 16-9-16 1Lond p245 CR France785

DICKINSON,Raymond Scott 2LtTCapt kia 2-10-15 16Lond p249 CR Belgium44

DICKINSON,Ronald Francis Bickersteth.MID Capt kia 16-6-15 10Lpool p216 MR29

DICKINSON,Talbot.MC.Lt kia 31-7-17 8LancF p221 MR29,2/5Bn

DICKINSON,Thomas Arthur 2Lt kia 1-7-16 1/6SStaffs p229 MR21

DICKINSON,Thomas Malcolm.DFC.Capt ded 4-1-21 IA 16Cav attRFC p276 CR Egypt15

DICKINSON,Walter Stanley T2Lt kia 23-4-17 8Lincs p75 MR20

DICKINSON,William 2Lt kia 29-3-17 5LancF p221

DICKINSON,William Henry Egerton de Brissac Maj dow 19-10-18 113/25RFA p206 CR France725,29-10-18

DICKINSON,William Vicris.CMG.Col ded 28-10-17 Staff AAG GHQ3Ech p1 CR France145 lateWelchR

DICKISON,John Malcolm Lt dow 12-6-18 2RSuss p118 CR France10,DICKINSON,J.M.

DICKS,Francis James Neville 2Lt dow 27-5-18 2/8Worc p226 CR France31

DICKSEE,Lawrence Rowland Arthur 2Lt kldacc 2-5-16 3N&D D'Coy p133 CR Durham27,9-5-16

DICKSEE,Maurice John Lt kia 14-9-18 9Mddx att10RFus p236 CR France245

DICKSEE,Reginald Frank 2Lt kia 8-10-18 6N&D p233 CR France849

DICKSON,Alan James Lt kia 14-11-14 HLI p162 MR29

DICKSON,Angus Lt kld 15-10-16 1/5RLancs p213 CR Belgium4,14-10-16

DICKSON,Arthur TLtCol kia 1-7-16 1SLancs att10WYorks p125 CR France373

DICKSON,Arthur Francis Lt kia 14-7-18 IARO att34PoonaHorse p276 CR Palestine3

DICKSON,Arthur Herbert 2Lt ded 13-10-15 LNLancs p135 CR Lancs52,7-10-15

DICKSON,Ashley Gordon.MID Maj dow 18-6-17 RHA attC123RFA p206 CR France

DICKSON,Barrington Blomfield Capt kia 9-5-15 1Nhampt p137 MR22

DICKSON,Cyril Garlies Lt kia 4-11-14 2LNLancs p135 MR47

DICKSON,Edward John Quayle.MC.TCapt kia 26-10-17 RE 255TC 1stCps p44 CR Belgium11

DICKSON,Edwyn David Lt kia 28-4-17 10Lincs p75 MR20

DICKSON,George Lt kia 12-7-15 7HLI p240 MR4

DICKSON,George Arthur Hamilton.MVO.Maj ded 16-2-18 5Worc attLabCps p108 CR Mddx26

DICKSON,George Hubert Murray 2Lt kia 26-10-18 6BlkW p231 CR France1256

DICKSON,Henry Goudie 2Lt dow 5-2-17 IARO att82Punjabis p276 CR Iraq5

DICKSON,Hugh Barclay Lt kia 12-10-17 3 att8BlkW p128 MR30

DICKSON,J.A.Capt 4-4-17 IA CR Cornwall123

DICKSON,James 2Lt kia 16-9-16 21Lond p251 CR France385

DICKSON,John Gavin 2Lt kia 8-3-16 4 att1HLI p162 MR38

DICKSON,John Hamilton 2Lt kia 14-9-14 att1CamH p167 MR15

DICKSON,Mary C.Nurse ded 16-2-17 VAD p200 CR France145

DICKSON,Robert.DCM.ACapt kia 27-5-18 7DLI p239 CR France1753

DICKSON,Robert Adair 2Lt kia 2-8-17 4 att6RIrReg p89 MR29

DICKSON,Robert Cecil Capt ded 16-6-19 RAMC p267&254 MR65

DICKSON,Robert Maxwell T2Lt kia 22-3-18 11Lpool att8RB p71 CR France1061

DICKSON,Sam.MC.ACapt 20-10-18 1/5Manch p236 CR France287

DICKSON,Sigurd Ayton 2Lt kia 1-2-17 102RFA p27 CR Belgium72

DICKSON,Thomas Graeme Capt 27-4-20 RAMC CR Derby58

DICKSON,Walter Felix T2Lt kia 1-8-18 11Ess p131 CR Belgium3,dow 31-7-18

DICKSON,Walter Michael T2Lt kia 26-9-15 11A&SH p173 MR19

DICKSON,William Herbert 2Lt kia 7-6-17 2/4LNLancs p234 CR Belgium31

DICKSON,William Tillie Lt dow 9-7-16 6RInniskF p104 CR France1490,Capt &CR France1490,Lt

DIETRICHSEN,Frederick Christian Capt kia 26-4-16 2/7N&D p233 CR Ireland5,25-4-16

DIGBY,Charles 2Lt kia 10-7-18 RGA 123SB p39 CR France924

DIGBY,G.H Maj 20-11-14 DorsYeo CR Dorset28

DIGBY,John Kenelm Lt kia 4-8-15 1/7Norf p73 CR Belgium71

DIGBY-JONES,Charles Kenelm TCapt ded 25-9-18 RE p44 MR70 &CR Europe195

DIGGENS,Martin Charles TCapt kia 30-6/1-7-16 13RSuss p118 CR France924

DIGGES La TOUCHE,Averell Lt 25-9-15 5 att2RIrRif MR29

DIGGES La TOUCHE,Denis Capt kia 8-8-15 8WelshR p126 MR4

DIGGLE,Joseph T2Lt kia 23-8-18 2RWelshF p97 CR France41,24-8-18

DIGNAN,Albert Guy Lt kia 21-3-18 SIrHorse att7RIrReg p24 MR27

DIGNAN,Joseph Patrick 2Lt kia 16-10-16 4ConnRgrs att8RinniskF p172 CR Belgium17

DIGNEN,George William 2Lt kia 24-10-18 3 att1NumbF p60 CR France206

DILBEROGLUE,Augustus Lt kia 1-4-18 3Huss p21 CR France485,Lt

DILBEROGLUE,Richard Nicholas Lt kia 15-9-16 1CldGds p51 CR France374

DILL,John Rowe Lt&Adjt kia 6-6-15 IA 69Punjabis p276 CR France924

DILL,Robert Foster.DSO.Capt kia 11-4-15 IA 129Baluchis p276 CR France924

DILLING,John Francis TLt kia 10-8-18 15LancF p92 MR16

DILLIWAY,George Goldin TLtACapt ded 10-10-18 RASC attH'Coy CamelTransCps p192 CR Palestine3,Golden

DILLON,Charles Edward Maxwell 2Lt kia 31-7-17 10RWKent p141 CR Belgium88

DILLON,Edeveain Charles Barclay 2Lt kia 13-10-16 3RDubF p176 CR France374,2Bn

DILLON,George Charles Tracy 2Lt kia 23-7-16 6Glouc p225 MR21,Tracey

DILLON,Harry Chester Wentworth Lt kia 24-11-15 IA 26Punjabis att24 p276 MR38,22-11-15

DILLON,Henry Mountiforort.DSO.Maj ded 13-1-18 2 O&BLI p130 CR Oxford32

DILLWYN-VENABLES-LLEWELYN,John Lister Capt kia 10-7-17 3CldGds p51

DILNUTT,Eric William LtTCapt kia 2-3-16 8RFus p67 MR19

DILWORTH,Maclean Proctor Lt kia 20-10-14 1N&D p133 CR France924,20-11-14

DILWORTH,Robert Kildahl 2Lt kia 28-12-16 2RMunstF p175 MR21

DILWORTH-HARRISON,Douglas Roy 2Lt 27-3-18 10 att1/8DLI MR27

DIMENT,Harry Stanley T2Lt kia 23-5-17 GL &6RFC p7 CR Belgium11

DIMENT,William James Gregory T2Lt kia 26-9-17 8EYorks p84 CR Belgium125

DIMERY,George Wentworth T2Lt ded 4-4-17 15WYorks p81 CR Yorks373

DIMMER,John Henry Stephen.VC.MC.CaptTLtCol kia 21-3-18 KRRC att2/4RBerks p150 CR France725

DIMMOCK,James Bolton 2Lt dow 16-5-17 3RWSurr p55 CR France40,2Bn

DIMOND,Francis Robert 2Lt kia 31-7-17 17Lpool p71 MR29

DIMSDALE,Edward Charles Capt kia 8-5-15 RB p178 MR29

DINAN,Francis Arthur 2Lt kia 31-7-17 113RFA p27 MR29

DINAN,Frederick Charles Capt dow 29-9-17 1Ess p131 CR Belgium18

DINAN,George Albert T2Lt kia 9-9-16 6 att8RDubF p176 MR21

DINEEN,C.H.see DINNEN,C.H.

DINES,Joseph T2Lt kia 27-9-18 13Lpool p71 CR France358

DINES,Percy John Francis T2Lt dow 1-7-16 Dev p76 CR France513

DINGLE,Arthur James TLt kia 22-8-15 6EYorks p84 MR4,Capt

DINGLE,John Lt kia 10-9-16 2NumbF p60 CR Greece3

DINGLEY,Alfred Claude.MIDx3 TCapt kia 19-4-16 7NStaffs p157 MR38

DINGLEY,Norman Oliver TLt dow 5-5-17 6Worc att93MGC p108&182 CR France113,kia

DINGLEY,William T2Lt dow 29-4-17 7Suff p78 CR France113

DINGWALL,J.D.2Lt kld 21-4-18 GL &RAF p190

DINGWALL-FORDYCE,James Lt dow 27-9-15 2A&SH CR France98

DINNEN,Campbell Hackwood Capt kia 4-3-18 Lpool attKAR p71&p200 CR WAfrica28,DINEEN 4-3-15

DINNIS,George Hugh 2Lt kia 28-4-18 16Manch p154 CR Belgium115

DINSDALE,Frank 2Lt kia 1-7-16 12Y&L p158 CR France802

DINSLEY,Francis Hugill 2Lt ded 8-3-19 2CldGds p262 CR Beds29

DINSMORE,M.Edmund TCapt ded 12-11-18 SL RAMC DentalCps p201 CR Ireland196

DINSMORE,John Hastings 2Lt kia 3-5-17 3 att6EKent p57 MR20

DINWIDDIE,James Travers Blount LtTCapt dow 13-9-15 BordR p117 CR Glouc143

DINWIDDY,Conrad Hugh 2LtACapt dow 26-9-17 RGA 13SB p39 CR Belgium11,27-9-17

DINWOODIE,David Wallace 2Lt kia 19-4-17 8ScotRif p225 CR France1495

DIPLOCK,Douglas Gerard T2Lt dow 5-4-18 PoW 30MGC Inf p182 CR France1266

DIPPIE,Harry Peckham T2Lt kia 18-7-16 11GordH p166 CR France402

DIPPLE,Thomas Denis Lt ded 30-11-18 O&BLI BucksBn p231 CR Sussex144

DISNEY,Arthur William T2Lt kia 30-11-17 9RFus p67 MR17

DISNEY,Brabazon Thomas CaptAMaj kia 17-10-17 RGA 166SB p39 CR Belgium19

DITCHFIELD,Samuel Eric 2Lt kia 31-7-17 4 att7/8KOSB p224 MR29

DITMAS,Thomas Owen Bulteel Lt kia 14-1-15 1Dev p76 CR Belgium169

DIX,Cyril Bernard T2Lt kia 9-8-17 8ESurr p112 MR29,10-8-17

DIX,Geoffrey Stewart 2Lt dow 6-5-15 5NStaffs p238 CR France284

DIX,Herbert Golden,MC T2Lt kia 14-2-17 7RWKent p141 CR France314

DIX,Stephen Hamilton.MC.MajTLtCol kia 4-10-17 Leinst Cmdg12/13NumbF p174 CR Belgium125

DIXEY,Edmund Harry T2Lt dow 3-7-16 10Suff p78 CR France66,8Bn

DIXON,Albert Ernest Lucas T2Lt kia 8-5-18 3RSuss att23RFus p118 CR France214

DIXON,Alfred Charles 2Lt kia 4-2-16 19LancF p92 CR France1504

DIXON,Arthur Edward Basil Lt dow 6-6-15 5LNLancs p234 CR Belgium2

DIXON,C.Lt kia 19-9-18 NCycBn &RAF p253

DIXON,Cecil Hargreave TLt kia 28-11-17 GL &9RFC p7 CR Belgium18

DIXON,Charles George Lt kia 9-5-15 RlrReg attRlrRif p89 MR32

DIXON,Charles Howard Lt dow 12-9-17 RFA p27 CR Herts108

DIXON,Charles John(Ian) 2Lt kia 22-6-17 9DLI p239 CR France162

DIXON,Charles Penrose 2Lt dow 25-10-17 GL att9RFC p7 CR Belgium18

DIXON,Charles Ralph Capt dow 5-5-15 Ess p131 MR4

DIXON,Claude Dudley T2Lt dow 28-7-16 10 att6Leic p87 CR France145

DIXON,Clive MacDonnell Maj kia 6-11-14 16Lancers p23 CR Belgium170,5-11-14

DIXON,Cuthbert Stuart T2Lt kia 3-5-17 7ESurr p112 MR20

DIXON,Cyril Burton.MC.TLt dow 12-11-18 2/4Y&L p158 CR France332,14-11-18

DIXON,Cyril Masxfield Lt kia 30-8-15 4Y&L p238 CR Belgium85

DIXON,Ernest 2Lt kia 19-8-16 10RWelshF p97 MR21

DIXON,Ernest Edward 2Lt kia 9-6-17 RGA 168SB p39 CR Belgium4

DIXON,Frederick T2Lt kia 18-9-18 3Worc p108 CR France632

DIXON,Frederick John Cruse T2Lt dow 6-9-16 1BlkW p128 CR France66

DIXON,Frederick William T2Lt kia 9-10-17 5Y&L p158 MR30

DIXON,Geoffrey Francis Lt ded 1-8-18 IARO att72CamelCps p276 MR61

DIXON,George.MID 2Lt kia 20-10-14 2Manch p154 MR22

DIXON,George T2Lt kia 6-8-15 RE 170TC p44 CR France163 Ex CldGds

DIXON,George LtCol ded 24-4-17 RASC p267 CR Lond14

DIXON,H.O.Lt 8-11-18 4EKent CR Kent28

DIXON,Harold George 2Lt kia 4-11-18 3Dors &RAF p124 CR France521,Lt

DIXON,Harry TLt kia 6-10-18 9Yorks p90 CR France234

DIXON,Harry Yorston 2Lt kia 13-7-15 11Y&L att9Manch p158 CR Gallipoli2

DIXON,Henry Edward Otto Murray 2Lt dow 10-4-17 4SfthH p241

DIXON,Henry Eric TCapt kld 19-8-17 GL &62RFC p7 CR Yorks543

DIXON,Henry Oliver 2Lt kia 6-9-17 RGA 32HAG p39 CR Belgium24

DIXON,Henry Philip Norman T2Lt kia 4-9-17 26NumbF p60 MR21

DIXON,Hubert Bradshaw Capt kia 12-3-15 N&D p133 MR22

DIXON,James Capt&Adjt kia 10-3-15 2Mddx p146 CR France706

DIXON,James Alfred TLt kia 10-8-15 6BordR A'Coy p117 CR Gallipoli5,9-8-15

DIXON,James Evelyn Bevan TCapt kia 1-7-16 6RWar p214 CR France1890

DIXON,James Galloway T2Lt kia 12-10-16 17Lpool p71 MR21

DIXON,James W.2Lt kia 5-8-17 RE 152FC p44 CR Belgium17

DIXON,John Francis 2Lt kia 12-4-18 4Y&L p238 MR30

DIXON,John George T2Lt kia 16-6-17 13NumbF p60 MR20

DIXON,John Henry 2Lt ded 1-5-19 RE 85FC p262 CR Egypt2

DIXON,John Vibart 2Lt kia 6-3-17 3NMidRFA p208 CR France745

DIXON,John William T2Lt kia 22-10-17 Manch att23Bn p154 MR30

DIXON,Kenneth 2Lt dow 25-11-16 6WRid p227 CR France203

DIXON,Leonard Frederick T2Lt kia 21-5-18 11 att2SWBord p99 CR France24,Lt
22-5-18

DIXON,Norman Ferguson.MID ACapt dow 5-10-17 6BlkW attMGC p187&231 CR
Belgium72

DIXON,O.D.TLt ded 4-11-18 2YLI p143 CR Yorks323

DIXON,Peter Sydenham TLt kia 7-8-18 7RSuss p118 CR France196

DIXON,Robert Archibald 2Lt kia 12-4-16 2Dors p124 MR38

DIXON,Robert Harrison Maj ded 16-11-15 RASC 54Div p253 CR Europe1

DIXON,Robert William.MM.T2Lt kia 5-9-18 26RFus p67 CR Belgium37

DIXON,Sidney Thomas 2LtTLt dow 20-11-17 3 att4Worc p108 CR France439

DIXON,Thomas Herbert.MC.TCapt kia 25-8-18 12Manch p154 CR France402

DIXON,William H.2Lt dow 23-6-18 3SfthH att25RAF p164 CR France40

DIXON,William Alexander 2Lt kia 16-8-17 3 att8RlrFus p171 MR30

DIXON,William Francis Trevor T2Lt kia 20-7-16 15N&D p133 MR21

DIXON,William Hutton 2Lt kia 22-4-18 3 att8SfthH p164 CR France54,21-4-18

DIXON,William Stanton 2Lt kia 30-4-18 2/4Lincs attLeic p217 CR
Belgium11,Swanston

DIXON-NUTTAL,Frederick John Lt kia 21-5-15 RE 1FC p210 CR Belgium96,J.F.

DIXSON,Thomas Storie Lt kld 8-12-16 1CldGds p51 CR France1568

DOAKE,Samuel Henry.DSO.CaptAMaj kia 30-3-18 RFA 52ArmyBde p27 CR
France268

DOBB,Robert Alan Capt ded 22-12-17 30RFA p27 CR Iraq8

DOBBIE,Alexander Middleton 2Lt dow 13-4-18 6BlkW p231 CR France10

DOBBIE,Herbert William 2Lt kia 14-11-16 3 att1RBerks p139 MR21

DOBBIE,John Shedden Lt kia 5-10-17 3GordH C'Coy p166 MR30,Capt 2Bn

DOBBIE,Robert Shedden 2Lt dow 12-4-17 11A&SH CR France40

DOBBIE,Robert William ACapt kld 23-12-18 18HLI &RAF p162

DOBBIE,William James 2Lt kia 7-6-17 2RlrRif p169 Belgium43

DOBBIN,Fergus Le Fanu 2Lt kia 16-7-19 IAUL 2/6GurkhaRif att3/1 p276 MR43

DOBBIN,George Frederick T2Lt kia 16-8-15 6RlrFus p171 MR4

DOBBIN,Robert Alexander Sheridan Lt kia 25-9-15 RGA p39 MR19

DOBBIN,William Leonard Price.MC.Lt kia 21-3-18 3RlrRif p169 MR27,2Bn

DOBBS,Arthur Hugh Capt mbk 22-4-16 IA 76Punjabis att92 p276 MR38

DOBBS,George Eric Burroughs CaptBtMajALtCol dow 17-6-17 RE AD Sigs p44 CR
Belgium11

DOBBS,Hugh Cathcart Capt kia 25-5-18 IA 3/124Baluchis p276 CR Asia82

DOBBS,William Carey Capt kia 31-7-17 2Mddx p146 MR29

DOBBYN,Robert Newport 2Lt kld 23-11-16 GL &RFC p2&190 CR Eire215

DOBBYN,William Augustus Nelson 2Lt kld 4-1-17 18LancF p92 CR France813,4-
2-17 15Bn

DOBELL,Caleb Clifford Lt ded 17-11-18 RE 256TC p44 CR Sussex178

DOBELL,Colin Macpherson Lt dow 30-5-18 1 att9RWelshF p97 CR France622

DOBIE,James Jardine.DSO.MC.Capt kia 30-9-18 3Huss p21 CR France911

DOBIE,Kirkpatrick Smith.MC.MM.2Lt kia 26-10-17.3 att2GordH p166&258 MR30

DOBIE,William Findlay Robertson Lt kia 14-12-14 1GordH p166 CR Belgium155

DOBIE,William Murray Lt kia 9-4-16 3 att1RWKent D'Coy p141 CR France1182

DOBINSON,Stanley Raine TLt kia 31-3-18 10 att1/4Yorks p90 MR27

DOBINSON,Thomas William.MID TCapt ded 1-12-18 RE 183TC p44 CR
France717,183FC

DOBINSON,William.MC.T2Lt kia 22-10-17 18LancF p92 MR30

DOBSON,Alfred Frederic Otterbine Lt kia 15-6-15 8N&D p233 CR
Belgium17,Ottobine

DOBSON,Arthur Edward John T2Lt kia 7-6-17 GL &45RFC p7 MR20

DOBSON,Edward TCapt kia 10-7-17 17HLI p162 CR Belgium24

DOBSON,Eric Trist Lt ded 8-6-20 IA 74Punjabis att2/124Baluchis p276

DOBSON,Frank Rayner T2Lt kia 28-9-18 3Y&L att10EYorks p158 CR France262

DOBSON,G.M.Maj 17-9-19 RAMC CR Wales564

DOBSON,George Lt kia 11-4-18 4 att6BlkW p230 MR19

DOBSON,Harold Percy TLtACapt kia 16-10-17 20NumbF p60 CR Belgium83

DOBSON,Harold Pierce.MID Capt kia 5-4-16 9Worc p108 MR38

DOBSON,James Robinson T2Lt dow 19-2-17 9RlrFus p171 CR France285

DOBSON,John 2Lt dow 4-5-17 RlrFus p171 CR France95

DOBSON,Montague Charles BdeMaj kld 26-9-15 RFA 21Div p27 CR France423

DOBSON,Nathaniel George TLt dow 17-11-18 BordR att1Camb p117 CR
France146

DOBSON,Reginald Graham.MIDx2 Maj ded 4-1-19 6WYorks att75MGC
p218&187,4-1-18 CR Egypt2

DOBSON,Thomas Ernest T2Lt dow 11-4-15 3MGC p182 CR France40,11-4-18

DOCKER,George Arthur Murray Capt kia 17-11-14 RFus p67 CR Belgium32

DOCKING,Robert James TLt dow 10-2-17 9EKent &43RFC p7&p57 CR France31

DOCKREE,Gilbert Arthur 2Lt kia 15-9-16 6Lond p247 MR21

DODD,Ernest John 2LtTLt kia 17-7-17 C177RFA p27 CR Belgium6

DODD,F.Capt 14-2-20 RGA CR Lancs2

DODD,Francis Joseph T2Lt ded 31-10-18 63MGC Inf p182 CR Lincs61

DODD,Herbert 2Lt kia 23-10-18 5Ches p222 CR Belgium408

DODD,Herbert Robert T2Lt kia 21-3-18 10Ess p131 MR27

DODD,James Forrest 2Lt kia 28-2-17 1LancF p92 CR France216,7Bn

DODD,John O'Connell TLt kia 7-11-18 6RMunstF p175 CR France968,2Bn

DODD,Neville 2Lt kia 1-7-16 1/6WYorks p218 CR France1890

DODD,Percy Reed Capt kia 10-3-15 2ScotRif p103 CR France260

DODD,Stanley Preston 2Lt dow 25-11-17 1/7Ches p223 CR Egypt2

DODD,Walter De Courcy Lt ded PoW 31-10-17 5RMunstF &11RFC p7&p175 CR
France568,Courcey kia

DODD,Westgarth John 2Lt dow 19-9-18 RFA X38MidTMB p27 CR France415

DODDRELL,Kenneth Curling 2Lt kia 19-9-18 2 att1/4Wilts p153 CR Palestine9

DODDS,Benjamin William Pedley.MC.Lt kia 8-8-19 IARO att34ResMtnBty p276
MR38,7-8-19

DODDS,Cave Bradburne 2Lt kia 25-9-15 12NumbF p60 MR19

DODDS,Cecil T2Lt kia 5-10-18 13DLI p160 CR France844

DODDS,Cecil James Capt kia 22-9-16 6 att1RMunstF p175 MR21

DODDS,Herbert Alexandra Christopher 2Lt ded 13-6-16 3/5Y&L p238 CR
Surrey15

DODDS,Robert William Lee Lt kia 25-9-15 13NumbF p60 MR19,26-9-15

DODDS,Walter Milbourne TCapt dow PoW 14-10-18 8NumbF p60 CR
Europe149,Melbourne 23Bn

DODDS,William Henry T2Lt kia 6-11-16 20NumbF p60 CR France82

DODGE,Walter Robert.MM.T2Lt kia 2-10-17 20Manch p154 CR
Belgium308

DODGSHON,Angus John Charles Lt kia 10-11-17 5Glouc p225 CR France1190

DODGSHON,John Hampson 2Lt kld 2-10-16 SurrYeo &RFCp205 CR Wilts116,1-10-16

DODGSON,David Scott Lt kia 13-11-14 2RGA 1SB p39 MR22

DODGSON,Francis TCapt kia 10-7-16 8Yorks p90 MR21 CR France1890

DODGSON,Guy Capt dow 14-11-18 Herts p252 CR France658

DODGSON,John Henley 2Lt kia 7-6-17 5RWKent p235 MR29

DODGSON,Kenneth Vernon TLt kia 25-9-15 8Dev p76 MR19

DODGSON,Reginald Henry Lutwidge Lt ded 14-3-18 RDC p269 CR Shrop67

DODGSON,Vernon Colville TLt dow 5-3-16 14 att11Mddx p146 CR France423

DODINGTON,Thomas Marriott Lt kia 2-7-16 1SomLI p79 MR21

DODKINS,Lionel Claud FlOff ded 13-6-21 25Lond repostedBordR &31RAF CR Surrey6

DODS,John Ballantyne Lt dow 11-4-18 1/8RScots p211 CR France201

DODS,William Henry Gordon Lt kia 21-10-14 Leic p87 MR32

DODSON,Henry Howard 2Lt kia 27-6-17 8Hamps p229 CR France245

DODSON,Herbert Edwin 2Lt kia 28-4-17 5 att9Norf p217 CR France551

DODSON,Herbert Leigh Midelton Lt ded 25-8-18 RASC att73&46RFC p15&192,kia CR France421

DODSON,Joseph Edward T2Lt kia 10-10-18 RWKent att10EKent p141 CR France82

DODWELL,Oscar Wilfred 2Lt kia 10-5-15 1Y&L p158 MR29

DOE,Alfred Bramhill 2Lt kia 23-4-17 6BlkW A'Coy p231 CR France604

DOGGART,Norman Alexander Capt 10-10-18 RAF &ScotRif CR Oxford69

DOGGETT,George Patrick 2Lt dow 4-7-17 7WRid p227 CR Camb16

DOHERTY,John T2Lt kia 16-8-17 8RDubF p176 MR30

DOHERTY,Joseph 2Lt kia 3-7-16 RGA 113HB p39 CR France203

DOHERTY,Mary Agnes Sister ded 5-9-16 QAIMNS p200 CR Greece7

DOHERTY,Patrick T2Lt dow 1-8-17 1RIrRif p169 CR Belgium11

DOHERTY-HOLWELL,Raymond Vernon.DSO.MID Maj kia 9-1-17 RE AD Sigs 8CpsHQ p44 CR Belgium5,LtCol

DOIDGE,Reginald Chamberlain TCapt kld 2-3-16 17LancF p92 CR France356

DOIG,David Lt 3-4-19 RGA CR Scot14

DOLAMORE,Arthur William.MID Capt kia 14-4-17 10Mddx att5EKent p236 MR38

DOLAN,Stephen Christopher 2Lt kia 16-8-17 RInniskF att49TMB p104 MR30

DOLBY,Horace Adams Lt kia 7-5-17 3 att1Leic p87 CR France115,1 att3Bn

DOLD,Cedric Lewis.MC.TCapt kia 5-10-18 RAMC att1SWBord p195 CR France725

DOLL,Philip Walter Rudolph Lt kia 31-10-14 1/8Lpool p71

DOLLEY,Reginald Charles Francis 2Lt kia 30-6-17 6N&D p233 MR20,1-7-17

DOLLING,Caledon Robert John Radcliffe T2LtACapt kia 20-8-16 2RWelshF p97 CR France453

DOLMAN,Leonard 2LtTLt dow 31-12-17 8Beds p85 CR France518

DOLPHIN,Eric John Weston Lt kia 7-11-14 1Hamps p120 CR Belgium69,Capt

DOLPHIN,Harold Maximilian Burton 2Lt ded 31-8-20 2/56PunjabRif attSeistanLevyCps p276 MR43,Lt

DOLPHIN,Samuel 2Lt kia 24-3-18 4SStaffs p122 CR France307 Ex 1/6ScotRif

DOLPHIN,Vernon Ommanney Maj kia 7-6-17 17RFA p27 CR France1182,8-6-17

DOMAN,George Herbert Ryder 2Lt dow PoW 11-6-18 12/13NumbF p60 CR Europe149

D'OMBRAIN,Roland Maund 2Lt kia 8-3-16 IARO att53Sikhs p276 MR38,DOMBRAIN

DOMEGAN,Christopher Patrick Lt drd 10-10-18 RIrFus &RAF p171 CR Eire437

DOMELEO,Robert Frearson TLt ded 10-12-18 RE ROD p44 CR France34,DOMLEO

DON,Alexander Duff Brownlee Lt kia 21-10-16 RE 2FC p44 CR France374

DON,Archibald William Robertson TLt ded 11-9-16 10BlkW p128 CR Greece7

DON,Daird Fairweather T2Lt kia 1-7-16 14 att2N&D attSWBord p133 MR21

DON,Frederick Alexander LtCol ded 24-5-18 IA S&TCps p276 CR Asia60

DON,Reginald Gilbert 2Lt kia 15/16-9-14 1BlkW p128 MR15,15-9-14

DON,Robert Macpherson Lt kia 8-4-17 10BlkW p128 MR37,8/9-4-17

DON,Thomas Douglas 2Lt kia 21-7-18 5BlkW p231 CR France324

DON,Valentine Grantham Lt kia 26-8-15 8RWKent p141 MR19,26-9-15

DONAGHY,Robert Andrews 2Lt kia 28-5-18 RGA NRidHB p39 MR18,Andrew

DONAHOO,Malcolmson Gardiner.MC.TLt dow 31-1-17 8YLI p143 CR Belgium11

DONAHUE,P.Capt&QM 26-5-21 RGA CR Essex9

DONALD,Alan James Ingram 2Lt kia 4-6-15 6Manch p236 MR4

DONALD,Andrew Patrick 2Lt ded 1-2-18 RE 7PontConstCo p262 CR Lond1,Lt

DONALD,Colin George Hamilton 2Lt kia 8-8-18 2SfthH p164 CR France250

DONALD,George Lt 12-9-20 RE IWT MR65

DONALD,Ian Strathy 2Lt dow 7-8-16 5ScotRif p224 CR France85

DONALD,James 2Lt ded 15-10-16 IARO att2S&M p276 MR43

DONALD,Robert Capt ded 3-5-16 RAMC p269

DONALD,Robert.MC.TLt kia 28-4-17 24NumbF p60 MR20

DONALD,William Clark 2Lt kia 31-7-17 4CamH p243 MR29

DONALD,William Francis Maxwell.MC.Capt kia 19-9-18 9HLI p240 CR France1496

DONALDSON,Alexander Cleveland TCapt kia 6-8-15 8CamH att1Ess p167 CR Gallipoli6

DONALDSON,Alexander Howard Lt kia 12-10-18 9HLI p240 CR France230

DONALDSON,Cleweth Thomas Lee 2Lt kia 14-4-17 GlasgowYeo att52RFC p18&p203 CR France662

DONALDSON,Denis Harrison 2Lt kia 25-9-15 7Lond p247 CR France550

DONALDSON,Geoffrey Boley Capt ded PoW 19-7-16 7RWar p214 MR32

DONALDSON,George Lt kia 16-5-17 6GordH p242 CR France546

DONALDSON,Herbert Graham 2Lt kld 16-2-18 20Lond attRFC p18&251,ded

DONALDSON,James Capt kia 23-8-17 7 at9BlkW p231 CR Belgium8

DONALDSON,James TCapt ded 5-12-18 RAMC att2/22Lond p195 CR Egypt1

DONALDSON,John.MC.Lt kia 25-3-18 8Manch att5RWar p237 MR27

DONALDSON,John James T2Lt kia 1-7-16 20NumbF p60 MR21

DONALDSON,Norman.MID Lt kia 10-3-15 45RFA p282 MR22

DONALDSON,Stuart T2Lt kia 28-9-18 15HLI p162 CR Belgium101

DONALDSON,Wilfred Wallace Douglas 2Lt dow 19-4-17 1/4ScotF p222 CR Palestine2

DONALDSON,William T2Lt kia 5-6-17 12RScots A'Coy p54 CR France604

DONALDSON-SELBY,Victor Montague 2Lt ded 31-8-17 3Lincs p263 CR Lond8,dow

DONCASTER,Guy Capt kia 8-6-18 IARO attCpsofGuides Inf p276 CR Palestine9

DONCASTER,Robert Ivan T2Lt kia 1-7-16 15LancF p92 CR France293

DONE,Neville Savage 2Lt kia 10-3-17 6 att22RFus p67 MR21

DONE,Robert Lt dow 13-10-18 15Ches p96 MR30

DONELAN,William Lawrence T2Lt kia 5-4-17 8EKent p57 CR France161

DONGREY,Hayden Harry T2Lt kia 23-3-18 41MGC p182 CR France1896,DONGRAY

DONKERSLEY,Reynold.MC.2Lt kia 20-7-18 2/5WYorks p218 CR France622

DONKIN,Samuel Thornton 2Lt kia 25-12-15 7NumbF p214 CR Belgium127

DONLEY,David C.B.2Lt dow 3-9-17 2ELancs p110 CR France285

DONNALLY,Robert Charles TLt kia 21-10-16 RH&FA 147Bde97Bty p28

DONNAN,William LtCol ded 13-8-19 IA attStaff p276 CR Iraq6,Col Ex Lincs

DONNELL,Arthur Patrick 2Lt kld 5-12-16 NumbF &RFC p2&60 CR Norf247,Lt

DONNELLY,Gilbert TLt kia 21-3-18 1RMunstF p175 MR27

DONNELLY,James Alexander 2Lt dow 31-3-18 GL &59RFC p15 CR France62

DONNELLY,John Verney.MID ACapt kia 9-10-17 9Manch C'Coy p237 MR30

DONNER,Eric Robert TCapt kia 3-9-16 11RB p178 MR21,Robin

DONNOLLY,Robert Charles Lt 21-10-16 97/147RFA MR21

DONOHUE,Thomas 2LtTLt dow 8-2-17 8BordR p117 CR France285,2Lt

DONOVAN,Bridget SNurse ded 3-4-16 QAIMNS p200 CR Hamps11

DONOVAN,Cyril Bernard.MC.TLt kia 25-3-18 2RDubF p176 MR27

DONOVAN,John 2Lt kia 26-4-18 5YLI p235 MR30

DONWORTH,Thomas Francis TCapt drd 28-7-16 RAVC att109RFA p198 CR France34 &CR France30

DOONER,Alfred Edwin Claud Toke.MID Lt&Adjt kia 30-11-14 1RWelshF p97 CR Belgium112,30-10-14

DOONER,John Graham.DSO.LtCol kia 31-7-18 RFA Staff 34DivHQ p28 CR France524

DOOGAN,George William TLt kia 21-10-16 11RSuss p118 MR21

DOOLEY,Thomas 2Lt kia 1-5-15 2Leic p87 CR France727

DOOTSON,Herbert 2Lt dow 5-11-17 RFA 66Bty p28 MR38

DORAN,Edward Sheridan 2Lt kia 1-11-16 RFA p28 CR France374

DORAN,Frank Beecher Lt kia 13-9-17 20CanadaInf CR Belgium18

DORAN,Louis Godfrey T2Lt kia 23-10-16 7 att2RDubF p176 MR21

DORE,Alfred Clarence T2Lt kia 1-7-16 101MGC p182 CR France267 Ex Y&L

DORE,Sidney Arthur.MID T2Lt kia 24-4-18 11 att1/7Mddx p146 CR France54

DORE,William Hayward 2Lt kia 25-9-16 1WYorks p81 MR21

DORINGTON,Thomas Philip Maj kia 12-11-14 1Dragoons p214 CR Belgium57

DORMAN,Anthony Godfrey.MC.TLt kia 13-11-16 13EYorks p84 MR21

DORMAN,Edward Crump Capt kia 1-5-15 1RMunstF p175 MR4

DORMAN,Thomas Robert Hobart 2Lt dow 21-2-16 2RMunstF p175 CR France779

DORNTON,Harold Shafto 2Lt kia 1-7-16 1/5N&D p232 MR21

DORRELL,Evelyn Percy 2Lt dow 14-10-18 4RWSurr p212 CR France380,kia

DORRELL,Harold George Harcourt T2Lt kia 3-4-16 10DLI p160&257,H.G.Hugh CR France420,2-4-16

DORRINGTON,Percy 2Lt kia 12-10-17 10N&D p133 MR30,Lt

DOSWELL,Frank.MM.2Lt ded 29-2-19 6RWSurr p262 CR Surrey6

DOTHIE,Elvery Ashton 2Lt kld 9-5-15 ELancs p110 MR32

DOTHIE,John Howard T2Lt kia 27-6-16 2BordR p117 CR France394

DOUCET,Gerald Danby 2Lt kia 26-10-17 7NumbF p214 MR30

DOUDNEY,Charles Edmund Rev dow 16-10-15 RAChDept att18Bde6Div p199 CR Belgium11

DOUDNEY,Hugh Denham ACapt kia 31-7-17 12RFus p67 MR29,Densham

DOUGAL,John Braes T2Lt kia 1-7-16 15RScots p54 MR21

DOUGAL,Robert Joseph TLt kia 1-7-16 21NumbF p60 MR21

DOUGALL,Eric Stuart.VC.MC.LtAMaj kia 14-4-18 A88RFA p28 CR Belgium192

DOUGHTY,E.A.MM.2Lt kld 14-4-18 GL att4RAF p190 CR France31,Albert Edward

DOUGHTY,George T2Lt kia 20-11-16 13RScots &RFC p2&54 CR France518

DOUGHTY,George Harry 2Lt kia 25-4-17 18Manch p154 MR20

DOUGHTY,George Marbrook.MC.Lt kia 21-8-17 22Mddx att17MGC Inf p146&182 CR Belgium167

DOUGHTY,Gordon Gray T2Lt kia 11-4-18 1KOSB p101 MR32

DOUGHTY,John Henry Lt ded 25-8-19 RFA Ex RAOC p261

DOUGHTY,Robert Cecil T2Lt kld 26-2-18 101RFC p15 CR France1063

DOUGHTY-WYLIE,Charles Hotham Montagu.VC.CB.CMG.LtCol kia 28-4-15 RWelshF p97 CR Gallipoli15A,26-4-15

DOUGLAS,Alexander Gawain TLt kia 15-8-16 10 att1Leic p87 CR France220

DOUGLAS,Alexander Stark 2Lt dow 28-10-18 3 att1/6BlkW p128 CR France52

DOUGLAS,Alfred William.MM.2Lt dow 3-9-16 14RWar p64 CR France23

DOUGLAS,Allen Grant.MC.Capt dow 30-11-17 14Lond p249 CR France1496

DOUGLAS,Archibald 2Lt kld 16-10-16 RFA attRFC p2&28 CR France82

DOUGLAS,Archibald Halliday Lt kia 16-9-16 9RScots A'Coy p212 CR France922

DOUGLAS,Andrew T2Lt dow 19-2-16 3 att2BlkW p128 CR Iraq5

DOUGLAS,Brian Charles O'Driscoll Capt kld 21-10-18 ConnRgrs attRAF p172 CR Mddx66

DOUGLAS,Bruce Francis Sholto 2Lt kia 14-4-15 4 att2SStaffs p122 CR France80,Lt

DOUGLAS,Bryce Lt kia 13-11-17 IA 1/101Grens att58Rif p276 CR Palestine9

DOUGLAS,Charles Camelon Lt dow 25-5-16 1/4CamH p242 CR France157,Cameron

DOUGLAS,Charles Whittingham Horsley.GCB.ADC.Col ded 25-10-14 Ch of Staff CR Lond8

DOUGLAS,David Tocher T2Lt dow 1-11-17 3ELancs p110 CR Lancs472

DOUGLAS,G.S.Maj 10-2-16 ScotRif CR Scot263

DOUGLAS,George Archibald Percy Capt dow 30-11-15 10Lond p248 CR Egypt3,Adjt 1/6Ess

DOUGLAS,Henry Guy Stuart Capt ded 8-9-19 GL &3ScotRif p266 CR Mddx39

DOUGLAS,Ian Victor.MC.2Lt kia 25-10-17 RGA 180SB p39 CR Belgium124

DOUGLAS,James Capt&QM ded 11-2-19 RAMC 1/1FA p253 CR Scot235,11-12-19

DOUGLAS,John Charles Edward TMaj dow 18-12-15 10Yorks p90 CR France285

DOUGLAS,John Gordon Lt kia 12-4-18 7SfthH p164 CR Belgium124

DOUGLAS,John Norman Turnbull Capt mbk 12-4-18 23NumbF p256 MR32

DOUGLAS,Kenneth Mackenzie TLt ded 9-12-18 GL 7SfthH attKAR p164,202&266 CR EAfrica86,Capt

DOUGLAS,Leslie Hall Lt kia 9-7-15 RE 2FC p210 CR Belgium98

DOUGLAS,Malcolm TMaj ded 17-11-18 MGC p182 CR Shrop19

DOUGLAS,Norman Dighton 2Lt kia 12-12-19 IARO att3CpsofGuides p276 MR43

DOUGLAS,Percy T2Lt ded 25-5-17 7EYorks p84 CR Yorks81

DOUGLAS,Robert.MID Lt dow 15-7-15 1/5KOSB p224 MR4

DOUGLAS,Robert Greenshields 2Lt ded 14-8-16 1SuffYeo attSuffR p205 CR Egypt1

DOUGLAS,Robert Jeffray.CMG.TD.LtCol kia 3-7-16 5ScotRif p224 CR France80

DOUGLAS,Robert Morrison Wilson 2Lt kia 29-3-18 5GordH p242 MR27

DOUGLAS,Ronald Ross T2Lt dow 30-8-17 7/8KOSB p101 CR Belgium11

DOUGLAS,Sholto TCapt kia 28-1-16 16Mddx p146 CR France114

DOUGLAS,Stafford E.Maj ded 15-2-20 A&SH CR Somerset197

DOUGLAS,William Anderson Capt kia 24-8-16 5RScots p211 2entries 6Bn MR21

DOUGLAS,William Gurwood.MC.2Lt ded 26-2-19 111RFA p261 CR Scot674

DOUGLAS,William Sholto Maj dow 14-11-14 RE p44 CR France102

DOUGLAS,William Campbell 2Lt dow 17-8-17 3 att1KOSB p101

DOUGLAS,William Millar 2Lt kia 19-8-17 5KOSB p224 MR30

DOUGLAS,William Robert 2Lt kia 5-10-18 1/10Lpool p216 CR France1725,Robertson

DOUGLAS,W.R.B.CIE.Cdr drd 28-6-19 RIM MR64

DOUGLAS-CROMPTON,Sidney Harold Lionel 2Lt kia 7-6-17 5RFus p67 MR29

DOUGLAS-DICK,Archibald William John Joseph Lt kia 11-11-14 1ScotsGds p52 MR29

DOUGLAS-HAMILTON,Angus Falconer.VC.TLtCol kia 26-9-15 6CamH p167 MR19

DOUGLAS-HAMILTON,Leslie Reginald Coventry TCapt kia 25-7-16 7CamH attLancF p167 CR France630,Lesley 24-7-16

DOUGLAS-JONES,William Eric Vyvian 2Lt ded 15-1-15 33RFA p28 CR France768

DOUGLAS-PENNANT,Alan George Sholto.Hon.Lt kia 29-10-14 1GrenGds p49 MR29

DOUGLAS-PENNANT,Charles.Hon.Lt kia 29-10-14 CldGds p51 CR Belgium115

DOUGLAS-PENNANT,George Henry.Hon.MID Capt kia 11-3-15 1GrenGds RoO p49 MR22

DOUGLAS-WILLAN,Stanhope William Howard Sholto LtACapt kia 17-2-17 2SStaffs p122 MR21

DOUGLAS-WILLAN,Walter Gordon Maj kia 24-3-18 4DLI att22NFusGarrBn p160 MR27

DOUGLASS,Archibald Henry TLt dow 8-4-18 9ESurr p112 CR Mddx53,Capt

DOUGLASS,George Percival.MC.Lt dow 25-8-18 157RFA p28 CR France100 Ex AustInf

DOUGLASS-JAMES,William Lt dow 25-9-15 RGA p39

DOULL,Gilbert Laurie T2Lt dow 11-3-17 11ScotRif D'Coy p103 CR France164

DOUST,Charles Bowden 2Lt kia 1-7-16 5Lond p246 MR21

DOUTHWAITE,Robert Christopher Morris Lt ded 19-6-19 8Y&L p158 CR Europe58A

DOVE,Charles Bertram Capt kia 21-3-18 3 att8BordR p117 CR France563

DOVE,Edward Maddison.MC.TLt kia 23-3-18 8ESurr p112 MR27

DOVE,Etienne Howard T2Lt kia 30-3-17 1RWelshF p97 CR France616

DOVE,Lewis Lt dow 1-4-18 BedsYeo attOxfYeo p203 CR France185

DOVE,Patrick Edward Lt kia 14-6-17 1GordH p166 MR20

DOVE,Percy Matthew Maj kia 15-5-17 2N&D p133 CR Belgium451

DOVE,Sydney Ernest T2Lt kia 16-8-16 8RWKent p141 CR France294

DOVE,Tom.MC.TCapt kia 16-8-17 12KRRC p150 MR30

DOVER,William Lt kia 28-4-17 5 att7Norf p216 MR20

DOVETON,J.H.Maj 19-4-15 16Cav MR66

DOVEY,Wiliam Edward 2Lt kia 23-10-16 1RLancs p58 MR21

DOW,A.Lt 23-2-17 CamH CR Scot966

DOW,Allan Gladstone T2Lt kldacc 18-7-17 GL &RFC p7 CR Kent125

DOW,David Edward.MID 2Lt dow 17-5-17 1/6SfthH p241 CR France95

DOW,James Robertson T2Lt kia 11-4-18 2SLancs p125 MR32

DOW,John T2Lt kia 25-3-18 12Lpool p71 MR27,12KRRC

DOW,John Capt ded 5-11-18 IA IMS p276 CR Asia82

DOW,Samuel Hugh T2Lt kia 30-12-16 9ScotRif p103

DOW,Walter 2Lt kia 19-12-15 1/8ScotRif p225 CR Gallipoli3

DOW,William T2Lt dow 2-2-17 9BlkW p128 CR France177,kia

DOW,William John 2Lt kia 22-8-17 5A&SH p243 MR30

DOWDELL,Ernest George.MC.2Lt kia 22-3-18 3 att8BordR p117 MR20

DOWDEN,Reginald Stanley 2Lt kia 16-8-17 1Lond p245 MR29

DOWDESWELL,Horace Scott 2Lt kia 3-11-17 1/5WelshR p230 CR Palestine1

DOWDING,Charles Gordon.MC.Capt dow 17-11-17 IA 87Punjabis att2SigCo p276 CR EAfrica11 &CR Tanzania1

DOWDING,Lionel 2Lt kia 7-1-16 Leic p87 MR38

DOWEND,John Middleton 2LtACapt kia 24-11-17 26NumbF p60 CR France592

DOWENS,James Alexander 2Lt kia 17-10-18 4KOSB p224 CR Belgium157

DOWLING,Frederick Payne Lt kia 7-8-17 1RDubF p176 MR29

DOWLING,Geoffrey Charles Walter TCapt kia 30-7-15 7KRRC p150 MR29

DOWN,Charles Boileau.MID Maj ded 10-5-19 40RGA p39 p262 CR Beds23

DOWN,John Aubrey Maj ded 28-11-18 8Mddx p235 CR Mddx26

DOWN,John Eric Lt kia 29-9-18 6Mddx C'Coy att63Div MG'Bn p146 CR France602

DOWN,Robert Hayward Lt dow 17-8-16 4Glouc p225 CR France74

DOWN,William Oliphant.MC.Capt dow 23-5-17 4RBerks p234 CR France530

DOWNER,Frederick 2Lt kia 2-4-17 5Manch att2/7N&D p236 MR21

DOWNES,Arthur Chernocke 2Lt dow 20-11-14 2Ches p96 CR Belgium150

DOWNES,Benjamin 2Lt kia 2-6-18 18Lond p250 CR France887

DOWNES,Donald Litt 2Lt dow 5-10-18 4Worc p108 CR Belgium38

DOWNES,Gilbert George TCapt dow 11-8-15 Lincs p75 CR Greece10

DOWNES,Herbert Laidlow.MID Lt kia 15-6-15 8Lpool p215 MR22

DOWNES,Howard Gray 2Lt kia 12-3-17 RE 517FCp210 CR Belgium5,13-3-17

DOWNES,Oswald 2Lt 1-7-16 2DLI CR Hereford9

DOWNES,Villiers Chernocke Lt dow 18-10-14 3Beds p85 CR France134

DOWNES,W.D.MC.Capt 5-8-20 RSuss attNigR HQ CR WAfrica42

DOWNEY,George Jamieson T2Lt ded 24-4-18 11RLancs p262 CR Wilts115,25-4-18 3Bn

DOWNEY,Sydney James Livingstone T2Lt kia 7-6-17 14RIrRif p169 CR Belgium61,Livingston

DOWNEY,William Edmund Capt drd 19-7-17 RAOC p198 MR37,ded

DOWNHAM,Harold 2Lt dow 29-9-18 1/7LancF p221 CR France512

DOWNIE,Andrew Marshall Maj dow 20-7-15 1/5HLI p240 CR Egypt3

DOWNIE,James Maitland Capt ded 28-10-18 RAMC p195 CR Iraq6

DOWNIE,James Wallace 2Lt kia 22-10-17 6ScotRif p224.MR30

DOWNIE,Leslie E.V 2Lt 9-4-17 4SfthH CR France15

DOWNIE,Nelson 2Lt dow 17-5-17 IARO att1/4GurkhaRif p276 MR43

DOWNIE,Reginald Alexander Forbes 2Lt dow 24-3-18 1 att3CamH p167 MR27,att5Bn

DOWNIE,Robert.MC.DCM.Capt kia 6-11-18 5ScotRif p224 CR France937

DOWNIE,Robert Theodore Manners Lt ded 24-1-16 3/5HLI p240 CR Ches69

DOWNIE,William Kimmond Capt ded 3-2-20 RGA CR Hamps11

DOWNING,Alfred Edward 2Lt dow 27-5-17 9LNLancs p135 MR18

DOWNING,Ernest Gillespie TLt kia 3-5-17 4RFus p67 MR20

DOWNING,Francis Geoffrey Lt ded 27-10-16 5Mddx attRE p146 CR Eire160

DOWNING,George Guy Barry Lt kld 4-9-17 GL &RFC p7 CR Wales20

DOWNING,Henry Francis TCapt kia 3-9-16 7Leinst p174 MR21

DOWNING,Herbert George.MC.2Lt kia 6-11-17 GL &29RFC p7 MR20

DOWNING,James 2Lt kia 3-9-16 3 att6RIrReg p89 MR21

DOWNMAN,Bernard Vincent Ridout T2Lt kia 21-9-16 9 att13N&D p133 CR France296

DOWSE,Benjamin Thomas John Lt gunshotWounds 25-1-21 IA 2/30Punjabis p276 MR43

DOWSE,Henry Harvey 2Lt ded 10-11-18 RASC &139RAF p192 CR Italy12

DOWSE,Robert Joseph Gordon.MID LtTCapt ded 19-12-18 RASC VIIICps TrpsMTCoy p192 CR France1277

DOWSE,Thomas William T2Lt dow 7-9-16 RE 34DivSigs p44

DOWSE,William Arthur Clarence Lt kia 3-7-16 11Ches p96 MR21

DOWSON,Humphrey.MC.TCapt kia 15-9-16 9KRRC p150 CR France402

DOWSON,Oswald John Capt kia 3-5-17 1/4RBerks p234 MR21

DOWSWELL,Charles Victor 2Lt kia8-10-16 9Lond p248 MR21

DOYLE,A.A.K.C.Capt 1-11-18 1Hamps CR Hamps83

DOYLE,Christopher.J.G.2Lt kia 15-8-17 2RDubF p176&257 MR29,15-7-17 8Bn

DOYLE,Denis Rev kia 18-8-16 RAChDept att2Leinst p199

DOYLE,Edward Percival T2Lt dow 5-7-16 11WYorks p81 CR France833

DOYLE,Eric Douglas.MC.Lt kia 29-7-17 190RFA p28 CR Belgium154

DOYLE,Francis Hubert Lt dow 12-10-16 RAVC p198 CR Egypt9

DOYLE,Henry T2Lt kia 17-1-17 ACycCps attNFus p181 CR France82

DOYLE,Henry James 2Lt dow 11-10-17 2/9Manch p237 CR Belgium3

DOYLE,James Charles.MC.Capt kia 27-5-18 RGA p39 MR18

DOYLE,John Francis Innes Hay.CMG.DSO.BrigGen ded 19-2-19 RFA attStaff p28 CR Belgium316

DOYLE,John Joseph TLt kia 10-8-15 6RDubF p176 MR4

DOYLE,Michael William 2Lt kld 22-3-18 RFC p15 CR Hamps13

DOYLE,Thomas Walter T2Lt dow 9-8-16 17 att16RB p178 CR Belgium11

DOYLE,William Joseph.MC.Chap4Cl kia 17-8-17 RAChDept att8RDubF p199 MR30 &CR France141

DOYNE,Philip Denys Lt kia 29-12-15 4 O&BLI p231 CR France1327,28-12-15

DRABBLE,Charles Frederick Lt kia 13-8-18 19DLI att18RAF p160 CR France1483

DRAG,A.M.HonLt&Comm 3-10-18 IndPostalServ CR Iraq8

DRAGE,Arthur William.MM.T2Lt kia 26-9-18 18Mddx p146 CR France439

DRAGE,George T.Maj ded 19-10-18 RIrRif p169 CR Ireland137

DRAISEY,Edwin Rowland Watts TLt kia 15-9-16 8Beds p85 MR21

DRAKE,Ernest Francis TLt ded 10-12-18 Ches p263

DRAKE,Francis T2Lt kia 27-3-18 WYorks att2/4YLI p81 MR20

DRAKE,Frederic Augustus Capt drd 27-5-18 WarYeo p205 MR41

DRAKE,Gerald Edward T2Lt dow 26-1-18 att10Worc p108 CR France905

DRAKE,Godfrey Ward T2Lt dow 1-8-17 2Yorks p90 CR Belgium11,2WYorks

DRAKE,Henry Mackay 2Lt dow 16/18-6-15 8Lpool p215 CR France410,17-6-15

DRAKE,Leonard T2Lt dow 5-10-16 11N&D p133 CR France177

DRAKE,Percy Albert T2Lt kia 13-10-16 11Glouc p106 CR France293

DRAKE,Robert Edward Capt dow 8-9-14 1Lincs p75 CR France1117

DRAKE,Robert Flint Lt kia 17-11-14 10Huss p22 CR Belgium57

DRAKE,Walker 2Lt kia 26-6-16 RHA p28 CR France131

DRAKE,Wilfred Wallace T2Lt dow 16-8-17 2Dev att23TMB p76 CR Belgium8

DRAKE-BROCKMAN,Paris Villiers 2Lt kia 18-7-18 1EKent p57 CR Belgium40

DRAKE-BROCKMAN,Ralph Zouch.MC.2Lt dow 29-9-17 46RFA p28 CR Belgium42

DRAKE-CUTLIFFE,Bernard Henry Hamilton 2Lt 11-4-21 Dev CR Devon91

DRAKEFORD,Harold Arthur T2Lt kia 5-4-18 8SomLI p79 MR20

DRAKELEY,Reginald Kenneth T2Lt dow 19-4-16 9RWar p64 CR Iraq5

DRANFIELD,W.B.AssSurg 19-2-17 ISMD CR EAfrica38 &CR Tanzania1

DRAPE,Norman 2Lt dow 15-7-17 RGA 28SB p39 CR France95

DRAPER,Arnold Inman TMaj kia 21-10-17 17Lpool p71 CR Belgium17

DRAPER,Arthur Reginald Olley Lt&QM dow 16-4-18 18NumbF p60 MR32

DRAPER,Cecil Frederick Napier Lt dow 17-6-16 1Mddx p146 CR France80

DRAPER,Dudley Lt ded 21-2-18 RFA p28 CR Mddx26

DRAPER,James 2Lt dow 10-11-18 4 att2LNLancs p234 CR France34

DRAPER,Mark Denman T2Lt kld 7-2-17 GL &RFC p7 CR Derby3

DRAPER,Roger Francis TCapt kia 22-8-15 6Y&L att8WRid p158 MR4

DRAYCOTT-WOOD,William 2Lt kia 29-6-15 2SStaffs p122 CR France163

DRAYSON,John Douglas.MC.TLtACapt kia 10-4-17 93RFA p28 CR France548,9-4-17

DREDGE,Stanley TLt kia 15-6-18 23MGC p182 CR Italy4

DRENNAN,James Wilson TLt dow 12-8-17 10RInniskF p104 CR Belgium7

DRENNAN,Robert Hugh Capt 26-7-17 RAMC CR Kent129

DRESCHFELD,Henry Theodore Capt ded 19-2-15 13Manch p154 CR Lancs489

DRESSER,Bruce William.MC.Lt dow 20-9-18 27RFA p28 CR France13,120Bty

DRESSER,Harry Jex CaptAMaj kia 2-6-18 1 att15Ches p96 CR France60

DREW,Alan Appleby Lt kia 10-3-15 4ScotRif p103 CR France706,2Bn

DREW,Charles George TLt ACapt kia 12-4-18 1RIrFus p171 CR Belgium168

DREW,Frederick James 2Lt kia 29-3-18 RGA 230SB p209 CR France184

DREW,Frederick William T2Lt kia 5-11-16 9 att7EYorks p84 MR21

DREW,J.T Lt 3-9-19 ConnRgrs CR Devon92

DREW,Richard William 2Lt kia 25-6-18 3 att12Glouc p106 CR France352

DREWE,Abrian.MID T2LtACapt kia 12-7-17 RGA 262SB p39 CR Belgium10

DREWERY,Arthur Bancroft 2Lt kia 20-10-16 19RFC p2 CR France169

DREWERY,George William 2Lt kia 22-3-18 1/4EYorks p219 MR27

DREWETT,Charles T2Lt dow 29-6-16 12EYorks p84 MR21

DREWETT,Herbert Benn 2Lt kia 30-10-17 4EYorks p219 CR Belgium126,Ben

DREY,Adolphe.MC.TLt kld 9-5-17 RASC &58RFC p7&192,Adolph ded CR Egypt15

DRIFFIELD,Herbert George T2Lt dow 1-8-17 2Lond att10RWKent p141 CR Belgium5

DRINKILL,Frederick Maurice Lt dow 1-7-16 2RFus p67 CR France35

DRINKWATER,Leonard Wilfred 2Lt kia 3-10-17 RFA p208 MR30

DRISCOLL,D.O'Neill Lt ded 13-8-18 1/4Mddx &RAF p146 CR Surrey152

DRIVER,Bernard Henry.MC.2LtAMaj kia 4-10-17 2RWSurr p55 CR Belgium115

DRIVER,Graham Dudley TLt ded 5-5-15 RASC p192 CR Mddx26,George

DRIVER,Harry.DSO.MC.Capt dow 10-8-19 Beds att45RFus p254 MR70 &CR Europe179

DRIVER,Harry Farrant.MC.Lt kia 28-8-18 1/1Camb p244 CR France370

DRIVER,Percy Scott Lt kia 26-3-18 RASC attRFC p18&253 MR20

DRIVER,Thomas Stanley Lt ded 2-12-18 4RRofCav p261 CR Essex120

DRON,John Kent Lt kia 13-10-18 6HLI att1KOSB p240 CR Belgium157

DROUGHT,Charles Frederick TCapt dow 31-12-15 7Lincs p75 CR France40

DROUGHT,George Thomas Acton Maj dow 14-6-15 RFA p28 CR Eire533,15-6-15

DROUGHT,Robert Victor.MC.2Lt dow 9-6-17 3 att14RirRif p169 CR France285,3 att7Bn

DROVER,Charles Peacock TLt kia 23-3-18 8 att1GordH p166 CR France174

DRUERY,Dudley Victor 2Lt dow 18-10-18 13Lond p249 CR France146

DRUITT,Charles Lambert.MID TLt kia 13-10-16 9SfthH p164 CR France177

DRUITT,Joseph 2Lt kia 9-5-15 RBerks p139 MR32

DRUMMOND,Alexander Gilmour.MC.2Lt dow PoW 5-4-18 3 att6BlkW p128 CR Germany1

DRUMMOND,David Robert Lt kia 3-11-14 2ScotsGds p52 MR29

DRUMMOND,Douglas Torrie 2Lt dow 3-5-17 3 att5CamH p167 MR20,Torrel

DRUMMOND,Eric Grey Maj kia 14-11-14 IA 2/4 att2/3GurkhaRif p276 CR France80

DRUMMOND,Francis T2Lt kia 5-7-16 9NumbF p60 CR France

DRUMMOND,Harry T2Lt kia 31-10-18 17LancF p92 CR Belgium143

DRUMMOND,Harvey Gerald Binns.MC.Lt dow 3-9-18 1ScotsGds p52 CR France646

DRUMMOND,Henry Claude Capt kia 24-7-16 7A&SH p243 CR France453

DRUMMOND,Henry Murray T2Lt dow 26-5-16 8 att9BlkW p128 CR Hereford96

DRUMMOND,John Davidson 2Lt kia 9-10-17 YLI att5Bn p143 MR30

DRUMMOND,John Grey T2Lt kia 13-10-15 RE 176TC p44 CR France765

DRUMMOND,Keaisley Mathwin.MC.Capt dow 24-3-18 6NumbF p213 CR France650,Kearsley

DRUMMOND,Nigel Felton Lt kld 20-12-16 6 att1KRRC p150 CR France817,Capt

DRUMMOND,Patrick Campbell T2Lt kia 25-9-15 8KOSB p101 MR19

DRUMMOND,Robert Charles Crosbie 2Lt kia 28-11-17 2CldGds p51 CR France256

DRUMMOND,Robert Kenneth.MC&Bar.TCapt dow 24-7-18 6CamH p167 CR France1228

DRUMMOND,Samuel Frederick 2Lt kia 29-7-17 17RFus p67 CR France572

DRUMMOND,Spencer Hensage Capt kia 30-7-15 7RB p178 MR29,Heneage

DRUMMOND,William Young T2Lt kia 11-7-16 13A&SH p173 CR France630

81

DRUMMOND-FRASER,Haddo Reginald.MC.Capt 1-8-18 5Ches att1Hereford CR France524

DRUMMOND-FRASER,Murray 2Lt kia 3-6-15 1/5Ches CR Belgium28

DRURY,Alfred Aloysius T2Lt kia 16-11-16 161RFA p28 CR France1013

DRURY,Follett McNeil.MID Lt kia 7-1-18 1/1Herts p252 CR Belgium20

DRURY,Gordon Vallancy TMaj ded 19-11-17 O&BLI 35TrgRes p130&266,GL George CR Wilts3

DRURY,Harold Strickland Lt kia 1-7-16 3 att8YLI p143 MR21

DRURY,Leonard George.MC.T2Lt dow 11-9-18 YLI att9Bn p143 CR France13

DRURY,Philip Blackett TCapt ded 15-7-16 18NumbF p60 CR Numb4

DRURY,William Symes TLt kld 29-1-16 8RDubF p176 CR France178,6Bn

DRURY-LOWE,William Drury.DSO.TLtCol kia 25-9-16 1GrenGds p49 CR France374

DRYBURGH,Joseph T2Lt dow 26-6-18 1 att7/8KOSB p101 CR France95

DRYDEN,John Thomas Lt ded 28-7-17 RAOC p198 CR Iraq5

DRYDEN,Norman McLeod Capt ded 24-11-15 1/6NumbF p270 CR Yorks303,23-11-15

DRYDEN-SMITH,Henry Dalby TCapt kld 14-12-15 RFC p1

DRYERRE,Robert Henry T2Lt kia 1-10-16 11 att7DCLI p114 MR21

DRYNAN,James Hugh St.Clair 2Lt kia 8-5-18 5ScotRif p224 MR30

DRYSDALE,Alexander T2Lt kld 25-3-18 RFC p15 CR Lancs114

DRYSDALE,Alexander Icely Maj kia 28-7-16 A87RFA p28 MR21

DRYSDALE,Alexander Nicholson.MC.TCapt dow 15-4-17 17HLI p162 CR France583

DRYSDALE,Donald Roy Lt dow 25-9-16 5Dors p124 CR France145

DRYSDALE,Hamilton Dunbar Capt kia 1-9-15 IA 26Punjabis att11RScots p276 CR France114

DRYSDALE,Ian Staveley T2Lt kia 18-9-15 11RB p178 CR France924

DRYSDALE,John.MC.2LtACapt kia 11-4-18 4GordH p241 MR19

DRYSDALE,Joseph Dudley TLt kia 23-10-16 2Lincs p75 CR France307

DRYSDALE,Roger Gillespie 2Lt ded 15-4-15 RWar p263 CR Hamps28

DRYSDALE,William.DSO.BtLtCol kia 29-9-16 2RScots Cmdg7Leic p54 CR France432

DUBERLY,Grey William Maj kia 13-3-15 1GrenGds RoO p49 MR22

DUBERLY,Vernon Conrad Capt kia 6-2-16 IA 17Cav p276 MR50

DUBOIS,Latimer Ridley 2Lt kia 7-4-17 18Lond p250 MR20

DuBOULAY,Arthur Housse Mayne.DSO.MajBtLtCol ded 25-10-18 RE AQMG3rdArmy p44

DuBOULAY,Hubert Lionel Houssemayne 2Lt kia 3-9-16 3 att1Wilts p153 MR21

DUBS,Charles Edward Douglas Capt ded 6-11-18 17Lancers p23 CR Scot546

DuBUISSON,John Edmund 2Lt ded 11-10-16 99RFA p28 CR Greece7

DuCANE,Hubert John.CB.MVO.TBrigGen ded 15-6-16 RH&FA GenStaffSthArmy p28 CR Essex212

DUCAT,Richard Maj dow 11-11-14 IA 20Inf p276 CR Iraq6

DUCHESNE,Richard Ernest T2Lt kia 8-10-16 7Nhampt B'Coy p137 CR France81

DUCKERS,Margaret Ellison SNurse ded 16-5-18 QAIMNS p200 CR Greece9

DUCKETT,Harold Ager 2Lt dow 7-6-17 9HLI p240

DUCKETT,Kenneth Lees 2Lt dow 22-8-16 9HLI p240 CR France176

DUCKETT,Vincent George T2Lt kia 23-3-18 14 att11DLI p160 MR27

DUCKETT,William Garnard.MC.2Lt kia 27-3-18 300RFA p28 MR27,Barnard

DUCKITT,Charles Stanley TCapt kia 3-5-17 18WYorks p81 MR20

DUCKSWORTH,Walter Clarence T2Lt kia 8-10-18 WelshR att1KSLI p126 CR France235

DUCKWORTH,Bernard 2Lt kia 28-7-16 1Ches p96 MR21

DUCKWORTH,Eric 2Lt kia 7-8-15 6LancF p221 MR4

DUCKWORTH,Herbert Hartley Lt kia 24-3-18 3/6LancF att2/7War p221 MR27

DUCKWORTH,Percy Blezard 2Lt kia 9-4-17 WarwickRFA p208 CR France418

DUCKWORTH,William T2Lt kia 25-3-18 20 att18LancF p92 MR27

DUCKWORTH,William Henry T2Lt dow 21-4-16 20LancF p92 CR France1,14-4-16

DUDDELL,Arnold Leslie Lt dow 27-9-17 3SStaffs att6Yorks p122 CR Belgium23

DUDDLE,William Kearsley 2Lt kia 20-8-17 8LancF p221 MR30,19-8-17

DUDDY,George Lionel Alfred T2Lt kia 10-4-18 11Suff p78 CR France685

DUDER,Harvey Stevens Capt kia 31-7-17 8Lpool p215 MR29

DUDGEON,Arthur TLt ded 19-11-18 RGA attRE 4FldSurvCo p39 CR France134

DUDGEON,Frederick Charles 2Lt kia 28-10-18 8Huss p22 MR38

DUDGEON,Ralph de Seton Maj 29-4-18 MilAccDept MR67

DUDLEY,Arthur Walter T2Lt kia 30-3-18 2 att8Worc p108 MR27

DUDLEY,Bernard John Cherleton Capt kia 24-1-17 Dors att3NigR p124&201 MR50

DUDLEY,Charles Leonard 2Lt kia 14-6-15 1/7Manch p237 CR Gallipoli6,4-6-15

DUDLEY,David Capt kia 9-5-15 IA 91Punjabis att6Jats p276 CR France924

DUDLEY,Eric Whittington 2Lt kia 30-6-16 13RSuss p118 MR19

DUDLEY,Henry Pemberton 2Lt kia 3-9-16 3Leinst att2IrReg p174 CR France402

DUDLEY,Herbert Edward.MID T2Lt kia 23-8-17 6SomLI p79 CR Belgium165

DUDLEY,Leonard Gray Capt dow 24-11-14 IA 6Jats p276 CR France80,Grey

DUDLEY,Leonard Thomas.MC.Lt dow 8-10-18 10RFus p67 CR France398,Capt

DUDLEY,Noel Montague Charles 2Lt dow 11-10-16 1/5Lpool p215 CR France40

DUDLEY,Samuel Robert TLt ded 21-12-15 RAMC p267 CR Essex1

DUDLEY,Walter Joseph TLt kia 16-6-15 4RFus p67 MR29

DUDLEY-HILL,William Capt 13-5-15 1LNLancs CR France80

DUDMAN,David.MID Lt&QM ded 26-4-19 11Leic p87 CR Germany1

DUERDEN,Charles 2Lt dow 24-3-18 87RFA p208 CR France13

DUERDEN,Edgar Lt dow 17-8-17 A150RFA p28 CR Belgium8

DUERDEN,Henry T2Lt kld 27-7-17 GL &RFC p7 CR Lancs235

DUERDEN,John Lt dow 10-6-17 2/4 att2/5ELancs p226 CR France769,2Lt

DUERDON,George 2Lt kia 10-4-18 4LNLancs attRFC p234&258,5Bn CR France37

DUFF,Alexander 2Lt kia 28-6-15 7ScotRif p224 MR4

DUFF,Beauchamp Oswald Capt kia 7-11-14 IA 1/1GurkhaRif att2/2 p276 MR28

DUFF,Beauchamp Patrick T2Lt kia 25-9-15 5CamH p167 MR19

DUFF,Edward Algernon ACapt ded 22-9-19 8TankCps p266 CR Asia81

DUFF,Guy Leith Assheton Capt dow 2-9-16 RFA p28 CR Scot141

DUFF,Hugh John.DSO.MC.Maj kia 6-9-18 2LovatScouts p204 CR France518,10CamH

DUFF,James 2Lt dow 9-4-17 RGA 167SB p39 CR France120,69SB

DUFF,James Mitchell Lt ded 24-8-19 7ScotRif p255 CR Burma129A,John

DUFF,John 2Lt dow 25-8-18 3 att1RInniskF p104 CR France855

DUFF,John Creran Lt kia 10-6-15 2GordH p166 MR22,Crera 18-6-15

DUFF,Peter Tyrie T2Lt kia 20-9-18 1/5SLancs p125 CR France106

DUFF,Robert George Vivian.Bart.Lt kia 16-10-14 2LifeGds RoO p20 CR Belgium380,Robin

DUFF,Sidney Hamilton 2Lt kia 13-4-18 18WelshR p126 MR32,9-4-18

DUFF,William Lt kia 28-6-15 1/7ScotRif D'Coy p224 CR Gallipoli6

DUFF,William 2Lt kia 18-11-16 13HLI p162 CR France534

DUFF,William Peter.MC.2Lt kia 23-4-17 8N&D p233 MR20

DUFF-GORDON,Cosmo Lewis Lt kia 3-9-16 Hereford att13MGC Inf p187&252 CR France402

DUFFELL,James Henry 2Lt kia 22-3-18 5TankCps p188 MR27

DUFFIELD,Arthur Edward 2Lt kia 16-8-17 8Mddx p236 MR30

DUFFIELD,William Ernest Capt ded 7-2-19 Ex RASC p267 CR Lond1

DUFFIN,Charles Francis TLtACapt kld 13-3-18 GL 9RIrRif attLabCps 127PoWCoy p190 CR France134

DUFFUS,Gordon Charles 2Lt kia 16-1-17 A235RFA p208 CR Belgium28

DUFFUS,William Lt dow 1-12-17 1/6GordH p242 CR France398

DUFFY,Alexander Noel T2Lt kia 18-11-16 8NStaffs A'Coy p157 CR France284

DUFFY,D.J.P.Lt 20-2-20 RMunsF att3NigR CR WAfrica39

DUFFY,Joseph Vincent TCapt ded 7-12-18 RAMC p195 CR EAfrica36

DUFFY,Thomas Bryan TCapt dow 16-8-18 1/2 att15DLI p160 CR France4,17-8-18

DUFTY,Thomas Ernest Lt kia 19-5-15 5Yorks p220 CR Belgium4

DUGDALE,Charles Cyril Lt dow PoW 27-5-18 4DLI attYLI p160 MR18

DUGDALE,Daniel TCapt kia 28-9-18 10EYorks p84 CR France262

DUGDALE,James.DCM.T2Lt dow 7-7-18 ELancs att1Bn p110 CR France31

DUGDALE,John Ainscow Capt ded 22-10-19 Norf p263 CR Lancs86

DUGDALE,Joseph Warrior 2Lt ded 3-1-18 27LabCps p189 CR France145

DUGDALE,Richard William.MC.Rev kia 24-10-18 RAChDept att1Norf p199 CR France658

DUGGAN,Charles William Maj drd 10-10-18 RAMC p195 MR40

DUGGAN,Frederick Capt kia 21-3-16 RH&FA p28 CR France275

DUGGAN,George Grant TCapt dow 16-8-15 5RIrFus p171 MR4

DUGGAN,Herrick Stevenson TLt dow 21-10-15 RE 70Coy p44 CR France80,18-9-15

DUGGAN,J.HonMaj&Commy 27-2-21 IOD CR Yorks548

DUGGAN,John Rowswell Lt kia 16-8-15 5RIrReg p89 CR Gallipoli4

DUGGAN,Joseph Henry William 2Lt kia 6-11-17 14Glouc &20RFC p7&106 MR20

DUGGAN,Thomas Alphonsus T2Lt kia 13-11-16 7ELancs p110 CR France384

DUGMORE,William Francis Brougham Radcliffe.DSO.MajALtCol kia 12-6-17 1NStaffs RoO p157 CR Belgium127

DUGNOLLE,John Henry 2Lt kia 25-9-15 2RSuss C'Coy p118 CR France219

DUGUID,Alexander Ritchie 2Lt kia 3-5-17 4EYorks p219 CR France777

DUGUID,Charles Frederick.DSO.MC.Capt kia 13-5-17 22Manch p154 MR20

DUGUID,Clarence Donald.MM.T2Lt kia 18-9-18 13WelshR p126 CR France415

DUGUID,James T2Lt kia 9-4-16 7NStaffs p157 MR38

DUHAN,Francis Taylor Maj kia 26-4-15 IA 19Punjabis att57Rif p276

82

DUHEAUME,Herbert Thomas TCapt ded 5-8-16 RAMC p195 CR Dorset162

DUIRS,Mearns William T2Lt kia 25-9-15 7KOSB p101 MR19

DUKE,Alexander Leonard LtCol ded 27-2-18 IMS p276 MR43

DUKE,Barry Pevensey Lt kia 3-11-14 3 att2RSuss p118 MR29

DUKE,John.MC.TCapt dow 22-4-18 11Ess p131 CR Belgium18

DUKE,Valentine Gordon Capt kia 10-7-16 RGA 26SB p39 CR France188

DUKES,Samuel SubCdr ded 21-10-16 IA S&TCps p276 CR France300

DULEY,Edwin Joseph T2Lt kia 2-11-16 7BordR p117 CR France744

DULSON,Matthew Harvey 2Lt kia 11-4-17 3DragGds p21 MR20

DUMARESQ,Herbert William Maj ded 14-1-16 RB p178 CR Surrey27

Du MAURIER,Guy Louis Busson.DSO.LtCol kia 10-3-15 3RFus p67 CR Belgium17,9-3-15

Du MOULIN,Francis Louis.MC.CaptALtCol kia 7-11-18 RSuss Cmdg1EYorks p118 CR France935

DUMSDAY,Cyril Robert Capt kia 27-4-15 8Mddx p236 CR Belgium152

DUMVILLE,E.2Lt kia 26-6-18 6WRid &RAF p227

DUN,Leslie Finlay Capt kia 28-9-15 10Lpool p216 CR Belgium6

DUNBAR,Arbuthnot John Capt kia 17-3-15 RFA 114Bty p28 CR France705

DUNBAR,John Campbell 2Lt kld 18-9-18 1/5HLI &RAF CR Egypt9

DUNBAR,William John Lt ded 20-11-17 RE p262

DUNBAVANO,Hubert 2Lt kia 25-8-16 RE p210 CR France400

DUNCAN,Alexander Lt kia 25-3-18 4Manch att40MGC p154&r182 CR France927

DUNCAN,Alexander Bell 2Lt dow 5-8-16 IARO att28Cav p276 CR Asia82

DUNCAN,Alexander John Farquharson 2Lt dow 31-3-18 4 att8/10GordH p242 CR France40

DUNCAN,Alick Thomas 2Lt kia 2-3-17 12ESurr p112 CR Belgium28

DUNCAN,Arthur Paul 2Lt ded 26-5-18 1Mon p270 CR Mon52

DUNCAN,Arthur Seymour 2Lt kia 9-4-18 17Mddx p146 CR France298

DUNCAN,Charles Eric T2Lt kia 24-11-16 3RB p178 CR France115

DUNCAN,Charles Walter T2Lt kia 22-11-17 att6Nhampt p137 CR Belgium106

DUNCAN,Christopher William.MC.2LtTLt kia 20-11-17 4NStaffs attA'TankCps p157,188&258 MR17

DUNCAN,Daniel McFie T2Lt kia 2-10-18 1/2KOSB p101 CR France699

DUNCAN,David Cyril 2Lt kia 21-8-18 14Lond p249 MR30

DUNCAN,Edward Francis.MC.Chap4Cl kia 11-3-17 RAChDept att103InfBde p199 CR France1182

DUNCAN,Edward Henry 2Lt dow 24-3-18 93RFA p28 CR France62,25-3-18

DUNCAN,Emile Horace George TCapt ded 28-10-16 RAMC p195 CR Surrey2

DUNCAN,Garnet George Lt kia 15-12-16 SL attGoldCoastR p254 CR EAfrica38 &CR Tanzania1

DUNCAN,George Balfour 2Lt kia 30-7-16 3 att2RScotsFus p94 MR21

DUNCAN,George Stewart Lt kia 23-9-17 6GordH p242 MR30

DUNCAN,H.Capt 20-6-21 RAMC CR Scot935

DUNCAN,Harold Forrester.MC.Lt dow 29-3-17 3/5HLI attRFC p18&240 CR France169

DUNCAN,Harry T2Lt kia 23-4-17 18Manch p154 MR20

DUNCAN,Henry John Maj kia 8-8-16 5Lpool p215 CR France630

DUNCAN,Herbert Richard Lt ded 26-4-19 RASC p192 CR Scot359

DUNCAN,Isabella Lucy May Sister ded 1-3-17 QAIMNS 13StatHosp p200 CR France64

DUNCAN,J.M.T2Lt ded 6-6-18 RE IWT p44 CR Scot495,20-11-17

DUNCAN,James 2Lt ded 19-4-19 TankCps p266 CR Scot840

DUNCAN,James Athol Gordon T2Lt kld 15-2-18 RFC p15 CR Hunts83

DUNCAN,John TLt kia 31-7-17 10HLI p162 MR29

DUNCAN,John Donald Parland 2Lt kia 16-6-17 13NumbF p60 MR20

DUNCAN,John Francis TCapt&adjt kia 25-9-15 10ScotRif p103 MR19

DUNCAN,Leonard George Capt ded 15-6-21 RE 136RlyConstCoy MR43

DUNCAN,Kenneth 2Lt kia 9-5-17 6Dev p217 MR20

DUNCAN,Kenneth William Allen 2Lt kia 8-5-18 10Lpool att6SfthH p216 MR20

DUNCAN,Malcolm 2Lt dow 21-9-17 1/7Lpool p215 CR Belgium3,Capt

DUNCAN,Philip Courtnay 2Lt kia 30-10-17 8Lond p247 CR Belgium126

DUNCAN,Robert Gordon Campbell 2Lt kia 3-5-17 10A&SH p173 CR France924

DUNCAN,Ronald Wingrave Capt kia 9-3-16 RAMC attLeic p195 MR38

DUNCAN,Stuart Capt kia 13-11-14 Glouc RoO att2SLancs p106 MR29

DUNCAN,W.A.TD.LtCol 18-12-17 MddxHuss CR Mddx26

DUNCAN,Walter.MIDx2 Lt ded 19-12-18 8Lpool p215 CR Lancs2

DUNCAN,William Balfour Bethune Lt kia 3-9-16 4BlkW p230 CR France701

DUNCAN,William Williamson Kerr Lt ded 29-2-16 RAMC p270 CR Scot877

DUNCANSON,Ian Ferguson 2Lt kia 12-10-17 8A&SH p243 CR Belgium126

DUNCANSON,Roy 2Lt kia 7-7-16 3 att9WRid p115 MR21

DUNCANSON,Stuart Ray 2Lt kia 11-8-17 1Mon att11Ches p244 CR Belgium125

DUNCANSON,Una Marguerite Nurse drd 31-12-17 VAD p200 CR Egypt1

DUNCOMBE-SHAFTO,Arthur.DSO.Capt kia 12-9-14 RScots p54

DUNCUM,Eric Cundy Lt 7-12-20 B84RFA CR Africa81

DUNDAS,Cecil Henry Lt dow 2-3-15 1WelshR p126 CR Belgium58 20-2-15

DUNDAS,David George Minden.MID 2Lt ded 10-2-18 IA 17Inf p276 MR66,Maj

DUNDAS,George.MC&Bar.Lt dow 2-9-18 161RFA p28 CR France119,kia A61RFA

DUNDAS,Henry Lancaster Neville.MC&Bar.LtACapt kia 27-9-18 1ScotsGds p52 CR France530,Nevill

DUNDAS,Richard Charles LtCol kia 25-9-15 11RScots p254 CR France924

DUNDERDALE,William Henry T2Lt kia 11-1-17 21Manch p154 MR21

DUNDON,James St.John TLt ded 17-6-16 RAMC p195 CR Iraq6

DUNDON,Sydney Jack 2Lt kia 16-8-16 13Lpool p71 MR21

DUNFORD,Ernest Thubron T2Lt dow 23-4-17 PoW GL &12RFC p7 France1276

DUNFORD,Roy Craig.DSO.Capt dow 10-11-16 1/6NumbF p213 CR Numb3

DUNGEY,Francis Herbert T2Lt kia 3-5-17 1EKent p57 MR19

DUNGLISON,William T2Lt dow 21-8-18 1NumbF p60 CR France745

DUNHILL,Carlos Miguel Guillermo Capt kia 1-12-15 RE att17S&M p44 MR38

DUNKERLEY,Harold TCaptAMaj dow 23-3-18 RAMC att95FA p195 CR France924

DUNKIN,Alfred Davy Hosking T2Lt kia 3-10-18 N&D att1/8Bn p133 CR France375,Davey

DUNKLEY,Alexander 2Lt kia 9-4-16 12 att9Worc p108 MR38

DUNKLEY,Henry Newman T2Lt kia 21-9-17 1/2 att12ESurr B'Coy p112 MR30

DUNLOP,Alesander Hamilton 2Lt kia 6-11-17 AyrYeo p203 CR Palestine1,12RScotsF

DUNLOP,Archibald Ballantine Henderson.MC.Capt dow 20-9-18 1Camb p244 CR France194

DUNLOP,Brian John 2Lt kia 31-7-17 3GrenGds p49 CR Belgium13

DUNLOP,Charles 2Lt dow 22-10-14 RInniskF p104 CR France473,Lt

DUNLOP,Christian Dolymythe Hamilton 2Lt kia 16-6-15 10Lpool p216 MR29,Dalrymple

DUNLOP,Colin Edward 2Lt kia 3-2-17 IARO att1/2GurkhaRif p276 CR Iraq5

DUNLOP,Frederick Cleave Strickland Capt kia 8-11-14 1Manch p154 CR France706

DUNLOP,George Harry Melville TMaj ded 3-7-16 RAMC 4GH p195 CR France40

DUNLOP,George Malcolm Capt kia 25-4-15 RDubF p176 CR Gallipoli15

DUNLOP,Harry Holmes Kerr Lt ded 12-2-19 RASC 1034 MT Coy p192 CR Italy15

DUNLOP,James Lt dow 1-11-18 4RScots p222 CR Belgium159,2-11-18

DUNLOP,James Wilkie TLt ded 5-3-17 5IrrReg p89 CR Surrey18

DUNLOP,John Francis Logan Lt dow 7-5-18 RGA 139HB p39 CR France71

DUNLOP,John Gunning Moore 2Lt kia 27-8-14 2RDubF p176 CR France660

DUNLOP,Julian Silver Strickland.MID Capt kia 24-10-14 1SStaffs p122 MR29

DUNLOP,Kenneth Strickland 2Lt kia 26-9-15 4 att1SStaffs p122 CR France423

DUNLOP,Launcelot Lindsay Brook T2Lt kia 3-7-16 11Ches p96 MR21

DUNLOP,William.MC.MM.2Lt kia 30-10-18 39RFA p28 CR France1270,51RFA

DUNLOP,William Eric Brook 2Lt kia 19-5-17 5BordR p228 MR20

DUNLOP,William James T2Lt kia 21-9-16 RFA p28 CR France430

DUNLOP-SMITH,R.Capt 12-6-17 33Punjabis CR EAfrica38 &CR Tanzania1

DUNMAN,Charles Norman Innes 2LtTLt kia 31-7-17 15Mddx attMGC Inf p146&182 CR Belgium112

DUNMAN,Victor William TLt dow 19-9-17 SL att2/2KAR p202 CR EAfrica52

DUNN,Arthur Gibson TLt kia 5-9-17 RAMC 129FA p195 CR Belgium83

DUNN,Clifford Martyn.MIDx2TCapt kia 25-11-17 17WelshR p126 CR France256,24-11-17

DUNN,Ernest George 2Lt kia 10-6-17 10Lpool attMGC Inf p187&216 CR France777

DUNN,Francis William Morgan 2Lt kia 10-8-15 5WelshR p230 MR4

DUNN,Frank Mewborne T2Lt kia 23-9-17 10DLI p160 CR Belgium78

DUNN,Frederick Charles Robert TLt kia 9-7-16 11LancF p92 MR21,10-7-16

DUNN,Frederick Oswald TLt kld 19-3-16 23NumbF p60 CR France275

DUNN,Gerald Morton 2Lt kia 13-10-18 RGA 140SB p209 CR France147

DUNN,Godfrey Lawrence Capt 21-9-20 1/1KentCycBn CR Kent268

DUNN,Gwynne Morgan T2Lt dow 23-2-17 9WRid p115 CR France105

DUNN,Harold Black T2Lt kia 30-8-18 1/5Dev p76 CR France1484

DUNN,Henry Joseph 2Lt kia 26-11-17 4RWKent p234 CR France1461

DUNN,Herbert 2Lt ded 25-10-15 8ScotRif p225 CR Egypt3

DUNN,Herbert Harman TLt ded 26-9-16 12Lpool B'Coy p71 MR21 &CR France1890

DUNN,Hugh Aubrey Fairfield 2Lt drd 21-5-16 RE p44 CR Wales37

DUNN,James 2Lt ded 14-11-18 IARO att2S&M p276 MR40,Lt

DUNN,James Shannon T2Lt kia 4-10-17 2KOSB p101 MR30

DUNN,John 2Lt kia 21-6-17 7ScotRif p224 CR Belgium115

DUNN,John 2Lt.MM.dow 1-2-18 3Suff p78 CR Frnce518,kia

DUNN,John.MM.2Lt kia 20-9-18 56RFA p28 CR France484

DUNN,John Cragg Lt dow 25-3-16 3Dors att59TMB p124 CR Belgium11

DUNN,John Hubert Malcolmson 2Lt kia 25-9-16 18RFA p28 CR France832

DUNN,John Robert Collard 2Lt kia 20-8-15 5WelshR p230 MR4

DUNN,John Valentine TCapt kia 15-8-15 7RMunstF p175 MR4,7RDubF

DUNN,Malcolm T2Lt kia 9-4-18 22NumbF p60 CR Belgium451

DUNN,Martin 2Lt kia 16-5-17 5BlkW p231 CR France97

DUNN,Philip Morgan TCapt kia 3-2-17 8RWelshF p97 CR Iraq5

DUNN,Ralph Ellis T2Lt dow 1-7-16 1SomLI p79 MR21

DUNN,Ralph John 2Lt kia 25-9-15 RE p44 MR19

DUNN,Robert James Armstrong Capt kia 23-4-17 4GordH p241 CR France1194

DUNN,Robert William Henry Brighen Col ded 8-1-17 Staff RFus 13ResInfBdeCdr p1 CR Wales613

DUNN,Robin Gaspar Lt kldacc 19-3-19 1/5Lincs p255 CR Kent268,Capt 18-3-18

DUNN,Spottiswoode Robert.TD.LtCol dow 29-6-15 1/4RScots p211 MR4

DUNN,Thomas Capt kia 19-4-17 1/5KOSB p224 CR Palestine8

DUNN,Thomas Edward Doncaster Lt dow 21-12-14 2ScotRif p103 CR France768,22-12-14

DUNN,William T2Lt kia 24-3-18 7Lincs p75 CR France216

DUNN,William John T2Lt kia 17-7-16 6KOSB p101 CR France744

DUNN-PATTISON,Richard Phillipson Capt kia 8-3-16 6Dev p217 MR38

DUNNACHIE,William James Nimmo Lt kia 15-4-16 RE 250TC p44 CR Belgium37,2Lt

DUNNAGE,Arthur 2Lt kia 1-9-16 5 att3RB p178 CR France402

DUNNE,Arthur Sydney Lt kia 2-7-17 6Drags p22 CR France1495

DUNNE,John Geoffrey David Baird Lt ded 12-11-18 3RDubF p176 CR France1028,1 Ex3Bn

DUNNE,Walter Edwin 2LtTLt ded 18-10-15 2LancF p92 CR France167

DUNNET,Donald 2Lt kia 15-6-15 5SfthH p241 MR22

DUNNETT,Raymond Frederick.MC.Lt kld 17-11-17 5Worc &RFC p7&108 CR Hamps153

DUNNING,Reginald Percy 2Lt kia 21-3-18 2/6N&D p233 MR20

DUNNINGTON-JEFFERSON,Wilfred Mervyn 2Lt kia 22/29-4-15 7 att3RFus p67 MR29,27-4-15

DUNPHY,K.P,MC Lt 19-5-20 2Leinst CR Eire381

DUNSCOMBE,Charles William TLtACapt dow 14-3-17 13Ess p131 CR France177

DUNSCOMBE,George 2Lt ded 6-11-18 PoW 17Manch p154 CR Europe149

DUNSFORD,Reginald Martin Capt ded 18-10-18 RGA 397SB p270 CR Hamps57

DUNSHEE,Ernest Rowland T2Lt dow 11-8-18 1/2 att5WRid p115 CR France40

DUNSMURE,Colin Hamilton Terrot 2Lt kia 25-9-15 5CamH p167 MR19

DUNSMURE,Henry Alexander Henderson Lt kia 20-2-15 2CamH p167 CR Belgium28,Alistair

DUNSTAN,Guy Pierce T2Lt kia 1-7-16 11BordR p117 CR France293,Peirce

DUNSTAN,Hedley T2Lt kia 18-8-17 Y&L &55RFC p7&158 CR France285

DUNSTAN,John Leonard Lt ded 28-10-18 GL &RAF CR Lond14

DUNSTAN,Sidney Chap4Cl ded 16-7-18 RAChDept p199 CR Notts68

DUNSTERVILLE,Graham Eardley Lt kia 30-10-14 1Dev p76 MR22

DUNVILLE,John Spencer.VC.2Lt dow 25-6-17 1Drags p21 CR France363,26-6-17

DUNWELL,Frederick Leslie 2Lt kia 4-1-16 5RFus p67 CR Belgium28,Fredrick

DUNWOODY,Hugh Henderson T2Lt kld 31-7-16 10 att9RIrFus p171 CR Belgium48

DUNWOODY,John Myles 2Lt kia 4-5-17 4RDubF p176 CR Italy14

DUNWOODY,Samuel T2Lt kia 5-10-18 17RIrRif p169 CR Belgium157

DUPE,Cyril Harry 2Lt dow 21-3-18 C149RFA att30DAC CR France1203

Du PLERGNEY,Victor Wilder 2Lt dow 18-4-18 1 att2/5Lincs p75 CR Belgium38,DuPLERGNY

DUPLOCK,Marten Cave TLt kia 2-4-18 7Beds p85 MR27

DUPRES,Ernest Cruzick TLtACapt kia 29-8-18 9RFus p67 CR France630

DUPUIS,Alfred 2Lt dow 8-8-16 1Lincs CR France46

DURAND,Francis William Capt kia 21-12-14 3 att2RMunstF p175 MR22,22-12-14

DURAND,Reginald Heber Marion Lt dow 29-6-17 IA 38CentIndHorse p276 CR France446

DURANT,Christopher Gilbert T2Lt kia 18-10-16 13 att4Worc p108 MR21

DURANT,Hugh.DCM.MID 2Lt kia 20-1-16 9Lancers p22 CR France423

DURANT,Noel Henry Colin Fairfax Lt kia 30-11-17 1IrGds p52 MR17

DURANT,Norman Lt kia 12-3-16 1Glouc p106 CR France149

DURBAN,Percy 2Lt kia 25-3-18 3GrenGds p49 CR France214,DURBIN

DURDLE,Reginald William Lt kia 18-9-18 4EKent p212 CR France369

DURHAM,Edward Lt kia 26-11-14 RB p178 MR22

DURHAM,William Elyrin Wakeman Maj kia 19-9-19 IA 27LightCav p276 MR43,Glynn

DURINGTON,Thomas Philip Maj kia 12-11-14 1Drags p21

DURLACHER,Eric Alexander Ogilvie.MC.2LtACapt kia 20-5-17 5 att2Worc p108&258 MR20

DURLACHER,Philip Alfred.MC.Lt ded 12-5-18 148MGC p266 CR Surrey160

DURNAN,Edward T2Lt kia 16-10-17 14Y&L p158 CR France184

DURNFORD,Richard Selby TCapt kia 31-7-15 9KRRC p150 MR29

DURNFORD,Robert Chichester.DSO.Capt kia 21-6-18 1/4Hamps p228 CR Asia82

DURNO,Ronald Walpole 2Lt kia 24-2-17 RFA attY41TMB p28 CR Belgium21

DURNO-STEELE,Frederick Arthur Lt kia 9-5-17 7 O&BLI p130 MR37

DUROSE,Sydney Truman Capt kia 2-4-17 7N&D p233 CR France366

DURRAD,Francis Albert Capt kia 8-11-17 RASC &22RFC p7&192 MR20

DURRANT,Alec William TLt kia 13-11-16 184RFA p28 CR France1013

DURRANT,Arthur Michael.MC.TLtACapt kia 5-12-16 RE 257TC p44 CR France705,257FC

DURRANT,Christopher Martin TLt kld 31-7-18 SL p201

DURRANT,Dudley Garton 2Lt kia 16-8-16 1/5Glouc p225 MR21

DURRANT,John TLt ded 17-10-18 3N&D p133 CR France1858

DURRANT,Lombe Atthill 2Lt kld 6-6-18 GL &65RAF p190 CR France71,kia

DURRANT,T.Capt ded 16-5-18 SL &RAF p201

DURRANT,William Blencowe 2Lt kia 9-5-15 6 att2RB p178 MR32,8-5-15

DURRANT,William Henry Gilbert T2Lt kia 26-9-15 6Dors att2Wilts p124 CR France423,Heinz

DURSTON,Charles Giles 2Lt kia 7-10-16 12Lond p248 MR21

DURTNELL,Richard Neville.MID T2Lt kia 28-4-17 11Suff p78 MR20

DURWARD,Andrew.MC.LtTCapt kia 16-10-18 6KOSB p101 CR Belgium157

DURWARD,Ronald Gibson Stewart Lt kia 11-8-18 1RScots p54 CR France360

DUSGATE,Richard Edmund T2Lt ded PoW 19-12-17 RE &46RFC p7&p44 CR France1142,dow

DUSSEE,Arthur Norman 2Lt kia 1-7-16 4 att19LancF p92 CR France296

DUST,Frank William.MC.Maj kia 23-4-17 RFA p206 MR20

DUTCH,Ernest James T2Lt dow 6-1-17 14 att25/7RFus p67 CR EAfrica39,25Bn

DUTHIE,Bertie T2Lt kia 23-10-18 GordH p166 CR France206,Bert 24-10-18 3 att1NumbF

DUTHIE,D.O.2Lt kia 23-8-18 GL &2RAF p190 MR20

DUTTON,Alfred Laurence T2Lt kia 11-4-17 RE 95FC p44 CR France568

DUTTON,Charles T2Lt kia 7-7-16 10LancF p92 MR21

DUTTON,Charles TCapt dow 28-7-16 2SStaffs p122 CR France141,29-7-16

DUTTON,Geoffrey 2Lt dow 8-9-17 4 att8RSuss p228 CR Belgium16

DUTTON,Gerald Alexander 2Lt ded 5-5-16 4SStaffs p122 CR Dorset160

DUTTON,John Gordon.MC&Bar.TCaptAMaj dow 5-4-18 D107RFA p28 CR France1233

DUTTON,Joseph Issacher 2Lt kia 21-3-18 82RFA p28 MR27

DUTTON,Richard T2Lt ded 19-8-17 GL &48RFC p7 CR Belgium132

DUTTON,Thomas Dutton Capt kia 3-11-17 5 att2/4RWKent p235 CR Palestine1,Daniel 4-11-17

DUVALL,John Richard Rev dow 6-10-17 RAChDept att13Manch p199 CR Greece1,att7Wilts

DUVOISIN,John Hurll 2Lt kia 15-7-16 9HLI p240 MR21

DUXBURY,Andrew Marshall Lt kia 30-3-18 1 att6 O&BLI p231 MR27

DUXBURY,Arthur T2Lt kia 9-4-18 5RLancs p58 CR France98

DUXBURY,Herbert Cecil T2Lt ded 11-5-17 GL &54RFC p7 MR20

DWYER,Charles Henry.MID TCapt kia 17-11-16 10Worc p108 MR21

DWYER,Harold Beecher 2Lt kia 16-4-16 IARO att103Mahrattas p276 CR Iraq1

DWYER,J.O.2Lt 10-9-16 7RIrF &TMB CR France66

DWYER,James Jameson.DSO.Capt ded 19-2-19 RAMC p195 CR France65

DYCHE,John TLt dow 28-1-17 8RWelshF p97 CR Iraq5

DYE,George Harry Gordon TLt dow 21-11-17 9Norf p73 CR France398

DYE,Norman Sawford 2Lt kia 25-3-18 N&D att16Bn p133 MR27

DYER,Arthur Francis Rayner TCapt&Adjt kia 30-9-17 GL att1KAR p202 CR EAfrica11 &CR Tanzania1

DYER,Cecil MacMillan 2Lt kia 9-4-15 6 att4RB p178 MR29

DYER,Charles James 2Lt kia 7-3-17 RGA 150SB p39 CR France550

DYER,Charles Nettleton Capt ded 14-7-16 HAC A'Bty p206 CR Egypt15,Chester

DYER,Edward Arnold Lt kia 28-6-15 9KSLI p144 CR Gallipoli6

DYER,Francis Lloyd Capt kldByArabs 15-4-15 IA 83BurmaInf p276 CR Asia82,Frank 93Bn

DYER,Frederick Vivian Alma LtTCapt kia 25-9-15 1Mddx p146 CR France114

DYER,Harry Frank 2Lt dow 28-8-17 1/6WRid p227 CR France102

DYER,Herbert Arthur 2Lt kia 7-12-17 GL &65RFC p7 MR20

DYER,James Edward Stanley 2Lt kia 9-10-17 6LancF p221 MR30

DYER,John Swinnerton.Bart.MC.Capt kia 31-7-17 1ScotsGds attDAQ MG GdsDiv p52 CR Belgium12

DYER,Laurence Charles Lt kia 19-4-17 4EKent att2/10Mddx p212 CR Palestine8

DYER,Percy Maitland Lt kia 1-9-17 RE 208FC p44 CR France366

DYER,R.MM.Lt ded 30-12-18 SL p201

DYER,Ralph Gibb T2Lt kia 23-2-17 RE 92FC p44 CR France832

DYER,Stewart B.B.DSO.Maj ded 26-1-17 3Wilts CR Europe42 Ex2LifeGds

DYER,Sydney Beresford Hope 2Lt dow 10-7-18 104LabCps p189 CR Staffs61

DYER,William Oscar 2Lt dow 28-10-17 RGA 276SB p39 CR France193

DYKE,Cyril John 2Lt kia 7-11-17 24 att2/22Lond p252 CR Palestine1

DYKE,E.P.W.2Lt kld 30-10-18 8Y&L &RAF p158 CR Belgium205

DYKE,Francis Hart 2Lt kia 27-9-17 RWKent att7LNLancs p141 CR Belgium20

DYKE,George Bewsey TLt kia 26-4-16 RGA 18SB p39 CR Belgium15

DYKE,Walter Ball TCapt kia 10-4-18 RGA 155SB p39 CR Belgium90

DYKES,Alfred McNair LtCol kia 26-8-14 RLancs p58 MR15

DYKES,James Johnstone Capt kia 12-7-15 5KOSB p224 CR Gallipoli2

DYMOCK,Robert Townsend Vaughan Lt dow 27-10-15 1KSLI p144 CR Belgium2

DYMOKE,Walter George T2Lt dow 3-10-16 6RBerks p139 CR France62

DYMOND,John Jordan 2Lt kia 12-4-18 1/5SLancs p230 CR France260

DYMORE-BROWN,Hugh Patterson 2Lt ded 21-2-19 9RBerks Ex att5Bn p265 CR Berks117

DYSON,Charles Capt kia 6-4-17 2/8WYorks C'Coy p219 CR France568

DYSON,Charles Bertram Lt kia 25-3-18 1/5ELancs p226 CR France560

DYSON,Harold Edward 2Lt kia 31-7-16 4Y&L p238 CR France246

DYSON,Hubert Archibald.MID LtACapt kia 18-11-16 7EKent A'Coy p57 CR France314

DYSON,S.G.2Lt ded 1-6-18 GL &RAF p190

DYSON,Stanley William TLtACapt dow 5-10-17 11Manch p154 CR Belgium16

DYSON,William Hubert 2Lt dow 14-7-16 16Lond p250 CR France1512

DYSON,William Webster 2Lt kia 26-8-16 1RIrFus p171 CR Belgium127

E

EADE,Aylmer 2Lt kia 9-10-17 3 att2Yorks p90 CR Belgium83

EADDY,Charles Thomas 2Lt kia 9-7-16 4 att8NStaffs p157 MR21

EADIE,David 2Lt kia 10-5-18 5ScotRif p224 MR30

EADIE,James 2Lt kia 15-5-17 5SfthH p241 MR20

EADIE,James Albert Lt kia 27-5-18 9A&SH attMGC p187&244 MR18

EADIE,Robert Allan T2Lt kia 6-8-16 7Lincs p75 CR France399

EADIE,William TCapt kia 18-10-16 5CamH p167 CR France385

EADON,Alfred Mitchell 2Lt dow 21-8-15 6Yorks p90 MR4

EAGAR,Denis Geoffray 2Lt kia 28-9-18 160RFA p28 MR30

EAGAR,Francis Russell 2Lt kia 9-5-15 RFA 36Bty p28 CR France525

EAGAR,Rowland Tallis.MID 2Lt kia 8-8-18 RFus att9Bn p67 CR France141

EAGAR,William George Massy Capt kia 21-8-15 3 att1RMunstF p175 MR4

EAGLE,Frank Walter Lt kia 6-6-16 RE 2/1FC p210 CR France281

EAGLE,Gerald Charles T2Lt kia 12-10-16 7Suff p78 MR21

EAGLESFIELD,William James.MM.MSM.2Lt ded 15-11-18 8LancF p221 CR France146

EAGLETON,John Ronaldson Lt dow 3-9-18 C291RFA p207 CR France177

EAITCH,Ernest 2Lt dow 2-11-18 1/17Lond p250 CR France1887

EAKIN,Robert Andrew Capt dow 24-9-17 1KSLI p144 CR Mddx49

EALAND,Frederick John Arthur T2Lt kia 26-9-15 8SomLI p79 MR19

EALES,Charles Wilfred Lt kia 27-9-18 2Dev p76 MR16

EALES,Francis Daw Sherbrooke 2Lt kia 3-5-17 9Leic p87 MR20

EALES,Frank 2Lt ded 2-3-19 12RB p266 CR Durhan64,Lt

EALES-WHITE,Henry Hewlett Capt mbk 25-7-15 6RScotF p256 MR19,27-9-15

EAMES,Arthur Horwood 2Lt kia 1-7-16 1EYorks p84 MR21

EAMES,Fred 2Lt kia 19-9-18 1/3Yorks att1/5Ess p90 CR Palestine9

EAMES,William Stanley Lt dow 16-2-16 7 att12RFus p67 CR Belgium11

EARDLEY,George Arthur T2Lt kia 27-11-17 RLancs att2/5YLI p58 MR17

EARDLEY-WILMOT,F.L.Lt 19-3-15 EOntarioR CR Belgium111

EARDLEY-WILMOT,Gerald Howard T2Lt dow 10-3-16 20MGC p182 MR21 CR France22,9Dev MGSect

EARDLEY-WILMOT,Theodore.DSO.MajTLtCol kia 22-3-18 Y&L att12Suff p158 MR20

EARL,Agnes Kerr Sister 19-3-19 ScotWomensHosp CR Europe57

EARL,Harry Walter T2Lt kia 18-9-18 2RSuss Res p118 MR16

EARLAND,Reginald John T2Lt dow 30-1-17 2SWBord p99 CR France105

EARLE,Cedric 2Lt kia 4-9-18 4EYorks p219 CR France298,Lt

EARLE,Charles Edward LtCol ded 11-8-17 16Ches p96 CR Lond14

EARLE,Ernest Clifford Lt kia 27-5-18 D250RFA p207 MR18

EARLE,John Vincent Lt kia 20-6-15 1N&D att WAFF p201&133 CR WAfrica6

EARLE,Noel Vansittart 2Lt ded 9-3-16 EKent attN&D p57 CR Surrey160,Capt

EARLE,Walter Colby Capt ded 7-4-15 Ches p96 CR Ches28

EARLE,Wallace Sinclair T2Lt kia 16-4-16 GL &9RFC p2&190 MR20

EARLE,Wilfrid Antony 2Lt kia 23-4-17 4EYorks p219 MR20

EARLEY,William T2Lt kia 11-10-18 Mddx att13Bn p146 CR France270

EARLY,Egbert Edward 2Lt kia 13-10-15 5Lincs p220 MR19

EARLY,Frank D.Capt ded 15-5-18 LdStrathconasHorse CR Canada1595

EARNSHAW,Oscar T2Lt kia 2-6-16 RE p44 MR29

EARY,Frederick Charles.MC.TCapt kia 24-3-18 7DCI p114 MR27

EASDON,A.R.SubAssSurg 10-9-18 IMS CR Iraq8

EASON,Alan 2Lt ded 20-1-16 9RBerks p139 CR Berks93

EASON,Raymond Praed TLt dow 1-7-16 10Lincs A'Coy p75 CR France267

EASON,Sampson TLt kia 7-8-15 5Dors p124 MR4

EASSON,David Lt kia 21-3-18 19Lond p250 MR20

EASSON,David,Ernest Craik Maj kia 13-7-15 6HLI p240 MR4

EAST,Alfred Tomlin 2Lt dow 25-12-15 IARO 1 att3S&M p276 CR Iraq1,25-9-15

EAST,Gordon Doulton LtTCapt kia 30-7-17 RAMC att3GrenGds p195 CR Belgium12,31-7-17

EAST,Herbert Hinton Rev kia 5-8-17 RAChDept att3Ches p199 MR29

EAST,Hubert James Capt kia 10-5-15 1Y&L p158 MR29

EAST,John TCapt kia 1-7-16 15DLI p160 MR21

EAST,Kingsley Dunmore TLt kia 27-5-16 18LancF p92 CR France632

EAST,Lionel William Fellow.CMG.DSO.ColTBrigGen kia 6-9-18 RFA Staff Cmdg X111C HvyArt p28 CR France88,Pellow

EAST,Sydney Clark 2Lt kia 9-10-17 HAC Inf p206 MR30

EAST,William Frederick Ernest T2Lt kia 16-11-16 12 att8ELancs p110 CR France153

EASTERBROOK,Henry George Lt dow 25-4-18 9Lond p248 CR France13

EASTERBROOK,William Reginald.MC.Lt dow 17-7-18 3Ches p96 CR France31,1Bn

EASTGATE-SMITH,Charles William TLtACapt kia 27-8-18 2Manch p154 CR France526

EASTHAM,Clement Vincent T2Lt kia 3-5-17 KSLI att7Bn p144 MR20

EASTMAN,William Viviash T2Lt kia 4-10-17 KRRC att13Bn p150 MR30,Vivaish

EASTON,Arthur Aitken.MID T2Lt kia 2-3-16 10HLI p162 CR Belgium30

EASTON,Cyril.MC.Capt kia 23-4-17 4EYorks p219 CR France162

EASTON,Jack Leslie 2Lt kia 21-3-18 RGA 277SB p39 MR27

EASTON,Percy Thomas Capt&QM ded 26-11-18 Mddx att8NigR p146,26-11-16&201&265 CR Lond5

EASTOP,David Lt dow 14-2-20 RFA CR Kent127

EASTWOOD,Benjamin.MC.TCapt kia 30-5-18 8Glouc p106 CR France1410

EASTWOOD,Donald Capt kia 20-9-17 6Lpool p215 MR30

EASTWOOD,Edmond Patrick 2Lt kia 22-3-18 2Leinst p174 CR France1494

EASTWOOD,Frank Molyneux Lt dow 30-10-14 1RWSurr p55 MR29

EASTWOOD,Frederick Arthur Jervis TLtACapt dow 6-6-17 D103RFA p28 CR Belgium1

EASTWOOD,John William T2Lt kld 28-1-18 10N&D p133 CR France530

EASTWOOD,Leslie T2Lt ded 19-9-15 6RLancs p58 CR Egypt3

EASTWOOD,Ronald.MID Lt kia 5-12-17 RE 42ELancsFC p210 CR France765

EASTWOOD,Sam Lt dow 10-5-18 2/5LNLancs p234 CR France84

EASTWOOD,Thomas Capt 10-1-17 RAVC CR Ches127

EASTWOOD,William.MID TMaj kia 11-8-15 RIrRif att6Bn p169 MR4

EATHORNE,Francis John T2Lt kia 31-7-16 24RFus p67 MR21

EATON,Alexander Robert Charles TLt kia 23-8-18 1Beds p85 CR France239,Alexandra

EATON,Charles William TCapt dow 9-8-17 11Leic p87 CR Belgium19

EATON,Clifford Gwatkin 2Lt kia 24-4-17 1/8Worc p226 MR21

EATON,George Hubert TLt kia 25-3-18 6MGC Inf p182 CR France1893

EATON,Guy Wellesley TCapt kia 6-9-16 8RIrF p171 MR21

EATON,Harold T2Lt kia 31-7-17 13Glouc p106 CR Belgium20

EATON,James Willcox T2Lt kia 1-7-16 20Manch p154 CR France397

EATON,John Rodman Lt dow 8-9-17 RASC p192 CR Belgium16

EATON,William T2Lt kia 6-9-18 18RIrRif p169 CR Belgium42,2Bn

EATON-JONES,Stafford Thomas T2Lt kia 28-10-16 22 att4Lpool p71 MR21

EATON-RICHARDS,Julian David 2Lt kia 25-9-15 2RSuss p118 MR19

EAVES,Alfred Thomas TLt kia 3-10-16 10RWSurr p55 MR21

EAVES,Frederick William D.2Lt kia 21-3-18 1 att7RIrReg p89 MR27

EAVES,Wilberforce Vaughan.MBE.Capt 10-2-20RAMC CR Lond29

EBBUTT,John Horace Lt ded 21-2-19 HuntsCycBn p253 CR France40,1Camb

EBDEN,Francis Thomas Powney Maj ded 9-10-19 IA 73CarnaticInf p276 CR Iraq8

EBERHARDIE,Donel Clemons ACapt ded 7-4-18 IARO RecruitgOff p276 MR66,EBARHARDIE

EBERLI,John Frederick 2Lt dow 16-8-17 3 att2RIrReg attTMB p89 CR Belgium8

EBERLIN,Frederick Harold Maden 2Lt kld 25-7-17 3YLI &RFC p7&143,ded CR Notts84

EBERY,Wilfred T2Lt kia 14-2-16 10N&D p133 MR29

EBORALL,John Arthur T2Lt dow 25-2-17 32RFus p67 CR Belgium21

EBSWORTH,Alexander E.MC.CaptALtCol kia 21-9-18 SLancs att9NumbF p125 CR France255

ECCLES,Arthur John Tolcher.MC.Lt ded 26-11-18 4ESurr attRE p112 CR France289

ECCLES,Charley Gordon TCapt kia 25-5-17 GL &41RFC p7 CR Belgium168

ECCLES,David Roderick T2Lt kld 5-12-17 GL &RFC p7 CR Glouc60

ECCLES,Henry T2Lt kia 28-2-17 3 att7 O&BLI p130 CR Greece6

ECCLES,Horace Dorset Capt kia 16-8-17 RAMC att13RIrRif p195 CR Belgium96

ECCLES,John Dennison.MC.Capt dow 27-9-16 9Lond p247 CR Mddx16

ECCLES,John Vivian William T2Lt drd 4-5-17 RLancs p58 CR Italy14

ECCLES,Robert Col ded 30-10-15 9Lpool p270 CR Lond8

ECCLES,Walter 2Lt kia 30-5-16 4LNLancs p234 CR France175

ECCLESTONE,James T2Lt dedacc 14-5-17 1LifeGds p23 CR Staffs135

ECHIN,C.P.SubCdr 27-10-17 S&T Cps MR43

ECHLIN,Frederick St.John Ford North Lt dow 27-9-16 5RFus &RFC p2&67 CR France518

ECKERSLEY,Herbert T2Lt kia 15-11-17 731LabCps p189 CR Belgium92

ECKLEY,Frederick George 2Lt kia 27-11-17 F'TankCps p188 CR France357

ECKSTEIN,L.A.Lt dow 23-11-16 1/2KARif p268 CR EAfrica38 &CR Tanzania1,L.W.

EDDEN,Henry Stewart Capt kia 21-8-15 RInniskF p104 CR Gallipoli5

EDDIE,George Richard Lt ded 3-11-18 1/4Y&L p238 CR France34

EDDISON,John Radley 2Lt kia 22-4-15 1/8N&D p233 CR Belgium17,21-4-15

EDDISON,Richard de Paiva Lt kia 10-8-17 2/4LNLancs p234 CR France922

EDDISON,Tom Denton Lt kia 30-7-16 14 att19Lpool p71 MR21

EDDY,Charles T2Lt kia 9-10-17 Mddx att16Bn p146 MR30

EDE,Edward Dickens 2Lt dow 13-6-18 5NStaffs p238 CR France145,9Bn Ex 9Lond

EDE,Edwin William.MC.T2LtACapt kia 30-8-18 11RFus p67 CR France786

EDEN,Arthur George 2Lt kia 21-5-18 7Ess p232 MR34

EDEN,Bernard Lt kia 9-5-15 att2Nhampt p137 MR32

EDEN,John Lt kia 17-10-14 12Lancers p22 CR Belgium132

EDEN,William Alfred Morton.Hon.Lt kia 3-3-15 4KRRC p150 MR29

EDENS,Lionel George T2Lt kia 3-9-16 8RBerks p139 CR France389

EDEY,Sydney T2Lt kia 28-4-18 8Leic p87 MR30

EDEY,William John T2Lt kia 1-2-18 1Ess p131 CR Belgium22

EDGAR,Bernard Roy T2Lt kia 31-7-17 23MGC Inf p182 CR Belgium167

EDGAR,Elizabeth SNurse drd 26-2-18 QAIMNS p200 MR40

EDGAR,George Geoffrey TLt dow 28-8-16 9KRRC p150 CR France145

EDGAR,John Hammond Lt dow 24-2-16 9DLI p239 CR Belgium127

EDGAR,John Maxwell LtACapt kia 22-3-18 4SStaffs p122 MR20

EDGAR,Robert Gerald Capt kia 4-6-15 1/6Manch p236 CR Gallipoli2

EDGAR,Surrey 2Lt kia 7-10-16 7Lond p247 MR21

EDGE,Edward Holden 2Lt kia 22/23-3-18 8Lond p247 CR France1893,22-3-18

EDGE,Frank Goodair 2Lt dow 10-8-17 4LNLancs p234 CR Belgium11,9Bn

EDGELER,Percival Lt 17-8-18 MilLabCps(EA) CR Surrey102

EDGELL,Richard Fayrer Arnold Lt kia 5-5-15 3 att2KOSB p101 MR29

EDGHILL,Arthur Richard Lt kia 9-10-17 ChesYeo p203 MR30

EDGHILL,Ashley Gay.MC.LtACapt dow 15-4-18 15LancF att96TMB p92 CR France62,kia

EDGINGTON,William 2Lt kia 8-5-15 RFA p28 MR29

EDGINTON Robert Walter Lawrence Lt kia 3-6-15 1/5RWar p214 CR Belgium339

EDINGBOROUGH,Noel Duncan T2Lt kia 1-7-16 15Mddx att109MGC p146&182 MR21

EDINGER,Frank Harrison Chap4Cl kia 26-2-18 RAChDept p199 MR40,drd

EDINGER,Walter Mark Valentine T2Lt kia 23-8-18 1 att4RWar p64 CR France239

EDIS,Robert Wilkie Henderson Capt ded 5-5-16 9Mddx 5SupplyCo p270 CR Mddx25

EDIS,Walter Owen Lt kia 29-3-18 BedsYeo p203 MR27

EDKINS,Charles 2Lt kia 29-10-18 4Lond p246 CR Belgium406,30-10-18 7Bn

EDKINS,Harrison 2Lt kia 16-9-16 1/21Lond p251 CR France239,15-9-16

EDKINS,Philip Eric 2Lt dow 16-7-16 7RWar p214 CR France833

EDLMANN,Ernest Elliot.DSO.Maj dow 17-4-15 RGA 23MtdBty p39 CR Iraq6

EDMANDS,Francis Douglas T2Lt dow 1-12-17 RASC 952MT attRGA p192 CR Palestine9

EDMANSON Joe Lt kia 2-7-16 7 att13YLI p143 CR Belgium101,2Lt

EDMETT,Arthur William TLt dow 16-3-18 10RWKent p141 CR Kent232

EDMISTON,Allan John 2Lt dow 16-8-18 4ScotRif CR Scot812

EDMOND,James 2Lt kia 20-8-17 HLI p162 MR34

EDMOND,John Adamson Capt kia 30-11-17 RAMC att60FA p195 MR17

EDMOND-JENKINS,William Hart TMaj dow 1-7-16 25NumbF p60 CR France430

EDMONDS,Albert Henry Lt dow 30-5-18 4Glouc p225 CR France145,2-6-18

EDMONDS,Edward Peregrine Pell 2Lt ded PoW 18-3-18 3RFC p15 CR France1252

EDMONDS,Harold Sylvester.MC.T2Lt dow 20-4-17 2Wilts p153 CR France40

EDMONDS,Leonard 2LtTLt kia 3-11-17 2/4RWKent p141 CR Palestine1

EDMONDS,Walter T2Lt kia 14-7-16 9ScotRif p103 MR21

EDMONDS,Walter John LtACapt ded 19-5-19 1/6Dev p217 CR Devon91

EDMONDSON,Frank Capt kia 11-4-17 1 att8ELancs p110 MR20

EDMONDSON,Percival Henry,MC.Lt dow 28-6-18 RHA attRGA 309SB p207 CR France116

EDMONSON,Kenneth James TCapt kia 4-6-16 3 att1Lincs p75 CR France188

EDMONSTONE,Norman Stuart Lt dow 7-11-17 2/16Lond p249 CR Palestine1

EDMONSTONE,William George TLt kia 14/16-9-16 2CldGds p51 CR France374,15-9-16

EDMUNDS,Cecil Harry Lt kia 23-3-18 21Lond p251 CR France439

EDMUNDS,Charles Vincent 2Lt kia 26-3-17 1/5Ess p232 CR Palestine8

EDMUNDS,David Gwynne TLtACapt kia 25-11-17 18WelshR p126&257 MR17

EDMUNDS,Guy Victor 2Lt kia 23-5-16 21Lond p251 MR20

EDMUNDS,Gwynne Rhys Lt kia 20-7-16 18 att2RWFus p97 MR21

EDMUNDS,Vivian Spence T2Lt kld 6-9-17 GL &37RFC p7 CR Sussex55

EDMUNDS-DAVIES,John Charles 2Lt dow 12-4-17 18 att10RWFus CR France52

EDMUNDSON,Charles Robert Eubank.MC.TCapt kia 1-7-16 8Y&L p158 CR France239

EDRIDGE-GREEN,Henry Allen 2Lt ded5-11-18 23RWFus &RAF p97

EDSELL,George Alfred Lt ded 15-8-15 RAMC p270 CR Surrey148,LtCol

EDWARD,Bernard Joseph.MC.2Lt dow 18-4-18 3 att9LNLancs p135 CR France65,Lt

EDWARD,Borlase Maj kia 18-3-17 RGA 247SB p39 CR France1182,EDWARDS

EDWARD,James Daniel 2Lt dow PoW 26-4-18 6HLI p240 CR Germany3

EDWARDES,Cecil.Hon.Capt kia 20-11-17 ScotHorseYeo attTankCps p189&205 MR17

EDWARDES,George D'Arcy TMaj kia 10-7-16 1Drags att13WelshR p21 CR France397

EDWARDES,Henry Arthur T2Lt kld 16-2-18 RFC p15

EDWARDES,Henry Frederick Edgcumbe 2Lt kia 6-3-17 3 att1DCLI p114 CR France80,6-2-17

EDWARDES,Owen 2Lt kia 1-7-16 2KRRC p150 MR20

EDWARDES,Thomas Lt kia 11-4-18 5Y&L p238 MR30

EDWARDES-CRATE,Ian Ronald.MC.T2Lt dow 10-10-18 9Yorks p90 CR France528,EDWARDS

EDWARDS,Alfred Ford Collins AssSurg2Cl 12-3-15 IMS MR28 CR France31

EDWARDS,Albert Campbell T2Lt kia 24-3-18 6 att7DCLI p114 MR27

EDWARDS,Albert John 2LtTLt kia 2-8-17 26RFus p67 MR29

EDWARDS,Alfred Cecil.MC.TCapt dow 25-7-17 RAMC att1/4YLI p195 CR France13

EDWARDS,Alfred Joseph 2Lt dow 10-4-16 3RScots att6LNLancs p54 MR38

EDWARDS,Algernon Stuart TLt kia 31-7-17 17RWFus p97 MR29

EDWARDS,Anthony Hepburn Lt kia 1-4-18 5 O&BLI p130 MR27

EDWARDS,Arthur 2Lt kia 16-6-17 4EKent p212 MR29

EDWARDS,Arthur T2Lt kia 17-9-17 3Y&L p158 MR30

EDWARDS,Arthur Corbett Capt kia 25-9-15 8RWKent p141 MR19

EDWARDS,Arthur Ernest T2Lt kia 1-9-18 7EYorks Ex8Bn p84 CR France307

EDWARDS,Arthur Joseph T2Lt kia 27-9-18 RWar att16Bn p64 CR France415

EDWARDS,Arthur Noel Capt dow 24-5-15 9Lancers p22 CR France285,25-5-15

EDWARDS,Arthur Strother Capt ded 2-5-18 MGC &RAF p182

EDWARDS,Arthur Webb 2Lt kia 10-10-17 GL &41RFC p7 CR France421

EDWARDS,Bernard Wallace TCapt kia 14-8-17 10RB p178 MR29

EDWARDS,Bert.MID Lt kia 2-9-18 D281RFA p28 CR France214

EDWARDS,Brian Wallie 2Lt ded 10-11-18 4RDubF &59RAF p176 CR Mddx46,Lt Ex RE

EDWARDS,C.H.Capt 27-8-20 RAMC CR Scot359

EDWARDS,Charles 2Lt kia 29-1-17 6EYorks p84 CR France150

EDWARDS Charles O'Reilly.MC.Capt kia 13-12-15 RE 57FCp44 CR Belgium1

EDWARDS,Clement Edward Alexander 2Lt ded 5-12-18 5 att11Worc p108 CR Devon247

EDWARDS,Colin Hyde 2Lt dow 22-5-17 1ESurr p112 CR France1276

EDWARDS,Cuthbert LtTCapt dow 17-4-18 RASC att7RWKent p192 CR France185,Glouc

EDWARDS,Donald William.MC.Capt kia 6-4-17 RASC att45RFC p7&192 CR Belgium406

EDWARDS,Edward Capt kia 17-8-16 1/2Mon p244 CR Belgium4

EDWARDS,Edward T2Lt kia 30-5-17 4Worc p108 MR20

EDWARDS,Edward.MC.ACapt kia 21-3-18 1Lincs p75 MR27

EDWARDS,Edward Ernest T2Lt kia 17-12-17 3Ches att1/4RSuss p96 CR Palestine3

EDWARDS,Edward Walter TCapt kia 23-11-17 18WelshR p126 MR17

EDWARDS,Edwin Allen James Lt dow 31-12-14 3 att1Beds p85 CR Surrey95

EDWARDS,Eric 2LtTLt kia 22-11-17 12SWBord p99 MR17

EDWARDS,Eric Lea Priestley Capt kia 20-9-14 1EYorks p84 MR15

EDWARDS,Eric Wilson.MC.TLtACapt kia 30-11-17 6RWSurr p55 MR17

EDWARDS,Ernest Victor 2Lt kld 16-2-18 GL attRFC p15 CR Egypt8

EDWARDS,Evan Chap4Cl ded 27-11-18 RAChDept p199 CR Lancs2

EDWARDS,Francis Andrew Lloyd T2Lt dow 10-8-16 5RBerks p139 CR France74

EDWARDS,Francis William Lloyd.OBE.MID LtCol 19-12-20 KRRC CR Wales677

EDWARDS,Frank Glencairn de Burgh Lt kia 12-10-14 I/12RHA p28 CR France350

EDWARDS,Frederick Thomas.MC.T2Lt kia 20-10-18 8Lpool p71 CR Belgium406

EDWARDS,Geoffrey Otto Charles 2Lt kia 7-7-16 9WRid p115 MR21

EDWARDS,George T2Lt ded 24-9-16 GL &RFC p2&190 MR20

EDWARDS,George Eric.DSO.ACapt kia 20-11-17 6SforthH p241 CR France1498

EDWARDS,George Percy.MC.Lt dow 2-10-18 D155RFA p28 CR France214

EDWARDS,George Richard Owen.DSO&Bar.TMaj dow 17-6-17 C173RFA p28 CR Belgium97

EDWARDS,Gerald John Capt dow 9-6-17 20Lond attKRRC p251 CR France518

EDWARDS,Gordon Stafford TCapt kia 28-9-16 8WRid p115 MR21

EDWARDS,Griffith Oliver.MC.T2Lt kia 20-9-17 11NumbF p60 CR Belgium84

EDWARDS,Guy Thulkeld TCapt kia 31-7-16 24RFus p67 MR21,Threlkeld

EDWARDS,Harold Ethelstan Lt kia 25-9-15 3 att2RWar p64 MR19

EDWARDS,Harold Thomas Capt kia 8-5-15 1Mon p244 CR Belgium96,Thorne

EDWARDS,Harold Welleson Hurst 2LtACapt kia 18-11-16 8Glouc p106 CR France215,Wellstone

EDWARDS,Harri Willis 2Lt kia 28-4-17 1/5ELancs p226 MR21

EDWARDS,Harry 2Lt kia 7-10-16 12Lpool p71 MR21

EDWARDS,Harry T2Lt ded 17-2-18 SStaffs p264 CR Staffs4

EDWARDS,Henry Arthur 2Lt 16-2-18 RFC CR Essex9

EDWARDS,Henry Laidley Garland Lt dow 16-5-15 3 att1RWFus p97 CR France260

EDWARDS,Howard Joseph 2Lt kia 9-10-17 7Worc p226 MR30

EDWARDS,Hywell 2Lt dow 22-11-17 2SWBord p100 CR France398

EDWARDS,J.Maj 23-5-16 RGA CR Ireland12

EDWARDS,James Harry TLt kia 7-1-17 14DLI p160 CR France114

EDWARDS,James Tudor 2Lt kia 13-9-15 3Lpool p71 CR France924

EDWARDS,John T2Lt kia 22-3-18 3RB p178 MR27

EDWARDS,John Francis Coster LtACapt dow 10-11-18 3 att24RWFus p97

EDWARDS,John Henry 2Lt kia 21-9-18 6 att25RWFus p223 CR France924

EDWARDS,John Hugh Evan Lloyd 2Lt kia 20-9-17 34/139RFA p28 CR Belgium102

EDWARDS,John Ivor Jones T2Lt kia 31-10-18 2 att24RWFus p97 CR Belgium140,Ivon

EDWARDS,John Kelvin Lt ded 28-11-18 7Ches p222 CR France1142,5Bn

EDWARDS,John Llewelyn 2Lt kia 7-9-17 C75RFA p28 CR Belgium12

EDWARDS,John Rathbone 2Lt kia 6-7-16 7DCLI p114 CR Belgium4

EDWARDS,John Robert T2Lt ded 15-11-18 704LabCps p189 CR France40

EDWARDS,John Stanley.MC.ACapt dow 24-4-18 LancHussYeo p204 CR Belgium38

EDWARDS,John Wesley.MC.2Lt kia 8-11-17 1/1WorcYeo p206 CR Palestine8

EDWARDS,Kenneth Grenville TLt kia 8-5-18 13RWFus p97 CR France60

EDWARDS,Lancelot Maj dow 15-4-15 1Lincs p75 CR France102

EDWARDS,Leo 2Lt ded 8-6-16 1Norf p73 MR20

EDWARDS,Leslie Edward.MC.TCapt dow 6-12-17 6 att8RFus C'Coy p67 CR France145

EDWARDS,Lewis George T2Lt kia 20-9-17 KRRC att11Bn p150 MR30

EDWARDS,Llewllyn Albert Lt ded PoW 21-3-18 7RWar p214 CR France672,Capt

EDWARDS,Llewllyn Foster.MC.TLt dow 12-4-18 8SLancs p125 CR France139

EDWARDS,Norman Roy 2Lt kia 19-4-17 8ScotRif p225 MR34

EDWARDS,Osborne Montague TLt kia 23-8-18 37MGC Inf p182 CR France577,25-8-18

EDWARDS,Oswald James T2Lt ded 10-12-18 RE 456FC p44 CR France146

EDWARDS,Percival Charles.DCM.TMaj kia 27-9-18 15RWar p64 CR France245

EDWARDS,Percy Howarth Lt kia 24-5-15 5NumbF p214 MR29

EDWARDS,Philip Arthur CaptTMaj kia 18-3-16 1LNLancs p135 CR France149

EDWARDS,Philip Percival 2Lt kia 25-4-17 7Worc p226 MR21,Perceval

EDWARDS,R.2Lt ded 15-6-15 6RB p266 CR Surrey95

EDWARDS,Reginald Howard 2Lt kia 22-9-16 19RFC p254 MR20

EDWARDS,Robert Maj ded 26-5-20 RAMC CR C'land&W'land17

EDWARDS,Robert Amor Lt dow 14-7-18 1WYorks p81 CR Belgium11

EDWARDS,Roland Frederick.MC.TLt dow 8-10-18 11RWSurr p55 CR Belgium11

EDWARDS,Roy 2Lt dow 30-11-17 10RB p178 MR17

EDWARDS,Spenser Ernest 2Lt ded 9-3-17 4EKent p212&270 CR Surrey160

EDWARDS,Stanley Robert TLt kia 24-9-15 8SStaffs p122 CR Belgium111,25-9-15

EDWARDS,W.E.CMG.Col 25-7-21 RA CR Lond28

EDWARDS,Walter 2Lt kia 26-4-16 6Lond p247 CR France924

EDWARDS,Wilfred William.MC.T2Lt dow 22-1-17 17RFus p67 CR France41

EDWARDS,William TCapt dow 28-3-18 RASC p192 CR France62

EDWARDS,William Armino Lt dow 1-11-17 GlamYeo p203 CR Palestine1,2Lt 24WelchR

EDWARDS,William Augustus Spencer Maj dow 30-4-16 NStaffs att7Bn p157 CR Iraq5

EDWARDS,William Francis Boucher Capt kia 14-4-15 IA 24Punjabis p276 CR Iraq6

EDWARDS,William Hardinge Colvin.MC.MID TCapt kia 9-5-15 1BlkW p128 CR France632

EDWARDS,William Ian.MC.TCapt&Adjt kia 5-8-17 11LancF p92 MR29

EDWARDS,William Victor Capt kia 29-12-17 7RDubF p176 CR Palestine3

EDWARDS-TROLLIP,John 2Lt kia 27-8-18 7Lond p247

EDYE,Charles Vivian de Grete Lt kia 30-10-14 2DCLI p114 MR29

EGAN,Pierce John Chap4Cl ded 6-4-16 RAChDept p199 CR Egypt3,att1BWIndR

EGERTON,Arthur George Edward MajTLtCol kia 29-9-15 1CldGds p51 CR France423

EGERTON,Arthur Oswald 2Lt kia 25/26-9-15 att5KSLI p144 MR19

EGERTON,Bertram Gustavus T2Lt dow 8-9-16 9N&D p133 CR France296

EGERTON,Brian Raleigh Lt kia 23-10-18 RE 87FC p44 CR France1296 &CR France1080

EGERTON,Charles Caledon Lt kia 18-4-15 2WRid p115 CR Belgium59

EGERTON,Edward Brassey TCapt dow 1-9-16 17Lancers D'Sqn p23 CR France158

EGERTON,George Algernon Maj dow 13-5-15 19Huss p23 CR France284,LtCol

EGERTON,James Boswell.MIDx2 Maj kia 27-10-18 IA 23Cav p276 MR38

EGERTON,John Frederick T2Lt dow 3-4-16 8KRRC ADC p150 CR France62

EGERTON,Louis Edward William Capt kia 1-8-17 BucksYeo p203 CR Belgium12,Edwin

EGERTON,Philip de Malpas Wayne LtACapt kia 8-10-18 19Huss p23 CR France341

EGERTON,Philip Graham Capt dow 18-10-18 3BlkW att2/19Lond p128 CR Egypt1

EGERTON,Phillip John Lt dow 17-10-14 BordR p117 CR Belgium57,Philip

EGERTON,Robert.MC.CaptTMaj kia 23-12-17 2RIrF &59RFC p7&171 CR France518

EGERTON,Robert Randle Lt kia 15-11-14 RE 1FC p44 CR Belgium96,16-11-14

EGERTON,Rowland Le Belward 2Lt kia 30-11-14 RWFus p97 MR32

EGERTON-GREEN,Charles Scroop Lt kia 1-7-16 2KRRC p150 MR20

EGERTON-GREEN,John William Capt dow 9-10-17 1RB p178 CR France102

EGERTON-WARBURTON,John Capt dow 30-8-15 ScotsGds p52 CR Ches136

EGGLESTONE,Ernest 2Lt ded 2-6-19 20DLI p160 CR Germany1

EGGLETON,Frank.MID Lt kia 21-10-17 17RFA p28 CR Belgium12

EGGLETON,Robert 2LtTLt dow 15-11-17 33RFA p28 CR Belgium16

EGLINGTON,Ferdinand Capt kia 1-7-16 1/5SStaffs p229 MR21

EGLON,H.E.Lt 19-7-17 SL attNigR CR EAfrica38 &CR Tanzania1

EGNER,Frederick Albert 2Lt kia 6-1-18 GL &6RFC p15 CR France62

EGREMONT,Godfrey Leonard Hobart Lt ded 2-5-18 8Manch p237 CR France1439

EHRHARDT,John Albert T2Lt kia 26-3-18 1TankCps p188 MR27

EICKE,E.C.LtCol 29-3-18 APD CR Mddx26

EICKE,Owen Macaulay.MC.TLt kia 5-11-16 62RFA p28 CR France374

EILLS,William.MC.Maj kia 9-4-18 C275RFA p206 CR France98,dow

EILOART,Cyril Howard T2Lt kia 26-9-18 IrGds att4GdsMGReg p52 CR France756

EILOART,Frank Oswald ACapt kia 3-5-17 1/1Lond p245 MR20

EINEM-HICKSON,Samuel Vernon Lt kia 4-11-14 2LNLancs p135 MR47

EISTOB,Wilfrith.VC.DSO.MC.TLtCol kia 21-3-18 16Manch p154

EKIN,James 2Lt kia 1-7-16 8Y&L p158 CR France293

EKIN,Leslie Montrose.MC.kia 1-7-16 8Y&L CR France246

EKINS,Franklin George.MC&Bar.Lt ded 27-1-19 1RIrReg p89 CR France1849

EKINS,Willingham Richard 2Lt kia 3-5-17 3 att11EYorks p84 MR20

ELAM,Charles Lt kia 1-7-16 12Y&L p158 CR France744

ELBOROUGH,Alfred Charles Ernest TCapt dow 30-7-15 6YLI p143 CR Belgium11

ELCHO,Hugo Francis Charteris, Lord LtTCapt kia 23-4-16 GloucYeo p203 MR34

ELD,Arthur William TLt kia 19-4-17 2Lincs p75 CR France407

ELDER,Alexander T2Lt kia 1-7-16 15RScots p54 CR France267

ELDER,James Capt kia 29-12-17 13RScots p54 CR Belgium94

ELDER,James 2Lt kia 21-3-18 6BlkW p231 MR20

ELDER,William Gardner Lt ded 10-2-18 2/20Lond p251 CR Lond32

ELDERFIELD,Henry T2Lt ded 11-11-18 NumbF att163ChineseLabCps p61 CR France52

ELDERKIN,John Victor 2LtALt dow 23-9-17 59RFA p28 CR Belgium23

ELDERS,John Francis 2Lt kia 28-10-17 16Lond p250 CR France646

ELDERTON,Fothergill Rex.MID Lt kia 25-9-15 3 att2RWar p64 MR19

ELDRED,John Sturgess 2Lt dow 27-11-14 2Leinst att2RIrRif p174 CR France102

ELDRIDGE,John Thomas T2Lt kia 18-9-18 2KRRC p150 CR France1700

ELEY,Ralph Corben 2Lt kia 24-3-18 19Lond p250 CR France216,Corban,dow

ELEY,William Arthur Derrick 2Lt kia 17-2-17 5 att1KRRC p150 CR France314

ELFORD,Arthur Douglas TLt kia 13-11-16 12EYorks p84 MR21

ELGEE,Hugh Francis Capt kia 6-7-15 SWBord attEgyptArmy p100 CR Gallipoli6

ELGEY,Eric 2Lt kia 19-3-17 RFA attRFC p18&208 CR France614

ELIAS,Hywel James T2Lt kia 5-6-17 21NumbF p61 MR20 &CR France1059

ELIFFE,M.Sister ded 25-5-16 QAIMNS p200

ELIOT,Geoffrey Lionel T2Lt kld 2-7-17 GL &RFC p7 CR Mddx17

ELIOT,Peter Douglas Colin Capt kia 25-2-17 IA 14Lancers p276 MR38

ELIOT,William Lawrence Lt kia 20-9-14 1WYorks p81 MR15

ELIOTT,Hugh Russell Capt kia 12-10-14 3Worc p108 CR France260

ELIOTT-LOCKHART,Percy Clare.DSO.LtCol dow 12-3-15 IA 59Rif p276 CR France632,kia

ELKINGTON,Thomas Garrett T2Lt dow 4-3-16 2Suff p78 CR Belgium11

ELKINGTON,Walter Henry T2Lt kia 22-3-18 11Hamps p120 MR27

ELLA,Alfred Newsam 2Lt ded 18-11-18 RGA 180HB p39 CR Greece9

ELLEN,Arthur Charles 2Lt dow 6-6-17 RGA 156HB p39 CR France297

ELLEN,Eric Adrian TLtACapt kia 30-1-17 2ELancs p110 CR France624

ELLEN,Harry John.MC.2Lt kia 14-9-18 2/20Lond p251 CR France755

ELLER,Cyrus Radcliffe Lt dow 30-5-17 8Manch p237 CR France1266

ELLERAY,Robert Lincoln T2Lt kia 18-4-18 2/6N&D p133 MR32

ELLERBY,Harry T2Lt kia 11-9-18 A122RFA p28 CR France398

ELLERINGTON,Robert.MC.TLtAMaj dow 29-3-18 39MGC p182 CR France185

ELLERKER,W.T Capt 14-12-21 RGA attIntel GHQ CR Germany1

ELLERSHAW,Wilfrid TBrigGen drd 6-6-16 RA p28 MR40,5-6-16

ELLERTON,Charles Fleetwood TCapt kia 21-5-16 10Ches p96 CR France68,19-5-16

ELLICE,Alexander TCapt dow 18-10-16 5CamH p167 CR France177

ELLICE,Andrew Robert Lt dow 29-9-16 4GrenGds SR p49 CR France105,2Lt

ELLICOTT,Frederick Arthur John 2Lt kia 8-7-16 6KOSB p101 CR France400,dow 9-7-16

ELLIFFE,Margaret Sister 24-5-16 QAIMNS CR Surrey160

ELLIKER,William Harold ACapt ded 19-2-19 RE p254 CR Staffs183

ELLINGHAM,Victor Edward 2LtTLt kia 1-10-17 Leic p87 MR30,2-10-17

ELLIOT,Alexander Shiels Lt kia 28-6-15 8HLI p240 MR4

ELLIOT,Edward John Capt kia 23-5-18 RAMC att10StyHosp p195 CR France134

ELLIOT,Gavin William Esmond.Hon.Lt dow 6-8-17 2ScotsGds p52 CR Belgium18

ELLIOT,Henry Gratten Capt kia 20-9-14 Dev p76

ELLIOT,Hugh Maj kld 26-7-15 11Lpool p71 CR Belgium84

ELLIOT,Hugh Lt ded 21-6-16 1 att14Lpool p71 CR Greece7

ELLIOT,James Brown T2Lt kia 22-11-17 RScots p54 CR Palestine3

ELLIOT,John Lt kia 3-8-17 108RFA p28 MR29

ELLIOT,Nichol T2Lt kia 9-7-17 1Nhampt att2TMB p137 MR31,10-7-17 Ex28Lond

ELLIOT,Thomas Archibald Scott T2Lt dow 6-8-17 CamH att7Bn p167 CR Belgium18

ELLIOT,Thomas Victor Guppy Lt dow 16-10-15 1RFA p207 CR France200

ELLIOTT,Charles Allen.CMG.DSO.LtCol 15-8-19 RE MR43 &CR Pakistan50A

ELLIOTT,Charles Arthur Boileau 2Lt dow 12-4-17 1SomLI p79 France113

ELLIOTT,Charles Howard Capt kia 27-4-15 IA 58Rif p276 CR France924,ELLIOT

ELLIOTT,Clarence William T2Lt kia 14-4-18 1RWSurr p55 MR32

ELLIOTT,Clifford Wilfrid 2Lt kia 12-8-17 23RFC p7 MR20

ELLIOTT,Duncan Lt kia 15-4-18 3BordR &4RAF p264 MR20

ELLIOTT,Edward Lt dow 25-10-18 B181RFA p28 CR Dorset53

ELLIOTT,Elizabeth Nurse 27-10-18 TFNS CR Durham109

ELLIOTT,Eric Cuthbert John TLt kia 22-11-17 GL &27RFC p7 CR France95

ELLIOTT,Eustace Trehane T2Lt kia 9-4-17 9 att8EYorks p84 MR20,10-4-17

ELLIOTT,F.Lt 2-2-16 3Lincs CR EAfrica61

ELLIOTT,Frank Phelps T2Lt kia 23-8-18 1Manch p154 CR France643

ELLIOTT,Frederick 2Lt dow 2-8-16 1/6SfthH attMGC p187&241 CR France176

ELLIOTT,Frederick Guy TLt kia 22-3-18 3Worc p108 MR20

ELLIOTT,Frederick William 2Lt kia 19-7-16 B166RFA p28 MR21

ELLIOTT,Geoffrey Edmund 2Lt kia 12-10-16 3 att2WRid p115

ELLIOTT,Geoffrey Faber 2Lt kia 31-8-16 4 att8SStaffs p122 MR21,ELLIOT

ELLIOTT,George Edward T2Lt dow 20-5-16 13RSuss p118 CR France80

ELLIOTT,George Keith Lt kia 8-9-18 3 att25RWFus p97 CR France365

ELLIOTT,Gerald Even Capt kia 21-7-16 6Glouc p225 MR21,Ewen

ELLIOTT,H.G.Capt 20-9-14 1Dev CR France1107

ELLIOTT,Harold Seymour Lt RegMutiny 17-2-15 IA 5LightInf p276 CR Asia45,kia 15-2-15

ELLIOTT,Henry Christopher T2Lt dow 20-12-17 RE 150FC p44 CR France52

ELLIOTT,Henry Ernest.MC.ACapt ded 2-3-19 RGA 152HB p39 CR Germany1

ELLIOTT,Herbert John 2LtTLt kia 2-11-17 1RWarGarrBn att1/4Nhampt p64 CR Palestine8

ELLIOTT,Horace William 2Lt kia 13-11-17 3SomLI p79 CR Palestine9

ELLIOTT,J.C.Rev 5-10-20 Chap4Cl CR Derby30

ELLIOTT,James Dunsmore T2Lt kia 22-10-17 16Ches p96 MR30,John Dunsmoor

ELLIOTT,James Harold 2Lt kia 29-11-16 2RWar p64 CR France221

ELLIOTT,John Benjamin George 2Lt kia 16-8-17 4Lond p246 MR29

ELLIOTT,John Forster TCapt ded 30-9-17 RAMC p267 CR Ireland146,Lt

ELLIOTT,John MacCreary Lt 16-4-17 LdStrathconasHorse &60RFC MR20

ELLIOTT,John William 2Lt kia 21-3-18 12/13NumbF p61 MR27

ELLIOTT,Leila Mabel Nurse 2-3-20 TFNS CR Scot241

ELLIOTT,Oswald Carr Finnes T2Lt kia 14-10-16 10GordH p166 CR France515,Fiennes

ELLIOTT,Phillip Lloyd 2Lt kia 21-10-14 1DCLI p114 CR France279

ELLIOTT,Philip Maurice T2Lt kia 1-7-16 3Mddx p146 CR France239

ELLIOTT,Reginald William Sidney kia 24-11-14 IA 1/7att2/8 GurkhaRif p276 CR France80

ELLIOTT,Robert Chambers Macdonald T2Lt kia 24-8-16 5KSLI p144 MR21

ELLIOTT,Thomas Brignall T2Lt kia 1-7-16 10RIrRif p169 MR21

ELLIOTT,Thomas Nichol 2Lt kia 11-4-18 7Lpool p215 MR32

ELLIOTT,Vere Arthur Edmonstone LtACapt kia 25-3-18 B165RFA p28 CR France745

ELLIOTT,Walter 2Lt kia 13-11-16 7RFus p67 CR France220

ELLIOTT,Walter Leonard Lt ded 21-11-16 9RB p178 CR France46

ELLIOTT,Wilfrid Edmund 2Lt kia 26-9-16 5Dors p124 MR21,ELLIOT

ELLIOTT,William LtACapt dow 3-9-18 RGA 374 att309SB p39 CR France833

ELLIOTT,William Herron,MBE Capt ded 28-1-20 RAMC 36CCS CR Germany1

ELLIOTT,William James.MC.2Lt dow 30-6-18 6RWKent p141 MR27

ELLIOTT-COOPER,Neville Bowes.VC.DSO.MC.TLtCol dow PoW 11-2-18 8RFus p67 CR Germany2

ELLIS,Basil Herbert Lt kia 16-6-15 5KSLI p144 CR Belgium115

ELLIS,Bryan Grogan Langley 2LtTCapt kia 13-10-17 RGLI att50BallSect 5WingRFC p7&200 CR Egypt9

ELLIS,Ceredig T2Lt dow 19-7-16 15RWFus p97 CR France51

ELLIS,Clifford Walker 2Lt kia 1-7-16 9 att2YLI p143 CR France267,3 att9Bn

ELLIS,Cyril Brooks 2Lt kia 13-11-16 HAC p206 CR France339

ELLIS,David Ithel.MC.Maj dow 9-4-18 285RFA p28 MR32

ELLIS,Douglas Quirk Lt ded 8-2-18 RFC CR Canada1667

ELLIS,Douglas Wilmshurst TLt kia 24-5-17 13Ches p96 CR Belgium43

ELLIS,Edward Charles TLt kia 7-8-15 11Glouc att15MunstF p106 CR Gallipoli6

ELLIS,Edward Miller.MC.Capt kia 7-8-18 HAC att5Lond p206 CR France44

ELLIS,Ernest Dennis TLt kia 27-9-18 4Beds p85 CR France1496 Ex10Bn

ELLIS,Evelyn Charles 2Lt kia 3-5-17 HAC p206 MR20

ELLIS,Francis Bevis TCapt kia 25-9-16 10NumbF p61 CR France239,26-9-16

ELLIS,Frederick Alfred T2Lt kia 22-3-18 11Ess p131 MR20

ELLIS,Frederick William 2Lt kia 3-3-18 1/13Lond p249 CR France184

ELLIS,G.R.Capt 28-6-18 RAMC CR Glouc126

ELLIS,George Adams Maj kia 10-3-15 ScotRif p103 CR France260

ELLIS,George Barker TLt kia 21-7-16 D51RFA p28 CR France399

ELLIS,George Frederick 2Lt kia 30-3-15 RE 173MinCoy p44 CR France706

ELLIS,Guy Stuart T2Lt kia 12-7-17 GL &57RFC p7 CR Belgium10

ELLIS,Harry T2Lt kia 9/12-4-17 8RLancs p58 MR20

ELLIS,Herbert Dudley 2Lt kia 25-9-15 RGA p39 MR19

ELLIS,Herbert Pearce.MC.Lt dow 1-12-17 GloucYeo p203 MR34

ELLIS,Horace Nickson.MC.T2Lt kia 9-10-18 6MGC Cav p182 CR France190

ELLIS,Hughie Lodwick Maldwyn T2Lt dow 5-5-17 1/2RWFus p97 CR France518

ELLIS,James Capt dow 24-4-17 7GordH p242 CR France113

ELLIS,James Clive T2Lt ded PoW 21-4-18 4TankCps p188 CR France364,dow

ELLIS,James Graves St.John T2Lt dow 11-10-15 RE p44 CR Gallipoli27

ELLIS,James Norman 2Lt kia 2-12-17 3 att2YLI p143 CR Belgium125,1-12-17

ELLIS,John Chute 2Lt dow 6-6-17 106RFA p28 CR Belgium11,Lt

ELLIS,John William 2Lt kia 27-5-18 4RWFus p223 CR France215,24-5-18 10Bn attRNDiv

ELLIS,Philip Challinor Lt kia 17-10-16 14HLI &1RFC p2&162,ded CR France705

ELLIS,Rae Adam Capt dow 22-9-18 25RWFus p204 CR France194

ELLIS,Reginald Denni Capt kia 8-6-17 1/4Lincs p217 CR France550,Dennie

ELLIS,Reginald Walter TLt kia 18-6-17 GL &9RFC p7 MR20

ELLIS,Robert Bruce.MC.Capt&Adjt dow 21-11-16 6BlkW p231 CR France40

ELLIS,Robert Charles T2Lt ded 31-5-18 PoW 2RB p178 CR France1755

ELLIS,Robert Percy 2Lt dow PoW 6-4-18 3RDubF p176 CR France934,2Bn

ELLIS,Robert Thomas Hugh 2Lt kia 13-10-17 19RWFus p97 CR Belgium168,12-10-17

ELLIS,Shirley Duncan.MC.T2Lt ded 19-3-16 RE 173Coy p44 CR France80

ELLIS,Thomas Arthur Capt 20-11-18 Min of Muns &RAF CR Ches28

ELLIS,Thomas Martin Capt kia 18-4-15 WRid attWYorks p115 CR Belgium115

ELLIS,Trevor Edgar.MID T2Lt kia 10-4-18 40MGC Inf C'Coy p182 MR32

ELLIS,Victor Richard Helps.MC.T2Lt kia 28-4-18 11RSuss p118 MR30,Help

ELLIS,William 2Lt kia 29-7-18 7Lpool p215 CR France745

ELLIS,William Ewart Simpson 2Lt kia 13-1-17 4SomLI p218 CR France785

ELLIS,William Forrest 2Lt kia 9-9-16 1/8Lpool p215 MR21

ELLIS,William John 2Lt kia 23-3-18 4 att9RWFus p223 MR20

ELLIS,Yvo Lempriere TLt kia 29-5-16 13Hamps p120 CR France114

ELLISON,Cuthbert Joseph ACapt ded 18-2-19 RGA p270 CR Berks2

ELLISON,Douglas Heins Capt dow 14-1-20 IA 95Inf att1/109 p276 MR43,Hems

ELLISON,Frederick John Gwynn 2Lt kia 16-8-17 1 att13RIrRif p169 MR30

ELLISON,Samuel T2Lt dow 25-3-18 2ELancs p110 CR France987

ELLISON,Samuel Charles TLt ded 17-7-17 RAMC p195 CR Egypt1

ELLISON,Stanley John 2Lt kia 1-7-16 5SStaffs p229 CR France644

ELLISON,Theodore Tarleton T2Lt kia 14-3-16 12 att1/6WelshR p126 CR France149

ELLISON,William Ronald 2Lt dow 20-6-15 RFA p28 CR Lancs164

ELLWOOD,Albert.MC.Capt kia 14-4-18 4RLancs p213 CR France1106

ELLWOOD,Charles Hugh Lt kia 2-6-15 4Lincs p217 CR Belgium98,1-6-15

ELLWOOD,Francis James Lt kia 4-10-17 1EYorks p84 CR Belgium167

ELLWOOD,Goeffrey Thomas Lovick TLt kia 17-7-16 6Leic p87 MR21,14-7-16

ELLY,Cyril John T2Lt dow 6-9-18 N&D att1/8Bn p133 CR France10

ELMES,King TCapt kia 28-9-18 RAMC att2/16Lond p295 CR Belgium42

ELMHIRST,Ernest Christopher 2Lt kia 7-8-15 8WRid p115 MR4

ELMHIRST,William TCapt kia 13-11-16 9EYorks p84 CR France742,8Bn

ELMITT,Austin Joyce,MC ACapt kia 24-11-17 17WelshR p126 MR17

ELMITT,George Carleton Brooksley 2Lt kia 16-8-17 7RIrRif p254 MR30,Brooksby

ELMITT-BROWNE,Austin T2Lt dow 15-6-16 2WRid p115 CR France10,15-6-18

ELMSLIE,Ernest George T2Lt kia 26-9-17 2RScots p54 MR30

ELMSLIE,Kenward Wallace Lt kia 4-11-14 4DragGds p21 MR29

ELPHICK,Kevin 2Lt dow 28-9-16 4 att2RIrRif p169 CR France44

ELPHICK,William Roy 2Lt ded 7-6-16 IA 108Inf p276 MR65,Lt

ELPHINSTONE,Arthur Percy Archibald.MID TLtCol kia 1-7-16 22NumbF p61 MR21

ELPHINSTONE,Montague TMaj kia 22-3-17 RASC attRFC p7&192 CR France833

ELRINGTON,Gerard Gordon Clement 2Lt kia 2-11-14 EYorks p84 MR29,31-10-14

ELRINGTON-BISSET,Walter Faviere T2Lt kia 25-9-15 9GordH p166 MR19

ELSE,William Edwin TLtACapt kia 3-1-18 17N&D p133 CR Belgium10

ELSMIE,George Edward Douglas LtCol murdered 18-6-17 IA 25Cav p276 MR43

ELSOM,Harold 2Lt kia 28-4-17 10Lincs p75 MR20

ELSON,Edwin Arthur 2Lt kia 9-9-16 9Mddx p236 MR21

ELSON,George Henry.MM.T2Lt ded 8-12-18 1/2 att14Leic p87 CR France1027

ELSTOB,Wilfrith.VC.DSO.MC.LtCol 21-3-18 16Manch MR27

ELSTON,Charles Douglas Capt dow 22-11-17 Nhampt p137 CR Lond4

ELSWORTH,George Herbert 2Lt ded 27-6-16 IARO att62Punjabis p276 CR Iraq6

ELSWORTH,Harold Lt kia 21-8-18 4RScotF p222 CR France214

ELTHAM,Charles William Lt kia 3-11-16 1RWSurr p55 MR21

ELTON,Alfred George Goodenough Col ded 17-11-19 ConnRgrs p266 CR Hereford191

ELTON,Arthur Bayard Maj ded 12-1-16 Ex Yorks p263

ELTON,Arthur Charles Lt kia 24-7-15 2RWKent p141 CR Iraq6

ELTON,Frederick John T2Lt dow 11-9-15 C48RFA 14Div p28 CR Belgium11

ELTON,George Kenward 2Lt kia 18-10-16 5Hamps p228 MR21

ELTON,Gordon Daubeney Gresley,DSO.MC Capt kia 5-11-17 RIrF p171 CR Belgium20

ELVERSON,Ronald Whidborne Lt kia 25-9-18 9ESurr p112 MR16

ELVEY,Charles Leslie 2Lt kia 9-4-17 5Suff p217 CR France581

ELVIDGE,Jabez Gordon 2Lt kia 17-11-17 3 att1/7WYorks p81 MR30

ELVIDGE,Laurence T2Lt dow 9-8-16 5ConnRgrs attRInniskF p172 CR Belgium165

ELVIN,Arthur George 2Lt ded 13-10-17 1/4Suff p217 CR Egypt2

ELVIN,Sydney James.MID 2Lt dow 13-4-18 1/4EYorks C'Coy p219 CR France31

ELWELL,Ernest Edward 2LtTLt kia 6-10-17 17 att21Manch p154 MR30

ELWIN,Frank Harold 2Lt kia 14-3-15 3 att2Wilts p153 MR22,12-3-15

ELWOOD,Robert Vernon T2Lt kld 17-11-17 GL &RFC p7 CR Yorks38

ELWORTHY,Edward Pearce 2Lt kia 11-8-15 RE 67FC p44 CR Gallipoli5,Lt 9-8-15

ELWORTHY,Thomas.MID T2Lt kia 3-5-17 1RLancs p58 CR France604 Ex RE

ELY,Denis Herbert James TCapt kia 1-7-16 15DLI p160 MR21

ELY,Percy Alfred Lt ded 17-11-18 1KEdwsHorse attNZEF CR Lond8

EMANUEL,Oliver Lt 25-9-15 1Wilts MR29

EMBERTON,Percival Harvey T2Lt kia 1-7-16 1SStaffs p122 CR France397

EMBLEM,Harold.MC.2Lt 23-4-18 8 att1N&D MR27

EMBREY,Cyril Stewart.MC.MIDx2 2Lt kia 12-10-18 1/6SStaffs p229 CR France847

EMERSON,Frank 2Lt kia 26-8-18 5Lond p246 CR France630

EMERSON,Harold Theodore T2Lt kia 10-7-16 8LNLancs p135 MR21

EMERSON James Samuel.VC.T2Lt kia 6-12-17 9RInniskF p104 MR17

EMERSON,John Miller T2Lt dow PoW 8-4-18 8MGC Inf p182 CR France526 Ex 1NumbF

EMERSON,Max William Pailthorpe 2Lt kia 5-7-16 5YLI p235 CR France702

EMERTON,Harry Burton.MC.TLtAMaj kia 27-9-18 B178RFA p28 CR France686

EMERY,Burkett John Lt kia 11/13-10-15 RE p210 MR19

EMERY,George William T2Lt kia 20-11-17 F'TankCps p188 MR17

EMERY,Ewart Arthur Edwin T2Lt kia 23-3-18 RE 16SigCoy p44 MR27

EMERY,Walter Herbert Vernon T2Lt ded 26-10-18 7ELancs p264 CR Lond4

EMINSON,George 2Lt kia 1-9-18 21Lond p251 MR16

EMINSON,Robert Astley Franklin 2Lt kia 20-7-16 6KRRC attMGC Inf p150&182 CR France515

EMINTON,Frederick Arthur 2Lt kia 23-4-17 18Manch p154 MR20

EMLEM,Harold,MC 2Lt kia 23-4-18 8N&D p233

EMMANUEL,Oliver Lt kia 25-9-15 Wilts p153

EMMENS,Richard Reeve 2Lt kia 4-9-16 GL attTMB p190 CR France432,Lt

EMMERSON,Alfred 2Lt dow 4-4-17 5Leic attRFC p18&220 CR France120

EMMERSON,Henry Hetherington TMaj kia 25-9-16 10Leic p87 MR21

EMMERSON Jabez.MID 2Lt kia 13-10-15 4Leic p220 MR19,Joseph Son of Jabez

EMMET,Frederick Herbert TCapt kia 14-7-16 9Leic p87 MR21

EMMET,Robert 2Lt ded 30-10-15 1LifeGds p20 CR Lond9,29-10-15

EMMETT,Alexis Renwick Lt kia 12-2-16 ISMD att2LNLancs MR50

EMMETT,Charles Percival LtACapt dow 28-6-18 1 att8ESurr p112 CR France31

EMMOTT John Barlow Lt kia 4-6-15 10Manch p237 CR Gallipoli6

EMMOTT,Rennie.MM.2Lt kia 31-7-17 7ELancs p110 MR29

EMMS,Harry T2Lt kia 6-8-16 8SomLI p79 CR France549

EMPEY,Simeon Robert Franks 2Lt ded 17-8-16 3RIrRif att9LNLancs p169 CR France4

EMSLEY John Alfred Capt ded 1-12-18 6WYorks p270 CR Yorks408

EMSLIE,Alexander 2Lt 16/17-5-17 6GordH p242 MR20

EMSLIE,Herbert Robertson 2Lt kia 24-10-17 6 att11A&SH p243 CR France545

ENDEAN,Frank Edgar T2Lt kia 24-3-18 15RIrRif p169 MR27

ENDERBURY,Frederick Albert 2Lt kia 9-2-16 10HLI p162 CR Belgium30

ENDERBY,Arthur Aaron TLt dow 2-8-17 4RFus p67 CR France512

ENGALL John Sherwin 2Lt kia 1-7-16 16Lond attMGC p187&250 MR21

ENGINEER,G.S Lt 30-5-16 IMS CR Egypt13

ENGLAND,Edward Parker.DCM.LtCol ded 10-1-21 RFA CR Devon29

ENGLAND,Ernest William Lt kia 26-9-16 3 att7YLI p143 MR21

ENGLAND,John Humphrey.MID T2Lt kia 31-7-17 14WelshR p126 MR29

ENGLAND,John Kenneth T2Lt dow 5-9-18 4ESurr p112 CR France145,8Bn

ENGLAND,Raymond Maj kia 26-8-14 88RFA p28 CR France1354

ENGLISH,Alfred Cecil 2Lt kia 30-12-17 28Lond p252 MR21

ENGLISH,Charles Arthur 2Lt kia 6-5-17 4BordR p228 MR20

ENGLISH,Eric T2Lt kia 7-8-15 13WYorks att1/8Manch p81 CR Gallipoli2

ENGLISH,Frederick Garnet 2Lt kia 13-11-16 3 att13Ess p131 CR France1890

ENGLISH,Richard Cornforth TLt ded 25-7-16 RASC p192 CR Lincs100

ENGLISH,Robert Ernest Capt kia 13-5-15 NSomYeo p205 MR29

ENNIS,Charles Francis 2Lt kia 20-11-17 1RMunstF p175 CR France689

ENNIS,Edward Armstrong 2Lt dow 30-10-18 3Leinst p174 CR Ireland12

ENNIS,Reginald Joseph 2Lt kia 16-8-17 1RIrRif p169 MR30

ENRIGHT,Anthony Basil 2Lt dow 11-5-17 D17RFA p28 CR France40

ENRIGHT,Thomas 2Lt dow 20-4-18 RIrRif p169 CR Lond9

ENRIGHT,Thomas Louis TCapt ded 19-3-18 RAMC p195 CR Greece7

ENSOR,Charles Edward James Lt ded 18-10-19 RGA p270 CR Hamps57

ENSOR,John Collen Lt dow 26-11-17 17WelshR p126&257 CR France512

ENSOR,William James Alfred 2Lt kia 3-10-18 1/6NStaffs p157 CR France1706

ENTWISTLE,Charles Egerton Lt dow 22-3-18 8Manch p237 CR France987

ENTWISTLE,Charles Herbert TLt kia 9-4-18 231MGC Inf p182 CR Palestine9

ENTWISTLE,Frederick 2Lt kia 9-10-17 1Norf p73 CR Belgium112

ENTWISTLE,John Edward T2Lt kia 24-10-18 24Manch A'Coy p154 CR Italy9

ENTWISTLE,John Maurice Binley Capt ded 2-12-18 Worc p108 CR Egypt1,1-12-18

EPPSTEIN,William Reginald TCapt dow 4-9-18 20DLI p160 CR Belgium11

EREAUT,Harold John Capt 8-6-16 EAMS CR EAfrica58

ERICSON,Eric Charles.MM.T2Lt kia 18-9-18 RSuss att7Bn p119 CR France369

ERLE,Christopher TCapt ded 10-2-17 1Nhampt GarrBn p137 CR Egypt1

ERLEBACH,Arthur Woodland T2Lt kia 5-7-17 GL &57RFC p7 CR France134

ERLEBACH,Edward Eustace 2Lt kia 7-2-17 45RFC p7 CR France1032

ERMEN,Godfrey Henry Capt ded 4-5-15 6WRid p227 CR Yorks481

ERRINGTON,A.H.P.2Lt kia 30/31-11-14 YLI p143 MR32

ERRINGTON,James Capt kia 30-8-15 7DLI p239 CR France681

ERSKINE,Neil 2Lt dow 23-8-18 1Lpool p71 CR France103

ERSKINE,Ralph TCapt ded PoW 1-1-18 GL &66RFC p15 CR Italy9,kia

ERSKINE,Thomas Barrie.MC.2LtTCapt dow 20-7-15 4A&SH att1GordH p173 CR Belgium6,kia

ERSKINE,Walter Augustus Capt kia 24-5-15 108RGA p39 CR Belgium135

ERVINE,Charles James T2Lt dow 6-4-16 27NumbF p61 CR France285

ERWOOD,Cecil Victor T2Lt kia 17-2-17 19 att1KRRC p150 CR France314

ESDAILE,Arthur James Lt kia 7-11-18 1Dev p76 CR France937

ESDAILE,George Augustus Churchill 2Lt kia 10-8-17 281RFA p208 CR Belgium19

ESDALE,Robert Blair T2Lt kld 13-11-17 GL &RFC p7 CR Canada256

ESMONDE,Geoffrey 2Lt kia 7-10-16 26NumbF p61 CR France922

ESMONDE,John Joseph TCapt ded 17-4-15 RAMC p195 CR Eire205

ESPIE,Thomas Fletcher Lt ded 6-2-19 5RIrF p171 CR Ireland79

ESSEX,Percy Clifford 2Lt kia 9-9-16 2/5LancF p221 MR21

ESSEX,Robert Charles Lt dow 14-5-18 B162RFA p207 CR France142

ESSON,Alfred Charles T2Lt dow 23-10-17 17LancF p92 CR Belgium16

ESTALL,Arthur Cecil TCapt dow 8-8-17 RASC p192 CR France102

ESTEN,Gerald Philip TLt kia 6-8-15 9RWSurr attEss p55 MR4

ESTRIDGE,Edward Wilfred 2Lt kia 13-11-16 3 att12EYorks p84 MR21

ETCHES,Alfred Joseph Edward TLt kia 11-4-17 GL &52RFC p7 CR France415

ETHELSTON,Herbert Wicksted Lt kia 14-3-15 1GrenGds p50 MR22

ETHERIDGE,Cecil Norbert Lt kia 29-3-18 2RB p178 CR France544

ETHERIDGE,Eckley Oxtoby 2Lt kia 12-7-17 149RFA p28 CR Belgium15,ETHEREDGE

ETHERIDGE,Hugh Dimsdale,MC.MM T2Lt dow 2-10-18 17RFus p67 CR France512

ETHERINGTON,Herbert Field 2Lt dow 8-1-16 2DragGds p21 CR France80,8-1-15

ETLINGER,Henry Capt dow 27-4-15 IA 9BhopalInf p276

EUSTACE,Thomas George Lt kia 28-6-15 4 att1RMunstF p175 MR4

EVAN-JONES,Hilary Gresford.MID Lt kia 16-2-15 1WelshR p126 MR29

EVANS,Albert Ashley 2Lt kia 24-9-18 1KSLI att2Y&L p144 CR France835

EVANS,Albert Aylward TCapt kia 16-6-17 13NumbF p61 MR20

EVANS,Albert Illtyd 2Lt kia 17-8-17 RFA 85Bty att92Bde p28 CR Belgium5

EVANS,Albert John 2Lt kia 15-6-17 19Lond p250 MR20,att2/2Bn

EVANS,Alfred Henry Courtenay T2Lt kld 22-3-18 11ELancs att107RFC p15 CR Wilts3

EVANS,Arthur 2Lt ded 31-3-15 18WelchR p126 CR Wales203

EVANS,Arthur 2Lt kia 18-10-16 3 att9Ess p131 MR21

EVANS,Arthur Ernest TCapt kia 24-6-17 19WelshR p126 CR Belgium23

EVANS,Arthur Frederick Lt kia 30/31-10-18 4RWFus &RAF p255,Frederic p223,5Bn

EVANS,Arthur John TLtACapt kia 2-7-18 10SWBord p100 CR France41

EVANS,Arthur Leslie 2Lt kia 20-7-16 2Suff p78 MR21

EVANS,Arthur Stuart LtCol ded 2-1-20 RE MR43

EVANS,Bernard T2Lt ded 8-4-17 GL &55RFC p7 CR France481,Lt

EVANS,Bertram Trevor T2Lt kia 22-4-18 13RWFus p97 MR27

EVANS,Charles Edward Maj kia 6-8-18 RE 82FC p44 CR France33

EVANS,Charles Heyland 2Lt kia 26-10-14 2BordR p117 MR29

EVANS,Charles Wilmot.MC.Capt kia 1-7-16 1 att4SStaffs p122 MR21

EVANS,Christmas Richard.MC.Capt ded 11-4-19 WelshR p264

EVANS,D.M.W.Lt 10-4-19 Mon CR Wales195

EVANS,David.MC.Capt kia 20-7-16 1ScotRif p103 MR21

EVANS,David 2Lt kld 14-9-16 1RE S'Coy p44 CR France1106

EVANS,David T2Lt dow 24-9-17 NumbF att1Bn p61 CR Belgium18

EVANS,David Edgar Lt kia 18-9-18 14WelshR p126 MR37

EVANS,David Edward 2Lt kia 26-8-18 3RWFus p97 CR France432

EVANS,David Owen TLt kia 12-2-16 17RWFus p97 CR France631

EVANS,David William T2Lt kia 8-10-18 1/2 att14RWFus p97 CR France1345,Williams

EVANS,Dennis Leslie 2Lt dow 15-12-17 21Lond F'Coy p251 CR Palestine9

EVANS,Douglas Houghton 2Lt kia 13-8-16 7ESurr p112 MR21

EVANS,Douglas Lane TCapt dow 26-9-16 6Nhampt p137 CR France41

EVANS,Douglas Osmond 2Lt kia 8-8-16 1Lpool p71 MR21

EVANS,Edward TLt kia 9-4-17 RAMC att10RWFus p195 CRFrance418

EVANS,Edward TCapt ded 21-5-18 RAVC p268 CR Wales713

EVANS,Edward Herbert Sandford LtTCapt kia 22-7-16 18LancF p92 CR France630

EVANS,Edward Juson T2Lt kia 3-7-16 9 att8Glouc p106 CR France393

EVANS,Edward Meredyd Lloyd Capt kia 14-3-16 5RLancs p213

EVANS,Edward Tilney T2Lt kld 19-2-18 GL &RFC p15 CR Essex1

EVANS,Edward Williams.MID Rev ded 10-2-19 RAChDept p268 CR Cornwall135

EVANS,Edwin T2Lt dow 22-11-16 2Mddx p146 CR France40

EVANS,Emrys T2Lt kia 29-4-16 RE 253TC p44 CR France423

EVANS,Eric Ben T2Lt kia 11-11-17 1/2 att2/8LancF p92 CR Belgium45

EVANS,Eric Charles Lt kia 23-3-18 5RWSurr p212 CR France1893

EVANS,Ernest 2Lt dow 21-9-18 RGA 91SB p39 CR France194

EVANS,Fisher Arthur Haslett Freke TLtACapt kia 11-1-17 RLancs p58 MR38

EVANS,Forrest Dinnett 2Lt kld 27-3-18 RFC p15 CR Wilts1

EVANS,Francis Bernard T2Lt kldacc 17-2-18 RFC p15 CR Norf61

EVANS,Francis Graham Lt ded 26-9-16 4RWFus p223 CR Wales609,25-9-16

EVANS,Frank Dudley 2Lt kld 9-6-16 4RWar &RFC p2&64 CR War65

EVANS,Frank Montague 2Lt kia 4/5-4-16 3RWSurr att9RWar p55 CR Iraq5,5-4-16

EVANS,Frederick Henry TLt kia 9-10-17 9 att15WYorks p81 MR30

EVANS,Frederick William T2Lt dow 28-10-16 13WelshR p126 CR Belgium11

EVANS,Frederick Woodham T2Lt dow 26-5-17 21Mddx &20RFC p7&146 CR France705 Ex 16Lond

EVANS,Frew Ferguson T2Lt kia 13-2-17 8 att4SWBord p100 MR38

EVANS,Geoffrey Maynard.MC.Chap4Cl kia 11-8-17 RAChDept p199 CR Belgium310

EVANS,George.MID 2Lt kia 3-10-18 1/6SStaffs p229 CR France443

EVANS,George Edwin T2Lt kia 26-3-18 1 att8ESurr p112 MR27,25-3-18

EVANS,George Ernest Knightly 2Lt kia 3-9-16 3Leinst att2RIrRif p174 CR France402

EVANS,Godfrey Stanton Lt ded 30-6-17 RDC p253 CR Essex255,Thomas

EVANS,Griffith William 2Lt kia 22-4-18 6RWFus &RAF p223&258 CR Lincs181,21-4-18

EVANS,Harry TLt kia 26-3-18 11WYorks p81 CR France745,Capt

EVANS,Harry Charles T2Lt kia 23-8-18 32MGC Inf p182 CR France526

EVANS,Henry Cope,DSO.2Lt kia 4-9-16 GL &RFC p2&190,ded 3-9-16 MR20

EVANS,Henry Robert Noel 2LtTCapt kia 16-8-17 8 att7DCLI p114 MR30

EVANS,Herbert Theodore Penrhys Lt kia 4-10-16 98RFA p28 CR Greece3

EVANS,Hew Reginald Lt ded 15-12-16 RDC p253 CR Kent61

EVANS,Horace Thomas Royston 2Lt kia 8/9-5-17 4 att15RWar p64 CR France777

EVANS,Hubert William T2Lt dow 24-5-17 6EKent p57 CR France40

EVANS,Hugh Arthur TLt ded 3-6-15 RAMC p195

EVANS,Hugh Elwyn.MC.Lt kia 26-3-18 5Yorks p220 MR27

EVANS,Hugh George 2Lt kia 4-9-18 5Lpool att16Dev p215 CR France511

EVANS,Hugh Robert 2Lt kia 19-9-18 18 att9WelshR p126 MR19

EVANS,Hugh William T2Lt kld 30-8-17 GL &35RFC p7 CR Essex48

EVANS,Humphrey Pennefather TLt kia 1-7-16 2SWBord p100 MR21

EVANS,Hywel Llewellyn 2Lt kia 26-9-17 7 att2RWFus p223 MR30,Llywelyn

EVANS,James Bansall TLt kia 20-8-16 20RFus p67 MR21

EVANS,James Reginald T2Lt ded 19-10-18 RE 3ResBn p44 CR Staffs52

EVANS,Jane Sister drd 26-2-18 QAIMNS p200 MR40

EVANS,John 2Lt ded 29-10-18 EYorks &13RAF p84 CR France332

EVANS,John.MC.MID 2Lt kia 19-9-18 1RWFus p97 CR France660

EVANS,John Arthur 2Lt kia 27-1-17 4RWFus att1/2Lond p223 CR France924

EVANS,John Baynes Lt kia 23-3-18 4Lond p246 MR20

EVANS,John Edward Martin Lt dow 9-2-18 8Manch &48RFC p237 CR France987

EVANS,John Eric Capt dow 9-5-15 4RWFus p223 CR France80,kia 10-5-15

EVANS,John Ewart 2Lt kia 27-9-18 Dev p76 CR France245
EVANS,John Harold Lt ded 12-12-19 WelshR p264 CR France1142,7RWFus
EVANS,John Henry Grant.DCM.2Lt dow 7-2-17 1DCLI p114 CR France80
EVANS,John Owen 2Lt kia 23-11-17 TankCps p188 MR17
EVANS,John Rayner Lt kia 8-10-18 1Mon p244 CR France1710
EVANS,John Trevor Stuart TCapt dow PoW 7-5-18 GL &19RWFus p190 CR France742
EVANS,John William T2Lt dow 10-4-17 11N&D p133 CR Belgium11
EVANS,Kenneth George Ogle 2Lt kia 31-3-18 6KSLI p144 CR France988
EVANS,Lawrence Picton Lt 21-8-18 6 att4RFus p67 CR France618
EVANS,Leonard Austin T2Lt ded 27-3-18 1TankCps p188 CR France52,dow
EVANS,Leslie Morier T2Lt kia 12-11-17 RASC p192 CR Belgium10
EVANS,Lewis Lt&QM ded 28-10-18 8Glouc p106 CR France34
EVANS,Margaret Ellen Miss ded 22-7-17 VAD att83GH p200 CR France64
EVANS,Neville Vernon 2Lt kia 16-8-17 3SWBord p100 CR Belgium106
EVANS,Noel Everard 2Lt dow 11-11-18 RFA 121Bty27Bde p28 CR France146
EVANS,Norman 2Lt kia 25-7-16 1SWBord p100 CR France832
EVANS,Norman Edward T2Lt kia 4-11-18 17RWFus p97 CR France735 Ex RFC
EVANS,Norman Emryn T2Lt dow 3-10-16 2SLancs p125 CR France74,Emrys
EVANS,Norman Harden Lt dow 19-4-17 2/4RWKent p234 CR Palestine8
EVANS,Oscar James T2Lt kia 5-1-16 8RWFus p97 MR4
EVANS,Percival Richard TLtAMaj dow 6-9-17 D74RFA p28 CR Belgium16
EVANS,Percy Charles David TCapt dow 22-12-15 13WelshR MGOffr att114Bde p126&182
EVANS,Philip T2Lt kld 24-1-17 GL&RFC p7&190,12-1-17 CR Hamps1
EVANS,Philip Henry 2Lt kia 3-5-17 2Ess p131 MR20
EVANS,Raymond T2Lt kia 12-1-17 9 att4SWBord p100 CR Iraq5
EVANS,Rees Tudor Capt kia 10-8-15 5WelshR p230 MR4
EVANS,Rhys Trevor 2Lt kia 1-9-17 4 att14RWFus p223 MR30
EVANS,Richard Lt dow 10-8-17 1/6N&D p233 CR France80
EVANS,Richard Hellier Agard Lt kia 5-11-17 IA 127BaluchiLI att2/124Baluch MR38
EVANS,Richard Parry T2Lt kia 14-5-17 1RWFus p97 CR France644
EVANS,Richard Stanley Lt kia 10-8-15 5WelshR p230 MR4
EVANS,Richard William Picton.MID Maj ded 13-9-18 4WelshR p229 CR Palestine8
EVANS,Robert Cecil Lt kia 6-4-18 4RWFus A'Coy p223 CR France232
EVANS,Robert Charles T2Lt kia 24-8-18 15WelshR p126 CR France832
EVANS,Robert Prichard T2Lt dow 11-4-17 14WelshR p126 CR Belgium18,Pritchard
EVANS,Roy Galloway TLt kia 26-8-18 9 att2SWBord p100 CR France28
EVANS,Rupert Ancrum 2Lt ded 25-1-16 3WYorks p81 CR Hereford162
EVANS,Samuel Houching Maj&QM ded 7-7-17 RASC p192 CR Scot764
EVANS,Stewart Nicholson Lt kld 9-7-17 2/6Suff attRFC p18&218 CR Suff83
EVANS,Thomas George T2Lt kia 20-9-17 SLancs att1/4Bn p125 CR Belgium10
EVANS,Thomas Richard.DSO.TMajALtCol kia 3-10-18 RWFus att1/6NStaffs p97 CR France375
EVANS,Tudor Eglwysbach 2Lt kia 1-7-16 8ESurr B'Coy p112 CR France513
EVANS,Walter George 2Lt ded 14-12-17 1Norf p263 CR Herts37
EVANS,Walter Richard Capt ded 15-12-16 Leic p263 CR Wales30,Maj
EVANS,William HonLt&QM ded 27-5-16 5Leinst p174
EVANS,William Ashton T2Lt dow 16-11-16 9Ches p96 CR France62
EVANS,William David Russell Lt kia 10-8-15 5WelshR C'Coy p230 CR Gallipoli5
EVANS,William Edwards 2Lt kia 1-5-17 3 att13RWFus p97 CR Belgium73
EVANS,William Henry Lt kia 2-11-17 1/5Ess p232 CR Palestine8
EVANS,William James,DCM Lt 27-5-16 5Leinst CR Eire322
EVANS,William Jones TCapt dow 13-9-17 RAMC att2/1SMidFA p195 CR Belgium10
EVANS,William Laurence TLt kia 11-8-16 RAMC att1/6I.pool p195 CR France630
EVANS,William Pearce.MM.Lt 31-7-20 B307RFC CR France113
EVANS,Willie Herbert TMaj kia 14-8-15 11RScots p54 CR France727,William
EVANS-FREKE,Percy Charles.Hon.LtCol kia 13-5-15 LeicYeo p204 CR Belgium35,Cecil
EVANS-JONES,William Rev kia 8-10-18 RAChDept att2RWFus p199
EVANSON-JONES,Tom Alec Edward 2Lt 7-8-15 11Manch MR4
EVATT,George Raleigh Kerr Capt kia 14-11-14 1Mddx A'Coy p146 CR France347
EVATT,James Millar Capt kia 21-3-18 RAMC att330RFA p195 MR27
EVE,Frederick Samuel.Sir.LtCol ded 15-12-16 RAMC CR Essex56
EVE,William Henry Capt kia 5-3-17 13Huss p22 CR Iraq8
EVELEGH,Rosslyn Curzon Capt kia 19-9-14 O&BLI p130 CR France1111
EVERARD,Christopher Philip Capt kia 11-1-17 3HLI p162 MR38
EVERARD,Clement Charlie TLt kia 7-9-16 9N&D p133 CR France296

EVERARD,Ernest Victor T2Lt dow 23-6-17 8LNLancs A'Coy p135 CR France40
EVERARD,John Guy Lt kia 12-3-15 3HLI p162 CR France279
EVERED,Henry Robert Hastings T2Lt kia 1-7-16 27NumbF p61 MR21
EVERETT,Charles Alfred Stanley 2Lt dow 17-6-17 2/4Lincs p217 CR France1468
EVERETT,George Gordon Capt kia 1-5-17 IA 2/67Punjabis p276 MR43
EVERETT,Walter Reginald T2Lt dow 4-9-17 Ess att11Bn p131 CR France179,Lt kia
EVERETT,William Thomas 2Lt kia 6-11-18 4RWSurr p212 CR France979
EVERETT,William Wallis TCapt kia 9-10-18 9 att2Norf p73 CR France443,8-10-18
EVERINGHAM,Guy T2Lt kia 8-4-17 GL 16RFC p7 CR France1321
EVERITT,John Paxman T2Lt kia 1-7-16 15WYorks p81 MR21
EVERITT,John Wilson 2Lt ded PoW 12-4-18 5KRRC C'Coy p150 CR France652,dow 12Bn
EVERITT,Rupert Edward 2Lt kia 24-6-17 RGA 299SB p39 CR Belgium1
EVERITT,William Needham,MC Lt kia 3-9-16 4WRid p227 MR21
EVERS,Bertram Saxelbye TCapt kia 14-9-16 9WYorks p81 MR21
EVERS,Ernest William.MC.TCapt kia 23-11-17 15 att21Mddx p146 MR17
EVERS,Hugh Lancelot.MC&Bar.Capt kia 1-11-18 2/8Worc p226 CR France290
EVERS,Leslie Montague 2Lt kia 30-3-18 6Yorks p90 Mk19
EVERSDEN,Robert Ernest Capt kld 5-8-19 3SuffYeo att47RAF p270 CR Asia81,15-8-19
EVERSFIELD,Charles John T2Lt kia 25-9-16 10YLI p143 MR21
EVERSHED,Albury Lt kia 1-7-16 1/6NStaffs p238 MR21
EVERSHED,Ernest Bernard 2LtTLt kia 27-9-17 GL RFus att1/2KAR p202 CR EAfrica11 &CR Tanzania1,28-9-17
EVERSHED,Philip Douglas Lt kia 22-8-18 7 att19Lond p247 CR France210
EVERSON,Charles Percy 2Lt kia 7-10-16 5DCLI p227 MR21
EVERSON,Harry Thomas T2Lt kia 7-11-18 8RWKent p141 MR16
EVERTON,Bird.MID Lt kldacc 19-4-20 2Dors B'Coy CR Ireland196
EVERTON,Maryon Jeffrey T2Lt kia 9-7-16 13 att10SWBord p100 CR France453,Jeffreys
EVERTON,Robert Frederick Lt ded 8-4-19 RGA 61Coy p39 MR65
EVERTON,Walter Hassell T2Lt ded 30-5-18 RASC attCamelTransport p192 CR Palestine9
EVEZARD,George LtACapt dow 9-5-17 1RWar p64 CR France95
EVILL,Chetwode Percy.MC.TCapt ded 17-7-18 IARO attS&M p276 MR69
EWEN,George Thomas.MC.Capt kia 8-3-16 3Manch p258&154 MR38
EWART,Archibald John T2Lt kia 28-9-16 11 att8WRid p115 CR France1170
EWART,Cecil Frederick Kelso TCapt kia 1-7-16 11RIrRif p169 MR21
EWART,James Henry HonBrigGen ded 1-1-16 4SfthH p270 CR Scot199,Col
EWART,Keith Penicuik 2Lt kia 4-1-18 27RFC p15 CR France920
EWART,Richard Henry Charles TLt dow 16-10-18 10 att14BlkW p128 CR France769
EWART,William Grieve Lt kia 30-3-18 Fife&ForfarYeo att13RScots p203 MR20
EWBANK,John Walter,MC &Bar LtTCapt kia 30-11-17 1BordR p117 MR17
EWBANK,Leonard 2Lt kia 23-2-16 5BordR p228 CR Belgium127
EWEN,Edgar Hunter Lt kld 1-5-17 5RScotF p222 CR Scot517
EWEN,Guy Cuthbert Lt kia 24-1-17 SL att3NigR MR50
EWEN,Henry Spencer.MC.Lt kia 5-4-18 1/23Lond p252 MR20
EWEN,Philip Keith Somerville TLt kia 3-9-16 17KRRC p150 CR France701
EWEN,William James LtACapt kia 25-3-18 3 att8RWKent p141 MR27
EWENS,G.W.F.Col 9-9-14 IMS MR67
EWENS,Thomas William T2Lt kia 30-3-17 13NumbF p61 CR France927
EWIN,Arthur.DCM.HonLt&QM kia 7/11-8-15 9N&D p133 MR4
EWING,Arthur Harold.MC.LtACapt&Adjt dow 8-9-18 1EYorks p84 CR France84
EWING,Douglas James.MM.2Lt ded 24-6-18 4 att2/6RWar p263 CR France1161
EWING,Douglas Ramsay Maj ded 31-5-17 ScotRif att66Bde HQ p103 MR37
EWING,Gordon Craig.MC.2Lt kia 20-9-18 4Lond p246 CR France369
EWING,Harold Gordon T2Lt kia 9-4-17 18Lpool p71 MR20
EWING,James.MID Capt dow 12-4-17 RAMC att8RWFus p195 MR38
EWING,James Adie T2Lt kia 31-7-17 11A&SH p173 MR29
EWING,James Robert Capt ded 19-5-15 RSuss p119 CR Sussex201
EWINGS,John George Vivian Lt kia 3-10-18 1YLI p143 CR France234
EXELL,Noel Jardine TCapt dow 31-7-15 9KRRC p150 MR29
EXLEY,A.T.2Lt kld 22-4-18 11NumbF &RAF p61
EXLEY,Charles Lt ded 11-10-15 RIM p276 CR Iraq6
EXLEY,George Allan 2Lt kia 14-1-17 5YLI attRFC p18&235 CR France158,Lt
EXLEY,John Henry TCapt ded 11-3-19 RAOC p267 CR Yorks361
EYDEN,Herbert.MC.Lt kld 7-4-18 RGA &21RAF p39 CR Belgium18,Capt
EYKYN,Gilbert Davidson Pitt Capt kia 25-4-15 RScots p54 MR29
EYLES,Harold Morley Lt kia 6-11-18 6Worc p108 CR France432
EYNAUD,P.A.M.Lt kia 21-3-18 MaltaR attRMunstF p201 CR France369

EYRE,Arthur Noel 2Lt kia 26-9-18 6N&D &57RAF p233&258,Lt MR20

EYRE,Charles Howard Lt kia 25-9-15 6 att2KRRC p150 CR France219

EYRE,Harry 2Lt kia 17-9-18 2N&D p133 MR16

EYRE,Henry Joseph Bagshawe Lt dow 14-7-17 1IrGds p52 CR Belgium115,Harry

EYRE,Henry Wright Capt dow 29-7-16 2/6Glouc p225 CR France134

EYRE,Sebert Henry Robert 2Lt kia 14-4-17 1Ess p131 MR20

EYRE,Thomas Herbert T2Lt kia 17-7-17 1/2 att7Yorks p90 CR France97,16-7-17

EYRE,William TCapt dow 19-8-15 12WelshR attLancF p126 CR Egypt6

EYRE-POWELL,John William Alcock Rev kia 16-4-18 RAChDept attHQ 27LabCps p199 MR30

EYRES,H.T.2Lt ded 9-11-18 RWSurr &101RAF p55 CR France1754

EYTON,Robert William.MID TLt kia 22-3-18 7RB att41TMB p178 MR27

EYTON-Lloyd,John Wathen T2Lt kia 24-6-17 GL 10RFC p7 CR France98

EZARD,Herbert Henry T2Lt kld 30-5-17 24RFC p7 CR Wilts4

EZRA,David Lt kia 6-8-18 RGA 192SB p39 CR France247

F

FABER,Cecil Valdemar T2Lt kia 30-7-15 9KRRC p150

FABER,John Benbow.MC.Capt kia 18-9-16 RE 1/3FC p210 MR20

FABER,Stanley Colt Maj kia 30-3-17 47RFA p28 CR France1182

FABER,Walter Louis TLt kia 24-8-16 5KSLI p144 MR21

FABIAN,Arthur Stanley LtTCapt kia 3-9-16 8 att13RSuss p119 CR France701

FAGAN,James Edward T2Lt dow 5-10-16 6 att8RInniskF p104 CR Belgium17,6-10-16

FAGAN,Jasper Gilbert Lt dow 22-11-15 IA 119Inf p276 MR38

FAGAN,Niel 2Lt dow 20-7-16 6 att1RB p178 CR Sussex4

FAILES,Gerald Watson.DSO.MC TCapt kia 15-4-18 9Norf p73 MR30

FAIR,Arthur Edward Balfour Maj kia 16-8-17 122RFA p28 CR Belgium12

FAIR,George Lt kia 1-10-18 1/4KOSB p223 CR France403,dow

FAIR,George Patrick Conroy 2Lt kia 1-7-16 1SomLI p79 CR France643

FAIR,James Conroy 2Lt kia 25-9-15 1CldGds p51 MR19,27-9-15

FAIR,James Gerald 2Lt kia 19-3-17 D of LancsYeo attRFC p18&204

FAIR,V.A.MC.Lt kld 29-9-18 KRRC att212RAF p265 CR Belgium140

FAIRALL,Harry Gustavus.MC.2Lt ded 5-11-18 4Leic p270 CR Leic63

FAIRBAIRN,Andrew Hubert 2Lt ded 5-6-15 3 att2RIrReg p89 CR Belgium125

FAIRBAIRN,George Eric 2Lt dow 20-6-15 10DLI p160 CR France285

FAIRBAIRN,Harry Lawson 2Lt kia 2-8-17 4CamH p243 MR29,att10Lpool

FAIRBAIRN,Maurice T2Lt kia 7-7-17 11RLancs p58 CR France379

FAIRBAIRN,W.R.Lt 12-1-17 11ESurr CR Surrey38

FAIRBAIRNS,Arnold.MID TLtACapt kia 14-10-18 10Yorks att13WRid p90 CR France347

FAIRBAIRNS,Joseph Maurice 2Lt kia 20-8-17 RFA 8DAC p28 CR Belgium5

FAIRBANK,Stanley Reginald T2Lt kia 4-4-18 8ESurr p112 MR27

FAIRBURN,Herbert Francis Lt dow 15-9-20 RFA CR Sussex110

FAIRBURN,William Ross Lt ded 12-1-17 ESurr p264

FAIRCLOUGH,Egerton.MID LtCol kia 10-4-18 Cmdg1/4SLancs p229 CR France80

FAIRCLOUGH,Eric Montague T2Lt dow 25-2-17 10RWSurr p55 CR Belgium11

FAIRCLOUGH,Robert Justice Capt dow 31-5-15 5Lpool p215 CR France102,30-5-15

FAIRCLOUGH,Robert Leslie 2Lt ded 5-5-17 RE 218Coy p262 CR France609

FAIRE,Reginald Alfred Capt kia 14-10-15 4Leic p219 MR19

FAIRER-SMITH,Aubrey TLt kia 25-4-18 RASC att182SBAC p192

FAIRGRIEVE,Alexander Oman Lt ded 25-12-18 IA 41Dogras p276 MR43,25-10-18 37Bn

FAIRGRIEVE,Robert 2Lt dow 24-11-17 RGA 86SB p39 CR Essex13

FAIRHURST,Lambert Supt 9-12-18 CombLabCps MR65

FAIRLEY,Duncan Lt kia 1-7-16 14Y&L p158 CR France156

FAIRLEY,Gilbert 2Lt kia 9-4-17 1RScotF p94 CR France418

FAIRLEY,James Fairburn TCapt ded 9-11-15 RAMC att11GH p195 CR France102

FAIRLEY,Philip Ernest.DCM.Capt ded 2-4-19 18Lond p250 CR Ireland68,dow

FAIRLEY,William Kerr T2Lt kia 12-8-18 1/2 att12RScotF p94 CR France19

FAIRLEY,Frank Capt kia 23-10-14 RScotF p94 MR29

FAIRLIE,Edward TCaptAMaj kia 30-3-18 7 att17KRRC p150 MR27

FAIRLIE,James Gordon TLtCol kia 22-4-16 Cmdg6LNLancs p135 MR38

FAIRLIE,Jno Ogilvy TCapt kia 27-9-15 10HLI p162 CR France98

FAIRLIE,Norman Edwin 2Lt kia 21-10-14 3 att2A&SH p173 MR32

FAIRTLOUGH,Frederick Howard.CMG.TLtCol kia 25/27-9-15 8RWSurr p55 MR19,26-9-15

FAIRTLOUGH,Gerald Harold.MC.Capt dow 13-6-18 RE 423FC p210 CR France40,Gerard Howard

FAIRWEATHER,Cyril John 2Lt kia 22-3-18 4 att14Hamps p228 MR27

FAIRWEATHER,Joseph CaptTMaj kia 15-1-17 4SWBord p100 CR Iraq5

FAIRWEATHER,Leslie John Edgar Cuthbert TLt dow 19-3-16 3Lincs p75 CR France922

FAIRWEATHER,William Lyall T2Lt kia 22-3-18 8RB p178 CR France1061

FAITHFUL,Eric Basil Francis Capt kia 10-3-18 3ConnRgrs att1RIrReg p172 CR Palestine3

FAITHFULL,Florence Mary Nurse drd 15-1-18 VAD BRCS p200 CR Iraq6

FAITHFULL,Francis William Alexander 2Lt kia 3-7-15 3 att2SfthH p164 CR Belgium23

FAITHFULL,Sidney Leigh T2Lt ded 15-8-16 RE 256TC p44 CR France15

FAKER,Frank Leonard T2Lt kia 13-11-16 12EYorks p84 MR21

FALBY,Edward Frederick 2Lt kia 9-9-16 1/4LNLancs p234 MR21

FALCK,Jack Randell 2Lt kld 7-12-17 GL &RFC p7 CR Hamps57

FALCOMER,William Meek 2Lt kia 13-5-16 3 att11RScots p54 CR Belgium71,FALCONER

FALCON,Francis Capt kia 6-8-15 12Worc p108 MR4

FALCON,Geoffrey William Lockhart TLt kia 6-8-15 11ESurr p112 MR4

FALCONAR-STEWART,Ian Stewart 2Lt dow 24-7-16 10A&SH p173 CR France145

FALCONAR-STEWART,Ronald Dundas.DSO.CaptTLtCol kia 19-9-18 12A&SH p173 CR Greece5

FALCONER,James Page Lt kia 5-8-18 4RScots p210 CR France26

FALCONER,James Rankin T2Lt kia 25-9-15 10HLI p162 CR France114

FALCONER,John Keith Lt kia 31-7-17 HampsYeo att14Hamps p203 MR29

FALCONER,Robert Whitfield TLt kia 1-7-16 16NumbF p61 MR21

FALCONER,William Keay Lt kia 26-4-15 7A&SH p243 CR Belgium129,25-4-15

FALCY,Humphrey Ned.MC.T2Lt kia 21-11-16 23NumbF p61 CR France275

FALKINER,Frederick Ewen Baldwin.MC.2Lt kia 21-8-17 15RIrRif &57RFC p7&169 CR Belgium125,17Bn

FALKINER,George Stride 2Lt kia 16-8-17 2RDubF p176 MR30

FALKNER,Arthur Newstead TCapt dow 20-7-16 8LNLancs p135 CR France145

FALKNER,Clarence Beach Capt kia 25-10-17 2/2Lond p245 MR30

FALKNER,Leonard Lt kia 25-9-15 8Lincs p75 MR19

FALKNER,William Harold 2Lt kia 20-10-17 RFC p7 CR France62,Lt kld

FALKONS,Robert TCapt kia 1-7-16 30 att27NumbF p61 MR21

FALL,Patrick Joseph Lt dow 15-11-16 15 att17Mddx p146 CR France203

FALLE,Bertram Vernon TCapt kia 16-8-15 6RIrF p171 MR4

FALLOON,T.SubAssSurg 3-1-20 IMS CR Iraq8

FALLOWES,John Tyrrell Champion TLt kia 15-9-16 9Suff p78 MR21

FALLOWFIELD,William Gordon T2Lt kia 25-9-15 2A&SH p173 CR France114

FALLOWS,Ernest Hamilton 2Lt kia 25-3-18 IrGds attGdsDivMGR p52&53 MR20

FALLOWS,James Albert.TD.LtCol kia 7-6-15 8LancF p221 CR Gallipoli1,6-6-15

FALSIDE,William James Chap4Cl ded 7-10-18 RAChDept p199 CR Italy19

FALVEY-BETTS.J.DSO.LtCol kia 5-10-17 15DLI CR Belgium96

FANE,Horatio Alfred.MC.Capt dow 11-8-18 OxfYeo p205 CR France587

FANE,Octavius Edward.DSO.MC.CaptAMaj dow 18-9-18 RGA 128HB p39 CR France836,SB

FANGHANEL,Frederick Charles 2Lt kia 1-7-16 1/4Lond p246 MR21

FANNING,Vivian Edward LtACapt kia 14-11-16 2 O&BLI p130 CR France152

FANSHAWE,Harvey Vernon 2Lt dow 11-10-17 1IrGds p52 CR Belgium16

FANSHAWE,Leighton Dalrymple TLt kia 3-8-17 7MGC p182 MR29

FARADAY,Roy Lt kia 7-6-17 2/6Lond att74MGC p187&246,Ray CR Belgium43

FARAGHER,Edward Sayle 2Lt kia 9-10-17 2LancF p92 MR30

FARDELL,Gervase.MC.Capt kia 29-9-18 5 att1KRRC p150 CR France1483

FARDELL,Hubert George Henry Lt kia 23-4-15 3 att2ESurr p112 CR Belgium167

FAREBROTHER,Harcourt Sutcliffe TCapt dow 24-7-16 Norf p73 CR Lincs162,Lt

FAREIRA,John E.AssSurg 21-5-18 ISMD MR68

FAREY,Cecil Victor.MC.2Lt dow 11-8-17 4 att7ESurr p112 CR France113

FARGUS,Frederick Brian Arthur Lt kia 1-1-15 9Lond p248 MR29

FARIE,Claude Allan Gilbert Lindsay Hamilton Capt dow 15-3-16 1HLI &RFC p2&162 CR Iraq5

FARIS,Sturton Johnston T2Lt kia 30-7-16 17Lpool p71 CR France294

FARISH,Samuel TLt kia 24-4-17 1KOSB p101 MR20

FARLEY,Ernest Harold T2Lt kia 3-7-16 9Ess p131 MR21

FARLEY,Frederick Albert 2Lt kia 1-7-16 1/2Lond p245 MR21

FARLEY,George Herbert 2Lt kia 16-8-17 3RInniskF p104 MR30

FARLEY,Harry William Lt kia 24-4-18 RWKent att8Bn p141 MR20

FARLEY,Joseph Thomas T2Lt ded 1-9-18 16Manch p154 CR France40

FARLEY,M.Matron ded 1-6-18 QAIMNS p200 CR Ireland24

FARLEY,William T2Lt kia 15-6-16 15RWar p64 CR France1182

FARMAR,Cyril Herbert Berkeley Capt kia 19-4-17 1/10Lond p248 CR Palestine8

FARMAR-COTGRAVE,Christopher Russell Capt 29-12-17 2Worc att100TMB CR France1371

FARMER,Arthur William 2Lt kia 7-6-17 5BordR p228 MR29

FARMER,Charles George Edgar TLt kia 18-8-16 7KRRC p150 MR21

FARMER,Cyril.DSO.MC.Maj dow 3-8-17 RGA 183Bty83Bde attRFA p39 CR Belgium18

FARMER,Frederick George 2Lt ded 1-5-15 IARO MR43

FARMER,Frederick Stanley T2Lt dow 20-7-17 1/2 att14Worc p108 CR France184,kia

FARMER,George Barten 2Lt kia 14-6-18 5ELancs p226 CR France5,15-6-18

FARMER,Henry Charles Maclean 2Lt kia 10-5-15 6 att4KRRC p150 MR29

FARMER,Henry Gamul TCapt dow 12-11-15 7SfthH p164 CR Germany1

FARMER,James Douglas Herbert 2Lt kia 4-11-14 9/41RFA p28 MR29

FARMER,James Inglesby 2Lt kia 9-5-15 2KRRC p150 MR22,Ingleby

FARMER,Roland Devonport Capt kia 22-3-16 5Leic p220 CR France68

FARMER,William McDowall Lt kia 9-4-16 14RScots att8RWFus p54 MR38

FARMILOE,George Frederick 2Lt kia 26-6-17 2HAC p206 CR France614

FARNES,Henry Charles T2Lt kia 6-7-17 GL &48RFC p7 CR France421

FARNHAM,Frank Jefferson 2Lt kld 15-4-17 RGA 239SB p39 CR France593

FARNHAM,Ralph Capt dow 31-10-18 6LancF p221 CR Belgium11

FARNWORTH,James 2Lt kia 9-8-16 1/5LNLancs p234 MR21

FARQUARSON,James T2Lt kia 23-4-17 11A&SH p173 CR France531,FARQUHARSON

FARQUARSON,John Charles Lancelot Lt kia 31-10/1-11-14 14Lond p249

FARQUHAR,Dean Maj ded 11-10-20 1A att7MGC Motors p276 MR43,12-10-20

FARQUHAR,Francis Douglas.DSO.LtCol kia 20-3-15 CldGds attPrcessPatCanLI p51

FARQUHAR,Hobart Brooks Capt kia 21-5-16 15Lond p249 MR20,22-5-16

FARQUHAR,James Edward Mainwaring TMaj kia 15-9-16 6CamH p167 CR France432

FARQUHAR,John Oswald Lt kia 23-3-18 RGlasgowYeo att10Ess p203 MR27

FARQUHAR,Ronald George T2Lt kia 29-3-17 9RWar p64 MR38

FARQUHAR,Rupert,MC Lt dow 17-9-17 4GrenGds p50 CR Belgium12

FARQUHAR,Walter Randolph Fitzroy.Bart Capt kia 15-10-18 RFA 59Div p207 CR France570

FARQUHAR,W.R.Lt ded 23-3-18 RFA p28 CR Surrey1

FARQUHAR-THOMPSON,Douglas T2Lt kia 13-10-15 10GordH p166 MR19

FARQUHARSON,Francis David Capt dow 11-4-18 5RScots att4Yorks p210 CR France1094

FARQUHARSON,Frank Lumsden Lt kia 4-6-15 6GordH p242 MR22,3-6-15

FARQUHARSON,Hugh Joseph T2Lt ded 27-8-16 2Norf p73 CR Iraq6

FARQUHARSON,John(Ian) 2Lt dow 23-8-18 4 att1GordH p242 CR France226

FARQUHARSON,John Charles Lancelot Lt 31-10/1-11-14 LondScot MR29

FARQUHARSON,Lewis Shaw Capt kia 12-5-18 1RScots p54 CR Belgium4

FARQUHARSON,Norman Kenneth T2Lt kia 29-8-18 2/5RLancs D'Coy p58 CR France568

FARQUHARSON,Peere William Nesham 2Lt kia 7-10-16 26RFus p67 CR France744

FARQUHARSON-ROBERTS,Donald.MC.TCapt kia 20-11-17 7 att4ESurr p112 MR17

FARR,Charles Gordon.MID 2Lt dow 25-3-18 4 att6KOSB p224 CR France40

FARR,Percival Ward Lt kia 31-7-17 4Mddx p146 MR29

FARRAN,Charles T2Lt kia 24-8-16 9KRRC p150 MR21

FARRAN,Edmond Baker 2Lt drd 8-8-15 5BlkW p255 CR Scot118,18-8-15

FARRAN,Edmond Chomley Lambert Capt kia 16-6-15 3 att2RIrRif p169 MR29

FARRAN,George Francis Maj kia 18-7-16 98RFA p28 CR France515,A88RFA

FARRANT,Archibald William TLt ded 6-11-18 87MGC p182 CR Berks23

FARRANT,George T2Lt kia 9-2-17 6RLancs p58 MR38

FARRANT,Robert George Capt ded 18-12-17 MilLabCps E Africa58

FARRAR,Ernest Bristow 2Lt kia 18-9-18 3 att16Dev p76 CR France1463

FARRAR,Fred T2Lt dow 4-10-17 8Lincs p75 CR Belgium132

FARRAR,Herbert Ronald 2Lt kia 24-12-14 3Leic att2Manch p87 CR Belgium97

FARRAR,John Frederick T2LtACapt ded 2-11-18 2WYorks p81 CR France1277

FARRAR,John Harold.MIDx2 Capt kia 9-5-15 3 att1Nhampt p137 MR22

FARRAR,Julian Gordon Knowles TCapt kia 14-9-16 12LancF p92 MR37

FARRAR,Valentine Anstruther TLt dow 15-3-16 17LancF p92 CR France495,17-3-16

FARRAR,William Watt TLt ded 10-8-16 RAMC p195 MR65

FARRELL,Adrian Lt dow 23-8-16 4EYorks p219 CR Yorks5

FARRELL,Bede Capt kia 24-4-15 4EYorks p219 MR29

FARRELL,Bryan Usher Lt 27-6-21 RASC 11MT MR43

FARRELL,Francis 2Lt ded 23-2-19 15RIrRif p265 CR Ireland33,Lt

FARRELL,J.E.J.Capt 19-11-17 5Ches CR Yorks256

FARRELL,John Leo T2Lt kia 16-3-18 17RIrRif p169 CR France1061

FARRELL,Joseph.DCM.MID TCapt ded 28-7-18 1Dev p263 CR Devon1

FARRELL,Reginald T2Lt kia 14-7-16 6Nhampt p137 MR21

FARRELL,Stanley Knox 2Lt kia 20-7-18 1/6BlkW p231 CR France1695

FARREN,John 2Lt kia 13-11-16 7RWSurr attSuff p55&263,Suff att7RWKent CR France802,Lt 3 att2Suff

FARREN,William Ignatius George Lt ded 29-3-17 3RWFus p97 CR Wales497

FARRER,Fred 2Lt kld 28-11-17 RFC p7 CR Kent231,Lt

FARRER,Henry Wyndham Francis Blackburn.MC&2Bars.CaptAMaj kia 30-10-18 30RFA p28 CR France1270

FARRER,Lyonel Henry St.George T2Lt ded 28-10-15 5 O&BLI p130 CR France102,9Bn

FARRER,Richard Bracken Lt kia 8-6-17 1/5Leic p220 CR France161

FARRIER,Archibald Manaton 2Lt dow 29-12-14 SWBord p100 CR France765

FARRIER,Douglas Towry 2Lt kia 1-10-17 RGA 219SB p39 CR Belgium124

FARRIMOND,Harry Carrington TLt ded 14-3-19 ELancs p264 CR Lancs368

FARRIMOND,Joseph T2Lt kia 21-7-16 8Nhampt att 1/5Glouc p137 MR21

FARRIN,Stuart Thomas 2Lt dow 7-12-17 RE 263RlyCo p44 CR Belgium84

FARRINGTON,Alfred Jack Lt kia 27-8-17 5RWar p214 CR Belgium126,John

FARRINGTON,F.L.Lt 16-12-20 S&M MR67

FARRINGTON,George William 2Lt kia 28-6-18 3 att12Glouc p106 CR France352

FARRINGTON,William Bowker 2Lt kia 25-3-18 6Manch p236 MR20

FARROW,Brian 2Lt kia 1-7-16 4 att2LancF p92 CR France742

FARROW,Charles Oswald 2Lt ded 2-12-18 RFA p261 CR Durham59

FARROW,Clifford Willis 2Lt dow 9-4-18 3 att4Dors p124 CR Palestine9

FARROW,Eric Tom 2LtTCapt kld 7-2-17 GL &RFC p7 CR Mddx34

FARROW,Jack TCapt kia 9-4-16 4SWBord p100 CR Iraq5

FARTHING,Leonard.MC.LtACapt kia 16-11-16 2ELancs p110 CR France744

FARTHING,William Edgar 2Lt dedacc 8-2-17 RGA 159HB p209 CR Devon1

FARWELL,John Edmund T2Lt kia 30-5-18 NumbF att4Bn p61 MR18

FASKALLY,Percy Blake Capt ded 18-12-19 RFus p263 CR Lond14,17-12-19

FAST,William Jack 2LtACapt kia 24-3-18 3 att12RSuss p119 MR27

FAULDER,Eric Amyas Wareing 2Lt kia 18-9-18 10WYorks p81 MR16

FAULDER,Harold.MIDx2 LtTCapt kia 26-4-18 3 att1/4Y&L p158 MR30

FAULKE,William James TLt kia 21-3-18 9Norf p73 MR20

FAULKNER,Charles Edward Arthur 2Lt dow 19-9-18 5Lpool p215 CR France530

FAULKNOR,Robert Sylvester John Capt kia 25-9-15 1LNLancs p135 CR France1723

FAULKS,Edgar TLt dow 26-9-15 RAMC att95RFA p195 MR19

FAULKS,Levi T2Lt kia 14-4-18 1Leic p87 MR30

FAUNCH,Ernest Alfred 2Lt kia 4-5-17 RGA 212SB p39 CR France557

FAUSSET,Charles Reginald 2Lt kia 3-5-15 3 att1/2RIrReg p89 MR29,2-5-15 1Bn

FAUSSET,Stewart Simon Lt kia 31-7-17 9Lpool p216 MR29

FAUSSET,Robert Clifford TLt dow 16-11-16 C74RFA p28 CR Lond4

FAUSSET,William Willoughby Bernard Capt ded 6-12-18 GL p190&257 CR Lond4

FAVELL,William Reginald 2Lt kia 2-7-16 4Y&L p238 CR France702

FAWCETT,Bertram James Acton.MID Capt dow 24-4-17 8ELancs p110 CR France95

FAWCETT,Edward Bertram.MID Capt kia 22-4-16 IA 92Punjabis p276 MR38,21-4-16

FAWCETT,Frank Aldridge 2Lt kia 1-7-16 1/5SStaffs p229 MR21

FAWCETT,Fred 2Lt ded 12-11-18 D of LancsYeo &RAF p255

FAWCETT,Geoffrey Lt kia 14-6-18 RASC p253 CR France62,8Lond

FAWCETT,John 2Lt kia 8-5-18 3 att2Yorks p90 CR Belgium111

FAWCETT,John Bellars 2Lt kia 21-3-18 RGA 233SB p39 MR27

FAWCETT,Joseph John 2Lt kia 23-3-18 9RInniskF p104 CR France1203

FAWCETT,Leopald George Frederick Elliot Capt kia 6-11-17 LanarkYeo p204 CR Palestine1,12RScotsF

FAWCETT,Richard Wilfrid 2Lt dow 26-9-15 4 att2SStaffs att15TMB p122 CR France80

FAWCETT,Robert Heath 2Lt kia 26-4-15 4 att1Beds p85 CR Belgium133

FAWCETT,Woodford T2Lt kia 21-3-18 5 O&BLI p130 CR France1061

FAWCUS,Walter.MC.TCapt kia 25-3-18 19NumbF p61 MR27

FAWDRY,Alfred George 2Lt kia 4-5-17 2RWar p64 MR20

FAWKNER,Leslie Charles 2Lt kia 26-10-16 15RFC p2 CR France156 See FOCKEN,L.C.true name

FAWSITT,Thomas Ruby 2Lt kia 16-9-16 3 att9Y&L p158 MR21

FAYLE,Barcroft Joseph Leech Capt kia 24-10-16 RAMC att2WYorks p195 CR France390

FAYLE,Gerald Leigh Bleeck Lt kia 22-7-16 RE 59FC p44 MR21

FAYRER,J.O.S.LtCol 19-10-18 5GurkhaRif CR Lond4

FAYRER,Joseph Steward 2Lt kia 21-1-16 IA 37Dogras p276 CR Iraq5

FAZACKERLEY,Harold.MC.T2Lt kia 25-8-18 LNLancs att1/4Bn p135 CR France106

FAZACKERLEY,Joseph 2Lt dow 24-10-18 13Manch p154 CR France13

FAZACKERLY-WESTBY,Gilbert Basil Joscelyn Capt kia 21-4-15 9Lond p247 MR29,J.B.

FAZAN,Roy 2Lt kia 9-5-15 5RSuss p228 MR22

FEAR,Edgar Leslie Brinsdon T2Lt dow 11-4-18 SomLI 3Coy p79 MR34

FEAR,Robert Stanley T2Lt dow 5-3-18 5Worc att15RFC p15&108 CR France398

FEARN,Charles Frederick 2Lt kia 4-7-15 4RInniskF att2MunstF p104 CR France80

FEARN,Herbert T2Lt kia 12-10-18 8ESurr p112 CR Belgium126

FEARNHEAD,John Hayes 2Lt dow 13-8-16 1/7Lpool p215 MR21

FEARNLEY,Ethel SNurse 23-11-14 QAIMNS CR France102

FEARNLEY,William 2Lt kia 1-7-16 2GordH p166 CR France331

FEARNLEY-WHITTINGSTALL,George Herbert TLt kia 3-8-16 11NumbF p61 CR France430

FEARNSIDE-SPEED,Ronald Nelson de Dieskan Lt kia 25-9-15 7Lond p247 MR19

FEASBY,Harold T2Lt kia 11-4-18 Y&L att1/5Bn p158 MR30

FEATHER,Reginald Albert 2Lt kia 16-8-17 9Hamps p229 MR30

FEATHERSTONE,Cecil Frederick Lt kia 25-4-15 3 att2ESurr p112 MR29

FEATHERSTONE,George Herbert T2Lt kia 1-7-16 9YLI p143 MR21

FEATHERSTONE,Marshall Breckon T2Lt kia 2-9-17 RE 2SpecCoy p44 CR Belgium88

FEATHERSTONE,Reginald Benjamin Capt kia 18-12-14 2Dev p76 MR22

FEATHERSTONE,Thomas.MC.T2Lt kia 25-4-17 12 att11Worc p108 MR37

FEATHERSTONE,Walter 2Lt ded 3-10-17 GL &RFC p7 CR Bucks36

FEATHERSTONE,William Lt kia 13-9-16 5Yorks p220 CR France453

FEATHERSTONE,William Davies.MC.Lt kia 23-3-18 D77RFA p207 CR France307

FEATHERSTONHAUGH,Edwyn Maj dow 27-4-15 1RDubF p176 MR4 See FETHERSTONHAUGH,E.

FEATHERSTONHAUGH,Harry TCapt kia 8-7-16 8RFus p67 MR21

FEATHERSTONHAUGH,Richard Collingwood Lt dow 14-5-15 KRRC p150

FEAVERYEAR,Albert George 2Lt kia 5-9-18 7 att19Lond p247 CR France511

FEDDEN,Cecil Olchar Lt acckld 7-1-18 IARO attRFC p276 CR Numb34 lost at sea

FEDDEN,Raymond Henshaw 2Lt kia 3-5-17 2HAC p206 MR20

FEETHAM,Alan 2Lt kia 18-9-16 5BordR p228 CR France453

FEETHAM,Edward.CB.CMG.TMajGen kia 29-3-18 Staff Commdg39Divn p1

FEGGETTER,John Halifax,MC TLt kia 4-10-17 12/13NumbF p61 MR30

FEHILY,Thomas TCapt kia 13-4-18 RAMC att2RFus p195 MR32

FEILD,John Forbes 2Lt kia 16-9-16 7DCLI p114 MR21

FEILDEN,Oswald Henry Capt dow 29-9-17 2/5Leic p220 CR Belgium18

FEILDEN,Granville John Henry 2Lt kia 25-4-15 2SfthH p164 CR Belgium129

FEILING,Hubert St.Lawrence.MID 2Lt kia 20-11-16 1BlkW p128 CR France397

FELIX-BROWN,Claud A kia 26-12-16 GL attRFC CR Belgium4

FELL,David Malcolm 2Lt kia 17-7-16 166RFA p28 CR France188

FELL,George Charles Huntley 2Lt dow 24-7-17 C82RFA p208 CR Belgium29

FELL,Harold 2Lt kia 5-11-16 6DLI p239 MR21

FELL,Matthew Henry 2Lt kia 17-9-16 5Yorks p221 CR France239

FELL,Sidney Fitzroy T2Lt kia 10-7-16 12 att3Worc p108 MR21

FELLOWES,A.H.G.Capt ded 2-4-18 att54RFC p261 CR France446,11-3-18

FELLOWES,Coulson Churchill.Hon.Capt ded 22-10-15 1LifeGds p20 CR Hunts102

FELLOWES,Cyril Walter 2Lt kia 21-3-18 att2/6NStaffs p157 MR20

FELLOWES,Hedworth George Ailwyn.MC.Capt kia 12-5-17 IA 11Lancers p276 CR France730

FELLOWES,Robert 2Lt kia 10-3-15 1KRRC p150 MR22

FELLOWES,Rupert Caldwell Butler LtACapt kia 21-8-18 1CldGds 4Coy p51 CR France103

FELLOWS,Arthur Simpson 2Lt kia 1-4-17 7Worc p226 CR France369

FELLOWS,Basil Hamilton Abdy 2Lt dow 22-3-17.3 att5RBerks p139 CR France46,FELLOWES

FELLOWS,Mervyn 2Lt dow 25-8-17 C173RFA p28 CR Belgium11

FELLOWS,Richard Woodhouse TLt kia 15-9-16 14 att2N&D p133 CR France374

FELTON,Hubert Ratcliffe 2Lt kia 9-10-17 7Worc p226 MR30,17Bn

FELTS,Percival Claude T2Lt kia 23-7-17 GL &6RFC p7 CR Belgium11

FEMNER,Cyril Frederick Hamilton 2Lt kia 24-9-16 2ScotGds p52

FENCHELLE,George John T2Lt dow PoW 30-6-16 12RSuss p119 CR France924

FENDALL,Charles Magrath TLt kia 14-12-15 RFA p28 MR29

FENDALL,Denis John 2Lt dow 8-8-17 RFA att4RFC p28&7,kia 7-8-17 CR Belgium19

FENDER,Edward Henry LtACapt kia 9-10-17 7WYorks p218 MR30

FENERAN,Frank Edward Capt kia 10-3-15 Lpool p71 MR22

FENN,Edward Gerald Palmer T2Lt kia 19-9-18 3RWFus GarrBn att1/5Ess p97 CR Palestine9,6Bn

FENN,John Edmund.MC.Lt kia 9-4-18 1/8Lpool p215 CR France260

FENN,Roland Pitt 2Lt kia 25-3-18 GL &18RFC p7 MR20

FENN-SMITH,Warren Kemp T2Lt kia 18-1-18 20RFC p15 CR France98

FENNELL,Frederick Vibond Lt kld 30-6-18 GL &8RAF CR France1564

FENNELLY,James Philps T2Lt kld 24-12-17 GL &RFC p7 CR Mddx17

FENNEMORE,George Charles T2Lt ded 3-11-18 RE p44 CR Iraq6

FENNER,Alan Thomas T2Lt dow 8-12-17 NStaffs att2/6Bn p157 CR France52

FENNER,Arthur.MC.LtTCapt ded 20-11-18 RASC HT25DivTrn p192 CR France146

FENNER,C.F.H.2Lt 24-9-16 2ScotsGds MR21

FENNER,Claude Cambridge LtCol kia 23-11-14 IA 59Rif p276 CR France727

FENNER,John Prebble T2Lt dow 8-8-17 7EYorks p84 CR France113

FENNER,Thomas 2LtACapt kia 22-3-18 3RB p178 MR27

FENNER,Walter Noel Lt dow 2-7-17 RFA p207 CR France13

FENNING,Algernon Esme Hal Maj kia 6-8-15 6Y&L p158 MR4

FENTIMAN,Frederick William 2Lt dow 24-3-18 BordR att8Bn p117 MR20

FENTON,Alan Hughes 2Lt mbk 4-3-17 43RFC p256 MR20

FENTON,Arthur Edward T2Lt kia 14-6-17 RWKent att11Bn p141 MR29

FENTON,Bede Liddell CaptTMaj kia 15-7-16 1Dors p124 MR21

FENTON,Charles Edwin T2Lt ded 19-8-17 12RIrRif p169 CR France40

FENTON,David Houston 2Lt kia 8-9-15 4WRid p227 CR Belgium167

FENTON,Douglas Annand Lt kia 9-9-16 3 att2ScotRif p103 CR France423,10-9-16

FENTON,Geoffrey Russell Lt kia 20-9-14 2ConnRgrs p172 MR15

FENTON,Gilbert Francis Rowland TLt kia 4-7-16 16RB p178 MR19

FENTON,William Vernon T2Lt dow 16-9-15 8Yorks p90 CR France684

FENWICK,Anthony Lionel.MID TLtACapt kia 16-2-18 6Lincs p75 CR France115

FENWICK,Maurice Edward Edmonds T2Lt kia 2-4-17 8Dev p76 CR France568

FENWICK,Percival Fenwick 2Lt kia 1-7-16 RFA p28 CR France700

FENWICK,William 2Lt dow 22-5-18 PoW 5 att10RWSurr p212 CR Germany1

FENWICK,William Cecil 2Lt ded 7-10-16 21RFC p2 MR20

FENWICKE-CLENNELL,Thomas Percival Edward Capt ded 20-2-19 Loth&BordHorseYeo p270 CR Greece9

FERARD,George Deas Lt kia 21-2-18 2Dev p76 MR30

FERGIE,Alexander Bancroft T2Lt kia 20-9-17 LNLancs att1/4Bn p135 MR30

FERGUSON,A.2Lt 22-9-18 EAfrMilLabCps APD CR EAfrica90

FERGUSON,Adam Lt dow 1-9-18 AustMGC 2Coy CR France119

FERGUSON,Alan TLt dow 4-7-16 9WRid p115 CR France207

FERGUSON,Alexander Crichton Capt ded 12-2-19 2RScots att8TMB p54&257,2Lt CR Germany1,Crighton

FERGUSON,Alexander Lundie Hunter TLt kia 23-7-16 8 att1/4GordH p166 MR21,22-7-16

FERGUSON,Alexander Robertson 2Lt kld 14-6-16 1/3ScotHorse p205 CR Egypt2

FERGUSON,Alva John T2Lt kld 4-8-17 127MGC p182

FERGUSON,Arthur Douglas Lt kia 12-10-17 6SforthH p241 MR30

FERGUSON,Arthur Alexander Lt dow 26-9-15 7Lond p247 CR France178,25-9-15

FERGUSON,Charles Edgar 2Lt kia 18-10-17 GL &22RFC p7 CR Belgium453

FERGUSON,David Raeside TLt kia 17-11-17 RE 135ArmyTrpsCoy p45 CR Belgium12

FERGUSON,Donald Francis 2Lt kia 7-5-17 ScotHorse att2GordH p205 MR20

FERGUSON,Douglas Chalmers T2Lt dow 26-1-17 10HLI p162 CR France145

FERGUSON,Duncan MacIntyre Grant Lt dow 14-5-15 3 att2KOSB p101 CR France102

FERGUSON,Fritz Eberhard.MC.Capt kia 7-10-19 IA 3CpsofGuides p276 MR43

FERGUSON,George Douglas.DSO.TCapt dow 23-4-17 RAMC att27RFA p195 CR France1325

FERGUSON,Harold Gowan.MC.Maj ded 30-11-18 RE p209 CR Lond14,Gowans

FERGUSON,Henry Horatio Edward TCapt dow 23-9-17 14HLI D'Coy p162 CR France398

FERGUSON,Henry Innes TCapt kia 14-7-16 17HLI p162 MR21

FERGUSON,Hugh Mortimer TCapt kia 11-6-17 9SStaffs p122 CR Belgium127

FERGUSON,Ian Alexander Grant TCapt kia 11-5-16 13RScots p54 CR France423

FERGUSON,J.Engr ded 12-7-17 IndLabCps attRE IWT Iraq6

FERGUSON,James Maj kia 22-7-16 9RScots p255 MR21

FERGUSON,James T2Lt kld 12-3-17 GL &RFC p7 CR Bucks51

FERGUSON,James Capt ded 9-10-18 SL IAUL RAMC p268 MR43

FERGUSON,James Arthur Ross Lt kia 9-5-15 3RSuss att1YLI p119 MR29

FERGUSON,James Ernest 2Lt kia 20-4-17 4 att10RDubF p176 MR20

FERGUSON,James Duncan.MID TLt dow 27-10-16 11Ess p131 CR France105

FERGUSON,James McKee TCapt kia 22-12-17 RAMC att6ConnRgrs p195 CR France1463

FERGUSON,John 2Lt kia 23-10-16 4 att2ScotRif p103 MR21

FERGUSON,John Capt kia 30-11-17 RAMC att1/12Lpool p195 MR17

FERGUSON,John 2LtTLt ded 8-7-18 14HLI p162 CR Scot167,3Bn

FERGUSON,John James Moore TCapt ded 19-11-18 7 att2Beds p85 CR France146,Charles

FERGUSON,Leonard R.C.T2Lt dow 20-7-16 13RScots p54 CR France134,Lt

FERGUSON,Norman Douglas 2Lt ded 1-7-19 LabCps 8Coy p266 CR France446

FERGUSON,Percy Grant 2Lt kia 10-3-15 Wilts p153 MR22

FERGUSON,Peter 2Lt kia 28-10-18 3A&SH p173 CR France1196

FERGUSON,Philip TCapt ded 27-1-19 RAMC p267 CR Surrey91

FERGUSON,Philip Hew.MC.CaptAMaj kia 22-10-17 152RFA p28 CR Belgium12

FERGUSON,Rachel SNurse ded 26-6-18 QAIMNS p200 CR Italy16

FERGUSON,Robert George.MC.T2LtACapt ded PoW 11-6-18 1RScotF p94 France924

FERGUSON,Robert William 2Lt kia 13-11-16 5GordH p242 CR France1501

FERGUSON,Roderick Mackenzie 2Lt kia 13-11-16 4GordH p242 CR France1490

FERGUSON,Samuel Cranswick 2Lt kia 8-9-18 8Lond p247 CR France511

FERGUSON,Stanley McEwan Lt ded 15-9-18 IA 17Cav p276 MR67 Ex 2Lt SfthH

FERGUSON,Thomas Capt kia 13-11-16 6BlkW p231 CR France35

FERGUSON,Thomas Jenkins T2Lt kia 30-8-18 15TankCps p188 CR France214

FERGUSON,Victor John Lt kia 21-8-18 2LifeGds att2GdsMGReg p20&53,21/22-8-19 CR France116

FERGUSON,William.MC.TCapt kia 1-11-16 12 att2Worc p108&258 MR21

FERGUSON,William Percival 2Lt kia 9-4-17 9RScots p212 CR France184

FERGUSON-DAVIE,Arthur Francis.CIE.DSO.LtCol dow 12-4-16 IA 51Sikhs p276 MR38

FERGUSON-POLLOCK,Robert Cuthbert Maj kia 11-4-17 IA 32Lancers p276 MR38

FERGUSSON,Douglas Hubert Lewin Lt dow 2-2-16 1CamH p167 CR Lond14

FERGUSSON,Edward Keith Ogilvy.MID TCapt kia 26-1-16 8SfthH p164 CR France178

FERGUSSON,Fitz-James Shillington T2Lt kia 22-3-18 12RB p178 CR France672

FERGUSSON,James Adam Hamilton 2Lt kia 20-9-14 HLI p162 MR15

FERGUSSON,James Grant T2Lt kia 14-7-16 8BlkW p128 MR21

FERGUSSON,James Scott Elliott Gillon Lt kia 27-4-15 5 att3Mddx p146

FERGUSSON,Kenneth Mountney James Lt kia 31-7-17 2Lincs p75 MR29

FERGUSSON,John Wright TLt ded 9-5-17 2SfthH p164 CR France40 Ex 9RScots

FERGUSSON,Robert Allan Arklay LtACapt kia 14-9-16 CldGds p51 CR France374,15-9-16

FERGUSSON,Robert Arthur 2Lt kia 15-4-17 6 att17RFus p67 CR France1321

FERGUSSON,Robert Frank Lt kia 12-7-15 1/5RScotF D'Coy p222 CR Gallipoli2

FERGUSSON,William Albert 2Lt dow 15-5-17 4Leic p220 CR France178

FERNALD,Van Dyke Lt ded 23-7-18 3RWSurr att139RAF p15&55 CR Italy9,kia

FERNANDES,Dudley Luis De Tavora.MID 2Lt kia 23-10-14 Beds p85 MR29

FERNIE,Andrew John T2Lt kia 12-10-17 11RScots p54 MR30

FERNIE,Roy Mackenzie Lt kia 16-8-15 RE 6SigCoy p210 CR Belgium59

FERNYHOUGH,Samuel Lt ded 7-5-18 4 att18Manch p154 CR Ches184

FERRABY,Robinson Lt ded 7-4-18 4EYorks p219 CR France64,dow

FERRAR,Walter Hughes Capt kia 2-11-14 2WelshR p126 CR Belgium57,31-10-14

FERRIE,Robert Leighton Moore.MC.2Lt kia 3-1-18 46RFC p15 CR France49

FERRIER,Gilbert Colin Cunninghame 2Lt kia 11-11-14 7 att4RFus p67 MR29

FERRIER,John Kinmont T2Lt dow 23-8-18 13RB D'Coy p178 CR France518

FERRIER,Robert Ernest 2Lt kia 15-10-16 4BlkW p230 CR France293

FERRILL,Tom Archibald 2Lt kia 16-8-17 3 att2WYorks p81 MR30

FERRIMAN,Frederick Samuel T2Lt kia 7-6-17 GL 6 O&BLI att25RFC p7 CR Belgium140

FERRIS,Alfred William 2Lt dow 5-3-17 2/3Lond p245 CR France120

FERRIS,Henry Norman 2Lt kia 9-10-17 4Glouc p225 CR Belgium126

FERRIS,James T2Lt kia 2-12-17 16HLI att97TMB p162 MR30

FERRIS,Samuel Bernard Clutton 2Lt ded 6-4-15 10Huss att11ResCavR p22 CR Wilts176

FERRIS,William Small T2Lt kia 7-6-17 12RIrRif p169 CR Belgium62

FERRYMAN,William Edward LtACapt dow 12-10-18 2ScotsGds p52 CR France337

FESTING,Arthur Hoskyns.CMG.DSO.Maj kia 9-5-15 RIrRif p169 MR32

FESTING,Hubert Wogan.DSO.MajTLtCol kia 21-3-18 15DLI att10YLI p160 MR27

FETHERSTONHAUGH,Ashly Elliot Herbert Maj kld 20-3-19 14KHuss p261 CR Eire510

FETHERSTONHAUGH,Edwyn Maj 27-4-15 1RDubF MR4 See FEATHERSTONHAUGH,E.

FETHERSTONHAUGH,George Rupert Alexander 2Lt kia 25/27-10-14 RFus p67 MR22

FETHERSTONHAUGH,John Lennox 2Lt kia 10-11-14 2A&SH p173 MR32

FETHERSTONHAUGH-FRAMPTON,Philip Tregonwell Lt kia 3-5-15 RWar att2EKent p64 MR29,Tregenwell

FEURER,Sydney Moss 2Lt kia 22-7-18 RBerks att27RAF p254 CR France1107

FEVERSHAM,Charles William Reginald.Earl LtCol kia 15-9-16 21KRRC attYorkHussYeo p150&206 CR France744

FEW,Robert James Donald Lt dow 27-10-18 1Dors p124 CR Oxford69

FEWELL,Charles William T2Lt ded 6-11-18 O&BLI p130 CR Essex50

FFOLKES,William Rupert Compton 2Lt kia 30-12-17 5 att1KRRC p150 CR France530

FFRENCH,Edward Fulke.Hon.2Lt ded PoW 13-11-18 296RH&FA p28

FFRENCH Ernest Dudley 2Lt kia 16-7-19 IA CpsofGuides att3/1GurkhaRif p276 MR43,ffRENCH

FFRENCH,Evelyn Wilson Capt kld 23-12-18 RFA &RFC p28 CR Mddx26

FIDLER,Canel Watt 2Lt dow 19-5-17 7A&SH attRFC p18&243,Carrell CR France297

FIDLER,Frederick Capt kia 26-4-15 1Hamps p120 MR29

FIDOE,Norman Godfrey T2Lt kia 21-3-18 1Leic p87 MR20

FIELD,Alfred John Lt kia 11-4-18 1/5NumbF p213 MR32

FIELD,Arthur Clarence Henley T2Lt dow 4-4-16 14RFus att4SWBord p67 MR38,5-4-16

FIELD,Arthur Dudley Lt kia 4-7-16 RGA 61SB p209 CR France430

FIELD,Arthur Montague 2Lt mbk 22-3-18 4Leic D'Coy p257&270,dow 13-4-18 CR France716

FIELD,Arthur Roland.MC.2Lt kia 17-9-18 C70RFA p28 CR France179

FIELD,A.W.Capt kia 9-1-18 48RFC p15 CR France238

FIELD,Charles Abel T2Lt dow 12-11-18 RWSurr att8Bn p55 CR France40

FIELD,Charles Cecil T2Lt kia 30-3-16 RWKent att2Suff p141 CR Belgium124

FIELD,Cyril Decimus 2Lt kia 4-6-15 5Worc p108 MR4

FIELD,Dave Hamilton Lt 22-4-15 RGA 2HB MR29

FIELD,Edwin Arthur T2Lt kia 14-9-16 14 att9WYorks p81 CR France293

FIELD,Francis Morgan TLtACapt kia 31-3-18 7EYorks p84 MR20

FIELD,George Walton T2Lt kia 25-9-15 10Glouc p106 CR France1723

FIELD,Gordon Stewart T2Lt kia 16-6-17 12NumbF p61 MR20

FIELD,Harold William T2Lt kia 27-5-18 9ACycCps p181 CR France1894

FIELD,Hassel Dyer.MID TCapt dow 28-9-17 RAMC att134FA p195 CR France139,Hassell

FIELD,Henry Lionel 2Lt kia 1-7-16 6RWar p214 CR France1890

FIELD,Howard LtTCapt kia 6-8-15 4Worc p108 MR4

FIELD,John Alan Francis TLtCol ded 23-4-18 13SWBord p100 CRKent179 Ex 13Ches

FIELD,John Archibald Capt kia 13-7-16 RE 92FC p45 CR France164

FIELD,John Morton T2Lt kia 11-4-16 7RSuss p119 CR France423

FIELD,John William 2LtTCapt kia 20-9-15 1RIrRif p169 CR France924

FIELD,Kenneth Douglas.DSO.LtCol kia 30-11-17 RGA 38SB p39 MR17

FIELD,Leslie Jack T2Lt kia 4-11-18 RBerks att8Bn p139 CR France230

FIELD,Linwood.DSO.MC.CaptAMaj kia 26-10-17 RFA p28 CR Belgium25

FIELD,Norman Lt kia 14-8-17 5Manch att25RFC p18&236 CR France924

FIELD,Oliver 2Lt kia 18-7-16 9DLI p239 CR France683

FIELD,Reginald George 2Lt dow 6-4-18 10Huss p22 CR France145

FIELD,Robert Alister.MC.LtACapt kia 2-4-17 2Yorks p90 CR France1186

FIELD,Samuel Hatten 2Lt kia 31-7-17 4SLancs p230 MR29

FIELD,Stephen Capt ded 10-4-15 PoW RAMC p195 CR Germany4

FIELD,Sydney Hubert 2Lt dow 9-8-16 4 att1RInniskF p104 CR Belgium165

FIELD,Vincent Alfred 2Lt kia 20-9-17 10RWSurr p55 MR30

FIELD,William Christian T2Lt kia 31-7-17 2RB p178 MR29

FIELD,William James.MC.2Lt kia 31-7-17 1RFus p67 MR29

FIELDEN,Gilbert Sutcliffe T2Lt ded 18-7-17 9RLancs p58 CR Greece1

FIELDEN,Norman Leyland Lt ded 22-2-19 RGA p254 CR Herts110

FIELDER,Charles Lt mbk 22-9-18 11WelshR p256 CR Greece5

FIELDER,Edgar John T2Lt kia 9/12-4-17 RLancs p58 CR France1182,Lt 8-4-17

FIELDHOUSE,Walter Benjamin T2Lt ded 1-11-18 2Lpool p71 MR43

FIELDING,Alexander.MC.T2Lt dow 26-10-18 26RFus att124TMB p67 CR Belgium158

FIELDING,Arthur William T2Lt kia 16-4-18 Y&L att6Bn p158 CR France163,15-4-18

FIELDING,Edward Fleming TLt kia 24-10-15 SomLI attKAR p200 CR WAfrica28

FIELDING,Francis Willoughby 2Lt kia 1-7-16 9Lond p248 CR France798

FIELDING,Frank T2Lt kia 4-10-17 1 att7LancF p92 MR30

FIELDING,George Rudolf TMaj kia 24-7-15 9N&D p134 CR Gallipoli14

FIELDING,Gerald Trueman 2Lt ded 27-5-18 B88RFA 19DAC p261 CR Belgium11,17-4-18

95

FIELDING,Henry Crossley Capt kia 12-9-15 IA 3A8Dogras att59Rif p276 CR France355 &CR France1887

FIELDING,Henry Simon.Hon.LtACapt dow 9-10-17 2CldGds p51 CR FEILDING 11-10-17

FIELDING,Herbert Hilton 2Lt kia 28-3-17 6Manch p236 CR France616

FIELDING,Joseph.MID 2Lt ded 16-12-17 GL RE attIWT p190 CR Iraq6

FIELDING,Joshua Maj ded 20-1-17 BRCS Ex 4DragGds CR Egypt8

FIELDING,S.Lt&QM ded 12-11-14 N&D p134 CR Derby97

FIELDING,F.Thomas.MID Capt&QM ded 31-10-18 4WRid p270 CR Yorks619

FIELDS,Edward Cotman T2Lt dow 22-6-16 27NumbF p61 CR France23,Cotnam

FIENNES,John Eustace Capt dow 18-6-17 2GordH p166 CR France113

FIFE,Alexander John LtCol ded 7-2-17 4Yorks attMGC p90,182,187&220 CR France40

FIFE,Gilbert 2Lt dow 16-7-16 9HLI p240

FIFIELD,Percival T2Lt kia 22-3-18 17KRRC p150 MR27

FIGG,Donald Whiteley.DSO.LtCol dow 5-3-17 24Lond &RFus p252 CR France624

FIGGINS,Henry Francis 2Lt kia 16-9-16 6Lond p247 MR21

FIGGIS,Lenox Paton.MC.TLtACapt kia 27-8-18 6EKent p57 CR France370

FIGGIS,Neville Johnstone TLt kia 10-8-15 6Leinst p174 CR Gallipoli18

FIGGURES,Douglas Lionel.MM.2Lt dow 15-10-18 C46RFA p28 CR France25

FILE,Harold William T2Lt kia 13-7-16 7RWKent p141 MR21

FILGATE,Thomas William Capt dow 29-9-15 8RMunsF p175 CR France178

FILLEUL,Leonard Amaurie 2Lt kia 21-10-14 SomLI attO&BLI p79 MR29,Amauri

FILLINGHAM,Reginald John.MC&Bar.LtAMaj dow 29-9-18 RGA 41SB p39&258 CR France194

FILMER,Robert Marcus.Bart.MC.TCapt dow 27-1-16 4GrenGds p50 CR France345

FILMER,Vivian Reginald Royal 2Lt kia 25-11-17 2Drags p21 CR France379

FILMER-STRANGEWAYS-ROGERS,Arthur Edmund 2Lt dow 4-11-18 3GrenGds p50

FILTNESS,John.MIDx2 Lt dow 22-5-18 D161RFA p28 CR France103,Capt

FINCH,Aubrey Malcolm Cecil Capt kia 7-7-19 4SfthH p241 MR70 &CR Europe179

FINCH,Ernest Wilfred Rupert Lt dow 7-8-16 4SfthH A'Coy p241 CR France74,kia

FINCH,Frank Marshall 2Lt kia 22-9-18 2RBerks p139 CR France604

FINCH,Frederick George Capt 3-7-21 IndOrdDept MR67

FINCH,George Capt ded 8-10-18 RAMC p253 CR Iraq6

FINCH,Herbert Marshall.DSO.LtCol kia 9-5-15 1RBerks p139 MR22

FINCH,Hugh Adair 2Lt kia 27-8-18 2GrenGds p50 CR France614

FINCH,Philip Gerard.MC.Lt kia 28-3-18 1NumbF p61 MR20

FINCH,Russell Claude 2Lt ded 5-11-18 22Lond p270 CR Essex209

FINCH,Tom 2Lt dow 20-10-17 6N&D p233 CR Derby98

FINCH,William Capt ded 22-2-19 RE CR C'land&W'land17

FINCH-NOYES,Charles William Fabin 2Lt kia 3-9-16 9LNLancs p135 MR21

FINCHAM,George Edmund Heygate 2LtTCapt kia 9-3-16 6RFC p2 CRBelgium11,Lt

FINDLATER,Percival St.George TCapt kia 28-3-18 RASC 21DivTrn p192 CR France79

FINDLAY,Arthur Bertram Lt kia 30-7-15 15 att7KRRC p150 MR29

FINDLAY,Cyril Olney 2Lt dow 17-10-17 4SomLI p218 CR France193

FINDLAY,Edward John 2Lt dow 9-5-15 14Lond p249 CR France80,Lt

FINDLAY,Ernest Robert 2Lt dow 5-10-17 255RFA p208 CR Belgium36

FINDLAY,Ian Caulcutt 2Lt dow 10-8-15 3Y&L p158 CR Belgium5,Calcutt 2Bn

FINDLAY,James T2Lt kia 16-6-17 12NumbF p61 MR20

FINDLAY,John 2LtACapt kia 25-4-18 6KOSB p101 MR30

FINDLAY,John Alexander.DSO.MIDx3 Maj kia 8-11-17 1/5HLI p240 CR Palestine8

FINDLAY,John Tulloch Lt kia 28-6-15 8ScotRif p225 MR4

FINDLAY,Lorimer TCapt kld 14-6-17 HLI GL &RFC p7 CR Scot398

FINDLAY,Neil Douglas.CB.BrigGen kia 10-9-14 Cmdg1Div RA p28 CR France1107

FINDLAY,Robert de Cardonnel Capt kia 11-3-15 4SfthH p241 MR22

FINDLAY,Robert Scott Capt kldacc 22-5-15 9A&SH p243 CR Scot76

FINDLAY,Ronald James T2Lt kld 24-12-17 RFC p7 CR Wilts3,FINLAY

FINDLAY,Scott T2Lt kia 8-5-18 19Manch p154 MR30

FINDLAY,Struthers 2Lt kia 4-8-16 ACycCps 52LowlandDiv p244 CR Egypt2

FINDLAY-HAMILTON,John Eric Lt kia 16-6-15 3 att2RScotF p94 MR22

FINDON,Robert TLt kia 18-4-18 RE 9FC p45 CR France250

FINE,S.2Lt kld 18-5-18 GL &RAF p190

FINEGAN,Herbert Marion Capt kia 16/18-6-15 8Lpool p215 MR22

FINIGAN,Wilfred James T2Lt kia 28-3-18 15MGC p182 MR20

FINK,Lawrence Alexander Lewis,MC 2LtACapt kia 5-10-17 2Beds p85 CR Belgium17

FINK,Sydney Lt dow 20-4-17 2/5SLancs p230 CR France769

FINKE,Richard Fenwick Capt kia 9-5-15 RSuss p119 MR22

FINLAY,A.TCapt ded 7-6-18 RAMC p267 CR Surrey41,5-6-18

FINLAY,Edward Norman Alison 2Lt kia 4-7-16 16RB p178 MR19

FINLAY,Eric Lionel 2Lt dow 20-3-16 6Dev p217 CR Iraq6

FINLAY,George Guy Lt kia 14-7-18 3 att2RIrReg p89 MR27

FINLAY,George Malcolm TCapt kia 5-11-17 14Hamps p120 CR Belgium105,Malcolme Ex 1Leinst

FINLAY,James Nelson 2Lt kia 28-3-18 14Lond att7CamH p249 MR20

FINLAY,John Cuthbert Capt kia 23-11-16 26NumbF B'Coy p61 CR France922

FINLAY,Robert Alexander Lt kia 9-5-15 5RDubF att1RIrRif p176 MR32

FINLAY,Thomas Pretsell Lt kia 25-9-15 3 att2GordH p166 MR19

FINLAYSON,Alexander.MID ACapt kia 22-3-18 6HLI att4NumbF p240 CR France34 &CR France834

FINLAYSON,Alexander Cunningham 2Lt dow 9-4-17 4RFC p7 CR France832

FINLAYSON,Alexander Moncrieff T2Lt dow 23-7-17 10 att7SLancs p125 CR France183

FINLAYSON,Bernard Stuart 2Lt dow 13-4-18 1 att1/4SfthH p164 CR France88

FINLAYSON,John T2Lt kia 23-3-18 5 O&BLI p130 CR France1061

FINN,Bernard William 2Lt kia 13-11-16 12 att13Ess p131 MR21

FINN,Francis William Lt kia 5-10-17 C74RFA p28 CR Belgium12,4-10-17

FINN,Michael AssCommsyHonLt ded 15-4-18 IA IOD p276 CR Iraq6

FINN,Thomas Joseph 2Lt ded 20-11-18 5RInniskF p104 CR France85,4Bn

FINN,William Joseph Rev kia 25-4-15 RAChDept p199 CR Gallipoli15

FINNEMORE,Henry James T2Lt dow 27-3-18 RSuss &RFC p16&119

FINNEMORE,Percival Edward Lt kia 26-10-17 Dev p76 MR30

FINNERTY,Wilfrid Edward 2Lt kia 22-3-18 10Lincs p75 MR20

FINNEY,Edwin Newland 2Lt kia 19-5-17 Leinst att6CycBn p174 CR France452

FINNEY,John.MC.2Lt ded 8-2-19 11RInniskF p257&104 CR France1028

FINNEY,Thomas 2Lt kia 21-3-18 3Y&L p158 MR20,2Bn

FINNIE,Bertram Knott Capt kia 1-10-15 5Lincs p220 MR29

FINNIMORE,David Keith Lt ded 10-5-17 RE 2PontoonPk p45 CR Hamps1

FINNIMORE,Henry James 2Lt 27-3-18 7Suss attRFC CR France300

FINNIS,John Fortescue LtCol dow 14-1-16 IA 53Sikhs p276 MR38

FINNIS,William Frank 2Lt dow 2-5-17 RGA 250SB p39 CR France924

FIPPARD,Richard Clift TCapt kia 4-6-15 14WYorks attLancF p81 MR4

FIRBANK,Godfrey Benjamin Joseph 2Lt kia 11-9-16 23RFC p2 MR20

FIRMIN,John Eric Robert T2Lt kia 10-8-15 5Wilts p153 MR4

FIRMIN,Maurice Harold Cuffe TLt kia 26-2-16 11LNLancs p135 MR20

FIRMINGER,Thomas T2Lt kia 3-9-16 9 att8EKent p57 CR France372

FIRTH,Arnold 2Lt kia 15-4-17 RFA p208 CR France568

FIRTH,Charles Ronald 2Lt ded 9-11-18 1/5WYorks p218 CR Germany3

FIRTH,Edwin Norris Lt ded 16-3-18 8WYorks p219 CR Yorks469,dow

FIRTH,Ernest Hartley TCapt kia 1-7-16 13Y&L p158 CR France156

FIRTH,Fred TLt kia 24-8-18 12 att10WYorks p81 MR16

FIRTH,Harold Lt kia 9-10-17 6Yorks p90 CR Belgium 126

FIRTH,James William Lt 1-10-18 Norf &108RAF MR20

FIRTH,John Stanley 2Lt kia 9-10-17 2 att3RWar p64 MR30,3 att2Bn

FIRTH,Joseph Oliver 2Lt kia 18-11-17 4LNLancs p234 CR France364

FIRTH,Percy 2Lt dow 28-7-18 2Yorks att2/8WYorks p90 MR18

FIRTH,Richard Charles Dundas Lt ded 21-12-14 9SLancs p125 CR Scot921

FISCHEL,Claude Henry Capt kia 14-9-18 RAMC att7Leic p195 CR France398

FISCHER,Alexander William.MID TLt dow 12-5-16 8Dev p76 CR France67,2Lt

FISCHER,John Bosman Capt kia 7-8-15 10NStaffs att8LancF p157 MR4

FISH,Barrow Edmondson T2Lt kia 3-9-16 11RSuss p119 CR France339

FISH,Benjamin Leslie TLt dow 30-10-18 12 att18Mddx p146 CR France332

FISH,Frank Edward Capt kia 17-5-15 3 att2Yorks p90 CR France279,Francis

FISH,Jack T2Lt kia 22-7-16 10Worc p108 CR France744

FISH,John Leslie T2Lt kia 3-7-16 7Suff p78 CR France393

FISH,Robert John 2Lt kia 30-9-17 4Lincs p217 CR France1723,Lt

FISH,W.R.MC.Capt kld 2-6-18 GL &RAF p190

FISHBOURNE,Charles Edward TLtCol dow 6-10-16 1 Cmdg8NumbF p61 CR France145

FISHBOURNE,Charles Eustace Lt ded 10-6-15 RE p45 CR Wales619,Capt 6-10-15

FISHBOURNE,Derrick Haughton Gardiner 2Lt kia 6-5-17 RGA 99SB p39 CR France1182

FISHBOURNE,Morgan 2Lt drd 1-1-17 2Co LondYeo p204 CR Greece16,FISHBURNE

FISHER,Alexander McEwan T2Lt kia 24-4-17 10ScotRif p103 MR20

FISHER,Arthur James 2Lt kia 25-10-16 GL &21RFC 14Wing p2&190 CR France306

FISHER,Arthur Maxwell TCapt kia 12-10-17 RAMC p195 CR Belgium23,58FC

FISHER,Cecil Eric Haig 2Lt dow 24-7-15 RE 15FC p45 CR France254

FISHER,Charles Heath.MC.2Lt kia 14-10-18 4 att12ESurr p112 CR Belgium157

FISHER,Charles John.DCM.2Lt dow 28-7-17 2Nhampt p137 CR Lond14

FISHER,E.J.SubAssSurg3Cl 27-1-16 IMS CR Iraq6

FISHER,Edmund 2Lt kia 16-11-16 3 att8ELancs p110 CR France153,Eddie

FISHER,Edmund Montague Prinsep 2Lt ded 31-3-18 RFA 36DAC p28 CR Hamps30

FISHER,Edward Henry 2Lt kia 9-4-18 KEdwHorse p24 MR19

FISHER,Edward Humbert 2Lt kia 19-5-15 Yorks p90 MR22

FISHER,Eric Whitmore Capt ded 14-10-18 IARO att119Inf p276 MR65

FISHER,Frank Capt kia 13-9-14 RWKent p141 MR15

FISHER,Frank Maj kia 26-9-17 RE 470FC p209 CR Belgium10

FISHER,Geoffrey Herbert 2Lt dow 25-10-15 8N&D p233 CR France40

FISHER,George Kenneth Thompson Capt kia 3-9-17 1/4Norf p216 CR Palestine8

FISHER,George William 2Lt kia 18-11-17 1/4Suff C'Coy p217 CR Belgium125,17-11-17

FISHER,Harold.DSO.Capt kia 15-12-14 1Manch p154 CR France571

FISHER,Harold TLt dow 14-4-18 RE 184TC p45 CR France180

FISHER,Harry Laireate 2Lt kia 27-10-18 10DLI p160 CR Italy9,Laureate 12Bn

FISHER,Henry Bruges ALtCol kia 3-10-16 Wilts att12Y&L p153 CR France727

FISHER,Henry Mornington.MC.2Lt kia 31-10-18 RFA attY31TMB p28 CR Belgium143

FISHER,Herbert 2Lt kia 11-4-18 NumbF att1/5DLI p61 MR32

FISHER,Henry Brean Lt dow 24-7-16 9MGC Inf p182 CR France833

FISHER,Herbert Learoyd Hammond Lt kia 8-8-16 1/8Lpool attMGC p187&215 MR21

FISHER,Herbert George.DSO.ALtCol ded 29-7-19 RFA p261 CR Wales26

FISHER,Hubert Patrick T2Lt kia 9-7-16 9KSLI p144 CR France643

FISHER,Hugh Bell TLt dow PoW 23-11-17 2RMunstF p175 CR Belgium140

FISHER,James Capt ded 23-2-19 4Lancs CR Lancs40

FISHER,John 2Lt dow 17-4-18 1 att2/5Lincs p75 CR France285

FISHER,John ACapt ded 17-4-19 5BordR p270 CR Surrey2

FISHER,John Campbell.MID ACapt dow 6-5-17 6RScotF p94 CR France1182,Maj 1Bn

FISHER,John Hammond.MC.2Lt dow 7-9-18 6WYorks att2/4YLI p218 CR France85

FISHER,John Hylton 2Lt kia 29-11-16 1/5WRid p227 CR France281

FISHER,John Joseph T2Lt dow 2-5-16 1NStaffs p157 CR France285

FISHER,John Wilfred.DSO.TCapt dow 8-7-16 10N&D p134 CR France833

FISHER,Leslie Benito TLt kia 14-8-15 12KRRC p150

FISHER,Mortimer Capt kia 20-9-14 1WYorks p81 MR15

FISHER,Norman Hill Lt dow 16-4-17 2/4LNLancs p234 CR France769

FISHER,O.G.Chap4Cl 4-11-20 CR Iraq8

FISHER,Percy Harold T2Lt dow 4-7-16 10RSuss attMGC p182&119 CR France203

FISHER,Percy Watkins.DCM.2Lt kia 12-9-16 22RFus p67 CR France1326,Watkiss

FISHER,Raymond Wadhams TCapt kia 13-9-16 NumbF p61 CR Greece6

FISHER,Robert 2Lt kia 14-11-16 3SStaffs att10Y&L p122 MR21

FISHER,Thomas Edward Coney Lt kia 1-7-16 1ELancs p110 MR21

FISHER,Wilfred T2Lt kia 9-5-15 1LNLancs p135 CR France80

FISHER,Wilfrid Frederick 2Lt kia 24-7-17 3 att12RSuss p119 MR29

FISHER,William Horace Arthur 2Lt kia 4-10-17 1/6RWar p64 MR30

FISHER,William Sefton Capt kia 23-3-18 4 att6Nhampt p234 MR27

FISHER-BROWN,Charles George Cranleigh.MID2Lt kia 10-8-15 5Wilts p153 MR4

FISHER-BROWN,Douglas Gordon 2Lt dow 28-6-18 RGA 2ArmyA/ASect p39

FISHER-BROWN,Kenneth Cuthbert 2Lt kia 13-11-16 1/7WRid p227 CR France281

FISHER-ROWE,Laurence Rowe LtCol dow 12-3-15 1GrenGds p50 CR France768,13-3-15

FISHER-SMITH,Alan Archibald Lt kia 1-8-17 CldGds att1GdsBdeMGC p53 CR Belgium106

FISHLOCK,Albert Ernest T2Lt dow 7-9-18 10Hamps p120 CR Greece6

FISKE,Dudley Lt dow 22-8-18 C86RFA p28 CR France119

FISKE,Harold Lt kia 20-12-16 GL &18RFC p2&190,ded CR France518

FISON,Frank Henry Lt kia 19-7-16 6Norf p217 CR France567,2/6Glouc

FISON,James Frederick Lorimer.MC.MIDx2 LtTCapt dow 2-11-17 6Suff p218 CR Suff133,4Bn

FITCH,Alfred Cyril T2Lt kia 2-4-17 2RWSurr p55 CR France1489

FITCH,Aubrey Sugden 2Lt kia 26-3-17 4RSuss p228 MR34

FITCH,Cecil Alexander Gordon 2Lt dow 18-9-18 RGA 260SB p39 CR France327

FITCH,Christopher John TLt kia 16-2-16 6Dors p124 CR Belgium131,Jack

FITCH,Conrad William TLt kia 3-7-16 6RWSurr p55 CR France251

FITCH,Douglas 2Lt kia 16-10-17 162RFA p28 CR Belgium21

FITCH,Louis Cifford.MM.T2Lt kia 28-7-18 1RFus p67 CR France161

FITCH,Matthew Craig.MC.Lt ded 9-12-18 RScots att2/10Bn p54 MR70 &CR Europe179,Capt

FITCH,Philip Henry Burt.MC.Lt kia 23-7-17 D177RFA p207 CR Belgium6

FITCH,W.S.Cdr 13-1-18 IA MiscList MR65

FITCH,Walter Frederick.MC.TCapt ded 1-11-18 GL 7Suff attBrMilMission p190 CR USA234

FITCH-JONES,Owen Edward TLt kia 13-5-17 13/275RFA p28 CR Belgium4

FITNESS,William John TLt ded 22-11-16 RAOC p198 CR Greece9

FITT,Charles William TLt kia 19-5-17 207MGC Inf p182 CR Belgium136

FITT,Norman Eric Lloyd 2Lt ded PoW 26-6-17 RIrF p171 MR20

FITTON,Hugh Gregory.CB.DSO.ADC.TBrigGen dow 20-1-16 Staff Cmdg101InfBde p1 CR Belgium11

FITTON,Norman 2Lt kia 14-11-16 7 att22RFus p67 MR21

FITTON,W.2Lt.MM.kldacc 19-8-18 1/2LancF &6RAF p92 CR France1525

FITTON,Walter Verdi 2Lt dow 29-9-16 2RFA p208 CR France74

FITZ-GIBBON,John Augustus TMaj ded 25-1-16 RGA p39

FITZBROWN,Eric 2Lt 1-7-16 18Lpool MR21

FITZBROWN,Geoffrey T2Lt dow 24-10-16 23DLI p160 CR France105

FITZCLARENCE,Augustus Arthur Cornwallis.MID Capt kia 28-6-15 2RFus p67 MR4

FITZCLARENCE,Charles.VC.BrigGen kia 12-11-14 Staff p1 MR29,IrGds

FITZE,Gerald Gadsden Lt kia 25-11-14 RHA p28 MR29,28/31-10-14

FITZGERALD,Alfred Edward TLtCol dow 13-7-16 ESurr att15DLI p112 CR Bucks50

FITZGERALD,Gerald 2Lt kia 1-7-16 26NumbF C'Coy p61 CR France150,Lt

FITZGERALD,Gerald Hugh Capt kia 13-9-14 4DragGds p21 CR France1339

FITZGERALD,Gerald Thomas TCapt kia 3-12-15 15DLI p160 CR France1140,30-12-15

FITZGERALD,Herbert 2Lt kia 9-4-18 6Lpool p215 CR France98,Lt

FITZGERALD,John Desmond Lt drd 10-10-18 4SLancs p230 MR40

FITZGERALD,Loftus de Vallentin MajALtCol kia 16-9-18 RIrF att2RInniskF p171 CR France285

FITZGERALD,Lord Desmond Maj&Adjt ded 3-3-16 1IrGds p52 CR France8

FITZGERALD,Maurice Robert Lt ded PoW 19-4-18 2IrGds p52 CR Belgium409

FITZGERALD,Oswald Arthur Gerald.CMG.LtCol drd 5-6-16 IA 18Lancers &Staff CR Sussex144

FITZGERALD,Robert William T2Lt dow 4-10-18 10RDubF p176 CR France1184

FITZGERALD,Roy James.MC.MID Lt kia 1-7-18 12Glouc att35RAF p106 CR France71

FITZGERALD,Thomas David T2Lt kia 30-7-16 8Glouc p106 MR21

FITZGERALD,William Wilks T2Lt kia 27-7-17 GL &25RFC p7

FITZGIBBON,Brian Normanby.MID TLt kia 21-8-16 6RIrReg p89 CR France178

FITZGIBBON,G.J.LtTCapt kia 20-11-17 10RDubF p176 CR France616

FITZGIBBON,John Augustus Maj 26-1-16 RGA CR Lond9

FITZGIBBON,Harold T2Lt kia 27-3-18 12RFC p16 CR France62

FITZGIBBON,John.MC.Chap3Cl kia 18-9-18 RAChDept att17FA p199 CR France835

FITZGIBBON,Michael Joseph TLt kia 15-8-15 7RDubF p176 MR4

FITZ GIBBON,Richard Apjohn.MID Lt dow 4-2-15 IA 128Pnrs p276 CR Egypt8

FITZHERBERT,Gilbert Clare.MC.Lt kia 18-9-18 2Y&L p158 MR16

FITZHERBERT,Harold Lancelot TLt kia 30-6-16 13RSuss p119 CR France924

FITZHERBERT,Wyndham Waterhouse Capt kia 7-7-17 13RSuss att55RFC p7&119 MR20

FITZHERBERT-BROCKHOLES,Thomas Joseph Capt&Adjt dow 14-3-15 2RB p178 CR France768

FITZHUGH,Godfrey Capt kia 31-10-17 MontgomeryYeo p204 CR Palestine1,25RWFus

FITZHUGH,Harold T2Lt kia 31-7-17 8ELancs p110 MR29

FITZMAURICE,Archibald Hamilton Lt kia 12-3-18 RFC p16 MR20

FITZMAURICE,John Herbert 2Lt kia 25-3-18 6KSLI p144 MR27

FITZMAURICE,Lindsay TLtAcapt kia 18-11-16 8SomLI p79 CR France339

FITZMAURICE,Maurice Alexander Ross Geraldine Lt kia 5-8-15 RE 21FC S&M p45 CR France924,6-8-15

FITZPATRICK,Dudley Thomas Francis Lt kia 27-10-14 3 att2SStaffs p122 MR29

FITZPATRICK,Gabriel Roy Capt kia 14-9-14 3WelshR p126 MR15

FITZPATRICK,John Joseph 2Lt kia 30-7-16 2 att8RMunstF p175 CR France223,29-7-16

FITZPATRICK,Thomas Gordon.MID TCapt kia 6-9-16 8RIrF p171 CR France1890

FITZROY,Michael Algernon 2Lt kia 15-4-15 4SfthH D'Coy p241 CR France924,Capt 17-4-15

FITZSIMONS,Terence 2Lt kia 4-4-16 3 att7RSuss p119 MR19

FITZWILLIAMS,John Kenrick Lloyd.MC.Maj kia 30-8-18 Z5A'RFA p28 CR France421,25ArmyBde

FLACK,Wilfred George.MC&Bar.Lt dow 7-9-17 1RFus p67 CR France40

FLACK,William Arthur.DCM.2Lt dow 19-12-15 RGA 27TMB p39 CR France102

FLAGG,Allston TCapt kia 26/27-9-15 10Norf att1/58Rifs p73&276,Alston 25-9-15 CR France705

FLAHERTY,John Ernest T2Lt ded 12-7-18 6Mddx p146

FLANAGAN,George Anton T2Lt kia 30-6-18 6RWSurr p55 MR27

FLANAGAN,Joseph Samuel Lt kia 23-8-18 20Lond p251 CR France1170,22-8-18

FLANEGAN,Lionel Christopher TLt kia 20-11-17 Ess &TankCps p188&264,Flanagan MR17

FLANIGAN,Edmund Hughes Lt ded 17-6-16 RAMC 102FA p195 CR Ireland105

FLATAU,A.Theodore TCapt kia 1-7-16 8ESurr p112 CR France513

FLATT,Harry T2Lt kia 28-11-17 6Y&L C'Coy p158 CR France551

FLAVELL,Alfred Victor 2Lt ded 4-5-18 Worc &RAF p264

FLAXMAN,Alfred Edward 2Lt kia 1-7-16 1/6SStaffs p229 MR21

FLAXMAN,Walter James 2Lt ded 27-5-17 RASC attS&TCps p192 MR38

FLECKNOE,Percy James Deane Lt dow 25-11-17 64RFA p28 CR Belgium3

FLEET,Aylmer Louis Elliot.MC.CaptAMaj kia 10-9-18 B56RFA p28 CR France433

FLEET,Leonard T2Lt kld 27-10-17 GL &RFC p7 CR Lancs33,Leanord

FLEET,Vernon Jesse Lt dow 10-9-18 RFA att3SpCoy RE CR Berks125

FLEET,William Alexander 2Lt kia 18-5-18 1GrenGds 3'Coy p50 CR France120

FLEET,William Henry.MC.2Lt dow 19-4-16 6BlkW p231

FLEETWOOD,Cyril Percy 2Lt dow PoW 12-7-16 9Lond p248 CR France716,Lt

FLEMING,A.2Lt dow 29-4-18 GL &RAF p190

FLEMING,Alfred.MC.T2Lt dow 1-7-18 27MGC Inf p182 CR France134

FLEMING,Charles Christie.DSO.Col dow 24-12-17 RAMC ADMS51DivStaff p195 CR France512

FLEMING,Charles Elphinstone Maj ded 2-3-15 RAMC p195 CR Scot812

FLEMING,Ernest Cole.MC.MID Maj kia 18-7-17 C121RFA p28 CR Belgium23

FLEMING,Ernest William T2Lt kia 4-11-18 13KRRC p150 CR France1480

FLEMING,Frank 2Lt kia 11-4-18 4SfthH p241 MR30

FLEMING,Frederick Nelson 2Lt ded 22-6-18 RGA 321SB p39 CR Germany3

FLEMING,Frederick William Oswald 2Lt dow 20-12-15 4WRid p227 CR Belgium11

FLEMING,Geoffrey Montagu Mason Lt kia 16-6-15 RAMC att2Beds p195 CR France279

FLEMING,George TLt dow 18-7-16 7 att1RScotF p94 CR France51

FLEMING,George 2Lt kia 29-5-18 3 att2ScotRif p103 CR France924

FLEMING,George Eric Pearce Lt 1-6-18 IARO att3/39GarwhalRif CR Pakistan50A

FLEMING,Harold Winning 2Lt kia 6-10-17 1/2Beds p85 MR30,5-10-17 1Bn

FLEMING,Henry Roland 2Lt kld 24-11-14 RFC p1 CR Wilts1

FLEMING,Hugh Lt kia 30-9-18 5HLI p240 CR Belgium116

FLEMING,Hugh Joseph T2Lt kia 24-8-16 7 att6Dors p124 CR France342

FLEMING,Ian Grant.MC.MID Capt kia 31-7-17 6GordH p242 CR Belgium27

FLEMING,James.MC.Lt kia 21-3-17 11RScots p54 CR France1182

FLEMING,James Hamilton Capt kia 13-10-15 1/5NStaffs p237 CR France258

FLEMING,James Sword T2Lt dow 29-9-17 1GordH p166 CR France40

FLEMING,James Wellington 2Lt kia 12-7-17 29RFC p7 MR20

FLEMING,John Allister 2Lt dow 22-7-16 1RWKent p141 MR21

FLEMING,John Joseph.MID TCapt kia 13-10-17 26NumbF p61 MR30

FLEMING,Joseph 2Lt kia 15-9-16 6HLI p240 CR France387

FLEMING,Malcolm James Henderson Lt dow 14-7-15 5A&SH p243 MR4

FLEMING,Reginald Henry T2Lt kia 11-7-16 15RWFus p97 MR21

FLEMING,Robert Alexander 2Lt dow 31-7-16 1/7BlkW p231 CR France833

FLEMING,Robert John T2Lt kld 29-1-18 RFC p16 CR Scot237

FLEMING,Richard Thomas Cyril Willis 2Lt dow 4-8-16 RH&FA p208

FLEMING,Thomas.MID T2Lt dow 20-10-18 RGA 71Bty21Bde p39 CR France725

FLEMING,Valentine.DSO.Maj kia 20-5-17 OxfYeo p205 CR France1495

FLEMING,Wilfrid Allan.MC.Capt kia 10-8-17 1Dev &56RFC p7&76 CR Belgium140

FLEMING,William James Calbard Capt ded 2-12-18 6GordH p270 CR Scot835

FLEMMING,Douglas Sidney T2Lt dow 1-6-17 9RLancs p58 CR Greece7

FLEMMING,Herbert Otto Capt dow 7-5-15 9Lond p247 CR Lond12

FLENLEY,Edmund Bernard 2Lt kia 9-4-17 5 att13Lpool p215 CR France581

FLESHER,Frederick Arthur Lt dow 27-9-16 6RWar p214 CR Yorks361

FLETCHER,Amiraux Silver.MID 2Lt kia 7-8-15 IARO att1/5GurkhaRif CR Gallipoli17

FLETCHER,Arnold Lockhart TLt dow 30-4-17 4Leinst att193MGC p174&182 CR France145

FLETCHER,Arthur TCapt ded 14-2-18 2GarBnRIrF attGarBnLpool p171 CR Greece3

FLETCHER,Arthur Frederick T2Lt kia 12-5-18 Nhampt att6Bn p137 CR France177

FLETCHER,Arthur Henry Felix 2Lt kld 22-5-17 13Huss &RFC p7&22,11Bn CR Surrey2

FLETCHER,Arthur Joseph T2Lt kia 23-4-17 13RFus p67 MR20

FLETCHER,Arthur Philip T2Lt kia 1-10-15 RE p45 CR Belgium132

FLETCHER,Arthur Stanley T2Lt kia 11-7-16 11SWBord p100 MR21

FLETCHER,Charles Alexander 2Lt kld 20-10-18 Worc &RAF p264

FLETCHER,C.W.Maj&QM 19-4-17 Ex ESuss CR Hamps7

FLETCHER,Donald Lockhart 2Lt ded 28-4-17 4 att6Leinst p174 CR Greece3,dow

FLETCHER,Edward Stewart 2Lt kia 3-5-17 6WYorks p218 MR20

FLETCHER,Eric Graham Lt kia 3-7-16 SLancs att2Bn p125 CR France402

FLETCHER,Ernest 2Lt kia 15-9-16 15Lond p249 CR France402

FLETCHER,Franklyn Haward Capt ded 5-6-18 RDC CR Sussex4

FLETCHER,Gareth Hamilton 2Lt kia 25-1-15 GrenGds SR p50

FLETCHER,George Herbert 2Lt kia 2-6-17 WYorks &4RFC p7&81 MR20

FLETCHER,George William 2Lt dow 9-8-16 3 att1RInniskF p104 CR Belgium11

FLETCHER,Gilbert Harding Capt kia 1-7-16 5NStaffs p237 CR France281

FLETCHER,Guy Verney Lt ded 24-4-16 RAMC att19DAC p195 CR France31

FLETCHER,Henry Mungles 2Lt kia 7-6-17 RFA attY30TMB p28 CR Belgium127

FLETCHER,Herbert Philips.DSO.Maj ded 3-8-16 1Co of LondYeo attRFC p18&204 CR Lond12,kld

FLETCHER,Herman T2Lt kia 13-11-16 7LNLancs p135 MR21

FLETCHER,Horace William 2LtTLt dow 26-3-17 9 att7RWFus p97 MR34

FLETCHER,Jack Haslip 2Lt kia 20-10-18 2ScotsGds p52 CR France320

FLETCHER,John T2Lt kia 28-9-18 LNLancs att2/4Bn p135 CR France256

FLETCHER,John Harwood Cash 2Lt kia 1-7-16 1/7N&D p233 MR21

FLETCHER,John Holland Ballett Lt dow 13-5-15 7Lond p247 CR France80

FLETCHER,Joseph Harold TCapt kia 25-11-17 RWFus att19Bn p97 MR17

FLETCHER,Leslie Morley 2Lt kld 5-7-17 GL &RFC p7 CR War67

FLETCHER,Malcolm 2Lt dow 8-9-17 9 att17HLI p240 CR France1361

FLETCHER,Maurice.MC.TCapt dow 9-9-16 9RMunstF C'Coy p175 CR France197

FLETCHER,Noel William Scott 2Lt dow 7-3-17 11DLI p160 CR France374

FLETCHER,Reginald William 2Lt kia 31-10-14 118/26RFA p28 MR29

FLETCHER,Robert Henry TLt kia 27-7-16 14 att17RFus p67 MR21

FLETCHER,Robert Ronald Radcliffe Lt ded 29-10-19 3 att6SLancs p264 MR65

FLETCHER,Roland Sackville Capt kia 1-11-14 1NumbF p61 MR29

FLETCHER,Thomas May.MC.Lt kia 1-8-17 20DLI p254&258 MR29

FLETCHER,Thomas Murray Kilpin T2Lt kia 23-4-17 1Beds p85 MR20,Kelpin

FLETCHER,Tom Walter 2Lt kia 26-9-17 N&D att2/5Bn p134 MR30

FLETCHER,Walter George.MIDx2 2Lt kia 20-3-17 2RWFus B'Coy p97 CR France684

FLETCHER,William Alfred Littledale.DSO.MIDx2 LtCol ded 14-2-19 Res 2/6Lpool p270 CR Lancs181,dow

FLETCHER,William George T2Lt kia 3-7-16 11NStaffs att2SLancs p157 MR21

FLETCHER,William Guy T2Lt dow 14-10-16 11SLancs p125 CR Kent129

FLETCHER,William Henry Anthony 2Lt ded 2-7-16 11 att7NStaffs p157 CR Iraq6

FLETT,Arthur David Lt kia 9-4-17 7RScots p211 CR France644,16Bn

FLETT,Frederick T2Lt kld 9-3-18 1SfthH p164 CR Egypt8,accded

FLETT,John Edmund Lt kia 15-11-15 7RScots p211 CR Gallipoli3

FLETT,William Henry.MC.Lt 19-4-16 6BlkW CR France95

FLEWITT,Edward Luke 2Lt kia 7-1-18 1/7N&D p233 CR France115,Lake

FLEXEN,Harold Augustus T2Lt dow 29-7-16 1Mddx p146 CR Mddx48

FLIN,Richard Valentine 2Lt kia 8-8-18 Ess att10Bn p131 CR France141

FLINDT,Leighton Harold Richard Edward 2Lt dow 4-10-16 3NStaffs att8Leic p157 CR France145

FLINN,Cyril Herbert 2Lt kia 14-4-17 1Ess p131 MR20

FLINN,Edgar Wormald 2Lt kia 13-11-16 34RFA &RFC p2&28 MR21

FLINN,Philip Woolven Lt kia 20-9-17 5SLancs p230

FLINT,Charles William T2Lt kia 1-7-16 26NumbF p61 MR21

FLINT,Harvey Priestman.MC.2Lt kia 27-5-18 9 att8Leic p87 MR18

FLINT,Ralph Stacey.MSM.MIDx3 2Lt kia 27-3-18 6RWSurr p55 MR27

FLINT,Robert Bradford.DSO.Lt dow 23-1-15 RE p45 CR Belgium98

FLINT,Wilfred Ernest 2Lt kia 1-7-16 1/7N&D p233 CR France281

FLINT,William Henry Maj ded 2-11-17 RAMC Res p270 CR Hereford110

FLINTOFF,A.Sister 9-11-18 TFNS att3GH CR Lond1

FLINTOFF,Randolph Alex TLt kia 25-6-16 10EYorks p84 CR France5,24-6-16

FLITCROFT,Joseph 2Lt ded 2-11-18 RGA p39&257 CR Lancs438

FLITCROFT,S.2Lt ded 17-2-19 SLancsF CR Lancs256

FLOOD,Dundas Charles TLt ded 27-10-18 8Leinst p174&263,8Leic CR Lond14,8Leic

FLOOD,Robert Samuel.MC.TCapt kia 5-12-17 9RIrF p171 CR France711

FLORY,Percival James T2Lt kia 22-8-18 4Beds p85 CR France745

FLORY,Robert James.MC.2Lt kia 28-6-17 2HAC p206 CR France614

FLORY,William Henry 2Lt kia 21-3-18 2/4 O&BLI p231 MR27

FLOWER,Alfred Chegwin Lt kia 25-9-16 4GrenGds SR p50 CR France374

FLOWER,Frederick Godfrey T2Lt kia 18-12-17 GL &21RFC p7 CR Belgium16

FLOWER,H.J.DSO.Maj ded 31-1-19 Ex KRRC p265

FLOWER,Leopold Arthur Lacon Capt kia 7-10-16 7Lond p247 CR France385

FLOWER,Oswald Swift TLtCol dow 12-7-16 13RWFus p97 CR France633

FLOWER,Victor Augustine.DSO.Maj kia 15-8-17 13Lond p249 CR Belgium115,LtCol

FLOWER,Wilfred Joseph 2Lt dow 18-8-17 1/7Worc p226 CR Belgium18

FLOWERS,Herbert T2Lt kia 1-9-16 8RWKent p141 CR France402

FLOWERS,Humphrey French Lt kia 14-10-18 RFA att82RAF p207 CR Belgium157

FLOWERS,John Arthur T2Lt kia 1-9-16 10 att7RSuss p119 MR20

FLOWERS,William Henry Field T2Lt dow 15-4-18 1/5Y&L p158 CR France324

FLOYD,Hayden T2Lt dow 11-7-16 PoW GL &11RFC p2&190 CR France927

FLOYD,Henry Murrell Capt kia 28-6-15 2RDubF p176 CR Gallipoli6

FLOYD,Howard Grimley T2Lt kia 9-4-18 1/5Dev p76 CR Palestine9

FLUCK,Harold Graham T2Lt dow 3-11-17 6Mddx att1/4Nhampt p146 CR palestine1,2/10Bn

FLUKE,Arthur Charles.MID 2Lt kia 10-1-15 116/26RFA p28 MR22

FLUKE,Samuel TLtACapt kia 16-8-17 11RInniskF p104 MR30

FLUX,George Belben Capt ded 18-3-18 RAMC p267

FLUX,Leonard Taylor T2Lt kia 1-11-16 12 att2Worc p108 MR21

FLUX,L.G.T2Lt ded 18-6-18 13TankCps p188 CR Hamps41,16-6-18

FLYNN,George Axen Wallace T2Lt kia 25-9-15 10ScotRif p103 MR19

FLYNN,Horace Justice Dillon Capt bombAcc 23-10-17 IARO att1/101Gren p276 CR Egypt8

FLYNN,John Hoskins T2Lt kia 30-9-17 GL &60RFC p7 CR France134

FLYNN,Joseph Michael T2Lt dow 11-5-18 25NumbF p61

FLYNN,Percy 2Lt kia 10-11-17 5 att2RMunstF p175 MR30

FLYNN,Thomas Lt&QM ded 23-7-18 LabCps p266 CR Yorks294

FOALE,William Ernest Lt ded 1-5-19 RGA A/ABty CR Lond8

FOCKEN,Leslie Charles 2Lt kia 26-10-16 15RFC p2 CR France156 see FAWKNER,L.C.

FODEN,Frank Joseph 2Lt kia 9-9-16 1/4Lond p246 MR21

FOGARTY,Gerald Joseph Lt kia 26-8-17 3RIrReg &9RFC p7&89 CR Belgium18

FOGARTY,William Joseph Capt kia 21-3-18 SIrHorse att7RIrReg p24 MR27

FOGERTY,John Frederick Cullinan Lt kia 25-9-17 RE 227FC p45 CR Belgium124

FOGERTY,William Perrott Lt ded 19-10-19 IA 58att57Rif p276 CR Egypt1,57att58Rif

FOGG,Thomas Holt TLt kia 26-3-18 RE 288ArmyTrpsCo p45 CR France526

FOGGIN,G.W.2Lt 14-7-18 NthCycBn att48RAF CR France71

FOGGO,Watson Henry TLt ded 20-5-18 5LancF p92 CR Ches3

FOISTER,Percy Reuben.DCM.2Lt kia 13-1-16 2Leic B'Coy p87 MR38

FOIZEY,Harold Egbert TLt kia 1-7-16 18WYorks p81 CR France156

FOLEY,Alfred Montague 2Lt kia 9-9-16 11 att2RSuss p119 CR France345,dow 3-8-16

FOLEY,F.Y.Capt&QM 12-5-18 RASC attRAF CR Hamps64

FOLEY,Geoffrey Robert T2Lt dow 17-5-17 7SomLI p79 CR France95,Lt

FOLEY,John TCapt kia 1-7-16 25NumbF p61 MR21

FOLEY,Michael Alphonsus Lt ded 25-4-19 6Leinst p174 CR Egypt9

FOLEY,Michael James Aloysius Capt kia 10-8-15 10Mddx p236 MR4

FOLEY,Thomas Algernon Fitzgerald Lt kia 25-10-14 Norf p73 MR22

FOLEY,Thomas William Winspear Lt kia 9-9-16 3 att7Leinst p174 MR21

FOLEY,William Alfred LtACapt dow 1-11-17 RIrF p171 CR France398

FOLINGSBY,Thomas Grueber 2Lt dow 23-6-17 7RFA p208 CR France480,22-6-16

FOLJAMBE,Hubert Francis Fitzwilliam Brabazon Maj kia 14-9-14 2KRRC p150 MR15

FOLJAMBE,Josceline Charles William Saville.Hon.MIDx3 CaptBtMaj kia 6-4-16 1 O&BLI p130 MR38

FOLKER,Edgar Reginald 2Lt kia 20-2-15 3Y&L p158 MR29

FOLLETT,George 2Lt kia 19-9-18 6RB att1/10Lond p178 CR Palestine9

FOLLETT,Gilbert Burrell Spencer,DSO.MVO BtLtColTBrigGen kia 27-9-18 CldGds 3GdsBdeHQ p51 CR France756

FOLLIOTT,Charles Russell Hastings Lt kia 10-3-18 RFC p15 CR France525,FFOLLIOTT

FOLLIOTT,John 2Lt kia 19-9-18 2DLI p160 CR France835

FOLLIS,Thomas 2Lt dow 24-2-17 7DCLI p114 CR France105

FOLLIT,Charles Albert Roy.DSO.MC.TCapt dow 20-8-16 10RWFus p97 CR France23

FOLLIT,John Fraser Lt ded 21-10-18 IARO att29Lancers p276 CR Syria2

FOLLIT,Reginald William 2Lt dow 28-4-17 GL &13RFC p7 MR20

FOOKS,Edward Luckham 2Lt kia 31-10-16 129RFA p28 MR37

FOORD,Charlton Willoughby Hougham T2Lt dow 19-12-16 60MGC p182 CR France67

FOORD,George Howard T2Lt dow 13-10-15 RASC 176Depot p192 CR Gallipoli1,Lt

FOORD-KELCEY,John Mordaunt 2Lt kia 1-7-16 2RWSurr p55 CR France397

FOORD-KELCEY,William Beverly.MC.Lt kia 24-9-18 C104RFA p207 CR France446

FOOT,David Victor T2Lt kldacc 4-5-17 GL &RFC p7 CR Scot721

FOOT,Douglas Eric 2Lt kia 13-10-15 8RBerks p139 MR19

FOOT,James Stanley Capt kia 30-7-16 1/7WelchR att2/4Glouc p230 CR France1887

FOOT,Victor Edward 2Lt ded 25-11-18 1WelshGds p53 CR France289

FOOT,William John Hawken Lt ded 28-10-19 IARO att109Inf p276 MR69

FOOTE,Trevor Maudsley AMaj kia 10-7-17 8LNLancs p135 CR Belgium10

FOOTNER,Arthur Henry T2Lt kia 6-8-15 1Ess p131 MR4

FOOTNER,Harry Erlegh TCapt kia 1-8-16 RGA 35HB p39 CR France515

FOOTT,Alexander Boyd Capt ded 21-7-18 RAMC att49FA p195 CR Palestine3

FORAN,Edward Cornelius 2Lt kia 28-12-17 5RMunstF p175 CR Palestine3

FORBES,A.J.Lt kia 21-10-17 3KAR attLovatScouts

FORBES Albert.MID Capt kia 30-8-18 8Manch p236 CR France308

FORBES,Alec.MID Capt kia 3-9-16 2RWar p64 CR France402

FORBES,Alexander 2LtACapt dow 22-3-18 HLI att17Bn p162 CR France512

FORBES,Alexander Bruce 2Lt dow 29-10-18 1/88A&SH p243 CR France241

FORBES,Alexander Stewart TLt dow 17-8-16 10SfthH att181MGC p182 CR France95

FORBES,Arthur Maj kia 17-4-16 IA 128Pnrs p276 MR38

FORBES,Arthur T2Lt kia 27-9-17 RE 11FC p45 CR Belgium19

FORBES,Arthur John Lt kia 21-10-17 1LovatScouts att1/3KAR p204&268 CR EAfrica11 &CR Tanzania1

FORBES,Beatrice Georgina Frederica SNurse 12-5-18 TFNS CR War7

FORBES,Douglas Tulloch 2Lt dow 17-1-16 17Lond p250 CR France201

FORBES,Donald Keith Lt kia 15-2-15 Suff p78 MR29

FORBES,Duncan T2Lt kia 28-3-18 13RScots p54 MR20

FORBES,Fergus George Arthur.Hon.Capt dow PoW 23-8-14 RIrReg p89 CR Belgium242

FORBES,Fergus Robert TLt kia 25-9-15 RE p45 MR19

FORBES,George Francis Reginald.MID LtCol dow 17-3-15 RIrReg p89 MR29 &CR France284

FORBES,Gordon Stewart Drummond.CMG.DSO.Maj dow 21-7-15 7KOSB p101 CR France109

FORBES,Gordon William 2Lt ded PoW 18-10-17 24RFC p7 CR Belgium132,kia

FORBES,Harry Seymour Capt ded 3-11-18 2/1StaffsYeo p205 CR France40

FORBES,Henry James 2Lt kia 18-8-18 3 att1KOSB p101

FORBES,Hunter Capt kia 6-4-16 IA 51Sikhs p276 MR38

FORBES,James T2Lt kia 12-12-15 RE 67FC p45 CR Gallipoli27

FORBES,Joel Scott Lt kia 1-4-17 RGA 78SB p209 CR France518

FORBES,John Donald T2Lt dow 29-9-15 10LancF p92 CR Belgium11

FORBES,Kenneth 2Lt kia 10-2-15 5Lond p246 CR Belgium136

FORBES,Lawrence Lt dow 9-7-17 5Lond p246 CR Lond12

FORBES,Leonard Noel Lt kia 19-9-18 6Ess p232 CR France369

FORBES,Leslie Alexander 2Lt kia 27-5-17 4 att1ScotRif p103 CR France568

FORBES Muirton Warrand Lt kia 24-5-18 2AustInf CR France28

FORBES,Noel Edmund 2Lt dow 12-5-15 20RFA p28 CR France80,Lt

FORBES,Robert Struthers 2Lt kia 24-4-17 8A&SH p243 CR France415

FORBES,William Alexander Stanhope 2Lt kia 3-9-17 3DCLI p114 CR France294

FORBES,William Guthrie.MC.Maj dow 26-9-18 RGA 135HB p209 CR France278

FORBES-MENZIES,Alastair.DSO.Capt 4-5-18 17RFus CR France924

FORBES-ROBERTSON,Kenneth Capt kia 8-11-14 1 att2SfthH p164 MR32,7-11-14

FORBES-ROSS,Ralph Morison 2Lt 20-2-15 2Lancs MR29

FORBES-SEMPHILL,Robert Abercromby.Hon.Lt dow 2-6-15 5GordH p242 CR France727,kia

FORD,A.2Lt kia 9-5-15 RFus p67 MR29

FORD,Alfred Murnie 2Lt dow 28-7-18 8SfthH p164 MR18,Marnie

FORD,Alfred Winn.MC.2Lt kia 18-9-18 45/42RFA p28 CR France530

FORD,Arthur Llewelyn T2Lt kia 27-9-15 12Lpool p71 CR France525

FORD,A.V Maj 13-12-18 RAMC CR Hamps 217

FORD,Cecil George 2Lt drd 10-10-18 NorfYeo p204 MR40

FORD,Charles Bell Capt kia 30-9-19 IA 103MahrattaLI att1/7GurkhaRif p276 MR38

FORD,Clement Charles LtTCapt kia 2-7-16 1SomLI p79 CR France643

FORD,Clement William 2Lt kia 31-7-17 5RLancs p213 CR Belgium125

FORD,David Milne 2Lt dow 3-11-18 7ScotRif p224 CR France332

FORD,E.G.Capt 7-10-15 RAMC CR War96

FORD,Francis William.MC.2LtACapt kia 26-9-17 1Camb p244 MR30

FORD,Frank Stephen.MID Capt&QM ded 24-3-18 1Ess p131 CR France64

FORD,Frederick Austin 2Lt kia 27-8-18 RE DivSigCo p45 CR France927

FORD,Herbert Alfred.MC.2Lt kia 11-8-18 1Dors p124 MR16

FORD,Herbert Walter 2Lt kia 10-8-17 5RWSurr p212 MR29

FORD,James Ernest T2LtACapt kia 4-10-17 1KOSB p101 MR30

FORD,John T2Lt ded 16-6-16 25RFus p67 CR EAfrica13

FORD,John Ballard Berkley Capt dow 16-2-17 2 att7RWKent p141 CR France177

FORD,Kenneth George Haslam TLt dow 1-12-15 11Ches p96 CR France285

FORD,Lawton Stephen 2Lt kia 1-7-16 2RWSurr p55 MR21

FORD,N.2Lt kld 5-4-18 RE &RAF p45

FORD,Norman Stanley.MC.2Lt kld 19-7-18 11RWSurr &RAF p55 CR Wilts116

FORD,Reginald James TCapt kia 2-7-16 17Manch p154 CR France397,1-7-16

FORD,Richard 2Lt kia 3-2-17 C177RFA p28 CR Belgium10,3-8-17

FORD,Richard Jellard.MC.Capt kia 9-5-15 1Worc p108 CR France566

FORD,Richard Nagle.MC.CaptTMaj kia 6-1-18 11RFus p67 CR France62

FORD,Robert Englefield ACapt dow 3-4-17 5LNLancs att55TMB p234 CR Belgium11,1Bn

FORD,Robert Willoughby Lt ded 10-5-19 1/11Lond p270 CR Essex275,Capt

FORD,Royston Dearmer 2Lt kia 15-3-15 1RIrReg p89 MR29,Royster

FORDE,Henry Rawson.MC.LtACapt kia 2-12-17 2YLI D'Coy p143 CR Belgium125

FORDE,John Patrick 2Lt dow 16-8-17 9RDubF p176 MR30

FORDE,Kenneth Rowley Lt kia 23-7-15 3EKent p57 CR Belgium98

FORDE,Lionel Winnington 2Lt kia 8-6-18 Dors att6Bn p124 MR27

FORDER,Charles Frederick 2Lt kia 9-9-16 3 att2RSuss p119 CR France389

FORDHAM,Charles George Harry Lt&QM ded 29-10-17 GL p190 p266 CR Numb4,Henry George

FORDHAM,Reginald Frederick 2LtACapt kia 5-11-17 5Ess p232 CR France522

FORDYCE,Ernie Lawrence Dingwall Capt ded 5-12-16 IA 84Punjabis attAssamMilPolice p276 MR66

FORDYCE,James Dingwell T2Lt dow 27-9-15 A&SH p173

FOREMAN,Granado Walter 2Lt kia 14-7-17 SR 22RFC p7 CR France95

FOREMAN,Harry Clennell TLt kia 24-10-18 3 att9NumbF p61 CR France739

FOREMAN,John Eugene TLt ded 9-7-17 RAMC p195 CR Egypt1

FORESHEW,Henry John Hulbert 2Lt kia 15-4-17 6 att3RB p178 MR20

FORESTIER,Walter Waldorf.MC.TCapt kia 12-3-18 1 att1/4DCLI p114 CR Palestine9

FORGE,Arthur Fyfe T2Lt kia 4-10-17 8Lincs p75 MR30

FORGE,Henry Noel Francis 2Lt kia 20-11-17 5Beds p219 CR France667

FORGE,William Frederick 2Lt kia 1-7-16 2Mddx p146 MR21

FORMAN,Francis 2Lt kia 14-7-16 3Dors att7RWar p124 MR21

FORMAN,Moses TLt dow 11-4-17 8ELancs p110 CR France581

FORMBY,Myles Lonsdall Capt kia 26-10-14 Wilts p153 MR22

FORMBY,Richard William Lt kia 16-2-17 RE p45 CR France294

FORMBY,Thomas Hope Capt kia 13-10-16 1Camb p244 MR21

FORREST,Austin Lancelot T2Lt kia 3-9-16 11KRRC p150 MR21

FORREST,Bertram Thomas Alexander 2Lt kia 27-12-17 LanarkYeo att14BlkW p204 CR Palestine3

FORREST,Charles Evelyn.DSO.Maj kia 22-11-15 O&BLI p130 MR38

FORREST,Evelyn Arthur Atherley TLt ded 9-12-15 11 att7Glouc p106 CR Europe1

FORREST,Frank Capt dow 13-9-14 RAMC p195 CR France1107

FORREST,Henry Dacre T2Lt kia 7-4-18 WYorks att5WRid p81 CR France745

FORREST,James Capt ded 6-10-15 RWKent attASC p265 CR Lond7

FORREST,John William T2Lt kia 27-10-15 7SfthH p164 MR19,27-9-15

FORREST,Laurence Bernard 2Lt kia 20-5-17 16KRRC p150 MR20

FORREST,Percy Huskinson 2Lt dow 21-3-18 7Leinst att16MGC Inf p174&182 CR France1495,16Bn

FORREST,R.F.Lt 17-1-19 GL &1/1WAfrServBde CR WAfrica53

FORREST,Reginald Lt kia 27-9-16 5LNLancs p234 CR France744

FORREST,Thomas Lt ded 28-5-18 RAMC attPatialiaLancers p195 CR Iraq8

FORREST,Walter Torrie Maj kia 19-4-17 1/4KOSB p223 CR Palestine8

FORREST,William Robinson 2Lt kia 12-9-18 7DLI p239 CR France530

FORRESTER,Cecil James K.TLt ded 13-1-19 RASC attRAMC 28DivFA p254 CR Greece9

FORRESTER,Hugh Fielding 2Lt kia 22-4-16 2BlkW p128 MR38

FORRESTER,James.MC.T2Lt kia 8-5-18 13RB p178 MR27

FORRESTER,James David TCapt kia 15-11-16 RAMC attRNavyDiv p195 CR France701,14-11-16

FORRESTER,Patrick Hamilton T2Lt dow 11-10-15 8BlkW p128 CR Scot231

FORRESTER,Robert Edgar Capt kia 16-6-15 1BlkW p128 CR France720

FORRET,David James T2Lt dow 28-12-15 9 att1KOSB p101 CR Gallipoli1

FORRET,Robert Smith Leiper.MC.2Lt dow 15-5-18 7ScotRif p224 CR France102,5 6Bn

FORRETT,Percival Donald Capt kia 5-2-16 5NumbF p213 CR Belgium309

FORRYAN,Donald T2Lt kia 16-9-16 9YLI p143 MR21

FORSAITH,Hugh John 2Lt kia 18-8-17 55RFC p7 CR France285

FORSDIKE,Charles William 2Lt dow 13-6-18 129/42RFA p28 CR France10

FORSDIKE,Harold Brooke TLt kia 1-7-16 14Y&L p158 MR21

FORSELL,Alan Richard Lt kia 14-10-15 4Leic p219 MR19

FORSHALL,John Lt kia 12-4-18 C123RFA p28 CR France204

FORSHAW,George Leslie Fresson T2Lt kia 19-11-17 LancF att3/5Bn p92 CR Belgium115

FORSHAW,Joseph 2Lt dow PoW 4-10-18 1/5LNLancs p234 CR France612

FORSTER,Alfred Henry Lt dow 10-3-19 2Drags p21 CR Hamps43

FORSTER,Arthur Paul TCaptAMaj ded 24-9-18 47MGC p182 CR France88,25-9-18

FORSTER,Christopher Jack ALt kia 21-7-17 RFA att3RE 3CoSpecBde p28 CR Belgium11

FORSTER,Eric Murray 2Lt kia 3-5-17 3 att2Ess p131 CR France451

FORSTER,Francis Arthur 2Lt dow 6-4-19 RGA 443SB p39 CR Germany1,Lt

FORSTER,Frederick Albert Capt dow 23-8-15 RFus p67 CR Belgium242

FORSTER,Frederick Richard.MC.2Lt dow 3-10-17 159RFA p28 CR France145

FORSTER,George Norman Bowes.CMG.DSO.BrigGen kia 4-4-18 RWar attStaff42InfBde p64 MR27

FORSTER,George Richardson.MID TCapt kia 25-8-17 19DLI p257&160 CR France363

FORSTER,Harold Ker 2Lt dow PoW 8-12-17 6Lond p247 CR France924

FORSTER,Harold Thomas.DSO.MC.LtAMaj dow 29-5-18 RBerks att2Nhampt p139 CR France1693 &CR France34

FORSTER,Henry William Broderick Lt ded 22-1-19 7Mddx p270 CR Mddx68,dow

FORSTER,Herbert Cyril Capt kia 25-5-15 3RFus p67 MR29

FORSTER,Hugh Murray TCapt dow 28-9-15 8KOSB p101 CR France178,Maj 26-9-15

FORSTER,James Ernest HonMaj kia 29-9-15 3 att1Y&L p158 CR France550

FORSTER,James Henry Lt kia 29-9-15 RE 2/1FC p210 CR France423,dow

FORSTER,John 2Lt kia 14-9-14 KRRC p150 MR15

FORSTER,John.MC.CaptAMaj dow 2-10-18 7RFus p67 CR France1184

FORSTER,John Percival TCapt kia 1-7-16 22NumbF p61 MR21

FORSTER,John Stanley Capt dow 23-8-18 B285RFA p207 CR France504,22-8-18

FORSTER,Lionel Archibald Capt ded PoW 4-11-14 Ches p96 CR France1276,dow

FORSTER,Ralph T2Lt ded 22-11-18 MGC p182 CR War81,Lt

FORSTER,Ralph Louis Francis 2Lt kia 3-5-17 1EKent p57 MR19

FORSTER,Thomas T2Lt ded 26-2-19 6Y&L p265 CR Ches128

FORSTER,Thomas Burton 2Lt kia 10-6-16 3 att2RIrReg p89 CR France394,dow

FORSTER,Thomas Foreman.MID ACapt kia 31-10-17 7DLI p239 CR Belgium13

FORSTER,Walter Johnson Capt kia 31-5-17 3 att8ELancs p110 MR20

FORSTER,William Edward Blake 2Lt ded 12-6-15 RFA p28 CR Eire49

FORSTER,William Oxley Lt dow 22-9-16 8DLI C'Coy p239 CR France177

FORSTER-BROWN,James Cameron TLt dow 27-8-16 12RB p178 CR France141

FORSTER-MORRIS,Herbert Gloyne Forster 2Lt dow 10-10-15 1SWBord p100 France1

FORSYTH,Andrew Alexander T2Lt kia 12-10-18 12 att9RScots p54 CR France1896

FORSYTH,Cusack Grant.DSO.TLtCol kia 14-9-16 NumbF 2 att6Yorks p90 CR France246

FORSYTH,David 2Lt ded 17-5-15 7HLI p270 CR Scot812,17-6-15

FORSYTH,Gordon Amhurst 2Lt kia 27-8-16 8RFus p67 CR France420

FORSYTH,Gordon Oliver TLt kia 11-10-18 37MGC Inf p182 CR France1396

FORSYTH,James T2Lt kia 13-7-16 7RWKent p141 MR21

FORSYTH,James Corson T2Lt kia 31-8-17 1Worc p108 CR Belgium54,30-8-17

FORSYTH,John 2Lt dow 28-3-18 3 att17HLI p162 CR France225

FORSYTH,John Alexander Stewart Lt ded 5-11-19 RB att517LabCps p266 CR France113

FORSYTH,John Charles 2Lt kia 11-10-18 ScotHorse p205 CR France660,13BlkW

FORSYTH,John Cusack.MID Lt&Adjt kia 22-9-14 23RFA p28 CR France1110

FORSYTH,Maxwell Hanton.DSO.MC.TMaj dow 11-3-18 9ScotRif p103 CR France1066 Ex 8GordH

FORSYTH,Roy Anderson 2Lt kia 28-11-17 RFA att7RFC p7&28 CR Belgium162

FORSYTH,Samuel Sanford.MID Lt kia 25-9-15 RFA 43TrHowBty p28 MR29

FORSYTH,W Lt 28-10-18 IA MiscList CR Pakistan50A MR43

FORSYTH,Walter William T2Lt ded 7-12-18 HLI att2Bn p162 CR France289

FORSYTH,William Capt dow 20-10-15 1/7GordH p242 CR France300

FORSYTH,William 2Lt dow 1-4-16 6A&SH p243 CR France95

FORSYTH,William Allan Capt kia 27-6-18 56RFA &79RAF p28 CR Belgium31

FORSYTH,William Forbes 2Lt kia 15-9-18 10RScots p212 CR France179

FORSYTH,William James Samuel 2Lt kia 13-5-17 3KOSB p101 CR France777

FORSYTH,William Laing 2Lt kia 22-3-18 5 att4SforthH p241 MR20

FORSYTH,William Matthew T2Lt dow 20-4-17 16Mddx A'Coy p146 CR France40

FORSYTH,William Walker 2Lt ded 1-3-19 3A&SH p266 CR Scot684

FORSYTH-GRANT,Ivor.MID Lt dow 19-10-15 2LovatScouts p204 CR Gallipoli26

FORT,Lawrence Capt kia 16-2-15 2EKent p57 MR29

FORTH,Charles 2Lt kia 30-7-17 2/10Manch p237 CR Belgium24

FORTESCUE,Grenville TCapt kia 4-9-15 11RB p178 CR France707 Ex 4Bn

FORTESCUE,William Aubrey Lt kia 12-10-16 3 att2LancF p92 CR France390

FORTUNE,Henry George 2Lt kia 17-1-17 3/6WelshR att132MGC Inf p187&230 CR Iraq5

FORTUNE,John TCapt ded 27-12-18 RAMC att27CCS p195 MR61

FORTUNE,Rutherford Lamond T2Lt dow 15-1-17 16RScots p54 CR France275

FORTUNE,Stanley Welsh 2Lt kia 13-3-16 10RB p178 MR29

FORWARD,Charles Arthur 2Lt kia 25-9-15 2Beds p85 MR19

FORWOOD,Thomas Brittain Capt kia 8-5-15 RLancs p59 MR29

FOSBERY,Frank Sidney Thomas T2Lt kia 21-3-18 21MGC p182 MR27

FOSBROOKE,Cuthbert 2Lt kia 19-7-17 6DLI p239 CR Belgium29,22Bn

FOSDICK,John Hyland TLt dow 31-7-15 7RB p178 CR Belgium11

FOSKETT,Herbert Edward 2Lt kia 28-4-17 5 att6Beds p219 MR20

FOSS,Frederick George Lt kia 6-11-17 1/6RWFus p223 CR Palestine1

FOSS,Gilbert Harry T2Lt kia 3-7-16 8BordR p117 MR21

FOSSETT,Reginald Graham T2Lt kia 3-10-18 5TankCps p188 CR France375

FOSTER,Alfred 2Lt kia 14-4-17 27/32RFA p28 CR France451

FOSTER,Alfred David.MC.2LtTCapt kia 5-5-17 8RSuss p119 CR France592

FOSTER,Archibald Courtenay Hays Lt kia 20-9-14 Hamps attKAR p120&202 MR50,18-9-14

FOSTER,Arthur Cedric 2Lt dow 12-3-15 1GrenGds SR p50 CR France500

FOSTER,Arthur Edward 2Lt kia 10-4-17 3 att7YLI p143 CR France905,9-4-17

FOSTER,Bernard La Trobe Lt kia 24-7-16 19Manch p154 CR France744,23-7-16

FOSTER,Charles Clifford Lt kia 29-7-18 5Ches p222 CR France524

FOSTER,Charles Finch Lt kia 27-3-18 9Lancers p22 CR France424

FOSTER,Douglas Cameron Capt kia 14-4-17 ScotRif p103 CR France434

FOSTER,Edward T2Lt kia 23-4-17 10RFus p67 MR20

FOSTER,Ethelbert Harold(Bert) Lt kia 8-10-18 4WelchR p230 CR France1345

FOSTER,Frank 2Lt ded 23-9-19 RGA 155SB SR p262 CR Lancs34

FOSTER,Frank Hawley T2Lt kia 3-6-17 GL &45RFC p7 MR20

FOSTER,Franklin James T2Lt kia 23-8-17 GL &11RFC p7 CR France120,Frank

FOSTER,George T2Lt kia 16-5-17 102RFA p28 CR Belgium127

FOSTER,George Haslewood T2Lt kia 21-3-18 RE 179TC p45 CR France1182

FOSTER,George Major Solloway T2Lt kia 3-7-16 10Worc p108 CR France393

FOSTER,H.Capt 29-6-17 IOD MR66

FOSTER,Harry Langton 2Lt kia 7-6-17 4WKent p234 CR Belgium154

FOSTER,Harold John Brittain Capt kia 14-4-17 Beds att1Ess p85 MR20

FOSTER,Heaton 2Lt kia 16-4-18 1EYorks p84 MR30

FOSTER,Hedley Roy Capt kia 22-8-17 BucksBn O&BLI p231 MR30

FOSTER,Herbert Knollys 2Lt kia 30-10-14 1Glouc p106 MR29

FOSTER,James Sloman T2Lt drd 13/14-8-15 9SomLI p79 MR4,13-8-15

FOSTER,John Capt kia 23-4-17 5SStaffs p229 MR20,8Bn

FOSTER,John 2Lt kia 25-4-18 4RScots p211 MR30

FOSTER,John Bowden T2Lt kia 11-10-18 7WYorks p81 CR France612

FOSTER,John Cecil.MC.MID TCapt kia 20-8-17 6Lincs p75 CR Belgium10

FOSTER,John Maurice 2Lt kia 23-7-16 4GordH p242 CR France432

FOSTER,John Rowland Maj 22-2-20 RAMC CR Lancs233

FOSTER,Joseph T2Lt dow 14-10-18 20DLI p160 CR Belgium11

FOSTER,Laurence Talbot Lisle TLt kia 5-8-15 16DLI att5Manch p160 CR Gallipoli6,7-8-15

FOSTER,Leonard T2Lt dow 13-8-16 15WYorks p81 CR Yorks388

FOSTER,Leslie Arthur Clifford T2Lt kia 12-4-18 13Lpool p71 CR France88,13-4-18 Lt

FOSTER,Norman Kessen TCapt ded 2-12-18 RAMC p195 MR41

FOSTER,Norman Rae Lt kia 26-3-17 1/7Ches p223 CR Palestine8,Roe

FOSTER,Percy George T2Lt dow 2-4-16 7RSuss p119 CR Sussex178

FOSTER,R.D.Lt mbk 7-8-15 6Lincs p256 MR4

FOSTER,Reginald T2Lt kldacc 3-1-18 RFC p16 CR Yorks368

FOSTER,Robert Clow T2Lt kia 10-4-18 11Suff p78 MR32

FOSTER,William Arthur Lt ded 20-2-19 5Manch &RAF p270 CR Dorset50

FOSTER,William Augustus Portman Lt dow PoW 11-11-14 1SStaffs p122 CR Germany3,Capt

FOSTER,William Leo Gorrill TCapt kia 2-7-18 RASC p192 CR France

FOTHERGILL,Reginald Alfred Lt ded 20-7-20 2/5Glouc CR Glouc11

FOTTRELL,Brendan Joseph 2Lt kia 15-3-15 3 att1RIrReg p89 MR29

FOUBISTER,John Leask 2Lt kld 8-10-17 GL &31RFC p7 CR Surrey6

FOUCAR,James Lewis Maj kia 8-5-15 12Lond p248 MR29

FOULDES,Thomas John.MID Capt kia 25-6-18 A114RFA p28 CR Greece6

FOULDS,Maurice Frank 2Lt kia 30-10-17 19 att2/6Lond p250 MR30

FOULGER,Maurice T2Lt kia 9-8-15 KSLI p144 MR29

FOULIS,James Bell TCapt kia 18-10-16 5CamH p167 MR21

FOULKES,Charles Henry Lt 11-9-20 6WRid CR Eire166

FOULKES,George Boyd TCapt kia 12-8-16 6RScotF p94 MR21

FOULKES,Thomas Howard.CIE.LtCol kldByTribesmen 14/15-11-20 IMS p276 MR43,15-11-20

FOULKES-WINKS,Oswald Woodward T2Lt kia 20-7-16 13Mddx att75TMB p146 CR France285

FOULSHAM,Arthur Percy 2Lt kia 20-7-17 RGA 245SB p39 CR Belgium29

FOUNTAIN,John Alfred Arnott T2Lt kia 1-7-16 10YLI p143 CR France267

FOURMY,William Reginald T2Lt dow 28-1-18 28MGC Inf p182 CR France439

FOWELL,John 2Lt kia 12-10-17 4 att8SStaffs p122 MR30

FOWKE,Mansergh Cuthbert Capt kia 30-8-14 2Manch p154 MR15

FOWLE,Michael Randolph 2Lt kia 24-11-14 2Wilts p153 MR29,24-10-14

FOWLE,Louis Richard.MID Lt kia 4-6-15 IA 14Sikhs p276 MR4

FOWLE,William Ernest Lt ded 1-5-19 RGA p262

FOWLE,William Meade Capt dow 16-3-16 RE p45 CR Sussex112

FOWLER,Alan Arthur Capt kia 28-4-15 2CamH p167 MR29

FOWLER,Alexander George.MID TCapt kia 1-1-18 GL &1KAR p202 CR EAfrica77

FOWLER,Bernard Edwin Lt kia 22-3-18 19MGC p182 MR20

FOWLER,Cecil Dashwood Melman Lt kia 25-9-15 1RWSurr p55 MR19,Milman

FOWLER,Charles Jefford T2Lt dow 1-6-16 22RFus p67 CR France95

FOWLER,Christopher George Capt kia 6-4-17 1/6Norf p217 CR France568

FOWLER,Claude Oliver 2Lt kia 23-10-18 5Beds p219 CR France1476

FOWLER,David Dennys 2Lt kia 16-3-17 RFC p7 CR Sussex114,17-3-17

FOWLER,Edward Wareham Lt kia 15-7-16 1/7RWar p214 MR21

FOWLER,Evelyn Philip Lt ded 5-10-17 BlkW p264

FOWLER,F.W.Capt 8-6-19 RE CR Mddx70

FOWLER,Francis Reginald 2Lt kia 18-10-16 3Leinst att2RIrRif p174 MR21

FOWLER,Frank Archibald 2LtACapt kia 28-7-17 RGA 295SB p39 CR France922

FOWLER,George Edward T2Lt kia 28-10-17 1 att12Glouc p106 MR30

FOWLER,George Glyn Lt dow 26-9-15 2KRRC p150 CR France88

FOWLER,George Herbert LtCol kia 15-10-15 Cmdg1/8N&D p233 CR France109

FOWLER,Horace Vernon Lt 15-7-17 RIM MR65

FOWLER,John Dudley 2Lt kia 30-11-14 5Lancers p21 MR29

FOWLER,John Edward.Sir.Capt kia 22-6-15 4SfthH p164 CR Scot936

FOWLER,John Orr 2Lt kia 19-8-17 GL &45RFC p7 MR20

FOWLER,Kenneth Ryeland T2Lt kia 3-6-15 RFA p28 CR Belgium28

FOWLER,Norman John T2Lt kia 23-4-17 1RWSurr p55 MR20

FOWLER,Ralph 2Lt kia 16-9-16 6DCLI p114 MR21

FOWLER,S.H.SubCondr 5-2-15 S&T Cps MR66

FOWLER,Valentine TMaj kia 2-6-17 10Yorks p90 CR France1489

FOWLER,William 2Lt kld 16-11-16 RFC p2 CR Scot398

FOWLER,William Maurice T2Lt dow 26-9-18 2RSuss p119 CR France673

FOWLIE,Charles Wilson Lawson Maj kia 30-5-15 5GordH p242 CR France705

FOWLIE,James Lawrence Lt kia 23-4-17 1 att10HLI p162 CR France1182,24-4-17

FOWNES,Henry Harley Maj dow 17-3-17 210 att174RGA p209 CR France120

FOX,Alan Geoffrey Capt kia 9-5-15 RE attRFC p1&45 CR France163

FOX,Albert Victor 2Lt kia 3-9-16 10RB p178 MR21

FOX,Andrew J.TLt kia 1-9-18 6 att4RBerks p139 CR France346

FOX,Andrew Stewart 2Lt kia 13-10-15 6NStaffs p238 MR19

FOX,Arthur.MC.ACapt kia 8-5-17 3 att1KSLI A'Coy p144 CR France115

FOX,Arthur Clause.DSO.LtCol drd 15-4-17 RAMC p195 MR35

FOX,Cecil Croker TLt kia 15-9-16 12ESurr p112 MR21

FOX,Charles Alexander Newcombe.MC.Lt kia 26-9-17 4NStaffs att2Worc p157&258 CR Belgium19,Capt 25-9-17

FOX,Charles James T2Lt kia 22-7-16 1RWKent p141 MR21

FOX,Charles Joseph 2Lt kia 29-6-16 16 att2RFus p67 CR France35

FOX,David T2Lt kia 15-10-17 11WYorks p81 MR30

FOX,Douglas Charles 2Lt kia 23-7-16 1NumbF p61 CR France432

FOX,Francis Nevil Wilson T2Lt kia 31-7-17 14WelshR p126 CR Belgium96

FOX,Francis Parker T2Lt kia 1-7-16 9RInniskF p104 MR21

FOX,Frank Herbert T2Lt kia 23-8-18 1Beds p85 CR France518

FOX,Frederick Donald T2Lt kia 5-11-16 19 att17N&D p134 MR21

FOX,G.H.Lt 6-5-21 RASC CR Lancs34

FOX,Geoffrey Noel Storrs 2Lt kia 28-3-18 5 att2WYorks p218 MR27

FOX,George 2Lt dow 24-5-15 RFA p28 CR Belgium4,Lt kia

FOX,George Herbert 2Lt kia 23-4-16 RFA att G'HQ Intelligence p28 MR34

FOX,Gerald Vincent TLt kia 10-7-18 4MGC Inf p182 CR France411

FOX,H.A.AssSurg 19-10-18 IMD MR65

FOX,Harold Sidney George 2Lt kia 8-4-17 4SfthH p241 CR France15,9-4-17

FOX,Harry Norton T2Lt kia 23-4-17 1Norf p73 MR20

FOX,James John T2Lt kia 11-9-18 Norf att12Bn p73 CR Belgium451

FOX,James Joseph.MID T2Lt kia 1-9-18 11RInniskF p105 CR France297

FOX,John T2Lt ded 18-11-17 5ConnRgrs p172 CR Egypt7

FOX,John Robert 2Lt ded 16-8-18 10Manch &RAF p270

FOX,Lawrence Anselm Storrs TLt dow 27-4-18 21WYorks p81 CR France102

FOX,Leslie Herbert 2Lt kia 11-7-16 4 att2Beds p85 MR21

FOX,Leslie William Capt kia 31-7-17 10Lpool p216 MR29

FOX,Maurier James 2Lt ded 10-1-19 4 att17Hamps p270 CR Kent27,Maurice John

FOX,Michael Stanley T2Lt kia 20-11-17 RWSurr att6Bn p55 MR17

FOX,Owen Gurney 2Lt kia 6-2-17 3 att1Dors p124 CR France221

FOX,Ralph Talbot 2Lt kia 25-8-18 4YLI p235 CR France614

FOX,Reginald Wilson LtCol kia 8-3-16 6Dev p217 MR38

FOX,Sidney Thomas 2Lt kia 21-9-17 RGA 230SB p39 CR Belgium113

FOX,Thomas Herbert LtACapt kia 31-3-18 17/41RH&FA p28 CR France41

FOX,Thomas Noel 2LtTLt ded 12-12-18 SomLI att79MGC Inf p79&182 CR Europe20

FOX,Vincent Lt kia 26-8-14 RAVC p198 CR France658

FOX,Victor William Darwin Lt kia 18-5-15 1IrGds SR p52 CR France727

FOX,Walter Henry Lt kia 16-6-15 4SStaffs att2Beds p122 MR22

FOX,Wilfred Armstrong 2Lt kia 29-7-15 4Lincs p217 CR Belgium98

FOX,William Archibald.MC.Lt kia 6-11-17 4RSuss p228

FOXALL,Thomas William T2Lt kia 2-10-18 RWFus 3GarrBn att25GarrBnLpool p97 CR France1887

FOXELL,Edward William Lanchester TCapt ded 11-6-17 7EKent att3ArmyGasSchl p57 CR France225

FOXON,Harold Richard Lt kia 28-8-18 7 att9Ess p232 CR France397

FOY,Ernest Reginald 2Lt kia 11-4-17 1SomLI p79 MR20

FOY,Martin Victor Capt kia 13-10-14 1RWSurr p55 CR France1329

FOY,William Archibald.MC.Lt 6-11-17 1/4RSuss CR Palestine1

FOYSTER,Ellen Lucy Sister drd 10-4-17 QAIMNS p200 CR France85

FOYSTER,Philip Tillard LtTCapt dow 11-12-16 RE 86FC p45 CR France40

FRADD,Kingsley Meredith Chatterton 2Lt kia 1-7-16 2Lond attMGC p187&245

FRAME,Robert T2Lt kia 28-3-18 RLancs p59 CR France452

FRAMPTON,John Guy Lt dow 11-10-18 1Mon p244 CR France725.4-10-18

FRAMPTON,John Reginald T2Lt kia 3-7-17 13Glouc p106 CR Belgium10

FRAMPTON,William John Goulbourn Shipdern Capt kia 24-4-18 2ELancs p110 MR27

FRANCE,Arthur Alderson T2Lt dow 7-10-16 RE p45 CR France513

FRANCE,Errol Martin T2Lt kia 30-7-16 10Worc p108 CR France432,Lt

FRANCE,John Galbraith 2Lt kia 12-4-17 8 att9ScotRif p225 MR20

FRANCE,William T2Lt kia 8-10-18 12/13NumbF p61 CR France1345

FRANCE-HAYHURST,Frederick Charles LtCol kia 9-5-15 4RWFus p223 CR France924

FRANCIS,Ainslie Norman.MC.MM.2Lt dow 30-4-18 1LancF p92 CR Lancs475

FRANCIS,Alan Buller T2Lt kia 24-8-16 9 att7DCLI p114 CR France390 &CR France399

FRANCIS,Basil Hugh 2Lt kia 4-2-15 3RScots att2HLI p54 CR France765

FRANCIS,Christopher Thomas TCapt dow 26-5-16 13RScots p54 CR France8

FRANCIS,Dudley Collins 2Lt kia 13-11-16 5Y&L A'Coy p238 CR France1327

FRANCIS,Edward Griffith 2Lt kia 21-5-16 8Lond p247 MR20

FRANCIS,Francis Gustave 2Lt kia 6-8-15 3 att1Ess p131 CR Gallipoli6

FRANCIS,Hugh Gordon.MC.MID TLtACapt kia 22-3-18 RE 104Coy p45 MR27

FRANCIS,John Capt kia 2-6-15 1/5RWar D'Coy p214 CR Belgium339

FRANCIS,Philip Arthur 2Lt kld 1-6-18 4Manch p154 CR France1416,kia att10Ches

FRANCIS,Richard John Lt dow 31-3-15 2Y&L p158 CR France922

FRANCIS,Vere T2Lt dow 20-4-17 3 att2Suff p78 CR France40

FRANCIS,William George 2Lt kia 10-3-18 66RFC p16 CR Italy75

FRANCIS,William Joseph 2Lt kia 22-3-18 11RFus p67 MR27

FRANCIS,William Pollock 2LtTLt kia 22-10-17 12RScots p54 MR30

FRANCKE,William Henry Lt ded 10-12-19 GL &LabCps 399PoW Coy 270 CR Scot235

FRANK,Edward T2Lt kia 7-8-15 6Yorks p90 MR4

FRANK,Robert James Brownlaw Lt dow 6-6-16 1/4RSuss p228 CR Egypt8,Brownlow

FRANKAU,Paul Ewart Lt kia 2-11-17 20RB p244 CR Palestine8

FRANKENSTEIN,Cyril Joseph T2Lt kia 23-8-18 13TankCps p188 CR France1170

FRANKENSTEIN,Oscar Reginald 2Lt kia 26-3-17 5WelshR p230 MR34

FRANKHAM,A.A.Lt ded 17-2-19 RGA 218SB p262 CR Hamps 4

FRANKLAND,Edgar 2Lt kia 24-10-18 9 att15DLI p239 MR16

FRANKLAND,John Cecil 2Lt kia 10-1-17 5LNLancs p234 MR29

FRANKLAND,Robert Cecil Colville Capt kia 7-8-15 3NStaffs att8LancF p157 MR4

FRANKLAND,Thomas Hugh Colville BtMaj kia 25-4-15 RDubF p176 MR4

FRANKLAND,Thomas Pemberton T2Lt kia 29-7-16 RGA 51 att109SB p39 CR France397

FRANKLEN-EVANS,George Philip 2Lt dow 18-9-18 4DLI p160 CR France327

FRANKLIN,Arthur John 2Lt kia 9-4-18 18WelshR p126 MR32

FRANKLIN,Benjamin Lester TLt kia 4-5-17 12Mddx &70RFC p7&146,dow CR France285

FRANKLIN,Cyril Edward Lt dow 20-2-17 RE p210 CR France251,kia

FRANKLIN,Edgar John LtTCapt drd 17-4-17 C58RFA p28 MR40

FRANKLIN,Francis 2Lt kia 3-5-15 3RFus p67 MR29

FRANKLIN,Frederick Robert 2Lt kia 9-12-17 10RIrRif p169 MR21

FRANKLIN,George T2Lt kia 20-10-18 3 att2NStaffs p157 CR France658

FRANKLIN,L.C.Lt 20-4-19 RASC CR Hunts65

FRANKLIN,Leslie Willoughby Lt dow 16-10-18 10/147RFA p28 CR France686

FRANKLIN,Percival George Capt kia 18-7-17 8Manch att1/8Lpool p236 MR29 CR Belgium10

FRANKLIN,Rodney Vernon TLt kld 24-6-17 GL &16RFC p7 CR Egypt15

FRANKLIN,Thomas Alderman.MC.Capt dow 27-11-17 1/5Beds p219 CR Palestine1

FRANKLIN,William Ernest T2Lt kia 1-4-18 10Worc p108 CR Belgium48

FRANKLIN,William Hyslop TLt kia 25-9-15 6KOSB p101 MR19,26-9-15

FRANKLIN,William Joseph T2Lt kia 5-10-16 11ESurr att7Suss p112 MR21

FRANKLYN,George William 2Lt kia 7-6-17 23Lond C'Coy p252 CR Belgium112

FRANKLYN,Henry TCapt kia 8-7-17 8RFus p67 MR21

FRANKLYN,William Edmund.KCB.Sir LtGen 27-10-14 Yorks CR Mddx39

FRANKS,Braham Alfred T2Lt kia 24-10-15 11 att8WRid p115 CR Gallipoli27,23-10-15

FRANKS,George Despard.CMG.DSO.LtCol kia 8-10-18 19Huss p22 France848

FRANKS,Harold Cooper T2Lt kia 15-6-18 2Suff p78 CR France33

FRANKS,John Ferguson.MC.Capt&Adjt dow 22-9-15 3KRRC p150 CR France692,kia

FRANKS,Lionel 2Lt dow 5-5-17 4 att8EYorks C'Coy p219 CR France145

FRANKS,Rolland Sutton 2Lt kia 12-10-17 8 att1ESurr p112 MR30

FRANKS,Spencer Capt kia 22-3-18 2SLancs p125 CR France481,28-3-18

FRASER,Alan Cumming.MC.2Lt kia 31-8-18 7Lond p247 CR France630

FRASER,Alan Simon 2Lt kia 24-3-18 RE HighlandFC p210 CR France1063,Lt

FRASER,Alexander.VD.LtCol kia 17-5-15 4CamH p242 MR22,18-5-15

FRASER,Alexander 2Lt kia 13-10-15 1BlkW p128 MR19

FRASER,Alexander 2Lt kia 30-11-17 att1/5LNLancs p135 MR17

FRASER,Alexander Evan Lt kia 2-5-15 2Mon p244 CR Belgium92

FRASER,Alexander Roderick 2Lt dow 26-4-17 3 att6SLancs p125 CR Iraq8

FRASER,Andrew.MC&Bar.Capt dow 20-4-18 2CamH p167 CR France95

FRASER,Andrew Knowles.MC.Capt kia 20-11-17 4SfthH p241 MR17

FRASER,Angus McIntyre Lt dow 19-6-18 1/6A&SH p243 CR France65

FRASER,Arthur Cecil T2Lt kld 22-1-18 RFC p16 CR Lincs61

FRASER,Arthur Ian.DSO.MID Maj kia 30-11-17 IA 9HodsonsHorse p276 CR France364,Ion

FRASER,Arthur Leslie 2Lt dow 1-7-17 RGA 27SB p39 CR France88

FRASER,Arthur William.DSO.T2Lt kia 1-7-16 1BordR p117 CR France1501

FRASER,C.Lovat Capt 18-6-21 14DLI CR Herts24

FRASER,Campbell Robertson 2Lt kia 17-4-18 1Lpool D'Coy p71 MR32,Lt 4Bn

FRASER,Charles Douglas 2Lt kia 22-3-18 3Lond p245 MR27

FRASER,D'Arcy Mackenzie TMaj kia 7-8-15 IA 75Carnatic att6Lincs p75&276 CR Gallipoli5

FRASER,Donald TCapt kia 1-7-16 RE p45 CR France68

FRASER,Donald.DSO.Chap2Cl kld 2-6-18 RAChDept p199 CR France204

FRASER,Donald Charles 2Lt kia 3-5-17 5 att9RFus p67 MR20

FRASER,Duncan McNeill 2Lt ded 16-10-19 9HLI p270 CR Scot752

FRASER,Eldred Leslie T2Lt kia 20-11-17 H'TankCps p188 MR17

FRASER,Frederick Gordon.MC.MID TCapt kia 14-6-17 12 att11RWKent p141 MR29

FRASER,Geoffrey Norris 2Lt kia 12-3-15 3 att2BordR p117 MR22

FRASER,George Allan 2Lt kia 15-5-17 2HAC p206 MR20

FRASER,George Dick T2Lt dow 3-6-18 13RB p178 CR France145

FRASER,Harold Reginald Drummond.MC.LtACapt kia 1-8-18 5Ches p222

FRASER,Henry Hubert Lt kia 27-5-18 3 att5Yorks p90 MR18

FRASER,Herbert Heron T2Lt dow 18-10-17 SfthH att8Bn p164 CR France40

FRASER,Herbert Ross T2Lt kia 24-8-16 17RScots p54 CR France630

FRASER,Hugh 2Lt kia 13-11-16 9A&SH p244 CR France131

FRASER,Hugh Crawford TCapt kia 5-8-15 2 att6RScotF p94 CR France727

FRASER,Hon Hugh Joseph.MVO.Maj kia 28-10-14 2ScotsGds p52 MR29

FRASER,Ian Catto T2Lt kia 25-9-15 2A&SH p173 CR France114

FRASER,J.R.CMG.LtCol 11-6-20 1LNLancs CR Mddx26

FRASER,James 2Lt dow 28-3-18 4BlkW p230 CR France145

FRASER,James 2Lt dow 20-5-18 330RFA p28 CR France142

FRASER,James Carstairs Lt kia 21-3-18 5SfthH p241 MR20

FRASER,James Herbert Lt dow 9-7-16 2Mon att107MGC p187&244 CR France74

FRASER,James Howie Lt kia 29-10-14 2GordH p166 MR29

FRASER,James Leslie Lt ded 1-4-19 3SfthH p265 CR Ches181,31-3-19

FRASER,James Lovat Hasack TLt dow 18-2-17 75MGC p182 CR France263

FRASER,James Scholfield.MID Maj kia 13/14-1-16 1/5EKent p212 CR Iraq5

FRASER,John T2Lt dow 6-4-18 47MGC p182 CR France169,5-4-18

FRASER,John Alexander Capt dow 28-8-14 2A&SH p173 CR France1394

FRASER,John Courtenay.MC.Lt drd 9-9-18 GrenGds attGdsMGR p50&53 MR40

FRASER,John Irwin see FRAZER,J.I.

FRASER,Kenneth John.MC.T2Lt kia 27-5-18 10DLI p160 MR18

FRASER,Lachlan Henry Veitch.MID Lt kia 24-2-15 4Mddx p146 CR Belgium104

FRASER,Lachlan Ronald 2Lt kia 25-9-15 IARO att69Punjabis p276 MR28

FRASER,Laureston Ross 2Lt kia 21-3-18 14Lond p249 CR France184,Lauriston

FRASER,Mackenzie Hamilton Capt ded 28-6-19 SfthH p254&266,A&SH CR EAfrica49

FRASER,Madge Neill Nurse 8-3-15 ScotWomensHosp CR Europe57

FRASER,Malcolm Goulding 2Lt kia 1-7-16 2ScotRif p103 MR21

FRASER,Oswald Campbell T2Lt kia 9-4-17 9BlkW p128 CR France924

FRASER,Owen Alan Denholm 2Lt ded 1-11-19 ULIA att3CpsofGuides p276 MR43

FRASER,Patrick Grant 2Lt kia 3-5-17 3GordH att8BlkW p166 MR20

FRASER,Patrick Neill TLt kia 1-7-16 1NStaffs att2BordR p157 CR France394

FRASER,Percy William Norman.DSO.Capt kia 22-2-15 2CamH p167 CR Belgium28

FRASER,Peter Campbell 2Lt dow 23-7-16 1NumbF p61 MR21

FRASER,R.A.2Lt kld 18-5-18 GL &RAF p190

FRASER,Rowland TCapt kia 1-7-16 6 att1RB p178 MR21

FRASER,Hon Simon 2Lt kld 29-10-14 3 att2GordH p166 MR29

FRASER,T.P.27-8-14 WAfrMedServ CR WAfrica58

FRASER,Thomas Lt kia 1-7-16 2Ess p131 MR21

FRASER,Thomas Francis TCapt kia 7/11-8-15 9WYorks p81 MR4,8-8-15

FRASER,Victor Murray Drummond 2Lt dow 3-6-15 5Ches p222

FRASER,Wallace TCapt kia 30-7-16 19Lpool p71 CR France294

FRASER,William T2Lt dow 29-9-15 1BlkW p128 CR France88

FRASER,William 2Lt kia 25-10-16 RFC p2 MR20

FRASER,William 2LtACapt kia 9-4-17 1GordH A'Coy p166 CR France581

FRASER,William Alan TCapt ded 7-7-17 RE 26DivHQ p45 CR Greece7

FRASER,William Augustus Cumming Maj ded 14-6-15 1Dors p124 CR Iraq6

FRASER-CAMPBELL,William Baillie 2Lt kia 23-3-18 8A&SH p243 MR27

FRASER-TYTLER,Patrick Seton TCapt kia 3-8-16 D36RFA p28 CR France630

FRATER,David George.MC.2Lt kia 17-4-18 A255RFA p208 CR France202,16-4-18

FRAYLING,Herbert Joseph T2Lt kia 30-8-18 1DCLI p114 CR France518

FRAYLING,Michael Stapleton 2Lt kia 16-9-16 C183RFA p28 MR21

FRAYNE,Ernest TLt dow PoW 17-5-18 16 att2Mddx p146 CR Germany3

FRAZER,Alexander.MC.T2Lt kia 13-8-16 10HLI p162 CR France151,10/11Bn

FRAZER,Douglas Villers Capt kia 16-8-17 RFA p207 MR30

FRAZER,John Irwin Lt kia 14-9-14 2ConnRgrs p172 CR France1107,FRASER

FRAZER,John Gordon LtCol ded 1-8-16 1Dev GarrBn p76

FREAKES,Alexander John 2Lt dow 3-9-18 RFA p208 CR Surrey1

FREAM,William Lt kia 21-7-16 1/5Glouc p225 MR21

FRECHVILLE,William Ralph.MID Capt kia 9-1-20 RE p262 CR Asia81,FRECHEVILLE

FREDERICK,Thomas.MC.TCapt dow 14-12-17 9Norf p73 CR France13

FREE,Ernest Robert 2Lt ded 16-7-18 RGA X'SB p209 CR Camb2

FREEAR,Eric Charles T2Lt kia 13-4-17 4Beds p85 CR France644,15-4-17

FREEDMAN,Bertie T2Lt kia 3-7-17 15Lpool att1/9Manch p71 CR France755

FREEDMAN,Phineas T2Lt kia 3-10-17 6EKent p57 CR France154

FREELAND,Hugo Wharncliffe Lt kia 14-8-16 RGA p39 CR Belgium113

FREELAND,John Buchan 2Lt kia 26-7-17 2Yorks p90 MR29

FREEMAN,Arthur Cyril Bruce Lt kia 27-9-18 3Huss &2RScotF p94 CR France530

FREEMAN,Douglas Lt kia 26-9-17 16AustInf CR Belgium88

FREEMAN,Edward TMaj kia 3-3-16 10RWFus p97 CR Belgium131

FREEMAN,Eric Allen TLt kia 18-8-16 9 att6DCLI p114 MR21

FREEMAN,Eric Payne TCapt ded PoW 23-3-18 14Hamps p120 CR France511

FREEMAN,Francis Basil 2Lt kia 1-7-16 1/8RWar p215 CR France700

FREEMAN,Francis Hubert T2Lt kia 1-7-16 19LancF p92 CR France393

FREEMAN,Frank Albert 2Lt kia 1-7-16 2KRRC p150 MR20

FREEMAN,Frank Ernest Allien 2Lt kia 21-3-18 RFA 18DAC att83Bde p28 MR27

FREEMAN,Frederick John 2Lt dow 3-7-16 4 att2WYorks p81 CR France74

FREEMAN,George Cyril TLtACapt kia 1-10-16 6RBerks p139 CR France246

FREEMAN,H.P.Lt 21-1-18 RFC CR Mddx26

FREEMAN,Herbert Joseph TCapt dow 29-10-18 142RASC 16DivTrain att13InniskF p192 CR France1034

FREEMAN,James 2Lt kia 20-8-17 RGA 225SB p39 CR Belgium124

FREEMAN,James Edward Hutton 2Lt kia 24-4-16 7RWSurr att29RFC p2&55 CR Belgium11

FREEMAN,John Bentley 2Lt kia 20-9-17 3 att11RWKent p141 MR30

FREEMAN,John Roland.MID T2Lt dow 12-2-17 23NumbF p61 CR France285

FREEMAN,John William 2LtTLt kia 24-9-17 RE X CpsSigCo p45 CR Belgium102

FREEMAN,Joseph.MC.T2Lt dow 9-4-18 21Mddx p146 MR32

FREEMAN,Noel 2Lt kia 5-4-18 3RWSurr p55 CR France1170

FREEMAN,Noel William.MC.TCaptAMaj kia 21-3-18 68/14RFA p28 MR20

FREEMAN,Peter 2Lt dow 19-9-18 RGA 284SB p39 CR France835,Lt

FREEMAN,Robert Stuart Lt ded 29-8-19 RASC MT p267 CR Mddx15

FREEMAN,Russel Herbert.MC.Maj kia 21-7-18 Worc &73RAF p264 CR France524

FREEMAN,Tom T2Lt kia 17-2-17 6Nhampt att54TMB p137 CR France314

FREEMAN,Tristram Lt kia 12-3-15 6Worc p108 CR Belgium17,3Bn

FREEMAN,William Thomas LtCol ded 23-12-18 RAMC CR Berks86

FREEMAN,William Winter T2Lt kia 30-11-17 11DLI p160 CR France415,Winters

FREEMAN-COWEN,Cecil 2Lt kia 23-6-16 175RFA p28 CR France430

FREEMAN-THOMAS,Gerald Frederick.Hon.2Lt kia 14-9-14 1CldGds p51 MR15,Gerard

FREEMANTLE,Ronald Percy Cowen 2Lt kia 30-4-17 9RFC p7 CR France1483

FREEMANTLE,William George Lt kia 4-6-15 7Manch p237 MR4

FREENEY,Patrick Joseph T2Lt kia 8-10-18 6RDubF att198L TMB p176 CR France845

FREER,Arthur Martin 2Lt dow 12-4-18 3DLI p160 CR France298

FREER,John William Lt dow 29-6-15 10Leic p87 CR Greece10

FREESTON,Cecil James T2Lt kia 18-9-17 7Yorks p90 CR France1190

FREESTONE,William Herbert Rev kia 14-12-16 RAChDept p199 CR Greece9

FREETH,Richard Victor Canston Lt kia 13-7-16 4RBerks p234 CR France631

FREMANTLE,Thomas Francis Halford T2Lt dow 17-10-15 5 O&BLI C'Coy p130 CR France40

FRENCH,Albert Anthony T2Lt kia 3-9-16 11RSuss p119 MR21

FRENCH,Allan George 2Lt kia 23-5-16 15RWar p64 MR20

FRENCH,Bertram St.George TCapt kia 1-7-16 15Lpool attRInniskF p71 CR France339

FRENCH,Cecil John.MC.Lt 28-9-18 4CanadaMGC CR France256

FRENCH,Charles John TMaj dow 2-7-16 5KSLI attRE 255TC p144 CR France178

FRENCH,Charles Stockley Lt kia 25-4-15 2RDubF p176 MR29

FRENCH,Claude Alexander Capt dow 1-6-15 2RIrReg p89 CR France64

FRENCH,Digby Manifred Capt kia 11-9-18 4Suff p217 CR France511,FFRENCH

FRENCH,Edward Fulke.Hon.2Lt ded 13-11-18 PoW 296RFA p28 CR Egytp3

FRENCH,Ernest Aloysius.Hon.Lt dow 16-8-17 2SWBord p100 CR Belgium16

FRENCH,Ernest Shaw Lt kia 12-9-18 5YLI p235 CR France755

FRENCH,G.H.2Lt 26-6-19 RFA CR Ches97

FRENCH,George Philip.Hon.Lt kia 9-5-15 3 att1SWBord p100 CR France924

FRENCH,John Lawson TLt ded 26-9-17 RASC 1ColGHQ p192 CR France95,2Lt

FRENCH,Percival Vincent T2Lt dow 19-7-16 16DLI p160 CR France630

FRENCH,P.H.Capt ded 12-11-14 RE p45 CR Eire57

FRENCH,Robert Douglas 2Lt kia 15-9-16 6Lond p247 MR21

FRENCH,Robert Mason Jackson Capt dow 19-2-16 3RWFus p97 CR Hamps13

FRENCH,Sidney Arthur TLt kia 20-3-18 7RWKent p141 MR21

FRENCH,Thomas Hugo T2Lt kld 13-1-17 GL &RFC p7 CR Essex231

FRENCH,Valentine Douglas 2Lt dow 17-6-15 5KSLI p144 CR Belgium80 &CR Belgium187

FRENCH,Victor James Somerset 2Lt kia 10-10-18 1IrGds p52 CR

103

France337

FRENCH,William Alexander Smith 2Lt kia 12/16-5-17 6SfthH p241 MR20

FRENCH,William Cotton Maj kia 12-3-15 IA 2/3GurkhaRif p276 CR France727

FRENCH-BLAKE,St J.L.O'B.A,MC Maj 19-4-17 21Lancers attWorcHuss CR Palestine18

FRENCH-BREWSTER,Robert Abraham Maj ded 17-2-17 IrGds SR p52 CR Lond8

FREND,Hugh Palliser T2Lt kia 20-3-17 6Nhampt p137 CR France420

FREND,John Arthur Edward 2Lt kia 17-1-17 281RFA p28 CR France705

FREND,William Reginald Capt&Adjt kia 21-9-14 2N&D p134 MR15 &CR France1893

FRERE,Bartle Laurie Stuart.MID Lt kia 13-11-16 4Beds p85 CR France220

FRERE,Edgar 2Lt dow 22-5-16 8Lond p247 MR20

FRERE,Frederick John Henry Tobias.MC.Capt kia 10-6-17 RAMC att6Lincs p195 CR Belgium17,9-6-17

FRERE,Gilbert Raper TLt&Adjt dow 26-10-15 10RB p178 CR France345,Capt

FRERE,Lionel Basil 2LtTLt dow 29-9-15 DLI att2EYorks p160 MR19

FRESTON,Charles Albert Edward 2Lt dow 25-3-18 5 att23RFus p67 MR20

FRESTON,Hugh Reginald 2Lt kia 24-1-16 3 att6RBerks p139 CR France515

FRETTINGHAM,Arthur Cyril 2Lt ded 27-2-17 19WelshR p264 CR Notts84

FRETWELL,Arthur Richard Lt dow 1-4-18 5SomLI p218 CR France62,5WYorks

FREW,David Thomas Crichton TCapt ded 29-9-16 RAMC att2RIrR p195 CR Scot764

FREW,James Robertson TLtACapt dow 23-11-16 RFA 63Bde12Div p28 CR France177

FREW,John William.MC.TCapt dow 8-10-18 RAMC att2/3WRidFA p195 CR France146,Williamson

FREW,Robert Dunlop Black Capt kia 3-8-17 RAMC 1/3FA p253 CR Belgium11

FREY,Emile 2Lt kia 26-8-18 5Lond p246 CR France214

FRICKER,Albert Charles T2Lt kia 27-2-17 10EYorks p84 CR France156

FRICKER,Arthur Warwick TLt kia 29-5-16 1Nhampt p137 CR France149

FRICKER,Edwin T2Lt kia 29-9-16 7RWKent p141 MR21

FRIEAKE,Gordon Minter 2Lt ded 1-8-16 1/4 O&BLI p231 CR France145

FRIEDBERGER,William Sigismund Capt kia 24-5-15 3 att5RFus p67 MR29

FRIEND,Charles Philip Lt ded 15-10-18 RFA p28 CR Europe41

FRIEND,Frank Howard TLt dow 29-9-15 2Wilts p153 CR France201,Haward

FRIEND,George Burton Taddy TCapt kia 25-7-15 6EKent p57 CR Belgium33,26-7-15

FRIEND,Henry John T2Lt kia 4-10-17 8SomLI p79 CR Belgium116

FRIEND,James Bertie T2Lt kia 21-8-18 17 att13Lpool p71 MR16,Joseph

FRIEND,Joshua J.T2Lt kia 9-9-17 NumbF att20Bn p61 CR France1461

FRIEND,Philip Emlyn 2Lt kia 7-7-16 MGC p182 CR France267

FRIEND,Stanley John 2Lt dow 22-4-18 7RWSurr p55 CR France145

FRIPP,George 2Lt dow 4-6-18 1Dors p124 CR France924

FRIPP,John Trude 2Lt kia 13-10-15 3Lincs p75 MR19

FRIPP,Joseph Harry T2Lt ded 12-3-18 12RFus p67 CR Lancs164

FRIPP,Tom Olphert 2Lt kia 30-6-18 RGA 177SB p39 CR Belgium2

FRISCH,Charles 2Lt kia 17-4-16 IARO att1/9GurkhaRif p276 MR38

FRISCH,Maurice 2Lt kia 25-8-16 5 att2RB p178 MR19

FRISCHLING,Geoffrey Hepworth T2Lt kia 14-8-18 9 att12ESurr p112 CR Belgium11,Lt

FRITCHLEY,Joseph Bertram 2Lt kia 27-8-18 6Lond p247 MR16

FRITH,Henry George T2Lt kia 31-7-17 17Manch p154 MR29

FRITH,Reginald William Lt ded 7-2-18 Herts p270 CR Essex83

FRITH,William Wesson LtACapt kia 3-11-17 RGA 169SB p39 CR Belgium176

FRITZBROWN,Eric T2Lt kia 1-7-16 18Lpool p71

FRIZELL,Richard Alexander TCapt kia 10-11-17 2RMunstF p175 MR30

FRIZELLE,Archibald 2Lt kia 1-5-16 75RH&FA B'Bty p28 CR Belgium4

FRIZELLE,Edwin Samuel 2Lt kia 3-8-15 5LancF p221 CR Gallipoli1

FRIZONI,Oscar Lorenzo Lt kia 13-11-16 12EYorks p84 MR21

FRODSHAM,William Thomas Lt kia 9-9-16 5SLancs p230 CR France402

FROLICH,John Charles Cecil 2Lt kia 15-9-16 21Lond p251 CR France385

FROMANT,Herbert Dudley Sands T2Lt kia 29-4-17 26NumbF p61 CR France451

FROST,Alan Capt kia 17-10-17 28Lond att259MGC Inf p187&252 CR EAfrica11 &CR Tanzania1

FROST,Alfred Iago 2Lt kia 1-7-16 2Mddx p146 MR21,Ingo

FROST,Arthur 2Lt dow 23-3-18 2 att8Worc p108 MR27

FROST,Arthur Byfield.MC.Lt kia 23-3-18 4RWSurr p212 MR27

FROST,Arthur Colin T2Lt kia 25-9-15 11A&SH p173 MR19

FROST,Charles Dale Capt kia 22-11-15 IA 110MahrattaLI p276 MR38

FROST,Colin Blomfield TLt kia 24-7-18 44RFA p28 CR France248

FROST,Cyril Haddon TLt kia 26-10-18 RFA 403HB p29 MR38

FROST,E.H.Capt 8-9-20 MGC Inf CR War129

FROST,Edmund Lionel Lt kia 16-6-15 4SLancs p230 MR29

FROST,Eric George Capt kia 26-1-16 1/7Mddx p235 CR France768

FROST,Evelyn Fairfax Meadows Capt dow 20-12-15 5HLI p240 CR Gallipoli1

FROST,Francis Conrade Shenstone 2Lt kia 21-3-18 4 att8EKent p212 MR27

FROST,George SubCdr drd 1-1-17 IA S&TCps p276 MR35

FROST,George Jesse T2Lt dow 9-9-15 7Suff p78 CR France285

FROST,James John TLt kia 7-7-16 11NumbF p61 MR21

FROST,John Wiliam.MC.Lt ded 23-3-19 2Nhampt p137 CR Oxford69

FROST,Joshua 2Lt dow 29-9-16 8DLI p239 CR France453

FROST,Kenneth 2Lt kia 22-2-15 1RWKent p141 MR29

FROST,Kingdon Tregosse Lt kia 4-9-14 3Ches p96 MR15

FROST,Percy Causton T2Lt kia 8-9-18 KSLIatt10Bn p144 CR France364

FROST,Robert Wall 2Lt kia 3-7-16 10 att7Suff p78 MR21

FROST,Ronald William.MC.Lt kia 10-10-17 94RFA p29&258 CR Belgium19

FROST,Thomas Lawrence Capt&Adjt kia 28-3-15 1Ches p96 CR Belgium165,Laurence

FROST,William Edward.MM.2Lt ded 9-10-19 1Lincs p263 CR Ireland14,Lt 8-10-19

FROST,William Frank 2Lt kia 17-10-18 21RFA p208 CR France341

FROUD,Harold William Lt dow 27-7-17 5DLI p238 CR France518

FROWD-WALKER,R.S.CMG.LtCol 16-5-17 10Glouc CR Kent97

FRY,Alfred Andrew Capt ded 27-6-19 3Mon &RAF p244

FRY,Alfred Harold 2Lt dow 30-10-16 1/22Lond C'Coy p251 CR France40

FRY,Arthur Charles 2Lt dow 28-2-17 2/4 O&BLI D'Coy p231 CR France164

FRY,Charles Augustus Capt kia 1-4-18 6Ess att2GarBnSuff p232 CR France65,2-4-18

FRY,Charles Edward Lt kia 17-11-17 D23RFA p29 CR France266,17-4-17

FRY,Edward Meaburn.MC.Lt kia 23-8-18 D211RFA p207 CR France643

FRY,Edwin Harries Sargood Maj dow 25-5-18 RGA 126SB p209 CR France84

FRY,Horace Charles 2Lt ded 24-2-17 10RWKent attRFC p7,kld p18&235,5Bn p141,p212 CR Kent127,23-2-17

FRY,John Desford Lt kia 15-9-16 1Lond p244 CR France785

FRY,John Libby 2Lt kld 20-2-17 RFC p7 CR Wilts116

FRY,John Thomas Lt&QM ded 3-10-15 RAMC p195 CR France8

FRY,Leonard 2Lt kia 19-7-16 6Glouc p225 CR France525

FRY,Leslie.MC.2Lt dow 9-11-18 3RScotF attMGC p94&182

FRY,Leslie Harrington.MID Lt kia 9-8-18 19Huss p23 CR France652

FRY,Stephen Gabriel 2Lt kia 22-5-15 IARO att1/1GurkhaRif p276 MR28

FRY,Walter Burgess Maj ded PoW 17-3-15 RAMC p195 CR Germany4

FRY,Wilfred 2Lt dow 3-11-18 10Lond p248 CR France146

FRY,William Henry TLt dow 26-5-17 88MGC p182 CR France113

FRYE,Lionel Henry 2Lt kia 16-6-18 1/2 att1/5Glouc p106

FRYER,Charles William 2Lt dow 1-8-18 1/12LNLancs p135 CR France248

FRYER,Christopher John Gwynne.MC&Bar.Lt kia 4-11-18 1Herts p252 CR France206

FRYER,Eric Hamilton Lt kia 3-8-16 4 att2/5LancF p92 MR21

FRYER,James Whaley 2Lt kia 1-7-16 22NumbF p61 MR21

FRYER,John Maj ded 2-3-20 7Huss p261 CR Dorset53

FRYER,John Percival T2Lt kia 22-3-18 8BordR p117 MR20

FRYER,Stanley Phillipps 2Lt kia 27-10-18 30RFA attY1TMB p29 CR France1270

FRYER,William Arthur TLt kia 3-10-18 KRRC att4Bn p150 CR France234

FRYER,William Basil 2Lt kld 26-12-16 3/5SStaffs attRFC p18&229 CR Egypt1

FUDGE,Alfred TLt dow 22-2-18 9Suff att101RFC p16&78 CR France1063

FUGE,Frederick Henry TLt kia 13-8-16 6SomLI p79 MR21

FUGEMAN,William Alfred TCapt kia 1-12-17 23RFus C'Coy p67 CR France1496

FULLALOVE,George Young 2Lt 13-8-17 55RFC CR France134

FULLARD,Norman 2Lt dow 22-5-18 5 att2YLI p235 CR France226

FULCHER,Bernard Vincent.MC.MIDx2Lt kia 17-11-14 2SLancs p125 MR29

FULCHER,Oliver Arthur 2Lt ded 29-6-16 RGA p39 CR Iraq6

FULFORD,Reginald Hardwick Chap4Cl kia 15-12-16 RAChDept p199 MR38

FULKES,John Greville 2Lt kia 13-11-16 3 att13Ess p131 MR21

FULLER,Bernard T2Lt kia 4-11-18 7RWKent p141 CR France660

FULLER,Charles Stephen.MC.T2Lt kia 11-11-17 GL &r1RFC p7 CR France285

FULLER,Cyril John T2Lt dow 22-7-16 6RBerks p139 CR France141

FULLER,Dunstan Milley.MC.TCapt kia 10-8-17 11RFus p67 MR29

FULLER,Edward James.MC&Bar.MM.Lt ded 28-7-19 RGA 3Bty p262 CR Surrey99

FULLER,Ernest Paget 2Lt kia 20-9-17 4 att10RWSurr p212 MR30

FULLER,Gardner Henry 2Lt ded 26-2-15 RASC p192&257

FULLER,Gordon Howard 2LtACapt kia 7-7-18 3 att2 O&BLI p130 CR France745

FULLER,H.2Lt 24-2-15 RASC CR Staffs108

FULLER,Henry Arthur.MID Lt dow 26-4-18 RE 490FC p210 CR France29

FULLER,Herbert Foster Maj ded 8-11-19 IA S&TCps p276 MR43

FULLER,Herbert Walter 2Lt kia 21-8-18 14Lond p249 CR France285

FULLER,Hugh William 2Lt kia 18-9-18 5Suff p217 CR France369

FULLER,John Henry Middleton Capt kia 4-11-14 IA 83Inf att63PalamcottahLI p276 MR47,WallajahbadLI

FULLER,John Severn.MID LtTCapt ded 15-3-19 177RFA p29 CR Asia33

FULLER,Leonard Arthur Lt kia 17-5-17 8DLI att11RFC p18&239 CR France604

FULLER,Leslie Thomas Easterbrook 2Lt kia 18-9-16 24Lond p252 MR21

FULLER,Morris Richard T2Lt kia 11-4-17 10RFus p68 MR20

FULLER,Oliver Lionel 2Lt ded 18-10-18 PoW 20Lond p251 CR Germany1

FULLER,Percy D.2Lt kia 18-8-16 6DCLI p114 CR France402

FULLER,William Lt&QM 3-1-20 GL att1GarBnSomLI CR Europe5

FULLER,William Blyth Capt kia 16-5-15 2RWSurr p55 CR France279

FULLER-MAITLAND,William Alan Capt dow 19-9-14 1CldGds p57 MR15

FULLERTON,Frank T2Lt kia 31-7-17 LNLancs att1/4Bn p135 MR29

FULLERTON,James Basil Lt kia 9-8-17 A240RFA p207 CR Belgium10

FULLERTON,John Kenneth Capt dow 15-8-17 1/6Glouc p225 CR Belgium20

FULLERTON,William Francis Hannan 2Lt kia 22-10-16 GL &RFC p2&190,ded CR France598

FULLIN,John Francis.MC.2Lt kia 22-3-18 5RMunstF p175 MR27

FULTON,Alexander T2Lt kia 19-8-16 13RScots p54 CR France515

FULTON,Andrew 2Lt kia 23-4-17 6A&SH p243 CR France434

FULTON,Andrew Wilfred TMaj kia 12-8-16 1/9Lpool p216 MR21

FULTON,Cecil John TLt dow 29-4-16 7RIrF p171 CR France80

FULTON,Charles Mathew Capt ded 23-7-20 IA 33Cav p276 MR67,24-7-20 23Cav

FULTON,D.T.MC.MID Capt 11-8-20 RE IWT CR Egypt2

FULTON,Ernest Alan T2Lt kia 3-10-16 25 att19Mddx p146 MR21

FULTON,George Koberwein.DSO.TCaptALtCol kia 14-4-18 9Ches p96 MR30 Ex6Wilts

FULTON,Harry Townsend.CMG.DSO.BrigGen dow 29-3-18 IA Cmdg3NZRifBde p276

FULTON,Hugh 2Lt kia 9-10-18 9HLI p240 CR France550

FULTON,James Fleming T2Lt kia 12-10-16 5CamH att26TMB p167 CR France385

FULTON,John Duncan Bertie.CB.MajTLtCol ded 11-11-15 RFA &RFC p1&29 CR Lond4

FULTON,Samuel Duff 2Lt ded 21-10-19 RGA p262 CR Scot288

FUNNELL,Cecil Herbert Michael Capt dow 30-4-16 RGA 128HB p39

FUNNELL,Harry Edward.DSO.TMaj ded 10-12-18 MGC attGHQ Italy p182 CR Italy65

FURBER,Gilbert George 2Lt dow 22-7-17 12Y&L p158 CR France113,Lt kia

FURLEY,Bernard Edward.MID TMaj kia 13-10-15 6EKent p57 MR19

FURLEY,Francis Edward Lt kia 22-3-18 1/4EYorks p219 CR France836

FURLEY,Percival Henry Biddulph 2Lt kia 1-6-19 IA 1/41Dogras p276 MR43

FURLEY,Robert Basil 2Lt kia 25-1-16 O&BLI BucksBn p231 CR France1327

FURLEY,Wolseley Haig.MID Lt kia 26-4-18 3RScots p54 MR30

FURLONG,Philip James T2Lt kia 30-7-16 19Lpool p71 MR21

FURMSTON,Clement Barrington T2Lt kia 9-4-17 154MGC Inf p182 CR France184

FURNEAUX,Phillip Templer Lt kia 26-10-14 1Lpool p71 MR29

FURNEAUX,William Edington.MC.TMaj kia 24-3-18 9SfthH p164 CR France511

FURNELL,Cecil Herbert Michael Capt 30-4-16 RGA 128HB CR Belgium11

FURNELL,Thomas Capt dow 31-7-18 1/7Ches p222 CR France145

FURNESS,Godfrey Gordon 2Lt kia 9-2-17 3 att2N&D p134 CR France423

FURNESS,James Collins LtCol kia 26-2-18 RAMC p195 MR40,drd

FURNESS,Montague Smith 2Lt kia 29-6-17 3/45RFA p29 CR Belgium115

FURNISS,Charles Frederick T2Lt dow 16-4-18 14Y&L p158 CR Belgium38

FURNISS,James 2Lt kia 31-7-17 4RIrRif p169 MR29

FURNISS,Kevin Robert Lt dow 29-4-17 PoW StaffsYeo att23RFC. p18&205 CR France403

FURSE,Edmund William LtCol kld 19-5-18 88RFA p29 CR France1410

FURSE,George Armond Capt dow 16-9-14 44RFA p29 CR France1329,Armand

FURSE,William Henry T2Lt kia 1-7-16 21NumbF p61 CR France150,dow

FURZE,Alfred TCapt&Adjt kia 16-9-16 7YLI p143 MR21

FURZE,Claude Capt dow 6-4-18 5Lond p246 CR France2

FURZE,Frederick Capt kia 20-9-17 5Lond p246 MR29

FURZE,Nevil Ford 2Lt kia 14-3-17 2RWSurr p55 CR France514

FUSSELL,James Gerald Lt kia 1-7-16 1/8RWar p215 MR21

FUSSELL,John William Hugo 2Lt kia 19-7-16 3 att6 O&BLI p130 CR France525

FUTERS,Norman Ratcliffe LtACapt kia 27-9-18 1NumbF p61 CR France357

FYFE,Austyn James Claude 2Lt kia 23-3-17 RFA &55TMB p208 CR Belgium4

FYFE,Charles Clarke 2Lt kia 21-3-18 6BlkW p231 MR20

FYFE,Gilbert 2Lt 16-7-16 9HLI CR France833

FYFE,Thomas Alexander.MC.Capt dow 29-8-18 1/5HLI p240 CR France145

FYFE,William Quentin Lt kia 21-3-18 5GordH p242 MR27

FYFFE,John James T2Lt kia 14-9-16 13WYorks p81 CR France293

FYLDES,Aubrey William 2Lt kia 9-8-15 1/4ELancs p226 CR Gallipoli2

FYNN,Robert Charles T2Lt kia 25-3-18 4Beds p85 MR20 &CR France390

FYNNEY,Frederick Adolphus TLt ded 27-11-18 TankCps p266 CR Kent175,Capt ExLpool

FYSH,Charles Edward.DSO.MC&Bar.Maj kia 28-7-18 6SfthH p241 CR France1697

FYSON,Geoffrey Lt dow 4-9-18 3 att1RScots p54 MR37

FYSON,George Dumill 2Lt kia 20-4-16 11Glouc p106 MR38,Dumillo 7Bn

FYSON,Harold George 2Lt kia 12-10-16 2Beds p85 MR21

FYVIE,William 2Lt kia 26-8-17 3RScots p54 CR France1461

G

GABAIN,William George.MC.Capt kia 24-3-18 Inns of CourtOTC SL att 2RB p201&252 CR France605

GABB,Richard George T2Lt dow 6-8-15 12 att1Ess p131 CR Gallipoli6

GABB,Stanley Frederick T2Lt dow 8-12-16 76MGC p182 CR France169

GABBETT,Pulteney Charles LtCol ded 11-7-16 IMS p276 CR Iraq5

GABBETT,Richard Edward Phillip LtCol kia 16-5-15 1RWFus p97 CR France279,Phillips

GABBETT-FAIRFAX,Thomas Oliver 2Lt kia 14-8-17 11RB p178 MR29

GABELL,Douglas Ridley Clunes 2Lt kld 12-7-18 Glouc &RAF p264

GABRIEL,Allan TLt dow 23-8-16 15N&D att105TMB p134 CR France23

GADDUM,Russell Charles Sydney T2Lt kia 10-9-16 17RFus p68 CR France344

GADNEY,Gilbert Sims T2Lt kia 3-7-16 8Glouc p106 MR21

GADSDEN,Crawford Cunningham Lt dow 16-10-17 4RWSurr att101RFC p18&212 CR France134

GADSDON,Frank Bannatyne T2Lt kia 7-6-17 9Ches p96 CR Belgium153

GAFFIKIN,George Horner TMaj kia 1-7-16 9RIrRif B'Coy p169 CR France396

GAFFNEY,James.MC.TCapt kia 8-10-18 RDubF p176 CR France844

GAFFNEY,Leon Arthur T2Lt dow 12-8-15 6RMunstF p175 CR Gallipoli27

GAGE,Brenton Albert Hamilton.MC.MIDx2 LtTCapt dow 29-5-15 7/4RFA p29 CR France631

GAGE,John Capt ded 7-11-16 11RDubF p176

GAGE,John Munro TCapt ded 29-11-18 RAMC p195 CR Greece2,att57RFA

GAGE,John Stewart Moore 2Lt kia 1-7-16 9RInniskF p105 MR21

GAGLIARDI,Louis Patrick.MID Capt accdrd 5-9-17 IARO att37Lancers p276 CR Iraq5

GAGNE,John 2Lt kia 24-5-17 GL &43RFC p7 MR20

GAILLIE,O.E.DSO.MC.Capt kia 7-12-17 RH&FA p29

GAINEY,Henry Charles T2Lt kia 14-7-16 8Dev p76 CR France453

GAIR,Henry Burgh 2Lt dow 15-5-18 4Dors att14PnrCoy p229 CR France84,13-5-18,1Bn

GAIR,Thomas Lt kia 10-9-17 A276RFA p207 MR30,9-9-17

GAISFORD,Lionel Lt kia 23-11-14 IA 58Rif WAFF p276 CR France80

GAISFORD,Robert Sandeman Lt kia 30-1-18 RFA att34RFC p16&29 CR Italy9,Capt

GAISFORD,Walter Thomas MajTLtCol kia 25-9-15 7SfthH p164 MR19

GAITSKELL,Cyril Egremont Lt dow 19-10-14 2Leinst p174 CR France922

GALBRAITH,Alexander Norman Capt 16-2-15 CeylonPlantersRifCps CR Eire541

GALBRAITH,Alfred Hugh T2Lt kld 24-2-18 57TrSqnRFC p16 CR Egypt8

GALBRAITH,Arthur Hugh Courtney Lt dow 9-9-18 RGA 285SB 83Bde p39 CR France145,Courtrey 284SB

GALBRAITH,David Boyd 2Lt kia 20-8-15 7HLI p240 CR Gallipoli1

GALBRAITH,Donald James Findlay Lt kia 25-1-15 9HLI p240 CR France765

GALBRAITH,James Robert 2Lt ded 20-9-17 A64RFA p29 CR Belgium8

GALBRAITH,Norman Dunlop Lt kia 22-8-18 7HLI p240 CR France113

GALBRAITH,William Brodie Lt dow 14-7-15 7HLI p240 CR Gallipoli1

GALBRAITH,William Thomas T2Lt kld 26-2-18 RFC p16 CR Scot214

GALE,Arthur Witherby.DSO.TCapt kia 10-4-16 2LifeGds attRFA RoO p20 CR Belgium11

GALE,Charles William Lt ded 20-2-19 Ex16GarrBn YLI p265 CR Surrey57

GALE,Harold William T2Lt kia 8-8-18 7RSuss att5RBerks p119 CR France141

GALE,Henry James 2Lt kia 21-3-18 1Lincs p75 MR27

GALE,Henry John Elliott.MC.MM.T2Lt kia 7-6-18 RE 1SpCoy p45 CR France31,8-6-18

GALE,Herbert Anthony.MC&Bar.ACapt dow 12-8-18 6 att2Wilts A'Coy p153 CR France31

GALE,John Hugh 2Lt kia 14-9-16 70RFC p2 CR France374

GALE,Marmaduke Henry Littledale Maj kia 28-6-15 IA 8Cav p276 MR66

GALE,Ralph George 2LtTLt kia 12-10-17 8SStaffs p122 MR30

GALE,Ralph Goulstone TLt kia 26-3-18 RE B SpecCo p45 CR France570

GALE,Robert Grafton TLt kia 24-4-18 RASC 24DSC att2/5Glouc p192 CR France248

GALE,William Newlyn Capt kia 3-5-17 4Y&L p238 MR20

GALL,Campbell McKenzie Lt kia 18-8-18 6KOSB p101 MR32

GALL,Grant Lt kia 21-3-18 3RScots attRE 3FdSurvCo p54 CR France245

GALL,William John Reid 2Lt dow 18-4-18 RGA 346SB p39 CR France31

GALLAGHER,Roland Henry Capt ded 25-6-15 MGC p182 CR France102

GALLAGHER,William Augustine.MID Capt kia 12-3-15 2ELancs p110 CR France1106,10-3-15

GALLAUGHER,Henry.DSO.Capt kia 7-6-17 11RInniskF p105 CR Belgium62

GALLAUGHER,Robert Rankin T2Lt ded 23-2-17 4Worc p108 CR France300

GALLETLEY,Ian Lt kia 3-8-16 C258RFA p207 CR France188

GALLEY,Ralph Rowlands 2Lt kia 22-3-18 11DLI A'Coy p160 CR France1206

GALLICHAN,Francis Ernest 2Lt kia 28-7-16 10NStaffs att99MGC p157 CALLICHAN &182 MR21,27-7-16

GALLIE,Arthur Lockhart Maj ded 23-9-15 Dors p124 CR Devon237

GALLIE,Charles 2Lt kia 22-8-15 RScotF attRFC p1&94 CR France924

GALLIE,Edward Archibald TLt kia 1-7-16 17HLI D'Coy p162 CR France293

GALLIE,Oscar Eugene.DSO.MC.Capt kia 7-12-17 A156RFA CR Belgium10

GALLIERS,Richard Sidney 2LtACapt kia 31-5-18 2Wilts p153 CR France1689

GALLIMORE,Henry Burrows Capt kia 26-5-17 D312RFA p207 CR France568

GALLIMORE,Hubert Thomas Keith Lt kia 29-3-18 4KSLI att6Ches p235 MR27

GALLINGER,George Harry T2Lt kia 31-10-17 GL &18RFC p7 CR France88

GALLO,Antonio Marie.MC.2Lt kia 31-7-17 5Beds p219 MR29

GALLOWAY,Bernard Thomas 2Lt kia 6-10-16 8Mddx p236 MR21

GALLOWAY,Frederick Philip TLt dow 12-11-17 27RFC p7 CR France40

GALLOWAY,Graeme Stuart Montgomerie T2Lt kia 4-7-16 4Lpool p71 CR France114

GALLOWAY,Harold Bessemer CaptTMaj kia 25-9-15 7SforthH p164 MR19

GALLOWAY,James Blyth 2Lt ded 17-11-18 RFA p208 MR65

GALLOWAY,Reginald Edgar Charles TCapt ded 11-2-19 RAOC 121Coy p198 CR France40

GALLOWAY,Robert Herbert 2Lt kia 24-3-18 8TanksCps p188 CR France245

GALLOWAY,Ronald Moncrief Lt kia 28-6-15 7RScots p211 MR4

GALLOWAY,William Ernest 2Lt kia 6-11-17 1/4WelshR p230 CR Palestine1

GALSWORTHY,Edgar T2Lt kia 27-9-18 11TankCps p188 CR France379

GALSWORTHY,Lionel Richmond Lt 8-3-21 RFA CR Norf101

GALTON,Francis William Joseph.MID Lt kia 23-4-17 1Dev p76 MR20

GALTON,Theodore Hugh 2Lt kia 21-10-14 Worc att3Bn p108 MR22

GALTRY,Raymond T2Lt kia 9-10-17 1/2 att6Yorks p90 MR30

GALWAY,Edgar Seaman SubCdr kia 7-5-15 IA S&TCps p276 CR Gallipoli30

GALWAY,Reginald Hugh Maj dow 15/17-2-15 RGA 80Coy p39 CR Asia45,15-2-15

GAMBELL,Dennis Clayton Lt kia 30-4-18 2/19Lond p250 MR34

GAMBLE,Frank Burfield 2Lt kia 1-7-16 1/7N&D p233 CR France281

GAMBLE,George T2Lt dow 24-9-17 2RB p178 CR France262

GAMBLE,Hugh Valentine Lt kia 3-5-17 2SfthH p164 CR France546

GAMBLE,James Frederick 2Lt kia 24-6-16 1RWar p64 CR France35,Lt 25-6-16

GAMBLE,John Walcote TLt dow 22-5-16 2DLI B'Coy p160 CR Belgium11,14Bn

GAMBLE,Ralph Dominic.MC.Lt kia 22-8-18 1CldGds p51 CR France103

GAMBLE,Richard Maurice Brooks 2Lt kia 16-5-15 7Lpool p215 CR France279

GAMBLE,Richard Sumner 2Lt kia 22-5-15 7ELancs att1/1GurkhaRif p264&276 MR22

GAMBLE,Walter Rayes.MC.TCapt dow 12-6-17 9Yorks p90 CR Belgium11,Raynes

GAMBLIN John Louis 2Lt kia 8-5-15 RFA p29 MR29

GAME,Hubert John TLt kld 8-6-17 RFA &RFC p7&29 CR Norf247

GAME,Reginald Francis 2Lt ded 10-10-18 3BlkW att60MGC Inf p128 CR Palestine9

GAME,Walter Harold 2Lt kia 23-4-17 5Yorks p221 MR20

GAMESON,George Henry Molyneux 2Lt dow 14-3-17 3 att8NumbF p61 CR France514

GAMLEN,Robert Arthur Winnington LtACapt kia 30-11-17 4Worc p108 CR France1483

GAMMAN,Edward 2Lt kia 26-10-17 RGA 306SB p39 MR30

GAMMAN,Gilbert T2Lt kia 10-8-15 5Wilts p153 MR4

GAMMELL,Henry Stobart.MC.LtACapt kia 31-8-18 1GordH p166 CR France927

GAMMIE,Herbert Forsyth TLt kia 14-9-18 1CamH att7NStaffs p167 CR Asia81

GAMON John Lionel Percival Lt kldacc 4-6-18 1BordR att51NumbF p117 CR Ches30

GAMON,Maurice Partridge TCapt kia 1-7-16 2LancF p92 CR France1890

GAMON,Sidney Percival Capt kld 23-3-18 5Ches attRFC p18&222 CR Ches117,Sydney

GANDAMALL,James Rev ded 10-10-18 IA CR Iraq6

GANDAR-DOWER,Leonard Francis 2Lt ded PoW 3-5-17 2HAC p206 MR20

GANDER,Leslie Stephen T2Lt dow 5-6-18 SfthH att1/4Bn p164 CR France40

GANDON,Ralph T2Lt kia 26-9-16 Dors att7Bn p124 MR21

GANDY,Clement Joseph.MC.2Lt kia 31-7-17 RE 234FC p45 CR Belgium96

GANDY,George Joseph 2Lt kia 15-5-17 2Leic p87 CR France727

GANDY,William Hendry.MID Capt kia 12-7-15 7HLI p240 MR4,Henry

GANE,Wilfred Errol.MC.Lt dow 8-12-17 D301RFA p207 CR Palestine3

GANLY,Roger.MC.Capt kia 29-9-16 LancF att11Bn p92 MR21

GANNON,John Howard T2Lt kld 9-10-17 3 att11RWFus p97 CR Greece6,8-10-17

GANSON,Andrew T2Lt kia 14-12-16 10HLI p162 CR France392

GANT,Alfred Claude T2Lt kia 17-10-18 2KRRC p150 CR France341

GANT,Harold Holden 2Lt kia 1-9-18 2Lond p245 CR France216

GANT,Leslie John Lt ded 15-7-19 RH&FA 19BdeAmmCol p261 CR Egypt1

GANTSMAN,Ernest T2Lt kia 10-11-17 KRRC att9Bn p150 CR Belgium10

GARBETT,Ronald Vivian T2Lt kia 5-1-18 10RFC p16 CR Belgium11

GARBUTT,James Reston Gardiner TLt kia 1-12-15 RAMC att8KOSB p195 CR France423

GARBUTT,Lawrence Mark T2Lt dow 10-8-18 3Ess att9Norf p131 CR France142

GARD,Frederick TLt kia 28-6-18 1DCLI p114 CR France20

GARDEN,Charles Robert John 2Lt ded 5-5-16 B69RFA p29 CR Iraq5

GARDEN,John James 2Lt kia 3-5-17 5RWSurr p212 CR France357

GARDINER,Alec Maj kia 20-12-14 RE p45 MR22

GARDINER,Alexander Anson 2Lt kia 26-1-17 IARO att13/2S&M p276 CR Iraq5

GARDINER,Archibald Macalister T2Lt dow 24-5-16 12A&SH p173 CR France80,11Bn

GARDINER,Arthur Lt dow 26-3-18 19Lond p250 CR Palestine9

GARDINER,Ashley James T2Lt dow 24-10-18 1SomLI A'Coy p79 CR France241

GARDINER,Charles Lt kia 25-4-18 4 att6KOSB p223 MR30

GARDINER,Charles Thomas 2Lt dow 1-6-15 3RFus p68 CR France102

GARDINER,Ellis Hubert Lt dow 7-10-18 1/7Ches A'Coy p223 CR Belgium11

GARDINER,Eric John Lt kia 19-4-17 5Norf p216 MR34

GARDINER,Ernest.MID Maj kia 2-3-15 RE 1FC p209 MR29

GARDINER,Evelyn Francis.MC.Lt kia 30-7-16 3SfthH att90MGC p182 MR21

GARDINER,Francis John 2Lt ded 28-3-17 IARO att40Pathans p276 CR EAfrica38 &CR Tanzania1

GARDINER,Frederick Thomas LtACapt kia 31-7-17 HLI att12Bn p162 MR29

GARDINER,Godfrey Dernan T2Lt kia 13-9-16 9Suff p78 MR21,GARDNER Dernan

GARDINER,Ivan Jephson Lt drd 27-5-18 5Norf &RAF p216 MR41

GARDINER James Totton 2Lt dow PoW 1-11-18 RIrRif p169 CR Belgium342

GARDINER,Kenneth Edward MacAlpine T2Lt ?? 17-10-15 14RFus att8Lond p68 CR France219

GARDINER,Kenneth John Rattray LtTCapt ded 1-2-17 SL RE att2/3KAR SL p202 MR46

GARDINER,Paul Wrey Lt kia 27-5-18 4Manch att1Worc p154 MR18

GARDINER,Robert Edward 2Lt kia 26-7-17 RGA 285SB p39 CR Belgium17

GARDINER,Stanley Tysol T2Lt kia 27-6-16 RE 55FC p45 CR Belgium6,Tysoe

GARDINER,William Edward Mansfield 2Lt kia 20-7-16 5Lond p246 CR France283

GARDINER,William MacPherson T2Lt kia 16-1-18 RB p178 MR30

GARDNER,Albert Abercrombie T2Lt kia 23-4-17 8SfthH p164 CR France536

GARDNER,Alex Young Fraser Lt ded 15-11-18 RASC p253 CR Scot237

GARDNER,Alfred Ernest 2Lt kia 13-1-17 1/4YLI p235 CR France504

GARDNER,Alfred Linton TCapt kia 9-4-18 RAMC 107FA att4NStaffs p195 CR France41,10-4-18

GARDNER,Andrew Abercrombie Lt kia 6-9-18 6A&SH att57MGC Inf p187&243 CR France309

GARDNER,Arnold 2Lt ded 13-7-19 10RSuss p264

GARDNER,Burnett Gilroy Craufurd 2Lt ded 7-5-15 RE 171TC p45 CR France1,Crawford

GARDNER,Caldwell Lt kia 11-9-16 6A&SH p243 CR France394

GARDNER,Cyril Gower Lt kia 14-9-16 2 att3GrenGds p50 MR21

GARDNER,Eric Mawdsley 2Lt kia 10-4-17 3SomLI p79 MR20

GARDNER,Eric Melford 2Lt kia 27-9-18 8 att28Lond p247 CR France1496

GARDNER,Francis Henry T2Lt dow 17-10-18 1/2Leic p87 CR France847

GARDNER,Frederick George Benjamin T2Lt kia 25-7-16 D166RFA p29 CR France188

GARDNER,George Capt kia 21-8-15 21Lancers attBucksYeo p23 CR Gallipoli5

GARDNER,George Ryding Sankey Maj ded 26-6-16 B265RFA p206 CR Egypt8,Sanky

GARDNER,Henry Montfort LtCol 28-10-18 4Lincs CR Glouc27

GARDNER,James 2Lt kldacc 27-11-16 RFC p2 CR Scot810

GARDNER,John.MC.TCapt dow 27-9-17 6/7RScotF p94 CR Scot674

GARDNER,Leonard Clement Lt dow 2-6-18 RGA 139HB p39 CR France69

GARDNER,Maurice Leigh 2Lt kld 19-1-15 RFC p1 CR Mddx26

GARDNER,Maurice Reginald George 2Lt kia 27-5-18 1Worc p108 MR18

GARDNER,Norman T2Lt kia 2-10-18 3WRid att16LancF p115 CR France237,Capt

GARDNER,Richard Pringle McKay 2Lt kia 18-8-16 2A&SH p173 CR France393,GARDENER

GARDNER,Robert 2Lt kia 5-5-15 5RLancs p213 MR29

GARDNER,Robert Bell 2Lt kia 7-1-18 5HLI p240 CR Palestine9

GARDNER,Robert MacGregor Stewart Maj kld 31-10-14 1Glouc p106 MR29

GARDNER,Robert Oswald Capt kia 8-5-15 3Mon B'Coy p244 CR Belgium152

GARDNER,Sidney T2Lt kia 27-3-18 11ELancs p110 MR20

GARDNER,Thomas Lt kia 22-7-16 2/20Lond p251 CR France68,28-7-16

GARDNER,Wedderburn Mackenzie T2Lt dow 23-8-17 8SfthH p164 CR Belgium11

GARDNER,William T2Lt kia 24-3-18 10 att15DLI p160 MR27

GARDNER,William Bristow.MC.T2LtACapt kia 28-3-18 2Wilts p153 MR27

GARDNER,William James 2Lt dow 26-9-16 1Leic attWYorks p87 CR France329

GARDNER,William Sutton 2Lt kia 6-3-17 RFA att57RFC p29&7 CR France46

GARDNER,Wilie T2Lt dow 17-10-17 WYorks att1/8Bn p81 CR France64

GARDOM John Charles TLt kia 6-8-15 12 att1Ess p131 CR Gallipoli6

GARFIT,Thomas Noel Cheney Lt kia 30-4-15 2DLI p160 CR France1140

GARFORTH,William Godfrey Willoughby Lt kia 16-5-15 2ScotsGds p52 CR France705

GARLAND,Cecil William Robert 2Lt kia 20-2-18 Lpool att1/7Bn p71 CR France765

GARLAND,Francis Henry 2Lt kia 23-10-18 4 att8Glouc p225 CR France270

GARLAND,George Arthur T2Lt kia 16-9-16 21DLI p160 MR21

GARLAND,George Harry Charles 2Lt ded 4-3-17 RFA 113Bty 25Bde p29 CR France833

GARLAND,James Harvey Lt dow 12-11-15 5GordH p242 CR France43

GARLAND,James Richard TCapt kia 1-7-16 2Lond p245 CR France798

GARLAND,John Jeffrey T2Lt dow 9-7-18 1/2Glouc p106 CR France21,James

GARLAND,Wilfred.MID T2Lt kia 8-5-17 7 O&BLI p130 MR37,Wilfrid

GARLICK,Charles Sidney T2Lt dow 16-7-16 8Wilts p153 CR France141,20KRRC

GARLICK,Frank Arthur 2Lt kia 20-2-16 13RFC p2 CR France448

GARLICK,Hilda Mary SNurse ded 12-8-17 TFNS CR War7

GARLICK,John Munro Lt dow 2-12-17 4A&SH p173 CR France398

GARLICK,Vivian Lt kia 15-6-18 O&BLI 1/4BucksBn p231 CR Italy2

GARMENT,Leonard Charles T2Lt kia 21-3-18 10LancF p92 MR20

GARNER,A.E.C. Sister ded 12-3-17 QAIMNS p200 CR Mddx13

GARNER,Edward Harold 2Lt kia 27-8-18 4Lond p246 MR16

GARNER,Frank Leslie T2Lt kld 20-12-16 GL &RFC p2&190

GARNER,Reginald William T2Lt kia 13-11-16 MGC p182 CR France156

GARNER,Robert Leonard 2Lt kia 24-8-18 11Lond p248 MR16

GARNER,Walter Percy 2Lt kia 13-4-18 18WelchR p264 CR France1059

GARNER-SMITH,Eric John Lt kia 25/26-5-15 1/24Lond MR22

GARNET,Grosvenor 2Lt kia 9-10-17 3LancF p92 CR Belgium83

GARNETT,Alfred Edward 2Lt kia 29-9-17 3Y&L p158 CR France550,30-9-17 2Bn

GARNETT,Claude Lionel Capt dow 31-12-15 RGA 86HB p39 CR Iraq1,30-12-15

GARNETT,Errol Russell 2Lt kia 18-10-16 2Wilts p153 CR France385

GARNETT,Ewanda Berckeley T2Lt kld 27-1-18 RFC p16

GARNETT,Harold Gwyer CaptAMaj kia 3-12-17 SWBord p100 MR17

GARNETT,Henry Knowles Lt ded 6-11-15 RFA p207

GARNETT,Ivan William T2Lt kia 12-2-16 6KSLI p144 CR Belgium101

GARNETT,Jerry Knowles Lt ded 6-11-15 3ELancsRFA p207 CR Europe1

GARNETT,Kenneth Gordon.MC.TLt dow 22-8-17 RH&FA p29

GARNETT,Laurence Henry TLt kia 7-8-17 A117ORFA p29 CR Belgium6

GARNETT,Phillip Nigel Lt dow 11-10-14 RBerks att1KAR p139&268 CR EAfrica80

GARNETT,William Herbert Stuart TLt kld 21-9-16 GL &RFC p2&190 CR Wilts116

GARNETT,William Patrick Lt dow 30-3-17 3RBerks attRFC p7&139 CR France81

GARNETT-BOTFIELD,Alfred Clulow Fitzgerald Lt kia 9-5-15 SWBord p100 MR22

GARNETT-BOTFIELD,Charles Sidney.MID Capt dow 14-12-14 2Beds p85 CR Shrop100

GARNHAM,Percival 2Lt ded 25-10-18 6Glouc p225 CR Italy11

GARNIER,Denys Keppel Capt dow 7-12-16 2Glouc p106 CR Greece3,6-12-16

GARNIER,John Warren Capt dow 29-5-15 3RWSurr p55 CR Sussex178,28-5-15

GARNONS-WILLIAMS,A.Aylmer Curtis.MC.Capt ded 14-5-18 SWBord &RAF p100 CR Sussex27

GARNONS-WILLIAMS,Richard Davie LtCol kia 25-9-15 12RFus p68 MR19,Davies

GARRAD,Edward Victor T2Lt kia 22-4-16 14RFus att6LNLancs p68 MR38

GARRARD,Frederick George.MC.2Lt dow 22-5-18 2GordH p166 CR Italy10

GARRARD,Harry Vernon Lt kia 2-11-14 BordR p117

GARRARD,Percy.DCM.Maj ded PoW 18-9-18 4KAR att24Lond p252,202&268 CR EAfrica77,24Lond att2/4KAR

GARRARD,Reginald Herbert T2Lt kia 23-4-17 16KRRC p150 CR France568

GARRARD,Stanley Charles T2Lt kia 28-8-15 14 att8RB p178 CR Belgium84

GARRARD,William Garth Blackall Lt kld 19-10-17 2NumbF p61 CR Greece1

GARRATT,Leslie Thomas T2Lt dow 3-7-16 32RFus p68 CR France285

GARRATT,Reginald Horatio 2Lt kia 29-9-17 GL &1RFC p7 MR20,GARRATT-REED 20-9-17

GARRAWAY,Wilfrid Fletcher 2Lt accdrd 5-11-16 IA 82Punjabis p276 CR Iraq5

GARRETT,Arthur Dale 2Lt kia 17-4-18 RE 456FC p45 MR30

GARRETT,Arthur ffolliott.OBE.Maj 28-3-20 RE CR France1571

GARRETT,Charles Harold Rev kia 26-9-17 RAChDept att2/6SStaffs p199 CR Belgium8

GARRETT,Dalton Gilbert Knox Lt kia 30-9-18 RAMC att133FA p195 CR France511

GARRETT,Henry Fawcett TCapt kia 22-8-15 6EYorks p84 CR Gallipoli5

GARRETT,Henry William 2Lt kia 24-3-18 20Lond p251 MR20

GARRETT,Hubert Frederick Lt kia 4-6-15 6EYorks p84 MR4,9Bn att1RDubF

GARRETT,Hyde Tregillas 2Lt kia 20-5-17 GL &23RFC p7 MR20,Tregellas

GARRETT,Maurice Humphris 2Lt kia 2-9-18 15Lond p249 MR16

GARRETT,Stephen Capt kia 12-3-15 4Suff p217 CR France768

GARRETT,William Oakley 2Lt kia 24-11-15 IARO att3S&M p277MR38,22/24-11-15

GARRETT,William Robert 2Lt ded 6-5-19 11N&D p134 CR Nhampt1

GARRETT-SMITH,Louis 2Lt dow 31-7-15 RE 61FC SR p45 CR Belgium5

GARRETY,J.F.T2Lt kia 21-9-18 ScotRif att1Bn p103 CR France666

GARRIOCH,John Thomas LtAMaj dow 3-4-18 RGA 173SB p39 CR France169,GARRIOCK

GARRITT,John Crossland 2Lt kia 30-5-18 7WYorks att1/6DLI p218 CR France622,1-6-18

GARROD,Alfred Noel TLt kia 25-1-16 RAMC att100FA p195 CR France80

GARROD,Basil Rahere Lt ded 4-2-19 1LNLancs &149RAF p135 CR Germany1

GARROD,Ronald Percival 2Lt kia 22-5-15 6Lond p247 CR France260

GARROD,Thomas Martin 2Lt dow 10-5-15 3LNLancs p136 CR France80,Lt

GARRUD,Owen Henry Lt kia 24-8-18 8Lond p247 CR France1187

GARRY,John Lt kia 12-2-17 IARO att102Gren p277 CR Iraq5,2Lt

GARRY,Kenneth T2Lt dow 18-6-17 13NumbF p61 CR France512

GARSIA,Oliver Dunham Melville Lt dow 18-9-14 2 att1DCLI p114 MR15

GARSIDE,Frank Gerald Lt kia 27-8-18 9Lond p248 CR France560

GARSIDE,Thomas Oughtibridge 2Lt kia 5-4-17 4RBerks p234 CR France1495

GARSTIN,Charles William North 2Lt dow 24-8-14 9Lancers p22 CR Belgium197

GARSTIN,Denys Norman.DSO.MC.TLtACapt kia 15-8-18 MGC p182 MR70 &CR Europe179,Denis 10Huss

GARSTIN,William Fortescue Colborne TMaj kia 7-8-15 5RIrF p171 CR Gallipoli ,9-8-15

GARTON,Arthur T2Lt kia 24-9-18 2RSuss p119 CR France375

GARTON,Arthur Richmond,MID Lt kia 26-4-15 6NumbF p213 MR29

GARTON,Edward Clive 2Lt dow 2-9-18 5RB p178 CR France1182

GARTON,Herbert Westlake TCapt kia 15-9-16 9RB p178 MR21

GARTON,Reginald William TLt kia 1-7-16 11SLancs p125 MR21

GARTON-SPRENGER,H.A Lt 25-7-21 4Beds CR SAfrica72

GARTSIDE-TIPPINGE,Francis 2Lt kia 6-11-17 GL &19RFC p7 MR20

GARVAN,Edmund William Lt kia 23-4-17 RFA 80Bty p29 CR France557

GARVEY,Ivan Harold.MC.Capt dow 20-2-17 3 att6ConnRgrs p172 CR Belgium17

GARVIE,Alexander Cockburn 2Lt kia 23-4-17 1/6BlkW p231 CR France604,Coburn

GARVIE,Ernest Leonard,MC 2Lt ded 15-6-18 9HLI attTMB p240 CR France142

GARVIE,James Alexander.MC.Lt kia 21-8-18 2KOSB p101 CR France798

GARVIE,Peter Thomas TLtACapt kia 25-6-17 RGA 13SB p39 CR Belgium29

GARVIN,Gerard Capt 22-7-16 7SLancs MR21

GARVIN,Roland Gerard TCapt kia 22-7-16 7SLancs p125 MR21

GARVIN,Samuel 2Lt kia 27-3-17 9 att1/7RWFus p97 CR Palestine8

GARVIN,William Myles Frederick T2Lt kia 23-9-17 1Ess p131 MR30

GARWOOD,Gerald Dennis 2Lt kia 13-11-16 4 att15RWar p64

GASCOIGNE,Ivo Clifton Lt dow 12-4-18 1GrenGds p50 CR France225

GASCOYNE,Charles Capt dow PoW 8-5-17 2/7N&D p233 CR France716

GASCOYNE,Francis Paul 2Lt kia 22-3-18 8 att11RWar p215 MR27

GASCOYNE,William Elhanan 2Lt kia 22-8-17 2/4 O&BLI p231 CR Belgium125

GASCOYNE-CECIL,John Arthur.MC.Capt kia 27-8-18 75RFA p207 CR France214

GASCOYNE-CECIL,Randle William Lt kia 1-12-17 RH&FA p207 MR17

GASCOYNE-CECIL,Rupert Edward Lt kia 11-7-15 1Beds Belgium127

GASELEE,Alec Mansel 2Lt kia 24-5-15 15Huss p22 MR29

GASHION,Stanley Michael 2Lt kia 8-5-17 1ESurr p112 MR20

GASKAIN,Cecil Stavley Lt kia 7-5-17 RA attRFC p18&207 MR20

GASKELL,Arnold Joseph 2Lt kia 2-11-18 12NorfYeo D'Coy p204 CR Belgium140

GASKELL,David Lyndsay Stranack T2Lt dow 12-1-16 16WelshR p126 CR France495,Lt dedacc

GASKELL,Frank Hill TLtCol dow 17-5-16 16WelshR p126 CR France345

GASKELL,John Charles Temple Capt kia 5-8-17 IA 69Punjabis att129Baluchis p277 CR EAfrica38 &CR Tanzania1,Maj

GASKELL,Joseph Lt&QM ded 5-4-17 NSomYeo p205 CR Essex146

GASKELL,Reginald Robinson Lt kld 15-12-16 RE attRFC p18&210 CR Yorks3

GASKELL,Lawrence Norris T2Lt dow 1-3-18 RFC p16 CR France15

GASKELL,Wallis William Penn 2Lt kia 25/26-5-15 24Lond p252 MR22,25/26-6-15

GASKIN,Robert Bertram T2Lt kia 9-9-17 23NumbF p61 CR France1461

GASPER,Horace Le Geyt Lt kia 20-12-19 IA 2/119Inf att1/103MahrattaLI p277 MR43,19-12-19

GASSON,R.S.Lt 25-12-17 6Mddx CR Lond10

GASTON,James.MC.TCapt dow 5-11-18 RAMC att4Suff p195 CR France1059

GATACRE,Edward George Capt dow 20-2-16 2WRid p115 CR France3

GATACRE,John Kirwan.MID Capt kia 12-10-14 IA 11Lancers att4Huss p277 CR France324,13-10-14

GATCHELL,James Harcourt Cecil.MC.TCapt kia 27-9-17 RAMC att11Suss p195 CR Belgium167

GATE,Leslie Charles Thomas 2Lt kia 30-10-17 10Beds p86 MR30

GATEHOUSE,John 2Lt ded 25-3-16 IARO att6Jats p277 CR Iraq6

GATEHOUSE,Richard Francis Capt kia 13-9-14 NumbF p61 CR France864

GATELY,John Edward Lt ded 13-6-16 IARO att2Lancers &MGC p277 CR Lancs169,3-6-17

GATENSBY,Samuel TLt ded 24-11-18 10RIrrRif p169 CR Ireland33,5-11-19 15Bn

GATES,Alan Ferrier 2Lt dow 20-8-17 B307RFA p29 CR Belgium8,21-8-17

GATES,Alfred William.MC.MID 2Lt kia 3-7-16 3 at2SLancs p125 MR21

GATES,Arthur Noel T2Lt kia 1-3-17 RE 176TC p45 MR20

GATES,Douglas Leslie 2Lt kia 1-10-15 1Suff p78 MR19

GATES,Eric Chasemore Lt kia 14-3-15 13Lond p249 CR France710,Capt 12-3-15

GATES,Henry T2Lt kia 18-10-18 RE 23FC p45 CR France1268

GATES,Horace John T2Lt kia 19-11-17 EKent &RFC 16Wing p57 CR Greece 3

GATFIELD,Reginald Alfred Lt dow 7-6-17 16Lond attMGC Inf p187&249 CR France297

GATH,Charles Henry 2Lt kia 30-10-14 3Huss p21 MR29

GATHORNE-HARDY,Alfred Cecil TCapt kia 25-9-15 9ScotRif p103 MR19

GATRELL,Reginald James Hurst.MC.Lt kia 1-7-16 3 att1EYorks p84 MR21

GATTENS,Charles Lt kld 15-6-19 RE &RAF p45

GATWARD,Frederick James.MM.T2Lt dow 25-4-18 13TankCps p188 CR Belgium11

GAUKROGER,Hubert T2Lt kia 2-4-17 1Manch p154 CR France672

GAUL,Ernest T2Lt kia 23-10-18 Lincs att6Leic p75 CR France1477,Capt

GAUL,Lawrence John Littlewood TLt ded 12-4-17 ArmyPayDept CR France88

GAULD,Alexander George Capt kia 15-9-16 19Lond p250 CR France390

GAULD,George ALt ded 24-6-19 RB APM attKRRCp178&254 CR France65

GAULD,Gordon Smith Mellis.MC.Lt kld 25-3-18 RFA &RFC p16&29 CR Lincs61

GAULT,Arthur Alexander T2Lt dow 10-10-18 11DubF D'Coy p176 CR France380

GAULT,John Victor 2Lt kia 23-10-16 5 att1RIrRif p169 CR France307

GAULT,Robert Anderson Lt kia 16-9-16 4GrenGds SR p50 MR21

GAULTER,Charles Pendrick 2Lt kia 18-8-16 3 att4Lpool p71 MR21

GAULTER,Cuthbert Vivian Lt kia 7-5-17 5RLancs att7RFC p18&213 MR20

GAUNT,Benjamin William Lt kia 7-9-18 3Y&L att63TMB p158 CR France745

GAUNT,Edward 2Lt dow 28-9-16 5WYorks p218 MR21

GAUNT,Eric Thomas Capt kia 9-10-17 RAMC p195 MR30

GAUNT,Kenneth MacFarlane 2Lt kia 25-9-15 2 att4RWar p64

GAUSSEN,Arratoon William David Capt kia 17-5-15 HLI p162 MR22

GAUSSEN,David Newbold T2Lt kia 31-7-16 9 att1Beds p86 CR France176

GAUSSEN,John Samuel.CBE.Col ded 13-10-19 ArmyPayDept p268 CR Hamps7

GAVAGHAN,Colin 2Lt kia 13-3-18 55RFC p16 CR Germany3

GAVIN,Neil Murphy TLt dedacc 12-3-16 RAMC 6FA p195 CR France88

GAVIN,Noel John Hay.MC.TCapt ded 2-11-17 RAMC p195

GAVIN,Robert Fitzaustin Lt kia 25-9-15 2RIrRif p169 MR29

GAWAN-TAYLOR,Francis 2Lt kia 9-8-15 3Y&L p158 MR29

GAWAN-TAYLOR,Norman 2Lt kia 24-4-17 3 att8Y&L CR Belgium116

GAWN,Thomas 2Lt kia 6-8-15 2Hamps p120 MR4

GAWNE,William Zacharias T2Lt kia 9-4-17 8BlkW p128 CR France729

GAY,Edgar Percy T2Lt dow 6-1-17 6DCLI p114 CR France158

GAY,Edmund 2LtACapt kia 12-8-15 1/5Norf p216 MR4

GAY,Frederick Hollington 2Lt dow 25-3-17 16RFC p7 CR France32

GAY,John(Jock).2Lt kia 10-10-15 RFC p1 CR France924

GAY,John TCapt ded 29-5-16 30NumbF p61

GAYER,Alexander Edward Capt&Adjt ded 23-11-18 6ELancs p110 CR Surrey1

GAYER,Edward John 2Lt kia 4-10-17 1Lincs p75 MR30

GAYES,Thomas Samuel 2LtACapt kia 10-4-18 11BordR p117 CR France214

GAYFORD,Thomas Frederick Marter 2Lt kia 23-11-17 RE 203FC p45 CR Belgium20,204FC

GAYFORD,William George T2Lt dow 26-9-15 69RFA p29 CR Egypt6

GAYNER,William John Lt ded 9-5-17 2/4SomLI attRFC p218 p261 CR France270,kld

GAYNOR,Brian Seymour Capt ded 1-11-20 IA 23Cav p277 MR65

GAZE,Geoffrey Atkinson Capt kia 15-9-16 Cmdg15Lond B'Coy p249 CR France432

GEAKE,Boyd Burnet T2Lt kia 1-7-16 9Y&L p158 CR France246,Lt

GEARD,Reginald Cheniston Capt murderedByTribesmen 27-7-20 IA 15Lancers attPoliticalDept p277 CR Asia82

GEARD,Walter Leslie Maj kld 26-6-16 C282RFA p206 MR21

GEARE,William Duncan Rev kia 31-7-17 RAChDept att165InfBde p199 CR Belgium10

GEAREY,Albert Edward.MC.Capt dow 17-10-18 8N&D p233 CR France847

GEAREY,Edward 2Lt kia 1-1-15 CamH attHLI p167 MR22,20-12-14

GEARY,Ronald Fitzmaurice 2Lt kia 15-1-16 21Lond p251 CR France149

GEARY-SMITH,Alexander Capt kia 7-8-15 9WYorks p81 MR4

GEBBIE,James Francis Roy Lt dow 4-10-14 SLancs p125 CR France1839

GEDDES,Alastair Cosmo Burton.MC.TMaj kia 19-4-17 GL &RFC 17KiteBallCo p7 CR France1485

GEDDES,Alistair Alexander Francis 2Lt kia 16-6-15 3 att2RScotF p94 MR22

GEDDES,Arthur Alexander TCapt ded 5-7-16 28RASC MotorAmbConvoy p192 CR Pakistan50A MR43

GEDDES,Augustus David LtCol kia 28-4-15 2EKent p57 CR Belgium84,Col

GEDDES,David Scott T2Lt kia 26-10-17 3Manch p154 CR Belgium116

GEDDES,Donald 2Lt kia 5-4-16 1SfthH att7Bn p164 MR38

GEDDES,John Gordon.CB.CMG.Col ded 26-8-19 RFA p261 CR Sussex55

GEDDES,John Rowland Lt 3-11-17 1CenOntario att23RFC CR Belgium16

GEDDES,Robert Stirling T2Lt kia 9-10-16 12MGC Inf p183 CR France294

GEDDES,William Murray Capt kia 27-9-15 2Wilts p153 CR France423

GEDDIE,George Alexander 2Lt kia 19-9-16 4CamH p243 CR France374,20-9-16

GEDDIS,Samuel McKee TLt kia 19-9-18 1Leic p87 CR France835

GEDGE,Basil Johnson Rev dow 25-4-17 RAChDept attRAMC 78FA p199 CR Greece5

GEDGE,Cecil Bertie 2Lt kia 25-9-15 3Lond p245 MR19

GEDGE,Edward Leonard.MID Lt kia 23/24-8-16 RH&FA p207 CR France251,GEDYE

GEDGE,Peter TLt kia 13-10-15 7Suff p78 MR19

GEE,Albert Edwin 2Lt ded 14-12-17 RGA p262 CR Lond33,dow

GEE,Donald T2Lt kld 31-1-18 RFC p16 CR Hamps192

GEE,Edward Topping Lt ded 12-2-19 12Lpool CR Lancs2

GEE,Ernest Desmond Farrell Maj kia 25-4-18 RGA 263SB p39 CR Belgium21

GEE,Frank Lionel T2Lt kia 5-9-17 RE 203FC p45 CR France364

GEE,Geoffrey Richard Dudley 2Lt kia 4-6-17 3RSuss &21RFC p7&119 MR20

GEE,George Edward TCapt dow 27-7-16 15RScots p54

GEE,Herbert Lt kia 10-7-15 16Lpool p71 CR Gallipoli6

GEE,Reginald Claud Moline.MC.TLtACapt kia 7-11-18 15DLI p160 CR France930

GEE,Robert Francis McLean 2Lt dow 27-10-14 3 att5Wilts p153 CR Sussex144

GEE,Thomas.MID Lt dedacc 13-11-17 B122RH&FA p29 CR Wales165

GEEN,William Purdon 2Lt kia 31-7-15 9KRRC p150 MR29

GEERE,Douglas Joseph 2Lt kia 23-2-16 D71RFA p29 CR France554

GEERING,S.Capt 20-10-19 RFus CR Surrey15

GEERING,Sydney Cecil 2Lt dow PoW 3-5-18 4Lond p246 CR France425

GEESON,Leslie Frederic T2Lt kld 15-6-17 GL &RFC p7 CR Surrey2

GEFEALL,George 2Lt kia 23-3-18 2/4 O&BLI p231 MR27

GEGGIE,William Millar McG.T2Lt kia 4-10-17 227MGC p182

GEIDT,Charles Uppleby Lt kld 10-4-18 GL CamH &RAF p190,C.W. CR Egypt1

GELDER,George Douglas TCapt kia 4-11-18 9WRid p115 CR France206

GELDERD-SOMERVELL,Roger Frederick Churchill 2Lt dow 13-3-15 1GrenGds SR p50 MR22,11-3-15

GELIOT,William Henry 2Lt kia 1-7-16 4Lincs p217 CR France281

GELL,Christopher Stowell 2Lt kia 18-9-16 1WYorks p81 MR21

GELL,James Bainton Stowell T2Lt kia 9-10-18 56RFA p29 CR France332

GELL,Philip 2Lt ded 5-9-17 3Ches att217InfBn p96 CR Eire94

GELLATLY,John Stewart 2Lt kia 31-7-17 9RScots p212 CR Belgium36

GELLATLY,Robert 2Lt kia 23-4-17 13RScots p54 MR20

GELME,Reginald William T2Lt ded 27-7-16 RE p45 CR Iraq6

GEMMELL,Alexander Capt ded 4-1-19 SL antiGas School p268 CR Scot239

GEMMELL,Andrew Steveson Lt ded 5-3-19 5HLI p240 CR Scot674

GEMMELL,Cecil Woodburn 2Lt kia 24-4-17 8 att10ScotRif p225 MR20

GEMMELL,George Manners 2Lt kia 13-11-16 13Ess p131 CR France1890

GEMMELL,James Brown Richardson 2Lt kia 16-7-17 2HLI p162 CR France721

GEMMELL,John TCapt kia 25-9-15 12HLI p162 CR France219

GEMMELL,Kenneth Alexander Lt kia 16-6-15 10Lpool p216 MR29

GEMMELL,Stewart Armour Capt dow 22-7-15 6HLI p240 CR Egypt3

GEMMELL,Stuart Sterling 2Lt kia 21-3-18 3 att7CamH p167 CR France1182

GEMMELL,Thomas 2Lt dow PoW 7-5-18 7A&SH D'Coy p243 CR France1142

GEMMELL,Wallace Alexander Capt ded 29-3-16 RASC p253 CR Egypt2

GEMMILL,John Adshead T2Lt kia 1-7-16 16HLI p162 CR France293

GEMMILL,William.DSO.LtCol kia 25-3-18 8RScots p211 MR20

GENGE,John T2Lt dow PoW 24-3-18 2Y&L p158 CR France568

GENNINGS,Cecil Samuel 2Lt kia 13-8-16 7ESurr p112 MR21 &CR France390

GENT,Alfred Harry Thomas.MC.2Lt dow 3-10-18 1/5N&D p232 CR France446

GENT,Frank Ernest Lt kia 7-8-15 9WYorks p81 MR4,9-8-15

GENT,George Edward 2Lt kia 14-9-17 379RFA p29 CR France275

GENT,Thomas Samuel T2Lt kia 24-7-15 7RB p178 MR29 CR Belgium453

GEOGHEGAN,James Randolph Capt kia 7-11-14 RInniskF p105 CR Belgium451

GEOGHEGAN,Stannus 2Lt dow 18-3-18 2A&SH p173 CR Belgium3,Lt kia 17-3-18

GEOGHEGAN,William George Richard 2Lt dow 13-4-17 2RInniskF p105 CR France583

GEORGE,Alan Lee T2Lt dow 14-4-18 15RWar p64 CR France21

GEORGE,Athelstan Key Durrance Lt dow 14-9-14 1Dors p124 CR France1429

GEORGE,Edward Barcroft 2Lt kia 16-9-16 4 att15DLI p160 CR France744

GEORGE,Edward Royston TLtACapt ded 12-8-17 RE 264Co p45 CR Belgium18

GEORGE,Elmor Wright T2Lt kia 10-5-18 15WelshR p126 CR France232

GEORGE,Eric Coe T2Lt ded 15-9-15 10Glouc p106 CR France98

GEORGE,Frank Alfred 2Lt kia 17-10-18 6WelchR p230 CR France1269

GEORGE,Frank William.MID T2Lt kia 22-8-15 5Dors p124 MR4

GEORGE,Frederick Ralph Lt kia 5-11-14 1ConnRgrs p172 CR France1157

GEORGE,Henry William Hotton 2Lt dow 19-3-19 10RWKent p265

GEORGE,Herbert Duncan King Lt ded PoW 6-4-17 2RDubF &48RFC p7&176 CR France1276

GEORGE,Ion Barry Maj ded 5-5-18 RIrReg p89 CR Surrey1

GEORGE,L.Lt ded 12-5-18 RASC &RAF p192

GEORGE,Laurence Edgar Capt kia 28-6-15 9SomLI p79 MR4

GEORGE,Thomas T2Lt kia 27-8-18 16RWFus p97 CR France432

GEORGE,Thomas William T2Lt kld 18-10-17 GL &RFC p7 CR Scot963

GEORGE,William 2Lt kia 12-3-15 BlkW p128 CR France924

GEORGE,William King Capt kia 25-1-15 3Glouc p106 CR France279

GEORGESON,Dan Horace.MIDx2 TLtACapt kia 9-3-18 8SfthH p164 CR France1182

GEORGESON,William 2Lt kia 3-4-18 5HLI p240 CR France745

GEPP,Nicholas Melvill TCapt kia 6-8-15 11YLI att1Ess p143 CR Gallipoli6

GERAGHTY,Thomas 2Lt kia 26-9-17 8EYorks p84 MR30

GERALD,Harold T2Lt kia 2-12-17 Worc att2/8Bn p108 MR17

GERARD,Gilbert Meade Capt ded 3-5-16 HLI p162 MR38

GERARD,Tom Overton T2Lt kia 10-7-16 MGC 112Coy p183 MR21

GERDS,Frederick Niven T2Lt kia 1-6-15 RE 176TC p45 CR France631

GERMAIN,Harry Gordon 2Lt 12-7-16 17NumbF p61 MR21

GERMAN,Frederick Francis TCapt ded 27-3-16 RAMC p195 CR Lancs149

GERMAN,Hugh Bernard.MC.TCaptAMaj kia 18-9-18 RAMC att17FA p195 CR France835

GERMAN,Ivon Hector.MC.TLtACapt ded 1-12-18 1Hamps p120 CR France40

GERMAN,William Henry Capt dow 16-3-16 1/6Dev p217 CR Iraq5

GERMANY,Ernest Albert Capt&QM ded 13-5-19 RAVC p268 CR Lond28

GEROW,Albert Augustus T2Lt kld 28-2-18 RFC p16 CR Hamps98

GERRARD,Harry Vernon Lt kia 2-11-14 2BordR p117 MR29

GERRARD,James Spinks Lt ded 13-2-19 RASC p267 CR Scot247

GERRARD,John Maurice Harold 2Lt dow 28-8-18 74RFA p29 CR France927

GERRARD,Robert Finlay Capt kia 18-4-17 4RScots att1/6Glouc p211 CR France363,Maj

GERTSON,Frederick.DCM.2Lt kia 16-4-18 12/13NumbF p61 MR30

GETHIN,Percy Francis 2Lt kia 28-6-16 3 att8Dev p76 CR France330

GETHIN,Richard Patrick Wilmot Lt kia 25-9-15 2RMunstF D'Coy p175 CR France219

GETHING,Hugh Bagnall 2Lt kia 21-8-15 1/1GloucYeo D'Sqn p203 CR Gallipoli5

GETHING,William Gordon 2Lt kia 22-9-17 2/6SStaffs p122 MR30,23-9-17

GETTING,Eric Noel Capt kia 28/29-9-15 1RBerks p139 MR19

GETTY,James Houghton Capt kia 3-5-17 12WYorks p81 MR20

GHOSH,N.Capt 22-12-19 IMS MR43

GIBAUD,Ernest John 2Lt kia 24-4-17 12Hamps p120 MR37,25-4-17

GIBB,Alexander Lt kia 5-6-17 RFA V63H TMB p207 CR France184

GIBB,Alexander Reid Capt kia 12-10-16 105RFA p207 CR Belgium137

GIBB,C.L.G.Capt 23-1-20 RE CR Ches31

GIBB,George Blaikie Capt kia 1-9-18 17Lond p250 CR France785

GIBB,George Calder 2Lt kia 17-4-18 3 att4Lpool p71 MR32

GIBB,George Eben TLt kia 25/26-10-18 HLI p162 MR38

GIBB,James Robertson 2Lt kia 4-11-18 6A&SH p243 CR France521

GIBB,James Shirra Capt kia 29-7-18 1/5A&SH p243 CR France524

GIBB,John Hardie T2Lt kia 31-7-17 KRRC att18Bn p150 MR29

GIBB,Richard 2Lt kia 11-5-15 1A&SH p173 MR29

GIBB,Robert Andrew 2Lt kia 19-4-17 1/5KOSB p224 CR Palestine8

GIBB,William Lt 19-2-17 APD CR Scot277

GIBB,William Alexander LtCol ded 10-3-15 RAMC att6Suff CR Suff83

GIBB,William Ian 2Lt kia 14-4-17 11Lond p248 MR20

GIBBENS,George T2Lt dow 2-4-18 2Mddx p146 CR France185

GIBBES,Frederick William T2Lt ded 13-10-17 GL &54RFC p8 CR Belgium132

GIBBINGS,Frank 2Lt kia 2-12-17 RBerks att2Bn p139

GIBBINS,Gwynn Gilbert TLt kia 26-7-17 RE 107FC p45 CR Greece6

GIBBINS,Roland Bevington Capt kia 3-12-17 2/8RWar p214 MR17

GIBBON,Frederic T2Lt kia 8-10-18 12/13NumbF p61 MR16

GIBBON,Frederick William T2Lt kia 25-8-18 1NumbF p61 CR France239

GIBBON,John Taylor T2Lt kld 6-2-17 GL &20RFC p8 CR Belgium115

GIBBON,Oliver Vernon T2Lt kia 3-4-16 12WYorks p81 CR Belgium124

GIBBON,Wilfrid St.Martin Lt ded 24-4-18 IA 2/89Punjabis p277 MR43

GIBBONS,Alfred St.Hill.MID TLtCol dow 15-7-16 13Lpool p71 CR France119

GIBBONS,Charles Barry 2Lt kia 24-8/1-9-14 2RIrReg p254 CR Belgium242,24-8-14

GIBBONS,Edward Ingram Lt kia 29-4-17 20LancF p92 MR21

GIBBONS,Edward Stephen.DSO.MajALtCol kia 19-9-18 Mddx Cmdg7HLI p146 CR France686

GIBBONS,James Bryan Lt kia 10-3-20 RGA p262 MR43

GIBBONS,John T2Lt dow 6-6-17 Dors att6Bn p124 CR France40

GIBBONS,Percy James T2Lt kia 7-10-16 3 att1ESurr att11RWKent p112 MR21

GIBBONS,Thomas Pilling.MC.Capt kia 22-3-18 1Herts p252 CR France528

GIBBONS,Wilfred Ernest Capt ded 20-12-17 RAMC p270 CR Leic63

GIBBS,Archibald Edward T2Lt kia 25-4-17 11Worc p108 MR37

GIBBS,Bernard.MC.MID 2Lt kia 6-7-15 6 att1RB p178 CR Belgium85

GIBBS,Cecil Charles T2Lt kia 27-3-17 GL &14RFC p8 CR Egypt2

GIBBS,Cecil Thomas T2Lt kia 9-4-17 9Ess p131 CR France531

GIBBS,David Angus 2Lt 24-3-18 6 att2RB p178 MR27

GIBBS,Edward Reginald Chap4Cl kia 29-3-18 RAChDept att1GrenGds p199 CR France1183

GIBBS,Eustace Lyle Capt dow 11-2-15 NSomYeo p205 CR Belgium57,kia

GIBBS,Gilbert Fincher T2Lt kia 28-4-17 8SomLI p79 MR20

GIBBS,Harold Walter Lt dow 25-3-18 158RFA p207 CR France113

GIBBS,Henry Sampson Capt&Adjt ded 9-2-18 DLI p265 MR66

GIBBS,Horace Austen 2Lt kia 29-4-17 1RBerks p139 CR France777

GIBBS,Ivan Richard TCapt kia 25-9-15 10Glouc p106 CR France1723

GIBBS,John Angel.DSO.TMaj kia 20-9-17 9WelshR p126 CR Belgium17

GIBBS,Lawrence Henry.MC.TLtACapt kia 18-9-18 10LancF p92 CR France415

GIBBS,Leslie Lt kia 26-9-15 8RWKent p141 MR19

GIBBS,Percy Roland T2Lt ded 17-3-16 14Worc p108 CR Devon69

GIBBS,Philip Henry Samuel Lt ded 25-10-19 RE CR Sussex111

GIBBS,Ronald Charles Melbourne 2Lt dow 29-10-14 2ScotsGds p52 MR29,28-10-14

GIBBS,Stanley Gordon Maj kia 20-9-17 RASC DAQMG 1AnzacCpsHQ p192

GIBBS,Thomas Charles.MC.Lt kia 31-8-18 7 at9Ches p223 MR18,31-5-18

GIBBS,Walter Septimus T2Lt kia 17-10-18 2KRRC p150 CR France341

GIBBS,Walter William T2Lt kia 22-4-18 RE 1FldSurCo p45 CR France268

GIBBS,William Alexander Lt ded 10-3-15 RAMC p270

GIBBS,William Beresford.MID TLtCol kia 3-9-16 3Worc p108 CR France246,dow

GIBBS,William Henry Herbert.MC.T2Lt kia 21-8-18 RASC 329SBAmmCol p192 CR France31

GIBLIN,Eric Lewis Capt kia 28-9-15 RAMC att24Lond p253 CR France107,Louis

GIBSON.A2Lt 13-12-15 IARO att110MahrattaLI CR Iraq5

GIBSON,Albert Fisher 2Lt kia 24-3-17 4Leinst att4RFC p8&174 CR France561

GIBSON,Albert Henry T2Lt kia 1-7-16 12 att9RInniskF p105 MR21

GIBSON,Alexander Douglas Lt kia 11-9-18 9Lpool p216 CR France482

GIBSON,Alwyn Morland 2Lt dow 27-9-16 6WYorks att1/6TMB p218 MR21,Alcwyn

GIBSON,Arthur 2Lt dow 6-7-17 RH&FA attY29TMB p29 CR Belgium16

GIBSON,Arthur Douglas T2Lt kia 9-4-17 22NumbF p61 CR France644

GIBSON,Arthur Ferrall Lt ded 29-10-18 RASC 14DivnTrain p193 CR Lond29

GIBSON,Arthur Lionel 2Lt kia 8-8-15 1/7WRid p227 CR Belgium67

GIBSON,Athol Thomas Capt kia 21-10-14 3 att2SLancs p125 MR22

GIBSON,Bertrand Dees.DSO.MID LtCol kia 27-5-18 4NumbF p213 CR France1753

GIBSON,Cecil Mervyn 2Lt kia 5-5-17 1/5Y&L p238 CR France705

GIBSON,Charles Leslie.MC.Lt dow 3-9-18 17Lond p250 CR France177

GIBSON,Charles Methven 2Lt kia 14-10-16 4BlkW p230 CR France215

GIBSON,Charles Sydney 2Lt kia 1-7-16 4RWar attMGC p183 CR France638,2War att22MGC Inf

GIBSON,Edgar Daniell T2Lt kia 9-10-17 GL &2RFC p8 CR France98

GIBSON,Franklin Reginald TLt ded 20-9-18 RGA 80Bde 176SB p39 CR Berks116

GIBSON,Frederick James Lt 28-12-20 6LNLancs CR Iraq8

GIBSON,George Henry 2Lt kia 27-8-17 2 att9WYorks p81 CR Belgium96

GIBSON,Gerald Dudley 2Lt dow 16-8-18 5Lancers p22 CR France145

GIBSON,Griffiths Ifor 2Lt 12-8-17 11WYorks att6RFC CR Belgium11

GIBSON,Harold.DSO.Capt dow 17-10-17 RAMC att71FA p195 CR France40

GIBSON,Harold Wolfe Lt kia 24-3-18 1Wilts p153 MR20

GIBSON,Harry Olivier Sumner Lt kia 19-4-17 11Lond p248 CR Palestine8

GIBSON,Henry T2Lt kia 30-9-18 Y&L att13Bn p158 CR Belgium451

GIBSON,Henry William T2Lt dow 27-11-16 2RDubF p176 CR France8

GIBSON,Herbert Edwin 2Lt kia 7-8-17 4 O&BLI p231 MR29

GIBSON,Horsburgh 2Lt dow 22-12-16 7A&SH p243 CR France62

GIBSON,Howard Graeme Maj ded 12-2-19 RAMC p195 CR France52

GIBSON,Hugh Stuart LtTCapt ded 19-2-19 5SStaffs p270 CR Lond12

GIBSON,Ivor Griffith T2Lt dow 11-8-17 11WYorks &6RFC p8&81

GIBSON,James TLt kia 5-10-17 13MGC Inf p183 MR30

GIBSON,James 2Lt kia 12-10-17 9A&SH p244 MR30

GIBSON,James Douglas Lt kia 25-3-18 RE 401FC p210 CR France385

GIBSON,James Guthrie 2Lt dow 12-9-17 PoW 3 att6CamH p167 CR Germany3

GIBSON,James William T2Lt kia 9-8-18 8TankCps p188 CR France526

GIBSON,Jesse Lt ded 7-3-19 RDC p270 CR Leic24

GIBSON,John 2Lt kia 19-6-16 2/7Dev attRFC p18&217 CR France120

GIBSON,John TLt kia 5-7-16 9Yorks p90 MR21

GIBSON,John Anthony 2Lt dow PoW 27-8-18 9RInniskF p105 CR Germany1,27-9-18

GIBSON,John Auchenlosh 2Lt kia 27-5-18 RGA 116SB p39 MR18

GIBSON,John Lancelot Lt kia 27-5-18 D251RFA p207 MR18

GIBSON,John Seear T2Lt dow 15-10-16 8Beds att16TMB p86 MR21

GIBSON,John Thomas T2lt kld 10-2-18 RFC p16 CR Wilts 28

GIBSON,Leonard TCapt ded 1-8-18 GL p190 CR Devon 69

GIBSON,Malcolm Reginald TLt kia 8-10-15 7ESurr p112 CR France423,8-10-16

GIBSON,Margaret Annabella Campbell.MM.UnitAdmintr ded 17-9-18 QMAAC p200 CR France13

GIBSON,Matthew Henry.MC&Bar.TLtACapt dow 28-10-18 RIrRif att12Bn p169 CR Belgium20,kia 29-10-18

GIBSON,Norman James Lt kia 21-11-17 4GordH p241 CR France256

GIBSON,Ollyett Archibald M.2Lt dow 27-8-16 RH&FA p29

GIBSON,Pendarves Christopher Foll TLt kia 10-4-17 13RFus p68 MR20

GIBSON,Percy Montague.MC.MM.2Lt dow 6-9-18 5Mddx att17Lond p146 CR France833

GIBSON,Reginald James 2Lt kia 28-6-15 4RScotF p211 MR4

GIBSON,Robert Lt kia 5-5-15 2KOSB p101 MR29

GIBSON,Robert 2Lt 23-7-16 1/9RScots CR France402

GIBSON,Robert Bowness Lt kia 11-7-16 3 att2Beds p86 CR France630

GIBSON,Robert Gray Nicol Lt kia 21-3-18 6 att2RScots p211 MR20

GIBSON,Ronald 2Lt dow 12-12-15 IARO att110Mahrattas p277

GIBSON,Samuel Archibald Gibson.MC.2Lt dow 26-8-17 3Wilts att2/1 O&BLI p153 CR Belgium11,Currie 3/1Bn

GIBSON,Thomas Ernest 2Lt kia 28-11-17 2/5WYorks p218 MR17

GIBSON,Walter Reginald 2Lt kia 4-10-17 8Lincs p75 MR30

GIBSON,William 2Lt kia 1-7-16 14 att15RScots p54 MR21

GIBSON,William Ramshaw 2Lt ded 16-6-18 8LNLancs p264 CR Lancs111,17-6-18

GIBSON-CRAIG,Archibald Charles.Bart.Lt kia 13/17-9-14 2HLI p162 MR15 14-9-14

GIDDINGS,Frank.MM.2Lt kia 2-12-17 att2Berks p139 MR30

GIDDY,Napier Llewellyn 2Lt kia 15-8-16 1Nhampt p137 CR France387

GIDLEY,Frederick William Lt kia 27-3-17 1 att4Ess p131 MR34

GIELGUD,Henry Lex Francis Adam.MC.MajALtCol kia 30-11-17 7Norf p73 MR17

GIERRIER,Elias George T2Lt drd 30-11-18 GL &IWT p190

GIFFARD,Colin Hay Capt kia 8-3-16 IA 1/1GurkhaRif p277 MR38

GIFFARD,Edmund Hamilton LtAMaj dow 10-11-18 2RFA p29 CR France332

GIFFARD,Robert Capt dow 1-11-14 RFA p29 CR Belgium57

GIFFARD,Sydney Lt kia 3-5-15 RFA p29 CR Gallipoli1

GIFFARD,William Carter.DSO.BrCol 25-4-21 WelchR CR C'land&W'land45

GIFFEN,James.MC.LtACapt dow 22-12-16 2CamH p167 CR France177

GIFFORD,Gordon Arthur Lt kia 10-7-17 LNLancs att2TMB p136 MR31

GIFFORD,Harry William.MID TCapt kia 15-7-16 1LNLancs p136 MR21

GIFFORD,Norga Ernest TCapt kia 14-7-16 7Leic p87 MR21

GIFFORD,William Roy 2Lt kia 7-10-16 4Lond p246 CR France744

GIFFORD-WOOD,Leslie Keith 2Lt mbk 22-8-15 6Yorks p256 MR4

GILBANKS,Richard Parker TLt kia 10-8-15 6BordR p117 MR4

GILBART,William Stuart T2Lt dow 26-9-16 9Leic p87 CR France833

GILBERT,Archibald Holmes T2Lt kia 21-9-17 GL &22RFC p8 CR Belgium46

GILBERT,Bernard Ryland Joseph 2Lt kia 1-12-17 1/5SStaffs p229 CR France115,30-11-17

GILBERT,Bertram Thomas Chesterton Lt kia 22-4-17 4Leic p219 MR29

GILBERT,Christopher Choaler TLt kia 28-9-16 11 att8WRid p115 MR21,Chowler 29-9-16

GILBERT,Edward Burton T2Lt kia 21-3-18 25RFus p68 CR France245

GILBERT,Frank Charles Henry TLt dow 23-4-16 14Hamps p120 CR France279,2Lt

GILBERT,Frank William 2Lt kia 11-10-17 2Ess p131 MR30

GILBERT,Gilbert Garnet T2Lt kia 18-3-18 9RLancs p59 CR Greece5

GILBERT,Herbert James.MID T2Lt kia 22-3-18 16RB p178 MR27

GILBERT,George Hewitt 2Lt kia 15-6-18 7Worc p226 CR Italy3

GILBERT,James Ponsonby Capt drd 30-12-15 IA 6Jats p277 MR41

GILBERT,John Driffield Lt kia 18-10-17 SussYeo attRFC p18&205 MR20

GILBERT,John Ewart TCapt ded 6-11-18 24RFus p68 CR Cornwall40

GILBERT,Joseph Plumptre 2Lt kia 11-4-17 4Hamps p228 CR France1193,dow

GILBERT,Kenneth Nigel Wilson.MC.ACapt ded 15-10-18 32RFA &RAF p29 CR Norf138

GILBERT,L.S.T2Lt kia 4-4-16 13RFus att8RWFus p68 MR38

GILBERT,Reginald Herbert 2Lt dow 8-8-18 6SfthH p241 CR Oxford69

GILBERT,Reginald William,MC T2Lt dow 21-7-16 53MGC p183 MR21

GILBERTSON,Graham Sydney 2Lt kia 28-11-17 4 att7Beds p86 MR30

GILBEY,Eric Lt kia 10-3-15 5RB p178 CR France709

GILCHRIST,Alexander Arthur T2Lt kia 3-9-16 A&SH att1CamH p173 CR France453

GILCHRIST,Archibald 2Lt kld 3-10-18 1/4RB &RAF p178 CR France234,Lt kia

GILCHRIST,Ivan Hamilton Learmouth 2Lt kia 2-10-15 2NumbF p61 CR France423,Lt 2/5Bn

GILCHRIST John TCapt dow 29-8-15 9BlkW p128 CR France98

GILCHRIST,Robert Crooks Capt kia 19-12-14 IA 46Punjabis att59Rif p277 CR France571

GILDEA,John Arthur Knox 2Lt kia 11-7-16 2RWar p64 MR21

GILDER,Tom Norman 2Lt ded 4-11-18 IA 47Sikhs p277 MR66

GILDERTHORP,Ellwood TLt dow 11-4-18 29MGC p183 CR France25

GILDERTHORP,Guy 2Lt kia 12-4-18 8RWar p215 CR France248

GILES,Edward Victor T2Lt kia 3-7-16 9 att5RBerks p139 MR21

GILES,Eric Capt dow 16-7-16 4Lond p246 CR France1

GILES,Geoffrey T2Lt kia 1-7-16 2GordH p166 CR France331

GILES,George Edward TLt kld 11-11-16 RFC p2 CR Glouc9,2Lt

GILES,Thomas William T2Lt dow 14-12-17 7EYorks p84 CR France134,Wilfred

GILES,Victor Marshall T2Lt kia 28-6-16 7RIrRif p169 CR France423

GILES,Walter Lt kia 13-7-16 RGA 32SB p39 CR France630

GILES,William Charles 2Lt kia 12-10-17 11 att8SStaffs p122 MR30,Lt

GILES,William James.DCM.T2Lt kia 6-4-18 6RWSurr p55 CR France296

GILES,William Stanley T2Lt kia 2-11-17 3RWar att1/4Norf p64 CR Palestine8

GILFILLAN,Arthur Wayland Lt ded 7-11-18 RFus &RAF p263

GILFILLAN,Donald Roy T2Lt kia 26-2-17 11Mddx p146 CR France1182

GILHESPIE,Charles Salkeld T2Lt dow 12-12-17 3LNLancs att1/5SLancs p136 CR France145

110

GILHESPY,Henry White Capt ded 3-11-19 RASC MT CR Asia53,Harry

GILHESPY,John William T2Lt kia 20-7-16 12 att1ScotRif p103&167 MR21

GILKINSON,Donald Stewart Capt kia 20-9-14 5ScotRif p103 CR France1329,Dugald

GILKINSON,James David Lt kia 26-8-14 2A&SH p173 CR France716

GILL,Basil Every Capt kia 18-10-16 2Yorks p90 MR21

GILL,Charles Treverlyn 2Lt kia 1-7-16 4 att22Manch p154 CR France630,Treverbyn

GILL,Colin 2Lt kia 31-7-17 12RFus p68 MR29

GILL,Daniel Aloysius T2Lt kia 24-10-16 18WYorks p81 CR France342

GILL,Eric Longden 2Lt kia 30-11-17 4Y&L p238 CR France245

GILL,Erold Waring TLt dow 25-7-16 86RH&FA p29

GILL,Francis Edwin Capt ded 28-2-15 RE p45 CR Lancs380

GILL,Frank Brooks 2Lt kia 3-9-16 6WRid p227 CR France293

GILL,Frank Hubert T2Lt kia 16-8-17 2WYorks p81 MR30

GILL,Frank Malcolm Capt kia 25/26-5-15 24Lond p252 MR22

GILL,George AssSurg 22-9-17 IMS MR66

GILL,Gordon Evans Maj ded 12-3-19 RE p254

GILL,Hugh Goddard Lt kia 12-3-18 13WYorks attRFC p16&81 CR France660,10Bn

GILL,Jack Woodward T2Lt kia 19-11-15 6YLI p143 CR Belgium101

GILL,John Brown Lt ded 20-1-21 6A&SH CR Scot874

GILL,John Ignatius T2Lt kia 7-6-17 11WYorks p81 MR29,7-6-16

GILL,Kenneth Carlyle.MC.MID Capt dow 22-10-18 1Camb &22RAF p244&258 CR France1512,23-10-18

GILL,Leonard Edward 2Lt kia 17-9-17 7N&D attMGC p233&187 CR France545

GILL,Noel Brendan 2Lt kia 23-4-17 18Manch p154 MR20

GILL,R.Capt 6-3-20 RAMC CR Hamps64

GILL,Rowland.MC.MM.2Lt kia 19-4-18 17Lpool p71 MR30

GILL,William Gerald Oliver 2Lt kia 27-3-17 1/7Ess p232 CR Palestine18

GILL,William Hutton Pridmore TCapt ded 26-1-17 RASC p193 CR France300

GILL,William Rey 2Lt kia 21-8-17 O&BLI 2/1BucksBn p231 CR Belgium96

GILLARD,Frederick T2Lt kia 24-8-18 9YLI p143 MR16

GILLENDER,Alfred Williamson 2Lt dow 10-4-17 3SStaffs att7Lincs p122 CR France97

GILLESPIE,Alexander Douglas 2Lt kia 26-9-15 4 att2A&SH p173 MR19

GILLESPIE,Charles Lt dow 20-9-15 4 att2HLI p163 CR France98

GILLESPIE,David Andrew 2Lt dow 24-1-17 3 att2BordR p117 CR France41

GILLESPIE,D.V.2Lt kia 5-4-18 GL &RAF p190

GILLESPIE,Francis Sydney TCapt dow 18-6-16 13RSuss p119 CR France345

GILLESPIE,Franklin Macaulay.MID TLtCol kia 9-8-15 4SWBord p100 MR4

GILLESPIE,Gordon Wood 2Lt kia 13-4-17 9Mddx attRFC p18&236 MR20

GILLESPIE,James Capt kia 30-7-16 1/7BlkW p231 CR France1890

GILLESPIE,John Lt ded 9-7-19 IndianMGC p266 CR Iraq8,9-8-19

GILLESPIE,Rollo 2Lt kia 25-9-15 3 att2SLancs p125 MR29

GILLESPIE,Thomas T2Lt kia 14-3-17 2BlkW p128 MR38

GILLESPIE,Thomas Cunningham 2Lt kia 18-10-14 2KOSB p101 MR22

GILLESPIE,William TCaptAMaj dow 9-4-18 RE 218FC p45 CR France169,206FC

GILLESPIE,William Edward T2Lt kia 11-9-18 7RB att12Londp178 CR France415

GILLESPIE,William Robert Beauchamp.MID TMaj kia 8-9-17 7RBerks p139 MR37

GILLETT,Edward Francis T2Lt dow 29-9-15 53RGA p39 CR France80,Lt

GILLETT,Frederick Tremlow T2Lt kia 22-7-16 1RWKent p141 MR21

GILLETT,George Maurice Gerald TCapt kia 26-9-16 6Leic p87 MR21

GILLETT,Herbert Edward Lt ded 23-11-18 1/1DerbyYeo p203 CR Greece9

GILLETT,Richmond Edward T2Lt dow 29-4-16 5RInniskF p105 CR France423

GILLHAM,Reginald George William 2Lt kia 26-9-17 RSuss att13Bn p119 MR30

GILLIAT,Cecil Glendower Percival Capt dow 14-10-14 RWar p64 CR France200

GILLIAT,Reginald Horace Crosbie Capt kia 6-4-15 5Leinst att1ConnRgrs p174 CR France1137

GILLIAT,Robert Vincent Lt dow PoW 25-5-18 10Manch p237 CR France1615

GILLIAT-SMITH,Arthur Lt 1-11-14 RE 26FC MR29

GILLIATT,Francis Ralph 2Lt kia 26-7-17 1/5Lincs p220 CR France223

GILLIATT,Otho Claude Skipwith Capt kia 30-10-14 1RB p178 CR Belgium32

GILLIES,Charles Percival.MC.TLt dow 5-5-16 MGC p254 CR France40,Percivale Capt

GILLIES,Forbes T2Lt kia 27-8-16 89MGC Inf p183 CR France765

GILLIES,Halliday Gordon Lt kia 13-11-16 3 att1RScotF p94 MR21

GILLIES,James T2Lt kia 1-7-16 2RWSurr p56 CR France630

GILLIES,James Brown Capt dow 14-11-16 4GordH p241 CR France131,kia 13-11-16

GILLIGAN,John Joseph 2Lt kia 25-4-18 B123RFA p29 CR France204

GILLILAND,Valentine Knox Capt kia 8-5-15 RIrRif att2Bn p169 MR29

GILLILAND,William Miller LtAMaj kia 28-4-15 RInniskF p105 CR Gallipoli3,W.M.M.Lt

GILLISON,Andrew.MID Rev 22-8-15 RAChDept att14AustInf CR Gallipoli18

GILLMAN,Angus George.MC.Maj kia 29-4-17 52/15RH&FA p29 CR France68

GILLON-FERGUSSON,James Scott Elliot Lt 27-4-15 5Mddx MR29

GILLOT,Oswald Cronek T2Lt kia 7-6-17 RE 68FC p45 CR Belgium168

GILMAN,Ronald John Lt ded 15-7-18 WarYeo p205 CR France40

GILMAN,William Harold 2Lt kia 14-6-18 8Lond p247 CR France62

GILMER,Ernest Richard T2Lt kia 12-10-16 1RIrF p171 MR21

GILMON,John Charles AssSurg 1-7-15 IMS CR India97A

GILMORE,Alexander William Francis.MC.2Lt kia 23-11-17 15RIrRif p169 MR17

GILMORE,Andrew 2Lt kia 11-3-15 1RIrRif p169 MR22

GILMORE,John Kenneth TCapt kia 22-8-16 6Glouc p225 MR21

GILMORE,Thomas Francis.MC.Lt kia 8-11-18 4 att5ConnRgrs p172 MR16

GILMOUR,Alastair Stuart T2Lt kia 15-9-16 11A&SH p173 CR France453

GILMOUR,Allan Capt ded 16-12-17 1LovatScts p204 CR Greece4,10CamH

GILMOUR,Archibald Keltie TCapt kia 16-8-16 7KOSB p101 CR France188

GILMOUR,D.Capt ded 19-8-16 RAMC CR Scot237

GILMOUR,Douglas TLt dow 16-2-16 7SfthH attTMB p164 CR France285

GILMOUR,Elphinstone Forrest 2Lt kia 28-3-18 1/4RScotF att8TMBp222 MR20

GILMOUR,G.L.T2Lt ded 12-8-17 RE IWT p45 CR Scot228

GILMOUR,Herbert James Graham Lt kia 19-9-14 3Worc p108 MR15

GILMOUR,James Lt kia 30-3-18 8 att9ScotRif p225 MR27

GILMOUR,Robert Wallace T2Lt kia 21-3-18 9RinniskF p105 MR27

GILMOUR,William T2Lt kia 4-12-16 13ScotRif att6Lancs p103 MR38,9-4-16

GILMOUR,Willis John Oberlin 2Lt kia 15-5-15 ScotHorse p205 MR37,Williejohn 15-5-17 13BlkW attSNottsYeo

GILPIN Albert John T2Lt kia 17-9-16 11KRRC A'Coy p150 CR France374

GILPIN,Ernest Henry Capt kia 21-3-18 2DLI p160 MR20,Harry

GILPIN,George Lt dow 7-10-18 1/8Manch CR France40

GILPIN,Norcliffe William Bernard 2Lt ded 1-6-17 RDC p253 CR Wilts115

GILPIN,Robert Lt dow 3-7-15 63RFA p29 CR Iraq6

GILROY,George Bruce.MC.TCapt dow 15-7-16 8BlkW p128 CR France23

GILROY,Kenneth Reid Lt dow 12-3-15 2BlkW p128 CR France727

GILSON,Alexander Ivan 2Lt kia 17-3-17 GL &RFC p8 MR20

GILSON,Edward Norman 2Lt dow PoW 5-11-18 2Y&L p158 CR Germany3

GILSON,Francis Gerald Maj dow 17-9-20 6Worc CR Hereford201

GILSON,George 2Lt kia 1-9-18 5Lond p246 MR16

GILSON,Leo Herbert TLt dow 29-7-16 7Suff p78 CR France51

GILSON,Robert Quilter TLt kia 1-7-16 11Suff p78 CR France515

GIMBLETT,Raymond John 2Lt ded 20-2-19 RFA 15DAC p29 CR Belgium316

GIMINGHAM,Charles Henry.MID Capt kia 9-11-17 1Herts attRFC p18&252 CR Greece3

GIMSON,Rupert Maj 10-3-21 6Ches CR Ches98

GIMSON,Walter Stanley.MC.T2LtACapt kia 16-8-17 GL YLI att61TMB p190 CR Belgium23

GINDER,Thomas Wilfred T2Lt kia 21-3-18 13Ess p131 MR20

GINN,Harold Etridge T2Lt kia 8-7-16 3Worc p108 CR France1890

GINN,S.W.Capt&Adjt 21-8-21 2EYorks CR Iraq8

GIOVANETTI,Albert Harcourt T2Lt kld 3-2-18 57ResSqnRFC p16 CR Egypt8

GIPPS,Reginald Nigel Lt kia 7-11-14 ScotsGds p52 MR29

GIRARD,Geoffrey Marcus Erskine T2Lt kld 16-11-17 7Leinst p174 CR France689

GIRARDOT,Markham Henry Capt kia 30-4-15 Ess p131 CR Gallipoli2,28-4-15

GIRARDOT,Paul Charcowt 2Lt kia 17-9-14 2 O&BLI p130 CR France1111,Chancourt

GIRDLESTON,Morrell Andrew Capt kia 25-3-15 IA 41Dogras p277 CR France924,GIRDLESTONE

GIRDLESTONE,H.W.Lt kld 30-4-18 RH&FA &4RAF p29 CR France134,RGA

GIRLING,Charles John 2Lt kia 23-10-16 1Hamps p120 MR21

GIRLING,Stephen Eastough TLt kia 29-9-18 9 att7DCLI p114 CR France379

GIROD,Milton 2Lt kld 19-3-16 3Ches &RFC p2&96,ded

GIRVAN,Frederick William LtACapt kia 26-10-17 8Dev p76 MR30

GIRVIN,Colin Bertram TCapt ded 5-11-18 3RDubF p176 CR Yorks181,dow

GISSING,Alexander 2Lt ded 9-10-18 3 att2SStaffs p122 CR France146

GITTINGS,Charles T2Lt kia 21-3-18 2 att2/5ELancs p110 CR France528

GITTINS,Albert.MC.TLt kia 25-5-17 5KSLI p144 CR France162

GITTINS,Henry Neville Capt ded 20-3-17 RGA 170SB p209 CR France169,Harry

GITTINS,Herbert 2Lt dow 2-6-17 5LNLancs p234 CR France255

GIUSANI,see GUISANI,S.J.J.V.A. CR France220

111

GIVEN,Robert 2Lt kia 27-5-18 19RIrRif att4EYorks p169 MR18

GJEMS,Albert Ole M ller 2Lt kia 8-8-17 5 att2RFus p68 MR29

GJERS,Lawrence ACapt kia 4-10-17 3 att2SfthH p164 MR30

GLACKEN,Hugh Frank Capt 16-1-18 MilWksServ MR65

GLADDEN,Leslie Charles Lt kia 20-4-18 3 att2Ess p131 CR France250

GLADSTONE,Elsie Mabel.ARRC.Sister ded 24-1-19 QAIMNS p200 CR Belgium265

GLADSTONE,John Ravenhill TCapt kia 23-8-18 6Leic p87 CR France742

GLADSTONE,Ralph Oscar T2Lt kia 2-11-17 RE 421WLancsFC p45 CR Belgium23

GLADSTONE,William Glynne Charles Lt kia 13-4-15 3RWFus p97 CR Wales637,1Bn

GLADSTONE,William Herbert.MC.LtACapt kia 27-9-18 1CldGds p51 CR France1497

GLADWELL,John Henry T2Lt kia 12-10-17 1 att7RWKent p141 CR Belgium20,dow 14-10-17

GLADWIN,Ralph Hamilton Fane Lt kia 26-10-14 2ScotsGds p52 MR29

GLAISBY,Kenneth Lt kia 1-11-17 2Bde att134Bty RFA p207 CR Belgium83

GLAISTER,George Lt kia 31-7-17 1/5LNLancs p234 CR Belgium10

GLAISTER,George Frederick TLt kia 1-8-18 2TankCps C'Coy p188 CR France300

GLANCY,Hugh G.2Lt kia 30-9-18 3RMunsF attMGC p183&175 CR France348

GLANFIELD,Barnard St.John Capt dow 31-8-16 4Suff p217 CR France397,Bernard

GLANFIELD,Gordon T2Lt kia 12-11-15 9Norf p73 CR Belgium92,11-11-15

GLANVILL,Ernest Mure Capt kia 2-11-14 RAMC attRScotsGreys p195 MR29

GLANVILLE WEST,Herbert T2Lt kia 19-8-18 Norf att12Bn p73 CR France193

GLASFURD,Duncan John TBrigGen dow 12-11-16 A&SH HQ 12AustInfBde p173

GLASGOW,William James Nesbitt.MC.MID TCapt dow 7-10-16 RE 93FC p45 CR France203,Nesbit

GLASIER,Philip Mannoch.DSO.LtCol kia 2-6-18 16Lond p249 CR France54,Mannock

GLASS,A.Lt 24-11-19 RGA CR Durham113

GLASS,David William Capt kia 18-9-16 5BordR p228 CR France239

GLASS,James Fraser 2Lt dow 26-4-15 2SfthH p164 CR Belgium151

GLASS,John Meldrum T2Lt kia 25-10-18 SfthH p164 CR France1256

GLASS,Leonard George 2Lt kia 9-10-17 1/2LancF p92 MR30

GLASS,William 2Lt kia 23-4-17 6BlkW p231 CR France924

GLASSCOCK,Sydney Frederick TLt kia 20-11-17 TankCps p188 MR17

GLASSON,Donald Havelock 2Lt dow 12-3-17 47RFC p8 CR Europe58

GLASTONBURY,Harold Mynett 2Lt dow 1-7-16 5 att1RIrRif p169 MR21

GLAZE,Donald Stuart T2Lt kia 26-10-17 SStaffs att1Bn p122 MR30

GLAZEBROOK,Philip Kirkland.DSO.Maj kia 7-3-18 1/1ChesYeo p203 CR Palestine

GLEAVE,Fergus 2Lt kia 22/23-7-16 10Glouc p106 MR21

GLEAVE,Harold Mason.MID Capt kia 6-3-17 3 att1N&D A'Coy p134 MR21 CR France624

GLEAVE,Thomas Reginald Lt kia 11-10-16 1/5SLancs p230 CR Belgium4

GLEDHILL,Annie Sister ded 17-10-18 QAIMNS p200 CR Palestine8

GLEDHILL,George Richard 2Lt kia 3-9-18 2/5WRid p227 MR21

GLEDSDALE,Arthur 2Lt kia 31-7-17 10Lpool p216 MR29,Arnold

GLEDSDALE,Irving Lt kia 13-7-17 3 att15Ches p96 CR France363

GLEDSTANES,Sheldon Arthur Capt dow 9-5-15 Beds p86 CR France284

GLEDSTONE,Herbert Reginald ACapt kia 25-5-18 NumbF att4Beds p61 MR27

GLEED,George Alfred.MID Lt dow 6-9-16 1Ches p96 CR France66,Capt

GLEED,John Victor Ariel 2Lt ded 7-7-17 45RFC p8 CR Belgium74

GLEESON,John Francis.MC.HonLt dow 2-2-18 8RMunstF p175 CR Eire167,Capt

GLEESON,Timothy TCapt&QM ded 22-12-18 SL Sch of Musk p201 CR Surrey148,28-12-18 ESurr

GLEGG,Arthur Livingstone 2Lt kia 10-8-15 6 att2KRRC p150 CR France114

GLEGG,Cuthbert Kemp TCapt kia 19-5-16 10ScotRif p103 CR France219,Charles

GLEGG,Robert.MID Lt kia 19-7-15 RE 1/2HighlandFC p210 CR France924

GLEGG,Walter Scott 2Lt kia 15-9-16 6 att9KRRC p150 MR21

GLEN,Alec 2Lt kia 29-12-15 Manch att8RFC CR France274

GLEN,Alexander Lt ded 21-9-16 RAMC p267 CR Yorks294,GLENN

GLEN,David 2Lt dow 24-4-17 4Suff p78 CR France120

GLEN,David Alexander 2Lt kia 28-12-15 Manch &RFC p1&154

GLEN,David Corse TLt kia 25-9-15 8RBerks p139 CR France219

GLEN,David Robert 2Lt kia 28-3-18 1/4 att1RScotF p222 MR20

GLEN,Donald Roy T2Lt kld 12-2-18 RFC p16 CR Kent25,GLENN

GLEN,James Capt 16-9-18 5ScotRif &70RAF MR20

GLEN,John Todd 2Lt kia 27-11-15 4ScotRif att1RMunstF p103 MR4

GLENCROSS,Andrew 2Lt kia 18-4-18 BlkW att1TMB p128 CR France279

GLENDAY,Alexander Goncalves Capt kia 8-8-15 RE 21S&M p45 CR France924

GLENDAY,Ferdinand Goncalves Capt kia 15-9-16 12NumbF attRFC p2&61 CR France167,dow

GLENDINNING,Arthur William Frederick T2Lt kia 14-7-16 12RScots p54 MR21

GLENDINNING,Duncan Retallick Lt kia 16-11-17 1/7Mddx p235 CR France307

GLENDINNING,James Graham 2Lt dow PoW 16-12-17 3Mon att57RFC p18&244 CR Belgium140,2-12-17

GLENDINNING,Thomas Henry TCapt kia 19-4-17 ACycCpsLowlandDiv p244 MR34,Clendinning

GLENIE,George Richard 2Lt kia 11-9-16 1/4RLancs p213 MR21

GLENIE,Julian William Lt accShotByServant 26-9-20 IA 3/70BurmaRif p277 CR Iraq6 Ex1KEdwHorse

GLENN,Archibald Patrick T2Lt kia 14-9-16 15WYorks p81 CR France631

GLENN,Cecil William TLt kia 28-1-17 RASC att1RInniskF p193 MR21

GLENNIE,John Herbert 2Lt kia 1-7-16 1KOSB p101 CR France220

GLENNON,Francis Henry T2Lt kia 16-11-16 10 att8ELancs p110 MR21

GLENNY,Ernest Howard Lt ded 9-10-18 RAMC p195 CR Iraq6

GLENNY,H.Q.Lt 18-11-14 SL attNigR CR WAfrica33

GLENNY,Thomas Alexander Maj kia 25-9-15 7KOSB p101 MR19

GLENTWORTH,E.W.C.G.de V.Viscount.Capt ded 18-5-18 WarYeo &RAF p205

GLIDDON,Ernest Frank Leslie Nevill 2Lt dow 5-6-18 4 att1Dors p229 CR France84

GLIDDON,G.C.Capt 11-5-15 MO 10CanadaInf CR France284

GLIDDON,Maurice.MC.TLtACapt dow 16-8-17 B108RFA p29 CR Belgium8

GLIDDON,Reginald Arthur 2Lt kld 9-5-18 13Mddx &RAF p146 CR Lond33,Lt

GLORNEY,Ernest Edward 2Lt kld 25-10-16 RFC p3 CR Ireland5,Lt

GLOSSOP,Bertram TLt kia 4-9-16 9Dev p76 MR21,6-9-16

GLOSSOP,Ernest Edward 2Lt dow 4-5-15 SomLI p79 CR France284

GLOSSOP,Walter George Cave Lt kld 20-6-21 RFA CR Surrey11

GLOSTER,Francis Beresford Lt kia 3-12-17 RASC &20RFC p8&193 MR20

GLOSTER,Gerald Charles Edward Lt kia 6-11-17 1Dev p76 MR30

GLOSTER,Henry Colpays Lt kia 13-3-15 6GordH p242 MR22

GLOVER,A.C.SubCdr 22-7-20 S&T Cps MR43

GLOVER,Alexander Milligan Thomson Lt kia 17-8-17 KOSB &70RFC p8&101 MR20

GLOVER,Ben Hilton 2LtACapt kia 1-7-16 7RWKent att50TMB p141 CR France397

GLOVER,Brian Edward.DCM.T2Lt ded 13-3-16 GL &8RFC p3&190 CR France421,kia

GLOVER,Clifford Lee Lt kia 18-5-18 Ches &48RAF p263 MR20

GLOVER,Cyril John 2Lt dow 8-10-16 10Lond p248 CR France105

GLOVER,G.M.MC.Capt 24-7-20 2Manch MR38

GLOVER,George Wright.DSO.Lt dow 31-8-18 6 att1RB p178 CR France95,1-9-18

GLOVER,John Bertram 2Lt kia 16-6-18 RGA 309SB p39 CR France116,HAC

GLOVER,John Grenside 2Lt kia 8-11-15 4YLI p235 MR30

GLOVER,Leonard James 2Lt dow 1-11-17 B82RH&FA p29 CR Belgium16

GLOVER,Richard Bowie Gaskell.MID Capt kia 5-11-15 1Lond p245 CR France254

GLOVER,Ronald Howard 2Lt kia 25-9-17 RFA X19TMB p208 CR France285,dow

GLOVER,Samuel Lawrence T2Lt ded 12-1-16 10WRid p115 CR France924,kld

GLUCKMAN,Philip Lt kia 8-10-16 25Lond p252 MR21

GLYKA,Anthony Isidore 2Lt kia 12-10-16 1RWar p64 MR21

GLYN,Charles Reginald 2Lt kia 9-1-17 IA 110MahrattaLI att105 p277 MR38

GLYN,Guy Godfrey TLt ded 16-8-15 RE 109Co RlyConSect p45 CR France51

GLYN,Richard Spencer Lt kia 20-10-14 1EKent p57 MR32

GLYNN,Alfred Henley 2Lt dow 12-2-17 15Lond p249 CR France41

GLYNN,Bernard James 2Lt kia 29-5-17 34RFC p8 CR France1170

GLYNN,Martin T2Lt kia 29-9-18 10 att2Worc p108 CR France665

GOADBY,John Clifton 2Lt kia 28-8-18 13Lond p249 CR France568

GOATCHER,Fred TLt dow 31-10-17 9Suff p78 CR France179

GOATER,Horace Benjamin Capt kia 10-8-18 8RDC att2/4Berksp253 CR France346

GOBEY,Alfred John Lt 19-11-20 2DLI CR Durham1

GOBY,James Henry ACapt ded 29-10-20 IARO attS&M att122RlyConstCoy p277 MR43

GODBER,Hugh Gerald TCapt kia 11/18-7-16 13NumbF p61 CR France188,12-7-16

GODBY,Thomas Stanley T2Lt kia 20-11-17 6Mddx att8Lpool p146 MR17

GODDALL,Cecil Clarence 2Lt kia 7-7-16 3 att6Dors p124

GODDALL,Clarence William 2Lt kia 15-11-16 2SStaffs p122

GODDARD,Alec Spencer 2Lt kia 30-11-17 7Norf p73&257 MR17

GODDARD,Eric 2Lt kia 4-7-16 1/7WRid p227 MR21

GODDARD,Frederick Sidney 2Lt kia 15-12-17 4RFus p68 CR France614

GODDARD,Gordon Cecil T2Lt kia 16-10-18 9ESurr p112 CR France206

GODDARD,Harold 2Lt kia 9-10-17 5WYorks p218 MR30

GODDARD,John Lister TLt kia 15-9-16 9Norf p73 MR21

GODDARD,Kenneth Aquinas McKenzie 2Lt kia 11-7-16 5Worc p108 CR France430,Acquinas Lt

GODDARD,Norman Molyneux T2Lt dow 2-7-17 SStaffs att9Bn p122 CR France285

GODDARD,Philip Henry Thomas T2Lt kia 26-9-16 11RFus p68 MR21

GODDARD,Ralph Garnett 2Lt kia 9-10-17 1HAC p206 MR30

GODDARD,Sydney George 2Lt kia 30-6-16 2RSuss p119 MR20

GODDARD,Sydney Vernon Lt dow 23-3-18 2/17Lond p250 CR Palestine3

GODDARD,William Neale TLt kia 13-6-17 1/2LancF p92 CR France765

GODDARD,William Thomas 2Lt dow 13-10-17 12/35RFA p29 CR France40

GODET,L.De G.2Lt kia 1-6-18 GL &RAF p190

GODFREY,Arthur Pole TLt kia 11-4-17 HouseHoldBn RHGds p20 MR20

GODFREY,Edward T2Lt kia 31-7-17 RWKent att10Bn p141 MR29,GODFERY

GODFREY,Frederick 2LtTCapt kia 16-8-16 4RFus p68 MR21 CR France1890

GODFREY,Harry Frederick 2Lt kia 1-7-16 1/5N&D p232 MR21

GODFREY,Henry 2Lt kia 9-9-16 5LancF p221 CR France402,8/9-9-16

GODFREY,Herbert Arthur T2Lt kia 12-5-17 11Mddx p146 MR20

GODFREY,Hugh 2Lt kia 1-7-16 2RBerks p139 MR21

GODFREY,John Leslie 2Lt dow 7-5-18 C113RFA p29 CR France180

GODFREY,Leonard George 2Lt kia 20-7-16 10RWFus p97 MR21

GODFREY,Leonard Powell TCapt dow 23-8-17 14WelshR p126 CR Belgium18

GODFREY,Norman Carter T2Lt kia 16-4-18 5TankCps p188 MR32

GODFREY,Oliver Cyril 2Lt ded 23-9-16 27RFC p3 CR France452,kia

GODFREY,Stephen Mervyn Lt kia 30-12-17 28Lond p252 MR21

GODFREY,Victor 2Lt kia 1-7-16 2RScotF p94 MR21

GODFREY,William Frank 2Lt kia 3-9-16 4NStaffs att72TMB p157 CR France402

GODFREY,William John 2Lt kia 3-9-16 1BlkW p128 MR21

GODFREY-FAUSSETT,Owen Godfrey.DSO.LtCol kia 2-5-15 Ess p131

GODFREY-PAYTON,Arthur Capt dow 29-8-16 7RWar p214 CR France74

GODLEE,John T2Lt kia 19-7-16 RFC p3

GODLEY,Gerald Annesley George Lt kia 26-3-18 RASC 15DivTrain p193 CR France113

GODLEY,John Lindley 2Lt ded 31-8-19 RB att286MGC Inf p266 MR43

GODMAN,Frederick Tyrell TCapt ded PoW 12-10-17 9RSuss p119 CR Germany3

GODMAN,Lawrence.DSO.MajALtCol dow 30-9-17 46RFA p29 CR France285

GODMAN,Walter Williams Wynn 2Lt kia 24-1-15 KRRC p150 CR France727

GODOLPHIN-OSBORNE,Maurice Capt dow 25-2-15 RB p178 CR France284

GODSAL,Alan T2Lt kia 30-7-15 7RB p178 MR29

GODSAL,Walter Hugh.DSO.MC.Maj dow 26-3-18 2DLI p160 CR France300

GODSILL,Stanley Lt kia 23-12-17 18Lond p250 CR Palestine3

GODSON,Albert Bernard Lawrence 2Lt kia 3-8-17 NStaffs att9Bn p157 CR Belgium17

GODSON,William Curry TLt kia 3-5-17 46RFA p29 CR France1185,1-5-17

GODWARD,Eric James 2Lt kia 25-8-15 7Mddx p235 CR France525

GODWIN,Charles Cayley 2Lt mbk 17-10-16 1RFC p256 CR France705

GODWIN,Colin Harold 2Lt kia 1-7-16 15Y&L p158 MR21

GODWIN,George 2Lt kia 28-9-18 17RFA p29 CR Belgium84

GODWIN,Harold North T2Lt dow 31-7-17 Lpool att209LabCps 209EmplCoy p189 CR France200

GODWIN,John Charles Raymond T2Lt kia 7-7-16 10 att7RSuss p119 MR21

GODWIN,Leslie Wentworth 2Lt kia 10-10-16 3 att16N&D p134 CR France215

GODWIN,Louis Vionnet T2Lt kia 23-10-16 2RB p178 MR21

GODWIN,Philip Edgar 2Lt kia 7-1-16 IARO att6Jats p277 MR38,6-1-16

GODWIN,Sidney William 2Lt kia 2-10-16 19Lond p250 MR21

GODWIN,Thomas Ernest Lt kia 21-8-17 GL &RFC CR Belgium140

GODWIN,William Bernard 2Lt kia 17-2-17 9 att12Mddx p236 MR21

GODWIN-WILLIAMS,Frederick James HonCapt ded 23-11-18 RWSurr p56&262 CR Nhampt151

GOEPEL,Robert Mackie Lt kia 17-9-16 5SfthH att123MGC p187&241 MR21

GOFF,Alfred Laurence 2Lt kia 16-1-17 14RFus att6LNLancs p68 MR38,Lawrence

GOFF,Charles Edward.MC.LtCol kia 8-8-16 1Lpool p71 MR21

GOFF,R.W.Lt 13-12-16 Leinst CR Kent217

GOFF,William Setten.MC.Lt kia 22-4-18 7RWFus p223 CR France296

GOFFE,William Reginald T2Lt kia 30-7-16 2 O&BLI p130 MR21

GOFFEY,John Graham 2Lt kia 3-9-16 12KRRC p150 CR France339,23 att17Bn

GOING,Charles Henry Bernard Lt kia 18-8-17 2RhodR C'Coy attKAR p202 CR Tanzania1

GOLBY,Arthur Hugh 2Lt dow 13-8-17 4RSuss p228 CR Belgium18

GOLD,Cecil Argo TLt&Adjt kia 3-7-16 5RBerks p139 CR France251

GOLD,Charles Read.DSO.Capt kia 21-11-17 DerbyYeo attDLI p203 CR France1266

GOLD,George Rome 2Lt kia 27-5-18 Hamps att2Berks p120 MR18

GOLD,Percy 2Lt kia 19-7-16 2ScotsGds p52 CR Belgium6,2-7-16

GOLDBERG,Frederick William 2Lt kia 3-10-16 3RWSurr att7RDubF p56 CR Greece3

GOLDBERG,Herbert Walter 2Lt dow 31-7-15 3RWSurr p56 CR France145

GOLDBY,William Charles T2Lt kia 22-8-18 18KRRC p150 CR Belgium11,21-8-18

GOLDEN,Alfred William T2Lt kia 25-3-18 9RSuss p119 MR27

GOLDEN,Frank Charles Allen TLt kia 26-12-15 12DLI p160 CR France83

GOLDER,William TLt kia 5-10-18 13DLI p160 CR France844

GOLDIE,Amyas Leigh TLt kia 6-8-15 11Glouc att4Worc p106 MR4

GOLDIE,Barre Herbert 2Lt dow 29-4-15 IARO att32Lancers attPatialaLancers p277 CR Egypt8

GOLDIE,George Henry Lt kia 14-9-14 1LNLancs p136 MR15

GOLDIE,Mark Leigh.DSO.MVO Maj ded 5-3-15 V'RHA p29 CR France31

GOLDIE,Paul Francis T2Lt kia 25-9-15 1LNLancs p136 MR19

GOLDIE-TAUBMAN,Gerald TCapt ded 15-9-15 RGA ComdtDetnBks p39 CR Lancs410

GOLDING,Edgar Lt kia 19-9-17 RASC attRFC p18&253 CR France658

GOLDING,Eric.DCM.2Lt kia 15-7-16 1Mddx p146 MR21

GOLDING,Frank 2Lt kia 21-5-17 17 att2/1Lond p250 MR20

GOLDING,Frank Alfred T2Lt kia 1-7-16 9YLI p143 CR France267

GOLDING,Harold T2Lt dow 25-8-17 7RWSurr p56

GOLDING,Harold Gordon Lancelot Lt ded 3-12-20 IA 1/35Sikhs p277 CR Palestine9 Ex 8SLancs

GOLDING,Harold William.MID TCapt kia 31-10-18 RASC att8SomLI p193 CR France206

GOLDING,Thomas James LtTCapt kia 26-9-17 RAMC p195 CR Belgium34

GOLDRICK,A.C.Lt kia 30-8-17 1KAR &SL p268 CR EAfrica90

GOLDRING,Frank Carter TLt kia 13-11-16 8RLancs p59 MR21

GOLDS,Frank T2Lt kia 5-10-16 11ESurr att7RSuss p112 CR France374

GOLDS,Gordon Brewer T2Lt kia 1-7-16 18Lpool p72 CR France397

GOLDS,Ingram Thomas ACapt kia 30-11-17 7ESurr p112 MR17

GOLDSELLER,Leon David Lt dow 14-4-17 5WRid p227 CR France614

GOLDSMID,Sidney Alexander 2Lt ded 7-11-14 3Worc p108 CR France924

GOLDSMITH,Amy Alice Victoria SNurse ded 5-3-19 TFNS att57GH p254 CR France1571

GOLDSMITH,Bertie Lt dow 13-10-18 30/39RFA p29 CR France146

GOLDSMITH,Frank.MC.TMaj dow 27-9-17 14Hamps p120 MR30

GOLDSMITH,Herbert Francis Lt kia 27-9-18 6LancF att63MGC p187&221 MR16

GOLDSMITH,Henry Mills Lt kia 9-5-15 Dev att2Lincs p76 MR32

GOLDSMITH,Lewis Wilberforce TCapt kia 5-11-16 7Yorks p90 MR21

GOLDSPINK,Edward Newell T2Lt kia 31-7-17 Lpool p72 MR29

GOLDSTEIN,Selwyn TLt ded 8-6-17 RE 173Coy p262 CR Belgium5

GOLDSWORTH,Duncan William Lt kia 25-9-15 3 att2SLancs p125 MR29

GOLDSWORTHY,Thomas.MID Lt kia 12/14-4-18 5DCLI attMGC p227 MR32,12-4-18

GOLDTHORP,Guy TCapt kia 23-4-17 10RFus p68 MR20

GOLDTHORPE,Arthur Francis T2Lt kia 12-5-17 7EYorks p84 MR20

GOLIGHTLY,George Frederick T2Lt dow 7-5-17 19DLI p160 CR France610

GOLLIN,Edgar Bearman T2Lt dow 14-5-17 13Lpool p72 CR France113,Capt

GOLLOP,R.J.Capt 28-5-20 3Dors CR Devon206

GOMERSALL,William Ellis TLt kia 1-7-16 22Manch p154 MR21

GOMME,Edward Elfred Coote TLtACapt kia 18-6-17 2Suff p78 CR France421

GONNE,Michael Edward.MC.Capt kia 7-8-18 RFus &54RAF p68&257 CR France526,8-8-13

GONNER,Edward Dermot Leslie 2Lt ded 2-7-18 5RWar p214 CR Ches198

GONNER,Edward Maurice.MC.TCapt kia 23-4-17 16KRRC p150&258 MR20

GONSALVES,D.R.Maj 15-3-21 IMD MR66

GOOCH,Edward Sinclair.MID Maj dow 21-9-15 BerksYeo p203 CR Scot430 Ex7Huss

GOOCH,Geoffrey Fulthorpe TLtACapt kia 19-9-18 RGA 25SB p39 MR16

GOOD,Thomas Henry TCapt dow 8-9-16 9RDubF p176 CR France23

GOOD,William Henry T2Lt kia 16-8-15 7RMunstF p175 MR4

GOOD,William Knight Lt kia 27-2-18 5RScots p211 MR30

GOODACRE,Harry 2Lt ded 29-5-19 3Lincs p263 CR Lincs61

GOODALE,Arthur William 2Lt kia 9-8-15 1KSLI p144 MR29

GOODALL,Albert James Gill TLt kia 1-7-16 2RBerks p139 CR France251

GOODALL,Arthur 2Lt dow 20-2-18 12Lond p248 CR Lond1

GOODALL,Arthur Charles T2Lt kia 6-11-16 7Yorks p90 MR21

GOODALL,Cecil Clarence 2Lt 7-7-16 3 att6Dors CR France1890

GOODALL,Clarence William 2Lt kia 15-11-16 2SStaffs p122 CR France1890,13-11-16

GOODALL,Edward Orme Clement TLt dow 9-11-17 23RFA p29 CR Belgium18

GOODALL,Frank Basil Lt kia 21-8-15 3BordR p117 MR4

GOODALL,Garnett Arthur Cumberland 2Lt kia 20-7-16 4Suff p217 MR21

GOODALL,George Mortimer Langdon 2Lt kia 9-5-15 3 att2ELancs p110 CR France566

GOODALL,George Percy TCapt kia 14-2-16 N&D p134 MR29

GOODALL,Harold Armitage 2Lt kia 22-3-18 RFA attZ16TMB p29 MR27

GOODALL,Marcus Herbert Capt dow 14-7-16 1/5Y&L p238 CR France74

GOODALL,Robert Leslie T2Lt kia 18-9-18 12Manch p154 CR France415 Ex 7HLI

GOODALL,William David Lt ded 11-5-21 6RScots CR Canada155

GOODBAN,Montague Sidney T2Lt kia 19-5-17 ESurr &22RFC p8&112 CR France439

GOODBODY,Henry Edgar Capt kia 12-5-15 4Leinst p174 MR29

GOODBODY,Owen Frederick T2Lt ded 20-10-15 RE 72FC 13Div p45 CR Egypt3,Lt

GOODCHILD,Stanley Cecil 2Lt kia 1-7-16 2Ess p131 MR21

GOODCHILD,Stewart John 2Lt kia 28-3-18 3 att7KSLI p144 MR20

GOODCHILD,Victor George Lt ded 31-10-18 GL &RAF p190

GOODDEN,Frank Widenham LtTmaj kld 28-1-17 RFC p8 CR Hamps1

GOODDEN,Henry William Lt kia 9-5-15 RAMC att2RIrReg p195 MR29

GOODE,Alfred T2Lt kia 29-3-17 NStaffs p157 MR38

GOODE,George Mortlock Lt kia 24-5-17 GL &43RFC p8 MR20

GOODE,Thomas Lord 2Lt kia 15-6-18 5RWar p214 CR Italy3

GOODES,George Leonard.MC&Bar.Capt kia 6-10-16 4Lond &140TMB p246 CR France453

GOODEVE,Lionel TMaj kia 26-8-15 6RScotF p94 CR France423,1Bn

GOODEVE,S.M.Lt 20-11-17 21RFC CR Belgium 16

GOODEVE,Thomas Edward.OBE.TCaptAMaj kld 26-1-19 RE p45&257 CR Syria2

GOODFELLOW,Arthur James Capt dow 7-8-15 8LancF p221 CR Gallipoli3

GOODFELLOW,Edward Arthur Fitzherbert 2Lt kia 21-2-16 3ConnRgrs att60TMB p172 CR Belgium23

GOODFELLOW,Eric Hector.MID TLt kia 9-3-16 28/9RFA p29 MR38

GOODFELLOW,Hugh Douglas TCapt dow 17-12-15 D49RFA p29 CR Belgium11

GOODFELLOW,James Gordon.MC.LtAMaj kia 23-3-18 RE 416FC p209 CR France184

GOODFORD,Charles James Henry.MC.Lt kia 1-7-16 1Hamps p120 CR France643

GOODHAND,Reginald Frederick SubCdr ded 16-7-17 IA IndOrdDept p277

GOODING,Herbert Robert Withom Lt kia 13-5-15 5Lond p246 MR22

GOODING,Samuel Jewell 2Lt dow 11-12-17 15ImpCamCps CR Egypt9

GOODING,William Thomas 2Lt kia 22-3-18 1/2 att6/7RScotF p94 MR20

GOODISON,Frank Bowler Lt dow 26-5-17 PoW 5SStaffs attRFC p18&229 CR Germany3

GOODLER, Cdr 19-2-15 S&T Cps CR Iraq6

GOODMAN,Basil Harris 2Lt kia 25/27-9-15 9Norf p73 MR19

GOODMAN,Claude Pendarvis 2Lt kia 18-8-16 4Lpool p72 CR France432

GOODMAN,Douglas Lt dow 24-11-17 RASC att12SWBord p253 MR17

GOODMAN,Eric George T2Lt kia 12-4-17 6Dors p124 MR20

GOODMAN,Gilbert Anthony 2Lt kia 28-10-18 10LNLancs att66RAF p136 CR Italy9,Lt 1Bn

GOODMAN,Geoffrey Thomas Lt kia 1-6-17 RFA p207 CR Belgium21

GOODMAN,Harold Harry 2LtACapt kia 16-8-17 3 att2Dev p76 MR30,Henry

GOODMAN,James 2Lt kia 11-4-17 NhamptYeo p204 MR20

GOODMAN,John Everatt T2Lt kia 14-8-17 GL &53RFC p8 CR France285

GOODMAN,Joseph 2Lt kia 11-4-17 5RLancs att10LNLancs p213 MR20

GOODMAN,Percy Nathaniel TCapt kia 3-3-16 13RFus 1Coy p68 CR France501

GOODMAN,Reginald Moon.MID 2Lt kia 16-5-15 SL att2BordR p201 CR France279

GOODRICH,Frank Edward.MC.TCapt kia 12-9-16 60RFC p3 CR France95,kldacc

GOODRICH,Walter Michael 2Lt kia 25-3-18 8 att6Manch p237 CR France1472

GOODRICK,John William 2Lt drd 26-2-18 GL RE HR17 &rIWT p190 MR38

GOODRICK,Walter Robert.MC.Capt kia 1-1-17 7DLI p239 CR France453

GOODSON,Harold Walter.MC.2LtTCapt kia 11-10-18 3 att6Dors A'Coy p124 CR France

GOODWAY,James T2Lt kia 27-12-17 7Yorks p90 CR France1498

GOODWILL,Goodwill,Cyril 2Lt kia 3-9-16 5WYorks p218 CR France383

GOODWIN,Cecil Herbert 2Lt dow 13-10-18 D189RFA p29 CR France686

GOODWIN,Cecil Stanley TCapt kia 31-8-16 A109RFA p29 CR France370

GOODWIN,Dudley Fletcher 2LtACapt dow 7-3-17 157RFA p29 CR France699

GOODWIN,Eric Lindsey TLt kia 12-10-16 13 att17Manch p154 MR21

GOODWIN,George 2Lt ded 19-10-17 1/7Ches p223 CR Egypt1

GOODWIN,Harold Desborough Lt kia 1-7-16 16Mddx p146 CR France1500

GOODWIN,Harold James 2Lt kia 24-4-17 RGA 135SB p39 CR France1182

GOODWIN,John T2Lt kia 29-11-17 1KRRC p150 MR17

GOODWIN,John TCapt&QM ded 22-2-19 RAMC p254 CR Lancs98

GOODWIN,John Stanley 2LtTLt kia 28-3-17 1SStaffs att22Manch p122 MR20

GOODWIN,Norman William 2Lt kia 16-9-17 1Mddx attRFC p8&146 CR Belgium383

GOODWIN,Stuart Wycliffe.MC.T2Lt kia 31-3-18 11BordR p117 CR France745

GOODWIN,William Alexander Delap TLt kia 1-7-16 11Y&L p158 CR France246

GOODY,Geoffrey Riddel TLt kld 14-7-18 9KRRC att10TrResBn p150 CR France34

GOODY,Gilbert Alexander T2Lt dow 6-11-16 22 att16KRRC p150 CR France105

GOODYEAR,Duncan Matheson TLt kia 29-6-17 GL &57RFC p8 CR Belgium6

GOODYEAR,Frank Percy.MSM.2Lt ded 8-2-19 RASC p193 p267 CR Wilts194

GOODYEAR,Frederick T2Lt dow 23-5-17 Ess att2Bn p131 CR France95

GOODYEAR,Frederick George.MC.Lt dow 18-12-17 24Lond p252 CR Egypt7

GOODYEAR,Raymond Norman 2Lt kia 24-4-17 6ESurr p226 CR France415

GOODYEAR,Roland 2Lt kia 12-4-18 9MGC Inf p183 MR30

GOOLD,Louis 2Lt dow 11-5-18 122/52RFA p29

GOOLDEN,Alexander Wood Capt kia 15-7-19 IA 3/124BaluchistanInf p277 MR43

GOOLDEN,Donald Charles 2Lt kia 15-8-16 6 att4RFus p68 CR France630,14-8-16

GOOSENS,Adolphe Anthony Lt dow 17-8-16 7Norf p73 CR France74

GOOSEY,H.2Lt kld 8-8-18 3NumbF &RAF p61

GOPSILL,Kenneth Lloyd TLt kia 15-2-18 ESurr att43RFC p16&112 CR France345,Capt

GORBUTT,Isaac Lt ded 19-3-19 11WYorks p263 CR Lincs156

GORBUTT,Martha Sister 28-7-20QAIMNS CR Lond29

GORDON,Adam Fraser 2Lt dow 11-8-16 10LNLancs p136 MR21

GORDON,Adrian Charles.DSO.LtCol kia 12-12-17 RFA 235Bde p206 CR France755

GORDON,A.E.Maj ded 19-12-16 RGA p39 CR Wales372

GORDON,Albert William 2Lt dow 12-8-17 32RFC p8 CR France40

GORDON,Alec McDougall.MC.MID Capt dow 7-11-17 246RFA p207 CR Belgium10

GORDON,Alec William.MC.CaptAMaj kia 6-8-18 RE 56FC p45 CR France33

GORDON,Alexander John Maxwell Capt kia 27-11-17 1/16Lond p249 CR France530

GORDON,Alexander Maurice Lt kia 23-1-16 1RFus p68 MR29,20-1-16

GORDON,Alexander Weston LtCol ded 20-12-18 3RIrF p171 CR Glouc27

GORDON,Alistair Campbell Miller T2Lt dow 1-3-17 6RScotF p94 CR Lond14

GORDON,Alister Fraser.CMG.DSO.TBrigGen dow 31-7-17 GordH Cmdg153Bde Staff p166 CR Belgium11

GORDON,Arthur Forbes T2Lt dow 18-4-18 1CamH p167 CR France10

GORDON,Bernard Vernon 2Lt kld 14-12-16 RFC p3 CR Numb86

GORDON,Bertram Gorges Reginald.DSO.TLtCol kia 20-7-16 2GordH p166 CR France176

GORDON,Cecil Philip George Capt kld 21-3-18 4SStaffs attRFC p16&122 CR Glouc67

GORDON,Charles Campbell Boswell 2Lt kia 28-4-17 3SomLI p79 MR20

GORDON,Charles Cecil CaptAMaj kia 4-6-17 110RH&FA p29 CR Belgium42

GORDON,Charles Ewan Lt kia 27-8-18 5RScots att1/5RScotsF p211 MR16 CR France162

GORDON,Charles William Eric BrigGen kia 23-7-17 BlkW 123InfBde p128 CR Belgium15

GORDON,Colin.MID Capt kia 16-8-17 2Lond p245 MR29

GORDON,Colin Graham 2Lt kia 1-7-16 3GordH p166 CR France331

GORDON,Cosmo George 2Lt dow 17-9-14 1Nhampt p137 CR France1107

GORDON,David Elder 2Lt kia 15-7-16 12RScots p54 CR France399

GORDON,Donald 2Lt kia 17-7-17 256RFA p208 CR Belgium5

GORDON,Donald Jervis Gordon T2Lt kia 3-7-16 8BordR p117 CR France233

GORDON,Douglas Lt kia 14-8-17 7A&SH att10RFC p18&243 CR France924

GORDON,Douglas Neave 2Lt kia 21-2-17 1/6SStaffs p229 CR France502

GORDON,Douglas Stanley 2Lt kia 21-2-18 RFA &2RFC SR p16&29 CR France98

GORDON,Elizabeth Marjorie Miss died 11-9-17 VAD StJAB p200 CR Greece9

GORDON,Eldred Pottinger 2Lt kia 22-11-15 IARO att104Rif p277 MR38

GORDON,Eric Alexander T2Lt kia 21-3-18 HLI att10/11Bn p162 MR20

GORDON,Ernest Arthur Woodhall 2Lt dow 29-7-17 4YLI p235 CR France13

GORDON,Geoffrey Lt kia 30-4-15 12Lancers p22 MR29

GORDON,George Duff TLt kia 12-3-15 2Nhampt p137 CR France768

GORDON,George Strachan 2Lt kia 19-8-17 7ScotRif attRFC p18&224 CR France1495

GORDON,Gerald Montague TCapt&Adjt kia 9-6-17 5 att12RFus p68 CR Belgium15

GORDON,Gilbert Thomas T2Lt dow 28-9-15 8GordH p166 CR France98

GORDON,Harold Eastly 2Lt kia 23-2-17 5Lond p246 CR Belgium11

GORDON,Henry Lt dow 19-12-15 3 att2KOSB p101 CR Gallipoli1,Harry 3 att1Bn

GORDON,Henry Bernard TLt kia 7-7-16 7RSuss p119 MR21

GORDON,Ivan Hugh Maj accShot 2-9-17 IA 56Rif attKapurtalaInf p277 CR EAfrica13

GORDON,J.C.H.2Lt 23-1-21 3GordH CR Scot341

GORDON,James Gaspar 2Lt kia 5-3-17 5 att6GordH p242 MR20

GORDON,James Willison Nugent Lt kia 22-2-15 5BlkW p231 CR France706,William

GORDON,John Cameron 2Lt kia 21-3-18 8RBerks p139 MR27

GORDON,John Frederick Strathearn Capt dow 19-11-14 ScotRif att1RScotF p103 CR Belgium150

GORDON,Lewis.DSO.Capt dow 18-10-15 GordH p166 CR Gallipoli3,BdeMaj 129Bde

GORDON,Maitland Lockhart Capt kia 7-5-17 3 att2GordH p166 MR20

GORDON,Michael Patrick Rev dow 27-8-17 RAChDept p199 CR Belgium24

GORDON,Peter,T2Lt kia 24-8-18 12 att18KRRC &4CamH p150 CR Belgium11,9Bn

GORDON,Reginald Clegg.DSO.Maj kld 26-3-18 RGA Lowland HB p209 CR France156,R.G.

GORDON,Robert T2Lt dow 4-12-16 99MGC p183 CR France40

GORDON,Robert Charles Lowther T2Lt dow 30-9-15 8GordH p166 CR France64

GORDON,Robert Eddington Capt kia 15-9-14 Nhampt p137 MR15

GORDON,Robert Hope Lt kia 8-8-16 1/8Lpool p215 MR21

GORDON,Robert Norman Capt kia 28-10-14 2BordR p117 MR29

GORDON,Roland Elphinstone.MC.CaptAMaj dow 30-8-18 C251RFA p29 CR France119

GORDON,Ronald Granville 2Lt kia 19-9-18 3 att2RSuss p119 CR France699

GORDON,Ronald Henry Capt kia 18-7-16 3 att1GordH p166 MR21

GORDON,Ronald Steuart Capt kia 2-11-14 IA 57Rif p277

GORDON,Sidney Eustace Laing Lt kia 13-3-15 6 att4RFus p68 MR29

GORDON,Sidney George T2Lt kia 20-9-17 16RB p178 MR30

GORDON,Thomas Seton T2Lt dow 22-1-16 11BordR p117 CR France43

GORDON,W.D.Lt 7-2-20 S&T Cps MR66

GORDON,W.H.Lt 30-10-16 CanadaFldArt 2DAC CR France133

GORDON,William Lt kia 9-5-15 CamH p167 MR22

GORDON,William Bonnalie.MID Capt ded 2-11-19 RAMC p267 CR Yorks474

GORDON,William Hyde Eagleson TLt dow 30-9-15 8GordH p166 CR France40

GORDON,Victor Frederick.MC.Lt dow 1-7-18 GL YLI attTMB p190 CR Mddx9

GORDON,Vivian TCapt kia 25-9-15 8GordH p166 MR19

GORDON-DUFF,Lachlan Capt kia 24-10-14 3 att1GordH p166 CR France348

GORDON-IVES,Victor Maynard Gordon Lt dow 16-9-14 3CldGds p51 CR France1107

GORDON-JONES,Eric 2Lt dow 1-8-17 2Mddx p146 CR Belgium11

GORDON-KIDD,Arthur Lionel.DSO.LtTCapt dow 27-8-17 4DragGds attRFC p8&21 CR Belgium18

GORDON-LENNOX,Lord Bernard Charles Maj kia 10-11-14 2GrenGds p50 CR Belgium134

GORDON PATCHETT,Reginald Lt 7-3-18 MilLabCps CR EAfrica53

GORDON-RALPH,Philip James Gordon Capt kia 6-8-17 2RIrReg p89 CR Belgium7

GORDON-SALE,H.Lt kia 9-3-15 3KAR p268

GORDON-SMITH,Gordon TLtACapt kia 24-10-18 RWKent att10Bn p141 CR Belgium408

GORDON-SMITH,Norman 2Lt kia 19-12-15 HLI attRFC CR Belgium379

GORDON-STEWARD,Charleton William TMaj kia 12-4-17 NumbF Staff198InfBde p61 CR France765

GORE,Annesley Charles Edward St.George Capt kia 26-6-15 IA 2/9 att1/9GurkhaRif p277 CR France631

GORE,Arthur Holmes Capt kia 12-8-15 8Hamps p229 MR4

GORE,Francis T2Lt dow 26-3-17 23Mddx p146 CR Belgium11

GORE,Gerard Ribton 2Lt dow 20-12-14 3 att2RWFus p97 CR France345,kia 1Bn

GORE,Leonard Joseph Capt kia 3-5-17 7 att12Mddx p235 MR20

GORE,Robert Clements.CB.CMG.BrigGen kia 14-4-18 A&SH Cmdg101InfBde p173 CR Belgium11,13-4-18

GORE,Sidney Kingston Lt kia 28-10-14 1RWKent p141 MR22

GORE,William Frederick.MM.T2Lt kia 27-9-18 2RIrReg att1RMunstF p89 CR France256

GORE-BROWN,Harold Thomas Thirlwall 2Lt dow 23-8-16 6 att7KRRC p150 CR France833

GORE-BROWNE,Eric Antony Rollo Maj drd 3-7-18 Dors att2/3KAR p124&268 MR46

GORE-JONES,Stanley Fox Lt kia 7-6-17 1Wilts CR Belgium43

GORE-LANGTON,Montague Vernon.MC.Capt kia 9-10-15 1IrGds p52 CR France423

GORELL,Henry Gorell.Lord.DSO.Maj dow 16-1-17 RFA 19Bty47Div p206 CR Belgium11

GORELL-BARNES,Charles Roper.DSO.MC.TCapt dow 21-4-18 GL att8RB p190 CR France52

GORFUNKLE,Isaac TLt kia 12-8-18 13 att1LancF p92 CR France193

GORING-Jones,Michael Derwas.CMG.DSO.TBrigGen ded 19-5-19 Staff 57InfBde p261 MR65

GORMAN,D.T.MC.LtACapt dow 22-6-19 2Hamps p120 MR70 &CR Europe179

GORMAN,Gerald Francis 2Lt kia 30-7-16 12RWar p64 MR21,14Bn

GORMLEY,Thomas 2Lt mbk 12-6-18 1 att7/8KOSB p156 MR20

GORNALL,George 2Lt kia 27-3-18 16RFC p16 MR20

GORNELL,Noel Christopher T2Lt kia 21-3-18 RE 157FC p45 CR France364,dow

GORRIE,Alexander Keith T2Lt kia 26-4-16 11HLI p163 CR Belgium137

GORRIE,John William 2Lt kia 19-7-16 7Worc p226 CR France832

GORRINGE,Arthur Arnold Capt ded 3-5-20 Ex RASC CR SAfrica63

GORRINGE,Edward Clifton.MC.TCapt kia 5-9-18 7RSuss p119 CR France511

GORRINGE,Noel Rupert Lt kia 10-4-18 4Nhampt attMGC p234&187 MR32

GORRINGE,Wilfred Stuart Capt dow 10-6-18 RE 82FC p210 CR France622

GORST,E.W.2Lt kia 25-10-14 1RFus p68 MR32

GORST,James 2Lt ded 29-5-17 42RFA p29 CR France113

GORT,Albert Henry 2Lt ded 6-11-18 RDC p253 CR Suff55

GORTON,Arthur Llewellyn Lt kia 20-10-18 IARO att1/10GurkhaRif p277 MR38,29-10-18

GORTON,George Herbert T2Lt kia 10-7-16 11 att9Yorks p90 MR21

GORTON,Lionel John 2Lt kia 16-4-18 1Lincs p254 MR30

GOSCHEN,Christopher Gerard TCapt kia 25-9-16 4GrenGds SR p50 CR France374

GOSCHEN,Hon George Joachim.MID 2Lt dow 19-1-16 1/5EKent p213 CR Iraq5

GOSDEN,Dudley Walter TLt kia 6-7-16 1Wilts p153 MR21,8-7-16

GOSLETT,John Southcote 2Lt ded 11-11-15 1/1NorfYeo p204 CR Egypt3,Lt

GOSLEY,George Andrew Hay 2Lt dow 16-10-16 1/9A&SH att1/14Lond p244 CR France145

GOSLING,Charles.CMG.ColTBrigGen kia 12-4-17 Staff &KRRC p1 CR France729

GOSLING,Douglas Edward Lt kia 20-5-15 RE p210 CR Belgium98

GOSLING,Frank T2Lt kia 26-4-18 5Y&L p158 CR Belgium102

GOSLING,Frederick Horace 2Lt kia 7-6-17 32RFus p68 CR Belgium111

GOSLING,Frederick William TCapt kia 20-7-16 23Manch p154 MR21

GOSLING,Gerald Noel.MC.Lt kia 7-7-19 1Glouc p106 MR70 &CR Europe179

GOSLING,Leonard Buchanan T2Lt ded 27-10-18 10TankCps p188 CR Dorset94

GOSLING,William Robert.MM.2Lt kia 21-3-18 2Wilts p153 MR27

GOSNELL,Harold Clifford 2Lt kia 1-7-16 1/2Lond p245 MR21

GOSNEY,Reginald Wilkie 2Lt kia 23-11-15 IARO att76Punjabis p277 MR38,22-11-15

GOSS,Edward Herbert Allan.MID TLt kia 1-7-16 7EKent p57 CR France397

GOSS,Edward Oliver 2Lt dow 14-10-18 4 att10RWSurr p212 CR Belgium112

GOSS,Hubert John.MC.2Lt kia 15-7-16 10Ches p96 MR21

GOSS,Raymond George Frederic 2Lt kia 13-8-15 1/5NStaffs p238 CR Belgium127,Frederick

GOSSAGE,Guy Winwood Maj ded 24-12-17 RFA p206 CR Shrop145

GOSSCHALK,Edward Meyer Lt kia 28-8-16 3 att6YLI p143 CR France402

GOSSE,Robert Buchanan Wilkes 2Lt dow 1-4-17 7Ches att1/6War p223 CR France511

GOSSE,William Hay.MC.TCaptAMaj kia 5-4-18 A79RFA p29 CR France41

GOSSELIN,Alwyn Bertram Robert Raphael.DSO.Capt kia 7-2-15 GrenGds p50 CR France720

GOSSET,Claude Butler Gosset Maj ded 16-2-16 Ches attRE 19SigCoy p96 CR France134

GOSSET,René Frankland ACapt kia 25-9-16 1EYorks p84 CR France1890

GOSSETT,William Beresford 2Lt kia 1-11-14 RFA p29 CR Belgium57

GOSSLING,Donald Foley 2Lt dow 10-6-17 2/9Manch p237 CR France80

GOSTLING,Thomas Harold 2Lt ded 2-8-19 Leic p263 CR War32

GOSWELL,Oliver Owen 2Lt kia 30-4-18 15Lond p249 MR34

GOTCH,Duncan Hepburn 2Lt kia 11-3-15 1Worc p108 MR22

GOTCH,Geoffrey William Lt ded 22-10-18 RGA &RAF p39

GOTCH,Roby Middleton Capt kia 1-7-16 7N&D p233 MR21,Myddleton

GOTELEE,Geoffrey Harris TLtACapt kia 18-9-18 7SWBord p100 MR37

GOTHE,Cecil Rudolph Lt ded 10-2-19 RGA p270

GOTT,Albert Ernest T2Lt kia 18-11-16 10RWar p64 MR21

GOUDIE,Alexander Currie T2Lt kia 20-9-17 9ScotRif p103 MR30

GOUDIE,Alexander Malcolm Lt dow 18-8-16 3Leinst att17MGC Inf p174&183 CR France329,2Bn

GOUDIE,Humphrey Blaikie T2Lt kia 17-8-16 7CamH p167 MR21

GOUGH,Bernard Bradley TLt kia 17-2-16 RAMC att8SStaffs p195 CR Belgium120

GOUGH,Bert Harold 2Lt kia 9-4-18 4RLancs p213 CR France1106

GOUGH,Cyril Lt ded PoW 8-9/9-11-18 4EYorks p219 CR Belgium353,11-10-18

GOUGH,Dermot Humphrey.MC.Lt ded 7-10-19 10Huss p261 CR Glouc40

GOUGH,Eric John Fletcher Capt kia 30-12-14 IrGds p52 CR France727

GOUGH,George Henry Waldron.MID Lt kia 15-12-17 1/7Ches p223 CR Palestine3

GOUGH,George William Blanthorne TLt kia 10-8-15 6Leinst p174 CR Gallipoli18

GOUGH,Harold Stuart TLt kia 17-6-16 11KRRC p150 CR Belgium4,16-6-16

GOUGH,Harry Stanley Lt ded 13-3-18 8Manch &RFC p237 CR Wilts115

GOUGH,Henry Percy Bright.MC&Bar.TMaj dow 22-4-18 17WelshR p126 CR France100,Harry

GOUGH,Horace Frederick.DSO.2Lt kia 21-9-17 NStaffs att8Bn p157 CR Belgium22

GOUGH,John Bloomfield.MID Lt kia 9-9-14 RHA p29 CR France1445,8-9-14

GOUGH,John Bolle Tyndale Maj kia 22-3-18 1Herts p252 CR France365

GOUGH,John Edmond.VC.ADC.KCB.CMG.BrigGen dow 21-2-15 Staff p1 CR France768,22-2-15

GOUGH,John Noel 2Lt kia 8-3-18 RFA attY29TMB p29 CR Belgium22

GOUGH,Leo Walter THon2Lt ded 23-4-18 GL IntelCps p190&257 CR France1571

GOUGH,Norman Lt kia 19-7-16 7Worc p225 CR France832

GOUGH,Owen Lt drd 30-12-15 IA 12Cav p277 MR41

GOUGH,Roland Ivor.DSO.TCapt dow 14-10-16 15RWar p64 CR France145

GOUGH,Rupert.MC.2Lt dow 28-10-17 RH&FA 71Bty p29 CR Belgium16

GOULD,Arthur Edmund T2Lt kia 13-5-16 13Ches p96 CR France68,14-5-16

GOULD,Cecil Arbuthnot Capt kia 26-3-17 5Ess p232 MR34

GOULD,Chalkley Vivian TLtAMaj kia 9-6-17 115/25RFA p29 CR Belgium102

GOULD,Clifford.MC.Lt kia 24-8-18 14RFA p29 CR France1014

GOULD,Eric Melville 2Lt kia 1-7-16 3 att2Dev p76 MR21

GOULD,Ernest William 2Lt kia 10-4-18 4SLancs att1/5SomLI p230 CR Palestine9

GOULD,Francis Hunt Capt kld 6-6-15 1Mddx p146 CR France922

GOULD,Francis William 2Lt kia 9-10-17 7Worc p226 MR30

GOULD,Frank Allan Capt ded 17-4-19 Res p270 CR Surrey160

GOULD,Frederick James 2Lt ded 12-12-18 RGA 143HB p39 CR Greece2

GOULD,Gerald Oscar Alan 2Lt dow 25-6-16 13KRRC p150 CR France120,George

GOULD,Henry Charles Hamerton 2Lt dow 15-4-17 32RFA p29 CR France95,27RFA

GOULD,James Robertson Sabiston.MID T2Lt dow 15-4-18 268MGC p183 CR France64

GOULD,Jay.CBE.LtCol ded 1-6-19 ADMS IMS p277 CR Asia60,2-6-19

GOULD,Joseph William T2Lt kia 13-10-18 1Y&L p158 CR France316

GOULD,Patrick Wallace T2Lt kia 24-8-16 9KRRC p150 MR21

GOULD,Ralph Bohn 2Lt dow 20-12-16 4SWBord p100 CR Iraq5

GOULD,Roy Ernest 2Lt kia 27-3-17 7Ess p232 MR34

GOULD,Walter Harvey Russell Lt kia 26-9-17 GL &70RFC p8 MR20

GOULD,William Justin TLt kia 23-8-15 5Nhampt p137 CR Belgium137

GOULDBY,James Henry 2Lt kia 25-8-16 5 att7Lincs p220 MR21

GOULDEN,E.C.Capt drd 28-3-15 NigR MR40

GOULDEN,Frederick Charles Capt drd 28-3-15 NigForces CR Eire58

GOULDEN,William Charles T2Lt kia 12-2-18 Mddx att2Bn p146 CR Belgium125,Wilfred

GOULDING,Frederick Ernest T2Lt ded 5-8-18 9RIrRif p169 CR France100

GOULDING,George Percival Kimber 2LtTLt dow 31-7-17 7ELancs p110 CR Belgium152

GOULDING,Reginald T2Lt kia 27-9-17 YLI att2Bn p143 CR Belgium24

GOULDSBURY,Henry Cullen TCapt ded 27-8-16 9RBerks EAUL att1KAR p139 CR EAfrica19,2Bn

GOUNDRY,John Firth 2Lt kia 16-8-17 9 att1/19Lond p248 MR29

GOURD,Percy TCapt kia 18-4-16 3SLancs p125 MR38

GOURLAY,Alexander Smith Forrest 2Lt kia 24-3-18 3 att2ScotRif p103 MR27

GOURLAY,George T2Lt kia 14-11-17 73MGC Inf p183 CR France528

GOURLAY,John Norman 2Lt kia 1-7-16 3SfthH p164 CR France605,2Bn

GOURLAY,William Norris TCapt dow 6-6-17 5CamH p167 CR France64

GOVAN,Douglas Moncrieff.MID Maj kia 28-6-15 IA 1/5GurkhaRif p277 MR4

GOVER,William Arthur Capt kia 3-3-15 IA 7Rajputs p277

GOW,James Lightfoot T2Lt kia 1-7-16 9 att1KOSB p101 CR France220

GOW,John Halley T2Lt kia 15-7-16 1Mddx p146 MR21

GOWAN,Arthur Blackmore Lt kia 14-7-16 RE 1/3DurhamFC p210 MR21,Blackwood

GOWAN,J.C.Capt 16-8-15 1/4Ess CR Gallipoli4

GOWANS,Alexander Douglas Stuart 2Lt dow 27-4-17 6BlkW p231 CR France95,Lt

GOWANS,William Maj dow 2-5-15 2YLI p143 CR France200

GOWANS,William Ireland T2Lt kia 13-10-17 25NumbF p61 MR30

GOWAR,Lancelot John T2Lt kld 1-5-17 GL &RFC p8 CR Mddx53

GOWER,Francis John Harman 2Lt kia 23-11-17 E'TankCps p188 MR17

GOWER,John Richard.MBE.MIDx2 Capt&QM 24-4-20 23WelchR att7SWBord CR Wales76

GOWING,William Lee 2Lt dow 12-12-17 1/4Norf p216 CR Palestine9

GOWSELL,Leonard Lt dow 20-4-18 GL &4RAF CR France134

GOZNEY,Charles Marsh.MC.Capt 15-8-20 RAMC MR38

GRACE,Alfred Alexander Gordon T2Lt kld 26-6-17 GL &22ResRFC p8 CR Egypt1

GRACE,Frank LtACapt dow 5-11-17 RFA 19Bty p29 MR38

GRACE,Handley Carleton TCapt dow PoW 2-9-17 6Nhampt A'Coy p137 CR Belgium393

GRACE,Joseph 2Lt kia 19-8-17 15Ches p96 CR France363

GRACE,Mervyn Bruce Lt kia 8-5-17 6NStaffs p238 CR France1495

GRACEY,Horace Charles Capt kia 18-10-16 1RB p178 CR France1891

GRACIE,Hugh Colin Stuart T2Lt dow 26-11-17 18WelshR p126 CR France398

GRACIE,John James.MC.Lt kia 17-9-18 1 att7/8KOSB p101 MR19

GRACIE,William James T2Lt kia 26-4-17 9NStaffs p157 CR France924

GRADON,F.M.Capt ded 18-9-20 RE IWT HQ Staff CR Iraq6

GRADWELL,Charles Edward Lt 21-3-18 RB att59MGC p178&183 MR27

GRADWELL,George Francis 2Lt kia 28-2-17 1RDubF p176 MR21

GRADY,Walter Henry 2Lt kld 22-4-15 RFus att3Bn p68 MR29,25-4-15 6Bn

GRAEME,Laurence Oliphant.CMG.MIDx3 TLtCol kia 10-3-16 1CamH p167 CR France178,GRÆME Lawrence

GRAFTON,William Salter T2Lt kia 15-8-18 9YLI p143 CR France233

GRAFTON-GRATTON,Thomas Walter 2Lt ded 24-2-19 RGA p254 CR Surrey148,24-1-19

GRAFTON-WIGNALL,John Dighton Capt kia 26-1-17 IA 82Punjabis p277 MR38

GRAHAM,Alan Moir Capt kia 20-12-14 IA 2/5GurkhaRif att2/2 p277 MR38

GRAHAM,Alec George Malcolm Capt kia 22-12-14 6Worc attNLancs p108 MR22

GRAHAM,Alexander.MID Capt dow 19-10-15 RAMC att1/7Ess p253 MR4

GRAHAM,Alexander Cecil Capt kia 10-9-16 1GrenGds SR p50 CR France394,12-9-16

GRAHAM,Andrew TLt kia 30-12-17 9BlkW att44TMB p128 CR France1182

GRAHAM,Andrew James Lt kia 26-9-17 6ScotRif p224 CR Belgium45

GRAHAM,Archibald Foster.MID 2Lt kia 11-11-15 RGA 6SB p39 CR Belgium84,Forster

GRAHAM,Archibald Stuart Bullock Lt kia 31-10-14 2GordH p166 MR29

GRAHAM,Arthur Thomas T2Lt kia 27-3-18 42MGC p183 MR20

GRAHAM,Austin Graham MajTLtCol dow 11-4-18 14 att5Yorks p220 CR France1094,5 att4Bn

GRAHAM,Bertram Robert LtCol kia 11-3-16 3KAR CpsofGuides p277&268 CR EAfrica56

GRAHAM,Cecil Erskine Capt kia 1-7-17 2BordR att1/5NStaffs p117 MR29

GRAHAM,Cecil Hollingsworth 2Lt kia 19-9-16 3RDubF attTMB p176 CR Belgium4,20-9-16

GRAHAM,Cedric Kenny Onslow T2Lt kia 16-9-16 15DLI p160 MR21

GRAHAM,Charles Hamilton Malise Lt kia 12-4-17 1RLancs p59 CR France604,17-4-17

GRAHAM,Cyril TLt kia 27-5-15 5BordR p228 MR29 CR Belgium45

GRAHAM,Donald Hatt Noble TCapt kia 27-9-15 9BlkW A'Coy p128 CR France219,25-9-15

GRAHAM,Duncan.DCM.2Lt kia 30-9-18 7A&SH p243 CR France236

GRAHAM,Duncan Charles Capt kia 28-4-17 7Norf p73 MR20

GRAHAM,Edwin Michael T2Lt kia 4-10-17 1DCLI p114 MR30

GRAHAM,Eric Clive 2Lt kia 9-1-17 3 att1Manch p154 CR Iraq5

GRAHAM,Eric Montrose Lt dow 2-4-15 SWBord p100 CR Lond8

GRAHAM,Ernest William 2Lt kia 18-10-16 12BordR att1ELancs p117 MR21

GRAHAM,Fenton Weiss Lt kia 4-10-15 4DLI att1YLI p160 CR France924,14-10-15

GRAHAM,Francis.DSO.MC.CaptAMaj kia 28-3-18 71RFA p29 CR France1182

GRAHAM,Francis Noel TCapt dow 16-11-16 11RWar p64 CR France62

GRAHAM,George Humphrey Irving Maj kia 7-2-16 IA 44Merwaralnf MR38 p277

GRAHAM,George Lionel Capt ded PoW 11-4-18 7RWar D'Coy p214 CR France1061

GRAHAM,George Lyons T2Lt kia 17-8-17 6RDubF p176 MR30

GRAHAM,George Stanley TLt ded 19-6-16 RAMC p195 CR Iraq5

GRAHAM,George William T2Lt kia 20-9-17 Mddx att5LancF p146 MR30

GRAHAM,Hamilton Carruthers 2Lt kia 26-8-18 8Lond p247 CR France626

GRAHAM,Harry Capt&QM ded 10-1-16 HLI p265 CR Lond35

GRAHAM,Henry 2Lt kia 28-6-17 IA 74Punjabis att67 p277 MR38

GRAHAM,Henry Balfour 2Lt kia 9-5-17 3 att10BlkW p128 MR37

GRAHAM,Hugh Christison 2LtTLt kia 9-6-17 9RScotF att33MGC p183&94 CR Belgium60,8-6-17

GRAHAM,Hugh Colborne T2Lt kia 1-10-17 1/2 att9Yorks p90 MR30

GRAHAM,James Lawson TLt dow 30-9-18 9RInniskF p105 MR30

GRAHAM,John Capt kia 16-6-15 10Lpool p216 MR29

GRAHAM,John 2Lt kia 16-9-16 10DLI p160 MR21

GRAHAM,John Arthur.MC.MID TMaj kia 20-3-16 7Lincs p75 CR France922

GRAHAM,John Frederick TMaj kia 1-7-16 A150RFA p29 CR France630

GRAHAM,John Hamilton Thom TLt kia 6-7-16 6KOSB p101 MR21,4-7-16

GRAHAM,John Robertson.MC.2Lt dow 22-9-16 C96RH&FA p29 CR France145,Roberson

GRAHAM,John Stanley 2Lt kia 30-8-18 4WelshR p230 CR France217

GRAHAM,John Wilfrid Lt kia 21-12-14 1CamH att3HLI p167 MR22,22-12-14 HLI attCamH

GRAHAM,Kenneth Stuart 2Lt kia 24-3-18 9SfthH p164 CR France785

GRAHAM,Lachlan Seymour 2Lt dow 29-8-17 7HLI p240 CR Belgium11,Lt 12Bn

GRAHAM,Lionel Lovell Capt kia 26-9-17 1Camb p244 MR30

GRAHAM,Malcolm G.MC.2LtACapt kia 26-10-17 2GordH p166 MR30

GRAHAM,Malcolm Hewley Lt kia 15-6-15 3 att2Yorks p90 MR22

GRAHAM,Marmaduke Whitaker Capt kia 24-7-15 2RWKent p141 CR Iraq6

GRAHAM,Percy Gordon TCapt kia 1-7-16 16NumbF p61 MR21

GRAHAM,Peter Capt kia 30-8-18 GL CamH att1KAR p167,202&266 CR EAfrica90

GRAHAM,P.N.Capt 28-11-20 NumbF CR Berks1

GRAHAM,Richard 2Lt kia 10-1-15 2ScotRif p103 CR France567

GRAHAM,Robert Lynedoch.MID Lt kia 16-9-17 GL &19RFC p8 CR Belgium125

GRAHAM,Robert Main T2Lt kia 4-10-16 10WRid p115 MR21

GRAHAM,Ronald McLeod 2Lt kia 12-3-15 Ess attRScotF p131 MR22

GRAHAM,Thomas Eric.MC.2Lt kia 24-3-18 2ScotRif p103 CR France1890

GRAHAM,Thomas Harold T2Lt dow 25-10-16 17RB p178 CR France105,2Bn

GRAHAM,Thomas Leslie.MC.Lt ded 23-5-19 3SfthH p265 CR Kent268

GRAHAM,Walter Ap.S.J. Maj ded 23-2-18 RAMC p267

GRAHAM,W.L.C.Capt 14-7-15 IARO CR Scot208

GRAHAM,William Capt kia 3-5-17 6DLI p239 MR20

GRAHAM,William LtCol ded 5-11-17 RAMC p267 CR Ireland57

GRAHAM,William George.MID Capt kia 24-6-15 5NumbF p213 CR Belgium43

GRAHAM,William James T2Lt kia 31-7-17 18Lpool p72 MR29

GRAHAM,William John T2Lt kia 22-11-17 18RIrRif p169 MR17

GRAHAM,William Rennie TLt kia 1-10-18 9RIrF p171 CR Belgium157

GRAHAM-CLARKE,John Altham Stobart 2Lt kia 1-7-16 9KOSB att6BordR p101 CR France339

GRAHAM-KING,Reginald 2Lt kia 23-3-18 4 att6Dors p229 CR France385,25-3-18

GRAHAM-MENZIES,Alastair Lt 1-1-15 1ScotGds MR22

GRAHAM-MONTGOMERY,Graham John Early Capt kia 24-4-17 12Hamps p120 MR37

GRAHAM-ROE,Archibald Chaceley T2Lt kia 29-4-17 KRRC att1Bn p150 MR20,28-4-17

GRAIL,Clifford George TCapt dow 23-7-15 7NStaffs p157 MR4

GRAINGER,James Francis Stuart TCapt dow 12-8-15 11BlkW att1KOSB p128 CR Gallipoli6

GRAINGER,John Henry 2Lt kia 15-9-16 4EYorks p219 CR France239

GRAINGER,John Scott 2Lt kia 1-7-16 1/2Lond p245 MR21

GRAMSHAW,Hugh 2Lt ded 28-2-16 3SStaffs p122 CR Numb49,Lt

GRAMSHAW,Robert Wilfred Raleigh 2Lt dow 27-1-15 3 att2RSuss p119 CR France80

GRAND,Hugh Stevenson.MID T2Lt kia 28-4-17 11Suff p78 CR France604

GRANDAGE,William Briggs LtCol dow 14-5-17 235RFA p206 CR Belgium11

GRANDIN,Richard John 2Lt kia 18-5-17 RASC &60RFC p8&193 MR20

GRANET,Edward John.CB.TBrigGen ded 22-10-18 RA p29 CR Europe51

GRANGE,James Burness T2Lt kia 20-4-18 21WYorks X'Coy p81 CR France250

GRANGER,Ernest Every Wyatt.MID TCapt kia 16-8-17 att9LancF p92 MR30

GRANGER,Frank T2Lt dow 15-12-16 20Manch p154 CR France74,14Bn

GRANGER,Frederick Collins.MC.MID T2Lt dow 30-3-17 1Glouc p106 CR France145

GRANGER,Harold Mossman 2Lt 29-5-15 1/7Manch CR Gallipoli2

GRANGER,William Thomas Lt dow 21-9-17 4Wilts p236 CR Belgium154

GRANSDEN,Victor Eric T2Lt kia 26-4-18 10RIrRif p169 CR Belgium64

GRANSMORE,Rodney Capt kia 28-9-15 Mddx p147 MR19

GRANT,Alan.MID 2Lt dow 3-9-18 1RScotF p94 CR France103,Allen

GRANT,Alan Francis Montague T2Lt dow 18-6-16 9RWSurr p56 CR France285

GRANT,Albyn Evan Powell 2Lt kia 14-8-15 7RWFus p223 MR4

GRANT,Alexander Capt kia 13-11-16 6GordH p242 CR France131

GRANT,Alexander 2Lt dow 24-4-17 7HLI p240 CR Palestine2

GRANT,Alexander 2Lt kia 27-9-18 1GrenGds p50 CR France1497

GRANT,Alexander George William LtCol kia 25-9-15 8Dev attWAfrR p76&200 MR19

GRANT,Arch TLtACapt kia 30-11-17 1Ess p131 MR17

GRANT,Charles Bruce 2Lt dow 8-12-17 9HLI p240 CR France64,Lt

GRANT,Charles William TLtACapt dow 12-10-17 11RScots p54 CR Belgium20

GRANT,Clifton Brown.MID TCapt kia 27-7-16 99MGC Inf p183 CR France1890

GRANT,D.2Lt kia 28-4-15 7CamH p168 MR29

GRANT,Daniel Menzies T2Lt dow 4-8-18 1/5A&SH p173 CR France1225

GRANT,Donald 2Lt kia 20-11-17 6SfthH p241 CR France1498

GRANT,Douglas Lt kia 30-11-17 1KOSB p101 MR17

GRANT,Edmund Henry T2Lt dow 2-8-16 16KRRC p150 CR France145

GRANT,Edward Macpherson Capt kia 14/15-4-16 HLI p163 MR38

GRANT,Ferris Nelson Capt kia 9-5-15 5RSuss p228 MR22

GRANT,George Campbell TLt dow 14-10-15 RE 96FC p45 CR France345

GRANT,George Leonard TCapt kia 11-10-15 RAMC attLondonScottish p195 CR France222

GRANT,Harold Allan 2Lt ded 27-9-18 4SStaffs att7NStaffs p122 CR Asia82

GRANT,Harold Duncan 2Lt ded 27-3-19 1Dev p76 CR France34

GRANT,Harold Edward T2Lt kia 3-9-16 17 at16RB p178 MR21

GRANT,Henry Norman 2Lt kia 1-7-16 1LancF A'Coy p92 CR France1492

GRANT,Hubert Anthony Capt kia 24-11-14 2Leic p87 CR France727

GRANT,Humphrey de Butts Capt kia 3-10-15 A63RFA p29 CR France219

GRANT,Ian Alan William Lt kia 24-4-17 70RFA p29 CR France1188

GRANT,Ivan Thorold T2Lt kia 9-10-16 10RWKent p141 CR France432

GRANT,James.MC.T2Lt kia 23-10-18 16N&D att8RBerks p134 CR France716

GRANT,James Gibson 2Lt ded 19-2-19 10Lpool p270 CR Lancs14

GRANT,John T2Lt kia 1-7-16 15RScots p54 MR21

GRANT,John 2Lt ded 24-11-18 5DLI attMGC p187&239 CR Greece2

GRANT,John Anderton 2Lt kia 14-5-18 3 att8RSuss p119 CR France196

GRANT,John Cardross.MC.TCapt kia 27-1-16 10ScotRif p103 CR France178

GRANT,John Mann.DCM.T2Lt kia 9-4-17 11RScots p54 CR France645

GRANT,John Russell 2Lt kia 8-5-18 6ScotRif p224 CR Belgium111

GRANT,John Spence.MC.2Lt kia 9-4-17 6GordH p242 CR France728,Capt Rev

GRANT,Joseph Brabazon Theobald Capt kia 16-8-15 6RMunstF p175 MR4

GRANT,Kenneth Henry T2Lt kia 26-8-16 10 att8SfthH p164 CR France453

GRANT,Nigel Alexander James 2Lt dow 24-4-17 1/4GordH p242 CR France40

GRANT,Noël 2Lt kia 25-5-17 B156RFA p29 CR France311

GRANT,Percy Kenmure.MID TLt ded 6-11-18 RASC attGHQ p193 CR France1027

GRANT,Percy Victor 2Lt kia 3-4-18 10Glouc att9RB p106 MR27

GRANT,Philip Thomas Wilson T2Lt kia 15-10-15 8 att5Wilts p153 CR Gallipoli5

GRANT,Reginald Walter Capt ded 26-11-18 8RWKent p265 CR Mddx39

GRANT,Richard Craven Capt kia 2-9-18 3ScotRif &209RAF p264 MR20

GRANT,Robert T2Lt kia 13-6-17 GL &29RFC p8 CR Belgium375

GRANT,Robert William Gordon Capt kia 24-5-17 7Manch p237 CR France905

GRANT,Ronald Cameron TLt ded 16-10-16 RE p45 CR France62

GRANT,Sidney Robert T2Lt kia 18-4-18 1MGC Inf p183 CR France765,Sydney

GRANT,Stanley Chadwick T2Lt kia 3-9-16 2RIrReg p89 MR21

GRANT,Stanley Kenneth TLt kia 26-3-18 9ESurr p112 MR27

GRANT,Stuart.MC.LtACapt kia 3-12-17 2/5RWar p214 MR17

GRANT,Theodore.MC&Bar.Capt kia 28-5-18 3Worc attSAfrDefForce p108 MR18

GRANT,Thomas Francis.MC&Bar.Lt kia 11-4-18 1/5SfthH p241 CR France201,10-4-18

GRANT,William Gordon 2Lt 17-4-17 1/7HLI p240 CR Palestine8

GRANT,William Hugh 2Lt kia 29-9-15 7SfthH p164 MR19,30-9-15

GRANT,William St.Clair.MC.TCapt&Adjt kia 26-9-18 5CamH p168 CR Belgium36

GRANT-DUFF,Adrian.CB.LtCol kia 21-9-14 BlkW p128 CR France1341,14-9-14

GRANT-PETERKIN,Cosmo Gordon Capt dow 12-9-17 ScotHorse att1/5GordH p205 CR Belgium16

GRANT-SUTTIE,Archibald Ronald Lt dow 23-7-17 L15RHA p29 CR Belgium16

GRANTHAM,Charles Alpe Lt kia 3-3-15 IA 33Cav p277 CR Iraq6

GRANTHAM,Edward Rodney Hasluck 2Lt dow 31-3-17 1NumbF p61 CR France1182

GRANTHAM,Edward Mason Capt kia 27-2-15 3Lincs p75 CR Belgium166,1Bn

GRANTHAM,Ernest Joel LtACapt ded 6-12-18 RAOC attRGA p198 CR France65

GRANTHAM,Ernest Russell T2Lt kia 27-11-17 9ESurr p112 CR France1461

GRANTHAM,Frederick William Capt kia 9-5-15 2RMunstF p175 MR22

GRANTHAM,Hugo Frederick 2Lt kia 28-6-15 3Ess p131 CR Gallipoli6

GRANTHAM,Percy William 2Lt kia 26-9-17 5Lincs p220 CR Belgium123,W.P.Lt

GRANTHAM,Richard Aubrey Fuge T2Lt kia 4-3-17 2Lincs p75 CR France439

GRANTHAM,William Capt dow 30-11-18 PoW 4WRid p227 CR Germany3

GRANVILLE,Basil Rayond 2LtACapt kia 23-4-17 7RFus p68 MR20

GRANVILLE,Clifford Paul McGarry Capt kia 5-5-18 1Mddx att3/1KAR p147&268 MR52

GRAPES,John Wellington 2Lt dedacc 24-7-17 8AustInf CR France251

GRASETT,Elliot Blair Lt kia 25-9-15 IA 28Punjabis att33 p277 MR28

GRASSICK,Peter TLt kia 25-10-18 A&SH p173 CR France1258

GRASSICK,William Henderson 2Lt ded 9-2-19 A86RFA p29 CR France34

GRASSIE,John Ainslie Aymer 2Lt kia 21-3-18 5BlkW p231 MR27

GRATTAN,John LtCol dow 26-4-17 IA 55Rif att53Sikhs p277 CR Iraq8

GRATTAN-BELLEW,William Arthur.MC.2LtTMaj dow 24-3-17 ConnRgrs &29RFC p8&172,GRATTON CR France46

GRATTON,Albert.MM.2Lt kia 20-11-17 RGA 211SB p39 CR Belgium84

GRATTON,George Harry T2Lt kld 4-3-18 RFC p16 CR Mon67

GRATTON,Reginald Ernest 2Lt kia 31-7-17 5LancF p221 MR29

GRATWICK,Harold Duncan Lt ded 18-2-19 4Dev p270

GRATWICK,Philip Charles Lt 30-3-18 9ACycCps p243 MR27

GRAVES,Adrian Hubert.MC&Bar.TLtACapt kia 22-3-18 40MGC p183 MR20

GRAVES,Algernon Frederick Charles TCapt dow 26-8-17 PoW 7RInniskF p105 CR Belgium140

GRAVES,Evelyn Paget CaptTmaj kia 6-3-17 RFA Cmdg60RFC p8&29 CR France46

GRAVES,Francis George 2Lt kia 20-9-17 4 att16N&D p134 MR30

GRAVES,George Henry T2Lt ded 22-2-19 5 att7RFus p263 CR Kent7,Lt

GRAVES,Harry Steele Lt dow 24-11-17 1/6BlkW p231 CR France145

GRAVES,Horace Jocelyn.MC.TLt dow 14-10-18 13Yorks att8WYorks p90 CR France146

GRAVES,James Singleton Lt kia 15-6-18 6 att2Worc p254 MR32,6 att4Bn

GRAVES,John TCapt dow 16-4-17 MGC IA 36JacobsHorse p183&277 CR France512

GRAVES,Lionel Percival 2Lt ded 24-12-18 9KOSB p264 CR Wales536,Lt 21-12-18

GRAVES,Robert James TLt ded 28-1-17 2RIrReg HS 2GarrBn p89 CR Ireland14 &CR Eire77

GRAVES,Thomas Molyneaux Lt dow 22-4-16 IA 76Punjabis att56Rif p277 MR38

GRAVES,Walter Francis Lt kia 9-11-14 3 att1Beds p86 MR29 &CR Belgium167

GRAVES-KNYFTON,Reginald Barrett Maj ded 29-10-18 4SomLI p218 MR66,Benett

GRAVES-SAWLE,Richard Charles Lt kia 2-11-14 2CldGds p51 MR29

GRAY,Alexander Allen.MC.T2Lt kld 3-2-17 GL &RFC p8&190 CR Mddx66

GRAY,Alexander Jackson Maj kia 7-11-17 10RScots att2/19Lond p212 CR Palestine1

GRAY,Alexander Tudhope 2Lt kia 21-4-17 6 att10ScotRif p224 MR20

GRAY,Andrew 2Lt kia 9-5-15 1BlkW p128 MR22

GRAY,Anthony Frederick Lt kia 26-8-18 1/1Camb p244 CR France196

GRAY,Arthur Frederick 2Lt drd 10-10-18 SuffYeo p205 MR40

GRAY,Arthur John Capt kia 31-7-17 1/1Camb p244 CR Belgium94

GRAY,Cecil Edward Patrick 2Lt dow 11-10-17 RFA attL'RHA p29 CR Belgium106,10-10-17

GRAY,Charles Dixon Lt kia 9-9-18 1ELancs p110 CR France1887

GRAY,Charles Rutherford T2Lt dow 23-11-17 11A&SH p173 CR France545

GRAY,Charles Shortland Capt kia 13-10-15 4Lincs p217 MR19

GRAY,Charles William T2Lt dow 4-12-17 23Manch p154 CR Belgium63

GRAY,Cyril Seaton 2Lt dow 21-4-17 1Ches p96 CR France40,2Wilts

GRAY,Cyrus Keswick 2Lt kia 14-4-17 18Lond p250 MR20

GRAY,David 2LtACapt kia 6-6-17 RGA 234SB p39 CR Belgium4

GRAY,David Gordon 2Lt kia 31-7-17 4RWKent p234 CR Belgium88

GRAY,David William T2Lt kia 18-7-16 5CamH p168 MR21

GRAY,Douglas Huon Lt kia 3-7-16 GL &RFC p3&190 MR20

GRAY,Douglas William 2Lt kia 18-11-16 111MGC Inf p183 MR21

GRAY,E.B.Lt 20-12-17 RGA CR Lond28

GRAY,Edis John William 2Lt kia 27-9-15 14DLI p254 MR19

GRAY,Edmund Trevennin T2Lt kia 22-10-15 15DLI p160 CR Belgium70

GRAY,Edward Cecil TCapt dow 2-5-17 11Manch p154 CR France512

GRAY,Edward Jasper 2Lt kia 31-3-18 6RB p178 CR France544

GRAY,Edward Leadbetter T2Lt kldacc 22-3-18 13RFC p16 CR Scot569

GRAY,Francis Henry Tower TLt drd 21-7-18 GL RASC attWAFF p190&201 CR Devon96

GRAY,Frederick Hodskinson 2Lt kia 1-4-17 HAC Inf p206 CR France568

GRAY,Frederick William.MC.2Lt kia 21-8-15 DorsYeo p203 CR Gallipoli5

GRAY,Geoffrey Thomas 2Lt kia 24-3-17 RE att8RFC p8&45 CR France120

GRAY,George 2Lt kld 28-4-16 4RDubF p176 CR Ireland14,kia

GRAY,George T2Lt ded 8-2-19 LabCps p189 CR France65,Lt

GRAY,George Donald TLt ded 5-5-17 2/4Y&L p158 CR France518

GRAY,George Ernest Marshall T2Lt kia 14-7-16 14NumbF p61 MR21

GRAY,George Godfrey T2Lt dow 10-4-17 5 O&BLI p130 CR France120

GRAY,George Robert TLt dow PoW 31-10-17 GL &84RFC p8 CR France1029

GRAY,Gerald Montague 2Lt kia 7-10-16 3 att6RWKent p141 MR21

GRAY,Harry Albert.MC.TLt dow 15-7-18 1RWKent p141 CR France31

GRAY,Hubert James Stirling Capt kia 27-3-17 4RSuss p228 MR34

GRAY,Hubert McKenzie ACapt kia 10-8-17 11RFus p68 MR29

GRAY,James Maj kia 28-6-15 1/4RScots p211 CR Gallipoli6

GRAY,James Blackhall 2Lt kia 27-10-18 4GordH p242 CR Italy9

GRAY,James Cook.MC.ACapt kia 22-12-17 11BordR p117 CR Belgium9

GRAY,James Roy ACapt ded 18-2-19 10TankCps p266 CR Surrey1

GRAY,John Capt kia 12-4-16 IA 36Sikhs p277 MR38

GRAY,John T2Lt kia 24-3-18 8TankCps p188 CR France307

GRAY,John Lt kia 21-9-18 5 att2A&SH p243 CR France666

GRAY,John 2Lt ded 26-11-18 18WYorks p81 CR Numb3,3Bn

GRAY,John Arthur.DCM.2Lt kia 4-3-17 2RBerks p139 CR France216

GRAY,John Hunter Wood TCapt&QM ded 17-11-18 17RFus p68 CR France289

GRAY,John James Enslie 2Lt kld 18-3-17 1DCLI p114 CR Hamps234,17-3-17

GRAY,John Parnwell 2Lt ded 13-9-18 D47RFA 14DAC p29 CR Lincs100,Lt

GRAY,John Purves T2Lt dow 1-10-18 12 att1RInniskF p105 CR France262

GRAY,Julian Frederick.MC.Capt dow 10-7-17 RE att1S&M p45 CR Palestine9,10-7-18

GRAY,Leonard Capt ded 31-7-17 1/5Ess p232 CR Egypt1

GRAY,Leslie Austin T2Lt kia 12-10-16 13 att4Worc p108 CR France390

GRAY,M.2Lt 16-8-16 3DubF att10RIrRif CR Belgium48

GRAY,Magnus Nigel.MID Lt dow 21-6-15 3 att1ScotRif p103 CR France83

GRAY,M.Nurse 23-1-16 ScotWomensHosp CR France1866

GRAY,Martin Kenion T2Lt kia 28-8-16 6YLI p143 CR France402

GRAY,Maurice LtACapt kia 8-8-18 7MGC Cav att2DragGds p21&183 CR France652

GRAY,Meredith 2Lt kia 16-8-16 3RDubF att10RIrRif p176

GRAY,Norman McNeil Maj dow 9-2-16 45/42RFA p29 CR Lond8,Macneill

GRAY,Patrick Walworth 2Lt dow 9-5-17 153RFA p29 CR France113

GRAY,Peter 2Lt kia 18-6-18 10Lpool p216 CR France266

GRAY,R.M.McC.MC.Lt 30-9-18 46CanadaInf CR France113

GRAY,Roderick Hubert.MC.2Lt dow 2-12-17 I'7RFA p29 CR France518

GRAY,Thomas Robert 2Lt dow 24-11-17 4Yorks att7YLI p220 MR17

GRAY,Victor Samuel Lt kia 8-8-18 4Suff &48RAF p270 MR20

GRAY,Vivian 2Lt kia 18-8-16 3 att9Lpool p72 MR21

GRAY,William Harrington TCapt ded 23-11-19 RAMC p267

GRAY,William Leslie 2Lt dow 28-9-18 4Suff p217 CR France512

GRAY-BUCHANAN,Walter Bruce Capt&Adjt kia 10-3-15 2ScotRif p103 CR France260

GRAY-CHEAPE,Hugh Annesley.DSO&Bar.LtCol drd 27-5-18 WorcYeo p206 MR41

GRAYFOOT,Blenman Buhot.CB.ded 30-9-16 IA IMS p277 CR Egypt1

GRAYSON,Ambrose Dixon Holdrege Capt kia 13-10-14 1RFA p29 MR22

GRAYSON,George 2Lt dow 24-12-18 155RFA p29 CR Durham102

GRAYSON,John Henry TLt kia 20-11-17 6RIrReg p89 CR France689

GRAZEBROOK,Charles Alvery Capt kia 10-3-15 6 att1KRRC p150 MR22,Alverey

GREANY,John Wingate.DSO.Capt&Adjt kia 9-4-16 5Wilts p153 MR38 mbk

GREATHEAD,Alan TCapt dow 20-11-17 9RFus p68 MR17

GREATHEAD,John Harding T2Lt kld 11-1-18 GL &RFC p16 CR Herts87

GREATHEAD,John Rivers T2Lt kia 23-10-16 2RB p178 CR France307

GREATHED,Robert Napier LtCol 26-3-20 RFA CR Devon207

GREATOREX,Janet Mary Sister ded 2-4-16 TFNS CR War151

GREATOREX,Thomas Anthony Capt 17-1-19 4EKent CR Devon230

GREATWOOD,F.S.2Lt ded 12-4-18 1/2RSuss &RAF p119 CR Kent7,drd

GREATWOOD,Harold 2Lt dow 20-10-17 36RFA p29 CR Belgium63

GREATWOOD,Walter Capt kia 8-3-16 IA 123Rif att1/1GurkhaRif p277 CR Iraq5

GREAVES,Eric.MC.TLt dow 21-11-18 7RDubF p176 CR France146

GREAVES,Frederic T2Lt kia 1-6-18 7RLancs att1/4LNLancs p59 CR France106

GREAVES,George Harold T2Lt kia 5-3-17 2WYorks p81 CR France439

GREAVES,John 2Lt dow 31-3-18 2/7RWar p214 CR France185

GREAVES,Reginald Lt ded 22-2-19 RGA 12SB p39 CR France1029

GREAVES,Thomas Capt dow 1-7-18 1/6N&D p233 CR France10

GREAVES,Victor T2Lt dow 28-11-17 WRid att2/5Bn p115 CR France398

GREEN,Alan Edward 2Lt kia 2-10-15 5SStaffs p229 MR19,13-10-15

GREEN,Alan Herbert T2Lt dow 26-2-18 RE &32RFC p45&16,25-2-18 CR Italy7

GREEN,Alfred TLt kia 19-9-17 5RFus att2/2KAR p202 CR EAfrica8 &CR Tanzania1,1/4Bn

GREEN,Allan T2Lt kia 19-8-17 21WYorks p81 CR France97,Lt

GREEN,Arthur Lt kia 26-3-18 9Manch p237 MR27

GREEN,Arthur Lt ded 3-12-19 SL RE &rIWT p268 CR Iraq6

GREEN,Arthur Dowson.DSO.Maj kia 28-9-14 Worc 17 InfBde p108 CR France1112

GREEN,Arthur Fairbrother 2Lt kia 21-3-18 2/6NStaffs p238 MR20

GREEN,Arthur Knowles 2Lt kia 30-9-17 148RFA p29 CR Belgium17,Knolles

GREEN,Arthur Percival TLt kia 6-7-16 7Norf D'Coy p73 CR France430,Perceval

GREEN,Arthur Vivian 2Lt kia 17-8-17 5RDubF p176 MR30

GREEN,Basil.MC.2Lt kia 1-7-17 5NStaffs p238 MR19

GREEN,Benjamin Cecil 2Lt kia 24-4-17 5ELancs att126MGC Inf p187&226 MR21

GREEN,Cecil Ernest 2Lt kia 26-8-18 5Lond p246 CR France329

GREEN,Cecil Henry T2Lt dow 9-10-16 6 O&BLI p130 CR France105

GREEN,Charles Arthur.MC.2Lt kia 13-7-17 RGA 2/3LowlandHB p39 CR France592,2/1Bn

GREEN,Charles Ernest T2Lt kia 14-7-16 9 att7KSLI p144 MR21

GREEN,Charles Henry.MID CaptAMaj dow 8-11-17 1SStaffs att3NigR p122&201 CR EAfrica33 &rCR Tanzania1

GREEN,Charles James LtACapt kia 16-4-18 13RSuss p119 CR Belgium21

GREEN,Charles Layton T2Lt kia 9-6-17 GL 11Ess att53RFC p8 CR France285

GREEN,Charles Taylor 2Lt kia 26-10-17 2RWSurr p56 MR30

GREEN,Clifford Whittington LtTCapt dow 27-6-15 RBerks p139

GREEN,Cuthbert 2Lt kia 15-10-16 2DLI p160 MR21

GREEN,Cyril Mortimer Lt kia 6-11-17 16RSuss p119 CR Palestine1,Capt

GREEN,Daniel Abbott 2Lt kia 13-11-16 3 att1Lpool p72 MR21

GREEN,Daniel Cottle 2Lt kia 25-2-17 22Lond attMGC Inf p187&251 MR38

GREEN,David T2Lt kia 1-8-17 23MGC p183 MR29

GREEN,Demetrius Frederick Edward Joseph.MID Lt ded 15-10-18 GL 9NumbF p190 CR France457

GREEN,Edward Scott Waring 2Lt kia 28-8-16 1Mddx p147 CR France399,27-8-16

GREEN,Edward Unsworth.MC.TCapt kia 10-8-17 9LNLancs p136 MR29

GREEN,Edwin Charles 2Lt kia 26-3-18 4NStaffs p157 CR France300

GREEN,Eric De Wilde T2Lt dow 15-4-18 1RWSurr p56 CR France102

GREEN,Ernest Arthur James Capt kia 21/22-10-20 2/67Punjabis MR43

GREEN,Ernest Michael TLt kia 3-9-16 14Hamps p120 CR France742,Capt

GREEN,Ernest Newham Chap4Cl ded 26-3-16 RAChDept p199 CR Mddx42

GREEN,Frank T2Lt kia 17-9-16 5RIrF p171 CR Greece3

GREEN,Frank 2Lt kia 3-11-16 4YLI p235 CR France1327

GREEN,Frank Lt dow 28-12-17 5Yorks p220 CR Belgium11

GREEN,Frank Clifford 2Lt kia 16-6-15 1Lincs p75 MR29

GREEN,Frederick George.MC.T2Lt kia 3-10-18 LNLancs att1/4Bn p136 CR France242

GREEN,Geoffrey George Miers T2Lt kia 28-3-18 WYorks att5YLI p81 CR France798

GREEN,George Birch T2Lt kia 11-6-18 1RWFus att7KSLI p97 CR France33

GREEN,George Owen TCapt kia 23-8-15 9WelchR p126 CR France1157

GREEN,Gilbert Pitcher T2Lt dow 25-10-16 13Ches p96 CR France44

GREEN,Geoffrey Walter Ashdown 2Lt kia 8-3-18 RFA &r59RFC p16&29 CR France518

GREEN,Harold T2Lt kia 28-2-17 1RDubF p176 MR21

GREEN,Harold Stewart.DCM.2Lt kia 4-4-18 4DragGds p21 CR France196

GREEN,F.Harold Syddal 2Lt dow 1-5-17 12SWBord p100 CR France85

GREEN,Henry Arthur 2Lt kia 9-10-18 4RWKent p234 CR France332

GREEN,Henry Edwin Capt dow 13-10-16 22Lond p251 CR France177

GREEN,Henry Morris TCapt kia 4-8-16 9RFus p68 CR France446

GREEN,Herbert.MC.Rev kia 24-8-17 RAChDept att41MGC p199 CR Belgium19

GREEN,Herbert John T2Lt kia 4-3-17 GL &r43RFC p8 CR France924

GREEN,Herbert Walter.DSO.MajBtLtCol dow 31-12-18 EKent attRWSurr p57 CR France146

GREEN,Herbert William 2Lt kia 16-8-17 5RSuss p228 CR Belgium10

GREEN,Herbert William T2Lt kia 12-10-17 2ScotsGds p52 MR30

GREEN,Horace Salkeld.MID Maj kia 20-9-17 7Lond p247 CR Belgium125

GREEN,Hubert Bishop 2Lt kia 13-4-18 7 att2Worc p226 MR32

GREEN,Hugh James Bernard Chap4Cl ded 8-12-18 RAChDept att20DivDetls p199 CR France134

GREEN,Hugh Mortimer Capt kia 10-8-15 4WelshR p230 MR4

GREEN,James T2Lt dow 21-7-16 7SLancs p125 CR France188

GREEN,James 2Lt dow 27-9-18 2Mddx p147 CR France268

GREEN,James Archer Capt kia 23-3-17 16Lond p249 CR France419

GREEN,John Alexander TLt ded 18-8-18 8SStaffs attAnsonBnRNDev p122 CR France69

GREEN,John Berks 2Lt kia 11-1-17 8Manch p237 MR21

GREEN,John Feetham 2Lt kia 5-11-16 7DLI p239 CR France385,Frettiam

GREEN,John James HonCapt&rQM ded 9-12-17 10WYorks p81 CR Essex1

GREEN,John Leslie.VC.Capt kia 1-7-16 RAMC att5N&rD p253 CR France281

GREEN,Joseph George Airey 2Lt kia 23-11-17 TankCps p188 MR17

GREEN,Leslie Alan 2Lt kia 13-11-16 6 att23RFus p68 CR France131,Lt

GREEN,Malcolm Charles Andrew LtCol kia 17-11-14 SLancs p125 MR29

GREEN,Norman T2Lt kia 25-1-17 7NStaffs p157 CR Iraq5

GREEN,Norman Wilson 2Lt kia 23-4-17 4EYorks p219 MR20

GREEN,Oswald Robert John TLt dow 5-7-16 9WelchR p126 CR France833

GREEN,Percy T2Lt kia 9-9-18 9YLI p143 CR France415

GREEN,Percy Harold T2Lt kia 26-3-18 9RInniskF p105 MR27

GREEN,Philip Louis Samuel 2Lt kia 18-9-16 4 att1WYorks p81 MR21

GREEN,Philip Sydney TCapt ded 13-11-18 RAMC 32SH p195 CR France34

GREEN,Phillip 2Lt kia 28-3-18 1/4EYorks p219 MR27,Philip

GREEN,Reginald Cumberland Lt dow 18-5-16 1Beds p86 CR France1182

GREEN,Richard Scott Lt kia 14-10-15 4Leic p219 MR19

GREEN,Richmond Edward Ormond Lyttleton T2Lt kia 19-2-16 6KSLI p144 CR Belgium73

GREEN,Robert Edward 2Lt kia 21-3-17 20Lpool p72 MR20

GREEN,Rupert Anthony Lt kia 25-3-18 Mddx att23Bn p147 MR20

GREEN,St.John T2Lt kia 6-12-17 12 att9RInniskF p105 MR17

GREEN,Thomas.DCM.22489 2Lt dow 28-10-16 RGA 10SB p39 CR France515

GREEN,Thomas Claud Erskine T2Lt kia 31-7-17 8RWSurr p56 MR29

GREEN,Thomas Seaman TLt kia 13-2-17 GL &r3RFC p8 CR France833

GREEN,Thomas William T2Lt dow 14-8-18 2TankCps p188 CR France34,Lt

GREEN,Vivian Unsworth 2LtTLt kia 26-3-17 15 att10Mddx p147 MR34

GREEN,William Bruce T2Lt kia 29-3-18 11Mddx p147 CR France266,Willie

GREEN,William Eddowes Lt dow 6-7-16 1Dors p124 CR France74,3Bn

GREEN,William Osmond T2Lt kia 1-7-16 10RIrRif p169 MR21

GREEN,William Wesley 2Lt kia 9-4-17 1EYorks p84 CR France162

GREENALL,Jack Eckersley D.Capt kia 31-3-18 LanarkYeo attRAF p255&204 CR France300

GREENALL,James Mackintosh Capt died /-11-19 RASC p267

GREENE,Aldrich Wells 2Lt kia 17-2-18 27RFC p16 CR France1887

GREENE,Charles Kendall Capt 25-3-16 EKent CR Ireland14 &rCR Eire77

GREENE,Ernest Alfred Jeffries Capt kia 22-10-20 IARO att2/67Punjabis p277

GREENE,Godfrey Robert 2Lt kia 3-9-16 116MGC Inf p183 MR21

GREENE,Henry.MIDx2 Lt kia 21-8-15 IA 92Punjabis att1/6GurkhaRif p277 MR4

GREENE,Henry Caldwell 2Lt kia 29-4-18 5RMunstF att1RIrRif p175 CR Belgium96,Harry

GREENE,Henry Roundell Capt ded 27-6-18 Hamps attGCR WAAF p120 CR Hamps10

GREENE,John 2Lt kia 3-11-16 Wilts att6Bn p154 MR21

GREENE,Quincey Shaw LtACapt kia 28-3-18 3CldGds p51 MR20

GREENE,Richard Ernest 2Lt dow 3-2-19 9RInniskF p105 CR France34,Lt

GREENE,Robin TCapt ded 21-9-18 RE PostalServ p45 MR65

GREENER,Arthur Stephen.MC.LtACapt dow 18-4-18 1NumbF p61 CR France10

GREENER,Francis Pemberton 2Lt kia 15-2-15 2ESurr p112 MR29

GREENER,Henry 2Lt kia 14-4-17 6DLI p239 CR France162

GREENER,Leysters Llewellyn.MC.Capt kia 5-12-17 2/6RWar p214 MR17

GREENER,Noel Hindmarsh TLt kia 25-9-15 6KOSB p101 MR19

GREENFIELD,Benjamin Lt ded 28-11-18 RFA p254 CR Scot862

GREENFIELD,Eric Frank T2Lt kld 13-2-17 2KRRC p150 CR France145

GREENFIELD,Fredk 2Lt kia 2-5-17 GL attRAOC p266

GREENFIELD,Gerald Henry 2Lt dow 17-8-17 B242RFA Bde p29 CR Belgium11

GREENFIELD,Richard Mentieth.CB.BrigGen ded 25-4-16 RInniskF GenStaff IrishCommand p1 CR Herts84

GREENFIELD,Ronald William Lt kia 23-10-16 1RB p178 MR21

GREENFIELD,Thomas Bevil T2Lt kia 19-9-15 RE 1/2FC p45 CR Gallipoli17

GREENHALGH,Harold Fifield T2Lt kia 9-4-18 RAOC p198 CR Belgium3

GREENHALGH,Hugh Charles T2Lt kia 5-5-17 20Mddx p147 CR France439

GREENHALGH,James Arthur 2Lt kia 22-10-14 Ches p96 MR22

GREENHALGH,Maurice Lomax T2Lt kia 25-9-15 15Lpool p72 CR France625

GREENHILL,Campbell.MC.TLt kia 10-8-17 3Worc p108 MR29

GREENHILL,Frederick William Ridge Lt kia 10-10-17 3GrenGds p50 MR30

GREENHILL,Reginald Fowler Capt dow 1-1-18 15LancF p92 CR France64

GREENHILL,Thomas Watson Lt kia 11-2-16 4DragGds p21 CR France423

GREENHOUS,Ernest Brereton TLt kia 26-8-17 1RScotF &r9RFC p8&94,T2Lt CR Belgium18

GREENHOW,Denys Edward T2Lt kia 6-3-17 45RFC p8 CR Belgium11

GREENLAND,Charles Stirling Walter Lt kia 9-5-15 2Glouc p106 CR Belgium167

GREENLAND,Richard 2Lt kia 13-4-17 9DLI p239 CR France420

GREENLEES,Charles Fouracres T2Lt kia 1-7-16 9RWSurr p56 CR France35

GREENLESS,George Dickson 2Lt kia 1-12-17 4BlkW p230 CR Palestine3

GREENOP,Garnet Arthur Claude 2Lt kia 9-7-16 RFA 172Bty p29 CR France701,8-7-16

GREENOUGH,William Gladstone 2Lt kia 21-10-18 4 att1/6Manch p154 CR France287

GREENSHIELDS,John Arthur.MC.2Lt kia 27-5-18 5 att9YLI p235 CR France622,Capt

GREENSHIELDS-LEADBETTER,Alan Edmonstoune.MID Maj kia 4-8-17 L15RHA CR Belgium12

GREENSLADE,Francis Harold 2Lt kia 31-5-18 A52RFA p29 CR France268

GREENSMITH,J.Cdr 29-5-20 IA MiscList CR Asia60

GREENSTED,Walter 2Lt dow 22-10-18 A50RFA p29 CR Belgium147

GREENSTREET,Ernest Henry T2Lt ded 15-2-19 19Mddx p147&257 CR Germany1

GREENSTREET,Frederick George Maj kia 9-1-17 IA 103MahrattaLI att105 p277 MR38

GREENUP,John Bertram 2Lt kia 12-10-17 5 att1RB p178 MR30,13-10-17

GREENWAY,Douglas Howard Wilson T2Lt kia 17-10-15 13 att4Worc p108 CR Gallipoli4

GREENWAY,Frederick Charles Garton T2Lt kia 14-7-16 8Leic p87 MR21

GREENWAY,Kenneth T2Lt kia 27-11-15 13 att4Worc p108 CR Gallipoli4,18-11-15

GREENWELL,John T2Lt kia 24-10-18 12/13NumbF p61 MR16

GREENWELL,Thomas William Maddison Lt kia 19-7-18 6NumbF att17LancF p213 CR France139

GREENWELL-LAX,Anthony William Capt kia 11-10-16 RGA 43SB p39

GREENWOOD,AMaj 10-6-19 IMD MR65

GREENWOOD,Arthur Donald T2Lt kia 30-8-18 2Beds p86 CR France397

GREENWOOD,Cecil James Lt kia 9-8-18 10Lond p248 CR France1170

GREENWOOD,Charles 2Lt kia 22-3-18 RLancs att6Wilts p59 MR20

GREENWOOD,Charles Norman.MC.2Lt dow 5-9-18 A70RFA p29 CR France95

GREENWOOD,Charles Stuart 2Lt ded 21-7-16 11RFus p68

GREENWOOD,Cyril Stewart T2Lt kia 20-8-16 1Nhampt p137 CR France387

GREENWOOD,Ernest 2Lt ded 31-10-18 4LNLancs p270 CR Yorks730

GREENWOOD,Gerald Wyatt Capt ded 17-11-18 B210RFA p207 CR Lancs381

GREENWOOD,Harold Sutcliffe T2Lt kia 22-7-16 14RWar p64 CR France432

GREENWOOD,Henry Smith.VD.LtCol 4-5-16 RE CR Surrey160

GREENWOOD,Herbert T2Lt dow 8-6-17 122MGC p183 MR29

GREENWOOD,Isidore Herbert Lt dow 6-7-18 10 att8Mddx p236 CR France54

GREENWOOD,James Barton Lt kia 13-10-18 19LancF att1/4Y&L p92 MR16

GREENWOOD,James Hurst.MC.TLt dow 24-7-18 11RWKent p141 CR Hamps13

GREENWOOD,John Exley T2Lt ded 11-9-17 GL &RFC p8 CR Yorks583

GREENWOOD,John Francis Bernal Lt kia 2-5-15 1RLancs p59 MR29

GREENWOOD,Joseph LtCol 27-12-15 RE CR Lond9

GREENWOOD,L.A.2Lt dow 13-4-18 GL &RAF p190

GREENWOOD,Leonard Montague.DSO.MC&Bar.TMaj ded 17-10-18 13DLI p160 CR France146

GREENWOOD,Tom 2Lt kia 31-8-18 5Lpool p215 CR France433

GREENWOOD,Tom Stanley T2Lt kia 7-7-16 14 att12Manch p154 MR21

GREENWOOD,Victor John Maj kia 18-4-18 D275RFA p206 CR France109

GREER,Donald Allister Lt ded 12-7-16 1ConnRgrs p172 CR Iraq5,Alister

GREER,Eric Beresford.MC.MajALtCol kia 31-7-17 2IrGds p52 CR Belgium12

GREER,Francis St.Ledger.MC.Lt ded 1-2-17 2IrGds p52 CR France833

GREER,James Kenneth Macgregor.MC.Lt dow 3-10-16 1IrGds p52 CR France145

GREER,Morrice Capt kia 16-6-17 RAMC attRWFus p253 CR Palestine8

GREEVES,Arthur Frederick Wellesley T2Lt dow 20-9-17 8NStaffs p157 CR Belgium21,Frederic

GREEVES,John 2Lt kia 1-7-17 5NStaffs p238 MR19

GREG,Arthur Tylston Capt kia 23-4-17 3Ches &55RFC p8&96 CR France1074

GREG,Robert Phillips 2Lt dow 3-5-18 4Ches p222 CR Belgium11,11Bn

GREGERY,James Langdale T2Lt kia 13-5-17 8Yorks attRE 101FC p90

GREGG,Charles Edward 2Lt kia 15-6-17 1/5RLancs p213 CR Belgium10

GREGG,George Philip 2Lt kia 26-3-17 7Ches p223 MR34

GREGG,Reginald Lt kia 1-10-18 6Manch p236 CR France376

GREGG,Robert Lt kia 9-8-15 2DLI p160 MR29

GREGG,William Henry 2Lt kia 1-7-16 5 att1RIrRif p169 MR21

GREGGE-HOPWOOD,Edward Byng George.DSO.MajALtCol kia 20-7-17 1CldGds p51 CR Belgium12

GREGOR,George Trevor.VD.LtCol kia 1-7-17 RFA 1WelshHB p206 CR Belgium1

GREGORY,Alfred John Reginald.DSO.Maj ded 4-12-18 RGA 120HB XIXCps p39 CR France717

GREGORY,Arthur Skelton T2Lt kia 22-9-18 3LNLancs att2ELancs p136 CR France184

GREGORY,Fleming Clement.MC.Capt dow 29-11-17 3County of LondYeo p204 CR Palestine9

GREGORY,Frank TLt kia 16-4-18 19LancF p92 MR30

GREGORY,Geoffrey Francis Gregory Lt kia 25-9-15 RBerks p139 MR32

GREGORY,George T2Lt kia 26-9-17 7Y&L p158 CR Belgium13

GREGORY,Godfrey Levinge Capt ded 5-1-18 6DLI CR Berks125

GREGORY,Henry Vincent Lt kia 15-3-17 3 att12Lpool p72 CR France513

GREGORY,Herbert Capt&QM ded 23-10-19 MGC Inf CR Lancs179

GREGORY,Herbert Thomas T2LtACapt dow 13-10-17 7RWKent p141 CR Belgium64

GREGORY,James Alfred TLt dow 13-4-17 RAMC 52FA att12Manch p195 CR France113

GREGORY,James Langdale 2Lt 13-5-17 8Yorks attRE 101FC CR Belgium127

GREGORY,John George 2Lt dow 8-1-16 6Lond p247 CR France178

GREGORY,John Sheridan TCapt kia 19-2-18 RASC attRFC p16&193 CR France369

GREGORY,Kenneth Stuart Lt kia 10-11-17 2/7RWFus att3MGC Inf p187&223 MR30

GREGORY,Percy John T2Lt kia 4-10-17 12/13NumbF p61 MR30

GREGORY,Reuben Henry.MC.TCapt kia 9-6-17 10N&D p134 MR29

GREGORY,Robert.MC.LtTMaj kia 23-1-18 4ConnRgrs att66RFC p16&172 CR Italy48

GREGORY,Stanley T2Lt kia 8-6-18 1/10Manch p154 CR France5

GREGORY,Stanley Harris T2Lt kia 13-11-16 15 att24RFus p68 CR France152

GREGORY,Stephen Barnes Lt ded PoW 3-6-16 4Dev p220 MR38

GREGORY,Sydney Maurice 2Lt kia 18-5-15 6Lond p247 CR France260

GREGORY,Thomas William Capt dow 22-3-18 4 att16NumbF p213 MR20

GREGORY,Walter Stanley T2Lt kia 30-4-17 5Wilts p153 MR38

GREGSON,Alan Herbert T2Lt kia 19-4-17 RWKent att2/4Bn p141 CR Palestine8

GREGSON,Edward Maurice Capt kia 28-6-16 4LNLancs p233 MR20

GREGSON,Francis Robert Capt dow 15-5-17 SL att4AustDiv p201 CR France13,Maj

GREGSON,Herbert 2Lt kia 30-11-17 35MGC p183 MR17

GREGSON,William Pilkington T2Lt dow 18-10-18 16TankCps p188 CR France725

GREGSON-ELLIS,Reginald George TCapt dow 17-4-17 O&BLI BucksBn p231 CR France511

GREIFFENHAGEN,Norman T2Lt dow 24-12-18 1EKent p57 CR Belgium11,24-12-15

GREIG,Hugh Irwin Maj kia 2-11-17 RGA p39 CR Belgium176

GREIG,James Gordon Hamilton 2LtTLt dow 13-8-15 6EKent D'Coy p57 CR France285

GREIG,John William Henry 2Lt kia 26-3-15 IARO att25Cav p277 MR43

GREIG,Morland John Maj kia 17-10-15 1RNDevYeo p203 CR Gallipoli27

GREIG,Ronald Henry.DSO.Maj kia 28-8-16 RE 54FC p45 CR France372

GREIG,Roy Scott Capt kia 28-3-18 14Lond att6CamH p249 CR France924,dow

GREIG,William Ewing Capt dow 27-5-15 5Lpool p215 CR France102

GRELL,Louis George Neville Lt ded 5-6-18 10WYorks att27Punjabis p81&p277 MR66

GRELLIER,Arthur Bertean 2Lt kia 26-3-18 LancF att2/7Bn p92 MR27,Berteau

GRELLIER,Gordon Harley 2Lt kia 31-10-18 RGA 51SB p39 CR France737

GRENFELL,Francis Octavius,VC Capt kia 24-5-15 9Lancers p22 CR Belgium4,dow

GRENFELL,Gerald William.Hon.T2Lt kia 30-7-15 8RB p179 MR29

GRENFELL,Julian Henry Francis.DSO.Hon.Capt dow 26-5-15 1Drags p21 CR France102

GRENFELL,Riversdale Nonn Capt kia 14-9-14 BucksYeo att9Lancers p203 CR France1328,Nonus

GRENNAN,Gerald Lismore T2Lt kia 12-10-16 20Lpool p72 MR21

GRENVILLE-GREY,Wilfred Hanbury Lt dow 16-5-15 1KRRC p150 CR France632,Wilfrid

GRENVILLE WELLS,Nigel Lt 9-10-19 WeldhGds CR Palestine3

GRESHAM,Gordon 2Lt dow 18-6-16 4EYorks p219 CR France285

GRESHAM,John Francis Lt ded 16-2-19 4EYorks p219 CR France377

GRESHAM,Leonard Stanley 2Lt dow 7-5-17 1/1Yorks ERidYeo p206 CR Egypt2

GRESLEY,Roger.MC.LtAMaj dow 6-9-18 A119RFA p29 CR France298

GRESLEY-COX,Edward Louis T2Lt kld 22-2-18 17/16RFC p16 CR Greece3

GRESSON,John Edward 2Lt kia 24-5-15 3 att2Ches p96 MR29

GRESWELL,Eric Walter Lt kld 9-6-18 8Ches att111RAF p96 CR Palestine9,kia

GRESWELL,H.G.Capt dow 18-8-16 RE 154FC p45 CR France88

GRESWOLDE-WILLIAMS,Francis Humphrey John Lt kia 3-8-17 SL att3/4KAR p202 CR EAfrica10 &CR Tanzania1,F.H.T.3/2Bn

GRETTON,Horace Edward Capt kia 16-8-17 2Lond p245 MR29

GRETTON,Rupert Harold TCapt kia 17-12-15 8Beds p86 MR29

GREVELINK,Edward James Yzenhoed Lt ded 6-6-17 2WRid &RFC p8&115 CR France403

GREVES,Thomas Samuel 2Lt ded 28-6-19 3 att11Hamps p264CR Sussex72

GREVILLE,David Onslow 2Lt kia 3-5-17 16WYorks p81 MR20

GREVILLE,George Gordon Francis Lt dow 31-3-18 4Huss p21 CR France988

GREVILLE,Sydney T2Lt kia 19-4-17 NStaffs p157 CR France366

GREW,Hubert 2Lt kia 2-7-15 7KRRC p150 CR Belgium165

GREW,Walter Ernest T2Lt kia 7-10-17 16RWar p64 MR30

GREY,Alice Annie Sister 21-8-16 ScotWomensHosp attSerbianArmy CR Greece7

GREY,Charles Joscelyn Eden(Robin).DSO.Maj 15-5-21 2GrenGds CR Lond4

GREY,Gordon Louis 2Lt ded 3-6-17 SNottsHuss p270 CR Lond8

GREY,John Ivor 2Lt kia 15-9-16 7NumbF p214 CR France387

GREY,Norman Lt kia 26-10-17 5LNLancs p234 CR Belgium126

GREY,Patrick Riddle T2Lt kia 26-9-16 15 att8NumbF p61 MR21

GREY,Sidney James 2Lt kia 1-8-18 14Lond att6Ca p249 CR France878

GREY-SMITH,Melville Capt kia 19-11-17 IARO att2/3GurkhaRif p277 CR Palestine9

GRIBBELL,Arthur Frank TCapt ded 13-3-16 RFA p29 CR Sussex128

GRIBBELL,Leslie Terrell T2Lt ded 31-3-16 3Dev p76 CR Dorset52

GRIBBEN,James Grenfell 2Lt kia 12-6-17 1/6SStaffs p229 CR France149,11-6-17

GRIBBLE,Charles Ethelburt.MC.LtACapt dow 15-10-18 3 att7Leic p87 CR France560

GRIBBLE,Charles Herbert Lt kia 30-11-17 4EKent p212 att1RGLI

GRIBBLE,Horace Dewey TLt ded 13-7-18 SL att1NigR p201&268 CR WAfrica41

GRIBBLE,Julian Royds.VC.Capt ded PoW 25-11-18 1 att10RWar p64 CR Germany3,kia

GRIBBON,John Stewart 2Lt kia 27-5-18 7YLI att2RB p143 MR18

GRIBBON,Montagu Claude Capt kia 9-12-15 IA 67Punjabis p277 MR38

GRICE,Harold George Lt dow 27-3-18 4RScots p211 CR France145

GRICE,Howard Thomas 2Lt kia 25-3-18 2ScotRif p103 CR France1203

GRICE,Lawrence Victor TLt kia 13-4-18 21NumbF p61 MR32

GRICE,Leslie Clark 2Lt dow 20-4-17 23/40RFA p208 CR France1185

GRICE,Maurice Chuma Lt accdrd 4-7-18 14ACycCps p244 CR Italy8

GRICE,Percival Samuel Henry Lt kia 2-9-18 2/17Lond p250 CR Belgium89

GRICE,Thomas Gerald CaptTMaj dow 15-6-16 3 att2ScotRif p103 CR France203

GRIDLEY,F.SubCdr 30-6-15 S&T Cps MR66

GRIER,Francis Nemo Lt&QM ded 30-4-18 SL p201 CR Egypt1

GRIER,William TLt drd 15-4-17 RAMC p195 MR35

GRIERSON,James Moncrieff.KCB.CVO.CMG.ADC.Sir.LtGen ded 17-8-14 Staff RA p1 CR Scot756

GRIERSON,John T2Lt kia 21-3-18 13Lpool p72 MR20

GRIERSON,John Henry Clifford 2Lt kia 31-7-17 3GordH p166 MR29

GRIERSON,John Livingstone Hailes T2Lt kia 1-7-16 3 att2RScotF p94 MR21

GRIERSON,Robert Lt&QM ded 14-2-16 2/5KOSB p270 CR Scot621

GRIERSON,Stanley Virtue 2Lt kia 31-8-18 3 att2SfthH p164 CR France421

GRIESBACH,Claude Walter 2Lt kia 23-10-16 2RBerks p139 MR21

GRIEVE,Alan Edward 2Lt kia 3-7-16 2SLancs p125 MR21

GRIEVE,C.C.Maj 22-9-20 2CamH CR Ireland14 &CR Eire77

GRIEVE,David Harley T2Lt ded 31-10-18 12LabCps p189 CR France34

GRIEVE,James TLt kld 21-2-17 3SLancs &RFC p8&125 CR Lancs149

GRIEVE,James Ross.MC.TCaptTMaj kia 4-4-18 C107RFA p29 CR France988

GRIEVE,Nicholas Harrington 2Lt kia 13-11-16 3 att1RScotF p94 CR France742

GRIEVE,William Percival 2Lt kia 16-2-15 Mddx att3Bn p147 MR29

GRIEVE,William Robertson Capt kia 28-4-17 7HLI p240 MR20

GRIEVES,James 2Lt kia 20-9-18 5NumbF p213 CR France530

GRIFFEN,Harold Samuel T2Lt dow 9-4-17 KSLI att5Bn p144 CR France418,GRIFFIN

GRIFFIN,Basil Walker T2Lt dow 2-12-17 2Lincs p75 MR30

GRIFFIN,Cecil Scott James Capt kld 11-10-17 1GordH attRFC p8&166 CR Devon76

GRIFFIN,Charles John T2LtACapt kia 1-9-16 2RWSurr p56 MR21

GRIFFIN,Clive.MC.Lt dow 11-11-16 3RFA p207 CR Greece7

GRIFFIN,Douglas Morley T2Lt dow 16-7-16 18Lpool p72 CR France51

GRIFFIN,Edward Stanley 2Lt kia 31-7-17 6Lpool p215 MR29

GRIFFIN,Edward William Lt kia 16-9-18 6Glouc attRAF p225&258 CR France792

GRIFFIN,George Edward TCapt kia 1-7-16 9YLI p143 MR21

GRIFFIN,Hedley Saunders 2Lt dow PoW 31-8-17 4RBerks p234 CR Belgium140 Ex HAC

GRIFFIN,Innes Edward Capt dow 19-2-16 1/4 O&BLI p231 CR France167,18-2-16

GRIFFIN,John James Wahal T2Lt kia 15-11-16 6Beds p86 CR France533,James John W.

GRIFFIN,Leslie Stuart Herbert.MID TLt kia 18-8-16 10Glouc p106 CR France386

GRIFFIN,Lilian Sister ded 5-9-16 TFNS p254 MR37

GRIFFIN,P.G.DSO.Maj 26-3-21 16RFA CR Palestine9

GRIFFIN,Reginald Herbert 2LtACapt dow 7-7-17 RFA attRGA 21SB p29 CR Belgium18,kld

GRIFFIN,Sidney James Capt dow 26-3-18 1 att3 O&BLI p130 CR Iraq8

GRIFFITH,Allex James William 2Lt kia 25-3-17 2Dors G'Coy p124 MR38,Allix Lt

GRIFFITH,Arthur Charles Fleming Lt kia 8-10-18 2 att17RWFus p97 CR France234

GRIFFITH,Edward William Collisson Capt dow 1-2-19 10RIrRif p254&257 CR Sussex185

GRIFFITH,Frank.VD.Col ded 4-1-17 R6FA p206 CR Kent91

GRIFFITH,Geoffrey Foster.MID Capt kia 26-9-17 9Lond p247 MR30

GRIFFITH,George Herbert Col ded 20-9-17 RE DepDir ofWorks p45 MR65

GRIFFITH,Gerald Lt kia 26-8-14 1Hamps p120 MR15

GRIFFITH,Henry Hall TCapt kld 2-11-17 45RFC p8 CR Sussex139,63Sqn

GRIFFITH,Henry Rathbone TLt ded 21-5-16 RAMC p267 CR Shrop93

GRIFFITH,John Gwynne Maj kia 24-5-15 IA 32Lancers attHQ9CavBde p277 CR Belgium57

GRIFFITH,John Herbert 2Lt kia 27-3-18 15WYorks p81 CR France927

GRIFFITH,Oswald 2Lt kia 27-2-15 80RFA p29 CR Belgium170,Lt

GRIFFITH,Rupert Varden De Burgh Lt kia 12-3-15 3RFus p68 CR Belgium17

GRIFFITH,Thomas Comber Lt dow 8-7-19 LNLancs p257&136 See GRIFFITHS.T.C. MR70 &CR Europe179

GRIFFITH,Trevor Llewelyn ALt kia 30-10-17 D82RFA p29 CR Belgium10

GRIFFITH,Walter Stanley Currie T2Lt kia 10-8-15 6Leinst p174 CR Gallipoli18

GRIFFITH,William Henry.MC.T2Lt dow 5-7-17 15RWFus p97 CR Belgium18

GRIFFITH,William Henry Lt 14-12-17 MilWksServ MR65

GRIFFITH,William Key 2Lt kia 26-9-17 12Lond p248 MR30

GRIFFITH,William Llewelyn T2Lt dow 22-9-17 WelshR att9Bn p126 CR Belgium183

GRIFFITH,William Starbuck Maj ded 23-7-15 RAMC p270 CR Wales389

GRIFFITH,William Walter Gilbert LtCol kia 22-4-17 IA 32Lancers p277 MR38

GRIFFITH-JONES,William Lionel Phillips.MC.Lt kld 12-7-16 3 att2DLI p160 CR Belgium5,dedacc

GRIFFITHS,Allen Rhys T2Lt kia 9-8-15 53/2RFA p29 CR Belgium59

GRIFFITHS,Arthur Ivor T2Lt kia 3-8-17 12Suff p78 CR France439

GRIFFITHS,Charles Jewell Thomas Lt ded 7-11-18 RDC p270 CR Hamps7

GRIFFITHS,Charles Ridley T2Lt dow 1-5-17 7RFus p68 CR France95

GRIFFITHS,Christopher William TLt dow 7-11-18 RE 123FC p45 CR France146

GRIFFITHS,D.H.Chap4Cl 15-12-15 CR Mon89

GRIFFITHS,David George.MC.Lt dow 15-12-18 84RFA p29 CR Wales231,17-12-18

GRIFFITHS,Edwin Arthur TLt kia 27-2-18 11SWBord att115TMB p100 CR France275

GRIFFITHS,Edwin Harold 2Lt dow 23-10-18 6RWFus attTMB p223 CR Italy9,kia 22-10-18

GRIFFITHS,Edwin John T2Lt kia 28-2-18 111LabCps p189 CR Belgium20

GRIFFITHS,Egbert Clarence T2Lt ded 27-2-19 5KRRC p265 CR Surrey2

GRIFFITHS,Francis Noot Gifford Lt dow 2-6-15 10Manch p237 CR Gallipoli1

GRIFFITHS,Frank Calvert 2Lt dow 14-2-17 3 att7Yorks p90 CR France105

GRIFFITHS,Frederick James Capt kia 1-9-18 20 att4Lond p251 CR France216

GRIFFITHS,George Clement TCapt kia 28-6-15 13 att1LancF p92 CR Gallipoli6

GRIFFITHS,George Richards TLt dow 15-9-16 1KRRC p150 CR France203

RIFFITHS,Gwyn Arthur TLt kia 2-6-17 15WelchR &35RFC p8&126 CR France839

GRIFFITHS,Harry James T2Lt dow 9-8-16 9 att1SomLI p79 CR Belgium11

GRIFFITHS,Henry Hingley TLt ded 26-10-18 SStaffs p264 CR Hereford186

GRIFFITHS,Hugh T2Lt ded 1-12-18 RE 310RdConstCo p45 CR France13

GRIFFITHS,Iorworth T2Lt kia 5-7-16 7ELancs p110 MR21 Iorwerth

GRIFFITHS,J.L Sister 30-10-15 QAIMNS CR Egypt3

GRIFFITHS,John.MID TCapt kia 1-7-16 12RIrRif p169 CR France339

GRIFFITHS,John Enos 2Lt kia 23-4-18 5Glouc p225 CR France248

GRIFFITHS,John Herbert 2Lt dow 29-5-18 B175RFA p29 CR France504,A174RFA

GRIFFITHS,John Joseph T2Lt kia 23-3-18 11Lpool p72 MR27

GRIFFITHS,John Llewelyn T2Lt kia 26-6-16 15 att12NumbF p61 CR France188

GRIFFITHS,John Neville TCapt kia 30-11-17 RAMC att58HAG p195 CR France245

GRIFFITHS,Leon David T2Lt dow 29-4-17 24RFus att5TMB p68 CR France95,Lt

GRIFFITHS,Lewis Herbert T2Lt kia 11-9-18 Norf att12Bn p73 CR Belgium451

GRIFFITHS,Nicholas T2Lt kia 10/11-7-16 7 att6SWBord p100 CR France150,11-7-16

GRIFFITHS,P.R.LtCol 13-7-20 RAMC CR Mddx26

GRIFFITHS,Reginald Hopkins Hill.MC.2Lt kld 17-10-18 9WelshR &RAF p126 CR Belgium140,Hopkin

GRIFFITHS,Royston Swire TLtAMaj ded 17-3-17 RGA 123SB p39 CR France1182

GRIFFITHS,Thomas Comber Lt dow 8-7-19 LNLancs att1SlavoBritLegion p136 SeeGRIFFITH.T.C.

GRIFFITHS,Walter 2Lt kia 21-11-17 1LancF p92 MR17

GRIFFITHS,Walter Edward Lambourn TCapt kia 26-4-17 9Glouc p106 CR Greece6

GRIFFITHS,Walter Harold T2Lt kia 4-10-16 7RWKent p14 CR France383,30-9-16

GRIFFITHS,William Charles TLt kia 21-10-18 10RInniskF p105 CR Belgium140

GRIFFITHS,William Dillwyn 2Lt kia 18-9-18 4WelshR p230 CR France1463,dow

GRIFFITHS,William George T2Lt kia 9-3-16 1 att1/5RWFus p97 CR Palestine3

GRIFFITHS,William Henry Capt&QM kia 7-8-15 6LancF p221 MR4

GRIFFITHS,William John.MC.Capt kia 24-11-17 17WelshR p126 MR17

GRIFFITHS,William Percival TCapt kia 30-3-16 10RWFus p97 MR29

GRIGG,George Irving 2Lt dow 21-7-17 RGA 234SB p39CR Belgium16

GRIGG,Harry Hasting Capt kia 16-5-15 IA 1/3GurkhaRifatt2/3 p277CR France631,Hastings

GRIGG,John Capt ded 14-10-18 EAfrSupplyCps CR EAfrica47

GRIGG,Lionel Francis T2Lt kia 29-7-16 1ESurr p112 MR21,28-7-16

GRIGG,Malcolm Howard 2Lt kia 9-7-16 26Manch p154 MR21,17Bn

GRIGGS,Horace Edward TCapt kia 5-10-15 9Ess p131 MR19

GRIGSON,Francis Henry T2Lt kia 9-8-15 9RWar p64 MR4

GRIGSON,Kenneth Walton.MC.Capt kia 20-7-18 7Dev att2/5WYorks p217 CR France622

GRIGSON,Lionel Henry Shockforth 2Lt kia 9-5-17 3Dev p76 MR20,Shuckforth

GRIMBLE,Henry T2Lt kia 28-9-16 8Suff p78 MR21

GRIME,Joseph Crookes 2Lt kia 26-3-18 17LancF p92 MR27

GRIMES,John Arthur.MC.T2Lt kia 7-3-18 1RBerks p139 CR France662

GRIMMOND,Alfred 2Lt kia 14-7-16 2RScots p54 CR France164

GRIMSDELL,Gerald Lucien.MC.TCapt ded 6-7-18 8SLancs p125 CR Mddx15,28-7-18

GRIMSDELL,Reginald Edward 2Lt kia 25-9-16 4Lond p246 MR21

GRIMSELL,Gerald Lucien.MC.Capt ded 6-7-18 SLancs p264

GRIMSEY,Walter James Lt drd 3-10-18 RFus attNigR CR Lond2 Served as SINCLAIR,F.

GRIMSHAW,Cecil Thomas Wrigley.DSO.Maj kia 26-4-15 1RDubF p176 CR Gallipoli15

GRIMSHAW,Ewing Wrigley LtCol kia 21-6-16 IA 62Punjabis p277 CR Iraq5,21-1-16

GRIMSHAW,Geoffrey Harrison T2Lt kia 10-7-16 6 att8LNLancs p136 MR21

GRIMSHAW,Harold Shrieves T2Lt dow 24-5-17 Manch att21Bn p154 CR France518

GRIMSHAWE,Charles Ronald Vaughan Lt mbk 28-5-18 22DLI p256 CR France1331

GRIMSLEY,William Henry TLt kia 6-10-18 14 att9Yorks p90 CR France844

GRIMSTON,Horace Sylvester Lt kia 23-10-14 2Wilts p153 CR Belgium308,21-10-14

GRIMWADE,Arthur Macrae Capt 6-9-20 RASC CR Hamps11

GRIMWADE,Edward Ernest 2Lt kia 17-9-16 3 att9LancF p92 MR21,Lt

GRIMWOOD,Bertie Constantine Ruffell.MC.Lt kia 7-11-17 RHA attRFC p8&29 MR20

GRIMWOOD,John Chisnell Lt kia 3-12-17 5Suff p217 MR17,att2/5RWar

GRINDELL,John Flint Lotherington Capt kia 20-6-17 7DLI p239 CR Belgium29,22Bn

GRINDLAY,Alexander Brown T2Lt ded 24-3-17 11RScots p54 CR France787

GRINDLAY,William T2Lt kia 30-5-18 DLI p160 MR18

GRINDLEY,Herbert Taylor Lt kia 19-10-15 RE p45 CR Belgium6

GRINHAM,Philip Richard John Lt kia 3-5-17 10Mddx p236 MR20

GRIPPER,Edward Cutbush Capt dow 5-12-17 7YLI p143 CR France40

GRIPPER,Walter Vincent Thomas Capt kia 24-7-16 3 att1ESurr p112 CR France397

GRISEWOOD,Francis 2Lt kia 30-6-16 11RSuss p119 MR19

GRISEWOOD,George Maria Joseph Alphonsus Capt ded 27-3-16 11RSuss p119 CR France345

GRISOT,Reginald T2Lt kia 6-8-18 11RFus p68 CR France209

GRISSELL,Bernard Salwey.DSO.MajTLtCol kia 19-4-17 Cmdg1/5Norf p73 CR Palestine8

GRISSELL,Francis Lt kia 15-9-16 1CldGds p51 MR21

GRIST,Cecil Howard 2Lt kia 3-5-17 7RWKent p141 MR20

GRIST,Henry Noel T2Lt kia 27-5-17 RE 173TC p45 CR Belgium23

GRIST,Percival Charles Hugh Lt kia 18-9-18 25Lond p252 CR France369

GRIST,Ronald Lt ded 15-5-18 18RB p244 CR Burma122A

GRISTWOOD,George Harry 2Lt dow 16-9-16 3 att1Leic p87 CR France105

GRITTON,S.Lt 5-10-18 IndPostalServ CR Iraq8

GROBEL,Peter,Rev ded 1-1-17 RAChDept p199 CR France102

GROCOTT,Frederick William 2Lt kia 17-7-17 3 att6RWKent p141 MR20

GROGAN,Gerald Forman TLt kia 8-1-18 RE 183Co p45 CR Belgium23

GROGAN,Hubert Lawrence.MC.LtACapt kia 6-5-18 4Worc p108 CR France24,5-5-18

GROGAN,James Colin Lt kia 4-6-15 KOSB p101 CR Gallipoli6

GROGAN,Richard Lawrence Renny 2Lt kia 30-1-17 RE 183Coy p210 CR France374

GRONOW,Charles David T2Lt dow 18-4-18 55MGC p183 CR France88

GROOM,Cyril Lt kia 30-12-17 28Lond p252 MR21

GROOM,Noel TLt kia 20-9-17 9Yorks p90 MR30

GROOMBRIDGE,Clement Thomas 2Lt ded 23-11-15 4Leic p270 CR Essex86

GROOME,Robert Edward Charles 2Lt dow 4-3-15 65RFA p29 CR Belgium151

GROOME,Thomas Mason Capt ded 1-6-16 6Manch Res p270 CR Ches182

GROSART,William David 2Lt dow 15-4-17 5LNLancs p234

GROSE,Albert George 2Lt ded 9-11-17 GL &4RFC p8 MR20

GROSE,Guy Charles George 2Lt kia 9-10-17 9WYorks A'Coy p81 CR Belgium126

GROSE-HODGE,Dorrien Edward 2Lt kia 24-4-15 3Suff p78 CR Belgium152,27-4-15

GROSER,Arthur Geoffrey Lt kia 7-10-16 7Mddx p235 CR France374

GROSER,Arthur Hugh 2Lt kia 22-9-16 3 att1RWFus p97 CR Belgium54

GROSS,Geoffrey Yates Capt kia 9-4-16 1RWKent p141 CR France1182

GROSS,Herbert George 2Lt kia 16-9-16 9YLI p143 MR21

GROSS,Robert John T2Lt kld 26-2-18 GL &RFC p16 CR Essex185,25-2-18

GROSS,William Henry Bright 2Lt kia 3-11-16 1RWSurr p56 MR21

GROSSART,Archibald Campbell 2Lt kia 23-7-18 10Lpool att1/5SfthH p216 CR France1697

GROSSART,Robert Dykes T2Lt kld 9-2-17 18WelchR &RFC p8&126 CR Scot608

GROSSART,William David 2Lt 15-4-17 4/5LNLancs CR France255

GROSSMAN,Victor David T2Lt kia 17-9-16 24NumbF p61 CR France515,15-9-16

GROSVENOR,Hugh Williams.Lord.Capt kia 25-10-14 1LifeGds p20 MR29,30-10-14

GROSVENOR,Richard Eustace.Hon.Capt kia 13-10-15 RFA p29 CR France423

GROSVENOR,Thomas TLt kia 17-9-17 7Lincs att57RFC p8&75 CR Belgium175

GROSVENOR,Thomas Robert 2Lt kia 14-8-17 13Lond p249 MR29

GROTE,Arthur Lloyd TCapt ded 9-7-18 RE IWT p45 CR Iraq6

GROUND,Edward George Lt kia 15-8-15 11Lond p248 MR4

GROUND,Francis William T2Lt kia 25-4-17 44MGC p183 MR20

GROUND,John Kingston T2Lt kia 19-6-16 10RWKent p141 CR Belgium137

GROUNDS,Keble 2Lt dow 15-9-16 4 att2N&D p134 MR21

GROUTAGE,Joseph Harry 2Lt kia 29-3-18 8RWar att61DivHQ p215 MR27,2/5Bn

GROVE,Charles Frederick Smith.MC.TLtACapt kia 8-8-18 1TankCps p188 CR France589

GROVE,Ernest Richard 2Lt kia 10-2-18 7Lpool p215 CR Belgium112

GROVE,James Percival 2LtTCapt kia 31-7-17 9Manch p237 MR29

GROVE,John Archibald.MID TMaj kia 10-8-18 RASC HT 32DivTrn p193 CR France692

GROVE,Percival Allen 2Lt dow 7-7-16 1/5RWar p214 CR France145,5-7-16

GROVE,Philip Cranston 2Lt kia 11-4-17 2SfthH p164 CR France604,Cranstoun

GROVER,Alice Jane Sister ded 6-2-19 QAIMNS 21GH p200 CR Egypt1

GROVES,Ernest 2Lt kia 31-3-18 7EYorks p84 MR20

GROVES,Francis Neville Lt kia 8-5-15 3Mon p244 MR29

GROVES,Harold Rienzi Milton T2Lt dow 14-10-17 28MGC p183 CR Belgium23,Rienzie

GROVES,Joseph Capt ded 19-10-18 6WRid p227 CR France377

GROVES,Leonard Alloway Lt kia 3-9-15 11RSuss p119 CR France1890

GROVES,Reginald Edward T2Lt kia 9-4-18 20Mddx p147 MR32

GROVES,Richard Lt dow 24-10-17 6 att11N&D p233 CR France64

GROVES,Robert Harry.MC.2Lt dow 12-4-17 3Lond C'Coy p245 CR France120

GROWSE,John Hartley LtTCapt dow 1-4-18 2Nhampt p137 CR France145

GROWSE,Robert Henry Maj ded 12-2-19 RASC F'Cps MT Coy p193 CR Germany1

GRUBB,Donald James T2Lt kia 15-8-15 5RInniskF p105 MR4

GRUBB,Lawrence Ernest Pelham 2Lt kia 18-11-14 YLI p143 MR29

GRUBY,Thomas William T2Lt dow 19-7-16 8BordR p117 CR France40

GRUCHY,Francis Le Maistre Capt kia 22-10-14 Leic p87

GRUMMITT,Hugh Cecil 2Lt ded 25-3-19 4EYorks p270 CR Yorks46

GRUMMITT,Joseph Roland Lt ded 14-11-18 4EYorks p219 CR Yorks46

GRUNDTVIG,Humphrey Halgrim.MC.TLt dow 22-3-18 11Leic p87 CR France512

GRUNDY,Cecil Boyce 2Lt dow 16-11-15 6 att1Mddx p147 CR France80

GRUNDY,Edwin Bosworth TLt dow 19-8-18 3LNLancs att11ELancs p136 CR France134

GRUNDY,Frederick William David T2Lt dow 26-2-17 9RIrF p171 CR France145

GRUNDY,George Edward Lt kia 22-7-15 9RWar p64 MR4

GRUNDY,Ronald Edwin 2Lt kia 1-7-16 2Mddx p147 CR France393

GRUNE,Gilbert Dennis James Lt kia 13-3-16 RFA attRFC p207 CR France421

GRUSELLE,Henri Ernest John 2Lt kia 30-11-17 1/13 att1/2Lond p249 MR17

GUBBIN,John Richard Francis 2Lt dow 20-11-17 PoW 47RFC p8 CR Europe58

GUBBINS,Richard Rolls.DSO.BtLtCol drd 25-1-18 KSLI p144 CR France85,SomLI

GUDGEON,Frederick Gustavus TCapt kia 28-6-15 16 att2RFus p68 MR4

GUDGEON,Robert Eustace.MC.Capt dow PoW 2-4-18 RFA p207 CR France1266

GUDGEON,Sidney 2Lt kia 14-5-15 3 att2Manch p154 CR Belgium56,Lt

GUDGEON,Thomas Wallace Lt kia 25-8-18 5RScotF attTankCps p189&222 CR France614

GUERNSEY,Heneage Greville Finch.Lord.Capt kia 14-9-14 1IrGds p52 CR France1112

GUERRIER,Elias George TLt drd 30-11-18 GL attRE IWT p190 CR Iraq5

GUEST,Cyril Stuart T2Lt dow 5-8-16 10SStaffs att9ELancs p110 CR Greece6

GUEST,Ernest William 2Lt kia 26-2-18 RLancs att25RFC p16&59 CR France88

GUEST,Frederick Charles Herbert Lt dow 3-6-17 RASC p253 CR France1182

GUEST,Ivor Arthur Melville Lt kia 6-11-17 1CapeCps CR EAfrica1

GUEST,John Aloysius T2Lt dow 27-7-16 24 att17Mddx p147 MR21

GUEST,John Eric Cox 2Lt dow 20-9-18 7RWar CR Italy10

GUEST,Reginald Victor 2Lt dow 28-8-16 2/8RWar p215 CR France134

GUEST,Sidney 2Lt kia 11-4-18 4SLancs p230 MR19

GUEST,Thomas Heald TMaj kia 1-7-16 13Y&L p158 MR21

GUEST-WILLIAMS,Wynne Austin Capt kia 25-9-15 RBerks p139 MR32

GUILDING,John 2Lt kia 18-8-17 8Worc p226 MR30

GUILDING,Sidney Cecil Lansdowne 2Lt ded 4-11-18 106RH&FA p29 CR Italy12

GUILLEBAUD,E.C.2Lt 3-6-15 11Worc CR Somerset33

GUILLIBAND,Geoffrey Peter Lt kia 10-8-15 6LNLancs p136 MR4,GUILLEBAUD

GUINEY,Edward Castray Capt drd 14-2-18 SL attNyassalandFieldForce p201&202,KAR

GUISANI,St.John Joseph Vincent Anthony T2Lt kia 13-11-16 10RDubF p176 CR France220,GIUSANI

GUISE,Henry George Christopher Lt kia 6-5-15 5Glouc p225 CR Belgium70

GUISE,James William T2Lt dow 19-8-17 5 O&BLI p130 CR Belgium8

GUISE,Reginald Edward.MC.Lt kia 29-6-18 12GloucYeo p203 CR France352

GULBENKIAN,Krikor T2Lt kia 20-9-17 Mddx att23Bn p147 MR30

GULL,Francis William Lindley CaptAMaj kia 25-8-18 1 att13RB p179 CR France518

GULL,Leonard Joseph T2Lt kia 24-7-17 90MGC p183 MR29

GULLAND,Alexander Falkland Lt dow 16-6-17 3EKent p57 CR Belgium11,Capt 8Bn

GULLICK Arthur Louis TLt kia 3-10-15 EKent p57 CR France552

GULLILAND John Hutchison TCapt dow 18-7-16 11Ess p131 CR Belgium11

GUMBLEY,Donald Charles Beric 2Lt kia 3-9-16 3 att1Wilts p153 MR21

GUMMER,Basil Austin 2Lt kia 12-8-16 1/9Lpool p216 MR21

GUMMER,Fred T2Lt kia 9-8-18 15TankCps p188 CR France526

GUMMER,Stanley Capt kia 9-10-17 5Y&L p238 MR30

GUNDILL,Robert Percy 2Lt kia 2-10-18 YLI &108RAF p265 MR20

GUNDLE,G.W.Lt kia 27-9-17 KAR p202

GUNDRY,William Lt&QM ded 19-1-18 GL p190 CR Lancs179

GUNINGHAM,William John Lt&QM 18-5-15 ShropYeo CR Lond4 Ex RHG

GUNN,Arthur T2Lt kia 5-5-15 2WRid p115 MR29

GUNN,Charles Mortimer Austin Capt kia 20-5-17 5ScotRif p224 MR20

GUNN,David TLt kia 13-10-17 SfthH att7Bn p164 CR Belgium123

GUNN,Edmond Alan 2Lt ded 13-2-19 RGA 77SB p39 CR Belgium265

GUNN,James Campbell T2Lt kia 27-5-18 Hamps att2RBerks p120 MR18

GUNN,Kenneth Lt kia 14-4-16 3 att1BlltW p120 CR France178,4-4-16 2 att1Bn

GUNN,Marcus Sinclair..C Lt dow 6-9-16 1BlkW p128 CR France833

GUNN,Murray Grant 2Lt kia 7-12-17 23RFC p8 MR20

GUNN,Ronald William Craig 2Lt kia 6-1-17 3 att12N&D p134 CR France115

GUNN,Walter Roderick Hamilton 2Lt kia 1-9-18 3Lond p245 CR France216

GUNN,Wilfred Herbert 2Lt kia 26-3-18 331RFA p29 MR27

GUNNELL,J.F.R Lt 8-4-20 Dors att51War CR Germany1

GUNNER,Arthur Henry Edmund T2Lt kia 26-3-18 11RSuss p119 CR France402

GUNNER,Benjamin George,MC LtTCapt kia 7-10-15 1NumbF p61 CR Belgium6

GUNNER,Frank Lt kia 14-4-18 4 att12ScotRif p103 MR32

GUNNER,John Hugh Capt dow 9-8-18 HampsYeo att15HampsR p203 CR Belgium21

GUNNER,William Henry.MC.2Lt kia 29-7-17 GL &60RFC p8 CR France924

GUNNERY,Cedric Leopold T2Lt kia 22-5-17 GL &46RFC p8 CR France354

GUNNING,Edward George Francis TCapt ded 10-6-19 RFA attRAOC p254 CR France65,acckld

GUNNING,Frank Douglas 2Lt kia 1-7-16 6 att11RInniskF p105 MR21

GUNNING,John Walter 2Lt kia 24-3-18 1Wilts p153 MR20

GUNNING,Orlando George.CMG.DSO.MID BrigGen ded 14-11-17 IA 36Sikhs p277 CR SAfrica172

GUNNING,William Herbert 2Lt dow 31-10-16 3 att10Hamps p120 CR Europe1

GUNNIS,Geoffrey George.MC.TCapt dow 13-10-16 3GrenGds p50 CR France145

GUNNIS,Ian Fitzgerald Stuart 2Lt kia 4-7-17 2GrenGds p50 CR Belgium84

GUNSON,Henry Edward Rev ded 23-8-18 RAChDept p199 CR Hamps10

GUNSON,Leslie Robert Schrader TLt kia 18-7-16 RGA 31HB p39 CR France399

GUNSTON,Frederic John Dover.MC.LtACapt dow PoW 14-7-18 6Worc p108 CR France1027,2Bn

GUNTER,Francis James Lt kia 24-5-15 11Huss p22 MR29

GUNTER,Robert Benson Nevill.Bart.LtCol ded 16-8-17 SL 3Yorks p201 CR Belgium5,Benyon

GUNTHER,Charles Emil TLt kia 24-9-18 2LifeGds att2GdsMGReg p20&53 CR France1701

GUNTHER,Geoffrey Robert.MC.2Lt kia 4-11-18 3GrenGds p50 CR France1080

GUNTHER,Norman Otto Frederick.MC.2Lt kia 11-7-17 att6REKentYeo p204 MR20,12-7-17

GUNTON,John Welby 2Lt kia 9-8-16 9SomLI &70RFC p3&79 MR20

GUNTON,Reginald Oliver 2Lt kia 21-3-18 3Lond p245 CR France1893

GURDON,Philip Norman Lt kia 9-10-16 IA 14Sikhs attJindInf p277 CR EAfrica36,Capt

GURNELL,Robert Matthew T2Lt kia 21-5-17 18RIrRif p169 CR Belgium100

GURNEY,Elizabeth Shepherd SNurse drd 10-4-17 QAIMNS p200 CR France85

GURNEY,Frederick Arthur T2Lt ded 23-3-16 5Nhampt p137 CR France40

GURNEY,Kenneth Gerard 2Lt ded PoW 17-12-17 5Glouc p225 CR France660,dow

GURRIN,Reginald Wells 2Lt dow 5-8-17 3 att12ESurr p112 CR Belgium167

GUSH,William George T2LtACapt kia 23-4-17 RFus p68 CR France777

GUTHE,Cecil Rudolph Lt 10-2-19 RGA CR Durham180

GUTHE,Thomas Percival Maj dow 13-1-16 1DurhamRFA p206 CR France40

GUTHRIE,Albert John Lt kia 30-7-16 5GordH p242 MR21

GUTHRIE,Alexander Capt ded 29-12-16 RDC 35ProtCoy p253 CR Scot386

GUTHRIE,Alexander Lt kia 12-7-17 1HighlandRFA Y32TMB p207 CR Belgium173

GUTHRIE,Arthur Calderwood 2Lt kld 9-8-18 RE att42RAF p45 CR France31

GUTHRIE,Charles Wilford 2Lt kia 1-8-17 13RScots p54 CR Belgium125

GUTHRIE,David Michall Chap4Cl dow 21-11-16 RAChDept att8ELancsp199 CR France41

GUTHRIE,George Watson TLt kia 13-11-16 RAMC RNDiv p195 CR France220

GUTHRIE,Hector MacLennan Lt kia 4-6-15 3 att1LancF p92 MR4

GUTHRIE,Hugh Smith 2Lt ded PoW 31-3-18 7BlkW p231 CR France924,dow

GUTHRIE,John Mack.MC.Capt kia 28-7-18 6BlkW p231 CR France1689

GUTHRIE,John Noel Capt kia 18-5-15 IrGds p52 CR France727

GUTHRIE,Robert Forman Capt kia 9-8-16 10Lpool p216 MR21

GUTHRIE,Robert Gilbert Lt ded 7-11-18 3RFA p207 CR Yorks3

GUTHRIE,Stuart 2Lt kia 4-4-18 5 att2/6Lond p246 MR20

GUTHRIE,Thomas T2Lt dow 27-6-18 6CamH p168 CR Scot752

GUTHRIE,Thomas Errol Capt kia 3-7-16 RAMC attNZ MedCps p195

GUTHRIE,William Colville 2Lt ded 7-11-18 C52RFA p208 CR France403

GUTHRIE,Willie Forrester Lt kia 26-4-18 4 att9ScotRif p103 CR Belgium74

GUTHRIE-SMITH,Ronald Cameron 2Lt kia 19/22-12-14 1HLI p163 CR France644,Lt 20-12-14

GUTMANN,Walter 2Lt dow 7-5-17 D71RFA p29 CR France40

GUTTERIDGE,Eric Lancelot T2Lt kia14-7-16 10Leic p87 MR21

GUTTERIDGE,Richard Charley Lt kia 28-5-18 2/6 att15DLI p239 CR France1331

GUTTERIDGE,Richard Howard 2Lt kia 2-10-16 9Lond p248 MR21

GUY,Christopher Godfrey Capt dow PoW 12-8-17 1/4Nhampt C'Coy attRFC p18&234 CR Belgium5

GUY,Norman Glass 2Lt kia 27-5-18 3 att7Leic p87 MR18

GUY,Reginald Churchill T2Lt kia 24-8-18 8RBerks p139 CR France177

GUY,Ronald Litterdale Lt kia 26-10-17 6 att1/7NumbF p213 MR30,Lidderdale

GUYON,George Sutherland LtCol kia 1-7-16 2RFus p68 MR21

GWYER,Alexander Grant Capt kia 22-10-14 6DragGds RoO p21 CR Belgium74,Alastair

GWYER,Charles Percy Capt kia 8-8-15 1 att8WelshR p126 MR4

GWYER,Cyril Lt kia 27-8-18 2GrenGds p50 CR France614

GWYN,Reginald Augustine Jerome 2Lt dow 3-3-16 2Lincs p75 MR29,Jermy

GWYNN John Chap4Cl dow 12-10-15 RAChDept att1IrGds p199 CR France80

GWYNNE,Henry Stanley 2Lt kia 24-11-17 6RWar p214 CR Belgium111

GWYNNE,Hubert Llewellyn 2Lt kia 18-11-16 8NStaffs p157 MR21

GWYNNE,John Fitzgerald.MC.MID Capt kia 9-7-15 RAMC p195 CR Belgium85

GWYNNE,L.H.Lt 10-3-18 EAUL CR EAfrica10 &CR Tanzania1

GWYNNE,Owen Perrott 2Lt kia 7-1-16 IARO att92Punjabis MR38 p277

GWYNNE,Roderick Thynne Sackville 2Lt dow 23-5-15 4YLI p235

GWYNNE-GRIFFITH,Gilbert Digby Mansel TLtACapt dow 2-7-18 RE attSPersiaRif p45 CR Asia82

GWYNNE-VAUGHAN,Kenneth Duncan T2Lt kia 6-9-16 15RFus att33MGC Inf p68&183 CR France296

GWYTHER,Edwin Thomas T2Lt dow 28-5-18 SStaffs att1/6Bn p122 CR France40

GWYTHER,Guy Llewelyn T2Lt kia 6-1-16 2Leic p87 MR38

GYE,Denison Allen TLtACapt kia 28-2-17 15RHA p29 CR France786

GYLE,Ernest Woods 2Lt kia 18-10-18 7BlkW p231 CR France1271

GYLLENCREUTZ,James Randolph TMaj drd 10-4-17 RAMC p195 CR France85

GYVES,John James T2Lt kia 3-6-18 11RDubF p176 CR France24,1Bn

H

HAARER,Philip McLellan 2Lt kia 28-11-16 15RFC p3 CR France41,22-11-16

HAASE,Edward George Louis T2Lt kia 3-7-16 9 att5RBerks p139 MR21

HABERSHON,Kenneth Rees TCapt kia 12-2-16 12RB p179 CR Belgium5

HABERSHON,Leonard Osborne TCapt kia 13-11-16 12EYorks p84 MR21

HABERSHON,Philip Henry T2Lt kia 25-9-15 9KRRC p150 MR29

HABERSHON,Sidney Heathcote 2Lt kia 8/13-4-18 12Suff p78 MR32

HABLUTZEL,George Rudolph 2Lt kia 1-7-16 1RLancs p59 MR21

HACK,Adrian Henry TLt kia 1-7-16 8YLI p143 CR France246

HACK,Charles Edward Capt kia 5-11-14 ConnRgrs p172 MR22

HACK,John Frederick Charles Lt kia 26-9-16 RGA 117HB p39 CR France401

HACKER,Norman Capt kld 26-10-17 2Dors p124 CR Iraq8

HACKETT,David Frederick Mackness.MM.Lt kia 22-8-18 1Leic p87 CR France383

HACKETT,Eric Adrian Nethercote T2Lt kia 9-9-16 6RIrReg p89 MR21

HACKETT,Harry Osborne 2LtTLt dow 28-8-17 11WelchR p126 CR Belgium16,Osbourn 16Bn

HACKETT,Henry Robert Theodore 2Lt kia 2-11-15 1RDubF p176 CR Gallipoli4

HACKETT,Learo Aylmer Henry.MC.TCapt kia 24-4-18 10RIrRif p169 CR Belgium64

HACKETT,Venice Clementine Henrietta Miss ded 13-10-18 VAD BRCS p200 CR Eire476

HACKETT,Walter Ralph TLt kia 3-10-16 7RWKent p141 MR21

HACKETT,William TLt ded 15-11-18 RE Ex 8SStaffs p45 CR Staffs67

HACKFORTH-JONES,Arthur Lt kia 8-8-18 3Glouc att7RWKent p106 MR16

HACKING,Walter William 2Lt kia 21-3-18 N&D att2/8Bn p134 MR20

HADDEN,Archibald Robert Capt kia 25-4-18 9Lond p247 CR France425

HADDEN,Arthur.MC.2Lt kia 8-3-16 IARO att53Sikhs MR38 p277

HADDEN,Cyril Martin ACapt kia 28-3-18 3 att1RScotF p94 MR20

HADDEN,Eustace Waller Russell Maj ded 11-6-16 1/4 O&BLI p231 CR France51

HADDEN,Francis Albert Lt 22-6-19 RAMC CR Mddx42

HADDEN,Frank John TLt ded 5-5-16 RemountServ 42RASC p24 CR Egypt9

HADDEN,John Hazlett Millar T2Lt kia 31-10-16 20RIrRif p169 CR Greece3

HADDEN,Nigel Clement Charles TCapt dow 9-4-16 RFA 14Bty p29 MR38

HADDER,Robert 2Lt kia 19-7-16 5Glouc attMGC p225

HADDOCK,Joseph Henry T2Lt kia 24-3-18 14RIrRif p169 CR France1203

HADDOCK,Wilfrid Spencer T2Lt dow 16-7-17 9SLancs p125 CR Greece7,Spence

HADDOCK,William.MC.TLt kia 24-9-18 1WYorks p81 CR France835

HADDOCK,William Theodore TLt ded 30-1-16 1/5Suff p217 CR Egypt3

HADDON,Harold Esmond.MIDx3 Lt kia 24-12-15 IA 119Inf p277 CR Iraq1

HADDON,Harwood Albert T2Lt kia 26-9-17 att2/8N&D p134 CR Belgium125

HADDON,Hugh Reid Capt ded 12-7-15 5RScotF p222

HADDON,Thomas Capt dow 20-4-18 PoW 2/7Ches p222 CR France934

HADDON,Vernon 2Lt kia 10-8-17 11RFus p68 MR29

HADDON,Walter T2Lt dow 27-9-15 7KOSB p101 MR19,25-9-15

HADDON-SMITH,Walter Basil Capt kia 16-5-15 RWSurr p56 MR22

HADDOW,H.R Capt 12-7-15 5RScotF CR Egypt

HADDY,Stephen Edgar 2Lt dow 16-8-17 4Hamps p228 CR Belgium16

HADEN,Frederick Haughton 2Lt kia 4-11-17 1RB att11TMB p179 CR France154

HADENHAM,Lawrence George T2Lt dow 18-7-16 9ESurr p112 CR France285,Lt

HADFIELD,Edgar T2Lt kia 22-3-17 10WelshR p126 CR Belgium23

HADFIELD,James Robert TLt ded 9-3-16 13Manch p154 CR Greece7

HADFIELD,Wilfred John Mackenzie Lt ded 10-9-14 SLancs p125 CR France1845 &CR France34,dow

HADINGHAM,Roy Matthew Lt kia 22-6-16 4Glouc p225 MR19,26-6-16

HADLAND,Spencer Austin Capt kia 24-3-18 2RB p179 MR27

HADLEY,Cyril Vernon 2Lt kia 3-7-16 10Worc p108 MR21

HADLEY,Ernest Sidney 2Lt kia 27-8-17 4Glouc p225 MR30

HADLEY,Peyton Sheldon.MC.TLtACapt ded 24-10-18 7Nhampt p137 CR Norf60,25-10-18

HADLEY,Reginald Bracebridge Lt mbk 31-10-14 1/2SWBord p256 MR29

HADOW,Arthur de Salis BtCol kia 27-9-15 10Yorks p80 CR France551,15Bn

HADOW,Erlan Godfrey.MC.TCapt kia 29-5-17 17WYorks p81 CR France415

HADOW,Gerald Francis Lt kia 15-6-15 2Yorks p90 MR22

HADRILL,Arthur William TLt kia 12-8-15 9Lincs attRMunstF p75 MR4

HADWEN,Charles Eugene.MM.T2Lt kia 12-9-18 RB att13Bn p179 MR16

HADWEN,Noel Waugh Capt kia 1-7-16 2WRid p115 MR21

HAEFFNER,Frederick Wilfred 2Lt kia 9-7-16 149RFA p29 CR France699,151RFA

HAGGAR,Harry Douglas Fox Lt kia 17-8-16 3LNLancs p136 CR France630

HAGGARD,Mark Capt dow 15-9-14 2WelchR p126 CR France1329

HAGGART,David Lt kia 14-6-18 1SfthH p164 CR Palestine9,3Bn

HAGGART,James 2Lt dow 3-1-18 4 att14BlkW p230 CR Palestine9

HAGGART,William Jackson Lt kia 31-8-18 4Glouc p225 CR France518,12Bn

HAGGARTY,John Joseph T2Lt dow 11-9-16 29 att22NumbF p61 CR France275,kia

HAGGER,William Alexander Capt ded 12-7-15 126Baluchis MR43

HAGGO,Aubrey Paxton 2Lt kia 18-8-16 4RScotF p222&221 CR France832

HAGON,Charles Douglas 2Lt dow 3-8-17 4SomLI p218 CR France52,8Bn

HAGUE,Albert Edward 2Lt kia 5-8-16 1/4LNLancs p234 MR21

HAGUE,Harold William 2Lt kia 16-6-18 D47RFA p29 CR France98

HAGUE,James Herbert 2Lt kia 23-4-17 7Manch p237 MR20

HAGUE,Leonard 2Lt kia 26-4-18 13Glouc p106 MR30

HAGUE,Sydney George.MC.TLt dow 21-9-18 1/2Beds p86 CR France194

HAGUE,Walter 2Lt dow 31-3-18 PoW 2/5N&D p232 CR Belgium241

HAHN,Benno Oscar Linsengen T2Lt kld 13-10-17 GL &RFC p8 CR Wilts116,Linsingen

HAIG,Alexander Weir.MM.2Lt dow 17-10-18 1 att1/5GordH p166 CR France163,Lt

HAIG,David T2Lt kld 5-7-18 4/5BlkW p128 CR France145

HAIG,Ernest Herman LtCol ded 28-12-14 RE p45 CR Essex81

HAIG-BROWN,Alan Roderick.DSO.LtCol kia 25-3-18 23Mddx p147 CR France518

HAIG-SMELLIE,Herbert Hamilton T2Lt dow 26-4-17 7Norf p73 CR France113,kia

HAIGH,Allen Mortimer T2Lt kia 13-4-18 RLancs att1/4YLI p59 MR30

HAIGH,Arthur Gordon 2Lt kia 15-2-16 RE 172Coy p45 MR29

HAIGH,Charles Roderick Lt 7-11-14 RWSurr p56 MR29

HAIGH,Edward 2Lt kia 19-12-15 5YLI p235 CR Belgium23

HAIGH,James Aspinall Lt dow 22-11-17 2/5WRid p227 CR France398

HAIGH,John Caleb 2Lt kia 2-10-18 3RDubF attRIrRif p176 CR Belgium157

HAILE,Robert.MC.TLt dow 29-10-18 10Ess p131 CR France1392

HAILES,Joseph HonCapt kia 1-9-15 RAOC p198 CR Gallipoli18,DADOS 54EAngliaDiv

HAILSTONE,Dudley William T2Lt kia 7-7-18 1DCLI p114 CR France20

HAILSTONE,George Rupert Capt kia 6-11-17 1/7RWFus p223 CR Palestine1

HAILSTONE,Ralph Puroglove T2Lt kia 18-10-16 13 att2Hamps p120 MR21,Pursglove

HAILWOOD,John 2Lt kia 15-10-18 1/4LNLancs p234 CR France1725,16-10-18

HAIN,Edward Capt kia 11-11-15 1DevYeo p203 CR Gallipoli27

HAIN,Edward Sydney T2Lt kia 21-11-17 KRRC att11Bn p150 MR17

HAINES,Alec C.Lt dow 8-5-15 RDubF p176

HAINES,Alexander Crichton Cooper 2Lt dow 8-5-15 2RDubF CR France102

HAINES,Alfred Godfrey Victor TLt dow 22-4-17 15N&D p134 CR France674,G.A.V.

HAINES,Ernest Andrade T2Lt kia 3-9-16 11 att9ESurr p112 MR21

HAINES,Ernest Edward.MC.T2Lt ded 11-2-17 14Lpool p72 CR Berks125

HAINES,Frank Percy Lt kia 15-6-17 8Leic p87 MR20,16-6-17

HAINES,Herbert Henry 2Lt kia 15-5-17 3Lond p245 CR France536

HAINES,Stephen Gilbert 2Lt dow 4-5-17 C70RFA p29 CR France40

HAINING,William John 2Lt kia 28-1-17 3 att1KOSB p101 MR21

HAINING,William Stobo T2Lt kia 20-11-17 TankCps p188 CR France712

HAINSBY,Fernley Winter 2Lt kia 26-3-18 RFC p16 MR20

HAIR,Donald Campbell 2Lt kia 3-10-16 6KSLI p145 MR21

HAIR,Eric Francis Wilson T2Lt dow 27-8-17 2Mddx p147 CR Lond28,Edwin

HAIRE,George TLt dow 7-1-16 6ConnRgrs p172 CR Belgium17

HAIRSINE,Owen.MC.LtTCapt kia 7-6-17 RAMC p195 CR Belgium2

HAIST,Orville Dwight T2Lt kld 5-7-17 GL &37TrSqnRFC p8 CR Lincs181

HAIZELDEN,Benjamin 2Lt dow 30-8-18 2/10Lond p248 CR France119

HAKE,Osmond George 2Lt kld 14-5-16 GL &RFC p3 CR Hamps15,Ormond

HAKEWILL,Thomas George T2Lt kldacc 11-2-16 11NStaffs att17RFC p3&157 CR Egypt3

HALCOMB,Leslie Broughton Maj kia 25-10-18 B295RFA p206 CR France1044

HALCOMBE,Norman Marshall TMaj ded 13-2-19 RE attRAF p255 CR Egypt7

HALCROW,Arthur Palmer Lt kia 23-4-17 3 att2Hamps p120 MR20

HALCROW,John William 2LtTLt kia 7-7-16 3Dors &4RFC p3&124 CR France44

HALCROW,Thomas Tulloch 2Lt kia 3-5-17 1 att2RScots p54 MR20

HALDANE,Arthur Cuthbert T2Lt kia 14-8-16 10SforthH p164 CR Belgium23

HALDANE,Colin Kennedy 2Lt dow 18-10-16 26Manch attMGC p154&183 CR France513

HALDANE,Douglas William 2Lt dow 9-4-17 9HLI p240 CR France1182

HALDANE,James Oswald 2Lt dow 9-8-16 6RB p179 CR Belgium73

HALDANE,Laurence Aylmer.DSO.TMaj kia 2-4-17 2Nhampt &Staffs p137 CR France480

HALDANE,Robert Patrick Lt dow 13-6-15 6BlkW p231 CR France1106

HALDEN,Alexander 2Lt drd 26-2-18 GL RE &IWT p190 MR38

HALDINSTEIN,Frank Worlfe Capt dow 7-3-17 RE p210

HALE,Alfred LLewellyn TCapt kia 8-7-18 10RWSurr p56 CR Belgium11

HALE,Frank Ernest T2Lt kia 25-8-18 13KRRC p150 CR France578

HALE,George Edwin T2Lt kia 22-3-18 39MGC p183 MR27

HALE,Harold John 2Lt kia 24-3-18 15DLI p160 MR27

HALE,Herbert Charles Lt dow 2-11-17 4Yorks p220 CR Belgium16

HALE,S.F.Lt ded 31-5-19 12Hamps p120

HALE,William T2Lt dow 9-8-18 2Worc p108 CR France34,1Bn

HALE,William John Douglas TCapt kia 28-4-17 10RWFus p97 CR France531

HALE,William Webb Lt ded 12-4-17 2/6ESurr attRDC p253 CR Surrey 83

HALES,Arthur Hoare.MC.TCapt kia 6-7-16 1Wilts p153 MR21

HALES,Charles Edward Hoare 2Lt ded 22-11-17 1Wilts p265 CR Somerset30

HALES,Eli George LtCol ded 23-11-18 RE Res p270 CR Sussex112

HALES,Walter Percy Capt ded 1-11-18 IARO att3/124BaluchistanInf p277 CR Asia82

HALES,William Clifford T2Lt kia 23-10-16 8 att2RBerks p139 CR France307

HALEY,Arthur 2Lt kia 1-6-18 3Ess &55RAF p131 CR France1667

HALFACRE,Cecil William T2Lt ded 19-10-16 7RBerks attTMB p139 CR Greece1

HALFHIDE,Charles Edward Nelson TLtAMaj kia 24-5-18 7ELancs attMGC p110&183 CR France41

HALFORD,Arthur Henry.DCM.2Lt dow PoW 30-5-18 RB att7Bn p179 CR France1615

HALFORD,Edward Frederick TLt ded 10-10-18 RE p45&257 CR Surrey104,Frederic

HALFORD,William Stanley 2Lt kia 15-9-16 20Lond p251 CR France432

HALFPENNY,William Henry 2Lt dedacc 24-11-18 11LancF att49RAF p92 CR Lancs2,Lt

HALL,Alan Ryder Lt kia 30-5-18 6NumbF p213 MR18

HALL,Albert Loader TCapt kia 4-4-18 8ESurr D'Coy p112 CR France424

HALL,Alexander Kilburn Capt kia 7-10-16 6RWKent p141 MR21

HALL,Allan Bernard Lt kia 3-5-17 ACycCps att11EYorks p181 MR20

HALL,Allan Gordon Maj kia 24-4-18 C210RFA p206 CR France745

HALL,Arthur Ernest Lt mbk 22-8-15 6Yorks p256 MR4

HALL,Arthur Gordon.MID Capt kia 26-10-14 2Beds D'Coy p86 CR Belgium115

HALL,Arthur Henry.MC.TLtACapt kia 19-11-16 2 att8SomLI p79 CR France339

HALL,Arthur James Melville 2Lt kia 15-9-16 20Lond p251 MR21

HALL,Aubrey Frederick TLt kia 8-8-18 RE 92FC p45 CR France209

HALL,Basil Claude Capt kia 25-8-18 8Manch p237 CR France643

HALL,Bruce Lt kia 25-9-15 SStaffs p122 MR19

HALL,Burton Howard Capt kia 4-11-14 IA 98Inf p277 MR47

HALL,Cecil Charles Hatfield.DSO.MIDx2 Maj kia 27-5-18 22DLI p160 MR18

HALL,Charles 2Lt dow 13 8 16 O&rDLI DucksBn p231 MR21

HALL,Charles 2Lt kia 28-3-17 8EKent attM'LTMB p57 CR France161

HALL,Charles Sidney T2Lt kia 7-4-17 GL &60RFC p8 CR France581

HALL,Charles Stuart 2Lt kia 12-1-17 1Mon p244 CR France1014

HALL,Charles William Lt dow 10-8-17 465/65RFA p29 CR France139

HALL,Clarence Espent Lyon TLt kia 7-7-16 5SWBord p100

HALL,Clifford Sheppard T2Lt kia 3-7-16 6RWSurr p56 CR France251

HALL,David Henry TCapt dow 14-5-18 RAMC att2SfthH p195 CR France10

HALL,David Sidney.MC.Capt kia 20-11-17 9A&SH attRFC p18&243 CR France134

HALL,Douglas Alexander TLt kia 25-4-17 10Y&L p158 CR France1193,Capt 23-4-17

HALL,Durham Donald George.MC.2LtTCapt dow 27-3-18 Yorks att80RFC p16&90 CR France62,kia

HALL,Edward Charles 2Lt kia 30-11-17 13Ess p131 MR17

HALL,Edward Henry TLt kld 27-11-16 DCLI attRFC p3 CR Yorks38

HALL,Edward Lawrence 2Lt kia 30-11-17 att1/5LNLancs p136 MR17

HALL,Edward Lionel T2Lt kia 27-3-18 9RSuss p119 MR27

HALL,Edwin Lincoln.MC.2Lt kia 22-4-17 3 att2Leic p87 MR38

HALL,Eric Watson.MBE.Capt kia 26-9-17 2/4Lincs p220&270 CR Belgium101

HALL,Ernest Leslie 2Lt kia 21-3-18 att2Wilts p153 MR27

HALL,Ernest Louis T2Lt dow 6-11-17 11Leic p87 CR Belgium11,5-11-17

HALL,Frances Mary.RRC.MID Matron ded 7-7-19 QAIMNS p268 MR43

HALL,Francis Edward Charles 2Lt kia 16-8-16 2Suff p78 MR21

HALL,Francis Henry T2Lt kia 30-9-18 1 att9RIrF p171 CR Belgium157 ExRIrRif

HALL,Frank Leslie Lt kia 27-8-17 4Glouc p225 MR30

HALL,Fred 2Lt kia 22-9-16 Dors attRFC p3&124 CR France294

HALL,Frederick Grainger TCapt kia 7-7-16 13Ches p96 CR France1890,Frederic

HALL,G.L.D.2Lt kld 2-5-18 GL &RAF p190

HALL,Geoffrey T2Lt kia 23-10-16 2Mddx p147 MR21

HALL,Geoffrey.MC.TLt kia 20-11-17 9RFus p68 MR17

HALL,Geoffrey Evans T2Lt kia 25-4-17 1 att9Norf p73 CR France149

HALL,George.MID Capt dow 23-4-18 14Lond p249 CR France39

HALL,George Dorrington Lt dow 17-9-18 1/5Dev p217 CR France1184

HALL,George Elliott 2Lt dow 29-5-18 RGA 196SB p39 CR France95,kia

HALL,George Ferrier Mansfield Lt kia 28-9-15 RBerks p139 MR19

HALL,George Foden Rooking T2Lt kia 28-6-17 RE 103FC p45 CR Belgium29

HALL,George Hanney Lt ded 6-12-19 IARO att4/39GarhwalRif p277 MR40,Capt

HALL,George Henry.MSM.T2Lt kld 24-12-17 RFC p8 CR Nhampt

HALL,George Wilfred 2Lt kia 20-11-17 GL &3RFC p8 CR France336

HALL,Gerald Percy 2Lt kia 13-11-14 4 att2HLI p163 CR Belgium126

HALL,Gilbert Sudbury 2Lt dow PoW 30-11-16 RFC p3 CR France598

HALL,Gordon William 2Lt kld 21-8-16 GL &3RFC p3&190 CR Norf209,Lt

HALL,H.W.Lt 24-12-20 Manch CR Sussex110

HALL,Harford Greville 2LtTLt kia 4-3-17 1N&D p134 MR21

HALL,Harold T2Lt kia 15-2-16 7Lincs p75 MR29

HALL,Harold Platt.MC.2Lt dow 9-11-18 C83RFA p29 CR France146

HALL,Harry Herbert 2Lt kia 2-12-17 6N&D p233 CR France668

HALL,Harry Spencer Lt ded 14-3-15 RAMC p195 CR Staffs125

HALL,Harry Sydney Hopton Hadley Capt ded 24-10-18 3RWKent p141 CR India97A

HALL,Henry Capt kld 25-9-18 RFA 18AC p207 CR Palestine3,kia

HALL,Henry Armstrong.CBE.Rev 12-5-21 CR Yorks381

HALL,Henry Cecil T2Lt kia 4-10-17 Hamps att1Bn p120 MR30

HALL,Henry Charles T2Lt kia 4-9-18 Wilts att15Hamps p153 MR30

HALL,Henry Guy Fitzwilliam TLt kia 13-11-16 10DCLI p114 CR France1491

HALL,Henry John 2Lt kia 19/20-7-16 54AustInf CR France82

HALL,Henry Lewes.MM.2Lt kia 30-11-17 KRRC att10Bn p150 MR17,Lewis

HALL,Henry Leonard Lt kia 27-10-18 RGA 14SB p39 CR France1271

HALL,Herbert Cecil Victor TLt kia 13-6-17 12DLI p160 CR Belgium127

HALL,Herbert John 2Lt kia 7-4-17 5GordH p242 CR France15

HALL,Herbert John Elliott Lt ded 7-2-19 RFA p254 CR Lond3

HALL,Hugh.MC.Lt kia 15-9-17 9DLI p239 CR France538

HALL,Hugh Wilfred 2Lt kia 15-5-17 2/3Lond p245 MR20

HALL,Humphrey Evans LtTCapt kia 27-11-15 2Norf p73 MR38,23-11-15

HALL,J.W.H.Capt ded 19-10-18 TankCps 776RFA CR Essex75

HALL,James Henry 2Lt kld 26-7-18 6LancF &RAF p255

HALL,James Herbert William TLtACapt ded 19-10-18 TankCps p188&261,RH&FA

HALL,James Hervey Lt 25-8-18 LancF &RAF CR Lancs263

HALL,James Muir 2Lt dow 23-4-17 51RFA p29 CR France1182

HALL,James Thomson T2Lt dow 9-6-17 9YLI p143 CR France40,8Bn

HALL,John Edward Kenyon 2Lt dow 22-9-15 3 att2SWBord p100 MR4

HALL,John Francis Ashley 2Lt kia 14-8-18 1EYorks &21RAF p84 CR France88

HALL,John Gilbert 2Lt kia 3-5-17 6WYorks p218 MR20

HALL,John Martindale 2Lt kia 28-8-16 3 att8BordR p117 CR France246

HALL,John McRobb T2Lt kia 1-7-16 21NumbF p61 MR21

HALL,John Pearson Herbert T2Lt kia 1-11-18 19NumbF p61 CR Belgium143

HALL,John Ramsay Fitz-Gibbon 2Lt kia 24-5-15 2RDubF p176 MR29

HALL,John Reginald T2Lt kia 10-7-16 15WelshR p126 MR21

HALL,John Smith Lt kia 21-3-18 7RB p179 MR27

HALL,Joseph T2Lt kia 31-7-17 72MGC p183 MR29

HALL,Joseph Stanley 2Lt kia 5-5-17 12EYorks p84 MR20

HALL,Kenneth Stuart TLt kia 25-1-16 15NumbF att21DivACycCps p61 CR France922

HALL,Louis Sylvester Lt kia 27-5-18 RE 490FC p210 MR18

HALL,Luther T2Lt kia 22-9-16 22RFA p29 CR France397,21-9-16

HALL,M.E.A.2Lt ded 27-3-15 14WYorks p81

HALL,Malcolm Wilfrid Forrester Lt kia 20-5-17 5 att1RInniskF p105&257 MR20,Wilfred

HALL,Mark Walter 2Lt kia 5-12-17 2/7N&D p233 CR France1498

HALL,Miles Arthur 2Lt kia 23-4-17 150MGC p183 MR20

HALL,Norman Bodger.MC.TLt dow 2-11-18 12DLI att68TMB p160 CR Italy9

HALL,Norman de Haviland T2Lt dow 7-10-16 1Suff p78 CR Greece7

HALL,Percy George T2Lt kia 30-6-16 23 att26NumbF p61 CR France430

HALL,Percy Mark Capt ded 4-1-19 13Beds p86

HALL,Percy Shene Bernard Capt kia 9-8-16 1EKent p57 CR Belgium47,Sheen

HALL,Peveril Austin 2Lt ded 5-11-18 RE p45 CR Nhampt31

HALL,Ralph Gordon T2Lt kld 23-1-18 GL &RFC p16 CR Canada256

HALL,Ralph Prescott TLt ded 22-3-19 RAOC p267 CR Yorks98

HALL,Reginald 2Lt kia 8-10-18 4Wilts p236 CR France234

HALL,Reginald Clifford.MC.LtACapt kia 20-11-17 5Y&L p238 CR France530

HALL,Robert Lane 2Lt kia 27-5-18 2Nhampt p137 MR18

HALL,Robert Macpherson Maj ded 8-7-15 IA 25Cav att6 p277 MR43

HALL,Roger Holinsworth TLtACapt dow 11-7-17 RFA AntiAircraftGrp p29 CR Belgium24,12-7-17

HALL,Samuel Lt kia 4-6-15 8Manch p237 MR4

HALL,Sidney LtACapt dow 21-3-18 RGA146Bty p39 MR20

HALL,Stanley Alexander Lt dow 10-4-18 RE 156Coy p210 CR France145

HALL,Sydney Lt kia 18-10-18 Manch &RAF p154

HALL,Theodore Newman Lt dow 15-8-16 4 O&BLI p231

HALL,Thomas Lt&QM ded 21-10-17 HLI p265 CR Scot525

HALL,Thomas 2Lt kia 27-3-18 4NumbF p213 MR27,1/6Bn

HALL,Thomas 2Lt dow 19-6-18 4 att11Ess attTMB p232 CR France142

HALL,Thomas Kershaw 2Lt kia 9-10-17 RFA 6/241Bde p29 MR30

HALL,Thomas Storey Inglis 2Lt kia 9-4-16 5 att6RLancs p59&p270,9-4-15 MR38,11-4-16

HALL,Thomas Peter Moubray T2Lt ded 12-12-18 5RRofCav p23 CR Egypt15

HALL,Walter 2Lt dow 15-11-18 5 att2Yorks p221 CR France34

HALL,Warwick Lt dow 1-7-16 SStaffs p122 CR France397

HALL,Wilfred Rodenhurst.MC.TLt kia 21/22-3-18 11Suff p78 MR20

HALL,William.MC.2Lt kia 21-3-18 6 att2/8Worc p108 MR27

HALL,William Brown Lt dow 25-8-18 ACycCps att24Lond p181 CR France119

HALL,William Charles TMaj ded 17-12-17 19RIrRif p169 CR Ireland146,17-12-18

HALL,William Ernest Lt kia 23-5-15 5RFus p68 CR Gallipoli6

HALL,William Francis TLt kia 7-10-17 20Manch p154 MR30

HALL,William Hingston 2Lt kia 5-4-18 6Nhampt p137 MR27

HALL,William Holden 2Lt kia 26-9-17 D51RFA p208 CR Belgium20

HALL,William Hubert TLt kia 19-2-17 53MGC p183 MR21

HALL,William Stephen Lt drd 10-10-18 5SLancs p255 CR Ireland14

HALL,William Teesdale 2Lt kia 19-5-17 24RFC p8 CR France1061,Teasdale Capt

HALL-BROWN John TMaj kia 7-7-16 10N&D p134 CR France397

HALL-WATT,Richard 2Lt kia 13-10-17 1GrenGds p50 CR Belgium106,13-11-17

HALLAM,Alice Violet Sister541 ded 18-12-16 VAD StJAB p200 CR France40

HALLAM,Horace George Searle Lt kia 1-12-17 RASC attImpCamelCps p253 CR Palestine9

HALLAM,Howard T2Lt kia 4-10-17 RWar att1/6Bn p64 MR30

HALLAM,Robert Samuel 2Lt kia 20-7-16 15N&D p134 MR21

HALLAM-BOTHAM,G.TMaj kia 3-8-16 10NumbF p61 CR France430

HALLARAN,William Col ded 23-1-17 RAMC p195 MR65

HALLER,Edward Denison T2Lt kia 3-6-17 GL &45RFC p8 MR20

HALLER,John Henry Lyle.MID Capt kia 12-3-15 3ESurr p112 CR Belgium17

HALLETT,Arthur Mapleton Capt kia 2-6-16 D125RFA p29 CR France745

HALLETT,Henry William Percy TCapt dow 12-10-18 Mddx att2Bn p147

HALLETT,Samuel William Lt dow 15-7-16 1Mddx p147 MR21

HALLEWELL,George Noble T2Lt dow 10-10-16 167MGC p183 CR France513

HALLEY,Clifford Richard Brice T2Lt kia 2-10-17 GL &57RFC p8 CR Belgium140

HALLEY,Edward Harland TLt kia 26-11-17 RFA att12TMB p29 CR France407

HALLEY,Jack Jacob TLt kia 26-7-16 13Worc att25MGC Inf p108&183 CR France423,HALLE

HALLEY,James Mitchell White,MC TCaptAMaj kia 24-10-18 RE 62FC p45 CR Belgium442

HALLEY,William Carr 2Lt ded 28-5-17 RGA 327SB p209 CR France113,Curr

HALLEY-JONES,Percival.MC.Capt kia 9-8-18 7Lond p247 CR France1170

HALLIDAY,Balfour 2Lt dow 4-7-17 1/7WYorks p218 CR France769

HALLIDAY,Charles Graham Rivers 2Lt kia 13-6-17 RE 225FC p45 CR Belgium10

HALLIDAY,Charles Walter Alexander 2Lt dow 17-11-16 53/2RFA p29 CR France105

HALLIDAY,Hugh Maclean LtCol ded 10-12-20 IA SuppList p277 CR India97A ExYLI

HALLIDAY,John 2Lt kia 8-5-18 2Yorks p90 MR19

HALLIDAY,John Alexander Capt ded 13-11-14 11Huss p22 CR Wilts145,dow

HALLIDAY,Leigh Hales 2Lt kia 31-7-17 8 att7Nhampt p137 MR29

HALLIDAY,Morrice Frederick John 2Lt kia 7-6-17 Glouc &RFC p8&106 CR Belgium126

HALLIDAY,Thomas Owens T2Lt kia 21-3-18 9RIrRif p169 CR France1061

HALLIFAX,John Dampier Lt kia 17-5-15 2Yorks D'Coy p90 CR France279

HALLIGAN,Matthew Lt kia 18-11-17 RDubF &RFC p8&176 CR France62

HALLIWELL,Eric John Lt kia 11-9-17 RFA SR &57RFC p8&29 CR Belgium158

HALLIWELL,Fred T2Lt kia 22-4-18 11Manch p154 CR France115

HALLIWELL,Frederick T2Lt kia 12-10-18 17Manch p154 CR France192,12Bn

HALLIWELL,Wilfrid Newbold T2Lt dow 21-9-16 9Yorks p90 CR France177

HALLMARK,Percy Harold T2Lt kia 2-9-18 24Y&L p159 CR France646

HALLORAN J SubCdr 17-1-21 IA S&TCps CR Pakistan50A MR43

HALLOWES,Alexander Boyle T2Lt ded 31-5-17 RASC p193 CR Lond8

HALLOWES,Geoffrey Blackwood 2Lt kia 4-9-17 1RWKent p141 CR France294

HALLOWES,John Chaworth LtACapt kia 28-10-18 7Huss p22 MR38

HALLOWES,Rupert Price.VC.MC.T2Lt kia 30-9-15 4Mddx p147 CR Belgium167

HALLPIKE,Christopher George 2Lt kia 6-4-18 RGA 68SB p39 CR France196

HALLUM,Howard George.MC.2Lt dow 12-1-18 2/5Hamps p228 CR Egypt7

HALLUMS,E.C.SubAssSurg 12-3-16 IMS CR Iraq1

HALLWARD,Basil Murray TLt kia 9-4-18 B79RFA p29 CR France704

HALLWARD,Kenneth Leslie TLt kia 28-5-16 3Worc p108 CR France

HALLY John Capt kia 30-7-16 6BlkW p231 MR21

HALPIN,William Oswald TCapt dow 10-8-18 RAMC att4Huss p195 CR France1170

HALSALL,Donald Court T2Lt kia 9-10-17 1/2 att3/5LancF p92 MR30

HALSE,Clive Harold 2Lt kia 24-4-17 GL &70RFC p8 CR France660

HALSE,Lionel William T2Lt ded 17-10-18 12Glouc p106 CR Yorks22,dow

HALSEY,Eric Charles 2Lt kia 19-6-17 7Lond p247 CR France689

HALSEY,Francis William T2Lt kia 14-11-15 RGA att3TMB p39 CR France423

HALSEY,Frederick 2Lt kia 10-8-17 7Beds p86 CR Belgium112

HALSTEAD,Arthur.MC.TLt ded 1-8-17 10WRid p115CR France134,dow

HALSTEAD,Arthur Frederick Lt kia 28-6-15 15RB p179 MR4

HALSTEAD,James Thornton T2Lt kia 7-12-16 LNLancs attTMB p136 CR Belgium136

HALSTEAD,John James T2Lt kia 21-3-18 7BordR p117 CR France245

HALSWELLE,Wyndham.MID Capt kia 1-4-15 1HLI p163 CR France706,HALSWELL 31-3-15

HALY,Andrew Stuart 2Lt dow 8-7-15 3RLancs attELancs p59 CR Belgium85

HALY,William Hele 2Lt kia 14-10-16 2Hamps p120 MR21,Heli

HAM,Frank Livingstone 2Lt ded 13-2-16 KEdwHorse p24 CR Eire322

HAM,Frederick William T2Lt ded 6-5-17 GL &158ResRFC p8 CR Egypt15

HAMAR,Alfred John Lt dow 8-4-17 RFC 55Sqd 9Wing p8 CR France300

HAMBLETON,H.R.Cdr 24-8-15 IndMilWksServ MR66

HAMBLETON,Walter Edwin 2Lt kia 21-3-18 4 att10Ess p232 MR27

HAMBLEY,Francis William T2Lt kia 31-7-17 2ELancs p110 MR29

HAMBLIN John Edward TLt kia 24-3-18 12Suff p78 MR20

HAMBLIN,William Ebb Lt kia 24-5-16 RE 5FC p45 CR France573

HAMBLY,Alan Gordon 2Lt dow 22-5-17 1Dev p76 CR Devon2

HAMBLY,Dudley Charles T2Lt kia 14-5-17 6Dors p124 MR20

HAMBRO,Percival 2Lt dow 23-3-18 1KRRC p150 CR France177

HAME,Arthur William LtACapt kia 21-5-18 RFA attX21TMB p29 MR18

HAMEL,H.P.J.G.T2Lt kia 10-1-18 RFC p16 CR France113

HAMEL,Robert Sydney 2Lt kia 12-4-18 1RGLI p200 MR32

HAMER,Arthur Derrick Capt kia 6-11-18 NCycBn p253 CR France957

HAMER,Frank Capt kia 7-6-15 9Manch p237 MR4

HAMER,Harold TLt ded 6-6-17 GL 3LNLancs &56RFC p8 CR France383

HAMER,Hubert James Tudor Lt kia 4-11-14 IA 108Inf att101Grens p277 MR47

HAMER,John T2Lt kia 22-3-18 6KSLI p145 MR27

HAMER,Maurice T2Lt kia 27-3-18 WYorks att5YLI p81 MR20

HAMER,Samuel T2LtACapt kia 14-4-17 26NumbF p61 CR France644

HAMER,Thomas Pryce TLt kia 7-7-16 11SWBord p100 MR21

HAMILL,William Lt kia 16-8-17 7Manch p237 MR30

HAMILTON,Albert Edward T2Lt kia 18-8-17 26RFus p68 CR France855

HAMILTON,Alexander Beamish.CB.BrigGen ded 30-12-18 Staff p261 CR Dorset95

HAMILTON,Alexander Turnbull Rossell TLt kia 9-5-17 5BordR p228 MR20

HAMILTON,Andrew Douglas Lt ded 26-4-19 310RFA p29 CR Germany1

HAMILTON,Archibald Charteris Capt kia 28-6-15 7KOSB p101 CR Gallipoli6

HAMILTON,Archibald Gilbert Capt ded 15-2-19 RE p45&257 CR France40

HAMILTON,Archibald Hamilton Capt ded 4-11-18 13RIrRif p265 CR Ireland33

HAMILTON,Archibald James Rowan Lt dow 21-10-15 2IrGds SR p52 CR France423

HAMILTON,Archibald Lindsay T2Lt kia 10-6-17 13DLI p160 CR Belgium127

HAMILTON,Archibald Samuel LtCol dow 13-10-15 14DLI IA Retd p160 CR Mddx29

HAMILTON,Arthur Anson Shirley 2Lt dow 24-11-16 3 att1Berks CR France40

HAMILTON,Arthur Donald T2Lt kia 20-10-17 RE 101FC p45 CR Belgium21,19-10-17

HAMILTON,Arthur John Lord Capt kia 6-11-14 IrGds SR p52 MR29,L.A.J.

HAMILTON,Arthur Leslie Lt kia 25/26-10-18 3HLI p163 MR38

HAMILTON,Arthur Percival.MC.TLtCol kia 15-9-16 RWSurr att19Lond p56 CR France453

HAMILTON,Bernard St.George TLt kia 28-6-17 15MGC p183 MR20

HAMILTON,Cecil Claude 2Lt kia 16-8-17 3ConnRgrs att2RIrF p172 MR37

HAMILTON,Cecil Fife Pryce Capt dow 27-10-14 1ScotsGds p52 CR Belgium57

HAMILTON,Charles Gough 2Lt ded 12-10-19 Norf p263 CR Hereford51,11-10-19

HAMILTON,Chatham Anson Shirley 2Lt dow 24-11-16 3 att1RBerks p139

HAMILTON,Claud William T2LtACapt dow 6-11-17 RGA 287SB p39 CR Belgium72

HAMILTON,David Love 2Lt kia 21-3-18 BlkW att6Bn p128 MR20

HAMILTON,Douglas 2Lt kia 9-5-15 RIrRif att1Bn p169 MR32

HAMILTON,D.R.T2Lt kld 23-1-18 RFC p16 CR War5

HAMILTON,Edward TLt kia 14-4-18 GL att9RIrRif p190 MR30

HAMILTON,Eric T2Lt kia 15-2-17 GL &54RFC p8 CR France927

HAMILTON,Francis Walker Douglas Capt ded 24-2-19 RFA Res p254 CR France457,WRid attDirShipReprs

HAMILTON,Francis William T2Lt dow 3-3-17 8RWKent p141 CR Belgium11

HAMILTON,Geoffrey Cecil Monck T2Lt kia 7-9-17 8RDubF p176 CR France294

HAMILTON,George Lt dow 26-11-17 2ScotsGds p52 CR France398

HAMILTON,George Cyril Rae Lt kld 18-6-16 RFC CR Canada 256

HAMILTON,George Edward Archibald Fitzgeorge 2Lt kia 18-5-18 1GrenGds p50 CR France120

HAMILTON,George John T2Lt kia 9-6-17 16RScotsF p54 MR21

HAMILTON,Guy Stanley Gerald TLt&Adjt kia 1-8-17 3RWSurr p56 MR29

HAMILTON,Harold Gerard Hans TCapt dow 27-7-17 7BordR C'Coy p117 CR France1182

HAMILTON,Harry Austin Maj kia 25-1-16 23RFA p29 CR Belgium11

HAMILTON,Hector Macdonald 2Lt kia 22-3-18 3 att1RInniskF p105 MR27

HAMILTON,Henry McCartney T2Lt kia 14-5-16 7KOSB p101 CR France423

HAMILTON,Herbert Otho Lt kia 25-9-15 12NumbF p61 MR19

HAMILTON,H.J.Capt ded 13-6-18 DCLI &RAF p114

HAMILTON,Hubert Ian Wetherall.CB.CVO.DSO.MajGen kia 14-10-14 Staff p1 CR Kent179

HAMILTON,Hugh Wallace LtTCapt dow 20-3-18 4A&SH p173 CR France145

HAMILTON,James 2Lt kia 5-11-16 4BordR p228 CR France385

HAMILTON,James Capt kia 3-1-17 6ScotRif p224 CR France392,1-1-17

HAMILTON,James Montgomery.MC.T2LtACapt dow 19-9-18 10LancF p92 CR France278

HAMILTON,James Russell T2Lt kia 22-10-17 17LancF p92 MR30

HAMILTON,John 2Lt kia 1-7-16 11RInniskF p105 MR21

HAMILTON,John 2Lt kia 23-3-18 4 att6NumbF p213 MR27

HAMILTON,John Alfred.DSO.Maj 19-7-21 RASC MR43

HAMILTON,John Dundas Lawrie Maj acckld 22-5-15 7RScots p211 CR Scot249,James

HAMILTON,John Guthrie 2Lt kia 21-3-18 2/7LancF p221 MR27

HAMILTON,John Percy T2Lt acckld 8-3-18 GL &RFC p16 CR Egypt1

HAMILTON,John Stewart T2Lt kia 21-3-18 10 att3RB p179 MR27

HAMILTON,Leslie d'Henin.Hon.MVO.Maj kia 29-10-14 1CldGds p51 MR29

HAMILTON,Mervyn James Capt dow 28-11-14 1GordH C'Coy p166 CR Belgium150

HAMILTON,Noel Crawford T2Lt kia 14-7-16 6Nhampt p137 MR21

HAMILTON,Norman Butler Lt kia 24-7-18 5Lancs p213 CR France261

HAMILTON,Ralph Gerard Alexander.Hon.LtCol kia 31-3-18 Cmdg106RFA p206 CR France1008

HAMILTON,Richard Marchbank 2Lt ded 7-12-18 IARO attMGC Inf p277 MR65

HAMILTON,Robert Ainslie TLt kia 28-3-18 RASC att5YLI p193 MR27

HAMILTON,Robert Gordon 2Lt kia 27-9-16 D77RFA p29 CR France630

HAMILTON,Robert Peyton 2Lt dow 25-9-15 20Lond p251 CR France178,Lt

HAMILTON,Robert Victor T2Lt kia 1-7-16 9RIrRif p169 MR21

HAMILTON,Ronald Eric 2Lt kia 23-4-17 1Dev p76 MR20

HAMILTON,Ronald Millie 2Lt kld 3-6-17 5Ches p222 CR France417

HAMILTON,Thomas Lt kia 12-5-17 7WYorks p218 CR France646

HAMILTON,Thomas T2Lt kia 8-12-17 10RInniskF p105 CR France379

HAMILTON,Tom Knox Lt kia 1-6-15 3 att1RWar p64 CR Belgium96,Ion

HAMILTON,Vyvyan Lodwick 2Lt kia 14-6-17 6 att18KRRC p150 MR29

HAMILTON,Wallace Bernard T2Lt kia 9-8-16 10 att6Beds p86 MR21

HAMILTON,William LtACapt ded 13-8-17 RE 183TC p45 CR Belgium16,14-8-17

HAMILTON,William Lt kia 30-9-18 3ConnRgrs att1InniskF p172 CR Belgium157

HAMILTON,William Arnold T2Lt kia 4-6-17 6ConnRgrs p172 CR Belgium60

HAMILTON,William Lees T2Lt kia 20-9-17 RE 237FC p45 CR Belgium102

HAMILTON,William Robert 2Lt kia 12-10-17 CldGds att4GdsMGReg p51&53 MR30

HAMILTON-AGNEW,A.E.Capt 3-11-18 RDubF CR Bucks32

HAMILTON-COX,A.F.OBE.Col 5-3-21 SthnCommdArmyPayDept CR Wilts129

HAMILTON-COX,Cecil Francis T2Lt kia 27-8-17 8WRid p115 MR30

HAMILTON-DALRYMPLE,John Raphael.MID Lt dow 23-4-15 2KOSB p111 MR29

HAMILTON-FLETCHER,Gareth 2Lt 25-1-15 3GrenGds att1ScotsGds MR22

HAMILTON-GRACE,Raymond Sheffield CaptBtMaj ded 4-8-15 13Huss p22 CR France353

HAMILTON-GRIERSON,James Gilbert 2Lt kia 12-7-15 5RScotF p222 CR Gallipoli2

HAMILTON-JOHNSTON,Douglas Charles Capt kia 21-1-16 2BlkW p128 MR38

HAMILTON-JOHNSTON,Ewen Colquhoun Richardson Lt kia 1-9-18 2 att1/4KOSB p101 CR France646

HAMILTON-JONES,Charles Nugent T2Lt kia 20-9-17 Mddx att9Lpool p147 MR30

HAMILTON-TEMPLE-BLACKWOOD,Lord Ion Basil Gawen Temple ded PoW 4-7-17 2GrenGds p50 MR29

HAMLETT,George Froude 2Lt kia 13-8-17 3 att1BordR p117 MR29

HAMLEY,W.S.Capt 28-10-19 IARO CR Lond4

HAMLEY,William Walter T2Lt dow 26-3-18 6Dors p124 CR France62

HAMLYN,Alfred Ernest T2Lt kia 16-7-16 9DCLI p114 CR Belgium11,7Bn

HAMLYN,Wilfrid Stephen T2Lt kia 24-8-17 6DCLI p114 MR30

HAMM,William George.MC.T2Lt kia 2-5-17 13EYorks p84 CR France777

HAMMANS,A.W.Maj 13-6-16 DCLI CR Oxford44

HAMMANS,Arthur John Spencer.MC.CaptAMaj kia 3-7-17 1DCLI p114 CR France184

HAMMERSLEY,Alan George 2Lt kia 14-3-17 5NStaffs p238 CR France579

HAMMERTON,Gilbert TLt kia 4-9-16 MGC p183 MR21

HAMMETT,Noel Henry Franklin Lt ded 7-9-17 IARO attASC 258MT p277 CR Europe51

HAMMICK,Ernest Lumley 2Lt ded 16-5-16 IARO 1/73CarnaticInf p277 MR66

HAMMICK,Eustace.MC.Capt dow 8-10-18 IA 17Inf p277 CR Egypt9

HAMMICK,Stephen Frederick.MID Capt dow 18-4-16 O&BLI p130 CR Iraq6

HAMMOND,Anthony Edgar 2Lt kia 28-11-17 12Lancers p22 MR17

HAMMOND,Douglas William 2Lt kia 24-5-17 2EKent p57 MR29

HAMMOND,Edward William 2Lt ded 2-10-18 1Worc p108 CR Glouc86

HAMMOND,Ernest William Frost.MC.2Lt kia 3-5-17 HAC p206 MR20

HAMMOND,Frederick Robert Cyprian 2Lt kia 6-7-15 2Lond p245 CR Belgium11,5-7-15

HAMMOND,Gilbert Philip 2Lt kia 10-9-14 2KOSB p101 MR15,26-8-14

HAMMOND,Guy Neville Lt 19-7-16 SL &2NigR CR WAfrica52

HAMMOND,Hugh Jerrold TLtACapt ded 23-3-18 2Glouc p106 CR Greece9

HAMMOND,Jack Cecil T2Lt kia 11-4-17 7Nhampt A'Coy p137 CR France570

HAMMOND,John Martin Richard Lt kia 25-9-15 11Ess p131 MR19,26-9-15

HAMMOND,John Maximilian.DSO.TLt dow 15-3-17 RAMC att10Dev p195 CR Greece1

HAMMOND,Kenneth Lowton Charles T2Lt kia 22-3-18 23NumbF p61 MR20

HAMMOND,Leonard TLt kia 5-7-16 10WRid p115 CR France515

HAMMOND,Paul TCapt dow 25-2-16 8ELancs p110 CR France121

HAMMOND.R.W.LtCol 26-8-18 RE CR Ireland24

HAMMOND,Richard Martin Lt dow PoW 20-5-18 RFA attX66TMB p29 CR Germany3

HAMMOND,Robert Whitehead.MC.TCapt dow 30-9-17 26RFus p68 CR France1361,LtCol

HAMMOND,Thomas Hill T2Lt kia 31-10-18 35MGC Inf p183 CR Belgium143

HAMMOND,Thomas Percival 2Lt dow 15-6-18 RGA 137SB p39 CR Italy5

HAMMOND,William Cecil Capt kia 24-4-17 8DCLI p114 CR Greece5

HAMMOND,William Walter Maj kia 5-5-18 RGA 139HB p39 CR France44,Walker

127

HAMMOND-CHAMBERS,Henry Borgnis Baret TCapt kia 21-7-16 7RLancs p59 MR21

HAMMONDS,Denys Huntingford.DSO.MC.CaptAMaj kia 30-3-18 RE 225FC p45 MR27,125FC

HAMNETT,Frederick George T2Lt ded 15-11-18 GL KRRC &XV CpsHQ IntelCps p190 CR France1027

HAMPE-VINCENT,Percival Campbell Capt dow 26-10-14 IA 129Baluchis p277

HAMPSALL,E.SubCdr 23-2-21 S&T Cps MR65

HAMPSHIRE,Stanley Lt kia 9-10-17 2/4ELancs p226 CR Belgium125

HAMPSON,Alfred Eric T2Lt kia 8-7-16 10Ches att7TMB p96 MR21

HAMPSON,Edgar TLt kia 1-7-16 15 att16LancF p92 MR21

HAMPSON,Frank 2Lt kia 30-11-17 3 att1Lpool p72 MR17

HAMPSON,Harold Norman 2Lt dow 8-4-17 4SLancs att&RFC p18&230 CR France285

HAMPSON,James Stanley 2Lt kia 21-5-18 4SLancs att1/4LNLancs p230 CR France106

HAMPSON,Norman T2Lt kia 15-2-17 11LNLancs p136 MR38

HAMPTON,F.A.F.2Lt ded 23-8-18 15NumbF &RAF p61 CR Mddx17,Lt

HAMPTON,George Kenneth Lt kia 16-8-15 1/4Norf p216 CR Gallipoli4

HAMPTON,George William Betts 2Lt kia 11-3-17 4Suff att2RFC 1Wing p18&217 CR France423,Lt

HAMPTON,William Orr 2Lt kia 1-7-16 3Norf &70MGC Inf p73&183 CR France293

HANAFY,Sydney Reginald T2Lt dow 24-11-17 GL &46RFC p8 CR France512

HANBURY,Claude Everard Robert Capt kia 9-10-17 1IrGds p52 CR Belgium12,2Bn

HANBURY,Evan Robert Maj kia 24-3-18 LeicYeo att14MGC p187&204 MR27

HANBURY,Herbert Wood Capt kia 15-11-16 1/7Mddx p235 CR France785

HANBURY-SPARROW,Brian.MC.Capt kia 26-8-18 3KSLI att7NStaffs CR Asia 81

HANBURY-TRACY,Algernon Henry Charles.Hon.CMG.TMaj ded 3-12-15 RHGds p20 CR Surrey151

HANBURY-TRACY,Hon Felix Charles Herbert Lt kia 19-12-14 att2ScotsGds RoO p52 MR32,Hubert

HANBURY-WILLIAMS,Charles Ferdinand Reiss Lt ded 16-12-16 2 O&BLI p130 CR Mon9,19-12-16

HANBY,Edward Wrey 2Lt ded 30-4-17 6 att23Mddx p147 CR Sussex178

HANBY,Francis James 2Lt kia 30-6-16 12RSuss p119 MR19

HANCOCK,Albert Leslie 2Lt kia21-5-16 1/7Lond p247 MR20

HANCOCK,Arthur T2Lt kia 17-10-18 50MGC Inf p183 CR France1386

HANCOCK,Francis De Berckem Maj ded 6-5-16 IARO attPoliticalDept p277 CR Asia60

HANCOCK,Frank Pine 2Lt kia 16-8-18 KRRC att2Bn p150 MR19

HANCOCK,Harold T2Lt kia 19-9-18 16RWFus p97 CR France415

HANCOCK,John Eliot.DSO.TCapt kia 21-3-18 9Norf p73 MR20

HANCOCK,John Henry TLt kia 9-6-17 RE 129FC p45 CR Belgium28

HANCOCK,John Maurice T2Lt kia 7-3-18 65RFC p16 CR Belgium18

HANCOCK,Ralph Escott.DSO.Lt kia 26-10-14 Dev p76 MR22,29-10-14

HANCOCK,Ralph Longhurst Lt kia 27-8-17 8Worc p226 MR30

HANCOCK,Robert David 2Lt kia 21-3-18 24MGC p183 MR27

HANCOCK,William T2Lt kia 28-9-17 14NumbF p61 CR Belgium19

HANCOCK,William Reginald Lt kia 24-4-17 RNDevYeo p203 MR37

HANCOCKS,William Capt kia 9-10-17 7Worc p225 MR30

HAND,Maurice William Lt kia 25-6-15 1Ches p96 CR Belgium107,25-1-15

HAND,Moreton Capt kia 31-7-17 20DLI p160 MR29

HANDCOCK,Henry R.2Lt kia 18-8-16 3Leinst p174 CR France630

HANDCOCK,Reginald Henry Birbeck HonLt drd 17-2-17 RAOC p198 CR France300

HANDFIELD-JONES,Neville Montague 2Lt kia 25-9-15 108RFA p29 CR Belgium112

HANDFORD,Everard Francis Sale 2Lt kia 15-10-15 8N&D p233 MR19

HANDFORD,Frederick Stanley 2Lt kia 27-1-16 4 att9ESurr p112 MR29

HANDFORD,Henry Basil Strutt Capt kia 15-10-15 8N&D p233 MR19

HANDFORD,John Willis T2Lt dow 24-3-18 20N&D p134 CR France177

HANDFORD,Reginald Stuart 2Lt dow 9-8-16 6RB p179 CR Belgium11,1Bn

HANDLEY,Guy Frederick Beckham.MC&Bar.Lt kia 27-8-18 2CldGds 3Coy p51 CR France615

HANDLEY,Herbert Eustace 2Lt kia 25/26-5-15 23Lond p252 MR22,25-5-15

HANDLEY,Walter T2Lt kia 25-3-18 9RWFus p97 MR20

HANDS,Cecil T2Lt kia 12-10-17 13DLI p160 MR30

HANDS,Frederick ACapt kia 27-5-17 RE 1SigConstCoy p45 CR France201

HANDS,Reginald Harry Myburgh TCaptAMaj dow 20-4-18 RGA attSAfrHvyArt73SB p39

HANDYSIDE,Arthur Cruikshanks 2Lt dow 17-4-18 1/4SLancs p230 CR France88

HANDYSIDE,Arthur John T2Lt kia 24-10-18 1NumbF att4RFus p61 CR France1082

HANDYSIDE,John T2Lt dow 18-10-16 16 att18Lpool p72 CR France389

HANDYSIDE,Percy James Alexander Capt kia 1-7-16 2Lond p245 CR France798,2-7-16

HANDYSIDE,Thomas Fosbery Lt kia 29-12-17 4RDubF p176 CR Palestine3

HANEWINKEL,Ernest Eberhard Capt kia 31-8-15 19Lond p250 CR France80,30-8-15

HANFORD,Albert William TLt kia 23-4-18 15Ches p96 CR France41,22-4-18 18Bn

HANHAM,P.B.Col 20-2-17 RFA CR Surrey106

HANKEY,Donald William Alers 2Lt kia 12-10-16 1RWar p64 MR21

HANKIN,E.M.Lt&QM 17-5-20 GL &CentIndRlyBn MR65

HANKINSON,Richard Hooton Lt kia 21-6-17 14 att1/6Manch p154 CR France755

HANKINSON,Robert Prothero 2Lt dow 23-2-17 IARO att56Rif p277 CR Iraq5

HANLAN,Edward Gordon Lt dedacc 9-8-17 RFC CR Canada1689

HANLEY,Alfred T2Lt dow 24-5-18 DLI p160 CR Lancs33

HANLEY,Bartholmew 2Lt kia 23-8-17 4RScots p211 CR Belgium115

HANMER,Alexander John.MC.2Lt dow 7-10-16 3 att6EKent p57 CR France145

HANMER,Lambert Alfred Graham.DSO.MIDx2 LtCol dow 29-4-18 IA 21Cav p277 MR38

HANN,Cecil Collins 2Lt kia 22-10-16 GL &3RFC p190&3 CR France833

HANNA,David Wishart.MC.T2Lt dow 24-6-16 8RFus p68 CR Surrey150

HANNA,Douglas Murray TCapt kia 25-9-15 8RBerks p139 CR France219

HANNA,Frank Leslie Lt ded 26-7-18 RASC p267 CR Ireland137,3A&SH ExRASC(HorseTransport)

HANNA,John Henry 2Lt kia 20-9-17 19Lond p250 MR29

HANNA,William Neil 2Lt ded 20-11-18 RH&FA &RAF p261

HANNAFORD,Ida Durant SNurse 14-3-18 QAIMNS CR Surrey160

HANNAFORD,Stanley John Lt kia 5-10-17 1ELancs p110 CR Belgium83,2Lt

HANNAFORD,William Allan T2Lt kia 23-11-17 5SomLI p79 CR Palestine3

HANNAH,Charles William Cooper 2Lt kia 28-9-16 3 att2Dev p76 CR France115

HANNAH,Edward Meale.MC.T2Lt dow 16-8-17 1 att6KSLI p145 MR30

HANNAH,Henry William 2Lt kia 10-2-17 5RScots p211 CR France131

HANNAH,James 2Lt drd 21/22-4-16 2/4RGA p209 CR Scot677,21-4-16

HANNAH,John George 2Lt dow 30-11-17 1Lpool p72 CR France364

HANNAH,R.L.MC.TCapt kia 25-3-18 12HLI p163 CR France630

HANNAH,Robert 2Lt kia 16-8-17 7RIrRif p169 MR30 Ex Tpr W'land &C'landYeo

HANNAM,Francis John Capt kia 5-7-16 2/4Glouc C'Coy p225 CR France1887

HANNAM,Sydney Philip.MC.Lt kia 11-7-16 161RFA p29 CR France702

HANNAN,George Giles T2Lt dow 17-8-17 8Suff p78 CR Belgium8

HANNAN,George Madder TMaj ded 13-10-15 9ScotRif p103 CR Kent234

HANNAN,Henry Monteith LtCol kia 21-6-15 8ScotRif p224 CR Gallipoli6

HANNAN,James Maxwell Adair T2Lt kia 23-7-18 9TankCps p188 CR France987

HANNAN,Stanley Livingstone LtACapt kia 30-11-17 D275RFA p207 MR17

HANNAN,William David.MC.Capt kia 14-10-18 1/8ScotRif p225 CR Belgium157

HANNAY,David TCapt ded 17-1-18 RAVC att7RHA p198 CR France145

HANNAY,Herbert Thomas 2Lt kia 28-3-18 1/4Lond p246 MR20

HANNING,James Henry Rowland 2Lt kia 26-9-15 8Lincs p75 MR19

HANNING,James Talmage 2Lt kia 27-11-16 9RFC p3 MR20

HANNON,John Coulson 2Lt kia 18-8-16 3Lpool p72 CR France432

HANNON,Norman Leslie 2Lt kia 16-5-15 7Lpool p215 CR France279

HANNON,Thomas James 2Lt dow 1-12-17 4KSLI p235 CR France398

HANNYNGTON,John Arthur BrigGen.CB.CMG.DSO.ded 21-8-18 IA 129Baluchis p277 CR Egypt8

HANSARD,Arthur John St.Leger Capt S/InflictGunshot 7-10-20 IARO 2/89Punjabis att98Inf p277 MR66

HANSELL,Kenneth Joyce Nelson Lt kia 21-3-18 4Leinst &26MGC att1RIrRif p169&183 MR27

HANSELL,William Booth Capt kia 27-5-18 6DLI p239 MR18

HANSEN,Carl Frederick Vilhelm Lt dow 31-7-17 9Lpool att165MGC p187&216 CR Belgium46

HANSEN,William George 2Lt kia 25-9-16 1/9Lpool p216 MR21

HANSFORD,John Scriven Lt ded 21-12-18 2/8Lpool p270 CR France788

HANSON,Harold Capt dow 1-12-17 5WRid p227 CR Belgium3,1/4Bn

HANSON,James Arthur 2Lt kia 14-4-18 att1/5WYorks p81 CR France193

HANSON,Norman.MM.2Lt dow 12-10-18 9WYorks p81 CR France214

HANSON,Sydney Capt drd 27-5-18 NottsYeo p205 MR41

HANSON,Wilfred Clements Lt dow 15-9-17 A232RFA p207 CR Belgium18

HANSON,William Edward T2Lt kia 28-4-17 NumbF att26Bn p61 MR20

HANSTOCK,John Walter 2Lt dow 30-10-18 RE 12FC p210 CR France1266

HANWRIGHT,Thomas.DCM.2Lt kia 3-10-16 2DCLI p114 CR Greece3

HARBEN,Kenneth Tucker 2Lt kia 13-8-18 5Lond p246 CR France23,dow 9-8-18

HARBISON,Robert 2Lt kia 28-9-18 5HLI p240 CR Belgium124

HARBORD,Cecil Gordon TLt kia 1-9-16 14Y&L p159 CR France631

HARBORD,Frank Robert Rev dow 8-8-17 RAChDept p199 CR Belgium7

HARBORD,George Alfred Lionel Lt kia 1-7-16 3 att1RInniskF p105 MR21

HARBORD,John.MC.Capt dow 10-7-18 NorfYeo p204 CR France65

HARBORD,Philip Anthony Asshelin.MC.Lt dow 1-12-17 2GrenGds p50&257 CR France439,Assheton

HARBORD,Stephen Gordon.MC.LtACapt kia 14-8-17 D153RFA p29 CR Belgium10

HARBOTTLE,John LtACapt kia 21-3-18 1Leic p87 MR20

HARBOTTLE,Stanley James Lt kia 26-10-17 91MGC Inf p183 MR30

HARCOURT,Howard Leslie 2Lt dow 18-3-17 5RWar A'Coy p214 CR France164

HARCOURT,Joseph 2Lt dow 5-10-18 Leic att12NStaffs p87 MR32

HARD,William Thomas 2Lt kia 23-3-18 3Lond p245 MR27

HARDAKER,Harold 2Lt kia 19-12-15 1/5Y&L p238 CR Belgium23

HARDCASTLE,John Balfour Capt 30-7-16 2 O&BLI MR21

HARDCASTLE,Sydney Philip TCapt kia 30-7-16 3 att2 O&BLI p130

HARDEN,Allen Humphrey Capt kia 21-10-14 2 O&BLI p130 MR29

HARDEN,Arthur James Victor 2Lt kia 25-9-15 RSuss p119 CR France219

HARDER,John Charles Victor.MID 2Lt dow 26-4-18 D50RFA p29 CR Belgium185

HARDEY-MASON,Harold Victor 2Lt kia 3-5-17 4EKent p212 CR France427

HARDICKER,James Ogden CaptHonLtCol ded 7-4-19 7Manch Res p270 CR Lancs30

HARDIE,David Whyte T2Lt kia 18-11-17 48RFC SR p8 CR Belgium176

HARDIE,Frederick Capt dow 20-9-17 RAMC p253 CR France297

HARDIE,John T2Lt kld 7-2-18 RFC p16 CR Kent127,5-2-18

HARDIE,Norman T2Lt kia 27-3-17 RE 2FC p45 CR France511

HARDIE,William 2Lt dow 18-4-17 4 att13LancF p92 CR France610,4 att15Bn

HARDIMAN,Wilfred James 2Lt ded 4-12-18 4ELancs p270 CR Lancs381,J.W.

HARDING.Arthur Dennis Lt dow 30-10-14 4 att1Glouc p106 CR Belgium57

HARDING,Arthur Keith.MC.TCapt kia 24-10-18 10RWKent p141 CR Belgium408

HARDING,Charles Egerton Hugh CaptBtMaj ded 10-12-17 RFus p68 CR France40

HARDING,Claude Stephen TLt ded 22-1-18 GL Norf att4/4KAR p190&202 CR EAfrica8 &CR Tanzania1

HARDING,Clive Scotland Lt kia 6-8-15 11ESurr att2Hamps p112 MR4

HARDING,Donald Stanley.MC.T2LtACapt kia 10-4-17 13RFus 3Coy p68 CR France311

HARDING,Eric Stanley Milthrop Lt kia 6-7-17 2/5Lpool p215 CR France922

HARDING,Francis Edward Basil Capt dow 1-12-15 RFA 21Bty p29 CR France145

HARDING,Frederick John T2Lt dow 22-9-17 12ESurr p112 CR Belgium116

HARDING,Geoffrey Harold 2Lt ded 3-9-17 13RWar attRFC p261&263 CR Berks71

HARDING,George Clifford Capt 14-4-19 RAVC 14MobileSect att3Huss CR Shrop37

HARDING,George Helliwell 2Lt kia 27-3-18 79RFC p16 CR France141

HARDING,George Herbert Capt ded 23-5-18 GL RAMC p266 CR Lancs2

HARDING,Henry George.MC.Lt kia 4-10-17 1Hamps p120 MR30

HARDING,Homer 2Lt ded 3-10-18 IARO TC p277 MR66

HARDING,Isabel Lois ded 15-2-19 VAD CR War7

HARDING,Jack Maynard 2Lt kia 26-10-14 1RWKent p141 MR22

HARDING,James Golding Lt kia 30-10-17 RFA att21TMB p29 CR Belgium112

HARDING,James Philip Capt dow 10-11-17 2RMunstF p175 MR30

HARDING,John (Jack) Samuel TLt kia 8-11-15 11NumbF p61 CR France83

HARDING,Joseph 2Lt kia 6-10-17 3 att2BordR p117 MR30

HARDING,Lionel Cox Lt dow 18-6-15 RGA 5MtnBty p39 CR France285

HARDING,Lionel Henry Powys.MC.2Lt kia 23-10-18 1/2 att6Leic p87 CR France1477

HARDING,Norman Ernest Jasper MajTLtCol ded 10-8-16 RAMC att12SH p195 MR65

HARDING,Reginald.MC.2Lt kia 28-3-18 3 att6RWSurr p56 CR France233

HARDING,Reginald William Fowler Capt kia 7-11-17 18Lond p250 MR34

HARDING,Robert Denis Stewart Lt kia 9-11-14 4 att1Beds p86 MR29,7-11-14

HARDING,Samuel Collis.MM.T2Lt kia 22-8-17 F'TankCps 18Coy p188 MR30

HARDING,Sydney Allen.MID T2Lt dow 3-9-17 1AircraftDepotRFC SR p8 CR France134,Lt

HARDING,Wilfred John.MC.Chap4Cl kia 31-10-17 RAChDept attDrakeBn p199 MR30,Wilfrid

HARDING,William Arthur Capt kia 8-8-15 8WelshR p126 MR4

HARDING,William Kesterton 2Lt died 26-6-19 5Beds p219 CR France146

HARDINGE,Edward Charles.Hon.DSO.MID Lt dow 18-12-14 15Huss p22 CR Kent141

HARDINGE,Henry Ralph.Hon.2Lt kia 9-5-15 2RB p179 MR32

HARDINGE,Patrick Robert.MC.TMaj dow 17-6-16 1 att10ScotRif p103 CR France80

HARDINGHAM,Robert Cecil.MC.CaptTMaj dow 18-9-17 1Mddx att3/2KAR p147&268 CR EAfrica10 &CR Tanzania1,2Bn

HARDMAN,Adrian Thomas Lt dow 30-3-16 4RFus p68 CR Belgium11

HARDMAN,Archibald TLtACapt kia 4-10-17 9YLI p143 MR30

HARDMAN,Basil Brocas Lt kia 29-10-18 IARO att1/10GurkhaR p277 MR38

HARDMAN,Cecil William TLt kia 21-9-16 23Manch att70RFC p3&154 CR France169

HARDMAN,Frederick McMahon 2Lt kia 29-10-14 4RFus p68 MR22

HARDMAN,Hudson Beauford Lt kia 17-8-16 3 att7CamH p168 MR21

HARDMAN,Kenrie Capt kia 25/26-10-18 3HLI p163 MR38,Kenric

HARDMAN,Robert Taylor T2Lt kia 1-7-16 RE p45 MR21

HARDMAN,Tom Walker T2Lt kia 18-7-17 11Lpool p72 CR Belgium102

HARDMAN,Wallace George.MID T2Lt kia 9-1-17 13Manch p154 CR Iraq5

HARDMAN,William Frederick Kerr.MC.T2Lt dow 28-10-17 RE 171Co p45 CR Belgium3

HARDS,E.2Lt ded 10-6-18 RGA p262 CR Kent191,Lt

HARDWICK,Nathaniel Charles 2Lt dow 15-9-17 10DCLI p114 CR Belgium173

HARDWICK,Oswald William T2Lt kia 9-5-17 1Dev p76 MR20

HARDWICK,Philip Edward,DSO LtCol dow 9-6-19 10Huss p22

HARDWICK,William West 2Lt dow 11-6-15 5 att2Mddx p147 CR France345

HARDWICK-TERRY.Leonard Alfred TLtACapt kia 31-8-17 RE att24RFC p8&45 CR France251

HARDY,Alan Herbert 2Lt kld 14-10-15 REKentYeo attRFC p18&204 CR Kent191

HARDY,Charles Edwin TCapt kia 13-4-18 22NumbF p61 MR32

HARDY,Charles Eric T2Lt kia 23-10-18 19MGC Divl p183 CR France270

HARDY,Edgar Leslie TLt dow 7-10-18 WYorks attRE p45&81 CR France272

HARDY,Ferdinand H.TLt kia 4-9-16 2RFus att22MGC p68&183 MR21

HARDY,Frederick 2Lt kia 9-9-17 3 att21NumbF p61 CR France1461

HARDY,Gathorne T2Lt dow PoW 30-4-18 10RIrFus p171 CR France393

HARDY,Geoffrey 2Lt dow 27-5-17 D312RFA p208 CR France518

HARDY,Guy John Meredith Lt dow 1-8-17 3CldGds p51 CR Belgium16

HARDY,Harold TCapt kia 15-4-18 13RIrRif p169 MR30

HARDY,James Henry Chap4Cl kia 5-5-18 RAChDept RGA att1/1WelchR p199 CR Belgium3

HARDY,Leonard Basil Lt kia 11-2-15 2Worc p108 CR France765

HARDY,Ralph Miller Lt kia 4-11-18 5 att16HLI p240 CR France940

HARDY,Reginald Herbert William Lt ded 4-11-18 3WelchR p126 CR Mon34

HARDY,Richard Luard TCapt&Adjt kia 24-8-17 KRRC att8Bn p150 CR Belgium112,Luord

HARDY,Ronald Montagu Capt kia 23-7-15 7RB p179 MR29

HARDY,Theodore Bayley.VC.DSO.MC.Rev dow 18-10-18 RAChDept att8Lincs p199 CR France146

HARDY,Victor Harriott Lt kia 25-10-14 Y&L att1Lincs p159 MR22,26-10-14

HARDY,Walter John 2Lt ded 21-8-17 15RFA L'Bty p29 CR Staffs84

HARDYMAN,John May Maitland.DSO.MC.MIDx2 TMaj kia 24-8-18 8SomLI p79 CR France745,LtCol

HARDY-SMITH,Arnold Capt ded 16-5-19 16RWar p64 CR Greece9,1Bn

HARE,Alexander Balfour 2Lt kia 31-10-16 2RH&FA p29 CR France396

HARE,Bernard Urmston.MID T2Lt kia 25-9-15 14 att1Mddx p147 MR19

HARE,Edward Henry 2Lt kia 23-7-19 6RDubF att1Yorks p176 MR43,Lt

HARE,Edward John T2Lt kia 24-3-17 GL &15RFC p8 CR France518

HARE,Evan Alfred Amyas 2Lt kia 10-3-15 2Mddx p147 CR France706,E.Amyas Alfred

HARE,George TLt kia 27-12-17 7RDubF D'Coy p176 CR Palestine3

HARE,Harry Vivian Capt kia 20-9-14 2DLI p160 MR15

HARE,John Alfred T2Lt kld 1-3-17 10Suff &RFC p8&78 CR Camb103

HARE,John Maxwell 2Lt kia 24-5-15 6DLI p239 MR29

HARE,Robert Stuart MacLaine Capt kia 6-8-15 1Ess p131 CR Gallipoli6

HARE,Stanley Grant T2Lt kia 19-4-17 15Mddx p147 CR Palestine8

HAREL,Louis Octave 2Lt kia 18-8-17 GL &11RFC p8 CR France1295

HARES,Vincent Colin TLt kia 30-11-17 6KSLI p145 CR Palestine3

HARFORD,Edward Bridges.MID Capt ded 15-7-18 4SomLI p255 CR Sussex144

HARFORD,George Lawrence Lt kia 17-2-15 2RLancs p59 CR Belgium133,16-2-15

HARFORD,John Henry Lt kia 25-10-16 3 att7SWBord p100 MR21,26-10-16

HARGER,Edwyn Oscar T2Lt dow 23-9-18 RE 171TC p45 CR Belgium192

HARGER,Frank Eric T2Lt kia 16-12-15 C49RFA p29 CR Belgium58

HARGRAVE,Ernest Lawton T2Lt kld 22-9-17 GL &79RFC p8 CR Hamps31

HARGRAVE,W.G.2Lt kia 17-4-18 GL &RAF p190

HARGREAVE,Frederick Parker TLtACapt kia 20-11-17 7YLI p143 MR17

HARGREAVES,Alan Knyveton.DSO.Capt kia 9-5-15 2RB p179 CR France566

HARGREAVES,Clifford.MIDx2 2Lt kia 22-8-18 22Lond p251 CR

129

France247

HARGREAVES,Cyril Augustus T2Lt dow 15-8-17 43RFC p8 CR France178

HARGREAVES,Frank.MID TLt kia 12-7-16 19RWFus p97 CR France550

HARGREAVES,Harold 2Lt kia 23-8-18 4YLI p235 CR France526,2Bn

HARGREAVES,James Pater 2Lt kia 9-10-17 126RFA p29 MR30

HARGREAVES,Leopold Reginald.MC.Capt dow 25-9-16 IrGds p52 CR France294

HARGREAVES,Norman Lt kia 23-11-16 4ELancs att29RFC p18&226 CR France158

HARGREAVES,Ralph Walter TLt kia 1-12-17 1WelshGds p53 MR17

HARGREAVES,Reginald Anthony Lt kia 28-6-17 4DLI p160 MR19

HARGREAVES,Sydney Jasper 2Lt dow 19-5-18 1GrenGds p50 CR France84

HARGREAVES,Thomas Charles.DSO.Maj kia 23-3-18 23Lond p252 MR20

HARGREAVES,William Henry Lt 8-5-18 15Mddx attRAF CR Palestine3

HARGREAVES,Willoughby Frankland T2Lt kia 21-2-18 66RFC p16 CR Italy7

HARIES-JONES,Llewelyn Albert 2Lt kia 30-7-16 27Manch p154

HARINGTON,Herbert Hastings LtCol kia 8-3-16 IA 84Punjabis att62 p277 MR38,HARRINGTON

HARINGTON,William Guy.DSO.Maj kia 28-9-17 IA 2/5GurkhaRif p277 CR Iraq8

HARKER,E.K.2Lt dow 18-4-18 RGA &RAF p39 CR Belgium38

HARKER,George Cuthbert Warburton Capt dow 1-12-17 12Lond p248 CR France518

HARKER,George Ernest 2LtTLt kia 19-5-17 23/40RFA p29 CR France1182

HARKER,Herbert Charles 2Lt dow 25-3-18 393RFA p30 CR France103

HARKER,John Gordon 2Lt dow 28-9-18 SussYeo p205 CR France278

HARKER,Lewis T2Lt kia 1-10-18 2YLI p143 CR France375

HARKER,Robert Percy 2Lt kia 20-3-15 1NStaffs p157 CR France681

HARKNESS,Percy Yarborough Capt kia 1-7-16 2WYorks p81 MR21

HARKNESS,Raymond TLt kia 23-11-17 119MGC Inf p183 CR France1498

HARLAND,Hugh Baxter T2Lt ded 28-10-17 RE BaseDept p45 CR France285

HARLAND,Reginald Wickham Capt kia 30-10-14 1Hamps p120 CR Belgium69

HARLAND,Richard 2Lt kia 16-6-18 RGA 254SB p40 CR France18

HARLAND,Sidney 2Lt kia 25-5-18 RGA 214SB p40 CR France247

HARLE,Richard John Patterson.MC.2LtTLt ded 26-4-17 KOSB att2A&SH p101 CR France40,Paterson Capt dow

HARLEY,Albert Edward T2Lt kia 15-4-18 NStaffs p157 CR France298

HARLEY,Arthur Darent Lt kia 1-7-16 6SStaffs p229 MR21

HARLEY,Benjamin Chapman 2Lt kia 1-7-16 14RIrRif p169 MR21

HARLEY,Frederick William 2Lt kia 3-6-17 7BlkW att70RFC p18&231 CR Belgium410

HARLEY,George Melven TCapt kia 25-9-15 12HLI p163 MR19

HARLEY,John Lt kia 4-6-15 13Worc p108 MR4

HARLEY,Katherine Mary 7-3-17 IntDept attSerbianMinister CR Greece7

HARLEY,Robert Alexander TMaj ded 20-10-17 24RWFus p270 CR Lancs1,19-10-17

HARLING,Tom Lough T2Lt kia 26-10-17 Manch att21Bn p154 MR30

HARMAN,Arthur.DCM.Capt&QM kia 26-6-15 1KRRC p150 CR France80

HARMAN,Arthur George 2Lt kia 20-10-18 1/6Manch p237 CR France287

HARMAN,Brian Relton Lt ded 4-11-19 IA 110MahrattaLI att125Rif p277 CR Egypt9,3-11-19

HARMAN,Cecil Rochfort 2Lt kia 10-11-17 1Glouc p106 CR Belgium26

HARMAN,Charles Edward Col ded 5-1-15 9RDubF p266 CR Ireland5

HARMAN,George Malcolm Nixon.DSO.Maj kia 27-11-14 RB p179 CR France1095,28-11-14

HARMAN,John Augustus TLt kld 18-11-17 RFC p8 CR Lincs136,17-11-17

HARMAN,John Bower 2Lt kia 26-8-14 29/22RFA p30 CR France657

HARMAN,L.W. Lt ded 27-10-18 RH&FA &RAF p207

HARMAN,William 2Lt kia 27-3-18 A106RFA p30 CR France588

HARMER,Gerald T2Lt kia 11-8-16 9NStaffs p157 MR21

HARMON,Wilfred Baldwin T2Lt kia 1-8-17 21KRRC p150 MR29

HARMOOD-BANNER,Walcot TCapt kia 30-8-15 3 att1SWBord p100 CR France114,29-8-15

HARMS,William T2Lt kia 4-3-17 21NumbF &59RFC p8&61 CR France502

HARMSWORTH,Cecil John 2Lt dow 9-1-17 2Suff att3Mddx p78 CR Greece3

HARMSWORTH,Harold Alfred Vyvyan St.George.Hon.MC.Capt dow 12-2-18 2IrGds p52 CR Lond12

HARNETT,Donald Alfred 2Lt kia 7-10-16 3 att6EKent p57 MR21

HAROLD,John Peter Bevan Lt dow 16-2-18 RFA attRFC p16&30 CR France40

HAROLD-BARRY,J.Capt kia 24-5-15 3RDubF p176 MR29

HAROLD-BARRY,John Gerard 2Lt kia 7-7-16 5RMunstF p175 CR France115,1Bn

HARPER,Alan Gordon T2Lt kia 1-6-17 187RFA p30 CR Belgium29

HARPER,Alexander Simpson TLt kia 12-10-17 8BlkW p128 MR30

HARPER,Alfred George Montague Norton Capt kia 16-10-17 SL att41L NigR p201,2entries

HARPER,Arthur 2Lt dow 1-4-17 2BordR p117

HARPER,Charles 2Lt ded 27-11-18 2KSLI p145 CR Greece2

HARPER,Charles Croke 2Lt kia 3-5-17 3 att5 O&BLI p130 MR20

HARPER,Clarence Rucil 2Lt kia 15-7-16 6WYorks p218 CR France246

HARPER,Edgar Henry TLt kia 10-7-16 8SStaffs p122 MR21

HARPER,Ernest Macowan TLt kia 9-8-15 7RMunstF p175 MR4

HARPER,Frederick Henry TLt dow 20-4-18 RE 11FC p45 CR Belgium38

HARPER,Gordon Philip 2Lt kia 29-9-18 4Lpool p72 CR France407

HARPER,Hal 2Lt kia 19-7-16 6RWar p214 MR32

HARPER,Harold Raymond T2Lt kia 4-11-18 1/2 att2/4WRid p115 CR France1081

HARPER,Hugo Alfred 2Lt kia 15-4-18 3 att2SforthH p164 CR France407

HARPER,James 2Lt kia 28-6-18 3 att1Ches D'Coy p96 CR France21

HARPER,John Alexander.MC.TCapt kia 14-2-17 RAMC att7Yorks p195 CR France786

HARPER,John Boughton T2Lt kia 12-10-17 7Lincs p75 MR30

HARPER,Owen Tannett 2Lt kia 22-3-18 1Leic p87 MR20

HARPER,Reginald Alexander 2Lt dow 16-9-17 2/1Lond p245 CR Belgium16

HARPER,Rennie T2Lt kia 14-10-18 1LancF p92 CR Belgium157

HARPER,Robert Charles Middleton 2Lt kia 19-4-17 GL att1/5Norf p190 MR34

HARPER,Tom T2Lt kia 4-6-17 1/2 att7LancF p92 MR29

HARPER,Walter Lacon Lt kia 1-7-18 3 att6Nhampt p137 CR France44,30-6-18

HARPER-SMITH,Septimus William 2Lt ded 19-10-19 RFus attLabCps p266 CR Yorks294,Lt

HARPLEY,Robert Ableson 2Lt kia 5-7-16 5YLI att148MGC Inf p235 MR21

HARPUR,Edward Percival H.TLt dow 11-9-16 7RIrRif p169 CR France66,RIrF

HARRAGIN,William Piercy Lt ded 1-11-18 A&SH attKAR CR EAfrica36

HARRIES,Eric Guy Capt dow 17-8-15 1/7RWFus p223 CR Greece10

HARRIES,Frederick Ebenezer Melville T2Lt kia 26-2-17 12KRRC p150 CR France744

HARRIES,Gilbert James St.Clair T2Lt kia 24-8-17 10DLI p160 MR30

HARRIES,Howard Lock T2Lt kia 13-11-16 18 att10RWFus p97 CR France156,Locke

HARRIES,James Francis Lt ded 30-6-18 6ESurr p226 CR Ches182

HARRIES,John Elvet 2Lt kia 23-4-17 3 att2SWBord p100 MR20

HARRIES,William Frank Reginald T2Lt kia 26-9-18 MGC Cav p183 MR34

HARRIES,Wyndham Trevor T2Lt kld 21-8-17 GL &3RFC p8 CR Sussex55

HARRIES-JONES,Llewelyn Albert 2Lt 30-7-16 27Manch MR21

HARRIGAN,William Piercy TLt ded 1-11-18 GL 11A&SH attKAR p173,202&266

HARRIMAN,Charles Henry T2Lt kia 29-10-17 GL &43RFC p8 CR France88

HARRIMAN,Horace William.MC.TCapt kia 1-9-18 8 att9WRid p115 CR France744

HARRINGTON,Charles Stanley Lawrence Lt ded 27-5-17 3ConnRgrs p172 MR38.drd

HARRINGTON,E.HonLt&QM ded 28-7-15 RASC p193 CR Lond9

HARRINGTON,George Christmas 2Lt ded 30-10-17 6DragGds p21 CR Kent232,Lt

HARRINGTON,Herbert Andrzey Biernaski Lt dow 9-12-14 3 att1Hamps p120 CR Hamps11,HARINGTON MR32,Andrzer

HARRINGTON,Philip William 2Lt kia 13-1-17 5Worc p108 CR Iraq5

HARRINGTON,Walter 2Lt kia 22-6-17 5WelshR p230 CR Belgium43 13Ches 21-6-17

HARRINGTON,Walter John 2Lt ded 18-5-19 LabCps att20RB p266 MR40

HARRIS,Albert James 2Lt kia 17-10-16 1RLancs p59 MR21

HARRIS,Albert Hansen 2Lt kia 26-9-15 8RWKent p254 MR19

HARRIS,Alfred Abraham 2Lt kia 9-9-16 10Mddx C'Coy p236 CR France294

HARRIS,Alfred Edward T2Lt kia 2-7-18 12MGC Inf p183 CR France704

HARRIS,Alfred George 2Lt kia 11-4-17 7WelshR p230 MR20,att2/6WYorks

HARRIS,Antrobus Taft 2Lt kia 19-3-16 4Beds att1Lincs p86 CR France922,Lt

HARRIS,Arthur Edward Crawford 2Lt dow 11-9-17 2/7RWar p214 CR Belgium18

HARRIS,Arthur Harold 2Lt dow 4-7-18 1 att16RWFus p97 CR France169,Lt

HARRIS,Arthur Lea Capt kia 31-7-17 4LNLancs p234 MR29

HARRIS,Arthur Stanley 2Lt kia 31-7-17 6Lpool p215 MR29

HARRIS,Aubrey TLt kia 4-9-16 21Manch A'Coy p154 MR21

HARRIS,C.B.Lt 3-3-19 6WelchR attMGC Inf CR Wales168

HARRIS,Cecil Alfred 2Lt dow 3-11-16 4RWSurr att4Suff p212 CR France105

HARRIS,Cecil St.John 2Lt ded 10-9-15 5SomLI p218 CR Somerset173

HARRIS,Charles Cecil 2Lt kia 13-6-17 4NStaffs p157 CR Belgium127

HARRIS,Charles Henry 2Lt dow 19-9-18 RWFus att1Bn p97 CR Greece6

HARRIS,Charles Montagu TLt dow 28-8-15 RAMC att7RScotF p195 CR France51

HARRIS,Charles Noel 2Lt kia 21-4-17 IA 123Rif p125 p277 MR38

HARRIS,Christopher Samuel 2Lt kia 27-5-17 6WYorks p218 MR19

HARRIS,Claude Leslie(Jim) Capt dow 2-5-18 HAC A'Bty p206 CR Palestine3

HARRIS,Edward.MC.Capt dow 25-4-18 RGA p209 CR Belgium38

HARRIS,Edmund George 2Lt dow 26-6-17 2/7WRid p227 CR France518

HARRIS,Eric Wallace Lt dow 4-11-17 RGA 213SB p40 CR Belgium11

HARRIS,Ernest Charles TCapt kia 23-10-16 12WRid p115 CR France400

HARRIS,Ernest Edward 2Lt ded 21-4-17 6 att1RIrF p171 CR Germany1 dow

HARRIS,Frank 2Lt kia 15-7-16 3 att10Ches p96 MR21

HARRIS,Frederick James Lt kia 13-4-18 6HLI C'Coy p240 CR Belgium89,9Bn

HARRIS,Frederick T.2Lt dow 19-9-15 B49RFA p30 CR Belgium5

HARRIS,F.W.Davie LtCol ded 20-6-17 RAMC p195 CR Surrey64

HARRIS,Hamilton Snow TCapt kia 1-7-16 13 att11N&D p134 CR France246

HARRIS,Harold Cecil Dunstan Lt 4-11-19 1Mon CR Ireland33

HARRIS,Harold Maltby 2Lt kia 16-6-17 3Co of LondYeo p204 MR29,Malthy

HARRIS,Henry TLt kia 4-10-16 10WRid attNhampt p115 CR France239,Harry,5-10-16 attNumbF

HARRIS,Henry James Fraser drd 27-2-16 IARO p277 CR Kent8

HARRIS,Henry James Lawrence TLt kia 6-11-16 16 att14Hamps p120 CR France293,Capt

HARRIS,Henry Lionel T2Lt dow 1-12-15 RE 105FC p45 CR France285

HARRIS,Herbert Brutus Aubrey Lt mbk 10-8-17 7RWSurr p256 MR29

HARRIS,Herbert Cecil TCapt kia 3-7-16 6RWKent p141 MR21

HARRIS,Howard Kilbourne.MC.Capt kia 22-2-18 3 att11Ess p131 CR France568

HARRIS,Hubert Alfred TCapt kia 31-7-17 RAMC att61RFA p195 CR Belgium13 74RFA

HARRIS,Hugh Ripley Lt ded 20-11-18 RH&FA att1TMB p30 CR France1858

HARRIS,Jack St.Clair Gainez 2Lt kia 22-2-15 SStaffs p122 CR France924,Gainey

HARRIS,John Anthony.MC.Capt kia 26-11-17 12Yorks p90 MR17

HARRIS,John Lionel 2Lt kia 7-4-16 IARO att125Rif p277 MR38,6-4-16

HARRIS,Johnny Stringer Lt kia 23-3-18 4SforthH p241 MR20

HARRIS,Joseph Cecil Capt kia 16-8-17 RAMC 3FA att A'CCS p253 CR Belgium8

HARRIS,Joseph Walter Lt kia 2-6-15 1Lincs p75 MR29

HARRIS,Leslie George Hamlyn 2Lt kia 2-11-14 N&D p134 MR29

HARRIS,Lyn Arthur Philip TCapt&Adjt kia 10-7-16 16WelshR p126 CR France397,11-7-16

HARRIS,Nathan Leonard.MC.TCapt kia 28-8-18 9RWFus p98&258 CR France98

HARRIS,Percy Cuthbert Capt kia 17-2-15 Suff p78 MR29,16-2-15

HARRIS,Percy George T2Lt kia 11-8-17 17RWFus &21RFC p8&98 MR20

HARRIS,Philip Dawson Capt kia 21-3-18 1NStaffs p157 MR27

HARRIS,R.D.AssSurg 16-7-21 IMS MR43

HARRIS,Reginald Arthur 2Lt kia 9-10-17 4 att9WYorks p81 CR Belgium83

HARRIS,Reginald Samuel 2Lt dow 24-6-17 5Mddx p147 CR Belgium11,13Bn

HARRIS,Reginald William TLt kia 3-9-16 4WYorks attZ1TMB p81 MR21

HARRIS,Robert Arthur TCapt drd 21-11-17 GL p190 MR40

HARRIS,Robert Edward TLt kia 4-11-18 8NStaffs p157 CR France984,2Lt

HARRIS,Robert Hugh 2Lt kia 28-9-16 11 att8WRid p115 MR21

HARRIS,Roland James Lt kia 16-9-16 6DLI p239 MR21,17-9-16

HARRIS,Roland Milton 2Lt kia 7-6-17 2Yorks &60RFC p8&90 CR France46

HARRIS,Rowland Hanwell.MC.2Lt kia 27-12-17 2/15Lond p249 CR Palestine3,Roland

HARRIS,Sydney Ernest T2Lt dow 15-5-18 2/4LNLancs p136 CR France145

HARRIS,Theodore Trevor 2Lt dow 4-10-16 2/7Mddx p235 CR France105

HARRIS,Thomas William.MID 2Lt kia 27-3-18 19DLI p160 MR27

HARRIS,Vernon T2Lt kia 9-4-16 12 att9RWar p64 MR38

HARRIS,Walter Lewis 2Lt kia 10-2-17 10Dev p76 MR37

HARRIS,Walter Read 2Lt ded 10-10-18 1/5Suff att1/1Camb p217 CR France123

HARRIS,Wilfred Ernest Lt kia 15-9-17 RFA 62TMB p207 CR France538

HARRIS,William Edward 2Lt dow 19-12-15 2DLI p160 CR Belgium11

HARRIS,William Gregory T2Lt kia 3-2-17 7Glouc p106 MR38

HARRIS,William Handel T2Lt kia 26-8-18 16RWFus p98 CR France432

HARRIS,William Lawson.MC.Lt kia 30-7-16 2RScotF C'Coy p94 MR21

HARRIS,William Robert Capt ded 15-2-19 RASC p193 CR France52

HARRIS,William Trengweath Lt drd 15-4-17 RAMC p195 MR35

HARRISON,Alfred Herbert Maj ded 3-11-18 RFA p30&257 CR Essex81

HARRISON,Bernard Percy Bartlan T2Lt kld 6-1-18 RFC p16

HARRISON,Brian T2Lt kia 10-7-16 14RWFus p98 CR France397

HARRISON,Brian Charles TCapt dow 12-8-18 11 att5BordR p117 CR France649

HARRISON,Cecil Eustace Maj kia 14-3-15 2RB p179 CR France709,12-3-15

HARRISON,Cecil George Bradford T2Lt kia 13-8-16 8RBerks p139 MR21

HARRISON,Charles Augustus LtCol ded 28-10-16 RE p270

HARRISON,Charles Geoffrey Lt kia 27-11-17 2/4Y&L p238 MR17

HARRISON,Charles Gordon.MC.T2Lt dow 26-9-18 3 att2SLancs p125 CR Belgium192

HARRISON,Charles Hibbert Lt kia 31-7-17 RFA D91HB p30 CR Belgium85

HARRISON,Christopher Rene Lt dow 23-5-15 3 att2Leic p87 CR France102

HARRISON,Cyril Cazalet Lt kia 19-9-14 3Worc p108 MR15,20-9-14

HARRISON,Cyril Henry T2Lt kia 6-9-17 10SLancs att1/5LancF p125 MR30

HARRISON,Dennis Riley T2Lt kia 3-5-17 BlkW att8Bn p128 MR20

HARRISON,Donald Howard Lt kia 16-9-18 C306RFA p207 CR France768

HARRISON,Douglas Roy Dilworth T2Lt kia 27-3-18 10DLI p160

HARRISON,Edgar Brooks 2Lt dow 28-9-16 7WYorks p218 CR France74,29-9-16

HARRISON,Edward 2Lt kia 28-4-17 RGA 158SB p40 CR France729

HARRISON,Edward Lt 17-5-18 RE &24RAF MR20

HARRISON,Edward Donald 2Lt kia 25-7-16 3RWKent att19Manch p141 MR21

HARRISON,Edward Frank.CMG.DSO.TLtCol ded 4-11-18 RE p45 CR Lond4

HARRISON,Edward Rainsford.MID Capt ded 25-12-18 RASC 524Coy 61DivTrn p253 CR France52

HARRISON,Eric Lt kia 30-6-15 3 att1Leic p87 CR Belgium44

HARRISON,Ernest Hesketh ACapt kia 18-9-18 5ESurr p226 CR France511,8Bn

HARRISON,Everard Capt kia 18-4-17 RAMC att1/6Gloucp253 CR France363

HARRISON,Francis Harold Lt kia 2-9-16 3Yorks att85RE SpBde p90 CR France150,att5RE

HARRISON,Francis Ingleby LtACapt dow 8-5-18 3 att1RWKent p141 CR France31,kia

HARRISON,Frank T2Lt drd 25-4-17 NStaffs p157 MR38

HARRISON,Frank Cecil Capt dow 13-10-18 RAMC p195 CR France612

HARRISON,Frank Cyril T2Lt dow 4-5-18 Lpool att1/5Bn p72 CR France88

HARRISON,Frank Talbot T2Lt kia 3-5-17 8ESurr p112 MR20

HARRISON,Frederick Alfred 2Lt kia 9-9-163Leinst att6RIrReg p174 CR France402

HARRISON,Frederick William,MC 2Lt kia 27-5-18 8DLI p239 MR18

HARRISON,Geoffrey T2Lt kia 1-7-16 MGC Inf p183 CR France393

HARRISON,George Carmichael TLtACapt dow 10-1-17 RGA 6A/ABty 24HAG p40 CR Belgium11

HARRISON,George Frederick Whitby T2Lt dow 30-9-17 3RRofCav attWiltYeo att6Wilts p23CR Belgium17

HARRISON,George Herbert.MC.2Lt dow 21-8-16 3 att1LNLancs p136 CR France833

HARRISON,George Launcelot Godwin 2Lt kia 7-11-17 4 att11RSuss p228 MR30

HARRISON,George Victor.MC.Lt dow 26-8-18 3 att1Lpool p72 CR France84

HARRISON,H.G.Capt &Adjt 24-7-20 2Manch MR38

HARRISON,Halford Claude Vaughan MajTLtCol ded 1-4-16 RFA 16HAG p30 CR France201

HARRISON,Henry Malcolm Lt dow 19-3-15 3 att2Glouc p106 CR Belgium28 28-3-15

HARRISON,Henry Neville Baskcombe.MVO.Capt dow 16-3-15 2DCLI p114 CR Belgium151,kia

HARRISON,Herbert Le Grew TLt ded 12-3-18 GL RE p266 CR Mddx16,Greu

HARRISON,Herbert William 2Lt dow 9-6-17 3 att1Lincs p75 CR France145

HARRISON,Henry Leslie Lt ded 28-10-18 4Yorks attRAF p220 CR Lond14

HARRISON James Spink T2Lt dow 28-5-18 2DLI p160 CR France142

HARRISON,James Molyneux LtCol ded 10-3-19 RASC p254 CR Yorks361,13-3-19

HARRISON John,MC Lt kia 16-4-17 6RWar p214 CR France669

HARRISON,John.VC.MC.2Lt kia 3-5-17 11EYorks p84 MR20,mbk

HARRISON,John 2Lt kia 31-7-17 4 att11LancF p92 CR Belgium34

HARRISON John Adshead T2Lt kia 12-4-18 31MGC p183 CR France352

HARRISON John German Capt ded 11-4-18 RFA X32TMB p207 CR France145,dow

HARRISON John Henry T2Lt kldacc 31-8-16 11 att7Lincs p75 CR France1014

HARRISON John William 2Lt kia 7-6-17 18Lond attRFus p250 CR Belgium154

HARRISON,Leonard Arthur T2Lt kia 17-7-16 12DLI p160 MR21

HARRISON,Leonard John Harrison 2Lt kia 24-5-15 IAUL att2LancF p277 MR29

HARRISON,Leonard John T2Lt dow 17-4-18 18 att1RIrF p171 CR Germany3

HARRISON,Lionel Joseph Briggs TCapt kia 27-3-18 5 att16N&D p134 CR France526,3 att16Bn

HARRISON,Maurice Cazalet TCapt kia 12-10-16 1RWar p64 MR21

HARRISON,Noel Stuart TLt kia 30-7-16 9 att2 O&BLI p130 MR21

HARRISON,Osmond 2Lt ded 5-2-19 RGA p270 CR Durham26,Lt

HARRISON,P.W.CBE.LtCol 5-3-20 3LNLancs CR C'land&W'land107

HARRISON,Percy Day 2Lt ded 12-3-17 4RSuss p228 CR Hamps15,HARRISSON

HARRISON,Percy Pool Capt dow 20-10-17 5N&D p232 CR France145

HARRISON,R.Lt ded 17-5-18 RE &RAF p210

HARRISON,R.A.2Lt 9-2-19 RMunstF CR Eire78

131

HARRISON,Richard Scorer Molyneux Maj kia 16-8-15 IA 51Sikhs att7RDubF p277 MR4

HARRISON,Ronald 2Lt kia 18-9-16 11 att16Lond p248 CR France402

HARRISON,Ronald TLt kia 10-11-17 11BlkW att1/5A&SH p128 CR Palestine8

HARRISON,Roland Damer.DSO.Maj kia 16-9-17 RFA p30 CR France369,HARRISSON

HARRISON,Roland Edgar TLt kia 27-2-16 1DLI p160 CR Belgium127,2Lt 8Bn

HARRISON,Samuel Dunlop Henderson TLt dow 29-10-18 1 att11RInniskF p105 CR France1034,kia 11 att13Bn

HARRISON,Stanley T2Lt kia 23-10-16 1Hamps p120 MR21

HARRISON,Stanley Sextus Barrymore.MC.AMaj dow 10-10-18 RAMC att1/3NMidFA p195 CR France34

HARRISON,Thomas Charles 2Lt kia 21-3-18 43MGC p183 MR27

HARRISON,Thomas Percy 2Lt kia 9-4-18 RFA p208 MR19

HARRISON,Thomas Walter Lt drd 10-10-18 1/4Lincs p217 MR40

HARRISON,Tom Marriott TCapt dedacc 3-4-17 3 att13NumbF p61 CR France40

HARRISON,W.M.Sister 3-4-20 QAIMNS MR66

HARRISON,Wilfred Ernest.MC.TCapt dow 10-4-18 11Suff p78 MR32

HARRISON,William 2Lt dow 5-7-16 3GordH att2SfthH p166 CR France62

HARRISON,William Lt dow 17-9-16 7Lpool p215 CR France23

HARRISON,William Lt kia 29-9-18 7ScotRif p224 MR30

HARRISON,William Henry TLt kia 24-1-17 4Ess p232 MR50

HARRISON,William Sandilands LtCol ded 12-4-15 RAMC p195 CR Lancs284

HARRISON,William Stanford Bennett T2Lt kia 7-7-17 9LNLancs p136 MR29

HARRISS,Reginald Edmund TCapt kia 12-5-17 10LancF p92

HARROP,James Allinson T2Lt kia 8-10-18 KSLI att1Bn p145 MR16

HARROP,James Lawton 2Lt dow 13-9-18 LNLancs att4Bn p136 CR France686

HARROP,Tom T2Lt kia 28-4-18 17Lpool p72 MR30

HARROP,Tom Lt ded 31-3-20 LabCps CR Lancs42

HARROP,William Henry Lt kia 9-10-17 4ELancs p226 MR30

HARROW,Leonard Phillip.DCM.Lt kia 28-8-18 16Lond p249 CR France214

HARROWER,Alan Pat TLt dow PoW 26-3-18 12NumbF p61 CR France528

HARROWER,James.VD.TCapt dow 15-9-16 14HLI p163 CR France188,kia 10/11Bn Ex 14Lond

HARROWER,Peter.MC.T2Lt kia 17-10-18 16 att12RScots p54 CR Belgium140

HARROWING,John Stanley.MC.TLt kia 4-5-17 2RWar ExRASC p64 MR20,Capt

HARRUP,Frederick Charles Leonard.MC.T2Lt kia 21-9-18 9RFus p68 MR16

HARRY,Alfred Edward Capt kia 3-1-16 3 att1Ches p96 CR France394

HARRY,Reginald Charles 2Lt kia 29-8-16 ACycCps SthMidDiv p244 CR France220

HARRYMAN,Geoffrey Charles T2Lt dow 8-8-16 25Manch p154 CR France145,16Bn

HARRYMAN,Sydney T2Lt dow PoW 24-3-17 13Glouc att88RFC p8&106 CR France924

HARSTON,Frank Northey.MC.MIDx2 LtTCapt kia 22-4-18 ELancs attStaff 11InfBde p110 CR France250,Maj

HARSTON,William Harvey 2Lt kia 23-11-17 8Nhampt &52RFC p8&137 CR France1361,7Bn

HART,A.F SubAssSurg2Cl 31-8-15 IA IMD CR Asia60

HART,Albert TLt kia 30-6-18 RASC att6RWKent p193 CR France61

HART,Andrew Chichester 2Lt kia 1-7-16 109MGC p183 CR France215,Lt Ex 11RInniskF

HART,Arthur Charles Capt kia 7-5-15 2NumbF p61 MR29

HART,Cecil Lyon Capt kia 1-7-16 3WRid p115 CR France643

HART,Charles Crowther 2LtTLt kia 14-11-17 3WRid att3/3KAR p115&202 CR EAfrica11 &CR Tanzania1

HART,Clarence Herbert Lt kia 23-10-18 5 att2Beds p219 CR France190

HART,Clifford John TCapt kia 9-8-16 Worc &RFC p3&108 CR France525,RFC attWorc

HART,Conway John TLt kia 10-10-16 16N&D p134 CR France383

HART,Cornelius Henry 2Lt kia 17-10-18 RGA 130SB p40 CR France340

HART,David Provan.MC.Lt 27-12-18 LNLancs CR Scot807 Served as PROVAN,D.H.

HART,Edgar Oswald T2Lt kia 10-7-16 13 att9Yorks p90 MR21

HART,Edward Alexander TCapt kia 9-4-16 7NStaffs p157 MR38

HART,Ernest 2Lt kia 26-10-18 2Ess p131 CR France1266

HART,Ernest George Lt kia 30-8-18 13Lond p249 CR France308

HART,Francis Henry Lt ded 4-7-18 10Manch att42MGC Inf p187&255CR Lancs34

HART,Frank Arthur Squire T2Lt kia 16-9-16 9SomLI p79 MR21

HART,Frederick Reginald.MC.Lt dow 28-1-17 1Herts p252 CR Mddx39

HART,George Washington TLtAMaj kia 15-3-17 189RFA p30 CR Belgium28

HART,H.J.Capt 1-5-17 EAfrRlys CR EAfrica47

HART,Howard Victor.MC.Lt kld 23-3-19 6Lond p246 MR70 &CR Europe180,6Yorks Ex6Lond

HART,Hyla Padgham TLt kia 5-10-18 13DLI p160 MR16

HART,James.MC.LtACapt kia 1-11-18 1/6WRid p115 CR France1256

HART,James Arthur 2Lt ded 18-12-19 5Nhampt p265 CR Europe51,Lt

HART,James Wilson.MC&Bar.Capt kia 24-3-18 10RWSurr p56 MR20

HART,John Gordon Lt kia 28-8-17 7HLI p240 MR34,Capt

HART,John Harcourt Welby.MIDx2 TLt kia 20-9-18 Dev att1Manch p76 MR34

HART,John Sidney 2Lt dow 18-4-18 1 att1/5ELancs p110 CR France84

HART,Neil Lancefield T2Lt kia 31-7-17 218MGC p183 MR29

HART,Laurence George Capt kia 3-11-14 IA 61Pnrs p277 MR47

HART,Percival Frank Lt dow 3-5-17 3 att1Beds p86 CR France64

HART,Reginald Munro Lt dow 25-7-16 1Glouc p106 CR France703

HART,Richard George 2Lt kia 30-7-16 3 att10RWar p64 CR France390

HART,Robert Arthur 2Lt dow 1-8-17 6 att1Worc p108 CR Belgium7

HART,Samuel Edward 2Lt dow 30-4-17 7GordH p242 CR France40

HART,Thomas T2Lt kia 5-4-18 63MGC p183 CR France41

HART,Walter 2Lt kia 7-6-17 4Y&L p238 MR29

HART,William Cecil Frederick Nicol Lt kia 1-4-18 11RLancs &57RAF p59 MR20

HART-DAVIES,Ivan Beauclerk Lt kld 27-7-17 RFC SR p8 CR War

HARTE,George William 2Lt kia 5-3-18 2RMunstF p175 CR France364

HARTE,Irvine William Bagot Maj kia 21-6-17 IA 2/6GurkhaRif p277 MR43

HARTE,Joseph 2Lt kia 6-6-17 5RScots p211 CR France546

HARTE,Michael Joseph Capt kia 21-3-18 RASC att2/6N&D p193 MR20

HARTE-MAXWELL,Percival Maxwell Lt kia 11-4-16 4ConnRgrs att1RIrRif p172 CR France515,2Lt

HARTER,Clements Jesse Lt kia 16-6-15 3 att4RFus p68 MR29

HARTER,Herbert Hatfield Lt kia 9-10-17 GrenGds att2GdsMGReg p50&53 CR Belgium106,Hatfeild

HARTER,John Collier Foster T2Lt kia 28-11-17 3RRofCav attNottsYeo p23 CR Palestine9,James

HARTER,John George Capt dow 3-4-16 1DLI 151Bde p160 CR Belgium11

HARTERT,Joachim Charles TLt kia 28-10-16 8EYorks p84 CR France133

HARTFORD,Hugh Irving St.John Capt kia 22-10-14 Ches p96 MR22

HARTIGAN,Edward Patrick T2Lt kia 20-11-17 RMunstF att57RFC p8&175 CR France134,kld

HARTIGAN,Jeremiah Austin Chap4Cl ded 16-7-16 RAChDept p199 CR Iraq5

HARTIGAN,Kenneth Leslie Stewart Lt ded 2-11-19 IA 35ScindeHorse att36JacobsHorse p277 CR Egypt1

HARTIGAN,Thomas Jerome T2Lt kia 18-8-16 8Nhampt p137 CR France402

HARTILL,John Harry TCapt ded 25-1-16 GL 3Ches p96 CR War100

HARTINGTON,John Ernest Lt dow 13-7-17 5LancF att164MGC p187&221 CR Belgium11

HARTLE,Julian Walter Leslie 2Lt ded 10-3-20 IARO attMilWorksServ p277 MR43

HARTLEY,Alfred Lt dow 9-10-18 RGA 263SB p40 CR France725

HARTLEY,Arthur Rowland 2Lt dow 9-11-17 5SStaffs p229 CR Yorks719

HARTLEY,Bernard Harold TLt kia 4-11-16 20LancF p92 CR France924

HARTLEY,Charles Fletcher.MID 2Lt kia 27-11-17 CldGds att2GdsBde MGC p51 MR17

HARTLEY,Christopher Lt kia 1-9-17 C210RFA p207 CR Belgium84

HARTLEY,D'Arcy John Joseph Lt kia 14-7-16 7DragGds attMGC p21&183 MR21

HARTLEY,Edmund Lt kia 18-5-18 2LancF p92 CR France412

HARTLEY,Frederick Lynn 2Lt dow 23-8-18 3 att1ESurr p112 CR France239

HARTLEY,Herbert Henry T2Lt kia 14-3-18 48RFC p16 CR France446

HARTLEY,Horace Neville 2Lt kia 13-10-15 1/6NStaffs p238 MR19

HARTLEY,James Ernest 2Lt kia 26-10-17 5LNLancs p234 MR30

HARTLEY,James Harold 2Lt kia 22-7-17 RMunstF &45RFC p8&175 CR France285

HARTLEY,John Armitage 2Lt kia 19-12-15 4WRid p227 CR Belgium11

HARTLEY,John Bernard Capt kia 4-6-15 1KOSB p101 MR4

HARTLEY,Noël Thomas.MC.TCapt kia 5-11-18 9WYorks p81&258 CR France1142

HARTLEY,Norman Curtis 2Lt dow 20-1-18 RFA 19DAC p30 CR France905

HARTLEY,Reginald TLt kld 26-10-15 10Worc p108 CR France260

HARTLEY,Reginald Humphrey 2Lt kia 3-5-17 7 att1Mddx p235 MR20

HARTLEY,Richard T2Lt kld 11-11-16 8EYorks p84

HARTLEY,Walter John TCapt kia 16-8-15 5RIrrF p171 MR4

HARTLEY,Walter Lockwood Lt kia 13-10-15 5Lincs p220 MR19

HARTLEY,William Edwin T2Lt kia 2-10-15 2Ches p96 MR19,1-10-15

HARTLEY,William Garfield Capt dow 9-8-16 48AustInf CR France74

HARTLEY,William Guest.MM.T2Lt dow 8-8-18 9Ess p131 CR France888

HARTLEY,William Holliday.MC.Lt dow 22-3-18 8Huss p22 MR27

HARTLEY,William Ismay Spooner TLt kia 1-7-16 8YLl p143 CR France246

HARTLEY,William John Capt kia 21-5-17 2/6Lond p246 MR20

HARTLEY,William Reginald 2Lt dow 20-12-15 7LancF p221 CR Gallipoli6

HARTLEY,William Stuart.MC.TCapt dow 8-10-18 9Manch att1LNLancsp237 CR France380

HARTMANN,Carl Herbert Lt kia 2-7-18 5RWKent p235 CR France516

HARTNALL,Archibald John Maj ded 6-3-17 2RFA p206 MR65

HARTNELL,Cuthbert LtACapt kia 16-7-15 8WYorks p219 CR Belgium96

HARTNELL,Edward Bush Capt ded 25-4-16 RAMC 1/4LondMtdBdeFA p253 CR Egypt9

HARTNELL-SINCLAIR,St.John Leslie 2Lt kia 25-9-15.3ESurr att2WelshR p112 MR19

HARTNETT,Joseph Mary Patrick SubCdr ded 18-2-15 IA S&TCps p277

HARTNETT,Michael Charles Lt kia 19-9-17 RMunstF attRFC p8&175 CR Belgium

HARTNOLL,Herbert Nicholas Lt&QM ded 28-5-16 RE p45

HARTNOLL,Hugh Peter Lt kia 12-12-14 1Worc p108 MR22

HARTNOLL,James Capt ded 20-5-17 RFA 1/1BerksBty p207 CR Egypt2

HARTNOTT, SubCdr 19-2-15 S&T Cps CR Iraq6

HARTOPP,Charles William Liddell 2Lt kia 13-10-15 7Suff p78 MR19

HARTREE,Cyril 2Lt kia 29-5-18 RGA 201SB p40 CR France25

HARTREE,Eric Mursell TLt kia 8-8-18 RASC att8RBerks p193 CR France247

HARTSHORN,Arthur William TLt dow 9-1-18 98MGC p183 CR Belgium11

HARTSHORN,Laurence Alec Lt dow 26-3-18 2DLI att18LTMB p160 CR France1483,4Bn

HARTT,Harold 2Lt kia 5-5-17 9Lpool p216 CR Belgium4 7Bn

HARTWELL,Barry Capt kia 30-10-14 IA 2/8GurkhaRif p277 MR28

HARTY,James Johnson TLt ded 6-3-17 RAMC p195 CR Eire88

HARTY,John Joseph 2Lt dow 27-9-16 1RMunstF att10RIrRif p175 CR France285

HARTY,Wilfrid A.2Lt kia 8-8-17 11RDubF p176 CR Belgium115

HARTY,William David T2Lt kia 30-9-18 KSLI att1/4Bn p145 CR France80

HARVARD,Kenneth O'Gorman Lt kia 1-8-17 2GrenGds p50 CR Belgium106

HARVARD,Lionel de Jersey LtACapt kia 30-3-18 1GrenGds p50 CR France1183

HARVEST,G.Maj 14-10-18 5Lond CR Lond13

HARVEST,Gordon Lindsay.MC.Lt dow 20-6-17 5Lond p246 CR France518,21-6-17

HARVEY,Albert Henry T2Lt kia 7-10-16 9RFus p68 MR21

HARVEY,Alec Wright Capt dow PoW 27-3-18 8ScotRif p225 CR France660

HARVEY,Alexander Scott TLt dow 29-3-18 2GordH A'Coy p166 CR France95

HARVEY,Alfred Wallace TCapt dow 7-9-16 RAMC att55RFA AmmCol p195 CR Iraq5

HARVEY,Austin Mozart.MBE.Lt mbk 27-10-18 5Dev p257

HARVEY,Bernard Sydney Capt kia 1-7-16 1/5Lond p246 MR21

HARVEY,Charles Claud Lt dow 3-4-16 7A&SH p243 CR France95,Cleland

HARVEY,Charles Lewis Capt dow 10-5-17 2/4Lincs p220&270 CR Lincs29

HARVEY,Charles Milne Lt kia 25-11-14 2Mddx p147 CR France1157,23-11-14

HARVEY,Claude Lindsay 2Lt kia 23-3-18 4 att7RWSurr p212 MR27

HARVEY,Douglas.DSO.Capt kia 10-2-17 IA 31Punjabis attStaff 35InfBde p277 CR Iraq5

HARVEY,D.S.Capt 29-10-21 RAMC CR War7

HARVEY,Douglas TLt kia 27-3-18 2GrenGds p50 CR France214

HARVEY,Douglas Lennox 2Lt kia 2-11-14 9Lancers p22 CR Belgium98

HARVEY,Douglas Preston.MC.T2Lt kia 20-11-17 164MGC p183 MR17

HARVEY,Edward Byron Atkins T2Lt kia 15-4-17 8RWKent B'Coyp141 CR France149

HARVEY,Edward George Capt kia 16-6-15 1Wilts p153 MR29

HARVEY,E.H.Capt 31-7-16 RE CR Hamps7

HARVEY,Eric Howard.MC&Bar.Capt kia 30-9-18 2/5Glouc A'Coy p225 CR France769

HARVEY,Ernest Anthony 2Lt ded 14-11-17 IARO att29Lancers p277 MR65,15-11-17

HARVEY,Frank Lennox Lt kia 30-10-14 9Lancers p22 MR29

HARVEY,Frederick William TLt kia 9-8-15 10SLancs att6LancF p125 CR Gallipoli1

HARVEY,George LtTCapt kia 21-6-17 RGA 336SB p40 CR France163

HARVEY,George Denis 2Lt kia 9-10-17 3CldGds p51 MR30

HARVEY,George Winfred.MC.LtACapt kia 12-4-18 A169RFA p207 CR France881,13-4-18

HARVEY,Gerald Franklyn Lt kia 8-11-15 RFA attRFC p1&30 CR Belgium11

HARVEY,Gilbert Aberdein Capt dow 25-11-17 RAMC att1RLancs p195 CR France113

HARVEY,Harry Thomas Lt kia 31-7-17 5Suff att23MGC p187&217 MR29

HARVEY,Henry Burnett T2Lt kia 30-3-18 13Glouc p106 MR27

HARVEY,Herbert Lt 23-5-20 IARO MR66

HARVEY,Herbert Alexander TLt kia 12-10-16 Beds att1Ess p86 MR21

HARVEY,James Capt kia 16-5-15 7Lpool p215 MR22,17-5-15

HARVEY,James.MID 2Lt kia 1-7-16 2SfthH p164 MR21

HARVEY,James T2Lt dow 26-2-17 2SfthH p164 CR Iraq5

HARVEY,James Walter TLt ded 25-8-17 RASC p267 CR Norf30,2Lt

HARVEY,John 2Lt dow 10-9-18 1RB p179 CR France13

HARVEY,John Alan T2Lt kia 20-11-17 11RDubF p176 CR France1489

HARVEY,John Albert T2Lt kia 4-4-18 7RWSurr attTMB p56 MR27

HARVEY,John Alexander 2Lt kia 25-9-15 6GordH p242 MR19

HARVEY,John Forsyth TCapt kia 23-3-18 9RInniskF p105 MR27

HARVEY,John Lawrence T2Lt kia 24-4-17 4SfthH p164 CR France545

HARVEY,John William Lt ded 26-12-18 IARO att2/56Regt p277 CR India97A

HARVEY,Kenneth Watson Lt dow 27-9-15 RFA 19A/Asect p30 CR Belgium11

HARVEY,Leslie 2Lt kia 25-4-15 8Mddx p236 MR29

HARVEY,Oliver Colin 2Lt kia 4-7-16 3 att7SLancs p125 MR21

HARVEY,Phillip Parmenter 2LtACapt kia 8-8-18 10Ess p131 MR16

HARVEY,Ralph de Warenne 2Lt dow 7-6-16 3Dors att1KRRC p124 CR France145,Warrenne

HARVEY,Richard Ernle TCapt&Adjt dow 27-10-15 9BlkW p128 CR France554,25-9-15

HARVEY,Richard Prentice Maj kia 9-5-15 3 att2RBerks p139 MR32

HARVEY,Robert Clive Lt kia 14-10-15 1/4Leic p219 MR19,13-10-15

HARVEY,Robert George Bosworth 2Lt kia 25-12-17 1/5Lincs p220 CR France163,kldacc

HARVEY,Rollo d'Aubigne ACapt kia 9-9-16 2RSuss p119 CR France432

HARVEY,Ronald Marmaduke Dawnay 2Lt kia 20-4-15 4NStaffs att1Beds p157 MR29 CR France453

HARVEY,R.W.2Lt ded 22-10-18 17RFus &RAF p68

HARVEY,Sidney Lancelot,DSO.MC Maj ded 8-1-19 RE 500FC p209 CR Asia81

HARVEY,Stanley 2Lt kia 9-4-17 4NStaffs att9YLI p157 CR France162

HARVEY,Stanley Alfred George TLt kia 21-3-18 8RBerks p139 MR27

HARVEY,Thomas 2Lt ded 29-4-17 3RLancs p59 CR Iraq8

HARVEY,Thomas Daniel.MC.TLt ded 17-10-18 MGC att2/1NigR p183&201 CR WAfrica54

HARVEY,Thomas Francis Lt kia 7-6-18 6SfthH &49RAF p270 MR20

HARVEY,Wickham Leathes Lt kia 3-3-15 IA 7Rajputs p277 MR61

HARVEY,William 2Lt kia 25-9-15 3Lpool p72 CR France163,1Bn

HARVEY,William 2Lt dow 14-10-16 NumbF att27Bn p61 CR France297

HARVEY,William Anthony Lt ded 7-11-17 4Norf attRFC p18&216 CR Europe51

HARVEY,William Clayton TLt kia 14-7-16 20KRRC p150 CR France513

HARVEY,William Henry T2Lt kia 23-10-18 A88RFA p30 CR France323,22-10-18

HARVEY,William James St.John TBrigGen dow 1-2-16 BlkW p128 CR Iraq5

HARVEY,William Mitchell 2Lt kia 10-7-16 13WelshR p126 MR21

HARVEY,William Reginald TLt dow 23-9-17 B95RH&FA p30

HARVEY JAMES,A.K.MID Capt 15-4-17 1EKent CR France551

HARVEY-JONES,F.M.MC.2Lt 18-6-17 3Worc att8BordR p285 CR France285

HARVEY-KELLY,Hubert Dunsterville,DSO CaptTMaj kia 29-4-17 RIrReg &19RFC p89&8 CR France604

HARVIE,Eric Fulton.MC.Lt kia 15-6-18 2GordH p166 CR France33,Capt 1Bn

HARVIE,James 2Lt dow 8-6-16 D92RFA p30 CR France40

HARVIE,Patrick Joseph TLt kia 16-4-17 9NumbF p61 CR France1188

HARVIE,Stuart McLaren 2Lt dow 1-6-18 2 att6KRRC p150 CR France10

HARVISON,Robert Albert Lt ded 9-2-19 3RMunstF p266

HARWOOD,Colin Crisp T2Lt ded 6-11-17 2MGC Inf p183 CR Notts68

HARWOOD,Gerald.AFC.Lt kldacc 1-5-19 3Suff attRAF p78 CR Kent103

HARWOOD,Percy Gregory Shelley Lt dow 31-12-17 1/4RSuss p228 CR Palestine3

HASELDEN,Cyril Gerrard TLt ded 27-11-18 RE attAustCpsHQ p45 CR France931,Capt

HASELDEN,Edgar Adolphus TCapt dow 9-7-16 11WYorks p81 CR France833

HASELDINE,Frederick HonLt&QM ded 2-12-14 8WRid p115 CR Leic13

HASELER,Maurice Noble 1Lt dow 4-7-16 2RWar p64 MR21

HASELER,William Hereward TLtACapt kia 20-11-17 'B'TankCps p188 MR17

HASELGROVE,Bertram Thorpe 2Lt dow 3-9-18 9Lond p248 CR France833

HASKINS,Victor Bradshaw 2Lt kia 20-11-15 3ESurr att5KSLI p112 CR Belgium84

HASLAM,Arthur Dixon TLt dow 2-11-18 9NumbF p61 CR France398

HASLAM,Bernard John.DSO.Maj kia 26-8-18 RE p45 MR61,LtCol

HASLAM,Charles Stanley Lt kia 10-11-17 YorkHussYeo p206 MR20,9WYorks

HASLAM,Herbert 2Lt kia 16-9-17 14Manch &6RFC p8&155 MR20

HASLAM,James Lt kia 30-10-17 28Lond p252 MR30

HASLAM,Robert T2Lt ded 29-3-18 12LancF p92 CR Greece1

HASLAM,Wilfred Henry Wescott Lt kia 7-2-16 4RWKent p234 CR Iraq6

HASLAM,William T2Lt kia 21-3-18 Manch att2/7Bn p155 MR27,24-3-18

HASLAM,William Kenneth Seale Capt kia 27-4-17 4RFA p207 CR France581

HASLER,Algernon 2Lt dow 18-9-16 2GrenGds SR p50 CR France833

HASLER,Arthur Thomas.MC.Lt&QM drd 4-5-17 RAMC att40CCS p195 CR Italy14

HASLER,Gordon Beverley T2Lt kia 26-7-16 9 att7Beds p86 CR France513

HASLER,Julian BrigGen kia 26-4-15 EKent p57 CR Belgium101

HASLER,Leonard Melsome TLt dow 21-9-17 2Ess att17MGC p131&183

HASLETT,Thomas Sinclair.MC.TLt kia 22-11-17 10RIrRif p169 MR17

HASLOCK,John Charles Simeon T2Lt dow 2-11-15 att7Glouc p106 MR4

HASLUCK,Sidney Vandyke.MID 2Lt kia 4-6-15 IARO att89Punjabis p277 MR4

HASSARD,Edward John,MC Lt ded 7-11-18 B110RH&FA p30

HASSELL,Robert De Bray.CMG.LtCol 22-2-20 RA CR Sussex225

HASSLACHER,James Alfred Charles Capt kia 29-12-17 2/20Lond p251 CR Palestine3

HASTINGS,Aubrey Joseph T2Lt kia 5-10-15 7ESurr p112 CR France108

HASTINGS,George Herbert Capt kia 5-2-15 1Mddx p147 CR France922

HASTINGS,George William 2Lt kia 1-8-17 3Mon att10Ches p244 CR Belgium8,Williams

HASTINGS,H.M.Sister 23-7-18 TFNS CR Scot613

HASTINGS,James Smith 2Lt ded 25-6-16 4GordH p270 CR Scot281

HASTINGS,Joseph Edward T2Lt kia 18-7-16 11 att8BlkW p128 MR21

HASTINGS,Joseph Lorton T2Lt kia 12-5-17 10LancF p92 MR20

HASTINGS,Leslie Lt kia 21-1-16 IA 102Grens p277 CR Iraq5,Capt

HASTINGS,Noël Henry Bruce TCapt kia 7-6-17 8Glouc p106 CR Belgium102

HASTINGS,Percy Maj dow 2-9-14 RWKent p141

HASTINGS-MEDHURST,Francis Leslie 2Lt kia 17-10-14 2Worc p108 MR22

HASTWELL,Hugh Norman 2Lt kia 30-6-18 10AustInf CR France193

HASTWELL,Wilfrid Maurice T2Lt kia 7-4-17 MGC p183 CR France266

HASWELL,Frederick 2Lt dow 23-4-15 3EYorks p84 MR29

HASWELL,Gordon TCapt kia 1-7-16 9YLI p143 CR France189

HATCH,Andrew Basil 2Lt ded 10-10-14 9Mddx p255 CR Mddx58,Lt

HATCH,George John Lt kia 6-4-17 17Lond attRFC p18&250 MR20 &CR France924

HATCH,Henry Bertram William T2Lt kia 18-11-16 57MGC Inf p183 MR21

HATCH,Jesse.MC.DCM.MM.Lt dow 23-10-18 RGA 95SB p40 CR France270

HATCH,Laurence Collier Lt kia 27-9-15 11DLI p160 MR19,14Bn

HATCH,Nicholas Stephen 2Lt kia 1-7-16 13RIrRif p169 CR France744

HATCH,Norman Claud 2Lt kia 21-10-16 2SLancs p125 CR France832

HATCH,Philip Randall TLt kia 7-10-16 6EKent p57 MR21

HATCH,Reginald William Lt kia 3-9-16 17 att10RB p179 MR21

HATCH,William Leonard Ringrose Lt kia 25-1-15 2RIrF p171 MR29

HATCHER,Reginald Gordon Lt dow 20-9-17 1/4RLancs p213 CR Belgium18

HATFIELD,Alfred Charles.MC.2LtACapt dow 21-9-17 8Y&L p159 CR Belgium11

HATFIELD,Arthur Percival Chap4Cl ded 9-7-18 RAChDept 1stBGH p199 CR Iraq5

HATFIELD,Charles Eric.MC.Capt kia 21-9-18 10EKent p204 CR France1462

HATFIELD,Roy Berriman Lt dow 24-5-15 8Lond p247 CR France80,kia

HATHAWAY,Sidney T2Lt kia 12-1-16 11RFC p3 CR France518

HATHAWAY,Thomas Hervey 2Lt kia 17-2-15 3RLancs p59 MR29

HATHERELL,Eric James 2Lt mbk 25-4-17 9WRid p256 MR20

HATHORN,Charles Nicholls 2Lt kia 10-8-15 6LNLancs p136 MR4

HATHORN,Noel McDonall.MID 2Lt kia 14-7-15 IARO att76Punjabis p277 CR Iraq6,McDouall

HATT,Arthur Beach TCapt kia 1-7-16 8SomLI A'Coy p79 CR France267

HATT,Edward Beach TCapt kia 26-8-16 7SomLI C'Coy p80 CR France400

HATT,Harold Ernest Lt drd 23-3-19 RASC p270 CR Oxford36,29-1-19

HATTAM,Harold Colin Lt kia 26-9-17 5 att1/4Suff p217 MR30

HATTE,Edward Stokes T2Lt kia 16-8-17 7RIrRif p169 MR30

HATTER,Bernard 2Lt kia 25-9-15 2 att3Leic p87 MR19

HATTON,Bryan 2Lt kia 23-4-16 1/1WorcYeo p206 CR Egypt2,Brian

HATTON,Christopher 2Lt 9-12-15 SStaffs CR Lincs69

HATTON,Ernest Robert.MID 2Lt kia 8-5-18 2Wilts p153 MR30

HATTON,Frederick Charles 2Lt kia 30-10-14 2Yorks p90 MR29

HATTON,Horace Walter Smeathman LtACapt kia 23-8-18 3 att2SStaffs p122 CR France927

HATTON,John Alfred 2Lt kia 3-5-17 7 att12Mddx p235 MR20

HATTON,Robert Andrew Maj dow 23-10-18 RFA 123SB p206 CR France332

HAUGHTON,Alfred John 2LtTLt kia 23-6-15 9DLI p239 CR Belgium17 24-6-15

HAUGHTON,Charles Stanley Lt ded 4-2-19 23RB p244 CR Ches8,5-2-19

HAUGHTON,Thomas Greenwood TLt kia 1-7-16 12RIrRif p169 CR France701

HAVELOCK,Beresford Arthur Jardine TMaj kia 14-9-18 1 att7NStaffs p157&265,14-9-15 Y&L CR Asia81

HAVELOCK,Ernest Wilfrid TLt dow 18-9-16 26RFus p68 CR France833,Wilfred

HAVERFIELD,John Campbell Lt dow 14-7-15 IARO att24Punjabis p277 CR Iraq6

HAVERS,Frederick Charles 2Lt kia 27-5-18 5Lincs p220 MR18

HAVERSON,James Blain Lt dow 25-6-16 RAMC 104FA p195 CR France430

HAVILAND,John Doria TLt dow 16-7-16 10RFus p68 CR France833

HAWARD,Godfrey TLt kia 15-11-16 99MGC Inf p183 MR21

HAWARD,Hereward Warren T2Lt dow 1-7-18 7 att2Beds p86 CR France69,Lt

HAWARDEN,Robert Cornwallis.Viscount.Lt dow 26-8-14 3CldGds p51 CR France932

HAWDON,Cecil 2Lt kia 27-6-16 4Yorks p220 CR Belgium182

HAWDON,Noel Elliot Chap4Cl ded 16-11-18 RAChDept CofE att45TMB p199 CR France34

HAWDON,Rupert Ayrton.MIDx2 TLtACapt kia 4-11-18 RGA 35SB p40 CR France1081

HAWES,Adrian Lancelot TLt kia 8-10-18 52MGC Inf p183 CR France602

HAWES,Ernest Harington T2Lt kia 5-6-17 20NumbF p61 MR20

HAWES,Frederick Maxwell 2Lt kld 14-9-17 RGA &RFC p8 CR Camb37

HAWES,Godfrey Charles Browne TCapt drd 10-4-17 RAMC p195 CR France85

HAWES,Herbert TLt kia 20-10-18 11 att1ESurr p112 CR France1388

HAWES,Robert Frank Capt dow 23-9-14 1Leic p87 CR France1107

HAWKE,Albert Edward Mountain Aysh T2Lt dow 11-9-16 19 att2KRRC p150 CR France833

HAWKE,Edward Anthony Francis Lt ded 27-12-18 20/7RFA p261 CR Cornwall106 9Bde

HAWKE,Ernest William 2Lt kia 11-5-17 7 att1Hamps p229 MR20

HAWKE,William Baldwin 2Lt kia 7-10-16 7Mddx p235 MR21

HAWKEN,Alfred George WO explosion 8-11-20 RIM p277

HAWKEN,G.W.2Lt 18-5-18 GL &RAF CR Hamps192

HAWKEN,William Victor Lt kia 26-4-16 2/7N&D p233 CR Mddx53

HAWKER,Albert Victor TLt ded 23-12-18 8 att9Glouc p106 CR France1571

HAWKER,Charles William Seymour Lt ded 13-3-18 13Hamps p264 CR Europe51

HAWKER,Frederick James T2Lt dow 16-7-16 8Glouc p106 CR France40

HAWKER,Gilbert Victor Lt ded 1-7-20 IARO attS&TCps p277 MR65

HAWKER,Lance George.VC.DSO.TMaj ded 23-11-16 RE &24RFC p3&45 MR20

HAWKER,Reginald Sudlow Capt dow 9-11-17 1DevYeo attMGC p203 CR Egypt2

HAWKES,Gerald Arthur 2Lt dow 3-7-18 RGA att521SB p40 CR France31

HAWKES,John Aubrey T2Lt dow 11-9-18 7Leic p87 CR France439,kia

HAWKES,John Cornock TLt kia 30-7-15 RAMC att8KRRC p195 CR Belgium35 Cornick

HAWKES,Percival Warburton Capt kia 9-4-18 5Lpool p215 MR19

HAWKES,Septimus James LtACapt ded 10-7-18 3RBerks p139 CR Berks86

HAWKESWORTH,Francis Henry Stanley 2Lt kia 25-1-15 3BordR attWelshR p117 MR22

HAWKINS,Alexander Edward CaptAMaj dow 12-12-17 B181RFA p30 CR France398

HAWKINS,Charles Francis Maj kia 25-4-15 RFA 46Bty p30 CR France1106

HAWKINS,Clarence Vincent Tom Capt kia 26-9-17 5SStaffs p229 MR19

HAWKINS,F.C.Lt dow 15-11-17 2KAR p268

HAWKINS,George Arthur LtCol ded 2-6-19 IA attS&TCps p277 CR Surrey1

HAWKINS,Gilbert William TLt dow 15-11-16 15 att13KRRC p150 CR France701

HAWKINS,Harold George T2Lt dow 24-7-15 11Mddx p147 CR France922

HAWKINS,Harold Ingleby Capt mbk 16-6-17 2Lond p257 MR20

HAWKINS,Herbert Edward 2Lt kia 11-5-17 1/14Lond p249 CR France537

HAWKINS,Herbert Edwin TCapt kia 1-7-16 10Ess p131 CR France513

HAWKINS,Humphrey Caesar.MC.2Lt kia 23-4-18 B121RFA p30 CR Belgium11

HAWKINS,John Bawtree TCapt&Adjt ded 30-8-16 SL 18InfBaseDepot p201 CR France40

HAWKINS,John Henry T2Lt dow 8-2-18 WYorks att8Bn p81 CR France266

HAWKINS,John Noel Capt dow 30-7-16 27Manch p155 CR France742

HAWKINS,John Stephen 2Lt kia 23-7-17 22Lond p251 CR Belgium122,24-7-17

HAWKINS,Kenneth Edwards.MC.LtACapt kia 22-3-18 7RFus p68 MR20

HAWKINS,Kenneth James T2Lt kia 8-8-18 1TankCps A'Coy p188 CR France587

HAWKINS,L.H.Lt 8-10-19 2Suff CR Surrey148

HAWKINS,Lionel Hope Lt kia31-10-14 1DragGds p20 MR29

HAWKINS,Oliver Luther 2Lt dow 26-4-15 3EYorks p84 CR France200

HAWKINS,Stanley.MC.Capt kia 29-5-18 HAC p206 MR18

HAWKINS,Walter Elmslie 2LtTLt dow 8-6-17 8Glouc p106 CR Belgium11

HAWKINS,Wilfred Francis Capt 21-4-21 RAMC CR Ireland33

HAWKINS,William Percy TLt dow 12-10-15 6KSLI p145 CR France40

HAWKRIDGE,Joseph Arnold T2Lt dow 6-11-16 15RFus att9RSuss p68 CR France12

HAWKS,Albert John Everdale 2Lt dow 15-6-17 79RFA p30 CR France113

HAWKS,Aubrey Meldrum Wood Lt kia 27-9-18 4RScots p211 CR France484

HAWKSEY,Bernard Richard Lt kia 28-9-18 5LancF p221 CR France658

HAWKSLEY,George Lt kia 22-3-18 4 att7/8RInniskF p105 CR France329

HAWKSLEY,John Plunkett Verney.DSO.MIDx3 TLtCol kia 8-8-16 110RFA p30 CR France515

HAWKSLEY,Walter Linney Maj kld 3-4-16 RAMC 98FA p253 CR France300

HAWKSWELL,Lewis Bertram Lt dow 18-9-18 6WYorks &RAF p255

HAWKSWORTH,Henry Charles Harold.MC.Lt kia 21-3-18 10Ess p131 MR27

HAWKSWORTH,Stanley Harcourt T2Lt kia 20-9-17 7Lpool p72 MR30

HAWLEY,Cyril T2Lt kld 23-7-17 GL &RFC p8 CR Yorks547

HAWLEY,Cyril Francis Capt kia 2-11-14 2KRRC p150 MR29

HAWLEY,F.SNurse 20-6-18 QAIMNS CR Staffs153

HAWLEY,Nellie MilProb Nurse drd 31-12-17 QAIMNS p200 CR Egypt1

HAWLING,Thomas Albert T2Lt kia 4-11-17 RLancs att9YLI p59 MR30

HAWORTH,Arthur T2Lt kia 19-7-16 16Lpool attMGC p72&183 CR France1157

HAWORTH,Harold Stanley Lt kia 13-8-16 4YLI p235 CR France293

HAWORTH,Herbert TLt kia 7-6-17 11 att8LNLancs p136 CR Belgium102

HAWORTH,Montague Burgess Lt kia 23-3-18 5ESurr p226 CR France1893

HAWORTH,Percy Geoffrey du Val Lt kia 30-7-16 18Manch p155 CR France402

HAWORTH,Philip Theodore 2Lt dow 3-5-17 D86RFA p30 CR France40,Capt

HAWORTH,Thomas Eldred Curwen T2Lt dow 2-12-17 9Ess p131 CR France398

HAWORTH-BOOTH,Benjamin Booth Maj 8-11-19 ERidYeo CR Mddx26

HAWTHORN,William T2Lt dow 31-12-15 RE 172TC p45 CR France40,Lt

HAWTREY,John James Alexander 2Lt ded PoW 17-9-17 GL 60RFC p8 CR Belgium140

HAWTREY,Ralph TLt kia 3-9-16 RE 179TC p45 CR France430

HAY,Alfred Chalmers 2Lt kia 9-4-17 3 att8/10GordH p166 MR20

HAY,Andrew Peter T2Lt kia 29-4-16 1KOSB D'Coy p101 CR France35

HAY,Archibald MajTLtCol kia 3-2-17 8RWFus p98 CR Iraq5

HAY,Arthur Leslie 2Lt dow 26-4-17 4 att10/11HLI p163 CR France113

HAY,Arthur Vincent.Lord Capt kia 14-9-14 1IrGds p52 CR France1112

HAY,Charles Edward Erroll Lt dow 9-8-18 17Lancers p23 CR France29

HAY,Donald Yalden Lt kia 11-8-17 2/5RWKent att20RFC p18,235&212,Malden RWSurr CR France134

HAY,Douglas Woulfe.MC.Lt kia 29-9-18 6 att1Mddx p147 CR France407

HAY,E.J.A.Lt 5-9-18 IA 2/41Dogras MR65

HAY,Edward Hutton 2Lt dow 11-6-17 1/7GordH p242 CR France113

HAY,Frank Tochetti TLt kia 26-9-15 7RScotF p94 MR19

HAY,Geoffrey William.MID Capt kia 9-5-15 3 att1LNLancs p136 MR22

HAY,James Barromew.DSO.TLtCol ded 2-8-19 SL GHQ p268 CR Egypt8

HAY,James Blackwood 2Lt ded 29-10-18 4Y&L p238 CR Italy12

HAY,James Duncan T2Lt dow 15-12-17 1/5RLancs p59 CR France145

HAY,James Henry Webster TCapt&Adjt kia 30-11-15 9SfthH p164 CR Belgium5

HAY,James Lyle T2Lt kia 3-7-16 12NumbF p61 CR France267

HAY,J.M.Lt mbk 24-3-18.MID Ches &62RFC p256 MR20

HAY,John 2Lt kia 23-1-17 40RFC SR p8 CR France31

HAY,Robert T2Lt kia 28-7-18 5Dev p76 MR18

HAY,Robert TLt ded 9-10-18 RASC MT p193 CR France34

HAY,Robert TLt ded 7-1-19 9 att2NLancs p254 CR Belgium302

HAY,Roger Bolton.MC.Lt dow PoW 17-7-17 3WYorks att48RFC p8&81 CR Belgium175,2Bn

HAY,William T2Lt dow 1-4-16 12ScotRif att1RScotF p103 CR Belgium11

HAY,William George TCapt ded 7-8-16 11 att8BlkW p128 CR France12

HAY,William Stevenson Brown TCapt kia 5-10-18 RAMC att53RFA p195 CR Belgium44

HAY-JAN,Henry Gordon 2Lt 15-2-17 8Wilts CR Iraq5

HAY-WEBB,A.B.Capt 23-8-15 1/5GurkhaRif MR4

HAY-WEBB,Charles Robert Forbes TCapt kia 28-12-16 235RFA p30 CR Belgium28

HAY-SMITH Alan Douglas 2Lt 26 3 17 1Ess MR31

HAYBITTLE,Richard William Lt dow 8-1-18 185MGC p183 CR Iraq5

HAYCRAFT,Alan Montague Lt kia 1-7-16 6 att2RFus p68 CR France1501

HAYCRAFT,Leonard Courtenay 2Lt kia 7-10-16 4Lond p246 MR21

HAYCROFT,Frank Alexander T2Lt kia 10-8-17 KRRC att10Bn p150 MR29

HAYDEN,Leon Anthony 2Lt dow 14-1-17 2RIrReg p89 CR France200

HAYDEN,William Clarence Capt kia 19-9-15 1HAC p206 CR Belgium6

HAYDOCK,Tom Lt dow 2-9-18 1/7ScotRif p224 CR France103

HAYDON,Alan TLt ded 28-12-18 RE 71FC p45 CR Surrey1

HAYDON,Edgar Frederick Bewes 2Lt kia 19-7-16 51/39RFA p30 MR21

HAYDON,Geoffrey Miles TLtACapt kia 16-8-17 8SWBord p100 CR Belgium106,dow

HAYDON,George Francis 2Lt kia 19-8-16 C175RFA p30 CR France1890,18-8-16

HAYE,Basil Lt drd 10-10-18 2RBerks p139 CR Ireland14

HAYE,Philip Lt ded 2-4-19 3RBerks att82MGC p183&139 CR Asia81

HAYES,Arthur 2Lt kia 25-3-18 3 att4Beds p86 MR20

HAYES,Cedric George Lt kia 9-4-18 RE 422FC p210 CR France260

HAYES,Charles Bianconi Capt kia 10-8-15 10Hamps p120 MR4

HAYES,Charles Robert 2Lt ded 25-3-19 IARO p277 CR India97A

HAYES,Claude Julian Patrick ACapt kia 9-8-16 1RFus p68 CR France164

HAYES,Ernest de Launoy Maj kia 10-3-15 ScotRif p103 CR France260,Lannoy

HAYES,Gordon Stanley T2Lt kia 15-6-18 1/2RWKent att5Glouc p141 CR Italy2

HAYES,Harry Urmston 2Lt kia 13-10-15 1BlkW p128 MR19,Urmson

HAYES,Herbert Henry TCaptAMaj kia 1-10-18 RGA 409SB p40 CR France439

HAYES,John Carolin.MC.Lt ded 19-11-18 2CldGds p57 CR France85

HAYES,John Henry 2Lt kia 31-7-17 5 att17RWFus p223 MR29

HAYES,Leo John 2Lt kia 10-10-18 3 att18Lpool p72 CR France190

HAYES,Leonard Frank 2Lt kia 29-4-18 1/5SStaffs p229 CR France572,Capt

HAYES,Marshall HonLt ded 23-3-19 15Ches p263 CR Sussex19

HAYES,Mortimer Frederick TLt kia 10-7-16 8EYorks p84 CR France531,Capt 29-4-17

HAYES,Reginald 2Lt kia 22-7-17 GL &45RFC p8 MR20

HAYES,Reginald Pole 2Lt kld 12-3-16 3SomLI p80 CR France55,Lt 6Bn

HAYES,Richard Johnson(Dick) T2Lt kia 4-11-18 7Wilts p153 CR France929

HAYES,Robert Harnett 2Lt dow 1-8-17 4ConnRgrs att2Leinst p172 MR29,Lt

HAYES,W.Rice Maj 19-2-19 RFA CR Yorks417

HAYES,William.DSO.Capt ded 20-10-18 RWSurr p56 CR Italy12

HAYES,Willie 2Lt dow 25-9-18 RGA 143SB p40 CR France146

HAYES-NEWINGTON,Charles Wetherell.MID TCapt kia 11-5-15 2Ches p96 MR29,8-5-15

HAYES-NEWINGTON,Harold May 2Lt kia 10-3-15 1Lpool p72 CR France1106

HAYES-SADLER,Edwin John Berkley Lt kia 28-10-14 RE p45 MR22

HAYES-SADLER,Ernest Reginald Capt kia 30-10-14 IA 2/8GurkhaRif p277 CR France1887

HAYES-SADLER,Gerard Ralph Lt kia 3-9-16 2RWar p64 CR France402

HAYES-SHEEN,George Edward Capt ded 19-2-15 6RIrRif CR Ches8

HAYFIELD,Allan Sydney T2Lt dow 6-10-16 7EKent p57 CR France74

HAYHOE,Alfred Charles 2Lt kia 27-7-16 1Beds p86 MR21

HAYHURST,John 2Lt kia 19-4-18 2Ess p131 CR France250,18-4-18

HAYHURST,Thomas Lt drd 13-8-15 RAMC 2/1FA p254 MR4

HAYLETT,Newman T2Lt dow 19-8-16 166RFA p30 CR France197

HAYLEY,Cyril William Seafort Burrell TCapt dow 18-9-15 10HLI p163 CR France98

HAYLOCK,Henry Capt kia 11-5-15 1/4Leic p219 CR Belgium99

HAYLOR,Charles Alexander Lt kia 17-2-17 10Mddx p236 CR France314

HAYMAN,Alfred George.MC.Capt kia 8-9-16 2WelshR A'Coy p126 CR France432

HAYMAN,J.H Lt dow 18-7-17 ASC 29MT att29SB p30 CR Belgium16

HAYMAN,William Deacon T2Lt kia 13-8-17 1/11Hamps p120 CR Belgium10

HAYMAN,William Muir.DSO.TMaj dow 13-7-17 RE 92FC p45 CR France145

HAYMES,George Noel 2Lt mbk 19-8-18 IA 1/89Punjabis att125Rif p277 MR34

HAYNE,Moreton 2Lt ded PoW 10-10-16 LancF &25RFC p3&92 CR France604

HAYNES,Albert TCapt ded 20-7-17 7NStaffs p157 CR Iraq8

HAYNES,Charles Graham.MC&Bar.Lt kia 23-10-18 4KRRC &RAF p265 CR France349,Capt

HAYNES,Charles Henry 2Lt kia 26-3-18 3 att8NStaffs p157 CR France798,Lt

HAYNES,Bernard Hamer 2Lt ded 20-12-17 RFA p261 CR Lancs40

HAYNES,Clifford Skemp T2Lt kia 1-7-16 15DLI p161 MR21

HAYNES,Francis Edmund Lt kld 20-4-18 1/5Suff p217 CR Palestine9

HAYNES,George James T2Lt kia 16-6-18 17 att13Mddx p147 MR20

HAYNES,George John TCapt ded 30-9-17 RASC p193 CR Scot557,LtCol

HAYNES,G.W.N.R.Capt kld 30-5-19 6RMunstF attRAF p254 CR Germany1

HAYNES,James 2Lt kia 29-3-16 11NumbF p61 CR France160

HAYNES,John Eustace Tarleton 2Lt kia 23-3-18 1 att2/8Worc p108 MR27

HAYNES,John Lorenzo Patrick Lt mbk 11-3-18 4LNLancs attRFC p257 CR France1277

HAYNES,Samuel 2Lt dow 4-10-18 4SomLI att58MGC p187&218 CR France146

HAYNES,William Charles 2Lt kia 3-5-17 3 att5 O&BLI p130 MR20

HAYNES,William George 2Lt kia 27-6-17 1/4Suff p217 CR France593

HAYNES,William Gray TLt kia 25-9-15 8RBerks p139 CR France552

HAYNES,William Harold Capt kld 26-9-18 6Yorks &RAF p90

HAYS,Samuel Copping Athanasius Capt ded 19-7-19 RASC p267 CR Lond2

HAYTER,Arthur Cecil Thomas Lt dow 1-11-14 Norf p73 MR29

HAYTER,Eric Francis Seafourth 2Lt kia 21-3-18 RFA 87Bty27Bde p30 CR France435

HAYTHORNTHWAITE,Rycharde Mead 2Lt kia 24-5-15 2EKent p57 MR29

HAYTON,Walter James 2Lt kia 16-9-16 4Yorks p220 MR21

HAYWARD,Bertram Richard 2Lt kia 6-6-15 RFA p30 MR4

HAYWARD,Cecil Bernard TCapt kia 27-7-16 23RFus p68 MR21

HAYWARD,Charles Oswald TLt kia 17-1-16 7Lincs &RFC p3&75 CR Belgium140

HAYWARD,Edward John 2Lt kia 12-11-15 5 att2RFus p68 CR Gallipoli4,Lt

HAYWARD,Edward Ronald 2Lt kia 20-12-16 RFA 99Bty p30 CR Greece9

HAYWARD,Ernest Frank Walton T2Lt kia 5-10-16 11Hamps p120 CR Belgium5,2Bn

HAYWARD,Ernest Harold Lt kia 24-4-17 7Wilts p153 MR37

HAYWARD,Herbert William.MID 2Lt kia 23-7-16 6YLI p143 MR20

HAYWARD,Herbert William T2Lt kia 26-9-16 8 att6Nhampt p137 MR21

HAYWARD,John Stratton T2Lt kia 7-7-16 11Wilts p153 MR21,1Bn

HAYWARD,Kenneth Alfred Capt ded 22-11-18 RH&FA p30

HAYWARD,Marcus Henry Hugh 2Lt dow 26-3-18 3 att7SomLI p80 CR France587

HAYWARD,Milward Cecil Lt ded 23-8-16 RAMC p255 CR Berks1

HAYWARD,Robert Edward T2Lt kia 27-3-18 att1NStaffs p157 MR27

HAYWARD,Walter 2Lt kia 21-3-18 1 att5NStaffs p157 MR27

HAYWARD,William Hugh T2Lt kia 31-8-18 12Manch att52TMB p155 CR France374

HAYWOOD,Charles Oswald TLt kia 18-1-16 7Lincs &RFC p75

HAYWOOD,Ernest.DCM.2Lt kia 27-5-18 5SLancs p230 MR18

HAYWOOD,Philip 2Lt kia 22-11-17 2/6WYorks p218 MR17

HAYWOOD,Sydney TLt kld 26-10-16 ELancs&RFC p3 CR Iraq5

HAYWORTH,Frederick 2Lt kia 12-5-17 7A&SH p243 MR20

HAYWORTH,Harry Asher 2Lt kia 15-4-17 7A&SH p243 CR France1182

HAZARD,Charles Piper 2Lt kia 21-4-16 1KSLI p145 CR Belgium73

HAZARD,Douglas TLt dow 17-10-18 RASC attMddx p193 CR France113

HAZARD,Douglas George Lt kia 23-5-15 3 att2KSLI p145 MR29 CR France453

HAZARD,William Noel T2Lt kia 26-8-18 14WelshR p127 CR France402,27-8-18

HAZEL,Dudley David Fraser Lt dow 25-4-17 6WRid p227 CR Mddx16

HAZELDENE,John Turner Clough 2Lt kld 9-5-15 4RWFus p223 CR France632,HAZLEDENE

HAZELL,Dudley Howard Lt kld 27-9-18 2RLancs attRFC p59&16 CR France924

HAZELL,Frederick Pung T2Lt dow 19-5-18 101LabCps p189 CR France145 Ex 12Nhampt

HAZELTON,Edwin Hills TBrigGen ded 25-7-16 RAVC IndVetCps p198 MR65,24-7-16

HAZZARD,William.MC.T2Lt dow 28-3-18 15WYorks p81 CR France62

HEAD,Albert Everest TLt kia 1-7-16 20NumbF p61 CR France267

HEAD,Arthur.MM.2Lt dow 6-9-18 44RFA p30 CR Fance177

HEAD,Arthur William George T2Lt kia 1-8-17 117MGC Inf p183 CR Belgium126

HEAD,Basil William Lt kia 31-7-17 Herts p252 MR29

HEAD,Bernard Maj kia 12-8-15 5RWFus p223 MR4

HEAD,Edward Keith Lt dow 11-12-16 4Y&L p238 CR Nhampt144

HEAD,Frank William.MID Lt dow 17-10-18 RE p210 CR France375

HEAD,Herbert George 2Lt kia 18-12-15 IARO att117Mahrattas p277 CR Iraq1

HEAD,Henry d'Esterre Lt dow 1-6-15 RDubF p176 CR France285

HEAD,Leslie Dymoke TCapt kia 1-7-16 9YLI p143 CR France267

HEAD,Mark T2Lt kia 28-12-15 8RFC p1 CR France1205

HEAD,Raymond Evelyn.MC.LtACapt ded 24-11-18 3Lpool p72 CR Esex13

HEAD,Reginald Capt kia 28-4-15 BordR p117 CR Gallipoli3

HEADEN,Herbert Harry Lt 6-5-20 3RMunstF CR Egypt9

HEADING,William Henry Chap4Cl ded 21-11-18 RAChDept p199 CR Camb84

HEADINGTON,Arthur Hutton Lt kia 27-11-17 BerksYeo p203 MR34,Capt

HEADLAM,J.2Lt kld 30-5-18 GL &RAF p190

HEADLEY,Herbert Marshall T2Lt kia 11-3-17 RFA att18RFC p8&30 CR France614

HEAGERTY,Richard Browne 2Lt kia 3-5-17 1/2Lond p245 MR20

HEAGERTY,William Thomas TMaj dow 31-1-17 13RSuss p119 CR Belgium11

HEAL,Cecil Ambrose 2Lt dow 3-7-15 3 att1Wilts p153 CR Belgium11

HEAL,Charles Henry 2Lt dow 9-5-15 SWBord p100 CR Gallipoli6

HEAL,Walter George 2Lt ded 23-10-18 RFA p261 CR Hamps7

HEALD,Douglas 2Lt dow 6-10-17 6RB p179 CR Belgium16

HEALD,Geoffrey Yates TCapt kia 1-7-16 15LancF p92 CR France293

HEALD,Thomas Penrose T2Lt kia 13-10-17 GL &6RFC p8 CR Belgium84

HEALD,William Margetson Lt dow 8-9-18 RAMC att16LancF p195 CR France145

HEALE,Arthur George.MC.Lt dow 23-4-18 41/42RFA p30 CR France40

HEALE,Ernest Newton LtCol ded 12-6-16 IA 121Pnrs att14NumbF p277 CR France1

HEALE,George Reginald Charles Capt dow 3-5-17 10WRid p115 MR29

HEALEY,Arthur Wilfred T2Lt kia 1-9-18 att1Wilts p153 CR France560

HEALEY,Philip 2Lt kia 25-9-15 3Manch att1LNLancs p155 MR19

HEALEY,Richard Elkanah Hownam Lt&Adjt kia 22-7-16 1RWKent p141 MR21

HEALING,George William 2Lt kia 4-10-18 22Lond p251 CR France161,3-10-18

HEALING,Kenneth 2Lt kia 27-4-17 6N&D p233 CR France1495

HEALY,Dermott Joseph 2Lt kia 5-8-17 5RMunstF att74TMB p175 MR29

HEALY,Edward Lt kia 7-6-17 6 att8BordR p117 MR29

HEALY,George Ernest HonLt ded 3-3-19 RASC Retd p267 CR Eire63

HEALY,Guy Rambant Lt kia 11-3-16 4RMunstF att3KAR p175&202 CR EAfrica56,3Bn

HEALY,John Frederick Lt kia 1-7-16 3 att9RIrRif p169 CR France383,2-7-16

HEANEY,Paul.DCM.MID 2Lt kia 21-10-14 RLancs p59 MR32

HEAP,Frederick William 2Lt kia 23-4-17 5DLI p239 CR France487

HEAP,Wilfred Herbert T2Lt kia 25-2-17 RB att12Bn p179 CR France744,Wilfrid

HEAPE,Brian Ruston LtACapt kia 16-5-17 RH&FA 162BdeA/Bty p30 CR France1182

HEAPS,Norman Costine.MID 2Lt ded 10-2-19 5Lpool p270 CR Belgium316,Normand

HEARD,Charles Miller 2Lt kia 10-4-17 1 att8ELancs p110 MR20

HEARD,Francis George Lt ded 15-3-17 RAMC p267

HEARD,Geoffrey Richard TCapt kia 3-7-16 RAMC att10RWar p195 CR France150,2-7-16

HEARD,Robert James Bannatyne Capt dow 5-5-15 1LancF p92 CR Egypt6 4-5-15

HEARD,Robert Rankin 2Lt kia 23-4-17 7BlkW p231 CR France604

HEARD,Robert H.Warren.MC&Bar.Lt ded 3-3-19 IrGds p254 CR Eire114

HEARN,Albert Henry 2Lt kia 1-10-17 1/2 att1/8Leic p87 MR30

HEARN,Edward Thomas Hills 2Lt kia 11-9-17 RFA &57RFC p8&30 CR Belgium140,kld

HEARN,George Harold 2Lt dow PoW 12-5-17 1ESurr p112 CR France924

HEARN,John Stanley T2Lt kia 12-10-16 7Suff p78 MR21

HEARN,Leonard Webb 2Lt kia 18-10-17 6DCLI p114 CR Belgium84

HEARN,Robert Cecil.MC.Capt kia 30-4-18 2/20Lond p251 CR palestine3

HEARNDEN,Harry Crespin Stephens TLt kia 6-8-15 9RWKent att2Hamps p141 MR4

HEARSCH,Edward 2Lt ded 28-6-15 RFA p30 CR Mddx40

HEARSON,Richard Philip TLt kia 23-3-18 1RR ofCav att5Lancers p23 MR27

HEASMAN,George Harry TLt kld 20-1-18 RFC p16 CR Sussex165

HEASTEY,George Rodney 2Lt kia 20-7-16 3RWFus p98 CR France397

HEATH,Alfred Chap4Cl kia 30-6-18 RAChDept att9WRid p199 CR France76

HEATH,Arthur George TLt kia 8-10-15 6RWKent p141 MR19

HEATH,Arthur Morris 2Lt kia 12-4-18 33MGC p183 MR32

HEATH,Edmund Griffith Capt kia 25-9-15 97RFA p30 CR France219

HEATH,Geoffrey Capt kia 10-8-15 1/7Ches p222 MR4

HEATH,Gerard Bower 2Lt dow 22-5-18 2CldGds p51 CR France84

HEATH,Henry Newport Charles.CB.MajGen ded 22-7-15 Staff CmdgSMidDiv p1 CR Surrey160,29-7-15

HEATH,Henry James Lt kia 17-7-16 16Mddx p147 CR France1500,1-7-16

HEATH,John Lionel 2LtTLt kia 2-10-15 1YLI p143 MR19,1-10-15

HEATH,John Oswald TLt kia 7-10-16 11RWKent p141 MR21

HEATH,Leonard George Capt dow 14-3-16 NottsYeo p205 CR France1,NhamptYeo att1Lancers IA

HEATH,Maurice Gordon.MID LtCol kia 25-9-15 2RWSurr p56 MR19

HEATH,Percy Macclesfield LtCol ded 14-7-17 IA 110MahrattaLI att105 p277 CR Iraq8

HEATH,Percy Voltelin Lt dow 1-9-15 RHGds p20 CR France1419,4-9-14

HEATH,Raymond Leopold Greig Capt kia 25-9-15 2RWSurr p56 MR19

HEATH,Roger Meyrick T2Lt kia 15-9-16 6SomLI p80 MR21

HEATH,Sidney Stuart 2Lt kia 23-4-17 7BordR p117 MR20

HEATH,Walter Rowland TLt kia 23-8-16 O&BLI 1/1BucksBn p231 MR21

HEATH,William Charles T2Lt kia 22-5-18 1/2 att10DCLI p114 CR France502

HEATH,William Hutsby 2Lt kia 1-7-16 1/6NStaffs p238 MR21

HEATH,William Rufus Kennard 2Lt kia 25-2-16 1Glouc p106 CR France551

HEATH-CALDWELL,Martin Frederick 2Lt kia 16-5-15 RHA p30 CR France80

HEATHCOAT-AMORY,Ludovic.MID Capt dow 25-8-18 1DevYeo att32DivHQ p203 CR France119

HEATHCOCK,Ethelbert Agnew Lt dow 29-9-17 1/4DCLI p226 CR Palestine2

HEATHCOCK,Thomas TCapt kia 10-7-16 7EYorks p84 CR France453

HEATHCOTE,James Shirley 2Lt dow 28-8-17 1CldGds p51 CR Lond8

HEATHCOTE,Martin Arthur.MC.T2Lt dow 18-7-16 10RFus B'Coy p68 CR France833

HEATHCOTE,Ralph Noel T2Lt dow 17-11-16 12EYorks p84 CR France203

HEATHCOTE,William Godfrey T2Lt kia 23-11-17 GL &29RFC p8 CR Belgium3

HEATHER,Percy Arthur Lt kia 12-7-17 1Nhampt p137 MR31

HEATHERINGTON,Eric 2Lt kia 4-5-17 2RWar p64 MR20

HEATLEY,Leonard TCapt dow 17-8-17 12Lpool p72 CR Belgium16

HEATLY,Charles Frederick T2Lt dow 17-4-18 16RWFus att38DivSnipingCoy p98 CR France134

HEATLY,Henry Francis Lt kia 22-2-15 2Yorks p90 CR France924

HEATLY,John Firth 2Lt kia 21-3-18 RWKent att7Bn p141 MR27

HEATON,Charles Darrell T2Lt kia 26-8-17 143MGC Inf p183 CR Belgium125

HEATON,Eric Rupert T2Lt kia 1-7-16 14 att16Mddx p147 CR France1500

HEATON,Harold Sinclair T2Lt kia 22-4-18 13 att17RWFus p98 CR France516

HEATON,Herbert Walker Lt kia 5-9-17 7LancF p221 CR Belgium84,Walter

HEATON,Ivon.MID TLtACapt dow 14-10-17 7RWKent p141 CR France13

HEATON,Lionel James 2Lt kia 29-8-18 3 att17RWFus p98 CR France374

HEATON,Norman Child 2Lt kia 3-5-17 1/1Lond p245 MR20

HEATON,Philip Ralph.DCM.TLt ded 4-1-17 1/2KAR p202 CR EAfrica38 &CR Tanzania1

HEATON,Robert Capt kia 25-9-17 5SLancs p230 CR Belgium22

HEATON,Stanley Tomlinson 2Lt kia 27-9-16 6WYorks p218 MR21

HEATON,William 2Lt kia 3-5-17 2/5WRid p227 MR20

HEATON-ELLIS,Charles Edward Robert TLt kia 19-3-16 6YLI p143 CR France420

HEATON-ELLIS,David.MC.Capt kia 27-5-18 2RB p179 MR18

HEAUMANN,Richard Capt kia 8/10-9-16 2Lond p245

HEAVEN,George Frederick Victor TCapt kia 25-1-16 16RWar p64 CR France394

HEAVEN,Norman Edwin 2Lt kia 21-3-18 66MGC p183 MR27

HEAVER,Douglas Cams T2Lt kia 4-8-16 8RFus p68 MR21

HEBBERT,Robert Francis Capt ded 19-3-16 IA IMS p277 CR Iraq6

HEBBES,Arthur Ernest Lt kia 28-11-17 4Suff attNigR p217 MR40,drd

HEBBLETHWAITE,Abraham Rhodes T2Lt kia 3-10-15 RFA 88Bty p30 CR France727

HEBBLETHWAITE,C.J.Lt 7-4-15 GL &NigR CR WAfrica47

HEBBLETHWAITE,George T2Lt kia 7-7-16 10LancF p92 MR21

HEBBLETHWAITE,John Christopher TLt kia 26-6-16 RFA p30 CR Belgium4 22-6-16

HEBDEN,Alan 2Lt kia 8-5-17 6BlkW p231 MR20

HEBDEN,George Spencer T2Lt kia 22-4-17 2Leic p87 MR38

HEBDEN,Robert Coke TCapt ded 25-2-16 RE 201Coy p45 CR France22

HEBELER,Roland Stuart TCapt dow 16-9-15 7RWSurr C'Coy p56 CR France22

HEBERDEN,Arthur Clements 2Lt kia 10-7-17 5 att2KRRC p150 MR31,6 att2Bn

HEBRON,William T2Lt kia 25-10-18 20DLI p161 MR30

HECKFORD,Percy James 2Lt kia 31-10-16 RGA 114HB p209 CR France393

HECKROODT,Benjamin TMaj ded 6-10-18 6RSuss p228 CR Iraq8

HECHT,Marcus Francis TMaj kia 3-9-16 17KRRC p150 CR France220

HEDDERWICK,Charles Stuart 2Lt kia 28-2-15 2RScots B'Coy p54 CR Belgium104

HEDDERWICK,Guy 2Lt kia 22-9-16 1RRofCav &RFC p3&23 CR France306,Lt

HEDDERWICK,James Alexander Lt ded 6-11-18 RGA 56A/ACoy p40 CR Mddx26

HEDDING,James Lawrence 2Lt dow 28-3-16 3Dors att1Mddx p124 CR France80,Lt

HEDGCOCK,Frederick Leslie T2Lt kia 30-9-18 D57MGC Inf p183 CR France256,29-9-18

HEDGES,Charles Cuthbert.MC.Lt kia 8-10-18 4Berks p234 CR France338

HEDGES,William Herbert.MC.Capt ded 21-8-16 RE 1FC p210 CR France120,dow 22-8-16

HEDGES,William Robert.MC.2Lt kia 18-9-18 2TankCps p188 MR16

HEDGLAND,Charles Samuel.MID TLt kia 17-4-18 33MGC Inf p183 CR Belgium167

HEDLEY,Gerald Montague.MID TCapt ded 4-10-18 RE 29Coy p45 CR France146

HEDLEY,James Frederic TLt ded 13-1-16 RASC p193 CR Wilts142

HEDLEY,John Hunt 2Lt kia 8-3-18 5 att4Mddx p147 CR Belgium112,4 att8Bn

HEDLEY,John Ralph.DSO.LtCol ded 15-7-17 6 Cmdg5NumbF p213 CR France214

HEDLEY,Joseph Walton Capt dow 13-9-16 2/5LancF p221 CR France833,12-9-16

HEDLEY,William Alexander Cosgrave.MID TLt dow 19-7-18 8 att1EKent p57 CR Belgium40

HEDLEY,William James TLtACapt kia 7-6-17 11RWSurr p56 CR Belgium29

HEDWORTH,Thomas Hedworth 2Lt drd 10-10-18 1Worc p108 MR40

HEENAN,Michael Cornelius Capt kia 12-1-16 Leinst att2Wilts p174 CR France513

HEENAN,Thomas George Graudon 2Lt kia 21-3-18 4RDubF p176 MR27

HEFFERMAN,William T2Lt kld 25-10-17 GL &RFC p8 CR France790

HEFFERNAN,Francis Joseph Christopher LtCol ded 16-7-17 RAMC p196 CR Iraq5

HEFFERNAN,William Patrick 2Lt kia 9-5-15 3RIrReg att1Glouc p89 MR22

HEGARTY,Andrew TLt kia 16-12-15 RAMC &RFA p196 CR Belgium58

HEGARTY,Edward 5432.MC.ACapt kia 3-9-16 3 att2RIrReg p89 CR France402

HEGGIE,David Rev ded 23-10-17 RAChDept att2/7RScots p199 CR Eire322

HEGGIE,David Alexander 2Lt kia 3-8-15 9 att1RScotF p94 CR Belgium82

HEGGS,Frederick William 2Lt kia 21-8-16 2Y&L p159 CR France156

HEIGHAM-PLUMPTRE,L.G.2Lt dow 4-6-18 1Beds &RAF p16&86 CR France1564

HEINEMANN,John Walter TCapt dow 6-3-16 20RFus p68 CR France114

HEINING,Wilfred Hardinge Capt kia 6-4-16 1A 54Sikhs att51 p277 MR38,HEINIG

HELBY,John Alfred Hasler 2Lt dow 3-8-16 2RDubF p176 CR Belgium11

HELDMAN,Harry Randolph TLt kia 27-9-15 9RSuss p119 MR19

HELE-SHAW,Henry Rathbone Lt kia 19-7-16 GL &RFC p3&190 CR France366

HELLARD,John Alexander 2Lt kia 2-7-16 3 att1SomLI p80 CR France1890

HELLIAR,Leonard Jeffrey 2Lt kia 14-5-17 236RFA p208 CR Belgium11

HELLICAR,Geoffrey Theodore 2Lt kia 27-7-16 2/20Lond p251 CR France68,26-7-16

HELLIER,Fred ACapt kia 12-10-16 3 att14DLI p161 MR21

HELLIER,Leonard Gordon T2Lt dow 16-12-17 3 att11BordR p117 CR Belgium18

HELLMERS,Alfred 2Lt dow 11-5-15 1RIrRif p169 CR France345

HELLYER,George Edgcombe TCapt dow 22-8-15 10Hamps p120 MR4

HELLYER,Sidney Hannaford 2Lt dow 8-5-15 4EYorks p219 CR Devon47

HELM,Frank 2Lt kia 4-6-15 8Manch p237 MR4

HELM,Henry Paul Dundas.MID Capt ded 6-11-18 2BordR &RAF p117 CR C'land&W'land17

HELME,Guy Masterman Lt dow 30-10-17 1CldGds p51 CR France40

HELME,Harold Lutwyche Capt kia 18-9-14 1LNLancs p136 MR15,14-9-14

HELME,Richard 2Lt kia 25-9-15 1LNLancs p136 MR19

HELME,Robert Barnard Lt kia 25-6-17 1Drags p21 CR France363

HELME,Thomas Herbert Capt dow 3-11-18 16Lond p249 CR Surrey88

HELMORE,Ernest Creswell 2Lt dow 1-1-17 1 att15N&D p134 CR France1182

HELMORE,Stanley Thomas John 2Lt kld 14-5-18 23RFus &18RAF p68 CR France21,kia

HELMS,Percy T2Lt dow 5-10-18 9Yorks p90 CR France194

HELSDON,Harold Leofric 2Lt kia 26-11-16 3Dors att1/7RWar p124 MR21

HELYAR,Maurice Howard Capt kia 24-1-15 RB p179 CR France285

HEMANS,George Willoughby Maj kia 4-3-17 1A 29Lancers p277 CR France430

HEMELRYK,Eugene John Vincent 2Lt kia 23-4-18 2LancF p92 CR France412

HEMING,Charles Leonard Parlett Lt dow 12-2-17 2Leinst p174 CR Kent177,ded

HEMING,Maurice Ivory T2Lt kia 1-7-16 2RBerks p139 MR21

HEMINGWAY,Horace Vincent T2Lt dow 2-10-18 36MGC p183 CR Belgium38

HEMINGWAY,James 2Lt kia 9-5-15 3 att1SforthH p164 CR France721

HEMINGWAY,Kenneth Stanley LtACapt kia 21-3-18 Worc att10Bn p108 MR20

HEMINGWAY,Maurice William,MC Lt mbk 27-5-18 33RFA p256 MR18

HEMINGWAY,Ralph Eustace 2Lt kia 15-10-15 8N&D p233 MR19

HEMINGWAY,Stewart TLt dow 6-4-16 4SWBord p100 MR38 ExSthIrHorse

HEMMANT,Maurice TLt kia 14-8-17 5 att11RB p179 MR29

HEMMERDE,Charles Eric.MC.Lt kia 27-9-18 6RWKent p141 CR France415

HEMMING,Francis William Capt kia 24-4-17 1/8Worc p226 CR France1495

HEMMING,Frank James.MC.Lt kia 13-4-18 5 att2Worc p108 MR32

HEMMING,Jesse Clifford 2Lt kia 27-8-17 8Worc p226 MR30

HEMMING,William Norman T2Lt ded 15-11-17 GL &65RFC p8 CR France285,dow

HEMPHILL,Richard Patrick T2Lt ded 24-3-17 6Leinst attaRFC p8&174 CR Egypt9,Capt acckld

HEMPSON,Claude Dawson.DSO.TCapt kia 8-3-17 10Suff att6RLancs p78 CR Iraq8

HEMSLEY,Ernest James.MC.T2Lt kia 4/5-9-18 12RSuss att10RWSurr p119 CR Belgium185,4-9-18

HEMSLEY,Godfrey Hamilton 2Lt kia 12-10-17 C255RFA p30 CR Belgium10

HEMSLEY,James Mortimer 2Lt ded 28-7-17 RFA attDerajatMtnBty p30 CR Africa38 &CR Tanzania1

HEMSTEAD,John 2Lt kia 16-4-17 106RFA p30 MR20,HEMSTED

HEMSWORTH,Augustus Hethersett 2Lt ded 6-6-15 YLI p265 CR Norf288

HEMUS,Cyril Harcourt.MC.2Lt dow 27-3-18 B87RFA p30 CR France62,28-3-18

HEMUS,Donald George TLt kia 22-3-18 3Worc p108 MR20

HENDERSHOT,Charles Cecil T2Lt kld 6-2-18 RFC p16 CR Canada1114

HENDERSON,Albert N.Maj kia 23-7-16 10RWar p64 MR21

HENDERSON,Alec Stewart Capt dow 25-4-15 1Lond A'Coy p245 CR France254

HENDERSON,Alexander Rennie Lt kia 25-9-15 4GordH p241 MR29

HENDERSON,Alfred Roche T2Lt kia 28-4-17 Mddx att17Bn p147 MR20

HENDERSON,Andrew Hubert Millin 2Lt kia 12-7-15 4KOSB p224 MR4

HENDERSON,Andrew William TCapt kia 1-7-16 1RB p179 MR21

HENDERSON,Angus 2Lt kia 3-5-17 1RScotF p94 MR20

HENDERSON,Archibald Wright T2Lt kia 30-12-17 223MGC p183 MR21

HENDERSON,Arthur Lt kia 4-8-16 9HLI p240 CR Egypt2 ACycCps 52Div
HENDERSON,Arthur.VC.MC.2LtACapt kia 24-4-17 4A&SH p173 CR France591
HENDERSON,Arthur Francis Maj kia 12-9-14 IA 27LtCav Staff p277 MR28
HENDERSON,Arthur Gordon Lt kia 18-5-19 IA 1/9GurkhaRif p277 MR43
HENDERSON,Arthur Percy 2Lt dow 19-6-17 RGA 49SB p40 CR France40,18-6-17
HENDERSON,Benjamin Hall Blyth 2Lt dow 18-6-18 5CamH p168 CR France134
HENDERSON,Bertram Mackay.MC.MID LtACapt dow 7-4-18 PoW GordH att7Bn p166 CR Germany3
HENDERSON,Cecil Ivanhoe T2Lt kia 26-11-17 1 att13ESurr p112 CR France481
HENDERSON,Charles Edward Piercy.MC.Capt kia 17-11-16 B71RFA p30 CR France453
HENDERSON,David Capt kia 15-9-16 8Mddx att19Lond p236 CR France390
HENDERSON,David.KCB.KCVO.DSO.Sir LtGen 17-8-21 A&SH CR Scot520
HENDERSON,Donald 2Lt kia 11-1-15 6 att1KRRC p150 CR France727
HENDERSON,Duncan Frank Capt kia 8/9-8-16 1InniskF p105 CR Belgium47,9-8-16
HENDERSON,Edward Elers Delaval.VC.Lt kia 25-1-17 NStaffs att7Bn p157 CR Iraq5,Delavel Cmdg9War
HENDERSON,Edward Francis Lt kia 27-3-18 4 att6EKent p212 CR France233
HENDERSON,Elmes Pollock Capt&Adjt kia 25-6-16 IA 106Pnrs p277 MR43,29-6-16
HENDERSON,Eric 2Lt kia 7-6-17 8Lond p247 MR29
HENDERSON,Eric Joseph.MC.2LtTCapt kia 25-3-17 70RFC SR p8 CR France518
HENDERSON,Eric Lockhart Hume Capt dow 21-5-15 RMunstF p175 CR Egypt3,20-5-15
HENDERSON,Everard Francis Scott Maj kia 6-7-16 2Leic p87 MR38
HENDERSON,G.A.F.Lt ded 4-7-18 GordH attRAF p166
HENDERSON,Geo.Ballingham 2Lt ded 31-10-18 63MGC p266 CR Scot127
HENDERSON,George Gartly T2Lt kia 6-8-16 17HLI p163 CR France114
HENDERSON,George Stuart.VC.DSO&Bar.MC.MIDx5 Capt 24-7-20 2Manch MR38
HENDERSON,George York.MC.Lt kia 22-11-17 RIrRif att10Bn p169 MR17
HENDERSON,Graeme Von Hope Lt kia 16-6-17 2/2Lond p245 MR20,Bonhote
HENDERSON,Harold Winfred Lt ded 13-11-18 3 att24Manch p155 CR Italy7
HENDERSON,Henry May MajALtCol kia 10-3-17 RE 18Div p45 CR France251
HENDERSON,Ian Henry David.MC.Capt ded 21-6-18 A&SH attRAF p173 CR Scot520
HENDERSON,J.SurgGen 12-4-19 IMS CR Kent83
HENDERSON,J.Capt 22-11-20 IOD MR65
HENDERSON,Jacob Johnson Lt dow 17-10-18 15SuffYeo p205 CR France769,16-10-18
HENDERSON,James LtTCapt ded 16-7-17 RAMC p196 CR Canada1691
HENDERSON,James.MC.AMaj kia 11-4-18 4GordH p241
HENDERSON,James Angus Smith Lt kia 25-3-18 7 att1/8A&SH p243 MR27
HENDERSON,James Francis Lt kia 27-3-18 4EKent p212
HENDERSON,James Fuller TLtACapt kia 26-4-18 7RWSurr p56 CR France489
HENDERSON,James Graeme T2Lt kia 3-12-17 1 att1/5RLancs p59 CR France658
HENDERSON,James Greig Mitchell.MC.MID 2Lt kia 18-8-16 4RB p179 CR France402,3Bn
HENDERSON,James Hugh T2Lt kia 7-11-15 11 att8WRid p115 CR Gallipoli27,2-11-15
HENDERSON,James Macdonald.MC&Bar.Maj 11-4-18 4GordH att7A&SH MR19
HENDERSON,James Norman Maj kia 28-6-15 1/4RScots p211 CR Gallipoli6
HENDERSON,James Percy T2Lt kia 11-9-17 21NumbF p61 MR21
HENDERSON,James Richard 2Lt ded 29-11-14 2/4BlkW p128&270 CR Scot386,28-11-14
HENDERSON,James Sowers 2Lt kia 22-3-18 RGA 33SB p40 CR France439
HENDERSON,John Easton TLt ded PoW 26-4-18 14NumbF p61 CR France716
HENDERSON,John Thomas Capt kia 15-9-16 4NumbF p213 CR France239
HENDERSON,Kenneth Selby Capt kia 2-6-18 SL &1RAF p268 MR20
HENDERSON,Michael William MajTLtCol kia 27-9-15 9BlkW p128 CR France219
HENDERSON,Neil Emslie Nelson 2Lt kia 11-4-18 1KOSB p101 MR32
HENDERSON,Noel Charles 2Lt kia 25-9-15 2BlkW D'Coy p128 CR France347,9-10-15
HENDERSON,Norman William Arthur Lt kia 10-11-14 RScotF p94 MR29
HENDERSON,Patric Gordon T2Lt dow 2-5-18 2WRid p115 MR19
HENDERSON,Raymond Montgomerie Hume Lt kia 20-9-14 2ConnRgrs p172 MR15
HENDERSON,Robert 2Lt dow 16-4-17 4GordH p242 CR France95
HENDERSON,Robert Francis Watt Lt dow 15-10-18 1/6RScots p211 CR France40,Capt
HENDERSON,Robert Morley Chap4Cl ded 3-2-19 RAChDept p199 CR Belgium265

HENDERSON,Robert Stanley Lt kia 13-10-18 1/6GordH p242 CR France271,Stanislaus Robert
HENDERSON,Thomas T2Lt kia 6-8-17 8RIrRif p169 MR29
HENDERSON,Thomas 2Lt kia 23-11-17 'B'TankCps p188 MR17
HENDERSON,Thomas Adam.MID 2Lt kia 25/27-9-15 6GordH p242 MR19
HENDERSON,Thomas Eric 2Lt kia 3-8-16 1SStaffs p122 CR France402,31-8-16
HENDERSON,Thomas Harvey.MC.TCapt kia 30-11-17 6 att10RB p179 MR17
HENDERSON,Walter 2Lt kia 8-3-18 9HLI att13RFus p240 CR Belgium112
HENDERSON,Walter TLt ded 29-10-18 RE attGHQ p45 CR France457 Ex 9RScots
HENDERSON,William 2Lt kia 21-3-18 1 att2DLI p161 MR20
HENDERSON,William 2Lt kia 9-4-18 14HLI p163 MR32
HENDERSON,William Alexander Capt kia 10-11-14 D/2A&SH p173 MR32
HENDERSON,William Douglas 2Lt kia 18-11-16 8NStaffs p157 CR France384
HENDERSON,William Fraser 2Lt kia 8-8-16 17Mddx p147 MR21
HENDERSON,William George 2Lt kia 23-4-17 4GordH p242 MR20
HENDERSON,William James.MC.MID TCapt kia 6-7-16 9LNLancs p136 MR21
HENDERSON,William James 2Lt kia 3-5-17 4 att12RScots p211 MR20
HENDERSON,William Lewis.MID TCapt dow 3-5-16 10WYorks C'Coy p81 CR France40
HENDERSON-BEGG,John Henderson Capt kia 23-7-16 4GordH p241 MR21
HENDERSON-HAMILTON,Charles Campbell TCapt kia 21-8-15 12ScotRif att1KOSB p103 MR4
HENDERSON-HAMILTON,James Campbell TLt kia 27-9-15 9BlkW p128 CR France219
HENDIN,Harold Percival Lt kia 28-4-17 10Lincs p75 MR20
HENDRIKS,Augustus Mark Capt kia 25-5-15 RFus att1WYorks p68 MR32
HENDRY,Alistair 2857.MID Lt kia 27-9-17 189RFA p207 MR30
HENDRY,Archibald Thomas 2Lt ded 23-10-16 3CamH p168 CR Scot501,Thomson
HENDRY,Charles Arthur 2Lt kia 27-3-18 9RFus p68 MR27
HENDRY,Hector Victor Baird 2Lt ded 6-10-16 7BlkW p270 CR Scot136
HENDRY,James.MC.TCapt dow 6-9-16 16RScots p54 CR France145
HENDRY,John B.Maj ded 28-8-19 RASC p267 CR Scot754
HENDRY,John Taylor ACapt ded 16-6-19 4RLancs p213 CR France65,2/5Bn
HENDRY,William T2Lt kia 27-7-16 17Mddx p147 MR21
HENDRY,William 2Lt kia 5-3-17 19Lond p250 CR Belgium56
HENEKER,Frederick Christian Maj kia 1-7-16 Leinst att20NumbF p174 CR France393,Cmdg21NumbF
HENERY,Hewett Walter Lewis Lt kia 19-4-17 5KOSB p24 CR Palestine8
HENLEY,Anthony Warton 2Lt dow 21-1-17 C156RFA p30 CR France40
HENLEY,Frederick T2Lt kia 27-10-16 20RFus p68 MR21
HENLEY,Frederick Louis T2Lt kia 1-10-16 13 att11N&D p134 MR21
HENLEY,Henry Thomas T2Lt kia 8-3-17 7RIrRif p169 CR Belgium17
HENMAN,Herbert Cecil 2Lt dow 25-9-17 RGA att18CpsHQ 3SB p40 CR Belgium16
HENMAN,Richard Mox.MC.LtAMaj ded 3-11-18 RFA p30 CR Berks85
HENMAN,Sydney TLt kia 10-8-17 RE 86FC p45 CR Belgium23
HENN,Edward Henry Lovett T2Lt kia 25-9-15 9RB p179 MR29
HENNA,John Ramsey 2Lt kia 9-9-16 3 att6RIrReg p89 MR21
HENNELL,Arthur T2Lt kia 3-1-18 14Worc p108 CR France668
HENNELL,Robert Alexander 2Lt kia 28-8-18 4 att1/7A&SH p173 MR16
HENNEY,Herbert Norman 2Lt kia 25-4-17 17RFA p30 CR France1182
HENNINGSEN,Cecil Eric 2Lt kia 30-11-17 ShropYeo p205 CR Palestine3,Lt
HENRI,Frank TCapt kia 15-6-18 11NumbF p61 CR Italy3
HENRIQUES,Philip Brydges Gutterlz T2Lt dow 24-7-15 8KRRC p150 CR Belgium11
HENRIQUES,Ronald Lucas Quiand Lt kia 14-9-14 2 att1RWSurr p56 CR France1329,Quixano
HENRY,Arthur Richard T2Lt kia 23-4-17 5 att1Mddx p147 CR France434
HENRY,Charles Lennox 2Lt kia 16-8-17 3 att7RIrF p171 MR30
HENRY,Charlotte E.SNurse drd 26-2-18 QAIMNS p200 MR40
HENRY,Claude Lt kia 19-9-14 3Worc p108 CR France1107
HENRY,Cyril Charles Lt kia 26-9-15 Worc att2nd p108 MR19
HENRY,Dermot Jepson T2Lt kia 9-7-17 5 att1RIrF p171 CR France546
HENRY,Douglas John Luther Martin 2Lt dow 25-9-17 4GordH p242 CR Belgium16
HENRY,George Cecil 2Lt dow 9-12-17 3Suff p78 CR Palestine3
HENRY,John Lt kia 13-4-18 9ACycCps p244 CR France324
HENRY,John Allan.MC.TCapt kia 14-7-16 11RScots p54 MR21
HENRY,Norman.MC.TCapt kia 8-5-18 17Lpool p72 MR30
HENRY,Walter T2LtACapt kia 8-10-16 RFA attW40TMB p30 MR20
HENRY,William Ernest Lt kia 1-5-16 1RIrF p171 CR France283
HENSHALL,Charles TCapt kia 8-7-16 18Manch p155 CR France630

HENSHALL,Donald Edward 2Lt dow 14-9-16 D238RFA p208 CR France177
HENSHILL-WOOD,Alexander Russell Lt dow 27-9-16 9Lpool p216
HENSHAW,A.H.SubCdr 11-4-21 S&T Cps MR43
HENSHAW,Isabel Sister ded 11-8-19 RAMC CR Canada116
HENSLEY,Wilfrid Henry Capt kia 21-3-18 6SomLI p80 MR27
HENSMAN,Henry John.MC.2Lt kia 18-9-18 1Herts p252 MR16
HENSON,Albert Cecil Maj kia 22-8-15 4Nhampt p234 MR4
HENSON,Stanley Benskin 2Lt kia 19-12-14 1SomLI p80 CR Belgium70
HENSTOCK,Arthur Frank Newman.MC.Capt kia 22-3-18 15N&D p134 MR27
HENSTOCK,Kenneth Parnell Lt kia 23-8-14 4Mddx p147 CR Belgium242
HENTY,Arthur Frank TCapt kia 4-3-16 11Mddx p147 MR19
HENTY,George Herbert Maj kia 30-11-17 7Suff p78 MR17
HENWOOD,John Edwin T2Lt dow 1-7-16 9RWSurr p56 CR Egypt9,acckld
HEPBURN,Andrew Munro 2Lt kia 3-9-16 6 att11RB p179 MR21
HEPBURN,Archibald James Capt kia 29-5-15 8Manch p237 CR Gallipoli2
HEPBURN,Arthur Jacobs 2Lt kia 30-3-18 RGA 173SB p40 CR France156
HEPBURN,David Laughton Inkster 2Lt kia 25-4-18 6WYorks p218 MR30
HEPBURN,George TLt kia 22-3-18 RE 98FC p45 CR France511
HEPBURN,Malcolm Arnold 2Lt kia 30-11-14 2SfthH p164 CR France339
HEPBURN,Reginald Lt ded 14-6-19 38RFA p30 MR43
HEPBURN,Reginald Victor 2Lt kia 16-9-18 GL &RAF CR France365
HEPBURN,Roger Paul.MC.T2Lt dow 3-8-17 RE 30DivSigCo att21InfBde p45 CR Belgium11
HEPBURN,William Duncan Capt kia 28-4-15 SfthH att5RScots p164 MR4
HEPBURN-STUART-FORBES-TREFUSIS,John Frederick.DSO.Hon.BrigGen dow 24-10-15 IrGds20InfBde p52 CR France279
HEPBURNE-SCOTT,Alexander Noel 2Lt kia 16-5-15 2ScotsGds p52 MR22
HEPNER,Herman 2Lt kia 8-5-17 4 att11ScotRif p103 MR37
HEPPELL,Harry Denby 2Lt kia 5-4-17 4Berks p234 CR France1495
HEPPELL,Thomas Reginald Capt kia 15-9-16 21Lond p251 CR France385
HEPPENSTALL,George Percival 2Lt kia 24-4-18 1Glouc att2Mddx p106 MR27 &CR France390
HEPPLE,Francis James TLt kia 28-4-17 11NStaffs att5MGC p157&183 MR20
HEPPLE,John TMaj drd 30-12-16 RAMC YorksFA p255 CR Yorks591
HEPTON,Arthur Lt dow PoW 13-4-18 5Yorks p220 CR France328
HEPTON,William TLt ded 9-11-18 4RRofCav att5DragGds p23 CR France1278
HEPWORTH,Arthur Montagu.MC.Lt kia 4-5-18 4RWSurr &RAF p212&258 CR Palestine9
HEPWORTH,Frederick Joseph 2Lt kia 20-5-17 3RMunstF attRInniskF p175 CR France155,19-5-17
HEPWORTH,George Percy Capt dow 27-10-18 RFA 4TrnDepot p207 MR65
HEPWORTH,Henry James Jephson 2Lt kia 16-8-17 12Lpool p72 MR30
HEPWORTH,Laurence Frederic Capt ded PoW 9-3-17 2Suff p78 CR Germany3
HEPWORTH,W.J.H.Capt 11-6-18 RAMC CR Durham62
HERALD,James Herbert Crossland Lt dow 24-1-15 8DLI p239 CR Belgium4,24-1-16
HERALD,Thomas T2Lt kld 20-10-17 GL &RFC p8 CR Wilts28
HERAPATH,Alfred Maltravers 2Lt kia 1-7-16 8Y&L attMGC p159 CR France156
HERAPATH,Norman Finnis 2Lt kia 11-4-17 1SomLI p80 MR20
HERAPATH,Randolph Fitz Roy Boehm LtACapt kia 3-7-16 1Lincs p75 CR France267
HERBERT,Alfred James Anthony 2Lt dow 17-9-17 ACycCps 2LdnDiv p244 CR Belgium16
HERBERT,Allan Douglas 2Lt dow 29-9-15 4Mddx p147 CR Belgium11
HERBERT,Charles Stanley.MC.Capt kia 27-5-18 15DLI p161 CR France1331
HERBERT,Cyril Joseph T2Lt kia 13-3-18 7Leinst p174 CR France365,23-3-18
HERBERT,Edmund Widdington T2Lt kia 16-10-18 1 KSLI att1/4Ches p145 CR Belgium112
HERBERT,Edward Grafton.MC.2LtACapt kia 9-4-18 10War attMGC p65&183 CR France1092,10-4-18
HERBERT,Elidye John Bernard.Hon.Capt kia 12-11-17 GloucYeo att19MGC p187&203,Elidyr CR Palestine8
HERBERT,Harry Bentley 2Lt kia 22-5-15 IARO att1/1GurkhaRif p277 MR28
HERBERT,Hubert Leslie TLt kia 7-8-15 8GordH p166 CR France727,Hugh
HERBERT,John William Lt ded 2-7-18 5RSuss p228
HERBERT,Johnstone Erskine Galway Lt kia 23-4-17 5Yorks p220 MR20
HERBERT,Malcolm Cavagnari Norton Lt dow 2-1-15 1Glouc p106 CR France202
HERBERT,Owen William Eugene 2Lt kiaAbout 27-10-14 23RFA p30 MR22
HERBERT,Reginald Strickson Lt kia 21-5-17 2/11Lond p248 MR20
HERBERT,Robert Bingley Capt kia 30-9-15 RE p210 CR France149
HERBERT,Ronald Crouch T2Lt kia 1-7-16 7RWSurr p56 CR France397
HERBERT,Ronald Young.MID Lt kia 23-9-17 RFA p207 CR Belgium21
HERBERT,Thomas William Percy TLtACapt kia 1-8-17 9WelshR p127 CR

Belgium111
HERBERT,William Alfred 2Lt kia 1-10-16 9DCLI att8YLI p114 MR21
HERBERT-SMITH,Vere 2Lt kia 22-3-15 5RB p179 CR France681,3Bn
HERBERT-STEPNEY,Herbert Arthur Maj kia 7-11-14 1IrGds p52 MR29
HERBERTSON,Andrew Hunter Lt kia 16-5-17 KRRC att7Bn Res p150 MR20
HERBERTSON,John.TD.Maj kia 12-7-15 4KOSB p223 MR4
HERBERTSON,William Gray T2Lt kia 25-9-15 8KOSB p101 MR19
HERBISON,Charles William TCapt dow 17-9-16 1Leic p87 CR France23
HERD,Horace Falkland Capt kia 27-12-14 WelchR p127 CR France260
HERD,James Semple T2Lt kia 16-10-17 52MGC p183 CR Belgium83
HERD,John 2Lt dow 23-9-17 1/4GordH p242 CR Belgium18
HERD,Oswald Alexander TCapt kia 24-9-16 14DLI p161 CR France374
HERDMAN,Arthur Widdrington Lt kia 25-10-14 1KSLI p145 MR32
HERDMAN,George Andrew T2Lt kia 1-7-16 18Lpool p72 MR21
HERDMAN,James Lt dow 9-5-17 5RScots att4NumbF p211 CR France40
HERDMAN,Thomas Anderson Lt kia 21-9-18 7RScots p211 CR France1496
HERINGTON,Percy Godfrey T2Lt kia 15-2-17 8RWFus p98 CR Iraq5
HERIOT,George Edward 2Lt ded 11-12-15 3Co ofLondYeo p204 CR Egypt9,13-12-15
HERISTON,Frank TLt kia 5-7-16 9Yorks p90 MR21
HERITAGE,Audrey Nurse ded 31-10-18 VAD CR Sussex178
HERITAGE,H.A.2Lt ded 28-6-18 14Lond &RAF p249
HERIZ-SMITH,Ambrose Joseph Cocks Lt kia 8-3-16 6Dev p217 MR38
HERIZ-SMITH,Denzil Mitford Heriz T2Lt dow 17-2-17 6Nhampt A'Coy p137 CR France314
HERMAN,George Alfred Lt kia 20-7-16 1Camb p244 MR21
HERMAN,Robert Douglas 2Lt ded PoW 22-9-16 2/5SLancs attRFC p18&230 CR France368,dow
HERMGES,Arthur Cyril Gustave T2Lt dow 19-5-17 5RInniskF p105 MR20
HERMON,Edward William.DSO.TLtCol kia 9-4-17 KEdwHorse &24NhamptF p24 CR France184,Cmdg24NumbF
HERMON-HODGE,George Guy Capt dow 7-7-16 RHA att165RFA p30 CR France169
HERMON-HODGE,John Percivald 2Lt kia 28-5-15 1/4 O&BLI p231 CR Belgium71
HERN,William Stanley TMaj kia 10-8-15 3Wilts p153 MR4
HERNE,David Joseph 2Lt kia 27-5-18 RGA 116SB p40
HERON,Ernest Stewart Lt kia 28-3-18 1/5Ches p222 CR France184
HERON,James T2Lt kia 28-3-18 2LancF p92 MR20
HERON,Jon Maxwell Maj kia 26-3-17 1/5Ess p232 CR Palestine
HERRICK,Harry Eustace Capt kia 11-5-17 RIrF p171 CR France546
HERRICK,John Riversdale Warren Capt dow 4-10-20 IA 3/2GurkhaRif att1/11 p277 CR Iraq6,24-10-20
HERRIES,Fred T2Lt dow 19-12-17 3BordR att10DLI p161 CR Belgium3
HERRING,Horner Reginald Capt kia 23-4-17 5DLI p238 MR20,Homer
HERRINGHAM,Geoffrey Wilmot Capt kia 31-10-14 6Drags att5DragGds p22 MR29
HERRIOTT,John.MC.T2Lt ded 17-2-19 41MGC p183&257 CR France40,Lt
HERRISON,Roger Orme LtCol ded 18-9-17 6RRofCav att4AustFABde de23
HERRON,Alec Rowan 2Lt kia 10-3-15 6 att1KRRC p150 MR22
HERRON,Cyril Douglas 2Lt kia 13-5-15 2DragGds p21 CR Belgium45
HERRON,Kenneth Chester Lt kia 24-4-18 EssYeo &RAF p203&258
HERRON,Reginald Maurice T2Lt dow 12-6-17 13RSuss p119 CR Belgium11
HERRON,Walter Fitzroy.MID TLt ded 3-4-16 4DragGds p21 CR France40,kldacc
HERSCHELL,Ernest Capt dow 26-9-16 6Lpool p215 CR France833
HERSEE,Charles Patrick Allen T2Lt kia 3-3-16 9RFus p68 MR19,2-3-16
HERTSLET,Harold Cecil 2Lt kia 1-7-16 6 att16Mddx p147 CR France35
HERTSLET,Warren Eccles Lt kia 15-8-15 10Lond p248 CR Gallipoli5
HERVEY,Douglas Frederick Lt dow 17-5-17 1/5Norf p216 CR Egypt9
HERVEY,Gerald Arthur Lt kia 8-8-17 1/1RGA p209 CR Belgium19
HERVEY,Thomas Percy Arthur T2Lt kia 15/17-9-16 21KRRC p150 CR France374,15-9-16
HESELTINE,William Wasney Lt dow 20-10-18 RGA 284SB p40 CR France146
HESELTON,George Robert TLt kia 2-6-17 13DLI p161 CR Belgium127
HESELWOOD,George Robert Fettes Lt ded 15-4-15 ArmyPayDept p200 CR Kent61
HESKETH,James Ernest Bytheway T2Lt kia 22-4-17 GL &11RFC p8 MR20
HESKETH,John.MIDx2 T2Lt kia 14-10-18 WYorks att1/6Bn p81 CR France761,dow
HESKETH,Thomas Humphrey Lt ded 28-1-19 1RRofCav p261 CR Scot674,21Lancers
HESKETH,William T2Lt dow 9-6-17 10Ches p96 CR France285
HESKETH,William Cecil TLt kia 9-10-16 149RFA p30 CR France744
HESKETT,John 2Lt kia 15-4-18 3 att2WRid p115 CR France98

HESLOP,Fred T2Lt kia 26-4-18 1WYorks p81 CR Belgium101

HESLOP,George Henry TCapt kia 1-7-16 16Mddx p147 CR France1500

HESLOP,Harold Linton Capt ded 30-10-17 RAMC att7DLI p270 CR Belgium38

HESLOP,William T2Lt kia 5-11-16 16DLI att64TMB p161 CR France114

HESLOP,Walter Lt ded 5-4-18 8SWBord p100 CR Durham88

HESS,Arthur Frank Maj dow 14-7-16 8WYorks p219 CR Yorks361

HESS,Augustus George 2Lt dow 25-2-15 RFA N'Bty p30 CR Belgium165

HESS,Henry.MID 2Lt&Adjt dow 28-10-16 5 att2Mddx p147 CR France105

HESS,Ivan Henry 2Lt kia 15-11-16 3EKent p57 CR France314,16-11-16

HESSELTINE,William T2Lt kia 21-8-16 9RB p179 CR France402

HESSLER,Jacob Andrew Norman Capt kia 27-5-18 5DLI p238 MR18

HESSLER,Jacob Kruse Müller.MID Capt kia 23-3-18 5DLI p238 MR27

HESTER,Edgar Hazel Capt&Adjt kia 16-8-17 2 att7RInniskF p105 CR Belgium167

HETHERINGTON,Arthur TLt kia 22-3-18 9YLI p143 MR27

HETHERINGTON,Guy Capt kia 27-3-17 7Ess p232 MR34

HETHERINGTON,John TLt ded 24-11-18 MGC Inf p183 CR Lincs69

HETHERINGTON,Stephen Owen T2Lt kia 29-9-16 11LancF p92 CR France383

HETHERINGTON,Thomas Alexander 2Lt kia 1-11-18 8RWar p215 CR France1079

HETHERINGTON,Thomas William TLt kia 17-7-16 12DLI p161 MR21

HETT,Roland Thorsten TLt dow 26-10-16 RASC att2Lincsp193 MR21

HETTERLEY,H.C.SNurse 30-5-17 QAIMNSCR Nhampt164

HEUMANN,Richard Capt kia 10-9-16 2Lond CR France218

HEUSTON,Fred Gibson 2Lt kia 15-8-15 6RIrFus p171 MR4

HEVENINGHAM,Lionel Joseph.MID 2Lt kia 7-10-18 C158RFA p30 CR France115

HEWART,Gordon Morley T2Lt kia 9-5-15 6Lincs p75 CR Gallipoli5,9-8-15

HEWAT,Anthony Morris Coates Capt kia 8-9-14 RScots p54 CR France1443,Coats

HEWAT,Bertie Barron.MC.2Lt kia 1-12-17 246RFA p30 MR30

HEWAT,George Michael Fitz Gerald 2Lt kia 10-3-15 IAUL att2SStaffs p122&277,mbk MR28

HEWAT,James Govan Argyll Capt dow 16-4-18 6BlkW p231 CR France88

HEWER,Charles 2Lt kia 23-8-18 1/1Camb p245 CR France196

HEWER,Charles William Lt kia 22-8-17 9A&SH p244 MR30

HEWER,Richard Tuckey 2Lt kia 21-11-17 1BerksYeo p203 CR Palestine3

HEWETSON,Arthur T2Lt kia 24-3-18 8Lancs p59 CR France174

HEWETSON,Charles Herbert Maj kia 23-7-16 11Glouc p106 MR21

HEWETSON John Dixon.MID TCapt dow 30-5-18 10 att1SStaffs p122 CR France1693 &CR France34,8Bn

HEWETSON John Jervis Lt murderedByLanceNaik 2-4-21 IA 1/8GurkhaRif p277 MR43

HEWETSON,Richard John Philip Capt dow PoW 3-7-18 3 att9LNLancs p136 CR France1329

HEWETT,Edmond Geoffrey Capt kia 2-12-15 2/4RWSurr p212 CR Gallipoli26

HEWETT,Ernest Arthur Frederick 2Lt kia 28-3-18 18Lpool att2Ess p72 MR27

HEWETT,George Edward Capt kia 12-3-15 Worc RoO att6Bn p108 CR Belgium17 WIndR att3Worc

HEWETT,Harold Capt kia 4-1-18 RBerks &113RFC p16&139 CR Palestine3,Harald

HEWETT,Henry Walter O'Connell Capt kia 25-9-15 IA 41Dogras attStaffBareillyBde p278 MR28

HEWETT,Herbert Arthur TCapt dow 20-10-18 10RWar p65 CR France403

HEWETT,Stephen Henry Philip 2Lt kia 22-7-16 19 att14RWar p65 MR21

HEWETT,William John.MID Capt kia 9-5-15 3RMunstF p175 CR France924

HEWISON,Charles Runciman TLt drd 4-5-17 RE p45 CR Italy14

HEWISON,Geoffrey Joseph 2Lt kia 15-7-16 3RMunstF p175 CR France267

HEWISON John Edward 2Lt dow 19-4-17 4RScots p211 CR France97,9Bn

HEWITSON John T2Lt kia 11-11-17 23NumbF p61 CR France536

HEWITT,Hon Archibald Rodney.DSO.Capt kia 25-4-15 2ESurr p112 MR29

HEWITT,Arthur Kidman T2Lt kia 20-9-17 3Norf att1/8Lpool p73 MR30

HEWITT,C.J.Maj 21-7-21 S&T Cps MR65

HEWITT,Cedric Atkinson Lt kia 27-10-18 11NumbF p61 CR Italy9

HEWITT,Denis George Wyldborn.VC.2Lt kia 31-7-17 2 att14Hamps p121 MR29,Wyldbore

HEWITT,Ernest Henry.MID Lt kia 15/16-6-15 4RLancs p213 MR22

HEWITT,Frederick Whitmore Chap4Cl kia 28-9-15 RAChDept att20InfBde p199 CR France423,27-9-15

HEWITT,George Alfred Guest Capt kia 27-11-17 2/5Y&L p238 MR17

HEWITT,Gordon Hughes Lt dow 24-9-14 2SLancs p125 CR France473

HEWITT,H.D.Lt dow 27-10-18 3EKent &RAF p57

HEWITT,Holt Montgomery TLt kia 1-7-16 109MGC p183 CR France383

HEWITT,Humphrey St.John 2Lt kia 9-7-18 5Lond p246 CR France177

HEWITT James Francis Lt kia 26-10-14 1ScotRif p103 MR32

HEWITT,James Gordon T2Lt ded 14-11-18 WYorks att2/7Bn p81 CR Yorks410

HEWITT,James Percy 2Lt kia 5-4-18 4 att8SomLI p218 MR20

HEWITT,Robert Edward Talbot 2Lt kia 7-6-17 3 att6RIrReg p89 CR Belgium17

HEWITT,Robert Westbrooke.DSO.MajTLtCol dow 30-9-17 14Huss p22 CR Iraq8

HEWITT,Sydney Rangeley.OBE.MIDx2 Chap4Cl ded 16-2-19 RAChDept attRAMC 6FA p199&257 CR Germany1

HEWITT,Thomas 2Lt kia 27-3-18 7Norf p74 MR27

HEWITT,William Arthur T2Lt kia 1-7-16 9RInniskF p105 MR21

HEWITT,William George 2Lt kia 14-10-14 3RScots p54 CR France1106

HEWITT,William Taylor T2Lt dow PoW 16-4-18 36MGC Inf p183 CR France34

HEWLETT,Harold Alcester Tom Capt kia 23-8-18 4Lond p246 MR16

HEWLETT,Harry Campbell T2Lt kia 28-4-17 7Suff p78 MR20

HEWSON,Charles Victor 2Lt kia 9-7-16 21RFC p3 CR France598

HEWSON,Falkiner Melton Capt ded 22-10-18 RAMC p196 MR65

HEWSON,Henry Holland Capt died 7-11-19 RASC p267 CR Surrey1,Hilliard

HEWSON,Joseph Edward T2Lt kia 10-7-16 8ELancs p110 CR France515

HEWSON,Stanley Barton 2Lt kia 27-8-18 6Lond p247 MR16

HEWSON,Wilfrid John.MID TLt dow 25-10-18 9NumbF p61 CR France332,Wilfred

HEXT,Charles Wilfred Maj ded 21-7-19 IA S&TCps p278 CR Egypt1

HEXT,Francis John.DSO.MC.CaptAMaj dow 9-5-18 41/42RFA p30 CR Cornwall13

HEXT,Thomas Madewood 2Lt kia 29-4-17 5 att12KRRC p150 MR20,Marwood 28-4-17 att1Bn

HEYCOCK,Edwin T2Lt kia 27-8-18 2 att14RWFus p98 CR France432

HEYES,A.E.2Lt dow 14-4-18 GL &21RAF p190 CR Belgium38

HEYES John Peter Capt ded 6-7-16 RAVC att42Div p253 CR Europe1

HEYES,William 2Lt kia 27-2-17 2Worc p108 CR France511

HEYGATE,Claud Raymond Capt kia 1-7-16 2 att10YLI p143 CR France267

HEYGATE,Reginald 2Lt kia 11-6-18 2KOSB p101 MR32

HEYLAND,Arthur Alexander Lt kia 22-5-15 IA 2/5GurkhaRif att1/1 p278 MR28

HEYLAND,J.R.L.MC.Capt 11-3-15 9GurkhaRif CR France727

HEYMAN John Archibald TCapt ded 2-2-19 RASC p267 CR Lond12

HEYMAN,John Henry TLt dow 18-7-17 RASC p193

HEYNES,Dudley Hugo 2Lt kia 16-5-18 402/14RFA 14ArmyBde p30 CR France889

HEYS,William George.TD.LtCol kia 4-6-15 8Manch p237 CR Gallipoli1

HEYWARD,Harvey Heale T2Lt kia 10-10-16 15DLI p161 CR France400,Harry Neale Ex 2Bn

HEYWARD,Maurice 2Lt kia 20-7-16 3 att8Dors p124 MR21

HEYWOOD,Albert Bertine T2Lt kia 4-10-17 10YLI p143 MR30

HEYWOOD,Arthur George Percival Maj dow 12-9-18 1/6Manch p236 CR France145

HEYWOOD,Aubrey Talley Lt kia 3-9-17 GL &45RFC p8 MR20

HEYWOOD,Bertram Charles Percival.TD.Col ded 28-10-14 Manch CR Staffs177

HEYWOOD,Charles Clement Lt kia 25-4-18 RFA p207 MR30

HEYWOOD,F.K.Lt kld 1-10-18 RASC &RAF p193

HEYWOOD,Herbert 2Lt kia 25-9-15 1Manch p155 CR France924

HEYWOOD,Herbert Capt dow 22-8-17 8Mddx attMGC p147&183 CR Belgium16

HEYWOOD James George Cross Lt kia 30-8-15 B1/4Nhampt p234 CR Gallipoli17,dow

HEYWOOD,Robert Myles Lt dow 15-2-15 3EKent p57 CR Belgium151

HEYWOOD,Stanley Lt kia 4-6-15 8Manch p237 MR4

HEYWOOD,Thomas Aston 2Lt dow 6-6-15 4ELancs p226 CR Gallipoli6

HEYWOOD,W.H.V.Capt 7-9-20 IndDefForce CR Derby98

HEWORTH,Frederick James.CB.DSO.TBrigGen kia 9-5-16 Comdg3ScotGds p1 CR Belgium6

HEYWORTH,Heyworth Potter Lawrence Capt kia 6-8-15 7NStaffs p157 CR Gallipoli31

HEYWORTH,J.P.Lt 27-2-20 RFA CR Ches74

HEYWORTH,Peter George 2Lt dow 12-5-17 10Worc att57TMB p108 CR Belgium11,Capt 50TMB

HEYWORTH,Wilfred Alexander 2Lt kia 23-5-16 5Lpool p215 CR France927

HIBBARD,Edmund John 2Lt kia 9-4-17 12Lond p248 CR France1185

HIBBARD,Nelson Stuart 2Lt kia 14-7-17 1LNLnacs p136 CR Belgium173

HIBBARD,Richard 2Lt kia 6-11-18 KSLI att4Bn p145 CR France521

HIBBERT,Arthur James 2Lt ded 14-8-17 B79RFA p30 CR France102

HIBBERT,Cyril Gordon Reuss Capt kia 16-6-15 1/4LNLancs p234 MR22

HIBBERT,Howard Morley 2Lt kia 1-7-16 1/5N&D p232 MR21

HIBBS,Laurence Bosdet T2Lt ded 21-3-16 RJerseyMil att7RIrRif p201 CR France88

HIBBS,Richard John Walmsley Lt kia 8-10-18 3 att22Manch p155 CR France846

HICHENS,James Bryan TLt kia 16-7-16 16KRRC p150 MR21,Byrn 15-7-16

HICHENS,William Thomas 2Lt kia 3-9-16 9 att1DCLI p114 CR France294

HICK,Harold Crispen T2Lt kia 12-7-16 19Lpool p72 CR France630

HICK,Joseph Marsden 2Lt kia 17-4-18 7WRid p228 CR France139

HICK,Pantland Capt ded 17-4-15 RAMC p270

HICKEY,Arthur Aidan 2Lt kia 25-10-18 2/5LancF p221 CR Belgium420

HICKEY,Denis.MC.T2Lt ded 7-11-18 2Leinst p174 CR France1028

HICKEY,Eugene Francis Lt ded 10-3-21 RDubF CR Europe51

HICKEY,Robert Francis 2Lt dow 16-8-17 9RDubF p176 MR30

HICKFORD,Albert T2LtACapt dow 10-5-17 14DLI p161 CR France8

HICKIE,Charles Sinclair Lt dow 1-10-17 6RFC SR p8 CR Belgium11

HICKING,Francis Joseph T2Lt kia 1-7-16 13 att1WYorks p81 CR France373

HICKING,George Graham TLt kia 1-7-16 6Y&L p159 MR21

HICKLENTON,Donald Stuart 2Lt kia 24-8-18 86RFA p30 CR France1170

HICKLEY,Henry Dennis Capt mbk 18-4-16 1A 2/7GurkhaRif att1/9 p278 MR38

HICKLEY,Richard Trollope North Lt kia 24-3-18 Herts p252 MR27

HICKLING,Edward Robert Eyre 2Lt dow 27-10-14 3Glouc attNLancs p106 CR Belgium150,Lt 26-10-14

HICKLING,John Christopher 2Lt kia 11-4-16 9Mddx p236 MR38

HICKMAN,Arthur Kendrick Lt kia 5-4-16 3 att8WelchR p127 MR38,RWFus

HICKMAN,Ernest John 2Lt kia 16-8-15 1/4Ess p232 CR Gallipoli4

HICKMAN,Harry Claude 2Lt kia 23-3-18 13RSuss p119 CR France365,Lt

HICKMAN,John George 2Lt kia 4-10-17 C50RFA p30 CR Belgium10

HICKMAN,Philip Gregory 2Lt dow 31-10-17 6SStaffs p229 CR France102

HICKMAN,Poole Henry TCapt kia 15-8-15 7RDubF p176 MR4

HICKMAN,Terence 2Lt kia 26/27-6-16 2Leinst p174 MR29,26-6-16

HICKMAN,William Christie 2Lt kia 1-7-16 175RFA p30 CR France393

HICKMOTT,Sydney Richard 2Lt dow 1-10-18 4RWKent p234 MR30

HICKOX,Edwin Baskerville.MC.TMaj dow 15-8-17 9Ess p131 CR France113

HICKS,Arthur Supt ded 16-6-19 NWFProvPolice MR43

HICKS,Arthur Leslie TLt ded 4-4-18 11Leic p87 CR France924,dow

HICKS,Basil Perrin TLt kia 25-9-15 8RBerks p139 CR France219

HICKS,Charles Albert T2Lt kia 3-10-18 6RInniskF p105 CR France375

HICKS,Charles Hubert Lt kia 21-7-18 8N&D p233 CR France28

HICKS,Edwin Theodore Capt ded 12-5-17 2/4Lincs p220&270 CR France833

HICKS,Eric Raymond.MC.Lt ded 25-12-18 RFA 60DivHQ p207 CR Egypt1

HICKS,Ernest 2Lt kia 9-10-16 2/18Lond p250 CR France68

HICKS,Frank Alan.MC.Lt kia 21-8-18 4RFus p68 CR France214

HICKS,Frederick Richard LtCol dow 12-6-15 Hamps p121 CR Cornwall128

HICKS,Harleigh Lionel Adrian Oswald 2Lt kia 12-4-18 5 att1/8Mddx p147

HICKS,Harry Ronald 2Lt kia 12-10-17 GL &19RFC p8 CR Belgium157

HICKS,Lawrence Frederick Lt dow 5-11-18 2Wilts p153 CR France321

HICKS,Robert 2Lt kia 26-5-18 23Lond p252 CR France177,25-5-18

HICKS,Walter Gerald T2Lt dow 12-8-15 8RFus p68 CR France12

HICKS,William Goss 2Lt dow 3-7-17 RGA 260SB p40

HICKSON,Horace Grant T2Lt kia 6/12-8-15 6Leinst p174 MR4

HICKSON,James Ferguson 2Lt dow 31-7-17 1/9Lpool p216 CR Belgium7

HICKSON,Reginald Davies.MC.TCapt dow 30-4-17 9Ess p131 MR20

HIDDINGH,Stephen Van Der Poel LtACapt kia 3-5-17 4RFus p68 MR20

HIDER,Arthur Leslie George 2LtTLt kia 27-5-17 8SStaffs A'Coy p122 CR France544

HIELD,John Hamer Capt kia 3-9-16 16RB p179 MR21

HIGGERTY,Frederick Charles 2Lt mbk 30-11-17 8Lond p257 MR17

HIGGIN,Harold Sinclair Capt ded 11-1-19 IARO att75CarnaticInf p278 MR65

HIGGIN,James Laurence.MID Capt kia 30-6-15 1A 1/10 att1/9GurkhaRif p278 MR4,29/30-6-15

HIGGIN-BIRKET,William Capt mbk 2-12-14 1/2LancF p256 MR32,28-10-14

HIGGIN-BOTHAM,Charles Egerton 2Lt kia 5-11-16 9DLI p239 MR21

HIGGINBOTHAM,Charles Ernest Maj kia 11-3-15 2Nhampt p137/ MR22

HIGGINBOTHAM,Robert Edward 2Lt kia 29-9-18 B115RFA p30 CR Greece5

HIGGONBOTTOM,Frederick T2Lt ded 6-4-17 9Ches &23RFC p8 MR20

HIGGINS,Arthur Aken TCapt ded 25-10-18 RAVC att115RFA p198 CR Greece5

HIGGINS,Arthur Henry 2Lt ded 29-10-19 RGA 258SB p262 CR Staffs61

HIGGINS,Claud Wilfred 2Lt drd 25-4-17 NStaffs p157 MR38

HIGGINS,Claude D.2Lt kia 22-9-16 21RFC p3 CR France446

HIGGINS,Cuthbert George 2Lt dow 1-7-16 6WYorks p218 MR21

HIGGINS,Douglas Stanley TLt kia 9-4-17 9 att5 O&BLI p130 CR France581,Capt dow

HIGGINS,Frederick 2Lt kia 27-7-18 1/7GordH p242 CR France622

HIGGINS,George Frederick TMaj kia 10/12-7-16 17Lpool p72 MR21,10-7-16

HIGGINS,Harry Vincent 2Lt kia 3-9-16 116MGC Inf p183 CR France1890

HIGGINS,Herbert Edward Powell Capt kia 10-8-15 6RLancs p59 MR4

HIGGINS,Hugh Stevenson 2Lt kia 28-3-18 13RScots p54 MR20

HIGGINS,John WO ded 2-8-16 RIM p278

HIGGINS,Michael Aloysius Lt kia 31-3-17 3Leinst p174 CR France480,2Bn

HIGGINS,P.J.Lt 18-2-20 RGA CR Ches18

HIGGINS,Percy Clynton Capt kia 22-9-17 1KSLI attNigR p145&201 CR EAfrica8 &CR Tanzania1

HIGGINS,Stanley T2Lt kia 28-9-18 2/7Lpool p72 CR France686,27-9-18

HIGGINS,Thomas,MC TLt dow 15-11-16 RE 130FC p45 CR France40

HIGGINSON,Ernest George T2Lt kld 4-10-17 GL &73RFC p8 CR Scot235

HIGGINSON,George Neale TLt kia 23-11-16 16LancF p92 CR France153

HIGGINSON,John Herbert 2Lt kia 30-11-17 5RHA p30 CR France1483

HIGGINSON,John Thomas Gordon T2Lt kld 1-11-17 GL &RFC p8 CR Ches51

HIGGINSON,John Victor.MC.Capt ded 23-9-19 2RWFus p263 CR Shrop97

HIGGINSON,Robert 2Lt kia 15-8-16 5RLancs p213 MR21

HIGGINSON,Thomas Cecil Lt kia 15-9-16 GrenGds attMGC SR p50 MR21

HIGGINSON,Tom Arthur TCapt kldacc 19-9-15 6KSLI p145 CR France706

HIGGINSON,William Clifton Vernon T2Lt kia 20-11-17 GL &3RFC p8 MR20

HIGGINSON,William Frederick Capt kia 25-4-15 1RDubF p176 CR Gallipoli15

HIGGITT,Leonard Henry Lt dow 30-10-17 4NStaffs att9YLI p157 CR France40

HIGGON,Archibald Bellairs Maj kia 10-9-15 RFA p30 CR Gallipoli20,9-9-15

HIGGON,John Arthur Maj kia 20-7-16 PembYeo p205 CR France82

HIGGS,Harry Leonard 2Lt kia 25-3-18 5Lond p246 MR20

HIGGS,John Phillip Lt dow 14-4-18 OxfYeo attMGC p205 CR France185

HIGGS,Lucien Herbert T2Lt kld 8-6-17 RFC SR p8 CR War65

HIGGS,Marcus Webb T2Lt kia 23-10-18 att9Dev p76 MR16 CR France231

HIGGS,Reginald Frank T2Lt kia 22-9-18 1RWSurr p56 CR France407

HIGH,Gilbert Cecil 2Lt kia 14-3-17 2/6Norf att2/5YLI p217 CR France239

HIGH,Robert Donald 2Lt kia 22-3-18 4GordH p242 MR20

HIGHAM,Percy Harrowell.MC.2Lt kia 17-2-17 6Nhampt p137 MR21

HIGHAM,Wilfred T2Lt kia 27-9-18 2/5RLancs p59 CR France530,Capt

HIGHFIELD,George Harold 2Lt dow 4-7-15 3Y&L p159 CR Belgium17

HIGHMORE,Charles Bowyer 2Lt ded 26-2-19 MGC p254 CR Surrey154

HIGHT,Norman Dudley John.MC.2Lt kia 24-3-18 3 att10Ess p131 CR France1893

HIGHTON,Harold Victor 2Lt kia 25-3-18 RFC p16 MR20

HIGMAN,Frederick James 2Lt dow 17-10-18 3 att1YLI p143 CR Scot764

HIGMAN,Michael T2Lt kia 18-8-16 6DCLI p114 MR21

HIGNETT,William Rowland 2Lt kia 3-5-17 4 att12EYorks p219 MR20

HIGSON,Frederic Stewart.MC.TLtACapt kia 31-8-17 17WelshR p127 CR France415

HIGSON,John Turnbull T2Lt dow 4-8-18 Nhampt att2Bn p137 CR Germany3

HIGSON,Richard Henry 2Lt kia 23-10-16 16 att2LancF p92 MR21

HIGSON,William Marsh T2Lt dow 9-4-17 8RLancs p59 CR France113,kia

HILARY,Henry Jephson 2Lt dow 3-6-17 17RH&FA p30 CR France113,2-6-17

HILDAGE,Harry 2Lt kia 15-4-17 27RFA p30 CR France1325

HILDER,Harold Sutton 2Lt kia 3-5-17 att7EKent p57 MR20

HILDER,Maurice Lake.MC.LtTCapt kia 3-5-17 5 att23RFus p68 MR20

HILDERSLEY,Stanley Kentfield Edwards T2Lt kia 12-9-16 6Yorks p90 CR France246

HILDITCH,Charles Henry 2Lt kia 23-10-18 27RFA p30 CR France206

HILDITCH,Richard.MID TLt kia 14-9-16 14Lpool p72 MR37

HILDITCH,Victor Cadifer.DSO.MC.ALtCol ded 11-2-19 RFA p261 CR Wales166,Cadifor

HILDRETH,Ernest T2Lt kld 18-10-16 14Yorks attRFC p3&90 CR Norf247

HILDYARD,Robert Aubrey 2Lt kia 20-12-16 1RLancs p59 CR France630

HILEY,Frank TCapt kld 13-2-18 8Yorks p90 CR Italy7

HILL,Adam Cyril Darley 2Lt kia 16-8-17 RIrRif CR Belgium125

HILL,Albert Charles Leonard 2Lt kia 27-5-18 4Berks p234 CR France248

HILL,Alec Leslie 2Lt kia 26-12-17 4 att1Dev p220 CR Italy48,kld

HILL,Alexander Lt kia 12-10-18 9HLI p240 MR16

HILL,Alexander Sidney 2Lt kia 9-10-17 6Glouc p225 MR30

HILL,Alan Purdie Dunlop Capt ded 8-2-19 RGA att59RAF p30&40 CR Belgium330,Maj

HILL,Alfred 2Lt kia 13-9-17 1/5NStaffs p238 CR France115

HILL,Alfred Saunders 2Lt kia 20-11-17 RGA 109SB p40 CR Belgium92

HILL,Andrew Bruce 2Lt kia 27-9-18 7RWar p214 CR France415

HILL,Arthur James 2Lt kia 8-7-16 2Wilts p153 MR21

HILL,Arthur Lionel T2Lt kia 25-9-15 1Mddx p147 MR19

HILL,Arthur Moberly 2Lt kia 9-4-17 NSomYeo att1SomLI p205 MR20

HILL,Arthur Rowland Maj kia 3-10-15 2Ches p96 MR19

HILL,Austen Shelbourne 2Lt dow 3-6-17 6Lond p247 CR France614

141

HILL,Barry Lt kia 1-7-16 10RIrRif p169 MR21

HILL,Benjamin Godlonton.MC.2Lt dow 5-6-17 RFA p208 CR Belgium102

HILL,Beresford Winnington TLt kia 4-3-17 GL 10RB &59RFC p8 CR France502

HILL,Bertram Gilbert 2Lt kia 25-9-15 3 att2RWar p65 CR France260

HILL,Brian Edward TCapt dow 2-10-18 RASC att1TankCps p188&193 CR France446

HILL,Cedric Lloyd Graham 2Lt kia 5-11-16 5 att8DLI p239 MR21

HILL,Charles Douglas Lucas T2Lt kia 14-2-16 9RSuss p119 CR Belgium72

HILL,Charles Edward HonLt ded 16-3-18 LabCps p266 CR Mddx46

HILL,Charles Edward TCapt kia 28-9-15 13Mddx p147 MR19

HILL,Charles Edward Cecil Lt kia 17-4-16 HLI p163 MR38

HILL,Charles Glencairn,CMG.DSO TLtCol kia 26-6-15 1RBerks p139 CR France1106

HILL,Charles Herbert TCapt kia 21-8-15 11Y&L att1RInniskF p159 MR4

HILL,Charles Percy Capt kia 19-8-16 4NStaffs p157 CR France513

HILL,Douglas Agar Worsley TLt dow 14-8-16 6EKent p57 CR France13

HILL,Edwin Arundel TMaj dow 26-10-18 8RSuss p119 CR France1170

HILL,Eric Alfred TLt kld 12-1-17 SL p201 CR Asia81,ded

HILL,Eric Battley 2Lt ded 19-11-16 5Ess attTMB p232 CR France121,1/6Bn

HILL,Ernest Hatton Capt ded 11-4-18 7WRid p227 CR Yorks619

HILL,Frederick.DCM.Capt kia 8-8-18 15Lond p249 CR France141

HILL,Frederick Thomas Cecil TMaj kia 7-8-15 6Y&L p159 CR Gallipoli26

HILL,Gerald Leader Capt kia 26-9-17 5Lincs p220

HILL,Gerald Stanley 2Lt kia 15-9-16 1Lond p245 MR21

HILL,George SubCdr ded 26-11-18 IA MilWksServ p278 CR EAfrica36 Ex 9Lancers

HILL,Guy Charles Dunlop 2Lt drd 4-5-17 2KSLI p145 CR Italy14

HILL,Harold Belfit Lt kld 6-9-18 3RWKent attRAF p141

HILL,Henry Hamp TCapt dow 8-3-16 11WYorks p81 CR France924

HILL,Henry Oswald William.MC.TCapt ded 21-10-17 GL &52RFC p8 MR20

HILL,Henry Tavener 2Lt kia 18-10-14 2RWar p65 MR29

HILL,Henry William T2Lt kia 10-8-15 6BordR p117 MR4

HILL,Horace Frederick.MC.TCapt dow 5-9-17 18Mddx p147 CR Belgium37

HILL,Hugh.MVO.DSO.BtLtCol kia 10-9-16 RWFus Staff p98 CR France80

HILL,James 2Lt ded 21-10-16 RGA 16HB p40 CR France64

HILL,James Alfred LtTCapt kia 17-4-18 1Leic p87 MR30

HILL,James Macgregor T2Lt dow 10-11-16 2NumbF p61 CR Greece9

HILL,Jeremiah Charles Holmes T2Lt dow 2-5-17 9Ess p131 CR France113

HILL,Jesse Adolphus Henry Capt ded 1-3-19 RFA p254 CR Essex14

HILL,John Edward TCapt dow 24-3-18 PoW 9Norf p74 CR France274

HILL,John Newton T2Lt ded 11-8-16 SL CamelTransportCoy 1CamCps p201 CR Egypt2

HILL,John Robertson Lt kia 2-6-15 3DLI p161 CR Belgium44

HILL,John Robertshaw T2Lt kia 6-5-17 RE P'SpCoy p45 CR France560

HILL,John Rowland T2Lt kia 5-8-16 13YLI p143 CR France643

HILL,Joseph T2Lt ded 23-11-18 MGC Inf p183 CR Wales78,Lt

HILL,Leonard Coulthard.MC.LtACapt ded 10-10-18 RFA att4ArmyArtySchool p30 CR France52,Maj

HILL,Leonard Grenville 2Lt kia 9-11-16 48RFA p30 CR France174

HILL,Lional George Capt kia 17-2-15 2EYorks p84 MR29

HILL,Maurice Cridland Lt kia 24-5-15 5NumbF p213 CR Belgium96

HILL,Michael.DCM.T2Lt kia 19-7-16 RE 3SigCo p45&259 CR France513

HILL,Nicholas Weatherby.MC.LtACapt kia 16-1-17 2 O&BLI p130 CR France280

HILL,Norman Ernest Albert 2Lt ded 27-3-15 14WYorks p254 CR Dorset141

HILL,Oldham Cyril Darley 2Lt kia 16-8-17 4 att7RIrRif p169

HILL,Percy Joseph TLt kia 3-10-18 1YLI p143 CR France234

HILL,Phillip Aubrey Capt kia 23-4-17 att2SWBord BrecknockBn p223 MR20

HILL,R.Lt 24-11-20 Glouc CR Devon68

HILL,Ralph Grenfell Lt kia 20-2-17 1KAR p202 CR EAfrica40,19-2-17

HILL,Reginald Byng Tower LtTCapt kia 3-6-17 8Ess p232 CR France115

HILL,Reginald Gordon.MC.TLt kia 11-10-17 RAMC att1CldGds p196 CR Belgium12

HILL,Reginald Percy 2Lt dow 25-8-18 A72RFA p30 CR France924

HILL,Richard Maj ded 17-2-15 3Yorks p90 CR Yorks171

HILL,Richard Alexander TLt kia 10-4-17 RGA 138HB p40 CR France480

HILL,Richard Alexander Gathorne Lt kia 12-8-18 SomLI &204RAF p263 MR20

HILL,Robert William Capt dow 31-7-17 1Camb p244 CR Belgium101

HILL,Stanley Frederick.MC&Bar.Capt kia 4-11-18 4Glouc p225 CR France933

HILL,Sydney Moir-Byres 2Lt kia 25-9-15 3GordH attCamH p166 MR19

HILL,Thomas Edward 2Lt dow 21-4-18 RGA 156B47HABde p40 CR France145

HILL,Thomas Hooton 2Lt kia 13-11-16 4Beds p86 CR France220

HILL,Thomas Wilson T2Lt kia 10-7-17 HLI att16Bn p163 CR Belgium24

HILL,Tom Warner T2Lt ded 14-10-17 4MGC Inf p183 CR Yorks543

HILL,Victor Baillie.MC.Capt dow 15-1-18 6KRRC p150 CR France64

HILL,Walter Edward Lt kia 23-9-14 3NStaffs p157 CR France1111,25-9-14

HILL,Walter Henry T2Lt kia 20-11-17 RB att10Bn p179 MR17

HILL,Wilfred Stuart T2Lt kia 31-7-17 RB p179 CR Belgium167

HILL,Wilfrid Dudley Capt dow 13-5-15 3 att1LNLancs p136

HILL,Wilfrid James T2Lt dow 17-9-16 6DCLI p114 CR France833

HILL,William.MID HonLt&QM ded 11-10-15 8RWFus p98 CR Gallipoli26

HILL,William TLt kia 30-10-17 RFA 86ArmyBde p30 CR Belgium19

HILL,William Alfred TLtACapt kia 23-3-18 7DCLI att61TMB p114 CR France1061

HILL,William Carlisle.MC.TLt kia 7-6-17 2RIrRif att74TMB p169 MR29

HILL,William Ernest TLt kia 8-8-18 9RFus B'Coy p68 CR France247

HILL,William Henry Ostler 2Lt dow 25-9-15 2Yorks p90 MR19

HILL,William Reginald.MC&Bar.Lt ded PoW 6-11-18 4 att12DLI p161 CR Germany4

HILL,William Robb 2Lt dow 24-8-18 4BlkW p230 CR France266,kia

HILL,William White Lt dow 20-4-17 ImpCamelCps CR Palestine2

HILL-TREVOR,Hillyer George Edwin Lt kia 21-12-14 1ScotsGds p52 MR22

HILL-WILLIAMS,J.Lt 3-3-17 PoliticDept CR EAfrica46

HILLAS,Arthur Benedict Edward Capt kia 23-4-17 7GordH p242 CR France644

HILLBROOK,Wallace Capt 22-7-16 UgandaMS CR EAfrica52

HILLEBRANDT,Frederick Edmund T2Lt kld 22-3-17 GL &RFC 5Wing p8 CR Essex48,HILLEBRANT

HILLER,Alan Menzies.MID 2Lt kia 16-5-15 3RWSurr p56 CR France279,2Bn

HILLERNS,Hero Wilhelm Oswald.MID Maj kia 14-4-17 B251RFA p206&207 CR France418

HILLIAR,Gordon Edward 2Lt kia 26-9-15 3SLancs attELancs p125 CR France276,dow

HILLIER,Cyril Anthony Hudson 2Lt dow 27-2-15 2Mon p244 CR Suff138,26-2-15

HILLIER,Frederick William 2Lt ded 2-12-19 IA 8Cav p278 MR43,3Lancers att27LtCav

HILLIER,Geoffrey Stuart Drummond TCapt kia 30-3-18 13Glouc p106 MR27

HILLIER,Maurice 2Lt kia 9-4-17 6KOSB p101 CR France645

HILLIER,Sidney Napier T2Lt kia 25-3-18 6SWBord p100 MR20

HILLIER,W.D.Capt 15-11-18 20DLI CR Ches147

HILLING,Sophie.ARRC.Sister ded 12-10-18 QAIMNS p200 CR France123

HILLMAN,Harold Alexander Moore TLt kia 1-7-16 11 att7Yorks p90 CR France397

HILLMAN,Horace James T2Lt ded 25-3-19 RE SpBde p262 CR Mddx68,Lt

HILLMAN,Leslie Harris Lt kia 31-7-17 2RB p179 MR29

HILLMAN-MILLER,James TLt dow 10-8-15 4SWBord p100 MR4

HILLS,Arthur Edward TCapt kia 28-5-18 14NumbF p61 MR18

HILLS,Arthur Hyde 2Lt kia 19-4-17 8Hamps p229 MR34

HILLS,Charles Herbert 2Lt dow 5-9-16 3Manch p155 CR France188

HILLS,Cyril.MC.T2Lt kia 30-8-18 2Suff p78 CR France433

HILLS,Ernest Leslie TLt dow 26-11-15 12RWFus att1NigR p98&201 CR WAfrica58

HILLS,Frederick Mervyn 2Lt kia 27-7-17 3 att7Nhampt p137 CR Belgium115,3 att2Bn

HILLS,Geoffrey Wilfrid 2Lt kia 14-6-17 10Lond p248 CR France568

HILLS,Laurence Clifford T2Lt kia 3-7-16 1Lincs p75 MR21

HILLS,Malcolm Arthur T2Lt kia 15-9-16 1EKent p57 MR21

HILLS,Maud Ellen Sister ded 22-7-18 TFNS p254 CR Surrey160

HILLS,Walter Edward.MID T2Lt kia 26-6-17 KRRC att16Bn p150 CR France1489

HILLS,William Frederick Waller TLt kia 6-3-17 GL RFA att57RFC p8 CR France46

HILLYARD,Noël Hardcastle Lt dow 23-4-17 223RFA p207 CR France95

HILLYER,James Excelsior 2Lt kia 27-10-17 RGA 186SB p40 MR30

HILLYER,Philip Charles T2Lt kia 31-8-18 13Lpool p72 CR France433

HILLYER,William Harold,MC Capt kia 22-5-16 RE 1/4FC p210 CR France80

HILTON,A Maj 4-3-15 RAMC CR Egypt9

HILTON,Arthur T2Lt kia 9-10-17 5Y&L p159 MR20

HILTON,Clarence Stuart Capt kia 1-7-16 2Mddx p147 MR21

HILTON,Fawcett T2Lt kia 3-7-16 1Lincs p75 MR21

HILTON,George 2Lt kia 8-8-16 4RLancs p213 MR21

HILTON,Harold 2Lt kia 26-11-17 14HLI p163 MR17

HILTON,Henry Denne 2Lt kia 19-12-14 5 att4Mddx p147 CR Belgium17,20-12-14

HILTON,Herbert Philip Capt kia 16-2-15 3Mddx p147 MR29

HILTON,Murray Venables BtColTCol kia 20-10-15 Cmdg7ELancs p110 CR France727 Ex Worc

HILTON,Oscar.MC.ACapt dow 14-11-18 RFA p254

HILTON,Reginald Musgrave 2Lt kia 23-4-17 6 att4Mddx p147 MR20

HILTON,Robert 2Lt ded 29-4-18 16Manch &13RAF p155 MR20,6-4-18 5Bn

HINCHCLIFFE,Frank Beatson 2Lt kia 4-11-18 5WRid p227 CR France206

HINCHLIFF,Cyril Stanley T2Lt kld 4-9-17 GL &RFC p8 CR Sussex9

HINCHLIFFE,Charles Ernest.MM.2Lt kia 20-7-18 YLI att4Bn p143 MR18

HINCHLIFFE,George William 2Lt kia 26-6-18 15WYorks att93TMB p81

HINCKLEY,Douglas Roy 2Lt kia 13-1-17 12Y&L att5RFC p9&159 CR France927

HINCKLEY,John 2Lt kia 27-3-18 RGA 24SB p40 CR France1170

HINCKS,Bertram 2Lt kia 18-12-16 5 att10KRRC p150 CR France402

HIND,Arthur Charles Sinclair Capt kia 14-4-15 IA 110MahrattaLI p278 CR Iraq6

HIND,Charles Raymond.MID Lt kia 30-5-16 2SStaffs p122 CR France924,29-5-16

HIND,Ernest William Gayles 2Lt kia 1-7-16 15IrRif p169 MR21

HIND,Frank Capt dow PoW 29-10-14 EYorks p84 CR France1887

HIND,Frank Farmer T2Lt kia 16-7-16 6Leic att110TMB p87 CR France453

HIND,Henry Basil Lindsay Lt kia 22-11-15 3SomLI attO&BLI p80 MR38

HIND,I.F.Capt ded 12-8-18 SL &RAF p201

HIND,Jesse Francis Montague TLt kia 27-9-16 9N&D p134 MR21

HIND,Lawrence Arthur.MC.LtCol kia 1-7-16 1/7N&D p232 MR21

HIND,Reginald Charles 2Lt kia 6-2-18 A160RFA p30 CR France592

HINDE,Cyril de Villiers.MC.Lt ded 11-1-17 2RBerks p139 MR29,11-7-17

HINDE,Kenneth 2Lt kia 3-2-17 5RLancs p213 CR France624

HINDE,William Henry Rousseau LtTCapt ded 22-10-18 RASC p193 CR Yorks361

HINDLE,Alfred Herbert 2Lt kia 12-5-18 26/17RH&FA p30 CR Belgium36

HINDLE,Harold Burn TLt kia 27-3-18 G'RHA p30 MR27

HINDLE,Ralph.DSO.LtCol kia 30-11-17 4LNLancs p233 CR France212

HINDLE,Stephen T2Lt kia 26-3-18 4TankCps p188 CR France395

HINDLEY-SMITH,Evelyn Hay Capt 16-5-18 5Manch CR Hamps214

HINDMARSH,George Edwin 2Lt ded 16-6-17 23RB p244 MR67,G.E.S.

HINDS,Ralph William Gore.MID Lt kia 16-5-15 2RInniskF p105 CR France279

HINDS,William Pugh TLt dow 2-2-16 15RWFus p98 CR France345

HINDSLEY,Eric TLt dow 11-4-17 1SStaffs p122 CR France64

HINDSON,Leslie Reginald Probyn Lt kia 10-6-17 A187RFA p30 CR Belgium15 Lesley

HINDSON,Reginald Gordon 2Lt ded 13-9-14 RFA p30 CR C'land&W'land17

HINE,Claude Annesley T2Lt dow 16-10-16 2 att10RWSurr p56 CR France833

HINE,Godfrey Valentine Brooke Lt kia 6-10-15 2IrGds SR p52 CR France423,2Lt

HINE,Harold Bowman Egerton Lt ded 31-8-18 7Hamps p229 CR Iraq5

HINE,Herbert Josiah.MM.T2Lt kia 25-8-18 6EKent p57 CR France430

HINE,T.C.2Lt kia 20-7-16 20RFus p68 MR21

HINE-HAYCOCK,Ralph Hugh Capt kia 3-5-17 1 att10YLI p143 CR France1186

HINES,Austin T2Lt dow 15-12-15 10DLI p161 CR Belgium11

HINES,Charles William Maj kia 24/25-6-15 7DLI p239 MR29,26-5-15

HINES,Harold William.MC.DCM.2Lt kia 7-10-17 RFA 113ArmyBde p30 MR30

HINGSTON,Edward Maj kia 28-3-15 RE 54FC p45 CR France768

HINGSTON,Frank Leonard Capt kia 26-4-15 1DCLI p114 CR Belgium151,Frederick

HINGSTON,George Bennett LtCol dow 16-6-15 RE p45 CR Egypt3

HININGS,Frederick William Crowther Capt kia 25-9-16 3 att1EYorks p84 MR21

HINKLEY,Arthur 2Lt kia 7-8-15 1/5LancF p221 MR4

HINKLEY,Siegfried Thomas T2Lt kia 3-7-16 6EKent C'Coy p57 CR France393

HINNELL,Thomas Squier 2Lt kia 12-8-15 5Suff p217 MR4

HINTON,Charles Allan.MC&Bar.Capt&Adjt kia 22-5-18 RE 46Div p210 CR France109

HINTON,Godfrey Bingham.CMG.LtCol kia 21-3-18 RFA 26ArmyBde p30 CR France518

HINTON,Norman Charles 2Lt dow 4-4-18 6RFus p68 CR France62,Lt 13Bn

HINTON,Walter Reginald T2Lt kia 14-7-16 2BordR p117 CR France453

HINXMAN,Alfred James TLt kia 10-8-15 5Wilts p153 MR4

HIPKIN,Henry James T2Lt kia 17-7-18 att7SfthH p183 MR32

HIPKINS,Fredk Wystan.MC.Capt kia 3-10-18 6N&D D'Coy p233 CR France375

HIPKINS,Norman.MID Capt kia 28-9-18 6NStaffs p238 CR France375

HIPPISLEY,Harold Edwin 2Lt kia 23-10-14 att1Glouc SR p106 MR29

HIPWELL,Charles Stanley.MC.Lt kia 14-10-16 16Lond p249 CR France15,15-10-16

HIPWELL,H.Reginald 2Lt kia 23-4-17 4SfthH attMGC p187&241 CR France604

HIRD,Christopher T2Lt kia 19-4-17 8WRid att1/4Nhants p115 CR Palestine8

HIRD,Frederick TLt kia 29-7-16 GL WRid att10TMB p190 MR21,dow

HIRD,Joseph William Smith T2Lt dow 26-1-17 7NStaffs p157 CR Iraq5

HIRE,Frederick TLt ded 12-10-18 RE p262 CR Belgium38

HIRONS,William John T2Lt kia 21-3-18 7Lincs p75 MR20

HIRSCH,David Philip.VC.MID Capt kia 23-4-17 4Yorks p220 MR20

HIRSCHBEIN,served as HURSTBOURNE,Walter Hirsch

HIRSCHORN,Cecil T2Lt ded 21-2-18 1Wilts att9Dev p153 CR Italy12,HIRSCHHORN

HIRST,Alfred Edison 2Lt kia 3-9-16 4WRid p227 MR21

HIRST,Cecil Pollock T2Lt kia 1-7-16 8Dev p76 CR France397

HIRST,Charles Capt kia 3-9-16 1/4WRid p227 MR21

HIRST,Fred Philip Lt ded 19-2-19 RGA p209 CR Europe1

HIRST,Gerald William 2Lt kia 26-2-17 3Lpool p72 CR France744

HIRST,Harold Capt kia 24-6-15 1/4YLI p235 CR France684

HIRST,Harold Hugh Lt ded 24-2-19 GL 21Manch attRE p266 CR Berks117

HIRST,Henry Denne LtCol ded 16-5-18 3EKent p57&251 CR Kent164

HIRST,James.MM.2Lt kia 14-9-18 20Lond p251 MR16

HIRST,Leonard George.MC.TLt ded 18-10-18 RE p254 CR France52

HIRST,Stanley Ewart 2Lt kia 24-10-17 RGA 200SB p40 CR Belgium19

HIRST,Wilfred Bertram 2Lt dow 22-4-15 4Lincs p217 CR Belgium98

HIRST,William T2Lt kia 1-7-16 14Y&L p159 CR France5

HIRST,William Henry T2Lt kia 1-8-18 WYorks att10Bn p81 CR France61

HISCOCK,Ernest Henry TCapt kia 25-1-17 9Worc p109 CR Iraq5

HISCOCK,Leonard Ernest T2Lt kia 10-8-15 9Worc p109 CR Gallipoli13

HISLOP,Alec Herbert 2Lt ded 24-12-17 14Lond p249 CR France95

HISLOP,Arthur Fowler Maj ded 19-3-19 IA S&TCps p278 MR43

HISLOP,Frederick Laurence 2Lt kia 23-4-17 6A&SH p243 CR France546

HISLOP,George Capt dow 28-11-17 RAMC N&D FA p253 CR Egypt9

HISLOP,James.MC.TLtACapt kia 31-7-17 CamH att6Bn p168 CR Belgium125

HISLOP,James Ambrose Lt kld 9-9-15 RAMC p254 CR Scot776,8HLI

HISLOP,John.MC.TLtACapt kia 22-9-17 8Beds p86 MR30

HISLOP,John Arthur TCapt ded 8-7-16 19Manch p155 CR Lancs464

HISLOP,John Hogben T2Lt dow 11-4-17 15RScots p54 CR France95

HISLOP,Percy Robert T2Lt dow 7-12-17 17Mddx p147 CR France145

HISLOP,Robert Wallace TLtACapt kia 22-7-17 RE 251TC p45 CR France163

HISLOP,Robert Wilson Lt 4-7-17 1/4 att1/6SfthH CR Belgium11

HISLOP,Walter Balmer 2Lt kia 28-4-15 5RScots D'Coy p211 CR Gallipoli2

HISSEY,Maurice Henry ACapt kia 26-10-16 2RBerks p139 MR21

HITCH,George Stuart Lt ded 9-11-18 5Lpool attRAF p215&258 CR Ches182,Stewart

HITCH,Gerald Henry Sibbald TCapt ded 10-2-19 RASC p254

HITCHCOCK,Cyril Augustus T2Lt kia 21-4-16 1KSLI p145 CR Belgium73

HITCHCOCK,Edward Arthur Lt dow 29-9-18 1/6HLI p240 CR France1184

HITCHCOCK,Herbert William TLt kia 13-11-16 MGC Inf att11TankCps p183 CR France383

HITCHCOCK,Reginald Francis 2Lt kia 14-4-18 25MGC p183 MR32

HITCHEN,Stanley Lucas T2Lt kia 6-6-16 17WYorks p81 CR France727

HITCHIN,George Robert Capt kia 14-8-16 RAMC 2/1FA p253 CR France141

HITCHINGS,Francis Noel Wells Lt kld 3-12-18 5RWSurr att6EKent p212 CR France1196,ded

HITCHINGS,Henry Mayne 2Lt kia 18-8-16 GL 7RIrRif att48TMB p190 CR France423,HITCHINS

HITCHINGS,Richard Gordon LtACapt kia 10-7-17 RFA 38DAC p30 CR Belgium16

HITCHINS,Henry William Ernest LtCol kia 28-4-15 1Manch p155 CR Belgium101,26-4-15

HITCHON,James Foldys Lt kia 1-7-16 10 att11ELancs Y'Coy p110 CR France802

HITNER,Victor Jacob TLt ded 20-7-18 RASC attLabCps p193 CR France145

HOADE,Reginald William 2Lt kia 15-7-16 2/7 att1Mddx p235 MR21

HOARD,Henry Herbert Hoare 2Lt kia 9-9-17 3 att21NumbF p61 CR France366

HOARE,Allen Brodie Capt kia 26-10-17 5LNLancs A'Coy p234 MR30,Alan

HOARE,Archibald Capt dow 27-11-17 12KRRC p150 CR France446

HOARE,Charles Morgan Lt kia 24-8-15 15Huss p22 MR15,24-8-14

HOARE,Edward 2Lt kia 9-5-17 1GrenGds SR p50 CR Belgium84

HOARE,Eric Sutherland 2Lt dow 11-11-16 53/2RFA p30 CR France105

HOARE,Evelyn Melville Shovell T2Lt kia 28-3-18 6EKent p57 MR27

HOARE,Frank William 2Lt kia 23-4-17 1Norf p74 MR20

HOARE,Frederick William Ernest Capt kia 10-8-17 HAC att11RFus p206 MR29 &CR France453

HOARE,George Henry 2Lt dow 1-6-17 RGA 93SB p40 CR Belgium11

HOARE,Gerard Croft 2Lt ded 1-8-18 6RB p179 CR Essex167

HOARE,Henry Colt Arthur Capt dow 20-12-17 DorsYeo p203 CR Egypt1,B Sqn

HOARE,Henry James Rev ded 5-8-17 RAChDept p268

HOARE,Henry Joseph 2Lt kia 15-8-15 10Lond p248 MR4

HOARE,Percival Hugh Trench Lt dow 8-1-15 3 att1ELancs p110 CR Belgium68,kia 2-1-15

HOARE,Percy James T2Lt kia 18-9-18 A117RFA p30 CR France528

HOARE,Reginald Arthur Capt kia 19-9-18 PembYeo att KSLI p205 CR France1701

HOARE,Richard Lennard Capt kia 1-7-16 12Lond p248 CR France798

HOARE,Robert Victor 2Lt ded 10-5-17 IA 22Cav p278 CR Iraq8

HOARE,Robert William Capt kia 9-10-17 7Worc C'Coy p225 CR Belgium126

HOARE,Vincent Robertson Maj kia 15-2-15 12Lond p248 CR Belgium58

HOARE,Walter John Gerald.DSO.TCapt kia 25-10-16 11RFus p68 CR France280

HOARE,Wilfred Gurney Capt kia 10-3-15 3DLI att2Wilts p161 MR22

HOARE,William George 2Lt kia 16-6-15 HAC p206 MR29

HOATHER,Harold Lt ded 4-5-19 WYorks p263 CR Sussex190

HOBART,Hobart Douglas Capt dow 21-4-16 IA 24Punjabis att53Sikhs p278 MR38,Lt 20-4-16

HOBART,Joseph Claud Antonie 2Lt ded 3-12-16 1/5RSuss p228 CR Lond9

HOBART-HAMPDEN,George Miles Awdry 2Lt kld 17-9-17 O&BLI &RFC p130&9 CR Bucks116,Lt

HOBBES,Narelli Sister ded 10-5-18 QAIMNS p200 MR38,Narrelle

HOBBS,A.S.Capt 16-10-18 IARO MR66

HOBBS,Alan Victor T2Lt kia 15-12-15 GL &RFC p17&190 CR France1144

HOBBS,Arnold William.MM.2Lt kia 9-4-17 3 att10YLI p143 CR France1186

HOBBS,Arthur Edward Singleton TCapt ded 16-10-18 IARO attArmyRemountDept p278

HOBBS,Arthur Harold Capt kia 2-10-15 1WelshR p127 MR19

HOBBS,Cecil William St.John 2Lt ded 31-5-16 RASC p267 CR Mddx29

HOBBS,Charles James Willoughby.DSO.Maj dow 16-10-16 2N&D p134 CR France105,LtCol

HOBBS,Eric 2Lt kia 1-7-16 2RWSurr p56 CR France397

HOBBS,Frank Matthew 2Lt kia 16-9-14 4RFus p68 MR15,14-9-14

HOBBS,Geoffrey Brian TLt kld 7-9-15 10NumbF att9RFC p61&1,Bryan CR Kent15,2Lt

HOBBS,Geoffrey Harold Chapman 2Lt kia 16-9-16 7Dors att6SomLI p124 MR21

HOBBS,Gerald Parker 2Lt dow 15-10-17 2Ess p131 CR Belgium16

HOBBS,H.E.2Lt kia 25-5-15 2NumbF p61 MR29

HOBBS,Henry Bede Lt kia 15-3-17 10Lpool p216 CR France513,Bedo

HOBBS,Herbert Victor T2Lt kia 7-4-17 17Manch p155 CR France214

HOBBS,John.MC.2Lt dow 28-6-15 1RScots p54 CR France285

HOBBS,Joseph Spencer Lt ded 8-6-18 1RFA p270 CR Herts87

HOBBS,Reginald George T2Lt kia 20-9-17 11KRRC p150 CR Belgium8

HOBBS,Victor William John Lt kia 9-8-18 4EKent p212 CR France209

HOBBS,William George TLt kia 25-9-15 8RBerks p139 MR19

HOBBY,Grenville Howard.MM.T2Lt kia 20-10-18 17 att14WelshR p127 CR France230

HOBDAY,Charles Frederick ACapt dow 1-12-17 3 att1Ess p131 CR France398

HOBDAY,Victor Maitland 2LtTCapt kia 7-6-17 11WYorks p81 CR Belgium127

HOBDAY,William Edward.DCM&Bar.T2Lt kia 11-4-17 13RB p179 CR France154

HOBDELL,Arthur Bert Falvey 2LtACapt dow 16-4-18 3 att6Wilts p153 CR Belgium18,Birt Falwey

HOBDEN,Charles Frank T2Lt ded 16-9-15 RGA p40 CR Europe23

HOBDEN,Ernest 2Lt kia 20-10-18 RGA 328SB p40 CR France319

HOBHOUSE,Paul Edward.MID Capt kia 21-3-18 6SomLI p80 MR27

HOBKINSON,Charles Wilfred T2Lt dow 23-8-15 6Y&L p159 MR4

HOBLYN,Walter Frederick 2Lt dow 1-10-15 att4CldGds p51 CR France88,Lt 2-10-15

HOBSON,Allen Faber.DSO.MIDx2 Maj kia 28-8-16 RE 2/1FC p209 CR France296,Alan

HOBSON,Alwyne Chadwick Lt kia 13-5-15 2LifeGds p20 MR29

HOBSON,Andrew John Hay Lt kia 9-10-17 8WYorks p219 MR30

HOBSON,Archibald Campbell LtCol ded 19-12-17 IA 99Inf att2/10Jats p278 MR66

HOBSON,Charles Cuthbert Lt ded 20-2-19 2Co ofLondYeo p204 CR Lond28

HOBSON,Edgar Charles T2Lt dow 20-5-17 PoW 15RWar p65 CR Germany1

HOBSON,Geoffrey Hamilton 2Lt dow 14-4-17 1Hamps p121 CR France40

HOBSON,John Alfred.MC.T2Lt kia 2-12-17 175MGC p183 CR France177 &CR France711

HOBSON,John Collinson TLt kia 31-7-17 1/6MGC p183 MR29

HOBSON,Leslie Faber 2Lt ded 12-7-15 4Y&L p238 CR Belgium1 dow

HOBSON,Nathaniel James Fennel Lt drd 10-10-18 5Lpool p215 MR20

HOBSON,Owen Ellis.MID TCapt kia 27-9-18 6 att4Beds p86 CR France1496

HOBSON,Robert Carl.MC&Bar.MID TCapt ded 10-11-18 GL NumbF 50Div p190 CR Devon2

HOCKADAY,Harold Francis Henry Legg 2Lt kia 10-10-17 4Dev 2Coy p220 MR30,Lugg

HOCKADAY,Sidney Reginald Capt dow 2-9-16 2Mon p244 CR Belgium11

HOCKEN,Stephen Lotan T2Lt kia 3-9-16 10KRRC p150 MR21

HOCKEY,Jessie Olive Sister 14-8-17 QAIMNS Res CR France64

HOCKIN,George Chamberlain Lt kia 24-11-15 IA 1/7 att2/7GurkhaRif p278 MR38,22-11-15

HOCKING,Edward Cuthbert 2Lt kld 28-10-18 RFA &151RAF p30 CR France646,Lt

HOCKING,Herbert Victor LtACapt kia 13-4-18 1DCLI p114 CR France18

HODDER,Charles William Rev ded 21-10-18 RAChDept p268 CR Surrey152

HODDING,Cuthbert Francis Capt ded 8-12-18 4Wilts CR Wilts129

HODDING,Frederick Capt ded 21-10-19 IARO att118LabCps p278 CR Pakistan50A MR43

HODDING,Henry Ellis.MC.TLt dow 8-11-18 10N&D p134 CR France332

HODDING,James Douglas T2Lt dow 10-7-16 10RFus A'Coy p68 CR France833

HODES,Francis Percy T2Lt dow 24-7-16 14RWar p65 CR France44,Lt

HODGART,Matthew.MC.Maj kia 9-10-17 RE 406FC p209 CR Belgium23

HODGE,Andrew Buckland Lt dow 31-7-17 3Leinst p174 MR29

HODGE,Arthur Egerton Lt kia 13-6-17 1NStaffs p157 CR Belgium127

HODGE,Frederick George 2Lt kia 31-10-17 2/21Lond p251 CR Palestine1

HODGE,George William 2Lt kia 27-4-18 2/4Lincs p217 MR30

HODGE,Jack Wheaton Lt kia 12-10-16 2WRid p115 CR France374

HODGE,Leslie Richard 2Lt kia 17-7-17 4Ess p232 MR20

HODGE,Lionel Bryant Capt dow 10-11-17 2/22Lond p251 CR Egypt2

HODGE,Lionel Clifford 2Lt kia 30-11-17 6RWKent p141 MR17

HODGE,William Bardo TLt ded 4-11-18 6 att11RScotF p94 CR France40

HODGES,Albert Rowland Cortis 2Lt kld 20-3-18 Mddx &RFC p16&147 CR Norf73

HODGES,Alfred John Carter 2Lt kia 23-8-18 20Lond p251 CR France119,Lt dow

HODGES,Archibald Gordon TLt kia 15-9-16 8Beds p86 MR21

HODGES,Arthur Thomas 2Lt ded 2-3-19 Ches p263 CR Glouc86

HODGES,Bernard T2Lt dow 16-4-18 KRRC att16Bn p150 MR32

HODGES,Charles Edward 2Lt kia 16-6-15 4RFus p68 CR Belgium116

HODGES,Daniel Alfred 2Lt kia 5-5-17 3 att10RWKent p141 CR Belgium152

HODGES,Edward Norman.MC.TCapt ded 22-6-18 RASC p193 CR France788

HODGES,Eric Colpoys 2Lt dow 15-7-16 2RIrReg p89 CR France833

HODGES,Harold Augustus.MID Capt kia 22-3-18 3Mon att11SLancs p244 CR France987,24-3-18

HODGES,Harold Henry T2Lt kia 13-7-16 7Leinst p174 CR France423,Henry Harold

HODGES,Harold Wardale 2Lt kia 9-5-15 6 att2KRRC p150 MR22

HODGES,Henry Burden 2Lt kia 18-4-15 2YLI p143 MR29

HODGES,James William T2Lt kia 21-3-18 ELancs att5Bn p111 MR27

HODGES,John Cyril Lt kld 17-9-16 RGA attRFC p3&40 CR War67

HODGES,John Percy 2Lt kia 25-4-18 6KOSB p101 CR Belgium21

HODGES,Sydney Howard 2Lt kia 17-10-14 4RFus p68 CR France567

HODGINS,Charles Francis Burgoyne 2Lt kia 25-9-15 2Wilts p153 CR France924

HODGKINS,James Percy 2Lt dow 26-9-17 2/4Leic p220 CR Belgium16

HODGKINSON,Alan.MID Lt kia 1-7-16 2RWar p65 CR France397

HODGKINSON,G.Lt dow 18-10-17 3/2KAR p202

HODGKINSON,Geoffrey Still Lt kia 24-7-17 A277RH&FA p30 CR Belgium7

HODGKINSON,George Cedric TLt dow 4-7-16 Yorks att8Y&L B'Coy p90 CR France833

HODGKINSON,Harry 2Lt kia 9-9-18 Manch att12Bn p155 CR France415

HODGKINSON,Hans Gerald 2Lt dow 18-10-17 5WRid att3/2KAR p255 CR EAfrica11 &CR Tanzania1,Lt

HODGKINSON,James Percival TCapt kia 2-11-16 15N&D p134 CR France1182

HODGKINSON,John T2Lt kia 17-4-18 18NumbF p61 MR32

HODGKINSON,John Francis Capt dow 10-11-14 3DragGds p21 CR France102

HODGKINSON,William Lt kia 9-10-18 6Lpool &RAF p270

HODGKISS,Frederick.MC.2Lt dow 8-10-18 3 att2/4LNLancs p136 CR France1184

HODGSON,Albert Hodgson T2Lt kia 22-1-17 GL &52RFC p9 CR France134

HODGSON,Alec Edmund Smart 2Lt kia 12-10-16 3Y&L p159 MR21

HODGSON,Arthur Dawson TLt kia 20-7-16 15N&D p134 MR21

HODGSON,Charles T2Lt dow 9-8-16 18 att15RScots p54 CR France74

HODGSON,Charles Basil Mortimer Capt dow 1-4-18 3RWSurr att2/24Lond p56 CR Egypt9

HODGSON,Charles Edward.DCM.T2Lt kia 2-10-18 KRRC att18Bn p150 CR Belgium112

HODGSON,Christopher Anthony Rowlandson Capt kia 18-12-14 3RWar p65 MR32

HODGSON,Christopher Michael Lt dow 17-6-17 B276RFA p207 CR Belgium10

HODGSON,Clarence Mortimer TCapt kia 18-9-16 14DLI C'Coy p161 CR France374

HODGSON,Cyril Arthur Godwin Capt ded 20-3-18 RNDevYeo p203 CR Egypt9

HODGSON,Cyril Francis 2Lt kia 11-1-17 IA 2/124BaluchistanInf p278 CR Iraq5

HODGSON,Evelyn Mary Sister ded 21-12-18 QAIMNS att28GenHosp p200 CR Greece9

HODGSON,Eric Godfrey 2Lt dow 22-5-15 IARO att40Pathans p278 CR France102

HODGSON,Francis Faith.MID Capt dow 17-5-15 IA 84Punjabis att58Rif p278 CR France924

HODGSON,Frederick James TLt ded 5-5-18 GL &1KAR p202 CR SAfrica144

HODGSON,George Bailey TCapt kia 13-4-17 GL &59RFC p9 MR20

HODGSON,George Graham Lt kia 9-5-15 2RBerks p139 MR32

HODGSON,George William Houghton Lt dow 6-11-14 2BordR p117 CR France102

HODGSON,Hamilton Capt kia 6-5-15 Lincs attHamps p75 MR4

HODGSON,Isaac Harvey TLt dow 20-4-16 1BordR p117 CR France67,2Bn

HODGSON,John T2Lt kia 27-10-18 12DLI p161 CR Italy9

HODGSON,John TLt ded 16-11-18 RE TransStores p45 CR France134

HODGSON,John Charles Capt kia 28-6-15 10BordR p117 MR4

HODGSON,John Edward.OBE.LtCol ded 5-11-18 RAMC att12ArmyCps attStaff p196 CR Greece19

HODGSON,John Henry.MM.TLt kia 30-4-18 4Mddx p147 CR France204

HODGSON,John Joseph T2Lt kia 13-8-17 RE 184TC p45

HODGSON,John Solomon Riddell Lt kia 25-3-17 2Dors p124 MR38

HODGSON,Maurice Kirkham Capt dow 12-3-15 1N&D p134 CR France768,kia 13-3-15

HODGSON,Michael Reginald Kirkman Capt kia 17-3-15 RFus attYLI p68 MR29

HODGSON,Oswald Arthur T2Lt kia 16-4-17 28 att9NumbF p61 MR20

HODGSON,Philip Ormiston 2Lt dow 13-3-15 2ELancs p111 CR France768,kia

HODGSON,Reginald T2Lt kia 27-6-16 7Leinst p174 CR France423

HODGSON,Reginald Drury TCapt kia 21-3-18 82RFA p30 MR27

HODGSON,Richard Everleigh Lt kia 16-9-18 4Lpool &204RAF p72 CR Belgium24,Eveleigh 15-9-18

HODGSON,Richard Victor T2Lt kia 20-6-17 22DLI att5DCLI p161 CR Belgium29

HODGSON,Rupert Ernest Lt kia 31-8-16 1NStaffs p157 CR France397

HODGSON,William Hope TLt kia 17-4-18 RFA 11ArmyBde p30 MR30

HODGSON,William Noel TLt kia 1-7-16 9Dev p76 CR France330

HODGSON-JONES,Douglas Sacre.MID TCapt ded 13-2-19 RE p262 CR Lancs34

HODKIN,Wilfred Capt kia 14-1-20 IA 1/109Inf p278

HODKINSON,Harold Hale T2Lt kia 8-8-16 10 att1/4RLancs p59 MR21

HODKINSON,Leonard T2Lt kia 14-9-17 15RWFus &53RFC p9&98 CR France285

HODKINSON,Peter 2Lt kia 23-10-18 7 att20DLI p239 MR16

HODSON,Bertie John TLt kia 21-3-18 5RIrReg att1RIrRif p89 MR27

HODSON,Edward Hutchinson TLt kia 24-3-18 15Ches p96 MR27

HODSON,George Benjamin.CB.DSO.BrigGen dow 29-1-16 IA Cmdg33Inf p278 CR Europe1,25-1-16

HODSON,Robert Charles T2Lt kia 8-5-17 RE 279RlyCo p45 CR France523

HODSON,Sydney 2Lt kia 21-3-18 5 att9KRRC p150 MR27

HODSON,Thomas George Smith Capt drd 10-4-17 RAMC p196 CR France85

HODY,Edmund Hody Maj ded 15-3-19 RASC VI Cps MT Coy p254 CR Germany1,15-6-19

HOEY,Fredk Cyril T2Lt kld 7-6-17 GL &RFC p9 CR Wilts28

HOFFA,James Michael Crosby Lt ded 28-7-17 1/3KAR p202 CR EAfrica38 &CR Tanzania1

HOFMEYER,Robert Ernest Murray 2Lt kia 24-4-17 5Yorks attMGC p221

HOFMEYR,Jan Hendrik T2Lt kia 27-10-17 N&D att1/8Bn p134 CR France115

HOFMEYR,Richard TLt ded 11-9-17 YLI &RFC p9&143 MR37

HOFMEYR,Robert Ernest Murray 2Lt kia 24-4-17 5Yorks att63MGC p187 MR20

HOG,Archibald Swinton Capt dow 20-8-17 5ConnRgrs p172 CR Europe1

HOGAN,Arthur Alan TLt kia 24-1-18 N&D att15Bn p134 CR Belgium83,2Lt

HOGAN,Edmund James Patrick Lt ded 11-2-20 IARO attS&TCps p278 MR67,13-2-20

HOGAN,Jack Graham 2Lt kia 28-3-18 1Hamps p121 MR20

HOGAN,Robert Garret Roche 2Lt kia 12-3-15 2RBerks p139 MR22

HOGAN,Robert James Lt ded 10-6-20 IARO attFollowersCentDept p278 MR69

HOGARTH,Archibald McDonald Lt dow 9-7-16 A104RFA p30 CR France188,Archie

HOGARTH,John Scott 2Lt kia 25-3-17 4KOSB p224 CR France68

HOGBEN,Frank T2Lt kia 12-10-16 7Norf p74 MR21

HOGBEN,Frederick 2Lt kia 23-10-16 3SStaffs att8Lincs p122 MR21

HOGBEN,Henry Francis Thomas Lt kia 22-11-15 10Mddx p236 MR38

HOGBEN,Leslie Thomas T2Lt kld 23-10-17 RFC p9 CR Kent177

HOGBEN,William Iggulden 2Lt kia 18-8-16 12WYorks p81 MR21

HOGBIN,Raymond T2Lt kia 20-9-17 32RFus p68 MR30

HOGG,Archibald TLt ded 14-10-18 RAMC p267 CR Scot685

HOGG,Clement Stuart T2Lt dow 6-4-17 RE Z SpCo p45 CR France95

HOGG,David Adams T2Lt kia 9-2-17 15HLI p163 CR France131

HOGG,Frank Alexander T2Lt dow 17-6-16 10 att1NStaffs p157 CR France285

HOGG,Hardinge Monteith Maj kia 22-4-17 IA 32Lancers p278 MR38

HOGG,Ian Graham.DSO.LtCol dow 2-9-14 4Huss p21 CR France1129

HOGG,Ivan Dayrell Meredith Capt kia 4-11-14 IA 101Grens p278 MR47

HOGG,J.S.Capt 12-8-17 RE 2FC CR Scot674

HOGG,James TCapt kia 24-9-16 14A&SH p173 CR France115

HOGG,James T2Lt kia 2-12-17 5RB p179 MR30

HOGG,Lewis Stephen Capt&Adjt kia 25-9-15 9RWFus p98 MR19

HOGG,Robert Morrison T2Lt dow 1-4-18 2DLI p161 CR Germany1

HOGG,Theodore Alan TCapt kia 21-3-18 2NStaffs p157 MR20

HOGG,Walter Gordon TLt kia 24-5-17 15RIrRif p169 CR Belgium100

HOGGE,Thomas Henry.MC.Lt kia 5-10-17 24RFA p30&258 CR France179

HOGGAN,Claude Ashley Rien Lt kia 30-5-18 46MGC p183 CR France109,Rieu

HOGGARD,Ernest John 2Lt kia 5-11-16 3RWSurr attMGC Inf p56&183 CR France385

HOGGARTH,Norman Scott T2Lt dow 30-5-18 PoW 6Leic p87 CR Germany3

HOGGETT,Frank Reginald T2Lt dow 18-7-16 10RWSurr p56 CR Lancs34

HOGHTON,Frederick Aubrey BrigGen ded 12-4-16 IA Cmdg17Inf p278 CR Iraq1

HOHLER,Arthur Preston LtCol ded 7-3-19 10Mddx p270 CR Bucks76

HOILE,George Vincent.MBE.Capt&QM 29-5-20 GL Ex RFA CR Surrey15

HOJEL,J.G.LtCol 21-3-19 IMS MR65

HOLAWAY,Charles Edmund 2Lt kia 11-8-17 ChesYeo attRFC p18&203 MR20

HOLBECH,David T2Lt kia 8-4-17 18KRRC p150 CR Belgium28

HOLBECH,William Hugh Lt dow 1-11-14 2ScotsGds RoO p52 CR War57

HOLBERTON,Philip Vaughan.MIDx5 ALtCol kia 26-3-18 6Manch p155 CR France518,2Bn

HOLBOROW,Frederick Bernard T2Lt kia 16-4-18 16KRRC p150 MR32

HOLBROW,Thomas Leonard Stanley.MC.Capt kia 28-3-18 RE 156FC p45 CR France899,Maj

HOLCROFT,Gilbert Culcheth 2Lt kia 9-8-15 2DLI p161 MR29

HOLCROFT,Raymond Boycott T2Lt kia 1-7-16 9Dev p76 CR France330

HOLDCROFT,Eric Crane T2Lt kia 4-10-17 RFus Res att13Bn p68 CR Belgium125

HOLDCROFT,Walter Leigh.MC&Bar.2Lt kia 5-8-18 1 att6NStaffs p157 MR19

HOLDCROFT,William Lawrence T2Lt kia 29-7-16 2SStaffs p122 MR21,28-7-16

HOLDEN,Cecil Alexander Nalorett 2Lt kia 28-5-19 22Punjabis p278 MR43,Lt 27-5-19 &CR Ireland24,Capt 22-11-18 2Leins

HOLDEN,Edward Charles Shuttleworth.DSO.LtCol 18-5-16 DerbyYeo CR Surrey160

HOLDEN,Ernest Airlie T2Lt dow 17-10-16 8LNLancs C'Coy p136 CR France59

HOLDEN,H Maj 3-3-20 IndOrdDept CR Burma129A

HOLDEN,Harold 2Lt kia 20-9-17 5LNLancs p234 CR Belgium96,1/4Bn

HOLDEN,Hyla Napier.DSO&Bar.LtCol kia 26-10-18 IA 5Cav attLancers p278 CR Lebanon1

HOLDEN,John 2Lt kia 28-9-18 4ELancs p226 CR Belgium50

HOLDEN,Joseph Rogers 2Lt kia 5-8-16 RE p210 CR France513,Roger

HOLDEN,Leigh 2Lt kia 9-6-15 4SLancs p230 MR29 &CR France453

HOLDEN,Leonard Neil TLt kia 9-7-16 11LancF p92 MR21

HOLDEN,Norman T2Lt dow 29-10-18 5SWBord p100 CR France380

HOLDEN,Norman Victor Lt&QM dow 4-6-15 6LancF p221 CR Gallipoli1

HOLDEN,Oswald Addenbrooke Chap4Cl kia 1-12-17 RAChDept att60InfBde p199 CR France379

HOLDEN,Vernon.DSO.MC.TMaj dow 2-10-18 10RWKent attWSurr p141 CR Belgium188

HOLDEN,William Leak 2Lt kia 4-1-17 19Manch p155 CR France927

HOLDER,Charles Vincent T2Lt kia 24-8-16 5KSLI p145 MR21

HOLDER,Tom S.TCapt ded 26-11-18 DCLI p114&257 CR Cornwall40

HOLDERNESS,William Harold 2Lt kia 17-4-16 6N&D p233 CR France68

HOLDICH,Godfrey William.VC.DSO.LtCol 13-4-21 RGA MR69

HOLDING,Alfred William TLt&QM ded 27-7-16 RAMC p196 CR Sussex144

HOLDING,James Capt&Adjt kia 1-8-18 1/4Ches p222 CR France524

HOLDROYD,Percy T2Lt kia 5-5-17 YLI att2/5Bn p143 MR20

HOLDSWORTH,Arthur Mervyn.MID LtCol dow 7-7-16 2RBerks p139 CR France40

HOLDSWORTH,Charles John T2Lt kia 8-5-17 Dev p76 CR France568

HOLDSWORTH,Ernest T2Lt kia 23-9-17 GL &29RFC p9 CR Belgium18

HOLDSWORTH,Godfrey Edward LtACapt kia 24-3-18 1 att4SStaffs p122 MR20

HOLDSWORTH,Henry Bernard Capt kia 10-4-18 8DLI p239 MR32

HOLDSWORTH,Joseph Arthur.MC.LtACapt ded PoW 17-6-18 5LancF p221 CR Germany4,2/8Bn

HOLDSWORTH,Vavasour Mervyn 2Lt kia 20-12-15 22Lond p251 CR

HOLE,Ernest George T2Lt ded 10-12-18 RASC p193 CR France1830

HOLE,Michael T2Lt kia 19-9-17 10KRRC p150 MR30

HOLE,William Arthur TLt kia 1-7-16 15RScots p54 MR21

HOLFORD,Leonard Brocklesby 2Lt dow 20-2-19 10Lpool p216 CR Ches181,1/16Bn

HOLGATE,Harold Arthur T2Lt kia 25-9-16 14 att1ESurr p112 MR21

HOLLAND,Albert Capt kia 21-9-18 6RSuss &RAF p158&228

HOLLAND,Archibald Clare 2Lt kia 27-7-16 1Beds p86 MR21

HOLLAND,Arthur Leslie 2Lt kia 21-4-17 6 att2RB p179 CR France407

HOLLAND,Basil Thomas 2Lt kia 10-3-15 2BlkW p128 MR22

HOLLAND,Charles.MC.Capt kld 25-1-18 8RFC p16 CR Sussex27

HOLLAND,Charles Stewart Maj kia 24-8-14 RFA p30 CR Belgium201,23-8-14

HOLLAND,Charles Trevenent T.Lt kia 9-5-15 33RFA p30 CR France348

HOLLAND,Clarence Jennings T2Lt kia 14-8-18 RLancs att1/4Bn p59 MR19

HOLLAND,Cyril Capt kia 9-5-15 RFA p30 CR France631

HOLLAND,Edward.MC.2Lt kia 13-9-16 1ScotsGds p52 MR21

HOLLAND,Edward Hugo T2Lt kia 23-4-17 4Worc p109 MR20

HOLLAND,Edward Matthew Lt kia 6-11-16 2Worc p109 MR21

HOLLAND,Ernest T2Lt kia 19-7-17 9SStaffs p122 CR Belgium29

HOLLAND,Frank Sidney Lt kia 27-11-17 2/6WRid p227 MR17

HOLLAND,Frederick 2Lt dow 22-8-17 3 att1N&D p134&257 CR France40

HOLLAND,George Percival T2Lt kia 18-3-18 RWar att7Norf p65 CR France255

HOLLAND,Gerald Edward.CB.CMG.CIE.DSO.MIDx2 TBrigGen ded 26-6-17 RE IWT Staff p1 CR Wales460

HOLLAND,Harold Richard 2Lt kia 12-4-18 Mddx att1/8Bn p147 MR20

HOLLAND,Jack Harold 2Lt ded 16-6-18 22RFus attRAF p68 CR France1233

HOLLAND,John Dixon Cuyler T2Lt kia 13-11-16 2 O&BLI p130 CR France152

HOLLAND,Ralph TLt&QM ded 21-8-16 RAMC p196 CR Eire322

HOLLAND,Ralph Bertram TCapt kia 2-10-16 7RWKent B'Coy p141 CR France383

HOLLAND,Ralph Lingard 2Lt kia 8-2-17 RGA 255SB p40 CR France285

HOLLAND,Reginald Capt kia 4-4-18 2/4 att8Berks p234 MR27

HOLLAND,Richard Edward T2Lt kia 24-10-18 1Mddx p147 CR France230

HOLLAND,Samuel Clifford.DSO.Maj ded 13-9-19 1KDragGds RoO p261

HOLLAND,Thomas Welsby Lt kia 18-9-18 4 att16RWFus p223 CR France415,2Lt

HOLLAND,Tyrrel Evelyn.MC.Capt ded 11-1-19 GL att12RB p254 CR Lond4

HOLLAND,Vivian Ernest Capt dow 8-11-18 7Huss p22 CR Iraq8

HOLLAND,Wallace Derry Ayre Capt ded 13-8-17 IA 11Lancers p278 MR43

HOLLAND,William Francis Claude TCapt ded 8-11-17 GL &4DLI p190&265 CR Essex261

HOLLAND,William Rawlinson Garside.MC.T2Lt dow 18-9-17 10WYorks att50TMB p81 CR France1190

HOLLAND-MARTIN,Geoffrey Robert 2Lt kia 26-3-18 16Lancers p23 MR27

HOLLANDS,Wilfrid George 2Lt kia 12-10-16 7 att4RFus p68 CR France156

HOLLES,Frederick Tetherley Noel 2Lt ded 11-9-16 3ELancs p111 CR Iraq5

HOLLICK,Percy Hood.MID 2LtACapt kia 8/9-5-17 3 att15RWar p65 MR20

HOLLIDAY,Alfred Rowland 2Lt kia 20-11-17 5Lond p246 CR France379

HOLLIDAY,Henry Lowther 2Lt kia 15-12-17 3 att9BordR p117 CR Greece5

HOLLINGBERY,Raymond Archibald Robert Lt kia 6-7-16 2 att3RWFus p98 CR France765

HOLLINGS,John Herbert Butler Lt kia 30-10-14 21Lancers p23 MR29

HOLLINGSHEAD,Amos Lt&QM ded 26-7-17 Yorks p90 CR Yorks176

HOLLINGSWORTH,F.Lt 26-4-15 1RhodR MG Sect CR SAfrica18

HOLLINGSWORTH,Frank Edwin 2Lt kia 15-9-16 A&SH &RFC p3 CR France1896 &CR France382

HOLLINGSWORTH,John Frederick T2Lt dow 2-10-16 14RSuss att7ESurr p119 CR France105

HOLLINGSWORTH,John Gordon Lt kia 12-8-15 10Mddx p236 MR4

HOLLINGWORTH,Leonard T2Lt kia 28-9-16 11 att1Dev p76 MR21

HOLLINGWORTH-BROWN,Robert Lt ded 27-12-19 RFA p261 MR65,28-12-19

HOLLINS,Edward Ralph Lambert TCapt dow 3-3-16 9RLancs p59 CR Belgium11,8Bn

HOLLINS,Herbert Francis TMaj ded 19-8-17 RGA 157HB p40 CR Iraq6

HOLLINS,James Piggott TLt&QM ded 3-2-16 13Lpool p72 CR Belgium15

HOLLINS,William Humphrey 2Lt kia 15-6-15 8N&D p233 CR Belgium17

HOLLINS-FISHER,Sydney Capt ded 28-9-18 9Mddx p236 MR65

HOLLINSHEAD,Shadrach 2Lt kia 27-3-18 3 att11ELancs p111 MR20

HOLLIS,Arthur Reginald TLt kia 12-9-18 10DCLI p114 CR France530

HOLLIS,Basil Lt kia 31-7-17 5BlkW p231 MR29

HOLLIS,Charles Frederick Griffith.MC.Lt kia 2-8-18 1EKent p57 CR Belgium40

HOLLIS,Frederick Alwin 2Lt ded 17-12-16 2/6BlkW p270 CR Norf209,16-12-16

HOLLIS,John Gordon.MID TLt kia 14-7-16 7Leic p87 MR21

HOLLIS,Percival Claude 2Lt kia 21-3-18 RGA 146SB p40 MR20

HOLLIS,Victor William.MC.2Lt kia 22-8-17 281RFA p30 CR Belgium19

HOLLIS,Walter Henry Lt kld 22-7-16 RDC p253 CR Sussex 189

HOLLIST,Anthony May Capron Capt kia 25/27-9-15 8EKent p57 MR19

HOLLMAN,George Leslie T2Lt dow 5-3-18 DLI p161

HOLLMAN,William Harold 2Lt kia 16-10-18 4RWKent p234 MR16

HOLLOM,Ernest Albert Bruce TLt kia 24-7-16 53RFA p30 CR France399

HOLLOMAN,Arthur TLt&QM kia 12-12-16 RAMC p196

HOLLOWAY,Arthur Grayston 2Lt kia 24-3-18 6 att16N&D p233 MR27

HOLLOWAY,Bernard Henry TCapt kia 27-9-15 9RSuss p119 MR19

HOLLOWAY,Claude Abrey Marseille Capt 19-12-19 RWKent &RAF CR Kent289

HOLLOWAY,Henry Francis.MC.2LtACapt kia 11-4-18 7ELancs att9WelshR p111&258 MR30

HOLLOWAY,James T2Lt kia 27-9-18 MGC Inf p183 CR France905

HOLLOWAY,James Clinton.MID LtCol ded 11-1-17 RDC Staff p1&253,Hollway CR Nhampt60 Ex Lincs&IA

HOLLOWAY,Leonard T2Lt kia 9-4-17 20NumbF p61 MR20

HOLLOWAY,Robert James.MID Lt&QM ded 14-8-16 5NumbF p213 CR Numb5,dow

HOLLOWAY,William Robert T2Lt kia 20-9-17 69MGC Inf p183 MR30

HOLLOWELL,Francis John 2Lt kia 7-7-16 3Worc p109 CR France1890

HOLLYWOOD,Arthur Carson TLt kia 1-7-16 9RIrF p171 MR21

HOLLYWOOD,James T2Lt kia 1-7-16 18 att12RIrRif p169 MR21

HOLM,Frank Diederick T2Lt/TLt kia 14-5-17 RE &27RFC p9&45 CR France62,2Lt

HOLMAN,Arthur Vincent Capt ded 9-1-17 Hereford p252 CR Glouc32

HOLMAN,Cecil Graham 2Lt dow 5-9-17 KOSB &8RFC p9&101 CR France214

HOLMAN,Donald TLt kia 8-8-18 11Mddx att7RWSurr p147 CR France247

HOLMAN,Geoffrey Lt kia 9-4-15 2KSLI p145 MR29

HOLMAN,Gerald Chaplin Lt kia 17-9-17 GL &41RFC p9 CR France1277

HOLMAN,Guy Henry Wallis Lt dow 6-7-16 1Wilts p153 CR France296

HOLMAN,John Lt dow 29-10-14 4DragGds p21 CR France102

HOLME,Alexander Charles Lt kia 6-9-14 Glouc att3NigR p106&268 CR WAfrica49

HOLME,Bertram Lester TLt dow 25-4-16 12RWFus p98 CR Iraq5

HOLME,George Weston 2Lt kia 22-12-16 RFA 50DAC p208 CR France388,23-12-16

HOLME,James Edward Capt kia 9-10-17 16RWar p65 MR30

HOLME,Ronald Henry Paull Lt dow 9-11-14 KOSB p102 CR Scot567

HOLMES,Akehurst Wilson 2Lt dow 28-7-17 RGA 295SB p40 CR France297

HOLMES,Albert Arundel Capt ded 19-5-15 2/5RSuss p228 CR Essex45

HOLMES,Albert Edward 2Lt kia 18-9-18 2Y&L p159 MR16

HOLMES,Alfred Raymond Cdr ded 26-6-16 IA MilWksServ p278 CR Iraq6

HOLMES,Andrew T2Lt dow 24-10-18 13DLI p161 CR France231

HOLMES,Archibald 2Lt kia 4-2-18 RFC p16 MR20

HOLMES,Aubrey T2Lt kia 1-7-16 2Ess p131 CR France1491

HOLMES,Basil Ralph Gardiner 2Lt kia 2-10-17 A38RFA p208 CR Belgium8

HOLMES,Bryan Hanby 2Lt ded 9-11-18 5RFA p30 CR Scot235

HOLMES,Cecil Crampton.MID LtTCapt dow 26-8-14 1Lincs p75 CR Belgium202,Crompton

HOLMES,Charles James Maj ded 5-4-16 RAMC p196 CR Lancs76,LtCol

HOLMES,Cuthbert Blace 2Lt dow 28-9-17 1/4LNLancs p234 CR Belgium18,Blacow kia

HOLMES,Cyril TLt ded 21-12-15 WelshR att8Bn p127 CR Greece11,Capt

HOLMES,Cyril Ernest Jackson 2Lt kia 24-6-17 3/5ELancs att2/5Lpool p226 CR France922

HOLMES,Duncan McPherson Studdert T2Lt kia 4-3-16 9Ches p96 MR19

HOLMES,Eric Cecil Lt dow 3-4-18 5DLI p238 CR France145

HOLMES,Ernest Cameron T2Lt kia 14-11-16 13KRRC p150 CR France701

HOLMES,Francis Lennox Lt kia 23-10-14 1SStaffs p122 MR29

HOLMES,Frederick 2Lt dow 10-5-15 RInniskF att4LNLancs p105 CR France80

HOLMES,George 2Lt kia 9-4-17 1EYorks p84 CR France162

HOLMES,George Francis Edwin T2Lt kia 25-10-16 15N&D p134 CR France1182

HOLMES,Henry Ball Maj dow 27-11-15 RIrF p171 CR Eire286

HOLMES,Hubert Lee Maj ded 22-4-18 IA 122Inf p278 CR Surrey11

HOLMES,James Fyfe.MC.2Lt mbk 23-3-18 9ScotRif p256 MR27

HOLMES,John Alexander 2Lt dow 26-4-16 4Leinst p174 CR France285

HOLMES,Leslie Stuart 2Lt ded 14-12-18 3SomLI p80 CR Lond12

HOLMES,Oswald Matthews T2Lt dow 25-8-17 6YLI p143 CR Belgium11

HOLMES,O.W.2Lt kia 16-8-17 7RInniskF p105 MR30

HOLMES,Reginald Eden LtACapt kia 4-6-18 1ScotsGds p52 CR France1014

HOLMES,Robert T2Lt ded 16-2-18 6RLancs p59 MR66

HOLMES,Robert Bryan 2Lt dow 1-7-16 5 att2KRRC p150 CR France178,Brian

HOLMES,Robert Reginald John Capt ded 26-3-16 RAMC 81FA p253 CR Europe1

HOLMES,Thomas George Lt kia 6-5-17 100RFC SR p9 CR France1277

HOLMES,Thomas Gerald 2Lt kia 27-3-18 A16RFA p30 CR France588

HOLMES,Thomas Symonds 2Lt kia 12-11-14 RWSurr attEKent p56 CR
France276,11-11-14

HOLMES,Vernon Raines.MC.Lt kia 14-10-16 6Ches p222 CR France293

HOLMES,Wilfred Bertram 2Lt kia 20-8-17 4Ches p222 MR30,Wilfrid 20-9-17

HOLMES,William.CMG.DSO.VD.MajGen ded 2-7-17 SL Staff AustDivHQ Ex AIF p1

HOLMES,William Henry T2Lt kia 15-12-17 7SfthH p165 CR France415

HOLMES,William James Maj 5-2-21 RAOC attIACC CR Germany1

HOLMS,Andrew Stuart TLt kia 1-7-16 RE 177TC p45 CR Belgium4,Lt

HOLMS,John Cyril Capt dow 10-9-15 9Lond p247 CR France513

HOLMS,William T2Lt kia 16-9-16 10/11HLI p163 CR France239

HOLNESS,Frederick Reginald T2Lt ded 2-2-19 6Lincs p263 CR Essex7,4Bn

HOLOHAN,P.Capt dow 19-8-15 1RMunstF CR Egypt6

HOLROYD,Benjamin 2Lt kia 13-11-16 1/5SfthH p241 CR France131

HOLROYD,Clifford 2Lt kia 3-5-17 2/6WRid p227 MR20

HOLROYD,Lister TCapt dow 12-9-16 7EYorks p84 CR France121

HOLROYD-SMYTH,Charles Edward Ridley.DSO.MC.CaptTLtCol dow 23-9-18
3DragGds att15DLI p21 CR Somerset37

HOLROYDE,John Sheffield 2Lt kia 10-5-17 EYorks &55RFC p9&84 CR France288

HOLT,Arthur Edward 2Lt dow 25-10-17 RGA 233SB p40 CR Belgium72

HOLT,Denis Ralph William Capt ded 31-12-19 IA 3/34SikhPnrs p278 MR43,31-1-
20

HOLT,Follett Hallett Lt kia 22-8-18 3 O&BLI attTankCps p130&188 CR
France370

HOLT,Fredk George Bradley 2Lt kia 5-4-18 24Lond p252 MR20

HOLT,Geoffrey Vesey 2Lt kia 2-9-17 91RFA p30 CR Belgium23

HOLT,Herbert Wilfred 2Lt kia 23-8-14 RE p45 CR Belgium242

HOLT,Hubert Granville,MC TLt kia 6-10-17 GL &9RFC p9 CR Belgium18

HOLT,John Leonard 2Lt kia 16-3-18 88RFC p16 CR France1266

HOLT,John William Capt kia 27-8-17 4WRid p227 CR Belgium126,8Bn Ex 4Bn

HOLT,Joseph Capt kia 4-6-15 6Manch p236 MR4

HOLT,Laurence Guy.MC.TCapt kia 27-9-16 1LNLancs p136 CR France385,3Bn

HOLT,Leslie Capt kia 11-3-18 2/10Lond p248 CR France1893

HOLT,Percy James T2Lt dow 6-9-18 6Beds att1/1Herts p86 CR France145

HOLT,Wilfred T2Lt kia 16-8-17 12Manch p155 CR Belgium96

HOLT,Wilfrid 2Lt kia 3-5-17 18WYorks p81 MR20

HOLT,William Frederick Sloane T2Lt ded 1-7-18 19Manch p155 CR Lancs474

HOLT,William Leslie T2Lt kia 23-12-17 10Y&L p159 CR Belgium131,22-12-17

HOLT,William Parkinson Capt kia 24-6-17 RASC attRFC p18&253 CR France1310

HOLTOM,Charles Cecil TLt kia 31-10-17 181MGC p183 CR Palestine1

HOLTOM,Charles Fifield 2Lt dow 4-8-16 1/5NStaffs p238 CR France120

HOLTOM,John Nicholson 2Lt ded 22-10-16 RFC p3 MR20

HOLTON,Francis Keatley Lt kld 27-10-17 1Mddx att98TMB p147 CR
Belgium48,2Lt

HOLTON,George James Paul 2Lt dow 16-9-18 1Co ofLondYeo p204 CR
France1184

HOLTON,John Arthur 2Lt kia 4-10-17 103RFA p30 CR Belgium21 Ex EssYeo

HOLWILL,William Bertram 2Lt dow PoW 16-5-18 66MGC Inf p183 CR France928

HOLYMAN,Leslie Edward 2Lt kia 9-3-17 1/5EKent p213 MR38

HOLYOAKE,Ralph LtCol ded 18-5-19 RAMC p267 CR Mddx48

HOMAN,Arthur Douglas CaptAMaj dow 9-5-17 RIrReg att70HLI p89 CR Greece1

HOMAN,Claude Knox TLt kia 18-9-15 6Dors p124 CR Belgium111

HOMAN,H.B.2Lt kld 4-4-18 GL &RAF p100

HOMAN,Henry Leslie Capt kia 10-3-15 2Mddx p147 CR France706

HOMAN,Ralph William LtTCapt dow 11-8-15 1EKent p57 CR Belgium11

HOMAN,Russell Charles TLt kia 22-3-18 15N&D p134 MR27

HOME,Robert TCapt kia 23-4-17 RAMC p196 17FA CR France80,22-4-17

HOME,Walter Gabriel.MID Maj dow 13-11-14 6DragGds p21 MR29,31-10-14

HOMER,Charles William T2Lt kld 27-10-17 GL &RFC p9 CR Suff173

HOMER,William Howard Claude.MC.Lt kia 26-4-18 6Glouc p225 MR30

HOMERSHAM,Arthur Jones Lt kia 18-2-18 25Lond attRFC p18&252 CR
France765,Alfred

HOMERSHAM,Ronald 2Lt kia 30-4-18 4EYorks att4RAF p219 CR France134

HOMFRAY,John Richards Lt kia 11-11-14 1SWBord p100 MR29 CR
France453,1Worc

HOMFRAY,Richard Pophin Capt ded 3-3-18 7Worc p225

HONAN,Matthew TCapt kia 14-11-16 10SLancs p125 CR France384

HONE,Gilbert Bentoit 2Lt kia 18-8-17 121RFA p30 CR Belgium23,17-8-17

HONE,Nathaniel Frederick Lt kia 1-7-16 3 att9RIrRif p254 CR France446

HONER,Douglas James Lt ded 4-6-17 RFA attRFC p18&207 MR20

HONESS,Albert Edward T2Lt kia 9-4-18 Mddx att21Bn p147 MR32

HONEY,Alexis Cowper 2Lt dow 10-2-18 5 att4Worc p109 CR France40

HONEY,Geoffrey Henry Le Sueur T2Lt kia 21-10-16 5 att17KRRC p150 MR21

HONEY,George Ronald.MC.TLt dow 25-9-18 9 att8RLancs p59 CR Greece5

HONEYBALL,Wilfred Chennell 2Lt kia 21-3-18 14MGC p183 MR27

HONEYMAN,Herbert Tom Allan 2Lt kia 10-12-17 RScotF &15RFC p9&94 MR20

HONEYMAN,Norman Stark 2Lt kia 22-10-17 8RScots p212 MR30

HONEYWILL,Stanley Ross 2Lt kia 8-10-18 4RFus p68 CR France912

HONYCHURCH,Terence William 2Lt dow 22-9-16 1/7Mddx att167TMB p235 CR
France105

HOOD,Andrew Smith Lt ded 24-7-18 RE p210 CR Scot395

HOOD,Charles Ivo Sinclair Chap4Cl dow 15-4-18 RAChDept att41RGA p199 CR
Belgium11

HOOD,Douglas Edward 2Lt kia 14-4-17 1Beds p86 CR France549

HOOD,Edward Thesiger Franklin.DSO.LtCol dow 15-5-18 LincsYeo Cmdg38RFA
p204 CR France180,Frankland

HOOD,Ernest William 2Lt kia 25/27-9-15 5Yorks p221 MR19

HOOD,Gilbert Brackenbridge 2Lt kia 19-2-18 2/19Lond p250 CR Palestine3

HOOD,James Minto Lt 23-2-20 GL RE attIWT CR Europe5

HOOD,John Lt kia 18-8-17 8A&SH att57RFC p18&243 CR Belgium140

HOOD,John William.MID Lt ded 15-11-18 RGA 39SB p40 CR France1142

HOOD,Oswald T2Lt kia 1-9-16 10 att11RSuss p119 CR France1013

HOOD,Percy Charles 2Lt dow 20-9-18 3 att1/5Norf p74 CR Palestine9

HOOD,Richard Edward.MIDx2 Lt ded 7-8-19 1/2RFA p270 CR Lancs149,Maj

HOOD,Ronald Paton 2Lt kia 28-9-17 GL &43RFC p9 MR20

HOOD,Thomas 2Lt kia 12-10-16 3 att7Suff p78 MR21

HOOD DANIEL,Arnold Frost Capt 28-1-17 2/5EKent C'Coy CR Ches62

HOOD-ROWAN,Maxwell 2Lt kia 12-8-16 1/9Lpool p216 MR21

HOOK,Cyril Walter Keenan TLtACapt kia 23-4-17 16Manch p155&257 CR
France162

HOOK,Duncan TLt kia 7-8-15 9LancF p92 CR Gallipoli27

HOOK,F.M.L.AssNurse 10-11-18 QAIMNS CR Dorset111

HOOK,Gerald Francis 2Lt kia 13-4-18 8BordR p117 MR32

HOOK,Robin T2Lt kia 9-8-15 9LancF p92 CR Gallipoli27,7-8-15

HOOK,Valentine.MID TCapt kia 3-5-17 7RWSurr p56 CR France538

HOOKE,Alfred Douglas 2Lt kia 28-4-17 4Mddx p147 MR20

HOOKE,Utten Lamont LtCol dow 21-6-17 3/4RWSurr p212 CR France545

HOOLE,Geoffrey 2Lt kia 15-9-16 1/15Lond C'Coy p249 CR France432,Geoffry

HOOLE,Ronald Herbert T2Lt kia 21-8-16 8RWSurr p56 MR21

HOOLEY,Arthur Wellesley.MC.MID Lt ded 9-2-19 RASC att11RWSurrp193 CR
Belgium267

HOOLEY,Basil Terah.MC.Maj ded 28-10-18 7N&D p233 CR Derby146

HOOLEY,Tom Williamson T2Lt dow 3-9-17 45LabCps p189 CR France139

HOOPER,Alfred Henry Capt kia 10-3-15 2Mddx p147 CR France706

HOOPER,Arthur James 2Lt kia 26-8-17 8Lond att7KRRC p247 MR30

HOOPER,Bernard Keith 2Lt kia 26-9-17 12Lond p248 MR30

HOOPER,Charles Frederick Aubrey Albert Anderson.MID TCapt ded 11-11-18
Wilts p254 CR Durham124,Frederic

HOOPER,Charles Winsmore.MID Capt kia 25-9-15 2HLI p163 MR19

HOOPER,Colin Holt Lt dow 28-9-15 20Lond p251 CR France1

HOOPER,David Ernest 2Lt kia 30-4-15 3 att2ELancs p111 CR France566

HOOPER,Ernest Jesse Joseph TLt dow 24-11-17 12SWBord p100 MR17

HOOPER,Eustace Woodrow Noel T2Lt kia 7-1-18 15DLI p161 CR France369

HOOPER,Henry H.Hoskin T2Lt kia 28-8-18 Lincs p75 CR France385

HOOPER,John Hamilton Morris 2Lt kia 30-11-17 1/16Lond p250 CR
France1496,Morriss

HOOPER,Leonard John T2Lt kia 26-9-16 5Dors p124 CR France832

HOOPER,Ronald Morley Lt kia 21-3-18 RGA 3FldSurCo p40 CR France245

HOOPER,Sidney Frederick Lt kia 12-3-15 3Wilts attDCLI p153 CR Belgium17

HOOPER,Stuart Huntly HonLtCol ded 31-5-15 RHA DAAG p30 CR Hamps19

HOOPER,William T2Lt kia 3-10-18 1 att1/5SStaffs p122 CR France341

HOOPS,Guy Staveley T2Lt ded 27-2-17 RFA p30 CR Hamps15

HOOPS,Harry Albert Mostyn 2Lt kia 16-8-17 4RIrF attRIrRif p171 MR30

HOOTON,Edward Cedric Lt kia 26-6-16 2/8RWar p215 MR19,27-6-16

HOOTON,Henry Hurst TLt dow 5-5-16 14RIrRif p169 CR France40,5-8-16

HOOTON,Nelson Mackrow 2Lt kia 16-8-17 17Lond p250 MR29

HOPE,Charles Edward T2Lt kia 22-3-18 17Manch p155 MR27

HOPE,Charles Bateman 2Lt kia 26-2-16 1/1DorsYeo p203 CR Egypt6

HOPE,George Everard.MC.LtCol kia 10-10-17 GrenGds att1/8LancF p50 CR Belgium173

HOPE,Herbert Alfred T2Lt dow 28-7-17 25RFC p9 CR France88

HOPE,Humphrey Brian Thompson Lt kia 26-4-17 4Nhampt attRFC p18&234 MR20 Thomasson

HOPE,James Horatio Maj kia 18-4-16 HLI p163 CR Iraq5

HOPE,John Angus 2Lt kia 22-10-17 16RScots p54 MR30

HOPE,Percy Beckett TLt ded 25-12-17 RASC p193 CR France40

HOPE,Reginald Addison TLt kia 31-7-17 1NStaffs p157 CR Belgium20

HOPE,William Edward Lt kia 6-11-14 1IrGds SR p52 MR29

HOPE,William Henry Webley.CMG.LtCol ded 13-5-19 RGA p40 CR Mddx6,kldacc

HOPE-EVANS,Timothy Idwal TCapt kia 23-11-17 19RWFus p98 MR17

HOPE-JOHNSTONE,Henry Murray.MC.CaptAMaj dow 31-7-17 att12RFus p68 CR Belgium15

HOPE-JOHNSTONE,William Gordon Tollemache Lt kia 25-10-14 RFus p68 MR22

HOPE-LUMLEY,Reginald Lewis TLt kia 11-10-17 2RBerks att37TrainingRes p139 CR France297

HOPE-WALLACE,James Lt kia 15-9-17 4NumbF p213 CR France594

HOPES-HEELIS,E.Capt 29-3-20 EAfrMilLabCps CR EAfrica47

HOPEWELL,Charles 2Lt kia 24-3-18 YLI att64TMB p143 MR27

HOPEWELL,James Handley Lt kia 14-7-16 6Leic p87 MR21

HOPEWELL,Robert George TCapt kia 3-9-16 17N&D p134 MR21

HOPGOOD,John Lambert T2Lt dow 17-8-16 8RWSurr p56 CR France66

HOPKIN,Robert Thomas T2Lt kia 20-9-17 16RB p179 MR30

HOPKINS,Arthur Emlyn.MC.LtACapt kia 21-3-18 2/5ELancs p226 MR27

HOPKINS,Arthur Maskern TLt dow 18-11-16 7SLancs p125 CR France215

HOPKINS,Arthur Martyn T2Lt kia 28-3-18 11KRRC p150 MR27

HOPKINS,Charles Randolph Limes Lt kia 18-12-14 2ScotRif p256 CR France706,Innes

HOPKINS,Daniel Idwal 2Lt kia 23-4-17 2SWBord p100 MR20

HOPKINS,Edward Favill George 2Lt kia 30-3-17 181RFA p30 CR France448

HOPKINS,Eric Arthur 2Lt kia 5-5-15 3 att1Beds p86

HOPKINS,Francis Gethin TLt ded 2-2-16 RAMC p196 CR Devon2

HOPKINS,Frederick Lt ded 17-6-19 GL attIA p254&266 MR65

HOPKINS,George Henry Stanton T2Lt kia 31-7-17 45MGC p183 MR29

HOPKINS,Gerald Broughton TLt kia 17-9-18 7/8KOSB p102 MR19

HOPKINS,Henry Greenfield Berkeley TLt dow 29-7-17 MGC HB p183 CR Belgium18

HOPKINS,Herbert Leslie.MID Lt kia 19-9-14 RAMC p196 CR France1107

HOPKINS,Lawrence Hilton Capt kia 7-10-18 HuntsCycBn p253 CR France547

HOPKINS,Lewis T2Lt kia 26-9-15 8SomLI p80 MR19

HOPKINS,R.W.Chap4Cl 24-4-18 RAChDept CR Belgium11

HOPKINS,Trevor 2Lt ded 13-9-19 WelshR p264 CR Wales76

HOPKINS,William Jones T2Lt dow 8-10-16 11EYorks p84 CR France495

HOPKINSON,Charles Reginald Thompson Capt kia 6-9-14 ESurr att3NigR p112 CR WAfrica48

HOPKINSON,Edward.MC.Lt mbk 23-4-17 8N&D p257 MR20

HOPKINSON,Eric Humphrey.MC.MID Lt ded 2-6-15 1Camb p244 MR32

HOPKINSON,George Silkston 2Lt kia 18-1-18 5N&D p232 CR Belgium20,Silkstone

HOPKINSON,Hugh James Pearson TLt dow 6-11-15 RE 67FC p45 CR Gallipoli27

HOPKINSON,James Garland Capt kia 25-9-15 4GordH p241 MR29

HOPKINSON,Rudolph Cecil.MIDx2 Lt dow 9-2-17 RE 12DivCycCo p45 CR Camb3

HOPLEY,Geoffrey William Vanderbyl 2Lt dow 18-5-15 GrenGds SR p50 CR Mddx19,12-5-15

HOPLEY,Thomas Henry 2Lt kia 10-10-18 RGA 132HB p40 CR France1392,Lt 11-10-18

HOPPER,James Arthur.MC.T2Lt kia 10-4-17 26NumbF p61 CR France644

HOPPER,Raymond T2Lt kia 11-1-17 GL &60RFC p9 CR France95

HOPPER,Robert Edward 2Lt kia 28-4-17 5WYorks p218 MR19

HOPPER,William Joseph Lt kia 6-9-18 6DLI attMGC p239&187,15DLI CR Belgium89

HOPPS,William Leonard T2Lt dow 22-5-16 25NumbF p61 CR France67

HOPSON,Albert Edward Lt kia 11-4-18 7DLI p239 MR32

HOPTON,Edward Michael Lt ded 17-3-16 1/1ShropYeo p205 CR Egypt6

HOPTON,Guy William Capt kia 27-7-15 RBerks att5Bn p139 CR Belgium71

HOPWOOD,Alan Clement T2Lt dow 18-9-18 RE 152FC p45 CR France755

HOPWOOD,Edwin John TLt kia 9-4-16 10 att6ELancs p111 CR Iraq5

HOPWOOD,Frederick Ernest TLt ded 26-10-18 RE ROD p45 CR France770

HOPWOOD,Frederick William.MM.2Lt kia 27-8-18 RBerks att8Bn p139&259 CR France399

HOPWOOD,Marcus 2Lt kia 3-9-16 10 att13RSuss p119 MR21

HOPWOOD,Norman T2Lt kia 23-10-18 19MGC Inf p183 CR France270,15Bn

HOPWOOD,Robert Gerald Capt kia 24-8-16 RB &70RFC p3&179 MR20

HOPWOOD,Robert Hervey TLt kia 5-2-16 16Mddx p147 CR France114,4-2-16

HORAN,Charles Robert.MC.TLt kia 10-11-17 8 att2RMunstF p175 MR30

HORBRUGH,Robert Patrick LtCol ded 5-9-14 IA Bera&CentProvComm Ex MadrasLancers

HORBURY,George Squire T2Lt kia 21-5-16 4Lpool p72 CR France163

HORE,Cecil William 2Lt kia 26-4-17 A47RH&FA p30 CR Belgium15,26-8-17

HORE,Charles Owen.CMG.Col ded 14-2-16 SL p201

HORE,Kennett Scarborough Lt kia 25-9-15 1/19Lond p250 CR France219

HORE,Percy Standish Capt kia 12-3-15 IA 52Sikhs att59Rif p278 CR France727

HORE,Ruthven Pomfret 2Lt dow 2-10-15 3Dors att1WelchR p124 CR France80

HORE,William Barras Capt kia 7-8-15 IA 120Inf att9WYorks p263&278 MR4

HORGAN,Matthew SubCdr 13-7-18 IOD MR66

HORKINS,Richard Earl TCapt kia 27-9-16 RAMC attRFA 77HB p196 CR France630

HORLER,Edwin T2Lt kia 31-7-17 122MGC Inf p183 CR Belgium124

HORLEY,Engelbert Lutyens Rothwell T2Lt kia 4-9-17 Manch att16Bn p155 CR Belgium24

HORLICK,Gerald Nolekin.MID Maj ded 5-7-18 GloucYeo attMGC p187&203 CR Egypt1

HORN,Arthur Henry Harvey 2Lt kia 2-9-18.24Lond p252 MR16

HORN,Edmund Eric T2Lt kia 4-3-17 2Mddx &8RFC p9&147 CR France120

HORN,Francis Cuthbert Lt dow 28-5-18 4 att2Manch p155 CR France622

HORN,John Bernard T2Lt kia 26-10-17 LNLancs att2/4Bn p136 MR30

HORN,John Cyril T2Lt kia 29-4-17 13EYorks p84 CR France777

HORN,John Hetherington T2Lt kia 13-10-18 1LNLancs att4Y&L p136 CR France316,6Bn

HORN,Robert.DSO&Bar.MC.TLtCol kia 18-4-18 7SfthH p165 CR Belgium11

HORNABROOK,Leonard Charles 2Lt dow 21-5-18 3 att1/4Leic p87 CR France40

HORNBEAK,George Henry 2Lt kia 2-10-17 22RFA p30 CR Belgium112

HORNBY,Cecil Geoffrey.OBE.MC.MajTLtCol ded 30-12-18 ELancs attWAFF p111&201 CR WAfrica4

HORNBY,Cyril Blurton S.2Lt kia 15-4-15 KSLI p145 CR Nhampt79

HORNBY,Geoffrey Phipps 2Lt kia 10-5-15 3Suff p78 MR29,8-5-15

HORNBY,Gerald Barford T2Lt kia 12-7-16 10Yorks p90 CR France397

HORNBY,Hugh Langton HonCapt dow 5-6-18 RInniskF Ex 8Bn p105 CR Sussex112

HORNBY,Joseph Henry.MID Lt kia 7-11-18 RE 94FC p45 CR France521

HORNBY,Richard Arthur Capt kia 9-4-18 Mddx att21Bn p147 MR32

HORNBY,William T2Lt kia 12-10-16 17Lpool 1Coy p72 CR France385

HORNBY,William Raymond 2Lt kia 4-6-15 4ELancs p226 MR4

HORNCASTLE,Cyril Charles Schubert Lt ded 8-1-19 RH&FA p30&257 CR Egypt9 10Div Staff

HORNCASTLE,Edward Henry Lt kia 27-5-18 10Manch p237 MR18

HORNCASTLE,Leonard Harry.MC.Capt kia 20-5-17 1Wilts &11RFC p9&153

HORNE,Alexander Capt kia 14-9-14 1CamH p168 MR15

HORNE,Charles Walter Capt ded 27-12-19 IARO att38CentIndHorse p278 CR Devon258

HORNE,Cyril Henry Morton TCapt kia 27-1-16 7KOSB p102 CR France222

HORNE,David Douglas TCapt kia 1-7-16 29 att21NumbF p61 MR21

HORNE,Herbet George McMillan 2Lt kia 13-4-17 19Lond attRFC p18&250 MR20

HORNE,James Anthony 2Lt kia 1-7-16 16Lond p250 CR France798

HORNE,John Austen T2Lt ded 2-11-18 6RRofCav p23 CR Kent298,6DragGds

HORNE,Leonard John Lt kia 15-6-18 2/4YLI p235 CR France745

HORNE,Robert Stevenson 13051 Lt ded 29-7-18 7A&SH &5/4KAR p243&268 CR EAfrica12 &CR Tanzania1,9Bn

HORNE,Thomas Wardlaw 2Lt kia 22-8-17 3 att8SfthH p165 MR30

HORNER,Bernard Lt ded 5-3-17 8LancF p221 CR France164

HORNER,Edward William Lt dow 21-11-17 18Huss p23 CR France398,kia

HORNER,Frederick Julian.MC.TLtACapt dow 15-4-18 RWar att2Ches p65 CR Greece3

HORNER,Karl Christian 2Lt dow 4-4-17 8WYorks attRFC p18&219 CR France46,7Bn

HORNER,Walter Aitken 2Lt ded 24-3-15 15Lpool p72 CR Lancs11

HORNER,William Arthur TLt dow 13-12-17 10KRRC p150 CR France40

HORNER,William Jackson 2Lt dow 15-7-17 RGA attV39TMB p40 CR Belgium11,RFA

HORNSBY,George Westome 2Lt kia 4-6-15 IARO att14Sikhs p278 MR4

HORNSBY,Harold Gibson T2Lt kia 1-7-16 7Yorks p90 CR France372

HORNSBY,John Philip Skipworth TCapt kia 2-9-18 10SWBord A'Coy p100 CR France216

HORNSBY,Ridiard Lionel T2Lt kia 7/11-10-15 Lincs p75 MR4,7-10-15

HORNSBY,William T2Lt kia 21-8-17 6SomLI p80 MR30

HORNSEY,John Frederick Lt kia 24-3-18 RAMC att6KSLI p196 MR27

HORNUNG,Arthur Oscar 2Lt kia 6-7-15 3 att2Ess p131 MR29

HORNUNG,John Peter.MC.T2Lt dow 20-2-16 95RFA p30 CR France922

HORRABIN,Maurice Pinney 2Lt mbk 30-11-17 4 att6EKent p257 MR27

HORRELL,? 9-1-20 VAD CR Egypt10

HORRIDGE,Robert Lt kia 17-11-14 3 att2Manch p155 CR Belgium98,4 att2Bn

HORROCKS,John HonLt&QM ded 23-10-15 1EYorks p84 CR Belgium5

HORROX,Henry M.T2Lt kia 1-7-16 24NumbF p61 MR21

HORSBRUGH,Boyd Robert TLtCol ded 11-7-16 RASC p193 CR Surrey32

HORSER,Stanley Cottrell Seymour TCapt kia 12-10-16 17Lpool p72 MR21

HORSEY,Cyril James T2Lt dow 22-11-16 7SLancs p125 CR France145

HORSEY,Thomas Frederick Charles SudCdr 7-3-16 IA MiscList CR India48

HORSFALL,Alfred Garnett.DSO.MajALtCol kia 9-10-17 2WRid p115 CR Belgium23

HORSFALL,Arthur Mendelssohn 2Lt kia 9-5-15 2RMunstF p175 MR22

HORSFALL,Basil Arthur.VC.2Lt kia 27-3-18 1 att11ELancs p111 MR20

HORSFALL,Cuthbert T2Lt dow 17-2-18 Worc att2/8Bn p109 CR France1204

HORSFALL,Cedric Fawcett Capt kia 18-9-16 6WRid p227 CR France246

HORSFALL,George Rowland T2Lt kia 20-11-17 14Y&L att48RFC p9 CR France1361

HORSFALL,Henry Francis Coghlan TCapt dow 22-4-16 6LNLancs p136 CR Iraq6,kia

HORSFALL,John Brown T2Lt kia 25-7-17 124MGC p183 MR29

HORSFALL,John Joseph TCapt dow 19-1-17 8WRid p115 CR France41

HORSFALL,Robert Elcum TCapt kia 20-11-17 12Lpool p72 MR17

HORSFALL,Vernon Adams 2Lt kia 3-9-16 4WRid p227 CR France1890

HORSFIELD,John Francis Lt kia 26-7-17 6Manch p236 CR Belgium24

HORSFORD,Harry Curwin Capt dow 8-4-17 5RBerks p139 CR France1182

HORSFORD,Thomas Gavin Moor Lt kia 16-6-15 2Beds p86 MR22

HORSFORD,Thomas Herbert O'Bryen Lt dow 14-3-15 2WYorks p81&257 CR France768

HORSLEY,Claude Cressy Lt dow 29-11-17 4NStaffs p157 CR France64,28-11-17

HORSLEY,Ernest T2Lt kia 14-8-17 10KRRC att59TMB p150 CR Belgium23

HORSLEY,John TCapt kia 16-5-15 3 att2BordR p117 CR France279

HORSLEY,Oswald.MC.Capt kld 19-8-18 GordH &RAF p166 CR Hamps179

HORSLEY,Ralph Neville 2Lt kia 27-8-17 7Worc p226 MR30

HORSLEY,Sir Victor Alexander Haden.Bart.CB.Col ded 16-7-16 RAMC p196 CR Iraq5

HORSLEY,Wilfred Palmer.MC.TCapt kia 2-7-17 GL &53RFC p9 CR France285

HORSNELL,Alick George T2Lt kia 1-7-16 7Suff p78 MR21

HORST,George Phillip 2Lt kldByTribesmen 18-4-16 IARO att24Punjabis p278 MR43

HORT,Courtenay Randell Lt ded 10-5-16 RGA 49SBp209 CR France145,Randall

HORTON,Frank.MC.2Lt drd 10-10-18 3Lpool p72 MR40

HORTON,H.F.MC.Lt 27-2-21 1WYorks CR Yorks38

HORTON,James Henry.DSO.MIDx2 LtCol ded 23-7-17 IMS DADMS III Cps p278 CR Iraq8

HORTON,Stanley Tom T2Lt kia 9-4-17 2Wilts p153 CR France595

HORTON,Victor John 2Lt kia 3-12-17 D161RFA p30 CR Belgium20,2-12-17

HORWITZ,Samuel Salmen Lt kld 21-10-16 3N&D attLNLancs p134 CR France390,Sydney

HORWOOD,Archibald Alfred 2Lt kia 28-3-18 1/6DLI p239 MR27

HORWOOD,Richard George 2Lt dow 8-5-18 20Lond A'Coy p251 CR France88

HORWOOD,Ronald Bentall 2Lt kia 1-7-16 3 att1Ess p131 CR France339

HOSE,Cyril Arthur Sparling 2Lt kia 10-9-16 1/5Lpool p215 CR France198

HOSE,Robert Henry 2Lt kia 18-3-17 5Beds p219 CR France420,2Bn

HOSEGOOD,Archibald Harding T2Lt kia 26-11-17 86MGC p183 CR France667

HOSEGOOD,Gilbert 2Lt kia 10-9-16 2Dev p76 CR France123

HOSEGOOD,Henry Arnold 2Lt kia 24-2-15 5RFus p68 CR Belgium17 3Bn

HOSEGOOD,Ralph T2Lt kia 23-7-16 12Glouc attTMB p106 CR France397

HOSEGOOD,William Leman Lt ded 15-8-18 4SomLI att4KAR p218&268 CR EAfrica36

HOSKEN,Ernest Dryden 2Lt kia 14-10-17 7CamH p168 MR20

HOSKEN,Henry Richard 2Lt kia 11-8-17 54MGC p183 MR29

HOSKEN,Victor Frederick 2Lt kia 7-10-16 7Lond p247 MR21

HOSKEN,Wilfrid 2Lt kia 21-8-15 6EYorks p84 MR4

HOSKIN,Alfred TCapt dow 4-7-17 RAVC att10Cps p198 CR France285

HOSKING,Cyril Gordon Lt kld 26-10-14 102RFA &4RFC p1&30 MR20

HOSKING,Herbert Edward Capt kia 3-2-17 IA 66 att62Punjabis p278 CR Iraq5,62 att66

HOSKING,Herbert John Roy 2Lt kia 23-7-16 7 att3LNLancs p136 MR21,3 att7Bn

HOSKINS,Cyril Lt kia 1-7-16 1/8RWar p215 MR21

HOSKINS,Francis Desmond 2Lt dow 2-10-15 1NStaffs p157 CR Belgium5,30-9-15

HOSKINS,George 2Lt kia 5-11-16 3 att10LancF p92 CR France401

HOSKINS,George Chandos.MC.T2Lt kia 11-3-17 GL 2RFC 1Wing p9 CR France423

HOSKINS,Joseph Capt died 7-10-18 4Dors p270 CR Dorset33,6-10-18

HOSKINS-ABRAHALL,Christopher Henry 2Lt kld 22-12-17 RFA attRFC p9&30,Hoskyns CR Devon237

HOSKYN,Frank Hebden 2Lt ded 19-11-19 IA TC att1/109Inf p278 MR43 2/102Grdrs Ex 1/109Inf

HOSKYN,John Henry 2Lt kia 20-9-17 9Lpool p216 MR30

HOSKYNS,Edwin Cecil Leigh Lt kia 20/21-10-14 1RWFus p98 MR29,20-10-14

HOSKYNS,Henry Charles Walter,DSO Maj kia 25-9-15 1Lincs p75 MR32

HOSKYNS-ABRAHALL,Bennet Edmund 2Lt dow 25-4-18 RGA 242SB p40 CR Belgium11

HOSLER,Albert Edward T2Lt kia 26-8-17 att7RB p179 MR30

HOSLEY,William James Seymour.MID Maj kia 25-9-15 6KOSB p102 CR France114

HOSSACK,Allan John.MM.T2Lt dow 27-4-18 14DLI p161 CR France144

HOSSELL,Leslie Cartmell Capt kia 8-8-16 1/8WYorks p219 MR21

HOSTE,George Michael Lt kld 7-10-16 16Lond p249 2entries1 kia MR21

HOSTE,William Graham.Bart 2Lt kia 9-5-15 RB p179 MR32

HOTBLACK,G.T.2Lt 22-3-21 Ess CR Sussex187

HOTCHKIN,Lambert Annesley 2Lt kia 8-10-16 21Lond p251 MR21

HOTCHKIS,Gilbert T2Lt kia 23-4-17 GordH p166 CR France162

HOTCHKISS,Felix James Bishop Lt kia 3-5-17 10 att13Mddx p236 MR20

HOTCHKISS,Henry TLt ded 19-6-18 RASC 17MT SP p193 CR France95,kia

HOTSON,Herbert Charles 2Lt kia 18-11-16 3 att2YLI p143 MR21

HOTSON,William Hugh McIntosh T2Lt kia 10-9-18 11N&D p134 CR Italy5,9-9-18

HOUFTON,Charles Morley Lt dow 12-11-15 8N&D p233 CR France924

HOUGH,Eric Bernard Capt kia 29-4-18 19Lpool p72 MR30

HOUGH,Geoffrey Goadsby TLtACapt ded 8-9-18 KRRC OC 214PoW Coy p150 CR France833

HOUGH,Topham Becher Dabridgecourt T2Lt kia 17-1-16 8EYorks p84 CR Belgium28

HOUGHAM,Bertram William.MC.LtACapt kia 6-9-18 3RWKent att5RBerks p141 CR France

HOUGHTON,Albert William 2Lt dow 31-3-18 10EYorks p84 CR France40

HOUGHTON,Arthur T2Lt kia 22-3-18 3Worc p109 MR20

HOUGHTON,George T2Lt kia 27-8-18 12WYorks att6Dors p81 CR France385

HOUGHTON,John.MM.T2Lt kia 14-12-17 18Manch p155 MR30 Ex 21Bn

HOUGHTON,John Reginald.MC.ACapt kia 21-3-18 1Lond p245 MR20

HOUGHTON,John Reginald Capt dow 22-3-18 6Manch attMGC Inf p187&236 CR France528,Maj

HOUGHTON,Noel.MID TMajALtCol kia 13-9-17 16N&D p134 CR Belgium21

HOUGHTON,Philip Squarey Capt kia 1-7-16 9Lond p247 MR21

HOUGHTON,Ralph 2Lt kia 20-3-18 6RWar p214 CR France1701,21-3-18

HOUGHTON,Tom Whitfield 2Lt ded 21-4-19 MGC Motors p183 CR Syria2

HOUGHTON,William T2Lt kia 9-4-16 11 att15RFus att8RWFus p68 MR38

HOULDSWORTH,William Gillbert Lt dow 23-9-14 ScotsGds p52 CR France462,Gilbert

HOULSTON,Edgar Charles Chap4Cl drd 4-5-17 RAChDept p199 CR France1571

HOULT,Alfred John LtAMaj ded 2-11-18 RGA 181HB p40 CR palestine11

HOULT,Arthur T2Lt ded 17-11-16 12EYorks p84 CR France74

HOULT,Robert Percy T2Lt kia 16-8-16 2WYorks p81 MR30

HOUNAM,George Leslie 2Lt kia 5-3-18 19DLI CR Belgium83

HOUNSON,George James T2Lt ded 20-9-17 Dev attLabCps p76 CR Devon2,19-9-17

HOURIHANE,Thomas Cormac Lt kia 1-2-20 IA 1/26Punjabis att4/39GarhwalRif p278 MR43,2-2-20

HOURSTON,David William Lt kia 11-8-17 7ScotRif p224 CR France25,9Bn

HOUSE,Horace George T2Lt kia 28-3-18 1Hamps p121 MR20

HOUSE,Joseph Francis T2Lt kia 24-3-18 Wilts att2RBerks p153 MR27

HOUSE,Malcolm Hutchinson T2Lt kia 3-5-17 8RB p179 MR20

HOUSECROFT,Harold 2Lt kia 19-11-14 4 att1ESurr p112 CR Belgium89

HOUSEHOLD,Ernest Scott 2Lt ded 22-7-17 5Ess p232 CR France113,dow 21-7-17

HOUSSEMAYNE DUBOULAY,Arthur.DSO.MajBrLtCol 23-10-18 RE 3Army GHQ CR France1512

HOUSTON,Arthur Oswald T2Lt kia 26-3-18 9RInniskF p105 MR27

HOUSTON,Cyril Thomas Lt ded 22-7-18 GL &RAF p190

HOUSTON,Frederick Neville.MC.Capt kia 1-7-16 Y&L p159 MR21

HOUSTON,Hugh TLt kia 24-10-17 17RScots Z'Coy p54 CR Belgium126

HOUSTON,John Cunningham T2Lt kia 14-10-18 1/2NumbF att9MGC Inf p61&183 CR Belgium157

HOUSTON,Kenneth D'Aguilar Capt kia 24-3-18 18Lond p250 MR20

HOUSTON,Thomas Cameron Capt dow 25-8-16 RAMC p253 CR France176

HOUSTON,William Houston TCapt dow 28-3-16 12RScots att1RScotF p54 CR Belgium11,Robertson

HOUSTON,William Wylie T2Lt kia 17-8-17 RE 226FC p45 CR France163,18-8-17

HOUSTON-BOSWALL,George Reginald.Bart.Capt kia 27-9-15 4GrenGds RoO p50 MR19

HOVELL,Mark T2Lt kia 12-8-16 1N&D p134 CR France423

HOVENDEN,Arthur Lester 2Lt kia 3-5-17 3 att7ESurr p112 MR20

HOW,Henry James 2Lt kia 14-4-17 9Lond p248 MR20

HOW,John Christian 2Lt kia 2-4-17 2RWSurr p56 CR France1489

HOW,William Alexander 2Lt kia 12-4-18 1RScotF p94 MR19

HOWARD,Addison James Lt kia 4-9-16 3 att1Beds p86 CR France294

HOWARD,Albert Leonard TLt kia 18-9-18 1LNLancs p136 CR France375

HOWARD,Alfred Heywood Capt kia 10-8-15 4WelshR p230 MR4

HOWARD,Alfred Lewis 2Lt kia 21-11-17 City of LondYeo p204 MR34

HOWARD,Arthur James 2Lt kia 30-4-15 2Hamps p121 MR4

HOWARD,Bernard Henry Maj kia 8-3-16 IA 47Sikhs p278 MR38

HOWARD,Cecil Cunningham T2Lt dow 23-5-16 8LNLancs A'Coy p136 CR France95

HOWARD,Cedric Stewart T2Lt kia 28-9-16 7Beds F'Coy p86 CR France383

HOWARD,Charles Reginald.OBE.TCapt kia 6-9-18 RAMC attKAR p196 CR EAfrica90

HOWARD,Dennis Brook.MC.T2LtACapt kia 22-10-17 35RFA p30 CR Belgium19,12RFA

HOWARD,Edgar Stacey T2Lt kia 9-8-18 6TankCps p188 MR16

HOWARD,Edward Douglas 2Lt kia 20-9-17 4RLancs p213 MR30

HOWARD,Eric Stanley T2Lt kia 18-5-17 RE att60RFC p9&45 CR France46

HOWARD,F.G.SNurse 18-11-14TFNS CR Wales135

HOWARD,F.J.C.Maj 6-6-20 8Huss CR Yorks335

HOWARD,Francis Stanley Capt kia 28-11-15 3Lond p245 MR19

HOWARD,Frederic George.MVO.DSO.MajTLtCol kia 19-10-15 RE p46 CR Belgium1,9-10-15

HOWARD,George Blake Lt ded 10-6-20 IARO attFollowersCentDept p278 MR66

HOWARD,George Oscroft 2Lt ded 14-11-18 5SStaffs p229 CR Yorks561

HOWARD,Gilbert Gordon Lt dow 29-10-18 6Glouc p225 CR France528

HOWARD,Guy Robert.DSO.Maj ded 23-10-18 1/2Ess &18RAF p131 CR France113

HOWARD,Harry Elsmore T2Lt dow 8-4-17 25NumbF p61 CR France265

HOWARD,Henry Charles Mowbray.MID Lt kia 29-9-15 Y&L p159 MR19

HOWARD,Herbert Arthur T2Lt dow 29-9-18 GordH att1Bn p166 CR France512,kia

HOWARD,Herbert Quey.DCM.2Lt kia 8-8-18 2Lond p245 MR16

HOWARD,James Kelvey Lt kia 11-2-17 5N&D attRFC p18&232 CR France924

HOWARD,John Allan Lt dow 9-5-18 3 att1Ess p132 CR France745

HOWARD,John Brereton Capt dow 6-4-18 4RWFus A'Coy p223 CR France232

HOWARD,John Turner TLt ded 18-6-18 RE 5FldSurCoy p46 CR France13

HOWARD,Kenneth Salwey LtTCapt kia 6-10-18 N&D att1Bn p134 CR France184

HOWARD,Leslie Rayner TLt kia 27-3-16 4RFus p68 MR29

HOWARD,Lewis Charles.DSO.TLtCol dow 23-12-15 8SomLI p80 CR France922

HOWARD,Lionel George T2Lt dow 12-4-17 5RBerks p139 CR France40 see HOWARD-GREEN true name

HOWARD,Louis Meredith TLtCol dow 2-7-16 24NumbF p61 CR France393

HOWARD,Lyulph Walter Mowbray TLt kia 15-9-15 7RWSurr p56 CR France189

HOWARD,Michael Francis Stafford Pte 10246 2HAC MR30 Ex Lt 18Huss attScotsGds

HOWARD,Norman TLt dow 1-8-15 5Nhampt p137 CR France922

HOWARD,Percy Edward TCapt ded 21-10-18 GL RAMC p266 CR Bucks51

HOWARD,Percy Edward Napier 2Lt kia 27-10-14 RIrReg p89 MR22

HOWARD,Philip Granville James Fitzalan.Hon.Lt dow 24-5-18 1WelshGds p53 CR France103

HOWARD,Richard Jackson T2Lt kia 17-3-16 9BlkW p128 CR France1723

HOWARD,Robert Henry Palmer.Hon.2Lt kia 9-5-15 4 att2ESurr p112 CR Belgium46,8-5-15

HOWARD,Victor Charles 2Lt drd 15-4-17 4ESurr p112 MR35

HOWARD,Walter Leslie TLt dow 16-8-17 48MGC p183 CR Belgium16,176MGC

HOWARD,William TCapt dow 8-10-15 8EKent p57 CR France1

HOWARD,William T2Lt kia 24-4-18 18Mddx att2Nhampt p147 MR27

HOWARD,William Aloysius T2Lt kia 24-4-17 7/8KOSB p102 MR20

HOWARD,William George 2Lt dow 20-12-17 RGA 119SB p40 CR Belgium3

HOWARD,William Hyson 2Lt kia 11-9-18 2Manch attX32TMB p155 CR

France1061

HOWARD-GREEN,L.G.2Lt served as HOWARD,L.G.

HOWARD-VYSE,Richard Capt kia 14-9-14 1LNLancs p136 MR15

HOWARTH,Alfred Doran Capt ded 26-3-18 6LancF p270 CR Lancs30,2/4Bn

HOWARTH,Charles Thomas.DCM.2Lt dow 28-5-18 149MGC Inf p183 CR Derby97 Ex N&D

HOWARTH,Frederick Ewart 2Lt kia 31-5-18 74RFA X'GdsTMB p30 CR France745

HOWARTH,Gilbert Lt kia 29-3-18 RGA 60SB p209 CR France644,2Lt 28-3-18

HOWARTH,Harold Victor Lt dow 2-5-18 1/5Dev p217 CR Palestine9

HOWARTH,J.Lt 6-5-20 LabCps CR Lancs112

HOWARTH,John 2Lt dow 10-9-16 RE 1FC p210 CR Derby26

HOWARTH,John Dearden T2Lt dow 1-8-17 9LNLancs p136 CR Belgium11,Lt 8Bn

HOWARTH,Norman 2Lt kia 13-7-16 3SLancs p125 CR France150,2Bn

HOWARTH,Norman 2Lt kia 22-3-18 2Yorks p90 MR27

HOWARTH,Norman Capt died 6-9-18 3RLancs &RAF p59 MR20

HOWARTH,Tom Hartley 2Lt dow 6-12-17 59MGC Inf p183 CR France716

HOWARTH,Wallace 2Lt kia 16-8-17 49MGC Inf p183 CR Belgium167

HOWAT,George T2Lt kia 26-8-18 ScotRif att2KOSB p103 CR France239,25-8-18

HOWATT,James Capt kia 28-6-15 7ScotRif p224 CR Gallipoli6

HOWATT,William Howatt 2Lt kia 3-5-17 7ScotRif att9RB p224 MR20,Henry

HOWCROFT,Laurence Walter TLt kia 20-11-17 1/2Hamps p121 CR France1483

HOWDEN,Francis William T2Lt dow 30-3-18 11 att1RDubF p176 CR France64,Frank

HOWDEN,George Bruce 2Lt ded 8-5-16 2DCLI p114 CR Devon152

HOWE,Arnold Ewart 2Lt kia 30-10-17 28Lond A'Coy p252 CR Belgium126

HOWE,Charles Kingsley T2Lt kia 1-7-16 6RBerks p139 CR France513

HOWE,Claude Arthur Capt kia 20-11-17 4RWFus att1/5LNLancs p223 MR17,30-11-17

HOWE,Edward Lt ded 4-1-17 22WYorks p81 CR Numb36

HOWE,Ernest TLt dow 14-12-16 RAMC att83FA p196 CR Greece9

HOWE,Frederick Norman.MID 2Lt kia 25-4-18 84/11RFA p30 MR30

HOWE,George Herbert 2Lt kia 28-3-18 RGA 151SB p40 CR France1182

HOWE,James Ashwell T2Lt kld 13-2-18 14RFC p16 CR Derby57

HOWE,James Roche Lt kia 18-10-18 3RMunstF B'Coy p175 CR France190

HOWE,Robert Ernest 2Lt kia 4-10-17 1EYorks p84 CR Belgium84

HOWE,Thomas Sydney Curzon.MC.2Lt kld 17-4-18 ConnRgrs &54RAF p266 MR20

HOWE,William Thomas.MM.2Lt kia 4-11-18 5 att9WYorks p218 CR France1142

HOWELL,Arthur Anthony.CMG.BrigGen ded 15-1-18 3Lond p270 CR Surrey160

HOWELL,Aubrey Hamilton Lt kia 6-1-16 2Leic p87 MR38

HOWELL,Augustus William 2Lt kia 15-4-17 6 att3RB p179 MR20

HOWELL,Charles Joseph Lt kia 25-1-17 Y&L attMGC Inf p159 CR Iraq5

HOWELL,Douglas Bert T2Lt kia 24-3-18 2HLI p163 MR20

HOWELL,Edmund Lally.MID TCapt kia 27-7-16 5 att1KRRC p150 MR21

HOWELL,Evan Idres Lt ded 21-4-18 4Nhampt att72RAF p234 CR Wales135

HOWELL,Ernest Alfred Russell LtCol drd 30-12-15 IA S&TCps p278 MR41

HOWELL,Francis Slinger 2Lt kia 2-8-17 GordH att8/10Bn p166 CR Belgium58,dow 31-7-17

HOWELL,George Woodbourne.MSM.2Lt kia 22-6-18 17 att1/2RWFus p98 CR France4,1/2att17

HOWELL,Herbert Edgar 2Lt kia 9-5-15 2ELancs p111 MR32

HOWELL,John T2Lt kia 25-9-15 9KRRC p150 MR29

HOWELL,John Edwin 2Lt 7-7-16 3 att16WelshR MR21

HOWELL,Maurice Ives Berthon 2Lt kia 25-9-15 1RWSurr p56 MR19

HOWELL,Norman Asquith T2Lt kia 23-12-16 6KSLI p145 CR France744

HOWELL,Norman Bulmer.MID Lt kia 24-7-15 2RWKent p141 CR Iraq6

HOWELL,Norman Eliott.MID Capt kia 7-1-16 IA 82Punjabis attStaff 35Bde p278 MR38

HOWELL,Philip.CMG.TBrigGen kia 7-10-16 4Huss Staff p21 CR France41

HOWELL,Reuben Harrison T2Lt dow 29-3-18 11 att2RDubF p177 CR France145

HOWELL,Richard David.MC.2Lt kia 15-9-18 3 att2WelshR p127 CR France673

HOWELL,Roland Basil 2Lt kia 2-10-15 4NStaffs p157 MR19

HOWELL,Thomas Chap4Cl kia 1-12-17 RAChDept att6KSLI p199 CR France379

HOWELL,Wilfred Symonds T2Lt kia 25-4-16 9ESurr p112 CR Belgium97

HOWELLS,Courtney Philip T2Lt kia 30-9-18 3Yorks att5YLI p90 CR France912

HOWELLS,David Geoffrey T2Lt ded 1-12-18 52RFus p68 CR Ches3

HOWELLS,Denzil 2Lt dow 13-4-18 5ELancs attY&L p226 CR Belgium183

HOWELLS,Edmund Sydney TLt kld 27-3-18 RFC p16 CR Wales389

HOWELLS,F.A.C.Lt 24-3-20 5Worc CR Glouc109

HOWELLS,George Davey 2Lt kia 28-2-18 1Mon att15Ches p244 CR Belgium83

HOWELLS,George James 2Lt kia 23-11-17 GL &8RFC p9 CR France403,kld

HOWELLS,Graham TCapt dow 2-5-16 14WelshR A'Coy p127 CR France345,kia

HOWELLS,Hugh T2Lt kld 10-4-17 GL &RFC p9 CR Mon76

HOWELLS,James T2Lt kia 21-3-18 RWSurr att8Bn p56 MR27

HOWELLS,John Edwin T2Lt kia 20-11-17 E15TankCps p188 CR France711

HOWELLS,John Hubert 2Lt kia 9-10-17 RFA att15RHA p30 CR Belgium12

HOWELLS,John Wesley 2Lt kia 23-7-17 7LancF p221 MR34

HOWELLS,Phillip George Herbert T2Lt kia 18-11-16 10NStaffs p157 CR France384

HOWELLS,Reginald Lt dow PoW 30-5-18 1Hereford p252 CR Germany3,HOWELL 1/3Bn

HOWELLS,William John TCapt dow 10-8-15 8WelshR p127 MR4

HOWES,Charles William TCaptAMaj kia 22-4-18 19DLI p161 CR France296

HOWES,Edward 2Lt kia 2-8-16 9NumbF p61 CR France397

HOWES,Harold Edward Lt kia 1-8-18 1/6Ches p222 CR France524

HOWES,Henry Edward.MM.Lt 18-1-21 ESurr CR Surrey107

HOWES,Hugh Gilbert 2Lt kia 8-3-16 IARO att2Rajputs p278 MR38

HOWETT,William T2Lt kia 18-9-18 RSuss att7Bn p119 CR France369

HOWFIELD,John Arthur.MC.2Lt kia 1-9-18 75RFA p30 CR France214

HOWIE,David Dickie 2Lt ded 19-1-16 2RFA p270 CR Egypt9,Lt

HOWIE,George Francis 2Lt kia 21-3-18 3 att16RScots p54 MR20

HOWILL,John Edwin 2Lt kia 7-7-16 16WelshR p127

HOWIS,Francis Thackeray T2Lt dow 8-12-15 12Ess att6Lincs p132 CR Gallipoli27

HOWITT,Adam Gordon.MC.TCapt kia 5-8-17 12ESurr p112 MR29

HOWKINS,Ernest Lt kia 4-8-16 1/5RHA p207 CR Egypt2,M.

HOWKINS,George Addington T2Lt kia 25/27-9-15 12NumbF p61 MR19

HOWLETT,Charles Wilfred T2Lt kia 1-7-16 9YLI p143 CR France189

HOWLETT,John Harold T2Lt kia 26-9-17 215MGC Inf p183 MR30

HOWLEY,Jasper Joseph.DSO.Maj kia 11-3-15 1Lincs p75 CR France525,2Bn

HOWMAN,Henry Roger TMaj kia 25/26-4-18 13Glouc p106 CR Belgium115

HOWSE,Basil Thomas 2Lt ded 18-9-16 C99RFA p30 CR Greece7

HOWSE,Harold Edward.MID ACapt kia 16-8-17 3 att2RBerks p139 MR30

HOWSON,C.J.Lt ded 5-7-18 Lpool &RAF p72

HOWSON,Frederick John Lt 18-10-18 126/29RFA MR65

HOWSON,George Rowland Paget T2Lt kia 9-4-17 1RLancs p59 CR France729

HOWSON,John Frederick Lt ded 18-10-18 RH&FA p30

HOY,Andrew Burn Lt dow 2-6-18 4RScots p211 CR France95

HOY,Arthur 2Lt kia 3-11-16 RE p210 CR France1327

HOY,John Leonard 2Lt kia 21-3-18 2/7N&D p233 MR20

HOY,William Capt ded 17-9-16 RAPC p200 CR Yorks98

HOYLAND,Godfrey Algernon.MC.LtACapt dow 3-10-18 36RFA p30 CR France

HOYLAND,John Fraser Capt kia 26-9-16 4 att9LancF p92 MR21

HOYLE,Basil William Edmond TCapt kia 25-9-15 9RWFus p98 MR19

HOYLE,Frederick Harold T2Lt dow 20-4-18 2WYorks p82 CR France145

HOYLE,Geoffrey Morgan Lt kia 9-8-15 3 att2N&D p134 MR29

HOYLE,Harold T2Lt kia 23-7-16 7LNLancs p136 CR France432

HOYLE,Humphrey King 2Lt kia 1-5-15 5LancF p221 MR4,7-5-15

HOYLE,John Baldwin.MC.TLt kia 1-7-16 7SLancs p125&258 CR France393

HOYLE,Walter Maynard 2Lt ded 11-5-17 Norf p263 CR Mddx26

HOYLE,William T2Lt kia 9-4-17 8EYorks p84 CR France581

HOYLES,Arthur Harry Child 2Lt dow 2-12-17 5HLI attRFC p18&240,Henry MR20

HOYNE-FOX,Leslie Vincent Capt ded 14-10-18 IA 120Inf p278 CR Iraq8,13-10-18

HOYS,Cecil Thomas Gray T2Lt kia 15-9-16 150MGC Inf p183 CR France239

HOYTE,Raymond Wilson Lt kia 21-3-18 2/7N&D p233 MR20

HUBBACK,Francis William 2Lt dow 12-2-17 2/6Lond p247 CR France120

HUBBARD,Adrian George T2Lt dow 30-8-16 9 att8EKent p57 CR France23

HUBDARD,Alfred T2Lt kia 17-2-17 8Suff p78 CR France314

HUBBARD,Alfred William.MID T2Lt kia 25-1-17 8RWFus p98 MR38

HUBBARD,Archibald Charles 2Lt kia 8-11-17 5 att2KRRC p150 MR30

HUEBARD,Bertram John.MC.2Lt kia 1-12-17 4GrenGds p50 CR France415,Lt

HUBBARD,Leslie Victor T2Lt kia 31-8-16 13Mddx p147 CR France432

HUBBARD,Percy William(Peter).MM.T2Lt kia 6-6-18 16LancF p92 CR France924

HUBBARD,William Dickenson Lt kia 8-7-16 3 att2Yorks p90 MR21,Dickinson

HUBBERT,Francis Stanley William 2Lt kia 23-5-15 2EYorks p84 MR29,23-4-15

HUBBLE,Frederick Richard T2Lt ded 2-8-18 RASC MT 36Div p193 CR France134

HUBBLE,Harry Leonard 2Lt kia 15-4-18 4Lincs p217 MR30

HUBBLE,Harry Ronald 2Lt kia 20-5-17 3 att4Lpool p72 MR20

HUBER,Edgar William T2Lt kld 2-11-16 1MaltaReg p201 CR Greece7

HUBER,H.W.Lt kia 7-1-16 MaltaReg attRInniskF p201 MR4

HUBERT,Donald Franklyn Lt kia 14-3-17 IA 9BhopalInf p278 MR38,Capt

HUBY,O.M.2Lt ded 11-9-18 5RWar &RAF p214

HUBY,Owen Meredith Lt kld 23-10-18 5RWar attRAF p255 CR Yorks1

HUCKER,Wilfred Thomas 2Lt dow 23-12-17 3 att8SomLI p80 CR France285

HUCKETT,Arnold Walter Lt kia 10-8-15 5Wilts p153 MR4

HUCKLE,Henry William 2Lt kia 5-9-18 1Camb p245 CR France511

HUCKLEBRIDGE,Sidney Eames Lt ded 7-3-19 21WYorks p82 CR Belgium243

HUCKS,B.C.Capt ded 7-11-18 GL &RAF p190

HUDDART,Cuthbert Edmund Arnold TCapt ded 29-1-17 RAMC p267 CR Lond8

HUDDART,Lindow Hereward Leofric TLt ded 5-2-17 GL RE att1NigR p201 CR EAfrica39

HUDDART,Robert Edward Thorne 2Lt kia 30-6-16 5 att2RB p179 CR France251

HUDDLESTON,Maurice Louis T2Lt kia 1-7-16 15DLI p161 CR France267

HUDDLESTON,Purefoy Gauntlett Capt kia 25-3-16 RE 84FC p46 CR Belgium1

HUDDLESTONE,Sydney Chantler 2Lt kia 25-1-15 3 att2BlkW p128 MR22

HUDDY,Edward T2Lt kia 30-7-16 11Glouc p106 MR21

HUDLESTONE,Harold Robert T2Lt dow 2-7-16 14Mddx p147 CR France513

HUDSON,Alban John Benedict.MC.Lt kia 7-6-17 3Worc p109 CR Belgium62

HUDSON,Allan Harrison 2Lt dow 13-6-15 1/9Manch p237 CR Gallipoli1

HUDSON,Arthur Cyril TMaj dow 2-10-16 3 att11RFus p68 CR France102

HUDSON,Arthur Henry William 2Lt kia 1-7-16 1RLancs p59 MR21

HUDSON,Arthur Hensley TCapt kia 31-7-17 6RBerks D'Coy p139 CR Belgium112

HUDSON,Arthur Thomas Rawlings Lt kia 12-4-18 2/7DLI p239 MR32,11-4-18

HUDSON,Aubrey Wells Lt dow 20-9-14 5 att2Worc p109 MR15

HUDSON,Austin Patrick Capt kia 1-9-17 5LancF p221 MR30,31-8-17

HUDSON,Charles Edward 2Lt dow 18-12-16 3/7Mddx p235 CR France59

HUDSON,Charles Herbert 2Lt kia 16-5-15 Lpool p72 CR France279

HUDSON,Cuthbert Newton Lt kia 29-3-17 2/5Lpool p215 CR France82

HUDSON,Edward Stanley T2Lt dow 13-2-17 10Dev p76 CR Greece1

HUDSON,Elijah Rennison 2Lt ded 18-1-19 RGA 46A/ACoy p262 CR Lond14

HUDSON,Ernest LtCol ded 14-10-16 IA IMS p278

HUDSON,Francis Reginald LtTCapt kld 21-3-18 RFC p16 CR Devon248

HUDSON,Frank TLt kia 12-10-18 12Manch p155 CR France192

HUDSON,Frank Hobbs T2Lt dow 26-4-18 1Worc p109 CR France39

HUDSON,George Trevor T2Lt kia 2-10-16 7RWKent p141 CR France383,29-9-16

HUDSON,Godfrey.MC.Maj kia 12-4-18 MGC p183 MR32

HUDSON,Godfrey Burnside 2Lt kia 18-4-18 3 att1Glouc p106 CR France765

HUDSON,Harold Baldwin T2Lt kia 13-11-16 10 att4Beds p86 CR France220,14-11-16

HUDSON,Harold Edwin T2Lt kia 27-9-15 10Ess p132 CR France430

HUDSON,Harry 2Lt dow 25-4-18 RGA 177SB p40 CR Belgium38 26-4-18

HUDSON,Harry T2Lt kia 21-9-18 RScots att1/4Bn p54 CR France646

HUDSON,Henry Erris.MC.2Lt kia 18-6-18 N&D att9Bn p134 MR19

HUDSON,Horace Sayer 2Lt ded 17-11-18 9Manch att2MGC Inf p187&237 CR France289

HUDSON,Jocelyn Hope TLt dow 12-1-16 C49RFA p30 CR Belgium11

HUDSON,John Burgoyne 2Lt kia 25-10-16 4Yorks p220 MR21

HUDSON,John William Willoughby Lt kld 30-11-15 1/5RWar A'Coy p214 CR France281,kia

HUDSON,Leslie Sidney 2Lt kld 28-10-17 3Glouc att49RFC p106&9 CR Kent7 1Bn

HUDSON,Robert Arthur.DSO.MajALtCol kia 9-10-17 8WYorks p219 MR30

HUDSON,Robert Dennis T2Lt kia 25-1-16 109RFA p30 CR Belgium28,Denis

HUDSON,Roland Burton 2Lt kia 19-7-16 O&BLI BucksBn p231 MR19

HUDSON,Thomas Heylyn Capt&Adjt kia 13-10-15 5RBerks p139 CR France149

HUDSON,Thomas James 2Lt kia 20-5-17 GL &11RFC p9 CR France481

HUDSON,Wilfred 2Lt dow 8-2-16 RE ERidCoy p210 CR Belgium11,Wilfrid

HUDSON-KINAHAN,Cecil Barton TLt ded 30-12-15 SL att4KAR p202 CR EAfrica52

HUDSON-KINAHAN,Daniel Dickinson Lt kia 9-4-16 2IrGds SR p52 CR Belgium72

HUDSPETH,Arthur 2Lt kia 19-9-16 10SStaffs att13DLI p122 MR21

HUDSPITH,Walter Leonard.MC.TLt kia 7-11-18 1Mddx p147 CR France941

HUFFINGTON,Thomas ACapt dow 8-2-17 7Yorks p90 CR France329

HUGGAN,James Laidlaw Lt kia 16-9-14 RAMC att3CldGds p196 MR15

HUGGAN,Robert Elliott Lt ded 29-5-18 9HLI att3/1KAR p240&268 CR EAfrica77

HUGGAN,Thomas T2Lt kld 24-7-17 RFC p9 CR Yorks383

HUGGARD,Hewitt Lt kia 7-8-15 6EYorks p84 MR4,9-8-15

HUGGARD,Lewis Dudley Richard TLtACapt kia 26-6-17 13Y&L p159 CR France1191

HUGGETT,Sidney George T2Lt kia 18-9-18 RSuss att7Bn p119 CR France369

HUGGETT,William Wyndham T2Lt dow 24-4-16 4SWBord att10Bn p100 CR France354

151

HUGGINS,Douglas Frank Capt kia 29-8-18 1Lond p245 CR France924

HUGGINS,R.H.Capt ded 27-6-19 3KAR p268

HUGH-JONES,Kenneth Herbert 2LtACapt kia 20-9-17 5 att12RB p179 CR Belgium83

HUGHES,Alan Stuart T2Lt kia 18-11-16 8NStaffs p157 CR France384

HUGHES,Albert Edward 2Lt kia 4-8-18 Lpool att1/9Bn p72 CR France261

HUGHES,Alexander Arbuthnot Capt kia 1-7-16 2SWBord p100 CR France1490

HUGHES,Alfred 2Lt kia 1-7-18 RE 526FC p210 CR France250

HUGHES,Arthur Maj kia 16-5-17 7Lpool p215 CR France279

HUGHES,Arthur.DCM.TCapt&QM ded 11-2-19 GL 18LancF att2Sch of Cookery p190 CR Germany1

HUGHES,Arthur Price Capt 31-3-21 17RWFus CR Wales535

HUGHES,Aubrey Noel T2Lt kia 26-9-16 5Dors p124 MR21

HUGHES,Benjamin Thomas T2Lt kia 17-3-18 13RWelshR att13RWFus p127 CR France275

HUGHES,Bryan Desmond.MC.TCapt kia 6-8-18 8RDubF p177 CR France28,1Bn

HUGHES,Burroughs Maurice Maj kia 15-9-15 4Norf p216 CR Gallipoli17

HUGHES,Charles Henry T2Lt kia 30-8-18 14WelshR p127 CR France217

HUGHES,Charles Walter TCapt dow 1-10-18 14RWar p65 CR France512

HUGHES,Christopher James Capt ded 13-5-16 4ConnRgrs p172 CR Iraq6

HUGHES,Cyril Rodyk TLt kia 4-7-16 7LNLancs p136 MR21

HUGHES,Daniel 2Lt kia 23-7-16 8GordH p166 MR21

HUGHES,Douglas Duncan 2Lt kia 10-7-16 11 att8SStaffs p122 MR21

HUGHES,Edward TCapt dow 16-9-16 2DLI p161 CR France329

HUGHES,Edward John.MC.Lt kia 20-10-18 3Lpool att13RWFus p72 CR France228,2Lt

HUGHES,Edward Malcolm LtCol ded 11-9-16 IA 14JatLancers p278 CR Iraq6

HUGHES,Edward Phillip T2Lt kld 27-7-17 RFC p9 CR Shrop145

HUGHES,Edward Reginald Graham 2Lt kia 25-9-15 2 O&BLI p130 CR France279

HUGHES,Edward William TLt ded 30-1-18 RAVC att23VetHosp p198

HUGHES,Eric 2Lt kld 14-11-17 RFC SR p9 CR Scot235

HUGHES,Eric James Walrond 2LtACapt kia 20-9-17 MGC Inf att4N&D p183 MR30

HUGHES,Ferdinand T2Lt kia 29-5-18 25MGC p183 MR18

HUGHES,Frederick TLt kia 12-10-16 1SLancs attY&L p125 CR Greece3,3Bn

HUGHES,Frederick Deeton Lt kia 21-10-14 1ELancs p111 CR Belgium451

HUGHES,Frederick Gordon 2Lt kia 26-6-16 3 att12NumbF p61 CR France188

HUGHES,Frederick Lee Maj kia 2-3-17 IA 20Inf attSWaziristanMil p278 MR43

HUGHES,Frederick Peter.MC.Lt dow 6-8-18 RE 511FC CR France71

HUGHES,Fred Micklewright 2Lt kia 23-3-18 1/1 att5 O&BLI BucksBn p231 MR27

HUGHES,Geoffrey Lt dow 5-8-18 1GrenGds p50 CR France502

HUGHES,George 2Lt kld 12-8-17 7KSLI p145 CR France256,kia

HUGHES,George Augustus.MC&Bar.2Lt dow 4-11-18 6WRid p227 CR France658

HUGHES,George William Victor 2Lt kia 27-11-17 YLI att2/5Bn p143 MR17

HUGHES,Gladys Corfield SNurse 6-11-18 QAIMNS CR Shrop101

HUGHES,Gordon McGregor 2Lt kia 8-8-16 9 att5RBerks p139 MR21

HUGHES,Guy Ferguson Lt ded 21-12-15 HP IA EmpCycCo GdsDiv RHGds p20 CR France1106

HUGHES,Guy Wiley 2Lt dow 31-12-14 Mddx p147 CR France284

HUGHES,Harold 2Lt kia 11-4-18 GL &7RAF p190 CR Belgium18

HUGHES,Harold 2Lt dow 23-4-17 27RFA p30 CR France1325

HUGHES,Harold Bickley Drewe Capt kia 16-5-15 3RWar attHLI p65 MR22

HUGHES,Harold George.MC.TLt kia 4-5-17 197MGC p183 CR France1193

HUGHES,Henry Kent Capt kia 9-5-15 1YLI p143 MR29

HUGHES,Horatio Clement T2Lt kia 18-9-18 1 att11RWFus p98

HUGHES,Hugh Darrell 2Lt kia 14-1-17 3 att8RWFus p98 MR38,High

HUGHES,Irvin John Lt kia 13-1-16 IA 1/9GurkhaRif p278 CR Iraq5

HUGHES,John.MC.Lt kia 9-10-17 4 att16RWar p65 CR Belgium125

HUGHES,John Arthur.MID Lt dow 26-1-15 4RWFus p223 CR France80

HUGHES,John Edwyn T2Lt dow 19-8-16 10RWFus p98 CR France141

HUGHES,John Gwilym TLt kldacc 3-11-16 20 att9RWFus p98 CR France52

HUGHES,John Henry T2Lt kia 3-7-16 8RWKent p141 CR France393

HUGHES,John Hugh Edward 2Lt kia 10-7-17 RGA 156SB p40 CR France591

HUGHES,John Lawrence TLt kia 1-10-17 17WelshR &25RFC p9&127 CR France88

HUGHES,John Meirion Lt 16-6-18 4SLancs &103RAF MR20

HUGHES,John Norman.MC&Bar.2Lt dow 2-8-18 4Ches p222 CR France1225

HUGHES,John Richard Hammond 2Lt ded 29-6-18 5RFA p208 CR France145

HUGHES,John Walter 2Lt kia 8-10-18 3 att1Ess p132 CR France1345

HUGHES,John William.MC.TLt kia 15-4-18 2WRid p115 CR France98

HUGHES,Lestocq 2Lt kia 26-9-16 5 att12Mddx p147 MR21

HUGHES,Lewis Reginald 2Lt dow 19-5-15 4NStaffs attRScotF p157 CR France80

HUGHES,Lionel Holford 2Lt kia 29-10-14 3 att1NStaffs p157 CR France82

HUGHES,Maurice Thomas T2Lt kia 30-5-16 20 att13RWFus p98 CR France1157

HUGHES,Myrddin McKelvie.MC.Lt kia 16-5-18 402/14RFA 14ArmyBde p30 CR France889

HUGHES,Norman Alfred TCapt kia 18-9-18 11WelshR p127 CR Greece5

HUGHES,Norman Labrey 2Lt kia 26-9-19 Dev att1 O&BLI p76&257 MR70 &CR Europe180,27-6-19

HUGHES,Oscar Cecil Lawrence Lt kia 18-8-17 RAMC att2KAR p196 CR EAfrica11 &CR Tanzania1

HUGHES,Owen T2Lt kia 30-11-15 RE 54FC p46 MR19

HUGHES,Percy Canynton T2Lt dow 3-10-18 11WelshR attSWBord p127 CR Greece6,3RWFus att7SWBord

HUGHES,Peter Capt kia 25-3-18 KRRC att11Bn p150 MR27

HUGHES,Peter Fredk.MC.Lt dow 7-8-18 RE 511FC p210 MR27

HUGHES,Rhys T2Lt dow 1-8-16 20LancF p92 CR France51

HUGHES,Robert Baskerville T2Lt kld 31-5-17 GL &RFC p9 CR Staffs153

HUGHES,Robert Charles 2Lt kia 17-8-18 15Lond p249

HUGHES,Robert Maurice Lt 1-8-19 EYorks CR WIndies36

HUGHES,Robert Peyton Lt kia 4-11-14 IA 101Grens p278 MR47

HUGHES,Sam T2Lt kia 6-11-17 WelshR att10Bn p127 MR32

HUGHES,Sidney Russell T2Lt kia 30-9-18 23 att11RFus p68 CR France212

HUGHES,T.O.AssPoliticAgent 16-4-16 MakranLevy Cps MR43

HUGHES,Tegerin TCapt dow 1-4-16 10RWFus p98 MR29

HUGHES,Thomas 2Lt kia 8-10-18 4WelshR p230 CR France1346

HUGHES,Thomas T2Lt ded 14-12-18 6ELancs p111 MR65,Lt

HUGHES,Thomas Derfel 2Lt kia 3-5-16 4 O&BLI p231 CR France1327

HUGHES,Thomas Hector Capt kia 15-10-14 Worc p109 CR France279

HUGHES,Thomas McKenny.MIDx2 TLt kia 5-2-18 KRRC att53RFC p16&150 CR Belgium11,6-2-18

HUGHES,W.2Lt kld 19-11-18 RH&FA &RAF p30

HUGHES,Walter 2Lt kia 8-3-18 3 att2YLI p143 CR Belgium12

HUGHES,William T2Lt kia 3-3-16 10RWFus p98 MR29

HUGHES,William 2Lt kia 26-3-18 10 att1/9Manch p237 MR27

HUGHES,William.MC.T2Lt dow 14-9-18 8 att2Beds p86 CR Surrey18

HUGHES,William Francis.MC.MM.T2Lt dow 7-9-18 17RFus p98&254 CR France103

HUGHES,William Frederick TLt kia 20-11-17 10RIrF p171 CR France1489

HUGHES,William George T2Lt kia 23-7-18 12Lpool p72 MR20

HUGHES,William Price T2Lt kia 24-8-18 10SWBord p100 CR France246

HUGHES,William Sladen Lt kia 14-9-14 RSuss p119 MR15

HUGHES,William Thomas ded 8-4-17 IARO CR India48

HUGHES-DAVIES,Arthur Gwynne.MC.Lt kia 20-9-18 7RWFus att53MGC Inf p187&223 CR Palestine3

HUGHES-DUDLEY,Robert Charles 2Lt PoW 17-8-18 CivServRif MR16

HUGHES-GAMES,Joshua Brewer.MC.Capt ded 17-10-18 18DLI p265 CR Shrop19

HUGHES-GIBB,Charles Pomery Capt dow 25-7-16 158RFA p30 CR France23

HUGHES-GIBB,Harold Francis TLt kia 18-4-17 B62RFA p30 CR France731,19-4-17

HUGHES-HALLETT,Harold Hereward Maj ded 16-6-19 NStaffs p265 CR Sussex184

HUGHES-HUGHES,William Montagu TCapt kia 25-9-15 9WelshR p127 CR France260

HUGHES-JONES,Harry Llewelyn TLt kia 3-3-16 11Mddx p147 MR19

HUGHES-ONSLOW,Arthur Maj ded 17-8-14 10Huss RoO p22 CR France87

HUGHES-ONSLOW,Denzil TMaj kia 10-7-16 6Dors p124 CR France370

HUGHESDON,Arthur Hamilton Lt kia 27-9-18 59RFA p30 CR France274

HUGHMAN,Cecil Mackenzie Capt dow 18-9-16 1/8Mddx C'Coy p236 CR France66

HUGHMAN,Leopold Alexander Capt kia 5-3-16 11Mddx p147 MR19

HUGHSTON,Johnston.MID TCaptAMaj dow 14-9-18 RAMC att68FA p196 CR Greece1John

HUGILL,Edwin Abbot TCapt ded 25-9-17 17RFus p68

HUGILL,Valentine Francis Herbert 2Lt kia 16-10-16 16RFus &42RFC p3&68 CR France82

HUGO,Reginald Graeff TLt dow 28-3-18 10/11HLI p163 CR France40

HUGO,Stephen Hofmeyr Capt kia 21-8-16 2RBerks p139 CR France423

HUIE,Henry William Richard Lt kia 11-8-18 9RScots p212 CR France360

HUISH,Francis T2Lt kia 28-7-18 Dev p76 CR France1689

HUITT,Richard Henry William 2Lt ded 13-12-17 RGA 77HAG p40 CR Belgium84

HULEATT,Francis Hugh.MC.CaptAMaj dow 28-2-17 C83RFA p30 CR France177

HULBERT,George Dodson 2Lt kia 9-8-18 18Huss p23 CR France652,Dodgson

HULE-KELLY,George Harvey Capt kia 20-10-14 NStaffs p157

HULKS,Henry John TCapt kia 3-9-16 17KRRC p150 CR France701,Harry

HULL,Edward Cecil Gordon Lt dow 26-8-17 30/39RFA p30 CR Belgium24

HULL,Edwin Charles T2Lt kld 17-3-18 RFC p16 CR Beds23

HULL,Joseph Laurence T2Lt dow 19-10-16 13Worc p109 CR France188

HULL,Lyonel Hyde Rochfort Lt kia 25/26-5-15 21Lond B'Coy p251 CR France279,25-5-15

HULLEY,Arthur Henry Booth TLt ded 4-12-18 RFA p30 p261 CR Hamps64

HULLETT,William Ernest T2Lt dow 7-12-17 Norf att7Bn p74 CR France446

HULM,Glynn TLtACapt ded 28-11-18 7 O&BLI p130 CR Greece9,WO

HULM,Wynne Odyerne TLt dow 25-9-15 8Dev p76 CR France88

HULME,Arthur T2Lt kia 23-10-18 20Manch p155 CR France231

HULME,Clarence Waller.MC.2Lt kia 16-9-18 317RH&FA p30 CR France245

HULME,Wilfred Lt ded 14-11-18 3Lpool att6TMB p72 CR Lancs463,Wilfrid 5Bn

HULSE,Edward Hamilton Westrow.Bart Capt kia 13-3-15 2ScotsGds p52 CR France347,12-3-15

HULTON,Alan Edward Grey TLt dow 6-5-15 RASC 173HTCoy p193 CR Glouc9

HULTON,Benjamin William T2Lt dow 5-7-18 13TankCps p188 CR France29,Wright Lt kia

HULTON,Cecil Harry Joy.MC.T2LtACapt kia 4-11-18 16LancF p92 CR France1479

HULTON-HARROP,Hugh de Lacey Lt kia 12-5-15 1LifeGds RoO p20 MR29,Lacy CR France453 Ex5Lancers

HULTON-SAMS,Frederick Edward Barwick TLt kia 30-7-15 6DCLI p114 CR France453

HUMBERSTON,Herbert Lt ded 20-10-18 Leic p263 CR Bucks80,2Lt

HUMBERT,Ernest Graham Johnston Lt dow 8-6-15 9RBerks att2Hamps p139 CR Gallipoli1

HUMBLE,Robert 2Lt kia 7-9-15 9A&SH p244 CR Belgium6

HUMBLE-CROFTS,Cyril Mitford TCapt kia 30-6-16 13RSuss p119 MR19

HUMBLY,William Leeuwin kia 23-8-18 RBerks att1Bn p139 CR France927 HUMBLEY

HUMBY,Frederick Harry Lt dow 9-11-18 6 att2/7RWar p214 CR France13

HUME,Arthur James T2Lt dow PoW 21-5-18 1TankCps p188 CR France1076

HUME,Arthur Sinclair Vernon Maj ded 21-9-15 3ScotHorse p205 MR4

HUME,Charles Geoffrey Lt kia 20-10-14 1SStaffs p122 MR29,26-10-14

HUME,Edward Archibald TCapt dow 27-8-15 7SStaffs p122 MR4

HUME,George Minchin 2Lt kia 12-6-15 RE 2FC p210 MR29 &CR France453

HUME,Robert Anseley Cuthbert LtCol dow 1-5-15 1BordR p117 MR4,Ouseley

HUME,Ronald TLt kia 6-4-17 20RFus &20RFC p9&68 p68 MR20

HUME-GORE,Gustavas Lt kia 17-10-17 7A&SH att4KAR p243&268 CR EAfrica30 &CR Tanzania1

HUME-KELLY,George Harry Capt 20-10-14 1NStaffs CR France681

HUME-WRIGHT,Maurice Gabriel TLt kia 10-7-16 8Yorks p90 CR France515

HUMFREY,B.J.H.LtCol 1-9-15 IA ArmyRemountDept CR Hamps245

HUMFREY,Douglas Herbert Washington Lt kia 16-5-15 3 att2 O&BLI p130 MR22

HUMFREY,John Edward Hampinstall T2Lt ded 28-7-18 3SLancs att18Y&L p125 CR France134

HUMFREY,Wiliam Knox Lt kia 26-8-14 2LancF p92 MR15

HUMMEL,Raymond T2Lt kia 19-5-16 18WYorks p82 CR France643

HUMMERSTONE,Lawrence George Lt kia 21-8-18 5Lond &12RAF p255&246,2Lt CR France103

HUMPHREYS,David Virgil T2Lt kia 24-4-17 14A&SH p173 MR21

HUMPHREY,Elsie M.Sister 19-4-20 TFNS CR Cornwall168

HUMPHREY,Eric Sutherland Capt kia 5-6-15 8LancF p221 CR Gallipoli1

HUMPHREY,Ernest Graham 2Lt dow 29-3-18 48RFC p16 CR France62

HUMPHREY,Idwal Ben T2Lt dow 14-9-16 14Lpool p72 CR Greece6

HUMPHREY,Joseph Herbert T2Lt kia 20-9-17 1/2 att8Glouc p107 CR Belgium22

HUMPHREY,Richard Ronald 2Lt kia 31-8-18 5Yorks p221 CR France777

HUMPHREY,Thomas Albert 2Lt kia 3-5-18 8RWSurr att205RAF p56 CR France425

HUMPHREY,Vincent Ernest TLt ded 26-10-18 RASC 3ArmyEFC p193 CR France1512

HUMPHREY,William.MC.2Lt dow 24-10-18 4 att3RDubF p177 CR France40

HUMPHREY,William Pryn 2Lt kia 27-5-18 1/4Lond p246 CR France54,Pryor

HUMPHREY-DAVY,Darrel Norman O'Neale T2Lt kia 12-2-17 att14 Hamps p121 CR Belgium4,1-2-17

HUMPHREY-JONES,Cecil TCapt kia 24-11-17 19RWFus p98 MR17

HUMPHREYS,Arthur Cecil Capt kia 10-5-15 7LancF p221 MR4

HUMPHREYS,Dashwood William Harrington.DSO.Maj kia 17-2-17 IA 1/8GurkhaRif p278 MR38

HUMPHREYS,Dudley Francis 2Lt dow 16-5-15 2RWSurr p56 CR France80

HUMPHREYS,Frederick Charles.MC.TCapt kia 4-10-17 8SomLI p80 MR30

HUMPHREYS,George Geoffrey Prendergast Maj dow 30-10-14 IA 127BaluchistanLI att129Baluchis p278 CR Belgium186

HUMPHREYS,John Alan 2Lt kia 31-8-17 C64RFA p30 CR Belgium8

HUMPHREYS,John Theodore Gordon 2Lt kia 19-7-17 IA 40Pathans p278 CR EAfrica38 &CR Tanzania1

HUMPHREYS,Laurence Olsen T2Lt dow 13-11-15 7RLancs p59 CR France98

HUMPHREYS,Noel Forbes.MC.MID TCapt dow 27-3-18 10TankCps p188 CR France40

HUMPHREYS,Percy Lloyd TCapt kia 31-7-17 15WelshR p127 CR Belgium66

HUMPHREYS,Richard Grain 2Lt kia 28-9-17 13KRRC p150 MR30

HUMPHREYS,Roy Lt kia 4-9-18 RASC p193 MR30

HUMPHREYS,Spencer Noel.MC.2Lt kia 10-2-17 116RFA p30 MR37

HUMPHREYS,Stanley Howard 2Lt kia 20-11-17 4 att7ESurr p112 MR17

HUMPHREYS,Victor Richard 2Lt kia 24-9-16 2RBerks p139 CR France423

HUMPHREYS,William George 2Lt kia 9-9-16 2RSuss p119 MR21

HUMPHREYS,William Thomas LtCapt&QM kia 4-10-18 3RFus p68 CR France234

HUMPHREYS-JONES,Shon Theodore Lt kia 14-11-17 RFA 86ArmyBde p30 MR30

HUMPHRIES,Cecil Frederick George.DSO.MC&Bar.DCM.TCaptALtCol dow 22-8-18 1DCLI att1Norf p114 CR France281,kia

HUMPHRIES,Leslie Glendower T2Lt kia 16-9-17 GL &4RFC p9 CR Belgium112

HUMPHRIES,Thomas T2Lt kia 1-7-16 15WYorks p82 MR21

HUMPHRIES,Walter Rawleigh T2Lt kia 27-7-16 18WYorks p82 CR France631

HUMPHRISS,Edward Victor 2Lt kia 11-4-17 NhamptYeo p204 MR20

HUMPHRY,Laurence Maj ded 5-2-20 RAMC p270 CR Camb2,LtCol

HUMPHRYS,Edward Thomas TCapt ded 3-5-16 2ScotRif GarrBn p103 MR65,BtMaj

HUMPHRYS,Leslie Palmer 2Lt dow 13-12-16 1HAC p206 CR France40

HUMPHRYS,Stewart Francis.MID T2Lt kia 26-8-16 20 att14RFus p68 CR France389

HUNKIN,William Burrows Clement.MC.TLt kia 3-11-18 14RWFus p98 CR France1478,4-11-18

HUNNYBUN,Gerald Norman.MC.MID TMaj kia 23-10-18 9Yorks p90&258 CR France231

HUNSTON,John Norman T2Lt dow 15-7-16 6Beds p86 CR France515,Lt

HUNSTON,Robert Donald T2Lt kia 28-9-16 10 att7Beds p86 CR France383

HUNSTONE,George Neil T2Lt kia 28-6-17 11RFC p9 CR France120

HUNSTONE,William Henry TMaj ded 18-2-19 GL p266 CR Yorks185

HUNT,Alfred John 2Lt dow 28-11-14 30RFA p30 CR France102

HUNT,Alfred Stanley 2Lt kld 20-8-17 GL &RFC p9 CR Wilts28,FltLt

HUNT,Alfred Thomas Lt ded 31-10-18 RFA p30&261 CR Lond29

HUNT,Arthur George 2Lt kia 4-11-18 IrGds att4GdsMGR p52&53 CR France1080

HUNT,Arthur Warner 2Lt dow 28-4-18 Ess att11Bn p132 CR France142

HUNT,Benjamin Owen T2Lt dow 23-5-17 10WRid p115 CR Belgium11

HUNT,Cecil Edwin Capt mbk 19-12-14 IA 34SikhPnrs p278 CR France705,dow

HUNT,Charles Francis 2LtACapt kia 25-9-15 2RB p179 CR France276

HUNT,Claude Holdsworth TCapt dow 2-4-17 RFA att18CpsHQ p30 CR France120

HUNT,D.A.DSO TCapt dow 30-11-17 SL att1/4KAR p202 MR52

HUNT,Edward Wallace Alleyne.MC.2Lt kia 1-5-17 GL &18RFC p9 CR France243

HUNT,Francis Henry Walter TCapt dow 27-9-15 5KSLI p145 CR Belgium140

HUNT,Frederick Arthur Lt ded 21-11-18 RHA p30 CR Wilts115

HUNT,Frederick Frank 2LtTLt kia 27-6-15 4Lond p246 CR France631

HUNT,Frederick William Capt kia 31-10-14 IA 19Lancers att4Huss p278

HUNT,George Ede 2Lt kld 21-7-18 5YLI &RAF p255 CR Yorks172

HUNT,Geoffrey Albert T2Lt kld 6-9-17 GL &RFC p9 CR Mddx28

HUNT,George Ward Capt kia 9-5-15 2Nhampt p137 MR32

HUNT,Gerald Ponsonby Sneyd.CMG.DSO.MajALtCol kia 23-3-18 1RBerks p139 CR France41

HUNT,Harold Montague 2Lt dow 27-8-18 3 att6EKent p57 CR France119

HUNT,Henry Hope 2Lt kia 26-10-18 10Lond &RAF p248&258

HUNT,James T2Lt kia 16-11-16 10 att8ELancs p111 CR France153

HUNT,James Charles Marjoribanks Lt kia 10-8-16 B47RFA p30 CR France453

HUNT,John Goldsworth TLt dow 11-3-19 RASC p255

HUNT,John Henry Sneyd 2Lt kia 16-9-16 23Lond p252 MR21

HUNT,John Reginald Lilly 2Lt kia 1-7-16 5N&D p232 CR France576

HUNT,John William Reynolds 2Lt kia 28-4-17 11Suff p78 MR20

HUNT,Lawrence Herbert Lt kia 4-12-17 21Lond p251 MR17

HUNT,Louis Gordon 2Lt kia 22-9-18 9Lond p248 CR France369

HUNT,Noel Guy Lt dow 5-4-17 4Berks p234 CR France511

HUNT,Percival George Havelock Lt kia 8-11-17 GL RFA att92TMB p190 CR France184

HUNT,Ralph Leslie T2Lt kia 15-10-16 11Ess p132 MR21

HUNT,Reginald Frank Lt ded 29-5-18 RFA Y8TMB p207 CR France1755,dow

HUNT,Reginald Thomas Headley 2Lt dow 12-4-18 10DLI p161 MR32

HUNT,Robert Lancelot Gibbs TCapt kia 7-10-16 6 O&BLI p130 CR France432

HUNT,Roger Victor Cecil T2Lt dow 1-10-18 B155RFA p31 CR France40

HUNT,Ronald Francis 2Lt kia 25-4-15 3RWar p65 MR29

HUNT,Sidney Herman 2Lt kia 22-8-17 19Lond p250 MR29

HUNT,Sidney William T2Lt kia 26-10-16 12 att13Ess p132 CR France643

HUNT,T.H.Maj 29-4-18 RAMC CR Yorks619

HUNT,William George Philip.MC.TCapt dow 15-8-17 10Ess p132 CR France40

HUNT,William Julian T2Lt kia 11-7-16 112MGC p183 MR21

HUNT,William Victor Lt dow 17-10-18 MGC att82RAF p183 CR Belgium20

HUNTER,A.H.Lt&QM 16-2-17 1Dors CR Hamps219

HUNTER,Albert Richmond.MC.Lt ded 11-2-19 23NumbF p61 CR France34

HUNTER,Alexander 2Lt kia 20-11-17 2/5LancF p221 MR21

HUNTER,Alexander Forbes 2Lt kia 23-5-16 21Lond p251 MR20

HUNTER,Alfred James 2Lt kld 6-8-18 1/4Mddx att101RAF p147 CR France29,Lt kia 7-8-18 17Bn

HUNTER,Archibald T2Lt kia 2-7-16 14 att9Ches p96 MR21

HUNTER,Archibald.MC.TMaj ded 10-10-18 5CamH p168 CR Ireland24

HUNTER,Archibald T2Lt kia 7-11-18 9YLI p143 CR France930

HUNTER,Archibald 2Lt ded 15-9-19 KOSB p264 CR Scot746

HUNTER,Archibald Douglas 2Lt kia 23-4-17 9Lond p248 CR France1193

HUNTER,Archibald Smith.MC.Capt dow 29-8-18 1/7A&SH p243 CR France145

HUNTER,Arthur David Capt kia 7-8-15 6Manch p236 CR Gallipoli2,Douglas

HUNTER,Arthur Lawrence T2Lt kia 8-8-18 9RFus p68 MR16

HUNTER,Atholl Gunning Capt kia 22-4-17 IA 32Lancers p278 MR38

HUNTER,Bentley Moore TCapt kia 31-7-17 RAMC att1/1Camb p196 MR29

HUNTER,Charles Gawain Raleigh Lt kia 24-4-15 2YLI p143 MR29

HUNTER,Charles James TLtACapt ded 4-11-18 LabCps p189 CR Lond14,4-11-19 Ex Beds

HUNTER,D.F.Capt 29-3-20 RAMC CR Ches182

HUNTER,David Maj ded SRussia 18-10-19 SL p268 CR Asia81

HUNTER,Douglas William.DSO.TCapt kia 25-3-18 RAMC att10WYorks p196 MR20

HUNTER,Eric Hamilton.MID 2Lt kia 7-8-15 IARO att1/5GurkhaRif p278 CR Gallipoli17

HUNTER,Frederick Lt ded 9-12-19 SL RE attIWT p268 CR Wales564

HUNTER,George Arnold Lt ded 3-8-17 ScotHorse att265MGC Inf p187&205 CR Egypt7

HUNTER,George Edward Capt kia 26-4-15 6NumbF p213 MR29

HUNTER,George Frederick Gordon Lt 9-2-19 EAfrMilLabCps CR Scot308

HUNTER,George Stuart.MC.TLt dow 10-11-18 RASC att13RB p193&258 CR France658

HUNTER,Godfrey Jackson 2Lt kld 26-4-16 5Lancers p22 CR Ireland14

HUNTER,Harry T2Lt dow 5-11-17 GL &RFC p9 CR France64

HUNTER,Herbert 2Lt kia 26-4-18 1/4RLancs p213 CR France106

HUNTER,Herbert.MC.Lt dow 23-10-18 1EKent p57 CR France924,Capt 6Bn

HUNTER,Hope Capt ded 3-12-17 14Lond p249 CR Egypt2 2LondScot

HUNTER,Howard Tomlin Capt kia 27-4-15 6NumbF p213 MR29,26-4-15

HUNTER,Hugh Michael Lt dow 6-4-15 3 att2Wilts p153

HUNTER,Hugh Swinterton Forsyth T2Lt kia 29-4-16 1KOSB p102 CR France35

HUNTER,Jack Lt&QM drd 27-5-17 NottsYeo p205 MR41,27-5-18

HUNTER,James Cecil 2Lt dow 2-9-18 5Lond p246 CR France833

HUNTER,James Gladstone 2Lt kia 14-3-17 4RScots att1/5SStaffs p211 CR France281

HUNTER,James Kenneth Lt kia 6-9-17 RE 427FC p210 CR Belgium125

HUNTER,James MacMillan T2Lt kia 17-10-18 KRRC att2Bn p150 CR France341

HUNTER,James Whitaker T2Lt dow 9-7-16 5Nhampt p137 CR France23,8-7-16

HUNTER,James Williamson 2Lt dow 14-11-16 2RScots p54 CR France74

HUNTER,John Maurice T2Lt kia 2-7-16 6Wilts p153 CR France267

HUNTER,Johnston Shaw Kirker 2Lt kia 30-6-16 D/157RFA p31 CR France631

HUNTER,Leslie Aubrey William Lt ded 3-11-18 4SfthH p255 CR Norf209

HUNTER,Leslie Whitaker Lt kia 14-8-16 4 O&BLI p231 CR France832,13-8-16

HUNTER,Martin Lt dow 11-4-18 9Lancers p22 CR France64

HUNTER,Melville Adrian Cecil 2Lt dow 15-11-15 4HLI att7SStaffs p163 CR Gallipoli27

HUNTER,Nigel Duncan Ratcliffe.MC&Bar.Capt kia 26-3-18 RE 228FC p46 CR France560

HUNTER,Norman Archbold T2Lt kia 3-9-17 26NumbF p61 CR France1461

HUNTER,Norman Frederick Lt dow 16-6-15 4RWar att4RFus p65 MR29

HUNTER,Patrick Colin T2Lt dow 16-10-17 2NStaffs attRFC p9 CR Greece1

HUNTER,Percy Talbot Langley Lt ded 19-7-16 1/14Lond p249 CR

France40,Lungley 2Lt

HUNTER,Peter T2Lt kia 17-4-16 RE 251TC p46 CR France163

HUNTER,Philip Needham Chap4Cl ded 14-3-19 RAChDept p268 CR Kent180

HUNTER,Richard Jocelyn Capt dow 25-8-18 5 att21Lond p246 CR France141

HUNTER,Robert Lt kia 5-6-17 RFA p207 CR Belgium127

HUNTER,Robert Gibson Lt kia 23-4-17 7A&SH A'Coy p243 CR France545

HUNTER,Ronald Gordon 2Lt dow PoW 25-4-18 1RDubF p177 CR Germany4

HUNTER,Thomas Lt kia 16-7-17 RE 474FC p210 CR Belgium36

HUNTER,Thomas Murray Capt ded 22-5-16 5SfthH p270 CR Scot975

HUNTER,Thomas Vicars Capt kia 5-12-17 RB &66RFC p179&9 CR Italy45

HUNTER,Thomas William.MC.Lt dow 24-10-18 113/25RH&FA p31 CR France1266

HUNTER,Wilfred Cleaver 2Lt kia 29-12-15 RGA 121HB p40 CR Belgium35

HUNTER,William 2Lt dow 10-10-16 10Ches p96 CR France44,Lt kia

HUNTER,William Alexander Dobson Lt kia 1-10-18 3 att8BlkW p128 CR Belgium157

HUNTER,William John Kenny T2Lt ded 26-10-17 3HLI p163 CR Scot235

HUNTER,William Mortimer 2Lt kia 29-6-17 4RInniskF p105 CR Belgium23

HUNTER,William Samuel T2Lt ded 1-2-16 9RWKent p141 CR Wilts142,Wallace

HUNTER,William Scott T2Lt kia 1-8-17 10ScotRif p103 MR29

HUNTER,William Stuart T2Lt kia 31-7-17 8Lincs p75 MR29

HUNTER-BLAIR,Alister 2Lt kia 9-5-15 CamH p255 MR22

HUNTINGTON,George Waldeof 2Lt kia 24-7-16 8 att6KRRC p150 MR21,24-8-16 6 att8Bn

HUNTINGTON,John.MC.Lt dow 12-8-18 5BordR p228 CR France29

HUNTINGTON,Nigel Jocelin Searanche Lt kia 17-11-14 Lincs p75 MR22

HUNTLEY,Edward Kenneth 2Lt kia 20-9-17 3 att6 O&BLI attRB p130 CR Belgium126,HUNTLY

HUNTLEY,John Fenwirk TLt kia 9-4-17 25NumbF B'Coy p61 CR France265,Capt

HUNTLY,Louis Francis 2Lt kia 26-4-17 1GordH p166 MR20

HUNTON,Frederick Capt kia 4-5-17 RAMC p253 CR Palestine2

HUNTRISS,Cyril John.MC.MID TCapt kia 1-7-16 1EYorks p84 MR21

HUNTRISS,Harold Edward Capt kia 17-5-15 2Beds p86 CR France279

HUNTRISS,William TLt ded 23-10-18 9WRid attWAFF p201&115 CR WAfrica3

HUNTSMAN,Benjamin Canning Capt kia 7-4-17 2/8N&D p233 MR21

HUNWICK,Edward Noel T2Lt kia 30-8-18 1/2ELancs p111 CR France307

HURD,Angier Percy Lt kia 30-3-18 1Herts p252 CR France425

HURD,Douglas William Capt dow 17-9-16 7Mddx p235 CR France329

HURD-WOOD,John Grahame TCapt kia 4-8-16 GL 68InfBdeHQ p190 CR France430

HURDMAN,Cyril 2Lt kia 19-7-16 3SStaffs att2/6RWar p122 MR32

HURLBATT,Edgar Simon.MC.Maj kia 27-3-18 7 att2/8Manch p237 MR27,Simm LtCol

HURLBUTT,Percivald.MC.HonCapt ded 8-6-18 7RWFus p223 CR Wales637

HURRELL,Colin John Richard Capt kia 2-11-17 10Lond p248 CR Palestine8

HURST,Aubrey Clive 2Lt dow 22-1-18 39RFC p16 CR Belgium18

HURST,Charles Ernest T2Lt kia 14-9-16 11 att6Yorks p90 CR France293

HURST,Henry Cubbin T2Lt kia 28-9-16 6Yorks p90 MR21

HURST,Herbert William 2Lt dow 10-10-17 C295RFA p31 CR France40

HURST,John Julius Lt kia 31-10-17 2/22Lond p251 CR Palestine1,Jules

HURST,Richard Henry 2Lt kia 29-9-18 9Lpool att12Norf p216 CR Belgium451

HURST,Sydney Bailey 2Lt kia 26-8-18 5RScotF p222 CR France1185

HURSTBOURNE,Walter Hirsch 2Lt kia 23-6-17 4WessexRFA p208 CR Belgium152

HURST-BROWN,Cecil 2Lt dow 26-9-15 2 O&BLI p130 CR France80,25-9-15

HURST-BROWN,Dudley 2Lt dow 15-6-15 129/30RFA p31 CR Belgium28

HURT,Seymour Frederick Aukland Albert Capt kia 18-10-14 RScotF p94 MR22

HURWORTH,Charles Reginald Lt kia 26-3-18 5Yorks p220 MR27

HUSBAND,Donald Irons 2Lt kia 16-8-16 4A&SH p173 CR France515

HUSBAND,George Staunton.DSO.Capt ded 21-2-17 IA IMS p278 MR61

HUSBAND,Joseph Sim.MIDx2 TLtAMaj dow 11-4-18 C59MGC p183 CR France262

HUSBAND,Kenneth D'Ombrian 2Lt kia 28-3-18 2Wilts p153 MR27,D'Ombrain

HUSBAND,Peter,Ross T2Lt kia 25-9-16 1BlkW p128 MR21

HUSBAND,William T2Lt dow 25-6-18 NumbF att15DLI p61 CR Derby76

HUSEY,Ralph Hamer.DSO&Bar.MC.MIDx4 BrigGen dow PoW 30-5-18 5Lond Cmdg25InfBde p246 CR France1329

HUSK,Frederick John.MID 2Lt dow 21-3-18 RGA 301SB p40 MR27

HUSKINSON,Frederick John Capt kia 1-7-16 RInniskF p105 MR21

HUSKISSON,Claude Alexander 2Lt kia 15-6-17 6 att1Hamps &TMB p229 CR France546

HUSKISSON,Herbert George 2Lt dow 27-1-17 6Hamps p229 CR Iraq5

HUSSEY,Charles Francis T2Lt kia 5-10-18 Glouc att1/5th p107 CR France375

HUSSEY,Edmund Dobson 2Lt kia 9-4-18 Mddx att21Bn p147 MR32

HUSSEY,Edmund Thornber 2Lt kia 7-6-17 1RMunstF p175 CR Belgium155

HUSSEY,Frank.MM.2Lt kia 4-10-17 8RWar A'Coy p215 MR30

HUSSEY,Frank William Lt kia 24-9-18 4Leic p219 CR France375

HUSSEY,Harold Edward T2Lt kia 25-3-17 3Dev att1Manch p76 MR38

HUSSEY,Hubert Murray.MC.2Lt kia 6-8-18 2 att1/6SStaffs p122 CR France98

HUSSEY,Michael Edward 2Lt 4-9-15 att81Pars MR67

HUSTON,William TCapt kld 6-12-17 RAVC attRASC 37DivTrn p198 CR France285

HUTCHEON,Samuel Wyness T2Lt dow 4-9-16 11 att12HLI p163 CR France40

HUTCHEON,Thomas T2Lt dow 12-8-16 7RScotF p94 CR France23,13-8-16

HUTCHESON,Andrew Guy.MC.TCapt&Adjt kia 14-7-16 9ScotRif p103&258 CR France399

HUTCHESON,Gordon James Lt ded 27-5-18 GL &RAF p190 CR France102

HUTCHESON,James McLeod T2Lt kia 21-9-17 12ESurr p112 MR30

HUTCHESON,John T2Lt kia 8-9-15 10N&D p233 CR Belgium112

HUTCHESON,Norman Heber Lt kia 12-3-15 RIrRif p169 MR22

HUTCHINGS,Edgar John 2Lt ded 9-11-15 10Lond p248 CR Europe1,dow

HUTCHINGS,Kenneth Lotherington Lt kia 3-9-16 4 att12Lpool p72 MR21

HUTCHINGS,Thomas Clifton TCapt dow 19-7-17 1LancF p92 CR Belgium16

HUTCHINS,Alfred John Avalon T2Lt dow PoW 22-3-18 2RSuss p119 CR Belgium140

HUTCHINS,C.F.MM.2Lt 15-1-19 RGA CR Glouc176

HUTCHINS,Cedric Page TLt kia 14-11-17 SL att1/3KAR p202 CR EAfrica11 &CR Tanzania1

HUTCHINS,Douglas Markham 2Lt dow 2-8-16 5Mddx att1/4 O&BLI p147 CR France167

HUTCHINS,Frederick Charles T2Lt kia 22-4-18 13RWFus p98 MR27

HUTCHINS,Ralph 2Lt ded 3-6-16 8Mddx p236 CR Surrey78

HUTCHINS,Richard Capt ded 13-5-15 4RMunstF p175 CR Eire48

HUTCHINSON,Albert T2Lt kia 8-10-18 att2Y&L p159 MR16

HUTCHINSON,Ambrose Lt kia 19-1-18 6Lpool attRFC p18&215 CR Belgium132

HUTCHINSON,Andrew Levy Lt kia 21-3-18 7RSots att31MGC p211&187,Hutchison MR20

HUTCHINSON,Anthony Christopher Campbell TMaj ded 18-11-18 30MGC p183 CR Surrey1,Clark

HUTCHINSON,Arthur George T2Lt dow 10-3-18 1/2SStaffs att1/4Ches p122 CRPalestine3

HUTCHINSON,Arthur Norman 2Lt kia 21-3-18 7Worc p226 MR37

HUTCHINSON,Basil Stewart Cayley Lt kia 20-9-14 EYorks p84 MR15

HUTCHINSON,Benjamin.MC.2Lt kia 3-5-17 11EYorks p84 MR20

HUTCHINSON,Bert 2Lt dow 12-8-18 3 att15LancF p92 CR France145,3 att5Bn

HUTCHINSON,Cecil Dunbar TLt dow PoW 12-8-17 7SStaffs &57RFC p9&122 CR Belgium140

HUTCHINSON,Cecil Leigh 2Lt kia 31-7-17 3 att2ELancs p111 MR29

HUTCHINSON,Edgar Francis 2Lt dow 24-5-15 4Yorks p220 CR Belgium165

HUTCHINSON,Edwin Octavius.MID TLt dow 21-9-18 RE 78FC p46 CR France906

HUTCHINSON,George Hanley Lt kia 2-3-16 4Yorks Y'Coy p220 CR Belgium5

HUTCHINSON,George Russell 2Lt kia 26-11-17 2/8WYorks p219 MR17

HUTCHINSON,Hanley Lt dow 1-9-17 2/5WYorks p218 CR France512

HUTCHINSON,Harry T2Lt kia 30-9-18 9 att3YLI p143 CR France375,att2Bn

HUTCHINSON,Henry William T2Lt kia 13-3-17 2/4Leic p87 CR France1472

HUTCHINSON,Herbert 2Lt kia 27-9-18 1 att3Beds p86 MR16

HUTCHINSON,Hugh Maxwell T2Lt dow 29-11-17 26NumbF p61 CR France214,HUTCHISON

HUTCHINSON,Ivan 2Lt kia 22-8-18 5EYorks p219 CR France514,Lt

HUTCHINSON,Jack Clifforde Lt kia 22-3-18 6ESurr p226 MR20,att4Leic

HUTCHINSON,James Gwynne Lt kia 10-11-17 246RFA p207 CR Belgium10

HUTCHINSON,James Walter LtTCapt dow 25-9-15 2Beds p86 MR19

HUTCHINSON,John Cayley Lt kia 5-8-15 IA 3 att1/3GurkhaRif p278 CR France1157

HUTCHINSON,John Summerscales Capt kia 3-9-14 2SLancs p125 CR France206,26-8-14

HUTCHINSON,Leslie Gwynne TLt kia 10-9-18 10EYorks p84 CR France297

HUTCHINSON,Peter 2Lt kia 11-9-18 4LNLancs p234 CR France1496

HUTCHINSON,Tom 2Lt kia 18-9-18 YLI att9Bn p143 CR France407

HUTCHINSON,Tom Macintosh T2Lt kia 13-11-16 13EYorks p84 CR France802

HUTCHINSON,William 2Lt kia 22-11-17 5 att2/8WYorks p218 MR17

HUTCHINSON,William John T2Lt kia 25-5-17 88MGC Inf p183 CR France311

HUTCHINSON,William Stanhope.MC&Bar.T2LtACapt dow 8-9-18 12/13NumbF B'Coy p61 CR France41

HUTCHINSON,W.J 2Lt 24-1-17 WRid attWIndR CR SAfrica171

HUTCHISON,Andrew Levy Lt kia 21-3-18 7RScots attMGC p187&211,HUTCHINSON

HUTCHISON,David Fancourt.MID 2LtACapt kia 29-8-18 3 att2YLI p143 CR France327

HUTCHISON,Donald Herbert 2Lt kia 9/10-8-15 16Lond p250 CR Belgium112,10-8-15

HUTCHISON,Edward TMaj kia 1-7-16 17HLI p163 CR France296

HUTCHISON,Innes Owen.MID T2Lt kia 7-1-16 2BlkW p128 MR38,Capt

HUTCHISON,James T2Lt kia 26-7-16 27Manch p155 CR France513

HUTCHISON,John McMaster TLt kia 22-10-16 9GordH p166 CR France239

HUTCHISON,John William 2Lt dow 26-11-17 1/8RScots p212 CR Palestine3

HUTCHISON,Robert Hamilton TLt kia 13-10-15 8 att1BlkW p128 MR19

HUTCHISON,Seton Marshall TLtACapt ded 8-1-18 Hamps att2WIndR p121

HUTCHISON,Thomas T2Lt kia 20-5-16 10/11HLI p163 CR France423,21-5-16

HUTCHISON,Thomas Walter Capt dedacc 22-11-15 10RScots p212 CR Scot725

HUTCHISON,William Murray.MC.MID Capt dow 27-4-16 1Lpool p72 CR France32

HUTCHISON,William Ramsay TCapt kia 22-3-18 6/7RScotF p94 MR20

HUTH,Austin Henry Capt kia 20-4-15 4ESurr p112 MR29,1Bn

HUTLEY,Horace Abrey 2Lt kia 2-4-18 7WRid p228 CR France298,12-4-18

HUTSON,Douglas Bertram Lt ded 23-7-18 RASC p193 CR Lond28

HUTSON,Harold T2Lt dow 26-3-18 10 att9YLI p143 CR France364

HUTSON,Harry Austen Capt kia 28-5-18 GL attLancF p190 MR18

HUTSON,William Cecil 2Lt kia 21-3-18 C51RFA p31 MR27

HUTT,Ernest Reginald 2Lt kia 25-9-15 6RScotF p94 MR19

HUTT,Francis Rodes TCapt kia 25-9-15 7KOSB C'Coy p102 CR France219

HUTT,Harold Vernon 2Lt kia 26-1-15 2RSuss p119 CR France720

HUTT,Walter Beresford 2Lt dow 29-9-18 RGA 527SB p40 CR France113

HUTTON,Alexander TCapt kia 8-7-16 2HLI A'Coy p163 CR France924

HUTTON,Andrew Donald TCapt kia 3-7-16 15HLI p163 CR France296

HUTTON,Frederick Robert Hughes Lt kia 12-5-15 9A&SH p244 MR29,10-5-15

HUTTON,George Adolph Lt drd 19-9-14 RE 3SigCoy p46 CR France1110

HUTTON John Barnabas Lt kia 13-10-15 5SStaffs p229 MR19

HUTTON,Lorne de Hutton T2Lt kia 24-3-18 41MGC Inf p183 CR France518

HUTTON,Richard 2Lt kia 7-11-14 3Leic att2RWar p87 MR29

HUTTON,Robert Capt kia 22-8-17 ScotHorse p205 MR30

HUTTON,Stanley Fell T2Lt kia 9-11-18 12Yorks p90 MR32,11-4-18

HUTTON,Walter Forbes T2Lt kia 14-7-16 8 att11BlkW p128 MR21,11 att8Bn

HUTTON,William Wallace 2Lt kia 28-10-17 7Lond attRFC p18&247 MR20

HUTTON-BALFOUR,Archibald Gibson T2Lt dow 22-3-18 3 att6KOSB p102 CR France511

HUTTON-SQUIRE,Robert Henry Edmund.DSO.MID Maj dow 8-4-17 RGA att85RFA p40 CR France12

HUXLEY,John Scott T2Lt kia 16-7-16 100MGC p183 MR21,15-7-16

HUXLEY,Joseph T2Lt kia 22-4-18 10 att14RWFus p98 CR France296

HUXLEY,Robert Charles 2Lt kia 7-5-18 8RWar p215 MR19

HUXTABLE,Geoffrey.MBE.2Lt 10-12-18 MilLabCps CR EAfrica36

HUYTON John 2Lt kia 28-5-17 4N&D att51TMB p134 CR France544

HYAMS,Alec Hallenstein Lt kia 3-5-15 9 att3RFus p68 MR29

HYATT,Valentine 2Lt kia 24-3-18 RFC p16 MR20

HYATT,William Joseph Lt mbk 24-10-18 4LabCps att9Dev p256&189,kia MR16

HYDE,Arthur Clarendon Maj kia 22-11-15 O&BLI p130 MR38

HYDE,Charles Stuart T2Lt kia 1-7-16 16WYorks p82 MR21

HYDE,Cyril 2Lt kia 1-12-17 RGA &35RFC p9&40 MR20

HYDE,Eustace Emil Lt kia 12-10-16 4 att1RIrF p171 CR France744

HYDE,Francis Cecil Lt kia 9-4-17 1RWKent p141 CR France523

HYDE,Gilbert Arthur T2Lt kia 4-10-17 YLI att9Bn p143 MR30

HYDE,Herbert Walter T2Lt dow 20-5-16 16RWar p65 CR France1182,kia

HYDE,Herbert William 2Lt kia 17-5-15 RSuss att2RInniskF p119 MR22

HYDE James Charles 2Lt kia 1-7-16 1/5N&D p232 MR21

HYDE,Leslie Arthur 2Lt ded 26-10-15 RHA p31 CR Eire356

HYDE,Patrick George Maj ded 2-3-15 RAMC p267 CR Hamps1

HYDE,Percival G.Lt ded 15-11-18 GL attIWT Ret p266

HYDE,William Frederick T2Lt kia 8-11-18 10RWar att2Lincs p65 CR France965

HYDE,William Nelson Capt&QM dow 16-10-16 2RWar p65 CR France264

HYDE,William Sisson 2Lt dow 7-11-18 5Lincs p220 CR France658

HYDER,Alfred William T2Lt kia 2-9-18 15ACycCps p181 CR France285

HYETT,Frank 2Lt kia 30-11-17 RGA 52HAG p40 CR France245

HYLAND,Albert Clive LtTCapt dow 10-8-18 RASC att6EKent p193 CR France69

HYLAND,Frederick Hunter 2Lt kia 23-5-15 Yorks &RFC p1&90 CR France350

HYLAND,Herbert Bright T2Lt kia 19-7-16 100MGC p183 MR21

HYMAN,Ezra Herbert 2Lt dow 1-11-18 3Glouc att11SLancs p107 CR France528

HYMAN,Robert Leslie T2Lt kia 23-8-17 6DCLI p114 MR30

HYMAN,Walter William 2Lt kia 1-7-16 26NumbF p61 MR21

HYNE,Charles Godfrey Haggas Cutcliffe Lt dow 21-11-16 2IrGds attTMB p52 CR Yorks482

HYNES,Ernest Stanley Patrick 2Lt kia 10-11-16 EKent &25RFC p3&57 CR France88,Lt

HYNDMAN,James Valentine TCapt dow 7-7-16 14RlrRif p169 CR France64

HYRONS,Francis Austin T2Lt kia 13-9-16 13 att2N&D p134 MR21

HYSLOP,James.MM.Lt kia 5-11-18 14Lond p249 CR France1142

HYSLOP,James T2Lt ded 15-2-19 RE p255 CR Scot510

HYSLOP,John Wallet 2Lt kia 26-10-17 3 att2GordH p166&257 MR30

HYSLOP,Ninian Steele T2Lt kld 30-10-17 RFC p9 CR Iraq6

HYSLOP,Thomas Anderson.MC.T2Lt kia 22-3-18 10 att4Yorks p90 MR27

HYSLOP,William Douglas T2Lt dow 25-3-18 8BlkW p128 CR France62

HYTTEN,Edwin Christopher 2Lt kia 12-11-15 8Hamps p229 CR Belgium182,12-11-16 11Bn

--------------------- **I** ---------------------

I'ANSON,John Francis Capt kia 20-9-14 3WYorks p82 MR15

I'ANSON,Leonard Percy Lt kia 25-4-15 4Yorks p220 MR29

IBBERSON,Henry Joseph 2Lt kia 5-10-17 220MGC Inf p183 CR Belgium308

IBBITSON,William Beveridge T2Lt kia 1-7-16 10WYorks p82 CR France373,Lt

IBBOTSON,Arnold Lt kia 13-10-18 1/4Y&L p238 CR France316

IBBOTSON,Edwin.MC.2Lt kia 11-4-17 10LNLancs p136 MR20

IBBOTSON,George Sharples 2Lt kia 14-5-18 5LNLancs p23 MR19

IBBOTSON,Roskell Lt kia 2-5-17 4 att2RlrF p171 CR Greece3 Ross

IBBOTSON,Robert 2Lt kia 28-4-17 5 att13Ess p232 MR20

IBBOTSON,Tom T2Lt kia 25-9-16 7Leic p87 CR France402

IBBS,John Thomas 2Lt dow 20-3-17 7Worc p226 CR France164

IDDON,Harold 2Lt dow 23-8-18 D173RFA p31 CR Lancs114

IDE,Thomas Norman 2Lt kia 2-7-16 2Ess p132 CR France643

IDESON,Joseph Henry T2Lt kld 13-3-17 N&D &RFC 12TrainingBn p134&9 CR Yorks438

IDLE,Wilfrid Ernest 2Lt kia 25-2-17 26RFus att17Lond p250 CR Belgium102,Wilfred 24-2-17

IEVERS,Oliver Goldsmith LtCol ded 12-2-16 SL IA Censor p268 CR Eire406

IKIN,Alfred Edward T2Lt kia 11-3-18 GL att93RFC p16 CR France88

ILBERY,Oscar Reginald 2Lt kia 1-7-16 2YLI p143 CR France1890

ILES,Charles Cochrane Lt dow 19-12-14 RAMC att2ELancs p196 CR France768

ILES,John Francis TLt kia 2-6-17 B165RFA p31 CR France644

ILES,John Owen Lt kia 25-9-15 1SStaffs att1RWFus p122 MR19

ILES,Percy Henry 2Lt kia 11-4-17 16 att1RWar p65 MR20

ILIEVE,William Arthur 2Lt kia 9-10-17 Ess att2Bn p132 CR Belgium126

ILIFF,Frederick John 2Lt kia 13-10-15 1/6SStaffs p229 MR19

ILIFFE,Thomas Dealtrey T2Lt kia 10-9-18 1 att2YLI p143 CR France672,Dealtry

ILLING,Francis 2Lt dow 8-5-18 5 att13RFus p68 CR France84

ILLINGWORTH,Frank T2Lt kia 15-12-16 2EYorks p84 CR Greece3

ILLINGWORTH,Fred Donald Roberts TLt kia 23-4-17 1Beds p86 MR20

ILLINGWORTH,Frederick William Lt ded 6-2-19 4ScotRif &RAF p264

ILLINGWORTH,Guy Russell ACapt ded 21-1-21 IA 1/91Punjabis p278 MR65

ILLINGWORTH,Harold Locke 2Lt kia 23-3-18 17Lond p250 MR20

ILLINGWORTH,John.MC.Lt dow 3-6-18 8WYorks p219 CR Belgium188,1/6Bn

ILSLEY,Alfred Lewis T2Lt ded 23-11-17 ELancs p111 CR Berks27

IMBER,William Arthur 2Lt kia 27-8-17 7RWar p214 MR30

IMPEY,John Eugene Lt kia 27-3-16 1Lincs attMGC p75&183 MR29

IMRIE,Arthur Leslie 2Lt kia 30-11-17 D275RFA p208 MR17

IMRIE,Daniel McLachlan 2Lt dow 16-11-17 GlasgowYeo p203 CR Belgium18

INCE,Hugh Ethelred McCarthy.MID LtAMaj kia 4-11-16 52/2RFA p31 CR France374

INCE,William Campbell Lt kia 2-6-16 8CanadaMGC CR Belgium106

INCH,George Edward 2Lt kia 22-9-17 1/2 att6Beds p86 MR30

INCH,John 2Lt kia 20-6-16 1/9 att1/8A&SH p244 CR France15

INCH,Robert Stuart Mark.MC.TLt kia 22-10-17 8Norf p74 MR30

INCHBALD,John Chantry Elliot.MID TLtACapt kia 2-4-17 9Dev p76 CR France568,Chantrey

INCHBOLD,Gerald Lt kia 31-5-17 4N&D &55RFC p9&134 CR France134

INCHES,Robert Kirk.DFC.2Lt kia 26-8-18 RE &RAF p46

INCHLEY,William Lt kia 19-12-15 3 att9WRid p115 CR Belgium84

IND,William Ernest.MC.Capt&Adjt dow 7-6-17 15Lond p249 CR Belgium11

INESON,James Walker T2Lt kia 18-5-17 18DLI p161 CR France644,19-5-17

INGERSOLL,James Hamilton 2Lt kia 29-9-16 2Lincs p8&75 CR France251

INGESTRE,Charles John Alton Chetwynd.Viscount.MVO.Capt ded 8-1-15 RHGds p20 CR Staffs143

INGHAM,Alan T2Lt kia 14-3-17 32Manch p155 CR France576,22Bn

INGHAM,Clarence 2Lt kia 21-8-18 RGA 65SB p40 CR France1182

INGHAM,Claud Mary Leo 2Lt kia 19-11-16 4ConnRgrs att9InniskF p172 CR Belgium100

INGHAM,Horace.MC.TLtAMaj kia 24-4-18 2WYorks p82 MR27

INGHAM,Major T2Lt kia 13-4-18 WYorks att1/7Bn p82 MR30

INGHAM,Robert John Fitzgerald.DSO.MajALtCol dow 1-7-17 RGA 58HAG HQ p40 CR Belgium11

INGLE,Aubrey Charles Bertram CaptHonMaj ded 8-1-17 4HLI attScotRif p163 MR65

INGLE,Roland George T2Lt kia 1-7-16 Lincs p75 CR France515

INGLEBY,Norman Ward.MID Capt kia 27-5-18 4EYorks p219 CR France1329

INGLES,Alexander Wighton Maj kia20-9-14 1WYorks p82 MR15

INGLES,Robert Adam 2Lt kia 21-3-18 16RScots p54 MR20

INGLESANT,Thomas George 2Lt kia 20-8-16 7N&D p233 CR France504

INGLETON,Hubert John Lt dow 2-11-18 4 att1/8LancF p92 CR France146

INGLIS,Alexander TLt kia 11-4-17 8GordH p166 CR France531

INGLIS,Alexander Alves 2Lt kia 26-9-16 RE att126FC p46 MR21

INGLIS,Arthur McCulloch.DSO.TMaj ded 12-5-19 Glouc p255 CR Glouc32

INGLIS,Charles North Dalrymple Lt kia 25-9-15 IARO att2/8GurkhaRif p278 MR28

INGLIS,David Capt kia 19-2-14 IA 1/4GurkhaRif p278 MR28

INGLIS,Douglas Ian 2Lt kia 7-2-17 3RDubF p177 CR Belgium17

INGLIS,Henry Montgomery 2Lt kia 13-3-15 6GordH p242 MR22

INGLIS,Herbert McClelland LtCol kia 17-9-17 MedCps CR NZ194

INGLIS,James HonLt&QM ded 28-11-15 GL p190 CR Scot799

INGLIS,James Arthur Chetwynd Lt kia 9-5-15 4HLI attSfthH p163 MR22

INGLIS,James Malcolm T2Lt dow 26-10-18 9RlrF p171 CR France34

INGLIS,James Normand.MC.Capt kia 22-4-16 BlkW p128 CR Iraq5

INGLIS,John Alfred Pigon Lt kia 26-9-15 RE p46 CR France554

INGLIS,Maurice Paterson TCapt kia 17-9-16 RAMC att1/5BordR p195 CR France453

INGLIS,Robert.MC.Lt dow 5-10-18 13BlkW p205 CR France194

INGLIS,Robert Anderson T2Lt kia 21-9-17 GL &19RFC p9 CR France705,ANDERSSON Lt

INGLIS,Rupert Charles Lt dow 29-6-15 3SWBord p100 MR4

INGLIS,Rupert Edward Rev kia 18-9-16 RAChDept p199 MR21

INGLIS,Sidney Herbert T2Lt dow 5-6-17 GL &16RFC p9 CR France12

INGLIS,William Logan 2Lt kia 2-10-17 4RScotF attRFC p18&222 CR Belgium383,Lt

INGLIS,William Wiley TLt kia 20-11-17 11DLI p161 CR France379

INGLIS,William Raymond Col ded 30-3-16 33RFus p68 CR Essex258

INGOLDBY,Roger Hugh.MID T2Lt kia 1-7-16 2RDubF p177 CR France744

INGOUVILLE-WILLIAMS,Edward Charles.CB.DSO.MajGen kia 22-7-16 Commdg34Div p1 CR France44

INGPEN,Norman Cecil TCaptAMaj dow 4-12-17 175MGC Inf p183 CR France446

INGRAM,Arthur Charles LtACapt kia 26-3-18 4Beds att4ELancs p86 MR20

INGRAM,Arthur Herbert Lt kia 6-9-18 Glouc att8Bn p107 MR19

INGRAM,Edgar Charles 2Lt kia 27-3-18 RWar att7Norf p65 MR27

INGRAM,Edith A.Nurse 13/14-8-18 VAD 55GH p200 CR France34,14-8-18

INGRAM,Eric Talbot Allan.MC.Lt kia 4-11-18 2RInniskF attX32TMB p105 CR France190

INGRAM,Gerald Sclater Lt kia 21-10-14 RWSurr p56 MR29

INGRAM,Henry John T2Lt dow 22-9-17 RB att16Bn p179 CR Belgium15

INGRAM,John Aldred 2Lt kia 23-4-17 6 att16Manch p237 MR20

INGRAM,Thomas Lewis.DSO.MC.TCapt kia 16-9-16 RAMC att1KSLI p196 CR France374

INGRAM,William Harold Lt kia 4-6-15 8Manch p237 MR4

INGRAM-JOHNSON,Reginald James Theodore 2Lt dow 10-7-15 DLI attELancs p161 CR France297

INGRAMS,Frank Ridley.MC.T2Lt kia 3-9-16 9ESurr p112&258 MR21

INGS,John Walter Lt kia 18-9-18 RE 56FC p46 CR France756

INIGO-JONES,Henry Richmond Lt kia 4-9-14 1ScotsGds p52 MR15,14-9-14

INKPEN,Wilfred T2Lt kia 26-10-17 2BordR p117 MR30

INKSTER,Walter 2Lt kia 25-9-15 4GordH p242 MR29

INMAN,Arthur Walter Patrick Col 17-6-20 RAMC CR Ireland5

INMAN,Desmond Hague TLt kia 17-2-17 RE 80FC p46 CR France314

INMAN,Edwin Lt kia 1-7-16 10Lincs p75 CR France150

INMAN,Leslie Yardley 2Lt dow 5-4-16 3RScots attWilts p54 MR38,6-4-16

INMAN,Richard Hugh TLt kia 28-6-18 11ELancs p111 CR France352

INNES,Albert James Langlands Lt ded 11-3-20 RAMC CR Scot241

INNES,Alexander Berowald Lt kia 16-6-15 1/7GordH p242 CR France727,18-6-15

INNES,Alfred James 2Lt kia 3-5-17 13Lpool p72 MR20

INNES,Donald McLeod 2Lt dow 7-10-18 BlkW att14Bn p128 CR France52,6-10-18

INNES,Edgar Arthur.CMG.LtCol kia 1-7-16 1/8RWar p214 MR21

INNES,Edward Arthur Robert(Jack) Lt d ed 15-7-19 IARO att4Cav p278 MR43

INNES,Frederick Arthur.MC.2Lt kia 3-9-16 4WRid p227 CR France293

INNES,Ian Charles Lt kia 2-11-14 IA 2/2GurkhaRif p278 MR28

INNES,James Brydon Lt kia 20-7-15 4KOSB p223 MR4

INNES,James David T2Lt dow 5-8-17 24NumbF p61 CR France446

INNES,James Stuart d'Anvergne.MC&Bar.Lt kia 5-8-17 189RFA p31 CR Belgium29 34RFA

INNES,John Alfred 9-9-18 BRCS CR France34

INNES,Patrick McLeod 2Lt kia 30-4-17 RGA 111SB p40 CR France268

INNES,Robert Prentice T2Lt kia 21-9-18 1/7RScots p54 CR France1496

INNES,Ronald Stewart T2Lt kia 7-8-15 11Manch p155 MR4

INNES,William Robert Capt kia 13-11-16 6Ches p222 CR France293

INNES-BROWN,Ambrose Robin.CMG.DSO.TMajALtCol kia 10-4-18 5KOSB p102 CR Belgium21

INNES-CROSS,Sydney Maxwell 2Lt kia 27-10-14 RIrRif p169CR France525

INNES-HOPKINS,J.R.Capt 25-5-15 5CanadaInf CR France727

INNOCENT,Edward John TLt kia 3-7-16 9RWKent p141 CR France397

INSKIPP,Douglas T2Lt kia 16-4-17 143MGC p183 CR France669

INSOLE,George Claude Latham.MC.MID LtACapt kia 12-4-18 1WelshGds p53 CR France745

INSTONE,Edwin Lloyd T2Lt dow PoW 4-8-17 SStaffs att7Bn p122 CR Belgium383

INWARDS,Horatio 2Lt kia 15-6-17 2Lond p245 CR France1489

INWOOD,Charles Hawkins T2Lt kia 16-8-17 145MGC Inf p183 MR30

IONIDES,Ambrose Constantine TLt kia 16-10-15 15 att9KRRC p150 MR29

IONIDES,Theodore Alexander 2Lt dow 16-11-16 3 att2 O&BLI p130 CR France203

IPSWICH,William Henry Alfred Fitzroy.Viscount.Lt kldacc 23-4-18 5CldGds attRAF p51 CR Suff173

IRA-SMITH,Herbert William Edwin Capt ded 7-12-20 1/5Beds &RAF CR Asia82

IRELAND,Albert 2Lt dow 9-7-16 D50RFA p31 CR France66

IRELAND,Arthur George T2Lt dow 19-10-17 5ResRofCav att1/1NumbHuss p23 CR Belgium16

IRELAND,Arthur William 2Lt kia 23-11-17 D256RFA p31 CR France711

IRELAND,Cubitt Austen.MC.Lt kia 14-10-17 6 att7Norf p217 MR20

IRELAND,de Courcy Maj ded 28-1-15 IA 36Sikhs p278 CR Asia20

IRELAND,Herbert Victor Lt&QM ded 13-11-18 1BordR attMGC p117&183 CR Yorks1

IRELAND,Herbert Richard Hall.MC.Maj dow 28-3-18 3Leinst att2MunstF p174 CR France145,LtCol

IRELAND,H.F.Lt dow 22-7-17 1/3KAR p202 CR EAfrica38 &CR Tanzania1

IRELAND,James 2Lt ded 24-7-18 RFA p31 CR Ireland33

IRELAND,James Balleny TLt kia 5-5-17 1 att7Glouc p107 MR20,11 att12Bn

IRELAND,James Reginald 2Lt kia 28-10-16 3 att2A&SH p173 MR21

IRELAND,John Balfour 2Lt kia 8-9-16 9BlkW p128 CR France402

IRELAND,John Thomas Craig Chap4Cl drd 4-5-17 RAChDept p199 CR Italy14

IRELAND,Joseph Knowles Capt kia 7-10-16 26RFus p68 MR21

IRELAND,Leslie Woodhouse Cubitt T2Lt kia 12-2-17 Manch p155

IRELAND,Robert Clifford 2Lt dow 7-11-16 133RFA p31 CR France832

IRELAND,Robert Megans.Sir.KBE.CB.CMG.Col ded 3-9-19 APD p268 CR Hamps8,Megaw

IRELAND,Samuel James T2Lt kia 12-10-16 17Lpool p72 MR21

IRELAND,Walter Ernest 2Lt kia 26-3-17 1/6RWFus p223 CR Palestine8

IRELAND,William 2Lt kia 25-9-15 2RSuss p119 CR France219

IRELAND,William Farquhar T2Lt kia 9-4-17 8GordH p166 CR France265

IRISH,Edward 2Lt kia 20-6-15 1/5WYorks p218 CR France566

IRISH,Edwin Charles 2Lt kia 26-12-17 2ELancs p111 MR30

IRLAM,George Arthur 2Lt kia 21-6-17 Manch att2/8Bn p155 CR France258

IRONS,William Morley T2Lt dow 13-4-18 5Y&L p159 CR Belgium11

IRONSIDE,Arthur Douglas 2Lt kia 22-9-17 D295RFA p208 CR Belgium84

IRONSIDE,Harold Allan TMaj ded 15-10-16 96MGC p183 CR France80

IRONSIDE,James Paul T2Lt dow 29-10-17 GL &28RFC p9 CR Belgium18

IRONSIDE,John Gladstone 2Lt ded 17-12-17 5GordH attMGC Inf p242 CR EAfrica11 &CR Tanzania1

IRONSIDE,Oliver Dalton Lt ded 1-4-19 RFA p207 MR65

IRONSIDE,William Stewart.DSO.MC.LtAMaj kia 2-11-18 24RFA p31 CR France717

IRVIN,Thomas William Lt dow 20-5-16 5GordH p242 CR France225

IRVINE,Charles 2Lt kia 24-8-18 4 att2RScots p211 MR16

IRVINE,Charles Knowles TCapt kia 14-8-17 10RB p179 MR29

IRVINE,Charles Wallace T2Lt kia 14-10-18 1RInniskF p105 CR Belgium157

IRVINE,Christopher Theodore Corrie.MID Lt dow 28-6-15 IA 25Punjabis att29InfBde p278 CR Gallipoli3 att69Punjabis

IRVINE,Edward White 2Lt kia 27-3-18 186RFA p31 MR20

IRVINE,Francis Duncan Maj kia 1-5-15 RE p46 MR4

IRVINE,Fred Catterson 2Lt kia 19-5-18 RGA 297SB p40 CR France113

IRVINE,Gerard Byrom Corrie Maj dow 15-5-17 IA 9BhopalInf p278 CR Iraq5

IRVINE,Gerard Foster TCapt dow 24-10-16 1RWar p65 MR21

IRVINE,Harold TLt dow 29-6-15 13Worc attRMunstF p109 MR4

IRVINE,John Laird Gallwey Capt kia 8-7-15 A&SH p173 CR France82

IRVINE,Paget George Capt dow 26-11-15 6Glouc p225 CR France1327

IRVINE,Robert 2Lt kia 1-9-18 12 att7/8RInniskF p105 CR Belgium89

IRVINE,Robert Charles.MID TCaptAMaj ded 10-11-18 RAMC 63FA p196 CR France13

IRVINE,Thomas Walter LtCol drd 26-1-19 IMS MR43

IRVINE,William Henry T2Lt kld 25-10-16 RFC p3 CR Wales119

IRVINE,William Magnus 2Lt kia 22-3-18 NumbF att12RFC p16&61 MR20

IRVINE-WATSON,John 2Lt kia 14-8-17 B110RH&FA p31

IRVING,Alexander AMaj ded 15-2-19 A&SH attCamH p266 CR Surrey160,1SfthH

IRVING,Alfred 2Lt kia 26-10-18 IA 15Sikhs att14 p278 MR38

IRVING,Archibald Denys 2Lt dow 16-9-18 82RFA p31 CR France511

IRVING,Aubrey Gordon Lt kia 10-3-15 RE attRFC 2Wing p1&46 CR France706

IRVING,David Piercy 2Lt kia 30-7-16 3 att2RScotF p94 MR30

IRVING,Ernest T2Lt kia 5-10-17 BordR att2Bn p117 CR Belgium125

IRVING,Herbert Rufus Evelyn.MC.T2Lt kia 31-10-18 1/2 att17LancF p92 CR Belgium143

IRVING,Robert 2Lt kia 2-8-16 2/5RLancs D'Coy p213 CR France630,Richard

IRVING,Thomas Henry 2Lt kia 19-8-16 3Lpool p72 CR France432

IRWIN,Andrew Herbert 2Lt kia 18-4-15 IAUL att8Rajputs p278 MR43

IRWIN,Aubrey Joseph T2Lt kia 3-9-18 2Hamps p121 MR32

IRWIN,Charles Patrick Michael Lt kia 9-9-16 3 att7RIrF p171 CR France402,10-9-16

IRWIN,Eric Conway.MC.Maj dow 19-7-17 IA 20Inf att40Pathans p278 CR EAfrica38 &CR Tanzania1

IRWIN,Frederick T2Lt kia 16-8-17 9RInniskF p105 CR Belgium96

IRWIN,Herbert Quintus Capt kia 26-4-15 1ConnRgrs p172 CR Belgium92

IRWIN,Horace Charles.MM.T2Lt kia 20-7-18 10A&SH att1/4SfthH p173 CR France622

IRWIN,James Ross T2Lt kia 2-9-18 2 att7RIrReg p89 CR Belgium89

IRWIN,Lancelot Bolton Lt ded 11-8-14 IA 52Sikhs p278 MR43

IRWIN,Richard Nynian TLt kia 6-3-17 9Glouc p107 CR Greece6,Nyniau

IRWIN,Thomas Whitmore Crommelin Lt dow 31-10-18 2N&D p134 CR Surrey1

IRWIN,W.H.SNurse 18-11-18 TFNS CR Surrey160

IRWIN,William Hetherton 2Lt dow 12-2-17 7HLI p240 CR France164

IRWIN,William James 2Lt kia 16-8-17 RIrRif att7Bn p169 MR30

ISAAC,Arthur Whitmore 2Lt kia 7-7-16 5Worc p109 MR21

ISAAC,Dudley Charles.MIDx2 TCapt kia 10-4-17 NStaffs att41MGC Inf p183 CR France1185

ISAAC,Frank Philip T2Lt kia 9-8-15 1KSLI p145 MR29

ISAAC,George Duncan ACapt ded 13-12-17 RGA 77HAG HQ p40 CR Belgium84,dow

ISAAC,George Gower Maj ded 31-7-16 RASC p253 CR Lond12

ISAAC,John Edmund Valentine.DSO.Capt kia 9-5-15 2RB p179 CR Belgium96

ISAAC,William Jones 2Lt kia 26-4-16 1/19Lond p250 MR20

ISAACS,Bernard Clifford T2Lt dow 1-8-17 89MGC p183 CR France64

ISAACS,Francis Harold T2Lt kia 30-9-18 1Suff att11RScotF p78 CR France1106

ISAACS,Henry Rowland 2Lt kia 9-4-17 4 att7Suff p217 MR20

ISAACS,Vincent Harcourt 2Lt kia 21-9-18 9RFus p68 CR France369

ISAACSON,Colin de Slutevalle.MC.Capt dow 11-6-17 SL &Staff EAfrUL p190&268 CR EAfrica10 &CR Tanzania1,Stuteville

ISARD,Cyril Bickford Capt kia 15-8-15 10Lond p248 MR4

ISBISTER,Leonard Stanley 2Lt kia 9-9-16 1/12Lond p248 MR21

ISHAM,John Vere 2Lt ded 3-6-16 5DragGds p21 CR France40

ISHERWOOD,Arthur 2Lt kld 8-12-16 6NumbF att149TMB p214 CR France1568

ISHERWOOD,Francis Edmund Bradshaw.MIDx2 LtCol kia 8-5-15 2Y&L Cmdg1Bn p159 MR29 &MR32

ISHERWOOD,H.2Lt 23-10-18 RAF &LNLancs CR Lancs257

ISHERWOOD,Norman Lt kia 6-9-17 1/6LancF p221 CR Belgium125

157

ISHERWOOD,Norman George T2Lt kia 8-10-15 RE 174TC p46 CR France637
ISHERWOOD,Samuel Guy Lt dow 20-9-18 7WYorks p218 CR France278
ISHMAEL,Henry Plummer 2Lt kia 4-11-14 IA SpServOff p278 MR47
ISLE,William Collinson Lt dow 13-8-15 7SStaffs p122 CR Greece10
IUNG,Henry Adolph 2Lt dow 9-5-15 3 att1NumbF CR France102
IVATT,Harold Alfred.MC.Capt kia 21-5-18 1/5SStaffs p229 CR France109
IVATTS,Selwyn.MC.2Lt kia 8-10-17 B93RFA p31 CR Belgium12
IVE,David 2Lt kia 23-10-14 RWSurr p56 MR29
IVE,Frank T2Lt kia 7-10-16 6 O&BLI p130 MR21
IVENS,Frank Harold Howe 2LtACapt kia 21-10-16 11RSuss p119 MR21
IVES,Henry James Mansfield 2Lt dow 28-4-17 C255RFA p31 CR France95
IVES,Kenneth Hill 2Lt ded 9-12-14 8WYorks p219 CR Yorks361
IVESON,Frank Taylor Lt kia 30-6-15 16DLI p161 CR Gallipoli2
IVESON,James Henry TLtACapt kia 23-3-18 20DLI p161 MR20
IVESS,Thomas Francis Capt ded 5-11-18 4RBerks p270 CR Surrey157
IVEY,Thomas.OBE.Capt&QM ded 23-10-19 O&BLI p264 CR Surrey1
IVORY,John Arthur TLt kia 27-9-18 MGC Inf p183 CR France1496
IZARD,Francis Vallance Capt kia 17-2-15 RGA p40 CR Asia45,16-2-15
IZARD,George Henry T2Lt kia 10-8-18 7Norf att35L TMB p74 CR France196 Ex RWar
IZAT,Alan.MC.Capt kia 2-1-17 RE 103FC p46 CR France177
IZON,Edgar Godfrey ACapt kia 27-9-18 RWar att14Bn p65 CR France518

J

JACK,Christina Sister ded 22-10-18 QAIMNS p200 CR Scot862
JACK,Douglas Peacock 2Lt kia 18-9-18 4EKent p212 CR France365
JACK,Gavine 2Lt kia 25-9-15 2RScots p54 MR29,Gavin
JACK,Henry Claude 2Lt kld 1-9-16 HLI &RFC p3&163 CR Hamps4
JACK,James Charles.DSO.MC&Bar.MID Maj dow 31-5-18 D150RFA SR p31 CR France71
JACK,Robert Lawrence Munro 2Lt dow 27-2-17 5GordH att16RFC p18&242 CR France95,26-2-17
JACK,Thomas 2Lt kia 9-4-17 6RScots p211 CR France184
JACK,Thomas Barclay TCapt dow 24-8-18 RASC att10Lond p193 CR France119
JACK,William Boyd.MC.TCapt dow 11-10-18 RAMC att1/5Leic p196 CR France847
JACKMAN,Gerald Radcliffe T2Lt kia 21-4-17 17WelshR p127 CR France439
JACKMAN,Harold.MC.T2LtACapt kia 21-3-18 7KRRC p150 MR27
JACKMAN,Henry Croome T2Lt ded 28-11-15 9EKent p57 p262 CR Glouc182
JACKMAN,John Robinson Lt kia 22-7-18 6WRid &RAF p227 CR France518,17-6-18
JACKMAN,Osbert William,MM T2Lt dow 7-11-18 1RWSurr p56 CR France952
JACKS,Edmund Cecil 2Lt kia 25-10-16 3Dev p76 MR21
JACKS,Harold Capt ded 27-1-19 7DLI att4NigR p239 CR WAfrica41,26-1-19
JACKSON,Alan James 2Lt kia 27-4-15 att3Mddx p147 MR29
JACKSON,Albert Leslie 2Lt dow 18-3-17 4Mddx p147 CR Lond10,Lt
JACKSON,Alexander Maclean.MC.Lt dow 27-4-17 RE 12FC p46 CR France80,Maj
JACKSON,Arthur T2Lt kia 2-11-16 7BordR p117 CR France307
JACKSON,Arthur T2Lt kld 7-2-17 GL &24RFC p9 CR Mddx1
JACKSON,Arthur Frederick 2Lt kia 27-8-18 10Lond p248 MR16
JACKSON,Arthur Gordon 2Lt kia 25-2-17 3 att6SLancs p125 MR38
JACKSON,Arthur Graham Lt kia 6-10-18 13Lond p249 CR France149
JACKSON,Arthur Lloyd TLtACapt kia 24-4-18 409/96RA p31 MR27
JACKSON,Arthur Rushton T2Lt kia 25-4-18 23RFus C'Coy p68 CR France214
JACKSON,Arthur Selby T2Lt kia 16-9-16 9YLI p143 MR21
JACKSON,Arthur Thomas T2Lt dow 8-11-18 8 att1/5Glouc p107 CR France341
JACKSON,Bertram Rolfe TCapt kia 15-9-16 1CldGds p51 CR France372
JACKSON,Bertram Washington Lt kia 14-9-14 2KRRC p150 MR15
JACKSON,Cecil Thomas Lt kia 31-8-18 1/12LNLancs attRAF p255 CR Egypt1
JACKSON,Cedric Arthur TLt kld 5-11-17 12Y&L &RFC p159&9 CR Derby127
JACKSON,Charles 2Lt kia 10-10-18 1/2LancF p92 CR France190
JACKSON,Claude Stewart Capt kia 9-10-17 3CldGds p51 MR30
JACKSON,Crosby 2Lt kia 1-8-18 4RScots p211
JACKSON,Cyril Compton LtCol kia 22-11-15 IA 103MahrattaLI p278 MR38
JACKSON,Daniel Talbot T2Lt kia 30-9-18 1 att2/5Glouc p107 CR France1887
JACKSON,David Capt ded 3-9-15 6RScots p211 CR Lancs34
JACKSON,David T2Lt kia 16-12-17 8BlkW p128 CR France415
JACKSON,Donald Lt ded 20-9-19 RASC p267 CR Scot52
JACKSON,Donald Fisher.MIDx2 Lt kia 11-10-18 20Huss p23 CR France341

JACKSON,Donald Richard Field Lt kia 27-8-17 5WRid p227 MR30
JACKSON,Douglas William TLt dow 18-5-17 att1KSLI p145 CR France178
JACKSON,Dudley William Gerald Capt dow 13-4-16 1 att10RWFus p98 CR France40
JACKSON,Edward Cecil TLt kia 30-5-16 15N&D p134 MR19
JACKSON,Edward Fergusson.MC.LtTCapt dow 22-9-18 7SfthH p165 CR Palestine9,Lt
JACKSON,Edward Philip 2LtACapt kia 30-11-17 1RBerks p139 CR France924
JACKSON,Edward Phillips 2Lt kia 9-5-15 3RWar attSWBord p65 MR22,Lt
JACKSON,Ernest 2Lt kia 1-7-16 3LancF p92 MR21
JACKSON,Ernest.DSO.MC&Bar.LtAMaj dow 15-4-18 RE 458FC p209 CR France64
JACKSON,Ernest Alexander 2Lt kia 27-5-18 6 att8BordR p117 MR18
JACKSON,Francis 2Lt kia 27-9-18 25 att2/20Lond p252 CR France755
JACKSON,Frank Wigmore.MC.Capt kia 9-6-17 RE 421FC p210 CR France922
JACKSON,Frederick Charles.DCM.Lt&QM dow 11-8-17 21Lond p251
JACKSON,Frederick Howard Capt kia 28-10-14 4 att2ConnRgrs p172 MR29
JACKSON,Frederick John 2Lt kia 14-10-18 1/3Lond &RAF p270 CR Belgium157
JACKSON,Frederick Vyvyan Milbourne Maj kia 13-4-18 A245RFA p206 CR Belgium10 14-4-18
JACKSON,George TLt kia 26-9-15 11A&SH p173 MR19
JACKSON,Geoffrey Laird.MID LtACapt kia 9-4-17 1RB p179 CR France728
JACKSON,George TCapt kia 25-8-17 18HLI p163 CR France363
JACKSON,George Conway TLt kia 25-9-15 6KOSB p102 MR19
JACKSON,George Dewar 2Lt kia 14-9-16 3GrenGds p50 MR21,15-9-16
JACKSON,George Henry.MC.2Lt kia 31-7-17 att2RB p179 MR29
JACKSON,George William TLt kia 7-5-17 7NumbF attRFC p18&214 MR20
JACKSON,Godfrey Lt dow 15-9-17 1/4ELancs p226 CR Belgium8
JACKSON,Hamilton Ray T2Lt dow 26-7-17 RASC attRGA 245SB p193 CR Belgium11,kia
JACKSON,Harold TCapt kia 7-6-17 GL 41RFC p9 CR Belgium56
JACKSON,Harold Edward 2Lt kia 12-6-17 6WYorks p218 MR19
JACKSON,Harold James T2Lt kia 4-6-18 10LancF p92 CR France220
JACKSON,Harold Willows Lt dow 14-5-17 4EYorks p219 CR France113
JACKSON,Harry T2Lt kia 9-10-17 WRid att1/7Bn p115 MR30
JACKSON,Harry 2Lt ded 25-10-18 RGA 4SAR Bde p40 CR Hamps1
JACKSON,Henry Douglas.MC.2Lt kia 26-10-16 4EYorks p219 CR France387
JACKSON,Henry Hall.MC.Capt ded 28-11-18 15Huss p22 CR Yorks256
JACKSON,Henry Medland T2Lt kia 19-9-18 RASC att1/10Lond p193 CR Palestine9
JACKSON,Henry Stewart TLt kia 1-7-16 8YLI p143 MR21
JACKSON,Henry Teasdale T2Lt kia 8-10-17 13NumbF att8Leic p61 MR30
JACKSON,Herbert T2Lt kia 21-3-18 11 att2RDubF p177 MR27
JACKSON,Herbert Meynell T2Lt kia 18-6-17 GL 53RFC p9 MR20
JACKSON,Herbert Percival Lt kia 25-9-17 A296RFA p207 CR Belgium84
JACKSON,Herbert William Lt kia 20-1-18 12/13NumbF p61 CR France439
JACKSON,Horace T2Lt kia 21-3-18 16MGC p183 CR Belgium45
JACKSON,James Battle T2Lt kia 23-4-18 2RWFus p98 CR France162
JACKSON,James Crosby 2Lt kia 1-8-18 4 att9RScots p211 CR France524
JACKSON,John Lt kld 22-5-15 9A&SH p244 CR Scot80
JACKSON,John 2Lt kia 19-8-16 3Dors att2/5Glouc p124 CR France1887
JACKSON,John T2Lt kia 20-9-17 26RFus p68 MR30
JACKSON,John Alfred 2Lt kia 4-5-16 6ScotRif p224 CR France114
JACKSON,John Bell Lt kia 7-6-17 RScots &43RFC p9&54 MR20
JACKSON,John Cooper 2Lt kia 31-7-17 3 att16Manch p155 MR29
JACKSON,John Edward.DSO.Capt ded 25-10-17 1/8Lpool p270 CR Lancs7
JACKSON,John Henry 2Lt kia 9-9-16 5LancF p221 MR21
JACKSON,John Male 2Lt ded /-9-17 DLI p265
JACKSON,John Montague Hammick TLt dow 18-8-15 5 O&BLI p130 CR Devon72
JACKSON,John William TLt kia 17-10-17 11N&D p134 CR Belgium72
JACKSON,Lancelot 2Lt kia 1-7-16 1BordR p117 MR21
JACKSON,Leonard 2Lt kia 22/23-7-16 15RWar p65 MR21
JACKSON,M.MIDx2 Lt&QM ded 23-5-18 RE 3Army Spec Coy p46 CR Sussex30
JACKSON,Malcolm Race T2Lt kia 25-3-18 Manch att1/6Bn p155 MR20
JACKSON,Martin de Carle 2Lt kia 5-11-16 RFA p31 MR21
JACKSON,Nicholas William Goddard 2Lt kia 9-9-16 1Nhampt p137 CR France432
JACKSON,Noel Bower 2Lt kia 6-12-17 2/5N&D p233 CR France711
JACKSON,Patrick Arthur Dudley 2Lt kia 4-1-17 2RIrRif p169 CR Belgium53
JACKSON,Raymond Wilfred 2Lt kia 9-10-17 4Y&L p238 MR30,Raymund
JACKSON,Robert T2Lt kia 13-4-18 9SfthH p165 CR Belgium21
JACKSON,Robert Cameron T2Lt kia 24-9-17 233MGC Inf p183 MR30

JACKSON,Robert Raimes.MC.Capt dow 1-11-17 105/29RFA p31 CR Belgium16

JACKSON,Robert William.MC.DCM.T2Lt kia 23-10-18 1 att16WYorks p82 CR France1266

JACKSON,S.S.Lt 29-9-15 EAfrTransCps CR EAfrica52

JACKSON,Samuel Lt kia 20-3-18 3 att2RIrReg p89 MR21

JACKSON,Sidney Douglas 2Lt kia 3-5-17 31/35RFA p31 CR France616

JACKSON,Sidney Foster Lt kia 17-11-17 7WYorks p218 CR Belgium308

JACKSON,Stanley T2Lt kia 10-11-17 12Manch p155 MR30

JACKSON,Stanley Foster Capt kia 4-6-15 1/6Manch D'Coy p236 Gallipoli6,dow

JACKSON,Stanley Richardson TMaj dow 31-12-15 19Lond p250 CR France88

JACKSON,Stewart Spiers.MC.2Lt kia 21-3-18 1 att2/8Worc p109 MR27

JACKSON,Theodore Walter TCapt ded 4-10-18 RASC HT p193 CR France25,Walton

JACKSON,Theophilus Rudolph.MC.TCapt dow 25-3-18 7DCLI p114&258 CR France987

JACKSON,Thomas Lt kia 12-7-15 5RScotF p222 MR4

JACKSON,Thomas Leslie.MC.TCapt kia 2-7-16 9Ches p96 CR France267

JACKSON,Walter 2Lt kia 9-10-17 7WYorks p218 MR30

JACKSON,Walter Lt dow 8-11-17 LanarkYeo p204 CR Palestine1,9-11-17 12RScotF

JACKSON,Wilfred Flower Lt kia 28-10-18 IARO attCpsofGuidesCav p278 MR38

JACKSON,Wilfred George Lt kia 27-4-15 1EKent p57 MR32

JACKSON,William.MC.T2Lt dow 26-8-18 3NumbF att15DLI p161 CR France84

JACKSON,William T2Lt kia 30-9-18 11RDubF att23RFus p177 CR France914

JACKSON,William Brabazon Mather Capt kia 27-4-17 2/6N&D p233 CR France1495,dow 28-4-17

JACKSON,William Ewart Capt kia 9-1-17 3 att1Manch p155 CR Iraq5

JACKSON,William Hickin T2Lt kia 3-5-17 15WYorks p82 MR20

JACKSON,William John Humphrey 2Lt dow 26-3-18 12 att6RInniskF p105 MR34

JACKSON-BARSTOW,John Eric Capt 27-1-19 NSomYeo &RAF CR Somerset197

JACKSON-TAYLOR,John Curzon 2Lt kia 21-3-18 1KSLI p145 MR20

JACOB,Anstey Ross 2Lt dow 18-9-16 4DLI p161 CR France833

JACOB,Arthur Henry Augustus Lt dow 16-7-16 4RFus p68 CR France40

JACOB,Arthur Leslie Hamilton TLt kia 25-9-15 18Lond p250 MR19

JACOB,Cecil Otway Reed Capt kia 29-11-17 2Dev att2/5Lincs p77 MR21 &CR France1498,3Dev

JACOB,Donald Allen 2Lt dow 13-11-17 1/4Lincs p217 CR France90,Lt 12-11-17

JACOB,Gwynne.DCM.MM&Bar.Lt kia 1-8-19 EYorks att45RFus p255 MR70 &CR Europe179

JACOB,Henry William James 2Lt kia 26-10-17 16Lond p250 MR20

JACOB,John Victor Reed Lt ded 16-3-19 RGA &RAF p255

JACOB,Victor Vivian Lt kia 25-9-15 2 O&BLI p130 MR19

JACOBI,Walter Thomas T2Lt dow 21-10-16 14RWar p65

JACOBS,Alan Edward Aflalo.MC.2Lt kia 7-8-16 8ESurr p112 MR32

JACOBS,Daryl.MID 2Lt kia 10-4-17 4SLancs p230 MR32

JACOBS,Henry 2Lt kia 6-7-18 5 att8RLancs p213 CR France98,Harry

JACOBS,Henry Houston 2Lt kia 25-9-15 8Lincs p75 MR19

JACOBS,Joel 2Lt kia 20-7-16 5Yorks p221 CR Belgium60

JACOBS,John Harry.MC.ACapt kia 11-10-18 1RFus A'Coy p68 CR France270

JACOBS,Robert Capt dow 20-7-18 RAMC p253 CR France46,kia

JACOBSON,Lyonel Hugh.MC.TLt kia 29-4-17 D50RFA p31 CR France96

JACOT,Conrade William T2Lt kld 23-6-17 GL RFC p9 CR War67

JACOT,Edward Lt kia 6-6-17 42RFC p255 MR20

JACQUES,David Wright 2Lt dow 1-12-16 1 att10RWSurr p56 CR France200,kia

JACQUES,Edward William Rigbye Lt kia 17-8-16 1Nhampt p137 CR France387,16-8-17

JACQUES,Francis Augustus LtCol kia 4-6-15 IA 14Sikhs p278 MR4

JACQUES,Geoffrey Plateras Lawson 2Lt kld 5-10-16 RFC p3 CR Essex50

JACQUES,George Sheriff Harkus 2Lt kia 27-6-16 6NumbF p214

JACQUES,William Gladstone 2Lt kia 17-10-18 5N&D p233 CR France847

JACSON,Mainwaring George ColTBrigGen ded 2-6-15 RoO Staff p1 CR Shrop95

JAFFE,Joseph TCapt kia 1-8-18 RAMC att2/4SomLI p196 CR France524

JAFFRAY,John Henry.Bart.2Lt kia 23-4-16 WorcYeo p206 MR34

JAFFREY,William.MC.Lt kia 23-3-18 6 att8A&SH p243 MR27

JAGGER,Arthur Stannus T2Lt dow 1-10-18 9RWFus p98 CR France98,Lt 30-9-18

JAGGER,Harry 2Lt kia 10-6-18 1LancF p92 CR France24

JAGGERS,William John 2Lt kia 20-9-17 RFA B277ArmyBde p31 CR Belgium112

JAGO,Edward Arthur 2Lt kia 1-7-16 3 att2Dev p77 MR21

JAGO,Henry Harris.MC.LtACapt kia 24-4-18 2Dev p77 MR27

JAGOE,Charles Bateman T2Lt kia 26-7-17 16RIrRif p169 CR Belgium5

JAKINS,Walter Vosper T2Lt kld 10-7-17 GL &54RFC p9 CR Essex40

JALLAND,Boswell Victor 2Lt kia 9-4-17 3EYorks p84 CR France162

JALLAND,Henry Herbert Lt 18-10-18 3 att1BlkW p128 CR France1271

JALLAND,Robert Miles T2Lt kia 26-8-18 6Leic p87 CR France385

JALLAND,Stephen Lt kia 9-8-15 6EYorks p84 MR4

JAMES,Albert TLt dow 28-3-18 10MGC p183 CR France169

JAMES,Albert Hazlewood H.2Lt ded 20-12-18 RH&FA p208 CR Wilts142

JAMES,Albert John Stanley.DSO.MC.TMajALtCol kia 28-3-18 10RWFus Comdg8RLancs p98 MR20

JAMES,Alfred 2Lt dow 8-3-18 1/4SLancs p230 CR France88

JAMES,Archibald Hugh.DSO.ALtCol kia 26-3-18 8NumbF att8WYorks p61 CR France745

JAMES,Alyn Reginald Capt kia 24-3-18 24RWFus &RFC p203 MR20

JAMES,Arthur Lt kia 3-1-17 7Yorks p90 CR France374

JAMES,Arthur Keedwell Harvey TCapt kia 15-4-17 GL p190

JAMES,Arthur Ling Capt kia 8-8-16 7Suff p78 MR21

JAMES,Baron Trevinnen.MIDx2 LtCapt kia 13-7-15 RE &RFC p1&46 MR20,Trevenen

JAMES,Basil Lister 2Lt dow 25-11-16 4EKent p212 CR France177

JAMES,Bernard Ashworth TCapt kia 18-8-16 13Mddx p147 MR21

JAMES,Bernard William Austin 2Lt kia 14-10-17 18 att6Lond p250 CR France644

JAMES,Burnet George Lt kia 26-9-15 RFA att7RFC p18&207 CR Belgium83

JAMES,Charles Kenneth.DSO&Bar.ALtCol kia 19-5-18 6BordR p117 CR France745

JAMES,Charles Llewellyn T2Lt kia 10-5-18 WelchR att15Bn p127 CR France232

JAMES,Clement Wilbraham 2Lt kia 1-7-16 15WYorks p82 MR21

JAMES,Donald Croft 2Lt kia 19-7-16 2/4Glouc p225 MR21

JAMES,Douglas Attwood Lt kia 25-4-15 BordR p117 CR Gallipoli3,Capt

JAMES,Douglas Charles 2Lt dow 1-10-15 1SStaffs p122 CR France473,Douglas Lt 30-9-15

JAMES,Edward Scott TCapt ded 19-8-17 B102RH&FA p31

JAMES,Enoch Lewis T2Lt kia 18-2-17 14RWFus p98 MR29

JAMES,Eric Gwynne.DSO.MID TCapt&Adjt dow 15-10-16 1KSLI p145 CR France145

JAMES,Eric Samuel Pennant Kingsbury Capt kia 17-3-15 6KRRC p150 CR Belgium28 4Bn

JAMES,Evan T2Lt kia 27-7-17 3 att15WelshR p127 CR Belgium23

JAMES,Francis Arthur TCapt dow 18-9-15 5Manch p236 CR Gallipoli3

JAMES,Frank Lt kia 1-11-18 3 att1SWBord p100 CR France1268

JAMES,Frank Clifford 2Lt dow PoW 4-5-17 1RBerks p139 CR France1276,Lt

JAMES,Frederick T2Lt kia 20-5-17 4Lpool p72 CR France434

JAMES,George Henry 2Lt dow 8-5-17 3 att2Hamps p121 CR France40

JAMES,George Millais Capt kia 3-11-14 EKent 1 att2InfBde p57 MR29

JAMES,George Sidney Lt kia 4-6-15 5Manch p236 CR Gallipoli2

JAMES,Gwilym T2Lt dow 8-10-18 13RWFus p98 CR France398

JAMES,Gwilym Christopher Bowring Lt dow 23-11-17 3 att2SWBord p100 CR France398

JAMES,Gwilym Gregory Maj ded 19-12-19 IMS p278 CR Iraq8

JAMES,Gwynne Lewis Brodhurst Lt kia 18-7-17 IrGds attTHB p52 CR Belgium12

JAMES,Henry John T2Lt kia 9-4-17 24NumbF p61 CR France184

JAMES,Henry Stoddart 2Lt kia 23-4-17 5BordR p228 CR France1185

JAMES,Henry Vernon Lt dow 12-4-18 41/42RFA p207 CR France201

JAMES,Herbert Walter 2Lt kia 4-10-17 13NumbF att9YLI p61 MR30

JAMES,James Wright TCapt kia 7-10-16 15Hamps p121 MR21

JAMES,Joe Conquest TCapt dow 14-7-16 5RBerks p139 CR France64

JAMES,John Capt dow 8-10-18 RAMC att18HLI p196 CR Belgium157,kia

JAMES,John Stephen Harvey 2Lt kia 16-5-15 1KRRC p150 MR22

JAMES,Kenneth Lister 2Lt kia 3-5-17 4 att6EKent p212 MR20

JAMES,Merridith Charles Clifton T2Lt dow 27-10-16 1Worc p109 MR21,Meredith

JAMES,R.A.Capt kia 16-7-18 5Mddx &RAF p255

JAMES,Ralph Lionel 2Lt died 3-8-17 7RWFus attRFC p223 CR Surrey157

JAMES,Reginald Arthur Capt 16-6-18 5Mddx &54RAF MR20

JAMES,Reginald Valpy ded 15-7-19 IARO attRailways p278 MR67

JAMES,Richard Arthur Brodie TCapt kia 13-9-16 9ELancs p111 MR37

JAMES,Richard Walter T2Lt kia 8-5-17 11ELancs p111 CR France1191

JAMES,Robert Kenneth Lt kia 27-5-18 4YLI p235 MR18

JAMES,Roy Francis T2Lt kia 2-9-18 18Manch p155 CR France308

JAMES,Rupert Frederick Lt kia 27-3-18 11EYorks p84 CR France927

JAMES,Samuel Forest T2Lt kia 18-11-16 8Glouc p107 MR21

JAMES,Vivian Gwynne Lt kia 26-3-17 12att1/7RWFus p98 MR34

JAMES,W.Douglass Lt 24-9-15 RGA TMB CR France98

JAMES,Walter Capt kia 25-6-15 10DLI p161 CR Belgium165

JAMES,Walter Ibbe Lt kia 25/27-9-15 3RWFus p98 MR19

JAMES,Wilfred Sydney T2Lt kia 24-11-17 19RWFus p98 MR17

JAMES,Wilfred Rowland TLt kia 16-9-16 23DLI p161 MR21

JAMES,William David T2Lt kia 23-5-18 9LNLancs p136 MR20

JAMES,William David.MM.2Lt kia 8-10-18 13RWFus p98 CR France1346

JAMES,William Maynard Capt&Adjt kia 8-10-18 1Mon p244 CR France1710

JAMESON,Alan Battersby 2Lt kia 21-7-16 1Camb p245 CR France765

JAMESON,Anthony Mildmay 2Lt kia 1-9-16 2Leinst p174 CR France399,Antony

JAMESON,Edmund James.DSO.TLt.Col dow 27-3-17 5Leinst Cmdg1/4Ess p174 CR Palestine2,John

JAMESON,Francis John TLt kia 25-9-15 12 att9ScotRif p103 CR France114

JAMESON,Harold.MC.DCM.2Lt kia 5-1-17 6RFC SR p9 CR Belgium11,42Sqdn

JAMESON,Harold Gordon 2Lt kia 16-8-15 RE 65FC p46 MR4

JAMESON,Harry Roderick Victor 2Lt kia 11-4-17 2SfthH p165 MR20

JAMESON,Horace Armytage.MC&Bar.Maj kia 24-3-18 311RFA p206 MR27

JAMESON,Ian Herbert Sydney TCapt kia 23-4-17 8SfthH p165 CR France536

JAMESON,James Leslie.MC.Lt kia 2-7-16 1/5WYorks p218 MR21

JAMESON,John 2Lt kia 30-8-18 1Dev p77 CR France1484

JAMESON,John Louis SubCdr 10-2-16 MilWksServ MR65

JAMESON,Robert Alexander 2Lt kia 21-7-18 1/8RScots p212 CR France622

JAMIESON,Colin Miller 2Lt kia 21-5-17 15Lond p249 MR20

JAMIESON,Crawford Lt kia 23-4-17 9RScots p212 CR France604

JAMIESON,Douglas Lt kia 9-7-17 RE 401FC p210 CR Belgium10

JAMIESON,Eric Liew Ellen 2Lt kia 22-8-17 A&SH p173 CR Belgium128,Lieuellen

JAMIESON,George William Lt kia 28-3-18 5 att10ScotRif p224 CR France57

JAMIESON,Gerald Alister.MID Maj dow 28-2-16 IA 9BhopalInf p278 MR65

JAMIESON,Jessie Smith SNurse ded 30-12-18 TFNS CR Scot236

JAMIESON,John T2Lt kia 3-4-18 9 att16LancF p92 CR France804

JAMIESON,John.DCM.2Lt kia 29-4-18 23NumbF p61 MR20

JAMIESON,John Melvill 2Lt kia 28-4-17 7N&D p233 CR France1495

JAMIESON,John Prior Capt dow 13-10-17 3 att1RLancs p50 CR Belgium16

JAMIESON,Leonard Foster TLt ded 27-6-18 RAMC att302RFA p196 CR Egypt1

JAMIESON,Nicol Capt kia 13-8-15 4RScotF p222 MR4

JAMIESON,Robert Lindsay T2Lt kia 3-9-16 12A&SH att1CamH p173 MR21

JAMIESON,Thomas 2Lt ded 5-9-19 4 att6WYorks p263 CR Germany1,drd

JAMIESON,William Patterson TLt kia 6-4-17 MGC HB p183 CR France581

JAMISON,James Clawson Capt kia 22-11-17 10RIrRif p169 MR17

JAN,Henry Gordon Hay T2Lt kia 15-2-17 8Wilts p153

JANASZ,James George Gee 2Lt kia 15-6-15 3Dors att2Wilts p124 MR22

JANE,William Maj dow 24-4-18 RE p209

JANES,Edmund 2Lt kia 13-5-18 RGA 70HAG 161SB p40 CR Fraance523,13-5-17

JANES,George Frederick HonMajT/QM ded 13-8-18 RASC p193&257

JANES,Willis T2Lt dow 22-1-17 6KOSB p102 CR France1

JAPP,William Neville 2Lt kia 25/26-9-15 1/20Lond p251 MR19,25-9-15

JAQUES,Arthur TCapt kia 27-9-15 12WYorks p82 MR19

JAQUES,George 2Lt kia 25-9-17 B236RFA p31 CR Belgium21

JAQUES,George Sheriff Harkus 2Lt kia 27-6-16 6NumbF CR Belgium17

JAQUES,John Barclay.MC.AFC.FlOff 1-4-20 DLI att216RAF CR EAfrica116

JAQUES,Joseph 2Lt kia 26-9-17 1NumbF p61 MR30

JAQUES,Joseph Hodgson Maj kia 27-9-17 12WYorks p82 MR19

JAQUES,William 2Lt dow 30-12-17 1RMLI CR France398

JARAH,Charles T2Lt dow 20-6-17 22DLI p161 CR Belgium29

JARDINE,Charles Hunt TLt kia 3-5-18 13RScots att2/2KAR p54&202 CR EAfrica92

JARDINE,Douglas Graeme Burness.MC.Capt ded 5-8-18 1/2HLI &RAF p163 CR Europe74,kia

JARDINE,Graham Brymmer Thomas 2Lt kia 18-10-16 13A&SH p173 CR France385,Brymner

JARDINE,Henry Marshall Lt kia 23-7-16 6 att2RScots p211 MR21

JARDINE,J.A Capt 19-3-20 RAMC CR Egypt2

JARDINE,Richard Webster 2Lt kia 23-7-16 7LNLancs p136 MR21

JARDINE,Robert Gordon 2Lt kia 20-7-17 56RFC SR p9 MR20

JARDINE,Ronald James 2Lt kldacc 13-9-17 2Drags attRFC p9&21 CR Scot582

JARDINE,William.Bart.TMaj ded 13-12-15 3KOSB p102 CR Scot582

JARINZOFF,Dmitri.MC.MID TLtACapt kia 8-10-17 10 att6ELancs p111 MR30

JARMAN,Andrew Hatch T2Lt kia 1-7-16 20NumbF p61 CR France393

JARMAN,Harry Love TCapt kia 15-1-17 RAMC att7SWBord p196 CR Greece6

JARRED,Geoffrey William 2Lt ded 30-12-17 3RBerks p139 CR Egypt1,drd

JARRETT,Aylmer Vivian.DSO.Capt dow 22-6-15 2Y&L p159 CR Belgium2

JARRETT,Charles Harry Brownlow Maj kia 25-4-15 1RMunstF p175 CR Gallipoli1

JARRETT,Herbert Horace 2Lt dow 6-12-17 5NStaffs p238 CR France145

JARRETT,Hubert Cecil Delacour LtCol ded 21-12-19 IA 1/19Punjabis p278 CR India48

JARROTT,Samuel Fox Armitage TLt dow 12-10-16 2DLI p161 CR France105,2Lt

JARVIE,John T2Lt dow 17-4-17 7/8KOSB p102 CR France787

JARVIE,Thomas Russell 2Lt kld 9-10-17 RFC p9 CR Scot780

JARVIS,Alan Bishop Capt kia 10-8-17 10Mddx att1RFC p18&236 CR Belgium140

JARVIS,Archibald Thomas TLt ded 24-9-16 12Ess att1YLI p132 CR Greece7

JARVIS,Arthur Bernard T2Lt kia 3-8-17 C177RFA p31 CR Belgium10

JARVIS,Arthur Septimus Guy 2Lt kia 31-10-14 1Nhampt p137 CR Belgium132

JARVIS,Charles Edward TLt kia 18-7-17 10WYorks p82 France97

JARVIS,Charles Wemyss Barron 2LtACapt kia 30-7-16 3RWKent att7RDubF p141 MR21 att1Bn

JARVIS,E.MacD.2Lt kld 6-6-18 GL &RAF p190

JARVIS,Edwin Leonard T2Lt kia 4-9-18 Hamps att2Bn p121 CR Belgium451

JARVIS,Ernest Cory TCapt kia 28-8-16 6 att8SLancs p125 MR21

JARVIS,Frederick Charles T2Lt kia 7-7-16 2Nhampt p137 MR21

JARVIS,George Frederick Jervaulx.MC.TLt dow 28-9-18 5RRofCav att9WYorks p23 CR France113

JARVIS,James Warden TLt dow 26-9-15 7KOSB p102 CR France88

JARVIS,John 2Lt kia 21-3-18 5NStaffs p238 MR20

JARVIS,John Baxter Capt ??? 10-4-19 RAOC p267

JARVIS,Louis Archibald Lt kia 16-5-15 2ScotsGds p52 CR France279

JARVIS,Ralph Himsworth.MC.LtTCapt kld 27-2-18 RFC p16 CR Surrey157

JARVIS,William Simpson T2Lt kia 8-11-18 7Lincs p75 CR France930,Simpkin

JAVES,John Walter Capt 3-11-20 ImpWarGravesComm CR Greece9

JAVES,Robert Charles T2Lt kia 15/17-9-16 10RWSurr p56 MR21,16-9-16

JAY,Arthur Palmer T2Lt kia 21-3-18 2RRegofCav att7BordR p23 MR20

JAY,Frank Goldsmith T2Lt kia 29-9-18 KRRC att18Bn p150 CR Belgium116

JAY,H.B.maj 20-8-17 DCLI CR Mddx26

JAY,William Oak Lt kia 25-4-17 8RLancs p59 MR20

JAYE,Harold Conway T2Lt dow 9-7-16 11WYorks p82 CR France833,13Bn

JEAKES,John William TLt dow 12-10-17 RBerks att6Bn p139 CR Belgium126

JEAL,Walter T2Lt kia 1-7-16 GL att15RScots p190 MR21

JEAVONS,Rechab Vivian 2Lt kia 30-8-17 RFA p208 MR30

JEBB,Arthur Beresford T2Lt kia 17-6-16 RFA attX16TMB p31 CR France223,Lt

JEBB,Hope Emile 2Lt dow 21-3-18 2DLI p161 MR20

JEBSON,George James 2Lt kia 23-1-17 RGA 113HB p40 CR France133

JECKS,Albert Edward Lt 15-5-21 RASC MR65

JEEVES,Charles Anthony Victor.MM.T2Lt kia 20-9-17 Dev att9Lpool p77 MR30

JEFF,Andrew Russell T2Lt kia 13-8-16 12HLI p163 CR France1170

JEFFARES,Richard Thorpe.MID Capt dow 6-10-17 4 att2RIrRif p169 CR France80

JEFFCOAT,Stanley Ferns T2Lt dow 29-4-17 22RFus p68 CR France184

JEFFCOCK,Harold Charles Firth Lt dow 30-5-17 8N&D p233 CR France446,Capt

JEFFCOCK,Robert Salisbury 2Lt kia 1-7-16 1/6SStaffs p229 MR21

JEFFERIES,James Leslie TLt kia 9-9-16 11Hamps p121 CR France1890

JEFFERIES,Maurice Arnold T2Lt kia 19-7-16 10SLancs p125 MR19

JEFFERIES,Richard Oliver Geary.MC.TLtACapt kia 29-9-18 8TankCps p188 CR France375

JEFFERIES,Stanley Saunders 2Lt kia 10-8-18 8TankCps p188 CR France526

JEFFERSON,Elgie Blyth Barwise Capt kld 15-5-19 1Lpool attRAF p72 CR France1359,15-5-16

JEFFERSON,Hamilton Lt kia 16-8-17 4 O&BLI p231 MR30

JEFFERSON,Ralph James 2Lt kia 25-2-17 3 att6SLancs p125 MR38

JEFFERY,Charles Launcelot 2LtACapt dow 23-9-17 1 att10RB p179 MR30

JEFFERY,Claud Gifford Capt dow 23-10-14 2Yorks p90 CR Belgium57,Giffard 24-10-14

JEFFERY,George Reginald T2Lt kia 13-2-16 20Huss p23 CR France423,Lt

JEFFERY,Harold Greensmith 2Lt kia 4-7-18 GL &58RAF CR France223

JEFFERY,John T2Lt kia 20-9-18 18 att9WelshR p127 CR France631

JEFFERY,Ronald Edward 2Lt kia 25-5-17 GL 55RFC p9 CR France421,Roland

JEFFERY,Tom Forbes 2Lt dow 17-4-18 156RFA p31 CR Belgium18,16-4-18

JEFFERY,William T2Lt dow 7-10-17 att10RB p179

JEFFERYS,Charles Thomas Claude Rev ded 20-11-18 RAChDept p199 CR Somerset26

JEFFERYS,Montagne Gane Lt kia 18-1-17 10Mddx p236 MR38

JEFFORD,William Arthur 2Lt kia 8-5-15 12Lond p248 MR29

JEFFREE,Johnson Vivian 2Lt kia 10-8-18 3Lond p245 CR France1170 Ex HAC

JEFFREY,Ernest Lt kia 24-3-TA 4RScots p211 MR20

JEFFREY,Joseph Hunter 2Lt kia 23-10-18 2DLI p161 CR France1266

JEFFREY,Reginald Harry 2Lt kia 11-4-17 4 at1RWar p65 CR France544

JEFFREYS,Alexander Harry ACapt kia 6-11-16 20NumbF Ex 19Bn p61 CR France82,19Bn

JEFFREYS,Charles Thomas Claude Rev ded 20-11-18 RAChDept p268

JEFFREYS,Charles Wilfred 2Lt kia 17-10-17 KSLI att5Bn p145 MR30

JEFFREYS,Darell Richard Capt kia 11-7-15 1Dev p77 CR Belgium56

JEFFREYS,Hubert Leslie 2Lt kia 29-4-17 13RFus p68 MR20 JEFFERYS

JEFFREYS,William Stanley TLt kia 10-7-16 13WelshR p127 MR21

JEFFRIES,Harold John Fotheringham Capt kia 26-9-15 1/5Leic p220 CR Belgium11,Maj

JEFFRIES,Herbert TLt dow 20-9-18 Yorks att12MGC attYorks p90&183 CR France194

JEFFRIES,Philip TLt ded 3-12-18 15MGC Motors p183 MR43

JEFFRIES,Thomas 2Lt kia 14-8-17 3Lond p245 MR29

JEFFRYS,James Herbert 2Lt mbk 27-5-18 7 att2ELancs p256 CR France1894

JEHU,John Howard Lt kia 28-11-17 1Co of LondYeo p204 CR Palestine3,MddxHuss

JEKYLL,Arthur Cyril Albert TCapt kia 11-5-16 RAMC att13RScotsp196 CR France423

JELF,Charles Gordon T2Lt kia 13-10-15 6EKent p57 CR France423

JELLEY,William Frederick.MC.2Lt dow 2-11-17 6Yorks p90 CR France145

JELLICOE,Eric Maitland Lt kia 1-7-16 6N&D p233 CR France281

JEMMETT,Charles William Lt kia 15-3-18 5EKent p213 CR France1712

JEMMETT,George Elwick 2Lt dow 17-12-17 13Lond p249 CR France13

JEMMETT-BROWNE,Antoney Edward Capt kia 11-9-14 2RSuss p119 CR France1113,Antony 10-9-14

JENINGS,George Pierce Creagh Lt kia 6-11-14 1KSLI p145 MR32

JENKIN,Louis Fleeming.MC&Bar.Capt kia 11-9-17 GL 9LNLancs &1RFC p9 MR20

JENKINS,Aneurin 2Lt kia 13-4-18 6SWBord p100 MR32

JENKINS,Arthur Emlyn TLt kia 4-12-16 20MGC p183 CR France131

JENKINS,Arthur Lewis Lt kld 31-12-17 4DCLI attRFC p18&226 CR Surrey152

JENKINS,Charles T2Lt kld 21-3-18 RFC p16 CR Wales367

JENKINS,Christopher Hutchinson LtTCapt dow 22-5-17 3RSuss &45RFC p9&119 CR France285

JENKINS,Cyril Donald Thomas Lt kld 2-10-16 3RWFus &RFC p3&98 CR Wales171

JENKINS,Cyril Frank Bingham TCapt dow 13-10-17 11SWBord p100 CR France64

JENKINS,David Chap4Cl ded 6-3-19 RAChDept p255 CR Wales118

JENKINS,David Lewis Lt kia 26-9-17 5RWFus p270&230,WelchR MR30,5 att10Bn

JENKINS,David Roy Capt kld 21-1-17 RFA attRFC p18&207 CR Wales7

JENKINS,Donald Fraser.MC.2Lt kia 13-11-16 6SfthH p241 CR France131

JENKINS,Edgar Ernest.MC.TLt.ACapt kia 25-3-18 RWar att1/5LancF p65 MR20

JENKINS,Edgar Kynnersley TCapt dow 23-9-16 2DCLI p114 CR Greece3

JENKINS,Edward Geoffrey T2Lt dow 26-10-18 1NumbF p61 CR France40

JENKINS,Edward Tuberville Llewellin Lt dow 25-7-16 RE 59FC p46 CR France23,2Lt

JENKINS,Edwin Walter Capt ded 9-11-16 Hamps CR Hamps13

JENKINS,Ernest 2Lt kia 2-9-18 40RFA p31 CR France214

JENKINS,Ernest Stanley 2Lt kia 24-11-17 5WelchR p230 CR France256

JENKINS,Francis Howard T2Lt kia 2-9-18 12SomLI p80 CR France439

JENKINS,Frederick John TMaj ded 22-1-19 RASC p267 CR Mddx13,23-1-19 dow

JENKINS,Garrett Primrose 2Lt kia 7-9-17 C75RFA p31 CR Belgium12

JENKINS,George Cliffe 2Lt kia 3-5-17 att2/5Y&L p159 MR20

JENKINS,James Temple 2Lt kia 20-9-17 4SfthH p241 MR30

JENKINS,John.MC.TMajALtCol dow 9-10-18 20KRRC att1Mon p150 CR France446

JENKINS,John Ernest TCapt dow 25-11-17 12SWBord p100 CR France398

JENKINS,Kenneth Gordon Lt dow 31-3-18 NSomYeo p205 CR France62

JENKINS,L.DSO.MC.LtCol ded 20-11-18 RGA &RAF p209

JENKINS,Llewellyn Maynard T2Lt dow 2-12-16 10WelshR p127 CR Belgium1

JENKINS,Patrick Graham 2Lt kia 9-4-17 4CamH p243 CR France924,7Bn

JENKINS,Ralph Conway T2Lt kld 2-12-17 GL RFC p9 CR Hamps4

JENKINS,Ralph George Lt ded 21-5-16 RGA p270 CR Wales35

JENKINS,Richard 2Lt kia 11-11-16 7Manch p237 MR21

JENKINS,Richard Borlase 2Lt dow 17-1-16 2SWBord att9RFC p3&100 CR France34,18-1-16

JENKINS,Richard Owen.MC.2Lt dow 21-9-17 1/5Lpool p215 CR Belgium3,Lt

JENKINS,Robert Alfred Capt kia 21-1-16 IA 97Inf p278 MR38

JENKINS,Robert Henry Charles 2Lt dow 19-10-16 8Lond p247 CR France145

JENKINS,Samuel Clifford T2Lt dow 21-8-18 2Wilts p153 CR France10

JENKINS,Sidney Emlyn T2Lt kia 22-4-18 NStaffs att16RWFus p157 CR France296,Sydney 15 att16RWFus

JENKINS,Sidney Oswald 2Lt kia 22-8-18 3RWFus att10KSLI p98 MR19

JENKINS,Sydney Randell Lt dow 26-9-15 3 att2WelshR p127 MR19

JENKINS,Thomas Frederick TMaj ded 26-2-19 GL 16WelchR att1ArmyMSch p190 CR France788

JENKINS,W.W.L.2Lt dow 25-6-18 1/2DCLI &RAF p114

JENKINS,William T2Lt kia 11-10-18 Dors att6Bn p124 CR France230

JENKINS,William Alexander 2Lt dow 14-4-17 7A&SH p243 CR France95

JENKINS,William Charles 2Lt kia 4-10-17 RGA 66SB p40 CR Belgium101

JENKINS,William Edwin Capt kia 1-10-15 2NumbF p61 MR19

JENKINS,William Edwin 2Lt kia 23-11-17 ESurr &60RFC p9&112 CR Belgium125

JENKINS,William Marenday TLt kia 3-10-16 23WelshR p127 CR Greece3,Marendaz

JENKINSON,John Capt kia 13-10-15 6NStaffs p238 MR19

JENKINSON,John Banks.MID Capt kia 14-9-14 RB p179 CR France1329

JENKINSON,John Wilfred Capt kia 4-6-15 12Worc attRFus p109 MR4

JENKS,Alan Robert Constantine.MC.TLt.AMaj kia 31-7-17 RE 61FC p46 CR Belgium17

JENKS,Arthur Leslie Lt dow 7-10-18 3 att2Dors p124 CR Egypt2

JENKS,John Edward TCapt dow 4-7-16 12RIrRif p169 CR France74

JENNER,George Reginald 2Lt dow 2-8-16 1/3 att1EYorks p84 CR France46

JENNER,John Thomas Russell 2Lt kld 21-12-17 GL 43RFC p9,R.J.CR Canada1143

JENNER-CLARKE,John William TLt kia 16-9-16 GL 6DCLI att43TMB p190 MR21

JENNINGS,Alexander LtTCapt ded 7-4-17 PoW RFA att29RFC p9&31 MR20

JENNINGS,Arnold John Capt kia 2-2-17 1 att6Leinst p174 CR France149

JENNINGS,Basil Spencer T2Lt dow 7-11-15 14 att6WYorks p82 CR Gallipoli27

JENNINGS,Charles Francis T2Lt kia 8-4-17 13Yorks p90 CR France439,Lt

JENNINGS,Francis Henry Cuthbert TLt ded 7-2-18 201MGC p183 CR Hamps11

JENNINGS,Francis Montgomery Capt ded 11-11-18 8Huss &2RRofCav p22&261 CR Eire148

JENNINGS,Francis William TLt kld 26-3-16 3Leics p87 CR Yorks63

JENNINGS,Gouldbourne Hayward 2Lt kia 10-8-16 20 att10RWFus p98 MR21,18-8-16

JENNINGS,H.A.K BrigGen 15-1-21 RA Staff CR India48

JENNINGS,Harold Victor Edgar 2Lt kia 29-5-18 14NumbF p61 MR18

JENNINGS,Henry Arthur 2Lt kia 29-4-16 6 att3Worc p109 CR France68,30-4-16

JENNINGS,Herbert Blake Lt dow 25-7-17 RGA 240SB p209 CR France398

JENNINGS,Hugh Cotton 2Lt dow PoW 3-5-17 RASC att12EYorks p193 CR France1277,Cotter

JENNINGS,H.W.McIvor T2Lt ded 29-2-16 RFA p31 CR Eire506

JENNINGS,Isaac Gaitskell 2Lt kia 21-3-18 5BordR p228 MR27

JENNINGS,John Gilderdale Maj mbk 10-8-15 IA 66Punjabis att6RDubF p278 MR4,Jack

JENNINGS,Richard William.MID TLt dow 3-7-16 10Worc C'Coy p109 CR France370

JENNINGS,Sidney James 2Lt kia 30-3-18 3ESurr attRE FldSur p112 CR France425,Sydney

JENNINGS,Thomas Edward ACapt kia 11-12-17 4Norf p216 CR palestine9

JENNINGS,William 2Lt dow 31-7-18 5Yorks p221 CR France1333

JENNINS,Harry T2Lt kia 12-11-16 8SStaffs p122 CR France307

JENNISON,Alfred Denzil 2Lt ded 17-9-16 14Lpool p72 CR Europe1

JENNISON,James Leonard 2Lt kia 3-5-17 15WYorks p82 MR20

JENNISON,Norman Lees.MC.TLt.ACapt ded 30-10-18 20Manch attTMB p155 CR Italy12

JENNS,Frank Arthur T2Lt dow 6-4-18 13Ess p132 CR France41

JENSON,Cyril Thornton T2Lt kia 10-5-16 25Manch attTMB p155 CR France625

JEPHSON,Charles Mitchell Warren Lt kia 27-12-17 5RWSurr p212 CR Palestine3

JEPHSON,Edward Jermy TCapt kia 15-9-16 10 att9Norf p74 MR21

JEPHSON,Howard 2Lt kia 23-4-17 6SStaffs p229 MR20

JEPHSON,John Noble.MID Maj dow 29-8-15 6RMunstF p175 CR Greece10

JEPHSON,William Jermy T2Lt kia 26-9-18 C175RFA p31 CR France451

JEPSON,Albert Clarence Leonard 2Lt kia 12-10-16 3Y&L p159 CR France432

JEPSON,Arthur George Leslie.MID Capt kia 16-9-16 2Lond p245 MR21,15-9-16

JEPSON,Joseph Jordan 2Lt kia 2-10-18 6LancF p221 CR France237

JEPSON,Norman Richard T2Lt kia 15-10-15 14 att2RFus p68 CR Gallipoli4,14 att2Bn

JEPSON,Stanley Capt ded 24-2-19 4NStaffs p157 CR France1028

JERGENSON,E.T.Lt kia 4-5-18 GL attKAR p266

JERRARD,Charles Frederick.MC.Capt ded 15-5-19 1Dors RoO p124&257 CR Germany1

JERRETT,Sidney(Jim) 2Lt dow 8-5-17 28RH&FA p31 CR France95,123RFA Ex H'RHA

JERVIS,Arthur Cyril LtTCapt kia 3-7-18 3Lpool att2/3KAR p72&202 CR EAfrica90

JERVIS,John Cedric TLt kia 26-10-16 5RFC p3 CR France133

JERVIS,Percy William 2Lt kia 3-4-17 5RWFus p223 CR France616
JERVIS,Robert Norrie TLt kia 5-1-16 RE 83FC p46 CR France525
JERVOIS,Philip Harding Lt dow 28-10-17 RGA 177SB p40 CR Belgium84,2Lt
JERWOOD,John Hugh.MC.Maj kia 21-3-18 10DLI att6SomLI p161 MR27
JESSON,Arthur 2Lt kia 16-11-16 6Beds p86 MR21
JESSON,Robert Witford Fairey.MID TCaptAMaj kia 22-2-17 5Wilts p153 MR38
JESSOP,Frederick Devereux.MC.TCapt kia 16-9-16 12ESurr p112 CR France277,15-9-16
JESSOP,George Edward Lt kia 10-4-18 8WYorks att6NumbF p219 MR32
JESSOP,John William LtCol kia 4-6-15 4Lincs p217 CR Belgium98
JESSOPP,Augustus John TLt kia 12-5-17 GL RFC p9 CR France777
JESSOPP,Walter Leverton TLt kia 31-7-17 MGC p183 MR29
JESSUP,Francis Reginald TCapt kia 1-7-16 1BordR p117 MR21
JESSUP,William Henry Gray.DSO.HonCapt dow 24-12-18 6DCLI p114
JESTIN,Martin T2Lt kia 7-6-17 7RIrF p171 MR29
JEUDWINE,Spencer Henry Capt kia 1-7-16 att2Lincs p75 MR21
JEUNE,Hugo St.Helier TCapt dow 12-5-17 9Glouc p107 CR France32,12Bn
JEWELL,Dudley Mark Hayward T2Lt kia 20-1-16 RE att18RFus p46 CR France279,RFus attRE
JEWELL,Edward Herbert T2Lt kia 15-5-16 11LancF B'Coy p92 CR France68,16-5-16
JEWELL,Frank Ernest T2Lt kia 15-12-17 RLancs att1/4YLI p59 CR Belgium101
JEWELL,J.B.Lt 6-4-18 GL &RFC CR Mddx34
JEWELL,William John T2Lt kia 1-9-18 12 att10SWBord p100 MR16
JEWHURST,George Stanley 2Lt dow 19-2-18 20Lond p251 CR France755
JEWITT,Dermod Patrick 2Lt kia 23-4-16 WorYeo p206 MR34
JEWITT,Joseph T2Lt kia 1-11-17 WYorks att1/7Bn p82 CR France1254
JEWSON,William Henry TMaj kia 19-4-17 4Norf p216 MR34
JEYNES,Harry.MC.MM.T2Lt kia 22-3-18 1Lincs p75 MR27
JICKLING,Frank T2Lt kld 23-10-17 GL RFC p9 CR Shrop52
JINKS,Mary Nurse 29-9-19 TFNS CR Scot358
JOACHIM,B.I.H.Lt 20-10-18 IMS MR67
JOB,Bernard Craig Keble 2Lt kia 18-4-15 3RWKent p141 MR29
JOB,Ernest Dalzel Capt kia 11-7-16 28Lond attMGC p187&252 CR France453
JOBLING,Ernest.MID ACapt kia 23-10-18 6ACycCps p181&257 CR France206
JOBLING,Harold Edward 2Lt dow 9-9-17 7Leinst p174 CR France593
JOBLING,Henry Douglas 2Lt dow 22-1-18 RFA p208 CR Yorks428
JOBLING,John Beresford TCapt ded 4-11-18 17LabCps p189 CR France332
JOBLING,Joseph Higgin TLt kia 1-12-17 10LancF p92 MR30
JOBSON,McGregor Maj dow 3-5-18 PoW 4KOSB p223 CR France1029
JODE,Gordon Robert Lovelace 2Lt kia 19-8-18 12Norf p204 CR France193
JOEL,Harold Walter ACapt kia 7-6-17 21Lond p251 CR Belgium122
JOFFE,William.DSO.2Lt kia 1-10-18 5YLI &RAF p270
JOHN Hugh Graham 2Lt mbk 16-6-15 3Y&L att1NumbF p256 MR29
JOHN,Iorwerth Glyndwr 2Lt kia 24-2-16 3 att1SWBord p100 CR France1723,25-2-16
JOHN Lennox William McClure 2Lt dow 24-9-16 1Lincs p75 CR France833,ded
JOHN,Wilbur Arnold Lt kia 1-8-18 SussYeo &RAF p205&258 CR Belgium112
JOHNS,Arthur T2Lt kia 25-9-17 RE 183TC p46 CR Belgium16
JOHNS,Arthur Hugh TLt kia 1-9-16 10 att11RSuss p119 CR France344
JOHNS,Bernard Digby TCapt kia 17-2-16 10RWFus p98 MR29
JOHNS,Bradley Cooper 2Lt ded 23-10-18 RGA 43A/ACoy p40 CR Essex122,22-10-18
JOHNS,Edward Tregonwell 2Lt dow 3-4-18 3 att6Dors p124 CR France103
JOHNS,Graham Lt kia 27-9-18 1ScotsGds att2TMB p52 MR16
JOHNS,Harold Thomas T2Lt kia 11-1-17 9 att8WelshR p127 MR38
JOHNS,Herbert 2LtACapt kia 11-4-18 1RGLI p200 MR32
JOHNS,Hubert Hilditch 2Lt ded 29-5-17 3BordR p117 MR65
JOHNS,Owen Llewellyn.MC.T2Lt kia 28-6-16 RFA attY33TMB p31&258 CR France296
JOHNS,Stephen T2Lt kia 14-3-16 RE 255Co p46 CR France705
JOHNSON,Alan Barrie.MC.Lt kld 27-1-18 45RFC CR Lincs181
JOHNSON,Alec.MC.Capt kia 18-9-18 1Camb p244 CR France369
JOHNSON,Alexander Downing 2LtTCapt kia 25-9-15 3 att2SStaffs p122 CR France163
JOHNSON,Alfred William.MC.TLtACapt dow 17-4-18 RE 1FldSur p46 CR France40
JOHNSON,Anthony.MC&Bar.2Lt kia 13-4-18 6 att2Worc p109 CR Belgium42,14-4-18
JOHNSON,Arnold Leslie Capt kia 14-10-18 5NStaffs p237 MR30
JOHNSON,Arthur Dennis 2Lt ded 16-10-17 RFA p270 CR Wales171
JOHNSON,Arthur Ellis T2Lt kia 20-7-17 Y&L att2Bn p159 MR19
JOHNSON,Arthur Graham MajTLtCol kia 17-9-17 RFA 33DAC p31 CR Belgium15

JOHNSON,Bernard Copestake 2Lt kia 14-5-17 2/7WRid p228 CR France690
JOHNSON,Charles Maj ded 15-1-17 RAMC p267
JOHNSON,Charles Cuthbert 2Lt kld 9-6-15 RE 1FC p210 MR4,6-6-15
JOHNSON,Clive Armstrong 2Lt kia 22-1-16 IARO att6Jats p278 MR38,Capt 21-1-16
JOHNSON,Cecil Marland 2Lt kld 6-6-18 GL &2RAF p190 CR France12
JOHNSON,Cyril Benton LtCol kia 21-9-17 1/6N&D p233 CR France258
JOHNSON,Cyril Goode 2Lt kia 7-6-17 149RFA p31 CR Belgium6
JOHNSON,Derrick Sivewright 2Lt kia 4-12-16 ACycCps HomeCountDiv attRFC p18&244 CR France924
JOHNSON,Donald Frederick Goold TLt dow 15-7-17 2Manch p155 CR France296
JOHNSON,Edmund George 2Lt kia 24-8-18 1 att12Lond p245 MR16
JOHNSON,Edward Fielder TCapt kia 7-12-17 B310RFA p31 CR France530,6-12-17
JOHNSON,Edward Francis 2Lt dow 7-11-18 5 att1Mddx p147 CR France930
JOHNSON,Eric Guildford 2Lt kia 25/26-9-15 8RWSurr p56 MR19
JOHNSON,Eric Hope Lt kia 22-12-17 8LancF p221 MR30
JOHNSON,Ernest Edward Chap4Cl ded 1-12-18 RAChDept att15LancF p199 CR France717
JOHNSON,Evelyn Walter James T2Lt dow 20-7-16 7Beds p86 CR France145
JOHNSON,Francis Hugh 2Lt kia 15-9-16 1/19Lond p250 CR France1890
JOHNSON,Frank L.Lt 6-9-17 BrWIndR attRFC CR Egypt1
JOHNSON,Fred Blacktin T2Lt kia 31-5-17 13RB p179 MR20
JOHNSON,Frederick Henry.VC.TCaptAMaj dow 26-11-17 RE 231FC p46 MR17 73FC
JOHNSON,Frederick Stansfield T2Lt kia 4-11-18 C92RFA p31 CR France
JOHNSON,G.J.J.Lt 17-5-15 IA 32Lancers CR EAfrica60
JOHNSON,Geoffrey Barham TCapt kia 23-11-15 7Norf p74 CR France423
JOHNSON,Geoffrey Robert T2Lt dow 7-8-15 7Glouc p107 MR4
JOHNSON,George Arthur Moxey Tuker 2Lt kia 21-5-17 19Lond p250 MR29
JOHNSON,George Bernard.DSO.Maj kia 18-4-18 A275RFA p206 CR France109
JOHNSON,George William TLt kia 24-4-18 8MGC p183 MR27
JOHNSON,Gilbert Ernest TLtACapt ded 4-7-18 14ACycCps p181 CR Italy8,drdacc
JOHNSON,Harold T2Lt dow 14-7-16 75MGC p183 CR France44
JOHNSON,Harold George Lt kia 7-8-17 1GrenGds p50 CR Belgium106
JOHNSON,Harold Richard Lt kld 19-1-16 3RFC p3 CR France88
JOHNSON,Harry Lt&QM 27-5-18 GL att9CpsCycBn MR19
JOHNSON,Harry Cecil.DSO.BtMaj dow PoW 1-1-15 KRRC p150 CR France598
JOHNSON,Henry Lt&QM kia 27-5-18 GL p254
JOHNSON,Henry Earlam 2Lt kia 4-6-16 5KRRC p150 CR France149
JOHNSON,Henry Norman Lt kia 2-11-17 5Manch p236 CR Belgium175
JOHNSON,Horace 2Lt kia 28-4-17 5SStaffs p270 MR20
JOHNSON,Horace James.DSO.LtCol kia 7-8-15 8WRid p115 CR Gallipoli27 JOHNSTON
JOHNSON,Horace Samuel T2Lt kld 9-3-18 RFC p16 CR Lincs181
JOHNSON,Howard Fife 2Lt kia 9-3-17 1/5EKent p213 MR38
JOHNSON,Hubert Alfred T2Lt kia 27-2-17 GL &8RFC p9 CR France120
JOHNSON,James Alexander Campbell Capt kia 21-8-18 8Lpool p215 CR France618
JOHNSON,James William Lt kia 30-11-17 8Mddx p236 MR17
JOHNSON,John T2Lt kia 9-1-17 133MGC Inf p183 MR38
JOHNSON,John Burgoyne LtCol ded 9-1-20 8DLI Res p270 CR Durham140
JOHNSON,John Chapman 2Lt kia 8-7-15 3 att1RWar p65 CR Belgium23
JOHNSON,John Frederic 2Lt kia 9-4-16 9RLancs p59 MR38
JOHNSON,John Frederick Lt dow 30-10-15 4Leic p219 CR France201
JOHNSON,Joseph John Claud 2Lt dow 5-4-18 SR att48RFA p31 CR France62
JOHNSON,Laurence Bertrand 2Lt dow 15-4-18 3 att1SomLI p80 CR France10
JOHNSON,Laurence Frederick T2Lt kia 16-6-17 8Dev p77 MR20
JOHNSON,Leslie Nethercote.MC.2Lt kia 3-6-17 6N&D p233 CR France570
JOHNSON,Luther Vincent Burgoyne Capt kia 26-4-15 8DLI p239 MR29,See BURGOYNE-JOHNSON
JOHNSON,Malcolm Johnson Williams Lt ded 18-2-19 RFA p207 CR War47
JOHNSON,Malcolm Thomas 2Lt kld 16-11-17 4 att12ESurr p112 CR Italy56
JOHNSON,Maurice Richard Wheatley Lt kia 28-6-18 IARO att21KohatMtnBty p278 CR Asia82
JOHNSON,Mervyn-Taylor Lt dow 17-10-14 2SWBord p100 CR France1329,14-9-14
JOHNSON,M.H.SNurse 5-9-15 QAIMNS CR Egypt9
JOHNSON,Newton Farring T2Lt kia 16-8-16 15 att26RFus p68 CR Belgium54 17-8-16
JOHNSON,Norman Alfred Power.MID 2LtTCapt kia 27-11-15.1LancF p92 MR4,Nelson
JOHNSON,Norman Teasdale 2Lt kia 16-4-17 3 att8RWKent p141 MR20,Leasdale
JOHNSON,Owen Bennett Goold T2Lt kia 9-4-17 11Suff p78 CR France265

JOHNSON,Percy Clarkson 2Lt kia 16-5-15 8Manch p237 MR4

JOHNSON,Phillip Norman.MC.Capt dow 16-10-18 1/4Y&L p238 CR France214

JOHNSON,Philip Walter 2Lt dow 18-5-15 3RWSurr p56 CR France632

JOHNSON,Pieter Cedric Earlam 2Lt kia 28-1-17 GL &RFC p9 MR20

JOHNSON,Raymond Albert.MC.TLt kia 24-4-18 1N&D p134 CR France144

JOHNSON,Rayner Harvey.MC.LtAMaj kia 26-9-18 RGA 122HB p40 CR France759,27-9-18

JOHNSON,Reginald Travernor Capt kia 13-10-15 5NStaffs p237 MR19

JOHNSON,Richard Colling TLt kia 31-7-17 RE SpCo p46 CR Belgium96

JOHNSON,Richard Digby.MID Maj kia 24-5-15 3RDubF p177 MR29

JOHNSON,Richard Ethelbert MajHonCol ded 29-10-15 GL p270 CR Yorks5 Ex EYorkRGA

JOHNSON,Robert 2Lt kia 24-4-17 4NumbF p213 MR20

JOHNSON,Robert Blissett Powell.MC.TLt kld 19-9-18 RGA 109HB p40

JOHNSON,Robert Deane TCapt kia 6-7-16 23RFus p68 CR France924

JOHNSON,Robert Harold Jervis 2Lt kia 13-3-17 2Ess p132 CR Belgium33

JOHNSON,Ronald Gordon Mayson Maj 30-9-20 RGA CR Berks73

JOHNSON,Ronald Lindsay TLtACapt kia 29-5-17 RFA HQDiv 23TMB p31 CR Belgium6

JOHNSON,Russell Lowell T2Lt kld 12-11-17 GL &RFC p9

JOHNSON,Samuel.MC.Lt kia 24-9-18 RFA attRGA 303SB p207 CR France421

JOHNSON,Samuel Clement Lt ded 8-2-19 RFA p270 CR Hamps15

JOHNSON,Sidney Frederick LtTCapt kia 10-1-17 3 att2BordR p117 CR France534

JOHNSON,Stanley T2Lt kia 20-7-16 2Suff p78 MR21

JOHNSON,Stanley Morrell T2Lt kld 25-5-17 GL &RFC p9 CR Yorks22

JOHNSON,Stephen Henry ACapt kia 20-5-17 GL att19TMB p190 MR20

JOHNSON,Sydney 2Lt dow 30-8-18 5WRid p227 MR16

JOHNSON,Thomas TLt kia 1-7-16 16HLI p163 MR21

JOHNSON,Thomas.MC.Lt kia 4-9-16 1BlkW p129 CR France432,3-9-16

JOHNSON,Thomas T2Lt dow 4-8-17 217MGC p183 CR Belgium18

JOHNSON,Thomas Henry Fielder.DSO.Maj ded 9-3-19 6Dors p264 CR Norf101

JOHNSON,Thomas Pelham.DSO.LtCol ded 12-6-18 RASC 15DivTrn p193 CR France113

JOHNSON,Victor Reginald William Lt dow 28-3-15 3 att2Wilts A'Coy p153 CR France706

JOHNSON,Walter Charles Littley 2Lt 30-7-17 6 att16Mddx MR20

JOHNSON,Wilfrid Lloyd T2Lt kia 19-4-16 2BordR p117 CR France394

JOHNSON,William 2Lt dow 16-5-15 2Leic p87 CR France727

JOHNSON,William T2Lt dow 12-11-16 8SStaffs p122 MR21

JOHNSON,William Charles Littley T2Lt kia 30-5-17 6 att16Mddx p147

JOHNSON,William Godfrey Easlam Capt dow 13-10-17 1/5Manch p236 CR France1361

JOHNSON,William Herbert 2Lt dow 28-6-17 4LNLancs p234 CR Lancs381

JOHNSON,William Inglis Capt dow 15-10-15 4Lincs p217 CR France80

JOHNSON,William Morton TCapt kia 2-7-16 16Manch p155 MR21

JOHNSON,William Roland 2Lt kia 1-7-16 1/6SStaffs p229 MR21

JOHNSON,William Stanley T2Lt dow 17-3-17 7ESurr p112 CR France158

JOHNSON-SMYTH,Edward Chap4Cl ded 10-2-17 RAChDept p199 CR France145

JOHNSTON,Adrian Alexander Hope Lt kia 2-7-16 5 att4Mddx p147 CR France267

JOHNSTON,Alec Leith TLt kia 22-4-16 1KSLI p145 CR Belgium73

JOHNSTON,Alexander 2Lt kia 25-3-18 10EYorks p84 MR20

JOHNSTON,Alexander Maj ded 22-9-18 RAMC p267 CR Scot80

JOHNSTON,Alexander Francis 2Lt kia 10-9-16 11 att1/6Lond p248 MR21

JOHNSTON,Alexander Vyvyan TLt kia 18-8-17 12Lpool p72 MR30,17-8-17

JOHNSTON,Alfred Roy T2Lt kia 24-4-17 GL &RFC p9 MR20

JOHNSTON,Andrew 2Lt kia 30-10-17 RFA &RFC p9

JOHNSTON,Andrew Robert 2Lt kia 29-7-18 5HLI attD'Coy 5KOSB p240 CR France866

JOHNSTON,Andrew Yaill Pollok 2Lt kia 5-10-17 5KOSB p224 CR Belgium112,Yuill

JOHNSTON,Arthur Annan 2Lt dow 16-4-17 B291RFA p208 CR France145

JOHNSTON,Basil 2Lt kia 3-9-16 6 att11RB p179 CR France294

JOHNSTON,Benjamin 2Lt ded PoW 3-11-18 11KRRC p150 CR Europe149

JOHNSTON.C.E.L.Maj 18-3-21 RGA CR Beds70

JOHNSTON,Charles Ernest.DSO.TD.Maj kia 23-3-18 6SfthH p241 MR20

JOHNSTON,Charles Moore TCapt kia 1-7-16 9RIrF C'Coy p171 CR France233

JOHNSTON,Charles Wright T2Lt kia 12-10-17 11RScots p54 MR30

JOHNSTON,David Ernest T2Lt ded 12-11-17 RASC 954MT p193 CR Iraq8

JOHNSTON,Donald Clark Capt dow 13-9-18 1 att1/8ScotRif p103 CR France145

JOHNSTON,Edward John Farquharson Capt kia 12-4-15 1RScots p54 CR Belgium151

JOHNSTON,Elliott Capt kia 1-7-16 13RIrRif p169 MR21

JOHNSTON,Evelyn Sandiland Capt 14/15-5-20 RGA 27MtnBty MR43

JOHNSTON,Foster Crampton 2Lt dow 23-4-17 13ESurr p112 CR France164,Forster

JOHNSTON,Francis Earl.CB.MIDx4 TBrigGen kia 7-8-17 NStaffs att3NZealandBaseHQ p157 CR France285,att1NZ

JOHNSTON,Francis WO ded 16-2-18 RIM p278

JOHNSTON,Frank.MID CaptTMaj dow 31-5-18 7KSLI p145 CR France33

JOHNSTON,Geoffrey Stewart Lt kia 14-5-15 EssYeo p203 MR29

JOHNSTON,George Mitchell Capt kia 3-4-16 RJLI att7RIrRif p201 CR France423,1-4-16

JOHNSTON,Gilbert Henderson T2Lt kld 15-12-17 GL &RFC p9 CR Scot228

JOHNSTON,Godfrey Julius Jeppe Lt ded 17-5-15 IA 32Lancers p278

JOHNSTON,Gordon Black Lt ded PoW 22-10-18 1/4RSuss p228 CR Iraq8

JOHNSTON,Henry Edward.DCM.2Lt dow 16-3-18 SussYeo p205 CR Palestine3

JOHNSTON,Herbert Augustus 2Lt kia 4-3-16 1RFC p3 CR France922

JOHNSTON,Hugh Bertie Henriques.DSO.Maj dow 27-10-16 RH&FA p31 CR France453,RGA 21HB

JOHNSTON,Hugh McColl Capt dow 4-4-18 RAVC att1RDrags p198 CR France37,kia

JOHNSTON,James Annandale 2Lt kia 2-7-16 3 att1SomLI p80 MR21

JOHNSTON,James Cecil TCapt kia 9-8-15 6RIrF p171 MR4

JOHNSTON,James MacCormac Caldwell TLt kia 27-5-16 RAMC att3Worc p196 CR France68

JOHNSTON,James Tait TLt kia 28-9-16 6BordR p117 CR France293,JOHNSTONE

JOHNSTON,James Valentine 2Lt kia 3-4-17 7HLI p240 CR France672

JOHNSTON,John 2Lt kia 10-4-18 RE 81FC p210 MR30

JOHNSTON,John Edwin T2Lt kia 10-7-16 4 att10SStaffs p122 MR21

JOHNSTON,John Henry Capt ded 18-5-18 6LancF p270

JOHNSTON,John Leslie 2Lt kia 12-5-15 O&BLI p130 MR22

JOHNSTON,John Lionel Lukin TCapt dow 21-6-16 2Leinst p174 CR France285,Lyonel

JOHNSTON,John Thomas Capt kia 27-5-17 10 att1/9RScots p212 MR20

JOHNSTON,Joseph Allen TCapt kia 18-2-17 9RIrF p171 CR Belgium43

JOHNSTON,Leslie.MC.2Lt dow 25-7-16 7Worc p226 CR France345

JOHNSTON,Octavius Ralph Featherston Capt kia 1-7-16 4Mddx p147 CR France267

JOHNSTON,Paul Headley 2Lt dow 11-6-18 C74RH&FA p31 CR France103,Lt

JOHNSTON,Percy Ellwood LtACapt dow 12-9-16 3DLI att2NumbF p161 CR Greece4

JOHNSTON,Richard George Mann Maj kia 25-8-16 C162RFA p31 CR France188

JOHNSTON,Robert Graham Lt kia 18-7-16 7SfthH p165 MR21

JOHNSTON,Robert London T2Lt kia 13-12-15 17Manch p155 CR France281,Loudon

JOHNSTON,Robert Neilson 2Lt kia 22-7-16 8ScotRif p225 MR34

JOHNSTON,Rowland Ivan 2Lt dow 28-8-18 2 att3RIrRif p169 CR France34

JOHNSTON,Sinclair Beatty 2Lt died 27-5-17 3 att7EKent p57 MR20

JOHNSTON,Stuart TLt kia 12-8-16 B70RFA p31 CR France703,dpw

JOHNSTON,Thomas James T2Lt kia 21-3-18 12 att7/8RInniskF p105 MR27

JOHNSTON,Thomas McKinnon 2Lt kia 13-11-16 3 att1RScotF p94 CR France742

JOHNSTON,Thomas Peacock Lt kia 20-5-17 ShropYeo attRFC p205&18 CR France120,2Lt

JOHNSTON,Walter Robertson Lt kia 6-9-18 A112RFA p207 CR France511

JOHNSTON,William Henry.VC.Maj kia 8-6-15 RE p46 CR Belgium115

JOHNSTON,William Holden 2Lt kia 30-7-16 17Lpool p72 CR France294

JOHNSTON,William Saville Lt dow PoW 23-3-18 7A&SH p243 CR France256

JOHNSTON,William Tardiff T2Lt kia 13-4-17 12Manch p155 CR France581,Tordiff

JOHNSTON,William Vincent TCapt ded 12-12-17 RAMC p196 CR Eire322

JOHNSTON-STEWART,Herbert Eustace Hathorn Capt kia 17-5-15 2HLI p163 MR22

JOHNSTON-STUART,Cyril George Lt kia 16-4-18 13EYorks p84 MR30

JOHNSTONE,Arthur James 2Lt kia 5-4-17 5RScotF p222 CR France1182

JOHNSTONE,Frederick John Lawrie.MC.Lt dow 29-8-16 2KRRC p150 CR France51,Capt

JOHNSTONE,George Dreyer 2Lt kia 19-12-16 7Lond p247 CR France1157

JOHNSTONE,George Smith Lt kia 26-8-18 3 att2KOSB p102 MR16

JOHNSTONE,Gilbert Lumley TCaptAMaj kia 4-10-16 96RFA p31 CR France389

JOHNSTONE,Godfrey Gleeson T2Lt kia 30-1-18 2RFC p16 CR France345

JOHNSTONE,Henry Archer TCaptAMaj kia 21-3-18 152RFA p31 CR France162

JOHNSTONE,Hugh Bertie Henriques Maj dow 27-10-16 RGA p262

JOHNSTONE,Hugh Noel 2Lt 1-6-21 2/8WYorks CR C'land &W'land54

JOHNSTONE.J.H.MC.Capt 18-5-18 Lpool&LancF CR Ches182

JOHNSTONE,James 2Lt dow 17-4-18 9HLI p240

163

JOHNSTONE,James Lt ded 20-10-19 LabCps p266 CR Scot238,CamelTransCps

JOHNSTONE,James Henry Walter Maj kia 15-9-14 115/25RFA p31 CR France1328,Waller

JOHNSTONE,John TCapt kia 9-9-16 7Leinst p174 MR21

JOHNSTONE,John Andrew Lt kia 20-5-18 RFA attRFC p31 CR France200

JOHNSTONE,John Douglas Lt kia 31-7-17 4RLancs p213 MR29

JOHNSTONE,John Pultney Hope Lt accDrd 15-2-18 IA 66Pujabis p278 MR66

JOHNSTONE,Melville 2Lt kia 16-7-17 27RFC SR p9 CR France134,Capt

JOHNSTONE,Nelson Lt ded 9-12-15 RAMC p270 CR Camb16

JOHNSTONE,Nelson Gordon.MC.2Lt kia 30-12-17 9BlkW att44TMB p129 CR France1182,Capt att22

JOHNSTONE,Reginald Fitzroy Lews Lt kia 8-9-14 1CamH p168 CR France1425

JOHNSTONE,Richard TCapt ded 8-4-19 NumbF p262 CR Durham26

JOHNSTONE,Richard Michael TCapt kia 25-3-18 12HLI p163 CR France630

JOHNSTONE,Robert Maj 6-10-17 7ScotRif CR Scot237

JOHNSTONE,Robert Brown Whylock 2Lt kia 19-7-18 51RFA p31 MR32

JOHNSTONE,Robert James Halliday Lt kia 26-9-17 5BlkW p231 MR30

JOHNSTONE,William 2Lt kia 30-3-16 8BlkW p129 CR Belgium71

JOHNSTONE,William James 2Lt kia 28-6-15 4RScots p211 MR4

JOHNSTONE,William Jeffray.MC.Lt kia 28-12-17 Fife&ForfarYeo p203 CR Palestine3

JOHNSTONE,William Joseph Capt dow 18-12-17 7Lond p247 CR France398

JOHNSTONE,William McCall T2Lt kia 13-2-16 152RFA p31 CR France275

JOHNSTONE,William Rutherford Mushet 2Lt kld 20-8-21 IAUL att1Leinst p278 MR66

JOICE,Philip Sidney T2Lt dow 1-12-17 16Ches p96 CR Belgium16 1Bn

JOICE,Reginald John TLt kia 30-4-17 60RFA p31 CR France96,1-5-17 C50RFA

JOICEY,Clive Montague LtTCapt kia 5-6-17 4NumbF p213 CR France604

JOICEY,Sidney James Drever.Hon.TCapt&Adjt kia 20-3-16 10NumbF p61 CR France557,Sydney

JOICEY-CECIL,John Francis James Lt kia 25-9-16 4GrenGds p50 CR France374

JOLLEY,John Andrew Benjamin T2Lt kia 11-10-15 2 att5Lincs p75 MR19

JOLLEY,Robert James 2Lt dow 22-8-18 1Ches p96 CR France84

JOLLIE,Francis Ormonde Holden Capt kia 25-4-15 2ESurr p112 MR29

JOLLY,Benton Ord T2Lt dow 9-2-17 7Yorks p90 CR France105

JOLLY,Frederick Capt ded 20-8-18 HertsYeo p204 CR Herts91

JOLLY,Percy 2Lt kia 13-7-17 4RLancs p213 CR France759,JOLLEY

JOLLY,R.2Lt 26-11-19 4GordH CR Scot500

JOLLY,Trevor Blake 2Lt kia 20-9-17 3 att12ESurr p122 MR30

JONAS,Frank Charlton Capt kia 31-7-17 1Camb p244 MR29

JONES,A.Capt 17-4-17 RE CR Surrey97

JONES,A.A.Col 23-9-15 MysoreImpServTrps MR66

JONES,A.E.Capt 9-4-18 1/6Lpool CR France88

JONES,Albert Capt kia 9-4-18 6Lpool p215

JONES,Alfred Cotton.MC.TCapt kia 2-7-16 8Lincs p75 MR21

JONES,Alfred Ivan Noel Lt ded 22-11-19 Norf att19Lond p263 MR34

JONES,Alfred Gwilym Capt ded 27-1-16 RAMC p196 MR43 &CR Pakistan50A

JONES,Alfred Roy 2Lt kia 23-3-18 RWar att2/7Bn p65 MR27

JONES,Archibald Wilson LtCol ded 22-2-17 4HLI attRemounts p163 CR Wales658

JONES,Arnold Seymour Lt dow 27-3-15 4SLancs p230

JONES,Arthur 2Lt kia 27-5-18 11LancF p92 MR18

JONES,Arthur T2Lt kia 23-8-18 8DCLI att3MGC p114&183,22-8-18 CR France927,5MGC

JONES,Arthur Ewart T2Lt kia 8-8-15 8WelshR p127 MR4

JONES,Arthur Godman T2Lt dow 1-7-17 10EYorks B'Coy p84 CR France113

JONES,Arthur Henry 2Lt ded 15-3-16 RFA p208 CR Shrop111

JONES,Arthur Leslie Gwynne 2Lt kia 4-5-18 RGA 252SB p40 CR Belgium8

JONES,Arthur Lloyd.MC.TCapt dow 3-9-18 14RWFus p98 CR France703

JONES,Arthur Mervyn Lt dow 21-11-16 1ScotsGds p52

JONES,Arthur Meredydd.MC&Bar.Lt dow 10-4-18 50MGC p183 MR32

JONES,Arthur Trevor TLt dow 19-6-17 17WelshR C'Coy p127 CR France439,Capt

JONES,Arthur Vernon.MID TCapt ded 16-2-19 GL &RWFus p255 CR France40

JONES,Arthur William 2Lt kia 31-3-17 HAC p206 CR France568

JONES,B.M.Lt kld 28-9-18 RE &RAF p256

JONES,Barham Ivor Lewis 2Lt kia 22-6-15 3SWBord p100 CR Gallipoli6,B.J.L.

JONES,Basil Rev ded 25-10-18 RAChDept p199 CR France85

JONES,Basil Gordon Dawes.MC.Lt kia 23-9-16 1 att2WelshR p127 MR21,23-10-16

JONES,Beatrice Isabel Matron I/C 14-1-21 QAIMNS CR Iraq8

JONES,Bryan John.DSO&Bar.Maj kia 20-10-18 1Leinst att15RIrRif p174 CR Belgium140,LtCol

JONES,Brynley Lewis Capt ded 26-12-18 3Mon p270 CR Mon4

JONES,Cecil Hughes TCapt kia 18-9-18 11RWFus p98 CR Greece5,Hugh

JONES,Cecil Norman 2Lt ded 9-11-17 3 att15WelshR p127 CR France255

JONES,Charles Arnold T2Lt dow 1-5-18 RASC att2Berks p193 CR France29

JONES,Charles David T2LtALt ded 7-3-18 8WRid attBritPortugueseMission p115 CR France345

JONES,Charles Douglas TLt kia 28-10-16 9YLI p143 CR France114

JONES,Charles Edward Coursolles TCapt kia 4-7-16 10RWar p65 MR21

JONES,Charles Henry Lt kia 10-4-16 RE 1/2FC p210 CR France68

JONES,Charles Lambert TLt kld 15-6-16 10Glouc p107 CR France149

JONES,Charles Taylor.MID T2Lt kia 25-9-15 2RWSurr p56 MR19

JONES,Cledwyn Lloyd 2Lt kia 21-3-18 2/7N&D p233 MR20

JONES,Clifford T2Lt kia 2-8-17 15RWFus p98 MR29

JONES,Cyril Gordon TLt kia 20-11-17 9Norf C'Coy p74 CR France379

JONES,Cyril Hammond Montague LtACapt ded 14-11-18 RGA p40 CR Wilts142,14-11-17

JONES,Dan Llewellyn T2Lt dow 14-3-16 9WelchR p127 CR France345

JONES,Daniel Thomas 2Lt kia 4-5-17 3 att1RWFus p98 MR20

JONES,David TCapt kia 12-7-16 10WelshR p127 MR21

JONES,David T2Lt kia 24-7-18 3SWBord att1KSLI p100 CR Belgium40

JONES,David 2Lt kia 18-9-18 3WelchR att11RWFus p127 CR Greece5 att11RFus

JONES,David 2Lt kia 8-10-18 10SWBord p100 CR France845

JONES,David John.MC.T2Lt ded 4-12-16 RE 178TC p46 CR France102

JONES,David Raymond Lt kia 17-4-18 RE p210 CR Belgium102

JONES,David William Llewellyn Lt dow 2-7-16 3Lond p245 CR France120,1-7-16

JONES,Douglas Grainger 2Lt kia 4-6-15 6 att4Worc p109 MR4

JONES,Douglas Llewellyn TLt kia 22-8-17 6Lincs B'Coy p75 MR30,Capt

JONES,Edward Earle 2Lt dow 1-8-17 4Yorks Y'Coy p220 CR France285

JONES,Edward Pitcairn 2Lt dow 13-5-17 5 att9RB p179 CR France46

JONES,Edward Stanley Lt ded 28-11-18 RAOC p198 CR Wales107

JONES,Edwin 2Lt dow 14-4-18 RGA 1/1NMidlandHB p40 CR Belgium183

JONES,Edwin 2Lt kia 23-8-18 5Mddx att2/16Lond p147 CR France139

JONES,Edwin Evan 2Lt ded 25-9-19 LabCps p266 CR Wales725,Lt

JONES,Edwin Jones TCapt kia 13-6-17 2/6LancF p221 CR France765,James

JONES,Edwin Tudor Capt kia 3-9-16 3 att1RWFus p98 MR21

JONES,Emyr Griffiths.MM.2Lt dow 18-9-18 3 att7SWBord p100 MR37

JONES,Eran Brindle HonCapt ded 10-11-18 19RWFus p263

JONES,Eric 2Lt kia 2-7-16 1/9Lpool p216 CR France174

JONES,Eric Arthur Owen 2Lt kia 18-9-16 16Lond p250 MR21

JONES,Eric Irvine 2Lt kia 22-3-18 2/19Lond p250 CR Palestine3

JONES,Ernest Hugh T2Lt kia 26-10-17 188MGC Inf p183 CR Belgium126

JONES,Ernest Kerrison TCapt kia 3-7-16 8 att9RWFus p98 MR21,2-7-16

JONES,Ernest Rae Capt kia 2-9-14 1Ches p96 CR Belgium216,24-8-14

JONES,Ernest William T2Lt ded 9-11-15 8WelchR p127 CR Europe1

JONES,Evan 2Lt kia 6-11-17 1/6RWFus C'Coy p223 CR Palestine1,Capt

JONES,Evan Brindle Capt ded 10-11-18 B'Coy 19RWFus CR Wales462

JONES,Evan Gwilym T2Lt dow 31-8-18 13WelchR p127 CR France84

JONES,Evan Harries.MC&Bar.2Lt kia 25-4-18 87RFA p31 MR30

JONES,Evan Lawrence TCapt kia 30-9-18 RAMC att2HLI p195 CR France1483

JONES,Evan Lewis T2Lt kia 13-11-16 10NStaffs att76MGC p157&183 CR France

JONES,Evelyn Llewellyn Hustler 2Lt kia 26-3-17 12 att1/5RWFus p98 MR34

JONES,F.D. Lt kia 7-7-16 10LancF p92 MR21

JONES,Felix Ernest.MC.Lt kia 16-8-17 4 O&BLI p231 MR30

JONES,Francis George.MID LtCol dow 9-5-15 Cmdg 1RInniskF p105 MR4,5-5-15

JONES,Francis Leonard Clarence.MC.MM.2Lt kia 1-9-18 2RWFus p98 CR France216

JONES,Francis Maynard Harvey.MC.2Lt dow 18-6-17 6Worc p109

JONES,Frank Riddell T2Lt kia 18-11-16 17HLI p163 CR France534

JONES,Fred 2Lt kia 24-5-15 9Manch p237 CR Gallipoli2

JONES,Frederick James.MM.2Lt kia 26-10-17 21Lond p251 MR20

JONES,Frederick S.C.2Lt kia 30-11-16 1LancF attMGC p92&183 CR France630

JONES,Frederick Thomas Averay 2Lt dow 5-12-17 3/1Hereford p252 CR France145

JONES,Frederick Wigan Lt dow 21-12-16 8RWar p215 CR War10

JONES,Frederick William James.MC.2Lt ded 24-10-18 RFA p261 CR Glouc5

JONES,G.M.Lt 13-12-18 W'land &C'landYeo CR Wales684

JONES,Geoffrey Anthony St.John Lt kia 14-6-17 4Mddx p147 CR France397

JONES,Geoffrey Brian T2Lt kia 18-9-18 SWBord att13WelshR p100 CR France415

JONES,George 2Lt kia 21-5-18 1/5SStaffs p229 CR France109

JONES,George Alfred Prime Capt kldacc 28-5-16 8EKent attRFC p3&57 CR Kent269

JONES,George Frederick.MC.T2LtACapt kia 28-3-18 7KSLI p145 MR20
JONES,George Harold Price Lt kia 30-5-18 7KSLI p145 CR France33
JONES,George James LtTCapt kia 7-4-17 GL RFC p9
JONES,George Morris 2Lt dow 14-7-18 4LNLancs p234 CR Lancs342
JONES,George William T2Lt kia 15/16-5-16 11Ches att6SWBord p96 CR France68
JONES,George William 2Lt dow 12-4-18 12Y&L p159 MR32
JONES,George Worthington.MC.Maj dow 10-11-17 RH&FA p206
JONES,Gerald.MC.Capt kia 2-11-17 7Ess p232 CR Palestine8
JONES,Gertrude Ellen Sister drd 10-4-17 QAIMNS p200 CR France85,Eileen
JONES,Gladys Maud Miss ded 21-8-17 VAD BRCS p200 CR Greece9
JONES,Griffiths Vaughan 2Lt dow PoW 24-4-18 4KSLI p235 CR Germany1,Griffith
JONES,Gwilym T2Lt kia 10-9-18 8Lincs p75 CR France530
JONES,Gwilym Rhys 2Lt kia 10-8-15 6RWFus p223 MR4
JONES,Gwilyn Arthur Tegid 2Lt kia 25-10-17 RGA 41SB p209 CR Belgium13
JONES,Harold 2Lt ded 26-12-17 RDC p253 CR Lancs463
JONES,Harold Edward T2Lt kia 22-11-17 GL &41RFC p9 CR France62
JONES,Harold Garfield 2Lt kia 8-10-18 A286RFA p31 CR France482,A288RFA
JONES,Harold Madoc.MIDx2 TLt kia 31-7-17 17RWFus p98 MR29
JONES,Harold Vivian TLt kia 10-7-16 13RWFus p98 CR France453
JONES,Harry.MID Lt kld 15-5-18 4Lond p246&270,ded CR Hamps1
JONES,Harry Edward 2Lt ded 12-10-17 22RFC p9 CR Surrey1
JONES,Harry Reynolds T2Lt kia 17-3-18 80RFC p16 CR France987
JONES,Henry John Rutherford TCapt ded 26-2-16 RAMC p196 CR Mddx51
JONES,Henry Myrddin.MID T2Lt kia 13-11-16 10RWFus p98 CR France156
JONES,Henry Paul Mainwaring TLt kia 31-7-17 MGC p183 MR29
JONES,Herbert 2Lt dow 4-11-18 5SLancs p230 CR France716
JONES,Herbert Francis T2Lt kia 10-7-16 10WelshR p127 MR21
JONES,Herbert Japson.MC.Capt dow 12-11-18 RH&FA p207
JONES,Herbet Joaquin 2Lt dow PoW 29-3-18 4 att7RIrReg p89 CR France658
JONES,Herbert Thomas 2Lt kia 4-11-18 3 att10SWBord p100 CR France34 &CR Frnce734
JONES,Herbert Wynn Lt dow 24-3-18 WelshHorseYeo attMGC p187&205,Wyman CR France650,25RWFus
JONES,Hilda Lilian Sister ded 28-10-18 QAIMNS p200 CR Devon1,L.H.
JONES,Horace Birchall 2Lt kia 1-7-16 1/6NStaffs p238 MR21
JONES,Horace Edwin 2Lt kia 21-3-18 SStaffs att2/6Bn p122 MR20
JONES,Hubert Victor Edward T2Lt kia 25-10-18 12RIrRif p169 CR Belgium140
JONES,Hugh T2Lt kia 3-9-16 10RWFus p98 MR21
JONES,Hugh T2Lt kia 27-9-16 11SStaffs att7Leic p122 MR20
JONES,Hugh.MC.TCapt ded 10-11-18 13Glouc p107 CR Glouc109
JONES,Hugh Ivor 2Lt ded 22-6-18 B51RFA attRE p31 CR France134
JONES,Hugh Laurie T2Lt ded 29-4-18 RASC attS&TCps p267 MR66,Lt
JONES,Hugh M.TLt kia 30-7-16 19Lpool p72 MR21
JONES,Hywel Herbert Saunders 2Lt kia 4-3-17 3RWSurr p56 CR France511
JONES,Ivor Cynric Salusbury Lt dow 21-9-16 5YLI p235
JONES,Ivor Dryhurst TLt kia 10-4-18 5SWBord D'Coy p100 MR30
JONES,Ivor Wyn 2Lt dow 9-6-17 7RWFus att1/24Lond p223 CR Belgium11,Wynne Lt
JONES,Jaffrey Fryer Selous 2Lt dow 26-8-16 2SpBde RE F'Coy CR France145
JONES,James Andrew.DSO.MC.MajALtCol dow 14-10-18 2DLI att17LancF p161 CR Belgium112
JONES,James Arthur.MID TCapt kia 8-10-18 10SWBord D'Coy p100 CR France845
JONES,James Brinley TLt kia 31-5-17 10WelshR att25LabBn p127 CR Belgium73
JONES,James Forbes.MID Maj dow 29-3-17 7A&SH p243 CR France40
JONES,James Melville Lt kia 27-8-17 RFA p207 MR30
JONES,James Richard Tudor 2Lt kia 23-7-18 3LNLancs p136 CR France524,2Bn
JONES,James Thomas 2Lt dow 24-8-17 20Lond p251 CR Belgium11
JONES,Jesse 2Lt kia 11-11-14 2O&BLI p130 MR29
JONES,John Arllwyd 2Lt kia 20-9-17 WelchR att9Bn p127 MR30
JONES,John Daniel Lt ded 21-2-16 RFA p31 CR France85
JONES,John Harold T2Lt kia 1-10-17 1RWFus p98 MR30
JONES,John Harold Ryle T2Lt kia 4-7-16 7SLancs p125 MR21
JONES,John Humphrey 2Lt kia 8-10-18 SWBord att5RWFus p223 CR France1346,15WelchR
JONES,John Langdale Maj ded 14-5-17 RAMC p196 MR43
JONES,John Lewis T2Lt ded 13-8-17 3WelchR p127 CR Wales278
JONES,John Llewelyn Thomas Capt kia 16-8-17 3Lond D'Coy p245 CR Belgium112
JONES,John Myddleton T2Lt kia 1-7-16 17DLI p161 MR21
JONES,John Owen T2Lt kia 6-6-17 WelshR att16Bn p127 MR29

JONES,John Sydney 2Lt died 27-8-17 189RFA p208 CR France139
JONES,John Thomas.MC.TCapt ded 28-3-18 RASC HQ DivTrn p193 CR France65
JONES,John Victor 2Lt kia 14-7-16 3Dors att7RWar p124 MR21
JONES,John Wilfred T2Lt kia 16-11-16 20 att9WelshR p127 CR France246,Wilfrid
JONES,John William T2Lt kia 8-8-18 10KSLI attImpCamelCps p145 MR34
JONES,John Ynys Palfrey T2Lt kia 30-8-18 14WelchR p127 CR France217
JONES,Joseph Maurice 2Lt kia 15-2-17 6 att9Worc p109 CR Iraq5
JONES,Joseph Stephen Lt 27-8-20 GL &RE IWT MR38
JONES,Kenneth Champion T2Lt kia 1-7-16 1ELancs p111 MR21
JONES,Kenneth James Devison TLtACapt kia 3-5-17 SStaffs att6Leic p122 MR20
JONES,Kingsmill William.DSO.Capt kia 2-8-18 RAMC attEKent p253 CR Belgium40
JONES,Lilian Kate Nurse ded 6-6-16 VAD p200 CR Mon67
JONES,Lawrence Henry Capt kia 4-10-17 2 att1ESurr p112 CR Belgium112
JONES,Lawrence Bertram 2Lt kia 23-10-16 2Lincs p75 MR21,Laurence
JONES,Leonard 2Lt kia 16-5-15 3 att1RWFus p98 MR22
JONES,Leslie Philips Lt dow 6-6-15 9RBerks att2Hamps p139 CR Gallipoli2,kia
JONES,Leslie Seymour Ross 2Lt kia 7-10-18 3Dev &65RAF p263 CR Belgium371,6-10-18
JONES,Lewis Farewell.MID Maj kia 1-7-16 1/12Lond p248 MR21 &CR France390
JONES,Lewis Jeremy Capt mbk 29-10-14 1A 9BhopalInf p278
JONES,Llewellyn James Capt dow 16-3-16 WIndR att7ESurr p112 CR France80
JONES,Llewellyn Price T2Lt kia 20-9-17 3 att9WelchR p127 MR30
JONES,Loftus Edward Percival TCapt kia 3-8-15 7Yorks p90 CR Belgium166,Perceval
JONES,Louis Gueret Walter Southwell 2Lt dow 20-6-17 1Mon B'Coy p244 CR France178
JONES,Lumley Owen Williames.DSO.TBrigGen ded 14-9-18 Cmdg13Ess Staff p132 CR France84
JONES,Max Greville.MC.Lt kld 12-6-18 1/2NumbF &55RAF p61 CR France1678
JONES,Maurice TLt dow 27-9-17 ELancs att14RWar p111 CR France568
JONES,Merfin Harman Salisbury T2Lt kia 11-8-18 YLI att8Bn p143 MR16,Merfyn Salusbury
JONES,Mervyn Lt 21-11-16 1ScotsGds SR CR France105
JONES,Oliver Saint Michael TLt kia 4-10-17 N&D att9Bn p134 MR30
JONES,Otto Hamilton T2Lt dow 23-11-17 15RIrRif p169 MR17
JONES,Owen Cecil Maj dow 30-12-17 1/7RWFus p223 CR Palestine3
JONES,Owen Gwilym 2Lt kia 26-3-17 7RWFus p223 MR34
JONES,Owen Morris Lt kia 31-10-18 6RWFus p223
JONES,P.H.MC.Capt&QM 23-1-21 Lincs CR Lincs181
JONES,Penry T2Lt kia 20-9-17 1/2 att10Worc p109 MR30
JONES,Percy.DCM.VD.Capt dow 3-11-17 IARO att13Lancers p278 CR Iraq8
JONES,Percy Barrett Capt kia 28-9-15 3Mddx p147 MR19
JONES,Percy Griffith 2Lt kld 2-7-18 RE &RAF p46
JONES,Philip Allsworth T2Lt dow 27-9-16 21KRRC p150 CR France833
JONES,Raymond John TLt kia 10-7-16 RAMC att129FA p196 CR France513
JONES,R.Colville 2Lt kld 4-11-18 13RB &RAF p179
JONES,Reginald George Capt kia 30-8-18 2/20Lond C'Coy p251 CR France617
JONES,Reginald George T2Lt kia 20-10-18 10WYorks p82 CR France658
JONES,Reginald Rees,DSO 2Lt dow 25-8-17 1WelshGds p53 CR Belgium18
JONES,Rhys Harris TLt kia 8-10-18 1/2 att6SWBord p100 CR France845
JONES,Richard T2Lt kia 21-10-16 2SLancs p125 MR21
JONES,Richard Alum T2Lt kia 20-11-17 D'TankCps p188 CR France1483
JONES,Richard Archibald TMaj kia 21-5-16 15RWar p65 CR France1182
JONES,Richard Basil Brandram.VC.TLt kia 21-5-16 8LNLancs p136 MR20
JONES,Richard Harold 2Lt kia 14-1-17 6LancF att1Lond p221 CR France1887
JONES,Robert Arthur Capt kia 10-9-14 122/28RFA p31 MR15,26-8-14
JONES,Robert Carl Molsch 2Lt dow 13-11-16 3 att5SWBord p100 CR France74,Moesch
JONES,Robert Henry T2Lt kia 29-9-16 13 att18WYorks p82 CR France134
JONES,Robert Nelson Lt kia 31-7-17 4Nhampt attMGC p187&234 MR29
JONES,Robert Roland Akrill 2Lt kia 9-4-17 4YLI p235
JONES,Rowland T2Lt dow 13-10-18 1/2 att9WRid p115 CR France398
JONES,Russell Shedden 2Lt kia 3-9-16 6 att3Worc p109 CR France246
JONES,Russell Hafrenydd 2Lt kia 10-8-15 7RWFus p223 MR4
JONES,Samuel Victor Charles Lt dow 23-9-16 3 att6RDubF p177 CR Greece3
JONES,Sidney Herbert 2Lt kia 28-7-18 4GordH p242 CR France1689
JONES,Simon James TLt dow 5-6-18 8SLancs p125 CR France622,2Bn
JONES,Stanley Capt kia 16-5-15 1RWFus p98 CR France279
JONES,Stanley T2Lt dow 25-2-17 14RWFus p98 CR Belgium23
JONES,Stanley Cottmore 2Lt kia 3-9-16 RE 2/1FC p210 MR21,Cotmore

JONES,Stanley Fox Gore T2Lt kia 7-6-17 Wilts p153

JONES,Stuart Kirby Lt dow 17-9-14 RAVC att25RFAp198 CR France473,18-9-14

JONES,Sydney Douglas Selborne 2Lt kia 2-9-16 26RFA p31 CR France397

JONES,Sydney Everard T2Lt kia 8-8-15 8WelshR p127 MR4

JONES,Sydney James TLt kia 15-9-16 11RWKent p141 MR21

JONES.T.H.Maj 18-3-16 QueensBays CR Kent27

JONES,Tom Bright Capt kld 11-4-18 GL &RAF p190 CR France95

JONES,Thomas 2Lt kia 31-7-17 161RH&FA p31 CR Belgium24

JONES,Thomas Alex Evansen T2Lt kia 7-8-15 11Manch p155

JONES,Thomas Capel Lt kia 26-10-17 3Lond p245 MR30

JONES,Thomas Edward Painton Capt kia 15-9-16 1/6Lond p246 MR21

JONES,Thomas Esmor Lt kia 6-4-18 4RWFus p223 MR27

JONES,Thomas Glasfryn Chap4Cl dow 12-4-17 RAChDept att11SWBord p199 CR Wales238

JONES,Thomas Idwal.MM.Lt kia 31-8-18 18Lond p250 CR France785

JONES,Thomas John.MC.TLtACapt dow 22-4-18 A122RFA p31 CR Belgium11

JONES,Thomas Lewis.MC.Lt dow 10-10-18 1/8Worc p226 CR France446,9-10-18

JONES,Thomas Lloyd Rees Lt 29-9-19 SWBord CR Wales306

JONES,Thomas Luke.MC.T2Lt dow 9-10-18 RASC attRGA 27SB p193 CR France214

JONES,Thomas Mozart 2Lt ded 6-7-18 RGA 262SB p40 CR Wales177,26SB

JONES,Thomas Stephen 2Lt kia 26-9-17 1/2 att10RWFus p98 MR30

JONES,Thomas William TLt kia 11-3-17 RAMC att27NumbF p196 CR France1182

JONES,Thomas William Allen 2Lt kia 31-7-17 4Ches p222 CR Belgium96

JONES,Thomas William Hathway.OBE.Maj 7-4-19 IARO CR EAfrica54 Ex 94Inf

JONES,Titho Glynne Lt kia 20-4-17 1/7RWFus p223 CR Palestine8

JONES,T.L.R.Lt ded 29-9-19 SWBord p263

JONES,Tom Wason T2Lt kia 8-10-18 SWBord att15WelshR p100 CR France1346

JONES,Trevor Benjamin TLt kia 18-9-18 16WelshR p127 CR Greece5,6Bn

JONES,Vavasor 2Lt kia 19-5-15 7RWFus p223 CR France427

JONES,Victor Trevor T2Lt kia 18-9-18 WelshR att17Bn p127 MR16 17 att14Bn

JONES,Wallace.MC&Bar.LtAMaj dow 15-10-18 C174RFA p31 CR France760

JONES,Walter George Cotterell T2Lt kld 17-3-18 RFC p16 CR Hunts104

JONES,Walter Joseph TLt dow 15-10-17 7Norf p74 CR France13

JONES,Walter Truran T2Lt kia 12-10-16 17Manch p155 MR21

JONES,Watkin Morgan Lt kia 29-3-18 RE 258TC p46 MR27

JONES,W.H.A.Capt 17-11-17 RWFus CR Surrey152

JONES,Wilfrid Griffith Lt kia 6-4-18 7RWFus p223 CR France232

JONES,William Bartholomew 2Lt kia 27-5-18 134MGC p183 MR18

JONES,William Edgar Lt kia 10-4-18 10RWar p65 MR30

JONES,William Edgar Chap4Cl dow 24-10-18 RAChDept att9Yorks p199 CR France234,kia 8-10-18 att2RWFus :-

JONES,William Henry 2Lt kia 27-5-18 1 att4Yorks p90 MR18 [&CR France528,24-10-18 att9Yorks

JONES,William Hugh 2Lt kia 21-6-17 7RWFus p223 CR Belgium23,16Bn

JONES,William James Lt kia 28-6-16 6Lpool p215   CR France506

JONES,William Orlando Maj kia 26-8-17 10SWBord p100 CR Belgium23,Capt

JONES,William Saville Lt kia 27-5-18 4NumbF p213 MR18

JONES-BATEMAN,Francis Capt kia 4-11-18 13RWFus p98 CR France521

JONES-BATEMAN,Llewelyn Capt dow 19-3-16 A103RFA p31 CR France88

JONES-BATEMAN,Lloyd Newton.CMG.LtCol ded 25-7-17 1Norf p74 MR65

JONES-MANLEY,David Henry George Capt kia 6-11-17 6RWFus p223

JONES-NOWLAN,Thomas Chamney 2Lt dow 27-5-17 3 att1RDubF p177 CR France113

JONES-PARRY,Ivor Norman Lt dow 12-5-17 RGA 171SB p209 CR France614

JONES-PARRY,John Jeffreys Bulkeley TMaj kia 30-7-15 6DCLI p114 CR Belgium35

JONES-ROBERTS,Peter Chap4Cl 23-6-21 CR Wales491

JONES-SAVIN,John Savin T2Lt kia 27-3-17 ACycCps att11RWFus p98 CR Greece6

JONES-VAUGHAN,Evan Nanney Capt kia 26-10-14 2RWFus C'Coy p98 CR France82

JONES-VAUGHAN,Hugh Thomas Charles Maj ded 20-11-18 RB p179 CR Asia60

JORDAN,Edward 2Lt kia 9-4-18 7ESurr p112 MR32

JORDAN,Francis Hugh Dormer 2Lt ded 23-7-18 RGA p262 CR Scot241

JORDAN,Hugh Stewart Latimer 2Lt kld 20-8-17 RFA attRFC p9&31 CRMddx37

JORDAN,James.MC.Lt kia 8-8-18 5DragGds p21 CR France526

JORDAN,John Edward 2Lt ded 9-2-16 1/7Worc p226 CR France3,10-2-16

JORDAN,Leslie Tiel.MID Lt kia 6-6-16 RE 2/1FC p210 CR France281

JORDAN,Louisa Sister ded 6-3-15 ScotWomensHosp CR Europe57

JORDAN,R.A.A.Y.Maj 14-6-20 KSLI CR Somerset31

JORDAN,William T2Lt kia 8-11-16 GL &45RFC p3&190 CR France134,Willie

JORDON,John Lt dow 19-6-15 9 att2SWBord p100 CR Gallipoli1,JORDAN

JORDON,Leonard Owen.MC.Capt kia 4-11-18 Hereford p252 CR France1087,JORDAN

JORDON,Percy Thomas Lt kia 21-8-15 3 att15RInniskF p105 MR4,att1Bn

JORDON,Victor Harry Capt kia 7-10-16 7Lond p247 MR21

JOSCELYNE,Arthur Kennett T2Lt dow 26-6-17 RBerks att5Bn p139 CR France1182

JOSCELYNE,Clement Percy 2Lt dow 10-10-17 3 att11Suff p78 CR Belgium16

JOSCELYNE,Frank Henry Tremlett TLtACapt kia 19-11-16 8SomLI p80 CR France339

JOSCELYNE,Lawrence Arthur.MC.T2Lt dow 1-10-17 7SomLI p80 CR Belgium11

JOSELAND,Arthur Noel Lt kia 22-9-17 4ESurr attNigR p112&201 CR EAfrica22 &CR Tanzania1

JOSELAND,Frederick Osborn 2Lt kia 10-9-16 12Lond p248 MR21

JOSEPH,Alan Edward TLt dow 10-5-17 14RWar p65 CR France8

JOSEPH,Cyril John Gadalja 2Lt ded 13-10-14 21Lond p251&270 CR Mddx40,Gedaliah

JOSEPH,Horace 2Lt kia 20-7-16 Dev p77

JOSEPH,Jack Benjamin T2Lt kia 8-1-17 RE 185TC p46 CR France53

JOSEPH,John Herbert TCapt kia 1-8-17 17Lpool p72 CR Belgium116

JOSEPH,John Rhys 2Lt ded 23-4-17 GL RFC p9 CR Scot235,Lt

JOSEPH,Stewart Hugh LtAMaj dow 18-8-17 RE 227FC p46 CR Belgium124

JOSEPH,Wilfred Gordon Aron T2Lt kia 19-4-17 1Nhampt att1/5Norf p137 CR Palestine8

JOSEPH,William Franklin George T2Lt kia 27-5-18 6 att2RBerks p139 MR18,att7Bn

JOSEPHI,Ernest Henry TLt ded 23-1-17 8RASC p193 MR21 CRMddx40

JOSEPHS,Joseph 2Lt kia 1-7-16 12Lond p248 CR France798

JOSLIN,Francis John Maj kia 18-4-15 RWKent p141 MR29

JOTCHAM,Fred T2Lt dow 27-9-18 RE 4SpCo p46 CR France298

JOTCHAM,Walter Morse 2Lt kia 19-8-17 1/8Worc p109 CR Belgium96

JOTHAM,Eustace.VC.Capt kia 7-1-15 IA 51Sikhs attNWaziristanMil p278 MR43

JOURDAIN,Charles Edward Arthur.DSO.LtCol kia 29-7-18 2LNLancs p136&258 CR France524

JOURDAIN,Ernest Nevill Capt kia 16-2-15 1Suff p78 MR29

JOWERS,Joseph Frank Lt kia 24-3-18 5 att6SomLI p218 MR27

JOWETT,Alan 2Lt kia 29-6-17 2/10Lpool p216 CR France705

JOWETT,Eric Craven Lt dow 9-7-16 GL &RFC p3&190 CR France514 Ex 12NumbF

JOWETT,Harold Crossley 2Lt kia 1-9-18 7LancF p221 CR France307

JOWETT,John Sutcliffe ACapt dow 22-9-18 4 att1/5Manch p155 CR France13

JOWETT,Sydney Ferguson 2Lt kia 27-5-18 12 att5Yorks p90 MR18

JOWETT,William Hall T2Lt dow 28-6-16 20Lpool p72 CR France67

JOWITT,Arthur Lt kia 25-4-15 1RWar p65 MR29

JOWITT,Thomas Lawrence Maj dow 17-7-15 5HLI p240 CR Greece10

JOY,Edward Sydney T2Lt kia 19-8-16 8RBerks A'Coy p139 CR France432

JOY,Frederick Charles Patrick 2Lt kia 16-6-15 3 att2RIrRif p169 MR29

JOY,George Bruce Lt dow 21-5-15 3WelchR att1HLI p127 MR22

JOY,Gwyn.MC.2Lt dow 16-7-17 2/10Lond p248 CR France145,

JOY,Thomas Cyril Bruce LtTCapt kia 11-12-15 2Dev att2Dors p77 CR Iraq1,1Bn

JOYCE,Alexander Hugh Sinclair.MM.T2Lt dow 20-8-18 12Norf p74 CR France134

JOYCE,Eric Gordon 2Lt kia 31-10-16 4Suff A'Coy p217 CR France294,30-10-16

JOYCE,Frank Bernard.MC.TCapt kia 21-4-18 10N&D p134 CR France252

JOYCE,Frank Postlethwaite TLt kia 29-5-17 7BordR p117 CR France604

JOYCE,Frederick George Lt kia 29-9-17 3 att2SWBord p100 CR Belgium106

JOYCE,George Edgar TLt kia 20-9-16 10 att7Leic p87 MR21

JOYCE,James T2Lt kia 22-8-15 9LancF p92 MR4

JOYCE,Norman Roy Lt kld 1-4-18 GL &23RAF p190 MR20

JOYCE,Philip Solomon Lt mbk 6-3-17 60RFC p256 MR20

JOYCE,Walter Herbert 2Lt kia 22-3-18 8Lond p247 MR27

JOYCE,William Alfred T2Lt kia 28-3-18 4MGC p183 MR20

JOYNSON,Leonard Charles Billingsley Lt kld 6-5-15 1/6SStaffs p229 CR Belgium170

JUBB,James Critchley 2Lt kia 23-7-16 1/4YLI p235 MR21

JUCKES,George Francis 2Lt kia 6-7-15 6 att1RB p179 CR Belgium85

JUCKES,Thomas Roland Lt kia 9-5-15 3 att2RSuss p119 MR22

JUDD,Alan Cecil.MC.Rev kia 21-3-18 RAChDept att2/5N&D p199 MR20

JUDD,Frank King T2Lt kia 30-11-17 5RBerks p139 MR17

JUDD,Frederick George Kerridge T2Lt kia 24-5-15 2RDubF p177 MR29

JUDD,Morris Stanley T2Lt acckld 18-8-17 RWKent att7Bn p141 CR France134

JUDD,William Bush TMaj ded 2-2-18 RASC 15DivTrain p193&257 CR Hamps221

JUDE,Leo Gerald Simon TLtACapt kia 15-11-16 10LNLancs p136 CR France534

JUDGE,Charles Harland Lt dow 17-5-15 4EYorks p219 CR France1

JUDGE,Leopold James T2Lt kia 3-5-17 GL 7Leic att110TMB p190 MR20

JUDGE,Wilfred Justice 2Lt dow 21-8-16 5 att1RFus p68 CR France66

JUDGE,William Spencer 2Lt dow 26-7-16 A105RFA p31 CR France145

JUKES,Andrew Monro Capt ded 18-10-18 IMS p278 CR Egypt15

JUKES,Arthur Starr 2Lt ded 6-3-17 10Lond p248 CR Egypt15

JUKES,Frederick T2Lt kia 20-9-17 9WelchR p127 MR30

JUKES,Michael Egerton Ewart TLt kld 4-9-15 14Manch p155 CR Staffs125

JULER,George Critchett Lt kia 31-8-14 5Lancers p22 MR15

JULIAN,Ernest Lawrence TLt dow 8-8-15 7RDubF p177 MR4

JULIUS,Cecil Herbert 2Lt kia 9-4-16 3 att6ELancs p111 MR38

JULL,Leslie Hubert Lt kld 3-1-18 NStaffs &RFC p16&157 CR Kent243

JUMP,John Herbert.MC.Lt kia 15-9-17 4LNLancs p234 CR France275

JUNG,Henry Adolph 2Lt ded 9-5-15 3 att1NumbF p61

JUNIPER,John Harvey 2Lt kia 30-4-17 7RFus p68 MR20

JUPE,Charles Eric ACapt kia 26-10-17 8Dev p77 MR30

JURGENS,Sydney George TLt dow 17-8-15 6RLancs p59 CR Egypt3

JURGENSON,Emil Theodore Lt kia 4-5-18 GL att1KAR p268 MR52

JURY,George Risehieth 2Lt kia 14-9-16 7Lond p247 MR21

JURY,Reginald 2Lt dow 6-10-17 4WRid p227 CR France1360

JUSTICE,George Hercules ACapt dow 31-7-17 7RInniskF att7NLancs p105 CR Belgium111,kia

K

KAHN,Edgar 2Lt kia 5-5-15 1Leinst p174 MR29

KANE,Augustine George 2Lt mbk 24-6-18 8SWBord attRAF p99&100,kia CR Greece6 3Bn

KANE,Frederick Paul 2Lt kia 1-11-16 GL &29RFC p3&190 CR France95

KANE,James Gabriel T2Lt kia 22-10-18 8 att10SWBord p100 CR France190

KANE,John Francis Aloysius Capt kld 22-3-15 Dev &RFC p1&77 CR Lond9

KANE,Robert Romney Godred.DSO.CaptALtCol dow 1-10-18 1RMunstF p175 CR France1184

KANE-SMITH,James.MC.Lt kia 27-5-18 110RFA p31 MR18

KANN,Edward Henry TLt kia 21-10-17 102RFC p9 CR Belgium383

KANN,Raymond Victor Lt RScotsF &RAF CR Lond12

KARNEY,David Noel T2LtACapt kia 21-3-18 11 att2RDubF p177 MR27

KARRAN,John Bowler T2Lt kia 1-7-16 9 att2SWBord p100 CR France1490

KARSLAKE,Harry Howard T2Lt kia 23-4-17 Dev att1DCLI p77 MR20

KARSLAKE,William Reginald Lt ded 29-12-17 PembrokeYeo p270 CR Devon53

KATINAKIS,Francis Beresford.MC.Lt dow 27-3-18 3DragGds p21 CR France1422

KATON,Arthur Robert.DCM.Capt 6-9-15 8SStaffs CR Staffs109

KATZ,Sampson Goldston TLt ded 19-7-18 8RLancs p262 CR Mddx40,Goldstone

KAUFFMAN,Albert Edward T2Lt ded 17-10-18 RASC p193 CR Palestine11

KAUNTZE,Cedric Ernest Wheldon Lt kia 1-10-15 3Worc p109 CR Belgium112

KAVANAGH,Bernard Chap4Cl dow 21-12-17 RAChDept p199 CR Palestine3

KAVANAGH,Edward 2Lt kia 30-7-16 18Manch p155 MR21

KAVANAGH,John William 2Lt ded 11-3-18 RFC p16 CR Kent28,FltLt 10-3-18

KAVANAGH,Thomas Osborne Joseph Lt kia 24-8-18 3 att1RIrFus p171 CR France855

KAY,Albert T2Lt kia 1-8-17 26RFus p68 CR Belgium88

KAY,Charles William Lt ded 3-11-18 4 att2LNLancs p234 CR France34

KAY,Collin Lowther 2Lt dow 12-10-16 12MGC Inf p183 MR21

KAY,Geoffrey Clarkson AMaj kia 29-3-18 5LancF attMGC p187&221 CR France644

KAY,George Alexander T2Lt kia 9-8-15 N&D p134 MR29

KAY,George Frederick 2Lt ded 16-9-19 LabCps p264 CR Scot241 Ex BordR

KAY,George Philip.MC.2Lt ded 21-10-18 172RFA p31 CR Egypt7

KAY,George Pollard 2Lt dow 29-6-17 46RFC p9 CR France354

KAY,Henry Norman Lt kia 21-8-18 7Manch p237 CR France514

KAY,John T2Lt kia 30-9-18 10 att1LNLancs p136 CR France516

KAY,John Alexander ACapt kia 9-10-17 6LancF p221 MR30

KAY,John Calvert 2Lt kia 15-7-16 11LancF p92 MR21

KAY,Lawrence Herbert T2Lt kia 18-11-15 12 att9RWar p65 CR Gallipoli4

KAY,Maurice Alfred 2Lt kia 30-4-17 GL &56RFC p9 MR20

KAY,Melville Herbert 2Lt kia 5-11-16 8DLI p239 CR France385

KAY,Noel Rawstone Wilkinson Lt dow 5-7-18 15RHA L'Bty p31 CR France102,Rawstorre

KAY,Robert Roland 2Lt kia 23-3-18 5DLI p239 MR20

KAY,Stanley Burnett Capt ded 28-1-18 7Yorks &RFC p16&90 CR Yorks361

KAY,Walter Haddow T2Lt kia 23-3-18 att6GordH p166 CR France757

KAY,William Lt dow 21-3-18 8LancF attMGC p187&221 MR27

KAY,William Algernon Ireland.Bart.CMG.DSO.MIDx6 BrigGen kia 4-10-18 KRRC Cmdg3InfBde p150 CR France725

KAY,William Henry.MC.Chap4Cl kia 5-4-18 RAChDept att5Dors p199 CR France223

KAY,William Joseph O'Neill Beaumont T2Lt ded 19-11-18 2BlkW p129 CR Lebanon1

KAY-ROBINSON,Hugh Thomas.DSO&2Bars.LtCol 26-4-18 12 att13RSuss MR30

KAY-SHUTTLEWORTH,Edward James.Hon.TCapt kld 10-7-17 GL 7RB 218InfBde p190 CR C'land &W'land86

KAY-SHUTTLEWORTH,Lawrence Ughtred.Hon.ACapt kia 30-3-17 D11RFA p31 CR France81

KAYE,Eric Priestley 2Lt kia 3-5-17 7WRid p228 MR20

KAYE,Frank Leon T2Lt dow 11-4-17 5 att9RFus p68 CR France113

KAYE,Frederick William Capt 8-1-19 IndOrdDept CR India97A

KAYE-BUTTERWORTH,George Saintow TLt kia 4-8-16 13DLI p161

KEABLE,Harold Charles Linford T2Lt kia 25-9-15 8RBerks p139 CR France552

KEAN,Francis John TLt dow 25-11-18 RASC p193 CR Lond9,ded

KEAN,James Rankin 2Lt dow 1-10-18 1/4RScotF p222 CR France34

KEAN,John Herdman Capt kia 1-12-17 1/5RLancs p213 MR17

KEANE,Albert Graham 2Lt dow 8-5-17 7 att2ScotRif p224 CR France1468

KEANE,Edward Dawson TCapt ded 31-10-18 RAMC att689MT Coy ASC p196 CR Europe58

KEANE,William May Augustine 2Lt kia 4-11-16 3 att8RIrF p171 CR Belgium17,Mary

KEARLEY,Harold 2Lt kia 3-2-18 15Lond attRFC p18&249 CR Belgium18

KEARNEY,Arthur Joseph Lt kia 9-9-16 att1RMunstF p175 MR21

KEARNEY,I.M.Sister ded 25-12-16 QAIMNS forIndia p278 CR Iraq6,26-9-16

KEARNS,Arthur Clark Rose Lt ded 7-6-16 1Glouc attWorc p107 CR France85,Clarkson

KEARNS,Reginald Arthur Ernest Holmes.CMG.LtCol ded 24-11-18 RASC p253 CR Surrey93

KEARNS,Thomas Joseph.CB.CMG.MIDx3 Col 30-6-20 RASC CR Kent24

KEARSLEY,John Stewart Lt kia 22-11-15 O&BLI p130 MR38,Steuart

KEARTON,Frank T2Lt kia 21-11-17 11KRRC p150 MR17

KEARTON,James Linton Graham Lt dow 3-12-17 1WelshGds p53 CR France398

KEAST,William Reginald 2Lt kia 21-8-17 66RFC SR p9 MR20

KEATES,Richard John.MC.2LtACapt kia 20-8-18 RGA 23BdeHQ p40 CR France177

KEATING,David Timothy TLt dow 21-4-18 1/4Y&L p159 CR Belgium38

KEATING,George 2Lt kia 17-2-15 2Ches p96 CR Belgium131

KEATING,George Henry Lt kia 18-9-18 2/1Camb p244 CR France369

KEATING,Harold Francis Amboor Lt kia 28-6-18 RE 210FC p46 CR France19

KEATING,Henry Sheehy Lt kld 20-1-15 IrGds p52 CR France727

KEATING,John Lt kld 17-2-15 2Ches p96 CR Belgium131

KEATING,John Baker T2Lt kia 20-7-16 15 att7N&D p134 MR20

KEATING,Robert Pears Capt kia 18-7-17 1/8Lpool p215 CR Belgium10 Richard

KEATING,Thomas Joseph TLtACapt kia 14-6-18 RFA att63RAF p31 CR Iraq8

KEATING,William Britten.MC.TCapt ded 11-10-18 9SfthH p165 CR Belgium11

KEATINGE,Eustace Gabriel Lawrence Lt kia 13-4-18 NumbF p61 CR Belgium307

KEATS,Frederick Thorold TLt kia 25-5-16 8Suff p78 CR France513

KEAY,C.H.Capt 9-5-21 RAMC CR Cornwall1

KEAY,James Gordon Lt dow 2-7-16 2/5RWar p214 CR France345

KEAY,Robert Naismith 2Lt dow 30-11-16 6BlkW p231 CR France102

KEAY,Wilfrid Farrar TLt&Adjt kia 16-9-16 9YLI p143 MR21

KEBBLEWHITE,Fred Edgar 2Lt kia 14-8-17 8N&D attRFC p18&233 CR France285

KEBLE,Eustace Charles 2Lt kia 21-3-18 att1NStaffs p157 MR27

KEDGLEY,Alfred Edmund.MM.2Lt kia 17-10-18 C83RFA p31 CR France1392

KEDIE,William Thomas Capt kia 21-8-15 1BlkW p129 MR22

KEE,William.MC.ACapt dow PoW 24-3-18 7 att1RDubF p177 MR27

KEE,William John TCapt ded 20-12-18 RAVC attRHA14ArmyBdeHQ p198 CR Canada1028

KEEBLE,Alfred Ernest TCapt dow 5-8-18 6MGC Inf p183 CR Belgium11

KEEBLE,Arthur Theodore T2Lt dow 28-6-17 RE 8SigCo p46 CR Belgium11

KEEBLE,John Harold T2Lt kld 27-10-17 GL &RFC p9 CR Suff121

KEEFE,Cecil Henderson TCapt kld 5-2-18 RFC p16 CR Norf207,FltCmdr

KEEFE,Ronald Conray Murray.MC.TCapt kia 27-3-18 19Manch p155&258 MR27 Raymond Conrad

KEELE,Charles Acland TCapt kia 12-7-16 14RB p179 CR Belgium5,12Bn

KEELER,Oscar Alan.MC.2Lt kia 20-9-17 7Lond att17KRRC p247 MR29

KEELEY-AYRES,H.Maj&QM 26-6-20 GL CR Iraq8

KEELIHER,William John 2Lt kia 25-7-18 1BordR p117 CR France40

KEELING,Bertram Francis Eardley.OBE.MC.Lt 20-9-19 RE CR Egypt9

KEELING,Charles Henry 2Lt ded 28-10-18 A15RFA H'Bty15Bde p31 CR France40

KEELING,G.B Lt ded 19-3-16 RIM MR64

KEELL,Herbert Alfred 2Lt kia 9-10-17 3 att2Ess p132 MR30

KEEN,Arthur Clive Capt kia 10-5-17 1/7Mddx p235 CR France531

KEEN,Aubrey Owen TLt dow 4-8-18 11RScots p54 CR France134

KEEN,Edward William 2Lt ded 5-7-18 IARO att1/6GurkhaRif p278 CR Iraq1

KEEN,James Raglan Lt dow 19-10-17 5RSuss p228 CR Belgium20,8Bn

KEEN,Stephen Whitworth.MC.Lt dow 21-8-18 2Lond &RAF p245&258

KEEN,William Allan Capt dow 6-9-18 7Mddx p235 CR France833

KEENAN,John TCapt ded 26-3-17 11RDubF p177 CR Ireland12

KEENE,Alfred.CMG.DSO.BtCol ded 21-4-18 RGA p255

KEENE,Hector Conway Lt 11-7-18 2/112Inf MR43

KEENE,John Pearce 2Lt kia 24-11-15 IARO att2/7GurkhaRif p278 MR38,22/24-11-15

KEENLYSIDE,Cecil Alexander Headlam Capt kia 20-7-15 1Camb p244 CR France922

KEENLYSIDE,Guy Francis Headlam Capt dow 29-10-14 1RWKent p141 CR France102

KEENLYSIDE,Thomas Edward Lt dow 21-4-18 18NumbF p61 CR Belgium38

KEEP,Douglas Scrivener Howard.MC.TCapt kia 14-7-17 7Beds p86 CR Belgium15

KEEP,Douglas William T2Lt kia 16-10-18 9ESurr p113 CR France206

KEEP,John Drummond 2Lt kia 13-10-18 5Lond p246 CR France273

KEEP,Walter Fischer T2Lt kia 7-6-17 15Hamps p121 CR Belgium154

KEEPFER,William Robert Cyril 2Lt kia 4-11-16 3 att2RWFus p98 CR France230 Ex 3DragGds

KEEPING,Claude Jeffery Capt kia 24-8-18 8Mddx p236 CR France927

KEESEY,George Ernest Howard TCapt kia 24-8-16 8RB p179 CR France1890

KEEVIL,Cecil Horace Case TCapt kld 13-6-17 18WYorks &RFC p9&82 CR Lond12

KEHOE,William Charles 2Lt dow 24-4-17 70RFA p31 CR France1182

KEIGHLEY,Linden Raynes 2Lt dow 3-12-17 4RLancs p213 CR France446,Rayner

KEIGHLEY,Richard Ernest Clayton Capt kia 1-8-17 RGA 1SB p209 CR Belgium34

KEIGHLEY,William Munkley TLt kia 1-7-16 10WYorks p82 CR France373

KEIGHTLEY,Philip Charles Russell Lt ded 2-3-19 RGA 262SB p255 CR Ireland56,Capt

KEIGWIN,Henry David 2Lt kia 20-9-16 3 att19LancF p92 CR France296

KEIL,Alexander Peter McLennan EngLt ded 11-10-16 RIM p278 CR Iraq5

KEILLER,George William Capt ded 9-3-19 RE RlySubComm p46 CR Germany1,Weston

KEIR,Edward Hugh T2Lt kia 28-10-17 GL 3Lancs att16RFC p9 CR France95,Lt

KEITH,Alexander Gill TCapt kia 26-11-15 11 att1GordH p166 CR Belgium21,27-11-15

KEITH,Alexander Graham T2Lt ded 18-12-18 HLI p265 CR Scot245,Lt

KEITH,Alexander James T2Lt kia 14-7-16 12Mddx p147 MR21

KEITH,Douglas Hay T2Lt kia 31-8-17 18HLI att18DLI p163 CR France268,17Bn

KEITH,George Elphinstone TCapt ded 6-12-18 RAMC p196 CR Italy16

KEITH,Malcolm T2Lt kia 26-9-17 8EYorks p84 CR Belgium16

KEITH,Noel Lt kia 22-5-17 8Lpool p215 CR France922

KEITH,Patrick Hay Lt kia 15-6-15 6ScotRif p224&225,8Bn MR22

KEITH-BRUMBY,Harry Catherall 2Lt ded 31-10-16 13DLI IARO att98Inf p161&278 CR EAfrica12 &CR Tanzania1,Lt

KEITH-MURRAY,Alastair William 2Lt kia 8/9-5-17 3BlkW p129 MR37,8-5-17

KEKEWICH,Arthur St.John Mackintosh.MID Capt kia 25-9-15 8Dev p77 MR19

KEKEWICH,George Capt dow 28-10-17 1Lond p204&245 CR Palestine1

KEKEWICH,Hanbury Lewis Maj kia 6-11-17 SussYeo p205 CR Palestine1,Capt

KEKEWICH,John Capt kia 25-9-15 8EKent p57 MR19

KEKEWICH,Robert George.CB.MajGen 5-11-14 EKent CR Devon185

KELK,Arthur Frederick Hastings,MC T2Lt kia 9-3-17 14WelshR p127 CR Belgium23

KELL,Douglas Fearn 2Lt dow 24-4-17 1/7GordH p242 CR France95

KELL,Waldegrave Frank Sydney 2Lt dow 23-7-17 10 att1/5Suff p78 CR Palestine2

KELLAGHER,Sydney Arthur.MC.Lt dow 4-8-17 34RFA p31 CR France13

KELLAS,Arthur Capt kia 6-8-15 RAMC 89FA p253 CR Gallipoli1,Maj

KELLEHER,Bartholomew TLt kia 27-9-18 RASC att8Lancs p193 CR France357

KELLER,Francis Frederick Lt dow 22-5-17 2/6Lond p246 MR20

KELLER,Roderick Leopold.MC.2Lt kld 15-8-18 RWar attRAF p65 CR Herts10,Capt

KELLETT,Richard Henry Villiers 2Lt kld 21-8-16 B74RH&FA p31 CR France203,Lt dow

KELLETT,William T2Lt kia 22-1-17 8SomLI att10RFC p9&80 CR France98

KELLIE,Esmond Lawrence 2Lt kia 19-4-15 Beds p86 MR29

KELLIE,John.MID Rev ded 1-8-17 RAChDept att6CamH p199 MR29

KELLIE,Kenneth Harrison Alloa TCapt kia 25-6-16 RAMC 104FA p196 CR France430

KELLIE,Leslie Lawrence 2Lt kia 1-2-17 102RFA p31 CR Belgium72

KELLIE,William Reid 2Lt kia 18-6-18 10Lpool p216 CR France279

KELLOCK,Harold Plumer Lt dow 6-10-18 NIrHorse att13/17RFA p24 CR France34

KELLY,Alfred George Lt ded 18-3-20 RASC CR Lond3

KELLY,Brian Edmund T2Lt kia 2-12-17 2Y&L p159 MR17

KELLY,Charles Leonard 2Lt kia 20-9-18 LNLancs &204RAF p264 MR20 &CR Belgium452

KELLY,Charles Patrick TLt kia 2-7-16 RAMC 96FA p196 CR France141

KELLY,Edward Denis Festus Capt kia 30-10-14 1LifeGds p20 MR29

KELLY,Edward Rowley 2Lt kia 7-7-15 3BordR attLancF p117 MR29

KELLY,George Henry Fitzmaurice LtCol kia 23-11-14 IA Cmdg34SikhPnrs p278 CR France571

KELLY,Harry Holdsworth Capt kia 24-10-14 RE 38FC p46 CR France82

KELLY,Henry John T2Lt kia 20-9-17 KRRC att21Bn p150 MR30

KELLY,Henry Newton Maj kia 25-9-15 IA 33Punjabis p278 CR France705

KELLY,James Sheil 2Lt dow 29-3-18 2/8LancF p221 CR France145

KELLY,John James T2Lt dow 12-4-17 7Leinst p174 CR France557,Capt kia 2Bn

KELLY,John Lawson.MC.Lt kia 4-11-18 RE 407FC p210 CR France1272

KELLY,Joseph Cresswell Lt ded 28-9-17 IARO att4/3GurkhaRif p278 MR43

KELLY,Joseph Francis Mary LtCol ded 22-8-16 RAMC p196 CR Wilts129

KELLY,Kenneth George Lt kia 27-5-18 MGC Inf p183 CR France1753

KELLY,Oscar Raphael T2Lt kld 2-5-17 GL NumbF &53RFC p9 CR Belgium152

KELLY,Percy Ewart 2Lt kia 27-4-15 8Mddx p236 MR29

KELLY,Percy Patrick T2Lt kia 1-7-16 10ESurr A'Coy p113 CR France513,8Bn

KELLY,Philip Edward TLtCol kia 10-10-18 1 att9RIrFus p89&265 CR Belgium157

KELLY,Robert Houston Lt kia 1-1-18 6A&SH att1KAR p243&268 CR EAfrica77

KELLY,Robert Maitland Lt kia 11-1-17 RNDevYeo att5Dors p203 MR21

KELLY,Terence O'Neil William 2Lt dow 2-5-15 4GordH p242 CR France40

KELLY,Thomas.MC.TMaj kia 26-6-17 11RWSurr p56 CR Belgium111

KELLY,Thomas Aloysius.MC.Capt kia 2-10-16 24Lond p252 CR France453

KELLY,Thomas Cameron T2Lt kia 27-3-16 19HLI p163 CR France515,16Bn

KELLY,Thomas Joseph Lt kia 7-11-17 IARO attMysore&HyderabadImpSerCav p278 CR Palestine8

KELLY,William John 2Lt kia 25-9-15 6GordH p242 MR19

KELLY,William Peter TCapt dow 12-11-16 26NumbF p61 CR France285

KELLY-LAWSON,George McFarquhar 2Lt 9-8-17 RGA CR Belgium23

KELSALL,John Lindsay TLt kia 28-8-17 86RFA p31 CR Belgium19

KELSEY,Arthur Edward Capt drd 26-2-18 RAMC p196 MR40

KELSEY,Herbert Burleigh T2Lt kia 17-2-17 12Mddx p147 MR21

KELSEY,Leon de Barr 2Lt kia 16-9-16 23Lond p252 MR21

KELSEY,Pryce Atwood Clive TCapt dow 26-7-15 EKent p57 CR France285

KELSEY,William TLt dow 23-9-16 RH&FA p31 CR Yorks575

KELSON,Gerald Miles.MC.Capt ded 27-12-19 KEdwsHorse p261 CR SAfrica144

KELWAY-BAMBER,Claude Herschel 2Lt kia 11-11-15 GL RFC p1&190 CR Belgium140

KELYNACK,Richard Henry 2Lt kia 4-10-17 1DCLI p114 MR30

KEMBER,Walter 2Lt kia 1-9-17 7LancF attRFC p18&221 Belgium140

KEMBER,Walter Herbert TCapt kia 7-6-17 8SLancs p125 MR29

KEMBER,Cyril Stewart 2Lt kia 27-5-18 3Suff att2/4RBerks p78 CR France248

KEMBLE,Harold William Capt 2-1-20 GloucHuss CR Glouc61

KEMBLE,Henry Herbert.DSO.MC.LtCol dow 7-6-17 15Lond p249 CR Belgium11,23Bn

KEMBLE,Henry Noel Lt kia 20-7-16 2Suff p78 CR France513,Capt

KEMISH,Charles Lt&QM kia 14-7-15 RASC AdvHorseTrans p193 CR Gallipoli1

KEMP,Albert 2Lt kia 1-7-16 10RInniskF A'Coy p105 MR21

KEMP,Alexander.MC.Lt dow 26-7-18 RE 34DivSigs 101BdeHQ p210 CR France145

KEMP,Alexander Gordon 2Lt dow 7-5-17 4GordH C'Coy p242 CR France40

KEMP,Alfred Greatrex T2Lt kia 10-8-15 9RWar p65 MR4

KEMP,Ambrose Ernest William 2Lt dow 10-12-17 1/19Lond p250 CR France13

KEMP,Basil Aubrey 2Lt kia 3-5-17 9 att7Mddx p236 MR20

KEMP,Bernard Herbert 2Lt ded 23-10-19 Ex MGC Inf p266 CR SAfrica52

KEMP,C.M.F.SNurse ded 4-7-18 QAIMNS 40GH p200 CR Iraq6

KEMP,Charles George T2Lt kia 24-9-17 1RWSurr p56 MR30

KEMP,Charles John 2Lt kia 25-5-15 5RScots p211 MR4

KEMP,Charles Matthew.DSO.TMaj dow 9-10-17 21Manch p155 CR Belgium308

KEMP,Douglas Gordon.MC.2Lt kia 21-3-18 RE p210 CR France568,dow

KEMP,Elsie Margaret Sister kia 20-10-17 TFNS 58CCS p254 CR France139

KEMP,Eric Arthur T2Lt kia 30-11-17 7ESurr p113 MR17

KEMP,Ernest Charles 2Lt kia 6-9-16 9Yorks &RFC p3&90,ded MR20

KEMP,Frank 2Lt kia 22-7-16 11YLI att56MGC Inf p143&183 MR21

KEMP,Frederick Owen T2Lt kia 23-10-16 2Mddx p147 CR France390

KEMP,George Arnold.MID 2LtTLt ded 12-1-18 3YLI att3/3KAR p202&143,9YLI CR EAfrica10 &CR Tanzania1

KEMP,George Hubert 2Lt kld 1-6-18 15DLI att20RAF p161 CR France134,kia

KEMP,Godwin Francis Lt kia 23-4-17 3 att1BordR p117 MR20

KEMP,Harold George 2Lt kia 21-10-15 2RB p179 CR France276

KEMP,Horace Douglas Meadows T2Lt dow 31-8-16 8RSuss p119 CR Oxford69

KEMP,James Ogilvie Capt ded 12-12-17 5RScots p211 CR C'land &W'land45

KEMP,John Thomson 2Lt kia 11-4-18 25MGC p183 MR32

KEMP,Kenneth Reginald Flint T2Lt ded 18-10-18 RASC p193 CR Devon68

KEMP,Louis Augustus T2Lt dow 22-3-18 9LNLancs p136 CR France512

KEMP,Norman 2Lt kia 9-9-16 5LancF p221 MR21

KEMP,Percy Vickerman LtACapt dow 31-5-18 4 att11DLI p161 CR France40

KEMP,Reginald 2Lt kia 26-8-18 8Manch p237 CR France832

KEMP,Sydney Frank.MC.2Lt kia 16-4-18 O&BLI BucksBn p231 CR France248

KEMP,Thomas T2Lt kia 1-7-16 20Manch p155 CR France397

KEMP,Thomas Norman Cameron.MC.Capt kia 17-5-19 IA 1/9GurkhaRif p278 MR43

KEMP,William Meadows 2Lt kia 28-2-17 5 att16Mddx p147 CR France216,3 att16

KEMP-WELCH,Maurice T2Lt kia 11-4-17 10Yorks p90 MR20

KEMPE-ROBERTS,John Archer Clinton 2Lt kia 10-3-18 RFC p16 MR40

KEMPSEY-BOURNE,Frank Leonard T2Lt kia 11-7-16 11RWar p65 MR21

KEMPSTER,Alec Albert Dresden Lt kia 25-9-15 66/4RFA p31 CR France705

KEMPSTER,Stephen Alec T2Lt kia 8-6-17 17Mddx p147 CR France184

KEMPSTON,Noel Chester 2Lt kia 12-10-16 4ConnRgrs att9InniskF p172 CR Belgium100

KEMPSTON,Robert James Lt kia 24-5-15 2RDubF p177 MR29

KEMPTHORNE,Harold Sampson Lt kia 24-8-17 RFA p207 CR Belgium72

KENCH,Leonard Sheldon Capt dow 29-6-16 2/7RWar p214 CR France134

KENDALL,George 2Lt ded 15-10-18 3WYorks &RAF p263 CR Ches56

KENDALL,John Haywood 2Lt kia 14-4-15 Dors p124 CR Iraq6

KENDALL,Locke Francis William Angerstein TLt dow 22-11-17 9Norf att21MGC Cav p74&183 CR Palestine9

KENDALL,Percy Dale 2Lt kia 25-1-15 10Lpool p216 CR Belgium186,Lt

KENDALL,Rose Elizabeth Sister drd 26-2-18 QAIMNS p200 MR40

KENDALL,Thomas Linaker 2Lt kia 1-8-16 3BordR &MGC p183 CR France513

KENDEL,Benjamin 2Lt kia 14-6-18 21Lond p251 CR France59

KENDERDINE,Tom Herbert Gordon TLt kia 9-9-16 LancF att2/5Bn p92 CR France402

KENDLE,Robert Hastings Maj ded 12-8-15 5Suff p217 CR Gallipoli4

KENDRICK,Arthur Percy Lt dow 9-10-17 1KAR p202 CR EAfrica40

KENDRICK,Frederick Howard 2Lt dow 16-10-15 5SStaffs p229 CR France201

KENDRICK,Haden Mostyn 2Lt kldacc 18-9-16 5SStaffs &RFC p229 CR Staffs47,Lt

KENEALLY,W.Cdr 6-9-20 IndMiscList MR65

KENEALY,John William Kierman 2Lt ded 21-8-15 4RIrReg p89 CR Eire350

KENION,Hugh Cyril T2Lt kia 1-7-16 2LancF p92 CR France742

KENNA,Paul Aloysius.VC.DSO.ADC.BrigGen dow 30-8-15 3MountedBde Staff p1 CR Gallipoli26,21Lancers

KENNARD,Arthur Molloy.DSO.TLtCol ded 2-1-17 179RFA p31 CR Scot214

KENNARD,Lionel Edward Maj ded 10-12-19 15KHuss RoO p261 CR Hamps19

KENNARD,Maurice Nicholl.MC.MIDx3 TLtCol kia 1-7-16 18WYorks p82 MR21 Ex 6DragGds

KENNARD,Patrick Noel Capt kia 14-7-16 1EYorks p84 MR21

KENNARD,Robert 2Lt kia 7-7-16 2RSuss p119

KENNARD,Terence Evelyn Lt kia 26-2-18 RFA &5RFC p16&31 CR France95

KENNARD,Willoughby Arthur.DSO.Capt ded 30-10-18 13Huss p22 CR France40,Maj

KENNARD,Winwood Read T2Lt kia 30-6-16 54MGC p183 CR France513,Reade

KENNAWAY,Arthur Lewis Lt kia 21-8-15 1DorsYeo p203 CR Gallipoli5

KENNEDY,Alastair McKinnon Lt ded 18-10-18 2/2RE p256 CR Scot442

KENNEDY,Alexander.MC.T2LtACapt kia 26-3-18 11RScots p54 MR27

KENNEDY,Andrew Macpherson T2Lt kia 26-3-18 20 att18LancF p92 MR27

KENNEDY,Archibald Edward Capt kia 26-8-14 2A&SH p173 CR France716

KENNEDY,Arthur St.Clair 2Lt ded 6-3-15 3RDubF p177 CR Ireland14 &CR Eire77

KENNEDY,Charles TLt dow 16-11-16 D102RFA p31 CR France145,D113RFA

KENNEDY,Charles Noel Jardine Capt kia 30-7-16 RScotF p94 MR21

KENNEDY,Charles Seccombe Craufurd.MC.Capt kldacc 22-8-16 1N&D attRE p134 CR France200

KENNEDY,David Hew.MC.T2Lt kia 31-7-17 2RScotF p94 MR29

KENNEDY,D.C.2Lt kia 16-10-14 HLI p163

KENNEDY,Donald 2Lt kia 30-8-18 1GordH p166 CR France927

KENNEDY,Douglas Stewart.MC.Capt kia 12-3-18 62RFC p16 CR France660

KENNEDY,Duncan Cameron Lt kia 9-9-16 9HLI att47MGC Inf p240 MR21

KENNEDY,Edwin Alfred 2Lt kia 12/16-5-17 6SfthH p241 MR20

KENNEDY,Gilbert Capt ded 11-12-18 1RMunstF p175 CR France65

KENNEDY,Gilbert McClelland 2Lt kia 16/18-6-15 6ScotRif p224 MR22,15-6-15

KENNEDY,Gilbert Stuart.MID Capt kia 12-3-15 IA 1/9GurkhaRif p278 MR28

KENNEDY,H.A.Lt 22-8-17 GL &RFC CR France924

KENNEDY,Herbert Alexander Capt dow 28-10-14 2RIrRif p169 CR France80

KENNEDY,Horas Tristram TLt kia 6-6-17 2RScotF attRE p94 CR France263

KENNEDY,Hugh Victor Strain T2Lt kia 16-8-17 14RIrRif p169 MR30

KENNEDY,Humfrey Hays MajALtCol kia 29-7-18 2 att8SfthH p165 CR FRancr524

KENNEDY,James T2Lt dow 26-9-15 1CamH p168 CR France178,Lt

KENNEDY,James T2Lt kia 21-3-18 8 att1RIrRif p169 CR France1061

KENNEDY,James Joseph TLt dow 17-10-18 6 att11RInniskF p105 CR France846

KENNEDY,James Patrick 2Lt kia 19-6-18 18Lond attMGC p187&250 MR32

KENNEDY,James Robert LtCol ded 3-8-17 IA 96Inf att90Punjabis p278

KENNEDY,James Wallace.MID ACapt kia 27-5-17 4 att1ScotRif p103 MR20

KENNEDY,John 2Lt kia 23-4-17 ScotRif att7BordR p103 MR20

KENNEDY,John T2Lt kia 20-4-18 BordR att15DLI p117 CR Belgium15

KENNEDY,John Alexander Capt dow 6-8-16 6SfthH p241 CR France74

KENNEDY,John Edwin TLt kia 25-9-15 8SfthH p165 MR19

KENNEDY,John Gilbert T2Lt kia 14-9-16 1Leic p87 MR21

KENNEDY,John Horace 2Lt kia 10-1-15 2SomLI attScotRif p80 CR France567

KENNEDY,John Murray Stewart TLt kia 10-8-15 9SfthH p165 CR France765

KENNEDY,John Patrick Francis Capt kia 24-4-18 5 att2RB p179 CR France424

KENNEDY,John Pitt Capt kia 10-3-15 2ScotRif p103 CR France260

KENNEDY,J.N.C.Maj 20-4-15 RE CR Hamps1

KENNEDY,Miles Arthur Claude.DSO.Capt ded 2-11-18 IA 1/8GurkhaRif p278 CR Pakistan50A

KENNEDY,Nigel.MID Lt kia 22-10-14 RScotF p94 MR29,25-10-14

KENNEDY,Norman 2Lt dow 31-10-17 1/2RScotF p94 CR France134

KENNEDY,Paul Adrian Capt kia 9-5-15 4 at2RB p179 MR32

KENNEDY,R.B.C.2LtTLt ded 10-8-17 Ches p96 CR Eire234,RDubF

KENNEDY,Robert 2Lt dow 10-7-16 2 att3RScotF p94 CR France66

KENNEDY,Rolf Darab T2Lt kia 27-3-18 23RFC p16 MR20

KENNEDY,Ronald Sinclair.MC.TCapt kia 17-4-18 RAMC att76FA p196 CR France856,Sinclaire

KENNEDY,Samuel Lancelot Richard Alexander Edgar 2Lt kia 15-9-16 8Lond p247 CR France432

KENNEDY,Thomas Christian 2Lt kia 25-11-15 C97RFA p31 CR France922

KENNEDY,Thomas James TLt kia 9-9-16 8RInniskF p105 MR21

KENNEDY,Tristram Gervias Lt dow 28-3-18 A301RFA p31 CR Palestine3

KENNEDY,Walter Douglas Lt kia 19-4-17 5RScotF p222 MR34

KENNEDY,Walter Louis 2Lt kia 3-9-16 12RSuss p119 CR France339

KENNEDY,William HonMaj&QM ded 29-5-15 KEdwHorse p24

KENNEDY,William.MC.MajALtCol kia 23-11-17 18HLI att18WelshR p163 MR17

KENNEDY,William Robert T2Lt kia 25-9-15 2A&SH p173 CR France114

KENNEFICK,Edward Hamerton Capt kia 8-7-16 Ess p132 MR21

KENNEFICK,John George Hamerton Capt kia 20-4-18 3 att2Ess p132&257 CR France250

KENNELLY,Leslie William TLt dow 9-10-15 9RSuss p119 CR France134

KENNETH,Archibald Capt kia 12-7-15 4RScotF p222 MR4

KENNINGTON,Harry Lt kia 27-10-17 52RFA p207 MR30

KENNY,Cecil John Lt kia 24-3-18 3RIrReg attMGC Inf p89&183 CR France1203

KENNY,Cecil Stacpoole 2Lt ded 11-11-15 KSLI p265 MR40,drd

KENNY,Francis Joseph Leo T2Lt kia 9-8-16 5ConnRgrs attRInniskF p172 CR Belgium47

KENNY,John Mary Joseph TLt kia 23-9-16 RASC &RFC p3&193 MR20

KENNY,Laurence Henry T2Lt kia 26-6-16 10 att8Suff p78 MR21

KENNY,William David.VC.Lt kia 2-1-20 IA 4/39GarhwalRif p278 MR43

KENNY,William George Stanhope Capt kia 10-3-15 IA 1/39GarhwalRif p278 CR France355 &CR France1887

KENRICK,Herbert William Mascall Capt ded 24-3-19 RoO att11Huss p22 CR Germany1

KENT,Alan Williamson 2Lt dow 27-4-15 7NumbF p214 CR Belgium4

KENT,Charles Ronald.MC.T2Lt kia 20-10-18 6 att5Dors p124 CR France192

KENT,Charles Stuart 2Lt kia 24-10-18 4BlkW p230 CR France1258

KENT,Edward Montague Wayne Lt kia 26-8-14 1Hamps p121 MR15,Swayne

KENT,Ernest TLt dow 8-4-17 2Ess &24RFC p9&132 CR France699

KENT,Frederick Charles 2Lt kia 5-7-17 7Worc p226 CR Belgium34

KENT,George Edward Lt kia 24-3-18 3 att8RLancs p59 MR20

KENT,George Herbert Stanton Capt kia 24-3-18 RE 490FC p46 MR27

KENT,Harold 2Lt kia 4-8-17 3 att8SWBord p100 CR Belgium101

KENT,Harold 2Lt dow 16-11-17 A50RH&FA p31 CR France1361

KENT,James Maddison Lt dow 5-8-15 3DLI p161 CR Belgium11,2Bn

KENT,Lionel Victor 2LtTLt dow 31-7-17 3SWBord p100 CR Belgium84 Ex 28Lond

KENT,Percival Naylor MajALtCol ded 8-4-18 3DragGds p21 CR France40,18-4-18

KENT,Peter Francis 2Lt kia 6-2-18 3RFC p16 CR France568

KENT,P.J.2Lt ded 2-9-16 N&D p264 CRWales17,P.G.

KENT,Ralph E Dawson LtCol kia 27-5-18 4Yorks att81TrainResBn p90 MR18

KENT,Sidney T2Lt kia 13-12-17 43MGC Inf p183 MR30

KENT,W.J.SubCdr 17-3-18 MilWksServ MR43

KENT,Walter John 2Lt kia 24-8-18 17Lond p250 MR16

KENT,William James Capt kia 7-8-15 13WYorks attManch p82 MR4

KENT,William John 2Lt kia 12-3-15 RFA 53Bty p31 France1106

KENT,William Morley 2Lt kia 21-2-18 RFC p16 CR Belgium158,Lt

KENTFIELD,Edwin Nelson T2Lt kia 17-2-17 23RFus p68 MR21

KENTISH,Ernest George 2Lt ded 27-2-18 B'RHA p31 CR Iraq8

KENTISH,Harold Edward Capt kia 30-3-18 RE 281ArmyTroopsCo p46 MR27

KENWARD,Robert 2Lt 7-7-16 2RSuss MR21

KENWORTHY,Donald LtTCapt kia 17-5-17 1SomLI p80 CR Belgium96,17-5-15

KENWORTHY,Stanley TCapt kia 1-7-16 17Manch p155 CR France397

KENYON,Charles Wilton T2Lt kia 16-3-16 10RSuss attT47TMB p119 CR France924

KENYON,James T2Lt kia 21-3-18 Manch att2/6Bn p155 MR27

KENYON,James Maj ded 22-12-18 Res 5LancF p270 CR Lancs321,22-11-18

KENYON,James Henry Turner Capt ded 28-9-18 RAVC p268 CR Derby98

KENYON,John De Winton 2Lt kia 16-5-15 4 att1Lpool p72 MR22

KENYON,William Douglas Capt dow 16-9-18 1/7Ches p222 CR France25

KEOGH,Alfred Alexander T2Lt kia 12-5-17 Mddx att11Bn p147 CR France1188

KEOGH,Frederick Bertram.MC.Capt kia 8-8-18 4ConnRgrs att1TankCps p172&188 CR France360

KEOGH,Henry Claude 2Lt kia 4-4-17 3 att13RSuss p119 CR Belgium127

KEOGH,James Lynch.MID Capt&QM ded 18-1-19 RAMC 83FA p253 CR Asia81

KEOGH,John 2Lt kia 22-3-18 3 att2Leinst p174 CR France365,Lt

KEOGH,Thomas T2Lt ded 16-12-18 RE IWT p46 CR India97A

KEOGH,William Gerald TLt ded 12-10-18 6Leinst att2/4NumbF p174 CR EAfrica116

KEPPELL,Albert Edward George Arnold.Hon.MID Lt kia 31-7-17 2RB p179 CR Belgium88

KEPPELL-PALMER,Stuart Leslie.MC.TLtACapt kia 3-10-18 3TankCps LtBn p188 CR France234

KEPPIE,Charles Browning T2Lt dow 27-3-18 2RB p179 CR France145

KER,Arthur Milford Capt kia 14-10-14 GordH p166 CR France1106

KER,Bruce Ralph Capt ded 28-11-19 SL p268

KER,Cecil Howard Capt kia 15-9-14 1Beds p86 MR15

KER,Frederick Roxburghe 2Lt kia 20-9-17 6Lond p247 MR29

KER,Laurence Arthur 2Lt ded 4-4-15 9RScotF p94 CR Scot677,kldacc

KER,Thomas Darling 2Lt kld 1-6-16 RE p46 CR Egypt2

KER-GULLAND,Reginald Glover 2Lt dow 12-11-14 14Lond p249 CR Belgium135

KERFOOT,Edwin Capt ded 8-3-20 5Manch p270 CR Lancs443

KERKHAM,Francis Leslie 2Lt kia 14-10-17 3 att7Norf p74 MR20

KERLEY,Bertram Frederick 2Lt kia 10-9-17 6SWBord p100 CR Belgium23 Fredrick

KERMODE,Edgar Marsden.DSO.MC&Bar.DCM.2Lt dow 27-7-18 2/5WYorks p218 CR France1697,26-7-18

KERNAGHAN,Graham Hemery TLt kia 1-7-16 8YLI p143 CR France246 &CR France1890

KERNAGHAN,John T2Lt dow 1-10-18 9RIrF p171 CR Belgium84

KERNICK,Charles Sylvester TLt dow 1-12-17 14MGC Inf p183 CR France446

KERR,Adam TCapt dow 3-11-18 10N&D p134 CR France1478

KERR,Alan Graham Lt kia 26-10-18 5ScotRif p224 CR France206

KERR,Alexander Lt dow 30-4-15 5RScots p211 MR4

KERR,Alexander Crerar T2Lt kia 1-1-17 RE 91FC p46 CR France515

KERR,Andrew Alan 2Lt kia 26-3-18 16KRRC p150 MR30

KERR,Arthur Douglas Garnett Odell 2Lt kia 3-8-16 10Mddx att1/5LancF p236 MR21

KERR,Daniel Lt kia 6-7-15 14Ches attSWBord p96 MR4

KERR,Daniel Eugene.MID Lt kia 10-6-18 RFA 87Btyp31 CR Belgium18

KERR,David.MC.T2Lt kia 12-8-16 6/7RScotF p94 CR France151

KERR,David Anselm 2Lt kia 13-10-14 3RScots p54 CR France708 &CR France1158,13-10-14 2Bn

KERR,David,Bryce TCapt kia 1-7-16 16HLI p163 MR21

KERR,David Chesne 2Lt kia 12-10-17 4RScots p211 MR30,Chesney

KERR,Donald 2Lt kia 1-7-16 14Lond p249 MR21

KERR,Edward Bournes TLt dow 26-5-16 12RB p179 CR Belgium11

KERR,Finlay 2Lt kia 4-7-16 2RIrReg p89 MR21,Lt 5-7-16

KERR,Frederick Walter.DSO.Col kia 31-10-14 1Div HQ Staff p1 CR Belgium58 1GordH

KERR,George Augustus L'Estrange 2Lt kia 30-6-18 2Beds p86 CR France516

KERR,Harry Smellie 2Lt dow 25-4-18 4RScots p211 MR30

KERR,Henry Thomas Frederick.MC.2Lt kia 25-9-15 2A&SH p173 CR France114

KERR,Henry Grace 2Lt dow 1-7-17 9Lancers p22 CR France178

KERR,Henry Thomas Ross 2Lt ded 3-7-16 PoW 8att6CamH p168 MR19

KERR,Hubert Rainsford Gordon Lt kia 21-12-14 1HLI p163 MR22,19-12-14

KERR,James 2Lt kia 1-7-16 4 att16HLI p163 MR21

KERR,James 2Lt kia 13-11-17 1/5KOSB p224 CR Palestine9

KERR,James Lt kia 21-3-18 3 att1RIrRif p169 MR27

KERR,James Campbell 2Lt ded 30-3-19 9HLI p240 CR Iraq6

KERR,James Elkin TLt dow 10-9-17 202MGC Inf p183 CR Belgium173

KERR,James Melrose 2Lt drd 4-9-16 1/5RScotF p222 CR Egypt7,3-9-16

KERR,John Murdoch 2Lt kia 13-11-16 8 att1RScotF p94 CR France742,1 att8Bn

KERR,John Robert Capt ded 7-11-17 12RDC p253 CR Lancs98

KERR,John William T2Lt kia 28-3-18 10ScotRif p103 CR France57

KERR,Leslie Henry Fox TLt dedacc 24-11-16 RASC 9DivTrain 106Coy p193 CR France169

KERR,M.T.SNurse 17-1-15 TFNS 2ScotGH CR Scot501

KERR,Norman James T2Lt dow 20-12-16 97MGC p183 CR France40

KERR,Peter Campbell T2Lt kia 18-8-18 1 att1/7LancF p93 CR France5

KERR,Robert 2Lt dow 7-6-17 19Lond p250 CR Belgium165

KERR,Robert Goodman.MC.TMajALtCol kia 11-7-18 7RInniskF att9RIrF p105 CR France855

KERR,Robert Thomas 2Lt kia 23-10-16 4Y&L p238 CR France927

KERR,William Walton.DSO.MC.CaptALtCol kia 3-5-18 2BordR p117 CR Italy2

KERR,William TLt kia 2-9-18 6RScotF att4MGC Inf p94&183 CR France1182,4MGC att6RScotF

KERR,William John Lt dow 10-3-15 2ScotRif p103 CR Gloucl24

KERR,William Niven 2Lt ded 26-11-18 19Lond p250 CR France1030

KERR-CLARK,St.Ruan Robertson TCapt kia 25-9-15 7SfthH p165 MR19

KERRICH,Henry Latham Lt dow 27-9-17 3N&D p134 CR Belgium93

KERRICH,John Herbert Capt kia 14-9-14 2WelshR C'Coy p127 CR France1329,Maj

KERRIDGE,Oswald Alfred T2Lt dow 23-7-16 16DLI p161 CR France145

KERRISON,Roger Orme LtCol ded 18-9-17Suffyeo CR France64

KERRY,Albert 2Lt kia 22-3-18 1RFus p68 MR27

KERRY,Arnold John St.Ledgier.MID Lt ded 14-2-18 16Manch p155 CR Camb16,Legier dow

KERSEY,William Henry Myddleton Capt kia 17-10-17 RGA 166SB p209 CR Belgium19

KERSHAW,Ellis T2Lt kia 1-7-16 13 att1LancF p93 MR21

KERSHAW,Henry Valder Capt kia 15-9-16 19Lond p250 MR21

KERSHAW,Joseph Harrison Lt ded 16-9-19 10Manch p256 CR Egypt2

KERSHAW,Kenneth Robert Beresford T2Lt kia 25-9-15 9GordH p166 CR France554

KERSHAW,Milton 2Lt kia 7-11-14 att2Glouc SR p107 MR29

KERSHAW,Ryder Samuel 2Lt kia 11-5-17 7LancF SR att1/1Lond p221 CR France581

KERSHAW,Thomas James T2Lt dow 23-1-17 11LancF p93 CR France264

KERTLAND,Edwin Blow 2Lt kia 16-6-15 3RIrF att2RIrRif p171 MR29

KERWOOD,Lionel Maj kia 21-10-16 1/8Worc p226 MR21

KERWOOD,Philip Malcolm Lt kia 25-6-15 8Worc p226 CR France285

KESBY,Thomas Herbert TCapt kia 15-9-16 EKent att70MGC Inf p57&184 CR France390

KESSACK,James O'Connor TCapt kia 13-11-16 25 att17Mddx p147 MR21

KESSLER,Edgar Capt kia 4-6-15 1/6Manch A'Coy p236 CR Gallipoli2

KESTELL-CORNISH,Robert Vaughan.MC&Bar.MIDx3 LtTCapt dow 17-6-18 Dors attStaffDivHQ p124 CR France102

KESTEVEN,Thomas Carew.Lord.Capt dow 4-11-15 LincsYeo p204 CR Somerset199,5-11-15

KETTLE,Rupert Arthur Lt kia 26-3-18 3Huss p21 CR France1063

KETTLE,Thomas Michael TLt kia 9-9-16 9RDubF p177 MR21

KEVILL-DAVIES,William Albert Somerset Herbert Lt dow 15-5-15 9Lancers p22 CR France285

KEW,George Richard ACapt dow 8-11-17 8SLancs p125 CR France98

KEWLEY,George Raymond T2Lt kia 20-5-16 8LNLancs p136 MR20

KEWLEY,John Tasker TLt dow 16-1-17 6LNLancs p136 CR Iraq5,Capt

KEY,Douglas Polson Lt dow 25-8-15 RE 78FC p46 CR Belgium82

KEY,Frederick Bertram 2Lt kia 1-7-16 8RWar p215 MR21

KEY,Hart Reginald 2Lt kia 13-4-18 6WRid p227 MR30

KEY,William Partridge Lt kia 11-9-15 1 att11YLI p143 CR France1059

KEYES,Cleveland.MC.TCaptAMaj dow PoW 24-3-18 C83RFA p31 CR France1703

KEYMS,Thomas Booth 2Lt kia 19-7-16 B84RFA p31 CR France402

KEYS,Joseph Nicholas Douglas.MC.LtACapt kia 21-9-17 11Ess p132 CR France149

KEYS,Malcolm T2Lt dow 31-8-16 8BordR p117 CR France44

KEYSER,Richard Norman Lt kld 22-8-17 3ELancs attRFC p9&111

KEYZOR,Herbert Louis Abraham T2Lt kia 9-3-18 1SWBord att25RWFus p100 CR Mddx66,kldacc CR Palestine3,2Bn

KHALAF,E.Capt ded 1-10/31-12-19 MO 3EgyptStatHosp CR Egypt2

KIBBY,H.C.2Lt ded 27-10-18 10Mddx &RAF p236

KIDD,Alastair Wilson TLt ded 26-10-18 RE 1BaseParkCo p46 CR France65,MiningCoy

KIDD,Balmer T2Lt dow 19-3-18 137MGC Inf p184 CR France98

KIDD,Cecil Christian.MID TCapt drd 28-2-18 RE 8FldTrpCo p46 CR Palestine2

KIDD,Charles Roland Capt 8-7-20 RAMC CR Hamps64

KIDD,Claude Bernard.MC.TCapt kia 24-3-18 15Ches p96 MR27

KIDD,Edward John Cecil 2Lt kld 10-4-18 5WYorks &RAF p270 CR Yorks474

KIDD,Guy Egerton.DSO.Maj kia 26-9-16 A70RFA p31 CR France453

KIDD,Herbert Dickie 2Lt kia 17-5-15 4CamH p243 MR22

KIDD,James Forrest 2Lt ded 1-11-18 12KRRC &20RAF p150 CR France937,Lt kld

KIDD,J.G.Capt 24-9-14 Cps of Army Schlmstrs MR67

KIDD,John Newman Capt kia 19-1-16 6DragGds p21 CR France423

KIDD,Leonard Cameron.MC.Lt kia 12-10-16 3RFC p3 MR20

KIDD,Philip Chabert 2Lt kia 30-10-14 Yorks p90 MR29

KIDD,Robert John Lt dow 24-4-21 IA 1/1 att1/11GurkhaRif p278 MR43,2/1Bn

KIDD,Vivian Norval.MC.TMaj ded 21-3-17 8WRid.Staff p115&258 CR France169

KIDD,William Sidney Lt kia 21-3-18 att2RMunstF p175 MR27

KIDDELL,George Bartam Pearce 2Lt ded 27-2-17 1RIrF p171 CR France67

KIDDER,Milton Ellory T2Lt kld 19-5-17GL RFC p9 CR Norf209,Elroy

KIDDIER,Ernest 2Lt kia 17-9-18 RGA 244SB p40 CR France686

KIDDLE,Cyril Frank 2Lt kia 25-4-18 4 att1/5WYorks p82 MR30

KIDDLE,Geoffrey Capt ded 29-7-16 7RFA p31 CR Iraq6

KIDDS,George Frederick T2Lt kia 25-7-17 11Mddx p147 CR France581

KIDNER,Thomas Clatworthy Capt kia 26-10-16 RAMC att2Mddx p196 MR21

KIDSON,Charles Wilfrid Lt kia 17-10-18 5 att2RDubF p177 CR France190

KIDSTON,William Hamilton Campbell Capt ded 8-8-17 9A&SH p243 CR France40,1/8Bn

KIELY,Florence Patrick 2Lt kia 24-6-17 4 att9RIrF p171 MR29

KILBORN,Leslie Bertram 2Lt dow 10-4-17 6GordH p242 CR France95,1/8Bn

KILBY,Arthur Forbes Gordon.VC.MC.Capt kia 25-9-15 2SStaffs C'Coy p122 MR19 CR France1059

KILBY,John T2Lt dow 21-8-16 10Glouc att7TMB p107 CR France2

KILBY,William Watson Capt ded 19-2-19 SL p268

KILGOUR,Alexander Lt kia 18-4-18 7BlkW p231 CR France279

KILGOUR,Arthur Wilson TLt/Capt kld 27-7-17 RFC SR p9

KILGOUR,Charles David Winton T2Lt dow 4-11-18 RFA 25ArmyBde p31 CR France1266

KILGOUR,Henry LtCol ded 24-11-15 2/5Dev p217 CR Egypt9

KILKELLY,John George Joseph Capt kia 24-3-18 RMunstF &RFC p16&175 MR20

KILKENNY,Edward Charles Randolph.MC.LtAMaj kia 26-6-17 A186RFA p31 CR Belgium5

KILLBY,Chester Winterbon Lt kia 21-3-18 C307RFA p207 MR27

KILLEN,Edward Osborne Brice TLt kia 15-1-17 RE 71FC p46 CR Iraq5

KILLICK,R.N.Lt 8-12-19 RWKent CR Kent289

KILLICK,Richard 2Lt kia 18-5-15 1/6Manch p237 MR4,15-5-15

KILLICK,Sidney Herbert Capt dow 18-11-16 1SLancs attHQ Staff p125 CR Iraq5

KILLICK,Sydney Howard 2Lt ded 16-5-18 8ESurr attMGC p113&184 CR France145

KILLINGBACK,Stanley Gordon Lt kia 10-8-16 RE p210 CR France15,11-8-16

KILLINGLEY,Hastings Grewatt Lt kia 23-10-16 2RDubF p177 MR21,Grevatt

KILMISTER,Harold Howard Linsdell.MC.Lt kia 22-8-18 5 att9RFus p68 CR France370

KILNER,Charles Ussher T2Lt dow 8-10-16 1Suff p78 CR Greece3

KILNER,Thomas Richard Burgess.MM.T2Lt kia 18-6-18 9N&D p134 CR France115

KILPIN,Franklin James 2Lt kia 16-4-18 RGA 250SB p40 CR Belgium21

KILPIN,Thomas Bennett 2Lt dow 15-6-17 RFA attY25TMB p31 CR France262

KILROE,Francis Joseph T2Lt dow 28-8-18 1HLI attRInniskF p163 CR France134

KILSBY,George Alfred 2Lt kia 18-9-18 4Nhampt p234 CR France212

KILVERT,Harry T2Lt dow 1-8-17 9RWFus p98 CR France285

KIMBELL,Harry John Sullings TLt ded 28-5-16 RAMC p196 CR Lond10

KIMBELL,Richard Evison 2Lt kia 16-4-17 14Huss &60RFC p9&22 CR France604

KIMBER,Basil Liddon T2Lt kia 10-7-16 7Lincs p75 MR21 Ex 5Lond

KIMBER,Henry Cyril Dixon Lt dow 22-6-16 19/7RFA p207 CR France12

KIMBER,John William Lt dow 11-5-18 4BlkW p230 CR France40,1Bn

KIMBER,Reginald Ernest T2Lt kia 20-9-17 8Glouc p107 MR30

KIMBERLEY,W.R Lt 26-9-20 GL &RASC CR Egypt6

KIMPTON,Frank Capt ded 14-3-19 RE p46&257 CR Iraq6

KIMPTON,Norman Herbert 2Lt dow 14-7-17 1RFA p208 CR Belgium12

KINAHAN,James T2Lt dow 8-10-18 23RFus p68 CR France407

KINCAID,Andrew Duncan 2Lt dow 23-3-18 BlkW att8Bn p129 MR27

KINCAID,James Brown TLt kia 23-4-17 13RScots p54 MR20

KINCAID,John Brown 2Lt kia 3-5-17 1RScotF p94 MR20

KINDER,Geoffrey George.MC.Capt kia 20-7-18 8WYorks p219 MR18

KINDER,Richard Clement TCapt kia 20-9-17 GL att26RFus p190 MR30

KINDER,Thomas Harry Capt kia 3-7-16 7Suff p78 MR21

KINDERSLEY,Douglas Cumming Paget.DSO.Capt kia 22-6-17 3HLI att2KOSB p163 CR France184

KINDERSLEY,Lionel Nassau 2Lt kia 25-11-17 15Huss p22 MR17

KINDLEYSIDES,Charles Frederick T2Lt dow 4-10-18 ACycCps att22NumbF p181 CR France106,5-10-18

KING,Alan Howard T2Lt kia 22-8-18 9RFus p68 CR France370

KING,Albert TLt kia 23-8-16 RFA p31 CR France833

KING,Albert 2Lt kia 31-5-17 3Mon p244 MR20,2Bn

KING,Alexander Duncan Campbell 2Lt kia 24-5-15 18Huss SR p23 CR Belgium2

KING,Alexander Lindsay T2Lt kia 9-4-18 HLI att10/11Bn p163 CR France705

KING,Alfred John 2Lt dow 17-6-18 6 att4NStaffs A'Coy p238 CR France122

KING,Alfred Nelson TLt kia 10-5-16 C53RFA p31 CR Belgium71

KING,Andrew Buchanan Maj dow 28-5-15 7A&SH p243 CR France200

KING,A.P.Lt ded 12-10-16 12Suff p263 CR Suff224

KING,Arthur Bernard T2Lt kia 7-7-16 12Manch p155 MR21

KING,Arthur Montague Maj kia 15-3-15 RB p179 MR29

KING,Arthur Philip 2Lt kia 24-11-17 2Mddx p147 CR Belgium126 Ex 1Lancs

KING,Arthur Towers Lt kia 17-11-17 1/1LincsYeo p204 CR Palestine9

KING,Arthur William 2Lt kia 17-9-16 17Lond p250 CR France432,15-9-16

KING,Berry 2LtTLt kia 3-5-17 3YLI &25RFC p9&143 CR France88,6Bn

KING,Bertie Allen T2Lt dow 29-4-17 7EYorks p84 CR France113

KING,Charles Lt dow 10-5-17 1/1GlamorganRHA p207 CR France1182

KING,Charles Arthur Cecil.MIDx2 Col kia 30-10-14 2Yorks p90 MR29

KING,Charles Eustace Dickson.MC.Capt&Adjt kia 11-10-16 2YLI p143 CR France114

KING,Charles Frederick 2Lt kia 20-9-17 Dev att1/6Lpool p77 MR30

KING,Charles Leonard 2Lt kia 22-3-18 Herts p252 CR France528

KING,Charles Sealy Lt kia 9-5-15 RMunstF p175

KING,Charles William 2Lt kia 25-9-15 2SStaffs p122 MR19

KING,Cuthbert TMaj kia 11-4-17 44MGC attRWSurr p184 CR France924

KING,Cyril Henry Marshall 2Lt kia 30-9-16 GL &60RFC p3&190 CR France95

KING,Cyril William T2Lt kia 9-11-17 52MGC Inf p184 CR Belgium126

KING,Daniel Arthur TLt ded 22-7-17 RE IWT p46 CR Iraq5

KING,David T2Lt kia 31-7-17 15RWFus p98 MR29

KING,David Taylor T2Lt kia 1-7-16 2GordH p166 CR France331

KING,Douglas Reid.MC.MID Capt kia 7-6-17 RAMC att74FA p196 CR Belgium152

KING,Ebenezer.MC.2Lt kld 17-3-17 3KOSB attRFC p9&102 CR Lincs181

KING,Edmund Harold T2Lt dow 3-7-16 6Wilts p153 CR France833

KING,Edward Gordon Macgregor 2Lt kia 17-7-16 KSLI attGlouc p145 CR France246

KING,Edward Roly Capt dow 23-4-18 3Norf A'Coy p74 MR38,Roby

KING,Edward Westcott 2Lt dow 20-10-18 B79RFA p31 CR France332

KING,Eric George T2Lt kia 21-3-18 8RBerks p139 MR27

KING,Eric George Lauder Lt kia 22-7-17 1GrenGds p50 CR Belgium12 Lander

KING,Frank Maxfield TMaj kia 22-3-18 KRRC att9LNLancs p150 MR20

KING,Frank Radcliffe T2Lt kia 14-9-16 14Lpool p72 MR37

171

KING,Frederick Cross T2Lt kia 23-10-16 17RIrRif att25MGC Inf p184 CR France307

KING,Frederick Harvey Lt kia 12-10-16 1WIndiaR att2WRid p192 MR21

KING,George 2Lt kia 12/13-2-17 3 att9Suff p78 MR19

KING,George Charles.MID Capt ded 4-7-21 RAMC 2FA CR Ches62

KING,Gilbert Stewart TCapt kia 3-4-17 15WYorks p82 MR20,3-5-17

KING,Gordon Wick 2Lt kia 9-4-16 8Ches p96 MR38

KING,Hamilton Boyd 2Lt kia 7-6-17 22Lond p251 CR Belgium120

KING,Harry T2LtACapt kia 3-9-16 11 att3Worc p109 CR France246

KING,Harry Garfield T2Lt kia 26-4-18 Ess att10Bn p132 MR27

KING,Harold Dudley 2Lt kia 6-10-18 Worc att1/8Bn p109 CR France1462

KING,Henry Alfred 2Lt ded 4-11-18 IA TC attS&TCps p278 MR61

KING,Henry Arthur.MC.2Lt kia 1-7-17 RFA D'Bty121Bde p31 CR Belgium1

KING,Henry Frederick T2Lt dow 7-5-17 9Leic p87 CR France120

KING,Henry Frederick Irwin Lt ded 5-11-18 D165RFA p31 CR Belgium159

KING,Herbert TLt dow 6-10-17 RAOC p198 CR Belgium8

KING,Herbert Garner T2Lt kia 10-9-16 2NumbF p61 CR Greece3

KING,Herbert Grenfell.MC.Capt kia 22-3-18 16NumbF p61 CR France34 &CR France834

KING,Horace Reginald Edward Lt kia 28-3-18 4Ess p232 MR20

KING,Hubert Weston 2Lt kia 10-11-18 10 att1Lond p248 CR Belgium256

KING,Hugh Denham 2Lt kia 13-3-17 2/10Lond p248 CR France175

KING,Humphrey Stuart.MC.TLtACapt kia 4-10-18 2NumbF p61 CR France375,3-10-18

KING,James Lt&QM drd 14-6-16 RAVC 20VetHosp p198 CR Egypt9,13-6-16

KING,James Norman 2Lt kia 18-4-18 4LNLancs p234 CR France1106

KING,John Alexander 2Lt kia 12-9-16 4GordH p242 CR France922

KING,John David.DCM.2Lt ded 30-6-18 242RFA attSigSubSect p31 CR France95

KING,John Francis BtMaj ded 26-9-19 Suff att3Ech GHQ p263 CR Egypt1

KING,John Rose.MC.TLt kia 22-4-18 18 att10WYorks p82 CR France2

KING,John Skelton Clarke.DCM.2Lt kia 3-5-16 1/4 O&BLI p231 CR France1327

KING,Joseph 2Lt kia 4-10-18 3ConnRgrs att2RMunstF p172 CR France1495

KING,Kerry.DCM.2Lt dow 25-9-18 RGA 7Bty 3BdeMtnArty p40 CR Greece5

KING,Leonard.MC.Lt kia 18-4-17 1/6Glouc p225 CR France363

KING,Lucas Henry St.Aubyn Lt kia 8-5-15 4KRRC p151 MR29

KING,Maurice T2Lt ded 24-6-17 GL attEgyptLabCps p190 CR Egypt2

KING,Maurice Edmund T2Lt kia 15-3-16 13Mddx p147 MR29

KING,Nathaniel Walter Ryder Lt kia 21-2-15 16Lancers p23 CR Belgium57

KING,Nita Madeline Miss ded 25-5-17 VAD p200 CR France64

KING,Noel Gilbet Bryan Lt kia 7-6-17 1Wilts p153 MR29

KING,Norman 2Lt dow 26-5-18 IrGds att4GdsMGR p53 CR France63 see OLIVER,H.A.B.true name

KING,Norman Toynbee Lt kia 22-3-18 3DragGds p21 MR27

KING,Percy T2Lt dow 5-8-17 7ESurr p113 CR France113,kia

KING,Percy James Church.MM.2Lt kia 24-10-17 RFA p208 CR Belgium21

KING,Percy Reginald 2Lt kia 30-7-16 18Manch p155 MR21

KING,Philip Douglas Atwood 2Lt kia 18-12-16 2RSuss p119 CR France744

KING,Reginald 2Lt dow 15-9-18 1Mon att1SWBordp244 CR France526

KING,Reginald Duncan 2Lt kia 19-4-17 8Hamps p229 MR34

KING,R.F.C.Maj 19-3-18 RFC 6Mddx CR Sussex125

KING,Richard T2Lt dow 18-4-16 6SLancs p125 CR Iraq5

KING,Richard Henry T2Lt kia 27-6-17 N&D att12Bn p134 CR Belgium115

KING,Robert T2Lt kia 29-9-18 1SWBord p100 CR France672

KING,Robert Anderson Ferguson Smyly 2Lt dow 23-5-15 2RDubF p177 CR France102,Andrew

KING,Robert Neal Capt kia 1-11-14 Lincs p75 MR29

KING,Robert Thomas 2Lt kia 31-7-18 6SfthH p241 CR France27

KING,Robert William 2Lt kia 27-3-18 1Camb p245 MR27

KING,Samuel Perston Lt kld 13-10-17 LincsYeo p270 CR Oxford1

KING,Soloman T2Lt kia 13-10-16 23NumbF p61 CR France275,Solomon

KING,Stewart William LtCol ded 25-12-15 IA 17Inf p278

KING,Sydney Lt kia 31-7-17 Herts p252 MR29,Simmonds

KING,Sydney Robert HonCapt ded 19-11-16 RAOC p198 CR Lond14

KING,Sydney William Thacker 2Lt kia 10-8-15 4Ches p222 MR4

KING,Thomas Shirley Capt kia 3-5-17 4 att7ESurr p113 MR20

KING,Victor Algernon Robert T2Lt kia 29-9-17 233MGC Inf p184 MR30

KING,Victor Reginald TLt dow 13-5-18 GL Nhampt attRE Sigs p46&190 CR France180

KING,Wilfred Frank T2Lt kld 4-11-17 GL RFC p9 CR Kent90

KING,William 2Lt mbk 11-4-18 1LancF p256 MR32

KING,William T2Lt dow PoW 26-6-18 6 att7DCLI p114 CR Germany4

KING,William BRCS 19-10-18 CR Dorset50

KING,William Albert de Courcy.DSO.MajALtCol kia 27-5-17 RE 36DivHQ p46 CR Belgium97

KING,William Galbraith T2Lt kia 7-7-16 9RScotF att1MunstF p94 CR France115,6-7-16 8Bn

KING,William Hugh Lt kia 11-4-18 8Ess att7RAF p258&232 CR Belgium18,kld

KING,William Oliver Redman Lt ded 28-2-19 SL p268

KING,William Thomas 2Lt kia 29-8-18 5RWKent p235 CR France1484

KING,W.J.Lt ded 16-5-18 1/2NStaffs &RAF p157

KING-CHURCH,Cyril Edward Capt dow 25-9-15 7Lond D'Coy p247 CR France107

KING-HARMAN,Lawrence Hope Capt kld 26-10-16 RHA att30RFC p3&31 CR Iraq5

KING-MASON,S.D.Capt 10-06-20 RFA attNigR CR WAfrica3

KING-SALTER,Nigel Henry.MIDx2 Capt kia 3-6-19 IA 1/6GurkhaRif attStaff 55InfBde p278 CR Iraq8

KING-STEPHENS,Lionel Eustace 2Lt dow 20-12-16 8N&D p233 CR France120

KINGCOMBE,Alexis Randolph Lt dow 28-6-15 11Yorks p90 CR Gallipoli6

KINGDON,Arthur Francis TCapt kia 9-10-17 6Y&L p159 MR30

KINGDON,Leonard 2Lt kia 12-1-16 Worc &RFC p3&109 CR Belgium406

KINGDON,Oliver.MC.MID TCapt kia 24-4-18 7Beds p86 MR27

KINGDON,Robert Claude Hawker 2Lt kia 9-4-17 123RFA p31 CR France68,19-4-17

KINGHAM,Albert Edward.MID TLt kia 6-9-16 8RIrF p171 CR France1890,KINGHAN

KINGHAM,George William Ambrose 2Lt drd 9-11-17 3EKent attWAFF p57&201 CR Mddx39,Lt 1Bn

KINGHAM,Leonard Arthur Lt kia 11-8-17 1 att6RBerks p139 CR Belgium113,10-8-17

KINGHAM,Rolland Hill T2Lt kia 23-3-18 7MGC p184 MR20,17MGC

KINGSBURY,Edward Harrison TLt ded 17-8-17 GL RE IWT p190 CR Egypt8

KINGSFORD,Reginald John T2Lt kia 1-7-16 10Y&L p159 MR21

KINGSLEY,Albert Thomas 2Lt kia 26-4-18 4SStaffs p122 CR Belgium21

KINGSLEY,Eric T2Lt dow 7-7-16 12Manch p155 MR21

KINGSLEY,Gerald Cecil Lt kia 23-10-14 LNLancs p136 CR Belgium126

KINGSMAN,Roland Walter 2Lt kia 12-10-17 10MGC Inf p184 CR Belgium167

KINGSTON,Harold William Fellemans Lt kia 21-8-15 9RWSurr attRInniskF p56 MR4

KINGSTON,Nugent Arthur T2Lt kia 1-4-18 1RWar p65 CR France924

KINGSTON,William Lt 16-8-17 7RIrRif MR30

KINGSTON,William.MC.MID 2Lt kia 16-8-17 3RMunstF att1RIrRif p169&175 MR30

KINGSTON-BLAIR,Oliphant Philip Laurence.DSO.TLtCol dow 8-4-18 11RIrRif p169

KINGSWELL,Frank Alford TLt kia 22-3-18 RB att8Bn p179 MR27

KINGSWELL,Leonard William TLtACapt kia 26-3-18 14 att1Hamps att7CpsReinf p121 MR20

KINGTON,Edwin Lt dow 17-9-16 11RFA p31 CR France74

KINGTON,William Miles.DSO.Capt kia 20-10-14 1RWFus p98&127,WelshR MR29

KINGWELL,Francis Robert 2Lt dow 14-10-16 11Mddx p147 CR France833

KINGWELL,Hugh Robert TLt dow 24-8-18 11TankCps p188 CR France927

KINKAID,David Brown Lt 23-4-17 13RScots MR20

KINKAID,John Brown 2Lt 3-5-17 1RScotsF MR20

KINKEAD,Richard Crofton George Moore Capt kia 31-10-14 RAMC att10Huss p196 CR Belgium57,30-10-14

KINKEAD,Thompson Calder T2Lt kld 4-9-17 GL 3RFC p9 CR Sussex55,3-9-17

KINLOCH,James Moncrieff Thompson 2Lt kia 11-7-15 RE p46 MR29

KINMONT,John Collie Capt ded 18-11-17 3CamH attI'TankCps p168&188 CR France398

KINNA,James Eckersley.MC.TLt ded 12-9-17 16LancF p93 CR France40,Charley

KINNACH,Samuel James T2Lt kia 15-7-16 10Yorks p90 MR21

KINNAIRD,Hon Arthur Middleton.MC.Lt kia 27-11-17 1ScotsGds p52 CR France755

KINNAIRD,David T2Lt kia 5-12-17 26NumbF p61 CR France592

KINNAIRD,Douglas Arthuron.Hon.Capt kia 24-10-14 1ScotsGds p52 CR Belgium104

KINNAIRD,Francis Joseph Capt dow 6-6-15 4 att2SStaffs p122 MR22

KINNAIRD,John Kay T2Lt ded 6-11-18 LabCps p189 CR Scot252

KINNEAR,Alexander Hope T2Lt dow 19-7-17 6CamH p168 CR Belgium16

KINNEAR,Charles Annesley 2Lt kia 16-10-16 50RFA p31 CR France397

KINNEAR,J.L.DSO.MC.Maj kld 28-4-18 1/2Lpool &RAF p72

KINNEAR,Katherine Ferrars Nurse ded 3-9-17 VAD CR France1360

KINNELL,Guy Reeve BtMaj ded 9-12-19 4WYorks p263 CR Dorset110

KINNIBURGH,John Donaldson T2Lt kia 6-11-17 GL att14BlkW p190 CR Palestine1 Ex A&SH

KINRADE,Edward T2Lt kia 23-10-18 22NumbF att2Lincs p61 CR France1475

KINROSS,George Irvine Lt kia 12-9-16 2/22Lond p251 CR France157

KINSEY,Albert Thornley T2Lt kia 16-8-17 7SomLI p80 CR Belgium453

KINSLEY,Lawrence Millais 2Lt kia 15-10-16 11Ess p132 CR France307

KINSMAN,Cecil Henry 2Lt dow 28-3-16 RE p210

KIPLING,John Lt kia 27-9-15 2IrGds p53 MR19

KIPPAX,Arthur Hadden T2Lt kia 1-7-16 7EYorks A'Coy p84 CR 372

KIPPAX,James Elliott 2Lt kia 22-9-18 4ELancs p226 CR France758

KIPPS,George Stewart TLt kia 22-8-18 RASC att4Worc p193 CR France28

KIRBY,Alexander Claude 2Lt kia 24-7-18 3 att1/5N&D p134 CR France109

KIRBY,Alister Graham Capt ded 29-3-17 5Lond p246 CR France1571

KIRBY,Arthur Maurice Lt kia 25-9-17 5DLI attMGC Inf p187&238 MR30

KIRBY,Francis Emile Capt ded 6-12-15 RAOC CR Lond35

KIRBY,Frederick William T2Lt kia 21-9-17 GL 19RFC p9 CR France705

KIRBY,George TLt dow 8-5-18 1LancF p93 CR France65,2Lt

KIRBY,George Ernest T2Lt kia 23-7-16 10Glouc p107 MR21

KIRBY,James Sabey 2Lt kia 10-2-17 10Dev p77 MR37

KIRBY,Kenneth Cameron Lt kia 18-9-18 4Norf p216 CR France369

KIRBY,Richard Elston LtTCapt kldacc 1-6-18 RGA 22CpsHvyArty attStaff p40 CR France1367

KIRBY,Robert Arthur T2Lt kia 11-5-17 11MGC p184 MR20

KIRBY,Sidney Henry T2Lt kia 19-12-15 10BordR att5HLI p117 CR Gallipoli3

KIRBY,Walter Ernest 2Lt mbk 10-7-15 IARO att15Sikhs p278 MR28

KIRBY,William Howard Lee TLt ded 11-12-16 2Suff GarrBn p78

KIRK,Alfred Charles 2Lt kia 31-3-18 13Lond p249 CR France44

KIRK,Arthur T2Lt dow 12-8-16 9SWBord att1/4RScotF p100 CR Egypt7

KIRK,Arthur 2Lt kia 28-6-18 4EYorks p219 CR France352

KIRK,Charles Edmund 2Lt kia 6-8-17 6Beds p86 CR Belgium17,5-8-17

KIRK,Charles Gordon TCapt kia 20-7-18 14Y&L p159 CR France1693 &CR France34

KIRK,Gerald 2Lt dow 24-4-15 1/5RLancs p213 CR Belgium151

KIRK,Gerard Arthur Lt dow 20-7-16 3 att1Lincs p75 CR Lincs98,Garard

KIRK,Harold Raymond 2Lt kia 31-7-17 4SomLI p218 MR29

KIRK,Henry Buchanan TBrigGen ded 12-5-16 A&SH 93InfBde p173 CR France1

KIRK,James.MC.Chap4Cl dow 1-4-18 RAChDept att2SfthH p199 CR France64

KIRK,James.VC.2Lt kia 4-11-18 10 att2Manch p237 CR France1479

KIRK,John Alexander 2Lt kia 13-10-18 5KOSB p224 CR Belgium112

KIRK,John Thomas.MC.2Lt kia 28-3-18 15MGC p184 MR20

KIRK,Joseph Lingard 2Lt ded 10-2-16 1/10Manch p237&270 CR Ches160

KIRK,Leslie Christiern TCapt kia 9-10-17 9WYorks p82 MR30

KIRK,Percival Gordon Capt kia 13-8-17 1Camb attRFC p18&244 CR France134

KIRK,Richard.MC.Capt kia 13-11-16 6Ches p222 CR France293

KIRK,Ronald Leslie 2Lt kia 2-9-18 7 att1Lond p247 MR16

KIRK,Thomas James 2Lt dow 2-7-16 2Ess p132 MR21

KIRK,Tom 2Lt kia 4-6-15 1/10Manch p237 MR4

KIRKALDY,John Givens Capt drd 13-8-18 GL attRE p46 MR41,Maj

KIRKBY,John Nevil 2Lt kia 25-9-16 3 att2Y&L p159 MR21

KIRKBY,William TLtACapt ded 1-11-18 5MGC p184 CR France332

KIRKCALDY,Charles Henry 2Lt kia 10-3-15 1SfthH p165 CR France706,KIRKALDY

KIRKCALDY,Ray H.2Lt mbk 25-3-18 24RFC p256 MR20

KIRKHAM,William Laben T2Lt dow 21-10-16 9RWKent p141 CR France59

KIRKHOUSE,George Capt kia 9-4-18 6DLI p239 CR France346

KIRKLAND,Frederick William 2Lt kia 1-7-16 att1RB p179 MR21

KIRKLAND,James Towers.MC.TCapt kia 18-9-18 RAMC 141FA att1Glouc p196 CR France836

KIRKLAND,William Harrison Capt kia 25-9-15 7CamH p168 MR19

KIRKLEY,Frank Robson.MC.Lt ded 13-11-18 B102RFA p31 CR Italy11

KIRKNESS,Thomas Robert 2Lt kia 18-8-17 GL &32RFC p9 MR20

KIRKPATRICK,Athol 2Lt kia 3-5-17 3 att6EKent p57 MR20

KIRKPATRICK,Edward Hartley Maj kia 15-5-15 2 O&BLI p130 MR22

KIRKPATRICK,Harry Fearnley.DSO.ALtCol dow 27-3-18 EKent attRN Div"Anson" p57 CR France62

KIRKPATRICK,Hugh Cunningham Bruce.DSO.MC.CaptTMaj kia 1-10-18 KOSB StaffGHQ p102

KIRKPATRICK,John Crighton TLt kia 10-12-17 GL &20RFC p9 CR Belgium11

KIRKPATRICK,Robert Buist 2Lt kia 23-6-18 3 att1DCLI p114 CR France20,dow

KIRKPATRICK,Samuel T2Lt ded 30-9-18 PoW LancF att2/5Bn p93 CR Germany3

KIRKUP,Philip Austin.MC.TMaj kld 11-4-17 7DLI attRFC p18&239 CR Durham28

KIRKUS,Cuthbert Hayward 2LtACapt kia 31-7-17 RGA 283SB p40 CR Belgium17

KIRKWOOD,Robert Patrick Lt kia 5-10-17 2 att1KOSB NStaffs p102 MR30

KIRKWOOD,William John T2Lt kia 11-11-15 Yorks att6Bn p90 CR Gallipoli27

KIRKWOOD,William Lithgow 2Lt kia 4-10-18 4KOSB p224 MR16

KIRSH,Charles Sidney 2Lt kia 19-4-15 Beds p86 CR Belgium165

KIRSOP,Conrad Robert John Capt ded 13-10-17 262RFA p207 CR Palestine2

KIRTLAND,John 2Lt kia 12-3-15 2ESurr p113 CR Belgium168

KIRTON,Ralph Imray.AFC.2Lt ded 22-11-18 KOSB &RAF p102 CR Lond3

KIRTON,William Henry 2Lt 1-11-20 2/24Lond CR Herts30

KIRWAN,Laird 2Lt ded 20-8-18 6SLancs &30RAF p125 CR Iraq8,Lt

KIRWAN,R.M.Chap4Cl 23-5-16 CR Mddx51

KIRWAN,Theodore James 2LtACapt ded 11-6-19 RASC p193 CR Asia82

KITCHEN,Fred Tudor 2Lt kia 28-5-18 6SWBord p100 MR18

KITCHEN,George Rowland 2Lt kia 9-4-18 3 att4SomLI p80 CR Palestine9

KITCHEN,Harold Rosslyn Lt kia 27-9-16 3 att8WRid p115 MR21,KITCHIN

KITCHENER,Cecil Lt ded 30-10-18 RGA 94Coy p40 MR43 &CR Pakistan50A

KITCHENER,Horatio Herbert.Earl.KG.KP.GCB.OM.GCSI.GCMG.GCIE.FldMar drd 6-6-16 Staff p1 MR40,5-6-16

KITCHER,Henry Ernesy TCapt kia 7-8-16 5Dors p124 CR France174

KITCHIN,Anthony Walter Brook T2Lt kia 24-9-15 7RWSurr p56 CR France189

KITCHIN,Ernest Harold TCapt kia 21-10-16 17 att15KRRC p151 MR21,21/22-10-16 15 att17Bn

KITCHIN,Francis Leslie TLt kld 11-4-17 11Glouc &4RFC p9&107,kia MR20

KITCHIN,John Buchanan LtACapt dow 5-5-17 6EKent p57 CR France113

KITCHING,Edward Allen 2Lt ded 8-9-15 2/2RFA p208 CR Yorks159,Lt

KITCHING,Fred 2Lt kia 10-7-18 4Yorks p220 CR Belgium188,5Bn

KITCHING,George Allenby 2Lt kia 22-4-18 4 att10N&D p134 CR France41

KITE,Ralph Bertram.MC.Capt dow 10-12-16 3 att2 O&BLI p130 CR France1

KITHER,James Frederick T2Lt kld 12-12-17 GL RFC 62Aerodrome p9 CR Kent7

KITSON,Edward Gerard Templeman 2Lt dow 3-9-16 3DCLI p114 CR France329

KITSON,Frederick Neill Edmonstone Lt dow 15-8-17 5BlkW p231 CR France922,14-9-16

KITSON,Harold 2Lt dow 21-10-18 5Yorks p221 CR France1287

KITSON,John Henry 2Lt kia 14-4-18 5WRid p227 MR30

KITSON,Richard Buller.MID Capt kia 13-11-17 IA 58Rif p278 CR Palestine9

KITTERMASTER,Arthur Noel Colley TCapt kia 4/5-4-16 9 att12Worc p109 MR38

KITTLE,Ernest Arthur Lewis TLt dow 10-10-18 6RRofCav att3DragGds p23 CR France528

KIVER,Herbert William 2Lt kia 17-4-17 6ESurr p226 CR France161,9Bn

KLEAN,Michael Graham T2Lt kia 1-7-16 16NumbF p61 CR France293

KLEE,Arthur Milton T2Lt kia 8-8-18 10TankCps p188 MR16

KLEIN,Albert John 2Lt kia 14-10-18 5Ess p232 CR France550

KLEMANTASKI,Louis Arthur.MID T2Lt kia 27-5-16 8RBerks p139 CR France161

KNAGGS,Francis Henry TCapt ded 24-6-17 RAMC p196 CR Yorks643

KNAGGS,Kenneth John 2Lt kia 16-3-18 4RWar attRFC p16&65 CR France1281

KNAGGS,Victor St.George Lt dow 12-8-18 G5RFA p31 CR France69

KNAPP,Arthur Douglas TLt ded 27-5-17 NyasaFldForce p201 CR EAfrica15 &CR Tanzania1

KNAPP,Oswald Reed 2Lt dow 13-9-16 2WelchR p127 CR France833

KNAPP,Percival Ernest Maj kia 7-1-16 IA 51Sikhs p278 CR Iraq5

KNAPP,Simon Stock.DSO.MC.Rev dow 1-8-17 RAChDept att2IrGds p199 CR Belgium16

KNAPP,Valentine Powell T2Lt kld 18-7-16 7ESurr p113 CR France3

KNAPP-FISHER,Cyril Edward Holme T2Lt dow 31-7-15 6YLI p143 CR Belgium11

KNAPPS-FISHER,S.B.2Lt ded 6-10-14 3NStaffs p265 CR Lond14

KNAPTON,Odber Augustus Lt kia 18-9-14 RWar p65 CR France864

KNATCHBULL,Reginald Norton.DSO.LtCol ded 24-7-17 2Leic p87 CR Iraq8

KNATCHBULL-HUGESSEN,Maurice Astley.MC.Lt kia 25-9-16 2GrenGds SR p50 CR France394

KNEALE,John Francis T2Lt kld 21-12-17 GL RFC p9 CR Shrop145

KNEATH,David John 2Lt dow 3-8-18 5Ches p222 CR France145

KNEE,George Creasy Lt kia 3-5-17 4 att8EYorks p219 CR France421 Capt

KNELL,Edward Charles.MC.2Lt kia 9-8-18 8Lond p247 MR16

KNELL,William HonMaj&QM ded 22-7-17 Lincs attRFC p75 CR Mddx66

KNELLER,Frederick Kneller 2Lt kia 21-3-18 8RFC p16 MR20

KNIFTON,Charles William McKinley 2Lt kia 23-11-17 2RSuss p119 MR30,22-11-17 McKinlay

KNIFTON,James McKinley 2Lt kia 21-7-18 3 att2RSuss p199 MR19

KNIGHT,Arthur Gerald.DSO.MC.TCapt kia 20-12-16 RFC p3 CR France927

KNIGHT,Alan Collingwood Lt dow 29-6-15 14RB attRDubF p179 CR Gallipoli3,28-6-15

KNIGHT,Albert James.MC.2Lt dow 2-6-17 3 att11N&D p134 CR Belgium11

KNIGHT,Alexander William T2Lt dow 14-10-15 12 att9RWar p65 CR Gallipoli27

KNIGHT,Alfred Howard Capt ded 10-12-15 1/5RSuss p228 CR Kent86

KNIGHT,Allan 2Lt kia 23-3-18 5 att11SLancs p230 MR27,24-3-18

KNIGHT,Arthur George Lt kia 29-6-15 9RFus p68 CR Belgium33

KNIGHT,C.R.Wentworth Lt ded PoW 21-6-19 SL p201

KNIGHT,Edgar Frederick 2Lt kia 28-5-16 3Lond p245 CR France1014

KNIGHT,Edward 2Lt kia 20-9-18 4RScotF p222 CR France646

KNIGHT,Edward James 2Lt kia 12-5-17 7 att10LancF p221 MR20

KNIGHTM,E.F.Maj 5-7-17 8Lpool CR Sussex125

KNIGHT,Ernest Alexander T2Lt kia 24-9-17 233MGC Inf p184 MR30

KNIGHT,Francis Ernest T2LtACapt kia 4-3-17 2Nhampt p137 MR21

KNIGHT,Frederick Thornton 2Lt kia 13-5-15 3 att1ELanc p111 MR29

KNIGHT,Geoffrey St.John Lt dow 10-9-18 4RInniskF att14TankCps p105&188 CR France34

KNIGHT,George Gordon Lt dow 17-6-18 1/1DorsYeo p203 CR Palestine3

KNIGHT,George Harold T2Lt kia 6-10-17 RFC GL 11BallCo p9 CR Belgium20

KNIGHT,Gerald Fetherston Lt ded 30-10-19 Dev &RAF p263

KNIGHT,Gerald Robert Frank Capt dow 17-8-17 6Ess att1/1 O&BLI p232 CR Belgium16

KNIGHT,Guy Cunninghame LtCol dow 11-9-14 1LNLancs p136 CR France1134

KNIGHT,Harold Harrison Lt kia 27-3-18 1/9Manch p237 CR France927

KNIGHT,Henry James Capt kia 21-3-18 6BlkW C'Coy p231 CR France646,dow

KNIGHT,Herbert William 2Lt ded 6-6-18 6N&D p270 CR Essex1

KNIGHT,Hugh Eric Coleraine Capt kia 11-4-18 3 att1ELancs p111 MR32

KNIGHT,James Matthew 2Lt kia 20-5-18 C165RFA p31 CR France504

KNIGHT,James William T2Lt dow 12-12-17 10Y&L p159 CR Wilts115

KNIGHT,James Burghleigh Caxton 2Lt kld 15-4-18 GL &RAF p190 CR Egypt9

KNIGHT,John Hall.VD.LtCol kia 13-10-15 5NStaffs p237 MR19

KNIGHT,John Oswald 2Lt kia 2-11-16 3 att11RWKent p141 CR Belgium152,31-10-16

KNIGHT,John Owen Coldhan T2Lt kia 30-11-17 6RWSurr p56 CR France415

KNIGHT,John Peake.DSO.MIDx2 TCapt kia 31-8-16 35RFA p31 CR France397 Ex RHA

KNIGHT,John Percival Lt kia 26-3-18 1/7DLI p239 MR27

KNIGHT,Maynard Mansfield Lt ded 28-1-19 IARO att1MadrasLabCps p278 CR Iraq8

KNIGHT,N.T.CIE.Capt 18-10-18 RIM MR66

KNIGHT,Osbert Richmond.MC.Lt kia 6-4-17 4RWSurr attRFC p18&212 CR France522

KNIGHT,Philip T2Lt kia 28-5-17 6 att7Nhampt p137 CR Belgium28

KNIGHT,Phillip T2Lt kia 29-9-18 16KRRC p151 CR France212

KNIGHT,Philip Clifford 2Lt kia 1-7-16 SomLI p80 MR21

KNIGHT,Raymond Edward.DCM.2Lt kia 21-7-16 1/5Glouc p225 CR France150,22-7-16

KNIGHT,Richard Brodnax Capt dow 5-9-18 3 att4Beds p86 CR France145

KNIGHT,Robert Halley Capt kia 19-9-18 4Wilts p236 CR Palestine9

KNIGHT,Robert Valentine Harold 2Lt kia 19-7-16 1Nhampt p137 CR France703

KNIGHT,Walter Foster TLt kia 27-2-17 14 att16WYorks p82 CR France580,Forster

KNIGHTM,William Bernard 2Lt kia 21-4-15 4NStaffs p157 MR29

KNIGHT,William Leonard TLt ded 26-2-19 2Ess p132 CR France34

KNIGHT-BRUCE,Algernon James Lewis 2Lt kia 10-3-15 33RFA p31 CR France706

KNIGHTON,Gerald Godfrey.MID TMaj dow 30-4-17 5 O&BLI p130 CR France214

KNIGHTS,Henry Thorne TCapt kia 19-10-16 2Yorks att21TMB p90 CR France385

KNIGHTS-SMITH,Bernard Arthur T2Lt kia 5-9-15 12RB C'Coy p179 CR France1157

KNIPE,Edward Arthur 2Lt dow 26-9-16 2KOSB p102 CR France630,kia

KNOCKER,Arthur Paget LtTCapt kia 7-2-15 1Hamps p121 CR Belgium69,8-2-15

KNOLLYS,Frederick Roger Alexander Nicholas Maj dow 24-9-15 CityofLondYeo p204 CR Lond14

KNOTT,Archibald Sherbrooke.MC&Bar.T2Lt dow 25-4-18 2RBerks p139 CR France71

KNOTT,Charles Singleton 2Lt kia 23-3-18 11RFus p68 MR27

KNOTT,Donald James Vivian T2Lt kia 7-10-16 12 att11RWKent p141 CR France744

KNOTT,Ernest Capt kia 22-3-18 6Manch p236 MR27

KNOTT,Frederick Vernon TLt kia 21-3-16 19ACycCps p181 CR France705

KNOTT,Frederick William T2Lt kia 7-6-17 9Yorks p90 MR29

KNOTT,Henry Basil TCapt dow 7-9-15 9NumbF p61 CR Blegium84

KNOTT,James Leadbitter.DSO.TMaj kia 1-7-16 10WYorks p82 CR Belgium84

KNOTT,Ralph Leonard Lt 25-9-15 12NumbF p61 MR19

KNOTT,Robert Cecil TCapt dow 14-8-16 28 att20NumbF p61 CR France924

KNOTT,Stanley T2Lt ded 1-2-18 RASC p267 CR Suff45

KNOTT,Stuart Wallace 2Lt kia 24-4-18 3Lond p245 MR27

KNOTT,Sydney James 2Lt dow 8-7-16 5 att3Worc p109 CR France44

KNOTT,Thomas Albert 2Lt dow 25-11-14 1RBerks p139 CR France102

KNOWLES,Andrew Brooks 2Lt kia 11-6-16 IARO att17Cav p278 CR EAfrica29,Lt

KNOWLES,Arthur Yalden Lt dow 26-8-17 RFA 2ReinfCo 5thArmy p31 CR France40

KNOWLES,Eustace Oliver.OBE.Capt 11-3-20 GL attRE IWT CR Iraq6 Ex RIM

KNOWLES,F.2Lt 26-5-20 5RRofCav CR Ches114

KNOWLES,Frank Henry Capt kia 3-5-17 5WYorks p218 MR20

KNOWLES,Gavin Tenison Royle Lt kia 1-7-16 1/5SStaffs p229 MR21

KNOWLES,George Clarence 2Lt dow 10-6-17 3 att9Yorks p90 CR Belgium11

KNOWLES,Harold Leslie 2Lt kia 30-1-17 10GordH p166 MR21

KNOWLES,Harry Wilfred.MC.2LtTLt kia 8-6-17 1 att1WYorks p82 CR Belgium127

KNOWLES,Hedley Lt kia 30-5-15 1/6WRid p227 CR France82

KNOWLES,Henry Rylands.MC.TCapt kia 30-7-16 RAMC att7RLancs p196 MR21

KNOWLESJ.C.B.Lt 3-4-20 5ELancs CR Lancs193

KNOWLES,John Lyndon 2Lt kia 18-8-16 5 att7RB p179 MR21

KNOWLES,Jonathan Edward Capt kia 23-8-14 Mddx p147 CR Belgium244

KNOWLES,Richard Arthur Lees.MC.Lt kia 25-2-18 KRRC att4Bn p151 CR Greece3

KNOWLES,Richard Cameron TLt kia 10-7-16 114MGC Inf p184 MR21

KNOWLES,Stephen 2Lt dow 24-10-16 5 att2RB p179CR France105

KNOWLES,Vincent Lt&QM ded 14-10-15 RE p46 CR Yorks5

KNOWLES,Walford Vernon 2Lt kia 31-12-17 3 att2RBerks p139 CR Belgium126

KNOWLES,William Scott.MC.Capt kldByRobbers 26-11-20 IA 1GurkhaRif attSPersiaRif p278 CR Asia82

KNOWLING,Francis John Dobree.MC.TCapt kia 8-3-18 10A&SH p173 CR Belgium12

KNOWLSON-WILLIAMS,Henry William T2Lt kld 11-7-17 GL RFC p9

KNOX,Alexander William Coningham Capt kia 19-10-14 2RIrReg p89 MR22

KNOX,Andrew Ronald T2Lt kia 12-12-15 RE 185TC p46 CR France430

KNOX,Arthur Rice.DSO.Maj dow 22-4-17 RFA p261 CR Lond29,23-4-17

KNOX,Arthur Victor Lt kia 6-6-17 5 att1NumbF p213 MR20

KNOX,Charles Duncan 2Lt kia 17-3-17 Suff &43RFC p9&78 MR20

KNOX,George 2Lt kia 9-4-16 8RLancs p59 MR29

KNOX,Hubert LtCol kia 13-10-16 Manch att16Bn p155 CR France432

KNOX,James Meldrum.DSO&Bar.LtCol dow 23-9-18 1/7RWar p214 CR Italy

KNOX,John.MC&Bar.T2Lt dow 23-10-18 13RIrRif p169 CR France34

KNOX,John Laurence T2Lt kia 20-11-17 7RSuss p119 MR17,Lawrence

KNOX,John Stanley 2Lt dow 11-7-16 7RInniskF p105 CR France115

KNOX,John Vesey Lt kld 4-1-18 18Lond attRFC p18&250 CR Ireland145

KNOX,Robert TCapt kia 17-4-16 1HLI p163 MR38

KNOX,Thomas Cowe 2Lt kia 19-8-18 7Lpool att12Norf p215 CR France19,Cowl

KNOX,William Capt ded 20-2-16 3CamH &13RFC p3&168 CR France448

KNOX,William 2Lt kia 24-3-18 54RFC p16 MR20

KNUBLEY,Robert Leavitt.MC.MID LtACapt dow 9-7-16 3Wilts p153 CR France44,7-7-16

KOCH,Marcus Addison T2Lt kia 22-9-15 2KSLI p145 CR France1472

KOE,Archibald Stephen LtCol dow 25-4-15 1KOSB p102 MR4,26-4-15

KOE,Philip Stephen 2Lt kia 31-7-16 1/4Y&L C'Coy p238 CR France246

KOEBEL,Charles Edward Capt dow 24-8-15 RWSurr attLancF p56 MR4

KOHN,Wilfred Arthur T2Lt kia 1-7-16 11ELancs p111 CR France156

KOHNSTAM,Oscar Jacob Charles 2Lt kia 29-6-16 4NStaffs attMGC Inf p157&184 CR France513

KOHNSTAMM,Norman Mortimer Joseph Capt kia 22-3-18 18Manch &RFC p16&155 CR France511,23-3-18

KORTRIGHT,Mountney Coesvelt William Lt kia 21-5-17 1Ess p132 CR France311,Mounteney

KRAMER,Gerald.MM.Lt kia 31-8-18 5ESurr p226 CR France563

KRAUSS,Dennis Hillel 2Lt dow 7-4-17 5NStaffs p238 CR France1

KRIEKENBECK,Ronald Edward Elliott Maj mbk 18-4-16 IA 128Pnrs p278 MR38,KOIEKENBEEK

KROENIG-RYAN,Alexander Charles Thomas Lt kia 24-10-18 8Mddx p236 CR France190,23-10-18

KROG,Eustace John.MC.TLt kia 7-9-18 1EYorks p84 CR France262

KROHN,Edmund Otto 2Lt kia 1-3-18 84RFC p16 CR France1893,Lt

KROHN,Nicholas Adolf 2Lt kia 16-5-15 2BordR p117 MR22

KROLIK,Elliot.MC.TCapt kia 23-10-17 16RB p179 CR Belgium124

KRUGER,Dirk Jacobus T2Lt kia 1-4-18 23Manch p155 CR France44,Lt 2-4-18

KUHN,Alfred Edgar Lt dow 18-5-15 2Beds p86 CR France80

KURTEN,Gaston Pierre Peter TLtAMaj kia 24-4-18 RGA 291SB p40 CR France304

KYD,Frank Proctor T2Lt kia 18-8-16 11ESurr attRWar p113 CR France293

KYDD,Chester Bishop T2Lt kia 3-5-17 3 att7Beds p86 MR20

KYDD,Henry John Naysmith Lt ded 13-5-18 LabCps p266 CR Numb96 Ex 2WYorks

KYDD,John William Albert T2Lt dow 26-3-18 19LancF p93 CR Belgium72

KYLE,David Logan 2Lt kia 19-5-15 RE p46 CR Belgium115

KYLE,Hugh Gavin 2Lt kia 12-7-15 4RScotF p222 MR4

KYLE,John Stott.MC&Bar.Lt dow 22-5-18 D123RFA p31 CR France63

KYNASTON,John Oswald Maurice TLt kia 21-9-18 74MGC Infp184 CR France1462

KYNCH,Harold Egerton Vivian Maj ded 31-5-19 Ches att183LabCps p189 CR France268

KYNOCH,Alexander Bruce TCapt kld 8-3-18 RFC p16 CR Mddx15

KYNOCH,Alfred Stewart T2Lt kia 13-3-18 52RFC &GL p16 CR France1203

KYNOCH,Colin Smith 2Lt kia 26-4-15 6DLI p239 MR29

KYRKE-SMITH,Arthur Kyrke Capt dow 23-9-14 1Lpool p72 CR France1110,kia

KYSH,Claude James Anthony Lt ded 27-11-18 1RWKent p141 CR Norf26

KYTE,Henry Edward T2Lt dow 22-11-17 14RIrRif p169 CR France512

L

LABERTOUCHE,Guy Neal Landale Maj dow 14-4-15 IA 122Inf att119 p278 CR Iraq6

LABETT,John William Hooper T2Lt kia 25-1-17 9Lincs p75 MR38

LABDON,Percy Miller T2Lt kia 26-9-17 RE 469FC p46 CR Belgium130

LABOUCHERE,Arthur Maxwell.DSO.TMaj dow 30-4-18 5 O&BLI p130 CR France1142

LACAITA,Francis Charles.MC.LtTCapt kia 3-4-18 17Lancers att1MGC p23&184 MR20

LACE,Walter Henry.MC.Maj kia 8-11-18 RE 439FC p209 CR Belgium406

LACER,see LACEY,E.A.

LACEY,Edred Severs 2Lt kia 21-10-16 17 att11Ches p96 MR21

LACEY,Everitt Arthur 2Lt ded 16-5-19 4Lpool p270 CR Wales671,LACER 7Bn

LACEY,Frank Philip Sleigh T2Lt ded 29-3-18 RASC MT &RFC p193 CR Egypt15

LACEY,Gordon Herbert.MC.2Lt dow 29-9-18 9Lond p248 CR France146

LACEY,Thomas Henry T2Lt dow 4-9-16 17KRRC p151 CR France169

LACEY,Wilfred Lt kia 31-3-18 RFA 59DAC attY59TMB p207 MR20

LACEY,William George.MC.Lt kia 4-11-18 RASC &27RAF p267 CR France154

LACEY,William Stocks TLt dow 11-10-16 RAMC att11RWKent p196 CR France833

LACHLAN,Cecil George.MIDx2 2Lt kia 31-8-17 17WYorks p82 MR21

LACK,Frederick George 2Lt kia 30-3-18 21Lond p251 CR Syria2

LACK,John Westlake TCapt dow 26-7-16 8Suff p78 CR France51

LACK,Reginald Walter.MM.MID 2Lt kia 29-9-16 13 att1RWFus p98 MR32

LACK,Reg Lambert T2Lt dow 18-7-16 14RIrRif p169 CR Surrey96

LACON,Sidney John Boileau Maj kia 12-4-18 RWar attVIIICps MT RASC CR Belgium3 see LOCON,S.J.B.

LA COSTE,Charles John Constable.MC.TCapt kia 9-10-17 GL att1/8WYorks p190 MR30

LACY,Francis Prior.MC.2LtTCapt kia 13-8-15 W'land&C'landYeo attRE 170TC p206 CR France163

LACY,Thomas Joseph 2Lt kia 7-4-18 48A'RFA p31 CR France2,8-4-18 B48

LACY,Wilfrid Henry TCapt kia 7-10-16 15Hamps p121 CR France744

LACY,William Braithwaite 2Lt dow 14-12-17 15Lond p249 CR France398

LADD,Alfred Caldier Maj kia 25-3-18 14Worc p109 MR20

LADE,John Harvey 2Lt dow 5-10-17 WarYeo att1/5WarR p205 CR Belgium16

LADELL,John Francis TLt kia 20-7-16 20Mddx p147 CR France149

LADLER,Ernest George T2Lt ded 3-12-18 700LabCps p189

LAFERLA,H.G.Capt 4-7-19 2MaltaR CR Europe4

LAFERRIERE,L.S.Capt.MC.29-5-20 RGA CR Lond9 served as MARTIN,L.S.

LAFONE,Alexander Malins.VC.Maj kia 27-10-17 1MddxHuss p204 CR Palestine1

LAFONE,Claude Alexander.DSO.Capt kld 14-3-15 2Dev D Coy p77 CR France706,12-3-15

LAFONE,Eric William.MC.TCapt kia 15-6-18 12DLI p161 CR Italy4

LAGDEN,Ronald Owen Capt kia 3-3-15 6KRRC p151 MR29

LAIDLAW,Andrew T2Lt kia 9-9-18 2Manch p155 MR16

LAIDLAW,James Clelland T2LtACapt kia 6-11-17 3ScotRif p103 CR Belgium13

LAIDLAW,John Leslie T2Lt dow 20-7-16 10A&SH p173 CR France23

LAIDLAW,Walter Sibbald TLt kia 23-11-17 RE 203FC p46 CR Belgium20

LAIDLAW,William Simpson 2Lt kia 30-8-18 250RFA p31 MR16

LAILEY,Eric Lillywhite T2Lt kia 29-2-16 7DCLI p114 CR Belgium23

LAINE,Charles Janion T2Lt kia 30-7-16 89MGC Inf p184 MR21

LAINE,Thomas de Jersey T2Lt kia 21-11-17 1RGLI p201 MR17

LAING,Alexander Arthur Lt kia 28-11-17 RE p210 CR France364

LAING,Alexander Torrance TCapt dow 24-7-16 13NumbF p61 CR France145

LAING,Charles William 2Lt kia 24-4-15 2EKent p57 MR29

LAING,David Patrick Lt kia 20-10-15 2RIrReg p89 MR22

LAING,Dudley Ogilvie TCapt kia 1-7-16 22NumbF p61 MR21

LAING,Ernest Edward T2Lt kia 29-7-17 7EYorks p84 CR France604

LAING,George T2Lt dow 10-4-17 9ScotRif p103 CR France95

LAING,Gerald Ogilvie TCapt kiaa a 5-6-17 20NumbF p61 MR20

LAING,Gilbert James 2Lt kia 12-3-15 ULIA att1RIrRif p169 p278 MR28

LAING,Henry Davidson Capt kia 13-3-15 6GordH p242 MR22,Harry

LAING,Harry Needham 2Lt kia 17-9-16 4Yorks p220 MR21

LAING,Ivan.MC.Lt kia 30-11-17 2CldGds p51 CR France662

LAING,James Alexander T2Lt kia 14-10-18 10RWSurr p56 CR Belgium157

LAING,James Gordon Maj kia 3-10-18 28Lond attMGC p187&252 CR France1887

LAING,James MacDougall Lt kia 23-3-18 25MGC p184 MR20

LAING,John Darg T2Lt kia 24-10-17 GL 19RFC p9 CR France1032

LAING,John Spence 2Lt ded 12-6-19 RASC p267

LAING,N.P.Capt 31-10-19 RAMC CR Lancs387

LAING,Robert MacLeod 2Lt kia 20-7-16 4 att1ScotRif p103 MR21

LAING,St.Clair King Nixon T2Lt ded 2-4-17 7RMunstF p175 CR France285

LAING,William McClymont Black 2Lt dow 21-6-16 1RScotF p94 CR Belgium11

LAIRD,Andrew Clark 2Lt kia 22-11-16 5BlkW att15RFC p18&231 CR France41,22-12-16

LAIRD,Arthur Donald T2Lt kia 1-7-16 17HLI p163 CR France246

LAIRD,Colin TLtACapt kia 20-9-17 19Lpool p72 MR30

LAIRD,Frank 2Lt mbk 25-3-18 8NStaffs att56TMB p256 MR20

LAIRD,Homer Warring T2Lt kia 8-10-17 GL RFC p9 CR France285

LAIRD,Hugh Blackhall 2Lt kia 8-7-16 3 att2Yorks p90 MR21

LAIRD,James Duncan T2Lt kia 25-3-18 12KRRC p151 MR27

LAIRD,James Ritchie 2Lt dow 22-7-16 5ScotRif p224 CR France44

LAIRD,Louis Wilfred T2Lt kia 2-9-18 NumbF att23LancF p61 CR France298

LAIRD,Matthew James Donald Capt kia 23-4-16 RE 2/2FC p210 CR Egypt2

LAIRD,Ninian Parker T2Lt kia 26-3-18 1 att7/8KOSB p102 MR20,28-3-18 3 att7/8Bn

LAIRD,William 2Lt kia 1-12-17 3CldGds p51 CR France662

LAIRD,William Allan Lt dow 18-9-15 3 att1RScotF p94 CR France64

LAIRD,William Weir 2Lt kia 4-11-16 5GordH p242 CR France131

LAIT,Wilfrid Francis James T2Lt kia 3-8-17 3 att8BordR p117 MR29

LAITHWAITE,John TLt kia 22-2-16 20Manch p155 CR France370

LAKE,Frank Gilbert Lt kia 31-7-17 Herts p252 MR29

LAKE,James Louis Engelburt Rey 2Lt dow 24-8-15 3 att1BordR p117 CR Greece10

LAKE,John Stephen Raymond Capt kia 16-6-16 1 att3SWBord p100 CR France550,3 att1Bn

LAKE,Noel Graham Lt kia 25-3-18 2/5Glouc p225 MR27,24-3-18

LAKE,Reginald St.George Lt kia 17-11-16 4 O&BLI p231 CR France392

LAKE,Thomas Ashton 2Lt kia 13-8-18 6N&D p233 MR19

LAKE,William TCapt kia 28-7-16 3 att2SStaffs p122 CR France390

LAKE,William Martin 2Lt dow 28-6-16 RGA attP34MedTMB TMB p40 CR France515

LAKEMAN,Arthur Frederick 2Lt kia 5-8-18 4BlkW att15TankCps p189&230,kld CR France300

LAKEMAN,Harold Leslie T2Lt kia 22-8-18 RASC att7LancF p193 CR France514

LAKEMAN,John Pearce T2Lt dow 20-4-17 NumbF att20Bn p61 CR France40,Pearse

LAKEMAN,Reginald Noel 2Lt kia 3-10-18 5N&D p233 CR France375

LAKIN,Charles Lt dow 21-8-16 4 O&BLI p231 CR France74

LAKIN,H.W.Mech 27-9-16 RIM CR Iraq5

LALONDE,Lionel Victor Pollock 2Lt ded 31-3-16 9SomLI p80 CR France1,45MGC

LAMAISON,Leonard William Henry Lt kia 2-7-16 2/5RWar p214 CR France1157

LAMAISON,Wilfrid Lawrence MID Lt dow 23-8-18 16Lond att1/6NStaffs p249 CR France10,Laurence

LAMB,Cameron.DSO.Capt dow 29-12-14 2BordR p117 CR France64

LAMB,Cecil Walter TCapt ded 15-11-15 RFA p31 CR Hamps17

LAMB,Dudley William Lt kia 22-3-18 14Lond p249 MR20

LAMB,Eric Robert Lt ded 2-11-18 5Manch p236 CR France341

LAMB,Ernest Edwin 2Lt kia 26-9-16 3RWKent att9LancF p141 MR21

LAMB,Everard Joseph Capt kia 1-11-14 3NumbF attYLI p61 MR29

LAMB,Edward Woolard Penistone 2Lt kld 24-4-18 GL &11RAF p190 CR France62,kia

LAMB,Francis Cardno 2Lt kld 7-9-16 RFC p3 CR Mddx17

LAMB,Francis James Ongley 2Lt ded 24-7-18 RGA attArmyAmmoPark p40 CR Iraq8

LAMB,Frank Muller Lt kia 21-3-18 7N&D p256 MR20

LAMB,George Ross 2Lt kia 20-4-17 7HLI p240 MR34

LAMB,Harold Alfred 2Lt kld 9-7-18 12Lancers att98RAF p22 CR France31,Lt kia 1Bn

LAMB,Harold George Wellesley 2Lt kia 8-10-18 6 att10RFus p68 CR France1345

LAMB,James Scott T2Lt kia 10-9-18 RB att2Bn p179 CR France369

LAMB,John 2Lt ded 28-7-17 5RScots p211 CR Scot 235

LAMB,John T2Lt dow 17-10-17 RE 179TC p46 CR Belgium16

LAMB,John Albert 2Lt kia 14-10-18 4WYorks att13WRid p82 CR France82,Lt

LAMB,John McNair T2Lt kia 4-11-18 A82RFA p31 CR France1478

LAMB,Joseph 2Lt dow 16-8-17 153RFA 36DAC p31 CR Belgium10

LAMB,Launcelot Rupert TLt kia 25-5-17 2RLancs p59 CR Greece5

LAMB,Patrick James TLt dow 31-7-18 RGA 14DAC p40 CR France33

LAMB,Raymond Wildman.MC.TLt ded 14-11-18 60MGC Inf p184 CR Egypt9

LAMB,Thomas 2Lt ded 30-6-16 4YLI p235 CR Numb20

LAMB,Walter TLt kia 1-7-16 22NumbF p62 MR21

LAMBARDE,B.A.Nurse 5-3-19 VAD RNHosp CR Kent147

LAMBART,Gerald Edgar Oliver Fortescue CaptAMaj dow 28-3-16 1RScotF p94 CR Belgium11

LAMBDIN,John Reginald.MC.Lt dow 24-9-18 7WYorks p218 CR France327

LAMBE,Frederick William TLt dow 10-11-16 5Norf p216 CR France515

LAMBE,Percy TLt kia 7-11-15 9 att6EKent p57 MR19

LAMBERT,Arnold Stuart.MC&Bar.MID LtAMaj ded 25-12-18 RE 459FC p46 CR Belgium330

LAMBERT,Arthur Frere MajALtCol kia 2-11-17 3RWSurr att10Lond p56 CR Palestine8

LAMBERT,Charles Henry TLt ded 17-8-15 RAVC attRFA p198 CR Egypt3

LAMBERT,Cyril John Noël.MC.Lt kia 2-9-18 103/40RFA p31 CR France214

LAMBERT,Douglas T2Lt kia 13-10-16 6EKent p57 MR19

LAMBERT,Eric Noel.MC.TCapt dow 7-6-17 3 att8Yorks p90 CR Belgium127

LAMBERT,Ernest Charles TLt dow 30-6-16 RAMC att12ESurrp196 CR France102

LAMBERT,Francis Courtenay Maj ded 29-3-16 RAMC p196 CR Iraq1

LAMBERT,Francis Henry Lt dow 14-6-15 3 att1Hamps p121 MR29

LAMBERT,Frederick Charles 2Lt kia 28-3-18 5YLI p235 MR20

LAMBERT,Frederick William Manley T2Lt ded 25-2-19 2SStaffs p264 CR Surrey15

LAMBERT,Geoffrey Fontaine 2Lt dow 15-4-16 1Herts p252 CR France145

LAMBERT,George 2Lt kia 22-4-15 3RFus p68 MR29

LAMBERT,George T2Lt kia 23-4-17 7CamH D'Coy p168 CR France1182

LAMBERT,George T2Lt kia 29-9-18 1 att2Worc p109 CR France665

LAMBERT,Harry Redcliffe 2Lt kia 21-3-17 RE 476SthMidFC p210 CR France1472

LAMBERT,Henry McLaren Capt kia 13-5-15 1Drags p21 CR Belgium2

LAMBERT,Henry Stuart 2Lt kia 11-1-16 5Yorks A'Coy p221 CR Belgium5

LAMBERT,Jack Fellowes 2Lt kia 30-7-15 9KRRC p151 MR29

LAMBERT,James Edward Downes TLt kia 2-11-15 6Nhampt p137 CR France637,1-11-15

LAMBERT,John Henry TCapt dow 9-8-16 25NumbF p62 CR France12

LAMBERT,John Lewis TMaj ded 20-10-16 4RASC ArmyAuxHorseCo p193 CR France300

LAMBERT,John Mounsey Capt kia 28-10-14 3 att1NumbF p62 CR France924

LAMBERT,Kenneth Capt kia 9-5-15 1YLI p143 CR Belgium152

LAMBERT,Leonard Walter T2Lt kia 28-3-18 RFus att4Bn p68

LAMBERT,Marie Louise Benjamin Hector Maj ded 24-8-19 RASC p267 MR70 &CR Europe180,Louis

LAMBERT,Maurice Borington TLt kia 7-8-15 6Yorks p90 MR4,Bovingdon

LAMBERT,Maurice Gustave Louis 2Lt kia 5-1-17 10Worc att7Berks p109 MR37

LAMBERT,Montague Arthur T2Lt kia 2-10-18 KRRC att18Bn p151 CR Belgium112

LAMBERT,Percy Gerald T2Lt kia 21-3-18 25NumbF p62 MR20

LAMBERT,Philip Felix 2Lt kia 3-5-17 2WRid p115 MR20

LAMBERT,T.S.CB.CMG.BrigGen kld 20-6-21 Staff CR Surrey1

LAMBERT,Walter Col ded 20-12-14 RAOC p267 CR Lond28,24-12-14

LAMBERT,William T2Lt dow 2-6-16 18HLI p163 CR France80,kia

LAMBERT,William Fairlie 2Lt kia 23-3-16 3 att9ScotRif p103 CR France390 &CR France1160

LAMBERT-SHEA,Joseph Patrick.MC&Bar.DCM.Capt&QM dow 1-12-17 2DCLI CR France398

LAMBOURNE,Reginald Bertram 2Lt dow 5-1-16 3 att2Hamps p121 CR Gallipoli1

LAMBOURNE,William 2Lt kia 9-8-18 23Lond p252 MR16

LAMBROUGHTON,Hugh T2Lt dow 12-4-18 1RScotF p94 CR France202

LAMBROUGHTON,Matthew T2Lt ded 16-11-18 3SfthH p165 CR France1027

LAMBTON,Edward Capt ded 28-3-16 PembrokeYeo p205

LAMBTON,Francis.Hon.2Lt kia 25-10-15 RHGds p20 MR29,30-10-14

LAMBTON,Geoffrey Lt kia 1-9-14 CldGds p51 CR France1108

LAMBTON,L Capt 28-3-16 PembrokeYeo CR Egypt9

L'AMIE H.St Clair Lt 5-10-20 WRid att2Ches CR Ireland14

LAMMERT,Rennie Dean T2Lt kia PoW 23-3-18 10 att8Glouc p107&257,dow 29-3-18 CR France403

LAMOND,George Alexander Walker TLtCol ded 25-2-18 RE IWT p46 CR Asia9

LAMONT,Alexander 2Lt drd 10-10-18 9Lpool p216 CR Ireland14

LAMONT,Geoffrey Simpson.DSO.2Lt kia 5-11-18 1GrenGds p50 CR France1080

LAMONT,James Kenneth Lt kia 27-10-17 RFA 4HB p207 CR Belgium101

LAMONT,John 2Lt kia 11-5-16 7KOSB p102 CR France423,12-5-16

LA NAUZE,George Mansfield Lt kia 9-5-15 4RIrRif p169 MR32

LA NAUZE,William Lt kia 16-5-15 4RIrRif p169 MR29

LANAWAY,Francis Charlton T2Lt kia 21-8-18 RSuss att7RFus p119 CR France518

LANCASTER,Alice Hilda SpMilProbat drd 3-6-18 TFNS p254 CR France64

LANCASTER,Arnold Busk.MM.T2Lt dow 11-4-18 29MGC p184 CR France1094

LANCASTER,Charles Edward TLt kia 21-3-18 3 att1Leic p87 MR20

LANCASTER,Dudley Wood 2Lt ded 23-1-18 SStaffs p264

LANCASTER,Ernest Randolph T2Lt kia 12-10-16 16MGC Inf p184 MR21 Ex 7Dors

LANCASTER,Gerald William.MC.Capt dow 14-9-18 3Mon att15WelchR p244 CR France34

LANCASTER,Henry Robert 2Lt kia 2-11-17 1/4Ess p232 CR Palestine8

LANCASTER,Howard Vincent T2Lt dow 21-11-17 3 att1Leic p87 CR France398

LANCASTER,James Capt kia 8-5-15 3Mon p244 MR29

LANCASTER,James Norman T2Lt kia 10-8-15 9Worc p109 MR4

LANCASTER,John Cecil Maj kia 8-5-15 1RWar p65 MR29 &CR Belgium152

LANCASTER,Joseph Clement 2Lt kia 29-4-18 3 att9LNLancs p136 MR30

LANCASTER,Joseph William Lt&QM ded 1-1-16 7LancF p270 CR Kent268

LANCASTER,Percy T2Lt kia 15-9-16 122MGC Inf p184 MR21

LANCASTER,Robert T2Lt kia 28-4-17 7Norf p74 CR France531

LANCASTER,Thomas Erwin 2Lt kia 1-7-16 2SfthH p165 MR21

LANCASTER,William Oliver T2Lt kia 26-10-17 21Manch p155 MR30

LANCASTER-BELL,A.Ray Lt kia 17-5-15 2DubF CR Belgium4

LAND,Ronald John Lt kia 20-3-18 3Y&L attMGC p159&184 MR20,21-3-18

LANDALE,Cyril TCapt kia 21-8-18 13KRRC p151 CR France1014

LANDALE,Douglas Blackwood Lt kia 23-10-14 3RB p179 CR France681

LANDALE,James Russell Capt kia 8-3-16 IA 2Rajputs p278 MR38

LANDELL,William TLt dow 22-7-17.14A&SH p173 CR France398

LANDERS,George Maxwell 2Lt kia 28-3-18 8RLancs p59 MR20

LANDON,John Robert LtACapt kia 3-9-16 15RWar p65 MR21

LANDON,William Henry Fitz Roy Capt kia 15-2-15 3Suff attBeds p78 CR Belgium98,Fitzroy

LANDREY,Cecil Thorpe TLt kia 21-4-18 RE 251TC p46 CR France88

LANE,Arthur Bloomfield TCapt kia 20-11-17 10RB p179 MR17

LANE,Charles Henry 2Lt dow 21-8-18 2 att10RIrRif p169 CR France100,kia

LANE,Charles Willington Tremayne.MC.CaptAMaj dow 4-4-18 7DragGds p21 CR France185

LANE,Edward Alfred Joseph Ardan Lt kia 1-7-16 1/9Lond p248 MR21

LANE,Edward Dion.MC.T2Lt dow PoW 8-12-17 59MGC Inf p184 CR France658

LANE,Edward F.Capt ded 13-4-19 3Hamps p121 CR Staffs140

LANE,Edward George Arthur Campbell 2Lt kia 30-9-18 Leinst att12RIrRif p174 CR Belgium157

LANE,Eric Arthur Milner 2Lt kia 8-3-16 3Manch p155 MR38

LANE,Ernest Albert 2Lt kia 1-9-18 3 att2Ess p132 CR France531

LANE,Frank 2Lt kia 16-5-17 17Lond p250 MR20

LANE,Frank Ashton T2Lt kia 31-7-17 18Lpool p72 MR29

LANE,Frank Nowell.MID Capt ded 11-8-18 IA 2/7GurkhaRif p278 CR Palestine9

LANE,Frederick William 2Lt dow 19-5-17 8Lond p247 CR France40,Frederic

LANE,Geoffrey Horsburgh Capt kia 19-12-19 IA 1/103MahrattaLI p279 MR43

LANE,George James.MID 2Lt dow 29-6-16 1RBerks p139 CR FRance40

LANE,George Ronald Capt&Adjt kia 16-9-16 2CldGds p51 CR France374,15-9-16

LANE,Harold Frank 2Lt kia 14-10-15 11RScots p54 CR Belgium122

LANE,Hector Allan Lt kia 13-5-15 ELancs p111 MR29

LANE,Henry Clarence Horsburgh T2Lt kia 10-7-17 1BordR p117 MR29

LANE,Jocylyn Henry Cambridge 2Lt ded 16-10-18 4CldGds p51 CR France40,Jocelyn

LANE,John Austen T2Lt ded 27-10-17 542LabCps p189 CR Sussex144,RGA

LANE,John Boyd Armstrong T2Lt dow 13-9-16 6RIrF p171 CR France145

LANE,John Elston 2Lt kia 3-5-17 4 att7EKent p212 MR20

LANE,Maurice.MC.MM.LtACapt kia 29-12-17 2/20Lond p251 CR Palestine3

LANE,Reginald William 2Lt kia 9-11-18 1/2Hamps &RAF p121 CR France276

LANE,Shales Frederick TCapt kia 18-9-18 9Norf p74 CR France1701

LANE,Sydney Henry TLtACapt kia 5-4-18 RGA 38HB p40 CR France924

LANE,Thomas Edward Moore TMaj ded 17-4-19 5KSLI p265 CR Lancs410

LANE,William George 2Lt dow 7-11-17 1/1WorcYeo p206 CR Egypt2

LANE-FOX,George Henry Capt 29-10-20 GL CR Surrey1

LANE-JOYNT,Albert William Lt kia 26-2-16 Dors attMGC p184 CR France279

LANE-MULLINS,James Brendan 2Lt kia 14-6-17 RFA att29DAC p31 CR France1182

LANE-NICHOLS,Douglas William TCapt kia 20-8-16 8RWSurr p56 MR21

LANES,Ewart Reginald.MC.Capt kia 22-3-18 8Lond p247 MR27

LANG,Arthur Lt kia 29-8-16 6A&SH p243 CR France394

LANG,Arthur Horace 2Lt kia 25-1-15 2GrenGds attScotGds p50 MR22 &CR France1896

LANG,Frederick Murray Capt dow 18-12-15 6A&SH p243 CR France43,17-12-15

LANG,Graeme Gordon T2Lt kia 11-4-17 7KOSB p102 MR20

LANG,Henry Astell Maj kia 9-6-15 4Worc p109 CR Gallipoli6,6-6-15

LANG,James Corbet Capt kia 12-7-15 1KOSB p102 MR4

LANG,John Capt ded 15-4-17 GL Res CR Scot717

LANG,Norman TLt kia 24-8-18 MGC DivBn p184 CR France393

LANG,Sidney Drummond 2Lt dow 26-2-17 5YLI p235 CR France177,kia 23-2-17

LANG,William Brymner LtTCapt kia 12-7-15 6A&SH p243 2entries Bryner 5Bn MR4

LANG-BROWNE,John Agnew Capt kia 16-5-15 2RWSurr p56 CR France279

LANGDALE,Edward George.MC.MID Lt kia 13-10-15 5Leic p220 MR19

LANGDALE,Harold Carthew Lt kia 26-9-17 13RSuss p119 MR30

LANGDALE,Mary Agnes Nurse 9-2-17 VAD CR Wilts115

LANGDON,Arthur Charles 2Lt dow 27-10-18 7 att15Hamps p229 CR Belgium158

LANGDON,Cecil Rev kia 31-10-17 RAChDept att11BordR p199 CR Belgium36

LANGDON,Douglas Eckley 2LtACapt kia 23-4-17 1DCLI p114 CR France547

LANGDON,John Henry.MC.Lt kld 5-6-18 2Glouc att195RAF p107 CR Egypt8

LANGDON,John Stafford T2Lt ded 24-10-18 RE IWT p46 CR France65

LANGDON,Lawrence TLt dow 14-3-16 14Hamps p121 CR France254,Laurence

LANGDON,Wilfrid Max TCapt kia 21-5-16 10Ches p96 CR France68

LANGDON,William Chappell Croeder.MID TLt dow 10-3-17 RGA attRE 3FldSurCoy p40 CR France120,Crocker

LANGFORD,Albert Frederick 2Lt kia 10-7-16 3Worc p109 MR21

LANGFORD,Arthur Hector Allan T2Lt dow 1-8-16 17N&D p134 CR France80

LANGFORD,Claude Charles 2Lt ded 23-2-18 6DragGds p21 CR War7

LANGFORD,Colin Cecil CaptAMaj dow 9-4-18 295RFA D'Coy p31 CR France169

LANGFORD,John Joseph T2Lt kia 15-9-16 18KRRC p151 CR France277

LANGFORD,Wallace George T2Lt dow 27-6-16 18KRRC p151 CR France285

LANGFORD,William John Lt kia 19-7-16 6Glouc p225 MR19

LANGHAM,Cecil Richard Capt kia 16-8-17 5RSuss p228 CR Belgium10

LANGHAM,John 2Lt kia 18-9-18 TA 7 att10N&D p233 MR16

LANGLANDS,Alan 2Lt kia 9-5-15 3 att1SWBord p100 CR France631

LANGLER,John Bickford.MC.Lt ded 31-10-18 RFA p31 CR Lond29

LANGLEY,Alfred 2LtACapt kia 20-9-17 6Wilts D'Coy p153 MR30

LANGLEY,Arthur Cecil Lt kia 23-9-17 34RFA p207 CR Belgium102

LANGLEY,Eric Erskine Lt ded 22-1-20 IARO att114LabCps p279 MR43

LANGLEY,Francis Jasper 2Lt kia 27-8-18 2GrenGds p50 CR France614

LANGLEY,Harry Gustave Lt ded 28-1-19 RDC p256 CR Ches74

LANGLEY,S.TD.Maj 20-1-21 GlasgowYeo CR Scot764

LANGRISHE,Hercules Ralph Lt kld 16-2-17 MontgomeryYeo attRFC p204&18 CR Eire362 &CR Ireland14

LANGSDALE,William Anthony.MM.MID T2Lt kia 22-3-18 12N&D p134 MR27 CR France390,22-3-16

LANGSTONE,Arthur 2Lt dow 19-5-17 20Lond p251 CR Belgium11,19Bn

LANGSTONE,Frederick Herbert Lt kia 17-4-18 88RFA 19DAC p31 MR30

LANGTON,Arthur Henry Brodie Lt dow 12-9-16 2KRRC p151 CR France23

LANGTON,David Elland T2Lt dow 10-4-17 36MGC p184 CR France113

LANGTON,Hugh Gordon 2Lt kia 26-10-17 4Lond p246 CR Belgium126

LANGTREE,Charles Henry Lt dow 3-8-16 159RFA p31 CR France23

LANGWILL,Trevor 2Lt ded 17-4-17 GL 60RFC p9 CR France1276,dow

LANGWORTH,Harold Samuel T2Lt dow 9-9-17 BordR att8Bn p117 CR Belgium34

LANGWORTHY,William Southmead Lt kia 4-10-17 7Dev p217 MR30

LANHAM,Walter James 2Lt kia 21-8-18 1/6SStaffs p229 CR France109

LANSDALE,Ernest Conway Lt ded PoW 30-9-16 RASC attRFC p18&253 CR France306,kia

LANSDALE,William Morris Capt kia 26-8-18 RAMC att5RBerks p196 CR France370

LANSDOWN,Francis Arthur Stanley T2Lt ded 14-8-17 SL att1BrWIndR p201 CR Palestine2,Lt

LANSTRY,Reginald Redfern Lt dow 27-9-15 11A&SH p173 CR France51

LANT,Edwin 2Lt kia 8-9-17 88RFA p208 CR France179

LANT,Thomas 2Lt kia 1-11-16 6NumbF p214 CR France388

LANYON,William Mortimer Capt kia 5-4-15 1RIrRif p169 CR France707

LAPP,Austin Ross T2Lt kld 9-3-18 RFC p16

LAPTHORN,Owen Heckford 2Lt kia 29-5-17 D102RFA p31 CR Belgium127,28-5-17

LARCOMBE,Archibald Herbert T2Lt ded PoW 26-10-18 2WRid p115 CR Germany3

LARCOMBE,Henry Reginald Reader 2Lt kia 2-9-17 6RFus p68 CR Kent7

LARCOMBE,Reginald Fred 2Lt kia 10-9-18 CityofLondYeo att2/2Lond p256 MR16

LARDNER,Dion Albert T2Lt kia 4-9-16 9 att1Beds p86 MR21

LARDNER,Roland 2Lt kia 26-5-18 Y&L &RAF p265

LARGE,Charles Edward Lt kia 27-5-18 45RFA p31 MR18

LARGE,Ernest T2Lt ded 8-3-19 RASC 13FldBakerySD p255 CR France40

LARGE,Ernest L.Capt dow 21-5-15 5Lond p246 CR France102

LARGE,Harold Bowater T2Lt kia 10-3-17 9RWar p65 MR38

LARGE,Harold Emmott TCapt dow 9-10-15 10RB p179 CR France706,8-10-15

LARGE,Herbert Edward Capt kia 16-2-15 3Mddx p147 MR29

LARGE,John Gerald Lt ded 4-6-18 RE p210 CR Lincs115

LARGE,Percy Francis T2Lt dow 28-6-17 3DLI p161 CR France285

LARGE,Philip Martin Maj kia 27-4-15 Mddx p147 MR29

LARGE,Ronald Murray LtACapt kia 4-11-18 7RFus p68 CR France521,3Bn

LARGEN,Edward Charles 2Lt kia 23-7-16 3 att1DCLI p114 MR21

LARKEN,Frederick James 2Lt kia 15-11-16 7NumbF p214 CR France430,14-11-16 1/4Bn

LARKEN,John Savage 2Lt kia 21-9-18 10EKent p204 CR France364

LARKIN,Frederick Joseph.MC.2Lt kia 7-11-17 2/22Lond p251 CR Palestine1

LARKIN,J.P.D.DSO.DCM.Maj 4-11-19 7KOSB &RAF CR Durham28

LARKIN,William James 2Lt kia 25-12-16 1Lincs p75 CR France423

LARKING,Ronald Guy.MC.Capt kld 1-4-18 RE 38DivSigCoy p46 CR France297,dedacc

LARKINS,Charles Horace T2Lt dow 21-11-17 16Mddx p147 MR17

LARKINS,Edward Arthur Malcolm Lt kia 18-7-15 2ELancs p111 CR France924,18-1-15

LARKINS,John Colin TLt kia 4-6-16 15RWar p65 CR France1182

LARKINS,L.H.TCapt kia 4-7-18 13TankCps p188 CR France1170

LARSEN,Hubert Victor 2Lt dow 23-8-18 3 att2SLancs p125 CR Belgium184,Herbert

LASCELLES,Arthur Moore.VC.MC.TCapt kia 7-11-18 3DLI p161 CR France930

LASCELLES,Edward Rowley Lt kia 2-9-18 25Lond p252 CR France624

LASCELLES,Francis Hope TLt kia 22-8-17 42MGC Inf p184 MR30

LASCELLES,Guy Ernest 2Lt kia 24-3-18 5RB p179 CR France605

LASCELLES,Harold Leslie TLt kld 11-3-17 GL RFC p9 CR Lond8

LASCELLES,John Frederick.MC.MID Lt kia 31-7-15 RB &RFC p1&179 CR France167

LASCELLES,Ronald Hastings.DSO.MajALtCol ded 16-2-19 RHA p261 CR Lond28

LASENBY,Searlin 2Lt kia 20-9-17 3 att1Surr att127BdeHQ p113 MR20,Scarlin MR30,Scarlin,12Bn

LASH,Augustus Oliver Maj dow 11-9-16 7RIrRif p169 CR France40

LASKEY,George.MM.T2Lt kia 16-10-18 RWKent att8Bn p141 CR France206

LASLETT,Henry Clinton.MC.T2Lt dow 2-8-16 D149RH&FA p31 CR France23

LASSEN,Reginald Capt ded 18-10-19 RASC MT p267 CR Yorks408

LASSETTER,John James Wilder T2Lt kia 8-3-17 11 att6LNLancs p136 MR38

LAST,Arthur James 2Lt dow 9-12-18 RH&FA p31

LAST,Basil Herbert T2Lt kia 23-4-17 17Mddx p147 CR France728

LAST,Ernest Reginald.MC.Capt kia 24-3-18 att1Lpool p72 MR20

LAST,Leonard Walter 2Lt kia 22-8-18 1Norf p74 CR France281 Ex HAC

LAST,Leslie Sydney 2Lt kld 21-2-18 RFA &RFC p16&31

LATER,Joseph Oswald TLt dow 13-7-16 MGC Inf p184 CR Lancs37

LATHAM,Arthur James T2Lt ded 4-2-16 RE 185TC p46 CR France430

LATHAM,Edgar Rettef 12Lt kld 20-10-17 GL 72RFC p9 CR Wilts4

LATHAM,Francis Pulsford Maj ded 26-2-17 3WelshR att1GarrBnWelshFus p127 CR Europe23

LATHAM,Percy 2Lt kia 20-8-15 8Hamps p229 MR4

LATHAM,Stephen Grey.DSO.MC&Bar.CaptALtCol kia 24-4-18 3 att2Nhampt p137 CR France144

LATHAM,Thomas Jones TLt kia 3-10-15 RAMC attRE p196 CR France423

LATHAM,Thomas Selby Lt dow 29-11-17 A18RFA p207 CR Belgium11

LATHAN,William T2Lt kia 24-9-18 RSuss att17Bn p119 CR France276

LATHBRIDGE,Staughton Charles Archelas 2Lt dow 31-10-15 RE 1/4FC p210 CR France80,Lt

LATHBURY,George Lionel Lt ded 24-2-19 6NStaffs p270 CR Staffs85

LATHEY,Arthur Richard T2Lt ded 25-10-18 GL RE p266 CR Surrey1

LATIMER,Alfred.MM.kia 4-10-18 RFA &RAF p261 CR Italy2

LATIMER,Francis T2Lt kia 7-7-16 12Manch p155 MR21

LATIMER,Hugh 2Lt kia 3-7-16 8RWKent p141 MR21,3 att6Bn

LATIMER,Kenneth T2Lt kia 27-2-18 9NStaffs p157 CR Belgium17

LA TOUCHE,Averell Digges Lt kia 25-9-15 5 att2RIrRif p169

LATTA,Alexander James Jobb 2Lt kia 5-8-16 62RFA p31 CR France296,Jopp

LATTA,Charles Keith Lt kia 29-11-15 2GordH p166 MR29,29-10-14

LATTA,Robert William Campbell T2Lt dow 22-10-17 2SfthH p165 CR France64,Lt

LATTER,Francis Robinson Capt dow 3-5-17 7RWKent p141 MR20

LATTER,George Walter William T2Lt kia 11-7-16 3RB p179 CR Belgium100

LATTEY,James Cumming Maj kia 5-5-18 RFA attRGA 1/1WelshHB p31 CR Belgium3,RFA att1/1WelchR

LATTO,William Duncan 2Lt ded 21-2-18 4GordH p242 France512

LAUDER,George Gordon 2Lt kia 30-7-16 1Lpool p72 MR21

LAUDER,John Currie Capt kia 28-12-16 1/8A&SH p243 CR France393

LAUDERDALE,John Maitland 2Lt kia 18-9-16 1/8DLI p239 MR21,17-9-16

LAUGHLAND,George Thomson T2Lt dow 21-6-17 15HLI p163 CR Belgium24

LAUGHLIN,James Courtney T2Lt kia 1-7-16 20Lpool p72 CR France699

LAUGHLIN,Philip Herbert TLt dow 21-12-17 1RWSurr p56 CR Palestine3

LAUGHTON,Geoffrey T2Lt kia 5-12-17 26NumbF p62 CR France592

LAUGHTON,H.P.W.Lt kia 28-5-18 10Mddx &RAF p236

LAUGHTON,Hubert Henry Schomberg TLt ded 25-11-18 2Worc attMGC p109&184 CR Surrey91

LAUGHTON,Joseph Thornton T2Lt dow 29-9-18 1Beds p86 CR France146

LAUNCETON,Roy.MC.TCapt kia 24-3-18 16 att2Mddx p147 CR France1472,24/25-3-18

LAURENCE,Bertie Standish 2Lt kia 9-9-15 1/2Co ofLondYeo p204 CR Gallipoli5

LAURENCE,Dudley Sydney 2Lt kia 23-10-16 6 att1RB p179 CR France432

LAURENCE,Stuart 2Lt kia 17-9-16 10RWKent p141 CR France400

LAURENSON,Laurence Capt ded 14-7-16 7GordH p270 CR Scot1014

LAURIA,Jack Victor T2Lt dow 18-6-16 14N&D attRE p134 CR France285

LAURIE,Alfred William 2Lt dow 22-11-16 RGA 42SB p40 CR France388

LAURIE,Donald Saunders.OBE.Capt ded 11-2-19 RE p46 CR Belgium406

LAURIE,Eric Unwin.MC.Lt kia 24-3-18 58MGC Inf p184 CR France1893

LAURIE,George Brenton.MID LtCol kia 12-3-15 RIrRif p169 CR France705

LAURIE,James Alexander Lt kia 3-5-17 6KOSB p102

LAURIE,John William TLtACapt kia 12-8-18 6EKent p57 CR France209,9-8-18

LAURIE,Wilfrid Walter LtACapt kia 19-5-17 3 att2KOSB p102 CR France184

LAURIE,William Joseph Cornwall 2Lt kia 6-1-17 IARO att2/124Baluchis p279 CR Iraq5

LAVARACK,Adolph Keith TLt kia 5-7-16 10WRid p115 CR France515

LAVELLE,James Delargey T2Lt kia 20-8-15 12HLI p163 CR France550

LAVELLE,Patrick Joseph Aloysius.MIDx2 Capt kia 4-10-18 5RScots p211 CR France602,RScotF

LAVELLE,William James 2Lt kia 21-3-18 4 att1/8RInniskF p105 MR27

LAVENDER,Frank Ashley 2Lt kia 14-3-17 1/5SStaffs p229 CR France281

LAVENDER,Harry Richard 2Lt kia 28-8-18 5RSuss p228 CR France630

LAVENDER,John Elliott 2Lt kia 28-4-17 10Lincs p75 MR20

LAVER,Francis Reynell Lt kia 9-4-18 4SStaffs p122 CR Belgium451

LAVERICK,Frederick Gordon T2Lt kia 23-7-17 7ELancs p111 CR Belgium102

LAVERS,Victor Alfred.MC.T2Lt dow 22-4-17 1RBerks p139 CR France145

LAVERTON,Frederick King 2LtTLt kld 19-12-17 3Glouc &RFC p9&107 CR Glouc88,3/9Bn

LAVERTY,Joseph T2Lt kia 16-8-17 13RIrRif p169 MR30

LAVILLE,Samuel Eustace Blythe TCapt kia 18-8-16 3Leinst p174 CR France630,2Bn

LAW,Alan Drummond TLt dow 3-5-17 4 att10A&SH p173 MR20

LAW,Alan Hugh T2Lt kia 4-11-18 16LancF p92 CR France231

LAW,Cecil Edward T2Lt kia 30-9-18 1LancF p92 CR Belgium20

LAW,Charles Arkley T2Lt kld 19-2-18 RFC p16 CR Norf247,13-2-18

LAW,Charles John Lt kia 19-4-17 3KOSB p102 CR Palestine8

LAW,Charles Lindsay Qwyder T2Lt kia 30-9-15 2Suff p78 CR Belgium167,Lindsey Gwydr

LAW,Charles Orlando TCapt ded 29-12-18 RE p262 CR Lond4,2-1-19

LAW,Edgar Felix Lt kia 5-4-18 6Nhampt p137 MR27

LAW,Edward Michael Fitzgerald 2Lt kia 11-8-18 Dors att1Bn p124 CR France360,Lt

LAW,Harry.MIDx2 Lt dow 7-7-15 1RWFus p98 CR Lincs14,21-7-15

LAW,Henry Merrick Burrell 2Lt kia 8-8-16 18RFC p3 CR France32

LAW,Henry Milner 2Lt kia 9-4-17 6SfthH p241 CR France15

LAW,James Kidston Capt kia 21-9-17 RFus &60RFC p9&68 MR20

LAW,John Gordon T2Lt kia 20-10-18 1ESurr p113 CR France1388

LAW,Malcolm Colin McGregor Lt dow 29-12-15 6WRid p227 CR Belgium1

LAW,Robert Archibald Fitzgerald.MC&Bar.2LtACapt dow 31-10-18 1 att7Wilts p153 CR France146

LAW,Thomas Pakenham 2Lt dow 27-8-15 IrGds SR att2Bn p53 MR22

LAW,William John.MID TLtCol kia 19-12-15 7LancF p221 CR Gallipoli6

LAWDER,Arthur William Charles 2Lt dow 15-4-17 155RH&FA p31 CR France120,A.G.

LAWDER,Noel Wilfred TMaj kia 4-9-16 1Beds p86 MR21

LAWES,Charles Gilbert TLt kia 27-10-16 9RWFus p98 MR21

LAWES,Thomas Eric 2Lt kia 18-6-17 3Suff p78 CR France421

LAWFORD,Edward Er.field Lt mbk 13-6-17 IARO att20DeccanHorse p279 MR28

LAWFORD,Herbert Martin Benson TCapt kia 7-10-16 9RFus p68 MR21

LAWLEDGE,Francis Mott 2Lt kia 10-10-16 RE attRFC p3&46 CR France644,Matt

LAWLER,Guy Feinagle Lt kiaWithArabs 22-4-20 IA 2Lancers C'Sqdn p279 CR Palestine11,Feinaigle

LAWLER,Lionel Alfred Ballantyne Lt ded 8-3-19 RASC p193&257 MR40

LAWLESS,Barry Joseph Anthony 2Lt kia 17-7-17 12Lond att56TMB p248 CR Belgium12

LAWLOR,Edward Fredk 2Lt kia 27-11-16 2Mon p244 CR France744

LAWRANCE,John Henry 2Lt kia 20-8-17 3 att2DCLI p114 CR France184

LAWRENCE,Alexander TCapt&Adjt dow 19-9-16 1GordH att10RWSurr p166 CR France833

LAWRENCE,Bertram Capt kia 27-10-14 1EYorks p84 CR France82,28-10-14

LAWRENCE,Brian Lightly 2Lt kia 1-6-15 att2Mddx p147 MR32

LAWRENCE,Charles Alfred.MC.TLtACapt kia 24-4-18 7Beds p86 MR27

LAWRENCE,Charles Philip 2Lt dow 29-4-16 IARO att27Punjabis p279 MR38

LAWRENCE,Christopher Hal 2Lt kia 13-10-14 6 att2KRRC p151 MR15,4 att2Bn

LAWRENCE,Edward.MC.DCM.LtACapt kia 28-3-18 10 att1NumbF p62 MR20

LAWRENCE,Edward William TCapt kia 10-7-16 RAMC att13RWFus p196 MR21

LAWRENCE,Francis Alfred John 2Lt kia 12-4-18 10Ess p132 MR27

LAWRENCE,Frank Helier 2Lt kia 9-5-15 3Glouc p107 MR22

LAWRENCE,Frederic Wilson Capt ded 9-12-15 Res GL 3/5Lpool p270 CR Lancs381

LAWRENCE,George Aubrey Kennedy.DSO.CaptTLtCol kld 28-1-17 RFA attRFC p10&31 CR Surrey160

LAWRENCE,Guy Francis Lt kia 27-8-18 2GrenGds p50 CR France924

LAWRENCE,Harold Raymond Lt ded 28-10-18 12NStaffs attTMB p157 CR Lancs381

LAWRENCE,Harold Roy 2Lt dow 12-7-17 2/6Lond p247 CR France398

LAWRENCE,Harry Joseph 2Lt kia 26-4-18 4Ess p232 CR France425

LAWRENCE,Henry 2Lt kia 17-1-17 5 att6Yorks p221 MR21

LAWRENCE,Humphrey Richard Locke Lt drd 30-12-15 IA 34SikhPnrs p279 MR41,Capt

LAWRENCE,James Linton TCapt dow 3-7-16 15RScots p54 CR France119

LAWRENCE,John George.MC.2Lt ded 15-2-18 Norf att2WIndiaR p74&192 CR EAfrica35 &CR Tanzania1

LAWRENCE,John James T2Lt kia 23-10-18 11RFus p68 CR France190

LAWRENCE,Joseph Reginald Mark 2Lt kia 16-8-16 3 att9ESurr p113 CR France294

LAWRENCE,Lawrence Arthur 2Lt kia 16-8-17 83/122RFA p31 CR Belgium23

LAWRENCE,Malcolm Eyton Lt kia 10-1-15 6 att2KRRC p151 MR22 &CR France1059

LAWRENCE,Michael Charles TCapt dow 16-9-16 1CldGds p51 CR France105

LAWRENCE,Norman Alan 2Lt kia 30-4-17 RFus &16RFC p10&68 CR France557

LAWRENCE,Oliver John 2Lt kia 26-5-15 8Lond p247 CR France261

LAWRENCE,Percy 2Lt kld 9-8-18 7Leinst &RAF p174

LAWRENCE,Rudolph Russell 2Lt kia 24-8-16 5KSLI p145 MR20

LAWRENCE,Thomas Edward 2Lt dow 22-9-18 7RSuss p119 CR France194

LAWRENCE,Walter Capt kld 2-1-15 7Ess attRFC p18&232 CR France284

LAWRENCE,William George 2Lt kia 23-10-15 O&BLI &RFC p1&130 CR France1266

LAWRENCE,Lawrence,William Lyttleton.DSO.Maj kia 31-10-14 1SWBord p100 MR29

LAWRENCE-TOWNSEND,Robert Edward Capt 2-3-18 5Mddx CR Kent61

LAWRENSON,Harold 2Lt kia 25-5-18 RGA 214SB p40 CR France247

LAWRENSON,Raymond Fitmaurice Lt dow 5-9-17 16Ches p96 CR France446

LAWRENSON,Reginald Robert.DSO&Bar.MajTLtCol dow 27-4-18 WIndia att18HLI p192 CR France40

LAWRIE,Allan James Capt kia 16-5-15 6ScotRif p224 CR France348

LAWRIE,Andrew Ralph TLt kia 22-8-17 D'TankCps p188 MR30

LAWRIE,Edward LtCol 22-8-15 IMS CR Sussex183

LAWRIE,Francis Allan TCapt ded 25-9-18 1ScotRif GarrBn attManch p103 MR66,26-9-18

LAWRIE,James Alexander Lt 3-5-17 6KOSB MR20

LAWRIE,James Hunter 2Lt kia 9-8-16 3 att7KOSB p102 CR France188
LAWRIE,John Charles CaptHonMaj ded 7-5-15 3Ess p132 CR Essex185
LAWRIE,Norman Ernest 2Lt kia 9-5-15 13Lond p249 MR32
LAWRIE,Robert Rossiter 2Lt dow 8-4-18 22Lond E'Coy p251 CR Palestine9
LAWRIE,Thomas Helm 2Lt kia 25-7-18 9RScots p212 CR France865
LAWS,Alfred Victor 2Lt kia 25/27-10-14 1NumbF Z'Coy p62 MR22
LAWS,Bernard Courtney Lt dow 25-5-15 3 att1Y&L p159 CR Belgium165
LAWS,Cecil William TLt kia 27-5-18 N&D p134 MR18,Willie
LAWS,Philip Umfreville.MC.TCapt kia 20-9-17 16N&D p134 CR Belgium124
LAWS,Selwyn Vernon T2Lt dow 25-5-18 9Ches p96 CR France31
LAWSON,Alexander Sutherland 2Lt kia 11-11-14 1BlkW p129 MR29
LAWSON,Alfred 2Lt kia 16-9-16 9DLI p239 MR21
LAWSON,Arthur Ashley T2Lt ded 19-3-18 TankCps p266 CR Hamps13
LAWSON,Arthur Bertram.DSO.BtMajALtCol kia 24-6-18 11Huss att2/5Glouc p22 CR France248
LAWSON,Arthur Cresswell T2Lt kia 19-11-16 11GordH attScotRif p166 CR Greece6
LAWSON,Arthur Cyril T2Lt dow 6-7-17 7RB p179 CR Lond4
LAWSON,Arthur James.MIDx3 TLtACapt kia 22-3-18 8Leic att110TMB p87 CR France669
LAWSON,Arthur James 2Lt ded 17-12-18 SL att1RdCps p201 CR EAfrica52
LAWSON,Cecil David Norton T2Lt kia 26-9-15 8RWKent p141 MR19
LAWSON,David T2Lt kia 9-10-17 5Y&L p159 MR30
LAWSON,Edward Grey 2Lt kia 14-11-16 7NumbF p214 CR France385
LAWSON,Frank Harry Reginald Lt ded 19-11-19 BucksHuss p270 CR Lond8
LAWSON,Frederick Henry Capt kia 24-5-15 5NumbF p213 MR29
LAWSON,Gavin T2Lt kia 4-8-16 12 att1/8ScotRif p103 CR Egypt2
LAWSON,George McFarquhar Kelly 2Lt kia 9-8-17 RGA 5SB p40
LAWSON,George William 2Lt kia 11-4-18 10 att5Yorks B'Coy p90 MR32
LAWSON,Harry Sackville Lt kia 5-2-18 RFA p207 CR France1066
LAWSON,Henry Heaton Chap4Cl kia 24-3-18 RAChDept att2NhamptR p199 CR France692
LAWSON,James Burnett TLt kia 27-3-18 2ScotRif p103 MR27
LAWSON,James McKercher T2Lt kia 1-7-17 1/2KOSB p102 CR France184
LAWSON,John Lawson T2Lt kia 14-10-16 10SfthH p165 MR21
LAWSON,John Low Maj ded 15-6-16 RASC p267 CR Hamps15
LAWSON,John Wilson.MC.TLtACapt kia 24-3-18 41MGC p184 CR France927
LAWSON,Joseph TLtACapt kia 22-3-18 18Lpool p72 MR27 21-3-18
LAWSON,Joseph Percy 2Lt kia 8-8-16 4RLancs p213 MR21
LAWSON,Norman Wilfrid Lt kia 14-11-16 5NumbF B'Coy p213 CR France385
LAWSON,Oswald Head Maj dow 17-3-16 IA 26Punjabis p279 CR Iraq5
LAWSON,Reginald Hugh.MC.MID TLt kia 24-8-16 7RB p179 CR France397
LAWSON,Robert Lt kia 27-5-18 7DLI p256 MR18
LAWSON,Robert Wybergh Gordon T2Lt kia 18-7-16 1GordH p166 MR21
LAWSON,William TLt kia 27-3-16 1DLI p161 CR Belgium56,2Lt 17 att8Bn
LAWSON,William TLt kia 24-4-17 14A&SH p173 CR France415
LAWSON,William T2Lt kia 19-9-18 1 att8RScotF p94 CR Greece5
LAWSON,William Bernard Webster Lt kia 22-10-14 1ScotsGds p52 MR29
LAWSON-JOHNSTON,Arthur McWilliam.MC.Lt dow 22-2-17 2GrenGds p50 CR France105
LAWSON-SMITH,John Lt kia 20-10-14 1WYorks p82 MR22
LAWSON-SMITH,Thomas Edward Lt kia 1-11-14 13Huss p22 MR29
LAWSON-WALTON,J.E.Capt 31-12-19 GL att4KAR CR EAfrica51
LAWTHER,Arthur Leonard 2Lt dow 23-5-16 RFA 22Bty 8HB p208 CR France12
LAWTON,Arthur 2Lt ded 4-9-19 RGA p262 CR Staffs105
LAWTON,Edward Gerald Capt dow 12-4-18 2ESurr p113 CR EAfrica116
LAWTON,Eric Reginald T2Lt kia 10-8-17 12Manch p155 CR France604
LAWTON,Robert Charles Lt dow 16-10-15 5Leic p220 CR France98,17-10-15
LAWTON,William T2Lt kia 3/6-7-16 8NStaffs p157 MR21
LAWTON,William Victor TLt dedacc 8-7-18 RE 7PontoonPk p46 CR France142
LAX,Anthony William Greenwell.MID Capt kia 11-10-16 RGA 43SB CR Greece6
LAX,Donald T2Lt kia 25-10-18 4 att20DLI p161 MR30
LAXTON,Archer Benjamin 2Lt dow 21-7-17 C110RFA p31 CR Belgium11
LAXTON,Reginald Earl T2Lt kia 10-6-16 16WYorks att93/1TMB p82 CR France5
LAY,Harold Frank Douglas 2Lt kld 7-3-18 RFC p16 CR France64,dedacc
LAY,John Frederick Lt 28-10-18 IARO att2/67Punjabis MR43 &CR Pakistan50A
LAYARD,Arthur Austen McGregor Maj ded 5-6-17 RE p46 CR Essex146
LAYARD,Frank Stanley.MC.2Lt kia 19-5-17 1BordR p117 CR France427,Stanlie dow
LAYARD,Peter Clement Lt kia 23-8-18 4Suff p217 CR France927
LAYBOURNE,John Oscar 2Lt kia 26-3-17 1/7Ches p223 CR Palestine8
LAYCOCK,Donald Stanley 2Lt dow 24-3-18 70/34RFA p208 CR France560

LAYCOCK,Joseph Harold 2Lt kia 7-10-16 2 att18KRRC p151 MR21
LAYCOCK,Lewis James Penard TLt kia 31-7-17 7Nhampt p137 MR29,Louis
LAYMAN,Douglas Arthur Campbell T2Lt dow 22-2-16 17LancF p92 CR France80
LAYMAN,F.H.Maj 2-10-17 RDC CR Surrey162
LAYNG,George Reginald Stuart T2LtALt dow 18-8-16 GL 10Glouc att1TMB p190 CR France44
LAYTHORPE,Roger Marmaduke 2Lt dow 8-7-16 3 att7SLancs p125 CRKent7,10-7-16
LAYTON,Roland Churchill Capt kia 30-4-18 NottsYeo p205 MR34
LAYTON-BENNETT,Geoffrey Ernest 2Lt 1-7-16 2Yorks CR France630
LAZARUS,Cyril Henry Lt kia 27-5-18 7Leic p87 CR France1755
LAZONBY,Julian Cecil 2Lt kia 23-11-17 B'TankCps p188 MR17
LEA,Gerald Ernest Capt kia 16-9-14 2Worc p109 CR France1329
LEA,Hilda Louisa SNurse 10-5-16 QAIMNS CR Surrey160
LEA,John T2Lt dow 15-7-16 8Leic p87 CR France207
LEA,Maurice Bertram T2Lt kia 18-8-16 7Nhampt p137 MR21
LEA-SMITH,Leslie Arthur TLt kia 7-7-16 6EKent p57 CR France251
LEACH,Edward Savory Wykeham Capt kia 3-5-17 1 att7ESurr p113 MR20
LEACH,Eric Thomas 2Lt dow 14-10-18 1Worc p109 CR Belgium406
LEACH,Ernest Walter Vindin ACapt kia 2-1-17 3 att2RIrRif p169 CR Belgium53
LEACH,Errol William Carlisle ALt kia 15-5-17 11ELancs p111 CR France777
LEACH,Francis James Capt dow 26-4-15 KSLI p145 CR Devon10
LEACH,Fred Lt kld 16-6-18 1/8Manch &RAF p256 MR65
LEACH,George.MM.2Lt kia 28-4-18 3 att19Manch p155 MR30,17Bn
LEACH,Gerald Kimball TLt kia 10-8-15 6BordR p117 MR4,Kemball
LEACH,Gordon Pemberton Capt kia 20-8-15 B66RFA p31 CR Gallipoli3,19-8-15
LEACH,Grey de Leche 2Lt ded 3-9-16 1ScotsGds p52 CR France23
LEACH,Herbert Lt kia 22-4-17 2Y&L p159 CR France551
LEACH,J.Capt 28-2-20 RFA CR Hamps4
LEACH,Robert Edward TCapt dow 29-11-17 RAVC att64RFA p198 CR Belgium10
LEACH,Sidney 2Lt kia 10-8-18 4TankCps p188 MR16
LEACH,Walter John T2Lt kia 11-10-18 RE 4FldSurBn p46 CR Belgium84
LEACH,William Alfred 2Lt ded 5-3-19 RFA 96BdeAC p31 CR France1029
LEACHMAN,Gerald Evelyn.CIE.DSO.LtCol 12-8-20 RSuss CR Iraq8
LEACROFT,Richard Frederick T2Lt kia 10-11-15 12Worc p109 CR France114,2Bn
LEACROFT,Ronald John Ranulph.MC.Capt kia 1-7-16 1SomLI p80 CR France1491
LEADBETTER,Alan Edmonstoun Greenshields LtAMaj kia 4-8-17 RH&FA L'Bty15Bde p31
LEADBETTER,Duncan 2Lt dow 6-8-17 82RH&FA p31 CR France71,7-8-18
LEADBITTER,Francis John Graham T2Lt kia 5-3-17 11KRRC p151 CR France374
LEADBITTER,Geoffrey George 2Lt mbk 19-4-17 4Nhampt p257 MR34
LEADER,Benjamin Eastlake Capt kia 12-10-16 3RWSurr att2WRid p56 MR21
LEADER,Francis William Mowbray Capt kia 26-8-14 2ConnRgrs p172 CR France943
LEADER,Reginald John Carey T2Lt kia 28-4-16 14DLI p161 CR Belgium23
LEAH,Wilfred Reginald 2Lt kia 10-9-16 1/4RLancs p213 CR France393
LEAHY,Eugene Patrick TCapt dow 18-9-16 RAMC att61FA p196 CR France105
LEAHY,Noel Edward Joseph Lt kia 10-8-18 5RH&FA p31
LEAHY,Percy Edward.MID TMajALtCol kia 17-7-18 6Y&L p159 CR France223
LEAK,Charles Henry Capt&QM ded 24-9-17 RE p46 CR Surrey15
LEAK,Reginald 2Lt dow 26-8-15 6LancF p221 MR4
LEAK,Reginald T2Lt dow 14-7-16 13Lpool p72 CR France141
LEAKE,Eric Gilbert.MC.Capt dow 31-7-18 7Manch att59RAF p258&237,Lt CR France84
LEAKE,Eric Larkin Wheadon Lt kia 4-6-15 LancF p92 MR4
LEAKE,George Dalton Capt kia 13-5-15 1ELancs p111 CR Belgium96
LEAKE,George Ernest Arthur.DSO.Capt dow 2-6-17 2/4Lond p246 CR France145
LEAKE,Russell Madley.MC&Bar.LtACapt kia 18-9-18 3 att1LNLancs p136 CR France375,Medley
LEAKEY,Herbert Nettleton Chap4Cl ded 24-7-17 RAChDept p199 CR EAfrica35 &CR Tanzania1
LEAL,George Lt kia 7-8-17 RFA att9RFC p10&31 CR Belgium20
LEAMAN,Mark Reginald 2Lt kia 5-4-18 42MGC p184 MR27,6-4-18
LEAMAN,Douglas Arthur 2LtTLt dow 14-8-17 4Norf p216 CR Belgium11,8Bn
LEAN,Hugh Henry.MC.Capt kia 29-7-17 153HLI p163 CR Belgium5
LEANING,Reginald William 2Lt kld 31-5-18 9Lpool p216 CR France40
LEAPINGWELL,Henry Byng Capt mbk 21-1-16 IA 97Inf p279 MR38
LEARED,Paul Lupus Maj ded 7-3-18 IA 1/7GurkhaRif attStaff 53Div p279 CR Iraq8
LEARMOUTH,Eric Charles Allan Lt kia 9-10-17 7WYorks p218 MR30
LEAROYD,Digby Guy TLt ded 13-12-17 GL RE IWT p46 CR Iraq6
LEAROYD,Ernest Smith T2Lt kia 23-11-17 20Mddx p147 MR17 CR France1059

LEAROYD,Geoffrey Ernest Douglas Capt ded 29-10-18 21Lancers p23 MR43

LEARY,Eric Lt dow 21-6-15 RIrReg p89 CR France1140

LEARY,Ernest Richard 2Lt dow 23-7-16 3Y&L attMGC p159&184 CR France300

LEARY,George Godfrey Whitney TLt kia 25-9-18 10Glouc p107 CR France1723

LEASK,James Cunliffe.MC.Capt kia 30-3-18 5NumbF p213 MR27

LEASK,John T2Lt kld 26-3-17 GL RFC p10 CR Scot876

LEASON,Thomas Herbert T2Lt dow 16-9-16 9YLI p143 CR France188

LEAT,Edwin John 2Lt dow 8-6-18 Dors att6Bn p124 MR27

LEAT,Frederick Charles 2Lt kia 27-5-18 2Dev p77 CR France1332

LEATER,Henry.MID Lt kia 21-3-18 2/9Manch p237 CR France1464,Capt

LEATHAM,Bertram Henry.DSO.MajALtCol kia 26-9-15 2Yorks att2Wilts p90 CR France423

LEATHAM,Edward Hubert Lt kia 31-10-14 12Lancers p22 MR29

LEATHER,Christopher Lt kia 25/27-10-14 3 att1NumbF p62 MR22

LEATHER,Ernest Arthur TMaj kia 10-2-16 15 att27NumbF p62 CR France347

LEATHER,Edward Wilberforce Capt kia 18-4-15 3Yorks att2YLI p90 MR29

LEATHER,J.Capt 18-9-14 IOD MR66

LEATHER,John Francis.MID Capt ded 16-10-18 RASC att1/4KSLI p253 CR France123

LEATHERDALE,Donald Ryan 2Lt kia 22-7-16 1RWKent p141 MR21

LEATHERLAND,Frederick Arthur T2Lt kia 7-8-18 11RFus p68 MR27

LEATHERLAND,Percy John T2Lt drd 10-10-18 3Lpool p72 CR Ireland14,Lt

LEATHES,Robert Herbert de Mussenden 2Lt kia 18-4-17 B62RFA p31 CR France731

LEATHLEY,William George T2Lt kia 1-7-16 8SomLI p80 MR21

LEAVER,Stanley Horace T2Lt kia 9-4-18 17Mddx p147 MR32

LE BAS,Owen Vincent Lt kia 7-11-15 RWSurr &RFC p1&56 CR France604

LEBISH,Frank Roland 2Lt dow 25-7-17 D173RFA p31 CR Belgium11

LE BLANC-SMITH,Charles Ralph TLt kia 27-11-15 8RB p179 CR Belgium73

LE BLOND,Robert Cecil Gamage du Plessis Capt ded 17-5-15 12RB p179

LE BRASSEUR,Robert Henry Hubert Lt ded 24-5-16 RFC p261 CR Norf209,Robin

LE BRETON,Vivian Bertram Lt kia 9-8-18 10Lond p248 CR France1170

LE BRUN,Lewis Appleby T2Lt kia 31-10-18 3Hamps att11SomLI p121 CR Belgium406

LEBY,Maitland Benn.MC.ACapt kia 12-4-18 2IrGds p53

LE CHAVETOIS,Grantley Adolphe ACapt dow 21-1-18 22Lond p251 CR Lond3,22-1-18

LECHE,Arthur Victor Carlton 2Lt kia 1-7-16 3SomLI p80 CR France1890

LE CHEMINANT,Cyril T2Lt kia 9-8-17 7Suff p78 MR20

LECHERTIER,Jacques Alfred 2Lt kia 4-11-18 D211RFA p31 CR France1082

LECHLER,Frederick Gordon 2Lt ded 24-9-16 IARO att62Punjabis p279 CR Iraq6

LECHLER,Henry Nicholson T2Lt kia 4-4-16 10 att6SLancs p125 MR38

LECHMERE,Nicholas George Berwick Lt kia 17-10-15 2ScotsGds p52 MR19

LECKENBY,Harold T2Lt kia 9-4-17 26NumbF C'Coy p62 CR France184

LECKIE,Graham 2LtTLt kia 7-7-17 RGA &21RFC p10&40 CR Belgium115

LECKIE,John.MC.TLtAMaj dow 29-8-18 56MGC Inf C'Coy p184 CR France103

LECKIE,John Harvey Lt kia 13-5-15 1Drags p21 MR29,13-6-15

LECKIE,Malcolm.DSO.Capt dow 29-8-14 RAMC p196 CR Belgium202,28-8-14

LECKIE,Otway Trevor MacRitchie Capt dow 13-4-15 IA 104Rif p279 CR Iraq6

LECKIE,Walter Alan TLt dow 21-2-16 RE 90FC p46 CR Belgium137

LECKY,Averell Lt dow 19-10-14 2Leinst p174 CR France681,20-10-14

LECKY,John T2Lt kia 16-7-16 18RIrRif p169 MR21

LECKY,John Rupert Frederick Capt kia 28-9-15 7RFus att2Norf p68 MR38

LECOMBER,Philip Hebdon Lt kia 27-3-18 2/7Manch p237 MR30

LEDBITTER,Herbert Peter Rev ded 28-2-17 RAChDept attAMTD Base p199 CR France1

LEDGARD,Frank Cooper Lt kia 23-10-14 2Yorks p90 CR Belgium140

LEDGER,Harold Partington T2Lt kia 20-11-17 GL 3RFC p10 CR France911

LEDGER,Horace Martin Capon 2Lt kia 22-12-15 IARO attFrenchSeaplaneFlight p279 MR34

LEDGER,Raymond Kerwood Lt kia 13-4-15 6RB attRWFus p179 CR France348,dow

LEDGER,Robert John 2Lt dow 11-3-17 7RSuss p119 CR France46,dedacc

LEDINGHAM,Andrew 2Lt kia 22-3-18 4GordH p242 MR20

LE DOUX,Vietch,Dallas Gerard 2Lt kia 4-8-16 3 att7RSuss p119 MR21

LEDUC,John Charles Romuald T2Lt kld 7-11-17 GL RFC p10 CR Kent125,Jean-Charles Lt

LEDWARD,George William Capt ded 12-8-15 5Suff p217 MR4

LEE,A.M.Capt 2-11-20 LNLancs CR Lond14

LEE,Arnold Thomas 2Lt kia 1-9-18 RGA 87SB p40 CR France419

LEE,Arthur Basil 2Lt kia 2-7-16 5WYorks p218 MR21

LEE,Audley Andrew Dowell.MC.TCapt kia 1-10-17 9Leic A'Coy p88 MR30

LEE,Bernard George TLt dow 22-3-18 D180RFA p31 CR France987,Capt

LEE,Charles Alexander Cmdr ded 6-2-18 RIM CR Italy6

LEE,Charles Frederick 2Lt dow 27-4-17 9Lpool p216 CR France95

LEE,Charles Harold 2Lt kia 20-9-17 RGA 249SB p40 CR Belgium112

LEE,Charles Henry.MC.Maj ded 26-2-20 24Manch CR Lancs95

LEE,Charles Percy 2Lt kia 22-10-18 3Lond &RAF p246&258

LEE,Charles Stuart 2Lt kia 30-12-15 RE 126FC p46 CR France1140

LEE,Edgar Charles T2Lt kia 1-6-16 17Mddx p147 CR France924

LEE,Edward Capt kia 14-10-16 Herts p252 CR France293

LEE,Eric Hanson T2Lt dow 19-9-16 9 att1KSLI p145 CR France105

LEE,Ernest Lt kia 11-7-15 4WRid p227 CR Belgium106

LEE,Ernest William 2Lt kia 28-9-16 1/5WYorks p218 CR France383

LEE,Frank Stanley TLt kia 22-3-18 13RB p179 MR30

LEE,Frederick Gurdon Driffield TLt ded 1-3-16 2/6Norf p217 CR Norf172

LEE,Frederick Henry Norris Lt dow 4-7-16 IrGds SR att1Bn p53 CR France102

LEE,George Jonston Capt ded 29-8-20 IARO attMechTrans p279 CR Dorset85,attRB

LEE,George Thomas Hutteman Lt ded 26-10-18 IARO attS&TCps p279 MR66

LEE,Harry Norman Capt kia 19-12-14 IA 59Rif p279 MR28

LEE,Hector McLean T2Lt kia 18-10-16 5CamH p168 MR21

LEE,Henry Lt dow 22-11-17 1RInniskF p105 CR France300

LEE,Henry Duncan 2Lt kia 5-8-17 42/5RFA 5ArmyBde p31 CR Belgium12

LEE,Herbert Malachi T2Lt kld 26-9-17 GL 62RFC p10 CR Kent7

LEE,Herbert Victor 2Lt dow 17-11-16 3 att1Suff p78 CR Greece3

LEE,Holdsworth T2Lt dow 31-5-17 8Lincs p75 CR Belgium97,31-7-17

LEE,J.S/AssSurg 6-8-20 IMS MR67

LEE,Jack.MC.Capt kia 31-7-17 6Ches p222 MR29

LEE,James Clifford 2Lt dow 1-8-17 2RBerks p139 CR Belgium11

LEE,James Denton 2Lt dow 22-1-18 10Manch p237 CR Yorks606

LEE,James Francis 2Lt kia 11-9-18 8Lpool p216 MR16

LEE,John Arthur 2Lt kia 16-9-16 3 att5KSLI p145 MR21

LEE,John Mitchell 2Lt kia 27-9-15 7BordR p117 MR29,25-9-15

LEE,John William 2Lt kld 31-3-18 2SWBord attRFC p16&100 CR Egypt1,Lt 8Bn

LEE,Joseph Bagnall TLt kia 8-8-15 6RMunstF p175 MR4

LEE,Kenneth Willoughby.MC.Capt dow 27-9-18 A95RFA p32 CR France40

LEE,Lennox Cleland Lee 2Lt kia 1-2-15 1IrGds SR p53 CR France720

LEE,Leonard Bernard 2Lt kia 30-11-17 RE 83FC p46 CR France1483

LEE,Leonard Harry Capt bombAcc 23-10-17 IA 110Mahrattas att2/101Grens p279 CR Egypt8

LEE,Lionel Shaw 2Lt kia 25-9-15 5 O&BLI p130 MR29

LEE,Michael Philip Edward.MC.Lt kia 26-3-18 6DragGds p21 MR28

LEE,Noel.VD.BrigGen dow 22-6-15 6Manch Cmdg42Div p236 CR Europe1

LEE,Noel Esmond TCapt kia 24-8-17 8KRRC p151 MR30

LEE,Percy William T2Lt kia 9-4-17 KSLI att5Bn p145 MR20

LEE,Philip Warburton LtAMaj kia 11-10-17 29RFA 3ImpDivArty p32 CR Belgium10

LEE,Richard T2Lt kia 13/16-10-15 10 att7Suff p78 MR19

LEE,Richard Henry Driffield Capt kld 23-6-17 1/6Norf attRFC p217&19 CR Norf172,FltCmdr

LEE,Robert Carswell T2Lt kia 4-11-18 18Lpool att10LancF p72 CR France206

LEE,Robert Ernest TCapt drd 10-10-18 RAMC p196 CR Ireland5

LEE,Sidney Edward 2Lt kia 11-4-17 3 att1GordH p166 MR20

LEE,Thomas 2Lt kia 9-4-18 50MGC Inf p184 MR32

LEE,William Lt kld 19-8-18 5RIrF &RAF p171 CR Egypt15

LEE,Walter Noel Oliff T2Lt kia 25-9-15 1SStaffs p122 MR19

LEE,William Melbourne 2Lt kia 21-3-18 RFA 298ArmyBde p32 MR27

LEE,William Robert Charles Paul 2Lt kia 10-7-15 7RFus attRWFus p68 CR France684

LEE-KIRBY,W.H Lt 11-12-16 1GarBnEss CR Egypt1

LEE-STEERS,John Henry Gordon Lt kia 17-11-14 GrenGds p50 CR Belgium134,STEERE

LEE-WOOD,Alfred Capt 1-7-16 15LancF MR21

LEEB,Mercer Eric Capt ded 10-7-19 LNLancs &RAF p264 CR Sussex144

LEECE,Edwin Stanley TLt dow 24-11-17 18WelshR p127 MR17

LEECE,Francis Ballantyne 2Lt kia 12-10-16 2WRid p115 MR21

LEECH,Arthur Charles Capt kia 4/5-6-15 5Manch p236 CR Gallipoli2

LEECH,Arthur William.MC.Lt dow 12-4-18 6NumbF p213 CR France134

LEECH,Bernard Jack T2Lt kia 9-10-17 148MGC Inf p184 MR30

LEECH,Cecil Darley Farran LtTCapt ded 2-3-18 2NStaffs p157 MR67

LEECH,Geoffrey Charles Martyn TLt dow 9-4-17 5KRRC p151 CR France120,9Bn

LEECH,Harry Maj kia 31-7-17 8Lpool p215 CR Belgium125,Henry

LEECH,James Alexander T2Lt kia 10-10-18 12 att5RInniskF p105 CR France1394

LEECH,Norman Black 2LtTCapt dow 10-5-17 10EYorks p84 CR France40,Bleeck

LEECH,Percy Leonard T2Lt kia 27-8-18 13WelshR p127 CR France432

LEECH,Robert Edward Holt T2Lt kia 30-9-18 KSLI att1/4Bn p145 CR France80

LEECH,William Frederick.DSO.T2Lt dow 18-8-17 GL &9RFC p10 CR Belgium18

LEECHMAN,Colin Barclay Lt kia 26-9-14 3Huss p21 MR15,24-9-14

LEED,David 2Lt kia 12-8-18 1/2Hamps &209RAF p121 MR20

LEEDHAM,Richard Walter 2Lt kia 24-10-18 6RWar p214 CR France321

LEEDHAM,William T2Lt kia 4-9-18 Hamps att15Bn p121 MR30

LEEDS,John Stanley 2Lt kia 19-9-15 HAC p206 CR Belgium6

LEEK,Major Frederick William T2Lt kia 20-11-17 TankCps p188 MR17

LEEKE,Charles Lt dow 11-4-16 1GrenGds MGC SR p50 CR France40

LEEKE,Henry Alan Lt ded 29-5-15 9RWar CR Hamps1 see LEERE,H.A.

LEEKE,Ralph Henry CaptTMaj ded 5-11-15 RB att4KAR p178&202 CR EAfrica56

LEEMING,Alfred Johnson,MID 2LtACapt kia 31-7-17 6RFus p68 CR Belgium167

LEEMING,James Arthur.OBE.TLt ded 4-10-18 RE 170TC p46 CR France146

LEERE,Henry Alan Lt ded 29-5-15 9RWar p65 CR Hamps1,LEEKE

LEES,A.G.H.Capt 6-8-14 RDubF CR Ireland2

LEES,Algernon Henry.MIDx2 Maj ded 8-11-19 RASC p267 CR Wilts190

LEES,Clifford.MC.Lt dow 5-11-18 3WRid att15LancF p115 CR FRance441

LEES,Edmund Hastings Harcourt Capt kia 28-10-14 2BordR p117 MR29

LEES,Eric Brown Maj kia 31-7-18 W'land&C'landYeo p206 CR France61

LEES,Frank Priestman 2Lt kia 17-6-16 4NumbF p213 CR Belgium60

LEES,James Lowry.MC.TLtACapt kia 23-8-18 6TankCps p188 CR France745

LEES,James Malcolm Lt kia 22-8-16 1NStaffs p157 CR France513

LEES,Jasper 2Lt drd 28-3-15 4HLI attNigR p163&201 MR40

LEES,John Capt kia 19-4-17 5RScotF p222 MR34

LEES,Paul Beveridge Lt ded 18-6-19 SL 12GravesReg p255&268 CR Germany1

LEES,Percival Booth T2Lt kia 19-7-16 16Hamps att14Glouc p121 MR21

LEES,Percy Beresford 2Lt kia 11-3-15 3Nhampt p137 MR22

LEES,Robert Milne T2Lt kia 21-3-18 80RFC p16 CR France987

LEES,Robert Wallace T2Lt kia 3-9-16 7 att2KOSB p102 MR21

LEES,Thomas Evans Keith.Bart.Lt dow 24-8-15 DorsYeo p203 MR4

LEES,Thomas Prior Maj kia 21-4-15 9Lond p247 MR29

LEES,William Henry 2Lt ded 25-6-19 9Ches p96 CR Lancs475

LEESE,Cecil Francis Winton Lt kia 30-5-19 IA 27Punjabis attSWaziristanMil p279 MR43,31-5-19 29Bn

LEESON,Alexander Neve.DSO.Lt kia 22-10-17 RHA &30RFC p10&32 CR Iraq8

LEESON,Ian Alister Capt kia 10-7-17 97MGC p184 CR Belgium24 11-7-17

LEESON,James Thomas Chap4Cl kia 23-4-17 RAChDept att13RFus p199 CR France452

LEETCH,Ernest Ashley.MM.Lt ded 19-3-19 RH&FA p261 CR Yorks528

LEETE,Frank Evelyn 2Lt dow 10-12-17 9Lond p248 CR Herts81

LEETE,Sydney John 2Lt kia 28-7-17 8Worc att57RFC p19&226 CR Belgium140

LEETE,William John Hurthwaite TCapt kia 21-1-16 11LancF p93 CR Belgium30,Hurstwaite

LEETHAM,Reginald LtACapt kia 12-10-17 5 att1RB p179 MR21

LEFAUX,John Faulkner 2Lt dow 15-10-18 15RHA p32 CR Belgium20

LEFEBORE,R.H.2Lt kld 13-4-18 GL &RAF p190

LEFEBVRE,Henri Homer TLt ded 15-12-17 RAVC p198 CR Surrey1

LE FEUVRE,Walter Tom TLt ded 8-1-17 RE p46 CR Wales498

LE FLEMING,Lawrence Julius.MID BtLtCol kia 21-3-18 ESurr att9Bn p113 MR27

LE FRANC,Guy Antoine Lt kia 16-7-21 IA 99LabCps p279 MR43

LEFROY,Bertram Percival.DSO.TLtCol dow 27-9-15 2RWar p65 CR France109,25-9-15

LEFROY,Francis Percival 2Lt kia 28-4-16 RE 73FC p46 CR France223

LEFROY,Frazer Kent 2Lt dow 8-4-17 11RFA p32 CR France12,Keith 7-4-17 85RFA

LEFROY,Gerald 2Lt kia 24-8-16 5 att2RMunstF p175 MR21

LEFROY,Tracy Edward.MIDx2 Maj kia 5-12-17 8RWar p214 CR France379

LEFTWICH,Nigel George Lt kia 15-4-18 Ches att2Bn p96 MR37

LEGALLAIS,Reginald Walter TLt kld 15-9-17 RFC p10 CR Dorset162

LEGARD,Geoffrey Philip Lt kia 8-5-15 2NumbF p62 MR29

LEGARD,George Bruce.MIDx2 Capt&Adjt kia 27-10-14 1RWKent p141 CR France924

LEGARD,Ralph Hawksworth Capt kia 9-8-15 4 att2DLI p161 MR29,Hawkesworth

LEGARD,Reginald John Lt dow 9-5-15 2WYorks p82 CR France345

LEGAT,Andrew Ronald.MC.Lt kia 28-3-17 A317RFA p207 CR France924

LEGATE,Francis Lt kia 27-8-18 5HLI p240 MR16

LEGG,Charles T2Lt ded 15-9-18 RE 203FC p46 CR France100

LEGG,Frederick William T2Lt kia 9-10-17 1Ess p132 MR30

LEGG,Horace Gordon Lt kia 24-3-18 22DLI p161 MR27,25-3-18

LEGG,William Norman TLt dow 24-3-16 7KSLI p145 CR France40,2Lt

LEGGAT,William 2Lt dow 2-7-15 7ScotRif p224 CR Europe1

LEGGAT,William 2Lt kia 13-10-18 3CamH p168 CR France271

LEGGATT,Ashley Gordon Scott T2Lt kia 16-9-16 C47RFA p32 CR France389

LEGGATT,Eric Gerard 2Lt kia 15-7-16 4 att10A&SH p173 MR21

LEGGATT,Jack T2Lt kia 5-4-16 6LNLancs p136 MR38,LEGGAT

LEGGATT,Logie Colin 2Lt kia 31-7-17 2CldGds p51 CR Belgium106

LEGGATT,Matthew 2Lt kia 26-3-18 5LancF attRFC p19&221 MR20,LEGGAT

LEGGE,David St.Clan 2Lt kia 14-7-16 7RWSurr p56 MR21

LEGGE,Gerald.Hon.TCapt kia 9-8-15 7SStaffs p122 MR4

LEGGE,Hugo Molesworth Lt kia 5-5-15 RFus p68 MR29

LEGGE,Reginald Charles Lt kia 16-9-16 MGC D'Coy HB p184 MR21

LEGGE,Ronald George Capt kia 18-12-14 2Dev p77 MR22

LEGGE,W.H.Lt 11-2-17 RFC CR Essex40

LEGGE-BOURKE,Nigel Walter Henry Lt kia 30-10-14 2CldGds p51 MR29

LEGGE-WILKINSON,Benjamin Claude T2Lt ded 4-1-16 RWar 1GarrBn p65 CR EAfrica116

LEGGETT,Alan Randall Aufrère.MID Lt kia 30-10-14 1NStaffs p157 CR Kent179,31-10-14

LEGGETT,Eric Henry Goodwin.DSO.Maj ded 30-7-16 188RFA p32 CR France134

LEGGETT,Wilfred Noël Maj kia 14-7-16 RGA 77SB p40 CR France232

LEGGOTT,Joseph Parkinson TLt dow 16-8-17 14RFA p32 CR France178

LEGGOTT,William Evers T2Lt kia 29-7-16 21Mddx p147 CR France115,30-7-16

LEGROVE,Walter 2Lt kia 25-4-18 12Lond p248 MR28

LEHFELDT,William Robert Alexander TLt dow 11-10-16 16N&D p134 CR France40

LEHMANN,Frederick Hope Maj ded 3-10-17 RDC p253

LEICESTER,Donovan Nicolas T2Lt kia 8-5-17 12Glouc p107 MR20

LEICESTER,James 2Lt ded 27-5-19 1Ches p263 CR Ches127,Lt 26-5-19

LEIGH,Benjamin Hilton TCapt ded 9-10-18 RAMC p267 CR Surrey91

LEIGH,Bernard Henry TLt kia 18-8-17 9RBerks att159LabCps p189 CR Belgium23

LEIGH,Chandos.DSO.Maj ded 29-8-14 KOSB p102&258 CR Belgium201

LEIGH,Edward Maj kia 1-5-15 2Hamps p121 CR Gallipoli2

LEIGH,Edward Henry Lt kia 9-5-15 2RB p179 MR32

LEIGH,Harvey Tunstill 2Lt kia 14-10-18 17LancF p93 CR Belgium157,Harry

LEIGH,Henry Clifford Capt kld 24-10-16 RFC p3 CR Lancs24,25-10-16

LEIGH,Henry Godfrey Thomas T2Lt ded 11-11-18 LabCps p189 CR France34

LEIGH,Herbert ACapt kia 14-10-18 1/7Ches p223 CR Belgium112

LEIGH,John Charles Thomas TCapt kia 3-7-16 EKent p57 CR France393

LEIGH,John Egerton TCapt kia 4-4-17 10KRRC p151 CR France662

LEIGH,Percy Lemprière Capt dow 29-8-16 RGA 29SB p40 CR France203

LEIGH,Robert Graham Lt ded 6-2-18 SL RecDuty p268 CR Berks125,6Nhampt

LEIGH,Rupert.Hon.Maj ded 14-8-19 Ex 4RIrDragGds p261

LEIGH,William Booth 2Lt kia 30-11-17 LNLancs att1/5Bn p136 MR17

LEIGH-BENNETT,Arthur.DSO.MC.Capt kia 3-10-15 2CldGds p51 CR France423

LEIGH-BENNETT,Olliph Spencer Lt dow 17-11-18 1CldGds p51 CR Sussex112

LEIGH-PEMBERTON,Percy Lt dow 27-7-16 4Mddx CR France145

LEIGH-PEMBERTON,Thomas Edward Geoffrey Lt kia 11-1-15 13Lond p249 CR France706

LEIGHTON,Archibald TCapt kia 2-9-18 RASC att1/5Lond p193 CR France511

LEIGHTON,Arthur 2Lt kia 14-11-16 3 att7SLancs p125 MR21

LEIGHTON,Bryan Baldwin Mawddy.Bart.TD.Maj ded 19-1-19 W'land&C'landYeo Res p270

LEIGHTON,George Roger Lt kia 7-8-18 6HLI &RAF p270

LEIGHTON,Harold.MC.TLt dow 26-5-17 88MGC Inf p184 CR France1182

LEIGHTON,John Burgh Talbot.MC.CaptTMaj dow 7-5-17 ScotsGds &23RFC p10&52 CR France41

LEIGHTON,Roland Aubrey Lt dow 23-12-15 1/7Worc p225 CR France3

LEISHMAN,Thomas Hugh 2Lt kia 23-4-17 5RScotF p222 MR20

LEISHMAN,Walter Algernon Lt ded 19-2-19 Dors p255 CR Hamps7

LEITCH,Alexander Harold Percival T2Lt dow 22-5-18 10RB p179 CR France81

LEITCH,Andrew J.Capt 11-2-19 RAMC CR Berks125

LEITCH,Eoin,Capt kia 31-7-17 5A&SH p243 MR29

LEITCH,George Fraser T2Lt kia 26-4-16 12 att9ScotRif p103 CR Belgium30

LEITCH,Neil TCapt kia 20-5-16 11HLI p163 CR France257

LEITCH,Vivian Bissett 2Lt kia 16-4-15 10Lpool p216 CR Belgium111

LEITH,Douglas Meldrum Watson.MC.Lt kia 21-3-18 4GordH p241 CR France245

LEITH,John T2Lt kia 23-8-18 16 att14RWar p65 CR France239

LEITHAM,Herbert Wilson 2Lt dow 17-10-18 5 att8BlkW p231 CR Belgium370

LELAND,John Henry Frederick 2Lt kia 10-8-15 5RWFus p223 MR4

LELAND,Walter Alfred 2Lt kia 4-6-15 10Beds att1RDubF p86 MR4

LELEU,Sydney Francis T2Lt dow 11-4-17 7KSLI p145 CR France46

LELIEVRE,Albert Frederick Henry T2Lt dow 4-8-16 17RFus p68 CRFrance23,14Bn

LEMAN,Douglas Walter Capt kia 28-3-18 21Lond p251 CR Syria2

LEMAN,Thomas Henry Capt kia 1-7-16 1/7N&D p233 CR France281

LE MARCHAND,John Wharton Jones Lt kia 9-8-15 IA 56Rif att1/6GurkhaRif p279 MR4

LE MARCHANT,Edward Herbert Charlie Lt dow 29-10-16 1Hamps p121 CR France145,Capt

LE MARCHANT,Henry Neville Capt kia 7/11-8-15 5Dors p124 MR4

LE MARCHANT,Louis St.Gratien.DSO.LtCol kia 14-9-14 1ELancs p111 CR France1445

LE MARCHANT,S.H.2Lt dow 25-5-15 6 att3RFus p68 CR Surrey62

LEMASS,Herbert Justin 2Lt kia 23-10-16 2RDubF p177 CR France432

LE MAY,Algernon Edward Lt dow 24-7-17 A235RFA p207 CR Belgium11

LE MAY,Lionel Henry LtACapt ded 24-2-19 SL att6KAR p202&257 MR46

LE MESSURIER,Cecil Cooper T2Lt kia 15-11-16 6Beds p86 CR France534

LEMESSURIER,Thomas T2Lt kld 30-1-18 RFC p16 CR Hamps90

LE MESURIER,Algernon Paul 2Lt mbk 9-3-17 IA 6GurkhaRif att27Punjabis p279 MR38,Arthur Edward

LE MESURIER,Clive 2Lt kia 29-4-15 IARO att33Cav p279 MR61,Lt

LE MESURIER,Frederick Neil Capt kia 25-4-15 att2RDubF p177 MR29

LE MESURIER,Havilland T2Lt kia 29-8-16 9KRRC p151&257 MR21,24-8-16

LEMMY,Frederick George TLt kia 14-7-16 11RScots p54 CR France399

LEMON,Adrian Leigh Lt kia 29-11-16 6DragGds att4MGC p21&184 CR France256

LEMON,Archie Dunlop TLt kia 1-7-16 12RIrRif p169 MR21,Dunlap

LEMON,David Wardlow.MC.T2Lt kia 22/23-3-18 7Leinst p174 CR France528,22-3-18

LEMON,Lionel Theodore T2Lt kia 12-4-17 6Dors p124 CR France531

LE MOTTEE,Edward D'Albert Maj kia 25-9-15 Glouc DivStaff p107 MR19

LEMPRIERE,Henry Anderson.DSO.LtCol kia 23-12-14 7DragGds p21 MR22

LENDON,Penry Bruce.MVO.Capt kia 21-10-14 3RLancs p59 CR Belgium32

LENDRUM,A.C.MC&Bar.Capt kld 27-10-20 RInniskF CR Ireland239

LENDRUM,Charles James William Kane.MID AMaj dow 13-11-16 3 att1RInniskF p105 CR France145

LENDRUM,Harold Bruce Lt dow 1-8-17 1/6SfthH p241 CR Belgium16

LENDRUM,James Herbert Reginald Chap4Cl kia 22-8-18 RAChDept att8Lancs p199 CR France745

LENKE,Ernest Capt ded 2-6-15 RFA p207 CR France102

LENNARD,Edward Stuart Russell T2Lt kia 14-9-17 GL 9RFC p10 CR Belgium18

LENNARD,Edward Wood 2Lt kia 30-11-17 4 att1RIrRif p169 MR30

LENNARD,Richard Granger T2Lt ded PoW 6-5-17 24NumbF p62 CR Belgium266

LENNARD,Samuel Frederic 2Lt kia 30-3-16 1/4Leic p220 CR France68,Lt

LENNOX,Alexander Dick 2Lt kia 18-10-17 5RScotF attRFC p222&19 CR Belgium453

LENNOX,Alfred James T2Lt kia 20-1-17 2RIrRif p169 MR32

LENNOX,Frederick William Lt ded 1-11-18 9DLI p239 CR Durham15

LENNY,Lancelot Arthur TLt kia 20-12-17 5RIrF att9ELancs p171 CR Greece6

LENOX-CONYNGHAM,Hubert Maxwell.DSO.MID BtLtCol ded 15-3-18 RAVC p198 CR Ireland17

LENOX-CONYNGHAM,John Staples Molesworth LtCol kia 3-9-16 Cmdg6ConnRgrs p172 CR France513

LENTAIGNE,Victor Aloysius 2Lt kia 14-9-14 2ConnRgrs p172 MR15

LENTON,Gerald T2Lt dow 27-7-17 2Beds p86 CR Belgium11

LENTON,Harold Bertram 2Lt kia 30-10-17 7RFus p68 MR30

LENZ,William Adolph Philip 2Lt kia 6-11-17 RGA 148SB p40 CR Belgium19,Ardolph

LEON,Edward Joseph 2Lt kia 7-10-16 8Lond p247 CR France385

LEON,John Temple Capt ded 30-3-16 RAMC p270 Surrey162

LEONARD,Denis.MM.T2Lt kia 6-11-18 2Yorks p90 CR France949

LEONARD,Francis 2Lt ded 4-7-15 RGA p40 MR43

LEONARD,Francis Patrick Mapletoft TLt dow 29-4-16 8RInniskF p105 MR19

LEONARD,George.DCM.TLt&QM ded 1-9-16 8SStaffs p122 CR France1

LE PAGE,George William TMaj kia 26-1-16 6RIrReg D'Coy p89 CR France178

LE PETON,Clive Alfred Lt kia 15-8-17 8 att7RInniskF p105 MR29

LE PETON,Desmond Alexander 2Lt dow 9-8-16 1SomLI p80 CR Belgium11

LE POER TRENCH,Nugent Charles 2Lt kia 16-1-17 9ESurr CR France115 see TRENCH,N.C.Le P.

LEPPER,Harper Mervyn.MC.2Lt kia 9-4-16 Mddx att8RWFus p147 MR38

LERESCHE,Alfred Sunderland 2Lt kia 3-9-16 1/7WYorks p218 CR France1890

LERMITTE,Henry James LtCol ded 20-6-18 EssYeo &RScotF p261 CR Essex196

LE SAUVAGE,Ernest Davies.MID 2Lt kld 30-5-16 1Dors att&RFC p3&124 CR Dorset149

LESLIE,A.F.Capt 25-8-21 RE CR Wales17

LESLIE,A.M.Maj 21-4-19 Suff CR Sussex95

LESLIE,Alexander William 2Lt dow 23-4-17 4Leic p220 CR France12

LESLIE,Cecil George.MC.Maj ded 11-8-19 3DragGds p261 CR Eire260

LESLIE,Charles Joseph 2Lt dow 24-4-18 5 att2WYorks p218 MR27

LESLIE,Donald Wilfred Russell Lt ded 20-2-21 IARO att41MuleCps p279 CR India48,D.R.W.

LESLIE,Edwin Victor Downie 2Lt kia 8-4-17 4SfthH p241

LESLIE,Frank King Capt kia 25-4-15 2RFus p68 MR4

LESLIE,George Constable Lt dow 15-8-17 5BlkW p231 CR France40,9Bn

LESLIE,George Muir T2Lt kia 3-10-15 2HLI p163 CR France423,2-10-15

LESLIE,Leslie Francis Ellington 2Lt kia 20-8-17 1KAR p202 CR EAfrica40,Lt

LESLIE,Norman Jerome Beauchamp Capt kia 19-10-14 3RB p179 CR France681

LESLIE,Richard Fitzgerald William Ferris Maj kia 22-8-15 5Dors p124 MR4

LESLIE,William Capt kia 12-1-16 70RGA p40 CR Asia62,dow

LESLIE,William Robert Norman 2Lt kia 25-1-15 3Glouc p107 CR France260,Lt 1Bn

LESLIE-SMITH,Gilbert Capt kia 14-7-15 IA 24Punjabis p279 CR Iraq6

LESSELS,Robert Murray 2Lt kia 29-7-18 RWSurr p56 CR France524

LESTER,Albert Edward.MC.2Lt kia 8-5-18 13Lond p249 MR27

LESTER,Ernest Charles Lt kia 3-7-15 10 att1BordR p117 CR Gallipoli6

LESTER,Eric Peter T2Lt kia 13-10-15 13 att2Worc p109 MR19

LESTER,Frank Capt dow PoW 25-3-18 6ESurr p226 CR France375

LESTER,Gerald James Rev ded 16-12-18 RAChDept attCMELocoWorks p199 CR France146

LESTER,John Beaumont TCapt kia 15-9-16 18KRRC p151 CR France277

LESTER,William Owen Ernest 2Lt kia 4-4-18 4 att8ESurr p113 MR27

LESTER-SMITH,Henry 2Lt kia 15-7-17 4Ches p222 CR Belgium152,14-7-17

LE STRANGE,Roland Capt ded 20-2-19 Staff CmdgChinLabCps CR Norf61

LE SUEUR,Ernest Geoffrey Carrington LtTCapt kia 26-7-17 1Yorks p90 MR29

LE TALL,Cyril Herbert Capt kia 30-8-18 1Lond p245 CR France646

LETHBRIDGE,Brian Hugh Bridgeman TLt dow 19-7-17 8Beds p86 CR France115,kia

LETHBRIDGE,Cecil Augustus Lt kia 3-5-17 8RFus p68 MR20

LETHBRIDGE,Fred.DCM.2Lt kia 24-4-18 2Dev p77 CR France144

LETHBRIDGE,Patrick Lionel TCapt&Adjt kia 25-9-15 7KOSB p102 MR19

LETHBRIDGE,William Bernard Lt ded 14-5-20 61Pnrs CR Devon12

LETHBRIDGE,William Henry T2Lt kia 4-10-17 12/13NumbF p62 MR30

LETHEBE,Herbert Thomas TLt kia 2-9-18 11TankCps p188 CR France924

LETHEM,John 2Lt kia 1-12-17 246RFA p208 MR30,Lt

LE THICKE,Gerald Mann 2Lt ded 23-7-15 5SWBord p100 CR Berks28

LETT,John Millard T2LtACapt kia 22-3-18 3Worc p109 MR20

LETTERS,Thomas Arthur Lt kia 13-3-15 3GordH p166 MR22

LETTS,Arthur Kingdon Maj ded 5-6-20 RWFus attMGC Inf

LETTS,Bertram Chiene TLt ded 21-10-15 RAMC 13CCS p196 CR Egypt3

LETTS,John Herbert Towne.MC.Capt kldacc 11-10-18 1/2Lincs &64RAF p75 CR France103

LEVACK,George MacLeod Capt kia 7-10-16 RAMC att6 O&BLI p253 MR21

LEVASON,Desmond George Granville Capt dow 27-3-17 1/1Hereford p252 CR Palestine8

LEVENE,Nathan Neville 2Lt kia 8-8-16 1/8Lpool p216 MR21

LEVENTHORPE,John Algernon.MID Lt kia 22-1-15 RE p46 CR Belgium74,23-1-15

LEVENTON,Raymond Sylvester T2Lt drd 5-11-17 GL 49RFC p10 CR Kent7

LEVER,Harold Brasington 2Lt ded PoW 23-10-18 5Beds p219 CR Belgium406

LEVER,Harrie,Reginald.OBE.LtCol ded 16-11-20 RASC MT MR43

LEVER,Harry Marshall.DCM.Lt 23-5-20 1RScots Ex Capt KAR CR Burma129A

LEVER,Joseph.MC.T2Lt dow 1-10-18 1KRRC p151 CR France512

LEVERETT,John Ivison 2Lt ded 27-3-19 LovatScts p270 CR Mddx26,Lt

LEVESON,Rudolph Marcus TLt kia 18-12-17 10DLI p161 MR30

LEVESON-GOWER,Ronald Charles Granville Gresham Lt dow 1-8-17 2CldGds p51 CR Belgium16

LEVESON-GOWER,William George Gresham Lt kia 9-10-18 1CldGds p51 CR France332

LEVETT,Richard Henry 2Lt ded 20-8-16 3RWKent p141 CR Kent279

LEVETT,Richard William Byrd 2Lt kia 10-3-17 6 att1KRRC p151 CR France430

LEVI,Albert 2Lt dow 12-6-19 4Beds p86 CR Mddx40,LEVY

LEVI,Frederick Joseph 2Lt kia 21-3-18 1 att2/5Lincs p75 MR20

LEVI,Harry T2Lt kia 30-11-17 9RFus p68 MR17

LEVICK,Arthur Lascelles 2Lt kia 15-9-16 3 att6YLI p143 CR France402

LEVICK,Percy TCapt kld 15-3-18 RAMC attGdsDAC p196 CR France266

LEVIE,Peter MacLeod.MC.Capt kia 24-10-18 1/4BlkW p230 CR France1258

LEVIN,Charles Norton.MC.Capt kia 21-3-18 21NumbF att102TMB p62 MR27

LEVINGE,Henry George.MIDx2 LtCol kia 10-8-15 6LNLancs p136 MR4

LEVINGE,Richard William.Bart.Lt kia 24-10-14 1LifeGds RoO p20 CR Belgium101

LEVINSTEIN,Gerald Edward TLt kia 12-10-16 26 att17Manch p155 MR21

LEVIS,James Henry Bruce T2Lt kia 12-8-15 6RIrRif p169 MR4

LEVITA,Francis Ellison Lt kia 12-10-14 4Huss p21 CR France324

LEVITT,Robert TLtACapt dow 7-7-17 6LNLancs p136 CR Iraq8

LEVITT,Sydney Neville T2Lt kia 29-9-18 16KRRC p151 CR France212

LEVY,A.2Lt 12-6-19 4Beds CR Mddx40

LEVY,Arthur Herbert Lt kia 31-7-17 232RFA p208 CR Belgium7

LEVY,Josiah 2Lt kia 19-4-17 1/4Norf p216 CR Palestine8

LEVY,M.B.MC.Capt 12-4-18 2IrGds MR32

LEVY-TEBBIT,Isaac 2Lt ded 4-12-15 19Lond p270

LEWER,Richard Roy TLt dow 21-7-16 16KRRC p151 CR France833

LEWES,Frederick Henry Meredith Capt dow 2-7-16 5N&D p232 MR21,1-7-16

LEWIN,Cecil Charles Humphreys.MC.Capt kia 2-11-18 4SomLI p218 CR France1257

LEWIN,Edward Chaloner TLt kia 27-9-18 RWKent att1Bn p141 CR France415

LEWIN,Edward Hale Capt kia 8-3-16 IA 46Punjabis att82 p279 MR38

LEWIN,Francis Harold.MC.MIDx2 TCapt kia 12-10-17 7RWKent p141 CR Belgium23

LEWIN,Frederick Henry Capt ded 8-12-15 3ConnRgrs p172 CR Eire432 &CR Ireland14

LEWIN,John Wesley 2Lt kia 24-9-18 LabCps att5Leic p88 CR France699

LEWIN,Kenneth Robert TLt kia 9-3-16 7DCLI p114 CR Belgium23

LEWIN,Rex Richard Lt kia 25-9-15 3 att2RSuss p119 MR19

LEWINGTON,Frank Samuel T2Lt kia 21-3-18 9Norf p74 MR20

LEWINGTON,George Longley T2Lt kld 23-12-17 GL RFC p10 CR Mddx6

LEWINSTEIN,Harry 2Lt kia 22-7-16 1RWKent p141 CR France432

LEWIS,Alfred Drysdale TLt kia 24-3-18 RE 62FC p46 MR27

LEWIS,Alfred Ernest George TLt kia 6-9-17 195MGC Inf p184 CR Belgium112

LEWIS,Alfred John T2Lt kia 1-8-18 1 att7/8KOSB p102 CR France864

LEWIS,Archibald Ernest T2Lt kia 28-9-17 1KSLI p145 CR France550

LEWIS,Arthur Glanmor 2Lt kia 11/13-10-15 3SWBord att1Mon p100 CR France550,12-10-15

LEWIS,Arthur Glynne Lt ded 10-7-17 IARO att13Lancers p279 CR Iraq8

LEWIS,Arthur Milton.MID Capt kia 8-8-19 IA 1/52Sikhs p279 MR38

LEWIS,Arthur Ralph Pollard 2Lt kia 23-3-18 93RFA SigSubSec p32 CR France518

LEWIS,Arthur Starkey TLt kia 4-5-17 1RWFus GarrBn p98 MR20

LEWIS,Benjamin Alfred T2Lt kia 8-11-18 YLI att2Bn p143 CR France928

LEWIS,Brinley Richard TLtAMaj kia 2-4-17 B122RH&FA p32 CR Belgium1

LEWIS,Cecil Hallowes Maj ded 28-5-15 RASC 1DivTrn p193 CR France145

LEWIS,Charles HonLt&QM ded 14-6-17 RASC p193 CR Egypt1

LEWIS,Charles 2Lt kia 21-3-18 6 att16Manch p237 MR27

LEWIS,Charles Edward 2Lt kia 9-9-16 1/4Lond p246 MR21

LEWIS,Charles Vernon TLt ded 18-8-15 11SWBord att3Dors p100 CR Wales491

LEWIS,Clifford Stanley Lt dow 19-9-16 2/6Glouc p225 CR France345

LEWIS,Cuthbert Preston T2Lt kia 8-6-17 RE 2SpCoy p46 CR France297

LEWIS,Cyril William Victor Lt kld 3-10-17 6 att1Mddx p147 CR Wales289

LEWIS,David Elwyn 2Lt dow 18-9-18 16RWFus p98 CR France415

LEWIS,David Jacob T2Lt kia 28-2-17 2RFus p68 MR21

LEWIS,Denys Mervyn 2Lt kia 25-4-17 1/7Worc p226 MR21

LEWIS,Donald Swain.DSO.TLtCol kia 10-4-16 RE attRFC p3&46 CR Belgium11

LEWIS,Douglas David Raymond 2Lt dow 22-4-17 8DLI p239 CR France418

LEWIS,Edgar Capt kia 0-3-16 1/4SomLI p218 MR38

LEWIS,Edmund Llewellyn 2Lt kia 26-12-16 1/7Ess att24RFC p19&232 MR20

LEWIS,Edward Pugh 2Lt kia 6-10-17 GL 9RFC p10 CR Belgium18

LEWIS,Edward Richard Hampton T2Lt dow 25-4-17 4Worc Z'Coy p109 CR France113,Edwin

LEWIS,Edwin Maj dow 30-9-18 1/6SStaffs p229 CR France327

LEWIS,Ernest Hastings Maj kia 12-8-15 8Hamps p229 MR4

LEWIS,Francis Alexander 2Lt kia 5-2-18 53RFC p16 CR Belgium11,Frank Arthur

LEWIS,Frank T2Lt dow 31-7-17 7MGC p184 CR Belgiu19

LEWIS,Frank Arthur T2Lt kld 28-3-18 RFC p16 CR Scot398

LEWIS,Frederic Homer T2Lt kia 29-4-18 10 att1RIrRif p169 MR30

LEWIS,George Arthur Dunally 2Lt kia 8-7-15 4SStaffs attRWFus p122 MR29

LEWIS,George Hardy LtTCapt dow 28-9-16 4 att2ESurr p113 CR France98,27-9-15

LEWIS,George Herbert Lt 9-12-16 APDept CR Lond29

LEWIS,Gerald Sidney TCapt kia 7-7-16 11Mddx A'Coy p147 CR France296

LEWIS,Gordon T2Lt dow 18-4-18 10WelshR p127 CR France765

LEWIS,Graham Knight TLt dow 1-11-18 1HLI p163 CR Iraq8

LEWIS,Graham Lawson Lt dow 9-7-16 4 att2LancF p92 CR France1

LEWIS,Granville Vernon Loch T2Lt kldacc 5-10-17 RFC p10 CR Mddx17

LEWIS,Harold LtCol kia 1-7-16 IA 37Lancers Cmdg20Manch p279 CR France397

LEWIS,Harold 2Lt dow 29-4-17 151MGC p184 CR France145

LEWIS,Harold Lockwood T2Lt kia 23-10-17 24NumbF p62 MR30

LEWIS,Harold Nicholson.MM.T2Lt kia 18-10-17 1/2 att17LancF p92 MR30

LEWIS,Harris 2Lt kia 25-9-16 1/7Lpool p215 MR21,Harry

LEWIS,Harry Arthur.DCM.MID Maj kia 1-7-16 9Y&L p159 MR21

LEWIS,Harry Blundell 2Lt kia 2-12-17 1/7Lond p247 MR17

LEWIS,Henry Clifford Capt kia 4-10-17 10Mddx p236 MR30

LEWIS,Henry William T2Lt kia 12-10-18 RE 154FC p46 CR France287

LEWIS,Herbert 2Lt drd 5-5-17 RASC 917&MT Co p193 MR37

LEWIS,Herbert Morice 2Lt kia 4-11-15 10Mddx p236 MR4

LEWIS,Herbert Owen Roland.MC.T2Lt kia 1-10-17 1/2 att9Yorks p90 MR30

LEWIS,Hugh Berwyn T2Lt ded 12-2-19 LabCps 775AreaEmployCoy p189 CR France1142

LEWIS,Hugh Frederick.MID Capt kia 19-10-14 2RWSurr p56 CR Belgium160

LEWIS,James Windsor Lt kia 6-6-16 1WelshGds CR Belgium6

LEWIS,John Charles Capt kia 20-11-17 1Mon att6KSLI p244 MR17

LEWIS,John Clifford 2Lt dow 27-3-18 RGA 24SB p209 CR France185

LEWIS,John Dunning Gaunt Lt kia 24-9-18 3KSLI p145 CR France725

LEWIS,John Emrys T2Lt kia 1-7-16 8SomLI p80 CR France267

LEWIS,John Nicholas Lt kia 8-8-15 8WelshR p127 MR4

LEWIS,John Thorpe TCapt kia 9-8-15 Lincs p75 MR4

LEWIS,John Walter Lt kia 6-6-16 1WelshGds p53

LEWIS,John Walter 2Lt dow 15-7-16 3 att8Dev A'Coy p77 CR France119

LEWIS,Joseph Henry T2LtACapt kia 8-10-18 17RWFus att1/7Ches p98 CR France234

LEWIS,Lance Will T2Lt kia 9-8-16 7KRRC attMGC Inf p151&184 CR France294

LEWIS,Lawrence Reddrop TCapt kia 11-7-16 11SWBord p100 MR21

LEWIS,Leonard Geoffrey 2Lt mbk 31-8-18 1 att2Wilts p256 MR29,31-7-17

LEWIS,Leonard Glynne.MC.T2Lt kia 24-11-17 18WelshR p127 MR17

LEWIS,Llewelyn T2Lt kia 1/12-7-16 17RWFus p98 MR21

LEWIS,Lloyd Edward Lt kia 24-9-18 5N&D p232 CR France375

LEWIS,Ludwig T2Lt kia 6-7-17 2MGC Inf p184 CR Belgium173

LEWIS,Morgan Henry Lt dow 20-6-15 4RScotF p222 CR Gallipoli1

LEWIS,Nevill Graham Nuscomb Hart Capt kia 17-9-17 3Mon p244 CR Belgium20,Newcome

LEWIS,Norman George Lt ded 12-2-19 18KRRC A'Coy p265 CR Glouc5

LEWIS,Norman Victor TLt kia 13-11-16 15 att13EYorks p84 MR21

LEWIS,Reginald Cameron.MC.TCapt kia 1-7-16 2RBerks p139 CR France393

LEWIS,Reginald Walter Morton TLt ded 3-10-18 1 att9Worc p109 CR Asia82

LEWIS,Richard Percy MajALtCol kia 8-9-17 Dev attManch p77 CR Belgium84,7-9-17

LEWIS,Robert Frederick T2Lt kia 20-9-17 17KRRC att117TMB p151 MR30

LEWIS,Robert George TLt kia 23-9-18 74MGC Inf p184 CR France1494

LEWIS,Stephen Henry Lt kia 28-8-15 5ConnRgrs p172 MR4

LEWIS,Thomas William T2Lt dow 20-10-17 1RWFus p98 CR Belgium112

LEWIS,Trefor 2Lt dow 27-5-18 RFA att37TMB p32 CR France63

LEWIS,Trevor Edward TCapt kldacc 28-8-15 5SWBord p100 CR France345

LEWIS,Wallenstein Ryan.MC.TCapt dow 25-3-18 RE 284AT Co p46

LEWIS,Walter Henry.MID Lt dow 4-8-17 D107RFA p32 CR France40,2Lt

LEWIS,William Owen 2Lt mbk 27-5-17 4 att2WelshR p257 MR20

LEWIS,William Thomas 2Lt kia 27-3-17 1/7Ess p232 CR Palestine8

LEWTAS,Oscar Capt kia 9-7-16 3 att2Manch p155 MR21

LEWTHWAITE,Charles Gilfred.MC.Lt kia 29-7-17 231R FA p208 CR France570,Gilfrid

LEWTON-BRAIN,James Andrew T2Lt dow 14-8-17 8Norf p74 CR Belgium11

LEWTY,Thomas Edmund.MID 2Lt kia 14-3-17 5NStaffs p238 CR France579

LEY,Christopher Francis Aden Capt kld 16-3-18 NottsYeo attRFC p19&205

LEY,Geoffrey Arthur Henry 2Lt kia 30-7-17 3Dev attTankCps p77 CR Belgium126

LEY,James Wickham.DSO.Maj ded 22-10-18 2NStaffs p157 CR Asia82,7Bn

LEY,John Howard 2Lt kia 9-9-16 1RMunstF p175 MR21

LEY,Maurice Aden Lt kia 1-11-14 EKent att1Lincs p75&262 CR Belgium101

LEY,Maurice Carew 2Lt kia 1-7-16 2Dev p77 CR France393

LEYBOURN,Frederick Percy.MM.MID T2Lt ded 1-11-18 17Manch att6Ches p155 CR France276,19Bn

LEYBOURNE,Philip Edwin.MC&Bar.Capt kia 4-9-18 8Hamps p229 CR Belgium111

LEYLAND,Herbert Edward T2Lt dow 17-10-17 RE 179TC p46

LEYLAND,Reginald Hamilton ALtCol kia 24-9-18 2RB p179 CR France184,Rex

LEYS,Colin McLaren T2Lt kia 15-9-16 8Beds p86 MR21

LEZARD,Arthur Gower Capt kia 31-1-16 13RB p179 CR France745

LIARDET,Frederick Charles Evelyn Lt ded 13-12-17 5Dev attRFC p217&19,dow CR Devon128

LIAS,Ronald John Mortlock TLt kia 23-2-16 9RSuss p119 CR Belgium72

LIBERTY,John Ince Lt kia 28-11-17 RFA 38ArmyBde p32 CR Belgium19

LIBBY,Alfred Thomas TLt kia 20-9-17 12ESurr p113 MR30

LIDDELL,Arthur John T2Lt dow 5-10-17 YLI att8Bn p143 CR France8

LIDDELL,John TLt kia 30-3-18 RE 144ArmyTroopCo p46 MR27

LIDDELL,John Aidan.VC.Capt dow 31-8-15 A&SH &RFC p173&1,Adrian CR Hamps106

LIDDELL,John Henry Tandy Lt dow 17-11-16 6 att1KRRC p151 CR France120

LIDDELL,John Robert Hugh T2Lt kld 10-11-17 GL RFC p10 CR Lancs421

LIDDELL,Lily Nurse ded 29-9-18 VAD BRCS p200 CR Egypt9

LIDDELL,Mathew Henry Goldie 2Lt ded 17-4-16 7ScotRif &54RAF p224&256,17-4-18 MR20,no date

LIDDELL,Robert 2Lt ded 24-1-19 Ess att1/7Bn p132 CR Italy6

LIDDLE,Horace Septimus HonCapt ded 1-6-18 Ex LabCps p266 CR SAfrica53 RFus

LIDDLE,William Capt ded 27-9-18 9RScots attRE 11DivSigs p212 CR France95

LIDGETT,John Cuthbert TLt kia 23-3-18 11SLancs p125 CR France1203,24-3-18

LIDIARD,Richard John Abraham 2Lt kia 1-7-16 3Lond p246 CR France1327

LIDINGTON,Norman Herbert T2Lt kia 15-9-16 1Nhampt att11Ess p137 MR21

LIDSEY,William John 2Lt dow 22-3-17 4 O&BLI &16RFC p19&231 CR France95

LIEBENTHAL,Louis George Lt kia 4-6-15 8CamH att1Ess p168 MR4

LIEBERT,Bernard Robert Maj kia 13-5-15 LeicYeo p204 MR29

LIEBERT,Frederick Alexander Charles Capt kia 17-11-14 NSomYeo p205 CR Belgium57 Ex 3DragGds

LIFETREE,Ernest Henry T2Lt kia 20-5-16 16N&D p134 CR France279

LIGHT,Eric 2Lt mbk 26-3-18 40MGC p256 MR20

LIGHT,George Joseph 2Lt kia 8-11-17 RGA 142SB p40 CR France777

LIGHTBODY,James Gordon Lt ded 27-4-19 IA 36Horse p279 MR65

LIGHTBODY,Wilfred Petre TLt kia 26-9-15 9Norf p74 MR19

LIGHTBOURN,Robert T2Lt kia 26-7-17 8Glouc p107 CR Belgium60 Lt

LIGHTFOOT,Francis Bertram 2Lt kia 30-12-17 28Lond p252 MR21

LIGHTLEY,Albert 2Lt kia 31-3-18 7EYorks p84 MR20

LILICO,Percy T2Lt kld 16-2-18 RFC p16 CR Numb58,Lt

LILLEY,Edmund Arthur Howe TLt kia 31-7-18 6Beds att112TMB p86 CR France1014,Capt

LILLEY,William David Hetherington 2Lt dow PoW 11-8-16 8Lpool p216 CR France1266

LILLEY,William Fred.MM.2Lt kia 24-4-18 6RWar p214 MR19

LILLIE,Frank William T2Lt kld 18-12-16 9YLI p143 CR France423,Capt

LILLIE,Frederick Sutherland Maj kia 15-3-15 1RIrReg p89 CR Belgium28

LILLINGTON,Conrad Ivan 2Lt kia 8-3-16 1/4SomLI p218 MR38

LILLIS,Martin Michael Arthur TLt kia 11-4-17 RIrReg &3RFC p10&89 CR France833

LILLY,Arthur John 2Lt kia 4-4-17 6RWar p214 CR France669

LILLY,Thomas Maj 24-9-19 RAOC CR Yorks361

LILLYWHITE,Frederick Thomas Sherwood T2Lt dow 26-5-17 2Mddx p147 CR France145

LILLYWHITE,Robert John TCapt kld 26-11-16 GL &RFC p190&3,LILLYWHILTE CR Sussex88

LIMB,Harry TLtACapt ded 23-10-18 RE IWT p46 CR France1359

LIMBERY,Charles Roy.MC.Capt kia 1-7-16 1SStaffs p122 CR France397

LIMBERY,Kenneth Thomas.MC.TCapt kia 26-9-17 RAMC att133FA p196 CR France139

LIMBRICK,Arthur William Wentworth 2Lt kia 14-3-17 3 att2RWSurr p56 CR France514

LIMERICK,Victor 2Lt ded 20-8-19 RFA &5RAF p256&258 CR Germany1,Lt

LIMONT,William Eric T2Lt kia 14-7-16 15 att12NumbF p62 MR21

LIMRICK,Paul Osborne Lt kia 12-9-16 8Lpool p215 CR France402

LINAKER,Archibald Frederick Richard TLt kia 9-9-18 SLancs att2LNLancs p125 CR Belgium15,Fredrick 2LNL attSL

LINCEY,Charles Edgar 2Lt kia 31-7-16 1/4RLancs p213 CR France453

LINCOLN,C.Joseph AssSurg 23-7-21 IMD MR66

LINDBERG,Thomas Henry TMaj ded 24-4-15 SL p201 CR Yorks245

LINDE,Henry Eyre T2Lt dow 24-6-17 7RInniskF p105 Cr Belgium60

LINDEN,Norman Eric T2Lt dow 4-9-18 10TankCps p188 CR France34

LINDEN,Samuel McCullagh.MID 2Lt kia 31-7-17 RGA 90HAG p40 MR29

LINDLEY,Ernest William 2Lt ded PoW 18-2-17 9Manch attRFC p19&237 CR France604

LINDLEY,Foster 2Lt dow 5-9-18 7EYorks p84 CR France41,Lt

LINDLEY,Harry Lt&QM ded 27-1-16 6Leic p88 CR Leic63

LINDLEY,John Bennett 2Lt dow 19-5-17 RFA V2HvyTMB p208 CR France265

LINDLEY,Thomas Grenville 2Lt dow 24-9-17 1/20 att2/10Lond p251 CR Belgium18

LINDOP,Eugene Lancelot Erskine.MC.Capt dow 30-1-16 IA 41Dogras p279 CR Iraq6

LINDOP,Herbert Cyril Lt kia 20-9-17 5NStaffs att10KRRCp238 MR30

LINDOW,Edwin 2Lt dow 11-8-16 3 att6Dors p124 CR France397

LINDREA,George Patrick Maj kia 18-7-16 B305RFA p206 CR France1887

LINDREA,Wilfred George 2Lt kia 30-3-18 4Glouc p225 CR France1170

LINDSAY,Adam 2Lt dow 1-8-18 10RScots p212 CR France1225

LINDSAY,Alexander Cuthbert TLt ded 10-2-18 GL RE IWT p46 CR Iraq6

LINDSAY,Archibald Thurston Thomas Lt kia 26-3-18 RE 7ATCoy attMon p46 CR France281

LINDSAY,Bernard Wilfred Capt dow 22-11-18 B187RFA p207 CR France34

LINDSAY,Charles Stephen Capt dow 11-4-16 IA 55Rif att53Sikhs p279 MR38

LINDSAY,Claud Frederic Thomas.MID Capt kia 31-3-18 RFA 33Bty p32 CR France1003,Maj

LINDSAY,Courtenay Traice TLt ded 28-4-16 RASC p193 CR Bucks57

LINDSAY,David Lt kia 15-4-17 7HLI p240 MR41

LINDSAY,David Paton TCapt ded 2-12-18 RAMC p196 CR EAfrica36

LINDSAY,Douglas Alexander Capt kia 15-5-15 5RScots p211 CR Gallipoli2

LINDSAY,Douglas Alexander T2Lt kia 25-9-15 10ScotRif p103 MR19

LINDSAY,Francis Howard Maj kia 1-7-16 14Lond p249 MR21

LINDSAY,George Lt kia 7-5-17 5 att11RScots p211 CR France97

LINDSAY,George Walter Thomas Capt kld 26-6-17 RFA attRFC p10&32 CR Wales16

LINDSAY,Henry.MC.Capt kia 8-8-16 1/4LNLancs p234 MR21

LINDSAY,James T2Lt kia 12-4-18 23NumbF p62 MR32

LINDSAY,James Arthur Capt ded 24-6-15 RGA p270

LINDSAY,James Basden T2Lt ded 8-8-18 RASC BaseSupplyDepot p193 CR Iraq6

LINDSAY,T.H.Capt 24-6-15 RGA CR Scot237

LINDSAY,William 2Lt kia 31-7-17 3 att2RScotF p94 MR29

LINDSAY,William Alexander Hewes 2Lt kia 31-7-16 4 att2HLI p163 MR21

LINDSAY,William Henry.MC.TCapt kia 3-9-18 9ESurr p113 CR France480

LINDSAY,William Horn 2Lt dow 30-5-19 6BlkW p129&257 CR Scot385

LINDSAY-SMITH,Campbell Lt 10-11-15 11 att8GordH CR Belgium125

LINDSAY-YOUNG,Laurence Hingston Capt dow 25-12-18 1RScotF &RAF p95 CR Hamps7

LINDSEY,Douglas Lt kia 17-12-17 3 att5Dors p124 CR France550,Capt

LINDSEY,Paul 2Lt kia 2-6-17 4 O&BLI p231 CR France162

LINDSLEY,George Vincent 2Lt dow 16-3-17 3 att2RWFus p98 CR France145

LINE,Eric Alfred Thiselton T2Lt ded 16-12-16 RASC 26DivTrain p193 CR Greece7

LINE,John Young Alexander T2Lt dow 13-3-16 8NStaffs D'Coy p157 CR France345

LINES,Francis Leonard Lt kia 19-4-17 1/4Nhampt p234 CR Palestine8

LINES,Herbert T2Lt kia 20-9-17 KRRC att10Bn p151 MR30

LINES,Sidney Martin 2Lt kia 13-5-15 1/5Lond p246 MR29 CR Belgium453

LINES,Thomas.MC.DCM.T2Lt dow 5-4-18 16LancF p92 CR France804

LINFORD,Ivor Hutchison.MC.TCapt kia 21-3-18 12Ess p132 MR27 10Bn

LING,Arthur Leonard 2Lt dow 3-11-18 5Lancs p213 CR France52,Lt

LING,Fergus Graham Capt ded 16-12-18 KEdwsHorse p24 CR W'land&C'land25

LING,Frederick William TCapt&Adjt kia 27-6-17 8RFus p68 CR France154

LING,Godfrey Frank Mackwood.MC&2Bars.Capt kia 23-5-18 2/7WYorks att185TMB p218 CR France798

LING,Leonard Simpson 2Lt kia 23-4-17 3 att1Norf p74 MR20

LINGARD,John Reginald Lt kia 21-8-15 6Manch p236 MR4

LINGEMAN,John Florris 2Lt dow 28-4-17 1EssYeo p203 CR France102

LINGWOOD,Edward St.Hilary T2Lt kia 3-5-17 7Beds p86 MR20

LINK,F.L.C.2Lt kld 7-6-18 GL &RAF p190

LINK,Horace Arthur 2Lt kia 9-9-16 1HAC p206 CR France161

LINKLATER,William Irvine 2Lt kia 5-4-18 B77RFA p32 CR France232

LINN,Peter 2Lt kia 22-10-17 16RScots p54 CR Belgium126

LINNELL,Robert McCheyne Capt ded 17-3-15 RAMC p196 CR Beds34

LINNING,John HonMaj&QM ded 16-9-14 1BlkW p129 MR15

LINSELL,Johnson Hugh T2Lt kia 25-9-15 Mddx p147 MR19

LINSTEAD,Douglas Walter T2Lt kia 6-5-16 12RFus 3Coy p68 CR Belgium339

LINTON,Charles Strangways.DSO.MC.MajALtCol kia 20-11-17 4Worc p109 CR France439

LINTON.F.P.Surg 18-10-18 IMS MR61

LINTON,Frederick Tom.MC.T2Lt kia 22-4-18 16RWFus p98 CR France296

LINTON,Henry McEwan TLt dow 28-9-15 12HLI p163 CR France178,kia 26-9-15

LINTOTT,Evelyn Henry TLt kia 1-7-16 15WYorks p82 MR21

LINTOTT,Harry Chamen Lt dow 22-3-18 5Lond p246 CR France398

LINTOTT,Richard 2Lt kia 3-5-15 5Lond p246 MR29

LINZELL,Harold Harding.MC.T2Lt kia 3-7-16 7BordR p177 CR France397

LINZELL,Stanley James.MC.Capt kia 3-4-17 RAMC p196 CR France1204

LIPP,Charles Napier 2Lt kia 31-7-17 6SfthH p241 MR29

LIPP,Frank 2Lt dow 30-5-16 2ScotRif att8RWFus p103 MR43

LIPP,Vernon Robertson 2Lt kia 17-6-16 5 att12RFus p68 CRBelgium339

LIPPIATT,William George T2Lt kia 10-8-18 6RWSurr p56 CR France636

LIPSCOMBE,Eric Lancelot Lt kia 9-5-15 3 att2RBerks p139 MR32

LIPSETT,Louis James.CB.CMG.TMajGen kia 14-10-18 RIrReg Staff DivHQ 18/1 p89 CR France686

LIPTROTT,Eric Carr.MID Lt dow 26-11-14 IA 6Jats p279 CR France102

LISBY,Leslie Norman Lt dow 5-11-17 4RSuss p228 CR Palestine1,2Lt

LISH,John Robertson 2Lt kia 4-10-17 3Lincs p75 MR30

LISLE,John Wynne 2Lt kia 3-5-17 15WYorks p82 MR20

LISLE,Robert Ernest Bentham Capt kia 30-3-18 8 att9DLI p239 MR20

LISMER,Alfred Bass TLt ded 26-10-18 RE CR Nhampt32

LISSAMAN,Arthur John TLt kia 13-4-17 23RFus p68 MR20

LISTER,Arthur Hugh.CMG.LtCol ded 17-7-16 RAMC p253 MR41

LISTER,Charles Alfred.Hon.MID 2LtLt ded 26-8-15 1Co ofLondYeo p204 CR Greece 10,28-8-15

LISTER,Frederick William.MC.Maj ded 24-2-19 WorcYeo attTankCps p189&206 CR War22

LISTER,Herbert Dixon 2Lt kia 4-9-18 4WelchR p230 MR30

LISTER,Herbert Henry Holden 2Lt kia 4-5-17 2RWar p65 MR20

LISTER,John Curtis T2Lt kia 20-5-17 17RFA p32 MR20

LISTER,John Raymond T2Lt kia 15-12-15 11 att8WRid p115 CR Gallipoli27

LISTER,Matthew William Capt kia 19-7-17 5 att9SStaffs p229 CR Belgium29

LISTER,Philip Thomas T2Lt dow 10-4-17 10YLI p143 CR France214,9-4-17

LISTER,Thomas Frederick T2Lt kia 28-4-17 27NumbF p62 MR20

LISTER,William Howard.DSO.MC&2Bars.TCapt kia 9-8-18 RAMC att21FA p196 CR Italy3

LISTON,William Prosper Lt kia 12-4-17 5Leinst p174 CR France557 see PROSPER LISTON

LITCHFIELD,Frederick George TLt kld 24-9-17 GL &RFC p10 CR Kent109

LITCHFIELD,Thomas 2Lt kia 31-7-17 3 att7Nhampt p137 MR29

LITHFIELD,John 2Lt kia 22-10-14 Beds p86 MR29

LITSTER,Hugh Sinclaire 2Lt dow 20-4-16 3Dors p124 CR Iraq5

LITTEN,Raymond TCapt kia 1-7-16 6RBerks p139 CR France513

LITTLE,Adam T2Lt kia 21-7-18 1/6SfthH p165 CR France1697

LITTLE,Andrew 2Lt kia 25-4-15 9DLI p239 MR29

LITTLE,Charles Hope LtCol ded 18-6-18 Cmdg4Wilts p236 CR France1571

LITTLE,Donald Alexander Duncan 2Lt ded 22-8-17 LanarkYeo att14BlkWp270 CR Egypt7

LITTLE,Harry Ewart T2Lt kia 18-9-18 2RSuss p119 CR France725

LITTLE,Henry James T2Lt kia 20-9-17 EKent att5SLancs p57 CR Belgium125

LITTLE,Herbert James Lt kia 26-3-18 1/7DLI p239 MR27

LITTLE,Henry Walter 2Lt kia 30-8-18 5WRid p227 CR France421

LITTLE,John.DCM.T2Lt kia 24-4-17 8GordH p166 MR20

LITTLE,John.MC.Capt dow 17-10-18 RE 90FC p46 CR Belgium405

LITTLE,John Russell 2Lt kia 3-5-17 KOSB att6Bn p102 MR20

LITTLE,John Wishart Maj ded 7-5-18 IA IMS p279 MR43

LITTLE,Norman James Richard T2Lt kia 13-3-17 11RFus p68 MR21

LITTLE,William 2Lt kia 1-10-16 6DLI p239 MR21

LITTLE,William 2Lt kia 24-4-18 RFA p208 CR France196

LITTLEBOY,Frederick Graham TLt dow 7-12-15 RWKent att9Worc p141 CR Gallipoli4

LITTLEBOY,Wilfrid Evelyn TLt kia 9-10-17 16RWar p65 CR Belgium112

LITTLEDALE,Arthur Charles.MID Maj dow 9-5-15 RFA 19Bty p32 CR France924,kia

LITTLEDALE,Robert TCapt kia 30-11-17 5Nhampt p137 CR France662

LITTLEDALE,Willoughby John Lt kia 23-3-18 2 O&BLI A'Coy p130 CR France307,Capt

LITTLEJOHN,John T2Lt kia 26-10-16 2WYorks p82 CR France1891

LITTLEJOHN,Stanley William 2Lt kia 23-9-17 RGA 142SB p40 CR Belgium94

LITTLER,Frank T2Lt kia 23-7-17 2 att8SLancs p125 CR Belgium11

LITTLER,James Tattock Lt kia 7-8-15 8LancF p221 MR4

LITTLER,John Edward T2Lt dow 4-5-18 11LancF p92 CR France100

LITTLER,Tom T2Lt kia 3-7-17 GL 1RFC p10 CR France285

LITTLETON,Cecil Francis Henry TLt dow 6-5-17 1 att5CamH p168 CR France95,Capt

LITTLEWOOD,Charles William Stephen.MC.2Lt kia 10-7-17 RE 7FC p46 CR France1185

LITTLEWOOD,Frederick William TLt kia 5-3-16 8Y&L p159 CR France347

LITTLEWOOD,George Patrick TCapt kia 3-9-16 17N&D p134 CR France339

LITTON,Reginald T2Lt kia 8-9-16 10 att2ELancs p111 CR France423

LIVERMORE,Ernest Bernard 2Lt kia 15-9-16 24Lond p252 MR21

LIVERSEDGE,Alexander Frederick 2Lt kia 25-3-18 Mddx att2Bn p147 MR27

LIVERSIDGE,Albert T2Lt dow 2-7-16 15WYorks p82 CR France62

LIVERSIDGE,Harold 2Lt kia 23-7-16 1DCLI p114 CR France402

LIVESAY,George Augustus Bligh Lt kia 28/29-5-16 5SWBord p100

LIVESEY,Alan George Hilton Lt kia 25-9-15 3 att1LNLancs p136 CR France1723,2Lt

LIVESEY,Cyril Joseph Glanville T2Lt kia 4-1-18 2Mddx p147 MR30

LIVESEY,Harry TCapt kia 1-7-16 11ELancs p111 MR21

LIVESEY,Joseph Harold 2Lt kld 30-11-17 1/4LNLancs p234 MR17

LIVINGSTON,William Montgomery T2Lt dow 15-4-17 6RIrF p171 CR France95,Lt

LIVINGSTONE,Frank Darley TCapt dow 22-3-18 RASC 15DivTrn p193 CR France113,kia

LIVINGSTONE,Frederick James H.T2Lt kld 12-1-18 RFC p16 CR Lincs136

LIVINGSTONE,Frederick Maurice T2Lt dow 4-11-18 16LancF p92 CR France341

LIVINGSTONE,Harold Gordon 2Lt kia 1-5-15 64RFA p32 CR Belgium20,5-5-15

LIVINGSTONE,Robert TLt ded 10-11-16 RE p46 CR Essex10

LIVINGSTONE-LEARMOUTH,Nigel James Christian Capt kia 22-8-15 15Huss attDorsYeo p22 CR Gallipoli5,21-8-15

LIVOCK,Eric Stuart Lt kia 8-11-17 4RWSurr attRFC p19&212 CR Belgium18

LIVSEY,Ernest Claude T2Lt kia 13-11-16 12EYorks p84 MR21,13-9-16

LIVSEY,William Mylrea 2Lt drd 2-6-17 RFA 5ResBde p32 CR Eire506

LLANGATTOCK,John McLean.Lord Maj dow 31-10-16 RFA p206 CR France102

LLARENA,Eustace Fernando 2Lt kia 18-6-15 2Suff p78 MR29

LLEWELLIN,C.H.OBE.MC.DCM.Capt 26-11-20 RE CR War16

LLEWELLIN,William Mervyn Johnes 2Lt kia 17-8-18 2SWBord p100 CR France1723,1Bn

LLEWELLYN,Arthur.OBE.LtCol 27-4-20 Comdg 3SomLI CR Somerset10

LLEWELLYN,Edward Thomas TLt dow 18-5-18 RWFus 4GarrBn att9Bn p98 CR France40

LLEWELLYN,Gwenyth Miss ded 4-11-18 VAD BRCS p200 CR France146,Gwynedd 3-11-18

LLEWELLYN,Harold Alfred TLt kld 14-6-16 8SWBord p100 CR Greece1

LLEWELLYN,John Herbert TCapt kia 24-8-16 5KSLI p145 CR France402

LLEWELLYN,John Horace TLt dow 9-10-17 RFA A/ABty p32 CR Belgium165,kia

LLEWELLYN,Thomas Edward.MM.2Lt kia 27-10-18 30RFA p32 CR France1270

LLEWELLYN,Vivian T2Lt kia 3-11-18 14RWFus p98 CR France1478,4-11-18

LLEWELLYN-JONES,Vivian Bruford Lt kia 4-5-15 2Suff att1WelshR p78 CR Belgium96

LLOYD,Alan Scrivener TLt kia 4-8-16 C78RFA p32 CR France188

LLOYD,Arthur Lt ded 4-2-18 2Ches p96&257 CR Ches8

LLOYD.C.M.C.Capt 25-4-16 2Hamps CR Lond12

LLOYD,Charles Edward MajHonLtCol ded 8-10-15 6RIrReg p89 CR Hamps1

LLOYD,Charles Gordon Lt ded 9-6-15 10RWFus p98 CR Hamps1,7-6-15

LLOYD,David Rhys Cadogen TLt kia 16-6-17 GL RFC p10 CR France568,Cadwgan

LLOYD,Dennis Montford Anthony 2Lt kia 22-3-18 6RWar p214 MR27

LLOYD,Duncan Ian Dowes Lt kia 14-8-15 IA 1/5Gurkhas att1/6 p279 MR4

LLOYD,Edward Raymond.MID Capt&Adjt kia 3-12-14 2RInniskF p105 CR France598,dow

LLOYD,Edward Stanley.MC.Lt ded 23-11-18 RH&FA HQ312Bde p32 CR France717

LLOYD,Ernest Alfred Collyer Lt kia 31-7-17 1ScotsGds p52 CR Belgium106

LLOYD,Ernest Henry TCapt dow 2-4-15 5RBerks p139 CR France145,2-4-18

LLOYD,Ewan Christian 2Lt dow 5-10-18 1SWBord p100 CR France725

LLOYD,Francis Burrows T2Lt kia 3-10-16 2Dev p77 CR France115

LLOYD,Francis Charles Aylmer TLt dow 8-10-15 12 att2HLI p163 CR France40

LLOYD,Francis Oswald T2Lt kia 12-2-16 9 att6KSLI p145 MR29

LLOYD,Frank 2Lt kld 1-2-19 5Worc &RAF p264

LLOYD,Frank Lewis Capt kia 1/4-10-15 Ches p96 MR19

LLOYD,Frank Stuart TMaj dow 5-9-17 13RWFus p98 CR Belgium16

LLOYD,Gerald Aylmer LtTCapt kia 16-2-15 1WelshR p127 CR Belbium166

LLOYD,Gilbert Kingsley 2Lt ded 21-2-16 3KSLI p145 CR Greece9,2Bn

LLOYD,Gilbert Lewis 2Lt kia 30-11-17 21Lond p251 MR17

LLOYD,Gwion Llewelyn Bowen Capt kia 7/11-8-15 5Dors p124 MR4,11-8-15

LLOYD,H.TLt kia 19-7-17 1/3KAR p202 CR EAfrica38 &CR Tanzania1

LLOYD,Harvey Richard.MID TCapt dow 6-9-16 6RIrReg p89 CR France66,Rickard

LLOYD,Henry John Graeme TCaptHonMaj ded 13-4-19 DCLI p264

LLOYD,Herbert T2Lt kia 12-8-16 7Nhampt p137 MR21 18-8-16

LLOYD,Hesperus David Watkins Maj kia 12-3-15 2ScotRif p103 CR France708,Watkiss 10-3-15

LLOYD,Hugh Clifford Chetwode LtTCapt ded 25-2-17 1DCLI p114 CR France64

LLOYD,Ira Cyril T2Lt ded 24-11-18 1/2Worc p109 CR France146

LLOYD,James.MC.LtTCapt dow 21-4-18 Glouc att8Bn p107 CR France40

LLOYD,James Percival T2Lt kia 25-7-17 1/2 att16RWFus p98 CR Belgium66,att15Bn

LLOYD,John Francis Selby Maj kia 18-6-15 6NStaffs p238 CR Belgium89

LLOYD,Lewis John Bevenall Lt kia 25-4-15 9KSLI p145 MR29

LLOYD,Llewellyn T2Lt dow 1-8-17 11SWBord p100 CR Belgium16

LLOYD,Lyndsey 2Lt kia 9-10-17 3 att2Hamps p121 MR30

LLOYD,Marteine Kemes Arundel Capt kia 15-9-16 2GrenGds SR p50 CR France402

LLOYD,Meyricke Entwisle Capt kia 23-10-14 RWFus p98 MR29,24-10-14

LLOYD,Mervyn Capt dow 15-3-15 3NumbF p62 CR Surrey106

LLOYD,Owen Robert.MC.2LtACapt dow 20-9-17 3 att7KSLI p145 CR Belgium83

LLOYD,Reginald Conway T2Lt kia 3-11-16 1RWSurr p56 MR21

LLOYD,Richard Glyn Lt kia 13-9-16 19Lpool p72 MR19

LLOYD,Richard Serjeantson 2Lt kia 18-6-17 GL 1RFC p10 MR20

LLOYD,Robert Arthur 2Lt kia 27-4-15 Lpool p72 CR Belgium101

LLOYD,Robert Courtois 2Lt kia 22-8-18 4 att7RIrReg p89 CR France139,dow

LLOYD,Robert Love.MID Maj dow 9-12-15 RWFus 158BdeHQ p98 CR Gallipoli26

LLOYD,Samuel Ernest Lt kia 16-3-16 1/7Worc p225 CR France3

LLOYD,Thomas Glyn TCapt kia 10-5-18 15WelshR p127 CR France232

LLOYD,Thomas Lancelot T2Lt ded 8-4-19 3RRofCav p261 CR Lincs44

LLOYD,Thomas Newburn Chetwoode Capt ded 25-4-16 Hamps p121

LLOYD,Thomas Richard Beamish T2Lt ded 20-2-16 RASC p193 CR Ireland14 &CR Eire161

LLOYD,Thomas Yale T2Lt kia 12-7-16 10WelshR p127 CR France453

LLOYD,Valentine.MC.Lt kia 23-10-18 3 att11Leic p88 CR France1475

LLOYD,Walter.MID Capt kia 7-8-15 8RWFus p98 CR Gallipoli31

LLOYD,Walter Henry Capt kia 4-8-18 RAMC att1/20Lond p253 CR France59

LLOYD,Walter Reginald LtCol kia 14-9-14 1LNLancs p136 MR15

LLOYD,William Benjamin 2Lt kia 10-8-17 3 att7Nhampt p137 MR29

LLOYD,William Henry Aloysius Capt kldBySepoy 16-7-16 IA 122Infatt101Grens p279 CR EAfrica2 &CR Tanzania1

LLOYD,William Merrick Ellis 2Lt kia 19-5-17 40RFA p32 CR France1182

LLOYD,William Robert T2Lt kia 12-7-18 15 att2RWFus p98 MR27

LLOYD,Wymond Howard Capt ded 9-3-16 Hereford p252

LLOYD,Wynell Hastings T2Lt kld 17-4-18 RE 123FC p46 CR France44

LLOYD-BAKER,Michael Granville Lloyd.MID Capt 23-4-16 GloucYeo MR34

LLOYD-EVANS,Edward Meredydd Capt 14-3-16 5Lancs CR France504

LLOYD-JONES,Edward Wynne.MID Capt kia 10-8-15 1/7RWFus p223 CR Gallipoli5

LLOYD-JONES,Harold 2Lt ded 1-7-18 RWFus p263 CR Wales227

LLOYD-JONES,Ivor Thomas.MID Capt kia 26-3-17 1/7RWFus p223 CR Palestine8

LLOYD-JONES,John TCapt ded 11-3-16 2Yorks p90 CR Wales531

LLOYD-JONES,Percy Arnold.DSO.MID Maj dow 22-12-16 RAMC p196 CR France120,LtCol

LLOYD-WILLIAMS,David Gray 2Lt kia 10-8-15 6RLancs p59 MR4

LLOYD-WILLIAMS,Kelyth Pierce T2Lt kia 17-10-16 17WelshR p127 CR France149

LLOYDS,Cyril Edwin Fowler 2Lt ded 9-1-19 RGA p262 CR Oxford51

LLUELLYN,Raymond Chester TCapt kia 13-8-18 7Lincs p75 CR France526

LOADER,Ernest Stanley 2Lt kia 4-11-18 2RSuss p119 CR France1272

LOADER,Graham Chard Capt kia 12-8-15 8Hamps p229 MR4

LOAM,Ernest Harold T2Lt kia 7-5-18 RE 56FC p46 CR France33

LOCH,Alex Arthur Francis.DSO.MID Capt kia 22-7-16 1SWBord p100 MR21

LOCH,Arthur Cuthbert 2Lt ded PoW 1-8-16 IARO att104Rif p279 CR Iraq8,LOCK

LOCHEED,R.W.2Lt kld 28-5-18 GL &RAF p190

LOCHRIN,Michael James Capt kia 23-10-14 RAMC att1Nhampt p196 MR29,Joseph

LOCK,A.S. see LOCH,A.S.

LOCK,George Maj 11-9-20 3LNLanc CR Hereford113

LOCK,James Alexander 2Lt kia 25-9-16 10NumbF p62 CR France239

LOCK,James Palmer 2Lt dow 2-2-18 63RFA p32 CR France769

LOCK,Thomas Henry Lt&QM ded 9-11-18 RNDevYeo p256 CR Eire398,19-11-18

LOCK,William Absalom TLt kia 25-9-15 6Wilts p153 CR France260

LOCKE,Frank William 2Lt 13-10-15 RE 1ArmyHQSigCoy CR France80

LOCKE,Harold Capt drd 10-10-18 RIrReg p89 MR40

LOCKE,Robert Douglas T2Lt kia 2-3-16 2Suff p78 CR Belgium131,Lt

LOCKERBIE,Herbert T2Lt kia 21-8-18 3MGC Inf p184 CR France924

LOCKET,George Eimer 2Lt kia 28-6-18 3 att1Suff p78 CR Belgium37,28-6-15

LOCKETT,Clifford Vincent Lt ded 12-2-19 5Ess p270 CR Mddx80

LOCKETT,Garstang Bradstock.MC.LtACapt dow 4-11-18 ChesYeo att1Ches p203 CR France380

LOCKETT,William Henry T2Lt kia 7-10-16 16 att12DLI p161 MR21

LOCKEY,Ernest William 2Lt kia 8/10-9-16 2Lond p245 CR France402

LOCKHART,Alan Ross T2Lt ded 7-12-17 13Manch p155 CR Greece9

LOCKHART,George Barclay Capt kia 14-4-17 HighCycBn attRFC p19&253 CR France58

LOCKHART,Gerald Bevis TLt kia 10-8-15 6LNLancs p136 MR4

LOCKHART,James Herbert 2Lt kia 30-7-16 7BlkW p231 CR France785

LOCKHART,John Sutherland Lt kia 10-5-16 3RScots p54 CR Belgium21,Jack 2Bn

LOCKHART,Reginald Frank 2Lt dow 10-7-17 13Lond attMGC p187&249 CR Belgium24

LOCKHART,Robert Hamilton T2Lt kia 11-11-15 9 att7RScotF p95 CR France423

LOCKIE,James.MC.Capt kia 22-3-18 12/13NumbF att2Lincs p62 MR27

LOCKING,Thomas Edgar Lt dow 20-1-18 RGA p209 CR France64

LOCKLEY,Henry James T2Lt kia 22-3-18 11LancF p92 MR20

LOCKLEY,Rupert Edward Holder Maj ded 21-10-15 GordH attWAFF p201&265 CR Berks43,20-10-15

LOCKTON,George Woodhams TCapt dow 21-10-17 RGA 153SB p40 CR France193

LOCKWOOD,Albert 2Lt kia 7-10-18 RGA 93SB p40 CR France375

LOCKWOOD,Frank T2Lt kld 4-11-17 GL RFC p10 CR Yorks652

LOCKWOOD,George T2Lt dow 3-11-17 10YLI E'Coy p143 CR France145

LOCKWOOD,Joshua Capt&QM ded 16-12-18 GL att4Dev p270 CRYorks677,YLI

LOCKWOOD,Reginald Ughtred Lt ded 10-1-19 IARO att14LabCps p279 MR66

LOCKWOOD,Richard William Mark 2Lt kia 14/15-9-14 2CldGds p51 CR France1112,14-9-14

LOCKYEAR,Horace 2Lt kia 20-5-18 6Lincs p75 CR France115

LOCKYER,Felix Courtenay 2Lt kia 12-2-17 8Dev p77 MR21

LOCON,Sidney John Boileau CaptTMaj kia 12-4-18 4RWar attRASC MT VIIICps p65 CR Belgium3,LACON

LODER,Robert Egerton Capt dow 2903017 1/4Suss CR Palestine2

LODER,William Victor 2Lt kia 10-5-18 4Wilts p236 CR Palestine9

LODER-SYMONDS,John Frederick Maj kia 31-11-14 1SStaffs p122 MR29,1-11-14

LODER-SYMONDS,Robert Francis Capt ded 3-3-15 1Ches p96 CR France145

LODER-SYMONDS,Thomas Lenthall Lt kia 9-5-15 2ScotRif p103 CR France525

LODER-SYMONDS,William Crawshay Capt ded 30-5-18 Wilts &RAF p153 CR Berks56

LODGE,Bernard Grime.MID 2Lt kia 24-8-17 4 att10DLI p161 MR30

LODGE,Gerald Aylmer Bleackley 2Lt kia 5-6-15 8LancF p222 CR Gallipoli2,6-6-15

LODGE,John 2Lt dow 18-3-18 RGA 190SB p40 CR Belgium11

LODGE,John William HonCol ded 23-8-17 3Yorks Cmdg2HSGarrBn p90 CR Yorks100

LODGE,K.A.2Lt ded 5-11-18 1LancF p92 CR Ches31,4Bn

LODGE,Ralph Nesbit 2Lt kia 1-7-16 3 att15LancF p92 MR21

LODGE,Raymond 2Lt dow 14-9-15 2 att3SLancs p125 CR Belgium113

LODGE,Richard Cuthbert TLt kia 27-8-17 16RScots p54 MR21

LODGE,Ronald Edward Somerville Lt kia 25-9-15 2Leic p88 MR19

LODGE,Tom.MC.T2Lt dow 21-5-18 2/4 O&BLI p130 CR France248

LODGE,William Wass 2Lt dow 17-4-18 6 att1Mddx p147 CR Belgium18

LODGER,Robert Egerton Capt dow 29-3-17 4RSuss p228

LODWICK,John Thornton.DSO.Capt drd 30-12-15 IA 2/3GurkhaRif p279 MR41

LOE,Harold Charles.MC.T2LtACapt kia 27-9-18 1Beds p86 MR16

LOEWE,Leopold TCapt kia 6-4-16 23RFA p32 CR Belgium28,107Bty

LOFT,A.A.Capt 15-6-16 RFA CR Yorks705

LOFT,Percy Trotter 2Lt kia 24-3-18 6 att18KRRC p151 MR20

LOFTHOUSE,George Hood 2Lt kia 23-4-17 4EYorks p219 MR20

LOFTING,Charles Edgar T2Lt dow 10-1-17 8NumbF p62 CR France701

LOFTUS,Henry Gordon TCapt kia 26-9-15 10Y&L p159 MR19

LOFTUS,Kenneth 2Lt ded 9-11-18 RFA p208 CR Surrey1

LOFTUS,William.MC.MID LtTCapt&Adjt dow 25-4-17 11RScotF p95&262 CR France40

LOGAN,Alexnder Taylor 2Lt kia 23-3-18 5CamH p168 MR27

LOGAN,Alfred Thomas.MID Capt kia 16-9-16 RAMC att3GrenGds p196 MR21

LOGAN,Arthur Capt kia 11-6-15 4RScotF p222 MR4

186

LOGAN,Crawford Randolph Capt kia 3-7-16 7Suff p78 CR France393

LOGAN,David Herbert Hosken 2Lt kia 1-7-16 2BordR p117 CR France394

LOGAN,Edward Townshaw.DSO.LtCol kia 25-9-15 15DLI att3Ches p161 MR19,Townshend 26-9-15

LOGAN,George Baillie Lt dow 6-5-17 2/8N&D p233 CR France122

LOGAN,Gordon Christie Lt kia 31-7-17 4BlkW p230 MR29

LOGAN,Hubert Henderson TCapt kia 15-9-16 10RWKent p141 CR France432

LOGAN,Hugh Lt ded 24-2-19 LeicYeo p204 CR Belgium406

LOGAN,John 2Lt kia 19-4-17 4RScotF p222 MR34

LOGAN,John Francis T2Lt kia 12-4-18 1RScotF p95 CR France410

LOGAN,John Hastie.MC.2LtACapt kia 1-8-17 13RScots p54 MR29

LOGAN,Joseph LtTCapt ded 21-4-18 2HLI p265 CR Scot798

LOGAN,Lionel Stuart Maj accShot 2-11-14 IA S&TCps p279 CR France354

LOGAN,Richard T2Lt kia 10-7-16 15HLI p163 CR France296

LOGAN,Robert 2Lt kia 12-10-17 3 att7SfthH p165 MR30

LOGAN,Robert 2Lt kia 20-10-18 4KOSB p224 CR France658

LOGAN,Rowland Octavius Capt kia 17-10-15 O&BLI att5Bn p130 CR Belgium113,Roland 16-10-15

LOGAN,Walter 2Lt kia 13-12-16 5ScotRif att1/6SStaffs p224 CR France745

LOGAN,William Alexander Ross 2Lt ded 19-2-19 MGC Inf p255 CR Scot503,Lt

LOGIE,Alexander Graham Spiers Capt ded 1-2-19 RAMC p270 CR Scot627

LOGIE,James Paton T2Lt kia 1-10-18 BordR att1GordH p117 CR France359

LOGSDAIL,Hugh 2Lt kia 19-9-18 RGA 99SB p40 CR France276

LOGSDON,Frank Lionel de Marche 2Lt kia 4-10-17 YLI att9Bn p143 MR30,Manché

LOMAS,Frank 2Lt kia 4-6-15 7Manch p237 MR4

LOMAS,George Archibald Colin.DCM.2Lt kia 22-5-16 20Lond p251 CR France924

LOMAS,George Guest TLt kia 22-3-18 Manch att2/6Bn p155 MR27

LOMAS,Harold TLt kia 1-7-16 20Manch p155 CR France397

LOMAS,John Henry T2Lt kia 30-8-16 4Lpool att98TMB p72 CR France402

LOMAX,Edward Harold TLtACapt kia 13-8-17 8SLancs p125 CR Belgium34

LOMAX,Gerald David 2Lt dow 11-5-15 3WelshR att2RBerks p127 CR France768

LOMAX,John 2Lt kia 18-8-16 3DCLI attRWar p114 CR France832

LOMAX,John Herbert TCapt dow 22-11-15 9RWar att9EKent p65 MR4

LOMAX,Samuel Holt.CB.LtGen dow 10-4-15 Staff p1 CR Hamps1

LOMAX,William Sinnott Lt kia 30-7-16 3 att7RScotF p95 MR21

LOMER,Henry Charles TCapt kia 5-5-17 GL 10RFC p10 CR France98

LONDON,Stanhope Francis.DCM.T2Lt kia 18-11-16 8NStaffs p157 CR France384

LONES,Percy East Capt kia 28-4-17 RAMC att5FA p196 CR France184

LONEY,Robert 2Lt kia 1-7-17 5N&D p233 MR19

LONG,Alfred Pocock Lt kld 23-3-17 7Mddx attRFC p19&235 CR Wilts25

LONG,Arthur Glanville Holland 2Lt dow 13-8-17 9Lond p248 CR Belgium7

LONG,Arthur Trevor D'Arcy Lt kia 21-8-15 1RInniskF p105 MR4

LONG,Arthur William Emanuel T2Lt kia 24-8-16 8 att1RWSurr p56 CR France390

LONG,Austin Theodore Lt kia 22-8-17 10RScots p212 MR30

LONG,Basil Andrew TCapt ded 10-2-17 11RLancs p59 CR France833

LONG,Bernard Wilfrid T2Lt kia 16-8-17 16WYorks p82 CR Belgium308

LONG,Charles Bernard 2Lt ded /-/-19 CldGds SR p262

LONG,Charles Henry T2Lt ded 19-2-18 HLI 1GarrBn p163 CR Scot235

LONG,Charles Percy T2Lt kia 13-4-17 RE att46RFC p10&46 CR Belgium11

LONG,Cyril Edwin Arnold Capt kia 27-3-18 15WYorks p82 CR France927

LONG,Daniel Edward 2Lt kia 28-5-18 1Lond p245 CR France54,Dennis

LONG,Francis Stuart Lt 8-9-16 1/5SLancs MR21

LONG,Francis William 2Lt dow PoW 28-6-16 94RFA p32 CR Belgium140

LONG,Frank Stevenson TLt kia 26-9-15 11Ess p132 MR19

LONG,Frederick Edward.MC.TCapt kia 24-8-17 11pool p72 CR Belgium19,11Bn

LONG,Frederick Joseph John Lt kia 31-7-17 RFA 37Bty p208 CR Belgium34

LONG,Guy Steer T2Lt kia 28-9-16 8Suff p78 CR France1170

LONG,Harold Dudley 2Lt kia 21-5-16 7Lond p247 MR20

LONG,Henry Archibald 2Lt kia 15-9-16 4NumbF p213 MR21

LONG,Horace Victor T2Lt dow 28-6-17 13NumbF C'Coy p62 CR France145

LONG,James William Capt kia 8/10-9-16 1/2Lond p245 MR21

LONG,John.MM.T2Lt kia 12-4-18 18DLI p161 CR France298

LONG,John T2Lt kia 4-11-18 RBerks att8Bn p139 CR France738

LONG,John Thomas 2Lt kld 10-10-17 53RFC &17Mddx p10 CR France285,dow

LONG,Leslie Paul Lt kia 25-9-15 1/20Lond p251 MR19 &CR France924

LONG,Reginald Stuart Lt kia 9-9-16 5SLancs p230

LONG,Violet Alice Lambton.OBE.DepChContr drd 2-8-18 QMAAC p200 MR40,3-8-18

LONG,Walter.CMG.DSO.MIDx2 TBrigGen kia 28-1-17 2Drags Cmdg56InfBde p21 CR France203

LONG,William Charles.MC.T2Lt dow 31-8-18 9RFus p68 CR France145

LONG,William Herbert Berkeley 2Lt dow 31-5-18 RGA 261SB p40 CR France84

LONG-INNES,Selwyn Lt kia 4-8-15 3RLancs p59 CR Belgium97,2Bn

LONG-PRICE,Cecil Evelyn Capt kia 7-8-15 9WYorks p82 MR4

LONGBOTHAM,Cyril Murgatroyd Capt ded 12-1-20 IA 1/72Punjabis p279 CR Europe51,dow

LONGBOTTOM,Donald Hough 2Lt kia 8-8-16 5Lpool p215 CR France630,Haigh

LONGBOTTOM,Edward Brooke Lt kia 9-10-17 7WYorks p218 CR Belgium123

LONGBOTTOM,Henry 2Lt kia 9-8-15 6SLancs p125 MR4

LONGBOTTOM,Robert T2Lt kia 31-7-15 7KRRC p151 MR29,30-7-15

LONGBOURNE,Hugh Richard.DSO.Capt kia 3-5-17 3RWSurr p56 CR France538,7Bn

LONGBOURNE,William Louis Jennings Lt kia 9-8-15 5 att2/4RWSurr p212 MR4

LONGCROFT,Thomas Roy 2Lt kia 25-9-15 3 att2Leic p88 MR19

LONGDEN,Alfred Henry Capt ded 2-3-19 5N&D p232 CR Notts32

LONGDEN,Ernest William Maj ded 21-8-18 4Y&L p238 CR Yorks543

LONGDEN,Frederick Cecil Capt kia 24-8-18 4 att15DLI p161 MR16

LONGFIELD,Charles Edmund.MID TCapt kia 10-3-18 6RMunstF p175 CR Palestine3

LONGFIELD,John Percival.MVO.Capt kia 30-9-15 3Norf p74 CR France166

LONGFORD,Thomas.KP.MVO.Earl BrigGen kia 21-8-15 HQ Cmdg2Mtd Bde Staff p1 CR Gallipoli5

LONGHURST,C.R. TMaj ded 8-3-18 NumbF p62 CR Numb74

LONGHURST,Harold George Fairfax TMajALtCol kia 12-10-17 6RBerks p139 MR30

LONGHURST,Seaward T2Lt kia 1-7-16 11N&D p134 CR France232

LONGLEY,Frank Arthur John 2Lt kia 18-6-17 7Lond att17KRRC p247 CR Belgium10,19-6-17

LONGLEY,Leslie Gordon T2Lt kia 12-7-16 15Lpool att19LancF p72 CR France296,Lt

LONGMAN,Frederick Lt kia 18-10-14 4RFus p68 MR22

LONGMAN,Valentine Sandford TLtAMaj kia 1-9-18 19RFA p32 CR France568

LONGMORE,Charles Gerard LtACapt ded 24-11-18 270RFA p207 CR Lebanon1

LONGRIDGE,Archibald Owen Carwithen Rev ded 12-10-18 RAChDept att11GH Boulogne p199 CR Devon200

LONGRIDGE,James Atkinson.CMG.LtCol kia 18-8-16 IA 43Erinpura attStaffHQ p279 CR France430

LONGSHAW,Charles Henry 2Lt dow 21-7-17 5SLancs p230 CR France345,2/4Bn

LONGSTAFF,Jack Campbell 2Lt kia 7-7-16 1/5Y&L p238 MR21

LONGSTER,William Ernest T2Lt kia 28-7-16 10Ches p96 CR France220

LONGTHORPE,Frederick T2Lt dow 20-9-18 TankCps p188 CR France278

LONGTON,Edward John 2Lt kia 6-6-15 3 att1Ess p132 MR4

LONGTON,John Lt kia 31-7-17 RASC &4RFC p10&193 MR20

LONGUEHAYE,James Stanley T2Lt kia 7-10-16 12 att6RWKent p141 MR21

LONGWORTH,Eustace Counsellor TCapt kia 26-9-16 9LancF p92 MR21

LONGWORTH-DAMES,Thomas Dudley Lt ded 28-11-19 6CarabDragGds p261 CR Eire475 &CR Ireland14

LONNEN,Leslie Edgar John Lt kld 16-8-16 RFC p3

LONSDALE,Arthur Carr Glyn Lt kia 10-3-15 6KRRC att2RScotF p151 CR France525

LONSDALE,James Raymond McLintock Lt ded 29-10-14 4Huss p21 CR Ches198

LONSDALE,Thomas Wilkes.MC.TCapt dow 5-6-16 7DCLI p114 CR France134,kia

LOOBY,Patrick Chap4Cl kia 26-10-17 RAChDept p199 CR Belgium1216

LOOK,John Leopold TLt dow 1-9-18 1Glouc att1/5Dev p107 CR France84,2Lt

LOOKER,Arthur Donald T2Lt kia 8-10-18 Suff 1GarrBn att15Ess p78 CR France1092

LOOKER,Leonard Davies 2Lt kia 1-8-17 5RWSurr p212 MR29

LOOMES,Herbert Rueben Lt kia 14-9-14 1LNLancs p136 MR15

LOOS,Cecil George Bertram Lt kia 13-3-15 3Worc p109 CR Belgium17,12-3-15

LORD,Arthur John Harry.DCM.2Lt kia 18-9-18 1/2 att7Leic p88 CR France415

LORD,Albert Edward.MM.T2Lt dow 29-4-18 12Yorks p90 CR Yorks467

LORD,Arthur Capt dow 12-2-17 3WelshR p127 CR Belgium18

LORD,Arthur George 2Lt kia 20-7-16 3 att2RWFus p98 MR21

LORD,Charles Henry TMaj ded 30-12-14 10RWFus p98 CR Hamps13

LORD,Cuthbert Edward HonMaj dow 23-6-15 3 att1SStaffs p122 CR France102

LORD,Douglas Frears Lt kia 26-5-17 RFA X27TMB p208 CR Belgium167,27-5-17

LORD,Ernest Joseph T2Lt kia 21-3-18 4TankCps p188

LORD,Eustace Charles Gabriel 2Lt kia 8-5-18 1IrGds p53 CR France925

LORD,Evelyn Geoffrey TLt ded 25-6-18 37MGC Inf p184 CR Lancs491

LORD,Frank Samuel 2Lt dow 12-3-15 2Dev p77 CR France768

LORD,George Hammond Lt kld 30-11-17 256RFA p208 CR Belgium18

LORD,Henry Otto TLt kia 1-7-16 26Manch p155 CR France397

LORD,Hugh Cecil 2Lt kia 26-10-17 Dev p77 MR30

LORD,John Frederick Wilson 2Lt kia 9-4-17 5YLI p235 CR France1185

LORD,Reginald Hollins.MC.Capt dow 25-11-18 B245RFA p207 CR France146

LORD,Roland Capt kia 8-10-18 3 att2NumbF p62 CR France338

LORENZEN,Olto Hans Hermann 2Lt dow 2-7-16 7Mddx p235 CR France120

LORIMER,Hugh Cowan Lt ded 27-11-18 5DCLI p270 CR Devon153

LORIMER,James Bannerman Capt kia 3-5-17 5CamH att8RB p168 MR20

LORIMER,John Scott.MC.2LtTCapt kia 5-11-17 1Norf att95TMB p74 MR30

LORIMER,Robert 2Lt kia 14-3-17 4RScots att1/5SStaffs p211 CR France281

LORING,Charles Buxton Maj kia 21-12-14 IA 37Lancers att34PoonaHorse p279 MR28

LORING,Charles Michael 2Lt kia 3-9-16 2RWar p65 MR21

LORING,Robert Nele 2Lt kia 16-6-15 5 att3Worc p109 MR29

LORING,Walter Latham LtCol kia 23-10-14 1RWar p65 MR29

LORING,William Capt dow 24-10-15 ScotHorse p205 MR4

LORY,J.J.Capt 12-12-18 MilLabCps CR EAfrica36

LOSH,James Norman Merryweather 2Lt kia 4-10-17 3Lincs p75 MR30

LOTAN,William Desmond Guthrie T2Lt kld 10-12-16 RFC p3 CR Eire319

LOTT,John Cyprian.MC.2Lt kia 13-4-18 3 att11ELancs p111 CR France193

LOTT,John English.MC.T2Lt dow 21-8-17 RE 4FldSurCo p46 CR France1468,21-5-17

LOTT,William T2Lt kia 7-10-16 14RSuss p119 MR21

LOUDON,James Brugh Livingstone Lt kia 13-4-18 6ScotRif p224 MR32

LOUDON,Robert TLt kia 13-9-18 13RScots p54 CR France179

LOUDON,Robert Gavin Morton Lt kia 12-5-16 6ScotRif p224 CR France114,11-5-16

LOUDON-SHAND,Stewart Walter.VC.TMaj kia 1-3-17 10Yorks p90 CR France189,1-7-17

LOUDOUN,Thomas 2Lt kia 8-6-18 2BlkW p129 CR Palestine9,LOUDON

LOUGH,Frederick George 2Lt kia 21-3-18 B88RFA p32 CR France905

LOUGHER,Gwylym Robert Lt&QM ded 21-9-17 RAMC WelshCCS p254 CR Egypt9

LOUIS,Gerald John TCapt dow 23-5-16 RASC 19MT AuxCoy p193 CR France924,22-5-16

LOUSADA,Bertie Charles Capt kia 9-5-15 1Y&L p159 MR29

LOUSADA,Edward Arthur Lt kia 2-11-14 2RSuss p119 MR29

LOVATT,Charles.MC.T2Lt kia 12-4-18 26NumbF att4Beds p62 CR France252

LOVE,Henry John.MM.T2Lt dow 2-11-18 RBerks Resatt2/4Bn p139 CR France332

LOVE,James Ellis T2Lt kia 2-9-18 18Manch p155 CR France308

LOVE,James Robert T2Lt kia 17-8-17 3RMunstF p175 MR30,18-8-17

LOVE,Reysom 2Lt kia 3-12-17 8 att2/5RWar p215 MR17

LOVE,Ronald Andrew 2Lt dow 1-11-18 9RInniskF p105

LOVE,Ronald Barclay T2Lt kia 15-3-16 8Lincs p75 CR France922.Lt

LOVEBAND,Arthur.CMG.LtCol kia 25-5-15 2RDubF p177 MR29

LOVEBAND,Arthur Reginald TCapt kia 6-12-14 1WYorks p82 CR France82

LOVEDAY,Charles Norton T2Lt kia 12-10-17 54MGC Infp184 MR30

LOVEDAY,Claude Godfrey 2Lt kia 10-10-16 2N&D p134 CR France374

LOVEDAY,Francis William.DSO.BtLtCol ded 15-9-19 RA p261 CR Devon207,16RGA

LOVEGROVE,Sidney Joseph Capt dow 14-3-16 NStaffs att3KAR p157&202 CR EAfrica52

LOVEITT,Alan Percy Charles 2Lt kia 25-7-16 7RWar p214 MR21

LOVELACE,Ronald Desmond Weston(Dick) 2Lt kia 26-10-17 1RWKent p141 MR30

LOVELACE-TAYLOR,Arthur George T2Lt kia 9-10-16 1RWar p65 MR21

LOVELL,Charles Ernest TLt dow 21-3-17 RE 62FC p46 CR France46

LOVELL,Clarence John 2Lt kia 19-10-17 RGA 274SB p40 CR Belgium84

LOVELL,Cyril Thomas T2Lt kia 14-6-18 9MGC &RFC p184 CR France27,15-6-18

LOVELL,Edward Caton 2Lt kia 12-11-17 5LancF p221 CR Belgium128

LOVELL,John Anthony T2Lt kia 22-1-16 2LifeGds B'Sqdn p20 CR France423

LOVELL,John Cuthbert TLt kia 1-8-17 10ScotRif p103 CR Belgium7

LOVELL,Leslie Graham T2Lt kia 11-4-17 GL 48RFC p10 MR20

LOVELL,Robert Clifford T2Lt kia 26-1-18 101RFC p16 CR France200,kld

LOVELL,William Leslie 2Lt kia 27-7-17 8RWKent &25RFC p10&141 CR France88

LOVELOCK,Clifford Andrew 2Lt ded 20-11-18 5 att26RWFus p223 CR France34,LOVELUCK

LOVER,Charles TLt ded 1-9-18 NStaffs attY&L p157 CR Ches19

LOVEROCK,Harold George 2Lt dow 5-8-16 1/1WarYeo p205 CR Egypt2

LOVETT,Alfred Crowdy.CB.CBE.TBrigGen ded 27-5-19 1Glouc p107&257 CR Yorks185

LOVETT,Owen.MID Capt kia 24-4-17 10Dev p77 MR37,25-4-17

LOVETT-THOMAS,Richard Sackville.MC.2Lt dow 12-3-17 165RFA p32 CR France1327

LOW,Alexander Petrie Capt kia 14-7-16 RAMC att7SfthH p253 MR21

LOW,Alexander Sturrock T2Lt kia 23-6-17 10ScotRif p103 CR Belgium6

LOW,David Carmichael 2Lt kia 18-7-16 1GordH p166 MR21

LOW,David Finlay 2Lt kia 26-10-17 16RScots p54 MR30

LOW,Eustace Bertram T2Lt kia 24-3-17 GL 4RFC p10 CR France561

LOW,George 2Lt kia 25-9-15 4GordH p242 MR29

LOW,George Alexander 2Lt kia 28-9-18 2RScotF p95 CRBelgium112

LOW,James Morrison Lt kia 1-7-16 2SfthH attMGC p165&184 MR21

LOW,John 2Lt kia 10-1-18 13KRRC p151 MR30

LOW,John Jackson.MC.MM.T2Lt kia 3-12-17 RE F'SpCo p46 CR Belgium307

LOW,John James 2Lt kia 3-8-17 1 att13NumbF p62 MR20

LOW,Joseph Davidson McKenzie 2Lt kia 13-7-16 6RScots p211 MR21

LOW,Thomas Cartrae Capt ded 30-10-19 MGC Inf p266 MR43,Carfrae

LOWCOCK,R.J.DSO.MC.Maj ded 22-7-18 N&D &RAF p134 CR Wilts4

LOWDEN,Norman.MID 2Lt kia 21-3-18 9RInniskF att109TMB p105 CR France672,Lt

LOWDER,Noel Reginald 2Lt kia 3-5-17 1RWar p65 MR20

LOWE,Albert Frank TLt ded 23-2-19 TankCps p266

LOWE,Alexander Lt kia 24-11-17 10SWBord Brecknock p223 CR France922

LOWE,Arthur Cecil.CMG.DSO.TLtColBrigGen kia 24-11-17 RFA p206 CR Belgium84

LOWE,Arthur Denis Worsley.MC.2Lt kia 4-10-17 3SWBord p100 MR30

LOWE,Ernest Archer 2Lt kia 26-9-17 5Lincs p220 MR19

LOWE,George Alexander T2Lt kia 4-12-16 15RScots p54 CR France83,Lt

LOWE,George Ernest.MC.2Lt kia 28-10-18 15WelshR p127 CR France230

LOWE,George Stanley 2Lt kia 18-9-18 8RFus att9Bn p68 CR France212

LOWE,Henry Griffith Pagan.DCM.T2Lt kia 8-11-16 GL &45RFC p3&190 CR France134,kld

LOWE,Henry Shanten Lt dow 21-10-14 2Worc p109 CR France477,Stanley

LOWE,James William TLt ded 3-8-19 RE p262 CR Lebanon1

LOWE,John Edmund.MC.2Lt kia 1-7-17 5NStaffs p238 MR19

LOWE,Joseph T2Lt kia 26-3-18 8 att1RDubF p177 MR27

LOWE,Maurice Lt kia 27-6-17 GL 19RFC p10 CR Belgium115

LOWE,Norman McGregor.DCM.2Lt kia 10-1-16 14Lond p249 CR France423

LOWE,Richard Conway.MC.MID TCapt kia 18-8-16 6RWar p214 CR France832

LOWE,Richard Heath Capt kia 9-10-17 6Ess p232 MR30

LOWE,Ronald Charles Lt dow PoW 18-8-18 8Lpool p215 CR France525

LOWE,Thomas Henry T2Lt kia 23-4-17 7BordR p117 MR20

LOWE,William TLt kia 5-7-16 7ELancs p111 CR France267

LOWE,William Erl Bridson.MC&Bar.ACapt kia 28-5-18 2ELancs p255 MR18

LOWE,William James T2Lt kia 27-4-16 8CamH attTMB p168 CR France480

LOWE,William Norman ACapt kia 24-11-17 14HLI att13ESurr p163 MR17

LOWENSTEIN,Jack Charles 2Lt kld 9-5-18 GL &RAF p190 CR France102

LOWER,Neil Eustace T2Lt kia 30-6-17 9MGC Inf p184 CR France550,Lt

LOWERY,Allan Maxwell TCapt dow 24-3-17 GL 70RFC p10 MR20

LOWERY,Thomas.DCM.T2Lt kia 3-8-17 15DLI p161 CR France1489

LOWES,Ernest Ion 2Lt dow PoW 2-6-18 5DLI p239 CR France1753

LOWIS,John Rollo Capt kia 4-9-18 HampsYeo p203 CR Belgium111

LOWNDES,Charles Arthur 2Lt kia 13-10-15 5NStaffs p238 MR19

LOWNDES,Richard Forbes 2Lt kia 14-11-16 5 att1KRRC p151 CR France533

LOWNDS,Reginald Herbert T2Lt ded 17-3-17 GL 43RFC p10 MR20

LOWRIE,James Harold T2Lt dow 25-1-17 9 att7EYorks p84 CR Europe1

LOWRIE,John Edward T2Lt kia 18-6-17 HouseholdBn p20 CR France546,17-6-17

LOWRY,Auriol Ernest Eric.DSO.MC.CaptALtCol kia 23-9-18 2WYorks p82 CR France268

LOWRY,Cyril John Patrick Lt kia 25-3-18 2WYorks p82 MR27

LOWRY,Henry Cooke Capt ded 11-7-16 RAVC p198 CR Iraq6

LOWRY,John T2Lt ded 4-5-17 9 att2KSLI p145 CR Greece7

LOWRY,Joseph Ewart TLt kia 25-8-18 2RIrReg p89 CR France239,2Lt

LOWRY,Sidney Henry.MC.Capt kia 31-7-17 Herts p252 MR29

LOWRY,Vyvyan Charles Lt kia 9-4-18 5ESurr attMGC p187&226 CR France1092

LOWRY,William Augustine Harper 2Lt mbk 4-6-15 IARO att14Sikhs p279 MR4

LOWRY COLE,Arthur Willoughby George.CB.DSO.BrigGen dow 9-5-15 Staff 25InfBde CR France566

LOWRY-CORRY,A Maj 12-2-21 RAOC CR Egypt3

LOWRY-CORRY,A.V.MC.Lt kia 12-9-16 1GrenGds CR France394

LOWRY-CORRY,Frederick Richard Henry TLt dow 30-9-15 C47RFA p32 CR France40

LOWSON,Courtenay Patrick Flowerdew Lt kld 3-11-17 1RB attRFC p10&179 CR Scot187

LOWSON,Matthew Stewart 2Lt kia 14-7-16 2BordR p117 CR France432

LOWSON,Norman Coutie.MC.TCapt dow 6-3-17 RE 7DivSigs p46 CR France41

LOWSON,Wilfred Robert 2Lt kia 16-9-16 5Yorks p221 CR France239,15-9-16

LOWSON,William 2Lt dow 17-11-16 8RScots p212 CR France74

LOWTH,Francis Robert Leslie.MID Capt mbk 22-8-18 2 att9LancF p256 MR4

LOWTH,John Leslie T2Lt kia 4-10-17 12/13NumbF p62 MR30

LOWTHER,Carl T2Lt kia 16-8-17 11Manch p155 MR30

LOWTHER,Ernest Frederick T2Lt kia 14-6-18 2Manch att96TMB p155 CR France924,4-6-18

LOWTHER,Rowland TCaptAMaj ded 10-11-18 RASC MT p193 CR France1028

LOWTHER,Thomas Beresford Lt kia 4-6-15 2LancF att1NumbFp92 MR29

LOWTHER,William 2Lt kia 27-5-18 Yorks p90 MR18

LOWY,Walter Albert TCapt dow 3-9-18 13 att10Hamps p121 CR Greece6

LOXLEY,Arthur Harry 2Lt kia 9-4-17 4NStaffs att6YLI p157 CR France581

LOXLEY,Charles Eric Smart.MID TCapt ded 18-12-18 Ess attMGC Inf p132&184 CR Egypt9

LOXTON,Charles Edward Holden 2Lt dow 23-5-15 1/5NStaffs p238 CR Belgium170

LOXTON,Lionel D'Estelle T2Lt kia 29-8-18 10SWBord p100 CR France217

LOY,Martin William TLt kia 28-8-16 RAMC p196 CR France246

LOYD,Alfred William Kirkman Maj ded 13-2-19 1RSuss p264 CR Kent280,2Bn

LOYD,Alwyne Travers Capt kia 28-9-17 5EKent att32RFC p19&213 CR Belgium11

LOYD,Geoffrey Archibald.MID Lt dow 13-11-14 2ScotsGds p52 CR Belgium150,kia

LOYD,Godfrey Beaumont.MC.Capt dow 1-12-17 12KRRC D'Coy p151 CR France446

LOYD,Lewis Frederick Innes AMaj ded 21-9-18 2/1LovatScouts attWorcHuss p204 CR Essex242

LOYD,Reginald Percy.MC.LtACapt kia 1-12-17 3CldGds p51 CR France662

LUARD,Charles Elmhurst.DSO.Maj kia 15-9-14 1Norf p74 MR15

LUARD,Edward Bourryan.DSO.TLtCol dow 24-4-16 KSLI p145 CR Belgium11,Bourryua

LUARD,Peter Dalbiac Lt mbk 19-9-18 3 att11ScotRif p256 MR37

LUBBOCK,Eric Fox Pitt.Hon.MC.TCapt kia 11-3-17 GL &45RFC p10 190&258 CR Belgium11

LUBBOCK,Harold Fox Pitt.Hon.Lt kia 4-4-18 2GrenGds p50 CR France1183

LUBY,Thomas William 2Lt kia 5-10-16 6 att3Worc p109 CR France246

LUCAS,Aberon Thomas.Lord Capt kia 3-11-16 HampsYeo &RFC p203 CR France568,Auberon

LUCAS,Albert James T2Lt dow 16-5-17 GL 66RFC p10 CR France120

LUCAS,Algernon 2Lt kld 28-4-16 KEdwsHorse p24 CR Ireland14,29-4-16

LUCAS,Arthur Geoffrey.MC.Lt dow 25-11-17 IA 127Baluchis att2/124 p279 CR Iraq8

LUCAS,Charles Lucas Clement 2Lt dow 30-6-17 Nhampt att7Bn p137 CR Belgium11,Leslie

LUCAS,Christopher Hollins T2Lt kia 11-4-18 8NStaffs p157 MR30,10-4-18

LUCAS,Clifton Malet T2Lt kia 10-7-16 4SWBord att15WelshR p100 MR21

LUCAS,Ernest Lt kia 18-9-18 2 att7SWBord p100 MR37

LUCAS,Ernest Henry Austin Lt kia 7-6-17 5Y&L p238 MR29

LUCAS,Frederick Gerald Bazalgette.MC.TCapt dow 10-8-17 6Beds p86 CR France285,Frederic

LUCAS,Frederick Richard 2Lt kld 21-10-16 RFC p3 CR Essex1,20-10-16

LUCAS,Gerald Blunt Capt dow 16-5-16 IA 38CentIndHorse att13RFC p279 CR France15

LUCAS,Harold Clement Montagu Lt mbk 2-11-14 IA 2/2GurkhaRif p279 MR28

LUCAS,James Edward T2LtACapt kia 5-5-17 10DLI p161 CR France581

LUCAS,John T2Lt dow 28-12-17 17RFus p68 CR France512

LUCAS,Keith Capt kld 5-10-16 attRFC p19 CR Hamps1

LUCAS,Lord Alberon Thomas Capt kia 3-11-16 HampsYeo attRFC p19

LUCAS,Malcolm Hugh.DSO.LtCol ded 2-8-20 IA 37Lancers InspGenSPersiaRif p279

LUCAS,Norman Carey T2Lt dow 2-10-16 6RIrRif p169 CR Greece4

LUCAS,Perceval Drewett 12Lt dow 6-7-16 10 att2BordR p117&257 CR France51,Percival

LUCAS,Reginald Blockley Capt kia 3-7-16 RAMC att7Norf p196 MR21

LUCAS,Robert Capt ded 1-11-18 52/15RFA p32 CR France40

LUCAS,Roy Herbert Charles TLt kld 25-12-15 RAVC att20RFA p198 CR France816

LUCAS,Sidney Richard 2Lt ded 6-11-18 RASC p193 CR Nhampt55

LUCAS,Thomas Charles Harvey Lt kia 6-2-17 Suff &20RFC p78&10 CR Belgium115

LUCAS,Thomas Farquhar Lt kia 16-6-17 3RWar att20BallCoRFC p10&65 CR Belgium6

LUCAS,Thomas Henry Lt kld 15-5-18 Hamps &RAF p121 CR Egypt9

LUCAS,Victor Carrington.MC.Lt kia 7-6-17 A236RFA p208 CR Belgium167

LUCAS,Wilfrid 2Lt kia 23-12-16 100RFA p32 CR Greece6 23/24-12-16

LUCAS,William Herbert TLt dow 21-1-16 8NStaffs p157 CR France345

LUCAS-TOOTH,Archibald Leonard Lucas.Bart Maj ded 12-7-18 2/1B'HAC p206 CR France95

LUCAS-TOOTH,Douglas Keith Lucas.DSO.Capt kia 13-9-14 9Lancers p22 CR France1340,dow 14-9-14

LUCAS-TOOTH,Selwyn Lucas Capt kia 20-10-14 LancF p263 CR Belgium32

LUCHFORD,Harry George Ernest.MC.Capt kia 2-12-17 20RFC p10 MR20

LUCIE-SMITH,Evan Lt kia 25-4-15 RWar p65 CR 32,Euan

LUCK,John Lewis T2Lt dow 6-9-18 WYorks att1/7Bn p82 CR Kent285

LUCK,Nelson Amos T2Lt kia 15-6-18 1RWKent att1/10 O&BLI p141 CR Italy2

LUCK,Percy 2Lt 4-11-19 Lincs CR Beds75

LUCKETT,John Spokes Lt dow 24-5-15 RIrReg p89 CR France285

LUCKHURST,William 2Lt kia 24-4-17 4Yorks p220 MR20

LUCKING,Frank Horatio 2Lt kia 28-4-17 3 att10Lincs p75 MR20

LUCKMANN,Harold John.MC.T2Lt kia 10-4-18 11 att10Worc p109 MR30,LUCKMAN

LUCY,Reginald Eric Lt dow 20-3-15 2Nhampt p137 CR Devon1,19-3-15

LUDLAM,Eric Wollaston 2Lt kia 28-3-18 7Manch p237 MR20,8Bn

LUDLOW,Ernest.MC.Capt kld 16-2-18 4GrenGds p50 CR Surrey160

LUDLOW,Frank Hubert Charles 2Lt kia 23-11-17 1/20 att1/2Lond p251 MR17

LUDLOW,John Coape ACapt dow 15-12-16 1RInniskF D'Coy p105 CR France145

LUDLOW,Leonard Gordon Sutton Lt kia 11-8-18 4YLI p256 MR30

LUDLOW,Lionel 2Lt kia 8-10-16 9Lond p248 MR21

LUDLOW,Stratford Walter Capt kia 1-7-16 1/8RWar C'Coy p214 CR France1890

LUFF,Edgar William Guy Lt kia 25-3-18 63MGC p184 MR20

LUGARD,Edward March 2Lt kld 30-7-18 1RLancs &RAF p59 CR Lond8

LUGER,Arthur LtACapt dow 13-8-18 1Leinst p174 CR Palestine3

LUGTON,George Deane 2Lt kia 30-11-17 8ScotRif p225 CR France647,Deans 30-11-18

LUIS,Eric George Vincent T2Lt kia 6-10-16 6 O&BLI p130 MR21

LUKE,John Norman 2Lt kia 9-9-18 5DLI p239 CR France908

LUKER,Frank Percy 2Lt ded 1-11-18 1GarrBn Worc &RAF p264 CR Bucks39

LUKEY,Charles Ximis 2Lt kia 24-6-16 1RWar p65 CR France35,Charley Ximines

LUKIS,Charles Pardy.Hon.Sir.KCSI.VD.SurgGen ded 21-10-17 IA IMS p279 MR65

LUKIS,Leofwin Collings Fellowes 2Lt kia 6-1-17 Ess &27RFC p10&132 CR France808

LUKIS,Theodore Stewart Capt dow 15-3-15 13Lond p249 CR France102

LUKYN,Stanley Edward.MC.2Lt kld 10-4-17 3RWSurr attRFC p56&10,ded CR Mddx76,1Bn

LUKYN-WILLIAMS,Herbert Temple TCapt dow 26-3-18 RAMC att15N&D p196 CR France

LUMB,Herbert T2Lt ded 8-10-15 A66RFA p32 MR4

LUMB,Joseph William.MC.2Lt dow 30-10-18 1/4WRid p227 CR France40

LUMGAIR,Robert Robertson Morrison Capt kia 19-4-17 1/4KOSB p223 CR Palestine8

LUMLEY,Corale Nurse 25-11-18 VAD CR NZ243

LUMLEY,Frederick William 2Lt kia 10-4-17 27NumbF p62 MR20

LUMLEY,Henry Ralph 2Lt kia 11-3-18 RFC p16 CR Lond12

LUMLEY,Richard John 2Lt kia 17-10-14 11Huss p22 CR Belgium69

LUMMIS,Ralph 2Lt kia 4-10-17 Lincs att12/13NumbF p75 MR30

LUMSDEN,Alfred Forbes.DSO.BrigGen kia 24-6-18 RScots Staff 46InfBdeHQ p54 CR France113

LUMSDEN,Bertie Noel Capt kia 23-4-15 SfthH p165 CR Belgium128

LUMSDEN,Carlos Barron TMaj ded 8-3-16 18HLI p163 CR France354

LUMSDEN,Charles Ramsey Capt kia 26-8-14 1GordH p166 MR15

LUMSDEN,David Aitken Capt kia 1-5-15 4Lpool p72 MR29

LUMSDEN,Henry Tailyour Capt ded 21-6-15 CamH &RFC p168&1,kld CR Scot294

LUMSDEN,Joseph Charles T2Lt kia 11-10-18 2NumbF p62 CR France1392

LUNAN,George Harold Lt kia 13-5-15 RAMC p196 CR Belgium126

LUNAN,James 2Lt kia 20-9-17 4GordH p242 CR Belgium126,Lt

LUND,Charles Lt kia 19-2-20 IA 1/8GurkhaRif att3/11 p279 MR43

LUND,Clifford Bullen Lt ded 31-12-19 RASC p267 CR Surrey1

LUND,Gilbert William T2Lt kia 9-10-17 WYorks att1/7Bn p82 MR30

LUND,Tom Clough Lt kia 23-3-18 1/4NumbF p213 MR27

LUND,William Bullen TLt drd 13-8-15 RASC p193 MR4

LUNDIE,Eric Balfour 2Lt kia 12-9-17 3CldGds p51 MR30

LUNDIE,James Edward 2Lt dow 29-3-18 4/5BlkW p230 CR France145

LUNDIE,Robert Charles.DSO.MIDx2 CaptAMaj kia 15-10-18 RE 93FC p46 CR France658,14-10-18

LUNDIUS,James Philip Lt kia 28-5-16 1/5GordH p242 CR France15

LUNN,Frank Victor 2Lt kia 31-5-18 8Lpool p216 CR France204

LUNN,Gilbert Alfred Lt ded 15-10-18 2/6RSuss p228 MR67

LUNN,Henry Anderson Capt ded 5-3-17 RAMC attColabaSHospBombay p196 MR65

LUNN,Herbert Charles Lt kia 22-3-17 3 att1RScots p54 MR20

LUNN,Ralph William 2Lt dow 17-6-17 B15RFA p32 CR France1182

LUNNON,George John 2Lt kia 27-4-15 2DCLI p114 MR29

LUNO,Evanston Holt Lt kia 20-7-18 4GordH p241 CR France622

LUNT,Arthur Towers T2Lt dow 17-8-16 15Lpool p72 CR France66,13Bn

LUNT,Christopher 2Lt kia 10-8-17 3 att9LNLancs p136 MR29

LUNT,Douglas Gordon Capt kia 16-7-16 5RWar p214 CR France832

LUPTON,Francis Ashford Maj kia 19-2-17 8WYorks p219 CR France514

LUPTON,Frank T2Lt kia 25-4-17 10Y&L p159 MR20

LUPTON,Frank William T2Lt kia 4-8-16 att9RFus p68 MR21

LUPTON,Joseph Brookes 2Lt kia 20-11-17 2/5LancF p221 CR France924

LUPTON,Lionel Martineux Lt kia 16-7-16 RFA p208 CR France296

LUPTON,Maurice Capt kia 19-6-15 7WYorks p218 CR France525

LUPTON,Reginald TCapt dow 22-8-15 9WYorks p82 MR4,8-8-15

LUPTON,Reginald Banister T2Lt ACapt kia 1-8-17 12RSuss p119 CR Belgium20

LUSCOMBE,Gridland John T2Lt kia 3-5-19 9 att7Beds p86 MR20

LUSCOMBE,Henry Lt kia 11-4-17 3Lond p245 CR France1185

LUSH,Charles William T2Lt kia 14-11-16 11RWar p65 CR France156

LUSH-WILSON,Herbert Geoffrey Maj kia 21-7-16 Y15RFA p32 CR France131

LUSHINGTON,Cecil Henry Gossett Lt kia 3-7-16 10Worc p109 MR21

LUSHINGTON,Sydney Edward James Chippendale TLt dow 25-9-16 GL 11Hamps att41Div ADC HQ p190 CR France40

LUSK,James Capt dow 28-12-15 1/6ScotRif p224 CR France300

LUTENER,George Arthur T2Lt kia 31-1-17 RE 15FC p46 CR France624

LUTENER,Richard Arthur Maurice T2Lt kia 6-4-16 6KSLI p145 CR Belgium73

LUTYENS,Charles Grae Capt dow 8-8-15 6ELancs p111 CR Gallipoli20,9-8-15

LUTYENS,Charles John Lionel Lt dow 3-10-17 A156RFA p32 Belgium131

LUTYENS,Cyril Arthur George Lt kia 9-10-17 3CldGds p51 MR30

LUTYENS,Lionel Gallwey.MC.CaptAMaj dow 6-1-18 123/28RFA p32 CR Belgium12

LYALL,Archibald Lt kia 2-7-16 15HLI B'Coy p163 CR France296,3-7-16

LYALL,Charles Genie Capt kld 18-10-14 1Lincs p75 MR22,George

LYALL,David Ivor 2Lt kia 18-10-16 3 att2Wilts p153 MR21

LYALL,Francis Gerald 2Lt kia 9-12-16 1BordR p117 CR France374

LYALL,George William 2Lt ded 7-12-17 6ResRegofCav p24 CR Wilts115 6-12-17

LYALL,James T2Lt dow 14-11-16 1GordH p166 CR France203

LYALL,James Thomson TLt kia 2-7-16 15HLI D'Coy p163 CR France296,3-7-16

LYBURN,John Jardine 2Lt ded 13-10-16 116RFA p32 CR Greece7

LYCETT,Lawrence Henley 2Lt dow 31-5-18 3 att1SStaffs p122 MR18,att4Bn

LYCETT,Timothy.DSO.LtTCapt dow 5-10-18 12KRRC p151 CR France106

LYCETT,William Bernard T2Lt dow 24-7-16 8Nhampt att1/5Glouc p137 CR France169,kia 3Bn

LYDDIARD,Francis Alfred 2Lt ded 22-4-19 RGA p262 CR Surrey15

LYDDON,Ernest Hugh Capt kia 31-10-14 Beds p86 MR29

LYDDON,Frederick Cyril 2Lt dow 26-4-15 ULIA att4Lpool p279 CR Belgium4

LYDEKKER,Cyril Richard Lt kia 15-8-15 5Beds p219 CR Gallipoli4

LYDEKKER,Gerard Owen Lt&QM ded 14-6-17 1/5Beds p219 CR Egypt1

LYDE-MALCOLM,Sackville Malcolm Berkeley Capt ded 17-10-18 NumbF p262 CR Mddx66

LYE,Gilbert 2Lt dow 27-7-16 4 att23Manch p155 CR France23,Lt kia 21-7-16

LYE,Robert Cobb.DSO.LtCol ded 28-6-17 IA 2/34SikhPnrs p279 MR67,27-6-17

LYELL,Charles Henry.Hon.Maj ded 18-10-18 RGA p209 CR USA234

LYELL,David 2Lt kia 12-7-15 7RScots p211 MR4

LYELL,James Francis Ronaldson Lt kld 25-11-17 3 att2RScots p54 CR France563

LYLE,Geoffrey Samuel La Warre 2Lt dow 29-4-17 2 O&BLI p130 CR France95

LYLE,Hedley Robert T2Lt kia 24-5-16 9GordH p166 CR France423,23-5-16

LYLE,James Vernon T2Lt kia 23-1-17 GL 45RFC p10 CR Belgium140

LYLE,John Clevendon Capt ded 6-12-16 RASC p253 CR Cornwall148

LYLE,Thomas Basil 2Lt kia 9-5-15 1BlkW p129 MR22

LYLE,William TLtCol kia 1-7-16 23NumbF p62 CR France150

LYNAM,James Michael.MC.Lt ded 29-12-17 RAOC p198 CR Ireland12

LYNCH,Bartholomew Patrick TLt kia 15-9-16 RB att9Bn p179 MR21

LYNCH,Colmer William Donald.DSO.TLtCol kia 2-7-16 9YLI p143 CR France189,1-7-17

LYNCH,Denis T2Lt kia 23-3-18 10 att15WYorks p82 MR20

LYNCH,Francis William 2Lt kia 27-4-15 4 att1ConnRgrs p172 CR Belgium92,26-4-15

LYNCH,Gilbert Edwin Lt kia 21-3-18 7DLI att7RIrRif p239 MR27

LYNCH,Harold Francis 2Lt kia 16-5-15 1RWFus p98 CR France279

LYNCH,James Meacher 2Lt kia 1-10-18 4RScots p211 CR Belgium160

LYNCH,James Stewart Lt kia 30-11-17 1RGLI p201 MR17

LYNCH,James Walker T2Lt kia 31-7-17 MGC HB p184 CR Blegium63,TankCps

LYNCH,Jasper Beverley Capt kia 5-3-17 IA 12Cav attStaff 6CavBde p279 MR38

LYNCH,John 2Lt kia 3-5-15 RFA p32 MR29

LYNCH,Joseph Edward TCapt kia 26-9-15 10Yorks p90 MR19

LYNCH,Michael John Lt ded 15-10-18 IARO att100LabCps p279 MR43,2Lt

LYNCH,Palric Stephen.MC.ACapt kia 27-12-16 7 att2Leinst p174 CR France149

LYNCH,Reginald Francis.MID Capt kia 8-3-16 2Manch p155 MR38 Ex 1Bn

LYNCH,Thomas 2Lt dow 29-4-17 20LancF p92 CR France610

LYNCH-STAUNTON,Eric Margrave 2Lt kia 9-5-17 3Lond p246 MR20

LYNCH-STAUNTON,Geoffrey 2Lt kia 5-3-17 13Huss p22 MR38

LYNCH-STAUNTON,Reginald Kirkpatrick.DSO&Bar.MIDx5 BtLtCol dow 7-11-18 220RFA p32 CR Iraq8

LYNDALL,Joseph Gwynne T2Lt kia 3-5-17 8KRRC p151 MR20

LYNDEN-BELL,Donald Percival Lt kia 25-4-15 1RIrF p171 CR Belgium96

LYNDEN-BELL,Colin Sutherland Lt ded 21-2-17 IA 99Inf att13Rajputs p279 CR Iraq6

LYNE,Charles Vyvyan TCapt kia 18-10-16 17WelshR p127 CR France149,19-10-16

LYNE,Cyril Lionel Bishop 2Lt kia 13-11-16 11Ess p132 MR21,13Bn

LYNES,Arthur Cecil D'Arcy 2Lt kia 10-7-15 1RBerks p139 CR Belgium121

LYNES,Wynne Parr Capt ded 8-10-16 5KRRC p151

LYNESS,Harold T2Lt dow 2-9-16 9RIrF p171 CR France285

LYNN SHAW,Henry Capt kia 3-7-16 10War CR France150

LYON,A.Maj 21-1-20 BordR CR Ches143

LYON,Alexander Patrick Francis.MID Lt kia 9-9-14 1GordH p166 CR France1391,27-8-14

LYON,Charles James Lt kia 13-1-14 1RScotF p95 MR29,13-11-14

LYON,Claude Edward T2Lt kia 27-5-17 B165RFA p32 CR France5

LYON,Claude Stuart.MC&Bar.LtAMaj kia 21-3-18 53/2RFA p32 CR France563

LYON,Donald Halliday 2Lt kia 20-9-17 10WRid p115 MR30

LYON,Edward Lycett TMaj dow 17-9-16 18Huss att7SomLI p23 CR France23

LYON,Eric T2Lt kia 4-11-18 1/2WRid att15LancF p115 CR France940,1/3Bn

LYON,Francis Charles Lt kia 13-4-18 4GrenGds p50 MR32

LYON,George William.MC.Lt kia 16-4-18 RE 511LondFC p210 CR France880

LYON,Reginald Anthony Lt kia 13-8-17 ACycCps att6Norf att1/7WRid p217 CR Belgium24

LYON,Robert Capt kia 30-7-16 5GordH p242 MR21

LYON,Robert 2Lt kia 17-3-17 5A&SH att1/8MGC p187&243 MR20

LYON,Walter Scott Stewart Lt kia 8-5-15 9RScots p212 MR29,Stuart

LYON-HALL,Clarence Espeut Capt dow 29-3-17 1/4Suss CR Palestine2

LYONCLARK,Basil L.TCapt dow 9-7-17 3/3KAR p202 CR EAfrica38 &CR Tanzania1

LYONE,Alexander Martin.MC.T2Lt dow 26-9-17 11NumbF p62 CR France8

LYONS,Basil 2Lt kia 19-7-17 5RBerks p139 MR20

LYONS,Denis James 2Lt kld 15-11-16 4 att6ConnRgrs p172 CR Belgium17

LYONS,Edward Thomas T2Lt kia 4-10-17 1/2Lancs p111 MR30

LYONS,Henry James T2Lt kia 23-9-17 7RLancs p59 CR Belgium20

LYONS,Robert Victor T2Lt kia 24-3-18 14 att23RIrRif p169 MR27

LYONS,Vincent Aloysius T2Lt dow 23-8-17 18HLI p163 CR France446

LYONS,W,Maj 26-10-16 RASC CR Hamps1

LYONS,William Barry CaptBtMaj dow 4-9-16 2RIrReg p89 MR21 CR France51,LtCol 2RMunstF

LYONS,William Holmes St.John Lt ded 1-11-18 6Mddx att2/4 O&BLI p147&257 CR Ireland137

LYONS,William Thomas.MID TCapt&Adjt kia 3-3-16 10RWFus p98 CR Belgium131

LYONS,William Thomas.MC.TCapt kia 19-7-16 8RLancs p59 MR21 18-7-16

LYS,Francis George Bryan T2Lt kia 14-7-16 6Nhampt p137 MR21

LYSONS,Nigel Lucius Samuel Maj kia 21-10-14 RLancs p59 CR Belgium32

LYTE,Owen Nevill TLt ded 31-10-18 RASC 6DivMTCoy p193 CR France441

LYTHGOE,Jeffrey Wentworth T2Lt kia 22-7-16 14RWar p65 CR France432

LYTTLE,E.Cdr 6-2-17 S&T Cps MR65

LYTTON,Percy Arthur Bertram 2Lt kia 4-2-18 RIrReg att58RFC p16&89 MR20

LYWOOD,Kenneth Primrose Gifford Lt kia 24-3-18 RFA O'Bty p32 MR27

M

MAASDORP,C.R.T2Lt ded 28-3-18 PoW RFC p16 MR20

MAASDORP,Norman TCapt dow 28-8-16 RFA p32 CR Lond8

MABEN,James Armstrong TLt kia 23-8-18 DorsR att6Bn p124 CR France215

MABEY,John Hume Capt dow 18-11-17 2/23LondR p252 CR Egypt9

MABON,John Craig Ferrie T2Lt kia 14-10-18 ScotRif att1/8Bn p103 CR Belgium112,11-10-18

MABY,Lionel Bruce 2Lt kia 12-9-18 2ScotGds p52 CR France1484

MACADAM,James Ferrier Lt ded 19-11-18 1/4EssR p232 CR Egypt9

MACADAM,John Lt dow 18-8-15 4EssR p232 MR4

MACALEVEY,William Francis TCapt kia 27-9-16 RAMC att54FA p196 CR France293

MACALISTER,George Howden 2Lt 24-8-16 5RScotF att78MGC MR37

MACALISTER,William Grierson Maj kia 20-7-16 5ScotRif p224 MR21

MACALLEN,James Capt dow 9-2-17 RAMC att6ELancR p196 CR Iraq5

MacALPINE-DOWNIE,James Robert LtCol dow 21-3-18 1/8A&SH p243 CR France1203

MACAN,Hugh O'Donoghue LtACapt dow 1-9-18 4ESurrR p113 CR France833

MACAN,Hugh Turner TLt kia 23-3-18 21MiddxR p147 MR20

MACAN,Robert Basil Capt kia 13-6-15 IA 28Cav att30Lancers p279 CR Belgium4

MACANDREW,Colin Geen Orr 2Lt kia 2-10-17 AyrYeo att29RFC p19&p203 CR Belgium140

MACANDREW,Henry John Milnes.Sir.KCB.DSO.MajGen ded 16-7-19 IA Comdg5CavDiv p279 CR Lebanon1

MACANDREW,Ian Maclean.MID Lt kia 25-12-14 1SfthH p165 MR22

MacANDREW,John McLean Capt ded 11-10-17 GL 3SfthH p190 CR Scot886,Maj

MacANDREW,Ronald TLt kia 16-8-15 5RIrReg p89 MR4

MacARTHUR Alaster Capt kia 13-11-16 8A&SH p243 CR France131

MacARTHUR,Daniel Reid 2Lt kia 21-9-18 7ScotRif p224 CR France666

MACARTHUR-ONSLOW,Arthur William Capt kia 5-11-14 16Lancers p23 CR Belgium89

MACARTNEY,Hussey Burgh George Capt kia 24-6-15 1RFus p68 CR Belgium92

MACARTNEY,Thomas Hendry 2Lt kia 7-6-17 19LondR attMGC p187&p250 CR Belgium48 attTankCps

MACASKILL,George Hasken 2Lt ded 4-7-18 EssR &RAF p132

MACAULAY,Bruce Wallace 2Lt kia 3-5-17 att2SfthH p165 MR20

MACAULAY,Colin Alexander T2Lt kia 9-4-16 12ScotRif p103 MR38

MACAULAY,George Cecil Gordon 2Lt kld 2-5-17 3EYorks p84 CR France777

MACAULAY,Horace Lt kia 25-4-18 3 att7SfthH p165 MR30

MACAULAY,James 2Lt kia 4-11-18 13RB p179 CR France733

MACAULAY,John B.Lt 8-2-19 Leinst CR Ireland14

MACAULAY,John Shaw 2Lt dow 4-1-18 25RFC p16 CR France134

MACAULAY,Maxwell Stanley 2Lt kia 7-5-18 Loth&BordHorse p204 CR Palestine3

MACAULEY,William Ingham.MIDx2 CaptTMaj RAVC kld 14-5-17 p198 CR France564

MACAUSLAND,Oliver Babington 2Lt kia 9-5-15 ULIA att1RIrF p279 MR28

MACBEAN,Duncan Gillies Forbes TCapt kia 18-6-15 2GordH p166 CR France765

MACBETH,Harold John 2Lt kia 15-9-16 17LondR p250 CR France432

MacBETH,John Duncan Gilmour 2Lt kia 19-4-17 5HLI p240 MR34

MacBETH,Margaret Ann 2ResM1009 SNurse 30-10-18 QAIMNS CR Scot200

MacBETH,Stanley Lt kia 15-9-16 1/18Lond p250 CR France432

MacBETH,Thomas Mcbeth Mathieson Lt 5-9-17 2Lond CR Belgium27

MacBETH,William David 2Lt kia 23-4-17 1/5BlkW p231 CR Lond1,18-2-19 Worc &CR France604,23-4-17

MACBEY,George Munro.MC.Lt kia 22-3-18 6SfthH p241 MR20

MacBRAYNE,D.C.H.2Lt 21-6-17 GL &11RFC CR France1277

MacBRAYNE,John Burns TLt kia 1-7-16 17HLI p163 CR France1890

MacBRYAN,Edward Crozier Lt kia 2-7-16 3 att1SomLI p80 MR21,1-7-16

MACCABE,Robert Maxwell 2Lt kia 23-4-15 8LondR p247 CR France80,Lt dow

MacCALL,Henry Dobree Capt kia 25-9-15 IA 33Pujabis p279 CR France1157

MacCALLUM,William Hay 2Lt kia 27-8-18 7HLI p240

MacCARTHY,Cornelius Aloysius 2Lt drd 19-7-17 9RDubFus p177 MR38

MacCARTHY-O'LEARY,William Felix Lt kia 6-9-16 1RMunstFus p175 MR21,7-9-16

MacCOLL,George Edwardes TMaj kia 5-8-17 8RIrRif p170 MR29

MacCOMBIE,William John TCapt kia 17-7-16 6KOSB p102 MR21

MacCORMAC,Meriotte Campbell Capt kia 16-5-17 7GordH p242 CR France604,Menotti

MacCORMICK,Alexander Campbell 2Lt kia 11-10-16 4A&SH C'Coy p173 CR France115,14Bn

MacCULLOCH,William Bruce TCapt kia 11-4-17 10HLI p163 MR20

MacCULLOCK,Sigurd Harold 2Lt dow 20-12-15 2SfthH p165 CR France344,Lt

MacCUNN,John Francis TCapt dow 25-9-15 6CamH p168 MR19,F.J.

MacDANIEL,Francis George Vernon Lt kia 20-11-17 2RMunstFus p175 CR France689

MacDANIEL,James Robertson 2Lt kia 18-8-17 3RDubFus att57RFC p10&177 CR Belgium140

MacDERMID,Donald Russell T2Lt kia 28-6-16 16HLI p163 CR France296

MACDERMOT,Hugh Maurice T2Lt kia 7-8-15 6RIrFus p171 MR4,9-8-15

MacDERMOTT,Robert Wilson T2Lt kia 9-1-16 8RIrRif p170 CR France35,8-1-16

MacDONALD,Alexander 2Lt 14-7-16 13Lpool MR21

MACDONALD,Alexander Lindsay.MC.LtTCapt kia 26-8-17 BlkW &9RFC p10&p129 CR Belgium18

MacDONALD,Alexander Robert,MC 2Lt kia 28-3-18 7CamH p168 MR20

MACDONALD,Alan Leslie 2Lt kia 19-5-17 2/8ManchR p237 CR France258

MACDONALD,Andrew Moffat TCapt kia 11-5-16 13RScot p54 CR France423

MACDONALD,Angus MacGillivray.DSO.ACapt kia 21-11-17 4SfthH p241 CR France1498

MACDONALD,Archibald Alexander 2Lt dow 17-4-16 4CamH p243 CR France285

MACDONALD,Archibald Hillcoat.DCM.T2Lt dow 5-3-16 ScotRif att1Bn p103 CR France163

MacDONALD,Charles Gordon 2Lt kia 15-6-15 6ScotRif p224&p225,8Bn MR22

MACDONALD,Charles Hodgson Barrington 2Lt kia 23-3-15 RFA 44Bty p32 France706,25-3-15

MACDONALD,Charles Philpot Lt kia 7-1-16 IARO att102Grens p279 MR38

MacDONALD,Claude Keith 2Lt kia 27-9-15 10A&SH p173 MR19

MACDONALD,Colin Capt kia 24-11-15 IA 1/7 att2/7GurkhaRif p279 MR38,22-11-15

MacDONALD,David Johnston Lt kia 29-10-17 RGA p209 CR Belgium12

MACDONALD,Donald Theodore.MC.Capt dow 15-3-20 IA 125Rif p279 CR Iraq8,14-3-20

MACDONALD,Edgar.MC.Capt dow 3-1-20 RFA CR Scot675

MacDONALD,Evan Ronald Horatio Keith 2Lt kia 20-9-14 2HLI p163 MR15

MacDONALD,George Anderson 2Lt kia 18-8-17 10A&SH p173 MR21,McDONALD

MacDONALD,George Cockburn 2Lt ded 17-11-18 5HLI p240 CR Scot530

MACDONALD,George Harper T2LtACapt kia 5-9-16 2GordH p166 MR21

MACDONALD,George Mortimer 2Lt ded 8-8-17 IARO att5Cav p279 MR43

MACDONALD,Godfrey Evan Hugh.Hon.Lt dow 2-11-14 1ScotGds p52 MR29

MacDONALD,Guyon Kenneth Capt ded 21-11-19 3N&D &RAF p264

MacDONALD,Hamish.MC.Lt kia 14-7-19 13Huss p22&p257 MR38

MACDONALD,Hector Robert 2Lt kia 22-2-17 1SfthH p165 CR Iraq5

MACDONALD,Hugh T2Lt kia 5-6-17 22NumbFus p62 MR20

MACDONALD,Hugh Ferguson T2Lt ded 20-5-18 11RScot p54 CR Scot752,kldacc

MACDONALD,James Cecil T2Lt ded 27-4-16 1CamH p168 CR France88

MACDONALD,John Capt 13-7-15 5HLI MR4

MacDONALD,John TCapt dow 23-7-16 5CamH p168 CR France51

MacDONALD,John 2Lt kia 29-10-16 5ScotRif p224 MR21

MacDONALD,John TCapt dow 11-4-17 16RScot p54 CR France95

MacDONALD,John 2Lt kia 27-5-18 RGA 286SB p40 MR18

MACDONALD,John Alexander TLt kia 30-11-17 1WYorks p82 MR17

MacDONALD,John Doran TCapt dow 18-3-16 SL GravesRegn p201 CR France285

MacDONALD,John McPhail.MC.2Lt kia 23-9-17 6ScotRif p224

MACDONALD,John P.Capt ded 20-11-20 RAMC CR Canada547

MACDONALD,John Row Mackenzie 2Lt kia 3-3-17 9RScot p212 CR France15

MACDONALD,John Stewart 2Lt kld 5-7-18 15LondR att2/5LancF p249 CR France106,kia

MacDONALD,Kenneth Lt kia 16-8-18 5NumbF &21RAF p270 MR20

MACDONALD,Malcolm TLt kia 10-10-16 10BlkW p129 MR37

MacDONALD,Murdock Donald T2Lt kia 18-7-16 7CamH p168 CR France423,Murds

MacDONALD,Neil.MC.2Lt kia 25-4-18 RGA 263SB p40 CR Belgium21 McDONALD

MACDONALD,Neville Douglas Maj ded 19-1-18 2Wilts CR Dorset51

MACDONALD,Percy 2Lt kia 21-4-17 7DLI p239 CR France594

MacDONALD,Percy Brooming Capt ded 19-5-17 8Yorks p263 CR Mddx26,McDONALD

MACDONALD,Robert Brown Aitchison T2Lt kia 17-8-16 9BlkW p129 CR France703

MACDONALD,Roderick T2Lt kia 1-7-16 23NumbFus p62 MR21

MacDONALD,Roderick John Macpherson 2Lt dow 20-4-17 4SfthH p241 CR France40

MacDONALD,Ronald.TD.Maj dow 10-6-16 4CamH D'Coy p242 CR France1571

MACDONALD,Ronald.DCM.Lt 29-2-20 2Yorks CR Lancs43

MACDONALD,Ronald Duncan 2Lt kia 31-10-17 82RFA p32 CR Belgium23

MacDONALD,Ronald Hugh Charles T2Lt kia 10-12-16 14DLI p161 MR19

MacDONALD,Ronald Ian.Hon.Capt ded 17-10-18 3CamH attGenStaff CR France1848

MACDONALD,Ronald Mosse Lt kia 3-11-14 1CamH p168 MR29

MACDONALD,Simon TLt kia 1-7-16 23NumbFus p62 CR France700

MACDONALD,Somerled Lt ded 30-11-19 IA 1/54Sikhs p279 CR Scot359

MACDONALD,Sydney Lt kia 2-9-18 8RScot p211 CR France646,1/4Bn

MACDONALD,Sylvester Patrick Joseph.MC.2LtACapt kia 7-6-17 3WorcR p109 CR Belgium89

MacDONALD,Thomas HonLt&QM ded23-11-14 5RIrReg p89 CR Eire186,McDONALD

MACDONALD,Walter Halli-Burton TLt ded 22-1-16 RAMC attNo2Sec ForthDefs p196 CR Scot237

MACDONALD,Wilfred Ferguson T2Lt kia 23-5-17 GL &18RFC p10 CR France381

MacDONALD,William Alexander Capt kia 23-7-18 1/5SfthH p241 CR France1697

MacDONALD,William Alexander LtACapt ded 18-2-19 RAOC p267 CR Essex88 Ex 14Lond

MacDONALD,William Forbes 2Lt kia 23-11-17 RFA p208 CR France415

MACDONALD,William Francis.MC.2Lt kia 1-9-18 3 att2SfthH p165 CR France421,31-8-18

MacDONALD,W.S.2Lt ded 28-1-18 RFC CR Canada1667

MACDONALD-BROWN,Ian Capt kia 15-11-16 RAMC att109RFA CR Belgium28

MACDONALD-MORETON,Norman Charles Henry.MC.TCapt kia 13-10-15 5KRRC p151 CR France692,3Bn

MacDONELL,Alastair Somerled 2Lt kia 13-10-15 3CamH p168 MR19,Alasdair 1Bn

MacDONNAGH,William John 2Lt kia 11-9-16 8MddxR p236 MR21

MacDONNELL,Colla Ion 2Lt kia 9-10-17 4Glouc p225 MR30

MACDONNELL,Francis William Joseph TMaj ded 4-10-15 14 att9WYorks p82 CR Europe4,4-12-15

MACDONNELL,Herbert Creagh Capt dow 24-5-15 RIrReg attRFC p1&p89 CR France200,23-5-15

MacDONNELL,Hugh Edward EdmundCapt ded 22-1-17 4ESurr p264 CR Devon2

MACDONNELL,John Henry O'Connell de Courcy Lt dow 14-10-18 6ConnRgrs attLeinst p172 CR Belgium157,kia

MACDOUGALD,Llewellyn George Duncan T2Lt kia 16-8-17 8RInnisFus p105 MR30

MACDOUGALL,Alastair Lt 30-4-18 CamH att2/14Lond CR Palestine3

MacDOUGALL,Alexander Lt kia 30-4-18 CamH p242

MacDOUGALL,Alexander 2Lt ded 26-10-18 LancF p263

MacDOUGALL,Allen TCapt kia 4-8-16 22RFus p69&p257 CR France394,Allan

MacDOUGALL,Archibald LtACapt kia 31-10-18 8ScotRif p225 CR Belgium140

MacDOUGALL,David Graham Mather Lt kia 27-7-17 5KOSB att1/3KAR p224 CR EAfrica38 &CR Tanzania1

MacDOUGALL,D.C.Lt kia 27-7-17 1/3KAfrR p202

MacDOUGALL,Dugald 2Lt ded 8-2-18 6A&SH p270 CR Scot677

MacDOUGALL,Edward Greaves TCapt kia 26-10-15 6CamH p168 MR19

MACDOUGALL,Finlay Neil Lt kia 18-8-16 3BlkW p129 CR France432

MacDOUGALL,Iain Capt&Adjt 1-9-14 2GrenGds CR Scot41

MACDOUGALL,Ian Capt kia 13-9-14 GrenGds p50

MACDOUGALL,Stewart of LUNGA TLtCol kia 21-7-15 10GordH p166 CR France107

MacDOWEL,Benjamin George Lt kia 22-9-15 3ConnRgrs p172 CR France924,1Bn

MACDOWELL,Charles Michael Vere Capt dow 28-4-17 1/6BlkW p231 CR France102

MacDOWELL,M.Miss 3-7-18 ScotWomensHosp CR Greece9

MACDOWELL,Robert T2Lt kia 25-2-17 NStaffR p157 MR38

MacDUFF,Alexander Capt kia 24-4-15 2CamH p168 MR29

MacDUFF,William Brown 2Lt kia 2-12-17 5BordR p228 MR30

MACE,Alban Bodley Rev 3-10-16 RAChDept 3 att2DCLI p199 CR Greece3

MACE,Alfred Reginald Lt ded 18-10-19 RASC MT p267 CR Essex1

MACE,Ernest 2Lt kia 10-8-17 4Nhants p234 CR Belgium125

MacEWAN,Maxwell 2Lt kia 5-7-17 5ESurrR p226 CR France439

MACEY,Clifford James T2Lt kia 25-5-15 Dors p124 CR France285

MACFADYEN,John Dennis Goulty.MC.TLt kia 8-8-18 1MGC p187 CR France485,1TankCps

MacFADYEN,Neil Douglas 2Lt kia 6-5-15 3 att2CamH p168 MR29,5-5-15

MacFADYEN,R.Lt 8-10-19 1CamH CR Scot808

MACFADYEN,Walter.MID Lt kia 7-5-17 RScot p54 CR France1182,Capt

MACFARLAND,George Adams TCapt dow 17-10-17 RAMC att23StnHos p196 CR Mddx16

MACFARLANE,Alastair Hunter Lt kia 12-5-15 8RScot p211 MR29 2Lt 9Bn

MACFARLANE,Alexander 2Lt kia 2-12-17 91RFA p32 CR France662

MACFARLANE,Donald McIntyre T2Lt kld 18-4-18 9ScotRif &RAF p103 CR Egypt9,McFARLANE Lt

MacFARLANE,Harold Embleton T2Lt kia 14-7-17 GL att55RFC p10 CR France134

MacFARLANE,Ian TCapt ded 18-7-17 RAMC attEgyptHospl p196 CR Egypt2

MacFARLANE,Ian Cameron T2Lt kia 14-9-16 11 att6YorkR p91 MR21

MacFARLANE,John Tennant Lt 26-9-15 MGC p184 MR19

MACFARLANE,Keith Dix Lewis TLt kia 14-4-17 9ScotRif p103 MR20

MACFARLANE,Kenneth Capt ded 7-12-16 5HLI p240 CR Scot764

MACFARLANE,Leslie Kerr 2Lt kia 23-8-18 8RScot p212 CR France927 2Bn

MACFARLANE,Robert.MC.Capt kia 21-4-17 3 att2BlkW p129 MR38

MACFARLANE,Robert George 2Lt 6-3-16 177RE CR Belgium11

MACFARLANE,Ronald Wallace 2Lt kia 3-9-16 RGA 152HB p40 CR France232

MacFARLANE,Wallace Bird 2Lt kia 10-3-15 5 att2Middx p147 MR22

MacFARLANE,William Barr 2Lt kia 20-7-15 5KOSB p224 MR4

MacFARLANE,William Cargill Stuart 2Lt kia 27-8-16 4A&SH p173 CR France239

MacFARLANE,William MacCallum.DSO.TMaj kia 19-2-17 15HLI att1/5SfthH p163 CR France15

MacFARLANE,William Smith.MC.Lt kld 20-6-18 5RScots CR Scot237

MacFARLANE,William Walter 2Lt kia 12-4-18 D256RFA p208 CR France1106,McFARLANE

MacFARLANG-GRIEVE,Alwyn Ronald 2Lt kia 17-3-17 1/8A&SH p243 CR France728,Lt

MacFARQUHAR,Murdo Mackenzie T2Lt kia 15-9-16 9 att7/8KOSB p102

MacFARREN,Ernest T2Lt dow 8-11-16 7RIrRif p170 2entries CR France285

MacFAYDEN,Robert Lt ded 8-10-19 CamH p265

MacFIE,Claud William 2Lt kia 16-6-15 3SStaffs att2Beds p122 MR22

MacFIE,Robert Alexander 2Lt kia 20-11-17 2/5LancFus p221 MR21

MacGEORGE,Henry Warwick LtTCapt kia 25-9-15 1SStaffs p122 MR19

MacGEORGE,William Henry LtCol ded 16-12-16 RDC p253

MACGEOUGH-BOND,Ralph Shelton 2Lt dow 22-8-17 D46RFA p32 CR Belgium124

MACGILL,Mary Mitchell Matron 11-3-15 QAIMNS CR Hamps1

MACGILVARY,Alexander Renfrew 2Lt kia 29-11-17 1/7ScotRif p103&p224,MACGILVRAY CR Palestine9,McGILVRAY

MacGILVRAY,John Duncan 2Lt kia 18-2-17 4CamH att2/10Lpool p270 MR32

MacGILVRAY,Martin Lt drd 10-11-17 RE attWAFF CR Scot50

MacGLASHAN,Alexander 2Lt kia 27-9-18 7ScotRif p224 CR France686,McGLASHAN

MacGRATH,Roger.MC.TCapt dow 5-5-18 RAMC att28FA p196 CR France102,McGRATH

MACGREGOR,Alexander Henry Campbell Maj kia 15-3-15 RIrFus p171 CR Belgium111,14-3-15

MacGREGOR,Alexander John Lindsay Capt dow 8-10-18 3/13BlkW D'Coy p205 CR France446

MacGREGOR,Alfred Horace.MID Capt kia 11-9-16 14LondR p249 MR21 10-9-16

MACGREGOR,Amyas.MC.Lt dow 13-10-16 RE 1LondFC p210 CR France513,Capt

MacGREGOR,Andrew Hamilton.MID Capt kia 13-11-16 6SfthH p241 CR France131

MacGREGOR,Andrew Steven 2Lt kia 23-4-17 RFA p208 CR France1188

MacGREGOR,Colin Alexander T2Lt kia 26-9-15 9GordH p166 MR19

MacGREGOR,Cortland Richard Lt kia 5-5-15 2SWBord p100 MR4,Cortland

MacGREGOR,Donald Alastair Capt dow 15-8-15 2RBerkR p139 CR Germany2

MacGREGOR,Donald Argyle Douglas Ian TLt kia 30-11-17 GL &41RFC p10 MR20

MacGREGOR,Douglas 2Lt kia 13-11-16 8A&SH D'Coy p243 CR France131,McGREGOR

MacGREGOR,George 2Lt kia 25-9-15 8SfthH p165 MR19

MACGREGOR,James.MC.T2Lt kia 10-4-18 11RScot p54 MR30

MACGREGOR,James Lt 12-7-18RFA CR Scot752

MacGREGOR,James Hamilton 2LtTLt kia 10-1-17 3BedR att132MGC Inf p138&184 CR Iraq5

MacGREGOR,John Atholl 2Lt kia 21/26-9-16 2CldGds p51 CR France218 &CR France374,Lt 26-9-16

MacGREGOR,John Campbell Rev ded 4-11-16 RAChDept p268

MacGREGOR,Kenneth Cortlandt 2Lt kia 26-2-15 2KOSB p102 MR29

MacGREGOR,Peter Maj 15-11-17 RAMC CR Yorks644

MacGREGOR,Ralph Alexander Montgomery Lt dow 26-9-18 RGA 136SB p40 CR France1484,Montgomerie

MacGREGOR,Reginald Kinloch TCapt kld 23-4-16 RAMC p196 CR France1372

MacGREGOR,Rhoderic 2Lt dow 23-7-17 RASC SR MT attT'CpsSiegePk 76SB DAC p193 CR France40

MACGREGOR,Robert Murray Lt dow PoW 9-5-15 1/13LondR p249 MR32

MacGREGOR,Ronald Lt ded 1-5-17 1LovatScts att2/2KAR p204 CR EAfrica47,3-5-17

MacGREGOR,Thomas Charles Stuart T2Lt kia 8-6-17 GL &53RFC p10 MR20

MACGREGOR-WHITTON,Percy William Thomas TCapt kia 9-7-16 2RScotFus p95 MR21

MacHAFFIE,John T2Lt kia 21-9-17 GL &29RFC p10 CR Belgium84

MacHARDY,David Scott T2Lt kia 1-7-16 16HLI p163 MR21

MACHARG,Ebenezer Maitland Capt kia 23-10-16 3 att1ScotRif p103 MR21

MACHARG,James Anthony Boyd 2Lt kia 29-10-16 6ScotRif p224 MR21

MACHELL,Humphrey Gilbert 2Lt ded 12-6-18 3BordR p117 CR France145,8Bn

MACHELL,Maurice Irving 2Lt kia 16-9-16 3 att5KSLI p145 MR21,15-9-16

MACHELL,Percy Wilfrid.CMG.DSO.LtCol kia 1-7-16 11BordR p117 CR France43

MACHEN,Frederick James 2Lt kia 3-6-17 1/20LondR p251 CR Belgium56

MACHON,C.F.E.Lt 16-9-20 3Glouc CR Glouc9

MacHUTCHEON,John Chisholm T2Lt dow 2-8-16 15N&D p134 CR France23

MACHUTCHISON,William Frederick Lt kia 26-3-18 7RDubFus p254 MR27

MacILDOWIE,Edward John Howard 2Lt kld 1-11-16 9HLI p240 MR21

MacILWAINE,Julian Mackay Capt kia 22-3-18 5RIrRif att12RFC p16&p170 MR20

MACINDOE,Cecil Alexander Dunn Capt kia 28-6-15 8ScotRif p225 CR Gallipoli2

MACINDOE,J.G.Maj 5-10-16 RAMC CR Devon74

MACINDOE,Ronald Christian Black Capt kia 28-6-15 8ScotRif p225 MR4

MacINNES,Duncan Sayre.CMG.DSO.BrigGen dedacc 23-5-18 RE p46 CR France40

MACINTOSH,Eric Lt kld 31-7-17 Herts p252 MR29

MacINTOSH,Henry Maitland TCapt dow 26-7-18 A&SH p173 CR France1225

MACINTOSH,John T2Lt kia 23-7-16 14RWarR p65 MR21

MacINTOSH,John Douglas Capt kia 6-5-15 5RScot p211 MR4

MacINTOSH,John Hill 2Lt kia 14-4-17 6HLI p240 MR21

MACINTOSH,Kenneth Alexander 2Lt kia 24-8-18 6HLI p240 CR France162

MACINTOSH,Kenneth John.MC.Lt dow 16-1-20 1/5 att2/5GurkhaRif p279 MR43

MACINTOSH,Thomas Gordon Gall T2Lt kia 18-8-18 11RScot p54 CR France26

MACINTOSH,William Henry Lt ded 9-11-18 4GordH p270 CR Scot244

MacINTYRE,Charles Frederick Davis T2Lt kia 6-11-18 27RFA 37HB p32 CR France937

MacINTYRE,D.Capt 30-5-19 2GurkhaRif CR Europe51

MacINTYRE,George Duncan TLt kia 10-7-16 15 att7YorkR p90 CR France267

MacINTYRE,Ian Campbell Lt kia 22-11-17 CamH att108MGC Inf p168&p184 CR France529

MacINTYRE,John Taylor 2Lt kia 25-8-17 9 att18HLI p240 MR21

MACINTYRE,Peter Brown Capt dow 3-8-17 4SfthH p241 CR Belgium23

MacINTYRE,Robert Cochran.MC.Lt kld 30-9-18 6A&SH p243 CR France236,6/10Bn

MacINTYRE,Thomas Lt kia 1-7-16 16N'umbFus p62 MR21

MacIVER,Andrew Tucker Squarey Capt kia 24-4-15 RE p210 CR Belgium21

MacIVER,Donald Lt 24-3-18 3SLancs att2/7RWar MR27

MacIVER,Donald John 2Lt dow 14-10-15 TA 4CamH p243 CR France1,McIVER

MACIVER,Duncan T2Lt kia 11-10-16 5CamH att26TMB MR21

MacIVER,Ian Lt kia 11-8-16 5RFA p32 CR France267,10-8-16

MacIVER,Kenneth TCapt kia 27-3-18 CamH Res att5Bn p168 MR27

MacIVER,Kenneth Ogg Mackenzie TLt kldacc 30-10-18 KRRC att1KAR p151&266 CR EAfrica77

MacIVER,Reginald Squarey Lt kia 1-7-16 4LancF p93 CR France643,2Bn

MacIVER,Robert Troutbeck 2Lt kia 11-9-15 1RScot p54 CR France82

MACK,Arthur Stanley Lt kia 9-4-17 3RLancs p59 CR France729,1Bn

MACK,Arthur Paston TLtCol kia 15-9-16 9Suff p78 CR France294

MACK,Edward Geoffrey 2Lt kia 27-9-15 3 att2Wilts p153 CR France423,Edgar

MACK,Isaac Alexander TLt kia 1-7-16 Suff attTMB p78 CR France267,Capt

MACK,Thomas T2Lt kia 26-1-16 DLI att9Bn p161 CR Belgium115

MACK,Thomas Arthur 2Lt kia 9-4-17 6GordH p242 CR France184

MACKADAM,Harold James T2Lt kia 30-12-17 7RFus p69 MR21

MacKAIN,Henry Fergus T2Lt kia 27-2-17 GL &13RFC p10 CR France95,Lt

MacKAIN,James Fergus Capt kia 23-11-14 IA 34SikhPnrs p279 CR France279

MacKAY,Alexander Rinnison T2Lt kia 13-3-16 13 att15HLI p163 CR France430,Kinnison

MACKAY,Alexander William.MC.TCapt dow 28-9-17 26RFus p69 CR France1361

MACKAY,Angus 2Lt dow 16-11-16 5SfthH p241 CR France102

MACKAY,Angus T2Lt dow 10-5-18 24RFus p69 CR France84

MacKAY,Arnold Langley 2Lt dow 31-10-16 3 att2RScotF p95 CR France40

MacKAY,Charles SubCdr ded 15-6-16 PoW IA S&TCps p279

MacKAY,Charles Alexander.MID Capt kia 21-3-18 5SfthH p241 MR20

MacKAY,Charles William Donaldson 2Lt kia 17-8-16 8CamH p168 CR France239

MacKAY,Claude Lysaght 2Lt dow 7-6-15 2WorcR att2ManchR p109 CR France102

MACKAY,Donald 2Lt dow 17-11-18 5SfthH p241 CR France40

MacKAY,Donald Paley Maj kia 9-10-17 5WYorks p218 MR30

MacKAY,Douglas Duncan Anderson Lt kia 14-10-18 RE &RAF p270

MacKAY,Eric Reay Capt kia 13-6-15 13A&SH p173 MR4

MacKAY,Frederick William.MC.Capt dow 24-10-18 1/4YLI p235 CR France146

MACKAY,George Douglas Lt dow 23-4-17 IARO att56Rif p279 MR38,2Lt

MACKAY,George Lawrence Forbes Lt kia 11-4-17 Leinst p174 CR France570,12-4-17

MacKAY,George Newton.MC.Lt 24-7-18 GordH att6MGC CR Belgium11

MACKAY,Gordon T2Lt kia 16-8-17 24Middx att16MGC Inf p147&184 MR30,44MGC

MACKAY,Hamish Strathy Lt kia 9-9-16 RGA 1HampsHB att22RFC p19&p209 CR France882

MACKAY,Harry William Mackintosh Lt kia 6-3-18 6GordH att18RFC p19&242 CR France31

MACKAY,Henry Neil T2Lt kia 28-11-16 12A&SH p173 CR Greece6

MACKAY,Ian.MID CaptTMaj kia 28-3-18 4CamH p242 MR20

MacKAY,Ian Darrock T2Lt kia 21-3-18 14A&SH p173 MR20

MacKAY,Ian Forbes TCapt kia 25-9-15 8GordH p166 MR19

MacKAY,James Lt kia 25-9-15 3 att1GordH p166 CR Belgium453

MACKAY,James Alasair Culbard.MC.Capt dow 22-7-16 6SfthH p241 CR France66

MACKAY,James Bruce TCapt dow 3-5-17 21WYorks p82 CR France97

MACKAY,James Ivan 2LtTCapt kia 5-10-17 3WRid att70RFC p115 CR Belgium11

MacKAY,John 2Lt kia 23-4-17 5BordR p228 CR France1185

MacKAY,John Alexander 2Lt kia 11-9-17 57RFC p10 CR Belgium158

MACKAY,John Mitchell.MID T2Lt kia 10-8-17 RE 130FC p46 CR Belgium112

MACKAY,John William TLt dow 20-8-17 7CamH p168 CR France64

MACKAY,Kenneth.MC.Capt dow 7-11-18 6GordH p242 CR France40,6/7Bn

MACKAY,Malcolm 2Lt dow 7-4-18 7A&SH p243 CR France113

MACKAY,Mark Sprot T2Lt kia 23-4-17 7CamH p168 CR France1182

MACKAY,Philip Storrs 2Lt kia 14-4-17 3 att1KOSB p102 CR France162

MACKAY,Samuel Francis Henderson Capt kia 13-6-17 5ELancs p226 MR19

MACKAY,Terence Faulkner T2Lt kia 3-10-18 KRRC att4Bn p151 CR France234

MacKAY,William Gidden 2Lt kia 25-9-15 3GordH p166 MR29

MacKENNA,Peter Fraser Maj ded 26-11-18 3/5RScotF Res p270 CR Scot520

MACKENSON,Christopher 2Lt dow 16-8-17 RB p179

MacKENZIE,Adrian Somerset T2Lt kia 1-4-17 GL 10HLI att15RFC p10 CR France41,Lt

MACKENZIE,Alan Keith Capt dow 16-9-16 3GrenGds p50 CR France23,Allan

MACKENZIE,Albert James.MC.2Lt dow 13-12-17 4 att2ScotRif p103 CR France64

MACKENZIE,Alexander Alan LtACapt kia 23-3-18 4SfthH p241 MR20

MACKENZIE,Alexander Kenneth 2Lt kia 1-9-18 2SfthH p165 CR France427

MacKENZIE,Alexander Ritchie Doughty 2Lt kia 22-3-18 4GordH p242 MR20,McKENZIE

MACKENZIE,Alistair 2Lt kia 24-3-18 3 att9SfthH p165 MR27,Alastair

MACKENZIE,Archibald TCapt dow 4-6-18 1NumbFus p62 CR France10

MACKENZIE,Bernard Francis Lt kia 28-6-18 4SLancs p230 CR France352

MACKENZIE,Boyce Mackey Scobie TLtACapt kia 22-3-18 8RWSurr p56 MR27

MACKENZIE,Charles Alexander Chandos Capt mbk 21-12-14 IA 20DeccanHorse p279 MR28

MACKENZIE,Colin Landseer 2Lt kia 20-9-14 2HLI p163 CR France1329

MACKENZIE,Cortlandt Graham Gordon Lt kia 25-10-14 RScotFus p95 MR29,29-10-14

MACKENZIE,Cyril Atkinson Capt kia 24-12-17 2/7Lpool p215 CR Belgium12

MACKENZIE,David Ferguson Capt kia 17-5-15 4CamH p242 MR22

MACKENZIE,Donald Lt&QM kia 30-9-18 5N&D p232 CR France375

MACKENZIE,Donald Charles Lt dow 20-1-15 1SfthH p165 CR Surrey112

MACKENZIE,Donald Lawson 2Lt kia 1-10-18 5SfthH p241 CR Belgium157,McKENZIE

MACKENZIE,Donald Stamford Forth Lt dow 31-7-17 177RFA p32 CR Belgium7

MACKENZIE,Duncan T2Lt ded 7-1-17 BlkW p264 CR Wales664,4-1-17

MacKENZIE,Edward Forbes 2Lt kia 14-12-14 RScot p54 MR29

MacKENZIE,Eric James Bethune Capt kia 8-7-16 29/42RFA p32&257 CR France513,Maj

MACKENZIE,Francis Edgar 2Lt kia 23-4-17 8ScotRif att13KRRC p225 MR20

MACKENZIE,Francis Ramsay 2Lt kia 1-7-16 2SfthH p165 MR21

MACKENZIE,Frederick Boyce ACapt ded 4-7-18 RGA 71HB p262 CR Hamps23

MACKENZIE,Frederick Obrè Capt kia 3-3-15 IA 7Rajputs p279 CR Iraq6

MACKENZIE,Frederick Thomas Lt 23-3-18 169RFA MR20

MacKENZIE,Frederick Wallace Capt ded 30-7-17 RAMC CR Scot591

MacKENZIE,George Arthur T2Lt kia 25-9-15 8GordH p166 MR19

MACKENZIE,George Laing.MC.T2Lt dow 13-4-18 SfthH att1/4Bn p165 CR France10

MACKENZIE,Gilbert Marshall Capt kia 21-4-16 SfthH p165 MR38

MACKENZIE,Henry Deedes Nutt TCapt kia 4-10-17 RAMC att95RFA p196 CR Belgium19

MACKENZIE,Henry Pierce.MID TCapt kia 25-9-15 9ScotRif p103 CR France114

MacKENZIE,I Nurse 2-11-18 QAIMNS CR Scot990

MACKENZIE,Ian.MC.Capt 21-3-18 5SfthH MR20

MACKENZIE,Ivan Emilio Mario TCapt kld 12-10-17 RFC p10 CR Hamps4

MACKENZIE,Jack Ronald Lewes Lt kia 21-4-17 SfthH p165 MR38

MACKENZIE,James Lt kia 16-5-15 ScotGds att2Bn p52 CR France279

MACKENZIE,James Alexander 2Lt kia 20-9-17 4SfthH p241 MR30

MACKENZIE,James Graham Lt kia 4-8-16 16RScot p54 MR21

MacKENZIE,John.VC.Maj kia 17-5-15 1Beds p86 CR France279

MACKENZIE,John TLt kia 26-9-16 8NumbF p62 MR21

MACKENZIE,John 2Lt kia 28-10-17 RGA 11SB p40 CR Belgium23

MacKENZIE,John 2Lt kia 1-12-17 GL &RFC p10 MR20

MACKENZIE,John Gladstone Capt kia 21-5-16 AustAMC 6FA CR France275

MACKENZIE,John Kincaid T2Lt kia 27-5-18 BordR att8Bn p117 MR18

MACKENZIE,Keith Bethune Capt kia 12-11-14 2SforthH p165 MR29

MacKENZIE,Keith Ingleby 2Lt kia 8-4-17 A&SH &RFC p10&p173 CR France1321

MACKENZIE,Kenneth TCapt kia 1-7-16 24NumbF p62 MR21

MacKENZIE,Kenneth Capt kld 9-9-18 9RScot p212 CR France541,27-8-18

MACKENZIE,Kenneth Fitzgerald 2Lt 14-7-16 SfthH att26MGC MR21

MACKENZIE,Kenneth Lee Warner Maj ded 27-11-14 IA 62Punjabis p279 CR Egypt15

MACKENZIE,Lynedoch Archibald LtACapt dow 19-10-15 RE p210 MR4

MACKENZIE,Mark Kinkaid Lt kia 1-2-16 4KRRC att3RB p151 CR France1894,Kincaid 25-9-14

MACKENZIE,Maurice.MID TLt kia 28-11-15 RAMC att2RIrRif p196 CR France921

MacKENZIE,Murdo John 2Lt kia 28-6-15 RFA p208 CR Gallipoli6

MACKENZIE,Murdock T2Lt kia 5-11-15 9BlkW p129 MR19

MACKENZIE,Murray Mitchell.MID T2Lt dow 21-11-16 10 att1/4SfthH p165 CR France59

MacKENZIE,Noel Olliffe Compton 2Lt kia 1-7-16 1/13LondR p249 MR21

MacKENZIE,Percy Melville Capt kia 6-10-18 2GordH p166 CR France686

MACKENZIE,R.H.Col 19-1-16 4ScotRif CR Scot237

MACKENZIE,Richard Devon Samuels T2Lt dow 1-7-17 8SfthH p165 CR Belgium2,Devern

MACKENZIE,Roderick Ian 2Lt dow 11-4-15 1BlkW p129 CR France80

MACKENZIE,Ronald Angus Hugh Lt kia 7-2-15 1Leinst p174 CR Belgium80,McKENZIE

MACKENZIE,Ronald Patrick 2Lt kia 19-4-17 1/5RScotFus p222 CR Palestine8

MACKENZIE,Simon 2Lt kia 7-12-16 4SfthH p241 CR France1182

MACKENZIE,Thomas Graham T2Lt dow 31-8-17 13 att5/6RScot p54 CR Belgium24

MACKENZIE,William Alexander Lt kia 17-5-17 9KOSB att167MGC Inf p102&184 CR France537

MACKENZIE,William Archibald 2Lt dow 29-9-18 2/5Lancs p213 CR France1184

MACKENZIE,William Sinclair 2Lt 28-4-17 4 att16RScots p211 MR20

MACKENZIE,William Stuart Capt ded 22-8-21 IA 1/124Baluchis p279 MR43

MACKEOWN John Harold T2Lt kld 5-10-17 5 att1ConnRgrs p172 CR Iraq8

MACKESON,Christopher.MID 2Lt&Adjt dow 16-8-17 2RB CR Belgium7

MACKEY,Edward Reeves.DCM.Lt kld 15-3-17 GL &RFC p10 CR Herts87

MACKIE,Alexander Mackay 2Lt kia 21-10-18 4DLI C'Coy att9MGC Inf p161&p184 CR Belgium140

MACKIE,Frank James T2Lt kia 29-5-17 19Lpool p72 CR Belgium4

MACKIE,George 2Lt dow 12-4-17 9RScot p212 CR France266

MACKIE,George Neville Capt kia 26-4-15 IA 54Sikhs att57Rif p279

MACKIE,Harold Lt dow 18-11-17 9RB p179 CR Belgium16

MACKIE,James D.TCapt kia 10-4-16 12LpoolR p72 CR Belgium23

MACKIE,James Logan LtACapt kia 27-12-17 1/1AyrYeo p203 CR Palestine3

MACKIE,Norman Lindsay LtACapt dow 28-9-15 14LondR attMGC p187,Lindsey&p249,25-9-15 MR19

MACKIE,Reginald Ernest Capt kia 28-6-15 4RScot p211 MR4

MACKIE,Thomas Sinclair Lt kia 18-11-16 3 att8NStaffs p157 MR21,Thomson

MACKIE,William 2Lt ded 29-4-16 6RScot p211 CR Scot722,Lt

MACKILLOP,Donald TLt kia 20-7-16 3 att1ScotRif p103 MR21

MACKINDER,H.J.H.WO accdrd 14-6-16 RIM p279

MACKINLAY James Lt ded 17-1-19 RDC p256 CR Lancs170

MACKINLAY,Robert Wallace.MC.Capt ded 6-2-19 RE 3SiegeCoy p210 CR Belgium316

MACKINNON,Alastair Lt ded 14-10-16 8A&SH attMGC p187&243,kld CR France397

MACKINNON,Alexamder Hood 2Lt kia 14-9-14 1CamH p168 MR15

MACKINNON,Archibald Donald T2Lt kia 13-10-18 51MGC Inf p184 CR France271

MACKINNON,Brice Bunny.MC.Lt ded 5-8-18 3 att10BlkW p129 CR France145

MacKINNON,Bruce Lt dow 2-10-18 4HLI att97TMB p163 CR France528

MacKINNON,Charles Frank Capt ded 14-6-19 1/6KAR CR SAfrica30

MACKINNON,Colin Alexander John 2Lt kia 25-9-15 1Middx p147 MR19

MACKINNON,Duncan Lt kia 9-10-17 1ScotGds p52 MR30

MACKINNON,Duncan TCapt dow 12-4-18 RAMC att9HLI p196 CR France324

MACKINNON,Farquhar Donald Lt dow 4-10-17 IARO att129Baluchis p279 CR EAfrica38 &CR Tanzania1

MacKINNON,Francis James Ogilvie Capt kia 16/17-5-15 3 att2GordH p166 CR France279

MacKINNON,Frank Irvine TCapt ded 30-12-18 RAMC p196 CR Syria2

MacKINNON,Gordon.MC.Lt kia 8-11-17 KOSB att1/5Bn p102 CR Palestine8

MacKINNON John T2Lt kia 21-4-18 8SfthH p165 CR France57

MacKINNON,John Angus 2Lt kia 22-8-17 4Berks p234 MR30

MacKINNON,Kenneth Lt kia 7-4-17 8N&D p233 CR France725

MACKINNON,Lachlan T2Lt kia 30-6-16 8CamH p168 CR France423,6Bn

MACKINNON,Lionel Neil Alexander Capt kia 6-11-15 CldGds att5NigR p51&201 CR WAfrica58

MACKINNON,Louis Charles Bowden Fuller 2Lt kia 21-3-18 RE 518FC p210 MR20,Fullarton

MACKINNON,Mary SNurse drd 26-2-18 TFNS p254 MR40

MacKINNON,Neil Alexander Lt kia 19-9-18 3SuffR p78 CR Palestine9

MacKINNON,Ronald Fullerton.MC.TLt kia 21-10-16 11LancF att9LNLancs p93 MR21

MACKINNON,Roy Livingston.MID Capt dow 15-4-21 4GordH CR Scot280

MACKINNON,Vincent Walter Kenneth.MID Lt kia 21-7-15 IA 53Sikhs p279 CR Asia60

MacKINNON,William Capt kia 11-5-17 1/14LondR p249 CR France537

MACKINTOSH,Alastair Hugh Capt kia 14-9-14 CamH p168 MR15

MACKINTOSH,Angus Alexander Capt ded 14-10-18 RHGds p20

MACKINTOSH,Charles Gustave Rochefort T2Lt kia 5-4-17 GL &RFC p10 CR France1484

MACKINTOSH,Donald.VC.Lt kia 11-4-17 3SfthH p165 CR France604

MACKINTOSH,Douglas Bruce Capt kia 24-7-16 BlkW att1KAR p129&268 CR EAfrica40

MACKINTOSH,Douglas Fraser Lt 2-10-17 50RFA att55RFC served as MATHEWS,G.

MACKINTOSH,Edwin Hampson TLt kia 25-9-15 8BlkW p129 MR19

MACKINTOSH,Ewart Alan.MC.Lt kia 21-11-17 5SfthH p241 CR France1498

MACKINTOSH,Gerard 2Lt ded 26-3-17 IARO attS&TCps p279 CR Iraq6

MACKINTOSH,Henry Leith 2Lt dow 5-3-15 1SStaffs p122 CR France254,Harry

MACKINTOSH,James Lawton 2Lt kia 1-5-15 ULIA att 1HLI p163&279 CR Belgium101,Lt

MACKINTOSH John Capt kia 23-7-18 6SfthH p241 CR France1697

MACKINTOSH John James TLt ded 1-4-16 RAMC att1GarrBn Ess p196 CR Egypt8

MACKINTOSH John Lachlan Lt 9-1-16 ArabRifs CR EAfrica50

MACKIRDY,Charles David Scott Lt dow PoW 22-3-18 11Huss p22

MACKNIGHT,Thomas William Finglan TLt ded 4-9-16 RAMC p196 MR65,Fingland

MACKLE,Augustine Mary 2Lt dow 16-8-17 5BordR att1/6Lond p228 CR Belgium19,Austin

MACKLIN,David Harold 2Lt kia 27-3-18 5BedR p219 CR France393,4Bn

MACKLIN John James Malcolm TLt kia 12-3-18 RLancs att12LancF p59 CR Greece5

MACKPHERSON,Donald 2Lt dow 11-11-17 RH&FA p208

MACKRETH John TLt kia 15-9-16 RE 41DivSigCo p46 MR21

MACKRIDGE,Ralf Leslie 2Lt kia 26-4-18 4 att1WYorks p82 MR30

MacKRORY,Ernest William T2Lt kia 14-7-16 1SStaffs p122 MR21

MACKWORTH,Arthur Christopher Paul TLt ded 25-11-17 RB p266 CR Oxford71

MACKWORTH,Francis Julian Audley Maj kia 1-11-14 RA p32 CR France1106

MacLACHLAN,Alexander Fraser Campbell.CMG.DSO.MajTLtCol kia 22-3-18 KRRC p151 CR France672

MACLACHLAN,David Corson T2Lt ded 18-5-17 MGC HB p184 CR France40

MacLACHLAN James Menzies.MC.T2LtACapt kia 2-12-17 GL att97/LTMB p191 MR30

MacLACHLAN,Kenneth Douglas Mackenzie Capt dow 27-4-15 SfthH p165 CR France134

MacLACHLAN,Kenneth Gilbert 2Lt kia 23-4-17 8 att13RScot p212 MR20

MACLACHLAN,Peter Malcolm.MC.TCapt dow 26-3-18 RAMC att15Hamps p196 CR France62,McLACHLAN

MACLACHLAN,Robert Hugh Muir dow 2Lt kia 23-3-18 4 att12RScots p211 MR27,McLACHLAN

MACLACHLAN,Ronald Campbell.DSO.TBrigGen kia 11-8-17 RB Staff Cmdg112InfBde p179 CR Belgium183

MacLACHLAN,Walter Miller 2Lt ded 11-7-16 13HLI att6SLancs p163 CR Iraq5,12 att6Bn

MacLACHLAN,William Smith 2Lt kia 29-8-18 1/14LondR p249 CR France646,McLACHLAN

MacLAGAN,Gilchrist Stanley Lt kia 25-4-15 3 att1RWar p65 MR29

MACLAGAN James Graham Lt kia 1-8-18 1/5LNLancs p234 CR France113

MacLAGAN,Philip Whiteside.MID Lt kia 16-4-16 5Bord p228 CR Belgium37

MacLAGAN,Thomas Duncan Ogilvie.MC&Bar.Capt kia 30-4-18 2/14Lond p249 CR Palestine3

MACLAREN,Frank Nairne Capt kia 15-4-16 IA 1/9GurkhaRif p279 MR38,14-4-16

MacLAREN,Donald Graeme 2Lt kia 29-6-17 10Lpool p216 MR32

MacLAREN,Ernest Cecil Capt kia 1-7-16 15LancFus p93 CR France215,McLAREN

MacLAREN,Robert T2Lt dow 24-7-16 16Ches p96

MacLAUGHLIN,Alexander Wilson Lt mbk 29-10-17 1RFC p256 MR20

MACLAVERTY,Colin Johnston Capt kia 18-9-16 1KSLI p145 MR21

MACLAY,Ebenezer Lt dow 11-4-18 1ScotGds p52 CR France62

MACLAY,James Webster 2Lt kia 28-6-15 7ScotRif p224 CR Gallipoli6

MACLAY,William Strang 2Lt dow 25-6-15 8ScotRif p225 MR4

MacLEAN,Alec Clarkson TLt kia 9-4-18 RE 296RlyCo p46 CR France1094

MacLEAN,Alexander Harvie Maj kia 26-8-14 2A&SH p173 CR France716

MacLEAN,Alexander Murchison TCapt kia 12-4-18 ScotHorse &10RAF MR20

MacLEAN,Alfred Knowles T2Lt kia 27-9-18 8NumbF p62 MR16,McCLEAN

MacLEAN,Alfred Peter Lt kld 17-9-18 4RScot &RAF p211&p258 CR Egypt15

MacLEAN,Alistair Fitzhugh Capt kia 8-8-15 IA 33Punjabis att14Sikhs p279 MR4

MacLEAN,Andrew De Vere Capt kia 19-9-14 ESurr p113 CR France864,17-9-14

MACLEAN,Archibald T2Lt kia 18-8-18 1KOSB p102 CR France28

MacLEAN,Arthur Kirkpatrick Lt kia 26-8-14 2A&SH p173 CR France716

MacLEAN,David 2Lt kia 14-7-18 1GordH p166

MacLEAN,Donald T2Lt dow 12-10-16 6CamH p168 CR France385

MacLEAN,Donald 2Lt kia 21-9-18 6ScotRif p224 CR France666

MacLEAN,Donald Frederick Durant TMaj ded 10-12-17 10RFus p69 CR Berks83

MacLEAN,Donald Lewis Lt 21-11-20 RB CR Ireland14

MACLEAN,Dugald Black.MC.TCapt kia 29-8-16 RAMC att8ELanc p196 CR France115

MACLEAN,Dugald Fitzroy 2Lt dow 23-7-16 KSLI att1/4Glouc p145 MR21

MACLEAN,Frederick William T2Lt dow 14-6-17 GL &29RFC p10 CR France46,McLEAN

MACLEAN,G.H.MC.Capt 30-8-20 Ches CR EAfrica116

MACLEAN,Ivan Clarkson.DSO.MC&Bar.TCapt dow PoW 4-4-18 RAMC att2RB p196 CR France441

MACLEAN,Henry Chevers TCapt kia 1-7-16 9RInnisF p105 MR21

MacLEAN,James Acheson.MC.Lt kia 30-9-17 D148RFA p32 CR Belgium17,2Lt

MacLEAN,Kemp T2Lt kia 28-3-18 13RScot p54 MR20

MacLEAN,Malcolm Alexander 2Lt kia 13-10-15 3CamH p168 MR19

MacLEAN,Moira Francis Allan Capt kia 17-2-15 RGA p40 CR Asia45,15-2-15

MacLEAN,Raymond Alastair T2Lt kia 13-11-16 3 att6SfthH p165 CR France131,McLEAN

MACLEAN,William Archibald Lt kia 12-3-15 3HLI p163 CR France279,1Bn

MACLEAN,William Macfarlane.MC.2Lt 24-3-18 5 att1/8A&SH MR27

MacLEAR,Basil Capt kia 24-5-15 2RDubFus p177 MR29

MacLEAR,Basil George Hope.MC.2Lt kia 26-7-16 4GrenGds p50 CR Belgium73

MacLEAR,Harry.DSO.LtCol kia 15-3-16 ELanc att3RScots p111 CR France222

MacLEAR,Percy Maj kia 30-8-14 RDubF Cmdg2NigR p177 CR WAfrica57,LtCol

MacLEAY,George Cameron T2Lt kia 17-8-16 8CamH p168 MR21,McLEAY

MacLEHOSE,James Colin T2Lt kia 14-2-17 16RB p179 CR Belgium6

MACLEHOSE,Norman Crawford Lt kia 26-5-15 8LondR p247 CR France261

MacLELLAN,George Douglas 2Lt kia 28-4-17 5HLI p240 MR20

MacLELLAN,Lewis.MC.Lt kia 30-11-17 1/5HLI p240 CR Palestine9

MacLELLAN,Malcolm TCapt kia 25-9-15 11A&SH p173 MR19,26-9-15

MacLENNAN,Iain Donald Forrest 2Lt kia 12-5-17 3 att1GordH p166 CR France1182

MacLENNAN,John Maj ded 9-8-16 1GordH p265 CR Scot287

MacLENNAN,Roderick Ward T2Lt kia 23-12-17 GL &60RFC p10 CR France200

MACLEOD,Alastair Roderick Lt kia 25-4-15 15RHA p32 MR4

MacLEOD,David.DSO.TLtCol ded 19-12-17 8GordH p166 CR France113

MacLEOD,Daniel Mackay 2Lt ded 9-7-18 7NumbF p214 CR Scot674

MACLEOD,Donald Capt kia 28-9-15 1/10Lpool p216 CR Belgium6

MACLEOD,Donald Lt drd 10-5-17 RE GL attIWT p191 MR38

MACLEOD,Donald.MC.T2Lt kia 1-7-17 BordR att1Bn p117 CR Belgium23

MACLEOD,Donald Angus 2Lt dow 5-10-17 3KOSB p102 CR France139

MACLEOD,Donald Kerr 2Lt kia 18-10-17 86RFA p32 CR Belgium19

MacLEOD,George Calder T2Lt kia 19-4-17 9 att1/5KOSB p102 CR Palestine8

MacLEOD,George Charles Sholto Capt dow 13-5-15 2BlkW p129 CR France80

MacLEOD,Ian Breac Lt kia 17-4-15 2BlkW p129 CR France924

MacLEOD,Ion Keith Falconer Capt kia 27-4-18 RAMC 75FA CR Belgium11

MACLEOD,John TLt kia 6-1-16 1SfthH p165 MR38

MACLEOD,James Herbert Negnoe TLt kia 29-6-16 8KOSB p102 CR France423,Neynoe 2Lt

MACLEOD,John Capt ded 12-7-19 RAMC att11Lancers p267 CR Iraq8

MACLEOD,Victor Charles Augustus T2Lt kia 18-7-17 10 att1/8ScotRif p103 CR Palestine8

MACLEOD,William Bannatyne Capt kia 12-1-17 IA 121 att34SikhPnrs p279 CR Iraq5,McLEOD 11/12-1-17

MacLUCKIE,Reginald William TCapt kia 11-8-16 3A&SH att9WYorks p173 CR France158

MACLURE,Gordon Stanley 2Lt dow 16-6-16 RFA attZ32TMB p32 CR France145

MACMAHON,Charles Edward Valentine 2Lt ded 9-3-16 1LNLancR p136 CR Lancs102,McMAHON 13-3-16

MacMAHON,John Aquila Lt dow 12-5-15 RAMC att3SomLI p196 CR Mddx80

MacMASTER,Donald Cameron Deford TLt kia 26-9-15 6CamH p168 CR France219,25-9-15

MacMEEKEN,Guy Steel Peebles.MC.TLtACapt dow PoW 5-5-18 12RScot p54 CR France1142

MacMEEKEN,James T2Lt kia 27-5-18 NumbF Res att5Bn p62 CR France1753

MACMICHAEL,Michael William Annesley Capt dow 16-9-16 11Ess A'Coy p132 CR France66,Lt

MACMILLAN,Cameron TLtACapt kia 22-8-17 8SfthH p165 MR30

MACMILLAN,Edwin James 2Lt kia 12-1-17 4 att8RIrF p171 MR29

MacMILLAN,James Alexander(Sandy) 2Lt kia 20-7-18 1/4SfthH p241 CR France622

MacMILLAN,James Bonthron.DSO.TMaj kia 30-11-17 7DCLI p114 MR17

MacMILLAN,John 2Lt 24-3-18 LanarkYeo att9RScots MR27

MACMILLAN,John 2Lt dow 24-9-18 8ScotRif p225 CR France278,McMILLAN 1Bn

MacMILLAN,Robert Alexander Cameron T2Lt kia 11-4-17 2SfthH p165 CR France604

MacMILLAN,Stephen Alexander Lt dow 9-5-15 IARO att58Rif p279 CR France80

MACMILLAN,Thomas 2Lt kld 12-2-17 GL &RFC p10 CR Scot675

MACMILLAN,Thomas Muir 2Lt 19-8-17 4SAInf CR France662

MacMULLEN,E.R.Lt 30-6-16 EAUL CR EAfrica2 &Tanzania1

MACMULLEN,Frederick Charles Kendall LtCol ded 19-6-16 IA 27Cav attStaff GenHQ p279 CR Iraq5,12Bn

MacMULLEN,George Reade Maj ded 28-1-16 SL IA Retd p201 CR War75

MacMURCHY,Ian Ure T2Lt kia 9-10-17 GL &9RFC p10 MR20,McMURCHY

MacNAB,Alexander 2Lt dow 24-10-18 D186RFA p32 CR France241

MACNAB,Angus Capt kia 1-11-14 RAMC att14Lond p254 MR29

MACNAB,Colin Lawrence.CMG.BrigGen ded 13-10-18 Staff p254 CR Essex254 Ex Suss

MACNAB,James T2Lt kia 19-8-15 8NumbF p62 MR4

MacNAE,Robert.MC.2Lt kia 10-10-16 10Lpool p216 CR Belgium4

MacNAGHTEN,A.C.R.S.Lt 29-11-14 1BlkW MR29

MacNAGHTEN,Arthur Douglas.Bart T2Lt kia 15-9-16 8RB p179 CR France432

MACNAGHTEN,Edward Harry.Bart.2Lt mbk 1-7-16 1BlkW att12RIrRif p256 MR21

MacNAGHTEN,Stewart Cecil Capt ded 9-11-18 RASC p253 CR Norf210,Steuart

MacNAGHTON,Arthur Edward Harry T2Lt kia 31-7-16 13RSussR p119 CR France727,MACNAGHTEN Hay

MACNAMARA,Charles Carroll Maj dow 15-7-16 1RIrRif p170 CR Herts29,Carroll Charles LtCol 16-7-16

MACNAMARA,Colin George Herbert Rawdon 2Lt kia 17-8-15 IARO Inf attCpsofGuides p279 MR43

MACNAMARA,George CaptAMaj dow 25-5-17 2Wilts p153 CR France178,kia 27-5-17

MACNAMARA,George Frederick 2Lt kia 17-8-16 4 att8RDubF p177 CR France115

MacNAMARA,Joseph Bernard 2Lt kia 19-10-16 3 att2WRid p116 CR France374,McNAMARA

MacNAMARA,Kevin Parnell 2Lt kia 29-6-16 RFC p3 MR20

MACNAMARA,Maccon John 2Lt kia 26-3-18 2RDubF p177 MR27

MACNAUGHT,Frederick Clement TLt kia 25-9-15 RE 91FC p46 MR19

MACNAUGHTON,Angus Charles Rowley Stuart Lt kia 29-10-14 BlkW p129

MacNEECE,James Douglas Gaussen Capt kia 16-8-16 39RFA p32 MR21

MACNEILL,Andrew Duncan TCapt kia 29-7-17 RGA 21HB p40 CR Belgium9

MacNEILL,Archibald 2Lt kia 25-3-16 6A&SH p243 CR France15,26-3-16

MACNEILL,William Mackinnon 2Lt kia 12-10-14 16Lancers p23 CR France324

MacNICOL,Angus John Bayne TLt dow 18-4-17 D50RFA p32 CR France95

MacNICOL,Douglas Oswald Lt kia 5-1-18 1/4RWSurr att57RFC p19&212CR Egypt8 2Lt RWKent

MacNICOL,Harry Mansfield TLt kia 19-7-16 8Norf p74 MR21

MACNICOL,Horatius Bonar 2Lt drd 30-7-15 10RScot p212 CR Scot239

MacNIE,George Francis T2Lt kia 5-9-16 5ConnRgrs att6RDubF p172 CR Greece3

MacNIVEN,Alister Orr Lt kia 5-9-17 7HLI attRFC p19&240,6Bn

MACONACHIE,Arthur Delano 2Lt kia 1-7-16 9YLI p143 CR France267

MACONCHY,George Alexander.MID Capt kia 14-1-20 IA 2/5GurkhaRif p279 MR43

195

MACOUAT,John T2Lt kia12-4-17 12RScots p54 CR France604

MacPHERSON,Arthur Vincent Claresholm TLt kia 25-8-15 14HLI att5RScots p163 CR Gallipoli4,McPHERSON Capt 4Bn

MacPHERSON,Donald William.MID Maj kia 16-11-16 IA 62Punjabis attStaffIndInfBde p279 CR Egypt15 McPHERSON

MACPHERSON,Duncan Stuart Ross Lt kia 24-11-14 IA 1/7 att2/8GurkhaRif p279 CR France80,23-11-14

MACPHERSON,Ewen Fergus Lord 2Lt kia 10-8-16 5RFA p32 CR France267

MACPHERSON,George TLt dow 15-9-16 MGC 4Sect p184 CR France105

MACPHERSON,George Denis Maj kia 27-9-15 13RScot p54 MR19 kld 26-9-15

MACPHERSON,Henry Douglas T2Lt kia 14-10-17 29RFC p10 CR Belgium18

MACPHERSON,Hugh Bannerman.MC.Lt kia 27-9-18 95RFA p32 CR France530

MACPHERSON,James Capt kia 10-3-15 4CamH p242 CR France1157

MacPHERSON,John Lt kia 1-7-16 1/7N&D p233 MR21

MacPHERSON,John Cook T2Lt kia 25-9-15 11 att1GordH p166 MR29

MacPHERSON,John Symon Lt dow 15-3-18 6GordH p242 CR France8

MACPHERSON,Maximillian.MIDx2 Capt kia 4-10-17 3 att1SfthH p165 MR30,3 att2Bn

MACPHERSON,Neil Maj kia 31-10-14 IA 2/2GurkhaRif p279 MR28

MacPHERSON,Robert Duncan Mearns 2Lt kia 25-10-15 7SfthH p165 MR19,25-9-15

MacPHERSON,Robert David T2Lt drd 6-6-16 8GordH p166 CR Scot900,5-6-16

MacPHERSON,Robert Nasmyth Maj kia 18-4-17 IA 40Pathans p279 CR EAfrica38 &CR Tanzania1

MacPHERSON,Ronald Charters Capt dow 18-4-18 B256RFA p207 CR France202

MacPHERSON,T.D.2Lt 11-11-18 RFA CR Scot253

MACPHERSON,William Meikle T2Lt kia 18-9-18 6MGC Inf p184 CR France1701

MacQUEEN,Alexander Norman 2Lt kia 25-3-17 6GordH attRFC p19&242 CR France568

MacQUEEN,John Ellison LtCol kia 25-9-15 6GordH p242 MR19

MACQUEEN,Roderick Reid TCapt kia 15-5-16 7RScotF p95 CR France423,Lt

MACQUEEN,Thomas Malcolm TLt kia 15-7-16 8ELancR p111 MR21

MACRAE,Alexander William Urquhart Capt kld 11-8-18 5RScot p211 CR France360,kia

MacRAE,Alfred Reginald AssComm ded 1-7-16 CR Iraq6

MACRAE,Archibald John Lt dow 5-10-18 4CamH att8SfthH p242 CR France106

MACRAE,Charles Alexander TLt ded 22-4-16 RASC p193 CR France1564,McRAE

MacRAE,Charles Eric 2Lt kia 10-11-16 1/4SfthH &RFC p19&241 CR France169

MACRAE,Charles Mackenzie Lt kia 5-7-15 1/4Hamp p228 CR Iraq6

MACRAE,Donald Alastair Lt ded 16-11-18 5SfthH att15MGC p187&241 CR Belgium406

MACRAE,Duncan Mackenzie 2Lt kia 4-10-17 3 att2SfthH p165 MR30

MACRAE,Frank Laing 2Lt kia 25-9-15 8SfthH p165 MR19

MacRAE,George Duncan T2Lt kia 27-3-18 31MGC Inf B'Coy p184 CR France745

MacRAE,George Pitt Taylor 2Lt kia 9-4-17 4SfthH p241

MACRAE,Ivor Alexander 2Lt dow 15-10-14 3 att2KOSB D'Coy p102 CR France80,14-10-14

MACRAE,John Nigel Capt kld 11-4-18 GL &83RAF p191 CR France88

MacRAE,John Alexander T2Lt kia 18-7-16 11 att8BlkW p129 MR21

MacRAE,John Harold 2Lt kia 25-8-16 4 att18ScotRif p103 CR France453,att1Bn

MACRAE,Joseph Nixon T2Lt kia 18-2-18 11BordR p117 CR Belgium126

MacRAE,Kenneth Matheson.MC.TMaj kia 1-11-18 124/28RFA p32 CR Belgiu140

MacRAE,Patrick Cameron Capt ded 5-3-17 RAMC 80FA p196 CR Scot458

MACRAE,William Charles Macintyre LtACapt kia 27-9-18 3RASC att14DivTrain p193 CR France429,29-9-18

MACREADY,Oscar Henry TCapt dow 3-12-17 16RIrRif p170 CR France512

MacREADY,William Capt kia 14-4-15 IA 120Inf p279 CR Iraq6

MACREIGHT,Arthur William James Lt ded 23-11-15 18Lond p250 CR Hamps15

MACREIGHT,Lionel Albert Lt kld 22-3-18 3 att2SLancs p125 MR27

MACRORIE,Roderick Douglas Capt kia 2-11-17 1/4RScot p211 CR Palestine8

MACROSTIE,Ernest James 2Lt kia 21-5-19 25Lond p252 MR43

MACROSTY,Henry Hugh TLt kia 19-12-15 C53RFA p32 CR Belgium84

MACRURY,Norman Lt kia 4-6-15 11BlkW attKOSB p129 MR4,McRURY

MacSHERRY,Dermot Joseph 2Lt kia 4-6-17 3 att6ConnRgrs p172 CR Belgium60

MacSWINEY,Joseph Ray.MC.Lt ded 2-11-18 10Lpool p216 CR Ches8,Capt

MacTAGGART,Murdoch Archibald.MID Capt kia 16-5-17 8A&SH p243 MR20

MacTAVISH,Hugh 2Lt kia 22-3-18 4ScotRif att8BordR p103 MR20

MacTAVISH,Roswell Murray.MC.TCapt ded 6-2-19 GL attStaff 45InfBde p191 CR France134

MACTIER,Henry MacKinnon Maj kia 12-3-15 IA 2/39GarhwalRif p279 CR France355 &CR France1887

MacVICAR,Neil T2Lt dow 4-5-17 2 att1/6SfthH p165 CR France40

MacVICKER,John Everard Churchill Lt ded 22-7-18 GL attRAF p191 CR France429

MacWALTER,Charles Christopher 2Lt kia 1-7-16 RLancs p59 MR21

MACWATT,Norman Ian Lt kia 1-7-16 2SfthH p165 MR21

MacWHIRTER,Thomas.MC.Maj kia 27-4-17 9GordH p166 MR20

MacWILLIAM,Frank T2Lt kia 2-6-18 7BordR p117 CR France4 McWILLIAM

MacWILLIAM,James Julian Gordon TLt kia 14-12-14 GordH p166

MADAN,Nigel Cornwallis TLt kia 3-3-16 8RLancs p59 MR29,2-3-16

MADDEN,Gerald Hugh Charles MajTLtCol dow 12-11-15 1IrGds p53 CR Eire468

MADDEN,Thomas Hylton 2Lt kia 10-3-15 1Lpool p72 CR France1106

MADDEN,William Henry TCapt dow 24-3-18 16RIrRif p170 CR France1063,kia

MADDEN,William Thomas TLt kia 14-4-18 1DCLI p114 CR France18

MADDER,Robert 2Lt kia 20-7-16 3/5GloucR att145MGC p187 CR France150

MADDERS,Hubert Franklin 2Lt kia 1-7-16 168RFA p32 CR France296

MADDEVER,Robert William Digory 2Lt dow 22-10-17 4SomLI p218 MR30

MADDICK,Herbert Capt dow 28-10-15 5Lancers p22 CR Surrey160

MADDICK,Sidney Alfred TLt ded 2-12-18 20Lpool att1/6KAR p72&202 CR EAfrica52

MADDISON,Bertram Lionel TLtCol kia 1-7-16 2Yorks att8Y&L p91 CR France246

MADDISON,Geoffrey T2Lt kia 28-8-18 7Norf p74 CR France370

MADDISON,George Lionel Temple Lt kia 17-7-17 RFA p208 MR29

MADDISON,Walter 2Lt ded 24-11-17 RFC p10 CR Lond10

MADDOCK,Owen Loftus 2Lt kia 7-10-16 9Lond p248 CR France374

MADDOCKS,John Onslow TLt kia 4-6-16 17 att15RWar p65 CR France1182,Anslow

MADDOX,Cecil Edwards Capt 16-4-17 63PalamcottaLI MR61

MADDOX,Cecil Richard Capt kld 6-4-17 IA 63LI p279

MADDOX,Cyril Percy T2Lt kia 20-11-17 Yorks att2/4YLI p91 CR France530

MADDOX,Edward Harry.MID TLt kia 27-8-18 RE 18DivSigCo p46 CR France515

MADDOX,John Mortimer 2Lt kia 12-8-16 3 att10LancF p93 MR21

MADDOX,Leonard George.MC&Bar.2Lt kld 30-8-18 1/22Lond p251 CR France785

MADDRELL,James Keggan TLt kia 23-4-17 90MGC p184 MR20

MADDRELL,John Denis Hugh Lt dow 13-12-16 1/5DCLI p227 CR France40

MADELEY,Claude Neville 2Lt kia 19-1-18 43RFC p16 CR France1316

MADELEY,Sydney 2Lt dow 11-3-15 KRRC p151 CR Belgium28

MADEN,Harold T2Lt kia 29-7-17 18Manch p155 MR29

MADEN,William Henry T2Lt dow 4-10-17 GL DCLI att95TMB p191 CR Belgium165

MADGE,Charles Albert.MID TLtCol kia 10-5-16 SL RWar p201 CR France80

MADLEY,Lewis George T2Lt kia 14-5-17 1RWFus p98 MR20

MADOCKS,Henry John TLtCol kia 25-9-15 9RWFus p98 CR France260

MADORE,William Douglas 2LtACapt dow 10-2-17 RE 254TC p46 CR France80

MAFFETT,Henry Telford Capt kia 20-10-14 2Leinst p174 CR France1140

MAFFEY,Henry TLt&QM dow 1-5-16 RAMC att139FA p196 CR France858,18-5-16

MAGAWLY CERATI DECLRY,Valerio Awby.DSO.CaptTLtCol kia 10-5-17 6Drags Cmdg7RB p22,10-8-17 CR France1185,de CALRY

MAGENIS,R.H.C.2Lt kia 15-9-14 3RIrRif p170 MR15

MAGER,William George 2Lt kia 1-7-16 13Lond p249 CR France1327

MAGGS,Eric William Bristow T2Lt kia 20-8-18 11KRRC p151 CR France547,Bristowe

MAGGS,George Ernest T2Lt dow 14-7-16 8RBerks p139 CR France176

MAGILL,Thomas Edmund 2Lt kia 3-9-16 6RIrReg p89 MR21

MAGINN,Philip Albert Charles.MC.Capt kia 15-9-16 18Lond p250 CR France453

MAGINNESS,Oscar Gladstone.MID TLt dow 15-12-15 RAMC attC51RFA p196 CR Belgium11

MAGNAY,John Christopher Frederick Lt kia 23-4-17 1Norf p74 MR20

MAGNAY,Philip Magnay.MIDx3 CaptTLtCol kia 13-4-17 RFus Cmdg12Manch p69 CR France924,Mathew

MAGNESS,Thomas Charles 2Lt kia 22-8-17 1/5RWar p214 MR30

MAGNIAC,Erskine.MID LtCol kia 28-4-17 IA 27Punjabis p279 MR38

MAGNIAC,Meredith.DSO.MajTLtCol kia 25-4-17 1/2LancF p93 CR France418

MAGOOKIN,William Douglas.DCM.2Lt kia 21-3-18 12RIrRif p170 MR27

MAGOR,Arthur Curgenven Capt kia 17-10-14 3 att2Wilts p153 MR29

MAGOVERNY,John Henry Capt ded 19-4-19 RAMC attCamH p267 CR Asia81

MAGRANE,George Fairfield 2Lt kia 7-6-17 RGA 161SB p40 CR Belgium451,261SB

MAGRATH,Beauchamp Henry Butler TMaj kis 2-6-16 8ELancs p111 CR France745,5Bn

MAGRATH,Meyrick Magrath.DSO.CaptAMaj kia 2-8-18 291RFA p32 CR France887

MAGUIRE,Cecil Augustine 2Lt kia 31-7-17 4 att2ScotRif p103 MR29

MAGUIRE,Edward Alphonsus T2Lt kia 8-10-18 RFus att4Bn p69 CR France338

MAGUIRE,Francis Patrick 2Lt kia 27-4-18 5Leinst p174 CR France24

MAGUIRE,Henry T2Lt dow 15-7-16 RE 124FC p46 CR France66

MAGUIRE,Hugh 2Lt kia 9-9-16 3ConnRgrs att7InnisF p172 MR21

MAGUIRE,John Reginald T2Lt kia 18-8-16 3 att12WYorks p82 MR21

MAGUIRE,M.2Lt 21-8-18 3Ches CR France239

MAGUIRE,Matthew Laurence.MC.2LtTLt kia PoW 28-4-17 1ConRgrs &30RFC p10&172 MR38,dow

MAHAFFY,Henry Irwin T2Lt kld 22-10-17 RFC p10 CR Ireland107

MAHER,Cyril Benjamin Lt ded 25-7-17 IARO att7IndLabCps p279 CR Iraq8,25-7-19

MAHER,John Charles Lt kia 14-4-18 2IrGds p53 CR France352

MAHOMED,Claude Atkinson Etty Lt kia 31-7-17 1ScotGds p52 CR Belgium106

MAHON,James Harold Capt dow 13-9-16 1/8Lpool p215 CR France66

MAHON,Oswald Sydney Wilson 2Lt dow 14-4-17 5 att7Lpool p214 CR France13

MAHONEY,Frank.MC.2Lt kia 6-10-17 2BordR p117 CR Belgium165

MAHONEY,Herbert James.MM.MID LtACapt dow 24-10-18 RGA 184SB p40 CR France1196

MAHONEY,Thomas.MC.MID Capt&QM ded 10-1-18 2RIrReg p89 CR France145,MAHONY

MAHONY,Brian Gerald 2Lt kld 3-9-18 1/2RMunstFus att189RAF p175 CR Lond4,MAHONEY

MAHONY,Edmund Joseph TLt kia 27-9-18 1RMunstF p175 CR France530

MAHONY,Edward Archibald Lt kia 16-8-17 3RIrRif p170 MR30

MAHONY,Frederick Henry.MID Capt dow 22-10-14 ChesR p96 CR France80

MAHONY,James TLt dow 4-3-17 11RWSurr p56 CR Belgium11

MAHONY,Norman T2Lt dow 23-6-18 LancF att1/2Bn p93 CR France10,2/5Bn

MAHONY,Thomas George T2Lt kia 13-7-16 19LancF p93 MR21

MAHONY-JONES,G.J.Capt 7-4-17 GL &RFC CR France285

MAHOOD,Charles Cleland T2Lt dow 16-9-16 9KOSB p102 CR France177

MAIBEN,W.SubCdr 2-3-15 IA S&TCps CR Asia60

MAIDEN,Albert Augustus T2Lt kia 16-9-16 6YLI p143 CR France329,dow

MAIDLOW,John Southern Maj dow 23-8-14 RFA p32 CR Belgium241

MAIL,Frank Oswald 2Lt kia 9-10-18 78RFA p32 CR France660

MAIN,Alfred Leonard Lt ded 3-10-19 2Worc p264 CR Staffs60,2Lt 5Bn

MAIN,Donald Alexander Mill.MC.Capt drd 6-9-18 6HLI p240 MR70 &CR Europe180,5-9-18 Ex9 att2/10RScots

MAIN,Eric Arthur 2Lt ded 26-2-18 6RRofCav attNSomYeo p24 CR France987

MAIN,George Ernest Lt kia 12-10-17 KOSB att6Bn p102 MR30

MAIN,John Capt dow 18-8-16 6ScotRif p224 CR France300

MAIN,John Alexander.MC.TLt kia 27-3-18 RE 278RlyCo p46 CR France174

MAIN,Percy Rowland 2Lt kld 28-9-16 15HantR attRFC p3&p121 CR Hamps9,23-9-16

MAINE,William John Samuel AssSurg drd 27-2-16 IMS RAMC p279 CR Kent8,W.J.C.

MAINPRISE,Bertie Wilmot.MIDx4 Maj kia 12-3-16 RE attHQBde p46 CR EAfrica56

MAINSTONE,James Francis 2LtACapt kia 4-10-17 1 att12Glouc p107 MR30

MAINWARING,Cyril Lyttleton Lt ded 16-2-19 RGA 422Bty p262 CR Surrey15,17-2-19

MAINWARING,Frank Harry George Carver Capt ded 6-1-19 3Co ofLondYeo att104MGC p187&204 CR France40

MAIR,Edward Millett 2Lt kia 3-9-16 3 att1CamH p168 MR21

MAIR,George Hay Lt ded 14-12-18 3RWFus attRSuss p98 CR Camb16

MAIR,John Gordon T2Lt dow 5-8-18 RE 150FC p47 CR France100

MAIR,William Craig.MC.Capt kia 22-3-18 4 att2RScotF p222 MR27

MAIS,Herbert Roxburgh.MID TLt dow 30-11-17 RE 70FC p47 CR France439

MAISEY,Albert Henry 2Lt dow 16-2-17 6Mddx p147 CR France164

MAISEY,Alfred George 2Lt kia 12-5-17 6RWSurr Inf p56 CR Belgium125 &CR France421

MAISH,William Edward.MC.T2Lt kia 12-10-17 27MGC p184

MAITLAND,Alexander 2Lt kia 20-5-17 9HLI p240 MR20

MAITLAND,Alexander McLean 2Lt kia 1-8-16 RE 1/2FC p210 CR France189

MAITLAND,Alfred Henry.Hon.Maj kia 19-9-14 1CamH p168 MR15,14-9-14

MAITLAND,Arthur Dudley TLt kia 1-7-16 13WYorks p82 CR France743,14 att16Bn

MAITLAND,Arthur James T2Lt kld 22-9-17 GL &RFC p10 CR Mddx5

MAITLAND,Edgar Francis Lt kia 24-9-17 6Manch p236 CR Belgium173

MAITLAND,Graham Macdonell 2Lt kia 26-1-16 1IrGds p53 MR29,Macdowall 1-11-14

MAITLAND,Henry Maitland.MC.TCapt ded 10-11-18 GL p191 CR France1848

MAITLAND,James Moule Hamilton T2Lt dow 23-4-17 2A&SH p173 CR France434

MAITLAND,John Dalrymple T2Lt kia 22-2-16 9WRid p116 MR29

MAITLAND,John Pelham Blanchard Capt ded 2-8-15 11YLI p143 CR Yorks321

MAITLAND,Keith Andrew Ramsay.MC&Bar.LtAMaj kia 4-10-17 A76RFA p32 Belgium12

MAITLAND,William Ebenezer 2Lt dow 24-12-14 3SfthH att2BlkW p165 CR France202

MAITLAND,William Renmure 2Lt kia 18-11-16 5Mddx attTMB p147 MR19

MAITLAND-ADDISON,Alec Arthur Creighton 2Lt dow 27-10-14 1ChesR p96 CR France102

MAITLAND-MAKGILL-CRICHTON,Charles Julian TMaj kia 25/27-9-15 10GordH p166 MR19

MAJOR,Arthur Oswald Capt kia 23-11-17 1/5SomLI p218 CR Palestine3

MAJOR,Charles William Wykeham Chap4Cl ded 19-3-19 RAChDept p199 CR Germany1

MAJOR,Cyril Birdee 2Lt kia 5-11-16 7EYorks p84 MR21 Bisdee

MAJOR,Harold TLt kld 19-10-15 14Mddx p147 CR Belgium82

MAJOR,Stanley T2Lt kia 3-3-17 3 att1EKent p57 CR France149

MAKANT,Angus Virtue Capt dow 14-3-15 5LNLancs p234 CR France922

MAKEHAM,Eric Noel T2Lt ded PoW 28-8-17 13Mddx p147 MR29,10-6-17

MAKIN,Stanley T2Lt kia 22-3-18 9YLI p143 MR27

MAKINNON,Charles Frank Capt mbk 14-6-19 SL att1/6KAR p257&p201,McKINNON ded

MAKINS,Geoffrey.MVO.Capt dow 23-8-15 3KRRC p151 CR France345

MAKINS,Hugh Capt dow 4-11-15 16LondR p249 CR Belgium2

MAKINSON,Frederick Valentine 2Lt kia 14-4-18 3Lpool p72 MR32

MALCOLM,Alan Alexander Lt kia 17-5-18 17Lancers &98RAF p23 MR20

MALCOLM,Albert Victor Sadler T2Lt kia 17-2-17 16 att11RFus p69 CR France314

MALCOLM,Archibald Houlder Lt kld 24-8-18 9HLI p240 CR France1186,kia

MALCOLM,Archibald Hugh T2Lt kia 16-5-17 1KOSB p102 MR20

MALCOLM,Geoffrey Cooper T2Lt kld 27-9-17 3YLI attRFC p10&p143,kia CR Essex73

MALCOLM,George John.MID TMaj kia 9-7-16 RFA attRFC p3&p32 CR France134

MALCOLM,Henry Alexander Drummond 2Lt dow 17-2-17 RFA Z33TMB p32 CRFrance624 Ex 2KEdwHorse

MALCOLM,James Waddell.MID 2Lt kia 12-7-15 5HLI p240 MR4

MALCOLM,John Evelyn LtACapt ded 19-2-19 RE 271RailCo p47 CR Belgium406

MALCOLM,Kenneth James Lt kia 19-2-18 2/20Lond p251 CR Palestine3

MALCOLM,Pulteney LtACapt kia 25-8-18 1GrenGds p50 CR France1487

MALCOLM,Robert James TCapt dow 15-7-16 2RScot p54 CR France23 true name STEWART,Malcolm Hector

MALCOLM,Sidney John TCapt kia 20-9-17 1/8A&SH p173 CR Belgium96,Sydney

MALCOLM,Stuart Renton Lt ded 22-11-18 RGA 38SB p40 CR France1725,39SB

MALCOLM,Thomas 2Lt dow 23-10-17 3 att18HLI p163 CR Belgium16

MALCOLM,William Aberdein Maj ded 3-10-15 RAMC att1/11Lond p253 CR Europe1

MALCOLM,William Noel 2Lt dow 12-6-15 RE 271RlyCoy p47 CR Europe7

MALCOLMSON,Hubert TLt&Adjt dow 16-9-16 6RIrReg p89 CR Eire185

MALCOLMSON,James Grant Capt ded 22-12-14 27/18Lond p250 CR Lond8

MALCOLMSON,John Joseph Maj ded 4-6-15 RFA p206 CR Hamps221

MALCOLMSON,Keith Grant Capt ded 30-8-21 RGA CR Lond8

MALCOLMSON,Thomas Stuart Capt kia 10-12-17 17RFA att15RFC p19&206 MR20

MALE,Arthur Ernest TLt ded 3-7-17 RMunstF att6ConnRgrs p175 CR France134,kldacc

MALE,Arthur Phillip TLt kia 23-11-17 121MGC p184 MR17

MALEHAM,Edgar Hubert T2Lt dow 29-3-18 2 att9Y&L p159 CR France62,23-3-18

MALEHAM,Stewart TCapt kia 1-7-16 13Y&L p159 CR France802

MALET,Frank Louis TLt kia 4-6-15 12RWar att2Hants p65 MR4

MALET,Hugh Arthur Grenville Lt kia 18-4-15 2KOSB p102 MR29

MALEY,Frederick 2Lt kia 14-10-18 4WRid p227 CR France612

MALEY,J.Cdr 30-12-19 IOD MR43

MALIGNY,H.A.Lt kia 5-3-21 RASC CR Surrey16

MALINS,Edward Francis T2Lt dow 12-4-18 2SWBord p100 CR France25

MALKIN,James Andrew 2LtACapt kia 4-9-16 2BordR p117 MR21

MALKIN,Norman Harry T2Lt dow 14-5-17 12Y&L p159 CR France113

MALLALIEU,Joseph 2Lt dow 7-11-17 1/7WRid p228 CR France8,6-11-17

MALLALUE,Maxwell.MC.MID Capt kia 24-8-16 9KRRC p151 MR21

MALLAM,Clifford Angus.MC&Bar.LtTCapt dow 29-10-18 3 att5RBerks p139 CR France1277

MALLANDAINE,Herbert Ernest 2Lt dow 9-3-16 IARO att97Inf p279 MR38,8-3-16

MALLEN,William James T2Lt kia 16-8-17 11 att8RDubF p177 MR30

MALLETT,Eric Sydney 2Lt kia 1-7-16 1ELancs p111 MR21

MALLETT,Hubert.MIDx2 Lt ded 3-2-19 5ESurr p271 CR Lond4,Capt Ex RWSurr

MALLETT,Phillip Henry John.MC&Bar.LtACapt dow 12-11-18 1Glouc p107 CR France146,P.F.H.

MALLETT,William James 2Lt kia 21-3-18 2/4 O&BLI p231 MR27

MALLETT,William Victor Lancelot Lt kia 22-3-18 5ESurr p226 MR20

MALLEY,F.L.Lt 19-7-21 RDubF att2/1KAR CR EAfrica36

MALLEY-MARTIN,J.MC.2Lt kld 30-10-18 1/2BordR &RAF p117 CR France332

MALLINS,Claude Joseph O'Conor Lt kia 2-11-14 2ConnRgrs p172 MR29

MALLINSON,Charles Heathcote Capt dow PoW 26/27-6-18 11ELancsR p111 CR Germany3,26-6-18

MALLINSON,Eric Lt kia 7-7-16 3 att9WRid p116 CR France267

MALLINSON,John Whiteley.MID 2Lt kia 14-2-16 6RB attMGC p179&184 MR29

MALLINSON,Richard Capt kia 1-8-17 ChesR p96 MR29,Maj

MALLOCH,David TLt kld 14-9-16 RE SpecBde p47 CR France74,2Lt dedacc

MALLOCH,Lyon Robert MacGregor.MC.Capt kia 18-11-17 5ScotRif p224 CR Belgium72

MALLOCK,Charles Herbert.DSO.Maj dow 5-11-17 23RFA p32 CR Belgium18

MALLONEY,John Charles T2Lt kia 9-4-17 1 att26NumbF p62

MALLORY,John Charles 2Lt kia 9-4-17 1 att26NumbF CR France265

MALONE,Brian Wilmot L'Estrange Lt kia 23-4-17 1Dev p77 MR20

MALONE,Briston Miniss 2Lt kia 16-8-17 9RIrF p171 MR30,Bristow

MALONE,Joseph James T2Lt kia 16-8-17 9RDubF p177 MR30

MALONE,M.P.SubCdr 4-3-19 IOD MR43 Ex ConnRgrs 6657

MALONE,Patrick Arthur 2Lt ded 13-2-19 RMunstF p266 CR Ireland12

MALONE,William Adolph 2Lt kia 16-5-17 13Ches p96 MR29,Adolphe

MALONEY,Francis Joseph ACapt dow 20-7-16 12RScot p54 CR France145

MALPAS,John Louis Lt kia 29-7-16 2SStaffs p122 MR21

MALPAS,Reginald Arthur 2LtTLt dow 18-11-17 3DorsR att7SomLI p124 CR Surrey160

MALPASS,Charles Edward.MC.ACapt kia 8-10-18 11RWKent att28Lond p141 CR France915

MALTBY,Alfred Henry 2Lt kld 4-6-18 GL &4RAF p191 MR20

MALTBY,Charles Robert Crighton TLt dow 27-8-16 12RB p179 CR France141

MALTBY,Charles Thomas T2Lt dow 27-3-18 Norf att7Suff p74 CR France62

MALTBY,E.W.Capt&QM 18-1-20 2/1LancHuss CR Lancs343

MALTBY,Gerald Capt ded 9-7-19 IARO attS&TCps p279 MR65,9-6-19

MALTBY,Phyllis May Nurse ded 6-12-18 VAD CR Surrey160

MALTON,Michael Innes T2Lt kia 22-8-18 7EKent p57 CR France430

MALTON,Paul Locock 2Lt dow PoW 3-9-18 1DCLI p114 CR France1027

MAN,Frederic Cecil Lt ded 21-2-19 3Hamps att3GurkhaRif p121 CR Egypt15 2/5Hamps att2/3GRifs

MANBY-COLGRAVE,Gerald Thomas TLt dow 21-4-17 RASC attRGA 221SB p193 CR France53

MANCE,Henry Eric 2Lt kia 15-9-16 10RWSurr p56 MR21

MANDALL,Harry 2Lt ded 18-5-19 RE p262

MANDER,Alfred Ernest Capt kia 9-10-17 4WRid A'Coy p227 MR30

MANDER,D'Arcy Wentworth Maj kia 20-9-14 2DLI p161 CR France1329

MANDER,Thomas James 2Lt ded 9-11-18 IARO attDir of Lab p279 CR Asia82

MANDERS,George Benjamin TLt dow 24-4-16 66/4RFA 66Bty p32 CR Iraq5

MANDERS,Neville Col kia 7-8-15 RAMC p196 CR Gallipoli20,9-8-15 DDMS AnzacAMedServ

MANDERS,S.G.Capt ded 9-12-18 9RWFus &RAF p98

MANDERSON,Horace Leslie 2Lt kia 9-4-16 11 att6LNLancs p136 MR38

MANDEVILLE,Pierce Capt kia 28-9-16 5WYork p218 CR France383

MANDLESTAM,Joseph 2Lt ded 6-3-16 RE p262

MANFIELD,Neville Phillip Lt kia 9-9-16 4Nhants attRFC p19&234 MR20

MANFORD,Reginald Valentine Lt kia 8-8-18 59/18RFA p208 CR France196

MANGER,Eric 2Lt kia 10-7-17 2MGC Inf p184 MR31 &CR Belgium173

MANGER,Gerald T2Lt kia 21-3-18 2RGLI p201 MR30

MANGER,John Kenneth 2Lt kia 8-5-15 2NumbFus p62 MR29

MANGIN,Frederick Meredyth LtCol ded 31-12-18 RAMC p196 MR69

MANGIN,Reuben Addison.MM.T2Lt dow 7-5-18 2WYorks p82 CR France145,7-4-18

MANIFOLD,William Herbert 2Lt kia 26-4-17 15/36RFA p32 CR France265

MANISTY,Henry Scott.MC.Lt kia 16-10-17 RE 18CpsHQ p47 CR Belgium11/5,14-10-17

MANKELOW,Archibald Henry.MC.Lt kia 14-5-15 IA 1/39GarhwalRif p280 CR France631

MANKTELOW,Walter Stanley T2Lt kia 21-3-18 2 att2/5ELancs p111 MR27

MANLEY,Charles Percival Henry.MC.T2Lt dow 4-10-18 8RWKent p141 CR France34

MANLEY,D.H.George Capt kia 6-11-17 1/6RWFus CR Palestine1

MANLEY,George Sydney 2Lt ded 30-11-18 3EYorks p84

MANLEY,Hamilton Douglas T2Lt kia 27-3-18 7RSuss p119 MR27

MANLEY,John 2LtTCapt kia 18-9-17 19RFC p10 CR France285

MANLEY,John Dundas 2Lt kia 26-9-14 RE SR p47 CR France1328

MANLEY,John Hunter Capt kia 9-1-17 IARO att59Rif p280 CR Iraq5

MANLEY,Terence Wood T2Lt kld 6-3-18 RFC p16 CR Kent180,2-3-18

MANLOVE,Leonard Cecil Tong 2Lt kia 3-8-16 3 att2Hamps p121 CR Belgium47

MANLY,Eric Cecil John Lt kia 18-7-17 B82RFA p32 CR Belgium29

MANN,Agnes Greig SNurse drd 10-4-17 QAIMNS p200 CR France85

MANN,Alexander David 2Lt kia 20-11-17 1/6SfthH p241 CR France1498

MANN,Alexander James T2Lt dow 10-4-17 8BlkW p129 CR France95

MANN,Arthur Longbottom TCapt kia 30-3-18 RE 328Co p47 MR27

MANN,Basil Stainforth Capt kia 27-11-17 2/6WRid p227 MR17

MANN,Charles Frederick Lt ded 4-12-18 22Lond CR Essex73

MANN,Charles Humphrey Dalla T2Lt kia 30-9-16 21 att13DLI p161 MR21

MANN,Charles Julian Lt kia 3-10-18 20Huss p23 CR France375

MANN,Frederick Christmas 2Lt kia 12-3-15 1NStaffs p157 CR France681

MANN,George Bertram 2Lt dow 29-9-19 9RFus CR Ches97

MANN,George William TCapt kia 24-7-17 MGC F'HB p184 CR Belgium16

MANN,Henry William.MID Lt kia 30-3-18 178RFA p32 CR France504,Harry

MANN,Horace Lt ded 25-12-18 3DorsR att1KAR p124&202 CR EAfrica86

MANN,Horace Walpole T2Lt kia 10-8-15 6LNLancs p136

MANN,Horatio Geoffrey Cornwallis.MC.2Lt kia 17-7-17 6RWKent p141 MR20

MANN,Horatio Gordon Capt kia 10-8-15 6LNLancs p136 CR Gallipoli19

MANN,Hugh Wallace TCapt dow 12-11-17 5CamH p168 CR France13

MANN,James Saumarez.MID Capt kia 22-7-20 6RWKent attPoliticDept CR Iraq8

MANN,John Anderson.MC.Lt kia 9-8-16 5ScotRif &RFCp224 CR France525

MANN,John Charles.MC.MID ACapt kia 26-9-17 2RWFus p98 MR30

MANN,John William 2Lt dow 22-8-18 4EKent p212 CR France209,7Bn

MANN,Lawrence John T2Lt kia 12-7-17 16NumbF p62 MR31

MANN,Nevill Swire Maj dow 12-4-16 LNLancs att6Bn p136 CR Iraq5

MANN,Osric Alwyn T2Lt kia 5-4-16 10RLancs p59 MR38,Lt

MANN,Percy Charles T2Lt kia 31-7-17 KRRC att17Bn p151 MR29

MANN,Robert Lamplough Lt kia 23-12-14 7DragGds p255 MR22,21-12-14

MANN,Robert Leonard 2Lt kia 9-10-16 3 att16RWFus p98&257 CR Belgium73

MANN,Robert Mathers.VD.TMaj ded 20-11-17 GL &ScotRif p191 CR Scot795

MANN,Stanley Walter 2Lt kia 1-11-19 9RFC p3 MR20

MANN,Stephen William.MM.T2Lt kia 27-3-19 GL att2Lond p191,255&257 MR70 &CR Europe179,kldacc

MANN,Theodore John Lewis 2Lt dow 28-4-18 173RFA p32 CR France142,Lt

MANN,Thomas Edward 2Lt kia 30-7-18 B10RFA p208 CR France865,31-7-18

MANN,William George 2Lt kia 28-11-17 GL &7RFC p10 CR Belgium162

MANNERS,Cecil Frederick T2Lt ded 17-6-17 692RASC MTC p193 MR43

MANNERS,Henry Fairholm T2Lt kia 28-4-17 7Norf p74 MR20

MANNERS,Hugh T2Lt kia 24-4-17 52MGC p184 MR20

MANNERS,James Herbert T2Lt ded 28-6-17 RE p47 CR France8

MANNERS,John Neville.Hon.Lt kia 1-9-14 2GrenGds p50 MR15

MANNERS,Lord Robert William Orlando.CMG.DSO.LtCol kia 11-9-17 Cmdg10NumbF p62 CR Belgium19

MANNERS,Richard Henry Hedges Maj ded 27-11-19 IA 106Pnrs att107 p280 MR43

MANNERS-SMITH,Frederick Maj dow 3-11-14 IA 2/3GurkhaRif p280 CR France80

MANNING,George 2Lt kia 28-1-16 ESurr p113 MR29,19-10-14

MANNING,George Alfred Lt kia 26-9-17 RE 438FC p210 MR30

MANNING,John Carlton T2Lt dow 17-2-17 3 att10Ches p96 CR France285

MANNING,Nicol Page 2Lt kia 6-10-18 4RScot p211 CR France1723

MANNING,Robert Charles.DSO.MC.TMaj dow 6-9-18 RE 170TC p47 CR France10

MANNING,Victor Lionel T2Lt kia 23-3-18 25MGC Inf p184 CR France307,dow

MANNOCK,Edward.VC.DSO.MC.Maj kia 26-7-18 RE &85RAF p47 MR20

MANOUKIAN,Zavern T2Lt kia 3-9-18 LancF att2/5Bn p93 CR France106

MANSBRIDGE,William Kenneth Elliott 2Lt kia 4-10-17 4Lond p246 MR30

MANSEL,Jestyn Llewelyn Capt kia 20-12-14 7DGds p255 MR22

MANSEL,John Delalynde Col ded 15-12-15 RemountService RB p24 CR Dorset102,11-12-15

MANSEL-CAREY,Spencer Lort Maunsel T2Lt dow 24-2-16 8 att9Dev p77 CR France22,Mansel kia

MANSEL-HOWE,Charles Iorworth Lt kia 9-8-18 23Lond p252 MR16

MANSEL-PLEYDELL,Edmund Morton Lt kia 12-3-15 3Dors attWorc p124 MR29

MANSEL-PLEYDELL,Henry Grove Morton.MC.Lt kia 17-5-16 1Dors p124 CR France1504

MANSEL-PLEYDELL,John Morton T2Lt dow 22-9-16 A107RFA p32 CR France300

MANSELL,Charles Paul T2Lt kia 3-9-16 16RWar p65 MR21

MANSELL,Harry Champion T2Lt kia 30-6-17 15MGC p184 MR29

MANSELL,Leslie Wyndham 2Lt kia 20-4-17 DerbyYeo p203 MR19,22-4-17

MANSELL,Walter Reynolds Capt dow 16-4-18 5SStaffs p229 CR France40,2Bn

198

MANSELL,William Du Pre TCapt kia 12-10-16 2LancF p93 MR21,MANSEL

MANSELL,William Stanley 2Lt kia 11-9-17 3ESurrR &22RFC p10&113 CR France705,1RFC

MANSER,William Edward Maj ded 8-4-17 RE p47 MR40

MANSERGH,Harry Read TLt dow 12-11-16 1 att1/9Lpool p72 CR France40

MANSERGH,John Loftus Otway Lt kia 25-9-15 RWar att2Bn p65 MR19

MANSERGH,Wilmsdorff George Lt kia 26-8-15 Manch p155 MR15,26-8-14

MANSFIELD,Eric Oswald T2Lt kia 24-8-18 8KRRC p151 CR Belgium11

MANSFIELD,George 2Lt kia 22-3-18 1Leic p88 CR France438

MANSFIELD,George Stanley 2Lt kia 22-3-18 1/4 att1EYork p219 MR27

MANSFIELD,Gerald Turner T2Lt kia 15-9-16 11RWKent p141

MANSFIELD,Harold T2Lt dow 12-4-16 1Ches p96 CR France40

MANSFIELD,Harold Barton T2Lt kia 13-11-16 10RDubF p177 CR France220

MANSFIELD,Harold Lawrie 2Lt dow 3-5-17 18WYorks p82 MR20

MANSFIELD,Harry John T2Lt kia 27-9-18 15TankCps p188 CR France357

MANSFIELD,John Roy 2Lt kia 18-6-17 RGA 121HB p40 CR Belgium29

MANSFIELD,Maurice Charles Lt ded 11-2-19 SL Intel Petrograd p268 MR70 &CR Europe180,11-2-16

MANSFIELD,Oscar Marshall T2Lt kia 14-3-17 2Leic p88 MR38

MANSFIELD,Reginald Horace T2Lt dow 1-10-18 121/27RFA p32 CR France512

MANSHIP,Charles Edward 2Lt kia 24-7-18 15N&D p255 MR30

MANSON,Bruce Edward Alexander Maj kia 3-11-14 IA 61Pnrs p280 MR47 Capt

MANSON,Charles Claude Edmonstoune.MC.2Lt kia 4-12-15 IARO att1/4GurkhaRif p280 MR4

MANSON,Gerald Patrick.MC.TCapt kia 24-8-17 6SomLI p80 MR30

MANSON,John Cochrane T2Lt kia 7-7-16 9RFus p69 CR France393

MANSON,Richard 2Lt kia 1-10-18 4GordH p242 CR France359,dow

MANTERFIELD,John Thomas 2Lt kia 21-9-18 Lincs attMGC p75&p184 CR France212

MANTLE,Alexander Lt kia 23-5-17 7Lond p247 CR France568

MANTON,Thomas T2Lt dow 22-10-17 7Y&L p159 CR Belgium25

MANTZ,Victor Frank T2Lt kia 25-10-18 1EssR p132 CR France1480

MANUEL,Vane Carrington T2Lt kld 18-12-17 GL &56RFC p10 CR Essex48

MANWARING,Jack Lancaster.MC.T2Lt ded 15-11-16 3 att9RWFus p98 CR Kent279

MAPLES,Kenneth James Capt kia 16-5-15 3 att2SStaffs p122 MR22

MAPLES,William Evelyn MajALtCol kia 14-12-16 WRid att6NLancs p116 MR38,15-12-16

MAPLESON,Gerald Horsley T2Lt kia 26-4-17 2 att2/4RWSurr p56 CR Palestine8

MAPPLEBECK,Gilbert William.DSO.LtCapt kld 24-8-15 Lpool &RFC p1&72

MAPPLEBECK,Gordon Whitfield ACapt dow 30-7-17 NStaffs att4Bn p157 CR Belgium15,4 att1Bn

MAQUIRE,Maurice 2Lt kia 21-8-18 3Ches p96

MARCH,Arthur John Jethro T2Lt ded 24-10-18 RE 50DivSig p47 CR France146

MARCH,Joseph Cyril Capt kia 14-1-20 IARO att2/5GurkhaRif p280 MR43

MARCH,William Francis George 2Lt dow PoW 24-10-17 GL &23RFC p10 CR Belgium140,Lt

MARCH-PHILLIPS,Spencer Leslie T2Lt kia 20-11-17 1TankCps p188 MR17

MARCHANT,Arthur Charles AssSurg kia 11-3-16 IA IndSubMedDept p280 CR EAfrica56

MARCHANT,Charles G.Capt kld 3-5-15 20Lond p251 CR France765,Silverlock

MARCHANT,Charles Stewart 2Lt kia 4-6-17 5 att9RDubF p177 CR Belgium182

MARCHANT,Charles Victor 2Lt kia 30-11-17 15Lond p249 MR17

MARCHANT,Francis George Wake 2Lt dow 25-10-16 RWKent &3RFC p3&141 CR France833,22-10-16

MARCHANT,Francis Scott Lt kia 22-3-18 5BordR att2TankCps p189&228 MR27 CR France307

MARCHANT,Frederick Louis 2Lt kld 20-11-17 7EssR p232 MR17

MARCHANT,Godfrey Maj ded 17-6-19 IA 29Lancers p280 MR43

MARCHANT,Harold Edgar T2Lt kia 5-6-16 Dev p77 CR France251

MARCHANT,Hugh Stephen Lt kia 7-1-16 1/5EKent p213 CR Iraq5

MARCHANT,Richard Henry 2Lt kia 26-1-16 9ESurr p113 CR Belgium125

MARCHANT,Sydney T2Lt dow 6-7-16 12NumbF p62 CR France119

MARCHETTI,Alexander 2Lt kia 15-3-16 5 att2RB p179 CR France348

MARCHETTI,Eustie 2Lt kia 8-11-16 149RFA p32 CR France374

MARCHMENT,William James LtACapt kia 4-11-18 RFA X32TMB p32 CR France190

MARDEN,Arthur Cecil 2Lt ded 11-12-17 RGA 117HB p40 CR Belgium101

MARE,Arthur Llewellyn TLtAMaj kia 27-5-18 33RFA p32 MR18

MARGERISON,Caleb Walden.MID TLt dow 6-7-16 11BordR p117 CR France44

MARGERISON,Thomas 2Lt kia 13-4-17 HuntsCycBn attRFC p19&253 CR France604

MARGERRISON,James T2Lt kia 14-4-18 10Yorks att150TMB p91 CR France40

MARGESSON,Edward Cuminghame Maj kia 25-4-15 2SWBord p100 MR4

MARGETSON,Emil Alexander 2Lt kld 16-6-17 GL &RFC p10 CR Mddx13

MARGETTS,Percy Alexander T2Lt kia 5-12-15 9 att6Lincs p75 CR Gallipoli4

MARGOLIOUTH,Alfred Henry 2Lt kia 2-4-17 5YLI &RFC p19&235 CR France924

MARILLIER,Frederick Charles Jennens 2Lt kia 30-10-14 2RSuss p119 MR29

MARILLIER-MILLER,Ralph T2Lt kia 30-7-16 25Manch p155

MARINDIN,Henry Eden Allan,MC T2Lt dow 8-10-18 KSLI att1/4Bn p145 CR France80

MARION,Donald 2Lt kia 9-5-15 SfthH p165

MARION-CRAWFORD,Harold Francis 2Lt kld 16-4-15 IrGds p53 CR France279

MARJORIBANKS,Alexander Capt&Adjt ded 28-9-14 52Sikhs attNWaziristanMil MR43

MARJORIBANKS,Marmaduke Edward 2Lt kia 21-11-17 1NumbF p62 CR France563

MARK,Hannah Dunlop Nurse 10-10-18 TFNS CR Wales4

MARK,James Wilson 2Lt dow 7-8-17 2RIrReg p89 CR Belgium7

MARKER,Raymond John.DSO.LtCol ded 13-11-14 GrenGds Staff p51 CR Devon87

MARKES,Thomas Maxwell 2Lt kia 1-10-17 1RLancs p59 CR Belgium23

MARKES,John Carlon.MIDx2 Maj kia 19-7-16 Leinst p174 CR France513 Ex LancF

MARKHAM,John Addis Capt kia 7-5-15 1EYorks p84 CR Belgium451

MARKHAM,Montagu Wilfred 2Lt kia 29-8-17 2ScotGds p52 MR30

MARKHAM,Ronald Anthony.MIDx2 Maj dow 26-10-14 2CldGds p51 CR Leic117,25-10-14

MARKHAM,Walter Henry James T2Lt dow PoW 27-3-18 NumbF att1/5Bn p62 MR27

MARKHAM-ROSE,Kenneth Lt kia 3-5-15 Ess attWAFF p132&201,3-5-16 CR WAfrica23

MARKS,Arthur Sampson Lt ded 25-10-18 Ex GL p267

MARKS,C.H. LtTCapt kia 23-10-15 Middx &RFC p1&147 CR France1266

MARKS,Charles Bernard.MC.T2Lt kia 23-10-18 ESurr att8Bn p113 CR France229

MARKS,Craig Royston T2Lt kld 3-5-17 GL &RFC p10 CR Lincs53

MARKS,George Frederick Handel LtCol ded 3-5-15 RAMC p196 MR65

MARKS,Horace Owen TLt kia 29-10-16 111RFA p32 CR France150,C110RFA

MARKS,Isidor David T2Lt kia 10-7-16 11WRid p116 CR France267

MARKS,James Albert 2Lt kia 25-2-17 NStaffs p157 MR38

MARKS,James Ganly Lt kia 23-3-18 5SfthH p241 CR France245

MARKS,John Hyman TLt kia 24-10-18 15DLI p161 CR France1477

MARKS,Nathaniel Capt ded 27-7-18 3/24Lond p252 CR Mddx40,Maj

MARKS,Philip Moses 2Lt kia 29-9-15 4 att5Middx p147 MR29

MARKS,S.A.Lt 16-2-20 RE CR Lancs9

MARKUS,Eugene Bernays.MC.2Lt dow 5-4-17 1RScotF p95 CR France40

MARKWICK,Frederick Thomas T2Lt kia 6-8-15 12 att1Ess p132 MR4

MARKWICK,William Percival Lt kia 5-9-18 5Norf p216 CR France511

MARLER,Wilfred Earlstone 2Lt dow 4-5-17 1SomLI p80 CR France95

MARLEY,Grace Margaret Prob 12-10-16 TFNS 2S GenHosp CR Wilts100

MARLEY,William Capt kia 23-4-17 5DLI B'Coy p238&239,6Bn CR France162

MARLIN,Harold James 2Lt kia 12-4-17 3SStaffs att1Lincs p122

MARLOR,Eric 2Lt kia 3-5-17 6WRid p227 CR France1489

MARLOW,Albert Leopold Craddock T2Lt dow 4-4-17 KRRC att10Bn p151 CR France364

MARLOW,Charles Dwyer T2Lt kia 17-8-17 8RDubF p177 MR30

MARLOW,George 2Lt dedacc 26-8-16 6LancF p221 CR Ches123

MARLOW,John Maj ded 29-2-16 3RIrReg p89

MARLOW,Kenneth Conway Lt ded 3-2-18 8RFus p263 CR Camb16,MARLOWE 3-12-18

MARLOW,Percy 2LtTCapt dow 7-6-17 Wilts att6Bn p153 CR Belgium102

MARLOW,Stanley John Lt kia 19-4-17 1/4Nhampt p234 CR Palestine8

MARLOWE,Cecil Arthur T2Lt dow 18-10-18 1/2Yorks att1/7WYorks p91 CR France94

MARMION,M.Sister ded 25-1-19 QAIMNS p200 CR Lond9

MARNER,George Lionel Stuart Lt kia 8-4-17 10Leic att2Bn B'Coy p88 MR38,Capt

MARNER,T.Cdr 24-5-19 IA OrdDept CR India164

MARNHAM,Hugh Cecil 2Lt kia 22-8-16 SussYeo attRFC p19&205 CR France727

MARNOCH,Margaret Bella SNurse 13-11-18 TFNS CR Scot333

MARONA,Charles Antonio RevChap ded 28-2-15 Suss RGA p271 CR Sussex134

MARQUARD,John TLtACapt kia 23-8-18 13RFus p69 CR France518

MARR,Frederick Sidney.MC.TLtACapt kia 30-8-17 B47RFA p32 CR Belgium15

MARR,Hugh Boyd 2Lt kia 16-12-16 19Lond p250 CR Belgium127

MARR,James Scott TCapt kia 18-11-16 17HLI p163 MR21

MARRABLE,Edmund Douglas Lt ded 25-4-18 1105RFA &RAF p208 CR Kent193,kld

MARRIOTT,Arthur Pelham.MC.LtACapt kia 7-4-17 11RFA 85Bty p32 CR France12

MARRIOTT,Frederick Ernest T2Lt kia 30-7-15 7RB p179 MR29

MARRIOTT,Geoffrey Vaughan 2Lt kia 22-4-18 N&D att1Bn p134 MR27

MARRIOTT,George Edward Joseph Capt ded 6-7-17 1/6LancF p271 CR France755

MARRIOTT,Herbert Norman TCapt kia 13-11-16 12EYorks p84 CR France1890

MARRIOTT,Hugh Digby T2Lt kia 9-10-15 15RB p179 CR Belgium84

MARRIOTT,John Douglas 2Lt kia 26-9-17 1ScotRif p103 CR Belgium112

MARRIOTT,John Francis Laycock 2Lt ded 26-1-15 7DCLI p114 CR Hamps1

MARRIOTT,Joseph Percy SubCdr ded 17-7-17 IA Cps of MilStaffClerks p280

MARRIOTT,K.M.H.Lt kia 28-9-18 1/2WRid &RAF p116

MARRIOTT,Norman Clarke Capt kia 17-8-17 5Leic p220 MR19

MARRIOTT,Osborne Delano TLtACapt kia 27-8-17 8WRid p116 MR30

MARRIOTT,Richard Henry.MC.Lt kia 18-9-16 KSLI p145 CR France374

MARRIOTT,Stanley George T2Lt kia 21-10-16 RE 2FC p47 CR France374

MARRIOTT,W.TMaj ded 26-12-15 16DLI p265

MARRIOTT-WATSON,Richard Brereton.MC.Lt kia 24-3-18 2RIrRif p170 MR27

MARRIS,Horace Frost.MC.TLt dow 12-12-17 RE 76FC p47 CR France446

MARROW,Edward Armfield Capt kia 25-4-15 1KOSB p102 CR Gallipoli6

MARRS,Frederick Mallinson 2Lt kia 4-3-17 1Worc p109 MR21

MARSDEN,G.DSO.Capt 24-9-16 12Ches CR Mddx26

MARSDEN,Harold 2Lt dow 14-8-17 6 att1/8Lpool p215 CR France134

MARSDEN,Harold 2Lt ded 5-6-18 8WRid p116,257&264,3Bn CR Yorks375

MARSDEN,Herbert William 2Lt dow 11-9-18 1/4LNLanc p234 CR France106

MARSDEN,Humphrey Miller 2Lt kia 11-10-18 7WRid A'Coy p228 CR France612

MARSDEN,James Alfred Capt kia 21-4-18 RE p210 CR France300

MARSDEN,John Horace.MC.Capt kia 27-4-17 6N&D p233 CR France1495

MARSDEN,John William 2Lt kia 20-11-17 2/5LancF p221 MR21

MARSDEN,Morris James T2Lt kia 20-9-17 214MGC Inf p184 MR30

MARSDEN,Philip Sidney Lt kia 30-5-17 9Manch p237 CR France905

MARSDEN,Reginald Lt kia 4-6-15 8Manch p237 MR4

MARSDEN,Wallis Austin Jonathan Lt dow 20-7-17 RFA p208 CR Wales251

MARSDEN,W.C.Capt 19-12-20 RAMC CR Hereford/Worc110

MARSDEN-SMEDLEY,George Futvoye 2Lt kia 18-8-16 5RB p179 MR21 3Bn

MARSH,Alford Stanley TCapt kia 6-1-16 8SomLI p80 CR France922,Alfred 5-1-16

MARSH,Bertie Cecil Capt gunshotWound 15-12-19 IA 1/69Punjabis p280 MR43 Ex 8Ches

MARSH,Charles Frederick William ACapt kia 22-9-18 12Ches p96 MR37

MARSH,Charles Walter Brockwell TLt kia 13-10-15 6EKent p57 MR19

MARSH,Clarence Eric Lt ded 31-10-18 RE p271 CR Staffs52

MARSH,Cuthbert Alban 2Lt dow 24-6-18 SLancs att42RAF p125 CR France31,dedacc

MARSH,Douglas Charles Earle 2Lt dow 8-4-18 6DragGds p21 CR France145,11-4-18

MARSH,Edward Waters Harbin Capt&Adjt drd 30-12-15 IA 13Rajputs att6SLancs p280 MR41

MARSH,Francis Bedford 2Lt dow 5-10-16 4RWSurr attMGC p187&212 CR France177

MARSH,Frederick Courtney Maj kia 7-8-15 BordR att6Bn p117 MR4 Francis Courteney

MARSH,Gilbert Howe Maxwell Capt kia 1-11-14 IA 41Dogras p280 CR France80

MARSH,Harold 2Lt kia 4-10-18 5 att3RFus p69 CR France234

MARSH,Harry Victor T2Lt dow 22-10-16 8Norf p74 CR France59

MARSH,Henry Francis Freke.MC.Capt&Adjt dow 2-2-17 IA 1/2GurkhaRif p280 CR Iraq5

MARSH,Henry Herbert TLt kia 12-2-16 10WelshR p127 CR France727,2Lt

MARSH,Henry Herbert Stanley Maj dow 2-4-15 RE 4FC p209 CR France80

MARSH,Henry Sidney 2Lt kia 13-11-16 78RFA p32 CR France430

MARSH,John Lt ded PoW 23-10-18 1WorcYeo p206 CR Iraq8

MARSH,John Edward Joseph 2Lt kia 24-9-17 1Camb p245 MR30

MARSH,John Lockwood.MID Capt kia 16-10-15 1/4Y&L p238 CR Belgium23

MARSH,John Theodore Templeman 2Lt dow 28-6-18 D15RFA p32 CR France31

MARSH,Joseph T2Lt kia 23-11-17 15RIrRif p170 MR17

MARSH,Nicholas Clayton T2Lt kia 25-9-15 16Lpool p72 CR France163,1Bn

MARSH,Philip Everard Graham.MC.Capt kld 20-12-18 RASC &RAF p193 CR Essex110

MARSH,Ralph Hedley T2Lt kia 12-4-18 7RWKent p141 MR27

MARSH,Robert Cecil T2Lt dow 19-9-18 2MGC p184 CR France40,17-9-18

MARSH,Robert Neville Caldicot 2Lt kia 3-7-16 3KOSB attMGC Inf p102 France1012,1Bn

MARSH,Victor Braine T2Lt kia 3-9-16 6 O&BLI p130 CR France513

MARSH,William Bernard T2Lt kia 21-3-18 12NumbF att1Lincs p62 MR27

MARSH,William John Grimstead Lt dow 7-11-17 IA 127Baluchis att2/124 p280 CR Iraq8

MARSH,Zacheus Stanley T2Lt kia 10-10-17 GL &52RFC p10 CR France1361

MARSHALL,Albert 2Lt ded 12-6-19 RFA p32 MR65

MARSHALL,Albert Herbert Bathurst T2Lt kia 22-5-18 GL att3RB p191 CR France81,Alfred Lt

MARSHALL,Alexander Balfour 2Lt kia 14-4-16 3ScotRif att5ConnRgrs p103 MR37

MARSHALL,Allan Gow TCapt kia 12-2-17 17HLI p163 CR France803

MARSHALL,Ambrose 2Lt kia 15-4-17 4Beds att1Hereford p252 CR Franmce644

MARSHALL,Andrew Fairlie Wilson 2Lt ded PoW 26-9-18 10EYorks p84 CR Germany3

MARSHALL,Archibald James 2Lt kia 26-10-17 LNLancs att2/5Bn p136 MR30

MARSHALL,Arthur Norris 2Lt kia 31-7-16 1Beds p86 MR21

MARSHALL,Arthur Raymond 2LtACapt&Adjt dow 2-2-18 RGA 34HAG p40 CR France145

MARSHALL,Augustus de la Pere 2Lt kia 9-5-15 8ELancs p111 MR32,22-5-15

MARSHALL,Bernard Gouldsmith 2Lt kia 5-4-16 1Nhants p137 CR France551

MARSHALL,Bernard Sanderson.MC.Lt kia 7-6-17 GL &20RFC p10 MR20

MARSHALL,Cecil Clyde 2Lt kia 24-6-17 RGA 21SB p40 CR Belgium1

MARSHALL,Charles Bertram Capt drd 13-8-15 RAMC p254 MR4

MARSHALL,Charles Samuel T2Lt dow 2-4-18 1Suff GarBn p78 France65

MARSHALL,Claud T2Lt kia 27-7-17 5SStaffs p122&p257,Claude CR Belgium73

MARSHALL,David.MC.2Lt kia 13-5-18 2/5LancF p221 CR France106

MARSHALL,Donald Ewan 2Lt kia 8-8-17 4WYorks &18RFC p10&p82 CR France201,7-8-17

MARSHALL,Douglas Cargill Lt kia 28-6-15 LancF p93 MR4

MARSHALL,Dudley 2Lt kia 26-9-17 6 att4RFus p69 MR30

MARSHALL,Duke 2Lt dow 22-2-19 A159RFA p32 CR Surrey1

MARSHALL,Edward Leslie.MC&Bar.TCapt dow 1-9-18 9RInnisF p105 CR France324

MARSHALL,Ernest William.MC.LtACapt kia 22-4-18 3SomLI p80 CR France98,1Bn

MARSHALL,Evelyn Saffery.MIDx2 TCapt dow 6-4-16 9RWar D'Coy p65 MR38

MARSHALL,Francis Capt dow 30-9-14 1Lpool p72 CR France473

MARSHALL,Frank TCapt kia 17-3-16 24Manch p155 CR France370

MARSHALL,Frederick Guy Lt kia 22-3-15 GrenGds p50 CR France279

MARSHALL,George Garth Lt kia 4-11-14 11Huss p22 CR Belgium57

MARSHALL,George Leonard Lt dow 26-9-15 3Lincs p75 CR France254,2Bn

MARSHALL,Harry T2Lt dow 5-11-18 1/5Lpool p72 CR France769

MARSHALL,Harold.MC.LtCol ded 10-9-18 7Hamp Cmdg1/4RFus p229 CR Hamps22

MARSHALL,Harold Sanders 2Lt kld 31-1-18 6NStaffs attRFC p19&238 CR Staffs84

MARSHALL,Harry TLt kia 30-9-18 15LancF p93 CR France376

MARSHALL,Harry Cecil T2Lt kld 23-12-17 GL &RFC p10 CR Surrey91

MARSHALL,Henry T2Lt kia 1-8-18 7RWSurr p56 CR France116

MARSHALL,Henry Turnbull Maj ded 21-9-15 IA 1Brahmans p280 MR43

MARSHALL,Herbert T2Lt kia 13-4-17 10WYorks p82 MR20

MARSHALL,Herbert William Hare TLt kld 26-8-17 GL &RFC p10 CR Somerset197

MARSHALL,Hubert Graham Hamilton T2Lt kia 2-9-18 TankCps p188 CR France427

MARSHALL,James Neville.VC.MC&Bar.LtCol 4-11-18 IrGds att16LancF CR France1479

MARSHALL,Jenner Stephen Chance 2Lt dow 21-10-14 2 O&BLI p130 CR Belgium57,23-10-14

MARSHALL,John Lt drd 15-4-17 RAMC p196 MR35

MARSHALL,John TLt kia 18-9-18 15WYorks p82 CR France285,Capt

MARSHALL,John Lt kia 24-10-18 4BlkW p230 CR France1258

MARSHALL,John Arthur Lt kia 6-4-17 HuntsCycBn att45RFC p19&253 CR Belgium406

MARSHALL,John Edward Capt kia 30-3-15 1DCLI p114 CR Belgium17

MARSHALL,John Hamilton T2Lt kia 23-10-16 8ELancs p111 MR21

MARSHALL,John Morice Maitland Lt dow 23-10-15 4Ess p232 CR Gallipoli18

MARSHALL,John Neville.VC.MC.LtALtCol kia 4-11-18 IrGds att16LancF p53

MARSHALL,John Percival Lt dow 4-11-17 B282RFA p32 CR Belgium20,D'Bty

MARSHALL,John Willoughby Hadfield 2Lt kia 21-3-18 3Y&L p159 MR20

MARSHALL,John Woodall.MC.TLt kia 1-7-16 27NumbF p62 CR France267

MARSHALL,Laurance Herbert T2Lt dow 22-4-18 RE 9FC p47 CR France145

MARSHALL,Louis 2Lt kia 23-11-17 GL &65RFC p10 MR20

MARSHALL,Mary P.MID SNurse kia 12-3-17 QAIMNS p200 CR Greece9,Bethia

MARSHALL,Matthew 2Lt kld 11-8-18 6RScot p211 CR France360,kia

MARSHALL,Philip Spencer Lt kia 15-8-17 B3/307RFA p208 CR Belgium10

MARSHALL,Robert Burnaby.MID Lt dow 14-9-19 1ESurr p255 MR70

MARSHALL,Robert Wilson 2Lt kia 27-5-18 7 att1A&SH p243 CR Palestine9,29-5-18

MARSHALL,Roger 2Lt kia 20-9-14 2DLI p161 MR15

MARSHALL,Roger Charles Lt ded 7-1-18 RFA p208 CR Camb97

MARSHALL,Stanley 2Lt dow 18-4-18 7LancF p256 CR France716

MARSHALL,Sydney James T2Lt kia 8-8-18 3RRofCav att15Huss p23 CR France649,Lt

MARSHALL,Theodore Samuel Simon 2Lt ded 31-7-17 RE p271 CR Cornwall140

MARSHALL,Thomas Frederick T2Lt kia 30-10-17 1ESurr p113 MR30

MARSHALL,W.E.Lt ded 27-6-18 RASC &RAF p253

MARSHALL,Wilfred Lt kia 4-6-15 10Leics p88 MR4 Wilfrid

MARSHALL,William Lt kld 27-4-15 8DLI p239 MR29

MARSHALL,William Cornelius T2Lt kia 29-9-18 11Lpool p72 CR France666,4Bn

MARSHALL,William Gainer Lt dow 19-8-15 RFA p208 MR29

MARSHALL,William Macandrew Capt kia 19-3-18 IA 37Dogras attPoliticalDept p280 CR Iraq8

MARSHALL,William Robert 2Lt kia 12-10-16 3 att7Suff p78 CR France560,Rowland

MARSHALL,William Thomas.VC.LtCol 11-9-20 19Huss CR Scot127

MARSHALL-LEWIS,Frank TLt kia 13-9-17 GL &43RFC p10 CR France88,2Lt

MARSHAM,John Ralph Theodore 2Lt ded 27-2-19 LabCps Ex 11Worc p266 CR Hamps202

MARSHAM-TOWNSEND,Ferdinand 2Lt kia 16-5-15 ScotGds att2Bn p52 CR France279

MARSHFIELD,Harold William T2Lt kia 14-8-18 9ESurr att10RWSurr p113 CR Belgium11

MARSLAND,Eric Forbes 2Lt kia 7-10-16 6 att8RFus p69 MR21

MARSLAND,James Francis.MC.Lt dow 18-8-15 2Leinst p174 CR Belgium11,15-8-15

MARSLAND,John.MC.TLt kia 23-7-17 8RSuss p119 CR Belgium29

MARSLAND,Sydney Hammond TLt kia 7-8-15 11Manch p155 MR4

MARSON,Eric Newton T2Lt kia 10-8-15 9RWar p65 MR4

MARSON,John Charles T2Lt kia 8-8-15 8WelshR p127 MR4

MARSON,William Henry 2Lt kia 1-7-16 1/6NStaff p238 MR21

MARSTERS,John Victor Harold TLt kia 25-9-15 6KOSB p102 MR19

MARSTON,Arthur Bright T2Lt dow 14-7-16 7RWSurr p56 CR France402,kia

MARSTON,Felix William T2Lt dow 24-7-16 10RWar p65 CR France300

MARSTON,Guy Eric Millett TLt dow 9-2-18 1War attRE 130FC p47 CR France512

MARSTON,Percy Ingram T2Lt dow 20-9-17 22DLI p161 CR France297

MARTEN,Charles Peter TLtCol kia 15-9-16 1WYorks Cmdg18KRRC p82 CR France1890

MARTEN,Harold Charles Capt kia 7-8-15 7SStaffs p122 MR4

MARTEN,Henry Humphrey.MID 2Lt kia 13-8-15 6KRRC att2Manch p155 CR France699,Lt

MARTEN-SMITH,Cecil Eugene T2Lt kia 13-11-17 2RSuss p119 MR30

MARTHEWS,Leonard Gordon 2Lt dow PoW 20-4-18 2SLancs p125 CR Germany1 Lt 22-4-18

MARTIN,Albert Emanuel 2Lt kia 2-9-18 3 att2/4YLI p143 CR france617

MARTIN,Albert Trever de Monteval Maj dow 10-12-17 2WIndR att5WelshR p192 CR Palestine3,Trevor Morteval RWFus

MARTIN,Alfred T2Lt kia 3-9-16 1RWKent p141 CR France294

MARTIN,Alfred John T2Lt dow 2-8-16 7 att10ESurr p113 CR France44

MARTIN,Alfred Stanley T2Lt dow 26-10-18 6RWSurr p56 CR France146,24-10-18

MARTIN,Algernon 2Lt kia 30-7-18 70RFA p32 CR France865

MARTIN,Arthur 2Lt kia 28-6-16 10Mddx att1/4Lancs p236 MR20

MARTIN,Arthur Derisley Capt kia 18-4-16 IA 36Sikhs att47 p280 MR38,17-4-16

MARTIN,Arthur Henry Col ded 27-8-18 RASC p253 CR Sussex111,24-8-18

MARTIN,Arthur Herbert T2Lt ded 5-3-19 RE 19RlyOpCo p262 CR Greece9

MARTIN,Arthur James Capt kld 15-5-15 8HLI p240 CR France727,kia

MARTIN,Arthur William 2Lt dedacc 14-3-17 61WelshR p127 CR Wales673

MARTIN,Aylmer Richard Sancton LtCol kia 9-5-15 RLancs p59 MR29

MARTIN,Basil Cuthbert Danvers 2Lt kia 4-6-15 13Worc p109 MR4

MARTIN,Bertram Charles.MM.T2Lt kia 13-4-17 4RFus p69 MR20

MARTIN,Cecil Hampson Capt kia 2-10-16 2ELancs p111 CR France423

MARTIN,Charles Andrew.MID Capt kia 6-12-15 6RDubF p177 MR37,8-12-15

MARTIN,Charles Herbert George Lt kld 2-5-15 1/3Mon p244 MR29 &CR Belgium453

MARTIN,Charles Stanley T2Lt kia 4-10-17 6Leic p88 CR Belgium165

MARTIN,Claude 2Lt kia 1-12-17 3CldGds p51 CR France662

MARTIN,Clive Victor LtCol kia 27-3-17 IA 29Lancers attStaff 10CpsHQ p280 CR Belgium11

MARTIN,Cuthbert Thomas.DSO&Bar.MIDx3 TBrigGen kia 27-5-18 HLI staff151InfBde p163 MR18

MARTIN,Cyril Basnett Lt kia 30-3-18 21Lond p251 CR Syria2

MARTIN,Cyril Stephen Bignold Capt dow 2-3-16 IA 90Punjabis p280 MR65,Cecil

MARTIN,David Archibald 2Lt kia 25-3-18 1 O&BLI p130 MR38

MARTIN,Douglas Bain 2Lt dow 9-10-18 C52RFA p32 CR France113

MARTIN,Douglas Francis de Renzy 2Lt kia 13-4-17 1NumbF p62 MR20

MARTIN,Duncan Lenox TCapt kia 1-7-16 9Dev p77 CR France330

MARTIN,Edward James T2Lt dow 21-12-17 att1/4SfthH p165CR France512

MARTIN,Edward Nugent Meredyth 2Lt kia 30-9-16 5Lancers RoO attMGC Cav p22 CR France630

MARTIN,Edward William Sidney.MID TCapt dow 16-2-17 RAMC att9Worc p196 CR Iraq5

MARTIN,Edwin John 2Lt kia 4-9-18 1Lond p245 CR Belgium89

MARTIN,Eldred Joseph Lt kia 1-7-16 3 att2RWar C'Coy p65 CR France189

MARTIN,Eric Tomlinson T2Lt kia 1-10-16 9DCLI att8YLI p114 MR21

MARTIN,Ernest 2Lt kia 18-7-16 D306RFA p32 CR France1887

MARTIN,Ernest 2Lt ded 16-12-17 RGA 15HB p40 CR Staffs84

MARTIN,Ernest Ivor T2Lt kia 18-8-18 6KOSB p102 CR France324

MARTIN,Ernest William T2Lt kia 27-7-16 1Norf p74 MR21

MARTIN,Fairlie Russell 2Lt kia 29-6-17 1RScotF att57RFC p10&p95 CR Belgium96

MARTIN,Felix William 2Lt dow 24-7-16 10RWar p65

MARTIN,Francis Henry 2Lt kia 24-11-17 RE 84FC p47 MR17

MARTIN,Frank Henry.MC.2Lt kia 28-3-18 2CldGds p51 CR France214,Lt

MARTIN,Frederick Arthur T2Lt dow 7-9-15 2N&D p134 CR Belgium2

MARTIN,Frederick Nathaniel 2Lt kia 24-10-18 3 att1RWar p65 CR France1260

MARTIN,G.J.Capt 1-3-20 6RIrReg attStaff APM CR Europe23

MARTIN,Geoffrey Clogstoun 2Lt kia 2-8-16 3RDubF p177 CR France423,Lt 9Bn

MARTIN,George Charles Russel Lt ded 12-9-18 Y&L attN&D p159 CR Kent203,kldacc

MARTIN,George Elvyn 2Lt kia 4-4-18 5 att7RWSurr p212 MR27

MARTIN,George Ernest Capt kia 2-8-17 11Ches p96 CR Belgium112

MARTIN,George Ernest T2Lt kld 29-11-17 GL &RFC p10 CR Wilts115

MARTIN,George Henry 2Lt kia 26-12-17 3 att2Nhants p137 CR Belgium125,27-12-17

MARTIN,George Johnston 2Lt kia 26-9-17 13RSuss p119 MR30

MARTIN,George Patrick Winfield TLt kia 2-10-18 8NumbF Y'Coy p62 CR France273

MARTIN,George Russell Courtney Lt kia 1-7-16 6RWar p214 CR France1504

MARTIN,George Styles Lt kia 23-4-17 5 att18Manch p236 MR20

MARTIN,Gordon Eric T2Lt kia 14-8-18 10RB p179 MR29

MARTIN,George William TMaj kia 17-9-18 17NumbF p62 CR France686

MARTIN,Harold TLt kia 31-7-17 12RFus p69 MR29

MARTIN,Harold James.MID Lt 12-4-17 3SStaffs att1Lincs CR France1186

MARTIN,Harold Young Capt kldacc 14-4-17 5Manch p236 CR Scot387,13-4-17

MARTIN,Harry Edward 2Lt kia 16-11-16 60RFC p3 CR France95

MARTIN,Harry Forster 2Lt kia 29-9-18 1SWBord p100 CR France672

MARTIN,Henry.DCM.2Lt ded 22-10-18 RGA p40 CR Derby2

MARTIN,Henry Lloyd TCapt kia 28-9-16 7RWSurr p56 MR21

MARTIN,Henry Yarde T2Lt dow 14-9-16 9Leic att9ELancs p88 CR Greece6

MARTIN,Herbert 2Lt dow 26-5-15 80RFA p32 CR France285,27-5-15

MARTIN,Herbert Ernest T2Lt kia 14-10-18 16 att1/8ScotRif p103 MR30

MARTIN,Horace Edmund Capt dow 19-6-16 8Mddx p236 CR France1

MARTIN,Hugh Waldyve Maj ded 2-6-18 IA 59Rif p280 MR65

MARTIN,James Adam 2Lt kia 12-7-15 6HLI p240 MR4

MARTIN,James Martin 2Lt kia 24-4-18 409/96RFA p32 CR France303

MARTIN,James Nelson 2Lt kia 21-3-18 RFA 61TMB p32 MR27

MARTIN,John.MC.Capt kia 9-4-17 8/10GordH A'Coy p166 CR France924

MARTIN,John 2Lt kia 19-12-17 RGA 229SB p40 CR Italy7

MARTIN,John Kingsley TCapt kia 1-8-15 10DLI p161 MR29

MARTIN,John Muir Lt kia 6-11-18 7ScotRif p224 CR France936

MARTIN,John Sinclair Lt kia 9-5-15 1RIrRif D'Coy p170 MR32

MARTIN,Joseph Skinner Capt&QM ded 13-2-19 GL 2/8Manch p254 CR Lancs34,Jonathan

MARTIN,Jules Stainmetz ACapt ded 15-12-18 RAMC att19SH p196 CR EAfrica92,Steinmentz

MARTIN,L.S.Capt see LAFERRIERE,L.S. true name

MARTIN,Lawrence Henry T2Lt kia 23-11-17 9RIrF p171 CR France1496,Laurence

MARTIN,Marcel James Capt&Adjt kia 9-5-17 16RWar p65 CR France184

MARTIN,Margery 0/1144 Trail AssAdmintr ded 17-5-18 QMAAC p200 CR Scot253,Marjorie

MARTIN,Marshal TLt ded 18-2-19 Dev 1GarBn p77&257 CR Palestine11

MARTIN,Norman.DSO.Lt kia 22-7-16 5 att1CamH p168 CR France515,23-7-16 3 att1Bn

MARTIN,Peter McEwan ACapt kia 2-12-17 11BordR p117 MR30

201

MARTIN,Rankin.MM.T2Lt ded 12-7-18 RE 176Co p47 CR France95

MARTIN,Reginald Frank 2Lt kia 30-6-17 1/5N&D p233 MR20

MARTIN,Reginald Poole TLt ded 2-12-18 RE p47 CR Devon36

MARTIN,Richard Archer Walcott 2Lt kia 16-8-17 3RDubF p177 MR30

MARTIN,Robert Lt kia 4-9-17 2/1ScotHorse att RFC p19&205 CR France134

MARTIN,Robert Douglas T2Lt kia 26-8-16 1Wilts p153 MR21

MARTIN,Ronald Hutton Capt kia 24-3-18 MunstFus &RFC p16&175 MR20

MARTIN,Ross T2Lt dow 25-10-18 12TankCps p188 CR France380

MARTIN,Rowland Hill.CB.CMG.CIE.BtCol ded 31-1-19 1Norf GarrBn p74 MR65

MARTIN,Sidney Grant 2Lt dow 18-4-17 13/17RFA p32 CR France581,Lt

MARTIN,Sidney Todd Lt kia 1-7-16 6 att 1RInnisF p105 MR21

MARTIN,Stanley.MM.2Lt kia 18-9-18 2Lond p245 CR France369

MARTIN,Stanley Charley James T2Lt dow 25-7-16 15Hamp att TMB p121 CR France285,Curley,26-7-16

MARTIN,Thomas.MC.Lt kia 31-10-18 5ScotRif p224 CR Belgium140

MARTIN,Thomas Dick 2Lt dow 18-6-18 119/27RH&FA p32 CR France20

MARTIN,Thomas Whittle.MC.Capt kia 9-4-17 RAMC att 11RScot p196 CR France645

MARTIN,Trice T2Lt kia 7-6-17 11RWSurr p56 CR Belgium29

MARTIN,Walter Percival T2Lt kia 24-8-16 7DCLI p114 CR France400

MARTIN,Wilfred Arthur T2Lt.ACapt kia 3-8-17 3RB p179 MR29,Wilfrid

MARTIN,William Francis Maj kia 13-5-15 LeicYeo p204 MR29 CR Belgium152

MARTIN,William Gerald TLt.ACapt kia 14-1-17 12KRRC p151 CR France785

MARTIN,William Harold 2Lt kia 14-9-16 24Lond p252 CR France453,Harrod

MARTIN,William Henry 2Lt ded 27-11-18 9 att 6KSLI p145 CR Ireland136,27-10-18

MARTIN,William Howard T2Lt kia 31-7-17 3 att 2RWFus p98 MR29

MARTIN,William Murdoch 2Lt kia 22-8-17 13RScot p54 MR30

MARTINDALE,Alfred Horace T2Lt kia 1-10-15 1YLI p143 MR19,4/5-10-15

MARTINDALE,John Ball TLt dow 1-8-18 LancF att 2LNLancs p93 CR France1225,Bell

MARTINDALE,Laurence 2Lt kia 31-3-18 2/4WRid p227 CR France924,21-3-18

MARTINDALE,Stanley 2Lt kia 4-9-16 2BordR p117 MR21

MARTINDALE,Warine Frederic Lt kia 15-9-16 1ScotGds p52 MR21

MARTINEAU,Alfred John Maj kia 17-4-17 RGA 19SB p209 CR France161

MARTINEAU,Clement Capt dow 5-5-18 PoW 10RWar p65 CR Belgium393

MARTINNANT,Archibald A.Maj 11-12-18 MadrasBarrackDept MR65

MARTINSON,Karl Ludwig TLt dow 1-6-17 RFA att RFC p10&32 CR France285

MARTLEW,Raymond Douglas Lt 4-6-21 TankCps CR Europe51

MARTYN,Cecil Radcliffe.MIDx2 Rev ded 3-3-19 RAChDept p199 CR France146

MARTYN,Edgar Spear Capt kia 30-11-17 6RWKent p141 MR17

MARTYN,Harold Henry Capt kia 21-3-18 3 att 2Wilts p153 MR27

MARTYR,John Francis Capt dow 11-8-17 1 att 6RIrRif p170 MR4

MARVIN,Donald 2Lt kia 9-5-15 1SfthH p165 CR France721

MARVIN,Henry Leslie 2Lt kia 27-10-17 GL &6RFC p10 CR Belgium116,26-10-17

MARWOOD,Charles Phillip Lysaght Capt dow 24-11-15 RWar att 1NigR p65&201 CR WAfrica58

MASCALL-THOMPSON,Cecil TCapt ded 21-1-16 RASC p193 CR Dorset139

MASCORD,Alfred Edgar 2Lt kia 6-5-18 6RWar p214 CR France1161

MASEFIELD,Charles John Beech.MC.2Lt dow PoW 21-8-17 1/5NStaffs C'Coy p238 CR France924,Capt 2-7-17

MASEFIELD,Robert Maj kia 24-10-14 KSLI p145 MR32

MASH,Oswald Nelson.MC.TLt kia 1-6-18 D174RFA p32 CR France504

MASHITER,Thomas Alexander Greenwood TLt kia 31-8-17 10Y&L att 1/5LancF p159

MASKELL,George Lt&QM kia 21-3-18 10ScotRif p103 CR France1182

MASKELL,Wilfred Fred 2Lt kia 22-11-17 1/4Lincs p217 CR France115

MASKELL,William Charles.DSO.MC.LtAMaj dow 15-12-17 C189RFA p32 CR France446

MASLIN,Leonard Frank,MC TLt ded 20-5-18 21MGC p184 CR France40

MASON,Albert Thomas T2Lt ded 1-3-18 LabCps att 66IndLabCo p189 CR France770

MASON,Allan Edward Glendinning T2Lt dow 30-6-16 7Leic p88 CR France62,Alan Glendenning

MASON,Arthur Edmund 2Lt kia 8-8-18 8Lond C'Coy p247 CR France141

MASON,Arthur Edward Wright Capt kia 2-3-16 7 att 8RFus p69 MR19,Knight

MASON,Arthur Humphrey Capt kia 21-8-15 NorfYeo p204 MR4,Humfrey 1/5NorfR

MASON,Arthur Pelham T2Lt kia 22-8-18 8 att 1SomLI p80 CR France250

MASON,Arthur Walton T2Lt kia 11-5-17 GL &7RFC p10 CR France528

MASON,Cecil Wyatt T2Lt kia 8-4-17 11RScot p54 CR France97

MASON,Charles 2Lt kia 27-9-18 3RWKent att 5MGC p141 MR16

MASON,Charles Douglas Forrest 2Lt 20-4-20 1/3Lpool CR Wales646

MASON,Charles Harold T2Lt kia 6-7-17 7RWSurr p56 CR Belgium29,7-7-17

MASON,Charles Henry.MC.2Lt dow 10-9-18 3Lond p246 CR France446

MASON,Derick Cecil 2Lt kia 10-11-17 1SWBord p255 MR30

MASON,Douglas Howard 2Lt kia 28-4-17 13Ess p132 MR20

MASON,Edward 2Lt kia 9-5-15 3 att 2Nhampt p137 MR32

MASON,Ernest TLt.ACapt dow 5-10-17 9YLI p143 CR France139

MASON,Fanny SNurse drd 10-4-17 QAIMNS p200 CR France85

MASON,George T2Lt kld 4-5-17 GL&RFC p11 CR Scot235 Ex 28Lond

MASON,George 2Lt kia 20-5-17 8 att 2Worc p226 MR20

MASON,George 2Lt kia 15-4-18 1 att 2/6NStaffs p157 MR32

MASON,George 2Lt kia 16-9-18 RGA Ex BSM 444SB p40 CR France161,15-9-18

MASON,George Sowersby T2Lt kia 8-10-18 2Y&L p159 CR France443

MASON,George William TLt kia 9-4-17 19Lpool p72 CR France592

MASON,Gerald Francis Lt kld 1-9-17 3Hamp att 12MGC p121&184,ded CR Hamps87

MASON,Godfey Jackson 2Lt kia 30-1-18 1/6 att 1/8LancF p221 CR France765

MASON,Gordon T2Lt kia 7-6-17 15 att 21KRRC p151 CR Belgium29

MASON,Herbert John.MC.Lt ded 16-12-18 Manch att 23Bn p155 CR Norf85

MASON,Hubert Harry Leslie 2Lt dow 12-10-17 1RWar p65 CR Belgium16

MASON,James Philip 2Lt kia 9-4-17 3 att 7ESurr p113 CR France96

MASON,John Norman.MC.TLt dow 13-10-18 2RRofCav att 1/1DorsYeo p23 CR Egypt1

MASON,Kenneth Ralph 2Lt kia 21-6-15 4Suff p217 CR France631

MASON,Lancelot William Hart 2Lt kia 14-4-17 5WYork p218 CR France115,1Bn

MASON,Norman George Minta.MC.Maj kld 13-9-18 RFA RNDivAmmCol p206 CR France560

MASON,Overton Trollope 2Lt kia 1-7-16 1/9Lond p248 MR21

MASON,Peter 2Lt kia 17-2-17 6 att 1KRRC p151 CR France314

MASON,Philip Granville.DSO.Maj kia 26-9-15 3DragGds p21 CR France423

MASON,Randall Stewart 2Lt kia 14-3-15 6RB p179 CR France709

MASON,Richard TLt.ACapt kia 23-11-17 13Yorks p91 MR17

MASON,Robert Brereton T2Lt kia 10-10-18 15MGC Inf p184 CR France705

MASON,Rowland Charles Lt dow 30-9-14 3LNLanc p136 CR War12

MASON,Royston Alfred Robson 2Lt dow 20-11-17 5 att 2RFus p69 CR France439

MASON,Stanley Hopkins T2Lt kia 26-9-16 8Suff p78 CR France314

MASON,Thomas Henry 2Lt dow 24-7-15 3Middx p147 CR France1

MASON,Vere Karsdale T2Lt kia 3-8-16 11Suff p78 MR21

MASON,Vernon T2Lt kia 1-4-18 1 att 9NumbF p62 CR France275

MASON,Wilfrid Howard T2Lt kia 9-3-17 RE 72FC p47 CR Iraq8

MASON,William James T2Lt kia 20-9-17 11RB p179 MR30

MASON,William John TCapt kia 3-7-16 8Glouc p107 MR21

MASON-MACFARLANE,Carlyon Will Capt kia 5-9-16 7Huss att 18ImpCamelCps p22

MASSEY,Albert Francis T2Lt kia 28-3-18 8MGC att 3Hamp p184 MR27

MASSEY,George Hocken 2Lt kia 27-6-16 A53RFA p32 CR France699

MASSEY,John Hamon.MC.MID Capt kia 27-5-18 5/45RFA p32 CR France1332

MASSEY,Louis Oger 2Lt kia 21-8-16 1RFus p69 CR France390

MASSEY,William Clayton 2Lt kia 5-11-18 4Lincs p217 CR Belgium204,6-11-18

MASSEY-LYNCH,Wilfrid John T2Lt kia 4-4-18 6RRofCav att 3DGds p24 MR27,Wilfred

MASSIAH-PALMER,Werner William Thomas.OBE.TMaj ded 17-2-19 GL &13NumbF p262 CR Mddx21,LtCol

MASSIE,A.H AssSurg 9-8-16 IMS CR Pakistan50A MR43

MASSIE,John Hamon.DSO.Maj dow 15-11-14 RGA 26HB p40 CR Belgium58

MASSIE,Sidney Edward 2Lt kia 8-5-17 att 1SomLI p80 MR20

MASSON,Alexander 2Lt dow 1-10-18 4SfthH p241 CR Belgium157

MASSON,Alex James 2Lt kia 23-3-18 9Manch p237 MR27

MASSON,J.HonMaj&QM ded 1-5-15 RScotF p95 CR Hamps7

MASSON,James 2Lt kia 28-7-18 7GordH p242 CR France1689

MASSON,James Alexander 2Lt dow 8-5-17 RGA 38HB p40 CR France1185

MASSY,Haworth Peel Capt ded 10-12-14 Leinst att 4NigR p174&201 CR WAfrica50

MASSY-BERESFORD,John Clarina Lt kia 28-8-18 310RFA p32 CR France5,23-8-18

MASSY-MILES,Henry Godfrey.MC.TCapt dow 26-4-18 RAMC att 1/8Lond p196 CR France145,Harry

MASSY-WHEELER,George Godfrey.VC. 13-4-15 IA 7Lancers CR Iraq6

MASTER,Charles Lionel.MID Capt kia 12-10-14 2RIrRif p170 CR France260

MASTER,George Gilbert Onslow Lt kia 25-7-16 1/4Glouc p225 CR France296

MASTERMAN,Frederick Michel 2Lt kia 1-7-16 3 att 10RIrRif p170 MR21

MASTERMAN,Robert Chauncey TLt kia 1-7-16 9LancF p93 MR21

MASTERS,Alexander Capt kia 23-11-14 IA 34SikhPnrs p280 CR France279

MASTERS,Charles William 2Lt kia 30-8-17 5 att8RFus p69 CR France154,5 att9Bn

MASTERS,Geoffrey T2Lt kia 9-4-17 9RFus p69 CR France531

MASTERS,George Edward Lt mbk 4-6-15 IA 89Punjabis att14Sikhs p280 MR4

MASTERSON,Christopher John 2Lt kia 2-9-17 10 att1Worc p109 CR Belgium50,Lt

MASTERSON,Frank 2Lt kia 5-4-18 9RFus p69 CR France516,MASTERTON

MASTERSON,George Cuthbert Dillon Capt ded 25-2-17 RLancs p262 CR Hamps8

MASTERTON,William Murray 2Lt dow 10-6-17 6RScot p211 CR France113

MASTIN,Frank T2Lt kia 2-11-17 1N&D 1stGarrBn att1/4Nampt p134 CR Palestine8

MATEAR,Norman Hirst Lawrence.MID TCapt kia 25-9-15 2RWar p65 MR19

MATHER,Alan William Lt ded 29-10-18 3BlkW &RAF p129 CR Lincs61

MATHER,Alfred Lushington 2Lt kia 7-1-17 3Y&L p159 CR Belgium4

MATHER,C.H.T2Lt dow 18-3-16 12NumbF p62 CR France285

MATHER,Donald 2Lt kia 2-11-17 5Manch p236 CR Belgium24

MATHER,Edward Noel 2Lt kia 26-4-15 6NumbFus p214 MR29

MATHER,Edward William 2Lt dow 13-10-16 RE 1FC p210 CR France300

MATHER,George 2Lt kia 8-10-16 25Lond p252 MR21,4-10-16

MATHER,John Wilfred TCapt kia 10-8-15 6LNLanc p136 MR4

MATHER,John Kearsley Lt kia 18-2-15 Y&L p159 MR29

MATHER,Norman 2Lt kia 9-8-16 1/10Lpool p216 MR21

MATHER,Robert T2Lt kia 27-3-18 20Lpool p72 MR27

MATHER,Volney 2Lt kia 31-7-17 12LNLanc p234 CR Belgium125

MATHERS,George Eric TLt kia 8-10-18 6MGC p184 CR France235

MATHESON,Alexander Percival Lt kia 13-7-17 GL &55RFC p11 CR Belgium344,Perceval

MATHESON,Andrew Scott T2Lt dow 10-4-17 7SfthH p165 CR France95,Lt

MATHESON,Archibald Angus T2Lt ded 20-12-17 RASC HQ BaseSupplyDepot p193 CR France145

MATHESON,Claude Bruce 2Lt kia 23-9-17 5 att2RB p179 CR Belgium52

MATHESON,George Hugh T2Lt kia 3-12-17 14DLI p161 MR17

MATHESON,Harry Mackay 2Lt ded 24/26-12-17 RFC attAust FC p11 CR Palestine8

MATHESON,Herbert 2Lt kia 23-3-18 13 att15Lond CR France716

MATHESON,Homer Lindsay T2Lt dow 16-8-16 9ESurr p113 MR21

MATHESON,Ian Kenneth LtACapt dow 13-5-17 3 att2SfthH p165 CR France40,Lt

MATHESON,James 2Lt kia 26-3-16 4A&SH p173 MR32

MATHESON,James Frederick.MC.TCapt dow 19-4-18 RAMC att7Norf p196 CR France145

MATHESON,James McDonald TCapt kia 30-11-17 RAMC att17Mddx p196 CR France530

MATHESON,John T2Lt kia 9-4-17 10HLI p163 MR20

MATHESON,John Hugh Capt dow 24-4-17 6GordH p242 CR France113

MATHESON,John James 2Lt dow 13-8-18 7CamH att1/5A&SH p168 CR France145,Lt

MATHESON,John MacLean 2Lt kia 26-6-18 4RScot p211 MR32

MATHESON,Malcolm Angus.MC.Capt dow 27-9-18 6GordH att 15TankCps p242 CR France433

MATHESON,Roderick Kyrle 2Lt dow 8-9-16 3RWKent att20Manch p141 CR France245

MATHEW.C.V.D.Waynflete T2Lt kia 21-8-17 RE 48DivSigCo p47 MR30

MATHEW,George Dudley Capt dow 10-5-15 IA 2/2GurkhaRif p280 CR Belgium140 &CR France924

MATHEW.J.D.Cdr 29-7-21 MilWksServ MR66

MATHEW,Murray Chamberlain Gervase.MID Lt dow 4-7-15 IA 28Punjabis att14Sikhs p280 CR Egypt3

MATHEWS,Anthony Edward T2Lt kia 19-7-16 11Dev att2/6Glouc p77 CR France1887

MATHEWS,Arnold.MID TLt dow 14-4-16 14Ches p96 MR38

MATHEWS,Award Yuill 2Lt dow PoW 26-10-18 1York att1WYork p91 MR16

MATHEWS,Edward Stanley TLt kia 2-10-18 1 att2Middx p147 CR France407,26-9-18

MATHEWS,George 2Lt kia 2-10-17 RFA att55RFC p11&32

MATHEWS,Hubert Victor 2Lt kia 26-8-16 135/32RFA p32 CR Belgium127

MATHEWS,Hugh Spencer Capt kia 22-7-16 14RWar p65 CR France432

MATHEWS,John Laurence Lt ded 28-12-17 3RSuss attRE DivSigs p264 CR France31,29-12-17 7Bn

MATHEWS,Joseph Henry T2Lt kia 27-3-18 5RBerks p139 MR27

MATHEWS,Robert Arthur Cecil Lt kia 18-10-16 3 att1ELancs p111 MR21

MATHEWS,Thomas Hugh Lt kia 2-11-14 1ELancs p111 CR Belgium68

MATHEWS,Walter Vivanti Dewar Maj dow 9-12-17 RGA 102SB p40 CR France398

MATHEWS,William Scott TLt kia 15-9-16 18KRRC p151 CR France1890

MATHEWSON,George Gillespie.MID TLt kia 27-3-18 RE 5FC p47 MR27

MATHEWSON,Hamilton TCapt dow 27-10-16 RAMC att2Nhampt p196 CR France105

MATHEWSON,James Kenneth 2Lt kia 14-9-18 D113RFA p32 CR Belgium188

MATHEWSON,Kenneth Lt kia 3-8-16 RFC p3 CR France161

MATHIAS,Charles Arthur Stirling,MC T2Lt kia 3-5-17 7EKent p57 MR20

MATHIAS,John Edmund 2Lt drd 11-10-16 5WelshR p230 CR Wales12

MATHIAS,John Harold Tudor 2Lt kia 25-11-17 5 att17WelshR p230 MR17

MATHIESON,Herbert Gerard Lt kia 10-3-15 3Lond p245 CR France706

MATHIESON,John T2Lt kia 5-8-18 3A&SH att7SfthH p173 CR France27

MATHIESON,Kenneth Ronald Lt kia 1-11-14 1IrGds p53 MR29

MATHIESON,Stanley 2Lt dow 16-8-18 7ScotRif p224 CR France85

MATHIESON,William 2Lt kia 25-5-18 4Beds p86 MR27

MATHIESON-MACBETH,Thomas McBeth Lt kia 5-9-17 8Lond p247

MATHVIN,Douglas Gatecliffe 2Lt kia 9-5-15 1/9Lpool p216 MR22,MATHWIN

MATON,Leonard Evelyn Leigh.MC.MIDx2Capt kia 9-5-17 1Dev p77 MR20

MATTESON,Leonard Maj ded 11-4-16 RASC SR p193 CR Lond8

MATTEY,Charles Percival T2Lt ded PoW 22-1-17 1Beds p86 CR France924

MATTHAMS,Lawrence T2Lt kia 13-10-18 49MGC Inf p184 CR France270

MATTHEW,Frank Henry 2Lt kia 9-10-15 RGA p40

MATTHEW,Wilfrid John 2Lt kia 19-5-18 5Lond p246 CR France196

MATTHEWS,Alfred Apsley T2Lt dow 12-9-16 9ESurr p113 CR France145

MATTHEWS,Arthur James TCapt ded 21-11-18 15SLanc p125

MATTHEWS,Bertram Cash TLt kia 24-3-17 2RScot p54 CR France645

MATTHEWS,Charles Henry 2Lt dow 22-3-18 1RFus p69 CR France987 Ex 2CldGds

MATTHEWS,David T2Lt kia 29-5-16 6ConnRgrs p171 CR France178

MATTHEWS,Ernest Alan 2Lt kia 2-4-18 8SomLI &RAF p255 CR France630,Lt 11Bn

MATTHEWS,Edward Alexander 2Lt kia 14-3-15 3Nhants p137 MR22,10-3-15

MATTHEWS,Edward Philip TLt dow 16-9-16 8RB p179 CR France66

MATTHEWS,Edwin Harold 2Lt kia 8-8-16 1/7Lpool p215 MR21

MATTHEWS,Edwin Martin Lt kia 8-11-16 1/4Glouc p225 MR21

MATTHEWS,Francis Harold T2Lt kia 24-7-17 266MGC p184 MR29

MATTHEWS,Frank Arthur TLt kia 24-4-17 10RSuss &9RFC p11&119 MR20

MATTHEWS,Frank Reginald Lt dow 23-3-18 12ESurr p113 MR20

MATTHEWS,George T2Lt dow 2-7-18 PoW WYorks att1/6Bn p82 CR Germany1

MATTHEWS,Godfrey Estcourt.CB.CMG.TBrigGen dow 13-4-17 198InfBde RMLI Staff p1

MATTHEWS,Harold Carey Maj kia 25-4-15 4York p220 MR29 CR Belgium453

MATTHEWS,Henry 2Lt kia 15-1-17 24RFus att47RFC p11 CR Greece7

MATTHEWS,Henry Arthur 2Lt dow 25-10-17 465/65RFA p32 CR Belgium16

MATTHEWS,Henry Aylmer Vallance.MC.TCaptAMaj ded 8-11-18 Cmdg14Div RASC MT p193 CR France1028

MATTHEWS,Herbert Lewis Lash 2Lt kia 9-9-16 11 att1/5Lond p248 CR France1890

MATTHEWS,John Brice TCapt kia 14-2-17 7RWKent p141 CR France314

MATTHEWS,John Bredel.MC.LtTCapt kia 1-10-17 3NStaffs att8Leic p157 MR30,Budel

MATTHEWS,John Edward Norman 2Lt died 4-8-19 1Suff att8N&D p263 CR Greece9

MATTHEWS,John Herbert Capt kia 13/14-9-14 1NumbF p62 MR15,Hubert 15-9-14

MATTHEWS,L.G.MID ChaplCl 26-5-16 CR Lond9

MATTHEWS,Leonard Mansfield TLt ded 25-6-18 RASC MT p193 CR France1358

MATTHEWS,Leslie Herbert 2Lt kia 28-3-18 RWar att2/6 p65 MR27

MATTHEWS,Lewis Joseph Rev ded 26-5-16 RAChDept p199

MATTHEWS,Mervyn Lt dow 28-1-15 RE p47 CR Glouc24

MATTHEWS,Myles Lewis Wyan TCapt kia 3-7-16 6RWKent p141 MR21

MATTHEWS,Noël Anwyl 2Lt kia 15-9-16 11Lond p248 CR France277,3 att8Bn

MATTHEWS,Richard Malcolm T2Lt kia 20-9-17 9York p91 MR30

MATTHEWS,Robert John Lt ded 2-11-18 4Norf p187&216 CR Lincs61

MATTHEWS,S.W.Capt 15-11-18 RAMC CR EAfrica8 &Tanzania1

MATTHEWS,Samuel Wauchope TLt ded 15-9-18 RAMC attMLB p196

MATTHEWS,St.John Bell T2Lt dow 25-11-15 6RBerks p139 CR France22

MATTHEWS,Thomas.MBE.LtACapt dow 27-6-18 RGA 521Household SB p40 CR France31,251SB

MATTHEWS,Walter Franey Capt kia 28-9-17 4Dors p229 CR Iraq8

MATTHEWS,Wilfrid Vernon.MC.T2Lt kia 1-10-18 11 att1/5BordR p117 CR France375

MATTHEWS,William Frederick Capt kia 18-8-18 1SWBord att1ELanc p100 CR France21

MATTHEWS,William Henry 2Lt kia 28-9-18 RGA 2/1Lowland HB p41 CR France446

MATTHEY,Edward Granville Capt kia 1-7-16 1LancF p93 CR France1492

MATTHYSSENS,Francis Alexander TCapt ded 23-6-16 1/4WelshR p230 CR Egypt1

MATTMAN,A.M.Lt 22-7-21 RFA SR CR Lond14

MATTOX,Charles Douglas Lt 15-6-20 RFA attIntCps CR Asia51

MATTS,Frank 2Lt kia 24-7-16 5War p214 CR France832

MATURIN,W.K.(Kay)Lt 29-1-15 UgandaPoliceBn CR EAfrica128

MAUBSELL,George Wyndham 2Lt kia 23-2-17 IARO att2S&M p280

MAUCHLINE,Allan Bryce T2Lt kia 14-10-18 SfthH att9Bn p165 CR Belgium157

MAUD,Charles Carns,DSO Capt kia 19-12-14 1SomLI p80 CR Belgium70

MAUD,Frederick T2Lt kia 20-9-17 124MGC Inf p184 MR30

MAUD,Frederick Stanley.MC.T2Lt kia 3-10-18 att2YLI p143 CR France375,Sidney

MAUDE,Frederick Stanley.Sir.KCB.CMG.DSO LtGen ded 18-11-17 Staff GOCinChief MEF p1 CR Iraq8

MAUDE,Gerald William Edward Capt ded 5-11-19 1Yorks p263 MR43

MAUDE,Gervase Henry Francis 2Lt dow 9-4-17 att8RFus p69 CR France113

MAUDE,John William Ashley T2Lt kia 24-8-15 10KRRC p151 CR France707,Achley 23-8-15

MAUDE,Louis Edward Joseph 2Lt kia 1-7-16 11YLI p143 CR France267

MAUDE,M.B.MC.Lt 24-1-21 4RFus CR Iraq8

MAUDE,Michael Day Wade Capt dow 14-10-17 3 att9Yorks p91 CR Yorks485

MAUDE,Robert Henry Ernest 2Lt ded 12-9-16 2WYorks GarBn att3NStaffs p82 CR Cornwall1

MAUFE,Statham Broadbent.MID TMaj dow 5-7-16 11WYorks p82 CR France833

MAUGHAN,Alfred William 2Lt kia 24-6-17 RGA 285SB p41 CR Belgium17

MAUGHAN,John.MID Capt kia 17-2-16 4Yorks p220 CR Belgium5

MAUGHAN,William Douglas T2Lt kia 19-11-17 17NumbF p62 CR Belgium23

MAUL,Richard Selby Lowndes 2Lt kia 30-7-16 2 O&BLI p130 MR21

MAULE,Edward Barry TLt kia 6-2-17 18HLI &20RFC p11&p163 CR Belgium112

MAULE,Geoffrey Lamb Capt ded 15-11-18 RAMC att27CCS p196 CR Iraq8

MAULE,Robert Lt kia 27-5-15 5RScot p211 CR Gallipoli3

MAULE-FRENCH,Eric Herbert Justus 2Lt kia 27-8-18 7Lond p247 CR France164,FFRENCH

MAULEVERER,Richard De Burgh 2Lt dow 13-11-17 3 att2ELancs CR Scot252

MAULKINSON,Harry Young T2Lt dow 4-6-17 7Lincs p75 CR Lincs202

MAULTSAIS,Wesley 2Lt 22-5-15 9RScots D'Coy CR Belgium453

MAUNSELL,Douglas Slade Lt kia 6-9-16 2RMunstF p175 MR21,5/6-9-16

MAUNSELL,Edwin Richard Lloyd Capt kia 1-7-16 1RDubF p177 CR France35

MAUNSELL,George Wyndham 2Lt 23-2-17 IARO attS&M MR38

MAUNSELL,Herbert Stofford Lt dow 1-9-15 3RWar p65 CR France98,2Bn

MAUNSELL,Marian Jane Nurse ded 7-1-19 VAD BRCS p200 CR Egypt9

MAUNSELL,Reginald Harcourt Proctor 2Lt kia 27-4-18 RGA 128SB p41 CR Belgium188

MAUNSELL,Robert George Frederick Capt drd 4-5-17 RE p210 CR Italy14

MAUNSELL,Thomas Bowyer-Lane Capt kia 1-5-15 1LancF p93 CR Gallipoli,25-4-15

MAUNSELL,Wilfrid Innocent Capt kia 8-2-15 2ScotRif p103 CR France567

MAURICE,Charles Henry Pryse 2Lt dedacc 24-1-17 3RBerks p139 CR France120

MAURICE,Francis Thomas 2Lt ded 29-10-18 1GrenGds p262

MAURICE,John Capel 2Lt kia 7-10-18 RBerks att2Bn p139 CR France184

MAURICE,Sterling 2Lt dow 11-5-15 RE 2FC p210 CR Belgium11

MAVETY,John Le Roy TLt ded 13-12-15 RAMC 46Div p196 CR France495

MAVOR,Robert George Innes.MC.2Lt kia 23-4-17 7A&SH p234 CR France545

MAW,Arthur Rogers Capt kia 21-3-18 10Manch p237 MR27

MAW,George Oliver TCapt dow 10-7-16 RAMC att13StatHospl p196 CR France430,attRB

MAW,Harry H.T2Lt kia 22-8-18 Beds p86 CR France239

MAWBY,Edwin George Lt kia 27-9-15 WelshGds p53 MR19

MAWBY,Thomas Henry 2Lt kia 24-6-18 4Lond p246 CR France1182

MAWDSLEY,Burton James Platt Lt kia 6-2-16 IA 17Cav p280 CR EAfrica42,Barton

MAWDSLEY,John Edmund T2Lt kia 24-4-17 10 att6RLancs p59 MR38

MAWDSLEY,Norman Hargreaves Lt ded 17-6-18 6RFus p69 CR Hamps15

MAWHOOD,Claude George T2Lt kia 14-9-16 8WRid p116 MR21

MAWSON,Alan John Lt ded 4-12-18 5NumbF p256 CR Numb5

MAXFIELD,Hugh Lt 8-12-18 MilLabCps CR EAfrica36

MAXTED,Spencer Edward Chap4Cl 19/20-7-16 AustInf CR France525

MAXWELL,Alexander Edward Lt dow 7-5-17 GL 20Mddx att121TMB p191 CR France1468

MAXWELL,Arthur Lt&QM ded 19-3-19 GL att4RWSurr p271

MAXWELL,Arthur Edwin Lt ded 18-3-20 RE attDORE Constantinople p271 CR Asia51

MAXWELL,Aylmer Edward Capt kia 9-10-14 1LovatSc CmdgCollingwoodBn RND p271 CR Belgium342,Aymer LtCol

MAXWELL,Charles William Lt kia 24-11-14 IA 2/8GurkhaRif p280 CR France279,23-11-14

MAXWELL,Clyde Fairbanks 2Lt kia 3-7-16 9Ess p132 MR21

MAXWELL,David.MC&Bar.Capt dow 3-8-18 5BlkW p231 CR France1225

MAXWELL,Eustace Lockhart LtCol mbk 20-7-16 IA 11Lancers att23Manch p280 MR28

MAXWELL,Francis Aylmer.VC.CSI.DSO.BrigGen kia 21-9-17 IA Cmdg27InfBde 9Div p280 CR Belgium84

MAXWELL,Harley Hyslop 2Lt dow 24-10-18 1CamH p168 CR France725

MAXWELL,Henry T2Lt kia 10-10-16 13Ches p96 CR France280,Capt 11-10-16

MAXWELL,Hon.Henry Edward.DSO.Col ded 2-3-19 SL BlkW p268 CR Eire251

MAXWELL,Ian Bouverie Capt kia 31-1-14 3 att1SWBord p100 MR29,31-10-14

MAXWELL,James Lt kia 21-8-15 11Lond p248 CR Gallipoli27

MAXWELL,James McCall Lt kia 1-6-16 459/118RFA p32 CR Belgium5

MAXWELL,John 2Lt kia 12-7-15 5RScotFus p222 MR4

MAXWELL,John.DSO.MC.CaptALtCol dow 4-12-17 7RB att8KRRC p179 CR Belgium84

MAXWELL,John Duncan T2Lt dow 18-7-17 11Suff p78 CR France446

MAXWELL,Joseph.MM.2Lt ded 26-3-18 3RScotF p263 CR Scot683

MAXWELL,Peter Benson Capt dow 24-9-14 EYorks late35Sikhs p84 CR France1110

MAXWELL,Power MacMurrough.MC.CaptAMaj dow 1-10-17 B95RH&FA p32 CR Belgium11

MAXWELL,Richard D'Arcy TLtACapt kia 23-10-18 2RScot p54 CR France292

MAXWELL,Richard Drummond Capt ded 3-6-16 RAMC p271 CR Scot239,6-3-16

MAXWELL,Richard Henry Perceval Lt kia 23-7-18 3 att10ScotRif p103

MAXWELL,Robert Greenwood TCapt kia 7-1-16 3SfthH p165 MR38

MAXWELL,Ronald Erskine Wilford TMaj kia 25-9-15 6KOSB p102 CR France550

MAXWELL,Stanley Woods T2Lt dow PoW 27-7-16 8RIrRif B'Coy p170 CR France1266

MAXWELL,Thomas T2Lt kia 9-9-16 8RDubF p177 CR France294

MAXWELL,Walter T2Lt ded 11-2-18 1SWBord p100 MR66

MAXWELL,Wellwood 2Lt dow 16-9-16 20Lond p251 CR France197,15-9-16

MAXWELL,William Francis John Lt kia 13-8-15 5KOSB p224 CR Gallipoli2

MAXWELL,William Gardner.MC.BtMaj ded 11-12-18 8GordH GSO att3CpsSchool p166 CR France13

MAXWELL,William Jardine Capt ded 26-8-16 2CamH att10SoudanInf EgyptArmy p168 CR EAfrica116

MAXWELL,William Leigh LtCol kia 12-5-15 IA 127Baluchis attRMLI p280

MAXWELL,William Nisbet 2Lt kia 12-10-16 3 att7SfthH p165 CR France489

MAXWELL,William Stewart 2Lt kia 21-3-18 56RFC p16 MR20,27-3-18

MAXWELL-HERON,Basil Charles Montague TCapt SL ded 22-9-16 p201 CR Lond4

MAXWELL-MOFFAT,Alexander Logan Nathan Lt ded 21-11-14 2Dors p124 CR Iraq6,dow

MAXWELL-STUART,Alfred Joseph 2Lt dow 24-8-18 1CldGds p51 CR France84,Lt

MAXWELL-STUART,Edmund Joseph TLt kia 26-4-16 RE 175Coy p47 CR Belgium5

MAXWELL-STUART,Henry Joseph Ignatius 2Lt kia 9-10-17 3GrenGds p51 CR Belgium106,CldGds

MAXWELL-STUART,J.J.Lt 2-3-16 9WRid CR Belgium15

MAY,Adrian Robson 2Lt kia 8-9-16 5Lpool p215 CR France188

MAY,Charles Campbell.MID TCapt kia 1-7-16 22Manch B'Coy p155 CR France397

MAY,Charles Richard Allen Lt ded 18-8-20 IA 56Rif p280 CR Egypt10

MAY,Claude Boyle.MC.TCapt kia 19-11-17 6BordR p117 CR France550

MAY,Ernest Bernard.DCM.T2Lt kia 4-10-16 30MGC p184 CR Greece3

MAY,Ernest Edward.DCM.2Lt kia 28-8-16 20Manch p155 CR France402

MAY,Francis Henry T2Lt kia 29-9-18 1TankCps p188 MR16

MAY,Frederick Wilson Laughton TCapt dow 8-6-17 11RIrRif p170 CR Belgium97

MAY,George Neville TCapt dow 29-5-18 RGA 243SB att87SB p41 CR France145,343SB

MAY,Harold Costwick 2Lt dow 27-3-15 3DorsR p124 CR France102,Gostwyck

MAY,Herbert Cecil 2Lt dow 29-9-18 6 att18KRRC p151 CR Belgium116

MAY,Herbert Edwin Lt drd 6-12-17 SurrYeo p205 MR37

MAY,James Percy Maj kia 12-2-17 IA 102Grens p280 CR Iraq5

MAY,John Hayes 2Lt kia 20-11-17 9Lond p248 CR France530

MAY,Leo Cuthbert 2Lt kia 27-6-18 3 att12Glouc p107 CR France352

MAY,Paul Archer 2Lt kia 15-4-17 1Dev p77 MR20

MAY,Percy William T2Lt kia 13-11-16 10 att7ELancs p111 MR21

MAY,Peter Langton 2Lt kia 13-2-16 2Drags SR p21 MR19

MAY,Ralph Edward 2Lt kia 12-7-15 5HLI p240 MR4

MAY,Richard Trelawney.MID TCapt kia 7-7-16 7RSuss A'Coy p119 MR21

MAY,Richard Wallis 2Lt kia 9-8-15 2DLI p161 MR29

MAY,Stanley Harris Lt kia 27-8-16 11LNLancs att2RWar p136 MR21

MAY,Thomas George T2Lt kia 6-8-17 143MGC p184 CR Belgium9

MAY,Walter Gould 2Lt kia 3-9-16 Hamps 1GarrBn p121 CR France339

MAY,Wilfred John.MC.T2Lt dow 1-8-17 2WYorks p82 CR Belgium11

MAY,William Clarence 2Lt kia 26-10-17 NumbF att1/5Bn p255 MR30

MAY,William Ernest Edward Frederick 2Lt kia 24-11-16 1/22Lond p251 CR Belgium167

MAY,William John T2Lt dow 23-3-18 Y&L p159 CR France177

MAYALL,James 2Lt dow 13-11-18 4KOSB p271 CR Lancs441

MAYBANK,John Gunter TLt kia 15-9-16 2YLI p143 CR France114,2Lt

MAYBERRY,Richard Lt kia 15-11-17 3RScotFus &70RFC p11&95 MR20 &CR Belgium167

MAYBERY,Richard Aveline.MC&Bar.Lt kia 19-12-17 21Lancers att56RFC p11&23 CR France1483,Capt

MAYBIN,James Johnstone TCapt kia 14-7-16 11RScot p54 CR France399

MAYBREY,Arthur James 2Lt kia 22-7-16 10Glouc p107 MR21

MAYBROOK,Walter Richard T2Lt kia 24-4-16 1Wilts p153 CR France68

MAYBURY,Arthur.DCM.2Lt kia 19-7-17 1 att5RBerks p139&257 MR20

MAYBURY,Francis Joseph 2Lt dow 5-10-18 5 att1RMunstF p175 CR France40,Lt

MAYBURY,Reginald 2Lt kld 23-4-17 6 att18Manch p237 MR20

MAYCOCK,Frederick William Orby.DSO.Maj kia 25-5-15 1Suff p78 CR Belgium125

MAYER,Frank TLt kia 3-10-18 RFus att4Bn p69 CR France338,8-10-18

MAYER,Frank Bertram Lt kia 13-10-15 5NStaff p238 MR19

MAYER,Frederick Percy Fry Lt ded 30-4-17 NigR CR WAfrica3

MAYER,Gerald Max.MID Lt dow 16-2-17 1Lond p245 CR France40,Capt

MAYER,John Stuart Lt kia 29-1-18 8Manch p237 CR Belgium72

MAYERSBACH,Jack Frederick T2Lt kia 4-5-18 13RB p179 CR France1014

MAYES,Robert Campbell.MC.2Lt dow 19-10-18 22Lond p251 CR France496,Capt

MAYES,Walter Herbert 2Lt kia 9-1-17 IARO att1S&M p280 MR38

MAYFIELD,Leonard Augustus T2Lt kia 27-9-18 NumbF att1Bn p62 MR16

MAYLIN,Bertram Henry 2Lt kia 11-4-18 8 att2/7Lond p247 MR32

MAYNARD,Frederick Creber Lt dow 20-9-18 RGA 119HB p41 CR France1184

MAYNARD,Frederick Owen Capt ded 12-1-20 RAVC CR Egypt2

MAYNARD,Hugh Charles Lt kia 15-9-16 1CldGds p51 MR21

MAYNARD,John Edwin.MC.Maj dow 17-10-18 6Lond p246 CR Hamps64

MAYNARD,John Wilmot 2Lt kia 24-4-15 3KRRC p151 MR29

MAYNARD,Michael James Lt kia 8-10-16 1/5Lond p246 MR21

MAYNE,Augustus Blair Maj ded 4-12-17 RH&FA 3DAC Ex CenIndHorse p32 CR Surrey113

MAYNE,Cecil Robert 2Lt kia 30-11-17 2/5 att7YLI p235 MR17

MAYNE,Denis John Heriot 2Lt kld 12-10-17 RIrRif &57RFC p11&170 CR Mddx16

MAYNE,George Rufane Talbot.MC.TLt dow 10-11-18 RASC p193 CR Eire394

MAYNE,Jasper Moone 2Lt kia 9-5-15 RFA p32 CR France525,Moore

MAYNE,Victor Charles Moore Lt kia 19-2-16 1SWBord p100 CR France1896 &CR France1723

MAYO,Percy Austin 2Lt kld 9-5-16 3Dors p124

MAYO,William Charles TLt kia 7/11-8-15 9N&D p134 MR4,7-8-15

MAYS,Alexander Walter 2Lt ded 14-11-16 IARO att14JatLancers p280

MAYS,Cecil Clarence 2Lt kia 30-3-18 1GrenGds p50 CR France1183

MAYS,Charles Cecil Wildman Lt drd 25-1-18 RAMC p196 CR France85,RASC

MAYS,Frederick William 2Lt ded 20-7-17 A69RFA p32 CR Iraq8

MAYS,W.H.2Lt 14-11-16 14Lancers MR65

MAYSON,Frank Eric Halton T2Lt kia 28-8-16 6YLI p143 CR France402,Hutton

MAYWOOD,James Henry LtTCapt kia 23-8-18 1DCLI p114 CR France239

MAZENGART,George Richard Bostock 2Lt kia 29-7-16 3 att1ESurr p113 MR21,MAZENGARB

McADIE,David Alister Alexander.MC.2Lt kia 22-8-17 5SfthH p241 MR30,MACADIE

McADIE,George 2Lt 22-3-18 14A&SH p173 MR20

McADOREY,John 2Lt dow 5-5-18 2/10Manch p155 CR France84

McAFEE,Lewis Alexander Capt kia 30-7-15 8RB p179 MR27

McALINDON,Thomas.MC.2LtACapt ded 17-9-18 2RIrRif p169 CR Ireland74

McALISTER,Clara SNurse drd 10-4-17 QAIMNS p200 CR France85

McALISTER,George Howden 2Lt kia 24-8-16 5RScotF &78MGC p187&222 MR37

McALISTER,Gordon Duncan 2Lt kia 10-4-18 4KSLI A'Coy p235 MR30

McALISTER,Hugh 2Lt ded 17-9-17 Y&L p159 CR Surrey1

McALLISTER,Angus TCapt ded 29-8-17 RE p46 CR Italy6,Andrew

McALLISTER,Charles ACapt kia 27-5-18 9DubF att2WYorks p177 CR France1753

McALLISTER,Robert 2Lt kia 30-10-17 8Lond p247 CR Belgium83

McALPIN,James Montgomerie T2Lt kia 11-4-17 8KOSB p102 MR20

McANDREW,Alister 2Lt kia 24-12-14 1BlkW p129 MR22

McANDREW,Charles Arthur Worthington 2Lt kia 26-4-17 24RFA p32 CR France257

McANDREW,Charles Roy 2Lt kia 21-9-18 WarYeo attMGC p187&205 CR France369

McANDREW,George Burbury LtCol kia 14-3-15 2Lincs p75 CR France525,10-3-15

McARA,Duncan 2Lt dow 29-4-17 3HLI p163 CR France95

McARDLE,Hugh Francis Lt kia 18-9-17 KEdwHorse &41RFC p10&24 MR20

McARDLE,Peter Paul T2Lt kia 26-4-18 1/2Ches att1/4Y&L p96 MR30

McARDLE,W.R.Capt 28-8-21 IMD MR65

McARTHUR,Dugald T2Lt dow 21-4-17 2BlkW p129 MR38

McARTHUR,John TCapt kia 27-2-17 GL &12RFC p10

McARTHUR,Lawrence William.MC.Capt kia 27-5-17 HAC att12RFC p19 CR Belgium140 &CR France46

McARTHUR,William Bell.MC.T2Lt kia 9-4-17 1RScotF p95 CR France418

McAULEY,Bernard Capt kia 7-8-15 6BordR p117 MR4

McAULEY,Francis Willmer TCapt kia 21-5-16 B230RFA p207 CR France281,McAULAY

McAULIFFE,Cornelius Rev ded 6-10-16 RAChDept p199 CR Eire167

McAULIFFE,George Henry 2Lt kia 29-10-14 CamH att2GordH p168 MR29

McBAIN,Frederick Thomas T2Lt kia 9-4-18 13Yorks p90 CR France82

McBAIN,John Mortimer 2Lt dow PoW 9-7-16 231RFA p32 CR France1484

McBEAN,Donald Lt kia 15-3-16 RWFus att10Bn p98 MR29

McBEAN,William T2Lt kia 12-5-16 11A&SH p173 CR France423

McBLANE,David McMurtrie 2Lt 12-10-17 4RScots MR30

McBRAYNE,David Cecil Hope T2Lt dow PoW 21-6-17 GL &11RFC p10

McBRIDE,Alfred Henry 2Lt dow 1-11-14 2HLI p163 CR Belgium58

McBRIDE,Andrew Best.MC.Capt kia 24-4-18 2/5Beds p219 CR France303

McBRIDE,Arthur King TCapt kia 7-6-17 12RIrRif p169 CR Belgium100

McBRIDE,John Gordon 2Lt kld 8-10-18 3Glouc &20RAF p107 MR20

McBRIDE,Joseph LtAMaj kia 23-4-17 27RFA p32 CR France1325

McBRIDE,William Wilson 2Lt dow 5-12-17 RGA 229SB p40 CR Italy7,kia

McBRIEN,Hubert John T2Lt kia 4-11-18 2DubF p177 CR France521

McBRINN,John Charles 2Lt kia 3-9-16 4RIrReg p89 CR France402,5Bn

McBURNEY,James Wilson T2Lt kia 16-8-17 14RIrRif p169 MR30

McCABE,Albert Peter Patrick.MID 2Lt kia 16/17-5-15 2RWSurr p56 CR France279

McCABE,Daniel.Sir Col 29-9-19 1Manch CR Lancs35

McCABE,Daniel James Bernard 2Lt kia 31-7-17 8Lpool p216 MR29

McCABE,John Bertram 2Lt kia 28-3-18 6LancF p221 MR27

McCAHON,Robert Lt dow 30-3-18 RE 69FC SR p46 CR France62

McCAIG,George Mann 2Lt dow 18-10-18 306RFA 61DAC p32 CR France403,kia

McCAIG,Peter Lt 27-9-18 ScotHorse att54RAF CR France147

McCAIG,William George 2Lt 1-10-18 13RAF CR France256

McCALL,Alfred Ward 2Lt kia 30-9-18 3 att11RScotF p95 CR France525

McCALL,Archibald.MC.2Lt dow 23-8-17 4KOSB p224 CR France40,7/8Bn

McCALL,Eric Hutchinson 2Lt ded 7-9-16 V'Bty RHA p32 CR Iraq6,Hutchison

McCALL,Gavin.MC.DCM.MM.ACapt kia 28-3-18 10ScotRif p103 CR France57

McCALL,Gilbert Stewart Lt dow 20-5-18 5SfthH p241 CR Scot112

McCALL,Mathew Brown Wright 2Lt kia 12-7-15 4RScotF p222 MR4

McCALL,Robert Alfred T2Lt kia 25-9-15 9Ches p96 CR France260

McCALL,William.DSO.LtCol ded 27-6-18 RAMC p253 CR Scot522

McCALLION,Frank Mungo.MC.TLt kia 20-7-18 4SfthH p165 CR France622

McCALLUM,Alexander Meikle TCapt dow 3-4-17 16HLI p163 CR France1204

McCALLUM,Charles 2Lt ded 6-11-18 1/10Lpool p216 CR Lancs4

McCALLUM,Donald T2Lt kia 25-9-15 10ScotRif p103 MR19

McCALLUM,Daniel Capt kia 3-9-16 51AustInf CR France516

McCALLUM,Duncan TCapt kia 22-9-17 12ESurr p113 MR30,21-9-17

McCALLUM,Edward 2Lt drd 30-12-17 13Lond p249 MR41

McCALLUM,George Lt 31-7-15 RAMC att5DCLI p196 MR29

McCALLUM,John 2Lt kia 15-9-16 3CamH p168 CR France239

McCALLUM,Malcolm Campbell 2Lt kia 18-11-16 7ScotRif att15HLI p224 CR France1890

McCALLUM,Norman 2Lt kia 31-7-17 11A&SH p173 MR29

McCALLUM,Rae Bruce T2Lt kia 2-9-17 4 att9RFus p69 CR France154,Ray

McCALLUM,William Hay 2Lt 27-8-18 7HLI MR16

McCAMMON,Charles Duncan 2Lt kia 3-7-16 9RWFus p98 CR France393

McCAMMON,Thomas Valentine Plaisted LtCol dow 28-4-17 5 att20RIrRif p169 CR France40,5RIrRif att2Hamps

McCANCE,Finlay 2Lt dow 22-5-15 2BordR CR France102

McCANCE,Robert 2Lt kia 21-11-17 5ScotRif p224 CR Belgium22

McCANDLISH,William Ewart 2Lt kia 24-3-18 20Lond p251 MR20

McCANN,Bertie Joseph 2Lt 12-11-16 18RIrRif p169 CR Belgium48,14-11-16

McCANN,Francis Lt&QM dow 27-1-16 RASC p193 CR Egypt6,24-1-16

McCANN,William Robert 2Lt dow 11-10-16 7DLI p239 CR France387

McCARTER,John Wylie T2Lt kia 6-12-17 12 att9RInnisF p105 2 entries MR17

McCARTHY,Alexander T2Lt kia 23-8-18 13RFus p69 CR France518

McCARTHY,David.MC.Lt kia 7-10-18 Lpool p72

McCARTHY,J.C.T.Lt 2-1-16 3ConnRgrs attTMB CR France721

McCARTHY,John Maj&QM ded 30-9-19 RASC RetPay p267 CR War135

McCARTHY,John Charles Thomas Lt kia 2-1-16 3ConnRgrs attTMB p172

McCARTHY,Noel Fisher 2Lt kia 18-10-16 2Yorks p90 MR21

McCARTHY,Terence Cormac.MC.Lt kia 7-7-20 IA 1/6Jats att1/99Inf p279 MR38

McCARTHY,Thaddeus Francis.MC.2Lt kia 14-4-18 4LNLancs p234 MR32,Lt

McCARTHY,William Offley Capt dow 26-8-16 2RhodR CR Tanzania1

McCARTHY,William Ronald Ware 2Lt kia 2-11-17 3BordR attPoW Camp p117 CR Palestine8 att3Norf

McCARTNEY,Hugh Lt ded 4-11-15 RAVC p270 CR Scot682

McCARTNEY,Robert Stuart 2Lt dow 9-1-18 WelshR att17Bn p127 CR France518

McCASH,John Watson Lt kia 22-11-16 6BlkW attRFC p19,231&208,23-11-17 MR20

McCASKIE,John T2Lt kia 23-3-18 6Dors p124

McCASKIE,Roy Whyte.MC&Bar.Lt dow 5-8-18 6SfthH p241 CR France85,White

McCASKILL,Kenneth TLt kia 27-9-18 1GordH p166 CR France1483

McCAUCE,Finlay 2Lt dow 22-5-15 3 att2BordR p117

McCAUL,Alexander Theodore Wigram Capt ded 8-8-15 RFA p261 CR Mddx43,21-8-15

McCAUSLAND,Arthur John Kennedy T2Lt kia 10-8-15 6BordR p117 MR4

McCAUSLAND,David Capt kia 22-11-17 12RIrRif p169 MR17

McCAY,James Frederick Daniel Lt kia 27-3-18 15RIrRif p169 MR27

McCAY,Thomas Fulton 2Lt kia 22-11-17 10RIrRif p169 MR17

McCLARENCE,Stanley T2Lt kia 10-4-17 27NumbF p62 CR France644

McCLATCHEY,Samuel Edward.MID Capt 25-3-18 RAMC att18WelshR p196 MR20

McCLATCHIE,Edward Alexander T2Lt dow 10-8-17 12RInnisF p105 CR Belgium18

McCLAY,J.Maj 17-1-17 RAMC CR Yorks38

McCLAY,Samuel Whitfield 2Lt dow 4-10-17 12 att1Lincs p75 CR Belgium112

McCLEAN,Angus Neil 2Lt 22-6-15 8 att1Wilts MR29

McCLEAN,J Lt 16-7-18 SL RE attIWT CR Asia82

McCLELLAN,Alfred 2Lt dow 13-10-17 5RIrRif p170 CR France297,McCLELLAND 1Bn

McCLELLAN,Allan John 2Lt kia 1-7-16 18 att15RIrRif p170 MR21

McCLELLAN,Greville Edward Gordon Capt kia 20-10-15 5 att2Worc p109 CR France114

McCLELLAND,Albert 2Lt 2-4-17 5HLI CR France164

McCLELLAND,Herbert 2Lt dow 2-4-17 5HLI p240

McCLELLAND,Samuel George 2Lt kia 25-9-15 8KOSB p102 MR19

McCLELLAND,Thomas 2Lt kia 16-5-15 7Lpool p215 CR France279

McCLELLAND,William Alan TMaj dow 18-1-18 N&D att15Bn p134 CR Belgium20

McCLENAGHAN,Arthur Bryant Phelps 2Lt kia 16-6-15 1Wilts p153 MR29

McCLENAGHAN,George Mayo Capt dow 8-11-18 1RWKent p141 CR France937

McCLEVERTY,Robert Jim Capt kia 29-10-14 IA 47Sikhs p279 MR28,28-10-14

McCLINTON,John Stuart TCapt kia 5-7-16 7SLancs p125 MR21

McCLOUGHIN,Robert James Capt dow 18-9-14 Beds p86

McCLOUGHLIN,Kenelm Rees.MID Capt kia 25-9-15 IA 14Sikhs att11RScots p279 MR28

McCLUGGAGE,William TLt kia 1-7-16 12RIrRif A'Coy p170 CR France1890

McCLUMPHA,Cyril Dudley Capt ded 9-7-21 IARO att1/112Inf p279 MR43

McCLURE,Charles Russell.MID Maj kia 21-10-14 19Huss p23 CR Belgium451

McCLURE,E.R.Lt 27-6-19 MilLabCps CR EAfrica51

McCLURE,Ernest.MID Lt kia 1-7-16 10RInnisF p105 MR21

McCLURE,Hugh Cecil 2Lt kia 23-10-18 RGA 146SB p40 CR France717,Lt

McCLURE,John 2Lt dow 24-11-17 4 att1RIrF p171 CR France398

McCLURE,John Richard Smyth.MID TLtACapt ded 29-10-18 RE 250TC p46 CR Lond13

McCLURE,T.A.2Lt ded 28-5-18 1/2ConnRgrs &RAF p172 CR Eire512

McCOLL,Duncan Colvin 2Lt kia 18-10-16 3 att5CamH p168 MR21

McCOLL,Ednor Ernest 2LtALt dow 24-10-17 3RScot p54 CR Belgium16,16Bn

McCOLL,William Laurence 2Lt dow 18-7-16 7EKent p57 CR France145,Lawrence Lt

McCOLLOCK,James T2LtACapt kia 22-8-17 7CamH p168

McCOMBE,William Joseph Pogue T2Lt kia 23-4-17 10N&D p134 MR20

McCOMBIE,Christian Nurse 15-1-19 TFNS CR Scot353

McCOMBIE,L.H.D.Lt 3-7-15 IntelDept CR EAfrica125

McCONAGHEY,Charles Jack Lt kia 22-4-16 2BlkW p129 MR38

McCONAGHEY,Maurice Edwin.DSO.MajALtCol kia 23-4-17 1RScotF p95 CR France1185

McCONAGHY,William.DSO.Maj ded 4-7-18 RAMC p196 CR Egypt15

McCONNAN,George Capt kia 9-8-16 10Lpool p216 MR21

McCONNAN,James T2Lt kia 20-9-16 14 att11Manch p155 CR France150,19-9-16 Lt

McCONNEL,Harold Jeffrey 2Lt ded 31-5-18 1RIrRif att98RAFp170 CR Belgium132,Lt 5Bn

McCONNEL,Merrick Hugh.MID Maj dow 14-9-17 B295RFA p32 CR Belgium11

McCONNELL,Frederick James T2Lt ded 10-3-18 RFC p16 CR France285

McCONNELL,Horace Lincoln Cyril.MC.Lt mbk 24-11-17 IARO attRFC p279 CR Syria2,dow PoW 22-11-17

McCONNELL,Primrose.MC.TCapt kia 18-9-18 101RFA DBty p32 MR37

McCONNELL,Reginald Bryan T2Lt kia 22-1-17 6KOSB p102 CR France1182,Brian

McCONNELL,Robert Wallace TLt kia 9-4-16 10RLancs p59 MR38

McCONNELL,William Clark Lt kia 9-7-16 3 att2RIrRif p170 MR21

McCONNELL,William Gardiner TCapt dow 13-10-17 RAMC att10Y&L p196 France285

McCONNOCHIE,Norman.MC.MID Capt kia 29-3-18 11HampR p121 MR27

McCONNOCHIE,William Jamieson 2Lt kia 8-11-15 5RFC p1 CR Belgium11,8-10-15

McCORMAC,Herbert Hood TLt kia 15-8-15 5RInnisF p105 MR4

McCORMACK,Campbell McNeill.MC&2Bars.CaptAMaj kia 22-9-18 RAMC att15FA p196 CR France562

McCORMACK,Edward 2Lt kia 1-11-18 4GordH p242 CR Belgium435

McCORMACK,George 2Lt ded 28-10-18 TankCps p188 CR Dorset109

McCORMACK,John Joseph TCapt kia 28-4-17 27NumbF p62 CR France604

McCORMACK,Joseph Francis TCapt kia 4-10-17 9N&D p134 MR30

McCORMACK,Thomas Lt kia 15-9-16 42MGC p184 MR21

McCORMICK,Edward John TLt kia 14-5-17 7RInnisF &12/8RFC p10&p105 CR France214

McCORMICK,Frank Pockell T2Lt dow 9-8-18 18 att9NumbF p62 CR France20,Pockett

McCORMICK,Gregory Day LtCol kia 21-12-19 IA 72Punjabis att2/122Inf p279 MR43

McCORMICK,Harry 2Lt dow PoW 8-5-17 5ELancs attMGC Inf p187&226 CR France1276

McCORMICK,James Gardiner 2Lt kia 16-5-15 2Worc p109 MR22,Lt

McCORMICK,John 2Lt dow 28-7-18 2/4YLI p235 CR France1693

McCORMICK,John Hugh Gardiner Capt kia 19-10-14 4 att2RWar p65 MR29

McCORMICK,Mark Huston 2Lt kia 23-4-17 RMunstF att1RInniskF p175 MR20

McCORMICK,William John T2Lt kia 8-11-17 RB att11Bn p179 CR France439

McCORQUODALE,Archibald Lt dow 25-7-16 RFA attA/ABty p32 CR France513

McCOSH,Edward.MC.Maj dow 26-9-18 9HLI p240 CR France906

McCOSH,Thomas.MC.Capt 16-4-17 RAMC att11WelshR p196 CR Greece6

McCOULL,William Sinclair Lt kia 3-5-17 MGC HB D'Bn attTankCps p184 MR20

McCOURT,Cyril Douglas 2Lt kia 8-10-16 21Lond p251 MR21

McCOWAN,Hew Lt kia 28-6-15 8ScotRif p225 MR4

McCOWAN,James T2Lt kia 16-6-18 SWBord att7KSLI p100 CR France33

McCOWAN,Robert McCaig.MC.2Lt dow 1-11-18 5 att2ScotF p222 CR France34

McCRACKEN,Benjamin Brayshan Victor T2Lt dow 23-8-17 10RInnisF p105 CR Belgium11,Lt 9Bn

McCRACKEN,Henry Joy 2Lt ded 17-10-17 GL &111RFC p10 CR Egypt2,Lt

McCRACKEN,James Henderson T2Lt kia 26-9-17 1RScotF p95 MR30

McCRACKEN,Peter Alexander Earle Lt kia 16-9-18 9HLI p240 CR France686

McCRAE,Alexander Bissett.MC.Lt kia 18-9-18 5ScotRif p224 CR France415

McCRAE,George Capt kia 28-6-15 4RScots p211 MR4

McCRAITH,Bernard Maj ded 29-1-19 RE 1BasePkCoy p209 CR France65,26-1-19

McCREA,Alexander 2Lt kia 27-6-17 RGA 58SB p40 CR Belgium1

McCREADIE,John 2Lt kia 21-3-18 255RFA p208 MR20

McCREATH,Andrew Berghans Lt dow 11-12-17 2/7NumbF att5KOSB p214 CR Egypt9

McCREDIE,John Forrest 2Lt kia 30-11-17 235MGC p184 MR17

McCREERY,Mona J.M.Capt ded 21-10-18 3RDubF p177 CR Eire355

McCREERY,Robert Bruce Lt kld 15-5-21 17Lancers CR Dorset87

McCRONE,John Milloy.MC.MID T2Lt kia 28-8-16 11A&SH p173 CR France515

McCROSTIE,Charles Hutchison T2Lt kia 1-7-16 GL 19HLI att14TMB p190 CR France1170

McCUBBIN,Percy Griffith 2Lt kia 23-4-18 7RB p179 MR27

McCUDDEN,John Anthony.MC.2Lt kia 18-3-18 84RFC p16 CR France1266

McCULLAGH,Alexander Henry T2Lt kia 16-8-17 11RInnisF att109TMB p105 CR Belgium96

McCULLAGH,Edwin Samuel T2Lt kia 7-6-17 14 att13Ches p96 CR Belgium168

McCULLOCH,Alexander Fenton T2Lt kld 16-8-17 GL &62RFC p10 CR Glouc67,McCULLOUGH

McCULLOCH,David French Capt ded 19-3-19 RASC p267 CR Lond32,Trench

McCULLOCH,Frederick James 2Lt kia 8-11-17 RGA &53RFC p10 &p40 CR Belgium111,McCULLOGH

McCULLOCH,James Arthur TCapt kia 27-9-18 1/8LancF p93 CR France712

McCULLOCH,John Capt 9-4-17 5GordH p242 MR20

McCULLOCH,John Allan 2Lt kia 21-12-17 RFA Z52DivMedTMB p32 CR Palestine9

McCULLOCH,John Wyndham Hamilton TCapt dow 21-10-15 8BordR p117 CR France285

McCULLOCH,Kenneth Lt kia 12-10-17 RFA p208 CR Belgium12

McCULLOCH,Kenneth Lionel Nevill 2Lt kia 1-6-17 6 att16Middx p147 MR20

McCULLOCH,R.C.S.Capt 1-3-19 RASC CR Scot228

McCULLOCH,Robert Arthur Douglas 2Lt kia 3-5-15 RLancs p262&93,LancF MR29

McCULLOCH,Robert Maxwell TLt kia 19-4-17 D106RFA p32 CR France149,20-4-17

McCULLOCH,Thomas LtCol 25-6-15 RAMC p196 CR Hamps64

McCULLOCK,James T2LtACapt kia 22-8-17 7CamH p168 MR30,McCULLOCH

McCULLOUGH,Robert James T2Lt kia 22-10-17 16Ches p96 MR30

McCULLOUGH,William John 2Lt kia 3-2-17 6DLI p239 CR France1182

McCURDY,John 2Lt dow 9-8-16 2Hamps p121 CR Belgium5

McCURRACH,Alexander 2Lt kia 18-10-16 CamH p255 CR France385

McCURRACH,George 2Lt 1-7-16 13HLI p163 MR21

McCURRICH,Laurence Oliphant Capt ded 25-10-18 IARO attRlyTrgCps p279 MR66

McCURRY,Alexander 2Lt mbk 25-4-18 9MGC Inf B'Coy p256 MR30

McCURRY,Walter Tennyson Lt kia 14-3-15 RAMC p196 CR Belgium59

McCUSKER,Patrick Joseph TLt kia 13-11-16 10DubF p177 CR France220

McCUTCHAN,Frank Marsh T2Lt dow 14-5-17 RE 212FC p46 CR France1186

McCUTCHEON,Hugh Edward 2Lt kia 3-9-16 7WorcR att4RFC p19&226 CR France44

McCUTCHEON,John Cecil Lt dow 2-10-16 6RIrF CR Greece4,ded RIrRif

McDERMOTT,Edward.MC.T2Lt kia 12-4-18 10EYorks p84 CR France193

McDERMOTT,J.W.Capt 8-5-19 IARO CIE CR Sussex111

McDERMOTT,Lawrence Alphonsus T2Lt kia 11-10-18 8RWSurr p56 CR France270

McDERMOTT,Robert Keith Capt 20-9-18 3 att1SfthH p165 MR34

McDIARMID,David Lt kia 10-8-16 164MGC p184 MR21

McDIARMID,Kenneth.MID Capt kia 18-4-15 3 att2KOSB p102 MR29

McDONACH,Patrick 2Lt kia 18-11-14 RWKent attSuff p141 CR Belgium89,McDONAGH

McDONALD,A.Lt 19-7-17 1/3KAR CR Tanzania1

McDONALD,Archibald Joseph Lt ded 3-11-18 1LovatScts p204 CR France34

McDONALD,Alexander T2Lt kia 14-7-16 13Lpool p72

McDONALD,Alexander T2Lt kia 30-7-16 9 att2KOSB p102 MR21

McDONALD,Angus George T2Lt ded 29-12-15 20KRRC p151 CR Lancs2

McDONALD,Archibald Lt kia 19-7-17 1/3KAR p202 CR EAfrica38

McDONALD,Charles 2Lt ded 28-11-18 14Lond attMGC Inf p270 CR Lond14,MACDONALD

McDONALD,Donald Alexander T2Lt kia 25-8-15 12ScotRif att5RScots p103 CR Gallipoli4

McDONALD,Edward Lawson Lt 22-11-17 12 RIrRif p170 MR17

McDONALD,Harold Stewart 2Lt kia 21-9-18 6ScotRif p224 CR France663

McDONALD,Harry Alexander Capt ded 5-2-18 ACycCps p243 CR Kent175,6-2-18

McDONALD,Henry Rhodes T2Lt kld 22-12-17 GL &RFC p10

McDONALD,James Vallence 2Lt dow 17-4-18 3 att6/7RScotF p95 MR30

McDONALD,John Capt kia 13-7-15 5HLI p240

McDONALD,John 2Lt ded 21-11-16 29 att22NumbF p62 CR Scot935,MACDONALD kldacc

McDONALD,John Mellis Capt mbk 20-7-16 1ScotRif p256 MR21

McDONALD,John Patrick CaptQM ded 25-3-15 RFA p32 CR Scot764

McDONALD,J.McP.MC.Lt 23-9-17 6ScotRif CR Belgium83

McDONALD,Kenneth William Lt dow PoW 4-9-17 RE LowlandFC attRFC p19&210 CR Belgium140

McDONALD,Lachlan John TLt kld 19-1-18 91RFC p16 CR Hamps192 MACDONALD

McDONALD,Mark William 2Lt drd 2-8-15 4RInnisF p105 CR Ireland45

McDONALD,Norman 2Lt dow 25-12-16 3LNLancs p136 CR EAfrica38 &CR Tanzania1,MACDONALD 2Bn

McDONALD,Ronald Graham.MC.TLtACapt dow 16-8-17 8NumbF p62 CR Belgium8

McDONALD,Samuel 2Lt 25-9-15 7CamH p168 MR19

McDONNELL,Archibald Clark Maj ded 4-10-16 Res RWSurr p270

McDONNELL,Charles Edward TLt kia 26-9-16 12Middx p147 MR21

McDONELL,Frank Joseph TLt ded 26-5-18 24 att9NumbF p62&257 CR Lancs169

McDONNELL,George Oscar Lt dow 18-3-18 RGA att12RFC p16&40 CR France214

McDONNELL,Herbert James Winter T2Lt kia 31-7-17 Middx att4Bn p147 MR29

McDONNELL,John de Courcy 2Lt ded 14-12-15 4GordH p270 CR Yorks294,MacDONNELL

McDONNELL,John LtCol kia 29-9-18 5Leinst att1InniskF p174 CR Belgium84

McDONNELL,John Joseph Chap4Cl kia 9-4-18 RAChDept att55MGC p199 CR France572

McDONNELL,Martin Joseph 2Lt dow 24-1-17 2RIrRif p170 CR France285

McDONNELL,Schomberg Kerr.Hon.GCVO.KCB.Maj dow 23-11-15 5CamH p168 CR Belgium11

McDONNELL,Thomas John T2Lt kia 1-11-17 1/2 att26NumbF p62 MR20

McDOUGAL,A.Lt 26-10-18 LancF CR Scot686

McDOUGAL,Ronald Lt kia 20-10-14 1EKent p57 MR32,McDOUGALL

McDOUGALL,Alexander Ernest 2Lt dow 20-2-18 10/11HLI p163 CR France145,Lt

McDOUGALL,Duncan Albert Herbert 2Lt 9-5-15 1SfthH p165 CR France721

McDOUGALL,George.MC.Capt 30-3-18 2/8Manch attMGC p187&237 MR27

McDOUGALL,John MacColl 2Lt kia 26-3-18 9SfthH p165 CR France343,MacDOUGALL

McDOUGALL,Lionel Robert 2LtACapt kia 8-4-17 2YLI Cmdg97TMB p143 CR France1701,8-8-17

McDOUGALL,Sydney Lt 7-8-15 6Manch p236 MR4 Sidney

McDOWALL,Archibald 2Lt kld 12-1-18 3ELancs attRFC p16&111 CR Essex50

McEACHRAN,Charles 2Lt kia 3-2-17 5Dev p217 CR Iraq5,Lt

McEACHRAN,Neil Lt kld 20-5-19 3HLI att59RAF p163 CR Germany1

McELNEY,Robert Gerald.MC.Capt kia 21-3-18 RAMC att77FA p196 CR France512

McELROY,Frederick William.DSO.Lt ded 16-11-18 7TankCps p188 CR France788,Capt

McELROY,George Edward Henry Capt kia 31-7-18 RGA &RAF p40

McELROY,John Oliver Capt ded 5-3-19 Relsd PoW 14Manch p255 CR Eire499 &CR Ireland14,4-3-19

McENERY,John Aloysius Capt kld 26-10-14 RE p46 MR29

McENTIRE,James Thomas LtCol 29-10-18 RAMC O/C 20StatHosp p196 CR Greece9

McENTIRE,James Virtue 2Lt ded 3-8-15 14Lond p270 CR Lond4

McERVEL,John Harold TMaj kia 8-8-16 1Manch attLpool p155 CR France400

McEUEN,James Stewart Capt kia 21-12-14 IA 20DeccanHorse p279 MR28

McEVOY,Frank Osmond T2Lt kia 9-4-17 3 att7ESurr p113 CR France96

McEWAN,David Grant T2Lt kld 23-1-16 10WelshR attTMB p127 CR France631

McEWAN,Donald Fraser 2Lt kia 30-7-16 6BlkW p231 MR21

McEWAN,Fraser 2Lt 24-3-18 GordH att44TMB p166 MR20

McEWAN,George Cameron T2Lt kia 9-4-17 1SfthH A'Coy p165 CR France924,2 att7Bn

McEWAN,George Edward 2Lt kia 15-11-16 9 att6Beds p86 MR21

McEWAN,George Lammie Lt 21-7-15 6HLI p240 MR4

McEWAN,James Robert Dundas Lt kia 12-10-16 2RScotF p95 MR21 McEWEN

McEWAN,Robert William Capt kia 14-4-17 5ScotRif p224 CR France162

McEWAN,William Gray TLt kia 27-10-18 22Manch p155 CR Italy9,2Lt

McEWEN,Charles James 2Lt kia 18-11-16 5HLI p240 CR France534

McEWEN,David Campbell 2Lt dow 10-4-17 1/9RScots A'Coy p212 CR France95,MacEWEN

McFADDEN,Robert Edgar 2Lt kld 12-10-18 10Mddx p236 CR France206

McFADYEN,John Craig 2Lt kia 6-6-17 RFA 11DAC p32 CR Belgium89

McFADYN,John Dennis Goulty.MC.TLt kia 8-8-18 1TankCps p188

McFALL,Thomas Lamont T2Lt kia 7-8-17 9RInnisF p105 CR Belgium45

McFARLAN,Arthur Keith 2Lt kia 15-5-16 11LancF p93 CR France68

McFARLAND,Foster Murray Lt kld 3-9-18 SL &RAF p268 MR20

McFARLAND,Francis John Elliott 2Lt kia 22-7-18 4RIrF p255 MR30

McFARLANE,Alexander Laidlaw T2Lt dow 2-9-18 1MunstF p175 CR France95

McFARLANE,George Capt&QM ded 23-9-17 RASC p193 CR Lond28

McFARLANE,James Arthur T2Lt kia 16-9-16 9HLI p163 CR France453,12Bn

McFARLANE,John.MC.2Lt kia 23-4-17 RFA p208 CR France266

McFARLANE,John Tennant TLt kia 26-9-15 MGC p184 see MacFARLANE,J.T.

McFARLANE,Robert George T2Lt dow 6-3-16 RE 177Co p46

McFARLANE,Robert Speedon 2Lt kia 3-7-16 15HLI p163 CR France1890,MACFARLANE

McFARLANE,Ronald Aitchison Lt kia 25-9-15 13RScot p54 MR19

McFARLANE,Walter T2Lt dow 15-1-17 RLancs att38MGC Inf p59&184 CR Iraq5

McFARLANE,William Capt&QM ded 1-1-19 7WRid p227 CR Egypt9

McFARLANE,William Arthur 2Lt ded 8-2-19 3CamH p168 CR Belgium329,7-2-19

McFARLANE,William Hannah Lt kia 27-5-18 1/8A&SH p243 CR France498

McFERRAN,Maurice Anderdon.MC.2Lt 21-3-18 5 att2RIrRif p170 MR27

McFERRAN,Thomas Malcolm T2Lt kia 21-6-17 GL &1RFC p10 MR20

McGAFFIN,Robert Clanrye 2Lt dow 5-7-16 RGA 10HSB p40 CR France251

McGAIN,Ashley Waterson T2Lt kia 1-7-16 11Suff p78 MR21

McGARRY,William Frederick Cecil 2Lt kia 10-8-15 6RDubF p177 MR4

McGARVIE,Hector Archer 2Lt kia 8-7-17 52RFA p32 CR Belgium29

McGAVIN,Charles Abercrombie 2Lt ded 24-11-17 7KRRC p265

McGAVIN,Peter Liddell 2Lt kia 14-8-17 GL &25RFC p3 CR France924

McGEAGH,William Morice Lt ded 10-2-19 3SLancs p255 CR Lancs405

McGECHAN,George Ross 2Lt 28-3-18 GordH att8/10Bn p166 MR20

McGEE,Thomas 2Lt kia 24-4-18 9 att2RB p179 MR27

McGEOCH,William T2Lt kia 13-10-16 KOSB att8TMB p102 CR France344

McGEORGE,Thomas Leslie 2Lt kia 7-8-15 5Manch p236 MR4

McGERGOW,Robert Dudley Wilson 2LtTLt kia 21-9-17 5DragGds &RFC p21

McGHEE,Harry TCapt kia 8-5-17 11ScotRif p103 MR37

McGHEE,Thomas Aloysius T2Lt kia 28-9-18 3CamH p168 CR Belgium46

McGHEE,William 2Lt kia 9-4-17 4 att7RScotsF p222 MR20

McGHIE,John Allen Lt 18-10-16 RIM MR65

McGIBBON,R.A.Sister 6-3-19 QAIMNS CR Ireland80

McGIBBON,Richard Forsyth T2Lt kia 23-4-17 10SfthH p165 CR France536

McGIBBON,Richard Forsyth T2Lt dow 16-11-16 15HLI p163 CR France74

McGIBBON,William Patrick 2Lt kia 23-9-17 4 att20DLI p161 MR30

McGIBNEY,Francis George 2Lt kia 3-5-17 4 att1RIrF p171 CR France604

McGILDOWNY,William.DSO.TMaj dow 27-5-17 RGA 124SB p40 CR France729,26-5-17

McGILL,Douglas T2Lt kld 27-10-17 GL &RFC p10 CR Scot523

McGILL,George Thomas.MC.LtACapt kia 3-5-17 2RScot p54 MR20

McGILLEWIE,Malcolm TLtACapt ded 24-5-18 RGA 390SB p40 CR Italy11

McGILLEWIE,Nigel T2Lt kia 12-10-17 6KOSB p102 CR Belgium126

McGILLICUDDY,John TLt kia 1-7-16 26NumbF p62 CR France150

McGILLICUDDY,Richard Hugh.MC.TCaptAMaj ded 20-10-18 RAMC p196 CR Hamps64,21-10-18

McGILLIVRAY,Charles Allister T2Lt kld 14-2-18 RFC p16 CR Wilts3

McGILLIVRAY,David T2Lt kia 29-9-18 15HLI p163 CR France375,dow

McGILLIVRAY,John 2Lt 14-7-16 7SfthH att2LovatScts p165 MR21

McGILLYCUDDY,Richard Hugh.MC.Maj 21-10-18 RAMC CR Hamps64

McGILTON,James 2Lt 23-3-18 8RIrRif p170 MR27

McGINITY,Henry Cuthbert ChapCapt ded 8-11-18 RAChDept att23FA p199 CR Italy7

McGINN,James Joseph AssCommsy&Lt ded 17-9-19 IA S&TCps p279 MR65

McGINN,Wilfrid Joseph T2Lt kld 18-2-18 34RFC p16 CR Shrop52

McGIVENEY,Philip.DSO.T2Lt dow 2-6-18 17LancF p93 CR France84

McGLASHAN,John Ewing Lt 12-7-15 5A&SH p243 MR4

McGONAGIL,Charles John.MC.TLt&QM ded 5-11-18 8Y&L p159 CR Italy9

McGOWAN,John Spence 2Lt 1-7-16 2Dev p77 MR21

McGOWAN,Joseph TLt ded 19-9-15 RAMC p196 CR Europe1,MacGOWAN,18-9-15

McGOWAN,Sidney.MC.Capt kia 25-5-17 5KOSB att1/6NStaffs p224 MR20

McGOWAN,William 2Lt kia 9-9-16 7Leinst p174 MR21

McGRANE,Peter Leo 2Lt kia 20-5-17 3RIrReg att1InnisF p89 MR20

McGRATH,Noel George Scott Lt dow 5-11-14 2DragGds p21 CR France102

McGRATH,P.N.AssSurg 22-2-17 IMD MR66

McGREGOR,Alexander 2Lt kia 11-4-18 4 att1/7BlkW p230 MR19

McGREGOR,Andrew William T2Lt kia 27-2-16 10 att9BlkW p129 CR France178

McGREGOR,Charles T2Lt kia 24-3-18 7DCLI p114 MR27

McGREGOR,David Capt kia 24-9-18 2A&SH p173 CR France666

McGREGOR,David Stuart.VC.Lt kia 22-10-18 6RScots att29MGC p187 CR Belgium141

McGREGOR,Donald Hamilton T2Lt kia 23-8-18 1GordH D'Coy p166 CR France618,MacGREGOR

McGREGOR,Ian Alexander T2Lt kia 10-9-16 2RFus att2NumbF p69 CR Greece3 15 att2NumbF

McGREGOR,Ian Lacy Lt 18-7-16 5CamH p168 MR21

McGREGOR,James 2Lt 20-5-17 9HLI p240 MR20

McGREGOR,Marcus 2Lt kia 3-10-15 att3Ches p96 MR19

McGREGOR,R.Lt ded 3-5-17 2/2KAR p202

McGREGOR,Robert Roy 2Lt ded 6-10-18 6SLancs p125 MR66

McGREGOR,Roderick Dear Capt mbk 9-4-18 RAMC att18WelshR p256 MR32,MacGREGOR

McGREGOR,Ronald Alexander Lt 9-4-18 6SfthH p241 MR19

McGREGOR,Ronald Malcolm 2Lt kia 24-5-15 2Ches p96 MR29

McGREGOR,W.2Lt 4-10-20 Worc CR Scot674

McGRIGOR,James Neil Grant 2Lt dow 7-11-14 GordH p166 CR Bucks55

McGRORY,John Joseph 2Lt kia 28-9-18 7A&SH p243 MR30

McGUFFIE,Arthur John Capt kia 29-11-17 1/7ScotRif p224 CR Palestine9

McGUINESS,John Norman 2Lt kia 21-3-18 11RDubF att2RMunstF p177 MR27

McGUIRE,Brian 2Lt kia 14-9-14 2DubF p177 CR France864

McGUIRE,Edward Lt 25-9-15 11HLI p163 MR19

McGUIRE,Robert Blayrey T2Lt kld 30-4-17 23Middx p147 CR Belgium15,Blayney

McGUSTY,Barry Edge 2Lt ded 15-5-18 3Leinst p266 CR Ireland24

McGUSTY,George Ross TLt dow 14-6-16 8RIrRif p170 CR France51

McHAFFIE,Arthur David 2Lt ded 4-10-17 IARO attS&TCps p279 MR43 &CR Pakistan50A

McHALE,George Nolan 2Lt kia 20-9-17 5Lpool p215 MR30

McHALE,John Richard Jarlath TLt kia 24-3-18 19Lpool p72 CR France1203,MacHALE

McHARDY,John Lt kia 24-7-18 1/5GordH p256 CR France865

McHARDY,Stewart John 2Lt kia 30-4-18 7Lond p247 CR Palestine3

McHARDY-YOUNG,James William T2Lt kia 19-8-15 RGA 6TMB p40 CR France721

McHARRIE,Robert Capt kia 9-6-18 5 att1RScotF p222 CR France33

McHATTIE,James William Lt kia 25-4-18 5Y&L att20RAFp238 CR France134

McHOUL,James Stewart T2Lt dow 26-8-17 16RScot p54 MR21,MacHOUL

McHUGH,Edward James Lt ded 31-10-18 4 att1RInnisF p105 CR France40,6Bn

McHUGH,Terence HonLt&QM dow 20-5-18 RAVC p198 CR France40

McILLVAINE,John Joseph Chap4Cl drd 26-2-18 RAChDept att2/7N&D p199 MR40

McILWAINE,Arthur Arnold 2Lt kia 5-3-16 1LNLanc p136 CR France551

McINDEOR,Malcolm Neil Lt dow 26-10-18 14Lond att7CamHp270 CR Wales168,26-10-19

McINDOE,William Reid 2Lt kia 6-8-18 5 att1GordH p242 CR France33,5-8-18

McINNES,John Edward 2Lt kia 1-7-16 1/5N&D p233 MR21

McINNES,Percy Norman Leopold 2Lt dow 20-7-16 3/5Yorks p221 CR France285

McINNES,Robert Donald T2Lt dow 30-3-18 17LancF p93 CR France44

McINNES,William Miller T2Lt kia 25-1-17 5Wilts p153 CR Iraq5

McINTOSH,Angus Alexander Capt 15-10-18 RHGds CR USA234

McINTOSH,Charles George Gordon T2Lt dow 28-9-15 8BlkW p129 CR France98,kia

McINTOSH,Daniel 2Lt dow 20-5-18 RGA 297SB p40 CR France95

McINTOSH,James 2Lt kia 13-11-16 1GordH p166 MR21

McINTOSH,James Marshall 2Lt kia 16-6-15 2RIrRif p170 MR29

McINTOSH,James Robert Hay.DCM.2Lt kia 22-3-18 7BlkW p231 MR20

McINTOSH,John 2Lt kia 22-3-18 16 att1/5NumbF p62 CR France834 Ex 19Huss

McINTOSH,John 2Lt kia 9-4-18 RGA 217SB p209 MR19

McINTOSH,Joseph Francis TLt drd 10-10-18 3 att2RWFus p98 CR Ireland14

McINTOSH,Robert Rae Lt kia 20-4-15 7CamH p168 MR29,24-4-15

McINTOSH,William TLt dow 6-7-16 23NumbF p62 CR France145,22Bn

McINTOSH,William Alexander 2Lt kia 26-9-17 2RScot p54 MR30,Lt

McINTOSH,William Matthew dow Lt 1-7-16 17HLI att97TMB p163 MR21

McINTYRE,Aaron 2Lt 29-7-16 25AustInf CR France1890

McINTYRE,Alexander Cameron.MC.Maj dow 24-3-18 8A&SH p243 CR France40,MACINTYRE

McINTYRE,Donald William 2Lt kia 28-6-17 Y&L att1/4Bn p159 MR20

McINTYRE,Francis T2Lt kia 3-5-17 8EYorks p84 MR20

McINTYRE,Frederick Malcolm T2Lt dow 2-5-16 RE 176TC p46 CR France224

McINTYRE,James Lennie 2Lt dow 14-5-18 10RFus p69 CR France145

McINTYRE,John Caldwell 2Lt dow 5-10-15 11 att2Yorks p91 CR France924,Lt

McINTYRE,John Watson 2Lt ded 30-3-17 4KOSB p224 CR France1182

McINTYRE,Malcolm T2Lt dow 21-9-16 6CamH p168 CR France40,Lt

McINTYRE,Reginald John TLt kia 25/26-10-18 HLI att1Bn p163 MR38

McINTYRE,Robert William.MBE.T2Lt kia 25-7-18 11EYorks p84 CR France19

McINTYRE,Sidney Colin 2Lt dow 25-3-18 6 att10DCLI p114 MR20

McINTYRE,Walter Graham T2Lt dow 21-8-18 att1BordR p117 CR France134

McIVER,Donald Lt kia 24-3-18 3 att2/7SLancs p125

McIVER,Hector Capt 30-4-21 RASC CR Palestine5

McIVER,James Noble 2Lt kia 25-8-17 8RScots p212 CR Belgium88

McIVER,Kenneth MacKenzie TLt kld 30-10-18 KAR &KRRC p202

McIVER,Kenneth Patrick John TLt dow 26-1-16 SL &NigRp201 CR WAfrica56

McJANET,Arthur William T2Lt kia 31-10-17 GL &18RFC p10 CR France88,McJANNET

McJANET,Walter Guy 2Lt dow 24-8-18 2Beds p86 CR Oxford69

McJANET,William Robert Benjamin Capt 14-7-16 10 att7SfthH p165 MR21,McJANNET Benny

McJANNET,Hector William.MID Capt ded 28-10-18 C261RFA p207 CR Egypt9,dow

McKAY,Alexander Matheson.MC.TLt dow 18-5-18 RE 179TC p46 CR France145

McKAY,Alfred Edwin Capt kia 28-12-17 RFC SR p10 MR20

McKAY,Alexander Steele 2Lt kia 10-4-18 3RScot p54 MR32

McKAY,Edward Horatio Lt dow 21-9-18 1SfthH p165 CR Palestine3

McKAY,Ernest Lt kia 19-9-15 1/7Ches p223 CR Gallipoli4

McKAY,Frederick.DCM. Lt dow 28-2-17 1RWFus p98 CR France204,MACKAY

McKAY,George Newton TLt kia 24-7-18 6MGC p184

McKAY,Harry.MC.Capt kia 10-4-18 4CamH p242 CR France260

McKAY,Henry Marshall Capt kia 13-11-14 RE p46 CR France706

McKAY,James Ivan 2LtTCapt kia 5-10-17 WRidR &RFC p10

McKAY,John Thomas Ralph Lt kia 30-3-18 IARO att58Rif p279 CR Palestine9

McKAY,William James 2Lt ded 29-9-19 LabCps CR Ireland183

McKEAN,Hugh Capt kia 7-7-16 12Manch p155 MR21

McKEAN,Kenneth Victor Lt ded 27-9-19 1MddxHuss att1/1DorsYeo p270 CR Lebanon1

McKEAND,David Gray TCapt ded 23-3-19 11WYorks p263 CR Yorks597

McKECHNIE,Alexander 2Lt kia 21-3-18 9KRRC p151 MR27

McKEE,Alexander Lt kia 22-11-17 10RIrRif p170 MR17

McKEE,John Albert T2Lt kia 1-12-17 2SStaffs p122 CR France530

McKEE,Patrick Joseph 2Lt kia 10-8-17 3 att2RIrRif p170 MR29

McKEE,William Dickson Lt kia 11-8-17 12RIrRif p170 MR29

McKEEVER,James Holden Lt dow 20-9-17 4Ches p222 CR France193

McKEEVER,Louis Lawrence.MC.Capt 8-11-17 RAMC att1/4RScotsF p196 CR Palestine8

McKELLAR,Archibald Peter 2Lt dow 22-7-18 7A&SH p243 CR France1415

McKELLAR Frederick Charles Marshall.MC.T2Lt kia 21-8-18 1Lincs p75 CR France514

McKELLAR,John Thomson 2Lt kia 13-11-16 8A&SH A'Coy p243 CR France131,Lt

McKENDRICK,David 2Lt kia 30-11-17 59MGC p184 MR17

McKENNA,John Charles Xavier TMaj ded 20-4-17 9NStaffs p157 CR France46

McKENNA,Justin Morell TLt kia 2-10-17 GL KRRC attRFC p10 CR France924

McKENNA,Reginald Talkington 2Lt kia 10-10-18 1 att8NumbF p62 CR France611

McKENNEY,William James 2Lt ded 9-5-16 6HLI p240 CR Scot237,16Bn

McKENNY,Edward Richard T2Lt kia 18-10-18 12 att6RInnisF p105 CR France660

McKENZIE,Alan A.Capt ded 3-11-19 RE IWT p262 CR Wales568,MACKENZIE Ex RNR

McKENZIE,Alexander TLt kia 7-6-17 11RWSurr p56 CR Belgium29

McKENZIE,Alexander Capt ded 25-5-19 RAMC p267 CR Scot286,Lt

McKENZIE,Angus.MC&Bar.Capt kia 4-11-18 2Manch p155 CR France1479

McKENZIE,Arthur Murdo.MC.TLtACapt ded 8-9-18 RE 6DivSigCo p46 CR France34

McKENZIE,Frederick Thomas Lt kia 23-3-18 RHFA p208

McKENZIE,Gordon William T2Lt kia 20-9-17 GL &RFC p10 CR Belgium18

McKENZIE,Ian.MC.Capt kia 21-3-18 5SfthH p241

McKENZIE,Ian Hume Townsend 2Lt ded 12-11-18 3HLI p265 CR Camb16,MacKENZIE

McKENZIE,James Kinnell T2Lt kia 30-10-15 10 att8SfthH p165 CR France423

McKENZIE,John Alexander.MC.Capt dow 10-4-18 RAMC att6DLI p196 CR France1094,MACKENZIE 9-4-18

McKENZIE,Kenneth Buchanan Capt kia 25-9-15 IA 123Rif att58 p279 MR28

McKENZIE,Kenneth Fitzgerald 2Lt kia 14-7-16 MGC p184

McKENZIE,Kenneth Fitzpatrick TLt kia 25-9-15 5CamH p168 CR France219,MACKENZIE

McKENZIE,Kenneth Nowell 2Lt kia 4-6-15 9EYorks p84 MR4

McKENZIE,Leslie TLt dow 2-4-18 9BlkW p129 CR France40

McKENZIE,Robert Andrew T2Lt kia 10-11-17 KRRC att9Bn p151 CR Belgium101

McKENZIE,William 2Lt dow 12-6-18 2/14Lond p249 CR Palestine3

McKENZIE,William Sinclair.DSO.2Lt kia 21-4-17 1SfthH p165 MR38

McKERGOW,Robert Dudley Wilson 2LtTLt kia 21-9-17 5DragGds &RFC p10 CR Belgium84

McKERRELL,Augustus De Segar.CB.TBrigGen ded 24-4-16 CommdgTayDefences Staff p1 CR Scot237 Ex CamH

McKERRELL,William Archibald Struthers Lt dow 10-4-18 8RScots att4RAF p211&258 CR France98

McKERROW,Charles Kenneth TCapt dow 20-12-16 RAMC att10NumbF p196 CR Belgium11

McKERSIE,Archibald James Lt dow 16-7-15 p240 CR Egypt6,Capt

McKEY,Hugh Aloysius 2Lt kia 25-3-18 5 att18HLI p240 MR27

McKIE,Douglas Hamlin 2Lt dow 11-4-17 3 att27NumbF p62 CR France184,kia

McKIE,Eric 2Lt kia 24-3-18 KRRC att11Bn p151 MR27

McKIE,William Purdon Lt kia 20-9-18 1/7HLI p240 CR France1496,MACKIE

McKIERNAN,Evelyn James SubCdr ded 14-6-16 IA S&TCps p279 CR Iraq6

McKIERNAN,Michael Vincent.MM&Bar.2Lt dow 11-5-18 6ConnRgrs p172 CR France145

McKIEVER,Victor Comley 2Lt dow 18-5-15 3 att2Manch p155 CR Belgium56,28-5-15

McKILLOP,James Bunting 2Lt kia 27-9-18 5RScotRif p224 CR France484

McKIMMIE,Alexander T2Lt kia 23-5-17 GL &6RFC p10 CR Belgium11

McKIN,John Nelson Burdette 2Lt kia 10-3-18 RFC p16 CR France525

McKINLAY,David Oliver 2Lt kia 21-10-17 28MGC p184 CR Belgium63

McKINLAY,Robert Galloway 2Lt kia 25-9-15 10HLI p163 MR19

McKINLEY,James Gordon 2Lt dow 3-6-15 RGA attRE p40 CR France200

McKINLEY,Samuel Brown.MC.Capt dow 7-2-19 12RScots p54 CR Scot757

McKINNEL,Bryden Capt kia 16-6-15 10Lpool p216 MR29,McKINNELL

McKINNEY,George TLt kia 16-8-17 13RIrRif p170 MR30

McKINNEY,Joseph James Moore 2Lt kia 27-3-18 12RIrRif p170 MR27

McKINNIE,Peter T2Lt kia 4-10-17 10MGC Inf p184 MR30

McKINNON,C.F.Capt ded 14-6-19 SL att1/6KAR p201&255

McKINNON,James Beaton T2Lt kia 7-6-17 23Middx p147 CR Belgium111

McKINNON,J.F.Lt mbk 28-11-17 65RFC p256 MR20

McKINSTRY,James McNeil T2Lt dow 2-12-16 2RInnisF p105 CR France44

McKINSTRY,Ronald William T2Lt kia 23-9-16 A48RFA p32 CR France399

McKINTY,Alexander Joseph(Allister) 2Lt drd 27-2-16 IARO p279 CR Scot280

McKIRDY,Gillies T2LtACapt kia 11-2-17 4Beds p86 CR France220,MACKIRDY

McKIRDY,Robert Fingland Capt kia 12-7-15 5A&SH p243 MR4

McKISACK,Lawrence Hill Wilson Lt kld 13-11-16 5Lancers attRFC p3&p22 CR Ireland33 Ex RGA &RE

McKNIGHT,Samuel TCapt kia 29-9-18 17RScots p54 CR Belgium72

McKNIGHT,Thomas T2Lt kia 21-2-17 10RInnisF p105 CR Belgium54

McLACHLAN,Berry.MC.Lt dow 11-10-18 C4RHA p32 CR France660

McLAGAN,James 2Lt kld 8-6-16 RE 61FC p270 CR Scot761

McLAGEN,Frederick Charles Albertus T2Lt ded 26-5-17 3LancF p263 CR Lond11

McLAGGAN,James Murray.MC.TCapt kia 4-10-18 RAMC att2RFus p196 CR France234,3Bn

McLAINE,Donald Lt dow 2-4-18 1/8LancF p221 CR France145

McLARDIE,Archibald 2Lt kia 25-12-15 5A&SH p243 CR Gallipoli3

McLARE,Alexander Vernon.MC.Lt kia 12-4-18 8DLI p239 MR32,Vernor Capt

McLAREN,Athole Stewart 2Lt kia 18-9-18 7Lond p247 CR France369

McLAREN,Donald Lt kia 3-5-17 1 att6KOSB p102 MR20

McLAREN,Eustace 2Lt kia 22-11-17 2/5Y&L p238 MR17

McLAREN,Hon Francis Walter Stafford T2Lt kld 30-8-17 GL &RFC p10 CR Surrey114

McLAREN,Frederic Monteath 2Lt kia 12-8-17 GL &RFC p10 MR20

McLAREN,James T2Lt dow 12-1-17 6KOSB p102 CR France1182

McLAREN,James Capt kia 21-11-17 7A&SH p243 MR17

McLAREN,John Francis Capt kia 28-9-15 4CamH p242 MR19

McLAREN,Malcolm Colquhoun.MC.TLt kia 22-10-18 7Leic p88 CR France192,MacLAREN Capt 23-10-18

McLAREN,Quentin 2Lt kia 26-10-16 6BlkW p231 CR France35

McLAREN,Richard Juson Maj dow 2-8-17 2WYorks p82 CR Belgium11

McLAREN,Robert T2Lt dow 24-7-16 16Ches p96 CR France141

McLAREN,Robert John Capt kia 1-7-16 14Ches att2SWBord p96 CR France1501

McLAREN,Samuel Bruce TLt dow 13-8-16 RE 35DivSigCo p46 CR France51

McLAREN,Thomas James 2Lt kia 25-1-16 RFA p32 CR Belgium101

McLAREN,William Somerville 2Lt dow 19-11-17 GL &48RFC p10 CR France1361

McLAUCHLAN,Alan Stewart Lt kia 28-3-18 RGA 405SB p209 CR France1182,MACLAUCHLAN

McLAUCHLAN,Andrew Youngson Greig 2Lt kia 28-9-18 8Manch p237 CR France379

McLAUGHLIN,Arthur Lt kia 9-5-15 3 att1RIrRif p170 MR32

McLAUGHLIN,Edmund Coldicoate Lt kia 18-5-15 6Lond D'Coy p246 CR France260

McLAUGHLIN,Edward Archibald Crofton T2Lt kia 9-11-15 7SfthH p165 CR Belgium127

McLAUGHLIN,Hubert Guy Bromilow 2Lt dow 12-10-16 3 att7SfthH p165 CR France385,Lt

McLAUGHLIN,Hubert James.DSO.LtCol ded 25-3-15 Remount Service p24 CR Hamps1,28-3-15

McLAUGHLIN,L.T.Lt 19-4-17 4WYorks attRFC CR Hamps4

McLAUGHLIN,William Pulteney Michael Dalzell Maj ded 6-12-19 IA 107Pnrs p279

McLAURIN,Robert 2Lt kia 7-6-17 10RIrRif p170 CR Belgium97,Lt

McLAY,Archibald.MC.2LtACapt kia 21-3-18 1/2 att6Leic p88 MR27

McLAY,Joseph T2LtACapt ded 9-10-18 16RB p179 CR France770

McLEAN,Angus Neil 2Lt kia 22-6-15 p153

McLEAN,Atholl Archibald T2Lt kia 1-7-16 11Suff p78 CR France515

McLEAN,Charles John Lt kia 20-9-17 9RScots p212 MR30

McLEAN,Colin LtCol kia 13-3-15 6GordH p242 CR France705

McLEAN,Donald 2Lt kia 14-7-18 1GordH CR France33

McLEAN,Donald Gordon TLt kia 4-2-18 GL &45RFC p16 CR Italy7

McLEAN,Gordon Davis TLt kia 21-8-18 7TankCps B'Coy p188 CR France514

McLEAN,Hugh Archibald Capt ded 7-11-18 RAMC p271 CR Scot756

McLEAN,James Monteith 2Lt kia 28-4-17 HLI p163 MR20

McLEAN,John Lt kld 16-7-18 GL RE attIWT p191 MR38

McLEAN,John Victor T2Lt dow 17-7-16 6RBerks p139 CR Mddx26,9Bn

McLEAN,Joseph Richard Garratt Lt kia 9-5-18 2A&SH p173 MR30

McLEAN,Robert TLt kia 11-7-16 RE 76FC p46 CR Belgium73

McLEAN,Robert Drysdale 2Lt kia 26-10-17 C64RFA p32 CR Belgium8

McLEAN,Thomas William 2Lt kia 21-9-17 GL &RFC p10 MR20

McLEAN,Walter Lt dow 17-11-17 6WYorks p218 CR Belgium72,Capt

McLEAN,William James 2Lt dow 12-8-16 1Ess p132 CR Belgium11

McLEAN,William Mcfarlane 2Lt kia 24-3-18 5A&SH p243

McLEAN,William Wood.MC.Lt kia 23-9-18 2A&SH p173 CR France666

McLEAN-RICHARDSON,Pelman Archibald Capt ded 19-11-18 IARO attS&TCps p279

McLEAR,Geoffrey D'Olier.MC.Lt died 29-1-19 IARO att2/39GarhwalRif p279 CR Kent177,MACLEAR

McLEAVY,C.E.SubCdr 17-11-15 IA CR Lond2

McLEAY,Duncan Matheson 2Lt kia 23-3-17 6A&SH attRFC p243 p19 CR France511

McLEISH,Gordon 2Lt 31-7-18 RAF CR Scot387

McLELLAN,Allan John 2Lt 1-7-16 18 att15RIrRif MR21

McLELLAN,Harold Noble 2Lt kia 9-7-16 2Manch p155 MR21

McLELLAN,James 2LtTLt kia 4-10-17 3HLI attMGC Inf p163&184 MR30

McLELLAN,Joseph Taylor TLt kia 21-3-18 55MGC Inf p184 CR France765,MacLELLAN

McLELLAN,Samuel TLt drd 16-10-17 GL RE &IWT p191 CR France1359

McLELLAN,Thomas Ancott Capt kia 25-9-16 9A&SH p243 CR France402

McLELLAND,Robert Carrick Lt dow 17-8-16 9HLI p240 CR Scot764

McLENNAN,Farquhar John 2Lt kia 18-8-16 1GordH p166 MR21

McLENNAN,John Lawrence.MC.Capt kia 28-8-19 RASC attRAF p267 CR Asia81

McLENNAN,William Ross 2Lt kia 21-3-18 5BordR p228 MR27

McLEOD,Alexander Lt drd 3-3-18 RE IWT CR France134

McLEOD,Angus 2Lt kia 20-11-17 4SfthH p241 CR France1498,dow

McLEOD,Archibald Alastair Capt kia 2-11-14 1Glouc p107 MR29

McLEOD,Daniel Edward 2Lt kia 1-12-16 B86RFA p32 CR France251

McLEOD,Douglas Keith 2Lt dow 21-10-18 24RFA 43Bty p32 CR France146

McLEOD,Elmer George T2Lt dow 23-11-17 GL &46RFC p10 CR France214

McLEOD,George MacFarquhar 2Lt kia 7-4-17 7GordH p242 CR France15

McLEOD,George Munro Lt ded 22-5-18 RAMC p271 CR Scot757,MacLEOD

McLEOD,G.M.2Lt 7-4-17 7GordH CR France15

McLEOD,John 2Lt dow 25-4-17 5ScotF p222 CR France1185

McLEOD,Ian Keith Falconer TCapt kia 27-4-18 RAMC att75FA p196

McLEOD,Matthew Paul 2Lt kia 14-11-16 6BlkW p231 CR France35

McLEOD,Roderick Patterson T2Lt ded 14-12-18 RE p46 CR Sussex112,MacLEOD Paterson

McLEOD,W.A.Rev ded 18-11-16 YMCA CR Greece7

McLEOD,William.MC.Capt dow 18-5-19 RAMC p196 MR43

McLERNON,Robert William 2Lt kia 8-5-15 RFA p32 CR Belgium132

McLINTOCK,Arnold.MIDx2 Capt kia 3-9-16 5WRid p227 CR France383

McLINTOCK,John Lawrie Lt kia 26-2-18 RFC p16 MR20

McLOUGHLIN,James Patrick Lt dow 24-5-15 4DubF attRIrRif p177 CR France285

McLURE,David T2Lt ded 8-3-18 2KRRC att4ArmyMuskSchool p151 CR France134

McMAHON,Bruce Metcalfe Capt ded 3-5-19 RAVC p198 CR Germany1

McMAHON,Norman Reginald.DSO.BrigGen kia 11-11-14 RFus attHQ10InfBde p69 MR32

McMAHON,Patrick 2Lt dow 11-6-17 4RIrRif p170 CR France285

McMAHON,Patrick Stan T2Lt dow 29-12-15 8MunstF p175 CR France80,Senon

McMAHON,T.SubCdr 19-12-20 MilWksServ MR65

McMAKING,Oscar Lennox 2Lt kia 11-9-17 LincYeo attRFC p19&204 MR20

McMANUS,Terence Joseph Lt ded 23-12-19 2Mddx p265 CR Sussex144,dow

McMASTER,Charles.MC.TLtACapt kia 16-8-17 7RIrRif attTMB p170 MR30

McMASTER,Hugh.DSO.MC.Maj dow 2-12-17 A46RH&FA p32 CR France64

McMASTER,John Wallace Lt dow 11-9-18 RGA att35SB p40 CR France103

McMASTER,Philip George TLt kia 20-6-18 18MGC p184 CR France196

McMICHAEL,Douglas William T2Lt dow 17-4-16 8Beds p86 CR Belgium73,20-4-16

McMICHAEL,John Edward Lt ded 12-5-17 EAUL 4/3KAR p202 CR EAfrica35 &CR Tanzania1

McMICHAEL,John Douglas Wield 2Lt kia 23-5-16 5Worc p109 CR France68,Wyld 3Bn

McMICHAEL,Walter Buchanan Lt kia 26-7-16 1/7GordH p242 CR France453

McMICKING,Gilbert Thomas Gore 2Lt ded 11-11-18 Camb p245 CR Europe97

McMILLAN,Donald Cameron 2Lt dow 11-3-16 12KRRC p151 CR France8,2Bn

McMILLAN,George T2Lt kia 31-7-17 2ELancs p111 MR29

McMILLAN,Hugh Dobie TLt kia 19-7-18 8BlkW p129 CR France324,dow

McMILLAN,John Lt dow 15-3-15 4SfthH p241 CR France102

McMILLAN,John 2Lt kia 24-3-18 LanarkYeo p204

McMILLAN,John Casely 2LtTCapt dow 6-2-17 RScotFus &4RFC p10&95 CR France59

McMILLAN,John Mackie 2Lt kia 1-8-18 7/8KOSB p102 CR France864,MACMILLAN

McMILLAN,J.S.TLt ded 12-3-18 GL RScots att3/3KAR p191&202 CR EAfrica35 &CR Tanzania1

McMILLAN,Neil T2Lt dow 29-11-16 1BlkW p129 CR France59,kia

McMILLAN,Kenneth Gregor 2Lt kia 16-8-17 33/33RFA p32 CR Belgium113

McMILLAN,William Calderwood SenAssSurg &Lt ded 24-10-17 IA ISMDept p279 CR Iraq8

McMILLAN,William McLeod Capt kia 25-9-15 11A&SH p173 MR19

McMINN,Hugh Bell TMaj ded 27-6-18 GL DAD RlyTrans p266 CR France40,27-7-18

McMINN,John Capt kia 27-5-18 14RIrRif p170 MR18

McMONNIES,Stuart Menzies 2Lt kia 20-11-17 4SfthH p241 MR17,21-11-17

McMORDIE,James Wilson 2Lt kia 18-11-16 9KSLI att2YLI p145 MR21

McMURDO,G.D.Capt 4-11-19 HLI CR Scot808

McMURDO,John Coke Capt kia 25-4-15 1Ess p132 MR4

McMURDO,John Hamilton T2Lt kia 27-5-18 NumbF Res att5Bn p62 MR18

McMURRAY,John Capt kia 12-10-17 12RScots p54 MR30

McMURRAY,Bertie Stedman Joseph Maj ded 12-6-18 IA 108Inf attSPersiaRif p279 CR Asia82

McMURRAY,Stuart 2Lt kia 7-8-17 2/2Lond attRFC p19&245 CR France201,8-8-17

McMURTRIE,John.MC.TCaptAMaj kia 26-7-17 RE 151FC p46 CR Belgium23

McMURTEIE,S.G.Chap4Cl 14-6-19 CR Ches178

McMUTRIE,Robert Lindsay TLtACapt kia 21-8-18 1RScotF p95 CR France618

McNAB,Alexander 2Lt dow 27-4-18 147RFA p32 CR France102

McNAB,J.B.McC.Lt 14-2-19 RE CR Belgium241

McNAB,James Fortune 2Lt dow 6-4-16 4A&SH att1KOSB p173 CR France35,MACNAB

McNAB,John Borrie McCulloch Lt kia 14-2-19 RE p210 CR Belgium241

McNAIR,Eric Archibald.VC.TCapt ded 12-8-18 9RSuss p119 CR Italy12

McNAIR,Robert Schemehorn T2Lt kld 17-3-18 RFC p16 CR Scot520,Schermerhorn

McNALLY,James Maj&QM ded 28-4-17 ConnRgrs p172 CR Eire301

McNALLY,Thomas Patrick 2Lt kia 30-9-17 10Y&L p159 CR Belgium17

McNALLY,William Wright.MC.2Lt kia 8-10-17 4Worc p109 MR30

McNAMARA,Joseph Charles 2Lt kia 2-6-17 GL &4RFC p10 MR20

McNAMARA,Vincent T2Lt ded 29-11-15 RE 136FortressCoy p46 CR Gallipoli1,dow

McNAMEE,John Joseph TLt dow 1-9-18 9RInnisF p105 CR France100,MacNAMEE 3-9-18

McNAUGHT,Douglas Ramson T2Lt kld 27-3-17 8GordH p166 CR Mddx15

McNAUGHT,Ernest Henry 2Lt kia 18-7-16 12RFus p69 CR Belgium116

McNAUGHT,James T2Lt kia 7-1-17 2RScots p54 CR France1890

McNAUGHT,James McGeogh Capt ded 13-11-19 4RWSurr p271

McNAUGHT-DAVIS,James Walden Fortune Lt 17-1-15 1SWBord CR France721

McNAUGHTON,Algernon 2Lt kia 30-9-18 10Lond p248 MR16

McNAUGHTON,Hamish Ian 2Lt kia 24-4-17 100RFA E'Bty p32 CR Greece6

McNAUGHTON,Norman George.MC.Capt kia 24-6-17 57RFC p10 MR20

McNAUGHTON,William James 2LtTLt dow 31-12-15 5ScotF p222 CR Gallipoli1

McNEIL,Francis George 2Lt kia 8-3-18 GL &70RFC p16 CR Belgium140

McNEIL,John Fraser 2Lt dow 9-9-15 D256RFA p32 CR France14

McNEIL,Robert T2Lt kia 6-2-16 6KOSB C'Coy p102 CR Belgium137

McNEILE,Henry Donald LtCol kld 20-12-15 1Drags p21 CR France1586

McNEILE,John LtCol kia 12-7-15 4KOSB p223 MR4

McNEILL,Alan Gordon.MC.CaptBtMaj dow 10-1-17 RE 2/2WLancFC p46 CR Belgium11

McNEILL,Donald Augustus 2Lt kia 16-11-16 7RFC p3 CR France742,MACNEILL

McNEILL,John 2Lt drd 26-2-18 GL RE &IWT p191 MR38

McNEILL,John Charles 2Lt kia 3-5-17 2Ess p132 MR20

McNEILL,Leslie Ernest TLt ded 25-3-19 4RlrDragGds p261 CR Surrey13

McNEILL,Malcolm.CMG.DSO.LtCol ded 3-6-17 11A&SH p173 CR France13

McNEILL,Neil 2Lt kia 11-11-14 1BlkW p129 MR29

McNEILL,Nigel Lorne 2Lt kia 1-7-16 3 att2GordH D'Coy p166 CR France331

McNEILL,Robert Archibald 2Lt kia 9-4-17 21NumbF p62 CR France265,MACNEILL

McNICHOL,James Percival 2Lt dow 20-6-18 4 att10A&SH p173 CR France84,Lt

McNICOL,John Hart.MC.TCaptAMaj ded 8-10-18 RAMC att86FA p196 CR Greece1,McNICHOL

McNICOLL,David Graham.DSO.MID LtCol dow 20-9-17 20DLI p161 CR Belgium15

McNICOLL,Godfrey Robert 2Lt kia 20-11-17 5BlkW p231 CR France712,Lt

McNICOLL,Malcolm David.MC.Capt dow 21-11-17 2/4YLI p235 CR France398,20-11-17

McNIFF,Francis Joseph 2Lt kia 13-3-18 24NumbF attRFC p16&62 CR France699

McNIVEN,Alastair T2Lt dow 1-5-17 7CamH p168 CR France113,MacNIVEN Lt

McNIVEN,Alister Orr Lt kia 5-9-17 7HLI &RFC p271 MR20

McNULTY,Michael John Lt kia 4-9-15 5 att9DubF p177 MR32

McPHAIL,Alexander Banks.MC.LtACapt dow 31-10-18 RGA 2SB p40 CR France146

McPHAIL,Peter John Stewart Lt ded 26-11-18 RGA p256 CR Scot239

McPHEE,Arthur David.MC.Capt 8-10-18 GL &CamH CR Scot246

McPHEE,Douglas 2Lt ded 21-2-19 RGA 1SB p40 CR Germany1

McPHERSON,Allen Ross T2Lt kld 26-1-18 RFC p16 CR Canada1688

McPHERSON,Archibald Austin Oliver Lt dow 26-5-18 RE 416FC p210 CR France95,MACPHERSON

McPHERSON,Ian Charles 2Lt kia 25-9-15 3 att2GordH p166 MR19

McPHERSON,Leonard Alfred T2Lt kia 28-7-17 GL &43RFC p10 CR France258

McPHERSON,Robert David 2Lt drd 6-6-16 8CamH p265 CR Scot900,5-6-16 see MacPHERSON.R.D.

McPHERSON,William Lt kia 8-5-17 A101RFA p208 CR Greece6

McQUAKER,George Wilson 2Lt kia 13-11-17 1/4ScotF p222 CR Palestine9

McQUEEN,John T2Lt kia 24-4-17 13HLI p163 CRFrance421,MACQUEEN

McQUESTIN,Matthew kia 28-3-18 1/4RScotsF att87TMB p222 MR20

McQUIBAN,William TCapt ded 2-5-18 RAMC p196 CR Egypt2

McQUINN,Wallace.MC.T2Lt de 6-8-18 PoW 16Manch p155 CR Germany4

McRAE,Archibald Douglas Lt ded 11-7-16 IA 80CarnaticInf p279 CR India164

McRAE,Archibald Ludovic T2Lt kia 12-10-17 5CamH p168 MR30

McRAE,Archibald William Capt kia 4-6-17 20RIrRif p170

McRAE,Peter McKay T2Lt kia 24-12-17 7Nhants attRE 129FC p137 CR France528,MACRAE

McRAE,Ronald Gwynnyd Montague T2Lt kia 28-1-18 24RFC p16 CR France1203

McRAE,William 2Lt kia 27-3-18 42MGC p184 MR20

McRAE,William Gordon 2Lt kia 26-10-17 GL &19RFC p10 MR20,21-9-17

McREADY-D'IARMID,Alistair Malcolm Cluny.VC.TLtACapt kia 1-12-17 4 att17Mddx p147 MR17

McREYNOLDS,John Bernard HonLt&QM kia 12-11-16 11EYorks p84 CR France203

McROBERTS,Thomas T2Lt kia 13-8-17 20RIrRif p170 CR Belgium125

McSHANE,John Chesterton T2Lt dow 28-7-16 RE 229FC p46 CR France80

McSHANE,Vincent TLt kia 21-8-15 15NumbF att2SWBord p62 MR4

McSHERRY,Bernard 2Lt kia 13-4-18 2Manch p155 CR France804,14-4-18

McSORLEY,Frederick William.MID 2Lt kia 5-4-17 20NumbF p62 CR France1182

McSWEENEY,Felix Joseph T2Lt kia 30-7-17 Middx att19Bn A'Coy p147 CR Belgium102

McSWEENY,Randal Roderick Lt ded 15-3-17 4HLI p163 CR France40,2Lt 10-3-17

McSWINEY,Eugene John Capt ded 26-12-16 RAMC p196 CR Eire122

McSWINY,Claude O'C T2Lt kia 14-7-16 9 att7KSLI p145 MR21

McTAVISH,I.A.B 2Lt kld 15-5-18 GL&RAF p191

McTAVISH,James Duncan 2Lt kia 23-4-17 GordH att7Bn p166 MR20

McVEIGH,Joseph 2Lt kia 28-3-18 3 att9BlkW p129 MR20

McVEIGH,William John TLt kia 28-12-17 7MunstF p175 CR Palestine3,6Bn

McVICAR,Thomas Graham 2Lt kia 28-3-18 4 att5BlkW p230 MR27

McVICAR,William Lt&QM ded 17-7-19 GL MGC Inf 116TrainingBn p266 CR Lincs61

McVICKER,Edgar Harold TLt kia 10-9-16 RAMC att2/5LancF p196 CR France397,9-9-16

McVICKER,John William T2Lt kia 14-7-16 13Lpool p72 MR21

McVITTIE,George Henry 2Lt ded 12-3-15 2/4BordR p228 MR40,8-3-15

McWHA,Archibald John 2Lt kld 2-1-17 RFC CR Kent180,Lt 5-1-17

McWHA,George Henry 2Lt kia 20-9-17 LNLancs att1/5Bn p136 MR30 see MEWHA

McWHAE,John Wilson Lt kia 21-6-17 189RFA p32 CR Belgium127

McWHANNELL,John.MC.2Lt dow 3-7-16 2Wilts p153 CR France23

McWHINNIE,Charles Routledge Lt dow 1-7-18 3 att6RWSurr p56 CR France41

McWILLIAM,Charles Thomas Lt kia 18-3-16 5GordH att51DivCycCoy p242 CR France157

McWILLIAM,Hamish Lt kia 29-5-16 2 att9BlkW p129 CR France423

MEACOCK,Robert Hugh T2Lt dow 19-10-16 21DLI p161 CR France46,19Bn

MEAD,Anthony George Lt ded 26-5-19 SL attRE p268CR Hamps186

MEAD,Bernard Wallace 2Lt dow 2-6-15 4RFus p69 CR France285

MEAD,Christopher.MID Lt kia 28-9-15 4 att2ESurr p113 MR19

MEAD,Edward 2Lt dow 22-4-18 6LancF p221 CR France145

MEAD,Evelyn Augustus Kew Capt 13-3-19 161/20RASC CR Surrey15

MEAD,George John 2Lt kia 22-2-17 IARO att92Punjabis p280 CR Iraq5

MEAD,Horace Warren TCapt kia 13-7-16 8RSuss p119 CR France630,MEADE

MEAD,John Robert Capt ded 15-12-17 RE 335RoadConsCo p47 CR Derby135

MEAD,Joseph Frederick 2Lt kia 23-8-14 4RFus p69 CR Belgium242

MEAD,Ralph Edward Culverhouse T2Lt kia 29-9-17 7EKent p57 CR Belgium3

MEAD,Robert John T2Lt dow 2-8-15 8RFus p69 CR France922

MEAD,Thomas Hallard T2Lt kia 24-7-16 72RFA p32 CR France423

MEADE,Alfred de Courcy.MC.Maj dedacc 15-12-18 RE p262 CR Ches18,14-12-18

MEADE,Cyril 2Lt kia 5-4-17 2/5Glouc p225 CR France674

MEADE,Evelyn Augustus Kew Capt ded 13-3-19 161/20RASC p255 CR Surrey15

MEADE,Michael.MC.Capt kia 9-4-18 5Lpool p215 CR France279

MEADE,Richard Gilbert Trevor T2Lt dow 10-10-17 MGC Cav p184 MR38 &CR Iraq8 Ex 14Huss

MEADE,Richard John Frederick Philip.MIDx2 Lt kia 4-6-15 IA 14Sikhs p280 CR Gallipoli3

MEADE,Robert Percy T2Lt kia 11-7-16 13RB p179 MR21

MEADE,Wakefield Waldo 2Lt kia 20-6-15 6 att3Worc p109 MR29 CR Belgium453

MEADOWCROFT,James T2Lt ded 7-11-18 RE 476FC p47 CR France332

MEADOWS,Albert Henry Capt kia 8-8-16 8Lpool p215 CR France402

MEADOWS,Chrisopher Bentley.MC.T2Lt kia 19-5-18 1RLancs p59 CR France412

MEADOWS,Daunt Capt 13-10-19 IndVetCps CR Pakistan50A

MEADOWS,Reginald Melville TLt kia 4-9-18 12ESurr p113 CR Belgium111

MEADS,John Arthur.MC.TCaptAMaj kia 10-10-17 10N&D p134 CR Belgium83

MEADWAY,Brian Wilton 2Lt ded 4-6-18 7Nhants att56RAF p137 CR Herts87,Lt

MEAKIN,Herbert Percy TCapt kia 25-9-16 3CldGds attGdsTMB p51 MR21

MEAKIN,Kenneth William Glenny 2Lt dow 16-5-15 5NStaffs p238 CR France285

MEAKIN,Sidney Arthur Lt kia 17-10-15 4 att1NStaffs p157 CR France681,17-12-14

MEAKIN,Thomas T2Lt kia 21-10-18 Leic att11Bn p88 CR France1266

MEAKIN,Walter Kendrick Capt kia 15-8-15 5Beds p219 MR4

MEAKINS,Robert William Spencam 2Lt kia 27-8-16 1RWKent p141 MR21

MEAL,William Capt ded 27-5-19 1Worc GarBn p264&255

MEALING,Maurice Edmund 2Lt kia 24-3-18 KSLI att56RFC p16&p145,ded MR20

MEARES,Cecil Stanley TCapt kia 30-7-16 19 att24RFus p69 CR France402

MEARES,Ellen Caroline Miss ded 24-2-19 VAD BRCS CR Surrey1

MEARNES,Henry Gould T2Lt dow 20-8-16 1GordH p166 CR France66,Gauld

MEARNS,Angus Hughes Lt ded 24-6-17 9BlkW &57RFC p129&11,Hughs kia MR20

MEARS,Edward de Quincey T2Lt kia 13-7-16 10Ess p132 MR21,14-7-16

MEARS,Francis Peel TCapt ded 22-2-19 RASC p255 CR Kent83,Perl

MEARS,James William 2Lt kia 12-11-14 HLI p163 MR29

MEARS-DEVENISH,John Augustus T2Lt dow 22-3-18 12 att1RFus p69 CR France987

MEASDY,Thomas Percy 2Lt kia 30-9-16 2Glouc p107 CR Greece3

MEASURES,John Charles T2Lt kia 30-9-16 6Y&L p159 MR21

MEASURES,Percy Lt kia 31-12-17 1/5Leic p220 CR France163,30-12-17

MEASURES,William Henry.MC.T2Lt kia 22-8-18 5 att11RFus p69 MR16

MEAUTYS,Denzil Hatfield Lt dow 7-5-17 3 att12WYorks p82 CR France40,1 att12Bn

MEAUTYS,Paul Raymond.MC.Capt kia 16-6-17 2NStaffs p157 CR France1185

MEAUTYS,Thomas Gilliat Lt kia 26-9-14 1WYorks p82 CR France1329,22-9-14

MEDCALF,Edwin Francis T2Lt dow 11-6-17 3 att8Leic p88 CR France518,kia

MEDCALF,William Archer T2Lt dow 15-10-17 15N&D p134 CR France139

MEDCRAFT,Alexander Raymond T2Lt kia 18-9-18 Hamps att12Bn p121 MR37 &end ofCR Greece1

MEDHURST,William Richard 2Lt ded 4-1-17 5RWKent p271

MEDLAND,James Edward Percy 2Lt kia 23-3-18 RE 64FC p210 MR20

MEDLEN,Leslie Lashbrook T2Lt kia 22-12-17 GL &16RFC p11 CR France95

MEDLEY,Bertram Anthony 2Lt kia 25-9-15 HLI p163 MR19

MEDLICOTT,Edward Morley TLt kia 11-4-16 2RBerks p139 CR France515

MEDLICOTT,Harold William 2Lt kld 21-5-18 RFC p16 MR20

MEDLICOTT,Sidney Neville T2Lt dow 6-10-15 A61RFA HB p32 CR France98

MEDWORTH,Frank Oswald.MC.TCapt kia 13-5-18 2Manch p155 CR France924

MEE,Ernest Campbell 2Lt kia 3-9-16 4WRid p227 MR21

MEE,George Hamilton TLt kia 22-8-15 6EYorks p84 MR4

MEECHAM,David Jeffreys T2Lt kia 27-3-17 11RWFus p98 CR Greece6,28-3-17

MEEK,Hubert Kingsley TCapt kia 15-9-16 14KRRC p151 CR France402

MEEK,John Lt kia 24/26-5-15 7DLI p239 MR29,24-5-15

MEEK,William T2Lt kia 17/19-9-18 2N&D p134 CR France835,18-9-18

MEEKE,William Stanley Capt kia 1-7-16 2Middx p147 CR France393

MEEKING,Norman Arthur 2Lt kia 1-7-16 9Lond p248 MR21

MEENAGHAN,John 2Lt kia 21-3-18 4ConnRgrs p172 CR France1495

MEERS,John Henry TCapt dow 9-10-15 RAMC attLNLancs p197 CR France178,10-10-15

MEERS,Philip James Lt ded 6-12-19 IA 2/69Punjabis p280 MR43,Capt

MEES,Rudolf Lt kld 14-11-18 GL&RAF p191

MEESON,Fitzalan Ridware Lt dow 4-11-18 13/17RH&FA p32

MEFF,William Blann Lt dow 14-11-16 1/7GordH p242 CR France41,kia

MEGAW,William Cecil Kennedy.MC.Capt&Ajt kia 31-3-15 1Norf p74 CR Belgium59

MEGENEY,Horace William LtACapt kia 21-9-18 72RFA p32 CR France439

MEGGS,Stewart Gordon 2Lt ded 3-3-17 RGA 213SB p209 CR France300

MEGGY,Frederick Arthur LtACapt kia 31-8-18 4Ess p232 CR France496

MEGSON,Robert Hargraves.MIDx2 Capt kia 23-4-17 16Manch p155 MR20

MEHARG,Robert John Lt ded 4-3-17 RIM attRE IWT p280 CR Iraq5

MEHEGAN,Daniel Joseph 2Lt kia 21-3-18 10 RDubF att2RMunstF p177 MR27

MEIKLE,James Drysdale T2Lt kia 4-11-18 13KRRC att111TMB p151 CR France1480

MEIKLE,Robert Jardine 2Lt kia 15-9-16 4DLI p161 CR France374

MEIKLE,William Reginald Dempster 2Lt kia 30-11-17 1KOSB p102 MR17

MEIKLEJOHN,Kenneth Forbes Lt&Adjt kia 26-9-14 1CamH p168 CR France1329,25-9-14

MEIKLEJOHN,Robert 2LtTCapt dow 15-11-15 7ScotRif p224 CR Gallipoli3

MEIN,Dudley Gerald.MC.Lt kia 26-10-18 IA 31Lancers attMysoreLancers p280 CR Lebanon1

MEIR,Wilfrid Ault.MID TLtACapt kia 11-4-18 8NStaffs p157 CR Belgium89,dow 10-4-18

MEIRE,Walter Herbert Geoffrey T2Lt kia 26-9-15 9Norf p74 MR19

MEISTER,Charles Gustave Clark.MC.Chap4Cl kia 18-4-18 RAChDept att10A&SH p199 CR Belgium21

MELDRUM,Ernest Alexander 2Lt kia 25-9-15 IARO att2/8GurkhaRif p280 MR28

MELDRUM,George Dundas 2Lt kia 16-12-16 5GordH p242 CR France832

MELDRUM,I.Sister 2-2-18 TFNS CR Scot677

MELDRUM,Ronald 2Lt kia 9-10-17 HAC Inf p206 MR30

MELHADO,Owen Stirling.MID T2Lt dow 7-12-15 6 att11Yorks p91 CR Europe9

MELHUISH,Alan George James 2Lt kia 21-3-18 7N&D p233 MR20

MELHUISH,Jan Vaughan Brenbridge T2Lt kia 27-10-15 7SomLI p80 CR France707,Ian Bremridge

MELHUISH,Leslie T2Lt kia 27-11-17 1/2Yorks att2/5YLI p91 MR17

MELLAND,Edward Guy Lt kia 30-6-15 8Ches attWYorks p96 CR Belgium96,1-7-15

MELLARD,Richard Bartlett 2Lt kia 1-7-16 5NStaffs p238 CR France576

MELLENFIELD,Cecil Beven T2Lt kia 23-10-16 7SLancs p125 CR France383

MELLER,Arthur William 2Lt kia 29-1-16 1EYorks p84 MR15,20-9-14

MELLERS,George Henry Reginald Capt kia 14-10-15 7N&D p233 MR19,13-10-15

MELLES,Gordon Frank Lt ded 6-11-15 2RFA HQ Staff p208 CR Egypt3

MELLING,Charles Flower.MC.ACapt mbk 13-5-18 1LancF p227 MR32

MELLING.Harold Lt kld 7-11-18 5Ches attRAF p256

MELLIS,Andrew Douglas John T2Lt kia 17-10-15 5 O&BLI p130 CR Belgium113,Lt

MELLIS,George Duncan Capt kia 30-11-17 C255RFA p207 CR France662

MELLIS,James 2Lt kia 15-6-18 5 att1GordH p242 CR France33

MELLIS-SMITH,Samuel Grant 2Lt kia 11-2-17 IARO 1/4 att2/4GurkhaRif p280 CR Iraq5

MELLISH,John George T2Lt kia 10-3-17 5Wilts p153 MR38

MELLISH,Henry Tupper Capt ded 4-10-17 RASC p267 CR Scot241

MELLISH,Richard Coppin T2Lt kia 25-9-15 1Middx p147 CR France114

MELLISH,Roy Thompson T2Lt kia 7-3-18 79RFC p16 CR France987

MELLISS,Montague Stanley CaptHonMaj ded 4-3-19 Res p271

MELLO,Arnold 2Lt dow 17-11-15 14Lond p249 CR France201

MELLOR,Francis Rigby TLt dow 15-1-17 10 att6ELancs p111 CR Iraq5,16-1-17

MELLOR,Frank Johnson Lt dow 19-9-16 2N&D p134 CR France105

MELLOR,Harold Welton TCapt ded 28-5-18 15RFus att2KAR p69 CR EAfrica90

MELLOR,John Lewis 2Lt kia 26-6-16 C163RFA att231TMB p32 CR France643

MELLOR,N.Lt drd 10-10-18 4WRid &RAF p256

MELLOR,Percy 2Lt kia 13-10-15 5NStaffs p230 MR19

MELLOR,Richard 2Lt kia 16-6-17 2/5Manch A'Coy p236 CR France163

MELLOR,Roy TLt kia 1-7-16 22Manch p155 MR21

MELLOR,Vincent Charles Serecold Lt ded 21-3-19 KRRC p255 CR Somerset161

MELLOR,Walton Capt kia 23-8-14 2RIrReg p89 CR Belgium242

MELLY,Hugh Peter Egeston Mesnard 2Lt kia 2-7-16 1Lancs p59 CR France643,Egerton 1-7-16

MELLY,Reginald Ernest Lt kia 30-7-16 20Lpool p72 MR21

MELROSE,James Douglas Leitch AMaj dow 25-4-18 RGA 29SB p271&206,RHFA CR Belgium40

MELROSE,Thomas Nelson 2Lt kia 14-11-16 5NumbF p213 MR21

MELTON,Arthur Francis Capt kia 27-11-17 2/6WRid p227 MR17

MELVILL,Melvill Leopold 2Lt kia 31-10-17 108/23RFA p33 CR Belgium11

MELVILLE,Alan Maj dedacc 8-8-16 IA 122Inf p280 MR43

MELVILLE,David.MC.ACapt kia 26-10-18 4 att5CamHp242 CR Belgium140

MELVILLE,David Charles T2Lt kld 21-1-18 RFC p16 CR Essex1

MELVILLE,David William 2Lt kia 21-3-18 14A&SH p173 MR20

MELVILLE,Harry George.DSO.CIE.Col ded 7-12-18 IMS p280 CR Iraq8

MELVILLE,Harry Taylor TLt kia 31-7-18 GL &RAF p191

MELVILLE,Hugh Colquhoun 2Lt kia 14-2-16 13 att10N&D p134 MR29

MELVILLE,John 2Lt kia 27-11-17 2/5WRid p256 MR17

MELVILLE,Joseph Thomson 2Lt kia 16-9-16 6HLI p240 CR France402

MELVILLE,Stuart Powis T2Lt kia 23-1-16 11N&D p134 CR France348,Bowie

MELVILLE,Sydney John Craig 2Lt kia 8-10-16 109RFA p208 CR France401

MELVILLE,William Woodfall Lt kia 9-5-15 6 att2KRRC MR22

MELVIN,Will Simpson 2Lt kld 23-8-18 1/4RB &RAF p179 CR France223

MENCE,William Charles Capt ded 25-7-19 RAMC CR Devon15

MENDEL,Reginald William Wynn 2Lt ded 19-9-17 RFA p33 CR Lond8

MENDS-GIBSON,Ollyett Archibald 2Lt dow 27-8-16 106/22RFA p33 CR France23

MENNIE,James T2Lt kia 18-9-18 7RSuss p119 CR France369

MENNIE,John Henderson 2Lt kia 10-4-17 4CamH att2/10Lpool p243 CR France705,11-4-17

MENZIES,Alastair Forbes.DSO.TLtACapt kia 4-5-18 17RFus p69

MENZIES,Alastair Graham TLt kia 1-1-15 ScotGds p52

MENZIES,Alexander Lawrence 2Lt dow 21-9-16 C48RFA p33 CR France145,Lt

MENZIES,Archibald Rudge Wilson Lt kia 25-11-17 2ScotGds p52 MR17

MENZIES,Arthur John Alexander.DSO.CaptAtCol kia 9-8-18 RAMC Cmdg3CavFA p197 CR France652

MENZIES,Harry 2Lt kia 29-4-17 23NumbF p62 MR20

MENZIES,Robert John.MID Capt kia 31-7-17 6BlkW p231 CR Belgium96

MENZIES,Vere Gordon Maj mbk 21-1-16 IA 97Inf p280 MR38

MENZIES,William Alan 2Lt dow 14-6-17 RGA 163SB p41 CR Belgium29

MEO,Giovanni Batista Lt kia 10-6-16 12Lond p248 CR France1327,Battista

MEPHAM,Horace Leslie 2Lt kia 11-4-18 6 att2RFus p69 MR32

MERCER,Alfred Stephen T2Lt kia 13-3-17 A155RFA p33 CR France133

MERCER,Andrew 2Lt dow 22-10-15 1BlkW p129 CR France40

MERCER,Archibald Ariel Maj kia 17-11-15 2Dors p124 CR Iraq6,17-11-14

MERCER,Eric Cameron 2Lt kia 13-10-14 ULIA att2LancF p93&280 CR France193

MERCER,Eric Dawson T2Lt dow 2-5-17 10LancFus p93 CR France40

MERCER,George Enos T2Lt kia 3-10-18 8 att1/4Leic p88 CR France375

MERCER,Hugh William Welch LtCol ded 14-6-18 IA p280

MERCER,John Edgar ACapt ded 3-12-19 RFA attHQ HejazOps p271 CR Egypt15,acckld

MERCER,S.Minchin Maj ded 27-6-19 RASC RetIA p267 CR Yorks438

MERCER,Thomas Milbourn 2Lt mbk 23-11-17 TankCps p256 MR17

MERCER,W.H.W.LtCol14-6-18 86CarnaticInf MR65

MERCER,William.MBE.TLt&QM ded 13-11-18 MontgomYeo p271 CR Greece9,13-12-18 RASC attExpForce

MERCER,William Malcolm Lt kia 28-11-17 4KOSB p223 CR Palestine9

MERCHANT,Alfred Douglas Lt kia 10-4-18 6 att11LancF p221 MR32

MERCHANT,Arthur Douglas Mount-Stephen T2Lt kld 13-5-17 GL &68RFC p11 CR Yorks38

MERCHANT,Herbert George T2Lt kia 28-9-16 9 att7Beds p86 MR21

MERCHANT,Reginald Frank 2Lt kia 21-3-18 36MGC Inf p184 CR France1061

MERCHANT,W.MC.Capt&QM 6-2-20 RAMC CR Hamps1

MERCHANT,William John 2Lt kia 7-10-16 7Lond p247 MR21

MERCIER,H.B.2Lt ded 3-11-18 RIrRif &RAF p170

MERCIER,Y.W.2Lt kia 25/27-9-15 3 att1RScotF p95 MR29

MERE,Colin Leigh TLt kia 10-8-15 6RLancs p59 MR4

MEREDITH,Arthur Llewellyn 2Lt dow 4-6-18 1Mon p243 CR France10

MEREDITH,E.M.2Lt kld 13-4-18 GL&RAF p191 CR Belgium38

MEREDITH,Eric Dunfee T2Lt kia 4/10-10-16 32RFus p69 MR21,7-10-16

MEREDITH,Gerald.MC.TCapt ded 27-3-18 11KRRC p151 CRFrance145

MEREDITH,John Collins 2Lt kia 23-9-18 43/24RFA p33 CR France835

MEREDITH,Malcolm Hereward 2Lt kia 10-11-15 4Worc p109 CR Gallipoli4

MEREDITH,Maurice Neville.MC.2Lt kia 26-10-18 IARO 1Lancers attMysoreLancers p280 CR Lebanon1,Lt

MEREDITH,Owen Watkin Wynn Hardinge T2Lt dow PoW 20-11-17 GL &64RFC p11 CR France421

MEREDITH,William John Lt dow 20-2-15 3MunstF attSLancs p175 CR Belgium182

MEREDITH,William Morris TCapt ded 7-12-18 Lpool p263 CR Norf128

MEREWETHER,Christopher Kerr Capt dow 19-12-17 1/4Wilts p236 CR Egypt7,Ken 20-12-17

MEREWETHER,John Alwarth TCapt kia 15-9-16 9RB p179 MR21

MERIVALE,Francis Lt ded 17-10-18 1/7NumbF p214 CR France146,17-11-18

MERIVALE,John William Capt kia 15-9-16 1/7NumbF A'Coy p214 CR France387

MERK,John William Albert 2Lt ded 15-4-17 IA 1/6GurkhaRif p280 CR Iraq8

MERRELL,Arthur Walter 2Lt kia 8-5-17 1/2 att12Glouc p107 MR20

MERRETT,Arthur Edwin T2Lt kia 18-12-16 15Hamps p121 CR Belgium28

MERRETT,Harold Edmund T2Lt dow 17-8-18 10N&D p134 CR France145

MERRICK,Herbert Frederick Rivers Lt kia 3-5-17 2RBerks p139 MR21

MERRICK,Thomas Barker.MC.TLtACapt kia 2-9-18 4MGC Inf p184 CR France421

MERRICK,Thomas James.DSO.MC.LtAMaj ded 8-11-18 87RFA p33 CR France13

MERRIFIELD,Percy 2Lt kia 21-3-18 Worc att2/8Bn p109 MR27,MERIFIELD

MERRIKIN,George Houlden 2Lt kia 27-8-18 2Lond p245 CR France1186

MERRILES,John Sutherland 2Lt kia 19-6-15 5RScots p211 CR Gallipoli6

MERRIMAN,Charles Henry T2Lt kia 9-4-17 2Wilts p153 CR France162

MERRIMAN,Gordon Holland Capt kia 12-5-15 95RFA p33 CR Belgium115

MERRIMAN,Sydney Thomas Lt ded 3-6-21 IA 1/97DeccanInf p280 MR65

MERRITT,Frederick Charles LtAMaj kia 17-6-17 B15RFA p33 CR France1182

MERRY,George William Henry 2Lt kia 21-3-18 16MGC Inf p184 CR France1495

MERRY,Norman Cuthbert TCapt kia 15-7-16 10Ches p96 MR21,14-7-16

MERRY,Ralph Valentine T2Lt kia 1-7-16 18Lpool p72 CR France397

MERRYFIELD,Leopold Reginald TCapt dow 28-8-16 13ESurr p113 CR France102

MERRYMAN,William Robert Hill.MID T2Lt kia 15-8-16 8RB p179 CR France399,MERRIMAN

MERRYWEATHER,Charles Walter TMaj kia 23-11-16 16LancF p93 MR21

MERSON,Marshall Lt kia 3-5-17 5RScotsF p222 MR34

MERSON,William Murison Smith Capt kia 13-11-16 7GordH p242 CR France131

MERTS,Walter Scott T2Lt ded 28-7-16 RE p47 CR Wales137,MERTZ

MESHAM,Robert Seymour TLt kia 19-4-18 SL MilLabCps WAAF p201&268 CR EAfrica92

MESSENGER,Henry Frederick Roy 2Lt kia 22-8-15 6Yorks p91 MR4

MESSENGER.L.W.2Lt ded 4-7-18 RH&FA &RAF p33

MESSENGER,Wilfred Chaundler TCapt dow 16-9-17 12RB p179 CR France145

MESSER,Allan Ernest Capt dow 17-2-16 1KRRC p151 CR France8

MESSERVY,Ernest Dyce Capt kia 20-7-17 21Lond attRFC p19&251 MR20

MESSERVY,Gerald.MC.CaptAMaj kia 9-10-18 16/41RFA p33 CR France914,8-10-18

MESSOM,Harold 2Lt kia 16-5-15 2RWSurr p56 CR France279

MESTON-REID,James Capt ded 6-11-18 RE p210 MR70 &CR Europe179

METCALF,Cecil David Lt kia 20-4-18 7Lond p247 CR France880

METCALF,George 2Lt dow 12-4-18 15RScots CR Belgium11

METCALF,Lister 2Lt kia 8-8-16 4Lancs p213 MR21

METCALFE,Francis.MID Capt ded 10-7-18 RAMC 1FA p256 CR Numb7

METCALFE,George 2Lt dow 12-4-18 10RScots p212

METCALFE,George Christopher TCapt ded 16-3-19 RAMC p267 MR66

METCALFE,Harry 2Lt kia 4-4-17 7N&D att11RB p233 CR France905

METCALFE,Ian Morehouse Lt dow PoW 1-11-17 3Worc p109 MR19

METCALFE,John Chaytor TMaj kia 7-7-16 13Ches p96 CR France393

METCALFE,Johnn Clifford.MC.Capt dow 20-3-16 RAMC 1/1FA p254 CR Belgium11,20-3-18

METCALFE,Joseph Stephen 2Lt kia 17-1-17 3Mon p244 MR19

METCALFE,Lawrence T2Lt ded 25-12-17 16WYorks p263 CR France184,Laurence Lt

METCALFE,Wilfred Charles TLt dow 19-8-16 11ESurr p113 CR France51,9Bn

METCALFE-SMITH,Bertram Cecil Lt dow 22-4-18 4 att21WYorks p82 CR France10

METGE,Randolph Cole Capt ded 4-10-19 Ex 5Leinst p266 CR Eire440

METHUEN,Cameron O'Bryen Harford Capt kia 20/21-10-14 RWar p65 MR29,20-10-14

METHVEN,David George Capt kia 20-10-14 SfthH p165 CR France1140

METHVIN,Donald Capt kia 12-9-18 2CamH p168 CR Greece6

METSON,Herbert Frank 2Lt dow 9-8-16 D70RFA p33 CR France23

METTAM,Athol Roy 2Lt kia 16-8-17 WYorks att217MGC Inf p82&184 MR30

METTHAM,John Arthur TLtACapt ded 12-11-18 RE p47 MR70 &CR Europe179

MEUGENS,Geoffrey Ellsworth Maj ded 30-10-18 TankCps p188 CR Kent268

MEVDELL,Colin Grant 2Lt kia 10-8-17 43RFC p11 CR France88,MEUDELL Ex AustImpF

MEWBURN,Simon William Richard Capt kia 20-5-16 14Huss p22 MR38,21-5-16

MEWHA,George Henry 2Lt kia 20-9-17 LNLancs att1/5Bn p136 MR30

MEWS,John Keith Capt dow 24-8-18 1Lond p245 CR France103

MEYER,Alan Wallace 2Lt ded 11-3-18 RGA 289SB p41 CR Italy7

MEYER,Constant Clifford William Lt dow 3-7-18 2Lincs p75 CR France119

MEYER,Herbert Frederick 2Lt kld 15-10-17 GL &RFC p11 CR Shrop52

MEYER,James Leopold Maj died 22-6-17 RE p47 MR65

MEYER,Llewellen 2Lt kia 11-6-16 6DLI p239 CR Belgium21

MEYER-GRIFFITH,Harold Walter Gooch Maj kia 28-5-15 LNLancs p136 CR WAfrica28

MEYERS,H.Deverell TCapt ded 30-10-18 RASC p193 CR Ireland24

MEYERS,Stanley Arthur 2Lt kia 26-10-17 1Lond p245 MR30

MEYNELL,Edward James Hugh.MC.Capt dow 4-10-18 1/5SStaffs p229 CR France446

MEYNELL,Hugo Charles T2Lt dow 27-9-15 12Ess p132 CR France80

MEYRICK,John Charles 2Lt kld 26-6-17 4LNLancs p234 CR Lancs92

MEYRICKE,Robert James Francis TMajALtCol kia 17-2-17 11RFus att6Nhampt p69 CR France251

MEYRICKE,Rupert John Chabert Maj ded 25-1-16 58RFA p261 CR Europe1,26-1-16

MEYSEY-THOMPSON,Claude Henry Meysey.Hon.Capt dow 17-6-15 3RB p179 CR Yorks249

MIALL-SMITH,George Eric.MC.Lt kia 25-9-17 8Norf &11RFC p258,11&74,25-3-17 CR France120

MIALL-SMITH,Ralph Arnold TLt kia 26-9-16 11RFus p69 MR21

MICALLEF,Paolo Capt ded 11-12-16 2MaltaR p201 CR Europe4

MICHAELIS,Grant Moritz Lt kia 23-9-15 RE 1/2FC p210 CR Gallipoli17

MICHELL,Arthur T2Lt kia 12-10-17 7RWKent p141 MR30

MICHELL,James Douglas T2Lt ded 9-10-18 2/4KAR &MGC p202 CR SAfrica144

MICHELL,John Colloryan Capt kia 28-8-14 12Lancers p22 CR France1715

MICHELL,Noel Burgess TCapt kia 22-3-18 11RFus p69 MR27

MICHELL,Robert Williams.MID TCapt dow 20-7-16 RAMC p197 CR Camb3

MICHELMORE,Jeffery Edwards Morton Lt kia 9-4-18 6 att13ESurr p226 MR32

MICHELMORE,Robert Frank 2Lt dow 7-7-16 16Middx p147 CR France245

MICHELSON,Arthur Conrad 2Lt kia 18-10-17 B64RFA p33 CR Belgium125

MICHELSON,Walter 2Lt dow 27-7-16 14DLI p161 CR Belgium11

MICHIE,Christopher Young Lt kia 21-11-17 7ScotRif p224 CR Belgium22

MICHIE,Henry George Lt kia 26-9-16 15 att8NumbF p62 MR21

MICHIE,John 2Lt kia 15-7-17 D15HLI p163 CR Belgium24

MICHIE,John Boyd TLt ded 31-12-18 RAMC p197 MR70 &CR Europe179

MICKLE,Kenneth Aubrey.DSO.Capt ded 30-7-19 4/22RGA p262 CR Australia307

MICKLETHWAITE,Harold Chandos T2Lt dow 25-3-18 1EYorks p84 CR France699

MICKLEWRIGHT,James T2Lt kia 3-11-18 RE 178TC p47 CR France1259

MIDDLECOTE,Edwin William Alfred George Lt kia 3-10-18 16KRRC attRAF p151 CR France915

MIDDLEDITCH,Archibald Milne Lt kia 1-7-16 12Ess p132 CR France1890

MIDDLEDITCH,Arnold Warden T2Lt ded 19-6-16 O&BLI p130 CR Herts30

MIDDLEHURST,John T2Lt kia 26-10-17 LNLancs att2/5Bn p136 MR30

MIDDLEMASS,Robert McGregor 2Lt dow 29-9-16 3 att7/8KOSB p102 CR France40

MIDDLEMIS,Herbert 2Lt kia 23-10-17 24/27NumbF p62 MR30

MIDDLEMISS,Thomas Elmslie Lt kia 17-10-17 RHFA p208 CR Belgium9

MIDDLETON,Alexander Samuel 2Lt dow 30-9-18 3 att1CamH p168 CR France145,30-9-15

MIDDLETON,Arthur Claud 2Lt dow 7-6-15 8LancF p221 CR Gallipoli1

MIDDLETON,Edward Geoffrey 2Lt kia 3-9-14 Suff p78

MIDDLETON,Edwin Relfe Barrett 2Lt kia 9-4-17 6SfthH p241 CR France15,9-4-18

MIDDLETON,Ernest Lt kia 26-2-16 DorsYeo p203

MIDDLETON,Frank Capt kia 17-11-14 Dors p124 CR Iraq6

MIDDLETON,George Hilton Lt kia 10-8-19 RAMC p255 MR70 &CR Europe180 Ex 2RFA

MIDDLETON,George North T2Lt kld 22-2-18 RFC p16 CR Scot398

MIDDLETON,Henry Capt kia 23-4-18 RE 456FC p210 CR Belgium15

MIDDLETON,James.MC.T2Lt kia 2-9-18 7KSLI p145 CR France1484

MIDDLETON,James Russell TLt dow PoW 21-6-17 GL &11RFC p11 CR Germany1 Ex CamH

MIDDLETON,John TCapt dow 2-10-17 8WRid p116 CR Belgium23

MIDDLETON,Leonard William T2Lt kia 8-11-17 GL &53RFC p11 CR Belgium111

MIDDLETON,R.MC.Capt 4-4-18 15Lond CR France1142

MIDDLETON,Reginald 2Lt kia 3-9-16 8WYorks p219 CR France383

MIDDLETON,Thomas Lt kia 1-7-16 16HLI att97TMB p163 MR21,Capt

MIDDLETON,Thomas Stanley 2Lt kia 19-5-17 3 att1BordR p117 MR20

MIDDLETON,William Archie Arbuthnot Capt kia 25-4-15 2SfthH p165 MR29

MIDDLEWOOD,Albert 2Lt kia 3-5-17 2WRid p116 MR20

MIDGLEY,Albert T2Lt dow 18-6-18 1/2Worc p109 CR Italy10,2 att1/7Bn

MIDGLEY,Arthur T2Lt dow 15-7-16 9MGC p184 CR France66

MIDGLEY,Ellis Reginald 2Lt kia 15-11-15 1/5YLI p235 CR Belgium23,17-11-15

MIDWOOD,Harry 2Lt dow 25-12-16 13Y&L p159 CR France74,Lt

MIDWOOD,Lilian Nurse drd 31-12-17 VAD p200 CR Egypt1

MIERS,Douglas Nathaniel Carleton Capel Capt kia 25-9-14 1CamH p168 CR France1339

MIERS,Maurice Colin Capel MajALtCol dow 9-8-17 5Middx att8SomLI p147 CR Kent61

MIERS,Richard Henry Probyn Capt kld 12-12-17 GlamYeo att31RFC p19&203 CR Hunts113,FlOff

MIGHELL,Philip T2Lt dow 12-10-17 GL &5RFC p11 CR France113,Lt

MIGNON,Jephson George TLtCol kia 15-7-16 8Leic p88 MR21,Jepson

MILBANK,Robert Charles Alfred Palso Edmund Capt dow 10-5-15 3 att2WRid p116 CR France102

MILBANKE,John Peniston.Bart.VC.LtCol kia 21-8-15 SherwoodRgrs p205 MR4

MILBOURNE,Leslie TLt dow 10-7-16 7LNLancs p136 CR France102

MILBURN,Richard Gerald 2Lt dow 10-2-15 4ESurr p113 CR Belgium115

MILBURN,Robert Norman T2Lt kia 20-7-18 YLI att2/9Bn p143 MR18

MILBURN,William Hudson 2Lt kia 15-7-16 4Suff p217 MR21

MILDMAY,B.W.StJ 2Lt kld 16-4-18 GL &RAF p191

MILEMAN,Vernon Wallace.MC.Capt kia 16-9-17 7Lond p247 MR29

MILES,Alfred Crosfield Vernor T2Lt kia 24-8-15 2WelshR p127 CR France114

MILES,Allan Oswald T2Lt kia 30-6-16 11 att13Glouc p107 MR19

MILES,Cyril Vernor Capt kia 25-9-15 2WelshR p127 MR19

MILES,Francis James Lt dow 6-11-17 366/268RFA p208 CR Palestine1,kia

MILES,George Henry 2Lt kia 13-9-17 1RWKent att6RFC p11&141 CR Belgium11,12-9-17

MILES,Gordon TLt kia 7-10-16 14 att9Yorks p91 MR21

MILES,Guy Ralph.MC.TLt dow 10-3-18 4RRofCav att5DGds p23 CR France446,George

MILES,Harold Gordon T2Lt kia 4or5-8-16 10DCLI p114 MR21,4-8-16

MILES,Henry Robert T2Lt kia 18-7-16 6ConnRgrs p172 CR France178,16-7-16

MILES,Herbert Francis T2LtACapt kia 3-9-16 2KOSB p102 CR France402

MILES,Herbert Talbot Lt dow 16-4-17 D291RFA p208 CR France518

MILES,Jesse Samuel 2Lt dow 19-6-18 1/2 att1/6Glouc p107 CR Italy11

MILES,John Guildford Capt kia 27-6-18 6Norf p217 CR France61

MILES,John Harris 2Lt kia 27-9-15 7 att4RFus p69 CR Belgium6

MILES,Leonard Percy 2Lt kia 7-10-16 6 att8RFus p69 CR France560

MILES,Maurice W.Holt Capt ded 25-11-18 Ex RAMC p267

MILES,Richard Douglas.MC.2Lt dow 17-8-17 4 att9RIrF p171 CR Belgium8

MILES,Robert Patrick Capt dow 30-12-14 KSLI p145 CR France768,Patric

MILES,Robert William TCapt kia 1-6-17 13 att11N&D p134 CR Belgium127

MILES,Roger Thomas William T2Lt kia 1-10-17 1/2 att7Leic p88 CR Belgium125,2-10-17

MILES,W.N.2Lt ded 24-7-18 14Worc &RAF p109

MILEY,Miles Lt dow 30-12-15 1RFA p208 CR France102

MILHOLLAND,Frederick Raymond TCapt dow 26-2-18 7 att6Yorks p91 CR France98

MILHOLM,David Archibald T2Lt kia 18-11-16 16HLI p163 MR21

MILL,James Drysdale 2Lt kia 15-10-15 3 att1KOSB p102 CR Gallipoli3

MILL,Leonard Binning Lt kia 9-8-16 10Lpool p216 MR21

MILL,Robert Cowper King Lt kia 3-9-16 5BlkW p231 CR France701

MILL,William Henry 2Lt kia 12-7-15 5RScotF C'Coy p222 CR Gallipoli2

MILLAIS,Geoffrey de Carteret TLtACapt dow 21-8-18 1Beds p86 CR France342

MILLAR,Arthur James Lt kia 25-4-15 3 att1RIrRif p171 MR29,Capt

MILLAR,Arthur Liberty Capt kia 15-4-18 6 att4RB p179 CR Greece3

MILLAR,Audley Charles Hyde.MC.TCapt dow 16-10-17 3 att9Yorks CR Belgium72,15-10-17

MILLAR,David Hopkin Lt dow 30-5-18 4 att5RScots p211 CR France84,kld

MILLAR,Douglas Archibald T2Lt kia 18-7-16 11 att1GordH p166 MR21

MILLAR,Duncan Crerar Reeve Lt dow 10-4-18 12Yorks att21TMB p91 CR France1094,13Bn

MILLAR,George Rev ded 26-8-17 RAChDept att13GenHosp CR France 102

MILLAR,George Inglis 2Lt kia 8-4-17 RFA p208 CR France266

MILLAR,G.R.SubCdr ded 1-1-18 IA RlyCps p280

MILLAR,Ian Arthur 2Lt dow 30-9-16 6RIrRif p170 CR Greece3

MILLAR,Ion Keith T2Lt kia 27-7-16 1ESurr p113 MR21

MILLAR,James T2Lt kia 25/27-9-15 3BlkW p129 CR France219

MILLAR,James 2Lt dow 25-4-18 Res att1/6WYorks p82 MR30

MILLAR,James T2Lt kia 24-9-18 13TankCps p188 CR France1701

MILLAR,James 2Lt ded 12-6-19 5RIrReg p263

MILLAR,James Ainslie 2Lt kia 25-9-15 RScotF p95 MR29,Anslie

MILLAR,James Joseph Francis 2Lt 12-6-19 5RIrRif CR Germany1

MILLAR,James Lytton 2Lt kia 29-7-16 5 att15RIrRif p170 CR France423,28-7-16 1Bn

MILLAR,James Roland TCapt kia 16-8-17 11DubF p177 CR Belgium45,16-8-18

MILLAR,James Steele Hair T2Lt ded 13-1-19 Mddx p265 CR Scot199

MILLAR,John Lt kia 29-7-18 6ScotRif p224 CR France524

MILLAR,John Pitcairn Lt kia 21-9-18 6ScotRif p224 CR France407 Ex14Lond

MILLAR,John Wilson Lt ded 14-10-18 6A&SH p271 CR Scot685,Willson

MILLAR,Leonard 2Lt dow 19-7-16 17DLI p161 CR France630

MILLAR,Robert Bain TLtACapt kia 24-7-18 17RScots attMGC p184 CR Belgium11

MILLAR,Robert Curle Lt kia 25-9-15 8SfthH p165 MR19

MILLAR,Robert Given T2Lt dow 16-8-16 9KOSB p102 CR France134,7/8Bn

MILLAR,Robert Gordon 2Lt dow 11-5-17 4 att11A&SH p173 CR France40

MILLAR,Robert Spiers Lt kia 18-9-18 6A&SH p243 CR France375

MILLAR,Stanley Gemmell TCapt kia 1-7-16 103MGC Inf p184 MR21

MILLAR,Walter Gordon Capt kia 8-7-16 3 att7EYorks p84 CR France453,7-7-16

MILLAR,William 2Lt kia 23-8-18 6TankCps p188 CR France927

MILLAR,William Linton TCapt ded 23-10-18 RAMC p197 CR France770

MILLAR,William McKay T2Lt kia 18-9-18 KSLI att10Bn p145 MR16

MILLARD,Albert Wardle Lt dow 25-2-18 A641RFA p33 CR France345

MILLARD,Alfred George T2Lt dow 7-8-17 9ESurr p113 CR Belgium88 See WILLARD

MILLARD,David Edward Hall 2Lt kia 23-4-17 3RWSurr p56 MR20

MILLARD,Edgar John T2Lt dow 31-7-17 8RWSurr p56 CR Belgium7,kia

MILLARD,Harold TCaptAMaj dow 11-4-17 7Nhants p137 CR France570

MILLARD,Henry Albert.MM.Lt dow 16-9-16 58/35RFA p33 CR France23,Harry

MILLARD,John Barnard T2Lt kia 25-6-17 8EKent p57 CR Belgium29 Ex HAC

MILLEN,W.D. See MILLER,William Donnell

MILLER,Alan 2Lt dow 14-10-16 3 att2Yorks p91 CR France188

MILLER,Albert Guy TCapt kia 29-12-15 RAMC att12Mddx p197 CR France370

MILLER,Andrew Lindsay 2Lt kia 12-10-17 9A&SH p243 MR30

MILLER,Andrew Richard Stuart 2Lt dow 21-4-18 3 att2KOSB p102 CR France31

MILLER,Archibald Craig Capt ded 3-10-15 RGA p271&209,kld CR Scot241

MILLER,Archibald Ingram TLt kia 11-3-17 RAMC att47RFA p197 CR France1182

MILLER,Archibald William Buchanan Lt ded PoW 13-7-17 1KOSB &RFC p11&102 CR Belgium140

MILLER,B.MC.2Lt kld 29-5-18 RGA SR &RAF p41 CR Belgium36

MILLER,Bertram Charles St.Clair 2Lt kld 29-11-17 RE attRFC p11&47 CR Kent231,Lt

MILLER,Charles Wilde 2Lt kia 7-6-17 11WYorks p82 CR Belgium127

MILLER,Clement Francis Patrick 2Lt ded 4-10-18 IARO att46DivSigs p280 MR65

MILLER,Cyril Rowland Eyre Lt dow 25-11-14 4ScotRif attKOSB p103 CR France102,23-11-14

MILLER,David Joseph 2Lt kia 12-4-18 3 att9RIrF p171 MR30

MILLER,Dudley Melville TLt kia 28-4-17 11Suff p78 CR France604

MILLER,Edwin George 2Lt kia 23-4-17 3 att7GordH p166 CR France604

MILLER,Ernest Cyril Capt kia 23-10-14 3 att1LNLancs p136 CR Belgium126,Ex 1Bn

MILLER,Francis John 2Lt kia 1-7-16 7RWSurr p56 CR France397

MILLER,Francis Samuel Lt dow 7-6-17 RE p210 CR Mddx25,2Lt

MILLER,Frank Edwin Commsy&Maj gunshotWound 11-10-20 IA IndOrdDept p280 MR65

MILLER,Frank Henry 2Lt kia 27-5-18 2RBerks p139 MR18

MILLER,Frederic Charles Lt kia 24-4-18 6Glouc CR France248

MILLER,Frederick David T2Lt dow 4-2-18 20RFC p16 CR Belgium11

MILLER,Frederick Richard Maj ded 4-2-16 RAMC p271 CR Hamps15

MILLER,Frederick William Joseph MacDonald Lt kia 24-10-14 2GrenGds p50 MR29,23-10-14

MILLER,George 2Lt dow PoW 31-3-18 RFC p16 CR Belgium241

MILLER,George Bell 2Lt kia 1-5-17 2HLI att18RFC p163&257 CR France244

MILLER,George Blair T2Lt kia 24-4-17 2HLI att18RFC p11 MR20,28-4-17

MILLER,George Clark Capt kia 26-8-18 5RScotF p222 CR France419

MILLER,George Frederick 2Lt kia 23-3-18 4 att11Ches p96 MR20

MILLER,George Gibbs.MID TLt ded 17-11-18 RE 8FldSurCo GHQ p47 CR Greece9

MILLER,George Gordon Darley 2Lt kia 15-9-19 RFA p255 MR70,1-9-19

MILLER,George James Capt dow 29-8-18 A56RFA p207 CR France103

MILLER,George James 2Lt kia 29-9-18 4Lincs p217 CR France407

MILLER,George Sefton TCapt kia 8-9-16 RAMC att1FA p197 CR France397

MILLER,George William 2Lt kia 15-12-17 2Ess p132 MR20

MILLER,Godfrey Lyall 2Lt kia 14-9-14 RE 11FC p47 CR France1107

MILLER,Gordon Stanley Reed 2Lt dow 24-12-16 6RSuss att11KRRC p228 CR France145

MILLER,Harold Patterson 2Lt dow 27-4-18 8ScotRif p225 CR France142

MILLER,Henry Thornton Lt kia 6-5-15 3EYorks att2WRid p84 MR29

MILLER,Henry William Waltson 2Lt kia 30-7-16 6BlkW p231 MR21

MILLER,Howard Todd Lt kia 21/26-3-18 LondIrRif p250 MR20

MILLER,Ian MacLeilain Lt kia 25-9-15 3A&SH p173 CR France114,Iain MacLellan 2Bn

MILLER,Inglis Francis Rowley Lt dow 13-9-14 RInnisF p105 CR France598

MILLER,Jack Humphrey Capt ded 25-8-17 3LNLancs attEgyptArmy p136 CR Egypt1

MILLER,James.MC.2Lt kia 11-3-18 6CamH p168 MR20

MILLER,James.DCM.2Lt kia 25-3-18 2SStaffs p122 MR20

MILLER,James Lt 31-7-18 5SfthH CR Scot862

MILLER,James Lt kia 14-10-18 3 att11Ches p96 CR Belgium157,3 att16Bn

MILLER,James Archibald Montgomerie 2Lt kia 16-4-17 7NumbF p214 MR20

MILLER,James Arthur T2Lt kia 28-3-18 GL &24RFC p16 CR France891,dedacc

MILLER,James Brand Scott 2Lt kia 14-3-18 RGA 252SB p41 CR Belgium19

MILLER,James Cooper Capt dow 24-11-17 14Lond p249 CR France512

MILLER,John Capt kia 19-8-15 6RWFus p223 MR4

MILLER,John.MC.T2Lt kia 1-8-17 10HLI p163 CR Belgium125

MILLER,John T2Lt kia 2-12-17 HLI att17Bn p163 MR30

MILLER,John.MC.Lt dow 12-11-18 7A&SH p243 CR France13

MILLER,John Austin Lt ded 3-4-20 4Ess p271 CR Essex50

MILLER,John Charles 2Lt kia 27-7-15 6DLI p239 CR France922

MILLER,John Donald Gardiner TLt dow 15-11-15 9BlkW p129 CR France423,Capt

MILLER,John Eric Hale 2Lt kia 11-1-16 3 att1NumbF p62 CR Belgium28 Hall

MILLER,John Kingsley Lt kia 19-9-18 24RWFus p203 CR France212

MILLER,John Lockhart Lt kia 21-5-16 8Lond p247 MR20

MILLER,John McGregor 2Lt kia 8-10-16 167MGC p184 MR21,7-10-16

MILLER,Joseph Ewing Bruce Lt dow 24-5-15 5 att1RIrRif p170 CR France134

MILLER,Kenneth Steven 2Lt kia 1-8-17 3ScotRif p103 MR29,4 att10Bn

MILLER,Maurice 2Lt ded 5-8-17 4RScots CR Scot242

MILLER,Neville 2Lt 28-6-17 5SStaffs 3RWar MR20

MILLER,Peter,Spence 2Lt drd 26-2-18 GL RE &IWT p191 MR38

MILLER,Ralph Marillier 2Lt 30-7-16 25 att17Manch MR21

MILLER,Reginald de Hochepied Marillier T2Lt dow 27-10-18 RWFus 3GarrBn p98

MILLER,Rex de Hochepied Marillier.MM.2Lt dow 27-10-18 3RWFus CR France1392

MILLER,Robert.MC.Lt dow 25-4-17 3 att10ScotRif p103 CR France113

MILLER,Robert Fordyce 2Lt kia 4-9-16 9Dev p77&235 CR France402

MILLER,Robert Goldie 2Lt kia 17-3-17 4A&SH att5RFC p11 CR France3

MILLER,Stanley 2Lt kia 1-7-16 11RInnisF p105 CR France526

MILLER,Thomas Alexander Grant Lt kia 27-4-15 1KOSB p102 MR4,26-4-15

MILLER,Thomas Murray T2Lt kia 27-1-16 7KOSB p102 CR France222

MILLER,Thomas Peacock T2Lt kia 26-3-18 LancF att6Bn p93 MR27

MILLER,Tom Drysdale.MC.TCapt kia 21-10-16 8BordR p117 MR21

MILLER,Walter T2Lt dow 30-4-17 11A&SH p173 CR France40

MILLER,Walter Douglas 2Lt kia 2-10-16 RGA attRFC p19&209 MR20

MILLER,Walter Roy 2Lt kia 15-9-18 1GrenGds att4GdsMGR p50 CR France1484

MILLER,William Donnell 2Lt kia 23-6-18 7GordH att4ResBn p242 CR France266,MILLEN

MILLER,William Edward 2Lt dow 17-7-16 7Lond p247 CR France224

MILLER,Wilfred Heard 2Lt kia 4-7-16 7SLancs p125 MR21,Wilfrid

MILLER,William Henry Capt kia 18-4-16 IA 74Punjabis att59Rif p280 CR Iraq5

MILLER,William Reginald Francis TLt kia 24/25-4-17 10Dev p77 MR37

MILLER-HALLET,Stewart Alexander T2Lt kia 11-7-16 11SWBord p100 MR21

MILLER-STIRLING,Edward George Bradshaw Lt dow 14-3-17 2BlkW p129 MR38

MILLER-STIRLING,H.J.G.S.Lt 16-10-17 GL attNigeriaR MR52

MILLETT,James Noble Layton 2Lt ded 13-3-18 73RFC p16 MR20

MILLICAN,John Stamper T2Lt dow 3-7-16 2WRid p116 CR France167,Lt

MILLICAN,Reginald Isaac 2Lt dow 23-3-18 4Middx p147 CR Belgium165

MILLICHAP,Frank Henry Lt dow 24-4-16 6SLancs attWRid p125 MR38 &CR Iraq5,WRid att6SLancs

MILLIGAN,Alastair T2Lt dow 30-4-17 5CamH att1/7A&SH p168 CR France40,3Bn

MILLIGAN,Donald Samuel Eccles Lt 9-10-17 RAMC 1/3FA att1/7Worc p197 CR Belgium20,12-10-17

MILLIGAN,Frank Joynt T2Lt dow 13-3-18 80RFC p16 CR France987

MILLIGAN,Frederick Albert T2Lt ded 29-4-16 7RInnisF p105 CR France115

MILLIGAN,George Berry Lt 24-3-18 152RFA p33 MR20

MILLIGAN,Herbert Ward TLt kia 21-11-17 16 att1LancF p93 MR17

MILLIGAN,James Henry.MID Lt mbk 25-9-15 IA 58Rif p280 MR28

MILLIGAN,John Richard 2Lt mbk 8-3-16 IARO att59Rif p280 MR38,att55Rif

MILLIGAN,Percy Bass TCapt kia 30-9-18 12HLI p163 CR Belgium116

MILLIKEN,Frank Stevens T2Lt dow 4-5-17 19Lpool p72 CR France13

MILLIKEN,James 2Lt kld 31-12-18 11RIrRif &RAF p170 CR Ireland42,MILLIKIN 12Bn

MILLIKEN,Joseph Dalton Lt 30-6-16 EAUL CR EAfrica123

MILLIN,Edward Job.MID TCapt kia 1-7-16 2YLI p143 MR21

MILLISHIP,William Griffin T2Lt kia 7-6-17 GL &1RFC p11 MR20

MILLNER,William Capt kia 13-10-15 5SStaffs p229 MR19

MILLS,Albert Edward 2Lt kia 16-8-17 3 att2RBerks p139 MR30

MILLS,B.A.J.Capt 23-2-21 6Dev CR Iraq8

MILLS,Ben Holt 2Lt dow 29-4-17 6Manch p237 CR France120,5Bn

MILLS,Charles Gordon 2Lt kia 26-1-15 1CldGds p51 CR France720,25-1-15

MILLS,Charles Thomas.Hon.2Lt kia 6-10-15 2ScotGds p52 MR19

MILLS,Edgar Edward.MC.Capt mbk 22-9-18 7SWBord p256 MR37,18-9-18

MILLS,Frank Symons Capt&Adjt kia 5-8-17 att7SomLI p80 CR Belgium23

MILLS,George Carlton Lt kld 4-11-17 RFC p11 CR Hamps4

MILLS,George Charles 2Lt kia 10-7-16 11WYorks p82 CR France832

MILLS,Gerald Desmond CaptTMaj kia 19-5-17 N&D &19RFC p11&134 CR France62

MILLS,Harry Forster Capt kia 21-3-18 46RFA p33 MR27

MILLS,Henry Jackson Lt dow 30-5-18 2Middx att19MGC p147&184 MR18

MILLS,Henry Valentine 2Lt kia 25-6-17 RGA 321SB p41 CR Belgium10

MILLS,John R.Lt&QM ded 11-8-14 RASC p193 CR Lond4

MILLS,John Birchell 2Lt dow 16-4-17 4RWFus p223 CR France64,Lt

MILLS,John Coleridge Lt kia 25-9-15 10HLI p163 MR19

MILLS,John Richard LtQM dow 7-5-18 11Huss p22 CR Kent179

MILLS,John Thomas HonCapt ded 22-12-14 RAOC p198 CR Lancs48

MILLS,Kenneth Le Gai T2Lt dow 11-11-17 GL &10RFC p11 CR France98

MILLS,Mansfeldt Charles Nightingale T2Lt kia 29-12-15 RE p47 CR France922

MILLS,Norman Hope Vandeleur T2Lt kia 17-9-17 146MGC p184 CR Belgium24

MILLS,Percy Trevenson Capt kia 8-2-15 3 att1RWKent p141 CR Belgium98

MILLS,Robert Cecil Lloyd TLt ded 28-2-19 6Nhampt att54TMB p265 CR Norf195,3Bn

MILLS,Robert Henry TMaj kia 10-7-16 14RWFus p98 CR France397

MILLS,Robert Nicholas Fenwick Capt kia 21-9-17 RASC attRFC p19&253 CR France705,23-9-17

MILLS,Samuel T2Lt kia 18-11-16 2YLI p143 MR21

MILLS,Tenlon Lewis TCapt dow 5-8-15 2 att11Middx p147 CR France922,Teulon kia

MILLS,Thomas Arthur Reginald Lt kia 26-9-17 5N&D p232 MR30

MILLS,Thomas Henry Lewis TCapt kia 14-7-16 8EYorks p84 CR France399

MILLS,Tom Rethanan Lt kia 4-6-15 6Manch p236 MR4

MILLS,Trevor Blake T2Lt ded 24-5-17 PoW 13ESurr p113 MR21

MILLS,William Checkley 2Lt kia 23-7-16 3 att2Yorks p91 MR21

MILLS,William Edward 2Lt kia 8-8-16 1/4SLancs p230 MR21

MILLS,William Henry 2Lt kia 5-10-17 1 att12Glouc p107 MR30,4-10-17

MILLS,William John 2Lt dow 4-9-18 20NumbF att20RAF p62 CR France142

MILLS,William Longley 2Lt kia 9-5-17 RFA &45RFC p11&33 CR France1039

MILLS,William Robert Granville 2Lt kia 16-2-17 103RFA p33 CR Belgium127

MILLS,William Thomas Capt 25-10-15 RAMC p197 CR Eire475 &CR Ireland14

MILLWARD,Charles T2Lt kia 22-3-18 11Leic p88 MR20

MILLWOOD,Frederick James T2Lt kia 23-10-18 186RFA p33 CR France1196

MILLSON,Avlan Ewen ACapt kia 9-4-17 6RFus p69 CR France418,4Bn

MILLSON,Edgar George Butlin 2Lt kia 18-6-16 4Beds p86 CR France1182

MILM,George Gordon.MC.TCapt kia 22-4-18 16 att15Ches p96 CR France41

MILN,William Wallace TLt kia 24-5-18 26NumbF att4Beds p62 MR18

MILNE,Alexander Lt kia 18-9-16 14DLI p161 CR France374

MILNE,Alexander James Bolton Lt kia 22-8-17 4 att9GordH p241 CR Belgium101

MILNE,Alexander Nichol Capt kia 7-8-15 6Manch p236 MR4,Nicol

MILNE,Alexander Richard Capt kia 31-7-17 Herts p252 MR29

MILNE,Allan Smith 2Lt kia 26-6-17 5GordH p242 CR Belgium5

MILNE,Clifford T2Lt kia 14-5-18 LNLancs att4Bn p136 MR19,13-5-18

MILNE,David 2Lt kia 21-9-18 HuntsCycBn att10Ess p253 CR France212

MILNE,Donald Farrow TLt kia 5-11-17 20 att1Manch p155 MR38

MILNE,Douglas Thwaite Capt dow PoW 28-3-18 4 att7CamH p242 MR20

MILNE,Eric Sutcliffe 2Lt kia 28-10-17 att12/13NumbF p62 CR Belgium127,12Bn

MILNE,Esmond William Capt dow 12-8-17 RGA 5SB p207 CR Belgium18

MILNE,George Smith Mitchell TLt kia 14-10-17 8/10GordH p166 CR France545

MILNE,George William T2Lt dow 22-10-17 22RFA p33 CR Belgium19 23RFA

MILNE,Helen Sister ded 23-11-17 QAIMNS p200 MR65

MILNE,Herbert Wardlaw Capt kia 27-9-15 IA 74Punjabis att6CamH p280 MR28

MILNE,Irvine McKenzie T2Lt kia 31-8-17 1RScotF p95 CR France245

MILNE,J.Lt 29-9-18 4A&SH CR France666

MILNE,James Gordon Capt kia 8-8-17 5HLI p240 MR34,10-8-17

MILNE,James Robertson.MID Capt ded 30-10-18 GL p191 CR France146

MILNE,James William.MIDx2 LtCol ded 21-6-19 IA Cmdg82Punjabis p280 MR43

MILNE,John Archibald Dickie 2Lt kia 12-10-17 2/1ScotGds p52 CR Belgium12,11-10-17

MILNE,John Theobald.MC.MID Capt mbk 24-10-17 48RFC p256 MR20

MILNE,John Vincent Percy 2Lt kia 25-9-16 NumbF att10Bn p62 MR21

MILNE,Joseph Lt kia 29-9-18 4A&SH p173 CR France666

MILNE,Joseph Ellis.DSO.MID Capt kia 22-2-17 RAMC p254 CR Belgium11

MILNE,N.L.Mabel Sister dow 2-10-17 TFNS 58GH p254 CR France134

MILNE,Patrick George TCapt kia 22-4-18 RAMC att93FA p197 CR France24

MILNE,Sydney Septimus Brown.DCM.Lt ded 29-10-18 5BlkW attMGC Inf p187&271 CR Scot396,dow

MILNE,William 2Lt kia 27-9-15 1GordH p166 MR29

MILNE,William TCapt dow PoW 25-7-18 49MGC Inf p184 CR Germany2 Maj

MILNE,William.MC.CaptTMaj kld 13-4-17 NLancs &25RFC p11&136 MR20 CR Scot239

MILNE,William Charles Lt ded 29-10-17 IARO att121Pnrs p280 CR Iraq8

MILNE-HENDERSON,James Young.MID Lt kia 31-7-17 11HLI p163 MR29

MILNE-HENDERSON,John Milne 2Lt kia 28-1-18 11RFC p16 MR20

MILNE-HOME,David William LtCol ded 27-7-18 RGA p41&257 CR Scot563

MILNER,Archibald Berry T2Lt kia 4-11-18 24MGC Inf p184 CR France521

MILNER,Archibald Donald LtACapt kia 23-3-18 1 att9Ches p96 MR20

MILNER,G.F.CMG.DSO.BrigGen 20-6-21 1ResCav CR Yorks305 Ex1LifeGds 5&17Lancers

MILNER,John Lt kia 26-4-16 1Wing 10RFC p3 CR France345

MILNER,John Lewis 2Lt kia 9-5-17 62/8RFA p33 MR29 CR Belgium453

MILNER,Lawrence Frank Lt kia 25-9-15 9Lpool p216 MR19

MILNER,Roy Denzil Pashley 2Lt kia 20-9-14 2N&D p134 CR France1893

MILNER-MOORE,Douglas Owen Capt ded 23-4-18 IA RE attEAMilRlys p280 CR EAfrica47

MILNES,Sydney Herbert Capt kia 7-8-15 5LancF p221 MR4

MILROY,Alexander Anderson 2Lt dow 4-7-18 6 att3Lpool p215 CR France10

MILROY,Eric 2Lt kia 18-7-16 8BlkW p129 MR21

MILROY,Peter 2Lt kia 30-11-17 1KOSB p102 MR17

MILSOM,Sidney Lt kia 30-7-15 8RB p179 MR29

MILTON,Edward Thomas TCapt kia 26-9-15 13NumbF p62 MR19

MILTON,Ernest Edward Lt kia 23-1-17 RGA 113HB p41 CR France133,2Lt

MILTON,George Herbert 2Lt kia 25-10-16 21/2RFA p33 CR France515

MILTON,John Munro 2Lt kia 25-9-15 13NumbF p62 MR19

MILWARD,Etienne Geoffrey TCapt dow 2-9-16 7DCLI p114 CR France66

MILWARD,Philip Henry TCapt dow 7-12-15 7RB p179 CR Belgium11

MILWARD,Stanley Reginald 2Lt kia 11-8-16 35MGC p184 MR21

MILWAY,Edwin Horace T2Lt kia 8-10-18 10RFus p69 CR France1185,Capt

MIMS,Harold Dickman Lt kia 27-9-18 4Dors p229 CR France274

MINCER,Frank T2Lt kia 23-10-18l 32MGC p184

MINCHIN,Hubert Charles Loder Lt mbk 20-12-14 IA 125Rif p280 MR28

MINCHIN,William Smith.MC.CaptQM kia 20-4-18 11RFus p69 CR France300

MINNAAR,C.W.R.2Lt kia 16-11-16 3 att8ELancs CR France153

MINOGUE,John O'Brien.CMG.LtCol ded 26-10-16 3 att9WYorks p82

MINOR,Philip.MID Lt kld 29-5-18 5DLI p239 MR18,kia

MINOR,Ronald 2Lt kia 1-7-16 2RLancs p59 CR France156,Roland 3Bn

MINORS,Ronald Towers Capt kld 27-3-19 7Worc attRAF p256 CR Belgium265

MINOT,Laurence.MC.Capt kia 28-7-17 57RFC p11 CR Belgium140

MINNAAR,Charles William Rorich 2Lt kia 16-11-16 3 att8ELancs p111

MINSHALL,Thomas Charles Wynn Capt dow 25-3-18 4RWFus p223 CR France267,Wynne

MINSHUALL,A.M.Sister ScotWomensHosp 21-4-15 CR Europe57

MINSHULL,George Henry.MC.T2Lt kia 20-10-18 15WelshR p127 CR France230

MINSHULL,John Lewis.MID Capt kia 2-4-17 3Lond p245 CR France420

MINTER,Charles Biron Capt ded 27-6-15 4/7Mddx p271 CR Mddx26

MINTER,F.2Lt kia 23-10-18 32MGC Inf CR France1266

MINTO,William Blair Griffiths.TD.dedacc 2-7-19 RGA p271 CR Scot280,Bain Ex 151SB

MINTOFT,Henry Stephen 2Lt kia 4-10-17 3EYorks p84 CR Belgium152

MINTY,George Capt kia 23-11-17 5GordH p242 CR France1498,6Bn

MINTY,Reginald T2Lt kia 22-5-18 RB att3Bn C'Coy p179 CR France81

MIRFIN,Joseph Colin T2Lt dow 17-8-17 6Y&L p159 CR Yorks543

MISELL,William 2Lt kia 20-10-18 ScotRif att10Bn p103 CR Belgium423

MISKIN,Maurice James.MC.TLtACapt kia 17-10-18 1TankCps p188 CR France660,Maj

MISSEN,Edward Roland Cecil 2Lt kia 4-10-18 2Lond B'Coy p245 CR France647

MISQUITH,Joan Charles 2Lt dow 4-2-17 A/102RFA p33 CR Belgium11,Juan Carlos

MITCHEL,Frederick David Capt dow 24-11-17 10RIrFus p280 CR France512

MITCHELL,Alexander Charles Oswald.MID Lt kia 30-4-17 att4SWBord B'Coy BrecknockBn p223 MR38

MITCHELL,Alexander Goble Lt kld 30-5-18 6 att4Middx p147 CR France84,4 att6Bn

MITCHELL,Andrew 2Lt dow 2-8-17 2Leinst p174 CR Belgium11

MITCHELL,Andrew Neill Lt kia 30-12-15 5RScotF p222 CR Gallipoli6

MITCHELL,Archibald 2Lt kia 25-4-18 4RScots p211 MR30

MITCHELL,Archibald McKerrow.MC.2Lt kia 6-7-17 1/23Lond p252 CR Belgium118

MITCHELL,Arthur Gorman 2Lt kia 13-5-16 5 att2RIrRif p170 CR France68

MITCHELL,Bertram Earnshaw T2Lt ded 4-2-17 12 att7ELancs p111 CR France40

MITCHELL,Charles Douglas 2Lt dow 26-3-18 4 att2HLI p163 CR France62

MITCHELL,Charles Henry 2Lt kia 3/4-9-16 1/6WYorks A'Coy p218 CR France383,3-9-16

MITCHELL,Charles Johnstone.DSO.Maj ded 16-10-18 O&BLI p130 CR Sussex183,16-11-18

MITCHELL,Charles Richard Gerald Lt kia 1-4-18 6DragGds p21 MR27

MITCHELL,Charles Wand Chap4Cl dow 3-5-17 RAChDept att8EYorks p199 CR France1182

MITCHELL,Clement Alexander TCapt kia 13-10-16 13Lpool p72 CR France156,14-10-16

MITCHELL,Edward Noel TLt kia 15-2-16 8Beds p86 CR Belgium92

MITCHELL,E.P.H.2Lt kld 7-5-18 BordR &RAF p117 CR Egypt9

MITCHELL,Eric Arthur 2Lt kia 27-10-14 2SLancs p125 MR22

MITCHELL,Eric Harrison TCapt kia 29-4-16 RA attRFC p3&33,Erik

MITCHELL,Francis James 2Lt kia 27-9-18 4RScots p211 CR France437

MITCHELL,Francis Sidney TLt kia 15-2-16 RAMC att9RSuss p197 CR Belgium72

MITCHELL,Frank 2Lt kia 12-5-17 50MGC p184 MR20

MITCHELL,Frank Warley 2Lt kia 7-6-18 2Manch p155 MR20

MITCHELL,Frank Kinniburgh 2Lt kia 8-5-18 8ScotRif p225 MR30

MITCHELL,Frederick McLellan.MC.LtACapt kia 2-5-18 18Huss attWorcYeo p23 CR Palestine3

MITCHELL,George 2Lt kld 22-7-15 3 att1BlkW p129 CR France109,dedacc

MITCHELL,George 2Lt kia 1-2-17 IA 45Sikhs p280 CR Iraq5

MITCHELL,George Alan Capt ded 29-11-19 RAMC p267 CR Asia51

MITCHELL,George Clarkstone 2Lt kia 21-3-18 3 att2N&D p134 MR20

MITCHELL,George Henry 23784 Lt kia 22-8-17 11A&SH p173 MR30,Capt

MITCHELL,George James T2Lt kia 19-7-16 11Dev att2/6Glouc p77 MR19

MITCHELL,Gordon T2Lt dow 17-8-17 RE 96FC p47 CR Belgium23

MITCHELL,Guy Spencer Tmaj kia 15-5-17 3 att11Lpool p72 CR France581

MITCHELL,Harry 2Lt dow 28-9-18 7Manch p237 CR France214

MITCHELL,Henry 2Lt dow 3-4-18 11EYorks p84 CR France102

MITCHELL,Henry Harrison TLt dow 23-2-16 11ELancs p111 CR Egypt7

MITCHELL,Henry Theophilus Kelly Lt kld 12-11-15 1RSuss p119 MR43,11-11-15

MITCHELL,Henry William 2Lt kia 22-1-17 5 att4DCLI p227 CR Palestine3,Lt

MITCHELL,Herbert Stanley Lt kia 21-3-18 4RWKent p234 MR27

MITCHELL,James T2Lt kia 26-4-16 GL &RFC p3&191

MITCHELL,James 2Lt 19-10-18 7 att13BlkW CR France982

MITCHELL,James 2Lt ded PoW 23-10-18 7BlkW p231

MITCHELL,James Alexander 2Lt kia 15-3-17 5BordR p228 CR France513

MITCHELL,James Arthur 2Lt kia 27-9-18 6NumbF p214 CR France439

MITCHELL,James Campbell Lt kia 13-1-16 IARO att56Rif p280 MR38

MITCHELL,James Douglas TLt ded 9-10-18 GL &KAR p191

MITCHELL,James Lawson Maj kia 16-3-16 24RFA p33 CR Belgium4

MITCHELL,James Marshall Lt kia 22-3-18 HLI att2Bn p163 MR20

MITCHELL,James Porter T2Lt dow 29-9-18 16HLI p163 CR France528

MITCHELL,James Thornburn ACapt dedacc 16-3-17 10 att7Leic p88 CR France80

MITCHELL,James Thomas Rankin.DSO.TMajALtCol dow 1-4-18 13RScots attA&SH p54 CR Scot808

MITCHELL,J.H Capt 26-10-17 7RScots p211 CR Belgium18

MITCHELL,John 2Lt dow 3-4-18 7ScotRif att25RAF p224&258 CR France52,Lt

MITCHELL,John Brine.MC.Capt kia 15-9-15 8Lond p247 CR France432

MITCHELL,John Halliburton Capt dow 26-10-17 7RScots p211

MITCHELL,John Harris 2Lt mbk 1-2-17 IARO 36Sikhs p280 CR Iraq5

MITCHELL,John Horsley 2Lt kia 19-5-17 RGA 305SB p41 CR Belgium138,Lt

MITCHELL,John Innes Lt ded 9-7-18 RGA p271 CR Scot60

MITCHELL,John Leischman 2Lt dow 4-6-17 18Lond p250 CR France52

MITCHELL,John Marshall TLt kia 9-5-17 11ScotRif p103 MR37

MITCHELL,John McGeorge 2Lt kia 25-9-15 5 O&BLI p130 MR29

MITCHELL,John Monfries Capt kld 22-5-15 7RScots p211 CR Scot249

MITCHELL,John Patrick Cameron 2Lt kia 21-4-17 4HLI &16RFC p11&163

MITCHELL,Joseph Spencer 2Lt dow 5-10-16 70RFC p3 CR France169,dedacc

MITCHELL,Julian Alan Spencer Capt dow 28-9-14 3KSLI p145 CR France1110

MITCHELL,Lawrence Adams.MC.LtTCapt kia 22-10-18 D123RFA p33 CR France287

MITCHELL,Leslie James T2Lt kld 22-12-17 GL &RFC p11

MITCHELL,Lewis Medcalfe 2Lt kia 11-8-18 1/5WYorks p218 CR Belgium188

MITCHELL,Norman R.Lt ded 6-6-18 RScot &RAF p54

MITCHELL,Norman Reid T2Lt kia 5-12-17 KRRC att20Bn p151 CR France1488

MITCHELL,Patrick James T2Lt dow 17-8-17 RE 83FC p47 CR Belgium16

MITCHELL,Percy Maschwitz Lt kia 6-11-17 1/1Herts p252 CR Palestine1

MITCHELL,Peter,Harper.MC.dow 14-9-17 1/4GordH p242 CR Belgium18

MITCHELL,Robert Clapperton T2Lt dow 26-7-18 7CamH p168 CR France1225,27-7-18

MITCHELL,Robert Thomas Lamont.MC.Lt ded PoW 29-11-18 4GordH p241 CR Belgium320

MITCHELL,Robert William Page T2Lt dow 10-10-17 16Middx p147 CR Belgium16

MITCHELL,Robert William Hamilton Capt ded 9-5-17 RoO 3 att2RInnisF p105 MR21 CR Ireland196

MITCHELL,Ronald Walter Lt dow 19-11-17 EKentYeo p204 CR Egypt7 10EKent

MITCHELL,Terence Hargreaves 2Lt dow 6-11-16 2/5DCLI att145MGC 48Div p187&227 CR France703,kia 5-11-16

MITCHELL,Thomas Maj dow 12-4-17 1Suss att8Ches p119 CR Iraq8

MITCHELL,Thomas T2Lt ded 4-11-18 14NumbF attGHQ LewisGSch p62 CR France40

MITCHELL,Thomas Frederick.MC.2Lt dow 4-10-18 5 att8N&D p233 CR France446

MITCHELL,Thomas Hume T2Lt dow 16-4-18 66MGC p184 CR France145

MITCHELL,Thomas James T2Lt kia 10-7-16 11Yorks p91 MR21

MITCHELL,Tom Illingworth CaptAMaj dow 12-4-18 16Middx p147 CR France40,13Yorks

MITCHELL,Walter Victor 2Lt kia 27-11-15 3Beds attTMB p86 MR19

MITCHELL,William 2Lt kia 28-4-17 25NumbF p62 MR20

MITCHELL,William TLt kia 24-3-18 RE 41DivSigCo p47 MR20

MITCHELL,William George 2Lt kld 23-3-18 RFC p16 CR Surrey6

MITCHELL,William Henry T2Lt kia 1-11-18 61MGC Inf p184 CR France290

MITCHELL,William Henry Lister 2Lt kia 20-9-17 5Lond p246 MR29

MITCHELL,William Holford Lt drd 15-4-17 4ESurr p113 MR35

MITCHELL-INNES,Gilbert Robert Lt dow 13-5-15 19Huss p23 CR Belgium4

MITCHELSON,George Stanley Lt 25-1-20 SLancs CR Ches3

MITCHISON,Malcolm Lt ded 4-11-18 13Lond p249

MITCHISON,William Anthony Lt kia 20-9-17 RE 19DivSigCo p47 CR Belgium124

MITCHLEY,Sydney Robert T2Lt kia 12-10-16 10 att7Norf p74 MR21

MITFORD,Hon Clement Bertram Ogilvy,DSO Maj kia 13-5-15 10Huss p22 CR Belgium4

MITTON,Harold Lt kia 29-7-17 RFA &10RFC p11 CR France98

MITTON,Thomas Ewart TLt kld 24-12-17 RE GHQ Sig p47 CR Belgium20

MOAKES,John Curtis TLt kia 5-9-16 RE 155FC p47 MR21

MOBBERLEY,Lionel Westwood.MC.Lt kia 11-9-16 24Lond p252 CR France453

MOBBS,Edgar Roberts.DSO.TLtCol kia 31-7-17 7Nhants p137 MR29

MOBBS,Edward Thomas 2Lt kia 7-5-17 1ESurr p113 MR20

MOBERLY,Henry Stuart Lt kia 25-9-15 IA 74Punjabis att69 p280 MR28

MOCATTA,F.E.Capt 26-8-19 RFA &RFC CR Mddx27

MOCATTA,Robert Menzies 2Lt kia 10-8-15 1/5RWFus p223 MR4

MOCKFORD,Joseph 2Lt dow 8-4-17 1Lond p245 CR France120

MOCKLER,Francis George Ross.MC.MID Capt kia 1-7-16 2RIrReg attMGC p89&184 MR21

MOCKLER-FERRYMAN,Hugh Lt kia 16-9-14 2 O&BLI p130 CR France1111

MOCKRIDGE,George Ewart Lt kia 1-7-16 64MGC p184 MR21

MOFFAT,Hugh Francis Baillie.MC.T2LtACapt dow 27-9-18 8RLancs p59 CR France756

MOFFAT,John Alexander T2Lt dow 11-8-18 RE 69FC p47 CR France69

MOFFAT,John Everard 2Lt kia 9-4-18 10Lpool p216 MR19

MOFFATT,Archibald Shirving Woolery LtCol kia 16-5-15 2BordR p117 MR22

MOFFATT,Cecil Henry T2Lt dow 1-8-16 2/5LancF p93 CR France66

MOFFATT,Durward Forbes 2Lt kia 30-11-17 7ESurr p113 MR17

MOFFATT,Edmund Craig Forbes Capt dow 30-5-17 8N&D p233 CR France446

MOFFATT,James Robert Capt kia 15-2-15 1Leinst p174 MR29

MOFFATT,Stanley L.T2Lt dow 13-8-16 2LancF p93 CR France630

MOFFETT,John Leeson 2Lt kia 11-3-15 RScotF p95 CR France279,10-3-15

MOFFITT,James Prior.MC.Capt kia 3-12-17 1 att14DLI p161 MR17

MOGGRIDGE,Charles Francis Blayney Lt kia 10-4-18 IARO att2/3GurkhaRif p280 MR34

MOGRIDGE,Basil Fullelove West 2Lt kia 13-10-15 4Leic p220 MR19

MOGRIDGE,Lewis 2Lt kia 12-4-18 8Lpool att5RAF p216&258 CR France95,Lt

MOHAN,Harry Deacon Capt kia 11-4-16 10RLancs p59 MR38

MOHAN,Thomas TCapt kia 23-3-18 RAMC att10SHosp p197 CR France134

MOIR,Archibald Gifford.MID Lt kia 26-4-15 7A&SH p243 CR Belgium167,25-4-15

MOIR,Douglas.MC.Lt dow 22-7-18 7CamH att1/2KAR p168&202 CR EAfrica90,kia

MOIR,Douglas Dana Drew Kinnaird 2Lt kia 23-7-16 2Yorks p91 MR21

MOIR,G.Capt 10-6-19 IARO att94Inf MR65

MOIR,George Andrew Christie Capt kia 7-4-17 5GordH p242 CR France15

MOIR,James McMurchy T2Lt kia 25-9-15 1BlkW p129 CR France115

MOIR,John Andrew Alexander 2Lt kia 16-6-15 2A&SH p173 CR France82

MOIR,John Elliot Maj ded 26-1-17 IA 10Lancers attStaff6CavBde p280 CR Iraq6

MOIR,Reginald Lt ded 9-11-15 RE SR p47 CR Surrey160

MOIR,Robert Bruce Oliphant 2Lt kia 9-4-17 3HLI att2DLI p163 MR19

MOIR-BYERS James Sandilands Lt ded 28-9-15 1/3ScotHorse p271 CR Numb4

MOKE-NORRIE,Geo Stuart Lt kia 7-10-16 3 att6EKent p57 CR France307

MOLAY,W.F.MSM.MID Lt 9-4-21 RASC CR Wilts115

MOLE,Harold Pearce 2Lt kia 3-9-16 11RSuss p119 MR21

MOLE,William.MID 2Lt dow 28-8-17 10DLI p161 CR Belgium18

MOLESWORTH,Charles Willoughby Murray.Hon.2Lt dow 15-4-17 1DCLI p114 CR France81,Lt

MOLESWORTH,Ernest Kerr Maj kld 31-1-15 RE att2S&M p47 CR France1169,31-12-14

MOLINEUX,Albert Ward Spencer 2Lt kld 28-7-16 RFC p3 CR Staffs78,MOLINEAUX

MOLINEUX,George King LtTCapt kia 5-5-17 2NumbF p62 MR29

MOLL,Albert Donald Campbell TLt kia 25-9-15 10ScotRif p103 MR19

MOLL,John Arnold Lt dow 21-9-19 RFA p255 CR Mddx26

MOLL,Tobias Mortimer T2Lt kia 15-7-16 9Leic p88 CR France207

MOLLARD,Alfred Edward.DCM.2Lt ded 7-11-18 10TankCps p188 CR Lancs34

MOLLETT,Frederick Norman Lt kia 18-7-18 9Hamps &107RAF p271 CR France1107

MOLLISON,William Allan Lt dow 1-10-18 2/6WRid att52MGC p227&187 CR France34

MULLMAN,Herbert Bernard ACapt kia 1-2-17 4 att2Leinst p174 CR France149

MOLLOY,Brian Charles Baskerville Capt kia 1-11-14 OxfHuss p205 MR29

MOLLOY,Henry Edward 2Lt kia 22-8-17 O&BLI 1/1BucksBn p231 MR30

MOLLOY,Joseph Geale.MC.T2Lt kia 2-9-18 1Norf p74 CR FRance512

MOLLOY,Michael Vallanery 2Lt kia 9-8-15 2N&D p134 MR29,Vallancey

MOLLOY,Wilfred Cyril 2Lt dow 10-5-18 PoW 16RScots p54 CR Germany3

MOLONEY,Bertram Weldon Capt kia 28-2-15 1ELancs p111 CR Belgium68

MOLONEY,Frank T2Lt kia 9-4-18 RB att6SomLI p179 CR Palestine9,att1/5Bn

MOLONY,Charles Albert TCapt kia 14-7-16 13Lpool p72 MR21

MOLSON,Eric Elsdale Lt kia 2-4-15 3RScots p54 CR Belgium104,1-4-15

MOLYNEUX,Benjamin,MC Lt dow 8-11-18 3 att11Ches p96 CR France332 att9Bn

MOLYNEUX,Eric Seymour.MID ACapt kia 30-11-17 Worc attIIICpsCycBn p109 CR France439

MOLYNEUX,Ian Moore Lt dow 10-7-18 1/7RScots p211 CR France95

MOLYNEUX,James Herbert 2Lt kia 16-8-17 12KRRC p151 MR30

MOLYNEUX-MONTGOMERIE,George Frederick Maj 22-10-15 3GrenGds CR France423

MOLYNEUX-SEEL,Edmund Harrington Maj ded 6-8-15 SL Lpool p201&268 CR Lancs152,5-8-15

MOLYNEUX-SEEL,Louis Edmund Harington Capt dow 6-1-15 BordR p117 CR Belgium140

MOMBER,Edward Marie Felin.DSO.MC.Capt dow 20-6-17 RE 177TC p47 CR Belgium11,Maj

MONAGHAN,Denis Laurence Capt kia 24-11-17 1TankCps p188 MR17

MONAT-BIGGS,Eric 2Lt kia 3-5-16 2Lincs p75

MONCK,Charles Henry Stanley.Hon.Capt kia 21-10-14 3CldGds p51 CR Belgium115

MONCKTON,Christopher 2Lt kia 1-7-16 RIrF &RFC p3&171 CR France839

MONCKTON,Francis Algernon Lt kia 8-11-14 1ScotGds p52 MR29

MONCKTON,Geoffrey Valentine Francis Lt kia 25-1-15 1ScotGds p52 MR22

MONCKTON,Marmaduke Henry Lt kia 9-7-15 RGA att8RFC p1&41 CR France285

MONCRIEFF,Charles George Conradi T2Lt dow 24-11-16 9 att12EYorks p84 CR France52

MONCUR,James Melville 2Lt kia 17-4-17 8RScots p212 CR France1182

MONCUR,William George T2Lt dow PoW 25-12-17 11RScots p54 CR France660

MOND,Francis Leopold Capt kia 15-5-18 RFA attRAF p207&258

MONDAY,Joseph Cyril 2Lt kia 3-5-17 3 att8BlkW p129 CR France1190

MONEY,Charles Arthur Gilbert Maj kia 13-12-16 IA 130Baluchis att129 p280 CR EAfrica38 &CR Tanzania1

MONEY,Duncan Goff 2Lt kia 16-2-18 4RFC p16 CR France525

MONEY,Eric William Lt kia 11-4-17 ACycCps attMGC HB D'Bn p181&183 MR20 1-4-17 TankCps

MONEY,George Russell 2Lt kia 1-7-16 4Middx p147 CR France267

MONEY,Gerald Hugh Kyrle 2Lt kia 27-7-16 18DLI p161 CR France631

MONEY,Henry Ironside.MID Capt kia 20-12-14 IA 1/1GurkhaRif p280 MR28

MONEY,Noel Campbell Kyrle Capt dow 6-9-15 IA 22Punjabis att5ConnRgrs p280 CR Europe1,Maj

MONEY,Roy Granville Kyrle 2Lt kia 9-4-17 3EKent p58 CRFrance531,Capt

MONIE,Roy Douglas John TLt kia 18-4-17 282RFA p33 CR France558

MONILAWS,Selwyn Macgeorge Lt kia 12-8-18 8RScots att12RScotFp211 CR France19

MONK,Alan Lt kia 26-10-17 att8Dev p77 MR30

MONK,Charles LtCol ded 11-7-16 RAMC p271

MONK,Ernest William Capt kia 29-3-18 1/4Lond attRFC p19&246 CR France167

MONK,George Bertram 2Lt kia 18-12-14 2RWar p65 MR32

MONK,Gerald Patrick Baillow Capt kia 3-10-15 1WelshR p127 CR France423,de Baillou

MONK,J.M.DSO.MC.Maj 24-10-20 Worc attEgyptArmy CR EAfrica116

MONKHOUSE,Alfred Ernest T2Lt kia 1-7-16 11BordR p117 MR21

MONKHOUSE,John Arthur Lt&QM ded 23-1-17 RAMC p254 CR Lond1

MONKHOUSE,Joseph Thompson Capt kia 27-4-15 6DLI p239 MR29

MONKHOUSE,Robert Alexander 2Lt kia 9/11-4-17 6GordH p242 CR France265

MONKMAN,Fred Kerbey T2Lt dow 28-9-17 26RFus p69 CR Belgium11

MONKS,Charles Phatean Lt kia 17-6-15 RH&FA p33 CR Belgium4,Phetean

MONKS,D.E.Maj 11-12-18 RlySurSiestanBengal NWRly MR61

MONREAL,George TMajALtCol dow 11-4-18 Res att6Wilts p153 CR Belgium183

MONRO,Harold Oswald 2Lt dow 21-5-17 9HLI p240 CR France214

MONRO,Kenneth Edward Lt dow 14-5-15 3 att1Nhants p137 CR France102

MONSELL,Henry Heacock Lt ded 3-12-19 1GarrBn RlrRif p265 CR Lond12

MONSON,Cyril Archibald 2Lt kia 18-5-15 Wilts p153 MR22

MONSON,Edward Charles Sutton.MC.Lt dow 15-6-18 A321RFA p33 CR France10 A331RFA

MONSON,William Herbert.MC.TCapt dow 7-9-16 8DubF p177 CR France66,kia

MONTAGU,Walter Philip Rev 31-10-18 RAChDept att22RGA CR France332

MONTAGUE,Albert Cecil 2Lt kia 16-6-17 117MGC p184 MR29

MONTAGUE,Felix David Lt kia 10/16-3-15 2Lincs p75 CR France525,10-3-15

MONTAGUE,Paul Denys Lt kia 29-10-17 20RB attRFC p19&243 MR37

MONTAGUE,Reginald Marcus Henry Cruise 2Lt kia 8-5-17 3EKent att8SWBord p100 CR Greece6

MONTAGUE,Richard Headley Lt kld 21-9-17 8Hamp p229 MR30,MONTAGU

MONTAGUE,Walter Philip Rev dow 31-10-18 RAChDept att22RGA p199

MONTAGUE-WILLIAMS,Edward Emanuel Lt 10-12-17 RGA 188SB CR Belgium19

MONTAGUE-WILLIAMS,Samuel Roger Thomas Aubon 2Lt dow 25-10-15 EKentYeo p204

MONTEITH,George Michael Capt kia 25-9-15 3 att1GordH p166 MR29

MONTEITH,Henry John Joseph Laurence Maj kia 27-12-15 LanarkYeo p204 CR Gallipoli3

MONTEITH,John Cassels TLtCol kia 1-10-15 2Beds p86 CR France423

MONTEITH,Matthew Rankin 2Lt kia 15-7-16 RE 64FC p47 CR France1890,16-7-16

MONTEITH,Patrick Rankin T2Lt dow 13-11-16 13 att2A&SH p173 CR France40

MONTEITH,Robert John Chap4Cl dow 27-11-17 RAChDept att70ArmyFldArtlyBde p199 CR France711

MONTEITH,William Albert Robertson 2Lt dow 2-9-18 2SfthH p165 CR France14

MONTEITH,William Neve Lt kia 25-9-15 6 att2RB p179 MR32

MONTESOLE,Eric Alfred T2Lt kia 4-3-16 7RSuss p119 MR19

MONTESOLE,Herbert Sarip Roy Lt kia 16/17-5-15 RSuss attBeds p119 CR France279,Sarif 17-5-15 att2Yorks

MONTFORD,Alfred Charles 2Lt kia 3-5-17 208MGC p184 MR20

MONTFORD,Douglas Raymond.MID Capt mbk 30-3-18 IA 98Inf att58Rif p280 MR34

MONTGOMERIE,George Frederick Molyneux Maj kia 22-10-15 GrenGdsResOff att3Bn p50

MONTGOMERIE,Robert 2Lt kia 1-10-18 5RScotsF p222 MR16

MONTGOMERIE,William Graham Capt dow 20-10-14 2Leinst p174 CR France922

MONTGOMERIE-FLEMING,James Brown TMaj dow 18-8-17 6EYorks p84 CR Belgium16

MONTGOMERY,Albert Barr.MID Capt dow 17-8-17 1/7Worc p225 CR Belgium8

MONTGOMERY,Andrew Graham 2Lt kia 6-9-18 3CamH att1/5SfthH p168 MR16

MONTGOMERY,Arnulf 2Lt kia 22-12-14 3 att2ConnRgrs p172 MR22

MONTGOMERY,Arthur Samuel TLt ded 21-6-16 5RInnisF p105 CR Greece7

MONTGOMERY,Edward Henry 2Lt kia 16-10-16 RFA X9TMB p33 CR France385 &CR France1890

MONTGOMERY,Frederick Alexander T2Lt kia 19-10-16 6KOSB p102 MR21

MONTGOMERY,George T2Lt dow 14-10-17 116MGC p184 CR Belgium132

MONTGOMERY,George Edward Capt kia 22-8-15 5Dors p124 MR4

MONTGOMERY,Hugh Lt kia 13-9-16 1IrGds p53 CR France374

MONTGOMERY,Hugh Bertram Capt kia 9-8-16 10Lpool p216 MR21

MONTGOMERY,Ignatius Diego 2Lt dow 8-11-17 7Lond att4DCLI p247 CR Palestine2

MONTGOMERY,Matthew 2Lt kia 20-7-18 5SfthH p241 CR France1697

MONTGOMERY,Norman Stevenson 2Lt kia 17-6-16 2CldGds p51 CR Belgium73

MONTGOMERY,Ralph Noel Vernon.DSO.Lt ded 1-4-19 D88RFA p33 CR France63,Maj

MONTGOMERY,Raymond Capt kia 25/29-9-15 RAMC p197

MONTGOMERY,Robert Capt 25/29-9-15 RAMC att1Glouc MR19

MONTGOMERY,Robert Taylor 2Lt kia 1-7-16 9RIrF p171 MR21

MONTGOMERY,William Sproat Capt dow 13-3-15 6Lpool p215 CR Belgium59

MONTRESOR,Ernest Henry LtCol kia 14-9-14 RSuss p119 MR15

MONTROSE-EKIN,Leslie.MC.2Lt kia 1-7-16 8Y&rL p159

MONYPENNY,Phillips Burnley Sterndale Gybbon.MC.Lt kia 28-6-18 3 att1RWKent p141&258 CR France20

MONYPENY,John Randolph Lt 22-6-20 LNLancs CR Kent61

MOODIE,Douglas Cameron 2Lt dow 15-3-17 1/4YLI p235 CR France345

MOODIE,Harry Morton 2Lt kld 16-9-18 9SfthH &RAF p165 CR France1359

MOODIE,John 2Lt dow 27-8-17 8SfthH p165

MOODIE,John Tully 2Lt dow 27-8-17 8SfthH CR France102

MOODIE,Ralph Wilson Capt kia 17-5-17 6 att1/5GordH p242 MR20

MOODY,Ambrose Capt kia 22-8-15 5Dors p124 MR4

MOODY,Charles Angelo 2Lt kia 21-8-17 GL &1RFC p11 CR Belgium125

MOODY,Henry Fred 2Lt kia 5-4-18 8Lincs p75 CR France798

MOODY,Leonard Leighton T2Lt kia 30-6-16 12RSuss p119 MR19

MOODY,Rowland Harry Mainwaring Capt kia ?-8-14 2LancF p93 MR15

MOODY,Thomas 2Lt kia 1-7-16 1/4Lond p246 MR21

MOODY,Thomas Lewis Vyvian 2Lt kia 21-3-18 1EKent p58 MR20

MOODY-WARD,Richard Guy Torrington Capt kia 9-5-15 2RBerks p139 MR32

MOOLMAN,L.J.H.Capt 21-11-18 EAfrIntelDept CR EAfrica36

MOON,Alfred Edward Capt ded 7-6-18 2RIrRif p171 CR Greece7

MOON,Basil Oliver.MID 2Lt kia 24-5-15 8Lond p247 CR France261

MOON,Clifford Abraham 2Lt kia 22-3-18 YLI att9Bn p143 MR27

MOON,Leonard James TLt ded 23-11-16 10Dev p77 CR Greece6

MOON,Roy Agnew.MC.TLt dow 28-4-18 61MGC p184 CR France145,27-4-18

MOON,Wilfrid James 2Lt kia 17-8-15 3Worc p109 CR Belgium91,Lt 19-8-15

MOON-ORD,Charles Denton 2Lt ded 1-12-16 7DLI p239 CR Durham28,dow 2-12-16

MOONEY,David George T2Lt kia 16-8-17 9DubF p177 CR Belgium45

MOONEY,Francis 2Lt kia 28-2-17 1RDubF p177 MR21

MOONEY,Reginald Herbert T2Lt dow 5-5-17 1Hamps p121 CR France95

MOOR,Christopher 2Lt kia 6-8-15 2Hamps p121 MR4

MOOR,Edward Lewis T2Lt dow 27-1-17 13 att9RWar p65 CR Iraq5

MOOR,George Raymond Dallas.VC.MC&Bar.Lt ded 3-11-18 2Hamps att30DivHQ p121 CR France276

MOOR-RAFORD,Leslie Claude Lt dow 26-10-14 1SStaffs p122 MR29

MOORAT,Francis Ferrers LtACapt dow 23-8-18 6 att4Middx p147 CR France745

MOORCOCK,Frederick Arthur 2Lt kia 3-5-17 YLI att2/5Bn p143 MR20

MOORCROFT,Alfred 2Lt ded 6-11-18 4SStaffs p122 CR Staffs78

MOORCROFT,Richard Lt ded 15-1-21 IA 57Rif p280 MR43 &CR Pakistan50A

MOORE,Alfred Arnold Lt kia 22-10-17 23Manch p155 MR30

MOORE,Albert James T2Lt kld 11-11-17 GL &RFC p11 CR Scot398

MOORE,Albert Reginald 2Lt kia 12-4-17 2/8WYorks p219 CR France568

MOORE,Alexander Holland TLt kia 26-3-18 5SWBord p100 MR20

MOORE,Andrew Douglas T2Lt kia 21-3-18 11Ess p132 MR20

MOORE,Archibald 2Lt kia 26-3-18 13 att22RIrRif p170 MR27

MOORE,Arthur Robert.MC.Capt ded PoW 1-7-16 1/4Lond p246 MR21

MOORE,Athelstan.DSO.MajBtLtCol dow 14-10-18 1DubF p177 CR Belgium84

MOORE,Beaufoi John Warwick Montressor,MC LtTCapt kia 10-6-17 RFC p11 CR Hamps4

MOORE,Brian Ponsonby Fitzgerald Lt dow 9-2-16 IA 62Punjabis p280 MR65,Capt

MOORE,C.2Lt 9-4-17 1/5SfthH CR France15

MOORE,Charles Arthur George 2Lt kia 19-4-18 5N&D p233 CR Belgium102

MOORE,Charles Francis Fitzgerald.MC.Capt 18-2-19 1/123OutramsRif att234Bde HQ CR Egypt2

MOORE,Charles Frederick 2Lt kia 12-3-15 3Worc p109 CR Belgium17

MOORE,Charles Ronald 2Lt 8-3-18 59RFC CR France518

MOORE,Claude Leighton 2Lt kia 26-8-18 7Lond p247 CR France164

MOORE,Clement,Selby Capt kia 19-7-20 IA 1/8 att1/10GurkhaRif p280 CR Iraq6

MOORE,Clifford 2Lt kia 9-4-17 5SfthH p241

MOORE,Clive Goulding Lt kia 15-8-17 GL &43RFC p11 MR20

MOORE,Cuthbert Alex 2Lt ded 25-9-17 14YLI attRFC p11 MR40,Alec

MOORE,Dacre William TLt kia 11-6-16 MGC Inf p184 CR France702

MOORE,Douglas Lewis Lt kia 22-4-18 1SomLI p80 CR France98

MOORE,Douglas Owen Milner Capt ded 23-4-18 RE attRailwayCps p47

MOORE,Edgar Noel.MC.Chap4Cl kld 5-1-18 RAChDept att20Lpool p199 CR Belgium127

MOORE,Edward Hayden.MC.Lt dow 25-4-17 2Y&L p159 CR France80,Capt

MOORE,Edward Kermish 2Lt dow 25-4-18 8Manch p237 CR France119,Kerruish Lt kia 9Bn

MOORE,Edward Patrick Aylett.MC.2Lt kia 4-11-18 1CldGds p51 CR France1080

MOORE,Ernest Francis Courtney.MC.2Lt kia 24-3-18 5RB p179 MR27

MOORE,Ernest Leonard 2Lt ded 4-7-16 2/4Glouc p225 CR France345

MOORE,Francis Hirst 2Lt kia 7-10-16 7YLI p143 CR France307

MOORE,Francis William.MC.MID TCapt dow 26-4-17 13/10Dev p77 CR Greece1

MOORE,Frederick T2Lt kia 3-7-17 GL &4RFC p11 CR Belgium11

MOORE,Frederick Harry Bedloe 2Lt kia 4-11-18 9Lond p248 CR France939

MOORE,Frederick Henry 2LtTCapt ded 17-5-17 RGA attRAOC p41 CR France46

MOORE,G.B.MC.Capt kld 7-4-18 GL &RAF p191 MR20

MOORE,Geoffrey William Broadbent Lt kia 14-10-18 2Leinst p174 CR Belgium157

MOORE,George Adams 2Lt dow 6-11-17 4Leinst p174 CR France446

MOORE,George Alexander 2Lt kia 2-5-18 14RWar p65 MR32 Ex 28Lond

MOORE,George H.J LtCol 14-3-21 9BhopalInf CR SAfrica26

MOORE,George William 2Lt kia 28-3-18 RGA 288SB p41 CR France729

MOORE,Gerald Alexander Clifford Lt dow 11-7-15 8ScotRif p225 CR Europe1

MOORE,Gerald Francis Hamilton 2Lt ded 12-8-17 3 att9BordR p264 CR Greece6

MOORE,Gillachrist 2Lt kia 7-11-14 2RSuss p119 MR29

MOORE,Harold Thomas Pelham.MC.Lt kia 4-11-18 210RH&FA p33 CR France1081

MOORE,Henry T2Lt kia 15-7-16 3 att2WelshR p127 MR21

MOORE,Henry.DSO.MC.TCaptALtCol dow 30-5-18 RAMC att16FA p197 CR France64

MOORE,Henry Geoffrey Hamilton 2Lt kia 19-5-15 RIrReg p89 MR22,20-10-14

MOORE,Henry Glanville Allen.MID LtCol kia 11-8-15 6EYorks p84 CR Gallipoli5,9-8-15

MOORE,Hugh Stirling 2Lt kia 1-10-17 7N&D p233 MR30

MOORE,Hugh Victor 2Lt kia 22-3-18 4ConnRgrs att48TMB p172 CR France365,21-3-18 Ex BlkW

MOORE,J.A.S.Capt 7-6-18 NyassaFF CR EAfrica90

MOORE,James George.MM.MID Lt 5-7-18 2RB attRAF CR Durham27

MOORE,James Voaden T2Lt kia 2-12-17 6 O&BLI p130 MR17

MOORE,John 2LtACapt kia 26-10-17 3 att2BordR p117 MR30

MOORE,John Aubrey T2Lt kia 7/11-8-15 7SStaff p122 MR4

MOORE,John Clark 2Lt kia 19-4-17 4KOSB p224 MR34

MOORE,John Clifford Dawson 2Lt kia/dow 20-7-18 7WRid p227 CR France1697

MOORE,John Davidson Lt kia 22-3-18 181RFA p208 MR27

MOORE,John Holmes Lyndon Lt kia 9-4-18 37RFA p208 CR Palestine9

MOORE,John O'Hara Capt dow 28-12-14 RE 55FC p46 CR France64,Maj

MOORE,John Ross 2Lt kia 9-9-16 3ConnRgrs att7RInniskF p172 MR21

MOORE,John Rushton.MC.LtAMaj kia 20/23-3-18 3Ches att71MGC p96&184 MR20,21-3-18

MOORE,John William TLt kia 27-8-18 RE 183FC p47 CR France251

MOORE,Keith Hayden Lt kia 26-11-15 1/4LNLancs p234 CR France702

MOORE,Kenneth Hartley T2Lt kia7-7-16 6Dors p124 CR France1890

MOORE,Kenneth William James 2Lt kia 15-9-17 3 att11Ess p132 CR France149

MOORE,Leonard Edwin 2lt kia 6-4-18 4Middx p147 MR27

MOORE,Lionel Watson Lt kia 27-8-16 5Glouc p225 MR21

MOORE,Lionel William Bentinck Lt kia 30-1-18 RFA att34RFC p19&208 CR Italy9

MOORE,Morgan Edward Jellett.MC.Lt dow PoW 27-3-18 2RIrRif p170 CR France1061,kia

MOORE,Percy T2Lt dow 5-5-17 12EYorks p84 CR France95,3-5-17

MOORE,Raymond Cecil Devereux 2Lt kia 9-10-17 HAC Inf p206 MR30

MOORE,Reginald Henry Hamilton Capt kia 11-6-15 1BordR p117 CR Gallipoli6

MOORE,Reginald John T2Lt kld 7-11-17 GL &62RFC p11 CR Kent7

MOORE,Richard 2Lt kia 15-7-16 6WYorks p218 CR France246

MOORE,Richard 2Lt ded 29-10-18 2RIrF p171 CR Greece2

MOORE,Richard Henry 2Lt dow 21-3-18 RFA 6DAC p33 CR France512

MOORE,Robert T2Lt dow 15-8-17 10RB p179 CR Belgium16

MOORE,Robert Chetwood Capt 16-9-15 S&T Cps MR65

MOORE,Robert Frank.DSO.MC.TLtALtCol kia 30-5-18 1N&D p134 MR18

MOORE,Robert McConnell.MM.2Lt kia 27-3-18 17RIrRif p170 CR France587,1Bn

MOORE,Roger Ludovic Lt dow 20-12-14 SomLI p80 CR Belgium136

MOORE,Ronald T2Lt kia 8-3-18 RFC p16

MOORE,Samuel Johnston 2Lt dow 18-3-17 5RScotF p222 CR France95

MOORE,Samuel Kerr T2Lt kia 25-2-18 2RB p179 CR Belgium22

MOORE,Saxon Weston LtACapt kia 23-8-18 1Herts p252 CR France281

MOORE,Thomas T2Lt kia 15-6-18 1 att1/4 O&BLI p130 CR Italy2

MOORE,Thomas George 2Lt kia 1-7-16 17 att8RIrRif p170 MR21

MOORE,Thomas Harold Lt kia 27-9-15 1/5Glouc p225 CR France742

MOORE,Thomas Sydney Lt dow 30-5-18 3NStaffs p157 MR18

MOORE,Ulick Augustus Lt kia 22-3-18 3 att6ConnRgrs p172 CR France365

MOORE,Victor Cuthbert 2Lt dow 4-9-16 3Leinst att6RIrReg p174 CR France23

MOORE,Waldo Alington Gwennap Capt kia 31-10-14 2WelshR p127 MR29

MOORE,Willfred Englebert Capt dow 11-3-16 1/5SStaffs p229 CR France808,Staffs

MOORE,William T2Lt kia 16-8-17 10RIrF p171 MR30

MOORE,William Addison Hone 2Lt kia 5-5-17 5Ess p232 CR France115

MOORE,William Ernest.MC.2LtACapt kia 14-11-17 86RFA p33 MR30

MOORE,William Henry Lt kia 8-8-16 5Lpool attMGC p215&187 CR France630

MOORE,William Henry Hilme TLt kld 19-10-15 10KRRC p151 CR France706,Helme

MOORE,William Henry Walker T2Lt kia 25-9-15 6Wilts D'Coy p153 CR France260

MOORE,William Joseph 2Lt kia 21-3-18 2RFA p33 MR20

MOORE,William Webb ALt dow 12-6-18 RE Z/SpecCo p47 CR France10

MOORES,Clive Guise Capt dow 30-11-14 RE p47 CR France284

MOORES,Henry Eustace 2Lt kia 7-7-16 3SStaffs att2ELancs p122 CR France267

MOOREY,William Edward 2Lt kia 26-10-17 3Lond p246 MR30

MOORHEAD,Arthur Henry BtCol ded 1-3-16 IA IMS p280

MOORHOUSE,Arthur 2Lt kia 16-11-16 8ELanc p111 MR21

MOORHOUSE,Arthur Edward 2Lt kia 15-11-16 5NumbF p213 CR France385

MOORHOUSE,Arthur John Maj ded 28-11-18 Manch p155 CR Berks42

MOORHOUSE,Harry.DSO.LtCol kia 9-10-17 4YLI p235 MR30

MOORHOUSE,Ronald Wilkinson.MC.Capt kia 9-10-17 4YLI p235 MR30

MOORHOUSE,Rowland Edward 2Lt kia 19-4-18 9Mddx p236 MR30

MOORHOUSE,Samuel LtCol ded 11-12-18 3A&SH p173 CR Hamps218

MOORHOUSE,W.Lt ded 22-8-18 1RWKent &RAF p141

MOORHOUSE,Walter T2Lt kia 22-11-17 1 att2/6WYorks p82 MR17

MOORHOUSE,William Barnard Rhodes.VC.Lt kia 26-4-15 RFC p1

MOORSE,Harold Henry Lt kia 18-3-15 Y&L p159 CR Belgium89

MOORSOM,Alfred Edgar Lt dow 3-8-16 4Suff p217 CR France51

MORAN,Francis TLt kia 22-8-16 9 att2MunstF p175 CR France453,Frank 23-8-16

MORAN,Gerald Charles Lt dow 26-5-15 5 att2DubF p177 CR France145

MORAN,H.J.Lt 24-9-15 8GurkhaRif CR France705

MORAN,John 2Lt kia 7-6-17 8Manch attLond p237 MR29

MORAN,John 2Lt kia 24-3-18 4CamH p243 MR20

219

MORAN,John 2Lt ded 7-6-18 8Lpool p216 CR France204

MORAN,Samuel Frederick T2Lt dow 1-10-18 9RIrF p171 CR Belgium38

MORAN,William Paul Lt dow 7-7-15 IA 1/10 att2/10GurkhaRif p280 CR Europe4,8-7-15

MORAN,Herbert James Lt dow 25-9-15 IA 1/8 att2/8GurkhaRif p280

MORAND-LEES,James Wright TCapt ded 5-11-18 Manch attBrWI p155

MORANT,Gerald Alexander Mackay.MC.TCapt kia 15-4-18 16 att2/5WYorks p82 CR France745

MORANT,Norman 2Lt dow PoW 27-3-18 2Yorks p91 CR France1266

MORANT,William Hedley T2Lt kia 25-10-16 1 att4NumbF p62 CR France423,12Bn

MORANT,William Miles Capt kia 12-4-18 7DLI p239 MR32

MORBEY,Charles Frederick William TCapt kia 9-8-17 7Suff p78 CR France154

MORBEY,J.S.2Lt ded 1-8-18 10Lond attRAF p248&258

MORCOM,Frank Clifford 2Lt kia 8-5-17 5 att18DCLI p227 MR20

MORCOM,Percival John Hosking Lt kia 11-4-18 5DCLI att1MGC Inf p227 MR32

MORDAUNT-SMITH,Lionel St.George 2Lt kia 15/16-5-15 RInnisF p105 MR22

MORDUE,Alfred George T2Lt dow 8-7-17 RE 268Co p46 CR France

MORE,Eric Roy Lt kia 27-10-18 3 att2GordH p166 CR Italy9

MORE,George Lt dow 2-10-17 7WelshR p230 CR France193

MOREHEAD,Robert Evans Capt ded 23-11-19 5RMunstF attGoldCoastR p266&268

MORETON,Ada SNurse ded 7-9-16 QAIMNS p200 MR65

MORETON,Cecil Harry 2Lt kia 17-9-18 RGA 22HB p41 CR France686

MORETON,Edgar.MC.LtAMaj kia 25-8-18 119/27RFA p33 CR France518

MOREY,Alan Wilson.MC.Lt kia 24-1-18 RFC p16 MR20

MORFEY,Kenneth Lt ded 20-5-18 IA 16Rajputs att1/97Inf p280 CR Iraq8

MORGAN,Alan Bertram 2Lt ded 22-4-17 RFC p11 CR France1276

MORGAN,Albert Ernest Capt kld 10-3-15 RFus attRFC p1&69 CR France706,Lt

MORGAN,Albert Sydney 2Lt kia 22-4-17 GL &RFC p261&267 CR France529

MORGAN,Alfred.MC.T2Lt dow 28-4-18 10SWBord p100 CR France41

MORGAN,Alfred Ernest 2Lt kia 29-10-16 Middx att12Bn p147 CR France832

MORGAN,Archibald John Lt ded 29-6-18 6BlkW p271

MORGAN,Arthur T2Lt kld 27-2-18 GL &RFC p16 CR Durham182

MORGAN,Arthur Conway Osborne.MID Lt kia 13-10-15 4/3RFA att5Lincs p208 MR19 &CR France1896,mbk

MORGAN,Arthur Dunbar TCapt ded 14-9-19 RAVC p268 CR Egypt9

MORGAN,Arthur Lewis 2Lt ded 11-9-16 1/5WelshR p271 CR Egypt8

MORGAN,Ashton TLt kld 4-2-18 RFC p16 CR Wilts4

MORGAN,B.Lt kld 16-10-18 6ScotRif &RAF p264

MORGAN,Basil Algernon Cecil 2Lt kia 28-3-18 1Hamps p121 MR20

MORGAN,Brinley Arthur 2Lt kia 4-3-17 RFA &RFC p11&33 CR France285

MORGAN,Cecil Buckley.CMG.DSO.MIDx3 TLtCol dow 29-3-18 22DLI p161 CR France145

MORGAN,Cecil Edward Lt drd 3-7-15 3Hamps p121 MR4

MORGAN,Charles Cecil Lt BombExplode 11-3-16 IARO att6Cav p280 CR France1564

MORGAN,Charles Joseph T2Lt dow 28-4-18 9TankCps p188 CR France145

MORGAN,Charles Sydney Stuart 2Lt ded 2-2-18 RFC p261 CR Lancs7,Sidney kldacc RFA

MORGAN,Clarence William Harding 2Lt kia 23-10-18 5Ess p232 CR France1480

MORGAN,Cyril Edward T2Lt kld 4-12-16 GL &RFC p3&191 CR Egypt9

MORGAN,Daniel Phillips 2Lt kia 26-9-17 1/2Worc p109 MR30

MORGAN,David Lloyd Pophen.MC.Capt kia 9-3-18 PembrokeYeo att2WelchR p205 CR Palestine3,Popkin

MORGAN,Douglas Noel 2Lt mbk 30-6-16 13RSuss p256 MR19

MORGAN,Edward Charles 2Lt kia 18-12-15 1 att5RBerks p139 CR France279

MORGAN,Edward Compton.MC.TCaptAMaj dow 29-9-17 76RFA p33 CR Belgium12

MORGAN,Edward Leslie 2Lt dow 9-11-17 23RFA p33 CR Belgium18

MORGAN,Emlyn Thomas TLt dow 7-2-16 15RWFus p98 CR France345

MORGAN,Ernest Alfred Lt dow 21-8-15 5WelshR p230 MR4

MORGAN,Fothergill Lewis 2Lt dow 3-12-17 1/7Lond p247 CR France398

MORGAN,Frank 2Lt kia 22-8-18 22 att1/24Lond p251 CR France370

MORGAN,Frederick James 2Lt dow 16-5-18 7RFus &18RAF p69 CR France31,Lt

MORGAN,Frederick Ernest.MC.T2Lt kia 23-11-17 12SWBord p100 MR17

MORGAN,Frederick Harold Lewis.MID Capt kia 4-5-15 RFA p33 CR Gallipoli2

MORGAN,Geffrey Evan Lt kia 7-9-17 4A&SH p173

MORGAN,Geoffrey Penney T2Lt kia 14-7-16 1RWFus p98 MR21

MORGAN,George Elton T2Lt dow 19-8-17 15WelshR C'Coy p127 CR Belgium16

MORGAN,George Hamilton.MID TCapt kia 23-11-17 19RWFus p98 MR17

MORGAN,Guy Williams Stuart Capt kia 25-9-15 RWFus p98 MR19

MORGAN,Henry Richard Lt kia 8-11-17 LancsYeo &RFC p204 CR Belgium18,kld

MORGAN,Herbert Glyn Rhys.MID T2Lt dow 31-7-17 17RWFus p98 MR29,1-8-17

MORGAN,Hubert Hoppin Lt kia 30-3-18 17Manch p155 MR27

MORGAN,Idris Anuerin TCapt kia 17-4-18 11 att2SWBord p100 CR France324

MORGAN,James Melvin T2Lt kia 4-3-17 2RE p47 CR France430

MORGAN,James White 2Lt dow 10-8-18 5LancF p221 CR France360,Lt

MORGAN,Jeffery Evan 2Lt 7-9-17 2A&SH CR Belgium15

MORGAN,John 2Lt kia 22-3-18 4GordH p242 MR20

MORGAN,John Cecil Capt kia 7-8-15 6Yorks p91 CR Gallipoli4

MORGAN,John Hywel 2Lt dow 22-11-17 1/4DCLI p227 CR Palestine3

MORGAN,John James 2Lt kia 7-4-17 77RFA p33 CR Belgium21

MORGAN,John Joseph Lee 2Lt dow 16-5-15 2RInnisF p105 CR France80,Leo Lt

MORGAN,John Parkinson 2Lt kia 27-5-18 112RFA p33 MR18

MORGAN,John Towlson Capt kia 29-10-18 1/2RWFus att70RAF p98 CR France263

MORGAN,John Walter Rees 2Lt kia 1-7-16 4 att2DubF p177 CR France643

MORGAN,John William Moore.DSO.LtCol ded 31-3-17 RASC p193 CR France102

MORGAN,Joseph TLt ded 6-10-18 RE attIWT p47 CR Asia66

MORGAN,Joseph Anthony TLt kia 30-5-17 9KSLI &RFC p11&145 CR Egypt2,2Lt

MORGAN,Leonard(Jack) Lt dow 1-12-17 4EKent p212 CR France439

MORGAN,Lewis Edward 2Lt kia 16-9-18 D275RFA p33 CR France106

MORGAN,L.L.MC.2Lt kia 28-4-18 6WelshR &RAF p230

MORGAN,Matthew Lt ded 8-11-18 4SWBord att4Mon p100

MORGAN,Morgan Hughes Buckley Maj ded 22-11-17 SLancs p264 CR Wales19

MORGAN,Oswald William LtTCapt kld 3-2-18 RFA attRFC p16&33 CR Hamps191

MORGAN,Ralph Lewis 2Lt kia 14-1-17 3 att13WelshR p127 CR Belgium73

MORGAN,Richard Croke.MID Capt ded 18-2-19 LabCps attStaff p266 CR Surrey43

MORGAN,Richard Godfrey T2Lt kia 13-11-16 12EYorks p84 CR France156

MORGAN,Ronald Charles Wybrow 2LtTLt dow 27-7-17 3SWBdrs &RFC p3&100 CR Belgium375,28-7-17

MORGAN,R.T.P.2Lt kia 9-7-16 8SLancs p125 MR21

MORGAN,Samuel Valentine Capt kia 10-8-17 2RIrRif p170 MR29

MORGAN,Sidney Herbert T2Lt kia 4-4-17 12ESurr att122TMB p113 CR Belgium28

MORGAN,Stephen Beverley 2Lt kia 14-5-15 3 att1Leic p88 CR France276

MORGAN,Thomas Augustus T2Lt kia 8-10-18 13WelshR attMGC p127 CR France234

MORGAN,Thomas Cyril T2Lt kia 12-8-17 11Ches p96 MR29

MORGAN,Vernon Leslie 2Lt kia 21-9-16 4EKent att70RFC p19&212 CR France169

MORGAN,Victor Harold TLt kia 6-9-17 1Lpool GarrBn att1/5LancF p72 MR30

MORGAN,Walter Bassett T2Lt kia 9-8-15 6SLancs p125 MR4

MORGAN,Walter Chapman T2Lt kia 19-7-16 8Norf p74 MR21

MORGAN,Walter Henry T2Lt kia 12-7-16 13 att15Hamps p121 CR Belgium54

MORGAN,Wilfrid T2Lt kia 18-9-18 1 att11RWFus A'Coy p98 CR Greece5

MORGAN,Wilfrid Gilbert T2Lt dow PoW 23-10-17 GL &4RFC p11 CR Belgium381

MORGAN,William T2Lt kia 9-9-16 7RInnisF p105 MR21

MORGAN,William 2Lt dow 23-7-18 62MGC p184 CR France1693

MORGAN,William Lt ded 19-11-18 RH&FA p33

MORGAN,William Alfred T2Lt kia 23-4-17 13RFus p69 MR20

MORGAN,William Anthony Capt ded 22-11-17 LanarkYeo p271 CR Scot803

MORGAN,William Donal T2Lt kia 13-10-15 RE 95FC p47 CR France114

MORGAN,William Hugh 2Lt kia 11-4-18 12SWBord attWelshR p100 MR32

MORGAN,William J.Lt 19-11-18 RFA CR Eire167

MORGAN,William Rich T2Lt kia 2-4-17 9 att1SWBord p100 CR France551

MORGAN,William Vanstone Capt kia 19-4-17 4Norf p216 MR34

MORGAN,W.J.DCM.Lt RFA p259

MORGAN-BROWN,Nigel Martin T2Lt ded 31-10-15 15 att8NumbF p62 CR Egypt3,Lt

MORGAN-GRENVILLE,Hon Richard George Grenville Capt kia 19-12-14 1RB p179CR Belgium71

MORGAN-OWEN,John Guith T2Lt kia 9-4-16 4SWBord p100 CR Iraq5

MORGANS,Thomas T2Lt dow 13-4-18 7KSLI p145 CR France98

MORHAM,Malcolm.MID 2Lt kia 7-3-16 IARO att120Inf p280 MR38

MORIARTY,Denis Joseph 2Lt kia 1-9-18 2RInnisF p105 CR France297

MORIARTY,James Henry.MID Lt kldacc 12-10-15 RGA 18SB p41 CR France80

MORIARTY,Redmond George Sylverius LtCol kia 24-5-18 att2RIrReg p89 MR29

MORICE,Norman Archibald TLt dow 11-3-16 7EYorks p84 CR France102

MORIN,John Archibald Scott Capt ded 4-11-18 RGA 149SB p41 CR France40

MORISON,Alfred James 2LtACapt kia 20-11-17 3 att1EssR p132 CR France1483

MORISON,Douglas Rutherford 2Lt kia 13-3-15 3 att2Wilts p153 CR France706

MORISON,Gerald Patrick John 2Lt kia 13-10-15 3 att1CamH p168 MR19

MORISON,John Sinclair T2Lt kld 13-10-16 GL &RFC p3&191 CR Scot398

MORISON,Robert McKenzie Capt ded 8-5-19 RAMC att31CCS p197 CR Lebanon1

MORITZ,Oscar Frank 2Lt dow 27-7-16 99MGC p184 MR21

MORKEL,Daniel Johannes Cecil 2Lt kia 16-11-16 3 att8ELancs p111 CR France152

MORKILL,Ronald Falshaw Lt kld 23-6-15 1WYorksR attRFC p1&82 CR Yorks462

MORLAND,Charles Bernard LtCol kia 31-11-14 WelshR p127 CR Belgium57,31-10-14

MORLAND,Kenneth Irvine Thomas T2Lt kia 3-9-16 6 O&BLI p130 CR France294

MORLAND,Leonard Mark TLt dow 3-5-16 12WYorks p82 CR France285

MORLAND,William T2Lt kia 2-12-17 17HLI att97L TMB p163 CR Belgium126

MORLEY,Arthur Selwyn.MC.2Lt kia 16-9-16 15DLI p161 MR21

MORLEY,David 2Lt kld 16-6-17 4EYorks p219 CR France644

MORLEY,Frank William T2Lt dow 9-10-18 10EKent p58 CR France80

MORLEY,Frederick Joseph.DSO.MC.CaptAMaj dow 24-4-18 6Dors p124 CR France64

MORLEY,George Thomas.MM.2Lt kia 24-3-18 1Wilts p153 CR France307

MORLEY,Gordon Harper.MID Lt kia 30-12-17 1/4KSLI p235 MR17 Harpur

MORLEY,Harold Lisle.MC.T2LtACapt dow PoW 2-12-17 6EKent p58 CR France660

MORLEY,John Killand Gulson Lt dow 15-5-18 RE E'SpecCo p47 CR France10 Kelland

MORLEY,John Norris Lt kia 25-9-15 7Nhants p137 MR19

MORLEY,Marmaduke Robert Hood TLt kia 1-7-16 8YLI p143 CR France246

MORLEY,William Lt kia 24-3-18 2/1SurrYeo att10RWSurr p205 MR27

MORLEY-BROWN,Alastair James T2Lt kia 29-4-16 9KOSB p102 CR France1182

MORPETH,Stanley Lt ded 22-10-18 PoW 6NumbF p214 CR Europe149

MORPHEY,Henry John Cdr ded PoW 23-12-16 IA IndOrdDept p280 CRIraq8,Lt

MORPHY,Arthur Albert 2LtTLt dow 29-11-17 RASC 42DivTrn p193 CR France98

MORRALL,Edgar Percy Basil TCaptAMaj kia 28-7-17 7BordR p117 CR France604

MORRALL,John Bernard 2Lt dow 23-3-18 10RWar p65 MR20

MORRAR,John Henry Maj kia 18-10-14 RLancs p59 CR Belgium32

MORRELL,Harold Frank TLt kld 19-3-18 3BWIndR &RFC p261 CR Greece3,Francis

MORRELL,Ralph D'Albin Capt kia 8-8-16 4Lancs p213 MR21

MORRICE,Charles Smith 2Lt kia 11-6-17 5SfthH p241 MR29

MORRICE,William Walter LtTCapt kia 30-12-17 3Wilts attabCps p153 CR France398

MORRILL,George Bertie T2Lt kia 23-10-18 KRRC att13Bn p151 CR France1480

MORRIN,William Arthur TCapt ded 1-8-18 RAVC att18RFA p198 CR France145

MORRIS,Albert Evelyn 2Lt kia 27-5-18 NumbF Res att4Bn MR18

MORRIS,Alexander Ramsey 2Lt kia 23/25-4-17 1/7BlkW p231 CR France604

MORRIS,Alfred Arthur Thomas.MC.TLt dow 24-10-18 21Middx p147 CR France661,1Bn

MORRIS,Alfred Ashurst Lt kia 27-9-18 1GrenGds p50 CR France1497

MORRIS,Alfred George 2Lt dow 10-6-16 4GordH p242 CR France95

MORRIS,Allan Duncan TLt kia 30-8-18 13WelshR p127 MR16

MORRIS,Andrew 2Lt dow 26-8-18 4 att12Manch p155 CR France832

MORRIS,Anthony George Attwood Lt kia 13-10-14 1RLancs p59 CR France855

MORRIS,Arthur Capt kia 18-9-18 12Ches p96 MR37

MORRIS,Arthur Cukelyn TLt kia 17-2-18 19RWFus att22RFC p16&98 CR France31,Cuhelyn

MORRIS,Charles 2Lt kia 8-3-16 1Manch p155 MR38

MORRIS,Charles Alan Smith CaptAMaj ded PoW 7-5-17 3Beds p86 CR France452

MORRIS,Charles Geoffrey Noel TLt kia 7-10-16 6 O&BLI p130 MR21

MORRIS,Charles Herbert Lt kia 13-4-17 RWelshFus &RFC p11&98 MR20

MORRIS,Christopher Mowbray Capt&Adjt kia 7/11-8-15 7SStaffs p122 MR4,9-8-15

MORRIS,Clive Wilson 2Lt kia 9-5-15 2KRRC p151 MR22

MORRIS,Colin Dwight T2Lt kia 14-3-16 9RFus p69 CR France423

MORRIS,Duncan Blackett Capt kia 11-9-18 IA 90Punjabis p280 CR Iraq6

MORRIS,E.Lt 24-3-21 RFA MR67

MORRIS,Edward Alan 2Lt dow 1-12-17 3SWBord att25RWFus p100 CR Palestine8,Edwin

MORRIS,Ellis Wayman T2Lt kia 9-11-17 5RFC p11 CR France1361

MORRIS,Ernest John 2Lt dow 17-6-16 1NStaffs A'Coy p157 CR Belgium97

MORRIS,Evan Price 2Lt kia 8-10-18 5NStaffs p238 CR France1345

MORRIS,Eyre Percival T2Lt kia 1-5-17 1EKentR attRFC p11&58 CR France120

MORRIS,Francis 2Lt kld 11-9-16 1/5WSurr p212 CR Iraq6,kia

MORRIS,Francis St.Vincent 2Lt dow 29-4-17 3N&D att3RFC p11&134 CR France145

MORRIS,Frank George Grier.DSO.MajALtCol kia 17-8-17 BordR att16Middx p117 CR Belgium12,Greir 16-8-17

MORRIS,Frederick Lt drd 27-5-18 3ScotHorse p205 MR41

MORRIS,Garfield Hughes T2Lt kia 17-8-17 12RB p179 MR30

MORRIS,George Henry.Hon.LtCol kia 1-9-14 1IrGds p53 CR France1108

MORRIS,George Henry 2LtACapt dow 3-6-17 RGA att2/8HvyTMB p41 CR Belgium11

MORRIS,George Mackelvey T2Lt dow 7-9-16 17Lpool p72 CR Lond4

MORRIS,George Tod Lt kia 11-4-17 RFA att59RFC p19&208 CR France777,RHA

MORRIS,Gilbert Willan TLt kia 1-7-16 8YLI p143 CR France246

MORRIS,Godfrey Maxwell LtCol dow 26-9-15 IA 2/8GurkhaRif p280 CR France705

MORRIS,Harold Henry Lt dow 22-7-17 D150RFA p33 CR Belgium6

MORRIS,Harry Capt kia 26-10-17 2/5LNLancs p234 CR Belgium167A

MORRIS,Henry T2Lt kia 28-9-15 3 att5Middx p148 MR19

MORRIS,Henry Gage Lt kld 23-4-15 DCLI p114 MR29

MORRIS,Hubert Marmaduke T2Lt dow 13-8-18 1/2 att15LancF p93 CR France34,17-8-18

MORRIS,Hugh Lt dow 14-7-15 2ScotRif p103 CR France254

MORRIS,Hugh Anthony Lt ded 18-10-17 RASC 782MT Coy p193 CR Greece4

MORRIS,Hugh Gwilym TCapt kia 14-7-16 RAMC att54FA p197 CR France630

MORRIS,Ian Russell Campbell 2Lt 7-8-15 HertsYeo att 1/8LancF p204 MR4

MORRIS,James Lt kia 27-12-17 GlamYeo att24WelshR p203 CR Palestine3

MORRIS,James Hulbert.OBE.Capt ded 1-6-19 RE p262 CR Wales152

MORRIS,John.MC.Maj kia 7-10-18 RAMC p253 CR France375

MORRIS,John Child TLt kia 8-8-15 8WelshR p127 MR4

MORRIS,John Clarke Lt kld 13-1-19 3WRid att19RAF p116 CR France1252

MORRIS,John Glynne T2Lt dow 23-9-17 N&D att16Bn p134 CR Belgium15

MORRIS,John Herbert 2Lt kia 21-9-16 6WelshR p230 CR France453

MORRIS,John Herbert Lt kia 6-3-18 RHA &49RFC p16&33 CR France120

MORRIS,John Torrington 2Lt kia 16-5-15 1RWFus p98 CR France279

MORRIS,John William Gibson Capt kia 1-4-16 12 att6Welsh p127 CR France551

MORRIS,Joseph T2Lt dow 4-11-18 16LancF C'Coy p93 CR France231,Lt

MORRIS,Leslie Tounsend T2Lt kia 1-6-18 Ches att5SWBord p96 MR18,Townsend

MORRIS,Lionel Alfred Harry Blackmore Lt kia 7-7-16 3 att1Wilts p153 CR France293

MORRIS,Lionel Bertram Frank 2Lt dow PoW 17-9-16 3RWSurr &4RFC p3&56 CR France598

MORRIS,Mansell John 2Lt kia 3-5-17 42RFC p11 CR France31

MORRIS,Michael Ambrose TLt kia 6-8-15 2 att13Hamps p121 MR4

MORRIS,Noel Dyke TLt dow 12-5-16 8SLancs p125 CR France40

MORRIS,Oscar David TCapt kia 21-4-17 12SWBord p100 CR France439

MORRIS,Philip Henry T2Lt kia 9-10-17 144MGC Inf p184 CR Belgium126

MORRIS,R.J.Lt ded 8-1-20 1Mon CR Wales85

MORRIS,Reginald Harry 2Lt kia 28-6-18 8RWar p215 CR France21

MORRIS,Reginald Martin 2Lt kia 17-2-17 14 att23Lond p249 MR21

MORRIS,Robert Cochrane MajTLtCol ded 25-3-17 RGA p41 CR France15

MORRIS,Robert Crowe Lt kia 23-9-18 RGA p209 CR Belgium11

MORRIS,Robert Parry.MC.Capt kia 27-10-17 RGA 1/4WelshSB p209 CR Belgium165

MORRIS,Sydney T2Lt kia 7-8-15 6Yorks p91 MR4

MORRIS,Sydney Herbert HonTCapt ded 11-1-18 RAMC p267 CR Surrey70

MORRIS,Thomas Ernest Lt&QM ded 9-1-16 RASC p193 CR Egypt6

MORRIS,Thomas Herbert Picton.MC.MID TLtCol dow 18-9-16 9RB p179 CR France105

MORRIS,Thomas Hodgkinson 2Lt kia 9-8-15 3Y&L p159 MR21

MORRIS,Tom Bernard.MID Lt dow 23-7-17 5RWFus p223 CR Belgium11

MORRIS,Wilfred Cyril 2Lt ded 15-12-18 IA 2/96Inf p280 MR65

MORRIS,William TLt dow 14-4-17 12WYorks p82 CR France40,Capt

MORRIS,William Albert.MC.Capt&QM ded 19-3-17 RInniskF p264 CR Ireland168

MORRIS,William Harold 2Lt ded 23-11-17 3Lincs p75 CR Staffs21

MORRIS,William Henry T2Lt kia 3-2-18 2SWBord p100 CR Belgium22

MORRIS,William James Lt ded 28-3-17 RGA p41 CR Canada742

MORRIS,William Norman 2Lt dow 25-5-16 8Wilts att106MGC p153&184 CR France8

MORRIS,William Oliver Ernest T2Lt kia 17-6-16 16 att12Lpool p72 CR Belgium47

MORRIS,William Percy Lt ded 20-12-18 11KRRC p151 CR France146

MORRIS,William Reginald T2Lt kia 25-9-15 7ELancs p111 CR France727

MORRIS,William Sydney LtTCapt kia 1-6-18 4 att18LancF p93 MR27

MORRIS JONES,O.Lt 31-10-18 14RWFus CR France1478

MORRISH,Donald Bernard T2Lt kia 18-8-16 1YLI att43TMB p143 MR21

MORRISON,Albert Victor 2Lt kia 30-7-16 2RScotF p95 MR21

MORRISON,Alexander Lt dow 25-7-15 RGA p209 MR4

MORRISON,Alexander Capt kia 25-9-15 5CamH p168 MR19

MORRISON,Archibald 2Lt dow 9-4-17 3 att15RScots p54 CR France95

MORRISON,Arnold 2Lt kia 26-10-17 3Lond p271&246 MR30

MORRISON,Arthur Stanley Lt kia 23-8-18 RGA 336SB p41 CR France103

MORRISON,Brian Harford Lt 9-6-19 22Punjabis MR43

MORRISON,Campbell Lt&QM ded 20-1-17 21Lond p251 CR Essex7

MORRISON,Colquhoun Grant.CMG.TBrigGen ded 23-5-16 PresClaimsCommission Staff p1 CR France300 Ex 1Drags

MORRISON,Donald TCapt dow 31-8-15 6RLancs p59 MR4

MORRISON,Douglas St.George Lt ded 3-9-17 RFA attR'A/A Bty p33 CR France518

MORRISON,Duncan Craig 2Lt kia 10-4-17 8A&SH p243 CR France924

MORRISON,Ernest Albert Augustus Lt ded 13-11-18 KRRC attRAF p151 CR Yorks172

MORRISON,Edwin Walter.MC.TLt ded 10-12-18 2DCLI p114 CR Greece2

MORRISON,Frederick Lansdowne.CB.DSO.VD.Col ded 22-12-17 1/5HLI p240 CR Egypt1

MORRISON,George T2Lt dow 25-10-15 12 att10ScotRif p103 CR France88,11 att10Bn

MORRISON,George James.MC.Lt dow 11-4-18 1/6SfthH p241 CR France88,ACapt

MORRISON,Gerard Humphrey Capt kia 31-3-15 5Lond p246 CR Belgium71

MORRISON,Haslett TLt,AMaj kia 23-4-18 61MGC p184 CR France248

MORRISON,J.H.I.Lt 31-3-16 EA Maxims CR EAfrica58

MORRISON,James Lt kia 25/27-9-15 4GordH p241 MR29

MORRISON,James Bough Lt dow 13-10-18 6A&SH &TMB p243 CR Belgium38

MORRISON,James Fyfe TCapt kia 18-11-16 17HLI p163 CR France534

MORRISON,James Ian TLt dow 28-9-16 GL 7RScotF att45TMB p191 CR France40,Iain

MORRISON,James McGregor.MC.TLt ded 15-2-19 GL Mddx att1NigR p201&191 CR WAfrica53

MORRISON,James William Sutton.MC.Lt kia 19-10-18 C'4Huss p21 CR France1287

MORRISON,John Lt kia 28-3-18 HighCycBn p253 CR France531

MORRISON,John TLt kia 24-9-18 1CamH p168 CR France725

MORRISON,John Gray Lt dow 19-8-17 6GordH p242 CR Scot832

MORRISON,John Stewart T2Lt dow 14-5-17 12ScotRif D'Coy p103 CR France145

MORRISON,John Woodley T2Lt dow 30-12-16 16RWar p65 CR France1

MORRISON,Joseph McLaren 2Lt dow 4-12-17 1/19Lond p250 CR France40

MORRISON,Kenneth Rae 2Lt kia 21-9-17 5 att18KRRC p151 MR30

MORRISON,Lechlan Allan 2Lt dow 6-1-16 3 att4SLancs p125 CR Belgium11

MORRISON,Leonard Graeme TLt kia 23-4-17 9BlkW p129 CR France536,Capt

MORRISON,Leslie.MC.Capt kia 25-3-18 1Lpool att1/7LancF p72&258 MR20

MORRISON,Lindsay 2Lt kld 28-7-17 GL &RFC p11 CR Wilts4

MORRISON,Norman Walter T2Lt kia 14-4-17 GL &RFC p11 MR20

MORRISON,Richard Fielding.MC&Bar.MIDx2 CaptAMaj dow 25-4-18 51RH&FA p33 CR Belgium38

MORRISON,Robert T2Lt dow 14-4-18 51MGC Inf p184 CR France924

MORRISON,Robert 2Lt kia 30-8-18 6LancF p221 CR France1484

MORRISON,Robert Cecil 2Lt kia 13-11-16 5Ches p222 CR France293

MORRISON,Robert Cochrane 2Lt ded 13-10-18 3RWar p263 CR Scot253

MORRISON,Robert Stevenson 2Lt kia 7-1-16 2BlkW p129 MR38

MORRISON,Robert Vernon T2Lt kia 13-5-17 Middx att11Bn p148 MR20

MORRISON,Ronald Macdonald 2Lt kia 9-4-17 1EYorks p84 CR France162

MORRISON,Rupert George 2Lt ded 24-8-18 RGA p262 CR Wales681,Lt

MORRISON,Samuel Rev 24-7-20 Chap4Cl CR Lancs34

MORRISON,Samuel Alexander 2Lt kia 3-5-17 7 att2SfthH p165 MR20

MORRISON,Stanley T2Lt kia 9-7-16 19LancF p93 CR France296

MORRISON,Thomas 2Lt kia 21-3-18 30MGC p184 MR27

MORRISON,Vernon MacDonald 2Lt kia 14-11-16 3 att7SLancs p125 CR France384

MORRISON,Walter Scott T2Lt kld 18-3-17 GL &RFC p11 CR Hamps4

MORRISON,William 2Lt kia 20-5-17 9HLI p240 MR20

MORRISON,William.MC.TCapt dow 25-10-17 RAMC att54FA p197 CR Belgium16,23-10-17 14FA

MORRISON,William T2Lt kia 2-12-17 2RB p179 MR30

MORRISON,William Fleming Oliphant Lt kia 2-9-18 9RScots p212 CR France646,8Bn

MORRISON,William Henry Stanley.MID Lt kia 26-5-15 24Lond p252 MR22

MORRISS,John Septimus Lt kia 5-10-17 1RWar p65 MR30

MORRISSEY,Walter George SubCdr mbk 6-5-16 1A IndOrdDept p280

MORRITT,William Graveley.MID Capt kld PoW 27-6-17 1ESurr p113 CR Germany2

MORROGH,Francis Mathew Dominick 2Lt 19-5-15 MunstF p175 CR Gallipoli6

MORROGH-BERNARD,Francis Anthony Lt kia 12-12-17 3MunstF p175 CR Palestinr3,11-12-17

MORROW,Hugh Gelston.MC.TLtACapt kia 22-10-18 15RIrRif p170 CR Belgium140

MORSE,Anthony Philip Lt ded 5-6-15 3 att2DCLI p114 CR France134

MORSE,Christopher TLt kia 7-12-17 RE 178TC p47 CR France439

MORSE,Christopher Charles T2Lt kia 14-11-17 GL &RFC p11 CR France1678

MORSE,Edward Hely Templeman 2Lt dow 8-5-17 6Dev p217 CR France512

MORSE,Eric Victor.MC.T2Lt kia 23-10-18 7EKent D'Coy p58 CR France206,Capt

MORSE,Ernest Frederick TLt kia 1-7-16 MGC Inf p184 CR France393

MORSE,Gerald Ernest 2Lt kld 31-10-17 4RWelshF att2RFC p19&223 CR France80

MORSE,Gordon T.H.2Lt kia 12-10-14 4Middx p148 CR France1106

MORSE,Gurth Stephen Lt dow 9-12-14 34RFA p33 CR France284,2Lt

MORSE,Percy Lapper 2Lt dow 20-11-17 1/4Glouc p225 CR France145

MORTEN,Galbraith 2Lt kia 16/19-5-15 Lpool p72

MORTEN,Lewis James 2Lt kia 4-11-18 O&BLI BucksBn p231 CR France1272

MORTENSON,Alfred T2Lt kia 15-4-18 59MGC p184 CR France285

MORTIBOY,William Woolly 2Lt kia 19-8-18 3 att2Manch p155 CR France526

MORTIMER,C.O.2Lt kia 1-4-18 6Dors p124

MORTIMER,Charles Gordon TLt ded 21-10-16 RFA att24A/A p33 CR Europe1

MORTIMER,Cyril Owen 2Lt kia 1-4-18 IARO att6Dors p280 CR France196

MORTIMER,Edmund Lt kia 26-4-15 6NumbF p214 MR29

MORTIMER,Edmund Alfred 2Lt kia 4-7-18 RGA 114HB p41 CR Belgium40

MORTIMER,Ernest George Smith Lt kld 3-4-18 GL &RAF p191 CR France169

MORTIMER,Gerald Henry Walter Capt kia 23-11-14 IA 10Jats att9BhopalInf p280

MORTIMER,Harry Limner LtACapt dow 21-9-17 6ESurr att18KRRCp226 CR France285

MORTIMER,James.CMG.LtCol kia 15-9-16 5Yorks attMGC p187&220 CR France453

MORTIMER,Leonard James TLt dow 24-11-17 9RFus p69 CR France415

MORTIMER,Robert T2Lt ded 27-10-18 10RIrRif p170 CR Ireland33

MORTIMER,W.B Lt 13-6-15 4DLI CR Belgium44

MORTIMER,William Brian Lt kia 13-6-15 4DLI p161

MORTIMER,William George Lt ded 22-3-19 IARO att28LightCav p280 MR66

MORTIMER,William Henry.MID Maj ded 21-2-21 DorsYeo CR Palestine9

MORTIMER,William Lionel Gueritz 2Lt dow 10-8-15 6RDubF p177 MR4

MORTIMORE,Owen John Capt kia 22-11-15 3Dev att2Dors p77 MR38

MORTIS,Eric John 2Lt kia 12-4-18 1RGLI C'Coy p201 CR France297

MORTLEMAN,Charles Ibbetson 2Lt kia 9-9-16 1/4Lond p246 MR21

MORTLEMAN,W.R.Lt 29-12-18 HAC

MORTLOCK,Percy George 2Lt kia 20-9-17 26RFus p69 MR30

MORTON,Albert Francis 2Lt kia 8-8-18 8Lond p247 CR France1170

MORTON,Alexander Capt 27-8-18 RAMC att1/7HLI p197 MR16

MORTON,Arthur Darley 2Lt kia 24-8-18 21Lond p251 CR France395

MORTON,Daniel.MID 2Lt kia 10-5-15 4KRRC p151 MR29

MORTON,Eric Lt dow 26-8-18 RE 247FC p210 CR France84

MORTON,Galbraith 2Lt 16-5-15 1Lpool CR France632

MORTON,George Capt kia 13-7-15 5HLI p240 MR4

MORTON,George TLt ded 23-11-18 18NumbF p62 CR Surrey1

MORTON,George Capt 13-7-15 5HLI MR4

MORTON,Gerald Arthur Capt kia 4-5-15 BordR p117 CR Gallipoli3

MORTON,Gordon Reid.MC.T2Lt kia 9-4-17 7CamH p168 CR France1182

MORTON,John Sydney TLt kia 25-4-17 2RScots p54 MR20

MORTON,John William TLt kia 10-4-17 3 att9Leic p88 CR France616

MORTON,Joseph Leonard Milthorpe TLtACapt kia 22-10-17 23Manch p155 MR30,Melthorp

MORTON,Leicester Charles T2Lt dow 19-5-17 1Leic p88 CR France178

MORTON,Norman Donald Rex Lt kia 22-4-17 2/17Lond p250 CR Greece6

MORTON,Percival Clare 2Lt dow PoW 13-4-18 5WRid p227 CR France225

MORTON,Philip Francis TMaj dow 11-8-16 11Suff p78 CR France145

MORTON,Robert Brooke Maj ded 10-2-19 RASC p267 CR Berks117,LtCol

MORTON,Scott Gladstone 2Lt kia 31-7-17 Manch p155 MR29

MORTON,Sidney.MID Maj kia 14-7-15 IA 24Punjabis p280 CR Iraq6

MORTON,Thomas Edward Capt dow 26-3-18 att7RIrReg p24 MR27

MORTON,William Lt kia 5-9-15 5 att2RIrRif p170

MORTON,William 2Lt ded 16-11-18 5SStaffs p229 CR Yorks361

MORTON,William Cattell.MC.Lt dow 22-7-17 C282RFA p208 CR Belgium11

MORTON,William John Edward Lt ?? 5 att2RIrRif MR29

MORTON,William Ronald Capt kia 4-5-17 2/8RWar p214 CR France672

MORTON,William Ross Col ded 21-11-17 RE p47 CR Asia40

MORUM,James Pearse 2Lt kia 1-7-16 6 att1RB p179 CR France643

MOSCROP,William Noel Jobson.MC.2LtACapt kia 27-5-18 RFus att5DLI p69&257 CR France1329

MOSELEY,Frederick Arthur Dudley Harris Capt ded 24-5-19 RWKent p265 CR Surrey1,53RSuss

MOSELEY,Henry Gwyn Jeffreys T2Lt kia 10-8-15 RE p47 MR4

MOSELEY,Herbert James Ritchie T2Lt kia 27-6-16 7RB p179 CR France1182

MOSER,Harold Wynn 2Lt ded 22-7-16 3/6ESurr p271 CR Sussex111

MOSES,Frank Samuel TLt dow 31-8-18 1/1WelshRGA p41 CR France1182

MOSES,James T2Lt kia 4-8-16 9LNLancs p136 CR France35

MOSES,Vivian Sylvester 2Lt kia 4-6-17 RFA 11DAC p33 CR Belgium60

MOSGROVE,Robert St.Patrick Capt ded 7-10-17 ArmyPayDept p268 CR Hamps13

MOSLEY,Arthur Roy Lt dow 23-11-17 2/4YLI p235 CR France398

MOSLEY,Geoffrey Kingdon Capt kia 10-4-18 6 att11Suff p217 CR France685,MOSELEY

MOSLEY,George Gordon Maj 7-8-18 IndDefF 37CalcuttaPresBn MR66

MOSLEY,Harold Drewell T2Lt kia 16-8-16 7RBerks p139 CR Greece6

MOSLEY,Nicholas Capt dow 1-8-15 NStaffs p157 CR Mddx26

MOSLEY,Percy 2Lt kia 28-3-18 5WRid p227 MR20

MOSMAN,Hugh 2Lt ded 12-2-16 4Yorks p271 CR Scot239

MOSS,Allan Maj 10-10-16 Worc CR Devon68

MOSS,Charles.MC.Capt kia 6-11-17 1/7Ches p223 CR Palestine1

MOSS,Charles William 2Lt kia 13-6-17 22Lond p251 CR France581

MOSS,Charles William T2Lt kia 8-8-18 RBerks att8Bn p139 CR France247

MOSS,Cyril James 2Lt ded 19-8-16 2Suff p78 CR Kent289

MOSS,Edward Hampton Capt kia 25-9-15 10Glouc p107 MR19

MOSS,Enoch Frank T2Lt dow 17-9-16 9RWFus p98 CR France285

MOSS,Ernest Sumner 2Lt kia 1-7-17 5NStaffs p238 CR France557

MOSS,Frederick Walter T2Lt kia 28-5-18 8Leic attRE 98FC p88 MR18

MOSS,George Percival T2Lt dow 22-12-17 12SWBord p100 CR France214

MOSS,Gerald Alex 2Lt kia 10-8-18 19 att2Manch p155 MR16,Alec

MOSS,Hamilton.MC.TCapt kia 31-5-18 9WRid p116 CR France35

MOSS,Hector Albert Lt kia 7-10-16 7Mddx p235 CR France374

MOSS,Herbert Frank 2Lt kia 30-8-18 RGA 132HB p41 CR France624

MOSS,Herbert Stanley T2Lt ded 4-8-18 2RRofCav attMddxHuss p23 CR Palestine8

MOSS,Howard James Harding 2Lt kia 13-10-15 5Leic A'Coy p220 CR France924

MOSS,John Miles T2Lt ded 6-9-15 RASC 258MechTransCo p193 CR France121

MOSS,John Stephen Noel 2Lt dedacc 24-11-16 RE 57FC p47 CR France169

MOSS,Leonard George 2Lt kia 21-3-18 1 att2/5Lincs p75 MR20

MOSS,M.E.2Lt 29-11-16 6Lpool CR Belgium4

MOSS,Morrice Edgar 2Lt kia 29-11-16 6Lpool p215

MOSS,Percy William T2Lt kia 23-8-18 59MGC Inf p184 CR France924,22-8-18

MOSS,Reginald Barnes Newton T2Lt kia 7-10-16 3 att6EKent p58 MR21

MOSS,Samuel Foden.MM.T2Lt dow 28-3-18 RE J'SpecCo p47 CR France40

MOSS,Sidney Cowan Lt ded 8-3-19 RE p271 CR Lancs1

MOSS,Thomas John.MC.MIDx2 LtAMaj kia 21-3-18 307RFA p33 MR27

MOSS,William Thomas Gregory T2Lt kld 5-7-17 GL &RFC p11 CR Lancs14,dedacc

MOSS-BLUNDELL,Cyril Bertram Lt kia 27-9-15 14DLI p161 MR19

MOSSCROP,Allan.MC.T2Lt dow 11-9-17 9ScotRif p103 CR Belgium19

MOSSE,John TLtCol ded 17-6-16 Leic Commdg Depot p88 CR Leic63

MOSSE,Philip Godfrey T2Lt kia 18-4-16 13RWar att6ELancs p65 MR38

MOSSE,William Oliver Matless Col drd 10-10-18 1GarBnMunstF Ret IA p175

MOSSMAN,Harold Alexander.MC.2Lt kia 25-4-18 3 att2RBerks p139 MR27

MOSSOP,William Nicholson.MC.Capt&Adjt dow 8-5-18 5WYorks p218 CR Belgium353,11-5-18

MOSTYN,Edward Henry Joseph David.VD.LtCol ded 2-8-16 4Suss p271 CR Sussex2,1-8-16

MOTHERSILL,James Neville T2Lt kia 7-6-17 10RWKent p141 CR Belgium29

MOTHERWELL,John Ernest 2LtACapt kia 21-10-16 3 att1RIrRif p170 CR France314,3RIrRif att9LNLancs

MOTHERWELL,William 2Lt dow 5-3-17 2 att7HLI p240 CR France300

MOTION,Sidney Howard.MID TLt dow 1-8-17 7Nhants p137 CR Belgium7

MOTLER,John Frederick 2Lt kia 30-7-16 4 att18Manch p155 MR21 &CR France1890

MOTT,Francis Stanley T2Lt dow 23-7-16 24RFus p69 CR France88

MOTT,Hugh Frederick.MC.Capt kia 1-7-16 16Lond p249 MR21,Fenwick

MOTT,Jacob Ernest T2Lt kia 23-12-17 1RIrFus &21RFC p11&171 MR20

MOTT,John Francis Capt kia 7-8-15 2 att6Y&L p159 CR Gallipoli27

MOTT,Lewes Woodham T2Lt kia 23-4-17 9EssR &RFC p11&132 CR France531

MOTTERAM,Arthur William 2Lt kia 21-5-18 6SStaffs p229 CR France 1/5Bn

MOTTERSHALL,Herbert Stanley 2Lt dow 9-10-17 2/9Manch p155 CR Belgium8

MOTTRAM,Frederick Capt&Adjt dow 9-9-17 RFA 48DAC p207 CR Belgium16

MOTTRAM,John Elliott Lt kia 9-10-17 7LancF p221 MR30

MOTTRAM,Osborne Arthur Capt kia 8-8-16 7Lpool p215 CR France630,9-8-18

MOTTRAM,Piercay John MacQueen Capt kia 6-10-19 1ARO att109Inf p208 MR43,Piercey

MOUAT,George Mouat Dundas Capt kia 9/10-5-15 1Lond p245 CR France254.9-5-15

MOUAT-BIGGS,E.2Lt 3-5-16 2Lincs CR France430

MOUATT-BIGGS,John Alborough Lt dow PoW 22-3-18 3 att2RIrReg p89 CR France660,Capt

MOUBRAY,Arthur Russell St John.MC.Maj dow 2-7-18 RGA 200SB p209 CR France29

MOUBRAY,Cyril Lloyd 2Lt kia 10-10-18 RE p210

MOUBRAY,Percy Lionel Capt kia 29-10-14 3 att1BlkW p129 MR29

MOUBRAY,Frank Capt 8-10-18 RFus att4Bn CR France338

MOUCK,Ernest Capt kia 7-8-15 15NumbF p62 CR Gallipoli2

MOUILLOT,Augustus de Thierry Capt dow 15-1-16 IA 51Sikhs p208 CR Iraq5

MOULD,Charles William TCapt kia 25-9-15 5KSLI p145 CR Belgium84

MOULD,David T2Lt kia 13-6-16 1RWar attTMB p65 CR France643

MOULD,Ernest Kingston 2Lt kia 2-9-18 4 att16RWar p65 CR France644

MOULD,James.DSO.MC.ACapt kia 3-9-16 3Worc p109 MR21

MOULDING,Sydney Dormer Lt kia 22-8-15 8Nhants attRInnisF p137 MR4

MOULE,Hugh Elliot Maj mbk 22-5-15 IA 1/4GurkhaRif p280 MR28

MOULSON,Samuel T2Lt kia 4-9-18 18WYorks p82 CR France245

MOULT,Samuel Walker 2Lt kia 15-9-16 2N&D p134 MR21

MOULTON,Charles Eric Lt kia 16-9-15 6Wilts p153 CR France260

MOULTON,William Ralph Osborne T2Lt kia 4-8-16 12Manch p155 CR France400

MOULTSAID,Wesley 2Lt kia 12-11-17 11RIrRif p170

MOUNT,Allan T2Lt kia 18-9-18 EKent p58 CR France369

MOUNT,Edward Alfred T2Lt kia 4-1-16 11RFus p69 CR Belgium28,9Bn

MOUNT,Francis TCapt kia 13-10-15 5RBerks p139 MR19

MOUNTAIN,Allan James 2Lt kia 23-7-16 1/4KLI p235 MR21

MOUNTAIN,Cyril Robert Wightman T2LtACapt kia 5-8-17 13Ches p96 MR29

MOUNTFIELD,Robert Noel Capt dow 5-11-17 8 att2/9Lpool p215 CR Belgium25

MOUNTFORD,Cecil TLt ded 3-3-19 RASC MT p267 CR Ches113,6-3-19

MOUNTFORD,Gordon Capt kia 12-6-17 5NStaffs attRFC p19&237 CR France200

MOUNTFORD,Stanley.MC.Capt kia 24-3-18 9RScots p212 MR 27

MOURITZ,Cecil John Hastings 2Lt kia 5-12-16 5 att2Leinst p174 CR France149

MOURITZEN,Roy Walter T2Lt kld 5-6-17 GL &RFC p11 CR Essex222

MOUSLEY,Alfred Charles 2Lt dow 30-9-17 162RH&FA p33 CR Belgium183

MOWAT,Charles James Carlton Capt kia 28-6-15 8ScotRif p225 MR4

MOWAT,James Maj drd 13-8-15 RAMC p253 MR4

MOWAT,James Dugald Lillie Lt kia 15-6-15 5SfthH p241 MR22

MOWAT,John Farquhar T2Lt dow 15-5-17 7Yorks p91 CR France95

MOWAT,John Graham.MC.Capt kia 27-6-17 1/4WRid p227 CR France258

MOWAT,John Maclellan T2Lt kld 5-1-17 NStaffs &RFC p11&157 CR Scot680

MOWAT,John William 2Lt kia 21-4-17 4 att14A&SH p173 CR France439,21-8-17

MOWAT,Morden Maxwell 2Lt dow PoW 16-5-16 RFC p3 CR France924

MOWAT,Robert James Dugald 2Lt kia 24-9-18 HampsYeo att101MGC p187&204 CR Belgium185

MOWAT,Sinclair Alexander 1917 RFC p257

MOWAT,Sydney Alexander T2Lt kld 2-7-17 GL &RFC p11 CR Scot858

MOWATT,Osmond TLt dow 22-4-17 10Huss p22 CR France113

MOWBRAY,James Seymour Strachan TCapt kia 25-9-15 8BlkW p129 MR19

MOWBRAY,John Leslie.DSO.Maj kia 24-7-16 41RFA p33 CR France630

MOWBRAY,Kenneth John Wharton 2Lt ltia 9-4-17 2 att7Suff p70 CR France581

MOWBRAY,Maurice Charles.MC.Lt kia 23-8-17 RE 89FC p47 CR Belgium19

MOWBRAY,William 2Lt dow 14-1-16 IARO att1/9GurkhaRif p208 MR38

MOWES,Alexander Barclay Lt kia 27-3-18 6Ches p222

MOWES,William Bernard 2Lt kia 7-4-17 6RScots p211

MOXLY,John Hewitt Sutton 2Lt kia 13-3-15 Beds p86 CR Belgium59,12-3-15

MOXON,Gerald John Mortimer TCapt kia 27-3-16 4RFus p69 MR29

MOXON,Hugh Cecil 2Lt dow 19-7-17 5 att8Beds p219 CR France80

MOXON,Tom Cyril Lt ded 19-11-18 RFA p271 CR Yorks361

MOYCE,George Herbert Stanley T2Lt dow 19-4-18 2/8Manch p155 CR France145

MOYES,A.B.Lt 27-3-18 6Ches CR France526

MOYES,John Lt dow 14-10-17 2CamH p168 CR Greece3

MOYES,William Lt 7-4-17 6RScots attRFC CR France285

MOYNA,Edward Gerald James TCapt kia 26-9-15 7RScotF p95 MR19

MOYNAN,Harold Otho William 2Lt kia 31-7-17 SWBord BrecknockBn p223 MR29

MOYNIHAM,Michael John Lt dow 3-6-18 8Lpool p215 CR France63

MOYSE,John Jenkins CaptAMaj dow 8-2-17 1Beds p86 CR France80

MOYSEY,Lewis Capt drd 26-2-18 RAMC p254 MR40

MOZLEY,Richard Inger Lt kia 21-3-18 3Y&L att36MGC p159&184 MR27

MUCHALL,George William Stuart 2Lt kia 10-5-15 RLancs p59 MR29

MUDDOCK,Jasper Milton Preston 2Lt kia 30-11-17 ShropYeo att10KSLIp205 CR Palestine3

MUDGE,Ernest Cecil Capt kia 25-9-15 2Wilts p153 CR France423

MUDIE,James Bolingbroke TCapt ded 6-1-16 RASC p193 CR France770,Harold

MUDIE,James T2Lt kia 30-9-16 9RScotF att1RScots p95 CR Greece3,30-9/1-10-16

MUDIE,Robert Allen Capt kia 20-9-17 8LancF p221 MR30,Alan

MUGFORD,Thomas George Lt kia 17-5-19 IA 1/35Sikhs p280 MR43

MUGGERIDGE,William 2Lt kia 14-5-17 RGA 112SB p41 CR France581,MUGGRIDGE

MUIR,A 2Lt 20-9-17 8A&SH CR Belgium83

MUIR,Allan Lt kia 15-5-19 10Lpool p216 MR70 &CR Europe180

MUIR,Alan Steele 2Lt dow 12-11-16 att98RScots p212 CR France41

MUIR,Alexander 2Lt dow 27-7-16 6HLI att4NumbF p240 CR France102

MUIR,Alexander 2Lt kia 20-9-17 8A&SH p243

MUIR,Andrew Lt kia 16-11-15 7ScotRif p224 CR Gallipoli3

MUIR,Andrew Christison Mitchell T2Lt dow 27-10-18 9 att1KOSB p102 CR Gallipoli14,27-10-15

MUIR,Andrew Reid 2Lt dow 7-11-17 B233RFA p33 CR France40

MUIR,Basil 2Lt kia 16-6-15 6 att3Worc p109 MR29

MUIR,Burleigh Leicester TCapt ded 4-11-18 RASC att3Cps HQ p193 CR France1725

MUIR,David Orrock 2Lt kia 20-5-17 9HLI p240 MR20

MUIR,Frederick Bennie Lt kia 15-11-16 3 att2HLI p163 MR21

MUIR,Harry T2Lt kld 18-4-16 11EYorks p84 CR France643

MUIR,Horace Wellesley 2Lt kia 24-4-17 4Beds p86 MR20

MUIR,James Hunter 2Lt kia 7-4-17 RFC p11 MR20

MUIR,James Lester T2Lt ded 11-8-16 10ESurr p264 CR Scot84 Ex 19RFus

MUIR,James Robert Grant Lt dow 17-9-18 1/7HLI p240 CR France686

MUIR,John Hugh TLt kia 26-9-17 1GordH p167 MR30

MUIR,John Huntly Maj dow 11-4-18 17Lancers att1KOSB p23 MR32

MUIR,John Wallace 2Lt kia 12-3-18 46RFC p255 MR20

MUIR,Matthew Andrew TCapt ded 18-7-16 15Huss att1KAR p22&202 CR EAfrica40

MUIR,Philip Denis Grahame 2Lt kia 6-12-16 2LovatScts att10CamH p204 MR37

MUIR,Stanley Keith.MC.T2LtTCapt kld 12-9-17 GL &RFC p11 CR Lincs67

MUIR,William Stewart 2Lt kia 25-9-16 6A&SH p243 MR21

MUIR-MACKENZIE,Robert Cecil.Sir.MC.Lt kia 12-4-18 att95DLI p239 CR France745

MUIRHEAD,Alexander Hugh 2Lt kia 31-7-17 1Camb p245 MR29

MUIRHEAD,George Wilson 2Lt dow 16-12-15 IARO att76Punjabis p280 CR Iraq1

MUIRHEAD,James Love LtTCapt kia 21-11-17 10RScots attTankCps p212&189 CR France1483

MUIRHEAD,John T2Lt kia 16-3-17 GL &59RFC p11 CR France120

MUIRHEAD,John Ritchie 2Lt kia 20-10-18 8ScotRif attTMB RFA p225 CR Belgium140

MUIRHEAD,Langdon 2Lt kia 29-9-18 59RFA p33 MR16

MUIRHEAD,Lennox Lt kia 21-9-18 7RScots p211 CR France1496,5Bn

MUIRHEAD,Phillips Quincy TLt kia 18-7-16 D25RFA p33 CR France453

MUIRHEAD,William 2Lt kia 28-3-18 3CamH att44TMB p168 MR20

MULCAHY-MORGAN,Edward Spread Lt kia 27-10-14 RIrRif p170 MR22

MULCAHY-MORGAN,Francis Campion Lt kia 6-9-16 7RIrRif p170 MR21

MULCUCK,Daniel Henry 2Lt kia 11-10-17 att8Lincs p75 MR30,MULCOCK

MULDOON,John Lt kia 13-9-18 2CamH p168 CR Greece6 2Lt

MULES,William George Horace Mainwaring Lt dow 12-2-16 IA 130Baluchis p280 CR EAfrica56,Capt

MULHALL,Frank Reginald 2Lt dow 15-10-18 RGA 25HB p41 CR France528

MULHOLLAND,Andrew Edward Somerset.Hon.Capt dow 1-11-14 1IrGds p53 CR Belgium57

MULKERN,Hubert Cowell Capt 1-7-16 RAMC att9RInniskF p197 MR21

MULKERN,Lionel Henry T2Lt kia 26-9-17 123MGC Inf p184 MR30

MULLALLY,Brian Desmond TCapt kia 1-7-16 26NumbF p62 CR France393

MULLALY,Charles Mylne Capt kia 9-5-15 IA 2/2GurkhaRif MR28 p280

MULLALY,Dennis Joseph St.Clair.MC.MID Lt kia 17-10-15 RGA 1SB p41 CR France423

MULLALY,Frederick Terence Hastings Capt kia 21-4-17 IA 2/6 att1/8GurkhaRif MR38 p280

MULLALY,Herbert Maj ded 19-1-20 IA 1/9 att2/4GurkhaRif p280 MR43

MULLANE,Bernard Patrick T2Lt dow 1-4-18 9RFus p69 CR France64

MULLEN,Arnold George Leighton Lt ded 15-2-19 5DLI &104RAF p239 CR France1633,kia 22-8-18

MULLER,Carl Wilhelm Albert 2Lt kia 5-10-16 5Worc p109 CR France423,Charles William 1Bn

MULLER,John Herman Lt kia 31-10-17 9Middx att113RFC p19&236 Cr Palestine1

MULLER,Norman Capt kia 28-7-18 6WYorks p218 CR France1689

MULLER-CHATEAU,James Lt ded 29-12-19 RH&FA p261

MULLER-CHATEAU,Leo Lt 27-2-19 RFA CR Norf209 Ex 1AustLtHorse

MULLETT,Walter Stephen 4835 Lt&QM ded 31-1-18 11RScots p54 CR Ireland33

MULLIGAN,Herbert Butler.MC.T2Lt kia 4-7-16 1 att12RScots p54 MR21

MULLIGAN,Sidney Gerald 2Lt kia 23-4-17 3 att4Beds p86 MR20

MULLIN,Archibald T2Lt kld 16-5-17 RAOC p198 CR France57,5-4-17

MULLINS,John Ollis 2Lt kld 30-3-15 Middx &RFC p1&148 CR Mddx29,dedacc

MULLINS,Richard Walter TCapt kia 1-7-16 10Y&L p159 CR France267

MULLIS,George Edwin LtACapt kia 30-9-16 RGA 14HB p41 CR France251

MULLOCK,Sidney Goss ALtCol kia 12-4-17 2Ess p132 CR France730

MULOCK,Edward Ross 2Lt kia 11-3-15 2GordH p167 CR France279

MULOCK,Henry Collister TLt kia 15-2-17 GL &52RFC p11 CR France105

MULROY,Thomas Bernard T2Lt ded 23-1-16 11Lpool p72 CR Yorks607

MUMBY,Harold Cheffings T2Lt kia 3-10-18 5TankCps p188 CR France375

MUMFORD,Arthur Green 2Lt kia 9-1-17 IARO att105Mahrattas p280 MR38

MUMFORD,Frank Richard Capt kia 8-7-16 2Wilts p153MR21 CR France390

MUMFORD,John Houston.MC&Bar.Lt kia 13-8-17 B110RFA p208 CR Belgium7

MUMFORD,Louis Richard 2Lt kia 21-10-18 23Lond attRAF p256 CR Mddx17

MUMFREY,B.J.H.LtCol See HUMFREY

MUMMERY,Harry Norman Samuel Capt ded PoW 6-8-18 HLI att14Bn p163

MUNBY,Ernest John Lt kia 31-1-15 RE 1EAngliaFC p210 CR France727

MUNCIE,Daniel McBeth 2Lt kia 3-12-17 2RFA p33 CR France711

MUNDAY,Edwin George Stanislaus 2Lt kia 20-2-17 3 att13Ess p132 CR France393

MUNDAY,Leslie William Crawford 2Lt kld 12-8-18 RGA p209 CR France1170

MUNDEN,John Arnold 2Lt kia 28-8-16 3 att6SomLI p80 MR21 &CR France1890

MUNDEY,Lionel Clement Lt kia 6-6-15 2RFus p69 MR4,5-6-15

MUNDEY,Walter Vivian Lt ded 30-9-19 19RHuss p621 CR Surrey136

MUNDS,Percy T2Lt dow 8-10-18 7RFus p69 MR16,1Bn

MUNDY,James TLt dow 26-11-16 19DLI p161 CR France1182

MUNDY,Jesse Ernest 2Lt dow 24-4-18 PoW Middx att2/2Lond p148 MR27

MUNDY,Lionel Frank Hasting.MID Lt dow 3-9-14 RHA p33 CR France1420

MUNDYE,Arnold T2Lt kld 29-7-16 1RWSurr p56 CR France176

MUNGALL,Robert 2Lt kia 23-4-17 7 att13RScots p211 MR20

MUNGEAM,Ernest George 2Lt dow 25-8-18 17MGC p184 MR6

MUNN,Leslie Vincent T2Lt ded 16-2-17 GL &RFC p11 CR France924 Ex 6Leic

MUNRO,Alexander T2Lt dow 5-11-16 10ScotRif C'Coy p103 CR France145

MUNRO,Alexander Douglas T2Lt kia 2-9-18 11 att1Ches p96 CR France1484

MUNRO,Baillie Chisholm.MC.2Lt kia 10-7-17 12 att2KRRC p151 MR31

MUNRO,Claud Bruce TLt kia 27-9-15 13RScots p54 MR19,26-9-15

MUNRO,Colin Cameron T2Lt dow 23-4-16 A122RFA p33 CR France345

MUNRO,Donald 2Lt kia 28-4-17 15RScots p54 MR20

MUNRO,Donald Rice 2Lt kld 28-7-17 RFC 37TrSqn p11 CR Lincs181,Lt

MUNRO,Duncan Leitch T2Lt dow 13-10-17 8BlkW p129 CR Belgium16

MUNRO,Fergus Fullerton T2Lt kia 20-9-17 att5CamH p168 MR30

MUNRO,Fred Ross 2Lt kia 18-11-16 7 att15HLI p240 MR21

MUNRO,Frederick John 2Lt dow 11-8-17 RGA 4SB p41 CR Belgium20,Lt

MUNRO,George William Lt dow 1-10-18 4 att5CamH p242 CR Belgium173

MUNRO,Guy Horace T2Lt kld 18-8-17 GL 26RFus attRFC p11 CR Mddx80

MUNRO,Hector Charles Seymour.MC.Capt kia 23-10-18 2SfthH p165 CR France1266

MUNRO,Hector William 2Lt kia 23-4-17 7A&SH p243 CR France545

MUNRO,Henry Fraser Capt dow 29-9-15 8SfthH p165 CR France1

MUNRO,Hugh Adam Lt kia 22-9-15 1/8A&SH A'Coy p243 CR France197,Capt

MUNRO,Hugh Donald.MID Lt kia 25-3-18 20DLI p161 MR20

MUNRO,Ian Duncan T2Lt kia 13-9-15 ACycCps att9DCC p181 CR France114,11-9-15

MUNRO,James Donald Sutherland 2Lt kld 17-7-17 RFC p11 CR Surrey150

MUNRO,James John T2Lt kia 31-10-18 1/2 att1/5KOSB p102 CR Belgium140

MUNRO,John.MC.2Lt kia 16-4-18 4SfthH p241 MR32

MUNRO,John Clegg T2Lt ded 10-11-18 3Worc p109 CR France332

MUNRO,John Sutherland Lt ded 16-7-17 RAMC att112FA p197 CR Iraq8

MUNRO,Murdo Simon 2Lt kia 26-4-17 12RB p179 CR France662

MUNRO,Ronald Lt kia 8-8-17 1/5A&SH p243 CR Palestine8

MUNRO,Ronald George.MC.Lt dow 19-9-16 18Lond p250 CR France145

MUNRO,Thomas Mackay 2Lt kia 25-9-15 7SfthH p165 MR19

MUNRO,William 2Lt kia 29-4-18 8Lpool p216 CR Belgium111,Lt

MUNRO,William Dawson Capt kia 16-5-17 8A&SH p243 MR20

MUNRO,William Pearce 2Lt dow 5-9-18 A70RFA p33 CR France421,Lt

MUNSEY,William Frederick 2Lt kia 16-8-17 12KRRC p151 MR30 Ex 28Lond

MUNSON,George Philip 2Lt kia 7-8-15 2Y&L p159 MR29 &CR Belgium453

MUNSTER,John Francis Lt kia 4-2-17 13Huss p22 MR38

MUNT,R.R.2Lt 11-5-16 1/1RFA CR Egypt1

MUNTZ,Joseph Oscar TCapt dow 4-9-18 16Dev B'Coy p77 CR France833

MURCHISON,Donald 2Lt kia 14-4-17 5ScotRif p224 MR20

MURCHISON,Kenneth Bickersteth 2Lt kia 22-8-17 2 att8SfthH p165 MR29

MURCHLAND,Charles TLt kia 26-5-15 RFA p33 CR Belgium101

MURDOCH,Barry Wilkie 2Lt kia 2-2-17 IARO att187MGC Inf p280 CR Iraq5,3-2-17

MURDOCH,James Gordon TLt dow 22-9-15 7SLancs p125 CR France345

MURDOCH,James Hunter George 2Lt kia 4-7-16 95RFA p33 CR France189,3-7-16

MURDOCH,John 2Lt kia 1-7-16 16HLI p163 CR France293

MURDOCH,Louis Farde Campbell 2Lt dow 19-9-16 2ScotGds p52

MURDOCH,Ronald Hamilton William T2Lt kia 28-10-16 21 att4Lpool p72 MR21

MURDOCH,Thomas John Carson TLt kia 6-2-16 24Manch p155 CR France637

MURE,Godfrey Arthur Stanhope Capt kia 3-1-17 ArabRifs CR EAfrica36

MURGATROYD,Ellison.DCM.TCapt kia 26-3-18 16WYorks p82 CR France798

MURGATROYD,Hugh Lester.MC.LtACapt dow 27-9-18 Leic att1/7LancF p88 CR France245

MURIEL,Sidney Herbert Foster Capt kia 30-4-15 BordR p117 CR Gallipoli3

MURLESS,Herbert Reginald.MC.TLt dow 7-2-17 1 att12RFus p69 CR France80

MURLY-GOTTO,James TLt dow 20-8-16 RE 70FC p47 CR France40,2Lt

MURPHY,A.G.Capt&QM ded 14-6-17 GL &RFC p11 CR Hamps1

MURPHY,Albert T2Lt kia 3-10-16 30 att24NumbF p62 CR France922

MURPHY,Alfred Durham.DSO.MC.BtMaALtCol kia 6-11-17 2Leinst p174 CR France528

MURPHY,Allen Ingham 23910 2Lt kld 30-3-17 RFC p11 CR Norf247

MURPHY,Bernard Joseph 2Lt dow 18-8-17 5MunstF attRIrRif p175 CR Belgium8

MURPHY,Christopher Fowler Lt kia 21-10-14 att2 O&BLI p130 MR29

MURPHY,Christopher John 2Lt kia 20-7-16 9MunstF p175 CR France115,1Bn

MURPHY,Christopher Trevor Elias.MID Lt dow 8-5-18 RGA 216SB p41 CR France40

MURPHY,Edward T2Lt kia 2-4-17 19Manch p155 CR France1186

MURPHY,Edward 2Lt kia 21-3-18 8 att1RDubF p177 MR27

MURPHY,Edwin Hale Capt dow 6-5-17 5Leinst p174 CR France1141,2Bn

MURPHY,F.Capt 13-3-20 RAMC CR Wilts64

MURPHY,G.F.L.Capt 22-11-18 RAMC CR Ireland24

MURPHY,George TLt kia 6-9-17 13RWar att1/5LancF Res p65 MR30

MURPHY,Harry Eustace Lt kld 22-4-18 1/4RFus &RAF p69 CR Eire78

MURPHY,Hugh Palmer TLt kia 6-8-16 10Lincs p75 CR France432

MURPHY,James 2Lt kia 15-4-18 2/5NStaffs p238 MR32 &CR France298

MURPHY,James Neville Herbert 2Lt kia 10-5-15 5 att2DubF p177 MR29

MURPHY,John.MID LtTCapt dow 17-8-17 D62RFA p33 CR France113,kia

MURPHY,John Lt kia 25-8-18 6NumbF p214 CR France239

MURPHY,Johnston Lt kia 2-7-16 6 att8RIrRif p170 MR21

MURPHY,Leonard Francis McCarthy2Lt ded 21-7-17 IARO att81Pnrs p280 MR43,121Bn

MURPHY,Lewis William Capt kia 9-4-16 2DCLI att5Wilts p114 MR38,3Bn

MURPHY,Matthew TCapt drd 10-10-18 RAMC p197 CR Eire75

MURPHY,M.J.MID 2Lt kia 12-3-15 3Worc p109 CR Belgium17,11-3-15

MURPHY,Philip Frederick T2Lt kia 2-7-16 RE 201FC p47 MR21

MURPHY,Reginald Graham Capt ded 4-10-18 RDC p256 CR Ches182

MURPHY,Robert T2Lt dow 1-10-18 1RIrRif p170 CR Belgium157

MURPHY,William 2Lt kia 10-3-15 2Leic p88 CR France727,11-3-15

MURPHY,William Joseph.MID TCapt kia 9-9-16 9DubF p177 CR France294

MURRAY,Alastair John Greville 2Lt dow 14-9-14 1CamH p168 CR France1894

MURRAY,Alexander Capt kia 14-8-17 ScotHorse p205 CR Belgium72

MURRAY,Alexander 2Lt kia 29-8-18 4GordH p242 CR France266

MURRAY,Alexander Gordon Wynch.MBE.Capt ded 15-2-19 ULCambUnivOTC p271 CR Kent34

MURRAY,Alexander Roxburgh 2Lt kia 18-11-16 4 att17HLI p163 CR France534

MURRAY,Andrew Lt kia 19-11-16 56MGC p184 MR21

MURRAY,Andrew Buchanan Lt kia 23-4-17 A&SH p173

MURRAY,Andrew Currie Capt kia 20-5-17 9HLI p240 MR20

MURRAY,Anthony Hepburn Poore Lt kia 9-4-17 3 att1RScotF p95 CR France581

MURRAY,Anthony Stoddart 2Lt mbk 22-3-18 1/8A&SH p257 CR France375,23-3-18

MURRAY,Archibald Capt&QM dow 13-9-14 KOSB p102 CR France870 &CR France1113

MURRAY,Arthur T2Lt kia 8-8-18 7RSuss p119 CR France1770

MURRAY,Cecil James Carruthers Capt kia 15-6-15 6ScotRif p224 CR France260

MURRAY,Charles.MC.2Lt kia 16-10-18 RGA 115SB p41 CR Belgium157,Lt

MURRAY,Charles John Lt kia 25-10-14 1CldGds p51 MR29,26-10-14

MURRAY,Charles Robinson T2Lt kia 18-9-16 9 att7KOSB p102 MR21

MURRAY,Charles Stephenson TCapt dow 1-7-16 12RIrRif p170 CR France44,2-7-16

MURRAY,Charles William 2Lt kia 25-9-15 9KRRC p151 MR29

MURRAY,Cyril 2Lt kia 16-8-17 2Lond p245 MR29

MURRAY,Edward Douglas TLt dow 20-7-16 8BlkW p129 CR France23,2Lt

MURRAY,Eric Dennys 2Lt kia 16-10-14 19Huss p23 CR France263

MURRAY,Ernest Francis Hume.MC.DCM.LtACapt&Adjt kia 9-10-17 2HAC p206 MR30

MURRAY,Fane Wright Stapleton Capt kia 30-11-14 12Lancers p22 MR29

MURRAY,Frederick Stanley Lt dow 19-11-17 3/2KAR &NStaffs p157&202 CR EAfrica11 &CR Tanzania1,NStaffs attKAR

MURRAY,George Capt kia 4-6-16 2Leinst p174 CR Belgium49

MURRAY,George Angus TLt kia 4-10-18 RE att310RFA p47 CR France910

MURRAY,George Anthony.MC.LtAMaj dow 4-4-18 D47RFA p33 CR France1173

MURRAY,George Ramsay Lt kia 23-12-16 IARO att13Lancers p280 CR Iraq5

MURRAY,Graham Dunmore.MID T2Lt kia 26-1-16 12NumbF p62 CR France922

MURRAY,Harold Gladstone Lt kia 16-12-16 1DivTMB attRFC CR France46

MURRAY,Henry Berkeley TLt kia 18-7-16 10A&SH p173 CR France162 &CR France513

MURRAY,Henry Francis Farquharson MajALtCol kia 23-8-17 9BlkW p129 CR Belgium8

MURRAY,Herbert.MC.Capt kia 25-7-18 1/4GordH p241 CR France622,20-7-18

MURRAY,James Brash T2Lt kia 21-5-16 8SfthH p165 CR France423

MURRAY,James Eric Capt kia 10-3-15 IA 89Punjabis att1/39GarhwalRif p280 CR France355 &CR France1887,87Bn

MURRAY,James McMillan 2Lt kia 24-6-17 8ScotRif p225 CR France1489

MURRAY,James Thomas Crockatt.DSO.Maj dow 16-2-15 1BlkW p129 CR France202,Crokatt

MURRAY,John 2Lt kia 16-8-17 5 att1KOSB p224 MR30

MURRAY,John Lt ded 30-10-17 1/6A&SH C'Coy p243 CR Belgium11,kia

MURRAY,John Claude 2Lt kia 9-7-16 2SWBord p100 MR21

MURRAY,John Congreve Lt dow 23-9-17 1/8RScots p211 CR Belgium16

MURRAY,John Robertson T2Lt dow 18-9-17 att9SfthH p165 CR Belgium46

MURRAY,Joseph Leonard T2Lt kia 29-5-17 GL &RFC p11 MR20

MURRAY,Kenneth Desmond 2Lt kia 25-9-15 9ESurr p113 MR19

MURRAY,Kenneth Hope 2Lt kia 18-6-16 6SfthH p241 CR France15,dow

MURRAY,Leonard Lt kld 13-3-17 LancHuss attRFC p204 CR Staffs176

MURRAY,Mabel SNurse ded 2-11-18 TFNS 3SGH CR Oxford69

MURRAY,Maurice Austin Lt kia 25-9-15 11Ess p132 MR19,26-9-15

MURRAY,Norman Cairns Capt kia 30-6-16 7War p214 CR France1327

MURRAY,Patrick Austin TCapt kia 1-7-16 25NumbF p62 MR21

MURRAY,Patrick Hallam Capt kia 25-9-15 61/131RFA p33 MR19

MURRAY,Patrick Maxwell Lt kia 20-9-14 2N&D p134 MR15

MURRAY,Percival William Lt dow PoW 2-2-17 6DLI attRFC p19&239 CR France1321

MURRAY,Peter Lt 13-1-20 25 att152Punjabis MR43

MURRAY,Randolph TLt dow 27-10-17 1CamH p168 CR France545,6Bn

MURRAY,Randolph Noel TLt dow 28-4-16 7RInnisF p105 CR France115,Capt

MURRAY,Raymond Hugh T2Lt kia 12-3-18 155MGC Inf p184 CR Palestine9

MURRAY,Robert Davidson T2Lt dow 2-10-18 11RScots p54 CR Belgium38

MURRAY,Robert Elder Lt kia 11-8-18 5 att5/6RScots p211 MR16

MURRAY,Robert Henry TCapt kia 7-7-16 11Yorks attRMunstF p91 CR France115

MURRAY,Robert Leslie.MID Capt kia 19-4-17 4Nhampt p234 MR34

MURRAY,Robert McDiarmid.MC.TLt dow 25-2-16 RGA 7SB p41 CR France102

MURRAY,Robert William Skinner Capt ded 6-5-19 RAMC att5FlSchl RAF p197 CR Egypt9

MURRAY,Ronald Alexander.MID TCapt dow 19-9-18 8RScotF p95 CR Greece6

MURRAY,Ronald Ernest.DSO&Bar.DCM.LtCol ded 29-6-20 BSAP CR Hamps161

MURRAY,Rupert Auriol Comaut Capt dow 11-3-15 1SfthH p165 CR France201,Conant

MURRAY,Thomas Capt kia 3-7-16 11Ches p96 MR21

MURRAY,Thomas Francis Maj kia 21-12-14 1HLI p163 MR22

MURRAY,Thomas William.MID Capt kia 19-7-20 IA 116Mahrattas p280 CR Iraq6

225

MURRAY,Victor Bickersteth Lt 28-2-21 2CamH CR Ches22

MURRAY,W.H.E.CB.BrigGen 2-2-15 Staff CR Scot967

MURRAY,William T2Lt kia 24-4-17 1Middx p148 CR France591

MURRAY,William 2Lt kldacc 30-7-18 RFA att17TMB p33 CR Irraq8

MURRAY,William Douglas Gillespie 2Lt kia 3-1-18 RFC p16 CR France285

MURRAY,William Dunmore TLt ded 23-1-16 RAMC p197

MURRAY,William Edward Capt kia 17-9-14 3GordH p167 CR France867,14-9-14 1Bn

MURRAY,William Grant 2Lt kia 16-4-18 7SfthH p165 MR30

MURRAY,William Raymond Croft Capt ded 25-2-17 5GrenGds p50 CR Europe28,26-2-17

MURRAY,William Roland T2Lt kia 11-11-17 GL &RFC p11 CR France44

MURRAY-DIXON,Henry Edward Otto Murray 2Lt dow 10-4-17 1/4SfthH CR France95

MURRAY-MENZIES,Clive William 2Lt kia 25-1-15 1BlkW p129 MR22

MURRAY-MENZIES,Duncan Innes.MC.LtACapt kia 22-8-17 BlkW attC'TankCps p129&188 MR30

MURRAY-SMITH,Arthur George Lt dow 2-11-14 2LifeGds p20 CR France1027

MURRAY-SMITH,Geoffrey Lt kia 29-9-15 6 att3RFus p69 MR19

MURTON,Charles Duncan.TD.Maj 7-9-19 5EKent CR Kent182

MURTON,Charles Evelyn 2Lt kia 30-11-17 35MGC Inf p184 MR17

MUSGRAVE,Cecil David TCapt ded 15-11-18 3RASC 8DivTrn p193 CR France1277

MUSGRAVE,Herbert.DSO.Maj kia 3-6-18 RE Staff 2CpsHQ p47 CR France142,2-6-18

MUSGRAVE,John James Nicholson T2Lt kld 27-2-18 RFC p16 CR C'land&W'land18

MUSGRAVE,Joseph Baxter.MC.Capt dow 16-3-20 4Ches CR Ches28

MUSGRAVE,Kenneth Lt kia 22-3-15 YLI p143 CR Belgium98

MUSGRAVE,Thomas Lt kia 6-2-15 1IrGds SR p53 CR France720

MUSGRAVE,William Martin 2Lt dow 15-4-17 5BordR att16Lond p228 CR France120,MUSGROVE

MUSGROVE,George Henry Stuart TLt kia 1-7-16 8ESurr p113 CR France513

MUSGROVE,John William 2Lt kia 19-7-18 4BlkW p230 CR France324

MUSKER,John Henry 2Lt kia 1-11-17 3 att1Ches p96 MR30

MUSKER,Joseph Walter T2Lt kia 30-7-16 20Lpool p72 MR21

MUSPRATT,Keith Knox.MC.2Lt TCapt kld 19-3-18 2DorsR &56RFC p16&124 CR Hamps15,16-3-18

MUSPRATT,Terence Petty.MC.Capt dow 29-5-18 3Worc p109 CR France1693

MUSSON,Alfred William TLt ded 10-9-18 RAMC p267 CR Lancs226

MUSSON,Graham 2Lt kia 25-3-18 8MGC p184 MR27

MUSSON,Harold Methuen.MC.2Lt dow 26-9-17 D149RFA p33 CR France40

MUSSON,John Henry 2Lt kia 19-7-15 2RWSurr p56 CR France631

MUSSON,Samuel Paynter Maj ded 2-6-17 IA S&TCps p280 CR Leic63

MUSTARD,Robert William 2Lt kia 31-3-18 12/13NumbF p62 MR27

MUTCH,George.DSO.TLt kia 6-7-17 GordH &4RFC p11&167 CR Belgium127

MYBURGH,John Adrian T2Lt dow 10-4-17 GL &55RFC p11 CR France300

MYCOCK,Sam.MM.2Lt kia 21-3-18 7 att2/6N&D p233 MR20

MYDDLETON,Edward Geoffrey 2Lt kia /-9-14 Suff p78 MR15,26-8-14

MYDDLETON-GAVEY,Francis Capt kia 26-9-15 2 att4Worc p109 MR4

MYER,T2Lt kia 14-2-17 GL &RFC p11

MYER,Denzil Grenville Alex T2Lt kia 25-2-17 Worc p109 MR38

MYER,Ernest Alex Maj kld 3-4-15 6Lond p246 CR France279

MYERS,Arthur Francis TLt kia 31-3-18 2RRofCav att4Huss p23 MR27

MYERS,Francis Michael.MC.T2Lt kia 14-2-17 GL 11Suff attRFC 11Wing p11 CR Belgium1

MYERS,Henry John TCapt ded 19-2-19 GL&RASC p255 CR Kent203

MYERS,James Wheatley.MID Capt dow 14-8-17 19Manch p155 CR France102

MYERS,John Coupar Capt kld 4-5-18 ScotHorse p205 MR19,Couper

MYERS,John Flesher TCapt kia 9-10-17 6Yorks p91 MR30

MYERS,John James 2Lt kia 22-10-17 11DLI p161 MR21

MYERS,Lawrence Benjamin 2Lt kia 9-6-16 IARO att130Baluchis p280 CR EAfrica19,8-6-16

MYERS,Thomas Wrighton T2Lt dow 19-11-17 1Nhants p137 CR Belgium16,Lt Wrightson

MYERS,Wilfrid Herman TCapt ded 10-4-16 12Lpool p72 CR Surrey160

MYLES,Alfred Thomas Charles 2Lt 2-7-18 10Lpool p216MR19,26-9-15

MYLES,Charles William Chester.MC.CaptAMaj ded 19-10-18 RAMC p253 CR Palestine9

MYLES,John Adam Whitson Douglas Capt ded 29-5-18 7HLI attKAR p240&268 CR EAfrica77

MYLES,Philip Henry Lt kia 13-1-16 IA 41Dogras p280 CR Iraq5,Capt

MYLES,R.S.Lt 22-10-19 S&T Cps MR65

MYLES,Thomas Booth.MC.Capt kia 2-8-17 12HLI p163 MR29

MYLES,William Whitson T2Lt dow 20-9-16 10ScotRif &TMB p103 CR France177

MYLIUS,John Kingsford.MID Lt dow 12-10-16 1KSLI p145 CR France105

MYLLES,James Robertson Jack 2Lt kia 30-7-15 3HLI p163 CR Belgium186,Lt 30-12-14

MYLNE,Edward Graham.MID Capt dow 12-6-15 1IrGds p53 CR France145

MYLNE,Euan Louis.MC.Lt dow 15-9-16 2IrGds p53 CR France374,kia

MYLNE,James Graham Lt kia 2-9-18 8RScots p211 CR France646

MYLREA,William Percy Garland TLtCol ded 25-8-15 RFA p271 CR Essex196

MYTTON,Percy Lt kia 2-5-15 8Mddx p236 MR29

MYTTON,Richard Devereux Hugh 2Lt dow 3-10-16 1Lond p245 MR21,1-10-16

N

NADAUD,Henry Louis Frederick Bonnetand.TD.Maj kia 21-3-18 24Lond p252 CR France439,Bonnetaut

NADIN,Trafford Capt ded 8-6-18 2/5N&D p232 CR Lond14

NAGLE,Gilbert.MC.TCapt&Ajt kia 5-7-17 7RSuss p119 CR France1182

NAILER,Edgar Ivan Fitzroy Lt kia 23-8-18 1Beds p86 CR France239

NAINBY,Whinfield Hamilton T2Lt kia 18-8-16 20KRRC p151 CR France513

NAINBY,William 2Lt kia 27-5-18 Lincs att62LTMB p75 MR18

NAIRN,Francis William EngLt ded 9-11-16 RIM p280 CR Iraq6

NAIRN,George 2Lt dow 28-9-16 70RFA 15Div p33 CR France177

NAIRN,Ian Couper.MC&Bar.Capt kia 2-9-18 Fife&ForfarYeo p203 CR France511,Cooper 14BlkW

NAIRNE,Lord Charles George Francis Mercer.MVO.Maj kia 30-10-14 1Drags p21 CR Belgium57

NAIRNE,James 2Lt kia 13-4-18 9HLI p240 MR32

NAIRNE,Ronald.MID 2Lt kia 3-4-18 5RScots B'Coy p211 CR France745,5/6Bn

NAIRNE,William Graham 2Lt dow 11-7-15 3SLancs att2LancF p125 CR Belgium11

NAISH,Alfred Herbert TLt kia 13-7-16 20KRRC p151 CR France513

NAISH,Edwin Athelstan T2Lt kia 22/23-7-16 10Glouc p107 MR21

NAISMITH,Noel Lings T2Lt kia 11-1-17 10 att7NStaffs p157 CR Iraq5

NALDER,Frank Shirley Capt kia 21-9-18 8KSLI p145

NANCARROW,John Vivian Capt kia 25-4-15 4Yorks p220 MR29

NANCARROW,William Thomas T2Lt kia 15-4-18 9Norf p74 MR30

NANGLE,Edward Jocelyn TCapt kia 26-9-15 RAMC att1LNLancs p197 CR France219

NANSON,Joseph T2Lt kia 1-7-16 25Manch p155 CR France397

NAPER,Frank Cornewall Capt kia 3-5-17 1RLancs p59 CR France544

NAPIER,Egbert Maj kia 13-11-16 1/5GordH RoO p167 CR France131

NAPIER,Guy Greville Lt dow 25-9-15 IA 35Sikhs att47 p280 CR France924,Capt

NAPIER,Henry Edward.MID TBrigGen dow 27-4-15 88Bde Staff p1 MR4,25-4-15

NAPIER,Henry Lenox Maj kia 17-11-15 11N&D p134 MR40

NAPIER,James 2Lt kld 7-4-18 GL &52RAF p191 MR20

NAPIER,John Chatt Lt kia 29-10-18 4NumbF p213 CR France1034

NAPIER,John Francis SubCdr ded 26-6-21 IA S&TCps 114Coy p280 CR Iraq8

NAPIER,Jonathan 2Lt kia 16-8-17 7YLI p143 MR30

NAPIER,Lennox Robert Murray Capt dow PoW 28-7-16 CamH E'Coy p168 CR France245

NAPIER,Maurice Alexander TMaj kia 27-5-16 Ches att10WelshR p96 CR France707

NAPIER,Rupert George Carrington Lt dow 2-8-17 2GrenGds p50 CR Belgium16,Carington

NAPIER,William Lennox.Bart.TMaj kia 13-8-15 4SWBord p100 CR Gallipoli17

NAREY,Vincent Gerald TLt dow 15-10-16 11 att8WRid p116 CR France145

NARRACOTT,Ronald William Lt kia 10-8-15 RE p210 MR29

NASBY,Frank Clementine 2Lt kia 1-9-17 4NumbF p213 CR France1461

NASH,Arthur James 2Lt kia 13-6-18 5N&D p233 MR19

NASH,Charles Frederic Wybrow.MC&Bar.Capt kld 27-3-18 7Norf p74 MR27

NASH,Edward Radcliffe Capt kia 21-2-15 16Lancers p23 CR Belgium57

NASH,Fountain O'Key Colbourne CaptTMaj kia 27-4-15 5NumbF p213 CR Belgium113

NASH,Francis Henry.MC.MID TCapt kia 18-7-17 9NStaffs p157 CR Belgium17,17-7-17

NASH,George 2Lt dow 29-6-15 6 att3Worc p109 CR Hereford166,Lt

NASH,Gordon 2Lt kld 7-5-18 GL &63RAF CR Kent156

NASH,Harold John Lt kia 24-3-18 4 att9RWelshF p223 MR20

NASH,James 2Lt kia 3-4-15 4 att1ESurr p113 CR Belgium17,2-4-15

NASH,James Haran Lt kia 27-3-18 1IrGds 1Coy p53 CR France214

NASH,Llewellyn Charles.MID Lt dow 29-9-15 2KRRC p151 CR France88,Capt 28-9-15

NASH,Manfred Victor Johnstone 2Lt kia 2-11-17 25 att1/10Lond p252 CR Palestine8

NASH,Phillip Geoffrey T2Lt kia 5-10-17 21Manch p155 CR Belgium308

NASH,William Fleetwood.DSO.TLtCol ded 28-12-15 BordR Maj RoO p117 CR C'land&W'land17

NASH,William Walter 2Lt kia 4-7-18 3 att2Ess p132 CR France412,2 att3Bn

NASMITH,Arthur Plater.DSO.TCapt kia 23-4-17 7BordR p117 MR20

NASMYTH,Alfred Wylie 12-10-17 AlbertaR attRFC CR Belgium140

NASON,John William Washington TCapt kia 26-12-16 GL 14Suss att46RFC p3&p191 CR Belgium4

NASON,Richard Philip 2Lt kia 16-4-18 SNottsHuss p205 MR32

NATHAN,David Lt kia 20-8-17 A155/2RFA p208 CR Belgium10

NATHAN,Leopold Charles T2Lt kia 14-9-16 8WWrid p116 MR21

NATHAN,Robert Percy.MC.LtACapt dow 22-3-18 RFA att36TMB p33 CR France1203

NATHAN,William Sylvester 2Lt kia 14-6-16 RFus att12Bn p69 MR29,14-6-17

NAUGHTON,H.F.Lt 10-11-17 IARO att7Lancers MR66

NAYLER,Frederick Augustus 2Lt ded 20-10-18 RASC p193 CR Mddx39

NAYLOR,Cyril Doughty.MC.T2Lt kia 25-8-18 7Lincs p75 CR France392

NAYLOR,Eric Lewin Lt kia 3-12-17 3SStaffs att2/6RWarR p122 MR17

NAYLOR,Frank 2Lt kia 23-3-18 LNLancs &59RFC p16&136,ded MR20

NAYLOR,Fred Lt kia 12-4-18 4EKent p212 MR32

NAYLOR,G.G.2Lt 8-6-20 GordH CR Yorks417

NAYLOR,Henry Charles 2Lt dow 24-9-17 3 att11RSuss p119 CR Belgium124

NAYLOR,Herbert William Eastwood Lt&QM kia 17-2-17 1ELancs p111 CR France624

NAYLOR,James Reginald 2Lt kia 26-10-17 1Lond p245 CR Belgium83

NAYLOR,John T2LtACapt kia 11-4-18 9Ches p96 MR30

NAYLOR,Joseph TLt kia 10-4-17 RAMC p197 CR France85

NAYLOR,Rowland Edmund Lt kia 16-5-15 1RWFus p98 CR France279

NAYLOR,Urmston Shaw TMaj kia 3-9-16 13DLI p161 MR21 &MR32

NAYLOR,Walter George 2Lt kia 31-8-18 7Lond p247 CR France218

NAYLOR,William Balme 2Lt kia 16-9-16 1/6WRid p227 CR France246

NAYLOR-LEYLAND,George Vyvyan.MID Lt dow 21-9-14 RHGds p20 CR France1328

NEAL,Harry Beecroft Lt ded 3-11-19 MGC Inf p266 CR Yorks22

NEALE,Algernon Hastings Campbell LtCol ded 7-1-20 8Lpool p271 CR WAfrica17

NEALE,Arthur Hill Lt kia 21-1-16 IA 1Brahmans att6jats p280 MR38

NEALE,Aubrey Charles T2Lt kia 1-8-17 1/2 att10Bn ScotRif p104 CR Belgium7

NEALE,Christopher Ernest T2Lt kia 29-9-18 10 att2Worc p109 CR France665

NEALE,E.A.C.Lt 26-10-20 1/39GarwhalRif MR43

NEALE,George Henry TLtCol.MID kia 28-9-15 3Mddx p148 MR19

NEALE,Guy Dalrymple 2Lt dow 18-5-18 1GrenGds p50 CR France84

NEALE,Herbert Cecil Thubron 2Lt dow 1-1-16 1Nhampt p137 CR France178

NEALE,John Everard Digby Capt kld 22-8-17 4Leic attRFC p19&219 CR Leic63

NEALE,Percy Reginald T2Lt kia 20-12-17 101MGC p184 CR France592 Ex GloucR

NEALE,Robert Edward 2Lt kia 18-3-18 29RFC p16 CR Belgium140

NEALON,Cedric Dunnill 2Lt kia 16-8-17 4RIrReg attRInnisF p89 MR30

NEALON,John Alfred 2Lt kia 4-3-17 10Mddx p236 CR France439

NEAME,Arthur Maj ded 17-3-16 RGA KentHB p209 CR Kent212

NEAME,Geoffrey.MC.TCaptAMaj kia 2-4-18 B190RFA p33 CR France745

NEAME,Gerald Tassell TCapt kia 1-7-16 EKent p58 CR France402

NEATE,Alan Burnaby 2Lt dow 23-4-17 B162RFA p33 CR France113

NEATE,Nelson Rayner.MC.Capt kia 3-5-17 11RFus attHAC p69 MR20

NEATE,William 2Lt kia 24-3-18 24RFus p69 MR20

NEAVE,Alexander Lionel William Capt kia 19-9-18 IA 110Mahrattas attCpsofGuidesInf p280 CR palestine9

NEAVE,Arundell Maj dow 21-2-15 16Lancers p23 CR Belgium57

NEAVE,Gerald Vansittart.MID Capt kia 16-8-17 2/1BucksBn O&BLI p231 MR30

NEAVERSON,Percy Charles 2Lt kia 15-4-18 6NStaffs p238 MR32

NEEDHAM,Arthur Charles TCapt kia 16-11-16 8ELancs p111 MR21

NEEDHAM,Benjamin Llewellyn TCapt kia 1-7-16 2Lincs p75 MR21

NEEDHAM,George Geoffrey.MC.MID Lt dow 22-8-15 LancF p93 CR Gallipoli27

NEEDHAM,Joseph Walter David T2Lt dow 12-11-17 48RFC p11 CR France40,kldacc

NEEDHAM,Pascall 2Lt kia 18-11-16 10RWar p65 MR21

NEEDHAM,Robert Lawrence Laurie Lt kia 21-1-16 5 att1/4Hamp p228 MR38,Laurence

NEEDS,Charles Richard 2Lt kldacc 27-2-17 RFC p11 CR Glouc11

NEELY,Clive William T2Lt ded 20-6-16 14RFus p69 CR Iraq5

NEELY,Hugh Bertram 2Lt kia 25-4-15 5Suff p78 CR Belgium4,23-4-15 1Bn

NEEMS,Percy Vincent Nigel T2Lt ded 9-10-15 10Glouc p107 CR Wilts86

NEGRETTI,Norman Charles Achille T2Lt kia 30-1-17 22Mddx p148 CR Belgium28 23Bn

NEGROPONTE,Jack T2Lt dow 29-10-16 8SLancs p125 CR France74

NEGUS,Arthur George 2Lt kia 1-7-16 16Lond p250 MR21

NEGUS,Ralph Albert T2Lt kia 18-4-16 11Glouc p107 CR France149

NEIGHBOUR,Leslie Gulliver 2Lt kld 16-8-15 5Lincs p220 CR Herts

NEIGHBOUR,Walter Bayard T2Lt dow 16-8-16 4RFus p69 MR21

NEIL,John.MC.Lt dow 28-3-18 7A&SH attMGC p187&243 CR Scot752

NEIL,Robert Donald 2Lt kia 26-10-16 1/5RScotF p222 CR France35

NEIL,Stanley Thomas Arthur TCapt kia 1-7-16 15WYorks p82 MR21

NEILAN,Gerald Aloysius TLt kld 24-4-16 10RDubF p177 CR Ireland12,kia

NEILL,David Taylor 2Lt kia 3-5-17 7 att12RScots p211 MR20

NEILL,Geoffrey William.MC.Lt acckld 8-6-18 6Leinst attRAF p174 CR Egypt8

NEILL,James Dermot TLt kia 1-7-16 108MGC p184 MR21

NEILL,Norman Capt kia 6-11-14 13Huss p22 CR Belgium134

NEILL,Reginald Henry Lt kia 14-7-16 11RIrRif p170 MR21,1-7-16

NEILL,Robert Kirkpatrick T2Lt kia 16-8-17 8NumbF attRes p62 MR30

NEILL,Robert Larmour Lt kia 9-5-15 5 att1RIrRif p170 MR32

NEILL,Rolfe Mayne 2Lt kia 3-6-17 70RFC p11 CR Belgium410

NEILL,Thom.W.R.T2Lt dow 3-7-16 9RScotF p95 CR France3

NEILL,William Proudfoot Lt ded 24-12-16 6 att9RScots p211 CR France169,2Lt

NEILSON,Douglas Francis.DSO.MC.LtACapt kia 16-4-18 3Lincs p75 MR30,Donald 15-4-18

NEILSON,John Towers Lt kia 2-11-17 1/8ScotRif p225 CR Palestine8,3-11-17

NEILSON,Malcolm Arthur Lt kia 9-4-17 Worc AMaj 2ndCanInf p109

NEILSON,Richard Clark T2Lt kia 27-8-17 16WelshR p127 MR309

NEILSON,Robert Rowland TLtAMaj kia 13-4-18 3MGC p184 CR France98

NEILSON,Somerville Montgomerie 2Lt kia 14-4-17 3 att1Dev p77 MR20

NEILSON,Thomas T2Lt kia 18-11-16 17HLI p163 CR France534

NEILSON,William Capt kia 21-11-17 7ScotRif att10KRRC p224 MR17

NEILSON,William 2Lt kia 30-5-18 87RFA p33 MR30

NEILY,Frederick Ernest T2Lt kia 22-12-17 GL &16RFC p11 CR France95

NEISH,A.Miss ded 18-10-18 VAD BRCS p200 CR Berks86

NEISH,Alexander Millar.MC.2Lt dow 24-3-18 7A&SH p243 CR France177

NEISH,Herbert Theodore Louis 2Lt kia 31-8-15 3 att1Nhampt p137 CR France423

NELDER,Gordon Charles Aldridge T2Lt kia 6-8-15 13 att2Hamp p121 MR4

NELIGAN,Geoffrey Hook Lt kia 8-11-18 1YLI p143 CR France981

NELIGAN,John.MID TLt ded 13-6-17 RAMC 9HospTr p197 CR Egypt7,Capt

NELIGAN,Maurice Alfred Bourke Lt kia 13-10-15 12DLI p161 CR France82

NELIS,James Edward Thornhill TLt kia 15-8-15 5RInnisF p105 MR4

NELL,Basil Frank.MID Maj ded 22-12-18 RE 519FC p209 CR Egypt9

NELLES,Norman Cummings 2Lt kia 29-1-15 1Nhampt p137 MR22

NELSON,Abercromby Anson Craven Maj ded 20-5-16 2/10RScots p271 CR Scot235

NELSON,Alfred Ralph LtCol drd 30-12-15 IA 83Inf p280

NELSON,Craig Capt kia 25-9-15 IA 3Brahmans att469Punjabis p280 MR28

NELSON,David.VC.LtAMaj dow 8-4-18 D59RFA p33 CR France201

NELSON,Ernest Bertram 2Lt dow 15-3-17 IARO att1/8GurkhaRif p280 MR38

NELSON,Ethelbert Horatio 2Lt kia 18-11-16 4WSurr p212 CR France535

NELSON,Graham Lt kld 30-8-17 5ScotRif attRFC p11,19,104&224 CR Scot674

NELSON,Harold Griffith 2Lt kld 22-1-18 RFC p16

NELSON,Harry 2Lt kia 15-9-16 20Lond p251 MR21

NELSON,Herbert T2Lt kld 19-3-18 RFC p16 CR War50

NELSON,James Reid 2Lt kia 23-4-17 1/7BlkW p231 CR France604

NELSON,John(Jack) 2Lt kia 1-7-16 8YLI p143 CR France246

NELSON,John Bell.MC.Capt dow 22-9-18 IA 73Inf att125Rif p280 CR Palestine9

NELSON,Joseph Lawrie T2Lt kia 8-3-16 18Manch B'Coy p155 CR France625

NELSON,Richard Owen LtTCapt drd 4-5-17 RASC p193 CR Italy14

NELSON,Thomas Arthur Capt kia 9-4-17 Lothian&BordHorseYeo attMGC p187&204 CR France1182

NELSON,Walter 2Lt kia 13-10-15 6SStaffs p229 MR19

NELSON,William Horace Vere TLt dow 8-7-16 10N&D p134 CR France833

NELSON,William Jackson T2Lt kia 27/30-9-18 Lpool att9Bn p72 MR16

NELSON-COOKES,Henry Capt ded 23-10-18 RGA p41 CR Hamps7

NEPEAN,Evan Cecil Lt kia 4-10-18 3RScotF att3RFus p95 CR France845

NEPEAN,Francis Molyneux Yorke Capt kia 16-9-15 7SomLI p80 CR France525

NESBIT,Henry George 2Lt kia 23-3-15 1EKent p58 CR France922,Lt

NESBITT,Arnold Stearns Capt kia 7-11-14 3Worc p109 MR29

NESBITT,Frank Wallace Rowland Lt dow PoW 19-4-18 7DLI p239 CR France1027,Rowlands

NESBITT,James Thompson Capt dow 25-3-18 A95RFA p207 CR France40

NESBITT,Terrence Beale 2Lt dow 24-4-16 3Dors p124 MR38

NESBITT,William Charles T2Lt kia 15-8-15 6RDubF p177 MR4,16-8-15

NESER,Frank Charles T2Lt ded 30-9-17 GL &RFC p11 CR Lincs181,François

NESHAM,Charles Frederick Maj ded 24-4-19 HAC p271 CR Surrey160

NESLING,Robert E.2Lt 4-3-18 KRRC &MGC CR Suff83

NESMITH,James Capt kia 12-7-15 5A&SH p243 MR4

NESS,Gordon Stuart Lt kia 10-11-14 3 att1RScotF p95 MR29

NESS,James Charles Alexander Lt kia 27-6-15 Beds p86 MR22

NESS-WALKER,William Percy.MC.Maj dow 31-12-17 B251RFA p206 CR Belgium11

NESSLING,J.D.Lt ded 30-11-20 RASC CR Sussex23

NETHERCLEFT,Hugh Kirk T2Lt dow 25-12-17 2SWBord p100 CR France145

NETHERSOLE,A.R.LtCol drd 30-12-15 83WallajahbadLI MR41

NETHERSÓLE,Timothy Lt kia 22-11-17 IA 87Punjabis att69 p280

NETTLESHIP,Mark T2Lt kia 1-9-18 1 att1/4KOSB p102 CR France646

NETTLESHIP,Thomas T2Lt kia 22-3-18 att1/5NumbF p6 MR27

NETTLETON,Roy TLt dow 9-10-18 7EKent attTMB p58 CR France146

NEVE,Harold.MID 2Lt kia 27-5-18 1 att7ELancs p111 MR18

NEVE,Rupert Ernest TLt kld 26-1-18 RFC p16 CR Berks71

NEVE,Walter Gregory 2Lt kia 25-8-17 2EKent p58 CR Greece1

NEVEY,Frank 2Lt kld 12-10-18 6WRid p227 CR France718

NEVILE,Bernard Philip TCapt kia 11-2-16 att7Lincs p75 MR29

NEVILE,Guy Lister Capt kia 15-6-15 2Yorks p91 MR22

NEVILE,Hugh George Lt kia 21-8-15 2SWBord p100 MR4

NEVILL,Cuthbert St.John Lt kia 18-4-18 C251RFA p208 CR France98

NEVILL,Edward James Lt 22-12-18 2/4Rajputs MR66

NEVILL,Frederick Pearson 2Lt kia 22-2-17 IARO att92Punjabis p280

NEVILL,Hugh Lewis.DSO.Maj kia 7-8-15 RFA p33 CR Gallipoli26

NEVILL,John Henry Caxthorne 2Lt kia 24-12-14 GrenGds SR p50 CR France727

NEVILL,Robert.MC&Bar.2LtACapt kia 10-4-18 2SLancs p125 MR32

NEVILL,R.W.Capt 3-11-18 RB CR Sussex203

NEVILL,T.Lt 22-11-17 87 att69Punjabis CR Asia62

NEVILL,Wilfred Percy TCapt kia 1-7-16 1EYorks att8ESurr p84 CR France513

NEVILLE,Charles TCapt dow 13-7-16 1N&D C'Coy p134 CR France51

NEVILLE,Frank Septimus TCapt dow 24-11-17 6Nhampt p137 CR Belgium16

NEVILLE,George Henry.MC.MID TCapt kia 2-7-16 1SomLI p80 CR France1890

NEVILLE,Henry George T2Lt dow 10-5-17 GL &20RFC p11 CR Belgium11

NEVILLE,Lionel John Neville Capt dow 17-12-14 RE 5FC p47 CR Norf235

NEVILLE,Philip Percy.MID TLt ded 27-2-19 APayDept p255 CR Italy12

NEVILLE,Robert Patrick.MC.Capt&QM dow 27-10-17 7NumbF p214 CR Belgium25

NEVILLE,Stanley Capt ded 6-11-18 2/8Ess p232 CR Essex146

NEVILLE,Stuart White 2Lt kia 21-9-18 7Lond p247 CR France155

NEVILLE,Thomas Villiers Tuthill Thacker Capt kia 13-5-15 3DragGds p21 CR Belgium167

NEVILLE,William Sim 2Lt kia 25-9-16 RGA p41 CR France374

NEVIN,Alex McDonald Lt ded 24-6-17 RAMC att36GH p197

NEVINSON,Humphrey Kaye Bonney 2Lt dow 5-6-15 10Manch p237 MR4

NEVITT,George Rothwell Capt kia 28-11-17 2/8WYork p219 MR17

NEW,Athelstan William Capt ded 15-5-18 4 att1Ess p232 CR France84

NEW,Brian Brooke 2Lt kia 16-8-17 7DCLI p114 MR30

NEW,Hedley Bruce Lt kia 31-10-17 4Ess attRFC p19&232 MR20

NEW,Paul Lt kia 19-5-17 3 att1BordR p117 MR20

NEWALL,Leslie 2Lt kia 2-9-15 1Lond p245 CR France347

NEWALL,Nigel Lt kia 12-10-17 1WelshGds p53 MR30,2Lt

NEWALL,William Osborne Lt kia 12-12-17 12WYork p82 MR20

NEWBERRY,William Frederick Capt kld 21-11-20 4RWSurr CR Mddx17

NEWBERY,Gilbert Leonard.VD.T2Lt dow 12-11-17 RASC p193 CR Belgium72

NEWBERY,Richard Fenton Theodore TLt kia 14-7-16 RAMC att6Nhampt p197 CR France630

NEWBIGGIN,John Prentice Lt ded 12-12-18 RGA p41 CR Hamps202

NEWBIGGING,Alexander Tweedie 2Lt kia 3-5-17 3 att1RScotF p95 MR20

NEWBIGIN,George Nesbitt 2Lt ded 6-4-16 RE 2FC p210 CR Durham15

NEWBOLD,George Harold Lt ded 12-2-19 C241RFA p271 CR Shrop89

NEWBOLD,Philip T2Lt dow 13-7-16 7RWKent p141 MR21

NEWBOROUGH,William Charles.Lord.TLt ded 19-7-16 WelshGds p53 CR Wales714

NEWBOULD,Henry James Frank TCapt kia 2-8-15 6KOSB p102 CR France727

NEWBURY,Fred Peirson 2Lt 22-2-17 92Pujabis CR Iraq5

NEWBURY,George Maj kia 11-3-16 IA 130Baluchis p280

NEWBURY,P.F.R.LtCol 25-5-18 Lincs CR Lond4 Ex Cmdg11Bn

NEWBURY,Sydney Eldridge 2Lt dow 30-6-17 7N&D p233 CR France178

NEWCOMB,Charles Stuart Lt dow 5-4-18 6EKent p58 CR France62

NEWCOMB,Harry Reed Lt died 30-6-18 4EKent p271 CR Kent27

NEWCOMBE,Charles Neil TLt kia 27-12-15 7YLI p143 CR France276

NEWCOMBE,Clark Charles Upham 2Lt kia 17-8-17 5 att10Worc p109 CR Belgium106

NEWCOMBE,Cyril T2Lt kia 25/28-9-15 12RFus p69 MR19

NEWCOMBE,Edgar 2LtACapt kia 15-4-18 16Lond p249 MR32

NEWCOMBE,John Carr T2Lt kia 21-3-18 RE 12FC p47 MR20

NEWCOMBE,Richard TLt kia 1-7-16 1ELancs p111 MR21

NEWCOMBE,William TLt kia 3-7-16 1Drags att8SLancs p21 CR France215,Capt

NEWCOME,Basil Rice Maj mbk 8-3-16 IA 1/2GurkhaRif p280

NEWCOME,George Maj kia 11-3-16 130Baluchis CR EAfrica56

NEWDIGATE,Richard Francis Capt kia 4-9-16 3 att1BordR p117 MR29

NEWELL,Arthur Francis ACapt dow 4-4-18 8RB p179 MR27,Frank

NEWELL,Charles TCapt dow 24-3-18 RE 3PontoonPk p47 CR France225,kia

NEWELL,Charles Edward TLt dow 25-5-16 8RInnisF p105 CR France80

NEWELL,Francis Allister 2Lt kia 24-3-18 5Lond p246 CR France245

NEWELL,Matthew Banks T2Lt kia 4/5-4-16 14Ches p96 MR38

NEWELL,Thomas Stanley 2Lt dow 5-7-15 3 att2Ches p96 CR France285

NEWELL,William Joseph LtCol ded 20-12-14 7KSLI p145 CR Mddx48

NEWEY,Reginald Harold Capt 2-11-20 RE MR43

NEWINGTON,Francis Reginald Hayes 2Lt dow 3-12-17 1/20Lond p251 CR France398

NEWINGTON,John Lt kia 22-5-15 3ESurr attChes p113 CR Belgium120,3 att1ESurr

NEWINGTON,Percy Wilmott Lt kia 21-3-18 1EKent p58 MR20

NEWLAND,Arthur Kenyon T2Lt dow 21-11-17 12RE p47 CR France379,Lt

NEWLAND,Cecil Dunbar Capt ded 9-7-20 IA 1GurkhaRif p280 CR Derby39 Ex 3A&SH

NEWLAND,Edward Albert T2Lt kia 23-10-18 24RFus p69 CR France320

NEWLAND,George Michael 2Lt kia 28-3-18 9Lond p248 MR20

NEWLAND,Henry John T2Lt kia 18-2-17 8ESurr p113 CR France314

NEWLAND,Herbert Basil T2Lt dow 18-3-16 1Lincs p75 CR France95,4Bn

NEWLAND,Norman Chester 2Lt dow 31-5-15 PoW 1Mon p244 CR Belgium383

NEWLANDS,Stewart Lindsay Leighton 2Lt kia 27-5-17 7 att1ScotRif p224 MR20

NEWLANDS,Sydney Barron T2Lt kia 1-7-16 16WYork p82 CR France1890

NEWLANDS,Thomas Capt kia 22-3-18 5 att2RScots p211 CR France174

NEWLOVE,John Francis 2Lt kia 25-6-17 9HLI p240 CR France1489

NEWLYN,Walter Tessier T2Lt kia 11-7-16 19WelshR p127 MR21

NEWMAN,Albert T2Lt kia 20-9-17 Suff att1/9Lpool p78 MR30

NEWMAN,Alfred TLt dow 1-7-16 12SWBord p100 CR France94

NEWMAN,Arthur Cecil T2LtACapt kia 20-9-17 23Mddx p148 MR30

NEWMAN,Cecil Harold T2Lt kia 12-5-17 6RWSurr p56 MR20

NEWMAN,Chafen Cecil.MC.TLtCapt dow 4-9-18 15Hamps attHampYeo p121 CR Belgium111

NEWMAN,Cuthbert Alan T2Lt kia 19-4-18 2 att15N&D p134 CR France232,18-4-18

NEWMAN,Cyril Arnell T2Lt dow 28-4-17 9NStaffs p157 CR France95

NEWMAN,Cyril Brown 2Lt kia 3-9-16 7WRid p228 CR France293

NEWMAN,Ernest John Lt ded 5-7-19 IARO att27LightCav MR43 &CR Pakistan50A

NEWMAN,Frederick Arthur TLt kia 31-7-17 GL 13RFus attX37TMB p191 CR Belgium100,Y37TMB

NEWMAN,John Sherwood T2Lt kia 7/11-8-15 6EYorks p84 MR4,9-8-15

NEWMAN,Leslie Cambridge Lt dow PoW 27-12-17 7RWelshF p223 CR France1027

NEWMAN,Neville T2Lt kia 27-6-16 10/11HLI p163 CR France423,28-6-16

NEWMAN,Reginald Bodman 2Lt kia 7-9-16 168MGC p184 MR21

NEWMAN,Reuben McCarthy Lt 23-11-18 IARO att3/2GurkhaRif MR67

NEWMAN,Robert 2Lt kld 27-5-16 RFC p3 CR Lond12

NEWMAN,Vernon William 2LtTCapt kia 25-9-15 4WYork att1NLancs p82 CR France219

NEWMAN HALL,Theodore Lt 15-8-16 1/4 O&BLI CR France145

NEWNHAM,Alfred Geoffrey 2Lt kia 11-11-14 att4RFus p69 MR29

NEWNHAM-DAVIS,Edward LtCol ded 27-2-16 99DeccanInf MR43

NEWNHAM-DAVIS,Nathaniel LtCol ded 28-5-17 RDC p253 CR Hamps120

NEWSAM,Arthur Fowler.MID TLt dow 30-3-18 SL attImpCamelCps p201 MR34

NEWSAM,Harry Brightstone T2Lt kia 8-8-18 3TankCps LtBn p188 CR France585

NEWSOME,Clifford William 2Lt kia 14-7-18 20Mddx att26RFus p148 CR Belgium89

NEWSOME,Reginald Horace Arthur.MC.MIDx2 Lt dow 30-8-18 8Lond C'Coy p247 CR France119

NEWSOME,Theodore Edward T2Lt kia 25-9-15 2RWar p65 MR19

NEWSON,Norman Alexander Lt kia 18-2-15 3Ches p96 MR29

NEWSON,Walter Alexander Maj ded 15-4-17 2/3Lond p245 CR France 13

NEWSTEAD,Frederick Lisle Capt kia 7-8-16 3DLI p161 CR France232,6-8-16 2Bn

NEWSTEAD,George Pope LtCol dow 4-3-15 Suff &WAAF p78&201 CR WAfrica28

NEWSTEAD,Rupert Randolph T2Lt kia 7-7-16 17 att13Ches p96 MR21

NEWSUM,Clement Neill Capt kia 26-9-17 5Lincs p220 MR30

NEWTH,Howard Rutherford 2Lt kia 14-4-17 5 att1Ess p232 MR20

NEWTON,Alan Herbert 2Lt dow 7-4-16 2Mddx p148 CR France197

NEWTON,Arthur Douglas.MID Maj kia 27-10-17 265RFA p206 CR Palestine1

NEWTON,Arthur John T2Lt kia 30/31-7-18 2/4SomLI p80 France524

NEWTON,Arthur Victor Capt kld 20-10-15 3SomLI att5RFC p1&80,28-10-15 CR Belgium11

NEWTON,Cecil T2Lt kia 15-9-16 6CamH p168 CR France239

NEWTON,Cecil Herbert T2Lt kld 11-3-18 RFC p16

NEWTON,Charles Hercules Augustus Francis TLt kia 13-3-16 10KRRC p151 CR Belgium73 C.H.F.A.

NEWTON,Charles Ronald 2Lt kia 20-9-18 D104RFA p208 CR France1495

NEWTON,Charles Thomas Kemp 2Lt kia 3-6-16 1WYork p82 CR Belgium73

NEWTON,Denzil Onslow Cochrane.MVO.Capt dow 9-1-15 Mddx p265 CR Belgium80 &CR Belgium187,PPCLI

NEWTON,Edwin Brierley Lt kia 10-4-18 RE 182TC p210 MR27

NEWTON,Eric TCapt dow 5-8-17 RAMC att129Baluchis p197 CR EAfrica38,kia CR Tanzania1

NEWTON,Frederick 2Lt kia 15-8-17 4Ches p222 CR Belgium19,1/5Bn

NEWTON,Henry Joseph 2Lt ded 2-8-16 Ches &RFC p3&96 CR France837

NEWTON,Horace Gerard Townsend Capt ded 25-4-17 13Huss p22 CR Iraq6,drd

NEWTON,John 2Lt kia 23-4-17 HAC p206 MR20

NEWTON,Joseph Edmund Lt ded 6-9-19 Ches p263 CR Ireland24

NEWTON,Leslie Abbott T2Lt kia 14-7-16 7Leic p88 MR21

NEWTON,Leslie Cuthbert.OBE.Capt ded 13-1-20 RAOC CR Surrey1

NEWTON,Murray Edell Lt kia 18-6-17 17Lond attRFC p19&250 MR20

NEWTON,Percy TCapt kia 25-9-15 7KOSB p102 MR19

NEWTON,Samuel Thomas Lt dow 13-12-19 1/5SStaffs attMGC CR Hereford186

NEWTON,Thomas.MC.TLtACapt dow 5-8-18 1LancF p93 CR France134

NEWTON,Vivian Frederic 2Lt dow 15-9-16 1RWFus p98 CR France145

NEWTON,Walter Claude Lt kia 4-7-17 4LNLancs p234 CR France525

NEWTON,Walter Kilshaw 2Lt kia 31-3-18 10WYorks p82 MR20

NEWTON,Wilfrid.MID Capt dow 28-9-16 1RWKent p141 CR France40

NEWTON,William Henry T2Lt dow 11-8-18 YLI att2Bn p143 CR France1170

NEWTON,William Howard Capt ded 22-2-19 RAOC p198 CR France1027

NEWTON,William John Maj ded 16-2-15 6Ches p222 CR Ches193

NEWTON,William Leslie 2Lt kia 14-4-17 5DLI p239 CR France162

NEWTON,William Savage Capt kld 6-1-15 HAC Inf p206 CR Belgium17

NEWTON,William Trafford Lt kia 1-7-16 6NStaffs p238 CR France576

NEWTON-DEAKIN,Charles Humphrey Lt kia 11-4-17 3DragGds p21 CR France1182

NEWTON-KING,Alexander Reginald 2Lt dow 12-4-15 2RIrReg p89 MR32,Lt

NEWTON-KING,Pierce Francis Lt kia 25-9-15 2 O&BLI p130 MR19

NIBLETT,Arthur Hilton T2Lt dow 21-9-16 RE p47 CR France833

NICCOL,George McLaughlan Capt ded 30-10-18 RH&FA p33

NICE,Cecil George Lt ded 9-2-20 5RWSurr p271

NICHOL,Anthony Thomas 2Lt dow 16-4-17 1NumbF p62 CR France113

NICHOL,Edward Frank.MC.Capt 24-9-19 3LNLancs &RAF CR Kent27

NICHOL,John Capt kld 3-4-18 1RScotF &RFC p58&95 CR Kent27

NICHOL,Robert C.TLt kia 11-10-17 7SfthH p165 CR Belgium126

NICHOLAS,Francis Mark 2Lt dow 28-9-17 2Manch p155 CR Belgium24

NICHOLAS,J.W.F.Lt drd 2803015 N&D attNigR MR40

NICHOLAS,James Lt&QM ded 5-1-17 RAMC p271 CR Mddx53,6-1-17

NICHOLAS,John Allen Capt ded 28-1-19 266RFA p207 CR France1849

NICHOLAS,Oliffe Richmond Lt kia 17-4-16 3RWKent att1ConnRgrs p141 MR38,18-4-16

NICHOLAS,Thomas Glyn.MID T2Lt kia 18-2-17 18 att14WelshR p127 CR Belgium23,19-2-17

NICHOLAS,Walter Wynne T2Lt kia 29-3-16 7DCLI p114 CR Belgium23

NICHOLAS,William John Worth 2Lt drd 3-4-15 3N&D attNigR p134&201 CR Cornwall20,3-3-15

NICHOLL,Alan Hope Smith 2Lt kia 21-3-18 24RFA p33 MR20

NICHOLL,Alfred Ernest T2t kld 3-2-17 13RIrRif p170 CR France285

NICHOLL,Arnold 2Lt kia 18-7-16 7WRid p228 CR France702

NICHOLL,B.R.Maj 8-3-16 IA 1/2GurkhaRif MR38

NICHOLL,Francis John TLt kia 25-9-15 12HLI p163 MR19,NICOLL

NICHOLL,John William Harford 2Lt kia 29-10-14 2WelshR p127 MR29,29-11-14

NICHOLL-CARNE,Osmond Whitlock T2Lt kia 1-8-17 9WelshR p127 CR Belgium152

NICHOLLS,Alfred John T2Lt dow 12-4-18 Y&L att1/4Bn p159 CR Belgium11

NICHOLLS,Clifford Capt kia 31-7-17 5RWelshF attMGC p187

NICHOLLS,Douglas William Arthur.MC.TCapt kia 10-4-17 7Suff p78 MR20

NICHOLLS,Edward Cecil Henry Robert Lt kia 20-9-18 RWSurr &41RAF p56 CR Essex222

NICHOLLS,Edwin Jesse.MC.T2Lt kia 18-10-18 1Worc p109 CR France1196

NICHOLLS,Ernest T2Lt kld 10-3-18 36RFC p16 CR Yorks546

NICHOLLS,Ernest James T2Lt kia 21-5-16 8LNLancs D'Coy p136 CR France68

NICHOLLS,George Arthur 2Lt kia 9-4-17 95RFA &15WarwickRHA p33 CR France418

NICHOLLS,Harold Mayne 2Lt ded 8-11-18 RFA p261CR Cornwall40,NICHOLAS

NICHOLLS,Harry George.DCM.2Lt dow 27-5-18 4 PoW att2RBerks p234 MR18

NICHOLLS,Henry King Capt kia 4-4-18 5 att8ESurr p226 MR27

NICHOLLS,Henry Lewin Faulconer Capt kia 25-2-15 1NumbF p62 CR Belgium166

NICHOLLS,Horace William.MC.2Lt kia 24-8-18 NumbF att1EYorks p62 CR France314

NICHOLLS,John Watson Lt kia 1-7-16 5 att2RFus p69 MR21

NICHOLLS,Leonard Harvey T2Lt kia 26-10-17 21Manch p155 MR30

NICHOLLS,Lionel 2Lt kia 26-8-16 8Lond p247 CR Belgium97

NICHOLLS,R.M.Lt dow 18-7-16 2WelshR p127 CR France833

NICHOLLS,Thomas Rocliffe Capt kia 26-9-17 Res 14Hamps p254 MR30

NICHOLLS,William Howard Capt ded 22-2-16 RAMC attMhowDiv p197 MR66

NICHOLLS,William Montague TLt kia 26-9-15 30/43RFA p33 MR19

NICHOLLS-JONES Thomas Cyril TLt kia 1-8-17 14RWFus p98 CR Belgium86,31-7-17

NICHOLS,Alselan Buchanan Lt kia 23-4-17 3Ess att1Bn 88TMB p132 MR20

NICHOLS,Arthur Robert.MC.Capt kia 23-10-18 4Lpool p72 CR France228

NICHOLS,Charles T2Lt ded 9-11-17 TankCps p188 CR Yorks543 Ex HAC

NICHOLS,Clifford Capt kia 31-7-17 5RWelshF att164MGC p223 MR29

NICHOLS,Cyril Robert Lt kia 23-9-18 3ESurr att5TMB p113 CR France755

NICHOLS,Eustace Alfred Morez T2Lt kia 20-7-16 12 att15N&D p134 CR France374

NICHOLS,Harold 2Lt dow 7-8-18 3 att8ESurr p113 CR France71

NICHOLS,Stanley Lawrence 2Lt kia 12-8-17 GL &19RFC p11 CR Belgium140

NICHOLS,Thomas Leslie T2Lt kia 8/9-5-17 15RWar p65 CR France777

NICHOLS,Walter Henry TMaj ded 15-10-15 8SomLI p80 CR Germany3

NICHOLSON,Alan Grifford Lt kia 10-8-15 4Ches p222 MR4,Gifford

NICHOLSON,Albert T2Lt kia 8-8-18 9RFus p69 CR France141

NICHOLSON,Alfred Francis James Steele 2LtACapt kia 16-8-17 5RIrRif p170

NICHOLSON,Arthur Davidson Maj dow 25-9-15 1CamH p168 CR Germany1,David dedacc

NICHOLSON,Arthur Harry T2Lt dow 9-4-17 19Manch p155 CR France104,10-4-17

NICHOLSON,Arthur Knight 2Lt kia 31-10-14 18Huss B'Sqn p23 CR Belgium118

NICHOLSON,Arthur Stuart Lt kia 4-9-14 1CamH p168 MR15

NICHOLSON,Basil Lee Lt kia 24-7-15 RFA p208 CR Belgium98

NICHOLSON,Bernard George Maurice TLt ded 29-10-18 13NumbF p62 CR Mddx53

NICHOLSON,Bruce Hills 2Lt kia 3-5-17 6 att4RFus p69 MR20

NICHOLSON,Edward Francis Dale Maj dow 12-10-17 1 att7SLancs p125 CR Belgium183

NICHOLSON,Edward Hills.DSO&Bar.MajALtCol kia 4-10-18 3RFus attESurr p69 CR France212

NICHOLSON,Eric N.Capt ded 20-6-17 12Lancers p22 CR Nhampt38

NICHOLSON,Geoffrey Arnold 2Lt kldacc 19-5-17 GL &RFC p11 CR Kent243

NICHOLSON,Geoffrey Alec Shield T2Lt dow 22-8-17 GL &6RFC p11 CR Belgium11

NICHOLSON,Geoffrey Douglas Lothian 2Lt kia 23-4-17 4Worc p109 MR20

NICHOLSON,George Crosfield Norris Capt kld 11-3-16 RFC p3 CR Berks33

NICHOLSON,Gordon Trevor 2Lt kia 28-9-15 IARO att119Inf p280 MR38

NICHOLSON,Harry Reid Lt ?? 24-4-17 1CanPnrs att20RFC MR20

NICHOLSON,Henry William.DCM.Lt kia 3-11-17 RGA 171SB p41 CR Belgium84

NICHOLSON,Harold Willison Capt kia 13-10-15 5Lincs p220 MR19

NICHOLSON,Hugh Hathorn 2Lt kia 24-5-15 2 att3Ches p96 MR29

NICHOLSON,Huntly Warwick Lt kia 17-11-14 1Ches p96 CR Belgium42

NICHOLSON,John Capt ded 16-11-15 RAOC p267

NICHOLSON,John Anthony Lt dow 5-10-18 48/36RFA p33 CR France512

NICHOLSON,John Edward Patrick 2Lt kia 16-9-18 3LNLancs att13KRRC p136 CR France245

NICHOLSON,John Maurice Leonard T2Lt kia 11-7-16 8SfthH p165 CR France423

NICHOLSON,Lancelot T2Lt kia 20-9-17 9Yorks p91 CR Belgium112

NICHOLSON,L.C.DSO.Lt dow 2-11-14 3 att1RBerks p139

NICHOLSON,Leonard Sampson 2Lt kia 2-5-15 12Lond p248 MR29

NICHOLSON,Maurice 2Lt kia 18-8-17 GL ACycCps &11RFC p11&181 MR20

NICHOLSON,Paul Cheesum 2Lt kia 26-4-18 9YLI p143 MR30

NICHOLSON,Randolph Renwick.MC.2Lt kia 18-9-18 4EYorks att2N&D p219 CR France672

NICHOLSON,Richard Le Brun.MC&Bar.TCaptAMaj kia 31-8-18 11 att1/6Ches p96 CR France139

NICHOLSON,T.HonCapt ded 6-11-15 RAOC p198

NICHOLSON,Thomas Edward TLt kia 1-7-16 25NumbF p62 MR21

NICHOLSON,Walter Alan T2Lt dow 27-9-15 2GordH p167 CR France1059

NICHOLSON,Walter Adams see NICOLSON.W.A.

NICHOLSON,William Dukinfield Lt dow 23-2-15 2CamH p168 CR Belgium28

NICHOLSON,William Herbert Hamilton Lt dow 13-4-18 RE p210

NICHOLSON,Winter T2Lt dow 16-3-17 RE 224FC p47 CR France624

NICKALLS,Edward Gilbert T2Lt kia 18-8-16 4Lpool p72 CR France432

NICKALLS,Hugh Quidhampton Lt kia 29-7-17 1DevYeo attRFC p19&202 MR20

NICKALLS,Norman Tom ColTBrigGen kia 26-9-15 BdeStaff 17Lancers p1 MR19

NICKEL,George Gaston T2Lt kia 31-7-17 20Lpool p72 MR29

NICKLIN,Harry John.MC.2Lt kia 16-4-18 2Worc p109 MR32

NICKLIN,William T2Lt dow 24-8-16 RE SpBde C'Coy p47 CR France453

NICKSON,Edmund Reginald T2Lt kia 29-4-18 64LabCps p189 CR Belgium101

NICKSON,Henry Maj kia 30-10-15 4LNLancs p233 CR France251,Harry

NICKSON,John Reginald T2Lt kldacc 2-1-18 35RFC p16 CR Oxford74

NICKSON,William Capt kia 30-7-16 19Lpool p72 MR21 &CR France1890

NICOL,Alexander 2Lt kia 12-7-15 5A&SH p243 MR4

NICOL,Andrew.MID TLt kia 22-5-16 6KOSB p102 CR Belgium136

NICOL,Anthony Thomas 2Lt dow 16-4-17 1NumbF p62

NICOL,C.Sister 6-2-17 QAIMNS CR Surrey160

NICOL,Charles Ashmore Capt kia 8-5-17 10BlkW p129 MR37,C.R.

NICOL,Charles Mill.MID Capt dow 23-10-16 RAMC DADMS 3Div p197 CR France203

NICOL,David TLtACapt dow 26-11-17 14A&SH p173 CR France256,kia 25-11-17

NICOL,Donald Ninian TLt ded 29-12-15 3ScotGds p52 CR Scot4,27-12-15

NICOL,George Moffat TLt kia 25-9-15 9ScotRif p104 CR France114

NICOL,Robert Lt kia 17-4-18 5A&SH attMGC p187&243 MR30

NICOL,Wilfred Edward.DSO.Maj dow 1-10-15 1GrenGds p50 CR France98

NICOLAI,Ronald Claud Lt kia 25-4-15 RWar p65 MR29

NICOLAY,Herbert Cleland Maj mbk 10-3-15 IA 2/2GurkhaRif p281 MR28

NICOLL,Eric Stanhope.MC.Capt kia 19-1-18 2/4RWKent p212&271 CR Palestine3,18-1-18

NICOLL,F.J. see NICHOLL.F.J.

NICOLL,James John McGregor 2Lt ded 9-7-18 RFA p261 CR Scot238,8-7-18

NICOLL,Leonard Orrick 2Lt kia 26-9-17 5BlkW D'Coy p231 MR30,Lt

NICOLLS,John Oliver Lt kia 25-9-15 IA 58Rif p281 MR28

NICOLLS,Richard Jeffreys TCapt kia 1-10-16 9N&D A'Coy p134 CR France151

NICOLSON,Alexander.MSM.T2Lt kia 13-5-18 2N&D p134 CR Belgium3,NICHOLSON Alick

NICOLSON,Donald McDonald 2Lt kia 19-4-17 GL att5KOSB p191 MR34 att3Bn

NICOLSON,Farquhar Murchison 2Lt kia 19-4-17 5HLI p240 CR France1701

NICOLSON,Walter Adams MajTLtCol kia 4-9-17 104RFA p33 CR Belgium183,NICHOLSON

NICOLSON,William T2Lt kia 13-8-16 6RScotF p95 CR France239

NICOLSON,William Alexander Capt ded 20-7-16 10ELancs p111 CR Iraq5

NICOLSON,William Hurst Maj kia 21-1-16 IA 37Dogras p281 CR Iraq5

NIELD,Wilfred Herbert Everard TLt kia 1-7-16 11RFus p69 CR France397

NIELSON,William Christian T2Lt kia 2-9-18 EYork att5YLI p84 France1484

NIGHTINGALE,Eric 2Lt kia 25-6-18 GL N&D &RAF p191 CR France526,Lt

NIGHTINGALE,Frank Leslie T2Lt kia 19-12-15 7Lt dow 27-4-17 2SWBord p100 MR20,23-4-17

NILSSON,Geoffrey Burbank T2Lt kia 18-9-18 Yorks att7EYorks p91 CR France415

NIMMO,Adam Prentice.MC.Capt dow 17-11-17 1/4KOSB p223 CR Egypt2

NIMMO,James Ronald 2Lt ded 1-5-17 7ScotRif p271 CR Scot675,kldacc

NIMMO,Stuart Henry TLt kia 19-9-18 8RScotF p95 MR37

NIMMO,William Leslie 2Lt kia 26-7-18 1NumbF p62&539 MR19 &CR France1896

NINIS,Francis Aubrey.MC.LtACapt dow 19-9-18 12Ches p96&257 CR Greece1

NINIS,George Elvey Howard 2Lt ded 29-11-18 RASC p267 CR Lond2

NISBET,Cecil Andrew TCapt dow 21-6-16 12Suff p78 CR France12

NISBET,David Joseph Lt dow 15-1-20 5RWKent p271

NISBET,Douglas Guille Lt kia 10-6-16 3 att5SWBord p100 CR France251

NISBET,Edwin TLt kia 6-9-18 59MGC Divl Inf p184 CR France309

NISBET,Frank Scobell.MID Capt kia 26-8-14 2Manch p155 MR15

NISBET,Frederic William 2Lt kia 14-2-17 YorkDrag att46RFC p19&206 CR Belgium5

NISBET,John 2Lt kia 15-4-15 3RScots p54 CR Belgium17

NISBET,John Andrew T2LtACapt kia 28-9-18 2RScotF p95 CR Belgium112

NISBET,Robert Douglas Morton Lt kia 9-5-15 2Lincs p75 MR32

NISBETT,Frank 2Lt kia 30-11-17 1/5SLancs p230 MR17

NIVEN,Alan Scott T2Lt kia 4-11-17 RLancs att9YLI p59 MR30

NIVEN,Allan Graham TMaj kia 1-7-16 21NumbF p62 MR21

NIVEN,Douglas Scott.DSO.Maj 12-2-19 25Cav MR43

NIVEN,James T2Lt kia 3-5-17 RE 253TC p47 CR France258

NIVEN,John 2Lt kia 13-5-17 RFA p208 CR France266

NIVEN,Kenneth James T2Lt kia 22-8-17 11A&SH p173 MR30

NIVEN,William Adam Mackie 2Lt kia 28-10-18 29RFC p3 CR France158

NIVEN,William Edward Graham Lt kia 21-8-15 BerkYeo p202 CR Gallipoli5

NIVISON,Robert Butler T2Lt kia 15/17-9-16 5 att21KRRC p151 MR21,15-9-16

NIXON,Arthur William Lennox T2Lt kia 1-6-17 GL &16RFC p11 CR France58,Lt

NIXON,Basil Northcote Capt ded 3-3-19 23Lond p271

NIXON,C.T.Lt 18-10-17 RFC CR Herts115

NIXON,Cyril John Lt ded 8-10-17 5Beds p219

NIXON,David 2Lt dow 29-7-18 5A&SH p243 CR France1225

NIXON,Gerald Ferrers Lt kia 24-10-14 RFA 129Bty p33 CR France706

NIXON,Harold Percival T2Lt kia 26-10-18 6Wilts p153 CR Belgium438,Perceval

NIXON,James Duncan 2Lt kia 11-4-18 4SfthH p241 MR19

NIXON,Lionel Philip T2Lt kia 15-9-16 23Mddx p148 MR21

NIXON,Montagu Alfred Capt ded 26-9-17 5RB p179 CR Hamps202

NIXON,Noel Charles Frederick Capt kia 24-3-18 8 att4Beds p86 MR20

NIXON,Oswald 2Lt kia 17-9-16 Ess &RFC p3&132,ded MR20

NIXON,Philip Henry 2Lt dow 18-12-16 2Glouc p107 CR Greece7

NIXON,Thomas William T2Lt dow 26-10-18 7Y&L p159 CR France214,1/4Bn

NIXON,Walter Henry 2Lt kia 19-9-15 RLancs &RFC p2&59 CR France834,19-7-15

NIXON,William Capt kia 1-7-16 20NumbF p62 MR21

NIXON,William Eric Capt kia 7-5-17 KOSB &40RFC p11&102 CR France1198

NIXON,William Gerald Lt kia 1-7-16 3Hamps att11TMB p121 MR21

NIXON,William Henry 2Lt kld 24-8-17 RGA 298SB p41 CR Belgium4

NIXON-ECKERSALL,Frederick Eckersall Maj kia 10-11-17 RGA 157SB p41 CR Belgium84,Frederic

NOAD,H.C.Maj 28-7-21 RASC CR Iraq1

NOAD,P.H.TCapt ded 3-7-18 RE p47&271 CR Wilts153

NOAKE,Arthur Stratford Maj drd 9-10-18 IARO S&TCps p281 MR40

NOAKES,Frederic Lt kia 25-11-17 1/1StaffsYeo p205 CR Palestine9

NOAKES,Harold Thomas T2Lt kia 23-7-17 GL &32RFC p11 CR Belgium11

NOAKES,James Edward Lt 23-10-20 4/7Mddx CR Surrey8

NOAKES,Stuart Bertram Capt drd 30-12-17 RASC MT p193 MR41

NOAKS,Geoffrey Vaughan 2Lt dow 18-8-16 1Nhampt D'Coy p137 CR France74

NOBLE,Archibald Francis.MID TCapt&Ajt kia 21-5-16 10Ches p96 CR France68

NOBLE,Bertram TLt ded 26-8-16 22 at16LancF att1ArmySch p93 CR France180,23-8-16

NOBLE,Harold Taylor T2Lt kia 28-9-17 GL &20RFC p11 CR France285

NOBLE,Henry Austin 2Lt dow 8-10-18 4Ess p232 CR France379

NOBLE,James Dickson Capt 12-10-14 RAMC 2FA CR Scot259

NOBLE,John Lt kia 28-9-18 5CamH att9MGC p184 CR Belgium58

NOBLE,John Stanley Lt dow 30-3-18 5RBerks p139 CR France62

NOBLE,John Wilson T2Lt kia 25-9-16 10NumbF p62 MR21

NOBLE,Marc Andrew Patrick 2Lt dow 1-7-17 C122RFA p33 CR Belgium1,C121Bde

NOBLE,Norris Heatley 2Lt dow 15-8-16 6 att1KRRC p151 CR France51

NOBLE,Thomas Gilson TMaj kia 1-7-16 20NumbF p62 MR21,Gibson

NOBLE,W.B.Lt 11-12-18 RScots CR Scot639

NOBLE,Walter Frederick T2Lt kia 3-7-16 12 att9Ess p132 CR France393

NOBLE,William Black Lt kia 26-4-15 6NumbF p214 MR29

NOBLE,William McDonald T2Lt dow 31-12-16 EKent attRE DivSig p58 CR France177

NOBLE,William Smyth Jackson T2Lt kia 21-3-18 15RScots p54 MR20

NOBLE-SMITH John 2Lt kia 9-4-18 165RFA p33 CR France1014

NOCK,Frederick John 2Lt dow 3-6-17 9YLI p143 CR France1184
NOCK,George Goodwin Rudgard T2Lt kia 5-9-18 7Suff att1/1Camb p78 CR France511,6-9-18
NODDER,Frederick May 2Lt kia 14-8-16 48RFA p33 CR France397
NODDER,Ruth Mary Nurse 24-5-18 TFNS MR43 &CR Pakistan50A
NODEN,Frank Hull 2Lt ded 3-12-18 RGA 319SB p41 CR Ches158
NOEL,Alfred 2Lt kia 3-5-17 2Lond p245 CR France537
NOEL,Hon Edward Col ded 9-11-17 SL Staff p268
NOEL,Francis Methuen 2Lt kia 26-10-17 4 att9Dev p77 MR30,Capt
NOEL,Hon,Robert Edmund Thomas More Capt ded 2-2-18 6RFus att1NigR p69&201 CR EAfrica11 &CR Tanzania1
NOEL,Tom Cecil.MC.Lt kld 22-8-18 3KOSB &RAF p102
NOKES,William Herbert 2Lt kia 26-10-17 6 att1SStaffs p229 MR30
NOLAN,Bernard T2Lt kia 21-3-18 2Y&L p159 MR20
NOLAN,Bevan John 2Lt kia 3-9-16 4 att2RIrReg C'Coy p89 CR France402
NOLAN,Howard Stanley T2Lt kld 27-7-17 GL &RFC p11 CR Wilts4
NOLAN,James.MC.DCM.2Lt dow 29-9-18 1RDubF p177 CR Belgium113
NOLAN,Leonard McNeill Lt ded 13-6-20 IA 58Rif p281 MR67
NOLAN,Maurice Edward T2Lt dow 25-9-15 RE p47 CR France554
NOLAN,Maurice Herbert William 2Lt dow 9-12-16 1RIrReg att10RIrRif p89 CR France285
NOLAN,Philip John Noel.DFC.Lt ded 7-4-18 RFA &RAF p33 CR France988
NOLAN,Raymond Philip Drummond Lt kia 3-11-14 3 att1BlkW p129 MR29
NOLAN,Rupert Henry Capt kia 21-10-14 RAMC p197 CR Belgium115
NOLAN,William Henry TLt kia 14-7-16 9Leic p88 MR21
NOLAN-MARTIN,Alfred John Capt dow 22-2-17 3RDubF attMGC Inf p177&184 CR Mddx16
NOON,Alfred Lewis Lt dow 2-4-18 2Dev p77 CR France185
NOON,Gilbert 2Lt kia 29-11-17 6N&D attRFC p19&233 MR20
NOONAN,Joseph Daniel T2Lt kia 24-8-16 6 att2RMunstF p175 MR21
NOOTT,Mervyn 2Lt kia 20-10-14 1EKent p58 MR32
NOPS,Thomas Waldegrave T2Lt kia 21-10-16 GL &RFC 9KiteBallSect p3&191 CR France297
NORBURY,Albert Maj 24-8-21 IndOrdDept CR India97A
NORBURY,Francis Campbell Capt kia 10-1-15 6 att1KRRC p151 CR France727
NORBURY,Philip Giesler TLt kia 1-7-16 7EKent p58 CR France397
NORBURY,Robert Fiddes TLt dow 4-10-17 1 att2SfthH p165 CR Belgium16
NORCOTT,Gerald Alfred Maj died 20-9-18 LNLancs p264
NORCROSS,Arthur Capt kia 9-10-17 4ELancs p226 MR30
NORCROSS,Frank 2Lt kia 30-7-16 23Manch p155 MR21
NORFOLK,Harold Maj kia 23-4-16 WorcYeo attTanks p206 MR34,23-2-16
NORIE,Evelyn William Meadows.ADC.Col ded 29-8-15 Staff AMS WarOff p1 CR Surrey135
NORIE-MILLER,Claud T2Lt drd 4-5-17 RASC p193 CR Italy14
NORKETT,Edward Lt ded 25-3-19 RASC p271 CR Berks29
NORMAN,Albert Edmund.MID Capt dow 11-5-15 3ESurr p113 CR France345
NORMAN,Arthur John T2Lt dow 29-9-16 8Leic p88 CR France145
NORMAN,Basil Chamberlin Qu'Appella Lt dow 30-9-18 4NStaffs p157 CR Belgium10,Qu'Appelle
NORMAN,Charles Capt dedacc 12-2-17 NthIrHorse att5RRofCav p23 CR France74
NORMAN,Edward John T2Lt kia 30-3-18 156RE p47 MR27
NORMAN,Garnet T2Lt dow 2-4-18 26RFus p69 MR27 11Bn
NORMAN,Gilford William T2Lt kia 25-9-16 19N&D att8Leic p134 MR21
NORMAN,Harold Henry Maj kia 10-11-14 Nhampt p137 MR29
NORMAN,Isaac Thomas Victor 2Lt dow 28-3-18 RE 121FC p47 CR France185
NORMAN,James Bertram.MC.T2Lt kia 10-4-18 40MGC Inf p184 MR32
NORMAN,Leonard Frank T2Lt kia 21-9-17 154MGC Inf p184 MR30
NORMAN,Lionel.MC.TCapt kia 15-9-16 1ScotGds p52 MR21
NORMAN,Percy William 2Lt ded 21-5-15 51RGA p41 MR66
NORMAN,Stanley 2Lt dow 16-9-16 7Mddx p235 CR France177,15/16-9-16
NORMAN,Stuart Sheridan Lt kia 23-12-14 Manch p155 MR22
NORMANSELL,John TCapt dow 10-3-17 13Y&L p159 CR France742,kia
NORQUOY,James TCapt kia 3-4-17 Mddx att13Bn p148 CR France570,2-4-17
NORRIS,Alfred James 2Lt kia 28-3-18 7KSLI p145 MR20
NORRIS,Arthur James Lt ded 10-1-17 HAC Inf p206 CR Surrey45
NORRIS,Bertie T2Lt kia 3-5-17 2LancF p93 MR20
NORRIS,Colin Chad Armstrong T2Lt kld 26-12-17 GL &RFC p11 CR Norf256
NORRIS,Cyril Norman T2Lt dow 19-8-17 26RFus p69 CR France855
NORRIS,Edward Fraser LtTCapt kld 15-3-18 RFC p16 CR Oxford74
NORRIS,Ernest Arthur 2Lt kia 22-3-18 21 att17KRRC p151 MR27
NORRIS,Frank Ernest Edwin TLt dow 2-10-18 10RWKent p141 CR Belgium111

NORRIS,Frederick T2LtACapt kia 7-6-17 23Mddx p148 MR29
NORRIS,Frederick George 2Lt kia 4-4-18 4Ches att7RWKent p222 MR27
NORRIS,Gilbert Hume TCapt dow 9-3-18 13KRRC p151 CR Belgium11
NORRIS,Harold Aubrey Blurton T2Lt kia 24-7-17 GL &57RFC 9Wing p11 CR France134
NORRIS,Kenneth Arthur Annesley 2Lt ded 16-6-16 RWKent p141 CR Iraq6
NORRIS,Leslie Archibald TLt kia 25-3-17 RE att70RFC p11&47 CR France245
NORRIS,Percy Walter T2Lt kia 29-7-18 34MGC Inf p184 CR France524
NORRIS,R.S.Cdr 16-7-15 IOD CR France354
NORRIS,Walter 2Lt kia 7-8-15 8Manch p237 MR4
NORRIS,William Eric 2Lt kldacc 14-1-18 MontgomYeo att17WelchR p204 CR France616
NORRIS,William Forbes Lt kia 25-8-15 5Norf attACycCps p216 MR4
NORRIS,William James George Capt kia 25-9-15 12WYorks p82 MR19
NORRIS,Sydney Frank 2Lt ded 28-4-19 RFA p33 CR Italy65
NORRIS,William John.MID Lt dow 14-10-18 1/10Manch p237 CR France13
NORRISH,Thomas Theodore 2Lt kia 13-9-16 1Dev p77 MR21
NORRISH,William 2LtACapt kia 27-8-17 10Mddx p236
NORSWORTHY,Harold Milford T2Lt kia 18-3-17 1EKent p58 CR France149
NORTH,Arthur Juvell.MC.Capt kia 27-9-18 4NumbF p213 CR France439,Jewell
NORTH,Charles Napier Maj kia 1-11-14 RE 5FC p47 MR29
NORTH,Francis Wilson 2Lt kia 9-9-16 3RIrReg att6ConnRgrs p89 CR France402,Frank
NORTH,Harry Lonsdale Lt kia 27-9-18 3 att2RIrReg p89 CR France1496
NORTH,Hugh Frederic Capt kld 21-1-16 1/4Hamps p228 MR38
NORTH,Julian Capt ded 14-10-16 IA IndTelegraphDept p281 CR EAfrica19
NORTH,Kenneth Croft Lt kia 31-10-14 4Huss p21 CR Belgium118
NORTH,Neville Marriott.MC.Capt kia 27-5-18 5NumbF p213 MR18
NORTH,Robert Dudley TLt kia 3-5-16 2 att13N&D p134 CR Belgium92,2 att14Bn
NORTH,Samuel Frost T2Lt kia 2-11-18 15LancF p93 CR France93
NORTH,Stanley 2Lt kia 16-8-17 19Lond p250 MR29
NORTHAM,John McClure 2Lt kia 15-9-17 15Lond p249 MR29
NORTHAM,Reginald Meek Lt ded 19-2-21 IARO attS&TCps p281 MR43,2Lt
NORTH-COX,Wilfrid Herbert Marshall 2Lt ded 2-3-16 3N&D p134 CR Numb2
NORTHCOTE,Douglas Horace Gilbert.MID Lt kia 12-3-15 3EKent attWilts p58 MR29
NORTHCOTE,Edward Stafford Capt kia 3-9-16 11RSuss p119 MR21
NORTHCOTE,George Barons Capt dow 4-12-15 2Norf p74 CR Iraq5
NORTHCOTE,James Fitz Gaulfield 2lt kia 9-10-17 5WYorks p218 MR30
NORTHCOTE,Hugh Farrar 2Lt kia 28-4-16 IARO att41Dogras p281 MR38
NORTHCOTT,Henry John T2Lt dow 18-10-18 Dors att1/5Glouc p124 CR Devon72
NORTHCROFT,Percival William Cordery Lt kia 31-7-17 6 at3RB p179 MR29
NORTHEY,Alfred.MID Lt kia 12-10-14 3Worc p109 CR France260
NORTHEY,George Evelyn Anson Lt kia 26-8-14 2Ess p132 MR15
NORTHEY,Mervyn Ackland Lt kia 28-10-18 3 att2RWKent p141 CR Iraq8
NORTHEY,William.DSO.Maj dow 22-10-14 2DLI p161 CR France102
NORTHLAND,Thomas Uchter Caulfield Capt kia 2-2-15 2ColdGds p51 CR France720,Ucher Caulfeild 1-2-15
NORTHOVER,Neville Evelyn T2Lt kia 4-9-18 Wilts att15Hants p153 CR Belgium111
NORTHROP,Harold 2Lt kia 9-10-17 8WYorks p219 MR30
NORTON,A.G.2Lt kia 9-5-15 2ELancs p111 CR France566
NORTON,Clement Edgar T2Lt ded 10-10-18 RASC p193 CR Palestine9
NORTON,Eric 2Lt kia 18-8-16 5Suff p217 CR France432,1/4Bn
NORTON,Frank Frederick T2Lt kia 20-9-17 21KRRC p151 MR30
NORTON,Frederick John Lt kia 23-3-18 D187RFA p33 CR France518
NORTON,Frederick William TCapt ded 14-10-16 RE 10LabBn p47 CR France52
NORTON,Hugh TLt kia 24-3-17 GL &8RFC p11 CR France120
NORTON,John Arnold TCapt dow 19-11-15 SL p201&268,ded CR Essex69
NORTON,Leopold Grantley Lt dow 20-10-14 2DLI p161 MR32
NORTON,Richard Conyers Lt kia 23-3-18 E'RHA p33 CR France360
NORTON,Richard Legge 2Lt kia 18-9-18 9Norf p74 CR France1701
NORTON,Tom Edgar Grantley 2Lt kia 20-4-15 4 att1ESurr p113 CR Belgium152
NORTON,William Lt kia 23-3-18 3 att7Leic p88 MR27
NORTON-FAGGE,Frederick Walter Langford Grantly.MIDx2 Lt ded 18-11-16 IARO SpServOff attGHQ p281 CR Iraq6,Frederic Grantley
NORTON-HARPER,Alfred George Montague Capt 16-10-17 SL att4NigR CR EAfrica11 &CR Tanzania1
NORVILL,Frederick Henry 2Lt dow 24-7-17 RGA 81SB p41 CR Belgium16
NORWAY.Frederick Hamilton 2Lt dow 4-7-15 2DCLI p114 CR France64

NORWELL,Herbert 2Lt kia 12-4-18 5 att2RFus p69 MR30

NORWOOD,John.VC.Capt kia 8-9-14 5DragGds RoO p21&204,2CountofLondYeo CR France1451

NORWOOD,John Norton 2Lt dow 22-7-16 11RInnisF p105 CR France169,4 att2Bn

NORWOOD,Reginald Harold 2Lt kia 29-9-18 TankCps p188 CR France375

NORWOOD,Robert Cecil Lt kia 18-7-16 BucksBn O&BLI p231 CR France832

NORWOOD,William James 2Lt kia 27-3-18 Mddx att2Nhampt p148 MR27

NOSS,Arthur Rex Hurden.MC.T2Lt dow 15-9-17 GL &48RFC p11 CR France1361

NOSWORTHY,Claude William Michelin Lt dow 6-12-17 RFA att10RFC p11 CR Belgium11

NOSWORTHY,Philip Chorlton 2Lt kia 11-5-15 3 att2Ches p96 MR29

NOTCUTT,Leonard Ernest Lt kia 3-5-17 7RFus att27MGC p69&184 MR20

NOTLEY,Albert Carr 2Lt kia 30-5-18 5RLancs p213 CR France106,31-5-18

NOTMAN,William Graham T2Lt kia 13-8-16 3 att12HLI p163 MR21

NOTT,Charles Lt kia 8-10-15 9Lpool p216 MR19

NOTT,Edward Ross T2Lt dow 13-7-16 9YLI p143 CR France51

NOTT,George Vincent TLt kia 18-8-16 7Nhampt p137 MR21

NOTT,Henry Paton Lt kia 27-4-16 6Glouc p225 CR France1327

NOTT,John Harley Lt ded 25-8-15 RASC 53Welsh DivTr p253 CR Egypt3

NOTT,Louis Cameron.MC.Capt&Adjt kia 18-4-17 1/6Glouc p225 CR France363

NOTT,Louis Phillip Maj ded 4-7-16 RE p271

NOTT,Saumarez Ewen T2Lt kia 9-9-17 13RSuss p119 MR30

NOTT,Thomas Walker.DSO.LtCol kia 18-4-17 1/6Glouc p225 CR France363

NOTT-BOWER,Charles Cecil 2Lt kia 16-5-15 IARO att2/3GurkhaRif p281 CR France631

NOTTIDGE,Edward Capt kia 8-11-16 D79RFA p33 CR France430

NOTTON,Cyril George 2Lt kia 3-12-17 NorfYeo att12Norf p204 CR Palestine3

NOTTON,Frank Gwyer 2Lt kia 27-8-17 5WelshR p230 MR30

NOVERRE,Arthur Kerr Maj ded 18-4-18 RASC 6DivA/C p193 CR Egypt1

NOWELL,Ernest Harold 2Lt kia 1-9-15 1Suff p78 CR Belgium89,Harry

NOWELL,Francis Percival T2Lt dow 2-7-16 18WYorks p82 CR France203

NOWELL,Joseph Kent 2Lt kia 16-8-17 8 att1Lond p247 MR29

NOWELL,Roger Emmett 2Lt kia 22-9-17 RFC p11 MR20

NOWELL,Wilfred James 2Lt kia 9-4-17 RFA 460HB p33 CR France182

NOYES,Claude Robert Barton T2Lt kia 1-7-16 15LancF p93 CR France293

NOYES,Harry Francis Golding TCapt ded 5-9-16 RAMC att17StHosp p197 MR65

NOYES,Ralph Elliot Maj kia 27-9-15 10Yorks p91 MR19

NOYES,Talbot Ronald Arthur Herbert TCapt kia 11-7-16 19NumbF p62 CR France430

NUDDS,Ronald Charles T2Lt dow 30-11-17 RE 219FC p47 CR Belgium3

NUGENT,Charles Capt ded 19-11-18 2RBerks p139 CR France1142

NUGENT,George Colborne.MVO.ColTBrigGen kia 3-5-15 Staff IrGds Cmdg141InfBde p1 CR France80,31-5-15

NUGENT,Gerald William Capt kia 10-8-15 GL Staff HQ29InfBde p191 MR4

NUGENT,Hugh Neville ACapt died 1-7-19 RASC

NUGENT,John Aloysius Joseph 2Lt kia 27-8-17 5Leinst p174 CR Belgium124,2Bn

NUGENT,Raymond Henry 2Lt kia 25-11-17 70RFA p33 CR France415,23-11-17

NUGENT,Richard Francis Robert 2Lt kia 18-12-14 ScotGds p52 MR32

NUGENT,William Andrew.Hon.Capt dow 29-5-15 15Huss p22 CR Lond9

NUNN,Edward Chamberland Lt ded 24-7-17 IARO att2/119Inf p281 CR Iraq8

NUNN,Frederick Arthur William Lt kia 2-4-18 1Lond &65RAF p271 MR20

NUNN,John Henry Maj dow 1-4-17 A149RFA p33 CR France120

NUNN,Mervyn Henry LtCol kia 10-8-15 9Worc Maj RoO p109 CR Gallipoli13

NUNNELEY,George Paterson.MC.CaptAMaj kia 27-3-18 4Beds p86 CR France393

NUNNELEY,Wilford Herbert.MC.2Lt kia 24-4-18 2Ess p132 MR19,Wilfred 23/24-4-18

NUNNELEY,Charles Francis Lt kia 25/27-10-14 3NumbF attYLI p62 MR22

NUNNERLEY,W.P.Lt 24-3-21 SL CR Scot142

NUNNERLEY,Willson Kenwick T2Lt kia 5-12-17 GL &13RFC p11 CR France113

NURSE,Reginald John Cecil 2Lt kia 25-3-18 4 att2/5Glouc p225 MR27,22-3-18

NUTCOMBE,Thomas Arthur 2Lt kldacc 2-8-18 ELancs &101RAF p111 CR France2

NUTHALL,John Constantine T2Lt kia 3-7-17 14MGC p184 CR Belgium24,13-7-17

NUTKINS,Vernon William Lt kld 19-2-18 RScotF att21RAF p16&95 CR Egypt8

NUTTALL,A.2Lt 11-5-16 1/1RFA CR Egypt15

NUTTALL,Albert Armitage Lt dow 15-8-16 1/7WRid p227 CR France2

NUTTALL,Eric John 2Lt kia 21-3-18 12WYorks att59MGC p82&184 MR20

NUTTALL,Harry Norbury T2Lt dow 5-7-17 RASC attMGC HQ HB p193 CR Belgium11

NUTTER,Alan Charles 2Lt dow 15-9-17 40RFC p11 CR France179

NUTTER,Geoffrey Hayward Elliot T2Lt kia 22-3-18 19MGC p184 MR20

NUTTER,Herbert Charles 2LtTLtACapt kia 16-6-17 5Suff p217 CR France421

NUTTING,Ernest Ralph 2Lt kia 18-11-16 3 att10RWar p65 MR21

NUTTLE,James Edward T2Lt ded 6-7-16 RE p47 CR Hamps245

NUTTRALL,Alfred 2Lt ded 11-5-16 RH&FA p209

NYE,Charles TLt kia 17-8-16 8Nhampt p137 CR France700,16-8-16

NYE,Reginald Rayner.MID Capt kia 17-12-15 3RScots p54 CR Belgium70

NYREN,Dudley Richard T2Lt kia 24-3-18 24RFus p69 MR20

O

OAKDEN,Arthur William Lt ded 29-6-18 A124RFA p261 CR France52

OAKDEN,Edward Ralph TCapt dow 22-3-17 10N&D p134 CR Notts84

OAKDEN,Ernest 2Lt kia 22-8-18 RGA 130HB p209 CR France526

OAKE,Douglas.MC.TCapt kld 8-8-18 GL RFA att92TMB p191 CR France19

OAKELEY,William Soulden TMaj ded 11-9-18 RASC MT p193 CR Lond8

OAKENFULL,Herbert Joseph 2Lt kia 7-10-16 10 att1/1Lond p248 MR21 CR France1890

OAKES,George Frederick Thomas.MID Capt dow 15-7-16 RE 130FC p47 CR France833

OAKES,Gerard Edmund Roseingrave Lt dow 19-4-18 1WYorks p82 CR Belgium8

OAKES,James Edwards Brooks.MC.Lt kia 10-7-17 RH&FA Z/1TMB p33 MR31

OAKES,Orbell Capt kld 13-3-15 Yorks p91 MR22

OAKES,Robert Claude 2Lt kia 19-7-16 RFA &RFC p2&33,ded CR France366,Lt

OAKES,Samuel T2Lt kia 6-5-17 RE Z'SpCoy p47 CR France560

OAKLEY,Christopher Herbert.MC&Bar.Capt dow 2-9-18 22Lond C'Coy p251 CR France630

OAKLEY,Henry Bernard 2Lt kia 3-5-17 8RB p179 MR20

OAKLEY,Reginald T2Lt kia 25-8-16 15 att8Yorks p91 CR Belgium54,Lt

OAKLEY,Reginald William Kennedy TLt kia 1-7-16 8YLI p143 MR21

OAKLEY-BROWN,Valentine Lt kia 9-10-18 3DragGds CR France341

OAKSHOTT,Albert Neville TLt kia 16-8-17 7RIrRif p170 MR30

OATES,Alfred Tennyson Lt dow 1-3-20 IA 10Lancers p281 CR Iraq8,kia

OATES,Herbert Prudent 2Lt kia 20-9-17 5Lpool p215 MR30

OATES,John Stanley TLtACapt dow 11-12-17 9 att6DCLI p114 CR Belgium84

OATES,Walter.MC.T2Lt kia 3-11-18 RE 218FC p47 CR France940

OATTS,Eric Pearce 2Lt kia 3-5-17 4RScotF p222 MR20

O'BEIRNE,Arthur James Lewis 2Lt dow 28-7-17 OxYeo att57RFC p19&205 CR Belgium24

O'BEIRNE,John Ingram Mullanniffe 2Lt kia 3-4-17 RWar att25RFC p11&p65 MR20

O'BRIAN,Walter Vincent 2Lt 20-9-16 1Ches MR21

O'BRIEN,Aubrey Ulick Marshall Capt kia 1-11-14 39RFA p33 MR29

O'BRIEN,Charles Stuart.MC.2Lt dow 27-9-18 11IrGds p53 CR France512

O'BRIEN,Daniel Joseph 2Lt kia 10-11-17 3 att2RMunF p175 MR30

O'BRIEN,Denis Patrick Capt ded 8-8-20 IARO 2EuphratesLevy attPolitcalDept p281 CR Iraq8

O'BRIEN,Dermot Lt kia 26-9-17 291RFA p208 CR Belgium23

O'BRIEN,Francis Joseph 2LtACapt kia 31-7-17 1Worc p109 MR29

O'BRIEN,Francis Pat T2Lt kia 16-8-16 10 att9ESurr p113 MR21

O'BRIEN,G.P.Capt 3-6-20 IMS MR65

O'BRIEN,Gerard.DSO.MID 2Lt kia 22-3-18 5RMunF att1InnisF p175 MR27

O'BRIEN,Henry Edward TCapt dow 8-9-16 RAMC att99FA No2GH p197 CR France85

O'BRIEN,Hugh Conor Henry Capt kia 21-12-14 2RMunF p175 MR22,22-12-14

O'BRIEN,Hugh Rivers Hamilton(Paddy) TCapt kia 1-6-16 112RFA 19AA Bty p33 CR Belgium127

O'BRIEN,Humphrey Donatus Stafford.MC&Bar.MID Capt kld 14-9-18 1Nhampt &63RAF p137 CR Iraq8

O'BRIEN,James Francis Lt kia 21-12-14 2RMunF p175 MR22

O'BRIEN,James Vincent Capt kia 10-8-16 RAMC att5Bde p197 CR France267

O'BRIEN,Jeremiah James Capt kia 10-3-18 4 att1RIrReg p89 CR Palestine3

O'BRIEN,John.MC.LtTCapt kia 6-10-18 2RMunF p175 CR France845

O'BRIEN,John Dwyer.MC.TLt dow 17-8-17 14RIrRif p170 CR Belgium8

O'BRIEN,Lucius James Francis.MID T2Lt dow 7-4-17 5Wilts p153 CR Iraq8,Frances Ex HAC

O'BRIEN,M.Nurse 21-2-17 QAIMNS CR Hamps1

O'BRIEN,Michael Patrick TLt ded 23-9-17 RAMC p197 CR Hamps1

O'BRIEN,Philip Anderson 2Lt dow 9-3-15 Leinst p174 CR France102

O'BRIEN,Robert Edward 2Lt ded 20-2-19 2 att3A&SH p255 CR Belgium316,2 att18Bn

O'BRIEN,Sidney Joseph Vincent 2Lt kia 7-6-17 5RMunF att2RIrRif p175 MR29

O'BRIEN,Terence Donough 2Lt kia 3-3-16 16Lancers att6RFC p2&23 CR Belgium11

O'BRIEN,Timothy John Aloysius Lt kia 7-8-16 27RFA CR France399

O'BRIEN,Thomas Augustine TLt ded 6-10-18 RAVC p199 MR65

O'BRIEN,Thomas Kevin TCapt kia 31-5-16 6ConnRgrs p172 CR France178,30-5-16

O'BRIEN,Walter Hubert Maj kldacc 7-2-17 RE IWT p47 CR France354

O'BRIEN,William Bartholomew Stevenson TLt ded 18-6-18 RE RTO p47 CR France145

O'BRIEN,William Donough TMaj dow 7-6-16 3ConnRgrs att20Manch p172 CR France23

O'BRIEN,William Vincent T2Lt kia 20-9-16 1Ches p96

O'BRIEN-BUTLER,Capel Desmond.MC.Capt kia 7-6-17 4 att6RIrReg p89 CR Belgium17

O'BRIEN-BUTLER,Charles Paget Capt dow 31-10-14 RAMC p197 CR France284

O'BRYEN,Myles Wheeler Lt kld 2-10-16 5RWar p214O'

CALLAGHAN,Duncan Mckay McDonald 2Lt kia 14-3-15 3 att2DCLI p114 CR Belgium28

O'CALLAGHAN,Gerard Arthur Capt dow 24-5-15 RIrReg p89 CR France285

O'CALLAGHAN,James T2Lt kia 21-10-16 13Ches p96 MR21

O'CALLAGHAN,John Charles.MC.TCaptAMaj kia 4-4-18 C190RFA p33 CR France745

O'CALLAGHAN,Thomas Francis 2Lt kia 13-10-15 4Leic p220 MR19

O'CARROLL,Francis Brendon T2Lt kia 10-8-15 6RDubF p177 MR4

OCHS,Ronald Philip 2Lt kia 27-9-15 5 att4Mddx p148 CR Belgium6,26-9-15

O'CONNELL,A.J.Lt ? 4NigR CR WAfrica56

O'CONNELL,C.W.MC.Lt kld 18-6-18 21Lond CR Essex9

O'CONNELL,Donald Charles 2Lt kia 9-9-16 4ConnRgrs att8RInnisF p172 MR21

O'CONNELL,J.M.Dr 7-11-18 SierraLeoneCivilServ CR WAfrica28

O'CONNELL,John Forbes Lt kia 20-9-14 RAMC p197 CR France1329

O'CONNELL,Maurice James Lt ded 30-7-18 222RFA attTMB p33 CR Iraq8

O'CONNOR,Arthur Cathal TCapt kia 27-7-16 1Norf p74 MR21

O'CONNOR,Arthur Patrick.CB.Col 25-1-20 RAMC CR Mddx77

O'CONNOR,Bernard Joseph TLt kia 4-10-18 3RFus p69 CR France234

O'CONNOR,Edward Victor 2Lt dow 12-5-18 RGA 29SB p41 CR Lond9

O'CONNOR,Frederick Henry Pomeroy Maj ded 1-2-16 RAOC p198

O'CONNOR,F.W.Capt&QM 17-10-19 RAMC CR Hamps232

O'CONNOR,Henry.VD.LtCol ded 1-12-15 RGA p209 CR Scot253

O'CONNOR,Hubert Michael.MC.TCapt dow 17-8-17 6KSLI p145 CR Belgium16

O'CONNOR,J.Capt 25-10-16 IA Ord Dept CR Hamps64

O'CONNOR,John McConville 2Lt kia 10-7-18 6ScotRif p224 CR France25,9Bn

O'CONNOR,Joseph Harris Lt dow 10-11-17 5 att2RMunF p175 MR30

O'CONNOR,Richard Dominick Capt kia 25-10-14 RAMC p197 CR France275

O'CONNOR,Roderic Alan Edward 2Lt kia 1-9-16 3Leinst p174 CR France399

O'CONNOR,Roderick Stratford 2Lt kia 28-4-17 4 att2SStaffs p122 MR20

O'CONNOR,William Moyle LtCol ded 21-1-16 RAMC p271 CR Ireland12

O'CONOR,Ronald Ramsay 2Lt ded 30-11-18 ColdGds 51 CR Berks45

O'CONOR,William Owen Rev&TMaj ded 24-1-19 IA IndEcclesEst p281 CR Asia82

O'DALY,Dominic Roe Dathy 2Lt kia 14-11-16 1/7NumbF p214 MR21

ODAM,Cecil Wilfred 2Lt kia 15-9-16 6Lond p247 MR21,Wilfrid

O'DEA,Lawrence Rev ded 4-11-17 RAChDept p199 CR Sussex15,Laurence

O'DEA Mathew Leo Brien Patrick Capt ded 4-6-19 IARO attS&TCps p281 CR Asia82

ODDIE,Francis Arthur Joseph TLt kia 23-10-16 2Mddx att2RBerks p148 MR21

ODDY,Alfred Edward T2Lt kia 27-9-18 8WYorks p82 CR France755,29-9-18

ODDY,James Leslie Capt dow 3-9-16 6WYorks p218 CR France44

ODELL,Oliver Henry Cecil 2Lt kia 10-9-16 3Lond p246 CR France453

ODELL,Philip Ralph Lt 30-4-21 2Beds &Herts MR66

ODELL,Robert Eric TLt dow 20-12-16 8BlkW p129 CR France158,kia

ODELL,William Capt.MC.kia 22-2-17 IA 123Rif att125 p281 CR Iraq5

ODELL,William Ward.MC.T2Lt kia 4-10-17 9N&D p134 MR30

ODGERS,Robert Blake Lt ded 31-8-17 RASC p271 CR Lond12,Capt

ODHAMS,Valentine Bernand TLt dow 5-10-15 15DLI p161 CR France1

ODLING,Eric Robert Meade Lt kld 25-3-15 RE p47 CR France765

ODLUM,William Henry Maj ded 25-11-20 IA IMS p281

O'DONAHUE,Thomas Henderson T2Lt kia 20-4-17 2/9Manch p155 CR France765

O'DONNELL,Anthony Patrick 2Lt kia 12-6-17 1/4Y&L p238 CR France705

O'DONNELL,Charles Vize Capt ded 12-5-19 SL LpoolRecruitStaff p268 CR Yorks185

O'DONNELL,George Boudrie LtCol ded 20-10-19 RetPay Ex RDC p271 CR Sussex111

O'DONNELL,Hugh Neil T2Lt dow 4-2-17 17WelshR p127 CR France145

O'DONNELL,Percy 2Lt dow 6-5-16 5RFA p33 CR Belgium11

O'DONNELL,Ralph T2Lt ded 25-3-18 61IndLabourCps p189 CR France770,28-3-18

O'DONAGHUE,Algernon Leopold 2Lt ded 22-5-17 RDC p253 CR Somerset25

O'DONOGHUE,Humphrey Patrick 2Lt kia 10-3-15 1Lpool p72 MR22

O'DONOGHUE,John Hamilton 2Lt ded PoW 27-6-16 IARO att110Mahrattas p281 MR38

O'DONOVAN,Miles Henry Capt kia 21-6-16 4 att8RMunF p175 CR France223,20-6-16

O'DOWD,Maurice Vernon 2Lt kia 25-5-15 3 att2NumbF p62 MR29

O'DUFFY,Kevin Emmet TLt kia 15-8-15 7RMunF p175 MR4

O'DWYER,Alfred Stanhope T2Lt kia 29-7-16 14RWar p65 MR21

O'DWYER,John T2Lt dow 11-9-16 GL attTMB p191

O'DWYER,Robert Martin T2Lt dow 18-10-15 D74RFA p33 CR France423

OERTLING,Lewis John Francis Lt dow 8-8-18 5Beds att5RAF p228&271 CR France71

O'FARRELL,Archibald Hugh 2Lt kia 27-9-18 1IrGds p53 CR France1497

O'FARRELL,Haward Patrick Austin TCapt died 6-12-16 SL p268

O'FARRELL,Howard Patrick Curtis LtCol died 6-12-16 14Hamps p121 CR Hamps7,14-12-16

O'FERRALL,Brendon Hynds 2Lt kia 16-8-17 A76RFA p33 CR Belgium12

OFFICER,Arnold Vincent T2Lt ded 10-5-17 12EYorks p84 CR France40

O'FFLAHERTIE,Godwin Joseph Anthony Swifte Lt kld 4-3-18 3KSLI att1Lpool p145

O'FIELD,Alfred T2Lt dow 11-11-17 RE 10CpsSig p47 CR Belgium11

OFIELD,Charles Henry 2lt dow 22-8-18 RGA 139HB p41 CR France119

O'FLAHERTY,Douglas Hill TCapt kia 1-7-16 15RIrRif p170 MR21

O'FLYNN,Dominick Thomas TCapt ded 16-6-18 RAMC att19DAC p197 CR France1415

O'FLYNN,Francis Joseph T2Lt kia 27-4-16 9RMunF p175

O'FLYNN,Michael Joseph TLt dow 24-9-18 RAMC att1Nhampt p197 CR France528

OGDEN,John Herbert 2Lt kia 31-7-17 5LNLancs p234 MR29

OGDEN,Percy 2Lt ded 7-6-17 RFC p261 CR C'land&W'land45

OGDEN,Walter Frederick T2Lt dow 2-12-17 11TankCps p188 CR France446

OGG,Lindsay Ross 2Lt ded 22-9-16 IARO attS&TCps p281 CR Iraq6

OGG,William Kelly Carmichael 2Lt kia 15-7-16 9HLI p240 MR21

OGILVIE,Alexander Walter TLt dow 30-10-18 RASC attRGA 60SB p193 CR Suff3

OGILVIE,Andrew Maxwell 2Lt kia 5-10-17 3 att2GordH p167 MR30

OGILVIE,James Roy 2Lt dow 22-8-18 RE 80FC p210 CR France119

OGILVIE,William Edmond T2Lt kia 27-9-15 9BordR p117 CR France425

OGILVY,Gilchrist Nevill.Bart.Lt kia 29-10-14 1ScotGds p52 MR29

OGILVY,Patrick Julian Harry Stanley.Hon.MC.ACapt kia 9-10-17 1IrGds p53 CR Belgium83

OGILVY,William Wickham Lt dow 23-3-18 20Huss p23 CR France1063

O'GIOLLAGAIN,John Gabriel T2Lt kld 5-9-17 GL &RFC p11 CR Wilts115

OGLE,Thomas Burton 2Lt kia 23-3-16 3Dors p124 MR38

O'GORMAN,E.M.Sister ded 20-11-14 TFNS CR Glouc6

O'GRADY,Amy Veda Sister 12-8-16 AustArmyNursServ MR65

O'GRADY,de Courcy 2Lt ded 14-2-15 ConnRgrs p266 CR Ireland24

O'GRADY,Standish de Courcy.CMG.DSO.LtCol 23-12-20 RAMC CR Europe1

OGSTON,James T2Lt dow 15-9-16 13RScots p54 CR France188

OGSTON,Kenneth Capt dow 12-4-18 6WRid p227 MR30

O'HALLORAN,John Fernan 2Lt kia 26-7-16 2HLI p163 MR21

O'HALLORAN-GILES,Robert 2Lt dow PoW 26-4-18 KEdwsHorse p24 CR Belgium406

O'HALLORAN,Sylvester North East ACapt kia 9-8-17 2Ess p132 MR20

O'HANLON,Sydney Esmond.MC.TLt kld 3-2-18 RFC p16 CR Lancs30

O'HARA,H.E.2Lt kld 25-5-18 GL &RAF p191

O'HARA,Henry Desmond.DSO.Lt dow 29-8-15 1RDubF p177 CR Europe23

O'HARA,Osborne Capt kia 13-2-15 2RIrF p171 MR29

O'HARA,Patrick Gilbert Warwick 2Lt kia 14-8-16 3ESurr att1/4RBerks p113 MR21

O'HARA,Thomas O.Lt ded 10-3-19 4RScots p211 CR Scot713

OHLMANN,Gerrard Alexander Louis 2Lt kia 29-9-15 3RFus p69 MR19

O'KANE,Paul Lt kia 21-3-18 4 att1RIrRif p170 MR27

OKE,Robert William Leslie LtTCapt kia 25-9-15 3 att2RBerks p139

O'KEARNEY-WHITE Ernest Francis 2Lt kia 9-9-16 9RDubF p177 MR21

O'KEEFE,Joseph Richard T2Lt kia 4-5-16 10LNLancs p136 CR France745

O'KEEFE,William Robert TCapt ded 21-11-18 RAMC 32CCS p197 CR Lebanon1

O'KEEFE,William Henry TLt kia 19-5-17 40RFA p33 CR France1182

O'KEEFFE,Marcus Menus.MC.LtAMaj kia 2-4-18 RFA 48ArmyBde p33 CR France2

O'KELLY,Henry Arundell de Pentheny Capt kia 18-5-15 18Huss CR Belgium4

O'KELLY,Patrick Joseph TLt kia 26-9-16 58RFA p33 CR France393

O'KELLY,Richard Capt ded 18-12-19 RAMC p267 CR Egypt9

OKEY,Leslie Alfred T2Lt kia 15-6-17 214MGC p184 MR20

OKEY,William Ewart T2Lt kia 21-1-16 1ConnRgrs p172 CR iraq5

O'LAND,Valentine T2Lt kia 1-7-16 15WYorks p82 MR21

OLDEN,Sidney Montague T2Lt kia 4-5-18 1BordR p117 MR32

OLDENDORFF,Friedrich Henrich Maj dow 1-9-16 7Mddx p235 CR France833,Frederick Henry

OLDERSHAW,Leslie Capt dow 2-10-17 RAMC att1/8Manch p254 CR Belgium24

OLDERSHAW,John Joseph Fritz 2Lt kia 1-7-16 9YLI p143 MR21

OLDERSHAW,Thomas Harold 2Lt kia 14-4-18 3 att2HLI p163 MR20

OLDFIELD,Edmund George William Capt kia 4-6-15 8Manch p237 MR4,5-6-15

OLDFIELD,Fred T2Lt kia 29-6-17 9NStaffs p157 CR Belgium17

OLDFIELD,Guy Christopher Ottley Lt kia 5-9-14 RWSurr attKAR p56&202 MR50

OLDFIELD,John Burleigh Maj&QM ded 9-12-14 7Ess p271 CR Lond14

OLDFIELD,John Burleigh.MC&Bar.T2LtACapt kia 16-8-17 2Nhampt p137 MR30

OLDFIELD,Laurel Cecil Francis TCapt kia 25-9-15 12RB p179 CR France768

OLDFIELD,William Henry 2Lt kia 17-5-15 4 att2HLI p163 MR22

OLDHAM,Joseph Haslope 2Lt kia 18-4-15 3DCLI att2YLI p114 CR Belgium152

OLDHAM,John 2Lt kia 19-4-18 6RWar p214 CR France248

OLDHAM,Leslie William Searles.MID Maj kia 28-7-15 RE 63Coy p47 CR France727

OLDHAM,Llewellyn Haslope T2Lt kia 26-9-15 2Worc p109 MR19

OLDHAM,Wilton Stransham Capt kia 22-11-15 IA 48Pnrs p281 MR38

OLDMAN,Harold Victor T2Lt kld 29-10-17 RFC p11 CR Herts30

OLDMAN,Wilfred Southey Deare TCapt kia 25-9-15 8RBerks p139 CR France552

OLDREY,Gerald Vivian Lt ded 19-2-19 1/1SNottsHuss p205 CR Egypt9,19-1-19

OLDREY,Montague 2Lt kia 26-10-17 3Lond p246 MR30

OLDREY,Robert John Blatchford Capt kia 29-10-14 4DragGds p21 MR22 &CR France1896

OLDREY,Vernon Roy Lt kia 31-8-18 4Lond p246 CR France646

OLDRIDGE,Peter Henry T2Lt kld 26-1-18 RFC p16 CR Hunts83

OLDS,Cyril Austin.DCM.2Lt kia 16-4-16 3Glouc p107 MR20

O'LEARY,Herbert Homfray Capt kia 14-1-20 IA 2/76Punjabis p281 MR43

O'LEARY,John Maj accdrd 9-9-15 IA IMS p281 CR Egypt8

OLIPHANT,Edward Havelock Maj kia 12-7-15 IA 95Inf p281 CR Asia82

OLIPHANT,Marcus Francis 2Lt kia 12-8-15 5Norf p217 MR4

OLIVER,Alfred Donald Capt dow 24-4-17 5/6Manch p236 CR Belgium11,21-4-17

OLIVER,Arthur Harold T2Lt kia 8-11-17 11EYorks p84 CR France184

OLIVER,Charles Gordon 2Lt dow 14-10-15 3Dev attYorks p77 CR France98

OLIVER,Cyril Francis Harrison TCapt kia 14-7-16 12WYorks p82 CR France453

OLIVER,Edgar Alexander T2Lt kia 27-7-16 23RFus p69 MR21

OLIVER,Edward Cole 2Lt kia 22-10-17 1/2 att16Ches p96 MR30

OLIVER,Ernest 2Lt kia 22-9-17 SuffYeo attNigeriaR p205 CR EAfrica22 &CR Tanzania1

OLIVER,Frank Lambton 2Lt kia 13-7-17 SomLI att55RFC p11&80 CR Belgium344

OLIVER,Frederick Richard 2Lt kia 1-7-16 1/6N&D p233 MR21,24-7-16

OLIVER,Frederick Ruddall Lt kia 3-5-17 8Leic p88 MR20

OLIVER,George Baxter T2Lt kia 17-6-16 157RFA p33 CR France631

OLIVER,George Eric 2Lt dow 31-7-17 8ScotRif p225 CR Belgium7

OLIVER,George Frank T2Lt kia 15-7-16 10Ches p96 CR France832

OLIVER,Guy Bertram Maj dow 29-9-16 189RFA p33 CR France400 Ex 116/26RFA

OLIVER,Guy Giffard Capt kia 21-1-16 IA 102Grens p281 CR Iraq5,G.C.

OLIVER,D.Hedley CaptAMaj ded 16-3-19 RE CR Surrey34

OLIVER,Harold Augustus Boyd 2Lt dow 26-5-18 IrGds att4GdsMGR CR France62,served as KING,Norman

OLIVER,Harry John T2Lt dow 23-4-18 13MGC p184 CR France31,Henry

OLIVER,Harry Percy Greenwood 2Lt kia 30-6-16 13RSuss p119 MR19

OLIVER,John Milner TLt kia 9-7-16 16Manch p155 MR21

OLIVER,Raymond Edward Creswick 2Lt mbk 28-8-16 2RB C'Coy p256 MR19

OLIVER,Robert.MID Lt mbk 25-9-15 12NumbF p256 MR19

OLIVER,Robert 2Lt kia 20-3-18 6BordR p117 MR19

OLIVER,Roderick Magrath Lt kia 27-8-18 2GrenGds p50 CR France614

OLIVER,Siddartha John 2Lt kia 10-8-17 GL &66RFC p11 MR20

OLIVER,Thomas Alfred Capt kia 14-8-17 GL &RFC p11 MR20

OLIVER,Thomas Frederick 2Lt ded 26-10-18 13N&D p264 CR Sussex183,Lt 12Bn

OLIVER,William Steele T2Lt kia 7/11-8-15 8NumbF p62 MR4

OLIVER-JONES,Alfred Vernon TLt ded 23-7-16 RFA attRFC p2&33 MR20

OLIVER-THOMPSON,John Herbert.MID TLtAMaj kia 21-3-18 40MGC p184 MR20

OLIVIER,Rosaire Henri TLt dow 11-10-17 GL &RFC 6BallCo p11 CR France102

OLIVIER,Jasper George 2Lt kia 16-9-16 3 att7DCLI p114 MR21

OLIVIER,Robert Harold Capt kia 14-9-14 1DCLI C Coy p114 MR15

OLLETT,Alfred Oscar T2Lt kia 27-4-16 13Ess p132 CR France160

OLLETT,Arthur Edmund William Lt ded 20-8-19 RE RlyOpDiv p262 MR66,Capt

OLLETT,Henry Wallace 2Lt dow 28-10-18 17RFA p209 CR France1725

OLLEY,Alfred.DCM.2Lt ded 1-7-19 WRid p264 CR Berks125

OLLIVANT,A.H.CB.CMG.MIDx2 GrigGen 31-8-19 RGA CR Kent217

OLLIVIER,Guy Lancelot CaptAMaj ded 20-1-18 RGA Commdg 65SB p41 CR France85

O'LONE,Robert James.MID 2LtTCapt kia 11-11-15 2RIrRif p170 CR Belgium137

O'LONE,Walter Percy.MID 2Lt kia 25-9-15 2RIrRif p170 MR29

O'LONGAN,Paul Charles Stacpoole 2Lt kia 1-6-17 RIrReg att41RFC p11&89 CR Belgium152

OLPHERT,Frederick John Lt dow 19-5-18 RE 940AreaEmpCoy p47 CR France770

OLPHERT,Hugh Montgomery Archdale 2Lt kia 9-9-16 3MunstF att7Leic p88 MR21

OLSEN,Sorën Bendix TCapt ded 20-4-18 RASC p193 CR Durham182

OLVER,John Denis Circuit.MC.2LtALt kia 27-4-17 123/28RFA p33 CR France68

O'MALLEY,Charles Lt kia 25-11-17 17WelshR p127 MR17

O'MALLEY,W.Lt 11-11-19 ConnRgrs CR Ireland12

O'MALLEY,William Joseph 2Lt kia 9-4-17 RFA Y47TMB p209 CR Belgium167

OMAND,Robert Stewart 2Lt dow 25-9-16 4Yorks p220 CR France177

O'MAY,William Shields.MC.LtTCapt dow 3-4-18 5 att15HLI p240 CR France169

O'MEARA,Bulkely Ernest Adolphus.DSO.Capt ded 31-8-16 EAUL CR EAfrica9 &CR Tanzania1

O'MEARA,Leon Alfred 2Lt kia 6-2-17 3 att6ELancs p111 MR38

O'MEEHAN,Isidore James Chap4Cl ded 19-12-19 RAChDept p268 CR Iraq5

OMEROD,James T2Lt ded 27-9-18 Manch att22Bn p155

OMMANNEY,Alfred Erasmus Stuart 2Lt kia 7-10-16 3 att6EKent p58 MR21

OMMANNEY,G.S.Col 21-3-18 58TrnResBn CR Lond4 Ex IA

OMMANNEY,Rupert Capt kia 31-10-14 RE 2DivStaff p47 CR Belgium58

OMMUNDSEN,Arthur Norman Victor Harcourt Lt kia 19-9-15 HAC p206 CR Belgium6

ONCKEN,William Gerrard TLt ded 17-2-19 46MGC Inf p184 CR France341,Gerhard Ex 2/23Lond

O'NEILL,Alfred Edward 2Lt dow 23-9-17 1/7Lpool p215 CR Belgium3

O'NEILL,Arthur Edward Bruce.Hon.Capt kia 6-11-14 2LifeGds p20 MR29

O'NEILL,Douglas Quirke 2Lt kia 26-4-18 10RWar p65CR Belgium185,Quirk

O'NEILL,Frederick 2Lt kia 13-11-16 5RDubF p177 CR France220

O'NEILL,Henry Dubois.MC.CaptAMaj ded 2-6-18 3Beds p86 CR Sussex107

O'NEILL,James Dominick 2Lt kia 24-8-16 5 att2RMunF p175 MR21

O'NEILL,John Teskey TCapt ded 10-10-16 17RIrRif p265 CR Ireland110

O'NEILL,Roderick Lt kia 3-5-17 6WRid p227 MR20

O'NEILL,Samuel Lt kld 12-6-15 6LancF p221 CR Gallipoli1,kia

O'NEILL,Samuel Lt kia 1-7-16 GL RA attTMB p191 MR21

O'NEILL,Thomas 2Lt ded 29-5-19 2RRofCav att1/1DorsYeo p23 CR Eire451

O'NEILL,Thomas Michael 2Lt kia 8-5-18 9RDubF &43RAF p266 MR20,O'NEIL

ONIONS,Wilfred 2Lt dow 25-4-15 3Mon p244 MR29

ONSLOW,Arthur Denzel.MC.2Lt kia 13-8-16 11RWar p65 MR21,Denzil

ONSLOW,Brian Watton.MID Lt kia 28-7-15 IA 11Lancers attAust NZ ArmyCps p281 CR Gallipoli30,Walton

ONSLOW,Milo-Richard Beaumont.MID Capt dow 5-11-17 IA 21Cav att33 p281 CR Iraq8

ONSLOW,Tom 2Lt kia 6-1-17 3 att5KSLI p145 CR France420

OPENSHAW,Edward Hyde LtCol ded 23-7-17 4SomLI p218 CR Iraq6

OPENSHAW,Fred T2Lt dow 8-10-18 1/2 att8Lpool p72 CR France256

OPENSHAW,Geoffrey Ormerod TCapt dow PoW 9-8-18 RASC p193 CR Germany3,Omerod

OPENSHAW,Harold Michael Lt dow 28-8-14 Norf p74 CR Belgium205

OPET,Isaac Harold 2Lt dow 22-3-18 PoW 7 att8Lond p247 CR France1893,Isidor

OPPE,Henry Sigismund TLt kia 6-11-15 11 att6Yorks p91 CR Gallipoli27

OPPE,Thomas Armin 2Lt kia 20-5-17 4 att1ScotRif p104 MR20

OPPENHEIMER,Lehmann James Lt ded 8-11-16 2/23Lond p252 CR France102

ORBELL,Douglas Lt kia 5-9-18 1Camb p245 CR France511

ORBELL,Ivan Scott 2Lt kia 25-10-17 att4RFus p69 MR22,25-10-14

ORCHARD,Ernest Frank Gordon Lt kia 31-7-17 8Lpool p215 MR29,1-8-17

ORCHARD,Hugh Thomas T2Lt kia 20-8-17 15N&D Y'Coy p134 CR France363

ORCHARDSON,Charles Moxon Quiller.MC.Capt dow 26-4-17 1CotyLondYeo p204 CR Egypt7,MddxHuss

ORCUT,Marcena Hitchcock T2Lt kia 1-3-18 3RFC p16 CR France345

ORD,Ord Ralph TLt kia 18-9-16 10RB p179 MR21

ORD-MACKENZIE,Douglas Allan 2Lt kia 24-9-16 9Lond p248 MR21

ORDE,John Barwick.MC.CaptTMaj dow 12-2-17 B99RFA p33 CR Greece6

ORDE-POWLETT,William Percy 2Lt kia 17-5-15 4Yorks p220 MR29

ORDE-WARD,A.P.Lt 11-11-18 Lincs attMGC CR Sussex144

ORDISH,Henry Thomas.MC.Capt dow PoW 21-3-18 6Lond B'Coy p246 CR France403,25-3-18

O'REILLY,Gerald Joseph T2Lt dow 30-11-16 Lincs p75 CR France297

O'REILLY,H.D.R.Capt 31-5-19 1/4RWSurr att1/5ESurr CR Iraq8

O'REILLY,Herbert Wilson 2Lt dow 20-1-16 4 att2RIrRif p170 CR France285

O'REILLY,Patrick Joseph.MC&Bar.TCapt kia 11-10-18 RAMC att7EYorks p197 CR France658

O'REILLY,Patrick Stanislaus.CMG.LtCol ded 18-11-18 RAMC p197 CR Lond29

O'REILLY,W.T.MC.Capt 19-9-20 Mddx CR Sussex95

ORETT,Claud Cecil Lt 25-9-18 14MGC Inf CR Belgium185

ORFEUR,Howard West Lt kia 23-8-18 8 att10Ess p232 CR France430

ORFORD,Charles Robert Hadfield T2Lt dow 18-7-17 1/2 att16LancF p92 CR Belgium24,19-7-17

ORFORD,Ernest Charles TCapt kia 30-7-16 20Lpool p72 MR21

ORFORD,Ernest Victor Molson 2Lt kia 23-10-16 14 att2Ess p132 MR21

ORFORD,Stephen Mewburn 2Lt kia 25-6-16 11KRRC p151 CR Belgium4

ORFORD,William Kirkpatrick T2Lt kia 1-7-16 GL 17Manch attTMB p191 MR21

ORGAN,Harold Charles 2Lt kia 9-10-17 4Glouc p225 CR Belgium126

ORGAN,Harold Percy TLt&Adj kia 1-7-16 10Y&L p159 MR21

ORGILL,Phillip Ronald T2Lt dow PoW 31-3-18 61MGC Inf p184&257,Philip CR France441

ORKNEY,Robert Lt kia 20-10-15 5A&SH p243 CR Gallipoli2

ORLEBAR,Basil John Capt kia 15-1-15 3 att1Beds p86 CR Belgium98

ORLEBAR,Robert Evelyn Lt kia 9-1-15 2Mddx p148 CR France1157

ORME,Alfred Lyth T2Lt kia 31-7-17 18Lpool p72 MR29,Lytn

ORME,Edward Leslie Lt kia 27-5-17 3 att1RWFus p98 MR20,att2Bn

ORME,Francis Reginald 2Lt kia 7-11-14 1RWFus p98 MR29

ORME,John McCallum.MC.Capt ded 3-4-17 RAMC p197 CR France31

ORME,Owen Felix LtTCapt kia 25-9-15 RSuss p119 CR France219

ORME,Peter William Merton 2Lt ded 7-5-17 11RSuss attRFC p261 CR Sussex183

ORMEROD,Andrew T2Lt kia 13-4-17 RH&FA att59RFC p11&33 MR20

ORMEROD,James 2Lt ded 27-9-18 22Manch CR Italy11

ORMESBY,Horatio Nelson Lt kia 4-6-15 12ScotRif attKOSB p104 MR4,ORMSBY

ORMESHER,Herbert TLt kia 4-10-15 7Lincs p75 CR Belgium56

ORMESHER,William TLt dow 7-12-15 16Lpool att2RFus p72 MR4,3-12-15

ORMISTON,Robert William T2Lt dow 25-3-18 6KSLI p145 CR France987

ORMOND,Alexander T2Lt kia 30-9-16 27 att11Manch p155 MR21

ORMROD,George Lt kia 18-9-18 5RSuss p228 CR France699

ORMROD,Harry TLt kia 1-7-16 8YLI p143 MR21

ORMROD,L.J.2Lt 3-5-15 12Lancers CR Wales664

ORMROD,Lawrence Moreland.MC.Capt ded 25-8-17 1RWFus p98 CR Wales664,dow

ORMROD,Oliver Hugh TCapt kld 12-9-16 RFA attRFC p2&33 CR Wales664

ORMSBY,Francis James T2Lt kia 3-9-16 14 att13RSuss p119 CR France701

ORMSBY,Harold Sydney.MID TLtACapt dow 18-2-17 14RWFus p98 CR Belgium23

ORMSBY,Horatio Nelson Lt 4-6-15 12ScotRif att1KOSB MR4

ORMSBY,Vincent Alexander.CB.BrigGen kia 2-5-17 IA Staff127InfBde p281 CR France363,1-5-17

O'RORKE,Benjamin Garniss.DSO.Rev ded 25-12-18 RAChDept p199 CR Cornwall40

O'RORKE,Denis Clifford.MC.Capt kia 24-3-18 att11KRRC p151 MR27

O'ROURKE,Daniel Lt kia 30-7-18 RGA 170SB p41 CR France343

ORPEN,Walter Selwyn 2Lt kia 6-7-16 2 att10LancF p93 MR21

ORPIN,Ralph Ernest 2Lt dow 6-8-17 A92RFA p33 CR Belgium12

ORR,Alexander Thomas TCapt ded 3-1-19 RE p47 CR Italy11,Thomson

ORR,Arthur James T2Lt kia 23-4-18 24Manch p155 CR Italy11

ORR,Arthur Roxboroughe Capt kia 17-11-15 2ScotGds p52 CR France257,Roxburghe 17-10-15

ORR,Edward Farquharson Burkitt Lt kia 23-3-18 HQ 173RFA p33 CR France1203,24-3-18

ORR,Hugh Brian T2Lt kia 22-3-18 HLI att10/11Bn p163 MR20

ORR,Jack Alexander Anderson Lt kia 12-6-18 3SfthH p165 MR19,2Bn

ORR,James Barbour Capt kia 31-7-17 4RScotF p222 MR29

ORR,James Henry T2LtACapt kia 30-11-17 RGA 210SB p41 MR17

ORR,James Kenneth T2Lt kia 1-7-16 16Mddx p148 MR21

ORR,John 2Lt ded 29-3-19 6DragGds p261 CR Scot525

ORR,John Arthur Capt kia 22-10-14 1CamH p168 MR29

ORR,John Boyd.DSO.Maj dow 24-8-14 1Norf p74 CR Belgium205

ORR,John Compton 2Lt kia 28-4-17 2 att5RBerks p139 CR France1182

ORR,J.L.Maj 10-2-18 IA 20DeccanHorse CR Devan238

ORR,Osborne John.DFC.Lt 23-10-18 204RAF MR20

ORR,Robert Baird Rowley Capt kia 3-7-17 9A&SH att4RFC p243 CR Belgium11

ORR,Robert Clifford Capt kia 19-12-14 3SomLI p80 CR Belgium70

ORR,Robert Duncan Lt kia 10-8-18 9A&SH p244 CR France649

ORR,Robert Watson 2Lt kia 25-9-15 18Lond p250 CR France219

ORR,Walter Leslie 2Lt kia 25-9-15 4 att2RIrRif p170 MR29

ORR,William Gilmour Moore 2Lt dow 12-1-17 3HLI p163 CR Iraq5

ORR-EWING,Ernest Pellew TCapt kia 15-9-16 ScotGds att1Bn p52 CR France374

ORRELL,John Turton 2Lt kia 2-12-17 GL &57RFC p11 CR Belgium140

ORRELL,Keith Faulkener Andrew 2Lt kia 13-1-17 10 att6SLancs p125 MR38

ORRETT,Claud Cecil TLt kia 25-9-18 14MGC p184

ORREY,Frederick William T2Lt dow 16-9-17 5 att3KRRC p151 CR Belgium140,att13Bn

ORRIN,William John T2Lt ded 12-11-18 5RBerks attLabCps p139 CR France85

ORRISS,Walter Gerald Lt dow 29-3-18 3GrenGds p50 CR France62

ORSON,John Tom 2Lt kia 21-3-18 4Leic p220 MR20

ORTON,Cecil Alfred Maj ded 30-9-17 RGA 22SB p41 CR Oxford45

ORTON,Ernest Henry 2Lt kia 9-5-15 2ScotRif p104 MR22

ORTON-SMITH,Geoffrey Ewing Lt ded PoW 1-3-17 6 att1/5RWar p214 MR21

O'RYAN,Francis Joseph T2Lt dow 23-8-18 8RLancs A'Coy p59 CR France103

OSBORN,Alfred Herbert 2Lt kia 23-10-18 8ESurr p113 CR France1478

OSBORN,Arthur Guy Capt kia 6-5-17 12SWBord p100 CR France439

OSBORN,Edward Stanley T2Lt kld 29-11-17 GL &RFC p11

OSBORN,Ernest John.MC.TLtACapt dow 13-4-18 24RFus att5TMB p69 CR France145

OSBORN,George Ashby Chadwick TCapt kia 24-4-17 7Wilts p153 MR37

OSBORN,Gordon Chadwick 2Lt kia 18-4-15 RE p47 CR Belgium165

OSBORN,Walter 2Lt kia 5-11-18 13Lond p249 CR France1142

OSBORNE,Albert John Francis 2Lt kia 10-7-17 3RWSurr p56 CR Belgium15,7Bn

OSBORNE,Alec Ferguson.MC.Capt ded 2-7-21 RASC CR Egypt9

OSBORNE,Archibald Edward Capt kia 21-3-18 5EKent p213 MR20

OSBORNE,Brian Lt kia 11-11-14 15Huss p22 MR29

OSBORNE,Brian Riversdale.MC.T2Lt kia 4-11-18 2GrenGds p50 CR France985

OSBORNE,Derrick Lt kia 21-3-18 3 att2DLI p161 MR20

OSBORNE,Edward Bertram T2Lt dowPoW 1-4-18 2 att2/5ELancs p111 CR France716

OSBORNE,Frank Louis 2Lt dow 21-3-18 2/5Lincs p220 MR20

OSBORNE,Frederick William 2Lt kia 23-4-17 5 att13KRRC p151 CR France1193

OSBORNE,George Edward Bell Maj kia 6-11-17 Fife&ForfarYeo p203 CR Palestine1

OSBORNE,Harold Lt kia 19-7-20 IA 105 att116MahrattaLI p281 CR Iraq6

OSBORNE,Harold John.MID Lt dow 4-8-15 1/4Hamps p228 CR Iraq6

OSBORNE,Harry Edgar Lt kia 10-8-18 5WelshR p230 MR4

OSBORNE,H.C.B.TMaj ded 28-6-16 27RFus p69 CR Kent28

OSBORNE,Henry Douglas 2Lt ded 24-2-19 5EKent p213 CR France34

OSBORNE,Hubert P.Capt kld 7-7-17 104CanadaInf attRFC CR Belgium115

OSBORNE,Hugh Corry T2Lt kia 23-7-16 12WYorks p82 MR21

OSBORNE,John T2Lt kia 2-12-17 17HLI p163 MR30

OSBORNE,John Sydney Lt kia 3-9-16 1/6HLI p240 CR Egypt2

OSBORNE,Leslie Hall TLt kia 7-8-15 9LancF p93 CR Gallipoli27

OSBORNE,Marcus Stuart Lt kia 24-4-18 8Huss att8MGC p22 MR27

OSBORNE,Robert Lionel T2Lt kia 7-7-16 14 att9RFus p69 CR France393

OSBORNE,Trevor Leonard Lt kia 30-9-18 Dev &RAF p77 CR France1483

OSBORNE,Victor Edward 2Lt kld PoW 7-4-18 3 O&BLI attMGC Inf p130&184 CR Germany3,Lt

OSBORNE,William Edward 2Lt dow 11-9-16 1/4Lond p246 CR France23,kia

OSBORNE,William John T2Lt dow 9-8-15 9LancF p93 MR4

OSBORNE-JONES,Noel 2Lt kia 8-5-16 15RWFus p98 MR19

OSBOURNE,Robert Capt kia 2-3-17 9HLI p240 CR France626

OSBURN,Francis Cecil Trousdale 2Lt dow 17-5-17 2 att9Ess p132 CR France113

OSGOOD,Thomas William TLt kia 19-7-16 D23RFA p33 CR France399

O'SHEA,Dermot Patrick Lt kia 11-9-17 IA 69Punjabis p281 CR Asia62

O'SHEA,Dermot Timothy T2Lt kia 10-8-18 14TankCps p188 CR France692

O'SHEA,Harry Arthur TLt kia 14-8-18 SL &92RAF p268 MR20

O'SHEA,Wilfred Bernard 2Lt dow 23-5-16 IA 1/8GurkhaRif p281 MR38

OSLER,Edward Revere 2Lt dow 30-8-17 A59RFA p33 CR Belgium16

OSMAN,Eric Edward 2Lt kia 20-5-17 3 att1InnisF p105 MR20,19-5-17

OSMASTON,Oswald Camplyon Hutchinson.MC.Lt kia 26-8-17 RE 12FC p47 CR France80

OSMASTON,Robert Shirley.MC.2Lt kia 24-9-16 3Suss attRFC p2&119 CR France167

OSMOND,Charles Frederick Squire T2Lt kia 28-11-17 6Yorks p91 CR France551

OSMOND,Cyril Thomas TLt dow 25-8-18 14WelshR p127 CR France84

OSMOND-WILLIAMS,Osmond Trahærn Deudraith.DSO.Capt dow 27-9-15 WelshGds p53

OSTLER,Alan.MC.2Lt kld 16-9-18 17RFA &13RAF p33 CR France481

OSTLER,Thomas T2Lt kia 7-6-17 11WYorks att69TMB p82 CR Belgium127

OSTREHAM,Duncan Haldane Lt kia 31-7-17 4LNLancs p234 MR29

O'SULLIVAN,John Anthony T2Lt kia 27-5-17 GL &1RFC p11 CR France551,O'SULLIVAN

O'SULLIVAN,Arthur Moore Capt kia 9-5-15 1RIrRif p170 CR France706

O'SULLIVAN,Donald Vincent Chap4Cl kia 5-7-16 RAChDept p199 CR France295,Donal

O'SULLIVAN,Fergus 2Lt kia 23-4-17 6NStaffs attRFC p19&238 CR France366

O'SULLIVAN,Gerald Robert.VC.Capt kia 21-8-15 1InnisF p105 MR4

O'SULLIVAN,Horace Alexander 2Lt kia 22-4-17 RGA 41SB p41 CR France68,Lt 24-4-17

O'SULLIVAN,Hugh Henry 2Lt kia 10-6-15 6NStaffs p238 CR France861

O'SULLIVAN,John Andrew Hamilton Lt kia 28-6-15 13HLI p163 MR4

O'SULLIVAN,Thomas George TLt kia 21-8-18 RE 4LtRlyOpCoy p47 CR France81

OSWALD,William Digby,DSO LtTMaj dow 15-7-16 5DragGds att12WYorks p21 CR France141,LtCol 16-7-16

OSWELL,Percy Vincent T2Lt kia 20-9-18 6RWSurr p56 CR France369

O'TOOLE,Daniel 2Lt kia 23-11-17 1RIrF p171 MR17

OTTER,Robert John Charles Capt dow 15-2-15 Norf p74 CR Belgium98,kia

OTTEY,Raymond Gascoyne 2Lt kia 28-7-17 3Leic att32RFC p11&88 MR20

OTTEY,Thomas William.DCM.Maj ded 3-12-18 RAOC p198 CR Kent175

OTTLEY,Algernon Glendower Capt dow 22-5-15 2EYorks p84 CR France102

OTTLEY,Geoffrey Claude Langdale.DSO.TLt dow 21-12-14 ScotGds p52 CR Scot430

OTTLEY,Glendower George.MID TMaj kia 3-9-16 RFus att9ESurr p69 MR21

OTTLEY,John Lawrence Young 2Lt kia 22-4-17 IA 56Rif p281 MR38

OTTLEY,Kendal Coghill Glendower Lt ded 31-10-16 WIndiaR p192

OTTLEY,Lionel Edward.MID Maj 20-8-21 NumbF CR Sussex200

OTTLEY,Reginald Benade Glendower 2Lt kia 23-12-17 9NStaffs att59RFC p11&157 CR France518

OTTON,Gilbert Charles 2Lt kia 20-9-16 5Y&L p238 MR21

OUCHTERLONY,John Palgrave Heathcote.DSO.Maj kia 7-6-17 RE 102FC p47 MR29

OUDIN,L'Eugene Capt dow 24-8-16 7DCLI p114 CR France141,E.L.

OUGHTON,Reginald 2Lt kia 11-10-18 6WRid p227 CR France612

OUGHTRED,Harold 2Lt kia 23-4-17 4EYorks p219 CR France162

OULTON,Henry Charles 2Lt kia 12-4-17 4Leinst p174 CR France557,Harry

OUTRAM,Edmund T2Lt kia 1-7-16 26Manch p155 MR21

OUTRAM,John 2Lt kia 6-11-17 1DCLI p114 MR30

OVANS,E.H.Capt 23-3-15 125NapiersRif

OVENDEN,Herbert Stephen Lt&QM ded 3-9-16 RASC p193 CR Kent5

OVENS,John Roberts Lt kia 5-11-14 1ConnRgrs p172 CR France1157

OVERMAN,John Gilbert T2Lt kia 9-9-18 9YLI HQ p143 CR France415

OVERTON,Charles 2Lt drd 20-5-17 RE IWT p47 MR38

OVERTON,John 2Lt kia 22-3-18 5 att9RWelshF p223 MR20

OVERTON,Thomas Darwin TLt kia 30-7-15 Lincs p75 CR Gallipoli2

OWEN,Arthur Adrian 2Lt kia 13-3-15 3RWar p65 CR France706

OWEN,Arthur Bankes 2Lt dow 26-10-18 7KSLI p145 CR France380

OWEN,Arthur Edmund Lt ded 18-10-16 1Nhampt att2/4Glouc p137 CR France345

OWEN,Arthur Percy Capt kia 8-3-16 Manch p155 MR38

OWEN,Augustus Charles.MC.TLt kia 6-8-18 8SomLI p80 CR France1014

OWEN,D.G.2Lt ded 23-11-16 3 O&BLI p130 CR Wales212

OWEN,Evan Richard TLtACapt kia 28-4-17 86RH&FA p33 CR France266,Maj

OWEN,Ernest Haddon 2Lt kia 21-12-14 3Lincs att1SWBord p75 MR22

OWEN,Frank LtCol 24-12-18 3/8Lond CR Essex107

OWEN,George Crompton Lt kia 9-4-18 1/4SLancs p230 CR France80

OWEN,George Webster Capt kia 6-6-15 10Manch p237 MR4

OWEN,Godfrey Felix TLt ded 21-10-18 3RIrReg p89 CR Wilts115,30-10-18

OWEN,Griffith Christmas T2Lt kia 31-7-17 11SWBord p100 MR29 &CR Belgium453

OWEN,Henry James T2Lt kia 24-8-18 16RWFus p98 CR France393

OWEN,Herbert Arthur Harold 2Lt dow 23-3-18 2ELancs p111 CR France987

OWEN,Herbert Ernest Malcolm T2Lt kld 18-7-17 GL &RFC p11 CR Wales692

OWEN,Herbert Morris T2Lt dow 25-3-18 9Ches p96 CR France300

OWEN,Horre Solle 2Lt kia 23-11-16 3Manch p155 CR France701

OWEN,Hugh Lt kia 16-5-15 3 att2BordR A'Coy p117 CR France279

OWEN,Humphrey Francis Lt kia 24-3-18 7RWFus p223 MR20,22-3-18

OWEN,Ifor Evan Lt dow 13-4-18 2Mon p244 CR Belgium18,Ivor

OWEN,Iorwerth Roland T2Lt dow 7-5-17 GL &13RFC p11 CR France96,ap Roland

OWEN,James 2Lt dow 20-5-17 5ScotRif p224 MR20

OWEN,John Morris TLtACapt kia 23-4-17 2RWFus p98 CR France593,Capt

OWEN,Leonard Sidney 2Lt kia 20-9-17 19Lond p250 MR29

OWEN,Malcolm de Brissac.MC.LtACapt kia 4-11-18 1Herts p252 CR France206

OWEN,Meredyth T2Lt kia 25-9-15 9WelshR p127 MR19 &CR France260

OWEN,Meurig T2Lt kia 1-8-17 WelshR att9Bn p127 MR29

OWEN,Norman Howell TCapt ded 1-3-19 RASC p267 CR Wales361

OWEN,Norman Moore 2Lt kia 13-9-14 RFA 49Bty p33 MR15

OWEN,Philip Charles T2Lt kia 25-9-15 9 att5KSLI p145 MR29

OWEN,Richard Frank T2Lt kia 30-4-17 102MGC attHamps p184

OWEN,Reginald Frank Leear LtTCapt kia 23-4-17 1Ess att88MGC p132&184 MR20

OWEN,Reginald Mansfield.MID TMaj dow 2-8-16 2 O&BLI p130 CR France141

OWEN,Reuben 2Lt ded 9-11-18 Suff att29Lond p263 CR Essex146

OWEN,Richard Frank T2Lt kia 30-4-17 Hamps att102MGC p121 MR20

OWEN,Rowland Hely Lt kia 18-4-15 3 att2WRid p116 MR29

OWEN,Thomas John 2Lt dow 19-2-17 3 att8RWFus p98 CR Iraq5

OWEN,Thomas John 2Lt kia 8-4-17 29RFC p11 CR France593

OWEN,Thomas Starr T2Lt kia 8-10-18 13RWFus p98 CR France1346

OWEN,Vernon Elias T2Lt dow 29-11-15 9RWFus p98 CR France40

OWEN,Wilfred Edward Salter.MC.Lt kia 4-11-18 5Manch p236 CR France1479

OWEN,William 2Lt dow 27-8-18 16RWFus p98 CR France84

OWEN,William David T2Lt ded 11-10-18 WelshR att15Bn p127 CR France1858

OWEN,William Henry Kenrick.MID TLt dow 1-10-15 9WelshR p127 CR France145

OWEN,William LLewellyn T2Lt dow 12-6-18 KSLI att1/4Bn p145 CR France145

OWEN,William Thomas Lt 14-10-18 213RAF MR20

OWEN,William Vandeleur 2Lt ded 12-11-18 3RScots p54 CR Hamps240

OWEN,Wynne Capt kia 10-3-15 IA 38Dogras att1/39GarhwalRif p281 CR France355 &CR France1887

OWEN-HOLDSWORTH,James Philip.MC.2Lt kld 12-4-18 GL &101RAF p191 CR France300

OWEN-JONES,Rhodri Deane Lt bombAcc 5-1-16 IA 36JacobsHorse p281 CR France51,Capt kia

OWENS,Arthur Owen 2Lt kia 22-4-18 15 att16RWFus p98 MR27

OWENS,Charles Arnold TLt dow 10-1-17 13 att10WYorks p82 CR France374

OWENS,Charles Percy.MID ACapt kia 14-4-17 3 att2SWBord p100 CR France162,15-4-17

OWENS,Edward.DCM.2Lt kia 27-6-18 10Ches B'Coy p96 CR France21

OWENS,Frederick Gordon.MID Maj ded 4-10-18 9Lpool p216 CR Egypt2

OWENS,John Philip Edmund 2Lt kia 13-10-15 6NStaffs p238 MR19

OWENS,William 2Lt kia 16-8-17 7RIrRif p170 MR30

OWENS,William Brabazon T2Lt ded 25-6-16 RE 56FC p47 CR Eire168,35FC

OWSTON,William Henry 2Lt dow 23-10-17 4Lincs p217 CR France32

OXENHAM,Gordon Vincent Lt 27-6-18 1Sqn AustFC MR34

OXLADE,Stanley T2Lt drd 4-5-17 RASC p193 CR Italy14

OXLAND,Nowell TLt kia 10-8-15 6BordR p117 CR Gallipoli5,9-8-15

OXLET,Alan Hayes 2Lt kia 10-12-17 149RFA p33 CR Belgium19

OXLEY,Edith Mary Sister 12-12-18 QAIMNS CR EAfrica101

OXLEY,Fergus Richard ALt kia 20-9-16 GL 10RSuss att1RDubF &TMB p119 CR Belgium4

OXLEY,Harry Alfred Lt kia 21-9-18 4 att10EKent p212 CR France1495

OXLEY,Harry Chamberlain TMaj dow 18-4-18 5SWBord att17NumbF p100

OXLEY,Herman Grant TLt kia 4-11-18 4 att2KRRC p151 CR France190

OXLEY,Malcolm Guy Macdonald 2Lt kia 19-9-17 GL &43RFC p11 CR France924

OXLEY,Richard Stephen T2Lt kia 18-4-18 13RSuss p119 MR30

OXLEY,Robert Duncombe CaptAMaj kia 6-9-16 1 att2GordH p167 MR21

OZANNE,Edward Graeme Capt dow 16-2-15 3RFus p69 CR Belgium59,kia 15-2-15

P

PACEY,Frederick Carman 2Lt 3-9-18 32 RAF MR20

PACEY,George William 2Lt kia 15-4-18 4Lincs p217 MR30

PACEY,Walter Ernest 2Lt dow 27-6-17 4Yorks p220 CR France518

PACKARD,Henry Norrington.DSO.LtCol kia 12-4-16 RFA p33 CR France1182

PACKARD,Walter Herbert 2Lt kia 15-7-16 4Suff p217 MR21

PACK-BERESFORD,Charles George Maj kia 10-9-14 RWKent p141 MR15,24-8-14

PACKER,Bertram Frith T2Lt kia 19-10-17 9Suff p78 CR France550,23-10-17

PACKER,Gilbert Lt 20-8-19 RE 337 Rd ConstCoy CR Yorks 159

PACKHAM,Eric Frank 2Lt dow 1-11-18 RASC att2Hamp p193 CR Hamps136

PACKMAN,Thomas Alfred Lt kia 10-9-16 RHA att7/8TMB p33 CR France423,9-9-16

PACKWOOD,I.MID Lt 5-1-19 IndianTelDept MR65

PACKWOOD,William Harry 2Lt kia 12-4-18 6RWar p214 MR32

PADDAY,William Hamilton Capt kia 21-12-14 IA 36Sikhs att47 p281 MR28

PADDISAN,Charles Waller Lt&QM kia 29-11-17 1/1LincsYeo p204 CR Palestine9

PADDISON,George Mitford TLt kia 30-7-15 6DCLI D'Coy p114 CR Belgium453

PADDISON,Henry Jepson.MC.2LtACapt kia 16-8-17 4Worc X'Coy p109 CR Belgium106

PADDOCK,Henry Leslie Maj kia 23-3-18 N&D att4ELanc p134 CR France528

PADDOCK,William Francis 2Lt dow 9-4-17 4RFus p69 CR France113

PADGETT,James Philip T2Lt kia 5-5-17 21WYorks p82 CR France97

PADLEY,Percy 2Lt kia 4-11-18 A112RFA p33 CR France231

PAGAN,Gavin Lang Capt kia 28-4-17 15RScots p54 MR20

PAGAN,George Hair Lt kia 30-7-16 1/7BlkW p231 CR France1890

PAGE,Alfred Cecil Dudley T2Lt kia 18-8-16 5 att7Nhampt p138 MR21

PAGE,Arthur Herbert T2Lt kia 19-7-16 8Suff p78 MR21

PAGE,Bernard Robert Lt kia 9-8-16 13Ess p132 MR21

PAGE,Cuthbert Frederick Graham.CMG.DSO.LtCol ded 6-12-19 RGA p262 CR Sussex93

PAGE,Donald Frederick Vincent Lt kia 21-9-18 7Suff &RAF p78 CR France256

PAGE,Dudley Alfred T2Lt dow PoW 14-8-17 Ches &56RFC p11&p96 MR20

PAGE,Francis Trafford 2Lt kia 9-5-15 att2RMunstF p175 MR22

PAGE,Frank.DSO&Bar.LtCol kia 31-7-17 Herts p252 MR29

PAGE,Frank.MC.MM.Capt dow 29-10-17 9Aust LH CR France8

PAGE,Gerald T2Lt dow 9-6-17 33MGC p184 CR France285

PAGE,Henry 2Lt kia 20-7-16 10RWFus p98 CR France744

PAGE,James Horn 2Lt ded 7-10-17 9HLI p240 CR Scot674

PAGE,John Canler 2Lt kia 18-10-16 9Norf p74 CR France307

PAGE,John Kenneth Samuel.MC.Lt dow 21-8-18 9RWar att1/5LancF p65 CR France643,22-8-18

PAGE,Lionel 2Lt kia 27-5-18 1Worc p109 MR18

PAGE,Lance Stallard March.MIDx2 Lt kia 20-8-18 10EKent &RAF p204&258,Capt CR Iraq8,St.Allard Capt

PAGE,Meaburn Staniland 2Lt kia 21-3-18 4Lincs p217 MR20

PAGE,Raymond Charles 2Lt 24-9-18 8SStaffs CR Staffs57

PAGE,Reginald 2Lt kia 1-7-16 1/6SStaffs p229 MR21

PAGE,Robert Burton Col ded 11-11-14 Staff LancF att7GenBaseDepot p1 CR France85

PAGE,Sydney Durrant Capt kia 19-4-17 1/4Norf p216 CR Palestine8

PAGE,Thomas Spencer T2Lt kia 19-10-16 9Norf att71TMB p74 CR France294

PAGE,Vernon.MC.2Lt dow 23-9-17 D315RFA p33 CR Belgium124,22-9-17

PAGE,Wilfred Frank TCapt dow 28-3-18 Ess att4Bn p132 CR Essex1,Wilfrid

PAGE-GREEN,Reginald Sebastian.MC.T2Lt kia 22-6-17 26RFus p69 CR Belgium154

PAGEN,Wilfred Robert TCapt kia 7-10-16 RAMC att6EKent p197 MR21

PAGET,Albert Edward.MVO.CaptBtLtCol ded 2-8-17 11Huss p22

PAGET,Colin Lt kia 1-9-18 RWar att9Bn p65 MR38

PAGET,Desmond Otho 2Lt kia 21-3-18 KRRC att7Bn p151 CR France1061

PAGET,George Godfrey Brandreth Lt kia 14-9-14 3 att1Nhampt p138 MR15

PAGET,Gerald Lewis Lt kia 13-7-17 RFC p11 MR34

PAGET,John Christopher LtACapt kia 26-4-17 RGA 157SB p41 CR France614

PAGET,Leslie Herbert 2Lt kia 27-9-18 9Manch p237 CR France712

PAGET,Michael Theodore 2Lt kia 17-8-17 3LancF p93 CR Belgium453

PAGET,Samuel James.MID Capt kia 26-3-18 GL attStaff 149InfBde p191 CR France526

PAGET,Wellesley Lyndoch Henr.CB.CMG.MVO.TBrigGen ded 11-6-18 RH&FA p261

PAIBA,Ellis James Alfred TLt kia 20-10-15 15 att2RFus p69 CR Gallipoli4

PAIGE,Jack Brian 2Lt kia 14-6-17 4EKent p212 MR29

PAIN,Edward Davy TCapt kia 18-8-16 6SomLI p80 MR21

PAIN,Wyndham Hackett LtCol 26-9-19 RWSurr CR Surrey134

PAINE,Ernest Louis Evelyn TCapt ded 8-4-17 17Bty MGC Motors p266 CR Palestine2

PAINE,George Gordon.MC.Capt dow 27-3-18 RBerks att6Bn p139 CR France41

PAINE,Harry Arthur 2Lt kia 29-9-18 6N&D p233 CR France375,Auther

PAINE,James Henry.DSO.LtCol dow 25-7-18 Cmdg76RGA p41 CR France209

PAINE,Walter Lionel TCapt&Adjt kia 4-6-15 10RLancs att1LancF p59 CR Gallipoli6

PAINE,William Thomas T2Lt kia 23-8-18 1Beds p86 CR France518

PAINTER,Albert Ernest 2Lt dow 14-4-17 RE 171TC p47 CR France297

PAINTER,Henry Septimus T2Lt kia 29-7-16 16 att12Glouc p107 MR21

PAINTER,John Sigley 2Lt dow 25-4-18 7Worc p226 CR Egypt2,Lt

PAISLEY,George William 2Lt kia 27-12-17 4BlkW p230 CR Palestine3

PAISLEY,Thomas T2Lt kia 25-9-15 10ScotRif p104 MR19

PAKEMAN,Herbert Lt 19-4-17 8Hamps MR34

PAKENHAM,Charles John Wingfield Lt kia 30-4-15 2Hamps p121 MR4

PAKENHAM,Herbert Lt kia 19-4-17 8Hamps p229

PAKENHAM,John Walter Beaven 2Lt kia 21-9-18 10Lond p248 CR France369

PAKENHAM,Robert Edward Michael Capt dow 17-1-15 2RMunstF p175 CR Lond8

PALARDY,G.2Lt dow 7-5-18 GL &RAF p191

PALETHORPE,Edwin Donald Lt kia 9-10-17 RFA p208 CR Belgium12

PALEY,George Maj kia 31-10-14 RB 1Div Staff p179 CR Belgium58

PALFREE,John William Bateman 2Lt dow 20-9-18 16N&D att8RBerks p134 CR France194

PALFREY,Reginald T2Lt kia 4/5-4-16 9RWar p65 CR Iraq5

PALFREYMAN,A.2Lt dow 9-10-18 RWFus att16Bn p98 CR France906

PALFREYMAN,George Alexander 2Lt kia 26-10-16 3EKent &RFC p3&58 MR20

PALGRAVE-SIMPSON,Evelyn Victor Craig Lt dow 25-11-18 C77RFA CR Lond12

PALIN,Oscar Ernest 2Lt kia 26-10-17 15Lond p249 MR30

PALK,Lawrence Charles Walter.Hon.DSO.TLtCol kia 1-7-16 Cmdg1Hamps p121 CR France643

PALLANT,Herbert Charles Capt ded 21-2-20 IARO attS&TCps p281 CR Asia82

PALLETT,Edward Roy Lt mbk 6-4-18 7RFus p256 CR France252,Capt

PALLING,William Lionel T2Lt kia 15-3-16 8RFus p69 CR France423

PALLISER,John Sylvester.MID Maj kia 9-8-18 5Yorks attMGC Inf p187&220 CR France1170,Silvester

PALMER,Albert Edgar 2Lt kia 27-9-18 8WYorks p82 CR France1483

PALMER,Albert Leslie 2Lt dow 6-3-17 5N&D p233 CR France120

PALMER,Alen Llewellen Maj ded 15-11-16 1WiltsYeo p206 CR France300

PALMER,Ambrose Henry Maj dow 2-5-17 RAMC attStaffsYeo p253 CR Egypt9

PALMER,Arthur Percy.DSO.Capt kia 27-9-15 1WelshGds p53 MR19

PALMER,Bertie William 2Lt dow 25-8-18 8ScotRif p225 CR France1358

PALMER,Cecil Howard.MID MajTLtCol kia 27-7-15 Worc Ex 9RWar p109 MR4,26-7-15

PALMER,Charles TCapt ded 15-1-16 5KSLI p145 CR Eire237

PALMER,Charles Walter 2Lt ded 29-3-16 PoW GL &RFC p3&191 CR France1276

PALMER,David Lt ded 26-2-18 RE IWT p47 MR38

PALMER,David Adams.MC.ACapt dow 25-3-18 3RDubF attTankCps p177&188 CR France177

PALMER,Derek William Onslow TLt kia 4-6-16 10EYork p84 CR France5

PALMER,Edward Anderson 2Lt kia 14-10-18 1Worc p109 CR France1277

PALMER,Edward Charles Maxwell 2Lt kia 23-4-17 13RFus att111TMB p69 MR20

PALMER,Eric George T2Lt kia 4-3-17 3 att2Nhampt p138 CR France439,Lt

PALMER,Francis Reginald T2Lt kia 23-4-17 6Dors p124 CR France531

PALMER,Frederick Edmund Corbett TMaj dow 28-8-15 7Y&L p159 CR Belgium11

PALMER,Geoffrey T2Lt kia 19-11-15 RE 153Coy p47 CR France281

PALMER,Geoffrey Raymond T2Lt kia 30-7-16 10WRid p116 MR21

PALMER,G.H.2Lt 31-10-18 RB CR Somerset186

PALMER,Harry 2Lt kia 27-5-18 8WYorks p219 MR18

PALMER,Henry Edwardes 2Lt dow 5-4-18 5RBerks p139 CR France516

PALMER,Henry John Lt kia 29-3-18 5 att1DCLI p227 MR27

PALMER,Herbert Lt kia 2-10-18 12Lancers p22 CR France375

PALMER,Herbert John TLt dow 21-12-16 RE 121FC p47 CR France285

PALMER,Horace John T2Lt kia 8-8-18 7RSuss p119 CR France247

PALMER,Horace Lewis 2Lt ktia 23-10-10 1/1Wilts p206 CR France1177,Harold

PALMER,Hugh Salisbury.MID Capt dow 25-4-18 RAMC FA p254 CR France29

PALMER,John Arthur Stuart 2Lt kia 16-12-17 RGA 343SB p41 CR Belgium20

PALMER,John Stanley Lt dow 18-10-16 2DLI p161 CR France105,2Lt

PALMER,John Walter Edmond 2Lt ded PoW 11-6-18 31MGC Inf p184 CR France1027

PALMER,John William T2Lt dow 25-9-17 12RB p179 CR Belgium16

PALMER,John William Henry TLt kia 20-7-16 20RFus p69 CR France1890

PALMER,Joseph Sidney Herbert 2Lt dow 27-9-16 1LNLancs p136 MR21

PALMER,Leslie Cowper 2Lt kia 26-9-17 4Suff p217 CR Belgium125

PALMER,Leslie Stewart Lt kia 20-9-17 4Dors attMGC Inf p187&229 CR Belgium112

PALMER,Lewis Arthur T2Lt kld 9-11-17 GL &RFC p11 CR Mddx15

PALMER,Percy Eric 2Lt kia 17-7-17 29RFC p11

PALMER,Percy Rogers.MC.2Lt kia 25-5-17 10Leic &55RFC p11&88 CR France421

PALMER,Reginald John Allen.MID Lt dow 22-7-16 1Wilts p153 CR France300

PALMER,Robert Stafford Arthur.Hon.Capt dow PoW 21-1-16 6 att1/4Hamp p228 MR38

PALMER,Roger Lt dow 13-8-15 2N&D p134 CR France40,2Lt

PALMER,Roland Gaskell Capt kia 25-4-15 2SWBord p100 MR4

PALMER,Ronald William Poulton Lt kia 4-5-15 1/4RBerks p234 CR Belgium53,5-5-15

PALMER,Samuel William Lt kia 27-3-18 10 att19RDubF p177 MR27

PALMER,Walter Gerard Capt kia 5-3-16 IA 113Inf attRFC p281 MR38

PALMER,Walter Harvey T2Lt kia 23-4-17 17Manch p155 MR20

PALMER,William Henry Eyre Hollingworth Capt ded 26-11-15 20RB p244 MR40

PALMER,William Lucius 2Lt kld 8-5-15 3Mon p244 MR29

PALMER,William Samuel Hudson T2Lt kld 15-9-17 GL &RFC p11 CR Surrey132

PALMES,Guy Nicholas Lt kia 9-5-15 YLI p143 MR29

PALMES,John Philip.MC.Capt kia 1-8-17 3 att2WYorks p82 MR29

PALMIERI,Alicia Mrs 15-5-17 VAD MR70

PANDFIELD,William Godridge.DCM.2Lt kia 21-8-16 2Worc p109 MR21

PANES,Ernest Philip Morris T2Lt kia 25-9-15 9KRRC p151 MR29

PANK,Adalbert Daniell Lt dow 18-6-15 RE 22FC p47 CR France134,2CavDiv

PANTER-DOWNES,Edward Martin Capt&BtMaj dow 26-8-14 2RIrReg p89 MR15

PANTING,Arnold Clement T2Lt kia 13-1-17 6RMunstF attRFC p175 CR Greece9

PANTON,Arthur William 2Lt kia 3-9-16 RE 234FC p47 CR France339

PANTON,John Gerald.CMG.Col ded 7-12-15 Staff RSuss p1 CR Surrey160

PANZERA,Francis William.CMG.TCol ded 4-6-17 SL p191&268

PAPE,Edmund Rogers 2Lt kia 27-3-18 5Manch p236 MR27

PAPPA,Armaud Francis 2Lt kia 5-5-17 8EYorks p84 MR20

PAPPRILL,Frederick Ernest T2Lt kia 3-6-17 9Leic att1/4ELanc p88 CR France905,Capt

PAPWORTH,Alfred Wyatt T2Lt kia 2-4-17 RE 129FC p47 CR France480

PARAMORE,Charles Gordon TCapt kia 25-9-15 8RBerks p139 CR France219

PARAMORE,Robert Edward Pynsent Lt kia 23-7-16 1Dev p77 MR21

PARBERRY,Ernest 2Lt kia 27-9-18 13Lpool att1NumbF p72 CR France,PARBERY

PARBURY,Frederick Nigel Maj kia 9-5-15 20RFA p33 CR France924,10-5-15

PARDOE,George Southey Rev ded 15-10-18 RAChDept p199 CR Palestine3

PARDON,Rolfe Buckland Lt ded 23-11-19 6RRofCav att13Huss p261 CR Mdd26

PARDY,Thomas Johnston 2Lt dow 7-5-17 4A&SH p173 CR france95

PARDY,William Leslie 2Lt dow 16-9-16 5SLancs p230 CR France,PARDEY

PARE,Charles Percy 2Lt kia 22-3-18 19MGC p185 MR20

PARFITT,Bertram Nowitt 2Lt ded 17-11-18 3Y&L p159 CR Yorks557

PARFITT,Ernest TCapt dow PoW 28-5-17 17Mddx p148 CR Germany3

PARFITT,F.A.2Lt 13-9-18 Y&L CR Yorks557

PARGITER,Henry Cdr ded 26-9-16 IOD p281 CR Iraq6

PARGITER,Reginald Amherst 2Lt kia 10-5-15 3 att1 Suff p78 MR29,PARGETER 8-5-15

PARGITER,William Herbert TLt kia 12-10-16 24RFA p33 CR France513

PARIS,Harold Graham.MC&Bar.Maj kia 6-10-18 RGA 138HB p41 CR France1461

PARISH,Albert Francis 2Lt kia 18-9-18 3 att9Ess p132 CR France369

PARISH,Jesse Hugh Lt ded 22-2-19 RGA p255 CR Lond3,28-2-19

PARISH,Robert.DCM.2Lt kia 10-9-16 2NumbF p62 CR Greece3

PARISH,William Harry T2Lt kia 30-11-17 7Norf p74 MR17

PARISOTTI,Luigi Lt kia 2-1-20 IA 4/39GurkhaRif p281 MR43,21-1-20

PARK,Adam St.John Lloyd.MC.Maj kia 21-4-17 A38RFA p33 CR France765,John

PARK,Alexander 2Lt kia 4-11-18 13RB p179 CR France733

PARK,Alexander Crabbe 2Lt dow 29-9-18 46MGC Inf p184 CR France327

PARK,Andrew T2Lt kia 14-7-16 26NumbF p62 MR21 16Bn

PARK,Archibald Kenneth Capt dow 9-5-15 IA 1/10 att2/2GurkhaRif p281 CR France924

PARK,Frederick Andrew Katchen Lt kia 3-10-18 46MGC Inf p184 CR France1710

PARK,George Alexander T2Lt kia 18-1-18 22RFC p16 CR France31

PARK,Herbert Sidney T2Lt kia 26-10-17 1Bord p117 CR France748

PARK,James Wilfrid Haynes.MID Capt kia 14-1-17 IA 22Cav p281 CR Iraq5

PARK,Victor Herbert Lt ded 4-3-19 2WellingtonR NZEF France85

PARK,Walter Williamson Lt kia 2-4-16 1Herts p252 CR France705

PARK,William 2Lt dow 21-3-18 15DLI p161 MR27

PARKE,Allan.MC.Capt kia 27-9-18 9 att1/8LancF p93 CR France712

PARKE,John Aubrey Lt kia 25-9-15 DLI att9RB p161 MR29

PARKE,Walter Evelyn Lt kia 13-10-14 DLI p161 CR France193

PARKE,William Henry TCapt kia 15-10-16 6ConnRgrs p172 CR Belgium17

PARKER,Allen Foggett 2Lt kld 31-5-18 1WYorks attRAF p82 CR Yorks294,Lt

PARKER,Alan Capt ded 1-4-17 12RLancs p271 CR C'land&W'land46

PARKER,Alan 2Lt kia 23-9-17 10Lond p248 MR29

PARKER,Albert Alfred.MID Capt kia 25-9-17 A296RFA p207 CR Belgium84

PARKER,Albert Victor 2Lt kia 19-11-16 19Lond p250 MR29

PARKER,Alfred Ernest Capt kia 7-11-14 3BlkW att2SfthH p129 CR France451

PARKER,Arthur Charles Lt ded 11-9-18 18Huss att13TankCps p23&188 CR Mddx83

PARKER,Basil Stewart Capt kia 6-8-15 2Hamps p121 CR Gallipoli6

PARKER,Cecil William Hannington Lt kia 27-12-16 WorcR &RFC p3&109 CR France203,Capt

PARKER,Charles Allen.MC.2Lt kld 19-2-18 RFA attRFC p16&33 CR Iraq6

PARKER,Charles Thomas Capt ded 11-7-18 2/4NumbF p213 CR Ches2 Ex 1lincs

PARKER,Colin 2Lt ded 25-10-18 PoW RWFus 3GarBn p98 CR France934

PARKER,Cyril Edmund 2Lt kia 1-1-15 1KRRC p151 MR22

PARKER,Edith Dorothy SpProb ded 7-4-18 QAIMNS p200

PARKER,Edward Thompson T2Lt kia 4-6-15 13WYorks att1LancF p82 MR15

PARKER,E.K.Matron ded 16-10-16 QAIMNS p200

PARKER,Erasmus Darwin Capt kia 20-3-15 2Manch p155 CR Belgium170

PARKER,Frank Bryan TCapt kld 23-3-19 7 att6Yorks p91 MR70 &CR Europe180

PARKER,Frederick Neville 2Lt kia 28-4-15 1KRRC p151 CR France80

PARKER,Frederick Richard 2Lt kia 19-7-16 3Wilts p153 MR19

PARKER,Geoffrey 2Lt kia 11-4-17 4 att10LNLancs p234 MR20

PARKER,George Alec.DSO.MC.Capt kia 27-11-16 Nhampt &RFC p3 MR20

PARKER,George Harvey 2Lt kld 24-3-18 RFC p16 MR20

PARKER,George Hastings Maj kia 19-12-14 1Hamps p121 CR Belgium69

PARKER,George Wilson 2Lt kia 9-10-17 6LancF p221 MR30

PARKER,Gerrard William TLt dow 29-9-15 8Lincs p75 CR France924

PARKER,Gilbert Edmund Anthony Lt kia 10-3-15 3 att2SStaffs p122 MR22

PARKER,Harold James 2Lt kia 15-4-18 Worc att2/8 p109 CR France248

PARKER,Harry Prevost England Maj ded 26-2-20 RIrReg Ex 129Baluchis CR Surrey1

PARKER,Henry 2Lt dow 30-4-15 Hamps p121 MR4,Harry Ex 2Worc

PARKER,Herbert John 2Lt kia 27-10-17 RGA 1/1WelshHB p41 CR Belgium115

PARKER,Herbert Proudfoot 2Lt ded 8-10-19 6Lond p271 CR Essex1

PARKER,James TCapt kia 16-6-16 RAMC att7SomLI p197 CR Belgium4

PARKER,James TLt kia 1-7-16 26NumbF p62 MR21

PARKER,James Stanley Lt kia 9-10-17 7WYorks p218 MR30

PARKER,Jeffery Wimpris TLt kia 7-8-15 RAMC att11Manch p197 MR4

PARKER,J.H.MajBtLtCol 29-6-17 RMLI CR Surrey37

PARKER,John 2Lt kia 21-7-15 RLancs &RFC p2&59 CR France518

PARKER,John Bradbery LtACapt ded 19-11-18 D84RFA p33 CR Sussex102

PARKER,John Caird T2Lt kia 1-7-17 11Bord p117 CR France293,1-7-16

PARKER,John Ernest Capt kia 8-5-15 12Lond p248 MR29

PARKER,John Norman T2Lt kia 8-9-17 2/6WYorks p82 CR France563

PARKER,John Vincent 2Lt ded 1-9-17 IARO att112Inf p281 MR65

PARKER,John Womersley.MC.T2Lt dow 13-11-17 3 att1/5WYorks p82 CR Belgium11

PARKER,Leonard Maj kia 7-1-17 15Huss att52RFC p11&22 CR France446

PARKER,Leonard George Capt kia 1-9-18 2Ess p132 CR France421,G.L.

PARKER,Leslie Rowland 2Lt kia 29-9-18 1SWBord p100 CR France672

PARKER,Leslie Walter Grosvenor 2Lt dow 20-7-17 6Ess p232 CR France

PARKER,Percy Dolph 2Lt kld 4-1-18 4RRofCav &RFC p16&23 CR Essex210

PARKER,Ralph Windsor Capt dow 28-3-18 3GrenGds p50 CR France225

PARKER,Robert Burton Capt kia 19-9-14 Nhampt p138 MR15

PARKER,Ronald Elphinstone Lt kia 9-9-14 RHA D'Bty p33 CR France1445,8-9-14

PARKER,Rupert Hardy Lt kia 2-12-17 2Lincs p75 MR30

PARKER,Samuel Lt&QM ded 1-11-15 5Norf p216 CR Europe23

PARKER,Sidney T2Lt kia 30-3-17 7ESurr p113 CR France1182

PARKER,Thomas 2Lt ded 11-12-18 2/4RWSurr att2/22Lond p212 CR Egypt1

PARKER,Thomas Cowper Lt kia 12-10-17 W'land&C'landYeo att7BordR p206 MR30

PARKER,Thomas Geoffrey Milsome TCapt ded 3-11-18 GL RAMC p191 CR Hamps17

PARKER,Victor Lt ded 5-3-16 1RFA p208 CR Belgium11

PARKER,Walter Henry LtACapt kia 15-6-17 RFus att2/4Lond p69 CR France1489

PARKER,Wilfred Horsley 2Lt kia 9-5-15 2RMunstF p175 MR22

PARKER,Wilfrid Ernest T2Lt kia 8/9-5-17 15RWar p65 MR20

PARKER,William T2Lt dow 31-12-17 10WYorks p82 CR France398

PARKER,William Brabazon Hallowes TLt dow 25-4-16 14 att8Ches p96 CR Iraq8

PARKER,William George John.DCM.2Lt ded 10-10-18 23Coy H'TankCps p188 CR Lond5

PARKER,William Harold.MC.Lt kia 26-4-18 3Worc p109 MR30

PARKER,William Lefevre Oxley Lt kia 31-10-17 11Huss att13RFC p12&22 MR20

PARKER,William Mackworth Capt&Adj kia 30-7-15 RB att8Bn p179 MR29

PARKER-JERVIS,C.E.LtCol 10-4-18 DLI CR Yorks230

PARKER-SMITH,Wilmot Babington Lt dow 12-9-15 1/3ScotHorse p205 CR Europe1

PARKES,Henry Gordon 2Lt kia 4-6-15 6 att4Worc p109 MR4

PARKES,Horace Frederick.MID 2Lt kia 12-3-15 1RWFus p98 MR22

PARKES,James Arthur Capt 29-3-17 3DLI CR Lancs34

PARKES,James Eric 2Lt kia 20-7-17 RE 69FC p47 CR France581

PARKES,Percy Reginald 2Lt dow PoW 4-4-18 18Lond D'Coy p250 CR France716

PARKES,Robert Lionel T2Lt kia 7-10-16 9RFus p69 MR21,Richard

PARKES,Samuel James 2Lt 13-8-18 205RAF MR20

PARKES,Theodore David TLtACapt kia 5-10-17 1SStaffs p122 MR30

PARKHOUSE,Frank Mayfield T2Lt kia 23-4-17 1Mddx p148 CR France434

PARKHOUSE,Oscar Lt ded 19-11-18 4Dev p220 CR Kent180

PARKHURST,George Henry 2Lt kia 3-6-18 3Manch att2/8Worc p155 CR France1693

PARKIN,Absalom Sydney 2Lt kia 3-5-17 15WYorks p82 MR20

PARKIN,Arthur LtCol kia 25-9-15 7Nhampt p138 MR19,27-9-15

PARKIN,George Frederic T2Lt kia 9-4-17 12WYorks p82 MR20

PARKIN,James Dowell 2Lt dow 27-5-18 DLI p161 MR18

PARKIN,Joseph Henry T2Lt kia 18-6-17 RE 529FC p47 MR20

PARKIN,Thomas Gregory T2Lt kia 9-8-15 6Lincs B'Coy p75 CR Gallipoli5

PARKIN,Thomas Henry LtTCapt dow 4-10-18 Lpool p72 CR France25,Lt 2/21MGC

PARKINSON,Albert 2Lt kia 9-4-18 Lpool att1/5Bn p72 MR19

PARKINSON,Alfred.MC.T2LtACapt kia 12-5-17 21Manch p155 CR France568

PARKINSON,Alfred Louis T2Lt ded 3-6-18 4ResCav att2DGds p23 CR Lancs2

PARKINSON,George Hartley Lt kia 13-4-18 6Norf p217 MR30

PARKINSON,Gilbert Maurice Capt ded 14-11-18 1NumbF att33ItalyDiv p62 CR Italy16

PARKINSON,Horace James Ankers 2Lt dow 1-7-17 4Leic p220 CR War97

PARKINSON,James Herring T2Lt kia 2-7-16 8Lincs p75 MR21

PARKINSON,Joe Anthony Francis Lt kia 13-10-14 Dors p124 MR22

PARKINSON,Leslie Gerard.MC.Maj kia 24-4-17 1/4Glouc p225 CR France365

PARKINSON,Oswald Wright 2Lt kia 1-2-17 3 att6ELancs p111 MR38

PARKINSON,Richard Frank.MC.MID Capt ded 7-11-18 RE 7FldTrp p47 MR38

PARKINSON,Thomas 2Lt kia 12-9-18 6RWFus p223 CR France415

PARKS,George Edwin Harold Lt dow 12-10-18 GL 12Manch p191 CR France1393,kia

PARKS,John Wynard.MC.Capt dow 12-8-19 1ELancs p255 CR Kent102

PARKS,William Francis.MID LtACapt ded 22-12-18 263RFA p33 CR Egypt9

PARKYN,William James 2Lt dow 12-10-18 6WRid p227 CR France214

PARLE,John Audley.MC.2LtACapt kia 30-11-17 12Lpool p72 CR France660

PARMENTER,Gordon William 2Lt kia 26-8-16 6 att12RB p179 CR France513

PARMETER,Francis Robert Bircham LtCol ded 16-10-19 LabCps p266 CR Surrey162,6-10-19

PARNELL,Geoffrey Brooke TMaj kia 15-7-16 1RWSurr p56 CR France4353

PARNELL,John Atherton Parnell TLt kia 8-9-16 1Glouc p107 CR France453,PARNELL PARNELL,J.A.

PARNELL,Leslie Reginald Lt kia 9-10-17 13Lond att2/4ELancs p249 MR30

PARNELL,Mervyn Edmund Capt kia 1-12-17 IA 36Horse p281 CR France417

PARNELL,William Alastair Damer.Hon.MC.Lt kia 25-9-16 att2GrenGds 4Coy SR p50 CR France374

PARR,Bertram Chambré Maj kia 3-9-18 O&BLI att2SStaffs p130 CR France1484

PARR,Denis Fillingham 2Lt kia 7-7-16 10N&D p134 MR21

PARR,Edgar Brian T2Lt dow 21-10-16 11SLancs p125 CR France188

PARR,George Roworth Lt kia 19-12-14 1SomLI p80 CR Belgium70

PARR,Hugh Wharton Myddleton Lt kld 15-5-15 5SStaffs p229 CR Belgium43

PARR,Jackson Webster 2Lt dow 29-3-18 YLI att2/4Bn p143 CR France169

PARR,Wilfred Alexander 2Lt kia 3-5-17 4RFus p69 MR20

PARR,Wilfred Wharton.MC.Capt kia 8-5-17 12Glouc p107 MR20

PARR-DUDLEY,John Huskisson T2Lt kia 1-7-16 11RFus p69 CR France397

PARR-DUDLEY,Walter 2Lt kia 5-4-18 9RFus p69 MR27

PARRIS,Walter Frederick 2Lt kia 15-3-15 3Mddx p148 CR Belgium17,PARRISS

PARRISH,George Lewis 2Lt kld 11-1-18 RFC p16

PARRISH,Harry Thorburn.MC.2Lt dow 23-11-18 Dors att6Bn p124 CR France13

PARROTT,Amy Maud Augusta Sister 24-10-18 VAD CR SAfrica53

PARROTT,Dennis Hele Lt kia 30-4-18 2/17Lond p250 CR Palestine3

PARROTT,Lionel Overton 2Lt kia 7-8-17 19RFA p33 CR France184

PARRY,Claude Frederick Pilkington.DSO.LtCol kia 20-8-18 34RFA p33 CR France745

PARRY,David Thomas 2Lt dow 24-3-17 1/5ELancs att5War p226 CR France145

PARRY,Donald George de Courcy LtAMaj kia 5-4-18 D78RFA p33 CR France41

PARRY,Francis Alexander.MC.Maj kia 27-9-18 16RWar p65 CR France415

PARRY,Frank Marden LtCol ded 2-12-19 RAMC p267 CR Mddx23

PARRY,Frank Meredith T2Lt kia 15-9-16 15Hamps p121 CR France277

PARRY,G.O.Lt 14-4-20 RWFus CR Wales497

PARRY,Harold T2Lt kia 6-5-17 17KRRC p151 CR Belgium4

PARRY,Henry Maysmor Lt dow 11-3-18 2/10Mddx p236 CR Palestine3,Maysmore

PARRY,James Hywell TLt dow 5-9-17 10RWFus p98 CR France512,Hywel

PARRY,John Stanley T2Lt kia 14-7-16 15 att13Lpool p72 MR21

PARRY,Norman Cecil Lt kia 27-7-15 3Y&L p159 CR Belgium96

PARRY,Robert 2Lt dow 26-3-17 1/7RFus CR Palestine8

PARRY,Robert 2Lt dow 23-3-18 7RWFus p223

PARRY,Robert Stephenson T2Lt dow 23-10-17 20LancF p93 CR Belgium106

PARRY,S.2Lt kld 3-5-18 RE &RAF p47

PARRY,Thomas Ellis T2Lt kia 23-10-16 2LancF p93 MR21

PARRY,Wilfred Seaton Bagott T2Lt kia 24-11-15 D53RFA p33 CR Belgium166

PARRY,William Henry Liddon T2Lt dow 29-11-16 24RFus p69 CR France1

PARRY,William Norman Maule 2Lt dow PoW 19-8-17 3Lond p246 CR Belgium140,Lt

PARRY-DAVIES,David Christopher T2Lt dow 10-5-16 9 att2SWBord p100 CR France167,6Bn

PARRY-JONES,Owen Guy.MID Capt dow 29-9-16 RAMC att3Suff p197 CR France74

PARSICK,Charles Edmund Lt sInflictGunshot 28-2-20 1ARO att99LabCps p281 MR43

PARSLOE,William Henry.MC.TCapt kia 8-11-18 7Lincs p75 CR France930

PARSLOW,A.J.Lt&QM 7-4-15 RE CR Ireland14

PARSLOW,Albert Jack 2Lt dow 10-10-16 9Lond p248 CR France105

PARSLOW,William Hunt ACapt dow 10-8-18 1Lond p245 CR France69

PARSON,Ernest Edward.MC.TLt dow 1-6-17 124RFA p33 CR France1184

PARSONS,Alfred Cyril Lt kia 29-3-18 3 att1SomLI p80 CR France53,Capt

PARSONS,Alfred Ernest 2Lt kia 3-5-17 4RFus p69 MR20

PARSONS,Alfred Henry Capt kia 8-3-16 IA 2/9GurkhaRif p281 MR38

PARSONS,Algernon George Maj kia 26-4-18 C149RFA p33 CR Belgium11

PARSONS,Arthur Oscar 2Lt dow 26-3-18 5DLI p239 CR France225

PARSONS,Beresford Frank T2Lt kld 23-1-17 GL &RFC p12 CR War10

PARSONS,Desmond Clere LtTCapt kia 15-9-16 2IrGds p53 CR France374

PARSONS,Douglas Montgomery.MID 2Lt kia 10-3-15 RE 5FC p47 MR22

PARSONS,Edgar Vincent Peter 2Lt dow 26-4-18 5 att2Worc p109 MR30

PARSONS,Edward Daniel TLt dow 20-9-15 RAMC p197 CR Surrey57,Daniell

PARSONS,Eric King TCapt kia 15-9-16 9RB p179 MR21

PARSONS,Ernest T2Lt ded 23-7-16 11WRid att1WelshR p116 CR Greece7,24-7-16

PARSONS,Forrest Gale 2Lt kia 26-10-16 RFC p3 MR20

PARSONS,George Jonathan 2Lt dow 31-8-18 4RFus p69 CR France103

PARSONS,Gilbert Newstead 2Lt kia 5-3-17 10Mddx att2RBerks p236 MR21

PARSONS,Hardy Falconer.VC.T2Lt kia 21-8-17 1/2 att14Glouc p107 CR France363

PARSONS,Herbert Lt kia 14-4-17 5 att10WYorks p218 MR20

PARSONS,Herbert T2Lt kia 14-7-16 2RScots p54 MR21

PARSONS,Herbert Mersfield 2Lt kia 13-4-18 50MGC Inf p185 MR32,Hubert Merefield mbk

PARSONS,Kenneth Templeton Jerrard TCapt ded 14-8-17 6RIrRif p170 CR Greece9

PARSONS,Leo Bernard T2Lt kia 12-8-16 EKent p58 CR France164

PARSONS,Maurice Harry Donne TCapt kia 18-7-16 O5RFA p33 CR France1887

PARSONS,P.H.Maj 27-4-20 LondScot CR Surrey9

PARSONS,Samuel Reginald Lt kia 9-4-17 2Wilts p153 CR France214

PARSONS,Septimus Eric Capt kld 14-4-18 8RWar p214 CR France248,kia

PARSONS,Walter Douglas 2Lt kia 13-4-18 7WRid p228 MR30

PARSONS,William Douglas Reynolds 2Lt kia 26-5-18 16RWSurr p56 CR Belgium36,Lt 11Bn See REYNOLDS-PARSONS

PARSONS,William Josiah Capt ded 27-10-18 5RLancs p213 CR Lancs80

PARSONS-SMITH,Eustace Macartney Capt ded 25-5-19 RAMC attEgyptArmy p197 CR EAfrica116,Maj

PARTEUR,William Raymond.MC.LtAMaj kia 10-7-17 102RFA p33 MR29

PARTINGTON,Cyril Walter 2Lt kld 30-8-18 1RWar att22RAF p65 CR France788,Lt

PARTINGTON,Harry 2Lt dow 25-8-18 5LancF att2/4Y&Lp221 CR France226

239

PARTINGTON,John Bertram Capt kia 3-2-17 4Dev p220 CR Iraq5

PARTINGTON,Leigh Capt kia 28-3-18 1NumbF p62 MR20

PARTON,Roland Thomas T2Lt dow 21-11-17 GL O&RLI att1/10Lond p191 CR Egypt1

PARTRIDGE,Alec John 2Lt kia 3-7-16 9 att5RBerks p139 MR21

PARTRIDGE,Ernest William T2Lt kia 19-11-15 5KSLI p145 CR Belgium84

PARTRIDGE,Geoffrey Dorman Lt kia 3-11-14 2WelshR p127 MR29

PARTRIDGE,Henry Treneman Lt kia 14-7-18 1/4RSuss attRAF p228&258 CR Egypt9,kld

PARTRIDGE,Hugh Roger.MC&Bar.Capt kia 24-7-18 RAMC 1/1WRidFA p254 CR Belgium188

PARTRIDGE,James Henry.MC.2Lt kia 24-3-18 1 att9RIrF p171 MR27

PARTRIDGE,Oswald 2Lt ded 22-10-18 RASC p193 MR41

PARTRIDGE,Richard Crawshay Bailey.MC.Capt kia 28-9-18 ShropYeo p205 CR France756

PARTRIDGE,Robert Charles Capt kia 8-9-14 5DragGds p21 CR France1451

PARTRIDGE,Robert Henry Capt kld 4-9-17 1/5Norf p216 CR Palestine9

PARTRIDGE,Wilfred Issell.MID Lt kia 24-4-17 10Dev p77 MR37

PASCALL,Paul Mervyn.MC.Lt 13-1-18 Mddx att1/2KAR CR EAfrica10 &CR Tanzania1

PASCO,John Crawford Claud 2Lt kia 4-9-18 15Hamps p121 CR Belgium111

PASCOE,Basil Conquest.MC.ACapt&Adj kia 27-5-18 2RB att25InfBdeHQ p179 CR France1753

PASCOE,Eric John 2Lt kia 14-4-17 GL &29RFC p12 CR France783

PASCOE,Frank Guy Buckingham T2Lt kia 2-7-17 9RIrF att53RFC p12&171 MR20

PASCOE,James Sidney.DSO.MIDx2 Maj 28-12-20 RAMC MR65

PASHBY,Frank Edwin 2Lt dow 13-4-18 RBerks att53RAF p139 CR Belgium11

PASHLEY,Eric Clowes.MID 2Lt kia 17-3-17 24RFC p12 CR France699

PASHLEY,Herbert Dudley 2Lt kld 25-12-16 29BallSect RFC p3 CR France397

PASK,Isaac Arthur James.DSO.MC.Capt kia 1-9-16 28RFA p33 CR France397

PASLEY,George Gerald T2Lt kld 19-12-17 RFC p12 CR Eire537

PASLEY,Thomas Edward Sabine 2Lt kia 11-4-18 1KOSB p102 MR32

PASLEY,William Ewart 2Lt kia 17-6-18 4SLancs att1/4LNLancsp230 CR France106

PASLOW,Alfred John Lt&QM ded 7-4-15 RE p262

PASS,Alfred Ernest 2Lt kia 26-8-18 10WRid p116

PASS,Charles Eric 2Lt kia 1-4-17 5BordR p228 CR France672

PASS,Joseph Albert Capt dow 20-5-15 19Lond p250 CR France80

PASSINGHAM,Edward George.MC.Lt kia 3-5-17 1NumbF p62 MR20

PASSMAN,Kenelm Granby Lt kia 30-8-18 12Suff p78 CR France927

PASSMORE,Arthur William 2Lt kia 4-4-16 9RWSurr p56 MR19

PASSMORE,John Edmund Saunders Capt ded 21-5-16 RAMC p271

PASSY,Cyril Hobart Deare Lt kia 8-3-16 IA 24Punjabis att53Sikhs p281 MR38

PASSY,DeLacy Wolrich Maj dow 12-8-15 IA 25Punjabis att8NumbF p281 CR Gallipoli1,Woolrich kia

PASSY,Logan Deare Capt kia 21-10-15 1DCLI p114 CR France279

PASTEUR,William Raymond.MC.Capt kia 10-7-17 D102RFA CR Belgium15

PASTFIELD,James Thomas Robinson 2Lt kia 21-12-14 5Mddx attNumbF p148 MR22,2-12-14

PASTFIELD,Joseph Victor Robinson Lt kia 9-9-18 5 att13Mddx p148 CR France10

PATCH,Aubrey Melchior William 2Lt kia 16/18-8-16 3 att8RLancs p59 MR21

PATCH,Henry Capt dow PoW 19-10-17 4SLancs attRFC p19&229 CR Belgium140

PATCH,Vernon Lane 2Lt kld 20-11-17 2/4WRid p227 CR France755

PATCHETT,William Ernest TLt kia 25-9-15 1CamH p168 MR19

PATE,George Clarence 2Lt kia 18-9-18 7Lpool p215 CR France530

PATEL,M.B.Lt 20-12-15 IMS att7Rajputs CR Iraq6

PATEMAN,Henry Lewis 2Lt kia 6-2-17 GL &15RFC p12 CR France41

PATER,Hugh 2Lt kld 17-4-17 3WYorks attRFC p12&82 CR Durham28

PATERSON,Alan Foster TLt kia 1-7-16 Mddx att2RFus p148 MR21

PATERSON,Alexander 2Lt kia 13-7-18 5ScotRif p224 MR30

PATERSON,Alistair Finlay 2Lt dow 5-6-15 4CamH D'Coy p243 CR France145

PATERSON,Andrew Melville.CBE.LtCol ded 13-2-19 RAMC p267 CR Lincs1

PATERSON,Arthur Cecil 2Lt kia 22-4-18 1/2 att19DLI p161 CR France296

PATERSON,Arthur Stanley Lt dow 2-10-18 8DCLI p114 CR Greece6

PATERSON,Charles 2Lt kia 28-6-15 4RScots p211 MR4

PATERSON,Charles James.MID Capt dow 1-11-14 1SWBord p100 CR Belgium57

PATERSON,Colin Campbell Lt kia 11-4-17 6CamH p168 MR20

PATERSON,David William Stewart 2Lt ded 20-6-16 RFC p3 CR France518

PATERSON,Douglas William 2Lt dow 31-3-18 1Bord p117 CR Belgium3

PATERSON,Edward Labarte 2Lt dow 23-10-18 10Lpool p216 CR France769

PATERSON,Frank T2Lt kia 1-7-16 9 att1KOSB p102 MR21

PATERSON,Gavin 2Lt ded 21-1-15 9RScotF p95 CR Scot810

PATERSON,Hugh Trevor T2Lt ded 13-5-16 10Suff p78 CR France40

PATERSON,Iain Rose 2Lt kia 12-10-17 3 att6CamH p168 MR30,att5Bn

PATERSON,Isla Scott.MC.Lt kia 1-11-17 4/5BlkW p231 CR Belgium21

PATERSON,J.H.2Lt 24-9-18 3 att1Ess CR France34

PATERSON,James 2Lt dow 20-9-17 8ScotRif p225 CR Belgium18

PATERSON,James.MC.ACapt ded 25-3-19 2ScotGds p262 CR Lond14

PATERSON,Jessie Jane SNurse ded 29-9-16 TFNS p254 CR Greece9

PATERSON,John Herbert Lt 21-6-18 IA 19Lancers &21RAF CR Egypt9

PATERSON,John Jamieson 2Lt kia 21-9-18 18 att10KSLI p145 CR France1495

PATERSON,Lamont Livingstone 2Lt kia 1-9-18 8Lond p247 CR France786

PATERSON,Leslie Arnott 2Lt dow 16-5-15 3Ess attRBerks p132 CR Herts72

PATERSON,Norman Keith TLt kia 29-6-16 A124RFA p33 CR France501

PATERSON,Robert Denzil TLt kia 12-10-16 20Lpool p72 CR France432

PATERSON,Robert Sanderson 2Lt kia 11-3-15 62RFA p33 MR22

PATERSON,Robert Walker.MC.MID 2Lt kia 21/23-3-18 2N&D p134&257 MR20,21-3-18

PATERSON,Stuart T2Lt dow 19-10-16 9KOSB att21MGC Inf p185 CR France389

PATERSON,Thomas Simpson Lt kia 10-11-16 RGA 95SB p209 CR France293

PATERSON,Wallace Campbell T2Lt kia 17-2-16 RE 173TC p47 CR France178

PATERSON,Walter Edward Wadbrook T2Lt ded 26-11-18 RFA p33 CR Kent217

PATERSON,Walter Herbert TLtCol kia 20-4-15 ESurr p113 CR Belgium165

PATERSON,Walter James 2Lt dow 30-10-17 4CamH p243 CR France113

PATERSON,William T2Lt kia 10-8-17 RE 92FC p47 MR29

PATERSON,William 2Lt kia 20-11-17 5 att6Sfth p241 CR France1498

PATERSON,William Brown.MC.2Lt kia 28-4-17 3 att13Ess p132 MR20

PATERSON,William Charles Dawson 2Lt kia 25-9-16 6RScots p211 CR France397

PATERSON,William Paterson TCapt kia 30-7-16 3 att2KOSB p102 MR21

PATERSON,William Wilson 2Lt kia 15-7-16 9HLI p240 MR21

PATERSON-BROWN,Ian Murray 2Lt kia 2-8-16 3A&SH p173 CR Belgium23

PATEY,Edward 2LtACapt kia 2-8-17 5 att3RB p180 MR29

PATEY,Robert Thomas.MC.LtACapt kia 20-5-17 1Lpool p72 CR France434

PATMAN,Harold George 2Lt kia 31-7-17 12RFus p69 MR29

PATON,David Moir Lt kia 24-9-17 GL &66RFC p12 MR20

PATON,Edward Kesson T2Lt dow 3-5-17 54MGC p185 MR20

PATON,George Alexander Lechmere 2LtTCapt kia 7/11-8-15 8NumbF p62 CR Gallipoli5,10-8-15

PATON,George Cyril Olquin TLt kldacc 20-6-16 9RScotF p95 CR Scot119,Olguin

PATON,George Henry Tatham.VC.MC.LtACapt kia 1-12-17 4GrenGds p50 CR France662

PATON,Henry Forsyth T2Lt ded 4-6-17 GL &21RFC p12 MR20

PATON,James Hill T2Lt ded 19-3-19 MGC Inf p266 CR Scot674

PATON,James Ley 2Lt kia 13-10-15 3 att1BlkW p129 MR19

PATON,John Edward.MID 2Lt kld 31-12-14 2Mon p244 CR Belgium33

PATON,John Marvin 2Lt kia 21-3-18 RE DivSigCo p47 CR France1182

PATON,Joseph Train Lt kia 30-5-18 5 att1RScotF p222 CR France33

PATON,Leslie 2Lt kia 21-3-17 11RScots p54 MR20

PATON,Malcolm David Rutter 2Lt dow 12-6-17 22Lond attRFC p19&251 CR France285

PATON,Morton Brown TCapt kia 7-8-15 10SLancs att6LancF p125 MR4

PATON,Norman Macalister 2Lt dow 16-7-17 3 att1GordH p167 CR France512

PATON,Robert 2Lt kia 23-10-18 4RScotF p222 CR France292,24-10-18

PATON,Thomas Howard Moore T2Lt ded 30-6-17 39LabCps p189

PATON,Walter 2Lt kia 26-10-17 LNLancs att2/5Bn p136 CR Belgium126,dow

PATON,Walter Storie T2Lt kia 1-7-16 11Bord p117 CR France293

PATON,William George TCapt kia 14-6-16 10ScotRif p104 CR France423

PATRICK,David Balfour T2Lt kia 18-7-16 11HLI att28MGC p163&185 MR21

PATRICK,Horace.DCM.2Lt kia 13-1-16 Leic p263 MR38

PATRICK,John Bonthrone 2Lt kia 12-7-15 1/4KOSB p224 MR4

PATRICK,Keith 2Lt kia 15-9-16 6HLI att4NumbF p240 2Entries CR France239

PATRICK,T.W.2Lt 25-5-19 EAULGravesRegistn CR EAfrica38 &CR Tanzania1

PATRIDGE,Basil George Nicholas Benedick 2Lt kldacc 27-1-15 IARO att2Rajputs p281 CR Egypt7,Benedict

PATRY,Hubert Francis 2Lt kld 13-9-14 NStaffs p157&265,ded CR Camb16

PATTEN,Charles Hill.MID Capt dow 3-10-16 1A&SH p173 CR Greece4

PATTEN,Francis Hope 2Lt kld 15-1-18 RFC p16 CR Scot237

PATTEN,Murray Gladstone.MC.Capt kia 14-4-18 9NumbF p62 MR32

PATTERSON,Alan Capt kia 14-3-16 71RFA p33 CR France554

PATTERSON,Arnott Andrew T2Lt dow 9-11-16 6Bord att34RFC p3&117 CR France882

PATTERSON,Arthur Henry Lt kia 14-10-18 RInnisF att109TMB p105 CR Belgium157

PATTERSON,Aubrey Frederick Albert T2Lt dow PoW 25-9-16 GL &RFC p3&191 CR France598

PATTERSON,Charles Capt ded 20-1-15 3LancF p93 CR Yorks361,19-1-15

PATTERSON,Charles Alfred Capt dow 8-10-16 5NumbF p213 CR France145

PATTERSON,Charles Cox Capt kia 21-10-16 1Ches p96 MR19

PATTERSON,Charles William Ernest Lt ded 12-2-19 RGA 503SB p41 CR France63

PATTERSON,Christian Bingley 2Lt kia 30-12-16 IARO att1/1GurkhaRif p281 CR Iraq5,Lt

PATTERSON,Douglas David John 2Lt kia 16-4-18 7SfthH p165 CR Belgium74

PATTERSON,George Capt kia 13-10-15 RE p210 MR19

PATTERSON,George Beatty 2Lt dow 22-6-18 D168RFA 32Div p34 CR France169,Beattie

PATTERSON,George Gordon 2Lt kia 25-9-16 7Lpool p215 MR21

PATTERSON,Hugh Cecil Lt kia 30-4-17 4Beds att38RFC p12&86 CR France120

PATTERSON John Agar 2Lt kia 30-11-14 2Beds p86 MR29

PATTERSON,John Hylton TLt kia 1-7-16 23NumbF p62 MR21

PATTERSON,John Keppel Priuli TLt dow 26-12-17 9ESurr p113 CR Sussex57

PATTERSON,Kenneth Scott 2Lt dow PoW 6-12-17 92RFA p34 CR France716,7-12-17

PATTERSON,Philip Leslie T2Lt kia 4-6-16 1NStaffs p157 CR Belgium97

PATTERSON,Robert Arthur 2Lt kia 12-4-17 6RB p180 CR France452

PATTESON,John Dossie 2Lt kia 13-10-14 5DragGds p21 CR France705

PATTINSON,Edwin Potter Lt kia 3-5-17 5YLI p235 MR20

PATTINSON,Ernest 2Lt kia 31-7-17 4 att1N&D p134 MR29

PATTINSON,George Foster 2Lt kia 27-5-18 DLI p161 MR18

PATTINSON,Hugh Lee Capt&Adj kia 4-8-15 3 att9RFus p69 CR France922

PATTINSON,Tom TLt ded 21/22-12-18 GL RE IWT p267 CR Iraq8,22-12-18

PATTINSON,William Graham TLt kia 25-4-17 76MGC p185 CR France531

PATTISON James 2Lt 27-2-19 10HLI CR Scot812

PATTISON John Herbert Lt accKld 21-6-18 IARO attRFC p281

PATTISON,John Howell Maj kia 28-4-15 RFA 26Bty 17Bde p34 MR4,PATTISSON

PATTISON,Peterswald Lt ded 22-2-16 RAMC p267 CR Scot253

PATTISON,Robert Capt kia 27-12-17 2/10Lond D'Coy p248 MR30

PATTISON,Robert Macfie 2Lt kia 28-6-15 8ScotRif p225 MR4

PATTON,C.R.Capt 6-11-18 RAMC CR Devon47

PATTON,David 2Lt dow 11-2-18 8 att2ScotRif p225 CR Belgium11

PATTRICK,Arthur Deverus Capt kia 12-8-16 5Norf p216 MR4

PATTRICK,John Harry 2Lt kia 30-11-17 Mddx att8Bn p148 MR17,PATRICK

PATTULLO,Hugh James Lt dow 30-9-18 28RFA p34 CR Belgium126,29-9-18

PATTULLO,Ronald Campbell 2Lt 15-9-18 204RAF MR20

PATULLE,Arthur J.WO ded 20-10-17 RIM p281

PAUL,Alexander Charles T2Lt dow 2-10-17 11RIrRif p170 CR France398

PAUL,Arthur Reginald 2Lt kia 22-1-18 20RAF p16 CR Belgium140

PAUL,Courtenay Talbot Saint.DSO.MID MajALtCol dow 31-7-17 36/45RFA p34 CR Belgium19

PAUL,Edgar.MC.Capt&Adj dow 10-9-18 1SomLI p80 CR France95

PAUL,Edgar Newton TLtACapt kia 28-12-17 6 att12KRRC p151 MR30

PAUL,Ernest Kenneth Montcrieff.MC.2Lt dow 18-4-18 RGA 252SB p41 CR France100

PAUL,Gavin 2Lt kia 30-10-14 2DragGds p21 MR29

PAUL,Herbert James T2Lt kia 20-11-17 12KRRC p151 MR17

PAUL,Jeffery William Ensor 2Lt kia 27-7-16 6 att1KRRC p151 MR21

PAUL,John Andrew Bowring.MC.T2Lt kia 10-10-16 10 att7ESurr p113 MR21

PAUL,Laird Irvine Cassan.MC.CaptAMaj dow 12-8-17 D82RFA p34 CR Belgium7

PAUL,Philip Reid Lt kia 1-10-18 BlkW att8Bn p129 MR30

PAUL,Thomas Bond Lt ded 19-9-15 IA IMS p281 CR Iraq6

PAUL,Thomas Guthrie 2Lt kia 9-4-17 25NumbF p62 CR France265

PAUL,William.DSO.MC.LtACapt dow 1-12-17 1WYorks p82 CR France398

PAUL,William Edgar TCapt kia 31-7-17 8RScotF p95 MR29

PAULET,Cecil Henry 2Lt kia 27-2-16 1/1DorsYeo p203 CR Egypt6,26-2-16

PAULET,Henry Monmouth Basing Lt ded /-/-19 Glouc p264

PAULINE,Victor Reginald 2Lt kia 8-5-18 GL &23RAF p191 CR France134

PAULING,George Francis.MC.Lt kia 25-3-18 3GrenGds p50 CR France924

PAULL,Bryan Dolphin 2Lt kia 30-9-16 RIrRif att8ESurr p170 CR France246,Capt

PAULL,Frederick Major T2Lt kia 27-11-15 14 att9N&D p134 CR Gallipoli4

PAULL,Henry Baynham T2Lt dow 21-8-16 6DCLI C'Coy p114 CR France833

PAULSON John Sydney 2Lt kia 17-9-14 2LancF p93 CR France874

PAUS,Oscar Lionel T2Lt dow 29-7-17 16WYorks p82 CR France95

PAUSCH,Arthur Walter Lt 16-7-18 GL &RAF CR France792

PAVITT,Charles Frederick.MC.Capt ded 17-8-18 RASC p193&259

PAVITT,Reginald James Lt kia 9-8-18 10EKent p204 CR France247 Ex Suss

PAWLE,Bertram TCapt kia 30-7-15 8RB p180 MR29

PAWLE,Derek Weatherall Capt kia 29-4-15 Bord att2NigR p117 CR WAfrica52

PAWLE,Malcolm Gerald TCapt ded 27-6-17 2BedsGarBn p86 MR67

PAWLEY.R.J.2Lt ded 28-11-18 RGA 92SB p41 CR Sussex200

PAWSEY,Harold Charles 2Lt kia 18-8-16 4Suff p217 CR France432

PAWSON,G.St.V.MC.Lt ded 6-11-18 Wmoreld&CumbYeo &RAF p206

PAXTON,Archibald Francis Campbell 2Lt kia 1-7-16 4Mddx p148 CR France267

PAXTON,Edward Hayton Capt ded 15-2-18 RDC p271 CR Staffs125

PAXTON,Gerald Arthur 2Lt kia 10-8-18 6RSuss att17RAF p228&258 CR Greece1

PAXTON,James William 2Lt kia 21-3-18 15RScot p54 MR20

PAXTON,Robert Michael Mill 2Lt kia 1-1-17 RGA 155SB p41 CR France347

PAXTON,Samuel Turven 2Lt kia 5-11-16 9DLI p239 MR21

PAYN,George Frederick Lt ded 10-8-19 SL p268 CR Essex146

PAYN,Reginald Wallace Capt kia 28-3-18 RE 253TC p47 MR27

PAYNE,Albert 2Lt kld 13-1-18 GL &RFC p16 CR Wales3

PAYNE,Albert James T2Lt ded 27-3-18 RASC p193

PAYNE,Cecil Brandon 2Lt kia 20-8-17 RFA att21RFC p12 CR Belgium36,Brannon

PAYNE,Cecil McKenzie T2Lt kia 22-9-17 GL &16RFC p12 CR France81,21-9-17

PAYNE,Charles Arthur Frank 2Lt ded 15-10-18 RASC 47Div MT Coy p193 CR France769

PAYNE,Charles Geraint Christopher 2Lt kia 12-3-15 HLI p163 MR22

PAYNE,Edward Geoffrey TCapt kia 25-9-15 9RWFus p98 MR19

PAYNE,Frederick Norman TCapt ded 14-11-17 GL attMilGovBaghdad p191 CR Iraq8

PAYNE,George Herbert Lt ded 26-8-14 2Suff p78 CR France716

PAYNE,Harold 2Lt kia 30-11-17 RFA 93ArmyBde p34 CR France755

PAYNE,Hedley Stuart.DCM.2Lt dow 21-2-19 4RWSurr p212 CR Lond1,Lt

PAYNE,Henry Drummond 2Lt kia 20-3-15 EYorks p84 CR Belgium98

PAYNE,Henry James 2Lt drd 4-5-17 6RSuss p228 CR Italy14

PAYNE,Henry Tomkin 2Lt kia 6-8-15 3 att1Ess p131 CR Gallipoli6

PAYNE,Henry William T2Lt kld 12-3-18 RFC p16 CR Surrey153

PAYNE,Horace Abraham 2Lt kia 18-3-18 GL &RFC p16 CR France1269

PAYNE,James Ralph Salisbury Lt kia 8-8-18 1TankCps &SfthH p188 CR France589

PAYNE,James William 2Lt kia 14-4-17 6DLI p239 MR20

PAYNE,John Oswald Lt kia 25-4-15 4 att1RWar p65 CR Belgium96

PAYNE,John Robert 2Lt dow 4-11-17 D82RH&FA p34 CR France145 Ex LCpl WKentYeo

PAYNE,Newman Hayes 2Lt kia 14-9-18 3MGC Divl p185 CR France1890,Inf

PAYNE,Osmond Guy TLt kia 1-7-16 2RBerks p139 MR21,Orsmond

PAYNE,Richard William Lt kia 19-8-15 RGA 6TMB p41 CR France721

PAYNE,Sydney Thomas Lt ded 6-4-18 GL &13RAF p191 MR20

PAYNE,Wilfred Stuart Lane.MC.Lt kia 4-9-17 RGA 13SB att7RFC p12&41 CR Belgium18

PAYNE,William Henry T2Lt kia 17-2-17 22RFus p69 CR France314

PAYNE,William Henry Capt ded 10-12-17 AustEngrs CavDivSigs CR Iraq8

PAYNE-GALLWEY,Maurice Hilton Frankland Lt kia 25-9-16 4GrenGds SR p50 CR France374,Hylton

PAYNE-GALLWEY,Philip Francis Lt kia 30-10-14 21Lancer p23 MR29 CR Belgium168

PAYNE-GALLWEY,William Thomas.MVO.Capt kia 14-9-14 GrenGds p50 MR15

PAYNTER,Francis Pendarvis Maj kia 10-1-16 RFA 4HB p206 CR Belgium127

PAYNTER,John T2Lt kia 8-10-15 RE 174TC p47 CR France637

PAYNTER,Reginald 2Lt kia 26-10-17 2Bord D'Coy p117 MR30

PAYTON,Charles Mervyn.MID Lt kia 18-4-15 3 att1RWKent p141 MR29

PAYTON John Leslie Lt kia 16-8-18 RFA &84RAF p271 MR20

PAYTON,Ralph Stuart TLt kia 22-7-16 14RWar p65 MR21

PEACE,Hubert Kirkby Lt dow 18-10-14 3Y&L att1Lincs p150 MR22

PEACH,Bertie Charles TLt kia 9-4-18 12Yorks p91 MR32

PEACH,Crugar Stanley 2Lt kld 24-4-17 1WYorks &16RFC p12&82 CR Surrey160

PEACH,Ernest James 2Lt kia 1-7-16 7N&D att139MGC p187&233 MR21

PEACH,Francis Edward T2Lt dow 23-2-19 N&D p255 CR Staffs135

PEACHE,William Wynter Lt ded 3-12-14 RE p47 CR Europe3

PEACOCK,Alfred Walter T2Lt kia 9-9-17RScots &24RFC p12 &54 CR France251 Ex AustImpForce

PEACOCK,David Ronald 2Lt kia 2-10-16 6DLI p239 MR21

PEACOCK,Frank 2Lt sInflictGunshot 3-12-18 IA TC att2/84Punjabis p281 MR66

PEACOCK,Frederick John ACapt kia 10-10-18 11Manch p155 CR France1301

PEACOCK,John Charles Millard 2Lt kia 27-5-18 5DLI p161 MR30

PEACOCK,John Luddington TLt kia 1-7-16 RE 150FC p47 CR France215

PEACOCK,John Thomas 2Lt kld 16-7-18 3DCLI &49RAF p114 CR France1437,Lt

PEACOCK,Lindsay Capt dow 19-9-18 IA 1/72Punjabis MR34 p281

PEACOCK,Percy Charles 2Lt dow 10-4-16 IARO att125Rif MR38 p281

PEACOCK,Reginald Howard Trees Lt kia 9-4-18 13ESurr p113 CR France924

PEACOCK,Robert Archibald T2Lt kia 27-1-16 12 att10ScotRif p104 CR France423

PEACOCK,Thomas Gordon TLt&Adj kia 25-9-15 8RBerks p139 MR19

PEACOCK,Thomas Harold 2Lt kia 27-6-18 1 att14Worc p109 CR France4

PEACOCK,Walter T2Lt kia 22-12-16 9RIrF p171 CR Belgium49

PEACOCK,William Hubert T2Lt kld 7-4-17 GL &45RFC p12 CR Lincs181

PEACOCK,William James Leonard T2Lt kia 18-8-16 EKent p58 CR France164

PEACOCK,William Webster TLt kia 16-8-16 RE 224FC p47 CR France149,15-8-16

PEACOCKE,Eric Forrester 2Lt kia 20-5-17 15 att16KRRC p151 MR20

PEACOCKE,Evelyn Jeffreys T2Lt kld 4-2-18 RFC p16 CR Wilts115

PEACOCKE,Herbert Parker 2Lt kia 3-7-16 8SLancs p125 MR21

PEACOP,Reginald Trevor 2Lt kia 2-9-17 RFA p208 CR Belgium24

PEADON,Harold Thomas 2Lt dow 27-3-17 1/4WelshR p230 CR Palestine2

PEADON,Percy Hewitt T2Lt dow 7-4-18 8Lincs A'Coy p75 CR France62

PEAK,John Harold Capt kia 16-6-15 4LNLancs p234 MR22

PEAK,Norman T2Lt kia 1-7-16 14Manch p155 CR France397

PEAK-GARLAND,George T2Lt kia 7-6-17 11RInnis p105 CR Belgium60

PEAKE,Arthur Lt kia 24-10-17 3 att11Ches p96 CR France163,2Lt

PEAKE,Cecil Gerald Wyatt.MID LtTCapt kia 10-3-15 2Lincs D'Coy p75 CR France525

PEAKE,Colin Lt kld 13-5-15 LeicYeo p204 CR Belgium152,kia

PEAKE,Henry Arthur Wyatt Capt kia 3-7-16 9Ess p132 MR21

PEAKE,John Lewis 2Lt kia 1-6-17 16Mddx p148 MR20

PEAKE,John Thelwal 2Lt dow 11-12-15 Nhampt p138 CR Kent289,11-5-15

PEAKE,Kenneth John Wyatt Lt kia 9-8-15 61Lincs D'Coy p75 MR4

PEAKE,Malcolm.CMG.TBrigGen kia 27-8-17 RA attStaff p1&34 France178

PEAKE,Raymond Lt dow 30-9-16 1ColdGds 1Coy p51 CR France105

PEAKE,William Francis Copson TLt dow 9-7-16 1RWSurr p56 CR France145,7-7-16

PEARCE,Arthur Carlton Lt kia 22-7-18 RASC att1/5N&D p193 CR France109

PEARCE,Charles Denison Fillis T2Lt kia 18-10-16 14Hamps p121 CR France798

PEARCE,Charles Stanley Capt kia 1-7-16 8ESurr p113 CR France513

PEARCE,Cuthbert James T2Lt kia 4-9-16 117MGC Inf p185 CR France220

PEARCE,Dudley George TCapt kia 3-9-16 8EKent p58 CR France1890

PEARCE,Edward Saxelby 2Lt kia 21-3-18 2/7Worc p226 MR20

PEARCE,Edward Sydney Charles Lt 31-3-18 57RFC MR20

PEARCE,Geoffrey Vincent 2Lt dow 18/19-12-14 RWar p65 MR32

PEARCE,George TLt kia 28-1-16 RFA p34 CR France625

PEARCE,Henry.MM.Lt ded 13-10-19 RFA 44ResBty p261 CR Dorset58

PEARCE,Henry Goold.MC.TLtACapt kia 15-7-17 RE 171TC p47 CR Belgium5

PEARCE,Herbert John Lt 24-3-20 RASC CamelTransCoy CR Egypt2

PEARCE,James.DCM.MM.2Lt ded 13-11-18 2WYorks p82 CR France40

PEARCE,James 2Lt ded 4-7-19 Worc 1GarrBn p264 MR67

PEARCE,John Francis Brice Capt kia 29-4-15 3KRRC p151

PEARCE,Maurice Leonard Lt dow 24-9-16 12Hamps attRSuss p121 MR37

PEARCE,Nathaniel Arthur Lt kia 25-11-17 4GrenGds p50 CR France713

PEARCE,Norman T2Lt kia 12-10-17 1RLancs p59 MR30

PEARCE,Richard.MC.Lt kia 27-9-18 23LancF attLabCps p189 CR France297

PEARCE,Robert Swayne 2Lt kia 9-5-15 RB p180 MR32

PEARCE,Sydney Martin Capt ded 7-12-18 4Leic &RAF p219&258 CR Sussex199,Maj 6-12-18

PEARCE,Walter Harry 2Lt dow PoW 24-4-18 RFA attX39TMB p34 CR France716

PEARCE,William Henry 2Lt kia 19-2-18 13Lond p249 CR France184

PEARCE,William James Lt kia 2-12-17 2/5Glouc p225 CR France667

PEARCE-BROWN,Richard 2Lt kia 17-7-16 4DLI p161 CR France832

PEARCE-FLEMING,George Eric Lt ded 1-6-18 IARO att3/39GarhwalRif p281 MR43

PEARCY,Albert 2Lt kia 30-11-17 Dev att7SomLI p77 MR17

PEARKES,Andre Mellard Capt kia 7-8-15 9WYorks p82 MR4

PEARMAN,Humphrey TLt kld 13-8-16 2Leinst attRFC p3&174,ded CR Surrey2

PEARMAN,James O'Hara T2Lt kia 25-1-17 13 att9RWar p65 CR Iraq5

PEARMAN,Thomas Henry 2Lt kia 4-11-18 4Wilts p236 CR France929

PEARS,Charles Martin T2Lt kia 23-11-17 GL &52RFC p12 CR France1361

PEARS,Maurice Loraine.CMG.TLtCol ded 20-10-16 17NumbF p62 CR Sussex112

PEARS,Norman 2Lt kia 24-4-17 4 att1/6Glouc p225 MR21

PEARSALL,Herbert George.MC.Capt ded 19-3-19 1TankCps p266 CR Staffs52

PEARSE,Alister Cullen.MC&Bar.Lt dow 16-9-19 Mddx att45RFus p255 MR70 &CR Europe179

PEARSE,Cecil George Lunnell Lt ded 20-10-18 RFA p208 CR Somerset197,Lunell

PEARSE,Frank Arthur T2Lt kia 2-7-16 1SomLI p80 MR21

PEARSE,Godfrey Maj ded 2-4-20 IA S&TCps p281 MR43

PEARSE,John Francis Brice Capt 29-4-15 3KRRC MR29

PEARSE,Kenneth Herbert T2Lt kia 6-8-15 11ESurr att2Hamps p113 MR4

PEARSE,Phyllis Ada SNurse ded 29-4-15 QAIMNS CR France85

PEARSE,Raymond Stanley T2Lt kia 23-8-16 71RFA p34 CR France239

PEARSE,Samuel LtCol ded 19-11-18 RE p47 CR Lond1

PEARSE,Walter Josiah.MC.2Lt kia 9-4-17 Z5RFA p34 CR France68

PEARSON,Alfred Christopher TCapt kld 4-4-19 9RWar p65 CR Iraq8

PEARSON,Angus John William T2Lt kia 1-7-16 14RFus att1RDubF p69 CR France35,Willans

PEARSON,Arthur James Balfour 2Lt kld 18-8-16 5Ess p232 CR France832

PEARSON,Arthur John.MC.2Lt kia 9-3-17 Nhants att29RFC p12&138 MR20

PEARSON,Athelstan 2Lt kia 13-6-17 5YLI p235 MR19

PEARSON,Bertram Walter Mockley Capt ded 25-10-18 RASC p193 CR France725

PEARSON,Cecil William Lt kia 3-1-18 4NumbF attRFC p19&213 MR20

PEARSON,Charles Hugh 2Lt kia 19-3-16 1/6SStaffs p229 CR France68,18-3-16

PEARSON,Charles Thornhill 2Lt dow 29-8-18 14RWar p65 CR France84

PEARSON,Cyprian Thomas 2Lt dow 6-10-17 A91RFA p34 CR Belgium23

PEARSON,David Easson 2Lt dow 4-9-18 RGA 112SB p41 CR France1484

PEARSON,Edward John 2Lt kia 2-8-17 83RFA p34 CR Belgium19

PEARSON,Ernest William TLt kia 6-8-15 17DLI att6Manch p161 CR Gallipoli1,7-8-15

PEARSON,Evelyn Henry Malcolm Paterson TCapt kld 8-1-16 12Lpool p72 CR France80

PEARSON,Francis Gilbert TLt dow 10-7-17 GL &10RFC p12 CR France98

PEARSON,Frank TCapt ded 5-2-18 GL LNLancs 49TrainingResBn &TMB p136&267 CR C'land&W'land83

PEARSON,Frederick George 2Lt kia 20-10-18 4 att16RWar p65 CR France1396

PEARSON,Frank Shakespeare LtCol ded 5-9-16 RASC p193 CR Dorset94

PEARSON,George Turney TLt kia 12-8-15 9Worc p109 MR4

PEARSON,Gerald T2Lt kia 29-10-17 45RFC p12 CR France200

PEARSON,Harold 2Lt kia 22-5-18 1 att7DCLI p114 CR France924

PEARSON,Harold 2Lt dow 27-9-18 1/7Manch p237 CR France712

PEARSON,Harry 2Lt dow 1-10-18 A/Bty14RFA p34 CR France146

PEARSON,Ignatius Gerald 2Lt kia 30-11-17 LNLancs att1/5SLancs p136 CR France658

PEARSON,James Lt dow 28-3-18 31MGC p185 CR France40

PEARSON,James Alan T2Lt kldacc 9-12-17 RFC p12 CR Norf58

PEARSON,James Bruce 2Lt mbk 25-3-17 IARO att93BurmaInf p281 MR38

PEARSON,John Lt kia 10-10-17 7LancF p221 MR30

PEARSON,John 2Lt dow 11-4-18 10RWar p65 CR Belgium11

PEARSON,John Ashworth TLt kia 4-8-16 8RFus p69 MR21

PEARSON,Joseph Sykes LtACapt ded 7-11-18 RASC MT p193 CR France65

PEARSON,Laumarin Saxe William T2Lt kia 19-7-16 13 att10Ess p132 MR21,Laumann

PEARSON,Maxwell Colquhoun TLt kia 23-11-15 7CamH p168 CR France423

PEARSON,Maurice Murray 2Lt kia 23-4-16 WorcYeo p206 MR34

PEARSON,Neil Mathieson 2Lt kia 17-8-16 5 att1RFus p69 MR21

PEARSON,Oliver Charles 2Lt kia 10-9-17 GL &70RFC p12 MR20

PEARSON,Reginald.MC.Capt kia 9-10-18 7Nhampt p138 CR France916

PEARSON,Reginald 2Lt kia 23-10-18 5WYorks p218 CR France1266,1Bn

PEARSON,Reginald Oswald 2Lt kia 16-6-15 1Lincs p75 MR29

PEARSON,Robert 2Lt dow PoW 7-8-18 1/2Yorks att8WYorks p91 CR France1615

PEARSON,Robert William Capt kld 15-5-15 5DLI p238 CR Belgium84

PEARSON,Stanley Osborne T2Lt kia 30-7-16 12 att10RWar p65 MR21

PEARSON,Stephen Hetley 2Lt kia 1-12-17 2GrenGds p50 CR France364

PEARSON,Sydney James Capt dow 15-8-16 1/8WYorks p219 CR France41

PEARSON,Terence Charles 2Lt kia 26-9-15 2Beds p86 MR19

PEARSON,Thomas Raleigh 2Lt dow 2-7-16 16KRRC p151 MR19

PEARSON,Walter Lt&QM ded 24-5-18 RAMC att41FA p197 CR Iraq8

PEARSON,Wilfred Hearne 2Lt kia 29-9-18 NCycBn ACycCps att57MGC Inf p187&253 CR France256

PEART,Leonard 2Lt dow 12-4-18 18DLI p161 CR France298

PEASE,Charles Capt ded 22-10-19 LNLancs p264 CR Lond28,Maj

PEASE,Christopher York Capt kia 9-5-18 YorkHuss p206 CR France223

PEASE,Cuthbert.MID Lt dow 18-9-16 1IrGds p53 CR France105,Capt

PEASE,Joseph Robinson Maj&HonLtCol ded 17-5-15 F'Res A'RGA Ex Yorks p41 CRYorks45

PEASE,Mark Robinson Lt kia 20-12-14 1EYorks D'Coy p84 CR France1140,20-10-14

PEASE,Ronald Herbert Pike Lt kia 15-9-16 1ColdGds p51 CR France374

PEASTON,Leslie Gordon 2Lt kia 21-3-18 1RFus p69 CR France366

PEATE,John Lt kia 8-9-16 3 att2Glouc p107 MR21 att1Bn

PEATFIELD,Stanley James T2Lt dow 2-7-16 9RBerks att60MGC p139&185 CR Belgium11

PEBERDY,Leonard Montague 2Lt kia 22-12-15 6DLI C'Coy p239 CR Belgium115

PECHELL,George Douglas 2Lt kldacc 21-12-16 IARO att108Inf &66RFC p281 CR Glouc9

PECK,C.W. Lt kia 29-9-15 6RScotF p95 MR19

PECK,Edwin Robert Richmond.MC.T2Lt kia 3-5-17 8Suff p78 CR France1185

PECK,Reginald Geoffrey Lt dow 29-2-16 4ScotRif att10HLI p104 MR32

PECK,Roland Henry.MID TLt kia 5-3-16 Dors &RFC p3 MR38

PECKER,Francis George ACapt dow 18-5-17 7KSLI p145 CR France40

PECKER,Henry Cyril 2Lt kia 20-4-15 3RScots p54 MR29

PECKHAM,Arthur Nyton Lt acckld 14-2-18 IARO att1/112Inf p281 CR Iraq8,Capt

PECKOVER,Reginald Kenneth Capt kia 7-6-17 IA 33Punjabis att7Rajputs p281 CR Asia62,Keith

PECKSTON,Cuthbert Joseph 2Lt kia 22-3-18 25NumbF p62 MR20

PECKSTON,Robert Henry 2Lt ded 22-10-17 7NumbF p214 CR Durham167

PEDDER,Edward Boynton Lt kia 17-1-16 18Huss SR p23 CR France423

PEDDIE,Alexander William Ponsonby Capt kia 13-9-14 1Lincs B'Coy p75 MR15,14-9-14

PEDEN,George Edward 2Lt kia 25-3-17 3Norf att133MGC Inf p74&185 MR38

PEDEN,Josef Kormendy Von Ikreny Lt kia 28-3-18 RFA attRFC p19&208 MR20

PEDLEY,Frederick Lewis 2Lt dow 24-8-17 24Lond p252 CR France64,23-8-17

PEDLOW,William.MC.ACapt kia 12-10-18 2RDubF p177 CR France660

PEDRICK,George Richard 2Lt kia 22-3-18 12Suff p78 MR20

PEEBLES,John Adair 2Lt kia 30-4-18 5ScotRif p224 CR Belgium3,9Bn

PEEBLES,John Reid Capt kia 28-6-15 1/7RScots p211 MR4

PEEBLES,Percy Norman 2Lt kia 9-4-17 12Lond p248 CR France1185

PEEBLES,Peter 2Lt kia 19-7-18 4BlkW p230 CR France324

PEEBLES,William Fleming T2Lt kia 30-4-17 5Wilts att113MGC p153&185 CR Belgium73,MGC attWilts

PEECOCK,Edward Gordon T2Lt kia 7-7-16 9RFus p69 MR21

PEED,Thomas Percy T2Lt dow 10-7-16 11 att8SStaffs p123 CR France833

PEEK,Alfred Taylor 2Lt kia 3-5-17 15WYorks p82 MR20

PEEK,Herbert Thain T2Lt kia 14-7-16 15DLI p161 MR21

PEEK,Roger Grenville Capt 23-3-21 9Lancers CR Devon100

PEEL,Alan Ralph Capt kia 17-11-14 SWBord att5NigR p100 CR WAfrica58

PEEL,Alfred T2Lt kia 5-5-17 6RBerks p139 CR France1185,17-5-17

PEEL,Ambrose Ethelstone 2Lt kia 27-4-18 1Beds p86 CR France346

PEEL,Charles William 2Lt kia 24-4-15 3RDubF p177 MR29

PEEL,Colin Nevill 2Lt kia 3-9-16 3 att14Hamps p121 MR21

PEEL,Geoffrey TLtACapt kia 17-7-17 6Beds p86 CR Belgium100

PEEL,Home.DSO.MC.CaptBdeMaj kia 24-3-18 8Lond p247 CR France374

PEEL,Lawrence Capt kia 24-10-14 Yorks OC 7DivCo p255 MR29,23-10-14

PEEL,Maurice Berkeley.Hon.MC&Bar.Rev kia 14-5-17 RAChDept p199 CR France646

PEEL,Robert Capt ded 7-12-17 Ches 2GarrBn p263 CR Mddx26

PEEL,Robert John De Neuville.MID T2Lt kia 29-3-17 9RWar p65 MR38

PEEL,Robert Lloyd.MC.Lt dow 3-9-17 A58RH&FA p34

PEEL,Thomas Alfred TLt dow 24-8-15 RAMC att5Dors p197 CR Greece10

PEEL,Tom T2Lt dow 21-4-17 2BlkW p129 MR38

PEEL,Walter Sidney.MC.Lt kld 27-9-18 3Lincs att59RAF p75 CR France 1Bn

PEER,Edmund Faithful 2Lt kia 23-4-17 4EYorks p219 MR20

PEERLESS,Cuthbert Henry 2Lt ded 12-5-18 8RSuss p119&257 CR Sussex112

PEERLESS,Charles Stephen T2Lt kia 14-8-16 C166RFA p34 CR France188

PEET,John Edward Grimston 2Lt kld 27-2-15 9RWSurr p56 CR Surrey131

PEFFERS,David Tweedie 2Lt kia 27-2-18 4A&SH p173 CR France162

PEGG,Conrad 2Lt dow 2-6-18 1/2 att6Leic p88 CR France145

PEGG,Hallam William T2Lt dow 3-7-16 8ESurr p113 CR France51

PEGG,Kenneth Hugh Lt kia 20-2-16 3 att2Leic p88 MR38

PEGG,William John T2Lt kld 18-3-18 10RWar p65 CR Norf103,18-3-19

PEGGIE,Alexander Wallace Bruce Lt kia 17-8-17 RGA p209 CR Belgium24

PEGLAR,Harry Sidney 2Lt kia 4-11-18 7RWKent p141 CR France660

PEGRAM,Charles Earnest.MC.TLtACapt ded 9-11-18 RB p180 CR Lond2

PEGUM,Joseph Patrick TCapt kia 26-9-17 RAMC att7KSLI p197 MR30

PEILE,John Selby Chadwick Lt kia 2-6-17 190RFA p34 CR Belgium28

PEIRCE,G.F.2Lt kld 26-5-18 GL &RAF p191

PEIRCE,Sydney Ernest.MC.26-12-15 1/4YLI CR France40

PEIRCE,William Gabriel King Capt kia 30-10-14 3Manch p155 MR22,26-10-14 2Bn

PELHAM,Herbert Lyttelton.Hon.Lt&Adjt kia 14-9-14 2RSuss p119 CR France1329

PELHAM-CLAY,Edward Cecil Granby Lt ded 17-10-19 IARO att3/150Inf p281 CR Egypt7 Ex 2/42Deoli

PELL,Albert Julian Maj ded 28-8-16 4Suff p217 CR Camb91,9Bn

PELL,Beauchamp Tyndall.DSO.LtCol dow 4-11-14 RWSurr p56 CR Belgium116

PELL,Harry Saxon 2Lt kia 6-4-17 40RFC p12 CR France783

PELLETIER,Charles Adolphe Lt 11-5-18 CanadaEngrs &1RAF MR20

PELLEW,James Edward Capt ded 15-12-19 RDC CR Cornwall142

PELLS,Charles Francis Robert Lt kia 11-4-17 6WYorks p218 MR20

PELLS,Cyril Elmore T2Lt kia 27-5-18 Dev p77 MR18

PELLY,Henry Gerald Maj ded 25-7-16 RH&FA p261

PELLY,Herbert Richard Lt kia 9-10-15 1/7Ess p232 CR Gallipoli17,Hubert

PELLY,William Francis Henry TCapt kia 1-7-16 9RInnisF p105 MR21

PELMORE,Bernard Julius TLt kia 18-7-17 RE 247FC p47 CR France184

PELTON,Kenneth Kemble.MC.2Lt kia 1-8-17 5Leinst att7RIrRif p174 MR29

PEMBER,Edward Horace Lt kia 30-9-17 RFA &5RFC p12&34 CR France95

PEMBER,Henry Cecil TCapt kia 3-5-17 HouseholdBn p20 CR France97 Ex 1LifeGds

PEMBERTON,Alan John MacDonald.MC.Capt ded 3-11-16 Leinst &RFC p3&174,Allan CR France614

PEMBERTON,Charles Oliver Paget Lt ded 4-4-16 RDC p253 CR Suff215,4-7-16

PEMBERTON,C.Warren 2Lt kld 25-4-16 RFC p3

PEMBERTON,Francis Percy Campbell Capt kia 19-10-14 2LifeGds p20 CR Belgium157

PEMBERTON,Frederick Despard Capt kia 21-8-17 RFA att50RFC p12&34 CR France660

PEMBERTON,Leigh T2Lt kia 25-9-15 9KRRC att9RB p151 MR29

PEMBERTON,Oswald Capt kia 21-12-14 2MunstF attDubF p175 MR22 1Munst attDubF

PEMBERTON,Percy Leigh 2Lt dow 27-7-16 4Mddx p148

PEMBERTON,Vivian Telfer.MC.Capt kia 7-10-18 RGA 216SB p41 CR France375

PEMBLE,Clarence Arthur Lyon 2Lt kia 1-8-18 RWSurr p56 MR20

PENDER,George.MID Capt dow 24-4-17 1/7RScots p211 CR Egypt2

PENDER,James(Hamish)Granger Gailes 2Lt kia 11-3-15 3 att2GordH p167 CR France525,Geils

PENDER,William Gordon.MC.Capt kia 15-8-17 40RFC p12 MR20

PENDEREL-BRODHURST,Bernard Richard 2Lt kia 1-10-18 RE 82FC p210 CR France631

PENDRIGH,Alexander Conrad Cuthbertson 2Lt dow 17-8-17 6Dev B'Coy p217 CR France145,2Bn

PENFOLD,Bernard Hugh T2Lt kia 20/23-10-17 N&D att15Bn p134 MR30,20-10-17

PENFOLD,Edward Norman Lt kia 29-5-18 2Lincs attLeic p75

PENFOLD,Jeffery Bradley TLt dow 28-1-16 7KOSB p102 CR France178

PENFOLD-WYATT,Hugh Graystone Lt ded 12-11-15 SussYeo p205

PENGELLEY,Rowland Donald.MID T2Lt kia 19-8-17 RE 153FC p47 CR Belgium111

PENGELLY,Edgar Ambrose.MC.Capt dow 31-3-18 RE 213ArmyTpsCo p47&259 CR France145

PENGELLY,William Augustus 2Lt kia 19-5-17 8Mddx p236 MR20

PENHALE,Thomas William T2Lt dow 15-4-17 13KRRC p151 CR France40

PENKETH,Alfred Thomas T2Lt kia 12-5-17 1SStaffs p123 MR20

PENKETH,Robert Charles Capt dow 16-4-17 6NumbF p213 CR France120

PENLINGTON,Arthur Berkeley.MC.2Lt kia 6-10-17 RFA 15ArmyBde p34 MR30

PENMAN,Geoffrey Evans TLt kia 9-5-17 11RWSurr att11MGC p56&185 CR France614

PENMAN,Rowland Arthur T2Lt kia 16-6-17 214MGC p185 MR20 att206Coy

PENN,Eric Frank 2LtTCapt kia 18-10-15 4GrenGds p50 CR France423

PENN,Geoffrey Mark 2Lt kia 11-12-15 6RB attSomLI p180 CR Belgium71

PENN,Thomas 2Lt kia 15-4-18 7Lincs p75 CR France41

PENN-GASKELL,Leslie Da Costa.MID 1Maj kld 4-2-16 Norf &RFC p3&74,Lt ded CR Mddx34,SqnCmdr

PENN-GASKELL,William TCapt kia 12-10-16 25Manch p155 MR21

PENNEFATHER,Charles Lewis TCapt kia 14-6-16 2RB p180 CR France251

PENNEFATHER,Somerset Edward Chap2Cl ded 29-8-17 13Lond p271 CR Mddx51

PENNEL,R.H.E.Maj 10-12-15 IAML AcntsDept MR65

PENNEY,Ian Campbell TCapt kia 27-9-15 13RScots p54 MR19,26-9-15

PENNEY,Nicholas Arthur Lt kia 10-4-21 IA 1/25 att28Punjabis p281 MR43

PENNEY,Reginald Harper T2Lt kia 9-11-17 11NumbF p62 CR France1858

PENNEY,Roland Lt kia 2-4-18 B190RFA p208 CR France745

PENNINGTON,Harold Cocking TLt dow 20-6-17 1RFus p69 CR France13

PENNINGTON,Harold Evelyn T2Lt kia 27-9-15 9RSuss p119 MR19

PENNINGTON,John.MID Lt kia 25-9-15 2RWar p65 MR19

PENNINGTON,Thomas T2Lt kia 28-9-15 2EKent p58 MR19,PENINGTON

PENNINGTON,William Henry 2Lt ded 2-3-15 14WYorks p82 CR Cornwall96

PENNINGTON William Herbert Maj kia 9-9-15 IA 12Cav att16 p281 CR Asia82

PENNY,Arthur Hugh Capt dow 1-7-16 1ELancs p111 MR21

PENNY,Arthur Taylor.MVO.Maj ded 28-9-15 2Hamps p264

PENNY,Bernard Willoughby 2Lt dow 18-8-17 2RFus p69 CR Belgium16

PENNY,George 2Lt kia 3-9-16 8WYorks p219 CR France383

PENNY,Stanley T2Lt dow 28-7-16 14RFus p69 CR France141

PENRICE,William Gordon T2Lt kia 7-6-17 20DLI p161 MR29

PENROSE,Algernon Fane Keane Lt kia 10-5-15 RInnisF p105 CR Gallipoli3

PENROSE,Claude Quayle Lewis.MC&Bar.MIDx2 Maj dow 1-8-18 RGA 245SB p41 CR France142

PENROSE,Edward John McNeill.MID Capt kia 25-4-15 1RIrF p171 MR29

PENROSE,Ernest Lt kia 5-4-18 12MGC Inf p185 CR France704

PENROSE,George Alwyn TCapt kia 9-4-17 8RWSurr p56 CR France161

PENROSE,Harold T2Lt dow 27-3-17 12 att8RFus p69 CR France113

PENROSE,Harold Wesley 2Lt kia 26-3-18 4RFus p69 MR20,Henry

PENROSE,Robert John Rowson 2Lt kia 26-4-18 Y&L att1/4Bn p159 MR32

PENROSE-FITZGERALD,Herbert James Cooper Lt kia 12-10-16 3 att1RIrF p171 MR21

PENROSE-FITZGERALD,Maurice J.TLt dow 26-7-16 7RWSurr p56 CR Eire81

PENROSE-WELSTED,Samuel Richard.DFC.Capt kia 17-7-18 5RIrReg &17RAF p89 MR37

PENRUDDOCKE,Charles.MID Lt kia 4-10-18 7Wilts C'Coy p153 CR France1495

PENRUDDOCKE,Cyril Powys Capt kia 3-9-16 11RSuss B'Coy p119 CR France1890

PENRUDDOCKE,Thomas T2Lt kia 25-4-17 8Wilts p153 MR37

PENSON,Thomas Edward 2Lt kia 18-9-18 25RWFus p98 CR France1494

PENTECOST,Charles Gordon 2Lt kia 27-3-18 25RFC p16 MR20

PENTELOW,Arthur Lenton 2Lt dow 28-7-18 62MGC p185 CR France622

PENTLAND,Robert Charles Maj ded 1-3-18 RDubF p266

PENTON,Arthur Herbert 2Lt kia 16-4-18 14Hamps att1/5Manch p121 CR France204

PENTON,E.G.Lt ded 29-5-18 RASC p193

PENWARDEN,William Francis 2Lt kia 31-8-18 4RFus p69 CR France568

PEPLER,Stanley James Lt 6-3-17 51CanadaInf &43RFC MR20

PEPLOE,Keith LtACapt kia 9-11-16 2 O&BLI B'Coy p130 CR France344

PEPPER,Alwyn Tayton Capt ded 6-11-18 RE 100FC 22Div HQ p47 CR Greece9

PEPPER,Cedric William 2Lt ded 21-10-15 3SomLI p80 CR Somerset219

PEPPER,Edith Dorothy SpProb ded 7-4-18 VAD QAIMNS p200&268 CR Egypt9

PEPPER,Enoch.MID 2Lt kia 26-4-18 4SStaffs p123 MR30

PEPPER,Robert Forsythe 2Lt kia 12-10-16 4 att1RIrF p171 MR21

PEPPER,Sydney Whitelock Capt kia 27-8-17 8RWar p214 MR30

PEPPER,William Bramwell Capt dow 4-8-16 RGA 3SB p41 CR France397

PEPYS,Francis.DSO.2Lt kia 12-11-14 2 O&BLI p130 MR29

PEPYS,John 2Lt kia 23-8-14 YLI p143 CR Belgium201

PEPYS,Reginald Whitmore Capt dow 21-9-14 2Worc p109 CR France1329

PERCEVAL-MAXWELL,R.H.Lt 23-7-18 3 att10ScotRif CR France865

PERCEVAL-MAXWELL,Richard Nigel Lt kia 30-3-18 16Lancers p23 CR France988

PERCIVAL,Alfred Jex Blake.DSO.TLtCol kia 31-11-14 NumbF 2DivStaff p62 CR Belgium58,Arthur 31-10-14

PERCIVAL,Anthony.MID TLt dow 15-10-17 95MGC p185 CR France145

PERCIVAL,Cecil Bernard TLtACapt kia 24-11-17 20 att18WelchR p127 MR17

PERCIVAL,Claude Victor Noble Maj kia 14-12-14 2RB p180 CR France158

PERCIVAL,George Stewart 2Lt kld 13-10-18 4Manch p155 CR France725,Stuart

PERCIVAL,John Lee 2Lt kia 30-9-18 8WYorks p219 CR France755

PERCIVAL,M.Lt att5NigR CR WAfrica58

PERCIVAL,Reginald Frank Lt kia 12-4-18 2Mon p244 MR32

PERCIVAL,Walter Lowe 2Lt dow 24-10-18 YLI att9Bn p143 CR France737

PERCY,George Clark.MC.MID LtACapt kia 31-7-17 3 att2ScotRif p104 MR29

PERCY,Harry Fortescue Lt ded 5-2-17 WiltsYeo p271 CR Surrey150

PERCY,Raymond.MC.LtACapt dow 12-8-18 12 att1Lpool p72&259 CR France84

PERCY,William Francis.MC.Maj ded 12-6-15 Norf p263 CR War143

PERCY-HARDMAN,William Henry Capt dow 1-3-17 4Dev attMGC Inf p187&220 CR Iraq5

PERCY-SMITH,Vernon Maj ded 29-9-20 SL IA 20DeccanHorse attRFC p281&268 MR65

PEREGRINE,John Pryor Puxton Lt kia 1-7-16 1EYorks p84 MR21

PEREIRA,Adrian O'Donnell TCapt kia 20-9-17 10WRid p116 CR Belgium112

PERFECT,Cyril St.Lawrence 2Lt dow 13-10-15 3RLancs att1RWSurr p59 CR France114

PERHAM,Edgar TCapt kia 23-7-16 12WYorks p82 MR21

PERHAM,Ernest Noble T2Lt dow 1-8-17 12 att4Worc p109 CR Belgium7

PERHAM,William Francis George Lt dow 10-3-18 3 att1Beds p86 CR Italy7,2Lt

PERKIN,Albert John T2Lt ded 23-12-17 RE p262 CR Devon73

PERKIN,Philip Kenneth 2Lt kia 1-7-16 12Y&L p159 MR21

PERKINS,Albert T2Lt kia 4-10-17 197MGC p185 CR Belgium20,149MGC

PERKINS,Æneas Charles Maj dow 28-4-15 IA 40Pathans p281 CR France284

PERKINS,Audley St.John Lt kia 2-4-17 9Dev p77 CR France568

PERKINS,Bernard St.George Lt kia 10-8-18 1 att9Ess p132 CR France247

PERKINS,B.T.Capt 14-6-16 N&D CR Somerset196

PERKINS,Cecil Howard Lt kia 22-7-18 2Yorks att21TMB p91 CR France65

PERKINS,Charles Henry Lt ded 14-9-19 11MGC Inf p266 CR Lancs263

PERKINS,Cyril John 2Lt dow 27-6-17 4Yorks p220 CR France518

PERKINS,Frank Arthur Capt dow 8-6-17 21Lond p251 CR Belgium11

PERKINS,Frank Bailey LtACapt kia 19-5-17 23/40RFA p34 CR France1182

PERKINS,George T2Lt kia 1-7-16 2WYorks p82 MR21

PERKINS,John Charles Campbell.DSO.LtCol 28-2-16 IAML AccntsDept MR65

PERKINS,Jukes Ford Rumsey Irving 2Lt kia 8-3-18 27RFC p16 CR France1061

PERKINS,Leonard T2Lt kia 3-11-16 1RWSurr p56 MR21

PERKINS,Reginald Gabriel Beale 2Lt kia 14-9-14 1RBerks p139 MR15

PERKINS,Thorold 2Lt kia 31-5-17 41RFC p12 CR Belgium18

PERKS,Maurice Case T2Lt kia 26-4-17 9LNLanc att74TMB p136 CR Belgium43

PERKS,Robert Clement.DSO.TCapt kia 27-10-18 10WRid p116 CR Italy9

PERKS,Wilfred Lawson 2Lt kia 24-8-16 3Worc p109 MR21

PERKS-MORRIS,Arthur Bois 2Lt dow 14-11-17 2RSuss p119 CR Belgium11

PERN,Montague Lt kia 9-5-15 RAMC att4RFus p197 CR France924

PERNEY,Erland Dauria 2Lt kia 23-11-17 11RFC p12 MR20

PERRAM,George Terrence Clements CaptAMaj kia 3-8-17 RGA att177RFA p41 CR Belgium10

PERRAM,Henry Charles Capt ded 17-2-19 IA 84Punjabis att66 p281 MR43

PERRATON,Frank Mayvour.MC.2Lt kia 29-4-17 22RFus p69 MR20

PERREAU,Gustavus Arthur LtCol kia 9-3-17 IA 2/4GurkhaRif p281 MR38

PERRET,Gerald Henry Lt kia 9-8-17 5RRofCav att10Huss p23 CR France652,PERRETT 8-8-18

PERRETT,Ernest Henry T2Lt kia 4-10-17 Hamps att1Bn p121 CR Belgium83

PERRETT,Fred Leonard 2Lt dow 1-12-18 17RWelshF p98 CR France34

PERRIER,Hargrave Carroll Lumley 2Lt kia 8-11-18 5RDubF p177 CR France1219,2Bn

PERRIER,William Samuel T2Lt kia 27-3-16 4RFus p69 MR29

PERRIN,Alfred John T2Lt kia 4-10-17 10YLI p143 MR30

PERRIN,Charles Louis Maj kia 23-11-15 IA 76Punjabis p281 MR38

PERRIN,Gilbert Dennis Lt kia 13/15-11-16 2SStaffs p123 CR France742,Capt

PERRIN,Maurice Nasmith Maj ded 28-4-19 RAMC attRAF p267 CR Surrey157

PERRIN,Reginald Percy.MC.Capt kia 27-5-18 GL att7InfBdeHQ p191 MR18

PERRIN,Thomas Frederick TCapt ded 24-7-17 RE IWT p47 CR Iraq6

PERRIN,Thomas Frood.MID Lt 24-5-20 3RIrReg CR Egypt6

PERRIS,Eric Loftus 2Lt kia 27-9-16 4Yorks p220 CR France515

PERRIS,Noel Felix 2Lt kia 20-7-18 2Lond &RAF p245&258

PERROTT,A.H. Lt kia 10-9-14 1RBerks p139 CR France866

PERRY,Alfred Frederick 2Lt 28-11-18 N Flight RAF MR20

PERRY,Arthur Ernest Cecil 2Lt dow 20-6-18 RGA 248SB p41 CR France343

PERRY,Benjamin Lewis Capt kld 26-4-15 1Mon p244 MR29

PERRY,Cecil Robert Lt ded 24-10-19 RASC p267

PERRY,Cecil Victor.MC.2Lt kia 23-4-17 120/27RFA p34 CR France1325

PERRY,Claude William T2Lt kia 1-7-16 7EYorks p84 CR France373,Charles

PERRY,Cullen Hay TLt kld 3-2-18 1/8RFus att23RFC p16&69,ded CR Egypt1

PERRY,Donovan Lt kia 22-3-18 Herts p252 MR27

PERRY,Evelyn Walter Copland 2Lt kldacc 16-8-14 RFC p2 CR France299

PERRY,Francis Ina Lowre Lt kia 2-5-15 1BordR p117 CR Gallipoli3

PERRY,Frank Burgess 2Lt kia 24-4-18 58MGC p185 MR27

PERRY,George Herbert Gresley LtTCapt dow 15-3-15 2WYorks p82 CR France102

PERRY,George Hugh 2Lt kia 31-3-18 9/41RFA p34 CR France41

PERRY,Henry Bernard.MID Capt kia 6-11-18 13Lond p249 CR France1142

PERRY,John 2Lt kia 23-7-16 3 att2Yorks p91 MR21

PERRY,Kenneth George T2Lt dow 1-11-16 11RSuss p119 CR France74

PERRY,Kenneth William 2Lt dow 8-12-17 1ColdGds p51 CR France40

PERRY,Lawrence Percy 2Lt 2-9-18 48RAF MR20

PERRY,Leslie Harold.MC.2Lt kia 6-10-18 4Glouc att2/6DLI p225 CR France1092,5-8-18

PERRY,Leslie Roy 2Lt kia 15-9-16 6Lond p247 MR21

PERRY,Percy Claude Lt kld 26-4-16 7N&D p233 CR Notts85

PERRY,Robert Proelss 2Lt kia 9-4-17 1/7Mddx p235 CR France420

PERRY,Roy Sinclair 2Lt kia 4-4-16 11 att6LNLancs p136 MR38

PERRY,Stephen Ralph TLt kia 18-9-16 12KRRC p151 MR21

PERRY,Sydney.MC.MM.2LtACapt kia 7-8-18 2RWSurr p56 CR Italy3

PERRY,Thomas 2Lt kia 25-9-15 1CamH p168 CR France553

PERRY,William 2Lt 24-8-20 NumbF CR Numb83

PERRY,William Charles T2Lt kia 30-12-17 GL attRFC p12 CR Egypt1

PERRY,William Claude T2Lt dow 13-7-16 20KRRC p151 CR France141

PERRY,William Everard Hill T2Lt kia 14-4-17 2Dev p77 CR France407

PERRY,William Johnstone 2Lt kld 21-5-16 1/6RWelshF p223 CR Egypt9

PERRY-AYSCOUGH,Henry George Charlie Capt kia 25-9-15 RMunstF p176 MR29,4ConnRgrs attRlrRif

PERRYMAN,Arthur Charles 2Lt kld 7-1-18 Mddx att16RFC p16&148 CR Mddx17

PERSSE,Cecil De Burgh Gordon 2Lt dow 19-7-15 7DragGds attIrGds p21 CR Hamps64

PERSSE,Dudley Eyre Lt dow 1-2-15 4RDubF p177 CR France284

PERSSE,Edward Aubrey Capt kia 14-10-18 A47RFA p34 CR Belgium100

PERSSE,Henry Wilfred.MC&Bar.CaptAMaj dow 28-6-18 2RFus p69 CR France134

PERSSE,Rodolph Algernon 2Lt kia 1-1-15 RB att2KRRC p180 MR22

PERSTON,George Fortescue 2Lt kia 12-2-17 B99RFA p34 CR Greece6

PERY,Cecil de Vere T2Lt kia 25-9-15 1Mddx p148 MR19

PESKETT,Guy Eastcoft Harry 2Lt kia 3-5-17 4WRid p227 MR20

PESKETT,Harry St.Hill Capt dow 13-4-17 10LNLancs C'Coy p136 CR France113

PETER,Alexander Gordon.MC.TCapt dow 5-7-17 RAMC att2/6SfthH p197 CR Belgium12,Alister

PETER,Alfred Edwin 2Lt kia 25-9-16 3NStaffs att9Leic p157 MR21

PETER,Pomeroy John 2Lt kia 19-9-18 10EKent p204 CR France364

PETER,Richard Henry 2Lt kia 30-4-18 16Lond p250 MR34

PETERS,Arthur Stafford 2Lt kia 30-11-17 13 att1/6Lond p249 MR17

PETERS,Albert Wallace 2Lt ded 20-11-18 TankCps p266 CR War23,MGC

PETERS,Ashley 2Lt kia 13-11-16 13EYork p84 MR21

PETERS,Charles Frederick 2Lt kia 18-3-18 6EKent p58 CR France922

PETERS,Charles Walter 2Lt kia 21-3-18 8 att7EKent p58 MR27

PETERS,Cyril Aubrey T2Lt kia 4-7-17 17Lpool p72 CR Belgium115

PETERS,Frank Wesley.MC.2Lt kia 18-7-17 1 att9Ess p132 MR20

PETERS,Gerard 2Lt ded 24-2-17 6Glouc p225 CR France692

PETERS,Henry TLt kia 12-10-16 26Manch p155 CR France744

PETERS,Joseph Henry Gervese Capt kia 10-1-20 IA 51Sikhs att2/152Punjabis p281

PETERS,Lionel Gordon Capt kia 25-3-18 10WYorks p82 MR20

PETERS,Owen Herbert Capt dow 5-8-16 RAMC 36SanitarySect p254 CR France23

PETERS,William John.MC.Lt kia 23-4-17 1Dev p77 MR20

PETERSEN,Aaron 2Lt kia 3-9-18 3EYorks &18RAF p84 MR20

PETERSON,George Benjamin 2Lt kia 31-3-18 4EYorks att6Dors p219 CR France196

PETERSON,J.Lt 20-5-19 14Dev CR Lancs14

PETERSON,William Sinclair 2Lt kia 6-11-14 RHA att2LifeGds p209 CR Belgium134,PETERSEN

PETHERBRIDGE,Henry B.Lt dow 24-7-16 NyasaVolRes att1KAR p268 CR EAfrica40,Victor 2Lt

PETLEY,Hugh Capt kia 16-9-16 1Lond p245 MR21

PETO,Clement Henry Capt kia 17-11-14 10Huss p22 CR Belgium57

PETO,James Archibald Lt kia 23-8-15 4Worc p109 CR Gallipoli4

PETO,Morton.MC.TCapt dow 22-9-16 RAMC p197 CR France177

PETRE,Lionel George Carroll.Lord.LtTCapt dow 30-9-15 4CldGds p51 CR Essex36

PETRIE,Alex Robertson 2Lt ded 13-2-19 3Manch p265 CR Lancs434

PETRIE,Alfred Hunt T2Lt kia 31-7-17 GL att72TMB p191 MR29

PETRIE,Allan Strachan 2Lt kia 11-9-16 14Lond p249 CR France294

PETRIE,Donald John 2Lt kia 9-9-16 1ORScots att2/5LancF p212 MR21

PETRIE,Henry Lawson T2Lt kia 30-7-16 9 att2KOSB p102 MR21

PETRIE,William Wilson LtCol ded 22-2-19 GL RFA p268 CR Norf11,27-2-19

PETT,Joseph 2Lt kia 21-3-18 2/4 O&BLI p231 MR27

PETTER,Harold Rupert 2Lt dow 3-5-17 1RScotF p95 MR20

PETTIGREW,Douglas St.George T2Lt dow 23-10-17 14 att17N&D p134 CR Belgium11

PETTIGREW,Gilbert Thomas Richardson Lt kld 12-9-17 1Hereford attRFC p19&252 CR War151,2Lt 12-8-17

PETTIGREW,John Lt ded 3-11-18 GL attSPersia Rif p191 CR Asia82

PETTIGREW,Robert McCalmont T2Lt dow 10-6-16 8RlrRif C'Coy p170 CR France702

PETTIGREW,Thomas Thomson 2Lt kia 28-7-18 8SfthH p165 CR France865

PETTINGER,Harold Sidney TLt kia 10-10-17 8YLI attHQ70InfBde p143 CR Belgium127

PETTINGER,James Wilson TCapt ded 6-10-17 RAMC p197 CR Somerset139

PETTIT,William Vaughan T2Lt kia 29-6-16 RE 173TC p47 CR France178

PETTITT,William 2Lt kia 19-4-18 1LNLancs p136 CR France1106

PETTS,Cyril Edward Lt ded 14-12-18 IARO att1/8GurkhaRif p281 MR66,C.F.Capt

PETTY,Alfred Hallam 2Lt dow PoW 17-7-16 5N&D p233 CR France1266

PETTY,Charles Henry Capt 2-6-21 6WRid CR Yorks483

PETTY,Eric Bateman Lt kia 23-3-18 5Ches p222 CR France512

PETTY,Nelson Widdup Lt kia 28-6-15 LancF p93 MR4

PETTY,Robert Leach 2Lt kia 31-8-18 WYorks att7NStaffs p82 MR61

PETYT,John Edward 2Lt kia 27-3-18 2/8Manch p237 MR27

PEYTON,Ernest T2Lt kia 1-7-16 4Mddx p148 CR France267

PEYTON,Henry Sydney Charles,MC LtCol dow 24-3-18 3RB Cmdg2Bn p180 CR France692

PEYTON,John Algernon Wynward Lt kia 22-8-18 7Norf p74 CR France196,Wyngard

PEYTON,Montagu Frank T2Lt kia 12-7-17 16NumbF Res p62 CR Belgium173

PHALEN,Ralph Uriel 2Lt kia 28-5-17 60RFC p12 MR20

PHARE,Dudley Gershom Lt kia 28-3-18 RASC p193 MR20 RAMC att7KSLI

PHAYRE,Charles Frederick 2Lt kia 27-8-14 2RMunF p176 CR France1751,Lt

PHAYRE,Richard Herbert Lt kia 26-10-14 2Yorks p91 MR29

PHEAR,Henry John Lt dow 17-10-17 RH&FA 14ArmyBde p34 CR Belgium172

PHEAR,Norman Carlyon T2Lt dow 20-11-17 GL &27RFC p12 CR France88

PHELAN,Albert Edward.MC.TLtACapt kia 20-11-17 1NumbF p62 MR20

PHELPS,Duncan 2Lt kia 29-9-18 RSuss attHamps p119 MR30

PHELPS,Leslie James 2Lt ded 3-11-18 1/2 att8Glouc p107 CR Wales149

PHELPS,Wilfred John Lt kia 15-9-16 9Norf p74 MR21,16-9-16

PHETHEAN,Charles Capt kld 30-3-18 5Manch p236 CR France425

PHIBBS,William Griffith Baynes Maj ded 8-11-14 RlrF p171 CR Wales462,5-11-14

PHILBRICK,Edward Hooper Lt ded 6-11-18 RFA 395Bty p34&257 CR Essex81

PHILBY,Denis Duncan Lt kia 12-11-14 RDubF attRMunF p177 CR Belgium96

PHILBY,Harold Payne.DSO.TMaj kia 17-5-16 2Y&L p159 CR Belgium2

PHILCOX,Cecil Ernest.MID TLt ded 24-5-17 1SStaffs p123 CR France518

PHILCOX,Percy Vivian Lt kia 1-11-18 RASC attRGA p193 CR France206

PHILIP,Andrew TLt dedacc 30-5-15 RAMC p197 CR Scot127

PHILIP,David Carswell 2Lt kia 29-4-17 23NumbF p62 MR20

PHILIP,Edgar Thomas 2LtTLt kia 18-6-17 RFA att9RFC p12&34 MR20 CR France451

PHILIP,Gerald Huntley 2Lt dow 11-11-16 3 att15Hamps p121 CR Hamps214

PHILIP,John Alexander 2Lt dow 7-5-18 D122RFA p34 CR France100

PHILIP,Kenneth Capt kia 27-3-18 1/4 att11EYorks p219 MR27

PHILIPPS,Ivor John Douglas TCapt ded 8-3-15 16Ches p96 CR Scot237 Ex 3BlkW

PHILIPS,Abraham Zadok TCapt dow 24-10-17 RAMC att56FA p197 CR Belgium18

PHILIPS,A.C.2Lt 7-7-16 6KOSB MR21

PHILIPS,Arthur Maxwell TCapt kia 11-11-15 11YLI att9WYorks p143 CR Gallipoli27

PHILIPS,Basil Edwin.MID LtCol kia 10-8-15 Cmdg5RWelshF p223 CR Gallipoli5

PHILIPS,Henry Charles T2Lt kia 7-12-17 10RWSurr p56 CR Italy7,PHILLIPS

PHILIPS,Herbert Stanley 2Lt kia 26-3-17 6Ess p232 MR34

PHILIPS,Mark Hibbert 2Lt kia 4-10-17 4 att1SStaffs p123 CR Belgium308

PHILIPS,William Theodore Caldwell 2Lt kia 2-5-18 9RScots p212 CR France33

PHILLIBROWN,Cyril George 2Lt dow 15-11-17 RGA 111SB p209 CR France446

PHILLIMORE,Hugh Bouchier Lt dow 16-6-15 8A&SH p243 MR22

PHILLIMORE,Jasper Prescott TLt kia 13-10-15 6EKent p58 CR France423

PHILLIMORE,Matthew Arden T2Lt kia 25-6-16 9Ess attRE 251TC p132 CR France163,11Bn

PHILLIPPO,Arthur James Cecil Eyre Lt kia 7-6-17 RASC att6RFC p12&193 CR Belgium410,dow

PHILLIPPS,Reginald William 2Lt kia 26-10-15 GrenGds 5R att1Dn p50 CR France423

PHILLIPPS,Rowland Erasmus.Hon.MC.TCapt kia 7-7-16 9RFus p69 CR France251,PHILIPPS Roland

PHILLIPS,Arthur 2Lt kia 23-4-17 2RWelshF p98 MR20

PHILLIPS,Arthur Blakeway 2Lt kia 19-6-16 12Lond p248 CR France1327

PHILLIPS,Arthur Cornwallis 2Lt dow 22-5-17 4 att1ScotRif p104 CR France1184

PHILLIPS,Azariah T2Lt kld 12-1-18 RFC p16 CR Wales690

PHILLIPS,Benjamin Wynford Lt kld 14-11-17 RGA &RFC p19&p209 CR Shrop89,PHILIPPS

PHILLIPS,Cecil Ivor 2Lt kia 27-10-17 Glouc att45RFC p12&107 MR20

PHILLIPS,Charles LtCol ded 10-1-19 RGA p262 CR Kent180

PHILLIPS,Charles Ernest.MC.Lt kia 22-10-18 4 att7RlrReg p89 CR Belgium143

PHILLIPS,Christian Gibson Maj kia 10-7-16 RLancs p59 CR France432

PHILLIPS,Colwyn Erasmus Arnold.Hon.MID TCapt kia 13-5-15 RHGds p20 MR29 PHILIPPS

PHILLIPS,Cyril Gordon 2Lt kia 10-11-17 3 att1SWBord p100 MR30

PHILLIPS,David Charles 2Lt kia 16-8-17 4RWelshF p223 CR Belgium106

PHILLIPS,Edward T2Lt dow 27-5-18 NumbF att5Bn p62 MR18

PHILLIPS,Edward George Dunscombe Masters LtACapt kia 13-11-16 2 att6RIrReg p89 CR Belgium17,14-11-16

PHILLIPS,Edward Hawkin.DSO.Maj dow 6-11-14 28RFA p34 CR France80,Hawtin

PHILLIPS,Edward Stone Lt kia 8-5-15 1Mon p244 MR29

PHILLIPS,Edwin Mann Lt dow 29-9-18 2RInnisF p105 CR France34

PHILLIPS,Eric Sutherland TCapt dow 21-2-17 8BordR B'Coy p117 CR France263

PHILLIPS,Ernest Arthur 2Lt kia 2-11-17 4RBerks att1/5Beds p234 CR Palestine8

PHILLIPS,Ernest James T2Lt kia 15-8-17 RE 170TC p47 CR France178

PHILLIPS,Eustace Edward Lovett T2Lt kia 30-10-15 6RBerks p139 CR France515

PHILLIPS,Fenton Ellis Stanley.MC.2Lt kia 13-10-16 3Dev &RFC p3,77&259 MR20

PHILLIPS,Frank Stewart T2Lt kia 23-11-17 13Yorks p91 MR17

PHILLIPS,Frederick Charles 2Lt dow 6-2-16 5NumbF p213 CR Belgium11

PHILLIPS,Frederick George LtACapt kia 25-4-18 5WYorks p218 MR30

PHILLIPS,Gilbert William TLt dow 20-11-17 TankCps p188 CR France415

PHILLIPS,Gwilym 2Lt kia 13-10-18 4Glouc att1/8LancF p225 CR France206

PHILLIPS,Guy Saggerson 2Lt kia 15-9-16 5Yorks p221 CR France239

PHILLIPS,Herbert 2Lt kia 13-10-16 2Yorks p91 MR21

PHILLIPS,Herbert Denis T2Lt kia 24-10-16 57MGC Inf p185 CR France535

PHILLIPS,Hubert Henry Lt dow 4-10-15 2 att3Leic p88 CR France345,7 att3Bn

PHILLIPS,J.Sister drd 20/21-3-17 QAIMNS p200 MR40,21-3-17

PHILLIPS,James Lt kia 1-11-18 RE 203FC p210 CR Belgium167

PHILLIPS,James William TCapt kia 30-5-18 9RWFus p98 MR ?

PHILLIPS,John 2Lt kia 20-7-16 5ScotRif p224 MR21

PHILLIPS,John Harold Montague 2Lt dow 25-1-16 RE 4FC p210 CR France80

PHILLIPS,John Henley Shawe Maj ded 28-9-19 RE p271 CR Mddx77

PHILLIPS,John Noel.MID Capt dow 18-4-15 1Lincs p75 CR France102

PHILLIPS,Joseph Alexander Lt kia 3-5-17 13Lpool p72 MR20

PHILLIPS,Joseph Douglas Lt kia 20-10-14 EKent p58 MR32

PHILLIPS,Joseph Leo T2Lt kld 20-7-17 GL &RFC p12 CR Norf209

PHILLIPS,Leonard Harry Perrins TLt kia 6-11-16 12 att2Worc p109 MR21

PHILLIPS,Leslie Capt kia 25-5-15 1WelshR p127 MR29

PHILLIPS,Maurice Aldcroft Capt kia 21-5-15 RFA 31Bty p34 CR France727

PHILLIPS,Norman Arthur 2Lt kia 25-3-17 54RFC p12 CR France1061

PHILLIPS,Norman Rutherford 2Lt kia 20-9-17 6Lpool p215 MR30

PHILLIPS,Owen Sherwood T2Lt kia 21-8-15 4SWBord p100 CR Gallipoli17

PHILLIPS,Patrick Tewan T2Lt kia 4/5-4-16 10 att6ELancs p111 MR38

PHILLIPS,Percy Montague TLt kia 25-9-16 13Yorks p91 CR France115

PHILLIPS,Philip Roy Capt ded 7-5-18 A55RFA p207 MR38

PHILLIPS,Ralph Aberdeen T2Lt kld 16-8-17 RFC 11TrnSqn p12 CR Lincs61

PHILLIPS,Ralph Noel Capt dow 27-12-14 RWFus p98 CR Berks42

PHILLIPS,Reginald 2Lt kia 23-4-17 2SWBord p100 MR20

PHILLIPS,Reginald Gurwen 2Lt kia 26-1-17 3EKent p58 MR19

PHILLIPS,Richard Glyndwr Lt dow 27-8-17 RGA p209 CR Belgium23

PHILLIPS,Richard Hill T2Lt kia 25-9-16 15RWar p65 CR France374

PHILLIPS,Stanley Cross Lt kia 15-9-16 4Y&L p238 CR France702

PHILLIPS,Sydney Capt kia 25-10-15 12RFus p69 MR19

PHILLIPS,Sydney Vernon T2Lt kia 14-8-16 10 att7Leic B'Coy p88 CR France1182

PHILLIPS,T.Capt 19-8-18 Lancs &RAF CR Lancs76

PHILLIPS,Thomas.MC.DCM.Lt kia 29-8-18 6Lpool p215 CR France106

PHILLIPS,Thomas Frederick 2Lt kia 29-7-18 3HLI p163 CR France397

PHILLIPS,Thomas Glynn Llewellyn Capt kia 26-3-17 5WelshR p230 MR34

PHILLIPS,Thomas McCann.MID Capt dow 4-11-14 RAMC p197 CR Belgium150

PHILLIPS,Tom Vaughan Wynne BtCol ded 29-9-16 RHA p271

PHILLIPS,Walter Ernest.MC.2Lt dow 23-3-18 23Lond p252 CR France177,22-8-18

PHILLIPS,Walter Henry Sherburn 2Lt kia 16-9-16 4EYorks p219 CR France387

PHILLIPS,William Charles Owen Capt kia 24-8-14 RWKent p141 CR Belgium201,23-8-14

PHILLIPS,William David 2Lt dow 28-9-18 15RWar p65 CR France512

PHILLIPS,William Ernest 2Lt dow 29-9-18 RGA 283SB p41 CR France1461

PHILLIPS,William James 2Lt kia 25-7-16 4SfthH p241 MR21

PHILLPOTTS,Brian Surtees.DSO.MajALtCol dow 4-9-17 RE Cmdg38Div p47 CR Belgium16

PHILLPOTTS,Fitzroy Charles TLt dow 9-8-18 7Glouc p107 MR4

PHILLPOTTS,Louis Murray.CMG.DSO.TBrigGen kia 8-9-16 RA Staff56Div p34 CR France394,Murr 24Div HQ

PHILP,Claude Hastings George Capt kia 28-3-18 RAMC att1/7Manch p197 CR France560,26-3-18

PHILP,Edgar Charles 2Lt ded 1-12-18 HAC Res CR Mddx76

PHILP,Richard William Manning Haigh TCapt kia 5-10-16 RFA 91Bde p34 CR France513

PHILPS,Andrew Christie T2Lt kia 17-7-16 6KOSB p102

PHILPOT,Godfrey Capt kia 1-9-16 RGA 25SB p41 CR France329

PHILPOT,John T2Lt kia 25-2-16 RE 253Co p47 CR France423

PHILPOTT,John Reginald.MC.TCapt ded PoW 15-1-18 63RFC p16 CR Iraq8

PHILSON,Samuel Cowell Col ded 4-11-18 RAMC p197 MR66

PHIPPARD,Dudley West T2Lt kia 4-10-17 1Hamps p121 CR Belgium83

PHIPPEN,Henry George Lt dow 9-11-16 4Glouc p225 CR France515

PHIPPS,Arthur Coryn 2Lt kia 13-4-18 9ACycCps p244 MR32

PHIPPS,Charles Percy Lt kia 19-7-16 O&BLI 2/1BucksBn C'Coy p231 MR19

PHIPPS,Christopher Leckonby Lt kia 14-8-17 RGA 118SB 7BallCo attRFC p12&41 CR Belgium19

PHIPPS,Constantine James.DSO.MC.MIDx3 LtAMaj ded 19-2-19 1Lpool att2DivSigCo RE p72&257 CR Germany1

PHIPPS,Lionel Lush TLt dow 28-9-15 7Nhampt p138 CR France178

PHIPPS,Robert Pickering 2LtACapt kia 13/15-11-16 4 att2SStaffs A'Coy p123 CR France1890

PHORSON,Douglas Stuart 2LtACapt kia 16-12-16 18DLI p161 CR France342

PHRIPP,Arthur Thornton T2Lt kia 19-10-17 WRid p116 CR Dorset67

PIBEL,Leo Maxse T2Lt drd 15-4-17 RASC p193 MR35

PIBWORTH,Frederick James Lt ded 20-12-19 IA TC att2/98Inf p281 MR43

PICK,Alfred James Lt kld 2-12-18 3DLI &RAF p161 CR Numb26

PICKARD,Donald Johnson T2Lt kia 17-7-16 6Leic p88 CR France432

PICKARD,Eugene Cuthbert Llewellyn Capt ded 24-11-18 RE 643FC p256 CR Sussex124

PICKARD,F.F.EngCmdr drd 30-12-15 RIM p281 MR64

PICKARD,Harry Lawson.MC.2Lt kia 20-10-18 1/2 att9RWelshF p98 CR France270

PICKARD,Lawrence Delapons 2Lt kia 10-8-17 5RWSurr p212 MR29

PICKARD,Reginald Gilbert 2Lt dow 2-3-17 1/7WelshR attYLI p230 CR France339

PICKARD,Rubie Mrs 13-4-16 BRCS CR France64

PICKARD-CAMBRIDGE,Herbert Evelyn Winn Lt kia 1-11-17 16Suss p205 CR Palestine1

PICKEN,Ronald Baynton Lt 6-9-18 RAF MR37

PICKER,Herbert Francis.MC.Lt ded 23-5-17 RE SigCo p47&210 CR France102

PICKERING,Albert Edwin.MC.2Lt kia 28-9-18 B165RFA p34 CR France285

PICKERING,Basil Horace 2LtTLt dow 1-12-15 8EKent p58 CR Germany1

PICKERING,Charles Leigh Lt kia 15-4-17 6Ches attRFC p19&222 CR Iraq8

PICKERING,Cyril Aubrey Lt kia 30-8-18 1RB p180 MR16

PICKERING,Edmund Charles 2Lt kia 15-9-16 6Lond p247 MR21

PICKERING,Francis Alexander Umfreville.DSO.MajTLtCol kia 23-12-17 2Drags att9RB p21 CR Belgium101

PICKERING,Frank Wells 2Lt dow 20-9-17 RGA 287SB p41 CR Belgium46

PICKERING,Freeman 2Lt dow 10-10-17 4Manch p155 CR France285,kia

PICKERING,George Anthony Raymond T2Lt kia 2-11-17 2 att1/4Nhampt p138 CR Palestine8,3-11-17

PICKERING,Harold Crosby 2Lt kia 7-7-15 NStaffs SR attLancF p157 MR29

PICKERING,Henry Earlam T2Lt ded 9-3-18 SLancs att1/5Bn p125 CR France765

PICKERING,Leonard Lt kia 9-4-18 RE 79FC p210 CR France490

PICKERING,Robert Hackney Lt kia 30-11-17 RFA N'A/ABty p34 CR France379

PICKERING,Thomas T2Lt ded 1-11-15 7Glouc p107 CR Egypt3

PICKERING,William Carrington Lt kia 11-10-18 6 att1RB p180 CR France270

PICKERING,William James 2Lt dow 7-6-17 RFA 113ArmyBde p34 CR France285

PICKERING-CLARKE,John Norman T2Lt kia 14-7-16 10 att7Leic p88 MR21

PICKERSGILL,John Henry.MC.Lt kia 28-8-18 10 att1/6Ches p96 CR France139,dedacc

PICKERSGILL-CUNLIFFE,John Cunliffe Capt kia 4-6-15 6 att1Worc p109 MR32

PICKERSGILL-CUNLIFFE,John Reynolds 2Lt kia 14-9-14 2GrenGds p50 CR France1112

PICKETT,Frederick Charles 2Lt ded 6-1-15 RScots p54 CR Mddx77

PICKETT,Gerald Molyneux 2Lt kia 9-9-16 3RIrF p171

PICKFORD,Herbert Thomas Reade 2Lt kia 25-4-17 O&BLI p130 MR37

PICKFORD,Howard Arthur T2Lt kia 14-7-16 21Manch p155 MR21

PICKIN,William Thomas TLt kia 25-9-15 2Leic p88 MR19

PICKLES,Clifford Crawshaw Capt 22-12-16 RAMC NumbFA CR Yorks361

PICKLES,Frederick Arthur.MC.Capt dow 5-9-18 12Manch p155

PICKLES,Harry 2Lt kia 14-4-17 4BordR att1/16Lond p228 MR20

PICKLES,Harry Thornton T2Lt kia 26-4-16 11 att9WRid p116 CR France922

PICKOP,James Taylor Greer 2Lt dow 21-6-17 4RFus p69 CR Lond8

PICKOP,William Bannister Augustus Lt dow 24-10-18 4RFus p69 CR France292,1Bn

PICKRELL,Leslie John 2Lt kia 29-3-18 RFA 29Bde MR20

PICKSTONE,Charles 2Lt kia 3-9-17 GL &1RFC p12 MR20

PICKSTONE,Dick T2Lt kia 12-10-16 14 att17Manch p155 MR21

PICKTHALL,Henry Clement Vaughan Capt ded 8-12-18 RGA 320SB p41 CR Greece1

PICKTHALL,William Roy 2Lt kia 16-9-18 A26RFA 26ArmyBde p34 CR France309

PICKUP,Alfred James T2Lt kia 26-9-15 2Yorks p91 MR19

PICKUP,George.MC.ACapt kld 20-8-18 6RLancs p59 CR Iraq1

PICKUP,William 2Lt kia 25-3-18 1ELancs p111 MR20

PICKUP,William Heys T2Lt kld 12-3-18 RFC p17&21 CR Lancs189

PICKWORTH,Arthur William 2Lt kia 28-9-18 16Lond p250 CR Belgium89

PICOT,Philip Simons Capt kia 11-7-15 14N&D p134 CR Gallipoli6

PICSTONE,Charles 2Lt kia 3-9-17 GL &1RFC p12

PICTON,F.J.L.MM.Lt ded 6-2-18 3 att1N&D p134 CR Mddx9

PICTON,James Allanson.MC.TLt kia 23-7-17 9ESurr p113 CR Belgium29

PICTON-WARLOW,Wilfrid Capt kia 20-12-14 WelshR attRFC p2&127,ded MR20

PIDCOCK,Frank Lt ded 17-2-19 RFA 296Bde p34 CR France146

PIDDUCK,Norman Andrews.MID T2Lt kia 1-7-16 102MGC p185 MR21

PIDSLEY,Hayward Gould 2Lt dow 21-5-17 RB ACoy p180

PIERCE,John Basil Lt 2-10-18 53RAF MR20

PIERCE,John Beresford Hudson T2Lt dow 27-4-17 RFA p34 CR France113

PIERCE,Robert Campbell TLtCol kia 1-7-16 1RInnisF p105 CR France339

PIERCE,Ronald Hugh MacGregor T2Lt kia 14-9-16 13 att9WYorks p82 MR21

PIERCE,Sidney Ernest.MC.2Lt dow 26-12-15 1/4YLI p235 CR France40,PEIRCE Sydney see PEIRCE,S.E.

PIERCY,George Bowmaker Lt 28-8-21 4RScots CR Scot561

PIERCY,Wilfred Ashton Lt kld 26-9-15 1/17Lond p250 MR19

PIERREPOINT,James H.TLt drd 4-5-17 RA p34 CR Italy14

PIERSON,Charles Frederick Leonard Capt kia 2-11-14 RGA 114HB p41 CR France260

PIERSON,Christopher Frank Kershaw T2Lt kia 10-10-17 GL &52RFC p12 CR France1361

PIERSON,Leslie Dilworth.MID Lt kia 30-10-16 10EYorks p84 MR21

PIERSON,Roy TLt kia 30-4-15 2Ess p132 CR Belgium20

PIERSON,William Henry Maxwell.MC.LtACapt kia21-11-17 3 att2SWBord p100 CR France911

PIERSSENE,Frederick Andrew Lt dow 6-9-18 4RSuss att26RFus p228 CR France142

PIGE-LESCHALLAS,Gilbert TCapt kia 15-8-15 7RDubF p177 MR4

PIGEON,John Walter Capt kia 3-9-20 IA IMS p281 MR38

PIGG,Bernard William 2Lt kia 3-7-16 6Worc p109 MR21,10Bn

PIGGIN,Frederick Loverseed Lt kia 20-12-16 RhodNatR CR Tanzania1

PIGGIN,Frederick William.MC.Capt drd 27-5-18 NottsYeo p205 MR41

PIGGOT,Arthur Alfred Lt kia 26-9-15 13NumbF C'Coy p255 MR19

PIGGOTT,Deighton Torre.MC.Lt kia 15-10-18 3 att8RWKent p141 CR France270

PIGGOTT,Frederick 2Lt kia 28-9-18 Y&L p159 CR France262

PIGGOTT,Frederick Cecil Holman TCapt ded 26-6-17 RAMC p197 CR Devon239

PIGGOTT,Gerald Wellesley 2Lt dow 14-5-15 127/29RFA p34 CR France284

PIGGOTT,G.F.Lt 23-3-18 5Ches MR27

PIGGOTT,William 2LtACapt kia 24-3-18 2Nhampt p138 MR27

PIGHILLS,John Arthur 2Lt dow PoW 29-5-18 WYorks att11LancF p82 CR France1331

PIGOTT,Christopher Devonshire 2Lt 26-8-16 1Wilts att8LNLancs MR21

PIGOTT,Eric John Keefe Pemberton Lt kia 24-6-15 1RIrReg p69 CR France1140

PIGOT,Ernest Borkman.MC.Lt dow 25-5-20 RGA p262 MR43,PIGOTT

PIGOT-MOODIE,Charles Alfred 2Lt kia 14-1-15 RB p180 CR Belgium17,13-1-15

PIGOTT,Christopher Devonshire T2Lt kia 26-8-16 1Wilts att8LNLancs p153 MR21

PIGOTT,Lancelot Boltry TLt kia 6-8-15 13 att2Hamps p121 MR4,Botry

PIKE,Cecil Francis Browne LtCol 15-3-20 RE Cornwall40

PIKE,Geoffrey Davies.MC.TCol acckld 15-8-18 IA 1/9GurkhaRif p281 CR Asia81

PIKE,Henry George 2Lt 30-8-18 65RAF MR20

PIKE,Richard Nicholson Capt kia 8-9-15 PolitcialOff att1NigR p201 CR WAfrica58

PIKE,Robert Maxwell.MID TCapt kia 9-8-15 RFC p2 MR20

PIKE,William.DSO.Capt kia 21-8-15 1RInnisF p105 MR4

PIKE,William Edward T2Lt kia 31-1-17 RE 77FC p47 CR France785

PIKE-STEPHENSON,Daniel Pike 2Lt dow 24-5-15 4NStaffs att1Ches p157 CR France102

PILCHER,Alfred Mark 2Lt dow PoW 6-6-18 15Lond p249 CR France1142

PILCHER,G.Maj 11-11-19 LNLancs CR Surrey160

PILCHER,Gerald Aubrey 2Lt dow 26-10-17 D159RFA p34 CR Belgium16,Lt

PILCHER,Thomas Percy Lt kia 10-3-15 2RB p180 CR France709,12-3-15

PILE,Cyril John 2Lt dow 29-4-17 RFA att12RFC p12&34 CR France531

PILGRIM,Harold Stephen 2Lt 17-2-19 6DCLI CR Leic55

PILGRIM,Henry Bastick 2Lt kia 1-7-16 13Lond p249 CR France1327

PILGRIM,Hugh Thomas.MC.Capt kia 25-8-18 9RFus p69 CR France578

PILGRIM,Stephen Argent Ffennell Lt dow 24-9-18 13TankCps p188 CR France327,2Lt

PILKINGTON,Hugh Brocklehurst.MID Capt kia 4-6-15 6Manch C'Coy p236 MR4

PILKINGTON,John Oscar TLt kia 6-9-17 20RFC p12 CR France285

PILKINGTON,Joseph Bernard Lt kia 20-4-18 1Nhampt p138 CR France260

PILKINGTON,Sam Capt kia 2-7-17 4Leic p219 CR France924

PILLEAU,Arthur Langston Maj kia 10-8-15 10Hamps p121 MR4

PILLEAU,Henry Charles.DSO.LtCol dow 21-9-14 RWSurr p56 CR France462

PILLINER,Rupert Colerick Leybourne 2Lt kia 4-11-14 127/29RFA p34 CR France297

PILLING,Doris Ellen Prob ded 29-3-19 QAIMNS CR Lond7

PILLING,Edgar 2Lt kia 23-4-17 460/15RFA 15Bde p34 CR France581

PILLING,J.E. 2Lt ded 1-7-18 5Lpool &25RAF p215 CR Belgium384

PILLING,Percy Cunliffe Capt dow 6-8-16 1/5LNLancs p234 CR France141

PILLING,Walter T2Lt kld 3-4-17 GL &RFC 5Res p12 CR Lancs211

PILLING,William.MC.2Lt ded 22-10-18 3 att2RWFus p98 CR France146

PILLMAN,Robert Lawrence TCapt dow 9-7-16 10RWKent p141 CR Belgium33

PILLOW,Henry Montgomery Scott T2Lt kia 8-8-17 7RFC p12

PILTER,Charles Lt dow 30-5-15 18Huss p23 CR France285

PIM,Thomas Lt kld 28-8-18 RFA &13RAF p34 MR20

PIMM,Charles William T2Lt kia 18-5-17 12Y&L p159 CR France644

PIMM,Victor Lionel 2Lt kia 10-11-16 2WYorks p82 MR21

PINCH,William 2Lt kia 31-7-17 1/5RLancs p213 CR Belgium10

PINCHES,Edward Harold 2Lt dow 16-11-17 3 att1LNLancs p136 CR Belgium16,Lt

PINCHIN,George Harold Lt dow 27-11-17 1/5Beds p219 CR Egypt1,2Lt

PINCHING,Minden Charles Cardigan.DSO.Maj ded 20-4-17 2DragGds p21 CR Surrey103

PINCKNEY,John William Lt kia 9-4-18 1KEdwHorse p24 CR France644,11-4-18

PINCOMBE,Lionel John T2Lt kia 20-9-17 32RFus p69 MR43

PINDER,Albert Humphrey.MID Lt kia 14-9-16 3 att1Leic p88 CR France374,15-9-16

PINDER,Reginald Maw Capt kia 7-10-17 5WRid p227 MR30

PINDER,S.R.Lt 19-2-18 GL &RFC CR Frnce924

PINE,Albert Arthur Lt kia 16-1-17 4Worc p109 CR Iraq5

PINE,Frank Youatt T2Lt kia 16-8-17 176MGC p185 CR Belgium12,15-8-17

PINE,Leslie William Tattersall 2Lt dow 18-8-17 2Hamps p121 CR Belgium16,Lt

PINE-COFFIN,John Edward.DSO.Maj ded 22-8-19 LNLancs 9264 CR Devon40

PINE-COFFIN,Tritram James Lt mbk 23-9-19 3Dev NR p256 MR70 &CR Europe180

PINFIELD,Guy Vickery TLt kld 24-4-16 8Huss p22 CR Ireland14,2Lt

PINFORD,William Herbert 2Lt ded 9-10-18 IARO attEmbnStaff p281 MR65,PINFOLD

PING,Alan Roy 2Lt kia 21-7-17 3Worc p109 MR29

PINHEY,Hammett Eardley 2Lt kia 19-4-15 3 att2DCLI p114 CR Belgium165

PINHEY,Kenneth Fleetwood Gordon Lt kia 2-8-17 RFA 83Bde p34 CR Belgium19

PINK,Alan Lins Lt kld 30-10-18 1/4RB &41RAF p180 CR Belgium441,Luis

PINK,Harold William 2Lt dow 7-10-16 RE 1/7FC p210 CR Greece4

PINKERTON,Eric Mitchell T2Lt kia 1-7-16 15RScots p54 MR21

PINN,Tyrrell Steventon T2Lt dow 12-10-15 8EYorks p84

PINNEGAR,John Arthur.MC.Capt kia 22-3-18 16RB p180 MR27,23-3-18

PINNEY,John Charles William Adderley.MID Lt kia 1-12-17 1RFus att30Horse C'Sqdn p69 CR France446

PINNIGER,Reginald Charles Lt ded 20-1-20 IARO att26Punjabis CR Devon72

PINNIGER,Wilfred James 2Lt kia 4-10-17 D91RFA 91Bde p34 CR Belgium86

PINNINGTON,Victor 2Lt kia 5-11-16 33 att23NumbF p62 MR32

PINNOCK,Carey T2Lt kld 30-11-17 RFC p12 CR Lincs136

PINSENT,Laurance Alfred.MID TLt dow 15-8-15 7NStaffs p157 CR Gallipoli19

PINSENT,Philip Ryland T2Lt dow 24-9-16 34RFC p3 CR France882

PINSENT,Richard Parker T2Lt kia 9-10-15 10RWar p65 CR France727

PINSON,Ivan Lapworth T2Lt dow 4-5-17 GL &70RFC p12 CR France1031

PIPER,Albert Benjamin Charles Lt ded 4-12-20 IA 120Inf p281 MR43,6-12-20

PIPER,Lawrence T2LtTLt kia 10-6-17 3Worc p109 CR Belgium43

PIPER,Reginald C.MID Capt&Adjt kia 29-4-18 1/6 att1/5SStaffs p229 CR France572

PIPER,Ronald Brandon 2Lt dow PoW 3-4-16 6RWar p214 CR France518

PIPER,Ronald Leslie.MC.MID Lt dow 11-10-17 IA 57Rif att129Baluchis p281 CR EAfrica11 &CR Tanzania1,Capt

PIPPET,John Gilbert.MM.2Lt kia 29-5-18 1Lincs p75 CR France1332

PIRDER,Sidney Rueben 2Lt mbk 19-2-18 80RFC p256

PIRIE,Alexander 2Lt dow 13-12-14 GordH p167 CR France284

PIRIE,Arthur Murray.DSO.ALtCol kia 21-11-17 21Lancers attBerksYeo p23 CR Palestine3

PIRIE,George Lawrence 2Lt ded 16-6-15 NhamptYeo p204 CR Surrey91

PIRIE,George Stephen LtTCapt kia 24-7-17 RAMC att9ESurr p197 CR Belgium29

PIRIE,William Shewan.DCM.Capt kia 19-4-17 5RScotF attMGC p187&222 MR34

PIRRET,James Kay 2Lt kia 4-4-17 11KRRC p151 CR France662

PIRRIE,Robert Bourn Lt kia 9-8-15 3BordR att1KSLI p117 MR29,10-8-15

PITCAIRN,Ellis Gledhill Capt ded 6-10-18 8BlkW p129 CR Belgium38

PITCAIRN,Hugh Francis T2Lt ded 3-6-17 RASC 47Div SplyColmnMechTrans p193 CR France95

PITCHFORD,Arthur Reginald 2Lt kia 17-9-18 att7KSLI p145 MR16

PITE,Horace Victor Walter 2Lt kia 10-4-18 3 att5Hamps p121 CR Palestine9

PITHER,Harold Francis 2Lt kia PoW 6-7-16 9 att5RDubF p177 CR France745,dow

PITHER,Sidney Edward Capt dow 11-6-18 1/2KOSB &RAF p102 CR Egypt15,dedacc

PITMAN,Arthur Frederick Edward Capt kia 3-1-18 5Sfth attRFC p19&241 MR20

PITMAN,Thomas Stuart TLt kia 28-9-17 6Y&L p159 MR30

PITOT,Maurice Leon 2Lt dow 8-10-18 RE &103RAF p47 CR France512,A.L.A.M.

PITT,Bernard T2Lt kia 30-4-16 10BordR attX47TMB p117 MR20

PITT,Bevan William 2Lt kia 10-5-17 55RFC p12 CR Belgium288

PITT,Douglas 2Lt kia 31-7-17 8ScotRif p225 CR Belgium7

PITT,Douglas 2Lt kia 24-3-18 8RWar p215 CR France1203

PITT,Geoffery Stanhope TCapt ded 11-2-19 26RFus p69 CR Lond12

PITT,George Llewllyn T2Lt kld 28-12-15 10Y&L &8RFC p2&159 CR France1205

PITT,James Maxwell Lt kld 13-10-14 1Dors p124 CR France260

PITT,J.H.Capt 16-4-17 SAfrSerCps MR46

PITT,John T2Lt kld 7-2-18 46RFC p17 CR Ches98,Jack

PITT,Robert Frederick Cadet 24-2-19 IndMiscList MR43

PITT,Stanley Lt kia 26-10-17 4RFA p208 MR30

PITT,Stanley Robert.MC.T2Lt kia 23-10-16 RFA 2Bde p34 CR France374

PITT,Vio Douglas Wallace 2Lt dow 24-8-16 8RBerks p139 CR France44

PITT,W.A.Maj 13-6-20 3RFus CR Lond12

PITT,William Neville TMaj dow 20-8-16 2Lincs p75 CR France98

PITT-PITTS,Edward Crewdson Pitt 2Lt kld 17-10-18 4EKent p212 CR France849

PITT-PITTS,Walter John Lt ded 9-8-18 GL &RAF p191

PITTAR,Charles Austin.MC.Lt 28-8-21 CldGds CR Oxford74

PITTIS,Charles Seymour.MC.Capt kia 19-4-17 8Hamps p229 CR Palestine8

PITTMAN,Cecil Frederick Lt kld 20-7-17 14RFC p12 CR Surrey2

PITTMAN,Frederick John 2Lt ded 20-8-18 RGA att14MtnBty p41 CR Iraq8

PITTMAN,Percy SubCdr ded PoW 28-2-17 IA MilWorksServ p281 CR Iraq8

PITTOCK,Herbert Frank Lt ded 27-8-19 MGC p266 CR Sussex107

PITTOCK,Percy Whittle Lt kia 27-9-18 7Lpool p215 CR France686

PITTOM,Wenn William Pratt 2Lt ded 10-10-14 4Nhampt p256 CR Nhampt27

PITTS,Francis Burton 2Lt dow 17-5-17 3 att8Leic p88 CR France924,Lt

PITTS-TUCKER,Cecil Mortimer Lt kia 21-12-14 HLI p163 MR22

PITTY,Thomas John 2Lt kia 25-3-18 10Mddx p236 MR20

PIXLEY,John Nicol Fergusson LtACapt kia 12-10-17 4GrenGds p50 CR Belgium106

PIXLEY,Reginald George Hewett.MC.Capt mbk 4-6-17 RFA &54RFC p257 CR France234

PIZA,Daniel ACapt kia 9-4-17 GL att64TMB p191 MR20

PIZEY,Noel Martin Lt dow 27-7-17 NDevYeo att75RFC p19&203 CR Belgium16

PLACE,Frank Clarke.MC.MM.2Lt kia 22-9-18 1/4RLancs p59&258 CR France109

PLACE,Philip Whiteley 2Lt kia 9-8-18 NumbF att12Norf p62 CR France19,19-8-18

PLAISTER,Geoffrey Ratcliffe TCapt kia 11-4-17 RAMC att10Y&L p197 MR20

PLAISTOWE,Alan ACapt kia 24-4-17 8Worc p226 CR France1495

PLAISTOWE,Richard Reeves Lt kia 19-4-17 1/5Norf p216 CR Palestine8

PLANT,Frederic George T2Lt kia 25-9-15 RWSurr p56 MR19

PLANT,George Bede Hornby.MC.Lt kia 18-9-18 NorfYeo p204 CR France369

PLANT,Herbert T2Lt dow 20-12-16 15 att14RWar p65 CR France80

PLANT,Herbert Stanley 2Lt ded 18-2-18 RE 181TC 52InfBde p47 CR France214,Lt

PLANT,Holford Charles Fourdrinier 2Lt kia 3-5-17 3NStaffs att9Leic p157 MR20

PLANT,Hubert Arthur 2Lt kia 24-5-17 6NStaffs p238 MR20

PLANT,John Blayney Llewellyn 2Lt ded 8-8-19 RASC p267 CR Germany1,RDubF att17RFus

PLANT,Percy William 2Lt kia 28-9-15 8RWKent p141 MR19

PLANT,Robert Sydney 2Lt kia 17-10-18 5N&D p233 CR France847

PLANT,Verner Lovelace Lt kia 5-4-18 8SomLI p80 MR20

PLANT,Wilfrid 2Lt kia 28-9-18 5NStaffs p238 CR France375,Wilfred

PLANTE,Arthur Gedge Lt kia 26-3-18 5ESurr att4NStaffs p226 MR27

PLASKITT,Sydney Vernon 2Lt kia 5-11-16 5 att9DLI p239 MR21

PLATER,Richard Henry Lt dow 3-5-17 9RB p180 MR20

PLATNAUER,Leonard Maurice 2Lt dow 3-5-17 16WYorks p82 MR20

PLATT,Charles Henry Morris 2LtTLt kia 23-11-17 RWar att52RFC p12&65 CR France1361

PLATT,Claud Lucien Francis 2Lt kia 27-5-18 RH&FA 25DAC p34 MR18

PLATT,Frank Lindsay Capt kia 21-3-18 3 att1KSLI p145 CR France646

PLATT,Henry Evelyn Arthur.MID Capt kia 15-5-16 19Huss att1CldGds p23 CR Belgium6

PLATT,John Rookhurst Lt dow 27-3-16 RFA 3Bde p208 CR Belgium127

PLATT,Lionel Sydney Capt kia 13-4-17 17Lancers att57RFC p12&23 CR France604

PLATTEN,Walter Henry T2Lt kia 10-9-16 14SWBord att19RWFus p100 CR France423

PLATTS,Arthur Leslie Capt kia 20-7-16 2Suff p78 MR21

PLATTS,Edgar Lovell Filmer Lt 28-4-17 RMLI MR20

PLATTS,John Carrick Capt kia 7-3-20 IA 17Cav att10Lancers p281 CR Iraq8

PLATTS,Reginald Hardy Lt ded 31-5-18 RGA p271

PLAYER,Alfred Edward Lt ded 10-7-19 LabCps attChineseLabCps p266 CR France65

PLAYER,Eric Noel TCapt kia 6-8-16 8Yorks p91 CR France515

PLAYER,Gilbert T2Lt dow 30-7-16 21DLI p161 CR France345

PLAYFAIR,A.L.MajGen 10-9-15 BengalStaffCps CR Sussex178

PLAYFAIR,Frank Capt kia 16-7-15 RScots p54

PLAYFAIR,Lambert Lt kia 6-7-15 1RScots att1RFC p2 CR Belgium9

PLAYFAIR,Lyon George Henry Lyon.Hon.Capt kia 20-4-15 RFA 69Bty31Bde p34 MR29

PLAYFAIR,Patrick Lyon Capt dow 11-4-18 7BlkW B Coy p231 MR19

PLAYFORD,Antony Boydell 2Lt kia 28-9-15 1SWBord p100 MR19

PLAYFORD,Patrick Randal Lt kia 1-7-17 A/1RFA p208 CR Belgium10

PLAYNE,Leslie Lt 27-3-18 16RFC MR20

PLEASANCE,Charles Joseph T2Lt kia 31-7-17 24NumbF p62 CR France725

PLEDGER,Earnest Charles 2Lt kia 10-10-17 16LancF p93 MR19

PLENTY,Edward Pellew Lt AMaj ded 21-11-18 1Manch &96RAF p265 CR Berks72,22-11-18

PLESTED,Horace George 2Lt kia 30-7-16 4 att16Manch p155 MR21

PLEWMAN,Charles Edward.MC.Lt kia 9-4-18 7Lpool p215 CR France261

PLEYDELL-BOUVERIE,Jacob Edward Lt ded 1-11-14 2KRRC p151 CR France102

PLEYDELL-BOUVERIE,Samuel Wilfred 2Lt kia 15-9-16 19Lond p250 CR France390

PLIMPTON,Robert Albert.MC&Bar.ACapt kia 27-9-17 A&SH att4BlkW p173 MR30,4/5Bn

PLOWDEN,Francis Charles Lt dow 22-8-18 ShropYeo att10KSLI C'Coy p205 CR France31

PLOWDEN,Godfrey Bruce A.Capt ded 2-2-17 1/7RWelshF p223 CR Egypt2

PLOWDEN,W.F.C.LtCol 28-12-18 CR Mddx77

PLOWES,Errol Sydney 2Lt kia 9-4-18 379/169RFA p209 CR France360,Sidney

PLOWMAN,Charles Hugh Lt kia 24-4-17 7Wilts 153 MR37

PLOWMAN,James.MC.TLtACapt dow 29-4-18 2Leinst p174 CR France24

PLUM,Robert Bagshaw 2Lt dow 2-10-17 RFA p209 CR Belgium183

PLUMB,Edward Stephen TLt dow 8-9-17 3WRid p116 CR France113

PLUMER,William Lt kld 7-2-15 YLI p143 CR Belgium98

PLUMMER,Arthur Henry 2Lt kia 17-5-15 5Lpool p215 MR22

PLUMMER,Charles Benjamin Chap4Cl kia 12-3-17 RAChDept att61InfBde p199 CR France513

PLUMMER,Frederick Charles T2Lt kia 23-9-17 215MGC p185 CR Belgium10

PLUMMER,Frederick Ryle Lt ded 2-11-18 RGA p209 CR France332

PLUMMER,John Humphrey 2Lt ded 10-8-18 3 att2GordH p167 CR Italy11

PLUMMER,John Scott 2Lt kia 17-8-17 Leic att1/5Bn p88 MR19

PLUMMER,Lionel Davey Capt kia 15-9-16 4NumbF p213 CR France239

PLUMMER,Sidney Arthur 2Lt kia 24-4-18 9Lond p248 CR France880

PLUMMER,William Francis 2Lt kia 15-9-16 18Lond p250 CR France390

PLUMPTON,Robert 2Lt ded 25-12-18 6Yorks p91 MR70

PLUMPTRE,Basil Pemberton.MC.Rev kia 16-7-17 RAChDept att1/21Lond p199 CR Belgium21

PLUNKET,Cedric John Lt kia 5-8-17 RFA 123Bde p34 CR Belgium62,6-8-17

PLUNKETT,Havelock Arthur Terence Lt kia 7-1-16 2BlkW p129 MR38

PLUNKETT,Patrick Lt&QM ded 7-9-16 RAMC p267

PLUNKETT,Reginald Frederick Desmond Lt Accdrd 6-9-18 IA 2/1GurkhaRif att 1/5 p281 MR38

POCHIN,Arthur Campbell T2Lt kia 26-9-16 10Ess p132 MR21

POCKETT,Walter Harold 2Lt kia 24-4-18 410/96RFA 96Bde p34 CR France300

POCKLINGTON-SENHOUSE,Oscar William 2Lt 18-6-15 2CldGds CR France114

POCOCK,Beril Edmund 2Lt kia 13-5-17 5Lond p246 MR29

POCOCK,Charles Arthur T2Lt kia 8-5-17 14RWar p65 CR France777

POCOCK,Charles Clarke 2Lt kld 14-3-16 1ESurr p113 CR France184

POCOCK,Malcolm Robertson.DSO.LtCol kia 5-11-17 IA 28Punjabis p281 MR38

POCOCK,Raglan Lionel Alfred T2Lt kia 25-8-17 8ELancs p111 CR Belgium17

POCOCK,Thomas Guy 2Lt dow 3-4-15 4Lpool p72

PODMORE,Edward Glanville 2Lt kia 25-9-15 9Lpool p216 MR21

PODMORE,Hubert.DSO.MIDx3 TMaj kld 31-12-17 6Nhampt att12Mddx p138 CR Belgium38,LtCol

POE,Charles Vernon Leslie Capt kia 3-3-15 4KRRC p151 MR29,2-3-15 Charley

POER,Hubert Piers Beresford CaptAMaj kia 24-4-18 RH&FA 91Bde p34

POGOSE,Ivor Reginald 2Lt kia 1-7-16 5Lond p246 CR France203,dow

POGUE,Reginald Thomas.MC.T2Lt dow 28-9-18 4TankCps p188 CR France194

POHL,Frederick Alfred Lt ded 22-10-18 A161RFA p34 CR Essex146,43RFA

POHLMANN,Reginald Peel 2Lt kia 5-2-18 25RFC p17 CR Belgium140

POINTER,Arthur James T2Lt kia 22-3-18 12Mddx att6Nhampt p148 MR27

POINTER,Henry John Lt ded 13-12-17 RH&FA 130Bde p34

POINTER,Reginald James 2Lt kia 21-3-18 3 att4ELancs p111 MR27

POLACK,Benjamin James T2Lt kia 9-4-16 9Worc p109 MR38

POLACK,Ernest Emanuel Lt kia 17-7-16 4Glouc p225 CR France293

POLAND,Guy Bernard 2Lt kia 21-3-18 24Lond p252 CR France439

POLAND,Henry Arthur 2Lt kia 18-4-15 C Coy 3 att1RWKent p141 MR29

POLE-CAREW,Wymond Nicholas Richard Lt kia 6-11-17 1DCLI p114 MR30

POLEHAMPTON,Frederick William 2Lt kld 26-4-15 8RFC p2 CR France134

POLGE,William Edwin 2Lt kia 16-8-17 7Lond p247 MR29

POLLAK,Harry Leopold TLt kia 23-10-16 17 att2RB p180 MR21

POLLAK,Otto Dennis Lt kia 8-7-16 17RFus p69 MR19

POLLARD,Alfred Gordon 2Lt kia 16-5-17 9A&SH p244 CR France604

POLLARD,Arthur 2Lt kia 21-3-18 2/6N&D C'Coy p233 MR20

POLLARD,Edward Branch TLt dow 26-7-15 KOSB attRE p102 CR Scot612

POLLARD,Ernest Madel T2Lt dow 16-8-17 KRRC att12Bn p151 CR Belgium23

POLLARD,Frank T2Lt dow 21/22-3-18 att2/4ELancs p111 MR27

POLLARD,Geoffrey Blemell.MID Lt kld 24-10-14 RFA 119Btyp34 CR France705

POLLARD,George Edward West 2Lt dow 3-9-18 5YLI p235 CR France103

POLLARD,George Herbert 2Lt dow 7-6-17 PoW 9A&SH attRFC p19&244 CR Belgium140

POLLARD,Gerald Evelyn Gustavus Capt kia 25-4-15 1RMunstF p176 MR4

POLLARD,Harold Ernest T2Lt dow 4-8-16 1KOSB p102 CR Egypt2

POLLARD,Herbert Edward TLt kia 26-6-17 RE 134ArmyTpsCo p47 CR Belgium1

POLLARD,Roger Thompson TLt kia 13-10-15 5RBerks p139 MR19

POLLARD,Stanley Madel T2Lt dow 12-4-18 RHA attAyrBty p34 CR Palestine3

POLLARD,Thomas Regester 2Lt ded 2-7-18 5 att2Lincs p220 CR France40

POLLARD,Thomas Whittaker TLt kia 16-5-17 10LancF p93 MR20

POLLARD,Wilfrid Downes T2Lt dow 26-4-18 15N&D p134 CR Yorks551

POLLARD,William Marcus Noel 2Lt kia 11-4-17 5NStaffs p238 CR France366

POLLARD-URQUHART,William Edward,MID Lt kia 18-4-15 1RSuss p119 MR43

POLLEY,Frank Clarence Capt ded 16-4-19 SL RE IWT p255&257 CR Asia81

POLLIN,Robert Kelly 2Lt kia 31-7-17 4RIrRif p170 MR29

POLLOCK,Charles Thomas Anderton Capt kia 31-3-18 Inns of Court OTC att1/1EYorks p252 CR France900,Anderton dow

POLLOCK,D.MM.TLtACapt kia 18-9-18 1CamH p168 CR France835

POLLOCK,Daniel TCapt drd 15-4-17 RAVC p199 MR35

POLLOCK,Douglas William Capt kia 6-5-15 4Worc Z'Coy p109 MR4

POLLOCK,Frederick Robert Lt kia 22-10-14 ColdGds p51 CR Belgium63

POLLOCK,George Henry 2Lt dow 18-6-15 4SStaffs att1RWar p123 CR Belgium9

POLLOCK,John Lt kia 1-7-16 13RIrRif p170 MR21

POLLOCK,John Dunbar Capt kia 28-6-15 4RScots p211 CR Gallipoli6

POLLOCK,Louis T2Lt kia 17-10-18 2DLI p161 CR France849

POLLOCK,Martin Viner Lt kia 9-5-15 3 att1SWBord p100 CR France924

POLLOCK,Max Kenneth TLtCapt kia 25-9-15 1RScotF A'Coy p95 MR29

POLLOCK,Sidney Geoffrey Lt ded 19-11-18 Glouc p264

POLLOCK-HODSALL,George Bertram Capt kld 9-11-14 3Suff p78 MR29,HODSOLL

POLSON,Geoffrey William 2Lt kia 14/15-9-14 1BlkW D'Coy p129 CR France1341,Lt

POMEROY,Granville George TCapt ded 30-3-17 GL 12Yorks attNigR p202 CR WAfrica54

POMEROY,Norman Ransch 2Lt kia 20-10-16 GL &RFC p3&191

POMFRET,Christopher 2Lt kia 27-3-18 1/4 att2/5ELancs p226 MR27

POMFRET,John William.MC.T2Lt kia 27-10-18 11NumbF p62 CR Italy9

POMFREY,James Arthur T2Lt dow 4-10-18 9Yorks p91 CR France364

POND,Frederick George 2Lt kia 5-9-18 RGA 144SB p41 CR France568

PONSFORD,Glyn George T2Lt kia 28-8-16 10RB p180 CR France400

PONSONBY,Ashley William Neville Capt kia 8-9-15 2 O&BLI p130 CR France279,M

PONSONBY,Cyril Myles Brabazon.Hon.MVO.Maj kia 27-9-15 3 att4GrenGds p50 MR19,28-9-15

PONSONBY,Cyril Thomas Lt kia 23-8-16 11KRRC p151 CR France397,24-8-16

PONSONBY,Gerald Maurice.MID Capt dow 31-8-14 2RInnisF p105 CR France1355

PONSONBY,Michael Henry Lt dow 27-8-18 2GrenGds p50 CR France927

PONSONBY,Spencer Lawrence TLt dow 12-1-16 12Mddx p148

PONSONBY,W.R.DSO.Capt 18-1-19 3DragGds CR Hereford129

PONTER,Harry William Francis Lt kia 3-9-18 4RWSurr p212 CR France646

PONTER,William Crossland Lt ded 27-11-18 23RB p244 MR66

PONTIFEX,Dudley Allen Capt kia 31-7-17 2ScotRif p104 MR29

PONTING,Cecil Arthur Lt 26-11-17 10SAfrHorse MR52

PONTING,Edward Frank T2Lt kia 5-10-18 21Manch p155 CR France234

POOL,James Williamson 2Lt kia 20-9-17 6ScotRif p224 MR30

POOL,Samuel.MC.TCapt kia 16-6-17 RAMC att8Leic p197 CR France1489

POOLE,Arthur George TLt ded 22-11-18 Glouc p264 CR Somerset71,28-11-18

POOLE,Bernard Goldsmith T2Lt kia 22-3-18 53RFC p17

POOLE,Edward Masters Rev ded 31-10-18 YMCA CR France13

POOLE,Eric Skeffington 2Lt dow 10-12-16 11Yorks CR Belgium5

POOLE,Esmond Randolph Lascombe Lt kia 25-5-19 IA 32Lancers p281 CR Iraq8

POOLE,Hugh Edward Algernon.MID 2Lt dow 2-6-15 11Huss p22 CR Berks84

POOLE,John Evered T2Lt dow 22-8-17 RE 33FC p47 CR Belgium11,73FC

POOLE,John Richard T2Lt kia 30-7-16 14RWar p65 MR21

POOLE,L.S.R.Lt ded 3-12-18 GL &RAF p191

POOLE,Richard William.MBE.Capt&QM 21-4-19 6ScotRif CR Scot764

POOLE,Robert Evelyn Sandford Lt kia 4-11-18 6 att13KRRC p151 CR France1480

POOLE,William Evelyn Stanley Lt kia 19-9-17 5NumbF p213 CR France538

POOLE,William John Rowland Ernest Lt kia 9-10-17 4Y&L p238 MR30

POOLEY,Charles.MC.LtTCapt kia 9-8-18 5DragGds p21 CR France652

POOLEY,Richard Sibthorpe T2Lt kia 23-4-17 8RScotF att1BordR p95 MR20

POOLEY,Robin Mark 2Lt kia 12-8-16 9Lpool p256 MR21

POORE,Roger TLt kia 19-9-15 A48RFA p34 CR Belgium20

POORE,Roger Alvin.DSO.Maj kia 26-9-17 WiltsYeo p206 CR Belgium126

POPE,Charles Alfred Whiting TCapt drd 4-5-17 RAMC p197 CR Italy14

POPE,Cicely Mary Legh Sister 25-6-21 VAD BRCS CR Europe57

POPE,Cyril Montague Lt dow 24-10-14 5 att2Worc p109 CR Belgium57 Montagu

POPE,Edward Alexander.DSO.LtCol ded 9-4-19 3WelshR p264 CR Dorset42

POPE,Edwin Albert T2Lt kia 27-2-17 GL &8RFC p12 CR France120

POPE,Ernest William TCapt kia 18-8-16 7RB p180 MR21

POPE,Harold Edward.MC&Bar.TLtACapt kia 24-8-18 21RGA 118HB Xfer to1/2LancsHB p41 CR France526

POPE,Henry William Capt kia 24-3-18 7DragGds att21MGC p21&185 CR France207

POPE,Herbert Arnold Lt kia 16-8-15 9Mddx p236 MR4

POPE,Howard John 2Lt 4-3-19 Glouc CR Glouc9

POPE,J.R.Capt 2-3-22 League of Nations Staff CR Europe150A

POPE,John Herbert 2Lt dow 11-4-17 1RIrF p171 CR France451

POPE,Percy Paris 2Lt kia 1-10-15 WelshR p127 MR19,1/2-10-15

POPE,Philip Gladstone Lt kia 16-10-17 RFA 35BdeHQ p34 CR Belgium19,31Bde

POPE,Reginald Thomas Buckingham Lt kia 16-2-15 1WelshR p127 CR Belgium166

POPE,William Archer TCapt dow 7-10-16 10RWSurr p56 CR France833

POPHAM,Edward Home TCapt kia 6-8-15 13 att2Hamps p121 MR4

POPHAM,John Francis Watson TCapt dow 3-10-16 8Leic p88

POPPLE,George Marsden T2Lt dow 26-6-16 15 att16NumbF p62 CR France702

POPPLESTONE,Archibald Harry 2Lt kia 6-12-17 7N&D p233 MR19

POPPLEWELL,Harry Bury Capt kia 22-7-18 3RIrRif att2/3KAR p170&268 CR EAfrica90

PORKESS,Walter Anderson Lt kia 10-2-17 NottsYeo att10RFC p19&205 CR France98

PORRITT,Edward Radcliffe T2Lt kia 30-7-16 17Lpool p72 CR France1890

PORRITT,John Ernest T2Lt kia 27-5-18 NumbF att5Bn p62 MR18

249

PORRITT,Thomas Handly.MC.2Lt dow 31-7-17 2ColdGds p51 CR Belgium16,Handley

PORRITT,William Murray 2Lt kia 25-9-15 3SLancs attNLancs p125 MR19

PORT,William Garfield 2Lt kia 4-10-17 1Dev p77 MR30

PORTAL,Oldric Spencer LtTCapt kia 3-5-17 1LifeGds attHousehdBn p20 CR France97

PORTEOUS,Dick MacDonald.DSO.Capt kia 10-5-15 1A&SH p173 MR29

PORTEOUS,Douglas Simpson T2Lt kia 20-10-16 6KOSB A'Coy p102 CR France432

PORTEOUS,Gilbert 2Lt kia 22-11-17 5ScotRif p224 CR Palestine3

PORTEOUS,Harry Morton T2Lt kia 25-9-15 12HLI p163 CR France219

PORTEOUS,James Hunter Capt kia 22-8-17 6A&SH p243 CR Belgium84

PORTEOUS,Thomas Williamson T2Lt kia 23-8-18 12TankCps p188 CR France502

PORTER,Alan Grey.MC.LtACapt dow 29-10-18 1 att6RIrF p171 CR France34

PORTER,Alex James 2Lt mbk 19-4-17 1Norf p256 MR34,Alec

PORTER,Alwyne Morton Francis Worsley Lt kia 25-4-15 1LancF p93 CR Gallipoli1

PORTER,Aubrey Blackwood Lt kia 3-10-15 4 att2HLI p163 CR France423

PORTER,Edgar George T2Lt kia 20-9-18 10EKent p58 MR16,18-9-18

PORTER,Edgar Wardle 2Lt dow 22-8-16 7Lpool D'Coy p215 CR France66

PORTER,Eric Henry TLt kia 17-2-16 8SStaffs p123 CR Belgium120,14-2-16

PORTER,Ernest James Lt dow 22-9-16 PoW 22Lond p251 CR France598

PORTER,Frederick Ernest Gilchrist TCapt dow 3-11-16 7LNLancs p136 CR France44

PORTER,Gavin Alexander LtTCapt ded 6-12-15 RFA 68Bty att13RFC p2&34 CR France518,5-12-15

PORTER,George Anthony Gordon T2Lt kld 9-3-18 RFC p17 CR Lincs100

PORTER,George Francis Lambert 2LtTCapt kia 8-6-17 11WYorks A'Coy p82 CR Belgium127

PORTER,Graham Hawksworth TLt kia 3-10-16 20RWFus p98 CR Belgium73,2-10-16

PORTER,Harold James TLt dow 15-8-15 5Manch p236 CR Egypt3,2Lt

PORTER,Hugh Gordon 2Lt kia 6-11-16 RGA 155HB p41 MR21

PORTER,John Charlton T2Lt kia 24-7-16 MGC F'HB p185 CR Belgium16

PORTER,John Edward T2Lt kia 23-7-16 7SLancs p125 MR21

PORTER,John Joseph Capt ded 3-8-18 RAMC p271 CR Norf209,kldacc

PORTER,John Thomas T2Lt kia 25-8-18 9 att2/4YLI p143 CR France568

PORTER,John William T2Lt ded 11-7-18 13TankCps p188 CR France300

PORTER,Leslie Capt ded 24-10-16 RFC p3 MR20

PORTER,Reginald Edward Lt kia 26-10-14 RAMC att3RB p197 MR32

PORTER,Robert 2LtACapt kia 25-11-17 1ScotRif p104 CR Belgium125

PORTER,Robert Ernest T2Lt dow 10-8-17 11RFus p69 CR Belgium19

PORTER,Robert Nuttall Lt ded 28-1-19 RAMC p267 CR Wales597,25-1-19

PORTER,Robert Wilson TLt kia 11-1-18 9 att4/5BlkW p129 MR30,Wilison

PORTER,Roderick Spicer Russell 2Lt kia 9-6-16 IARO att130Baluchis p281 CR EAfrica19

PORTER,Royden Spencer Bayspool 2Lt ded 6-2-17 2HAC Inf p206 CR France40

PORTER,Samuel TLt dow 7-8-15 11Y&L att8Manch p159 CR Gallipoli2,kia

PORTER,Stanley Fitzherbert 2Lt ded 6-6-17 GL &RFC p12 CR Lancs170

PORTER,W.2Lt ded 28-2-19 RH&FA attRAF p34

PORTER,William T2Lt kia 1-7-16 6 att1RInnisF p105 CR France339

PORTER,William Guthrie.DSO.Maj kia 8-6-17 C86RFA p206 CR Belgium15

PORTER,William James Lt dow 3-8-17 2Leinst p174 CR Belgium11

PORTER.Wilson 2Lt kia 24-3-18 RFA att56RFC p17&34 MR20

PORTERFIELD,Leonard Witherow TLt ded 1-11-18 167RFA p34&257 CR Mddx17

PORTLOCK,Alfred Edgar T2Lt kld 6-12-17 RFus &RFC p12&69

PORTWAY,Lionel Felix 2Lt kia 14-4-17 1Ess p132 CR France155

POSENER,Percy Julian T2Lt kia 8-7-16 8 att2Wilts p153 MR21

POSFORD,Benjamin Ashwell 2Lt dow 25-2-15 RASC p193 CR France102

POSNER,Philip Ernest 2Lt dow 27/28-4-17 3SStaffs att8Lincs p123 MR20,27-4-17

POSNETT,William Leonard 2Lt kia 22-6-17 1/13Lond p249 MR20

POSTLES,Charles Ernest 2Lt dow 21-8-18 KSLI att1Ches p145 MR16

POSTLETHWAITE,William T2Lt dow 14-3-18 15WelchR p127 CR France346

POSTLETHWAITE,Christopher Joyce TLt dow 9-1-18 12Suff p78 CR France518

POTTER,Charles Gordon Lt kia 15-9-16 8Hamps p229 MR21

POTTER,Donald Rolls Capt dow 21-12-17 2/4RWSurr p212 CR Palestine3

POTTER,Edward TLt ded 10-11-18 10RWar p65 CR France146

POTTER,Francis George 2Lt kia 24-4-17 7 att1/8Worc p226 MR21

POTTER,Francis John T2Lt kia 1-7-16 GL &RA att94TMB p191 MR21

POTTER,Fred.DCM.2Lt dow 22-9-17 7ELancs p111 CR Belgium183

POTTER,Frederick John 2Lt kia 21-5-16 8Lond p247 MR20

POTTER,Harold 2LtTLt kia 9-4-17 3 att7ESurr p113 CR France182

POTTER,Henry William Ross Maj mbk 20-12-14 IA 129Baluchis p281 MR28

POTTER,John.DSO.MID T2Lt dow 24-7-16 1SStaffs p123 CR France51

POTTER,John 2Lt kia 24-3-18 1/8 att1Worc p226 MR27

POTTER,Keith Erskine T2Lt dow 13-8-18 Hamps att1Bn p121 CR France10

POTTER,Kenneth Mitchell.DSO.Maj kia 8-7-17 52RFA p34 CR Belgium29

POTTER,Percy Walter 2Lt dow 21-5-17 5 att2Worc p109 CR France214

POTTER,Reginald 2Lt kia 9-5-15 1LNLancs p136 MR22

POTTER,Reginald Funge 2Lt dow 24-7-16 4NStaffs p157 CR France23

POTTER,Robert John T2Lt kia 16-8-17 9RDubF p177 MR30

POTTER,Robert William TLt kia 8-10-18 16RWar att1NumbF CR France338,16-10-18 12Bn

POTTER,Robert.MC.T2Lt kia 14-10-18 BlkW att8Bn p129 CR Belgium88

POTTER,William Rochester T2Lt dow 24-4-17 149MGC Inf p185 CR France120

POTTER,William Robert McCall 2Lt kia 17-9-18 C70RFA p34 CR France179

POTTERTON,Henry 2Lt dow 13-12-17 6WYorks p218 CR France52

POTTERTON,William Hubert TLt kia 24-7-16 RE 23FC p47 CR France430

POTTINGER,Charles Evan Roderick Lt dow 11-5-15 RE p47

POTTINGER,Robert Ormond Brabazon Lt kia 9-5-15 att2RMunstF p176 MR22

POTTS,Arnold Leslie Leopold 2Lt kia 5-11-16 7 att1/9DLI p239 MR21

POTTS,Charles 2Lt dow 11-6-17 4 att11Ches p222 CR France285

POTTS,Ernest Alexander.MC.T2Lt dow 15-10-18 24 att10RFus p69 CR France146

POTTS,Geoffrey Fildes TLt kia 23-4-17 17Manch p155 CR France162

POTTS,Henry 2Lt dow 1-10-16 7Beds att1Ess p86 CR France102

POTTS,Henry Herbert T2Lt dow 31-7-17 RE 254TC p48 CR Belgium11

POTTS,Norman Rhead T2Lt kia 19-7-17 SStaffs att9Bn p123 CR Belgium29

POTTS,Richard Harold Urwin T2Lt dow 2-12-18 1/2WRid att16LancF p116 CR Frnce441

POTTS,Robert William T2Lt dow 24-3-18 25MGC p185 CR France177

POTTS,William Edgar.MM.2Lt kia 13-4-18 5WYorks p218 MR32

POTTS,William Janson.MC.Lt kia 21-9-17 RFA att59RFC p19&208 CR France705

POULLETT,William John Lydston.Earl Capt ded 11-7-18 RHA p256 CR Somerset67,RWar

POULTER,Henry Chapman TCapt dow 29-11-17 8RDubF p177 CR France616

POULTER,Hugh Douglas Michael 2Lt kia 15-7-16 RE 68FC p48 CR France1182

POULTER,John Charles Archibald 2Lt kia 24-2-17 4Hamps p228 MR38

POULTER,Wilfred Forman 2Lt ded 6-3-18 24RFC p17 CR France660

POULTNEY,John Bernard 2Lt kia 18-2-17 3 att8SLancs p125 MR32

POULTON,Frederick James TLt kia 2-11-17 9RWSurr att1/8Hamps p56 CR Palestine8

POULTON,Harry Edward 2Lt dow 26-10-17 3 att1SStaffs p123 MR30

POULTON,Roy Roswell Capt kia 8-8-18 8Lond p247 MR16

POUND,Cecil Davison TLt kia 22-9-18 117MGC Inf p185 CR France836

POUND,John Russell Capt dow 27-4-15 3 att2KSLI p145 MR29

POUND,Murray Stuart 2Lt dow 7-11-14 RWSurr p56 CR Lond14

POUNDALL,William Arthur Lloyd.MC.TLtTCapt kia 31-10-17 SLancs att53RFC p12&125 CR Belgium101

POUNDER,Benjamin William Lt kia 9-10-17 1/5WRid p227 CR Belgium101

POUNTNEY,Percival TLt kia 7-6-17 75MGC p185 MR29

POVAH,Frank Capt kia 16-6-15 RScots p54 MR29 See POYAH

POWELL,Alfred Trevanion 2Lt dow 22-7-16 4CamH p243 CR France15

POWELL,Allan Wentworth.DCM.T2Lt kia 21-8-16 8RWSurr p56 CR France394

POWELL,Brian Baden 2Lt ded 11-1-20 ULIA att1/69Punjabis p281 MR43,Lt

POWELL,Cecil Henry 2Lt kia 15-6-17 O&BLI &RFC p256 MR20

POWELL,Charles.MC.Capt dow 21-3-18 RE 409FC p210 CR Belgium20

POWELL,Charles Swan T2Lt kia 17-7-16 6Leic p88 MR21,14-7-16

POWELL,David Bernard Lt dow 4-9-17 12SWBord p223 CR France398,2Lt

POWELL,David Emrys TLt kia 28-3-18 2DivMGC p185 CR France4,Dafydd Ex 14RWFus

POWELL,Edward Darley.DSO.MC.Maj kia 1-9-18 RE 468FC p48 MR19

POWELL,Edward Ingram Capt kia 22-3-18 6RSuss p228 CR France364

POWELL,Edward Watson 2Lt kia 31-10-17 84RFC p12 MR20

POWELL,Eric Layton T2Lt kia 16-4-17 20RFus p69 MR20

POWELL,Eric Limbery TLt kia 6-4-18 B17H&FA p34 CR France300

POWELL,Ernest Arthur 2Lt dow 15-9-18 7Ches p223 CR France88

POWELL,Eyre Burton Lt ded 4-8-15 3Wilts p153 CR Dorset110

POWELL,Frederick Gill.MC.CaptBtMaj ded 15-4-17 Dors p264 CR Lond8,14-4-17

POWELL,Frederick William 2Lt dedacc 20-1-17 5 att10RDubF p177 CR France74

POWELL,George Alexander Lt kia 28-6-15 15KRRC att1RInnisF p151 MR4

POWELL,George Aubyn 2Lt ded 7-12-16 RFC p261 CR Herts38

POWELL,George Henry T2Lt kia 29-4-17 MGC p185 MR20

POWELL,Gerald Frederick Watson Maj kia 29-7-17 KentCycBn att8RWKent p253 CR Belgium29,28-7-17

POWELL.Harold Osborne 2Lt kia 31-10-14 4DragGds p21 MR29

POWELL,Harry Stranger.MC.Capt dow 5-10-17 1/6RWar C'Coy p214 CR Belgium16,Stanyer

POWELL,Henry Mitchell Capt kia 9-12-14 2SStaffs att1Dors p123 MR29

POWELL,James Henry T2Lt kia 24-11-15 10 att2SStaffs p123 MR19

POWELL,John Allen T2Lt kia 14-1-17 NStaffs att2Y&L p157 CR France423

POWELL,John Harold Slade Maj ded 8-2-15 RH&FA p34

POWELL,John Stewart TCapt kia 2-7-16 11Hamps p121 CR France223,dow 3-7-16

POWELL,Leonard Maurice 2Lt kia 17-6-15 3 att1GordH p167 MR29

POWELL,Lindsay Carlton T2Lt kia 31-5-16 7RSFus &23RFC p3&95 CR France46,Lt

POWELL,Maurice TLt kia 5-7-17 14RFA p34 CR France570

POWELL,Patrick John Gordon Lt kia 2-4-17 RASC attRFC p12&193 MR20

POWELL,Percival 2Lt kia 1-8-15 9 att3RB p180 CR Belgium92

POWELL,Phillip Keith T2Lt kia 7-6-17 8YLI p141 MR29

POWELL,Reginald Walter T2Lt kia 10-7-16 3Worc p109 MR21

POWELL,Rendel 2Lt kia 20-8-18 2YLI p143 CR France526

POWELL,Rhys Campbell Ffolliot 2Lt kia 13-9-14 2HLI p163 CR France1329,14-9-14

POWELL,Richard TLt dow 22-8-17 153RFA p34 CR France13

POWELL,Richard Henry 2Lt kia 9-5-15 5RSuss p228 MR22

POWELL,Richard Oversby TCapt&Ajt kia 16-7-16 36/33RFA p34 CR France1887

POWELL,Robert Keal TLt kia 4-10-16 11NStaffs att2SLancs p157 CR France832

POWELL,Roland Rice 2Lt dow 29-8-18 1SomLI p80 CR France14

POWELL,Scott TCapt dow 4/5-4-16 8RWFus p98 MR38

POWELL,Sidney Lewis TCapt kia 12-7-17 16LancF p93 CR Belgium174,Sydney

POWELL,Thomas.DCM.TCapt ded 1-7-18 8RIrReg p89 CR Ireland14 Ex O&BLI

POWELL,Thomas Clark 2Lt dow 15-7-17 RGA 12HB p41 CR Belgium11

POWELL,Thomas Henry Norman 2Lt kld 24-4-17 RFC p12

POWELL,Thomas William 2Lt kia 25-4-18 4Mddx p148 CR France514

POWELL,Thomas William.MC.TCapt ded 24-11-18 TankCps p188 CR Oxford85

POWELL,Townsend George Capt kia 9-5-15 3 att2Nhampt p138 MR32

POWELL,Victor Edmund TLtACapt kia 26-9-17 3 att7KSLI p145 MR30

POWELL,Wilfred Guy 2Lt kia 26-3-18 7SomLI att61TMB p80 MR27

POWELL,Wilfred Roderick LtACapt kia 9-4-18 4Dors p229 MR34

POWELL,William Arthur 2Lt kia 5-10-18 7 att11N&D p233 CR France234

POWELL,William Edward George Pryce Wynne 2Lt kia 6-11-18 1WelshGds p53 CR France1211,Lt

POWELL,William Uniacke Perry TLt ded 20-10-16 EYorks &RFC p3 CR Hereford/W54

POWELL-AKROYD,Frank Allnutt 2Lt kia 24-8-18 3YLI p143 CR France314,23-8-18

POWELL-JOHNSON,R.B.MC.Lt 19-9-18 RGA 109HB CR Belgium192

POWELL-JONES,Percival Morgan Capt kia 22-4-16 SWBord BrecknockBn p223 MR38

POWER,Charles 2Lt kia 25-9-15 2Leinst att2RWar p174 MR19

POWER,George Henry Fosbrooke Lt dow 9-5-15 6Mddx p148 MR29

POWER,Henry Richard Lt kia 22-8-17 3RIrRif att48RFC p12&170 CR France1361

POWER,Herbert Capt kld 12-3-15 Nhampt p138 MR22

POWER,John James T2Lt kia 19-9-18 7RWSurr p56 CR France1495

POWER,John Wethered Lt kia 10-9-16 WelshGds 4Coy p53 CR France394

POWER,Joseph Leo T2Lt kia 14-2-18 8 att9WRid p116 CR France1483

POWER,Lawrence Henry 2Lt kia 22-3-18 2TankCps p188 MR27,Laurence

POWER,Pierce Michael Joseph Lt dow 2-3-15 RAMC att1Wilts p197 CR Belgium17

POWER,Raphael Joseph 2Lt kia 19-7-17 IA 46 att33Punjabis p281 CR EAfrica38 &CR Tanzania1

POWER,R.E.Lt kia 17-4-18 SL att4/4KAR p202 CR EAfrica92,Capt

POWER,William Boyle 2Lt kld 17-7-16 RFC p3 CR Hamps1

POWER,William Goodlake Capt kia 16-10-16 RAOC p198 CR France44

POWER-CLUTTERBUCK,James Edward T2Lt kia 25-6-17 RFA att52RFC p12&34 CR France451

POWERS,Bernard Alexander Lt kia 25-9-17 Mddx att19RFC p12&148 MR20

POWERS,Herbert Grendon.MC.Capt&Adjt kia 19-9-18 6Hamps p229&281 IARO att1/1GurkhaRif CR Palestine9

POWLES-CURTIS,Arthur John TCapt dow 11-9-16 17KRRC p151 MR21

POWLESLAND,John Northley Julian 2Lt dow 20-9-16 6Lond p247 MR21

POWLEY,A.D.Lt kia 10-6-16 1KAR p268 CR EAfrica40,2Lt

POWLEY,Joseph T2Lt kia 3-5-17 2Ess p132 MR20

POWLEY,Walter Harry Chap4Cl ded 23-2-19 RAChDept p268 CR Lond10

POWNALL,Allen Claude Morrison 2Lt kia 27-3-18 B104RFA p34 CR France281

POWNALL,Edward T2Lt kia 9-10-17 LancF att8Bn p93 MR30

POWNALL,Hubert Joseph 2Lt kia 23-7-16 4 att10RWar p65 CR France432

POWNALL,John 2Lt kia 30-10-16 6 att2Worc p109 MR21

POWNALL,Lionel Henry Yorke Lt kia 21-3-15 RWKent p141 CR Belgium165

POWNEY,Arthur John T2Lt dow 15-9-17 GL att9RFC p12 CR Belgium16

POWNEY,Joseph Thomas Maj ded 18-12-14 RE p48 CR France85

POWRIE,William T2Lt kia 27-9-18 Y&L att2/4Bn p159 MR16

POWYS,Geoffrey Mappleton TLt kia 19-6-17 1GarBn att8NumbF p62 CR Belgium75,Mappleton

POYAH,Frank Capt kia 16-6-15 RScots p54 MR29 See POVAH

POYNDER,Leopold Eliot Capt bombExplosion 26-6-16 IA 1/6 att2/6GurkhaRif p281 CR Iraq6

POYNDER,Robert Hamilton Lt kia 24-3-18 4 att2SStaffs p123 MR20

POYNTER,Leslie John T2Lt dow 25-10-18 20Manch p155 CR France521

POYNTING,Arthur Lt kia 26-7-16 6RWar att143MGC p187&214 CR France150,27-5-16

POYNTON,Charles Edward Lt kia 30-7-16 26Manch p155 CR France402

POYNTON,John T2Lt kia 4-10-17 RWar attRes 1/6Bn GHQ p65 CR Belgium126

POYNTON,Reginald James Lt ded 29-9-15 RE 2/2SigCoypp210 CR Lond12,kldacc

POYNTZ,H.A.SenAssSurg 5-6-18 IMS MR43

POZZI,Leonard Lambert 2Lt 8-5-15 6AustInf MR4

PRACY,Henry Reginald T2Lt dow 5-9-16 1RWKent p141 CR France23,kia

PRAETORIUS,Alfred 2Lt kia 27-5-18 C155RFA p34 CR France924

PRAGNELL,Archie Ernest 2Lt drd 30-12-17 21Lond p251 CR Egypt1

PRAGNELL,George Frederick TCapt kia 23-7-17 GL 11RWKent Staff 123InfBde p191 CR Belgium15

PRAIN,Theodore.MID Lt kia 21-10-14 1Leic C'Coy p88 MR32

PRALL,Cedric Barkley LtCol 5-4-16 IMS MR65

PRANCE,Arthur Christopher Norman.MC.Lt kia 29-5-18 SWBord p100 MR18

PRANGLEY,Charles Dean 2Lt kia 25-9-16 Lincs p75 CR France374

PRANKHERD,Richard Percy Lt kia 10-11-18 WarYeo attMGC p187&205 CR France937,PRANKERD

PRATKEY,Joseph Edward 2Lt kia 3-5-17 8Leic p88 MR20

PRATT,Alexander Stewart T2Lt kia 24-3-17 12 att10ScotRif p104 MR20

PRATT,Arthur Rev ded 29-6-17 RAChDept att6SStaffs p229&268

PRATT,Arthur 2Lt dow 11-2-18 5Beds p219 CR France1063,7Bn

PRATT,Arthur T2Lt dow 2-7-18 2Beds att6Nhampt p86 CR France516

PRATT,Arthur Victor.MID T2Lt kia 21-3-18 9ESurr p113 MR27

PRATT,Audley Charles.DSO.CaptTLtCol dow 16-8-17 11RInnisF p105 CR Belgium84

PRATT,Aylwin Murray 2Lt kia 21-8-17 186RFA p34 CR Belgium27

PRATT,Christopher T2Lt kia 18-10-16 8CamH p168 MR21

PRATT,Ernest Charles 2Lt kia 14-5-17 2/4RFus p246 MR20

PRATT,Ernest St.George.CB.DSO.BrigGen ded 24-11-18 DLI InspInf Staff p1 CR Lond4

PRATT,Ernest Victor 2Lt kia 25-9-17 C277RFA p34 CR France285

PRATT,Francis Norton Capt kia 18-9-18 2Y&L p159 CR France835

PRATT,Geoffry Cowper Spencer Lt dow 27-11-15 RH&FA 14A/ASect p34 CR France285,Geoffrey

PRATT,George Leslie 2Lt kia 16-5-15 3RWSurr p56 CR France279

PRATT,James Arthur CaptHonMaj ded 25-6-15 SL RecOff p268 CR Eire113

PRATT,John Curdie Lt dow 23-3-18 5 att14HLI p240 MR20

PRATT,John Armstrong.MC.Lt kia 23-8-18 3Lpool p72

PRATT,John Selby.MID TLt kia 11-4-17 10Yorks p91 France162

PRATT,Lionel Henry 2Lt kia 25-9-15 18Lond p250 CR France149

PRATT,Mervyn Dalles Capt ded 13-4-20 IA 121Pnrs p281 MR43

PRATT,Neville Herbert TCapt dow 8-7-16 10N&D B'Coy p134 CR France207

PRATT,Ralph Lewis Capt kia 18-10-16 2/4Glouc p225 CR France705

PRATT,William George James T2Lt kia 28-9-17 23RFus p69 CR France163

PRATT,William John Armstrong.MC.Capt kia 23-8-18 3 att1Lpool p72 CR France927

PRATTE,Arthur Williams Staples TLt kia 6-8-16 10Lincs p75 CR France390

PREBBLE,Cyril Edgar.MC.T2Lt dow 8-8-18 12Mddx att2/2Lond p148 CR France69

PREBBLE,John 2Lt kia 21-6-17 49/40RFA p209 CR France1182

PREDDY,Edward Fred Spencer LtACapt kia 8-12-17 RGA 36SB p41 CR France379

PREECE,Ellis 2Lt kia 2-10-18 1HLI &RAF p265

PREECE,Henry Raymond Lt kia 8-10-18 6 att4KRRC p151 CR France845

PREECE,P.J.LtCol 29-10-21 8Lond CR Wales497

PREECE,William Henry SubCdr ded 5-11-19 IOD p281

PREEDY,Alban TCapt kia 1-7-16 3Dev p77 MR21,2Bn

PREEDY,John Benjamin Knowlton Lt kia 26-10-17 2Lond p245 MR30

PREEDY,Lawrence Jack 2Lt kia 31-3-18 4 att1RWar p65 MR20

PREESTON,Philip Southwell 2Lt kia 28-3-18 1RFA p34 CR France582

PRENDERGAST,Charles Randolph Lt kia 21-1-16 IA 84 att28Punjabis p281 MR38,28 att84

PRENDERGAST,James Francis T2Lt kia 27-7-16 6RMunstF p176 CR France115,1Bn

PRENDERGAST,Matthew Vincent Chap4Cl ded 16-9-18 RAChDept p199 CR Egypt9

PRENDIVILLE,Lawrence Anthony 2Lt kia 31-7-17 7Lpool p215 MR29

PRENTER,Dalton T2Lt kia 21-3-18 9RIrF p171 MR27

PRENTICE,Alexander Reid.MC.TCapt kia 9-11-17 12 att10ScotRif p104 CR France1182

PRENTICE,James T2Lt kld 4-11-17 RFC p12 CR Scot503

PRENTICE,John Ridley 2Lt kia 18-6-15 3Suff p79 MR29

PRENTICE,John Robert 2Lt dow 17-4-18 4A&SH p173 CR France134

PRENTICE,Oliver 2Lt kia 27-3-18 1Lond att2/7LancF p245 MR27

PRENTICE,Thomas Alfred Maj kia 10-8-15 1/4Ches p222 MR4

PRENTICE,Walter Lowry 2Lt dow 3-8-17 4ConnRgs att2Leinst p172 CR Belgium11

PRENTIS,Horace Taylor 2Lt kia 27-4-18 17Manch A'Coy p155 MR30

PRESCOTT,Alec Frank Evelyn TLt kia 8-10-16 124MGC p185 MR21,Alex

PRESCOTT,Ernest Twiss 2Lt dow 26-2-18 34RH&FA p34

PRESCOTT,Lewis William 2Lt 22-4-18 23RAF

PRESCOTT,Reginald Julius 2Lt kia 15-4-17 18LancF p93 MR21

PRESCOTT,Robert Stewart T2Lt kia 1-7-16 10ELancs p111 CR France221

PRESS,George William LtACapt kia 26-10-17 1RWKent p141 MR30

PRESSLY,John Seymour 2Lt kia 15-11-15 1/5YLI p235 CR Belgium23

PREST,William Charles Seagar 2Lt kia 17-8-16 5WYorks p218 CR France702

PRESTIDGE,John Vernon FitzGerald Lt dow 2-5-17 1 att11Suff p79 CR France95

PRESTON,Arthur John Dillon.MID Capt kia 15-8-15 6RDubF p177 CR Gallipoli4

PRESTON,Alfred James T2Lt dow 21-9-18 8RBerks p139 CR France194

PRESTON,George Allen LtCol Acckld 6-5-19 IA 2/6GurkhaRif p281 CR Asia81

PRESTON,Herbert Stanley T2Lt dow 8-9-16 1BlkW p129 CR France66

PRESTON,Herbert William Lawson Lt ded 19-8-17 RFA M'A/ABty p34 CR France145

PRESTON,James Henry T2Lt ded 11-1-19 LabCps attLpool p266 CR Lancs313

PRESTON,John Abe Stanley Lt dow 6-10-16 11Glouc p107 CR Greece7,Alec

PRESTON,Leslie George.MC&Bar.TCapt dow 10-7-18 8RWKent att6Dors p141 CR France61

PRESTON,Philip Chamberlayne.DCM.TCapt kia 13-10-15 7Norf p74 MR19

PRESTON,Richard Amyas.MC.CaptALtCol dow 7-6-18 RAMC att58FA p197 CR France1415

PRESTON,Rudolph Arthur.MC.Lt kia 15-9-16 RFC p3 CR France1465

PRESTON,Sidney TLt kia 10-4-18 1Ess att98TrResBn p132 CR France745

PRESTON,Stanley CaptAMaj kia 25-9-17 1Mddx p148 MR30,12Bn

PRESTON,Thomas Frederick Lt kia 24-1-17 NorfYeo attRFC p19&204 CR Belgium152

PRESTON,Thomas Harry 2Lt dow 30-9-18 6NStaffs p238 CR Belgium11,4Bn

PRESTON,Thomas Haworth Capt kia 17-11-14 3ELancs p111 CR Belgium68,1Bn

PRESTON,Wilfrid 2Lt dow 4-7-16 7WRid p228 CR France296

PRESTON,William Carter 2Lt kia 10-4-18 8BordR p117 MR32

PRESTWICH,Joseph Lt dow 7-2-16 RASC DivTrn attRFC p19&253 CR Belgium5

PRETOR-PINNEY,Charles Frederick.DSO.TLtCol dow 28-4-17 13RB p180 CR France95

PRETSELL,William Gardiner.MC.T2Lt kia 20-7-18 YLI att5Bn p143 CR France1689

PRETTY,Donald 2LtTLt dow 11-5-15 4Suff p217 CR France80

PRETTY,Harold.MC.CaptAMaj kia 24-3-18 4Suff att10DCLI p217 MR20

PRETTYMAN,Frank Remington Lt kia 4-7-17 2ScotGds p52 CR Belgium12,PRETYMAN

PRETYMAN,Maurice William 2Lt kia 12-8-15 RE 10SigCo p48 MR4,10-8-15

PREVEL,James Alexander Emanuel.MC.TLt kia 29-9-18 2Nhampt p138 CR France212

PRIAULX,George Kendall.DSO.MajTLtCol kia 24-3-18 11KRRC p151 MR27

PRICE,Arthur T2Lt kia 13-11-16 7KSLI p145 CR France742

PRICE,Charles 2Lt dow 18-7-17 1/4SLancs p230 CR Belgium16

PRICE,Charles Lempriere.DSO.Capt kia 16-9-14 2RScots p54 CR France1107

PRICE,Charles Leslie 2Lt dow 15-3-18 1RIrReg p89 CR Egypt2

PRICE,Charles Thomas 2Lt kia 30-11-17 7HLI p240 CR Palestine9,5Bn Ex9HLI

PRICE,David Eleazer 2Lt kia 8-9-16 2WelshR p127 MR21

PRICE,David Leonard T2Lt kia 27-3-18 5 att3/7KSLI p145 CR France174

PRICE,Eric William Manning 2Lt dow 1-7-16 1Hamps p121 CR France5

PRICE,Ernest Dickenson Lt dow 19-3-16 3RIrReg att2RIrRif p89 CR France924,Dickinson kia

PRICE,F.J.Lt ded 29-11-18 RGA p262 CR C'land&W'land44

PRICE,Francis Maurice 2Lt dow 4-6-17 5Lincs p220 CR France214

PRICE,George Bernard Locking 2Lt dow 23-8-17 3 att8GordH p167 MR30

PRICE,Gordon William Bassett TLt kia 23-11-17 12SWBord p100 MR17

PRICE,Graham T2Lt kia 9-3-16 GL &6RFC p3&191 CR Belgium11

PRICE,Harold.MC.TCapt kia 26-6-16 26NumbF p62 CR France430

PRICE,Harold Strachan T2Lt kia 24-5-15 3RFus p69 MR29

PRICE,Henry Bertram Lt kia 3-5-15 5Lond p246 MR29

PRICE,Henry Wall 2Lt kia 4-7-16 4 att2Manch p155 CR France251

PRICE,Henry Wall Maj ded 19-6-19 4Manch p155 CR Ches53

PRICE,Herbert Allen.MC.T2Lt dow 30-11-17 3SomLI attMGC Cav p80&185 CR Palestine9

PRICE,Hugh 2Lt kia 11-10-18 3WYorks att1/7WRid p82 CR France270

PRICE,J.F.N.Maj 13-8-18 Beds att2NigR CR WAfrica35

PRICE,James Thirkell.MC.MIDx2 Capt kia 21-4-16 C77RFA p34 CR France423

PRICE,John Esmond T2Lt kia 1-7-16 14Manch p155 MR21

PRICE,John Thomas T2Lt kia 20-7-16 20RFus p69 MR21

PRICE,John Turner 2Lt kia 27-5-18 1/5RLancs p213 MR19

PRICE,Joseph William James 2Lt dow 22-4-17 3 att26NumbF p62 CR France40

PRICE,L.Capt 21-11-20 GL CR Hamps 220

PRICE,Leonard John Joliffe T2Lt dow 15-8-16 2KOSB p102 CR France51,Jolliffe

PRICE,Leonard Charles 2Lt kia 25-4-18 4 att16LancF p93 MR30,Lawrence Lt 4 att19Bn

PRICE,Montague Leonard 2Lt kia 26-6-16 1/7Mddx p235 CR France1327

PRICE,Owen Douglas Capt&QM ded 10-12-18 RAMC p267 CR Scot239,12-12-18

PRICE,Paul Adrian Edward 2Lt kia 23-4-17 RGA O'A/A Bty p41 CR France756

PRICE,Reginald 2Lt kia 1-7-16 1/6RWar p214 MR21

PRICE,Robert St.John Locke Capt kia 25-9-15 IA 33Punjabis p281 MR28

PRICE,Samuel Allen T2Lt ded 11-7-17 GL RE IWT p191 CR Iraq6

PRICE,Sidney James 2Lt kia 15-9-16 9Suff p79 MR21,Sydney

PRICE,Stanley Hastings.MC.T2Lt kia 24-1-18 15N&D p134 CR Belgium83

PRICE,Thomas John Lt 27-5-18 RAF MR34

PRICE,Thomas Joseph.MC.2Lt dow 25-4-18 1/10Lpool p216 CR France88

PRICE,V.M.Capt 15-12-19 3Ess CR Essex123

PRICE,Victor William TLt kld 7-11-17 11Worc attRFC p12&109,1Bn CR Hereford154

PRICE,W.H.Lt&QM 16-10-18 IndDefForce MR 66

PRICE,Walter Edgar Lt ded 31-5-19 3 att9RSuss p119&257 CR Germany1

PRICE,Wilfred T2Lt dow 3-5-17 8EYorks p84 CR France1182

PRICE,William Eric 2Lt kia 2-5-15 5RSuss p228 CR France249

PRICE,William Henry 2Lt kia 23-8-17 42MGC Inf p185 CR Belgium125

PRICE,William Henry TCapt kia 24-3-18 10Mddx p148 MR20 19Bn

PRICE-EDWARDS,Owen Capt kia 22-6-16 18RFus p69 MR21

PRICHARD,Arthur Douglas T2Lt dow 8-10-17 34MGC p185 CR Belgium16

PRICHARD,Edgar Albert CaptHonMaj ded 29-2-16 4Glouc p271 CR Glouc10

PRICHARD,Francis Hesketh Capt ded 1-2-20 RGA p262 CR Asia81

PRICHARD,Frederic Giles Lt dow 9-8-15 2EYorks p84 CR Essex267

PRICHARD,John Walter 2Lt kia 18-9-18 4RWFus p223 CR France365,Lt

PRICHARD,Richard Gerald Mannsell Maj dow 7-6-18 GlamYeo att38CentIndHorse p203 CR Palestine3,Mauncell

PRICHARD,Rowland George Lt kia 24-4-15 1Suff p79 MR29

PRICHARD,Thomas James.MC.TCapt kia 28-3-18 1RLancs p59 CR France452

PRICHARD,Thomas Lewis Capt dow 9-11-14 2RWFus CR France102

PRICKARD,Gerald Thornton 2Lt kia 4-6-15 3SWBord att1RDubF p100 MR4

PRICKETT,Lancelot Capt kld 2-6-16 RGA &RFC p3&41 CR Sussex93 Ex 71HB RGA

PRIDE,A.R.T2Lt kia 3-5-17 8RFus p69 MR20

PRIDE,Harry.MC.Capt kia 23-4-17 10Mddx p236 CR France581

PRIDEAUX,Edwin Ravenhill 2Lt 17-5-18 203RAF MR20

PRIDEAUX,Geoffrey Arthur.MC.TCapt kia 19-1-17 SomLI p80 CR France624

PRIDEAUX-BRUNE,Edmund Nicholas 2Lt kia 22-5-18 3RB p180 CR France81

PRIDHAM,George Frederick TLtCol ded 16-12-16 1 att1/5WelshR p127 CR Egypt8

PRIDHAM,William Albert Stanley TLt drd 5-1-16 12NumbF p62 CR France102

PRIDMORE,George Harry T2Lt kia 31-8-18 21WYorks att1Ess p82 CR France531

PRIDMORE,Percy Malin.MC.Capt kia 21-9-17 2/6RWar p214 CR Belgium10,2-9-17

PRIDMORE,Reginald George.MC.Maj kia 13-3-18 RH&FA p206

PRIEST,Benjamin.MC.2Lt dow 26-4-18 72/38RFA p34 CR Belgium38

PRIEST,F.T2Lt ded 22-5-18 O&BLI att3Bn p130 p264 CR Berks119

PRIEST,Robert Edgar Priest Lt kld 15-8-17 276RFA p208 CR Belgium41,Paul

252

PRIEST,Roy Simpson Capt kia 19-4-17 7/103 NZ Bn ImpCamelCps MR34

PRIEST,Walter Samuel Lt&QM ded 25-9-17 RASC p267 CR Hamps8

PRIESTLEY,Archibald Bertram Capt dow 12-9-14 Dors p124 CR France1429

PRIESTLEY,Charles Henry Ryland TLt ded 19-6-18 RGA 120HB p41 CR War23,Harry dow

PRIESTLEY,Charles Homans 2Lt kia 4-9-16 6/12RB p180 CR France294

PRIESTLEY,Charles Lacey 2LtACapt dow 11-11-17 1Glouc p107 CR Belgium22

PRIESTLEY,Douglas Bernard T2Lt kia 31-7-17 2/5LancF p93 MR29

PRIESTLEY,Dyker Stanton 2Lt kia 1-7-16 108MGC p185 MR21

PRIESTLEY,Frederick.MC.Lt kia 27-5-18 1 att5Wilts p153 MR37

PRIESTLEY,Frederick Nicoladies Maj ded 2-9-18 RFA p271 CR Yorks42

PRIESTLEY,Percival Thomas CaptAMaj ded 28-9-18 RAMC att25CCS p197 CR Greece7

PRIESTLEY,Stanley Noel Lt kia 23-7-16 8Glouc p107 MR21

PRIESTLEY-EVANS,Mansfield Capt kia 10-7-20 IARO att231Brahmans attPoliticalDept p281 CR Iraq8

PRIESTLY,Albert Edward 2Lt kia 3-5-17 4WRid p227 MR20

PRIESTLY,Ernest Neville 2Lt 8-5-15 10Jats MR65

PRIESTMAN,Edmund Yerbury T2Lt kia 19-11-15 6Y&L p159 CR Gallipoli27

PRIESTMAN,George Aloysius(Louie) TLt dow 15-5-18 19NumbF p62 CR France84,2Lt

PRIESTMAN,Kenneth Mallorie T2Lt kia 31-8-16 RE 105FC p48 CR France246

PRIESTNALL,William Eustace 2Lt kia 27-5-18 NumbF att5Bn p62 CR France1753

PRIME,Arnold 2Lt kia 21-3-18 4 att2/8Manch p155 MR27

PRIMEAU,Cecil Willibrod 2Lt kia 27-10-17 GL &70RFC p12 MR20

PRIMROSE,Neil James Archibald.Hon.MC.Capt kia 15-11-17 1/1BucksYeo p203 CR Palestine9

PRIMROSE,Nigel.MC.TLt ded 25-10-18 64RFA p34 CR France34,Capt

PRIMROSE-WELLS,James Bowen Lt dow PoW 4-4-18 4Beds p86 CR France246

PRINCE,Alfred George Maj 8-2-19 7Lond CR Surrey160

PRINCE,Alick Lancelot Capt kia 8-11-14 1LNLancs p136 MR29

PRINCE,Arthur Alec 2Lt kia 4-10-18 19Lond p250 CR France567

PRINCE,Claude Melnotle T2Lt kia 18-8-16 9RSuss p119 MR21,Melnotte

PRINCE,Frederick George 2Lt kld 18-5-19 2Lond &RAF p245

PRINCE,Frederick Harold T2Lt kia 9-4-17 8EYorks A'Coy p84 CR France581

PRINCE,George Reginald Dudley Lt ded 24-11-18 RE p210 CR Greece9

PRINCE,John Cecil Butter 2Lt kia 27-9-18 9 att16Lond p248 CR France429,Butler

PRINCE,Julius Sefton Lt kia 25-9-15 7Lond p247 MR19

PRINCE,Norman Charlesworth Capt kia 18-4-17 6WRid p227 CR France614

PRINCE,Victor Charles.MC.2Lt kia 1-9-18 4Lond p246 MR16

PRINCE,W.F.J.2Lt ded 30-5-18 9Lond attRAF p248

PRINCE,William T2Lt dow 28-8-17 6Y&L p159 CR Belgium16

PRINCE-SMITH,Donald St.Patrick TLt kia 24-10-17 RDubF att16RFC p12&177 CR France95,2Lt

PRING,Basil Crompton TLt kia 1-7-16 96MGC p185 MR21

PRING,Francis Raleigh Lt kia 25-9-15 9RSuss p119 MR19

PRINGLE,Arthur Stanley TCapt kia 25-9-15 10ScotRif p104 MR19

PRINGLE,Charles Eric T2Lt kia 10-7-16 8 att11LNLancs p136 MR21,11 att8Bn

PRINGLE,James 2Lt ded 8-2-15 14HLI p163 CR Scot253

PRINGLE,Lionel Graham(Leo).MVO.Capt dow 29-12-14 1HLI p163 CR France1027,Leonel

PRINGLE,Matthew 2Lt kia 27-8-17 86RFA p209 CR Belgium19

PRINGLE,Norman Douglas TCapt kia 7/11-8-15 6EYorks p84 MR4,7-8-15

PRINGLE,Norman Robert.Bart Capt ded 18-4-19 GL RE IWT p267 CR Lond4,24-4-19

PRINGLE,Robert Gray 2Lt kia 23-4-17 8HLI p240 CR France1730

PRINGLE,Robert Scott Lt dow 14-9-14 1RWSurr p56 CR France1341

PRINGLE,Robert William Hay TCapt kia 1-7-16 16WYorks p82 MR21 CR France156

PRINGLE,Walter Gerald.MID T2Lt kia 12-10-17 6KOSB p102 CR Belgium126

PRINGLE,William Rennie TLt kia 22-7-16 7SLancs p125 MR21,22/23-7-16

PRINGLE-PATTISON,John Ronald Seth 2Lt kia 5-9-16 2GordH p167 CR France402,6-9-16

PRINTER,Merwanji Dinsha Capt accdrd 2-10-20 IMS CR Egypt2

PRIOLEAU,William Louis St.Julian Maj ded 17-10-19 Norf p263 CR Egypt2

PRIOR,Charles Ronald 2Lt kia 22-8-19 3EKent p58 CR France430,7Bn

PRIOR,Edward Foss TCapt kia 15-9-16 8RB p180 CR France400

PRIOR,Edward Robert Seymour.DSO.MC.TMajALtCol kia 27-5-18 8SLancs att11Ches p125 MR18

PRIOR,Harry Leonard 2Lt ded 3-7-18 1/4RFus att117RAF p69 CR Kent71,kldacc 30Bn

PRIOR,Henry George Redmond TLt kia 7-10-16 11RWKent p141 CR France385,2Lt

PRIOR,Herbert 2Lt dow 27-8-18 5YLI p235 CR France832

PRIOR,John Peter T2Lt kia 9-4-17 24NumbF p62 CR France644

PRIOR,Leslie Montague Sidney T2Lt kia 26-7-16 B156RFA p34 CRFrance453

PRIOR,Leslie Percy Capt dow 7-6-17 10Lond attRFC p19&248 CR France285

PRIOR,Lewis Atkins 2Lt kia 30-6-16 13 att10RSuss p119 MR19

PRIOR,T.A.Lt 10-2-21 5Lond CR Lond14

PRIOR-WANDESFORDE,Christopher Butler 2Lt dow 27-6-17 4Yorks p220 CR France ,Lt

PRISMALL,Arthur Capt kia 14-3-15 13Lond B'Coy p249 CR France710

PRISMALL,Merrick Orville Lt kld 20-12-17 RFA attRFC p12&34 CR Mddx47

PRITCHARD,Andrew Baden Capt ded 26-10-18 StaffsYeo p205 CR Syria2

PRITCHARD,Charles Frederick 2Lt kia 17-9-17 GL &57RFC p12 CR Belgium175,drd

PRITCHARD,Charles Meyrick TCapt dow 14-8-16 12SWBord p100 CR France98

PRITCHARD,David 2Lt kia 19-3-16 1RWFus p98 CR France638

PRITCHARD,Douglas William Lindsay 2Lt kia 27-7-17 2/230RFA p209 CR France161

PRITCHARD,Francis James T2Lt kia 15-11-17 7Lincs p75 CR Belgium23

PRITCHARD,George.MC.Capt kia 3-12-17 2/8Worc p226 MR17

PRITCHARD,Gwynedd William Llewelyn.MC.MID T2Lt kia 23-10-18 20Manch p155 CR France231,Capt

PRITCHARD,Henry T2Lt kia 7-4-18 RWFus attHoodBn p98 MR27

PRITCHARD,H.T.Capt 3-2-20 KOSB CR Devon207

PRITCHARD,Joseph SubCdr ded 12-2-17 IA S&TCps p281 MR61

PRITCHARD,J.F.H Lt 4-9-17 SPersiaRif CR Asia82

PRITCHARD,John 2Lt kia 4-9-17 13RWFus p98 CR Belgium23

PRITCHARD,John Eric Stirling 2Lt dow 27-10-17 RFA 52Bty p34 CR Belgium11

PRITCHARD,John Harold Capt kia 15-5-17 HAC Inf p206 MR20

PRITCHARD,Osborn Brace LtCol ded 27-11-16 WelshR p127

PRITCHARD,Ralph Broomfield.DSO.MC.TCapt dow 26-4-18 14NumbF att2Lincs p62 CR Belgium18

PRITCHARD,Richard T2Lt dow 22-8-16 3 att2 p77

PRITCHARD,T.L.Capt dow 9-11-14 3 att2RWFus p98

PRITCHARD,Thomas Bradley.MC.T2Lt kld 5-12-17 RFC 39HDSqn p12 CR Mddx29 Ex 52MT RASC

PRITCHARD,Thomas Thompson T2Lt kld 30-8-17 GL &RFC p12 CR Wales440

PRITCHARD,Wilfred Dryden Capt dow 25-9-15 8RFA p3 MR19

PRITCHARD,William TCapt kia 21-6-16 9Y&L p159 CR France430

PRITCHARD,William Alwyn 2Lt kia 26-4-18 DLI att1Wilts p161 CR Belgium126

PRITCHARD,William Bridgett LtCol dow 29-6-15 RAMC attELancsFA p253 MR4

PRITCHARD,William Ernest TLt ded 29-10-18 6YLI p265 CR Suff207,2Lt

PRITCHARD-BARRETT,John Oscar Lt kia 15-6-15 3att2Yorks p91 MR22

PRITCHETT,Edward Guy Lt kia 16-5-18 Hereford att6KSLI p252 MR20

PRITCHETT,George Edgar Kenyon T2Lt dow 3-6-18 18LancF p93 CR France63

PRITCHETT,Walter Penrose Capt dow 26-12-14 1Glouc p107 CR France102

PRITTIE,Francis Reginald Denis.Hon.MIDx2 Capt kia 19-12-14 1RB p180 CR Belgium71,Dennis

PRIVETT,Arthur Bellman T2Lt dow 8-1-16 2Leic p88 MR38

PROBERT,Arthur James T2Lt kia 9-4-17 1 att25NumbF p62 CR France265

PROBERT,Sydney Lt kia 27-5-18 7DLI p239 MR18,ded PoW

PROBYN,John William 2Lt kia 12-4-18 5WRid p227 MR30

PROCKTER,Frederic Lt kia 2-10-16 7Mddx p235 MR21 CR France390,3-10-16

PROCTER,Alexander Duncan Guthrie T2L kia 7-7-16 8RFus p69 MR21

PROCTER,Arthur.MC.Lt kia 1-7-16 1/8RWar p215 MR21

PROCTER,Charles Austin 2Lt dedacc 24-4-18 GL &82RAF CR France52

PROCTER,Charles Edgecumbe TLt kia 2-8-15 1/7Norf p74 CR Belgium71

PROCTER,Harry Mettam 2Lt kia 27-8-17 1 att9WYorks p82 MR30

PROCTER,Herbert T2Lt ded 11-11-17 RE p48 CR France177,kldacc

PROCTER,John Norman William Atkinson.MC.MID Lt dow 2-5-18 1/6WRid p227 CR France142

PROCTOR,Charles Gordon T2Lt kld 20-2-16 10ESurr &RFC p3&113 CR Numb74

PROCTOR,Frank Goodheart 2Lt dow 2-11-17 4Ches p222 CR France40,PROCTER

PROCTOR,Frederick William TMaj ded 13-6-16 SL RWFus p201 CR Berks29,Frederic

PROCTOR,George TLt kia 17-4-18 LancF att19Bn p93 MR30

PROCTOR,George Vincent Lt kia 6-9-17 8LancF p221 MR30

PROCTOR,James Adolphus 2Lt dow 18-9-18 14RFA p34 CR France673,kia 402Bty

PROCTOR,James Claude Beauchamp TCapt kia 1-7-16 10RInnisF p105 CR France383

PROCTOR,John.MID Maj dow 12-8-18 RAMC att9CavFdAmb p197 CR France879

PROCTOR,Leslie Horner Lt kld 17-11-18 RASC &10RAF p193 CR Belgium393

PROCTOR,Maubray T2Lt kia 26-5-17 1Y&L p159 CR Belgium127,Mowbray

PROCTOR,Walter Alan 2Lt dedacc 25-6-19 2ELancs p264 CR Lancs205

PROCTOR,William Fife Capt dow 27-9-15 ScotHorse p205 CR Greece10

PROCTOR,William Harold T2Lt kia 9-4-17 6RWKent A'Coy p141 CR France513

PROCTOR,William Howard.DSO.Capt kia 23-4-17 10LNLancs p136 MR20

PROCTOR-BEAUCHAMP,Horace George.Bart.CB.LtCol kia 12-8-15 5Norf p216 MR4

PROCTOR-BEAUCHAMP,Montague Barclay Granville 2Lt kia 12-8-15 5Norf p216 MR4

PROFEIT,Leopold TCapt kia 25-4-17 8KSLI p145 CR Greece6

PROFFITT,John Thomas Read 2Lt 20-10-18 66Wing 224Sqn RAF MR37

PROFIT,Lodwig Tudor T2Lt dow 20-6-18 Lpool att2/6Bn p72 CR France204

PROPHET,Cecil 2Lt kia 9-10-17 20Lond p251 MR30

PROPHIT,George Craigie Lt ded 10-12-20 IA 1/39GarhwalRif att18Div HQ p281 CR Iraq8

PROSPER LISTON,William Capt 12-4-17 5Leinst CR France557 see also LISTON

PROSSER,Albert Victor TLt kia 26-11-16 Worc attBordR p109 CR France233,9N&D attWorc

PROSSER,Arthur Edward.MID TCapt ded PoW 23-10-18 1Worc C'Coy p109 CR Belgium342

PROSSER,John Lt ded 28-12-17 16Lancers p23 CR Surrey91

PROSSER,John Lt kia 28-9-18 4 att8BlkW p230 CR Belgium101

PROSSER,Walter T2Lt dow 9-10-18 1/6Glouc att38MGC Inf p185 CR France560,Lt

PROTHERO,Francis Isaac TLtACapt ded 13-2-19 LabCps p266 CR Wales135

PROTHERO,James Edward Douglas Capt ded 11-8-18 IA 90Punjabis attPoliticalDept p281 CR Asia82

PROTHERO,Philip Bernard LtTCapt kia 26-7-17 4A&SH &5RFC p12&173 MR20

PROTHERO,Rowland John Lt dow 8-11-18 7Huss p22 CR Iraq8

PROTHEROE,William Bertram TLt kia 12-6-17 GL &53RFC p12 MR20

PROUD,John Dover.MC.LtTCapt dow 1-8-18 RAMC att46FA p197 CR France1225,Maj

PROUD,John Reginald Stanhope TLt dow PoW 6-4-17 GL &RFC p12 CR Belgium406

PROUDFOOT,Colin Andrew Lt dow 7-1-16 IA 53Sikhs p281 MR38

PROUDFOOT,Cyril Dallas 2Lt kia 22-4-18 NottsYeo &RAF p205&258 CR France103

PROUDFOOT,Harold Heafford Capt kia 2-9-16 RAMC att26RFA p197 CR France397

PROUDFOOT,Thomas John Anderson T2Lt kia 23-2-18 54RFC p17 CR France987,kld

PROUGHTEN,Charles Ernest 2Lt kia 23-5-18 SurrYeo att10RWSurr p205 CR Belgium84

PROUT,Douglas William T2Lt kia 3-9-16 8RBerks p139 MR21

PROUT,William Thomas 2Lt kia 28-7-16 3 att1Ches p96 MR21

PROVAN,David Hart.MC.2Lt ded 27-12-18 5LNLancs p234 CR Scot807 see HART.D.P.true name

PROVAND,Dixon 2Lt kia 15-9-16 19Lond p251 CR France390

PROVIS,Ernest Snell 2Lt kia 16-6-16 4 att8RMunstF p176 CR France223

PROWSE,Charles Bertie.DSO.TBrigGen dow 1-7-16 SomLI 11InfBde p80&259 CR France3

PROWSE,Gerald Maurice Warren T2Lt kia 12-4-17 9RSuss B'Coy p119 MR20

PRUDEN,Walter Henry 2Lt ded 27-11-18 34MGC p185 CR Lancs14

PRUDHAM,Thomas Pearson T2Lt kia 28-4-17 25NumbF p62 MR20

PRUNTY,Patrick Gerald Fitzroy 2Lt ded 16-5-16 IARO att33Cav p281 CR Iraq5

PRUST,Henry Royston T2LtACapt kia 20-11-17 7YLI p143 MR17

PRYCE,Alfred Owen Challoner 2Lt kia 14-4-18 8ScotRif p225 MR32

PRYCE,Arthur Meurig Capt ded 21-2-19 RAMC 35GH p197 CR France65,att129FA 14RWFus

PRYCE,Hugh Beauclerk Mostyn Capt dow 19-3-15 4RB p180 CR France284

PRYCE,Thomas Tannatt.VC.MC&Bar.Capt kia 13-4-18 4GrenGds p50 MR32

PRYCE-JENKIN,Richard Douglas 2Lt kia 31-12-14 1SWBord p100 CR France260

PRYCE-JONES,Reginald T2Lt kia 19-10-17 8Y&L p159 CR Belgium308

PRYDE,James Watson Lt kia 5-5-18 7BlkW att1KAR p231&268,Capt MR52

PRYKE,Arthur.MC.2Lt kia 11-4-17 2Suff p79 MR20

PRYKE,Edgar King T2Lt kia 30-11-17 GL &3RFC p12 CR France177

PRYN,William Reginald TLt ded 27-6-15 RAMC 9FA p197 CR Belgium11

PRYNN,Norman LtACapt kia 28-3-18 3 att1Hamps p121 MR20

PRYNNE,Edgar George Fellowes TLtACapt kia 16-9-16 4RFus att1/23Lond p69 MR21

PRYNNE,Norman Fellowes 2Lt kia 24/25-4-17 10Dev p77 MR37

PRYOR,Arthur Henry T2Lt kia 10-4-17 27NumbF p62 MR20

PRYOR,Ferdinand William Lt dow 12-9-16 3RIrRif att6InnisF p170 CR Greece4

PRYOR,Joseph Stoneman 2Lt kia 25-3-18 RE 228FC p210 MR27

PRYOR,Robert Selwyn 2Lt kia 1-5-15 1RLancs p59 MR29

PUCKLE,John.DSO.MID LtCol drd 15-4-17 RASC p193 MR35

PUCKLE,Thomas Norman Capt kia 30-8-14 Leic att2NigR p88 CR WAfrica57,Maj

PUCKRIDGE,Christopher Francis Hewitt ACapt kia 28-3-17 3 att7DCLI p114 CR France907

PUCKRIDGE,Cyril Vincent Noel 2Lt kia 21-7-16 1/5Glouc p225 MR21

PUDDICOMBE,Donald Ramsay T2Lt dow 24-7-16 13EYorks p84 CR France345

PUDDICOMBE,Frank Cecil TLt kia 28-10-18 8Dev p77 CR Italy9

PUGH,Arnold Richard Capt dow 24-6-15 3SLancs p125

PUGH,Cyril Webster Lt kia 21-8-18 RFA att38MGC p34 CR France2

PUGH,David William 2Lt kia 7-10-18 YLI att15Bn p143 CR France1140,Williams

PUGH,Edward Rhodes Capt ded 2-12-18 30NumbF att1KAR p62,267,&202 CR EAfrica86

PUGH,Geoffrey Arthur 2Lt kia 10-10-16 26RFus p69 MR21

PUGH,George Morris 2Lt dow 2-9-18 RGA 91SB p41 CR France785

PUGH,Henry Loyn 2Lt dow 11-9-16 3SWBord p100 CR France833

PUGH,Herbert Elias 2Lt kia 22-7-16 3 att2SLancs p125 MR21

PUGH,Ronald George 2Lt kia 19-8-16 3KSLI att7NStaffs p145 CR France156

PUGSLEY,John Frederick 2Lt kia 30-8-18 1Dev p77 CR France1484

PULFORD,Harvey St.George James.MID Capt ded 28-6-16 IA MilGovNasiriyeh 4Rajputs p281 CR Iraq6,Maj

PULING,R.J.C.Capt 29-2-20 GL &RE IWT CR Iraq6

PULLAM,Frank T2Lt kia 19-6-18 1NStaffs p157 CR France480

PULLAN,Charles Ernest Arbuthnot T2Lt kia 30-12-15 16DLI p161 CR France1140,15Bn

PULLAN,Charles Maxwell 2Lt kld 21-3-17 2WRidRFA p209 CR France614

PULLAN,John Aynsley.MID 2LtTLt kia 28-11-17 DLI att9RFC p12&161 CR Belgium18

PULLAR,Thomas Hume 2Lt kia 24-8-18 8 att1/7HLI p240 MR16

PULLEIN,Thomas Harold 2Lt kia 21-3-18 25NumbF p62 MR20

PULLEINE,Robert Percy 2Lt kia 4-9-16 D18RFA p34 CR France515

PULLEN,Alan Collier 2Lt dow 19-8-16 3SomLI p80 CR France833

PULLEN,Charles Tease Lt kia 4-9-17 RGA att25RFC p19&209 MR20,Jesse

PULLEN,Frederick John Edward T2Lt kld 26-3-18 RFC p17 CR Somerset153

PULLEN,Guy Harper 2Lt kia 13-5-15 RHGds p20 MR29

PULLEN,Richard Standeford.MID T2Lt kia 26-10-17 SStaffs att1Bn p123 CR Belgium112

PULLEY,Charles Maj dow 20-7-15 Cmdg68RFA p34 CR Kent287,26-7-15

PULLEYN,Edward Henry 2Lt kia 25-11-17 1/20 att1/2Lond p251 MR17

PULLEYN,James Lewis T2Lt kia 17-10-16 6Dors &RFC p3&124 MR20

PULLIN,Bernard John.MC.Lt dow 21-10-17 D291RFA p208 CR Belgium16

PULLIN,John Henton TLt dow 21-1-16 9LNLancs p136 CR France285

PULLING,O.L.2Lt mbk 25-9-15 RGA att10TMB p256 MR19

PULLINGER,Harold Bessant T2Lt kia 1-9-18 att8ESurr p113 CR France400

PULMAN,Harry Robert Sauve Capt kld 10-3-15 3Lond p245 CR France706

PULVERMAN,Oscar Percy T2Lt dow 1-9-15 1Suff p79 CR Belgium97,Lt

PUMPHREY,Arnold.DSO.MID TCapt kia 21-9-17 20DLI A'Coy p161 MR30

PUMPHREY,Hubert T2Lt kia 26-4-18 10Ches p96 MR30

PUNCHARD,Alfred CaptAMaj kia 29-3-17 2NStaffs p157 MR38

PUNCHARD,Edmund Elgood.MID Lt kia 29-10-14 2Beds p86 MR29,31-10-14

PUNCHARD,James Septimus Lt ded 2-4-19 5RLancs p271 CR C'land&W'land83

PUNCHARD,R Hugh Lt ded 31-10-18 RGA attTankCps p41&188 CR Devon267

PUNTAN,Herbert Forbes 2Lt kia 9-4-17 3 att2GordH p167 MR20

PURCELL,Albert Joseph 2Lt kia 14-7-16 2RWar p65 MR21

PURCELL,Charles Francis Lt kia 15-9-16 2IrGds attMGC p53&185 MR21

PURCELL,Richard Guy.MC.CaptAMaj dow 28-3-18 RGA 31HB p41 CR France1182

PURCELL,Stanley Joseph T2Lt dow 26-3-17 RB p180 MR34

PURCHAS,Ernest Charles Lt dow 4-3-15 V'RHA p34 CR France31,3-3-15

PURCHAS,Geoffrey Thomas 2Lt kia 26-9-17 1RWSurr p56 MR30

PURCHASE,Arthur James Lt ded 4-12-19 WYorks attMGC p263 CR Surrey106

PURCHES,Clifford Arthur T2Lt kia 22-3-18 19MGC p185 MR20

PURDEY,M.Sefton TMaj ded 25-5-16 RemountSve 18Huss p24 CR Kent268

PURDIE,David Scott 2Lt dow 30-9-18 9Lpool p216 CR France256

PURDIE,Frank Phillip Maj ded 20-3-19 8Ess p271 CR War151

PURDIE,Peter Robertson 2Lt dow 17-8-17 RGA 14HB p41 CR Belgium24

PURDIE,Thos.Paterson T2Lt kia 10-7-16 13 att20WelshR p127 MR21

PURDON,George Hardress 2Lt kia 23-7-16 2KRRC p151 MR21

PURDON,Harold Reginald 2Lt dow 28-4-18 9Lpool p216 CR France62

PURDON,Robert Gordon 2Lt kia 16-8-16 13Lpool p72 MR21

PURDON,Theodore Oscar TCapt kia 9-9-16 7Leinst A'Coy p174 CR France402

PURDON-STOUTE,Henry T2Lt kia 10-11-17 2RMunstF p176 MR30

PURDY,Archer Kershaw T2Lt dow 20-11-17 1Leic p88 CR France379

PURDY,Harry Wilfred T2Lt kia 23-4-17 19Manch p155 MR20

PURDY,Richard Shaw T2Lt dow 11-9-16 6 att8RInnisF p105 CR France23

PURGOLD,Louis Joseph Lt kld 20-8-17 RFA attRFC p19&208 CR Lancs1

PURKESS,Arthur James T2Lt kia 27-6-18 12Y&L p159 CR France24,13Bn

PURKIS,Harold Arthur T2Lt kia 28-7-17 111MGC Infp185 CR Belgium100

PURKIS,John Nottage T2Lt kia 25-9-15 SomLI att6Bn p80 MR29,Nollidge

PURLL,William Albert George 2Lt kia 3-5-17 11EYorks p84 MR20

PURNELL,Alfred William Howard(Bert) 2Lt dow PoW 20-11-17 RGA CpsHA 120SB p41 CR Belgium140,Albert

PURNELL,Arthur Channing TCapt kia 1-7-16 16Mddx p148 MR21

PURNELL,Stanley George Hardy T2Lt kia 5-6-17 21NumbF p62 MR20

PURSER,Norman Frederick T2Lt kia 28-2-18 GL &12RFC p17 CR France214

PURSER,Philip Addison TLt dow 30-4-16 RASC p193 CR Ireland14

PURSER,Philip Warburton 2Lt ded 11-10-16 3Mddx p148 CR Mddx39

PURSGLOVE,Edwin James Lt kia 6-11-17 5BordR p228 CR Belgium106

PURSLOW,George 2Lt kia 12-10-18 5NStaffs p238 CR France230

PURVER,Bernard Arthur TCapt kia 7-10-16 11RWKent p141 MR21

PURVES,George Gordon de Burgh TCapt dow 8-11-15 2 att6RScotF p95 CR Germany1

PURVES,Harry de Burgh CaptTMaj kia 18-6-16 2A&SH p173 CR France80

PURVES,James Phillip 2Lt kia 11-4-18 6A&SH p243 MR19

PURVES,Thomas Henderson T2Lt kia 22-3-18 2TankCps p188 CR France307

PURVES,Thomas Warren TLt kia 7-6-17 23Mddx p148 CR Belgium111

PURVES,Walter Douglas Laidlaw TLtACapt kia 28-4-17 9ELancs p111 CR Greece6

PURVIS,Eyre Walter Molyneux Maj AccShot 4-3-15 IA 16Cav p281 CR Iraq6

PURVIS,George Bell Capt kia 8-6-17 5Yorks att56MGC Inf p187&220 CR Belgium102

PURVIS,John Ralph TCapt kia 25-9-15 9RB p180 MR29

PURVIS,John William T2Lt kldacc 2-5-17 GL &RFC p12 CR Durham19

PURVIS,Ronald Montague Capt dow 14-3-17 3 att2BlkW p129 MR38

PUSCH,Ernest John 2Lt kia 8-8-16 11RWar p65 CR France453

PUSCH,Frederick Leopold.DSO.Lt kia 27-6-16 IrGds att1Bn SR p53 CR Belgium73

PUTMAN,Edmund 2Lt ded 16-4-18 RGA 383SB p41 CR Egypt1

PUZEY,Arthur Kenneth Capt kia 11-11-14 4RFus p69 MR29

PYATT,Richard Goodwin Lt kia 13-10-15 1/7N&D p233 CR France423

PYBUS,Harold Robert Lt ded 24-7-16 4 att2DLI p161 CR Numb4

PYBUS,Robert 2Lt kia 14-7-16 8DLI p239 CR Belgium97,24-7-16

PYCROFT,Arthur Percival T2Lt kld 16-6-17 GL &RFC p12 CR Notts84,Lt

PYE,Colin T2Lt dow 8-10-18 KSLI att1Bn p145 CR France725

PYE,Francis John Capt kia 15-12-16 5RFus attGoldCoastR p69 CR EAfrica38 &CR Tanzania1

PYE,Walter George 2Lt kia 24-7-17 A277RFA p209 CR Belgium7

PYE,William Wakeley T2Lt kia 14-10-15 6RWKent p141 MR19

PYE-SMITH,Phillip Howson Guy TLt kia 15-5-17 11Lpool p72 CR France581

PYKE,William Edward 2Lt kia 9-9-16 1/4LNLancs p234 MR21

PYM,Claude John Lt ded 27-3-17 2IrGds p53 CR France105,26-3-17

PYM,E.H.Maj ded 11-11-19 RE p262 CR Devon258

PYM,Francis Leslie Melville Lt kia 2-7-16 2IrGds p53 MR29

PYM,John Scarlett T2Lt kia 5-12-16 2RWSurr p56 CR France174,6Bn

PYM,John Walter 2Lt kia 7-7-16 7Lond p247 CR France558

PYMAN,Allan Lt kia 15-6-15 3 att2Yorks p91 MR22

PYMAN,James Capt kld 18-11-14 3BordR attManch p117 MR29

PYMAN,Ronald Lee Lt kia 3-5-17 15 att12Mddx p148 MR20

PYNE,Ernest Sydney 2Lt dow 12-10-17 4 att9WYorks p82 CR Belgium16

Q

QUAIFE,Eric John 2LtACapt kia 30-6-17 RGA 294SB p41 CR Belgium339

QUAIL,Henry Charles T2Lt kia 18-2-18 RE 124FC p48 CR France922

QUAILE,Robert Ernest Browne 2Lt kia 3-10-18 4 att6RInnisF p105 CR France1495

QUALE,Charles Philip 2Lt kia 15-6-16 2/1BucksBn O&BLI p231 CR France706

QUARMBY,Frederick 2Lt kia 18-9-16 7WRid p228 CR France300

QUARMBY,James Scholfield 2Lt kia 2-12-17 7WRid p228 CR France530

QUARRELL,Charles Hubert T2Lt kia 16-6-17 13NumbF p62 MR20

QUARRIER,Edward John 2Lt kia 31-5-18 3 att2Hamps p121 MR32

QUARRY,Herbert TLt kia 2-8-16 RFA F8TMB p34 CR France114

QUARRY,St.John Shandon.MID Maj kia 14-4-18 3RBerks Cmdg14RWar p139 CR France346

QUARTERMAN,Percy Harold Lt kia 9-10-17 23Lond att2/4ELancs p252 CR Belgium125

QUARTLEY,Thomas Warner 2Lt kia 15-1-15 Lancs attSLancs p59 CR Belgium89

QUAYLE,Rupert Charles T2Lt kia 4-10-18 1 att1/4Leic p88 CR France441

QUEEN John 2Lt kia 7-6-17 12NumbF p62 MR20

QUEKETT,John 2Lt kia 31-7-17 5BlkW p231 CR Belgium96

QUELCH,Arthur Francis T2Lt kld 15-1-18 RFC p17 CR Kent129

QUENINGTON,Michael Hugh.Viscount Lt dow 23-4-16 1/1GloucYeo p203 CR Egypt10,kia

QUEST,Harold.MC.TCapt kia 3-11-16 14Y&L A'Coy p159 CR France1326

QUIBELL,George Edwin 2Lt kia 26-3-17 10Mddx p236 MR34

QUIBELL,Samuel Boyd.MID Maj dow 5-2-16 4EYorks p219 CR Belgium11

QUICKE,Edward Owen St.Ayres Godolphin.MID Capt kia 25-10-14 3Dev p77 MR22,Cyres

QUICKE,Henry Lt kia 23-3-18 4RWFus p223 MR20

QUIGLEY,Christopher T2Lt kia 21-3-18 11 att2RDubF p177 MR27

QUIGLEY,William Grainger 2Lt ded 2-11-18 IA TC attSchoolofInstrn RoO p281 MR65

QUILLER-COUCH,Bevil Brian.DSO.MC.AMaj ded 6-2-19 9/41RFA p34 CR Germany1

QUILLINAN,Lawrence Patrick Capt ded 14-1-20 IA 1/124BaluchistanInf p281 MR67

QUILTER,Frederick Walter 2Lt kia 31-8-15 6Lond p247 CR France149

QUILTER,John Arnold Cuthbert LtCol 6-5-15 GrenGds CR Gallipoli14

QUILTER,Roy Molyneux.MID TCapt kia 19-4-16 8Beds p86 MR29

QUIN,Desmond Hilary Lt kia 18-9-18 5RWSurr p212 CR Greece5

QUIN,Francis John 2Lt dow 2-5-18 50RFA p34 CR France142

QUIN James Davidson 2Lt kia 19-8-18 2RFus p69 CR France28,18-8-18

QUIN,Leslie William Whitworth.MC.TLtACapt kia 24-4-17 3 att27NumbF p62 MR20

QUIN,Walter Capt 11-7-21 GL CR Iraq6

QUINCEY,Thomas Edmund De Quincey 2Lt kia 9-5-15 6 att2RB p180 MR32

QUINE,Brian Howell TLt kia 27-6-18 2BlkW p129 CR Palestine9

QUINLAN,Charles 2Lt kia 31-7-17 5Leinst p174 MR29

QUINLAN,Harold Daniel Lt kia 26-3-18 4Huss p21 MR27

QUINLAN James Leonard 2Lt dow 28-12-17 7RWar p214 CR France52

QUINLAN John Francis Pembroke Boxwell 2Lt kia 3-7-16 RFA attRFC p2&34,ded MR20

QUINLAN,Louis T2Lt kia 27-4-16 8RInnisF p105 CR France219

QUINN James 2Lt dow 29-7-16 RGA 109SB p41 CR France430

QUINN James Ewart 2Lt kia 5-10-18 8Lpool p216 CR France256

QUINN John Henry 2Lt ded 11-8-19 RFA 220Bde AC p261 CR Iraq8,Lt

QUINN John James Patrick LtCol ded 26-9-15 IA 117Mahrattas p281 MR65,25-9-15

QUINN John Patrick TLt dow 20-6-17 11RDubF p177 CR France40,2Lt

QUINN,J.P.Lt 6-10-20 2RDubF CR Eire506

QUINN,Thomas Joseph T2Lt dow 18-6-18 9WRid p116 CR France84

QUINN,William Henry Corry 2Lt kia 21-4-18 A70RFA p34 CR France113

QUINT,Henry John T2Lt kia 24-9-18 3Glouc att5Leic p107 CR France699

QUIRKE,Amyas Septimus.MC.T2Lt dow 3-11-18 56MGC p185 CR France40

R

RABAN,Richard Bassett Cockburn LtCol kia 11-5-16 IA 1Lancers att13RScots p281 CR France423

RABONE,Arthur Brian Capt kia 1-7-16 6RWar p214 MR21

RABONE John Kenneth Capt ded 1-9-15 1/5RWar p214 CR France40,1-12-15

RABONE,Maxwell T2Lt dow 22-8-15 2RMunstF p176 MR4

RABY,William Donald T2Lt kia 8-10-18 1/2RWFus p98 CR France234

RACINE,Ernest Guy 2Lt kia 9-4-17 10Lpool p216 CR France581

RADCLIFF,Herbert Travers Capt kia 15-3-15 5Leinst p174 MR29

RADCLIFF,Robert Sussex Francis Derwentwater 2Lt kia 26-3-18 80RFC p17

RADCLIFFE,Arthur Philip Joseph LtACapt dow 18-8-17 71RFA p34 CR Lond6

RADCLIFFE,David TLt kia 18-3-16 24RFus p69 CR France161

RADCLIFFE,Dering John Jasper Lt kld 31-10-17 5GrenGds p50 CR France112

RADCLIFFE,E.B.Sister ded 10-3-19 QAIMNS p200 CR France65

RADCLIFFE,Ernest Charles Derwentwater T2Lt kia 31-7-17 15RWFus p98 CR Belgium106

RADCLIFFE,Ernest John T2Lt kld 20-2-16 GL &RFC p2&191,ded CR Mddx17

RADCLIFFE,Frederick TLt kia 10-4-17 35MGC p185 MR20

RADCLIFFE,George Amyas Lt kia 25-4-17 3A&SH att17RFC p12&173 MR37

RADCLIFFE,George Kan 2Lt kia 1-7-16 14RIrF p171 MR21

RADCLIFFE,James Lt kia 24-2-18 1/7WRid p227 CR Belgium34

RADCLIFFE,Jasper Fitzgerald.DSO.MIDx2 LtCol kia 31-1-16 Dev attEss p77 CR France515

RADCLIFFE,John Douglas Henderson Capt dow 30-7-15 7KRRC p151 MR29

RADCLIFFE,Miles TCapt kia 12-12-14 BordR attRScotF p117 CR Belgium186

RADCLIFFE,Percival Victor Alban Lt dow 25-11-17 5Yorks attMGC Cav p187&220 CR France256

RADCLIFFE,Samuel Roberts.DSO.MID Maj ded 30-4-18 172RFA p34 CR Egypt2

RADCLIFFE,William Thomas 2Lt kia 20-7-18 4A&SH p173 CR France622,7Bn

RADCLIFFE,William Yonge T2Lt dow 19-8-15 5Wilts p153 MR4

RADCLYFFE,Charles Edward.DSO.LtCol kia 25-9-15 11Ess p132 MR19,26-9-15

RADFORD,Amyas Leith Capt kia 12-5-15 9Lpool att8LancF p216 MR4

RADFORD,Basil Hallam TCapt kia 20-8-16 RFC p2 CR France203,dedacc

RADFORD,Charles Oates Lt ded 5-4-18 1KARif p268 CR EAfrica86

RADFORD,Francis Buckley 2Lt kia 25-3-18 3 att13RFus p69MR30

RADFORD,Maurice Clive.DSO.Capt kia 28-9-15 1RBerks p139 CR France423

RADFORD,Oswald Campbel TCapt dow 26-2-16 12KRRC p151 CR Belgium11

RADHILL,P.J.Lt ded 2-6-18 5Ches attRAF p222

RADLOFF,Heinrich Lt kia 14-9-18 1/11Lond &RAF p248&258 CR Palestine3,dedacc

RADMILOVIC,John TLt ded 3-11-18 15 att3WelshR p127 CR Wales17

RAE,Alfred Ian T2Lt kia 24-4-17 13RB p180 MR20

RAE,James TLt drd 13-4-17 RAMC p197 MR35,15-4-17

RAE,James T2Lt kia 4-10-17 SfthH att2Bn p165

RAE,James Albert T2Lt ded 4-9-15 10Beds p86 CR Herts110,kldacc

RAE,James Edmond Pringle TCaptAMaj kia 30-11-17 7DCLI p114 MR17

RAE,John Cairns.MC.LtACapt kia 10-4-17 86RFA p34 CR France266

RAE,Lindsay Leon de'Cram Clement Marsham 2Lt drd 10-10-18 YorkDragYeo p206 MR40

RAE,Reginald Wilson 2Lt kia 30-3-15 3ESurr attSStaffs p113 CR Belgium111,2Bn

RAE,Thomas Keith Hedley T2Lt kia 30-7-15 8RB p180 MR29

RAE,William Alexander 2Lt kia 31-7-17 6BlkW p231 CR Belgium65

RAE,William John Capt 27-3-17 3AustBnImpCamelCps MR34

RAE,William Kenneth T2Lt ded 8-11-18 RASC 1032MT Coy p193 CR Greece2

RAEBURN,Alfred Anthony Douglas 2Lt kia 15-7-16 9HLI p240 MR21

RAEBURN,Gordon Peter T2Lt dow 11-4-17 8ELancs p111 CR France581

RAESIDE,George Forrest.MC.T2Lt kia 9-4-18 1/4Lancs p59 CR France1106

RAFFERTY,John Capt 1-3-21 ConnRgrs CR Wilts115

RAFFIN,Archibald Franklin.MC.TLtACapt ded 30-11-18 9Dev p77 CR France717

RAFTER,James.MC.Capt ded 5-10-19 RAMC p267 CR Lancs169

RAGGETT,Bertram Robert 2Lt kia 5-1-18 RGA att10RFC p17&41 CR Belgium11

RAGHUBIR,Singh LtCol 18-1-15 2KashmirRif MR48

RAHILL,Peter Joseph kld 2-6-18 5Ches attRAF CR Ches28

RAHLES-RAHBULA,Arnold James 2LtTCapt kia 28-4-17 8Lincs p75 MR20

RAIKES,Frank Steward Waddington 2Lt kia 9-5-15 5 att2RB p180 MR32

RAIKES,Frederick Munro 2Lt kia 22-2-17 SWBord BrecknockBn attMGC p187&223,Monro CR Iraq5

RAIKES,John Francis 2Lt kia 11-10-16 3 att9Ess p132 MR21

RAIL,Richard Augwin Lt kia 9-10-17 3CldGds p51 MR30,Angwin

RAILSTON,Spencer Julian Wilfred Lt kia 1-11-14 IA 18Lancers att4DragGds p281

RAILTON,Arthur Temple TLt kld 9-5-15 4SfthH p241 CR France924,kia

RAIMES,Lancelot Capt dow 1-6-16 5DLI p238 CR France285

RAIMES,Leslie Robinson Lt 1-7-16 21NumbF MR21

RAINBOTH,Lawrence John T2Lt kld 24-12-17 GL &RFC p12 CR Canada261

RAINBOW,Albert Edward 2Lt kia 23-7-16 4 att10RWar p65 MR21

RAINBOW,George Lt kia 9-10-18 4SLancs p230 France256

RAINBOW,John 2Lt kia 7-8-15 6Manch p237 MR4

RAINBOW,Thomas Welford T2Lt kia 18-11-16 10Worc p109 MR21

RAINE,Charles William 2Lt kia 3-11-18 3WRid att16LancF p116 CR France933

RAINE,Foster Rev ded 7-12-18 RAChDept p268 CR Cornwall61

RAINE,George Kenneth 2Lt dow 2-7-16 16 att18DLI p161 CR France169

RAINE,George Stevenson T2Lt kld 15-3-17 26RFus attRFC p12&69 CR Lond12,56ResRFC attRFus

RAINE,Hubert TLt kia 23-3-18 RE 202FC p48 CR France1203

RAINE,Leonard T2Lt kia 15-8-16 6Y&L p159 CR France420

RAINE,William.MC.Capt&Adjt dow 7-9-18 9Lpool p216 CR France433

RAINES,Leslie Robinson TLt kia 1-7-16 21NumbF p62

RAINEY,Edmund Flower LtCol ded 20-7-16 IA 72Punjabis p281 MR67,30-7-16

RAINEY,Victor Thomas James 2Lt kia 30-9-17 2Dev p77 CR Belgium68

RAINEY,William 2Lt kia 23-11-17 2RIrRif p170 MR17

RAINIE,James Wilson McTurk kia 27-3-16 2RScots p54 CR Belgium15

RAINS,R.H.Capt 23-6-20 RAMC CR Lond14

RAINSFORD-Hannay,Ramsay.MID Capt kia 1-2-17 IA 45Sikhs p281 MR38,Maj

RAISTRICK,F.A.Lt 16-11-18 Leic CR Yorks418

RAISTRICK,John William 2Lt kia 19-5-17 1/8WYorks p219 CR France1887

RAIT-KERR,Sylvester Cecil Capt kia 13-5-15 RFA p34 MR29

RAIT-KERR,William Charles.DSO.Capt kia 10-11-14 RFA 57Bty43Bde p34 MR29

RAITT,Alexander Redmayne Lt kia 8-3-16 IA 3RajputLI p281 MR38,Capt

RALEIGH,George Hebden BtMaj kld 20-1-15 Ess &4RFC p2&132 CR France1359

RALEY,Walter Hugh 2Lt kld 14-5-15 5Y&L p238 CR France276

RALEY,William Henry George Capt kia 15-6-15 3 att2Yorks p91 MR22

RALFS,Francis Arthur Lt dow 16-9-16 5RFus att9LancF p69 CR France74

RALLI,Leonidas,Lucas TCapt ded 24-4-17 RASC p193 CR France1886,20-4-17

RALLI,Lionel Peter Lt dow 14-11-18 20Huss p23 CR France146

RALLISON,Victor Edward 2Lt kia 7-4-17 17Manch p155 CR France1185

RALLS,Frederic Hamilton.MC&Bar.Capt dow 24-8-18 9Lond D'Coy p247 CR France141

RALPH,Henry Bertie 2Lt dow 12-10-18 B255RFA p34 CR France241

RALPH,John Gray 2Lt kia 18-6-16 7Lond p247 CR France558

RALPHS,Arthur T2Lt kia 23-4-17 GL &12RFC p12 CR France531

RALPHS,Walter Joel TLt dow 15-7-16 12RFA p34 CR France399,Capt

RAM,George Edward Capt ded 25-3-16 4NStaffs A'Coy p157 CR Lond4

RAM,Percival John T2Lt kia 1-7-16 26Manch p155 MR21

RAMIER,L.S.Lt 14-9-18 IMS CR Mddx26

RAMNEY,Reginald Van Taerling Lt dow 28-3-18 3GrenGds p50

RAMPLEY,William Temple 2Lt kia 30-9-18 1LovatScts attKOSB p204 CR Belgium157

RAMSAY,Alexander Lt ded 28-4-15 5RFus att1RWar p69 CR Belgium383

RAMSAY,A.G.TCapt ded 6-1-19 KAR p202

RAMSAY,Alan Livingstone LtTCapt kia 24-4-16 3RIrReg p89 CR Ireland24

RAMSAY,Alexander 2Lt kia 28-3-18 4RScotF p222 MR20

RAMSAY,Alexander.MM.2Lt kia 20-10-18 5LancF p221 CR Belgium417

RAMSAY,Alexander Charles Marquis Lt ded 18-12-14 RASC p193 CR Mddx26

RAMSAY,Archibald Hamilton T2Lt kia 13-10-15 9 att2 O&BLI p130 MR19

RAMSAY,David James 2Lt kia 21-3-18 59MGC Inf p185 CR France568,18MGC

RAMSAY,David Winson TLt kia 14-2-16 10N&D p134 MR29,Derrick

RAMSAY,Duncan Gavin.MID 2LtTLt kia 19-12-14 2RSuss att2RWSurr p119 CR France924,18-12-14

RAMSAY,George Strachan Lt 8-8-18 49RAF MR20

RAMSAY,Herbert Cyril Lt dow 22-4-18 1Nhampt p138 CR France260

RAMSAY,John Marmaduke TLt dow 14-4-17 2 att10RB p180 CR France164,13-4-17

RAMSAY,John Richard Maj kia 6-1-17 RFA 160HB p34 CR Iraq5

RAMSAY,Keith Winton TLt kia 3-5-16 7KRRC p151 CR France924

RAMSAY,Louis Nail Griffitt 2Lt kia 21-3-15 3 att2GordH p167 CR France768,Neil

RAMSAY,Norman Lt dow 3-11-14 4DragGds RoO p21 CR Belgium98 Ex RFA

RAMSAY,Norman T2Lt kia 3-9-16 16RB p180 MR21

RAMSAY,Stuart.DSO.TCapt dow 3-6-17 8LNLancs p136 CR Belgium43,2-6-17

RAMSAY,William James Lt kia 27-3-18 RWFus &RFC p17&98 CR France300

RAMSBOTHAM,Geoffrey Bury.MID Lt kia 16-5-15 3RSuss attSStaffs p119 MR22

RAMSBOTTOM,Basil William Lt kia 19-8-18 12Norf p204 CR France19

RAMSBOTTOM,Reginald T2Lt kia 29-7-16 29 att17RFus p69 MR21

RAMSDEN,Edward.MM.T2Lt kia 21-3-18 NStaffs p157 MR27

RAMSDEN,Emsley T2Lt kia 15-9-16 MGC p185 CR France390

RAMSDEN,S.2Lt dow 12-4-18 GL &RAF p191

RAMSDEN,Walter Frederick Stewart T2Lt ded 15-11-18 LabCps att22PoW Co p189 CR France146

RAMSEY,Arthur William Lt kia 12-4-15 3EKent attRInnisF p58 MR29

RAMSEY,Charles Owen 2Lt kia 21-3-18 12/13NumbF Res p62 MR27

RAMSEY,George Bennett 2Lt ded 27-8-15 RE p210 MR4

RAMSEY,Harry Victor Lt ded 5-8-18 RFA p208 CR Beds74

RAMSKILL,William Bliss 2Lt dow 16-9-18 A119RFA p34 CR France34

RANBY,Harvey Lt kia 9-8-17 7Suff p79 MR20

RAND,Charles Herbert Sidney T2Lt kia 18-9-18 21NumbF att2Lincs p62 CR France415

RANDALL,Albert William 2Lt kia 8-8-18 3Lond p246 MR16

RANDALL,Charles Barton TLt kia 31-7-17 A74RFA p34 CR Belgium12

RANDALL,Charles Deschamps TCapt kia 7/11-8-15 9N&D p134 MR4, 9-8-15

RANDALL,Charles Edwin T2Lt kia 27-5-18 RBerks att2/4Bn p139 CR France248

RANDALL,Edwin Walter Lt kia 23-4-17 7RFus p69 MR20

RANDALL,Frank Horace T2Lt kia 18-7-17 9Norf p74 CR France258

RANDALL,Frederick Percival 2Lt kia 16-9-16 6SomLI p80 MR21

RANDALL,Geoffrey Victor 2Lt kia 30-7-16 ELancs &4RFC p2,261&264 CR France44,20-7-16 Deleted see MR

RANDALL,Guy Philip.MC.LtACapt kia 18-9-18 3KOSB p102 CR France415,2Bn

RANDALL,Herbert Ernest T2Lt dow 20-5-18 7KSLI p145 CR France33

RANDALL,John ACapt ded 17-2-19 RGA p255 CR Wilts156

RANDALL,John Beaufoy TCapt kia 31-10-17 RAMC att82RFA p197 CR Belgium10

RANDALL,Mervyn Gregory.MC.T2Lt kia 6-6-18 8NStaffs p157 CR France622

RANDALL,Reginald Wigmore Sancroft T2Lt kia 9-5-15 att2Nhampt p138 MR32

RANDALL,L.Richard William 2Lt ded 4-2-19 SNottsHuss p271 CR Essex1

RANDALL,Sidney Walter T2Lt ded 31-10-17 GL &11RFC p12 CR France568

RANDALL,Stanley.DCM.MM.MID 2LtTLt ded 31-12-18 EKent attWAFF p58&202 CR WAfrica1

RANDERSON,Robert TCapt kia 7-8-15 6Yorks p91 CR Gallipoli26

RANDLE,Thomas Henry 2Lt dow 11-8-17 3Worc p109 CR Belgium7

RANDLESOME,G.W.Gnr ded 30-11-16 RIM IWT p281

RANDOLPH,Julien TLt kia 27-9-15 1WelshGds p53 MR19

RANEY,Paul Hartley 2Lt kia 21-8-17 66RFC p12 MR20

RANK,Sydney Lt dow 23-10-18 RGA 216SB p209 CR France231

RANKEN,Dudleigh Chalmers TCapt kia 27-7-16 23RFus p69 MR21

RANKEN,Ernest Ford T2Lt dow 25-3-16 7KOSB p102 CR France134

RANKEN,George Lt kia 1-11-18 RGA 19SB p209 CR France521

RANKEN,Harry Sherwood.VC.Capt dow 24-9-14 RAMC p197 CR France1110,25-9-14

RANKIN,Franklin Sharp Lt 23-10-16 CanadaEngrs &18RFC MR20

RANKIN,Frederick Alan 2Lt kia 23-4-17 1/5BordR attD'TankCps p228 CR France162

RANKIN,James 2Lt kia 30-11-17 LNLancs att1/5Bn p136 MR17

RANKIN,James Thomson 2Lt kia 23-12-15 4A&SH att1RScots p173 CR Gallipoli1

RANKIN,John T2Lt kia 23-4-17 7Lincs p75 MR20

RANKIN,John Hall 2Lt ded 2-3-16 RH&FA p34

RANKIN,Robert Herbert T2Lt kia 23-11-17 15RIrRif p170 MT17

RANKIN,William TLt kia 18-2-18 RE HQ VIICps p48 CR France446

RANKIN,William John T2Lt kia 30-6-17 9Y&L p159 CR Belgium127

RANKINE,W.H.Chap2Cl 11-7-21 RE Scot528

RANKING,George Harvey Chap4Cl kia 20-11-17 RAChDept attIV Cps HvyArt p199 CR France529

RANKING,James Gabriel Lancaster Capt kia 12-7-15 IA AssPoliticResident PerianGulf p281 CR Asia82,G.J.L.

RANN,William Alfred.MID SubCdr ded PoW 25-6-16 IA S&TCps p281 MR38

RANNEY,Reginald Van Taerlingh Lt dow 28-3-18 3GrenGds CR France924

RANSDALE,Alfred Charles T2Lt kia 1-9-18 15LNLancs p136 CR Belgium188

RANSFORD,Clement Gascoyen Capt kia 26-10-14 1SStaffs p123 CR Belgium116

RANSOM,Frederick Charles 2Lt kia 9-4-18 5 att9Ess p232 CR France197

RANSOM,Henry Bayly Lt ded 30-10-18 3Wilts p265

RANSOM,Hubert William 2Lt kia 27-3-18 GL &70RFC p12 CR France232

RANSOM,John,MC Capt ded 4-9-19 RBerks attHQ LofC p265 CR France40

RANSOM,Richard Edward Croft TCapt dow 21-7-16 13EYorks p84 CR France345,RANSON

RANSOM,Robert Cyril Starling T2Lt dow 19-10-17 7Beds p86 CR Belgium64

RANSOME,Bertram Colby TLt ded 30-6-18 RASC MT p193 CR France85,Coleby

RANSOME,Cecil Talbot TLt&Adjt kia 1-7-16 16WYorks p82 CR France156

RANSOME,Frederick Ronald 2Lt kia 27-5-18 1RDubF att2WYorks p177 CR France1753,dow

RANSOME,Geoffrey Cyril TLt dow 15-1-18 13Yorks p91 CR France518

RANSOME,Herbert Fullarton TLt ded 14-11-17 RAMC p197 CR Lancs233

RANSOME,John Edwin T2Lt kld 12-12-17 GL &RFC p12 CR Lincs10

RANSON,Charles Sherriff 2Lt kia 16-8-17 13Lond p249 MR29

RANSON,Leslie Edward Lt kia 29-9-18 5 att2Worc p109 CR France665

RAPER,Frank Alexander D'Arbly.MC.T2Lt kia 11-12-17 122MGC p185 CR Italy7

RAPER,Robert George TMaj kia 2-7-16 8SStaffs p123 CR France372

RAPER,Sydney Ernest 2Lt kia 17-8-17 6SfthH attRFC p19&241 CR Belgium132

RAPHAEL,Henry George 2Lt kia 31-7-17 7ELancs p111 MR29

RAPHAEL,John Edward TLt dow 11-6-17 GL 18KRRC p191 CR Belgium11

RAPHAEL,Norman Henry 2Lt dow 8-6-16 2RWar p65 CR France67

RAPLEY,William Godfrey 2Lt kia 25-9-17 Mddx att1Bn p148 CR Belgium63

RAPOPORT,John Lindsay 2Lt kia 27-5-18 6 att12RB p180 MR20

RAPP,Ernest James T2Lt kia 9-4-17 GL attYorks p191 CR France1185

RAPP,Reginald 2Lt kia 18-6-15 7WRid p228 CR France347,Lt

RAPSON,Harold Thomas 2LtACapt dow PoW 23-3-18 3 att7RWKent p141 CR France1717

RASH,Arnold William 2Lt kia 31-7-17 5Suff p217 CR Belgium94

RASH,Ralph Reginald T2Lt kia 12-10-16 7Suff p79 MR21

RASTRICK,Urpeth Lt kia 14-12-14 Nhampt p138 CR France572

RATCLIFF,John Edward Lt kia 20-10-14 2RWar p65 CR Belgium140,19-10-14

RATCLIFF,Sidney Arthur 2Lt kia 31-3-17 C59RFA p34 CR France158

RATCLIFF-GAYLAND, Eric Ronald 2Lt kia 20-7-16 1/5DCLI p227 CR France1887,19-7-16

RATCLIFFE,Alfred Victor TLt kia 1-7-16 10WYorks p82 CR France373

RATCLIFFE,Clifford Stanley 2Lt kia 22-7-18 10RIrF p171 MR32

RATCLIFFE,Frederick Brockwall.MID LtACapt dow 30-3-18 1Drags att6MGC Cav p21&185 CR France145

RATCLIFFE,Frederick Frank T2Lt dow 10-9-17 8RWSurr p56 CR France139

RATCLIFFE,William Henry 2Lt kia 1-7-16 4 att1SStaffs p123 CR France397

RATHBONE,Arnold Richard Capt dow 24-6-15 3 att2SLancs p125 CR France1

RATHBONE,George Benson Lt ded 28-5-19 RGA 1/1HB p41 CR Germany1

RATHBONE,George Henry Lt 29-4-17 AlbertaR &12RFC MR20

RATHBONE,George Powell TLt kia 21-3-18 7Nhampt p138 MR27

RATHBONE,Guy Benson TCapt kia 21-4-16 11 att7Glouc p107 MR38

RATHBONE,John Ernest Vivian Lt kia 4-6-18 3 att1Dors p124 CR France502,Capt

RATHBONE,Thomas Ford 2Lt kia 26-9-17 5NStaffs p238 CR Belgium125

RATHMELL,E.AssMatron6286 ded 28-7-19 QAIMNS CR Yorks222

RATLIFF,Edward Francis.MC.Capt kia 2-12-17 6 att2RB p180 MR30

RATNAGAR,S.D.Capt 24-4-17 IMS att1/94Inf MR43

RATSEY,Clayton Capt kia 12-8-15 8Hamps C'Coy p229 MR4

RATSEY,Donald White Capt kia 12-8-15 8Hamps D'Coy p229 MR4

RATSEY,Stephen Gilbert Lt kia 19-4-17 8Hamps p229 CR Palestine8

RATTIGAN,Cyril Stanley Capt kia 13-11-16 7RFus p69 MR21

RATTON,Joseph Holroyd Maj 2-9-17 RGA 163SB p41 CR Belgium19

RATTON,Wilfrid Holroyd 2Lt ded 9-7-15 22Lond p251 CR EAfrica125

RATTRAY,David 2Lt dow 21-9-18 D23RFA p34 CR France327

RATTRAY,David Lindsay TCapt kia 17-2-17 23RFus p69 MR21

RATTRAY,Haldane Burney.DSO.LtCol kia 1-2-17 IA 45Sikhs p281 MR38

RATTRAY,Malcolm McGregor.DSO.LtCol ded 27-11-19 RAMC 3BritGH p267 CR Iraq6

RATTRAY,James Alec 2Lt kia 23-9-17 RGA 5SB p41 CR Belgium23

RAVEN,Frederick Gifford T2Lt dow 24-3-17 RE p48 CR France85,Frederic

RAVENHILL,Aleck George TCapt kia 25-9-15 8SfthH A'Coy p165 CR France219,Alex

RAVENOR,Geoffrey Paxton T2Lt kia 2-10-16 6RBerks p139 CR France246

RAVENSCROFT,Alan Paddock TLt kld 16-1-17 RFA attRFC p12&34,ded CR Lond29

RAVENSCROFT,Dudley Clement 2Lt 1-5-19 18Lond att81MGC CR Greece9

RAVENSCROFT,Guy TCapt kia 18-10-16 18Lpool p72 CR France385

RAVENSCROFT,Richard Birbeck Lt kia 16-8-17 Herts p252 MR30

RAW,Rowland T2Lt kia 7-8-15 9LancF p93 CR Gallipoli27

RAW,Rupert George.DSO.Capt kia 7-8-15 8NumbF p62 MR4

RAWBONE,Charles Robert T2Lt kld 18-12-17 GL &RFC p12

RAWDON-HASTINGS,Edward Hugh Hastings 2Lt ded 25-9-15 2BlkW p129 CR France64,15-9-15

RAWDON-HASTINGS,Paulyn Charles James Reginald Capt kia 13-10-15 5Leic A'Coy p220 MR19

RAWE,Charles Henry 2Lt kia 24-4-18 RFA SR attRGA 309SB p34 CR France210

RAWES,Douglas TLt dow 16-8-15 8KRRC p151 CR Europe28

RAWES,Jocoslyn Hugh Russell TLt kia 1-7-19 7Beds p86 CR France513,1-7-16

RAWLE,Charles William Forbes T2Lt kia 5-4-16 9Worc p109 MR38

RAWLE,William Richard Capt dow 8-8-18 1/2Lond p245 CR France95

RAWLING,Cecil Godfrey.CMG.CIE.DSO.TBrigGen kia 28-10-17 62SomLI p80 CR Belgium19

RAWLINGS,Charles William Ernest T2Lt dow 28-9-17 1Glouc p107 CR Belgium18

RAWLINGS,George Wilfred Harry Leslie TLt kia 27-1-17 4Hamps p228 MR38

RAWLINGS,Leonard Justly T2Lt kia 7-11-16 2Nhampt p138 CR France744

RAWLINGS,Thomas William T2Lt ded 8-10-18 RWSurr att39RFus p56 CR Palestine8

RAWLINS,Gerald Edmund Adair Capt kia 7-7-16 9RFus p69 CR France393

RAWLINS,Guy Vernon Champion Capt ded 30-1-19 RE att7TankCps p48&188 CR France63

RAWLINS,Hugh Penrose Cardozo 2Lt kia 4-10-17 10YLI p143 MR30

RAWLINS,John Bromley Capt kia 16-8-17 RAMC p254 CR Belgium96

RAWLINSON,Curwen Vaughan 2Lt kia 21-5-15 3 att1Dors p124 CR Belgium82

RAWLINSON,Godfrey Marshall 2Lt dow 16-7-16 1/4 O&BLI p231 CR France203

RAWLINSON,Guy Edward 2Lt dow 23-7-16 1/3Camb p245 CR France924

RAWLINSON,Harry Raymond T2Lt kia 26-9-17 118MGC Inf p185 CR Belgium112

RAWLINSON,Leonard Hugh Lt kia 10-5-15 2Lancs p59 MR29

RAWLINSON,Robert.MID 2Lt kia 25-9-15 3 att2BordR p117 MR19

RAWLINSON,William Gray Lt kia 14-3-15 2DCLI p114 MR29

RAWNSLEY,Gerald 2Lt kia 21-1-17 4WRid p227 CR France503

RAWSON,Arthur.MIDx2 Capt kia 6-10-13 13BlkW p205 CR France1495

RAWSON,Edward Douglas 2Lt kia 23-8-18 4 att2SStaffs p123 CR France214,23/24-8-18

RAWSON,Harry William Capt ded PoW 22-4-18 16RScots p54

RAWSON,Hubert Wyatt Hay Capt kia 15-11-16 3 att2 O&BLI p130 CR France152

RAWSON,Lionel Reginald.MC.LtACapt kia 23-10-16 6 att17KRRC p151 MR21

RAWSON,Philip Colin 2Lt kia 25-9-15 RBerks p139 MR19

RAWSON,Stuart Milner TLt kia 20-7-16 20RFus p69 MR21

RAWSON,Thomas Leonard HonLt ded 28-6-17 RAOC IOD p198 MR43 &CR Pakistan50A

RAWSTHORN,Eric 2Lt kia 15-6-15 4LNLancs p234 MR22

RAWSTORNE,Thomas Geoffrey Maj dow 31-7-17 1/1LancHussYeo p204 CR Belgium23

RAY,Archibald Douglas Hussey Capt kia 30-4-15 Worc p109 CR Gallipoli15

RAY,Frederick Lee 2Lt kia 16-5-18 1Beds p86 CR France21

RAY,Philip Oliphant T2Lt ded 13-4-17 8BlkW &59RFC p12&129 MR20

RAY,Reginald Morison 2Lt kia 27-9-18 7Manch p237 CR France712

RAY,Richard T2Lt dow 26-5-18 RASC MT att40RGA 196SB AC p193 CR France40

RAYMENT,Edward TLt ded 6-4-17 RE IWT p48 CR Scot112

RAYMOND,Arthur Augustus Lt kia 1-8-15 2RIrRif p170 MR29

RAYMOND,Bertram Seymour Maj ded 12-8-17 IA 97DeccanHorse p281 CR Asia82

RAYMOND,Edward Wetherall Hunter Lt dow 29-5-15 RInnisF p105 CR Lond4

RAYMOND,Frederick Charles Motley 2Lt kia 21-8-15 8Hamps p229 MR4

RAYMOND,John Brannan.MC.LtACapt&djt dow 4-10-18 6ESurr att 1/5N&D p226 CR France446

RAYMOND,Wynne Dudley.MID Lt kia 26-10-18 IA 2Lancers attMysoreLancers p281 CR Lebanon1

RAYMOND-BARKER,Cecil Langton T2Lt kia 25-9-15 12RB p180 CR France768

RAYMONT,William Clifton Lt kia 6-5-17 3Mon p244 CR Belgium4,5SWBord

RAYNER,Albert Stanley Lt dow 15-7-18 1/2Nhampt attRAF 21ssSect 2AirSupplyDept p138 CR France792

RAYNER,Arthur Tamplin T2Lt dow 6-7-16 44MGC Inf p185 CR France423,kia

RAYNER,Benjamin Harold Capt kia 14-6-17 1/5NStaffs p157 MR20

RAYNER,Cecil Arthur 2Lt dow 9-11-15 6Ess p232 MR4

RAYNER,Charles Oliver T2Lt kia 1-10-17 GL &25RFC p12 CR France88

RAYNER,Cyril Hood T2Lt kia 24-2-17 18LancF p93 CR France648

RAYNER,Donald Lt kia 8-8-18 1Camb C'Coy p245 CR France196

RAYNER,George Biddulph 2Lt kia 12-5-15 3Ess att2Glouc p132 CR Belgium167

RAYNER,Harold 2Lt kia 4-9-18 4EYorks p219 CR Belgium96

RAYNER,Harold Leslie T2Lt kia 1-7-16 9Dev p77 CR France330

RAYNER,Haydn Eric William 2Lt kia 17-3-17 3 att2 O&BLI p130 CR France786,3 att6Bn

RAYNER,Hubert William TLt dow 5-11-17 GL 10RWFus att76TMB p191 CR France563

RAYNER,James Ernest Robert.MC.2LtTLt dow 10-5-18 C91RFA p34 CR France71

RAYNER,John 2Lt dow 6-7-16 4/10Mddx att1/5EKent p236 CR Iraq5

RAYNER,Leonard Bramhall Capt kia 27-3-17 6Ess p232 MR34

RAYNER,Leslie King T2Lt kia 18-4-17 GL att13RSuss att116TMB p191 CR Belgium4

RAYNER,Noel Roderick Lt kia 27-7-17 WYorks &57RFC p12&82 CR Belgium24

RAYNER,Oliver Crossley Lt kia 18-11-16 3 att2Manch p155 MR21

RAYNER,Percy Thomas.MC&Bar.T2Lt kia 26-8-18 18KRRC p151 CR Belgium11,25-8-18

RAYNER,Roy Balfour Hodgson TLt dow 24-5-16 15WYorks p82 CR France169

RAYNER,Ryde Guild 2Lt kia 26-10-17 4NumbF p213 MR30

RAYNES,Albert Brainerd 2Lt kia 11-3-15 RSuss att2RBerks p119 MR22,10-3-15

RAYNES,Albert Herbert Lt kia 25-9-15 11Ess p132 MR19,Arthur 26-9-15

RAYNES,Frank Arthur.MC.2Lt kia 27-3-18 3ScotRif att17RScots p104 MR20

RAYNES,Robert T2Lt dow 17-10-15 14DLI p161 CR France1

RAYNHAM,Charles 2Lt dow 19-3-18 1Mddx p148 CR Belgium45

RAYNOR,Harold Arthur Livingston 2Lt dow 7-6-18 6RB D'Coy p180 CR Mddx66

RAYSON,William Humphrey Ronald TLtACapt dow PoW 27-3-18 C47RFA p34 CR France1266

REA,Frank Melton 2Lt kia 27-3-16 1NumbF p62 MR29

REA,Herbert Finlay Lt kia 16-8-17 14RIrRif p170 MR30

REA,Vivian Trevor Tighe Lt kia 25-10-14 4 att2RIrRif p170 CR France279

REACHER,Stanley William TCapt dow 4-7-16 16RB p180 CR France727,kia

READ,Anketell Moutray.VC.Capt kia 25-9-15 Nhampt &RFC p2&138 CR France219

READ,Arthur Beddome 2Lt kia 16-9-14 1SomLI p80 CR France1107

READ,Arthur Herbert TLt dow 28-4-18 1Worc p109 CR France29

READ,Charles TLt kia 5-10-18 1/2 att9Yorks p91 CR France844

READ,Charles Stanley 2Lt kia 6-12-17 GL &52RFC p12 MR20

READ,Clare Moore T2Lt kia 19-7-18 11MGC Inf p185 CR France223

READ,Cyril de Lacy TLt ded 5-3-19 6Lincs p75

READ,Edrick Hurdman Lt kia 26-12-17 16RFC CR France95

READ,Edward Macartney T2Lt kia 2-4-17 9Dev p77 CR France568

READ,Eric Oswald Chap4Cl kia 3-10-18 RAChDept att5Dors p199 CR France273

READ,George Averille Capt kia 8-3-17 3 att7Leinst p175 CR Belgium100,Averil

READ,George Chisholm 2Lt kia 4-1-18 RE attRFC p17&48 CR Belgium18

READ,Harry Esmond Capt kia 10-8-17 LincYeo att24RFC p19&204 CR France660

READ,John Frederick Cullingford T2Lt kia 28-9-15 11Ess p132 MR19,26-9-15

READ,Lawrence William TLt kia 9-12-16 1Ess p132 MR21

READ,Leonard St.Clair T2Lt ded PoW 20-12-16 11Ess p132 CR France924,Lt

READ,Phillips Towter 2Lt kia 23-10-17 2RFA p34 MR21,Towler

READ,Stanley.MC.T2Lt kia 28-4-17 17Mddx p148 MR20

READ,Stephen Tucker TLt ded 11-12-18 GL 15EYorks att1KAR p84,202&267 CR EAfrica77

READ,Terrance Capon T2Lt dow 22-4-17 Norf att1/5Bn p74 CR Palestine8

READ,Walter Felix Lt ded 14-9-15 1/8Hamps p229 CR Egypt6

READ,William Lister.MC.Capt kia 10-3-18 6Ches p222 CR Palestine3

READE,Arnold Baillie T2Lt kia 21-2-18 66RFC p17 CR Italy9

READE,Charlton Leverton Ridout 2Lt kia 9-9-16 2RSuss p119 MR21

READE,John Henry Loftus.MID Lt kia 28-10-14 Manch p155 MR22

READE,Leonard Edwin T2Lt kia 30-8-17 9SLancs p125 CR Greece5

READE,Reginald William TLt kia 4/5-4-16 9RWar p65 CR Iraq5

READER,Bertram Edward T2Lt kia 22-10-17 6SomLI p80 MR30

READER,William Howard 2Lt dow 30-7-16 5SfthH p241 CR France176

READING,Harold Leslie 2Lt kia 5-11-17 108RFA p34 CR Belgium12

READING,John Francis 2Lt kia 29-4-16 7Worc p226 CR France1327

READING,Vernon Jack 2Lt kia 26-3-15 15RFC p17 MR20

READMAN,Wilfred T2LtACapt dow 30-9-18 9 att2/4LNLancs p136 CR France1184

READY,Edward Charles 2Lt dow PoW 2-5-17 3 att1RBerks p139 CR France1276

READY,Nathaniel Henry Alter 2Lt dow 1-8-17 MGC F'HB p185 CR Belgium11

REAH,Kenneth Hudson T2Lt ded 25-11-18 3KRRC p151 CR Greece9

REANEY,Harold Agnew.MC.TLt ded 27-7-18 Beds p263 CR Hunts83

REANEY,Michael Foster Capt kia 2-7-15 IMS att 1/5GurkhaRif p281 CR Gallipoli3

REAVELL,Keith Watts TLt kia 9-12-16 12Hamps p121 CR Greece5,10-12-16

REAVIE,Wilfred Laurance 2Lt kia 16-8-17 3RDubF p177 MR30

REAY,Stanley 2Lt kia 28-1-18 11RFC p17 MR20

REAY,Thomas Stanley Lt dow 1-3-18 3 att10DCLI p114 CR France398

REAY,William Roland T2Lt kia 27-5-18 25MGC Inf p185 CR France1332

REBBECK,Edward William Wise T2Lt kld 24-4-16 KRRC &RFC p3&151 CR Hamps15

REBBECK,William Henry.MC.TLt ded 4-11-18 RE 50Div p48 CR France341

RECKENZAUN,Augustus Lt ded 28-1-19 SL EAfrUL p268 CR SAfrica30

REDDEN,George Herbert.MC.2LtTCapt kia 7-6-17 7ELancs p111 CR Belgium102

REDDIE,Francis Graham 2Lt 18-5-18 206RAF MR20

REDDING,Edward Joseph.DCM.2Lt kia 4-10-17 RWKent p141 MR30

REDDING,J.SubCdr 13-2-20 IA ExRFA CR Norf209

REDDING,John Hamilton Montford 2LtTLt ded 2-3-17 RMunstF p176

REDDING,John Wills T2Lt kia 24-4-18 7 att2ELancs p111 CR France304

REDDY,William George Lt ded 4-4-19 1CamH p168 CR France1357,Wilfred kldacc

REDFERN,Frederick Arthur Dudley TLt ded 15-7-17 GL attEmpS PersianRif p191 CR Iraq6

REDFERN,Samuel Lees Capt dow 2-3-17 1/5LNLancs p234 CR Belgium7,2-8-17

REDFERN,Wilfrid ACapt kia 22-3-18 3 att7EYorks p84 CR France560

REDGATE,Bernard Allan 2Lt kia 29-4-18 B15RHA p34 CR Belgium36

REDHEAD,Harold Arthur Lt kia 7-8-17 3 att6Nhampt p138 CR France141

REDMAN,Arthur Sidney 2Lt ded 27-11-19 IA IMS RoO att37Dogras p281 MR67,22-7-18

REDMAN,Wilfred George T2Lt kld 8-11-17 GL &RFC p12 CR Norf259

REDMOND,William Hoey Kearney TMaj dow 7-6-17 6RIrReg p89 CR Belgium183,7-6-16

REDPATH,Harold Edwin 2Lt kia 15-7-16 1NumbF p62 MR21
RADPATH,James Thomas 2Lt kia 25-4-15 KOSB p102 CR Gallipoli3
REDSHAW,Walter Geoffrey T2Lt kia 6-3-16 6EKent p58 MR29
REDWAY,Frank Mercer 2Lt kia 14-2-18 2/21Lond p251 CR Palestine3
REECE,F.B.Capt dow 20-4-18 RE &4RAF p48 CR France134
REECE,Humphrey Stanley TLt dow 2-4-16 1GordH p167 CR Belgium21
REED,Allan Thomas Lt kld 1-11-18 17Lond &RAF p256
REED,Andrew Gordon Capt kia 10-8-15 7RWFus p223 MR4
REED,Bernard TLt kia 12-4-18 10 att15WYork p82 MR32
REED,Bertram Lt kia 12-4-18 15WYorks p82 MR32
REED,Charles Napier TLt kia 24-11-17 12SWBord p100 MR17
REED,Charles Sydney Lt kia 8-5-15 3Mon A'Coy p244 MR29
REED,Charles Sydney T2Lt kia 14-7-16 7Leic p88 MR21
REED,Clifford Hugh.MC.Chap4Cl kia 7-6-17 RAChDept p199 CR Belgium152
REED,Dane Baron TCapt kia 18-8-16 14 att13Mddx p148 MR21
REED,Frederick Capt ded 28-4-15 A&SH p266
REED,Frederick William Carlton 2Lt kia 3-5-17 8RB p180 MR20
REED,George.MC.Lt ded 21-10-17 IARO attS&TCps 5Div p281 CR Iraq8,Capt
REED,Gerald Francis Woolterton.MID TLt kia 21-3-18 8BordR p117 MR20
REED,Gordon Vernon 2Lt kia 22-3-18 7N&D p233 CR France530
REED,Guy Baron Lt dow 23-8-18 8 att2Beds p86 CR France119
REED,Henry T2Lt kia 30-8-18 A57MGC Divl p185 CR France592,Inf
REED,Henry Gerrard Capt kia 29-10-18 IA 114Mahrattas p281 MR38
REED,Henry William Terrent 2Lt kia 2-5-15 2Mon p244 CR Belgium92
REED,Horace Alfred.MC.MID TLt dow 9-4-18 11Suff p79 MR32
REED,James Richard T2Lt kia 24-11-17 8RFus p69 MR17
REED,John Charles.MC.2Lt ded 14-12-18 D280RFA 56Div p34 CR France1142
REED,John Sleeman 2Lt ded 31-3-16 EKent &RFC p3&58,31-1-16 CR Norf131,kld
REED,Leslie Augustus Lt kia 27-8-15 1/4Lincs p217 CR Belgium127
REED,Paul Maurice T2Lt ded 27-12-15 8SomLI att&RFC p80&2,Maurier CR Egypt9
REED,Robert 2Lt kia 24-5-15 1Dev p77 CR Belgium56
REED,Russel Walter 2Lt kia 11-10-18 1RFus p69 CR France270
REED,Sydney George Herbert TLt ded 24-12-18 104MGC Inf p185 CR Belgium393
REED,Talbot.MID Capt kia 12-3-15 IA 67Punjabis att59Rif p281 CR France727
REED,Walter Nelson.MC.TLt kia 27-10-16 RGA 10SB p41 CR France453
REED,William John T2Lt dow PoW 28-10-17 8Dev p77 CR Belgium393
REED,William Percy 2Lt kia 15-9-17 RFA 232ArmyBde p34 CR Belgium34
REED-HARDING,Clarence Henry Lt kld 15-2-18 1/5SomLI attRFC p19&218 CR Egypt1
REEDER,Edward TLt kia 26-9-15 8EYorks p84 MR19
REEDER,Robert Capt kia 6-1-18 10Manch attRFC p19&237 CR France62
REEKS,Frederick Lt ded 7-8-21 IARO attLabCps p281 CR Staffs49
REEP,Alfred Mills T2Lt kia 16-9-16 6DCLI p114 MR21
REES,Albert Lloyd TLt kia 6-11-17 1RWFus p98 CR Palestine1,1/6Bn
REES,Alexander Armstrong TCapt ded 7-2-17 RAMC att7Suss p267 CR France57,4-2-17
REES,Andrew Montgomery Lt kia 18-10-16 9Ess p132 MR21
REES,David John Lt ded 7-7-19 11DLI p265
REES,David Melvyn 2Lt dow 12-4-17 2DLI p161 CR France98
REES,Edris 2Lt dow 27-10-17 3 att1RWFus p98 MR30
REES,Edward Davies T2Lt 49009 kia 13-6-17 RWFus att16Bn p98 CR Belgium73
REES,Edgar George 2Lt kia 23-11-17 19RWFus p98 MR17
REES,Eric Montague 2Lt kia 8-10-18 6 att13RFus p69 MR16
REES,Ernest Llewellyn T2Lt kia 22-10-18 B113RFA p34 CR Belgium141
REES,Henry Charles TMaj kia 5-8-16 12SWBord p100 CR France550
REES,Henry Hugh Tregarthen T2Lt kia 11-7-16 16RWFus p98 MR21
REES,Ivor Guest TLt dow 5-8-16 9WelchR p127 CR France145,2Lt
REES,John Cyril T2Lt ded 6-11-15 3 att8WelchR p127 CR Egypt6
REES,John Oswald T2Lt dow 8-11-17 SWBord att24WelshR p100 CR Egypt2
REES,John Trevor 2Lt kia 22-1-15 1RWFus p98 CR France684
REES,Kenneth David 2lt dow 29-8-17 4 att5Ches p222 CR France8
REES,Lawrence Sinclair T2Lt kia 10-7-16 13WelshR p127 MR21,Laurence
REES,Leofric Lt dow 4-10-17 4 att1RWar p65 MR30
REES,Morgan James TCapt dow 30-10-16 RAMC 132FA p197 CR France102
REES,Owen George 2Lt dow 20-9-18 10Lond p248 CR Palestine9
REES,Robert Griffith Lt 10-7-16 15RWFus MR21 CR France1890
REES,Roland Gwyn TLt dow 10/11-7-16 15RWFus p98
REES,Rowland.MC.Lt kia 25-3-18 6SfthH p241 MR20

REES,Thomas Stanley TLt ded 18-3-16 46MGC Inf A'Coy p185 CR France658
REES,Tom Lt kia 17-9-16 14RWFus &RFC p3&98 CR France667
REES-MOGG,Louis Leyson Lt kia 11-8-15 RE 68FC p48 MR4
REESE,Arnold.MC.2Lt kia 1-8-17 2WYorks p82 MR29
REESE,David William Capt ded 23-6-21 RAMC CR Devon72
REESE,Richard Tudor Capt kia 23/24-8-18 3Mon att1Lpool p244 CR France214
REESE,William TLt ded 2-2-17 15WelchR p127 CR Wales245
REEVE,Alan Lt 27-3-18 1CentOntarioR &11RFC MR20
REEVE,Charles d'Arcy Edmund Wentworth TCapt kld 18-7-16 Suff attRFC p3&79 CR Suff242,REEVES
REEVE,Charles Frederick T2Lt dow 13-5-17 GL &2RFC p12 CR France80,15-5-17
REEVE,Charles Simms Capt kia 14-2-15 2ESurr p113 MR29
REEVE,Ernest William.MC.Capt kia 3-5-17 11EYorks p84 MR20
REEVE,Garnett Norman Bray Lt kia 1-9-18 9Mach p237 CR France239
REEVE,George.MC.MM.Lt ded 14-10-18 1RIrF attKRRCp265 CR Nhampt ,15-10-18
REEVE,Gilford Montier Capt kia 8-7-16 12Ess p132 MR21
REEVE,Harry 2Lt kia 18-5-16 5Lpool p215 CR France927
REEVE,Herbert 2Lt ded 8-2-17 Ex 10RSuss p264 CR Mddx26
REEVE,Herbert T2Lt kia 30-11-17 9RFus p70 MR17
REEVE,Herbert Joseph 2Lt ded 24-9-15 1Hereford p252 CR Europe1
REEVE,John Stanley Lt kia 29-6-18 2HAC Inf p206 CR Italy8
REEVE,Walter James Lt ded 29-11-18 1/6Dev p217 MR66
REEVE,William Tankerville Monypenny.CMG.LtCol ded 28-9-15 Leinst att1Ess p175 CR Lond4
REEVES,Frank T2Lt dow 30-12-17 247MGC Inf p185 CR France285
REEVES,Geoffrey Browning Capt acckld 28-2- 17 IA 9Horse p281 CR France1564
REEVES,Geoffrey Frederick John 2Lt kia 6-6-15 3Hamps p121 CR Gallipoli2
REEVES,Harry Charles T2Lt kia 24-8-16 21 att2WelshR p127 MR21
REEVES,Harry Gosford TCapt kia 24-1-18 RFC p17CR France285
REEVES,Hugh Charles Maj ded 29-1-15 RGA 4MthBty p41 MR43
REEVES,Laurence 2Lt dow 25-8-18 1Herts p252 CR France84
REEVES,Leslie Leonhardt Capt ded 14-2-19 16/41RFA p34 CR Germany1
REEVES,Stafford Reichel Maj ded 26-3-19 RGA p41 CR India97A
REEVES,Victor Charles Methuen.MID Maj kia 26-2-16 1/1DorsYeo p203 CR Egypt6
REEVES-SMITH,Denys 2Lt kia 2-10-15 RE 87FC p48 MR19
REGAN,Ernest Charles T2Lt kia 21-3-18 9RSuss p119 CR France366
REGAN,James Herbert T2Lt kia 27-9-18 1NumbF p62 MR16
REHM,A.G.MC.Maj 12-4-21 SL &EAPayCps p EAfrica51
REICHARDT,Paul 2Lt kia 31-7-17 3ELancs p111 MR29
REID,Alex John 2Lt kia 26-4-16 1ESurr p113 CR France1182
REID,Alexander 2Lt kia 15-2-17 1/22Lond p251 CR Belgium127
REID,Alexander.MC.Capt dow 13-10-18 6GordH p242 CR France686
REID,Alexander Daniel.DSO.MajALtCol kia 31-7-17 1RIrRif p170
REID,Alexander William T2Lt kia 4-3-17 6KOSB att43RFC p12&102 CR France924
REID,Annie Campbell SNurse ded 4-3-19 TFNS p254 CR Egypt9,QAIMNS Res
REID,Archibald David 2Lt dow 8-8-17 5 att4Mddx p148 CR France285
REID,Bernard Joseph T2Lt kia 28-6-16 3RDubF p177 CR France423,9Bn
REID,Bruce Simpson 2Lt kia 6-8-18 RGA 192SB p41 CR France247
REID,Charles Douglas 2Lt kia 15-7-16 9HLI p241 CR France296
REID,Charles John Capt 10-8-15 9RWar MR4
REID,David Inglis 2Lt kia 25-8-15 2/5RScot p211 CR Gallipoli4
REID,Donald 2Lt kia 17-8-17 4 att2HLI p163 CR France163
REID,Douglas Leman 2Lt kia 21-9-17 6Ess p232 CR France149
REID,Edward Harington Capt kia 30-4-15 2Suff p79 MR15,26-8-14
REID,Ellis,Ramsay.CB.DSO.Col 14-10-18 RAPC CR Essex145 Ex Ess
REID,Eric Archdall 2Lt kia 29-3-18 1Hamps A'Coy p121 MR20
REID,Eric Bruce Capt kia 20-10-14 1NStaffs p157 CR France681
REID,Fergus Hamilton Capt kia 16-5-15 RGA 59SB p41 CR France260
REID,G.E.H.Lt kia 9-3-15 SL att4KAR p268 CR EAfrica12 &CR Tanzania1
REID,Geoffrey Percy Nevile Lt kia 14-5-15 EssYeo p203 MR29,13-5-15
REID,George 2Lt kia 9-4-17 1/6GordH p242 CR France184
REID,George Lt kia 12-4-18 8RScots B'Coy p211 MR32
REID,George Lt kia 25-8-18 27HQ RFA p34 CR France239
REID,George Leslie 2Lt kia 1-12-17 7DragGds p21 MR17
REID,George Robert T2Lt kia 15-9-16 1EKent p58 MR21
REID,George Whiteley Capt&Adjt kia 4-5-15 2Hamps p121 CR Gallipoli2,1-5-15
REID,Gerald Mortimer Lt kia 9-5-18 11Lond p248 CR France516

REID,Gordon 2Lt kia 3-5-17 9 att6KOSB p102 MR20

REID,Gordon Alexander T2Lt kia 8-10-18 1Ess p132 CR France611

REID,Guy Patrick Spence.MC.LtTCapt kld 16-10-17 1SfthH attRFC p12&165 CR Lincs181

REID,Hugh 2Lt kia 23-7-18 3 att1/6GordH p167 CR France622

REID,Ian Capt ded 13-6-19 RE CR Canada256

REID,James.MID TCapt kia 25-9-15 10HLI p163 CR France114

REID,James 2Lt kia 23-10-16 4 att2ScotRif p104 MR21

REID,James T2Lt dow 1-2-17 15HLI p163 CR France41

REID,James Lt dow 8-10-18 1LNLancs p136 CR France146

REID,James Archibald John 2Lt dow 16-10-16 1Camb p245 CR France59

REID,James Lestock Ironside Lt kia 2-11-14 IA 1/2 att2/2GurkhaRif p281 MR28

REID,James Robert Lt kia 27-7-16 1RBerks p139 MR21

REID,J.F.W.Lt 25-3-21 2RInnisF CR Dorset57

REID,John T2Lt kia 18-8-16 4Lpool p72 CR France432

REID,John LtACapt kia 4-4-18 15HLI p163 CR France745,Lt

REID,John 2Lt kia 16-9-18 5DLI p239 CR Belgium188,19Bn

REID,John C.M.Lt 12-5-18 213RAF MR20

REID,John Deighton Lewis Lt kia 9-5-18 23Lond p252 CR France516

REID,John Gardner TCapt kia 8-9-16 11Worc p109 CR Greece6

REID,John Lavens 2Lt dow 12-9-16 10Lpool p216 CR France23,13-9-16

REID,John Lawrie T2Lt dow 16-7-16 RFC p3 CR France203

REID,John Lindsay T2LtACapt dow 18-10-17 RE 179TC p48 CR Belgium16

REID,John Shute 2Lt dow 17-8-17 3SWBord att87TMB p100 CR Belgium16,2Bn

REID,Norman Malcolm TCapt ded 12-1-17 GL RASC p191 CR Glouc9

REID,Percy Cargill 2Lt kia 6-5-17 16Lond p250 CR France537

REID,Reginald Harper LtACapt kia 14-9-18 153RFA p34 CR France856

REID,Robert T2Lt kia 22-5-16 9GordH p167 CR France423,21-5-16

REID,Robert T2Lt kia 1-7-16 9 att1KOSB p102 CR France220

REID,Robert TLt kia 1-7-16 15RScots p54 MR21

REID,Robert 2Lt kia 30-7-16 1/7BlkW p231 CR France1890

REID,Robert Neill 2Lt dow 14-5-17 1/2 att4Lpool p72 CR France145

REID,Robert Heslop 2Lt kia 2-12-17 3HLI p163 MR30,Hislop

REID,Robert Logan T2Lt kia 8-8-15 RE 29DivSigs p48 CR Gallipoli1

REID,Robert Robertson 2Lt dow 13-7-16 RE 130Co p48 CR France833

REID,Robert Vernon Lt dow 26-3-18 5LNLancs p234 MR20

REID,Robert Walker TCapt kia 13-8-16 10/11HLI D'Coy p163 CR France151

REID,Robert William 2Lt dow 17-5-16 9BlkW p129 CR France80

REID,Robert William Kerr T2Lt kia 7-7-16 11 att9LNLancs p136 MR21

REID,Stuart Keppel.MC.Capt dow 29-7-18 1/4RSuss p228 CR France864

REID,Thomas Ernest 2Lt dow 18-4-17 3 att3BlkW A'Coy p129 CR France40,Capt

REID,Thomas Mayne,MC 2Lt kia 3-5-17 9 att6KOSB p102 MR20,Capt

REID,William Alexander Lt dow 27-12-17 2/9Lpool p216 CR Belgium13,26-12-17

REID,William Bacon Johnston Capt dow 20-5-15 3SfthH attGordH p165 CR Scot153

REID,William Douglas.MC.TCapt kia 5-10-17 RAMC att21Manch p197 CR Belgium72

REID,William George 2Lt dow 23-2-17 3ScotRif p104 CR France786

REID,William John T2Lt kia 26-11-17 6GordH p167 CR France398

REID,William Leonard Capt dow 17-4-15 Dors p124 CR Iraq6,15-4-15

REID,William Morison T2Lt dow 26-2-16 23Manch p156 CR France345,7Bn

REIDY,Edmund McAyliffe TCapt dow 23-7-16 11Manch p156 CR France46

REIDY,Harold St.John Q.TCapt ded 19-10-18 RASC p193 CR France52

REILLY,Alexander Maxwell T2LtACapt dow 26-11-16 9RInnisF p105 CRFrance285

REILLY,Arthur Frederick Capt kia 30-5-19 IARO attZhobMil p281 MR43

REILLY,Aubrey Spranger Townsend Capt kia 22-2-17 IA 69Punjabis att92 p281 CR Iraq5

REILLY,Henry Duncan Ryan Capt dow 30-5-19 4RWSurr p212

REILLY,James Miller T2Lt kia 20-9-17 12RScots p54 MR30

REILLY,Ralph Alec Lt kia 24-11-14 IA 31Punjabis att58Rif p281 CR France80,23-11-14

REINCKE,Leo Frederick TCapt kia 17-8-17 10WRid att48RFC p12&116 CR France1361

REISS,Stephen Lacy TLt kia 13-10-15 5RBerks p139 MR19

REISS,Willoughby Emil Lt dow 8-8-15 1/6Manch p236 CR Gallipoli1

REITH,Steven Donaldson.DCM.2Lt kia 20-9-18 IARO att2/42Deolali p282 CR Palestine9,21-9-18 Ex 17HLI

REITH,William Robertson T2Lt ded 17-2-19 9TankCps p188 CR France113

RELF,Thomas Joseph Lt kia 4-10-17 7Dev p217 MR30

RELTON,Douglas Edward Lloyd Lt dow 4-6-18 23Bty 40Bde RFA p34 CR France10

RELTON,Gerald Lyons 2lt dow 17-9-14 3ESurr p113

REMINGTON,Felix George 2Lt kia 11-5-17 RGA 3HAG p41 MR20

REMINGTON,Wallace T2Lt kia 23-3-18 24RFus p70 MR20

REMMER,Fred 2Lt kia 12-4-18 5NumbF p62 MR32

REMNANT,Percy Waterland Lt ded 25-12-20 RASC CR Europe149

RENDALL,Francis Holden Shuttleworth.DSO.TLtCol dow 9-7-16 DCLI att5Y&L p114 CR France245

RENDALL,George 2Lt kia 24-3-18 11KRRC p151 MR27

RENDALL,Robert Alexander.MC.TLtACapt kia 18-9-18 8DCLI p114 CR Greece6

RENDEL,Andrew James.MC.CaptAMaj dow 29-6-17 81/5RFA p34 CR France178

RENDEL,Reginald Dacres 2LtTLt kia 16-5-15 2 O&BLI p130 MR22

RENDELL,Leonard Wyndham.MID.2Lt dow 19-10-14 1Beds p86 CR France80

RENDELL-DUNN,Hubert Cecil T2Lt dow 24-11-16 11 att10LNLancs p136 CR France74

RENDLE,Anthony Darley Russell T2Lt kia 10-10-17 9Dev p77

RENDLE,Arthur Edward 2Lt kia 6-11-17 1DCLI p114 MR30

RENDLE,George 2Lt kia 1-10-18 4EYorks p219 MR30

RENNARD,Edward Marmaduke.MID Capt kia 8-8-16 1/4LNLancs p234 MR21

RENNICK,Frank R.LtCol dow 26-4-15 IA 40Pathans p282 CR France200

RENNIE,Cyril Thomas T2Lt kia 25-9-16 9Leic p88 MR21

RENNIE,David Lt 2-6-15 IAUL att25Cav MR43

RENNIE,Donald Williamson 2Lt kia 11-11-14 5RFus p70 CR France451

RENNIE,Edward Clement Lt dow 16-6-18 RGA attRAF p41 CR Greece4

RENNIE,F.Robert T2Lt kia 9-2-16 9ScotRif p104 CR France264

RENNIE,Guy Capt kia 26-10-14 1GrenGds p50 MR29

RENNIE,Hugh Robert 2Lt dow PoW 10-7-18 14Lond attCamH p249 CR Europe149

RENNIE,James Davidson 2Lt kia 9-4-17 1/5GordH p242 CR France184

RENNIE,James Francis.MC.2Lt kia 31-7-17 B70 RFA p34&259 MR29

RENNIE,John Archibald 2Lt dow 25-7-16 3Dev p77 CR Scot212

RENNISON,Harold Leslie Lt kia 12-11-17 IARO att2/3GurkhaRif p282 CR Palestine8

RENNISON,Walter Martyn Lt kia 30-12-16 3 att6RIrReg p89 MR29

RENNY,Gerald Mercer Lt kia 15-4-17 92RFA p34 CR France905

RENNY,James 2Lt kia 26-9-17 5BlkW p231 CR Belgium88

RENNY-TAILOUR,Henry Frederick Thornton 2Lt kia 11-11-14 RE p48 MR29,TAILYOUR

RENSHAW,Alfred Lt dow 7-6-15 5LancF p221 CR Gallipoli1

RENSHAW,Frank T2Lt kia 12-7-16 17N&D p134 CR France727

RENSHAW,Leonard TCapt kia 13-5-16 18Manch p156 CR France625

RENSHAW,Percy Connaught T2Lt dow 24-7-18 Lincs att2/5LancF p75 CR France10

RENTON,Alan John Capt kia 2-12-17 2Ess p132 CR Palestine9

RENTON,Charles T2Lt kia 6-3-17 8 att1Nhampt p138 CR France328

RENTON,Colin Campbell LtCol sInflictedGunshot 2-9-15 IA 98Inf p282 CR EAfrica54,kldacc

RENTON,Cyril William Lt ded 19-7-17 20Lond p251 CR Surrey38

RENTON,Elwyn George TLt ded 29-5-18 RASC attCamelCps p193 MR67

RENTON,Francis Wallace Home TLt kia 30-8-16 8BordR p117 CR France246

RENTON,Harry Noel Leslie TLt kia 30-7-15 9KRRC p151 MR29

RENTON,Stanley.MC.TLtACapt kia 6-5-17 8Dev p77CR France614

RENTON,William Gerald Forrester Capt kia 2-6-15 1 att2DragGds p20 CR Belgium4

RENTOUL,Alexander Lt kia 27-3-18 YorkHuss att25RFC p19&206 CR France514

RENWICK,Donald William Lt dow 14-6-17 3 att1NStaffs p157 CR Belgium127

RENWICK,Gidean Andrew Forrest 2Lt kia 22-8-17 13RScots D'Coy p54 MR30

RENWICK,Hugh Archibald Lt kld 19-8-18 SWBord &RAF p100 CR Hamps145

RENWICK,James Clarence T2Lt ded 21-3-18 10RIrRif p170&257 CR Numb87,Lt

RENWICK,Thomas Buchanan Lt kia 29-4-15 6RB att3Mddx p180 MR29

REPEN,Frederick Capt ded 13-6-19 RFA Lond DAC p34 CR Germany1,Frank

REPTON,C.T.Lt kia 25-4-18 NottsYeo &RAF p205 CR Palestine3

RERRIE,Errol Seymour.MC.Lt 12-5-17 3 att7EYorks p84

RESTALL,Kenneth.MID TLt kia 26-9-16 12Mddx p148 MR21

RETALLACH-MALONEY,Henry Richard Capt ded 17-12-18 6Ess p232 CR Essex1

RETTIE,William Philip 2Lt kia 1-7-16 1BordR p117 MR21

REVELL,Robert Arthur Capt dow 13-6-15 1Ess p132 CR Egypt3,Lt 12-6-15

REVELLE,Roy Cyril 2Lt kia 15-9-18 3RWKent &RAF p141 CR Palestine9,16-9-18 8 O&BLI

REVENE,Howard Stephen Lt ded 25-8-17 RGA 72HB p41 CR Iraq6

REVINGTON,John Huleatt 2Lt kia 4-9-16 9Dev p77 MR21

REW,Douglas Jolland 2Lt kia 28-6-17 5Ess p232 CR France115

REW,John Frederick George T2Lt kia 1-7-16 8Dev p77 CR France330

REX,Eustace Charles T2Lt kia 3-9-16 18HLI D'Coy p163 CR France402,2KOSB

REYMES-COLE,William Elmer.DSO.Capt kia 11-11-14 3RMunstF p176 CR Belgium96

REYNARD,Charles Frederick Capt ded 16-6-18 3EYorks p84 CR France772

REYNARD,Henry Corner T2Lt kia 25-9-15 1SStaffs D'Coy p123 MR19

REYNELL,Frederick Henry T2Lt kia 23-4-17 GL &35RFC p12 CR France95

REYNISH,Horace John Cook 2Lt kia 23-3-18 59RFC p17 MR20

REYNOLDS,Albert Stanley 2Lt kia 13-4-18 4DCLI p227 CR France100,1Bn

REYNOLDS,Alfred Slater 2Lt kia 25-7-17 70/34RFA p34 CR Belgium10

REYNOLDS,Arthur HonCapt ded 2-6-17 RAOC p198 CR France102

REYNOLDS,Benton William Richard.MID Lt ded 20-7-16 IA 103MahrattaLI p282 CR Iraq8,Benbow

REYNOLDS,Charles Edward Lt dow 23-10-18 21Lond &RAF p251&258

REYNOLDS,Douglas.VC.Maj ded 23-2-16 83RFA p34 CR France40

REYNOLDS,Eric Hindle 2Lt ded 26-12-17 10Ches att120PoWCo p96 CR Ches31

REYNOLDS,Francis Daniel.MC.T2Lt ded 9-9-17 8RWSurr p56 CR Kent83,Lt

REYNOLDS,Frank T2Lt kia 13-9-16 2N&D D'Coy att71TMB p134 CR France294

REYNOLDS,Frank Leslie T2Lt kia 20-7-16 11 att15N&D p134 MR21

REYNOLDS,George Hubbard T2Lt kia 9-4-16 10SLancs p125 MR38

REYNOLDS,Guy Beresford Eaton 2Lt kia 18-11-16 3 att2YLI p143 CR France152

REYNOLDS,H.C.Capt kia 20-9-14 3Wilts p153 MR15

REYNOLDS,Harold Henry T2Lt kia 4-10-17 1Beds p86 CR Belgium112 Ex Sgt 4Wilts

REYNOLDS,J.E.2Lt kld 18-5-18 GL &RAF p191

REYNOLDS,John James 2LtTCapt dow 31-12-15 1ScotRif p104 CR France80

REYNOLDS,John William 2Lt kia 7-8-15 4Y&L p238 CR Belgium85

REYNOLDS,Percival 2Lt mbk 19-9-18 10WYorks p256 MR16

REYNOLDS,Percy Basil TCapt ded 4-12-18 RASC p193 CR France34

REYNOLDS,Richard Frederick TLtACapt kia 2-10-18 6RRofCav att15Hamps p24 CR Belgium115

REYNOLDS,Robert Reynold 2Lt kia 31-5-18 41RFA p34 CR France266

REYNOLDS,Sidney Holdsworth Lt dow 16-4-18 1/4Y&L p238 CR Belgium38

REYNOLDS,Thomas James Capt kia 25-10-14 2RIrRif p170 CR France279

REYNOLDS,Thomas Josceline Gordon 2Lt dow 11-10-16 4 att2Beds p86 CR France389

REYNOLDS,Victor Eustace TCapt kia 4-5-16 10WYorks p82 CR France922

REYNOLDS,William Kingsley Lt kia 10-9-15 3 att1Leic p88 CR Belgium126

REYNOLDS-PARSONS,William Douglas Lt 26-5-18 11RWSurr CR Belgium36 see PARSONS

RHEAD,Charles Henry David 2Lt kia 28-3-18 7Manch p237 MR27

RHODES,Arthur Lt kia 25-5-15 7DLI p239 CR Belgium167,24-5-15

RHODES,Charles Frederick Stanley T2Lt kia 7-6-17 11Ches MR29

RHODES,Gerald Rudolph Lt ded 30-10-18 6Ches p256 CR Suff9

RHODES,Henry Capt kia 17-9-17 RFA 33DAC p34 CR Belgium15

RHODES,John Arthur 2Lt kia 24-8-18 6WYorks p218 CR France832

RHODES,John Kenneth T2Lt dow 17-7-16 10 att8BordR p117 CR France44,16-7-16

RHODES,Thomas George Lt 11-6-18 3WRid att57RAF p12 France792

RHODES,W.H.Lt 5-5-16 10Lond CR Wilts180

RHODES,William Marvell 2Lt kia 16-9-18 4YLI p235 MR21

RHODES-MOORHOUSE,William Barnard.VC.Lt 27-4-15 RFC CR Dorset6

RHUDE,Foster Weston 2Lt kia 30-11-17 GL &43RFC p12 CR France88

RHYS,Watkin Leoline Tom T2Lt dow 24-4-17 13RB p180 CR France113

RHYS-DAVIDS,Arthur Percival Foley.DSO.MC.2Lt kia 27-10-17 56RFC p12 MR20

RIACH,Gordon Pennington Lt kia 24-9-18 3CamH p168 CR France725,1Bn

RIACH,Walter Hamilton LtTCapt dow PoW 5-5-18 5CamH p168 CR France716

RICARD,Frank 2Lt kia 25-4-15 4 att1RWar p65 MR29

RICE,Arnold Hamilton T2Lt kia 29-11-17 GL &19RFC p12 CR France285

RICE,Arthur Henry TLt kia 20-9-17 17KRRC p151 MR30

RICE,Arthur Hugh Hamilton 2Lt kia 7-2-16 IARO att114Mahrattas p282 MR38

RICE,Bernard Neville TCapt ded 9-7-17 10EYorks p84 CR War83,dow 10-7-17

RICE,Cecil Vincent 2Lt kia 11-5-17 HouseHoldBn p20 CR France546

RICE,Edgar William 2Lt kia 9-8-16 5LNLancs p234 CR France400

RICE,Edward Felix 2Lt dow 18-2-17 5Lond att169TMB p246 CR France345

RICE,Ernest John T2Lt kia 20-11-17 Dev att7SomLI p77 MR17

RICE,Fred T2Lt kia 1-7-16 8 att2SWBord p100 CR France1490

RICE,Frederick Thomas T2Lt kia 12-9-18 13RB p180 CR France530

RICE,Gerard Beechey Howard BrigGen ded 7-5-16 IA Staff 35InfBde p282 CR Iraq5,31Punjabis

RICE,James Alfred.DCM.T2Lt kia 11-10-18 24MGC p185 CR France270

RICE,John Arthur Talbot.MC.Capt dow PoW 14-4-18 5Lancers p22 CR France1061

RICE-Jones,Alfred Theodore TCapt dow 23-3-18 12Lpool p72 CR France1063

RICH,Arthur Capt ded 29-2-16 SL RecOff p201&268 CR Mon67

RICH,Austin Frederick 2Lt kia 27-12-17 2/24Lond p252 CR Palestine3

RICH,Charles Bayard.MID Maj kia 16-8-17 45RFA p34 MR30

RICH,Christopher Stiles Capt kld 22-3-15 RFA attRFC p2&34,ded CR France284,Maj dedacc

RICH,Cyril Shirston 2Lt kia 7-8-16 164RFA p34 CR France80,Lt

RICH,Ernest Evelyn.DSO.Maj dow 1-12-17 U'RHA p34 CR France364

RICH,John Stanser Lt kia 16/19-5-15 3 att1Lpool p72 MR22,17-5-15

RICH,William Suttor Capt dow 9-11-14 Ches p96 CR France1276

RICHARDES,Roderick Alexander William Pryse 2Lt dow PoW 18-9-18 1 att11RWFus p98 MR37

RICHARDS,Arthur 2Lt dow 27-6-17 1Mon p244 CR France550

RICHARDS,Arthur Gough TLt kia 24-4-17 12Worc p109 CR France364

RICHARDS,Arthur Stanley Lt kia 25-6-17 RFA Y8TMB p208 CR Belgium29

RICHARDS,Arthur William Lt kia 28-3-18 A62RFA p34 CR France343

RICHARDS,Bruce Carlton Lt kia 11-7-17 RFA p34 CR Belgium173

RICHARDS,Charles Walter 2Lt kia 27-9-16 1/8Lpool p216 MR21

RICHARDS,Dudley Brookhouse 2Lt dow 20-9-16 6Glouc att15MGC p187&225 CR France105,29-9-16

RICHARDS,Ella Miss ded 14-10-18 VAD BRCS p200 CR Greece9

RICHARDS,Ernest Harry T2Lt kia 2-4-17 21Manch p156 CR France689

RICHARDS,Ewart Wilfred T2Lt dow 10-5-18 10RWar p65 CR France100,11-5-18

RICHARDS,Francis Graham.MIDx2 Maj kia 5-3-15 RAMC 14FA p197 CR Belgium170

RICHARDS,Frank 2Lt kia 14-5-15 2Hamps p121 CR Gallipoli2

RICHARDS,Gwilym Owen T2Lt dow 23-4-18 14RWFus p98 CR France44

RICHARDS,Henry Heaton 2Lt kia 2-4-17 3 att2RWSurr p56 CR France1489

RICHARDS,Henry Scotson T2Lt dow 3-4-17 15N&D att25RFC p12 CR France924

RICHARDS,Henry Stokes 2Lt ded 1-8-18 10Ess &RAF p132 CR Kent180,kld 12Bn

RICHARDS,Hubert Henry Lyster 2Lt kia 7-12-15 5ConnRgs p172 MR37

RICHARDS,Hugh Phelps Maj kia 18-5-16 21Lond p251 CR France924

RICHARDS,James Thomas TLt dow 27-9-16 D180RFA p34 CR France105

RICHARDS,John T2Lt kia 15-3-18 16RWFus p98 CR France275

RICHARDS,John T2Lt dow PoW 30-3-18 1NumbF p62 CR France924

RICHARDS,John Hywell.MC.TLt dow 19-4-18 6SWBord p100 CR France31

RICHARDS,John Leslie Hill TLt dow 15-4-18 1Dev p77 CR France31,2Lt

RICHARDS,John Thomas T2Lt kia 6-11-17 3 att24WelshR p127 CR Palestine1

RICHARDS,Joseph Arthur Capt kia 4-11-18 1/8RWar p215 CR France933

RICHARDS,Leslie John T2Lt kia 1-8-17 9RDubF p177 MR29

RICHARDS,Llewelyn Thomas T2Lt kia 4-9-15 17RWFus p98 CR France217

RICHARDS,Maurice Tom TLt dow 23-9-17 189MGC Infp185 CR France113

RICHARDS,Norman Frederick Kynaston T2Lt kia 24-7-16 12Glouc p107 MR21

RICHARDS,Paul.MC&Bar.TLtAMaj kia 3-10-18 61MGC Inf p185 CR France346

RICHARDS,Percival Morgan T2Lt kia 15-7-16 10RFus p70 MR21

RICHARDS,Peter Austin Willmott T2Lt kia 10-9-16 11Y&L p159 CR France246

RICHARDS,Richard John T2Lt dow PoW 12-5-17 5 O&BLI p130 CR France924

RICHARDS,Robert Ingram 2Lt dow 27-10-17 1Lond p245 MR30

RICHARDS,Roland TLt kia 7-12-15 16RFus att7RMunstF p70 MR37

RICHARDS,Ronald Henry T2Lt kia 2-6-16 11RSuss p119 CR France114

RICHARDS,Stanley Earl 2Lt dow 29-8-16 1Mon p244 CR France120

RICHARDS,W.H.Chap4Cl 19-2-20 CR Wales518

RICHARDS,Walter Edward 2Lt dow 11-12-18 3 att16RSuss p119 CR Sussex226

RICHARDS,William Beresford Lt kia 30-11-17 3 att7DCLI p115 MR17

RICHARDS,William Ernest Cdr ded 14-9-18 IndOrdDept p282

RICHARDS,William Jenkin TCapt kia 27-8-17 16WelshR p127 MR30

RICHARDS,William John TLt dow 12-10-18 15WelshR p127 CR France398

RICHARDS,William Reeves.MID TCapt&Adjt kia 15-8-15 6RDubF p177 CR Gallipoli5

RICHARDSON,Albert Edward Capt ded 24-11-18 RB attMGC Inf p180&185 CR Wales83

RICHARDSON,Alfred Terence Leatham Capt kia 6-11-17 WSomYeo p205 CR Palestine1,12SomLI

RICHARDSON,Allan William TLt kia 11-8-15 6RIrRif p170 MR4

RICHARDSON,Angus MacDonald 2Lt kia 25-9-15 2GordH p167 MR19

RICHARDSON,Archer Stuart 2Lt kia 25-6-17 RGA 13SB p41 CR Belgium29

RICHARDSON,Archie Pelham Lt 19-11-18 IARO CR Egypt2

RICHARDSON,Arthur Archibald Lt kia 26-9-15 11A&SH p173 MR19

RICHARDSON,Arthur Balfour 2Lt kia 21-3-18 8RWKent p141 MR27

RICHARDSON,Arthur Douglas 2Lt ded 12-1-15 10WYorks p82 CR Yorks208

RICHARDSON,Arthur Gordon T2Lt dow 19-9-18 7EKent p58 CR France1468

261

RICHARDSON,Arthur John Buchannan 2Lt ded 4-1-15 4Yorks CR Yorks126

RICHARDSON,Basil Hutton 2Lt ded PoW 31-5-15 8DLI p239 CR Germany3

RICHARDSON,Basil James 2Lt kia 9-10-17 8WYorks p219 MR30

RICHARDSON,Charles Frederick James TLt kia 23-3-18 RE 80FC p48 CR France1893

RICHARDSON,Daryl Stewart Lt kia 16-5-15 3 att2BordR p118 MR22

RICHARDSON,David Alexander 2Lt kia 21-3-18 7BlkW B'Coy p231 MR20

RICHARDSON,Douglas Birch Capt kia 29-7-16 RE att29RFC p19&210 CR Belgium11

RICHARDSON,Edric Hugh Barnstey Capt kia 15-6-15 3Wilts p153 MR22

RICHARDSON,Edward AssSurg3Cl 2-10-17 IA IMD MR43 &CR Pakistan50A

RICHARDSON,Edward Earle.MM.2Lt kia 9-11-18 1/2ESurr att15RAF p113 CR France1223

RICHARDSON,Ernest Benbow T2Lt ded 28-10-15 RE 67FC p48 MR4

RICHARDSON,Evan John Capt kia 25-9-15 2Yorks p91 MR19

RICHARDSON,Ewart 2Lt kia 27-9-16 4Yorks p220 MR21

RICHARDSON,Francis Aymer.MIDx2 Lt kia 27-5-18 RFA A Bty NumbrianBde p208 MR18

RICHARDSON,Francis James.DSO.Maj ded 11-12-17 4A&SH p173 CR Surrey75

RICHARDSON,Frank Capt kia 7-6-17 24Lond D'Coy p252 CR Belgium131

RICHARDSON,Frank Arnold 2Lt kld 25-4-18 EYorks att11Bn p84&263,died CR Wilts115

RICHARDSON,Frederick Edward John T2Lt kia 21-11-17 11KRRC p151 MR17

RICHARDSON,Garnet St.John Lt dow 7-12-15 IA 7Rajputs p282 CR Iraq5,Capt

RICHARDSON,Geoffrey Oliver 2Lt kia 26-3-17 1/4Ess p232 CR Palestine8

RICHARDSON,George Alvarez 2Lt kia 27-9-16 6Yorks p91 MR21

RICHARDSON,George Hugh.MC.TCapt kia 29-10-18 22Manch p156 CR Italy9

RICHARDSON,George Sydney TLtACapt kia 20-5-18 RASC MT p193 CR France882

RICHARDSON,Harold Stewart TLt dow 24-4-17 11Leic p88 CRFrance80,2Lt

RICHARDSON,Henry 2Lt dow 21-5-17 RGA 36SB p41 CR France1186

RICHARDSON,Henry Thomas Lt dow 23-8-15 1/5NumbF p213 CR Numb60

RICHARDSON,James Maj ded 24-8-17 7HLI p240 CR Scot683

RICHARDSON,James Freer Capt ded 27-11-19 IA IMS att49IndGH p282 MR43

RICHARDSON,Jasper Myers LtCol dow 30-3-18 RGA p209 CR France40

RICHARDSON,John T2Lt dow 9-9-17 NumbF Res att23Bn p63 CR France1461

RICHARDSON,John Cottier.DCM.Capt kia 4-10-18 2Manch p156 MR16

RICHARDSON,John Ernest Lt kia 7-5-15 2Lond p245 CR France1141

RICHARDSON,John Lowick 2Lt kia 21-8-17 3/4Glouc attRFC p225 CR France1059

RICHARDSON,John Sherbrooke T2Lt kia 9-4-17 26NumbF p63 CR France184

RICHARDSON,John Stanley Capt kia 28-10-14 RE p48 MR22,Maj

RICHARDSON,John Watson Maj kia 3-5-17 4Y&L p238 MR20

RICHARDSON,John William Capt 12-10-17 34Bn AIF MR29

RICHARDSON,Lancelot Lytton.MC.Capt kia 13-4-17 25RFC p12 CR France1321

RICHARDSON,Martin James.MID TLt dow 3-11-14 RAMC 21FA p197 MR29

RICHARDSON,Maurice Lewis George 2Lt kia 28-2-17 3SLancs att2/7RWar p125 CR France526

RICHARDSON,Mervyn Stronge.MID TCapt dow 19-3-16 1RWFus p98 CR France638

RICHARDSON,Percival Blythe L.TCapt ded 3-11-18 MGC 9 att10A/ACoy p185 CR France52

RICHARDSON,Percy William T2Lt ded 12-11-18 RE p262 CR Mddx42,11-11-18

RICHARDSON,Raymond Driver 2Lt dow 26-4-18 4GrenGds p50 CR France180

RICHARDSON,Richard Francis Lt dow 30-9-15 2RWar p65 CR France145

RICHARDSON,Robert 2Lt dow 26-7-18 4RScots p211 CR France134

RICHARDSON,Robert Cecil 2Lt kia 2-12-17 3 att11BordR MR30

RICHARDSON,Robert Harold 2Lt kia 6-11-17 18Lond att6RFC p250 CR Belgium11

RICHARDSON,Robert Scovell.MC.TLt dow 1-9-16 91MGC p185 CR France66

RICHARDSON,Rodney Francis 2Lt dow 31-7-17 3Manch p156 MR29

RICHARDSON,Roger Bryer 2Lt kia 27-5-18 3WYorks p82 MR18

RICHARDSON,Ruskin John Robert kia 25-9-15 3 att2SStaffs p123 MR19

RICHARDSON,Sidney Athelstone T2Lt dow 3-11-17 266RFA p34 CR Palestine1

RICHARDSON,Thomas Capt&QM ded 26-1-19 1/4BordR p271 CR C'land&W'land59

RICHARDSON,Thomas Charles.MC.TMaj dow 4-2-16 RE 185TC p48 CR France430

RICHARDSON,Thomas William.MC.DCM.2Lt kia 28-3-18 32RFA p34 CR France531

RICHARDSON,Thomas William Taylor 2Lt kia 21-3-18 12/13NumbF p63 MR27

RICHARDSON,Victor.MC.Lt dow 9-6-17 4RSuss p228 CR Sussex183

RICHARDSON,Walter Fairfax Capt kia 9-5-15 2ELancs p111 CR France706

RICHARDSON,Wilfrid Frank.MC.TCapt ded 27/28-9-17 7BordR p118 CR France225,Wilfred

RICHARDSON,William Arthur Ingham T2Lt dow 31-8-15 1RWKent p141 CR Kent89

RICHARDSON,William Francis TCapt ded 7-2-20 RE p262 CR Asia81

RICHARDSON,William Harold Lt kia 14-4-17 6DLI p239 CR France162

RICHARDSON,William Quintus Newsom 2Lt kld 6-10-17 RFC p12 CR Essex208

RICHARDSON,William Turner T2Lt kia 1-7-16 12RIrRif att108MGC p185 MR21

RICHARDSON-JONES,Charles Harry 2Lt kia 11-6-16 6RFus p70 CR Belgium28,4Bn

RICHENS,Richard Ivor 2Lt dow 14-4-17 18Lond p250 CR France1185

RICHER,C.E.McG.Lt 3-9-18 14CanadaFA CR France14

RICHER,Frederick Arthur Maj ded 9-2-19 15Huss p261 CR Lancs34

RICHES,George William T2Lt kia 8-10-17 7Suff p79 CR France154,7-10-17

RICHES,Percy William T2Lt ded 6-12-15 10Norf p74 CR Norfl10

RICHMAN,Alexander Woolacott 2Lt dow 26-9-17 1/9Lpool p216 CRFrance40,Lt

RICHMOND,Cuthbert Laurence 2Lt kld 24-5-15 5NumbF p213 MR29

RICHMOND,Frederick Robert T2Lt kia 13-3-17 22DLI p161 CR France402

RICHMOND,Harold Christopher Capt kia 25-1-15 Glouc p107 CR France279

RICHMOND,Harold Stedman TCapt kia 24-8-16 9KRRC p151 MR21

RICHMOND,Hugh Bowlin Lt kia 9-12-17 1/21Lond p251 CR France1483,Bowten

RICHMOND,Leslie Lt kia 10-9-14 1GordH p167 CR Belgium242,23-8-14

RICHMOND,Thomas Herbert Capt dow 1-11-14 3YLI p143 CR France102,2Bn

RICKARD,George Henry.MID Maj ded 6-2-19 RGA 79SB p262 CR Sussex4,6-2-18

RICKARD,Victor George Howard TLtCol kia 9-5-15 RMunstF p176 CR France924

RICKARDS,Arthur Traherne.MID LtTCapt kia 13-9-17 RGA &43RFC p12&41 CR France88

RICKARDS,David Logan 2Lt kia 19-12-15 1/4YLI p235 CR Belgium23,dow

RICKARDS,Hew Wardrop Brooke Lt kia 28-7-17 RFA &57RFC p12&34 CR Belgium149,51RFC

RICKEARD,William Christopher Lt kia 30-9-15 19Lond p250 CR France219,C.W. 25-9-15

RICKERBY,John Harold Ellerson.MC.Capt kia 22-3-18 5Glouc p225 CR France672

RICKETT,Rupert Alexis TCapt kia 9-7-16 8SLancs p125 MR21

RICKETTS,Clyde Robert TLt ded 11-10-18 RASC p193 CR Mddx9

RICKETTS,Frederick 2Lt kia 18-9-18 3EKent p58 CR France835,1Bn

RICKETTS,Harold Edwin T2Lt dow 14-7-16 RWSurr attMGC p56&185 CR France141

RICKETTS,Henry William Felix Maj kia 10-8-15 IA 93BurmaInf att5Wilts p282 MR4

RICKETTS,James Stuart 2Lt dow 3-10-18 RFA 122A Bty p34 CR France146,5-10-18

RICKETTS,William Falkland Geordie 2Lt kia 1-4-17 4Leinst p175 CR France480,2Bn

RICKMAN,Stuart Hamilton Maj dow 26-8-14 RB p180 CR France1348,27-8-14

RICONO,Martin Capt ded 5-3-17 RAMC attSALabCps CR France40

RIDDELL,David Moore T2Lt ded 23-9-17 16Lpool p72 CR Ireland33,dow

RIDDELL,Frederick James TLt drd 13-8-15 9Beds attEss p86 MR4

RIDDELL,Henry James Maj kia 22-11-15 IA 48Pnrs p282 MR38

RIDDELL,James Riddell 2Lt kia 6-9-15 IARO att2/3GurkhaRif p282 CR France1157

RIDDELL,James Foster BrigGen kia 26-4-15 Staff Cmdg1/1NumbInfBde p1 CR Belgium125

RIDDELL,John Dean 2Lt dow 17-4-17 1/5GordH p242 CR FRance40,RIDDEL

RIDDELL,Richard Cecil Hewat ACapt dow 14-1-20 5SomLI att1A2/76Pujabis p271&282 MR43,RIDDEL

RIDDELL,Robert Anderson 2Lt dow 25-8-16 5ScotRif p224 CR France453

RIDDELL,Robert Mackie T2Lt kldacc 1-7-16 10GordH p167 CR France257,RIDDEL

RIDDELL,Sydney.MC.TLtACapt kia 13-10-17 9Y&L p159&257 CR Belgium112

RIDDELL,Walter.MC.2Lt kia 29-4-18 3 att2RScotF p95 MR30

RIDDELL,William T2Lt kia 1-7-16 11Dev p77 CR FRance330

RIDDETT,Norman Lock 2Lt kia 12-10-17 4 att8ESurr p113 CR Belgium126

RIDDLE,Francis Edmund Langton 2Lt kia 16-5-15 2 O&BLI p130 MR22

RIDDOCK,James Keppie Capt ded 17-10-18 6Hamps p228 CR Iraq8

RIDEAL,Samuel 2Lt kia 27-6-17 1/6Lpool p215 CR Belgium10

RIDEHALGH,Harold Lt kia 23-9-18 1/10Lpool p216 CR France109,2Lt

RIDER,Alonzo Ward 2Lt kia 12-10-17 26MGC Inf p185 MR30

RIDER,Clifford Ernest T2Lt kld 10-10-17 RFC p12 CR Canada1688

RIDGE,Everard Vaughan TLt kia 10-4-17 153MGC p185 MR20,9-4-17

RIDGE,Percy Lt ded 21-2-19 RGA p262 CR Surrey16

RIDGE,Percy Brewster Capt ded 12-3-16 RAMC p254

RIDGEWAY,Edward William Crawfurd Maj kia 23-2-17 IA 1/2GurkhaRif p282 MR38

RIDGWAY,Edward Capt kia 30-11-17 2/6NStaffs p238 MR17

RIDGWAY,Harold Edwin TLt kia 7-6-17 7ELancs p111 CR Belgium102

RIDGWAY,Henry Akroyd Capt kia 13-10-15 5NStaffs p237 CR France550

RIDGWAY,Henry Collinson 2Lt kia 7-10-16 7Lond C'Coy p247 MR21

RIDGWAY,John Edwin Lt 20-11-17 2/5WRid p227 MR17

RIDGWAY,John Herbert.DSO.MajTLtCol kia 23-4-17 1NStaffs att10Y&L p157 CR France924

RIDGWAY,Richard Harry James Willis 2Lt kia 6-12-16 Glouc att1TMB p107 CR France385,H.R.J.W.Lt

RIDGWAY,William 2Lt kia 7-10-16 18KRRC p151 MR21

RIDGWAY,William Thomas 2Lt kia 2-12-17 BordR att11Bn p118 MR30

RIDGWELL,Sydney Causton 2Lt kia 2-11-17 3 att1/7Ess p132 MR34

RIDLEY,Alfred Edwin T2Lt ded 25-7-18 RE IWT p48 CR France65

RIDLEY,Charles Noel Capt dow 7-10-15 NumbYeo p204 CR France134

RIDLEY,Christopher Mellor TCapt kia 31-10-16 10Ess p132 MR21

RIDLEY,Hector 2Lt kia 9-8-15 2N&D p134

RIDLEY,Henry Mills 2Lt dow PoW 23-5-18 9DLI p239 CR Belgium140

RIDLEY,Herbert Leslie.MC.LtACapt kia 15-7-17 RDubF p177 CR Belgium12

RIDLEY,Joseph T2Lt kia 15-6-18 11NumbF p63 CR Italy3

RIDLEY,Lancelot Edwin Lt kia 19-8-16 1/4RBerks p234 MR21

RIDLEY,Pattison Reay.MC.Lt kia 3-5-17 NorthCycBn att5WRid p253 MR20

RIDLEY,Stewart Gordon T2Lt ded 18-6-16 RFC p3

RIDLEY,Thomas 2Lt kia 23-3-18 12/13NumbF p63 MR27

RIDLEY,William Hector Mather Wilson 2Lt 9-8-15 2N&D D'Coy MR29

RIDOUT,Clarence Grosvenor T2Lt dow 22-12-15 9 att1KSLI p145 CR Belgium11

RIDOUT,Gaspard Alweed Evelyn 2Lt kia 21-3-18 331RFA p34 CR France366,Alured

RIDOUTT,William Alexander Lt ded 19-2-19 7DLI p239 CR Hamps9

RIDPATH,Frederick Cecil Lacey Lt kia 27-12-17 2/4WSurr p212 CR Palestine3

RIDPATH,Geoffrey Lionel Chevalier 2LtTLt kia 1-7-16 Mddx p148 CR France267

RIDSDALE,Aubrey Haywood 2Lt kia 22-8-15 CityLondYeo p204 CR Gallipoli5

RIECKE,Arnold Francis Marshall.MID Maj ded 19-6-19 307RFA p34&257 CR Nhampt80,kldacc

RIEKIE,Harry Heatly Lt 4-7-18 9RAF MR20

RIELLY,William Ernest Capt ded 28-11-15 RAMC att3Lond p254 MR4

RIEPLE,Leopold Anthony T2Lt ded 30-10-18 RGA 51SB p41 CR France398

RIGBY,Arthur George.MC.Capt kia 12-10-17 8WYorks p219 MR30

RIGBY,Charles 2Lt kia 4-11-18 6RWar &62RAF MR20,RFus

RIGBY,Douglas Archibald.DCM.2Lt dow 24-4-17 5ScotRif p224 CR France120

RIGBY,Douglas Marshall Lt kia 4-9-18 6Ches p222 CR Belgium89

RIGBY,Edward William TCapt kia 14-7-16 7KSLI p145 MR21

RIGBY,Francis John Capt kia 21-1-16 3 att1SfthH p165 MR38

RIGBY,George.MC.TLt kia 7-6-17 3Y&L p159 CR Belgium127

RIGBY,J.2Lt ded 20-11-18 GL ExtraRegEmployList RAF p267

RIGBY,James Arthur Maj 25-12-16 RAMC CR Lancs111

RIGBY,James Richard Anderton Lt kia 26-9-15 3 att2Yorks p91 MR19

RIGBY,John 2Lt kia 21-3-18 6SStaffs p229 MR20

RIGBY,John H.Capt&QM ded 21-5-18 126MGC Inf p185 CR France1571,20-5-18

RIGBY,Thomas Frank 2Lt kia 27-3-18 3RFC p17 MR20,Franklin

RIGBY,William Geoffrey Morris TLt dow 7-7-16 69MGC Inf p185 CR France

RIGG,George Southerton.DSO.2LtTLt kia 31-7-17 3Y&L att52MGC Inf p159&185 CR Belgium106

RIGG,Samuel AMaj kia 25-3-18 5BordR p256 MR27

RIGG,Stanley 2Lt dow 21-6-18 5BordR p228 CR C'land&W'land74

RIGGENBACH,Frank Arthur Lt kia 19-9-18 1/6Ess p232 CR Palestine9

RIGGOTT,Robert Cyril 2Lt kia 20-9-17 5LancF p221 CR Belgium125

RIGGS,John Stephenson 2Lt dow 19-12-17 RGA 239SB p41 CR France214

RIGGS,Roy Robertson 2Lt kia 22-7-17 19RFC p12 CR France31

RIGHTON,Richard Harry 2Lt kia 27-9-18 6 att7RFus p70 CR France1496

RIHOY,Stanley Alfred 2Lt dow 12-4-18 1RGLI p201 MR32

RILEY,Albert Victor TLt kia 20-8-17 A155RFA p34 CR Belgium10

RILEY,Arthur Cecil Capt kia 25-9-15 19Lond p250 CR France219

RILEY,Ernest 2Lt kia 26-9-18 6SStaffs p229 CR France528

RILEY,George Harold Lt kia 21-8-18 RASC p193 CR France134

RILEY,H.J.Lt 5-4-20 2SLancs CR Lancs150

RILEY,Henry Davison TCapt kia 1-7-16 11ELancs p111 MR21

RILEY,Herbert Angus 2Lt kia 28-6-16 1/9Lpool p216 CR France174

RILEY,James Louis 2Lt kia 29-9-18 1/7Lpool p215 CR France109

RILEY,James Shutt TLt kia 10-8-18 1TankCps p188 CR France649,Capt

RILEY,James Trevor Lt kia 3-9-16 4WRid p227 MR21

RILEY,John Reginald Newton 2Lt kia 3-9-16 5WRid p227 CR France383

RILEY,Leslie T2Lt kld 5-2-18 RFC p17 CR Mddx15

RILEY,Nathaniel Edgar 2Lt kia 21-5-17 3 att2YLI p143 CR France502

RILEY,Paul T2Lt kia 10-10-17 LancF att8Bn p93 MR30

RILEY,Stanley James TCapt kia 12-10-16 1RWar p65 MR21

RILEY,Sydney T2Lt kia 20-9-18 1NumbF p63 CR France530

RILEY,Thomas Capt dow 5-8-16 C158RFA p34 CR France23

RILEY,Thomas Dickinson 2Lt kia 20-9-17 7ScotRif p224 CR Belgium125

RILEY-WATSON,Leslie 2Lt kia 4-7-16 C246RFA p34 CR France215

RIMER,James Cook 2Lt kia 17-3-17 43RFC p12 MR20

RIMER,William Marshall 2Lt kia 1-10-18 4Y&L p238 CR France406

RIMINGTON,Ernest Cameron Waterfield 2Lt kia 2-10-15 3Ches p96 CR France924

RIMMER,Samuel Gerard Lt kia 4-5-16 RFA p208 CR France927

RIMMER,William 2Lt kia 26-10-17 5LNLancs p234 MR30

RIND,Edward Seton.MID Lt kia 22-11-15 1A 24Punjabis p282 MR38

RINDER,Charles Henry 2Lt kia 16-8-17 7Lond p247 MR29

RINES,Edward Thomas 2Lt kia 22-8-17 4SomLI p218 MR30

RING,Charles Augustus Eamonson Capt ded 29-10-18 RAMC p267 CR War88

RING,Leslie Gordon Lt kia 18-9-18 3Lond p245 CR France369

RING,Norman Augustus Manders Lt kia 4-5-17 3 att2RWar p65 MR20

RINTOUL,David Wylie Lt kia 21-10-14 RAMC att3CldGds p197 MR29

RIODAN,Hubert De Burgh Capt kia 10-5-15 ESurr att2nd p113 CR Belgium46

RIORDAN,John Leonard 2Lt kia 8-9-18 5Lond p246 MR16

RIORDAN,Timothy Harold 2Lt dow 6-7-16 4YLI p235 CR France2

RIPLEY,Charles Roger.MID Lt kia 22-10-14 3Y&L p159 MR32,2Bn

RIPLEY,Eris Richard T2Lt kia 31-10-17 GL &53RFC p12 CR Belgium101,Eric

RIPLEY,George Eustace Col dow 16-10-16 6Nhampt p138 CR Nhampt67

RIPMAN,Helmut Armstrong 2Lt dow 16-5-18 RGA 47SB p41 CR France40

RIPPERGER,Harold Alvin Theodore.MC.Lt kia 23-10-18 4Glouc p225 CR France287

RIPPIN,James Harry 2Lt ded 9-3-16 4LNLancs p234 CR Lancs257,Henry 5Bn

RIPPINGILLE,Frank Alexander 2Lt kia 11-11-14 EYorks p84 MR29

RIPPON,Gilbert Harold Earle 2Lt kld 7-6-16 RFC p3 CR Somerset26

RIPPON,Norris 2Lt kia 18-11-15 1/5WRid p227 CR Belgium23

RISELEY,Stanley Maj ded 5-2-15 RAMC p271

RISHWORTH,Henry Holmes 2Lt ded 15-9-15 6WRid p271 CR Yorks439

RISHWORTH,James Lt kld 3-5-17 4EYorks p219 MR29

RISHWORTH,J.R Lt 15-6-15 1A S&TCps CR India164

RISHWORTH,Keith T2Lt kld 6-8-17 GL &RFC p12 CR Yorks3

RISING,Frederick 2Lt kia 15-8-15 5Beds p219 MR4

RISING,Robert Edward.DSO.Maj ded 7-11-14 1Glouc p107 CR Belgium134,dow

RISLEY,Nathan Bright.MC.TCapt dow 20-9-17 16RB p180 CR Belgium15

RISSIK,Bernard 2Lt kia 22-6-15 9RB p180 MR29

RISTEEN,Clifford Fraser 2Lt kia 26-9-17 GL &45RFC p12 MR20

RITCH,William Robertson TCapt kia 23-3-18 11 att9ScotRif p104 MR27

RITCHIE,Alexander 2Lt dow 28-4-17 2ScotRif att23TMB p104 CR France121

RITCHIE,Alexander Stewart.MC.TCapt kia 1-10-18 8BlkW p129 MR30

RITCHIE,Archibald Frederick Lt kia 10-9-14 2YLI p143 MR15.26-8-14

RITCHIE,Arthur Gerald Capt dow 22-11-14 1ScotRif p104 CR France102

RITCHIE,Francis James Dickson 2Lt kia 20-7-16 1ScotRif p104 MR21

RITCHIE,Frank Johnstone T2Lt kia 23-10-16 2Lincs p75 MR21

RITCHIE,Frank Robert 2Lt kia 15-8-15 3RScots att2HLI p54 CR France721

RITCHIE,George Lt ded 15-5-16 6HLI p240 CR Scot674

RITCHIE,Harold.Hon.DSO&Bar.TMajALtCol dow 28-10-18 11ScotRif att1RWSurr p104 CR France332

RITCHIE,Henry Deacon 2Lt dow 27-9-18 1CldGds p51 CR France756

RITCHIE,James Adam T2Lt dow 8-8-18 BlkW att4/5Bn p129 CR France1225

RITCHIE,James Garrick 2Lt ded 3-5-19 CamH p265 CR Scot280

RITCHIE,Jessie SNurse ded 13-8-16 QAIMNS p200 CR Greece7

RITCHIE,John 2Lt kia 25-4-17 6BlkW att66MGC p187&231 CR Greece6

RITCHIE,John Capt ded 28-10-17 6HLI p240 CR Scot674

RITCHIE,John James Austin 2Lt kia 29-9-18 9HLI p241 CR France663

RITCHIE,John Mearns T2Lt kia 15-7-16 12RScots p54 CR France402

RITCHIE,John Nevill 2Lt kia 21-4-16 3SfthH p165 MR38

RITCHIE,John Waugh T2Lt kia 23-4-17 2 att7GordH p167 MR20

RITCHIE,Leonard Albany Lt kia 24-3-18 RE 1/1EdinburghFC p210 CR France1063

RITCHIE,Louis Malcolm Lt kia 5-5-18 4RScots att1KAR p211&268 MR52

RITCHIE,Richard Ayres Lt kia 22-11-15 3 att2Norf p74 MR38

RITCHIE,Richard James Wallace LtACapt kia 20-5-18 4 att18HLI p163 CR France60

RITCHIE,Robin Blackwood LtACapt kia 20-7-16 1ScotRif p104 MR21

263

RITCHIE,Robert Richard TCapt kia 3-5-17 9ScotRif p104 MR20

RITCHIE,Thomas Arthur 2Lt kia 18-10-16 3 att1ELancs p111 CR France432

RITCHIE,Thomas Pearsall Ayres 2Lt kia 15-3-15 6 att4RB p180 MR29

RITCHIE,William Lancelot 2Lt dow 1-8-17 1Camb D'Coy p245 CR Belgium16

RITCHIE,William Smail 2Lt kia 29-7-18 5A&SH p243 CR France524

RITCHIE-BROWN,John Lt kia 7-11-16 RAMC attHQ 43HAG RGA CR France2

RITCHINGS,Albert Arthur William.MM.2Lt kia 27-9-18 11 att16Lond p248 CR France429,29-9-18

RITSON,Arthur Stuart 2Lt kia 5-11-16 5 att1/6DLI p271 MR21

RITSON,Claude Wilson T2LtACapt kia 28-4-17 13Ess p132 MR20

RITSON,Eustace Blackburne 2Lt kia 8-10-17 204MGC Inf p185 MR30

RITSON,Francis TCapt kia 17-6-17 Dors att5Bn p124 CR Belgium76

RITSON,John Andrew TCapt kia 22-7-16 7SLancs p126 CR France432,23-7-16

RITTER,William Henry TLt kia 2-6-17 GL &15RFC p12 CR France41,dedacc

RITTY,John.MC.TCapt kia 9-9-16 7RInnisF p105 MR21

RIVERS,George Claude T2Lt kia 21-8-16 9ESurr p113

RIVERS-SMITH,Edwin Lt 6-11-18 RGA CR Hamps219

RIX,John Cecil TCapt kia 6-7-16 RAMC att9Yorks p197 CR France515

RIX,Leslie Gordon.MID Capt dow 11-2-17 1/4Lond p245 CR France345

RIXON,Theodore Meredith.MC.TMajALtCol kia 19-9-17 6 att8KRRC p151 CR Belgium126

ROACH,Matthew TCapt kia 2-7-16 RE 255TC p48 MR20,225TC

ROADLEY,Thomas Stanley Lt kia 17-8-17 4SStaffs att8RFC p12&123 CR Belgium140

ROADS,Herbert William 2Lt ded 5-5-16 10Lond p271

ROAN,Walter Tait 2Lt kia 29-9-16 8DLI p239 MR21

ROBARTS,Henry Martyn 2Lt dow 26-9-17 4Norf p216 CR France113

ROBATHAN,Douglas Parker Capt kia 10-8-15 5WelshReg p230 MR4

ROBATHAN,Laurence.MID 2Lt kia 28-9-17 2/5Leic p220 CR Belgium16

ROBB,Albert Victor.MM.MID T2Lt dow 12-3-18 5CamH p168 CR France439

ROBB,Alexander Gentle.MC.Lt dow PoW 20-5-18 3ScotRif p104 CR Germany2,1Bn

ROBB,Alexander Kirkland.MID Maj kia 20-9-14 2DLI p161 CR France1329

ROBB,Harold Brindley.MID TLt ded 2-1-17 RASC p193 CR Lond1

ROBB,Henry Alexander Lt kia 10-7-17 3N&D att1LNLancs p134 MR31,Henri

ROBB,J.Lt 13-12-18 RFA CR Kent83

ROBB,John T2Lt kia 21-7-17 16WYorks p82 CR France268

ROBB,Ralph George Campbell TLt kia 25-9-15 10ScotRif p104 MR19

ROBB,Russell Edwin T2Lt ded 5-1-18 65RFC p17 CR Belgium140

ROBB,Thomas Douglas Lt kld 26-9-15 17 att20Lond p250 CR France550

ROBB,Victor Harold TLt dow 3-7-16 14RIrRif p170 CR Ireland33

ROBB,William John Mechan 2Lt kia 20-7-18 4 att6BlkW p230 MR18

ROBB-SMITH,Alexander TCapt ded 15-12-17 RAMC attRA &RFA BaseDepot p197&257 CR France85

ROBBINS,Arthur Hodder Capt&Adj kia 21-3-18 7/8RInnisF p105 CR France365

ROBBINS,George Latimer 2Lt dow 10-6-18 6WRid att25MGC Inf p187&227 CR France145,9-6-18

ROBBINS,John Laurence TLt kia 26-3-18 10Ches attStaff 26Div p96 CR France300,Lawrence 25Div

ROBERSON,Frank Hubert Langhorne 2Lt dow 12-8-17 7RWSurr p56 CR Belgium7

ROBERSON,George Lewis T2Lt dow 21-3-18 8RSuss p119 CR France1063

ROBERT,Annie Louise Sister 28-9-16 QAIMNS CR Ches8

ROBERTON,Charles Drinnan 2Lt kia 1-7-16 4LancF p93 CR France156

ROBERTON,David McCulloch SeeROBERTSON.D.M.

ROBERTON,James Leslie SeeROBERTSON.J.L.

ROBERTON,Robert Douglas Finch.MC.Lt dow 12-10-20 1Ess CR Yorks38

ROBERTS,Alan Sheriff T2Lt kia 10-7-16 14RWFus p98 CR France397

ROBERTS,Alfred Frank T2Lt kia 18-11-16 17HLI p163 CR France534

ROBERTS,Anthony Gerald Malpas 2Lt kia 20-10-14 2RInnisF p105 CR France451,Lt

ROBERTS,Archibald Maj dow 22-8-15 6Yorks p91 CR Europe1 Ex IA 95Inf

ROBERTS,Arthur Capt kia 15-9-16 15Lond p249 CR France700

ROBERTS,Arthur Colin.CMG.DSO.BrigGen ded 17-5-17 RFus Cmdg80InfBdeHQ p70 CR Mddx51

ROBERTS,Arthur Doricourt.MC.TLt kld 31-8-17 GL &RFC p12 CR Surrey60

ROBERTS,Arthur Hosbury Starkey Lt dow 4-11-18 3 att15WelchR p127 CR France1478

ROBERTS,Arthur Howell 2Lt kia 20-10-18 5RWelshF p223 CR France1391

ROBERTS,Arthur Wilmot 2Lt ded PoW 16-12-18 DLI p161 CR Germany4,15WYorks

ROBERTS,Benjamin Richard TLt kia 30-7-16 RAMC att98FA p197 CR France23

ROBERTS,Birdsell(Bert) T2Lt kia 9-10-17 WYorks Res att9Bn D'Coy p82 MR30

ROBERTS,Cadwalader Glyn TLt kia 3-7-16 9RWFus p98 CR France393

ROBERTS,Cecil Llewellyn Norton 2LtACapt kia 9-10-17 2RWar p65 MR30

ROBERTS,Cecil Quinlan 2Lt kia 16-5-15 RFA 113Bty p34 CR France727

ROBERTS,Charles Edward.MM.2Lt dow 10-10-16 7Lincs p75 CR France203

ROBERTS,Charles Henry Hill.MC.2Lt kia 15-9-16 21Lond p251 CR France385

ROBERTS,Charles William 2Lt kia 28-12-17 1Dev p77 CR Italy48,Willis

ROBERTS,C.J.Maj 6-11-18 4Hamps CR Hamps13

ROBERTS,Cyril Ainley T2Lt kia 25-4-18 13TankCps p188 MR30

ROBERTS,D'Arcy Granville St.Clair.MC.TCapt kia 26-4-18 4 att1Worc p109 CR France144

ROBERTS,David.MC.TCapt dow 23-4-17 7Lincs p75 CR France1182

ROBERTS,David Charles T2Lt kia 19-7-16 10SWBord p100 CR France643

ROBERTS,David Francis Lt kia 2-11-17 RE 410FC p210 CR Palestine8

ROBERTS.E.SNurse 12-8-17 QAIMNS CR Wales672

ROBERTS,Edgar 2Lt kia 31-8-18 DorsYeo p203 CR Belgium89

ROBERTS,Edmund Percy TLt kia 21-3-18 11Ess p132 MR20

ROBERTS,Edward Elwyn Lloyd 2Lt dow 20-9-18 2/6RWar p214 CR France194

ROBERTS,Edward Owen Lt ded 29-1-17 RDC p253 CR Ches28

ROBERTS,Elwyn T2Lt kia 10-2-17 GL &10RFC p12 MR20

ROBERTS,Eric James 2Lt kia 23-9-16 27RFC p3 MR20

ROBERTS,Ernest Woolley 2Lt kld 6-6-17 7LancF p221 CR Gallipoli2

ROBERTS,F.W.OBE.VD.LtCol 14-7-20 RE CR Norf209

ROBERTS,Francis T2Lt kia 27-10-16 20RFus p70 CR France374

ROBERTS,Francis Bernard TCapt kia 8-2-16 9RB p180 CR Belgium85

ROBERTS,Francis Watson 2Lt kia 14-10-15 14Lond p249 CR France219,ROBARTS 13-10-15

ROBERTS,Francklin Allender 2Lt kia 8-8-18 7Lond p247 CR France141

ROBERTS,Fred TLt kia 23-7-16 11 att6YLI p143 CR France1182

ROBERTS,Frederick John TCapt kia 28-9-15 3Lpool p72 CR France163,25-9-16 1Bn

ROBERTS,Frederick John TMaj dow 17-10-15 6RWSurr p56 CR France98

ROBERTS,Frederick Norman T2Lt dow 19-11-18 3RFus p70 CR Lancs14

ROBERTS,Frederick Roberts 2Lt dow 7-9-16 3GordH p167 CR France833

ROBERTS,Frederick Sheriff 2Lt kia 28-8-18 1 att9RWFus p98 CR France98,29-8-18

ROBERTS,Frederick Sleigh.The Rt Hon.Earl.VC.KG.KP.PC.GCB.OM.GCSI.GCIE.VD:- FieldMarshall ded 14-11-14 ColCommdt RA Col IrGds p1 CR Lond15

ROBERTS,Frederick William.MC.TCapt dow PoW 1-10-17 10RWKent p141 CR Belgium393

ROBERTS,Gavesen Brooke 2Lt kia 26-9-17 GL &19RFC p12 MR20,Gavern

ROBERTS,George Alfred.MM.2Lt kia 21-3-18 1Leic p88 MR20

ROBERTS,George Bradley 2Lt dow 7-5-15 ULIA att1Manch p156&282 CR France102

ROBERTS,George Jewell T2Lt dow 17-6-16 RE 250Co p48 CR France285

ROBERTS,George Peskett TLt dow 26-4-16 134RFA 61HB p35 CR Iraq5

ROBERTS,Gerald Chip-chase TLtCol kia 8-6-16 14Glouc p107 CR France705,Chipchase

ROBERTS,Griffith Evans T2Lt kia 7-6-17 6BordR p118 MR29

ROBERTS,Guy Hepworth LtACapt dow 22-11-17 2/4YLI p235 CR France398

ROBERTS,Harold.MC.TCapt dow 27-10-18 9SStaffs p123 CR Italy7

ROBERTS,Harold Owen Bodvel.MC.Lt dow 18-11-15 7Lond p247

ROBERTS,Harry Cureton Lt kia 27-12-17 MontgomYeo att25RWFus p204 CR Palestine3

ROBERTS,Harry Leslie T2Lt dow 10-9-16 189RFA p35 CR France197

ROBERTS,Henry Norman 2Lt kia 28-4-17 10LNLancs p136 MR20

ROBERTS,Henry Sheriff Capt kia 27-8-17 17RWFus p99 MR30 Ex 5Bn

ROBERTS,Howel Dilwyn T2Lt kia 31-10-18 14RWFus p99 CR France1478

ROBERTS,Idris T2Lt dow 3-9-18 17RWFus p99 CR France41,Lt kia 2-9-18

ROBERTS,Iorworth Cynon 2Lt kia 10-4-18 25MGC Inf p185 MR32

ROBERTS,Ivon L'Esterrre.MID Maj kia 8-6-15 RFA p35 MR4,d'Esterre

ROBERTS,James Roderick Trethowan 2Lt dow 3-3-15 3Suff p79 CR Belgium182,Lt 4-3-15

ROBERTS,James Thursby 2Lt dow 20-7-16 2RWSurr p56 CR Hamps64

ROBERTS,Jane SNurse drd 10-4-17 QAIMNS p200

ROBERTS,John T2Lt kia 14-9-18 1/9Lpool p72 CR France433

ROBERTS,John.MC.Lt ded 11-11-18 S158RFA p35 CR France34,A158

ROBERTS,John Ernest Bate.MID 2Lt dow 23-9-15 IARO att1/5GurkhaRif p282 MR4,WAFF

ROBERTS,John Harry T2Lt dow 11-4-18 EYorks attRes 2Y&L p84 CR Belgium11

ROBERTS,John Henry Charles 2Lt dow 2-5-15 Dors p124 CR France284

ROBERTS,John Herbert Lt kld 24-9-18 RFA &8RAF p35 MR20

ROBERTS,John Lambert.MC.Lt kia 21-3-18 1/2 att6Leic C'Coy p88 CR France212

264

ROBERTS,John Robert Bowden 2Lt kia 1-2-16 4NumbF p213 CR Belgium127,dow

ROBERTS,John William 2Lt dow 23-3-18 7 att1/4RWelshF p223 MR20

ROBERTS,Laurie Paterson T2Lt kia 23-2-18 20RFC p17 CR France134,Lawrie

ROBERTS,Leslie.MC.T2Lt kia 24-8-18 12ESurr att6RWSurr p113 CR France370

ROBERTS,Lionel John 2Lt kia 3-9-16 16RB p180 MR21

ROBERTS,Llewellyn Hilton 2Lt kia 13-8-16 11RWar p65 MR21

ROBERTS,Matthias Groves 2Lt kia 3-7-17 3 att1RBerks p139 CR France258

ROBERTS,M.C.MC.Capt dow 10-11-18 A Coy CanadaInf CR Belgium202

ROBERTS,M.D.SNurse drd 31-12-17 QAIMNS p200 CR Egypt1

ROBERTS,Noel Humphreys 2Lt kia 23-4-17 1KOSB p102 MR20

ROBERTS,Oscar Howard Salter 2Lt dow 28-9-17 21Lond p251 CR France113

ROBERTS,Philip Hugh Gore 2Lt dow 21-8-15 1/5GordH p242 CR France197

ROBERTS,Ralph Jennings TLt kia 31-10-17 179MGC p185 CR Palestine1

ROBERTS,Reuben TCapt kia 7-7-16 RAOC DADOS 25Div p198 CR France296

ROBERTS,Richard Bowen Lt ded 31-1-18 W'land&C'landYeo p271 CR Wales447,13-1-18

ROBERTS,Richard D'Esterre Capt ded 15-10-18 25DLI p161&266 CR Yorks294

ROBERTS,Robert James T2Lt kia 10-10-16 14 att13Ches p96 CR France280,11-10-16

ROBERTS,Robert Jesse Adams.DSO.TCapt dow 22-9-17 10WelshR att15LudhianaSikhs p127 MR67

ROBERTS,Robert John 2Lt dow PoW 28-10-18 6MGC Inf p185 CR France1211

ROBERTS,Rupert Edward TMaj dow 26-3-18 16Manch p156 CR France145

ROBERTS,S.T.C.Lt 30-7-18 52RAF CR France41

ROBERTS,Samuel HonCapt ded 6-12-14 RE Staff p48 CR France145

ROBERTS,Thomas 2Lt kia 25-5-15 3 att2Ches p96 CR Belgium165,24-5-15

ROBERTS,Thomas TLt dow 11-10-18 6Y&L p159 CR France214

ROBERTS,Thomas Owen 2Lt kia 18-9-18 RWFus att14Bn p99 CR France415

ROBERTS,Thomas William T2Lt kia 30-9-16 7RWKent p141 MR21

ROBERTS,Thomas Wilson T2Lt dow 1-9-16 1Ches p96

ROBERTS,Victor T2Lt kia 19-7-17 9WelshR p127 CR Belgium111

ROBERTS,Victor George 2Lt kia 27-7-17 4WelshReg p230 CR Belgium23

ROBERTS,Walter Rowland Southall Capt kia 16-8-15 RAMC p254 CR Gallipoli27

ROBERTS,William T2Lt dow 8-8-17 218MGC p185 CR Belgium7

ROBERTS,William Lt kia 27-12-17 6RWelshF p223 CR Palestine3

ROBERTS,William 2Lt kia 22-9-18 7SWBord p100 CR Greece5,18-9-18

ROBERTS,William Arthur TLt dedacc 20-8-17 GL RFus 30TrResBn p70&267 CR Kent7

ROBERTS,William John 2Lt kia 21-3-18 1RDubF p177 MR27

ROBERTS,William Lloyd Lt kia 6-11-17 1/7RWelshF p223 CR Palestine1,2Lt

ROBERTS,William Thomas 2Lt kia 28-9-18 3 att1DCLI p115 CR France245

ROBERTSON,Alexander 2Lt dow 17-8-17 RFA &34RFC p12&35 CR France1361

ROBERTSON,Alexander Lt dow 28-1-18 6SfthH att101MGC Inf p187&241 CR France214,kld

ROBERTSON,Alexander Myron Capt kia 4-8-16 1/6GordH p242 CR France1890

ROBERTSON,Alexander Stuart.MC.Lt kia 2-9-18 8RScots p211 CR France1486

ROBERTSON,Alexander Winton.MC.Maj dow 23-4-16 RGA 68SB p209 CR France62

ROBERTSON,Andrew 2Lt kia 13-11-16 7GordH p242 MR21

ROBERTSON,Angus Burns TCapt ded 8-11-18 RAMC p197 CR Scot270

ROBERTSON,Archibald 2Lt kia 9-4-18 20Mddx p148 MR32

ROBERTSON,Archibald Garden 2Lt kia 8-6-17 BlkW att66RFC p12&129 MR20

ROBERTSON,Archibald Watson T2Lt kia 9-6-18 RE 263Coy p48 CR France119,8/9-6-18

ROBERTSON,Athol Lt dow 26-3-16 2A&SH p173 CR France80

ROBERTSON,Battle Dow T2LtACapt kia 22-8-18 4RFus p70 CR France618

ROBERTSON,Charles.MC.Rev dow 3-10-18 RAChDept p199 CR Greece9

ROBERTSON,Charles Boyd 2Lt kia 16-10-17 A165RFA p35 CR France184

ROBERTSON,Charles Eric 2LtTCapt kia 12-7-17 Cmdg11RFC p12 CR France421

ROBERTSON,Charles Granville T2Lt kia 27-3-18 Ess att2Nhants p132 MR27

ROBERTSON,Charles John 2Lt kia 22-3-17 6BlkW p231 CR France15

ROBERTSON,Charles Thomas Andrews CaptAMaj dow PoW 23-3-18 1/5GordH p167&256 CR France1061

ROBERTSON,Charles William 2Lt dow PoW 22-8-16 3Manch p156 CR France716

ROBERTSON,Clement.VC.TLtACapt kia 4-10-17 3RWSurr attTankCps p56&188

ROBERTSON,David 2Lt kia 31-7-17 6RScots p211 MR29

ROBERTSON,David Hunter Henderson Lt kia 10-3-15 4ScotRif p104 CR France706,2Bn

ROBERTSON,David McCulloch 2Lt kia 13-2-17 1MGC p185 MR21,ROBERTON

ROBERTSON,David Norman 2Lt ded PoW 16-4-17 60RFC p12 MR20

ROBERTSON,David Stephen.OBE.BtLtCol ded 8-12-19 RScotF p263 CR Asia20

ROBERTSON,Douglas Forbes T2Lt dow 28-9-16 15 att8NumbF p63 CR France44,26-9-16

ROBERTSON,Douglas Hill T2Lt kia 14-4-17 1KOSB D Coy p102 MR20

ROBERTSON,Duncan Alexander T2Lt kld 11-11-17 GL &RFC p12 CR Scot677

ROBERTSON,Edmund John Macrory.MID Lt kia 22-5-15 70/34RFA p35 CR France571

ROBERTSON,Edward Craig Maj kia 29-9-15 Y&L p159 MR19

ROBERTSON,Eric Hume 2Lt kia 21-3-18 RDubF att48TMB p177 MR27

ROBERTSON,Ernest Cecil Leonard Lt kia 18-10-15 1/20Lond A'Coy p251 CR France219,Lennox

ROBERTSON,Ernest Guy TCapt ded 28-10-18 GL RAMC p191 MR19 Y&L CR Hamps12

ROBERTSON,Eustace James T2Lt dow 2-3-17 7Glouc p107 CR Iraq5,Capt

ROBERTSON,Fergus 2Lt ded PoW 3-12-18 3 att1/5BordR p118 CR Germany3

ROBERTSON,Frank Capt dow 25-6-15 12Worc p109 CR Egypt6

ROBERTSON,Frank Harding Lt FlyingAcc 22-2-18 IARO attRFC p282 CR Egypt15

ROBERTSON,Frederick Neal Lt kia 11-4-18 7 att1/4GordH p242 MR19

ROBERTSON,Frederick Percival TLt kia 4-3-16 20LancF p93 CR France631,3-3-16

ROBERTSON,George TCapt kia 1-7-16 21NumbF p63 MR21

ROBERTSON,George Arthur Norris TCapt kia 16-8-17 9 att3SWBord p100 CR Belgium106

ROBERTSON,George Cockburn 2Lt kia 21-7-15 6DLI p239 CR France683

ROBERTSON,George Hawthorn Minto TLt ded 10-3-19 GL 13HLI attNigR p202,255&267 CR Scot742,Minot

ROBERTSON,George Seaborn Hyssett 2Lt kia 18-11-16 5 att10Worc p109 MR21

ROBERTSON,Gilbert 2Lt kia 25-9-15 3 att1CamH p168 CR France219

ROBERTSON,Gilbert Swale TCapt kia 27-9-15 13RScots p54 MR19

ROBERTSON,Glagow Archibald William Capt kia 13-11-14 IA 2/39GarhwalRif p282 CR France727,ROBERTSON-GLASGOW

ROBERTSON,Glynn Cuthbert Lt kia 15-3-16 RE 1/2FC p210 CR France68,16-3-16

ROBERTSON,Gordon T2Lt kia 17-11-15 10GordH p167 CR France423

ROBERTSON,Haldane Stanford 2Lt kia 19-4-17 4Nhampt p271 MR34

ROBERTSON,Harold Hay.MC.T2Lt dow 11-9-18 7EYorks p84 CR France307,kia

ROBERTSON,Helenus Macaulay Capt kia 26-1-16 3 att2RWFus p99 CR France114

ROBERTSON,Henry William T2Lt dow 21-4-18 11A&SH p173 CR France95,kia

ROBERTSON,Herbert R.Capt ded 28-7-16 RAMC p271 CR Sussex216,29-7-16

ROBERTSON,Herbert.MC.Maj dow 5-4-18 C86RFA p206 CR France37

ROBERTSON,Herbert Charles Lt kia 1-11-18 135/32RFA p35 CR France1260

ROBERTSON,Herbert Johnston Graeme Lt kia 25-9-15 3 att1BlkW p129 MR19

ROBERTSON,Herbert Neville 2Lt dow 30-4-18 3 att10Ches p96 CR France13

ROBERTSON,Hugh Grant Capt kld 26-4-15 ConnRgrs p172 CR Belgium92

ROBERTSON,Ian Gordon Lt kia 13-11-16 7GordH C'Coy p242 CR France131,2Lt

ROBERTSON,James 2Lt ded 9-7-17 4HLI att19DLI p163 CR France122,dow

ROBERTSON,James LtCol kia 21-3-18 RAMC 2/1FA p253 CR France307

ROBERTSON,James 2Lt kia 21-8-18 4RScotF p222 CR France927

ROBERTSON,James 2Lt dow 5-10-18 19Lond p251 CR France106,7Bn

ROBERTSON,James Duncan.MC.LtTACapt dow 27-8-17 9GordH p167 CR Belgium11

ROBERTSON,James Horan TLt kia 18-7-16 8 att11BlkW p129 MR21,11 att8Bn

ROBERTSON,James Houldsworth Lt 11-3-18 48RFC p258 CR France987

ROBERTSON,James Leslie 2Lt kia 6-9-16 4Yorks attRFC p19&235 MR20,ROBERTON

ROBERTSON,James Whittingham 2Lt kia 23-4-17 1/7BlkW p231 CR France604,Whittingehame

ROBERTSON,John Capt kia 28-6-15 4RScots p211 CR Gallipoli2

ROBERTSON,John Alexander Tower Lt drd 30-12-15 IARO att2/3GurkhaRif p282 MR41

ROBERTSON,John Barclay T2Lt kld 13-11-17 ScotRif att2Bn p104 CR France262

ROBERTSON,John Brewis TCapt dow 17-9-16 9BlkW p129 CR France51

ROBERTSON,John Frederick Maj 12-3-15 11Hamps CR Eire505

ROBERTSON,John Gilfillan 2Lt kia 7-6-17 11RInnisF p105 CR Belgium155

ROBERTSON,John Henry TLt dow 11-3-18 RFC p17

ROBERTSON,John Johnston T2Lt kia 27-9-18 8NumbF p63 CR France272

ROBERTSON,John Keith Grant TLt kia 1-1-17 GL &RFC p12 CR France833

ROBERTSON,John Ross Lt kia 12-5-17 Fife&ForfarYeo attRFC p19&203 CR France272

ROBERTSON,John Stoddart.MID TLt kia 21-5-16 7CamH p168 CR France423

ROBERTSON,John Struan Carmichael 2Lt kia 31-3-18 B46RFA p35 CR France1061,21-3-18

ROBERTSON,Keith Forbes Lt kia 27-8-16 6 att1RB p180 CR Belgium115

ROBERTSON,Laurence Grant T2Lt kia 30-7-16 9 att2KOSB p102 MR21,Lawrance

ROBERTSON,Leonard Dougal.MC.Lt kia 13-11-17 1/4KOSB p223 CR Palestine9

ROBERTSON,Leslie Johnston Walker.MC.Lt kia 3-10-17 3GordH p167 CR Belgium112

ROBERTSON,Lewis Capt dow 7-11-14 1CamH p168 CR Belgium84,3-11-14

ROBERTSON,Magnus Rainer.MC.TCapt dow 22-8-18 2 att11Ess p132 CR France370,Rainier 9Bn

ROBERTSON,Matthew Struan TCapt kia 2-3-16 1GordH p167 CR Belgium21

ROBERTSON,Maxwell Alexander Capt kia 1-7-16 10RInnisF p105 MR21

ROBERTSON,Mowbray Mitcalfe T2Lt kia 31-8-16 9NStaffs p157 CR France397

ROBERTSON,Neil Wallace.MC&Bar.2Lt kia 2-9-18 1RScotF p95 MR16

ROBERTSON,Norman Bethune.DSO.Maj kia 30-11-17 2RFA p35 CR France379

ROBERTSON,Norman Cairns Capt ded PoW 20-6-17 2Hamps p121 CR Germany2

ROBERTSON,Norman McLeod Lt kia 17-10-16 GL RFA att60RFC p3,19,191&208 CR France80

ROBERTSON,Peter Lt ded 16-1-19 3CamH &RAF p168 CR Ches8

ROBERTSON,Ralph 2Lt kld 11-5-17 8Hamps attRFC p19&229 CR Egypt1

ROBERTSON,Robert Arthur Harvey LtCol ded 29-5-20 IA 1/30Punjabis p282

ROBERTSON,Robert Bruce Hope 2Lt kia 28-6-15 8ScotRif p225 MR4

ROBERTSON,Robert Hamilton 2Lt kia 30-11-17 3 att2Hamps p121 MR17

ROBERTSON,Robert Sergius 2Lt dow 20-7-16 1 att3KOSB p102 CR France145,Sergins

ROBERTSON,Robert Ward Shepherd Lt kia 27-5-17 4RWSurr att19MGC Inf p187&212 CR France593

ROBERTSON,Ronald TCapt ded 13-9-17 10HLI p163 CR Surrey9

ROBERTSON,Sydney T2Lt kia 29-7-18 KOSB att1/5Bn p102 MR18

ROBERTSON,Thomas Arthur TCapt ded 11-7-17 RASC p267 CR Ireland14,drd

ROBERTSON,Walter Raymond T2Lt kia 1-7-16 2BordR p118 CR France394

ROBERTSON,Walter Raymond T2Lt kia 5-3-18 RE p210

ROBERTSON,William 2Lt dow 3-5-17 1RScotF p95 MR20

ROBERTSON,William Adam Lt drd 30-12-15 IARO att4Cav p282 MR41,att2RRofCav

ROBERTSON,William Bethune Lt kia 25-3-18 RE 404FC p210 MR20

ROBERTSON,William Dickson 2Lt kia 28-7-17 3/5RScots att1/5ancs p212 CR Belgium10

ROBERTSON,William Ford.MIDx2 TCapt&Adjt kia 17-10-17 9NumbF p63 CR Belgium85

ROBERTSON,William George Lt dow 15-12-17 11GordH att156MGC Inf p167&185 CR Egypt9

ROBERTSON,William Haswell 2Lt dow 2-8-18 9RScots p212

ROBERTSON,William John.TD.Maj dow 11-3-15 4SfthH p241 CR France705,10-3-15

ROBERTSON,William Marr 2Lt ded 12-7-19 3NumbF att25Lpool p262 CR Palestine11,Lt

ROBERTSON,William Maxwell Lt ded 28-6-15 2Lincs p75 CR France705

ROBERTSON,William Maxwell 2Lt dow 2-8-18 9RScots CR France1225

ROBERTSON,William Moore.MC.Lt kia 12-11-17 5RScots p211 MR34,1/4Bn

ROBERTSON,William Stewart.DCM.MID 2Lt kia 31-10-14 8BlkW att2GordH p167&264 MR29

ROBERTSON,William Stewart.MC.TLt kia 3-9-16 10 att4/5BlkW p129 CR France701

ROBERTSON-DURHAM,William Hugh TCapt kia 25-9-15 10ScotRif p104 MR19

ROBERTSON-ROSS,Patrick Maitland TCapt kia 26-9-15 8RWKent D'Coy p142 MR19

ROBERTSON-WALKER,Arthur Murdoch Maxwell.MID TCapt kia 7-7-16 8RFus p70 MR21

ROBILLIARD,Francis Humphrey John 2Lt kia 4-10-17 3Lincs p75 MR30

ROBIN,Cecil 2Lt dow 24-5-18 86RFA p35 CR France29

ROBIN,Charles Harold Capt kia 11-5-17 2RJLI att13Y&L p201 CR France1191

ROBIN,John F.TLtAMaj ded 29-11-18 57MGC Inf p185 CR France1030

ROBINETTE,Caroline Amelia SNurse ded 30-3-17 QAIMNS p200 CR Kent38

ROBINS,Charles Frederick TLt dow 2-4-18 5MGC Cav p185 CR France145

ROBINS,George Upton Capt dow 7-5-15 3EYorks p84 CR Belgium127,5-5-15

ROBINSON,Albert Alexander TLt kia 20-7-16 RGA 59SB p41 CR France397

ROBINSON,Alec Maj dow 16-4-18 C177RFA p35 CR France31

ROBINSON,Alexander Joseph 2Lt dow 8-8-17 116/26RFA p35 CR Belgium5

ROBINSON,Alfred Elliot Somers 2Lt kia 16-6-15 2RScotF p95 MR22,Eliott

ROBINSON,Archibald Tyrell.DSO.MajTLtCol dow 11-5-17 ESurr att7 O&BLI p113 CR Greece1

ROBINSON,Arthur Gabriel T2Lt kia 9-3-16 11BordR p118 CR France515

ROBINSON,Arthur Gordon T2Lt kia 9-1-17 RE SpCo p48 CR France115

ROBINSON,Arthur Henry T2Lt kia 11-6-17 25RFus p70 CR EAfrica10 &CR Tanzania1

ROBINSON,Arthur Hine 2Lt kia 26-4-15 1Manch 1Coy p156 MR29

ROBINSON,Arthur Linnell T2Lt dow 25-2-16 8Nhampt attRE 173TC p48 CR France88,Limnell

ROBINSON,Arthur Owen 2Lt kia 21-3-18 N&D att2/8Bn p134 MR20

ROBINSON,Augustine Lt dow 15-3-15 4SStaffs attELancs p123 CR France768

ROBINSON,Benjamin Stanley 2Lt kia 1-7-16 2RBerks p139 CR France393,Lt

ROBINSON,Bernard Oates 2Lt kia 9-10-17 4Y&L p238 MR30

ROBINSON,Bertram Langhorn Capt ded 6-9-17 RASC 4Coy 50DivTrn p253 CRDurham42

ROBINSON,Birketh Waring 2Lt kia 18-9-18 7Lpool p215 CR France530

ROBINSON,Cecil Beaumont TLt kia 14-9-16 13 att9WYorks p82 MR21

ROBINSON,Cecil Rowland 2Lt kia 26-9-17 1Camb p245 CR Belgium116

ROBINSON,Charles TLtACapt kia 14-7-18 12WYorks p82 CR Belgium3,15-7-18 1Bn

ROBINSON,Charles Arthur Lt kia 9-4-17 4RInnisF att111MGC p105 MR20

ROBINSON,Charles Edward Lt ded 25-10-18 1/5WYorks p218 CR Yorks123

ROBINSON,Charles Eugene Barnes Maj kia 28-9-15 IA 117Mahrattas p282 MR38,27-9-15

ROBINSON,Charles Lawson.TD.LtCol kld 8-5-15 1Mon p244 MR29

ROBINSON,Charles Surtees.MID TCapt dow 13-9-16 9Norf p74 CR France23

ROBINSON,Claude Gladstone T2Lt kia 20-10-15 7SWBord p100 CR France1472

ROBINSON,Courtney Vyvyan Maj ded 22-1-19 RGA p209

ROBINSON,Cyril Charles Edward Lt kia 28-4-18 59RAF

ROBINSON,De la Pere LtCol 30-10-18 APDept CR Lancs263

ROBINSON,Daniel George Mark 2Lt kia 16-5-15 ULIA att1SStaffs p282 CR France705

ROBINSON,Donald TLt kia 3-5-17 15WYorks p82 MR20

ROBINSON,Douglas Eric 2Lt kia 17-9-16 1/5DLI p239 CR France1890,15-9-16

ROBINSON,Edgar Lt kia 14-9-14 1LNLancs p136 MR15

ROBINSON,Edgar Francis 2Lt kia 20-6-18 6EKent p58 MR27

ROBINSON,Edmond Capt kia 20-3-17 RAMC attSfthH p197 CR France1182

ROBINSON,Edward,Gnr ded 24-5-16 RIM p282

ROBINSON,Edward Lt kld 6-12-17 RFA &RFC p12&261,2entries MR43

ROBINSON,Edward Colston T2Lt kia 26-9-15 8SomLI p80 MR19

ROBINSON,Edwin Winwood Lt kld 25-10-14 5Lancers D'Sqn p22 MR29,erased Voorhezele &CR Belgium454,kia

ROBINSON,Eli Lt kia 1-7-16 1/5NStaffs p238 MR21

ROBINSON,Elizabeth.ARRC.Sister ded 14-7-19 TFNS 3BritGH p271 CR Iraq ,12-7-19

ROBINSON,Eric Arthur TCapt dow 10-9-16 12Glouc p107 CR France23

ROBINSON,Eustace Dixon Sharper 2Lt kia 4-9-17 GL &25RFC p12 MR20

ROBINSON,Francis Bradbury Capt dow 3-7-16 6N&D p233 CR France120

ROBINSON,Francis Edward Lt kia 27-10-14 3 att2SStaffs p123 MR29

ROBINSON,Francis Victor Lt ded 29-7-18 RGA 383SB 59HvyGrp p41 CR Egypt9

ROBINSON,Frank TLt dow 7-7-16 14NumbF p63 CR France23

ROBINSON,Frank Victor TLt kia 3-5-17 18WYorks p82 MR20

ROBINSON,Frank Wright.MC.Lt kia 13-5-17 14 att22Manch p156 MR20

ROBINSON,Fred 2Lt kia 26-1-18 GL att22RFC p17 CR Egypt1

ROBINSON,Frederick 2Lt kia 28-7-18 4GordH p242 CR France622,1/7Bn

ROBINSON,Frederick Andrew.MC.TCaptAMaj kia 4-11-18 10TankCps p188 CR France190

ROBINSON,Frederick Henry.MC.Lt kia 30-9-17 3Lincs att3NigR p75&202 CR EAfrica11 &CR Tanzania1

ROBINSON,Frederick Winwood.DSO.MID MajTLtCol dow 18-4-17 130/40RFA p35&258 CR France52,Maj

ROBINSON,Frederick Wilfred.DSO.MC.Maj dow 29-3-18 8MGC p185 MR27,28-3-18

ROBINSON,Gathorne Clegg 2Lt ded 6-6-18 YLI attRAF p143 CR Yorks570

ROBINSON,Geffrey Wathen TLt kia 25-9-15 10Glouc 4Coy p107 CR France1723

ROBINSON,Geoffrey Francis Capt kia 21-5-15 6KSLI att1/4Ghurkas p145&282,mbk IndVoltrs MR22

ROBINSON,George Whalley Capt kia 15-2-15 3Leinst p175 CR Belgium111

ROBINSON,George Thomas 2Lt kia 3-6-18 2SfthH p165 CR France412

ROBINSON,Gerald Duckworth.MID Capt dow 26-9-16 3 att1ESurr SR p113 CR France329

ROBINSON,Harold Arthur Maj ded 31-5-16 2LNLancs p136 CR SAfrica158

ROBINSON,Harold Fletcher TLt kia 1-7-16 15LancF p93 CR France215

ROBINSON,Harold Godfrey Capt kia 12-6-17 1NStaffs p157 CR Belgium127

ROBINSON,Harold Leefe 2Lt dow 10-4-16 IARO att103MahrattaLI p282 MR38

ROBINSON,Harold Percival 2Lt kia 31-7-17 6Lpool p215 MR29

ROBINSON,Harold Robert 2Lt kia 13-10-18 RGA 10SB p41 CR France716

ROBINSON,Harold William 2LtTLt kia 30-9-17 YLI att3Nigeria p143&202 CR EAfrica11 &CR Tanzania1

ROBINSON,Harry 2Lt kia 15-4-18 2/6NStaffs p238 MR32

ROBINSON,Harry Hesketh Kay 2LtACapt kia 26-3-18 5 att16RB p180 MR27

ROBINSON,Harry Ingham.MID Maj kia 13-10-15 5Lincs p220 MR19

ROBINSON,Harry Stanley Shepley Lt dow 9-6-15 3 att2KOSB p102 CR Belgium28

ROBINSON,Harry William TLtAMaj ded 9-11-18 O&BLI LabCps p266 CR Oxford69

ROBINSON,Henry HonLt&QM ded 3-11-15 RAMC att25GenHospl p197 CR France40

ROBINSON,Henry John T2Lt kia 21-9-17 10RWKent C'Coy p142 MR30

ROBINSON,Henry Awtry T2Lt kld 18-2-18 RFC p17 CR France1844,Harry Awty

ROBINSON,Henry Betham Maj ded 31-7-18 RAMC p253 CR Lond14

ROBINSON,Henry Ellis TCapt kia 25-4-18 RAMC att1/6WYorks p197 MR30

ROBINSON,Henry Harold.DSO.TCapt drd 4-5-17 RAMC p197 CR Italy13

ROBINSON,Herbert Edwin 2Lt kia 10-7-17 189RFA p209 CR Belgium29

ROBINSON,Hercules Edward Joseph.Hon.T2Lt dow 26-9-15 8EKent p58 CR France178

ROBINSON,Hugh Huntley.MC&Bar.Maj kld 3-5-19 RAMC &RAF p253 CR Belgium241

ROBINSON,Horace Victor George 2Lt kia 24-10-17 7Worc p226 MR20

ROBINSON,Hugh Thomas Kay.DSO.LtCol kia 26-4-18 12 att13RSuss p119

ROBINSON,Isaac T2Lt kia 23-10-16 12 att2ELancs p111 MR21

ROBINSON,Isaac Vincent T2Lt kia 14-7-17 RE 67FC p48 CR Belgium36

ROBINSON James 2Lt kia 20-5-17 9 att4Lpool p216 CR France434

ROBINSON,James Norman T2Lt dow 22-7-18 6LancF att13ELancs p93 CR France28

ROBINSON,James Thompson TLt kia 7-9-18 RWFus att24Bn p99 CR France285,8-9-18

ROBINSON,James Vernon TLt dow 13-8-18 1 att16LancF p93 CR France145

ROBINSON,John 2Lt kia 1-7-16 3 att2SWBord p100 CR France1501

ROBINSON,John Cecil T2Lt kia 5-6-17 YLI att2Bn p143 CR Belgium173

ROBINSON,John Cyril Charles Henry Capt kia 3-6-17 5ELancs p226 CR France905

ROBINSON,John Edward T2Lt kia 3-11-16 Lincs p75 CR France374

ROBINSON,John Henry 2Lt kia 30-11-17 4SomLI att2/6NStaffs p218 MR17

ROBINSON,John Holdsworth 2Lt kia 1-7-16 16WYorks p82 MR21

ROBINSON,John Hunter T2Lt dow 17-9-18 8 att12NumbF p63 CR France145,12/13Bn

ROBINSON,John Langley 2Lt kia 21-1-16 IARO att41Dogras p282 CR Iraq5,Lt

ROBINSON,John Singleton Henry TLt kia 24-9-18 13 att12WelshR p127 CR France673

ROBINSON,John Wilfred Capt kia 15-11-16 4NumbF p213 MR21

ROBINSON,John Yate.MC.TCapt&Adj dow 23-8-16 7NStaffs p157 CR Hereford/W154

ROBINSON,Joseph 2Lt dow 11-10-16 7NumbF p214 CR France145

ROBINSON,Kennett TLt kia 25-9-15 RAMC att12Manch p197 CR Belgium37,Kenneth

ROBINSON,Leonard TCapt kia 22-8-15 9LancF p93 MR4

ROBINSON,Leonard Herbert Frank TLt dow 18-3-16 7ESurr attTMB p113 CR France257,17-3-16

ROBINSON,Leslie Fergus.MC.Lt kia 27-9-18 RFA p208 CR France364,Feargus

ROBINSON,Leslie John Capt kia 12-3-15 Nhampt p138 MR22,1Bn &CR France1896,2Bn

ROBINSON,Louis Francis Woodward TLt kia 25-5-17 RE 153FC p48 MR20

ROBINSON,Max Louis 2Lt kia 22-7-16 2RScots p54 MR21,23-7-16

ROBINSON,Noel Stafford Maj dow 2-8-18 RFA p206 CR France888

ROBINSON,Osmond Cyril.MC.2Lt ded 24-5-18 181RFA p261 CR Yorks173,Lt

ROBINSON,Percy Dickson.MC.Capt kia 31-3-18 RFC MR20 p261

ROBINSON,Percy Douglas TCapt kia 7-7-16 9NumbF p63 MR21

ROBINSON,Ralf Hubert.MM.T2Lt dow 23-8-17 RB att2Bn p180 CR Belgium11

ROBINSON,Ralph Duncan TCapt kia 7-6-17 9LNLancs p136 CR Belgium43

ROBINSON,Raymond Cecil 2Lt dow 19-10-18 RGA 270SB p41 CR France725

ROBINSON,Reginald Humphries T2Lt kia 4-10-18 1/4RLancs p59 CR France109,Humphreys Lt

ROBINSON,Reginald William TCapt kia 15-8-15 5RInnisF p105 CR Gallipoli4

ROBINSON,Richmond Fothergill T2Lt kia 30/31-7-15 7KRRC p151 MR29,30-7-15

ROBINSON,Robert Ernest T2Lt dow 12-11-18 46MGC p185 CR France123

ROBINSON,Roland Weymouth 2Lt dow 9-9-15 IARO att96Inf p282 CR Asia82

ROBINSON,Sidney Furness 2Lt ded 10-3-15 RH&FA p35 p261

ROBINSON,Stephen Owen.MID Capt kia 5-11-17 13Huss att5DragGds p22 CR Iraq8

ROBINSON,Sydney Francis Lt kia 22-7-17 5SLancs p230 MR29

ROBINSON,Thistle.MC.TLt kia 25-10-18 RFus att26Bn p70 CR Belgium408

ROBINSON,Thomas Botterill 2Lt ded 25-1-20 RFA p271 CR Yorks62,23-1-20

ROBINSON,Thomas Edward Lt kia 18-10-16 11 att2Yorks p91 MR21

ROBINSON,Thomas Naylor T2Lt kia 25-9-16 19 att14DLI p161 MR21

ROBINSON,Walter 2Lt kia 29-9-18 5WYorks attTankCps p189&218 CR France212

ROBINSON,Walter de Horne.MC.LtACapt kia 27-1-17 3 att1BordR p118 MR21

ROBINSON,Wilfred Cane Lt kia 22-3-18 11Hamps p121 CR France365

ROBINSON,William T2Lt kia 1-8-18 1/2 at1/5KOSB p102 CR Frnce524

ROBINSON,William T2Lt kia 22-8-18 8 att12/13NumbF p63 CR France514

ROBINSON,William Alfred Layton 2Lt kia 26-6-17 3RWSurr p56 CR Belgium29,11Bn

ROBINSON,William Charles 2Lt kia 7-1-17 IA 30Punjabis p282 CR EAfrica39

ROBINSON,William Eardley T2Lt kia 26-9-16 11SStaffs attLeic p123 MR32

ROBINSON,William Edwin TCapt kia 18-11-16 16HLI p163 MR21

ROBINSON,William Ewart T2Lt kia 19-8-15 8NumbF p63 MR4

ROBINSON,William Frederick Rokeby Lt 24-9-18 8RAF MR20

ROBINSON,William George T2Lt kia 1-10-17 Leic att8Bn p88 MR30

ROBINSON,William John Lt ded 19-2-19 HAC p271 CR Scot726

ROBINSON,W.Leefe.VC.Capt ded 31-12-18 Worc &RAF p109 CR Mddx23

ROBLIN,Lewis George 2Lt kia 5-5-18 1NumbF p63 MR19

ROBSON,Alfred Styan 2Lt kia 5-11-16 6DLI p239 MR21

ROBSON,Albert Frank TCapt kia 24-3-18 10RWSurr p56 MR20

ROBSON,Alexander 2Lt dow 8-11-17 RIrFus p171

ROBSON,Charles T2Lt dow 2-12-18 18NumbF p63 CR Durham18

ROBSON,Charles Alexander Burleigh.DCM.2Lt dow 8-11-17 2RIrFus CR Palestine1

ROBSON,Charles Henry TCapt kia 1-12-17 RAMC 2/4FA att2/4Glouc p197 MR17

ROBSON,Edgar Capt dow 3-12-14 1SLancs p126 CR France284

ROBSON,Edward Fawcett 2Lt dow 18-5-18 B79RFA p35 CR France84

ROBSON,Edward Moore.MC.Capt kia 11-4-18 5Yorks A'Coy p220 MR32

ROBSON,Frederick William.DSO.LtCol kia 28-3-18 5Yorks p220 MR27

ROBSON,Frederick William.MM.T2Lt dow 22-8-18 5MGC Inf p185&259 CR France281

ROBSON,George Lt kia 20-9-17 4SfthH p241 MR30

ROBSON,George William 2Lt kia 5-11-16 8DLI p239 MR21

ROBSON,Gerald David TLt kia 24-8-17 9KRRC p151 CR Belgium72

ROBSON,Harry Stuart Lt kia 8-8-18 10Lond p248 MR16

ROBSON,Henry Crompton Lt kia 12-3-18 7 att2/10Mddx p235 MR34

ROBSON,John Matley 2Lt ded 17-7-15 9Manch p237 CR Egypt3

ROBSON,Joseph T2Lt kia 20-7-18 2/4Y&L p159 CR France1689

ROBSON,Ralph George Griffiths Capt kia 23-12-14 RE 3Coy p48 CR France768

ROBSON,Richard Ivan.MC.Capt dow 6-8-17 15RIrRif p170 CR Belgium11

ROBSON,Stanley 2Lt kia 31-3-18 4EYorks p219 CR France232

ROBSON,Tom Capt kia 22-8-18 19Lond p250 CR France210

ROBSON,William T2Lt ded 30-10-18 17KRRC p151 CR Scot596

ROBSON,William Friend 2Lt kia 3-5-17 296RFA p35 CR France366

ROBSON,William John 2Lt kia 30-11-17 NumbYeo p204 CR France415

ROBSON-SCOTT,Thomas Selby Lt kia 14-12-14 RScots p54 MR29

ROCH,George Powell Capt kia 21-5-18 PembrokeYeo att1KSLI p205 CR Belgium3

ROCH,William Protheroe LtACapt kia 11-3-18 WelshHorse p205 CR Palestine3

ROCH-AUSTIN,Sidney Leslie TLt dow 4-11-18 1/2 att1/4WRid p116 CR France1081

ROCHE,C.MC&Bar.Maj 14-3-21 RAMC CR Scot359

ROCHE,Francis Capt ded 30-6-17 RAVC 10VetHosp p199 CR France40

ROCHE,Francis Cavendish Chap4Cl ded 14-11-15 RAChDept p199 CR Egypt6

ROCHE,Hyacinth Joseph Albert Capt kld 19-1-15 RMunF attRFC p2&176 CR France1360,kia

ROCHE,James Patrick.MC.2LtACapt kia 7-6-17 GL RFA att47TMB p191 CR Belgium17

ROCHE,K.J.2Lt 21-11-18 1/2Madras&SMahrattaRifs MR66

ROCHE,Patrick Joseph.MC.Lt ded 25-8-17 IARO att1Sap&Min p282 CR Iraq8

ROCHE,Richard John Maj&QM ded 6-12-16 RWKent p265

ROCHE,Thomas Maj kia 17-11-14 1Wilts p153 CR Belgium106

ROCHE,Thomas.MC.Capt ded 26-9-19 RMunstF p266 MR40

ROCHE,William Henry T2Lt kia 27-3-18 10RIrFus p171 CR France987

ROCHELL,Alfred LtTCapt dow 14-4-18 1NumbF p63 CR France40

ROCHFORT,Arthur D'Oyly Lt ded 31-10-18 RGA &58RAF p41 CR Egypt15,13-10-18

ROCHFORT-BOYD,Henry Charles.DSO.MajTLtCol dow 4-12-17 16RHA 4CavDiv p35&258 CR France145

ROCHFORT-DAVIES,Wallis Rowland Henry 2Lt 8-3-16 3SomLI CR Somerset197

ROCKE,Charles Owen 2Lt kia 23-8-18 1GrenGds p50 CR France502

ROCKEY,Jim 2Lt kia 2-5-17 1/4Lincs p217 CR France551

ROCKLEY,William Lisle.MC.T2Lt kia 10-10-17 10Y&L p159 MR30,11-10-17

RODAKOWSKI,Raymond Juzio Paul LtACapt kia 9-10-17 1IrGds p53 MR30

RODD,Charles Bouchier 2Lt kia 30-10-16 2Dev p77 MR21

RODD,Frederick Trevor Lt kia 16-6-17 2/3Lond p245 MR20

RODDAM,Robert Collingwood.MC.Capt kia 16-6-15 3 att1NumbF p63 MR29

RODDAN,Reginald T2Lt kia 1-10-18 9TankCps p188 CR France375

RODDICK,Andrew Maj kia 14-5-15 EssYeo p203 MR29

RODDY,Edwin Louis Maj died 3-7-19 1Ches p263CR Dorset152

RODERICK,Allan Whitlock Nicholl Lt kia 10-8-15 4WelshReg p230 MR4

RODERICK,Francis TLt dow 31-7-17 14WelshR p127 CR Belgium23

RODERICK,Hume Buckley LtACapt kia 1-12-17 1WelshGds 3Coy p53 CR France415,15-12-17

RODERICK,John Victor Tweed Lt kia 27-8-18 1CldGds p51 CR France103,21-8-18

RODERIGUES,A.R.G.Maj 18-3-20 IMS MR65

RODGER,Douglas TLt kia 1-7-16 RAMC att90FA p197 CR France44

RODGER,George Swan 2Lt mbk 9-1-17 2Leic p256 MR38

RODGER,James Alexander Valentine 2Lt kia 3-9-16 13 att14Hamps p121 MR21

RODGER,Lawton Keir Lt ded 15-1-19 RE CR Scot812

RODGER,Matthew Freer Lt kia 23-10-16 1 att2ScotRif p104 MR21,4 att2Bn

RODGER,W.Lt ded 1-11-18 RE 57FC p48 CR Scot86

RODGER,Walter Washington Buchanan 2LtTLt kia 8-7-15 1/5A&SH p243 CR Gallipoli1

RODGERS,Albert Henry Lt ded 7-11-18 4Res RFA p35&257 CR Yorks551,7-10-18

RODGERS,Alan Evison Lt kia 5-6-15 5ELancs p226 MR4

RODGERS,Albert Henry T2Lt dow 17-10-18 50MGC Inf p185 CR France1386

RODGERS,Edward Joseph T2Lt kia 24-4-17 10ScotRif p104 MR20

RODGERS,Henry Frederick T2Lt kia 4-10-17 1/7RWar Res p65 MR30

RODGERS,John.MID LtACapt dow 8-3-18 2YLI p143 CR Belgium12

RODGERS,John.MC.Capt kia 2-9-18 2/4Y&rL D'Coy p238 CR France617

RODGERS,John Richard Lt kia 20-11-17 8Hamps attTankCps p189&229 MR17

RODGERS,Joseph Edward 2Lt dow 25-1-15 1CldGds 1Coy p51 CR France202

RODGERS,Robert William Christian Meyer Capt kia 29-7-17 RGA 1HB p209 CR Belgium9

RODHAM,Robert T2Lt kia 17-10-17 27 att9NumbF p63 CR Belgium85

RODNEY,Burnett William T2Lt kia 20-4-17 11RWKent p142 CR Belgium28

RODNEY,Hon William Francis 2Lt kld 9-5-15 RB &3RFC p2&180 CR France98

RODNEY-ANDERSON,Patrick Graham LtCol ded 14-6-16 IA 76Punjabis p282

RODNEY-RICKETTS,Stewart Arthur.MC.T2LtACapt kia 31-10-17 D82RFA p35 CR Belgium10

RODOCANACHI,Paul John T2Lt kia 27-7-17 GL &53RFC p13 CR Belgium76

RODRIQUES,Frank Capt ded 22-1-20 IA IMS p282

RODWELL,Hubert T2Lt dow 10-10-16 9 att11LNLancs p136 CR France85

RODWELL,Mary SNurse drd 17-11-15 QAIMNS p200 MR40

RODWELL,William Albert.MC.T2Lt kia 9-11-17 RE 171Co p48 CR Belgium3

ROE,Albert John Havilland T2Lt kia 9-8-15 7KRRC p151 MR29

ROE,Arthur Robert Montgomery Capt dow 16-9-14 1Dors p124 CR France1862

ROE,Cyril Charles Lt 28-4-17 RMLI MR20

ROE,Edward Allan.MC&Bar.TLtTCapt kia 2-9-18 ESurr att2/4RWSurr p113 CR Belgium15

ROE,Francis Leslie T2Lt dow 7-1-16 2SLancs p126 CR France40

ROE,Frank Edward Mervyn Capt dow 7-6-16 5 att12RB p180 CR Belgium11

ROE,Harold 2Lt kia 4-9-18 3 att2/5LancF p93 MR19

ROE,Heriot Baker T2Lt kia 23-8-18 1ESurr p113 CR France239

ROE,John George 2Lt kia 26-9-17 3 att2/8N&D p134 CR Belgium130

ROE,John Windsor Maj dow 7-8-16 C185RFA RABde IndianEF p35 CR France80

ROE,Samuel George Capt kia 20-10-14 2RInnisF p105 CR France451,21-10-14

ROE,Sidney Charles 2Lt kia 5-5-17 14Lond p249 CR France581

ROE,William Richard T2Lt ded PoW 11-5-17 11RFus attHAC p70 CR France1293

ROEBER,David Arnold 2Lt kia 14-8-16 3 att7Beds p86 CR France82

ROEBUCK,Alfred Eric Eaton TCapt kia 8-9-18 9WRid p116 CR France662

ROFFEY,Harold Bowyer.DSO.MajTLtCol kia 15-4-18 LancF att2/5Lincs p93 CR France285

ROFFEY,J Capt 16-10-16 IA MilWorksServ CR Burma129A

ROFT,Edwin John 2Lt kia 25-7-18 8Lond p247 MR27

ROGER,Edward James Pringle T2Lt kia 19-7-18 RASC 49DivTrn p193 CR Belgium18

ROGERS,Alan Stanley Clark TCapt kia 7-8-15 6EYorks p84 MR4

ROGERS,Albert Edward 2Lt kia 3-5-17 2LancF p93 MR20

ROGERS,Alfred Morris T2Lt kia 18-7-16 15Glouc p107 CR France114

ROGERS,Allen Stanley Clark Lt kia 8-8-15 IA 61Pnrs att6EYorks p282

ROGERS,Arthur 2Lt kia 26-3-17 6RWelshF p223 CR Palestine8,1/7Bn

ROGERS,Arthur Gerald TLt kia 26-9-16 12Mddx p148 CR France215

ROGERS,Arthur Norman Capt kia 24-11-17 1/7RScots p211 CR Palestine3

ROGERS,Benjamin Richard Corlay 2Lt kia 17-10-18 6 att3RFus p70 CR France190

ROGERS,Cecil Victor De Burgh 2Lt kia 21-4-17 GL &29RFC p13 CR France581

ROGERS,Cecil Walter T2Lt dow 28-12-17 7RWSurr p56 CR Surrey55

ROGERS,Charles Hunter 2Lt dow 9-11-14 RH&FA p35 CR Lond14,Lt

ROGERS,Clarence Elias 2Lt kia 18-6-16 RFC p3 CR France924

ROGERS,Denys Stutely 2Lt kia 21-3-18 189RFA p35 MR20

ROGERS,Edward.MC.CaptAMaj dow 8-12-16 RE 67FC p48 CR France62

ROGERS,Edward Ambrose Gordon Capt ded 9-4-16 RGA 93SB p271 CR Cornwall36

ROGERS,Esmond Hallewell T2Lt kia 3-7-16 10RWar p65 MR21

ROGERS,Francis Caryer Campbell.MVO.Capt kia 15-2-15 2DCLI p115 MR29

ROGERS,Francis Lyttelton Lloyd T2Lt kia 7-1-16 D75RFA p35 CR France705,6-1-16

ROGERS,G.C.MC.Capt 30-10-17 52RFC CR France1361 CR France383

ROGERS,George Murray TLt kia 1-7-16 13RIrRif p170

ROGERS,George Stanley 2Lt kld 10-8-16 RFC p3 CR Canada1602

ROGERS,Gerald 2Lt kia 1-9-18 126AC RFA p35 CR France421

ROGERS,Godfrey Marcus Lt dow 27-4-18 1 att12Glouc p107 CR France31,2Lt 28-4-18

ROGERS,Henry Milward Capt dow 26-5-15 5Manch p236 CR Greece10

ROGERS,Henry Peverell Lt kia 5-7-16 1N&D p134 MR21

ROGERS,Herbert George 2Lt kia 28-12-15 9SomLI p80 MR4,29-6-15

ROGERS,Hermoine Angela Nurse drd 31-12-17 VAD p200 CR Egypt1

ROGERS,John.DCM.Lt&QM ded 13-6-18 GordH p265 CR Scot758

ROGERS,James Archibald Lt kia 26-2-18 RE p48 MR38

ROGERS,James Joseph T2Lt kia 28-3-18 11 att2RDubF p177 CR France526,27-3-18

ROGERS,John Lewis Capt ded 15-11-18 1/4DCLI p226 CR Egypt9

ROGERS,Leonard Castel Campbell.MC.MID Lt dow 25-12-14 IA 1/7 att1/9GurkhaRif p282 CR France727

ROGERS,Leonard Neville TCapt dow 11-4-17 1 att18NumbF Res p63 CR France97

ROGERS,Maurice Croston 2Lt dow 25-2-15 RE 59FC p48 CR Belgium170

ROGERS,N.H.Capt ded 25-4-17 2/4GurkhaRif MR40

ROGERS,Percy Alexander MacKarness Lt kia 9-10-17 7WYorks p218 MR30

ROGERS,Percy Arden Lt kia 27-5-18 RE 170TC p48 CR France179

ROGERS,Reginald T2Lt kia 15-9-16 7RB p180 CR France1890

ROGERS,Richard Henry Lyster Lt kia 4-10-17 32RFA p35 CR Belgium86

ROGERS,Robert Carmichael TCapt dow 2-8-18 RAMC att18HAG p197 CR France34

ROGERS,Robert Maxtone T2Lt kia 25-9-16 9 att2KOSB p102 MR21,Maxton

ROGERS,Robert Murray 2Lt kia 2-7-16 8KRRC p151 MR20

ROGERS,Ronald Joseph Capt kia 28-6-15 14RB p180 MR4

ROGERS,Samuel.DCM.2Lt ded 24-11-17 6RWar p214 CR France1778

ROGERS,Sheffield Digby Kissane Lt kia 14-6-15 4RFus attNumbF p70 MR29

ROGERS,Sidney Frederick 2Lt kld 31-12-17 RE p210 CR Hamps8

ROGERS,Sidney Gilbert 2Lt kia 4-10-17 1Dev p77 MR30,3-10-17

ROGERS,Stanley T2Lt kia 4-10-18 Wilts att7Bn p153 MR16

ROGERS,Stanley Arthur Lt kia 21-3-18 2/6N&D p233 MR20

ROGERS,Thomas DepCommy&Capt ded 13-2-15 IA S&TCps p282 CR France356,Lt

ROGERS,Thomas Jerome 2Lt ded 30-10-18 IARO attLabCps p282 CR Pakistan50A,31-10-18

ROGERS,Trevor T2Lt kia 24-11-17 18WelshR p127 MR17

ROGERS,Wilfrid Frank.DSO.MID CaptAMaj kia 19-5-17 45RFA p35 CR France581

ROGERS,William Ewart Lt kia 31-7-17 6Ches p222 MR29

ROGERS,William Frederick 2Lt kld 28-12-15 RFC p2

ROGERSON,Andrew William Maj dow 6-10-17 8A&SH p243 CR Belgium16

ROGERSON,Ernest Sidney TCapt kia 19-8-16 9RSuss p119 MR21

ROGERSON,Harold T2Lt kia 1-8-17 13Mddx p148 MR29

ROGERSON,John Lilly T2Lt kia 5-10-18 9ScotRif att28TMB p104 CR Belgium157

ROGERSON,Noel 2Lt kia 28-2-18 3WYorks att2/4YLI p82 MR20

ROGERSON,William TCapt kia 27-8-18 RAMC att8RBerks p197 CR France515

ROHAN,Patrick Bernard 2Lt kia 16-3-15 2YLI p143 MR29

ROHDE,John Haughton Lt kia 28-10-14 RE att21S&M p48 MR22

ROHDE,Harold Turner Capt kia 12-4-16 IA 89Punjabis p282 MR38

ROLASON,Leslie Norton 2Lt kia 26-9-17 9Lond p248 MR30

ROLFE,Ernest Victor T2Lt kia 5-3-17 13Huss p22 CR Iraq8

ROLFE,John Shirley 2Lt ded 4-10-18 IARO att9HodsonsHorse p282 MR65,5-10-18

ROLFE,Philip TCapt kia 24-8-18 RASC att7Norf p193 CR France370

ROLFE,Raymond Harold Lt kia 23-4-18 4GrenGds attIrGds p50 CR France24,22-4-18

ROLFE,Wilfred Edwin 2Lt kia 22-8-17 2/1BucksBn O&BLI p232 MR30

ROLLAND,Frederick James Gordon TLt kia 25-9-15 8 att6KOSB p102 MR19

ROLLASON,Arthur Gilbert Capt ded 30-7-15 1/7Worc p225 CR France3,dow

ROLLASON,Charles Henry 2Lt dow 6-4-18 6N&D p233 CR France145,16Bn

ROLLESTON,Francis Launcelot 2Lt kld 26-4-15 2Lond p245 CR France1141,Lancelot kia

ROLLINS,Harold Victor Lt kia 24-4-18 12Lond p248 MR27 CR France1890

ROLLO,Thomas William T2Lt ded 4-11-18 LabCps p189 CR France34,Capt

ROLPH,Charles Colwyn Capt kia 15-10-15 2Leic p88 CR France765

ROLPH,George William Capt kia 10-8-15 Worc att9th p109 MR4

ROLSTON,Leslie Hicks Lt dow 1-4-18 RGA 182SB p41 CR France37

ROLSTON,William Edward Capt ded 9-8-21 2/5EKent att1D GHQ CR Germany1

ROMANES,Edmund Giles Radcliffe Lt dow 7-6-15 12Worc attRFus p109 MR4

ROME,Hubert Charlton Capt kia 18-12-14 IA 20Inf att129Baluchis p282 CR France571

ROME,James 2Lt kia 18-11-16 5HLI p240 CR France1890

ROMER,Frederick Charles.CB.CMG.HonColTLtCol kia 26-9-15 8EKent Ex LancF p58 MR19

ROMER,Guy Frederick T2Lt dow 3-5-16 13Mddx p148 CR France285

ROMER,Mark Leman Ritchie TCapt dow 20-9-16 7KRRC p151 CR Lond8

ROMILLY,Arthur Hovell Capt kia 21-10-14 DCLI p115 CR France279

ROMILLY,Cosmo George TLt kia 11-8-15 13N&D att1RInnisF p134 CRGallipoli6

ROMILLY,Francis Henry.DSO.Capt kia 25-9-15 2Leic p88 CR France1157

RONALD,James McBain Capt kia 23-4-15 2EKent p58 MR29

RONALDSON,Alexander T2Lt kia 9-6-16 12 att10ScotRif p104 CR France423

RONALDSON,Charles Rashleigh TLt kia 3-9-16 16RB p180 MR21

RONALDSON,James Gray T2Lt kia 20-9-17 10RWSurr attTMB p56 MR30

RONALDSON,John Stein 2Lt kia 9-4-17 3CamH p168 CR France1182

RONAYNE,James Andrew Lt kia 25-9-15 5RMunstF p176 CR France219

RONCA,Edward Henry T2Lt kia 17-10-18 1EKent p58 CR France849

ROOK,Frederick William 2Lt kia 21-7-17 40RFC p13 MR20

ROOK,Reuben Victor Capt kld 30-8-18 20Lond p251 CR France624,kia

ROOKE,Charles Douglas Willoughby.MID Lt kia 19-6-15 1ScotRif p104 CR France83

ROOKE,Claude Eugene 2Lt kld 21-1-18 3KOSB attRFC p17&102 CR Lancs14

ROOKE,Douglas Giles Capt ded 2-11-18 CldGds p51 CR Italy12

ROOKE,Giles Maj kia 9-5-15 IA 2/10GurkhaRif att2/2 p282 MR28

ROOKE,Henry Clive Lt kia 11-4-18 3 att1KOSB C'Coy p102 MR32

ROOKE,Sidney Austin Harold 2Lt dow 20-9-18 RWar att2/7Bn p65 CR France496

ROOKE,Wallace Mortimer.MID Capt ded 8-10-18 RWiltsYeo att2WiltR p206 CR Wilts29

ROOKE,William Albert T2Lt kia 29-7-16 7DCLI p115 CR France344

ROONEY,Bruno Martin Lt kia 25-6-15 9KOSB p102 CR Gallipoli6

ROONEY,Richard James TCapt dow 19-9-17 RE p48 CR France134

ROOPE,Charles Francis T2Lt kia 1-7-16 2RFus p70 CR France1501

ROOPER,Trevor Godolphin Hungerford 2Lt kia 18-1-17 1KSLI p145 CR France423

ROOPER,William Victor Trevor Capt kia 9-10-17 24RWFus attRFC p19&203 CR France285

ROOS,Gustav Oscar Capt kia 1-7-16 14Y&L p159 CR France927

ROOT,Harold Walter Lt dow PoW 22-3-18 36MGC Inf p185 CR France441,102MGC

ROOTH,Richard Alexander LtCol kia 25-4-15 1RDubF p177 CR Gallipoli15

ROOTS,Percy William 2Lt kia 11-6-17 7Lond p247 MR29

ROPE,John Arthur T2Lt kia 24-8-16 9 att1RWSurr p56 MR21

ROPER,Douglas Wingfield 2lt dow 11-11-17 RGA 279SB p41 CR Belgium10

ROPER,Eric Walter TLt&Adj dow 12-9-16 17RFus p70 CR France203

ROPER,Geoffrey Stapylton Rowe.MC.T2Lt kia 12-5-17 3 att7Yorks p91 CR France924

ROPER,George Fitzgerald 2Lt ded 18-5-19 RFA p262 CR Suff83,drd

ROPER,Oliver Stuart LtACapt kia 27-11-17 2/5YLI p235 MR17

ROPER,Reginald Trevor Maj kia 12-10-14 1Dors p124 CR France260

ROPER,William Edward Capt kia 31-7-17 1/5RLancs p213 CR Belgium10

ROPER,William Frank.MC.T2Lt kia 29-9-18 11RFus att54TMB p70 CR France511

ROPER,William Horace Stanley 2Lt dow 11-10-17 3GrenGds p50 CR Belgium16,Lt

RORIE,Thomas Handyside Baxter Capt kia 18-8-16 4BlkW p230 CR France387

RORISON,William Gilbert Don Gurdon Capt kia 9-4-18 3 att10/11HLI p163 MR32

ROSA,Herbert Charles 2Lt kia 31-7-17 RFA 8DAC p35 CR Belgium5

ROSCOE,Arthur.MC.T2Lt dow 5-9-16 8RWKent p142 CR France23

ROSCOE,Ernest 2Lt ded 26-6-15 17WYorks p82 CR Yorks361

ROSCOE,Richard Lang.MC.TCapt dow 4-2-17 22RFus p70 CR France59

ROSE,Alexander Lt kld 6-9-18 7HLI &RAF p271 CR Scot752,2Lt

ROSE,Alexander Daniel.MC.DCM.2Lt kia 31-8-17 17WYorks p82 MR21

ROSE,Algernon Winter.MC.Capt ded 29-10-18 EssYeo &RAF p256&271,2Lt CR Essex256

ROSE,Archibald John Gordon 2Lt kia 26-9-17 12Lond p248 MR30

ROSE,Arthur Hugh Percy Capt kia 23-11-14 3Ess p132 CR Belgium33,2Bn

ROSE,C.V.Lt kia 6-9-18 2KAR p268

ROSE,Eric Dudley Capt kia 30-3-18 22Lond p251 CR Syria2

ROSE,Eric William.MC.T2Lt kia 5-4-18 1/2LancF att1/8Bn p93 MR20

ROSE,Eric Wollaston.MID Capt kia 28-3-18 5Lond Ex SussYeo p246 MR20

ROSE,Frank Stanley D.Bart.Capt kia 26-1-15 10Huss p22 CR Belgium117,26-10-15

ROSE,Frederick Alexander Lt kia 10-8-15 4GordH p241 CR Belgium56,2Lt

ROSE,Geoffrey Craig 2Lt dow 13-2-15 3SfthH att1GordH p165 CR Lond13

ROSE,George 2Lt kia 28-6-18 7 att15RWar p214 CR France20

ROSE,George Douglas 2Lt kia 20-9-17 4GordH C'Coy p242 MR30

ROSE,Harold Emerson Capt dow 7-7-17 RAMC att2CldGds p197 CR Belgium12

ROSE,Herbert John.MID Capt kia 4-6-15 8Manch p237 MR4

ROSE,Hugh Alexander Leslie.DSO.Maj kia 18-4-18 RFA Staff DivHQ p35 CR Belgium11

ROSE,Hugh Price 2Lt kia 11-4-17 2SfthH p165 CR France604

ROSE,John Alexander TCapt kia 9-3-17 17WYorks p82 CR France648

ROSE,John Charles Reginald Lt dow 9-11-14 A&SH p173 CR France284

ROSE,Joseph Harold T2Lt dow 28-12-17 Worc Res att2/8Bn p109 CR Hereford/W110,4-1-18

ROSE,Launcelot St.Vincent.MID Maj kia 27-11-14 RE 55FC p48 CR France525

ROSE,Merton Alfred.MC.2Lt dow 19-9-18 2/5RWar p214 CR France31

ROSE,Osmond Arthur 2Lt ded 12-9-19 5Dors att1/4Wilts p264 CR Egypt2

ROSE,Phillip Vivian TCapt dow 25-4-17 GL 7 O&BLI BdeStaff p191 CR Bucks123

ROSE,Reginald Alfred 2Lt kia 2-8-17 2/7Manch CR Belgium24

ROSE,Reginald Vincent 2Lt kia 1-7-16 1/6RWar B'Coy p214 MR21

ROSE,Ronald Henry Evan TLt kia 28-4-17 6Beds p86 MR20

ROSE,Ronald Hugh Walrond.MID Capt kia 22-10-14 ScotRif p104 MR32

ROSE,Ronald Madoc Tierney.MID CaptTMaj kia 18-9-16 Y&L att2/3KAR p159&202 CR EAfrica39,19-9-16

ROSE,Stewart Alan Lt kia 28-3-18 3NumbF p63 MR20

ROSE,Theodore William Frank 2Lt kia 4-4-18 7RFus p70 MR20,Frederick

ROSE,Thomas Allen.DSO.Capt kia 23-8-14 RScotF p95 CR Belgium206

ROSE,William TLt kia 11-4-17 10HLI p163 MR20

ROSE,William Samuel T2Lt kia 2-12-17 ELancs att2/5Bn p111 MR30,22-12-17

ROSE-CLELAND,Alfred Middleton Blackwood Bingham Lt kia 1-7-16 4RDubF p177 CR France35,1Bn

ROSENBAUM,Laurence Braham Lt dow 17-4-18 3Mon p244 CR Belgium38,1/2Bn

ROSENTHAL,Arthur 2Lt kia 23-11-17 GL &65RFC p13 MR20

ROSEVEAR,Frank Rudolph Capt dow 23-8-18 13Lond p249 CR France103

ROSEVEARE,Francis Bernard Lt dow 9-11-17 IA CpsofGuides Inf att5ScindeInf p282 CR Iraq8

ROSEVEARE,Harold William 2Lt dow 20-9-14 1Wilts p153 MR15

ROSEVEARE,Ronald Chard T2Lt kia 8-8-16 9 att1SomLI p80 CR Belgium73

ROSEVEARE,Ernest William Capt kia 27-4-18 4DCLI p226

ROSEWARNE,Ernest William Capt 27-4-18 4DCLI CR Palestine9

ROSHER,Henry Louis LtCol kia 14-4-15 Cmdg2Dors p124 CR Iraq6

ROSHER,J.R.Capt&QM 19-3-19 23RWFus CR Wales491

ROSIER,James Erle Radcliff Lt dow 20-9-16 A245RFA p208 CR France296,kia

ROSINDALE,Herbert 2Lt kia 11-10-18 1/4EYorks p219 CR France612

ROSKELL,Gertrude Lucinda Nurse ded 31-10-15 VAD att17GH CR Egypt3

ROSKELLY,Wilfred Menadue Lt kia 29-7-17 32RFC p13 MR20

ROSKILLY,Alfred T2Lt kia 3-5-17 7RWSurr p56 MR20

ROSLING,Alan Percy 2Lt kia 4-3-17 1Worc p109 MR21

ROSLING,Charles Holbrook LtACapt dow 22-10-18 3 att7DCLI p115 CR France398

ROSS,A.D.AssSurg 5-6-21 IMS MR66

ROSS,Alaistair 2Lt kldacc 17-1-16 RFC p3 CR Scot280

ROSS,Alexander Aitkin LtCol ded 24-11-15 RAMC 3FA p253 CR Scot244

ROSS,Andrew Beaconsfield TLt kia 6-8-17 RAMC att2RIrRif p197 CR Belgium29

ROSS,Archibald Seymour 2Lt kia 9-5-15 1CamH p168 MR22

ROSS,Arthur Claude 2Lt dow 6-12-17 RScotsF att10RFC p13&95 CR Belgium11

ROSS,Arthur J.Capt kia 16-8-17 5 att1RIrRif p170 MR30

ROSS,Arthur Justin.DSO&Bar.Maj kldacc 2-8-17 RE &RFC p13&48 CR Lond4

ROSS,Cecil Goodall.MC.2Lt kia 23-4-17 3RScots att45TMB p54 MR20

ROSS,Claude Murray 2Lt kia 10-8-17 45RFC p13 MR20

ROSS,Colin 2Lt dow 25-10-18 7 att2A&SH p243 CR France40

ROSS,David.DSO.MC.LtACapt kia 6-11-18 2A&SH p173 CR France521

ROSS,David George 2Lt kia 5-9-15 3Worc p109

ROSS,D.E.2Lt 20-9-18 3Worc CR France632

ROSS,Donald TLt kia 13-11-16 2HLI B'Coy p163 CR France221,13/15-11-16

ROSS,Donald Neil Campbell 2Lt dow 30-11-17 D46RFA p35 CR Belgium18

ROSS,Donald Ord 2Lt kia 11-4-17 6CamH Ex NumbF p168 MR20

ROSS,Douglas Nicol.MM.Lt 17-2-18 BrColumbia &RAF MR20

ROSS,Douglas Stuart Lt kia 1-7-16 Lincs p75 CR France393

ROSS,Douglas William Robertson T2Lt kia 11-1-18 45RFC p17 CR Italy9

ROSS,Edric Crawford Ogilvie Maj AccGunwound 23-4-17 IA 44MerivaraInf p282 CR Iraq6

ROSS,Edward TLt dow 7-10-17 22Manch p156 CR France139

ROSS,Evan Nicholas TLt kia 27-6-18 2BlkW p129 CR Palestine9

ROSS,Findlay McFadyen.MC.Lt kia 1-8-18 1/9RScots p212 CR France524

ROSS,Fleetwood George Campbell Maj kia 2-11-14 IA 2/2GurkhaRif att34SikhPnrs p282 CR France1896

ROSS,Frederic Gordon T2Lt kia 1-7-16 20Manch p156 CR France397,Lt

ROSS,Geoffrey Henry 2Lt ded 18-10-18 Ex 7SomLI p263 CR Lond7,Lt

ROSS,George Augustus Bellair Lt kia 1-6-18 6Lpool attRAF p215&258 CR France1693

ROSS,George Alexander Sinclair Capt kia 28-6-15 4RScots p211 MR4

ROSS,George Duncan 2Lt kia 9-4-17 3GordH att8BlkW p167 CR France729

ROSS,George Harry Thornton 2Lt kia 9-8-16 13Ess p132 CR France402

ROSS,George James T2Lt kld 30-1-18 6/7RScotF p95 CR France57

ROSS,George Munro TLt kia 1-7-16 ACycCps attNumbF p181 MR21

ROSS,George W.2Lt ded 2-3-19 RE p262 CR Canada256

ROSS,Gwilliam Emanuel Henry T2Lt kia 3-7-16 8Glouc p107 MR21

ROSS,Harold 2Lt dow PoW 8-4-18 5LancF p221 CR France716

ROSS,H.E.Clunies Lt ded 27-9-18 2KAR p268 CR Sussex30,Capt See CLUNIES ROSS

ROSS,Hugh Alexander.DSO.MajALtCol kia 27-10-18 2GordH p167 CR Italy9

ROSS,James Andrew Lt kia 26-7-16 4SfthH p241 MR21

ROSS,James Graham T2Lt kia 30-12-17 SfthH att7Bn p165 CR France439

ROSS,James Hamilton 2Lt dow 19-4-17 5RScotF att155MGC p187&222 CR Palestine2

ROSS,James Hector T2Lt kia 23-4-17 8SfthH p165 CR France536

ROSS,James Kenneth T2Lt ded 9-4-17 GL &24RFC p13 CR France403,FltLt

ROSS,James Wilson TLt kld 26-3-18 GL &RFC p17 CR Scot249

ROSS,John Alexander 2Lt kia 26-10-15 17Lond p250 CR France219

ROSS,John Alexander T2Lt kia 13-8-16 RE 178TC p48 CR France453

ROSS,John Alexander T2Lt kia 31-8-18 10HLI p163 CR Belgium115

ROSS,John Edgar(Ian) Capt dow 25-4-16 4Lpool p72 CR France80

ROSS,John McKenzie 2Lt 12-4-17 2SAfrInf MR20

ROSS,Kenneth 2Lt kia 20-6-16 4RIrRif p170 MR29,25-9-15

ROSS,Kenneth Cameron 2Lt kia 11-3-18 7N&D p233 CR France614

ROSS,Kenneth McAlpine TCapt dow 17-9-18 RAMC att1/5HLI p197 CR France686

ROSS,Lawrence George T2Lt dow 30-5-17 7DragGds p21 CR France446

ROSS,Melbourne 2Lt kia 25-9-15 4 att2RIrRif p170 MR29

ROSS,N.M.Maj 5-1-20 18RScots CR Scot1

ROSS,Norman Leslie TCapt dow 15-4-18 8SLancs p126 CR Belgium38,2Bn

ROSS,Peter TCapt kia 1-7-16 16RScots p54 MR21

ROSS,Peter Cunningham T2Lt dow 26-6-17 GL &RFC p13 CR France113

ROSS,Ralph Morison Forbes 2Lt kia 20-2-15 RLancs p59

ROSS,Raymond Glenara Lt kia 4-4-18 RFA p208 MR27

ROSS,Richard(Dickon).MC.2Lt kia 25-9-16 1Dev p77 CR France374

ROSS,Robert.MC.Capt dow 18-4-17 1/7GordH p242 CR France95

ROSS,Robert Simmie T2Lt kia 3-9-16 9 att2KOSB p102 CR France402

ROSS,Robert Stewart T2Lt dow 24-9-17 9ScotRif p104 CR Belgium18

ROSS,Robert Thomas 2Lt dow 29-9-18 5RScotF p222 CR France262

ROSS,Robert Workman SchmasterCl3 11-12-18 Cps of Army Schmasters CR Devon86

ROSS,Ronald Campbell 2Lt kia ?-9-14 2RScots p54 CR France658,26-8-14

ROSS,Ronald Maynard 2Lt kia 4-3-17 1Worc p109 CR France439

ROSS,Simon Fraser Lt kia 23-4-17 4GordH p241 CR France545

ROSS,Thomas Stewart 2Lt dow 13-11-18 3CamH p168 CR France441,1Bn

ROSS,William 2Lt kia 12-4-18 9HLI p241 MR32

ROSS,William Munro Lt kia 11-3-15 2GordH p167 MR22

ROSS,William Samuel Baird 2Lt kia 21-3-18 15RIrRif p170 MR27

ROSS,William Stuart TLt kia 23-7-17 1BordR p118 CR Belgium92,Capt 6Bn

ROSS,Willie LtACapt kia 16-8-17 SWBord p100 CR Belgium106

ROSS-JENKINS,Maurice 2Lt kia 16-6-18 Glouc &RAF p107

ROSS-TAYLOR,Ian Henry Munro T2Lt kia 27-9-16 7Beds p86 MR21

ROSS-THOMPSON,Alexander.MID Lt kia 30-11-14 2RScotF p95 MR29

ROSSE,Martin 2Lt kia 22-2-17 IARO att53Sikhs p282 CR Iraq5

ROSSE,William Edward.Earl.Maj dow 10-6-18 IrGds p53 CR Eire480

ROSSER,Arthur T2Lt kia 10-7-16 14WelshR p127 MR21

ROSSINGTON,Arthur 2Lt kia 13-9-18 6WRid p227 CR France530

ROSSITER,Philip 2Lt kld 19-1-15 RBerks att2RWSurr p140 CR France924

ROSTERN,Joseph Norman Lt kia 26-3-18 2/7Manch p237 CR France511,28-3-18

ROSTRON,George T2Lt kia 21-3-18 59MGC p185 MR20

ROTCHELL,William SubEngr 22-10-18 GoutWatWks &RE MR65

ROTHBAND,Jacob Eustace TCapt kia 19-7-16 23Manch p156 CR France453,Jack

ROTHE,Sidney Ernest Orme 2Lt kia 13-11-16 15 att17Mddx D'Coy p148 MR21

ROTHERAM,Walter Sutton.MID 2Lt kia 29-9-17 A83RFA p35 MR30

ROTHON,Charles Francis T2Lt kia 1-7-16 1Dors p124 MR21

ROTHWELL,Henry.MM.T2Lt kia 2-12-17 14MGC p185 CR Belgium23

ROTHWELL,Reginald Fleetwood 2Lt kia 31-8-18 22 att8Lond p251 CR France624

ROTHWELL,Sidney 2Lt kia 7-1-16 1/5EKent p213 CR Iraq5,Sydney

ROTTMAN,Richard Charles Lt kia 24-4-15 3 att2ESurr p113 CR Belgium167

ROUGHSEDGE,William Lt kia 25-9-17 8Mddx p236 CR Belgium93

ROUGHT,C.G.Lt 31-1-19 RWSurr CR Surrey96

ROUGHTON,Thomas Hende.MC.LtACapt dow 24-3-18 4 att2LancF p93 CR Belgium22,1Bn

ROUILLARD,Charles Louis Amedee Lt kia 18-12-16 IARO att32Lancers p282 MR38

ROUND,Auriol Francis Hay Lt dow 5-9-14 2Ess p132 CR Essex285

ROUND,Edward T2Lt kia 21-4-17 4Worc p109 CR France531

ROUND,Harold Cecil.DSO.MC.TLtACapt kia 24-8-17 6 att9RB p180 MR30

ROUND,James Murray.MC.Capt kia 13-11-16 13Ess p132&259 CR France1890

ROUND,William George.MC.TLt kia 1-5-18 3Worc p109 CR Belgium11

ROUND,William Haldane Capt kia 1-7-16 7N&D p233 CR France281

ROUNSEFELL,Eric de Wolf.MC.2Lt kia 3-9-18 Leinst p175 CR Belgium170

ROUQUETTE,Douglas George 2Lt kia 26-9-17 GL &RFC p13 MR20

ROUQUETTE,John Hector 2Lt kia 17-7-16 1RWSurr p56 MR21,16-7-16

ROUS,Thomas.MID 2Lt dow 22-3-18 D296RFA p35 CR France40

ROUSE,Albert Charles.MID Lt dow 20-3-16 Worc attRE 32Sigs p109 CR France197

ROUSE,Alexander Ritchie Lt dow 31-8-18 C315RFA p208 CR France214,kia

ROUSE-BOUGHTON-KNIGHT,Thomas Andrew Greville 2Lt dow 18-10-16 1RB p180 CR France630,Lt kia

ROUSELL,William Stephen 2Lt kia 8-8-18 3 att7RSuss p119 CR France247,Lt

ROUT,William Owen Nelson TLt kia 25-9-15 10HLI p163 CR France114

ROUTH,John Cyril Capt kia 6-5-15 2Ches p96 MR29

ROUTLEDGE,Arthur Richard.MIDx2 Capt ded 27-6-18 RAVC p199&271 CR Lincs183

ROUTLEDGE,Calvert Capt ded 22-5-16 LNLancs & RDC p271 CR Surrey96

ROUTLEDGE,John T2Lt kia 16-4-17 1KOSB p102 MR20

ROUTLEDGE,John Frederick TLt kia 23-9-17 1NumbF p63 MR30

ROUTLEDGE,Joseph.MM.T2Lt kia 14-9-17 1/2 att15LancF p93 CR Belgium24

ROUTLEDGE,Phillip Charles Lytton LtCol kia 17-5-15 2SStaffs p123 MR22

ROUTLEY,Ernest George.MC.T2Lt kia 7-10-16 6EKent p58 MR21

ROUX,Frank T2Lt ded 26-4-17 RFC p13 CR France924

ROW,Arthur Leslie.MM.2Lt kia 5-6-18 1RBerks p140 CR France120

ROW,Harry Akers 2Lt kia 11-3-15 4Suff p217 CR France705

ROW,John Eric T2Lt kia 29-10-16 8Suff p79 MR21

ROW,Leslie Joseph T2Lt kia 4-6-16 10Norf p74 MR20

ROW,William Burnett T2Lt dow PoW 15-4-18 WYorks att1/5Bn p82 CR France285,14-4-18

ROWAN,John Leck Lt kia 12-7-15 5A&SH p243 MR4

ROWAN,Robert Lt kld 22-8-18 1/2ScotHorse attImpCamelCps p205 CR Palestine9

ROWAN-ROBINSON,William James Maj kia 12-5-15 2KSLI p145 erased from MR29 CR Belgium453

ROWAT,Maurice Alexander TLt kia 12-2-18 66RFC p17 CR Italy48,2Lt

ROWAT,Robert 2Lt kia 16-9-17 GL &8RFC p13 CR France214,Robin

ROWAT,Thomas Finlayson 2Lt 27-11-20 5DragGds CR Scot685

ROWATT,David T2Lt kia 1-7-16 A10RFA p35 CR France630

ROWBOTHAM,Howard Leeson Lt kia 30-11-17 61MGC Inf p185 MR17

ROWBOTHAM,John Edwin.MC.Maj kia 26-3-18 2/7Manch p237 CR France511

ROWBOTTOM,Joseph Arnold 2Lt kia 24-9-17 2/6Manch p237 CR Belgium173

ROWCROFT,E.C.DSO.Maj 27-7-16 IA GS MR65

ROWDEN,Cuthbert Roger.MC.Maj kld 20-4-18 5Worc &78RAF p109 CR Sussex114

ROWDEN,Edmund Percival Lt kia 6-9-17 RE p210 CR France219

ROWDEN,Reginald Colin George TLt kia 30-11-17 RFC p13 CR France446

ROWDON,Alfred William Lt 10-5-18 80RAF MR20

ROWE,Arthur Robert Reginald.DCM.T2Lt kia 7-2-17 17N&D p134 CR Belgium4

ROWE,Benjamin Franklin Lt kia 1-6-17 RFus &RFC p13&70 MR20

ROWE,E.F.Maj 14-4-18 1GarBnSuff CR Lond8

ROWE,Edwin Vivian T2Lt kia 1-9-18 13WelshR p127 MR16

ROWE,Gilbert James Burbery T2Lt dow 17-4-18 5RBerks p140 CR France65

ROWE,Harold Charles 2Lt kia 19-7-17 298RFA p209 CR Belgium131

ROWE,Harvey Wilfrid Warwick.MC.TLtACapt kia 20-8-17 10Ches p96 CR Belgium15

ROWE,Henry Price Capt ded 6-11-18 RE p256 CR Devon47

ROWE,Percy Trevelyan Capt dow 30-11-17 B306RFA p207 CR France1498

ROWE,Philip Henry 2Lt dow 17-9-16 7Mddx p235 MR20 &CR France1890

ROWE,Robert Ronald Lt 3-5-18 73RAF MR20

ROWE,Stafford Gordon Garnet Godfrey Thomas 2Lt kia 10-11-17 3 att6Dors p124 CR Belgium23

ROWE,Thomas 2Lt kia 23-5-16 5Lpool p215 CR France927

ROWED,Charles Henry Lt kia 8-9-16 1/5SLancs p230 MR21,9-9-16

ROWELL,T.MC.2Lt ded 20-5-18 RBerks &RAF p140 CR Nhampt79

ROWELL,William Cecil Capt ded 22-5-19 LNLancs &RAF p136

ROWLAND,Cecil Fred 2Lt kia 21-3-18 RGA 321SB p41 CR France581

ROWLAND,Cyril William.MC.Capt kia 23-8-18 1Lond p245 CR France593,1/4Bn

ROWLAND,John Walter Bruce 2Lt kia 1-11-18 175A D175RFA p35 CR France1257

ROWLAND,Maurice 2Lt kld 4-10-17 YLI att10Bn p143 CR Belgium112

ROWLAND,Rowland Evan Basil 2Lt kia 27-7-16 16RWar p65 MR21

ROWLAND,Stanley Jackson Lt kia 2-11-17 3RWFus att1/8ScotRif p99 CR Palestine8

ROWLAND,Sydney Domville TMaj ded 6-3-17 RAMC att26GenH p197 CR France40

ROWLAND,William Charles Roche TLt kia 4-11-18 9WRid p116 CR France1081

ROWLAND,William Henry 2Lt ded 22-2-19 RWFus att26Bn p99 CR France1359,6Lpool att165TMB

ROWLAND,William Lesingham Lt ded 15-8-19 123ChineseLabCps p266 CR France446

ROWLAND,William Ronald 2Lt kia 1-6-17 17Lond p250 MR29

ROWLANDS,Arthur William TLt kld 15-8-17 RFC p13 CR Lancs2 Ex 10Lpool &RASC

ROWLANDS,Charles William.MSM.T2Lt kia 26-9-17 10RWFus p99 MR30

ROWLANDS,Franklyn Theodore Rowland 2Lt kia 21-11-17 3 att2SWBord p100 CR France911

ROWLANDS,Helena May Nurse ded 10-5-19 TFNS CR Wales568

ROWLANDSON,Thomas Sowerby.MC.Capt kia 15-9-16 4Yorks p220 CR France515

ROWLES,Stanley Walter TLt dow 13-12-17 RASC att10RFC p13&193 CR Belgium18

ROWLETT,George Thomas 2Lt kia 30-7-16 RGA 137HB p41 CR France515

ROWLEY,Albert George T2Lt kia 26-4-18 DLI p161 CR France144

ROWLEY,Charles Edgar T2Lt kld 19-1-18 RE &RFC p17 CR Essex16,Lt

ROWLEY,Charles Pelham Maj kld 29-10-16 RGA p41 CR Hamps60

ROWLEY,Charles Ronald T2Lt kia 10-7-16 9 att1LancF p93 MR21

ROWLEY,Dalbiac Thomas Cotton Capt dow 2-7-16 2 att4Mddx p148 CR France44

ROWLEY,George Cecil.Hon.2Lt kia 17-2-17 5 att1KRRC p151 CR France314

ROWLEY,Gerald.MC&2Bars.Capt dow 15-10-18 6Ches p222 CR France25

ROWLEY,Harold George Lt ded 17-3-16 RE 61FC p48 CR France1182

ROWLEY,Hugh Travers TLt kia 1-7-16 9 att2RBerks p140 MR21,Capt

ROWLEY,John LtTLtCol ded 20-12-16 RFA p271 CR Surrey38

ROWLEY,John 2Lt kia 23-12-17 2Manch p156 CR Belgium126

ROWLEY,John Thomas Lt ded 15-2-21 IARO attLabCps p282 MR67,16-2-21

ROWLEY,Joseph 2Lt kia 1-7-16 1RLancs p59 MR21

ROWLEY,Joseph Albert T2Lt kia 26-10-18 Ess att10Bn p132 CR France521

ROWLEY,Joshua Robert Capt kia 2-11-17 HLI att1/5Suff p164 CR Palestine8

ROWLEY,Newton T2Lt kia 10-7-16 8Yorks p91 CR France515

ROWLEY,Reginald Frederick Lt kia 21-3-18 A179RFA p35 CR France1061,462Bty

ROWLEY,Walter Austin 2Lt kia 6-7-17 3 att8Leic p88 MR20

ROWLEY-CONWY,Geoffrey Seymour Maj kia 10-8-15 6LNLancs p136 MR4

ROWNTREE,Lawrence Edmund 2Lt kia 25-11-17 A26RFA p35 CR Belgium10

ROWSE,Richard Sidney 2Lt ded 2-9-15 2/5DCLI p227 CR Cornwall109

ROWSELL,Herbert Greaves TCapt kia 3-9-16 14Hamps p121 CR France1890

ROWSON,Stanley 2Lt kia 29-9-16 11LancF p93 MR21

ROWSON,Tom Hollingworth 2Lt kia 15-9-16 19Lond p251 CR France390

ROXBROUGH,William Henry.MC.T2Lt dow 13-4-18 11Suff p79 CR Belgium11,Lt

ROXBURGH,Alan Cameron Lt dow 28-11-17 NottsYeo attRFC p19&205 CR Palestine9

ROXBURGH,George Archibald Capt ded 25-2-20 IA 38CentIndHorse p282 MR67

ROXBURGH,John Capt kia 26-9-15 6RScotF p95 MR19

ROXBURGH,John Hewitt.MC.TMaj kia 2-10-18 MGC RN DivBn p185 CR France530

ROXBURGH,John Wood Lt kia 19-4-17 1/4RScotF p222 CR Palestine8

ROXBURGH,William Fletcher Lt kia 23-3-18 7HLI p240 MR20

ROY,David Charles 2Lt kia 25-8-18 49RAF MR20

ROY,James Ferrie 2Lt kia 30-7-16 6BlkW p231 MR21

ROY,John James 2Lt kld 13-3-18 7Worc p226 CR France398

ROY,Kenneth James.MID Capt kia 24-8-15 4Mddx p148 CR Belgium242 23-8-14

ROYAL-DAWSON,Oswald Sidney TCapt dow 25-8-17 5 O&BLI p130 CR Belgium11,Sidney

ROYCE,David Costa Lt kia 7-1-16 2Leic p88 MR38

ROYCE,Percival Francis 2Lt kia 10-9-18 2Lond p245 MR16

ROYDEN,Thomas Utting T2Lt kia 14-11-16 19 att1KRRC p151 MR21

ROYDS,John Ilted Lt kia 22-3-18 28Lond p252 MR20

ROYDS,Thomas Alington 2Lt kld 20-4-18 GL &59RAF p191 CR France76

ROYER,Harold Ernest T2Lt kia 27-9-18 4RFus p70 CR France358

ROYLANCE COURT,W.H Capt kia 24-5-15 9Lancers CR Belgium4

ROYLE,Arthur Clegg Fanshawe Lt dow 27-9-14 1NStaffs p157 CR France1110

ROYLE,Dennis Carlton.MC.TCapt kia 21-8-18 4RFus p70 CR France214

ROYLE,Frederick William TCapt dow 8-7-16 19Manch p156 MR21

ROYLE,John Bedward TMaj kia 15-1-17 7SWBord p100 CR Greece6

ROYLE,William 2Lt kia 5-7-16 5YLI p235 MR21

ROYLEY,Harry 2Lt kia 16-9-16 15DLI p161 MR21

ROYLEY,Joseph Holt 2Lt kia 25-4-18 WYorks att1/5Bn p82 MR30

ROYSTON,Basil Drage 2Lt dow 2-10-16 2/1RGA p209 CR France297

ROYSTON-PIGOTT,George Arthur.DSO.TLtCol kia 3-7-16 Nhampt att10Worc p138 CR France393

ROZELAAR,Samuel Louis TLt drd 10-10-18 RBerks att2Bn p140

RUANE,John Patrick T2Lt kia 2-11-17 9RWar att1/5Norf p65 CR Palestine8

RUBY,Joseph Bennett 2Lt kld 4-9-18 RGA attBase Depot Havre p41 CR France1571

RUCK,John Arthur T2Lt kld 25-5-16 GL &RFC p3&191,ded CR Kent232

RUCK,John Egerton TMaj kia 8-8-15 7Glouc p107 MR4

RUCK,Laurence Humphrey Lt kia 14-3-15 1Worc p109 MR22,11-3-15

RUCK-KEENE,Benjamin Corrie Chap4Cl kia 26-9-17 RAChDept att8EYorks p199 CR Belgium84

RUCK-KEENE,Ralph Edgar TLt kld 16-1-16 9RWelshF p99 CR France631,kia

RUDALL,Bertram Allen 2Lt kia 17-7-17 4RWKent p234 CR France421

RUDD,Arnold.MID T2Lt kia 27-3-18 RE 63FC p48 MR27

RUDD,Kenneth Sutherland TCapt kia 10-10-18 10WYorks p82 CR France658

RUDD,William Ferris Capt kia 13-11-16 12RWFus p99 CR France742

RUDDIMAN,William 2Lt kia 13-11-16 3RScots p54 CR France742

RUDDLE,Reginald.MC.T2Lt kia 24-7-18 12RB p180 CR France161,Lt 3Bn

RUDDOCK,Edgar Herbert Montague Capt kia 22-6-15 13Worc p109 MR4

RUDDOCK,Joseph John Lt dow 5-6-18 1/4RLancs att55DivHQ p213 CR France10

RUDDOCK,R.B.2Lt 6-4-18 5NumbF att4Beds MR27

RUDDOCK,Richard Fenwick 2Lt kia 18-6-16 6NumbF p214 CR Belgium17

RUDDOCK,Thomas Lt kia 7-8-18 4EKent p212 CR France116

RUDDY,Thomas Lt ded 1-7-16 1Manch p156 CR Iraq5

RUDDY,William 2Lt kia 26-10-17 4NumbF p213 MR30

RUDELL,Emil Arthur 2Lt dow 27-9-18 3 att16RWar p65 CR France905

RUDGE,Reginald Theodore T2Lt kia 5-11-16 7Yorks p91 MR21

RUDKIN,George Henry.MC.T2Lt ded 28-10-18 21MGC p185&257 CR Lincs34

RUDMAN,Harold Ewart Capt kia 19-7-16 6Glouc D Coy p225 MR19

RUEGG,Kenneth Stanes 2Lt kia 20-9-14 2N&D p134 MR15

RUFF,Samuel 2Lt kia 17-11-16 1/7WRid p228 CR France281

RUFUS,Thomas.MC.TCapt kia 14-4-18 11LancF A'Coy p93 MR32

RULE,John Lindon 2Lt dow 2-11-16 31AustInf CR France432

RUMBALL,George Thomas Sydney.MC.T2Lt kia 13-4-18 RFus att2Bn p70 CR France193

RUMBELOW,Albert 2Lt kia 16-4-18 5SWBord p100 MR30

RUMBOLD,Christian Franklyn Hales Maj kia 22-11-15 4ESurr att2Norf p113 MR38

RUMILLY,Alfred Henry Robinson 2Lt dow 28-6-17 7Worc p226 CR France795,kldacc

RUMSBY,Richard William.MC.Lt dow 9-5-18 9RSuss attRAF p119 CR France792

RUMSEY,Arthur Charles 2Lt kia 24-9-16 9Lond p248 CR France394

RUMSEY,Charles Gordon Lt 25-5-15 3SWBord att1WelchR MR29

RUNCIMAN,Edmund Inglis 2LtTLt kia 22-10-15 9KRRC p151 CR Belgium44

RUNCIMAN,Keith Stewart T2Lt kia 24-4-17 14A&SH p173 CR France379

RUNDALL,Arthur Montagu Capt kia 20-12-14 IA 1/4GurkhaRif p282 CR France279

RUNDALL,Lionel Bickersteth Lt kia 19-12-14 IA 1/1GurkhaRif p282 MR28

RUNDELL,Leslie Eric.MC&Bar.Capt dow 10-12-17 7Lond p247 CR France755

RUNDELL,Reginald Charles T2LtACapt kia 3-5-17 GL att10TMB p191 CR France

RUNDLE,Cubitt Noel 2Lt kia 19-5-15 2SWBord p100 CR Gallipoli6,19-6-15

RUNDLE,Horace Liberty 2Lt kia 20-7-16 8Dev p77 CR France432

RUNDLE,James Robson 2Lt kia 20-11-17 4RLancs p213 CR France364

RUNDLE,Raymond Wallis Lt kia 9-5-15 1N&D attRWar p134 CR France525

RUNDLE,Stanley TLt dow PoW 30-4-18 RASC p193 CR B201 ?

RUNGE,Oscar Julius Tolme.MC.Lt kia 15-10-16 Mddx att18MGC Inf p148&185 MR21

RUNNELS-MOSS,Cyril Gower Vincent 2Lt ded 5-12-17 GL &RFC p13 MR20

RUNNELS-MOSS,Eric Cross Arnold 2Lt ded PoW 9-7-18 2RFA p35 CR Germany3

RUPP,Frederick Albert Lt kia 1-7-16 6 att11BordR p118 MR21

RUSACK,Louis Amrhein TLt kia 4-7-16 7BordR p118 CR France397

RUSBRIDGE,Robert Thomas Smith TLt ded 11-11-18 RASC 55DivSupplyCol p193 CR Kent83,650MT Coy

RUSE,Edward Wallace Lt kld 31-12-15 RE 128FC p48 CR France275

RUSH,Clement Ward 2Lt kia 3-9-16 5WRid p227 MR21

RUSH,Ernest William 2Lt kia 28-4-17 7Suff p79 CR France312

RUSHBROOK,Sydney Herbert 2Lt kia 6-7-15 Norf attCycCps p74 MR29

RUSHBROOKE,Bartle Davers Capt kia 25-5-15 3 att2Suff p79 MR29

RUSHBROOKE,William Ewart 2Lt kia 26-8-17 7RB p180 CR Belgium125

RUSHBY,Frank Capt ded 26-2-15 RFA p35 CR Berks121

RUSHMORE,Ernest Reginald 2Lt kia 6-9-17 4 att11LancF p93 MR30

RUSHTON,Arthur 2Lt kia 27-7-18 8RLancs p59 CR France33

RUSHTON,Cecil George Capt kia 16-5-18 GL &RAF p191

RUSHTON,Edward Birley Leigh.MID Capt kia 25-9-16 2Nhampt p138 CR France423,Lever

RUSHTON,Frank Gregson T2Lt kia 1-7-16 GL 2Wilts att53TMB p191 CR France513

RUSHTON,Frederick Hornby Lever.MC.MID Lt kia 15-9-14 2RIrReg p89 MR15

RUSHTON,William Henry LtACapt kia 25-9-16 1Lincs D'Coy p75 CR France374

RUSHWORTH,Frederick Arthur 2Lt kia 29-9-16 6Yorks p91 MR21

RUSHWORTH,Henry T2Lt kia 11-8-18 18KRRC p151 CR Belgium21

RUSHWORTH,Tom.MID Capt kia 16-9-16 7Lond p247 CR France432

RUSS,S.H.Lt 28-10-20 RASC CR Somerset186

RUSSEL,Arthur Richard Lt kia 25-12-15 3Norf p74 CR Iraq1,2Bn

RUSSEL-RENDLE,Anthony Darley 2Lt kia 10-10-17 9Dev CR Belgium112

RUSSELL,A.M.SNurse 4-10-16 QAIMNS CR Berks86

RUSSELL,Alexander Christopher TCapt kia 10-10-15 11N&D p135 CR France680

RUSSELL,Alexander James TLt kia 15-8-15 7RDubF p177 MR4

RUSSELL,Arthur Lt dow 23-7-16 9HLI p240 CR Scot86

RUSSELL,Arthur Charles Lt dow 28-10-18 6RB p180 CR France113

RUSSELL,Arthur Claude Hamilton TCapt ded 27-10-18 RAOC p267 CR Europe51

RUSSELL,Arthur Henry Eric Lt dow 22-3-18 3 att6ConnRgrs p172 CR France987,Capt

RUSSELL,Bernard.MC.T2Lt kia 25-9-15 RBerks p140&257 MR32 See ABINGER true name

RUSSELL,Charles Lt kia 22-11-17 9EYorks IARO att3/3Gurkhas p84&282 CR Palestine3

RUSSELL,David Leslie Capt dow 23-5-15 8Lond p247 CR France80

RUSSELL,Edward Lt kia 1-7-16 11N&D p135 MR21

RUSSELL,Edward Stanley.MC.Capt kia 6-11-17 1/1Hereford p252 CR Palestine1

RUSSELL,Eleanor AssAdmtr ded 21-2-19 QMAAC p200 CR Leic63

RUSSELL,Ernest 2Lt kia 4-9-18 20DLI p161 MR30

RUSSELL,Francis George T2Lt dow 17-4-18 2EYorks p84 CR Belgium21,1Bn

RUSSELL,Francis Gerald 2Lt kia 28-1-17 RFA &RFC p13&35 CR France744

RUSSELL,Francis Wycliffe.MC.Lt kia 27-8-18 1/16Lond p249 CR France644

RUSSELL,George Launcelot Lighton Capt ded 1-3-18 RE p271 CR Sussex 220,1-3-19

RUSSELL,George Smith T2Lt kia 1-7-16 16RScots p54 MR21

RUSSELL,Glen 2Lt kia 18-3-18 54RFC p17 CR France333

RUSSELL,Guy Campbell Lt ded 21-2-19 16Lancers p261 CR Surrey1,21Bn

RUSSELL,Guy Edward Frank 2Lt kia 14-10-15 4Leic p220 MR19,13-10-15

RUSSELL,Hamish Galbraith 2Lt dow 16-8-15 1/7HLI p240 CR Egypt3,16-7-15

RUSSELL,Harley Raymond Lt kia 13-10-15 att1Glouc p107 MR19

RUSSELL,Henry TCapt dow 10-6-16 16WYorks p82 CR France5,Harry

RUSSELL,Henry.DCM.2Lt kia 12-7-16 RE 7FC p48 CR Belgium37

RUSSELL,Henry Branfill TLt dow 11-7-16 1Ess p132 CR France169

RUSSELL,Henry Freeman 2Lt kia 6-8-15 4Worc p109 MR4

RUSSELL,Henry Thornbury Fox.MC.Capt kld 18-11-18 6RWFus &RAF p256

RUSSELL,Hubert Leslie 2Lt ded 1-9-19 IA 27LightCav p282 CR Pakistan50A MR43,kldacc

RUSSELL,James.MC.TCapt ded 10-7-17 17HLI p164 CR Scot674

RUSSELL,James Cosmo.DSO.LtCol 31-7-17 IA 9HodsonsHorse att6CamH p282 CR Belgium7

RUSSELL,James Forteath Lt kia 2-7-15 IA 2/10GurkhaRif p282 MR4

RUSSELL,James Galloway 2Lt kia 3-5-17 2RScots p54 MR20

RUSSELL,John Maj kia 26-8-15 5RScotsF p222 MR4

RUSSELL,John TLtACapt kia 10-4-17 B76 RFA p35 CR France924,9-4-17

RUSSELL,John 2Lt dow 21-4-17 1/7ScotRif p224 CR Palestine2

RUSSELL,John 2Lt kia 9-8-17 3EKent D'Coy p58 MR29

RUSSELL,John Capt&QM dow 6-10-18 7HLI p240 CR Scot757

RUSSELL,John Fox.VC.MC.Capt kia 6-11-17 RAMC att1/6RWFus p254 CR Palestine1

RUSSELL,John Guy Harry Stebbing 2Lt dow 29-9-18 RWKent att10Bn p142 CR Belgium11

RUSSELL,John Hepburn T2Lt kld 12-11-17 GL &40RFC p13 CR Scot674

RUSSELL,John William Binfield TLt kia 7-7-16 9WRid p116 MR21

RUSSELL,Joseph Eric 2Lt kia 23-11-16 7RWSurr p56 CR France646

RUSSELL,Lawrence Dobrée 2Lt dow 2-9-16 7RFC 15Wing p3 CR France833

RUSSELL,Laurence Edward Lt kia 24-8-14 WRid p116 CR Belgium201 Lawrence

RUSSELL,Leonard Maj kia 9-5-15 2ELancs p111 CR France706

RUSSELL,Leonard Cosmo Bolles TCap kia 7-10-16 12RB p180 CR France307

RUSSELL,Leonard William Edward T2Lt ded 14-11-18 8 att2/4Leic p88 CR Germany3

RUSSELL,Lionel William Bowden 2Lt kia 20-9-17 6 att12ESurr p226 MR30

RUSSELL,Marcus Ralph TLt kia 22-3-18 2RRofCav att8Huss p23 MR27

RUSSELL,Noel John Gilbert 2Lt dow 27-9-18 A26RFA p35 CR France113

RUSSELL,Oswald Bede Plowden.MC.MID Capt kia 3-9-20 IA 10Lancers p282 MR38

RUSSELL,Patrick Alfred 2Lt kia 2-4-17 1LovatScts attRFC p19&204 CR France407

RUSSELL,Peter Currie Stuart Lt dow 19-12-15 5ScotRif attRFC p19&224 CR France285

RUSSELL,Robert Campbell.MID T2Lt dow 31-8-18 7NStaffs p157 CR Asia81

RUSSELL,Robert Ferguson TCapt ded 22-4-17 RAMC 10GH p267 CR France145

RUSSELL,Thomas Capt kia 19-4-16 5ScotRif p224 CR France163

RUSSELL,Thomas T2LtTCapt kia 12-10-16 13A&SH p173 MR21

RUSSELL,Thomas Edward Francis 2Lt kia 3-5-17 2/5Y&L p238 MR20

RUSSELL,Thomas Wallace T2Lt kia 13-11-16 10RDubF p177 CR France220

RUSSELL,Thomas Leopold TLtACapt kia 6-11-17 SL &3/2KAR p202 CR EAfrica33 &CR Tanzania1

RUSSELL,Walter Col ded 4-4-17 RE p48 CR Lond4

RUSSELL,Walter Edward 2LtALt kia 11-5-17 129/42RFA attX29TMB p35 CR Belgium12,13-7-17

RUSSELL,Walter Guthrie 2Lt kia 29-9-16 8DLI p239 MR21,Wallace

RUSSELL,Walter Nicol T2Lt dow 26-8-16 9 att1RScotF p95 CR France23

RUSSELL,Walter Oswald Lt kia 26-8-18 7NStaffs attDunsterforce p157 MR61,Capt

RUSSELL,Walter Russell Capt kia 21-10-14 Nhampt p138 MR29,23-10-14

RUSSELL,William Capt kia 5-5-15 5RScots p211 MR4

RUSSELL,William Lt kld 3-4-18 RE &RAF p256

RUSSELL,William T2Lt kia 27-9-18 15TankCps p188 CR France530

RUSSELL,William Black Lt kia 19-6-15 14RScots p54 CR Gallipoli6

RUSSELL,William Edward 2LtALt kia 13-7-17 129/42RFA attX29TMB p35 CR France538,12-5-17

RUSSELL,William George Mark Lt ded 8-10-15 4/7Mddx CR Surrey37

RUSSELL-SMITH,Hugh Francis Capt dow 5-7-16 1RB CR France145

RUSTON,Allan Maxwell.MM.2Lt kia 23-4-18 2LancF p93 CR France412

RUSTON,Arthur Cecil Maj kia 2-5-15 8Mddx p235 MR29,26-4-15

RUSTON,Cecil Harold Sowerby 2Lt kia 4-4-18 4 att7EKent p212 MR27,Somerby

RUSTON,Frederick Augustus Lt dow 21-3-18 94RFA p35 CR France987

RUTH,Tom Bertrand T2Lt ded 24-2-17 3BordR p264 CR C'land&W'land17

RUTHERFOORD,David Geoffrey Corry Capt kia 17-4-16 14RFA p35 MR38

RUTHERFOORD,Thomas Corrie.MID LtCol ded 18-10-18 IMS att11CavBde p282 CR Lebanon1

RUTHERFORD,Alfred Fletcher Corrie Capt kia 10-8-15 1 att6BordR p118 MR4,RUTHERFOORD

RUTHERFORD,David Alfred.MC&Bar.Lt kld 1-11-20 7RGA 115SB MR40

RUTHERFORD,George Sparkes 2Lt ded 22-2-19 2BordR p264 CR C'land&W'land17

RUTHERFORD,John Allen TCapt kia 24-8-16 7MGC Inf p185 MR21

RUTHERFORD,Mark T2LtACapt kia 23-7-18 9TankCps p188 CR France987

RUTHERFORD,Norman Edwin T2Lt dow 21-7-16 7RLancs p59 CR France833

RUTHERFORD,R.B.Maj 12-1-21 RAMC CR Scot239

RUTHERFORD,Ralph Baillie TCapt kia 3-7-16 6RWSurr p56 CR France251

RUTHERFORD,Robert Capt kia 15-9-16 9DLI p239 MR21

RUTHERFORD,Robert Witten Glendinning Capt kia 28-6-15 4RScots p211 MR4,Glendenning

RUTHERFORD,Thomas Wood T2Lt kia 22-8-15 6Yorks p91 MR4

RUTHERFORD,William Cecil 2Lt ded 10-3-19 19NumbF p63 CR France134,Lt

RUTHERFORD,William McConnell T2Lt dow 19-4-18 10EYorks p84 CR France64

RUTHVEN,James.MC.Capt kia 9-4-18 4EYorks p256 MR32

RUTHVEN,William Logan Maj kia 3-12-17 1EYorks Cmdg2/6Glouc p84 MR17,2-12-17

RUTLEDGE,John Bedell TCapt kia 1-7-16 7EYorks p84 CR France373

RUTLEDGE,Joseph Ward Lt 31-7-17 B103 RFA p35 MR29

RUTLEDGE,Laurence Hugh Nesbitt Capt dedacc 10-1-21 IA 8GurkhaRif attS&T Cps MT p282 MR43

RUTTER,Donald Campbell.MC.Capt kia 7-6-17 RSuss &43RFC p13&119 CR Belgium125

RUTTER,Eustace Frederick.MID Maj kia 13-5-15 1ELancs p111 MR29

RUTTER,Frank Lionel T2Lt kia 14-7-16 2RWSurr p56 MR21

RUTTER,W.R.Capt 27-6-16 UgandaVolRes CR EAfrica123

RUTTLEDGE,John Forrest TCapt kia 1-7-16 2WYorks p82 MR21

RUTTLEDGE,Victor John TCapt ded 3-11-16 RAMC att8MtdBrigFA p197 CR Egypt15

RUTTLEY,Percy Kemp TCapt ded 19-10-18 GL 17WelchR D'Coy p191 CR Wales149

RUXTON,W.H.Lt ded 29-8-18 3RIrReg &RAF p89

RUXTON,William Stewart Mitchell.MC.Lt kia 12-4-18 1BordR p118 MR32

RYALL,Robert William Lt dow 11-10-15 IA 2/8GurkhaRif p282 CR France40

RYAN,Alfred Eric.MC.2LtACapt kia 23-3-18 11RWSurr p56&259 MR20

RYAN,Bliss Wilberforce.MM.Lt kia 20-9-17 CanadaEngrs &RFC CR Belgium18

RYAN,Charles M.J.MC.Lt kia 4-10-18 3RMunstF p176 CR France1495

RYAN,Clement Ignatius Maj kia 8-7-16 Ess att9Bn p132 MR21

RYAN,Donald Whitmore 2Lt kia 9-5-15 Nhampt att2Bn p138 MR32

RYAN,Edward St.John Norwood.MC.TCapt kia 22-10-18 12ESurr p113 CR Belgium140

RYAN,F.D.Lt 18-10-17 SL att3NigR CR EAfrica11 &CR Tanzania1

RYAN,Finley Francis.MC.Capt kia 25-6-17 8Lpool p215 CR France765

RYAN,George Julian.DSO.TLtCol kia 22-1-15 2RMunstF p176 CR France279,23-1-15

RYAN James T2Lt kld 13-1-18 7Leinst p175 CR France145

RYAN James Henry Aloysius.MC.LtTCapt kia 25-9-15 1Lpool p72 CR France163

RYAN John Henry 2Lt dow 2-5-17 57RFC p13 CR France518

RYAN John Stanley TCapt kia 25-6-16 18KRRC p151 CR Belgium54

RYAN,Martin.MC.TCaptAMaj kia 18-10-17 25RFus p70 CR EAfrica11 &CR Tanzania1

RYAN,Michael Rev ded 1-11-16 RAChDept p199 MR65

RYAN,Patrick Cornelius T2Lt kia 13-10-18 2ELancs p111 CR France777

RYAN,Patrick Joseph 2Lt kia 21-3-18 RWar att6NStaffs p65 MR20

RYAN,Warwick John Norwood 2Lt kia 5-9-16 DorsYeo p202

RYAN-BELL,Hugh Randolph Lt dow 29-8-17 1/8Worc CR Belgium16

RYAN-LEWIS,Wallenstein.MC.Capt dow 25-3-18 RE 284Coy CR France1063

RYCKMAN,Edward Gurney 2Lt kia 4-5-16 7RFC p3 CR France1031

RYCROFT,Henry Frederick Capt kia 7-8-15 3 att2Y&L p159 erased from MR29 CR Belgiu453

RYCROFT,Nelson Wynne T2Lt kia 25-9-17 6Beds p86 MR30

RYCROFT,Robert 2Lt kia 11-10-18 3WRid p116 CR France612

RYDE,John Titcombe 2Lt dow 8-5-17 Beds Res att12Glouc p86 MR20

RYDER,Charles Ernest HonTLt&QM ded 6-11-15 17Lpool p72 CR Wilts115

RYDER,Leonard Charles T2Lt kia 25-4-17 11 att12Worc p109 MR37

RYDER,Reginald Victor T2Lt dow 28-6-17 13Glouc att4RFC p13&107 CR Belgium11

RYDER,Robert Nathaniel Dudley.Hon.Maj kia 30-11-17 8Huss p22 CR France364

RYDER,William Harold Lt kia 6-7-17 YorkHuss attRFC p19&206 CR France44

RYLANDS,Frank 2Lt dow 25-4-17 16Manch p156

RYLANDS,Harold Bertram T2Lt kia 23-11-16 16LancF p93 MR21

RYLANDS,Reginald Victor Capt kia 29-5-15 1/7Manch p237 CR Gallipoli2

RYLE,M.C.Nurse 21-2-15 RussianRedCraoss CR Europe57

RYLEY,Charles Maj ded 4-5-17 RAMC Staff DADMS 40Div p197 CR France446

RYLEY,Donald Arthur George Buchanan Lt kia 11-2-17 NStaffs p157 MR19

RYLEY,Harold Buchanan 2Lt kia 5-9-16 4 att1NStaffs p157 MR21

RYLEY,Harold Buchanan TLt kia 15-12-17 1/5Suff p79 CR Palestine9

RYLEY,Herbert Frank Brownlow Capt kia 2-11-14 att1LNLancs p136 MR29

RYMER,John Henry TCapt kia 7-8-15 11Manch p156 MR4

RYRIE,Arthur TLt kia 10-8-18 6TankCps p188 CR France360

S

SABIME,Gerald TLt kia 22-10-18 N&D att15Hamps p135 CR Belgium408

SABISTON,James Anderson 2Lt kia 22-8-17 4A&SH att7CamH p173 MR30

SACH,Charles Burleigh 2Lt kia 1-7-16 1/13Lond p249 MR21

SACHS,Rudolf Dinges 2Lt kia 20-10-18 1/5ELancs p226 CR France287

SACKVILLE-WEST,Kelvin Frederick.MIDx2 Capt ded 29-6-21 QueensBays CR Kent217

SADD,Philip George TMaj kia 15-9-16 18KRRC p151 MR21 CR France1890

SADLEIR,John Raymond T2Lt ded 26-11-18 MGC p266 CR Lincs61,SADLIER SomLI

SADLER,Charles Edward T2Lt kia 1-7-16 10 att1ELancs p111 MR21

SADLER,Ferrebee 2Lt kia 21-4-17 9DLI attRFC p19&239 MR20

SADLER,Gerald Gloag Capt ded 1-11-14 3DragGds p21 MR29,Gerard

SADLER,Hereward Pattison T2Lt dow 19-7-16 6RBerks p140 CR France513,kia

SADLER,Roland Albert James 2Lt kldacc 23-9-18 RWar &RAF CR Norf24

SADLER,Vyvyan Kendall TCapt kia 17-4-17 RAMC att29RFA p197 CR France97

SADLER,William Douglas 2Lt dow 3-8-17 4ESurr p113 CR Belgium11,9Bn

SADLER,William Edward 2Lt kia 8-5-15 3 att2SLancs p126 CR Belgium132

SADLER,William Harold 2Lt kia 24-8-18 24 att21Lond p252 MR16

SADLIER,Francis Arthur 2Lt kia 14-10-18 2InniskF p105 CR Belgium157

SAFFERY,Leslie Hall 2Lt kia 1-7-16 4RDubF p177 MR21

SAGE,Douglas Michael 2Lt kia 18-12-17 GL &65RFC p13 CR Belgium140

SAGE,Sidney Edward Bush Lt dow 13-9-18 6Glouc p225 CR France686

SAHA,N.N.Lt 7-12-19 IMS CR Lebanon5

SAIDLER,William Tweeddale Lt kia 26-3-18 RGA &RFC p19&209 CR France385

SAILLARD,Phillip 2LtTLt kia 22-8-17 1EYorks attC'TankCps p84 CR Belgium16,Philip

SAINES,Charles Edward T2Lt kld 22-10-17 GL &RFC p13 CR Mddx12

SAINSBURY,Charles.MC.TLt dow 7-6-17 1Wilts p153 CR Belgium43

SAINSBURY,Frederick Capt 26-2-19 EAfrLabCps MR46

SAINT,Edward Twelftree.DSO.MID LtCol dow 29-8-18 1Camb p244 CR France119

SAINT James Harcourt T2Lt kia 4-6-17 RE 428FC p48 CR France905

SAINT,William Bell Lt dow 15-9-16 1/10RScots att70RFC p19&212 CR Frnce446

St.AUBYN,Edward Stuart.Hon.Maj kia 30-12-15 Staff p1 MR41,drd Ex KRRC

St.AUBYN,Francis Joseph TLt kia 10-4-17 7KRRC A'Coy p151 CR France594

St.AUBYN,Morice Julian.MC.TMaj kia 22-3-18 7KRRC p151 MR27

St.AUBYN,Piers Stewart.Hon.2Lt kia 31-10-14 2KRRC p151 MR29

St.CLAIR,Charles Henry Murray.Hon.Capt kia 20-12-14 1SfthH p165 CR France279

St.CLAIR,C.H.D.Maj 31-3-21 RASC DADT CR Asia51

St.GEORGE,Guy Staniforth Wemyss Lt dow 28-4-15 IA 1/1GurkhaRif p282 CR France200

St.GEORGE,Harold Avenel Blight 2Lt kia 15-11-15 1LifeGds p20 CR Belgium134,Howard Bligh 15-11-14

St.GEORGE,Harold Edgar 2Lt kia 13-8-16 6Lpool C'Coy p215 CR France294

St.HILL,Ashton Alexander.DSO.TLtCol kia 27-10-18 1/2WRid att11NumbF p116 CR Italy9

St.HILL,George Herbert.MID LtCol kia 8-7-17 RNDevYeo p203 CR France905

St.JOHN,Esmée Barbara Miss ded 12-10-16 VAD p200 CR France64,B.E.

St.JOHN,Thomas.DCM.2Lt dow 2-7-16 1ELancs att11MGC p185 CR France35

St JOHN MILDMAY,Bouverie Walter 2Lt kldacc 16-4-18 GL &70RAF CR France169

St.LEGER,Dennis Claude Grant 2Lt mbk 21-3-18 295RFA p256 CR France568,22-3-18

St.LEGER,St.John Richard 2Lt kia 15/17-9-16 2Lond p245 MR21

St.LEGER,William Brett.MC.Lt kia 27-4-18 2ColdGds p51 CR France925

St.QUINTIN,Clifford Jack Lt kia 15-5-17 HAC Inf p206 MR20

St.VINCENT-RYAN,Edmond William LtCol ded 24-8-19 RAMC p256 CR Wales564

SAINTON,Francis Charles.MC.LtACapt kia 18-4-18 2RSuss p119 CR France721

SAKER,Frank Harrison Capt kia 30-10-14 4 att2ConnRgrs p172 MR29

SAKER,Richard Maj kia 25-4-15 4ConnRgrs att5AustralianInfDiv p266

SALAMAN,Euston Abraham 2Lt ded 18-2-16 RFA p209 CR Mddx40

SALAMONSON-SANGSTER,Henry Pryor Saltarn 2Lt mbk 26-9-17 3KOSB att14Hamps p256 MR30

SALATHIEL,Ewart Gladstone T2Lt dow 17-7-16 11SWBord p100 CR Mon83,4Bn

SALBERG,John Beaumont 2Lt ded PoW 30-6-16 12RSuss D'Coy p119 CR France924

SALE,Alexander Gordon Lt 9-3-15 SL att3KAR CR EAfrica12 & CR Tanzania1

SALE,Edward Hanson TCapt kia 25-9-15 10Glouc p107 CR France1723

SALE,Richard Crawford.MID Capt kia 26-3-17 1Hereford p252 MR34

SALE,Richard Lander TLt dow 15-1-18 RHGds p20 CR France446,Lauder

SALES,Norman Lt dow 30-6-18 2YLI &87RAF p143 CR France1525

SALISBURY,Cecil Roland T2Lt kia 7-5-17 14RWar p65 CR France

SALISBURY,Frederick James Lt ded 23-9-19 RE IWT p262 CR Iraq5

SALISBURY,Percy Harold T2Lt kia 27-8-16 10Leic att11Ches p88 CR France246

SALISBURY,Robert Cecil TCapt kia 22-3-18 19Lpool p72 MR27

SALISBURY,Walter Fredk 2Lt dow 30-12-17 28Lond p252 MR21

SALMAN,Clifford T2Lt kia 13-10-15 9 att8RBerks p140 MR19

SALMON,Andrew Frank 2Lt kld 16-8-17 4 O&BLI p231 MR30

SALMON,Bernard Bryant.MC.T2Lt kia 9-7-16 25 att8Manch p156 MR21

SALMON,Cecil Gordon Lt kia 14-6-15 3 att2N&D p135 CR Belgium44

SALMON,Claude Garrett Capt kia 9-5-15 3 att2ScotRif 104 CR France525

SALMON,Gilbert Henry Capt 28-8-20 1/6Dev CR Iraq8

SALMON,J.F.Maj 4-12-19 IA MiscList MilPrison CR Hamps64

SALMON,Reginald Thomas T2Lt kia 12-5-17 7EYorks p84 MR20

SALMON,Stanley Francis T2Lt kia 19-7-17 9WelshR p127 CR Belgium111

SALMON,Wilfred Graham 2Lt kia 7-7-17 RFC p13 CR Kent125,Lt

SALMONS,Harry T2Lt dow PoW 1-4-18 1WYorks p82 CR France1483

SALOMONS,David Reginald Herman Philip Capt drd 28-10-15 RE p210 MR4

SALT,Thomas Frederick Cyril Lt 3-4-15 11SWBord CR France284

SALT,Walter Petit C.TCapt kia 24-10-16 2LancF p93 MR21

SALTER,Albert Leonard 2Lt kia 21-3-18 RWar att2/6NStaffs p65 MR20

SALTER,Donald Sowerby 2Lt dow 22-3-18 RGA 126SB p41 CR France512

SALTER,Francis Henry T2Lt kia 21-10-16 11RSuss p119 CR France383

SALTER,Geoffrey Charles Tayler.MC.2Lt kia 18-3-16 EYorks &RFC p261&263 MR20,Lt 28-5-18 RAF

SALTER,Henry Albert 2Lt kia 7-6-17 7Lond p247 CR Belgium29

SALTER,John Henry Clavell 2Lt kia 9-4-18 att1/5Lancs p59 MR19

SALTER,John Henry Raymond T2Lt kia 13-10-17 GL &54RFC p13 CR Belgium125

SALTER,Reginald Charles Falconer LtTCapt kia 8-6-15 2SLancs p126 erased from MR29 CR Belgium453

SALTER,Robert Capt kia 26-8-16 7WYorks p218 CR France293

SALTER,William TCapt kia 9-8-16 17Mddx p148 MR21

SALTMARSH,John Henry Thomas T2Lt dow 30-12-17 3Ches att2/22Lond p96 CR Palestine3

SALTMARSHE,Oliver Edwin TLt kia 1-7-16 7RWSurr p56 CR France397

SALTREN-WILLETT,Archibald John.MID LtCol kia 11-10-17 RGA p41 CR Belgium10

SALUSBURY,Norman Horace Pemberton T2Lt kia 1-12-15 10BordR att1/7HLI p118 CR Gallipoli3

SALUSBURY-JONES,Ivor Cynric Lt dow 21-9-16 5YLI CR France74

SALVESEN,Edward Maxwell 2Lt kia 25-4-15 4RDubF p177 MR29

SALVESEN,Frederick Malcolm Ross Capt kia 22-12-19 IA 82Punjabis p282 MR43,21-12-19

SALVESON,Cristian Raymond Lt ded 22-5-15 7RScots attRFC p19&211,kld CR Scot249,SALVESEN

SALVESON,Eric Thomas Somervell 2Lt kia 23-4-17 7RScots p211 CR France421,SALVESEN

SAMARSINHA,Leonard Phillip Capt 1-4-20 IA IMS CR India97A

SAMES,Gilbert Fielding T2Lt dow 25-10-18 10TankCps p188 CR France441,24-10-18

SAMES,William Fielding Lt dow 31-5-15 4ELancs p226 MR4

SAMMUT,Herbert Joseph Maj kia 2-5-15 Ess p132 MR4

SAMPSON,Amyas Terrell Lt 8-8-18 3RAF MR20

SAMPSON,Arthur Henry Winn 2Lt kia 1-7-16 4Mddx p148 CR France267

SAMPSON,Bertram George T2Lt kia 12-2-17 11RFus p70 CR France251

SAMPSON,Carl Alexander Capt kia 9-8-18 25Lond p252 CR France1170

SAMPSON,Henry Charles DepCommsy&Capt ded 26-12-15 IA S&TCps p282 CR France85

SAMPSON,Horace William 2Lt kia 28-5-18 5Lond p246 CR France41

SAMPSON,Hugh Delaine T2Lt dow 2-9-17 RASC p193 CR Belgium11,Delane

SAMPSON,Richard Harry TLt ded 29-10-18 GL WelchR att114BdeHQ 30Div p191 CR France40

SAMPSON,Ronald Henry 2Lt kia 30-8-18 RGA 122SB p41 CR France593

SAMPSON,T.F.2Lt kia 18-9-18 12Ches p96 MR37

SAMPSON,Tom Burton TLt kia 20-11-17 KSLI p145 CR France379

SAMPSON,Walter Bladen TCapt kia 10-7-16 13RB p180 CR France832

SAMS,Charles T2Lt kia 7-6-17 11RWKent p142 CR Belgium56

SAMSON,Oswald Massey 2LtALt dow 17-9-18 RGA 143SB p41 CR France511

SAMSON,Arthur Legge.MC.Capt kia 25-9-15 2RWFus p99 CR France114

SAMSON,Phillip Edward Lt dow 21-10-18 1/5Lpool p215 CR France163,2Lt

SAMUDA,Cecil Markham Annesley Maj dow 2-7-17 SomLI p80 CR France285

SAMUEL.A.D.T2Lt ded 19-5-18 RASC p193 CR Mddx40

SAMUEL,Cecil Valentine 2Lt dow 6-10-17 4RWar p65 CR Belgium20,Lt 4-10-17 1/8Bn

SAMUEL,Edgar Barnett.MID T2Lt kia 30-1-16 16Mddx p148 CR France924,31-1-16

SAMUEL,George Christopher Capt dow 16-8-18 9/82RFA p207 CR France122

SAMUEL,Gerald George TLt kia 7-6-17 10RWKent p142 MR29

SAMUEL,Gerard Stuart T2Lt dow 14-7-16 8EYorks p84 CR France23,Steuart Lt

SAMUEL,James Frederick T2Lt kia 22-4-18 13RWFus p99 CR France516

SAMUEL,James Roscoe T2Lt kia 25-1-17 7NStaffs p157 CR Iraq5

SAMUEL,Wilfrid Gilbert LtACapt kia 21-9-18 6Suff p218 CR France212

SAMUELS,Arthur Molesworth 2Lt kia 13-10-14 1RIrF p171 CR France324

SAMUELS,Arthur Purfoy Irwin TCapt dow 24-9-16 11RIrRif p170 CR Belgium49,Purefoy

SAMUELS,George Bernard 2Lt kia 22-10-16 21DLI &RFC p3&161,ded MR20

SAMUELS,Lesser Joseph.MC.TLtAMaj kia 29-9-17 A83RFA p35 MR30

SAMUELS,Wilfred Templeton T2Lt dedacc 14-7-17 GL &RFC 47BallSect p13 CR France52

SAMUELSON,Geoffrey Bernard Fitzroy.MC.Lt kia 27-11-17 CldGds p51 MR17

SAMUELSON,Lelia Mathilda.Lady ded 18-6-15 VAD CR Scot80

SAMUELSON,William Denys.MID LtACapt dow 31-12-17 RGA 113SB p41 CR Belgium11

SANBORN,William Reginald T2Lt kld 7-2-18 RFC p17

SANBY,William Worthington T2Lt kia 1-7-16 20NumbF p63 MR21

SANCTUARY,Cecil Reginald 2Lt kia 22-9-18 9Lond p248 CR France665

SANCTUARY,Charles Lloyd.MC.TCapt dow 15-11-16 8Suff p79 CR France102

SANDALL,Horace Cecil Blandford T2Lt kia 9-3-18 12 att10RFus p70 CR Belgium113

SANDALL,James Hosking 2LtACapt dow 23-7-17 RGA 229SB p41 CR Belgium11

SANDALLS,Charles 2Lt kia 18-9-18 1LNLancs p136 MR16

SANDBACH,Frank Stainton 2Lt kia 29-7-17 C93RFA p209 CR Belgium12

SANDBACH,Gilbert Robertson Capt dow 3-7-17 Denbigh Yeo att24RWFus p203 CR Egypt9

SANDBACH,Hugh Handley Capt kia 3-11-14 1Drags Ex DragGds attEAfrForce p21 CR EAfrica28 &CR Tanzania1

SANDBACH,William TMaj kia 10-8-15 6RLancs p59 CR Gallipoli17

SANDBROOK,David Aubrey.MID TCapt kia 31-7-17 14WelshR p127 MR29

SANDELL,Robert Louis T2Lt kia 22-9-16 34MGC Inf p185 CR France832 Ex 13LancF

SANDEMAN,Albert Fitzroy TLtACapt kia 2-12-17 11BordR p118 MR30

SANDEMAN,Charles Vaughan T2Lt kia 4-7-16 RE 184TC p48 CR France1182

SANDEMAN,George Amelius Crawshay Capt kia 26-4-15 3 att1Hamps p121 MR29

SANDEMAN,Kenneth Charles TLt kia 1-9-18 11Hamps att2RInniskF p121 CRBelgium89

SANDEMAN,Sydney Robert Lt kia 22-4-15 RGA p209 MR29

SANDEMAN,William Alastair Fraser Lt ded 19-10-14 1GordH p167 CR France1887

SANDER,A.T.Lt 22-11-20 3GrenGds CR Lond4

SANDERS,Alvin Augustus Maj kia 12-3-15 2ELancs p111 MR22

SANDERS,Archibald Morton 2Lt dow 9-4-17 5KOSB p224 CR France95

SANDERS,Arthur Edward Capt dow 19-5-16 2Y&L p159 CRBelgium5

SANDERS,Arthur Richard Careless.CMG.DSO&Bar.MajTBrigGen kia 20-9-18 RE 50InfBde 17Div p48 CR france906

SANDERS,Charles Phillips T2Lt ded 15-9-18 RE p48 CR Iraq6

SANDERS,Clive ACapt kia 27-5-18 WYorks att2Bn p82 MR18

SANDERS,Frederick Egerton.MC.2Lt kia 10-10-18 5Lpool p215 CR France190,18 Ex19Bn

SANDERS,Frederick John T2Lt dow 6-8-18 23RFus p70 CR France169

SANDERS,George Edward 2Lt kia 19-7-17 2/1NCycBn att1/8Lond p253 CR Belgium118

SANDERS,George Ernest Lt kia 9-10-17 16RWar p65 MR30

SANDERS,Gordon Harry E.2Lt ded 15-5-19 21Lancers p23&257 MR69,14-5-19

SANDERS,Henry Sacheverel Lt kia 21-8-18 6RWar p214 CR France239

SANDERS,James Donald Gerhardt Capt kia 5-1-16 RFA &RFC p3p35 CR France285

SANDERS,John Emerton 2Lt kia 25-8-16 17LancF p93 MR21

SANDERS,John Harry TLt ded 19-1-19 RAOC BaseDepot p198&257 CR Italy15

SANDERS,John Henry T2Lt dow 27-10-17 GL &59RFC p13 CR France446

SANDERS,Joseph Henry T2Lt kia 23-6-17 10ScotRif p104 CR Belgium6

SANDERS,Leslie Yorath T2Lt kia 10-3-17 RGA attRE FldSurvCoy p41 CR France120

SANDERS,Sydney Elphick 2Lt kia 30-11-17 RWKent att6Bn p142 MR17

SANDERS,Vincent Stanton 2Lt kia 4-9-16 1Beds p86 MR21

SANDERS,William Alfred Thomas 2Lt kia 9-9-16 1/13Lond p249 MR21

SANDERSON,Albert Montague Lt 1-10-18 74RAF MR20

SANDERSON,Archibald James Capt dow 2-5-15 att1KOSB p102 MR4

SANDERSON,Arthur Keith 2Lt kia 25-9-15 5Mddx att7Lond p148 MR19

SANDERSON,Arthur Watson Maj kia 28-6-15 7RScots p211 CR Gallipoli6

SANDERSON,Charles Buswell 2Lt 25-9-18 27RAF MR20

SANDERSON,Christopher.DSO.T2Lt kia 18-6-17 GordH p167 MR20

SANDERSON,Clement Oliver St.John.MC.TLt kia 27-4-18 RE 58InfBde p48 CR Belgium18

SANDERSON,Eric Harvard 2Lt kia 24-9-18 D149 RFA p35 CR Belgium60

SANDERSON,Francis William TLt kia 2-9-16 RE SpecBde p48 CR France833 Ex28Lond

SANDERSON,Fred Borthwick 2Lt dow 10-8-16 C258RFA p209 CR France145

SANDERSON,Gerald Stanley 2Lt kia 22-7-16 11Lond p248 CR France283

SANDERSON,Geoffrey Evan TLt kia 1-7-16 MGC 107Coy p185 MR21,Euan

SANDERSON,George Edward Lt 30-3-18 1AustBn ImpCamelCps MR34

SANDERSON,Gordon 2Lt dow 13-10-15 IARO att2/2GurkhaRif MGCoy p282 CR France765

SANDERSON,Harold Scott TLt kia 25-9-15 8BlkW p129 MR19

SANDERSON,Harry TCaptAMaj kia 23-4-17 A63RFA p35 CR France1182

SANDERSON,Hugh Capt kia 12-7-15 1/4KOSB p224&271 MR4

SANDERSON,John Topping T2Lt kia 18-12-15 7BordR p118 CR Belgium72,12-12-15

SANDERSON,Philip Noel LtTCapt dow 25-4-15 att1KOSB p102 MR4

SANDERSON,Ronald Harcourt MajALtCol kia 17-4-18 148RFA p35 CR Belgium11

SANDERSON,Roy Broughton 2Lt dow 17-4-18 RGA 6SB p41 CR Belgium38

SANDERSON,Sidney Charles 2Lt kia 11-10-16 2/18Lond p250 CR France68,Sydney

SANDERSON,Thomas Edward.MID Lt kia 13-4-18 1/4Y&L p238 CR Belgium89

SANDERSON,Walter Kerr T2Lt kia 1-7-16 1BordR p118 MR21,Ker

SANDERSON,Wilfrid T2Lt dow 15-4-18 WYorks att1/7Bn p82 CR Belgium38

SANDERSON,William Howard Lt dow 28-9-18 4RIrReg p89 CR France1184

SANDFORD,Charles James Vavasour 2Lt dow 6-5-17 8Mddx p236 CR France113

SANDFORD,Clement Richard Folliot.MC.Capt kia 22-2-17 5YLI p235 CR France163

SANDILANDS,John George T2Lt kia 21-3-17 11RScots p54 MR20

SANDISON,Eric William Wright.MID 2Lt ded 18-11-16 3 att15RScots p54 CR France64

SANDLAND,William Maj&QM ded 12-11-18 NStaffs p265 CR Staffs125

SANDOE,Charles Frederick.MC.2LtACapt kia 30-8-18 1DCLI p115 CR France518

SANDOE,Montague William Augustus T2Lt dow 8-5-17 9Dev p77 CR France568

SANDOM,William Ernest TLt ded 10-11-18 32MGC p185 CR France146

SANDRY,James Ralph.MC.Capt dow 13-11-17 RGA 329SB p209 CR France40

SANDS,John William.MC.Lt kldacc 20-5-18 RE SigCoy att44RGAp48 CR France106

SANDS,Leslie Kelham TCapt dow 28-4-16 10LancF p93 CR France285

SANDYS,Edwin Thomas Falkiner.DSO.TLtCol ded 14-9-16 2Mddx p148 CR Lond4,13-9-16 dow

SANDYS,Mervyn Keats Capt kia 25-10-14 2Y&L p159 MR32,22/23-10-14

SANDYS,William Edwin TLt kia 5-9-17 GL &32RFC p13 CR Belgium11

SANDYS-THOMAS,Walter Jones 2Lt kia 4-2-17 3 att2SWBord p100 CR France744

SANER,Hubert Evelyn TCapt ded 17-11-18 RASC 372HorseTransCoy p193 CR France34

SANFORD,Walter Henry 2Lt ded 11-2-19 Dev att2/4DCLI p77&257 CR France1849

SANG,Alfred Frederick Joseph 2Lt dow 2-10-14 SL IntelCps p201 CR France16

SANGER,Henry Keith T2Lt kia 13-4-18 10EYorks p84 CR France193

SANGER,Thomas Rudolph 2Lt kia 1-7-16 1/5SStaffs p229 MR21

SANGER-DAVIES,Llewellyn Herbert TCapt kia 1-7-16 15DLI p161 MR21

SANGSTER,Albert Burnett 2Lt 13-8-18 206RAF MR20

SANGSTER,Frederick Charles TLt dow 6-9-16 16RWar p65 CR France23

SANGSTER,William John Campbell 2Lt kia 25-9-15 4GordH p242 MR29

SANIFORD,Noel Pendlebury 2Lt dow 3-4-17 5Ches p222 CR France120,SANDIFORD

SANKEY,C.M.MC.2Lt kld 15-5-18 3EKent &RAF p58 CR Mddx53

SANKEY,Sydney John Capt kld 25-9-15 6SStaffs p229 CR Belgium132,kia

SANKEY,Thomas T2Lt kia 13-12-17 2WYorks p82 CR France134

SANKEY,William Mandeville.MC.Lt dow 23-3-18 2Mon p244 CR Belgium84

SANSOM,Alfred John LtCol kia 5-7-17 5RSuss p228 CR France1182

SANSOM,Edwin Richard 2Lt dow 30-10-18 4EKent p212 CR France380

SANSOM,Roland Charles Lt 16-5-18 GL &55RAF CR Germany3

SANSOM,Walter Edwin Hammond T2Lt kia 16/18-8-16 8Lancs p59 MR21

SANSOME,Howard Victor 2Lt kia 26-10-17 14RWar p65 CR Belgium112

SANT,Edward Medley 2Lt kia 1-9-17 19RFC p13 MR20

SANTLER,William Amos T2Lt kia 13-6-16 8ESurr p113 CR France513

SANTS,Herbert Walter Lt ded 24-12-17 RFA attAOC p35 CR Iraq8

SAPHIN,Alfred Bridge 2Lt ded 15-8-17 3KRRC p265 CR France381,20Bn

SAPHIR,Max.MC.Capt 22-3-18 SAfrInf A'Coy MR27

SAPORTAS,Herbert Arnold Lt kia 17-7-15 2Manch p156 CR Belgium56,16-7-15

SAPTE,Anthony TCapt kia 1-7-16 4Mddx A'Coy p148 CR France267

SARCHET,Hugh le Gallienne.MC.ACapt kia 4-4-18 8RBerks p140 MR27

SARCHET,Leslie Lionel TLt kia 23-10-18 GL att55TMB p191 CR France716,Capt Hamps Xfer to 7EKent

SARDON,Herbert John S.TLt dow 31-10-18 3Dev p77 CR Mddx44

SARGAISON,William Henry T2Lt kia 6-12-15 5RIrF att5ConnRgrs p171 MR37,7RDubF att5CR

SARGEANT,Arthur Percival 2Lt kia 14-7-16 9Leic p88 CR France453

SARGEANT,Bernard Theobald 2Lt kia 11-4-17 8Lond p247 CR France1185

SARGEANT,Harold William 2Lt dow 4-4-18 18Lond p250 CR France37

SARGEANT,Ralph Leslie 2Lt kld 25-3-17 3 att8SomLI p80 CR France1180

SARGEAUNT,Arthur Frederick LtCol kia 31-7-15 RE p48 CR Belgium6

SARGEAUNT,Herbert Gaussen MajALtCol kia 15-6-17 RGA 16HAG p41 CR France285

SARGENT,Alfred George LtCol ded 14-5-18 IMS att25IndGH p282 CR Iraq6

SARGENT,Augustus Montague T2Lt dow 27-4-18 15N&D p135 CR France62

SARGENT,Ernest Vernon Lt kia 27-5-18 5NumbF p213 MR18

SARGENT,Henry Westbury 2Lt dow 6-7-16 1N&D p135 CR France430

SARGENT,Reginald William Fitzgerald T2Lt kia 5-10-17 220MGC Inf p185 CR Belgium308

SARGINT,Edward Eaton.MC.TCapt kia 16-8-17 7RIrF p171 MR30

SARGOOD,Hugh Frank T2Lt kia 10-5-17 16Mddx p148 MR20

SARJEANT,Douglas Leslie Lt kia 21-1-15 1/8RWar p215 CR France281,21-10-15

SARKIES,S.C.LtCol 7-3-17 IMS CR Mddx26

SARSBY,Reginald Ambler T2Lt kia 21-12-15 10Norf p74 CR France279,22-12-15

SARSFIELD,William Stopford Maj dow 20-9-14 2ConnRgrs p172 CR France1107

SARSON,Herbert William Phillips 2Lt dow 20-10-15 1/4YLI p235 CR Belgium11,Phillip

SARTORIS,Charles Frederick Lt kia 24-6-15 10 att7Leic p88 CR Gallipoli6,att2RFus

SARTORIUS,Euston Francis Frederick Capt dow 5-4-15 1GrenGds p50 CR France102

SASSE,Frederick Hugh Capt dow 8-5-15 2EYorks p84 CR Lond4

SASSOON,Hamo T2Lt dow 1-11-15 RE p48 MR4

SATCHWELL,Frank Henry Sandom Capt kia 3-5-17 HAC Inf p206 MR20

SATCHWELL,Henry Lt ded 8-12-18 Res GL p271 CR Numb4

SATCHWELL,Ralph William 2Lt kia 31-1-17 RGA 76SB p41 CR France393

SATTERTHWAITE,G.E.2Lt kld 11-6-18 GL &RAF p191

SATTERTHWAITE,William Herbert Capt kia 7-6-18 2/5RLancs p213 CR France204

SAUERBECK,Charles Theodore William TLt kia 11-9-17 13DLI p161 CR Belgium19

SAUL,Herbert Lepard T2Lt kia 24-10-18 7Suff p79 CR France1259

SAULEZ,Alfred Gordon Capt ded 5-7-21 RASC 83MT CR Iraq8

SAULEZ,Arthur Travers AMaj kia 22-4-17 D64RFA p35 CR France644

SAULL,Harold Truscott T2Lt died 2-10-18 LabCps p266 CR Surrey1,Lpool

SAUMAREZ,Reginald Stafford.MC.Capt kia 23-3-18 22Lond p251 CR France245

SAUNDBY,William Spencer FitzRobert 2Lt kia 17-11-16 Yorks &RFC p3,261&263 MR20

SAUNDER,George Bertram T2Lt kia 15-4-17 1EKent p58 CR France551

SAUNDERS,Albert James 2Lt kia 27-6-17 RGA 58SB p41 CR Belgium1,26-6-17

SAUNDERS,Alfred.MID TCapt dow 16-12-16 6Lancs 1Coy p59 CR Iraq5

SAUNDERS,Alfred George T2Lt kia 29/31-7-16 8NStaffs p157 MR21

SAUNDERS,Alfred Hewgill Lt kia 10-3-15 2RBerks p140 CR France709

SAUNDERS,Arthur Brain TLt dow 4-9-16 17KRRC p151 CR France169,Bryan

SAUNDERS,Arthur Courtenay Capt kia 14-3-15 2DCLI p115 CR Belgium28

SAUNDERS,Arthur Hugh Richard Capt mbk 8-3-16 IA 1/2GurkhaRif p282 MR38

SAUNDERS,Charles T2Lt kia 1-7-16 15WYorks p82 MR21

SAUNDERS,Charles Fabian T2Lt kia 18-8-16 7Nhampt C'Coy p138 CR France402

SAUNDERS,Charles Frederick 2Lt dow 18-4-18 2N&D p135 CR Belgium38

SAUNDERS,Charles Robert Edgar Capt dow 28-4-15 4Lond p246 CR France200

SAUNDERS,Clement 2Lt dow 11-2-17 66/4RFA p35 CR Iraq5

SAUNDERS,Claude Winstanley Capt kia 30-9-19 IA 108Inf att1/7GurkhaRif p282 MR38

SAUNDERS,Clifford William.MC.TLtACapt kia 16-10-17 6Dors p124 MR30

SAUNDERS,Cyril Page Gore ACapt kia 27-9-16 3 att1LNLancs p136 CR France385

SAUNDERS,D.M.LtCol ded 2-12-18 RAMC p267 CR Ireland5

SAUNDERS,Edwin Walter Lt kia 5-5-15 1Camb p245 MR29

SAUNDERS,Ernest Manners 2Lt dow 4-12-17 1/4Ess p232 CR Egypt2,Maurice

SAUNDERS,Ferdinand Ward 2Lt kia 25-1-18 WelshR &35RFC p17 CR France446

SAUNDERS,Francis William 2Lt kia 1-8-18 8A&SH p271 CR France866

SAUNDERS,Frank 2Lt dow 17-10-17 1/4Glouc p225 CR Belgium18

SAUNDERS,F.W.Capt ded 29-4-18 12RInniskF p105 CR Shrop93

SAUNDERS,George T2Lt kldacc 30-3-18 51RFC p17 CR Essex13

SAUNDERS,George James Rich LtTCapt kia 26-9-16 SLancs att7Leic p126 MR21

SAUNDERS,George Morley Maj ded 26-2-18 DLI p265

SAUNDERS,Gwilyn Essex T2Lt kia 18-9-18 RWFus att16Bn p99 CR France415

SAUNDERS,Harold Cecil Rich.DSO.CaptAMaj kia 30-5-18 EYorks p84 MR18

SAUNDERS,Harold Macleod T2Lt kia 25-6-18 11ELancs p111 CR France19

SAUNDERS,Horace Victor Bertram T2Lt kia 22-3-18 46MGC p185 CR France258

SAUNDERS,James Renault Lt kia 4-11-18 2CldGds p51 CR France1080

SAUNDERS,Kenneth 2Lt kld 31-12-14 16NumbF p63 CR Numb4

SAUNDERS,Louis Desormeaux T2Lt kia 26-9-15 1SWBord p100 MR19

SAUNDERS,Noel Martyn TCapt kia 20-10-18 7BordR p118 CR France1476

SAUNDERS,Reginald Arthur Lt kia 14-3-16 RFA att1RFC p19&207,TCapt CR Belgium21

SAUNDERS,Robert T2Lt kia 26-10-17 13MGC Inf p185 MR30

SAUNDERS,Robert Stratford Howard Lt dow 12-4-18 D330RFA p35 CR France145

SAUNDERS,Roy Llewellyn T2Lt kia 9-4-16 10 att6ELancs p111 MR38

SAUNDERS,Samuel George Yarrow 2Lt kia 3-11-17 1/4Ess p232 CR Palestine8

SAUNDERS,William Gilbert TCapt&Adjt kia 6-9-16 5Lpool p215 CR France188

SAUNDERS-JONES,Henry St.John Lt dow 3-8-17 IA 20Inf att30Punjabis p282 CR EAfrica10 &CR Tanzania1

SAUNDERSON,Robert de Bedick Lt 18-10-17 GL &NigR CR EAfrica11 &CR Tanzania1

SAUNDERSON,Samuel Treherne Capt kld 22-4-18 NIrHorse &RAF p24

SAVAGE,Alfred 2Lt ded 7-10-17 RFA 4Bde DAC p35 CR Iraq8

SAVAGE,Alfred Charles T2Lt kia 31-7-17 8Suff p79 MR29

SAVAGE,Alphonso Macardle Lt ded 8-3-19 3DragGds p261CR Wilts115,A.N.

SAVAGE,Arthur Raymond Boscawen Maj 18-5-21 RFA CR Ireland14

SAVAGE,Cuthbert Farrar Lt dow 20-6-17 10NumbF p63 CR Belgium11

SAVAGE,Donaldson Lizars 2Lt dow 15-11-16 RE 56FC p48 CR France133,kia

SAVAGE,Edward Hugh Noël Lt kia 29-6-18 RE 1Coy p48 CR France77

SAVAGE,Francis Vandry 2Lt kia 1-5-17 IARO att1/94Inf p282 MR43

SAVAGE,Frederick Quinton T2Lt kia 20-9-17 6Wilts p153 MR30

SAVAGE,George Henry.MM.T2Lt kia 21-10-18 att12ESurr p113 CR B449,C.H.

SAVAGE,Gerald Roderick LtTCapt dow 4-10-17 3 att11Ess p132 MR30

SAVAGE,Harold Wilson Capt kia 10-8-15 10Hamps p121 MR4

SAVAGE,Harry George ACapt kia 20-9-17 4Hamps p228 MR30

SAVAGE,Henry George 2Lt kia 17-10-17 17Lond p250 CR Belgium112,dow

SAVAGE,Henry Osborne Lt kia 26-10-16 RFA X32TMB p35 CR France35

SAVAGE,John Ardkeen Capt kia 18-9-14 1Nhampt p138 MR15,17-9-14

SAVAGE,John Brown 2Lt dow 16-5-15 1RWFus p99 CR France279

SAVAGE,John Geoffrey T2Lt kia 24-7-16 RGA 40 att109SB p41 CR France397

SAVAGE,John Raymond Boscawen 2Lt kia 18-6-16 25RFC p3 CR France161

SAVAGE,Tom Alixander Capt ded 26-6-19 RGA AC att10IndMA Bde p41&257 CR Egypt8,Alexander dow

SAVAGE,Thomas John T2Lt kia 11-10-18 RB att3Bn p180 CR France270 Ex NIrHorse

SAVAGE,Wilfred Clyde Richmond Capt ded 5-5-18 IA 32Lancers p282

SAVAGE,William Beck Lt kia 21-3-18 51MGC p185 MR20

SAVAGE,William Howard T2Lt kia 1-7-16 11RFus p70 CR France397

SAVAGE,William Leslie T2Lt kld 16-6-17 GL &RFC p13 CR Glouc67

SAVAGE-ARMSTRONG,Francis Savage Nesbit.DSO.MID MajTLtCol kia 23-4-17 1SStaffs Cmdg11War p123 CR France452

SAVATARD,Thomas Warner Capt kld 29-5-15 7Manch p237 CR Gallipoli2

SAVEALL,Garrett T2Lt kia 13-7-16 7RWKent p142 MR21

SAVEL,Harold Richard Lt kia 25-5-15 21Lond p251 CR France279

SAVERY,Roger de la Garde Capt kia 7-8-15 10SStaffs p123 MR4

SAVILE,Francis Ewart TLt ded 9-2-16 6RRofCav att9Lancers p24

SAVILE,George Keith 2Lt kia 20-6-15 1/4Glouc p225 CR Belgium48

SAVILE,William Henry Bouchier TCapt kia 14-8-16 70RFA p35 CR France453

SAVILL,F.E.Lt 9-2-16 9Lancers CR Dorset28

SAVILL,John Edward T2Lt kia 24-8-17 RB att9Bn p180 MR30

SAVILL,Ronald John 2Lt kia 30-4-17 3 att9Ess p132 MR20

SAVILL-ONLEY,Frederick Simerville Wroth Capt ded 9-7-20 IA S&TCps p282 MR43,Somerville

SAVILLE,Clifford Allen Capt kia 8-11-17 11EYorks p84 MR20

SAVILLE,Eric T2Lt kia 8-10-18 1RBerks p140 CR France338

SAVILLE,Robert TCapt kld 16-3-18 GL &RFC p17 CR Yorks447

SAVORY,Ernest Harley 2Lt kia 8-7-17 7RWSurr p56 MR29,10-8-17

SAVORY,Francis Richard Egerton Capt dow 5-12-15 2KSLI p145 MR37

SAVORY,Henry Lawrence Scott 2Lt dow 26-4-18 1Suff GarBn att3Worc p79 CR Belgium38

SAVORY,Maurice Jeffery TCapt dow 3-2-17 9WRid p116 CR France105

SAVOURS,Arthur William Lt kia 2-8-18 6 att11RFus p70 CR France209

SAW,Noel Humphrey Wykeham.MC.Capt kia 9-10-17 RAMC att4Worc p197 CR Belgium16

SAWARD,Harry Douglas.MID Capt kia 23-3-15 2RScots p54 CR Belgium104

SAWARD,Ralph 2Lt kia 29-4-17 22RFus p70 MR20

SAWDEN,William Wright Lt dow 5-6-17 RGA att20RFC p209 CR Belgium11

SAWDON,Arthur Tindale T2Lt kia 28-6-17 13EYorks p84 CR France777

SAWER,Edgar 2Lt kia 31-7-17 42/2RFA p209 CR Belgium12

SAWYER,Aleck Makson T2Lt dow 13-12-17 50MGC p185 CR France13,Mayson 12-12-17

SAWYER,Charles Quinton TCapt kia 14-7-16 8EYorks attTMB p84 CRFrance399,C.O.

SAWYER,Frederick William Campion TLt dow 4-4-17 RE 218FC p48 CR France1204

SAWYER,Gordon Stanley 2Lt kia 13-10-17 IARO att113RFC p282 CR Egypt9

SAWYER,Herbert 2Lt kia 12-10-16 7Suff p79 MR21

SAWYER,Maitland Lindsay T2Lt dow 27-4-17 2Y&L p159 CR France80

SAWYER,Robert Fulwell 2Lt dow 24-8-17 KRRC att17Bn p151 CR Belgium111

SAWYER,William Robert T2Lt dow 8-10-17 6EYorks p84 CR Belgium23

SAXBY,Eric Yardley 2Lt kia 9-9-16 9Mddx att2/5LancF p236 MR21

SAXBY,George Scrase 2Lt dow 22-4-17 9Lond p248 CR France113

SAXELBYE,Frank Norman Lt dow 11-5-15 4EYorks p219 CR France102

SAXON,Ethel Sister ded 3-9-17 TFNS p254 MR43

SAXON,Fredk Thomas 2Lt kia 8-12-17 RGA 143SB p41 CR France415

SAXON,Harry.MID TLt kia 30-11-16 8RLancs p59 CR France133,29-11-16

SAXTON,Arthur Cyril T2Lt kia 30-7-16 1 att2KOSB p102 MR21

SAXTON,Ernest Wilkinson Lt ded 19-12-19 LabCps p266 CR Notts60

SAYCE,George Ben TCapt kia 1-7-16 26Manch p156 CR France397

SAYE,Lancelot Hugo T2Lt dow 11-7-16 6RBerks p140 CR France40

SAYER,Cecil Oversley Lt dow PoW 7-6-15 7DLI p239 CR Belgium393

SAYER,Charles Melville T2Lt kia 17-6-17 GL &4RFC p13 CR Belgium10

SAYER,Harry 2Lt dow 24-10-15 1EKent p58 CR France80

SAYER,Hubert Lionel 2Lt kia 17-8-17 RFA &7RFC p13&35 CR Belgium18

SAYER,James Herbert 2Lt kia 3-4-17 15RFC p13 CR France646

SAYER,Leonard Charles T2Lt dow 4-7-16 17RFus p70 CR France12

SAYER,Robert Bramwell T2Lt dow 19-2-17 11RFus p70 CR France41

SAYER,Thomas Errington TCapt kia 25-9-16 11 att10YLI p143 MR21

SAYER,William Thomas T2Lt kia 5-6-16 RE 180FC p48 MR20

SAYERS,Charlie Ronald T2Lt kia 13-4-17 9Leic p88 CR France616

SAYERS,Horace George David Lt drd 2-6-17 23Lond p252 MR41

SAYERS,Keith Raymond Lt mbk 9-9-17 RWKent &23RFC p256 MR20

SAYERS,Leslie.MC&Bar.TCapt kia 23-8-18 16RWar p65 CR France579

SAYERS,Robert 2Lt kia 21-10-14 2Mddx p148 MR22

SAYES,John T2Lt kia 31-10-18 2Dev p77 CR France1142

SAYLE,George Randall Fysh Lt dow 10-5-15 33/33RFA p35 CR France254,9-5-15

SAYRES,Alexander Ward Fortescue Maj dow 10-10-17 RAMC 2/1FA p253 CR France52,LtCol

SAYRES,Hugh Wingfield Capt kia 1-7-16 1 att2LancF p93 CR France643

SAYWOOD,Charles 2Lt kia 5-7-16 95RFA p35 CR France189

SCAIFE,Joseph 2Lt kia 21-3-18 1WRid att2Y&L p116 MR20

SCAIFE,Thomas Earle Gordon.MC.2Lt kia 26-9-16 6DragGds &RFC p3&21,ded MR20

SCALE,George Devereux TCapt kia 20-7-16 10RWFus p99 MR21

SCALES,Edwin Herbert Lt dow 11-10-18 RASC att 1EKent p193 CR France446

SCALES,Edward Lionel Capt ded 11-11-18 4Mddx p148&258 CR Lancs472

SCALES,Patrick Joseph T2Lt kia 17-2-17 6Nhampt p138 MR21

SCALES,Walter Alexander.MC.Capt kld 6-1-18 6WYorks p218 CR France62,kia

SCALLAN,Richard Talbot 2Lt kld 31-5-18 RGA attLabCps EscortOffr 90PoWCo p41 CR France1822

SCAMELL,Reginald Frank TCapt kia 20-4-16 11 att7Glouc p107 MR38,21-4-16

SCAMMELL,Sydney John Alfred 2Lt kia 16-9-16 6SomLI p80 MR21

SCANDRETT,John Jackson T2Lt kia 15-5-16 6/7RScotF p95 CR France423,14-5-16

SCANDRETT,William Frederick T2Lt kia 27-6-16 att2RSuss p120 MR20

SCANLAN,William Jack 2Lt kia 1-9-17 6Lond p247 MR29

SCARBOROUGH,Edward Owen 2Lt ded 25-5-18 6Lpool attRAF p215&258

SCARBOROUGH,Gerald Capt dow 12-9-18 4WRid att15Ess p227CR France31

SCARBOROUGH,Haydn 2Lt kia 17-9-18 3 att1WYorks p82 CR France835

SCARBROUGH,Michael Claud.MID TMaj kia 26-9-16 12Mddx p148 MR21

SCARBROUGH,Reginald John Capt dow 2-11-17 3Dev att1/8Hamps p77 CR Palestine2

SCARLETT,Harold Ernest 2Lt kia 17-9-16 3Lond p246 MR21

SCARLETT,Robert Stubbs T2Lt kia 20-12-17 16RScots p54 CR France162

SCARLETT,Thomas Capt ded 31-1-19 SL attHQ Staff RTO p201 CR Belgium265

SCARR,Geoffrey Campbell Lt FlyingAcc 18-11-18 IARO attRAF p282

SCARR,Reginald Graham T2Lt kia 14-7-16 12WYorks p82 CR France432

SCARTH,Alan Edward Capt dow 22-4-17 IARO att53Sikhs p282 MR38

SCARTH,Isaac Hinton Lt kia 23-4-17 4Yorks p220 MR20

SCARTH,James Charles T2Lt kia 14-7-16 10 att7SfthH p165 MR21

SCATCHARD,Thomas Capt kia 8-9-14 RAMC p197 CR France1426

SCATTERGOOD,Tom Victor T2Lt dow 6-6-17 21NumbF p63 CRFrance113

SCAWIN,William Neville Lt kia 15-4-18 5Y&L attMGC Inf p187&238 MR30

SCED,Henry Forbes TLt kia 24-9-17 14NumbF p63 CR Belgium19

SCHAFER,Thomas Sydney Lt kia 26-9-15 13NumbF p63 MR19

SCHALL,Henry Frederick 2Lt dow 24-9-16 RGA 150RotherhamHB p41 CR France833

SCHELL,Frederick Stanley 2Lt kia 22-8-18 RGA 130HB p41 CR France526

SCHENKEL,F.J.Lt dow 19-11-17 EAIntelDept CR EAfrica35 &CR Tanzania1

SCHIFF,Alfred Sydney Borlase 2Lt kia 9-4-17 1RB p180 CR France604

SCHIFF,Martin Noel Lt kia 17-6-17 1ScotsGds p52 MR29

SCHIFF,Mortimer Edward Harold Capt kia 26-9-17 12Suff p79 MR21

SCHILL,Edward Melland TLt dow 25-8-16 21LancsF p93 CR France23,17Bn

SCHINCK,Roger Henry 2Lt ded 31-10-14 3RWSurr p56 CR Belgium57,dow

SCHINDLER,William Barron 2Lt kia 20-7-18 2/5WYorks p218 CR France622

SCHLOSS,Lionel Ernest 2Lt kia 31-7-17 44MGC p185 MR29

SCHLOTEL,Charles Henry Cooper.MC.MIDx2 Capt ded 21-3-19 10DCLI p114 CR Germany1

SCHMIDT,F.P.Acc 4-11-18 IA AccsDept MR61

SCHNEIDER,Alexander Capt kia 29-6-21 IA 2/21Punjabis p282 MR43

SCHNEIDER,Herbert Hugo Lt kia 5-12-14 RE p48 MR40

SCHNEIDER,Stewart Spearing 2Lt kia 1-7-16 2RBerks p140 MR21

SCHOFIELD,Alexander Traies Capt dow 10-11-18 ACycCps &KentCycBn p244&271,HighCycBn CR Iraq8,att2RWKent

SCHOFIELD,Cuthbert TLt kia 25-9-15 14 att12RFus p70 MR19

SCHOFIELD,Henry William Melles Lt ded 2-10-20 IA 123Rif att104 p282

SCHOFIELD,James Humphrey Clare TLt kia 26-9-16 1 att15DLI p161 MR21

SCHOFIELD,John.VC.T2Lt kia 9-4-18 2/5LancsF p93 CR France1106

SCHOFIELD,John 2Lt dow 24-9-18 5LancsF p221 CR Lancs266

SCHOFIELD,John Douglas Price T2Lt kld 26-5-17 RFC p13

SCHOLEFIELD,Arthur Hoyle 2Lt kia 18-5-17 19Lond att2LondRB p251 MR20

SCHOLEFIELD,Cyril Hamilton Reid CaptAMaj kia 28-3-18 RGA 69SB p41 CR France184

SCHOLEFIELD,Harry 2Lt dow 28-4-17 4YLI p235 CR France40

SCHOLEFIELD,Richard Powell T2Lt dow 25-7-16 16Ches W'Coy p96 CR France66

SCHOLES,Fredk W.2Lt kia 3-5-17 15WYorks p82 MR20

SCHOLES,Wilfred Paul 2Lt kia 13-10-15 4Leic p220 MR19

SCHOLES,William Robert Capt ded 14-7-18 LabCps p189 CR Scot15,12-7-18 HLI

SCHOLEY,Charles Harry Norman TCapt kia 25-9-15 9RB p180 MR29

SCHOLFIELD,Richard Denham T2Lt kia 10-8-15 6RLancs p59 CR Gallipoli17

SCHONFIELD,Edwin TCapt kia 20-9-16 2/19Lond p250 CR France68

SCHOOLING Cecil Herbert Rev dow 21-6-17 RAChDept att21InfBde p200 CR Belgium11

SCHOOLING,Eric Charles Capt kia 31-10-14 2RWar p65 MR29

SCHOOLING,Paul Sydney Bedford TLt kia 26-9-16 13 att9LancsF p93 MR21

SCHOOLING,Peter Holt 2Lt dow 30-3-16 9ESurr p113 CR France285

SCHREIBER,Owen Reginald.MC&Bar.CaptAMaj dow 22-10-17 106/22RH&FA p35 CR Belgium11

SCHRODER,Francis Thomas Lt kia 24-3-15 2Suff p79 CR Belgium103,2Lt 15-3-15

SCHRODER,Henry Dudley 2Lt kia 2-12-17 15LancsF p93 MR30,1/5Bn

SCHUH,Rudolf Oscar.MC.Lt ded 8-11-18 1Dev p77 CR France146

SCHULT,Edgar T2Lt dow 28-10-17 2RWSurr p56 CR Belgium11

SCHULTE,D.F.J.MC.Capt 30-7-18 Beds &60RAF CR France1564

SCHULTZ,George Edward TCapt dow 12-8-17 15Ches p96 CR France363,19-8-17

SCHULTZ,Leonard Elmslie T2Lt kia 27-9-15 2Wilts p153 MR19

SCHULTZE,Hugh Lees T2lt kia 20-10-18 Dors att6Bn p124 CR France192

SCHUR,Philip Lt kia 15-6-18 9N&D p135 CR France115,Phillip

SCHUSTER,Alfred Felix Lt kia 30-11-14 4Huss SR p21 MR29

SCHUSTER,Christopher John Claude 2Lt kia 10-8-18 5RB 1Coy p180 CR France412,1Bn

SCHUTE,John Hartley TLt kia 15-8-15 6RIrF p171 MR4

SCHWAGE,Sidney Philip T2Lt kia 7-9-18 6RWSurr p56 CR France439,SCHWABE

SCHWALM,Charles Edward Lt kia 22-11-17 6Glouc p225 CR France1327

SCHWARZ,Reginald Oscar.MC.CaptTMaj ded 18-11-18 6KRRC StaffConOfSalv attHQ 1Ech p151 CR France40,19-11-18

SCHWEDER,Archibald Alan.MC.TCapt kia 26-9-16 9N&D p135 MR21

SCILLEY,James Frederick 2Lt kia 22-1-18 10RIrRif p170 MR21

SCLANDERS,Charles Maclure Lt kia 12-4-18 16Lond p249 MR32

SCOBEY,Richard Campbell 2Lt kia 23-8-17 6DCLI p114 CR Belgium125,5Bn

SCOBIE,C.G.Lt kia 21-5-18 SL &88RAF p268 MR20

SCOBIE,James 2Lt dow 2-8-17 4 att9GordH p242 CR Belgium7,3-8-17

SCOBIE,John Allan Mackay.MC.MID Lt kia 8-3-16 IA 59Rif p282 MR38

SCOBIE,John Angus Nicholson MacEwen Lt kia 29-7-16 RE 225FC p48 CR France727,McEwen

SCOBIE,K.McD.2Lt kld 27-10-18 RGA &RAF p41

SCOGGIN,Harry Cumming 2Lt kia 9-8-16 2Hamps p121 CR Belgium47

SCOLDING,George Henry 2Lt kia 26-3-18 4 att7Norf p216 MR27

SCOLLARD,David Francis.MC.Capt kia 20-4-17 RIrRif att7Bn p170 CR Belgium17

SCOLLICK,Laurence Trevor T2Lt kia 26-6-17 2DLI p161 CR France149

SCOONES,Earl Foster T2Lt kia 23-11-16 13Lpool p72 CR France5

SCOONES,Fitzmaurice Valentine 2Lt ded 18-8-16 3BlkW p129 CR Scot926

SCORE,William Thomas T2Lt kia 27-3-18 6EKent p58 CR France233

SCORER,Herbert Selwyn Capt kia 13-10-15 5Lincs C'Coy p220 MR19

SCORER,Nicholas 2Lt dow 29-3-18 4Yorks p220 CR France64

SCORER,William Harold.MID TLt dow 6-10-18 7Wilts p153 CR France194,Capt

SCOT-SKIRVING,Archibald William Capt dow 9-8-15 5RIrF p171 MR4,Waller

SCOTLAND,David Lothian TLtACapt dow 5-10-18 21MGC p185 CR France13

SCOTT,Alan Dale Wyndham.MC.TLt dow 26-10-16 92RFA p35 CR France,T20RFA

SCOTT,Alexander.TD.CaptHonMaj ded 12-2-15 RGA p209 CR Scot237

SCOTT,Alexander 2Lt kia 24-4-17 10HLI p164 MR20,Capt

SCOTT,Alister Will Henderson Capt dow 16-5-15 6 att2Worc p109 CR France80,kia

SCOTT,Andrew Hamilton Lt kia 3-5-17 4 att6KOSB p223 MR20

SCOTT,Andrew Holmes.MC.Capt kia 31-7-17 RE p48 MR29

SCOTT,Andrew Riddell Lt dow 24-4-17 1/5KOSB p224 CR Egypt2

SCOTT,Archibald T2Lt kia 25-4-17 8/10GordH p167 MR20

SCOTT,Archibald MacDonald T2Lt kia 16-8-17 8NumbF p63 CR Belgium96

SCOTT,Arnold Charles Lt dow 9-6-18 3 att1RScotF p95 CR France10

SCOTT,Arthur Blake 2Lt kia 26-3-17 1/7Ches p223 CR Palestine8

SCOTT,Arthur de Courcy LtCol kia 6-5-15 1Ches p96 CR Belgium134,5-5-15

SCOTT,Arthur Earnshaw 2Lt 24-3-15 A'Coy 4SAfrInf Ex C'Coy 3rd MR27

SCOTT,Arthur Edward T2Lt kia 21-3-18 3RB p180 MR27

SCOTT,Arthur Ernest Mortimer Lt kia 7-11-16 7 att4RFus p70 MR21

SCOTT,Arthur George 2Lt kia 23-12-15 2WRid p116 CR France513,21-12-15

SCOTT,Arthur William Maj ded 23-9-15 RAMC p253 CR Yorks361

SCOTT,Basil John Harrison 2Lt kia 23-10-14 2SStaffs p123 MR29

SCOTT,Bernard Lt kia 21-5-16 15Lond p249 MR20

SCOTT,Campbell Lowe TLt kia 2-9-18 3RScots att81TMB p54 CR Greece6,1Bn

SCOTT,Cecil 2Lt kia 31-7-17 7Ess p232 MR29

SCOTT,Cecil Ewart.MC.TLtACapt dow 9-9-18 8TankCps p188 CR France34

SCOTT,Charles Brough Lt dow 20-11-17 1Drags p21 CR France439

SCOTT,Charles Edward LtCol dow 9-8-16 6WYorks p218 CR France40

SCOTT,Charles Gordon Lt kia 28-10-16 3A&SH p173 CR France744

SCOTT,Charles Lindsay Murray Capt kia 15-2-17 GL 3NStaffs att54RFC p13&157,ded CR France1489

SCOTT,Clarence Trebor 2Lt kia 20-9-17 5Ches p222 MR30

SCOTT,Clifford 2Lt kia 2-8-17 83RFA p35 CR Belgium19

SCOTT,David T2Lt kia 7-4-17 7 att1ScotF p95 CR France57

SCOTT,David Harden.MC.Lt kia 12-11-17 GL &65RFC p13 CR France705

SCOTT,David Lyon 2Lt kia 9-4-17 4GordH p242 CR France531

SCOTT,Desmond 2Lt kia 25-10-16 54/39RFA p35 CR France453

SCOTT,Douglas Brogden Lt kia 9-4-18 6DLI p239 MR32

SCOTT,Douglas Gordon T2Lt kldacc 13-12-17 RFC p13 CR Shrop52

SCOTT,Dudley Holme TLt dow 2-7-16 17Lpool p72 CR France526

SCOTT,Edward Claud 2Lt kia 21-11-14 RGA p41 CR France82

SCOTT,Edward Richard 2Lt kia 19-2-18 1EYorks p85 CR France530,1/7Bn

SCOTT,Elvin Alfred.MC.TL kia 8-4-16 RGA 111HB p41 CR France149

SCOTT,Eric Bertrand Ralph TLt kia 10-7-16 RE 25DivSigCo p48 CR France44

SCOTT,Eric Douglas 2Lt kia 30-10-17 GL &1RFC p13 MR20

SCOTT,Eric Farrow 2Lt kia 30-10-17 D317RFA p209 CR Belgium20

SCOTT,Francis Charles Dudley Lt kia 4-11-18 6DLI &52RAF p271 MR20

SCOTT,Francis Gordon.MM.T2Lt kia 20-10-18 1/5Manch p156 CR France287

SCOTT,Francis Sherwood Lt kia 17-10-18 3 att1YLI A'Coy p143 CR France190

SCOTT,Frank 2Lt dow 8-10-18 5Lpool p215 CR France380

SCOTT,Frank Alexander T2Lt kia 18-9-18 58MGC Inf p185 CR France511

SCOTT,Frank Edward 2Lt dow 4-4-18 RGA 405SB p41 CR France40

SCOTT,Frederick.MC.Capt kia 27-5-18 9Leic p88 MR18,Frederic

SCOTT,George Ernest 2Lt kia 13-4-18 4DCLI p227 CR France18

SCOTT,George Gordon Douglas Lt ded 22-4-18 157RH&FA p262

SCOTT,George Henry Hall TCapt kia 1-7-16 7RWSurr C'Coy p56 CR France397

SCOTT,George Jefferson.MID Capt kia 25-12-15 1/5Yorks p220 CR Belgium5

SCOTT,George Klassen TLt kia 24-2-17 RE 237FC p48 CR Belgium21,Klaassen

SCOTT,George Trotter T2Lt dow 6-5-17 2WYorks p82 CR France1468

SCOTT,George Gordon Douglas Lt ded 22-4-18 157RFA p35 CR Scot280

SCOTT,Gilbert Ernest Josiah Capt kia 25-3-18 12 att19KRRC p151 MR27

SCOTT,Gordon Lt kia 1-7-16 2Mddx p148 MR21

SCOTT,H.G.R.B.Lt 21-3-16 20Punjabis CR EAfrica13

SCOTT,Harold Donald 2Lt kia 16-10-18 3/45RFA p35 CR France1277

SCOTT,Harold George Capt kia 30-7-18 O&BLI &52RAF p264 MR20

SCOTT,Harold Vesey Capt ded 1-9-15 3RB p180 CR France64,Herbert

SCOTT,Henry Arthur 2Lt kia 8-4-17 RE 512FC p210 CR France420

SCOTT,Henry James 2LtTLt dow 29-9-15 4CamH p242 CR Scot581

SCOTT,Herbert Lawson 2Lt ded 6-6-17 2ScotF p95 CR France113

SCOTT,Hugh McLellan Capt kia 6-9-18 3HLI p164 MR30

SCOTT,Ian Archibald Sawers 2Lt kia 1-7-16 1KOSB p102 CR France220,2Bn

SCOTT,J.H.M.Capt 24-3-19 RAMC CR Scot566

SCOTT,James Lt kia 25-9-15 6GordH p242 MR19

SCOTT,James TLt kia 25-9-15 7KOSB p102 CR France219

SCOTT,James 2Lt kia 15-11-16 7A&SH p243 CR France533

SCOTT,James T2Lt drd 26-2-18 RE IWT p48 MR38

SCOTT,James.MC.Lt dow 10-3-18 B302RFA p208 CR Palestine3,9-3-18

SCOTT,James Angus Lt mbk 26-10-17 7NumbF B'Coy p257 MR30

SCOTT,James Francis 2Lt kia 23-4-17 3 att13RScots p54 MR20

SCOTT,James Hall TMaj kia 25-9-15 10ScotRif p104 MR19

SCOTT,James Huggan Lt ded 9-11-18 8RScots att9GordH p211 CR France34

SCOTT,James Robinson T2Lt dow 23-3-18 13KRRC p151 CR France987

SCOTT,James Thompson TLt dow 5-10-17 9Leic p88 CR France40

SCOTT,James Wood 2Lt kia 28-6-15 8ScotRif p225 MR4

SCOTT,James Yuill TLt kia 3-9-16 10RB p180 MR21

SCOTT,John T2Lt dow 27-3-18 22DLI p161 MR27

SCOTT,John Crossfield 2Lt kia 16-10-16 5 att4Worc p109 MR21

SCOTT,John Davie.DSO.CaptALtCol kia 21-3-18 5 att2RIrReg p89 CR France212

SCOTT,John Ellison Lt kia 27-5-18 7DLI 50Div p239 MR18

SCOTT,John George Alec T2Lt dow 15-3-16 16LancsF p93 CR France43

SCOTT,John Gordon 2Lt kia 9-5-15 1BlkW p129 MR32

SCOTT,John Hastings Folliott 2Lt kia 9-4-17 3 att5.O&BLI p130 CR France581

SCOTT,John James.MC.TLtACapt kia 28-6-18 1RWKent p142 MR32

SCOTT,John Kemp T2Lt kia 14-7-16 1ScotF p95 CR France453

SCOTT,John Michael Corse Maj ded 29-3-17 1RScots p54 CR Greece1

SCOTT,John Millar T2Lt kia 18-8-16 11 att1BlkW p129 MR21

SCOTT,John Murray 2Lt kia 2-4-18 295RFA p35 CR France745

SCOTT,John Willoughby.DSO.MIDx3 LtCol kia 23-4-17 OxYeo Cmdg8SomLI p205 CR France924

SCOTT,Jack Voung Lt dow PoW 26-7-18 1RRofCav att10RWSurr p23 CR Germany3,25-7-18

SCOTT,Kenneth Robert.MC.Capt kia 2-11-19 IA 31Punjabis attAdminStaffPostalDept p282 CR Iraq8

SCOTT,Kenneth William Laing 2Lt kia 21-10-16 11Ches p96 CR France383,Lairg

SCOTT,Leonard T2Lt kia 24-3-18 1 att12Suff GarrBn p79 MR20,22-3-18

SCOTT,Leslie TLt kia 12-10-17 HouseholdBn p20 MR30

SCOTT,Lindsay Buchannan TMaj ded 14-11-18 RAOC p198 CR France85,Buchanan

SCOTT,Lionel Keith TLt ded 4-7-16 RE 225FC p48 MR19

SCOTT,Maurice Douglas Guest.MC.LtTCapt kld 17-3-18 3LNLancs &RFC p17&136,ded CR Derby145

SCOTT,Munro Briggs T2Lt kia 12-4-17 12RScots p54 MR20

SCOTT,Nigel Dennistoun 2Lt kld 19-4-16 RWSurr &RFC p3&56 CR Norf255

SCOTT,Noel Edmund.MID Lt dow 21-9-17 RE 422FC p210 CR Belgium18

SCOTT,Norman Sawers 2Lt kia 23-4-15 2KOSB p102 CR Belgium167

SCOTT,Phillip Camm 2Lt kia 8-10-18 7 att1YLI p143 CR France234,Philip

SCOTT,Ralph 2Lt kia 12-4-18 C256RFA p35 CR France1106

SCOTT,Ralph Quintus Lt kia 16-4-17 3ESurr att20RFus p113 CR France434

SCOTT,Reginald Eric Edward Lt dow 13-10-15 7Mddx p235 CR France525

SCOTT,Richard Thomas Folliott Lt kia 16-3-15 1EYorks p85 CR France1140,16-3-18

SCOTT,R.J.2Lt dow 8-5-18 GL &RAF p191

SCOTT,Robert Edward Leslie.MC&Bar.Lt kia 14-9-18 RGA 129HB p41 CR France245,13-9-18

SCOTT,Robert Michael TLt ded 25-12-18 GL attRE Sigs p191 CR Egypt1

SCOTT,Robert Walter Theodore Gordon T2Lt dow 15-8-16 7SfthH p165 CR Scot319

SCOTT,Roger Douglas CaptAMaj kia 13-10-15 2Glouc p107 CR France219

SCOTT,Ronald Burrell Ind 2Lt kia 9-9-16 1Lond p245 CR France402

SCOTT,Ronald Mayne T2Lt dow 20-9-16 13A&SH p173 CR France833

SCOTT,Samuel Geoffrey TCapt ded 6-1-18 RAMC att7DivTrn p197 CR Italy7

SCOTT,Samuel Jervois Capt 27-5-20 RAMC 108FA CR Ireland85

SCOTT,Samuel Lackland T2Lt kia 8-8-18 3Ches att11MGC Inf p96&185 CR France1170,11Ches att58MGC

SCOTT,Sidney Maurice Lt kia 15-9-16 1ColdGds p51 CR France374

SCOTT,Sidney Towers 2Lt dow 12-4-17 5RLancs p213 CR France102,Sydney

SCOTT,Stanley.MC.TLtAMaj kia 6-6-18 19MGC p185 CR France1693

SCOTT,Tampler Henry Capt kia 26-4-15 IA 87Punjabis att47Sikhs p282 CR Belgium167,Templer

SCOTT,Thomas.MC.2Lt dow 21-5-17 4ScotRif p104 CR France214,1Bn

SCOTT,Thomas 2Lt kia 27-5-18 3DLI p255 MR18

SCOTT,Thomas McCreary T2Lt kia 3-9-16 9 att2KOSB p102 CR France402

SCOTT,Thomas Rennie Capt kia 9-5-15 RLancs p59 MR29

SCOTT,Thomas Walter 2Lt kia 13-10-16 1Camb p245 MR21

SCOTT,Victor William.MC.Lt kia 16-3-18 13ESurr attRFC p17&113 CR France924

SCOTT,W.C.Lt 13-3-19 RASC CR Lond14

SCOTT,Walter Lt ded 23-10-15 RFA p208 MR4

SCOTT,Walter Alexander 2Lt kia 22-11-17 10RIrRif p170 MR17

SCOTT,Walter Elvin 2Lt kia 7-5-15 SL 1Wilts p201 CR Belgium111,6-5-15

SCOTT,Walter Falconer Capt kia 25-10-14 IA 59Rif p282 CR France348

SCOTT,William Capt ded 11-11-17 RAVC p268 CR Ireland5

SCOTT,William T2Lt dow 8-10-18 SWBord att13WelshReg p101 CR France375

SCOTT,William David T2Lt kia 3-8-17 26RFus p70 MR29

SCOTT,William Douglas Lt kia 22-8-17 4 O&BLI p231 MR30

SCOTT,William Emiley Oscar Lt kia 29-9-16 9DLI p239 MR21

SCOTT,William Francis T2Lt kia 1-7-16 8SomLI p80 CR France267

SCOTT,William Henry TLt ded 20-11-17 LabCps p189 CR Italy57,RE

SCOTT,William James De Vere 2Lt kia 29-5-15 8Manch p237 MR4

SCOTT,William Leslie Lt kia 17-6-15 5GordH p242 MR22,16-6-15

SCOTT,William McDougall Woodward TLt ded 2-9-18 RASC p193 CR Italy16,2Lt

SCOTT,William Peach Lt dow 9-11-17 1/5HLI p240 CR Palestine8

SCOTT-DEAKIN,Reginald Lt kia 31-7-17 A74RFA p35 CR Belgium12

SCOTT-GATTY,Charles Comyn Scott Maj ded 24-7-16 1Herts p271 CR Herts116

SCOTT-HOGG,James ded 12-8-17 RE p271

SCOTT-HOLMES,B.T2Lt kld 24-10-16 KRRC attMGC p185 CR Somerset185

SCOTT-HOLMES,Henry Favil T2Lt kia 1-7-16 RE 208FC p48 MR21

SCOTT-MacKIRDY,Charles David 22-3-18 11Huss MR27

SCOTT-MILLER,Edward Lt kia 14-5-18 3RLancs p59 CR France106,1/4Bn

SCOTT-MILLER,Walter Dudley 2Lt kld 22-6-17 RFus attRFC p13&70

SCOTT-MONCRIEFF,William BrigGen kia 28-6-15 Staff 1/7ScotRif Commdg156Bde p1 CR Gallipoli6

SCOTT-PILLOW,H.M 2Lt 8-8-17 Mddx att7RFC CR Belgium18

SCOTT-SMITH,Eric Henry 2Lt ded 29-10-15 RE 14FortressCoy p48 CR Greece11

SCOTT-STEVENSON,John Lt dow 9-10-18 RE 90FC Ex 8RScots CR Belgium38

SCOUGAL,Alec Graham.MC.MajALtCol kia 18-9-18 17RScots p54 CR Belgium3

SCOUGAL,Alan Muir T2Lt dow 7-10-15 3Worc p109 CR Belgium11

SCOUGAL,Francis William.MC.TMaj kia 19-9-18 11ScotRif p104 CR Greece5

SCOUGALL,Douglas Muir 2Lt kia 4-5-17 4 att1/5Lond p246 CR France537

SCOVELL,Reginald Herbert Capt kia 16-8-15 RE 65FC p48 MR4

SCOWEN,Charles Henry T2Lt ded 25-9-17 TankCps p188 p266 CR Hamps13

SCRACE,John T.Lt ded 24-8-18 5EKent att21TrngDepotStn RAF p213&258,kia CR Kent44,kld

SCRACE,Reginald George Lt kia 19-7-16 2/4Glouc p225 MR21

SCRASE-DICKINS,Spencer William.CB.MajGen 23-10-19 Staff CR Sussex13

SCRATTON,Geoffrey Howell.MC.TLt kia 1-8-17 4/5A&SH p173 MR29

SCRIMGEOUR,Michael TLt kia 30-7-15 8RB p180 MR29

SCRIVEN,Arthur Cecil.MC.TLt kia 7-11-16 10Suff att47MGC p185 CR Belgium17,Capt 6-11-16

SCRIVEN,John Barclay LtCol kia 5-9-15 21Lancers p23 MR43

SCRIVENER,Alwyne Twyford.MID Capt ded PoW 5-7-17 5NStaffs p237 MR19

SCRIVENER,Arthur William.MC.Capt kia 2-11-17 1/10Lond p248 CR Palestine8

SCRIVENER,John Sydney 2Lt kia 2-12-17 8LancsF p222 MR30

SCRIVENS,Albert Victor Capt ded 11-1-19 RDC p253 CR Essex81 Ex MddxR

SCROGGIE,Vallentine.MC.T2Lt kia 4-11-18 1 att1/5Glouc p107 CR France933

SCROGGIE,William Robertson 2Lt kia 2-12-17 LNLancs att1/5SLancs p136 MR17,30-11-17

SCRUBY,William Samuel T2Lt kia 29-6-16 12Mddx p148 MR21

SCRUTTON,Hugh Urquhart TCapt dow PoW 10-9-16 2NumbF p63 MR37

SCUDAMORE,George Prince Mountford 2Lt kia 8-5-15 2RLancs A'Coy p59 MR29

SCUDAMORE,John 2Lt kia 25-9-15 2KRRC p151 CR France219

SCUDAMORE,John Venables Lt kia 25-4-15 2RFus p70 MR4

SCUDAMORE,Leonard George Lt ded 17-4-17 RAMC p197 p267 CR Wilts167

SCUDAMORE,Robert Capel.MC.TCapt kia 26-2-18 8RFus attRFC p17 CR France1678

SCULTHORPE,William Vaughan 2Lt kia 8-6-17 1/22Lond p251 CR Belgium120

SCURFIELD,Bryan.MC.Lt ded 30-9-18 4 att2ESurr p113 CR Greece9

SEABROOK,Harry Spencer 2Lt kia 12-7-16 16N&D p135 MR19

SEABROOK,James Herbert Lt kia 10-9-14 SL IntelCps 5SigTrp RE att5CavBde p201 CR France1128,2Lt

SEABROOKE,Alexander Stanger TCapt ded 1-7-16 RAMC att2BGH Basra p197 CR Iraq5

SEABURY,Edgar Raymond 2Lt kia 21-9-17 13Lond p249 MR29

SEAFIELD,James.Earl.Capt dow 12-11-15 3 att5CamH p168 CR Belgium11

SEAGER,William Henry T2Lt kia 7-2-16 10SWBord p101 CR France631

SEAGO,George William Edward TLt dow 6-10-18 O&BLI att1/5Glouc p130 CR France194

SEAGRAVE,P.2Lt kia 1-11-18 7Lpool &RAF p215

SEAHOLME,Max Knud T2Lt kia 30-3-18 7RFC p17 CR Belgium18

SEAL,George Hatcher.MC.Lt dow 29-10-18 15Hamps p204 CR Belgium158

SEALE,Theophilus T2Lt kia 22-8-16 7 att2RMunstF p176 CR France453

SEALE,William Henry.MC.2Lt dow 14-3-18 2 O&BLI att5TMB p130&259 CR France398

SEALY,Charles Frederic Noel Prince 2Lt kia 24-5-15 7RFus p70 MR29

SEALY,Edward Molesworth Walpole Capt ded 25-12-15 RE p48 CR Devon39

SEALY-KING,Charles Lt 9-5-15 2RMunstF MR22

SEAMAN,Charles William Frederick T2Lt kia 6-11-18 7Wilts p153 CR France929

SEAMAN,Edwin Charles.CB.CMG.10-5-19 RE CR Lond8

SEAMAN,Leonard James Cameron Lt kia 30-8-18 1RWar p66 CR France421

SEAMANS,Arthur Edward Lt dow 3-12-17 RGA p209 CR Belgium72

SEAR,Eric John Cecil 2Lt kia 8-9-16 2WelshR p127 MR21

SEARGINSON,John Capt kia 10-11-16 4Yorks p220 CR France385

SEARIGHT,G.G.Lt 12-11-20 4RDubFus attRE IWT CR Iraq6

SEARLE,Alec T2Lt kia 23-4-17 RE 202FC p48 MR20

SEARLE,Archibald Henry 2Lt 13-7-17 1AustFC MR34

SEARLE,Arthur Henry Lt ded 18-6-16 9Manch p271 CR Wilts186,11Lond

SEARLE,B.W 2Lt ded 3-10-15 10SStaffs p123

SEARLE,John Arthur T2Lt dow 4-5-17 1N&D p135 CR France122

SEARLE,Percy 2Lt ded 21-2-19 RASC p193 CR France65

SEARLE,Thomas George.MC.MSM.2Lt kia 20-9-17 1/2Beds p86 MR30

SEARLE,Valentine Lang Stuart 2Lt dow 22-6-16 D76RFA p35 CR Belgium11

SEARS,Joseph Patrick T2Lt kia 20-8-18 2 O&BLI p130 CR France214

SEARSON,Harold William 2Lt dow 17-6-17 12Ess att3KRRC p132 CR Greece9

SEATER,George Harold Lt kia 14-9-20 IA 2Rajputs att8 p282 MR38

SEATER,Percival John 2Lt kia 3-5-17 3 att8ESurr p113 MR20

SEATER,Thomas Rendall T2Lt kld 21-1-18 RFC p17 CR Wilts116

SEATH,Douglas Ambrose TLt kia 24-4-17 ScotRif p104 MR20,2 att6BordR

SEATON,Alexander Adam Capt dow 4-9-15 1Camb p244 CR France922

SEATTER,George T2Lt kia 9-9-18 15DLI p161 MR16

SEAVER,Charles TCapt dow 3-10-16 8RInniskF p105 CR France145

SEAVERNS,Joel Harrison Lt dow 10-5-15 1Lond p245 CR France345

SEBAG-MONTEFIORE,Robert Montefiore Capt dow 19-11-15 EKentYeo CR Egypt5, see SEGBAG-MONTEFIORE below

SEBASTIAN,Skinner Raymond.MC.MIDx2 LtTLtCol dow 27-3-18 3Hamps Cmdg5 O&BLI p121 CR France145

SECKER,Charles William TLt dow 4-11-18 RE 3SpCo p48 CR France658,3-11-18

SECKER,John Devereux 2Lt ded 12-12-16 3/4Ess att1Camb p232 CR Essex146,dow 13-12-16 Ex 5Lond

SECKHAM, Gerald Adair Lt kia 6-1-15 2ELancs p111 CR France924

SECKINGTON,Frank Lt kia 14-7-16 1SStaffs p123 MR21

SECRETAN,Reginald Herbert 2Lt kld 31-7-17 Herts p252 MR29

SECRETT,Albert George 2Lt kia 28-4-17 Mddx att17Bn p148 MR20

SEDDEN,Henry T2Lt kia 8-8-18 6TankCps p188 CR France652,SEDDON

SEDDON,Edward Macmahon.DSO.LtCol kia 24-6-17 RGA 45HAG p41 CR Belgium17

SEDDON,Frank Augustus 2Lt kia 30-11-17 Lpool att1/8Bn p72 MR17,Augustine 20-11-17

SEDDON,Horace 2Lt kia 25-8-18 5 att2/4LancF p221 CR France617

SEDDON,Max Hugo TLt dow 4-11-18 RASC MT p193 CR France206

SEDGLEY,Henry Frederick Lt kia 22-9-18 9Lond p248 CR France665

SEDGLEY,Lionel Edwin 2Lt ded 9-11-18 9Manch p271 CR Surrey156

SEDGWICK,Arthur Edward Lt kia 10-9-16 5Lond p246 CR France66,dow

SEDGWICK,Francis Balfour Capt kld 18-10-18 13Suff &RAF p263

SEDGWICK,Joseph T2Lt kia 9-10-17 2/4ELancs p111 MR30

SEE,Sydney Matthews 2Lt kia 10-10-16 A71 RH&FA p35 CR France453

SEEAR,Christopher Charles Capt ded 30-10-19 SL p268 CR Lond14

SEED,Harper T2Lt kia 20-9-17 17N&D p135 CR Belgium20,Lt

SEED,James Parrott T2Lt kia 17-6-18 2Hamps p121 CR France193

SEEDS,William Albert T2Lt kia 6/7-7-17 10RWSurr p56 CR Belgium111,6/7-6-17

SEEL,Horace Arthur Lt kia 7-12-15 7Ches p223 MR4

SEELY,Charles Grant Capt kia 19-4-17 8Hamps p229 CR Palestine8

SEELY,Frank Reginald 2Lt dow 13-4-17 1Hamps p121 CR France53

SEERS,Wilfrid.MID TMaj kia 20-9-17 15Hamps p121 MR30

SEFTON,Percy T2Lt kia 22-8-18 13ELancs p111 MR32

SEGAL,Marcus T2Lt kia 19-6-17 13Lpool p72 CR France1182

SEGBAG-MONTEFIORE,Robert-Montefiore Capt dow 19-11-15 REKentYeo p204

SEGGIE,Alexander 2Lt kia 1-7-16 9RIrrF B'Coy p171 CR France339

SEGNITZ,Hermann Ferdinand 2Lt kld 25-9-15 19Lond p251 CR France219

SEGRAVE,P.2Lt 1-11-18 7Lpool &RAF CR France937

SEGRAVE,William Henry TLt kld 12-2-17 GL &RFC p13

SEGUIN,Ubalde Hornidas 2Lt kia 6-4-17 16RFC p13 CR France522,Hormisdas

SELBIE,Colin Mackenzie T2Lt kia 14-7-16 11 att9ScotRif p104 MR21

SELBY,Beauchamp Henry Capt kia 20-9-14 1NumbF p63 MR15

SELBY,Gerrard Prideaux Capt kia 26-9-16 RAMC att9LancsF p197 CR France393,Gerard

SELBY,Herbert Richard.MSM.MID Lt 12-4-19 IOD MR65

SELBY,Millin 2Lt dow 29-9-15 3EKent p58 CR France257

SELBY,Millin John TLt kia 7-7-16 2Nhampt p138 MR21

SELBY,William.DSO.LtCol ded 8-9-16 IA IMS p282

SELBY-LOWNDES,Meyrick Edward Lt ded 27-10-18 3 att2SforthH p165 CR Surrey1

SELBY-LOWNDES,Richard Cecil Williams TLt ded 11-7-18 RASC p193 CR Bucks37

SELBY-SMITH,Miles Bury Capt kia 15-3-15 4RB p180 CR Belgium28,SMYTH

SELCH,Frederick William T2Lt kia 4-11-18 9Yorks att7EYorks p91

SELFE,Edgar Donald TCapt kia 7-8-18 9Norf p74 CR Belgium3

SELFE,Hugh Donald TCapt kia 9-7-17 8NStaffs p157 CR Belgium77,Ronald

SELLAR,James Arthur T2Lt kia 3-4-17 6 O&BLI A'Coy p130 CR France568

SELLAR,John Lt kia 9-4-18 6SforthH p241 MR19

SELLAR,John Mill TLt kia 25-9-15 7KOSB p102 MR19

SELLARS,Eric Francis.MC.Capt kia 18-9-18 12Ches p255 MR37

SELLARS,Herbert Whiteley.MC.Lt 15-5-18 11RAF MR20

SELLERS,John Harrison 2Lt kia 24-5-15 3 att2NumbF p63 MR29

SELLERS,Philip 2Lt kld 23-3-17 Worc attRFC p13&109,ded CR Wilts194

SELLERS,Thomas T2Lt kia 22-4-17 RE 173TC p48 CR France178

SELLERS,Vernon Guy Lt ded 27-10-18 RFA X48TMB p208 CR Italy7

SELLMAN,Edgar Nevill Newmark 2Lt kia 4-4-18 3Glouc att5 O&BLI p107 CR France1170,SELMAN Newmark

SELLON,Bruce Heckford 2Lt dow 16-8-17 11Lond attLondRB p248 Belgium8

SELLON,Marmaduke Heckford 2Lt kia 15-6-18 RGA att1/1War HB p41 CR Italy4

SELLS,Archibald Jenner TLt kia 26-10-16 2 att3RWSurr p56 CR Belgium54

SELLS,C.P.MC.Capt ded 4-7-19 RAMC attRAF p254 CR Dorset93

SELLWOOD John Dorey 2Lt kia 26-3-18 RE 2FC p48 MR20

SELOUS,Frederick Courteney.DSO.TCapt kia 4-1-17 25RFus p70 CR EAfrica23

SELOUS,Frederick Hatherley Bruce.MC.Capt kia 4-1-18 RWSurr &RFC p17&56 MR20

SELOUS-JONES,Jeffrey Fryer T2Lt dow 26-8-16 RE p48

SELWYN,A.H.2Lt ded 25-1-15 RASC p193 CR Lond4,Lt

SELWYN,Arthur Penrose Lt FlyingAcc 18-5-16 IA 11Lancers attRFC p282 CR Hamps4

SELWYN,Christopher Wakefield 2Lt dow 17-5-15 5Leic p220 CR France284

SELWYN,Colin Redgrave 2Lt kia 22-8-17 6SomLI p80 Cr Belgium112

SELWYN,George Vincent Carus Lt dow 25-10-18 106RFA p35 CR France146

SEMPLE,Henry Spencer.MC.LtAMaj kia 5-9-17 RE 203FC p48 CR France364

SEMPLE,Robert Edward Watson.MC.Capt dow 5-11-18 RFA attGdsDivTMB p35 CR France146

SEMPLE,Robert Woodburn Barnard.MC.T2Lt kia 9-4-17 7CamH p168 CR France1182

SEMPLE,William David 2Lt kia 29-6-16 13KRRC p151 CR France283

SENESCHALL,George Rhodely 2Lt ded 16-11-18 5N&D p256 CR Derby120

SENHOUSE,Oscar William Pocklington 2Lt kia 19-6-15 CldGds p51

SENIOR,Albert Morton Capt dow 22-4-16 IA 91Punjabis att92 p282 MR38

SENIOR,Edwin Capt ded 23-6-20 SL &RE IWT CR Iraq6

SENIOR,George Fairburn 2Lt kia 17-11-17 4 att1/7WYorks p82 CR Belgium308

SENIOR,Harold Frank.MC.TCaptAMaj dow 13-4-18 A75RFA p35 CR France40

SENIOR,Herbert Godbert Lt kia 28-5-19 8Manch p237 MR18

SENIOR,Joseph TLt dow 9-5-17 GL &45RFC p13 CR France285 Ex 11WYorks

SENIOR,Robert Mackenzie 2Lt kia 27-3-18 4 att8Norf p216 MR27

SENIOR,Thomas Hugh Sandford TLt kia 11-6-16 2Worc p109 CR France114

SENIOR,Walter Talbot 2Lt kia 3-9-16 6WYorks p218 CR France215

SENSICALL,George Edwin T2Lt kia 9-10-17 6Y&L p159 MR30

SENTER,John Watt TLt dow 9-6-18 RAMC att53FA p197

SEPPINGS-WRIGHT,Frank Thomas 2Lt BombAcc 21-7-15 IARO 113Inf att6Jats p282 CR France345

SERGIADES,John Nicholas Lt kia 30-7-16 19Lpool p72 MR21

SERGINSON,Harold.MC.T2LtACapt kia 27-2-18 16NumbF att96TMB p63 CR Belgium106

SERJEANT,Cyril Lawson TLt dow 21-6-16 1Nhampt p138 CR France149

SERNBERG,Allan TCapt kia 2-7-16 9Ches p96 MR21

SERVANTE,Alfred William T2Lt kia 18-9-18 7RWSurr p56 MR16

SERVICE,Alexander Cumming Lt kia 29-5-18 6A&SH att136MGC Inf p187&243 CR Palestine9

SERVICE,George Brown T2Lt kia 30-3-18 16MGC Inf p185 CR France1170

SESSIONS,F.H.N.Lt 5-6-18 RDubF &RAF CR Ireland24

SESSIONS,John Herford Vivian TLt dow 28-9-18 WelshR att13Bn p127 CR France278

SETCHELL,Alfred Knight 2Lt mbk 21-3-18 9Norf p256 MR20

SETON,Bruce Eglington 2Lt kia 13-1-16 IARO att53Sikhs p282 MR38,15-1-16

SETON-BROWNE,Montague William.MID Lt kia 24-11-14 2Leic p88 CR France727

SETTLE,Mellard Capt ded PoW 23-12-18 1/5NStaffs p237 CR Ches1

SETTLE,Reginald Henry Napier.DSO.MC.MIDx4 TLtCol kia 24-3-18 19Huss att21MGC p23&185 MR27

SETTLE,Reginald William T2Lt kia 23-7-16 GL attRFC p3&191 CR France167

SETTRINGTON,Charles Henry.Lord.Lt dow 24-8-19 IrGds attRFus p255 MR70 &CR Europe179

SEUTER,John Watt Lt 9-6-18 RAMC CR France4

SEVERNE,Henry Francis.MID 2Lt kld 10-5-15 1/6N&D p233 CR Belgium17

SEVERS,Alfred George 2Lt kia 28-3-17 GL &25RFC p13 MR20

SEVIN,Clifford Newton 2Lt dow 25-3-18 15Hamps p121 MR20

SEWARD,Robert Francis T2Lt kia 25-10-16 Bord att2ELancs p118 MR21

SEWARD,Stanley Richard LtACapt kia 30-10-17 7RFus att7RScotF p70 MR30

SEWART,Gerald Evelyn Spuldlam T2Lt kia 8-5-16 10DLI p161 CR France420

SEWELL,Cecil Harold.VC.Lt kia 29-8-18 RWKent att3TankCps p142&188 CR France1484

SEWELL,Douglas Clifford Campbell Lt dow 10-9-14 3RWKent p142 CR Belgium242

SEWELL,Edward John 2Lt dow 10-4-18 RGA 217SB p41 CR France88

SEWELL,Francis Brooke Lt kia 15-5-18 RGA 126HB p41 CR France343

SEWELL,Geoffrey Edward 2Lt dow 2-9-17 1EKent p58 CR France179

SEWELL,Harry Kemp Lt ded 20-8-17 21RFA p35 CR Lond28 Ex WKentYeo

SEWELL,Henry Edward Maj ded 4-6-18 RGA 524SB p262 CR France268

SEWELL.Herbert Victor T2Lt kia 13-11-16 186RFA p35 MR21

SEWELL,Norman Oscar Lt kld 9-5-15 1/13Lond p249 MR32

SEWELL,Sidney Davis Maj kia 18-2-15 RE 3FC p209 CR Belgium58,Davies

SEWELL,William Allan Lt kia 12-11-17 4BordR attRFC p19&228 MR20

SEWELL,William Tait TCapt kia 1-7-16 11RInniskF p105 France383,Maj

SEWILL,Arnold Waterlow T2Lt kia 23-7-16 12WYorks p82 CR France630

SEYMOUR,Bertram T2Lt kia 31-7-17 MGC p185 MR29

SEYMOUR,Charles T2Lt kia 13-4-18 61MGC Inf p185 CR France248

SEYMOUR,Charles Benjamin 2Lt 6-9-18 11RAF MR20

SEYMOUR,Constance Emily Mary SpProb ded 12-2-17 QAIMNS CR Hamps1

SEYMOUR,Francis TLt kia 30-7-15 7KRRC p151 MR29

SEYMOUR,Greville Crawford 2Lt kia 15-4-17 3 att1Dors p124 CR France1701

SEYMOUR,Harcourt T2Lt dow 9-11-18 4KRRC p151 CR France658

SEYMOUR,Lewis Thievry Lt kia 13-8-16 2Y&L p159 CR France1012,Thierry

SEYMOUR,William Matthew 2Lt kia 16-8-17 10RIrFus p171 MR30

SEYMOUR-ISAACS,Maurice T2Lt kia 26-10-17 2Bord p118 MR30

SEYMOUR-JONES,R.Arnold Lt dow 27-3-15 4SLancs CR Belgium28

SEYMOUR-URE,William Bruce T2Lt kia 4/10-10-16 32RFus p70 MR21

SEYS,Roger Cecil.DSO.OBE.Maj 10-4-21 RGA CR Lancs366

SHACKELL,Frank Charles Lt kia 23-5-17 ACycC attRFC p19&244 CR France381

SHACKLE,Frank Guy.MC.LtACapt kia 21-11-17 2Mddx p148 CR Belgium92

SHACKLEFORD,Alfred Edgar John 2Lt kia 9-5-15 1SfthH p165 CR France721

SHACKLES,Kenneth George 2Lt dow 11-5-17 4EYorks p219 CR France214

SHACKLES,Ronald Guy.MC.2Lt kia 19-9-18 KSLI att10Bn p145 MR16

SHACKLETON,Harold.MM.MID TLt kia 26-8-18 1 att9TankCps p188 CR France155

SHACKLETON James Ernest T2Lt kia 21-3-18 7Leic p88 CR France407

SHACKLETON James Sutcliffe Lt kia 16-4-17 2/4WRid p227 CR France568

SHACKLETON,Thomas Smith Lt kia 5-5-17 2/6WRid p227 CR France690

SHACKLETON,William Launcelot Collier TLt dow 24-4-17 26NumbF p63 CR France546

SHACKLOCK,George Miller 2Lt kia 12-3-15 1N&D p135 MR22

SHADDICK,Cecil George T2Lt kia 7-8-16 1Dors p124 CR France114

SHAFTO,Arthur Duncombe,DSO.Capt 26-8-14 2RScots D'Coy CR France658

SHAFTO,John Stanley Horsfall T2Lt kia 12-8-16 EKent p58 CR france164

SHAFTO,Thomas Duncombe Capt kia 2-5-15 RFus p70 CR Gallipoli2

SHAIL,William Archibald 2Lt kia 16-8-17 1Lond p245 MR29

SHAIRP,Norman.MC.Capt ded 13-10-18 AyrYeo p203 CR Syria2

SHAKERLEY,Arthur Cecil 2Lt kia 22-4-17 D64RFA p35 CR France644

SHAKERLEY,Eric Piers.MID Capt kia 10-3-15 6 att1KRRC p151 MR22

SHAKERLEY,Geoffrey Charles.DSO.MajTLtCol kia 15-5-15 1KRRC p152 CR France525

SHAKESPEAR,Everard Richard T2Lt kia 23-8-18 2SStaffs p123 CR France927

SHAKESPEAR,George Frederick Cortlandt.DSO.MC.Maj ded 24-2-19 IA 88Inf p282 CR Mddx26

SHAKESPEAR,William Henry Irvine.CIE.Capt kia 24-1-15 17IndCav PolitOff p282 MR53

SHAKLE,Hugh Philip Capt kia 21-11-17 4GordH p241

SHAND,Alexander 2Lt dow 9-5-15 1BlkW p129 MR22

SHAND,Frederick Gordon 2Lt dow 12-10-18 C311RFA p209 CR France113

SHAND,John James Fraser 2Lt kia 6-8-17 RGA 185HB p41 CR Greece6

SHAND,Wilfred 2Lt ded 11-2-19 4Lond p271 CR Kent83,Wilfrid

SHAND,William Gadrow TCapt dow 25-7-16 RAMC att20LancF p197 CR France23,Garrow

SHAND,William Kenwick Willoughby Lt ded 13-10-19 2Norf p263 CR France1571

SHAND-KYDD,William 2Lt kia 16-5-17 51RFA p35 CR France1188

SHANDLEY,Robert Newlyn 2Lt kia 22-8-18 3 att9Ess p132 CR France247

SHANKLAND,Llewelyn Ap Tomas TLt dow 25-11-17 19RWFus p99 CR France398,Aptomos

SHANKS,Daniel Albert 2Lt 21-9-18 108RAF MR20

SHANKS,Edward Ferrier T2Lt kia 21-10-16 5ConnRgrs attInniskF p172 MR21

SHANKS,John Arthur Gordon.MC.MID Capt kia 4-10-17 6A&SH attMGC p187&243 CR Belgium165,3-10-17

SHANKSTER,George TLt kia 9-10-16 6Nhampt p138 MR21

SHANKSTER,Stanley 2Lt kia 3-7-16 7Lincs p75 MR21

SHANLEY,Andrew 2Lt kia 25-9-16 MGC 64Coy p185 MR21

SHANN,Alan Webster 2Lt kia 27-11-17 2/8WYorks p219 MR17

SHANN,Albert 2Lt kia 8-5-18 2Yorks p91 MR30

SHANN,John Webster TLt kia 1-7-16 10WYorks p82 CR France373

SHANN,Kenneth 2Lt kia 8-5-15 3 att2NumbF p63 MR29

SHANN,Reginald Arthur Lt kia 21-3-18 3 att4ELancs p111 MR27

SHANNON,Cyril Richmond Capt kia 4-10-15 RE 101FC p48 MR19

SHANNON,George Strangman.MC.MID 2Lt kia 5-5-15 Dors p124 CR Belgium132

SHANNON,Jeremiah 2Lt kia 1-8-18 7/8KOSB p102 CR France864

SHANNON,John James TCapt kia 29-11-17 RAMC att1/1LincsYeo p197 CR Palestine9

SHANNON,John Paterson 2Lt ded 4-3-19 12RB p266 CR Scot596 Ex 5KOSB

SHANNON,Percy Roy TLt dow 3-11-18 RAMC att11FA p197 CR France613

SHANNON,Richard Bernard.Earl of.2Lt kia 13-4-17 4RFus p70 MR20

SHANNON,Robert Mortimer.MC.2Lt dow 29-4-18 50RFA p35 CR Belgium11

SHAPLAND,Adam Francis Terrell TLt kia 20-9-17 6Wilts p153 MR30

SHAPLAND,Herbert George 2Lt dow 2-3-18 36RFA p35 CR France398

SHAPLEY,Alfred Edward TLt kia 1-7-16 23NumbF p63 MR21

SHAPTER,Lewis Henry Capt kia 31-1-15 3Suff attBeds p79 CR France276

SHARER,George Short T2Lt kia 26-9-15 7RScotF p95 MR19

SHARKEY,Thomas 2Lt kia 26-3-18 att1/6DLI p161 MR27

SHARLAND,Frederick James 2Lt kia 24-10-17 23RFC p13 MR20

SHARMAN,Arthur Patrick 2Lt kia 20-9-17 5Lond p246 MR29

SHARP,A.G.TMaj kia 10-8-15 9RWar p66 MR4

SHARP,Albert George 2Lt dow 1-9-18 4BordR p228 CR France805

SHARP,Andrew T2Lt kia 27-9-15 9BlkW p129 MR19,25-9-15

SHARP,Arthur Augustus Charles T2Lt kia 22-3-18 2TankCps p188 MR27

SHARP,Arthur Granville.MC.Lt kia 23-8-18 D72RFA attGdsDivArtly p35 CR France924

SHARP,Beresford 2Lt kia 9-4-18 7Lpool p215 MR19

SHARP,Cecil Jervis Capt kia 9-1-20 IA 13Rajputs att4/39GarhwalRif p282 MR43

SHARP,Charles Gordon 2Lt dow 5-2-16 4NumbF p213 CR Belgium4

SHARP,Christopher Harold 2Lt ded 26-9-18 3Norf att99RAF p74 CR France1667

SHARP,Cyril Robert TCapt kia 14-7-16 3 att12WYorks p82 MR21

SHARP,Eric.MID Lt ded 22-5-17 EKent att2KAR p202&212 CR EAfrica15 &CRTanzania1

SHARP,Fred 2Lt kia 3-8-18 10Mddx p236 CR France522

SHARP,Frederick Arthur Hamilton Lt kia 30-10-18 51/39RFA attStaff p35 CR France1270

SHARP,Frederick Leonard.CMG.LtCol kia 13-8-16 39RFA p35 CR France397

SHARP,George T2Lt ded 29-10-18 GL attIntelCps p191 CR France13

SHARP,George Benjamin 2Lt kia 21-3-18 9ESurr p113 MR27

SHARP,Humphrey TLt kia 5-10-15 11RFus D'Coy p70 CR France637

SHARP,James Calrow 2Lt kia 12-10-16 2LancF p93 MR21

SHARP,John Stanley TMaj kia 17-3-17 5RBerks p140 CR France1182

SHARP,Leon Owen T2Lt kia 1-7-16 2Lincs p75 CR France293

SHARP,Lewis Frederick T2Lt kia 1-7-16 10YLI p143 MR21

SHARP,Matthew.MC.2Lt dow 11-2-18 2/7Lond p247 CR France64

SHARP,Reginald Archibald 2Lt kia 2-9-16 RGA 47SB p209 CR France630

SHARP,Stanley Ernest 2Lt ded 20-10-18 SomLI p80 MR61

SHARP,Stephen Oswald TLt kia 1-7-16 13Y&L A'Coy p159 CR France156

SHARP,William Dalton Colombo 2Lt kia 9-10-17 4Norf p216 MR30

SHARPE,Anthony Herbert LtACapt kia 25-9-17 3 att4Lpool p72 MR21

SHARPE,Arthur Noel Lt kia 3-9-16 5WRid p227 CR France383

SHARPE,Charles Lancelot Arden 2Lt kia 26-4-15 3Mddx p148 CR Belgium151

SHARPE,Douglas Staveley 2Lt kia 7-7-16 3 att1Wilts p153 CR France744

SHARPE,Gerald Norman 2Lt kia 31-7-16 1Y&L p230 CR France216

SHARPE,Henry Norman 2Lt kld 26-1-17 3Leic &RFC p13&88 CR Essex7

SHARPE,John Sutton 2Lt kia 8-8-16 1/8Lpool p216 MR21

SHARPE,Leonard Frederick Robert Lt ded 27-7-18 3Lincs p263 CR Ireland14 &CR Eire77

SHARPE,Maurice 2Lt kia 28-10-16 GL &RFC p3&191 MR20

SHARPE,Robert.MC.T2Lt dow 12-9-18 10 att2Leinst p175&75,Lincs CR France145,Lincs

SHARPE,Stanley Arthur TLtACapt kia 23-11-17 12SWBord p101 MR17

SHARPE,Sydney William T2Lt dow 25-3-18 25RFus p70 CR France103,26Bn

SHARPE,Thomas William.DCM.T2Lt ded 5-7-18 LabCps p189&258 CR Yorks548

SHARPIN,Frank Lloyd T2Lt dow 14-10-16 9 att8Beds p86 CR France105

SHARPLES,Evelyn Horace Guy TCapt kld 19-1-18 RFC p17 CR Yorks138

SHARPLES,George Woods T2LtALt kia 7-6-17 19Lpool p72 CR Belgium127

SHARPLES,Norman.MID TLt kia 20-9-17 7RFC p13 CR Belgium18

SHARPLES,Norman Capt&Adj kia 21-3-18 Manch att16Bn p156 MR27

SHARPLES,Philip Edmund TLt kia 7-6-17 9Y&L p159 CR Belgium127

SHARPLEY,Henry Lt dow 24-3-18 RFA A66TMB p208 CR France770

SHARPS,Herbert Charles Valentine T2Lt kia 22-4-18 RB att1Bn p180 CR France411

SHARPS,Robert T2Lt kia 18-4-18 61MGC p185 CR France202

SHARRATT,Robert Weetman TLt kia 10-3-16 16LancF p93 CR France702

SHATTOCK,Harry Edward TLtACapt dow 7-8-17 7RWKent p142 CR Belgium11

SHATTOCK,Montague Mancha Capt kia 8-1-15 16Lond p249 CR France1140

SHAVE,Leslie Harrie T2Lt kia 12-4-17 6Dors p124 CR France531

SHAW,Albert T2Lt kia 12-10-16 9Norf p74 MR21

SHAW,Albert Thomas T2Lt dow 13-6-18 1/7RWar p66 CR Italy11,Lt 18-6-18

SHAW,Alexander Jack 2Lt kia 12-10-16 4 att10A&SH p173 MR21

SHAW,Alexander James Mackintosh TCapt kia 9-7-16 1KOSB p102 CR France339

SHAW,Alexander Morton Capt kia 10-4-18 Yorks p255 MR32

SHAW,Alfred T2Lt kia 1-10-17 Leic att8Bn p88 MR30

SHAW,Alfred 2Lt dow 8-8-19 ACycCps p255 CR Lincs179,Lt

SHAW,Alfred John 2Lt drd 27-5-18 NottsYeo p205 MR41

SHAW,Arthur Gilbey TLt kia 24-12-15 10N&D p135 CR Belgium72

SHAW,Arthur James 2Lt kld 1-2-18 RFC p17 CR Surrey95

SHAW,Bernard Henry Gilbert Lt kia 18-12-14 2WYorks p83 MR22

SHAW,Bernard Hudson T2Lt kia 22-1-17 13Ches p96 CR Belgium54

SHAW,Bernard Lynton Lt kia 23-4-17 4RWFus att2SWBord p223 MR20

SHAW,Charles Athelstan Capt dow 9-1-16 1KEdwardsHorse p24 CR France80

SHAW,Charles Conway.MC.TLt kia 31-8-18 39MGC Inf p185 CR France421

SHAW,Charles Henry 2Lt dow 1-8-17 3Beds p86 MR29

SHAW,Charles Richard 2Lt kia 11-4-18 86WRid p227

SHAW,Charles Salisbury T2Lt dow 30-9-18 1/7Lpool p72 CR France106

SHAW,Clarence Gordon Lt kia 1-7-16 1Lincs p75 MR21

SHAW,Cuthbert Frank 2Lt kia 30-10-14 att2RSuss B'Coy p120 MR29

SHAW,Cyril Trevor Capt kia 23-11-15 IA 122Inf att120 p282 MR38,22-11-15 Rajputs

SHAW,David Perston Maj kia 15/16-6-15 6ScotRif p224 MR22

SHAW,Douglas Sinclair.MIDx2 Lt ded 7-8-17 IARO att61Pnrs p282 CR EAfrica38 &CR Tanzania1

SHAW,Dugald 2Lt dow 27-7-18 1/5SfthH p241 CR France1697

SHAW,Edward Alfred TCapt kia 7-10-16 6 O&BLI p130 MR21

SHAW,Edward Lockhart T2Lt kia 5-8-16 9RWSurr p56 CR France251

SHAW,Edward Wingfield.DSO.Capt dow 7-12-16 1Mddx p148 CR France145

SHAW,Ernest Vernon James 2Lt ded 10-11-18 IARO att2/56Rif p282 MR65

SHAW,Evelyn Fidgeon 24-8-18 FANYC CR France1415

SHAW,Eyre Massey Lt dow 30-7-16 5 att11Mddx p148 CR France44

SHAW,Francis Joseph Marshall 2Lt kia 5-7-16 1N&D p135 MR21

SHAW,Frank Aubrey.MC.Lt kia 16-7-18 6LancF &98RAF p271 MR20

SHAW,George T2Lt kia 12-4-18 2Lincs p75 CR Belgium74

SHAW,George Herbert.VD.LtCol kia 24-4-15 4EYorks p219 MR29,Hubert

SHAW,Gerald Alan Santor T2Lt kia 1-7-17 1/8Lpool p72 CR Belgium10,4-7-17

SHAW,Giles Havergal Lt kia 11-4-17 5Beds p219 MR20

SHAW,Gordon Thompson.MC.TCapt kia 28-8-18 1RMunstF p176 CR France592

SHAW,Guy Trevor TMaj kia 7-7-16 2Nhampt p138 MR21

SHAW,Harold Maj kia 4-6-15 1LancF p93 MR4

SHAW,Harold Lee T2Lt kia 9-6-16 1Lincs p75 CR France281,10-6-16 1/4Bn

SHAW,Harold Joseph T2Lt dow 11-4-18 KRRC att2Bn p152 CR France201

SHAW,Harry 2Lt ded 20-4-19 TankCps p188 CR Ches137

SHAW,Henry Lynn TCapt kia 3-7-16 10RWar p66

SHAW,Herman Lt dow 26-4-17 RE 248FC p48 CR France95

SHAW,Hugh James Capt kld 11-11-14 5 att1RFus p70 CR France348

SHAW,James Capt kia 9-4-16 IA 2Rajputs p282 MR38

SHAW,John T2Lt kia 26-4-18 Manch p156 CR France144

SHAW,John Donald Lt kia 26-7-16 9RScots p212 CR France864,13Bn

SHAW,John Fyffe T2Lt kld 19-2-18 RFC p17 CR Scot386

SHAW,John Herbert 2Lt kia 26-10-17 6NumbF p214 MR30

SHAW,John William T2Lt kia 21-3-18 7KRRC p152 MR27

SHAW,Joshua Harold 2Lt dow 1-5-18 3 att1WYorks p83 CR France142

SHAW,John Thomas Capt ded 8-5-18 20LancF p93&258 CR Lancs2

SHAW,Julius Brinkley 2Lt kia 25-3-18 18Mddx att7Nhampt p148 MR27

SHAW,Leslie Gardner 2Lt kia 13-10-15 5SStaffs p229 MR19

SHAW,Llewellyn William Emile TCapt kia 10-8-18 10A&SH p173 CR France649

SHAW,Marmaduke Marshall.MC.LtACapt kia 21-3-18 3 att2N&D p135 CR France646

SHAW,Maurice TLt dow 30-9-15 12HLI p164 CR France1

SHAW,Max Joseph TLt kia 15-9-16 16 att26RFus p70 MR21

SHAW,Patrick T2Lt kia 30-6-15 1Leinst p175 CR France1140

SHAW,Philip Lt kia 26-10-17 6 att5NumbF p214 MR30

SHAW,Philip Haldane 2Lt kia 25-9-15 8BlkW p129 MR19

SHAW,Ralph.DSO.Lt kia 28-4-17 RWar SR att11Bn p66 MR20

SHAW,Randolph Albert Maj dow 14-11-16 A62RFA p35 CR France188

SHAW,Raymond Pugh LtTCapt kia 28-11-15 5 att2RFus p70 MR4

SHAW,Reginald Thomas Lt kia 9-5-15 RSuss att2Bn p120 MR22

SHAW,Richard Joseph T2Lt dow 26-6-17 11SLancs p126 CR France40

SHAW,Robert Capt kia 20-9-17 7Lpool p215 CR Belgium128

SHAW,Robert Dykes Somerville TCapt kia 23-3-18 7SfthH p165 MR27

SHAW,Robert Edward Fredric.MC.LtCol kia 23-8-18 13Lond p249 CR France924

SHAW,Robert Henderson T2Lt kia 18-9-16 13NumbF p63 CR Belgium83

SHAW,Robert Ramsey Stewart Lt kia 1-7-16 1/6NStaffs p238 CR France576

SHAW,Ronald Percy T2Lt kia 22-3-18 66MGC p185 MR27

SHAW,Rowan T2Lt kia 22-2-16 9Ches p96 CR France705

SHAW,S.TLt ded 13-1-18 GoldCoastR p202 CR EAfrica10 &CR Tanzania1

SHAW,Sydney Thomas T2Lt dow 11-5-16 12 att10WYorks p83 CR France285

SHAW,Thomas 2Lt kia 2-4-18 4SLancs p230

SHAW,Thomas Charles Whitehall 2Lt kia 24-8-18 4Lond p246 CR France395

SHAW,Thomas Gordon 2Lt kia 17-3-18 94RFC p17 MR20

SHAW,Thomas Herbert Lt kia 8-8-17 7RInniskF p105 MR29

SHAW,Victor Charles 2Lt ded 16-10-16 3/1RFA attZ29TMB p209 CR France145

SHAW,Walter Douglas.MC.TLt dow 8-11-18 RFus att1/10Manch p70 CR France1211,7-11-18

SHAW,William 2Lt kia 1-7-16 2SfthH p165 MR21

SHAW,William Lt ded PoW 27-9-16 1Camb p245 CR France598

SHAW,William Bernard TLt kia 12-4-17 9RSuss B'Coy p120 MR20

SHAW,William Cobley T2Lt kia 6-9-17 2Wilts p153 CR Belgium17

SHAW,William Easterby Lt dow 18-5-15 2KSLI p145 CR France102

SHAW,William Henry 2Lt kia 2-11-17 1/5Norf p217 CR Palestine8

SHAW,William Hetherington TLt kia 8-10-18 3MGC Inf p185 CR France358

SHAW,William Lindsay.MC.TLtAMaj kia 16-4-18 RE 228FC p48 CR Belgium20

SHAW,William Maxwell.DSO.Maj kia 29-5-17 102RFA p35 CR Belgium127

SHAW-HELLIER,Arthur Joseph Bradney TLt kia 9-8-15 7SStaffs p123 MR4

SHAW-STEWART,Neil Lt kia 21-8-16 3RB C'Coy p180 CR France402,Niel

SHAW-TWILLEY,J.Lt 9-5-20 RFA CR Yorks38

SHAW-WOOD,Richard T2Lt kld 17-3-18 RFC p17&258,SHAW

SHAWYER,Maurice Arthur Pritchard 2Lt kia 12-10-14 5 att1Mddx p148 MR32,14-10-14

SHEA,Joseph Patrick Lambert.MC.Capt&QM dow 1-12-17 2DLI p161

SHEA,Richard Thomas Lt ded 12-11-18 RGA p41 CR Wales383,2Lt

SHEARBURN,Frank Alan 2Lt kia 14-9-16 4 att10ScotRif p104 CR France703

SHEARBURN,Herbert Henry SubCdr 17-11-15 IAOrdDept CR India164

SHEARD,Arthur William 2Lt dow 17-1-17 5Y&L p238 CR France41,5/6Bn

SHEARD,Fraser Morton.MC.TCapt dow PoW 2-4-18 18Lpool p72 CR France441

SHEARD,Geoffrey Senior 2Lt dedacc 26-6-17 3Ches p96 CR France113

SHEARD,Thomas William Maj ded 29-9-17 RDC p253 CR Ches53

SHEARER,George.MC.TLtACapt kia 24-8-18 13Y&L p159 CR France324

SHEARER,J.F.Capt 17-7-21 RASC CR Iraq8

SHEARER,William Lt kia 8-6-18 315RFA p208 CR France61

SHEARMAN,Ambrose Augustus Capt dow 20-4-18 2/7Lond C'Coy p247 CR France37,Augustine

SHEARMAN,Eustace Robert Ambrose LtCol kia 13-5-15 10Huss p22 CR Belgium4

SHEARMAN,Herbert Henry Lt dow 5-7-16 1 att2Lincs p75 CR France23

SHEARMAN,Valentine LtACapt dow 25-3-18 2RScots p54 CR France103

SHEARS,Arthur Cecil 2Lt kia 3-7-16 7Suff p79 MR21

SHEARS,Edward Hornby Lt kia 4-7-17 IrGds p53

SHEASBY,Edwin William 2Lt kia 15-9-16 1Lond p245 MR21

SHEAY,William 2Lt dow 16-5-15 2Yorks p91 CR France80,Lt

SHECKLETON,Richard 2Lt kia 8-6-17 8NStaffs p157 MR29

SHEDDEN,Graham Percival Capt dow 31-10-14 RGA 35HB p41 CR Belgium57

SHEDDEN-DOBBIE,Robert T2Lt dow 12-4-17 11A&SH p173

SHEDEL,Rupert Frederick 2Lt kia 12-10-16 3 att1Ess p132 MR21

SHEEHAN,Cornelius T2Lt kld 8-8-17 6MunstF att17RFC p13&176 CR Greece9

SHEEHAN,Desmond Joseph T2Lt ded 10-5-17 66RFC p13 CR France924

SHEEHAN,Gordon Keith Patrick Lt kia 28-8-18 2Nhampt p138 CR France268

SHEEHAN,Martin Joseph 2Lt kld 1-10-18 2RMunstF &RAF p266

SHEEN,Cyril Cross T2Lt dow 3-5-17 11Suff p79 CR France13,2-5-17

SHEEN,George Edward Hayes Capt ded 19-2-15 6RIrRif p170

SHEEPSHANKS,Charles John Harcourt TCapt kia 17-3-16 8Dev p77 CR France188

SHEEPSHANKS,William 2Lt kia 10-7-17 6 att2KRRC p152 MR31

SHEFFIELD,Edward Frederick T2Lt kld 17-5-16 GL &RFC 7KiteBallSect p3&191 CR France68

SHEFFIELD,George Alfred Charles T2Lt kia 26-10-17 1SStaffs p123 MR30

SHEFFIELD,George Nelson Maj ded 1-1-18 3Ess p132 CR Sussex178

SHEFFIELD,Harold Welford Lt kia 23-3-18 1EYorks p85 MR27

SHEFFIELD,Lancelot Hull 2Lt kia 25-3-17 3 att2Dors p124 MR38

SHEFFIELD,Ralph David 2Lt kia 16-6-17 2/3Lond p246 MR20

SHEFFIELD,Surtees TLt kia 6-8-15 13 att2Hamps p121 MR4

SHEGOG,Richard Wellington TCapt dow 1-8-17 RAMC att1/4LNLancs p197 CR Belgium11

SHEIL,Charles 2Lt dow 22-4-18 RMunstF &2RAF p176 CR France179

SHEKURY,Cecil.MC.TLt kia 16-4-18 2Beds p86 CR Belgium12

SHELDON,Archibald Edward 2Lt dow 23-8-15 5Ess p232 CR Gallipoli27

SHELDON,Charles Stanley Lt 27-6-18 70RAF MR20

SHELDON,Reginald Eley 2Lt dow 15-4-18 7N&D p233 CR France102

SHELDON,Robert.MM.Lt ded 3-6-20 1/5SStaffs p264 CR War9 Ex 26War

SHELDRAKE,Archibald Turner Lt kia 28-9-18 7HLI &RAF p271 MR20

SHELLEY,Cecil William Charles TLt kia 17-10-15 2ScotsGds p52 MR19

SHELLEY,Ernest Bowen LtACapt kia 12-9-18 1GrenGds p50 CR France1484

SHELLEY,Philip John 2Lt kia 31-7-17 C83RFA p35 CR Belgium115

SHELLINGTON,Percy Gordon T2Lt kld 26-8-17 RFC p13 CR Norf247 Ex CanadaEngrs

SHELTON,Charles Capt kia 21-10-16 8Norf p74 MR21

SHELTON,John Parker 2Lt kia 19-4-17 8Hamps p229 CR Palestine8

SHELTON,Kenneth LtTCapt dow 14-2-18 3EKent &RFC p17&58 CR France987

SHELTON,Lionel Cartlidge Lt 7-6-20 MGC Inf attRAOC CR Egypt6

SHENKEL,Frank J.HonLt dow 19-11-17 GL p191

SHENNAN,Douglas Francis Fairfax Lt kia 8-5-15 4KRRC D'Coy p152 MR29

SHENTON,Austin Kirk.MC.TLtACapt ded 26-7-18 RE 12SigCo p48 CR France29

SHEPARD,Bernard Anthony T2Lt dow 26-5-17 RFA attZ24TMB p35 CR Nhampt13

SHEPARD,Cyril Harry T2Lt kia 1-7-16 9Dev p77 CR France330

SHEPARD,Norbert Gerald TLt dow 2-8-16 103RFA D'HB p35 CR France44

SHEPHARD,Ernest Arthur 2Lt kia 11-1-17 5Dors p124 CR France744

SHEPHARD,Ernest Edward.MID 2Lt kia 6-6-18 4Glouc p225 CR France20,12Bn

SHEPHARD,Gordon Strachey.DSO.MC.MID BrigGen kia 19-1-18 RFusstaff Cmdg1RFC p17&70 CR France88

SHEPHARD,Stuart Norman T2Lt kld 17-2-18 GL &RFC p17 CR Essex1

SHEPHEARD,Philip Capt kia 13-6-15 1Ess p132 MR4

SHEPHERD,Alfred Seymour.DSO.MC.2Lt kia 20-7-17 29RFC p13 MR20

SHEPHERD,Arthur Lindesay Moore TLt ded 3-11-16 PoW 6KRRC &RFC p3&152 CR France604

SHEPHERD,C.H.CB.DSO.Col 2-1-20 1Lincs CR India97A

SHEPHERD,Charles Arthur T2Lt kia 12-10-16 7Norf p74 CR France294

SHEPHERD,Edward Alexander Capt kia 3-9-16 4BlkW p230 MR21

SHEPHERD,Edwin Alexander TLt dow 13-4-18 3MGC p185 CR France98,14-4-18

SHEPHERD,Gerald Alexander Gaselee Capt kia 20-12-14 IA 57Rif p282 CR France571

SHEPHERD,Harold Ernest Lt ded 30-12-18 RFA p256 CR Beds75

SHEPHERD,James Duncan.MC.AMaj kia 8-8-19 RE att1S&M p255 MR38

SHEPHERD,James Montague Edward Capt kia 15-2-17 RB &1RFC p13&180 CR Belgium115

SHEPHERD,John Cuthbert Lt kia 25-8-18 4 att10LancF p93 CR France239

SHEPHERD,Norman Robinson Capt kia 4-11-16 7DLI p239 CR France388

SHEPHERD,Richard Malcolm Sisnett 2Lt kia 9-8-16 4RIrReg &RFC p4&89,ded MR20

SHEPHERD,Stanley T2Lt kia 27-9-18 DLI att8Lpool p161 CR France1496

SHEPHERD,Stanley Le Fleming.MC&Bar.Maj kia 10-8-19 Nhampt att45RFus p255 CR Europe179,SHEPPERD

SHEPHERD,Tom Lt kia 17-10-18 4Y&L p238 CR France441,2Bn

SHEPHERD-CROSS,Cecil Herbert.MID Maj dow 15-10-17 DukeofLancYeo att197MGC p187&204 CR Belgium16

SHEPHERD-TURNEHAM,Thomas Percy TCapt kia 28-9-16 6Yorks p91 MR21 Norman

SHEPPARD,A.G.E.Lt kld 12-11-17 1/4KAR p202

SHEPPARD,Asa Frederick T2Lt kld 23-2-17 GL &27RFC p13 CR Lancs474

SHEPPARD,Charles 2Lt kia 27-9-18 16Lond D'Coy p250 CR France429

SHEPPARD,Charles Westcar Lt ded 29-10-18 RE p262

SHEPPARD,Frederick William T2Lt kia 12-6-17 12RSuss p120 CR Belgium126

SHEPPARD,Gordon 2Lt dow 3-11-17 RGA 309SB p41 CR France64,HAC

SHEPPARD,Hubert 2Lt dow 9-12-17 2/17Lond p250 CR Palestine3

SHEPPARD,Illtyd 2Lt ded 3-1-21 IA 1/15Sikhs p282 CR Iraq8

SHEPPARD,Joseph Henry T2Lt kia 24-8-18 7RWSurr p56 CR France116,Lt

SHEPPARD,Lewis Charles Burford 2Lt kia 21-4-17 3SomLI att32RFC p13&80 CR France41

SHEPPARD,Percy Howard.MM.2Lt dow 28-5-18 RGA 119SB p42 CR France1332

SHEPPARD,Reginald Thomas Lt kia 13-5-17 13Lond att2/10Manch p249 CR France163,dow

SHEPPARD,Richard Bellamy.MC.TCapt kia 22-4-18 14WelchR p127 CR France59

SHEPPARD,Samuel Gurney.DSO.LtCol dow 21-8-15 HertsYeo p204 CR Gallipoli5,kia

SHEPPARD,Sidney 2Lt kia 28-4-17 3/10Lond att17RFus p248 MR20

SHEPPERD,S.Le F.MC&Bar.Maj 10-8-19 6Nhampt att45RFus MR70

SHEPPEY-GREENE,Napier Guy Sheppey Lt dow 14-6-18 3 att7RWKent p142 CR France69

SHEPPHARD,W.Lt&QM 29-5-20 RASC CR Surrey115

SHEREK,Paul Lt kld 1-10-18 NStaffs &57RAF p265 CR France658

SHERER,Stephen Frank T2Lt kia 29-9-18 2SWBord p101 CR Belgium116

SHERIDAN,Daniel.MC.DCM.2Lt kia 24-3-18 2HLI p164 MR20

SHERIDAN,Henry Hamilton 2Lt kia 3-5-17 att1RIrFus p171 CR France1896

SHERIDAN,Henry Richards T2Lt kia 3-9-16 6ConnRgrs p172 CR France402

SHERIDAN,John Wilton Lt dedacc 27-9-18 CamH &54RAF CR Essex73

SHERIDAN,Leonard Capt kia 26-3-18 8 att2RDubF p177 MR27

SHERIDAN,Richard Brinsley TLt kld 7-3-16 8RDubF p177 CR France201

SHERIDAN,William Frederick Temple Capt kia 25-9-15 5 att2RB p180 MR32

SHERIDAN,William Nicholas T2Lt kia 1-9-16 17RIrRif p170 CR Belgium49

SHERIFF,Kenneth 2Lt dow 23-6-15 3RWKent att2BordR p142 CR France102

SHERIFF,Leo Frederick David 2Lt kia 13-11-16 4BlkW p230 CR France293,SHERRIFF

SHERIFF,Wilfred T2Lt kia 19-7-17 22DLI p161 CR Belgium29

SHERINGHAM,Hugh Valentine Lt ded 16-10-18 CamelTransCps attRASC p253 CR Egypt9,Capt

SHERLEY,James TCapt kia 27-11-17 RAVC att70RFA p199 CR France415

SHERLOCK,Charles Gregg Capt dow 14-11-17 RAMC DADMS p197 CR Iraq6

SHERLOCK,George Wright Stratford LtCol dow 30-6-21 IA 2/21Punjabis p282 MR43

SHERLOCK,Gerald T2Lt dow 21-4-18 55MGC p185 CR France88

SHERLOCK,Gerrard Loundes Edward Lt kia 25-8-14 3Huss att5NigR p21&202 CR WAfrica58,Capt

SHERLOCK,Ronald Francis Capt kia 23-7-16 2KRRC p152 MR21

SHERMAN,John James Lt kia 20-10-17 15/36RH&FA p35 CR Belgium94

SHERMAN,Palton 2Lt kia 30-4-17 GL &RFC p13 CR France1483

SHERMAN,Reginald TCapt dow 10-10-17 RAMC att4FA p197 CR Belgium12

SHERRARD,Bertram 2Lt kia 22-5-18 D92RFA p35 CR France547

SHERRARD,John Charles TCapt ded 28-3-19 SL p255&268

SHERREN,Arthur Oswald Capt kia 3-8-17 4EKent p212 MR29

SHERREN,Hugh Godwin.MID Maj ded 28-2-20 RAMC p267 CR Asia51

SHERRIFF,Alexander T2Lt kia 22-3-18 1/2 att6/7RScotF p95 MR20

SHERRIFF,Alexander Nimmo 2Lt kia 30-10-14 1Nhampt p138 MR29

SHERRIFF,John George Lt kia 26-4-15 7A&SH p243 MR29

SHERRY,Gerald.MID Lt dow 26-7-16 1Beds p86 CR France833

SHERSTON,Somerset Arthur Capt kia 9-5-15 RB p180 MR32

SHERVINGTON,Thomas Robert Munro Capt dow 25-9-15 8EKent p58 MR19

SHERVINGTON,William Hugh Byam T2Lt kia 18-7-16 9 att6Beds p86 MR21

SHERWELL,Ferdinand Nigel TLt kia 13-6-17 7Beds p86 CR France541

SHERWELL,Rex 2Lt kia 3-7-16 3Lincs &25RFC p4&75 CR France88

SHERWOOD,Charles Edward 2Lt kia 22-10-17 3 O&BLI p130 CR Belgium112

SHERWOOD,Clement Walter T2Lt kia 28-11-17 17RFus p70 MR17

SHERWOOD,Hamilton Stanley 2Lt kia 28-8-18 3 att1/4KSLI p145 CR France98,29-8-18

SHERWOOD,Robert T2Lt kia 26-2-18 GL &RFC p17 CR France95

SHERWOOD,William Bernard Lt kia 27-10-17 RFC p13 MR20

SHERYER,Harold John Lt dow 5-8-17 8Hamps p229 CR France139

SHEWAN,Alan Davidson TLt kia 15-9-16 11A&SH p173 CR France453,Capt

SHIEL,John Hubert Trevor 2Lt kia 8-3-18 1Dors p124 CR Belgium12

SHIELD,Clement Ridley.MC.Capt kia 7-10-16 4HLI att51DivHQ p164 CR France3,8-10-16

SHIELD,Frederick Dowson T2Lt kia 6-7-16 8 att5Nhampt p138 CR France251

SHIELD,William James 2Lt kia 2-3-17 6Lpool p215 MR29

SHIELDS,Donald De Vere Lt 10-11-18 42CanadaInf CR Belgium241

SHIELDS,George Hilliard TLt kia 3-2-17 GoldCoastR p202 CR EAfrica38 &CR Tanzania1

SHIELDS,Hugh John Sladen Lt kia 25/26-10-14 RAMC p197 MR29 Haden

SHIELDS,William TLt kia 5-9-17 14Manch &45RFC p13&156 CR Belgium124

SHIELDS,William Francis Waugh TLt kia 25-9-15 9 att5KSLI p145 MR29

SHIFFNER,John Bridger.Bart.2Lt kia 24-9-18 RSuss att2Bn p120 CR France375

SHILCOCK,John Winton Lt kia 22/24-11-15 5RWSurr p212 MR38

SHILLINGFORD,Stanley Charles Lt kia 16-6-18 2RFus &RAF p70 CR France324

SHILLINGTON,Thomas Graham TCapt ded 18-8-17 9RIrFus 108Bde 36Div p171 CR Belgium8

SHIMMIN,Thomas Edward 2Lt kld 22-4-17 NorthDivCyc attRFC p19&253 CR Egypt15

SHINE,Edward.DCM.2Lt kia 20-10-18 15RWar p66 CR France1396

SHINE,Hugh Patrick 2Lt kia 25-5-15 1RIrFus p171 MR29

SHINE,James Rev dow 21-4-18 RAChDept att21Mddx p200 CR France102

SHINE,James Owen Williams.MID Capt kia 16-8-17 2RDubF p177 MR30

SHINE,John Denis 2Lt ded 25-8-14 RIrReg p89 CR Belgium241,Denys

SHINGLER,John Stanley Marsh.MC.Capt dow 4-9-18 4RWFus p223 CR France177

SHINN,Stanley Gilbert Lt ded 13-12-18 20Lond p251 CR France146

SHINNER,William Goodwin Blake Lt dow 2-1-18 28Lond p252 CR France398

SHIPLEY,Arthur Hammond Butler T2Lt kia 27-9-16 6Yorks A'Coy 11Div p91 MR21

SHIPLEY,Harold TLtCol ded 2-10-18 11RLancs att11BrWIndR p59 CR Italy12

SHIPP,Robert Cyril Lt ded 11-1-18 RASC p193 CR Devon1

SHIPPARD,Sanford William Lt kia 10-7-17 1LNLancs p136 MR31

SHIPPEY,Cyril Shaw 2Lt dow 21-12-15 3 att8Beds p86 CR Belgium11

SHIPPEY,James Reginald 2Lt dow 14-10-14 4Beds p86 CR France80

SHIPPOBOTTON,Frank T2Lt dow 20-11-17 1/4LNLancs p136 CR France446

SHIPSTER,Walter Neville.MC.MID Capt dow 20-9-18 1Manch p156 CR Palestine9

SHIPTON,Cyril Herbert 2Lt kia 25-9-15 2HLI p164 MR19

SHIPWAY,Guy Maxwell Capt kia 23-8-14 1Glouc p107 CR France1752,26-8-14

SHIRLEY,Archibald Vincent 2Lt kia 8-6-17 WelshHorseYeo attRFC p19&205 MR20

SHIRLEY,John George Frederick 2Lt kia 22-4-18 1Hamps p121 CR France411

SHIRLEY,Samuel Myatt T2Lt dow 1-5-17 18Manch p156 CR France214

SHIRREFF,Francis Gordon 2Lt kia 1-7-16 2RBerks p140 MR21

SHIRTCLIFF,Fred T2Lt kia 9-4-18 10DLI p161 MR32,SHIRTLIFF

SHIVES,Robert Kilgour TCapt kld 29-9-16 RFC p4

SHOESMITH,Edward James 2Lt kia 7-6-17 1RFus p70

SHONE,Geoffrey Beville.MC.Lt dow 19-10-17 1SStaffs att56RFC p13,123&259 CR France13

SHONE,Harold Lonsdale T2Lt ded 9-7-18 6RRofCav p24&261 CR Ches,10-7-18

SHONE,Robert Francis 2Lt kia 14-2-15 ESurr p113 MR29

SHOOBERT,Neil TLt kia 31-7-17 23Mddx p148 MR29

SHOOSMITH,Frank Stewart Lt kia 21-8-15 5Beds p219 MR4

SHOOTER,John Harold.MC.2Lt kia 10-4-18 5Y&L &RAF p238 CR France303

SHORE,Florence Nightingale Sister 16-1-20 QAIMNS CR Mddx53

SHORE,Walter Francis LtCol ded 6-12-16 RAVC p199 MR66

SHOREMAN,James.MC.2Lt kia 27-9-18 7Lpool p215 CR France1498

SHORLAND-BALL,Leslie 2Lt kia 6-9-16 3RIrRif p170 SeeSHORTLAND-BALL

SHORROCK,Thomas Dudley Ralph T2Lt kia 20-9-17 26RFus p70 MR30

SHORT,Andrew David Aitkin 2Lt kia 26-3-18 18LancF p93 MR27

SHORT,Cuthbert William.MC.Lt kia 6-3-17 IARO 9HodsonsHorse attRFC p282 CR France833

SHORT,Francis Leslie Capt ded 3-6-16 1RWKent p142 CR Lond7,3Bn

SHORT,James 2Lt ded 8-4-19 LabCps attEgyptLabCps p189 CR Egypt15

SHORT,John TLt ded 28-10-18 11WelshR p127 CR Greec9

SHORT,Oliver James T2Lt dow PoW 3-4-18 10Worc p109 CR Belgium406

SHORT,Vere Dawson TCapt kia 25-9-15 7Nhampt p138

SHORT,Walter TCapt kia 20-7-18 YLI 7 att5Bn p143 CR France 1689

SHORT,William Ambrose.CMG.LtCol kia 21-6-17 286RFA p35&258 CR France922

SHORT,William Innes 2Lt kia 11-8-15 1KOSB p102 MR4

SHORTEN,Henry William 2Lt kia 16-10-18 RGA 19SB p42 CR France1392

SHORTER,Alfred George T2Lt kia 1-7-16 16DLI p161 MR21

SHORTER,Lewis Victor Henry Lt ded 14-11-19 1/4EKent p271 CR Asia60

SHORTER,Vernon Banbury Capt dow 28-9-17 Lincs att10RWSurr p75 CR France139

SHORTER,William John Lt kia 24-3-18 1/8Ess attRFC p19&232 CR France95

SHORTHOUSE,Algernon Geoffrey T2Lt ded 5-6-18 13Yorks p91 CR Camb16

SHORTLAND-BALL,Leslie 2Lt kia 6-9-16 3 att8RIrF p265 MR21 See SHORLAND-BALL

SHORTO,Martin Hubert Lt kia 27-7-17 RE p210 CR Belgium24

SHORTRIDGE,Arthur 2Lt kia 14-3-15 2RIrFus p171 MR29

SHORTT,Vere Dawson Capt 25-9-15 7Nhampt MR19

SHORTT,William Edward Dudley Lt kia 12-10-17 1ScotsGds p52 CR Belgium13

SHOTT,Henry Hammond.DSO.Capt kia 26-8-14 1RBerks p140 CR France944

SHOVEL,Thomas Jasper Rev dow 5-10-18 RAChDept att2/2WessexFA p200 CR France759

SHOWELL,Harold George T2Lt kia 16-7-17 27NumbF p63 CR France366

SHOWERS,H.L.LtCol.CSI.CIE.2-2-16 IA CR Mddx26

SHOWERS,St.George Swaine Lt kia 9-8-17 3 att2Ess p132 MR20

SHRAPNEL,Victor George Fleetwood TLtACapt kia 23-3-18 8ESurr A'Coy p113 MR27

SHREWSBURY,Carl Brannell 2Lt kia 13-10-15 5Lincs p220 MR19

SHRUBSOLE,Arthur Edward T2Lt kia 13-4-17 11Leic p88 CR France223

SHUBRICK,Richard Brian LtTCapt dow 28-4-15 1RInniskF p105 MR4

SHUFF,William Edward Lt&QM ded 20-12-16 SL 4RWSurr p201 CR Mddx66

SHUFFLEBOTHAM,Guy Mynors.MID TLtTCapt kia 3-9-16 7SomLI p80 CR France294

SHUFFLEBOTHAM,John T2Lt kia 25/27-9-15 12NumbF p63 MR19

SHUFFREY,Gilbert Lt kia 9-8-15 6SLancs p126 MR4

SHUMM,Brian Godfrey 2Lt 27-9-18 22RAF MR20

SHUREY,Charles TCapt dow 21-7-16 10RFus p70 CR France833

SHUREY,Edward TLt ded 18-7-18 16WelshR p127 CR Eire322

SHUTE,George Francis 2Lt ded PoW 13-10-17 4 att2/6Glouc p225 MR20

SHUTT,Herbert Cecil Lt kia 13-11-16 3 att1RScotF p95 MR21

SHUTTLEWORTH,Ernest Hebden T2Lt kia 20-7-18 WYorks att8Bn p83 CR France622

SHUTTLEWORTH,Ernest Ronald 2Lt kia 1-7-16 1/8RWar p215 MR21

SHUTTLEWORTH,Henry T2Lt kia 2-10-18 1/2 att16LancF p93 CR France237

SHUTTLEWORTH,Kingsley Christopher Lt kia 19-11-17 1/4Suff p217 CR Belgium125

SHUTTLEWORTH,Robert George Maj kia 10-8-15 IA 110Mahrattas att9RWar p282 MR4

SHUTTLEWORTH,R.W.2Lt ded 15-8-18 9LancF &RAF p93 CR Yorks487,16-8-18

SIBBIT,George Bertrand TLt kia 27-9-18 1NumbF p63 MR16

SIBBIT,Henry TMaj kia 1-7-16 22NumbF p63 MR21

SIBETH,Charles George Augustine 2Lt kia 9-8-15 RE p48 MR29

SIBLEY,Robert Dymond Gladman Maj 1-10-18 210RAF MR20

SIBOLD,Foster Moverley T2Lt kia 25-9-15 10HLI p164 MR19

SIBOLD,Sidney Sparkling Moverley.MC.LtACapt dow 12-4-18 C165RH&FA p35

SICHEL,Geoffrey Michael John Lt kia 9-2-15 3Mddx p148 MR29

SICHEL,Oliver Walter.MID Capt dow 25-10-18 5 att2/6RWar p214 CR France332

SIDDALL,David Henry 2Lt kia 16-9-18 5YLI p235 CR France97

SIDDALL,Douglas Hamblett T2Lt kia 11-4-18 51MGC p185 MR19

SIDDALL,Joseph Henry Lt 25-7-18 209RAF MR20

SIDDALL,Thomas Arthur 2Lt dow 17-4-17 25Lond p252 CR France120

SIDDLE,Joe 2Lt dow 14-10-17 3 att1/5YLI p144 CR Belgium3

SIDDONS,Henry Thomas Brandon 2Lt dow 24-8-16 5Leinst p175 CR France513

SIDEBOTHAM,Gerald Capt kia 9-3-18 1/4Ches p222 CR Palestine3

SIDEBOTHAM,James Nasmyth Wedgwood TCapt kia 12-10-16 17Manch p156 MR21

SIDEBOTHAM,John Frith TLt kia 12-2-16 6KSLI p145 CR Belgium101

SIDEBOTTOM,Robert Yardley Capt kia 26-8-14 2LancF p93 MR15

SIDEY,William Hepburn 2Lt dow 13-10-17 RGA 62SB p42 CR Belgium16,12-10-17

SIDGWICK,Arthur Hugh 2LtACapt dow 17-9-17 RGA 157SB p42 CR Belgium18

SIDLEY,John Witherington T2Lt dow 2-8-16 16/41RFA p35 CR France23

SIDNEY,Leicester Philip 2Lt kia 2-10-17 17KRRC &29RFC p13&152 CR Belgium140

SIDWELL,Albert Edward.MC.TLt kia 7-7-17 9RFus p70 CR France581,Capt

SIEBER,John Frederick Louis T2Lt dow 4-10-16 6EYorks p85 CR France64

SIEBER,John Lonsdale Lt kia 17-10-17 4A&SH att1/2KAR p173&202 CR Eafrica11 &CR Tanzania1

SIEBERT,Stanley Prentice T2Lt dow 21-9-17 16RB p180 CR France139

SIEDLE,Karl Otto.MC.TCaptAMaj dow 30-5-18 B174RFA p35 CR France84

SIEVERS,Nowell Johnstone TCapt kia 30-11-17 9Ess p132 MR17

SIFTON,William Alfred T2Lt dow 25-12-15 8SStaffs p123 CR Belgium11

SIKES,Robert Gordon Lt ded 22-2-19 LeicYeo att4Huss p204 CR France146

SILBY,Thomas Stanley.MC.TLt kia 12-9-18 10SWBord p101 CR France415

SILCOCK,Bertram Baker.MID 2Lt kia 10-8-15 7RWFus p223 MR4,Baker

SILCOCK,Percy Bryan T2Lt dow 11-8-17 14 att16Ches p96 CR Belgium7,13Bn

SILCOTT,William Henry Capt ded 9-9-19 RH&FA p262 CR Devon1,H.W.RGA

SILCOX,Baylis.MID T2Lt kia 29-12-17 GL att7RDubF p191 CR Palestine3

SILK,Norman Galbraith Lt kia 9-6-15 2SWBord p101 CR Gallipoli6

SILK,Thomas William Lt kia 26-10-17 9Dev p77 MR30

SILL,John Sutton Capt ded 8-12-18 2EKent p262 CR Hamps7

SILLAR,Tom Cameron TLt kia 30-9-15 9Y&L p159 CR France680

SILLARS,David Robertson TCapt kia 4-5-18 12HLI p164 CR France60,4-6-18

SILLARS,George Alexander 2Lt kia 1-12-17 5HLI p240 CR Palestine9

SILLARS,Harry Frederick Lionel 2Lt kia 1-7-16 4A&SH att2SfthH p174 MR21

SILLARS,Hugh Conn Lt ded 19-2-19 RE IWT p48 CR France85

SILLEM,Arthur Henry Lt kia 24-3-18 4 att8NStaffs p157 CR France380

SILLEM,Augustus Charles Herman T2Lt kia 18-7-16 52RFA p35

SILLEM,Stuart Charles 2Lt kia 12-8-17 GL &RFC p13 MR20

SILLEM,Thomas George TLtACapt kia 14-4-18 16WelchR p127 MR30

SILLENCE,James.MM.Lt dow 24-4-18 1Hamps p121 CR France88,2Lt

SILLERY,Charles Cecil Archibald TLtCol kia 1-7-16 Cmdg20NumbF p63 CR France150

SILLERY,John Jocelyn Doyne.MID Maj kia 7-8-15 11Manch RetIA p156 MR4

SILLS,Charles Caldwell 2Lt kia 26-9-14 1SWBord p101 MR15

SILMON,William Osman de Weld 2Lt kia 28-2-17 8WYorks p219 CR France514

SILVER,Edward 2Lt kia 1-5-18 2/14Lond p249 CR palestine3

SILVER,Humphrey William T2Lt kia 7-6-18 RSuss att2Bn p120 CR France163,W.H.8-6-18

SILVER,John Watt 2Lt kia 26-10-18 4GordH p242 CR France1196

SILVER,Keith T2Lt kia 18-11-16 8Glouc p107 CR France215

SILVER,Sidney Edwin.MC.Capt kia 20-11-17 3 att11Ess p132&259 CR France379,Sydney

SILVER,Thomas Samuel Harper 2Lt kia 16-4-18 RGA 80SB p42 CR Belgium74

SILVER,Walter Barrington Maj ded 4-10-14 RIrFus p171 CR Hamps234,3-10-14

SILVER,Walter Laurence Conningham TLt kia 12-10-16 7Suff C'Coy p79 CR France512

SILVERS,Frank Pitchford.MC.Capt dow 27-5-18 1/6SStaffs p229 CR France10

SILVERTON,Ernest George.MM.2Lt kia 26-7-17 RGA 303SB p42 CR Belgium10

SILVERTOP,Francis Somerled Joseph Lt kia 20-5-17 OxYeo p205 CR France1495

SILVERTOP,William Alexander.MC.Capt kia 27-11-17 20Huss p23 CR France256

SILVERWOOD,Hugh Fletcher Capt kia 27-3-17 6Ess p232 MR34

SILVESTER,Anson Lloyd 2Lt kia 1-1-15 2RSuss p120 CR France720,31-12-14

SILVESTER,Geoffrey Francis TCapt dow 17-7-16 7KSLI p145 CR France66

SILVESTER,Reginald 2Lt kia 7-6-17 20Lond p251 MR29

SILVESTER,William Hugh T2Lt dow 3-11-18 RWar att2/7Bn p66 CR France146

SIM,Alexander Taylor T2Lt kia 12-5-16 13RScots p54 CR France423

SIM,Bueth Vernon Capt dow 7-5-15 Mddx att4Bn p148 CR Belgium35

SIM,Herman Alexander Coysgarne Lt kia 9-5-15 2ScotRif p104 CR France525

SIM,James Robertson Gould 2Lt kia 5-6-17 3RScots p54 CR France1182

SIM,John Moir.MID 2Lt kld 25-3-17 6GordH att70RFC p242&261 CR France518,kia

SIM,Lancelot George Earle 2Lt kia 14-9-16 1GrenGds SR p50 CR France630

SIM,Louis St.George Leslie 2Lt ded 20-12-15 11BlkW p129 CR Lond8

SIM,Norman Young 2Lt kia 9-9-16 9Lond p248 MR21

SIM,William Capt kia 13-11-16 5ScotRif att6SfthH p224 MR21,6Bn

SIM,William George 2Lt kia 14-10-18 5 att8BlkW p231 CR Belgium157

SIMCOCK,Gilbert Alexander 2Lt kia 9-4-14 14Ches p96 MR38

SIMEONS,Edward Emil TCapt dow 17-2-16 8Beds p86

SIMKIN,Horace John TCapt dow 14-7-16 13Lpool C'Coy p72 CR France141,kia

SIMKINS,Walter Francis 2Lt kia 9-10-16 3 att2WRid p116

SIMMANCE,Allan James Spencer TCapt kia 18-8-16 4Lpool p72 MR21

SIMMONDS,Austin Gundry 2Lt drd 2-6-17 5A Res RFA p35 CR Eire506

SIMMONDS,Frederick Daniel T2Lt ded 18-2-19 4Beds p263 CR Lond1

SIMMONDS,Guy Bloxham T2Lt kld 29-12-16 76MGC Inf p185 CR France300,kia 86/5MGC

SIMMONDS,Harold 2Lt kia 31-7-17 18Manch p156 MR29

SIMMONDS,Leslie Bernard 2Lt 16-9-18 57RAF MR20

SIMMONDS,Percy Grabham 2Lt kia 1-7-16 9Lond p248 MR21

SIMMONDS,Richard George T2Lt accdrd 4-7-17 GL 1Worc attRFC X'Depot p13 CR Egypt1

SIMMONDS,Walter Sangster T2Lt kia 7-10-16 10RB p180 MR21

SIMMONS,Arthur George 2Lt kia 7-2-16 IARO att114Mahrattas p282 MR38

SIMMONS,Benjamin Howard TLt kia 29-10-18 14ACycCps p181 CR Italy9

SIMMONS,Eric Warr 2Lt kia 11-8-15 6Y&L p159 MR4,10-8-15

SIMMONS,Frank Wortley Capt kia 22-11-17 2/4Hamps p228 CR Palestine3

SIMMONS,Frederick William T2Lt kia 27-5-18 1 att7Leic p88 MR18,2 att7Bn

SIMMONS,John 2Lt kld 21-8-16 3RB p180 CR Hamps1

SIMMONS,John Marcus Rainsford Lt dow 28-8-20 IA 1/116Mahrattas p282 MR38

SIMMONS,Paul Emery May Capt dow 24-7-15 4Hamps p228 MR38

SIMMONS,Percy Marston 2Lt kia 20-10-18 4Wilts p236 CR France270,2Bn

SIMMONS,Richard Ernest 2Lt kia 5-12-17 RGA 232SB p42 CR Belgium25

SIMMONS,Robert Dendney 2Lt kia 23-9-18 7Lond p247 CR France155,Deudney

SIMMONS,Robert George T2Lt kia 22-3-18 11RFus p70 MR27

SIMMONS,Russell Louis Harry 2Lt kia 25-9-15 RBerks p140 MR32

SIMMONS,Sydney Noël Lt dow 27-10-16 RWiltsYeo p205 CR Surrey157

SIMMONS,Walter John.MC.Lt dow 27-8-18 17Lond p250

SIMMONS,William Aubrey TLt dow 3-11-18 B88 RFA p35 CR France332

SIMMONSI,B.H AssSurg2Cl 8-11-19 IMS MR67

SIMMS,Alexander Capt drd 13-9-18 RE p48 MR40,12-9-18

SIMMS,Alfred George Francis Lt ded 30-12-17 6ConnRgrs p172 MR41,drd

SIMMS,George Norman.MVO.Capt ded 27-8-14 2RMunstF p176 CR France1751

SIMMS,J.B.P.2Lt kld 4-6-18 3NumbF &4RAF p63 MR20

SIMMS,John Sibbald Capt kia 26-10-17 12Lond p248 CR Belgium20

SIMMS,William Capt kia 19-7-16 2/6RWar p214 CR France567

SIMON,Eric Conrad Capt dow 17-8-15 2/5LancF p221 CR France197

SIMON,Henry Hemrick Maj dow 8-9-17 C210RFA p206 CR Belgium11

SIMON,Marcel Andre T2Lt kia 29-4-17 6RBerks att2 O&BLI p140 MR20

SIMON,Norman T2Lt kia 14-7-16 8EYorks p85 MR21

SIMON,Robert M.Sir.LtCol ded /-/-15 RAMC p271

SIMON,Victor Herman.MC.Maj kia 5-6-17 RE 3FSqd p48 CR France363

SIMONDS,Charles Francis.MID TMaj kia 29-6-16 13KRRC p152 CR France501

SIMONDS,Charles Henville.MC.Lt dow 29-4-18 RE 126FC p48 CR Belgium11

SIMONDS,Ernest Hugh T2Lt kia 28-3-18 9RFus p70 MR27

SIMONDS,John De Luze.DSO.CaptAMaj kia 21-4-17 RGA 136SB p42 CR France223,22-4-17

SIMONET,Harold Keith.MC.Capt dow 29-4-18 1/8N&D p233 CR France88

SIMONET,Kenneth William Lee Capt kia 21-1-16 1Yorks p91 MR38

SIMONS,George Henry.DCM.T2Lt kia 26-8-17 10Lincs p75 CR France1462

SIMONS,John Henry Stuart 2Lt kia 10-7-17 3 att1Nhampt p138 MR31

SIMONS,Leon.MC.Capt kia 17-2-17 22RFus p70 MR21

SIMONS,Richard Frederick.MC.Capt ded 9-1-20 12LNLancs attSomalCamCpsp271 CR Egypt7

SIMPKIN,Arthur Wilson TCapt kia 30-9-18 13Yorks att8WYorks p91 CR France755

SIMPKIN,Harry Hargreaves TCapt kia 22-3-18 13Yorks p91 MR20

SIMPKIN,Norman Travers Lt 18-8-19 RFA CR USA13

SIMPKIN,Reginald John Henry 2Lt kia 16-7-16 1/5RWar p214 MR21

SIMPSON,Alexander McGregor 2Lt kia 5-9-18 8Lond p247 CR France511

SIMPSON,Allen Ross Fraser T2Lt kia 16-7-16 10YLI p144 MR21

SIMPSON,Anthony Bean Tracey 2Lt kia 6-5-15 2WRid p116 MR29

SIMPSON,Anthony Henry Lt ded 1-2-15 1RWar SR p66 CR France102

SIMPSON,Arthur Ernest 2LtTLt kld 25-1-15 RASC p193

SIMPSON,Arthur Guy 2Lt kia 23-11-17 B'TankCps p188 MR17

SIMPSON,Brian 2LtTLt kia 9-5-15 ScotRif p104 MR22

SIMPSON,Brian George Casson 2Lt dow 29-7-15 RHA p35 CR Belgium11

SIMPSON,Cecil Barclay 2Lt kia 7-10-17 4SfthH p241 CR France536

SIMPSON,Charles Vernon Martin Capt kia 31-7-17 1/5RLancs p213 CR Belgium10

SIMPSON,Christopher Byron TCapt kia 7-10-16 26RFus p70 MR21

SIMPSON,Claude Battwell 2Lt kia 6-11-17 GL &RFC p13 MR20

SIMPSON,Claude Frank Bell Capt dow 3-12-17 9 att14DLI p239 CR France711

SIMPSON,Clifford Sandford TCapt kia 10-7-16 8Yorks p91 CR France515

SIMPSON,Clive Lennox TLtTCapt ded 19-3-17 RE IWT p262 CR Asia45

SIMPSON,Colin.MID 2Lt kia 7-8-16 A79RFA p35 CR France765

SIMPSON,Cyril Woodhouse TLt kia 14-7-16 7Leics p88 MR21

SIMPSON,David.MC.2Lt kia 2-6-17 1WelshR p127 MR37

SIMPSON,David Kilgour 2Lt dow 2-11-16 9HLI p241 MR21

SIMPSON,David Thomson Lt ded 2-12-19 RFA p271 MR40

SIMPSON,Daniel Harrison Lt dedacc 21-12-16 GL Manch p267 CR Lancs30

SIMPSON,Donald.MC.2Lt dow 19-5-17 1/5SfthH p241 CR France95

SIMPSON,Douglas Alexander 2Lt dow 15-10-15 7GordH p242 CR France43

SIMPSON,Douglas Richard T2Lt kia 28-9-18 RE att108RFA p48 CR Frnce511

SIMPSON,Elizabeth Nurse ded 11-5-17 TFNS p254 CR Scot729,10-5-17

SIMPSON,Eric Cograve.MC.TCapt drd 4-5-17 GL p191 CR France1779

SIMPSON,Eric Hadley T2Lt kia 11-4-18 10Ches C'Coy p96 MR32 Ex 4CamH

SIMPSON,Eric Maudsley Capt ded 2-5-16 9Worc p109 CR Iraq5

SIMPSON,Ernest Herbert 2Lt dow 2-10-17 RGA attG'BtyAA AnzacCp p42 CR France134

SIMPSON,Evelyn Victor C.LtRet ded 25-11-18 C172 RH&FA p262

SIMPSON,Frank William Harris Capt kia 16-2-17 RGA att53RFC p13&42 CR France263

SIMPSON,Frederic TCapt dow 31-3-18 RAMC att2/1LondFdAmb p197 CR Kent127

SIMPSON,Frederick John Rayner 2Lt kia 31-7-17 5 att4Mddx p148 MR29

SIMPSON,Geoffrey Barnsley TCapt dow 12-11-15 7Y&L p159 CR France40

SIMPSON,George TLt kia 4-7-16 18DLI p161 CR France156

SIMPSON,George.MC.T2Lt kia 12-9-18 SWBord att10th p101 CR France415

SIMPSON,George Arnold 2Lt kia 2-7-16 5Leinst att64MGC p175&185,5Leics MR21

SIMPSON,George Duddington 2Lt kia 22-10-17 4RScots p211 MR30

SIMPSON,George Edward TCapt kia 22-10-17 23Manch p156 MR30

SIMPSON,George Fullarton 2Lt kia 29-7-18 5ScotRif p224 CR France864,Fullerton 10Bn

SIMPSON,George Kenneth.MC.TLt dow 7-3-17 RFC 4BallWing 14KiteBallSect p13 CR France164

SIMPSON,George Murdoch T2Lt kia 18-11-16 16HLI p164 MR21

SIMPSON,George Paterson T2LtACapt dow 2-8-18 10ScotRif p104 CR France1225

SIMPSON,George Ricardo Lt dow 30-8-18 3 att1Ches p96 CR France34

SIMPSON,Gerald William Ackroyd Lt died 26-1-19 RAOC p267

SIMPSON,Harry Graham Maj kia 27-5-18 1/4GordH att8MGC Inf p187&241 CR France1753

SIMPSON,Henry Delafosse TLt kia 24-8-17 8KRRC p152 MR30,Hugh

SIMPSON,Henry Gordon.MID 2Lt kia about 16-6-15 9DCLI att1RInniskF p115 MR4,6-6-15

SIMPSON,Henry Lamont 2Lt kia 29-8-18 8LancF p222 MR16

SIMPSON,Henry Leslie TLt ded 26-8-18 TankCps p266

SIMPSON,Henry Richard Deighton TLt kld 20-12-16 6DragGds &RFC p4&22 CR Kent105

SIMPSON,Herbert 2Lt dow 7-7-16 6N&D p233

SIMPSON,Herbert William ACapt kia 23-10-16 2RB p180 MR21

SIMPSON,James 2Lt dow 21-6-15 1/4GordH p242 CR France1

SIMPSON,James Alexander TLt dow 22-10-16 GL &10RFC p4&191 CR France98

SIMPSON,James Ashton 2Lt dow 25-7-16 RGA p42

SIMPSON,James Christian Capt ded 27-6-19 RAMC p271 CR Lond8

SIMPSON,James Francis T2Lt dow 27-10-17 20MGC p185 CR Belgium11

SIMPSON,James Harper Lt dow 12-10-17 8LancF p221 CR France193

SIMPSON,James Hawthorne Lt dow 3-7-16 RE 1/1FC p210 CR France35

SIMPSON,James Jamieson T2Lt kia 28-3-18 1NumbF p63 MR20

SIMPSON,James Kirk.MC.TLt kia 11-4-18 9SfthH p165 CR Belgium111

SIMPSON,James Marsden T2Lt kia 9-5-16 RE 173TC p48 CR France178

SIMPSON,James Cowie T2Lt kia 4-12-16 174RE p48 CR France251

SIMPSON,John Clark 2Lt kia 1-7-16 32RFC 10Wing p4 CR France423,Lt

SIMPSON,John Cornelius T2Lt dow 23-3-18 16RB p180 CR France119,23-8-18

SIMPSON,John Edmund.MID Capt kia 30-10-14 2YLI p144 MR29,31-10-14

SIMPSON,John Eric 2Lt kia 7-7-18 4Lincs att9Norf p217 CR Belgium3

SIMPSON,John Horace 2Lt kia 25-9-15 6 att2KRRC p152

SIMPSON,John Parker Norfolk 2Lt dow 27-5-15 5 att3RFus p70 CR Belgium140

SIMPSON,John Watt T2Lt kldacc 8-12-16 7BordR p118 CR France1568

SIMPSON,John Wyckliffe.MC.2Lt kia 1-8-17 9Lpool p216 MR29

SIMPSON,L.2Lt 5-4-20 3RWSurr CR Herts31

SIMPSON,Odo Mackay Lt kia 13-7-18 4N&D p135 CR Belgium3,2Bn

SIMPSON,Paul James Calvert 2Lt kia 1-10-15 3YLI p144 MR19,4-10-15

SIMPSON,Percy William TLt kia 1-11-16 9WRid p116 MR21

SIMPSON,Reginald Henry 2Lt kia 7-7-15 4 att2LancF p93 MR29

SIMPSON,Robert Arthur Abbs Lt dow 30-10-17 4NumbF p213

SIMPSON,Robert Fraser Lt kia 21-3-18 7 att1/6GordH p242 MR20

SIMPSON,Roger Cordy Capt ded 27-2-19 10WKentYeo p204 CR Surrey41

SIMPSON,Rolf T2Lt kia 26-5-17 18KRRC p152 CR Belgium152

SIMPSON,Rupert Victor Maj kia 28-9-15 1 O&BLI p130 MR38

SIMPSON,Stanley Ashe T2Lt kia 28-9-18 1Dev p77 CR France245

SIMPSON,T.E.2Lt kld 1-6-18 GL &RAF p191

SIMPSON,Thomas TLt kia 1-7-16 27NumbF p63 MR21

SIMPSON,Thomas Henry Capt&QM ded 10-8-19 RASC p267 CR Notts121

SIMPSON,Thomas Liddle.MC.T2Lt dow 30-11-18 DLI att64TMB p161 CR France658,Liddell ded

SIMPSON,Victor James 2Lt kia 24-8-16 5KSLI p145 MR21

SIMPSON,Vivian Samuel.MC.TCapt kia 13-4-18 12Y&L p159

SIMPSON,W.Cdr 14-11-15 IOD MR65

SIMPSON,William Drysdale 2Lt kia 3-10-15 5RScots p211 CR Gallipoli4

SIMPSON,William Herbert Mostyn Lt dow 19-12-14 3ESurr p113 CR France102,1Bn

SIMPSON,William Hugh Maj kia 17-4-16 IA 93BurmaInf p282 MR38

SIMPSON,William Norman TLt kia 31-3-18 YLI att16EntrenchBn p144 CR France1893

SIMPSON,William Ronald Carde 2Lt kia 16-5-15 2BordR p118 CR France279

SIMS,Charles Henry T2Lt kia 24-4-18 7 att2ELancs p111 MR27

SIMS,Donald Palmer 2Lt kia 23-10-18 2HAC Inf p206 CR Italy9,24-10-18

SIMS,Douglas Henry.MC.T2Lt dow 10-10-18 1Leics p88 CR France725

SIMS,Gordon Lawrence Lt ded 22-2-20 IAUL 1/36Sikhs p282 MR43,2Lt

SIMS,Heber Harold T2Lt dow 1-9-18 4RFus p70 CR France103

SIMS,Thomas Augustus HonCapt&RidgMr ded 19-5-15 RFA p35 CR France85

SIMSON,David Henry Ainsworth Cranstown 2Lt kia 18-9-18 111/24RFA p35 CR France835

SIMSON,Herbert Cyrus Lt ded 12-1-18 RFC p17 MR40

SIMSON,James Robert.DSO.MajTLtCol dow 9-11-17 HLI attKOSB p164 CR Scot237

SIMSON,Noel Charles Spicer Capt dow 26-9-15 RGA 21AA Sec p42 CR France40

SIMSON,Roderick Alexander 2Lt ded 11-11-18 RGA 259SB p42 CR France163

SIMSON,Ronald Francis Lt kia 15-9-14 16/116RFA p35 CR France1341

SIMSON,William Kingsbury T2Lt kia 5-6-17 22NumbF p63 CR France1182

SINCLAIR,Alexander Thomson T2Lt kia 10-9-17 239MGC Inf p185 CR Belgium112

SINCLAIR,Andrew Bremner 2Lt kia 10-12-17 5 att8SfthH p241 MR20

SINCLAIR,A.P.K Capt 19-12-20 RAPC CR SAfrica144

SINCLAIR,Archibald King T2Lt kia 5-12-16 11 att2BlkW p129 MR38

SINCLAIR,Colin Johnston 2Lt ded 30-11-16 27/32 A320RFA p35 CR Lond12,dow

SINCLAIR,Constance Miss ded 22-2-17 VAD p268

SINCLAIR,David Capt kia 20-7-16 7ScotRif p224 CR France432

SINCLAIR,David Williamson Lt dow 22-10-18 RAMC att11RScots p197 CR Belgium140

SINCLAIR,Donald 2Lt dow 18-12-17 7HLI attRFC p19&240 CR France200

SINCLAIR,Donald George Capt dow 15-7-17 RFA 51TMB p207 CR France134,17-7-17

SINCLAIR,Douglas Monteith Farquhar Lt kia 30-3-17 GL &40RFC p13 CR France777

SINCLAIR,Eric Alexander 2Lt kia 23-4-17 5 att2RScotF p222 MR20

SINCLAIR,Eric Russell.MC.Lt kia 13-10-18 7A&SH p243 CR France1196

SINCLAIR,Frank TLt drd 3-10-18 RFus attNigR p70&202 see GRIMSEY,W.J.

SINCLAIR,Gavin Wilson 2Lt dow 7-12-17 19Lond p251

SINCLAIR,George T2Lt kia 9-4-17 11Mddx p148 CR France96

SINCLAIR,George Stanley 2Lt ded 28-5-17 5 att1RIrRif p170 CR France511

SINCLAIR,George Walker 2Lt kia 27-9-18 4RScots p211 CR France484

SINCLAIR,Gerald.MC.2Lt kia 21-3-18 RMunstF att2RIrReg p176 MR27

SINCLAIR,Gerald John LtACapt kia 18-4-18 1BlkW p129 CR France1106

SINCLAIR,Harold Lt kia 17-2-17 4WRid p227 CR France1890

SINCLAIR,Herbert Spencer T2Lt kld 24-12-17 GL &199RFC p13 CR Scot674

SINCLAIR,James Johnston TCapt ded 14-11-18 RAMC p197 CR Scot764

SINCLAIR,John Mitchell T2Lt kia 6-12-15 13ScotRif att5ConnRgrs p104 MR37

SINCLAIR,John Norman.DSO.MajALtCol kia 24-3-18 RFA p35 CR France164

SINCLAIR,Kenneth Lt dow 12-10-18 RE p210 CR France398

SINCLAIR,Lachlan T2Lt kia 28-9-16 12NumbF p63 CR France400

SINCLAIR,Luke Taylor T2Lt kia 2-3-16 11GordH p167 MR29

SINCLAIR,R.B.Lt ded 22-3-19 RH&FA attRAF p35

SINCLAIR,Robert 2Lt kia 9-5-15 2BlkW p129 CR France924,Lt

SINCLAIR,W Lt 18-3-16 RIM MR64

SINCLAIR,William T2Lt kia 18-10-16 18Lpool p72 MR21

SINCLAIR,William Everitt T2Lt kld 15-3-18 GL &RFC p17 CR Wilts129,Everett

SINCLAIR-TRAVIS,Norman Brownlie Maj dow 26-3-18 RGA 297SB p209 CR France1182,kia

SINDALL,Richard Edward Capt dow 1-7-15 1/1Camb p244 CR France285

SING,Charles Millington 2Lt dow 7-7-16 7RSuss p120 CR France1890

SINGER,Ernest Henry Percy 2Lt kia 28-3-18 7Ess p232 MR20

SINGLE,Frederick Alexander.MC.Capt dow 30-3-18 2DragGds B'Sqn p21 CR France185

SINGLEHURST,Reginald LtACapt kia 21-3-18 24 att9KRRC p152 MR27

SINGLEHURST,Robert Bruce.MC.T2Lt kia 30-4-16 12NumbF D'Coy p63 CR France1890,Capt

SINGLETON,Frank Chester TCapt kia 3-9-16 17N&D p135 CR France220

SINGLETON,Harold James 2Lt ded 6-4-19 RFA p262 CR Lancs14

SINGLETON,Mark Rodney Lt kia 7-5-15 2YLI p144 MR29

SINGLETON,William James TLt drd 10-10-18 20 att3RWFus p99 CR Ireland14

SINKINSON,Evelyn Henry Le Mesurier Capt kia 14-7-15 IA 24Punjabis p282 CR Iraq6

SINKINSON,Francis Geoffrey 2Lt dow PoW 8-4-18 2TankCps p188 CR Belgium353,Lt

SINNETT-JONES,Gilbert Lloyd TCapt kia 4-4-16 8RWFus p99 MR38,9-4-16

SINNETT-JONES,James Victor 2Lt kia 10/12-7-16 3 att17RWFus p99 MR21

SINTON,Edwin.MC.LtACapt kia 21-8-18 RFA att4LtRlyOpCoy RE p35 CR France81

SINTON,William.MM.T2Lt kia 30-11-17 6BordR C'Coy p118 CR France550

SIORDET,Gerald Caldwell.MC.T2Lt kia 9-2-17 13RB p180 MR38

SISLEY,Arthur Jackson Smith 2Lt kia 10-9-17 GL &RFC p13 MR20

SISLEY,Donovan Laurier 2Lt kia 6-3-18 RFC p17 MR20

SISSON,George Lt dow PoW 20-12-17 RGA 71HB p42 CR France658

SISSONS,Norman Lea TLt kia 9-9-16 11EYorks p85 CR France727

SISSONS,Roland Edward Lt kia 2-6-16 8WYorks p219 CR France251

SISTERTON,Norman Hele 2Lt kia 16-4-18 12/13NumbF att1Lincs p63 MR30,SISTERSON

SITFORD,Leopold John T2Lt kia 2-9-18 1/4Manch p156 CR France.308,1/6Bn

SIVEWRIGHT,William George T2Lt kia 26-9-17 RSuss att13Bn p120 MR30

SIVEWRIGHT,William John LtACapt kia 2-11-17 7Manch p237 CR Belgium175

SIZELAND,Charles T2Lt kia 12-10-16 7Norf p74 MR21

SKAIFE,Arthur Frederick Capt kia 1-11-14 1Mddx p148 CR France347,Frederick

SKAKLE,Hugh Philip.MID Capt kia 21-11-17 4GordH CR France256

SKEEN,Oliver St.John.DSO.Maj kia 21-1-16 IA 62Punjabis p282 CR Iraq5

SKEET,John Richard Lt kia 27-4-18 2Lond att7RWSurr p245 MR27

SKEET,William Celington TCapt kia 9-4-17 12WYorks p83 CR France581

SKEFFINGTON,Herbert Neville Southwell 2Lt kia 28-7-17 57RFC p13 CR Belgium149

SKELSEY,Robert Max Lt kld 29-3-18 4WRid att186TMB p227 MR20

SKELTON,Benjamin Dowell T2Lt dow 7-11-18 att10Ess p132 CR France146

SKELTON,Charles George Gordon T2Lt kia 18-11-16 10SLancsatt17Bn p126 MR21,7Bn

SKELTON,Francis T2Lt kia 21-10-17 28RFC p13 CR Belgium18

SKELTON,Harry T2Lt dow 12-10-16 8RFus p70 CR France833

SKELTON,Henry T2Lt kia 2-10-18 11 att16LancF p93 CR France237 Ex 28Lond

SKELTON,Sydney Capt ded 20-3-18 1/5EKent p213 CR Iraq8

SKEMP,Arthur Rowland Lt kia 1-11-18 4Glouc p225 CR France190,1Bn

SKENE,Ian.MC.2Lt dow PoW 13-4-18 6LancF p221 CR France1142

SKENE,James Henry 2Lt kia 14-7-16 4RBerks p234 MR19

SKENE,Robin Reginald 2Lt kld 12-8-14 RFC p2 CR Surrey126

SKERRY,James Beadnell T2Lt kia 1-6-16 17Mddx p148 CR France924

SKETT,Arthur Edwin Pye 2Lt kia 11-11-16 2WYorks p83 CR France744

SKEVINGTON,Arthur Victor T2Lt kia 25-9-16 13 att10YLI p144 MR21

SKEVINGTON,William Percy T2Lt kia 8-9-18 11EYorks B'Coy p85 CR France297

SKEWES,Arthur Courtis T2Lt kia 19-7-16 11Dev att2/6Glouc p77 CR France1887

SKEY,Charles Harland Capt kia 18-8-16 1BlkW p129 MR21

SKIDMORE,John Henry T2LtACapt ded 7-11-18 LabCps att214PoW Coy p189 CR Hereford/W186,8-11-18

SKILL,Harold Jefferson TCapt dow PoW 7-4-18 Mddx att21Bn p148 CR Belgium353

SKILLINGTON,Harry 2Lt kld 18-8-16 4Nhampt p234 CR France832

SKINNER,Alfred Capt kia31-8-16 4SLancs att27RFC p19&229 CR France662

SKINNER,Charles Edwin TCapt ded 13-1-20 RFA p262 CR Asia81

SKINNER,Douglas Hilton TCapt dow 16-7-16 7RWKent A'Coy p142 CR France119

SKINNER,Edward Dudley T2Lt kia 9-9-17 1/8Manch D'Coy p156 CR Belgium84

SKINNER,Edward Howard 2Lt kia 25-9-16 Dev p77 CR France374

SKINNER,Ernest Archibald 2Lt dow 26-11-17 24MGC p185 CR Belgium3

SKINNER,Ernest Henry 2Lt kia or dow 21/31-3-18 1/1Camb p245 MR27

SKINNER,Frederick Tom TCaptAMaj kia 3-9-16 14Hamps p121 CR France742

SKINNER,Frederick William Fletcher 2Lt dow 13-8-17 2 attD108RFA p209 CR Belgium7

SKINNER,George Arthur TCapt ded 11-10-19 RAMC p267 CR Kent46

SKINNER,Harold Bazalgette Capt kia 8-3-16 IA 2Rajputs p282 MR38

SKINNER,Hilary Francis Cleveland 2Lt kia 25-7-16 1SWBord p101 MR21

SKINNER,James Stuart Capt drd 21-2-17 2KSLI p145,Steuart MR35

SKINNER,Lewis Samuel Corbett Lt ded 31-12-19 IA 39CentIndHorse att38 p282 CR Egypt2

SKINNER,Robert Leonard Grahame 2Lt ded 3-5-18 1/2BlkW &64RAF p129 MR20

SKINNER,Stephen William 2Lt kia 4-10-16 32RFus p70 MR21

SKINNER,Thomas Arnold T2Lt dow 10-8-17 7KOSB p102 CR France145,7/8Bn

SKINNER,Wilfred Henry 2Lt dow PoW 27-5-18 8MGC Inf p185 CR France928

SKINNER,William T2Lt kia 25-9-15 6KOSB p102 CR France114

SKINNER,William Lt ded 21-6-16 RIM p282 CR Iraq6

SKINNER,William.MC.TCapt kia 25-4-18 12RScots D'Coy p54 MR30

SKINNER,William Edward T2Lt kld 4-3-18 RFC p17 CR Lond28

SKIPWITH,Granville Arthur 2Lt kia 16-6-15 RFA 72Bty p35 CR Belgium165,Lt
SKIPWORTH,Bernard William.MC.Lt kia 25-4-18 3RSuss att9MGC Infp120&185 MR30
SKIPWORTH,Frank Peyton Maj kia 25-9-15 7RScotF p95 MR19
SKIPWORTH,Philip John TLt kia 7-8-15 11WRid att5Manch p116 MR4
SKIRROW,Arthur TLt kia 28-3-18 13Y&L p159 CR France745
SKIRROW,Geoffrey LtACapt kia 27-8-18 5WYorks p218 CR France614
SKITT,Harold George T2Lt kia 1-10-18 10 att1RIrFus p171 CR Belgium157
SKOTTOWE,Claude Mannering 2Lt kia 21-10-16 2SLancs p126 CR France384
SKOTTOWE,Gordon T2Lt dow 12-4-18 7RWKent p142 CR France185
SKOULDING,Alfred Cecil T2Lt dow 21-2-17 6 O&BLI p130 CR France105
SKRIMSHIRE,Herbert Eric 2Lt dow 28-3-18 RGA 116SB p42 CR France184
SKRINE,Henry Langton TCapt kia 25-9-15 6SomLI p80 MR29
SKRINE,Sholto Herries.MC.TLt dow 19-9-17 B95RFA p35&259 CR Belgium19
SKUCE,Arthur TLt dow 8-10-17 6 O&BLI p130 CR Oxford74
SKYRNE,Richard Edward Elcho 2Lt kia 6-2-17 3 att1Wilts p153 CR Belgium70
SLACK,A.E.Lt 31-12-20 RASC CR Iraq8
SLACK,John Barnett T2Lt kia 27-5-18 NumbF Res att5Bn p63 CR France1753
SLACKE,Charles Oven TCapt kia 1-7-16 14RIrRif p170 CR France215,Owen
SLACKE,Clulow Orme Capt mbk 12-11-16 12ESurr p256 MR29
SLACKE,Roger Cecil Maj kia 16-5-15 3EKent attRWSurr p58 CR France279,2BordR
SLADE,Charles Godfrey Mitford Maj kia 8-11-14 4WYorks attNLancs p83 MR29
SLADE,Ernest Cowper.DSO.MC.LtCol kia 4-5-18 4 att8Glouc p225 CR Belgium102
SLADE,Robert Blackmore Maj kia 10-7-18 RGA 123SB p209 CR France924
SLADE,Robert Gordon Lt kia 18-4-18 19DAC attA88RFA p35 CR Belgium11
SLADE,Stewart Harold TLt kia 21-8-18 15TankCps p188 CR France214
SLADE,Wilfrid Adolphus 2Lt kia 23-4-17 70RFA p35 CR France1188
SLADE BAKER,Robert Cunynghame.MC.Lt kia 19-8-17 1RBerks CR France572
SLADE-KING,Philip S.TLt ded 13-5-18 2Norf p263 CR Iraq8
SLADE-POWELL,John Harold Maj dow 8-2-15 52RFA CR Suff83
SLADEN,Charles St.Barbe Maj ded 2-9-17 RE p48 CR Hamps11
SLADEN,John Henry 2Lt ded 7-2-19 NumbF p262 CR Numb83
SLADEN,St.Barbe Russell.TD.LtCol kia 12-3-18 5 Cmdg1RWSurr p212 CR Belgium84
SLANEY,Albert Edward T2Lt ded 3-10-17 GL attLabCps p191 CR Yorks547
SLANEY,John Cobley Lt kia 17-2-16 76RFA p35 CR Belgium28
SLATER,Charles Hugh Hope TLt kia 31-7-17 10ScotRif att46InfBde p104 CR Belgium7
SLATER,Gilbert John Leigh Lt&Adjt kia 30-4-16 8Worc p226 CR France1327
SLATER,Harry Lt dow 28-5-18 1/6SStaffs p229 CR France40
SLATER,James 2Lt dow 16-11-16 9DLI p239 CR Yorks45
SLATER,John T2Lt dow 26-3-20 20 att17LancF p93 CR France177
SLATER,John Cyrus 2Lt ded 6-7-17 5Lond p246 CR France40,dow
SLATER,John Elwyn 2Lt kia 3-5-17 5ELancs att2LancF p226 MR20
SLATER,Leonard Capt kia 14-9-14 2RSuss p120 CR France1329
SLATER,R.A.Lt 12-8-19 RAMC CR Scot762
SLATER,Richard Henry.MIDx2 TCapt kia 27-7-16 1KRRC p152 MR21
SLATER,Ronald Mortimer Lt dow 21-11-14 1Worc p109 CR France345
SLATER,Thomas Alexander Fletcher 2Lt kia 16-9-16 3 att5Dors p124 MR21
SLATFORD,Clarence Douglas.MC.Lt ded 31-10-19 2Ess p264 CR Lond14
SLATTER,Roland Percy TCapt kia 15-7-16 1RWSurr p56 MR21
SLATTERY,Duncan Vincent 2Lt kld 3-3-17 Hamps &RFC p13&121 CR Essex43
SLATTERY,Francis James LtACapt ded 9-1-19 RE 8FC p48 CR Eire30
SLATTERY,Francis William 2Lt 17-9-16 3AustLH MGSqn MR34
SLAUGHTER,Arthur Charles T2Lt dow 23-8-16 16Lpool p72 CR France765
SLAUGHTER,Vivian Lt kia 27-9-18 2/20Lond p251 CR France358
SLAUGHTER,William Leonard 2Lt kia 6-9-18 HuntsCycBn attEss p253 CR France511
SLEATOR,Robert John T2Lt ded 8-5-17 9RIrFus C'Coy p171 CR Belgium97
SLEE,John Balhatchet Lt kia 24-3-18 3 att7DCLI p115 MR27
SLEEMAN,William Fraser T2Lt kia 31-5-17 GL &55RFC p13 CR France134
SLEIGH,William Ward TLt kia 25-2-17 18WYorks p83 CR France342
SLICER,Philip Sydney Lt dow 30-9-18 RGA 319SB p42 CR France327
SLICER,Walter Gordon 2Lt kia 13-4-18 8RWar p215 CR France248
SLIDE,G.H.Capt 14-7-18 ScotHorse CR Scot669 Ex 17Lancers
SLIDEL,Sydney Robert T2Lt dow 20-4-18 4Lincs p75 CR Belgium38
SLIGHT,William Hubert T2Lt kia 26-9-17 RE 212FC p48 CR Belgium37,26-9-19
SLINGER,Albert 2Lt 3-5-18 206RAF MR20
SLINGER,George Nicholas T2Lt kia 28-11-16 159RFA p35 CR France452
SLINGER,William TLt kia 23-7-17 12 att1ELancs p111 CR France730

SLINGSBY,Anthony Edward King Lt kia 16-7-15 1/6WRid p227 CR Belgium23
SLINGSBY,Arthur Morris.MC.Capt kia 8-3-16 1A 56Rif p282
SLINGSBY,Charles 2Lt kld 7-8-15 4A&SH p174 CR Yorks250,3Bn
SLINGSBY,Henry Laurence.MC.Capt dow 11-8-17 2YLI att10DCLI p144&259 CR Belgium172
SLOAN,Arthur James 2Lt kia 30-8-18 C315RFA p209 CR France214
SLOAN,Cyril Rennie 2Lt ded 13-5-17 29RFC p13 CR France1483,Cyrie
SLOAN,George Henry Capt dow 16-11-15 2ScotHorse p205 CR Gallipoli26
SLOAN,Harold Alexander 2Lt kia 21-1-17 RGA 198SB p42 CR France786
SLOAN,John Bruce 2Lt kia 23-7-18 5 att7/8KOSB p224 CR France865
SLOAN,Thomas Ian Thompson 2Lt kia 23-4-17 7A&SH p243 CR France545
SLOAN,Thomas William 2Lt kia 20-9-17 8Lond p247 MR29
SLOAN,Wilfred Scott Lt kia 28-4-17 8 att1ScotRif p225 CR France40,Wilfrid dow
SLOANE-STANLEY,Humphrey Henry.MC.LtACapt kia 13-4-18 4GrenGds 1Coy p50 MR32
SLOCOCK,Cyprian Henry Benson LtACapt dow 3-4-18 3 att2 O&BLI p130 CR France102
SLOCOCK,Lancelot Andrew Noel 2Lt kia 9-8-16 1/10Lpool p216 MR21
SLOCOMBE,Arthur Douglas 2Lt kia 30-7-16 8Glouc p107 CR France432
SLOLEY,Robert Hugh 2Lt kia 1-10-17 RGA att56RFC p13&42
SLOPER,Bruce James.MC.T2Lt kia 31-8-18 3MGC Inf p185 CR France614
SLOPER,Gerard Orby.MC.Capt ded 8-2-19 NumbF att5Bn p63 MR70
SLOPER,Victor Frederick 2Lt drd 10-10-18 4Wilts p236 CR Wilts16
SLOWE,Alfred T2Lt dow 25-8-17 YLI att6Bn p144 CR Belgium11,Abraham
SMAIL,Frank Weddell Lt dow 1-12-15 1/7NumbF D'Coy p214 CR Numb34
SMAILES,Frank Capt&QM ded 21-11-19 GL Yorks p267 CR Yorks159
SMAILES,George T2Lt kia 22-10-16 2WYorks p83 MR21
SMALE,Florence Emily Nurse 13-10-15 VAD 19GH CR Egypt3
SMALL,Alexander Couper.MC.T2Lt kia 23-10-16 2ELancs p111 CR France307
SMALL,Arnold T2Lt dow 12-4-17 8Mddx p148 CR France120
SMALL,Dudley Francis Capt kia 24-3-18 15Ches p255 MR27
SMALL,E.Capt 28-4-21 Beds CR Beds23
SMALL,Frank Gilbert Harrell 2Lt dow PoW 9-6-18 47MGC p185 CR Germany3,Lt
SMALL,Hugh Alexander.MC.T2Lt kia 10-7-16 20Lpool p72 MR21
SMALL,James Bruce Lt kld 2-8-18 1/4RB att101RAF p180 CR France29
SMALL,John TLt kia 29-4-16 9BlkW p129 CR France423
SMALL,John Bertram T2Lt kia 23-3-18 4SStaffs p123 MR20
SMALL,Walter 2Lt mbk 30-7-16 9 att2RScotF p256 MR21
SMALLEY,John Douglas Lt kia 15-3-15 1Camb D'Coy p245 CR Belgium111
SMALLEY,Robert Francis Lt ded 14-5-18 4SStaffs p123 MR32,14-4-18
SMALLEY,Walter Herbert T2Lt dow 28-10-18 2Nhampt p138 CR France113
SMALLEY,William Miles 2Lt kia 9-12-14 N&D p135 CR France924
SMALLMAN,Arthur Frederick Strong 2Lt kia 14-11-16 1HAC Inf p206 CR France339
SMALLMAN,Edward 2Lt ded 19-11-16 RE p210 CR Surrey152
SMALLWOOD,Eric Butter.MC.Capt kia 7-1-17 Herts p252 CR Belgium73,Butler
SMALLWOOD,Frank Graham.CVO.Col ded 30-12-19 RAOC p267 MR65 Ex RA
SMALLWOOD,George Baxter.MM&Bar.2Lt ded 2-11-18 RLancs attMGC p59&185 CR Lancs171
SMALLWOOD,James Fenemore.MC.MID TLt dow 22-5-17 11Mddx p148 CR France40
SMALLWOOD,Reginald 2Lt kia 18-4-17 5Ches p222 MR20
SMALLWOOD,Robert Henry Lt dow 27-5-18 PoW 4NumbF p63 MR18
SMALLWOOD,William Spencer T2Lt kia 25-1-18 GL &22RFC p17 CR France88
SMART,Claude Edward TLt kia 24-7-17 10Worc p109 CR France644,14Bn
SMART,David Lorimer 2lt dow 5-4-17 RE 430FC p210 CR France80
SMART,Edgar Herbert Lt kia 30-11-17 1/6Lond p246 MR17
SMART,Edward Treloar Lt mbk 27-3-18 RGA &2RFC p256 MR20
SMART,Eric Douglas 2Lt kia 18-11-16 10RWar p66 MR21
SMART,Eustace Fowler TLt kia 8-2-16 7Leic p88 CR France745
SMART,George Henry Capt kia 22-12-14 4WYorks attNLancs p83 MR22
SMART,George Orme T2Lt kia 7-4-17 GL &RFC p13 MR20
SMART,Norman Lt kia 16-10-17 1/8LancF attMGC p187&221 CR Belgium88
SMART,Walter TLt kia 3-10-18 6MGC Inf p185 CR France441
SMART,William Ellis 2Lt kia 11-10-18 3Yorks att7WYorks p91 CR France612
SMART,William Leonard T2Lt kia 29-8-18 1/2LancF att8RLancs p93 CR France615
SMARTT,William Francis Capt ded 15-1-16 RAMC p271 CR Norf15
SMEATHMAN,Cecil Lt dow 24-10-14 Leic p88 CR France284
SMEATHMAN,Julian Missensden Lt kia 24-10-14 RE p48 MR29
SMEDDLE,George Robert Graham TLt kld 11-3-18 RFC p17 CR Durham55
SMEE,Arthur Joseph 2Lt ded 28-10-18 3Wilts attRAF p153 CR Surrey15

SMEETH,H.G.2Lt 25-9-18 att2/4RWSurr CR Belgium192
SMEETH,William Sutton T2Lt kld 17-7-17 9RIrRif attRFC p13&170 CR Yorks475
SMELLIE,John Ormond Lt ded 8-8-17 MGC Inf p185 CR Essex86
SMERDON,John Geoffrey T2Lt kia 20-9-17 3SomLI att2/5LancF p80 MR30
SMETHAM,James Eric 2Lt kia 14-11-16 RWar att3MGC p66 MR21
SMETHURST,Frederick James.MC.LtACapt kia 30-11-17 1/5SLancs p230 MR17
SMETHURST,John T2Lt kia 16-9-16 12Lpool p73 CR France374
SMILES,Samuel T2Lt kia 16-8-17 13RIrRif p170 CR Belgium125,1Bn
SMILES,William Alan TCapt kia 9-7-16 2RIrRif p170 MR21
SMILLIE,George Sinclair 2Lt dow 13-8-17 C121RFA p35 CR Belgium16
SMITH,Adam Davidson 2Lt kia 2-10-18 4RScots p211
SMITH,A.H.T2Lt ded 16-8-18 LabCps p189 CR Essex5
SMITH,Alan Douglas Hay 2Lt kia 26-3-17 4Ess p232
SMITH,Alan Francis Broadley Maj kia 16-6-15 5BordR p228 CR Belgium167
SMITH,Alan Joseph 2Lt kia 9-7-18 RGA 49SB p209 CR France19
SMITH,Alan Langdale Capt ded 3-12-19 IA 63Inf att1/80CarnaticInf p282 CR Iraq8
SMITH,Alan Raymond Noel 2Lt ded 10-7-19 IA 130Baluchis p282 MR43 &CR Pakistan50A
SMITH,Alan Wenman Lt kld 18-3-17 6Lpool &RFC p215 p271
SMITH,Albert Edward 2Lt kia 22-3-16 1Lincs p75 MR32
SMITH,Albert Francis 2Lt mbk 9-9-16 9Mddx att13Lond p257 MR21
SMITH,Albert Gower Capt dow 20-5-16 3 att1Manch p156 CR Iraq5
SMITH,Albert Victor T2Lt kia 28-8-18 20Mddx p148 CR Belgium188
SMITH,Alec T2Lt kia 8-7-16 10LancF p93 MR21
SMITH,Alexander Cooper T2Lt kia 23-7-16 2RSuss p120 MR21
SMITH,Alexander Cyril T2Lt kia 23-11-16 10LNLancs p136 MR21,Ayre
SMITH,Alexander Joseph.MM.2Lt kia 31-7-17 11RWSurr p56 MR29
SMITH,Alexander Millar 2Lt dow 26-1-18 16KRRC p152 CR Belgium3
SMITH,Alexander Noel 2Lt dow 26-9-16 7NumbF p214 CR France102
SMITH,Alexander Will.MC.2Lt kia 21-3-18 GordH att1/5Bn p167MR27
SMITH,Alfred Archibald Lt kia 2-4-16 1/5SStaffs p229 CR France68
SMITH,Alfred Percy Capt kia 23-8-15 RAMC att32FA p197 MR4
SMITH,Alfred Victor.VC.2Lt kia 22-12-15 1/5ELancs p226 CR Gallipoli6
SMITH,Alfred William.MM.T2Lt dow 4-10-17 8Leic att8Lincs p88 CR Belgium11
SMITH,Algernon Lindsay Eric.MIDx2 Lt kia 31-11-14 1LifeGds p20 CR Belgium167,31-10-14
SMITH,Allan Bertram.MBE.Lt kia 27-5-18 5 att1/8A&SH p243&258 CR France498
SMITH,Allan Higson.MC.Capt kia 21-8-17 GL &21RFC p13 MR20
SMITH,Allan Wenman Lt kld 18-3-17 6Lpool &1RFC p261 CR Lancs170
SMITH,Allison Gould.MC.Capt kia 18-4-18 7LNLancs p136 MR19
SMITH,Andrew 2Lt kia 14-11-16 6NumbF p214 MR21
SMITH,Archibald MacBrayne 2Lt dow 31-7-17 9A&SH p244 CR Belgium7
SMITH,Arthur T2Lt kia 26-8-18 N&D att10Bn p135 MR16
SMITH,Arthur Lt drdacc 25-10-19 RE CR Lancs43
SMITH,Arthur Borland Lt kia 1-8-16 5ScotRif p224 CR France864,10Bn
SMITH,Arthur Charles Vaughan T2Lt kia 9-10-17 EYorks att8WRid p85 MR30
SMITH,Arthur Gilliat Lt kia 1-11-14 RE p48
SMITH,Arthur Harold T2Lt kia 27-3-18 18 att9Manch p156 MR27
SMITH,Arthur Herbert ACapt kia 6-10-16 2Dev C'Coy p77 MR19
SMITH,Arthur Hodson 2Lt dow 9-6-18 1/5N&D p233 CR France10
SMITH,Arthur Howard T2Lt kia 14-7-16 10Leic p88 MR21
SMITH,Arthur John TLt kia 25-9-15 7Lond p247 CR France550
SMITH,Arthur Jonathan T2Lt kia 28-3-18 36MGC Inf p185 CR France360
SMITH,Arthur Leslie Lt kld 22-8-17 1/4SfthH attRFC p19&241 CR Lond3
SMITH,Arthur Roughton 2Lt dow 22-7-16 1/6Glouc p225 CR France44
SMITH,Arthur William T2Lt kia 7-9-18 23RFus p70 CR France530
SMITH,Aubrey Fairer Lt 24-4-18 RASC MT CR France880
SMITH,Augustus William T2Lt kia 2-2-16 5 O&BLI p130 CR Belgium20
SMITH,Bernard Alfred 2Lt dow 16-4-18 3 att9Norf p74 CR Belgium38
SMITH,Bernard Ridley Winthrope Lt dow 15-11-14 ScotsGds p52
SMITH,Brian Rivers Capt kia 8-8-18 4Lond p246 MR16
SMITH,Burns Crawford 2Lt kia 31-10-17 4NumbF p213 CR Belgium11
SMITH,C.MC.Lt 5-6-20 2NumbF CR Iraq8
SMITH,C.SNurse 26-1-21 TFNS CR Yorks361
SMITH,C.F.2Lt kia 9-4-18 12Suff att121TMB p79 MR32
SMITH,Campbell Lindsay TLt kia 10-11-15 11 att8GordH p167
SMITH,Cecil 2Lt kld 12-10-18 ArmyCycCps NorthernCycBn p244&271
SMITH,Cecil 2Lt kia 14-10-18 18WelchR CR France258
SMITH,Cecil Owen 2Lt kia 20-8-17 36/33RFA p35 CR Belgium84

SMITH,Cecil Ramsden T2Lt kia 12-6-17 M'SpecCo RE p48 CR France922
SMITH,Cedric Harry.MC.2LtACapt kia 31-10-17 RGA 229SB p42 CR Belgium19
SMITH,Charles Alfred 2Lt kia 1-10-16 17Lond p250 MR21
SMITH,Charles Arthur.DCM.T2Lt kia 19-9-18 1/2Leic p88 CR France1701
SMITH,Charles Cyril 2Lt kia 25-9-15 5KSLI p145 MR29
SMITH,Charles Edgar Holton TCapt kia 16-9-16 RAMC att10/11HLI p197 CR France239
SMITH,Charles Emanuel Webb T2Lt kld 28-7-17 GL &RFC p13
SMITH,Charles Ernest Lt kia 13-4-18 1/6Lpool p215 CR France88
SMITH,Charles Francis Bateman Lt kia 15-2-15 1Suff p79 MR29
SMITH,Charles Henry T2Lt kia 19-3-16 13WelshR p127 CR France279 Ex 4Ches
SMITH,Charles Henry.MID TMaj kia 27-7-16 8Y&L p159 MR21
SMITH,Charles Hoyle 2Lt kia 23-4-17 9 att13RScots p212 MR20
SMITH,Charles Jervoise Dudley 2Lt kia 16-6-15 1GrenGds p50 MR22,15-6-15
SMITH,Charles John 2Lt mbk 27-5-18 7Worc p257 MR18
SMITH,Charles Jonsing Capt ded 20-12-19 5Mddx p265 CR Surrey84
SMITH,Charles Maxwell 2Lt kia 3-5-17 7Ess p232 MR20
SMITH,Charles Randolph 2Lt kia 22-4-17 RGA 244SB p42 CR France214
SMITH,Charles Sydney.MC.MID TMaj ded 28-11-18 97MGC p185 CR Derby98
SMITH,Charles Theodore 2Lt dow 22-5-15 3DragGds p21 CR France102
SMITH,Clement Roy Blackshaw 2Lt kia 28-4-17 3 att6Beds p86 MR20
SMITH,Clifford Day 2Lt kia 23-10-18 5 att9Norf p217 CR France190,Lt
SMITH,Clifford Thomas 2Lt kia 30-7-17 B122RFA p35 CR Belgium12
SMITH,Colin T2Lt kld 11-3-17 GL &48RFC p13 CR Lincs181
SMITH,David.MC.DCM.2Lt kia 18-10-18 1BlkW p129 CR France1271
SMITH,David Arthur 2Lt kia 26-10-17 4NumbF p213 MR30
SMITH,David Thorne T2Lt kia 3-12-17 14DLI p161 MR17
SMITH,Donald Graham 2Lt kld 10-4-18 1/4Mddx &42RAF Ex RAMC p148 MR20
SMITH,Donald Charnock TCapt kia 1-7-16 16WYorks p83 MR21
SMITH,Donald 2Lt ded 29-1-19 1SfthH p165 CR Egypt2
SMITH,Donald Claud T2Lt dow 13-10-15 7Suff p79 MR19
SMITH,Donovon Richardson McCallum 2Lt dow 27-5-18 4Manch att 1Worc p156 MR18
SMITH,Douglas George.MC.TLt dow 16-8-17 6KSLI p145 CR Belgium16
SMITH,Douglas Robert Capt ded 9-9-18 8Lond att47Div HQ p247 CR France788
SMITH,Douglas Tweedie 2Lt 10-4-16 RFC CR Essex86
SMITH,Douglas Wilberforce TCapt kia 1-7-16 RAMC att20Manch p197 CR France397
SMITH,Dugald T2LtACapt dow 8-10-18 4RFus p70 CR France338
SMITH,Duncan Galloway Capt dow 26-6-16 RE 1FC p210 CR France203
SMITH,Duncan Robertson Moir T2Lt dow 27-8-17 1RScots p55 CR France1461
SMITH,Duncan Vaughan.DSO.LtCol dow 13-4-17 1Lond p145 CR France145
SMITH,E.2Lt kld 29-4-18 GL &RAF p191 CR France184,28-4-18
SMITH,Edgar Ernest.MC.TLt kia 3-12-17 183MGC Inf p185 MR17
SMITH,Edmund Davidson MajGen ded 8-9-16 Staff AQMG p261 CR Lond8
SMITH,Edmund Percival Col kia 2-5-15 17RFA p35 CR Gallipoli2,Perceval
SMITH,Edward Capt 25-3-20 RDC CR Numb4
SMITH,Edward Corrigan Capt kia 30-9-15 2Suff p79 CR Belgium167
SMITH,Edward Frank T2Lt kia 7-7-16 12Manch p156 MR21
SMITH,Edward James TLt kia 28-9-16 8WRid p116 MR21
SMITH,Edward John.MIDx2 TCapt kia 5-10-18 GL &22NumbF p63 CR France163
SMITH,Edward Pelham 2Lt kia 16-8-18 9Lpool att12Norf p216 CR France19
SMITH,Edward Thompson T2Lt kia 19-10-15 8EKent p58 CR Belgium56
SMITH,Edwin Rivers 2Lt ded 6-11-18 RGA p262
SMITH,Eric 2Lt ded 15-10-16 8RWKent p142 CR France32
SMITH,Eric Arthur T2Lt kia 22-7-16 14RWar p66 CR France432
SMITH,Eric Drummond T2Lt kia 4-10-17 9N&D att6Y&L p135 MR30
SMITH,Eric John Garner Lt kia 26-5-15 24Lond p252
SMITH,Eric St.Clare Lt kld 2-7-17 RFA attRFC p13&35 CR Essex1
SMITH,Ernest Lt kia 12-7-15 5KOSB p224 MR4
SMITH,Ernest Edwin Lt ded 26-6-16 RIM p282
SMITH,Ernest Frederick William T2Lt dow 27-12-16 1Leinst attRFC p4&175 CR France833
SMITH,Ernest George Humphrey 2Lt kia 3-11-17 7Ess p232 CR Palestine8,Humphery 1/4Bn
SMITH,Ernest John TMaj dow 28-12-15 7YLI p144 CR France345
SMITH,Ernest Kennedy 2Lt dow 22-12-15 1EKent p58 CR Belgium11
SMITH,Ernest Stuart 2Lt kia 15-5-18 6RWar p214 MR19
SMITH,Ernest Wilson Marshall 2Lt kld 22-3-16 5Leinst attMGC p175&185 CR Lincs61
SMITH,Evelyn Hay Hindley TCapt ded 16-5-18 Ex 5Manch p271

SMITH,Everard Cecil Lt kia 23-8-14 RFus p70 CR Belgium242

SMITH,F.E.SNurse 1-7-18 QAIMNS CR Lancs32

SMITH,F.de Lisle Lt 30-10-18 RFA CR Ireland14

SMITH,F.J.CB.VD.BrCol 3-6-16 8ScotRif CR Scot756

SMITH,Fereday Fisher Lt kia 28-11-17 4Huss p21 MR17

SMITH,Francis Douglas Matthews 2Lt dow 25-1-16 7Mddx C'Coy p235 CR France525

SMITH,Francis Edwin Lt ded 18-11-18 1Camb p245 CR War151,Capt

SMITH,Francis Geoffrey John LtACapt ded 29-7-18 RASC 3Coy 59Div p253 CR France226,F.J.G.

SMITH,Francis John Lt ded 30-10-18 15Lond p271 CR Oxford24

SMITH,Francis Johnston.MC.2Lt kia 16-5-17 7 att6GordH p242 CR France604

SMITH,Francis Shingleton Capt kia 24-11-15 IA IMS att120RajputsInf p282 MR38

SMITH,Frank Harold T2Lt kia 2-9-18 9TankCps p188 CRFrance426

SMITH,Frank Redfern Lt dow 17-11-17 7Mddx attRE 66DivSigs p235 CR Belgium3

SMITH,Frank William Howard Lt dow 4-12-17 19Lond p250 CR France145

SMITH,Frederick Charles 2Lt kia 10-7-17 4Nhampt att2KRRC p234 MR31

SMITH,Frederick George.MID T2Lt kia 8-10-16 23DLI p161 CR France1182

SMITH,Frederick George T2Lt kld 8-2-18 RFC p17 CR War50

SMITH,Frederick George 2Lt kia 27-8-18 9HLI p240 CR France162

SMITH,Frederick Herbert Corbett Douglas 2Lt kia 10-12-17 RGA 52SB p42 CR France161

SMITH,Frederick John Capt dow 23-8-18 5Beds p219 CR France281

SMITH,Frederick Neville Cowran ALt dow 27-8-16 6Worc att100TMB p109 CR France833

SMITH,Frederick Seaton Chap4Cl ded 15-11-18 RAChDept att13Y&L p200 CR France34

SMITH,Frederick William TCapt kia 25-4-16 1WYorks p83 CR Belgium73

SMITH,Frederick William 2Lt dow 11-4-17 5Lincs p220 CR France113

SMITH,Geoffrey Bache TLt&Adjt dow 3-12-16 19LancF p93 CR France120

SMITH,Geoffrey Cholerton.MC.2LtTLt kia 31-7-17 RASC attRFC p13&193 CR Belgium11

SMITH,Geoffrey H.MC.ACapt mbk 16-10-18 1CldGds p256 CR Belgium242,22-10-18

SMITH,Geoffrey Harold 2Lt dow 10-7-17 1Nhampt D'Coy p138 MR31

SMITH,Geoffrey Herbert T2Lt dow 22-9-16 1EKent p58 CR France145

SMITH,Geoffrey Watkins TCapt kia 10-7-16 13RB p180 CR France832

SMITH,George.MID Capt kia 13-3-15 6GordH p242 MR22

SMITH,George T2Lt kia 15-9-16 10 att9RWKent p142 CR France277

SMITH,George Alan Campbell.MC.TCapt kia 28-9-18 14A&SH p174 CR Belgium185

SMITH,George Alexander.DSO.LtCol kia 28-7-18 4GordH p241 CR France524

SMITH,George Buchanan 2Lt kia 25-9-15 GordH att2Bn p167 MR19

SMITH,George de Ville TCapt kia 1-7-16 13Y&L p159 CR France156

SMITH,George Evanston Lt kia 25-9-15 3A&SH p174 CR France114,2Bn

SMITH,George Lawrence Lotinga T2Lt kia 19-7-17 10NumbF p63 CR Belgium29,Laurence

SMITH,George Maxwell Lt ded 13-9-19 3 att1N&D p264 MR65,10Bn

SMITH,George Morley T2Lt dow 6-10-17 7Leic p88 CR France139

SMITH,George Pringle TLt kia 12-4-17 14RScots p55 CR France604

SMITH,George William 2Lt mbk 28-3-18 8RLancs p257 MR20

SMITH,Gerald Howard.MC.Lt kia 29-3-16 6SStaffs p229 CR France95,dow

SMITH,Gerald Sydney TLt kia 13-11-16 153MGC Inf p185 CR France1502

SMITH,Gilbert Keppal TLt ded 13-3-16 5 att1Mddx p148 CR France423,Keppel dow

SMITH,Gilbert Parker 2Lt kld 5-1-18 2Yorks p91 CR Belgium127

SMITH,Godfrey Garrett 2Lt kia 11-5-17 2RWSurr p56 MR20

SMITH,Godfrey Michael.MC.T2Lt dow 28-10-18 D256RFA p35 CR Yorks438

SMITH,Godfrey Leveson 2Lt kin 29 9-15 1CldGds p51 MR19

SMITH,Gordon Hamilton T2Lt kia 9-5-17 8Dev p77 MR20

SMITH,Gordon Keith.MC.Capt kia 21-8-17 GL &RFC p13 CR France276,Keigh

SMITH,Granville Keith Falconer Lt kia 29-10-14 1CldGds p51 MR29

SMITH,Granville Roland Francis.CVO.CB.Col ded 4-3-17 Ex CldGds p262

SMITH,Harold 2Lt kia 12-10-16 7Norf p74 CR France512

SMITH,Harold.MC.Capt kia 22-11-17 2/6WYorks p218 MR17

SMITH,Harold.MC.TCapt&Adjt dow 28-3-18 15WYorks p83 CR France169

SMITH,Harold Andrew 2Lt kia 21-3-18 N&D att2/6Bn p135 MR20

SMITH,Harold Benjamin 2Lt dow 20-5-17 7Lond p247 CR France568

SMITH,Harold Henderson 2Lt kia 19-9-18 4 att1BlkW p230 MR16

SMITH,Harold Heyworth T2Lt kia 13-2-16 150RFA att1TMB SpBde RE p35 CR France275

SMITH,Harold Robert Lt kia 21-3-18 NStaffs p157 MR20,Rymer

SMITH,Harold Robert.MC.TLt kia 7-11-18 RWKent att8Bn p142 MR16

SMITH,Harold Spencer 2Lt kia 31-7-18 3Lond &53RAF p246&258 CR France20

SMITH,Harry Gordon 2Lt kia 13-3-18 4A&SH p174 CR Greece6

SMITH,Harry Graham TCapt drd 10-4-17 RAMC p197 CR Europe96

SMITH,Harry Leonard Chappell Lt kia 20-10-14 N&D p135 MR32

SMITH,Harry Marsden Lt dow 27-2-17 PoW 1LNLancs p136 CR France1266

SMITH,Harry Norman T2Lt kia 2-3-17 20LancF p93&258 CRBelgium20,23-11-17

SMITH,Headford 2Lt dow 14-9-18 119ArmyBde A119RFA p35 CR France34

SMITH,Henry 2Lt drd 1-1-17 WorcYeo p206 CR Greece16

SMITH,Henry T2Lt kia 19-10-18 13Manch p156 CR France1392,9Bn

SMITH,Henry Crawford 2Lt ded 10-10-16 1OxfHuss p271

SMITH,Henry Dalby Dryden Capt kld 14-12-17 DLI attRFC CR Hamps1

SMITH,Henry James T2Lt kia 4-10-17 8SomLI p80 MR30

SMITH,Henry Leslie 2Lt kia 17-8-17 RFA p209 CR France266

SMITH,Henry Thomas Bayard 2Lt kia 25-3-18 4Huss &9TankCps p21&189 MR27

SMITH,Herbert T2Lt dow 19-7-17 3 att2Manch p156 CR Belgium24

SMITH,Herbert Bennett 2Lt kia 17-7-17 WSomYeo p205 CR Belgium78,12SomLI

SMITH,Herbert Carington LtCol kia 25-4-15 2Hamps p121 MR4

SMITH,Herbert Dudley T2Lt kia 17-3-18 1/2 att2/7LancF p93 CR France528

SMITH,Herbert Evans 2Lt dow 18-6-17 1/5NStaffs p237 CR France178

SMITH,Herbert Fyfe T2Lt kia 23-4-17 2RScotF A'Coy p95 MR20

SMITH,Herbert George.MC.TCaptAMaj ded 16-2-19 RASC p267 CR Surrey160

SMITH,Herbert James T2Lt dow 29-4-16 10RLancs attRDubF p59 CR France551

SMITH,Herbert James 2Lt kia 9-4-18 7 att13ESurr p113 MR32

SMITH,Herbert Leslie TCapt kia 24-3-18 19Lpool p73 MR27

SMITH,Herbert Norman 2Lt kia 20-11-17 5WYorks p218

SMITH,Herbert Shaw 2Lt dow 12-4-17 9RScots p212 CR France40

SMITH,Herbert Stoney.DSO.LtCol kia 22-10-15 1Leic p88 CR Belgium5

SMITH,Horace 2Lt kia 8-10-16 5Lond p246 MR21

SMITH,Horace Claudian T2Lt kia 11-9-17 52RFC p13 CR Belgium173

SMITH,Horace Richard.MC.2Lt kia 5-11-17 9Lond p248 CR France939,Capt

SMITH,Horace Uchtred T2Lt kia 18-1-18 8SStaffs p123 CR France530

SMITH,Hubert Hector Capt kia 25-9-15 8KOSB p102 MR19

SMITH,Hugh Francis Russell 2Lt dow 5-7-16 1 att6RB p180

SMITH,Hugh Stewart TCapt kia 18-8-16 4 att2A&SH D'Coy p174 CR France432

SMITH,Isham Percy.DSO.CaptAMaj kia 30-11-17 RGA 102SB p42 CR France407

SMITH,Jacob Hardy.DSO.MC.Lt dow 29-8-16 3RB p180 CR France51,Capt

SMITH,James T2Lt kia 9-4-17 10GordH p167 CR France531

SMITH,James Lt ded 1-4-18 6SfthH attLabCps p266 CR Scot874,Capt

SMITH,James Albert 2Lt kia 21-3-18 RFA 30DAC p35 MR27

SMITH,James Bonner 2Lt kia 15-8-17 6BlkW att43RFC p19&231 MR20

SMITH,James Bowman T2Lt kia 28-6-18 7DCLI Ex ScotRif p115 MR20

SMITH,James Clement 2Lt kia 27-3-16 4RFus p70 MR29

SMITH,James Douglas LtACapt kia 27-9-18 ScotRif att1/7Bn p104 CR France484

SMITH,James Montague Lt&Adjt kia 2-5-15 RScots p211 MR4

SMITH,James Norman T2Lt kia 31-7-16 15Lpool att9Ches p73 CR France515

SMITH,James Osbourne Lt kia 2-11-17 1/7ScotRif p224 CR Palestine8

SMITH,James Rockcliffe.MC.TCapt kia 20-5-17 16KRRC p152 MR20

SMITH,James Salsbury Capt kia 17-12-17 LNLancs att 1/5Bn p136 MR17,2Lt 30-11-17

SMITH,James Tennant Capt kia 5-6-17 1/4ELancs p226 CR France905

SMITH,James William 2Lt kia 21-3-18 7GordH p242 MR20

SMITH,James William.MID 2Lt dow 30-11-18 RGA 251SB p42 CR Ches28

SMITH,Jeanie Barclay Sister 28-4-16 QAIMNS CR France40

SMITH,John 2Lt kia 14-11-17 6 att4/5BlkW p231 MR30

SMITH,John T2Lt kia 20-7-18 Lpool att5Dev p73 MR18

SMITH,John 2Lt ded 20-2-19 RGA 200SB p262 CR Scot758,Lt

SMITH,John Adams.MC.T2Lt dow 28-4-17 28 att20NumbF p63 CR France40

SMITH,John Alexander Hay T2Lt kia 14-8-15 11RScots p55 CR France410

SMITH,John Basil T2Lt dow 19-8-17 14RWar A'Coy p66 CR France113

SMITH,John Christie 2Lt kia 21-3-18 6N&D p233

SMITH,John Clarence 2Lt kia 2-12-17 1/20Lond p251 MR17

SMITH,John Dowse Lt ded 3-11-18 DLI CR Lancs43

SMITH,John Fletcher TLt ded 28-7-16 19N&D &RFC p4&135 CR Notts84

SMITH,John Frazer T2Lt kia 11-4-17 7CamH p168 CR France531

SMITH,John Gardiner T2Lt kia 20-9-17 O&BLI att6Bn p130 MR30

SMITH,John Godfrey Bradley TLt drd 15-4-17 RAMC p197 MR35

SMITH,John Grant Lt ded 27-2-19 RE p48 CR France40

SMITH,John Henry 2Lt kia 9-7-18 10Mddx att 103RAF p236&258 CR France31

SMITH,John Henry.MM.2Lt kia 28-8-18 Dev att7SomLI p77 MR16

SMITH,John Herbert Michael 2Lt dow 17-9-14 2Manch p156 CR France1113,10-9-14

SMITH,John Hobson 2Lt ded 24-11-18 78RH&FA p35 CR France658

SMITH,John Horne 2Lt kia 23-7-18 6ScotRif p224 CR Belgium3

SMITH,John Lancelot 2Lt kia 9-8-16 1/4SLancs p230 MR21

SMITH,John Macdonald T2Lt kia 12-5-16 12ScotRif p104 MR19

SMITH,John Marshall 2Lt dow 27-9-18 9HLI p241 CR France1184

SMITH,John Rankin Donald 2Lt kia 31-7-17 5RScotsF p222 MR29,2Bn

SMITH,John Richard Gutteridge T2Lt dow 30-12-16 32 att8NumbF p63 CR France40

SMITH,John Samuel 2Lt kia 28-4-17 5SStaffs p229 MR20

SMITH,John Selby Armstrong 2Lt mbk 25-4-17 3 att10WRid p257 MR20,att9Bn

SMITH,John Taylor T2Lt dow 29-3-18 18 att2WYorks p83 CR France650

SMITH,John Veere 2Lt dow 26-7-16 4/8Mddx p236 CR France80

SMITH,John Wilmhurst Grainger ACapt kia31-8-16.1SStaffs p123 MR21,Wilmshurst Granger

SMITH,Joseph 2Lt kia 14-3-17 6SStaffs p229 CR France281,1/5Bn

SMITH,Joseph Basil.MID T2Lt kia 18-9-18 SLancs att9Bn p126 MR37

SMITH,Joseph Cecil Lt kia 28-7-17 RFC p13 MR20

SMITH,Joseph Edward T2Lt kia 15-1-16 12HLI p164 CR France423,18-1-16

SMITH,Joshua Harold Lt kia 12-8-15 6LancF p221 CR Gallipoli2

SMITH,J.S.Lt30-4-20 RFA CR Cornwall140

SMITH,Julian Martin T2Lt ded 10-9-14 SL att9Lancers p201 CR France1441

SMITH,Kenneth Carrington Lt ded 26-3-19 RE p262 CR Staffs41

SMITH,Kenneth Leslie 2Lt kia 20-9-17 LancF p221 MR30

SMITH,Lawrence Brumwell T2Lt kia 14-9-18 10 att1/4LNLancs p136 CR France279,Lt

SMITH,Lawrence Oliver Lt ded 30-6-19 SL att1WT p268 CR Iraq6,GL

SMITH,Leon Walter Lt kia 12-4-18 4DCLI p227 MR32,1/5Bn

SMITH,Leonard George 2Lt kia 1-7-16 2Ess p132 MR21

SMITH,Leonard Hale Lt kld 3-11-17 6Ess attRFC p19&232 CR Essex1,2-11-17

SMITH,Leonard Hearne T2Lt kia 11-8-17 16Mddx p148 MR29

SMITH,Leonard William T2Lt kia 23-10-16 2Mddx p148 MR21

SMITH,Leslie Morgan TMaj ded 20-12-17 1BedsGarrBn p86 CR India48

SMITH,Leslie Phillips 2Lt ded 6-3-15 RGA p42 CR Kent231

SMITH,Leslie Tildero T2Lt kia 16-9-16 7YLI p144 MR21,Tilden

SMITH,Lothrop Lewis de Berniere Lt ded 3-9-16 6RB p180 CR Kent68,kldacc

SMITH,Louis Herbert Collin 2Lt kia 13-10-15 1Mon p244 MR19 CR France1896,Collen

SMITH,Martin Kirke Lt kld 14-12-15 RFA 99TMB p208 CR France637,kia

SMITH,Matthew Frederick.MC.TCapt kia 18-9-18 10WYorks p83 CR France415

SMITH,Neville Field TCapt kia 24-1-16 15DLI p161 CR France922

SMITH,Norman Edward T2Lt kia 20-7-18 1/2LancF att2/4Hamps p93 CR France622

SMITH,Norman Gordon 2Lt kia 19-12-15 HLI &RFC p2&164

SMITH,Norman Havelock 2Lt kia 23-3-18 20Lond att141TMB p251 MR20

SMITH,Norman Herbert 2Lt 20-11-17 2/5WYorks CR France1483

SMITH,Norman Louis Lt kia 30-12-17 1/4KSLI p235 MR17

SMITH,Norman McGaan Capt dow 12-12-17 RAMC 2FA p254 CR Palestine9

SMITH,Norman McNeill T2Lt kia 1-7-16 21NumbF p63 MR21

SMITH,Norman Spires Lt ded 1-2-19 RASC attRGA 27SB AC p193 CR France63,Spiers

SMITH,Olive Masseuse 24-9-16 ScotWomensHosp attSerbianArmy CR Greece7

SMITH,Patrick Leete TLt dow 27-9-15 10Y&L p159 CR France201

SMITH,Peter TLt kia 28-4-17 RE &12RFC p13&48 CR France46

SMITH,Percival Thomas Lt kia 26-9-15 8RWKent p142 MR19

SMITH,Percy T2Lt dow 13-5-18 1 att2/5LancF p93 CR France10

SMITH,Percy Claude Jacomb 2Lt kia 1-7-16 1EYorks p85 MR21

SMITH,Percy George Cecil 2Lt kia 18-8-18 11RScots D'Coy p55 CR France26

SMITH,Percy Kirk T2Lt kia 12-9-17 RE 212FC p48 CR Belgium37

SMITH,Percy Lloyd T2Lt kia 3-5-17 12WYorks p83 MR20

SMITH,Philip Golding T2Lt kia 5-10-18 13DLI p161 CR France844

SMITH,Quintin Livingstone T2Lt kia 1-7-16 13 att15LancF p93 MR21

SMITH,Ralph 2Lt kia 27-9-15 1WelshGds p53 MR19

SMITH,Ralph Eustace Capt kia 19-4-18 NumbYeo &RAF p204&258 CR France303,18-4-18

SMITH,Ralph Henry T2Lt kia 30-7-16 17Lpool p73 CR France294

SMITH,Ralph John TLt ded 31-7-18 GL RE IWT p48 CR Iraq6

SMITH,Ralph Leslie 2Lt murderedBySowar 16-7-16 IARO att126Baluchis p282 MR43,124Baluchis

SMITH,Ralph Pritchard T2Lt kia 5-8-17 8NStaffs p158 CR Belgium77

SMITH,Randolph Rae Lt ded 9-8-15 13N&D p264 CR Lond8,2Lt 12Bn

SMITH,Raymond TCapt kia 1-7-16 11BordR p118 MR21

SMITH,Raymond Alexander 2Lt kia 1-7-16 3Lond p246

SMITH,Reginald Lt kia 20-12-16 18RFC p4 CR France518

SMITH,Reginald Frederick 2Lt kia 14-5-17 15Lond p249 MR20

SMITH,Reginald George T2Lt kia 7-10-16 122MGC p185 MR21

SMITH,Reginald Iredale T2Lt kia 18-7-16 10A&SH p174 MR21

SMITH,Reginald John 2512 2Lt dow 1-4-18 D291RFA p35 CR France864

SMITH,Reston Alexander T2Lt kia 25-1-18 73RFC p17 CR France31

SMITH,Reuben Hinton Lt kldacc 10-1-18 4Dev p220 CR Kent38,14Bn Ex 15Bn

SMITH,Rex Johnston TCapt kia 1-7-16 15Y&L p159 CR France246

SMITH,Richard Alfred Capt ded 28-8-18 RAOC p198 CR Mddx77

SMITH,Richard Thomas 2Lt ded 3-5-15 4ELancs p226 CR Lancs193

SMITH,Robert 2Lt kia 1-7-16 2YLI p144 MR21

SMITH,Robert 2Lt dow 9-8-17 BordR att8Bn p118 CR Belgium112

SMITH,Robert 2Lt kia 20-11-17 1/4RLancs p59 CR France844

SMITH,Robert T2Lt kia 15-12-17 2RScotF p95 MR30

SMITH,Robert 2Lt kia 28-3-18 14Lond att7CamH p249 MR20

SMITH,Robert Campbell McIntyre 2Lt kia 20-6-16 8A&SH p243 CR France15

SMITH,Robert Cecil CaptALtCol dow 1-12-17 20DLI att11RWSurr p161 CR Italy76

SMITH,Robert Dunlop Capt kia 12-6-17 IA 33Punjabis p282

SMITH,Robert Fraser 2Lt kia 20-9-17 68MGC Inf p185 MR30

SMITH,Robert Gardner Paget 2Lt kia 15-9-16 9Suff p79 MR21

SMITH,Robert James 2Lt kia 13-11-17 6SfthH p241 CR France131

SMITH,Robert John TCapt kia 6-5-16 15LancF p93 CR France251

SMITH,Robert Paterson.MC.T2Lt dow 2-8-17 8SfthH p165 CR Belgium8

SMITH,Robert Rutherford T2Lt kia 20-9-17 196MGC p185 CR Belgium10

SMITH,Robert Wright 2Lt kia 12-2-17 6HLI p240 CR France35

SMITH,Robert Yearsley Clarke 2Lt kia 21-3-18 2/6N&D p233 MR20

SMITH,Roderick Franklyn.MC&Bar.TCapt kia 28-3-18 6KSLI p145 MR27

SMITH,Roger T2Lt kia 25-1-17 4SWBord p101 MR38

SMITH,Roland 2Lt kia 6-4-17 3YLI Inf &RFC p13&144 MR20

SMITH,Ronald Christian Sundius 2Lt kia 13-3-15 ULIA att2WYorks p282

SMITH,Rowland Siddons Capt ded 21-10-18 3WYorks p263

SMITH,Roy Samuel 2Lt kia 11-4-17 9Lond p248 CR France104

SMITH,Samuel Douard Irvine Lt kia 1-7-16 5 att1RIrRif p170 CR France246

SMITH,Samuel Percy Capt kia 28-2-17 1/5SStaffs p229 CR France502

SMITH,Sergius Holland 2Lt kia 24-11-15 4 att2SStaffs p123 MR19

SMITH,Sidney Lt kia 8-12-15 RGA 113Bty p42 CR France222

SMITH,Sidney Arthur T2Lt kia 10-8-15 10Hamps p121 MR4

SMITH,Sidney Fraser 2Lt dow 3-9-17 D256RFA p209 CR France40

SMITH,Sidney George.VD.TD.LtCol ded 8-10-17 7Hamps p229 CR Iraq8

SMITH,Sidney George 2Lt kia 21-3-18 59MGC p185 MR20

SMITH,Sidney Harold T2Lt kld 23-10-17 GL &RFC p13 CR Shrop52

SMITH,Sidney John Howard 2Lt kia 10-2-17 10Dev p77 MR37

SMITH,Sidney O'Connol 2Lt dow 25-8-16 9RB p180 CR France177,O'Carrol Lt kia

SMITH,Stanley 2Lt kia 18-11-15 1/5YLI p235 CR Belgium23

SMITH,Stanley Fenton Capt kia 9-10-17 5Y&L p238 MR30

SMITH,Stanley Herd T2Lt dow 27-5-18 2TankCps p189 CR France885

SMITH,Susie Marie Colbourn SNurse 12-2-16 QAIMNS CR Staffs78

SMITH,Sydney Capt kia 19-5-18 3 att1ESurr p113 CR France177

SMITH,Sydney Bicheno 2Lt ded 1-12-18 RGA p209 CR Lond3

SMITH,Sydney Ferrar 2Lt kia 7-5-15 1Ches p96 MR29

SMITH,Sydney John T2Lt kia 20-9-17 26RFus p70 CR Belgium22

SMITH,Sydney Newman 2Lt kia 9-8-17 7Suff p79 MR20

SMITH,Sydney Phillip Capt kia 6-4-18 RASC &RAF p271 MR20,Philip

SMITH,T.E.2Lt ded 11-6-18 1/4Worc &RAF p109 CR War60

SMITH,Theodore Thomas 2Lt 29-9-18 11RAF MR20

SMITH,Thomas TMaj kia 23-1-17 6RScotF p95 CR France151,6/7Bn

SMITH,Thomas TLt ded 23-5-17 RAMC p267 CR Mddx26,22-5-17

SMITH,Thomas 2Lt kia 16-5-18 13RScots p55 MR20

SMITH,Thomas Lt kia 28-10-18 NottsYeo p205 MR38

SMITH,Thomas Arthur Lt kia 7-10-16 15Lond p249 MR21

SMITH,Thomas Edmund 2Lt kia 14-7-17 GL &27RFC p13 CR France924

SMITH,Thomas Edward 2Lt kia 5-9-18 8Lond p247 CR France511

SMITH,Thomas Emanuel 2Lt kia 23-4-17 RGA 263SB p42 CR France777,Emmanuel

SMITH,Thomas Lawrie Lt kia 18-9-18 AyrYeo attMGC p187&203 CR France415

SMITH,Thomas Rowland T2Lt dow 30-3-18 N&D attCamelCps p135 MR34

SMITH,Thomas Sidney 2Lt kia 13-10-14 Dors p124 MR22,Sydney

SMITH,Thurston Boyd T2Lt kia 7-6-17 11RWSurr p56 CR Belgium29

SMITH,Valentine Herbert Capt ded 1-6-18 5RWSurr &1KAR p212&268 CR EAfrica77

SMITH,Victor Sidney 2Lt kia 6-10-17 44RFA att113RFC p13&35 CR Palestine2

SMITH,Vivian Norman TCapt kia13-11-16.6Wilts p153 CR France251

SMITH,W.E.2Lt 13-5-17 RFC CR Mddx66

SMITH,Wansey 2Lt kld 2-4-18 11ELancs att10RAF p111 CR Belgium11,kia

SMITH,Wallace T2Lt kia 23-11-17 RE 129FC p48 CR France528

SMITH,Walter Ernest LtACapt dow 5-7-17 8YLI TrainingRes p144 CR France512

SMITH,Walter Gordon 2Lt ded 5-3-19 RASC 9CpsTroopSplyCo p267 CR Lond12,Lt

SMITH,Walter Sydney T2Lt kia 9-1-18 49RFC p17 CR France238

SMITH,Walter Thomas 2Lt kia 3-3-17 8Beds p86 CR France163

SMITH,Walter Tyrrell 2Lt kia 14-10-16 4BlkW p230 CR France215,Lt

SMITH,Walter Wyville T2Lt kia 18-10-15 9RFus p70 CR France423

SMITH,Wilbraham Fremantle 2Lt dow 28-9-16 5Ches p222 CR France105

SMITH,Wilfred 2Lt dow 9-5-17 4 att6RSuss p228 CR France40

SMITH,Wilfred Robert Abel.CMG.LtCol dow 19-5-15 2GrenGds p50 CRFrance727,Wilfrid

SMITH,Wilfred Vincent 2LtTLt kia 8-8-17 3 att8Glouc p107 CR Belgium17,7-8-17

SMITH,William Lt dow 17-6-15 4LNLancs B'Coy p234 CR France201

SMITH,William 2Lt dow 8-6-17 A275RFA p209 CR Belgium11,Lt

SMITH,William 2Lt kia 1-9-18 20Lond p251 MR16

SMITH,William 2Lt 29-10-18 2/5Lpool CR Lancs193

SMITH,William Alexander TLt dow 3-6-17 RAMC att27RFA p197 CR France95

SMITH,William Alfred.MID TLtCol dow 9-7-16 18Manch p156 CR France23

SMITH,William Arthur Heseltine 2Lt kia 27-5-18 1EYorks p85 MR18

SMITH,William Byron T2Lt dow 25-10-18 YLIatt9Bn p144 CR France332

SMITH,William Cecil 2Lt kia 31-7-18 5Manch p236 CR France5

SMITH,William Charles 2Lt ded 8-2-18 1RFC p17 CR Devon258

SMITH,William Edward.MC.2Lt kia 29-8-18 Mddx att1/13Lond p148 MR16

SMITH,William George Rae TLt kia 25-1-16 ArmyCycCps p181 CR France922

SMITH,William George Richard 2Lt kia 16-8-17 Mddxatt2Bn p148 MR30

SMITH,William Gerald Furness Lt dow 5-7-15 3 att1NStaffs p158 CR Belgium44

SMITH,William Gordon.MC.2Lt dow 21-3-18 4 att8Leic p220 CR France716,Lt 22-3-18

SMITH,William Hammond.MID CaptAMaj kia 12-4-17 A52RFA p35 CR France451

SMITH,William Harold Vyvyan 2Lt kia 31-7-17 2ELancs p111 MR29

SMITH,William Henry 2Lt kia 23-4-17 281RH&FA p35 CR France591

SMITH,William Henry T2Lt ded 4-11-18 RBerks Res att2/4Bn p140 CR Essex13

SMITH,William James Capt drd 29-5-17 Dors attEgyptianArmy p124 MR34

SMITH,William James TLt kia 2-10-17 Y&L att8Bn p159 MR30

SMITH,William Joseph 2Lt kia 31-7-17 4Leinst p175 CR Belgium84

SMITH,William Kenneth Ord ded 2-5-17 BRCS 17AmbTrn CR France134

SMITH,William Leslie LtACapt dow 15-4-18 2Worc p109 MR32,kld

SMITH,William Reginald Sturston 2Lt ded 22-10-17 GL &RFC p13 MR20

SMITH,William Robson LtACapt ded 19-11-18 RFA X31TMB 2ndArmy p35 CR France134

SMITH,William Roy TLt kia 24-3-18 RASC att8RWSurr p194 CR France605

SMITH,William Spencer 2Lt kia 23-7-16 2KOSB p102 MR21

SMITH,William Stanley 2Lt kia 25-6-16 RMunstF p176 CR France550

SMITH,William Strain.MC.T2LtACapt dow 23-3-17 1RScotF p95 CR France57

SMITH,William Travers.MID 2Lt kia 20-11-17 RE 174TC p48 CR France689

SMITH,William Watson T2Lt dow 18-10-16 11GordH p167 CR France145

SMITH,Willoughby Willard T2Lt kia 9-7-16 19Manch att21TMB p156 CR France630

SMITH,Wyndham Alexander 2Lt kia 23-4-16 GloucYeo p203 MR34

SMITH-CUMMING,Alexander Mansfield Lt kld 3-10-14 1SfthH p165 CR France1437,Alastair dedacc

SMITH-GRANT,John Gordon Smith Cheetham Capt ded 30-5-18 9RScots att70RAF p212&258 CR France84,kld

SMITH-HOWARD,Kenneth Overend Howard T2Lt kia 16/17-10-16 12RSuss p120 MR21,18-10-16

SMITH-LEE,Jeannie Nurse ded 30-3-17 VAD 30Detachment att9GH p200 CR France145

SMITH-MASTERS,Bruce Swinton.MC.Capt kia 1-7-16 2Ess p132 CR France643

SMITH-MASTERS,George Arthur T2Lt kia 19-8-15 6Beds p86 CR Belgium97

SMITH-MAXWELL,Archibald Findlay TLt kia 1-7-16 17HLI p164 CR France1890

SMITH-REWSE,Henry Bingham Whistler Maj dow 21-11-14 51/36RFA p35 CR Belgium150,22-11-14

SMITH-RYLAND,Henry Dennis Capt dow 7-4-17 1/1WarYeo p205 CR Egypt2

SMITH-SLIGO,Archibald George Roderick Joseph 2Lt kia 14-9-14 1CamH p168 MR15

SMITHER,Charles 2Lt 22-11-18 RFA CR Mddx17

SMITHER,Harold T2Lt kia 6-7-17 GL &48RFC p13 CR France403

SMITHERS,Edward Henry Keith TLt kia 9-7-16 11 att16Manch p156 MR21

SMITHERS,Harold TMaj kia 4-11-16 RGA p42 CR France5

SMITHERS,Reginald Cuthbert Welsford 2LtACapt kia 16-8-17 YLIatt7Bn p144 MR30

SMITHETT,Arthur Cecil Hamilton LtCol dow 24-11-15 IA 76Punjabis p282 MR38

SMITHETT,Graeme Cecil East 2Lt kia 12-10-17 1Nhants &27RFC p13&138 CR Belgium383,Lt

SMITHIES,Ellen Louise SNurse ded 22-2-19 TFNS 3SthGH CR Essex1

SMITHWICK,James Arnold Capt ded 9-11-15 4 att2RIrReg p89 CR Eire350

SMOLLETT-YOUNG,Alexander CaptHonMaj ded 23-5-16 SL 9A&SH p268 CR Scot80

SMOOTHY,Albert Victor 2Lt dow 9-11-18 2Lond p245 CR France1033

SMURTHWAITE,Douglas Stuart Stirling 2Lt kia 26-10-14 1BlkW A'Coy p129 MR29,Donald

SMURTHWAITE,Oscar TLt kia 17-4-18 18NumbF p63 MR32

SMYLIE,Robert Stewart R.TLt kia 14-7-16 7 att1RScotF p95 CR France453

SMUTH,Algernon Beresford Capt kia 15-11-14 2YLI p144 MR29

SMYTH,Arthur Hugo T2Lt kia 13-3-18 RASC 69SB AmmCol p194 CR France15

SMYTH,Donald Seymour 2Lt kia 19-10-14 RIrReg p89 MR22

SMYTH,Edmund Fitzgerald.MC.AMaj kia 3-12-17 11RIrRif p170 CR France379,Fitz-Gerald

SMYTH,Edwin Percy TLt kia 28-6-18 7RWKent p142 CR France21,Percival

SMYTH,George Bostall Jenkinson TLtACapt kia 22-10-18 7RIrRif p170 CR Belgium140,6Bn

SMYTH,Gerald Brice Ferguson.DSO&Bar.MIDx4 LtCol 17-7-20 RE CR Ireland106

SMYTH,Gordon Dill Long T2Lt kia 16-8-17 13RIrRif p170 MR30

SMYTH,Irvine Johnston 2Lt kia 3-9-15 5RInniskF p105 CR Gallipoli5,6Bn

SMYTH,James Capt kia 9-7-15 3 att2LancF p93 MR29

SMYTH,James 2Lt kia 12-3-17 2RFC p13 CR France924

SMYTH,John T2Lt kia 23-11-17 9RIrRif p170 MR17

SMYTH,John Albert Gordon T2Lt kia 29-6-18 5MGC Inf p185 CR France346

SMYTH,John Fairfax Field 2Lt kia 22-7-17 1ScotsGds p52 CR Belgium12

SMYTH,John Hawkins T2Lt kia 12-4-17 6 att2Leinst p175 CR France557,10-4-17

SMYTH,John Ross 2Lt kia 20-10-14 3 att2RIrReg p89 MR22

SMYTH,Mary Grace AssAdmintr ded 22-2-19 QMAAC p200 CR War74

SMYTH,P.G.4-3-19 VAD CR Egypt9

SMYTH,Philip Joseph T2Lt dow 16-9-16 6ConnRgrs attRFC p4&172 CR France23

SMYTH,Richard Alexander Noel Capt dow 8-11-14 RGA 5SB p42 CR France297,7-11-14

SMYTH,Ross Acheson Maj ded 27-9-17 10RInniskF p105 CR Ireland201 Ex RIrReg

SMYTH,William Henry TLt kia 17-4-18 2Worc p109 MR32

SMYTH,William Houghton TCapt kia 1-7-16 13RIrRif p170 MR21

SMYTH-OSBORNE,Wilfred Lt kia 29-8-15 1Worc p109 CR France347,Wilfrid

SMYTH-PIGGOTT,Bernard Cecil BvtMaj ded 15-4-16 DLI p161 CR USA23

SMYTHE,Andrew Graham Cowan Maj kia 7-9-17 RGA 140SB p42 CR Belgium83,Conran

SMYTHE,Frederick Fleming 2Lt kia 18-9-14 2Worc p109 CR France1329,Fleming Fredrick

SMYTHE,Lee Gordon Fuller Lt ded 26-4-20 IA 2/70BurmaRif p282 MR40

SMYTHE,Patrick Evelyn Lt ded 30-11-18 3 att2BlkW p129 CR Egypt1

SMYTHE,Ralph Conran Maj dow 22-11-15 RGA 2SB p42 CR France1

SMYTHE,Rudolph Meade Capt dow 13-9-15 5Beds p219 MR4 13-10 15

SMYTHIES,Ernest Dudley TCapt ded 16-7-18 RE p48 CR Glouc27

SNAGG,B.C.K.Capt 27-2-19 RM CR Sussex197

SNAITH,Henry T2Lt kia 5-4-15 10KOYLI p144 CR France745,5-4-18 2Bn

SNAITH,William Ernest T2Lt kia 3-5-17 Ex 3Bn 4RFus p70 MR20

SNAPE,Frank William 2Lt kia 7-5-15 2YLI p144 MR29

SNEADE,Charles George.MC.Lt kia 14-10-18 4Worc p109 CR Belgium161

SNEAD-COX,Geoffrey Phillip Joseph 2Lt kia 20-10-14 att1RWFus p99 MR29

SNEAD-COX,Richard Mary 2Lt kia 28-10-14 3RScots p55 MR22

SNEATH,Claude Davis Lt kia 14-10-14 4Mddx p148 CR France1106

SNEATH,Wilfred Archer.MC.TLt dow 11-7-17 RAMC att2FA p197 CR Belgium24,12-7-17

SNEATH,Wilfred Harry Lt 6-4-18 208RAF MR20

SNEDDON,Andrew Beattie 2Lt kia 3-10-17 GL &RFC p13 MR40

SNELGROVE,Frederick Augustus T2Lt kia 24-8-18 6RWKent p142 CR France370

SNELGROVE,Herbert Davys Bernard 2Lt kia 15-8-17 RFC p13 CR France1732

SNELGROVE,Sidney Henry TLt kia 30-7-15 14 att7KRRC p152 MR29

SNELL,Arthur Cyril Everitt 2Lt kia 18-10-16 26MGC p255 MR21,Everett

SNELL,Christopher T2Lt dow 14-7-16 10WRid p116

SNELL,Cyril Herbert Lt mbk 9/10-11-17 DofLancsOwnYeo att12Manch p257 MR30,Hubert 9-11-17 MR34,9-10-17

SNELL,Eric Aylmer Goldney.MID TMaj kia 16-11-17 1Beds att1/4KAR p86&202 CR EAfrica15 &CR Tanzania1

SNELL,Francis Saxon T2Lt kia 11-7-16 8 att9RBerks p140 CR France372

SNELL,Herbert 2Lt kia 7-4-17 24Lond att2/6LancF p252 CR France260

SNELL,Norris TCapt kia 14-7-16 8EYorks p85 MR20

SNELL,Philip Sidney T2Lt kia 9-8-15 6RIrFus p171 MR4

SNELL,Stanley Saxon 2Lt dow 6-5-18 B159RFA p35 CRFrance41

SNELLING,Frederick John T2Lt kia 30-10-17 7RWar p70 MR30,7RFus

SNELSON,Victor Louis T2Lt kia 15-7-17 WelshR att12SWBord p127 CR France439

SNEYD,Dryden George Thompson.MC.Maj ded 7-4-19 RGA p262 CR Lond4

SNEYD,Thomas Humphrey Capt kia 2-11-14 4 att2LancF p93 CR Belgium168

SNITHER,Chas 2Lt ded 22-12-18 RH&FA p262

SNOW,Cecil Longville LtCol kld 11-12-15 IntelDepot CR Egypt19

SNOW,Charles Foote 2Lt kia 30-6-16 RFA p35 CR Belgium136

SNOW,George Wilkie 2Lt kia 20-4-17 8RScots p212 CR France1182

SNOW,Richard Aslin 2Lt kia 4-12-15 1/4Y&L p238 CR Belgium23

SNOW,Tom Cyril Capt ded 10-7-19 LabCps Ex SomLI p266 CR Dorset94

SNOWBALL,John Francis Lt ded 29-9-18 RASC p271 CR Numb43

SNOWBALL,John Hearn 2Lt dow 15-9-16 108RFA p35 CR France294

SNOWDEN,Harcourt John Lt kia 11-1-15 1Herts p252 CR Belgium632

SNOWDEN,Harold Jackson Lt dow 11-8-17 2SLancs attRFC p13&126 CR Lond12

SNOWDEN,Jasper Whitfield Lt kia 25-2-17 9Worc p109 MR38

SNOWDEN,Reginald Wallace TLt kia 10-7-17 8SStaffs p123 MR21

SNOWDEN,Stanley Jackson Capt kia 26-3-17 9Mddx p236 MR34

SNOWDON,Henry Frederick Lt kia 6-10-16 1Lond p245 MR21

SNOWDON,Ralph 2Lt kia 2-10-17 4EYorks p219 CR France162

SNOWDON,Sidney Frank 2Lt kia 15-9-16 1Lond p245 MR21

SNOWIE,George T2Lt kia 15-9-16 8KOSB p102 MR21

SNYDER,Lorne 2Lt kia 23-4-17 Hamps att2Bn p121 MR20

SNYDERS,Emanuel Leon 2Lt kia 17-3-19 RASC p194 MR70 &CR Europe180

SOAME,Everard Nixon Buckworth Herne Capt kia 21-3-18 2/5NStaffs p237 MR20

SOAMES,A.R.Capt 22-7-21 6RWKent CR Lond29

SOAMES,Alfred.DSO.TMaj kia 13-10-15 att6EKent p58 MR19

SOAMES,Arthur Henry Leslie.MC.TLtCapt ded 7-7-15 3Huss attRFC p2&21 CR Wales619

SOAMES,Gilbert Horsman Maj kia 9-6-17 1WYorks p83 France114,9-1-17

SOAMES,Harold Martin Lt kia 11-9-14 20Huss p23 CR Belgium201,23-8-14

SOAMES,Maurice Gordon Maj dow 24-9-16 A48RFA p35 CR France833

SOAMES,Oliver Jack T2Lt kia 27-3-18 4Beds p86 CR France516

SOAMES,Robert Eley TLt kia 1-7-16 8ESurr p113 CR France513

SOAMES,William Noel Lt ded 19-5-16 ChesYeo p203

SODDY,James T2Lt kia 23-4-17 Norf p74 MR20

SODEN,Harold Corbet Lt kia 22-5-16 4Lpool p73 CR France163,23-5-16

SOGNO,George Frank T2Lt dow 9-10-17 13RSuss attRFC p13&120 CR Belgium18

SOLLEY,Bernard John 2Lt kia 10-8-18 2Lond p245 CR Belgium79

SOLLY,Arthur Norbury TCapt kia 11-8-17 GL Manch att20RFC p13 CR France134

SOLLY,William Buckle.MC.Lt dow 19-10-18 3LancF att101TMB p93 CR Belgium450

SOLOMAN,Edmund John T2Lt kia 2-8-17 1 att8SLancs p126 CR Belgium34

SOLOMON,Arthur Meyer Capt kia 24-3-18 10 att1/19Lond p248 MR20

SOLOMON,Hubert Philip 2Lt kld 20-10-17 RFC p13&258 CR Lincs136

SOLOMON,Harry M.Lt ded 5-12-18 6Beds &RAF p86

SOLOMON,John Howard 2Lt dow 21-4-17 7Lond att18KRRC p247 CR Belgium11

SOLOMON,Kenneth Maurice Halpen T2Lt dow 18-9-15 11Glouc att11Worc p107 CR Mddx40,Keneth Halgren

SOLOMON,L.B.TLt kia 12-4-18 2RFus attRAF p70 CR France193

SOLOMON,Leonard T2Lt kia 23-4-17 1KOSB p102 MR20

SOMAN,Leon Asher 2LtTLt kia 8-3-17 6LNLancs p136 MR38

SOMERS,Cyril Dermott Fouace 2Lt dow 20-5-17 1RInnisF p105 CR France113

SOMERS-COCKS,Reginald.MC.TCapt kia 24-4-18 GL att7SomLI p191 CR Belgium1, Staff att261InfBde

SOMERS-SMITH,John Robert.MC.Capt kia 1-7-16 5Lond p246 MR21

SOMERS-SMITH,Richard William 2Lt kia 30-6-15 7KRRC p152 CR Belgium165

SOMERSET,Fitz Roy Aubrey.MC.TLt kia 7-7-16 13Ches p96 MR20

SOMERSET,Norman Arthur Henry 2Lt kia 25-10-14 1GrenGds p50 CR Belgium140,23-10-14

SOMERVAIL,William Fulton.DSO.MC.CaptBdeMaj kia 4-10-18 2ScotRif p104 CR France725

SOMERVILLE,Harold Aytoun 2Lt kia 17-6-20 IA 1/129Baluchis p282 MR43

SOMERVILLE,Henry Arthur.MC.2Lt kia 28-3-18 RSuss &82RFC p17&120 CR France1234

SOMERVILLE,Martin Ashwood 2Lt dow 21-9-18 6RB att1/10Lond p180 CR Palestine9,Ashworth

SOMERVILLE,Richard Newman 2LtTLt kia 9-10-15 RE 94FC p48 CR France631

SOMERVILLE,Stafford Dudley 2Lt kia 5-7-16 5YLI p144 CR France702,Lt

SOMERVILLE,Stafford James MajTLtCol dow 16-8-17 1RInnisF att9RIrF p105 CR Belgium8

SOMERVILLE,William 2Lt kia 25-4-18 4RScots p211 CR Belgium168

SOMMERVILL,John 2Lt dow 31-10-18 4RScotF p222 CR Belgium143

SOMMERVILLE,George Little Capt kia 16/18-8-16 3 att8RLancs p59 MR21,16-8-16

SOMMERVILLE,William Henry Lionel.MC.TLt ded 3-12-18 RAOC 550AS p198 CR France34

SONDHEIM,Walter T2Lt kld 4-3-18 RFC p17 CR Wilts28

SONES,Liba 2Lt kia 22-3-18 5 att2LNLancs p234 MR27,Ziba

SONGER,William Arthur T2Lt kia 15-9-16 9RB attTMB p180 MR20

SONGHURST,Charles Edward.MM.T2Lt kia 22-8-18 Ess Res att9Bn p132 MR16

SONNEX,Ernest James Harvey 2Lt kia 24-9-18 4RBerks p234 CR France234,Lt

SOPWITH,Frank Wesley.MC.Lt kia 27-5-18 251RFA att50NumbrianHB p208 CR France1329

SORBY,Charles Malin Clifton 2Lt dow 8-5-15 3Mon p244 CR France284

SORGE,Ivan Percival Campbell T2Lt dow 15-10-16 9 att6BordR Pnrs p118 CR France121

SORLEY,Charles Hamilton TCapt kia 13-10-15 7Suff p79 MR19

SORO,William T2Lt kia 16-4-17 20RFus p70 CR France434

SORRILL,Herbert 2Lt ded 22-5-19 O&BLI p264 CR Staffs52

SORTWELL,Arthur Robert Capt ded 28-3-18 RASC attRFC p267 CR Mddx53,28-2-18

SOTHAM,Ralph Clifford Lt kia 9-1-18 5WSurr attRFC p19,212,271&261,RWKent

SOTHEBY,Lionel Frederick Southwell 2Lt kia 25-9-15 A&SH p174 MR38

SOTHERS,Charles Gordon T2Lt dow 6-12-17 18Mddx p148 CR Belgium45

SOUCHOTTE,C.2Lt kld 23-4-18 GL &RAF p191

SOULE,Francis Lt&QM ded 23-11-19 RAMC p267 CR Hamps62

SOULSBY,Henry Stanley T2Lt kia 6-7-16 9 att6KOSB p102 CR France402

SOULSBY,William Dobson 2Lt kia 31-8-18 6Lond p247 CR France624

SOUNESS,Thomas 2Lt kia 7-9-18 116/26RFA p35 CR France309

SOUPER,Noel Beaumont T2Lt kia 1-7-16 6RBerks p140 MR21

SOUSTER,Albert Edward T2Lt kia 12-4-18 31MGC Inf p185 MR32

SOUTAR,Alexander Henderson.MC.LtAMaj ded 28-5-18 RE 98FC p48 MR18

SOUTAR,Alexander Smith.MIDx2 Capt 15-3-20 RASC CR Egypt9

SOUTAR,Frank Henderson.MID 2Lt kia 21-1-16 3 att2BlkW p129 MR38

SOUTER,George Lt dow 3-9-18 1/7ScotRif p224 CR France103

SOUTER,James Mitchell Lt 11-4-17 59RFC CR France777

SOUTH,Walter Burns Campbell Lt ded 13-10-18 9Mddx p236,189&258 CR Dorset94

SOUTHALL,William Percival Lt 28-5-18 64RAF MR20

SOUTHCOMB,Edward Hamilton 2Lt kia 31-7-17 3 att24Manch p156 MR29

SOUTHERN,Gerald Cameron Lt kia 21-7-15 IA 53Sikhs p282

SOUTHERN,Hugh 2Lt mbk 18-4-16 IARO att47Sikhs p282 MR38

SOUTHERN,Mathew T2Lt kia 12-9-17 10EYorks p85 CR France184

SOUTHERN,Thomas William.MC.2LtACapt kia 29-9-18 11 att4EYorks p219 CR France285

SOUTHEY,Harry Hartley Waite Maj dow 30-3-17 1/5WelshReg p230 CR Egypt2

SOUTHEY,Robert George Melvill Lt kia 23-7-16 1DCLI p115 MR21

SOUTHGATE,Charles Edward T2Lt kia 18-2-17 1RB p180 CR France216,19-2-17 Ex HAC

SOUTHGATE,Henry Albert 2Lt kia 8-4-18 3RWKent attAnsonBn p142 CR France252

SOUTHIN,Charles Alec.MC.2Lt kld 15-2-18 21Lond attRFC p19&251 CR Mddx5

SOUTHON,John Edward.MC.2Lt kia 3-12-17 1/17Lond p250 MR17

SOUTHWELL,Arthur Horace Steadman 2Lt kia 13-11-16 7KSLI p145 CR France1890

SOUTHWELL,Evelyn Herbert Lightfoot TLt kia 15-9-16 13RB p180 MR21

SOUTHWELL,Frederick Edward Granville Lt dow 10-4-17 4EYorks p219 CR France113

SOWELL,Arthur Donald TLt kia 24-8-16 7DCLI B'Coy p115 CR France630

SOWERBY,Frank Douglas 2Lt dow 1-8-16 4Huss SR att18LancF p21 CR France51

SOWERBY,Isaac 2Lt kia 4-9-17 6RWar p214 CR Belgium84,3-9-17

SOWERBY,Maurice Eden.CMG.DSO.Col 28-1-20 CR Egypt9

SOWERBY,Victor Holgate T2Lt dow 31-7-17 2Lincs p75 MR29

SOWINSKI,Joseph Ladislas.MC.Lt kia 28-11-17 RFA &49TMB p208CR Belgium10

SOWLER,F.Capt 8-7-21 RFA

SOWRY,Alfred Allan T2Lt kia 31-8-17 17WYorks p83 MR21

SOWTER,Francis Ingle 2Lt kia 9-8-17 4EKent p212 CR France421

SOWTER,Geoffrey Smart Capt kia 14-10-18 3 att15N&D p135 CR Belgium157,Maj

SOWTER,George Henry Joseph Capt kia 13-10-15 5Lincs p220 MR19

SOWTER,Unwin Henry Etches Lt dow 22-4-17 N&D p135 MR38

SPAFFORD,Alfred Douglas Dale 2LtACapt kia 13-11-16 2RScots p55 CR France742

SPAFFORD,Arthur Langworthy Capt&Adj kia 7-8-15 1 att6LancF p93 CR Gallipoli1

SPALDING,Albert Goodwill T2Lt kia 1-7-16 RInnisF att10th p105 MR21

SPALDING,Robert Gordon 2Lt dow 28-9-15 3 att2SLancs A'Coy p126 CR France40

SPALLE,Ernest James TLt ded 25-2-19 RAOC p268 CR Scot226

SPANKIE,David Noel Lt ded 7-3-19 RASC att1/5WYorks p253 CR France1142

SPANKIE,Dysart Watt T2Lt kia 5-6-16 104MGC Inf p185 CR France727

SPANKIE,Montague Douglas.MID Lt kia 14-5-15 IA 14Sikhs p282 CR Gallipoli3

SPANNER,Herbert TCapt kia 28-12-16 27RFC p4 CR France620

SPANTON,Cyril Holtby T2Lt ded 23-11-18 RASC MT p194 CR France34

SPANTON,John Woodfield T2Lt dow 13-6-17 13RB p180 CR Sussex178

SPANTON,Thomas Henry.DCM.2Lt kia 1-7-15 3KRRC p152 CR France1141,dow

SPARENBORG,Hans Robert Capt kia 26-8-17 1RLancs p59 MR15

SPARGO,Loris Stiles 2Lt kia 5-8-17 1/5N&D p233 CR France115

SPARGO,Richard Henry Arthur SubCdr dow 14-3-16 IA S&TCps p283 CR Iraq1

SPARK,Archibald Charles T2Lt kia 31-7-17 8GordH p167 CR Belgium101

SPARK,Archibald Graham.MC.TCapt kia 9-4-17 9YLI p144 CR France591

SPARKE,Errol 2Lt kia 22-3-18 20Mddx p148 MR20

SPARKES,Richard Abbot Maj ded 2-11-18 IA 1/54Sikhs p283 MR67

SPARKS,Clive TLt kia 1-7-16 12RSuss p120 CR France924,30-6-16

SPARKS,I.D.Capt 8-3-15 RFus CR Surrey152

SPARKS,James Elliot Lt kia 21-7-16 2RFus p70 MR21

SPARKS,James Frederick TLt kia 9-4-17 8RLancs p59 CR France1182

SPARKS,John Barnes.CBE.29-3-20 RN CR Lond4

SPARKS,Robert Lionel 2Lt kia 22-11-17 2RFus p70 CR France910

SPARKS,Robert William.MC.T2Lt kia 29-4-18 18Lpool 1Coy p73 MR30

SPARLING,Arthur Edward Lt ded 19-2-15 8Ess p271 CR Norf74

SPARLING,Norman Chalmers.MID Maj kia 25-9-15 IA 54Sikhs att6KOSB p283 MR28

SPARLING,Sidney James Belton Maj kia 4-6-15 IA 57Rif attRNDHoweBn p283

SPARROW,Benjamin Charles Capt kia 10-3-15 IA 1/39GarhwalRif p283 CR France355 &CR France1887

SPARROW,Brian Hanbury.MC.Capt kia 26-8-18 3KSLI att7NStaffs p145

SPARROW,Francis 2Lt kia 25-4-15 att2RDubF p177 MR29

SPARROW,Frank Edward TLt dow 13-8-16 RE 129FC p48 CR France141,kia

SPARROW,George Lewis Lt dow 23-12-15 3SWBord attKOSB p101 CR France284,23-12-14

SPARROW,George William Sparrow Capt kia 4-10-18 4KSLI p235 CR France82

SPARROW,Walter Burnaby Lt kia 1-9-18 3 att10Hamps p121 CR Greece6

SPARROW,William Gordon Morgan Capt kia 8-7-17 Nhampt &1KAR p138&268 CR EAfrica40

SPARTALI,Cyril T2Lt kia 13-10-15 8RBerks p140 MR19

SPARTALI,Michael 2lt kia 15-6-15 3 att2SWBord p101 MR4

SPARY,Fred Lt 25-11-20 RE CR Kent46

SPATZ,Walter T2Lt kia 1-7-16 2Mddx p148 MR21

SPAULL,Ernest Mayall Vaughan 2Lt kia 26-3-18 94RFA p35 CR France300

SPEAKMAN,Alan Edwards T2Lt kia 5-9-18 RFusatt2Bn p70 CR France298

SPEAR,A.E.Capt ded 8-3-18 Ex SL p268

SPEAR,Norman Victor T2Lt kld 29-8-17 RFC p13 CR Norf247

SPEAR-MORGAN,Basil Howard Lt ded 16-9-19 1BordR p264 CR Mddx16,Capt dow 16-9-16

SPEARES,Harold Thorne T2Lt kia 16-8-17 10RInnisF p105 MR30

SPEARING,Edward Lt kia 11-9-16 4RLancs p213 MR21

SPEARMAN,John Vanstone T2Lt kia 25-8-15 1KSLI p145 CR Belgium92

SPEARS,Alexander T2Lt kia 18-8-17 12Lpool p73 MR30

SPEARS,Alexander George 2Lt kia 22-8-18 23Lond p252 MR16

SPEARS,G.W.MC.Maj 11-3-21 RAOC CR Germany1

SPEARS,John 2Lt kia 23-4-17 2RScotF p95 CR France539

SPEDDING,Charles Rodney.DSO.Maj kia 19-9-14 2RIrRif p170 MR15

SPEDDING.George 2Lt kia 20-8-17 2/4YLI p235 CR France563

SPEDDING,John Carlisle Decv Maj ded 9-3-19 APD p255 CR Hamps115

SPEECHLY,Thomas Martindale T2Lt kld 8-2-18 RFC p17 CR Wilts129,5RRofCav

SPEED,Arthur Sydney 2Lt kia 4-6-17 1/5SStaffs p229 CR France149

SPEED,David Nelson 9106 T2Lt dow 2-5-17 A&SH att8BlkW p174 CR France113

SPEEDIE,John Gibson 2Lt kia 14-6-17 4RScots p211 CR France644

SPEEDY,Ralph Coggin 2Lt ded 4-12-18 19MGC Cav p185 CR Yorks222

SPEER,Alfred Henry Templeman Loraine Lt kia 9-7-16 RFA attRFC p19&208 CR France1185

SPEIGHT,James Leslie Lt dow 9-10-17 6WYorks p218 MR30,Capt

SPEIRS,George Patrick Maj kia 1-10-18 6HLI p240 CR France602

SPEIRS,Ronald Patrick 2Lt kia 23-4-17 2A&SH p174 MR20

SPEKE.Hugh Tmaj kia 12-8-15 10LancF Ex9SomLI p93 CR Belgium37

SPELMAN,Henry Harington 2Lt dow 22-9-18 YLIatt4Bn p144 MR16,Harrington

SPENCE,Alec William T2Lt kld 25-4-17 GL &51RFC p13 CR Kent197 Ex Mddx

SPENCE,Alexander.MC.Chap4Cl dow PoW 31-3-18 RAChDept attRInniskF p200 CR France987

SPENCE,Bertram T2Lt kia 21-9-18 9RFus p70 CR France369

SPENCE,Charles Bennett.MID Lt kld 9-5-15 RFA att3RFC p2&35 CR France98

SPENCE,David Stuart 2Lt kia 13-12-15 A66RFA p35 MR4

SPENCE,Geoffrey Shalders T2Lt ded 15-4-17 8SWBord p101 CR Beds23

SPENCE,Gilbert Chisholm Drever.MC.Capt kia 1-10-18 2HLI p164 CR France1483

SPENCE,Henry 2Lt kia 13-10-18 7A&SH p243 CR France1196

SPENCE,James Hamilton Lt kia 16-7-18 RGA &54RAF p262 MR20

SPENCE,John Robert Capt kia 9-4-18 RH&FA p207 CR France570,RGA 237SB

SPENCE,Joseph 2Lt dow 8-8-17 RFA p209 CR France285

SPENCE,Lyell Campbell.MC.Lt kia 25-5-18 CanadaFA &RAF CR France10

SPENCE,William Herbert John Shepherd T2Lt ded 23-9-17 GL RE att1WT p191 CR Iraq6

SPENCE,William Kenneth Mackay 2Lt kia 23-4-17 3RScots p55 CR France155,13Bn

SPENCE,William Samuel TLt kia 26-4-17 GL &RFC p13 CR France777

SPENCER,Alfred de Courboisier 2Lt kia 26-9-15 8WelshR att8RBerks p127 CR Gallipoli4

SPENCER,Arthur T2Lt kia 1-7-16 15Y&L p159 CR France246

SPENCER,Arthur Egerton Lt kia 2-7-16 10N&D p135 MR21

SPENCER,Arthur Max 2Lt kia 12-4-17 1RB p180 CR France728

SPENCER,Charles Herbert Slingsby 2Lt kia 5-10-18 C330RFA p35 CR France262

SPENCER,Charles James Capt kia 18-12-14 2Dev p77 CR France567

SPENCER,Edward Lt kia 24-10-14 2Wilts p153 MR29

SPENCER,Eliot Lt dow 18-2-18 5RWar p214 CR Staffs73

SPENCER,Francis 2Lt kia 26-9-17 4 att2/7N&D p135 CR Belgium125,Capt

SPENCER,Francis Leslie.MID Capt kia 2-12-17 2Mon p244 CR France1483

SPENCER,Frederick James Edmund T2Lt ded 9-11-18 PoW Wilts p153 CR Germany3

SPENCER,George Lt dow 5-12-17 20Lond p251 CR France446,4-12-17

SPENCER,George Barton T2Lt kia 25-7-18 13RB p180 CR Frnce614,25-8-18

SPENCER,Gerald Robert Maj ded 13-5-18 RDC p253 CR Sussex128

SPENCER,Gerald William Suckling T2Lt dow 24-2-16 8Norf p74 CR Lond28

SPENCER,Harry John Capt ded 17-11-16 9DLI p239 CR France177

SPENCER,Henry Beresford Capt kia 2-9-18 WSomYeo &TankCps p189&205 CR France646

SPENCER,Herbert 2Lt kia 11-7-16 7Leic p88 MR21

SPENCER,Henry Marston T2Lt kia 12-10-17 7EKent p58&258 CR Belgium126,Hugh Manning

SPENCER,Herbert Cecil Stanhope Lt 26-7-21 RFA CR Sussex183

SPENCER,Hugh Maitland Capt kia 25-4-15 SfthH p165 CR Belgium129

SPENCER,Jack Hamlyn.MC.T2Lt dow 5-6-18 1RDerks p140 CR France63,Capt

SPENCER,James Hilary L.ACapt dow PoW 16-7-18 1LancF p93 CR France1027

SPENCER,James Michael Jeslyn Lt kia 3-11-16 4NumbF attRFC p19&213 CR France927

SPENCER,James Sturtevant 2Lt kia 2-9-16 26RFA p35 CR France397

SPENCER,John Aldersley Craven 2Lt kia 9-8-15 9WYorks p83 MR4

SPENCER,John Clive Capt kia 22-3-18 11Leic p88 MR20,21-3-18

SPENCER,Mowbray Bertram Stovell 2Lt kia 4-8-15 7Worc p226 CR France1327

SPENCER,Richard Isaac Barré T2Lt kia 14-7-16 7 att1RScotF D'Coy p95 CR France453

SPENCER,Richard Martin Lt kia 22-1-16 1RWar p66 CR France643,2Lt

SPENCER,Shirley McTurk Lt kia 10-10-17 290RFA p208 MR30

SPENCER,Stanley 2LtTLt kia 3-5-17 2/5Y&L p238 MR20

SPENCER,Sydney.MC.Lt kia 24-9-18 5Norf p216 CR France369

SPENCER,Sydney Gurton TCapt kia 13-10-15 5RBerks p140 MR19

SPENCER,W.2Lt kia 10-5-18 GL &RAF p191

293

SPENCER,Walter George Capt dow 26-3-18 23Lond p252 CR France145

SPENCER,Willy Paton Berthold Lt kia 10-3-15 2Wilts p153 MR22

SPENCER-SMITH,Charles Owen Capt dow 3-8-17 16Lond p249 CR France139

SPENCER-SMITH,Gilbert Seymour Worsley Lt kia 9-4-18 5Hamps p228 CR Palestine9

SPENCER-SMITH,Henry.MC.Capt&QM kia 21-3-18 8Leic p88&259 MR27

SPENCER-SMITH,Martin 2Lt kia 10-9-16 16Lond p250 MR21

SPENDLOVE,Gervase Thorpe 2Lt dow 17-11-14 SLancs p126 CR Belgium57

SPENS,Walter Thomas Patrick Lt ded 18-2-17 9RScots p212 CR France95

SPENS,William Lt kld 17-5-15 9HLI p140 CR France413,kia

SPENSLEY,Frank Oswald Capt ded 23-10-18 RAMC attRAF p197&267 CR Dorset110

SPENSLEY,James Richardson TLt dow PoW 10-11-15 RAMC att8EKent p197 CR Germany3

SPERANZA,E.R.2Lt 10-12-18 RMaltaArtly CR Europe4

SPEYER,Cecil Arthur 2Lt kia 16-8-17 4Lond C'Coy p246 MR29

SPEYER,Frederick William Heurick T2Lt kia 14-6-17 att2Suff p79 CR France421,Lt

SPICE,Ernest Robert 2Lt kia 30-4-18 2/20Lond p251 CR Palestine3

SPICER,Cecil Wilfred T2Lt kia 23-11-16 2Lincs p75 MR21

SPICER,Edmund Daniell 2Lt kia 1-2-17 20RFC p13 CR Belgium158

SPICER,Eric Evan Capt kia 28-3-18 1/4Lond p246 MR20

SPICER,Filmer Blake 2Lt dow 6-10-16 3EKent attMGC 111Coy p58&185

SPICER,George Henry T2Lt kia 6-6-18 17RFus p70 CR France745

SPICER,Leonard Baker 2Lt kia 4-10-17 YLIatt9Bn p144 MR30

SPICER,Ronald Murray 2Lt ded 31-5-16 ERidYeo p206 CR Norf210

SPICER,Robert William Capt kia 26-3-17 4RWSurr p212 MR34

SPICER,Stanley Thomas TLt dow 9-8-16 2SStaffs p123 CR France397,kia

SPIEGELHALTER,Leo HonCapt ded 30-4-18 Insp of Army Schls CR Lond3

SPIELMAN,Harold Lionel Isidore Capt kia 13-8-15 10Manch p237 CR Gallipoli3

SPIERS,Archibald Lionel Clive TLt kia 26-9-17 7KSLI p145 MR30

SPIERS,D.2Lt 29-6-18 4RScots CR Scot674

SPIERS,Graham Kinloch 2Lt kia 22-7-18 5ScotRif p224 CR France25,23-7-18 9Bn

SPIERS,William Lt ded 3-8-19 RASC p267 CR Iraq8

SPILLER,Arthur James T2Lt kia 17-9-16 7SomLI p80 MR21

SPILLER,E.SchMstr 15-5-18 Cps of SchMstrs CR Scot288

SPILLING,Charles Nathaniel Jerald T2Lt kia 24-8-17 KRRC att8Bn p152 MR30

SPINDLER,Nellie SNurse kia 21-8-17 QAIMNS att44CCS p200 CR Belgium11

SPINK,Cecil Cooper T2Lt kia 4-6-16 10EYorks p85 CR France5

SPINK,Dennis Boucher 2Lt kia 30-10-17 6Lond p247 MR30

SPINK,Edward Wodehouse Lt kia 23-10-18 1/7LancF p221 CR France287

SPINK,Eric Minor TLt&ACapt kia 14-9-18 7NStaffs p158 CR Asia81

SPINK,Hubert Octavius Chap4Cl kia 9-8-16 RAChDept att55Div p200 CR France141

SPINKS,W.H.Rev ded 29-5-18 YMCA CR France40

SPINNEY,Frank T2Lt dow 2-10-16 2RScots p55 CR Greece4

SPINNEY,Kenneth Trim TLt kia 3-9-16 17KRRC p152 CR France220

SPINNEY,Robert Eric.MC.TLt dow 1-2-17 GL IntelCps &WRid p191 CR France74

SPINNEY,Ronald Henry Lt dow 2-7-16 2CldGds p51 CR Belgium11

SPITTAL,Robert Haig TCapt kia 4-10-17 RAMC att7LancF p197 MR30,att9Bn

SPITTLE,Thomas Stanley Capt dow 2-10-17 1Mon p244 CR France179

SPILSBURY,Francis James Capt ded 11-10-19 RAMC CR Lincs220

SPOFFORTH,Edward Reginald Lt kia 2-3-16 5Yorks p220 CR Belgium5

SPONG,Frederick William Edward 2Lt dow PoW 2-8-17 2Lond D'Coy p245 CR Belgium140,21-8-17

SPOONER,Charles Norman Capt kia 10-4-18 5Dev p217 CR Palestine9

SPOONER,George Piercy T2Lt kia 20/23-9-17 26RFus p70 MR30

SPOONER,Raymond Wilberforce 2Lt kia 8-6-17 RFC Ex RFA p13 MR20

SPOONER,Ronald Alan TCapt dow 23-9-16 11RWFus p99 CR Greece6

SPOOR,Herbert Mather.MC.TCapt ded 13-12-17 RAMC p198 CR Belgium84

SPOTTISWOODE,John Capt kia 31-10-14 6 att2KRRC p152 MR29

SPRAGG,Charles Edward Wright Capt kia 10-9-18 4EYorks p219 CR France415

SPRAGG,Westley Neal Lt kia 1-1-18 RFC SpSch of AerialGunnery p17 CR Egypt9

SPRAKE,George Harold TLt kia 18-7-16 8 att3BlkW p129 MR21

SPRAKE,Gilbert Edwin Lt kia 4-6-15 5ELancs p226 CR Gallipoli6

SPRANG,Frederick Williamson Lt&ACapt kia 12-4-17 6Dors D'Coy p124 CR France531

SPRATT,David Herbert T2Lt kia 20-9-17 Mddx att6Lpool p148 CR Belgium125

SPRAY,Arthur.MC.TCapt&Maj kia 5-5-18 5TankCps p189 CR Belgium11

SPREAT,Leicester Hulke.MC.2Lt dow 8-10-16 A91RFA p35 CR France105

SPRECKLEY,Arthur Freer Lt drd 30-12-15 IA 2/9 att1/9GurkhaRif p283 MR41,Capt

SPRECKLEY,Guy Lesingham T2Lt kia 23-4-17 22 att7KRRC p152 MR29

SPRECKLEY,Ralph Lesingham.MC.Lt kia 14-9-14 2ConnRgrs p172 CR France1107,Lessingham

SPRENGER Oliver Howard T2Lt kia 5-6-17 26NumbF p63 MR20

SPRIGG,Henry Aldwin Guildford TCapt kia 9-5-18 14 att2/5Hamps p121 CR Palestine9,9-4-18

SPRING,Harold Albert Arden T2Lt kia 15-9-16 10ScotRif p104 MR21

SPRING-RICE,Gerald TLt kia 26-5-16 11BordR p118 CR France702

SPRINGATE,Arthur Stephen T2Lt kia 25-3-18 2/4Leic p88 MR20

SPRINGFIELD,Arthur Lincoln T2Lt kia 9-4-17 3SomLI p80 CR France532

SPRINGFIELD,George Patrick Osborn Capt kia 12-9-14 2DragGds p21 CR France1110

SPRINGFIELD,Humphrey Osborn.MID 2Lt kia 5-8-16 1/1WarYeo p205 CR Egypt2

SPRINGMAN,Ralph Thomas James 2Lt dow 21-9-18 RGA 169SB p42 CR France1468

SPRINKS,Ralph Cecil 2Lt kia 7-8-17 B83RFA p209 CR Belgium19

SPROAT,Gerald Maitland TLt kia 1-7-16 11 att17Manch p156 MR21

SPROAT,James McCosh.MC.2Lt kia 17-7-16 17Lpool p73 MR21,11-7-16

SPROSON,William Wilson 2Lt kld 7-8-18 17LancF att101RAF p93 CR France29,Lt kia

SPROSTON,Frederick Alvin 2Lt dow 30-7-18 6Ches p222 CR France866

SPROSTON,William Norris.MC.T2Lt kia 4-4-18 8RB p180 MR27

SPROT,Ivan Boyd Lt kia 23-10-14 1CamH p168 CR Belgium115

SPROT,James William Lennox Capt kia 11-11-14 2 att1BlkW p129 MR29

SPROTT,Douglas Anderson Capt ded 4-1-18 4BordR attMGC p187 CR Iraq8

SPROTT,Douglas Andrew Capt ded 4-1-18 4BordR p228

SPROTT,Frederick William 2Lt ded 25-8-18 IARO att92Punjabis p283 CRIraq5,Lt

SPROTT,Maurice William Campbell.MC.TCapt kia 21-3-18 9Norf p74 MR20

SPROXTON,Charles.MC.Capt&Adjt kia 19-7-17 4Yorks p220 CR France592

SPRUNT,Alexander Dalzell 2Lt dow 17-3-15 4Beds SR att2SStaffs p86 CR France201

SPRUNT,Gerald Harper 2Lt ded 15-10-19 2Beds p263 MR40,Lt dow

SPURGE,Henry Wesley Lt&ACapt dow 17-9-17 3 att5 O&BLI p130 CR France40

SPURGEON,Donald Frank Parker Lt kia 10-9-18 20Lond att1/5Beds p251 CR Palestine9

SPURGEON,Percival TCapt dow 18-5-18 RASC att7RWSurr p194 CR Lond1

SPURLING,Francis Eyton TCapt dow 6-12-17 12RB p180 CR Belgium3,7Bn

SPURLING,Henry Stephen TCapt dow 21-8-16 10 att9ESurr p113 CR France66,Harry

SPURRELL,Frederick John Durnford T2Lt ded 19-2-15 9RSuss p120 CR Norf94

SPURRELL,Herbert George Flaxman TCapt ded 8-11-18 RAMC attRAF p197 CR Egypt1

SPURWAY,Douglas Capt kia 23-3-18 4Yorks p220 MR27

SPURWAY,George Vyvyan.MC.TLt kia 28-3-18 56MGC p185 MR20

SPURWAY,Richard Popham T2Lt drd 13-8-15 2SomLI attHamps p80 MR4

SPURWAY,Sidney Macdonald T2Lt kia 21-9-17 22RFC p13 CR Belgium46

SQUAIR,Robert Hay TLt dow 13-10-17 7SfthH p165 CR Belgium63

SQUIER,Harry Anderton T2Lt kia 19-4-16 10 att8Beds p86 CR Belgium73

SQUIRE,Basil Brett.MID Lt&ACapt kia 23-4-17 15RFA p35 CR France581,450RFA

SQUIRE,D.J.22-10-18 VAD CR Hamps1

SQUIRE,Frederick T2Lt&ACapt kia 31-7-17 11RWKent p142 CR Belgium111

SQUIRE,Leslie Charles Herman 2Lt dow 13-5-15 7Lond p247 CR France80

SQUIRE,Stanley Charles TLt kia 9-8-15 7Glouc p107

SQUIRE,Wallace Henry 2Lt dow 9-4-17 4EKent p212 CR France1182

SQUIRE,Wright Thomas 2Lt kia 30-6-18 RGA 78SB p42 CR France174

SQUIRES,Charles Arthur 2Lt kia 25-4-18 B162RFA p35 CR Belgium3

SQUIRES,Charles Thomas 2Lt dow 30-3-18 4RSuss p228 CR France144

SQUIRES,Edward Constable.MC.TCapt kia 18-8-16 12WYorks p83 CR France453,dow

SQUIRES,Francis Chavasse Capt dow 7-7-15 IA 1/23SikhPnrs p283 CR Asia60

SQUIRES,Francis William 2Lt kia 10-11-16 RGA 95SB p42 CR France294

SQUIRES,John Henry T2Lt kia 12-4-18 SfthH att1/5Bn p165 CR France202

SQUIRES,Reginald Alfred.OBE.Capt ded 25-4-19 16YLI APM 61Div p255&144 CR France52

SQUIRES,Roger Dewar TCapt kia 7-8-15 9N&D p135 MR4,Robert 9-8-15

SQUIRES,Sidney Charles Lt kia 29-10-18 5RWar p214 CR France290,28-10-18

SQUIRL,Montague Ernest Lt dow 15-12-18 2A&SH p174 CR France658,kia

SQUIRL-DAWSON Hugh Dawson Capt ded 31-1-18 1/1RHA p207 CR Palestine2

STABLE,Lascombe Law Capt kia 26-10-14 RWFus p99 CR France705,Loscombe

STABLE,Russell Colin 2Lt kia 9-10-17 2RWar p66 MR30

STABLES,Harold Rolleston Lt kia 15-11-14 5RFus attChes p70 MR29

STABLES,James Howard Lt mbk 17-2-17 IARO att1/8GurkhaRif p283 MR38

STABLES,Leonard Theodore Drury Lt kia 23-10-18 6Beds attNhants p86 CR France190

STABLES,Robert Cecil 2Lt kia 13-5-17 IARO att3Sap&Min p283 MR38

STACEY,Brian John 2Lt dow 26-4-17 B63 RFA p35 CR France40

STACEY,Charles Noble Lt dow 10-5-15 7Mddx A'Coy p235 CR France525

STACEY,Cyril Robert William 2Lt kia 8/9-8-16 3 att1RInniskF p105 CR Belgium47,9-8-16

STACEY,Dorothy Louise SNurse 5-10-18 QAIMNS CR Dorset87

STACEY,Douglas William T2Lt dow 20-6-17 20RFC p13 CR France200

STACEY,Gerald Arthur.DSO.Maj kia 9-10-16 2Lond p245 CR France294

STACEY,Harold 2Lt kia 4-8-18 5NStaffs p238 CR France109,1/6Bn

STACEY,Herbert Leonard 2Lt kia 31-7-17 7Lpool p215 CR Belgium125

STACEY,John Brewer T2Lt kia 19-11-16 8ESurr p113 MR21

STACEY,John Charles.MM.2Lt kia 10-4-18 2SfthH p165 MR19

STACEY,John Harold 2Lt kia 4-12-17 5ESurr attRFC p19&226 CR Egypt15

STACK,Edward Hugh Bagot Capt kia 30-10-14 IA 2/8GurkhaRif p283 MR28

STACK,George Hall.DSO.MIDx3 ALtCol ded 16-9-19 RE 3Div p262 CR Palestine9

STACK,James Charles 2Lt kld 30-4-18 LabCps att4RAF p189 CR France134,Lt

STACK,John Masfen Capt kia 1-7-16 6NStaffs p238 CR France576

STACKE,Oliver George Norman Lt kia 17-5-15 RInniskF p105 MR22,15-5-15

STACKHOUSE,William Thomas Capt kia 12-3-15 1N&D p135 MR22

STACPOOLE,George Eric Guy Lt kia 27-1-15 1RIrReg p89 CR Belgium80

STAFF-BRETT,Henry William T2Lt kia 24-3-18 14Y&L p159 MR32

STAFFORD,Arthur Darrell TLt dow 20-5-18 1RWar att1/3LancF p66 CR France145

STAFFORD,Charles Edward Trevor T2Lt kia 31-7-17 10/11HLI p164 CR Belgium58

STAFFORD,Claude Charles Lt kia 13-10-14 Beds RoO p86 MR22

STAFFORD,Cyril Francis 2Lt dow 14-4-17 24RFus p70 CR France53

STAFFORD,Frederick John Ewart 2Lt dow 22-4-17 8RFC p13 CR France52

STAFFORD,Henry Herbert Owen T2Lt kia 4-10-16 10WRid p116 MR21

STAFFORD,James Neilson Greenleer Capt kia 16-4-17 6RWar p214 CR France669,Greenlees

STAFFORD,Kenneth James.MC.Lt dow 14-11-18 37/27RH&FA p35 CR France146

STAFFORD,Thomas Colegrave TCapt ded 2-4-16 1Yorks GarrBn p91 MR65,4-4-16

STAFFORD-KING-HARMAN,Edward Charles Capt kia 6-11-14 1IrGds 1Coy p53 MR29

STAGG,Alfred Charles T2Lt kia 19-7-16 11Glouc p107 CR France633

STAGG,Arthur John T2Lt kia 27-5-18 2WYorks p83 MR18

STAGG,Edward Christopher T2Lt kia 18-7-16 14Glouc p107 MR21

STAGG,Harold William 2Lt kia 28-3-18 15MGC p185 MR20

STAGG,John Reginald .DCM.T2Lt kia 17-9-16 27 att17Mddx p148 CR France156

STAIGHT,Ralph Neville 2Lt kia 24-3-17 3SomLI p80 CR France418 Ex 10Huss

STAINBANK,Arthur Reeve 2Lt kia 20-7-17 113RFA p35 MR29

STAINBANK,William Dering 2Lt ded 8-4-16 RFA p35 CR Lancs103

STAINER,Claude Hamilton 2Lt kia 15-11-16 6ESurr att10LNLancs p226 MR21

STAINFIELD,Walter George Lt ded 18-11-18 RGA 115SB p42 CR Kent5

STAINFORTH,George T2Lt kia 14-7-16 13Lpool p73 MR21

STAINFORTH,Herbert Graham.CMG.LtCol ded 11-5-16 IA Cmdg4Cav p283 CR Iraq5

STAINFORTH,Richard Terrick Lt dow 19-10-14 2RWar p66 CR Belgium84

STAINSBY,John Addison TLt drd 26-2-18 RAMC p198 MR40

STAINSBY,Thomas Cecil T2Lt kia 1-10-18 9TankCps p189 CR France375

STAINTON,Ernest Lt dow 25-11-18 7Worc p225 CR Mddx51

STAINTON,Robert Meres T2Lt kia 1-7-16 10Y&L p159 MR21

STAINTON,Walter Adam Lt kia 14-9-16 3GrenGds p50 MR21

STALEY,Edward Vernon Lt kia 18-9-18 D290RFA p35 CR France364

STALEY,Francis Colin Lt kia 8-3-16 5SomLI p218 MR38

STALEY,Frederick Alexander 2Lt kia 25 10-18 3 att8ESurr p113 CR France1482,23-10-18

STALKER,Daniel TLt dow 12-4-18 169RFA p35 CR France300

STALKER,Francis Brown Douglas T2Lt kia 22-8-15 SL 6BordR p201 MR4

STALKER,James Johnston Harris TLtACapt kia 28-4-17 11RWar p66 MR20

STALKER,M.B.Sister S1326 18-1-21 1Res QAIMNS CR Scot169

STALKER,Robert Macallan Lt kia 8-9-15 5SfthH att22RFC p19&241 MR20

STALLARD,Arthur Dudley.VD.Capt 6-2-19 InnsOfCourt ResCps CR Surrey160

STALLWORTHY,Arthur Reynolds 2Lt kia 30-11-17 3EKent att1/5SLancs p58 MR17

STAMFORD,Gerald Morton 2Lt kia 15-6-15 2Wilts p153 MR22

STAMMAS,Thomas Laurence Capt 6-11-20 RFA CR Lond28

STAMMERS,Joseph Ralph T2Lt kia 9-4-17 5 O&BLI p130 CR France581

STAMP,Douglas Blatspiel Lt dow 10-4-16 EYorks SR p85 CR Belgium1

STAMPE,George Herbert TMaj kia 27-3-18 24MGC p185 MR27

STAMPER,Geoffrey 2Lt kld 25-3-18 4 att1N&D p135 MR27

STANANOUGHT,Richard Frederick TLt&Adjt dow 5-9-16 12WYorks p83 CR Frnce145

STANBOROUGH,Walter Thomas 2Lt dow 13-5-15 att2SWBord p101 MR4

STANBRIDGE,Arthur Christian Capt&Adjt kia 18-11-16 8NStaffs p158 MR21 STANDBRIDGE

STANBURY,Lional Duncan TLt kia 7-7-16 52MGC p185 MR21

STANCER,John William T2Lt dow 17-4-18 23NumbF p63 CR France134

STANDEN,Leslie James Denman Lt kia 18-3-16 5Lincs p220 CR France68,Capt

STANDERWICK,Edwin William 2Lt kia 20-4-18 7Ess p232 CR France250,Lt

STANDRICK,Jones Harold John.MC.Capt dow 21-2-18 2/18Lond p250 CR Palestine3,kia

STANDRING,Benjamin Arthur 2Lt dow 19-12-14 RWar p66 CR France253

STANDRING,Dudley Hethorn Capt dow 30-5-15 8Manch p237 CR Gallipoli2

STANDRING,Frederick John Lt kia 6-9-18 8RScots att57MGC p187&211 CR France309

STANDRING,William Shuttleworth 2Lt kia 30-7-16 12ELancs p111 CR France298

STANFIELD,Alfred Vivian 2Lt kia 16-8-16 2RWSurr attRFus p56 MR21

STANFIELD,Charles Cecil Capt ded 31-5-17 3EKent att1NHants p58 CR Hamps1

STANFIELD,Thomas William.MM.T2Lt kia 23-11-17 3Yorks p91 CR France256,13Bn

STANFIELD,William Bowman 2Lt dow 29-9-15 3 att1Nhampt p138 CR France178,Lt 26-9-15

STANFORD,Donovan Edward 2Lt kia 21-3-18 6RDubF att2RIrReg p177 MR27

STANFORD,James Vesey TLt kia 25-9-15 8SfthH p165 MR19

STANG,J.S.MC.Capt BlkW p259 See STRANG,J.S.

STANGE,George Nugent.MC.TLt kia 27-10-18 1 att2LancF p93

STANGER,Nevill Bentley 2Lt dow 5-10-15 4SLancs p230 CR France40,Bentlif

STANGER,Philip James Capt kia 8-11-15 1/20Lond p251 CR France219

STANHOPE,Colin Lundin.OBE.Capt ded 14-10-19 GL p267 CR France457,18-10-19

STANHOPE,Richard Philip.Hon.Capt kia 16-9-16 3GrenGds SR p50 MR21

STANHOPE,Talbot Fitzroy Eden Lt kia 9-5-15 2RB p180 MR32

STANIFORTH,William Moorwood 2Lt kld 23-3-17 YorkDragYeo &RFC p19&206,ded CR War65

STANILAND,Geoffrey 2Lt kia 14-4-15 4Lincs p217 CR Belgium98,13-4-15

STANILAND,Meaborn Capt kld 29-7-15 4Lincs p217 CR Belgium98

STANLEY,Ada SNurse 22-12-15 TFNS CR Yorks639

STANLEY,Arthur Kinnaird Lt kia 15-6-18 6Glouc p225 CR Italy2,1/5Bn

STANLEY,Charles Gordon 2Lt kia 19-9-18 RWar att34RAF CR Italy11

STANLEY,D.H.Lt 17-8-20 GL CR Iraq8

STANLEY,Edmond Talbot Maj ded 27-2-19 LabCps p266 CR France146,11Dev

STANLEY,George Hopkins 2Lt kia 31-10-14 1ELancs p111 CR Belgium68

STANLEY,Lawrence Aston 2Lt kia 30-11-17 9RFus p70 MR17,Laurence

STANLEY,R.B.Capt ded 17-2-19 RASC &RAF p253

STANLEY,Robert Oliver 2Lt kia 9-4-16 12RWFus p99 MR38

STANLEY,Sidney Edgar T2Lt ded 19-10-17 11RFC p13 CR France1185

STANLEY,James Arthur TCapt kia 27-9-18 RAMC att15RWar p198 CR France245

STANLEY,John Joseph 2Lt kia 9-12-17 2RIrRif p170 CR France379

STANLEY,John William 2Lt kia 7-6-17 4 att11LancF p93 MR29

STANLEY,Percy Douglas 2Lt kia 4-10-17 YLI att9Bn p144 MR30

STANLEY-BAKER,Richard Maj 13-11-18 IARO att3BurmaMTCoy MR43 &CR Pakistan50A

STANLEY-CREEK,Robert Forbes Stanley.DSO.Capt kia 29-10-14 RWSurr p56 MR29

STANNARD,Alexander Jewell LtAMaj kia 20-8-17 RGA 29SB p47 CR Belgium19

STANNARD,John Arnold.MC.Lt dow 23-4-18 6Hamps p229 CR France88,5Bn

STANNARD,W.L.Capt kia 4-5-15 5SLancs p230 CR Belgium125

STANNUS,Thomas Robert Alexnder.DSO.MajALtCol dow 17-6-17 4Leinst p175 CR France40

STANSELL,Lionel Brough.MM.2Lt ded 26-10-18 3RWKent &RAF p142 CR Kent232,10Bn

STANSFELD,H.A.HonMaj ded 8-12-14 Yorks p91

STANSFELD,Harold Hamer Grey Maj dow 25-9-15 IA 74 Cmdg69Punjabis p283 CR France705

STANSFELD-SMITH,Lyalph 2Lt kld 12-6-15 1Wilts p153 CR Belgium35,Lyulph 13-6-15

STANSFIELD,Frank 2Lt kia 31-5-15 5ELancs p226 CR Gallipoli6

STANSFIELD,Frederick Noel 2Lt kia 2-12-17 17Mddx p148 MR17,STANSFELD Capt 1-12-17

STANSFIELD,John Raymond Evelyn.DSO.MajTLtCol dow 28-9-15 2GordH p167 CR France98,STANSFELD

STANSFIELD,Sydney Pearce 2Lt kia 30-4-17 1/4WRid p227 CR France727

STANTIAL,Frank Evered 2Lt dow 4-5-15 3Suff p79 MR29

STANTON,Claude Wilfred Capt kia 8-5-15 1Mon p244 MR29

STANTON,Clifford.MID TLt kia 31-7-17 10WelshR p127 CR Belgium65

STANTON,Francis Stanislaus 2Lt kia 27-9-18 5RScotF p222 CR France530

STANTON,Gareth Marsh T2Lt dow 20-2-16 8RWKent p142 CR Belgium11

STANTON,George Capt dow 16-8-16 RAMC p198 CR Eire78 .

STANTON,Oswald Wilfred TCapt ded 6-11-18 15Mddx att10Lond p148&265 CR Lond12

STANTON,Robert 2Lt kia 7-8-15 6RDubF p177 MR4,9-8-15

STANTON,Roydon Ross Lt ded 18-10-18 CldGds p51 CR Berks84

STANTON,Victor George 2Lt ded PoW 29-3-18 RFC p17 CR France511

STANUELL,Charles Martin 2Lt kia 20-9-14 2DLI p161 MR15

STANWAY,Frank T2Lt kia 29-3-17 Glouc att1st p107 CR Iraq8,7Bn

STANWAY,Gerald 2Lt dow 5-10-17 5 att7SStaffs p229 CR Belgium16

STANWELL,William Alexander 2Lt dow 6-7-15 LancF p93 MR29

STANWORTH,Joseph T2Lt dow 11-7-17 2ELancs p111 CR Lancs219

STANYON,Terence George 2Lt dow 23-7-16 WelshR att 1ESurr p127 CR France630

STAPLES,Edmund 2Lt dow 20-8-18 17Lond att44TMB p250 CR France145

STAPLES,Osric Ormsund T2Lt kia 25-9-15 6RScotF p95 MR19

STAPLETON,Harold Edward Beaumont Capt dow 26-9-17 RGA p209 CR Belgium46

STAPLETON,Harold Frederick Lt kia 15-9-16 1Lond p245 CR France432

STAPLETON,Hubert Capt kia 15-9-16 15Hamps p121 MR21

STAPLETON,Nicholas Capt ded 6-12-18 25Lond p252 CR France146

STAPLETON,William Howell T2Lt kia 26-8-18 2Beds att5RBerks p86 CR France630

STAPLETON-BRETHERTON,Osmund Frederick Lt kia 22-3-18 9Lancers p22 MR27

STAPLETON-BRETHERTON,Wilfred Stanislaus Capt kia 8-11-14 4RFus p70 MR29

STAPLEY,Lawrence D'Arcy 2Lt kia 12-10-16 7Suff p79 MR21,D'Arcy Laurence

STAPYLTON,Granville Joseph Chetwynd Maj kia 25-8-14 RH&FA p36

STARES,Robert Percy Maj kia 30-10-14 Beds p86 CR Belgium115

STARFIELD,Baron T2Lt kia 19-1-18 RFC p17

STARK,James Duncan.MID T2Lt dow 3-9-18 PoW 2 att6KOSB p102 CR Germany1

STARKEY,Francis William T2Lt kia 25-10-17 Manch att21Bn p156 MR30

STARKEY,Joseph Bernard Collins Lt kia 13-11-16 3 att2HLI p164 MR21

STARKEY,Thomas Randle 2Lt ded 13-11-16 RDC p253 CR Notts96,Lt

STARKEY,Vivian George TLt kia 14-10-15 7YLI p144 CR France348

STARKY,James Baynton 2Lt kia 6-7-16 3 att1Wilts p153 MR21

STARLING,Benjamin Alfred 2Lt kia 23-3-18 2Lond p245 CR France184

STARLING,Frederick Leslie 2Lt kia 13-9-16 3Lond p246 MR21

STARR,Alfred 2Lt ded 27-10-18 22Lond p271 CR Lond10

STARR,Arthur James TLt kia 22-3-18 11 att9RInniskF A'Coy p105 MR27

STARR,Dillwyn Parrish Lt kia 14/16-9-16 2CldGds p51&258 CR France374,15-9-16

STARR,Philip Comfort Lt kia 20-2-18 RE 154FC p48 CR Belgium165

START,Lesingham Eden 2Lt ded 23-2-15 13DLI p161 CR Hamps1

STATHAM,Arthur Yates 2Lt kia 3-5-17 5ESurr att9RB p226 MR20

STATHAM,Hugh Kington Llewellyn Lt kia 6-9-17 3Dors p124 CR Belgium24

STATHAM,Noel Horner Lt kia 3-2-17 5ESurr p226 CR Iraq5

STATTON,Percival Graham T2Lt dow 18-4-17 18Lpool p73 CRFrance52

STAUGHTON,A.W.Capt 26-12-16 2RMLI CR France40

STAUNTON,Harvey Chap4Cl ded 14-1-18 RAChDept p200 CR Iraq8

STAVEACRE,James Herbert.MID Maj kia 4-6-15 7Manch p237 MR4 &CR Gallipoli2

STAVELEY,Arthur Godfrey.MID Maj ded 24-3-20 50RFA CR Germany1

STAVELEY,Frederick Simpson Capt kld 15-3-15 EYorks attWRid p85 CR Belgium96,14-3-15

STAVELEY,George Hendley Capt kia 14-4-17 1 att2YLI p144 CR France1890

STAVELEY,Hugh Sheardown TLt kia 3-5-17 11EYorks p85 MR20

STAVELEY,Miles.MC.CaptAMaj dow 29-9-18 340/44RFA p36 CR France194

STAVERT,Robert Elliott Capt kia 25-8-18 4Lond p246 CR France576

STEAD,Aubrey Arthur 2Lt kia 9-4-17 1SomLI attTMB p80 CR France581

STEAD,Brian Desmond Howland Lt kia 21-3-18 1ELancs p111 MR20

STEAD,Charles Brian.MC.Capt dow 28-9-18 8WYorks p219 CR France512

STEAD,Charles Henry 2Lt kia 27-4-15 8Mddx p148 MR29,25-4-15

STEAD,Geoffrey Henry.MC&Bar.TLt dow 22-7-18 Ches att74L'TMB p97 CR France65,Capt

STEAD,Horace Stuart 2Lt kia 26-3-18 1/2 att17LancF p255 MR27

STEAD,John 2Lt ded 15-11-16 5SLancs p230 CR Lancs179

STEAD,John Kenneth Capt dow 4-2-17 4Yorks att20RFC p19&220 CR France285

STEAD,Ralph T2Lt kia 1-7-16 16WYorks p83 CR France742 Ex 19RFus

STEAD,Willie Wouldhave TLt kia 25-8-17 17WYorks p83 CR France630

STEADMAN,William Milton TCapt kld 10-10-17 RE IWT p48 CR France8

STEARN,John Holder.DSO.MID TLt kia 3-12-17 14DLI p161 MR17

STEARNS,Eric Gordon T2Lt dow 7-8-15 4RFus p70 CR Belgium11,6-8-15

STEARNS,Patrick Chillingworth 2Lt kia 4-12-17 5 att7KRRC p152 CR Belgium22

STECKLEY,Ray Clarke 2Lt ded 24-2-19 8Lond p271 CR Hamps2

STEDMAN,Arthur Roy Lt 14-8-18 88RAF MR20

STEDMAN,Philip Bertram Kirk Lt dow 19-8-16 4Lond p246 CR Lond12,Capt

STEDMAN,Raymond Cecil 2Lt dow 20-5-18 4 att1ESurr p113 CR France31

STEDMAN,William Walter Thomas 2Lt kia 13-11-16 18Lond p250 CR Belgium120,10-11-16

STEEDMAN,Arthur Haldane T2LtACapt dow 30-3-17 10ScotRif p104 CR France113

STEEL,Arthur Edward Lt kia 3-5-18 21Mddx &206RAF p148 MR20

STEEL,Alan Ivo Lt kia 8-10-17 2CldGds p51 MR30

STEEL,Angus Murray Russell.MID 2Lt kia 9-6-18 7ScotRif p224 CR Belgium3,5Bn

STEEL,Anthony T2Lt kia 11-9-18 LabCps att8Lpool p189 CR France686

STEEL,Charles Ernest 2Lt ded 28-9-16 7Mddx p271 CR Mddx48,STEELE

STEEL,Douglas Graham.MC.2LtACapt kia 13-11-16 3 att2Suff p79 CR France802

STEEL,Edward Anthony.DSO.LtCol ded 14-10-19 RFA p262 MR70 &CR Europe195

STEEL,Edwin Bedford Maj dow 23-11-14 RAMC p198 CR France284

STEEL,Ernest 2Lt kia 21-3-18 1NStaffs p158 MR27

STEEL,Harold Ponsonby Capt kia 5-8-17 IA 129Baluchis p283 CR EAfrica38 &CR Tanzania1

STEEL,James.MC.Capt kia 2-9-18 RAMC 10FA att1SomLI p198 CR France421

STEEL,James Camplett Lt kld 13-3-15 1A&SH p174 CR Belgium28,Campbell

STEEL,John Gordon.MID 2Lt ded 24-5-17 9DLI p239 CR Numb3

STEEL,Norman 2Lt kia 16-8-17 1/5Glouc A'Coy p225 MR30

STEEL,Robert Archibald 2Lt kia 27-3-18 RB &16RFC p255&257,Lt mbk MR20

STEEL,Stanley Joseph Capt kia 19-6-18 1/4Norf p216 MR34,18-6-18

STEEL,Walter Frank Banfield 2Lt kia 20-10-17 9HLI p241 CR Belgium49

STEEL,Wilfred 2Lt kld 9-5-15 4Y&L p238 CR France276,Wilfrid

STEEL,William Henry Lt&QM kia 28-6-15 5RScots p211 MR4

STEELE,Alfred Charles John 2Lt kia 23-8-18 1RWKent p142 CR France239

STEELE,Alfred Harmer T2Lt dow 5-2-17 GL &16RFC p13 CR France95,4-2-17

STEELE,Allan Robert TCapt dow 6-4-18 9ScotRif p104 CR Scot730

STEELE,Arthur Joseph TLt kia 22-9-15 6EYorks p85 MR4

STEELE,Benjamin Harry 2Lt kia 20-11-17 1Worc p109,258&257,mbk MR30

STEELE,D'Arcy Walter Stewart 2Lt kia 1-10-15 3Dors p124 MR21

STEELE,Ernest Cecil TLt kia 18-9-18 21MGC Inf Divl p185 CR France417

STEELE,Francis Gardner 2Lt kia 18-11-16 4 att2HLI p164 MR21

STEELE,Frederick James 2Lt kia 13-10-15 3Dors att8RBerks p124 MR19

STEELE,Frederick Wilberforce Alexander.MIDx2 Lt dow 25/27-10-14 RFus p70 MR22

STEELE,George Frederick.CMG.LtCol dow 22-5-15 1Drags p21 CR France285

STEELE,Gilbert Bernard Edward Capt kia 5-9-19 3SLancs &IARO att2/3Brahmans p264&283 MR43

STEELE,Norman Leslie 2Lt 20-4-17 1AustFC MR34

STEELE,Oliver Capt kia 25-10-14 1RBerks p140 MR29

STEELE,Robert Balfour Lt dow PoW 22-10-17 IARO att84RFC p283 CR Belgium140,21-10-17

STEELE,Robert Kingsley 2Lt kia 24-5-15 5NumbF p213 CR Belgium96,STEEL Lt

STEELE,William 2Lt dow 27-9-18 LancF att1/7Bn p93 CR France712

STEELE-NICHOLSON,Alfred Francis James Capt 16-8-17 5RIrRif MR30

STEELE-NICHOLSON,William Herbert Lt dow 13-4-18 RE 2/2Div CR Mddx16

STEELE-PERKINS,Cyril Steele Lt kia 31-8/2-9-14 RLancs p59 CR France611,26-8-14

STEEN,Thomas 2Lt kia 1-3-17 5RScotF p222 CR France745

STEENEKAMP,Petrus Andries 2Lt kld 23-5-16 26RFC p4 CR EAfrica56

STEER,Gordon Pemberton Capt dow 26-12-15 3SomLI att2Wilts p80 CR France64

STEGGALL,Hubert Henry TLt kia 18-9-18 N&D att10Bn p135 CR France407

STEHN,Arthur Edward Capt kia 8-11-18 4 att10RWar p66 CR France965

STEIBEL,Charles Lt kia 2-2-17 IMS 11IndGH att62Punjabis p283 CR Iraq5

STEIBEL,Marie Louise AssAdmntr ded 1-12-18 QMAAC p200 CR Lancs34

STEIN,Colin Hunter 2Lt kld 24-5-15 7A&SH p243 MR29

STEIN,John Francis 2Lt kia 28-9-16 3RIrRif p170 CR France293

STEINBERG,George Kenneth.MC.TLt kia 22-3-18 34MGC Divl p185 MR20

STEINMAN,Bernard Puckle Capt ded 26-4-16 1EKent p58 CR France145

STELFOX,George Henry T2Lt kia 9-10-17 1LancF p93 CR Belgium126

STELL,Jack 2Lt ded 19-6-18 13RScots &RAF p55 CR Lancs206

STEMBRIDGE,Jim T2Lt kia 29-9-18 2Yorks p91 CR France273

STENHOUSE,Andrew TLt dow 27-9-15 10ScotRif p104 MR19

STENHOUSE,Herbert Wilson.DSO.Maj kia 26-6-16 RWSurr GSO DivHQ p56 CR France5

STENHOUSE,John Maitland.MC.TCapt dow 25-8-16 RAMC att96RFA p198 CR France145

STENNING,Bernard Clement 2Lt dow 26-7-17 5ESurr attRE 228FC p226 CR France139

STENNING,Leslie Gerald Lt dow 1-9-15 6Ess p232 CR Essex48

STENNING,Sidney Nelson 2Lt kia 21-3-18 189RFA p36 MR20

STENT,Harold Rudolph 2Lt kia 20-7-18 1/2WRid p116 CR France622,2/4Bn

STEPHEN,Adrian Consett.MC.MID LtAMaj kia 14-3-18 D242RFA p36 CR Belgium21

STEPHEN,Alan James 2Lt dow 18-10-18 6 att2KRRC p152 CR France725

STEPHEN,Albert Alexander Leslie.DSO.Capt dow 31-10-14 ScotsGds p52 CR Belgium57

STEPHEN,David James Shirres.MC&Bar.TCapt dow 24-10-17 RAMC att54FA p198 CR Belgium18

STEPHEN,Douglas Clinton Leslie Capt dow 10-9-14 GrenGds p50 CR France1805

STEPHEN,Fred'k Charles Lt kld 25-9-15 6GordH p242 MR19

STEPHEN,George Lt ded 26-10-18 4GordH p256 CR Scot287

STEPHEN,J.Lt kia 14-10-18 3EKent attlA p58 MR38

STEPHEN,James Anderson T2Lt dow 28-10-17 2BordR p118 CR Belgium11

STEPHEN,James Eliot Lt kia 14-10-18 IA 1/19Punjabis p283 MR61 Ex 3EKent

STEPHEN,James Howie Frederic Lt kia 11-1-17 3 att1HLI p164 MR38

STEPHEN,James Pedraza 2Lt kia 23-5-17 46RFC p13 CRFrance354

STEPHEN,John Stephen Lt kia 23-3-18 16Lancers p23 MR27

STEPHEN,Kenneth Travers.MC.LtACapt dow 22-4-18 RFA X2TMB p36 CR France95

STEPHEN,Lionel Henry York TCapt ded 22-5-18 RAMC p198 CR Hamps13,25-5-18

STEPHEN,William Capt kia 13-11-16 5GordH p242 CR France1490

STEPHEN,William Ian 2Lt ded 4-12-17 IA 18Lancers p283 CR Asia60,I.W.

STEPHENS,Alexander Augustus ACapt&Adjt died 25-11-18 RGA p42 CR Hamps11

STEPHENS,Arnold Melvill.MID T2Lt dow 30-12-15 11LancF p93 CR France285

STEPHENS,Cecil Hubert Lt kia 23-10-18 111/24RFA p36 CR France1266

STEPHENS,Dudley Eric 2Lt dow 29-3-18 B70RFA p36 CR France113

STEPHENS,Ernest Stanley T2Lt kia 6-7-17 1Lincs att62TMB p76 CR France593

STEPHENS,Francis John 2Lt kia 30-1-17 22Lond p251 MR37

STEPHENS,Fred Orlando Lt kia 24-4-18 5 att2WYorks p218 MR27

STEPHENS,Frederick Henry Lt 23-11-17 2CentOntarioR &3RFC MR20

STEPHENS,Geoffrey Duncan 2Lt kia 9-7-16 5 att1RFus att17TMB p70 CR Belgium97

STEPHENS,George Harold Lt ded 13-12-20 RGA 219SB CR Lancs1

STEPHENS,Godfrey Gwilyn Brychan T2Lt kia 7-7-16 9SWBord att3WelshReg p101 MR21

STEPHENS,Henry French.DSO.MC.TMaj dow 14-10-18 86RFA p36 CR Lond2

STEPHENS,Howell Charles 2Lt kia 31-7-17 1Worc A'Coy p109 MR29

STEPHENS,John Herbert T2Lt kia 3-5-17 16 att12Mddx p148 MR20

STEPHENS,John Lockhart Lt kld 10-3-15 3Lond A'Coy p245 CR France706

STEPHENS,John Parnall Lt 23-7-21 RFA CR Iraq8

STEPHENS,John Stanley 2Lt kia 23-4-17 8SStaffs p123 MR20

STEPHENS,Kyrle Nalder T2Lt ded 31-12-17 RASC p194 CR Dorset22

STEPHENS,Llewellyn T2Lt kld 12-6-17 GL &RFC p13 CR Lond4

STEPHENS,Nasson Barrington 2Lt dow 1-6-16 4EYorks attMGC p187&219 CR France285

STEPHENS,Norman Victor Lt ded 28-1-20 41MGC Inf CR Germany1

STEPHENS,Robert Miller Lt kia 27-9-18 5RWKent p235 CR France413

STEPHENS,Sidney Thompson.MC.2Lt kia 9-10-17 att9Dev p77 MR30

STEPHENS,Thomas Alexander T2Lt dow 22-9-17 RE 250TC p48 CR Belgium165

STEPHENS,William Head T2Lt kia 14-7-16 9Leic p88 MR21

STEPHENS,William Leslie T2Lt ded 19-6-17 RE 143ArmyTroopCo p48 CR Greece4

STEPHENSON,Arthur Frederick Vere Lt kia 23-7-16 4GordH p241 MR21

STEPHENSON,Arthur Thomas Lt kia 28-6-16 7Lpool p215 CR France576,Theodore

STEPHENSON,Charles Lindsay T2Lt kia 28-11-17 9NumbF p63 CR France592

STEPHENSON,Claudius TCapt dow 2-11-16 12Ches p97 CR Greece6

STEPHENSON,Cyril Seymour 2Lt ded 6-12-16 9Lancers p22 CR Sussex204

STEPHENSON,Denys George Lt kia 16-5-15 2ScotsGds p52 CR France279

STEPHENSON,Derek Charles.DSO.MC.Maj kia 23-3-18 CmdgZ5RHA p36 CR France1893

STEPHENSON,Douglas Buchanan.MC.Capt kia 21-3-18 9Manch p237 MR27

STEPHENSON,Erik 2Lt kia 1-7-16 3Y&L p159 CR France246

STEPHENSON,Eric Arthur 2Lt kia 7-2-19 Yorks att17Lpool p255 MR70 &CR Europe180

STEPHENSON,Eric Lionel 2Lt kia 18-3-16 4Lincs p217 CR France68

STEPHENSON,Eric Seymour.DSO.Capt ded 6-5-15 Glouc attEgyptArmy p107 CR Europe3,dow

STEPHENSON,Eric William Rokeby LtCol kia 27-4-15 3Mddx p148 MR29,Ernest 23-4-15

STEPHENSON,Ernest Cooper Apperly 2Lt kia 21-3-18 RFA 18DAC att83Bde p36 MR27

STEPHENSON,Francis Leaman T2Lt ded 6-2-18 att3DLI p161 CR Durham81

STEPHENSON,Gertrude Annie Sister 25-3-18 QAIMNS CR Surrey160

STEPHENSON,Hubert Victor T2Lt kia 8-5-17 1DCLI p115 MR20

STEPHENSON,J.L.Lt 28-12-17 RAMC CR Lancs246

STEPHENSON,John Roberts T2Lt kia 7-8-17 16NumbF p63 MR31

STEPHENSON,Kenneth Langton.MIDx2 T2Lt kia 26-9-15 2Beds p86 MR19

STEPHENSON,L.J.T.Capt 8-6-15 O&BLI CR Surrey2

STEPHENSON,M.Silvia 9-11-15 VAD CR Egypt9

STEPHENSON,Norman Masters 2Lt ded 1-5-16 2RGA p271 CR Kent129

STEPHENSON,Olaf Stephen 2Lt kia 1-7-16 8YLI p144 MR21

STEPHENSON,Rennie TLt kia 16-11-16 10RFus p70 CR France701

STEPHENSON,Robert Brewis.MC.2Lt dow 23-10-17 4 att22NumbF C'Coy p213 CR Belgium16

STEPHENSON,Selwyn Seymour Lt ded 13-3-15 RFA p271 CR Lancs381

STEPHENSON,Urban Arnold Lt kia 23-3-18 1Lincs p76 CR France511

STERLING,George Pomeroy.DSO.MC.TCapt kia 27-10-18 11NumbF p63 CR Italy9

STERLING,John Lockhart 2Lt kia 28-9-15 3 att2RScotF p95 MR19

STERLING,Robert Capt ded 16-10-17 RAMC p198 CR Numb60

STERLING,Robert William Lt kia 24-4-15 3 att1RScotF p95 CR Belgium28,23-4-15

STERLING,William Charles Lt 3-10-18 24RAF MR20

STERN,Leonard Hermann 2Lt kia 9-5-15 13Lond p249 MR32

STERN,Sidney Lt kia 19-7-17 8Mddx att3/3KAR p202&236 CR EAfrica38 &CR Tanzania1,Sydney

STERN,Sydney Lionel 2Lt kld 22-2-18 RFC p17 CR Scot764

STERNBERG,Edgar Adolph Joseph T2Lt kia 16-10-16 11 att2RLancs p59 CR France115

STERNBERG,Rupert Oswald 2Lt dow 1-7-16 83RFA p36 CR France102

STEUART,James William Harvie 2Lt 12-5-20 9RScots CR Scot723

STEUART,Norman Kennedy.MID Capt dow 15-9-16 ConnRgrs att6Bn p172 CR France300

STEUART,Walter Willox T2Lt dow 5-3-17 18HLI &46RFC p13&164 CR Belgium11

STEVEN,Archibald T2Lt kia 25-10-16 10Worc att8Glouc p109 MR21

STEVEN,George Gordon TLt kia 24-10-16 TankCps p189 CR France246 Ex MGC

STEVEN,Harvey Smith Lt kia 7-10-15 1/4BlkW p230 CR France765

STEVEN,Robert T2Lt dow 24-3-18 14HLI p164 MR20

STEVEN,Sidney Herbert Lt kia 25-9-15 4BlkW p230 MR19

STEVEN,William Struan Robertson Capt ded 1-7-19 RAMC p267 CR Devon1

STEVENS,Alexander.DCM.Capt&QM ded 10-4-17 1HLI p164 MR65

STEVENS,Alexander Mackay Lt 28-9-18 202RAF MR20

STEVENS,Alfred James 2Lt kia 21-9-18 1RWar att142RAF p66 CR Palestine9

STEVENS,Albert Charles Capt&QM ded 21-5-17 RE p48 CR Yorks551

STEVENS,Alfred Leslie Lt kia 18-4-17 1Leic p88 MR19

STEVENS,Arthur Eustace.MC.2Lt dow 16-7-15 1Hamps p121 CR France102

STEVENS,Arthur Reginald Ingram TLt kia 4-8-16 9RFus p70 CR France832

STEVENS,Cecil Robert LtCol ded 18-11-19 IA IMS p283

STEVENS,Cyril Stanley Geoffrey ACapt kia 9-10-17 1/2 att3/5LancF p93 MR30,Geoffry

STEVENS,Donald Eustace Lt kia 13-3-18 2/5Manch attRFC p19&236 CR France134

STEVENS,Douglas Alfred Stephen T2Lt kia 9-3-18 GL att76RFC p17 CR France95

STEVENS,Douglas Harcourt 2Lt kia 7-8-18 4EKent p212 CR France247,6-8-18

STEVENS,Edward Alfred Murtagh.MC.2Lt kia 16-6-18 1 att6EKent p58 CR France61,E.H.M.18-6-18

STEVENS,Edward Henry Lt dow 16-6-17 ELancs att25RFC p13&111,16-8-17 CR Belgium406

STEVENS,Ernest 2Lt dow 2-2-15 1SfthH p165 CR France727

STEVENS,Fenwick Charles Lt dow 7-9-18 2/5RLancs attTMB p213 CR France103

STEVENS,Frederick Charles.DCM.TCapt kia 31-7-16 D158RFA p36 CR France329,dow

STEVENS,Frederick George 2Lt dow 21-10-17 RFA p209 CR Belgium25

STEVENS,George Kellner 2Lt kia 4-6-16 3 att1Lincs p76 CR France188

STEVENS,George Percival Lt kia 21-3-18 232RFA attRE p208 MR27

STEVENS,Gorham Ninton 2Lt ded 18-1-18 1/5Lincs p220 CR France98,Vinton Lt

STEVENS,Henry Francis Bingham TLt kia 16-9-15 6RWKent p142 CR Belgium126

STEVENS,James T2Lt kia 9-4-17 5 O&BLI p130 CR France581

STEVENS,John Michael Stanilaus Gregory 2Lt dow 14-7-17 1RFC p13 CR France200

STEVENS,Lottie M.SNurse ded 15-3-16 QAIMNS p200 CR Egypt3

STEVENS,Leonard Frank Lt kia 25-3-18 6ESurr att4NStaffs p226 MR27

STEVENS,Lothian Basil 2Lt kia 9-5-15 SStaffs p123 MR32

STEVENS,Montague Lt kia 7-7-16 5 att1Worc p109 MR21

STEVENS,Norman Walter BtMaj ded 27-7-19 RAMC p267 MR65

STEVENS,Percival Charles 2Lt kia 6-4-17 8RWSurr p56 CR France161

STEVENS,Percy TLt kia 23-9-18 7RWKent p142 CR France364

STEVENS,Reginald Walter Morton.MID Capt dow 29-8-14 RIrRif p170 CR France1395,28-8-14

STEVENS,R.H.B.2Lt kld 30-5-18 GL &RAF p191

STEVENS,Robert LtCol ded 18-11-19 IA IMS CR Devon153

STEVENS,Ronald William.MM.2Lt dow 31-10-17 8Worc Ex 1/4 O&BLI p226 CR France547

STEVENS,Stephen Repton LtCol kia 8-3-16 IA 93BurmaInf p283 MR38

STEVENS,Thomas Tearle TLt kia 26-9-15 9Suff p79 MR19

STEVENS,Walter Sydney John T2Lt kia 7-7-16 11 att9LNLancs p136 MR21

STEVENS,William Philip 2Lt kia 3-8-18 1 att18Lond p245 MR16

STEVENSON,Alan TCapt kia 26-9-16 13 att9N&D p135 CR France296

STEVENSON,Alan McDonald Lt 5-4-18 GL&RAF CR Egypt9

STEVENSON,Alexander 2Lt kia 9-12-16 6GordH p242 CR France393

STEVENSON,Arthur 2Lt kia 27-4-18 RGA 152SB p42 CR Belgium188

STEVENSON,C.A.Lt 21-1-20 ConnRgrs CR Ches51

STEVENSON,Carlos 2Lt kia 2-1-17 20Lond p251 CR Belgium167

STEVENSON,David James 2Lt kia 22-6-16 5ScotRif p224 CR France765

STEVENSON,Douglas Baptiste 2Lt kia 11-3-17 DCLI &45RFC p13&115 CR Belgium11

STEVENSON,Frank Chown Lt kia 22-9-17 4Nhampt &NigR p234 CR EAfrica22 &CR Tanzania1

STEVENSON,Frederick 2Lt kia 29-4-17 22RFus p70 MR20

STEVENSON,George Arthur 2Lt dow 9-5-15 3EYorks p85 CR France102,2Bn

STEVENSON,George Hambly Capt kia 9-1-16 IA 125Rif p283 MR38,6-1-16

STEVENSON,George Herbert Maj kia 25-9-15 2WelshR p127 MR19,26-9-15

STEVENSON,Harold George 2Lt kia 25-6-17 13Y&L p159 CR France777

STEVENSON,Harry Burnett.MID Capt kia 7-8-15 IA 2Rajputs att2/10GurkhaRif p283 MR4,6-8-15

STEVENSON,Henry Fitzroy TLt kia 7-7-16 13Ches p97 MR21

STEVENSON,Hugh 2Lt kia 10-9-16 10 att16Lond p248 MR21 CR France1890

STEVENSON,Hugh Lt kia 9-10-17 6LancF p221 MR30

STEVENSON,Ilston Henry Lt kia 16-2-16 8 att7Nhampt p138 MR29

STEVENSON,J.Lt ded 15-5-18 RE p256

STEVENSON,James T2Lt kld 1-5-17 GL &RFC p13 CR Scot893

STEVENSON,John Lt ded 15-5-18 IARO att1Sap&Min p283 MR66

STEVENSON,John Connell.MID T2Lt kia 23-8-18 6RWSurr p56 CR France370,dow

STEVENSON,John Huntley Wickham 2Lt dow 5-2-17 IA 46 att26Punjabis p283 CR Iraq5

STEVENSON,John Scott Lt dow 9-10-18 RE p210

STEVENSON,Leonard William Hugh.MC.TLt kia 1-7-16 9RInniskF p105 MR21

STEVENSON,Marcus James Lt ded 10-9-15 RAVC attSherwoodRgrs p254 CR Egypt9

STEVENSON,Paul William John 2Lt dow 25-5-15 23Lond C'Coy p252 CR France414

STEVENSON,Philip Noel 2Lt kia 14-1-20 IA 1/109Inf p283 MR43

STEVENSON,Ralph Tapley 2Lt kia 3-8-18 5Lond 1Bn p246 MR16,31-8-18

STEVENSON,Richard John 2Lt dow 10-5-18 3 att1Hamps p121 CR France88

STEVENSON,Robert Capt kia 23-8-17 7 att9BlkW p231 CR Belgium8

STEVENSON,Robert Dennistoun TCapt kia 16-5-16 11A&SH p174 CR France423

STEVENSON,Robert Lyon Capt 9-8-17 EAUL CR EAfrica12 &CR Tanzania1

STEVENSON,Sampson Donald Lt dow 3-10-18 5Hamps p228

STEVENSON,Samuel Bristow 2Lt ded 29-9-16 RGA 138SB p42 CR Greece7

STEVENSON,Talbert.MC&Bar.Capt&Adjt kia 14-11-17 4/5BlkW p230 CR Belgium21

STEVENSON,Thomas Kerr T2LtALt kia 28-1-17 6/7RScotF att45TMB p95 CR France151

STEVENSON,Tom Lt kia 1-8-18 1/9RScots p212 CR France524

STEVENSON,Walter Henry T2Lt kia 5-6-17 29RFC p13 CR France46

STEVENSON,William 2Lt kia 11-6-18 3BordR att10N&D p118 MR27

STEVENSON,William.MC.2Lt kia 18-9-18 RGA 147HB p42 CR France647

STEVENSON,William Alexander Gibb.MID Capt dow PoW 20-12-17 14HLI p164 CR France1142

STEVENSON,William Henry 2Lt kia 21-3-18 11Leic p88 MR20

STEVENSON-HAMILTON,Olmar Charles John Maj ded 12-6-19 IA S&TCps p283 MR43

STEWARD,Arthur Amyot 2Lt kia 6-10-17 RFA &RFC 11BalloonCo p13&36 CR Belgium20,Lt

STEWARD,Charles 2Lt kia 25-5-15 3 att2KSLI p145 MR29

STEWARD,Harold N.Capt FlyingAcc 3-12-16 IA 6Cav &RFC CR Hamps180

STEWARD,John Henry Maj ded 10-5-15 4Norf p74&263 CR Norf139,3Bn

STEWART,Adrian Harry Lt kia 29-8-14 Glouc att3NigeriaR p107&202 CR WAfrica55

STEWART,Alan Dundas T2Lt kia 19-9-15 9RSuss p120 CR France1597

STEWART,Albert Lewis.DSO.TMaj kia 4-10-17 22MGC Inf p185 MR30

STEWART,Alexander Charles Capt kia1 2-4-18 9ACycCps p181 CR France193,12-4-18

STEWART,Alexander Dugald Lorn.MC.Capt dedacc 9-9-19 2GordH p265 CR Scot2

STEWART,Alexander James.MC.LtAMaj dow 30-4-18 2WYorks att59MGC Inf p83&185 CR France100,MGC attWYorks

STEWART,Alexander Leitch Capt kia 21-3-18 9 att1/7A&SH p244 MR20

STEWART,Alexander Vivian 2Lt kia 23-4-17 4GordH p242 MR20

STEWART,Algernon Brigham Anstruther.DSO.LtCol kia 24-5-16 1SfthH p165 CR France157,23-5-16 1/4Bn

STEWART,Alister Douglas TLt kld 13-10-17 GL &RFC p13 CR Wilts116,Alistere

STEWART,Andrew.MC.T2Lt kia 20-9-17 10NumbF p63 CR Belgium132

STEWART,Andrew Christie T2Lt drd 19-4-18 GL RE attIWT p191 MR38

STEWART,Andrew Philip.MC.TLt ded 2-6-18 KOSB p264 CR Scot764

STEWART,Bertrand Capt kia 13-9-14 WKentYeo p204 CR France1110,12-9-14

STEWART,Bryce.MID Lt kia 21-4-16 1SfthH p165 MR38

STEWART,C.G.HonLt&QM ded 26-2-18 Leic p263

STEWART,Charles Edward TLtCol kia 31-8-16 190RFA p36 CR France397

STEWART,Charles Edward 2Lt dow 10-9-16 20Manch p156 CR France51

STEWART,Charles Edward.CMG.TBrigGen kia 14-9-16 BlkW Cmdg154InfBde p129 CR France922

STEWART,Charles Edward.MC.TCapt dow 10-4-17 10DLI p161 CR France120

STEWART,Charles Frederick Somes.MC.TMaj kia 5-4-18 RMunstF att6Nhants p176 CR France587

STEWART,Christopher Codrington Capt kia 24-11-15 IA 20Punjabis attStaff 16Bde p283 MR38

STEWART,David Lt kia 14-6-15 6SfthH p241 CR France705

STEWART,Douglas Alexander T2Lt kia 7-7-16 13Ches p97 MR21

STEWART,Douglas Marshall S.Capt dow 3-1-19 4RScots p271 CR Scot239

STEWART,Duncan Hinshelwood 2Lt kia 20-4-18 9 att11A&SH C'Coy p244 CR France531

STEWART,Duncan John 2Lt kia 23-10-16 6ScotRif p224 CR France374

STEWART,Edward John T2Lt kia 30-11-17 140MGC Inf p185 CR France1496

STEWART,Elizabeth Grace SNurse 15-2-16 QAIMNS CR Hamps1

STEWART,Frederic Arnold TLt kia 16-9-16 10DLI p161 MR21

STEWART,Geoffrey Capt kia 22-12-14 1CldGds p51 MR22

STEWART,George TLtACapt kia 5-6-17 26NumbF p63 MR20

STEWART,George 2Lt kia 11-4-18 1/6WRid p227 CR France297

STEWART,George Lothian.MID 2Lt kia 9-4-17 6 att13RScots C'Coy p211 CR France924

STEWART,Gerald Capt kia 9-4-17 1/6SfthH p241 CR France15

STEWART,Gerald Charles Capt kia 13-5-15 10Huss p22 CR Belgium4

STEWART,George Pemberton.DCM.T2Lt kia 25-9-15 1CamH p168 CR France29

STEWART,George Soutar 2Lt ded 18-6-19 GL &RAF p267 CR USA184

STEWART,Guy Somerville 2Lt kia 28-3-18 49RFC p17 MR20

STEWART,Henry Edward TCapt kia 1-6-17 8RSuss p120 CR France1184

STEWART,Henry Ernest TLt kld 19-11-17 RScotF 55TrgResBn p95 CR Scot119

STEWART,Henry Warburton 2Lt ded 11-2-19 RGA 77SB p42 CR Germany1,Lt

STEWART,Herbert Lt kia 23-4-15 3DLI att2DCLI p161 MR29

STEWART,Herbert TLtACapt kia 9-4-17 9KRRC p152 CR France581

STEWART,Howard William 2Lt kia 27-8-18 GrenGds att4GdsMGReg p50&53 CR France614

STEWART,Hugh TLt kia 25-3-18 12HLI p164 CR France630

STEWART,Hugh.DSO.MC.MajTLtCol kia 12-4-18 RAMC att94FA p198 CR France857

STEWART,Hugh Duncan.MC.Maj kia 12-10-18 RFA p206 CR France612

STEWART,Humphrey.MID TCapt kia 3-7-16 5RBerks p140 MR21

STEWART,James 2Lt kia 28-10-16 22Lpool p73 CR France374

STEWART,James T2Lt dow 25-10-18 CamH Res att5Bn p168 CR Belgium143

298

STEWART,James Alexander Logan Lt kia 13-5-15 1RB p180 CR Belgium126

STEWART,James Aitchison TLt dow 12-10-16 GL &21RFC p4&191 CR France85

STEWART,James Augustus Lt kia 9-5-15 3RMunstF p176 MR22 2Bn

STEWART,James Henry 2Lt kld 21-12-17 413/302RFA p36 CR Palestine3

STEWART,James Robert Chap4Cl kia 2-1-16 RAChDept att2Worc p200 CR France80

STEWART,John Cecil Grahame 2Lt kia 25-9-15 2KRRC p152 CR France219

STEWART,John Charles Miller 2Lt kia 3-7-16 2/7WYorks att25RFC p19&218 CR France88

STEWART,John Ebenezar.MC.TCapt kia 26-4-18 8BordR attSStaffs p118 MR30

STEWART,John Houghton Lt kia 24-5-15 2RInniskF p105 MR22,15/16-5-15

STEWART,John James Erskine Brown 2Lt dow 12-6-17 7 att12RScots p211 CR France40

STEWART,John Kennedy 2Lt dow 2-11-17 4 att1/7RScots p211 CR Palestine8

STEWART,John Maurice 2Lt kia 1-4-15 IrGds SR p53 CR France279

STEWART,John Morley 2Lt dow 21-8-17 10 att2RScots p212 CR France103

STEWART,John Nelson 2Lt kia 9-4-17 5Lpool p215 CR France595

STEWART,John Robertson 2Lt kia 12-4-18 2/4RWKent p234 CR Palestine3

STEWART,John Stanley T2Lt kia 17-10-16 10 att1RLancs p59 MR21

STEWART,John Stewart 2Lt dow 15-7-15 5A&SH p243 MR4

STEWART,John Walcot.MC.TLt kia 21-3-18 16RScots p55 MR20

STEWART,Joseph 2Lt kia 16-8-17 4RDubF p177 MR30

STEWART,Joseph Charles 2Lt kia 7-2-16 IARO att33Cav p283 CR Iraq6

STEWART,Keith Anthony.Hon.Lt kia 9-5-15 2BlkW p129 CR France924

STEWART,Malcolm Hector Capt dow 15-7-16 2RScots CR France23 served as MALCOLM,R.J.

STEWART,Mungo.MID Lt dow 7-2-17 55RFA HQ Staff p36 CR Iraq5

STEWART,Murdock Sutherland Capt ded 22-9-20 RASC CR EAfrica116

STEWART,Nathaniel William Lt kia 23-1-17 7RScots attRFC p19&211 MR34

STEWART,Norman Sinclair.MID Capt kia 30-9-15 2RScots p55 CR Belgium4

STEWART,Osmer Noël.MC.2Lt kia 31-7-17 B71RFA p36 CR Belgium84

STEWART,Ralph Walker Maj kia 2-9-18 Fife&ForfarYeo p203 CR France511,14BlkW

STEWART,Robert T2Lt kia 1-7-16 1KOSB p102 MR21

STEWART,Robert Arthur Chap4Cl ded 3-11-17 RAChDept att57CCS p200 CR France787

STEWART,Robert Colin TCapt kia 1-7-16 8Y&L p159 CR France246

STEWART,Robert Locke 2Lt ded 18-10-18 IA TC attRGA 1BritMtnArtBde p283 MR66

STEWART,Robert Taylor T2Lt dow 27-9-15 7RScotF p95 CR France98,Lt 28-9-15

STEWART,Ronald TLt drd 15-4-17 RAMC p198 MR35

STEWART,Ronald James.MC.Lt dow 28-1-16 3 att1SfthH p165 CR Iraq5

STEWART,R.S.Maj 13-6-21 Lpool CR Devon50

STEWART,Samuel George.MC&Bar.MID LtAMaj kia 27-10-18 30/39RH&FA p36 CR France1270

STEWART,Sydney Douglas Maj ded 29-11-19 GL &Mddx p267 CR Surrey1

STEWART,Thomas.MC&Bar.Maj kia 12-9-17 8 att5/6RScots p211 CR Belgium24

STEWART,Vernon Forster Lt kia 13-5-17 8DLI att16RFC p19&239 CR France32

STEWART,Vernon Radcliffe Lt kld 5-12-17 RASC &19RFC p13&194 CR Lancs283,2Lt

STEWART,Walter Robert.DSO.MC.BtMajTLtCol kia 8-4-18 13RB p180 CR France203

STEWART,Walter Ross Taylor 2Lt kia 6-8-16 9A&SH p244 CR France1327

STEWART,Weston Capt dow PoW 27-3-18 1/4 att1/6SfthH p241 CR France560

STEWART,William Maj dow 12-7-15 4RScotFus p222 MR4

STEWART,William Alfred Lindsay.MC.Capt kia 25-9-16 GrenGds att4th p50 CR France374

STEWART,William Beardmore Capt kia 24-5-17 D/HB107RFA p207 CR Belgium15

STEWART,William Debenham McLaren Capt kld 23-9-16 1BlkW p129 MR21,Debnam

STEWART,William Johnston 2Lt kia 1-7-16 10 att9RIrFus p171 MR21

STEWART,William Malcolm.MID TCapt dow 27-10-16 23MGC p185 CR France105

STEWART,William Marshall 2lt kia 24-3-17 8 att10ScotRif p225 MR20

STEWART,William McEwan Henderson T2Lt kia 16-8-17 11RInniskF p105 MR30

STEWART,William Norman.DSO.LtCol kia 22-3-18 NSomYeo att6Leic p205 MR27

STEWART,William Victor 2Lt kia 8-5-15 1Mon p244 MR29

STEWART,Wilma Bridges SNurse ded 10-7-18 TFNS CR Surrey99

STEWART-CORRY,Eberhardt George Lt kia 26-6-17 5Yorks p220 MR20

STEWART-JONES,Thorold Arthur Capt kia 9-5-15 5RSuss p228 MR22

STEWART-MOORE,Henry TLt kia 10-9-16 6 att7RInniskF p105 CR Greece3

STEWART-MURRAY,Lord George Maj kia 14-9-14 BlkW p129 MR15

STEWART-RICHARDSON,Edward Austin.Bart.Capt dow 28-11-14 3 att1BlkW p129 CR Scot203

STEWART-RICHARDSON,John Lauderdale 2Lt kia 17-5-16 2CldGds p51 CR Belgium44

STEYN,Stephanus Sebastian Lombard TLt kia 8-12-17 B117RFA p36 CR Palestine3

STEYTLER,Edward Dickinson 2Lt kia 25-7-16 SLancs &7RFC p4&126 MR20

STICKLAND,William Alban Lt kia 23-5-16 84/11RFA p36 CR Belgium5

STIDSTON,William Popkiss 2Lt dow 3-8-17 5 att2Leinst p175 CR Belgium7

STIDWELL,Herbert Jenkins 2Lt kia 27-7-16 3 att1RBerks p140 MR21

STIFF,Charles Neville Carleton Capt kia 22-3-18 4Yorks p220 MR27

STIGAND,Chauncey Hugh.OBE.Maj kia 8-12-19 RWKent attEgyptArmy CR EAfrica116

STILEMAN,Cecil Herbert T2Lt kia 29-2-16 RFus &5RFC p4&70 CR Belgium11

STILEMAN,Frederic William Cheere Capt kia 23-7-16 8Glouc p107 MR21

STILES,Arthur James 2Lt kia 3-8-16 8RFus p70 MR21

STILES,Edgar Watson.MID Lt dow 13-4-18 7NumbF p214 CR France88

STILES,Edgcumbe Leopold 2Lt kia 14-4-18 4EKent p212 MR32

STILES,Vincent Harcourt Lt kia 20-9-17 24Lond attMGC p187&252 CR Belgium88

STILL,George 2Lt kia 3-4-18 4CamH &RAF p243 CR Europe20

STILL,Reginald Sidney Hewitt 2Lt kia 7-10-16 28 att9RFus p70 MR21

STILWELL,Montague James Lt dow 30-6-18 4RWKent p234 CR France516

STIMPSON,John Crockett 2Lt kia 2-7-16 1/8WYorks p219 MR21

STIMSON,Montague Adolph 2Lt kia 30-9-16 10 att8ESurr p113 MR21

STIRLAND,Joseph Lt kia 24-3-18 22DLI p161 MR27

STIRLING,Colin Robert Hoste.DSO&Bar.MC.CaptALtCol dow 29-5-18 ScotRif att2RBerks p104 CR France145

STIRLING,George Edward 2Lt kia 7-10-16 8Lond p247 MR21

STIRLING,Gordon.MC.Lt kia 15-9-16 ScotsGds attMGC Inf p52 MR21 CR France390

STIRLING,Gordon Sheffield.MC.Capt dow 26-12-16 RoO 1/3KAR attA&SH p202&259 CR EAfrica38 &CR Tanzania1 A&SH attKAR

STIRLING,Harry Francis Dundas.MC.Maj kia 9-1-17 IA 59Rif p283 CR Iraq5,Henry LtCol

STIRLING,James Capt kia 2-1-15 3 att1ScotRif p104 CR France83

STIRLING,John Hunt Lt dow 22-8-17 57/45RFA p208 CR Belgium11

STIRLING,Richard Kellock Lt kia 21-8-15 5 att1RFus p70 MR29 &CR Belgium453

STIRLING,Robert Lt kia 19-2-15 1A&SH p174 CR Belgium28

STIRLING,William Aeneas Capt mbk 14-10-16 2SfthH p257 MR21

STIRLING-COOKSON,Samuel Baillie Capt kia 17-5-15 1RScotF p95 CR Belgium28

STIRLING-STUART,James Lt dow 9-11-14 ScotsGds p52 MR29

STITT,Innes d'Auvergne Stewart 2Lt kia 28-3-18 16Lond p250 MR20

STIVEN,Albert T2Lt kia 24-1-17 2 att6/7RScotF p95 CR France151

STIVEN,Ronald Walter Sutherland Capt dow 15-9-15 RScotF p95 CR Germany3

STOALING,Thomas 2Lt kia 14-5-17 2/4Lond p246 MR20

STOBART,John Geoffrey 2Lt kia 15-3-17 6 att4RB p180 CR Belgium111

STOBART,William TLt kia 24-8-16 10DLI attRFC p4&161 CR Belgium11

STOBBART,Roland Walter T2Lt kld 6-3-18 RFC p17 CR Numb7,Walton

STOBBS,Henry 2Lt kia 26-10-17 4NumbF p213 CR Belgium126

STOCK,Arthur Boy Capt ded 12-12-15 AyrshireYeo p271 CR Surrey160

STOCK,Charles Herbert T2Lt ded 31-5-16 13Hamps att9Worc p121 CR Iraq5

STOCK,Hubert Reginald 2Lt kia 25-10-14 1EKent p58 MR32

STOCK,James Mulock Thompson TLt kia 16-11-16 8ELancs p111 MR21,15-11-16

STOCK,John Launcelot Walmsley 2Lt dow 3-5-17 3Dors att6SomLI p124 CR France581

STOCK,Sydney Albert Cdr ded 31-7-16 IA S&TCps p283 CR Iraq6

STOCKDALE,Arthur William Sinclair 2Lt kia 24-5-17 7DLI p239 MR29

STOCKDALE,Edward Leslie Johnson TLt kia 7-7-16 10LancF p93 MR21

STOCKDALE,Frank TCapt dow 19-9-18 11RWFus p99 CR Greece1

STOCKDALE,Guy Nelson.MC.Maj kia 21-3-18 WYorks att11Ess p83 MR20

STOCKDALE,Norman Henry T2Lt kia 18-9-16 Lincs p76 CR France251

STOCKDALE,Walter Edwin 2Lt kia 10-9-15 NottsYeo p205 CR Gallipoli5,Lt

STOCKDALE,William Lt kia 3-5-17 6WRid p227 MR20

STOCKEN,Kenneth Edger 2Lt kia 30-8-18 3SomLI att1Dev p80 CR France239

STOCKENSTROM,Andries Lars Lt 22-5-18 70RAF MR20

STOCKER,Arthur Rutterford.MC.ACapt ded 24-1-19 6SfthH attMGC Inf p187&241 CR Belgium316

STOCKER,Edward 2Lt kia 29-5-15 6KOSB p102 MR19,25-9-15

STOCKER,Frederick Luff TLt kia 23-8-18 28 att20RFus p70 CR France927

STOCKER,Harold Victor 2Lt kia 28-3-18 2/6RWar p214 MR27

STOCKER,St.John Crichton TCapt kia 12-3-15 2Nhampt p138 MR22

STOCKER,Thomas Fuller 2Lt kia 19-5-15 RE 171Coy p48 CR Belgium4

STOCKHAM,Thomas Alan Campbell Lt kia 22-3-18 1EYorks p255 MR27

STOCKHOUSEN,Ivan Lancelot 2Lt kia 3-10-17 BritWIndiesR att17RFC p13&192

STOCKINS,William James 2Lt kia 7-6-18 22Lond &RAF MR20,6-6-18

STOCKLEY,Harold Brodie 2Lt kld 22-7-18 2Lond &RAF p271

STOCKLEY,James Pearson Maj kia 7-1-16 IA 102Grens p283 MR38,6-1-16

STOCKLEY,Philip George TCapt ded 12-2-17 EYorks p85 CR Surrey36

STOCKLEY,Philip Lloyd TLtACapt kia 26-4-18 30MGC Inf p185 MR30

STOCKLEY,Walter Edwin TLt kia 9-8-18 14TankCps p189 CR France694

STOCKS,Harris Lawrence.DSO.Maj kia 1-7-16 15RScots p55 CR France296,Laurance

STOCKS,Michael George Lt kia 10-11-14 2GrenGds p50 CR Belgium134

STOCKS,Murdoch MacQueen T2Lt dow 10-4-16 11 att8GordH p167 CR France285

STOCKS,Tom Dixon T2Lt dow 16-4-18 3WRid p116 CR France249,15-4-18 2BN

STOCKTON,James Godfrey Capt kia 22-8-17 4 O&BLI p231 MR30

STOCKWELL,Charles Inglis Maj dow 21-10-14 2SfthH p165 CR France922

STOCKWELL,Eric Craig St.George Maj ded 20-1-19 YLI p265 CRYorks590

STOCKWELL,Frank Roland 2Lt kia 6-8-16 2/13Lond C'Coy p249 MR20

STOCKWELL,George TCapt kia 6-10-17 5Dors p124 MR30

STOCKWOOD,Lawrence Francis T2Lt dow 12-10-17 HouseholdBn p20 CR Belgium83,Finlay

STODDARD,A.A.Lt 27-11-18 IARO att S&M CR Hereford/W56

STODDARD,Ralph Cyril 2Lt ded 3-7-16 SLancs &4RFC p126&4,kia STODDART MR20

STODDART,Frederick William Capt kia 27-10-14 1Wilts p153 MR22

STODDART,George Benjamin Johnstone 89720 2Lt kld 10-4-18 GL 65RAF p191 CR France37,kia

STODDART-MacLELLAND,Chaltair Ruaridh Alwinn Domhnuill CaptHonMaj ded 30-11-14 3Ess p132 CR Scot54,MacLELLAN

STOER,Fred Charles T2Lt kia 17-3-16 6DCLI p115 CR France420

STOKER,Edward Alexander Morris.MC.Lt dow 12-9-16 4 att6RIrReg p89&170 CR France66

STOKER,George.CMG.23-3-20 RAMC CR Devon69

STOKES,Charles Leonard Lt kia 26-9-17 6Hamps att19MGC Inf p187&229 MR30

STOKES,Claud Harry.DFC.dow 7-11-18 RAF CR Belgium199

STOKES,Clifford 2Lt kia 18-2-17 13Ess p132 CR France314

STOKES,Guy Lennard T2Lt kia 5-7-17 D174 RFA p36 CR Belgium5

STOKES,Haldane Day.MVO.Lt kia 17-2-15 2RLancs p59 CR Belgium133

STOKES,Harold T2Lt kia 20-11-17 E'TankCps p189 MR17

STOKES,Herbert George T2Lt kia 25-3-18 RE 77FC p48 MR20

STOKES,Hugh Adrian Innys Blyth.MC.2Lt dow 28-11-18 3 O&BLI p130 CR Surrey1

STOKES,John Alan T2Lt kia 16-8-17 10RIrFus p171 MR30

STOKES,John Hill.MC.Capt dow 22-3-15 3RWKent att1RBerks p142&259 CR France102

STOKES,John Wilfred LtCol kld 10-2-16 RAMC 3WRidFA p253 CR Lond12

STOKES,Leicester Henry 2Lt kia 31-10-17 18Lond p250 MR30

STOKES,Oliver Chetwode 2Lt kia 5-3-17 2RMunstF p176 CR France1472

STOKES,Philip Durham 2Lt dow 10-4-17 6RB p180 CR France145,11Bn

STOKES,Reginald Alexander 2Lt kia 24-2-17 9YLI p144 CR France163

STOKES,Reginald George Maj kia 28-9-15 2LNLancs p136 CR EAfrica58

STOKES,Robert John 2Lt kia 20-8-16 6 att2KRRC p152 CR France402

STOKES,Terence Fuller Capt dow 7-2-17 IA 82Punjabis p283 CR Iraq5

STOKES,William Allen LtCol 27-8-20 RE attRAF CR Egypt6

STOKES,William Henry 2Lt kia 18-4-18 RGA 101SB p42 CR France200

STOKES-ROBERTS,Edward Rowland Bennett.CB.BrigGen ded 22-11-17 RE HQ Baghdad p48 CR Iraq8

STOKOE,Henry Bertram TCapt kld 12-10-15 6YLI A'Coy p144 CR Belgium105,dedacc

STOKOE,James Clarke T2Lt kia 11-12-15 14Manch att6LNLancs p156 CR Gallipoli5,Lt

STOLLARD,Gordon TMaj kia 3-9-16 17N&D p135 MR21

STOLLERY,John Cecil 2Lt kia 24-5-15 5RFus attRWar p70 MR29

STONE,Alfred Lt ded 17-10-19 3Suff p263 CR France40

STONE,Arnold Capt kia 29-4-17 1/5N&D D'Coy p232 MR19

STONE,Arthur.DSO.TLtCol kia 2-10-18 15LancF p93 CR France836,16Bn

STONE,Arthur Brabazon.MID Maj kia 10-5-15 Ches p97 MR29

STONE,Arthur Cuthbert 2Lt kia 1-2-17 IARO att45Sikhs p283 CR Iraq5

STONE,Arthur Edward Capt kia 24-7-15 A243RFA p207 CR France251

STONE,Charles Douglas Felgate 2Lt kia 9-9-16 4RIrReg att6ConnRgrs p89 MR21

STONE,Docksey 2Lt kia 21-7-16 2/8RWar p215 CR France1887

STONE,Ellis Robert Cunliffe 2Lt kia 26-10-14 2RWFus p99 CR France705,Lt 25-10-14

STONE,Frank Ablett T2Lt kia 20-9-17 Norf att1/8Lpool p74 MR30

STONE.Frederick James TLtACapt dow 29-12-16 7Glouc p107 CR Iraq5

STONE,George Morrison 2Lt kia 17-8-16 RE 1/1FC p210 MR21,Marrison

STONE,Harold 2Lt kia 7-6-17 23Lond p252 CR Belgium74

STONE,Harold George T2Lt kia 5-4-18 8SomLI p80 MR20

STONE,Henry Brassington Lt kia 18-2-15 RE 3FC p210 CR Belgium120

STONE,Henry Reginald 2Lt dow PoW 17-4-18 13Lond p249 CR France142,Lt

STONE,Herbert John T2Lt dow 15-11-17 19RFC p13 CR France285

STONE,Herbert William Degetan 2Lt kia 26-4-16 2IrRif att4ConnRgrs p172 CR France68,Degetau

STONE,Noel Herbert.MC.LtACapt kia 27-4-18 1Worc p109 CR France144

STONE,Oliver John 2Lt dow 22-9-16 4 att2/41RFA p209 CR France169

STONE,Robert Claude 2LtTLt kia 8-4-17 RLancs att9MGC Inf p59 CR France1701

STONE,Tom Pearce Griffith TLt dow 5-2-17 B66RFA p36 CR Iraq5

STONE,Walter Napleton.VC.ACapt kia 30-11-17 3 att17RFus p70 MR17

STONE,William.MM.2Lt kia 18-8-18 12NorfR &NorfYeo p204 CR France19

STONE,William Charles 2Lt dow 4-11-18 2RMunstF p176 CR France716

STONE,William Henry.DCM.2Lt kia 26-9-16 6Nhampt p138 CR France1890

STONE-WOOTEN,Frank 2Lt kia 21-9-17 KRRC att18Bn p152 MR30

STONEHAM,Charles.CMG.Col ded 31-1-16 RAMC p253 CR Mddx26,STONHAM

STONEHAM,Greville Cope 2Lt kia 14-11-16 1RBerks p140 CR France152

STONEHAM,Reginald Percy.DCM.2Lt kia 9-5-15 1N&D p135 CR France566

STONEHOUSE,Charles TLt kia 1-7-16 11ELancs p111 MR21

STONEHOUSE,Ronald Lt kia 1-4-18 RASC &101RAF p253 CR France62

STONEHOUSE,Robert Alfred 2Lt kia 28-4-17 4 att10LNLancs p234 MR20

STONEMAN,William Thomas 2Lt dow 26-7-17 14Lond p249 CR France139,ded

STONES,Francis Dawbarn.MC.Capt dow 28-9-17 2/6N&D p233 CR Belgium18

STONES,George Herbert Lee Lt dow 9-12-17 5 att11N&D p232 CR Italy7

STONES,George Lawden Boys.MC.Capt dow 30-3-17 IA 7Lancers attHQ 6CavBde p283

STONES,Shepherd 2Lt kia 3-11-16 5NumbF p213 CR France387

STONES,Thomas Frederick T2Lt kia 17-9-16 9 att10RWKent p142 CR France401

STONEX,Frank Hugh Tilney 2Lt ded 1-2-18 4RDubF p266 CR Ches182

STONEY,Francis George Duncan TLt dow 25-8-16 RE 204Coy p48 CR France141

STONEY,George Butler.DSO.MajTLtCol kia 15-10-15 KOSB p102 CR Gallipoli3

STONEY,Thomas Ramsay 2Lt kia 10-4-18 6KOSB p102 CR Belgium21,3Bn

STONEY,Thomas Samuel Vesey 2Lt kia 9-10-17 1IrGds p53 MR30

STONIER,William John Lt kia 27-4-17 2Beds att2RFC p13&86 MR20

STONNILL,Frank Roland 2Lt kia 24-3-18 Herts p252 MR27

STONOR,Cuthbert Anthony 2Lt kia 1-7-16 1RInniskF p105 CR France1490

STONOR,Howard Carew.Hon.Lt kia 10-3-15 4Beds att2SStaffs p86 MR22

STOODLEY,Percy Bennett 2Lt ded 9-11-16 7 att2Wilts p153 CR Greece5,Ballard

STOOKS,Herbert Drummond Sumner T2Lt dow 25-4-17 52MGC Inf p185 CR France113

STOPFORD,Frederick Duncan T2Lt kia 15-9-16 15Hamps p121 MR21

STOPFORD,Heneage Frank Maj kia 15-9-16 RFA p36 CR France277

STORAR,Robert Archibald T2Lt kld 16-12-15 18NumbF p63 CR Wilts115,19Bn

STORCH,Herbert.MC.T2Lt dow 24-8-18 13Yorks att1EYorks p91 CR France742

STORE,Albert Cash Lt kia 25-8-16 10 att5KRRC p152 MR21,5 att16Bn

STORE,Leonard 2Lt ded 31-8-15 5Lincs p272 CR Lincs123

STORER,John Young Maj kia 25-9-15 8Lincs p76 MR19

STORER,Patrick George Rawlings 2Lt dow 16-6-18 RH&FA 3DAC p36 CR France33,kia

STOREY,Fawcett 2Lt kia 23-4-17 5BordR p228 CR France1185

STOREY,H.P.2Lt 13-2-21 RASC CR Lancs401

STOREY,Harrison Leetham 2Lt dow 12-9-16 6WYorks C'Coy p218 CR Yorks410

STOREY,Harry Hilton 2Lt kia 13-10-14 DLI p161 MR32

STOREY,Kenneth Cothay Bonnell 2LtTLt kia 9-4-17 3 att5RBerks p140 CR France1182

STOREY,Robert William 2Lt kld 9-3-18 1DLI att37MGC p161&185 CR Belgium19

STORIE,John Capt ded 4-10-15 RAVC p272

STORK,William Henry 2Lt dow 11-1-18 3DragGds p21 CR France446

STORKEY,Gordon Coleman T2Lt kia 1-8-17 2Mddx p148 MR29,Colman

STORM,Jack Newton T2Lt kia 23-3-18 5TankCps p189 MR27,28-3-18

STORM,William George.MC.Capt kia 9-10-17 5Y&L p238 CR Belgium125

STORMONT,William Lundie 2Lt kia 31-8-18 5RFA p36 CR France592

STORMOUTH-DARLING,John Collier.DSO.TLtCol kia 1-11-16 1ScotRif att9HLI p104 CR France294,STORMONTH

STORR,Henry.DSO.MajTLtCol ded 15-8-18 18Mddx p148 CR Kent284

STORR,Leycester Benthyn.DSO.Maj mbk 29-3-18 12Lpool att7DCLI p257 MR27,Penrhyn

STORRAR,Andrew Wynne 2Lt kia 16-8-17 2RDubF att48TMB p177 CR Belgium45

STORRIE,Hugh Cochrane Capt kia 12-9-15 RAMC att2RWSurr p198 CR France423

STORRS,James Parker 2Lt dow 8-8-17 6Ches p222 CR Belgium7

STORY,B.C.Agent 22-3-16 EAForce CR EAfrica44

STORY,George Ernest TLt ded 9-9-17 RE 297FC p48 CR Lond1

STORY,Leslie Campbell 2Lt 1-7-18 209RAF MR20

STORY,Tom T2Lt kia 18-11-16 11BordR p118 CR France153

STOTHERD,Sidney Boyle Maj dow 19-10-15 7Suff p79 CR France80

STOTHERT,George Mervyn TLt dow 10-6-17 13WelshR p127 CR Belgium18

STOTON,H.B Capt 3-1-22 SL &IntptrAlliedComm CR Germany1

STOTT,Edward Henry Hussey T2Lt dow 3-9-17 218MGC Inf p185 CR France297

STOTT,Frank Gordon Lt dow 11-7-16 5Ches attMGC p187&222 CR France296,Gorden att14TMB

STOTT,George Whittaker 2Lt dow 8-11-18 6 att9WRid p227 CR France146

STOTT,James Lt kia 19-6-15 10Manch p237 MR4

STOTT,James T2Lt kia 11-10-18 LancF att2/5Bn p93 CR France525,2-10-18

STOTT,Philip Harle 2Lt kia 25-4-18 4 att1/5WYorks p83 MR30

STOTT,Philip Nicholson 2Lt ded 21-3-15 10Manch p237 CR Glouc214

STOTT,Robert Sebastian.MC.2Lt kia 12-10-18 5LancF attL'TMB p221 CR France192

STOTT,Ronald Howorth 2Lt kia 20-9-17 3LNLancs att7RB p136 CR Belgium42

STOTT,Walter Goodwin Lt kia 19-9-18 4Manch att15Ches p156 CR Belgium188,18-9-18

STOTT,William Charles Herbert Ernest T2Lt kia 29-9-18 3YLI p144 CR France357

STOTT,William Ernest 2Lt kia 8-8-18 5LancF p221 CR France156,Lt

STOURTON-LANGDALE,Edward Francis Joseph TLt kia 5-10-16 RE 233FC p48 CR France744

STOUT,George Frederick T2Lt kia 30-9-16 6Yorks p91 MR21

STOUT,George Ronald Yorston.MC.2Lt kia 30-4-17 8A&SH attRFC p19&243 CR France557

STOUT,Jnr.Thomas Lt kia 28-6-15 1/8ScotRif p225 MR4

STOVIN,Frederick Cecil Lt 24-4-18 209RAF MR20

STOVIN,George John Lucas Lt ded 2-2-17 IARO att37Dogras p283 CR Iraq5

STOVIN,John Thomas 2Lt kia 28-1-18 6RIrReg p89 CR France212

STOVIN,Lewis John Elliott Lt ded 22-8-17 127RFA p36 CR Kent28,2Lt

STOVOLD,Grosvenor Henry T2Lt kia 10-8-17 11RFus p70 MR29

STOVOLD,Percy Angel Capt kia 1-9-16 2RWSurr p56 CR France402

STOW,Basil T2Lt dow 22-10-18 15RIrRif p170 CR Belgium140

STOW,Montague Bruce TLtCol dow 2-7-16 1EYorks p85 CR France119

STOWE,William Hardwicke T2Lt ded 5-3-18 3Dev p263 CR Yorks447,Lt

STOWELL,Philip Charles Lt ded 12-6-20 IARO attS&TCps p283 MR65,Capt

STOWELL,Robert Cuthbert T2Lt kia 20-11-17 RLancs p59 CR France154

STOWELL,Thomas Brown.MC.2Lt dow 19-11-17 3 att8SLancs p126 CR France80

STOWELL,Wilfrid T2Lt kia 22-3-18 Leinst p175 MR27

STOYLE,A.P.Lt ded 27-2-19 4RFus attRAF p70

STRACEY,Reginald George.MID Capt kia 1-1-15 1ScotsGds p52 CR France644

STRACHAN,Albert T2Lt ded 30-10-18 LabCps attChineseLabCps p189 CR Devon258

STRACHAN,Alexander Macdonald 2Lt kia 20-7-18 4BlkW p256 MR34

STRACHAN,Andrew Robert 2Lt 20-9-18 20RAF MR20

STRACHAN,Aubrey Causton.MC&Bar.Lt kia 28-3-18 C70RFA p36&259 CR France1182

STRACHAN,Benjamin T2Lt kia 18-5-17 GL &12RFC p13 CR France1182

STRACHAN,David Livingston Capt ded 29-12-16 6WYorks p218 CR Yorks361

STRACHAN,Edward Stanley 2Lt kia 14-10-15 8N&D p233 MR19

STRACHAN,George Henry Lt ded 24-11-18 7GordH p242 CR France332

STRACHAN,Henry Lt dow 29-7-18 9DLI p230 CR France143

STRACHAN,James Capt kia 11-4-18 4GordH p241 MR19

STRACHAN,Wellesley Kendle Lt kia 24-8-18 8RScots p211 CR France214,Capt

STRACHAN,William Stead TCapt kia 18-2-18 RE p48 CR France446

STRAFFORD,Percy Belcher Maj kia 24-8-15 WRid p116 CR Belgium201

STRAHAN,Charles Eric Capt kia 28-11-14 2BlkW p129 CR France80

STRAHAN,Geoffrey Bennock 2Lt kia 31-8-15 10Lond p248 CR Gallipoli17

STRAIGHT,Marshall Stuart T2Lt kia 24-12-15 12 att1Ess p132 CR Gallipoli1

STRAIN,John London.MID LtACapt kia 31-7-17 RGA 214SB p42 MR29,Loudon

STRAIN,Thomas TCapt ded 16-9-16 RAMC 6MobLab p198 CR France201

STRAKER,Albert Gray 2Lt kia 3-10-16 7NumbF p214 MR21

STRAKER,Charles Constantine Lionel 2Lt dow 7-7-16 3Mon p244 CR France215

STRAKER,Frank T2Lt dow 16-7-16 RFA attZ39TMB p36 CR France80

STRAKER,Herbert 2Lt dow 9-11-18 6WYorks p218 CR France146

STRAKER,Kenneth Lt kia 23-7-16 3SfthH p165 CR Iraq5

STRANACK,Frederick George Lt kia 27-7-15 3 att1GordH p167 CR Belgium56,28-7-15

STRANG,James Buchanan T2Lt kia 30-7-16 17LancF p93 MR21

STRANG,John S.Capt kia 28-3-18 9BlkW p129&258 SeeStang,J.S.

STRANG,John Traquair 2Lt kia 18-5-18 B79RFA p36 CR France41

STRANG,Robert Capt kia 14-11-16 7A&SH D'Coyp243 CR France131

STRANG,Robert Brown T2Lt dow 12-8-16 6 att7RScotF p95 CR France703

STRANGE,Gilbert John Capt kia 24-9-18 Dors &40RAF p264 MR20

STRANGE,Hector Stanley 2Lt ded 7-10-18 2/4Dors &RAF p124 CR Egypt15

STRANGE,Lionel Cresswell 2Lt dow 22-7-17 9Ess p132 CR France113

STRANGE,Reginald Sydney T2Lt kia 17-10-18 1/2Beds att1Nhampt p86 CR France1270

STRANGE,William Hilbert Charles T2Lt kia 31-10-16 6RIrRif p170 CR Greece3

STRANGE,William Frederick 2Lt kia 1-7-16 2Lond p245 MR21

STRANGER,George 2Lt kia 11-4-18 1RGLI p201 MR32

STRANGER,Harry Easterbrook Knollys.MC.ACapt dow 11-5-18 1RGLI p201 CR France65

STRANGER,John Sercombe Capt kld 3-3-16 6Dev p217 MR38

STRANGER,Richard Henry Lt dow 13-3-15 1N&D p135 CR France102

STRANGWAYS-ROGERS,A.E.F.2Lt 4-11-18 3GrenGds CR France1080

STRANSOM,Norman G.Lt dow 10-5-18 GL &RAF p191

STRATFORD,Ernest Lt dow 21-4-15 RAMC p198 CR Berks112

STRATFORD Herbert Douglas 2Lt dow 13-4-18 2GrenGds p50 MR32

STRATFORD,Laurence TLt kia 28-3-18 15 att1RB p180 MR20

STRATHAIRN,Hubert William 2Lt dow 16-11-16 6BlkW p231 CR France41

STRATHERN,Tom Dalrymple 2Lt kia 8-7-16 3 att2Yorks p91 MR21

STRATTON,Frederick Arthur 2Lt dow 27-1-17 IARO att82Punjabis p283 CR Iraq5

STRATTON,George Bernard TMaj kia 10/11-8-17 10DCLI p115 CR Belgium173

STRAUGHAN,Thomas Arthur TLt ded 5-1-18 8NumbF p63 CR Numb11,5-2-18

STRAUSS,Bernard Lewis,MC AMaj kia 1-12-17 1EKent p58 CR France439

STRAUSS,Victor Arthur Lt kia 27-11-16 RASC &RFC p4&194 MR20

STRAW,Alexander TLt dow PoW 3-6-18 1N&D p135 CR France1755

STRAW,Frederick Walter 2Lt kia 7-11-16 3 att14Y&L p159 MR21

STRAWSON,Frank Gordon T2Lt kia 1-10-18 11RWSurr p56 CR Belgium112

STREAM,John Harvey TLt kia 19-2-18 7Lincs att20RFC p17&76 CR Belgium11

STREATER,John Wenban T2Lt dow 22-7-18 15RWar p66 CR France65

STREATFIELD,J.P.S.2Lt ded 3-6-15 6N&D p233&272

STREATFIELD,Thomas Basil Maryon 2Lt dow 7-11-17 3 att1RWKent p142 CR Belgium112

STREATFIELD-JAMES,Ralph.DSO.Capt dow 7-10-16 1ESurr p113 CR France,STREATFEILD

STREATHER,Edward Harry Parsons Lt mbk 11-9-17 70RFC p257 MR20

STREET,Brooks Henry Lt kia 6-8-17 2/7WelshR &34RAF p230&258 CR Italy11

STREET,Cyril TLt kia 26-6-17 GL &1RFC p13 MR20

STREET,Edmund Alger T2Lt kia 2-6-16 22Manch p156 MR21

STREET,Edmund Rochfort.DSO.TMaj dow 15-10-16 2N&D p135 CR France105

STREET,Frank TLt kia 7-7-16 9RFus p70 MR21

STREET,Harold Edward.CMG.MIDx8 LtCol kia 25-8-17 106RFA GenStaff p36 CR Belgium15

STREET,Harry Lt ded 5-10-19 RFA p262 CR Sussex143

STREET,Harvey Ferrington 2Lt mbk 3-5-17 7WRid p257 MR20,Farrington

STREET,Herbert.MM.T2Lt dow 24-11-18 1RBerks p140 CR France40

STREET,Herbert Duke 2Lt ded 26-3-18 4RSuss p272 CR Surrey38

STREET,Hewson.MC&Bar.Capt dow PoW 1-6-18 5Lincs att10Worc p220 CR France622

STREET,Norman Kingsley Capt kia 10-8-15 Worc att39InfBde HQ p109 MR4

STREET,Richard T2Lt kia 24-4-17 WYorks att86MGC p83&185 MR20

STREET,Samuel William Lt ded 9-11-15 IA S&T Cps CR WAfrica61

STREET,Thomas Anderson TLt ded 27-1-18 10Glouc p264 CR Belgium96

STREETEN,Basil Robert Chap4Cl ded 1-11-18 RAChDept att2/5LancF p200 CR France1725

STRETCH,Thomas Noel Heath.MC&Bar.TLt kia 25-3-18 MGC Inf attRASC p185&194 CR France630,2Lt

STRETTELL,William Michael Dashwood Stirling Capt kia 28-11-17 4HLI att1AircraftDepot RFC p13&164 CR France134

STRETTELL-MILLER,Charles Wallace Lt kia 6-10-18 7RScots att4/1MGC p187&211 CR Belgium18

STRETTON,Alexander Lynam De Courcy.MC.Capt kia 16-10-17 SLancs attNigR p126 MR52

STRETTON,John de Courcy.MC.2Lt kia 11-5-18 3 att1RWar p66&259 CR France411

STRETTON,Sidney TLt kia 27-3-17 GL &15RFC p13 CR France62,66Sqn

STRETTON,William Stapleton de Courcy Lt dow 4-9-16 3 att2RWar p66 CR France23,Capt

STRETTON,William Thomas Capt&QM ded 10-4-16 RFA p262 CR Eire49

STREVENS,George William.MC.LtACapt dow 27-9-18 1DCLI p115 CR France146

STRIBLING,Frederick George TLt dow 8-7-16 1N&D p135 CR France44

STRIBLING,Lewis James 2Lt dow 16-11-17 RGA 329SB p42 CR Belgium72,kia 13-11-17

STRICK,Edward Talfourd Capt ded 19-6-15 2/6WelshR p272 CR Wales171

STRICKLAND,Charles John 2Lt kia 5-4-18 1/12 att23Lond p248 CR France232

STRICKLAND,James Edward Trench TLt dow 8-8-16 2SLancs att100MGC p126 CR France40,3ResBn

STRICKLAND,Joseph Chap4Cl ded 15-7-17 RAChDept 12Bde 4Div p200 CR Europe4

STRICKLAND,Reginald 2Lt ded 25-12-15 3 att2 O&BLI p130 CR France80

STRICKLAND,Vincent Norman Lt ded 10-5-17 O&BLI CR Lond8

STRICKLAND-CONSTABLE,Frederick Charles LtCol ded 20-12-17 3EYorks attStaff p85&263 CR Yorks93

STRIEGLER,Henry William 2Lt kia 12-8-16 7ESurr p113 MR21

STRINGER,Albert Edward 2Lt kia 7-6-15 9Manch p237 MR4

STRINGER,Dudley 2Lt kia 3-5-17 10EYorks p85 MR20

STRINGER,Frederick William TLtCol ded 30-6-16 RASC p194

STRINGER,Gerald Moffatt 2Lt kld 15-3-15 13Ches p97 CR Hamps13

STRINGER,Guy Frederick Lt kia 17-6-15 RGA NMidHB p209 CR Belgium9

STRINGER,Henry Francis Godfrey 2Lt dow 3-5-17 RGA 36SB p42 CR France97

STRINGER,John T2Lt kia 7-10-16 26RFus p70 MR21

STRINGER,William Charles 2Lt ded 14-6-17 RFC p13 CR Mddx26

STRITCH,George Seymour Russell TCapt kia 7-2-16 6ConnRgrs p172 CR France178

STROMQUIST,Sydney Goodwin TCapt kia 26-9-15 8Lincs p76 MR19

STRONG,Arthur Penton Lt kia 26-10-17 7NumbF p214 CR Belgium126

STRONG,Cecil Verge.MC.LtAMaj kia 10-3-17 RE 15FC p48 CR Frnce624

STRONG,Edward George 2Lt kia 27-5-18 RE 15FC p48 MR18

STRONG,George Henry 2LtTLt kia 3-1-17 GL att2NigeriaR p202 CR EAfrica36

STRONG,Howard Bertie Lt kia 29-10-14 RWSurr p56 MR29

STRONG,James Mortimer T2Lt dow 26-7-17 23MGC p185 CR Belgium7

STRONG,James William TLt kia 11-6-16 18LancF p93 CR France632

STRONG,Oliver Arthur 2Lt kia 8-5-17 1ESurr p113 MR20

STRONG,Oswald Lucking T2Lt dow 5-8-17 1SomLI att2KSLI attTMB p80 CR Greece9

STRONG,R.Harold 2Lt kia 13-3-15 2ESurr p113 CR Belgium182,Lt 12-3-15

STRONG,Thomas William T2Lt ded 26-5-18 att4SStaffs p123 CR France622

STRONG,William Charles Capt&QM ded 26-7-18 2/4Wilts p236 MR66STRONGE,James Matthew Lt kia 16-8-17 9RIrFus p171 CR Belgium8

STROSS,David 2Lt kld 12-3-17 RFA attRFC attMGC p19,187&209 CR Yorks363

STROTHER,John Marmaduke.MC.2Lt kia 28-4-17 3 att10Y&L p159 MR20

STROUD,Arnold Lt kia 15-9-16 4 att1/7NumbF p213 MR21

STROUD,Eric HubertNoel Lt kia 21-4-18 Leic &53RAF p263 CR Belgium453

STROUD,Henry Clifford Capt kld 7-3-18 RE attRFC p19&210 CR Essex73

STROUD,Reginald Gordon T2Lt kia 1-7-16 9Y&L C'Coy p159 CR France246

STROUD,Stephen George T2Lt dow 13-10-18 Ess Res att9Bn p132 CR France58,Lt

STROUD,Sydney Hill LtACapt kld 20-10-18 78RFA HQ p36 CR France661

STRUBEN,Leicester Frederick 2Lt kia 16-11-16 7DragGds &70RFC p261 2entries CR France307

STRUDWICK,John Meredith Ker 2Lt dow 21-4-18 2 att6RWSurr p56 CR France40

STRUEBIG,Edwin Harold.MM.2Lt kia 8-8-18 10Lond p248 France1170

STRUGNELL,Alfred Charles 2Lt kia 1-7-16 2Yorks p91 MR21

STRUGNELL,H.F.H.Maj ded 21-3-19 RM CR Hamps242

STRUGNELL,L.W. 2Lt kld 16-6-18 1/4Mddx &RAF p148

STRUTH,James Scotland T2Lt kia 16-9-17 17RScots p55 CR France364

STRUTHERS,Andrew Craig T2Lt kia 14-9-16 10ScotRif p104 CR France703

STRUTHERS,James D.Lt ded 8-8-19 87RGA 19SB p262 CR Asia33

STRUTHERS,Kenneth 2Lt kia 7-10-16 14Lond p249 MR21

STRUTT,Anthony Herbert TLt dow 27-4-18 16N&D p135 CR Belgium8

STRUTT,Richard Neville T2Lt kia 25-9-15 12 att2RScots p55 CR Belgium115,dow 15-10-15

STUART,Alexander Rev kia 24-10-17 RAChDept att12RIrRif p200 CR France755

STUART,Alexander Davidson.MC.TLt kia 12-10-17 7SfthH p165 MR30

STUART,Alexander George LtCol kia 4-6-16 1A 40Pathans attHQ 50Div p283 CR Belgium191 Ex 2RScots

STUART,Andrew John.Viscount TLt kia 25-9-15 6RScotF p95 MR19

STUART,Atholl Archibald Capt kia 12-10-17 10 att11RScots p212 CR Belgium96

STUART,B.DSO.Maj 3-6-2- RFA attPoliticDept CR Iraq8

STUART,C.W.C.E.SubCdr 8-9-20 18DivTrain S&T Cps CR Iraq8

STUART,Cecil Edgar Lt kia 13-9-14 2LancF p93 MR15

STUART,Charles Lt kia 31-7-17 9A&SH p244 CR Belgium96

STUART,Charles Edward Cecil Wilmot SubCdr ded 8-9-20 1A S&TCps p283

STUART,Charles Erskine TCapt dow 15-3-17 2/6Suff p218 CR France41

STUART,David Aymery T2Lt kldacc 29-10-16 7CamH 7RFC p4&168 CR Scot239

STUART,Frank TCapt kia 10-4-18 GL att57TMB p191 MR30

STUART,George Douglas Gordon Lt kia 23-9-17 84/11RFA p36 CR Belgium13

STUART,Herbert Gordon 2Lt dow 7-3-19 3Lond p272 CR Essex86

STUART,James Capt kia 13-4-17 1RInniskF &59RFC p13&105

STUART,James Duff Maj 7-3-17 1CanadaPnrBn &43RFC MR20

STUART,James Maitland Capt 13-4-17 1RInnisF &59RFC MR20

STUART,James Ogilvie Grant.MC.Capt kia 30-3-18 5BlkW p231 MR27

STUART,John T2Lt ded 24-4-18 6RFus p70&258 CR Numb1,kldacc 29-4-18

STUART,John 2Lt kia 28-7-18 3 att9BlkW p129 CR France865,3 att4/5Bn

STUART,John Charles 2Lt dow 23-2-17 5ScotRif p224 CR Scot764

STUART,John Lachlan.MID Capt ded 23-10-18 5RFus p263 CR Camb16

STUART,Joseph Joachim Maxwell Lt kia 2-3-16 3 att9WRid p116

STUART,Karl Edwin Lt kia 25-3-18 2Mddx D Coy p148 MR27

STUART,Kenneth Bruce 2Lt kia 5-11-16 6DLI p239 CR France385

STUART,Maurice Stevenson 2Lt kia 15-6-18 8BlkW p129 CRFrance25

STUART,Morton Hollinshed Crawford 2Lt dow 8-3-16 IARO att2Rajputs MR38,Hollinshead Craufurd

STUART,Robert Alexander T2Lt kia 25-9-15 7CamH p168 MR19

STUART,Robert James Noel 2Lt kia 16-5-15 3 att2RScotF p95 CR France279,17-5-15

STUART,Robert Sheffield.Viscount Lt kia 2-11-14 RScotF p95 MR22

STUART,Vernon Douglas.MC&Bar.Lt kia 29-9-18 RGA 180SB p42 CR France212

STUART,W.A.Lt 30-10-16 RAMC CR Scot764

STUART,W.J.Lt ded 22-8-21 RE CR Canada180

STUART,William Aloysius T2Lt dow 26-5-17 18HLI p164 CR France1468

STUART,William Bruce George.MC.TCapt kia 22-11-17 2RIrRif p170 MR17

STUART,William Esme Montague 2Lt kia 7-10-16 6RWKent p142 MR21

STUART,William Grant Spruell.MC.Capt kia 23-4-17 7CamH p168 CR France1182

STUART-FRENCH,C.H.Maj ded 23-12-16 DAQMG 1MntedDiv p1 CR Herts20,5DragGds

STUART-RUSSELL,Cecil Henry TLt kia 7-9-16 RGA 17HB p42 CR France630

STUART-SMITH,Philip James Lt 8-5-18 CanadaCpsCavR &74RAF MR20

STUART-WORTLEY,John LtCol kia 21-3-18 6SStaffs p229 MR20

STUBBS,Alfred Joseph 2Lt kia 22-10-18 4RWKent p234 CR Belgium408,23-10-18

STUBBS,Cecil Arthur 2Lt dow 2-7-16 2Lond p245 CR France120

STUBBS,Charles Albert TLt ded 9-3-18 RAOC D66Bde p198 CR Greece7

STUBBS,Frank Percival T2Lt dow 25-11-16 15N&D att105TMB p135 CR France46

STUBBS,Frederick William Arthur.MC.2Lt kia 9-5-17 6N&D p233 CR France149,10-5-17

STUBBS,Herbert Edgar T2Lt dow 4-9-17 GL LabCps att65ChineseLabCps p191 CR France134

STUBBS,Lewis Robert.MC.2Lt dow 29-3-18 RGA 123SB p42 CR France40

STUBBS,Reginald Arthur 2Lt kia 8-6-16 4MunstF &RFC p4&176 CR France573

STUBBS,William Norman T2Lt kia 23-10-18 9 att1Ches p97 CR France206

STUCKLEY,Edwin Lane 2Lt kia 25-12-17 17 att4Lond p272 CR France184,STUCKEY

STUCLEY,Humphrey St.Leger Maj kia 30-10-14 GrenGds p50 CR Belgium116,29-10-14

STUDD,Francis Cyril Rupert.DSO.MajTLtCol kia 13-4-18 EKent att22NumbF p58 MR32

STUDD,Lionel Fairfax Capt kia 14-2-15 12Lond p248 CR Belgium58,15-2-15

STUDDY,Melvin Leslie T2Lt dow 22-10-16 1 att8NumbF p63 CR Durham19,15 att8Bn

STUDHOLME,Launcelot Joseph Moore.MID TCapt kia 9-9-16 7Leinst p175 MR21

STUDHOLME,Paul Francis William 2Lt kia 3-10-17 1Dev p77 CR Belgium112,4-10-17

STUDLEY,Charles Carr 2Lt kia 9-10-17 3 att1/8WYorks p83 MR30

STUDLEY,Harry Capt&QM ded 25-2-16 7BlkW p272 CR Scot142,Maj

STUDLEY,Logan 2Lt kia 25-10-14 Yorks p91 CR Belgium57,EYorks

STURDY,Arthur Carlile.MC.Capt ded 1-5-19 RAMC p198 MR65

STURDY,George T2Lt kia 9-10-17 6Y&L p159 MR30

STURGE,Edmund Capt ded 8-2-19 10Mddx attRE Sigs p236 CR Italy6

STURGES,Roland T2Lt kia 21-3-18 1 att2/7Manch p156 MR27

STURGESS,George Minshall 2Lt kld 5-4-18 Ess attRAF p132 CR Egypt8,Lt

302

STURGESS,Thomas George.MC.T2Lt dow 10-11-18 63MGC Divl p185 CR Belgium236,MM

STURRIDGE,Ernest Arthur Leland TCapt ded 30-12-15 6YLI p144 CR Belgium11

STURROCK,Andrew Lt kia 14-7-16 3 att1RScotF p95 CR France453

STURROCK,Arthur Hill TLt drd 4-5-17 31MGC Inf p185 CR Italy14

STURROCK,Bernard Silvester Lt kia 26-9-15 4BlkW p230 MR19,Sylvester

STURROCK,George Lt kia 12-7-15 4RScotF p222 MR4

STURROCK,Harry Douglas.MC.Capt ded 1-2-18 ACycCps 1/1HighCycBn p244&272 CR Scot386

STURROCK,Thomas Gibbs Gordon T2Lt dow 16-10-16 17RScots &RFC p4&55 CR France1032

STURT,Douglas Elliott TLt ded 30-10-18 20Mddx p148 CR Mddx66,31-10-18

STURT,Ernest Guy Maclean T2Lt kia 16-8-16 12Mddx att6Nhampt p148 CR France82

STURT,Hon Gerald Philip Montagu Napier Capt dow 11-11-18 CldGds p51 CR Dorset133

STURT,Humphrey Morriston Lt ded 17-1-18 1/8LancF p221 CR France765

STURT,Kate Rosina SNurse 13-12-16 QAIMNS CR Surrey160

STUTTARD,Harold Pierce T2Lt kld 30-10-17 GL &RFC p13 CR Lancs336

STYLES,Alfred Cornwall TLt kia 19-7-16 16Ches p97 CR France630

STYLES,Arthur Horatio TLt dow 26-7-16 17RWFus p99

STYLES,Frederick Ernest Lt kia 27-8-14 2RMunstF p176 CR France1751

STYLES,Harold Thomas T2Lt kia 22-10-17 Manch att23Bn p156 MR30

SUCKLING,Cornelius Vincent Capt kia 16-7-16 1/5RWar p214 MR21

SUDBURY,John Allen TLt kia 29-9-18 2Worc att1GarrBn p109 CR France665

SUDELL,Henry James TCapt dow 28-8-15 RASC 111Coy 10DivTrain p194 MR4

SUDLOW,Horace Stanley T2Lt kia 30-3-18 2 att2/8Worc p110 MR27

SUFFIELD,Ernest 2Lt dow 1-5-18 107RFA p209 CR France145

SUFFOLK &BERKSHIRE,Henry Molyneux Paget.Earl Maj kia 21-4-17 Cmdg1WiltsRFA p206

SUGDEN,Christopher Babington 2Lt kia 25-5-15 4YLI p235 CR France684

SUGDEN,Guy Hatton Lt kia 12-10-16 3 att2WRid p116 CR France374

SUGDEN,Harold Capt dow 20-6-15 9Manch p237 CR Greece10

SUGDEN,John T2Lt kia 29-3-18 1/2 att1/5WRid p116 CR France798,5 att1Bn

SUGDEN,John Edwin,DSO TCapt&Adjt kia 28-9-16 10RIrRif p170 CR Belgium43

SUGDEN,John Paget 2Lt kia 8-7-17 6WRid p227 MR29

SUGG,B.Capt 3-4-21 RE CR Cornwall 40

SULIVAN,Eugene Gilbert Capt ded 8-5-17 4 att1ESurr p113 CR France777,kia

SULIVAN,Philip Hamilton 2Lt kia 27-8-14 2RMunstF B'Coy p176 CR France1751

SULLEY,Alan Hereford T2Lt kia 3-9-16 9 att2KOSB p102 CR France402

SULLINGS,Stephen John Rev ded 21-11-15 RAChDept Chap4Cl attRAMC 54EAngDiv p200 CR War7

SULLIVAN,Arthur John 2Lt kia 15-9-16 2Lond p245 CR France402

SULLIVAN,Cyril Charles Loyola 2Lt ded 16-6-17 3 att1Lincs p263 CR France40

SULLIVAN,Francis Joseph T2Lt kia 28-5-18 2DLI p161 CR Belgium3,27-5-18

SULLIVAN,John Duncan 2Lt dow 26-8-18 24Lond p252 CR France119

SULLIVAN,Timothy 2Lt kia 4-5-15 1RMunstF p176 MR4

SULLIVAN,Walter Ernest.MC.T2Lt dow 19-4-18 13WelshR B'Coy att114Bde HQ38Div p127 CR France62

SULLY,Donovan Ernest T2Lt dow 9-8-16 9SomLI p80 CR Belgium73

SULMAN,Geoffrey 2Lt kld 20-6-17 GL &51RFC p13 CR Lincs181

SULMAN,Paul Loxton.MC.TCapt dow 28-4-18 11Hamps p121 CR Surrey160

SUMMERHAYE,Dudley Leycester 2Lt kia 21-4-15 9Lond D Coy 1Bn p248

SUMMERHAYES,John Alexander T2Lt&ACapt kia 27-8-18 13RInniskF p105 CR France353

SUMMERS,Alfred Spencer Mason Capt ded PoW 15-9-16 19Huss &RFC p4&23 CR France560

SUMMERS,Archibald Young 2Lt kia 22-3-18 12NumbF att11Leics p63 MR20,Archibold

SUMMERS,John Collings 2Lt kia 13-8-18 RGA 120HB p42 CR France1170

SUMMERS,Ranulph Augustus T2Lt kia 28-9-15 9 att1RBerks p140 MR19

SUMMERS,Walter Gordon TCapt kia 28-12-15 7RWKent p142 CR France189

SUMMERS,William Assheton.MC.Capt kia 1-8-16 18Huss &RFC p4,23&259 MR20

SUMMERSCALES,Claude Lt ded 22-7-16 3ConnRgrs p172 CR Iraq6

SUMMERSCALES,Frederick David 2Lt kia 9-3-17 5 att22DLI p239 MR21

SUMMERSON,Herbert Walker T2Lt dow 5-6-18 9LNLancs p136 CR France622

SUMMERTON,Harold TLt kia 29-7-15 7SStaffs p123 CR Gallipoli2

SUMMERVILLE,Joseph.MC.MM.T2Lt kia 29-10-18 8Yorks B'Coy p91 CR Italy9

SUMNER,Charles Maunoir Col ded 30-6-16 SLancs p264 CR Cornwall79

SUMNER,Geoffrey Lt ded 11-5-18 RFA &RAF p272 CR Lancs170

SUMPSTER,Frank Mariner Lt kia 21-3-18 8RBerks att53TMB p140 MR27

SUMPTER,George.DSO.MC&Bar.Capt 20-8-20 RFA CR Asia51

SUMPTION,Henry George 2Lt dow 15-10-18 HampsYeo att15HampsR p204 CR Belgium11

SUMSION,Francis Lt kia 4-11-18 3WelshR &RAF p127 CR Belgium218

SUNDERLAND,Alfred Joseph Elton.MIDx3 MajTLtCol kia 31-7-17 2Dev p77 CR Belgium34

SUNDERLAND,Geoffrey TLtACapt kia 24-9-18 2RSuss C'Coy p120 CR France1700

SUNDIUS-SMITH,Ronald Christian 2Lt 12-3-15 1ARO att2WYorks MR28

SUPPLE,Edward James Collis Lt dow 22-8-15 1/6WRid p227 CR France64

SURGEY,Henry Norris Capt kia 3-1-17 2RWar attArabRifs p66 CR EAfrica36

SURR,Rudolph Vincent 2LtALt kia 31-10-18 5Worc att24TMB p110 MR21

SURRY,Norman Frederick T2Lt kia 12-10-18 16KRRC p152 MR16

SURTEES,Charles Gordon Villiers Lt kia 26-10-14 2BordR p118 MR29

SURTEES,William Beverley TCapt dow 28-9-16 9WYorks p83 CR France59

SUSSEX,Edgar William.MC.LtACapt kia 25-8-17 3ScotRif p104 CR Belgium24

SUSSEX,Reginald Arthur 2Lt dow 20-3-17 4WYorks att1Y&L p83 MR37

SUTCLIFFE,Archibald Alfred Capt died 12-3-15 RAMC p198 CR Germany4,SUTCLIFF

SUTCLIFFE,Fred Malcolm 2Lt kia 29-5-17 8Lond A Coy p247 MR20

SUTCLIFFE,George Mitchele 2Lt kia 21-10-17 RGA 237SB p42 CR Belgium36,Mitchell

SUTCLIFFE,Herbert Richard Charles T2Lt kia 1-7-16 24NumbF att5/24TMB p63 CR France393

SUTCLIFFE,John TLt kia 12-5-16 27Manch p156 CR France370,24Bn

SUTCLIFFE,Kenneth Wilson T2Lt kia 16-9-16 9 YLI p144 MR21

SUTCLIFFE,Oswald 2Lt kia 3-11-16 4YLI p235 CR France1327

SUTCLIFFE,Robert 2Lt dow 5-7-16 16WYorks p83 CR Yorks737,Lt

SUTCLIFFE,Roland Pruett Lt ded 20-10-18 IA 2/53Sikhs Ex 6BnAustInf p282 MR67

SUTCLIFFE,Sydney.MM.2Lt kia 2-10-17 RWelshF &11RFC p13&99 CR France924,Lt

SUTHERLAND,A.N.Chap4Cl 16-1-18 CR Scot764

SUTHERLAND,Alan D'Arcy 2Lt 28-2-17 RAF CR Wilts116

SUTHERLAND,Alister Morphett Lt died 28-8-20 NZ StaffCps MR69

SUTHERLAND,Allan Newton 2Lt kia 22-3-18 7GordH p242 MR20

SUTHERLAND,Anderson.MC.TLtAMaj dow 7-11-18 RHA att51/39RFA p36 CR France441

SUTHERLAND,Andrew Ernest TLt kia 3-10-16 A67RFA p36 CR Greece3

SUTHERLAND,Bessie Gray Sister 26-9-15 ScotWomensHosp CR Europe57

SUTHERLAND,Colin Lt ded 7-11-18 RE p272 CR Scot760

SUTHERLAND,George 2Lt kia 9-4-17 4KOSB p224 CR France924,7/8Bn

SUTHERLAND,George Angus.MC.Capt kia 27-7-18 1/5SfthH p241 CR France1697

SUTHERLAND,George Harry 2Lt kia 21-3-18 2/4 O&BLI att177TMB p231 MR20

SUTHERLAND,George Hay TLt dow 2-11-18 9RInniskF p105 CR France34

SUTHERLAND,George King Lt ded 9-3-19 RE p262 CR Wales13

SUTHERLAND,Goodwin 2Lt kia 9-4-17 4GordH p167

SUTHERLAND,H.W.SubPM 14-5-16 IndP&TDept CR EAfrica56

SUTHERLAND,Hector John.MID TCapt dedacc 2-2-17 6 O&BLI p130 CR France105

SUTHERLAND,Hugh Lt kia 29-10-17 RFA p208 CR France592

SUTHERLAND,J.A.Lt 29-6-17 ELakeBordPolice MR52

SUTHERLAND,James Parker T2Lt kia 9-4-17 2RScots p55 CR France581

SUTHERLAND,James Gilbert T2Lt dow 11-8-15 11HLI p164 CR France727

SUTHERLAND,James Lawrence Cathcart.MC.Lt dow 13-8-18 1RWKent att104RAF p142 CR France1667,19-8-18

SUTHERLAND,James Lindsay T2Lt kia 31-7-17 23Mddx p148 MR29

SUTHERLAND,John 2Lt kld 21-3-18 1/6LancF p221 MR27

SUTHERLAND,John Alexander 2Lt kia 8-12-17 24Lond p252 CR Palestine3

SUTHERLAND,John McIntyre 2Lt kia 23-4-17 9RScots p212 CR France545,Macintyre

SUTHERLAND,Noel Lt kia 21-11-17 4SforthH p241 MR17

SUTHERLAND,Thomas Capt dow 14-6-20 2/6Lpool CR Lancs2

SUTHERLAND,Walter Riddle T2Lt kia 4-10-18 8SfthH p165 CR France106,Riddell

SUTHERLAND,William.MM.T2Lt kia 7-10-18 7RDubF p177 CR France234

SUTHERLAND,William Dunbar.CIE.LtCol ded 27-6-20 IA IMS p283 CR India97A

SUTHERLAND,William Henry.MC.2Lt kia 23-3-18 4GordH p242 MR20

SUTOR,Harry C.N.TCapt ded 23-9-16 GL p191 CR Lond2,SUTER

SUTTHERY,Dorian Melbourne 2LtTLt dow 19-5-17 11A&SH p174 CR Shrop82

SUTTIE,William Campbell 2Lt kia 24-5-15 7A&SH p243 MR29

SUTTON,Arthur Eldred Barker Lt ded 4-7-18 6Lpool &RAF p215&258

SUTTON,Alexander Gordon 2Lt kia 2-1-18 6 att2RB p180 CR Belgium22

SUTTON,Austin Ivor Spencer 2Lt dow 13-4-18 RFA Y31TMB p209 CR France169

SUTTON,Cyril John T2Lt kia 1-7-16 RFA att5RE p36 MR21

SUTTON,Eric Guy.MC.TLt kia 8-4-16 7RSuss p120 CR France423

SUTTON,Eustace Martin TLt kia 24-3-18 RE 35DivSigCo p48 MR27

SUTTON,Fergus Algernon Lt kia 26-2-15 2SLancs p126 CR Belgium17,27-2-15

SUTTON,Geoffrey Storrs.MC.TCapt kia 23-3-18 19Lpool p73 CR France672

SUTTON,George Nathaniel 2Lt ded 14-10-16 B95RFA p36 CR Lond8,dow

SUTTON,Horace Josiah T2Lt dow 24-11-15 13 att9N&D p135 MR4

SUTTON,Hubert Joselin Lt kia 27-9-15 1WelshGds p53 MR19

SUTTON,John William Wellesley.MC.2Lt kia 29-6-17 RGA att28RFA p42 CR France184

SUTTON,Oliver Joseph.MC.Capt kia 23-3-18 9Manch p256 MR27

SUTTON,Percy Turner Lt kia 24-8-18 RGA 283SB p42 CR France1170

SUTTON,Richard Thomas TLtACapt dow 3-10-18 7RInniskF p105 CR France1495

SUTTON,Sir Richard Vincent.Bart.MC.Capt ded 29-11-18 1LifeGds attGdsMGR p20&53 CR France34

SUTTON,Robert William 2LtTCapt kia 16-10-15 2RDubF p177 CR France35

SUTTON,Vivian Charles Woolfe T2Lt dow 14-9-18 RWKent att2/20Lond p142 CR France755

SUTTON,Wilfred Moschary Lt dow 17-9-16 2Y&L p159 CR France23

SUTTON,William Henry TLt kia 23-10-18 2WelchR p127 CR France1268

SUTTON,William Victor Ross 2Lt kia 13-11-17 1/1BerksYeo p203 CR Palestine9

SWABEY,Alan Maurice Eustace 2Lt kia 20-4-15 3SomLI attYLI p80 MR29

SWABY,Sydney Thomas TLt dow 31-8-18 WYorks att2/4YLI p83 CR France103

SWAIN,Basil Fitzroy Lt&QM dow 22-3-18 11RSuss p120 MR27

SWAIN,Charles Douglas Downs Lt kia 29-9-17 RGA 186SB p42 CR Belgium101

SWAIN,Clifford Maxwell 2Lt kld 4-4-18 GL &52RAF p191 CR France37,kia

SWAIN,Ernest George 2Lt ded 4-5-15 RASC p194 CR Hamps64

SWAIN,John George 2LtACapt kia 9-1-17 13N&D att93BurmaInf p135 CR Iraq5

SWAIN,John Henry Lt kia 9-1-17 IA 93BurmaInf p283

SWAIN,L.M SNurse 31-8-15 TFNS CR Egypt3

SWAIN,Robert Ernest T2Lt dow 8-7-16 13RWFus p99 MR21

SWAIN,Thomas T2Lt dow 25-7-16 8Yorks p91 CR Yorks159

SWAIN,William T2Lt kia 22-9-16 14 att8Yorks p91 CR France515

SWAINE,Henry Poyntz 2Lt kia 15-9-14 2RIrRif p170 MR15

SWAINE,S.W.2Lt kld 4-4-18 RH&FA &RAF p36

SWAINSON,Francis Gibbon.MC.Capt kia 1-7-16 16Lond p249 MR21

SWAINSON,John Anthony 2Lt kia 11-1-17 IARO att105MahrattaLI p283 MR38

SWAINSON,Joseph Leonard.DSO.TLtCol dow 9-8-16 6DCLI p115 CR France23

SWALE,Arthur Duncan Lt dow 5-10-18 6 att11N&D p233 CR France194

SWALE,J.V.2Lt 17-2-17 2RMLI CR France41

SWALES,George Middleton LtACapt kia 26-9-17 1RScotF att8/1TMB p95 CR Belgium188

SWALLOW,Arthur Reginald 2Lt kia 24-4-17 8Worc p226 MR21

SWALLOW,Bertie T2Lt kia 31-10-18 1/2 att18LancF p93 MR30

SWALLOW,Ernest Harold 2Lt kia 10-10-17 6 att4Mddx p148 CR Belgium56

SWALLOW,Hervey Lancelot St.George 2Lt mbk 25-9-15 10Y&L p257 MR19

SWALLOW,John Reginald 2Lt kia 8-8-16 1Lpool p73 MR21

SWALLOW,Luther James Lt kia 31-7-17 NStaffs p158 MR29

SWALLOW,William Hugh.OBE.TLtAMaj ded 21-2-19 RAOC DADOS 31Div p268 CR France134

SWAN,Donald Brian 2Lt kia 7-3-17 RHA p209 CR France786

SWAN,George Grieve 2Lt kia 1-7-16 4 att22Manch p156 MR21

SWAN,George Henry T2Lt kia 14-7-16 1RScotF p95 CR France453,Harry

SWAN,George Richard Lt dow 9-8-18 5 att8A&SH p243 CR France145

SWAN,Herbert Thomas 2Lt ded 22-8-18 58MGC p266 CR France16

SWAN,Joseph 2Lt kia 29-9-17 RGA 186SB p42 CR Belgium101

SWAN,Robert John 2Lt kia 29-3-18 A187RFA p209 CR France283,28-3-18

SWAN,William Capt kia 6-10-17 2/5N&D p232 CR France711,6-12-17

SWANN,Cecil Herbert Lt dow 27-8-18 2/6RWar p214 CR France398

SWANN,Gerald Huddart T2Lt kia 18-10-17 GL &41RFC p13 CR France41

SWANN,George William Lt dow 24-3-17 RASC &70RFC p13&194 MR20,SWAN

SWANN,Humphrey Nisbet Capt ded 4-4-17 Lincs Staff15Cps p76 CR France164

SWANN,T.Capt 18-1-17 6N&D CR Derby29

SWANSON,George William Capt drd 10-10-18 4Hamps attRAF p228 MR40

SWANSON,J.W.K.Capt dow 13-4-17 46CanadaInf CR France12

SWANSTON,Charles Oliver.DSO.LtCol kia 2-11-14 IA 34PoonaHorse p283 CR France525

SWANWICK,Russell Kenneth Lt kia 15-9-14 3Glouc p107 CR France1329,14-9-14 1Bn

SWARBRICK,W.Capt 6-9-20 LancF CR Lancs102

SWAYNE,Cecil Walter Harris Lt ded 25-5-17 2SomLI p80 MR43

SWAYNE,Stephen Cormack Lt kia 30-9-15 3EKent p58 MR19

SWEARS,Hugh Miller Lt kia 11-4-17 MGC attD'TankCps p185 MR20

SWEENEY,Gilbert Martin T2Lt kia 5-10-17 1Ches p97 MR30

SWEENEY,Walter Percy 2Lt 20-9-17 3Regt SAfrInf MR29

SWEET,Frederick Gordon Lt kia 26-3-17 3 att1/4Ess p132 CR Palestine8

SWEET,George Charles Walrond Rev ded 7-8-19 RAChDept p268 CR Somerset183

SWEET,Henry George T2Lt kia 25-9-18 RWSurr att2/4Bn p56

SWEET,John Lemon Leslie 2Lt kia 16-6-15 RScotF p95 MR22,Laxon

SWEET,Leonard Herbert TCapt kia 22-6-16 1Hamps att29RFC p4&121 CR Belgium11

SWEET,Roy Thornhill.DSO.Capt ded PoW 17-10-18 IA 2/7GurkhaRif p283 CR Iraq8

SWEET-ESCOTT,Leslie Wingfield TLt kia 25-9-18 5 O&BLI p130 MR29,25-9-15

SWEET-ESCOTT,Murray Robertson Lt kia 20-9-14 3Lpool p73 MR15

SWEET-ESCOTT,William Arthur Lt dow 14-10-18 RFA 50HQBde p36 CR Belgium157,kia

SWEETLAND,Rupert Girard 2Lt dow 26-1-17 3RWFus p99 CR Iraq5 Ex 29CanadaInf

SWEETMAN,Michael James Joseph Maj dow 27-11-15 2Worc att2Dors RoO p110 CR Iraq1

SWEETMAN,John Stephen T2Lt dow 27-4-16 8RIrFus p171 CR France423,SWEETNAM Lt

SWEETNAM,Richard Rodney Stephen TCapt kia 1-7-16 RFA 125Bty p36 CR France643

SWELL,Albert Ernest.DSO.ACapt kia 17-8-16 1Nhampt p138 CR France387

SWETENHAM,Edmund Lt kia 22-10-14 2DLI p161 MR32,27-10-14

SWETENHAM,Foster Maj kia 26-8-14 2Drags p21 CR France1715

SWIFT,Allen Richard 2Lt kia 10-11-17 A246RFA p36 MR30

SWIFT,Harold Heyes T2Lt kia 10-8-17 9LNLancs p136 MR29

SWIFT,Humphrey Morris 2Lt kia 16-11-17 2WelchR p127 MR30

SWIFT,James Herbert 2Lt kia 31-5-18 5Manch p236 CR France1689,Hubert

SWIFT,John T2Lt kia 9-1-17 12Manch p156 CR Iraq5

SWIFT,John 2Lt kia 22-11-17 2/7WYorks p218 MR17

SWIFT,Neville Cropley.DSO.MC&Bar.LtAMaj dow 28-3-18 3 att2ELancs p111 CR France185

SWIFT,Sydney Reginald T2Lt dow 4-12-16 2 att8NumbF p63 CR France59

SWIFT,Wilfred Harold Lt dow 22-4-17 IARO att51Sikhs p283 MR38

SWIFT,William T2Lt kia 1/3-7-16 8Lincs p76 CR France267

SWIFT,William T2Lt kia 11-10-18 WYorks Res att1/7WRid p83 CR France612

SWIFTE-O'FFLAHERTIE,Godwin Joseph Anthony Lt 4-3-18 3KSLI att1Lpool &RFC CR Egypt9

SWINBURNE,Matthew 2Lt dow 5-9-18 PoW 3RLancs p59 CR France1142

SWINBURNE,Thomas Anthony Stewart.DSO.MIDx3 CaptAMaj kia 1-4-18 RE 2FC p48 CR France880

SWINDALL,Arthur Cecil T2Lt kia 11-10-17 7RWSurr p56 MR30

SWINDELLS,Charles Geoffrey Rupert 2Lt kia 9-1-17 2Leics p88 MR38

SWINDELLS,Geoffrey Hillier LtCol kia 1-8-18 1/4Ches p222 CR Frnce524,Hilliers

SWINDELLS,Harold 2Lt kia 15-8-17 1/5SStaffs p229 CR France115

SWINDLE,Jackson 2Lt dow 14-10-16 14DLI p161 CR France52

SWINEY,Ernest Robert Rainier LtCol drd 30-12-15 IA 1/39GarhwalRif p283 MR41

SWINFEN,Percy Courtney 2Lt kld 20-9-17 GL &RFC p13 CR Yorks2

SWINHOE,Edmund Arthur Maj ded 27-10-18 IA S&TCps MR67

SWINLEY,George Dighton Probyn Maj dow 13-5-15 IA 14Sikhs p283 CR Gallipoli3,14-5-15

SWINLEY,Gordon Noël Balfour Lt kia 22-6-15 3 att2KOSB p102 CR Belgium96,dow 23-6-15

SWINNEY,James Herbert Cecil.MC.2Lt kia 16-4-17 7NumbF p214 MR20

SWINNEY,Norman Atkinson T2Lt kia 28-4-16 13NumbF p63 CR France188

SWINTON,A.J.Capt 7-9-20 RE MR65

SWINTON,Ernest.MID 2Lt dow 28-5-15 RFA p36 CR Lancs186

SWINTON,James Gibson 2Lt kia 25-3-18 4BlkW p230 MR27

SWIRE,Alexander Glen 2Lt kld 14-5-15 EssYeo p203 MR29,kia 13-5-15

SWORD,James Hubert 2Lt kia 10-9-14 4Huss p21 CR France1128,Lt

SWORDER,Charles Frederick 2Lt kia 3-7-16 7Suff p79 CR France393

SWORDER,Hubert Pelham Lt kia 2-4-17 RWSurr &57RFC p14&56 CR France924

SWORDER,John Perkins Lt dow 24-7-18 5RWSurr att1/1Hereford p212 CR France864,2/4Bn

SWYNNERTON,Frederick 2Lt ded 18-12-18 IARO attPostalCensorDept p283 MR65

SYDENHAM,Humphrey St.Barbe Lt ded 8-10-16 2/4 att1/4Dev p220 CR Iraq5

SYDES,Edward John Rev AustChap ded 15-11-18 att5FA CR Lond9

SYDNEY,Herbert Lt ded 26-5-17 RE IWT p48 MR38

SYER,Hubert Lionel.MC.Capt dow 18-11-16 1/14Lond p249 CR Lond12

SYERS,Thomas Scott.MC.CaptAMaj ded 14-11-18 D157 RFA p36 CR Sussex183

SYFRET,Edward Tristram Smyth 2Lt dow 17-8-16 3 att1Nhampt p138 CR France833

SYFRET,John Eustace Ridge 2Lt ded 17-1-19 RH&FA p262

SYKES,Arnold Walker TCapt kia 30-9-17 3Y&L A'Coy p159 CR Belgium165,9Bn

SYKES,Claude TLt kia 2-7-16 GL 10Y&L attTMB p191 MR21,Charles

SYKES,Douglas Collett.MC.TLt dow 26-7-17 7BordR p118 CR Belgium24,11Bn

SYKES,Edward Burton T2Lt kia 31-7-17 6/7RScotF p95 MR29

SYKES,Eric Turner Capt kia 3-5-17 2/5WRid p227 CR France644

SYKES,Ernest Edward.MC.Capt kia 4-7-16 4WRid p227 CR France702

SYKES,Frank William Lt kia 14-3-18 RFA p208 CR Belgium21

SYKES,Gerald Wolriche 2Lt kia 25-5-15 7WYorks p218 CR France525

SYKES,Harold Keith Lt dow 29-6-17 GL &42RFC p14 CR France285

SYKES,Harold Widdington TCapt ded 11-11-18 RAMC att14CCS p198 CR EAfrica87,Widdrington Maj

SYKES,Jabez 2Lt dow 25-6-15 4ELancs p226 CR Gallipoli1

SYKES,Jack A.2Lt kld 4-10-18 3GordH &RAF p167

SYKES,James Martyn Strickland 2Lt kia 13-11-16 5GordH p242 CR France1490

SYKES,John Spencer 2Lt kia 3-12-17 Worc att2/7Bn p110 MR17

SYKES,Leslie Gordon 2Lt kldacc 22-3-18 RFA attRFC p17&36 CR Yorks645

SYKES,Leslie Hindle Lt kia 3-10-18 6SStaffs p229 CR France375

SYKES,Mark.Bart.Col ded 16-2-19 4EYorks p272 CR Yorks35,5Yorks

SYKES,Oliver John TCapt dow 17-10-16 RGA 23SB p42 CR France296

SYKES,Ronald Arthur Lt dow 28-4-17 7RFus p70 CR France95,Capt

SYKES,Tom T2Lt kia 29-6-17 7Yorks p91 CR France97

SYKES,Walter Ernest Lt kia 20-11-17 5RWKent p235 CR France379

SYKES,William Lt ded 4-4-18 112Bty 6Div RFA p36 CR France102

SYKES,William Ernest MajTLtCol ded 8-1-15 9Worc p110 CR Sussex156

SYKES-BANKS,William Maj 19-2-16 Dors attGenStaff HQ CR France377

SYLVESTER,Charles Percival Haythorn T2Lt kia 3-10-18 SStaffs att1/6Bn p123 MR16

SYLVESTER,George Harry 2Lt dow 4-11-18 4Lond p246 CR France403

SYM,John Munro.Sir.KCB.3-10-19 IA CR Scot237

SYME,David.MM.2Lt dow 4-7-18 6BlkW p231 CR France95,Lt

SYMES,Charles William Capt ded 10-10-15 1/4 att2Dors p229 CR Iraq5,9-10-15

SYMES,Edward Douglas.MC.Capt kia 13-8-17 9Lond p247 CR Belgium112

SYMES,John Bond Capt kia 3-5-17 2Lond p245 CR France537

SYMES,Henry T2Lt kia 30-9-16 6Y&L p159 MR21

SYMES-THOMPSON,Cholmeley Capt kia 17-11-14 2GrenGds p50 CR Belgium134

SYMINGTON,George Charles 2Lt dow 1-8-17 3 att12RSuss p120 CR Belgium16

SYMINGTON,Percy George TLt kia 1-7-16 17HLI p164 CR France744

SYMINGTON,William.TD.SurgMaj ded 3-9-16 RAMC att4BordR CR C'land&W'land13

SYMON,John T2Lt kld 5-1-18 2Yorks p91 CR Belgium127

SYMONDS,Arthur 2Lt kia 17-2-17 23RFus p70 MR21

SYMONDS,Bertram Oliver T2Lt kia 21-8-18 34MGC p185 CR Belgium10,Bertan

SYMONDS,Frank James T2Lt kia 1-7-16 16WYorks p83 MR21

SYMONDS,Frederick George.DCM.MM&Bar.MID T2Lt kia 22-10-17 8Norf p74 MR30

SYMONDS,Kenneth Claud Lt 16-10-17 KSLI CR Shrop114

SYMONDS,Spencer Leslie Hatton Lt kia 12-11-17 GL &7RFC p14 CR Belgium88

SYMONDS,William Frederick John.DSO.LtCol dow 24-4-18 11Lond p248 CR France37

SYMONDS-TAYLER,Frederick Kingsley Capt dow 17-4-17 3 att1KSLI p145 CR France98

SYMONDSON,Vernon T.Capt kld 13-11-18 13Huss &RAF p22

SYMONS,Alfred Castell Lt ded 26-2-19 3RScots attTankCps p262

SYMONS,Arthur George.MC&Bar.TCapt&Adjt ded 23-10-18 21Mddx p148 CR Kent180

SYMONS,Charles Fleming Jelinger TLt kia 25-9-15 9RWFus p99 MR19

SYMONS,Charles Handley Lanphier 2Lt kia 20-11-17 5 att8RFus p70 MR17

SYMONS,Charles Leslie 2Lt dow 23-4-18 RE 63FC p48 MR30

SYMONS,Clement Aubrey TLt kia 25-9-15 10Glouc p107 MR19

SYMONS,Douglas 2Lt kia 1-10-16 20Lond p251 MR21

SYMONS,Eric Clarence T2Lt dow 1-9-16 98MGC Inf p185 CR France833

SYMONS,Frank Albert.CMG.DSO.LtColTCol kia 30-4-17 RAMC ADMS 9DivStaff p198 CR France97

SYMONS,Frederick Gordon Lt kia 22-5-16 3 att2RScotF p95 CR Belgium53

SYMONS,Herbert William.MID Capt kia 20-11-14 1YLI attSomaliCamelCps p144 CR EAfrica60,19-11-14

SYMONS,Hubert Maj dow PoW 22-3-18 D47RFA p36 MR27

SYMONS,Keith William Allardyce Lt 30-7-18 73RAF MR20

SYMONS,James Anthony 2Lt kia 18-7-16 5RSuss p228 CR France296

SYMONS,Rudolph Clifford Lt ded 13-9-17 RASC 3Coy p272 CR Somerset42

SYMONS,T.S.Capt kld 29-9-18 3RSuss &RAF p120 CR France379

SYMONS,Vivian Hood Maj 29-1-17 RAMC CR Wilts115

SYMS,Albert George Ernest.TD.LtCol ded 22-1-18 12Lond p248 CR Lond1

SYNGE,Allen Francis Lt kia 27-11-17 2IrGds p53 MR17

SYNGE,Francis Patrick Hamilton.MC.LtACapt kia 29-7-17 2IrGds SR p53 CR Belgium13

SYNGE,Mark.CIE.DSO.LtCol ded 11-7-21 IA S&TCps p283 CR Sussex200

SYNNOTT,Fitz Herbert Paget 2Lt kia 10-8-15 5RWFus p223 MR4

SYNNOTT,Walter Pierre 2Lt ded 11-10-18 6Drags attMGC p22&185 MR65

SYNYER,Richard Harold 2Lt dow 21-9-18 12Lond p248 MR16

SYRETT,Alfred Montague T2Lt kia 4-5-17 1RWFus p99 MR20

SYSON,Leslie 2Lt kld 17-9-16 RGA &RFC p209 CR War67

SYVRET,Stanley de Beaudenis Lt ded 14-5-18 3RScotF p263 CR Dorset156

<h1 style="text-align:center">T</h1>

TABBENER,Thomas Kemp Lt dow 9-12-17 2/19Lond p250 CR Palestine3,kia 8-12-17

TABER,Stacey James Hutley 2Lt kia 20-7-16 2Ess p132 CR France643

TABOR,John Morton T2Lt kia 21-9-17 KRRC att18Bn p152 MR30

TABUTEAU,Rupert Rochefort Moliere Lt kia 28-3-18 3CldGds p51 MR20

TACK,Eldred William.DCM.MM.T2Lt kia 28-9-18 NStaffs Res p158 CR France415

TACKABERRY,John Bailey Capt ded 25-3-17 IMS 83CombStatHosp p283 CR Iraq6

TACKNEY,J.J.Gnr ded 18-8-17 RIM p283

TACON,Ernest John Ballard 2Lt kia 9-10-17 LancHuss p204 MR30

TAFFS,Charles Reginald Lt kia 15-5-15 3 att1RBerks p140 CR France632

TAFT,Thomas Lt&QM dow 23-12-17 6DLI att4Yorks p239 CR Belgium10

TAGENT,Harold William 2Lt kia 24-3-17 4RIrF &8RFC p14&171 CR France120

TAGG,Charles Hirch 2Lt kia 15-2-15 2ESurr p113 MR29

TAGG,Harold Arthur Lt kia 12-10-14 Mddx p148 CR France1106

TAGGART,Henry Rawson 2Lt kia 24-7-18 3A&SH att1BlkW p174 CR France258

TAGGART,Herbert 2Lt kia 8-5-16 11 att15RWFus p99 MR19

TAHOURDIN,Philip Ramsay 2Lt kia 17-4-16 IA 47Sikhs p283 MR38,Lt

TAHOURDIN,Spencer Maxwell Maj dow 8-2-16 IA 12Cav p283 CR Iraq6

TAILFORD,John Wilson.MC.Capt kldacc 22-5-17 BordR &RFC p14&118 CR Kent7

TAIT,David Borthwick 2Lt kia 11-8-18 4 att5/6RScots p211 CR France360

TAIT,Evelyn Euphemia Worker ded 22-10-18 QMAAC CR France85

TAIT,Henry Forsyth T2Lt kia 1-9-16 10 att12ScotRif p104 MR21

TAIT,James Capt kia 16-6-17 7DLI att2/1Lond p239 MR20

TAIT,Kenneth James Capt kia 23-3-18 1/85MC AuklandMtdRif NZEF MR34

TAIT,Robert Andrew T2Lt kia 22-3-18 9LNLancs p136 CR France245

TAIT,Thomas Henderly Lt drd 15-4-17 3A&SH p174 CR Greece14

TAIT,Wilfred Webster Lt dow 19-12-15 10WelchR p127 CR France1106,Wilfrid

TAIT,William Bell T2Lt kia 15-12-17 2RScotF p95 MR30

TAIT-KNIGHT,Alec TCapt dow 27-10-16 22DLI p161 CR France105

TAITE,William Henry Jules 2Lt ded 27-9-18 3Mddx p148 CR Greece9

TALBOT,Ainslie Douglas Capt kia 3-6-15 1LancF p93 CR Gallipoli1,4-6-15

TALBOT,Arthur Aston Lt ded 29-10-18 SWBord BrecknockBn p223 CR EAfrica52

TALBOT,Arthur Charles 2LtTLt dow 17-7-15 2Ess p132 CR France102

TALBOT,Arthur Sydney TLt kld 27-9-17 48RFC p14 CR Essex73

TALBOT,Cecil Melliar T2Lt kia 20-9-15 14 att4Mddx p148 CR Belgium6,27-9-15

TALBOT,Claude Eustace Chetwynd T2Lt kia 25-9-15 6SomLI p80 MR29

TALBOT,Edward Charles.MID Capt dow 29-4-15 IA 47Sikhs p283 CR France200,Maj

TALBOT,Eric Lawrence Lt dow 23-10-14 RHA p36 CR Belgium57

TALBOT,Frank Henry T2Lt dow 15-7-16 RWar att1BordR p66

TALBOT,Frederick Charles ACapt kia 9-10-17 D'TankCps p189 MR30

TALBOT,Frederic Herbert T2Lt kia 20-7-16 15N&D p135 MR21

TALBOT,Gilbert Walter Lytleton TLt kia 30-7-15 7RB p180 CR Belgium453,Lyttleton

TALBOT,Humphrey Richard Lt dow 13-11-14 3DragGds p21 CR Belgium57,Humfrey kia

TALBOT,John Lionel Pemberton 2Lt dow 14-10-18 4Worc X'Coy p110 CR Belgium157,kia

TALBOT,Leonard Lane.MC.Capt dow 24-4-17 27RFA p36 CR France95

TALBOT,Norman Hale T2Lt kia 24-8-16 5 O&BLI p130 MR21

305

TALBOT,Ralph Frederick 2Lt 2-9-18 8RAF MR20

TALBOT,Reginald Fitzroy 2Lt kia 27-8-16 RFC p4 MR20

TALBOT,Rimell Smith 2Lt kia 23-4-18 A121RFA p36 CR Belgium11

TALBOT,Stanley Alfred T2Lt kia 19-10-16 NStaffs att9LNLancs p158 CR France446

TALBOT,Theophilus Edwin 2Lt dow 21-3-18 C160RFA p36 CR France512

TALBOT,William Caithness 2Lt ded 20-7-18 6Leinst &RAF p175

TALBOT-BOWE,Edward TCapt dow 1-11-17 12RBerks att188LabCps p140 CR France145

TALL,John Jeffery 2Lt kia 15-2-18 4Dev p220 MR30

TALLENT,Albert Cecil T2Lt kld 4-11-17 RFC p14 CR Lond10,Charles

TALLENTIRE,Arthur Tom 2Lt kld 20-10-15 28Lond &RFC p19&252 CR Belgium11

TALLON,Moses 2Lt kia 4-8-16 11Suff p79 MR21

TANBURN,Walter Louis 2Lt kia 13-4-17 IARO att1/2GurkhaRif p283 MR38

TANCOCK,Osborne George.MC.Lt kia 17-3-18 RFA att5RFC p17&36 CR France95

TANDY,Archdale Maurice Stratford Lt kia 20-10-14 RIrReg p89 MR22

TANDY,Arthur Jesse 2Lt ded 28-7-19 WYorks p263 CR Scot9

TANFIELD,Arthur Horace 2Lt kia 13-4-17 59RFC p14 MR20

TANKARD,William Joseph 2Lt kia 31-8-18 4 att5LancF p93 CR FRance239

TANNER,Arthur Edward T2Lt dow 10-7-17 16NumbF p63 MR31

TANNER,Charles Cyril Pontin Capt ded 5-10-18 RGA 157HB p42 CR Iraq8

TANNER,Charles Patrick LtACapt kia 30-11-17 59MGC p185 MR17

TANNER,David 2Lt kia 30-8-17 8N&D p233 MR19

TANNER,David Thomas TLt kia 31-8-16 16RWFus p99 CR Belgium73,Capt

TANNER,Edward Joseph Selby T2Lt kia 8-7-16 11Yorks attMGC Inf p91&185 CR France397

TANNER,Gerald Russell.MC.2LtTLt dow 8-4-18 Wilts p153 CR Camb3

TANNER,Harold Herbert TCapt drd 16-8-16 RAMC 13GH p198 CR France102

TANNER,Hubert John T2LtACapt kia 9-4-17 1SomLI p80 MR20

TANNER,John Arthur.CB.CMG.DSO.BrigGen dow 23-7-17 Staff RE 7Cps p1 CR France214

TANNER,John Frederick 2Lt ded 21-2-19 11N&D p264 CR Yorks686

TANNER,John Howard TLt kia 15-9-16 10Hamps p121 CR Greece3

TANNER,Morris Villiers Godwin T2Lt dow 7-4-17 3 att2/8N&D p135 CR France610

TANNER,Percy Valentine Capt kia 27-3-18 79RFC p255 MR20

TANNER,Ralph Eyre Capt dow 23-9-14 1Lpool C'Coy p73 CR France473

TANNER,Raymond Stuart 2Lt kia 31-8-16 3RLancs p59 CR Belgium120

TANNER,Thomas George TLt kia 14-10-17 RFA attRE p36 CR France154

TANNER,Thomas Lanfear Capt kia 18-9-18 4RWKent p234 CR France364

TANNETT-WALKER,Frederick William.VD.Col ded 6-3-17 4RE p48 CR Yorks372

TANQUERAY,Andrew Alexander Truman TCapt kia 30-7-15 9KRRC p152 MR29

TANQUERAY,Frederic Baron 2Lt kia 1-7-16 16Mddx B'Coy p148 CR France221,Lt

TANQUERAY-WILLAUME,F.G.Maj 11-2-19 RHA CR Hamps7

TAPLIN,Albert William 2Lt kia 1-7-16 1/12Lond p248 MR21

TAPP,George Norman T2Lt dow 28-3-16 14Ches p97 CR FRance300,2YLI

TAPP,Harold Donesthorpe Lt dow PoW 25-7-17 RE 3FC att70RFC p19&210 CR Belgium140,Donisthorpe

TAPP,Theodore Arthur.MC&Bar.Capt dow 21-10-17 CldGds att3GdsMGR p51 CR Belgium16

TAPP,William SubCdr ded 16-4-19 IA S&TCps p283

TAPPENDEN,Frank William T2Lt kia 2-7-18 18MGC p185 CR France44,1-7-18

TAPPENDEN,Herbert Frederick 2Lt kia 26-3-17 4RSuss p228 MR34

TAPSELL,William Algernon.DCM&Bar.MM.2Lt dow 18-9-18 1Lincs p76 CR France145

TAPSON-JONES,Herbert.MC.Capt dow 12-11-18 4RFA CR Mon67

TARBET,Arthur Kenneth 2Lt kia 21-8-15 1RInniskF p105 MR4

TARBET,Edmund Alex 2Lt kia 21-8-15 att1RInniskF p105 MR4

TARBET,Victor 2Lt kld 4-10-17 4Dev p220 MR30

TARBET,William Duncan T2Lt kia 9-4-17 7SfthH attC'MGC p165&186 MR230

TARBUTT,Fraser Coventry Lt 16-6-18 56RAF MR20

TARDUGNO,Ray T2Lt kia 7-7-17 17RWFus att57RFC p14&70 CR France134

TARGET,Noel Alexander TLt kia 4-8-16 13DLI p161 MR21

TARGETT,Ernest TLt ded 19-2-19 RASC p255 CR France1076

TARGETT,George Henry Lt kia 18-9-18 1/10Mddx attMGC p187&236 CR France1495

TARR,Francis Nathaniel Lt kia 18-7-15 1/4Leics p219 CR Belgium127

TARR,Henry Charles Hardman 2Lt ded 2-2-19 RASC p194 CR Egypt1

TARR,William Lt 31-10-15 7WYorks CR Belgium73

TARR,William Lt kia 14-7-16 7WYorks p218

TARRAN,Reginald Stuart.MC.2Lt kia 24-3-18 1Lpool p73 MR20

TARRANT,Arthur Ralph 2Lt kia 24-6-18 4RBerks p234 MR19

TARRANT,Henry Geoffrey Nelson.MC.T2Lt kia 31-7-17 6RBerks p140 CR Belgium112

TARRANT,Herbert Sutton Capt kia 27-4-15 HLI p164 CR Belgium101

TARRANT,Percival John TCapt kia 25-6-18 1/2 att11ELancs p111 CR France19

TARRAS,John Rae 2Lt kia 16-10-16 RFA X9TMB p36 CR France385 &CR France1890

TARRATT,Duncan McNeill Fox 2Lt kia 4-10-17 2SfthH p165 CR Belgium83

TART,Cyril James 2Lt kia 1-7-16 RE 219FC p48 MR21 CR France1890

TASKER,Field Pass T2Lt dow 6-10-17 16RWar p66 CR Belgium11

TASKER,Herbert Edwin 2Lt kld 22-8-18 6 att19Lond p247 CR France210

TASKER,Richard Greaves TCapt kia 3-7-16 10Worc p110 CR France393

TASKER,William 2Lt kia 27-5-18 4Leics p220 MR18

TATAM,Leslie Charles 2Lt kia 19-5-16 att8RLancs p59 MR20

TATE,A.C.R.2Lt kld 2-5-18 GL &RAF p191

TATE,Andrew T2Lt kia 20-1-18 NumbF att24/27Bn p63 CR France162

TATE,Charles Bernard Capt kia 1-7-16 15RIrRif p170 MR21

TATE,Frederick Herman.MID Capt kia 11-8-17 10KRRC p152 MR29

TATE,Gerald Charles 2Lt dow 21-3-15 3EYorks p85 CR France284

TATE,Harold Glen TCapt kia 17-2-17 2SStaffs p123 MR21

TATE,Herbert Lloyd T2Lt kia 12-6-16 RFA p36 CR Belgium136

TATE,John Martin TCapt kia 27-5-18 14NumbF p63 MR18

TATE,Johnston T2Lt kia 7-11-17 5RIrFus p171 CR Palestine8

TATE,Lionel Percy T2Lt kia 4-11-18 Res 8NStaffs C'Coy p158 CR France984

TATE,Tom Campbell T2Lt dow 2-9-16 12RSuss p120 CR France203

TATE,William Edward Lt kld 12-8-17 2/5N&D &RFC p232 CR Wilts28

TATE,William Lewis Lt kia 13-3-15 3RFus p70 CR Belgium17 Louis

TATEM,Rolland James.MC.Lt kia 27-9-18 42RFA p36 CR France530

TATHAM,Basil Owen Capt kia 23-4-15 3EYorks p85 MR29

TATHAM,Cautley Lt dow 18-6-15 1HAC D'Coy p206 CR France285,Capt

TATHAM,Geoffrey Bulmer.MC.Capt kia 30-3-18 3RB att116InfBde HQStaff p180 CR France652

TATHAM,George Henry Riley 2Lt dow 11-10-18 5Yorks att1/7WYorksp221 CR France611

TATHAM,Ion Mordaunt T2Lt kld 11-7-17 GL &RFC p14 CR Hamps30

TATHAM,John Savil 2Lt kia 9-2-17 9KRRC att6RLancs p152 MR38,Savill

TATHAM,Lawrence Castell Stanley T2Lt kia 10-1-18 GL &5RFC p17 CR France113

TATHAM,Sherman Trevor.MC.Lt ded 25-5-19 Ex 11Mddx p265 CR Lond14,dow

TATLOCK,Robert Reginald Lt ded 19-6-16 RASC p253 CR Greece7,Rattray 18-6-16

TATLOW,Archibald Henry TCapt kia 4-6-16 15RWar p66 CR France1182

TATTERSALL,Eric T2Lt dow 26-9-17 23Manch p156 CR France446

TATTERSALL,Harold Vaughan TLt ded 22-4-18 PoW 1NStaffs p158 CR Germany4,dow

TATTERSALL,Percival John T2Lt kld 9-1-18 RFC p17 CR Essex11

TATTERSALL,Philip Charles Paul.DSO.Capt accdrd 28-7-17 1/11Lond p248 CR Palestine2

TATTERSFIELD,Neville T2Lt ded 20-11-18 2TankCps p189 CR Dorset94

TATTON-TATTON,C.H.Lt ded 26-11-18 6RB p180 CR Surrey1

TATUM,George Edward 2Lt kia 30-11-17 15Lond p249 MR17

TATUM,Harold Maj kia 4-11-14 IA 101Grens p283 MR47

TAUNTON,Clive Warneford Capt kia 25-11-16 2Mon p244 CR France400

TAUNTON,Cuthbert Andre Patmore T2Lt kia 9-8-15 7SStaffs p123 CR Gallipoli5

TAUNTON,Oscar.MC.Lt dow 14-6-15 RE 1FC attELancs p210 CR Greece10

TAUNTON,Percy Charles James 2Lt kld 7-8-17 RGA 297SB p209 CR Belgium29

TAVERNER,Arthur Frederick 2Lt dow 11-10-16 1KSLI p145 CR France105

TAVERNER,Harold Percy Lt kia 27-3-17 6Ess p232 MR34

TAVERNER,Harold Tait 2Lt dow 12-4-18 B88 RFA p36 CR Belgium11,TAVENER

TAVERNER,Norman Henry Lt ded 4-12-18 GL P267 CR Lond10

TAWNEY,Robert Lionel.MC.2LtALt dow 30-11-17 7SomLI p80 MR17

TAWSE,James Gordon Capt dow 15-4-17 D291RFA p207 CR France518

TAYLER,Eric Hardwick Lt ded 9-2-15 1Y&L p159 CR France200

TAYLER,H.F.TLt ded 8-11-18 RE p48

TAYLER,Jervoise Graham 2Lt kia 15-5-15 3 att2Leic p88 CR France727

TAYLER,St.Cyprian Churchill.MC.Capt mbk 17-3-18 RSuss &80RFC p257 MR20

TAYLER,William Ulric Chevallier Lt kia 10-8-19 7RWKent att45RFus p255 MR70 &CR Europe179,1Bn

TAYLEUR,Charles Edward Lt kia 7-8-15 10NStaffs att8LancF p158 MR4

TAYLEUR,W.OBE.LtCol 8-7-21 ShropYeo Cmdt LabBn CR Shrop81

TAYLOR,A.D.TCapt kld 24-8-18 GL &RAF p191

306

TAYLOR,Adam 2Lt dow 22-3-18 RGA 210SB p42 CR France987

TAYLOR,Adrian Aubrey Charles Capt kia 28-6-15 RDubF attEgyptPolice p177 MR4

TAYLOR,Adrian Connell TLtACapt dow 24-9-17 15HLI p164 CR France1361,Cannell

TAYLOR,Albert Cecil 2Lt kia 20-7-16 Suff p79 CR France402

TAYLOR,Albert Edward.DCM.2Lt kia 9-4-17 2WRid p116 MR20

TAYLOR,Alexander Capt kia 21-4-17 9RScots p212 CR France545

TAYLOR,Alexander John 2Lt dow 8-8-18 16SussYeo p205 CR France31,kia

TAYLOR,Alexander Steven Bain 2Lt kia 23-7-18 1/5SfthH p241 CR France1697

TAYLOR,Alfred Cecil.MM.T2Lt kia 23-10-18 1DCLI p115 CR France1476

TAYLOR,Alfred Francis TLt kia 9-8-16 10 att7Suff p79 MR21

TAYLOR,Alfred Squire LtTCapt kia 31-7-17 RAMC att10/11HLI p198 CR Belgium58

TAYLOR,Alfred Thurston Lt kia 5-10-18 RE 423FC p210 CR France1723

TAYLOR,Andrew Leitch TCapt kia 12-5-17 6SfthH p241 MR20,13-5-17

TAYLOR,Archibald Cameron T2Lt kia 29-4-17 23NumbF p63 MR20

TAYLOR,Archibald McMillan Capt kia 10-8-15 4Ches p222 MR4

TAYLOR,Arnold Bradley T2Lt kia 12-7-16 9Leic p88 MR21

TAYLOR,Arthur Lt kia 10-4-18 4Ches p222 MR32

TAYLOR,Arthur Cuthbert Brooke Lt kia 4-6-15 6Manch p236

TAYLOR,Arthur George 2Lt dow 26-4-18 7RWSurr p56 MR27

TAYLOR,Arthur George Ernest LtACapt dow 26-5-17 7RFus attRN Div p70 CR France95,27-5-17

TAYLOR,Arthur Gilbert Vivian Lt ded PoW 17-10-17 IA 41Dogras attRFC p283 MR20

TAYLOR,Arthur Leonard T2Lt dow 16-11-18 10N&D p135 CR France52

TAYLOR,Arthur Martin T2Lt kia 1-8-17 2Dev p77 MR29

TAYLOR,Arthur McCutheon 2Lt kia 10-11-17 2RMunstF p176 CR Belgium126

TAYLOR,Arthur Montague Lt dow 25-9-15 IA 1Brahmans att2/8GurkhaRif p283 CR France705

TAYLOR,Arthur Rowland T2Lt kld 19-1-18 RFC p17 CR Hamps31

TAYLOR,Aucher Wilbraham 2Lt kia 26-9-16 5RBerks p140

TAYLOR,Bernard Arthur 2Lt kia 30-11-17 166MGC Inf p186 MR17

TAYLOR,Brook Wilbraham.DSO.Maj dow 2-4-16 RFA p36 MR65,8-4-16

TAYLOR,Bruce Mitchell.MC.DSO.Maj kia 6-11-17 1DCLI p115&258 CR Belgium37

TAYLOR,Charles 2Lt ded 9-5-18 C59RFA 11DAC p262 CR France224

TAYLOR,C.de B.Capt dow 24-12-18 RIrRif p265

TAYLOR,Cecil Frederick Lt dow 20-1-18 GlasgowYeo &RFC p203 CR France64

TAYLOR,Cecil Meakin 2Lt kia 7-10-16 4Lond p246 CR France744

TAYLOR,Cecil Salusbury LtCol dow 6-11-16 RGA 28HAG p42 CR France400

TAYLOR,Cedric Charles Okey Lt kia 3-12-16 3EKent attTMB p58 CR France1182

TAYLOR,Charles CaptTMaj kia 5-8-17 3RIrReg p89 MR29

TAYLOR,Charles Christopher Vassell TLt kia 26-12-17 301RH&FA p36 CR Palestine3

TAYLOR,Charles Edward Lt kia 1-11-15 1WYorks p83 MR29 CR Belgium101

TAYLOR,Charles Frederick 2Lt dow 18-2-17 19WelshR p127 CR Belgium18

TAYLOR,Charles Harry Lt drd 17-11-15 10WYorks p83 MR40

TAYLOR,Charles Harry T2Lt kia 25-1-17 9Worc p110 CR Iraq5

TAYLOR,Charles Livingstone LtACapt kia 24-3-18 3 att8ELancs p111 MR27,8 att2Bn

TAYLOR,Charles Manners T2Lt kia 9-4-18 RASC p194 MR32

TAYLOR,Charles Matheson 2Lt dow 20-4-17 121RFA p36 CRFrance68

TAYLOR,Charles Stanley T2Lt kia 3-11-17 1/7Ess p132 CR Palestine8

TAYLOR,Charles Tyerman Lt kia 24-8-14 18Huss p23 CR France206

TAYLOR,Clives Wailes.MC.2Lt dow 25-2-17 17RFus p70 CR France64

TAYLOR,Conrad Paul.MID TCapt kia 28-10-16 8EYorks p85 CR France133

TAYLOR,Coutart-de Butts.MM.Capt dow 24-12-18 RIrRif CR Sussex111 See SgtCOLLINS RFus

TAYLOR,Daniel Martin Lt kia 28-6-15 7ScotRif p224 CR Gallipoli6

TAYLOR,David George 2Lt kia 9-9-16 10Manch attRLancF p237 MR21

TAYLOR,Denis Percival Beauchamp.MC.Lt kia 14-3-16 3Huss att3RFC p4&21,ded CR France782

TAYLOR,Douglas Lt ded 26-7-18 RAMC 41GenHosp p198 CR Greece7

TAYLOR,Douglas John 2Lt kld 29-12-16 21RFC p4 CR Egypt9

TAYLOR,Douglas John Bulpin Capt kia 2-9-18 WSomYeo p205 CR France,12SomLI

TAYLOR,Douglas Merwyn 2Lt kia 4-10-16 3 att7EKent p58 MR21

TAYLOR,E.C.OBE.Maj 26-3-21 RE Staff CR Staffs109

TAYLOR,Edgar Lt 25-8-18 79RAF MR20

TAYLOR,Edmund T2Lt dow 26-9-17 GL &23RFC p14 CR Belgium16

TAYLOR,Edward 2LtTLt kia 13-5-15 18Huss p23 MR29

TAYLOR,Edward Algernon 2Lt kia 11-2-18 1Herts p252 CR France439

TAYLOR,Edward Graham T2Lt kia 25-9-15 7CamH p168 MR19

TAYLOR,Edward Graham 2Lt dow 23-5-17 4HLI p164 CR France40,Lt 2Bn

TAYLOR,Edward Roy.MC.TCapt kia 23-10-18 1SWBord p101 CR France1271

TAYLOR,Edward Shillingfleet Sodley 2Lt ded 9-6-18 4NStaffs p265 CR Essex130,Lt

TAYLOR,Edward Staveley 2Lt dow 19-8-16 7Lpool p216 CR France23

TAYLOR,Eric Francis Howard T2Lt kia 27-7-16 23RFus p70 MR21

TAYLOR,Ernest 2Lt dow 16-10-15 1/4WRid p227 CR Belgium9

TAYLOR,Ernest T2Lt dow 7-9-18 7Lincs p76 CR France41

TAYLOR,Ernest Albert Isaac TCapt dow 23-7-18 B98 RFA p36 CR Greece1

TAYLOR,Ernest George 2Lt kia 2-5-15 3 att2RLancs p59 MR29

TAYLOR,Ernest Reginald.MC.Capt kia 11-8-18 7Ess att18KRRC p232 CR Belgium11

TAYLOR,Ernie Rumbold Capt kia 18-4-15 WRid attEYorks p116 CR Belgium152

TAYLOR,Eustace Edmund Marshall TLt kia 1-1-17 169MGC Inf p186 CR France1157

TAYLOR,Ezra Dolphin 2Lt kia 30-4-15 RHA Y'Bty p36 CR Gallipoli14,28-4-15

TAYLOR,Forster T2Lt kia 16-10-18 9ESurr p113 MR16

TAYLOR,Francis Galloway 2Lt kia 23-7-16 12WYorks p83 CR France432

TAYLOR,Francis Henry 2Lt kia 30-11-17 3Mon B'Coy p244 CR France379,1/2Bn

TAYLOR,Francis Maurice TLt kia 15-7-16 10RFus p70 MR21

TAYLOR,Francis Mortimer.MC.Capt kia 17-3-19 RAMC p198 CR Europe180,Maj

TAYLOR,Frank TMaj kia 13-3-16 10Y&L p159 CR France922

TAYLOR,Frank Wilsher 2Lt kia 1-9-18 5Lond att1/20Lond p246 MR16

TAYLOR,Frederick Cecil LtACapt kia 22-8-18 13KRRC p152 CR France214

TAYLOR,Frederick George T2Lt ded 21-7-17 9NumbF p63 CR Mddx13

TAYLOR,Frederick George Lt kia 14-4-18 4EKent p212 MR32

TAYLOR,Frederick William.TD.LtCol ded 10-7-16 5Ess p272 CR Essex119

TAYLOR,Garth Smithies TLt kia 15-10-16 2N&D p135 MR21

TAYLOR,Geoffrey England 2Lt dow 26-9-18 RFA attY33TMB p36 CR France278

TAYLOR,George TLt drd 30-10-17 RAMC p198 MR38

TAYLOR,George Lt mbk 23-3-18 RE 517FC p257 CR France1472

TAYLOR,George Charles TCapt dow 6-9-18 RAVC att26RFA p199 CR France309,kld

TAYLOR,George Francis Woodland 2Lt kia 4-5-17 2Ess p132 CR France451

TAYLOR,George Gall Lt kia 29-9-18 9HLI p240 CR France663

TAYLOR,George Henry Recknett Capt kia 30-11-17 7Suff p79 MR17

TAYLOR,George Milburn TLt dow 25-5-16 A161RFA p36 CR France43

TAYLOR,George Ossory 2Lt kia 8-10-16 1/5Lond p246 MR21 CR France1890

TAYLOR,George Robert Marmaduke Stanbury Lt dow 30-9-17 295RFA p208 CR Belgium18

TAYLOR,George Stanley 2Lt drd 4-5-17 RASC 905MT Coy p194 CR France1571

TAYLOR,George Thomas T2Lt kia 2-11-17 att1/7Ess p132 CR Palestine8

TAYLOR,George William T2Lt kld 1-10-17 733LabCps p189 CR France285

TAYLOR,George William Lt dow 9-11-17 A150RFA p36 CR Belgium16

TAYLOR,Gerard Bardsley T2Lt kia 24-9-18 11Leic att9DLI p88 CR France835,dow

TAYLOR,Gilbert Elliott Lt ded 13-7-18 4Y&L p272 CR Lancs34

TAYLOR,Gilbert Leslie Frederick Capt dow 26-8-17 3Lond attKRRC p245 CR France64

TAYLOR,Gordon Annesley Capt kia 15-2-15 1Leinst p175 MR29,14-2-15

TAYLOR,Guy Collins Vernon Lt kia 2-10-17 1RWFus p99 MR30

TAYLOR,Guy Hastings Maj mbk 14-11-14 IA 2/39GarhwalRif p283 MR38

TAYLOR,Harold Charles Norman Capt kia 21-5-16 20Lond p251 CR France924

TAYLOR,Harold Harker T2LtACapt drd 11-8-18 LabCps att83ChineseLabCps p189 CR France65

TAYLOR,Harold James 2Lt kia 17-10-18 1EKent p58 MR16

TAYLOR,Harold Richard 2Lt dow 17-3-17 SurrYeo att77MGC p187&205 CR Greece1,Lt

TAYLOR,Harold St.George T2Lt ded 15-4-16 6 att11BordR p118 CR France295

TAYLOR,Harold Victor T2Lt kia 23-8-17 6DCLI p115 MR30

TAYLOR,Harry TLt kia 27-2-16 RE 98FC p48 CR France922

TAYLOR,Harry T2Lt kia 12-10-16 26 att18Manch p156 MR21

TAYLOR,Harry Vivian.MC.Lt kia 22-3-18 17Manch p156 CR France672,Capt

TAYLOR,Helen Batchelor Miss 12-11-15 VAD att4Beds CR Europe1

TAYLOR,Henry TLt dow 9-11-17 2Ess att179MGC p186 CR Palestine1

TAYLOR,Henry Arthur.MC.2LtTCapt kia 27-9-16 RWKent attRFC p4&142 CR France614

TAYLOR,Henry William T2Lt dow 29-5-17 8NumbF p63 CR Belgium102

TAYLOR,Henry Young Cameron Capt ded 25-8-17 RAMC p198 CR Scot241

TAYLOR,Herbert TCapt ded 11-10-15 16KRRC p152 CR Lancs261

TAYLOR,Herbert T2Lt kia 1-4-17 15LancF p93 CR France672

TAYLOR,Herbert Berwick 2Lt kia 31-7-17 4Lond p246 CR Belgium106

TAYLOR,Herbert George Brooks 2Lt kia 16-9-16 1/7Mddx p235 CR France785

TAYLOR,Herbert Hampden TCapt dow 3-4-18 RAMC att4RWFus p198 CR France62

TAYLOR,Herbert Samuel 2Lt kia 28-4-17 O&BLI BucksBn att2/4Bn p232 MR21

TAYLOR,Herbert William Lt ded 12-6-16 2RFA p208 CR Yorks2

TAYLOR,Hugh.MID Capt kia 19-12-14 ScotsGds p52 CR France566,18-12-14

TAYLOR,Hugh Mascie TMaj kia 7-8-15 6RIrFus Ex1Bn p171 MR4,9-8-15

TAYLOR,Ian Cleasby 2Lt kia 4-12-17 7RScots p211

TAYLOR,James T2Lt kia 31-7-17 9BlkW p129 MR29

TAYLOR,James Craik Maj dow 8-6-15 RAMC att4ScotsF p253 CR Gallipoli1

TAYLOR,James Irvine.MC.2Lt kia 28-4-17 3Lincs p76 CR France1194

TAYLOR,James McEwen Thomson.MC&Bar.Lt ded 27-2-19 6CamH p168 CR Scot752

TAYLOR,James Norman.MC.Lt dow 27-7-17 IARO att33Punjabis p283 CR EAfrica38 &CR Tanzania1

TAYLOR,James Wood Colin Lt kia 9-8-17 N&D att2Bn p135 MR29

TAYLOR,John.MC.T2Lt ded 20-9-16 3 att2RScots p262

TAYLOR,John T2Lt dow 13-5-17 RE 233FC p48 CR Belgium11

TAYLOR,John.MC.MM.TLt kia 29-9-18 35MGC Inf p186 MR30

TAYLOR,John Arthur Harold 2Lt kia 24-9-15 1RDubF p177 CR Gallipoli4

TAYLOR,John Birley 2Lt kia 24-12-17 1/4ELancs A'Coy p226 CR France765,25-12-17

TAYLOR,John Cameron.MC.2Lt kldacc 20-9-16 3 att2RScots CR Scot812

TAYLOR,John Edgar 2Lt kld 1-2-17 RE attRFC p210&19,TAYLER CR Staffs156,Lt 6-2-17

TAYLOR,John Edward Middleton T2Lt dow 24-4-17 18Manch p156 CR France214

TAYLOR,John Ogilvie Capt kia 3-5-17 4EKent att1/7Mddx p212 MR20

TAYLOR,John Oswald 2Lt kia 19-4-17 5Beds p219 MR20

TAYLOR,John Tyson 2Lt dow 17-10-18 4SLancs att1/4LNLancs p230 CR France163

TAYLOR,John William Lt kia 12-3-15 1/2Mon p244 CR Belgium33

TAYLOR,John Yates Lt kia 6-7-17 4ELancs attRFC p19&226 CR Belgium112

TAYLOR,Joseph Bertram Lt 28-3-18 GL &RFC MR20

TAYLOR,Joseph Macintyre Lt kia 24-10-18 2A&SH p174 MR16

TAYLOR,Kenneth 2Lt dow 17-6-17 RGA 184SB p42 CR Belgium18

TAYLOR,Leon Eric 2Lt kia 17-2-17 7Beds att54TMB p86 MR21

TAYLOR,Leonard 2Lt kia 27-8-18 3 att2Manch p156 MR16

TAYLOR,Leonard Frank 2Lt kia 14-3-17 1/5SStaffs p229 CR France281

TAYLOR,Leonard William TLtACapt kia 19-2-18 141MGC p186 CR France755

TAYLOR,Leslie Francis.MC.TLt kia 27-5-18 KRRC att8MGC p152&186 MR18

TAYLOR,Leslie Thompson TLt dow 3-6-18 8LNLancs p136 CR France95,Luke

TAYLOR,Matthew Neilson T2Lt kia 27-8-18 MGC Divl Inf p186 CR France1504

TAYLOR,Maurice 2Lt kia 23-3-18 RFus att11Bn p70 MR27

TAYLOR,Maurice Llewellyn 2Lt kia 26-8-16 6 att12RB p180 CR France513

TAYLOR,Maurice William.MC.2Lt kia 12-4-18 4RIrFus p171 MR30,11-4-18

TAYLOR,Merrill Samuel Lt 7-7-18 209RAF MR20

TAYLOR,Nellie Miss ded 27-6-18 VAD BRCS p200 CR France13

TAYLOR,Norman Austin.MC&Bar.Capt dow 26-3-18 1/21Lond p251 CR France40

TAYLOR,Norman Gawan 2Lt kia 24-4-17 3Y&L p159

TAYLOR,Norman Leopold T2Lt dow 18-9-16 19Lpool p73 CR France80

TAYLOR,Norman Robertson.MC.Capt kia 3-5-17 5BlkW p231 MR20

TAYLOR,Percival Harry 2LtTLt kia 13-6-17 2/6LancF p221 CR France765

TAYLOR,Percy Ezra Lt ded 30-3-19 SL RE IWT p201 CR France1571

TAYLOR,Peter 2Lt kia 8-8-16 4 att2ScotRif p104 CR France423,Lt

TAYLOR,Philip Charton Lt kia 15-9-16 2Lond p245 MR21

TAYLOR,Philip Gustave Adolphe T2Lt kia 25-7-17 RE 171Coy p48 CR Belgium5

TAYLOR,Ralph Paton 2Lt kia 10-7-16 3Nhampt att10SWBord p138 CR France397

TAYLOR,Raymond Brewitt.MC.TCapt dow 22-8-18 RAMC att7FA p198&259 see BREWITT-TAYLOR,R.

TAYLOR,Raymond Robert 2Lt ded 19-4-19 2Yorks p263 CR Scot674

TAYLOR,Richard Booksbank Capt kia 30-4-15 BordR p118 CR Gallipoli3,Brooksbank

TAYLOR,Richard Hayward 2Lt kia 20-9-17 8Lond p247 MR29

TAYLOR,Richard Neville T2Lt kia 26-5-16 12EYorks p85 CR France643

TAYLOR,Robert Edward 2Lt kia 17-9-17 41RFC p14 CR France1277,11-9-17

TAYLOR,Robert Edward 2Lt kia 12-10-18 7 att12Manch p237 CR France192

TAYLOR,Robert Fowler 2Lt dow 23-6-18 1/2 att3Glouc Res p107 CR Italy11

TAYLOR,Robert Henry T2Lt dow 13-6-17 RE 102FC p48 CR Lond1

TAYLOR,Robert Leslie 2Lt kia 30-11-17 12Lpool p73 MR17

TAYLOR,Robert Leslie T2Lt dow 11-9-18 Worc 1GarBn att11SLI p110 CR France31.Lester

TAYLOR,Robert Thomson T2Lt kia 22-10-17 6KOSB p102 MR30

TAYLOR,Robert Valentine Capt kia 29-7-18 8RWar att2LNLancsp215 CR France866

TAYLOR,Robert William.MC.Lt dow 24-10-17 8/83RFA p36 CR Belgium16

TAYLOR,Roger Cecil TLt kia 4-10-17 7SStaffs p123 CR Belgium23

TAYLOR,Ronald Francis T2Lt kia 8-8-15 5KSLI p145 MR29

TAYLOR,Ronald Woodhouse T2Lt kia 7-7-16 11NumbF p63 CR France267

TAYLOR,Samuel Alexander T2Lt kia 16-8-17 9RInniskF att109TMB p105 MR30

TAYLOR,Seymour George Frederick Capt kia 20-10-15 2CldGds p51 CR France423

TAYLOR,Sidney Arnold Turner T2Lt dow 17-4-17 12Worc att218MGC p110 CR France145

TAYLOR,Sidney Harold 2Lt kia 4-4-17 3Dors p124 CR France1701,1Bn

TAYLOR,Stanley Gordon 2Lt kia 21-10-16 72/38RFA p36 CR France513

TAYLOR,Stanley Waterman TLt kia 21-3-18 7EKent p58 MR27

TAYLOR,Stuart Campbell.DSO.BrigGen dow 11-10-18 3YLI attStaff 93InfBde p144 CR France25 Ex 15WYorks

TAYLOR,Thomas T2Lt kia 26-3-18 82RFC p17 CR France1242

TAYLOR,Thomas Jesse T2Lt kia 21-3-18 RWKent att52TMB p142 MR20

TAYLOR,Thomas Owen Lt dow 4-11-17 1/5Suff p79 CR Palestine2

TAYLOR,Thomas Ralph 2Lt kia 7-8-15 6LancF p221 MR4

TAYLOR,Thomas Reekie Morrison 2Lt kia 14-8-18 5RScotF p222 CR France184

TAYLOR,Thomas St Clair Gifford Lt kia 17-3-18 2/10Lond &35RFC p248 CR France446,FltOff

TAYLOR,Vernon TLt kia 15-9-16 7MunstF MGC Inf p186 CR France402

TAYLOR,Vicat Scott 2Lt kld 14-1-17 GL &RFC 10ResSqn p14 CR Lond1

TAYLOR,W.Lt 6-11-18 41MGC Inf CR France934

TAYLOR,Walford Charles Cdr ded 29-7-18 RIM p283 CR Asia82

TAYLOR,Walter 2Lt kia 30-7-16 5GordH p242 MR21

TAYLOR,Walter T2Lt ded 17-7-18 RASC p194 CR Iraq6

TAYLOR,Walter Douglas T2Lt kia 5-7-16 10WRid p116 CR France515

TAYLOR,Whitehead George Edward 2Lt kia 29-9-14 9Lancers p22

TAYLOR,William,Chap3Cl ded 19-10-16 RGA p209 CR Scot398

TAYLOR,William 2Lt kia 18-9-17 4EYorks p272 MR30

TAYLOR,William 2Lt kia 22-9-18 5Glouc p225 CR France1106

TAYLOR,William Alexander TLt kld 10-8-17 GL &RFC p14 CR Scot86

TAYLOR,William Aloysius Capt dow 11-5-15 5SLancs p230 CR France102

TAYLOR,William Anthony TLt kia 31-7-17 166MGC p186 MR29

TAYLOR,William Berrill T2Lt kia 31-7-18 10N&D p135&258 CR France61

TAYLOR,William Bruce T2Lt dow 17-4-17 15 att9Yorks p91 CR France40.2Bn

TAYLOR,William Crookenden TLt dow 5-11-18 13HLI attDivMGC p164&186

TAYLOR,William Currie LtACapt ded 7-11-18 RFA 14DAC p36 CR Scot249

TAYLOR,William Edward 2LtTLt drd 2-6-17 182RASC p194 MR41,482Coy

TAYLOR,William Edward Lt kia 31-7-17 55/33RFA p208 CR Belgium10

TAYLOR,William Ernest Ewart 2Lt kia 27-3-18 3 att13RSuss p120 CR France402

TAYLOR,William Frederick Lt kia 7-6-17 3EKent p58 CR Belgium115

TAYLOR,William Henry SubCdr ded 3-2-15 IA S&TCps p283 CR France145

TAYLOR,William Henry Capt&BtMajTMaj ded 11-2-19 RAVC attStaff p199 CR France134

TAYLOR,William John TCapt ded 1-8-17 8SfthH p165 CR Scot854

TAYLOR,William John Macdonald T2Lt kia 19-12-15 1BordR p118 CR Gallipoli1 Jack

TAYLOR,William Pike 2Lt kia 3-5-17 5Y&L p238 MR20

TAYLOR,William Wadman Capt kia 21-3-18 RASC att2/6N&D p253 MR20

TAYLOR-LOBAN,Gustavus TCapt kld 7-6-17 GL &RFC p14 CR Scot398

TAYLOR WHITEHEAD,George Edward 2Lt kia 29-9-14 9Lancers A'Sqn p22 CR France1337

TAYLOUR,George Ryfield Capt kia 19-10-14 2RWar p66 CR Belgium140

TAYTON,Wilfrid Edward 2Lt kia 10-8-17 Nhampt att6Bn p138 MR29,Wilfred

TEACHER,Norman McDonald.DSO.MajALtCol dow 26-9-17 1/2RScotF p95 CR Belgium84

TEACHER,William George T2Lt kia 14-5-16 15HLI D'Coy p164 CR France702

TEAGUE,Cyril T2Lt kia 4-10-17 SStaffs att1Bn p123 CR Belgium308

TEAGUE,John Gooden Lt kia 3-9-16 RASC att1DCLI p253 MR21 Godden

TEAHAN,John Patrick 2Lt kia 8-10-16 11N&D p135 MR21

TEALBY,Harold Edgar William 2LtACapt kia 5-4-18 6 att7RFus p70 MR20

TEALE,Guy Neville 2LtTCapt kia 20-7-16 20RFC p4 CR France787

TEALE,John Arthur T2Lt dow 27-9-16 11NumbF p63 CR France177

TEAPE,Charles Lewarne T2Lt kia 4-9-16 9Dev p77 CR France402

TEAPE,Cyrud Charles Tulloh Lt ded 26-4-20 IA 21Punjabis p283 MR43,1/26Punjabis

TEARE,John Stewart.MC.TLt kia 3-8-17 108RFA B'Bty p36 MR29

TEASDALE,Eric Henry Janson Lt drd 21-1-17 ASC att1MGC p187&253 CR France102

TEASDALE,Samuel Bird T2Lt kia 31-7-17 10Y&L p159 MR29

TEAZ,Homer Nevin.MC.TLtACapt kia 22-3-18 9YLI p144 CR France511,23-3-18

TEBBITT,I.L.2Lt 4-12-15 19Lond CR Mddx40

TEBBUTT,Arthur Brookes Lt kia 19-4-17 5Norf att163MGC p187&216 CR Palestine8

TEBBUTT,Oswald Nevelle Capt kia 15-3-15 1Camb p244 CR Belgium28,Neville

TEBBUTT,Roger Joseph Capt kia 24-8-18 1Camb p244 CR France430

TEDDER,Oswald Stanley 2Lt kia 27-4-18 8Lincs p76 CR France604,27-4-17

TEDMAN,Basil T2Lt kia 21-3-18 Mddx att13Bn p148 MR27

TEE,Albert Edward 2Lt kia 30-10-18 4Beds C'Coy p86 MR30

TEE,Clifford Vernon 2Lt dow 11-8-18 RGA 153SB p42 CR France34

TEE,Eric William Capt kia 27-3-17 6Ess p232 MR34

TEED,Edmund Maj 25-11-14 5RWSuss CR Sussex178

TEED,Henry Samuel 2Lt kia 24-7-16 1/4RBerks p234 MR21

TEELING,Ambrose Mary Anthony Twibide de Lone Lt kia 24-9-14 3Norf p74 CR France1107

TEELING,Humphrey 2Lt dow 13-10-16 7Norf p74

TEELING,Luke Joseph LtAMaj dow 8-11-18 B87RFRA p36 CR France521

TEESDALE,Frank Robinson Maj ded 17-3-16 IA 25Cav attStaff p283 CR Surrey52

TEETON,Percy Randolph.MC.Capt dow 17-10-18 1/6SStaffs p229 CR France146

TEGGART,Francis William Stuart Lt kia 26-10-17 A&SH attGordH p174 CR Belgium115

TEGGART,John Cameron Thomson TCapt kia 21-7-18 RAMC att256RFA p198 CR France1693

TEGGIN,Eugenie Elizabeth SNurse ded 25-12-18 QAIMNS p268 CR Shrop104

TEGLIO,Max T2Lt kia 11-4-17 Dev attWorcs p77 CR Iraq8

TEGNER,Augustus Alfred Becher 2Lt s/iGunshotWound 6-3-18 IARO attS&TCps p283 CR Iraq8

TELFER,Andrew T2Lt ded 15-11-18 Hamps att10Bn p121 CR Greece9

TELFER,Claude William TLt kia 8-11-18 1YLI p144 CR France981

TELFER,Henry Adam TLt kia 1-7-16 YLI att64TMB p144&255 CR France267

TELFER,Leslie Croom T2Lt dow 12-5-16 9 att8Beds p87 CR France102

TELFER,Robert Harold Cecil 2Lt kia 26-9-16 3KOSB attMGC Inf p102 CR France702

TELFER,Somerville Goodman 2Lt kia 8-5-15 12Lond p248 MR29

TELFORD,Carmont Owen 2Lt ded 7-2-19 IA 1/35Sikhs p283 MR43

TELFORD,Hilton Roberts Capt dow 9-9-17 21NumbF p63 CR France446

TELFORD,Robert Bernard Lt ded 21-2-19 RE p262 CR Numb1

TELPER,Richard Greenwell 2Lt kia 7-10-16 4 att12DLI p161,TELFER

TEMPERLEY,Harold Kenyon Lt kia 26-10-17 6 att1/7NumbF p214 MR30

TEMPERLEY,Jesse Hargreaves T2Lt kld 25-10-17 92MGC p186 CR France184

TEMPEST,Basil T2Lt dow 25-4-17 13Manch p156 CR Greece6

TEMPEST,Oswald Aldam Lt kia 28-3-18 RASC att2WYorks p194 MR27,Aidan

TEMPEST,Wilfred Norman TMaj kia 26-9-16 6YLI p144 MR21,2 att9Bn

TEMPEST-HICKS,Charles Edward Henry.MC.Capt dow 9-8-18 16Lancers p23

TEMPLAR,John Franklin Hopwood.MID Capt ded 8-2-19 2RFus p70 CR France34

TEMPLE,Arthur Hilliard William Capt kia 14-12-14 2Suff p79 MR29,Williams

TEMPLE,Edgar 2LtTLt kia 10-9-17 WYorks att12Yorks p83 CR France1461

TEMPLE,Ernest Nelson T2Lt dow 8-4-18 2/7WYorks p83 CR France62

TEMPLE,John Henry 2Lt dow 21-5-18 4EYorks p219 CR France102

TEMPLE,William 2Lt kia 7-6-17 17Lond p250 MR29

TEMPLE,William Arthur Mould Capt dow 23-10-14 1Glouc p107 CR Belgium11,21-10-14

TEMPLEMAN,John Watson 2Lt kia 25-3-18 1LancF p93

TEMPLEMAN,William Henry Lt ded 11-3-19 RAOC p268

TEMPLER,Claude Frank Lethbridge.MID LtACapt kia 4-6-18 1Glouc p107 MR19

TEMPLETON,Archibald Douglas Lt kia 28-6-15 8ScotRif p225 MR4

TEMPLETON,Godfrey Allan 2Lt dow 27-7-18 1/7A&SH p243 CR France1693

TEMPLETON,James Russell 2Lt kia 19-9-18 1 att8RScotF p95 MR37

TEMPLETON,William Fowler Capt kia 1-10-18 4RScotF p222 CR France602

TENCH,Montague Beavan 2Lt kia 10-3-16 9 att5Ess p132 CR France246,10-8-16

TENNANT,Alexander Smith TLt kia 27-9-18 LancF att1/7Bn p93 CR France758

TENNANT,Charles Alan Ramsay(Bunny) 2Lt kia 9-5-15 3Dors att2Dev p124 CR France566

TENNANT,Charles Grant 2Lt kia 9-5-15 4SfthH p241 MR22

TENNANT,Edward Martin Cookes 2Lt dow 16-10-16 4GordH p242 CR France5

TENNANT,Edward Wyndham.Hon.Lt kia 22-9-16 4GrenGds p50 CR France294

TENNANT,George Christian Serocold 2Lt kia 3-9-17 1WelshGds p53 CR Belgium12

TENNANT,Henry 2Lt kia 27-5-17 2Drags att52RFC p14&21 CR France1486

TENNANT,John Amherst TCapt dow 23-8-15 10Beds att1BordR p86 MR4,22-8-15

TENNANT,John Harold Anthony Lt kld 23-3-21 9Lancers CR Yorks335

TENNANT,Mark Lt kia 16-9-16 ScotsGds attMGC Inf p52 CR France374,Capt

TENNANT,Philip Eyre 2Lt kia 31-7-17 3ConnRgrs att2Leinst p172 MR29

TENNANT,Robert Edward TCapt kia 28-8-16 6YLI p144 CR France402

TENNENT,Bernard Charles.MC.TLtAMaj kia 22-8-18 RAMC att84FA p198 CR France504,7FA

TENNENT,Oswald Moncreiff 2Lt kia 16-6-15 1WYorks p83 CR Belgium58

TENNYSON,Alfred Aubrey.Hon.Capt kia 21-3-18 4 att9RB p180 MR27,23-3-18

TENNYSON-SMITH,John Alan TLt kia 7-3-17 10RWKent p142 CR Belgium28

TERRAS,James Sutherland T2Lt kia 11-1-17 133MGC Inf p186 MR38

TERRELL,Arthur Clive 2Lt dow 20-4-17 3Mddx p148 CR France40,5 att4Bn

TERRELL,Claud Romako a'Beckett.MC.2LtACapt dow 10-6-17 15RHA p36 CR France113

TERRELL,Frank William Lt kia 3-9-16 8Glouc att3Worc p107 CR France526

TERREY,Harry Leslie LtAMaj dow 22-3-18 RGA 126SB p42 CR France512

TERRIS,William T2Lt dow 3-4-17 2GordH p167 CR France156

TERRY,Charles Edward LtCol ded 11-2-20 Res 5Yorks p272 CR Kent279

TERRY,Harold Millard T2Lt kia 28-6-17 RE 4SpCo p48 MR20 Howard

TERRY,Henry Walter Seymer Lt 22-3-18 2SAfrInf MR27

TERRY,John DepCommsy&Capt ded 9-9-16 IA S&TCps p283 CR Iraq5

TERRY,John Elliott 2Lt ded 16-10-17 RFC p14 CR France145

TERRY,John Norman TCapt dow 20-9-16 6Lond p246 CR France833

TERRY,Leslie Ryder Lt ded 7-8-19 5RWar att1/5SomLI p256 CR Egypt9

TERRY,Robert Joseph Atkinson.MVO.DSO.Maj kia 3-10-15 2RSuss p120 CR France178,LtCol 1-10-15

TERRY,Sidney Frederic Capt kia 24-3-18 1Wilts p153 MR20

TERRY,Walter John TMaj kia 1-10-15 7Suff p79 MR19

TERRY,William Gregory Capt ded 28-10-16 RGA 36DivArt p42 CR Devon1,Gordon

TERRY,William Gregory Capt dow 27-8-17 2/8LancF p221 CR France1361

TESTI,George T2Lt kia 20-11-17 E'TankCps p189 CR France711

TETLEY,Arthur Calvert T2Lt kia 7-6-17 10WRid p116 CR Belgium127

TETLEY,Clarence Ernest Wand.MID Lt 22-8-15 9LancF MR4

TETLEY,Frederick Noel 2Lt kia 27-9-18 7RWar p214 CR France245

TETLEY,Harold Arthur 2Lt kia 12-4-18 6RWar p214 MR32

TETLEY,John Charlton Lt kia 11-4-18 7DLI D'Coy p239 CR France346

TETLEY,John Christopher Dodsworth Lt kia 9-10-17 3/3GrenGds p50 MR30,Charles

TETLOW,Cyril Lawson Lt kia 22-8-16 RASC attRFC p19&253 CR France727

TETLOW,Joseph TLt kia 25-8-18 KRRC att12Bn p152 CR France578,13Bn

TETLOW,Kenneth Burgess 2Lt kia 21-3-18 7 att2/8Worc p226 MR27

TETLOW,Luke Mallinson Lt kia 29-5-15 1/7WRid B'Coy p227 CR France347,dow 30-5-15

TEUNON,James M.2Lt ded 30-12-18 RFA &RFC p17

TEUNON,M.Lt 4-1-19 RGA attRAF CR Scot378

TEW,Percy T2Lt kld 16-6-17 RFC p14 CR War151

THAANUM,James Conrad T2Lt dow 12-8-15 19RGA 16SB p42 CR France167

THACKER,Herbert Lane 2Lt drd 15-4-17 RASC p194 MR35

THACKER,William Alfred T2Lt kia 12-5-17 7Yorks Ex 5SStaffs p91 MR20

THACKERAY,Frederick Rennel.MC.Lt kia 18-4-15 2WRid p116 MR29

THACKERAY,Frederick Rennell Col ded 15-10-15 RFA 75GdsDiv p36 CR France121

THACKRAY,William Hesling 2Lt dow 26-3-18 5Lancers p22 CR France1063

THAIN,William Skinner T2Lt drd 15-9-18 RWar Res att15Bn p66 CR France13

THARRATT,George Venes Lt drd 17-11-15 1Lpool p73 MR10

THATCHER,Francis Geoffrey.MC.Capt dow 1-6-18 RAMC DADMS HQ40Div p198 CR France134

THATCHER,George Robin.MC.Lt dow 1-4-18 RGA M'A/ABty p42 CR France103

THAYRE,Frederic James Harry.MC.LtTCapt kld 9-6-17 RFC p14 MR20

THEAK,Horace Leonard 2Lt dow 4-5-17 4Ess p232 CR France8

THEILMAN,Carl Erik Maj kia 24-4-15 4EYorks p219 MR29

THELWALL,Hubert Wallace Maj kia 23-4-16 1WIndiaR att15N&D p192 CR France727

THELWELL,Harry Rowland 2Lt dow 8-7-16 3 att2WRid p116 CR France40

THEOBALD,Arnold.MC.Lt ded 29-6-18 7RScots p211 CR France134

THEOBALD,Frederick George Capt kia 2-9-14 1RLancs p59 MR15,26-8-14

THEOBALD,Reginald.MC.Lt kia 10-4-18 3Suff C'Coy p79 CR France685,11Bn

THEOBALD,Ronald John MacIver Wilson 2Lt kia 21-3-18 5 O&BLI p130 CR France1061

THEODORE-SMITH,Dennis 2Lt kia 30-8-15 RE p48 CR France922

THERON,Lucas Cornelius T2Lt kld 15-7-17 GL &RFC p14 CR Lincs181,dedacc

THESIGER,Frederic Ivor.Hon.2Lt dow 8-5-17 RH&FA 87Bde p36 CR Iraq8,1-5-17

THESIGER,George Handcock.CB.CMG.ADC.MajGen kia 26-9-15 RB Staff Cmdg9ScotDiv p180 MR19

THEW,Frank Atkinson 2Lt kia 12-9-16 2/22Lond p251 CR France157

THEWLIS,Frank.MC.Lt kia 15-9-16 1CldGds p51 MR21

THEWLIS,Harold Darling Lt kia 4-6-15 1/7Manch C'Coy p237 MR4

THEXTON,Percival TCapt ded 20-11-18 RAVC 8MobileVetSec MEF p199 CR France1858

THICKE,Frank Vincent Lt kia 31-10-14 SL att22InfBde p201 MR29

THICKNESSE,Francis William.DSO.CaptAMaj dow 19-10-17 RGA 122HB p42 CR Belgium11

THICKNESSE,John Audley TLtCol kia 1-7-16 Cmdg1SomLI p80 CR France643

THICKNESSE,Raymond Samuel 2Lt kia 10-10-17 4 att2LancF p93 CR Belgium126,9-10-17

THIERRY,Frederick George 2Lt kia 17-9-16 GL &RFC p4&191 CR France439

THIERRY,Leonard Hubert 2Lt kia 10-12-17 GL &15RFC p14,261&267 CR France646

THIERRY,Paul Stanislas.MID Capt 18-2-20 RAVC att317RFA CR Asia9

THILL,John Joseph Lt kia 30-9-15 2Suff p79 MR29

THIMBLEBY,John Egremont 2Lt ded 29-8-15 5Lincs p220 CR Lincs225,Lt kldacc

THIRLBY,Stuart Longston 2Lt kia 22-3-18 6Leics p88 MR27

THIRLWELL,Thomas Albert TLt dow 1-10-17 RE 170TC p48 CR France8,Capt

THIRLWELL,Walter Houlden T2Lt kia 16-8-17 3ESurr att176MGC p186 CR Belgium12,15-8-17

THISTLEWOOD,Percival T2Lt kia 28-8-17 9RB p180 CR Belgium11,dow 25-8-17

THODAY,Albert Eric 2Lt kia 3-5-17 4RFus p70 MR20

THODY,Clarence James Capt kia 30-8-18 8Manch p237 CR France308

THOM,David T2Lt kia 14-9-16 10HLI p164 CR France453

THOM,James Flockhart.MC.Capt dow 27-9-18 Fife&FrfarYeo att17MGC Cav p187&203 CR Syria2

THOM,Laurence Wilson Lt dow 21-4-17 1/8ScotRif p225 CR Egypt2

THOMAS,Albert T2Lt kia 30-5-18 16 att9WelshR p127 MR18

THOMAS,Albert Edward 2Lt kia 17-2-17 3Mon att99MGC p187&244 MR21

THOMAS,Alec Vaughan TCapt kia 6-8-15 11ESurr att2Hamps p113 MR4

THOMAS,Alexander Reginald TCapt kia 3-7-16 10Worc p110 CR France832

THOMAS,Alfred Henry T2Lt kia 21-6-16 15LancF att196TMB p93 CR France702

THOMAS,Alma Cyril Lt dow 8-11-14 RWSurr p56 CR Belgium150,7-11-14

THOMAS,Aneurin Clement Lt ded 13-11-18 RHA p272 CR Wales29,Capt

THOMAS,Arthur Coke T2Lt kia 2-6-16 6 O&BLI D'Coy p130 CR Belgium165

THOMAS,Arthur Crichton AMaj 16-11-17 355RGA p42 CR Belgium85

THOMAS,Arthur Hanland,CB.DSO Col ded 8-11-19 RASC p267 CR Hamps146,Havieland

THOMAS,Arthur John Gordon Lt kia 31-5-16 6BlkW p231 CR France15

THOMAS,Arthur Lanham T2Lt kia 11-4-16 9 att7DCLI p115 CR Belgium23

THOMAS,Arthur Laurie Capt dow 30-8-18 20Lond p251 CR France630

THOMAS,Arthur Lewis 2Lt kia 24-4-18 3 att2Nhampt p138 MR27

THOMAS,Arthur Tuder Capt dow 29-9-18 GlamYeo att24RWFus p203 CR France262,Tudor

THOMAS,Arthur William 2Lt kia 8-2-17 IARO att2Sap&Min p283 CR Iraq5

THOMAS,Arthur William Maj ded 9-12-20 IMS p283 CR Iraq6

THOMAS,Aubrey Jocelyn Nugent Capt kia 1-5-15 1LancF p93 CR Gallipoli1,25-4-15

THOMAS,Basil Llewllyn Boyd TLt kia 9-4-17 15RWFus att27MGC p99&186 CR France265

THOMAS,Bryn Atherton Brodie T2Lt kia 16-8-16 13Lpool p73 CR France294

THOMAS,Cecil Rees T2Lt dow PoW 17-8-17 GL &57RFC p14 CR Belgium140

THOMAS,Charles Alexander TCapt kia 23-8-16 16KRRC p152 CR France399

THOMAS,Charles Harold Horatio TLt kia 20-9-17 214MGC Inf p186 CR Belgium310

THOMAS,Charles Herbert.MID Capt dow 5-11-14 2SStaffs p123 CR France102

THOMAS,Charles Humphrey Rittsen Lt dow 16-6-15 3 att2SLancs p126 CR Belgium58,Rittson

THOMAS,Cyril Llewellyn Seymour 2Lt kia 6-9-16 3BordR &RFC p4&118 CR France705,kld

THOMAS,Cyril Raymond T2Lt kia 18-8-18 11 att2SWBord p101 CR France28

THOMAS,Cyril Vaughan 2Lt kia 18-7-17 2RFA p36 CR France115,Lt 21RFA

THOMAS,Daniel Gwyn 2Lt kia 25-5-15 3RDubF p177 MR29

THOMAS,Daniel Morgan 2Lt 17-11-19 EgyptLabCps CR Europe5

THOMAS,David Arthur T2Lt kia 4-5-17 RWFus p99 MR20

THOMAS,David Cecil Sandby 2Lt kld 16-2-18 3WelshR att57RFC p17&127 CR Egypt8

THOMAS,David Cuthbert 2Lt dow 18-3-16 3RWFus p99 CR France638

THOMAS,David John T2Lt kia 22-4-18 15 att13RWFus p99 CR France339

THOMAS,David Lewis TLt kia 30-3-18 RE 253FC p48 CR France144,2Lt

THOMAS,David Morgan 2Lt ded 15-11-19 LabCps p266

THOMAS,Desmond 2Lt kia 28-6-18 4SLancs &RAF 14N'Wingp272 CR Italy9

THOMAS,Donald James 2Lt kia 21-12-17 2/7Mddx p235 CR Palestine3,Lt

THOMAS,Duncan Collison Willey Capt kia 12-11-14 4A&SH att1GordH p174 MR29

THOMAS,Edward Geoffrey Lt ded 10-10-18 7RWFus p223 CR Shrop93

THOMAS,Edward Palgrave 2Lt kia 9-8-16 7Lpool p215 CR France630,dow

THOMAS,Eric Hand T2Lt ded PoW 18-1-18 2WRid p116 MR20,8-12-17

THOMAS,Eric Lawrence(Dick) TLt kia 18-9-18 13WelshR p127 CR France415

THOMAS,Eric Rowland 2Lt kia 13-6-17 3Mon p244 CR Belgium42

THOMAS,Ernest William Noel T2Lt kia 20-11-17 O&BLI att6Bn p130 MR17

THOMAS,Evan David T2Lt dow 20-4-18 2SWBord p101 CR France180

THOMAS,Evan Llewellyn Lt kia 26-3-17 5RWFus p223 MR34

THOMAS,F.H.Lt 1-8-19 IndMilWksServ MR66

THOMAS,Francis Bernard Vivian Lt kia 22-9-16 4DCLI p227 CR France1887

THOMAS,Francis Stephen Capt kia 16-2-18 16RFC p17 CR France1724

THOMAS,Frank Hender T2Lt kia 1-10-15 RE 175Coy p48 CR Belgium132,Lt

THOMAS,Frank William Henry.MC.Lt dow 5-1-18 1StaffsYeo attRFC p19&205 CR Surrey1

THOMAS,Frederick George Byam Lt kia 6-8-15 1Ess C'Coy p132 CR Gallipoli6

THOMAS,Frederick James 2Lt kia 21-9-17 3 att11WYorks p83 MR30

THOMAS,Frederick Spriggs ACapt dow 21-4-17 1/4WelshR p230 CR Palestine2

THOMAS,Frederick William LtCol dow 26-1-16 IA 9BhopalInf p283

THOMAS,Geoffrey Lynn.MC.Capt kia 6-6-18 95RFA p36 CR France622

THOMAS,Geoffrey Owen 2Lt kia 25-4-18 19LancF p94 MR30

THOMAS,George T2Lt kia 13-11-16 10RWFus p99 MR21

THOMAS,George Oliver Capt kia 26-9-15 2RWFus p99 CR France114

THOMAS,Godfrey Vignolles.Bart.CB.CBE.DSO.MIDx2 BrigGen ded 17-2-19 RFA 24DivArtly p36 CR Essex167

THOMAS,Greville Wynn Lt kia 10-4-18 IA 2/4 att3/3GurkhaRif p283 CR Palestine9

THOMAS,Harold Morris 2Lt kia 10-11-16 4Yorks p220 CR France385

THOMAS,Harry Reid Capt kia 25-12-15 RGA 34SB p42 CR France1106

THOMAS,Heber 2Lt kia 12-10-17 4 att7EKent p212 MR30

THOMAS,Heinrich William Max TCapt kia 1-7-16 1ELancs p111 CR France152

THOMAS,Henry Evan Maj kia 18-4-18 Suff p79 CR Belgium191

THOMAS,Herbert Gordon 2Lt kia 13-11-16 3RWFus p99 CR France156

THOMAS,Honoratus Leigh Murron T2Lt kia 15-9-16 9Beds p87 MR21,8Bn

THOMAS,Horace Wyndham T2Lt kia 3-9-16 14 att16RB p180 MR21

THOMAS,Howard Victor Fraser.MC.Lt kia 22-10-18 3 att11RScots p55 CR Belgium140,Capt

THOMAS,Hugh TLt kia 2-3-17 RFA attY1stTMB p36 CR France692

THOMAS,Hugh 2Lt kia 30-7-16 8Glouc p107 MR21

THOMAS,Hugh Gareth T2Lt kia 10-5-17 142MGC Infp186 CR Belgium165

THOMAS,Ivan Arthur T2Lt kia 10-5-17 142MGC Infp186 CR Belgium165

THOMAS,James Grant Brandon 2Lt dow 17-11-14 RInniskF p105 CR Lond4

THOMAS,James Leonard Capt kld 28-2-17 3Lond attRFC p19&245 CR Wilts4

THOMAS,James Shepherd T2Lt kia 3-5-17 15WYorks p83 MR20

THOMAS,John Baron Rittson 2Lt kia 18-4-18 4 att2Manch p156 CR France804

THOMAS,John Boaz Lt kia 23-1-18 RFC p17 CR Asia62,Boase

THOMAS,John Clay Lt ded 25-12-19 11WelshR p264CR Asia51

THOMAS,John Dobson T2Lt kld 20-3-18 RFC p17 CR Hamps31

THOMAS,John Mewrig 2Lt kia 22-5-18 3 att2WelshR p127 CR France114,Meurig 23-5-18

THOMAS,John Simons T2Lt kia 27-8-17 Lincs p76 CR France1462

THOMAS,John Vick Lt ded 3-12-18 RE p210 MR40

THOMAS,Joseph Henry Lt&QM ded 25-6-19 Ex RWFus p263 CR Sussex93

THOMAS,Kenneth TCapt kia 3-6-16 12KRRC p152 CR Belgium96

THOMAS,Lilian SNurse 14-8-18 QAIMNS CR Lancs14

THOMAS,Lionel George Theophilus 2Lt kia 20-9-17 5WelshR attMGC Inf p187&230 CR Belgium112

THOMAS,Llewellyn 2Lt kia 27-12-17 DenbighYeo att12RWEFus p203 CR Palestine3

THOMAS,Llewellyn Maj&QM ded 29-11-15 6WelshR p230 CR Wales171

THOMAS,Matthew TCapt kia 30-12-15 7LNLancs p136 CR France727

THOMAS,Maurice Wotton Lt kia 5-8-16 RFA &RFC p4&36 MR20

THOMAS,Morgan Lt ded 26-7-19 2SWBord p263 CR Wales95,dow 16-7-19

THOMAS,Noel Lavender 2Lt kia 18-9-18 1 att11RWFus p99 CR Greece5

THOMAS,Oscar Clifford Lt kia 1-12-17 GrenGds att1GdsMGR p50 CR France417

THOMAS,Owen Redrupp 2Lt ded 4-3-19 RE 11DivSig p262 CR Europe51,Lt

THOMAS,Owen Richard Capt ded 21-8-17 WelshHorse 54Div p205 CR Palestine2

THOMAS,Philip Edward 2Lt kia 9-4-17 RGA 244SB p42 CR France420

THOMAS,Reginald Ernest 2Lt kia 13-9-18 RGA 193SB p42 CR France729

THOMAS,Reginald Ivor Victor Clifford 2Lt kia 24-11-17 3 att12SWBord p101 MR17

THOMAS,Reginald Percy TLt kia 24-8-18 11 att10SWBord p101 MR16

THOMAS,Reginald Spencer Dudley 2Lt kia 18-9-18 RWFus att25Bn p99 MR16

THOMAS,Rhys Ivor.MC.MID Lt kia 14-9-14 1ConnRgrs p172 CR France1107

THOMAS,Richard Nixon T2Lt dow 23-8-15 9RWFus p99 CR France345

THOMAS,Robert Alfred TMaj ded 3-6-15 15LancF p94 CR France169

THOMAS,Robert Edward Hon2Lt ded 27-11-18 Ex LabCps p266

THOMAS,Robert Newton TCapt kia 23-7-17 GL &RFC p14 MR34

THOMAS,Robert Stanley.MC.T2Lt kia 24-3-18 4Worc p110 CR Belgium22,25-3-18

THOMAS,Rufus Haydon TCapt kia 24-3-18 RAMC att2RScotsF p198 MR20

THOMAS,Rufus William T2Lt kia 9-5-18 16RWFus att113TMB p99 CR France296

THOMAS,Sidney John T2Lt kia 21-9-17 RWKent att10Bn p142

THOMAS,Stanley Meredith 2Lt ded 13-12-18 RFA p209 CR Wales171,Lt

THOMAS,Sydney T2Lt kia 1-7-16 11Suff p79 MR21,Sidney

THOMAS,Sydney Edwin Bailey TLt kia 3-9-16 10 att13RSuss p120 CR France339

THOMAS,T.W.LtCol 26-1-16 9BhopalInf CR Iraq5

THOMAS,Thomas T2Lt kia 10-1-16 16RWFus p99 CR France631

THOMAS,Thomas TLt kia 3-11-16 51MGC Inf p186 CR France374

THOMAS,Thomas TCapt kia 23-8-17 13WelshR p127 CR Belgium23

THOMAS,Thomas Oliver T2Lt kia 10/12-7-16 17RWFus p99 MR21

THOMAS,Trevor Sanby Lt kia 7-4-18 5WelchR p230 CR France804

THOMAS,Tudor T2Lt kia 25-11-17 19RWFus p99 MR17

THOMAS,Walter Edward T2Lt kia 21-9-18 RSuss att16Bn p120 CR France212

THOMAS,Walter Joseph Charles T2Lt dow 22-4-17 11RLancs p59 CR France164

THOMAS,Walter Saunders TCapt ded 15-9-17 NumbF att11GarBn p63 CR Europe1

THOMAS,Wilfred Patrick Otto T2Lt kia 1-7-16 9Y&L p159 CR France246,Wilfrid

THOMAS,William.MM.T2Lt ded 7-11-18 1/2 att1/5ELancs p111 CR France658

THOMAS,William Burton Lt kia 24-10-18 7Worc p225 CR France612

THOMAS,William Edgar.DSO.MC.TMajALtCol kia 20-10-18 7EYorks attBordR p85 CR France1476

THOMAS,William Eric 2Lt kia 31-7-17 118MGC p186 MR29

THOMAS,William Hope 2Lt kia 11-4-18 1Leics attX6TMB p88 MR20,21-3-18

THOMAS,William Humphrey.MC&Bar.MID Capt dow 28-11-17 1/1BerksYeo p203 CR Egypt2

THOMAS,William Norman 2Lt kia 8-4-16 GL KSLI att27RFC p4&191 CR France68,N.W.

THOMAS,William Stanley Lt kia 15-10-16 4 att11Ess p232 MR21

THOMAS-O'DONEL,George O'Donel Frederick.MC.MIDx2 Capt&Adjt kia 16-6-15 4RFus p70 MR29

THOMASIN,Arthur Lt drd 31-12-17 RIM p283 CR Egypt1

THOMASON,Herbert James Bateman T2Lt kia 26-9-17 1/2Leics p88 CR Belgium130

THOMASSET,Gurden Theodore Lt kia 25-9-15 20Lond p251 CR France526

THOMLINSON,John Robert T2Lt kia 8-8-18 4RRofCav att2DragGds p23 CR France526

THOMPSON,A.D.Lt kia 9-3-15 4KAR p268 CR EAfrica12 &CR Tanzania1 Ex DragGds

THOMPSON,Adam Howie 2Lt 7-9-18 4GordH att191RAF CR Hunts90

THOMPSON,Albert Martin T2Lt kia 21-12-15 RFus att1/15Lond p70 MR19

THOMPSON,Alberto Charles.DSO.Maj ded 30-7-19 RDubF p266 CR Lincs69

THOMPSON,Alfred Mussali T2Lt ded PoW 31-7-17 17LancF p94 CR France127,Mussalli dow 3Bn

THOMPSON,Andrew William T2Lt kia 30-5-17 9NStaffs p158 MR20

THOMPSON,Arnold Bosanquet Capt dow 25-12-15 RAMC 1/3ELancsFA p254 CR Gallipoli1

THOMPSON,Arnold Edward Lt 20-9-17 4BrWIndR att26RFus MR29

THOMPSON,Arthur TCapt kia 1-7-16 24NumbF p63 CR France393

THOMPSON,Arthur 2Lt kia 23-10-17 24NumbF attLincs p63 MR30

THOMPSON,Arthur Ernest T2Lt kia 3-9-16 12Lpool p73 MR21

THOMPSON,Arthur George T2Lt kia 2-6-16 14RWFus p99 CR France705

THOMPSON,Arthur Herbert TLtACapt kia 25-9-16 12 att10YLI p144 MR21

THOMPSON,Arthur Herbert 2Lt kia 1-10-16 17Lond D'Coy p250 CR France385

THOMPSON,Aubrey Lloyd Sinclair.MC.LtACapt ded 14-11-17 1Lpool p73

THOMPSON,Brian Wildman-Osborne Capt kia 10-8-15 6LNLancs A'Coy p136 MR4

THOMPSON,C.C.Capt 8-4-19 9Dev CR Staffs84

THOMPSON,Cecil Cuthbert Capt kia 14-7-16 2 att4RInniskF p105 CR France393

THOMPSON,Cecil Victor.MID T2Lt kia 6-2-17 8 att6ELancs p111 MR38

THOMPSON,Cecil William 2Lt dow 6-5-17 3/6LancF att63MGC p187&221 CR France40

THOMPSON,Charles Henry T2Lt kia 3-6-16 2DLI p161 CR Belgium73

THOMPSON,Charles Milburn 2Lt kia 26-8-17 3 att24/27NumbF p63 CR France1461

THOMPSON,Charles John McKinnon Lt dow 27-3-16 1NumbF p63 MR29

THOMPSON,Charles William 2Lt kia 29-6-18 3RWSurr att1EKent p56 CR Belgium3

THOMPSON,Conway Bennett TCapt ded 23-5-16 14Mddx p148 CR Sussex111

THOMPSON,Cyril T2Lt kia 1-6-18 20 att18LancF p94 CR France232

THOMPSON,Cyril James Ockelford Lt dow 25-12-17 18Lond p250 CR Palestine3

THOMPSON,Douglas Blaxland Lt kia 24-10-19 RFA att47RAF p262 CR Asia81

THOMPSON,Edward Homer Boxwell TLt drd 13-8-15 9SomLI attHamps p80 MR4

THOMPSON,Edward James Vibart Collingwood 2Lt dow 10-9-14 3RWFus p99

THOMPSON,Edward Medforth Lt kia 26-2-16 5Yorks p220 CR Belgium5,22-2-16

THOMPSON,Elizabeth Prob kia 1-10-17 TFNS p272

THOMPSON,Ellis T2Lt kia 18-5-17 18DLI D'Coy Ex 4NumbF p161 MR20

THOMPSON,Ernest Edward 2Lt dow 16-10-18 RGA 228SB p42 CR France1392

THOMPSON,Fendall Powney 2Lt kia 1-7-16 1Hamps p121 CR France643

THOMPSON,Francis Clement Lt dow 3-10-17 B59RFA p36 CR Belgium16

THOMPSON,Frank Arthur 2Lt dow 17-8-18 4SfthH p241 CR Surrey76

THOMPSON,Frank Dickinson 2Lt kia 13-1-17 15Lond att17KRRC p249 CR Belgium73

THOMPSON,Frank Samuel Capt kia 23-3-18 17Lond p250 MR20

THOMPSON,Frederic George T2Lt kia 10-4-17 7 att6Beds p87 MR20

THOMPSON,Frederick Charles Maj kia 2-7-16 1/5WYorks p218 MR21

THOMPSON,Frederick Vivian.DSO.MajTLtCol dow 14-10-17 RE att9Ess p48 CR France113

THOMPSON,Geoffrey 2Lt kia 3-9-16 1ARO 2S&M attRE 179TC p283 CR France430

THOMPSON,George Lt 16-1-15 RGA 2HB CR Devon2

THOMPSON,George Cyril 2Lt dow 24-10-15 6LancF p221 CR Gallipoli1

THOMPSON,George Eric T2Lt kia 3-9-16 12Lpool p73 MR21

THOMPSON,George Masterman Lt kia 22-8-14 1RScots attGoldCoastR p55&202 CR WAfrica5

THOMPSON,George Samuel Rodie 2Lt kia 14-9-14 2KRRC p152 MR15

THOMPSON,Gerald Pittis Newman Lt kia 4-5-18 1 att8RDubF p177 CR France353

THOMPSON,Gilbert Capt&Adjt kia 24-2-15 ConnRgrs att13Lond p172 CR France707

THOMPSON,Harold 2Lt kia 9-5-17 3 att1Nhampt p138 MR22

THOMPSON,Harold.DSO.TLtCol dow 22-4-17 1 att1/4RScotF p95 CR Egypt2

THOMPSON,Harold T2Lt kia 29-9-18 EKent p58 CR France212

THOMPSON,Harold Blundell Lt kia 2-10-17 RH&FA Staff Lt HQ 29Div Art p36 CR Belgium12

THOMPSON,Harold Eustace 2Lt dow 7-10-16 RFA 23Div X22TMB p36 CR France177

THOMPSON,Harold Francis TCapt kia 12-7-16 9 att12RB p180 CR Belgium5

THOMPSON,Harold Victor 2Lt kia 26-9-17 GL &29RFC p14 MR20

THOMPSON,Hector 2Lt dow PoW 18-9-16 RFC p4 CR France439

THOMPSON,Henry 2Lt 11-6-18 103RAF MR20

THOMPSON,Henry Cedric St.John.DSO.LtACapt dow 30-11-17 2CldGds p51 CR France439,1-12-17

THOMPSON,Henry Herbert Capt 2-1-18 ArmyPayDept Mid CR Hamps1

THOMPSON,Henry Norman 2Lt kia 22-3-18 9 att12RInniskF p105 MR27

THOMPSON,Herbert.MID Capt kia 28-3-18 7DLI p239 CR France700

THOMPSON,Herbert Balfe TCapt kia 18-9-16 Lincs p76 CR France251

THOMPSON,Herbert Henry Capt ded 2-1-18 ArmyPayDept p268

THOMPSON,Herbert Richard TLt ded 3-5-18 Beds 2GarBn p87 MR43,Capt

THOMPSON,Herbert William 2Lt kia 1-7-16 10 att11ELancs p111 MR21

THOMPSON,Horace Brockbank.MC.2Lt kia 24-4-17 7RBerks p140 MR37

THOMPSON,Hubert Roberts 2Lt dow 30-6-18 RGA 99SB p42 CR France31

THOMPSON,Ivan Frank Ross LtCol kia 26-1-17 1A Cmdg26Punjabis p283 CR Iraq5

THOMPSON,J.TLt kia 11-3-17 GL &45RFC p14 CR Belgium11

THOMPSON,J.Capt 20-11-20 Manch CR Ireland33

THOMPSON,James Ambrose 2Lt kia 18-10-16 3 att2Wilts p153 MR21

THOMPSON,James Reginald Walter T2Lt dow 22-3-18 RFC p17 MR20

THOMPSON,James William 2Lt dow 8-8-18 12/13NumbF CR France145

THOMPSON,John.DCM.Lt kia 16-10-16 GL &RFC p4&191 CR France245

THOMPSON,John Cecil Caster 2Lt kia 25-1-15 att1ScotsGds p52 MR22

THOMPSON,John Crawford 2Lt kia 21-3-18 5 att1RIrRif p170 MR27

THOMPSON,John Henry Louis Lt dow 17-9-14 WRid p116 CR Belgium201

THOMPSON,John Oscar 2Lt dow 9-8-16 1/5SLancs p230 MR21

THOMPSON,John Wycliffe 2Lt 5-7-18 7DragGds CR Essex132

THOMPSON,Jonah George 2Lt kld 19-5-17 RFC p14 CR C'land&W'land98

THOMPSON,Joseph.MC.TLtACapt kia 25-10-18 121RFA p36 CR France1391

THOMPSON,J.W.2Lt dow 8-8-18 12/13NumbF p63

THOMPSON,Leslie Northcote 2Lt kia 2-12-17 1/5Lond p246 MR17

THOMPSON,Lloyd Maurice 2Lt kia 25-1-17 7NStaffs p158 CR Iraq9

THOMPSON,M.H.2Lt dow 28-11-14 RWKent p142 CR Hamps173,29-11-14

THOMPSON,Matthew Arnold 2Lt kia 21-3-18 3 att2NumbF p63 MR27

THOMPSON,Morice Bell TLt kia 3-5-17 8MGC p186 MR20

THOMPSON,N.2Lt 5-8-16 17DLI CR France430

THOMPSON,Neville Rudd Lt kia 5-9-15 21Lancers p23 MR43

THOMPSON,Offley Charles Wycliffe Lt kia 20-9-14 1WYorks p83 MR15

THOMPSON,Patrick Stapler.MC.Lt kia 27-4-18 RE 466FC p210 CR France109

THOMPSON,Percy Laughorn T2Lt kia 16-6-17 14DLI p161 CR France115,Langhorn 12-6-17

THOMPSON,Peter Cleasby Lt ded 4-3-19 SL 1NigeriaR p201&202 CR WAfrica41

THOMPSON,Peter Lettice TLt kia 8-8-18 8NStaffs Res p158 CR France33,THOMSON 2Lt

THOMPSON,Philip Capt kia 23-3-18 22RFC p17 CR France245

THOMPSON,Philip Aloysius Xavier Murray 2Lt kia 21-8-15 3 att1RInnisF p105 MR4

THOMPSON,Reginald TLt kia 23-10-16 2ELancs att7Bn p111 MR21

THOMPSON,Reginald Paul 2Lt dow 9-8-16 3SomLI p80 CR Belgium11,1Bn

THOMPSON,Richard Lt dow 20-10-17 2/4ELancs p226 CR France64

THOMPSON,Richard Henry Vaughan.MID TCapt kia 26-9-16 11RFus p70 CR France702 see VAUGHAN THOMPSON,R.H.

THOMPSON,Richard Seward 2Lt kia 16-1-17 18Lond att2/2Lond p250 MR20,16-7-17

THOMPSON,Robert.MC.2Lt kia 26-10-17 7NumbF p214 MR30

THOMPSON,Robert Ellerton 2Lt 1-10-18 80RAF MR20

THOMPSON,Robert Lloyd.MC.LtAMaj kia 1-12-17 C173RFA p36&259 CR France530

THOMPSON,Roger Eykyn Capt kia 12-4-18 15 att2Hamps p203 MR32

THOMPSON,Ronald Fawcett Carrier 2Lt kia 11-9-16 GrenGds SR att4Bn p50 CR France294,TOMPSON Lt

THOMPSON,Ronald William 2Lt kia 11-4-18 1Mon p244 MR20

THOMPSON,Ross Col 5-12-19 RE att2S&M MR66

THOMPSON,Samuel Frederick Henry.MC.DFC.Capt 27-9-18 22RAF MR20

THOMPSON,Stanley TCapt kia 15-9-16 15Hamps p121 CR France188

THOMPSON,Sydney Richmond 2Lt 30-5-20 NumbF CR Durham19

THOMPSON,Thomas John Chichester Conyngham.DSO.Capt kia 24-3-18 4RIrF att2RIrRif p171 MR27

THOMPSON,Walter Capt kia 6-8-15 17DLI att6Manch p161 MR4

THOMPSON,Walter Albert 2Lt ded 8-9-17 10ELancs p111 CR Surrey150

THOMPSON,Walter Lincoln 2Lt kia 9-10-17 3 att2Ess p132 MR30

THOMPSON,Walton Downing Lt dow 2-9-18 3RWFus att1/6HLI p99 CR France145

THOMPSON,Warren Stanley Capt ded 2-9-19 RAVC CR Canada99 p268

THOMPSON,Wilfred Albert 2Lt dow 21-8-17 1/5Lincs p220 CR France80,24-8-17

THOMPSON,Wilfred Bernard T2Lt kia 8-10-18 LNLancs att1/4Bn p136 MR16 att5Bn

THOMPSON,Wilfred John 2Lt kia 31-7-17 7 att10Ess p232 CR Belgium310

THOMPSON,Wilfred Taylor TLt kia 26-9-15 14DLI p161 MR19

THOMPSON,William Frank TLt dow 1-1-16 RAMC 99FA p198 CR France80

THOMPSON,William George Lt kia 14-7-17 5Suff attRFC p19&217 CR France245,Capt

THOMPSON,William John T2Lt kia 26-3-18 6RInniskF p105 CR Palestine3

THOMPSON,W.S.Lt 16-4-20 2GurkhaRif CR Devon33

THOMPSON-HOPPER,James,MC.TLt kia 30-6-17 20DLI p161 CR Belgium137

THOMPSON-McLAUGHLIN,Lee 2Lt kld 19-4-17 4WYorks &RFC p14&83,ded

THOMPSON-SMITH,Kingsley 2Lt kia 23-3-18 11RWKent p142 MR20

THOMSON,Adam 2Lt kia 17-5-18 1/4RLancs p213 CR France106

THOMSON,Alan Graham Lt kia 26-9-17 7RScots p211 MR30

THOMSON,Alexander T2Lt dow 21-4-16 10SfthH p165 CR Iraq5,22-4-16

THOMSON,Alexander Lt kia 22-7-19 IA 3/9BhopalInf attJindInf p283 MR43

THOMSON,Alexander Henry Gouger.DSO.LtCol ded 2-8-18 IA 30Punjabis p283 MR66

THOMSON,Alfred Maurice.MID Capt kia 7-7-16 RAMC att7RSuss p198 MR21

THOMSON,A.L.C.MC.Capt 14-11-17 Lpool CR Hereford/W182

THOMSON,Archibald Walton TLt kia 3-5-17 12RScots p55 MR20,Walter

THOMSON,Arthur Stewart 2Lt dow 15-9-16 7Lond p247 MR21

THOMSON,Arthur Yalden Graham.MC&Bar.Capt kia 30-11-17 CamH attStaff p168 CR France1182

THOMSON,Charles.MC&Bar.Capt kia 2-9-18 7 att2ELancs p111 CR France184,1-9-18

THOMSON,Cyril Ground.MC.Capt kld 22-9-18 WSomYeo att12SomLI p205 CR France1495

THOMSON,David.MC.2Lt mbk 26-11-17 14HLI p257 MR17

THOMSON,David 2Lt ded 1-5-19 9RB p255 CR Notts106

THOMSON,Donald Godrid Campbell Lt kia 31-10-14 2Beds p87 MR29

THOMSON,Douglas Gordon 2Lt kia 30-11-17 10RB p180 MR17

THOMSON,Edmund Peel Maj kia 21-12-14 RMunstF attRIrReg p176 MR22

THOMSON,Edward B.Lt 17-4-20 116/26RFA MR66

THOMSON,Elizabeth Miss kia 30-9-17 VAD BRCS att58GH p200 CR France134

THOMSON,Elizabeth Robertson Sister ded 26-10-18 QAIMNS CR Scot249

THOMSON,Eric James Lt kia 28-6-15 7RScots p211 MR4

THOMSON,Ernest Anderson T2Lt kia 6-11-17 14BlkW p129 CR Palestine1

THOMSON,Francis Wishart 2Lt kia 28-6-15 7RScots C'Coy p211 MR4

THOMSON,Frederick Stanley Capt kia 1-7-16 14Lond att69MGC p187&249 MR21

THOMSON,George 2Lt kia 11-9-16 9A&SH p244 CR France294

THOMSON,George Alastair St.Clair Capt dow 21-7-16 3 att2A&SH p174 CR France23,Sinclair

THOMSON,George Burrell Lt dow 12-7-17 Nhampt p138 MR31

THOMSON,George Ewan Christian 2Lt kia 18-11-17 3 att1BlkW p129 MR30,19-11-17

THOMSON,George Frederick Maynard T2Lt dow 19-5-17 11Lpool p73 CR France214

THOMSON,George Vallance Bruce 2Lt kia 22-3-18 10 att15RScots p212 MR20

THOMSON,Haldane Lt kia 4-6-15 12ScotRif att1KOSB p104 CR Gallipoli2

THOMSON,Henry George Allen Maj dow 28-3-17 RWar Staff 15Div p66 CR France255

THOMSON,Henry Thomas TLt dow 26-9-15 7SStaffs p123 CR Lond4

THOMSON,James TCapt kia 25-9-15 10HLI p164 CR France114

THOMSON,James Capt kia 31-8-17 5BordR p228

THOMSON,James Capt&Adjt 31-10-17 1BordR CR Belgium13

THOMSON,James.MID Maj ded 26-11-17 RGA 130SB p42 CR Greece2

THOMSON,James Thomson HonMaj&QM ded 10-3-18 2NumbF p262 CR Numb7

THOMSON,James 2Lt kia 22-8-18 4GordH p242 CR France745

THOMSON,James Albert Raymond.DSO.LtCol kia 27-5-18 5Yorks p220 CR France1329

THOMSON,James Pringle TLt dow 15-8-16 6CamH p168 CR France44

THOMSON,James Scott Capt kia 5-5-17 14Lond A'Coy p249 CR France531

THOMSON,James Stein T2Lt kia 22-7-18 1/2WRid att1/7LancF p116 CR France5

THOMSON,James Walter Stewart Lt kia 12-4-18 4GordH att154TMB p241 MR19

THOMSON.J.H.2Lt 9-10-18 5A&SH &107RAF CR Belgium205

THOMSON,John 2Lt kia 18-6-17 5Lpool p215 CR Belgium10,17-6-17

THOMSON,John Lt 27-10-18 CanadaEngrs &N'Flt RAF MR20

THOMSON,John Lt ded 25-2-19 RE &RAF p255 CR Scot115

THOMSON,John Morrison Lt accdrd 26-3-21 1/3KAR CR SAfrica53

THOMSON,John Murray 2Lt kia 21-9-18 4RScots p211 CR France1496

THOMSON,John William Lt ded 4-2-19 RGA att55FdSurvey RE p262 CR Scot274

THOMSON,Kenneth Clarke.MID Lt dow 31-12-14 2RScotF p95 CR France345

THOMSON,Kenneth Douglas T2Lt kia 18-7-16 10A&SH p174 CR France164

THOMSON,Kenneth Sinclair Lt kia 3-3-15 IA 21Cav att16 p283 CR Iraq6

THOMSON,Leslie Charles TLt kia 31-7-17 4Mddx p148 MR29

THOMSON,Minnie Bailey SNurse 18-9-14 TFNS att2GH

THOMSON,Peter McLellan TMaj kia 24-12-15 5HLI p240 CR Gallipoli3

THOMSON,Peter Walls 2Lt kia 24-7-16 RGA 109SB p209 CR France397

THOMSON,Reginald Gresham.MC.MID LtACapt dow 18-9-18 1KSLI A'Coy p145&259 CR France327

THOMSON,Richard Edward John Lt kia 19-5-15 IA 15Sikhs p283 CR France924

THOMSON,Robert Lt dow 20-9-19 10RScots p256 CR Scot247,2Bn

THOMSON,Robert Thoresby 2Lt kia 8-6-17 7Mddx att4Lincs p235 MR20

THOMSON,Ronald T2Lt dow 27-1-17 RE 185TC p48 CR France1

THOMSON,Rowley Stuart Lt ded 1-11-20 IARO attIDForce p283

THOMSON,Samuel Andrew 2Lt 5-9-18 60RAF MR20

THOMSON,Samuel Pestell Donald Lt kld 13-5-15 1/1LeicsYeo p204 MR29 &CR Belgium453

THOMSON,Spencer.MC.TLt kia 24-4-17 14 att2RFus p70 MR20

THOMSON,Stewart Armour Lt dow 24-9-18 SNottsHuss att100MGC Inf p187&205 CR France194

THOMSON,Sydney James Kerr.MID 2Lt dow 12-10-15 3 att1RScotF p95 CR France64

THOMSON,Thomas Lt kia 25-4-17 7A&SH &RFC p19&243 CR France421

THOMSON,Walter Halton 2Lt kia 3-7-16 3HLI p164 CR France293

THOMSON,Wardlaw Ivor T2Lt kld 6-6-17 GL &RFC 27ResSqn p14 CR Lond3

THOMSON,Wilfrid Burrell.MC.Capt mbk 25-3-17 2Dors p257 MR38

THOMSON,William.MC.T2Lt dow 12-4-18 15HLI p164 CR France169

THOMSON,William Lt dow 26-8-18 4 att2KOSB p223 CR France84

THOMSON,William James 2Lt dow 18-11-16 3 att1CamH p168 CR France177

THOMSON,William Robinson Ketchen 2Lt kia 16-10-17 RGA 23HB p42

THONEMANN,Emil Howard 2Lt kia 3-5-17 RFA 13Bty 17Bde p36 MR20

THORBURN,Christopher Cowan 2LtTLt kia 14-6-17 1GordH p167 MR20

THORBURN,Edward Francis Capt kia 23-3-15 12RScots p55 MR27

THORBURN,Edward Francis Lt kia 10-6-15 6Manch p236 MR4

THORBURN,James Capt kia 11-2-17 RGA attRFC p19&209 CR France924

THORBURN,James Walker 2Lt dow 12-3-17 6CamH p168 CR France158

THORBURN,John Morgan TCapt dow 7-8-17 32RFus p70 CR France139

THORBURN,Thomas Orr Lt kia 13-4-18 6ScotRif p224 CR France324

THORBURN,V.TallyClk 16-10-17 S&T Cps CR Iraq6

THORBURN,Walter Ernest.TD.Capt ded 22-1-19 8RScots p256 CR Scot671

THORBURN BROWN,Thomas Elliot Lt dow 20-9-18 3KOSB CR France512

THORBY,Charles Frederick 2Lt kia 30-3-18 11/612NZBn ImpCamelCps MR34

THORLAND,V.S.T2Lt ded 22-7-18 RE 7CpsHQ p262 CR France134,Lt

THORLEY,Gordon Lt dow 7-11-18 1/10Manch p237 CR France929 &CR France955

THORLEY,Horace William 2Lt dow 8-10-18 17Lancers p23 CR France652,8-8-18

THORLEY,William Bowers T2Lt dow 20-4-18 8NStaffs p158 CR France64

THORMAN,Alan Marshall 2Lt kia 1-7-16 1/2Lond p245 MR21

THORMER,Harry T2Lt kld 30-12-17 90MGC p186

THORN,Dudley Oswald Lt kia 7-8-18 5Suff att2/4Berks p217 CR France346

THORN,Harold Lewis 2Lt kia 15-6-17 20Lond p251 CR France581

THORN,Humphrey 2Lt dow 13-10-16 3 att7Norf p74 CR France833

THORN-DRURY,J.G.Lt 12-3-20 1EKent CR Kent37

THORNALLAY,Allatt Barber 2Lt kia 1-7-17 6SStaffs p229 CR France662,THORNALLEY 2/5Bn

THORNBACK,Leonard Thomas Lt ded 2-5-18 29MGC p266 CR France24

THORNDIKE,Francis Herbert Lt dow 17-8-17 LincsYeo att11RFC p19&204 CR France113

THORNE,Charles Everard.MC.T2Lt dow 16-8-17 RE 150FC p48&258 CR Belgium8

THORNE,Cornelius TCapt kia 30-9-16 8ESurr p113 MR21

THORNE,Foster Newton MajTLtCol kia 18-4-17 1RSuss Cmdg6LNLancs p120 MR38

THORNE,Guy Stafford 2LtTCapt ded 18-3-17 13RFC p14 MR20

THORNE,Harold Underhill Hatton ALtCol kia 9-4-17 4Berks att12RScots p234 CR France97

THORNE,Henry Cyril TLt kia 27-6-16 1RBerks p140 CR France161

THORNE,John Parry Lt kia 1-7-16 5SStaffs p229 MR21

THORNE,Marlborough 2Lt kia 28-9-15 8ESurr D'Coy p113 CR France189,27-9-15

THORNE,Norman John 2Lt 12-5-17 8Hamps att52MGC CR France97

THORNE,Sigmund Alexander Oscar T2Lt ded 22-12-16 17WYorks CR Sussex111 p263

THORNE,Sydney Charles 2Lt kia 24-4-17 10Dev p77 MR37

THORNE,Thomas Bezly Houghton LtCol kia 21-3-18 2/6NStaffs p238 CR France690,Bezley

THORNE,Thomas Fleetwood Joseph Nicol Capt kia 27-9-15 4GrenGds p50 MR19

THORNE,William Anthony Laroque Capt ded 7-8-18 2RLancs p59 CR Greece4

THORNELY,Maurice T2Lt kld 3-12-16 Nhants &RFC p4&138 CR Yorks178

THORNER,H.A.M 2Lt 30-12-17 90MGC CR Belgium19

THORNHILL,Charles Massy.DSO.MC.Maj ded 19-6-19 IA 24Punjabis attStaff p283 MR67

THORNHILL,Geoffrey Holland Lt ded 10-5-17 3RWar att3LabCps p66 CR Herts84

THORNHILL,George Robert Lt kia 22-10-14 1EKent p58 MR32

THORNHILL,Hubert Burrington LtACapt ded 25-3-19 1Dev &TMB att2RWKent p77 CR Iraq6

THORNHILL,John Evelyn.DSO.BtLtCol ded 2-10-18 SfthH attStaff p165 CR Europe23

THORNHILL,William Ewart T2Lt kia 4-10-17 1/2ELancs p111 MR30

THORNILEY,Percy Arthur Henry.MC.TCapt kia 11-1-17 21Manch p156 CR France221

THORNLEY,Arthur Lincoln TLt ded 12-4-16 RAMC p198 CR Lancs256

THORNLEY,Henry TLt dow 19-12-16 11Manch p156 CR France339

THORNLEY,John Dales.MC.T2Lt kia 24-10-18 8 att6EKent p58 CR France1147,25-10-18

THORNLEY,Reginald Tom Lt kia 1-10-18 1/5LNLancs p234 MR16

THORNS,Francis Joseph T2Lt dow 31-5-16 5RBerks p140 CR France178

THORNSBY,Harold Stansfield T2Lt kia 24-8-18 10WYorks Ex 12Y&L p83 MR16

THORNTON,Claude Arthur Muir 2Lt kia 27-5-18 8WYorks att5DLI p219 CR France1753,Lt 7Bn

THORNTON,Cyril T2Lt kld 5-10-17 GL &RFC p14 CRWar7

THORNTON,Douglas Saville 2Lt kia 1-10-16 11N&D p135 MR21

THORNTON,Francis Arthur TCapt ded 18-11-17 RE 171TC p49 CR Belgium18

THORNTON,Frank T2Lt kia 1-7-16 7EYorks C'Coy p85 CR France373

THORNTON,Frank Cecil T2Lt kld 15-7-16 11Leics p88 CR Belgium1

THORNTON,Frederick Edward Maj kia 25-3-17 IA 105MahrattaLI p283 MR38

THORNTON,George Muir TCapt kia 22-8-17 8SfthH p165 MR30

THORNTON,George Rowland Hart 2Lt kia 9-4-18 RGA 16HB p42 MR19

THORNTON,Godfrey St.Leger.DSO.Maj ded 4-2-18 RFA p36 CR Notts84

THORNTON,Harold James 2Lt ded 25-9-17 RFC p14 MR40,23-9-17

THORNTON,Hedley Thomas 2Lt ded 25-1-16 5RWKent p235 CR Kent82

THORNTON,Herbert Boucher 2Lt kia 9-7-17 9Lond attMGC p187&248 CR Belgium77

THORNTON,James 2Lt kld 9-11-16 RScots &RFC p4&55 CR Scot279

THORNTON,John McLaren TLt kia 20-1-16 RE p49 MR32

THORNTON,John William T2Lt dow 27-3-18 2/4Y&L p159 CR France225

THORNTON,Joseph Henry Banks T2Lt kia 22-9-18 LabCps att23LancF p189 CR France263

THORNTON,Leonard Neville 2Lt kia 22-7-16 11 att10Glouc p107 MR21

THORNTON,Leslie Irvine Lumsden 2Lt kia 9-9-15 IARO att16Cav p283 CR Asia82

THORNTON,Noel Shipley.DSO.MC.LtTMaj dow 10-4-18 6 att7RB p180 CR France52

THORNTON,Reginald George 2Lt kia 5-9-17 20Lond p251 MR29

THORNTON,Robert West.MID Lt kia 16-6-15 4RFus p70 MR29

THORNTON,Sidney Percy TCapt dow 5-12-16 11Leics A'Coy p88 CR France80

THORNTON,Stanislaw Bonaventure T2Lt kia 29-7-16 2SStaffs p123 MR21,Stanislaus 28-7-16

THORNTON,Victor Hubert TCapt kia 24-10-18 GL 9NumbF p191 CR France739

THORNTON,Wilfred Thomas 2Lt kia 30-7-16 7BlkW p231 MR21

THORNTON-SMITH,Arthur Donald.DSO.MID TLtACapt kia 16-8-17 12KRRC p152 MR30

THORNTON-VARLEY,Charles Richard 2Lt dedacc 25-5-15 RGA p272 CR Yorks2

THORNYCROFT,Edward Gerald Mytton Lt kia 15-9-14 RLancs attKAR p59&202 CR EAfrica43,Capt 12-9-14

THORNYCROFT,John Ralph Mylton Capt kia 21-10-14 3 att1RWSurr p56 MR29

THOROGOOD,Edward Linford Lt kia 3-9-18 8LancF p221 CR France298

THOROWGOOD,Leslie Vernon TCapt kld 22-3-18 RFC p17 CR Wilts3

THOROWGOOD,Rowland William Theodore.MC.TLt kia 7-8-18 11RWar p66&259 CR France412,1Bn

THORP,Austin.CMG.DSO.LtCol kia 30-10-18 RGA att82RFA p42 CR France716

THORP,Edward Henry Courtenay LtACapt kia 21-8-18 1Dev p77 CR France798

THORP,Frederick Horace 2Lt dow 31-3-18 10Manch attRFC p20&237 CR France95,Lt

THORP,Henry Guy Hanwing 2Lt dow 13-3-15 3YLI p144 CR France284,Hanning

THORP,Henry Thomas TLt kia 21-2-18 RFC p17 CR Palestine3

THORP,John Eric 2Lt kia 3-5-17 7WRid &186LtTMB p228 CR France646

THORP,Leslie 2Lt kia 16-11-16 10RFus p70 MR21

THORP,Robert Oakley Vavasour.MC.2Lt kia 22-3-18 3NumbF att64TMB p63 CR France669,1Bn

THORP,Thomas Tudor 2Lt kia 16-8-17 D83RFA p36 CR Belgium125

THORP,Walter Twiss Lt kia 28-3-18 1/7Manch p237 CR France927,T.W.

THORPE,Albert Edward T2Lt ded 6-12-18 Yorks att11EYork p91 CR France134

THORPE,George Robert Capt dow 25-4-17 1HAC p206 CR France113

THORPE,Herbert Gordon.MC.2Lt mbk 24-3-18 1Lpool A'Coy p257 CR France307,Lt kia

THORPE,John Somerled.MC.Maj kia 15-9-16 ScotsGds att2Bn p52 CR France513

THORPE,Norman John 2Lt kia 12-5-17 8Hamps attMGC p187&229

THOULESS,Archibald Cecil T2Lt kia 26-4-16 10Norf &RFC p4&74 MR38,9Bn

THOYTS,Francis Gordon Grant Maj dow 26-8-14 1SomLI p80 MR15

THRELFALL,Herbert Edward 2LtTLt dow 4-11-17 266RFA p36 CR Palestine1

THRELFALL,John Alexander 2Lt dow 10-5-18 9Lpool p216 CR France100,Lt

THRESHER,Oswald Lt dow 2-10-18 RE p210 CR Palestine11

THRIFT,Sydney Henry 2Lt kia 15-7-16 10Ches p97 MR21

THRING,Ashton Edward 2Lt ded 9-2-17 D1RFA p209 CR Beds66

THROCKMORTON,Richard Courtenay Brabazon TLtCol kia 9-4-16 8RWFus Cmdg3Wilts p153 MR38,5Bn

THROSSELL,Horace Claude Sharman 2Lt kia 17-3-17 9Suff p79 CR France423

THRUPP,Maurice Lt kia 31-7-17 1GrenGds p50 CR Belgium106

THRUSTON,Bertie John.DSO.CaptTMaj ded 22-11-18 Lincs attWAfrR p76&202 CR WAfrica30

THUELL,William Johnson T2Lt kia 22-10-16 GL &RFC p4&191 MR20

THUILLIER,George Fleetwood.MC.LtACapt kia 26-3-18 2Dev p77 CR France1472

THUNDER,Michael Hubert Francis 2Lt kia 23-9-16 RFC p4 CR Kent29,24-9-16

THURBURN,Augustus Edward Charlie Sedgwick 2LtACapt kia 28-5-17 9Ess att3KRRC p132 CR Greece9 A.E.S.C.

THURBURN,Eric James Ptolemy 2Lt kia 9-4-17 3ScotRif att16RScots p104 MR20,Erik

THURGAR,Ralph William.MC.Capt kia 19-4-17 1/4Norf p216 CR Palestine8

THURGOOD,Ernest Fuller TCapt kia 31-5-18 16Ches p97 CR France1689

THURLOW,Arthur Geoffrey T2Lt dow 29-8-15 8WRid p116 CR Egypt3,Lt&Adjt

THURLOW,Geoffrey Robert Youngman 2LtTLt kia 23-4-17 13 att10N&D C'Coy p135 MR20

THURLOW,John Kennings 2Lt kia 24-4-18 10Lpool p216 MR19

THURNELL,William Cornelius Gibson 2Lt dow 16-9-16 7Lond p247 CR France177

THURSBY,Arthur Delves TCapt kia 15-2-15 KRRC p152 MR29

THURSTON,Arthur AssCommsy&Lt ded 29-7-16 IndOrdDept p283 CR Iraq6

THURSTON,Hugo Champneys.CB.CMG.Col ded 17-8-19 RAMC p267 CR Glouc190

THWAITES,Guy.DSO.Maj ded 30-5-17 RASC p194 MR34 &CR EAfrica116

THWAITES,Marmaduke LtTCapt kia 30-9-15 Yorks p91 MR19

THWAITES,Robert Capt dow 28-6-17 1/4ELancs p226 CR France755

THWAITES,Robert.MID TCapt kia 24-3-18 22DLI p161 MR27

THWAYTES,John 2Lt kia 18-3-17 BordR att4RFC p14&118 CR France614

THYNNE,Algernon Careret.DSO.LtCol kia 6-11-17 NDevYeo p203 CR palestine1

THYNNE,Lord Alexander George.DSO.LtCol kia 14-9-18 Cmdg6Wilts p206 CR France80

TIBBS,B.E.Lt ded 9-1-18 SL RE IWT p262 MR38

TIBBS,Robert Dunham Lt drd 30-12-15 IARO att39GarhwalRif p283 MR41

TIBBS,Thomas 2Lt kia 22-3-18 NumbF att1/4Bn p63 MR27

TICE,Ernest William T2Lt dow 1-8-17 17 att11RSuss p120 CR Belgium7,Wilfred

TICEHURST,Gordon Harry Lt kia 20-9-17 5Lond 2Bn p246 MR29

TICHBORNE,John Capt ded 6-4-20 RAMC CR Mddx48

TICHBORNE,Muriel Edith Elizabeth 24-10-18 VAD CR Hamps1

TICKLE,Andrew Brown Lt kia 14-7-17 9Lpool p216 CR Belgium10,1/8Bn

TICKLE,Ernest T2Lt ded 13-7-18 2SLancs p126 CR France806

TICKLE,Frederick Ralph TCapt ded 5-11-18 RAMC att7RB p267 CR Lancs164

TICKLE,Gordon Philip 2Lt dow 30-9-18 6Lond p247 CR France146

TICKNER,Thomas George TLt dow 1-9-18 8SLancs p126 CR France74

TIDD,Ernest George Capt kia 13-6-15 6HLI p240 MR4

TIDDY,Claude Julian 2Lt kia 11-8-18 1Dors p124 MR16

TIDDY,Hector Kingsley Portus T2Lt kia 26-7-17 GL &7RFC p14 CR Belgium18

TIDDY,Reginald John Elliott Lt kia 10-8-16 2/4 O&BLI p231 CR France1887

TIDMARSH,John Moriarty Lt ded 3-9-18 12WRid &RAF p116 CR Eire167,kld

TIDSWELL,Cecil Robert Capt kia 16-10-16 1Drags &RFC p4&21 CR France398

TIDSWELL,William Francis Howard Lt kia 31-10-16 88RFA p36 CR France251

TIDY,Percy Ernest 2Lt kia 24-4-17 12Hamps p121 MR37

TIERNAN,Edwin Lawrence 2Lt dow 29-9-16 C240RFA p36 CR France44

TIERNEY,Herbert Stanislaus 2Lt kia 9-4-16 8Ches p97 MR38

TIFFANY,Harry Waddington.MC.2Lt kia 15-11-16 12RFus p70 MR19

TIFFEN,Harold Vincent 2Lt kia 20-11-17 2/5LancF p221 MR21

TIGAR,Geoffrey Herbert T2Lt kia 13-10-17 6RBerks p140 MR30

TIGAR,Harold Walter Lt kia 9-5-15 3Mddx p148 MR29

TIGHE,James Patrick LtTCapt kia 15-7-16 2RIrReg p89 MR21

TIGHT,Arthur Sidney T2Lt kia 23-3-18 69MGC B'Coy p186 MR27

TILBROOK,Frank Calder Lt dow 10-4-18 7DLI attRE 231FC p239 CR France1094

TILBURY,Arthur TCapt drd 4-5-17 RAMC p198 CR Italy14

TILBURY,Augustus Capt kia 8-6-17 RFA p207 CR France614

TILBURY,Herbert Walter T2Lt kia 5-9-18 Lincs p76 CR France245

TILBURY,Robert William 2Lt ded 18-3-18 95RFC p17 CR Hamps7

TILDESLEY,Harold Vaughan 2Lt kia 14-3-17 1/5SStaffs p229 CR France281

TILEY,George Charles T2Lt kia 21-10-16 9LNLancs p136 CR France384

TILL,Henry T2Lt kia 4-10-17 1Gloucs p107 MR30

TILLARD,Arthur George Capt kia 20-10-14 3 att2Manch p156 MR22

TILLARD,Philip Algernon Capt kia 19-11-16 ShropYeo att8ESurr p205 MR21

TILLARD,Thomas Atkinson Lt kia 6-12-16 NorfYeo attRFC p20&204 CR France285

TILLETT,Albert Edward 2Lt dow 25-3-18 2Mddx p148 MR27

TILLETT,Alexander.DSO.MC.LtALtCol dow 3-12-17 2Dev p77 CR Belgium3

TILLETT,John Edward Lt kia 8-10-18 3 att1Lincs p76 CR France234

TILLETT,Reginald Alfred William 2Lt kia 24-3-17 GloucHuss attRFC p20&203 CR France120

TILLEY,Alan Herbert 2Lt dow 10-4-17 2/4 O&BLI p231 CR France610

TILLEY,Arnold Reid Capt kia 11-5-16 8ScotRif att16RFC p20&225 CR France680,TILLIE Reed

TILLEY,Frank Lewis Cdr 14-2-19 IndMilWksServ MR65

TILLEY,John TCapt kia 28-11-16 7Norf p74 CR France1182

TILLIE,Charles Gordon.MID LtTCapt dow 23-8-15 1RInniskF p105 MR24

TILLIE,John Archibald 2Lt kia 19-7-18 8BlkW p129 CR France324

TILLOTSON,John Lancelot.MID 2Lt kia 23-4-17 4Dors p229 CR France531

TILLY,Charles Wynn TLtCol kia 14-4-18 18DLI att15WYorks p161 MR32

TILLY,John,.MC.TCapt kia 8-6-18 8Yorks p91 CR Italy1

TILLYARD,Sidney Joseph T2Lt kia 2-3-16 35MGC Inf p186 CR France423,Sydney

TILLYER,Richard Bateson Blunt Lt kia 25-4-15 1RWar C'Coy p66 MR29

TILNEY,Leonard Arthur.MC.Maj kia 9-3-18 RHGds att40RFC p17&20 CR France924

TILSTON,John 2Lt kia 18-10-18 RGA 291SB p42 CR France1351,Jack

TILSTON,John Edward T2Lt kia 23-4-17 154MGC p186 MR20

TIMBERLAKE,Roy TLt kia 27-7-17 4Beds p87 CR France644,P

TIMMINS,Frank T2Lt dow 19-12-17 C265RFA p36 CR Palestine9,TIMMANS

TIMMINS,George Oswald T2Lt kia 23-10-18 Beds att1Nhants p86 CR France190

TIMMINS,William Benjamin.MID 2Lt dow 20-5-15 1SStaffs p123 CR France64,Lt

TIMMIS,Richard Sutton 2Lt dow 10-5-15 3KRRC p152 CR France284

TIMONY,Patrick Charles Laurence T2Lt kia 24-8-18 15HLI p164 CR France1170

TIMS,Frederick Maj ded 28-12-15 RAOC p198 CR Lond29

TIMSON,Percy Walter Johnson Lt 26-9-18 57RAF MR20

TINDAL,Archibald Arthur 2Lt kia 8-9-16 177RFA p36 CR France294

TINDAL,David 2Lt dow 18-7-16 11 att8BlkW p129 MR21

TINDALL,Alexander George T2Lt kia 8-10-18 att1/5GordH p167 CR France115

TINDALL,Eric Vickers 2Lt dow 12-9-14 4KRRC p152 CR France1107

TINDALL,Fanny Sister ded 15-1-18 QAIMNS p200 CR Iraq6

TINDALL,Howard Simson TLt kia 31-7-17 6RBerks p140 CR Belgium112

TINDALL,Lawrence.MM.2Lt kia 21-6-18 10WRid p116 CR Italy1,TINDILL

TINDALL,Louis Nicolas Lindsay.MC.Lt kia 27-5-18 2Dev p77 MR18

TINDALL,Richard Frederick 2Lt kia 25-9-15 3Lincs p76 MR32

TINDLE,Kirton 2Lt kia 26-3-18 1/7DLI p239 MR27

TINGLE,John 2Lt dow 16-6-18 23MGC p186 CR Italy11

TINKER,Alan Hirst Capt kia 28-3-18 1/7Manch p237 MR20

TINKLER,George Henry T2Lt kia 25-4-17 7SStaffs p123 MR20

TINKLEY,Horace Arthur 2Lt dow 1-4-18 C2/75RFA p36 CR France169

TINLEY,Gervase Francis Newport.CB.CMG.MIDx2 Col ded 18-2-18 IA BaseCommdtMarseilles p283 CR France1571 Ex 31Lancers

TINLEY,James 2LtACapt kia 20-7-16 1RScotF p95 CR France432

TINLING,George Evelyn.MC.LtACapt kia 4-10-17 1ELancs p111 MR30

TINN,Farquhar Gray Lt ded 6-11-16 5HLI p240 CR Scot508

TINNE,Stuart Christian Capt ded 1-3-18 1RWKent attRFC p261&265 CR Surrey110

TINNISWOOD,Alfred 2Lt kia 1-10-18 RE 412FC p210 CR France484,Lt

TIPLADY,Frank Ewart T2Lt dow 27-9-15 14Mddx att7Lond p148 CR France88,Lt 5Bn

TIPPET,Charles Henry TMaj kia 7-8-15 7RDubF p177 CR Gallipoli5

TIPPETT,Alexander Arnold 2Lt dow 19-8-15 2KSLI p145 CR France275

TIPPING,William 2Lt kia 8-8-16 1/8Lpool p216 MR21

TIPPING,Frank Blamphin Lt kia 19-8-17 RGA &56RFC p20&209 CR France363

TIPTAFT,William Rutherford 2LtTLt kia 21-9-17 62MGC Inf p186 CR Belgium102

TIPTON,Richard James Capt dow 12-3-18 RFA att40RFC p20&207 CR France12

TISDALL,Charles Arthur Maj kia 1-9-14 IrGds p53 CR France1108

TISDALL,Charles Henry T2Lt kia 13-2-16 9RSuss p120 CR Belgium72

TISDALL,Charles Richard.MC.2Lt kia 15-9-16 1IrGds p53 CR France394

TISDALL,John Theodore St.Clair 2Lt kia 8-8-16 1 att11Lpool p73 MR21

TISDALL,Michael Henry Capt kld 23-12-19 NSomYeo &RAF p272

TITCHENER,Leonard Raymond Lt kia 3-12-17 5RLancs att22RFC p20&213 CR France31

TITFORD,Claude Francis 2Lt dow 2-9-18 8 att1/9Lond p247 CR France833

TITJEN,Carsten Francis Henry Lt ded 12-9-16 14Manch p156 CR Sussex178,3Bn

TITLEY,Anthony Graham 2Lt kia 13-4-17 4 att10WYorks p83 CR France311

TITLEY,Richard Guy.MC.Capt dow 13-10-17 1/6Glouc p225 CR Belgium16

TIZZARD,George 2Lt kld 8-3-16 6Dev A'Coy p217 MR38

TOBIAS,Leslie Mark Capt ded 25-2-19 RWFus 2GarBn p99 CR Egypt5

TOBIN,Gerald Vere T2Lt ded 15-5-17 11Hamps p121&264 CR Lond9

TOBIN,Richard Patrick TCapt kia 15-8-15 7RDubF p177 MR4

TOBIN-WILLIS,John Galbraith 2Lt kia 17-8-17 RASC att7RFC p14&194 CR Belgium18

TOD,Alexander Revell.MC.Lt dow PoW 18-4-18 5ESurr p226 CR France651

TOD,Frederick Masefield Cockburn T2Lt kia 25-9-15 7KOSB p102 MR19

TOD,William Lennox TCapt dow 29-4-17 15RScots p55 CR France40

TODD,Alexander Findlater Capt dow 21-4-15 3Norf p74 MR29 CR Belgium151,1Bn

TODD,Alfred Guy Eric 2Lt kia 23-4-17 4ESurr att2Hamps p113 MR20

TODD,Alick.MC.Lt dow PoW 16-4-17 4DLI &18RFC p14&161 CR France429

TODD,Charles Bernard 2Lt kia 11-6-17 RGA 184SB p42 CR Belgium4

TODD,Charles Hatt T2Lt kia 12-10-17 att6RBerks p140 MR30

TODD,Charles Leslie Morgan 2Lt dow 4-8-16 4SLancs p230 CR France141

TODD,Chester William Maj kia 9-8-17 A1RFA p206 CR Belgium10

TODD,Frederick George T2Lt kia 12-2-18 2/3Glos attRFC p17&107 CR France1678

TODD,Harold George Winslow TLt kia 12-10-15 7Suff p79 MR21

TODD,Harry T2Lt ded 29-10-18 24MGC p186 CR France40

TODD,Herbert Stanley.MC&Bar.LtACapt kia 18-9-18 4 att8ESurr p113 CR France511

TODD,James Clark T2Lt kia 27-6-17 17HLI p164 CR Belgium173

TODD,James Farquar Capt mbk 30-10-14 IA 39CentIndHorse att2LifeGds p283

TODD,James William T2Lt kld 28-9-17 GL &RFC p14 CR Surrey15

TODD,John 2Lt dow 4-7-18 9HLI p241 CR France268,Lt

TODD,John George TCapt kia 1-7-16 23NumbF p63 CR France150

TODD,Oswald Erick Maj ded 10-7-16 IA 1/5GurkhaRif p283 MR67,Erik

TODD,Richard James Killingworth Lt kia 21-1-16 IA 93BurmaInf p283 CR Iraq5

TODD,Robert Victor.DCM.Lt kia 9-8-18 24 att7Lond p252 MR16

TODD,T.R.Maj 22-9-19 IndOrdDep MR67

TODD,Valentine Otto Capt kia 9-4-17 1RLancs p59 CR France777

TODD,William Capt dow 29-6-15 RGA 1/4MountainBde p209 MR4

TODD,William Drysdale 2Lt kia 15-9-16 6ScotRif att11A&SH p224 CR France453

TODD,William Henry Lt&QM ded 28-8-15 4Ess p232 CR Gallipoli27

TODD-NAYLOR,William Bryan T2Lt kia 24-8-16 8KRRC p152 CR France397

TODD-THORNTON,J.H.B.Maj ded 12-1-18 3NumbF GarBn p63 CR Sussex112

TODMAN,Charles Vincent Lt kia 3-8-18 10Lond att16RAF p248&258CR France95

TODRICK,Thomas.MID Capt kia 14-12-14 8RScots p211 CR France684

TOFTS,Charles Frank Lt kia 7-1-18 5ESurr &1KAR p226&268 CR EAfrica77

TOKELY,Reginald Cyrus 2Lt dow 23-12-16 2Ess p132 CR France105

TOLERTON,Lee TLt kia 15-8-15 6RIrFus p171 MR4

TOLHURST,Alfred Wilfred T2Lt kld 6-10-17 GL &RFC p14 CR Kent130

TOLHURST,Bernard Joseph Lt dow PoW 22-4-17 11WRid &11RFC p14&116 CR France421

TOLLEMACHE,Arthur Henry William 2Lt kia 19-7-16 RE &RFC p4&49,ded MR20

TOLLEMACHE,Bevil Douglas 2Lt kia 22-12-14 1CldGds p51 MR22

TOLLEMACHE,Horace Murray TLt kia 17-7-18 13Hamps p121 CR Belgium11,15Bn

TOLLEMACHE,John Eadred TLt kia 21-8-16 6 att8RWSurr p56 CR France394

TOLLEMACHE,Leo De Orellana Capt kia 1-11-14 1Lincs p76 MR29

TOLLEMACHE-TOLLEMACHE,L.S.D.O.Frandati-Filius Tollemache-Tollemache de Orellana Plantagenet Capt ded 20-2-17

TOLLER,Edward Northcote TCapt kia 20-7-16 20RFus p70 CR France432 [Leic p88 CR France177

TOLLER,George Reginald TLt ded 27-7-17 Lincs 1GarBn p76 CR Iraq8

TOLLER,Richard Arthur Lt ded 24-2-19 2WelchR attRAF p264 CR Lond4,27-2-19

TOLLITT,William Ernest Capt ded 15-5-19 IA 2/48Pnrs p283 MR65,W.G.18-5-19

TOLMIE,George Lester 2Lt dow 19-11-18 6Nhampt p138 CR Yorks11

TOLMIE,Robert 2Lt ktia 13-10-18 1/5SIthH p241 CR France271

TOLSON,George Henderson Lt dow 1-12-17 2/18Lond p250 CR Palestine3

TOLSON,Horace 2Lt kia 29-3-18 6RWar Ex RAMC 87FA p214 MR27

TOLSON,James Martin 2Lt dow 20-10-18 A74RFA p36 CR France319

TOLSON,Joseph Capt dow 28-10-17 1/6N&D p233 CR France98

TOLSON,Robert Huntries 2Lt kia 1-7-16 15WYorks p83 CR France742,Huntriss

TOMBAZIS,James Lyell.DSO.MC.2Lt kia 8-10-18 2N&D p135 CR France849

TOMBLIN,Harold Raymond Lt kia 10-7-16 3 att2Manch p156 MR21

TOMBLIN,James Douglas T2Lt dow 13-11-15 12/12MGC p186 CR Belgium11

TOMBLINGS,Eric Hunter Griffith TLt ded 21-1-16 RE p49&258 CR Yorks504,Honton

TOMBS,James Douglas T2Lt ded 18-2-16 7BordR p118 CR France134

TOMBS,Joseph Simpson McKenzie 2Lt dow 11-9-15 48RFA p36 CR Belgium11

TOMES,Geoffrey Capt kia 10-8-15 IA 53Sikhs att1/6GurkhaRif p283 MR4

TOMEY,Donald Stuart TLt kia 25-3-18 11EYorks p85 MR20

TOMEY,Wilfred T2Lt dow 9-10-18 1RBerks p140 CR France380

TOMKIES,Henry Lea 2Lt kia 25-4-17 RFC p14 MR20

TOMKINS,Albin George 2Lt kia 13-9-16 2IrGds p53 CR France294

TOMKINS,Charles Percy T2Lt dow 29-10-18 Mddx att1Lpool p148 CR Mddx16

TOMKINS,Frank Savell TLt kia 8-8-15 7Glouc p107 MR4 Savill

TOMKINS,Frederick Allen TCapt dow 14-7-16 RFA attTMB p36 CR France141,15-7-16

TOMKINS,Vigor TCapt kia 13-10-15 7ESurr p113 MR19

TOMKINS,William Henry Chap4Cl ded 28-9-18 RAChDept att7SStaffs p200 CR France647

TOMKINSON,C.W.Lt 19-10-18 14Ches CR Ches51

TOMKINSON,Percy Alexander 2Lt kia 4-10-18 6N&D p233 CR France441

TOMLIN,Charles Geoffrey Lt dow 9-7-16 22Lond p251 CR France12

TOMLIN,Harry Francis T2Lt kia 28-9-17 GL &20RFC p14 CR France285

TOMLIN,Reginald Arthur.MC.2Lt kia 1-9-18 1/22Lond p252 CR France785

TOMLINSON,Charles Valentine T2Lt kia 1-7-16 11N&D p135 CR France246

TOMLINSON,Charles William 2Lt kia 3-9-16 1/4WRid p227 MR21

TOMLINSON,Dan T2Lt kia 10-8-18 1Lpool p73 CR France266

TOMLINSON,David Mitchell.MID TMaj dow 13-5-16 13RScots p55 CR France80

TOMLINSON,Ernest 2Lt kia 5-9-18 4Lincs p217 CR France245,7Bn

TOMLINSON,Ferdinand Roger John 2Lt kia 26-10-14 SStaffs p123 MR29

TOMLINSON,Herbert Cecil 2Lt dow 21-3-18 RGA 39SB p42 CR Belgium3

TOMLINSON,Hugh.MC.Lt ded 2-4-17 57RFC p14 CR France924,Capt

TOMLINSON,James Ashworth T2Lt dow 22-11-15 13 att1LancF p94 CR Gallipoli4

TOMLINSON,James Freeman TLt kia 24-3-18 2HLI p164 MR20

TOMLINSON,Robert Henry T2Lt dow 19-7-16 18Lpool p73 CR France145

TOMLINSON,Thomas Harry 2Lt dow 23-7-16 1Dev p77 CR France390 &CR France399

TOMPKINS,Harold Arthur 2Lt dow 1-7-16 att1ELancs p111 MR21

TOMPSON,Alan Hawtree 2Lt kia 27-9-15 GrenGds SR att4Bn p50 MR19,Hawtin

TOMS,Arthur Woodland Lt kld 27-11-14 3Dev attScotRif p77 CR France768

TOMS,Horace James Henry T2Lt kia 9-4-17 11N&D p135 CR Belgium127

TOMS,Stanley Muir Lt dow 8-12-17 2/18Lond p250 CR Palestine3

TOMS,William Henry Capt kld 5-12-18 RAOC p198 CR Belgium400

TOMSON,James Wyndham.MID Capt kia 24-9-18 5Leic B'Coy p220 CR France699

TONG,George Lt kia 16-8-18 RE 422FC p210 CR France106,15-8-16

TONGE,Harry TLt ded 25-10-18 2NumbF GarBn p63 MR67

TONGE,John.MID LtCol dow 19-4-17 230RFA p206 CR France98

TONGE,John Richard TLt kia 16-12-17 15LancF p94 CR Belgium20

TONGE,Septimus TLtACapt ded 9-5-18 MGC p266 CR Wales537

TONGE,William Russell T2Lt kia 12-1-16 17Manch p156 MR21

TONGUE,Andrew Leslie 2Lt kia 28-5-18 C175RFA p36 CR France504

TONGUE,Claude Leslie T2Lt ded 26-10-18 Worc 1Res GarBn attLCB Depot p110 CR France34

TONGUE,John William Collis TCapt kia 25-9-15 10Glouc p107 CR France1723

TONGUE,Walter Edward Lt ded 1-5-18 RE p49 CR War10

TONKIN,Edith Mary Miss ded 14-10-18 VolAid BRCS att3GH p200 CR France13,13-10-18

TONKIN,Frederick Cuthbert.DSO.MC.LtTCapt dow 4-11-18 7EYorks p85 CR France1478

TONKING,David Wilson 2Lt dow 29-5-17 3DCLI att10RWar p115 CR France285

TONKS,Leslie Robert James 2Lt kia 11-4-18 4 att9SStaffs p123 MR32,9 att4Bn

TONKS,Samuel William Maj kia 13-10-15 RE p209 MR19

TONSON-RYE,John Reginald Capt ded 25-5-19 RASC MT p255 CR France1571

TOOGOOD,Henry Duncan.MC.T2Lt kia 21-3-18 9KRRC p152 MR27,Harry

TOOGOOD,Percival Frederick 2Lt dow 23-2-17 IARO att2/9GurkhaRif p283 MR38,T.F.24-2-17

TOOHEY,James Thomas T2Lt kia 18-1-17 6RIrReg p89 CR Belgium100

TOOK,Cyril Arthur 2Lt ded 14-8-19 12Suff p263 CR Suff2

TOOKE,Bernard TCapt kia 3-5-17 18WYorks p83 MR20

TOOLEY,Harold Augustus Rupert Lt mbk 20-12-14 RGLI attDCLI p257 MR22,att2Leic

TOOLIS,James Hollingworth Lt kia 1-7-16 2Lincs p76 MR21

TOOMEY,Archibald Roche T2Lt kia 10-8-15 6Leinst p175 CR Gallipoli18

TOON,Harold Phillips T2Lt kia 14-7-16 17 att15DLI p161 MR21

TOOTELL,Bernard 2Lt kia 23-6-17 7N&D att4RFC p20&233 CR Belgium11

TOOTILL,Edward Cecil T2Lt kia 22-8-17 10DLI C'Coy p162 MR30

TOOVEY,Arthur Wilfred TCapt ded 1-12-18 13Beds p87 CR Mddx25,30-11-18

TOOVEY,Kennedy St.Clair Hamilton 2Lt ded PoW 15-10-18 RLancs att166TMB p59 CR Germany3

TOPHAM,Albert Alfred T2Lt ded 7-12-18 GL attSARdCps p191 CR EAfrica36

TOPHAM,Alfred James Tudor 2LtACapt kia 26-9-17 3 att7KSLI p145 MR30

TOPHAM,Charles Henry 2Lt dow 21-10-16 RGA 115HB p42 CRFrance52

TOPHAM,Henry Augrave Cecil 2Lt dow 25-5-15 ULIA att1WelchR p283 CR France285,Angrave

TOPHAM,James Capt&Adjt kia 26-9-15 8Lincs p76 MR19

TOPHAM,Michael 2Lt kia 13-4-17 27RFC Ex 19RFus p14 MR20

TOPP,Richard William 2Lt dow 1-7-16 6 att11RInniskF p105 MR21

TOPPIN,Harry Stanley.MID Capt dow 13-9-14 1NumbF p63 MR15

TOPPIN,Sidney Miles.MC.Maj dow 27-9-17 RGA 151HB p42 CR Belgium11

TOPPING,Eric T2Lt dow 25-4-17 10Y&L p159 CR France113

TOPPING,J.2Lt kia 16-9-18 2BlkW attRAF p129 MR34

TORBIT,James TLt ded 10-9-18 RASC attRGA N'SiegePark p194 CR France34

TORIN,Richard Maynard Lt kia 24-4-15 RE p49 CR France279

TORKILDSEN,W.Cdr 6-11-18 S&T Cps MR43

TORKINGTON,Charles Coke Capt kia 25-5-15 1WelshR p127 MR29

TORKINGTON,John Elmsley Bourchier Capt drd 30-12-15 IA 63PalamcottaLI p283 MR41

TORNEY,Thomas Frederick Hastings Lt kia 3-9-18 3 att13WelshR p127 MR16

TORRANCE,Kenneth T2Lt kia 2-9-18 1RScotsF p95 CR France646

TORRENS,Attwood Alfred Maj kia 8-12-16 RFA p206 CR France832

TORRENS,Gerald Calverley TCapt ded 24-12-16 MGC p186 CR Surrey160

TORRENS,James Claude T2Lt kia 30-5-18 19MGC B'Coy p186 MR18

TORRIE,Louis Eric 2Lt 10-3-21 4KSLI CR Glouc9

TORRIE,Thomas George Jameson TLtCol kia 18-11-16 2LifeGds att7ELancs p20 CR France251

TORRY,Arthur James Dashwood.MC.Lt kia 9-10-17 RGA attRFC p14&42 CR Belgium18

TORRY,John Shirley Archibald T2Lt dow 19-9-15 12RB p180 CR France345

TORTOISHELL,George Henry 2Lt kia 14-3-17 1/5NStaffs p238 MR21

TOSDEVIN,William Cecil 2Lt kia 20-11-17 7Nhampt p138 CR France446

TOSETTI,Douglas.MC.TMaj kia 21-3-18 8RBerks p140 MR27

TOSH,Elmslie Maj kia 25-9-15 4BlkW p230 CR France705

TOSHACK,Thomas 2Lt kia 10-4-17 C'Bn MGC p186 MR20,11-4-17 TankCps Ex 9EYorks

TOSSWILL,Walter Roy Capt dow 12-8-16 1ELancs p111 CR Belgium11

TOTHILL,Geoffrey Ivan Francis 2Lt kia 27-3-16 4RFus p70 MR29

TOTTENHAM,Arthur Henry 2Lt kia 27-6-16 2RInniskF C'Coy p105 CR France296

TOTTENHAM,Charles Gordon Loftus Capt dow 30-3-15 RE att4S&M p49 CR France924

TOTTENHAM,Edward Lowry.MC.2Lt kia 9-4-16 11 att6LNLancs p136 MR38

TOTTIE,Eric Harold 2Lt dow 22-9-14 1NumbF p63 CR France1107,Harald Lt

TOUCHE,Eric Percy Johnstone 2Lt ded 17-5-18 Ess &RAF p132

TOUGH,Arnold Bannatyne TCapt kia 1-7-16 11ELancs p111 CR France802,dow

TOUGH,John James TCapt dow 6-10-18 RAMC att5FA p198 CR France1483

TOUGHILL,C.M.Nurse 14-11-15 ScotWomensHosp CR Europe58

TOULMAN,Philip Musgrave Lt kia 22-6-17 LeicYeo p204 CR France363

TOULMIN,Harold.MC.Lt kia 17-9-18 6LNLancs &46RAF p136 MR2

TOVEY,D.Lt 5-5-18 NRA SchOfMusketry CR Surrey131

TOVEY,Harry Turner LtMaj dow 22-4-18 A88 RFA p36 CR Belgium18

TOVEY,W.SubCdr 30-5-21 S&T Cps MR65

TOWELL,Gerald Wyman.MC&Bar.LtACapt dow 8-8-18 N'RFA p36 CR France23,kia

TOWER,Bertie Christopher Butler.MC&Bar.MIDx3 CaptAMaj dow 22-8-18 Cmdg4RFus p70 CR France504

TOWER,Christopher Cecil Lt kia 4-10-15 EssYeo p203 CR France178,2-10-15

TOWER,Frank TCapt&Adjt kia 13-4-17 12Manch p156 CR France924

TOWER,Hugh Christopher Capt kia 19-9-16 RFC p4 MR20

TOWER,William Claude Cecil Capt ded 30-11-18 10EKentYeo &RAF p256 CR Sussex144

TOWERS,Grainger Malcolm Lt dow 20-1-16 2Lpool p73 CR France80,1Bn

TOWERS,Wilfrid Goodwin 2Lt kia 2-4-17 4Manch p156 CR France616,Wilfred

TOWERS-CLARKE,John William Lt kia 1-7-16 2RScotsF p95 MR21,CLARK

TOWES,Norman Henry T2Lt kia 4-11-18 7RWSurr p56 CR France737

TOWGOOD,Arthur Cecil Carden T2Lt kia 13-5-17 27 att11Mddx Ex 12Lond p148 MR20

TOWLER,Cyril John 2Lt kld 4-9-18 3RWKent &RAF p142

TOWLER,F.S.2Lt ded 5-10-18 SWBord &RAF p101

TOWLSON,Albert John T2Lt kia 16-10-18 RE 122FC p49 CR Belgium157

TOWLSON,William Holland T2Lt dow 28-9-17 122MGC p186 CR France13

TOWN,Charles Aubrey.MC.TCapt kia 20-9-17 11WYorks p83 MR30

TOWNEND,Cecil Pelham 2Lt dow 24-9-16 1 att2/21Lond p245 CR France95

TOWNEND,Francis William Capt dow 29-3-15 RE 35SigCoy p49 CR France80,Whitchurch 28-3-15

TOWNLEY,Bertram Russell Capt ded 7-11-18 IARO attSPersianRif S&TCps p283 CR Asia82

TOWNLEY,Charles Richard BrigGen ded 15-5-18 Staff Comdg7Dist SuffR p261 CR Hamps13

TOWNLEY,Felix Lionel T2Lt kia 26-10-17 14RWar p66 MR30

TOWNLEY,John Lt ded 1-4-19 7Ches p272 CR Lancs34

TOWNROE,Geoffrey Charles Capt kia 8-9-17 D1/4SLancs p229 CR Belgium10

TOWNSEND,Arthur Eric 2Lt kia 15-2-17 5DLI attRFC p20&239 CR France424

TOWNSEND,Arthur Evans T2Lt kldacc 26-11-15 18Manch p156 CR France300

TOWNSEND,Arthur Gordon TLtACapt kia 5-9-17 2HLI p164 CR Belgium24

TOWNSEND,Charles Victor.MID T2Lt kia 21-3-16 7KSLI p145 CR Belgium28

TOWNSEND,Douglas William Ormond 2Lt kia 16-8-17 GL &7RFC p14 CR Belgium140,TOWNSHEND

TOWNSEND,Eric Lever 2Lt dow 17-9-16 15Lond p249 CR France188

TOWNSEND,Eric Travers Capt kia 8-11-17 1/5HLI p240 CR Palestine8

TOWNSEND,Francis Edward Steavenson Lt dow 30-9-16 5DLI p239 CR France52

TOWNSEND,George John Lt dow 26-11-15 IA 66Punjabis p283 CR Iraq1,Capt

TOWNSEND,Guy Storey Lt kia 23-8-18 5Yorks attMGC Inf p187&220 CR France210,2Lt

TOWNSEND,Harry 2Lt kia 19-7-16 MGC 53InfBde p186 MR21

TOWNSEND,Harry Lt ded PoW 23-2-19 RH&FA p262 CR Yorks361

TOWNSEND,Hugh Vere 2Lt kia 6-5-15 3Mon p244 MR29

TOWNSEND,Ivan Vesey Lt kia 3-2-15 2ELancs p111 CR France924

TOWNSEND,John T2Lt kia 14-7-16 12WYorks p83 MR21

TOWNSEND,John Vernon Lt kia 24-9-18 5Yorks p221 CR France1701

TOWNSEND,Joseph 2Lt kia 21-3-18 5NStaffs p238 MR20

TOWNSEND,Joseph Ernest T2Lt kld 2-1-17 1Worc att66RFC p14&110 CRGlouc9

TOWNSEND,Joseph Leslie T2Lt kia 2-10-17 1/2 att3/5LancF p94 MR30,9-10-17

TOWNSEND,Lionel George Oliver TCapt kia 7/11-8-15 7SStaffs p123 MR4.9-8-15

TOWNSEND,Martha SNurse ded 21-9-18 QAIMNS p200 CR Greece9

TOWNSEND,Richard Stepleton Barry TLt kia 1-7-16 10RIrFus p171 CR France339,9Bn

TOWNSEND,Robert Edward Lawrence TCapt ded 2-3-18 Mddx p265

TOWNSEND,Ronald Travis Robert Lt kia 30-11-17 5HLI attCanadianLocalForce &RFC p261&272 MR20

TOWNSEND,Sidney John 2Lt kia 13-5-15 2LifeGds p20 MR29

TOWNSEND,Thomas T2Lt kia 4-6-16 1EYorks p85 CR France189,Lt

TOWNSEND,Thomas Ainsworth.MC&Bar.Capt kia 24-3-18 RAMC p254 MR20

TOWNSEND,W.H.2Lt dow 23-4-18 GL &RAF p191

TOWNSEND-GREEN,Henry Russell Capt dow 3-3-15 1/16Lond p249 CR France922

TOWNSHEND,Arthur Fitzhenry TLtCol dow 16-9-16 11RWKent p142 CR France833

TOWNSHEND,Dudley Ryder TCapt dow 21-8-15 11LNLancs attLancF p136 MR4

TOWNSLEY,Bryan Hill T2Lt kia 14-9-16 12 att9WYorks p83 MR21

TOWNSON,Herbert Johnston 2Lt kia 21-4-18 15WYorks &RAF p83 CR France52,kldacc

TOWSE,Clifford Henry TCapt kia 8-11-15 6RWKent B'Coy p142 MR19

TOWSE,William Norman Capt kia 15-9-16 4Lond p246 CR France385

TOYE,Hubert Clarence 2Lt dow 15-10-15 2RSuss p120 CR France88

TOYE,Sydney Samuel 2Lt kia 10-10-18 C122RFA p209 CR France190

TOYNBEE,Geoffrey Percy Robert Capt kia 15-11-14 RB p180 MR32

TOZER,Harold Percy 2Lt kld 16-12-16 9DLI attRFC p20&239 CR Wilts128

TOZER,Horace Gordon 2Lt kia 1-10-15 3 att2Yorks p91 MR19

TOZER,John Henry Wallace TLt ded 3-8-17 RASC p194 MR65

TOZER,Sidney Prout TLt kia 8-10-18 Dev p77 CR France844,Sydney

TOZER,William Lt ded 5-5-16 RFA p208 MR38

TRACEY,Geoffrey Eugene TLt kia 25-9-15 9Dev p77 MR19

TRAFFORD,Edmond Thyrkel TLt ded 10-5-16 1Norf GarrBn p74 MR43

TRAFFORD,Geoffrey Thomas Lt kia 23-7-18 1LifeGds att9TankCps GdsMGR p20,53&189 CR France987,Capt

TRAFFORD-RAWSON,John Henry Edmund TCapt kia 18-9-16 1WYorks p83 MR21

TRAHERNE,George Gilbert Capt kia 6-8-16 RGA 15DivArtly p42 CR France44

TRAIL,Robert George Anthony Maj dow 1-12-17 IA CpsofGuidesCav attJodhpurLancers p283 CR France446

TRAILL,Anthony TCapt ded 25-8-17 RAMC att2/4WRid p198 CR France512,att2/4WYorks

TRAILL,Charles Harold.MC.Capt 9-11-20 RFA CR Surrey158

TRAILL,Colin Balfour.MC.TMaj dow 28-6-18 10EYorks p85 CR France19

TRAILL,Henry Rauthwells Capt kia 4-6-19 IA 87Punjabis attSWaziristanMil p283 MR43,Rauthmell 30-5-19

316

TRAILL,John Murray.MID Maj kia 30-10-14 2Beds p87 MR29,LtCol

TRAILL,Kenneth Robert TLt kia 1-7-16 6RBerks p140 CR France513

TRAILL,Sinclair George Capt kia 24-11-16 1CamH p168 CR France169,Maj kldacc 23-11-16

TRAN,David Rushton T2Lt kia 28-7-18 SfthH att8Bn p165 CR France865

TRAPP,Andrew Lt kia 23-4-18 41RFA p36 CR France266

TRASK,Charles William Trevor T2Lt kia 18-8-18 3SomLI att24WelshR p80 CR France248

TRASK,John Hedley T2Lt kia 20-11-17 Hamps att14Bn p121 CR Belgium21

TRASK,Sydney Robert T2Lt kia 8-8-16 10 att7Suff p79 MR21,9-8-16

TRATMAN,Harold Wigmore Lt 3-12-17 2/6Glouc p225 MR17,Arnold

TRATMAN,Francis Victor T2Lt kia 25-8-17 14Glouc p107 CR France363

TRATTLES,William Horace T2Lt kia 25-1-17 13Hamps att9Worc p121 CR Iraq5

TRAUNWEISER,G.N.2Lt kld 15-4-18 GL &RAF p191

TRAVERS,Hamilton Henry Lt dow 28-3-15 1SWBord p101 CR France80

TRAVERS,Horace Eden Kennedy T2Lt dow 8-11-16 14N&D att10LNLancs p135 CR France62,kldacc

TRAVERS,Hugh Eaton Frederick Capt mbk 7-8-15 2 att9LancF p257 MR4

TRAVERS,Hugh Mortimer.DSO.Capt kia 8-11-14 5RMunstF p176 MR29

TRAVERS,Hugh Price Maj kia 7-8-15 8WRid p116 CR Gallipoli27

TRAVERS,Spencer Robert Valentine.MID TLt kia 9-8-15 7RMunstF p176 MR4

TRAVERS,Tom Stockholm.MC.MID Capt kia 7-11-17 2/20Lond p251 CR Palestine1,Stockham

TRAVERS-SMITH,Robert Montgomery 2Lt drd 4-10-18 15MGC Inf p186 MR40

TRAVERSE,James Hector T2Lt kia 30-11-17 10RDubF p177 CR France1489

TRAYES,Frederic Kenneth Jackson 2Lt kia 22-3-18 11Ches p97 MR20

TRAYLEN,Norman Algernon.MC.Lt ded 4-11-18 RASC 61SB p253 CR France279

TRAYLOR,John Nelson Capt ded 27-11-15 Res 11Dev p272 CR Somerset71,TRAYLER

TREACY,Eric Henry 2Lt dow 14-12-16 12LNLancs p234 CR France131,kia

TREACY,Michael 2Lt kia 21-3-18 4 att1RMunstF p176 MR27

TREADWAY,Harold Ligonier T2Lt kia 8/9-5-17 15RWar p66 MR20

TREADWELL,George Reuben TCapt kia 5-2-17 6ELancs p111 MR38,Maj

TREADWELL,Robert Naylor.MC.TLt dow 9-9-17 GL 9Ess &22RFC p13 CR France95

TREASE,Reginald Ernest.DSO.MC.Lt ded 5-12-18 28Bde 124Bty RFA p36 CR Notts84

TREASE,Sidney Charles 2Lt mbk 19-9-18 3N&D att11ScotRif p257 MR37

TREASURE,James Herbert.TD.Maj ded 3-12-18 RGA p209 CR Egypt2

TREASURE,William Herbert 2Lt kia 1-7-16 1SomLI p80 MR21

TREBILCOCK,John Archibald.MC.Maj dow 21-5-18 76RFA p36 CR France103

TREBLE,James Noel Capt kia 18-10-15 4 O&BLI p231 CR France1327

TRECHMANN,Kuno Griffith 2Lt kia 2-7-16 12NumbF p63 MR21

TREDENNICK,John Archibald St.Leger Capt kia 23-7-18 2 att1/5SfthH p165 CR France1697

TREDGOLD,John Clarkson.MC.2Lt kia 12-4-17 3RScots p55 MR20

TREE,Charles James Lt dow 20-7-15 9Worc p110 CR Gallipoli1

TREE,Philip Bevan T2Lt kia 24-3-18 8MGC p186 MR27

TREE,Warren Francis TCapt kld 22-7-16 10Worc p110 MR21

TREFFRY,Dormer Kierulff de Bretton 2Lt kia 15-9-16 4CldGds p51 CR France294

TREFUSIS,Arthur Owen TCapt kia 7-7-16 9LNLancs p136 CR France832

TREFUSIS,Haworth Walter Capt kia 7-11-16 1Nhampt p138 CR France744

TREGARTHEN,Ernest William Lt kld 18-3-18 5RWFus &RFC p223 CR Wales17

TREGASKIS,Arthur T2Lt kia 7-7-16 16WelshR p127 CR France453,Lt

TREGASKIS,Leonard T2Lt kia 7-7-16 16WelshR p127 CR France453,Lt

TREGELLES,Geoffrey Philip.MID TCapt kia 1-7-16 8Dev A'Coy p77 CRFrance330

TREGLOWN,Charles Henry TLt kia 30-3-17 D47RFA p36 CR France1182

TREHEARNE,Leslie Llewellyn T2Lt dow 25-9-15 9WelshR A'Coy p127 CR France98,TREHARNE 24-9-15

TREHERN,Arthur Reginald 12Lt kia 27-7-15 5RBerks p140 CR Belgium71

TREHERNE,Claude William LtTCapt dow 12-8-17 RAMC DADMS 37Div p198 CR France40

TRELAWNY,Henry Wallace Lt kia 23-10-18 1DCLI p115 CR France1476

TRELEAVEN,Noel Houghton 2Lt kia 23-11-16 5WYorks p218 CR France283

TRELIVING,Arthur Stanley T2Lt kia 29-3-18 23Mddx attTMB p148 CR France745,Lt

TRELIVING,Walter Ricks T2Lt ded 11-10-18 RASC p267&194,Hicks CR Somerset43

TREMBATH,Allen Edward Capt kia 26-5-15 15Lond p249 CR France260

TREMBATH,Arthur Cecil Capt kia 22-12-16 5ESurr p226 CR Belgium127

TREMEARNE,Arthur John Newman TMaj kia 25-9-15 1/22Lond D'Coy att8SfthH p165&251 MR19

TREMEARNE,William Crew 2Lt kia 26-9-15 8SfthH p165 MR19

TREMEER,Sidney Charles T2Lt dow 17-5-17 7Beds p87 CR France13

TREMELLAN,Enner Thorney Capt ded 20-12-17 5WelshR p230

TREMELLEN,Donald Hargreaves 2Lt kia 23-4-17 3 att1DCLI p115 MR20

TREMLETT,Elias.DSO.MC.TLt dow 23-5-17 9Dev att208MGC Inf p77&266 CR France614

TRENBATH,Jack 2Lt kia 8-9-18 4ELancs p226 CR France262

TRENCH,Charles Reginald Chenevix.MID Maj kia 21-3-18 2/5N&D p232 MR20

TRENCH,David 2Lt 23-4-17 4 att2RScotF MR20

TRENCH,David Cunningham 2Lt dow 26-2-16 4RScotsF p222

TRENCH,Derrick Le Poer.DSO.MC.Maj kia 28-8-17 RFA HQ Staff p36 CR France178

TRENCH,Frederick Power Le Poer Lt dow 9-4-16 3Leinst att2RDubF p175 CR France745

TRENCH,Frederick Sydney.Hon.Lt dow 16-11-16 1KRRC p152 CR France131,ded

TRENCH,Nugent Charles Le Poer T2Lt kia 16-1-17 9ESurr p113 CR France115 see LE POER TRENCH

TRENCH,Percy Richard Oliver LtTCapt kia 25-1-17 1RWSurr attRWFus p56 MR38

TRENCHARD,Frederick Alfred Lt kia 24-5-15 RFA p36 CR Belgium92

TRENCHARD,John Wilfrid Hugh Lt dow 3-10-17 RGA 122HB p42 CR Belgium11,Capt

TRENCHMANN,Friedrich Otto T2Lt dow 15-10-16 94RFA p36 CR Durham165,Frederick 14-10-16

TRENERRY,Dudley Goodall 2Lt ded 21-1-18 RFC p261 CR Mddx42,Lt

TRENOW,Geoffrey Foveaux.MC.Lt kia 20-9-17 5Lond 2Bn p246 MR29

TRERISC,Walter Thomas Llewelyn T2Lt kia 15-4-18 1RWar p66

TRERISE,Robert 2Lt dow 13-6-18 RGA 237SB p42 CR France10

TRERISE,Walter Thomas Llewelyn2Lt 15-4-18 1War MR32

TRESIDDER,Charles Tolmie Capt dow 22-4-16 7Glouc p107 MR38

TRESIDDER,Thomas Arthur Capt kia 28-6-15 14RScots p55 CR Gallipoli6

TRESISE,Richard Arthur T2Lt dow 12-10-18 21Manch p156 CR France446

TREVARTHEN,Arthur Francis Vivyan Aubrey TLt kia 28-1-16 2SStaffs p123 CR France279

TREVELYAN,Walter Raleigh TCapt ded 19-4-16 RASC p194

TREVELYAN,Wilfred 2Lt kia 4-5-15 5 att4RB p180 MR29

TREVENEN,Sydney Vyvyan.MC.Capt dow 10-6-18 49/40RFA p36&259 CR France40

TREVES,Wilfred Warwick.OBE.Maj 18-5-20 RAMC CR Mddx26

TREVETHAN,R.SNurse ded 4-9-17 TFNS p254 CR Iraq5

TREVITHICK,Robert Percy 2Lt kia 23-4-17 232RFA p36 CR France536

TREVOR,Ernest Wilberforce Chap4Cl dow 14-11-16 RAChDept att13RB p200 CR France701

TREVOR,Frederick Pelham 2Lt kia 8-5-15 3 att2DCLI p115 MR29

TREVOR,Gruffydd Vaughan TLt ded 5-11-18 RE 256TC p49 CR France34,255TC

TREVOR,Harry Spottiswoode.MID Lt kia 15-8-15 RE att4FC S&M p49 CR France924

TREVOR,Herbert Edward CaptTLtCol kia 11-4-17 Nhampt att9Ess p138 CR France1182

TREVOR-JONES,Evan Edward 2Lt kia 1-7-16 6 att1RB p180 MR21

TREVOR-JONES,John Eric.MC.TCapt kia 22-4-18 6 att1RB p180 CR France411

TREVOR-ROPER,Charles Cadwaladr Capt dow 3-8-17 8Hamps p229 CR Belgium20,14Bn

TREW,John McCammon TCapt ded 28-3-18 RLancs p59 CR Yorks595

TREWARTHA-JAMES,Derric Vernon TLt kia 13-10-15 5RBerks p140 CR France219

TREWBY,Arthur Lt dow 17-5-15 RE 11Coy p49 CR France80

TREWEEKE,Frank Lesley T2Lt ded 7-11-16 RE p49 CR Camb2,Leslie,Lt

TREWHITT,Eric Gerald Lt dow 14-11-16 1HAC p206 CR France44

TREWMAN,Athol Benedict 2Lt dow 22-10-14 1Mddx p148 CR France1887,Lt

TRIBE,A.L.TCapt dow 17-11-17 3/2KAR 2RhodesianR p202 CR Tanzania1,Maj

TRIBE,Charles Walter LtCol kia 13-1-16 IA 41Dogras p283 CR Iraq5

TRICKETT,William Edwin Maj ded 21-11-17 5RWFus p223 CR Wales648

TRIER,Norman Ernest T2Lt dow 6-10-15 2EYorks p85 CR France98

TRIGG,H.F.E.2Lt 8-5-18 GL attRAF CR Hamps15

TRIMBLE,Alan Vincent 2Lt 25-8-18 41RAF MR20

TRIMBLE,Noel Desmond T2Lt dow 29-4-16 12 att8RInniskF p105 CR France115,kia

TRIMBLE,Robert Maxwell.MID Lt kia 21-3-18 5NStaffs p238 MR20

TRIMBY,Henry Thomas Maj&QM ded 19-6-16 RMunstF p266

TRIMBY,T.Maj&QM 19-6-16 RMunstF CR Eire159

TRIMINGHAM,Wentworth Gray T2Lt ded 4-1-18 11LancF att1Lincs p94 CR France512

TRIMMER,Edmund Howard.MID TLt dow 10-8-15 6ELancs p111 MR4

TRIMMER,Frederick George T2Lt kia 12-10-16 26Manch p156 CR France432

TRIMMER,George Ernest Lt ded 16-11-18 2LancF attRE p94

TRIMMER,T.Capt 18-11-18 RE att2FldSurCoy CR France1027

TRIMMER,William Charles 2Lt kia 21-7-16 O&BLI 1BucksBn p232 CR France832

TRIMMER,William Douglas Maclean Lt kia 30-10-14 1Hamps p121 CR Belgium69

TRIMMING,Henry William Noel 2Lt kld 15-5-15 RFA p36 CR Hamps13

TRINDER,Arnold James Lt kia 16-6-15 7NumbF p214 MR29

TRINDER,John Robert.MC.Maj kia 15-9-16 18Lond p250 CR France453

TRINDER,Samuel Louis T2Lt dow 17-8-17 9RIrFus p172 CR Belgium8,Levis

TRINGHAM,Llewellyn Watkins Howell Capt ded 22-11-18 21Lancers attRGA 51BdeHQ p23 CR France146

TRIPE,Alfred King Lt kia 23-11-17 RGA attTankCps p189&209 MR17

TRIPHOOK,Owen Leech.MIDx2 LtACapt ded 6-4-19 RFA attIndMilAccsDept p207 CR Iraq8,Maj

TRIPP,Arthur William Howard BrevCol ded 6-5-17 Lpool p73 CR Devon50

TRIPP,Cyril Claude 2Lt kia 13-11-16 3 att7LNLancs p136 CR France384

TRIPP,Donald Owen Howard.DSO.TCapt kia 18-8-16 1LNLancs p136 MR21

TRIPP,Harold LtACapt kia 16-8-17 3ESurr att1/4Berks p113 MR30

TRISTRAM,Eric Barrington 2LtTLt kia 6-9-17 RFus att1/5LancF p70 MR30

TRISTRAM,John Hutchinson Lt kia 11-3-15 1Worc p110 MR22

TRISTRAM,Lancelot Barrington Crofte Capt kia 31-10-14 2Leic p88 CR France727,Crofts

TRITTON,Alan George Capt kia 26-10-14 3CldGds p51 CR France727

TROLLOP,J.E.2Lt 27-8-18 7Lond CR France164

TROLLOPE,Cyril Harvey 2Lt kld 4-5-17 2/14Lond attRFC p20&249 CR Kent91

TROLLOPE,William Kennedy 2Lt dow 3-5-17 13RFC p13 CR France95

TROMAN,Thomas Joseph Barnsley T2Lt kia 14-7-16 62MGC p186 MR21,13/14-7-16

TRONTON,Frederick Thomas TCapt kia 25-9-15 10ScotRif p104 MR19

TROREY,George Alan 2Lt dow 21-3-18 177RFA p36 MR27

TROTER,Alexander Nigel Lt dow 12-10-14 3RScots p55

TROTMAN,Francis Henry Lionel T2Lt kia 7-11-18 1Dev p77 CR France937

TROTT,Henry George T2Lt dow 16-8-17 10WelshR p127 CR Belgium16

TROTTER,Alexander Nigel Lt dow 12-10-14 3 att2RScots p55 CR France705

TROTTER,Alexander William Lewis TMaj kia 12-7-16 9Leic p88 CR France397

TROTTER,Alick Dunbar.MC.Lt kia 18-9-18 9SLancs p126 MR37

TROTTER,Archibald Lt kia 31-12-14 CldGds p51 CR France727

TROTTER,Arthur Francis Capt ded 27-4-19 11Lpool p263 CR Berks125

TROTTER,Bertram Freeman T2Lt kia 8-5-17 11Leic p88 CR France223,7-5-17

TROTTER,Colin Liddell TLt ded 22-1-18 SL att3/2KAR p202 CR EAfrica10 &CR Tanzania1

TROTTER,Edward Henry.DSO.TLtCol kia 8-7-16 GrenGds att18Lpool p50 CR France630

TROTTER,Erle,Britt.MC.DCM.Lt ded 28-5-19 3RWKent p142&265 CR Kent46,dow

TROTTER,Henry Baron.MM.2Lt dow 10-9-18 1WelshGds p53 CR France145

TROTTER,James Keith Lt dow 26-8-14 1GordH p167 CR France658

TROTTER,Kenneth Stuart 2Lt kia 26-4-15 6 att1RB p180 MR29

TROTTER,Reginald Baird.MID Capt kia 9-5-15 2 att1CamH p168 MR22

TROTTER,Ronald Herbert Gillet Lt kia 25-9-15 3 att2RBerks p140 MR32

TROTTER,Warren Francis Col 19-6-16 OC HB RMA CR C'land&W'land100

TROUNCE,Frank 2Lt kia 4-9-18 11Lond p248 CR France439

TROUNCE,Sydney Abel 2Lt kia 5-5-17 5Suff p217 CR France162

TROUP,Frank Monck-Mason TLt kia 10-4-17 13RFus p70 CR France154

TROUP,John Guthie 2Lt kia 13-5-17 5ScotRif att16RFC p20&224 CR France32

TROUP,Stewart Houghton TLt kia 2-12-17 7 att2RBerks p140 MR30

TROUSDELL,Maurice George TCapt kia 6-8-17 RASC 436GdsDivTrain p194 CR Belgium12

TROUTON,Desmond Gardner ACapt kia 13-10-17 B102 RFA p36 CR Belgium19

TROUTON,Edmund Arthur Lt kia 1-7-16 3 att9RInniskF p105 MR21

TROWER,Alfred Bence 2Lt kia 29-5-18 1ScotsGds p52

TROWLES,Frederick Herbert T2Lt dow 13-9-18 7EKent p58 CR France122

TROWSDALE,Charles Robert 2Lt dow 2-10-18 KRRC att9Bn p152 CR Belgium112

TRUBRIDGE,R.W.Lt dow 6-5-18 GL &RAF p191

TRUBSHAWE,Eric James 2Lt dow 2-2-17 RE 460FC p210 CR France342,kia

TRUBY,George Edward T2Lt kia 31-7-17 2Lincs D'Coy p76 MR29

TRUEMAN,Albert Edward Mackrell 2Lt kia 30-5-18 2RB p180 MR18

TRUEMAN,Arthur Philip Hamilton MajTLtCol ded 26-11-18 EKent p58 CR Notts68

TRUEMAN,Charles Fitzgerald Hamilton Capt kia 26-8-14 2Manch p156 CR France716

TRUEMAN,William Ernest 2Lt ded 30-10-18 IARO att2S&M p283 MR65

TRUMAN,Alfred Holloway 2Lt kia 6-4-16 3 O&BLI p130 MR38

TRUMAN,Donald George Harding Lt kia 1-7-16 2/5RWar p214 CR France1157

TRUMAN,Thomas Archibald T2Lt ded 17-9-18 RASC 56DivTrain p194 CR France113,13-9-18

TRUMBLE,William Acton.DCM.2Lt ded 9-10-18 1/6Ess p232 CR Egypt2

TRUMP,Frederick Joseph.DSO.LtCol kia 2-12-17 1Mon attSStaffs p244 CR France258

TRUSCOTT,Francis George.MC.MIDx2 Lt dow 6-4-17 6Suff attRFC p20&218 CR Belgium406

TRUSLER,George Lt ded 17-7-18 IARO attIOD p283 MR66

TRUSS,George Marquand 2Lt kia 25-9-16 ScotsGds attMGC p52 CR France513

TRUSTRAM,Raymond Prince.MC.Lt dow 28-8-18 121/27RFA p36 CR France84

TRYHORNE,Mark William Lt ded 12-12-20 1/8Gurkhas MR43

TRYON,George Arthur.MC.CaptALtCol kia 7-11-18 6 att4KRRC p152 CR France978

TRYON,Henry TCapt kia 15-9-16 15 att8RB p180 MR21

TRYON,Richard Capt kia 10-1-15 6 att2RB p180 MR22

TUBBS,Seymour Burnell Capt kia 22-8-17 5Glouc p225 MR30

TUCK,Duncan Beresford.MID TCapt dow 30-3-18 16Mddx p148 CR France145

TUCK,Duncan Johnson Capt dow 3-7-16 3 att6 O&BLI p130 CR France46

TUCK,Henry Malpas T2Lt dow 26-10-18 21Mddx att26RFus p148 CR Belgium158

TUCKER,Alan Robert Lloyd 2Lt kia 18/20-12-14 ULIA attRWar p66&283,19-12-14 MR32

TUCKER,Albert Ruthven 2Lt dow 16-5-17 162RFA p36 CR France113

TUCKER,Alfred Capt kld 8-8-15 5YLI p235 CR Belgium85

TUCKER,Arthur Haines Lt kia 16-10-17 4RSuss att9KRRC p228 CR Belgium112

TUCKER,Cecil Hall 2Lt dow 7-9-15 10NStaffs att8LancF p158 CR Gallipoli2,7-8-15

TUCKER,Clifford Francis 2Lt kia 9-4-18 RLancs att1/5Bn p59 MR19

TUCKER,Donald Cecil 2Lt kia 24-3-18 GL &41RFC p13&191 MR20

TUCKER,Edwin George T2Lt kia 13-10-15 10Norf p74 MR19

TUCKER,Frederick Dennis 2Lt kia 25-9-17 1RWSurr p56 MR30

TUCKER,Frederick St.George TMaj kia 3-7-16 10Worc p110 CR France393

TUCKER,H.G.2Lt kld 4-4-18 GL &RAF p191

TUCKER,James Parke LtTCapt kia 23-4-17 3 att10N&D p135 MR20

TUCKER,John Ayre.MID 2Lt kia 1-11-14 115Bty RFA p36 CR Belgium57

TUCKER,Leslie Archibald 2Lt kia 22-3-18 2TankCps p189 MR27

TUCKER,Lionel Louis Clerici T2Lt kia 1-7-16 20NumbF p63 MR21

TUCKER,Samuel William Joseph Brocklehurst T2Lt dow 13-9-18 Norf att2/5Lancs p74 CR France31,att25Lpool

TUCKER,Sidney.MM.2Lt dow 11-8-18 20Lond p251 CR France69

TUCKER,Stanley Dawson Simm Lt kia 26-10-17 6NumbF p214 MR30

TUCKER,Tudor Henry St.George Maj ded 19-8-17 IA PoiticalDept att21Punjabis p283 MR43

TUCKER,William Henry 2Lt kia 1-7-16 1/12Lond p248 MR21

TUCKEY,Albert William TLt kia 25-9-15 1Nhampt p138 CR France219

TUCKEY,James Caulfield 2Lt kia 31-8-16 13Mddx p148 MR21

TUCKWELL,John Henry Graham 2Lt kia 23-3-18 7A&SH p243 MR20

TUDHOPE,Thomas 2Lt kia 25-9-15 3 att9ScotRif p104 MR19

TUDOR,Alan Roper T2Lt kia 5-6-17 9SfthH p165 CR France97

TUDOR,Percival Bradbury 2Lt ded 1-11-18 RH&FA 26JacobsMtnBty p36 CR Iraq8

TUDOR-JONES,Charles Edward Tudor 2Lt kld 15-12-15 ELancs attRFC p2&111 CR France1144

TUDSBERY,Lancelot 2Lt kia 22-8-17 B70RFA p36 CR Belgium8

TUDWAY,Hervey Robert Charles Lt dow 18-11-14 2GrenGds p50 CR France102

TUFF,Cecil Thomas Capt kia 18-4-15 3 att1RWKent D'Coy p142 MR29

TUFF,Frank Noel 2Lt dow 5-11-15 REKentYeo p204 CR Europe1

TUFFLEY,Victor Evelyn.DSO.MC.MID Lt dow 7-9-18 10Lond p248 CR France511

TUFFREY,Charles 2Lt ded 2-1-17 RDC p272 CR C'land&W'land17

TUFNELL,Carlton Edward Capt kia 15-9-16 3CldGds p51 CR France402

TUFNELL,Carlton Wyndham Lt kia 6-11-14 GrenGds p50 CR Belgium134,Carleton

TUFNELL,Gilbert Jolliffe 2Lt ded 22-2-18 RGA p262 CR Essex128,RFA

TUFNELL,A,W.CMG.DSO.Col IA 8Lucknow 17-5-20 CR India97A

TUFT,Gerald Hugh 2Lt kia 27-4-17 6N&D p233 CR France375

TUFTS,George Henry T2Lt kld 26-1-18 KRRC &RFC p17&152 CR Norf285

TUGBY,Leslie Andrew T2Lt kia 18-9-18 13WelshR p127 CR France415

TUGWELL,Claude Buchanan Capt 28-3-17 Dors CR Surrey160

TUGWELL,Frederick William 2Lt ded 2-3-19 RWSurr p262 CR Sussex143

TUGWELL,Geoffrey Arnold.MID Capt kia 23-4-17 4Yorks p220 MR20

TUGWELL,Oswald Norman 2Lt dow 22-4-17 4 att1WYorks p83 CR France80

TUITE,Henry Mark LtCol dow 24-3-18 RMunstF p176 MR20

TUITE,Mark Alan Wallace 2Lt dow 2-12-17 10Lond attTankCps p189&248 CR France398

TUKE,Arthur Harold Seymour 2Lt kia 7-5-15 3 att2NumbF p63&258,Harrington MR29

TUKE,Cyril Stratford TCapt kia 25-9-15 9BlkW attMGC p129&186,27-9-15 MR19

TUKE,Francis Henry Chap4Cl kia 20-7-16 RAChDept att53Bde p200 MR21

TUKE,Ottley TLt kia 17-10-18 7EYorks att1YLI p85 CR france190

TUKE,Percy George T2Lt dow 21-3-18 20MGC p186 MR27

TULETT,William John HonCapt ded 6-5-17 11N&D p264 CR Yorks561

TULL,Walter David 2Lt kia 25-3-18 5 att23Mddx Ex 17Bn p148 MR20,Daniel

TULLIDGE,Bernard Henry ACapt kia 27-8-17 6 att13Worc p110 MR30

TULLIDGE,Robert Milton 2LtACapt dow 25-1-17 13 att9RWar p66 CR Iraq5

TULLIS,John Drysdale Capt dow 18-11-14 1RScotsF p95 CR France64

TULLIS,Robert Ramsey Capt dow 25-5-15 7A&SH p243 CR France285

TULLIS,William Capt&Adjt kia 1-7-16 RScotsF att22NumbFp95 MR21

TULLOCH,Edith Sarah SNurse 8-10-18 QAIMNS CR Surrey160

TULLOCH,Ernest St.Clair TLt kia 7-7-16 11NumbF p63 MR21

TULLOCH,William T2Lt kia 20-7-16 53MGC Inf p186 CR France630,TULLOCK

TULLOH,Cecil Falconer Capt kia 13-10-14 Mddx p148 CR France1106

TULLOH,George Swinton LtCol kia 10-5-15 2Glouc p107 CR Belgium167,9-5-15

TULLY,Henry Robson 2Lt dow 27-5-18 8 att4NumbF p63 MR18

TULLY,James Kivas Capt dow 19-9-16 1/7Mddx p235 CR France23

TULLY,Richard Latimer 2Lt ded 22-7-18 4 att12NumbF p213 CR France84

TULLY,Thomas Michael T2Lt ded 9-10-18 GL RE IWT p49 CR Iraq6

TULLY-CHRISTIE,William Kerwin Capt ded 20-2-18 RAVC p199 CR Lond4

TUMILTY,Austin T2Lt ded 10-11-17 11RDubF p177 MR20

TUNBRIDGE,Arthur Thomas Hornby T2Lt kia 12-10-17 RBerks att6Bn p140 MR30

TUNBRIDGE,Gerard Charles 2Lt dow PoW 27-4-18 1Y&L p159 CR Greece3

TUNE,Charles Walter T2Lt kia 23-11-17 13Yorks p91 MR17

TUNKS,Edward Joseph Austin 2Lt kia 3-4-18 4Hamps p228 CR France924,14-4-18

TUNNAH,William T2Lt ded 28-4-18 PoW WYorks att1/6Bn p83 CR Belgium111

TUNNELL,Oliver T2Lt kia 24-10-18 12/13NumbF p63 MR16

TUNSTALL,James Charles Francis T2Lt kia 14-2-17 11KRRC p152 CR France744

TUPMAN,Arthur Lyon Lt kia 22-8-18 3N&D &80RAF p135 CR France329,2Lt 2Bn

TUPPER,Harold 2Lt dow 22-7-18 10RFus p70 CR Kent224,Lt

TURBUTT,Gladwyn Maurice Revell Lt kia 21-10-14 3 O&BLI p130 CR Belgium126

TURK,George Deane 2Lt dow 23-6-17 PoW 7 att1Ess p232 CR Germany1

TURK,Herbert Henry.MC.2Lt kia 3-11-16 11RFC p4 CR France46

TURNBULL,Alexander Miller 2Lt kia 25-4-17 GL &12RFC p13 CR France421

TURNBULL,Arthur Francis X.T2Lt kld 9-2-18 RFC p17 CR Dorset115

TURNBULL,David Stevens Lt kld 15-4-17 6BlkW attRFC p20&231 CR Scot237

TURNBULL,Derwent Christopher Lt dow 14-3-15 RAMC 84FA att1Ches p198 CR Belgium59

TURNBULL,Dudley Ralph.DSO.BrMajALtCol kia 1-10-17 GordH att20Manch p167 CR Belgium308

TURNBULL,Francis Egerton 2Lt kia 27-5-18 DLI att1Wilts p162 MR18

TURNBULL,George T2Lt kia 14-4-18 16RScots p55 MR32

TURNBULL,Gerald Illtyd.MC.TLt dow PoW 9-4-18 18WelshR p127 CR France1027,Gerard 20-4-18

TURNBULL,Henry James 2Lt kia 25-9-16 1/7Lpool p215 MR21

TURNBULL,Hugh McDiamid Lt kia 5-9-17 4RScots p211 CR Belgium24,Macdiarmid

TURNBULL,Hugh Vincent Corbett Capt kia 13-11-14 2KOSB p102 MR29

TURNBULL,John Oswin Capt kia 8-9-16 3 att2WelshR p127 MR21

TURNBULL,John Seymour Lt 17-6-18 Worc &41RAF MR20

TURNBULL,Laurence 2Lt kia 16-6-15 3 att2Beds p87 MR22

TURNBULL,Maxwell.MC.TCapt ded 18-10-18 3 att8BordR p118 CR France40

TURNBULL,Robert.MC.T2Lt kia 25-8-18 13RB p180 CR France518

TURNBULL,Robert Duncan 2Lt kia 5-9-18 RGA 144SB p42 CR France568

TURNBULL,Robert Henry MC.T2Lt dow 4-6-18 18LancF p94 CR France84,Hendry

TURNBULL,Stephen John.DCM.Lt 19-4-20 RAOC MR43

TURNBULL,Thomas Russell T2Lt kia 11-10-16 11 att9BlkW p129 CR France1059

TURNBULL,William T2Lt kia 12-6-17 53RFC p13 MR20

TURNBULL,William Andrew 2Lt kia 17-7-16 5Yorks p221 CR Belgium60

TURNBULL,William Arthur TLt kia 13-11-16 4Beds p87 CR France220

TURNBULL,William Elliot Lt kia 28-4-15 5RScots p211 MR4

TURNELL,Reginald Leaf T2Lt kia 23-11-17 13 att20Mddx p148 MR17

TURNELL,Robert Douglas.MM.T2Lt kia 27-3-18 52RFC p17 CR France300

TURNER,Alan Fletcher Lt kia 13-5-15 1/1LeicYeo p204 MR29 CR Belgium453

TURNER,Alan Joseph Chamerton 2Lt ded 5-10-18 RASC p267 CR Lancs34,Chamberlain 6-10-18

TURNER,Alan Macfarlane 2LtTLt dow 19-12-15 1/5HLI p240 CR Gallipoli3

TURNER,Alexander Buller.VC.2Lt dow 1-10-15 3 att1RBerks p140 CR France98

TURNER,Alexander Law Lt ded 12-3-16 A1/3RFA p208 CR Egypt3

TURNER,Arthur.TD.LtCol ded 11-8-15 RE p272 CR War

TURNER,Arthur 2Lt kia 26-6-17 4DLI p162 CR France149,2Bn

TURNER,Arthur Charlewood 2Lt kia 16-1-18 6RB p180 CR France154

TURNER,Bernard TLtACapt kia 8-5-17 14RWar p66 CR France777

TURNER,Bingham Alexander.DSO.Capt kia 2-11-14 6RB p180 MR29

TURNER,Charles Hampden.MID TMaj kia 30-9-15 2Suff p79 MR29

TURNER,Charles Rushton 2Lt ded 30-10-15 RH&FA 3C ResBde p36

TURNER,Crosby Russell Swanson 2Lt kia 27-7-16 3Dors attKRRC p124 MR21

TURNER,Cuthbert 2Lt kia 23-4-17 4 att7BordR p228 MR20

TURNER,David Fotheringham T2Lt kia 26-9-15 8EYorks p85 CR France1723

TURNER,David Thompson Capt kia 30-5-18 4NumbF p213 CR France1689

TURNER,Douglas William 2Lt ded 15-2-19 Ess p132 CR Nhampt79,17-2-19

TURNER,Duncan 2Lt ded 16-10-16 IA TC att80CarnaticInf p283

TURNER,Edgar Harold Holmes T2Lt dow 23-10-16 11WelshR p127 CR Greece6

TURNER,Edmund Sanctuary 2Lt kia 21-8-15 RGA 116SB p209 CR France397,21-8-16

TURNER,Edward Percy TLtACapt kia 19-3-17 2RFA p36 CR France115,42RFA

TURNER,Elliott Douglas 2Lt kia 24-8-18 5HLI p240 CR France162,Douglass

TURNER,Eric Walter Carpenter Lt dow 9-8-16 3 att2Hamps CR Belgium165

TURNER,Ernest Arthur Lt kia 3-9-16 1/6WYorks p218 MR21

TURNER,Ernest Augustus Lt ded 10-10-18 UnListEAfr p287 SAfrica69

TURNER,Ernest Gilbert.DSO.2LtTCapt kia 12-4-17 11RScots p55 MR20

TURNER,Ernest John 2Lt dow 3-4-18 10 att2/4YLI att20EntrenchBn p144 CR France145

TURNER,Evelyn Victor TLt kia 18-11-16 GL att8NStaffs p191 MR21

TURNER,Frederick Eley 2Lt ded 27-9-18 1/2WYorks &RAF p83 CR France1061

TURNER,Francis Ignatius T2Lt kld 27-9-18 att8WYorks p83 CR France755,8 att1Bn

TURNER,Frederick Harding Lt kia 10-1-15 10Lpool p216 CR Belgium186,2Lt

TURNER,Frederick Harry.MC.TLt kld 10-1-17 GL &RFC p13&191 CR Bucks51

TURNER,Frederick Richard 2Lt kia 15-1-17 A100RFA p36 CR Greece6

TURNER,Frederick Whitecross T2Lt kia 9-4-17 4 att10ScotRif p104 MR20

TURNER,Frederick William Robertson Lt kia 5-8-16 RE 2Coy p210 CR France158

TURNER,George Corrall Capt kia 13-9-17 2/6WYorks p218 CR France563

TURNER,George Henry T2Lt kia 15-10-18 YLI att1/4Bn p144 CR France316,13-10-18

TURNER,George Herbert T2Lt dow 14-6-16 13 att15RWar p66 CR France1

TURNER,George Perrior T2Lt kia 30-6-16 GL 14Hamps att116TMB p191 MR19

TURNER,Gerard Capt kia 4-6-15 IA 1/5GurkhaRif p283 CR Gallipoli3

TURNER,Gilbert Austin 2Lt kia 17-11-16 3RWKent att7LNLancs p142 MR21

TURNER,Harcourt Charles Lt kia 23-8-17 3 att6DCLI p115 MR30

TURNER,Harold Frank Barclay LtACapt dow 1-9-17 Wilts p153 CR Belgium72

TURNER,Harold Lake Compton Maj ded 14-6-18 IA 1/2GurkhaRif p283 MR43,2/9Bn

TURNER,Harold Runciman.MC&Bar.Maj kia 19-5-18 RGA 297SB p209 CR France113

TURNER,Henry Alfred.DCM.T2Lt kia 18-9-18 5 att8KSLI p145 CR Greece5

TURNER,Henry Hamilton Fyres LtCol kia 1-12-17 IA 2Lancers p283 CR France446

TURNER,Henry Scott 2Lt ded 11-3-15 BlkW p129 CR Mddx52

TURNER,Herbert Deacon 2Lt kia 20-8-17 GL &70RFC p13 MR20

TURNER,Herbert Duncan Bruce Lt ded 9-8-17 20/9RFA attRFC p13&36 CR Lancs34

TURNER,Herbert Ellery Capt kia 15-4-18 RGA 169SB p209 CR France881

TURNER,Herbert Guy Capt kia 2/3-3-15 2Ches p97 MR32

TURNER,Herbert Kersey TCapt kia 15-7-16 4Suff p217 CR France453

TURNER,Herbert Norman TLt kia 14-7-16 12WYorks p83 CR France453

TURNER,Herbert Stanley 2Lt kia 24-3-18 15DLI p162 MR27

TURNER,Hubert Samuel Alston 2Lt kia 1-8-17 2Yorks p91 MR29

TURNER,Humphrey Shewell Capt 7-12-15 46Punjabis attRE 31DivSigs MR43 &CR Pakistan50A

TURNER,James Alexander.DSO.MC.LtTLtCol kia 26-7-18 2RScots p55 CR France864

TURNER,James Clifford Lt kia 3-8-16 RFA &RFC p4&36 CR Belgium265

TURNER,John 2Lt kia 29-11-16 7GordH p242 CR France239

TURNER,John AssComsy&Lt ded 11-7-17 IndOrdDept p283 CR Iraq6

TURNER,John 2Lt dow PoW 13-4-18 2TankCps p189 CR Germany3

TURNER,John.MC.ACapt kia 22-10-18 8 att10RWar p215 CR Franxce270

TURNER,John Alvey 2Lt kia 24-2-17 7Mddx p235 MR19

TURNER,John Percival 2Lt kia 26-10-17 3 att14RWar p66 MR30,Capt

TURNER,John Reginald Lt kia 13-10-14 3Dors p124 CR France279

TURNER,Joseph Henry.MC.T2Lt dow 21-9-18 11 att6RWKent p142 CR France194

TURNER,Kenneth Leigh T2Lt kia 2-5-18 5RRofCav attWorcYeo p23 CR Palestine3

TURNER,Maurice Arthur TCapt kia 16-7-16 4Suff p217 MR21

TURNER,Miles Ransome Lt ded 13-1-20 IAUL 25Cav p283 MR43

TURNER,Noel Cuthbert 2Lt ded 29-6-16 IARO p283 CR Surrey34

TURNER,Noël Price James.MID Lt dow 10-5-15 3 att1SWBord p101 CR France80,9-5-15

TURNER,Percival Eric 2Lt dow 5-10-17 143MGC p186 CR Belgium16

TURNER,Percy Herbert 2Lt kia 6-7-15 3 att2SWBord p101 CR Gallipoli6

TURNER,Ralph Pool T2Lt ded 9-3-16 GL &1RFC p4&191 CR Belgium132

TURNER,Reginald T2Lt kia 20-11-17 KSLI att6th p145 CR France379

TURNER,Reginald Allison 2Lt kia 21-3-18 30MGC Inf p186 CR France1701

TURNER,Richard George 2Lt kld 4-5-17 RFC 37ResSqn p13 CR Hamps76

TURNER,Richard Radford 2Lt kia 3-2-17 3RSuss p120 CR Belgium4

TURNER,Robert Henry Lt dow 23-3-18 5Lincs p220 CR France177

TURNER,Roger Bingham Lt kia 9-4-16 3Ches p97 MR38

TURNER,Ronald 2Lt kia 15-8-16 1/5Ess p232 MR4

TURNER,Russell Sandon Capt kia 4-10-17 5RWar p214 MR30

TURNER,Thomas Alfred TLt kia 29-4-17 50RFA p36 CR France96,D5RFA

TURNER,Thomas Edwin Lt kia 9-5-15 13Lond p249 MR32

TURNER,Thomas James 2Lt kia 2-9-18 4RScots p211 CR France646

TURNER,Thomas Norman Leslie 2Lt murderBySepoy 26-3-16 IARO att48Pnrs p283 MR38

TURNER,Walter Gregory 2Lt kia 8-6-17 4Leic p220 MR20

TURNER,Warren Geoffrey Dalton Lt kia 24-5-17 GL &11RFC p13 MR20

TURNER,William Capt ded 6-4-18 RAMC p254 CR Scot501

TURNER,William Ernest 2Lt kia 27-8-17 7Worc p226 MR30

TURNER,William Joseph T2Lt kia 12-10-18 Mddx att4Bn p148 CR France206

TURNER,William Marlow 2Lt ded 28-10-18 IA LabCps att61BurmaLabCo p266 CR Lond8,28-10-16

TURNER,William Rowland.MC.TLt dow 10-11-17 RE 254TC p49 CR Belgium11,Roland MM not MC

TURNER,William Stewart Lt kia 16-6-15 10Lpool p216 MR29

TURNER,William Tom Capt kia 10-8-15 7Ches p223 MR4

TURNEY,Leonard William Maj kia 3-5-17 6 att8RFus p70 MR20

TURNEY,William 2Lt kia 10-7-16 8SStaffs p123 MR21

TURNLEY,John Francis T2Lt kia 16-4-17 9MGC Inf p186 MR30,TURNLY

TURNOR,Christopher Randolph Lt kia 26-10-14 10Huss p22 CR Belgium117

TURNOUR,Arthur William Winterton 2LtTLt kia 25-9-15 2RB p180 MR32

TURPIE,McKenzie Fleming 2Lt dow 23-7-16 7LNLancs p136 MR21

TURPIN,James Knowles Lt kia 14-8-17 A241RFA p208 CR Belgium10

TURPIN,James Stephen T2Lt dow 21-5-16 GL 8SomLI attTMB p191 CR France23

TURRELL,Henry Gifford 2Lt dow 3-11-17 4 O&BLI p231 CR Oxford71

TURTON,Alice Mary SNurse ded 7-5-17 QAIMNS SR att26StatHosp p200 CR Egypt8

TURTON,Cecil William Lt kld 4-2-16 6RSuss p228 CR Sussex112

TURTON,Edmund Spencer Lt kia 1-9-15 YorkHussYeo p206 CR Belgium11,31-8-15

TURTON,Ernest Francis LtACapt kia 27-10-17 RGA 117HB p42 CR Belgium101

TURTON,Richard Dacre TLt kia 24-9-17 9Y&L p159 CR Belgium19

TURTON,Robert Straker Maj ded 15-12-19 RAMC p267 CR CentralAmerica6

TURTON,Thomas Charles T2Lt kia 8-5-17 14Lpool p73 CR Greece6

TURTON,Zouch Austin Lt kia 23-4-15 Norf attEYorks p74 MR29

TUSON,William 2Lt kld 27-3-18 8Manch p237 MR20,26-3-18

TUSON,William.MBE.Capt ded 29-1-20 RAMC CR Hamps1

TUTIN,Guy Luntley Lt ded 27-1-19 3N&D att2/4RBerks p255 CR Notts66

TUTTIETT,Laurence William Capt kia 2-9-16 12RSuss p120 MR21,3-9-16

TUTTON,Francis James.MM.T2Lt dow 26-8-18 RBerks att5Bn p140 CR France630

TUZO,John Atkinson Capt ded 8-4-18 6RSuss attEARlys p228 CR EAfrica36

TWEDDELL,Thomas Lt dow 28-6-18 3 att7Yorks p91 CR France145,att7EYorks

TWEDDLE,William John 2Lt kia 16-4-17 7Ess p232 CR France423,4Ess att9Suff

TWEEDALE,Eric T2Lt kia 1-7-16 13 att16WYorks p83 MR21

TWEEDALE,Maurice Capt kia 16-5-15 7Lpool p215 CR France279

TWEEDIE,Alexander 2Lt kia 19-4-17 5KOSB p224 CR Palestine8

TWEEDIE,Cunningham Burnside.MC.TCapt dow 17-4-17 6KOSB p102 CR France40

TWEEDIE,David 2Lt dow 5-8-18 5RScotsF p222 CR France27,6-8-18

TWEEDIE,Gilbert TLt ded 21-4-18 RRofCav p261 CR Scot109

TWEEDIE,Leslie Kinloch T2Lt kia 17-1-16 C72RFA p36 CR France423

TWEEDIE-SMITH,Alan Morton.MID T2Lt kia 13-10-15 1RWSurr p57 MR19

TWEEDIE-SMITH,Douglas TLt ded 10-4-16 GL &RFC p4&191

TWEEDY,Cecil Mahon Lt kia 28-2-17 3RDubF p177 CR France215

TWEEDY,Francis Charles Lt kia 9-10-17 5LancF p221 MR30,C.F.

TWEEDY,Gerald Vincent T2Lt kia 13-4-17 BordR att11Bn p118 CR France672

TWEEDY,Maurice Willoughby TLt ded 29-10-17 APCps p268 CR France1180,TWEEDIE

TWEEDY,R.C.Maj 12-7-17 RAMC CR Cornwall163

TWEEDY,Trevor Carlyon Capt kia 15-9-16 6NumbF p213 CR France402

TWEEDY,William Wildman T2Lt kia 27-5-18 RE 3Workshop 3LabBn p49 CR France84

TWEEN,Alfred Stuart.DSO.TMaj kia 23-3-18 10Ess p132 CR France1893

TWELVETREES,Bernard T2Lt kia 4-10-17 RWKent att5Glos p142 CR Belgium128

TWELVETREES,Edward Dudley Lt kia 8-8-18 1Camb p245 CR France196

TWENLOW-ALLEN,William Alfred T2Lt kia 18-10-16 18Lpool p73 CR France385,TWEMLOW

TWENTYMAN,Arthur Capt kia 29-11-14 10Lpool p216 CR France525

TWENTYMAN,Denzil Clive Tate TCapt kia 1-7-16 10Y&L p159 CR France267

TWENTYMAN,Joseph Jefferson.DCM.T2Lt ded 11-2-19 HLI p255&265 CR C'land&W'land74

TWIDALE,Elfric Ashby 2Lt kia 22-4-17 RFA attRFC p13&36 CR France214

TWIGG,Albert Ransom Lt kia 12-4-18 8DLI p239 MR32,Ramsom

TWIGG,Ellis T2Lt kia 18-9-18 4RFus p70 MR16

TWIGG,Francis William LtACapt kia 24-9-18 1Nhampt p138 CR France375

TWIGGE,Francis 2Lt dow 9-4-17 3 att1NumbF p63 CR France418

TWINE,Harold William T2Lt kia 13-5-16 2Y&L p159 CR Belgium73

TWINING,Cecil Francis Harvey Capt kia 3-5-15 3 att1Hamps A'Coy p121 MR29

TWINING,Richard Wake 2Lt kia 1-7-16 1Dev p77 CR France174

TWISS,Arthur Montague Capt kia 17-11-14 RE att3S&M p49 CR Iraq6

TWIST,Francis Cecil Orr 2Lt kia 30-7-16 18Manch p156 MR21

TWITE,Harold Llewellyn Lt kia 1-12-15 RFA attRE 183TC p208 CR France394

TWOMEY,Francis Philip 2Lt kia 22-2-17 IA 54 att51Sikhs p283 CR Iraq5

TWYFORD,Lionel Thomas Campbell.MID ColTBrigGen 24-8-20 NStaffs CR Surrey58

TWYMAN,Percy Gedge T2Lt dow 15-4-17 10RFus p70 CR France40,Lt

TWYNAM,Cyril Francis Frederick Lt kia 15-4-18 3HLI p164 CR France924

TWYNAM,Godfrey 2Lt dow 18-11-16 11BordR p118 CR France153

TYACK,Richard Henry.MID TCapt dow 4-11-18 6DCLI p115 CR France332

TYACKE,Charles Noel Walker Capt kia 23-3-18 5DCLI p227 CR France1203

TYACKE,Edward Humphry TLt kia 29-5-18 25MGC p186 MR18

TYDD,William John Stern 2Lt dow 22-1-17 4ConnRgrs p172 CR France285

TYERMAN,Cyril Laurence Lt kia 9-4-18 6DLI p239 MR32

TYLDEN-PATTENSON,Arthur Dagnall TLt kia 5-1-15 2 O&BLI p130 CR France1106

TYLDESLEY,William Knowles Lt kld 26-4-18 5 att9LNLancs p234 CR Belgium21,kia

TYLEE,Jervis Moore Lt kia 24-8-14 15Huss p22 MR15

TYLER,Albert Lt kia 12-11-14 RE p49 MR29

TYLER,Alfred Herbert Maj kia 11-11-14 RE p49 MR29

TYLER,Cornelius George Capt dow 11-7-16 3 att2Beds p87 MR21

TYLER,E.W.MC.Capt 25-9-20 4RFus CR Iraq8

TYLER,Gilbert Edward.MC.2Lt dow 18-9-16 19Lond p251 CR France177

TYLER,Guy Cromwell TLtACapt kia 22-8-18 1Norf A'Coy p74 CR France281

TYLER,Harold Robert Capt kia 18-8-15 1/4Ess p232 CR Gallipoli4

TYLER,Herbert Henry.MC.Capt kia 17/19-9-18 6N&D p233 MR16

TYLER,John Collett 2Lt kia 18-4-15 RFA p36 MR29

TYLER,Roper Maxwell.DSO.LtCol ded 26-3-19 DLI p162 CR Germany1,26-2-19

TYLER,William Alfred 2Lt kia 27-8-18 7Lond p247 CR France164

TYLER,William Eric T2Lt ded 28-10-18 MGC p186 CR Somerset198

TYNDALE,George Stafford Hilliard Lt dow 13-3-15 WIndiaR att2Mddx p192 CR France102

TYNDALL,Arthur George T2Lt kia 18-11-17 2RB A'Coy p180 MR30

TYNDALL,James 2Lt dow 4-6-17 19Lond p251 CR France518

TYNDALL,Joseph Charles Lt kia 2-3-15 4RDubF attRIrRif p177 CR Belgium17

TYNDALL,William Ernest Marriott.DSO.BtLtCol dow 1-8-16 WRid p116 CR Surrey160

TYNER,Thomas Goodwin T2Lt kia 9-9-16 9RDubF p177 MR21

TYNTE,M.A.TMaj ded 7-12-18 6RMunstF p176 CR Eire532

TYRER,Christopher St.John T2Lt dow 24-7-16 15RWar p66 CR France833

TYRER,John Rawsthorne 2Lt kia 9-10-17 7Manch attRFC p20,8-10-17&p237,Lt CR Belgium23

TYRIE,David T2Lt kia 18-4-18 15DLI p162 MR30

TYRRELL,Arthur James 2Lt kia 7-3-17 10RLancs p59 MR38

TYRRELL,Francis Chichester Lt dow 15-2-15 3CldGds p51 CR France80,2Lt 16-2-15

TYRRELL,Gerald Ernest.DSO.MIDx4 LtCol ded 17-5-17 RGA 64HAG p42 CR Lond28

TYRRELL,John Marcus 2Lt kld 20-6-18 3RIrFus attRAF p172 CR France102,Capt

TYRRELL,John McIntosh T2Lt kia 9-4-17 8EYorks p85 CR France581,Lt

TYRRELL,Joseph Lionel Allanson T2Lt kia 3-3-16 8 att5Nhampt A'Coy p138 MR19,2-3-16

TYRRELL,Launcelot Adrian Hope T2Lt kia 13-11-16 8EYorks p85 CR France742,Lt

TYRRELL,Leonard Collin 2Lt kia 9-10-17 5WYorks p218 MR30

TYRRELL,Oscar 2Lt kia 9-9-16 10Lond p248 MR21

TYRRELL,W.A.Capt kld 9-6-18 GL &RAF p191

TYRRELL,Walter T2Lt dow 4-9-18 1/2 att17RWFus p99 CR France41

TYRRELL-GREEN,Dennis Noel Lt kia 26-3-17 4RSuss p228 MR34

TYRWHITT,Nathaniel Bridges Maj kia 28-12-15 16Lond p249 CR Belgium44,25-12-15

TYRWHITT-DRAKE,D'Urban John 2Lt kia 3-5-17 HouseholdBn p20 MR20

TYRWHITT-DRAKE,Thomas Victor 2Lt kia 29-1-17 1RB p180 CR France439

TYSER,George Beaumont TMaj kia 5-7-16 7ELancs p111 CR France150

TYSER,Henry Erskine T2Lt kia 9-4-17 8BlkW D'Coy p129 CR France729

TYSOE,Leonard T2Lt kia 31-5-17 39LabCps p189 CR France729

TYSON,Alexander Baird LtACapt kia 24-4-17 2A&SH p174 CR France434,23-4-17

TYSON,Claude Richmond 2Lt kia 22-8-17 O&BLI 2/1BucksBn p232 MR30

TYSON,Donald T2Lt kia 8-8-15 7YLI p144 CR France922,7-8-15

TYSON,Eric James.DSO.MC.TMaj dow 11-3-18 5RFC p17 CR France15,12-3-18

TYSON,John Tyson 2Lt mbk 25-9-15 IARO att2/3GurkhaRif p283 MR28

TYSON,Percy Eldin 2Lt kia 8-12-16 3 att2WelshR p127 MR21

TYSON,William Noel Dawson TLt kia 29-9-18 15Ches p97 CR Belgium116

TYTLER,James Hall 2Lt dow 16-9-16 9DLI p239 CR France188

TYTLER,Robert Adam Neilson Maj ded 5-6-19 GordH p255 CR Lond8

TYTLER,William Boyd TLt kia 1-7-16 22NumbF p63 MR21

TYZACK,Eric Delaney 2Lt kia 15-9-17 RE attRFC p20&210 CR France705

U

UDNY,George Richard Murray 2Lt dow 17-5-15 2GordH p167 CR France80

UINT,C.SubCdr 24-9-20 RIM MR65

ULLMAN,Douglas Maurice Jaques T2Lt kia 23-4-17 24RFus p70 CR France777

ULLYOTT,Cecil 2Lt kia 23-8-18 5EYorks p219 CR France215

ULOTH,Arthur Curtis Wilmot.MC.Lt dow 19-9-18 3RSuss p120 CR France194

UMNEY,Basil Charles Lovell 2Lt kia 22-7-16 4RFus p70 MR21,23-7-16

UMNEY,Cecil Francis T2Lt kia 26-9-16 7 att5Dors p124 CR France314

UNCLES,Charles William 2Lt kia 9-10-17 4YLI p235 MR30

UNDERHILL,Charles Bertram TLt kia 27-3-16 12WYorks p83 CR Belgium105

UNDERHILL,Cyril Scott T2Lt dow 21-1-16 9KSLI p145 CR Belgium1

UNDERHILL,Edward Samuel TCapt kia 12-10-16 8LNLancs C'Coy p136 CR France393

UNDERHILL,George TLt kia 6-9-16 9Dev p77 MR21

UNDERHILL,Hugh Caulfield 2Lt mbk 8-8-15 IARO att1/6GurkhaRif p283 MR4

UNDERHILL,Reginald LtACapt kia 18-11-16 11 att4Mddx p148 MR21

UNDERHILL,Thomas William T2Lt kia 19-8-16 EKent p58 CR France164

UNDERHILL,William Annesley Capt kia 21-10-14 Worc p110 MR22

UNDERWOOD,Alexander Russell.DCM.MID AssSurg4Cl drd 13-9-17 IMS att23IndGH CR Iraq5

UNDERWOOD,Cyril Charles 2Lt kia 4-2-17 1/7Worc att 1/8War p226 CR France1472

UNDERWOOD,Cyril Henry ACapt kia 2-5-18 17Lond p272

UNDERWOOD,Edmund Poole T2Lt kia 30-7-16 17 att29RFus p70 MR21,29 att17Bn

UNDERWOOD,Edward James 2Lt dow 8-6-17 RFA XIITTMB p36 CR Belgium11

UNDERWOOD,Francis 2Lt dow 18-4-17 4RWKent attYLI p234 CR France583

UNDERWOOD,George Milne 2Lt kia 6-3-17 GL &16RFC p14 MR20

UNDERWOOD,Harold Henry Capt kia 19-4-17 1/4Nhampt p234 CR Palestine8

UNDERWOOD,Harry.DCM.Lt&QM ded 18-10-17 RAMC att ADMS EgyptHospStaff p198 CR Egypt2

UNDERWOOD,John T2Lt dow 16-4-17 10Leics p88 CR France40,8Bn

UNDERWOOD,John Middleton 2Lt kia 10-11-16 3/45RFA p209 CR France374

UNDERY,John Alfred 2Lt kia 29-10-14 4RFus p70 MR29 26-10-14

UNGER,Michael James 2Lt drd 20-9-15 IARO att14FerozeporeSikhs p283 MR4

UNIACKE,Henry Percy.CB.LtCol kia 13-3-15 2GordH p167 CR France768

UNIACKE,Robie Fitzgerald MajTLtCol kld 28-5-15 RInniskF p105 CR France1091

UNSWORTH,Cyril Joseph TLt dow 7-7-16 7SLancs p126 CR France23,2Lt

UNWIN,Ernest Frederick.MID TMaj ded 22-3-16 RASC att10RFC ResSqn p4&194 CR Lond12,dow

UNWIN,Francis John Lt kia 17-9-19 3KSLI &RAF p265

UNWIN,George Ernest T2Lt ded 25-10-18 LabCps p266 CR Yorks547

UNWIN,George Stuart T2Lt kia 30-7-16 15 att11N&D p135 CR France515

UNWIN,Lancelot Urquhart Capt kia 27-4-15 Hamps p121 MR29

UNWIN,Reginald William 2Lt kia 8-10-16 11 att1/5Lond p248 MR21

UNWIN,Wilfrid Peyto T2Lt ded 16-5-16 16RIrRif p170 CR France167

UPFILL,Thomas Henry.MC.Lt kld 18-10-18 RFA att59RAF p36 CR France658

UPHILL,Reginald William James 2Lt kia 22-3-18 1RFus p70 MR27

UPJOHN,William Moon Lt kia 24-8-18 1WelshGds p53 CR France560

UPPERTON,C.B.Capt 31-3-17 SomLI CR Kent27

UPPLEBY,Wyvil Charles Spinola Capt dow 9-2-18 12RSuss p120 CR France1092

UPRICHARD,Henry Albert TMaj kia 1-7-16 13RIrRif p170 CR France383

UPSON,Humphrey Cyril TCapt kia 29-7-16 RGA 109SB p42 CR France397

UPSTONE,Cedric Donovan 2Lt ded 11-7-16 1/4Dev p220 MR65

UPTON,Hon Eric Edward Montagu John.MIDx2 Capt&Adjt kia 9-5-15 2KRRC p152 CR France632

UPTON,John Alberic Everard 2Lt dow 20-8-16 7KSLI D'Coy p145 CR France141,3Bn

UPTON,Ralph Hamon Weeley 2Lt kia 3-5-17 3 att8ESurr p113 CR France162

UPTON,Roger Maitland 2Lt kia 7-6-17 4DLI p162 CR Belgium111

UPTON,Thomas Francis Joseph Capt kia 8-11-18 1YLI p144 CR France981

UPTON,William Edwin Lt&QM ded 5-3-16 19N&D p135 CR Norf209

URBAN,Oscar Arthur T2Lt kia 3-9-16 11 att9ESurr p113 MR21

URCELL,William Lt ded 4-11-18 2Lond p272

URE,Ian.MC.Capt kld 2-2-18 9A&SH A'Coy att 1/6Bn C'Coy p244 CR Italy7

URE,James Mitchell T2Lt dow 16-8-16 8KOSB p102 CR France833

URE,John Andrew Capt kia 21-10-14 3 att2A&SH p174 CR France566

URE,William Alan Lt dow 3-11-17 B262RFA p208 CR Palestine2

UREN,Philip 2Lt kia 18-5-16 1LancF p94 CR France1504

URIDGE,Edgar John Gibbons 2Lt kia 26-6-17 A147RFA p36 CR France149

URINOWSKI,Alexander 2Lt dow 25-8-18 1/2Lpool &RAF p73

URQUHART,Angus Lt kld 26-9-15 4CamH p242 MR19

URQUHART,Alexander 2Lt kia 17-8-17 9HLI attRFC p20&241 MR20

URQUHART,Edward Frederick Maltby Capt kia 23-10-14 1BlkW p129 CR Belgium193

URQUHART,Francis Clement Lt dow 13-4-18 16RScots p55 CR Belgium38

URQUHART,James Lawrance Lt kia 25-9-15 7Nhampt p138 MR19,Lawrence

URQUHART,John TCapt kia 24-4-17 14A&SH p174 CR France662

URQUHART,William TLt kia 7-8-16 11 att1BlkW p129 MR21

URQUHART,William Thomas Bruce T2Lt kia 6-7-17 N&D att1Bn p135 CR Belgium10

URRY,Robert Alexander 2Lt ded 27-4-18 7EYorks p85 CR France62,Lt

URSELL,Victor George T2Lt kia 3-5-17 8 att7KSLI p145 MR20

URSELL,William Lt ded 4-11-18 2Lond CR Mddx53

URWIN,Thomas Alexander T2Lt dow PoW 15-1-18 RFC p17 CR France441

USBORNE,Alfred James TCaptAMaj kia 29-4-17 50RFA p36 CR France96

USHER,Arthur Norman.MC&Bar.2Lt kia 4-11-18 10RFus p70 CR France1480,Lt

USHER,Christopher Lancelot Lt dow PoW 23-4-18 3 att1Wilts p153 CR France987

USHER,Isaac William Lt kia 4-7-16 2RIrReg p89 CR France397

USHER,John Milne T2Lt kia 25-9-15 9GordH p167 MR19

USHER,Robert William Armitage Lt kia 2-5-17 1/7LancF p221 CR France363

USSHER,Beverley Capt kia 19-6-15 Leinst p175 CR Gallipoli6,Beverly

USSHER,Beverley William Reid Maj ded 5-2-16 17DLI p162 CR Mddx48

USSHER,Stephen Capt kia 16-12-14 IA 129Baluchis p283 CR France571

UTTERSON,Henry Kelso.DSO.MIDx3 LtCol kia 10-8-18 Dors att15LancF p124 CR France1022

UZIELLI,Valentine Leslie Douglas 2LtTLt kia 21-7-17 RFA p36 CR Belgium24

UZZELL,Francis Claude 2Lt dow 3-2-18 2/5RWar p214 CR France1203

V

VACHELL,Richard Tanfield.MID Capt dow 1-8-15 5NumbF att3RFC p2&63 CR France98,2-8-15

VACHER,George Herbert 2Lt kia 11-11-14 4 att2RWar p66 MR32

VADE-WALPOLE,Thomas Henry Bourke TLt kia 20-9-15 10GordH p167 CR France554

VAILE,Edward Ernest 2Lt kia 5-10-15 3Worc Ex 1HAC p110 MR29

VAILE,Lawrence Edward Stuart T2Lt kld 29-8-17 GL &RFC p14 CR Norf247

VAILE,Philip Amyas 2Lt dow 14-10-16 2/19Lond p251 CR France85,acckld

VAISEY,Charles Thomas Hilton 2Lt dow 30-6-16 RFC p4 CR France120, 1-7-16

VAISEY,Guy Maddison 2Lt dow 19-4-18 1Glouc p107 CR France10

VAISEY,Roland Maddison Capt kia 7-9-18 36RFA p36 CR France1484

VALE,Andrew Walter T2Lt kia 9-2-17 7EYorks p85 CR France785 Ex 2AustFA

VALENTINE,Guy Capt kia 15-9-16 6Lond p246 CR France277

VALENTINE,James.DSO.CaptTMaj ded 7-8-17 RFC p14 MR70 &CR Europe180

VALENTINE,Moss 2Lt kia 26-10-17 3RWSurr p255 MR30

VALENTINE,Robert Lepper TLt dow 30-4-16 8RDubF p177 CR France178

VALIENT,James Lt dow 28-10-17 7RWFus p223 CR Palestine1,VALIANT

VALINTINE,Rudolf.MC.Capt dow 12-11-17 1WarYeo p205 CR Palestine1

VALLANCE,Harold Leonard 2Lt dow 28-9-18 7HLI p240 CR France52

VALLANCEY,Henry Havelock Delachamps Capt dow 4-5-20 RFA p272 CR Surrey58,VALLENCEY De E

VALLANGE,Lancelot William 2Lt kia 31-10-16 21/2RFA p36 CR France394

VALLANS,Thomas 2Lt ded 28-4-19 RE IWT p49 CR Iraq6

VALLENTIN,John Franks.VC.Capt kia 7-11-14 1SStaffs p123 MR29

VALLINGS,Henry Alan LtCol kia 14-7-15 1A 29Punjabis p283 CR EAfrica56

VAN BUSKIRK,L.R.E.Lt 9-12-17 FortGarryHorse &RFC CR Wilts116

VANCE,Charles Richard Griffin 2Lt kia 10-3-15 3Ches p97 CR Belgium59,9-3-15 1Bn

VANCE,Ezekiel TLt dow PoW 15-7-16 11RIrRif p170 CR France657

VANCE,James Lt kia 21-10-14 Ess p132 CR France451

VANDELEUR,Alexander Moore Capt kia 30-10-14 2LifeGds p20 MR29

VANDELEUR,John Beauclerk Lt kia 7-11-14 3Leics attWorc p88 MR29

VANDELEUR,William Mountcharles Crofton Capt kia 26-8-14 2Ess p132 CR France1347

VANDELL,Henry Ivanhoe Lt kia 10-11-14 1Nhampt B'Coy p138 MR29,11-11-14

VANDENBERG,F.A.2Lt kld 20-5-18 GL &RAF p191

VAN den BERGH,James Henry Lt kia 21-5-16 6Lond RFA p208 MR20

VAN den BERGH,Seymour Jacob H.Lt kia 27-10-17 1MddxHuss p204 CR Palestine1,Capt

VAN-den-BOK,Frederick 2Lt kia 1-7-16 2Mddx A'Coy p148 MR21

VAN DER GUCHT,Rupert Lionel LtCol ded 14-8-16 1A S&TCps p283 MR66

VAN der HOFF,Clement Lewis Lt mbk 29-1-18 3RFC p257 MR20

VANDERLINDE,Morris John Thomas 2Lt kia 30-8-18 9Lond p248 CR France624

VANDER-LINDE,Simon T2Lt dow 18-10-17 6Beds p87 CR Belgium11

Van der MERWE,C.S.2Lt 8/9-1-17 EAUL AfrScts CR EAfrica39

VANDERSPAR,Edgar Roland Lt dow 24-6-15 2Manch p156 CR Belgium56

VANDOME,Joseph John 2Lt kia 4-10-17 1ELancs p111 MR30

VAN DUZER,Harry Norman T2Lt ded 25-3-18 RFC p17 CR War97

VANE,Henry Cecil.Hon.Capt ded 9-10-17 298AC RFA p207 CR France145

VAN EEGHEN,Esme Charles 2Lt kia 20-7-17 RGA 324SB p42 CR Belgium23

VANE-TEMPEST,Charles Stewart Lt dow PoW 25-3-17 DSLI att70RFC p20&239 CR France1349

VANGOETHAM,Henry Edward LtTCapt kld 11-7-17 RFC p14 CR Dorset51,VAN GOETHEM

VAN GRUISEN,Nicholas Albert Ray Capt kia 21-8-18 9 att13Lpool p216 CR France745

VAN GRUISEN,Wilfred.MC.Lt dow 1-11-16 1RFus p70 CR Ches8

VANN,Arthur Harrison Allard Capt&Adjt kia 25-9-15 12WYorks p83 MR19

VANN,Bernard William.VC.MC&Bar.LtCol kia 3-10-18 8N&D p233 CR France375,1/6Bn

VAN NECK,Charles Hylton Lt kia 20-10-14 1NumbF p63 CR France924

VAN NECK,Philip Lt kia 26-10-14 1GrenGds p50 CR Belgium116

VANNER,James Charles.DSO.MC&Bar.Capt ded 19-3-19 7Leic p255 CR Dorset49

VAN OPPEN,Pier William Lt dow 16-4-18 4EYorks p219 CR France102,Willem

VAN PRAAGH,Ralp Bertram T2Lt kia 9-4-17 9KRRC p152 CR France581

VANPRAET,Francis Lt kia 1-10-18 RFA p208 CR France375

VANRENEN,Arthur Saunders.MID TLtCol kia 15-8-15 5RInniskF Ex Lincs p105 MR4

VANSITTART,Arthur Bexley 2Lt dow 12-5-15 11Huss p22 CR Belgium6

VAN SOMEREN,Claud Donald 2Lt kia 21-3-18 6MGC p186 MR20

VANSTON,Henry William Frederick Mortimer Capt ded 4-9-17 RIrFus att1/4Ess p172 CR Egypt9

VANSTONE,Charles Douglas Howard 2Lt ded 7-2-17 15RB attTMB p180 CR Devon153

VANSTONE,Stanley Paul TLt dow 29-10-15 10RB p180 CR France345

VARDON,Evelyn Francis Claude 2Lt kia 10-5-16 5RDubF p177 CR France178,8Bn

VARDY,Albert Theodore 2Lt kia 4-7-16 2RWar p66 CR France397

VARDY,Harold Henry 2Lt ded 22-8-18 RE 96LtRlyOpCoy p49 CR Egypt1

VARDY,Marcel Capt kia 27-8-17 A'TankCps p189 CR Belgium72

VARIAN,Walter Osborne 2Lt kia 30-3-18 5RMunstF p176 CR France401

VARLEY,Ernest 2Lt ded 2-3-18 101LabCps p189 CR France512,dow Ex Lpool

VARLEY,John Samuel Lt&QM ded 25-2-19 LabCps p266

VARLEY,Leonard Lt kia 12-11-15 1/6WRid p227 CR Belgium23,11-11-15

VARLEY,William 2Lt kia 24-3-18 RGA 2/1LancHB p42 CR France430

VARNDELL,Charles Henry Essex TLt kia 13-3-16 6RWSurr p57 CR France423,2Lt

VARNDELL,Leslie John T2Lt dow 18-9-16 4Lpool p73 CR France833

VASEY,Sydney.MC.2Lt kia 10-8-18 9 att16LancF p94 MR16,Capt

VASS,Thomas McKenzie.MM.2Lt kia 4-5-18 8ScotRif p225 MR32

VASS,William Maj&QM ded 23-9-17 6Manch p236 CR Lancs34

VASSALL,Phillip Saumarez Capt kia 7-8-15 7Glouc p107 MR4,Saumerey

VASSIE,Charles Edward T2Lt kia 1-7-16 9YLI p144 CR France267

VASSIE,Richard Lt 13-4-18 Ches CR Scot805

VAUCOUR,Awdry Morris.MC&Bar.DFC.Maj kld 16-7-18 RA &RAF p36 CR Italy11,kia

VAUDREY,Claude Henry Slade Capt ded 2-5-16 3Manch RoO p156 CR Iraq5

VAUDREY,Norman TCapt kia 1-7-16 17Manch p156 CR France397

VAUDREY-BARKER-MILL,William Claude Frederick Capt 15-9-16 8RB CR France402

VAUGHAN,A.E.J.AssSurg 1-9-16 ISM MR66

VAUGHAN,Arthur Owen.DSO.OBE.DCM.LtCol ded 15-10-19 LabCps p266 CR Wales671,YLI

VAUGHAN,Charles.DCM.2Lt kia 6-11-17 1/1Hereford p252 CR Palestine1

VAUGHAN,Charles Alvarez 2Lt kia 25-9-15 7SfthH p165 MR19

VAUGHAN,Charles Davies.DSO.Maj kia 25-4-15 BordR p118 CR Gallipoli3

VAUGHAN,Donald 2Lt kia 30-10-17 3Lpool p73 CR Belgium83,6Bn

VAUGHAN,Edward Wilmot 2Lt kia 15-7-16 12RFA p36 CR France399

VAUGHAN,Evan James Stanley TCapt kia 18-8-16 13Mddx p148 MR21

VAUGHAN,Francis Seymour Lt kld 17-3-18 5RWKent attRFC p20&212 CR Greece3,2/4Bn

VAUGHAN,George Edward.MC.Maj kia 15-9-16 3CldGds p51 CR France402

VAUGHAN,George William T2Lt kia 21-11-17 7SStaffs p123 MR20

VAUGHAN,Guy Carleton TCapt kia 20-7-16 1Dev p77 CR France399

VAUGHAN,Harold TLt&Adjt kia 31-7-17 A74RFA p37 CR Belgium12

VAUGHAN,Harold John 2Lt kia 8-6-16 1Camb p245 MR19

VAUGHAN,Harry Robert 2Lt kia 27-10-14 ConnRgrs attDLI p172 MR32

VAUGHAN,Henry Humphreston Scott.MID Maj kia 24-4-16 83RFA p37 CR Belgium5

VAUGHAN,Horace William Henry Lt kia 4-6-15 10RLancs attRFus p59 MR4

VAUGHAN,James Henry Lionel Maj kia 12-5-18 GL attKAR p202 MR52,5-5-18

VAUGHAN,John T2Lt kia 30-7-16 20Lpool p73 MR21

VAUGHAN,John David.MC.2Lt dow 18-3-17 14WelshR p127 CR Belgium1

VAUGHAN,John Lindhurst.MC.TCapt kia 16-8-16 4 att9ESurr p113 MR21,Lyndhurst

VAUGHAN,John Montgomery 2Lt dow 25-5-15 RFus p70 CR France285

VAUGHAN,John Muir 2Lt dow 18-9-18 3 att2RSuss p120 CR France327

VAUGHAN,Kenelm Cuthbert 2Lt kia 13-9-16 2IrGds p53 CR France400

VAUGHAN,Leslie Howell 2Lt kld 23-4-17 4SomLI p218 CR France604

VAUGHAN,Percy Cecil 2Lt kia 26-9-17 RGA 294SB p42 CR Belgium19

VAUGHAN,Philip Edmund,DSO Maj ded 4-12-18 6Worc p264 CR Wales201,5-12-18

VAUGHAN,Richard Creswell T2Lt kia 16-4-17 8RWKent C'Coy p142 MR20

VAUGHAN-JONES,Edward Lt kia 11-5-18 3 att11RWFus p99 CR Greece5

VAUGHAN-JONES,Gerald Lt kia 26-2-17 RE att18RFC p20&210 CR France374

VAUGHAN-LEWES,Martyn Tulloch Lt dow 22-7-16 3WelshR &RFC p4&127 CR France285,kld

VAUGHAN-ROBERTS,Richard William TLt kia 30-7-16 19Lpool p73 CR France400

VAUGHAN-SAWYER,George Henry CaptInterpreter kia 29-10-14 1A att34SikhPnrs p284 CR France706,27-10-14 Ex 23Bn

VAUGHAN-SHEEHAN,George M.R.Capt 24-1-19 IARO attLabCps CR Surrey1

VAUGHAN THOMPSON,Richard Henry.mid Capt kia 26-9-16 11RFus CR Frnce702 see THOMPSON,R.H.V.

VAUGHTON,Guy Eglington 2Lt kia 20-11-17 8Ess p232 CR France911

VAULKHARD,John Vincent T2Lt kia 15-9-16 10 att8Beds p87 MR21

VAUSE,John Gilbert TLt kia 1-7-16 15WYorks p83 MR21

VAUSE,Thomas Christopher 2Lt kia 3-9-16 8WYorks p219 CR France383

VAUSE,Wilfrid.MC.Capt kia 23-4-17 5Yorks p220 CR France162

VAVASOUR,Lionel Ormiston Lt ded 24-7-15 2NStaffs p158 MR67

VAVASOUR,Rudolph Dunstan 2LtTLt ded 16-1-17 RFA attRFC p14&37 CR Lond6

VAWDREY,Gilbert Lloyd 2Lt kia 10-11-17 2WelshR p127 CR Belgium20

VAWSER,Thomas Edmund 2Lt kia 21/23-3-18 1Lond p245 CR France1893

VEACOCK,Stanley John TLt dow 17-10-17 1Hamps att20RFC p14&121 CR France200

322

VEALE,Allan Adolphus T2Lt kia 22-1-18 RFC p17 CR France285

VEASEY,John Sherard Lt kia 12-3-15 1Worc p110 MR22

VEEVERS,Edgar Samuel 2lt kia 10-7-18 1/4RLancs p213 CR France106

VEITCH,Alexander Gordon Lt kia 23-4-17 RFA p208 CR France777

VEITCH,Dawyck Moberly Veitch Capt kia 8-7-16 IA 1Lancers attRFC p284 MR20

VEITCH,James.MC.2Lt dow 19-8-18 5CamH p168 CR France25

VEITCH,John Leonard.MC.MID Maj kia 21-5-18 7 att1Dev p217 CR France20

VEITCH,Michael.MC.2Lt kia 11-8-18 5RScots p211 CR France360

VELLA,Arthur Henry.MID 2Lt kia 28-4-17 1ELancs attRIrFus p111 CR Greece6,att9RLancs

VENABLES,Alfred Ernest 2Lt kld 4-4-17 RFC p14

VENABLES,Aubrey William TCapt kia 2-10-16 RAMC att81FA p198 CR Greece3

VENABLES,Charles Edward T2Lt dow 12-10-16 14Yorks p91 CR France177,9Bn

VENABLES,Charles John.DSO.Maj kia 8-8-15 7Glouc RoO p107 MR4

VENABLES,Gilbert Rowland 2Lt kia 7-3-15 3KSLI p145 CR Belgium111

VENABLES,Vernon Wilson 2Lt dow 18-10-16 3 att2Wilts p153 MR21

VENABLES-LLEWELYN John Lister Dillwyn Capt kia 10-7-17 3/3CldGds CR Belgium12

VENIS,Arthur Raymond 2Lt kia 22-11-15 IARO att48Pnrs p284 MR38

VENMORE,James Frederick.MC.TLt kia 11-7-16 14RWFus p99 CR France397

VENN,Bertram Joseph T2Lt kld 11-7-17 RE &RFC p14&49 CR Glouc9

VENNER,Edgar William 2Lt kia 9-7-16 RWKent att16Manch p142 MR21

VENNER,Ernest Valentine(Nick) 2Lt kia 18-8-16 3RB p180 CR France402

VENNER,George Eric TMaj kia 8-7-16 1 att3N&D p135 CR France397

VENNER,William Frederick Fouracre TLt ded 5-12-16 GL 13Hamps attRE 49MotAir p191 CR EAfrica32

VENNING,Edwin Gerald Capt kia 6-8-15 3Suff B'Coy p79 CR Belgium182,1Bn

VENOUR,Walter Edwin LtCol kia 31-10-14 IA 58Rif p284 CR France80

VENTRIS,Alan Favel 2Lt kia 14-9-15 2SLancs p126 CR Belgium113,Favell

VENUS,Frederick Arthur T2Lt kld 1-7-16 20NumbF p63 CR France393,kia

VERAGUTH,G.F.2Lt ded 18-3-18 19RFA p37 CR Mddx26

VERCOE,Frederick Gordon.MID 2Lt ded 28-4-19 3RWKent p265 MR65,3RWSurr

VEREKER,Robert Humphrey Medlicott 2Lt kia 25-8-14 2GrenGds p50 CR France932,Humphry

VERELST,Harry Wilson.MC.CaptAMaj kia 26-9-16 CldGds p51 CR France374

VERESMITH,Daniel James Christopher Lt dow 14-4-17 1RFA p208 CR France95,Capt

VERESMITH,Evelyn Henry T2Lt dow 9-7-16 14 att9RFus p70 CR France23,Lt

VERGETTE,Samuel.MID 2Lt kia 4-10-17 4 att1Lincs p217 MR30

VERITY,Gilbert 2Lt dow 31-7-17 2/5LancF p221 CR Belgium11

VERLEY,Albert Stuart Leonard TLt kia 16-8-17 9RDubF p177 MR30

VERNALL,Arthur Humphrey.MC.2Lt dow 23-8-18 3 att6Leics p88&259 CR France84,kia

VERNEDE,Robert Ernest 2Lt dow 9-4-17 5 att12RB p180 CR France245

VERNER,Frederick Charles 2Lt kia 25-10-14 1KSLI p145 MR32

VERNER,George de Wet LtCol dow 10-10-15 7KOSB p102 CR France473

VERNER,James Hamilton TCapt kia 5 -12-17 9RInniskF p105 MR17

VERNER,Lancelot Guy T2Lt dow 27-8-16 115MGC p186 CR France145,105MGC

VERNHAM,Noel Mark Hodson T2Lt kia 4-2-17 GL &16RFC p14 CR France95

VERNHAM,Noel Marshall 2Lt kia 28-7-16 4 att1ESurr p113 MR21

VERNIEUX,C.O.Capt 12-3-20 IARO attLabCps MR65

VERNON,Charles Edward Granville TCapt kia 15-8-15 5RInniskF B'Coy p105 CR Gallipoli4

VERNON,Frank Lawson 2Lt kld 8-11-16 12LNLancs p234 CR France62,dedacc

VERNON,Frederick Lewis 2Lt kia 1-7-16 26NumbF p63 CR France393,Capt

VERNON,Frederick Travis 2Lt kia 30-8-15 5Ches p222 CR France625

VERNON,George Francis Augustus Capt 10-11-15 DerbyYeo CR Europe1

VERNON,Grenville Bertie Capt kia 25-4-18 3 att2Nhampt p138 MR27

VERNON,Herbert Douglas Lt kia 15-9-16 GrenGds attMGC p50&186 MR21,attGdsMGR

VERNON,Leonard Patrick.MC.TLt kia 18-6-17 10RWFus p99 CR France531

VERNON,Leslie Godfrey Harcourt 2Lt kia 11-9-16 RWFus &RFC p4,261&263 MR20

VERNON,Lord George Francis Augustus Capt ded 10-11-15 DerbyYeo p203

VERNON,Roger T2Lt kia 14-5-16 8SomLI p80 CR France924

VERNON,Ronald Cecil Lt ded 11-10-18 GenDepot Staff Wynberg CR SAfrica144

VERNON,T.T.LtCol 24-1-19 7Lpool CR Ches32

VERNON,William Hams Lt kia 7-10-16 4Lond p246 MR21

VERNON,William Henry Lovell 2Lt kia 7-10-16 OxfordYeo att6 O&BLI p205 MR21

VERNON,William Walter 2Lt dow 11-10-16 RE 90FC p49 CR France703,Lt

VERNON,William Wood 2Lt kia 7-7-16 4ConnRgrs attRIrF p172 MR21,att2RIrRif

VERNON-INKPEN,Robert Cecil T2Lt kld 21-10-16 12RWar attRFC p4&66 CR

Hamps7

VERRALL,Christopher Francis Lt kia 22-12-14 2RSuss p120 MR22

VERRAN,Frank Nicholas Lt kia 18-10-16 2Wilts p153 MR21

VERRILL,William Gibson T2Lt kia 26-10-17 1/5NumbF p63 MR30

VERSCHOYLE,Francis Stuart 2Lt kia 25-4-15 RE R Anglesey 2S'Coy p49 CR Belgium57

VERSCHOYLE,William Arthur Capt kia 11-4-17 1RIrFus p172 MR20

VERSFIELD,Vernon Ferris 2Lt kia 3-4-18 B190RFA p37 CR France745,VERSFELD 2-4-18

VERYARD,Albert Thomas Chap4Cl kia 28-6-17 RAChDept att15TMB p200 CR France184

VESEY,George Walter.MC.Capt dow 26-3-18 9RIrFus p24 CR France1235,Waller

VESEY,James.MC.Lt kia 25-9-15 RBerks p140&259 MR32

VESEY-FITZGERALD,William Herbert Leslie 2Lt kia 14-8-16 2Dev p77 CR France423

VESSEY,Frank Court.MC.MM.Lt ded 25-10-18 RGA 353SB p42 CR France34

VESSEY,John Arthur T2Lt kld 12-6-17 45RFC p14 CR France200

VETTER,H.E.Capt ded 12-1-18 3/4KAR p202 CR EAfrica15 &CR Tanzania1

VEYSEY,Stanley 2Lt dow 21-9-17 RGA 119SB p42 CR Belgium16

VICARS,W.G.Capt 3-10-18 NigR CR Mddx80

VICARY,Gilbert Dake Capt dow 10-11-17 1/5Dev C'Coy p217 CR Palestine2,Doke

VICARY,William Dallin 2Lt kld 8-3-16 6Dev p217 MR38,Lt

VICAT,Frederick Holland 2Lt kia 8-12-17 3 att2WRid p116 CR France155

VICAT,Horatio John Lt kia 18-9-14 RWKent p142 MR15

VICK,Arnold Oughtrad Lt kia 27-9-18 11 att6Yorks p91 CR France611

VICK,Donald Benjamin TLt dow 8-7-16 C162RFA p37 CR France134

VICK,Edward.DCM.T2Lt kia 9-7-17 8Glouc p107 CR Belgium152

VICK,Kenneth Jesson T2Lt kld 5-7-17 GL &RFC p14 CR Yorks12

VICK,Sidney Francis T2Lt kia 20-9-17 att1/7Lpool p73 MR30

VICKERS,Charles Goldthorp Capt kia 22-11-17 2/4Y&L p238 MR17

VICKERS,Eric Leslie.MID T2Lt dow 8-1-17 8RB p180 CR France145

VICKERS,Ernest Charles 2Lt kia 26-1-17 7Ess p232 MR21

VICKERS,Frederick TMaj kia 21-4-17 15N&D p135 CR France674

VICKERS,Godfrey Raymond T2Lt kia 6-1-18 27RFC p17 CR France201

VICKERS,Hugh Gordon Muschamp Lt kia 30-10-18 IARO att13Lancers p284 CR Iraq8

VICKERS,Noel Lt kia 24-3-18 1EYorks p85 MR27

VICKERS,Noel Muschamp TLt kia 3-8-16 13Yorks p91 CR France149

VICKERS,Robert 2Lt dow 10-12-17 C162RFA p209 CR Belgium18

VICKERS,Thomas Bernard Lt kia 16-7-21 IA 2Sap&Min attRE 14FC p284 MR43

VICKERS,Thomas Henry Capt ded 15-11-16 BordR p264

VICKERS,William Burnell T2Lt kia 21-6-17 RGA 184SB p42 CR Belgium10

VIDALL,Lancelot Andrews 2Lt kia 25-9-15 3 att2 O&BLI p130 MR19

VIDLER,Bertram Hall 2Lt kia 12-4-17 9RSuss p120 CR France480

VIDLER,George Holbrook Eric Lt kia 8-7-16 2Wilts p153 MR21,9-7-16

VIGAR,William Arthur Lt ded 26-10-20 IA TC att120Inf p284

VIGERS,Lancelot Leslie T2Lt kia 1-7-16 RE 30FC p49 CR France513

VIGERS,Robert Stanley Garrard 2Lt dow 5-4-17 6 att10KRRC p152 CRFrance630

VIGOR,William Petter 2Lt kia 13-8-16 4 att11RWar A'Coy p66 MR21

VIGORS,Arthur Cecil T2Lt kia 9-9-16 9RDubF attRMunstF p177 MR21,MunstF attDubF

VIGORS,Charles Henry.MC.Capt kia 18-9-18 12Ches p97 MR37

VIGORS,Philip Wilson.MVO.Capt ded 2-4-17 7Worc p110&272,RoO RIrR CR Hereford/W116

VIGORS,Philip Urban.MVO.Capt ded 2-4-17 7Worc p225

VILE,Herbert Leslie 2Lt kia 3-5-17 2WRid p116 CR France604,VILLE Hubert

VILLAR,Clement John Capt kia 19-9-18 8Hamps p229 CR Palestine9

VILLAR,Robert Peter Capt kia 22-3-18 18Lpool p73 MR27,Maj

VILLIERS,Algernon Hyde Lt kia 23-11-17 Lothian&BordHorseYeo att121MGC p187&204 MR17

VILLIERS,Edgar Fyfe.MID Lt ded 13-11-18 68RFA attSch of Instruct Zeitoun p37 CR Egypt9

VILLIERS,Henry Lister 2Lt kia 4-2-17 6InnisDrags att11RFC p14&22 CR France832,Harry dow

VILLIERS,William Earle LtACapt kia 10-11-17 5 att9KRRC p152 CR Belgium101

VILLIERS-STUART,Charles Herbert Maj kia 17-5-15 IA 56Rif attAust&NZ HQ p284CR Gallipoli30,Punjabis

VINCE,Arthur Neville.DSO.LtCol kia 21-3-18 12Lpool p73&258 MR27

VINCE,William John Douglas 2Lt kld 22-5-17 RFC p14

VINCE,William Lang TLt kia 8-5-17 14RWar p66 CR France777

VINCENT,Alfred Copplestone Waldon TCapt kia 26-9-16 5Dord p124 CR France280

VINCENT,Austin Ears Lt kia 7-11-18 RFA attZ91Bde p37 CR France521,8-11-18

VINCENT,Basil Britton T2Lt kia 23-7-16 8Glouc p107 MR21

VINCENT,Charles 2Lt kia 17-10-18 4EKent p212 CR France849

VINCENT,Charles,RIM EngLtCmdr ded 30-6-21 IA p284

VINCENT,Charles Issam Francis 2Lt kia 16-10-18 1CldGds p51 CR France337,Issard

VINCENT,Frederick Charles 2Lt kia 21-3-18 7KRRC p152 MR27

VINCENT,George Ernest.DCM.2Lt kia 17-2-17 9Mddx p236 CR France314

VINCENT,George Samuel T2Lt kia 4-10-17 13RFus p70 MR30

VINCENT,James Trevor Crawley 2Lt kia 9-5-15 2WelshR p128 CR France631

VINCENT,Leslie Arthur Walter 2Lt dow PoW 31-3-18 4Beds p87 CR France403

VINCENT,Lionel Charles Henry T2Lt kia 3-9-16 12Glouc p107 MR21

VINCENT,Mark Hamilton Capt dow 1-10-15 IA 33Punjabis p284 CR France345

VINCENT,Stanley T2Lt ded 28-3-18 RASC MT p194&258

VINCENT,Vivian 2Lt dow 31-5-18 22DLI p162 MR18

VINCENT,William Capt kia 30-10-14 3DCLI p115 MR29

VINCENT,William Jefferson 2Lt kia 1-10-18 1 att5Dors p124 CR France406

VINCENT,William Morris T2Lt kia 26-3-17 10Suff att 1/4Ess p79 MR34

VINCENT-JACKSON,Montagu John TLt kia 4-2-16 11N&D p135 CR France705

VINE,Christian Courtenay 2Lt dow 25-9-16 19N&D att8Leics p88 MR21

VINE,Christopher Nithsdale Vincent T2Lt kia 18-8-16 6DCLI p115 MR21,C.V.N.

VINE,Robert Saselby 2Lt kia 14-10-16 1Camb p245 MR21,Saxelby

VINE,Wilfred Harold.MC.T2Lt kia 12-10-16 2Y&L p159 MR21

VINER,Alan Bertrand 2Lt kia 7-4-17 8N&D p233 CR France725

VINER,Frank Hillidge.MC.2Lt dow 12-9-18 23NumbF att2/7Lpool p63&259 CR France433

VINER,George Noel(Rex).MID LtACapt kia 12-10-18 4Mddx p148 CR France206

VINER,Rollo Lee T2Lt kia 4-7-16 7SLancs p126 CR France393

VINER-JOHNSON,Percy Joseph Viner Capt kia 12-3-15 3Wilts p153 MR29

VINEY,Cecil Henry 2Lt kia 9-5-15 Nhampt p138 MR32

VINEY,Philip Ernest Capt dow 17-12-14 Leics p88 CR France284

VINEY,Reginald Austin Lt 27-7-18 GL attGoldCoastR MR52 CR WAfrica6

VINICOMBE,Lionel Frank T2Lt kia 29-6-16 8RWKent p142 CR Belgium97

VINNICOMBE,Leslie Lt ded 25-10-18 2Dev attRTE p77 CR Italy12

VINSON,Albert Higgs.MID LtTCapt kld 22-3-18 13RFC p17 CR Kent127

VINT,William Percival ACapt kia 5-8-18 6MGC p186 CR Belgium11

VINTCENT,Charles Aubrey 2Lt kia 13-4-15 5 att4RB p180 MR29

VINTER,B.SNurse 30-5-18 TFNS 2GH CR Lond3

VINTER,Robert Bagster Wilson.MC.2Lt kia 31-10-16 6 att2Worc p110 MR21

VIPOND,Hugh Lt kldacc 28-7-17 1/6Manch p236 CR France518

VIPOND,Sidney James T2Lt dow 20-4-16 8Beds p87 CR Belgium11

VIRGIN,William Job Farnham 2Lt kia 4-11-18 2Wilts p153 CR France521

VIVEAST,William Henry Capt kia 9-8-18 8TankCps p189 CR France526,VIVEASH

VIVERS,John Capt kia 27-10-15 1/5RScotsF p222 CR Gallipoli2

VIVIAN,Charles Augustus LtCol kia 27-4-15 IA 15Sikhs p284

VIVIAN,Gilbert 2Lt dow 22-7-16 4EYorks p219 CR France8

VIVIAN,Robert Trevor.MID Capt mbk 8-3-16 RAMC att1/6Dev p257 MR38,Richard

VIZARD,Harold Talbot.MC.LtACapt kia 1-9-18 ABty 71Bde RH&FA p37 CR France1182

VIZE,Stanley Reed Lt ded 11-10-18 9Hamps p229 CR Egypt1 2/5Bn att4TMB

VOELCKER,Harold Edward T2Lt kia 20-7-16 6SLancs p126 MR21

VOGAN,Lindsay Clarence T2Lt dow 28-4-17 13Mddx p148 CR France12

VOKES,Basil 2Lt kia 15-2-17 O&BLI BucksBn p232 CR France624

VOKINS,Kean Esse T2Lt kia 11-7-16 11RWar p66 MR21

VOLKERS,Frederick Cyril Stowell T2Lt kia 1-7-16 1RB p180 MR21

VOLLER,Herbert William T2Lt kia 6-12-16 10Glouc p107 CR France385

VON POELLNITZ,Herman Walter CaptTMaj kld 11-5-18 2Lincs &72RAF p76 CR Iraq8

VON TREUENFELS,Carl Otto,DSO Maj dow 24-6-17 285RFA p206 CR France8

VON WINCKLER,Myles William Lt kia 1-8-17 2Mddx p148 MR29

VORES,Geoffrey Bernard 2Lt kia 4-6-15 1LancF p94 MR4

VORLEY,Charles Archibald T2Lt dow PoW 13-9-16 11RSuss p120 CR France657,Lt

VORLEY,W.K.TLt ded 30-11-16 RFA 12A/A Bty p37 CR Lond12

VOSE,Thomas T2Lt kia 13-12-17 2 att12WYorks p83 CR France563,Lt

VOSS,Ernest William Thomas T2Lt kia 24-9-17 11RWar p66 MR30

VOUSLEY,Frederick TMaj ded 5-2-21 IARO attStaff p284 CR India48

VOWLER,Darrell Francis Stephen TMaj ded 28-2-19 N&D attMGC p135&186 CR Cornwall64

VOWLER,Edward Maxwell 2Lt kia 14-3-15 2DCLI p115 MR29 &CR Belgium453

VOWLER,John Arthur Geoffrey Lt ded 19-7-17 3Leinst attMGC p175 CR Hamps64

VOWLES,Stephen Foster 2Lt kia 28-4-17 3 att13Ess p132 MR20

VOYCE,Henry Eugène T2Lt kia 6-8-15 4Worc Y'Coy p110 CR Gallipoli6

VOYSEY,Alfred Ebenezer 2Lt kia 29-7-17 SR attRGA 21HB p42 CR Belgium9

VYNER,Cuthbert Jack Sigfrid Lt dow 24-7-15 4 O&BLI p231 CR France201

VYVYAN,Beresford Houghton TCapt dow 18-8-17 A121RFA p37 CR Belgium16,Haughton

VYVYAN,Walter Drummond Lt kia 2-3-15 2KSLI p145 MR29

VYVYAN,William Geoffrey Capt dow PoW 24-10-14 RWFus p99 CR Belgium167

VYVYAN-ROBINSON,Courtenay Maj ded 22-1-19 RGA 156SB CR France1030

W

WACE,Henry Edward Capt kia 14-4-18 4KSLI p235 MR30

WACE,Herbert Gordon T2Lt kia 21-8-15 RMunstF p176 MR4

WACE,Percival Beckwith Capt dow 3-7-16 5RBerks p140 MR21

WACHER,John Stewart 2Lt kldacc 5-8-16 1RWKent att7RDubF p142 CR Greece9

WACHER,Walter Ronald TLtACapt kia 12-10-17 2 att6RBerks p140 MR30

WADDAMS,Arthur Richard Lt AccBombExplos 22-11-17 IARO att44MerwaraInf p284 CR Iraq6

WADDAMS,Walter Herbert Leonard.MC.ACapt dow 12-4-17 1/1Lond p245 CR France120

WADDELL,David Adams.MID Lt kia 6-4-17 4GordH p241 CR France266

WADDELL,David Bruce 2Lt kia 21-3-18 2DragGds p21 MR27

WADDELL,James Douglas Capt kia 25-9-15 12RFus p70 MR19

WADDELL,James Hamilton 2Lt kia 5-6-17 11RScots p55 MR20

WADDELL,Thomas Bryson 2Lt kia 8-4-17 5SfthH p241 CR France184

WADDELL-DUDLEY,Robert Rowland Lt kia 15-4-15 3RFus p70 CR Belgium125

WADDINGTON,James Hubert T2Lt dow 6-7-16 16WelshR p128 CR France633

WADDINGTON,Walter Charles 2Lt dow PoW 3-7-18 1/4EYorks p219 CR Germany3

WADDY,John Raymond.MC.MID Lt kia 17-3-15 RAMC attSomLI p198 CR Belgium70

WADE,Albert Luvian TLt kia 28-4-17 17Mddx attTMB p148 MR20

WADE,Arthur Norman T2Lt dow 19-9-15 7YLI p144 CR France705,Lt

WADE,G.A.Maj 17-3-19 RAMC CR Devon239

WADE,George 2Lt drd 1-1-17 7A&SH p243 MR35

WADE,George Edward Ahern 2Lt kia 3-5-17 9RB A'Coy p180 MR20

WADE,Gordon Standley 2Lt dow 13-11-16 5 att17Mddx p148 CR France41

WADE,Graham Hardie Capt kia 26-4-15 1/7A&SH p243 CR Belgium129,25-4-15

WADE,Harold Walter Lt mbk 29-10-14 IA 3Brahmans att9BhopalInf p284

WADE,Herbert.MC.Lt kia 2-11-18 17MGC Inf p186 CR France1475

WADE,Herbert John Clark TLt dow 14-11-17 180MGC Inf p186 CR Egypt7

WADE,Hubert T2Lt kia 9-10-17 YLI att5Bn p144 MR30

WADE,John Mayall 2Lt kia 19-6-15 9Manch p237 MR4

WADE,Lawrence Frank 2Lt kia 28-8-18 9RFus p70 CR France370,Laurence 22-8-18

WADE,Oliver John T2Lt kia 22-10-16 9RWKent &RFC p4&142 MR20

WADE,Richard Curtis 2Lt kia 26-2-18 40RFC p17 CR France924

WADE,Samuel Shorten Arthur 2Lt kia 8-12-14 Lincs p76 MR22

WADE,Sidney T2Lt ded 26-10-18 Lincs p76 CR Notts85

WADE-GERY,Robert Hugh Capt dow 17-7-16 RGA 1SB p42 CR France189

WADESON,Edward Yeadon Lt kia 22-3-18 3 att10LNLancs p136 MR20

WADESON,Frederick William George,CB.MajGen ded 10-12-20 IA Ex KOSB CR Devon71

WADHAM,Vivian Hugh Nicholas.MID Capt kia 17-1-16 1Hamps &RFC p4&121 CR Belgium125

WADLOW,Bernard Victor T2Lt kia 3-4-17 13Mddx p148 CR France570,2-4-17 Ex 5Bn

WADLOW,Harold Maj kia 24-7-16 RGA 109SB p42 CR France397

WADLOW,Harry TCapt kld 1-5-17 GL &RFC p14 CR Glouc38

WADSON,Stanley Parker 2Lt kia 10-8-18 6RWSurr p57 CR France636

WADSWORTH,Ernest Hinchcliffe 2Lt ded 12-3-17 4WRid p227 CR Yorks411

WADSWORTH,Maurice Moxon Lt kia 9-7-15 5YLI p235 CR Belgium85

WADSWORTH,Percy 2Lt kia 22-3-18 1EYorks p85 MR27

WADSWORTH,Wilfred Howard 2Lt dow 22-3-18 RFA X16TMB p37 CR France987

WAGER,Arthur Howell Lt dow 17-7-16 C85RH& p37 CR France630,Capt

WAGER,Willson Stanley 2Lt kia 12-7-17 16NumbF p63 MR31

WAGGOTT,Garibaldi Matthewson 2Lt kia 11-4-18 16 att1/6NumbF p63 MR32,13-4-18

324

WAGHORN,Herbert Gilmore Capt dow 26-4-17 6NStaffs p238 CR France511

WAGHORN,Leonard Pengelly 2Lt kia 6-11-14 3RWKent att1RBerks p142 MR29

WAGHORN,Percy William 2Lt kia 7-10-16 8RFus p70 CR France512 Ex Sgt 1Drags

WAGHORNE,Harold Frederick 2LtTCapt dow 21-9-16 11YLI p144 CR France833

WAGNER,Ethelbert Godwin Stockwell 2Lt kia 7-1-17 RWar &32RFC p14&66 CR France518

WAGSTAFF,John Carleton T2Lt kia 12-10-17 SStaffs att8Bn p123 CR Belgium126

WAGSTAFF,Robert Arthur 2Lt kia 1-10-18 29MGC p186 CR Belgium84

WAHL,Bruno Wolfgang 2Lt kia 26-9-16 IARO att28Cav p284 MR61,29Cav

WAHL,Matthew Daniel 2LtAMaj kia 21-6-17 RGA 294SB p42 CR Belgium48,Mathew

WAIN,Richard William Leslie.VC.TLtACapt kia 20-11-17 25Manch attA'TankCps p156&189 MR17

WAINE,William Henry Capt kia 6-8-15 14Manch p156 MR4

WAINMAN,Ernest T2Lt kia 2-3-17 20Manch p156 CR France514

WAINMAN,Philip Stafford Gordon CaptBtMaj kia 26-9-15 6 att2Worc p110 CR France423

WAINWRIGHT,Clifford Ernest 2Lt dow14-10-18 KRRC att11RAF CR France375

WAINWRIGHT,Eric Lawrence Lt ded 15-9-15 IARO att59Rif p284 CR Lond14,2Lt dow 15Sikhs

WAINWRIGHT,Geoffrey Chauner 2Lt dow 22-12-14 3Nhampt p138 CR France727

WAINWRIGHT,Geoffrey Harry Lt dow 8-9-18 3 att2Suff p79 CR France13

WAINWRIGHT,Geoffrey Lennox 2Lt kia 25-9-15 3 att2RSuss p120 CR France219

WAINWRIGHT, Harry Arnold 2Lt kia 16-7-18 15Ches p97 CR Belgium40

WAINWRIGHT,Henry Carrey TLt dow 5-2-16 17Lpool p73 CR France300,Currey

WAINWRIGHT,Samuel Stewart Lt kia 11-3-17 6Norf p217 CR France314,12-3-17

WAISTELL,Walter Edmund T2Lt kia 4-10-17 12/13NumbF p63 MR30

WAIT,Charles Frederick Wells TLt dow 15-7-16 10YLI p144 CR France188

WAIT,Herbert Alfred Vincent 2Lt kia 2-12-17 2RBerks D'Coy p140 MR30,Lt

WAITE,Alfred.DCM.2Lt kia 5-4-18 5RBerks p140 CR France516

WAITE,Arthur Sydney 2Lt dow 25-9-16 1/4NumbF p213 CR France145

WAITE,Charles 2Lt dow 28-3-18 4 att2/8WYorks p83 CR France225

WAITE,Clement William.DSO.TMaj ded 31-1-19 11EYorks p255 CR Yorks22,30-1-19 13Bn

WAITE,Frederick Maxwell 2Lt kia 7-6-17 1/4Leic p220 CR Belgium9

WAITE,Hugh Conyers 2Lt kia 6-4-17 2/8WYorks p219 CR France568 Ex CanadaInf

WAITE,Joseph Thorpe Lt kia 21-1-16 1/5EKent p213 CR Iraq5

WAITES,Charles James 2Lt kia 10-10-18 6ConnRgrs p172 CR France230

WAITT,Reginald Charles 2Lt kia 27-8-17 11Suff p79 MR21

WAKE,Charles Baldwin Drury 2Lt kia 25-9-18 6 att2KRRC p152 CR France375

WAKE,Hugh St.Aubyn.MVC.Maj kia 30-10-14 IA 2/8GurkhaRif p284 MR28

WAKE,Thomas Frederick Henry 2Lt dow 10-4-18 1 att8NStaffs p158 CR Belgium11

WAKEFIELD,Arthur Gibbon Lt kia 29-5-19 IARO att144LabCps p284 MR43,2Lt 28-5-19

WAKEFIELD,Charles John Maj ded 1-7-20 RIrRifl att7KAR CR EAfrica36

WAKEFIELD,Frank Mahan Lt ded 2-1-18 DorsYeo attMGC p187&203,2-1-19 CR Hamps64

WAKEFIELD,Jessie Emily Sister ded 7-2-19 TFNS p254 CR France40

WAKEFIELD,Leonard John 2Lt kia 16-6-17 8Lond p247 MR20

WAKEFIELD,Montague Stephen Lt kia 20-11-17 3 att1N&D p135 MR30

WAKEFIELD,Oliver T2Lt kia 12-10-17 HouseholdBn p20 MR30

WAKEFIELD,Roger Owen Birbeck Lt dow 28-8-14 RIrFus p172 CR France657

WAKEFIELD,Sydney Clark 2Lt kia 22-3-18 2TankCps p189 MR27

WAKEFIELD,Thomas Butler T2Lt kia 8-9-17 2/6WYorks p83 CR France563

WAKEFORD,Charles Herbert Stanley Lt kia 7-9-18 GlamYeo p203 CR France446,24WelchR

WAKEFORD,Edward Francis Capt ded 23-2-15 6RSuss p272 CR Sussex58

WAKEFORD,Edward Kingsley TLt kia 14-7-17 7Leic p88 CR France453,16-7-16

WAKEFORD,F.R.S.Lt ded 25-12-18 GlamYeo &RAF p203

WAKEFORD,George Tarik 2Lt kia 23-7-16 4RBerks p234 MR21

WAKEFORD,Harold T2Lt kia 4-4-16 10 att6SLancs p126 MR38

WAKEFORD,Owen.MC.Maj dow 21-3-18 RGA 76SB p42 MR20

WAKEFORD,Robert Scott T2Lt ded 22-2-17 RFC p14 CR Berks85

WAKEFORD,Walter Thomas 2Lt kia 7-7-16 2ELancs p111 CR France744

WAKELEY,John Eric Stanley.MID T2Lt dow 9-9-16 1Glouc p107 CR France833

WAKELEY,William Norman 2Lt kia 8-5-17 15Lpool attMGC p73&186 MR37

WAKEMAN,Edward Offley Rouse 2Lt kia 16-5-15 att1GrenGds SR p50 MR22 &CR France1059

WAKEMAN,Frank Trevor Lt kia 30-10-17 5RWar attRFC p20&214 MR20

WAKERLEY,Arthur John Capt kia 8-6-17 1/4Leic D'Coy p219 CR France550

WAKLEY,Bertram Joseph Maj ded 11-2-17 1LNLancs p136 CR lond4

WALBEOFFE-WILSON,William Capt kld 2-8-15 3Mon p244 CR Belgium79

WALBAUM,William Frederick Lt dow 12-9-17 B276RFA p208 CR Belgium16

WALCH,Brian James Brett 2Lt dow 28-10-15 2/4Ess p232 Gallipoli18

WALCH,James Bernard Millard T2Lt kia 25-9-15 2RWSurr p57 MR19

WALCOT,Basil.DSO.Maj ded 14-9-18 RE p49 CR Surrey131

WALCOTT,Francis Sharpe TCapt kia 26-9-16 RAMC att8NumbF p198 CR France393

WALCOTT,John Henry Lyons 2Lt kia 2-11-14 IA 2/2GurkhaRif att34SikhPnrs p284 MR28

WALCOTT,Lyons George Edmund Lt kia 2-7-16 5Lincs p220 CR France576

WALDEGRAVE,Edmund John 2Lt kia 10-8-18 D286RFA p37 CR France266

WALDEN,Rand Edwin John T2Lt kia 16-11-17 2LancF p94 CR France154

WALDIE,Charles Percival 2Lt kia 26-9-15 8RWSurr p57 MR19

WALDIE,John Gray TLt kia 31-7-17 11BlkW attt25MGC p129&186 MR29

WALDRON,Benson T2Lt kia 31-7-17 19Manch C'Coy p156 MR29

WALDRON,Cecil Hamersley TLt kia 2-3-16 7Lincs p76 MR29

WALDRON,Fionn Thomas 2Lt kia 23-10-16 2Ess p132 CR France924

WALDRON,Francis Fitzgerald.MIDx2 TMaj ded 3-7-16 19Huss att60RFC p4&23 CR France568,kia

WALDY,Cuthbert Temple 2Lt kia 20-10-14 SLancs p126 MR22

WALE,Adie Capt dow 30-5-18 186RFA X39TMB p37 CR France84,kld 166RFA

WALE,Alan Ernest T2Lt kld 23-11-17 GL &RFC p14 CR Mddx9,23-7-17

WALE,Alick Arthur ACapt kia 8-11-17 2 att7LNLancs p136 CR Belgium183

WALE,C.C.Augustus Capt 4-4-20 IMS MR65

WALE,Clifford Hardwicke T2Lt kia 19-1-16 RIrRifl p170 MR32

WALES,Harold Robert T2Lt kia 14-7-16 9EYorks p85 MR21

WALEY,Aubrey John TLt kia 31-7-17 12RFus p70 MR29

WALFORD,Alexander Ellis TLt kia 16-8-16 2Suff p79 MR21

WALFORD,Alfred Sanderson LtACapt ded 19-1-19 2Ches p97 CR Gallipoli29

WALFORD,Garth Neville.VC.Capt kia 26-4-15 RFA p37 CR Gallipoli15

WALFORD,George Henry Maj kia 19-4-15 Suff p79 CR Belgium59

WALFORD,Hamilton Stewart Lt kia 27-5-18 12Worc att1/4WelshR p110 MR18

WALFORD,Leonard Nithsdale Lt kia 8-5-15 12Lond p248&249 MR29

WALFORD,Oliver Robson 2Lt kia 26-4-15 1Hamps p121 CR Belgium152

WALFORD,Percy Frederic T2Lt kia 11-4-17 7KRRC p152 CR France532

WALFORD,W.G.Capt kia 4-11-18 RE &62RAF p49 CR B218 ?

WALKDEN,Arthur Chamberlain 2Lt kia 28-4-17 4ELancs p226 MR21

WALKER,Adolphus 2Lt dow 15-4-18 1/2 att2/5WRid p116 CR France169

WALKER,Alexander Lamond LtCol ded 27-12-16 RHFA p262 CR Norf11

WALKER,Allan Dixon Lt mbk 16-6-15 2Lincs p257 MR32

WALKER,Alfred English TLt kia 22-8-16 20RFus p70

WALKER,Anthony Thornton T2Lt kia 30-7-15 8RB p180 MR29

WALKER,Archdale Gillam 2Lt kia 17-5-15 4NStaffs att2RScotF p158 MR22

WALKER,Arnold Henry Lt dow 17-9-18 3 att8Ches p97 CR Lancs14

WALKER,Arthur Lt kia 10-8-18 WRid attMGC Inf p116 CR Belgium192

WALKER,Arthur Dight 2Lt kia 18-10-16 7 att19Manch p156 MR21

WALKER,Arthur Dunbar LtCol kia 26-3-18 RE 24DivHQ p49 MR27

WALKER,Arthur John TCapt kia 7-8-15 11Yorks att6Manch p91 CR Gallipoli2

WALKER,Arthur Nimmo LtCol kia 24-9-16 RAMC attRHFA p198&206 CR France703

WALKER,Basil Scarisbrickle 2Lt kld 9-5-15 5Ches p222 CR Belgium35

WALKER,Charles Corbould Capt kia 26-8-14 2A&SH A'Coy p174 CR France716

WALKER,Charles Nigel Gordon TLt kia 7-8-15 10SStaffs att8Manch p123 MR4

WALKER,Clarence Howard T2Lt dow 28-9-16 10 att12Ess p132 CR France74

WALKER,Claud Arthur Leonard Lt kia 10-7-18 2RInniskF p105 CR France296

WALKER,Cornwall Nathaniel Brownlow Lt kia 16-8-17 7RInniskF p105 MR30,Capt

WALKER,Denham 2Lt dow 19-9-16 2/5ELancs att18MGC p187&226 CR France105

WALKER,Denis Henry Capt dow 26-1-16 5Yorks p220 CR Belgium11

WALKER,Edgar Wilmer Capt kia 27-10-14 3EYorks p85 CR France82,29-10-14 1Bn

WALKER,Edmund Basil.MID 2Lt kia 18-4-15 1RWKent p142 CR Belgium152

WALKER,Edward William.DSO.Capt kia 6-11-17 1/7RWFus p223 CR Palestine1

WALKER,Eric Alfred English Lt 22-8-16 20RFus CR France389

WALKER,Eric Arthur T2Lt kia 29-12-15 9 att6KSLI p145 CR France525

WALKER,Ernest James Capt dow 4-10-17 296RFA p207 CR Belgium11

WALKER,F.F.2Lt dow 14-4-18 GL &RAF p191

WALKER,Francis Hercules TLtCol kia 7-1-16 7NStaffs p158

WALKER,Frank Benjamin 2Lt kia 23-7-16 2 att6KRRC p152 MR21,6 att2Bn
WALKER,Frederick Cecil Banes 2Lt kia 9-5-15 Dev p77
WALKER,Frederick Charles T2Lt kia 25-11-15 8Suff p79 CR France430
WALKER,Frederick Clarkson Lt kia 20-9-17 5Lpool p215 MR30
WALKER,Frederick Leslie T2Lt kld 28-12-17 RFC p14 CR Herts30
WALKER,Frederick Ramsay.MC.2Lt ded 6-1-17 2A&SH p174 CR Scot236
WALKER,Frederick Rutley.MBE.Capt ded 26-11-19 31Punjabis attPoliticalDept p284 CR Iraq8
WALKER,Gavin Henry Capt kia 14-3-15 1HLI p164 CR France279
WALKER,George TLt dow 28-11-15 10Beds attNigR p87&202 CR WAfrica58
WALKER,George Bruce TLt ded 1-3-19 17HLI attRFC p265 CR Scot674
WALKER,George Ernest TLt ded 6-6-17 11RScots p55 CR France604
WALKER,George Francis 2Lt kia 7-12-16 5Y&L p238 CR France701
WALKER,George Henderson Lt kia 28-7-17 GL att45RFC p14 MR20
WALKER,George Henry Lt kia 16-6-15 4RLancs p213 MR22
WALKER,George Pybus 2Lt kia 9-8-18 10TankCps p189 MR16
WALKER,George Stafford Lt dow 20-11-17 B79RFA p37 CR France145
WALKER,George Stanley 2Lt kia 23-10-18 20Manch p156 CR France231
WALKER,George William Quarmby Lt kia 7-7-16 7WRid p227 CR France702
WALKER,Gervaise Mapletoft Lt kia 15-4-18 3 att1Leic p88 MR30,Capt
WALKER,Gideon.MC.TCapt kia 27-11-17 RAMC att3FA p198 CR France755
WALKER,Gordon Henry 2Lt kia 10-11-17 6Nhampt p138 MR30
WALKER,H.Col 26-7-17 WYorks CR Mddx26
WALKER,H.LtCol 3-6-19 1WelchR attRAF CR Devon1
WALKER,Harold Saxon.MID Capt dow 12-9-17 2/9Lond p247 CR Belgium16
WALKER,Harry.CMG.LtCol dow 27-9-15 4BlkW p230 CR France705
WALKER,Harry 2Lt kia 28-7-17 RGA 295SB p42 CR France922
WALKER,Harry Brampton LtACapt ded 24-9-17 RFA p37 MR65,Bampton
WALKER,Harry Cullis Steele 2Lt kia 12-3-15 1N&D p135 CR France1059
WALKER,Henry Gerald 2Lt kia 1-7-16 2YLI p144 MR21
WALKER,Henry John Innes Capt kia 25-4-15 att1RWar p66 MR29
WALKER,Herbert John Maj ded 25-9-16 RE Staff p262 CR Greece7,dow
WALKER,Herbert Newton 2LtTLt kia 6-6-17 11SStaffs attMGC p123&186 CR Belgium100,107MGC att11SStaffs
WALKER,Herbert William Capt ded 12-3-19 7N&D p233 CR Notts84
WALKER,Hercules Frank LtCol 7-1-16 7NStaffs MR4
WALKER,Howard Napier.OBE.MC.Lt ded 3-6-19 WelshR &RAF p255
WALKER,Hugh Percy Wonham 2Lt kia 23-4-17 5A&SH p243 CR France1182
WALKER,Ingham 2Lt kia 27-9-18 3MGC p186 CR France756
WALKER,Jack Bertram 2Lt dow 8-3-18 1/5RLancs p59 CR France88
WALKER,James Edward 2Lt kia 3-5-17 1RLancs p59 MR20
WALKER,James Hope 2Lt kld 16-3-17 GL &RFC p14 CR Herts38
WALKER,James Robert.MC.LtAMaj kia 20-3-17 B62RFA p37 CR France1182
WALKER,J.C.2Lt kld 18-10-18 GL &RAF p191
WALKER,Jerome Lennie T2Lt kia 6-5-16 14RIrRif p170 CR France702
WALKER,John T2Lt kia 1-7-16 14NumbF p63 MR21
WALKER,John Prentice 2Lt ded 18-9-16 7A&SH p272 CR Scot64
WALKER,John Alexander 2Lt kia 26-8-18 1RScotF att1/4KOSB p95 MR16
WALKER,John Arthur TCapt kia 19-2-16 10RWFus p99 CR Belgium15
WALKER,John Chinnery 2Lt kia 19/20-12-15 1/5WYorks p218 CR Belgium73
WALKER,John Croxton 2Lt kia 3-9-16 1Camb p245 CR France220
WALKER,John Edward Schlmaster 29-8-14 Cps of Schlmasters CR Kent7
WALKER,John Haslam T2Lt dow 2-11-17 GL att16RSuss p191 CR Egypt9
WALKER,John Henry 2Lt kia 18-9-17 4EYorks p219 MR30
WALKER,John Quintin Frederick 31-3-18 57RFC MR20
WALKER,John West Lt kia 11-4-17 2/5Lincs p220 MR21
WALKER,John Wickham Capt kia 5-7-16 5YLI p235 CR France744
WALKER,Joseph Noel Lt kia 4-7-16 1/5YLI p235 MR21
WALKER,Kenneth MacKenzie 2Lt kia 12-8-18 3Wilts att209RAF p153 MR20
WALKER,Lawrence Hale.MID 2Lt kia 12-10-16 2Beds p87 CR France432,Hall
WALKER,Leslie Bedford Capt dow 1-7-17 5Yorks p220 CR France145
WALKER,Louis Lt ded 22-10-19 IARO att1/10Jats p284 MR43 &CR Pakistan50
WALKER,Lewis Aubrey T2Lt kia 6-8-17 RASC attRGA 118SB p194 CR Belgium11
WALKER,Malcolm Reid 2Lt kia 23-4-17 7A&SH p243 CR France545
WALKER,Maurice John Lea 2Lt kia 3-5-17 6RWKent p142 MR20
WALKER,Miles Lt ded 3-12-18 RASC 29DivTrn p253&272 CR Lond8
WALKER,Norman Crawford Capt kia 25-9-15 4BlkW p230 MR19
WALKER,Norman Reginald Lt kia 23-8-18 RScots att10KOSB p55 CR France19
WALKER,Oscar Lt kia 3-5-17 5WRid p227 MR20
WALKER,Oscar Robert Capt kia 4-6-15 12Worc attRFus p110 MR4

WALKER,Oswald Bethell Capt kia 23-8-14 15Huss p22 MR15
WALKER,Percy Richard Samuel 2Lt kia 5-8-18 RE 103FC p49 CR France161
WALKER,Ralph T2Lt kia 21-4-17 11A&SH p174 MR38
WALKER,Reginald.MID Maj dow 5-9-16 RE 105FC p49 CR France59
WALKER,Reginald Lt kia 25-4-18 1/5WYorks p218 CR Belgium126
WALKER,Reginald Fydell 2Lt dow 21-10-14 2Manch p156 CR France279
WALKER,Reginald Selby.DSO.LtCol kia 30-9-18 RE VI CpsHQ p49 CR France1483
WALKER,Richard 2Lt kia 9-8-16 2/5LancF p221 MR21 Ex 28Lond
WALKER,Robert Coutts 2Lt 12-8-21 2RScots MR66
WALKER,Robert Hugh TLt kia 9-4-17 9SfthH p165 CR France96
WALKER,Robert Jardine.MID Capt kia 25-9-15 GordH SR att1Bn p167 MR29
WALKER,Robert Russell 2Lt kia 23-3-18 7Lond p247 CR France672
WALKER,Robert Sandilands Frowd.CMG.TLtCol ded 16-5-17 SL p201&268
WALKER,Roger Beverley.MC.Capt dow 13-11-18 YorkHuss att9WYorks p206 CR France34
WALKER,Stephen 2Lt ded 14-5-18 Camb &RAF p245 CR Essex246,kld
WALKER,Samuel Hugh T2Lt kia 16-8-17 14RIrRif p170 MR30
WALKER,Samuel Richard Ernest 2Lt dow 11-10-18 1NumbF p63 CR France380
WALKER,Stanley.MC.Capt kia 20-5-18 C246RFA p37 CR Belgium8
WALKER,Stanley Arthur TLt kia 14-10-16 RAMC att1/5Ches p198 CR France293,1/6Bn
WALKER,Sydney 2Lt kia 15-8-17 7DLI p239 CR France1186
WALKER,Sydney Stratton TCapt kia 19-7-16 12EYorks p85 CR France1157,Shatton
WALKER,Thomas Campbell T2Lt kia 14-2-16 10LancF p94 MR29
WALKER,Thomas Cartmel 2Lt kia 5-6-15 1/5Manch p236 CR Gallipoli2,6-6-15
WALKER,Thomas Kynaston Lt kia 24-4-16 1IrGds 1Coy p53 CR Belgium72
WALKER,Thomas Percival Patterson Capt kia 4-7-18 13TankCps p189 CR France1170
WALKER,Turner Russell T2Lt dow 2-7-16 18Lpool p73 CR France630,1-7-16
WALKER,Vernon Lee T2Lt kia 29-5-17 8ELancs p111 MR20
WALKER,Victor 2Lt kia 4-4-18 14Glouc att7RWKent p107 MR27
WALKER,William.DFC.Capt kld 8-10-18 GL &6RAF p191 MR20
WALKER,Walker 2Lt dow 25-8-18 6LancF p221 CR France927,Walter
WALKER,Walter Arthur Beaumont 2Lt dow 30-10-14 Beds p87 CR France80
WALKER,Wilfred Bertram Maj kia 29-10-14 Yorks p91 MR29
WALKER,Wilfred Harold 2Lt kia 3-5-17 Mddx att12Bn p148 MR20
WALKER,William TCapt kia 1-7-16 9YLI p144 CR France189
WALKER,William 2Lt kia 9-1-17 3Manch p156 CR Iraq5
WALKER,William Archibald Smail Maj kia 12-4-15 46Punjabis att130Baluchis p284 CR EAfrica56
WALKER,William Cleland Lt kia 16-4-18 1ScotRif att19TMB p104 MR32
WALKER,William Eaton Guy Capt kia 1-7-16 7N&D p233 CR France281
WALKER,William Francis 2Lt kia 9-4-18 3 att9NumbF p63 MR32
WALKER,William Gray Johnstone.MC&Bar.TLtACapt kia 18-7-17 GL attTMB 8Div p191 CR Belgium5
WALKEY,Francis Ashton 2Lt kia 17-10-18 2RDubF A'Coy p177 CR France190
WALKINGTON,Charles Edward Capt kia 14-10-18 2RIrRif p170 CR Belgium157
WALKINSHAW,James 2Lt kia 26-4-18 att5CamH p168 MR30
WALL,Arthur Geoffrey Nelson T2Lt kld 6-8-17 RFC p14 CR Ches182
WALL,Leonard Comer Lt kia 9-6-17 A275RFA p208 CR Belgium11
WALL,Michael Thomas 2Lt kia 7-6-17 3 att6RIrReg p89 CR Belgium17
WALL,Richard Ralph Baldwin Maj kia 8-6-17 378/169RFA p37 CR France922
WALLACE,Alexander Moultrie Capt kia 12-3-15 3Nhampt p138 MR22
WALLACE,Andrew Capt kia 12-7-15 4KOSB p223 MR4
WALLACE,Arthur Reginald TLt ded 18-1-19 GL RE attIWT p191 CR Iraq8
WALLACE,Charles Arthur Phin 2Lt kia 22-3-18 3 att6KOSB p102 MR27
WALLACE,Cyril John George Lt ded 9-9-18 14NumbF p63 CR France40,24Bn
WALLACE,Cyril Walter 2Lt kia 8-3-16 IARO att47Sikhs p284 MR38
WALLACE,David Stephenson 2Lt kia 19-9-14 2SLancs C'Coy p126 CR France1107
WALLACE,Denis 2Lt dow PoW 18-4-18 4 att9RScots p211 CR France1703,Lt
WALLACE,Dudley Whistler.MC.Lt kia 9-10-17 1/5WYorks p128 MR30,Capt
WALLACE,E.SNurse ded 6-6-16 QAIMNS p200
WALLACE,Geoffrey Robert.MC&Bar.MID Capt kia 27-8-17 7Worc p225 MR30
WALLACE,George Douglas T2Lt kia 26-10-17 21Manch p156 CR Belgium115
WALLACE,George Frederick T2Lt kia 23-5-17 20Mddx p148 CR France439, Capt
WALLACE,Harold Bruce 2Lt kia 26-10-14 3Lpool p73 MR29
WALLACE,Harry Herbert T2Lt dow 21-1-17 27NumbF D'Coy p63 CR France297,Henry
WALLACE,Henry Gilmour 2Lt kia 3-8-17 C86RFA p37 CR Belgium118

WALLACE,Houston Steward Hamilton TCapt kia 22-7-16 10Worc p110 MR21

WALLACE,John 2Lt kia 9-5-15 BlkW p129

WALLACE,John 2Lt kia 1-8-17 TA 4RScots p211 MR34

WALLACE,John Ernest Dudley Lt dow 7-8-17 RE 2FC p210 CR Belgium16

WALLACE,John James Rev dow 8-11-18 RAChDept att8NStaffs p200 CR France332

WALLACE,John Kennedy 2Lt kia 23-4-17 1/7BlkW p231 CR France604

WALLACE,John Robert 2Lt 9-5-15 1BlkW MR22

WALLACE,John Roger 2Lt kia 23-4-15 1RScotF p95 CR Belgium28,22-4-15

WALLACE,Joseph Stephen.MC&Bar.CaptAMaj kia 28-3-18 RAMC p253 CR France266

WALLACE,Kenneth Moss TLt dow 31-5-16 8RIrRif p170 MR19 CR France80

WALLACE,Lillie SNurse 6-6-16 QAIMNS CR Surrey160

WALLACE,Robert Capt ded 6-5-15 2EYorks p85 CR France102

WALLACE,Robert Nelson Capt ded 5-7-18 RAMC att6RScots CR Essex146

WALLACE,Robinson 2Lt dow 2-10-16 8DLI p239 CR France177

WALLACE,Stuart Annesley Lt kia 31-5-17 RGA 156SB p42 CR France1186

WALLACE,Thomas Victor Walter T2Lt dow 2-11-17 1/8Hamps p121 CR Palestine2,kia

WALLACE,Walter Mackenzie T2Lt kia 21-10-15 12Mddx p148 CR France188

WALLACE,William T2Lt kia 29-9-16 54MGC p186 MR21

WALLACE,William Lt kia 16-11-17 3 att1CamH p168 CR Belgium22,17-11-17

WALLACE,William Douglas 2Lt dow 22-8-16 5HLI p240 CR France176

WALLACE,William Edwin T2Lt kia 31-7-17 RE 254TC p49 CR Belgium5

WALLACE,William Ernest Lt kia 17-4-17 8RScots p211 CR France1182

WALLACE,William Middleton Lt kia 22-8-15 5RB attRFC p2&180 CR France924

WALLACE,William Thwaites.MC.TLt kia 12-4-17 B160RFA p37 CR France96,B16RFA

WALLACE-COPLAND,Reginald Capt 16-7-19 3/1GurkhaRif MR43

WALLER,Charles Raymond T2Lt kld 9-6-17 GL &RFC p14 CR Mddx66,9-8-17

WALLER,C.L.LtCol 14-1-15 42DeoliR MR67

WALLER,Francis Ernest.Bart.Capt kia 25-10-14 6 att4RFus p70

WALLER,Hardress Edmund Capt dow 22-11-17 2Y&L p159 CR France398

WALLER,Henry Norman Capt kia 3-7-17 2/4WRid p227 CR France1488

WALLER,Herbert William.MC.TCapt kia 10-4-17 21NumbF p63 CR France96

WALLER,John Raymond T2Lt kld 18-5-17 GL &RFC p14 CR Glouc9,dedacc

WALLER,Richard Alured 2Lt ded 1-11-17 5RFus p70 CR France446

WALLER,Richard Hope Capt kia 3-11-14 IA 38Dogras p284 MR47

WALLER,Thomas Henry Whalley TLt kia 22-10-17 14Glouc p107 MR30

WALLER,Thomas Jenkinson 2Lt dow 28-9-18 2NumbF att4Beds p63 CR France1184,3Bn

WALLEY,Geoffrey Stephen Lt dow 20-8-16 5 att2KRRC p152 CR France177,kia

WALLEY,George John 2Lt dow 25-8-18 7Lincs p76 CR France13

WALLEY,John Clifford 2Lt kia 23-3-18 5 att7Leic p220 MR27

WALLIKER,Lester Charles 2Lt dow 15-5-15 2ESurr p113 CR France102

WALLING,Ernest.MC.MIDx2 CaptAMaj kia 25-4-18 7WYorks p218 MR30

WALLINGTON,Charles Harold T2Lt kia 20-9-17 Dev att1/6Lpool p77 MR30

WALLINGTON,Frank Courtneay 2Lt kia 6-8-18 SomLI att1/5SLancs p80 CR France106

WALLINGTON,Geoffrey Stafford 2LtTCapt&Adjt kia 19-9-17 KRRC att10Bn p152 CR Belgium126

WALLINGTON,Nigel Hugh 2Lt kldacc 21-6-17 1SomLI p80 CR France729

WALLIS,Alfred Babbington Capt kia 21-3-18 2/6N&D p233 MR20,Bibbington

WALLIS,Alleyne Westaby 2Lt kia 7-6-17 10Lond p248 MR29

WALLIS,Arthur 2Lt dow 2-10-18 1/5LNLancs p234 CR France1184

WALLIS,Arthur Cecil Capt dow 17-9-18 2/5SLancs att4LNLancs p230 CR France13

WALLIS,Arthur Vincent.MID Lt ded 10-7-17 3L EgyptianLabCps p201 CR Iraq1

WALLIS,Harry Bertram T2Lt dow 11-7-16 11RB p180 CR Belgium11

WALLIS,Bertram Henry.MC.Capt kia 18-9-18 RASC att1/1Camb p194 CR France369

WALLIS,Charles William 2Lt kia 31-7-17 6 att13Mddx p148 CR Belgium112

WALLIS,Duncan Boyd Lt dow 23-7-15 3ConnRgrs att2RMunstF p172 CR France98,24-7-15

WALLIS,Edward Percy TCapt kia 17-10-16 RLancs att8RSuss p59 CR France150,18-10-16

WALLIS,Francis Herbert Guy Capt dow 17-5-18 11EYorks p85 CR France27

WALLIS,Frederick George TLt kia 30-11-17 EKent p58 MR17

WALLIS,George Arthur Edward.MC.2Lt dow 16-10-18 8RWKent p142 CR France380

WALLIS,George Herbert.DCM.Capt&QM dow 20-9-18 1RWSurr p57&259 CR France278

WALLIS,Harold Legh Lt kld 2-7-16 GL &RFC p4&191,Leigh CR Surrey160

WALLIS,Henry Digby Lt kia 21-10-14 3CldGds p51 MR29

WALLIS,John Buckridge 2Lt drd 10-10-18 4Wilts p236 CR Ireland14,Buckeridge

WALLIS,Nevill Hampton 2Lt dow 25-5-18 C50 RFA p37 CR France102

WALLIS,Noel Veder T2Lt kia 10-4-17 12 Ches p97 CR Belgium102,9Bn

WALLIS,Reginald Robert 2Lt kia 26-3-18 RWar att7Norf p66 MR27

WALLIS,Thomas Francis Capt kia 2-9-18 12SomLI p80 CR France511

WALLIS,Walter Kelburne Lt ded 17-7-18 Lincs attELancs p76 CR Iraq5

WALLIS,William Isaac 2Lt dow 10-10-18 2Hamps p121 CR Belgium38

WALLOND,William John 2Lt kia 22-3-18 13Mddx p148 MR27

WALLWORK,Herbert TLt kia 20-7-16 20RFus p70 MR21

WALMESLEY,Richard Lt kia 23-10-14 3 att2Yorks p91 CR Belgium88,21-10-14

WALMISLEY-DRESSER,Henry Joseph TMajALtCol dow 17-9-16 RWar attESurr p66 CR France833

WALMSLEY,James Blair T2Lt kia 8-8-16 7/8KOSB p102 CR France188

WALMSLEY,Sam Harold Capt kia 5-6-15 5ELancs p226 MR4

WALN,Edward Ashton 2Lt kia 21-10-18 2/6Lpool p215 CR Belgium406

WALNE,Horace George 2Lt kia 11-4-17 2Suff p79 CR France581

WALPOLE,Horatio Spencer Lt kia 9-4-18 1CldGds p51 CR France103

WALPOLE,John Robsart Capt kia 1-7-16 7RWSurr p57 CR France397

WALROND,Francis Hillier T2Lt dow 15-8-16 5 O&BLI p130 CR Sussex111

WALROND,George Basil Stuart TCapt kld 19-3-16 6SomLI p80 CR France420

WALROND,Victor.MIDx2 CaptAMaj kia 26-4-17 15/36RFA p37 CR France265

WALROND,Hon William Lionel Charles TLt ded 2-11-15 RASC p194 CR Devon243

WALSEN,C.W. TLt kia 4-8-17 4KAR p202 CR EAfrica5 &CR Tanzania1,WALSER

WALSH,Albert 2Lt dow 8-8-17 5ELancs att4RFC p20&226 CR Belgium18

WALSH,Archibald Charles Mark 2Lt dow 18-3-15 RHA X'Bty p37 CR Somerset157

WALSH,Arthur.MC.Capt kia 11-4-18 4SLancs p229 MR19

WALSH,Frank 2Lt kia 12-5-17 6 att18Manch p237 MR20

WALSH,Frank 2Lt kia 29-9-18 340/44RFA p37 CR France212

WALSH,Frederick William T2Lt dow 11-7-16 19KRRC att17RWFus p152 CR France833,11Glouc

WALSH,Geoffrey Christian Lansdale 2Lt kia 22-6-17 Ches att13Bn p97 MR29

WALSH,Geoffrey Pennell Lt kia 9-8-15 N&D att2Bn p135 MR29

WALSH,Gordon James Turnbull.MID Capt 2-7-19 IARO att13Lancers MR66

WALSH,Henry Alfred.CB.Col ded 25-11-18 SomLI Ex Cmdg No8District p263CR Somerset157

WALSH,Herbert T2Lt kia 30-12-17 46RFC p14 CR France49

WALSH,John.MID TMaj dow 19-2-17 22RFus p70 CR France393

WALSH,John Joseph 2Lt kia 8-10-18 5ConnRgrs p172 CR France846

WALSH,Lionel Henry.MC.DCM.ACapt dow 29-8-18 7Lond p247 CR France119

WALSH,Lionel Percy TMaj dow 4-7-16 2RDubF p177 CR France167

WALSH,Martin Oliver.MBE.2Lt kia 3-5-17 2/4YLI p235 MR20

WALSH,Michael Francis 24/1923 2Lt 23-12-16 3Bn 3(Rifle)Bde CR France923

WALSH,Patrick Joseph Lt kia 20-9-15 IA IMS p284 CR France354

WALSH,Percival TLt dow 8-7-16 8LNLancs p136 CR France74,2Lt

WALSH,Phillip James T2Lt kia 30-11-17 8RDubF p177 CR France1489,Lt

WALSH,Stephen Barry Lt ded 8-9-15 RAMC att1CavFA p198

WALSH,William TCapt ded 27-2-19 RAVC p268 CR Eire422

WALSH,William Leopold Hampson 2Lt kia 9-8-18 RWKent att8Bn p142 CR France634

WALSHA,Albert Arthur Lt kia 18-9-18 1Norf p74 CR France1701,9Bn

WALSHAM,Harold T2Lt dow 18-9-15 7KRRC p152 CR France40

WALSHAW,Frank Lt kia 20-9-18 IARO att1/101Grens p284 MR34

WALSHE,Francis Weldon.MC.TCapt kia 25-8-16 3 att1SWBord p101 CR France151

WALSHE,James D Lt kia 6-4-18 4RWFus p223 CR France232

WALSHE,M.A.SNurse 21-8-15 QAIMNS CR Europe4

WALTER,Alfred Ernest Henry U.T2Lt dow 13-5-17 2 O&BLI p130 CRLond14

WALTER,Arthur.MM.2Lt kia 21-3-18 1EYorks p85 MR27

WALTER,Bertram.DSO.Maj dow 16-9-16 106/22RFA p37 CR France23

WALTER,Cecil TLtACapt kia 8-10-17 9Dev p77 MR30

WALTER,Harold Ernest CaptTLtCol dow PoW 29-9-15 8Lincs p76 CR France1276

WALTER,Joseph Stanley TCapt kld 21-5-18 RWSurr p57 CR Germany3

WALTER,Raymond T2Lt kia 15-7-16 10Ches p97 MR21

WALTER,Stephen Reginald Parke Lt kia 31-7-17 RWSurr att32RFC p14&57 CR Belgium11

WALTER,Sydney 2Lt kia 25-10-14 1GrenGds p50 MR29

WALTER,William Frederick Maj kia 11-8-15 Staff LancF GSO 53Div p1 MR4

WALTERS,David T2Lt dow 22-5-17 15LancF p94 CR France145

WALTERS,Edward Charles 2Lt kia 22-12-14 3 att1Glouc p107 CR France260

WALTERS,Ernest Beauchamp TLt kia 30-7-16 8Glouc p107 MR21

WALTERS,Ernest Henry 2Lt kia 26-9-16 10Manch p237 MR19

WALTERS,Fred 2Lt kia 21-3-18 2/5N&D p233 MR20

WALTERS,Frederick William 2Lt kia 14-10-15 4Leic p220 MR19

WALTERS,Graham Yuille Laundy Lt dow 15-9-16 IrGds attMGC Inf p53 CR France374

WALTERS,Herbert Aidan 2Lt kld 7-4-18 GL &21RAF p191 CR Belgium18

WALTERS,Harold Victor TCapt kia 3-9-16 17N&D A'Coy p135 CR France339

WALTERS,Henry James.MID Lt kia 5-5-15 2Mon p244 MR29

WALTERS,Leslie Hadfield 2Lt dow 17-2-17 5Suff p217 CR France314

WALTERS,Sidney.MC.2Lt dow 4-10-18 SStaffs att1/6Bn p123 CR France446

WALTHER,Kurt Albert 2Lt kia 4-11-18 13KRRC p152 CR France1480

WALTHEW,Ernest John.MC.LtCol kia 22-5-18 RE Cmdg46Div p209 CR France109

WALTHEW,John Syers 2Lt kia 19-9-17 GL &4RFC p14 MR20

WALTON,Albert Bertie.MM.2Lt dow 16-9-18 KRRC att13Bn p152 CR France512

WALTON,Arthur James T2Lt dow 16-10-17 Y&L att9Bn p159 CR France139

WALTON,Charles Hindley T2Lt kia 23-7-16 19Manch p156 MR21 CR France390

WALTON,Eric Alfred 2Lt kia 16-9-16 9DLI p239 MR21

WALTON,Ernest 2Lt kia 27-3-18 18DLI p162 MR27,19Bn

WALTON,Francis John George T2Lt kia 1-7-16 18WYorks p83 CR France742

WALTON,Frank Arthur 2Lt kia 26-9-17 2Lond D'Coy p245 MR30

WALTON,Fred.MM.TCapt kia 15-9-16 18KRRC p152 MR21 &CR France1890

WALTON,Frederick Maxwell 2Lt ded 21-2-19 Worc att1/8Bn p110 CR France1849

WALTON,George Pears Lt kia 22-8-18 4NumbF att2Lincs p213 CR France514,dow

WALTON,Harold Arthur Gordon Lt ded 2-5-17 RFA 33DAC p37 CR France64

WALTON,Harold Foster 2Lt dow 11-4-17 27NumbF p63 CR France95

WALTON,Harold Henry.MC.Capt kia 13-10-15 7N&D A'Coy p233 MR19

WALTON,Harold William Lt dow 24-11-17 13Yorks p91 CR France398

WALTON,Hector Cyril T2Lt kia 9-9-17 Ess att8RWKent p132 CR Belgium19

WALTON,Henry.MC.Capt kia 27-3-18 1/6DLI p239 MR27

WALTON,Herbert Parlby Lt dow 7-12-17 2Yorks p91 CR Belgium165

WALTON,John Leigh Lt ded 22-7-18 21Lond p251 CR Lond14,dow

WALTON,Joseph Cyril Lt kia 29-4-18 4WRid p227 MR30

WALTON,Joseph Frank 2Lt dow 12-11-16 11 att12ESurr p113 MR29

WALTON,Leon Maitland 2Lt kia 17-11-16 1/4LNLancs p234 CR Belgium4,16-11-16

WALTON,Lewin Barlow BrigGen ded 24-5-17 IA Staff p284 MR65

WALTON,Oswald Thomas 2LtTLt kia 12-4-17 3SLancs &18RFC p14&126 CR France568

WALTON,Percy Jackson T2Lt kia 8-3-17 1WYorks p83 CR France115

WALTON,Reginald Frederick William T2Lt kia 26-9-17 12WYorks p83 CR Belgium45

WALTON,Richard Crawhall Lt kia 7-11-14 IA 1/9GurkhaRif p284 CR France705

WALTON,Robert Clare 2Lt kia 10-8-15 5RWFus p223 MR4

WALTON,William Knott 2LtTLt kia 31-7-17 20DLI p162 MR29

WALTON,William Lees Percival 2Lt kia 30-11-17 217MGC p186 MR17

WAND,Wilfred Ernest TLt kia 7-7-16 9NumbF p63

WAND-TETLEY,Charles Ernest Lt kia 22-8-15 9LancF p94

WANE,Hayward T2Lt kia 18-10-16 18Lpool p73 MR21

WANER,Gerald Richard Francis T2Lt dow 2-3-17 RE &25RFC p14&49 CR France88

WANLISS,Alexander.MID Lt kia 9-5-15 1BlkW p129 CR France924

WANKLYN,John Sudell.MC.Lt kia 29-5-18 29RFA p37&259 CR France202,Endell 128RFA

WANKLYN,Kenneth.MID Lt ded 15-11-18 98RFA p37 CR France1858

WANKLYN,William Hibbert T2Lt kia 11-5-17 HouseholdBn p20 CR France452

WANSBROUGH,William Evelyn Capt kia 29-7-16 3 att2SStaffs p123 MR21

WANSTALL,Elton Cyril 2Lt dow 25-9-15 EKent p58 MR19

WARBURTON,Fred Eric 2Lt kia 15-10-17 49RFA 3DivArtAnzacCpsTroops p37 CR Belgium10

WARBURTON,George Augustus Lowe T2Lt kld 1-10-17 GL &RFC p14 CR Norf247

WARBURTON,George Harold Edmondson.MC.LtACapt kia 17-4-18 4Lpool p73 CR Belgium40

WARBURTON,Henry Heap 2Lt dow 9-9-16 7LancF att48MGC p187&221 MR21

WARBURTON,Stanley T2Lt kia 14-9-16 12LancF p94 MR37

WARD,Albert 2Lt kia 28-6-18 15WYorks p83 CR France24

WARD,Albert Joseph 2Lt kia 13-6-18 2Leinst p175 CR France24,18-6-18

WARD,Alec 2Lt kia 28-6-18 15WYorks p83 CR France24

WARD,Alfred Claude Leonard TCapt&Adjt ded 18-11-15 5KSLI p145 CR France64

WARD,Allen Dudley Walter T2Lt ded 23-7-17 7RWSurr p57 CR France145,Allan

WARD,Andrew Rushworth T2Lt kld 21-1-18 RFC p17 CR Lond10

WARD,Arthur 2Lt kia 17-10-14 Lpool p73 CR Belgium126,20-10-14

WARD,Arthur Bowsher 2Lt kia 15-8-18 8 att1EYorks p85 CR France339

WARD,Arthur Claud.DSO.Capt kia 26-8-14 2LancF p94 MR15

WARD,Arthur Edward Martyr Capt&Adjt kia 12-8-15 1/5Norf p74 MR4

WARD,Aubrey Parker Orde Lt ded 11-11-18 4Lincs p217

WARD,Basil Mignot Capt kia 3-5-15 1Ess A'Coy p132 CR Gallipoli1,25-4-15

WARD,Bernard Michael T2Lt kia 20-11-17 11RDubF p177 CR France1489

WARD,Bertram Edmund LtCol ded 22-10-14 1Mddx p148 CR France102

WARD,Charles Albert John Lt ded 15-12-18 IARO attCensorsDept p284 MR34

WARD,Charles Cecil Brooks 2LtTLt dow 11-1-17 7NStaffs p158 CR Iraq5

WARD,Charles Francis Capt kia 15-5-15 RFA p37 MR29

WARD,Charles Sanford TLt kia 7-1-16 10RWar p66 MR19

WARD,Charles Wilson.MC.Capt kia 29-4-18 RHFA attStaff RGA HQ IIICps HAB p37 CR France1025

WARD,Cecil Wellesley 2Lt kia 11-9-17 A/148RFA p37 CR Belgium79

WARD,Cyril Bertram 2Lt dow 1-11-16 21Lond p251 CR France95

WARD,Cyril Richard 2Lt kia 14-7-16 RE 3/1 attChesFC p210 CR France399

WARD,Dacre Stanley 2Lt kia 1-7-16 12Lond p248 MR21

WARD,Dudley Theophilus 2Lt kia 20-9-17 5Lond p246 MR29

WARD,Edward Arthur Hunter Lt kia 11-8-17 6WYorks attRFC p20&218 CR France1314,FltCmdr

WARD,Edward Leslie 2Lt kia 14-7-16 1 att3SStaffs p123 MR21,3 att1Bn

WARD,Edward John.MC.2Lt kia 2-10-17 C50RFA p37&259 CR Belgium10

WARD,Eric 2Lt dow 27-2-18 10RFus p70 CR Belgium11

WARD,Eric Seth Lt kia 10-8-17 O&BLI &32RFC p255 MR20

WARD,Ernest.MC.2Lt ded 19-10-18 A56RFA p37 CR France85

WARD,Ernest Hawksworth Capt kia 30-11-17 1/5LNLancs p234 MR17

WARD,Errol Stephen Remson Lt 8-12-18 9TankCps CR Oxford69

WARD,F.M.2Lt kld 22-4-18 GL &RAF p191

WARD,Francis Welsford Capt kia 9-10-17 4Glouc p225 MR30

WARD,Frank Reginald T2Lt dow PoW 15-10-17 14HLI p164 CR France924,15-12-17

WARD,Frank Saxon Capt kia 31-7-17 8Lpool p215 MR29

WARD,Fred.MC.MID Capt kia 8-12-17 2/19Lond p250 CR Palestine3

WARD,Geoffrey Arthur T2Lt kia 30-9-16 12 att7RWKent p142 CR France383

WARD,George Arthur Ernest 2Lt kia 20-10-18 7Lincs p76 MR16

WARD,George Bernard.MC&Bar.T2LtTMaj kia 21-9-17 GL &10RFC p14 CR France98

WARD,George Cecil 2Lt kia 2-7-16 8WYorks B'Coy p219 CR France215,1-7-16

WARD,George Herbert 2Lt kia 4-6-15 7Manch p237 MR4

WARD,George Duval TCaptAMaj kia 18-5-17 B181RFA p37 CR France439

WARD,George Ernest 2LtTCapt kia 25-9-15 RSuss p120 CR France219

WARD,George Matthews T2Lt kia 24-8-16 7DCLI p115 CR France630,Matthew

WARD,Hon Gerald Ernest Francis.MVO.Capt kia 30-11-14 1LifeGds p20 MR29

WARD,Harold.MIDx2 Maj kia 21-3-18 2/4 att2/5Lincs p217 MR20

WARD,Harold Arthur 2Lt kia 20-4-18 7Worc p226 MR32

WARD,Harold Frederick.MC.TCapt kia 30-11-17 7ESurr p113 MR17

WARD,Henry Ernest Lt ded 13-12-18 RE p49 CR Yorks98

WARD,Hubert Henry T2Lt kia 19-9-18 1/4Ess p132 CR Palestine9

WARD,Jack Bouverie Mallam 2Lt kia 7-11-14 2 O&BLI p130 MR29

WARD,James Eyre Drummond Maj ded 20-6-16 11Mddx attRAOC p148 CR Yorks38

WARD,Jebusa Newton Lt kia 27-8-18 1IrGds p53 CR France214

WARD,J.G.2Lt ded 7-5-18 1/2LancF &RAF p94

WARD,John 2Lt ded 18-12-15 4RLancs p213 CR France22

WARD,John 2Lt kia 30-8-18 3 att2WRid p116 CR France421,31-8-18

WARD,Kenneth Hilary Wodehouse Capt dow 30-8-18 KRRC p152 MR61

WARD,Laurance 2Lt kia 10-4-18 4York p220 MR32

WARD,Maurice Arthur.MC.Capt dow 10-4-18 11LancF p94 CR France1094

WARD,Neville Lascelles 2Lt kia 23-8-14 ESurr p113 CR Belgium201

WARD,Noel Loftus Moore 2Lt kia 15-10-16 3/5Ess p232 MR21

WARD,Norman Hartley T2Lt dow 8-3-17 5Mddx att1LNLancs p148 CR France164

WARD,Norman John T2Lt kia 11-8-16 11RWar p66 MR21

WARD,Otho Charles Capt kia 11-1-17 IA 2/124BaluchisInf p284 CR Iraq5

WARD,Patrick Michael SubCdr ded 28-12-17 IA S&TCps p284

WARD,Paul Francis Seymour 2Lt kia 22-3-18 2/7 att2/8Worc p226 MR27

WARD,Percival Arthur 2Lt dow 16-5-18 50RFA p37 CR France102

WARD,Percy Duncan TCapt dow 11-10-16 11LancF p94 CR France59

WARD,Percy Harry Bavister 2Lt kia 19-5-17 GL &22RFC p14 CR France439,Percival Banister

WARD,Peter Womersley.MC.TCapt&Adjt dow 23-2-17 6SLancs p126 CR Iraq6

WARD,P.F.Lt ded 12-9-15 RAMC p198

WARD,Philip TLt kia 27-12-17 17Manch p156 MR30

WARD,Reginald Ibotson Lt dow 26-5-19 1DragGds p20 MR43

WARD,Reginald Lucian Lt kia 21-4-16 2Y&L p159 CR Belgium73,Lucien

WARD,Robert Oscar Cyril.MIDx2 TMaj kia 20-11-17 EKent attTankCps p58&189 CR France662

WARD,Samuel Leonard.MC.2Lt kia 22-3-18 RWar Res att2/6Bn p66 MR27

WARD,Stephen Remson T2Lt ded 8-12-18 TankCps p189

WARD,Thomas TLt kia 11-6-16 21NumbF p63 CR France515

WARD,Thomas Pillans Lt kia 31-7-17 Nhampt att7Bn p138 MR29

WARD,Thomas Pryce 2Lt dow 10-10-18 1SWBord att1/1Hereford p101 CR Belgium11

WARD,Walter Delay Capt ded 4-9-18 1/9Hamps p229 MR66

WARD,Walter Granby Lt kia 3-9-18 RGA 171SB p42 CR Italy1

WARD,Walter Wallace Capt ded 28-10-18 RASC p194 CR France1512

WARD,William 2Lt kia 4-3-17 5 att1Worc p110 CR France439

WARD,William Alfred Maj ded 30-8-18 RAMC p198 p267 CR Hamps1

WARD,William Arthur Bayford Kirivan.MID TLt dow 2-8-15 RE Sigs p49 MR4,Kirwan

WARD,William Ernest TLt ded 4-11-18 LancF p255 CR Lancs256

WARD,William Leigh 2Lt kia 22-12-17 4SomLI p218 CR Belgium111

WARD-JONES,Frederick Vivian.MC.2Lt kia 17-7-16 1 att9SWBord p101 CR France453,Lt 16-7-16

WARD-PRICE,Leonard Stanley Lt kia 25-3-17 2LifeGds att70RFC p14&23 CR France846,Capt

WARDE,Basil Charles Conroy 2Lt kia 30-7-16 2 O&BLI p130 CR France402

WARDE,Brian Edmund Douglas Lt kia 16-6-15 6 att4RFus p70 MR29

WARDE,C.A.Maj 14-2-20 15RFus CR Mddx66

WARDELL,Warren Henry Maj mbk 27-11-14 IA 1/39GarhwalRif p284 MR28,24-11-14

WARDELL,William Moss 2Lt kia 23-3-18 1MGC p186 MR27,1TankCps

WARDEN,Edmund Oscar Capt kia 28-6-15 12Ess p133 CR Gallipoli6

WARDEN,Walter George TCapt kia 1-7-16 8SomLI p80 CR France267

WARDILL,Charles Henry T2Lt kia 1-7-16 15 att12Y&L p159 MR21

WARDLAW,A.P.M.Maj 14-5-17 9Suss CR Mddx26

WARDLE,Cyril Ernest 2Lt kia 3-10-18 3 att1N&D p135 CR France441

WARDLE,Frank Lt selfInflictGunshot 2-9-20 IA TC att2/22Punjabis p284 MR65

WARDLE,James Kenneth TLt dow 30-4-16 15WYorks p83 CR France167

WARDLE,John Russell Maj kia 2-1-16 GlasgowYeo p203 CR Gallipoli3

WARDLE,Joseph Frederick TLt ded 14-2-19 RE 334RdConstCo p255 CR Staffs170

WARDLEWORTH,Douglas Lt ded 24-10-14 RAMC p198 CR France85

WARDLEY,Geoffrey Charles Norton TLt dow 24-7-16 RGA 24SB p42 CR France329

WARDLEY,Miles Edward T2Lt kia 29-4-17 22RFus p70 MR20

WARDROP,John T2Lt kia 3-8-16 8RFus p70 MR21

WARDROPER,James Marsh Maj ded 27-3-20 RWSurr CR Hamps241

WARE,Bertram Knight 2Lt kia 19-9-16 15Lond p249 MR21

WARE,Denys C.Capt kld 20-9-18 Lpool &RAF p73

WARE,Eric Wallace 2Lt kia 18-10-16 3 att2Wilts p153 CR France432

WARE,Francis Henry Capt kia 1-7-16 13Lond p249 MR21

WARE,John Wilson 2Lt kia 10-7-16 RE 74FC p49 MR19

WARE,Kenneth Charles Webb 2Lt kia 21-3-18 RGA 77SB CR France1188

WARE,William 2Lt mbk 27-10-18 2RWFus p257 MR16

WAREHAM,Frederick William Lt kia 1-7-16 1/8RWar p215 MR21

WAREHAM,Lawrence John 2Lt kia 21-7-16 1/7Worc p226 MR21

WAREING,Cecil Hooten Lt dow 1-11-17 4Beds p87 CR Belgium16

WAREING,William Robert Alexander Capt kia 23-3-18 11Lpool p73 CR France1061

WARHAM,Joseph T2Lt dow 7-5-17 8KRRC p152 CR France214

WARING,Edward Robert 2Lt kia 29-10-14 1KRRC p152 MR29

WARING,Frank 2Lt dow 24-8-16 5Y&L p238 CR France40,Lt

WARING,Frederick Royden 2Lt kia 7-7-16 10 att7RSuss p120 MR21

WARING,Holt Maj dow 15-4-18 NIrHorse attRIrRif p24 CR Belgium89

WARING,John.MC.Capt kia 6-10-18 20Manch p156 CR France234

WARINGGILL,Erold Lt 25-7-16 8RFA CR France207

WARK,Hugh Alexander Lt kia 14-3-18 6GordH p242 CR France381

WARLAND,Frederick Leslie 2Lt kia 25-3-18 3 att12ESurr p113 MR20

WARLAND,Maurice George T2Lt dow 20-1-17 8Wilts p153 CR Iraq5

WARLOW,Edmund Jarvis Leith TLt kia 6-11-16 11 att2Worc p110 MR21

WARLOW,Theodore William TLt dow 28-7-15 6YLI p144 CR France102

WARMAN,William Alfred 2Lt 13-10-18 RAF Ex1/4Ess CR Egypt9

WARMINGTON,Alfred Ernest TCapt kia 24-5-16 6RIrReg p89 CR Ireland14,24-4-16

WARMSLEY,Frank Walter 2Lt dow 22-11-17 1/5N&D p233 CR France179

WARN,Wallace Gordon Lt dow 23-9-16 10RSuss &RFC p4&120 CR France245,kia

WARNE,Bertie Joseph 2Lt dow 4-4-18 Mddx att21Bn p148 CR France40

WARNE,William Millar Lt kia 22-5-15 RGA 7SB p42 CR France260

WARNER,Archibald 2Lt kia 1-7-16 5Lond p246 CR France1327

WARNER,Arnold Ashton Justice 2Lt kia 24-8-18 1GrenGds p50 CR France1489

WARNER,Bernard Oldershaw Lt kia 19-5-17 3 att1Ess p133 CR France311

WARNER,Bertram 2Lt kia 12-4-17 1LondRB p246 MR20

WARNER,Charles Thornton Capt ded 12-9-20 IA 1/22Punjabis p284 MR43,30-9-20

WARNER,Clive Wynyard Lt ded 14-10-18 IA 3Lancers p284 MR43

WARNER,Cornwallis John Lt kia 16-5-15 3 att2 O&BLI p130 MR22

WARNER,Douglas Redston 2Lt kia 1-7-16 4RDubF p177 CR France1500

WARNER,Harry James 2Lt kia 3-6-17 6Nhampt p138 CR France541,Henry

WARNER,Herbert Moline Lt dow 16-11-14 1ELancs p111 CR France284,Capt

WARNER,Robert 2Lt kia 6-3-17 2/5Y&L p238 CR France514

WARNER,Samuel 2Lt kia 1-10-18 12RIrRif p170 CR Belgium157

WARNER,Thomas Lovell.DSO.TMaj ded 27-12-17 8Leic p88 CR France446

WARNER,Thornton Sparr Capt kia 23-7-16 11 att8Glouc p107 MR21

WARNER,William Henry 2Lt kia 21-8-18 5MGC Div p186 CR France281,Inf

WARNER,William James 2Lt kia 3-5-17 18WYorks p83 MR20

WARNES,David Hoggett Lt ded 10-6-17 RFA p208 CR EAfrica38 &CR Tanzania1

WARNINGTON,Charles 2Lt kia 3-5-17 6EKent p58 MR20

WARNOCK,Elizabeth MacMath(Daisy)Nurse ded 5-5-18 VAD 10Detachment BRCS 8GH p200 CR France145

WARNOCK,George Moir.MID Lt dow 29-3-18 6A&SH p243 CR Frnce145,Muir

WARNOCK,Hugh Adolphus Hector Lt dow 16-8-15 4 att1RIrF p172 CR France518,Hector A.Hugh

WARNOCK,Robert.MC.T2Lt kia 12-8-16 6/7RScotF p95 CR France151

WARR,Thomas Edward T2Lt dow 14-10-17 6Dors p124 CR France102

WARR,William Charles Samuel.DCM.2Lt kia 1-7-16 22RFA p37 CR France397

WARRAND,Alastair St.John Munro Capt kld 18-3-15 1BlkW &RFC p2&129,ded CRFrance1027,19-3-15

WARRE,Cecil Alberic Hardy T2Lt kia 24-4-17 88MGC Inf p186 CR France531

WARRE-CORNISH,Gerald Maj kia 16-9-16 6SomLI p80 MR21

WARRELL,Alfred 2Lt kia 9-10-17 5LancF p221 MR30

WARRELL-BOWRING,Walter John 2Lt kia 30-7-16 3 att6RWSurr p57 CR France251,29-7-16

WARREN,Alan John 2Lt dow 10-7-17 12Lond p248 CR France755

WARREN,Alan Rowland 2Lt kia 8-10-16 9Lond p248 MR21

WARREN,Albert T2Lt kia 17-3-18 Leic &35RFC p17&88 CR France446,Lt

WARREN,Archibald Alexander.MIDx2 TLt kia 20-1-16 8BordR p118 CR France924

WARREN,Charles Gordon 2Lt kld 28-8-18 21Lond p251 CR France214

WARREN,Dawson LtCol kia 17-9-14 RWSurr p57 CR France1342

WARREN,Edgar Cecil 2Lt kia 3-5-17 8 att1Lond p247 MR20

WARREN,Francis Purcell 2Lt mbk 14-7-16 2SLancs p257 MR21,3-7-16

WARREN,Fred Langford 2Lt kia 1-7-16 4 att2WYorks p83 MR21

WARREN,Frederick Robert Fulford TLtAMaj kia 22-10-16 14Hamps p121 CR France384

WARREN,Frederick John Maj ded 14-7-15 9WelshR p128 CR Wilts115

WARREN,Harry 2Lt kia 7-7-17 4Hamps p228 CR Belgium115

WARREN,Ivan John 2Lt dow 8-3-18 3 att1Glouc p107 CR Belgium38

WARREN,James Lionel East Capt kia 2-10-15 att1WelshR p128 MR19

WARREN,John Booker Brough Lt kia 28-10-14 1BordR p118 MR29,James

WARREN,John Crosby.MC.MID Capt kia 21-3-18 7N&D p233 CR France646,Maj

WARREN,Martin 2LtACapt kia 24-3-18 5 att1Worc p110 MR27,25-3-18

WARREN,Peyton Tollemache Capt dow 14-8-15 RAMC 3FA p254 CR Gallipoli27

WARREN,Richard Crawford.MC&Bar.28-6-21 1 O&BLI CR Hamps70

WARREN,Richard Dunn Maj kia 7-4-18 6Leinst p175 CR Belgium72,kld 11Leic

WARREN,Theodore Stewart Wolton T2Lt kia 17-7-16 17DLI p162 MR21

WARREN,William Duncan 2Lt kia 20-9-17 19Lond p251 MR29

WARREN,William Edward AMaj dow 29-3-18 RGA 81SB p42 CR France169

WARREN,William Stanley 2Lt ded 10-10-17 3 att2BordR p118 CR France139,dow

WARREN-SWETTENHAM,Thomas Robert Eaton Wybault Maj kia 6-2-15 2EYorks p85 MR29

WARRINER,Thomas Andrew Latimer 2Lt kia 10-10-16 5Worc p110 CR France631

WARRINGTON,Francis Arnold TLt kia 7-10-16 148RFA p37 CR France374

WARRINGTON,Garfield Lt kia 18-8-17 RASC p253 CR France855

WARRINGTON,Harold Gordon Lt dow 6-12-17 RFA 63A/ASect p208 CR Italy7

WARRINGTON,William Barrett Capt ded 2-2-19 RAMC p256 CRLancs12,Barnett

WARRY,John Lucas Capt dow 27-4-17 8N&D p233 CR France511

WARTER,Henry De Grey Capt kia 20-11-17 4DragGds p21 CR France711

WARTER,Joseph Gordon 2Lt kia 30-9-17 Wilts att66RFC p14&153 MR20

WARTER,William Henry Lt kia 9-5-17 168MGC Inf p186 CR France531

WARTNABY,Charles Richard Arnold Lt kld 11-3-15 NhamptYeo p204 CR France1106

WARWICK,Colin Winder.MC.2Lt kia 22-3-18 5 att8BordR p228 CR France1484

WARWICK,Douglas Charles.MC.LtAMaj ded 20-1-19 NStaffs att11MGC p194&265 CR France1252

WARWICK,John Cedric Geoffrey Lt drd 27-5-18 NottsYeo p205 MR41

WARWICK,John Douglas Barford Maj kia 10-3-17 HuntsCycBn att 1/1BucksBn O&BLI p253 CR France624

WARWICK,J.L.2Lt kld 14-6-18 GL &RAF p192

WARWICK,Thomas Harry.MC.2Lt kia 28-4-17 3 att9NStaffs &MGC p186 CR France924,Lt

WARWICK,William Robert St.Clair 2Lt dow 19-12-15 1/4Ches p222 CR Egypt3,WARRICK

WASBOROUGH,Spencer Vere Capt kia 12-4-17 1SomLI p80 CR France728,WASBROUGH

WASBROUGH,William Lewis 2Lt kia 25-9-15 1LNLancs p136 CR France1723

WASEY,Cyril Walter Carleton.MC.Capt kia 28-10-17 2RWar att16RFC p14,66&259 CR France95

WASHBROOK,Harry 2Lt kia 22-8-18 5Lpool p215CR France619

WASHBROOK,Mark Thomas 2Lt dow 21-11-18 5 att11ELancs p226 CR France34,Tomas

WASHINGTON,Frederick.MC.2Lt kia 22-8-18 4 att1RInniskF p105 CR France855

WASHINGTON,Jonathan Noel 2Lt dow 2-10-15 Manch &RFC p2&156 CR France518

WASON,Cyril Ernest T2Lt kia 30-11-17 9RFus p70 MR17

WASTELL,Kenneth T2Lt kld 23-3-18 RFC p17 CR Hunts83

WATERER,M.D.G.2Lt 25-11-19 37Lancers MR65

WATERER,Michael Anthony 2Lt dow 11-10-18 Mon RE &6RAF p49 CR France446

WATERFALL,Vincent 2Lt kld 22-8-14 3EYorks att5RFC p2&85 CR Belgium406

WATERFIELD,Frederick Charles Capt dow 21-5-15 IA 45 att15Sikhs p284 CR France80

WATERHOUSE,Alfred William.MC.MID Capt kia 12-1-16 1Drags p21 CR France423

WATERHOUSE,Arved 2Lt kia 13-10-14 RLancs p59 CR France324

WATERHOUSE,Gilbert 2Lt kia 1-7-16 Ess p133 CR France1890

WATERHOUSE,Gilbert Wilmot T2Lt dow 10-4-17 6RWKent p142 CR France113

WATERHOUSE,Irvin Preston T2Lt kia 8-11-16 10WYorks p83 MR21

WATERHOUSE,Kenneth Capt kia 9-8-16 2/5LancF Z'Coy p221 CR France294

WATERHOUSE,Rennie Capt kia 7-5-15 7LancF p221 MR4

WATERHOUSE,Richard Dalton LtCol kia 7-8-15 8LancF p256 MR4

WATERHOUSE,Robert Bentley Maskill 2Lt ded 26-3-19 5WYorks p272 CR Yorks311

WATERIDGE,Edgar Leake Lt kia 20-11-14 Leic p88 MR22

WATERLOW,Clive Maitland MajTLtCol kld 20-7-17 RE attRNAS p49 CR Lincs86

WATERMAN,Henry Richard Lt kia 28-8-16 3 att1Mddx p148 MR21 CR France1890

WATERS,Bernard Stanley 2Lt kia 3-5-17 4Lond p246 MR20

WATERS,Charles Louis.MC&Bar.CaptAMaj dow 19-10-17 RBerks att1NigR p140&202 CR EAfrica11 &CR Tanzania1

WATERS,Eric Gordon 2Lt kia 24-1-17 HampsYeo attRFC p20&204 CR Belgium11,Lt

WATERS,Eric Joseph Fitzgerald Lt kia 5-3-20 IA 10Lancers p284 MR38

WATERS,George Thorold Capt dow 29-3-18 7Suff p79 CR France64

WATERS,John Patrick T2Lt kia 18-11-17 56RFC p14 CR France177

WATERS,Kenneth Selby 2Lt murdered 30-5-17 IARO att1BritMtnBty p284 MR67

WATERS,Reginald Rigden ACapt dow 24-10-16 4 att1RWar p66 MR21

WATERS,Reginald William 2Lt kia 12-8-18 1LancF D'Coy p94 CR France193,13-8-18

WATERS,William Denne 2Lt kia 12-3-15 3N&D p135 CR France768,Lt dow 1Bn

WATERS,William Nisbet 2Lt kia 28-7-16 1/6A&SH p243 MR21 CR France1890

WATERSON,Frederick Paris T2Lt kia 31-7-17 17N&D p135 MR21

WATERTON,John Edward Mary Claude Pius Augustine 2Lt kia 29-11-17 5Beds p219 CR Palestine9

WATERTON,Joseph Charles Edmund Mary John Reginald ded 18-2-15 5Beds p272 CR Beds48

WATES,Leslie Charles T2Lt kia 9-10-17 GL &29RFC p14 CR Belgium18

WATHERSTON,G.F.Capt 27-11-16 UgandaPoliceBn CR EAfrica127

WATHERSTON,Robert James Henderson Fell 2Lt kia 3-12-17 1/5Leic p220 CR France163

WATHES,Thomas Sidney Capt kia 19-7-16 6RWar p214 MR32

WATKIN,Alfred Charles 2Lt kia 1-7-16 5NStaffs p238 CR France281

WATKIN,Ben Gerald Noel 2Lt dow 25-1-15 40RFA p37 CR France80,27-1-15

WATKIN,Harry Lt ded 21-10-18 1WRid p116 MR67

WATKIN,Henry George Maj kia 21-8-15 4Huss Staff 2MntdBde p21

WATKIN,Frank Ernest Capt kia 3-1-15 1NumbF p63 MR29,1-1-15

WATKINS,Charles Lt ded 30-1-15 GL Res p272 CR Essex1

WATKINS,Eric Leopold Charles Lt ded 2-3-17 2RFA p208 MR65

WATKINS,Eustace Arundel De St.Barbe Sladen Capt dow 31-1-15 3Dev p77 CR France345

WATKINS,Frederick Augustus 2Lt kia 24-3-18 7EYorks p85 MR20

WATKINS,David John George 2Lt kia 21-4-18 1SWBord p101 CR France109,Lt

WATKINS,Horace Holmes 2Lt kia 21-10-14 3 att1SWBord p101 MR29

WATKINS,Howell Cyril.MC.Lt dow PoW 23-10-18 PembrokeYeo p205 CR France716,Howel 24WelshR

WATKINS,Iltyd Edwin Maitland Capt kia 5-5-15 2Mon p244 MR29,7-5-15

WATKINS,Mervyn Holmes Lt kia 18-9-18 C100RFA p208 CR Greece5

WATKINS,Reginald Noel Lt kia 31-3-18 7EYorks p85 MR20

WATKINS,Thomas 2Lt kia 9-5-15 2RBerks p140 MR32 Ex 2GrenGds

WATKINS,Vivian Holmes Capt dow 20-2-15 2Mon p244 CR Mon69

WATKINS,William 2Lt kia 23-7-18 3WelshR att139RAF p128 CR Italy9

WATKINSON,Arthur T2Lt dow 3-8-16 12RScots p55 CR France40,14Bn

WATKINSON,John.MC.Lt&QM ded 10-12-18 18HLI p164 CR France34

WATKYN-THOMAS,Alwyn Capt mbk 13-11-16 2HLI p257 MR21

WATLINGTON,Henry Joseph 2Lt kia 6-7-17 GL &70RFC p14 MR20

WATMOUGH,John Cyril 2Lt kia 10-7-15 att2NumbF p63 CR Belgium37

WATMOUGH,Oscar Oswald 2Lt kia 1-9-18 2WRid p116 CR France421

WATNEY,Valentine Howell TLt dow 3-2-17 152MGC Inf p186 CR Surrey6

WATNEY,William Herbert Lt kia 10-5-15 2RB A'Coy p180 MR32

WATSON,Alastair Fisher T2Lt kia 23-4-17 9BlkW p129 CR France536

WATSON,Albert Edward Lt 6-11-20 20DLI CR Yorks547

WATSON,Alec Philip 2Lt dow 14-4-17 3 att2Hamps p121 CR France113

WATSON,Alexander Bruce 2Lt kia 28-4-17 7HLI p240 MR20

WATSON,Alfred Charles Capt kia 3-9-16 5WYorks p218 CR France293

WATSON,Alfred William T2Lt kia 1-5-17 GL &10RFC p14 CR France98

WATSON,Allan.DSO.Capt 18-1-20 RAMC CR EAfrica116

WATSON,Arthur Paton T2Lt dow 13-10-16 21Lpool p73 CR FRance833

WATSON,Arthur Toward TMaj dow 5-8-17 21KRRC p152 CR Belgium21

WATSON,Arthur Vivian Cradock.MC.Lt ded 21-12-19 7MGC p266 CR Egypt2 see CRADOCK-WATSON

WATSON,Benjamin T2Lt dow 17-6-16 5 att7RInniskF p105 CR France115

WATSON,Benjamin Alexander 2Lt kia 24-10-18 7 ATT12/13NumbF p214 MR16

WATSON,Cedric Gordon Lt kia 9-5-15 RBerks attESurr p140 MR32

WATSON,Charles Chap4Cl ded 22-7-18 RAChDept p200 CR Iraq6

WATSON,Charles Beaumont.MC.Lt dow 12-7-18 21MGC p186 CR France74,kia

WATSON,Charles Challinor.MID Lt dow 1-6-17 A21RFA p208 CR France570

WATSON,Charles Edward Stephen 2Lt kia 1-7-16 1ELancs p111 MR21,Stephens

WATSON,Charles John TLt dow 26-1-17 10Ches A'Coy p97 CR Iraq5

WATSON,Charles Reginald Lt kia 7-4-16 IA 28Punjabis p284 MR38,6-4-16

WATSON,Charles Victor Macgregor 2Lt kia 3-10-17 1Lothian&BordHorseYeo &RFC p204 CR Greece3

WATSON,Clifford Thomas 2Lt dow 3-12-17 7Lond p247 CR France512

WATSON,Cyril Pennefather 2Lt kia 1-7-16 3ELancs p111 MR21

WATSON,David Galloway Lt ded 5-6-15 RAMC att2Beds p198 CR France40

WATSON,Dominic MacAulay Lt dow 3-12-17 WSomYeo p205 CR France446,12SomLI

WATSON,Dorothy Mortimer SNurse ded 13-3-17 TFNS p254 CR Europe1

WATSON,Douglas Christian TCapt ded 16-6-16 RE attSerbianArmy p49 CR Greece21

WATSON,Elizabeth Harvey SNurse ded 5-11-18 QAIMNS p200 CR France658

WATSON,Ernest Guthrie 2Lt kia 19-9-14 2SLancs D'Coy p126 CR France1107

WATSON,Evan Philip 2Lt dow 28-3-18 8RIrRif p170

WATSON,Francis Lt kia 9-5-15 3 att2ESurr p113 MR29

WATSON,Francis George Stuart 2LtACapt kia 23-10-16 2LancF p94 MR21 CR France1890

WATSON,Francis Shuldham.DSO.Maj dow 2-5-18 RGA 276SB p42 CR France63

WATSON,Frank Lt kia 1-7-16 18WYorks att93TMB p83 MR21

WATSON,Frank TCapt kia 2-4-17 Manch att71TrainingRes p156 CR France616,22Bn

WATSON,Frank Fairweather T2Lt kia 4-8-16 14 att15RScots p55 CR France432

WATSON,Frank McEwan 2Lt kia 3-5-17 55MGC p186 MR20

WATSON,Frederick John 2Lt kia 24-3-18 7DCLI p115 MR27

WATSON,Frederick Johnston Lt 10-6-16 43CanadaInf CR Belgium134

WATSON,Geoffrey Lt kia 21-1-16 IA 28Punjabis p284 MR38

WATSON,Geoffrey Launcelot Capt kia 20-4-15 att13ESurr A'Coy p113 MR29

WATSON,Geoffrey,William T2Lt kia 1-8-17 11Ches p97 MR29

WATSON,George Carr Capt kld 8-3-16 6Dev p217 MR38

WATSON,George Douglas Lt dow 18-10-18 5ScotRif p224 CR Belgium11,1/8Bn

WATSON,George Edmund Borlase.DSO.MC.Maj kia 29-8-18 O'Bty RHA 5ArmyBde p37 CR France629

WATSON,George Henry Capt dow 18-9-16 RAMC 3FAp254 CR France177

WATSON,George Walker 2Lt kld 29-12-16 1/7RWFus attRFC p223 CR Egypt9

WATSON,George William Annakin T2Lt kia 7-3-18 RFC p17 CR France64,Lt

WATSON,Harry 2Lt kia 12-8-16 1/9Lpool p216 MR21

WATSON,Henry James Arthur Lt kia 23-8-18 5 att1Beds p219 CR France239

WATSON,Henry Trelss Capt dow 6-3-15 3Lpool attManch p73 CR Belgium165,att2YLI

WATSON,Herbert Sanderson TCapt kia 26-9-15 8GordH p167 MR19

WATSON,Ivan Philip 2Lt dow 28-3-18 12RIrRif CR France145

WATSON,Jack Cecil Lt kia 5-10-17 10Mddx p236 MR30

WATSON,James 2Lt kia 7-7-16 3 att2RIrRif p170 CR France150,9-7-16

WATSON,James TLt kia 30-7-16 27Manch p156 CR France397

WATSON,James Clarkson Lt dow 31-8-17 3 att6CamH p168 CR France40,2Lt

WATSON,James Frederick 2Lt ded 22-1-16 5BlkW p231 CR Scot398

WATSON,James Laverick T2Lt kia 29-4-17 23NumbF p63 MR20

WATSON,James Norman 2Lt dow 10-8-16 3 att1RInniskF p105 CR Belgium11

WATSON,James Roby T2Lt dow 2-12-17 175MGC Inf p186 CR France711

WATSON,James Stennett 2Lt kia 26-11-17 4EYorks att1/4WRid p219 CR Belgium20

WATSON,John T2Lt kia 7-4-17 16RScots p55 MR20

WATSON,John.Bart.2Lt kia 23-3-18 16Lancers p23 MR27

WATSON,John 2Lt kia 27-4-18 17RScots p55 CR France60

WATSON,John Allan 2Lt kld 31-1-19 RFA attRGA MtnBty p209 MR70 &CR Europe179

WATSON,John Christopher Capt kia 26-9-17 2GordH p167 CR Belgium8,1Bn

WATSON,John Eben T2Lt kia 26-9-15 7RScotF p95 MR19

WATSON,John Edmund Malone.MC.Chap4Cl dow 10-4-18 RAChDept att21Mddx p200&259 CR France1094

WATSON,John Frederick T2Lt dow 23-10-17 10NumbF p63 CR France102

WATSON,John Irvine 2Lt 14-8-17 B110RFA CR Belgium7

WATSON,John Lawrence Craig Lt kia 9-4-17 5GordH p242 MR20

WATSON,John Mitchell Capt kia 13-11-17 4KOSB p223 CR Palestine9

WATSON,John Mowbray Walter TLt kia 23-8-17 249MGC p186

WATSON,John Peirson 2Lt kia 29-7-17 3EYorks D'Coy p85 MR20

WATSON,Joseph St.John.MC.DCM.Lt&QM dow 30-4-18 2DLI p162 CR France100

WATSON,Joseph Harold 2Lt dow 3-10-18 1/2 att1/4Leic p88 CR France725

WATSON,Joseph James.DCM.2Lt kia 16-8-18 F99 RFA T'Bty 1TMB p37 CR Greece6

WATSON,Kenneth Charles Forrester.MC.Lt kia 12-4-18 3SLancs att2/7RWar p126 MR32

WATSON,Kenneth Clennell TLt kia 11-4-17 10LNLancs p136 MR20

WATSON,Laurence Charles 2Lt kia 12-8-15 8Hamps p229 MR4

WATSON,Laurence Stuart Lt kia 29-7-18 8ScotRif p225 CR France524

WATSON,Leslie Riley 2Lt kia 4-7-16 RHFA p209

WATSON,Lord Arthur James 2Lt kia 26-9-18 5Yorks att7EYorks p221 MR16

WATSON,Louis Talbot Capt kia 11-3-15 1Worc p110 CR France525

WATSON,Mark Sanderson 2Lt kia 11-1-17 4HLI p164 MR38

WATSON,Noel Alick Capt kia 22-4-17 IA 55Rif att56 p284 MR38

WATSON,Norman Campion 2Lt kia 24-4-17 6 att12HLI p240 MR20

WATSON,Norman John 2Lt kia 27-5-18 C246RHFA p37 CR Belgium8

WATSON,Oliver Cyril Spencer.VC.DSO.LtCol kia 28-3-18 1MddxHuss att2/5YLI p204 MR20

WATSON,Oswald Halley 2Lt kia 9-9-17 2PORif p247 MR29

WATSON,Peter Seton 2Lt kia 9-4-17 5A&SH p243 CR France728

WATSON,Raymond Victor T2Lt kia 16-8-17 8NumbF p63 MR30

WATSON,Reginald 2Lt kia 7-10-16 11RWKent p142 CR France385

WATSON,R.H.17-9-14 1LNLancs MR15

WATSON,Robert Lowson Capt ded 8-2-16 4BlkW p272 CR Scot386

WATSON,Robert Oke Carey Capt kia 26-3-17 2/10Mddx p236 MR34

WATSON,Roger Wentworth TLt kia 30-7-15 8KRRC C'Coy p152 CR Belgium453,20-7-15

WATSON,Samuel Meredith 2Lt kia 1-7-16 64MGC p186 CR France267

WATSON,Stanley John T2Lt dow 28-11-15 8 att2RScotF p95 CR France80,Lt

WATSON,Stanley Lee Capt kia 25-9-15 4BlkW p230 MR19

WATSON,Sydney Fairweather 2Lt kia 6-9-16 2GordH p167 MR21

WATSON,Sydney Towers 2Lt kia 1-7-16 16 att15DLI p162 MR21

WATSON,Thomas TCapt kia 11-4-17 6RScotF p95 MR20

WATSON,Thomas T2Lt kia 26-3-18 82RFC p17 CR France1242

WATSON,Thomas Colclough.VC.LtCol ded 15-6-17 RE p49 CR mddx26

WATSON,Thomas Hovenden.DSO.MC.ALtCol kia 23-3-18 2/1Worc att1N&D p110 CR France987

WATSON,Thomas Palmer.MC.TCapt kia 7-3-17 6ELancs p111 CR Iraq8

WATSON,Vesey Clayhills Capt kia 11-4-17 19RFA p37 CR Iraq8

WATSON,Walter 2Lt kia 27-5-18 EYorks att4Bn p85 MR18

WATSON,Walter John Mowbray Lt kia 22-8-17 249MGC Inf CR Belgium127 Ex NStaffs

WATSON,William.MIDx3 MajTLtCol kia 3-5-17 1SomLI att5YLI p80&235 MR20

WATSON,William Lt kia 21-3-18 4RBerks att184TMB p234 MR27

WATSON,William Lt&QM ded 18-6-18 SL DLI p201 CR Lancs450

WATSON,William Capt dow 22-8-18 24Manch att1EYorks p156 CR France131

WATSON,William.CMG.LtCol ded 3-3-19 RAMC p267 CR Mddx26,SomLI attGHQ

WATSON,William Baikie.MC.Lt dow 30-9-18 C95RFA p37 CR France357

WATSON,William Ernest.DSO.Maj kia 31-10-14 6DragGds p21 MR29

WATSON,William Erskine 2Lt kia 24-3-18 17Lpool p73 MR27

WATSON,William George Douglas Capt kia 19-4-17 5KOSB p224 MR34

WATSON,William John 2Lt kld 26-5-17 GL &RFC p14 CR Lond14

WATSON,William Norman.MC.TCapt ded 29-5-16 6KOSB p102 CR France285

WATSON,William Stanley Capt dow 11-8-18 RASC att15LancF p194 CR France879

WATSON,William Vernon Crowther 2Lt kia 15-10-17 6WYorks p218 CR Belgium126

WATSON,William Wallace T2Lt kia 13-10-16 2Yorks p91 MR21

WATSON-SMYTH,Edward Jeffray Capt kia 27-8-18 2CldGds p51 CR France615,Jeffery

WATSON-TAYLOR,Arthur Simon 2Lt kia 14-9-17 22Lond p252 CR Belgium72

WATSON-THOMAS,Walter Patrick 2LtACapt kia 21-10-16 8BordR p118 MR21

WATT,Alexander Capt dow 20-6-16 4BlkW p230 CR France134

WATT,Alexander 2Lt kia 18-8-18 3 att2RScots p55 CR France26

WATT,Alexander Lyle Capt kld 10-3-15 5BlkW p231 CR France279

WATT,Basil Harry T2Lt kia 25-9-15 7CamH p168 MR19 &CR France1896

WATT,Charles Cecil 2Lt kia 8-5-17 4 att2KOSB p224 CR France777

WATT,Colin Robert Jamieson T2Lt dow 14-8-16 RE 212FC p49 CR France833

WATT,Douglas Gordon.MID 2Lt kia 2-3-16 3 att1GordH p167 CR Belgium167

WATT,George Macdonald 2Lt kia 17-3-17 16RFC p14 CR France32

WATT,Hugo Burr Craig.MC.Lt kia 24-8-18 8DLI p239 MR16

WATT,J.Capt 22-12-18 SAfrPostalCps MR52

WATT,James 2Lt kld 2-5-17 4RScots attRFC p20&211 CR Greece1

WATT,John 2Lt dow 14-11-16 5GordH p242 CR France131

WATT,John Heigh 2Lt kia 12-4-18 6 att4Worc p110 MR32

WATT,John Grant 2Lt kia 27-8-18 7GordH p242 MR16

WATT,John Vade T2Lt dedacc 30-10-15 14Ches p97 CR Shrop147

WATT,Kenneth Murray 2Lt dow 1-10-17 PoW 3Beds p87 CR Palestine8

WATT,Norman Lindley 2LtTLt dow 27-7-17 KEdwHorse &RFC p14&24,Lindlay CR Belgium76,Lindsey

WATT,Percy Bryden MID Lt ktia 14-4-18 13GordH att13MGC p167&186,11GordH CR France21,13MGC

WATT,Robert 2Lt kia 10-8-17 11RFus p70 CR Belgium125

WATT,Robert Sherwin 2Lt kia 12-6-17 GL &45RFC p14 CR France200

WATT,Robert Stapleton T2Lt dow 20-11-16 13EYorks B'Coy p85 CR France40

WATT,Thomas Stevenson T2Lt kia 22-9-17 14HLI p164 MR21

WATT,William 2Lt dow 10-4-18 17LancF p94 CR Scot816 Ex 2GordH

WATT,William James 2Lt kia 25-9-15 6GordH p242 CR France219

WATTERS,John Rev ded 7-11-18 RAChDept att115InfBdeHQ p200 CR France332

WATTERSON,Gerald 2Lt kia 13-3-18 ELancs att1Bn p111 CR France616

WATTERTON,William Frederick HonLt&QM ded 2-1-17 RAMC p198 CR Hamps1,1-1-17

WATTHEWS,Harold Lt kia 8-6-17 3 att10WRid p116 MR29

WATTON,Stanley Victor 2Lt dow 27-11-16 3 att3/7SLancs p126 CR France40

WATTS,Albert Edward T2Lt kia 25-9-16 10YLI p144 MR21

WATTS,Albert Edward 2Lt ded 6-3-17 16RFC p14 MR20

WATTS,Albert Edward 2Lt kia 22-4-18 15WelchR p128 CR France59

WATTS,Charles Harold Reynell Capt kia 25-12-14 2Nhampt p138 MR22

WATTS,Cyril George CaptABdeMaj kia 1-10-18 GL 11EYorks Staff93InfBde p192 CR Belgium48

WATTS,Donald William Stuart 2Lt kia 12-10-16 3Y&L p159 CR France307,Stewart

WATTS,Dudley Haldane 2Lt kia 26-9-15 8RWKent p142 MR19

WATTS,F.W.VD.Capt 9-5-18 IndDefForce 26Rifs MR66

WATTS,Francis John 2Lt kia 17-7-17 RGA 9SB p42 CR Belgium29

WATTS,Frank Mansell Wall Lt 25-3-20 HLI CR Asia33

WATTS,Frederick Robert 2Lt kia 29-8-18 12Norf p204 MR32

WATTS,George Leonard T2Lt kia 17-10-16 88MGC p186 MR21

WATTS,Graham Harman 2Lt ded 11-7-18 1CamH att2/4KAR p168&202 CR EAfrica52

WATTS,Harland T2Lt dow 22-11-16 7SLancs p126

WATTS,Harold Vaughan Iremonger Capt dow 11-8-17 7 att2Dev p217 CR Belgium18

WATTS,Henry Leonard TCapt kia 20-10-15 9Ess p133 MR19

WATTS,Henry Rowland T2Lt kia 7-6-17 6EYorks p85 CR Belgium21

WATTS,Hubert Lt ded 8-2-19 3NumbF p262 CR Numb4

WATTS,John Howe 2Lt kia 6-11-17 1/1Hereford p252 CR Palestine1

WATTS,Leonard.MM.2Lt kia 9-10-18 3Lond p246 CR France647,Capt

WATTS,Norman Luther TMaj kia 25-9-16 9Lpool p216 CR France397

WATTS,Robin Kenelm 2Lt kia 23-8-18 3 att7RWKent p142 CR France177

WATTS,Ronald William Ailsa.MC.T2Lt dow 12-11-16 13 att2Worc p110 CR France105

WATTS,Samuel TLt ded 28-10-18 2Manch att96TMB p156 CR Ches154,Capt dow

WATTS,Stephen Lt dow 6-9-16 1RMunstF p176 CR France833

WATTS,Talbot Hamilton TCapt kia 1-7-17 16Mddx p148 MR21

WATTS,Thomas William 2Lt kia 25-9-15 9Lpool p216 CR France1723

WATTS,W.Spalding Lt 15-11-20 RE MR40

WATTS,Wilfrid(Val) T2Lt kia 17-1-16 GL &1RFC p4&192 CR Belgium140

WATTS,William John 2Lt kia 12-4-18 49MGC Inf p186 MR30

WATTS,William Kenworthy Capt kia 2-12-17 6Norf att2/6Glouc p217 MR17

WATTSON,Cyril Beaven.MC.2Lt kia 8-10-17 7RFC p14 MR20

WAUCHOPE,James Bourdillon Lt kia 10-3-15 2Mddx p148 MR22,Baurdillon

WAUD,Ernest Henry.MC.LtTCapt kia 16-8-17 22NumbF attRFC p14&63

WAUD,Harold Fenwick T2Lt kia 27-8-17 14DLI p162 CR France551

WAUD,Lionel Douglas Lt kia 8-11-14 ELancs p111 CR Belgium68

WAUD,Wilfred Ernest Lt 7-6-17 9NumbF MR21

WAUGH,Arthur John TCapt kia 17-8-16 RAMC att1NStaffs p198 CR France513

WAUGH,Edward Geoffrey T2Lt kia 4-4-16 10 att6SLancs p126 MR38

WAUGH,George Noel Capt dow 26-5-17 10/86NZ VetCps CR France769

WAUGH,Thomas Hall.MC.TCapt kia 6-6-17 22NumbF p63 CR France1182

WAVELL,Arthur John Byng.MC.Maj kia 9-2-16 1WelshR attArabRifEAfrProtForces p128 CR EAfrica50

WAWN,Frederick Middlemont Capt kia 25-5-15 7DLI p239 MR29

WAY,Frank.MC.Capt&QM ded 25-10-18 RASC p267 CR Hamps1

WAY,Frederick Henry Lt kia 11-9-15 RBerks p140 CR France349

WAY,George Currey TMaj kia 28-1-16 16Mddx p148 CR France114

WAY,Henry Stanley Capt kld 5-5-19 16TankCps p189 CR France788,6-5-19

WAY,Robert Edward Allen T2Lt dow 29-5-17 10LNLancs p137 CR France113

WAY,Roderick Norman 2Lt kia 13-1-16 28RFA p37 MR38

WAYET,Frank Merewether Lt kia 27-9-15 3 att1ScotRif p104

WAYLAND,Richard Bunster 2Lt dow 22-9-16 11ELancs p111 CR France260

WAYLEN,Arthur Francis Capt ded 19-12-19 RFA CR Surrey1

WAYMAN,Fawcitt.MC.TCapt&Adjt kia 31-7-17 20DLI p162 MR29

WAYMAN,William Ambler Capt kia 14-8-16 1/4 O&BLI p231 MR21

WAYMARK,William Ebenezer Capt ded 10-12-19 RAMC p267 CR Asia33,15-12-19

WAYTE,Samuel Wilfred.MC.2Lt dow 7-10-17 103RFA p37 CR France193,Wilfrid

WEAR,Albert Edward T2Lt kia 11-9-17 20RFC p14 CR France134

WEAR,Arthur TLtACapt kia 4-12-17 2Y&L p159 CR France711

WEARE,Albert James Bertram Capt ded 18-4-19 DLI p265

WEARE,Frederick John 2Lt dow 9-10-18 4RFus p70 CR France380

WEARING,Douglas George TCapt ded 11-11-18 SL &RAMC p201&255 CR Eire166,GL

WEARNE,Frank Bernard.VC.2Lt kia 28-6-17 3 att10Ess p133 MR19

WEARNE,Keith Morris Capt kia 21-5-17 3Ess p133 CR France311

WEARNE,Kenneth Martin 2Lt kia 20-9-17 5RWSurr p212 MR30

WEATHERBY,Thomas Capt ded 8-5-17 9WRid p116 CR Sussex138

WEATHERDON,Hugh Eric Capt ded 3-11-20 IA 2/11GurkhaRif p284 CR Iraq8

WEATHERDON,Sidney George T2Lt kia 19-9-17 11Ess D'Coy p130 CR France149

WEATHERHEAD,Andrew 2Lt kia 1-7-16 3 att1RLancs p59 MR21

WEATHERHEAD,George Ernest Capt&Adjt kia 8-5-15 2RLancs p59 CR Belgium58,9-5-15

WEATHERHEAD,Stanley Ernest William 2Lt kia 23-4-17 4Worc p110 MR20

WEATHERILL,Edward Theaker T2Lt kia 15-8-15 7RDubF B'Coy p177 MR4,16-8-15

WEATHERILL,William Brown 2Lt mbk 18-6-18 10 att1/4LNLancs p257 MR19,17-6-18

WEATHERLEY,Lawrence Edwin Martin Lt kia 19-2-18 20Lond p251 CR Palestine3

WEAVER,Augustus Henry 2Lt dow 12-4-18 6WRid attMGC p187&227 CR France185

WEAVER,Cecil Vivian Rupert 2Lt dow 9-8-18 RGA 66SB p42 CR France924

WEAVER,Humphrey Capt kia 7-2-16 IA 114Mahrattas p284 MR38

WEAVER,John James Capt kldacc 20-4-17 RAMC att2/4ELancs p254 CR Lancs381,later att65LowlandDiv

WEBB,Albert William.DCM.2Lt kia 24-7-16 RGA 109SB p42 CR France397

WEBB,Alfred Henderson 2Lt ded 4-5-16 3Leic p88 CR Iraq6

WEBB,Allan Bonville Hay Capt dow 23-8-15 IA 1/5GurkhaRif p284

WEBB,Arthur Henry 2Lt kia 23-6-17 4EKent p212 MR29,24-6-17

WEBB,Arthur Pelham T2Lt kia 8-4-17 5KSLI D'Coy p145 CR France581,9-4-17

WEBB,Athelstan Sylvester Kenshole Lt kia 21-3-18 7NumbF p214 CR France518

WEBB,Charles Parker.MC.2Lt kia 23-7-17 3 att11RWKent p142 CR Belgium154

WEBB,Cyril Francis Lt kia 25-9-15 2Yorks p91 MR19

WEBB,Dennis Henry TLt kia 10-11-17 2MGC p186 CR Belgium20

WEBB,Denys Stubbs T2Lt kia 21-10-16 13Ches p97 CR France535

WEBB,Duncan Vere.MC.Capt dow 16-10-18 3 att1Leic p88 CR France725

WEBB,Edward Charles Harry 2Lt kia 10-3-15 2Lincs p76 CR France525

WEBB,Edward Melvill Lt dow 1-5-15 4NStaffs attYLI p158 CR France102

WEBB,Ernest T2Lt dow 14-7-16 7Leic p88 MR21

WEBB,Ernest Charles 2Lt kia 17-2-18 8 att4Beds p87 CR France398

WEBB,Evelyn Maxwell Capt kia 23-7-16 2KRRC p152 MR21

WEBB,Frank Ralph 2Lt kia 9-9-16 1/12Lond p248 MR21

WEBB,George 2Lt kia 5-6-18 1/2SStaffs attRAF p123 CR France1235

WEBB,George Henry Duder Capt dow 29-3-18 RAMC p254 CR France62

WEBB,George Tudor T2Lt kia 21-4-16 24RFus p70 CR France559

WEBB,Gerald Vernon Tisdall Capt kia 6-8-15 2Hamps p121 MR4

WEBB,Gilbert Watson Capt ded 1-7-16 3RIrRif &RFC p4&170 CR France518

WEBB,Gordon Arthur TLt kia 20-9-17 10RWSurr p57 MR30

WEBB,Harold Oswald Capt kia 15-9-16 8Lond p247 CR France432

WEBB,Henry 2Lt kia 26-4-18 RGA 9HB p42 CR Belgium20

WEBB,Henry Carlyle Capt kia 19-9-17 5BordR p228 CR France453

WEBB,Henry Rees LtACapt dow PoW 7-5-18 4SStaffs p123 CR Belgiu140

WEBB,Henry Stanley 2Lt kia 21-3-18 4 att9ESurr B'Coy p113 CR France692

WEBB,Herbert Percy 2Lt dow 26-4-17 71RFA p37 CR France1182

WEBB,Horace Maitland Turner Lt kia 10-3-15 3Lpool p73 CR France1106

WEBB,Jack Purnell Capt dow 22-8-18 12Glouc p107 CR France84

WEBB,John Boyer Lt kia 21-4-15 4NStaffs attBeds p158 CR Belgium127

WEBB,John Clifford 2Lt kia 14-9-16 3 att1Leic p88 CR France374

WEBB,John Harold.MC.2Lt kia 9-10-18 21Manch p156 CR France341,dow

WEBB,John Timms 2Lt kia 9-5-15 6Lond p247 CR France260

WEBB,Joseph Gilbert.MC.Lt ded 9-5-18 14RFus p99&259 CR Wales368,dow 14RWFus

WEBB,Louis Victor 2Lt dow 10-1-17 IARO att1/1GurkhaRif p284 CR Iraq5

WEBB,Matthew 2Lt 22-3-18 1SAfrInf MR27

WEBB,Musgrave Maitland Lt kia 18-9-16 16Lond p250 CR France785,Capt

WEBB,Noel William Ward.MC&Bar.Capt kia 16-8-17 70RFC p14 MR20

WEBB,Oswald Brooke TCapt dow 3-7-16 11RIrRif p170 CR France44,4-7-16

WEBB,Philip Edward T2Lt kia 25-9-16 RE 59FC p49 MR21

WEBB,R.B.TMaj ded 26-7-16 25RFus p70 CR EAfrica6 &CR Tanzania1,27-7-16

WEBB,Reginald Brooke Holding 2Lt kia 9-1-17 IARO att53Sikhs p284 MR38

WEBB,Richard Howard 2Lt dow 10-10-18 A237RFA p37 CR France40

WEBB,Richard Joseph 2Lt dow PoW 1-6-18 25MGC Inf p186 CR France1753

WEBB,Samuel Cecil 2LtTCapt kia 3-10-16 6RMunstF p176 CR Greece3

WEBB,Stanley Horace 2Lt dow PoW 26-3-18 3 att7RWKent p142 CR France1707

WEBB,Thomas Frederick Capt kia 7-9-17 6Lond p246 MR29

WEBB,Thomas Henry Basil 2Lt kia 1-12-17 1WelshGds p53 CR France415

WEBB,Thomas Richard Henry T2Lt dow 31-7-17 18KRRC p152 CR Belgium5,1-8-17 14Bn

WEBB,Trevor 2Lt kia 10-5-17 GL &55RFC p14 CR France1266

WEBB-BOWEN,Hugh Ince Capt dow 23-5-15 RWFus p99 CR Gallipoli1

WEBB-WARE,Kenneth Charles 2Lt kia 21-3-18 RGA 77SB p42

WEBBER,Alan Frank Augustus 2Lt kia 24-8-18 5ELancs p226 CR France239

WEBBER,Frederick Henry.MC.2Lt dow 24-10-18 9Norf p74 CR France146

WEBBER,Frederick John T2Lt kia 30-11-17 235MGC p186 MR17

WEBBER,Harold Victor 2Lt kia 5/7-7-15 SomLI B'Coy p80 CR Belgium85

WEBBER,Henry.MID TLt dow 21-7-16 7SLancs p126 CR France188

WEBBER,Leonard Alexander T2Lt dow 9-7-16 9Dev p77 CR France40

WEBBER,Lynden TLt kia 9-8-15 6Lincs p76 CR Gallipoli5,7-8-15

WEBBER,Stanley Albert 2Lt kia 1-7-16 1SStaffs p123 CR France397

WEBBER,William Henry Lt ded 2-6-15 2/4Dev p220 CR Devon72

WEBBERLEY,Reginald Selwyn T2Lt dow 30-9-17 2/6NStaffs p158 CR Belgium16

WEBER,Harry Percy 2Lt kia 15-11-16 3 att7RLancs p59 CR France232,16-11-16

WEBER,Reginald Otho 2Lt dow 4-9-17 3 att8LNLancs p137 CR Belgium11,5-9-17

WEBER,Victor Joseph Lt kld 15-12-18 3BordR &RAF p118

WEBSDALE,Frank Capt 13-7-19 RE CR Ches182

WEBSTER,Alexander 2Lt kia 9-4-17 4GordH p242 CR France184

WEBSTER,Alfred Alexander 2Lt dow 24-8-15 3 att1GordH p167 CR France40

WEBSTER,Arthur Cecil 2Lt kia 3-5-17 4EYorks p219 MR20

WEBSTER,Aubrey Herbert Bower T2Lt kld 25-4-16 6Nhampt p138 CR France164

WEBSTER,Bruce 2Lt kia 5-9-18 RScots att1/9Bn p55 MR19

WEBSTER,Charles Alexander 2Lt kia 9-4-17 6SfthH p241 CR France15

WEBSTER,Donald Keir 2Lt dow 3-5-17 7ScotRif att10/11HLI p224 CR France40

WEBSTER,Douglas Gordon.MC.Lt kia 29-9-18 21MGC Inf p186 MR30

WEBSTER,Edward Lt 12-9-20 12Ches CR Asia51

WEBSTER,Edward Mackay 2Lt kia 1-8-16 2RBerks p140 CR France423

WEBSTER,Erwin Wentworth TCapt kia 9-4-17 13KRRC p152 MR20

WEBSTER,Frank Augustus.MC.2Lt kia 1-11-18 1/4Glouc p107 CR Italy4

WEBSTER,George Alan 2Lt kia 18-9-18 4 att1EYorks p219 MR16

WEBSTER,George Alexander Malcolm 2Lt kia 28-2-18 SLancs &RFC p17&126 CR France327

WEBSTER,George Thomas T2Lt dow 7-12-17 203MGC p186 CR France102

WEBSTER,George William.MID 2Lt kia 15-6-15 1RScotF D'Coy p95 CR Belgium126,16-6-15

WEBSTER,Godfrey Vassall George Augustus Lt kia 4-8-17 3GrenGds p50 MR29

WEBSTER,Harold Stanley Lt kia 7-8-17 4EYorks p219 CR France538

WEBSTER,Harold Wolstan Maj dow 12-4-18 RE 497FC p209 CR Belgium11

WEBSTER,Henry Hellyer 2Lt kia 14-4-18 1Lincs p76 MR30

WEBSTER,Hugh Maxwell T2Lt kia 5-7-16 7ELancs p111 CR France150

WEBSTER,John Alexander Croone 2Lt kia 21-4-17 1SfthH p165 CR Iraq8

WEBSTER,John Frederick 2Lt kia 24-8-18 9HLI p241 CR France1170

WEBSTER,John Philip Lt dow 24-10-18 9YLI p144 CR France332,Phillip

WEBSTER,John Ralph Ward 2Lt dow 11-8-16 5Lpool p215 CR France66

WEBSTER,John Richard Capt kia 9-9-16 1/4Lond p246 MR21

WEBSTER,John Ryrie.DSO.MC.LtCol kia 22-3-18 16N&D p135 MR27

WEBSTER,John William Capt dow 29-3-18 2Leinst p175 CR France145

WEBSTER,Joseph Frain.MID 2Lt kia 30-10-14 3BlkW att1/-GordH p129 MR29

WEBSTER,Michael Harold TLt kia 1-7-16 13 att16WYorks p83 MR21

WEBSTER,Robert Bell 2Lt kld 28-4-16 6Dors p124 CR France922

WEBSTER,Sidney Herbert 2Lt kia 30-11-17 3Lpool p73 CR France844,6Bn

WEBSTER,Thomas John 2Lt kia 8-10-16 7Mddx p235 CR France402

WEBSTER,Thomas William 2Lt kia 1-10-16 11 att1/16Lond p248 MR21

WEBSTER,Walter Henry.DSO.2Lt kia 10-2-17 4Lond p246 CR France525

WEBSTER-JONES,Alfred Owen Webster Lt kia 13-11-16 3 att2 O&BLI p130 MR21

WEDD,Charles Clifford Lt 11-10-17 3MGC AIF MR29

WEDD,Edward Parker Wallman.MC.Capt kia 13-7-18 EssYeo attRAMC p203 CR Belgium12

WEDD,Hermann 2Lt kia 30-4-17 3/1RGA p209 CR France

WEDD,W.S.Lt kia 14-7-15 SL att3KAR p268 CR EAfrica56

WEDDELL,Herbert Lt dow 8-10-16 RFA D4HB p208 CR France177

WEDDERBURN,George Herbert Lt kia 9-8-18 HampsYeo att15Hamps p204 MR30

WEDDERBURN,Robert Hamilton Maclagan 2Lt kia 3-2-15 3ScotRif p104 CR France83,Lt

WEDDERBURN-MAXWELL,James 2Lt kia 30-9-18 3 att6KOSB p102 CR Belgium157,1-10-18

WEDDERSPOON,John Henry Butcher Lt kia 6-4-17 RFA attRFC p20&208 CR Belgium406,Jack

WEDGWOOD,Allen 2Lt kia 19-8-15 8NumbF p63 MR4

WEDGWOOD,Arthur Felix Capt kia 14-3-17 1/5NStaffs p237 CR France800

WEDGWOOD,Cecil.DSO.Maj kia 3-7-16 8NStaffs p158 CR France150

WEDGWOOD,Gilbert Colclough TLt kia 1-7-16 109MGC p186 MR21

WEDGWOOD,Percy Ashworth Lt ded 24-1-18 RAMC att1/2MddxHuss p198 CR Palestine3

WEDGWOOD,Philip Egerton T2Lt kia 1-7-16 16RIrRif p170 CR France383

WEDGWOOD,William Armstrong 2Lt kia 9-7-16 RE attRFC p20&210 CR France1185

WEEDEN,Charles Harold 2Lt kia 25-3-18 23Lond p252 MR20

WEEDING,John Richard Baggalay.MID 2Lt kia 22-12-14 2WelshR p128 CR France260,Baggally

WEEDING,Thomas Maj kia 26-8-17 1RWSurr p57 CR Belgium24

WEEDON,Dudley Harry T2Lt dow 20-11-17 8NumbF p63 CR Lond14

WEEITCH,James John 2Lt dow 8-10-17 82RFA p37 CR Belgium20

WEEKES,Arthur Nelson Henry.MC.Capt kia 29-7-18 1/4RSuss B'Coy p228 CR France524,Hampton

WEEKES,Cyril Warner.MC.Capt kia 16-9-18 RFA p37 CR France309

WEEKES,Reginald Penkivil Olive T2Lt kia 7-5-17 GL &10RFC p14 CR France98

WEEKES,Sydney Charles Lt ded 28-11-18 IARO att2/72Punjabis p284 MR65,WEEKS

WEEKES,Walter T2Lt kia 23-4-17 Lincs p76 MR20

WEEKS,Francis Mathwin Capt kia 11-4-18 NumbF att8DLI p63 MR32

WEEKS,Henry Russell Capt dow 23-9-18 1WelshR p128 CR Greece5,18-9-18

WEEKS,Herbert Ward Meredith TLt dow 23-11-17 2SWBord p101 CR France446

WEEKS,John T2Lt drd 13-8-15 Dev attHamps p77 CR Greece14

WEEKS,Reginald Skinner 2Lt kia 9-10-16 10Mddx p236 CR France293

WEEKS,Stephen Frederick TLt kia 10-7-16 RE 130FC p49 CR France393

WEGG,Hugh Neville Capt kia 25-3-18 16 att2Mddx p148 MR27

WEGG-PROSSER,Cecil Francis T2Lt kia 3-9-16 15 att16RB p180 MR21

WEIGALL,Richard Edward Cromwell Lt kia 12-3-15 1N&D p135 MR22,11-3-15

WEIGHELL,Frank 2Lt kia 14-4-17 3 att4YLI p144 CR France616

WEIGHTS,James Herbert 2Lt kia 9-8-18 10TankCps p189 CR France1170

WEILL,Abraham T2Lt dow 9-8-16 1RB p180 CR Belgium73

WEINBURG,Philip David Lt kia 9-5-15 4BlkW A'Coy p230 CR France924,2Lt

WEINEL,Edward Eugene 2LtALt kia 7-6-17 RFA attY30TMB p37 CR Belgium127

WEINEL,George Henry 2Lt ded 28-10-18 1/8RWar p215 CR France528

WEIR,Charles Sutherland 2Lt kia 30-5-17 5 att18HLI p240 CR France60

WEIR,Charles William 2Lt kia 28-10-17 261RHFA p37 CR Palestine8

WEIR,Donald Lord.DSO.MC.Capt 21-4-21 2Leic MR43

WEIR,Genge Gordon.MC.Capt drd 9-9-18 7RScots p211 MR40

WEIR,George Lt ded 5-10-18 RFA p208 CR France1858

WEIR,Harold Llewellyn 2Lt kia 31-10-17 4NumbF p213 CR Belgium11

WEIR,Henry Keith Crichton T2Lt dow 3-5-16 10SStaffs att9N&D p123 CR Ireland124

WEIR,Henry Leabody 2Lt ded PoW 28-10-18 12RIrRif p170 CR Germany1,Harry

WEIR,Herbert James Lt dow 9-11-17 AyrYeo p203 CR Palestine1,12RScots

WEIR,John TCapt kia 1-7-16 9RInniskF p105 MR21

WEIR,Peter 2Lt dow 15-8-15 87RFA p37 CR France40

WEIR,Robert Lt kia 16-11-16 1/8RScots p211 CR France221

WEIR,Robert T2Lt kia 9-4-17 15DLI p162 CR France591 Ex 1/7A&SH

WEIR,Thomas Henderson.MC.LtAMaj kia 8-5-18 RE 526FC p209 CR France98

WEIR,William Logan TLt kia 22-10-17 23Manch p156 MR30

WEISS,Edward Stanley T2Lt kia 22-11-17 41RFC p14 CR France62

WEISS,Hubert Foreaux 2Lt dow 3-9-18 8Lond p247 CR France833,Foveaux

WEISS,Thomas Jessop T2Lt dow 27-6-16 151RFA p37 CR France699

WEITZMANN,Cecil Gothet 2Lt dow 25-9-15 4 att1SStaffs p123 CR France109,Goblet

WELBOURN,Ernest Cecil 2Lt kia 21-4-17 5Yorks p221 CR France504,WELBOURNE

WELBURN,Thomas Harold Lt ded 12-8-17 ASC p272

WELBY,Davis 2Lt ded 23-10-18 RGA p42 CR Yorks257

WELBY,Glynne Everard Earle Maj kia 27-9-14 1SWBord D'Coy p101 MR15,26-9-14

WELBY,John Arthur TCapt dow 17-3-17 11Worc p110 CR France41

WELBY,Richard William Gregory Lt kia 16-9-14 2GrenGds p50 CR France1112

WELCH,Arthur Sidney 2Lt kia 29-9-17 RGA 149SB p42 CR Belgium20,Lt

WELCH,Edward Ronald TCapt kia 16-9-16 RAMC att5DLI p198 MR21

WELCH,Eric Arthur T2Lt kia 23-4-17 GL &16RFC p14 CR France269

WELCH,George Frederick Lt planeAcc 11-2-18 IA attRFC p284 MR67,10-2-18

WELCH,Harold Echalaz.DSO&Bar.LtCol kia 29-3-18 6KSLI p145 CR France360

WELCH,Howard Vyse TMaj ded PoW 4-10-15 9ESurr p113 CR France1724 Ex 4Bn

WELCH,Hugh(Toby) Lt kia 28-3-17 RFA attRFC p20&208 CR France1059

WELCH,James Stanley Lightfoot TLt kia 1-7-16 12YLI p144 CR France802

WELCH,John Eric Haddon 2Lt kia 25-9-15 8Lincs p76 MR19,26-9-15

WELCH,Richard Sydney 2Lt kia 24-3-18 9Ches p97 MR20

WELCH,Stafford Leslie B.2Lt ded 20-7-17 4 att1RWar p66 CR France52

WELCH,Stephen Cocks T2Lt kia 29-4-16 7CamH p168 CR France423

WELCH,Vere Edward Osbaldiston Capt kia 30-8-18 1/5Lond A'Coy p246 CR France568,Osbaldeston

WELCH,Walter George Frederick Lt kia 30-10-14 117RFA p37 CR Belgium59

WELCHMAN,Edward Theodore.DSO.Capt dow 26-10-14 1WYorks p83 CR France102

WELCHMAN,Eric Llewelyn Lt kia 24-8-14 1Lincs p76 CR Belgium202

WELCHMAN,Gerald Harington Capt ded 17-4-19 IARO att1LabCps p284 CR India97A

WELCHMAN,John Charles St.George Lt kia 10-3-15 IA 1/39GarhwalRif p284 CR France355 &CR France1887

WELCHMAN,Patrick Elliot.MC.DFC.Capt dow 28-11-18 1/2KOSB &99RAF p102 CR France1678,Eliot

WELD,Edward Joseph 2Lt dow 27-9-15 72RFA p37 CR Belgium11

WELD,Hugh Edward 2Lt kia 25-1-15 1ScotsGds att28Lond p52 MR22,28Lond att1SGds

WELD,Thomas Joseph Wilfrid.MC.Capt ded 18-11-18 1LovatScts &2/2KAR p204&268 CR Eafrica52

WELD-BLUNDELL,Robert Shirburne 2Lt ded 1-1-16 6Lpool p215&272 CR Lancs168

WELD-FORESTER,Arthur Orlando Wolstan Cecil.Hon.MVO.Maj dow 1-11-14 GrenGds p50 CR Shrop143

WELDON,Anthony Arthur.Bart.CB.DSO.BtCol ded 29-6-17 4Leinst p266 CR Eire313

WELDON,Arthur Steuart Maj kia 25-3-17 2 att7NStaffs p158 MR38,Stewart

WELDON,Geoffrey Capt dow 25-9-16 D48RFA p37 CR France40

WELDON,Henry Walter Cecil T2Lt kia 26-4-16 7RIrRif p172 CR France423,Capt 27-4-16

WELDON,William Joseph 2Lt kia 4-6-17 72/38RFA p37 CR France451

WELDRICK,Wilfred 2Lt kia 12-4-18 25MGC Inf p186 MR32,11-4-18

WELFORD,Alice Sister ded 15-1-18 QAIMNS att65BritGH p200 CR Iraq6,drd

WELFORD,Frederick T2Lt kia 9-10-17 3 att6Yorks p91 MR30

WELHAM,Harry George.MC.TLt kia 4-11-18 3 att9RSuss p120 CR France985

WELINKAR,S.K.C.Lt kia 27-6-18 SL &RAF p201

WELLACOTT,Arthur Cecil Baber 2Lt ded 16-2-19 3RInniskF p264 CR Devon267

WELLBURN,T.A.Lt 12-6-17 RASC CR Yorks98

WELLDON,James Hoste 2Lt kia 30-11-17 6EKent p58 MR17

WELLER,Charles Capt kia 16-8-17 RAMC att1/1Lond p198 CR Belgium72

WELLER,Edward Arthur Walstone.MC.2Lt dow 22-10-18 7RWar attMGC p187&214 CR France146

WELLER,George Herbert LtTCapt kia 12-7-15 7HLI p240 MR4

WELLER,William Richard HonLt&QM kia 18-7-16 10A&SH p174 CR France164

WELLERD,George Godfrey T2Lt dow 15-4-17 1RB p180 CR France102

WELLESLEY,Cyril Gerald Valercan Capt kia 14-3-15 2Lincs p76 CR France525

WELLESLEY,Edmund Ernest Charles TCapt kia 30-4-16 9Norf p74 CR Belgium92

WELLESLEY,Edward Victor Colley William.MC.Capt ded 2-10-16 RE p262 CR Eire531,Maj

WELLESLEY,Eric George 2Lt kia 21-12-15 8Yorks p91 MR32

WELLESLEY,Lord Richard Capt kia 30-10-14 1GrenGds 3Coy p50 CRBelgium112,29-10-14

WELLESLEY-MILLER,John Leslie 2Lt kia 15-9-16 1EKent p58 CR France294

WELLINGS,Charles Henry Clifford T2Lt kia 11-8-17 152LabCps p189 CR Belgium12

WELLINGS,Henry William.DCM.T2Lt dow 20-6-18 KSLI att17MGC p145&186 CR France169

WELLINGS,Thomas Fitch 2Lt dow 16-7-18 RGA 297SB attCRA Bty p209 CR France95

WELLS,Alfred Langton 2Lt kia 9-10-17 1IrGds p53 CR Belgium83

WELLS,Arthur Scott TLt kia 26-9-16 33 att8NumbF p63 MR21

WELLS,Cyril Edward Elliott Lt kia 10-3-15 2ESurr p113 CR Belgium17

WELLS,Douglas Henry.MC.2Lt kia 3-5-17 5Y&L p238 MR20

WELLS,Frank Irving Pascoe Lt kia 9-5-15 2WelshR p128 CR France631

WELLS,Fred 2Lt kia 25-4-18 2/5LancF p221 CR France106

WELLS,Frederick 2Lt ded 1-8-15 2N&D p135 CR France102

WELLS,Frederick Bennett 2Lt dow 10-10-18 23RFus p71 CR France380

WELLS,Frederick Edward TLtACapt ded 13-10-18 TankCps p189 CR Surrey41

WELLS,Frederick Neville Lt ded 7-11-18 RASC p194 CR France85

WELLS,Guy Francy Capt dow 15-6-15 RE p49 CR Belgium165,Franey

WELLS,Henry Frederick 2Lt kia 21-9-18 8ScotRif p225 CR France663

WELLS,Henry Maurice Watkins Lt kia 15-9-16 4RBerks attRFC p20&234 CR France382 &CR France1896

WELLS,Herman Theodore T2Lt ded 2-4-16 RASC MT p194 CR France85

WELLS,Hurlestone Vesey Capt kia 12-4-18 2RFus p71 MR32

WELLS,James Ritchie T2Lt kld 17-11-17 1BlkW attRFC p14&129 CR Scot755

WELLS,Leonard Frank.MC.2Lt kia 11-10-18 9WYorks p83 CR France611

WELLS,Leslie Howard Elliott 2Lt ded 4-5-15 3 att2LancF p94 CR B94 ?

WELLS,Louis Conrad 2Lt kia 31-3-18 att2RBerks p140 MR27

WELLS,Maurice Godfrey 2Lt kia 28-3-18 C211RFA p37 CR France745

WELLS,Nigel Grenville Lt ded 9-10-19 WelshGds p262

WELLS,Norman T2Lt dow 25-9-17 1/2 att16LancF p94 CR France1361

WELLS,Norman Albert 2Lt dow 29-12-17 1/1Hereford p252 CR Palestine3

WELLS,Norman Lancaster Lt kia 10-8-15 6LNLancs p137 MR4

WELLS,Norman Septimus LtCol ded 20-4-20 IA IMS p284 CR Mddx26,Maj

WELLS,Reginald William 2Lt dow 3-10-17 1/2 att1ESurr p113 MR30

WELLS,Ronald Graham TLt kia 4-3-16 7RSuss p120 MR19

WELLS,Thomas William Maurice 2Lt kia 1-7-16 2SWBord p101 MR21

WELLS,Walter Neave Capt kia 27-10-14 3EKent att1KRRC p58 MR29

WELLS,William 2Lt kia 13-1-16 2Leic p88 MR38

WELLS,William Leslie T2Lt kia 21-5-16 D235RFA p37 CR France924

WELLS,William Lewis.MC.&Bar.Lt dow 6-5-18 8Mddx att48RAF p20,236,258&237 CR France145,Capt

WELLS-COLE,Neville William.MID Maj kia 6-1-18 28RFA p37 CR Belgium12

WELLS-COLE,William Francis 2Lt kia 31-7-17 1Lincs p76 MR29

WELLSTED,George Wormall TCapt kia 30-6-16 11Hamps A'Coy p121 CR France223

WELLWOOD,Frederick Paton.TD.Capt ded 6-2-17 SL LNLancs p201 CR Scot387,6-3-17

WELLWOOD,Robert Kemp.MC.Lt kia 23-7-18 6SfthH p241 CR France1697,Capt

WELMAN,Noel Yvon Loftus.DSO.Capt kia 25-9-15 1Mddx p148 CR France114,dow

WELSBY,Sydney Walter Humfrey 2LtTLt kia 30-4-17 14Ches p97 MR38

WELSFORD,Geoffrey Joseph Lightbourn 2Lt kia 30-3-16 2Mddx &RFC p4&148 CR France1412,Lightbourne

WELSFORD,George Keith T2Lt kia 20-10-16 11RFC p4 MR20

WELSH,Alexander Torburn 2Lt kia 3-5-17 4RWFus p223 CR France537

WELSH,Anthony Reginald 2LtTLt dow 19-2-16 4Yorks p220 CR France102

WELSH,Cyril Clifton Capt kia 17-7-17 D256RFA p37 CR Belgium5

WELSH,Robert Milne Ballantyne LtACapt kia 23-4-17 7BordR p118 MR20

WELSH,Tom Capt kia 12-7-15 5KOSB p224 CR Gallipoli2

WELSTEAD,Harry Marion TLtCol kia 17-8-15 9LancF p94 CR Gallipoli27

WELTER,Leslie Dingman 2Lt kia 18-6-17 17KRRC p152 CR Belgium10,19-6-17

WEMYSS,Norman Douglas 2Lt kia 27-7-16 1Beds p87 MR21 CR France390

WENBORN,Harold 2Lt dow 24-3-18 47MGC p186 CR France177

WENDEN,Charles Blade 2Lt kia 31-7-17 RGA 104SB p209 CR Belgium34

WENDEN,George TLtTCapt kia 16-3-17 BordR att35RFC p14&118 CR France120

WENDER,Louis.DCM.2Lt kia 16-6-18 Manch p156 MR27

WENDOVER,Albert Edward Charles Robert.Vicount Lt dow 19-5-15 RHGds p20 CR Bucks86

WENHAM,Edward Kimber 2Lt kia 30-10-18 1/7Worc p226 CR Italy4

WENN,William Capt dow 1-4-17 1/5Norf p216 CR Egypt2

WENSLEY,Frederic Martin T2Lt kia 5-8-16 10Lincs p76 MR21

WENSLEY,George Thomas 2Lt ded 31-1-18 1SLancs p126 MR43

WENSLEY,Harold William 2Lt ded 15-11-18 1Lincs p76 CR France658

WENTWORTH,Cyril John T2Lt dow 3-2-17 12RSuss p120 CR Belgium11

WENTWORTH,John 2Lt kia 4-7-18 179RFA p37 MR27

WENTZEL,Eric Francis LtACapt kia 23-3-18 3 att8ESurr p113 MR27

WERE,Cyril Narramore Chap4Cl ded 9-1-18 RAChDept p200 CR France193

WERNER,Charles Augustus Capt kia 9-5-15 6 att2RB p180 MR32

WERNET,William Edward ACapt kld 30-7-18 4SWBord attLightTMB p101 CR Iraq8

WERNHER,Alexander Pigott 2Lt kia 10-9-16 WelshGds p53 CR France394

WESCHE,Ernest Brocklesby Capt kia 19-10-14 SLancs attNigR p126 CR WAfrica56

WESLEY,Charles Wallace T2Lt ded 6-2-19 1SStaffs p123 CR France65,Lt

WESSELHOEFT,George Henri T2Lt kia 16-9-16 15DLI p162 CR France744

WEST,Alan Herbert Mainwaring Lt BombExplosAcc 7-1-18 IA 36Sikhs p284 CR Iraq5,dow

WEST,Archibald Stewart.MC.Maj kia 23-3-18 93RFA p37 CR France518

WEST,Arthur Eustace Lockley 2LtACapt dow 28-4-17 RGA 213SB p42 CR France1186,kia

WEST,Arthur Graeme T2LtACapt kia 3-4-17 6 O&BLI p130 CR France568

WEST,Charles Frederick Arthur 2Lt kia 4-10-17 1/2ESurr p113 MR30

WEST,Charles Henry Raymond Lt kia 3-6-15 6 att4Mddx p148 MR29

WEST,Corney.MC.Lt kia 27-5-18 5DLI p239 CR France1753

WEST,Cyril Frederick Ernest 2Lt kia 28-9-18 RSuss p120 CR Belgium115

WEST,Edward Lynn TCapt kia 31-7-16 1Norf p74 MR21

WEST,Francis Charles Bartholomew LtCol kia 28-9-16 243RFA p206 CR France251

WEST,George.MM.2Lt kia 22-3-18 9 att6Leic p88&259 MR27

WEST,George Arnold 2Lt dow 8-8-18 1ELancs attMGC p111&186 CR France141

WEST,George Clifford 2Lt kld 12-2-17 3 att7SStaffs p123 CR France818

WEST,George Cyril AssSurg4Cl kia 12-2-16 IMS attRFA 82Bty p284 CR Iraq1

WEST,Gerald William Lt kia 25-9-15 RSuss att2Bn p120 MR19

WEST,Harold 2Lt kia 9-5-15 1BlkW p129 MR22

WEST,Harold Douglas 2Lt dow 25-3-18 1KRRC p152 MR20

WEST,Henry Cave Capt kia 22/24-11-15 RFA att5RHA p37 MR38,22-11-15

WEST,Henry Meldrum Pelham TCapt kia 20-9-17 11NumbF p63 CR Belgium125

WEST,Herbert,John.MC.Capt dow 22-8-18 4 att1Beds p87 CR France84

WEST,Herbert St.John Carr Maj dow 27-10-18 12DLI p162

WEST,James Stafford 2Lt dow 20-7-16 RGA 116SB p42 CR France23

WEST,John Preston Sackville 2Lt kia 14-6-17 D189RFA p37 CR Belgium127

WEST,Leslie Gower 2Lt kia 24-10-18 5Lond p246 CR Belgium414

WEST,Lionel Reginald Everard Capt kia 23-4-17 8Lond p247 CR France279

WEST,Mortimer Sackville T2Lt kia 11-11-17 GL &11RFC p14 CR France120,dedacc

WEST,Nevile.MC.Capt kia 16-2-17 1RBerks A'Coy p140 CR France280,17-2-17

WEST,Percy Charles Warren Lt&QM ded 29-7-15 RFC p2 CR Lond8

WEST,Percy Francis 2Lt ded 24-3-18 RFC p17 MR65

WEST,Richard Arnsley.VC.DSO&Bar.MC.CaptALtCol kia 2-9-18 NIrHorse attTanks p24,189&259 CR France614,Annesley

WEST,Sidney T2Lt kia 1-4-17 11BordR p118 CR France672

WEST,Stanley James 2Lt ded 20-11-17 2RWSurr p57 CR Lond1

WEST,Sydney Albert T2Lt kia 30-8-17 7MGC p186 CR Belgium72

WEST,Theodore 2Lt kia 24-9-16 RE attRFC p20&210 CR France518

WEST,Walter Montague Lt dow 5-5-15 1Camb p245 CR Belgium102

WEST,Wilfrid Thomas 2Lt kia 25-3-18 9RInniskF p105 MR27

WEST,William T2Lt kia 7-8-15 9N&D A'Coy p135 CR Gallipoli5,9-8-15

WEST,William Anderson.MC.2Lt kia 21-6-18 3 att13RScots p55 CR France113

WEST,William James.MC.MM.2Lt&ACapt kia 3-9-18 2Hamps p121 MR32

WEST-THOMPSON,Maurice T2Lt kia 23-11-17 GL &60RFC p14 CR France139

WESTACOTT,Ernest George T2Lt dow 19-5-16 16RB p180 CR France279

WESTALL,Ronald Cameron Lt kia 12-11-14 2RSuss p120 MR29

WESTAWAY,Leslie Thomas T2Lt kia 1-7-16 2RFus p71 CR France1501

WESTBROOK,Edward Worsley 2Lt dow 8-11-15 8Manch p237 CR Gallipoli6

WESTBY,Edmund Henry Herbert Capt&Adjt kia 25-5-15 1WelshR p128 MR29

WESTBY,Edwin John Lt ded 4-1-19 RFA p262 CR Lond4

WESTBY,Percival St.George Charles Capt kia 23-9-17 A296RFA p207 CR Belgium8,Perceval

WESTCOTT,Edgar.MC.Capt dow 4-11-18 9WYorks p83 CR France1084

WESTERBERG,George Herbert 2Lt kia 5-9-16 106RFA p37 CR FRance397

WESTERBY,James Thomas 2Lt dow 5-6-18 7EYorks p85 CR France40

WESTERMAN,Harry 2Lt kia 11-8-18 KRRC att21Bn p152 CR Belgium21

WESTHEAD,John SubCdr accdrd 17-8-20 IA S&TCps p284

WESTHORP,William Hast T2Lt kia 28-4-17 27NumbF p63 CR France604

WESTLAKE,Albert Neave.MC.2Lt kia 4-1-18 4NStaffs att27RAF p17&158 CR France920,Lt

WESTLAKE,Algernon Maj ded 25-5-15 RAMC p253 CR Lincs158

WESTLAKE,Geoffrey Arthur Lt kia 7/8-10-16 1Lond p245 MR21

WESTLAKE,John 2Lt ded 5-12-19 IA S&TCps p284 MR61,T.

WESTLAKE,John Howard T2Lt dow 7-5-17 GL &12RFC p14 CR France113

WESTMACOTT,Frederick Charles 2Lt kia 31-7-17 3 att1RWKent p142 MR29

WESTMACOTT,Spencer Ruscombe Lt kia 0-5-15 2 att1Leinst p175 MR29

WESTMORE,Lawrence Arthur T2Lt kia 1-7-16 1Hamps p121 CR France643

WESTMORELAND,Ernest 2Lt dow 19-2-18 80RFC p17 CR France525

WESTOBY,Frank Durrant 2Lt kia 16-9-16 1/7Mddx attMGC p187&235 CR France785

WESTOBY,Reginald Herbert 2Lt kia 4-10-17 3Lincs p76 MR30

WESTON,Charles Guy TLt kia 1-11-15 7Yorks p91 MR29 CR Belgium35

WESTON,Edmund Culpeper Col ded 7-9-15 Staff Ex Lpool p261 CR Hamps132

WESTON,George Primrose.MC.Capt kia 1-10-16 20Lond p251 MR21

WESTON,John Archibald Lt&Adjt 23-5-20 1RFus CR Hamps1

WESTON,John Cecil 2Lt dow 6-6-17 16Lond p250 CR France518

WESTON,John Douglas 2Lt kia 1-7-16 13 att11Suff p79 MR21

WESTON,John Spencer Theodore,MC LtTCapt kia 20-8-15 3RWar attRBerks p66&259 CR France1106

WESTON,Joseph Capt 17-10-15 14 att9KRRC p149 MR29 Served as CRUIKSHANKS

WESTON,Kingsley Vale 2Lt dow 10-4-18 4WYorks attMGC Inf p83&186 CR Notts84,Lt

WESTON,Maurice Sydney T2Lt kia 27-4-17 N&D att6Bn p135 MR21

WESTON,Ronald John Maj ded 27-10-18 IARO attRE p284 MR43 &CR Pakistan50A

WESTON,Stanley Valentine.MM.T2Lt ded 18-2-19 MGC Inf p266 CR Kent83

WESTON,Wilfrid James TLt kia 22-8-15 6Y&L p159 MR4

WESTON-WEBB,Henry TLt kia 24-8-16 5 O&BLI p130 MR21

WESTPHAL,Benjamin Augustus 2Lt kia 23-4-17 18Manch p156 MR20

WESTRAY,F.E.2Lt ded 19-12-18 SL UgandaMedServ p255 CR EAfrica40,Lt

WESTRICK,Charles 2Lt kia 31-7-17 3 att1RWKent p142

WESTROPP-DAWSON,Walter Henry 2Lt 24-5-15 2Ches MR29

WESTWATER,Frederick 2Lt kia 28-4-17 3RScots p55 MR20

WESTWELL,Mary AssAdmintr ded 10-10-18 QMAAC p200 CR Ireland14,drd

WESTWOOD,Alexander Cleghorn Lt kia 16-6-15 7BlkW p231 MR22

WESTWOOD,Alfred Herbert Capt kia 21-9-18 10RWar att6Nhants p66 CR France511

WESTWOOD,James 2Lt kia 25-6-17 RGA 321SB p42 CR Belgium10

WESTWOOD,James Henry 2Lt kia 12-7-16 3SStafs att62MGC p123 MR21

WESTWOOD,Stanley Benjamin.MC.2Lt kia 15-4-18 4LNLancs p234 CR France1106

WESTWOOD,Walter Peter 2Lt kia 26-9-17 6Suff p218 MR30

WESTWOOD,Walter Raymond 2Lt dow 26-10-16 3RFA p209 CR France145

WETENHALL,William Thornton TCapt kia 17-7-16 6Leic p88 MR21

WETHERALL,Arthur Hewitt.DCM.2Lt ded 21-1-18 3 att9LancF p263 CR France40

WETHERALL,Eric Francis Cecil TLt ded 27-12-18 LabCps p266 CR France1041,2Lt 12NStaffs

WETHERALL,Francis Gyrth Johnston Lt kia 19-9-18 IA 1/72Punjabis p284 MR34

WEVELL,William Henry Lt kia 14-5-16 3Worc p110 CR France68

WEYMAN,Henry Morton Capt ded 26-8-16 RFA p207 CR Lancs33

WEYMAN,Percy Lt dow 16-10-17 7LancF p221 CR Belgium24

WEYMOUTH,John Alexander.Viscount 2Lt kia 13-2-16 2Drags p21 CR France423

WHALE,William John Lt&ACapt dow 14-6-17 RGA 163SB p42 CR Belgium29

WHALEY,Frank T2Lt kia 31-3-17 2Yorks p91 CR France1186

WHALEY,Oswald Stanley T2Lt kia 10-8-15 10Hamps p121 MR4

WHALL,Anna Marjorie AssAdmintr ded 6-12-18 QMAAC p200 CR France85

WHALL,Edwin Lionel Haversham T2Lt kia 18/21-9-17 1KRRC p152 CR Belgium125,20-9-17 18Bn

WHALL,Walter Edward.MC.Capt kia 6-5-18 7SomLI att11RWFus p80 CR Greece5

WHALLEY,Henry Worthington Capt kia 4-6-15 4ELancs p226 MR4

WHALLEY,Julian Lawson LtACapt dow 3-12-17 3 att9Ess p133 CR France658

WHALLEY,Leonard 2Lt kia 26-3-18 N&D att15Bn p135 MR27

WHALLEY,Reginald Livesey Capt kia 16-9-18 4ELancs &RAF p226&258 CR France403

WHARRAM,Charles Etherington Lt mbk 26-3-18 52RFC p257 MR20

WHARTON,Christopher Willis 2Lt kia 26-10-17 3Lond p246 MR30

WHARTON,Frank Hammond Lt kia 25-9-15 3 att1LNLancs p137 CR France1723

WHARTON,Guy Fitzgerald Lt dow 9-5-15 2DLI att1YLI p162 CR Belgium6

WHARTON,Herbert Lt ded 5-7-17 2/4WRid p227 CR France145

WHARTON,Sidney Alfred T2Lt dow 1-7-16 8Norf attTMB p74 CR France141

WHATELEY,Richard Herschel Lt kia 25-8-16 5 att2RB p180 MR19

WHATELEY,Stephen William Capt dow 25-10-18 1RMunstF p176 CR France528

WHATELY,Percival Vivian Victor TLt kia 27-12-17 179MGC Inf p186 CR Palestine3

WHATFORD,George Lumley Capt kia 22-11-15 IA 66Punjabis p284 MR38

WHATFORD,Stuart Lumley.CMG.DSO&Bar.TLtCol kld 30-8-19 Yorks att8Y&L p255 CR Italy15,30-9-19

WHATLING,Harold Wilfred T2Lt kia 26-6-16 8Suff p79 MR21

WHATMOOR,Donald Gurney T2Lt kia 17-1-16 7Beds p87 CR France370

WHEADON,James Hansford 2Lt dow 11-3-17 RGA 15SB p42 CR France164

WHEAT,Harold Arthur T2Lt kia 2-12-17 2Y&L p159 MR17

WHEATCROFT,Frederick George 2Lt dow 26-11-17 5 att13ESurr B'Coy p226 CR France256

WHEATCROFT,George Hanson T2Lt kia 13-8-15 RGA 16HB p42 CR France344,11-8-15

WHEATCROFT,Ronald Duncan Lt dow 2-7-16 6N&D p233 CR France120

WHEATCROFT,William Hands T2Lt kia 7-3-17 1NStaffs p158 CR France149

WHEATE,Arthur T2Lt dow 5-4-16 1 att6ELancs p111 MR38

WHEATER,Kenneth Ronald Maclaren T2Lt kia 6-5-17 RE 4SpecBn p49 CR France560

WHEATER,Sydney Capt kia 15-9-16 24Lond p252 MR21

WHEATLEY,Annie Sister ded 1-8-19 TFNS p272 CR Yorks583

WHEATLEY,Arthur.MM.2Lt dow 8-5-18 4RLancs p213 CR France88
WHEATLEY,Arthur Nevin.MID Maj dow 5-7-16 5WRid p227 CR France40
WHEATLEY,Frank Rees T2Lt kia 11-8-16 12Ess p133 CR Belgium44
WHEATLEY,John Charles 2Lt dow 3-10-18 N&D att1/5Bn p135 MR16
WHEATLEY,Joseph Horace Lyncham 2Lt kia 15-6-17 2/4Lond p246 MR20
WHEATLEY,Lionel Frank 2Lt kia 22-11-17 154MGC p186 MR16
WHEATLEY,Ralph Ruthven T2Lt ded 16-2-19 1KRRC p265 CR Scot231
WHEATLEY,Roland 2Lt kia 24-11-16 4 att15N&D p135 CR France1182
WHEATLEY,Rutland Villiers 2LtTLt kia 29-11-17 6EYorks p85 CR France184
WHEATLEY,William Clarke 2Lt kia 3-5-17 9RB p180 MR20
WHEATLY,Edward Richard 2Lt dow 10-10-17 156RFA p37 CR France139
WHEELDON,Frank Percy Capt kia 30-10-17 8Lond p247 MR30
WHEELDON,Thomas Victor 2Lt kia 12-7-17 16NumbF C'Coy p63 MR31
WHEELER,Alexander James Paterson 2Lt kld 9-5-18 GL &RAF p192 CR France102
WHEELER,Arthur Leslie Doble Lt kia 10-8-17 3RFA p208 CR Belgium7
WHEELER,Augustus Henry Maj kia 10-8-15 6RWFus p223 MR4
WHEELER,Charles Norman Capt kia 7-1-15 att2SLancs p126 MR29
WHEELER,Charles Palliser Capt kia 25-9-15 RBerks p140 CR France1106
WHEELER,George Godfrey Maj kia 13-4-15 IA 7Lancers p284
WHEELER,Harold Ernest.DCM.2Lt kia 3-9-16 1KOSB p102 CR France402
WHEELER,Harry Lloyd T2Lt dow 26-12-15 9EKent att6RWKent p58 CR France80
WHEELER,Henry Thornton Camden Capt ded 30-10-16 3Lpool CmdgGoldCoastR p73 CR WAfrica2
WHEELER,Howard Sidney 2Lt 5-2-19 3NStaffs CR War10
WHEELER,Hugh Graham 2Lt kia 28-4-17 25NumbF p63 MR20
WHEELER,Jack Douglas 2Lt kia 31-7-17 5Suff B'Coy p217 MR29
WHEELER,John Eric Capt kia 10-11-16 RGA p209 CR France294
WHEELER,John Piggott.MC.LtAMaj kia 30-10-17 D82RFA p37 CR Belgium10
WHEELER,P.F.C.d'Erf Capt 24-7-17 Dors attRFC CR Lond7
WHEELER,Russell Mervyn Lt kia 30-11-16 9 att1/7Mddx p236 CR France705
WHEELER,Wilfrid Henry 2Lt kia 26-4-18 SStaffs att4Bn p123 MR30
WHEELER,William Pierce 2Lt kia 2-7-16 1/6RWar p214 MR21
WHEELER-O'BRYEN,Myles Lt acckld 2-10-16 2/5RWar CR France1887
WHEELHOUSE,George William T2Lt ded 6-7-17 RASC p194 CR Iraq6
WHEELOCK,Charles Herbert T2Lt ded 19-3-18 RFC p17 CR Kent125,Lt
WHEELTON,William 2Lt kia 29-3-18 1 att1/7WYorks p83 CR Belgium72
WHEEN,John Capt kia 15-5-15 Lpool p73 MR22
WHELAN,George.MC.2Lt kia 16-8-17 2WYorks p83 MR30
WHELAN,Harry George,MC Lt ded PoW 11-4-18 2RMunstF p176&259 CR Germany3
WHELAN,John Percy Capt kia 11-12-14 RIrRif att2RIrReg p170 MR29
WHELAN,Joseph Lt 15-7-20 IARO attRGA 35MtnBty MR43
WHELDON-WILLIAMS,Victor TLt kldacc 6-7-16 13Mddx p149 CR France200
WHELTON,Daniel T2Lt dow 29-4-16 8RInniskF p105 CR France423
WHETSTONE,Walter Hugh Lt kia 28-3-18 3CldGds p51 MR20
WHEWAY,Frank Reginald 2Lt dow 14-11-17 RGA 183SB p42 CR Belgium173
WHICKER,Frederick Paul Lt dow PoW 12-4-18 1/22Lond p251 CR France563
WHIDBORNE,George Ferris.MC.Lt dow 24-10-15 2CldGds p51 CR France80
WHIDDETT,Horace 2Lt dow 27-8-18 3Lond p246 CR France119
WHIFFIN,Hartley Allen TLt kia 25-9-15 10Glouc p107 CR France1723
WHIKS,Charles T2Lt kia 10-10-15 9RLancs p59 MR21
WHILE,Frank Richard T2Lt kia 15-7-16 1Mddx p149 CR France432
WHILE,Charles Victor 2Lt kia 26-6-16 8RWar p215 MR19
WHILE,Ivor Austin 2Lt kia 31-8-16 4 att1NStaffs p158 MR21
WHILLIER,Leonard Alfred TLt kia 15-9-16 9Suff p79 MR21
WHILMORE-SEARLE,Bertram T2Lt ded 3-10-15 10 att4SStaffs p123
WHIMSTER,Thomas Forbes 2Lt kia 19-11-16 RE p210 CR France131,Lt
WHINCUP,Frank TLt drd 2-7-17 RAMC p198 CR France85
WHINNEY,Edward Maj kia 26-9-16 7Mddx p235 CR France215
WHINNEY,Frederick Stoddart.MC.Capt ded 17-3-19 Lincs 88InfBdeMaj p76 CR Germany1
WHINNEY,John Arthur Perrot 2Lt kia 22-6-17 OxfYeo p205 CR France212
WHINYATES,Harold Bennet 2Lt dow 14-8-17 3 att8SLancs p126 CR Belgium11,Bennett
WHIPPLE,Herbert Connell Capt dow 24-11-14 Dev p77 CR France284
WHISH,John Kenneth Tulloch Capt dow 8-9-14 1ESurr p113 CR France1445
WHISSON,William Henry 2Lt dow 6-5-17 10Mddx p236 CR France113
WHISTLER,Bertram Charles 2Lt kia 29-9-18 4NStaffs p158 CR Belgium116
WHISTLER,Ralfe Allen Fuller Capt dow 27-4-17 2HLI p164 CR France95,28-4-17
WHISTON,Philip Selwyn Lt kia 21-3-18 5N&D p232 MR19

WHITAKER,Arthur Cecil TCapt kia 1-1-16 11WYorks p83 CR France82
WHITAKER,Charles Frederick Lt kia 5-5-15 3 att2WRid p116 CR Belgium115
WHITAKER,Charles Warburton.MC.Lt dow 18-9-18 8Manch p237 CR France278
WHITAKER,Foster 2Lt dow 3-5-17 5 att2A&SH p243 CR France13
WHITAKER,Frederick TLt ded 28-10-16 RAMC p198 CR Egypt1
WHITAKER,George Capt kia 20-9-17 5Lond p246 MR29
WHITAKER,George Clifford TCapt kia 1-7-16 15WYorks p83 CR France342
WHITAKER,Harold Capt kia 30-11-14 2RB p180 CR France1158
WHITAKER,Harry Garratt.MC.Capt 15-1-20 1/5SLancs CR Lancs160
WHITAKER,Leonard T2Lt kia 16-8-17 YLI att7Bn p144 MR30
WHITAKER,Oscar Frederick TLt ded 10-11-18 5RB p180 CR Mddx83
WHITAKER,Owen.MID T2Lt kia 29-8-15 RGA 65SB p42 CR Belgium85
WHITAKER,Samuel 2Lt ded 26-2-19 10WRid p264
WHITAKER,Sydney George 2Lt kia 22-3-18 40MGC p186 MR20
WHITAKER,Thomas Saville 2Lt kld 7-11-15 1/6WRid p227 CR Belgium23,Savile
WHITAKER,Victor John Lt kia 6-4-17 3Lincs att2RFC p14&76 MR20
WHITAKER,William 2Lt kia 6-12-17 GL &23RFC p14 MR20
WHITBOURN,Walter.MC.2Lt kia 22-8-18 6 at2Beds p87 MR16
WHITBREAD,Basil 2Lt kia 22-7-16 14RWar p66 CR France432
WHITBY,Ernest Victor T2Lt kia 1-7-16 4Mddx p149 CR France267
WHITBY,Eustace Roland.MC.Lt kia 20-11-17 1RMunstF GarBn p176 MR20
WHITBY,Harry Alden TCapt kia 10-7-16 11WYorks p83 CR France832
WHITBY,James Hornby.MID Capt ded 16-3-16 19Lond p250 CR France88
WHITCHER,Charles Edwin 2Lt kia 22-4-17 4Leic p220 MR20
WHITCHURCH,G.Capt 26-5-20 RE 68SigCo CR Suff137
WHITCHURCH,Leslie Sedgwick Capt kia 31-10-14 IA 21Cav attDgnGds p284
WHITCUT,H.M. Lt kld 25-4-18 5SStaffs &RAF p229 CR Wilts115,28-4-18
WHITE,Alexander Maj dow 9-9-15 5RScots p211 CR Scot253
WHITE,Alexander Blair 2Lt kia 23-7-18 5 att8KOSB p224 CR France865
WHITE,Alfred William Lt ded 13-4-19 RASC 1034MTCoy p194 CR Italy15
WHITE,Algernon William 2Lt kia 9-8-18 15Hamps p121 MR30
WHITE,Arthur 2Lt kia 18-1-15 RE 2FC p210 CR France285
WHITE,Arthur Bryan Capt kia 16-8-17 5Lond p246 MR29
WHITE,Arthur Elimen Lt ded 22-7-17 SL IWT p201
WHITE,Arthur Gillmore Lt 15-7-17 RE IWT MR38
WHITE,Arthur Ingram 2Lt dow 23-3-18 KSLI att4th p145 CR France512
WHITE,Arthur Wilfred.MC.Capt kia 7-4-16 IA 117Mahrattas p284 MR38
WHITE,Aubrey Cecil T2Lt kia 1-7-16 8Y&L p159 CR France293
WHITE,Basil Walwyn 2Lt kia 8-4-17 Lpool att35RFC p14&73 CR France481
WHITE,Bernard Charles de Boismaison TLt kia 1-7-16 20NumbF p63 MR21
WHITE,Cecil Augustus 2Lt dow 4-10-17 3 att7SStaffs p123 CR Belgium16
WHITE,Cecil Godfrey.MC.Lt kia 21-4-18 RFA att53RAF p272 CR Belgium453
WHITE,Cecil Hayhoe.MC.T2Lt dow 24-9-17 23NumbF p63 CR France164
WHITE,Cecil William Keane.MC.LtACapt dow 29-7-17 X17RFA p37 CR France178
WHITE,Cecil Wilson Morton T2Lt kia 26-9-15 9Norf p74 MR19
WHITE,Charles Douglas 2Lt ded 10-5-16 12KRRC &RFC p4&152 CR Lond8
WHITE,Charles Kirbell 2Lt kia 1-9-18 8Leic att110TMB p88 CR France560
WHITE,Charles Ramsay.DSO.MIDx3 LtCol 31-3-21 3Yorks CR Yorks569
WHITE,Clement Wiliam.DSO.TMaj ded 31-1-19 11EYorks p255
WHITE,Clifford T2Lt kia 26-9-17 200MGC Inf p186 MR30
WHITE,Cyril Arthur T2Lt kia 28-4-17 17Mddx p149 MR20
WHITE,Cyril William 2Lt kia 4-10-17 1/5RWar p214 CR Belgium125
WHITE,Denis Atholl Pheaneas Terence T2Lt dow 23-11-17 15RWar p66 CR France40
WHITE,Dixon 2Lt kia 29-11-17 StaffsYeo p205 MR34
WHITE,Donald Edward Everard Surg1Cl 2-10-19 IMS att4BritStatHosp MR43
WHITE,Douglas Archibald 2Lt kia 23-3-18 7 att8ESurr p113 MR27
WHITE,Edward Beadon,T2Lt dow 1-7-16 11Yorks attMGC p9&186,kia CR France156
WHITE,Edward Erskine Capt kia 14-9-14 Nhampt p138 MR15
WHITE,Edwin Gordon.MC.LtACapt dow 7-5-18 8Dev p77 CR Italy11
WHITE,Edwin Thexton 2Lt kia 20-9-17 4RLancs p213 MR30
WHITE,Edwin Victor Lt kia 6-9-18 7SStaffs p123 MR16
WHITE,Eric 2Lt kia 6-5-16 RE 2/1WLancsFC p210 CR France504
WHITE,Ernest Lt kia 10-4-18 WSomYeo att55MGC p187&205 CR France279
WHITE,Ernest Norman Lt dow 24-9-17 5 att1Mddx p149 CR Belgium152,25-9-17
WHITE,Ernest William.MC.2Lt ded 20-10-18 RGA 290SB p42 CR France380
WHITE,Esmonde Ricarde Burke 2Lt kia 5-1-16 1/6NumbF p214 CR Belgium127

WHITE,Francis Capt kia 4-9-16 6Ches p222 CR France453,1Bn

WHITE,Francis Herbert.MC.Capt dow 16-4-18 12YLI p144&259 CR France180

WHITE,Francis Reginald 2Lt dow 23-1-17 RE att10RFC p14&49 CR France98

WHITE,Frederick George 2Lt kia 4-9-17 64RHFA p37 CR Belgium8

WHITE,G.C.Lt 17-10-18 1CapeCps CR Palestine8

WHITE,Geoffrey Stewart Augustus Lt kia 10-9-14 2SLancs p126 MR15

WHITE,Geoffrey Wilfred 2Lt dow 1-4-17 6 att10RB p180 CR France164,Capt

WHITE,George TCapt kia 1-7-16 1SStaffs p123 CR France397

WHITE,George Anderson 2Lt dow 30-3-18 3 att1RScot p95 CRFrance169

WHITE,Gerald John Davis 2Lt kia 6-7-16 2RIrReg p89 MR21,5-7-16

WHITE,Gilbert Clement Whit TLt dow 6-10-15 13Ches p97CR France285

WHITE,Harold Tom 2Lt kld 27-2-17 RE attRFC p20&210

WHITE,Harold Edward TLt dow 21-4-16 3Manch p156 MR38

WHITE,Harold Norton 2Lt kia 6-9-18 57MGC Div p186 CR France309,Inf

WHITE,Henry Thompson Lt kia 8-9-16 3 att1WelshR p128 MR34

WHITE,Herbert Beresford Lt kld 13-4-17 23RFA p37 CR France98

WHITE,Herbert Robert 2Lt kia 1-7-16 3 att2Ess p133 MR21

WHITE,Herbert Thomas T2LtACapt dow 4-10-16 26NumbF att103TMB p63 CR France297

WHITE,Hill Wilson Capt mbk 12-4-18 RAMC p257 MR32,kia

WHITE,Horace Arthur Lt dow 22-11-17 7/8RIrF p172 CR France214

WHITE,H.T.2Lt 27-2-17 RFC CR Surrey157

WHITE,Hugh 2Lt kia 27-8-18 2GrenGds p50 CR France924

WHITE,Hugh Reginald 2Lt kia 27-5-18 5Mddx p149 MR18

WHITE,James Mathew TLt ded 16-3-16 RAVC TC att126RA p199 CR France1016

WHITE,James Pringle 2Lt kia 28-4/26-5-15 10Lpool p216 MR29,16-6-15

WHITE,John Lt kia 4-6-15 2Hamps p121 MR4

WHITE,John 2Lt kia 1-7-16 3 att2GordH p167 CR France331

WHITE,John Finlayson T2Lt dow 7-8-15 6Yorks p91 MR4

WHITE,John Gardner Lt kia 26-8-17 5ScotRif attRFC p20&224 CR France375

WHITE,John Peregrine Robertson Capt ded 7-10-16 RFA p207 CR Scot280

WHITE,John Robert T2Lt kia 23-4-17 7Lincs p76 MR20

WHITE,John Stanley 2Lt kia 18-9-18 2RSuss p120 CR France699

WHITE,John Stephen Grantham TLt dow 31-7-17 12RWFus p99 CR Belgium12,17Bn

WHITE,John Vernon TCapt kia 1-7-16 20Manch p156 CR France397

WHITE,Joseph Wetherall T2Lt kia 26-9-15 8EYorks p85 MR19

WHITE,L.J.H.Lt 2-5-21 2SomLI MR66

WHITE,Leonard Thomas.MC.2Lt kia 21-9-18 RGA 133SB p209 CR France687

WHITE,Leslie Charles Walter 2Lt dow 29-9-18 2RInnskF p106 CR Belgium84

WHITE,Leslie Spencer 2Lt kldacc 15-3-15 1RWKent p142 CR Belgium165,Spender

WHITE,Lewis Scott.MC.TCapt kld 29-9-17 RFC p14 CR Somerset25

WHITE,Lionel TLt kia 19-3-16 10WelshR p128 CR France279

WHITE,Lynton Woolmer Lt dow 10-9-14 1 att2DragGds p20 CR France1420,3-9-14

WHITE,Malcolm Graham Lt kia 1-7-16 6 att1RB p180 MR21

WHITE,Matthew 2Lt dow 13-4-17 5 att1RScotF p222 CR France40

WHITE,Melville Arthur T2Lt kia 23-4-17 3RFC p14 CR France366

WHITE,Nathan T2Lt kia 1-7-16 29 att21NumbF p63 MR21

WHITE,Ralph Ernest 2Lt dow 28-9-17 12ESurr p113 CR Belgium11

WHITE,Richard Finch.DSO.Maj kia 8-12-19 Ess CR EAfrica116

WHITE,Richard Henry.MC.2Lt kia 6-8-17 25Lond p252 MR29

WHITE,Ritchie David T2Lt dow 24-2-18 4RFC p17 CR France98

WHITE,Robert Christian Lt dow 18-9-18 4BordR p228 CR France906,7Bn

WHITE,Robert Edward 2Lt ded 18-3-15 4ScotRif p104 CR Scot235

WHITE,Robert Stewart 2Lt ded 4-11-18 RFA p37 CR Surrey1

WHITE,Roger Wingate Maj kia 18-5-15 364RFA p37 CR Belgium115

WHITE,Ronald Edwin 2Lt dow 5-3-15 RE NumbDiv p210 CR Belgium59

WHITE,Samuel Walton T2Lt kia 16-6-17 13NumbF p63 MR20

WHITE,Sidney Herbert T2Lt dow 9-11-17 1Wilts C'Coy p153 CR France80

WHITE,Spencer John Meadows Capt kia 15-1-17 1/4Norf attRFC p20,216&220,2Lt 4Dev CR Greece7,Lt

WHITE,Stafford Charles Lt kia 31-7-17 1/7Lpool p215 CR Belgium167

WHITE,Stewart Alexander TCapt kia 3-7-16 21NumbF p63 MR21

WHITE,Thomas T2Lt dow 8-7-16 2 att11LNLancs p137 MR21,att8Bn

WHITE,Thomas Herbert.MC.T2Lt ded 24-1-19 7ELancs &RAF p111

WHITE,Thomas James.MC.Lt kia 20-11-17 255RFA p208 CR France662

WHITE,Thomas Leslie.MC.Capt ded 10-7-21 IA S&TCps p284

WHITE,Thomas Pate 2Lt dow 17-10-17 7ScotRif p224 CR France113

WHITE,Wilfred Appleton 2Lt kia 3-10-18 KRRC att4Bn p152 CR France234

WHITE,William 2Lt kia 25-4-15 4RDubF p177 MR29

WHITE,William.MC.Lt kia 12-10-16 2Beds p87 CR France432

WHITE,William Charles 2Lt kia 24-10-18 9TankCps A'Coy p189 CR France1274,Lt 23-10-18

WHITE,William Ewart Cecil 2Lt kia 27-8-18 6Lond p247 CR France329

WHITE,William Gurney 2Lt dow 23-9-16 281RFA p209 CR France105

WHITE,William Hawtrey.MID Maj kia 15-2-15 1RIrReg p89 CR Belgium80,14-2-15

WHITE,William Kenneth 2Lt kia 31-7-17 4ScotRif p104 MR29

WHITE-BELL,John William Capt kia 9-9-16 5RMunstF p176 CR France294

WHITE-BOWMAN,Alwxander 2Lt 25-9-16 EYorks attMGC Inf CR France785

WHITEFOORD,Charles B.Chap4Cl dow 30-5-18 RAChDept att6Lond p200 CR France84

WHITEFOORD,Lionel Cole Lt kia 15-9-16 IrGds attMGC p53 MR21

WHITEHEAD,Alfred Gordon Lt kia 29-1-18 6WYorks attRFC p20&218

WHITEHEAD,Charles Hugh Tempest Maj kia 25-9-15 IA 56Rif Ex 10HLI p284 MR28

WHITEHEAD,Charles James T2Lt kia 4-10-17 1/2 att1ESurr p113 MR30

WHITEHEAD,Edgar Joseph William Lt ded 17-2-19 RGA 312SB attRE p42 CR France40

WHITEHEAD,Eric Alfred 2Lt kia 13-3-18 GL &24RFC p17 CR France1893

WHITEHEAD,Eric Wilfred T2Lt kld 17-2-18 RFC p17 CR Surrey15,21-2-18

WHITEHEAD,Frank Brenand Lt kia 23-4-17 5Yorks p221 MR20

WHITEHEAD,Geoffrey Nield T2Lt kia 15-10-17 RFC 11BallonCoy p14 CR Belgium20

WHITEHEAD,George Stanley 2Lt kia 2-12-17 D153RFA p37 CR France530

WHITEHEAD,George William Edendale Lt kld 17-10-18 RFA &53RAF p37 CR Belgium140

WHITEHEAD,Henry 2Lt kia 13-6-16 RFA attX4TMB p37 CR France344

WHITEHEAD,Henry Lt ded 4-3-19 RASC p267 CR Yorks469

WHITEHEAD,Henry Montagu Lt kia 14-4-15 4ESurr p113 CR Belgium167

WHITEHEAD,Hugh MacGuire.MID Lt kia 21-3-18 5 att8RSuss p228 MR27

WHITEHEAD,James Edward 2Lt kia 16-9-16 1/7Mddx p235 CR France785,15-9-16

WHITEHEAD,James Hugh Edendale 2Lt ded 13-3-19 9RWKent p265 CR Kent122

WHITEHEAD,John Holberton LtCol dow 12-1-17 IA 93BurmaInf p284 CR Iraq5

WHITEHEAD,John Robert Gobertus T2Lt kld 3-8-16 RFC p4

WHITEHEAD,John Walton Capt kia 1-12-17 246RFA p207 MR30

WHITEHEAD,Lewis Ernest TCapt ded 20-5-19 GL &65RAF p267 MR20,Ewart 20-5-18

WHITEHEAD,Mark 2Lt kia 12-8-16 1/9Lpool p216 MR21

WHITEHEAD,Percy Neil.MC.Capt kia 21-3-18 RE 174TC p49 MR20

WHITEHEAD,Reginald Maurice 2Lt kia 22-11-17 41RFC p14 CR France62

WHITEHEAD,Walter 2Lt kia 6-9-16 3 att8RDubF p177 MR21

WHITEHORN,William Joseph Lt kia 18-9-18 7SWBord p101 MR37

WHITEHORNE-COLE,Arthur George Capt kia 20-9-17 RAMC p198 CR France285

WHITEHOUSE,Alfred Ernest 2Lt kia 8-5-15 12Lond p248 MR29

WHITEHOUSE,Arthur Leslie 2Lt kia 10-9-16 RGA 15SB p42 MR20

WHITEHOUSE,Augustus George Richard.MC.Maj kia 1-8-18 1Hereford p252 CR France524,Augustin

WHITEHOUSE,Charles Thomas 2Lt dow 15-1-15 15RFA p37 CR France80

WHITEHOUSE,Cyril Duncan 2Lt kia 26-5-18 1WelshGds p53 MR20

WHITEHOUSE,Eric 2Lt dow 5-9-18 RGA 144SB p42 CR France568

WHITEHOUSE,Herbert Maj kld 23-3-18 C34RFA p206 CR France245,dedacc

WHITEHOUSE,John Walter Glendenning Lt kia 21-3-18 RE 156FC p49 CR France511

WHITEHOUSE,Percy John 2Lt kia 31-10-14 3RWKent att1Nhants p142 MR29,2-11-14

WHITEHURST,Albert Percival.MID 2Lt kia 25-3-18 1Worc p110 MR27

WHITEHURST,George J Lt ded 23-12-19 RASC CR Canada180

WHITEHURST,Walter Harry T2Lt kia 22-4-17 NStaffs attY&L p158 MR19

WHITELAM,Lewis 2Lt kia 3-9-16 5WRid p227 MR21,WHITELAN

WHITELAW,Geoffrey Lacy T2Lt ded 14-4-18 HouseholdBn p20 CR Scot886

WHITELAW,James Weir 2Lt kia 11-4-17 6RScotF p95 MR20

WHITELAW,Robert Hilary Lockhart T2Lt dow 28-5-17 HouseholdBn p20 CR France145

WHITELAW,Thomas Capt kia 7-4-18 RAMC att2/7WYorks p254 CR France745

WHITELAW,Thomas Mitchell 2Lt dow 29-5-18 8ScotRif p225 CR Durham26

WHITELAW,William Alexander Lt ded 14-2-19 3A&SH p266 CR Scot240

WHITELEY,Benjamin Eric 2Lt kia 28-8-18 7WYorks p218 CR France268

WHITELEY,Charles Taylor Lt dow 1-7-18 2/8 att14RWar p215 CR France31

WHITELEY,Clifford 2Lt kia 18-9-17 8Y&L p159 CR Belgium96

WHITELEY,Edward Claude Capt kia 14-4-15 RE p49 CR Iraq6

WHITELEY,Hubert 2Lt dow 11-10-16 9DLI p239

WHITELEY,Laurence Lt kia 31-7-17 5BlkW attMGC Inf p187&231 CR Belgium93

WHITEMAN,George Worley 2Lt kia 31-7-17 RHFA 3/4HB p209 CR Belgium21,30-7-17

WHITEMAN,Harold Ernest 2Lt kld 23-10-16 8Hamps attRFC p20&229 CR Sussex107

WHITEMAN,John.MID Maj dow 25-4-17 4Mddx attRND CmdgHawkeBn p149 CR France95,LtCol

WHITEMAN,Ormonde Charles.MID TCapt kia 22-11-17 11RFus p71 CR Belgium13

WHITER,Bertrand Thomas 2Lt kia 27-1-17 10 att20Lond p248 MR21

WHITESIDE,Albert T2Lt kia 6-12-17 17RIrRif p170 MR17

WHITESIDE,Carrol Herbert Marston Lt&Adjt dow 1-11-16 7BordR p118 CR France105,Capt

WHITESIDE,Miles Bruce Dalzell 2Lt ded 13-6-18 1HLI &RAF p164 CR Wales31

WHITESIDE,Robert Borras Capt ded 20-4-15 RASC p194 CR France473

WHITESIDE,Robert Parkinson T2Lt kia 28-4-17 1Lpool p73 MR20

WHITESIDE,William Leslie T2Lt kia 5-7-15 RFA p37 CR Gallipoli6

WHITEWAY,Edward Victor.MC.Capt dow 28-4-18 13ESurr att122BdeHQ p113 CR France40,12Bn

WHITEWRIGHT,Alfred Rutherford 2Lt ded 11-5-16 4N&D p135 CR Glouc9

WHITFIELD,Arthur Henry Lt 14-1-21 TankCps CR Hamps8

WHITFIELD,Arthur Noel Lt kia 14-10-14 2RIrRif p170 CR France1106

WHITFIELD,Edward Hillyard Day 2Lt kia 7-8-15 6Y&L p159 MR4

WHITFIELD,Frederick Ashburnham Hooker 2Lt kia 23-4-15 att3Mddx p149 MR29

WHITFIELD,Gilbert Henry 2Lt mbk 8-8-15 IARO att14Sikhs Ferozepore p284 MR4

WHITFIELD,John T2Lt kia 2-12-17 16HLI p164 CR Belgium123

WHITFIELD,John Burrows Lt dow 20-1-16 RE 104FC p49 CR Belgium11

WHITFIELD,John Lawrence Capt dow 23-6-15 1/4LNLancs p234 CR France102

WHITFIELD,Lewis Hayes T2Lt dow 30-10-17 21RFC p14 CR Belgium16

WHITFIELD,Nigel Bernard Capt ded 7-7-18 RNDevYeo &RAF p203&257

WHITFIELD,Richard Houlbrook TLt kia 12-5-16 RE 104FC p49 CR Belgium138

WHITFORD,Myles T2Lt kia 29-4-16 7RIrRif p170 CR France423,dow 28-4-16

WHITGREAVE,Henry Egerton T2Lt kia 1-7-16 1SomLI p80 CR France1491

WHITHAM,Charles Lt kia 6-10-18 17Lond p250 MR16

WHITHAM,John Edmund 2Lt kia 20-10-16 RGA p209 CR France1327

WHITING,Arthur 2Lt kia 27-3-18 1NStaffs p158 MR27

WHITING,James Oliver Lt kia 22-9-17 60RFC p14 MR20

WHITING,Reginald Cunningham T2Lt dow 31-5-17 Lpool p73 CR Devon72,Cunnynghame

WHITING,Thomas TCapt kia 30-7-16 20Lpool p73 MR21

WHITLARK,Joseph Capt 27-4-16 EAMilLabBureau CR EAfrica44

WHITLEY,A.H.AssSurg 24-2-20 IMS MR66

WHITLEY,Alexander Fauvel Lt kia 23-7-16 RGA 49SB p209 CR France630

WHITLEY,Benjamin Heywood.MID 2Lt kia 17-7-16 3RScots p55 CR France399

WHITLEY,Charles.MC.TCapt kia 11-4-17 7KRRC p152 CR France594

WHITLEY,Harry 2Lt kia 27-3-18 1/2Yorks att2WYorks p91 CR France1472

WHITLEY,Walter Herbert.MID 2Lt kia 21-2-17 4KRRC p152 MR35

WHITLEY,William George T2Lt kia 16-8-16 13Lpool p73 CR France294

WHITLEY-BAKER,Edward.MC.Lt ded 16-12-20 RE attRCpsofS CR Dorset135

WHITLOCK,Frederick Walter 2Lt 25-9-15 6 O&BLI CR France706

WHITLOCK,Tom Oliver T2Lt kia 29-8-16 30 att22NumbF p63 CR France275,24-8-16

WHITMARSH,Alec 2Lt dow 8-9-18 8Lond p247 CR France833

WHITMARSH,Donald Lyle T2Lt kia 22-8-17 12 att2Hamps p121 CR Belgium125

WHITMORE,Harry Cyril 2Lt kld 8-8-18 3Norf att94TMB p74 CR France19,Lt dow 11-8-18

WHITMORE,Roger Searle.MC.Capt kia 20-11-17 1KSLI p145 CR France711

WHITMORE-SEARLE,B.2Lt 3-10-15 SStaffs CR Dorset151

WHITNEY,Thomas Geoffrey 2Lt ded 15-6-16 3RWar p262 CR Hamps240,Geffrey acckld

WHITROD,Roper Henry 2Lt kia 28-5-18 4Lpool p73 CR Belgium36

WHITSIT,John Reginald TLt dow 16-8-15 5RInniskF p106 MR4,WHITSITT

WHITSON,Harold White Lt kia 25-9-15 2HLI p164 MR19

WHITSON,Henry Thomas Capt dow 5-9-18 1/10Lpool p216 CR France10

WHITSON,Wilfred Robert CaptTMaj 30-11-17 HLI att9Suff p164 CR France439,Wilfrid

WHITTAKER,Charles Brown.MID Lt kia 22-7-16 12RScots p55 MR21,23-7-16 3 att2Bn

WHITTAKER,Herbert Leonard Charles Lt kia 21-9-18 1RWSurr p57 CR France369

WHITTAKER,James Russell T2Lt kia 29-8-16 6YLI p144 CR France402

WHITTAKER,John Chalton 2Lt kia 28-4-18 6WRid p227 MR30

WHITTAKER,Norman 2Lt kia 12-5-18 3RLancs p59 CR France88

WHITTAKER,Roger D'Arcy Capt&Adjt kia 30-6-16 13RSuss p120 MR19

WHITTAKER,William Gaylard 2Lt kia 22-10-17 3 att23NumbF p63 MR30

WHITTAKER,William Robert Lt 27-3-17 1Hereford p252 MR34

WHITTALL,George William.MC.Lt ded 30-12-19 3DragGds RoO p261 CR Surrey138

WHITTALL,Noel Charles T2Lt kia 13-9-17 7RFus att6RFC p14&71 CR Belgium11,12-9-17

WHITTALL,Roland William T2Lt dow 6-8-15 SL 52DivHQ p201 MR4

WHITTAM,Francis Joseph 2Lt kia 1-7-16 3 att1LancF p94 MR21

WHITTAM,Frederick T2Lt kia 7-8-15 GL att1/5LancF A'Coy p192 MR4

WHITTAM,Matthew John Goldsborough TLt dow 11-8-15 8WRid p116 CR Gallipoli1

WHITTARD,Harold Alfred 2Lt kia 13-8-17 22RFA p37 CR France1489 Ex HAC

WHITTEMORE,Frederick Lt kia 29-3-16 1Beds p87 MR20

WHITTEN,Francis Robert.MC.Maj dow 18-4-18 RE 458FC p209 CR Belgium38

WHITTERON,Claude 2Lt kia 25-4-18 WYorks att1/6Bn p83 MR30

WHITTET,Gilbert T2Lt kia 14-7-16 7RWSurr p57 MR21

WHITTING,Richard Harcourt Cadet 21-9-18 RMilCollCamberley CR Somerset17

WHITTINGHAM,Arthur William.MC.Lt kia 10-10-17 RFA p208 MR30

WHITTINGHAM,Clive Alan Capt kia 9-6-17 RAMC att12RFus p198 CR Belgium15

WHITTINGHAM,Leonard Buxton 2Lt dow 26-4-18 1 att3Worc p110 CR Belgium11,5Bn

WHITTINGHAM,Lewis Stuart 2Lt kia 28-2-17 7RWFus att1InniskF p223 CR France216

WHITTINGHAM,Thomas Lt kia 13-10-15 4Leic p220 MR19

WHITTINGTON,F.Capt 6-11-16 IndMilWksServ MR66

WHITTINGTON,George Edgar 2Lt kia 30-11-17 12Lpool p73 MR17

WHITTINGTON,George William Lt ded 9-6-20 IA 7Lancers p284

WHITTINGTON,William James 2Lt kia 16-5-15 3 att2RInniskF p106 MR22

WHITTINGTON-GREEN,Clifford Capt dow 27-6-15 1RBerks CR France98

WHITTINGTON-INCE,Ralph Piggott.MC.Lt dow 11-11-18 11EYorks p85 CR Belgium143

WHITTLE,Arthur Denton T2Lt kia 16-9-16 10DLI p162 MR21

WHITTLE,Cyril Herbert Spencer Lt kia 24-8-14 15Huss p22 MR15

WHITTLE,Eric Thomas 2Lt kia 23-4-17 7Manch A'Coy p237 MR20

WHITTLE,Walter Victor Patrick Charles 2Lt kia 13-4-15 1Worc p110 CR France684

WITTOCK,Frederick Walter T2Lt kia 25-9-15 6 O&BLI p130

WHITTOME,Arthur George Lt mbk 27-8-20 IA 2/123Rif p284 MR38

WHITTON,Peter Isles Capt kia 28-6-15 7ScotRif D'Coy p224 CR Gallipoli6

WHITTY,John Leo.MC.Capt kia 8-7-16 Leinst &70RFC p4&175 MR20

WHITTY,Michael Joseph LtCol ded 28-3-17 RAMC p198 CR Lancs156

WHITTY,Thomas 2Lt kia 5-10-16 RoO 8Norf p74 CR France215

WHITWAM,Harold Ernest Capt kia 9-10-17 7WRid p227 MR30

WHITWELL,Harry William Maj kia 15-8-20 IA 13Rajputs p284 CR Iraq8

WHITWELL,Patrick Henry 2Lt kld 25-4-18 1/2Yorks &4RAF p91 CR France28,kia

WHITWORTH,Arthur George Richard 2Lt dow 30-3-18 24 att19NumbF p63 CR France62

WHITWORTH,Charles Edward.MID 2Lt dow 22-8-15 6Yorks p91 MR4

WHITWORTH,Ernest Stanley TLt kia 20-12-15 10RWar p66 CR France631

WHITWORTH,Henry Capt kia 27-9-18 8Manch p237 CR France273

WHITWORTH,Henry Parker.MC.Capt dow 29-10-18 RAMC att6KOSB p198 CR Belgium20,Parks

WHITWORTH,Herbert Clifford Lt kia 26-3-18 7SomLI p80 MR27

WHITWORTH,James Frederick Capt kia 21-3-18 RFus Ex WYorks p71 MR20,2Lt 18 att1WYorks

WHITWORTH,James Melville 2Lt kia 6-6-15 9SomLI attEss p80 MR4

WHITWORTH,John Haworth.DSO.MC.MID Maj dow 31-3-18 2/6Manch p236 CR France145

WHITWORTH,Walter Haworth 2Lt dow 14-9-18 7LancF p221 CR France526

WHYATT,Albert Allen 2Lt kia 30-5-18 8Glouc p107 MR18

WHYATT,Percy.MC.TCapt kia 18-10-17 11N&D p135 CR Belgium72

WHYATT,Raymond Selwyn.MC.2Lt kia 13-10-18 10N&D p135 CR France1393

WHYBROW,Harry Thomson TCapt dow 21-3-16 MGC Motors p186 CR EAfrica13

WHUMAN,Richard David Lt&QM ded 10-3-17 5RScots p211 CR France95

WHYMAN,William Arthur 2Lt kia 16-9-16 1/7Mddx p235 CR France785

WHYMARK,William Emerson T2Lt dow 27-11-17 12Suff p79 CR France398

WHYTE,Alan Hill T2Lt kia 9-4-17 11A&SH p174 CR France924

WHYTE,Alexander Cumming TCapt ded 11-4-16 B159RFA p37 CR France254

WHYTE,Alexander Williamson.MC.Lt kia 25-10-18 6ScotRif p224 CR Belgium140,9Bn

WHYTE,Cecil Bertram 2Lt kld 3-5-18 RScots &98RAF p262 MR20

WHYTE,George Henry T2Lt kia 4-12-17 GL &49RFC p14 CR France120

WHYTE,George Herbert.MC.Lt kia 23-12-17 17Lond p250&272,18Bn CR Palestine3,2/18Bn

WHYTE,George Thomas Capt ded 9-6-19 RAMC p267 CR Eire76

WHYTE,John Lt dow 26-4-15 7A&SH p243 CR Belgium151,Capt

WHYTE,John Dudley TCapt kia 13/14-7-16 8RSuss p120 CR France630

WHYTE,John Francis Capt ded 20-10-18 RE IWT p49 CR France65

WHYTE,John Scott.MC.2Lt kia 23-10-18 7 att5ScotRif p224 CR France190,Lt

WHYTE,Mark Gilchrist 2Lt kia 19-8-18 2RFus p71 CR France28

WHYTE,Robert Lt kia 12-4-18 2RScots p55 MR32

WHYTE,Robert Barbour 2Lt kia 25-9-15 3 att1BlkW p129 CR France219

WHYTE,William Lt kia 28-9-18 4/5BlkW p231 CR France699

WHYTE,William Boyd 2Lt kia 21-9-17 9A&SH p244 MR30

WHYTEHEAD,Hugh Holton 2Lt kia 12-7-17 GL &29RFC p14 MR20

WHYTEHEAD,Hugh Richard Augustine Capt kia 12-5-15 IA 1/6GurkhaRif p284 CR Gallipoli6,Augustin 22-5-15

WIBBY,Edward John Lt 2-3-21 IA 73MalabarInf CR Glouc92

WICKETT,Thomas Pemberthy T2Lt dow 20-11-17 5RBerks p140 CR France664

WICKHAM,Anthony Theodore Clephane Lt kia 2-11-14 4 att2ConnRgrs p172 MR29 &CR Belgium453

WICKHAM,Bernard William Theodore.MC.TLt kia 14-4-17 9SStaffs C'Coy p123 CR Belgium127

WICKHAM,Charles Frederick Onslow T2Lt dow 26-6-16 15 att16NumbF p63 CR France702

WICKHAM,Cyril Henry Capt dow 15-1-15 RFus p71 CR France683

WICKHAM,Edmund Theodore Eugene di Christofero de Bourllon TCapt ded 26-6-18 4ConnRgrs att1GBnRWar p266

WICKHAM,John Dobree Durrell Capt dow 22-6-15 1Lincs p76 MR29

WICKHAM,John Seville Deacon T2Lt kia 31-7-17 7RLancs p59 MR29

WICKHAM,Lister Darell TCapt kia 3-7-16 6 att7Lincs p76 MR21

WICKHAM,Montagu Hill Clephane De Cristoforo De Bouillon.MID Capt dow 9-5-15 2ConnRgrs B'Coy p172 MR29

WICKHAM,Nigel John Latham TCapt kia 19-4-16 6ConnRgrs p172 CR France178,18-4-16

WICKHAM,Thomas Strange.DSO.Lt kia 25-8-14 Manch att5NigR p156&202 CR WAfrica58,Capt

WICKHAM,William Joseph Capt kia 31-10-14 1ScotsGds p52 MR29

WICKHAM,William Thomas Donald Lt dow 10-10-18 1 att11Manch p156 CR France113

WICKS,G.H.OBE.Maj 21-8-21 GL attRE CR Wilts14

WICKS,Harry Valentine Inwood T2Lt kia 14-4-17 11ESurr att11MGC p113 MR20

WICKS,William Charles.MC.2Lt kia 16-9-17 4 att10N&D p135 CR France604

WICKSON,Edward Arthur Capt kia 16-6-17 51CanadaInf &RFC CR Belgium6

WIDCOMBE,Charles Ingleton 2Lt kia 6-4-16 3 O&BLI p130 MR38

WIDDOP,Arthur Norman Lt kia 30-9-18 4 att7EKent p212 MR16

WIDDOWS,Archibald Lt ded 6-10-18 1/2DCLI att8Ches p113 MR67,7-10-18 11DCLI

WIDDOWSON,A.D.2Lt 18-2-19 RGA CR Notts84

WIDDOWSON,Alfred John Harold Ryder 2Lt kia 25-8-14 2SLancs p126 CR France286

WIDDOWSON,Joseph James TLt dow 23-10-16 1Wilts p153 CR France59

WIDGERY,Philip Henry Lt kia 24-3-18 5 att21Mddx p149 MR20

WIDOWFIELD,George 2Lt dow 14-10-15 1Mon p244 CR France201

WIGAN,William Lewis TLt dow 23-2-16 1 att8RWKent p142 CR Belgium11

WIGFALL,William Edmund Clare.MC.Lt dow 29-8-16 3EYorks p85 CR France102

WIGFIELD,Joshua Biram Crossley Lt dow 21-9-18 RE 74DivSigs p49 CR France194

WIGG,Sydney Harold Capt kia 13-10-18 C255RFA p207 CR France241

WIGGEN,Robert Harrison.MC.T2Lt kia 17-2-17 15 att23RFus p71 MR21,Royal

WIGGETT,Allan James T2Lt dow PoW 15-3-16 13KRRC D'Coy p152 CR France214

WIGGIN,Douglas Holme 2Lt dow 23-12-14 1Glouc p107 CR France202

WIGGIN,George Robert Lt kia 23-4-16 WorcYeo p206 MR34

WIGGIN,Noel Holme TLt kia 11-1-17 RFA 36BdeAmmCol p37 MR38

WIGGINS,Alec Henry 2Lt kia 22-8-18 20Lond p251 MR16

WIGGINS,H.C.2Lt kld 1-4-18 GL &RAF p192

WIGGINS,Thomas 2Lt kia 27-6-18 17LancF att99RAF p94 CR France1667

WIGGINS,Thomas ACapt kia 27-5-18 4 att5Yorks p256 MR18

WIGGINS,William Esmy 2Lt ded 19-8-16 LeicYeo p204 CR Oxford69

WIGGINTON,Arthur T2Lt kia 30-7-16 2EYorks p85 CR France727

WIGHT,Ernest Octavius Col dow 19-12-15 RAMC p198 CR Belgium1

WIGHT,John Guthrie 2Lt kia 1-11-16 6HLI p240 MR21

WIGHT,William Stewart Balmain 2Lt kia 9-4-17 3 att2RScots p55 CR France581

WIGHT-BOYCOTT,Thomas Andrew.DSO.BrigGen ded 30-3-16 WarYeo p205 CR Staffs45

WIGHTMAN,A.B.Capt.MC.2-5-21 2/9Manch CR Lancs471

WIGHTMAN,James.DSO.MC.Maj dow 9-4-18 8ESurr p113 CR France37

WIGHTMAN,John Francis 2Lt kia 4-9-17 GL &11RFC p14 MR20

WIGHTON,George Edwin T2Lt dow 11-3-16 10 att11ELancs p111 CR France631,11-8-16

WIGHTWICK,Sydney 2Lt dow 9-9-17 2/9Lond p248 CR Belgium26

WIGLESWORTH,Godfrey 2Lt kia 8-7-16 24RFC 14Wing p4 CR France46

WIGLEY,Frederick Gwyn Mackay Capt ded 26-3-21 IA 73CarnaticInf p284

WIGLEY,Herbert Henry TLt kia 31-7-17 7RLancs p59 MR29

WIGSTON,Geoffrey Herbert Capt kia 9-9-16 1ESurr at2Suss p113 CR France432

WIILOCK,Neville Gore LtACapt dow 22-11-17 1KOSB p102

WILBERFORCE,W.R.S.2Lt kld 2-6-18 7KRRC &RAF p152 CR Hamps130

WILBRAHAM-TAYLOR,Aucher 2Lt 26-9-16 5RBerks

WILCHER,Harold 2Lt dow 5-7-16 YLI p144 CR France833

WILCHER,Leslie Reginald Victor 2Lt ded 8-5-19 113RFA p37&255 CR Germany1

WILCOCK,Henry Blamires Lt kia 13-11-16 3 att13Ess p133 CR France1890

WILCOCK,Maurice Nettleton Lt kia 18-9-18 13RFus p71 CR France245

WILCOCKS,James Lt&QM ded 20-10-17 RAMC p198 CR Hamps34

WILCOX,Frederick Alexander Cumberland TLt kia 14-7-16 6Nhampt p138 MR21

WILCOX,Frederick Herbert Cumberland Capt kia 14-1-17 4LancF p94 MR38

WILCOX,Harold Ray Capt ded 13-2-19 18LancsF p263 CR Eire534

WILCOX,John Theodore Cumberland Capt kia 12-5-15 IA 2/39GarhwalRif p284 CR France631

WILCOX,Kenneth Theodore Dunbar T2Lt kia 8-11-15 9RWSurr p57 CR Belgium82 8Bn

WILCOX,Percy Stracey 2Lt kia 23-3-18 174RFA p37 MR27

WILCOX,Percy William T2Lt kld 31-12-17 RFC p14 CR Sussex111,FltLt

WILCOX,William 2Lt kia 18-5-18 11Manch att34TMB p156 CR France223

WILD,Arthur 2Lt kia 18-9-16 14DLI p162 CR France374

WILD,Basil Warren.MC.Lt kia 1-10-18 9TankCps p189 CR France375

WILD,Henry.MC.Lt kia 21-8-18 14NumbF att1Lincs p63 CR France514

WILD,Jack Douglas Lt ded 21-9-19 EKent att1/4Bn p262 MR67

WILD,Lionel Tudor Capt kia 30-11-17 7SomLI B'Coy p80 MR17

WILDBLOOD,William Arthur TLt kia 16-6-17 RASC 24DivTrain 195Coy p194 CR Belgium15

WILDE,Arthur William 2Lt kia 21-1-16 1Hamps p121 MR21

WILDE,Edwin Joseph Lt kia 1-9-18 3Leic att110TMB p88 CR France307

WILDE,Harold.MM.Lt 3-9-18 11TankCps MR16

WILDE,James Greaves Spencer 2Lt dow 1-11-18 5WYorks p218 CR France1256

WILDER,Arthur James 2Lt dow 23-3-18 32MGC p186 CR Belgium16

WILDER,Frank 2Lt kia 31-3-16 Q'RHA p37 CR France1182

WILDER,Reginald Connor Philip 2Lt kia 18-11-14 3 att2Suff p79 MR29,dow

WILDERS-LEWIS,Henry Charles T2LtACapt kia 31-7-17 10RWSurr A'Coy p57 CR Belgium115,WILLDERS Ex 19RFus

WILDGOOSE,Ernest Henry 2Lt kia 22-3-18 RE 104FC p49 MR27

WILDIG,George.DCM.Lt dow 6-11-18 1KSLI p145&258 CR Wales402

WILDING,Godfrey James 2Lt kia 20-12-16 3RLancs p59 CR France630

WILDING,Horace Holden 2Lt kia 13-9-18 12 att13KRRC p152 CR France245

WILDING,John 2Lt dow 7-12-15 4ELancs p226 CR Gallipoli6

WILDING-JONES,Hugh Wynn Lt dow 22-9-18 3 att11RWFus p99 CR Greece9

WILDMAN,Arthur Henry Lt kia 14-9-15 IA 130Baluchis p284

WILDMAN-LUSHINGTON,Percy John 2Lt kia 3-5-17 3 att6KOSB p102 MR20

WILDON,Edward Harold 2Lt kia 27-4-17 232RFA p209 CR France581,Lt

WILDSMITH,Leonard Charles 2Lt kia 2-3-15 12Lond p248 CR Belgium58

WILDSMITH,Raymond Charles 2Lt kia 7-6-17 25Lond p252 MR29

WILEMAN,Gerald Watkins Brett 2LtACapt kia 8-9-16 2SWBord p101 CR France151

WILES,H Lt 7-8-20 GL RE attArmySigServ CR Egypt2

WILES,John Davenport 2Lt kia 4-10-16 1Suff p79 CR Greece3

WILEY,Donald William 2Lt kia 12-10-18 SussYeo p205 CR France341,Lt

WILEY,Evelyn Otway Scarlett Lt ded 7-11-18 12 att2DLI p162 CR Italy9

WILEY,William.MIDx2 Maj ded 12-2-17 RAMC att42FA p198 CR Mddx48,12FA

WILFORD,Arthur Lucius.DSO.Maj dow 1-7-17 IA 5LtInf p284 CR EAfrica8 &CR Tanzania1,LtCol

WILFORD,Lionel Russell Lt ded 8-11-18 9SStaffs p123 CR France1571

WILFORD,Robert 2Lt kia 23-11-17 5 att13Yorks p221 MR17

WILFORD,William Frederick Shirley.MM.2Lt dow 25-10-18 5Beds p219 CR France441,2Bn

WILGERS-LEWIS,Henry Charles T2LtACapt kia 31-7-17 10RWSurr p57
WILKES,Albert Victor 2Lt kia 24-5-18 7N&D p233 MR19
WILKES,Clifford TLtACapt kia 28-4-17 GL 2SStaffs att6TMB p192 MR20
WILKES,George Lionel 2Lt kia 20-4-18 7Lond p247 CR France880
WILKES,Henry James Trevor 2Lt kia 28-2-18 GL &16RFC p17 CR France95
WILKES,James Alwyn 2Lt dow 24-3-18 6MGC Cav p186 MR20 Alwyne
WILKES,Norman Bayley 2Lt kia 29-4-18 1/5SStaffs p229 CR France572
WILKES,Sidney Archer 2Lt kia 24-8-18 4BlkW p230 CR France184
WILKIE,Alexander Buchan 2Lt dow 30-11-17 1RIrRif p170 CR Belgium84
WILKIE,Charles Joseph TLtCol kia 18-10-16 17WelshR p128 CR France149,19-10-16
WILKIE,David.MID Maj kia 24-4-17 5BlkW attRN Div p230 MR20
WILKIE,George Spence Mclean 2Lt dow 4-8-15 5BlkW p231 CR France345,Lt
WILKIE,John Hunter 2Lt dow 9-4-15 1Leinst p175 CR Belgium58
WILKIE,John Stewart TCapt kia 14-4-17 16HLI p164 CR France672,16-4-17
WILKIN,William White 2Lt kia 26-10-17 1/5NumbF p63 MR30
WILKINS,A.R.Lt 10-2-21 RFA CR NZ320
WILKINS,Alfred Henry 2Lt kia 1-7-16 1/7N&D p233 MR21
WILKINS,Archie Raymond Lt kia 8-3-16 3 att1Manch p156 MR38
WILKINS,Bernard Ivan T2Lt dow 6-1-16 9Yorks p91 CR France254
WILKINS,Frank Trevor T2Lt dow 3-7-16 15NumbF att1BordR p63 CR France169
WILKINS,Geoffrey T2Lt dow 4-10-15 2NumbF p63 CR France98
WILKINS,Herbert Jocelyn Ussher Capt kia 10-8-15 1 att6SLancs p126 MR4
WILKINS,John Christopher Martin Lt kia 24-3-18 10DCLI p115 MR20
WILKINS,Laurence Arnold Capt kia 25-8-18 4Y&L p238 CR France614
WILKINS,Mervyn Sydney Lt kia 16-6-18 1/6Glouc p225 CR Italy3
WILKINS,Vernon Spencer Lt ded 11-11-18 4 O&BLI p231 CR France52
WILKINSON,Ambrose Joseph T2Lt kia 26-9-16 6 att12Mddx p149 MR21
WILKINSON,Arthur Benjamin Lt dow 14-11-16 5RSuss p228 CR France515
WILKINSON,Arthur Wilfrid Capt dow 18-4-18 3WYorks p83 CR Belgium8,1Bn
WILKINSON,Arthur William 2Lt kia 12-7-17 5 att13Yorks p221 CR France439
WILKINSON,Bernard.MID 2Lt dow 6-6-17 1/6NStaffs A'Coy p238 CR France149,Lt
WILKINSON,Bernard Jocelyn 2Lt kia 8-7-16 3 att2Yorks p91 MR21
WILKINSON,Bernard Kedington Rodwell TCapt ded 24-1-18 7NStaffs p265 CR Surrey1
WILKINSON,Charles Bliss 2Lt kia 28-3-18 RFA att8RFC p17&37 CR France167
WILKINSON,Charles Harold.MC.2Lt ded 13-10-18 42RHFA p37
WILKINSON,Charles Leslie Lt kia 21-3-18 6 att2/5N&D D'Coy p233 MR20
WILKINSON,Charles Leyburn.DSO.Maj dow 7-4-18 B250/80RFA p206 CR France37
WILKINSON,Clarence Loftus Mason TLtACapt dow 6-11-16 C165RFA p37 CR France74
WILKINSON,Clement Arthur Maj kia 2-5-15 2KSLI p145 MR29 CR Belgium453,12-5-15
WILKINSON,David Stanley TLt ded 26-8-17 GL &56RFC p14 CR Belgium393
WILKINSON,Edmund.DCM.HonLt&QM kia 31-10-14 1LNLancs p137 CR Belgium57
WILKINSON,Edward Wilson T2Lt kia 7-7-16 11 att9WRid p116 MR21
WILKINSON,Eric Fitzwater.MC.MIDx2 Capt kia 9-10-17 8WYorks A'Coy p219 MR30
WILKINSON,Eric Russell.MC.TLt dow 7-10-17 GL &47RFC p14 CR Greece1
WILKINSON,Ernest Alexander 2Lt kia 25-9-15 2Leic p88 MR19
WILKINSON,Eyre Spencer Lt kia 12-1-16 1Lond attRFC p20&245 CR France682,Spenser
WILKINSON,Frank 2Lt kia 27-7-16 3Dors att2/5Glouc p124 CR France1157
WILKINSON,Frank 2Lt dow 13-9-18 2/4YLI p144 CR France1184
WILKINSON,Frank Capt ded 13-11-18 RHFA p272 CR Durham28,3RGA 276SB
WILKINSON,Frederick 2Lt dow 19-6-20 1GarBnYLI Ex 3Huss CR C'land&W'land82
WILKINSON,Frederick James T2Lt kia 9/12-4-17 8RLancs p59 MR20,11-4-17
WILKINSON,Frederick Richardson Lt ded 8-1-20 IA 1/23SikhPnrs p284 CR Asia51
WILKINSON,Geoffrey Ellison T2Lt kia 30-7-16 20Lpool p73 MR21
WILKINSON,Geoffrey Miles 2Lt kia 10-10-17 DCLI &56RFC p14&115 CR France705
WILKINSON,George 2Lt kia 9-4-18 5DLI p239 MR32
WILKINSON,Gordon Frederick Noble T2Lt kia 1-7-16 10YLI p144 MR21
WILKINSON,Harold Reid TLt dow 10-9-17 RFC p14 CR Canada1694
WILKINSON,Horace Capt dow 31-10-18 1/12LNLancs p234 CR France1033
WILKINSON,Hugh Wilmot T2Lt kia 18-7-16 12 att11Ess p133 CR Belgium44
WILKINSON,James Fisher.MC.Maj dow 29-10-18 54/39RFA p37 CR France1270,Fischer kia

WILKINSON,James Rendell 2Lt ded 20-5-16 PoW 3LancF p94 CR Germany4,Lt
WILKINSON,John 2Lt kia 19-9-18 4 att12A&SH p174 CR Greece5
WILKINSON,John Bright TLt dow 23-6-16 RE 225FC p49 CR France80
WILKINSON,John George T2Lt dow 25-10-17 15DLI p162 CR Belgium11
WILKINSON,John Graham Lt kia 20-7-18 1/4Hamps attDunsterforce p228 MR61
WILKINSON,John Henry Warburton Capt dow 5-5-17 5SStaffs p229 CR France134
WILKINSON,John Laurence T2Lt kia 30-6-16 RE 173TC p49 MR19
WILKINSON,John Rothes Marlow Lt kia 10-9-14 4Mddx p149 CR Belgium242,23-8-14
WILKINSON,John Yeardley 2Lt dow 23-12-17 1/8Manch p237 CR France80,kld
WILKINSON,Marcus Leonard T2Lt dow 8-7-17 10NumbF p63 CR Belgium11
WILKINSON,Maurice Hewson.MC.TLtAMaj kia 31-7-17 RE 177TC p49 CR Belgium5
WILKINSON,Norman Capt kia 21-3-18 9Manch p237 MR27
WILKINSON,Norman Cecil 2Lt dow 24-8-17 RGA 332SB p42 CR Belgium16
WILKINSON,Osborn Cecil Capt dow 5-2-15 5EYorks p85 CR France200
WILKINSON,Percy Lt kia 4-12-17 6LancF att2/7RWar p221 MR17
WILKINSON,Robert Bruce T2Lt dow 12-12-17 LNLancs att1/4Bn p137 CR France446
WILKINSON,Roger Leslie Stuart 2Lt dow 21-11-16 4Beds p87 CR France40
WILKINSON,Robert John LtACapt ded 2-7-18 RIrF p172
WILKINSON,Samuel William 2Lt dow 9-4-18 RGA 237SB p42 CR France201,Lt
WILKINSON,Sidney John.DSO.TLtCol kia 7-7-16 10SWBord p101 MR21
WILKINSON.Thomas Hill Lt 2-2-21 3Lpool CR Lancs149
WILKINSON,Thomas Orde Lawder.VC.TLt kia 5-7-16 7LNLancs p137 MR21
WILKINSON,Thomas William Musgrave Lt kia 20-7-18 8WYorks p219 CR France622,Capt
WILKINSON,Vaudelene Auguste Sydney 2Lt ded 7-6-18 6 att19Mddx p149 CR France1364,Vandeleur
WILKINSON,Walter Lightowler 2Lt kia 9-4-17 1/8A&SH p243 CR France728
WILKINSON,William 2Lt ded 24-2-19 RE p210 CR Germany1
WILKINSON,William Alfred 2Lt kia 2-12-17 256RFA p209 CR France711
WILKINSON,William Andrew 2Lt kia 21-3-18 4InnisF p106 CR France1495
WILKINSON,William Charlton Capt kia 9-4-18 2/5LancF p221 CR France260
WILKINSON,William Donald 2Lt kld 14-11-16 5 att13Ess p232 MR21
WILKINSON,William Jefferson 2Lt kia 25-9-15 Leic p88 MR19
WILKINSON,William Oscar Capt kia 5-8-17 7Ches p223 MR29
WILKINSON,William Thomas TCapt kia 5-7-16 9Yorks p91 CR France515
WILKINSON,W.S.2Lt ded 6-9-15 4WYorks p83 CR Yorks110
WILKS,Harold T2Lt kia 12-10-16 17Manch p156 MR21
WILKS,Harold Douglas Lt ded 18-2-19 4 O&BLI p272 CR Hereford/W58
WILKS,Percy Walter 2Lt drd 10-10-18 RASC p194 CRIreland14
WILKS,Richard Harold 2Lt kia 30-11-17 2/5NStaffs p238 CR France1498
WILKS,Sydney Lt kia 7-10-16 6RWKent p142 MR21
WILKS,Walter Charles.MC.Rev kia 4-10-17 RAChDept att7Staffs SenChapNCofE p200 CR Belgium23
WILL,Alfred William LtAMaj kia 25-5-18 SL attSPersiaRif p201 CR Asia82
WILL,George Kennedy Lt dow PoW 11-9-16 8WYorks p219 CR France245
WILL,John George TLt kia 25-3-17 GL &29RFC p15
WILLANS,Guy Russell 2Lt dow 29-3-18 3 att2LancF p94 CR France40
WILLANS,Robert St.John Lt kia 9-11-14 NumbF p63 MR29
WILLANS,William Alan Jenne ACapt kia 24-3-18 18KRRC p152 MR20,Jeune
WILLARD,Albert Ellis Lt kia 4-7-17 7RSuss D'Coy p120
WILLARD,Alfred George T2Lt dow 7-8-17 9ESurr p113 see MILLARD
WILLARD,Kenneth Hugh 2Lt ded PoW 12-10-17 Y&L att45RFC p159 CR Belgium140
WILLATS,Alton Henry TCapt kia 7-9-17 2/5Y&L p159 CR France563
WILLATS,Harry Ashley 2Lt ded 12-2-17 RFA p37&262 CR Lond10,Lt
WILLATS,Horace Lennan Capt ded 17-12-16 7EYorks p85 CR Lond14
WILLARD,Kenneth Hugh 2Lt ded PoW 12-10-17 Y&L &RFC p15
WILLBOURN,Horace Haynes 2Lt kia 8-5-18 8 att2WRid p116 CR France411
WILLBY,Frank Richard Bagg Lt kld 18-3-19 GL Staff Ex YLI p192 CR Egypt9
WILLCOCK,Frederick Norman T2Lt kia 10-7-16 8SStaffs p123 MR21
WILLCOCKS,Harold Francis CaptAMaj ded 7-5-19 RFA p262 CR Lond28
WILLCOX,Alan George T2Lt kld 14-2-18 GL &RFC p17 CR Egypt15
WILLCOX,Hugh Patterson 2Lt kia 30-11-17 7ESurr p113 MR17
WILLES,Patrick Dalrymple Lt ded 29-9-18 3RLancs &RAF p59
WILLES,William Frances George Capt ded 19-7-16 1Dors Cmdg11Div ACycCps p124 CR France46
WILLETT,John Arnold 2Lt kia 2-7-15 9SomLI att2RFus p80 MR4

WILLETT,Joseph Cyril 2LtTLt kia 15-5-17 19LancF att152MGC p94&186 CR France194

WILLETT,Nelson Herbert 2Lt kia 11-4-18 2RFus p71 MR32

WILLETT,Richard 2Lt kia 31-7-17 6LancF p221 MR29

WILLEY,Chester Matthew 2Lt ded 9-7-16 RGA CR Lond14

WILLEY,Rupert Harold Duncan Capt kia 14-7-19 SL attRE IWT p201 MR38

WILLEY,Henry Lowes TLt kia 22-10-17 23Manch p156 MR30

WILLEY,John Maj kia 3-4-18 A312RFA p207 CR France745

WILLEY,R.2Lt kld 20-5-18 GL &RAF p192

WILLEY,Thomas Arthur Raymond Robert Ellicott T2Lt kia 1-7-16 15WYorks p83 MR1

WILLIAM,John Rhonwy Capt dow PoW 13-8-16 10Lpool p216

WILLIAM-POWLETT,Oliver Richard Ferdinand 2Lt 30-4-21 7Huss MR65

WILLIAMS,Albert Stanley Gabriel TLt kia 28-10-17 RE 171TC p49 CR Belgium3

WILLIAMS,Alfred Richard T2Lt kia 16-8-17 49MGC Inf p186 MR30

WILLIAMS,Almericus John Falkiner de Courcy 2Lt dow 25-10-14 WIndiaR p192 CR France80,Lt 22-10-14 MddxR

WILLIAMS,Arthur Blount Cuthbert,CB BrigGen 11-7-18 IA MR67

WILLIAMS,Arthur Courtenay T2Lt kld 18-9-17 44RFC p15 CR Canada1694

WILLIAMS,Arthur Ivor Meakin.MID Capt dow 9-10-18 13RWFus p99 CR France906,Ifor 15 att13Bn

WILLIAMS,Arthur Jones T2Lt kia 3-11-17 1/4WelshR p128 CR Palestine1

WILLIAMS,Arthur Llewellyn 2Lt kia 26-3-17 1/6RWFus p223 CR Palestine8

WILLIAMS,Arthur Montague Lt kia 15-6-15 7N&D p233 CR Belgium17

WILLIAMS,Arthur Owen T2Lt kia 16/19-8-16 10RWFus p99 MR21

WILLIAMS,Arthur Trevor T2Lt dow 4-9-17 15RWFus att25RFC p15&99 CR France88

WILLIAMS,Aubrey 2Lt kia 25-4-18 WYorks att1/6Bn p83 MR30

WILLIAMS,Bernard Hallett 2Lt kia 31-7-17 5LNLancs p234 MR29

WILLIAMS,Bleddyn Capt kia 22-1-16 17RWFus p99 MR19

WILLIAMS,Brinley Jenkyn T2Lt kia 20-5-16 19NumbF p63 CR France1106

WILLIAMS,Burton Robert.MID.Bart.Lt kia 3-10-17 3 att1Dev p77 MR30,3/4-10-17

WILLIAMS,Cecil Arthur 2Lt kia 21-3-18 5 att9Norf p217 MR20

WILLIAMS,Charles Aubrey T2Lt kia 3-4-16 8RLancs p59 MR29

WILLIAMS,Charles Beasley TCapt kia 28-8-15 2RIrRif A'Coy p170 MR29A

WILLIAMS,Charles Beresford 2Lt kia 1-9-18 7Lond p247 CR France216

WILLIAMS,Charles Ellicombe.MID LtTCapt dow 27-5-17 7SWBord p101 CR Greece6

WILLIAMS,Charles James TLt dow 19-12-15 8Beds p87 CR Belgium11

WILLIAMS,Charles Montague T2Lt dow 29-7-16 25 att16Manch p156 CR France66

WILLIAMS,Charles Oswald Nicholson TMaj kia 2-12-15 8RLancs p59 CR Belgium15

WILLIAMS,Christopher Manners Capt&Adjt kia 24-3-18 HQ 66RGA p42 CR France1893

WILLIAMS,Claude Cuthbert Lt ded 24-6-21 IARO 2/2GurkhaRif p284 MR65

WILLIAMS,Colin Ernest T2Lt kia 17-10- 17 RASC p194 CR EAfrica38 &CR Tanzania1

WILLIAMS,Collingsby Philip 2Lt kia 26-8-17 GL &RFC p15 MR20,Phillip

WILLIAMS,Cyril Lt kia 30-7-16 HLI &60RFC p4&164 MR20

WILLIAMS,Daniel John 2Lt kia 5-10-17 13MGC Inf p186 MR30

WILLIAMS,Daniel Llewellyn 2Lt kia 15-10-18 1WelshR att1/1Hereford p128 CR Belgium157

WILLIAMS,David Aubrey T2Lt kia 25-7-16 1SWBord p101 MR21

WILLIAMS,David Jenkins 2Lt dow 20-9-17 1Mon att6KSLI p244 CR Belgium83

WILLIAMS,David Marmaduke Lt kia 25-9-15 2SStaffs p123 CR France924

WILLIAMS,David Ransome Vaughan T2Lt ded 20-11-18 1Hamps p121 CR Yorks244,21-11-18

WILLIAMS,Donald Mattieu T2Lt kia 9-4-16 12 att9RWar p66 MR38

WILLIAMS,Douglas T2Lt dow 10-7-16 11 att9YLI p144 CR France145

WILLIAMS,Edgar 2Lt kld 25-1-18 5Y&L p238 CR France184

WILLIAMS,Edward Albert 2Lt ded 31-12-18 GL EgyptLabCps &RAF p189 CR Egypt8

WILLIAMS,Edward Emanuel Montague 2Lt kia 10-12-17 RGA p42

WILLIAMS,Edward Ernest.DSO.TMaj kia 19-8-15 8NumbF p63 CR Gallipoli5

WILLIAMS,Edward Gordon Lt kia 12-8-15 2GrenGds SR p50 CR France495,kldacc

WILLIAMS,Edward Herbert T2Lt kia 31-8-16 2SWBord p101 CR Belgium73

WILLIAMS,Edward Stanley 2Lt kia 3-6-17 3 att8LNLancs p137 CR Belgium43

WILLIAMS,Edward Styant Maj kia 8-5-15 1Mon p244 MR29

WILLIAMS,Edwin Gordon 2Lt dow 13-5-17 10RWFus p99&258 CR France40

WILLIAMS,Einon Lt ded 28-10-18 RE p272

WILLIAMS,Eric Lt kia 27-3-18 18 att2WYorks p83 MR27

WILLIAMS,Ernest Joseph Lt kia 15-10-18 5 att2RIrF p170 CR Belgium157

WILLIAMS,Ernest Thurston Capt kia 3-5-17 6RWKent p142 MR20

WILLIAMS,Evan T2Lt kia 10-4-17 10RWFus p99 CR France531,11-4-17

WILLIAMS,Fawcett Thomas Capt ded 23-2-19 17WelshR attSWBord p264 CR Wales168

WILLIAMS,Felix George 2Lt kia 21-3-18 20Lond p251 MR27

WILLIAMS,Felix Roland T2Lt kia 10-4-17 7KRRC p152 CR France594

WILLIAMS,Francis Christopher Dallas 2Lt kia 19-7-16 3ESurr att2/4RBerks p113 CR France1887,Lt

WILLIAMS,Francis Slaney Lt kia 20-9-17 8N&D p233 MR30

WILLIAMS,Frank Emlyn.MC.Capt kia 7-4-18 1/5WelshR &57RAF p230&258 CR Egypt8

WILLIAMS,Frank Leonard.MC.LtACapt dow 30-5-18 8BordR att25MGC p118,186&259 CR France1693

WILLIAMS,Frederick Lt kia 24-6-18 7RWFus &62RAF p223&258 CR France924

WILLIAMS,Frederick Thesiger TLtCol dow 12-7-16 2Nhampt p138 CR France145

WILLIAMS,G.TLt dow 7-8-17 SL att3/2KAR p202 CR EAfrica10 &CR Tanzania1

WILLIAMS,G.2Lt 22-5-18 4SWBord CR Wales178

WILLIAMS,G.Capt 1-9-20 7WelchR CR Yorks222

WILLIAMS,G.J.2Lt ded 27-4-15 5Y&L p238

WILLIAMS,George Augustus Capt ded 6-2-19 Res p272 CR Lond8

WILLIAMS,George Ernest T2Lt kia 20-11-17 O&BLI att6Bn p130 MR17

WILLIAMS,George Gabriel Lt ded 21-2-19 RE AntiGasSch Etaples p49 CR France40,24-2-19

WILLIAMS,George Henry Spence de Meaker TCapt kia 13-5-16 1/8LancF p94 CR France631

WILLIAMS,George Jackson 2Lt ded 27-4-15 5Y&L p272 CR Wales659,Lt

WILLIAMS,George Stanley Lt kia 20-10-18 WelshR att14Bn p128 CR France230

WILLIAMS,George Stewart Louis Stanilaus Stevens 2Lt kia 8-9-18 6 att25RWFus p223 CR France365,Lt

WILLIAMS,George Trevor TLt ded 19-4-18 RFA 38Bty 9Bde p37 MR43,Capt kldacc &CR Pakistan50A

WILLIAMS,Gerald Leopold.MC.2Lt kia 15-10-18 12RInniskF p106 CR Belgium156

WILLIAMS,Gordon Lt kia 30-10-17 1/28Lond F'Coy p252 MR30

WILLIAMS,Gordon Capt ded 15-11-18 8WelshR p128 MR38

WILLIAMS,Gordon Percy 2Lt kia 16-4-18 1Lpool D'Coy &IntelStaff GHQ p73 CR France924

WILLIAMS,Gwilym T2Lt dow 21-5-16 12 att17RWFus p99 CR France345

WILLIAMS,Guy Grenfell T2Lt kia 6-6-16 9 att7DCLI p115 CR Belgium6

WILLIAMS,H.D.Lt 20-12-20 RE CR Kent95

WILLIAMS,H.I.2Lt kia 18-10-18 4KRRC p152

WILLIAMS,H.W.K.2Lt 11-7-17 RFC CR Glouc19

WILLIAMS,Harold LtTCapt kia 25-4-17 11Worc p110 MR37

WILLIAMS,Harold Edward 2Lt kia 7/8-10-16 1Lond p245 MR21

WILLIAMS,Harold Garnett 2Lt kia 27-9-18 8RLancs p59 CR France357

WILLIAMS,Harold Justus 2Lt 9-7-16 RFA attGdsTMB CR Belgium73

WILLIAMS,Harold Osborne 2Lt kia 21-1-17 13Mddx p149 MR19

WILLIAMS,Harold Sutton.MID Maj ded 21-3-15 1Dors p124 CR France102

WILLIAMS,Harry Benjamin.MC.2Lt kia 3-5-17 5 att13Lpool p215 MR20

WILLIAMS,Henry Aitken Capt ded 2-11-18 6 att4Mddx attMinofNatServ p265 CR Lond8,Harry

WILLIAMS,Henry Evan Vincent Lt dow 22-5-17 2Lond p245 CR France512

WILLIAMS,Henry Frederick Maj ded 2-5-16 9RMunstF p176 CR Lond28,1-5-16

WILLIAMS,Henry Vincent 2Lt kia 26-5-16 3Worc p110 CR France68

WILLIAMS,Herbert Henry.MID TCapt kia 20-9-17 6Wilts p153 CR Belgium17

WILLIAMS,Herbert Mainwaring.DSO.Maj dow 23-12-17 RAVC 63Div p199&258 CR France398

WILLIAMS,Hilary Evelyn Eccles T2Lt kia 30-9-15 11RB p180 CR France706

WILLIAMS,Horace George Lt kia 17-10-18 2Y&L p159 CR France849

WILLIAMS,Howard Glynne Lt ded 5-1-17 6KRRC p265 CR Wales706

WILLIAMS,Howard Oscar 2Lt kia 11-4-18 23NumbF p63 MR32

WILLIAMS,Howell 2LtTLt ded 21-2-17 RWFus attGoldCoastR p99 CR WAfrica3

WILLIAMS,Howell Morgan 2Lt kia 24-6-17 4WelshR p230 CR Belgium23,19Bn

WILLIAMS,Hubert Cracroft.MC.MID Lt kldacc 18-10-15 2RWSurr p57 CR France114

WILLIAMS,Hugh 2Lt kia 28-7-18 PembrokeYeo att7KSLI p205 CR France33

WILLIAMS,Hugh Osborne Lt dow 12-8-15 5RWFus C'Coy p223WILLIAMS,Hugh Powell TCapt kia 5-6-16 14RWFus p99 CRFrance1730

WILLIAMS,Hywel TCapt kia 10/12-7-16 17RWFus p99 MR21

WILLIAMS,Idris Havard Joseph Capt dow 3-6-15 RFus p71 CR Wales86

WILLIAMS,Idwal 2Lt kia 26-9-17 1/2RWFus p99 MR30

WILLIAMS,Ivor Phillips 2Lt kia 7-1-16 3KSLI att4SWBord p145 MR4

WILLIAMS,J.A.Maj 20-9-19 RGA CR Hamps11

WILLIAMS,J.J.2Lt 6-6-21 RWFus CR Wales725

WILLIAMS,James B.TCapt dow 22-7-16 18LancF p94 CR France66

WILLIAMS,James Alfred 2Lt kia 6-9-16 3RIrF p172 MR21,RIrRif

WILLIAMS,James Ezekiel TCapt ded 27-9-18 GL p267

WILLIAMS,James Griffith Lt kia 27-8-18 RWFus att17Bn p99 CR France432,29-8-18

WILLIAMS,James Hubert.DSO.Capt ded 30-11-20 IA 1/10GurkhaRif p284

WILLIAMS,James Morgan 2Lt kia 9-5-18 19 att17RWFus p99 CR France296

WILLIAMS,James Trevor 2Lt ded 7-6-18 IARO att30Punjabis p284

WILLIAMS,Jennie Miss ded 31-1-19 VAD p200 CR France85

WILLIAMS,John TCapt kia 30-6-17 19RWFus p99 CR France439

WILLIAMS,John T2Lt drd 22-10-17 11RDubF att1/5Hamps p177 MR66

WILLIAMS,John Alfred T2Lt kia 18-11-16 11 att2YLI p144 CR France152

WILLIAMS,John Bromfield T2Lt kia 25-9-15 5CamH p168 MR19

WILLIAMS,John Herbert TCapt ded 18-11-17 GL p192 CR Mddx26,6-11-17

WILLIAMS,John Herschell 2Lt kia 17-6-17 C84RFA p37 CR Belgium127

WILLIAMS,John Lewis TCapt dow 12-7-16 16WelshR C'Coy p128 CR France23

WILLIAMS,John Rhonwy(Ronnie) Capt 12-8-16 10Lpool CR France1266

WILLIAMS,John Ronald Watson.MC.Lt kia 12-4-18 RE p210 MR32

WILLIAMS,John Rowland Lt kia 27-9-17 2MonR attMGC p187&244 MR30

WILLIAMS,John Trevor 2Lt ded 7-6-18 IARO att1/30Punjabis MR43

WILLIAMS,John Tyler 2Lt kia 21-3-18 9 att11Lpool p216 MR27,Tytler

WILLIAMS,John Victor 2Lt kia 26-9-17 4Lpool p73 MR30

WILLIAMS,Joseph Stephenson.MC.LtACapt kia 25-9-17 3 att4Lpool p73 MR30

WILLIAMS,Justus Harold 2Lt kia 9-7-16 RHFA attGdsTMB p37

WILLIAMS,Katherine SNurse ded 6-8-19 QAIMNS p268 CR Wales571,4-8-19

WILLIAMS,Kenneth George TLt dow 21-10-16 74MGC Inf p186 MR21

WILLIAMS,Leigh Roslin Lt kia 27-5-18 B'Bty 251Bde RFA p208 MR18

WILLIAMS,Leonard Lt dow 11-9-15 3 att1SWBord p101 CR France423

WILLIAMS,Leonard Charles 2Lt dow 10-11-17 3Lincs p76 CR Belgium11,1Bn

WILLIAMS,Leonard Vincent TCapt kia 26-5-17 7SWBord p101 CR Greece6

WILLIAMS,Leslie T2Lt kia 1-7-16 23NumbF p63 CR France1890

WILLIAMS,Leslie Caradoc Lt kia 27-8-17 RFA D1/55Div p208 CR Belgium10

WILLIAMS,Lewis T2Lt kia 18-8-16 10RWFus p99 MR21

WILLIAMS,Lionel Murray Capt ded 9-4-17 6Mddx att2Ess p149 MR65

WILLIAMS,Lloyd Capt dow 2-8-17 17RWFus CR Belgium18

WILLIAMS,Lloyd Allison T2Lt kia 20-7-16 1DCLI p115 MR21

WILLIAMS,Martin Floyer TLt kia 11-8-16 A65RFA p37 CR France296

WILLIAMS,Maurice Dingwall 2Lt kia 22/24-10-14 RWSurr p57 CR Belgium83

WILLIAMS,Maxwell Henry 2Lt kia 19-9-17 17Lond p250 CR Belgium10

WILLIAMS,Meredyth Robert Owen T2Lt kia 14-3-17 25NumbF p63 CR France1182

WILLIAMS,Montgomery.MID Capt 23-8-16 RMA CR France296

WILLIAMS,Noel Dyson Lt kia 22-10-18 3 att5SLancs p126 CR Belgium406,dow

WILLIAMS,Norman Lt kia 21-3-18 8RBerks p140 MR27

WILLIAMS,Norman Ernest 2Lt kia 9-11-17 10Lond attRFC p20&248 CRFrance1361

WILLIAMS,Norman Stevens Lt kia 4-11-17 1/4RSuss p228 CR Palestine1,Steevens

WILLIAMS,Osmond Trahairn Deudraeth.DSO.Capt dow 30-9-15 WelshGds CR France88

WILLIAMS,Oswald Michael Maj kia 13-10-15 1Mon p244 MR29 Now known MR19

WILLIAMS,Oswald Morgan 2Lt kia 9-4-16 16WelshR B'Coy p255 MR19

WILLIAMS,Owen Edgar 2Lt kia 19-4-17 Worc att1/4WelshR p110 CR Palestine8

WILLIAMS,Owen Herd Spear LtCol ded 9-1-15 PembrokeYeo p272 CR Wales393,9-12-14

WILLIAMS,Percy John 2Lt dow 17-5-17 6ESurr p226 CR Greece7

WILLIAMS,Peter T2Lt kia 13-11-16 10RWFus p99 MR21

WILLIAMS,Philip Clarence TLt kia 10-8-15 10Hamps p121 MR4

WILLIAMS,Philip Ernest.MC.TCapt dow 24-11-17 19RWFus p99 CR France512

WILLIAMS,Ralph Eustace 2Lt kia 29-6-18 19NumbF attRE p63 CR France84,28-6-18

WILLIAMS,Raymond Burke.MC.TCapt kia 19-9-16 RE 176TC p49 MR20

WILLIAMS,Reginald Joseph T2Lt kia 25-9-15 9RWFus p99 MR19

WILLIAMS,Richard 2Lt dow 2-4-18 17RWFus att41MGC p99&186 CR France169

WILLIAMS,Richard Harte Keatings CaptBtMaj dow 12-12-16 RASC p194

WILLIAMS,Richard Henry T2Lt kia 13-11-16 10RWFus p99 MR21

WILLIAMS,Richard James 2Lt dow 29-4-18 12Lond p249 CR France145

WILLIAMS,Richard Lloyd TCapt dow 2-8-17 17RWFus p99

WILLIAMS,Richard White 2Lt dow 16-8-15 1/10Lond p248 MR4

WILLIAMS,Robert 2Lt kia 8-10-15 GrenGds SR att3Bn p50 CR France423,2Bn

WILLIAMS,Robert John 2Lt kia 31-8-18 3MGC Inf Div p186 CR France614

WILLIAMS,Robert Lukyn Lt kia 27-10-18 IA 23Cav p284 MR38

WILLIAMS,Robin A.W.Lt kia 18-4-15 2YLI p144 MR29

WILLIAMS,Roderick Mathafar Capt kia 12-8-17 2GarBnRWFus &32RFC p15&99 MR20,Rodric Mathafarn

WILLIAMS,Roderick Philip 2Lt ded 8-9-16 IA 72Punjabis p284 MR43.9-9-16

WILLIAMS,Roland Vaughan T2Lt kia 5-6-17 32RFC p15 CR France381

WILLIAMS,Rowland 2Lt kia 23-10-18 9RFus p71 CR France1296 &CR France1080

WILLIAMS,S.R.T.A.M.2Lt dow 25-10-15 REKentYeo CR Gallipoli1

WILLIAMS,Samuel Mervyn 2Lt kia 16-10-16 3 att2N&D p135 MR21

WILLIAMS,Selwyn Coldham TLt kia 18-1-17 B189RFA p37 CR Belgium102,C'Bty

WILLIAMS,Stanley Charles Howard TLt ded 14-10-18 GL att1NigR p192&202 WAfrica53

WILLIAMS,Stanley Norman T2Lt ded 25-10-16 GL &RFC p4&192 CR France514

WILLIAMS,Stuart Duncan 2Lt kia 3-5-17 HouseholdBn p20 MR20

WILLIAMS,Sydney Mansell 2Lt kia 15-6-17 20Lond p251 MR22,15-6-15

WILLIAMS,Theodore Cecil Ormonde.MC.Capt dow 24-3-18 16N&D p135 CR France177,Ormond

WILLIAMS,Theodore Edward 2Lt kia 1-7-15 1SomLI p80 CR Belgium85

WILLIAMS,Thomas Benjamin 2Lt kia 27-5-17 3 att2RWFus p99 MR20

WILLIAMS,Thomas Jones 2Lt kia 28-12-17 1/7LancF p221 CR France765

WILLIAMS,Thomas Langley 2Lt kia 1-9-18 1Lpool p73 CR France646

WILLIAMS,Thomas Rix 2Lt kia 20-7-18 8WYorks p219 CR France622

WILLIAMS,Thomas Wodehouse Lt kia 9-5-15 3Nhampt att1NLancs p138 MR22

WILLIAMS,Timothy Davies 2Lt dow 5-4-18 RGA 248SB p42 CR France41

WILLIAMS,Trevard Lewis 2Lt kia 30-10-17 7RFus p71 MR30

WILLIAMS,Vaughan Floyer 2Lt kia 3-4-17 GL &60RFC p15 CR France518,2-4-17

WILLIAMS,Vivian Pedr 2Lt kia 22-4-18 15RWFus p99 CR France296

WILLIAMS,Walter 2Lt kia 15-5-18 7Lpool p215 CR France106,1/6Bn

WILLIAMS,Walter Frank 2Lt kia 12-9-18 SWBord att10th p101 CR France415

WILLIAMS,Walter Patrick 2Lt kia 17-4-18 3 att4Lpool p73 MR30

WILLIAMS,Wilfred Brynmor T2Lt kia 5-7-16 20 att16WelshR p128 CR France397,dow

WILLIAMS,Wilfred Cyril Lt kia 24-9-16 12Hamps p121 MR37

WILLIAMS,William 2Lt ded 27-2-17 3 att1RWFus p99 CR Lancs4,dow

WILLIAMS,William 2Lt kia 29-8-18 281RFA p37 CR France214,30-8-18

WILLIAMS,William Bernard Lt kia 20-10-18 WelshR att14Bn p128 CR France230

WILLIAMS,William Frederick 2Lt kia 27-9-18 17RFus p71 CR France1497,Lt

WILLIAMS,William George TCapt dow 29-8-17 17RWFus p99 CR Belgium16

WILLIAMS,William George Bransby.MC.Capt kia 12-5-17 19RFC p15 MR20

WILLIAMS,William Harold Lt kia 9-11-18 RGA 326SB p42 CR Belgium214

WILLIAMS,William Harold Trant T2Lt ded PoW 22-8-17 29RFC p15 CR Belgium140,dow

WILLIAMS,William Henry T2Lt kia 6-11-17 9 att1/7RWFus p99 CR Palestine1

WILLIAMS,William Henry 2Lt kia 22-3-18 1/7Lpool p73 CR France765

WILLIAMS,William Henry Capt kia 30-5-18 3Mon att5SWBord p244 CR France622

WILLIAMS,William Humphrey Capt kia 3-5-18 6LancF &RAF p221&258 CR palestine9

WILLIAMS,William Hutton Capt kia 18-5-15 3ESurr att2Beds p113 CR France279

WILLIAMS,William Ifor 2Lt dow 18-3-18 1 att16RWFus p99 CR France275

WILLIAMS,William James.MC.2Lt kia 19-9-17 16RWFus p99 CR France275

WILLIAMS,William James Minister 2Lt kia 7-2-16 3 att2RWFus p99 CR France114

WILLIAMS,William John Lt dow 12-5-15 2Mon p244 CR France102

WILLIAMS,William John TLt kia 25-2-17 14RWFus p99 CR Belgium23

WILLIAMS,William Morley T2Lt kia 7-6-17 14WelshR p128 CR Belgium23

WILLIAMS-BULKELEY,Richard Gerard Wellesley.MC.Maj ded 28-3-18 1WelshGds p53 CR Mddx16,Gerrard

WILLIAMS-FREEMAN,Anthony Peere Capt dow 4/5-4-16 Lincs p76 MR38

WILLIAMS-FREEMAN,Harry Peere LtACapt kia 8-8-18 3 att1/5RWar p66 CR Italy1.9-8-18

WILLIAMS-MEYRICK,Edmund Oswald Griffith TLt ded 7-5-16 RWFus 1GarrBn p99 CR Europe23

WILLIAMS-VAUGHAN,John Christopher Arthur 2Lt kia 18-7-16 SWBord BrecknockBn att 100MGC Inf p187&223 MR21,15-7-16

WILLIAMS-WYNN,Charles Walkin 2Lt kia 29-10-14 1ColdGds p51 CR Belgium115

WILLIAMSON,Alan Kennedy 2Lt dow 20-4-17 8A&SH p243 CR France40

WILLIAMSON,Alexander T2Lt kia 31-1-16 9Suff p79 CR Belgium101

WILLIAMSON,Alexander John Neeve 2Lt kia 14-9-14 SfthH p165 CR France867

WILLIAMSON,Andrew Maj kia 21-3-18 RE 12FC p49 MR20

WILLIAMSON,Charles Harry.MC.Capt kia 27-3-17 7Manch attRFC p20&237 CR Egypt2

WILLIAMSON,Charles Percival Lt kia 12-3-17 RE 56FC p49 CR France1182

WILLIAMSON,Cyril George T2Lt kia 2-7-16 10RWar p66 MR21

WILLIAMSON,Edgar Rowe.MC.Lt kia 10-9-16 5Lond att169TMB p246 MR21

WILLIAMSON,Edward Benjamin Bickford 2Lt kia 19-2-17 ConnRgrs att6Bn p172 CR Belgium17

WILLIAMSON,Edward Maurice Lt kia 1-3-15 1N&D p135 CR France706

WILLIAMSON,Frank Lt kia 24-3-18 5Lond p246 MR20

WILLIAMSON,Frank Alfred 2Lt dow 4-6-15 ScotRif att1KOSB p104 MR4

WILLIAMSON,Frederick Lt kia 10-5-17 IARO att1/4GurkhaRif p284 MR43

WILLIAMSON,George Lt dow 12-11-14 3 att2WRid p116 CR Belgium84

WILLIAMSON,George Hamilton.MC.TCapt dow 12-4-17 7KRRC p152 CR France120

WILLIAMSON,Gerald Coutts 2Lt kia 9-10-17 4Ess p232 CR Belgium115

WILLIAMSON,Gerald Douglas T2Lt dow 1-1-18 7RFC p17 CR Belgium18

WILLIAMSON,Hugh Albert.MID 2Lt kia 2-7-16 3Manch &34RFC p4&156,ded MR20

WILLIAMSON,Harold 2Lt kia 27-5-18 25MGC p186 MR18

WILLIAMSON,Harold Godwin 2Lt kia 1-7-16 6NStaffs p238 MR21

WILLIAMSON,Hugh Henshall Clifford Lt kia 15-9-16 1CldGds p51 MR21,mbk

WILLIAMSON,John 2Lt kia 1-7-16 2SfthH p165 CR France643

WILLIAMSON,John 2Lt kia 24-9-17 246MGC Inf p186 MR30

WILLIAMSON,John Alexander Lt kldacc 10-4-17 10EKent attRFC p20&204 CR Kent34

WILLIAMSON,John Daniel 2Lt kia 15-7-16 1 att4SStaffs p123 MR21,4 at1Bn

WILLIAMSON,John George Joseph 2Lt kia 2-9-18 2 att7RIrReg p89 CR Belgium97

WILLIAMSON,John Maurice 2Lt kia 16-5-15 2GordH p167 CR France279

WILLIAMSON,John McLeod 2Lt kia 12-4-18 4A&SH p174 MR32

WILLIAMSON,John Stanley 2Lt kia 1-5-15 1LancF p94 MR4,25-4-15

WILLIAMSON,Kenneth Harper T2Lt dow 19-4-17 7KRRC B'Coy p152 CR France40

WILLIAMSON,Robert Burdett 2Lt kia 29-10-18 1/2RSuss &RAF p120

WILLIAMSON,Robert Hamilton Lt dow 27-12-14 RGA p42 CR Scot280,2Lt

WILLIAMSON,Stephen de Thierry Lt kia 10-3-15 3ScotRif p104 CR France260,2Bn

WILLIAMSON,Thomas Cockburn 2Lt kia 26-9-15 4BlkW p230 MR19

WILLIAMSON,Wilford Robert.MC.TLt dow 14-8-17 8Norf p74 CR Belgium11,Wilfrid

WILLIAMSON-NAPIER,Alfred Maxwell Lt kia 12-12-18 75RFA p37 CR France1484,12-9-18

WILLINGTON,James Vernon Yates T2Lt kia 6-8-16 6Leinst p175 MR4,10-8-15

WILLINGTON,Reginald Ernest.DCM.Lt dow 31-8-18 2YLI p144 CR France119

WILLINK,George Ouvry William.MC.MID Capt kia 28-3-18 2/4RBerks p234 CR France1170

WILLINK,Herman James Lindale Capt dow 5-11-18 1/6WRid p227 CR France402

WILLIS,Arthur Rhys 2Lt kia 28-7-17 4HLI att20DLI p164 CR Belgium29

WILLIS,Charles Frederick Maj kia 7-3-18 5Y&L p238 CR Belgium307,8-3-18

WILLIS,Cyril Louis 2Lt kia 7-10-16 12Lond p248 MR21

WILLIS,Edgar Reginald TLt kia 13/14-7-16 8RSuss p120 CR France630

WILLIS,Eric Fitzgeorge Lt kia 27-3-18 28Lond p252 MR20

WILLIS,F.A.Sister 15-12-19 TFNS 4LondGH CR Essex5

WILLIS,Frederick LtACapt kia 30-9-18 9 att1/5Dev p77&258 CR France1483

WILLIS,George Henry Lt dow 10-8-15 6SLancs p126 CR Gallipoli17

WILLIS,Henry George.MID 2Lt dow 22-12-15 2DLI p162 CR France102

WILLIS,Hugh Dudley TCapt dow 12-8-17 RAMC att3Worc p198 CR Belgium7

WILLIS,Justin Charles.MC.Maj dow 7-8-18 RE 18DivSigCo p49 CR France71

WILLIS,Oscar 2Lt kia 20-6-16 5NumbF p213 CR Belgium60

WILLIS,Raymond TLt kia 25-3-18 5RRofCav att18Huss p23 CR France513

WILLIS,Raymond Maurice T2Lt kia 6-11-17 1DCLI p115 MR30

WILLIS,Richard TLt kia 15-5-16 9LNLancs p137 CR France68

WILLIS,Russell 2Lt kia 25-10-14 Y&L att1Lincs p159 CR France705

WILLIS,Samuel Capt kia 1-7-16 14RIrRif p170 MR21

WILLIS,Sherlock Amyas.MID LtTCapt dow 15-5-17 4Mddx p149 CR France40

WILLIS,Thomas Ambrose Lt kia 8-12-17 18Lond p250 CR Palestine,2Bn

WILLIS,William Francis Bucknote T2Lt kia 23-7-16 1DCLI p115 MR21,Frederick Bucknole

WILLIS-FLEMING,Richard Thomas Cyril 2Lt dow 4-8-16 1/5RHA p209 CR Egypt2,kia

WILLISON,John Downie Lt kia 25-7-18 2/9RScots p212 CR France865

WILLMER,Arthur Franklin TCapt dow 20-9-16 9RB p180 CR France145

WILLMER,Walter TCapt kia 13-7-16 19Lpool p73 MR21,30-7-16

WILLMORE,E.G.MC.Lt 31-7-20 RGA CR Herts31

WILLMORE,John 2Lt 5-11-17 2/7Worc MR20

WILLMORE,William Albert 2Lt kia 26-4-18 13 att10Ches p97 MR30

WILLMOT,John Dyott Lt kia 3-7-15 6 att2Worc p110&258 CR France571

WILLMOT,Robert Dyott 2Lt kia 17-2-18 6 att2KRRC p152 CR Belgium63

WILLMOTT,Albert Mckenzie Lt ded 11-2-19 RASC p194 CR Belgium265

WILLMOTT,John Herbert Victor.MC.LtACapt kia 28-3-18 3 att2Ess p133 MR20

WILLNER,John Capt&QM kia 7-4-18 1/6SStaffs p229 CR France480

WILLOCK,Guy Charles Boileau Capt kia 25-9-15 18Lond p250 CR France219

WILLOCK,Neville Gore Capt 22-11-17 KOSB CR France398

WILLOUGHBY,Edwin Charles Capt dow 8-8-15 7Glouc p107 MR4

WILLOUGHBY,Francis George Godfrey TCapt kia 9-8-15 9RB p180 MR29

WILLOUGHBY,James Gerald Capt kia 3-3-15 IA 33Cav p284 CR Iraq6

WILLOUGHBY,John Christopher.Sir.DSO.Maj ded 16-4-18 RASC p267

WILLOUGHBY,Stanley Nelson Lt kia 1-8-17 B70RFA p37 CR Belgium7

WILLOX,George Martin Lt 8-12-18 MilLabCps CR EAfrica36

WILLS,Alban Noel Lt dow 7-3-18 1/5YLI p235 CR Belgium11

WILLS,Alfred James 2Lt kia 18-10-18 RGA 182SB p42 CR France190

WILLS,Alfred Leslie Lt kia 23-4-17 4Worc p110 MR20

WILLS,Arthur George Lt kia 7-8-15 9N&D p135 MR4,9-8-15

WILLS,Bertram Shera Capt 19-8-19 RAMC CR Leic63

WILLS,John Godfrey 2Lt kia 27-9-18 A93RFA p37 CR France759

WILLS,John Scott Lt kia 4-9-18 20DLI p162 CR Belgium111

WILLS,Mary Elizabeth SNurse 30-3-18 TFNS CR Durham13

WILLS,Oliver Byerley Walters Lt ded 10-11-18 GL &RAF p192

WILLS,Percy 2Lt dow 19-4-15 1DCLI p115 CR Belgium151

WILLS,Robert Bruce Melville.MID Capt kia 15-2-15 RE 2FC p210 MR29,Recommended for VC

WILLS,Robert Dixon.MM.2Lt kia 23-4-17 5BordR p228 CR France162

WILLS,Robert George.MC.MM.2Lt ded 3-12-18 RE 46DivSigs att230RFA p49 CR France717

WILLS,Thomas George Francis 2Lt kia 2-9-18 3SomLI p80 CR France511

WILLSON,Edgar Brian Lt kia 27-5-18 25MGC p186 MR18

WILLSON,Francis George Dudley Lt kia 24-9-18 3 att1Nhampt D'Coy p138 CR France375

WILLSON,Frederick James Lt dow 10-1-17 IARO att3/1Sap&Min p284 CR Iraq5

WILLSON,Harold Hilton 2Lt dedacc 10-1-17 5Suff D'Coy p217 CR France52,8Bn

WILLSON,Nellie SNurse 16-10-18 QAIMNS CR Lincs76

WILLSON,William Alick Parkinson.MID Lt dow 1-4-18 11RIrRif att22EntrenchBn p170 CR France988,12Bn

WILLSTEAD,Grahame Ernest Lord LtACapt kia 24-3-18 3SomLI p80 CR France1061,7Bn

WILLY,John Howard Cole T2Lt kia 25-11-17 2Dev p77 MR17

WILMER,Harold Gordon Maj kia 4-7-15 IA 14Sikhs Ferozepore p284 MR4,5-7-15

WILMOT,Ben.MC.TLtACapt kia 6-6-17 20NumbF p63 MR20

WILMOT,Edmund Sacheverell 2Lt kia 13/15-11-16 4 att2SStaffs p123 CR France1890,13-11-16

WILMOT,Paul Dominie Lt kia 25-3-18 3 att12RSuss p120 MR27

WILMOT,Ralph Henry Sacheverel.Bart.Capt ded 14-1-18 CldGds p262 CR Lincs60

WILMOT,Robert Coningby TCapt kia 29-10-17 10N&D p135 CR Belgium86,Coningsby

WILMOT,Sachevarel Darwin Capt ded 14-10-18 RGA 159SB p42 MR43,Sacheverel

WILMOT,Thomas Norbury.MC.2Lt dow 25-8-16 2Worc p110 CR France833

WILMOT-SITWELL,Jacinth Sacheverall Lt dow 9-7-16 3CldGds p51 CR Belgium73

WILMSHURST,Cecil Arthur 2Lt kia 5-4-18 4 att5RBerks p234 MR27

WILMSHURST,Edwin Roy TLt dow 1-12-16 29 att20RFus A'Coy p71 CR France145

WILSEY,Edward Henry 2Lt kia 11-1-17 IARO att93BurmaInf p284 CR Iraq5

WILSHAW,Eric James 2Lt ded 23-12-18 A233RHFA p37 CR Lancs209,dow

WILSHIN,John Howell 2Lt dow 25-4-18 6 att1RFus p71 CR France145,22-4-18

WILSHIRE,Laurence Stanley 2Lt kia 14-4-18 95MGC p186 CR France18

WILSON,Alec Capt kia 26-3-17 1Hereford p252 MR34

WILSON,Alan Hood 2Lt kia 17-3-15 6RB p181 CR Belgium71

WILSON,Alan Mowbray 2Lt kia 19-11-16 3 att8ESurr p113 MR21

WILSON,Alan Sydney Lt kia 23-4-17 2SLancs att51MGC p126&186 MR20

WILSON,Albert Cecil 2Lt dow 8-7-16 14Lond p249 CR France95

WILSON,Albert Knowles Lt kia 14-3-15 1Manch p156 MR22,12-3-15

WILSON,Alexander 2Lt kia 21-3-18 2/7LancF att1/6Bn p221 MR27

WILSON,Alexander LtCol&QM ded 18-9-19 RAMC p267 CR Kent67

WILSON,Alexander Gordon 2Lt kia 27-8-18 12 att13RInniskF p106 CR France353

WILSON,Alexander Newbigging 2Lt kia 24-11-17 5KOSB p224 MR34

WILSON,Alexander Philip Lt kia 14-4-17 GL &2RFC p15 CR France58

WILSON,Alexander Stewart T2Lt kia 20-4-17 10RDubF p177 MR20

WILSON,Alfred Cairns.MC.2Lt dow 25-9-16 14Lond p249 CR France329

WILSON,Alfred Clarke 2Lt mbk 6-11-18 3 att6Lincs p257 CR Belgium241

WILSON,Allan TLt ded 25-8-15 RE 79FC p49 CR France22

WILSON,Allan Clark 2Lt kia 28-4-17 15RScots p55 MR20

WILSON,Allan Stanley 2Lt dow 12-7-17 5BordR attMGC p187&228,Lt CR France102

WILSON,Andrew 2Lt kia 16-7-18 13RScots p55 CR France139

WILSON,Archibald 2Lt kia 27-3-18 LancF att6Bn p94 MR27

WILSON,Archibald Field TCapt kia 25-9-15 9ScotRif p104 CR France114

WILSON,Arnold 2Lt kia 3-5-17 5WYorks p218 MR20

WILSON,Arthur Alexander 2Lt kia 23-4-17 3A&SH p174 CR France434

WILSON,Arthur Desmond Lloyd TLt kia 1-7-16 9RWKent p142 CR France1490

WILSON,Arthur Dominic 2lt dow 10-9-16 3RMunstF p176 CR France66,1Bn

WILSON,Arthur Edward Lt ded 3-12-18 14RWar p263 CR War3

WILSON,Arthur Henry Capt kia 18-10-14 EYorks p85 MR32

WILSON,Arthur Henry Maitland Capt ded 29-1-18 IA 12Cav p284 CR Iraq8

WILSON,Arthur Holt.DSO.LtCol ded 18-11-19 7ESurr Ex 2Bn p264 CR Suff64

WILSON,Arthur Hone Lt dow 18-11-16 4 att7RFus p71 CR France40

WILSON,Arthur Leslie Lt kia 18-7-18 5CamH p168 CR France285

WILSON,Arthur Stafford T2Lt kia 25-8-16 2RB p181 CR France423

WILSON,Arthur Walker 2Lt dow 22-8-18 251RFA p37 CR France119,Lt

WILSON,Arthur Wesley 2Lt kia 30-7-17 ScotsGds att3MGC p52 CR Belgium20

WILSON,Belford Alexander Wallis.MC.2Lt kia 26-9-17 2 att14Hamps p121 MR30

WILSON,Brodie Wyatt Lt kia 23-9-18 19Lond att20RAF p272 CR France1061

WILSON,Cecil Eustace T2Lt kia 16-4-17 GL &7RFC p15 CR France672

WILSON,Cecil Fred 2Lt dow 27-7-18 4Hamps p228 CR France1693,Lt

WILSON,Cecil Vere TLt dow 31-7-16 1RBerks p140 CR France145,2Lt

WILSON,Charles 2Lt kia 9-5-17 2GordH p167 MR20

WILSON,Charles Edgar Andrew Capt dow 8-4-18 RAMC p198 CR France122

WILSON,Charles Edward Capt&Adjt kia 17-9-14 RWSurr p57 CR France1342

WILSON,Charles Edward T2Lt kia 16-8-16 1Nhampt p138 CR France387

WILSON,Charles George Gordon T2Lt kia 9-4-17 3 att9ScotRif p104 CR France265

WILSON,Charles Henry.MID Lt dow 30-9-18 5YLI p235 CR France512,Capt

WILSON,Charles Lindsay.DCM.2Lt kia 8-8-16 1/5Lpool p215 MR21,9-8-16

WILSON,Charles Oscar Lt kia 26-3-17 1/5Ess p232 CR Palestine8

WILSON,Charles Robert T2Lt kia 24-5-17 88MGC Inf p186 CR France545

WILSON,Charles Wyndham Lt kia 12-3-15 2BordR p118 MR22

WILSON,Christina Murdock A/Sister ded 1-3-16 QAIMNS p200 CR France64,Murdoch

WILSON,Clive Harry Adolphus.DSO.Maj 18-1-21 ERidYeo CR Yorks83

WILSON,Conrad Blackadder 2Lt kia 7-2-17 9HLI p241 CR France511

WILSON,Cornelius William 2Lt ded 25-11-18 A76RFA p37 CR France717

WILSON,Cyril Frederick Lt kia 13-5-15 5DragGds p21 MR29

WILSON,Cyril Spencer.MC.Maj ded 27-10-18 RGA p272 CR Somerset35,RE

WILSON,D.H.DSO.LtCol 3-3-20 GL RTO CR Mddx16

WILSON,David.MC.LtTCapt kia 30-7-16 24RFC p4 CR France300

WILSON,David 2Lt dow 28-12-16 2A&SH p174 CR France105,29-12-16

WILSON,David 2Lt ded 12-7-18 5SLancs att143RAF p230&258 CR Scot774,21-7-17

WILSON,David Oliver 2Lt dow 8-10-16 1/1Lond p245 CR France105

WILSON,David Rex Lt dow 30-10-14 RWSurr p57 CR Greece4 MR29

WILSON,Denis Erskine TMaj dow 24-9-16 7RDubF p177

WILSON,Denis Grey.MC.LtCol mbk 1-7-16 IA 17Cav att1/5N&D p284 MR28,D.D.

WILSON,Douglas Jonathan Rogers T2Lt kia 25-9-15 9WelshR p128 MR19

WILSON,Douglas Russell.MC.2Lt kia 25-10-17 6 att16KRRC p152&259 MR16

WILSON,Edward 2Lt kia 26-3-18 7DLI p162 MR27

WILSON,Edward Henry 2Lt kia 8-10-18 14WelchR p128 CR France1345

WILSON,Edwin 2Lt kia 4-11-18 Yorks att9WRid p91 CR France206

WILSON,Edwin Thomas 2Lt kia 23-3-18 10RWar p66 MR20

WILSON,Eric Crawcour 2Lt kia 28-10-18 2RWKent p142 CR Iraq8

WILSON,Eric Maurice T2Lt kia 1-7-16 17 att10RIrRif p170 MR21

WILSON,Eric Western 2Lt kia 20-9-14 1WYorks p83 MR15

WILSON,Ernest Albert 2Lt kia 6-9-18 3 att1Lpool p73 CR France518

WILSON,Ernest Edwin 2Lt kia 4-11-18 16 att10N&D p135 CR France735

WILSON,Evan Welldon 2Lt kia 23-4-17 4A&SH p174 MR20

WILSON,Evelyn Seppings TCapt kia 29-9-15 EYorks p85 MR19

WILSON,Ewen Holmes Humphries James Lt kia 8-9-14 1BlkW p129 CR France1451

WILSON,F.A Col 21-3-15 IndStaffCps PoliticDept CR Egypt9

WILSON,Frank 2Lt kia 3-6-16 3 att1Lpool p73 CR France924

WILSON,Fred T2Lt kia 15-9-16 9Suff p79 MR21 &CR France390

WILSON,Fred.MC.DCM.2LtTCapt kia 25-10-17 Manch att22Bn p156 MR30

WILSON,Fred 2Lt ded 13-11-18 10RWar p66 CR France13

WILSON,Fred Brookfields T2Lt dow 7-8-17 12Y&L p159 CR France95,Brookfield

WILSON,Frederick Lawrence 2Lt dow 23-11-16 6WRid p227 CR France120

WILSON,Frederick Thomas Austen 2Lt kia 12-3-18 5 att2RFus p71 MR32

WILSON,Frederick William Lt kia 24-3-18 RInniskF p106 MR27,25-3-18

WILSON,Gavin Laurie.DSO.MC.LtCol ded 16-2-19 11A&SH p174 CR France40,1/8Bn

WILSON,Geoffrey Lt ded 15-5-18 RASC 19DivTrain &209RAF p194 MR20

WILSON,Geoffrey Hutton Lt ded 23-12-18 RE p49 MR40

WILSON,Geoffrey Mervyn Underhill LtTCapt kia 26-9-15 3 att2Wilts p153 MR19

WILSON,George Andrew 2LtACapt kia 12-7-17 RGA 262SB p42 CR Belgium10

WILSON,George Andrew Glanville ACapt kia 31-7-17 6RSuss p228 MR29

WILSON,George Douglas Lt dow 13-9-16 2RFA p208 CR France145

WILSON,George Frederick T2Lt kia 1-7-16 21Manch p156 CR France397

WILSON,George Henry.MC.LtAMaj dow 4-11-17 D282RFA p207 CR Belgium36

WILSON,George Reginald Capt kia 10-8-15 4Ches D'Coy p222 MR4

WILSON,Gilbert John 2Lt kia 6-11-17 SussYeo p205 CR Palestine1,16Suss

WILSON,Gordon Chesney.MVO.LtCol kia 6-11-14 RHGds p20 CR Belgium134

WILSON,Gordon Ivor 2Lt kld 12-2-17 YorkDragYeo attRFC p20&205 CR Wilts116

WILSON,Gordon Javot 2Lt kia 12-3-15 NhamptYeo p204 CR France158,Jacob

WILSON,Guy Denis Capt kia 30-11-17 169RFA p207 MR17

WILSON,Hamish Blacklock Bowes Lt kld 18-7-18 GlasgowYeo &RAF p272

WILSON,Harold 2Lt kia 5-9-18 17Lond p250 CR France511

WILSON,Harold Algar 2LtTCapt kia 6-1-16 1KSLI p145 CR Belgium20,6-1-15

WILSON,Harold Benjamin 2Lt kia 7-4-17 18Lond p250 CR Belgium167

WILSON,Harold John Fossick T2Lt ded 17-2-19 LabCps p266 CR Surrey157,KEdwHorse

WILSON,Harry Stuart TMaj&Adjt kia 9-9-16 1RMunstF p176 MR21

WILSON,Henry T2Lt kia 15-9-16 23Mddx p149 MR21

WILSON,Henry A.MC.2Lt kia 9-5-18 A28RFA p37 CR France28

WILSON,Henry Foss 2Lt kia 21-3-18 16MGC p186 CR France212

WILSON,Henry Ivan De Burgh Capt kia 19-4-17 2/4RWKent p234 CR Palestine8

WILSON,Herbert 2Lt kia 8-11-18 6LancF p221 CR France937

WILSON,Herbert Hayden.DSO.TCapt kia 11-4-17 RHGds p20 CR France1182

WILSON,Herbert Lawson 2Lt ded 2-11-18 Mddx att18Bn p149 CR France332

WILSON,Herbert Raymond Capt dow 9-1-17 IA 114Mahrattas att105MahrattaLI p284 CR Iraq5,kia

WILSON,Herbert Stanley Capt dow 13-5-15 RGA A/ABty p42 CR Belgium102

WILSON,Herbert Villers Lt dow 15-12-19 10Hamps p264

WILSON,Humphrey Hamilton T2Lt kia 19-2-18 RFC p17 CR France369

WILSON,Horace Hayman Maj drd 30-12-15 2RLancs p59 MR41

WILSON,Hugh 2Lt kia 17-10-18 3CamH p168 CR France1268

WILSON,Hugh Russell.MC.Capt kia 11-9-16 5DLI C'Coy p238 CR France515

WILSON,Hugh Stanley 2Lt kia 14-9-15 8Worc p226 CR France1327

WILSON,Hugh Young 2LtTLt kia 14-6-17 2GordH p167 MR20

WILSON,Humphrey Worthington LtTCapt kia 4-10-15 Yorks p91 MR19

WILSON,Ian McLean Lt kia 7-8-15 6Yorks p91 MR4

WILSON,James ACapt kia 15-6-18 3 att1GordH p167 CR France33

WILSON,James 2Lt ded 12-7-18 CamH att52GordH p168 CR Essex146,Lt

WILSON,James Bannerman Gartly T2Lt dow 30-4-17 15 att12KRRC p152 CR France85

WILSON,James Boyd Lt kia 18-10-18 2NumbF p63 CR France1392

WILSON,James Ernest Studholme.MC.Capt dow 23-8-17 RAMC att2/1 O&BLI p254 CR Belgium11,24-8-17

WILSON,James Gilmour T2Lt dow 15-2-17 2RScotF p95 MR29

WILSON,James Herbert Gray Capt accdrd 7-12-15 IA 103MahrattaLI p284 MR38

WILSON,James Miller 2Lt kia 25-7-17 RGA 333SB p42 CR Belgium10

WILSON,John 2Lt kia 9-5-15 RE p210 MR22

WILSON,John TLt ded 16-10-15 5A&SH p243 CR Egypt3

WILSON,John TLt kia 9-3-16 RAMC att10WRid p198 CR France924

WILSON,John T2Lt kia 1-7-16 2Mddx p149 MR21

WILSON,John T2Lt kia 1-4-17 15LancF p94 CR France672,Lt

WILSON,John 2Lt kia 23-4-17 3 att9BlkW B'Coy p129 CR France536

WILSON,John 2Lt kia 22-3-18 RGA 120HB p42 MR20

WILSON,John Capt ded 30-12-18 RAMC att78GH p198 CR Palestine2

WILSON,John Alexander 2Lt kia 13-11-16 5GordH p242 CR France1502

WILSON,John Andrew Hackett 2Lt dow 19-9-18 9Ess p133 CR France194

344

WILSON,John Barclay 2Lt kia 15-6-15 6ScotRif p224 MR22

WILSON,John Boyd LtCol kia 28-6-15 7ScotRif p224 CR Gallipoli6

WILSON,John Cooper 2Lt kia 17-10-16 4BlkW attRFC p20&230 MR20

WILSON,John Dawson.MC.Lt ded 13-10-18 IA 38CentIndHorse p284 CR Syria2

WILSON,John Dykes Capt ded 16-2-16 IA IMS p284 CR Scot69

WILSON,John Edward Goodwin 2Lt kia 16-8-17 7RWFus p223 MR30

WILSON,John Furnevall TLt kia 29-9-16 RE 9FC p49 CR France246

WILSON,John Graham.MID Capt kia 1-2-17 IA 45Sikhs p284 MR38

WILSON,John Hardy 2Lt kia 7-4-17 8N&D p233 CR France725

WILSON,John Hutton Bowes LtCol kia 7-6-17 WRid att9Y&L p116

WILSON,John James Lt ded 3-1-19 MillLabCps CR EAfrica

WILSON,John Norman Capt dow 4-7-17 1/6BlkW p231 CR Belgium11

WILSON,John Robert.MID Capt kia 20-10-17 RE att9RFC p20&210 CR Belgium140,22-10-17

WILSON,John Soulsby.MID Lt dow 12-10-17 8SStaffs p123 MR30

WILSON,John Thomson T2Lt kia 28-1-17 SfthH att8Bn p165 CR France392

WILSON,John Victor 2Lt kia 27-4-17 5Ches p222 CR Palestine8

WILSON,John Victor 2Lt kia 17-11-17 7RScots p211 CR Belgium20,Lt

WILSON,John William.MM.2Lt kia 21-3-18 7N&D p233 MR20

WILSON,John Wilson T2Lt kia 27-12-17 15RIrRif p170 CR Palestine9

WILSON,Joseph.MC.TCapt kia 30-11-17 6CamH p168 CR France1182

WILSON,Joseph Alec T2Lt kia 14-11-16 149MGC p186 CR France1896

WILSON,Kenneth Felix Capt kia 2-11-17 1/7Ess p232 CR Palestine8

WILSON,Laurence Cecil 2Lt dow 12-8-15 3Norf p74 CR Norf26

WILSON,Laurence Farrer TCapt kia 23-4-17 16Manch p156 MR20

WILSON,Lawrence Trench T2Lt dow 9-8-15 RGA attRE 171TC p42 CR France922

WILSON,Lewis TCapt&Adjt ded 27-11-16 12 att9Ess p133 CR Lond8

WILSON,Lewis McIver T2Lt dow 27-3-16 11HLI p164 CR France285

WILSON,Lloyd 2Lt kia 24-3-18 15DLI p162 MR27

WILSON,Marshall Meredith Lt kld 29-1-18 4BordR attRFC p20&228 CR Greece1,kia

WILSON,Matthew.MC.Capt ded 12-10-18 11A&SH p174 CR Italy6,3Bn

WILSON,Myrtle Elizabeth SNurse ded 23-12-15 QAIMNS p200 CR France64

WILSON,Michael Connal 2Lt kia 20-7-16 8 att5ScotRif C'Coy p225 MR21

WILSON,Neville Inchbold.MC.Lt kia 6-4-18 3 att4RWFus p99 MR27

WILSON,Norman Lt kia 14-7-16 7WYorks p218 CR France702

WILSON,Oswald 2Lt kia 19-3-17 5NStaffs p238 CR France149

WILSON,Philip John Conning Lt kia 9-5-15 CamH att1Bn p168 MR22

WILSON,Philip Stanley 2Lt kia 20-8-16 3 att2RWFus p99 CR France453

WILSON,Ralph Aylmer.MC.2Lt kia 9-4-18 4DLI p162&259 MR32

WILSON,Ralph Edwyn Lt dow 28-9-15 2RScots p55 CR France40

WILSON,Raymond Ernest 2Lt kia 10-3-17 3 att7RWSurr p57 MR29,10-8-17

WILSON,Richard Nelson 2Lt kia 23-8-18 13Lond p249 CR France174,24-8-18

WILSON,Robert 2Lt kia 3-7-16 RBerks p140 MR21

WILSON,Robert.MM.T2Lt kia 30-6-17 9Y&L p159 CR Belgium127 Ex 12Bn

WILSON,Robert Capt ded 12-4-18 GL att6DLI p192&254 MR19 &CR Scot632,RScots

WILSON,Robert Alexander T2Lt kld 2-5-17 19DLI p162 MR21

WILSON,Robert Archibald Scarlyn 2Lt kia 12-10-16 3 att7SfthH p165 MR21

WILSON,Robert Armstrong TCapt kia 18-10-15 D74RFA p37 CR France423

WILSON,Robert Forsyth 2Lt kia 13-11-16 6GordH p142 CR France131

WILSON,Robert Gerald Aldin 2Lt kia 13-3-17 1CldGds p51 CR France786

WILSON,Robert Hamilton Birch Capt kia 1-3-20 IA 2/9GurkhaRif p284 MR43

WILSON,Robert Henry TCapt dow 15-5-17 RAMC att84RFA p198 CR France40

WILSON,Robert Meredith Lt kia 10-8-15 6LNLancs p137 MR4

WILSON,Robert Philip 2Lt kia 7-8-15 6FYorks p85 MR4

WILSON,Robert Sym Capt kia 8-11-14 SfthH p165 MR22

WILSON,Robert Victor Lt dow 13-4-18 1/2 att2/7RWar p66 CR France88,2Lt

WILSON,Ronald Edward 2Lt kia 11-3-16 IA BombayVolRif p284 CR EAfrica56,13-3-16 VolMGC

WILSON,Spence Ross T2Lt dow 13-10-16 13A&SH p174 CR France177

WILSON,Stanley Wright 2Lt kia 18-11-16 11BordR p118 MR21 Ex 8Bn

WILSON,Strawson Lieveslay TLt dow 21-7-16 15N&D D'Coy p135 CR FRance66

WILSON,Sydney Cunningham Maj ded 9-11-18 2RFA p207 CR Scot381

WILSON,Theodore Percival Cameron Lt kia 24-3-18 GL &10N&D p192 MR20,Capt

WILSON,Thomas.MC.TLt kia 29-6-17 RE p49 CR EAfrica38 &CR Tanzania1

WILSON,Thomas 2Lt kia 29-8-18 3 att2/4LNLancs p137 CR France568

WILSON,Thomas Douglas 2Lt kia 23-4-17 7A&SH p243 CR France546

WILSON,Thomas Irving Ward.MC.TCapt kia 28-11-16 21Manch p156 CR France339

WILSON,Thomas James 2Lt kia 21-3-18 295RFA p37 MR20

WILSON,Thomas Lewis 2Lt dow 27-9-18 10Manch B'Coyp156 CR France712

WILSON,Thomas Percy T2Lt kia 28-9-16 7Beds p87 CR France383

WILSON,Thomas Reginald 2Lt kia 20-11-17 E'TankCps p189 CR France711

WILSON,Thomas Wilson Lt kia 5-5-15 6Lpool C'Coy p215 MR29

WILSON,Tom Benholt 2Lt kia 18-7-17 2IrGds p53 CR Belgium12,Bonhote

WILSON,Tristram William Jourdain T2Lt kia 24-11-17 11RWar p66 CR Belgium111,Jordan

WILSON,Victor John Frackleton Lt kia 17-10-18 3 att6RInniskF p106 CR France190,2Lt

WILSON,Walton Ronald TLt dow 12-7-16 RAMC att2SfthH p198 CR France5

WILSON,Wilfred Charles 2Lt kia 9-8-16 1/5SLancs p230 MR21

WILSON,Wilfrid Gordon.MBE.TCapt ded 10-12-18 GL attRE p49&p192 CR EAfrica36

WILSON,William 2Lt dow 12-4-18 18DLI p162 MR32

WILSON,William ACapt ded 4-2-19 1ScotGds p255 CRMddx16

WILSON,William Alderice TLt ded 6-4-19 GL RIrRif att1/7KAR p202 CR EAfrica52

WILSON,William Andrew Rev ded 20-3-18 YMCA CR France85

WILSON,William Arnold T2Lt kia 22-10-17 Manch att23Bn p156 MR30

WILSON,William Charles Davidson Capt kia 18-9-18 RAMC att9SLancs p254 MR37

WILSON,William Clement T2LtTLt kia 25-9-15 1Worc p110 MR32

WILSON,William George 2Lt ded 3-5-18 RASC 17Div MT p194 CR France84,Lt 8-5-18

WILSON,William Graham T2Lt dow 24-8-17 14A&SH p174 CR France398

WILSON,William Harrison 2Lt kia 21-3-18 15DLI p162 CR France439

WILSON,William James 2Lt kia 24-4-17 10Dev p77 MR37

WILSON,William James 2Lt kia 28-3-18 3MGC p186 MR20

WILSON,William John Maj dow 20-6-18 5RFA p207 CR France102

WILSON,William Keates Harrison TCapt ded 12-4-16 Dev 1GarBn p77 CR Egypt9

WILSON,William Scott Banks Capt kia 19-9-18 6ScotRif p224 CR France686,Branks

WILSON-BARKWORTH,Kenneth Arthur.MC.Capt kia 25-10-17 4EYorks p219 MR30

WILSON-BROWNE,Rowland Murray 2Lt ded PoW 21-7-16 RFC p4 CR France543,kldFlying

WILSON ROBERTS,Thomas 2Lt 1-9-16 1Ches Ex 6Lpool CR France329

WILSON-WALKER,Alan Alexander Lt kld 20-3-16 13RFC p4 CR Kent7,2Lt

WILTON,Charles Innes 2Lt kia 21-10-16 3 att2SWBord p101 CR France307

WILTON,Ernest Parkin TLt ded 5-11-18 RFC &RASC p194 CR Yorks643

WILTON,Harold Capt ded 27-11-14 2RFA p272 MR66,28-11-14

WILTON,Richard Birkenhead 2Lt kia 1-10-17 15 att9Yorks p91 MR30,Birkinhead

WILTON,Samuel Brammer.MC.Capt kia 14-3-17 1/5NStaffs C'Coy p237 CR France800

WILTON,Thomas LtCol ded 26-6-16 12Lond Res p272 CR Mddx29

WILTSHIRE,Charles Robert 2Lt dow 13-7-16 BedsYeo p203 CR France176

WILTSHIRE,Healey James Armstrong 2Lt kia 19-4-17 1/7Ess p232 CR Palestine8

WILTSHIRE,Percy Maj dow 25-4-17 1RFA p207 CR France53,kia

WILTSHIRE,William George Earl 2Lt kia 31-3-18 3Wilts p153 CR France1211

WINBUSH,Edward Thomas 2Lt kia 24-9-17 RFA 33DAC p37 CR Belgium15

WINCH,Edmond Arthur 2Lt kia 19-10-15 4 att2WYorks p83 CR France525

WINCH,Edward Hadfield Lt kia 25-3-18 12HLI p164 MR27

WINCH,Edward Maurice 2Lt dow 25-3-15 6RB p181 CR France1,3Bn

WINCH,Edward Nightingale 2Lt dow 9-10-18 8RWKent p142 CR France912

WINCH,Gordon Bluett.DSO.MID Maj dow 10-4-18 A285RFA p207 CR France1094

WINCH,Harry Wilson 2Lt kia 2-4-17 ACycCps 2LondCycCoy att2Manch p244 CR France672

WINCH,Ronald Bluett 2Lt ded 16-4-15 10EKent p272 CR Kent235,18-4-15

WINCH,William Haffenden 2Lt dow 13-1-16 1/5EKent A'Coy p213 CR Iraq6

WINCHESTER,W.H.Capt 2-3-20 RE CR France65

WINCHESTER,William Charles Connor TLtACapt kia 21-10-16 10 att2SLancs p126 CR France384

WINCKLEY,Charles Reginald T2Lt kia 20-7-16 15N&D p135 MR21

WINDELER,Charles Francis Lt kia 10-5-15 4RWar p66 MR29

WINDELER,Herbert Wheelwright Lt kia 28-11-17 4GrenGds p50 MR17,27-11-17

WINDER,Harold 2Lt kia 15-5-17 10ELancs p111 CR France1191

WINDHAM-WRIGHT,John.OBE.Maj ded 14-2-19 5 att11RWSurr p212 CR Germany1

WINDLE,Michael William Maxwell TLt kia 25-9-15 8Dev p77 MR19

WINDRIDGE,E.A.Lt kiaAbout 9-6-18 9NStaffs p158

WINDSOR,Alfred Cooper Lt ded 15-7-15 8Ess attEAngCycCo p272 CR Lond10

WINDSOR,Harold George 2Lt kia 8-10-18 7RWFus p223 CR France1346

WINDSOR,Leslie St.Lawrence T2Lt kia 11-6-15 2Suff p79 MR29,10-6-15

WINDSOR,Mark Gilham 2Lt dow 10-3-15 2Dev p77 CR France1106

WINDSOR-CLIVE,Archer.Hon.Lt kia 25-8-14 3CldGds p51 CR France932

WINDUS,Charles Eric 2Lt kia 9-5-15 1RIrRif p170 MR32

WINES,Walter Wheeler T2Lt kia 24-8-17 8RB p181 MR30

WINFIELD,Frank 2Lt dow PoW 31-5-15 5NumbF p213 CR Belgium383,Lt 31-1-15

WING,Frederick Drummond Vincent.CB.MajGen kia 2-10-15 RA Staff 12Div p1 CR France178

WING,Vincent Sladen 2Lt kia 10-8-17 65/28RFA p37 CR France354

WINGARD,Hume Saunders T2Lt dow 20-9-16 7 att12SWBord p101 CR France178,Sanders Lt 26-9-16

WINGATE,Alexander 2Lt kia 13-10-15 9HLI p241 CR France114

WINGATE,Alfred Douglas Lt kia 16-5-15 ULIA att2RInniskF p264&284,2Lt MR22,15/16-5-15

WINGATE,Malcolm Roy.DSO.MC.CaptBtMaj kia 21-3-18 RE 459FC p49 MR20

WINGATE,Thomas Paterson Capt kia 18-4-15 1KOSB p102 MR29,2Bn

WINGFIELD,Cecil John Talbot Rhys Capt dow 29-4-15 4KRRC p152 CR Glouc138

WINGFIELD,Glanville Harry 2Lt kia 12-7-16 18KRRC p152 CR Belgium54,Granville 5Bn

WINGFIELD,Richard James Trench.MID T2Lt kld 27-4-16 28/9RFA p37 CR Iraq5

WINGROVE,George Frederick 2Lt kia 15-7-16 22Manch p156 MR21,13-7-16

WINGWORTH,Charles Henry Cecil T2Lt kia 25-9-16 10YLI p144 MR21,WINKWORTH

WINK,John Edward T2Lt ded 21-9-16 8SfthH p165 CR France145

WINKLEY,Charles.MC.TCapt kia 30-11-17 235MGC p186 MR17

WINKLEY,Sydney Joseph 2Lt kia 1-7-16 1/6RWar p214 MR21

WINKWORTH,Edwin John 2Lt dow 6-12-17 RGA 219SB p42 CR France518

WINKWORTH,Henry Edward Vernon T2Lt dow 18-2-17 6Nhampt p128 CR France177

WINKWORTH,Kenneth John T2Lt kia 12-8-17 8Suff p79 MR29

WINKWORTH,Walter 2Lt dow 26-8-15 5NumbF p213 CR France285

WINMILL,Thomas George Peyton Capt kia 11-6-18 U16RHA p37 CR France115

WINMILL,Westropp Orbell Peyton Lt kia 22-3-18 1Beds p87 MR27,23-3-18

WINN,Arthur Capt kia 9-9-14 3Suff p79 CR France1113,2Bn

WINN,John 2Lt kia 23-3-18 12Y&L p159 MR20,Yorks att7Y&L

WINNICOTT,Russell.MC.2Lt kia 6-12-17 5Dev att41RFC p20&217 CR France41,Lt

WINNINGTON,Charles 2Lt kia 14-10-18 Ches att1/7Bn p97 MR30

WINNINGTON,John Francis Sartorius.DSO.LtCol dow 22-9-18 1Worc Cmdg 1/4Nhampt p110 CR Palestine9

WINSER,Arthur Cecil.MID TLt dow 22-2-16 8ELancs p111 CR France62

WINSER,Basil Charles TCapt kia 15-2-16 10LancF p94 CR Belgium131

WINSER,Frank Edward 2Lt kia 20-8-17 GL &43RFC p15 MR20

WINSER,Frederick Herbert T2Lt kia 7-10-16 11WYorks D'Coy p83 CR France239

WINSER,Percy Ralph 2Lt kia 23-4-17 149RFA p37 CR France1186

WINSLOW,Benjamin Harmer 2Lt kia 30-11-17 1/6Lond p247 MR17

WINSPEAR,Arthur 2Lt kia 5-11-14 2ConnRgrs p172 MR29

WINSTANCE,William Allsop,DSO.MC LtCol kia 25-4-18 5SStaffs p229 MR30

WINSTANLEY,Bernard Joseph Lt ded 9-9-19 IARO att3S&M p284 MR43,10-9-19

WINSTANLEY,George Clement T2Lt kia 2-7-16 1SomLI p80 MR21

WINSTANLEY,Newnham Leibman Lt kia 13/15-11-16 4 att2SStaffs p123 CR France742

WINSTANLEY,Oswald Coke 2Lt kia 10-8-15 5WelshR p256 MR4

WINTER,James T2Lt kia 28-2-18 70RFC p17 CR Belgium3

WINTER,Laurence Amos Capt ded 15-11-18 RAMC 20GH p198 CR France40

WINTER,R.R.C.2Lt kld 9-8-18 DLI &54RAF p162 CR France526

WINTER,Robert Harold T2Lt dow 17-12-15 10 att7SStaffs p123 MR4

WINTER,Samuel Douglas 2Lt ded 21-11-18 11 att1/4Lond p248 CR France788

WINTER,Thomas Barron 2Lt kia 22-4-18 13RWFus p99 CR France516

WINTER,Wilfred Ormond,DSO CaptAMaj ded 30-11-18 RE p49 CR France1277

WINTERBOTHAM,Cyril William Lt kia 27-8-16 1/5Glouc p225 MR21

WINTERBOTTOM,Charles Percy 2Lt kia 2-8-17 3 att2SLancs C'Coy p126 CR Belgium112

WINTERBOTTOM,Cyril 2Lt kia 14-4-18 8RWar p215 MR32

WINTERBOTTOM,Dudley Dickson Capt kia 7-8-15 5Manch p236 MR4

WINTERBOTTOM,Guy Maj kia 9-8-17 DerbyYeo p203 CR Greece3

WINTERBOURNE,Frank Thomas Capt drd 10-10-18 2Lond p245 CR Ireland14

WINTERSGILL,Gerald Walker.MID Lt ded 26-11-18 RE attATS p49 CR Greece9

WINTERTON,William 2Lt kia 27-9-15 3 att11RScots p55 MR19

WINTHROP-SMITH,Bernard Lt ded 15-11-14 1ScotsGds CR Derby42

WINTLE,Armar Lowry-Corry.MC.Lt dow 22-8-17 9RInniskF p106 CR France64

WINTLE,Ernest de Vaynes LtCol kia 7-2-16 IA 12Cav p284 MR38

WINTLE,Fitzhardinge LtCol 23-3-16 87Punjabis MR65

WINTON,Ernest Walter 2Lt kia 15-12-17 RGA 2SB p42 CR Belgium13

WINTON,Harry George Denys Lt kia 3-5-15 Suff p79 CR Belgium74

WINTON,Harold Barkley 2Lt kld 21-4-18 GL &1RAF p192 CR France134,Lt dedacc

WINTON,John Hubert T2Lt kia 7-7-16 9NumbF p63 CR France393

WINTOUR,Reginald Prince Lt ded 15-12-16 SL RE RTO p201 CR Notts39

WINWOOD,Thomas Ralph Okeden.MC.TLtACapt dow 28-4-17 B199RHFA p37 CR Greece6,B99

WIPF,John Jacob 2Lt kia 8-10-18 3Lincs p76 CR France611,1Bn

WIRKHAM,Nigel John Latham TCapt kia 19-4-16 6ConnRgrs p172

WISE,Arnold Vincent Denys.MC.LtACapt kia 15-5-17 RE 2FC p49 CR France446

WISE,Colin Walter T2Lt kia 31-7-17 74RFA A'Bty p37 CR Belgium12

WISE,Francis Harry Varney TLt kld 13-1-18 RFC p17 CR Mddx77

WISE,Frederick Mortimer T2Lt kia 5-9-16 13Y&L p159 CR France631

WISE,George Edward Foster Lt kia 4-6-16 2/7RWar p214 CR France114

WISE,Henry Lupton Lt drd 30-12-17 6Dev p217 MR41

WISE,Lancelot Charles Lt ded 2-5-17 NIrHorse att3Lancers p24 MR43 &CR Pakistan50A

WISELEY,Francis Joseph TLt dow 14-9-15 RAMC p198 CR Egypt6

WISELY,Alfred Douglas 2Lt kia 12-9-16 4GordH p242 CR France922

WISEMAN,Phillip Henry Franklin Lt dow 27-10-17 2/4LNLancs p234 CR Belgium25

WISEMAN,Stanley 2Lt kia 10-3-17 4Ess p232 CR France624

WISEMAN,Vincent Harvey 2Lt kia 9-4-17 4YLI p235 CR France1186

WISEMAN,Willingham Franklin Gell Capt kia 1-7-16 2Lincs p76 MR21

WISEMAN-CLARKE,Charles Francis Ralph Lt kia 20-2-16 108RGA p42 CR Belgium135

WISHART,Edward George 2Lt dow 21-4-18 1/5GordH p242 CR France31,Lt

WISHART,William Ferguson 2Lt dow 17-6-15 6ScotRif p224 CR France201,Fergusson

WISHART,William Frederick 2Lt kia 15-6-18 4 att1GordH p242 CR France33

WISKAR,Joseph William Capt dow 7-3-17 6Lond p246 CR Lond14,6-3-17

WISSETT,John Noel 2Lt kia 4-6-18 4LNLancs p234 CR France204

WISSMAN,John Rudolph Lt kia 15-9-14 22/34RFA p37 CR France1329

WITCOMBE,Henry James 2Lt kia 23-8-18 Ess att1Bn p133 CR France281

WITHALL,John 2Lt kia 7-10-16 6 att8RFus p71 MR21

WITHEROW,Alexander Hunter T2Lt dow 3-7-16 17RIrRif p170 CR France74

WITHEROW,John Thomas T2Lt dow 5-8-17 9RIrRif p170 CR Belgium7

WITHERS,Charles Garnet T2Lt kia 3-7-16 9 att2SLancs p126 CR France215,10-7-16

WITHERS,Frank Dean T2Lt kia 1-7-16 8SomLI p80 MR21

WITHERS,Victor William T2Lt dow 6-7-16 MGC p186 CR France558

WITHERSPOON,John Clarence Lt kia 11-10-17 13DLI p162 MR30

WITHEY,Charles Elisha Capt kia 20-9-17 4RLancs p213 MR30

WITHEY,Ralph Wallace Lt ded 2-1-18 GordH p167 CR Iraq6

WITHY,Basil TLt dow 2-7-16 18Lpool p73 CR France66

WITT,Cecil Frederick T2Lt kia 28-2-18 KRRC &RFC p17&152 CRFrance327

WITT,Charles 2Lt kia 22-9-18 5N&D attMGC Inf p188&233 CR France836,46MGC att5N&D

WITT,Leonard Stanley 2Lt dow 2-5-17 A104RFA p37 CR Belgium11

WITTER,Harold 2Lt kia 26-4-18 13TankCps p189 MR30

WITTKUGEL,Adolf Frederick Capt dow 15-2-17 SL &SPersiaRif p284,T2Lt CR Asia82

WITTY,James Hannay 2Lt kia 15-4-17 3 att1Dors p124 CR France1701

WIX,Geoffrey Arthur Gibson Lt kia 12-10-17 3ESurr attRBerks p113 MR30

WIXCEY,Herbert Frank 2Lt kia 7-8-18 4RSuss p228 CR France247

WODEHOUSE,Arthur Powys Capt kia 22-11-15 IA PoliticDept att110MahrattaLI p284 MR38

WODEHOUSE,Edward.Hon.MC.2Lt kia 30-3-18 16Lancers p23 MR27

WODEHOUSE,Ernest Charles Forbes.DSO.LtCol kia 10/13-3-15 Worc p110 MR22,12-3-15

WODEHOUSE,Evelyn Charles Bradley T2LtTLt kia 4-10-17 1 att10Beds p87 CR Palestine8

WODEHOUSE,Francis John Ashburnham 2Lt kia 26-8-17 3DCLI att9RFC p15&115 CR Belgium18

WODEHOUSE,Philip.Hon.Lt ded 6-5-19 GL p192 CR Norfl18

WOLF,Percy Lt kia 4-6-15 4ELancs p226 MR4

WOLFE,Bernard.MID TLt ded 20-7-18 38RFus p71 CR Palestine3,WOLFFE

WOLFE,Bertram 2Lt dow 12-7-18 5LNLancs p234 CR Ches158

WOLFE,George Capt kia 2-6-15 10RScots p212 MR29

WOLFE,Sidney George TLt kia 22-10-17 18LancF p94 MR30

346

WOLFE-MURRAY,A.A.CB.LtCol ded 7-12-18 HLI Staff p164 CR Scot668,BrigGen

WOLFENDEN,John Hutton Bowes LtCol kia 7-6-17 WRid att9Y&L p116

WOLFENDEN,Laurence 2Lt kia 24-10-18 2WRid p116CR France1260,Lawrence

WOLFERSTAN,Stanley 2Lt kia 3-4-17 1Dors p124 CR France1701

WOLFF,Gustav Frederick.MID ACapt kia 21-3-18 3RWFus attMGC p99&186 CR France381,Maj

WOLFF,John Alfred LtCol kia 23-10-18 RFA 4HB att14RHA p206 CR France206

WOLLASTON,Frederick Hargreaves Arbuthnot.DSO.MajALtCol kld 8-3-18 4RB Cmdg1/5Suff p181 CR Leic87

WOLLASTON,Keith Roland Lt kia 10-10-18 20Manch CR France611

WOLLEN,Douglas Charles 2Lt kia 13-4-17 GL &25RFC p15 CR France1321

WOLLET-DODD,Frederic Hora 2Lt ded 24-7-19 1YLI p265 CR Asia52,WOLLEY Hova

WOLLEY-DOD,Douglas Kirk TLt kia 25-9-15 12Lpool p73 CR France525

WOLLOCOMBE,Francis T2Lt dow 10-9-16 9Dev p77 CR France66

WOLSELEY,William Bertie TLt dow 5-7-16 160RFA p37 CR France833

WOLSELEY,William Joseph 2Lt kia 11-3-15 2ELancs p111 CR France706,12-3-15

WOLSELEY-JENKINS,Charles Wolseley.MID Capt kia 25-9-15 2RB p181 MR32

WOLSTENCROFT,William Herbert Beau 2Lt kia 12-4-18 1RScotF p95 MR32,Bean

WOLSTENHOLME,Charles Skaife TCapt kia 17-7-16 12DLI p162 MR21

WOLSTENHOLME,George Mellor.MC.Lt kia 5-10-18 9Yorks p91 CR France341

WOLSTENHOLME,Richard Francis TCapt kia 28-11-16 15Ches p97 CR France1182

WOLTHERSPOON,James 2Lt kia 2-10-18 RScots att5/6Bn p55 CR France375

WOLTON,Owen Biddell 2Lt kia 12-8-15 5Suff p217 MR4

WOMAR,Frederick 2Lt kia 22-10-17 3Glouc p107 MR30

WOMERSLEY,David Norman TLt ded 1-2-17 11MGC p186 CR France13

WOMERSLEY,John William Lt kia 4-6-15 8Manch p237 CR Gallipoli2

WOMERSLEY,Sinclair Patterson 2Lt kia 15-4-18 59MGC Inf p186 MR32,Patteson

WONNACOTT,Thomas Henry 2Lt kia 9-5-17 3Dev p77 MR20

WOOD,Alan Salisbury.MID Lt dow 29-3-18 1/7 att2/9Manch p156 CR France169

WOOD,Alexander Maj dow 12-4-17 3RSuss p120 CR France1182

WOOD,Alfred Godfrey 2Lt kia 11-12-17 1/4Norf p216 CR Palestine9

WOOD,Alfred Lee TCapt kia 1-7-16 15LancF p94

WOOD,Algernon George Newcome.DSO.Maj kia 30-10-15 1Ess p133 CR Gallipoli4

WOOD,Almeric Watkins 2Lt dow 26-9-15 3 att5 O&BLI p130 CR Belgium5

WOOD,Archibald 2Lt kia 29-9-18 att5YLI p144 MR16

WOOD,Basil Vaughan 2Lt kia 3-7-16 6RWKent p142 MR21

WOOD,Brian Robert Philip 2Lt kldacc 2-7-15 7Lond p247 CR France222

WOOD,Bryce 2Lt dow 10-5-18 4 att1GordH p242 CR France10

WOOD,Cecil Gordon TLt dow 20-9-15 6ELancs p111 CR Europe1,Cyril 19-9-15

WOOD,Cecil Strachan Capt dow 3-12-14 3EYorks p85 CR France85,2-12-14

WOOD,Charles Edmund.MID Capt&Adjt kia 11-3-15 1RWFus p99 CR France1158

WOOD,Charles Harold 2Lt dow 25-8-16 8SWBord att8KRRC p101 CR France177,Harald

WOOD,Charles Pascoe 2Lt dow 18-4-18 4EYorks att7N&D p219 CR Belgium38,kia

WOOD,C.K.Lt ded 3-10-18 RASC p267 MR40,drd 3-8-18

WOOD,Claude Ernest TCapt kia 14-9-16 8WRid p116 MR21

WOOD,Clement Percy 2Lt kia 21-11-17 2ELancs p111 MR30

WOOD,Colin Richard Capt kia 18-1-15 5Mddx attGlouc p149 MR22

WOOD,Collingwood Lindsay Capt kia 24-5-15 18Huss A attB'Sqn p23 CR Belgium113

WOOD,Creighton Arthur Bell Lt kia 28-6-15 1Ess p133 MR4

WOOD,David Cardale 2Lt kia 23-7-16 8Glouc p107 MR21

WOOD,Donald TLtCol kia 1-7-16 1RB p101 MR21

WOOD,Donald Theodore.MC&Bar.2Lt dow 25-8-18 77RFA p37 CR France141

WOOD,Edwin Leonard 2Lt kia 26-9-17 1RScotF C'Coy p95 MR30

WOOD,Eric Arthur Walton T2Lt kia 25-2-16 9WRid p116 CR Belgium131

WOOD,Eric Horace 2Lt kia 23-10-16 1Hamps p121 MR21

WOOD,Ernest James Vivian 2Lt dow 9-11-18 36RFA p37 CR France332

WOOD,Ernest Richard Gardner Lt ded 20-7-18 1NStaffs p265 CR France161

WOOD,Frank 2Lt dow 23-10-17 8N&D att86MGC p188&233 CR France134

WOOD,Frank 2Lt kia 30-9-18 1LancF p94 MR30

WOOD,Geoffrey 2Lt kia 6-5-17 GL &2RFC p15 MR20

WOOD,Geoffrey Dayrell TLt kia 13-10-15 7Suff p79 MR19

WOOD,Geoffrey Kershaw Pemberton 2Lt kia 31-10-18 1LancF p94 CR Belgium140,1/2 att18Bn

WOOD,Harold William Chap4Cl ded 1-11-18 RAChDept attRGA 282SB p200 CR France34

WOOD,Harry Gordon,2LtTLt dow 9-6-17 11WYorks p83 CR Belgium127,7-6-17

WOOD,Harry Douty 2Lt kia 1-7-16 2Mddx p149 MR21

WOOD,Hector Frederick.MC.Capt kia 20-9-17 32RFus p71 MR30

WOOD,Henry T2Lt dow 2-1-16 19RFus p71 CR France80

WOOD,Henry George Capt kia 25-9-15 att1LNLancs D'Coyp137 CR France1723

WOOD,Henry George Westmorland.DSO.Capt kia 3-8-18 1/7Worc p225 CR Italy2

WOOD,Henry Percy 2Lt kia 22-3-18 21MGC p186 MR27

WOOD,Henry Stewart.MC.Lt kia 11-8-18 3Dors p125&259 CR France360

WOOD,Herbert Lt kia 1-9-18 20Lond p251 MR16

WOOD,Herbert Bertram TCapt ded 29-1-18 GL &RFA attPoW Coy p267 CR France8,Henry

WOOD,Herbert Frederick Maj ded 11-12-18 9Lancers &RAF p22

WOOD,Horace Lt dow 24-8-18 RASC p253 CR France141,2/10Lond

WOOD,Hubert Kenneth TLt ded 16-5-17 2/2KAR p202 CR EAfrica39

WOOD,James 2Lt kia 5-8-17 1Wilts p153 MR29

WOOD,James 2Lt dow 11-8-18 10Ess p133 CR France119

WOOD,James Capt ded 14-9-18 SL RAMC p201 CR Greece6

WOOD,James Alexander Scott 2Lt kia 12-6-17 1/6WYorks att146TMB p218 CR France1887

WOOD,James Buckley Capt kia 26-3-18 10LancF p94 CR France526

WOOD,James Patrick.MC.2Lt ded 30-3-16 IARO att119Inf p284 CR Iraq1,2/198Inf

WOOD,John T2Lt kia 13-11-16 13EYorks p85 CR France802

WOOD,John 2Lt kia 13-11-17 4KOSB p224 CR Palestine9

WOOD,John George.MC.LtACapt kia 4-10-17 3SfthH p165 MR30

WOOD,John Gervaise 2Lt kia 3-10-16 3Nhampt att149MGC Inf p138 CR France385,Gervase

WOOD,John Goldsmith 2Lt kia 8-12-16 5SLancs p230 MR21

WOOD,John Lockhart.DSO.Capt dow 11-6-15 RoO 18Huss p23

WOOD,John Patrick Hamilton TLtACapt kia 11-1-17 22Manch p156 CR France533

WOOD,John Sendal 2Lt kia 7-2-16 IARO att44MerwaraLI p284 MR38

WOOD,John William Massey.MVO.LtCol ded 9-12-16 Remount Sv SL RecStaff p24&268 CR Lond8 Ex 1DragGds

WOOD,Joseph 2Lt kia 27-9-17 6N&D p233 MR30

WOOD,Joseph Clark T2Lt kld 13-1-18 RFC p17 CR Hamps31

WOOD,Keith Eric.MID Lt dow 27-5-15 23Lond p252 CR France80

WOOD,Leslie John 2Lt kia 4-10-17 14RWar p66 MR30

WOOD,Leslie William 2Lt kia 19-7-16 SLancs att2/7RWar p126 MR19

WOOD,Lewis Ironside.CMG.LtCol kia 16-5-15 Cmdg2BordR p118 CR France727

WOOD,Llewellyn George Capt ded 22-11-18 CityLondYeo att103MGC Inf p188&204 CR France1277

WOOD,Matthew Rodney.MC.TCapt kia 22-10-17 18LancF p94 MR30

WOOD,Maurice Herbert Lt kia 13-4-17 4Lincs attRFC p20&217 MR20

WOOD,Maxmilian,David Francis.DSO.Maj dow 22-8-15 9WYorks p83 MR4,LtCol 21-8-15

WOOD,Noel Ernest 2Lt kia 27-9-15 3EKent p58 MR19

WOOD,Norman Clark.MC.Lt kia 2-9-18 17TankCps p189 CR France46

WOOD,Oswald Ireland Lt kia 3-10-15 1Suff p79 MR19

WOOD,Paul Barnard Lt kia 23-4-17 5 att7RFus p71 MR20

WOOD,Peter Norris T2Lt dow 19-1-17 10RLancs p59 CR Iraq5

WOOD,Philip Capt dow PoW 5-4-16 IA 89Punjabis p284 CR Iraq8

WOOD,Philip John 2Lt kia 25-5-17 4RWSurr attRFC p20&212 CR France62,dedacc

WOOD,Philip Lovel 2Lt kia 4-3-17 43RFC p15 MR20

WOOD,Ralph Lt ded 17-10-18 7WRid &RAF p256

WOOD,Ralph Miles T2Lt dow 9-11-16 9WRid p116 CR France105

WOOD,Reginald Ewart 2Lt dow 3-8-18 EKent p58 CR France209

WOOD,Reginald Harry 2Lt kia 1-4-16 1/5NStaffs p238 CR France68,2-4-16

WOOD,Reginald Nixon T2Lt kia 22-2-16 9RIrF p172 CR France701

WOOD,Richard Poingdestre.MC.CaptALtCol kia 9-10-16 2Y&L p159 MR21

WOOD,Richard Shaw T2Lt kld 17-3-18 RFC p17 CR Hamps31

WOOD,Richard Thomas 2Lt kia 25-4-18 9MGC Inf p186 MR30

WOOD,Robert Basil T2Lt kia 12-10-16 6 att2BordR p118 CR Belgium137

WOOD,Robert Howard TLt ded 27-2-19 RAOC p268 CR B84 ?

WOOD,Robert Smith T2Lt dow 24-11-17 2RScots p55 MR20 &CR France512

WOOD,Ronald Beaumont.MID CaptALtCol kia 21-8-18 12Lancers att6Tanks p22&189 CR France745

WOOD,Rowland Henry T2Lt ded 4-7-17 3Mddx p149 CR Greece7

WOOD,Russell Elliott LtCol ded 8-2-17 RAMC p256 CR Scot253

WOOD,Samuel Herbert 2Lt kia 26-10-17 5RLancs p213 MR30

WOOD,S.G.Lt 3-2-18 IA IMD MR43 &CR Pakistan50A

WOOD,Theodore Herbert Henry 2Lt kia 13-4-15 3Dors p125 CR Belgium59,1Bn

WOOD,Thomas Anthony Capt ded 16-7-18 9KRRC p152

WOOD,Thomas Basil 2Lt kia 13-10-15 4Lincs p217 MR19

WOOD,Thomas Leonard 2Lt dow 26-6-17 16Ches p97 CR France145

WOOD,Thomas Percival Lt kia 25-9-15 IARO att2/3GurkhaRif p284 MR28

WOOD,Thomas Theodore T2Lt dow 14-7-16 9Yorks p91 CR Ches4

WOOD,Thomas Victor T2Lt kia 4-8-16 7RSuss p120 MR21

WOOD,Tom 2Lt ded 17-7-17 RFA attRAOC p37 CR Iraq6,RAVC

WOOD,W.2Lt kia 8-5-15 RB p181

WOOD,Walter Bertram.MC&Bar.Lt kld 11-11-17 2/8Hamps &29 att44RFC p20&229 CR Lincs156

WOOD,Wilfred John TLt kia 1-7-16 6Mddx p149 CR France267

WOOD,Wilfred Thomas 2Lt kia 9-8-17 3 att2WRid p116 MR20

WOOD,William 2Lt 8-5-15 4RB MR29

WOOD,William Allan 2Lt kia 1-10-18 1Dors p125 CR France699

WOOD,William Anthony 2Lt kia 6-11-17 SuffYeo B'Coy p205 CR Palestine1,15Suff

WOOD,William Bertram.MC.2LtACapt kia 25-8-17 2Wilts p153 CR Belgium17

WOOD,William Bryan 2Lt kia 23-7-16 8Glouc p107 MR21

WOOD,William Edmond 2Lt dow 26-4-18 12Lond p248 CR France40

WOOD,William John T2Lt kia 7-11-15 Mddx att16Lond p149 CR Belgium44

WOOD,William Leslie 2LtACapt kia 7-5-17 15RWFus p99 CR Belgium73

WOOD,Williams TCapt kia 31-5-16 8RWKent p142 CR Belgium97

WOOD,Wilfred 2LtTCapt ded 15-3-19 RGA 120SB p262 CR Derby66

WOOD-MARTIN,Francis Winchester Capt kia 17-2-15 1Suff p79 MR29

WOOD-MARTIN,James Isidore Capt kia 12-3-15 2Nhampt p138 MR22

WOODALL,John F.MC.2LtTLt kia 8-11-17 157MGC p186 CR Palestine8

WOODBRIDGE,Austin Hale.MC.Capt ded 28-2-19 8Mddx p236 CR France806

WOODBRIDGE,Stanley George.MC.Capt dow 19-12-18 13NumbF p63 CR Mddx18

WOODBRIDGE,Stephen Antony Ruston T2Lt dow 15-9-16 10RWar p66 CR Mddx48

WOODBURN,Cecil George 2Lt kia 25-9-15 3 att2Leic p88 MR19,Cyril

WOODBURN,Leonard Holt Lt dow 28-8-18 8 att7HLI p240 CR France84

WOODCOCK,Alfred Taylor 2Lt dow PoW 4-6-18 4EYorks p219 CR Germany1

WOODCOCK,Arthur Douglas T2Lt kia 16-8-17 WYorks att10Bn p83 MR30

WOODCOCK,Cecil William Napier 2Lt kia 14-9-18 10RFus p71 CR France245

WOODCOCK,Frank Capt kia 15-9-16 5Yorks p220 CR France453

WOODCOCK,Frederick.MC.Capt kld 31-10-18 RGA &101RAF p42 MR20 &CR France528

WOODCOCK,Geoffrey Herbert 2Lt kia 6-4-18 6 att4RWFus p223&272 CR France232

WOODCOCK,Leonard Albert T2Lt dow 10-4-17 21NumbF p63 CR France95,11-4-17

WOODCOCK,Victor Joseph TLt kia 30-9-17 3RFC p15 CR France398

WOODCROFT,J.SubCdr 23-6-21 S&T Cps MR43

WOODD,Alex.Bethune Peter 2Lt dow 24-8-18 3 att10WYorks p83 CR France805,Alec 25-8-18

WOODERSON,Douglas Henry David TCapt kia 6-8-16 RAMC att6Lpool p198 MR21

WOODFORD,Arthur Francis Lt 29-6-21 2Beds &Herts MR66

WOODFORD,Charles Basil Stanley 2Lt kia 22-8-16 15Glouc p107 MR29

WOODFORD,Harold Vivian T2Lt kia 13-10-15 8RBerks p140 MR19

WOODGATE,Arthur Horace T2LtACapt kia 9-4-17 11Suff att101TMB p79 CR France581

WOODGATE,F.J.Lt 12-10-18 3RWFus CR Essex83

WOODGATE,Lionel Streatfield.MID Lt kia 8-9-14 1RLancs p59 CR France1113

WOODHAM,Charles Burnett.DSO.Capt kia 15-6-15 1DCLI p115 CR Belgium121

WOODHAMS,Eric William Lt dow 11-12-17 BedsYeo p203 CR France446

WOODHAMS,Geoffrey TCapt kia 19-3-16 7RSuss p120 CR France423

WOODHEAD,John William Lt ded 27-11-18 6WRid p272 CR Yorks361

WOODHEAD,Percival Lt kia 12-7-15 4KOSB p223 MR4

WOODHEAD,Robert Comber TCapt kia 17-7-16 12DLI p162 MR21

WOODHOUSE,A.F.Lt kia 13-4-18 SL att4/4KAR p202 CR EAfrica92

WOODHOUSE,Alfred James Capt kia 30-10-14 35RFA p37 MR29

WOODHOUSE,Bernard Capt dow 5-9-17 RAMC att10WelshR p198 CR Belgium18

WOODHOUSE,Cecil Herbert Lt kia 6-6-18 12Y&L p159 MR30

WOODHOUSE,Coventry William.MC.Capt 1-11-18 SL attEAfrForce CR EAfrica89

WOODHOUSE,Disney Charles Rev ded 6-10-16 RAChDept att12RSuss p200 CR France102

WOODHOUSE,Earn Faunce 2Lt kia 15-9-17 4ELancs p226 CR Belgium8

WOODHOUSE,Edward John Lt dow 18-12-17 IARO att38CentIndHorse p284 CR France446

WOODHOUSE,Frederick George T2Lt kia 10-7-16 10 att8SLancs p126 MR21

WOODHOUSE,Gordon Stafford T2Lt dow 14-10-15 D64RFA p37 CR France257

WOODHOUSE,Henry 2Lt kia 4-11-18 1/2 att9WRid p116 CR France206

WOODHOUSE,Hugh Egerton Lt ded 1-3-19 5Beds p272

WOODHOUSE,Leslie Douglas TLt kia 3-9-16 17N&D p135 MR21

WOODHOUSE,Lionel Mostyn.MC.DFC.Lt kia 27-9-18 EssYeo &RAF p203&258

WOODHOUSE,Percy Aspden 2Lt ded 11-9-15 9Manch p237 MR4

WOODHOUSE,Percy Wilfred 2Lt kia 28-3-18 5RFC p17 CR France58,Lt

WOODHOUSE,Reginald Courtenay Hulton Lt kia 14-1-16 IA 1/56Rif p284 MR38,13-1-16

WOODHOUSE,Robert Cecil Lt kia 14-8-15 RHA p208 CR Belgium113

WOODIN,Walter Guise T2Lt kia 30-7-16 20Lpool p73 MR21

WOODIWISS,Isaac Newton 2Lt kia 10-5-15 Lincs attRFC p2&76 CR France924

WOODLAND,Clement Arthur Lt ded 1-4-18 4NStaffs att6YLI p158 CR France40

WOODLAND,Herbert Lancelot 2Lt kia 9-8-16 10Lpool p216 MR21

WOODLAND,Leslie Frank 2Lt kia 21-3-18 180RFA p37 MR27

WOODLAND,Richard William Lt kia 9-8-15 1KSLI p145 MR29

WOODLEY,Ada Ann Sister 10-1-18 TFNS CR Essex254

WOODLEY,Charles Albert 2Lt kia 8-10-18 YLI att9Bn p144 CR France234

WOODLEY,Charles Benjamin T2Lt kia 8-10-16 124MGC p186 CR France744

WOODLEY,Stanley William T2Lt kia 22-1-17 GL &10RFC p15 CR France98

WOODLOCK,Francis Joseph T2Lt kia 13-8-17 KRRC att11Bn p152 MR29

WOODMAN,Douglas T2Lt kia 11-3-18 56RFC p17 CR France725

WOODMAN,James Edward Somerville.DSO.Maj kia 25/27-9-15 2LancF att12NumbF p94 MR19

WOODMASS,Kenrick Talbot Capt kia 23-4-15 2EYorks p85 MR29

WOODROFFE,Arthur Henry T2Lt kia 31-7-17 RWKent att10Bn p142 MR29

WOODROFFE,Charles Edward 2Lt kia 27-7-18 N&D att15Bn p135 CR Belgium184

WOODROFFE,Kenneth Herbert Clayton Lt kia 9-5-15 6 att3RB p181 MR22

WOODROFFE,Leslie.MC.TCapt dow 4-6-16 8RB p181 CR France12,14Bn

WOODROFFE,Neville Leslie.MID Lt kia 6-11-14 1IrGds p53 MR29

WOODROFFE,Sydney Clayton.VC.T2Lt kia 30-7-15 8RB p181 MR29

WOODROFFE,Walter Gordon Capt kia 16-9-16 7Mddx p235 CR France329

WOODROW,William Davidson 2Lt kia 23-4-17 5 att13RScots p211 MR20

WOODRUFF,Arthur Hamilton Winthrop Lt kia 28-9-17 4Dors p229 CR Iraq8

WOODRUFF,George Norman Cecil Lt ded 2-12-18 21 att2Lond p272 CR Kent83

WOODS,Alexander Richard Rolleston Lt kia 6-7-15 RE 56FC p49 CR Belgium101

WOODS,Alfred Marcus 2Lt kia 26-2-17 C78RFA p37 CR France785

WOODS,Basil Hamilton 2Lt drd 17-12-14 RE 2FC p210 CR Egypt15

WOODS,Charles Halkett Carson Lt 21-9-17 CanadaArmyServCps &20RFC

WOODS,Edmund.MID Lt kia 12-8-15 4ELancs p226 MR4

WOODS,Edward Hunter Thurtell 2Lt kia 15-7-16 4Suff p217 CR France432

WOODS,Eric Evelyn 2Lt dow 18-5-18 12Lpool p73 CR France145

WOODS,Eric Joseph 2LtTLt kia 9-10-17 9WYorks B'Coy p83 MR30

WOODS,Fletcher Hugh Lionel 2Lt kia 14-11-16 7NumbF p214 CR France385

WOODS,Frank Cecil Lt kia 2-4-17 3RWSurr p57 CR France1489

WOODS,Fred'k William Lt kia 28-8-18 4Dors B'Coy p229 CR France277

WOODS,George Capt kia 9-9-16 9Lond p247 MR21

WOODS,Harold Ernest T2Lt dow 1-5-17 PoW 9NumbF p64 CR France1276

WOODS,Harold Wallace 2Lt kia 23-4-17 4Suff p217 CR France591

WOODS,James Maj kia 9-5-15 IMS p284 CR France631

WOODS,James T2Lt kia 23-10-16 10 att1RLancs p59 MR21

WOODS,James Edwin Lt kia 6-12-17 9RInniskF p106 MR17

WOODS,J.C.TMaj ded 13-5-18 RASC p267 CR Lond28,3-5-18

WOODS,John James Lt ded 17-10-18 5N&D p232 MR65,2Lt

WOODS,John Russell TCapt dow 16-9-16 1CldGds p51 CR France105

WOODS,John William.MC.T2LtACapt kia 14-4-17 2YLI p144 CR France1701

WOODS,Leslie.MC.Capt ded 25-2-19 RHFA 15DAC p37 CR Belgium316

WOODS,Norman Hill Lt kia 16-8-17 3 att7InniskF p255 MR30

WOODS,Richard Cheetham TLt kia 18-10-17 GL &GoldCstR p202 CR EAfrica11 &CR Tanzania1

WOODS,Richard Hartland 2Lt kia 4-12-17 25Lond att8KRRC p252 CRBelgium125

WOODS,Thomas Cecil Hardwick Lt kia 22-3-18 4 att11Suff p217 MR20

WOODS,William John Peirce T2Lt kia 3-7-16 10Suff p79 CR France393

WOODS,William Thornley Stoker 2Lt dow 27-10-16 62RFA p37 CR France374

WOODS,Walter James TLt dow 24-4-17 1/2KAR p202 CR EAfrica8 &CR Tanzania1,Capt

WOODSIDE,Archibald Mitchell 2Lt dow 23-4-18 9HLI p241 CR France84

WOODSIDE,David Cunningham 2Lt dow 26-2-16 4RScotF p222 CR Scot764,Cunninghame

WOODSIDE,Hugh Marr 2Lt kia 15-7-16 9HLI p241 MR21

WOODSTOCK,Walter Percy TLt kia 1-7-16 8Y&L p160 MR21

WOODTHORPE,Arthur John 2Lt kia 9-10-18 RGA 276SB p42 CR France1355

WOODTHORPE,William Ernest 2Lt kia 13-10-15 3Dors att8RBerks p125 MR19

WOODVILLE-MORGAN,Eric Theodore 2Lt kia 20/23-9-17 6 att26RFus p71 MR30,20-9-17

WOODWARD,Arthur Frederick Albert T2Lt kia 19-11-17 RB att2Bn p181 MR30

WOODWARD,Charles Lt 30-10-14 1RWFus CR France80

WOODWARD,Charles Francis Lt dow 20-5-15 RWFus p99

WOODWARD,Edward Seymer Lt kia 6-1-16 IA 97Inf p284 MR38

WOODWARD,Ernest Harold Hamley T2Lt kia 24-12-16 10RWSurr p57 MR29

WOODWARD,George Ernest 2Lt kia 29-9-18 Worc att2nd p110 CR France665

WOODWARD,Henry Joseph Maj dow 22-8-18 RGA 336SB p42 CR France103

WOODWARD,Leslie.MC.2Lt kia 22-3-18 SLancs att2Bn p126&258 MR27

WOODWARD,Leslie Collins.DSO.Maj dow 3-9-18 63RFA p37 CR France833

WOODWARD,Reginald Rupert T2Lt kia 1-12-17 RLancs att1/5Bn p59 MR17

WOODWARD,Robert Capt kia 9-5-15 3 att1SWBord D'Coy p101 CR France279

WOODWARD,Robert William 2Lt dow 30-8-17 RGA 145SB p42 CR Belgium12

WOODWARD,Sydney Forest.MM.2Lt dow 19-10-18 1 att5Glouc p107 CR France528

WOODWARD,William Thomas 2Lt kia 14-6-17 3 att2Suff p79 MR20

WOODWARK,Ernest Reginald TMaj kia 21-8-15 5Norf p216 MR4

WOODYATT,Nigel Gresley Reginald Capt mbk 8-3-16 IA 1/2GurkhaRif p284 MR38

WOOKEY,Frederick Maurice 2Lt dow 19-3-15 1RIrReg C'Coy p89 CR France284

WOOKEY,Guy Richard Penny Lt dow 10-5-15 EYorks p85 MR29

WOOKEY,William Nehemiah TCapt kia 26-7-17 8Glouc att11TMB p107 CR Belgium60

WOOLASTON,Keith Roland Lt kia 10-10-18 20Manch p156

WOOLDRIDGE,Albert Edward 2Lt kia 19-8-17 6RWar p214 MR30

WOOLDRIDGE,Charles Reginald 2Lt ded 12-10-18 5N&D p233 CRFrance52

WOOLER,Charles Armytage T2Lt dow 20-7-16 12WYorks p83 CR Yorks257,Capt 10Bn

WOOLER,Herbert Sykes.MID T2Lt dow 28-3-16 12WYorks p83 CR Belgium11

WOOLER,Rupert Basil Lt dow 3-5-17 12WYorks p83 MR20

WOOLF,Cecil Nathan Sidney 2Lt dow 30-11-17 SR 20Huss B'Sqdn p23 CR France512,29-11-17

WOOLF,Walter Francis Lt kia 27-3-18 3 att7KSLI p145 CR France174,2Lt

WOOLF,Walter Richard Mortimer 2Lt dow 26-9-15 3 att2BordR p118 CR France98

WOOLF,William Lt kia 21-9-18 24WelshR p128 CR France365

WOOLL,George HonTLt&QM kia 19-8-15 8NumbF p64 MR4

WOOLLACOTT,Cedric Percy 2Lt kia 22-4-17 D64RHA p37 CR France644

WOOLLARD,G.F.Lt ded 3-9-18 6WRid attRAF p227

WOOLLATT,Claud Humpston TCapt kia 21-8-16 8RWSurr p57 MR21

WOOLLATT,Philip Reginald 2Lt kia 14-7-16 7RWSurr p57 MR21

WOOLLCOMBE,Charles Stephenson 2Lt kia 12-10-14 2KOSB p102 CR France260

WOOLLCOMBE,Walter Ley Maj ded 30-8-16 RAMC p272

WOOLLEN,Joseph Alfred 2Lt kia 27-4-18 Manch att17Bn B'Coyp156 MR30

WOOLLERTON,Frank.MC.2Lt kia 3-10-18 14 att2YLI p144 CR France375

WOOLLETT,J.C.Capt 16-11-18 RFC CR Kent230

WOOLLETT,William Charles Capt kia 16-9-16 11 att9YLI p144 CR France744

WOOLLEY,Charles Rupert Lt kia 28-7-16 5DLI p239 CR Belgium60

WOOLLEY,Henry George T2Lt dow 17-4-17 8RWKent p142 CR France80

WOOLLEY,Thomas Hugh Corbett Capt kia 27-4-17 2/8N&D p233 CR France1495

WOOLLEY,Wilfrid Edwin 2Lt kia 11-7-17 1Mddx p236 CR France604,3/10Bn

WOOLLEY,William Lawton 2Lt dow 18-9-18 3 att7SWBord p101 CR Greece5

WOOLLOCOMBE,John Morth Maj kia 3-2-17 1Dev p77 CR Iraq5,WOOLLCOMBE

WOOLLVEN,Gerald Clifton Lt kia 11-9-18 C290RFA p208 CR France369,10-9-18

WOOLLVEN,John Humphrey 2Lt kia 4-9-18 15Hamps p121 CR Belgium111

WOOLMAN,John Gray 2Lt kia 2-11-18 Y&L p160 CR France1196

WOOLMER,Stanley Herbert France T2Lt kia 3-9-16 17KRRC p152 MR21

WOOLNOUGH,Arthur Stanley T2Lt dow PoW 1-12-17 7DCLI C'Coy p115 CR France658

WOOLNOUGH,Charles Walter Fyffe T2Lt kia 22-3-16 10Beds att69MGC Inf p87&186 CR France559,21-3-16

WOOLNOUGH,Frederick Ullathorne Capt dow 22-3-18 3Dors att&6SomLI p125 CR France1203

WOOLNOUGH,George Morton 2Lt kia 7-4-17 159RFA p37 CR France672

WOOSNAM,Richard Bowen Lt kia 4-6-15 6 att4Yorks p91 MR29

WOOSTER,Clarence Daniel Henry.MC.Capt kia 9-8-18 6RWSurr p57 CR France636

WOOSTER,Reginald Joseph TCapt kia 15-9-16 RAMC att9RB p198 MR21

WOOTTEN,William John George 2Lt ded 24-4-19 IARO p284 MR65,WOOTTON

WOOTTON,Donald Herbert ACapt dow 25-8-18 20Lond p251 CR France119

WOOTTON,John Wesley TCapt dow 11-10-17 11Suff p79 CR France134

WORCESTER,Harold Paul TCapt kia 10-9-16 7SStaffs p123 CR France251

WORDINGHAM,Vincent Robert T2Lt kia 16-8-17 GL &Worc p192 CR Belgium106

WORDSWORTH,Alexander Gerald Capt kia 6-12-14 4Mddx p149 MR22

WORDSWORTH,John Lionel Lt kia 6-11-14 5Lancers p22 MR29,4-11-14

WORDSWORTH,Joseph Charles Ditch 2Lt kia 6-4-17 8DLI attRFC p20&239 CR France1321

WORDSWORTH,Osmund Bartle 2LtTLt kia 2-4-17 21MGC p186 MR20

WORKMAN,Edward.MID Lt dow 26-1-16 5 att2RIrRif p170 CR France40

WORKMAN,Charles Service.MC.2LtTLt kia 20-7-17 ScotRif att70RFC p15&104,dow CR Belgium393

WORMALD,Drury Frank Percy Capt ded 4-11-18 RGA p209 CR Shrop125

WORMALD,Frank.CB.LtColTBrigGen kia 3-10-15 12Lancers Cmdg5CavBde p22 CR France1745

WORMALD,Guy TCapt kia 14-9-16 12 att14LancF p94 MR37

WORMALD,Oliver Edward Capt ded 2-2-17 5Suff p217 CR Camb51

WORMULL,Charles Frederic TLt kld 5-10-17 GL &RFC p15

WORNER,Percival Seymour T2Lt kia 4-9-16 9Dev p77 CR France400

WORRALL,Ernest Arthur TCapt kld 20-3-18 51RFC p17 CR Lancs34,Lt

WORRALL,Herbert 2Lt kia 25-4-18 WYorks att1/6Bn p83 MR30

WORSLEY,Charles Sackville Pelham.Lord.Capt kia 30-10-14 RHGds MG Sect p20 CR Belgium58,Lt

WORSLEY,Evelyn Godfrey 2Lt dow 17-9-17 3GrenGds p50 CR France23

WORSLEY,Harold Rapley 2Lt kia 1-9-18 10LancF D'Coy p94 CR France307

WORSLEY,John Fortescue Lt kia 27-11-17 3GrenGds p50 MR17

WORSLEY,Reginald Eric Milne T2Lt kia 8-3-18 AlbertaR GL &RFC p17 CR France214

WORSLEY,Richard Stanley.DSO.MajBtLtCol drd 4-5-17 RASC p194 CR Italy14

WORSLEY,William Reginald 2Lt kia 1-8-17 4SomLI p218 MR29

WORSLEY-WORSWICK,Basil Henry 2Lt 29-4-16 2KEdwsHorse CR Ireland14

WORSNOP,Edgar TLt dow 7-8-15 9WYorks p83 MR4

WORSNOP,John William 2Lt kia 30-6-16 18WYorks p83 MR21

WORSTENHOLM,John 2Lt kia 25-9-17 GL &6RFC p15 CR Belgium11

WORSTER,Alexander Frederick.MC.2LtACapt dow 23-11-17 1EKent p58 CR France398

WORSTER,Frank Copeland,MC LtACapt dow 30-5-18 2Worc p110 CR France1693

WORSWICK,Henry Worsley 2Lt kld 28-4-16 KEdwsHorse p24

WORTH,Bertram Stanley 2Lt ded 8-12-19 LabCps p266 CR Surrey1

WORTH,James William.MC.DCM.2Lt dow 28-11-17 2/6WYorks p218 CR France398

WORTH,Leslie Lt ded 16-8-18 RE p210 CR Egypt2

WORTH,Stanley Seymour T2Lt kia 1-12-17 4RInnskF att14MGC p106 & 186, 2LtTLt CR Belgium23

WORTH,Thomas 2Lt kia 10-8-15 7Ches p223 MR4

WORTHINGTON,Claude Arthur.MID MajTLtCol kia 28-9-15 2EKent p58 MR19

WORTHINGTON,Claude Swanwick.DSO&Bar.TD.LtCol dow 14-10-18 6Manch att5Dors p236 CR France13

WORTHINGTON,Frederick TCapt kia 28-4-17 10Lincs p76 CR France581

WORTHINGTON,Noel Trevor Lt dow 8-8-15 6RLancs p59 CR Gallipoli18

WORTHINGTON,Ralph TMaj kia 17-5-17 16Ches p97 CR France1701

WORTHINGTON,Reginald George Lt kia 16-9-14 2 O&BLI p130 CR France1111

WORTHINGTON,Richard Fitzpatrick Capt dow 4-5-17 2/5Glouc p225 CR Glouc69

WORTHINGTON,Samuel Lt kia 28-11-17 1/1RIlA p208 CR Palestine3

WORTHINGTON,Walter Gustavas.MC.Maj dow 27-4-18 12Lond p248 CR France145

WORTHINGTON-EYRE,Lionel George.MID Lt kia 14-7-17 D78RFA p37 CR France418

WORTHINGTON-JONES,George.MC.Maj dow 10-11-17 293RHA CR Belgium18

WORTHINGTON-WILMER,Hugh Ferdinand Mansfield Capt kia 11-5-16 2 att13RScots p55 CR France423,Maj

WORTLEY,John Francis.MC.Capt kia 14-4-18 4Y&L p238 MR30

WORTLEY,Maurice Lester 2Lt kia 3-10-15 3Suff p79 MR19

WORTON,John Paton Lt kia 8-5-15 3Mon p244 MR29

WOTHERSPOON,Andrew Scott Capt kia 16-8-17 4 O&BLI p231 MR30

WOULFE,Gerald Lascelles T2Lt kia 14-7-16 6Nhampt p138 MR21

WRAGG,Frederick William.MID Maj kia 1-7-16 1/5N&D p232 MR21

WRAGG,Norman John Lt dow 18-7-16 3SStaffs att1N&D p123 CR France145

WRAITH,Alfred Osborn.MID TLtAMaj dow 13-6-17 RE 254FC p49 CR Belgium5,kia

WRANGHAM,D'Arcy George Maj 22-7-20 2EYorks MR43

WRAY,Cormac Patrick James T2Lt kia 15-7-16 5 att8InniskF p106 CR France115

WRAY,David Withers Lt died 16-12-19 RIrF 1GarrBn p265 CR Burma129A,Withersow 16-12-18

WRAY,Ernest Warneford Lt kia 23-8-17 RE 517FC p210 CR Belgium8

WRAY,Francis Alan 2Lt kia 31-7-17 8Lpool p216 MR29

WRAY,Harry T2Lt kia 29-12-17 Yorks att10Bn p91 CR France417

WRAY,John Leonard T2Lt kld 13-2-18 RFC p17 CR USA228 J.C.

WRAY,Kenneth Christopher George Capt kia 9-8-16 1/4SLancs p230 MR21

WRAY,Percy Hugh 2Lt kia 7-6-17 7RIrF p172 CR Belgium111

WRAY,Thomas Ernest T2Lt kia 4-9-17 GL &7RFC p15 CR Belgium18

WREFORD,Bertram William Heyman LtACapt kia 23-4-17 1Dev p77 CR France58

WREFORD,B.F.L.2Lt ded 11-5-18 4Lond &RAF p246

WREFORD,Leslie Warren 2Lt kia 16-8-17 4Lond p246 MR29

WREFORD-BROWN,Claude Wreford.DSO.Capt kia 25-5-15 2NumbF p64 MR29

WREFORD-BROWN,Oswald Eric TCapt dow 7-7-16 9NumbF p64 CR FRance23

WREN,Christopher Bray 2Lt kia 15-9-16 6Lond p247 MR21

WREN,Thomas Thorpe T2Lt dow 29-7-16 10LNLancs p137 CR Lancs464

WRENFORD,Arthur Leonard.MID CaptALtCol kia 21-3-18 Worc att4ELancs p110 CR France924

WRESSELL,Frank T2Lt kia 2-8-17 1YLI p144 CR Belgium173,1/5Bn

WRIGGLESWORTH,Alfred Gunn 2Lt kia 4-9-16 3Manch p156 MR21

WRIGHT,Aislabie Harcourt Nelson 2Lt kia 2-9-18 1SomLI p80 MR16

WRIGHT,Alan Austin Capt kia 6-9-18 3 att12ESurr p113 MR30,4-9-18

WRIGHT,Albert Harley 2Lt ded 13-1-20 IA 2/2GurkhaRif p284

WRIGHT,Alexander Allen.MC.Capt kia 8-8-16 1/4RLancs p213 MR21

WRIGHT,Alfred Kyrle Terrett 2Lt dow 10-12-17 16Lond p250 CR Egypt1,10-12-16

WRIGHT,Allan O'Halloran.MID Capt kia 13-3-15 1RIrRif p170 MR22

WRIGHT,Arthur T2Lt kia 15-9-16 10War att33MGC p186 CR France251

WRIGHT,Arthur Samuel 2Lt kia 15-8-18 8EYorks p85 CR France352

WRIGHT,Arthur William TCapt ded 13-10-17 GL &RE p192 CR Durham28

WRIGHT,Basil Charles.MC.Lt kia 24-9-18 2RSuss p120 MR16

WRIGHT,Cecil Keith Foyle 2Lt kia 21-8-18 10RFus p71 CR France927

WRIGHT,Cecil Laurence 2Lt kia 7-7-17 RGA 287SB p42 CR Belgium34

WRIGHT,Cecil Medwyn 2Lt kia 6-11-17 22Lond p252 CR Palestine8

WRIGHT,Charles Lt kia 29-11-17 1/1LincsYeo p204 CR Palestine9

WRIGHT,Charles.MC.Lt kia 27-5-18 3 att11Ches p97 MR18

WRIGHT,Charles James T2Lt kia 18-10-16 11SStaffs att26MGC p123&186 MR21

WRIGHT,Charles James Stewart TCapt kia 14-7-16 7Leic p88 CR France1890

WRIGHT,Claude Russell Lt kia 21-5-17 5Suff attMGC p188&217 CR France646

WRIGHT,Crossley 2Lt kia 21-11-17 2/6WRid p227 MR17

WRIGHT,Cyril Paul T2Lt kldacc 25-5-16 7RWKent att55/2TMB p142 CR France169,25-6-16

WRIGHT,Donald Samuel T2Lt dow 25-4-17 1 att8Beds p87

WRIGHT,Edmund Capt kia 3-7-16 6RWSurr p57 CR France251

WRIGHT,Edmund Lancelot T2Lt dow 16-7-16 7KSLI p145 CR France66,Capt

WRIGHT,Edward Dearden Lt kia 21-3-18 1/4ELancs p226 MR27

WRIGHT,Edward Frank Macer 2Lt kia 2-4-17 4NumbF p213 CR France1182

WRIGHT,Edward Martin Capt kia 10-4-17 5ELancs p226 MR20

WRIGHT,Edwin Capt kia 17-11-14 3DragGds p21 CR Belgium57

WRIGHT,Edwin George Englesby T2Lt kia 16-6-16 7SomLI p80 CR Belgium4

WRIGHT,Edwin Stanley T2Lt kia 3-7-16 7Suff p79 CR France393

WRIGHT,Egerton Lowndes.MC.CaptBdeMaj kia 11-5-18 O&BLI BucksBn p231 CR France749

WRIGHT,Eric Alfred TLt ded 21-6-15 RAMC p198 CR Egypt3

WRIGHT,Eric Tracey TCapt kia 13-3-17 20RFus p71 CR France114

WRIGHT,Ernest Granville Col ded 27-7-19 IA Staff p284

WRIGHT,Francis Beattie Lt 12-4-18 RFA &10RFC

WRIGHT,Francis John.MID Capt ded 26-9-19 SL attStaff p268 CR France457

WRIGHT,Frederick 2Lt kia 12-4-17 2/5Lincs p220 CR France1494

WRIGHT,Frederick Adams T2Lt kia 19-9-17 DCLI att9RFC p15&115 CR Belgium18

WRIGHT,Frederick Charles 2Lt kia 14-4-18 18Mddx p149 CR France324

WRIGHT,Frederick John T2Lt dow 4-8-17 1/8Lpool p73 CR Belgium7

WRIGHT,Frederick Wilfred TLtCol ded ??? RASC p267

WRIGHT,George 2Lt dow 19-9-16 1/6Lpool p215 CR France40,Georges

WRIGHT,George Bertram 2Lt kia 11-10-18 1RFus p71 CR France270

WRIGHT,George Clinton 2Lt kia 10-3-15 2Dev p77 CR France279

WRIGHT,George Darling Maj ded 26-5-20 IA 2/70BurmaRif p284 CR Hamps64,98Inf

WRIGHT,George Drennan Cron 2Lt kia 23-10-14 2Beds p87 CR Belgium157

WRIGHT,George Edward.MC.2Lt kia 9-10-18 RASC attRGA 276SB p194 CR France1355

WRIGHT,George William 2Lt kia 24-3-18 7Leic p88 MR27

WRIGHT,G.H.Lt ded 15-9-17 Cps of Guides CR Canada740

WRIGHT,Guy Powell 2Lt kia 2-7-18 9 att1Mddx p236 CR France745

WRIGHT,Hannah Elizabeth SNurse ded 22-10-18 QAIMNS p200 CR Italy12

WRIGHT,Harold TCapt dow 14-9-15 6LNLancs p137 CR Leic119

WRIGHT,Harold Ivan Lt kia 8-11-17 4EYorks p219 MR20

WRIGHT,Harold Reginald Lt dow 16-9-18 5WYorks p218 CR France34

WRIGHT,Harry Stevenson.CMG.LtCol ded 1-10-19 RASC p267 CR Hamps 64,30-9-19

WRIGHT,Harry William 2Lt kia 19-12-15 1GordH p167 CR Belgium21

WRIGHT,Henry Gordon Capt kia 6-6-15 8N&D p233 CR Belgium17

WRIGHT,Henry Gordon T2Lt kia 9-4-17 5 att11Mddx p149 CR France96

WRIGHT,Henry Thomas Richard Somerset Capt kld 21-12-16 Manch p156 CR EAfrica116

WRIGHT,Herbert Melville T2Lt kia 2-4-17 2Yorks p91 CR France1186

WRIGHT,Horace William 2Lt kia 3-5-17 7Mddx p235 MR20

WRIGHT,Howard Caldwell.MC.Capt dow 2-9-17 1/17Lond p250 CR Belgium18

WRIGHT,Hugh Stafford Northcote Capt kia 30-10-14 IA 2/8GurkhaRif p284 MR28

WRIGHT,James William Lt kia 10-10-17 5WRid p227 MR30

WRIGHT,John 2Lt kia 4-11-18 18NumbF att8NStaffs p64 CR France940

WRIGHT,John Armer.MC.Lt kia 18-9-18 11 att7RSuss p120 CR France369

WRIGHT,John Crosby Lt kia 10-4-17 RGA p209 MR20

WRIGHT,John George William 2Lt kia 11-5-17 2Lond p245 CR France646,1Bn

WRIGHT,John Major Stanley 2Lt kia 24-2-17 157RFA p37 CR Belgium23,Lt 24-2-18

WRIGHT,John Shilvock 2Lt kia 7-11-18 RGA 219SB p42 CR Belgium143

WRIGHT,Joseph Benjamin 2Lt kia 21-4-17 2DLI p162 MR29

WRIGHT,Joseph Herbert.MC.Capt kia 25-3-18 8Glouc p107 MR20

WRIGHT,Matthew John T2Lt kia 1-7-16 14RIrRif p170 MR21

WRIGHT,Neil James Robert 2Lt kia 15-9-14 15RFA p37 CR France1329

WRIGHT,Noel Tracey LtTCapt dow 1-10-15 3 att2Yorks p91 CR France257

WRIGHT,Norman George T2Lt kia 13-7-16 9RWSurr p57 MR21

WRIGHT,Norman Stanley T2Lt kia 15-9-16 26RFus p71 MR21

WRIGHT,Oscar Capt ded 13-10-17 IARO 31Punjabis attPoliticDept p284 MR66

WRIGHT,Percival Edward 2Lt kia 24-4-18 RFA p209 CR France144

WRIGHT,Percy Andrew T2Lt kld 21-12-16 GL &RFC p4&192,ded CR War7,TLt

WRIGHT,Peter.MC.Maj kia 11-1-18 B186 RHFA p37&258 CR Belgium10

WRIGHT,Reuben.DSO.TCapt dow 17-8-17 7YLI p144 CR Belgium16

WRIGHT,Richard Bertram 2Lt kia 8-7-18 RFus att1/6WYorks p71 CR Belgium188

WRIGHT,Richard Connett 2Lt kia 19-8-18 9 att3RB p181 MR16

WRIGHT,Robert T2Lt kia 7-11-17 18RIrRif attRIrF p170 CR Palestine8

WRIGHT,Robert Maj kia 29-11-17 1/1LincsYeo p204 CR Palestine9

WRIGHT,Robert Kenneth.MC.LtACapt kia 29-9-18 6Beds att2Worc p87 CR France665

WRIGHT,Robert Taylor 2Lt kia 1-11-17 4 att15N&D p135 CR Belgium106

WRIGHT,Samuel Donald 2Lt dow 25-4-17 1 att8Beds CR France8

WRIGHT,Samuel King TLt kia 7/11-8-15 8WRid p116 MR4

WRIGHT,Sidney Harry TLtACapt ded 10-2-19 LabCps att114ChineseLabCo p189 CR France113

WRIGHT,Stamford Walter Seppings Lt kia 9-9-16 1ConnRgrs p172 CR France294

WRIGHT,Stanley.MC.2Lt kia 24-10-17 RE attRFC 21KiteBalloonSect p15&49 MR20

WRIGHT,Sydney John 2Lt kia 23-8-18 Ess p133 CR France281

WRIGHT,T.Maj 19-12-18 attRASC CR Kent7

WRIGHT,Theodore.VC.Capt kia 14-9-14 RE p49 CR France1107

WRIGHT,Thomas 2Lt kia 1-5-15 RBerks att2Bn p140 CR France1158

WRIGHT,Thomas T2Lt kia 13-10-15 1/5Lincs p76&258 MR19

WRIGHT,Victor Albert 2Lt kia 15-4-18 10RWar p66 MR30

WRIGHT,Vivian Arthur Butler T2Lt kia 3-12-15 12Ess att6Lincs p133 CR Gallipoli4,2-12-15

WRIGHT,W.LtCol 13-5-16 RASC CR Kent91

WRIGHT,Walter Horace 2Lt kia 21-3-18 1WYorks p83 MR20

WRIGHT,Walter Tom Crosby Lt kia 8-8-18 2TankCps p189 MR16

WRIGHT,Walter Whitmore 2Lt kia 23-8-17 RGA 276SB p42 CR Belgium19

WRIGHT,Walter Herbert LtCol ded 8-11-15 1/4YLI Res p254&258 CR Yorks361

WRIGHT,Wilfred Eric Capt ded 3-11-18 5SStaffs p272 CR War1

WRIGHT,William TLt kia 7-7-16 6KOSB p102 CR France630

WRIGHT,William 2Lt kia 17-2-17 2SStaffs p123 CR France239

WRIGHT,William 2Lt kia 22-3-18 4GordH p242 MR20

WRIGHT,William 2Lt kia 8-8-18 RFA 175ArmyBde p37 CR France196

WRIGHT,William Clifford TLt kia 10/12-7-16 17RWFus p99 MR21

WRIGHT,William Edward Bellyse TLt kia 22-9-15 7YLI p144 CR France525

WRIGHT,William Gerald 2Lt dow 8-6-17 8Hamps p229 CR Belgium11

WRIGHT,William Joseph T2Lt kia 17-5-16 9Leic p88 CR France745

WRIGHT,William Lake 2Lt kia 20-10-18 17RSuss p120 CR France1054

WRIGHT,William Richardson 2Lt kia 20-4-16 1/4Lincs p217 MR20

WRIGHT,William Sidney 2Lt kia 21-3-18 9Norf p74 MR20

WRIGHT-INGLE,Cecil Hubert T2Lt kia 30-4-16 19RFus att2Leinst p71 CR Belgium49

WRIGLEY,Henry Neville 2Lt ded 30-8-17 RFA 53DAC p209 CR Egypt2,Harry

WRIGLEY,James 2Lt kia 29-9-17 RGA 289SB p42 CR Belgium102

WRIGLEY,Joseph Lt kia 1-7-16 1/5Y&L p238 MR21

WRIGLEY,Leonard Gordon 2Lt kia 9-10-17 2/9Manch p237 CR Belgium125

WRIGLEY,Percy Bernard 2Lt kia 23-3-18 RE 518FC p210 MR20

WRIGLEY,Ralph Mortimer Lt ded 6-11-18 RE 3RlyCoy attRMon Eng p49 CR France52

WRIGLEY,Willoughby Thornton.MC.MID Capt kld 15-8-20 C'Coy 5Wilts CR Iraq8

WRINCH,Harry Durrill TLt dow 20-8-16 BBty 115BdeRFA p37 CR Greece6

WRINCH,Stanley 2Lt kia 8-5-15 3Suff p79 MR29

WRIXON,Arthur Henry TLt kia 2-6-16 13 att11Suff p79 CR France515

WROE,Wilfred Dent TLt kia 13-10-15 10Lincs p76 CR France515,29-6-16

WRONG,Colin Bassett.MC.Lt kia 28-12-17 6RMunstF p176 CR Palestine3

WRONG,Harold Verschoyle Lt kia 1-7-16 15LancF p94 MR21

WROTH,Walter Adams Lt kia 31-5-18 SL &2/4KAR p202 CR EAfrica90

WROUGHTON,Herbert T2Lt kia 8-12-17 12Norf p74 CR Palestine3

WROUGHTON,John Henry Theodore Lt dow 9-5-18 RE 136Co p49 CR France100

WROUGHTON,Musgrave Cazenove.MID 2Lt dow 31-10-14 12Lancers p22 CR Belgium186,30-10-14

WROUGHTON,Philip Musgrave Neeld TMaj kia 19-4-17 1/1BerksYeo p203 CR Palestine8

WYAND,Edward Herbert TCapt kia 30-1-16 16KRRC D'Coy p152 CR France114

WYATT,Alfred John Lt kia 23-10-18 1 att8ScotRif p104 CR France190

WYATT,Arthur Thomas Elford Capt ded 19-2-17 3 att1Lincs p76 CR Lincs142

WYATT,Edwin Wellington 2Lt ded 21-6-19 IA TC attRGA 4MtnBty p284 MR43

WYATT,Esdaile Frederick Burkett.MID TCapt kia 8-1-16 2SLancs &MGC p126&186 CR Belgium28

WYATT,Felix Capt kia 2-7-17 5Suff &RFC p217 CR France439

WYATT,Francis Ogilvy.MVO.LtCol ded 16-12-19 RGA p262 MR43 &CR Pakistan50A

WYATT,Geoffrey Wilfred Penfold 2Lt kia 15-9-16 1EKent p58 MR21 CR France1890

WYATT,Godfrey Louis 2Lt dow 24-5-15 6LancF p221 CR Gallipoli1

WYATT,Henry Edward T2Lt kia 19-1-17 40MGC Inf p186 MR38

WYATT,H.G.P.Lt 12-11-15 1SussYeo CR Egypt3

WYATT,John 2Lt dow 25-10-18 4Glouc p225 CR France292

WYATT,Samuel John Livesley 2Lt kia 23-4-17 18Manch p156 MR20

WYATT,William Herbert 2LtTLt kia 4-5-16 1EYorks p85 CR France188

WYATT,William John T2Lt dow 26-10-17 8Dev p77 CR Belgium11,29-10-17

WYATT-SMITH,John Drummond T2Lt kia 17-3-18 28RFC p17 CR Italy48

WYBORN,Walter Samuel Lt ded 6-2-19 4RInniskF p264 CR Sussex185

WYBRANTS,John Holman 2Lt dow 30-7-18 3 att7Lond p246 CR France13

WYKES,Ernest Arthur Inns T2Lt kia 30-11-17 5RBerks p140 MR17

WYKES,Herbert Ivie TCapt dow 30-9-15 6Wilts p153 CR France145

WYLD,Cyril Garnet.MID T2Lt kia 5-7-16 9Yorks p91 MR21

WYLD,George Richard Capt kia 24-12-14 3Wilts attRBerks p153 CR France260,att1RBucksHuss

WYLDE,G.Maj ded 1-1-21 2SStaffs CR War7

WYLDE,Thomas Edgar Lt dow 27-6-17 4Norf attRFC p20&216 CR France113

WYLEY,Francis John Capt dow 23-4-15 1YLI p144 CR Belgium151

WYLEY,William Reginald FitzThomas Lt&Adjt kia 19-9-16 RFA p208 CR France251

WYLIE,Alan Lindsay.MC.T2Lt kia 20-11-17 GL &RFC p15 CR France379

WYLIE,Arrol Edmiston 2Lt kia 18-1-18 56RFC p17 MR20

WYLIE,Arthur William Lt kia 10/16-3-15 2Lincs p76 CR France525,10-3-15

WYLIE,Hamilton MacLaren T2Lt kia 7-1-16 SfthH p165 MR38

WYLIE,J.R.2Lt kld 23-4-18 RDubF &RAF p177

WYLIE,Percival Thomas Lt ded 27-4-19 ArmyPayDept p200 CR Asia81

WYLIE,Robert Downie Capt kia 23-8-17 3 att6CamH p168 CR Belgium7

WYLIE,William Gladstone.MC&Bar.Lt kia 28-3-18 9DLI p239 MR20

WYLIE,William Stanley Lt dow 10-5-15 3Y&L p160 MR29

WYLLIE,Alexander Capt ded 18-4-17 RScotF attEgyptArmy p95 CR EAfrica116

WYLLIE,Andrew Inglis Capt kia 2-9-18 4RScotF attTankCps p189&222 CR France614

WYLLIE,Hugh Alexander 2Lt kia 3-9-16 1/7WYorks p218 CR France252

WYLLIE,Hugh Tweed Walford Capt kia 24-5-15 4DragGds p21 MR29

WYLLIE,Hugh William TLt kia 26-10-16 7ELancs p111 MR21

WYLLIE,William W.Lt ded 6-4-17 LanarkYeo p272 CR Greece6,10-4-17

WYLLIE,William Thomas.MID Capt kia 19-7-16 1DLI p162 CR France397

WYLLY,Edward Vesey TLt ded 17-1-18 SL att2/3KAR p268 CR Tanzania1

WYNDHAM,George Heremon 2Lt kia 24-3-15 3Dev attNumbF p77 CR Belgium98

WYNDHAM,Percy Lyulph Lt kia 14-9-14 CldGds p51 MR15

WYNDHAM,William Reginald.Hon.Lt kia 6-11-14 LincsYeo att1LifeGds p20&272 CR Belgium134

WYNN,Arthur Ernest T2Lt dow 1-11-16 PoW GL &RFC p4&192 MR20

WYNN,Richard Alexander 2Lt kia 14-4-15 Norf p74 CR Iraq6

WYNN,William Alfred Lt ded 28-7-19 8Mddx p256 CR Iraq8

WYNNE,Arnold T2Lt kia 8-4-17 13Lpool B'Coy p73 CR France581,9-4-17

WYNNE,Charles Wyndham T2LtACapt dow 26-6-17 RGA 182SB p42 CR France134,24-6-17

WYNNE,Edward Ernest Capt kia 8-6-17 1/5Leic p220 CR France161

WYNNE,Edward Henry John Lt dow 16-9-16 3GrenGds p50 CR France66

WYNNE,Eric Ralph Lovatt Capt kia 26-10-18 IA 1/10GurkhaRif p284 MR38

WYNNE,Francis George.DSO.Maj kia 10-4-18 9LNLancs att1Wilts p137 MR32,2Bn

WYNNE,Gerald Mansfield Lt ded 22-10-19 RE 455FC p262 CR Germany1,Gerard

WYNNE,Maurice Okeover Mostyn Lt dow 28-8-15 132/1RFA p37 CR France922

WYNNE,Maurice St.Clair Patrick.DCM.MID Lt dow 11-10-18 1/2RInniskF p106 CR France398

WYNNE,William 2Lt kia 7-2-16 IARO att90Punjabis p284 MR38

WYNNE-JONES,Morys Lt kia 29-10-14 RE 36Co p49 MR29

WYNNE-WILLIAMS,Humphrey Evan T2Lt kia 30-3-16 10RWFus p99 CR Belgium15

WYNSTONE-WATERS,E.Capt 26-8-18 EAMS CR EAfrica52

WYNTER,Cecil Domville Lt dow 5-10-15 IrGds att2Bn p53 CR Leic24

WYNTER,Francis Constantine William Capt kia 22-11-15 O&BLI p130 MR38

WYNTER,Hugh Talbot.MID Maj kia 15-9-14 22/34RFA p37 CR France1329

WYNTER,Philip Cecil Capt dow 20-4-15 1ESurr p113 CR Belgium127

WYNYARD,Damer.MID TCapt&Adjt kia 20-4-15 1ESurr p113 MR29

WYPER,James 2Lt kia 23-7-18 7/8KOSB p102 CR France865

WYPER,James Stewart TLt dow 8-9-16 7/8KOSB p102 CR France145

WYTHES,Claude Aspinall Capt kia 28-4-15 4Worc p110 MR4

WYVILL,Marmaduke Ibbetson TMaj ded 6-3-16 RB p181 CR Yorks138

Y

YALLAND,William Stanley Lt kia 23-10-14 Glouc p107 MR29

YANDLE,Thomas T2Lt kia 10-4-17 13RFus p71 MR20

YANESKE,Walter T2Lt kia 30-7-16 8Glouc p107 MR21

YAPP,William Clarence 2Lt kia 7-8-15 5LancF p221 MR4

YARDE,John Tristram.MC&Bar.MIDx2 Capt dow 21-9-18 1/5Beds p219 CR Palestine9

YARDLEY,Eric Barnes 2Lt dow 20-7-17 5YLI p235 CR Sussex111

YARDLEY,Frederick George T2Lt dow 17-9-15 8NStaffs p158 CR France8,Frederic

YARDLEY,Frank T2Lt kia 7-8-17 246MGC p186 MR29

YARDLEY,William 2Lt dow 30-4-17 9Ess p153 MR20

YARROW,Eric Fernandez.MID 2Lt kia 8-5-15 7A&SH p243 CR Belgium73

YARROW,Henry Edwin Goodwin 2Lt kia 30-7-16 2KOSB p103 MR21

TATE,Charles Allix Lavington.VC.Maj ded PoW 20-9-14 2YLI p144 CR Germany4

YATES,Alec James.DCM.2Lt kia 28-3-18 4MGC DivBn p186 MR20

YATES,Arthur Gerald Vavasour 2Lt kia 1-7-16 16Lond p250 MR21

YATES,Charles Cecil TLt kia 15-5-16 9LNLancs p137 CR France68,16-5-16

YATES,Francis William Capt dow 25-4-15 3 att2YLI p144 CR Shrop111

YATES,Frank Dutton T2Lt kia 15-4-17 13Mddx p149 MR20

YATES,Frederick T2Lt kia 30-11-17 2Hamps p121 CR France910

YATES,George Herbert TLt ded 15-2-19 ArmyPayDept HQ 4Army p200 CR France34

YATES,James Stanley 2Lt kia 8-10-15 3 att6RWKent p142 MR19

YATES,John Carrington Lt kia 21-3-18 160RFA p208 MR20

YATES,John Edwin T2Lt kia 1-11-17 70RFC p15 CR Belgium18

YATES,Richard 2Lt kld 11-2-16 14 RFC p4 CR Egypt3

YATES,Richard 2Lt kia 24-4-18 1EYorks p85 MR30

YATES,Robert Charles Byam Capt mbk 20-10-14 IA 1/4GurkhaRif p284 MR28

YATES,Samuel Benjamin 2Lt kia 22-12-17 10 att8Manch p237 CR France80

YATES,William Grandage.MID 2Lt kia 9-1-17 1Manch p156 CR Iraq5

YATMAN,Dennistoun Hamilton Lt kia 11-4-18 1NumbF p64 MR19 &CR France1896

YAXLEY,Charles William T2Lt dow 23-4-17 8Dev p77 CR France518

YEAMAN,Charles Henry 2Lt ded 15-9-16 7DLI p239 CR Durham8

YEAMAN,Denis John T2Lt kia 5/10-10-16 24KRRC p152 CR France374

YEAMAN,Keith Sanger Capt ded 5-6-18 RFA p207 CR Camb16,Maj

YEARSLEY,Hubert Abram 2Lt kia 9-4-18 RE 79FC p49 CR France490

YEARWOOD,Carleton Douglas T2Lt kia 16-8-17 YLI att7Bn p144 CR Belgium152

YEATES,Stanley Charles Lt kia 14-4-17 16Lond B'Coy p250 MR20

YEATHERD,Motagu Locke Capt kia 11-4-17 12Lancers p22 CR France162

YEATHERD,Raymond Gilbert Hooker.MID Lt kia 15-9-16 2DragGds p21 MR21

YEATMAN,Bernard Joseph Pym Lt kia 23-10-18 9Dev p77 CR France231,2Lt

YEATMAN,Harry Farr Capt kia 21-11-17 DorsYeo p203 CR Palestine3

YEATMAN,Marwood Edwards Capt ded 15-9-14 1SWBord p101 MR15

YELD,Cyril de Clare Lt ded 24-10-18 IARO attS&TCps p284 MR43

YELL,Reuben Harold T2Lt kia 9-3-18 GL &16RFC p17 CR France95

YELLAND,Edward Jonathan 2Lt 15-12-16 4 att2WRid MR21

YELLEN,Cyril Francis T2Lt kia 30-11-17 RFus att17Bn p71 MR17

YEO,Everard Lisle T2Lt dow 7-10-16 36MGC Inf p186 CR France833

YEO,Frederick George T2Lt kia 26-10-16 8RWKent p142 CR France149,27-10-16 Ex HAC

YEO,Hubert Claud Cater T2Lt kia 24-8-17 6DCLI p115 MR30

YEO,James Frederick Jesse 2Lt kia 1-8-17 11HLI p164 MR29

YEO,Leslie Farquhar Lt dow 10-3-15 2SStaffs p123 CR France80,kia

YEOMAN,Bryan Frank Lawson 2Lt ded 11-5-18 1/4Lond &RAF p246&258,Lt kia CR Oxford97

YEOMANS,Howard William Capt kia 8-10-17 2/1Hereford attMGC p188&252 CR Belgium96,Haywood

YEOMANS,Walter Joseph George T2Lt kia 8-4-17 5KSLI D'Coy p145 CR France581,9-4-17

YEWDALL,Frederick George Lt ded 18-5-18 20DLI p162 CR Durham19

YIRRELL,Percy Tom Wilson 2Lt dow 30-3-17 B240RFA p209 CR France511

YONGE,Geoffrey Bowen 2Lt dow 21-11-18 1/5Dev p77 CR France146

YORATH,Glynne Lougher TLt kia 23-11-17 12SWBord p101 MR17

YORKE,Charles Henry T2Lt kia 7-10-16 11RWKent p142 CR France385

YORKE,David 2LtTLt kia 17-2-15 RLancs p59

YORKE,Frederick Lt kld 13-1-19 6Ches attRAF p256 CR Durham26

YORKE,James Hamilton Langdon.MC.Capt kia 27-12-17 PembrokeYeo p205 CR Palestine3,24WelshR

YORKE-JONES,Kenrick T2Lt kia 26-12-17 17Manch p156 CR Belgium126

YORKE-LODGE,Bryant Wynne.MC.2Lt kia 14-9-16 3 att12LancF p94 MR37

YOUDALE,Alfred Clarence.MC&2Bars.2LtACapt kia 23-12-17 SR 21RFC p15 MR20

YOUDEN,Sidney Edwin Capt kia 27-8-18 1DLI att1/7HLI p162 MR16

YOUENS,Frederick.VC.T2Lt dow 7-7-17 13DLI p162 CR Belgium127

YOULL,John Scott.VC.2Lt kia 27-10-18 11NumbF p64 CR Italy7

YOUNG,Ada Elizabeth Nurse 15-7-18 VAD CR Notts70

YOUNG,Alan Catchpole 2Lt kia 24-3-18 5Lond p246 MR27,Catchpool

YOUNG,Alan Edward Frushard 2Lt kia 25-7-17 RGA p42 CR Belgium24

YOUNG,Alan Emilius 2Lt kia 25-9-15 1/20Lond p251 MR19

YOUNG,Albert Maj dow 14-12-14 IA 2/1GurkhaRif attHQ GarhwalRif p284

YOUNG,Albert Meredyth Lt kia 3-3-16 IARO 16Cav p284 CR Iraq ,3-3-15

YOUNG,Alexander Aytoun 2Lt dow 14-3-17 3 att2BlkW p129 MR38

YOUNG,Alfred Gordon 2Lt ded 31-12-16 3/5RWKent p235 CR France787

YOUNG,Andrew 2Lt kia 27-12-16 3ScotRif att13RScots p104 CR France392

YOUNG,Andrew Gardyne Lt kld 13-10-17 1/6A&SH p243 CR Belgium165

YOUNG,Andrew Yates T2Lt kia 30-9-15 13ScotRif att2RScotF p104 MR19

YOUNG,Archibald Lt kia 28-6-15 4RScots A'Coy p211 MR4

YOUNG,Arthur Maj 14-12-14 1GurkhaRif CR France202

YOUNG,Arthur Cecil TCapt kia 6-7-16 16NumbF p64 MR21,1-7-16

YOUNG,Arthur Conway 2Lt kia 16-8-17 4 att7/8RIrFus p172 CR Belgium125

YOUNG,Arthur Cyril 2Lt kia 2-4-17 8RFC p15 CR France120

YOUNG,Arthur Ernest 2Lt dow 21-5-18 D108RFA p209 CR France196

YOUNG,Arthur John 2Lt dow 10-3-18 1 att7SWBord p101 CR Palestine3,1SWB att7RWFus

YOUNG,Arthur Webster TMaj kia 13-9-15 10N&D p135 CR Belgium6

YOUNG,Benjamin Poyntz TCapt ded 6-11-16 RAMC p198 CR Ireland14

YOUNG,Bertrand John 2Lt kia 5-10-18 5RWar B'Coy p214 CR France375,6Bn

YOUNG,C.Lt ded 20-7-18 GL &RAF p192

YOUNG,Charles Alan 2Lt kia 14-10-18 D256RFA p37 CR France241

YOUNG,Charles Edward Lt ded 17-12-18 MilLabCps CR EAfrica36

YOUNG,Claude Norman T2Lt dow 14-7-16 12RScots p55 MR21

YOUNG,Colin Turner.MID Capt kia 24-4-17 3WRid att17WelshR p116 CR France439

YOUNG,Cyril Rutherford Moffat Maj dow 1-7-17 RGA p209 CR Durham181

YOUNG,David Coley.MID LtCol kia 12-3-15 IA 2/4 att1/4GurkhaRif p284 CR France632

YOUNG,David Goldie TLt kia 25-9-15 10ScotRif p104 MR19

YOUNG,David Lindsay 2Lt kia 26-10-17 4NumbF p213 MR30

YOUNG,David William Laird T2Lt kia 6-1-17 GL 53RFC p15 CR France285

YOUNG,Douglas Campbell Lt ded 18-9-15 RFA p208 CR Egypt3

YOUNG,Edmund Taylor Lt kia 10-6-15 6Manch p236 MR4

YOUNG,Edward Thomas Capt dedacc 14-3-18 LabCps att6ChineseLabCoy p189 CR France134

YOUNG,Eric Templeton Capt kia 28-6-15 6ScotRif p224 MR22

YOUNG,Ernest Joseph 2Lt ded 7-11-18 Mddx att18Bn p149 CR France398

YOUNG,Fergus Hay TLt drd 23-10-15 RAMC att29DivAmmCol p198

YOUNG,Francis Chisholm.MID 2Lt kia 14-2-17 3RFC p15 MR20

YOUNG,Frank Edward.VC.2Lt kia 18-9-18 1Herts p252 CR France530

YOUNG,Frank Irwin 2Lt kia 24/25-7-16 1NumbF p64 CR France399

YOUNG,Frederick Dobell Lt dow 6-8-17 RGA p209 CR Belgium12

YOUNG,Frederick Henry.MC&Bar.LtACapt dow 25-8-18 3 att1Lincs p76 CR France131

YOUNG,Frederick Sydney Newman.MIDx2 CaptAMaj ded 1-3-18 RASC p194 CR Iraq8

YOUNG,Geoffrey Abbott 2Lt kia 4-3-17 3Nhampt att24TMB p138 CR France439

YOUNG,George Arnold Lt kia 4-10-17 50RFA p37 MR30

YOUNG,George Cooper T2Lt kia 17-3-18 GL &5RFC p17 CR France95

YOUNG,George Edward Savill Maj dow 31-3-17 1IrGds p53 CR France105

YOUNG,George James Taylor 2Lt kia 20-11-17 15RFC p15 CR France379

YOUNG,George Minchin Capt ded 10-3-16 RASC p194 CR France924

YOUNG,George Neville Gardiner.MC.Lt dow 25-7-15 2Leinst p175 CR France64,Patrick

YOUNG,George Walter Capt kia 27-5-18 8EYorks p85 MR18

YOUNG,George William Capt drd 26-2-18 RAMC p198 MR40

YOUNG,George William Lt dow 8-4-18 PoW 4BlkW p230 CR France934

YOUNG,Harold Farquhar 2Lt kia 20-8-17 3 att9N&D att43RFC p15&135 MR20

YOUNG,Harold Victor 2Lt dow 8-12-17 54RFC p15 CR France1359

YOUNG,Harry Capt ded 4-3-19 RGA p209 CR Belgium396

YOUNG,Henry Harman 2Lt kia 24-5-15 3RFus p255 p263 MR29

YOUNG,Herbert Nugent.DSO.MajALtCol kia 25-10-18 7RInniskF att11N&D p106 CR France231

YOUNG,Hugh Hutchinson 2Lt kia 26-5-18 6SfthH p241 CR France324,7Bn

YOUNG,Hugh Roxburgh Maj dow 21-4-17 1/4RScotF p222 CR Egypt2

YOUNG,James Lt kia 5-4-18 RE 258Co p49 CR France144

YOUNG,James 2Lt kia 24-8-18 5DLI p239 CR France314

YOUNG,James Alexander Y.Lt ded 12-8-15 8Hamps p229 MR4

YOUNG,James Cecil 2Lt kia 6-4-18 7RFus p71 CR France252

YOUNG,James Hill 2Lt dow PoW 17-1-18 14Lond attRFC p20&249 CR France441,Lt

YOUNG,James Logie.MC.Lt kia 19-7-18 8BlkW B'Coy p129&259 CR France324

YOUNG,James Vincent T2Lt kia 1-7-16 9 att8SomLI B'Coy p80 CR France267

YOUNG,John Lt kia 9-6-17 13DLI p162 CR Belgium28

YOUNG,John Lt ded 10-1-20 5HLI p272

YOUNG,John Arthur Capt kia 4-10-17 17N&D p135 MR21

YOUNG,John Edward Rostron T2Lt kld 7-7-17 GL attRFC p15 CR Essex84

YOUNG,John Edwards 2Lt 10-1-20 5HLI attIA CR Scot674

YOUNG,John Erskine Capt kia 24-8-14 RScotF p95 CR Belgium206

YOUNG,John Ferrers Harington LtTCapt kia 1-7-16 3 att1RLancs p59 CR France643

YOUNG,John Haddow 2Lt dow 9-6-18 NumbF att5Bn p64 CR France1437

YOUNG,John Stevenson T2Lt kld 3-2-18 RFC p17 CR Scot87

YOUNG,Leonard George Birmingham 2Lt kia 19-5-16 10Ches p97 MR20

YOUNG,Leslie Alexander Capt kia 21-5-16 20Lond p251 CR France924

YOUNG,Leslie Duncan 2Lt kia 7-10-17 2/7Manch p237 MR30

YOUNG,Lucian Albert 2Lt dow 26-10-18 1SomLI p80 CR France646,Lt

YOUNG,Malcolm Henry Lt kia 29-6-16 5LancF p221 CR France1512

YOUNG,Marcus Ernest 2Lt kia 21-3-18 RFA attX58TMB p37 CR France1893,24-3-18

YOUNG,Martin Cortlandt de Budé T2Lt dow 26-9-15 7KOSB p103 CR France178

YOUNG,Mary Ann Eliza ded 13-2-19 VAD att57GH p200 CR France1571

YOUNG,Margaret Cameron Nurse ded 30-7-18 VAD 2GH p200 CR France34

YOUNG,Mervyn Cyril Nicholas Radford 2Lt dow 25-5-15 RDubF p177 CR France200

YOUNG,Nevill Lindsay 2Lt kia 20-8-16 2RSuss p120 CR France402

YOUNG,Norman Mitchell Lt kia 25-4-15 RScots p55 CR Belgium4,23-4-15

YOUNG,Phillip Lt dow 21-8-18 6Mddx att31MGC p149&186 CR Surrey2,MGC attMddx

YOUNG,Philip Mortlock.MID Lt kia 10-3-15 3 att1Lpool p73 MR22

YOUNG,Reginald James.MC.Capt ded 14-2-19 2Mddx p265

YOUNG,Robert Asshelon 2Lt kia 21-12-14 RMunstF p176

YOUNG,Robert Percival.MC.Lt kia 17-12-17 1/4RSuss p228 CR Palestine3

YOUNG,Roger Assheton 2Lt 22-12-14 2RMunstF MR22

YOUNG,Rowdon Morris T2Lt kia 11-8-16 13RFus p71 CR France1890,Rawdon

YOUNG,Samuel Kenneth 2Lt kia 30-11-17 1LondIrRif p250 MR17

YOUNG,Stanley James Lt kld 23-12-17 RFC p15 CR Hamps57

YOUNG,Sydney Vernon 2Lt dow 25-9-15 RE 56FC p49 MR29

YOUNG,Thomas James.MM.2Lt kia 24-9-17 Mddx att1Bn p149 MR30

YOUNG,Wilfred Henry 2Lt dow 30-5-15 1/6Glouc p225 CR Belgium68,Wilfrid

YOUNG,William TLt kia 22-8-17 7CamH p168 MR30

YOUNG,William Alexander.MC.Capt dow 10-6-18 2BlkW p129 CR Palestine9

YOUNG,William Nicholas 2Lt kia 9-9-16 3RScotF p95 CR France727

YOUNG,William Steele Lt kia 2-11-17 RE att412FC p210 CR Palestine8

YOUNG,William Thomas Lt kia 12-7-17 RGA 12HB p209 CR Belgium6

YOUNG-FULLALOVE,George T2Lt kia 13-8-17 55RFC p15

YOUNG-HERRIES,Alexander Dobrée Capt kia 22-7-16 KOSB p103 CR France397,23-7-16

YOUNGE,Frederick George Patrick Lt dow 14-2-15 2Leinst p175 CR France284

YOUNGER,Charles Frierson Lt dow 21-3-17 Loth&BordHorse p204 CR France251,Frearson

YOUNGER,David George T2Lt kia 1-7-16 17HLI p164 CR France293

YOUNGER,John Malcolm Capt ded 31-8-18 CldGds p262 CR Scot608

YOUNGER,John Ramsay T2Lt kia 6-5-16 15LancF p94 CR France251

YOUNGHUSBAND,Harold.DSO.TLtCol kia 20-4-16 Beds Cmdg7Glouc p87 MR38,21-4-16

YOUNGMAN,John Marshall.MC.TLt kia 23-6-16 9ESurr p113 CR Belgium97

YOUNGS,James William Lt dow 12-4-18 3SStaffs att151MGC p123&186 CR France25,John

YULE,Charles Whitehead TCapt kia 11-5-16 13RScots p55 CR France423

YULE,George Udney.DSO.LtCol ded 22-12-18 RE p49 MR65

YULE,John Carmichael.MC.Lt dow 25-12-17 2GordH p167 CR France512

YULE,Louis William.MID 2Lt kia 29-9-15 RFC p2 CR Belgium82,26-9-15

Z

ZACHARIAS,Francis Herbert 2Lt kia 25-9-16 3 att1SWBord p101 MR21

ZACHARIUS-JESSEL,Victor Albert Villiers 2Lt kia 6-4-17 7 att15DLI p239 MR20,Lt

ZEALLEY,Eric Ralph Lt 30-8-18 Lancs attRAF CR France788

ZEDER,Joseph Herbert 2Lt dow PoW 3-7-16 4 O&BLI p231 CR France924,2Bn

ZEEDENBERG Eric 2Lt 20-7-16 20RFus MR21 Served as COVENTRY

ZEIGLER,Philip Harold T2Lt dow 23-9-16 9 att6EKent p58 CR France46,kia

ZELLAND,Edward Jonathan 2Lt kia 15-12-16 4WRid p227

ZIANI de FERRANTI,Basil.MC.TLtAMaj dow 12-7-17 RGA 21SB p42

ZIGOMALA,John Copeland MBE Lt kld 25 8 19 IrGds attRE p255 MR70 &CR Europe179

APPENDIX 1

A list of the memorials and cemeteries mentioned in the list of officers.

MEMORIALS

MR4   Helles Memorial,Gallipoli.
MR15   La Ferte-Sous-Jouarre Memorial,France.
MR16   Vis-En-Artois Memorial,France.
MR17   Cambrai Memorial,France.
MR18   Soissons Memorial,France.
MR19   Loos Memorial,France.
MR20   Arras Memorial,France.
MR21   Theipval Memorial,France.
MR22   Le Touret Memorial,France.
MR27   Pozieres Memorial,France.
MR28   Neuve-Chapelle Indian Memorial,France.
MR29   Ypres (Menin Gate) Memorial,Belgium.
MR30   Tyne Cot Memorial,Belgium.
MR31   Nieuport Memorial,Belgium.
MR32   Ploegsteert Memorial,Belgium.
MR34   Jerusalem Memorial,Israel.
MR35   Mikra Memorial,Salonica,Greece.
MR37   Dorian Memorial,Greece.
MR38   Basra Memorial,Iraq.
MR40   Hollybrook Memorial,Southampton,England.
MR41   Chatby Memorial,Egypt.
MR43   Delhi Memorial,India.
MR46   Mombasa British Memorial,East Africa.
MR47   Tanga British Memorial Cemetery,East Africa.
MR50   Nairobi British and Indian Memorial,East Africa.
MR52   Dar Es Salaam British and Indian Memorial,East Africa.
MR53   Aden Memorial,Arabia
MR59   Bardera Fort Memorial,Somaliland.
MR61   Tehran Memorial,Iran.
MR64   Bombay (St Thomas) Cathedral Memorial,India.
MR65   Kirkee Memorial,India.
MR66   Madras Memorial,India.
MR67   Karachi Memorial,Pakistan.
MR68   Taukkyan Memorial,Burma.
MR69   Delhi 1914-1918 War Memorial,India.
MR70   Brookwood (Russia) Memorial,England.

CEMETERIES

EAST AFRICA.

2   Handeni Cemetery.
6   Korogwe Churchyard.
7   Korogwe Military Cemetery.
8   Lindi Cemetery.
9   Mhonda Mission Cemetery.
10   Mingoyo Cemetery.
11   Mtama Cemetery.
12   Mwanza Cemetery.
13   New Moshi British Cemetery.
15   Songea European Cemetery.
19   Tanga Main Cemetery.
22   Bweho Chini Military Graves.
23   Chogowali Military Grave.
28   Longido Cemetery.
29   Luchomo Military Grave.
30   Mahiwa Military Graves.
32   Mikese Military Grave.
33   Mkwera Military Graves.
35   Dar Es Salaam (Sea View) Cemetery.
36   Dar Es Salaam (Upanga Street) Cemetery.
38   Kilwa Kivinje Cemetery.
39   Morogoro Cemetery.
40   Iringa Cemetery.
42   Kajiado Cemetery.

43   Kisii Boma Military Grave.
44   Kisumu Cemetery.
46   Molo Military Grave.
47   Mombasa Protestant Cemetery.
49   Mumias European Cemetery.
50   Mwele Ndogo Military Grave.
51   Nairobi Forest Cemetery.
52   Nairobi South Cemetery.
53   Naivasha Cemetery.
54   Nakuru Cemetery.
56   Taveta Military Cemetery.
58   Voi Cemetery.
59   Wajir Cemetery.
60   Hargeisa War Cemetery.
61   Mogadishu African War Cemetery.
66   Port Louis Western Cemetery.
77   Mangochi Town Cemetery.
78   Karonga Church of Central Africa Presbyterian Cemetery.
80   Karonga New War Cemetery.
86   Zomba Town Cemetery.
87   Beira Christian Cemetery.
89   Maputo Cemetery.
90   Lumbo British Cemetery.
92   Pemba Cemetery.
101   Harare (Pioneer)Cemetery.
116   Khartoum War Cemetery.
124   Entebbe European Cemetery.
125   Jinja Roman Catholic Churchyard.
126   Kabarole Mission Cemetery.
127   Kampala (Jinja Road) European Cemetery.
128   Mbarara (St James) Churchyard.

SOUTH AFRICA.

18   Trekkopjes Cemetery.
26   Durban (Ordnance Road) Military Cemetery.
30   Durban (Stellawood) Cemetery.
42   Benoni Cemetery.
52   Johannesburg (Braamfontein) Cemetery.
53   Johannesburg (Brixton New) Cemetery.
63   Potchefstroom European Cemetery.
69   Roberts Heights Military Cemetery,Pretoria.
72   Tzaneen Estate Cemetery,Selati Valley.
81   Rooidam Military Cemetery,Tempe.
144   Plumstead Cemetery,Cape Town.
158   Simonstown (Dido Valley) Cemetery.
171   Woltemade Cemetery,Cape Town.
172   Wynberg (Church Street) Cemetery,Cape Town.

WEST AFRICA.

1   Christiansborg Civil Cemetery.
2   Gambaga European Cemetery.
3   Kumasi European Cemetery.
4   Sekondi (Shama Road) European Cemetery
      now Takoradi European Cemetery,Ghana.
5   Chra Village Cemetery now Whala Cemetery.
6   Kumasi Memorial.
8   Elisabethville Cemetery.
17   Relizane Communal Cemetery.
23   Bathurst Memorial.
28   Freetown Memorial.
30   Freetown (King Tom) Cemetery.
33   Bakundi Military Grave.
35   Bauchi European Cemetery.
39   Enugu Military Grave.
40   Ibadan Mission Church Cemetery.
41   Lkoyi New Cemetery,Lagos.
42   Kaduna Cemetery.
45   Lokoja Town Cemetery.
46   Mamfe European Cemetery.

47	Maio Kalei Military Grave.
48	Nsanakang Cemetery Enclosure.
49	Nsanakang European Cemetery.
50	Udi Military Grave.
52	Yola Station Cemetery.
53	Zaria European Cemetery.
54	Zungeru Cemetery.
55	Calabar Memorial.
56	Ibadan Memorial.
57	Lokoja Memorial.
58	Zaria Memorial.
61	Duala Cemetery.

ASIA.

9	Colombo (Kanatte) General Cemetery,Sri Lanka.
20	Sai Wan Bay Memorial (UMA & UMB),Hong Kong.
33	Hong Kong Cemetery,Hong Kong.
40	Yokohama War Cemetery,Japan.
45	Kranji War Cemetery,Singapore.
51	Haidar Pasha Cemetery,Istanbul.
52	Chanak Consular Cemetery,Asiatic side of the Dardanelles.
53	Famagusta Military Cemetery,Cyprus.
60	Maala Cemetery,Aden.
62	Sheikh Othman Cemetery,Aden.
64	Horth Point Christian Cemetery,Kamaran Island.
66	Muscat Old Cemetery,Oman.
81	Haidar Pasha Memorial.
82	Tehran War Cemetery,Iran.

AUSTRALIA.

112	Sydney (Waverley) General Cemetery.
307	Brighton General Cemetery.

BELGIUM.

1	Ferme-Olivier Cemetery,Elverdinghe.
2	Hop Store Cemetery,Vlamertinghe.
3	Nine Elms British Cemetery,Poperinghe.
4	Vlamertinghe Military Cemetery.
5	Poperinghe New Military Cemetery.
6	Brandhoek Military Cemetery,Vlamertinghe.
7	Brandhoek New Military Cemetery,Vlamertinghe.
8	Brandhoek New Military Cemetery No.3,Vlamertinghe.
9	Hospital Farm Cemetery,Elverdinghe.
10	Vlamertinghe New Military Cemetery.
11	Lijssenthoek Military Cemetery.
12	Canada Farm Cemetery,Elverdinghe.
13	Bleuet Farm Cemetery,Elverdinghe.
15	Reninghelst New Military Cemetery.
16	Dozinghem Military Cemetery,Westvleteren.
17	Kemmel Chateau Military Cemetery.
18	Mendinghem Military Cemetery,Proven.
19	Huts Cemetery,Dickebusch.
20	Duhallow A.D.S. Cemetery,Ypres.
21	La Clytte Military Cemetery,Reninghelst.
22	Oxford Road Cemetery,Ieper.
23	Bard Cottage Cemetery,Boezinge.
24	Coxyde Military Cemetery.
25	Solferino Farm Cemetery,Brielen.
26	Divisional Collecting Post Cemetery,Boesinghe.
27	Track "X" Cemetery,St Jean-Les-Ypres.
28	Dickebusch New Military Cemetery.
29	Dickebusch New Military Cemetery Extension.
30	Gunners Farm Cemetery,Ploegsteert.
31	Motor Car Corner Cemetery,Ploegsteert.
32	Le Touquet Railway Crossing Cemetery,Ploegsteert.
33	Calvaire (Essex) Military Cemetery,Ploegsteert.
34	Belgian Battery Corner Cemetery,Ypres.
35	Divisional Cemetery,Dickebusch Road,Vlamertinghe.
36	Gwalia Cemetery,Poperinghe.
37	Ridge Wood Military Cemetery,Voormezeele.

38	Haringhe (Bandaghem) Military Cemetery.
40	Abeele Aerodrome Military Cemetery,Watou.
41	Watou Churchyard.
42	Kandahar Farm Cemetery,Neuve-Eglise.
43	St Quentin Cabaret Military Cemetery,Ploegsteert.
44	Potijze Burial Ground.
45	Potijze Chateau Grounds Cemetery.
46	Potijze Chateau Lawn Cemetery.
47	Potijze Chateau Wood Cemetery.
48	La Plus Douve Farm Cemetery,Ploegsteert.
49	Ration Farm (La Plus Douve) Annexe,Ploegsteert.
50	Underhill Farm Cemetery,Ploegsteert.
52	Prowse Point Military Cemetery,Warneton.
53	Hyde Park Corner (Royal Berks) Cemetery,Ploegsteert.
54	Berks Cemetery Extension,Ploegsteert.
56	Chester Farm Cemetery,Zillebeke.
57	Ypres Town Cemetery,Menin Gate.
58	Ypres Town Cemetery Extension,Menin Gate.
59	Ramparts Cemetery,Lille Gate,Ypres.
60	La Laiterie Military Cemetery,Kemmel.
61	Spanbroekmolen British Cemetery,Wytschaete.
62	Lone Tree Cemetery,Spanbroekmolen,Wytschaete.
63	St Julien Dressing Station Cemetery,Langemarck.
64	Minty Farm Cemetery,St Jan.
65	No Man's Cot Cemetery,Boezinge.
66	Welsh Cemetery (Caesar's Nose),Boezinge.
67	Colne Valley Cemetery,Boezinge.
68	Lancashire Cottage Cemetery,Ploegsteert
69	Ploegsteert Churchyard.
70	Ploegsteert Wood Military Cemetery,Warneton.
71	Rifle House Cemetery,Warneton.
72	Menin Road South Military Cemetery,Ypres.
73	Essex Farm Cemetery,Boesinghe.
74	Wytschaete Military Cemetery.
75	Derry House Cemetery No.2,Wytschaete.
76	Torreken Farm Cemetery No.1,Wytschaete.
77	Somer Farm Cemetery,Wytschaete.
78	Cabin Hill Cemetery,Wytschaete.
79	Lindenhoek Chalet Military Cemetery,Kemmel.
80	Dickebusch Old Military Cemetery.
81	Reninghelst Churchyard.
82	Reninghelst Churchyard Extension.
83	Clement House Cemetery,Langemarck.
84	Ypres Reservoir Cemetery.
85	Talana Farm Cemetery,Boesinghe.
86	Dragoon Camp Cemetery,Boesinghe.
87	Ruisseau Farm Cemetery,Langemarck.
88	Aeroplane Cemetery,Ypres.
89	Wulverghem-Lindenhoek Road Military Cemetery.
90	Westhof Farm Cemetery,Neuve-Eglise.
91	La Brique Military Cemetery No.1,St Jean-Les-Ypres.
92	La Brique Military Cemetery No.2,St Jean-Les-Ypres.
93	Wieltje Farm Cemetery,St Jean-Les-Ypres.
94	Buffs Road Cemetery,St Jean-Les-Ypres.
96	New Irish Farm Cemetery,St Jean-Les-Ypres.
97	Dranoutre Military Cemetery.
98	Dranoutre Churchyard.
99	Packhorse Farm Shrine Cemetery,Wulverghem.
100	Pond Farm Cemetery,Wulverghem.
101	White House Cemetery,St Jean-Les-Ypres.
102	Klein-Vierstraat British Cemetery,Kemmel.
103	Suffolk Cemetery,Vierstraat,Kemmel.
104	Godezonne Farm Cemetery,Kemmel.
105	Elzenwalle Brasserie Cemetery,Voormezeele.
106	Artillery Wood Cemetery,Boesinghe.
107	R.E. Farm Cemetery,Wytschaete.
111	Voormezeele Enclosure No.3.
112	Hooge Crater Cemetery,Zillebeke.
113	Birr Cross Roads Cemetery,Zillebeke.
114	R.E. Grave,Railway Wood,Zillebeke.

CANADA.

99 Deloraine Cemetery,Souris,Manitoba.
116 Winnipeg (Elmwood) Cemetery.
155 Gabriola Island Graveyard,Nanaimo,British Columbia.
256 Montreal (Mount Royal) Cemetery,Hochelaga,Quebec.
261 Aylmer (St Paul's) Roman Catholic Cemetery,Hull,Quebec.
423 Preeceville Cemetery,Mackenzie,Saskatchewan.
547 Edmonton Cemetery,East Edmonton,Alberta.
740 Halifax (Camp Hill) Cemetery,Nova Scotia.
1028 St John (Fernhill) Cemetery,New Brunswick.
1087 Kincardine Cemetery,Bruce,Ontario.
1114 Kingsville (Greenhill) Cemetery,Essex,Ontario.
1143 Chatham (Maple Leaf) Cemetery,Kent,Ontario.
1245 Ottawa (Beechwood) Cemetery,Carleton,Ontario.
1380 Peterborough (Little Lake) Cemetery,Peterborough,Ontario.
1430 Lindsay (Riverside) Cemetery,Victoria,Ontario.
1464 Brantford (Greenwood) Cemetery,Brant,Ontario.
1531 St Catharines (Victoria Lawn) Cemetery,Lincoln,Ontario.
1667 Hamilton Cemetery,Wentworth,Ontario.
1688 Toronto (Mount Pleasant) Cemetery,York,Ontario.
1691 Toronto (Prospect) Cemetery,York,Ontario.
1694 Toronto (St James's) Cemetery,York,Ontario.

CENTRAL AMERICA.

6 Quirigua Hospital Cemetery,Guatemala.

EGYPT.

1 Alexandria (Hadra) War Memorial Cemetery.
2 Kantara War Memorial Cemetery
3 Chatby Military Cemetery.
6 Chatby War Memorial Cemetery.
7 Port Said War Memorial Cemetery.
8 Ismailia War Memorial Cemetery.
9 Cairo War Memorial Cemetery.
10 Cairo New British Protestant Cemetery.
13 Cairo Civil International Cemetery.
15 Suez War Memorial Cemetery.
19 Mersa Matruh Military Cemetery.

EUROPE.

1 Pieta Military Cemetery,Malta.
3 Ta Braxia Cemetery,Malta.
4 Addolorata Cemetery,Malta.
5 Rinella Military Cemetery,Malta.
7 Pembroke Military Cemetery,Malta.
9 Marsa Jewish Cemetery,Malta.
17 Plovdiv Central Cemetery,Bulgaria.
20 Sofia War Cemetery,Bulgaria.
23 Gibraltar (North Front) Cemetery,Gibraltar.
28 Lisbon (St George) British Churchyard,Portugal.
42 Madrid British Cemetery,Spain.
51 Vevey (St Martin's) Cemetery,Switzerland.
56 Belgrade New Cemetery,Yugoslavia.
57 Chela Kula Military Cemetery,Nish,Yugoslavia.
58 Skoplje (Uskub) British Cemetery,Yugoslavia.
58a Kuzala Cemetery,Rijeka,Yugoslavia.
74 Vederso Churchyard,Denmark.
96 Noordwijk General Cemetery,Holland.
97 Orthen Protestant Cemetery,Hertogenbosch,Holland.
149 Poznan Old Garrison Cemetery,Poland.
150a Malbork Commonwealth War Cemetery,Poland.
179 Archangel Allied Cemetery,Russia.
180 Archangel Memorial,Russia.
193 Churkin Russian Naval Cemetery,Vladivostok,Siberia.
195 Vladivostok Memorial,Siberia.

FRANCE.

1 Le Treport Military Cemetery.
2 Forceville Communal Cemetery Extension.
3 Louvencourt Military Cemetery.

4 Acheux British Cemetery.
5 Bertrancourt Military Cemetery.
8 Calais Southern Cemetery.
10 Pernes British Cemetery.
12 Barlin Communal Cemetery Extension.
13 Mont Huon Military Cemetery,Le Treport.
14 Ligny-St Flochel British Cemetery,Averdoingt.
15 Maroeuil British Cemetery.
16 BoisGuillaume Communal Cemetery.
18 Morbecque British Cemetery.
19 Le Grand Hasard Military Cemetery,Morbecque.
20 Thiennes British Cemetery.
21 Tannay British Cemetery,Thiennes.
22 Corbie Communal Cemetery.
23 Corbie Communal Cemetery Extension.
24 Cinq Rues British Cemetery,Hazebrouck.
25 La Kreule Military Cemetery,Hazebrouck.
26 Le Peuplier Military Cemetery,Caestre.
27 Caestre Military Cemetery.
28 Borre British Cemetery.
29 Crouy British Cemetery,Crouy-Sur-Somme.
30 Crouy Communal Cemetery,Crouy-Sur-Somme.
31 Aire Communal Cemetery.
32 Bruay Communal Cemetery Extension.
33 Sandpits British Cemetery,Labeuvriere.
34 Terlincthun British Cemetery,Wimille.
35 Auchonvillers Military Cemetery.
37 Picquigny British Cemetery.
39 Longpre-Les-Corps Saints British Cemetery.
40 Etaples Military Cemetery.
41 Varennes Military Cemetery.
43 Warloy-Baillon Communal Cemetery.
44 Warloy-Baillon Communal Cemetery Extension.
46 Avesnes-Le-Comte Communal Cemetery Extension.
49 Izel-Les-Hameau Communal Cemetery.
51 Abbeville Communal Cemetery.
52 Abbeville Communal Cemetery Extension.
53 Haute-Avesnes British Cemetery.
54 Dainville British Cemetery.
55 Dainville Communal Cemetery.
57 Wanquetin Communal Cemetery Extension.
58 La Chaudiere Military Cemetery,Vimy.
59 Contay British Cemetery.
60 Harponville Communal Cemetery.
61 Harponville Communal Cemetery Extension.
62 Doullens Communal Cemetery Extension No.1.
63 Doullens Communal Cemetery Extension No.2.
64 Wimereux Communal Cemetery.
65 Les Baraques Military Cemetery,Sangatte.
66 La Neuville British Cemetery,Corbie.
67 La Neuville Communal Cemetery,Corbie.
68 Ecoivres Military Cemetery,Mont-St Eloy.
69 Pernois British Cemetery,Halloy-Les-Pernois.
71 Vignacourt British Cemetery.
74 Puchevillers British Cemetery.
76 Toutencourt Communal Cemetery.
77 Herissart Communal Cemetery.
79 Molliens-Au-Bois Communal Cemetery.
80 Bethune Town Cemetery.
81 Villers Station Cemetery,Villers-Au-Bois.
82 Ration Farm Military Cemetery,La Chapelle-D'Armentieres.
83 Brewery Orchard Cemetery,Bois-Grenier.
84 Bagneux British Cemetery,Gezaincourt.
85 Ste Marie Cemetery,Le Havre.
87 Sanvic Communal Cemetery.
88 Lapugnoy Military Cemetery.
94 Marles-Les-Mines Communal Cemetery.
95 Aubigny Communal Cemetery Extension.
96 Ste Catherine British Cemetery.
97 St Nicholas British Cemetery.

278 Thilloy Road Cemetery,Beaulencourt.
279 Guards Cemetery,Windy Corner,Cuinchy.
280 Courcelette British Cemetery.
281 Foncquevillers Military Cemetery.
283 Hannescamps New Military Cemetery.
284 Bailleul Communal Cemetery.
285 Bailleul Communal Cemetery Extension.
286 Briastre Communal Cemetery.
287 Belle Vue British Cemetery,Briastre.
288 Solesmes Communal Cemetery.
289 Solesmes British Cemetery.
290 Crucifix Cemetery,Vendegies-Sur-Ecaillon.
292 Vertain Communal Cemetery Extension.
293 Lonsdale Cemetery,Aveluy and Authuile.
294 Guillemont Road Cemetery,Guillemont.
295 Bouzincourt Communal Cemetery.
296 Bouzincourt Communal Cemetery Extension.
297 Trois-Arbres Cemetery,Steenwerck.
298 Le Grand Beaumart British Cemetery,Steenwerck.
299 St Acheul French National Cemetery,Amiens.
300 St Pierre Cemetery,Amiens.
303 Longueau British Cemetery.
304 Camon Communal Cemetery.
306 Bancourt Communal Cemetery.
307 Bancourt British Cemetery.
308 Manchester Cemetery,Riencourt-Les-Bapaume.
309 Sun Quarry Cemetery,Cherisy.
311 Orange Trench Cemetery,Monchy-Le-Preux.
312 Happy Valley British Cemetery,Fampoux.
314 Regina Trench Cemetery,Grandcourt.
315 Haspres Coppice Cemetery,Haspres.
316 York Cemetery,Haspres.
319 Quievy Communal Cemetery Extension.
320 St Hilaire-Les Cambrai British Cemetery.
321 Canonne Farm British Cemetery,Sommaing.
323 Montrecourt Churchyard.
324 Meteren Military Cemetery.
327 Brie British Cemetery.
328 Ennemain Communal Cemetery Extension.
329 Bronfay Farm Military Cemetery,Bray-Sur-Somme.
330 Devonshire Cemetery,Mametz.
331 Gordon Cemetery,Mametz.
332 Awoingt British Cemetery.
333 Awoingt Churchyard.
336 Estourmel Churchyard.
337 Carnieres Communal Cemetery Extension.
338 Forenville Military Cemetery.
339 Ancre British Cemetery,Beaumont-Hamel.
340 Busigny Communal Cemetery.
341 Busigny Communal Cemetery Extension.
342 Sailly-Au-Bois Military Cemetery.
343 Hedauville Communal Cemetery Extension.
344 Mailly-Maillet Communal Cemetery Extension.
345 Merville Communal Cemetery.
346 Merville Communal Cemetery Extension.
347 Rue-David Military Cemetery,Fleurbaix.
348 Rue-Du-Bois Military Cemetery,Fleurbaix.
349 White City Cemetery,Bois-Grenier.
350 Vieux-Berquin Communal Cemetery.
352 Aval Wood Military Cemetery,Vieux-Berquin.
353 Nieppe-Bois (Rue-Du-Bois) British Cemetery,Vieux-Berquin.
354 La Gorgue Communal Cemetery.
355 Lestrem Communal Cemetery.
356 Calonne-Sur-La-Lys Communal Cemetery.
357 Lowrie Cemetery,Havrincourt.
358 Grand Ravine British Cemetery,Havrincourt.
359 Ribecourt Railway Cemetery.
360 Bouchoir New British Cemetery.
363 Villers-Faucon Communal Cemetery.
364 Villeers-Faucon Communal Cemetery Extension.

365 Ste Emilie Valley Cemetery,Villers-Faucon.
366 Jeancourt Communal Cemetery Extension.
368 Epehy Communal Cemetery.
369 Epehy Wood Farm Cemetery,Epehy.
370 Meaulte Military Cemetery.
372 Fricourt British Cemetery (Bray Road).
373 Fricourt New Military Cemetery.
374 Guards' Cemetery,Lesboeufs.
375 Bellicourt British Cemetery.
376 Uplands Cemetery,Magny-La-Fosse.
377 Janval Cemetery,Dieppe.
379 Fifteen Ravine British Cemetery,Villers-Plouich.
380 Delsaux Farm Cemetery,Beugny.
381 Red Cross Corner Cemetery,Beugny.
382 Haplincourt Communal Cemetery.
383 Mill Road Cemetery,Thiepval.
384 Grandcourt Road Cemetery,Grandcourt.
385 Warlencourt British Cemetery.
386 Bazentin-Le-Petit Communal Cemetery.
387 Bazentin-Le-Petit Communal Cemetery Extension.
388 Bazentin-Le-Petit Military Cemetery.
389 Thistle Dump Cemetery,High Wood,Longueval.
390 London Cemetery and Extension,High Wood,Longueval.
392 Martinpuich British Cemetery.
393 Ovillers Military Cemetery.
394 Citadel New Military Cemetery,Fricourt.
395 Bray Hill British Cemetery,Bray-Sur-Somme.
396 Bray Vale British Cemetery,Bray-Sur-Somme.
397 Dantzig Alley British Cemetery,Mametz.
398 Rocquigny-Equancourt Road British Cemetery,Manancourt.
399 Quarry Cemetery,Montauban.
400 Bernafay Wood British Cemetery,Montauban.
401 Longueval Road Cemetery.
402 Delville Wood Cemetery,Longueval.
403 Cambrai East Military Cemetery.
404 Drummond Cemetery,Raillencourt.
406 Sucrerie Cemetery,Epinoy.
407 Villers Hill British Cemetery,Villers-Guislain.
410 Hinges Military Cemetery.
411 Le Vertannoy British Cemetery,Hinges.
412 Mont-Bernenchon British Cemetery,Gonnehem.
413 Mont-Bernenchon Churchyard.
414 Annezin Communal Cemetery.
415 Gouzeaucourt New British Cemetery.
417 Heudicourt Communal Cemetery Extension.
418 Beaurains Road Cemetery,Beaurains.
419 Achicourt Road Cemetery,Achicourt.
420 Agny Military Cemetery.
421 Vis-En-Artois British Cemetery,Haucourt.
423 Vermelles British Cemetery.
424 Crucifix Corner Cemetery,Villers-Bretonneux.
425 Hangard Communal Cemetery Extension.
426 Dury Mill British Cemetery.
427 Dury Crucifix Cemetery.
429 Sauchy-Cauchy Communal Cemetery Extension.
430 Albert Communal Cemetery Extension.
432 Caterpillar Valley Cemetery,Longueval.
433 Ecoust-St Mein British Cemetery.
434 Heninel-Croisilles Road Cemetery.
435 Lagnicourt Hedge Cemetery.
437 Morchies Australian Cemetery.
438 Morchies Military Cemetery.
439 Fins New British Cemetery,Sorel-Le-Grand.
441 Premont British Cemetery.
443 Montbrehain British Cemetery.
444 Calvaire Cemetery,Montbrehain.
445 High Tree Cemetery,Montbrehain.
446 Tincourt New British Cemetery.
448 Aizecourt-Le-Bas Churchyard.
451 Athies Communal Cemetery Extension.

452	Point-Du-Jour Military Cemetery,Athies.
453	Flatiron Copse Cemetery,Mametz.
457	City of Paris Cemetery,Pantin.
461	Levallois-Perret Communal Cemetery.
462	Neuilly-Sur-Seine New Communal Cemetery.
473	Les Gonards Cemetery,Versailles.
477	St Germain-En-Laye Old Communal Cemetery.
480	Aix-Noulette Communal Cemetery Extension.
481	Ontario Cemetery,Sains-Les-Marquion.
482	Triangle Cemetery,Inchy-En-Artois.
484	Moeuvres British Cemetery.
485	Hourges Orchard Cemetery,Domart-Sur-La-Luce.
487	Demuin British Cemetery.
489	Hangard Wood British Cemetery.
490	Gentelles Communal Cemetery.
495	St Venant Communal Cemetery.
496	St Venant Communal Cemetery Extension.
498	Berguette Churchyard.
500	Busnes Communal Cemetery.
501	Berles-Au-Bois Churchyard Extension.
502	Berles New Military Cemetery.
503	Berles Position Military Cemetery.
504	Bellacourt Military Cemetery,Riviere.
505	De Cuisine Ravine British Cemetery,Basseux.
506	Beaumetz-Les-Loges Communal Cemetery.
511	Peronne Communal Cemetery Extension,Ste Radegonde.
512	Grevillers British Cemetery.
513	Carnoy Military Cemetery.
514	Queens Cemetery,Bucquoy.
515	Becourt Military Cemetery,Becordel-Becourt.
516	Bouzincourt Ridge Cemetery,Albert.
518	Achiet-Le-Grand Communal Cemetery Extension.
521	Cross Roads Cemetery,Fontaine-Au-Bois.
522	Thelus Military Cemetery.
523	Nine Elms Military Cemetery,Thelus.
524	Raperie British Cemetery,Villemontoire.
525	Rue-Petillon Military Cemetery.
526	Heath Cemetery,Harbonnieres.
527	Roisel Communal Cemetery.
528	Roisel Communal Cemetery Extension.
529	Hermies British Cemetery.
530	Hermies Hill British Cemetery.
531	Feuchy Chapel British Cemetery,Wancourt.
532	Tigris Lane Cemetery,Wancourt.
533	Frankfurt Trench British Cemetery,Beaumont-Hamel.
534	New Munich Trench British Cemetery,Beaumont-Hamel.
535	Stump Road Cemetery,Grandcourt.
536	Guemappe British Cemetery,Wancourt.
537	Tank Cemetery,Guemappe.
538	Heninel Communal Cemetery Extension.
539	Bootham Cemetery,Heninel.
540	Cherisy Road East Cemetery,Heninel.
541	Rookery British Cemetery,Heninel.
543	Vis-En-Artois Communal Cemetery.
544	Fampoux British Cemetery.
545	Level Crossing Cemetery,Fampoux.
546	Crump Trench British Cemetery,Fampoux.
547	Sucrerie Cemetery,Ablain-St Nazaire.
548	Givenchy-En-Gohelle Canadian Cemetery,Souchez.
549	Zouave Valley Cemetery,Souchez.
550	Loos British Cemetery.
551	St Patrick's Cemetery,Loos.
552	Bois-Carre Military Cemetery,Haisnes.
553	Ninth Avenue Cemetery,Haisnes.
554	Fosse 7 Military Cemetery (Quality Street),Mazingarbe.
557	Lievin Communal Cemetery Extension.
558	Bois-De-Noulette British Cemetery,Aix-Noulette.
559	Tranchee De Mecknes Cemetery,Aix-Noulette.
560	Beaulencourt British Cemetery,Ligny-Thilloy.
561	Beugnatre Communal Cemetery.

562	Barastre Communal Cemetery.
563	Favreuil British Cemetery.
564	Bapaume Australian Cemetery.
566	Le Trou Aid Post Cemetery,Fleurbaix.
567	Aubers Ridge British Cemetery,Aubers.
568	H.A.C. Cemetery,Ecoust-St Mein.
570	Fosse No.10 Communal Cemetery Extension,Sains-En-Gohelle.
571	Beuvry Communal Cemetery.
572	Beuvry Communal Cemetery Extension.
573	Quatre-Vents Military Cemetery,Estree-Cauchy.
576	Gommecourt Wood New Cemetery,Foncquevillers.
577	Bucquoy Communal Cemetery.
578	Bucquoy Communal Cemetery Extension.
579	Shrine Cemetery,Bucquoy.
580	Owl Trench Cemetery,Hebuterne.
581	Tilloy British Cemetery,Tilloy-Les-Mofflaines.
582	Cayeux Communal Cemetery.
583	Cayeux Military Cemetery.
585	Le Quesnel Communal Cemetery Extension.
587	Mezieres Communal Cemetery Extension.
588	Beaucourt-En-Santerre Churchyard.
589	Beaucourt British Cemetery.
591	Cojeul British Cemetery,St Martin-Sur-Cojeul.
592	St Martin Calvaire British Cemetery,St Martin-Sur-Cojeul.
593	Boyelles Communal Cemetery Extension.
594	Hibers Trench Cemetery,Wancourt.
595	Neuville-Vitasse Road Cemetery,Neuville-Vitasse.
596	Henin Crucifix Cemetery.
598	Porte-De-Paris Cemetery,Cambrai.
602	Cantaing British Cemetery.
604	Brown's Copse Cemetery,Roeux.
605	Pargny British Cemetery.
609	Voyennes Communal Cemetery.
610	Nesle Communal Cemetery.
611	Naves Communal Cemetery Extension.
612	Wellington Cemetery,Rieux-En-Cambresis.
613	Villers-En-Cauchies Communal Cemetery.
614	Mory Abbey Military Cemetery,Mory.
615	Mory Street Military Cemetery,St Leger.
616	St Leger British Cemetery.
617	Gomiecourt South Cemetery.
618	Railway Cutting Cemetery,Courcelles-Le-Comte.
619	Warry Copse Cemetery,Courcelles-Le-Comte.
620	Ervillers Military Cemetery.
622	Marfaux British Cemetery.
624	Hem Farm Military Cemetery,Hem-Monacu.
625	Suzanne Communal Cemetery Extension.
626	Suzanne Military Cemetery No.3
629	Frise Communal Cemetery.
630	Peronne Road Cemetery,Maricourt.
631	St Vaast Post Military Cemetery,Richebourg-L'Avoue.
632	Rue-Des-Berceaux Military Cemetery,Richebourg-L'Avoue.
633	Morlancourt British Cemetery No.1
634	Morlancourt British Cemetery No.2,Ville-Sur-Ancre.
636	Ville-Sur-Ancre Communal Cemetery Extension.
637	Point 110 Old Military Cemetery,Fricourt.
638	Point 110 New Military Cemetery,Fricourt.
639	Chipilly Communal Cemetery.
643	Sucrerie Military Cemetery,Colincamps.
644	Bailleul Road East Cemetery,St Laurent-Blangy.
645	Bailleul Road West Cemetery,St Laurent-Blangy.
646	Queant Road Cemetery,Buissy.
647	Cagnicourt British Cemetery.
648	Rosieres Communal Cemetery.
649	Rosieres Communal Cemetery Extension.
650	Rosieres British Cemetery,Vauvillers.
651	Caix Communal Cemetery.
652	Caix British Cemetery.
657	Caudry Old Communal Cemetery.
658	Caudry British Cemetery.

660 Honnechy British Cemetery.	759 Louverval Military Cemetery,Doignies.
661 Inchy Communal Cemetery Extension.	760 Iwuy Communal Cemetery.
662 Metz-En-Couture Communal Cemetery British Extension.	761 Niagara Cemetery,Iwuy.
663 Targelle Ravine British Cemetery,Villers-Guislain.	765 Gorre British Cemetery,Beuvry.
664 Villers-Guislain Communal Cemetery.	768 Estaires Communal Cemetery.
665 Pigeon Ravine Cemetery,Epehy.	769 Estaires Communal Cemetery Extension.
666 Domino British Cemetery,Epehy.	770 Blargies Communal Cemetery Extension.
667 Villers-Plouich Communal Cemetery.	772 Forges-Les-Eaux Communal Cemetery.
668 Sunken Road Cemetery,Villers-Plouich.	777 Orchard Dump Cemetery,Arleux-En-Gohelle.
669 Saulcourt Churchyard Extension,Guyencourt-Saulcourt.	779 Lens Communal Cemetery,Sallaumines.
672 Savy British Cemetery.	782 Billy-Montigny Communal Cemetery.
673 Marteville Communal Cemetery,Attilly.	783 Izel-Les-Equerchin Communal Cemetery.
674 Vermand Communal Cemetery.	785 Combles Communal Cemetery Extension.
675 Roupy Communal Cemetery.	786 Guards' Cemetery,Combles.
680 "X" Farm Cemetery,La Chapelle-D'Armentieres.	787 St Pol Communal Cemetery Extension.
681 Chapelle-D'Armentieres Old Military Cemetery.	788 St Pol British Cemetery,St Pol-Sur-Ternoise.
682 Chapelle-D'Armentieres New Military Cemetery.	790 Hesdin Communal Cemetery.
683 La Chapelle-D'Armentieres Communal Cemetery.	792 Huby-St Leu British Cemetery.
684 Bois-Grenier Communal Cemetery.	795 St Georges Churchyard.
685 Suffolk Cemetery,La Rolanderie Farm,Erquinghem-Lys.	798 Gommecourt British Cemetery No.2,Hebuterne.
686 Queant Communal Cemetery British Extension.	800 Rossignol Wood Cemetery,Hebuterne.
687 Dominion Cemetery,Hendecourt-Les-Cagnicourt.	801 Luke Copse British Cemetery,Puisieux.
689 Croisilles Railway Cemetery.	802 Queens Cemetery,Puisieux.
690 Ecoust Military Cemetery,Ecoust-St Mein.	803 Ten Tree Alley Cemetery,Puisieux.
692 Fouquescourt British Cemetery.	804 Quesnoy Farm Military Cemetery,Bucquoy.
694 Vrely Communal Cemetery Extension.	805 Fienvillers British Cemetery.
699 Cerisy-Gailly Military Cemetery.	806 Pont-Remy British Cemetery.
700 Cerisy-Gailly French National Cemetery.	808 St Ouen Communal Cemetery.
701 Hamel Military Cemetery,Beaumont-Hamel.	813 Bonneville Communal Cemetery.
702 Authuile Military Cemetery.	816 Conde-Folie Communal Cemetery.
703 Contalmaison Chateau Cemetery.	817 Coulonvillers Communal Cemetery.
704 Senlis Communal Cemetery Extension.	818 Cramont Communal Cemetery.
705 Pont-Du-Hem Military Cemetery,La Gorgue.	832 Pozieres British Cemetery,Ovillers-La Boisselle.
706 Royal Irish Rifles Graveyard,Laventie.	833 Heilly Station Cemetery,Mericourt-L'Abbe.
707 Rue-Du-Bacquerot (13th London) Graveyard,Laventie.	834 Caulaincourt Communal Cemetery.
708 Euston Post Cemetery,Laventie.	835 Trefcon British Cemetery,Caulaincourt.
709 Neuve-Chapelle British Cemetery.	836 Hancourt British Cemetery.
710 Neuve-Chapelle Farm Cemetery.	837 Beaumetz Communal Cemetery.
711 Ribecourt British Cemetery.	839 Mons-En-Chaussee Communal Cemetery.
712 Ribecourt Road Cemetery,Trescault.	840 Tertry Communal Cemetery.
713 Trescault Communal Cemetery.	841 Vraignes Communal Cemetery.
714 Quarry Wood Cemetery,Sains-Les-Marquion.	844 Beaurevoir British Cemetery.
716 Le Cateau Military Cemetery.	845 Guizancourt Farm Cemetery,Gouy.
717 Le Cateau Communal Cemetery.	846 Serain Communal Cemetery Extension.
718 Selridge British Cemetery,Montay.	847 Fresnoy-Le-Grand Communal Cemetery Extension.
720 Cuinchy Communal Cemetery.	848 Brancourt-Le-Grand Communal Cemetery.
721 Woburn Abbey Cemetery,Cuinchy.	849 Brancourt-Le-Grand Military Cemetery.
725 Vadencourt British Cemetery,Maissemy.	855 Bertenacre Military Cemetery,Fletre.
727 Le Touret Military Cemetery,Richebourg-L'Avoue.	856 Mont-Noir Military Cemetery,St Jans-Cappel.
728 Highland Cemetery,Roclincourt.	857 Borre Churchyard.
729 Mindel Trench British Cemetery,St Laurent-Blangy.	858 Caestre Communal Cemetery.
730 Hervin Farm British Cemetery,St Laurent-Blangy.	860 Hondeghem Churchyard.
731 Bunyans Cemetery,Tilloy-Les-Mofflaines.	861 La Creche Communal Cemetery,Bailleul.
733 Ghissignies British Cemetery.	864 Vauxbuin French National Cemetery.
734 Englefontaine Churchyard.	865 Buzancy Military Cemetery.
735 Englefontaine British Cemetery.	866 Oulchy-Le-Chateau Churchyard Extension.
737 Poix-Du-Nord Communal Cemetery Extension	867 Crouy-Vauxrot French National Cemetery,Crouy.
730 Preux-Au-Bois Communal Cemetery.	870 Chacrise Communal Cemetery.
739 Bermerain Communal Cemetery.	874 Ste Marguerite Churchyard.
742 Serre Road Cemetery No.1,Beaumont-Hamel,Hebuterne and Puisieux.	878 Villemontoire Communal Cemetery.
743 Serre Road Cemetery No.3,Puisieux.	879 Boves East Communal Cemetery.
744 A.I.F. Burial Ground,Grass Lane,Flers.	880 Boves West Communal Cemetery.
745 Bienvillers Military Cemetery.	881 Boves West Communal Cemetery Extension.
747 Humbercamps Communal Cemetery Extension.	882 Allonville Communal Cemetery.
748 Bailleulmont Communal Cemetery.	885 Frechencourt Communal Cemetery.
749 Barly French Military Cemetery.	886 Bavelincourt Communal Cemetery.
755 Ruyaulcourt Military Cemetery.	887 Montigny Communal Cemetery (Somme).
756 Beaumetz Cross Roads Cemetery,Beaumetz-Les-Cambrai.	888 Montigny Communal Cemetery Extension (Somme).
757 Beaumetz-Les-Cambrai Military Cemetery No.1	889 Blangy-Tronville Communal Cemetery.
758 Bertincourt Chateau British Cemetery.	891 Bertangles Communal Cemetery.

904 Neuville-Bourjonval Communal Cemetery.
905 Neuville-Bourjonval British Cemetery.
906 Five Points Cemetery,Lechelle.
907 Ytres Communal Cemetery.
908 Manancourt Communal Cemetery.
910 Marcoing Communal Cemetery.
911 Marcoing British Cemetery.
912 Masnieres British Cemetery,Marcoing.
913 Noyelles-Sur-L'Escaut Communal Cemetery.
914 Noyelles-Sur-L'Escaut Communal Cemetery Extension.
915 Rumilly Communal Cemetery Extension.
916 Cagnoncles Communal Cemetery.
920 Niergnies Communal Cemetery.
921 Le Bizet Cemetery,Armentieres.
922 Cite Bonjean Military Cemetery,Armentieres.
924 Cabaret-Rouge British Cemetery.Souchez.
925 Ayette British Cemetery.
927 Douchy-Les-Ayette British Cemetery.
928 Avesnes-Sur-Helpe Communal Cemetery.
929 Fontaine-Au-Bois Communal Cemetery.
930 Dourlers Communal Cemetery Extension.
931 Maubeuge (Sous-Le-Bois) Cemetery.
932 Landrecies Communal Cemetery.
933 Landrecies British Cemetery.
934 Hautmont Communal Cemetery.
935 Berlaimont Communal Cemetery.
936 Berlaimont Communal Cemetery Extension.
937 Pont-Sur-Sambre Communal Cemetery.
938 Sebourg British Cemetery.
939 Sebourg Communal Cemetery.
940 Ors British Cemetery.
941 Aulnoye Communal Cemetery.
943 Grand-Fyat Communal Cemetery.
944 Maroilles Communal Cemetery.
948 Bermeries Communal Cemetery.
949 Brttrechies Communal Cemetery.
952 Ecuelin Churchyard.
953 Eth Communal Cemetery.
955 Gommegnies Communal Cemetery.
957 Hargnies Communal Cemetery.
965 Malplaquet Communal Cemetery,Taisnieres-Sur-Hon.
968 Monceau-St Waast Communal Cemetery.
978 St Remy-Chaussee Communal Cemetery.
979 St Waast-La-Vallee Communal Cemetery.
981 Semousies Churchyard.
982 Taisnieres-En-Thierache Communal Cemetery.
984 Wargnies-Le-Grand Churchyard.
985 Wargnies-Le-Petit Communal Cemetery.
987 Roye New British Cemetery.
988 Moreuil Communal Cemetery Allied Extension.
1003 Hailles Communal Cemetery.
1008 Rouvrel Communal Cemetery.
1012 Englebelmer Communal Cemetery.
1013 Englebelmer Communal Cemetery Extension.
1014 St Amand British Cemetery.
1016 Henu Churchyard.
1017 Mondicourt Communal Cemetery.
1022 Ignaucourt Churchyard.
1027 Lille Southern Cemetery.
1028 St Andre Communal Cemetery.
1029 Tourcoing (Pont-Neuville) Communal Cemetery.
1030 Ascq Communal Cemetery.
1031 Halluin Communal Cemetery.
1032 Linselles Communal Cemetery.
1033 Fretin Communal Cemetery.
1034 Cretinier Cemetery,Wattrelos.
1039 Bousbecques Communal Cemetery.
1041 Criox Communal Cemetery.
1044 hem Communal Cemetery.
1049 Mouvaux New Comunal Cemetery.

1050 Neuville-En-Ferrain Communal Cemetery.
1054 Sailly-Les-Lannoy Churchyard.
1058 Willems Communal Cemetery.
1059 Arras Road Cemetery,Roclincourt.
1061 Grand-Seraucourt British Cemetery.
1063 Noyon New British Cemetery.
1066 Montescourt-Lizerolles Communal Cemetery.
1071 Blerancourt Communal Cemetery.
1074 Jussy Communal Cemetery.
1076 Le Quesnoy Communal Cemetery.
1079 Preseau Communal Cemetery Extension.
1080 Villers-Pol Communal Cemetery Extension.
1081 Ruesnes Communal Cemetery.
1082 Capelle-Beaudignies Road Cemetery,Capelle.
1084 Artres Communal Cemetery.
1087 Maresches Communal Cemetery.
1091 Steenwerck Communal Cemetery.
1092 Croix-Du-Bac British Cemetery,Steenwerck.
1094 Haverskerque British Cemetery.
1095 Laventie Communal Cemetery.
1100 Steenbecque Churchyard.
1106 Vieille-Chapelle New Military Cemetery,Lacouture.
1107 Vailly British Cemetery.
1108 Guards' Grave,Villers-Cotterets Forest.
1110 Braine Communal Cemetery.
1111 Soupir Churchyard.
1112 Soupir Communal Cemetery.
1113 Montreuil-Aux-Lions British Cemetery.
1117 Bezu-Le-Guery Communal Cemetery.
1128 Gandelu Communal Cemetery.
1129 Haramont Communal Cemetery.
1134 Priez Communal Cemetery.
1139 Vieil-Arcy Communal Cemetery.
1140 Houplines Communal Cemetery Extension.
1141 Ferme Buterne Military Cemetery,Houplines.
1142 Valenciennes (St Roch) Communal Cemetery.
1144 Raismes Communal Cemetery.
1147 Bruille-St Amand Churchyard.
1154 Thivencelle Churchyard.
1157 Rue-Du-Bacquerot No.1 Military Cemetery,Laventie.
1158 Fauquissart Military Cemetery,Laventie.
1159 Quesnoy-Sur-Deule Communal Cemetery.
1160 Quesnoy-Sur-Deule Communal Cemetery,German Extension.
1161 Isbergues Communal Cemetery.
1169 St Hilaire-Cottes Churchyard.
1170 Villers-Bretonneux Military Cemetery,Fouilloy.
1172 Fouilloy Communal Cemetery.
1173 Aubigny British Cemetery (Somme).
1180 Neufchatel Churchyard.
1182 Faubourg-D'Amiens Cemetery,Arras.
1183 Boisleux-Au-Mont Communal Cemetery.
1184 Sunken Road Cemetery,Boisleux St Marc.
1185 London Cemetery,Neuville-Vitasse.
1186 Henin Communal Cemetery Extension.
1187 Summit Trench Cemetery,Croisilles.
1188 Feuchy British Cemetery.
1190 Sunken Road Cemetery,Fampoux.
1191 Albuera Cemetery,Bailleul-Sire-Berthoult.
1193 Chili Trench Cemetery,Gavrelle.
1194 Roeux British Cemetery.
1196 Auberchicourt British Cemetery.
1198 Masny Churchyard.
1202 Ham Communal Cemetery.
1203 Ham British Cematery,Muille-Villette.
1204 Foreste Communal Cemetery.
1205 Douilly Communal Cemetery.
1206 Eppeville Churchyard.
1211 Maubeuge-Centre Cemetery.
1216 Sains-Du-Nord Communal Cemetery.
1219 Floursies Churchyard.

1223 Solre-Le-Chateau Communal Cemetery.
1225 Senlis French National Cemetery.
1227 Compiegne South Communal Cemetery.
1228 Royallieu French National Cemetery,Compiegne.
1230 Verberie French National Cemetery.
1231 Nery Communal Cemetery.
1233 Marissel French National Cemetery.
1234 Dompierre French National Cemetery.
1235 Vignemont French National Cemetery.
1236 Annel Communal Cemetery,Longueil-Annel.
1242 Hardivillers Communal Cemetery.
1252 Denain Communal Cemetery.
1254 Famars Communal Cemetery Extension.
1256 Maing Communal Cemetery extension.
1257 Querenaing Communal Cemetery.
1258 Thiant Communal Cemetery.
1259 Vendegies Cross Roads British Cemetery,Bermerain.
1260 Verchain British Cemetery,Verchain-Maugre.
1266 St Souplet British Cemetery.
1268 Vaux-Andigny British Cemetery.
1269 La Vallee-Mulatre Communal Cemetery.
1270 La Vallee-Mulatre Communal Cemetery Extension.
1271 Wassigny Communal Cemetery.
1272 Le Rejet-De-Beaulieu Communal Cemetery.
1274 St Benin Communal Cemetery (Nord).
1276 Douai Communal Cemetery.
1277 Douai British Cemetery,Cuincy.
1278 Brebieres British Cemetery.
1279 Annoeullin Communal Cemetery German Extension.
1281 Arleux-Du-Nord Communal Cemetery.
1284 Auby Communal Cemetery.
1287 Brillon Communal Cemetery.
1293 Hem-Lenglet Communal Cemetery.
1295 Lallaing Communal Cemetery.
1296 Lecelles Churchyard.
1301 Paillencourt Churchyard.
1308 Somain Communal Cemetery.
1310 Beaumont Communal Cemetery.
1311 Corbehem Communal Cemetery.
1314 Noyelles-Godault Communal Cemetery.
1316 Quiery-La-Motte Communal Cemetery.
1321 Bois-Carre British Cemetery,Thelus.
1325 Vimy Communal Cemetery,Farbus.
1326 Hebuterne Communal Cemetery.
1327 Hebuterne Military Cemetery.
1328 Vendresse Churchyard.
1329 Vendresse British Cemetery.
1331 hermonville Military Cemetery.
1332 Jonchery-Sur-Vesle British Cemetery.
1333 Beaurepaire French National Cemetery,Pontavert.
1337 Longueval Communal Cemetery.
1339 Bourg-Et-Comin Communal Cemetery.
1340 Moulins Churchyard.
1341 Moulins New Communal Cemetery.
1342 Paissy Churchyard.
1345 Bois-Des-Angles British Cemetery,Crevecoeur-Sur-L'Escaut.
1346 Moulin-De-Pierre British Cemetery,Villeers-Outreau.
1347 Esnes Communal Cemetery.
1348 Fontaine-Au-Pire Communal Cemetery.
1349 Ligny-En-Cambresis Communal Cemetery.
1350 Haucourt Communal Cemetery.
1351 Becquigny Communal Cemetery.
1354 Selvigny Communal Cemetery.
1355 Wambaix Communal Cemetery.
1357 Bleue-Maison Military Cemetery,Eperlecques.
1358 Croix-Rouge Military Cemetery,Quaedypre.
1359 Dunkerque Town Cemetery.
1360 Malo-Les-Bains Communal Cemetery.
1361 Zuydcoote Military Cemetery.
1364 Buysscheure Churchyard.

1366 Houtkerque Churchyard.
1367 Ledeerzeele Churchyard.
1369 Steenvorde Communal Cemetery.
1372 Wormhoudt Communal Cemetery.
1374 Audruicq Churchyard.
1386 Quietiste Military Cemetery,Le Cateau.
1387 Beauvois-En-Cambresis Communal Cemetery.
1388 Bethencourt Communal Cemetery.
1391 Bertry Communal Cemetery.
1392 Maurois Communal Cemetery.
1393 Montigny Communal Cemetery (Nord).
1394 Reumont Churchyard.
1395 Troisvilles Communal Cemetery.
1396 Viesly Communal Cemetery.
1402 Nesles-La-Gilberde Communal Cemetery.
1404 Mailly-Le-Camp French Cemetery.
1410 Dormans French National Cemetery.
1415 Sezanne Communal Cemetery.
1416 Soulieres Churchyard.
1420 Baron Communal Cemetery.
1422 Creil Communal Cemetery.
1425 Bassevelle Churchyard.
1426 Bellot Communal Cemetery.
1429 Coulommieers Communal Cemetery.
1432 Fretoy Communal Cemetery.
1436 La Haute-Maison,Ferme Des Arceries.
1438 Meaux Communal Cemetery.
1439 Melun North Cemetery.
1440 Montereau Communal Cemetery.
1441 Nangis Communal Cemetery.
1443 Orly-Sur-Morin Communal Cemetery.
1445 Perreuse Chateau French National Cemetery,Signy-Signets.
1451 Sablonnieres New Communal Cemetery.
1461 Hargicourt British Cemetery.
1462 Hargicourt Communal Cemetery Extension.
1463 Ronssoy Communal Cemetery.
1464 Villeret Churchyard.
1465 Hesbecourt Communal Cemetery.
1468 La Chapelette British Cemetery,Peronne.
1472 Assevillers New British Cemetery.
1473 Foucaucourt Communal Cemetery.
1475 Vendegies-Au-Bois British Cemetery.
1476 Amerval Communal Cemetery Extension,Solesmes.
1477 Ovillers New Communal Cemetery,Solesmes.
1478 Forest Communal Cemetery (Nord).
1479 Ors Communal Cemetery.
1480 Beaurain British Cemetery.
1482 Bousies Communal Cemetery.
1483 Flesquieres Hill British Cemetery.
1484 Vaulx Hill Cemetery,Vaulx-Vraucourt.
1485 Vaux Australian Field Ambulance Cemetery,Vaulx-Vraucourt.
1486 Vraucourt Copse Cemetery,Vaulx-Vraucourt.
1487 L'Homme Mort British Cemetery,Ecoust-St Mein.
1488 Noreuil Australian Cemetery.
1490 Croisilles British Cemetery.
1490 "Y" Ravine Cemetery,Beaumont-Hamel.
1491 Redan Ridge Cemetery No.1,Beaumont-Hamel.
1492 Redan Ridge Cemetery No.2,Beaumont-Hamel.
1494 Templeux-Le-Guerard Communal Cemetery Extension.
1495 Templeux-Le-Guerard British Cemetery.
1496 Moeuvres Communal Cemetery Extension.
1497 Sanders Keep Military Cemetery,Graincourt-Les-Havrincourt.
1498 Orival Wood Cemetery,Flesquieres.
1499 Demicourt Communal Cemetery,Boursies.
1500 Hawthorn Ridge Cemetery No.1,Auchon-Villers.
1501 Hawthorn Ridge Cemetery No.2,Auchon-Villers.
1502 Hunter's Cemetery,Beaumont-Hamel.
1504 Miraumont Communal Cemetery.
1512 Fillievres British Cemetery.
1525 Wavans British Cemetery.

363

1553 Le Crotoy Communal Cemetery.
1564 Quend Communal Cemetery.
1568 Vaux-En-Amienois Communal Cemetery.
1571 Mazargues Cemetery Extension.
1586 Fruges Communal Cemetery.
1597 Rimboval Churchyard.
1615 Rethel French National Cemetery.
1632 Plaine French National Cemetery.
1633 Roppenheim Communal Cemetery.
1643 Neuf-Brisach Communal Cemetery.
1667 Chambieres French National (Mixed) Cemetery,Metz.
1678 Charmes Military Cemetery,Essegny.
1689 Chambrecy British Cemetery.
1690 Courmas British Cemetery.
1693 Epernay French National Cemetery.
1695 La Neuville-Aux-Larris Military Cemetery.
1697 St Imoge Churchyard.
1699 Vandieres Churchyard.
1700 Berthaucouer Communal Cemetery,Pontru.
1701 Chapelle British Cemetery,Holnon.
1703 Guise (La Desolation) French National Cemetery,Flavigny-Le-Petit.
1704 La Baraque British Cemetery,Bellenglise.
1706 Levergies Communal Cemetery.
1707 Ribemont Communal Cemetery.
1710 Sequehart British Cemetery No.1
1712 Brissay-Choigny Churchyard.
1715 Moy-De-L'Aisne Communal Cemetery.
1717 Sery-Les-Mezieres Communal Cemetery.
1723 St Mary's A.D.S. Cemetery,Haisnes.
1724 Carvin Communal Cemetery.
1725 Don Communal Cemetery.Annoeullin.
1726 Phalempin Communal Cemetery.
1730 Wicres Churchyard.
1732 Santes Churchyard.
1744 Monchy-Breton Churchyard.
1745 Nedonchel Churchyard.
1751 Etreux British Cemetery.
1752 Etreux Communal Cemetery.
1753 La Ville-Aux-Bois British Cemetery.
1754 St Erme Communal Cemetery Extension.
1755 Sissonne British Cemetery.
1766 Etroeungt Communal Cemetery.
1775 Nice (Caucade) British Civil Cemetery.
1778 Troyes Town Cemetery.
1779 Gruissan Communal Cemetery.
1788 Dijon (Les Pejoces) Cemetery.
1798 Conches-En-Ouche Communal Cemetery.
1799 Evreux Communal Cemetery.
1805 Maintenon Communal Cemetery.
1822 Talence Communal Cemetery.
1830 Champagnole Communal Cemetery.
1839 St Nazaire (Toutes-Aides) Cemetery.
1841 Orleans Main Cemetery.
1844 Vendome Town Cemetery.
1845 Angers West Cemetery.
1848 Tourlaville Communal Cemetery.
1849 Tourlaville Communal Cemetery Extension.
1856 Lyon (La Guillotiere) Old Communal Cemetery.
1858 St Germain-Au-Mont-D'Or Communal Cemetery Extension.
1862 Le Mans West Cemetery.
1866 Asnieres-Sur-Oise Communal Cemetery.
1886 Monaco Principality Cemetery,La Condamine.
1887 Laventie Military Cemetery.
1888 Haubourdin Communal Cemetery.
1890 Serre Road Cemetery No.2,Beaumont-Hamel and Hebuterne.
1891 Thiepval Anglo-French Cemetery,Authuile.
1893 Chauny Communal Cemetery British Extension.
1894 Montcornet Military Cemetery.
1896 Canadian Cemetery No.2,Neuville-St Vaast.

GALLIPOLI.
1   Lancashire Landing Cemetery,Helles.
2   Redoubt Cemetery,Helles.
3   Pink Farm Cemetery,Helles.
4   Azmak Cemetery,Sulva.
5   Green Hill Cemetery,Sulva.
6   Twelve Tree Copse Cemetery,Helles.
13   The Farm Cemetery,Anzac.
14   Skew Bridge Cemetery,Helles.
15   "V" Beach Cemetery,Helles.
17   7th Field Ambulance Cemetery,Anzac.
18   Embarkation Pier Cemetery,Anzac.
19   No.2 Outpost Cemetery,Anzac.
20   New Zealand No.2 Outpost Cemetery,Anzac.
26   Lala Baba Cemetery,Sulva.
27   Hill 10 Cemetery,Sulva.
29   Ari Burnu Cemetery,Anzac.
30   Beach Cemetery,Anzac.
31   Shrapnel Valley Cemetery,Anzac.

GERMANY.
1   Cologne Southern Cemetery.
2   Hamburg Cemetery,Ohlsdorf.
3   Niederzwehren Cemetery,Cassel.
4   Berlin South-Western Cemetery,Stahnsdorf.
9   Coblenz Jewish Cemetery.

GREECE.
1   Sarigol Military Cemetery.
2   Kirechkoi-Hortakoi Military Cemetery.
3   Struma Military Cemetery.
4   Lahana Military Cemetery.
5   Doiran Military Cemetery.
6   Karasouli Military Cemetery.
7   Salonika Anglo-French Military Cemetery,Lembet Road.
8   Salonika Protestant Cemetery.
9   Mikra British Cemetery,Salonika.
10   East Mudros Military Cemetery,Lemnos.
11   Portianos Military Cemetery,West Mudros,Lemnos.
14   Syra New British Cemetery.
16   Suda Bay War Cemetery,Crete.
18   Bralo British Cemetery.
21   Athens New Protestant Cemetery.

INDIA.
48   Delhi War Cemetery.
97a Calcutta (Bhowanipore) Cemetery.
164 Madras (St Mary's) Cemetery.

IRAQ.
1   Kut War Cemetery.
5   Amara War Cemetery.
6   Basra War Cemetery.
8   Baghdad (North Gate) War Cemetery.
9   Baghdad East Jewish Cemetery.

ITALY.
1   Barenthal Military Cemetery.
2   Boscon British Cemetery.
3   Magnaboschi British Cemetery.
4   Granezza British Cemetery.
5   Cavalletto British Cemetery.
6   Taranto Town Cemetery Extension.
7   Giavera British Cemetery.
8   Memorial to the Missing,Giavera British Cemetery.
9   Tezze British Cemetery,Vazzola.
10   Dueville Communal Cemetery Extension.
11   Montecchio Precalcino Communal Cemetery Extension.
12   Staglieno Cemetery,Genoa.
13   Savona Town Cemetery.

14   Savona Memorial.

15   Arquata Scrivia Communal Cemetery Extension.

16   Bordighera British Cemetery.

19   Faenza Communal Cemetery.

45   Carmignano Di Brenta Communal Cemetery.

48   Padua Main Cemetery.

56   Oneglia Town Cemetery.

57   San Remo Town Cemetery.

59   Testaccio Protestant Cemetery,Rome.

65   Turin Town Cemetery.

74   Altivole Communal Cemetery.

75   Conegliano (San Giuseppe) Communal Cemetery.

76   Falze Communal Cemetery,Trevignano.

LEBANON.

1   Beirut British War Cemetery.

NEW ZEALAND.

194   Purewa Cemetery.

243   Featherston Soldiers' Cemetery.

320   Suva Cemetery,Fiji.

PAKISTAN.

50a   Rawalpindi War Cemetery.

PALESTINE or ISRAEL.

1   Beersheba War Cemetery.

2   Deir El Belah War Cemetery.

3   Jerusalem War Cemetery.

5   Jerusalem Protestant Cemetery,Mount Zion.

8   Gaza War Cemetery.

9   Ramleh War Cemetery.

11   Haifa War Cemetery.

14   Richon-Le-Zion Jewish Cemetery.

SYRIA.

2   Damascus Commonwealth War Cemetery.

TANZANIA.

1   Dar Es Salaam War Cemetery,Bagamoyo Road.

U.S.A.

13   San Francisco (Cypress Lawn) Cemetery,California.

77   Avon (St Michael's) Cemetery (Norfolk),Massachusetts.

169   New York (Woodlawn) Cemetery,New York.

184   Akron (Glendale) Cemetery (Summit),Ohio.

187   Chillicothe (Grandview) Cemetery (Ross),Ohio.

228   Fort Worth (Greenwood) Cemetery (Tarrant),Texas.

234   Arlington National Cemetery (Arlington),Virginia.

234a   Newport News (Green Lawn) Cemetery (Warwick),Virginia.

WEST INDIES.

36   Kingstown (St George) Cathedral Close,St Vincent.

ENGLISH,IRISH SCOTTISH and WELSH COUNTIES.

BEDFORD & HUNTINGDON.

8   Higham Gobion (St Mary) Churchyard,Beds.

23   Bedford Cemetery,Beds.

34   Pavenham (St Peter) Churchyard,Beds.

48   Campton and Shefford Cemetery,Beds.

65   Biggleswade Cemetery,Beds.

66   Dunstable Cemetery,Beds.

70   Eaton Socon Churchyard,Beds.

74   Luton Church Burial Ground,Beds.

75   Luton General Cemetery,Beds.

78   Houghton Regis (All Saints) Churchyard,Beds.

83   Huntingdon Cemetery,Hunts.

90   Upwood Cemetery,Hunts.

102   Ramsey (St Thomas a Becket) Churchyard,Hunts.

104   St Ives Public Cemetery,Hunts.

113   Wyton (All Saints) Churchyard,Hunts.

BERKSHIRE.

1   Abingdon Cemetery.

2   Abingdon (SS Mary & Edmund) Roman Catholic Churchyard,
      St Helen Without.

19   Bradfield (St Andrew) Churchyard.

23   Stratfield Mortimer (St Mary) Churchyard.

27   Yattendon (SS Peter & Paul) Churchyard.

28   Bisham (All Saints) Churchyard.

29   Boyne Hill (All Saints) Chhurchyard,Bray.

33   Hurley (St Mary) Churchyard.

37   Stubbings (St James the Less) Churchyard,Bisham.

39   Ascot (All Saints) Churchyard Extension,Winkfield.

42   Cranbourne (St Peter) Churchyard,Winkfield.

43   Crowthorne (St John the Baptist) Churchyard.

45   Sandhurst Royal Military College Cemetery.

47   Warfield (St Michael) Churchyard Extension.

56   Hinton Waldrist (St Margaret) Churchyard.

71   Maidenhead Cemetery.

72   Newbury Old Cemetery.

73   Chieveley (St Mary) Churchyard.

83   Clewer (St Andrew)Churchyard.

84   Windsor Cemetery.

85   Reading (Caversham) Cemetery.

86   Reading Cemetery.

93   Long Wittenham (St Mary) Churchyard.

94   Sotwell (St James) Churchyard.

112   Wokingham (All Saints) Churchyard.

113   Wokingham (St Paul) Churchyard.

116   Bearwood (St Catherine) Churchyard,Hurst St Nicholas.

117   Earley (St Peter) Churchyard.

119   Hurst (St Nicholas) Churchyard Extension.

121   Sonning (St Andrew) Churchyard.

124   Wargrave (St Mary) Churchyard.

125   Wokingham (St Sebastian) Churchyard,Wokingham Without.

BUCKINGHAMSHIRE.

12   Penn Street (Holy Trinity) Churchyard,Penn.

32   Weston Turville (St Mary) Churchyard.

36   Beaconsfield Cemetery.

37   Bletchley (St Mary) Churchyard.

39   Buckingham Cemetery.

50   Twyford (The Assumption) Churchyard.

51   High Wycombe Cemetery.

55   Datchet Cemetery.

57   Dorney Burial Ground.

69   Wyrardisbury (St Andrew) Churchyard.

76   Long Crendon (St Mary) Churchyard.

80   Marlow Cemetery.

82   Marlow (St Peter) Roman Catholic Churchyard.

86   Moulsoe (St Mary) Churchyard.

91   Wavendon (St Mary) Churchyard.

96   Upton-Cum-Chalvey (St Mary) Churchyard.

116   Great Hampden (St Mary Magdalene) Churchyard,Great & Little Hampden.

120   Monks Risborough (St Dunstan) Churchyard.

123   Tylers Green (St Margaret) Churchyard,Chepping Wycombe Rural.

CAMBRIDGESHIRE.

1   Cambridge General Cemetery.

2   Cambridge (Mill Road) Cemetery.

3   Cambridge (SS Gile's & Peter's) Cemetery.

16   Cambridge Borough Cemetery,Fen Ditton.

19   Cottenham (All Saints) Churchyard.

21   Dry Drayton (SS Peter & Paul) Churchyard.

31   Horningsea (St Peter) Churchyard.

37   Stapleford (St Andrew) Churchyard.

39   Trumpington (SS Mary & Michael) New Churchyard.

51   Weston Colville (St Mary) Churchyard.

84   Chatteris General Cemertery.
91   Wilburton (St Peter) Church.
97   Doddington (St Mary) Churchyard.
103 Wisbech Borough Cemetery.

CHESHIRE.
1   Alsager (Christ Church) Churchyard.
2   Ashton-Upon-Mersey (St Martin) Churchyard.
3   Bebington Cemetery.
4   Bebington (St Andrew) Churchyard.
8   Birkenhead (Flaybrick Hill) Cemetery.
11   Bowdon (St Mary) Churchyard.
18   Northenden (St Wilfrid) Churchyard.
19   Over Peover (St Lawrence) Churchyard,Peover Superior.
22   Rostherne (St Mary) Churchyard.
28   Chester General Cemetery.
30   Christleton (St James) Churchyard.
31   Eccleston (St Mary) Churchyard.
32   Great Saughall (All Saints) Churchyard.
44   Church Lawton (All Saints) Churchyard.
51   Crewe Cemetery.
53   Ashton-Under-Lyne and Dunkinfield Joint Cemetery.
56   Altrincham Cemetery.
62   West Kirby (St Bridget) Churchyard.
72   Macclesfield Cemetery.
74   Alderley Edge Cemetery.
84   Prestbury (St Peter) Churchyard.
97   Middlewich Cemetery.
98   Mottram-In-Longdendale Cemetery.
111 Wybunbury (St Chad) Churchyard.
113 Nantwich (All Saints) Church Cemetery.
114 Nantwich General Cemetery.
117 Neston-Cum-Parkgate Cemetery.
123 Lostock Gralam (St John) Churchyard.
127 Northwich Cemetery.
128 Northwich (St Helen) Churchyard.
131 Appleton Thorn (St Cross) Churchyard,Appleton.
137 Halton Cemetery.
143 Stretton (St Matthew) Churchyard.
147 Sale Cemetery.
154 Heaton Mersey Congregational Churchyard.
158 Stockport Borough Cemetery.
160 Stockport (Willow Grove) Cemetery.
175 Waverton (St Peter) Churchyard.
178 Egremont (St John) Churchyard.
181 Woodchurch (Holy Cross) Churchyard.
182 Wallasey (Rake Lane) Cemetery.
183 Lindow (St John) Churchyard.
184 Wilmslow Cemetery.
186 Over (St Chad) Churchyard.
190 Bidston (St Oswald) Churchyard.
192 Eastham (St Mary) Churchyard.
193 Heswall (St Peter) Churchyard.
197 Thurstaton (St Bartholomew) Churchyard.
198 Willaston (Christ Church) Churchyard.

CORNWALL.
1   Bodmin Cemetery.
13   St Mabyn Churchyard.
20   Calstock Cemetery.
36   Mawnan (SS Mawnan and Stephen) Churchyard.
40   Falmouth Cemetery.
56   Ruan Minor (St Ruan) Churchyard.
61   St Martin's Churchyard.
64   Launceston Cemetery.
68   North Hill (St Torney) Churchyard.
79   Morval Church Cemetery.
96   Penzance Cemetery.
106 St Day (Holy Trinity) Churchyard.
109 Redruth Cemetery.

123 St Austell Cemetery.
128 St Columb Major Cemetery.
135 Maker (SS Macra,Mary and Julia) Churchyard.
140 St Stephens-By-Saltash (St Stephen) Churchyard.
142 St Ives Cemetery.
148 Launcells (St Swithin) Churchyard.
163 Kenwyn (St Kenwyn) Churchyard,Kenwyn Rural.
172 Gulval (St Gulval) Churchyard.
177 St Erth (St Ercus) Churchyard,St Erth Rural.

CUMBERLAND AND WESTMORLAND.
6   Aspatria (St Kentigern) Churchyard,Cumberland.
13   Brampton (St Martin) Old Churchyard,Cumberland.
17   Carlisle (Dalston Road) Cemetery,Cumberland.
18   Carlisle (Upperby) Cemetery,Cumberland.
25   Wetheral Cemetery,Cumberland.
40   Cockermouth Cemetery,Cumberland.
44   Silloth (St Paul) Churchyard,Cumberland.
45   Crosthwaite (St Kentigern) Churchyard,Cumberland.
46   Keswick (St John) Churchyard,Cumberland.
54   Great Salkeld (St Cuthbert) Churchyard,Cumberland.
59   Penrith Cemetery,Cumberland.
68   Allonby (Christ Church) Churchyard,Cumberland.
74   Wigton Cemetery,Cumberland.
82   Kendal (Parkside) Cemetery,Westmorland.
83   Kirkby Lonsdale (St Mary) Churchyard,Westmorland.
85   Arnside Cemetery,Westmorland.
86   Barbon (St Bartholomew) Churchyard,Westmorland.
91   Heversham (St Mary) Churchyard,Westmorland.
98   Selside (St Thomas) Churchyard,Whitwell and Selside,Westmorland.
100 Troutbeck (Jesus) Churchyard,Westmorland.
107 Bowness-On-Windermere Cemetery,Westmorland.
108 Windermere (St Mary's) Cemetery,Westmorland.

DERBYSHIRE.
2   Alfreton (Lea Brooks) Cemetery.
3   Alfreton (St Martin) Churchyard.
26   Tideswell (St John the Baptist) Churchyard.
29   Bakewell Cemetery.
30   Baslow (St Anne) Churchyard.
32   Crich (St Mary) Churchyard.
39   Mackworth (All Saints) Churchyard.
42   South Wingfield (Park) Burial Ground.
51   Bolsover (St Mary) Old Churchyard.
58   Fairfield (St Peter) Churchyard.
66   Edale (Holy Trinity) Churchyard.
76   Whittington (St Bartholomew) Churchyard.
97   Derby (Normanton) Cemetery.
98   Derby (Nottingham Road) Cemetery.
99   Derby (Uttoxeter Road) Cemetery.
120 Long Eaton Cemetery.
122 Cromford (St Mary) Churchyard.
127 Dore (Christ Church) Churchyard.
135 Newton Solney (St Mary) Churchyard.
145 Ockbrook (All Saints) Churchyard.
146 Risley (All Saints) Churchyard.

DEVONSHIRE.
1   Plymouth Old Cemetery.
2   Efford Cemetery,Plymouth.
3   Weston Mill Cemetery,Plymouth.
10   Hawkchurch (St John the Baptist) Churchyard.
11   Kilmington (St Giles) Churchyard.
12   Musbury (St Michael) Churchyard.
15   Axminster Cemetery.
29   Horwood Churchyard.
33   Morte Hoe Cemetery.
36   Westleigh (St Peter) Churchyard.
37   Bideford Church Cemetery.
39   Abbotsham Churchyard.

368

51 Brimpsfield (St Michael) Churchyard.
61 Quenington Cemetery.
67 Cirencester Cemetery.
69 Lower Cam (St Bartholomew) Churchyard,Cam.
72 Slimbridge (St John) Churchyard.
86 Gloucester Cemetery.
88 Barnwood (St Lawrence) Churchyard.
92 Hempsted (St Swithun) Churchyard.
102 Wotton Congregational Church Cemetery,Wotton St Mary With-Out.
109 Lydney (St Mary) Churchyard.

124 Newnham (St Peter) Churchyard.
126 Chedworth (St Andrew) Churchyard.
133 Whittington Cemetery.
138 Great Barrington Cemetery.
143 Amberley Church Cemetery,Minchinhampton.
159 Rodborough (St Mary Magdalene) Churchyard.
168 Stroud Cemetery.
176 Ashchurch (St Nicholas) Churchyard.
182 Berkeley Cemetery.
190 Thornbury Cemetery.
203 Eastington (St Michael) Churchyard.
214 Stanton (St Michael) Churchyard.

HAMPSHIRE.
1 Aldershot Military Cemetery.
4 Gosport (Ann's Hill) Cemetery.
7 Eastney Cemetery,Portsmouth.
8 Milton Cemetery,Portsmouth.
9 Portsea Cemetery,Portsmouth.
10 Portsdown (Christ Church) Cemetery,Portsmouth.
11 Portsdown (Christ Church) Military Cemetery,Portsmouth.
12 Wymering (SS Peter and Paul) Churchyard,Portsmouth.
13 Bournemouth East Cemetery.
15 Bournemouth (Wimborne Road) Cemetery.
17 Christchurch Cemetery.
19 Highcliffe (St Mark) Churchyard.
22 Throop Congregational Churchyard,Holdenhurst.
23 Fordingbridge Cemetery.
28 Lymington Cemetery.
30 Brockenhurst (St Nicholas) Cemetery.
31 East Boldre (St Paul) Churchyard.
34 Milton (St Mary Magdalene) Churchyard.
41 Eling (St Mary) Churchyard Extension.
43 Exbury (St Catherine) Church.
53 North Stoneham (St Nicholas) Churchyard.
56 Southampton (Hollybrook) Cemetery.
57 Southampton Old Cemetery.
58 Southampton (St Mary Extra) Cemetery.
60 Botley (All Saints) Churchyard.
62 Hound (St Mary) Churchyard Extension.
64 Netley Military Cemetery,Hound.
70 Cheriton (St Michael) Churchyard.
76 Bentley (St Mary) Churchyard.
83 Grayshott (St Luke) Churchyard.
85 Headley (All Saints) Churchyard Extension.
87 Kingsley (St Nicholas) Old Churchyard.
90 Andover Cemetery.
98 Penton Mewsey (Holy Trinity) Churchyard.
106 Basingstoke (South View) Cemetery.
115 Newnham (St Nicholas) Churchyard.
119 Sherfield-Upon-Loddon (St Leonard) churchyard.
122 Upton Grey (St Mary) Churchyard.
130 Shedfield (St John the Baptist) Churchyard.
132 Swanmore (St Barnabas) Churchyard.
136 Crofton (Holy Rood) Old Churchyard.
138 Porchester (St Mary) Churchyard.
144 Farnborough Abbey Roman Catholic Churchyard.
145 Farnborough Burial Ground.
146 Fleet (All Saints) Churchyard.

153 Hartley Wintney (St Mary) Old Churchyard.
159 Yateley (St Peter) Churchyard.
161 North Hayling (St Peter) Churchyard.
173 Highclere Cemetery.
179 Steep (All Saints) Churchyard.
180 Petersfield Cemetery.
182 Braishfield (All Saints) Churchyard,Michelmersh.
186 Rownhams (St John) Churchyard.
191 Nether Wallop (St Andrew) Churchyard.
192 Stockbridge Cemetery.
202 Winchester (West Hill) Old Cemetery.
205 Compton (All Saints) Churchyard.
214 Ryde Borough Cemetery,Isle of Wight.
216 East Cowes Cemetery,Isle of Wight.
217 Oakfield (St John's) Cemetery,Isle of Wight.
218 St Helens Churchyard,Isle of Wight.
219 Sandown (Christ Church) Churchyard,Isle of Wight.
220 Shanklin Cemetery,Isle of Wight.
221 Ventnor Cemetery,Isle of Wight.
232 Carisbrooke Cemetery,Isle of Wight.
234 Freshwater (All Saints) Churchyard,Isle Of Wight.
240 Parkhurst Military Cemetery,Carisbrooke,Isle of Wight.
241 Shalfleet Churchyard,Isle of Wight.
242 Shorwell (St Peter) New Churchyard,Isle of Wight.
245 Wippingham (St Mildred) Churchyard,Isle of Wight.
246 Whitwell New Burial Ground,Isle of Wight.

HEREFORD AND WORCESTER.
9 Whitbourne (St John the Baptist) Churchyard Extension,Hereford.
18 Hereford Cemetery,Hereford.
51 Bosbury (Holy Trinity(Churchyard,Hereford.
54 Colwall (St James the Great) Churchyard,Hereford.
56 Much Marcle (St Bartholomew) Churchyard,Hereford.
59 Ledbury Cemetery,Hereford.
96 Mansell Gamage (St Giles) Churchyard,Hereford.
110 Bromsgrove Cemetery,Worcester.
116 Martin Hussingtree (St Michael) Churchyard,Worcester.
129 Broadway (St Eadburgh) Churchyard,Worcester.
144 Kidderminster (St John the Baptist) Churchyard,Worcester.
154 Great Malvern Cemetery,Worcester.
162 Harpley (St Bartholomew) Churchyard,Lower Sapey,Worcester.
166 Martley (St Peter) Churchyard,Worcester.
182 Blockley Church Cemetery,Worcester.
186 Stourbridge Cemetery,Worcester.
189 Lower Mitton (St Michael) Churchyard,Worcester.
191 Tenbury (St Mary) Churchyard,Worcester.
201 Kempsey (St Mary) Churchyard,Worcester.
208 Worcester (Astwood) Cemetery,Worcester.

HERTFORD.
10 Shenley (St Botolph) Churchyard.
12 Chipping Barnet Church Burial Ground.
24 Layston Churchyard.
29 Chorley Wood (Christ Church) Churchyard.
30 Great Northern London Cemetery.
31 Great Birkhamsted (St Peter) Churchyard.
37 Harpenden (St Nicholas) Churchyard.
38 Bishop's Hatfield (St Etheldreda) Church Cemetery.
60 Tewin (St Peter) Churchyard.
72 Knebworth (St Mary) Churchyard.
81 Hitchin Cemetery.
84 Rickmansworth Cemetery.
87 St Albans Cemetery.
91 Redbourn (St Mary) Churchyard.
108 Wareside (Holy Trinity) Churchyard,Ware Rural.
110 Watford Cemetery. ·
115 Radlett (Christ Church) Churchyard,Aldenham.
116 Welwyn Cemetery.

369

KENT.

5	Charlton Cemetery.
7	Dover (St Jame's) Cemetery.
8	Dover (St Mary's) New Cemetery.
15	St Margaret's-at-Cliffe (St Margaret) Churchyard.
24	Birchington (All Saints) Churchyard.
25	Minster Cemetery.
27	Margate Cemetery.
28	Ramsgate Cemetery.
29	Ramsgate (St Augustine) Roman Catholic Churchyard.
30	St Lawrence Cemetery.
34	Walmer (St Mary) Old Churchyard.
37	Hackington (St Stephen) Churchyard.
38	Herne Bay Cemetery,Herne.
44	Luton (Christ Church) Churchyard.
46	Gillingham New Cemetery.
61	Fort Pitt Military Cemetery.
62	Frindsbury (All Saints) Churchyard.
63	Rochester (St Margaret's) Cemetery.
67	Isle of Sheppey General Cemetery,Minster-in-Sheppey.
68	Leysdown (St Clemeny) Churchyard.
71	Sittingbourne Cemetery.
82	Beckenham (St George) Churchyard.
83	Crystal Palace District Cemetery.
85	Bexley Heath Cemetery.
86	East Wickham (St Michael) Churchyard.
89	Bromley Hill Cemetery.
90	Bromley (London Road) Cemetery.
91	Plaistow (St Mary's) Cemetery.
95	Hayes Churchyard.
96	Keston Churchyard.
97	Knockholt (St Katharine) Churchyard.
99	Orpington (All Saints) Churchyard.
100	St Paul's Cray (St Paulinus) Churchyard.
102	Chislehurst Cemetery.
103	Chislehurst (St Nicholas) Churchyard.
105	Crayford (St Paulinus) Churchyard.
109	Darenth (St Margaret) Churchyard.
122	Wilmington (St Michael) Churchyard.
124	Dartford (East Hill) Cemetery.
125	Dartford (Watling Street) Cemetery.
127	Erith (Brook Street) Cemetery.
129	Gravesend Cemetery.
130	Northfleet Cemetery.
141	Fordcombe (St Peter) Churchyard,Penshurst.
147	Riverhead (St Mary) Churchyard.
153	Sevenoaks (Greatness Park) Cemetery.
154	Sevenoaks (St Nicholas) Churchyard.
156	Foots Cray Baptist Chapelyard.
157	Sidcup Cemetery.
160	Ashford Cemetery.
164	Bridge (St Peter) Churchyard.
175	Canterbury Cemetery.
177	Canterbury (St Martin) Churchyard.
179	Cheriton (St Martin) Churchyard.
180	Shorncliffe Military Cemetery.
182	Cranbrook Cemetery.
191	Chilham (St Mary) Churchyard.
197	Wye (SS Gregory and Martin) Churchyard.
203	Saltwood (SS Peter and Paul) Churchyard.
205	Faversham Cemetery.
212	Ospringe (SS Peter and Paul) Churchyard.
217	Folkestone Old Cemetery.
224	Harrietsham (St John the Baptist) Churchyard.
230	Hythe Cemetery.
231	Lydd (All Saints) Churchyard Extension.
232	Maidstone Cemetery.
234	Bearstead (Holy Cross) Churchyard Extension.
235	Boughton Monchelsea (St Peter) Churchyard.
239	Linton (St Nicholas) Churchyard.
243	Staplehurst (All Saints) Churchyard.
252	East Peckham (St Michael) Churchyard.
259	West Malling (St Mary) Churchyard.
261	New Romney (St Nicholas) Churchyard.
267	Rusthall (St Paul) Churchyard.
268	Tunbridge Wells Cemetery.
269	Southborough Cemetery.
279	Brenchley (All Saints) Churchyard.
280	Groombridge (St John) Churchyard,Speldhurst.
281	Hildenborough (St John the Devine) Churchyard.
282	Horsmonden (St Margaret) Churchyard.
284	Matfield (St Luke) Churchyard,Brenchley.
285	Paddock Wood (St Andrew) Churchyard,Brenchley.
287	Speldhurst (St Mary) Churchyard.
289	Tonbridge Cemetery.
298	Westwell Burial Ground.
301	Wrotham (St George) Churchyard Extension.

LANCASHIRE.

1	Allerton Cemetery,Liverpool.
2	Anfield Cemetery,Liverpool.
4	Everton Cemetery,Liverpool.
7	Kirkdale Cemetery,Liverpool.
9	Lingfield Road (Broad Green) Jewish Cemetery,Liverpool.
10	Much Woolton (St Mary's) Roman Catholic Cemetery,Liverpool.
12	St Jame's Cemetery,Liverpool.
14	Toxteth Park Cemetery,Liverpool.
18	Wavertree (Holy Trinity) Churchyard,Liverpool.
19	Birch-in-Rusholme (St James) Churchyard,Manchester.
24	Cheetham Hill Wesleyan Cemetery,Manchester.
30	Manchester Crematorium.
32	Manchester (Gorton) Cemetery.
33	Manchester (Philips Park) Cemetery.
34	Manchester Southern Cemetery.
35	Moston (St Joseph's) Roman Catholic Cemetery,Manchester.
37	Newton Heath (All Saints) Churchyard,Manchester.
40	Barrow-in-Furness Cemetery.
42	Bispham (All Hallows) Churchyard.
43	Blackpool Cemetery.
48	Fleetwood (St Peter) Churchyard Extension.
52	Lund (St John) Churchyard,Clifton-with-Salwick.
71	Grange-Over-Sands Cemetery.
76	Lancaster Cemetery.
77	Lancaster (Scotforth) Cemetery.
80	Bolton-le-Sands (Holy Trinity) Churchyard.
86	Warton (St Oswald) Churchyard,Warton-with-Lundeth.
92	Lytham (St Cuthbert) Churchyard.
95	St Anne's-on-Sea Churchyard.
98	Morecombe (Torrisholme) Cemetery.
102	Preston (New Hall Lane) Cemetery.
103	Broughton (St John the Baptist) Churchyard.
111	Longton (St Andrew) Churchyard.
112	Longton (St Oswald) Roman Catholic Churchyard.
114	Penwortham (St Mary) Churchyard.
149	Great Crosby (St Luke) Churchyard.
150	Great Crosby (SS Peter and Paul) Roman Catholic Churchyard.
152	Huyton (St Agnes) Roman Catholic Churchyard.
156	Liverpool (Yew Tree) Roman Catholic Cemetery.
157	Newton-in-Makerfield Cemetery.
160	Prescot (St Mary) Churchyard.
164	St Helens Cemetery.
168	Ince Blundell Roman Catholic Cemetery.
169	Liverpool (Ford) Roman Catholic Cemetery.
170	Sefton (St Helen) Churchyard.
171	Warrington Cemetery.
176	Hollinfare Cemetery,Rixton-with-Glazebrook.
179	Eccleston (Christ Church) Churchyard.
181	Halewood (St Nicholas) Churchyard.
186	Farnworth (St Luke) Churchyard.
189	Accrington Cemetery.

193	Blackburn Cemetery.
199	Mellor Wesleyan Methodist Chapelyard.
205	Burnley Cemetery.
206	Habergham (All Saints) Churchyard.
209	Briercliffe (St James) Churchyard.
210	Foulridge (St Michael) Churchyard.
211	Haggate Baptist Chapelyard,Briercliffe.
216	Newchurch-in-Pendle (St Mary) Churchyard,Goldshaw Booth.
219	Wheatley Lane Inghamite Chapelyard,Wheatley Carr Booth.
222	Church and Clayton-le-Moors Joint Cemetery.
226	Clitheroe (St Mary's) Burial Ground.
233	Whalley (Queen Mary's Hospital) Military Cemetery.
235	Colne Cemetery.
246	Padiham Cemetery.
255	Bolton (Astley Bridge) Cemetery.
256	Bolton (Heaton) Cemetery.
257	Bolton (Tonge) Cemetery.
261	Halliwell (St Peter) Churchyard.
263	Bury Cemetery.
266	Bury (St Paul) Churchyard.
267	Elton (All Saints) Churchyard.
277	Darwen Cemetery.
278	Hoddlesden (St Paul) Churchyard.
283	Haslingden Holden Hall) Cemetery.
284	Haslingden (St James the Great) Churchyard.
313	Rawtenstall (Longholme) Wesleyan Chapelyard.
321	Tottington (St Anne) Churchyard.
336	Whitworth Cemetery.
342	Ashton-in-Makerfield (St Thomas) Churchyard.
343	Ashton-in-Makerfield (St Thomas) Churchyard,Heath Lane Extension.
346	Chorley Cemetery.
366	Formby (St Peter) Churchyard.
368	Wigan Cemetery.
380	Southport (Birkdale) Cemetery.
381	Southport (Duke Street) Cemetery.
386	Aughton (Christ Church) Churchyard.
387	Aughton (St Michael) Churchyard.
401	Douglas Cemetery,Isle of Man.
403	Kirk Braddan (St Brendan) New Churchyard,Isle of Man.
405	Kirk Christ Lezayre (Holy Trinity) Churchyard,Isle of Man.
410	Kirk Malew (St Malew) Churchyard,Isle of Man.
413	Kirk Maughold (St Machut) Churchyard,Isle of Man.
416	Ashton-under-Lyne (Hurst) Cemetery.
421	Audenshaw (St Stephen) Churchyard.
427	Oldham (Chadderton) Cemetery.
434	Eccles (Peel Green) Cemetery.
438	Hindley (All Saints) Churchyard.
441	Hey (St John the Baptist) Churchyard Extension.
443	Leigh Cemetery.
450	Middleton New Cemetery.
463	Prestwich (St Margaret) Churchyard.
464	Prestwich (St Mary) Churchyard.
471	Higher Broughton (St John) Churchyard.
472	Kersal (St Paul) Churchyard.
474	Salford (Weaste) Cemetery.
475	Stretford Cemetery.
478	Pendlebury (St Augustine of Canterbury) Churchyard.
481	Swinton Cemetery.
483	Tyldesley Cemetery.
489	Whitefield British Jews' Cemetery.
491	Worsley (St Mark) Churchyard.

LEICESTERSHIRE.

13	Barrow-upon-Soar Cemetery.
24	Woodhouse Eaves (St Paul) Churchyard Extension,Woodhouse.
55	Burbage (St Catherine) Churchyard.
63	Leicester (Welford Road) Cemetery.
64	Loughborough (Leicester Road) Cemetery.
87	Shenton (St John) Churchyard.
97	Market Harborough (Northampton Road) Cemetery.

117	Sysonby Churchyard.
119	Quorn (St Bartholomew) Churchyard.
120	Shepshed Cemetery.

LINCOLNSHIRE.

10	Skirbeck Quarter (St Thomas) Churchyard.
14	Fleet (St Mary Magdalene) Churchyard.
25	Gosberton Cemetery.
29	Spalding Cemetery.
34	Folkingham (St Andrew) Churchyard.
44	Bourne Cemetery.
53	Waddington (St Michael) Churchyard.
60	Stubton (St Martin) Churchyard.
61	Grantham Cemetery.
67	Harlaxton (SS Mary and Peter) Churchyard.
69	Londonthorpe (St John the Baptist) Churchyard.
76	Billinghay Cemetery.
86	Leasingham (St Andrew) Churchyard.
98	Quarrington (St Botolph) Churchyard.
100	Stamford Cemetery.
115	Middle Rasen (St Peter) Churchyard.
123	Cleethorpes Cemetery.
136	Gainsborough General Cemetery.
142	Broughton Cemetery.
156	Grimsby (Scartho Road) Cemetery.
158	Scartho (St Giles) Churchyard.
162	Stallingborough (SS Peter and Paul) Churchyard.
179	Lincoln (Canwick Road) Cemetery.
181	Lincoln (Newport) Cemetery.
183	Louth Cemetery.
202	Mablethorpe (St Mary) Churchyard.
220	Hogsthorpe (St Mary) Churchyard.
225	Spilsby Cemetery.

LONDON.

1	Wandsworth Cemetery.
2	Nunhead (All Saints) Cemetery.
3	Camberwell (Forest Hill Road) Cemetery.
4	Brompton Cemetery,Kensington.
5	Fulham Old Cemetery.
6	Fulham (St Thomas of Canterbury) Roman Catholic Cemetery.
7	Hammersmith Cemetery.
8	Kensal Green (All Souls) Cemetery,Kensington and Hammersmith.
9	Kensal Green (St Mary's) Roman Catholic Cemetery,Hammersmith.
10	Abney Park Cemetery,Stoke Newington.
11	City of London and Tower Hamlets Cemetery,Stepney.
12	Hampstead Cemetery.
13	Hampstead (St John) Additional Burial Ground.
14	Highgate Cemetery,St Pancras.
15	St Paul's Cathedral.
28	Charlton Cemetery,Greenwich.
29	Greenwich Cemetery.
32	Eltham (St John the Baptist) Churchyard,Woolwich.
33	Plumstead Cemetery,Woolwich.
35	Woolwich Cemetery.

MIDDLESEX.

1	Edmonton Cemetery.
5	Enfield Chase Cemetery.
6	Enfield Highway Cemetery.
9	Southgate Cemetery.
12	South Mimms (St Giles) Churchyard.
13	Tottenham and Wood Green Cemetery.
15	Islington Cemetery.
16	St Marylebone Cemetery.
17	St Pancras Cemetery.
18	Harrow on the Hill (St Mary) Lower Churchyard.
19	Harrow on the Hill Cemetery.
21	Edgware (St Margaret) Churchyard.
23	Harrow Waeld (All Saints) Churchyard Extension.

25	Pinner Cemetery.
26	Golders Green Crematorium.
27	Golders Green Jewish Cemetery.
28	Hampstead Garden Suburb (St Jude) Church.
29	Hendon Park Cemetery.
30	Hendon (St Mary) Churchyard.
34	Ruislip (St Martin) Churchyard Extension.
37	Wembley Old Burial Ground.
39	Paddington Cemetery.
40	Willesden Jewish Cemetery.
41	Willesden Liberal Jewish Cemetery.
42	Willesden New Cemetery.
43	Willesden Old Cemetery.
44	Acton Cemetery.
46	Chiswick Cemetery.
47	New Brentford (St Lawrence) Churchyard.
48	Ealing and Old Brentford Cemetery.
49	Greenford (Holy Cross) Churchyard.
51	Kensington (Hanwell) Cemetery.
52	Perivale Cemetery.
53	Westminster City Cemetery.
58	Hampton Burial Ground.
62	Harlington (SS Peter and Paul) Churchyard.
66	Heston (St Leonard) Churchyard.
68	New Brentford Cemetery.
70	Ashford Cemetery.
76	Sunbury New Cemetery.
77	Teddington Cemetery.
78	Hounslow Cemetery.
80	Twickenham Parochial Cemetery.
83	Hillingdon Cemetery.

MONMOUTHSHIRE.

4	Abergavenny New Cemetery,Llanfoist.
9	Llanfoist (St Faith) Churchyard.
19	Trevethin (St Cadoc) Churchyard.
34	Caldicot (St Mary) Churchyard.
52	Newport (Christchurch) Cemetery,Christchurch.
67	Newport (St Woollos) Cemetery.
69	Panteg Cemetery.
76	Graig Congregational Chapelyard.
83	Rogerstone (Bethesda) Baptist Chapelyard.
89	Usk (St Mary Magdalene) Churchyard.

NORFOLK.

11	Heydon (SS Peter and Paul) Churchyard.
15	Stratton Strawless (St Margaret) Churchyard.
24	Redenhall (The Assumption) Churchyard,Redwnhall-with-Harleston.
26	Thorpe-Next-Norwich (St Andrew) Church Cemetery.
30	Cromer No.2 Burial Ground.
58	Docking (St Mary) Churchyard.
60	Heacham (St Mary) Churchyard.
61	Hunstanton (St Mary) Churchyard.
73	Marham (Holy Trinity) Churchyard.
74	Runcton Holme (St James) Churchyard,South Runcton.
77	Stradsett (St Mary) Churchyard.
85	Great Yarmouth (Caister) Cemetery,East Caister.
94	Aldborough (St Mary) Churchyard.
101	Mundesley (All Saints) Churchyard.
103	Overstrand (St Martin) Churchyard.
110	West Runton (Holy Trinity) Churchyard,Runton.
111	Weybourne (All Saints) Churchyard.
118	Kimberley (St Peter) Churchyard.
128	Little Massingham (St Andrew) Churchyard.
132	Great Yarmouth New Cemetery.
137	Colney (St Andrew) Churchyard.
138	Cringleford (St Peter) Churchyard.
139	East Carleton (St Mary) Churchyard.
151	King's Lynn Cemetery.
162	Hedenham (St Peter) Churchyard.

172	Woodton (All Saints) Churchyard.
179	Upwell (St Peter) Churchyard.
184	East Bilney (St Mary) Churchyard,Beetley.
195	Mileham (St John the Baptist) Churchyard.
207	Eaton (St Andrew) New Churchyard,Norwich.
209	Norwich Cemetery.
210	Norwich (The Rosary) Cemetery.
231	Hoveton St John Churchyard,Hoveton.
235	Sloley (St Bartholomew) Churchyard.
247	Narborough (All Saints) Churchyard.
254	Swaffham (SS Peter and Paul) Churchyard.
255	Thetford Cemetery.
256	Blo'Norton (St Andrew) Churchyard.
259	East Harling Cemetery,Harling.
261	Feltwell (St Nicholas) Churchyard.
285	Attleborough Cemetery.
288	Breckles (St Margaret) Churchyard,Stow Bedon.
301	Watton Nonconformist Burial Ground.

NORTHAMPTON.

1	Brackley (St Peter) Churchyard.
13	Church Brampton (St Botolph) Churchyard.
27	Barby (St Mary) Churchyard.
31	Yelvertoft (All Saints) Churchyard.
32	Daventry (Holy Cross) Churchyard.
38	Newnham (St Michael) Churchyard.
55	Castle Ashby (St Mary Magdalene) Churchyard.
60	Northampton (Towcester Road) Cemetery,Hardingstone.
67	Cottingham (St Mary Magdalene) Churchyard.
74	Kettering Cemetery.
76	Middleton Cheney (All Saints) Churchyard.
78	Abington (SS Peter and Paul) Churchyard.
79	Northampton General Cemetery.
80	Dallington Cemetery.
107	Raunds Wesleyan Methodist Chapelyard.
144	Wellingborough (London Road) Cemetery.
151	Peterborough Old Cemetery,Soke of Peterborough.
161	Hambleton (St Andrew) Churchyard,Rutland.
164	Oakham Cemetery,Rutland.

NORTHERN IRELAND.

33	Belfast City Cemetery,County Antrim.
40	Carrickfergus (Victoria) Cemetery,County Antrim.
42	Ballylinney Presbyterian Cemetery,County Antrim.
45	Glenarm New Cemetery,County Antrim.
56	Drumbeg (St Patrick) Church of Ireland Churchyard,County Antrim.
57	Dundrod Presbyterian Churchyard,County Antrim.
68	Kilmore (St Aidnan) Church of Ireland Churchyard,County Armagh.
71	Armagh (St Mark) Church of Ireland Churchyard,County Armagh.
74	Derrytrasna Roman Catholic Churchyard,County Armagh.
79	Seagoe Cemetery,County Armagh.
80	Lurgan (Dougher) Roman Catholic Cemetery,County Armagh.
85	Bessbrook (Christ Church) Church of Ireland Churchyard Extension, County Armagh.
105	Banbridge Roman Catholic Cemetery,County Down.
106	Banbridge Town Cemetery,County Down.
107	Bangor New Cemetery,County Down.
110	Belfast (Dundonald) Cemetery,County Down.
124	Down Cathedral New Cemetery,County Down.
136	Hillsborough (St Malachi) Church of Ireland Churchyard,County Down.
137	Knockbreda Church of Ireland Churchyard,Newtownbreda,County Down.
138	Holywood Cemetery,County Down.
145	Newcastle (St John's) Cemetery,County Down.
146	Colonallan Church of Ireland Churchyard,County Down.
165	kinawley Church of Ireland Churchyard,Derrylin,County Fermanagh.
168	Enniskillen New Cemetery,County Fermanagh.
181	Coleraine Cemetery,County Londonderry.
183	Killowen (St John) Church of Ireland Churchyard,County Londonderry.
196	Londonderry City Cemetery,County Londonderry.

201 Glendermot Church of Ireland Churchyard,County Londonderry.

229 Dungannon Borough Cemetery,County Tyrone.

231 Cappagh (St Eugenius) Church of Ireland Churchyard,
East Mountjoy,County Tyrone.

239 Kilskeery Church of Ireland Churchyard,County Tyrone.

248 Strabane Cemetery,County Tyrone.

NORTHUMBERLAND.

1 Newcastle-upon-Tyne (All Saints) Cemetery.

2 Newcastle-upon-Tyne (Byker and Heaton) Cemetery.

3 Newcastle-upon-Tyne (Old Jesmond) General Cemetery.

4 Newcastle-upon-Tyne (St Andrew's and Jesmond) Cemetery.

5 Newcastle-upon-Tyne (St John's,Westgate and Elswick) Cemetery.

7 Newcastle-upon-Tyne (St Nicholas) Cemetery.

11 Alnwick Cemetery.

11a Bolton Churchyard.

19 South Charlton (St James) Churchyard.

20 Warkworth (St laurence) Church Burial Ground.

26 Bedlington (St Cuthbert) Churchyard.

34 Berwick-upon-Tweed Cemetery.

36 Blyth Cemetery.

39 Horton (St Mary) Churchyard,Blyth.

43 North Gosforth Joint Burial Ground.

49 Earsdon (St Alban) Churchyard,Seaton Valley.

58 Wooler (St Mary) Church Burial Ground.

60 Gosforth (St Nicholas) Churchyard.

74 Longbenton (Benton) Cemetery.

75 Morpeth (SS Mary and James) Churchyard.

83 Newburn (Lemington) Cemetery.

86 Ancroft (St Anne) Churchyard.

87 Norham (St Cuthbert) Churchyard.

96 Tynemouth (Preston) Cemetery.

99 Whitley Bay (Hartley South) Cemetery.

NOTTINGHAMSHIRE.

2 Annesley and Felley Cemetery,Annesley.

32 Plumtree (St Mary) Churchyard.

39 East Retford Cemetery.

60 Hucknall Cemetery.

66 East Leake (St Mary the Virgin) Churchyard.

68 Mansfield (Nottingham Road) Cemetery.

70 Forest Town (St Alban) Churchyard.

84 Nottingham Church Cemetery.

85 Nottingham General Cemetery.

96 Halam (St Michael) Churchyard.

106 Southwell Minster (St Mary) Churchyard.

112 Sutton-in-Ashfield Cemetery.

121 Worksop (Retford Road) Cemetery.

OXFORDSHIRE.

1 Banbury Cemetery.

24 Bicester Cemetery.

32 Spelsbury (All Saints) Churchyard.

36 Dorchester Cemetery.

44 Goring (St Thomas of Canterbury) Churchyard.

45 Mapledurham (St Margaret) Churchyard.

51 Henley-on-Thames Cemetery.

69 Oxford (Botley) Cemetery.

71 Oxford (Holy Cross) Cemetery.

73 Oxford (Rose Hill) Cemetery.

74 Oxford (Wolvercote) Cemetery.

85 Brize Norton (St Brice) Churchyard Extension.

97 Witney Burial Ground.

SCOTLAND.

1 Applin Old Churchyard,Lismore and Applin,Argyll.

2 Applin (St Cross) Episcopalian Churchyard,Lismore and Applin,Argyll.

4 Ardmarnoch House Burial Ground,Filfinan,Argyll.

9 Campbeltown (Kilkerrean) Cemetery,Argyll.

14 Dunoon Cemetery,Dunoon and Kilmun,Argyll.

15 Dunoon (Holy Trinity) Episcopalian Churchyard,Dunoon and Kilmun,Argyll.

22 Kiells Old Churchyard,Jara,Argyll.

26 Kilbride Parish Churchyard,Kilfinan,Argyll.

41 Kilmohri Old Churchyard,Craignish,Argyll.

44 Kilmory Castle Burial Ground,Glassary,Argyll.

45 Kilmun Cemetery,Dunoon and Kilmun,Argyll.

50 Kilvickeon Old Churchyard,Kilfinichen and Kilvickeon,Argyll.

52 Lochgoilhead Parish Churchyard,Lochgoilhead and Kilmorich,Argyll.

54 Oban (Pennyfuir) Cemetery,Kilmore and kilbride,Argyll.

60 Tarbert Burial Ground,Kilcalmonell,Argyll.

64 Alloa (Sunnyside) Cemetery,Clackmannan.

69 Tillicoultry Cemetery,Clackmannan.

76 Boturich Castle Private Cemetery,Kilmaronock,Dumbarton.

77 Cardross Parish Churchyard,Dumbarton.

80 Dumbarton Cemetery,Dumbarton.

82 Helensburgh Cemetery,Row,Dumbarton.

84 Kirkintilloch (Auld Aisle) Cemetery,Dumbarton.

86 New Patrick Cemetery,Dumbarton.

87 New Kilpatrick Parish Churchyard,Dumbarton.

92 Abercrombie Old Chapelyard,Fife.

97 Ballingry Cemetery,Fife.

105 Cowdenbeath Cemetery,Beath,Fife.

109 Cupar New Cemetery,Fife.

112 Dunfermline Cemetery,Fife.

115 East Wemyss Cemetery,Wemyss,Fife.

118 Forgan (Vicarsford) Cemetery,Fife.

119 Inverkeithing Cemetery,Fife.

122 Kilconquhar Parish Churchyard,Fife.

127 Kirkcaldy Cemetery,Kirkcaldy and Dysart,Fife.

136 Newburgh Cemetery,Fife.

141 St Andrews Eastern Cemetery,Fife.

142 St Andrews Western Cemetery,Fife.

151 Kinross East Burying Ground,Kinross.

153 Orwell Parish Churchyard,Kinross.

167 Callander Cemetery,Perth.

169 Comrie Cemetery,Perth.

171 Crieff Cemetery,Perth.

180 Innerwick-in-Glenlyon Parish Churchyard,Fortingall,Perth.

187 Kinfauns Parish Churchyard,Perth.

199 Perth (Wellshill) Cemetery,Perth.

200 Pitlochry New Cemetery,Moulin,Perth.

203 St Madoes Parish Churchyard,Perth.

204 Scone Cemetery,Perth.

208 Trossachs Parish Churchyard,Callander,Perth.

211 Denny Cemetery,Stirling.

212 Falkirk Cemetery,Stirling.

214 Grangemouth Burial Ground,Stirling.

226 Stirling (Ballengeich) Cemetery,Stirling.

228 Stirling (Mar Place) Cemetery,Stirling.

231 Colinton Parish Churchyard,Edinburgh.

235 Edinburgh (Comely Bank) Cemetery.

236 Edinburgh (Dalry) Cemetery.

237 Edinburgh (Dean,Western) Cemetery.

238 Edinburgh Eastern Cemetery.

239 Edinburgh (Grange) Cemetery.

240 Edinburgh (Liberton) Cemetery.

241 Edinburgh (Morningside) Cemetery.

242 Edinburgh (New Calton) Burial Ground.

244 Edinburgh (Newington) Cemetery.

245 Edinburgh (North Merchiston) Cemetery.

246 Edinburgh (Piershill) Cemetery.

247 Edinburgh (Portobello) Cemetery.

249 Edinburgh (Rosebank) Cemetery.

252 Edinburgh (Seafield) Cemetery.

253 Edinburgh (Warriston) Cemetery.

259 Cranston Parish Churchyard,Midlothian.

262 Dalkeith (Eskbank) Cemetery,Midlothian.

263 Dalmahoy (Sr Mary) Episcopalian Churchyard,Ratho,Midlothian.

267 Inveresk Parish Churchyard,Midlothian.

269 Lasswade Old Churchyard,Midlothian.

270 Loanhead Cemetery,Lasswade,Midlothian.	627 Dirleton Parish Churchyard,East Lothian.
274 Penicuik Cemetery,Midlothian.	632 Haddington Cemetery,East Lothian.
275 Penicuik Parish Churchyard,Midlothian.	639 Prestonkirk Parish Churchyard,East Lothian.
277 Roslin Cemetery,Lasswade,Midlothian.	644 Tynninghame Burial Ground,East Lothian.
279 West Calder Cemetry,Midlothian.	660 Kirkbean Parish Churchyard,Kirkcudbright.
280 Aberdeen (Allenvale) Cemetery.	669 Innerleithen Cemetery,Peebles.
281 Aberdeen (Grove) Cemetery.	671 Peebles Cemetery.
286 Aberdeen (St Peter's) Cemetery.	674 Cathcart Cemetery,Renfrew.
287 Aberdeen (Springbank) Cemetery.	675 Eastwood Cemetery,Renfrew.
288 Aberdeen (Trinity) Cemetery.	677 Greenock Cemetery,Renfrew.
294 Belhelvie Old Cemetery,Aberdeen.	679 Kilbarchan Cemetery,Renfrew.
308 Ellon Cemetery,Aberdeen.	680 Kilmacolm Cemetery,Renfrew.
310 Folla-Rule (Sr George) Episcopalian Churchyard,Fyvie,Aberdeen.	682 Neilston Cemetery,Renfrew.
313 Fraserburgh (Kirkton) Cemetery,Aberdeen.	683 Paisley Abbey Cemetery,Renfrew.
319 Huntly Cemetery,Aberdeen.	684 Paisley (Hawkhead) Cemetery,Renfrew.
330 Kincardine O'Neil Old Churchyard,Aberdeen.	685 Piasley (Woodside) Cemetery,Renfrew.
333 Kintore Parish Churchyard,Aberdeen.	686 Port Glasgow Cemetery,Renfrew.
341 Lonmay Parish Churchyard,Aberdeen.	696 Kelso Cemetery,Roxburgh.
353 New Pitsligo Parish Churchyard,Tyrie,Aberdeen.	711 Ashkirk Parish Church,Selkirk.
357 Old Machar Cathedral Churchyard,Aberdeen.	713 Galashiels (Eastlands) Cemetery,Selkirk.
358 Peterculter Parish Churchyard,Aberdeen.	717 Selkirk Parish Churchyard.
359 Peterculter New Burial Ground,Aberdeen.	721 Bo'ness Cemetery,Bo'ness and Carriden,West Lothian.
378 Turriff Cemetery,Aberdeen.	722 Dalmeny Cemetery,West Lothian.
380 Arbroath Eastern Cemetery,Arbroath and St Vigeans,Angus.	723 Ecclesmachan Cemetery,West Lothian.
381 Arbroath western Cemetery,Arbroath and St Vigeans,Angus.	725 Kirkliston Burial Ground,West Lothian.
385 Dundee Eastern Necropolis,Angus.	726 Linlithgow Cemetery,West Lothian.
386 Dundee Western Cemetery,Angus.	728 Polkemmet Private Burying Ground,Whitburn,West Lothian.
387 Dundee Western Necropolis,Angus.	729 Uphall Cemetery,West Lothian.
395 Monifieth Cemetery,Angus.	730 Whitburn Cemetery,West Lothian.
396 Montrose (Rosehill) Cemetery,Angus.	742 Portpatrick Cemetery,Wigtown.
398 Montrose (Sleepyhillock) Cemetery,Angus.	746 Stoneykirk Parish Churchyard,Wigtown.
430 Fort William (St Andrew) Episcopalian Churchyard,Kilmallie,Inverness.	752 Glasgow (Craigton) Cemetery.
438 Insh (St Eunan) Churchyard,Kingussie,Inverness.	754 Glasgow Eastern Necropolis.
442 Inverness (Tomnahurich) Cemetery.	755 Glasgow (Lambhill) Cemetery.
447 Kilmallie Old Churchyard,Inverness.	756 Glasgow Necropolis.
455 Kilmuir Old Churchyard,Duirinish,Inverness.	757 Glasgow (Riddrie Park) Cemetery.
458 Kingussie Parish Churchyard,Kingussie and Insh,Inverness.	758 Glasgow (St Kentigern's) Roman Catholic Cemetery.
495 Laurencekirk Cemetery,Kincardine.	760 Glasgow (Sandymount) Cemetery.
500 St Cyrus Upper (Parish) Churchyard,Kincardine.	761 Glasgow (Sighthill) Cemetery.
501 Ardrossan Cemetery,Ayr.	762 Glasgow Southern Necropolis (Central Division).
503 Ayr Cemetery.	764 Glasgow Western Necropolis.
508 Colmonell Parish Churchyard,Ayr.	766 Tollcross (Central) United Free Churchyard,Glasgow.
510 Cumnock New Cemetery,Old Cumnock,Ayr.	774 Cadder Cemetery,Lanark.
514 Darvel Cemetery,Ayr.	775 Cambuslang (Westburn) Cemetery,Lanark.
517 Dundonald (Troon) Cemetery,Ayr.	776 Cambusnethan Cemetery,Lanark.
520 Girvan (Doune) Cemetery,Ayr.	780 Carluke (Wilton) Cemetery,Lanark.
522 Irvine Cemetery,Ayr.	783 Carnwath New Cemetery,Lanark.
523 Irvine Parish Churchyard,Ayr.	789 Culter Parish Churchyard,Lanark.
525 Kilmarnock Cemetery,Ayr.	795 East Kilbride Cemetery,Lanark.
528 Kirkmichael Parish Churchyard,Ayr.	798 Hamilton (Bent) Cemetery,Lanark.
530 Largs Cemetery,Ayr.	799 Hamilton Parish Cemetery,Lanark.
531 Mauchline Cemetery,Ayr.	803 Lanark (St Leonard's) Cemetery.
533 Monkton and Prestwick Cemetery,Ayr.	805 Lanark (St Nicholas) Cemetery.
546 Symington Parish Churchyard,Ayr.	807 Lesmahagow Cemetery,Lanark.
547 Tarbolton Parish Churchyard,Ayr.	808 New Monkland Cemetery,Lanark.
561 Greenlaw Parish Churchyard,Berwick.	810 Old Monkland Cemetery,Lanark.
563 Hutton Parish Churchyard,Berwick.	812 Rutherglen Cemetery,Lanark.
566 Lennel Old Churchyard,Berwick.	816 Strathaven New Cemetery,Avondale,Lanark.
567 Longformacus New Burial Ground,Berwick.	832 Gamrie Old Churchyard,Banff.
569 Mordington Burial Ground,Berwick.	835 Keith (Broomhill) Cemetery,Banff.
581 Annan Cemetery,Dumfries.	838 Macduff Parish Churchyard,Banff.
582 Applrgarth Parish Churchyard,Dumfries.	840 Martlach Parish Churchyard,Banff.
591 Dryfesdale Cemetery,Dunfries.	854 Halkirk Parish Churchyard,Caithness.
596 Dunfries (St Michael's) New Cemetery,Dumfries.	858 Olrig New Cemetery,Caithness.
608 Kirkpartick-Juxta Parish Churchyard,Dumfries.	862 Thurso Cemetery,Caithness.
612 Moffat Cemetery,Kirkpatrick-Juxta,Dumfries.	871 Duffus Cemetery,Moray.
613 Morton New Cemetery,Dumfries.	874 Elgin New Cemetery,Moray.
617 St Mungo Old Parish Churchyard,Dumfries.	876 Forres (Cluny Hill) Cemetery,Moray.
621 Troqueer New Burial Ground,Dumfries.	877 Grantown-on-Spey New Burial Ground,Cromdale,Moray.
625 Aberlady Parish Churchyard,East Lothian.	886 Nairn Cemetery,Nairn.

893 Evie Cemetery,Evie and Rendall,Orkney.
900 Lyness Naval Cemetery,Hoy and Graemsay,Orkney.
926 Cromarty Parish Cemetery,Ross and Cromarty.
935 Fodderty Old Churchyard,Ross and Cromarty.
936 Foich Burial Ground,Lochbroom,Ross and Cromarty.
963 Rosskeen Parish Churchyard Extension,Ross and Cromarty.
966 Suddie Old Churchyard,Knockbain,Ross and Cromarty.
967 Tain (St Duthus) Cemetery,Ross and Cromarty.
968 Tarbat Parish Churchyard,Ross and Cromarty.
975 Brora Cemetery,Clyne,Sutherland.
990 Melness Cemetery,Tongue,Sutherland.
1014 Lerwick New Cemetery,Zetland.

SHROPSHIRE.
19 Shrewsbury General Cemetery,Meole Brace.
37 Church Stretton (St Lawrence) Churchyard Extension.
52 Stoke-upon-Tern (St Peter) Churchyard Extension.
60 Little Ness (St Martin) Churchyard.
63 Petton Churchyard.
67 Ludlow New Cemetery.
74 Caynham (St Mary) Churchyard.
81 Little Drayton (Christ Church) Churchyard.
82 Market Drayton Cemetery.
89 Newport Cemetery.
93 Oswestry General Cemetery.
95 Haughton (St Chad) Churchyard,West Felton.
97 Knockin (St Mary) Churchyard.
100 Moreton (SS Philip and James) Churchyard,Llanyblodwel.
101 Nantmawr Congregational Chapelyard,Oswestry Rural.
104 St Martin's Churchyard.
111 Donington (St Cuthbert) Churchyard.
114 Shifnal (St Andrew) Churchyard.
125 Clive (All Saints) Churchyard.
130 Shawbury (St Mary) Churchyard.
138 Broseley Cemetery.
143 Willey (St John the Devine) Churchyard.
145 Tilstock (Christ Church) Churchyard,Whitchurch Rural.
147 Whitchurch Cemetery.

SOMERSET.
10 Burrington (Holy Trinity) Churchyard.
17 Uphill (St Nicholas) Churchyard.
19 Wedmore (St Mary Magdalene) Churchyard.
25 Bath (Locksbrook) Cemetery.
26 Bath (St James's) Cemetery.
30 Bathwick Church Cemetery.
31 Bathampton (St Nicholas) Churchyard.
33 Bathford (St Swithun) Churchyard.
35 Charlcombe (St Mary) Churchyard.
37 Lansdown Cemetery,Charlcombe.
40 Wellow Cemetery.
42 Bridgwater (Wembdon Road) Cemetery (Chapel Portion).
43 Bridgwater (Wembdon Road) Cemetery (Church Portion).
49 Middlezoy (Holy Cross) Churchyard.
67 Hinton St George (St George) Churchyard.
71 Clevedon (St Andrew) Churchyard.
96 Frome (St John the Baptist) Churchyard.
101 Corston (All Saints) Church.
118 Kingweston (All Saints) Churchyard.
126 Easton-in-Gordano (St George) Churchyard.
139 Minehead Cemetery.
153 Shepton Mallet Burial Ground.
157 Taunton (St Mary's) Cemetery.
161 Churchstanton (St Paul) Churchyard.
172 Staple Fitzpaine (St Peter) Churchyard.
173 Staplegrove (St John) Churchyard.
183 Sampford Arundel (Holy Cross) Churchyard.
185 Wells Cathedral Cemetery.
186 Wells Cemetery.
196 Wookey (St Matthew) Churchyard Extension.

197 Weston-Super-Mare Cemetery.
198 Carhampton (St John the Baptist) Churchyard.
199 Crowcombe (Holy Ghost) Churchyard.
210 Holford (St Mary) Churchyard.
219 Redlynch (St Peter) Church,Bruton.
222 South Cadbury (St Thomas A Becket) Churchyard.

STAFFORDSHIRE.
4 Brierley Hill (South Street) Baptist Churchyard.
6 Ogley Hay (St James) Churchyard.
21 Coseley (Christ Church) Churchyard.
41 Codsall (St Nicholas) Churchyard Extensions.
45 Pattingham (St Chad) Churchyard.
47 Pennfields (St Philip) Churchyard,Trysull and Seisdon.
49 Wombourn (St Benedict) churchyard.
52 Smethwick (Uplands) Cemetery.
57 Tetenhall Regis (St Michael) Churchyard.
60 Walsall (Bloxwich) Cemetery.
61 Walsall (Ryecroft) Cemetery.
67 Rushall (St Michael) Churchyard.
73 West Bromwich Cemetery.
78 Wolverhampton General Cemetery.
84 Burton-upon-Trent Cemetery.
85 Horninglow (St John) Churchyard.
91 Cheddleton (St Edward the Confessor) Churchyard.
93 Kingsley (St Werburgh) Churchyard.
105 Norton-in-the-Moors (St Bartholomew) Churchyard.
108 Lichfield (St Chad) Churchyard.
109 Lichfield (St Michael) Churchyard.
114 Cannock Chase Military Burial Ground,Brereton.
125 Whittington (St Giles) Churchyard.
134 Castle Church (St Mary) Chuhrchyard.
135 Stafford Cemetery.
140 Great Haywood (St Stephen) Churchyard,Colwick.
143 Ingestre (St Mary) Churchyard.
152 Normacot (Holy Evangelists) Churchyard.
153 Stoke-on-Trent (Burslem) Cemetery.
156 Stoke-on-Trent (Hartshill) Cemetery.
170 Rangemore (All Saints) Churchyard,Tatenhill.
176 Blithfield (St Leonard) Churchyard.
177 Denstone (All Saints) Churchyard.
180 Newborough (All Saints) Churchyard.
183 Uttoxeter Cemetery.

SUFFOLK.
3 Aldringham (St Andrew) Churchyard.
9 Dunwich (St James) Churchyard.
45 Bungay Cemetery.
54 Felixstowe New Cemetery.
55 Felixstowe (SS Peter and Paul) Churchyard.
64 Redgrave (St Botolph) Churchyard.
69 Badingham (St John the Baptist) Churchyard.
83 Ipswich Cemetery.
98 Oulton (St Michael) Churchyard.
106 Earl Soham Cemetery.
121 Brantham (St Michael) Churchyard.
126 East Bergholt Cemetery.
133 Stutton (St Peter) Churchyard.
137 Southwold (St Edmund) Churchyard.
138 Stowmarket Cemetery.
173 Euston (St Genevieve) Churchyard.
176 Bury St Edmunds Cemetery.
207 Nayland Cemetery,Nayland-with-Wissington.
215 Icklingham (St James) Churchyard.
224 Exning Cemetery.
225 Sudbury Cemetery.
242 Great Livermere (St Peter) Churchyard.

SURREY.

1   Brookwood Military Cemetery.
2   Barnes (East Sheen) Cemetery.
3   Barnes Old Cemetery.
4   Mortlake Burial Ground.
6   Bandon Hill Cemetery,Beddington.
8   Carshalton (All Saints) Churchyard.
9   Caterham Burial Ground.
11   Whyteleafe (St Luke) Churchyard.
13   Sanderstead (All Saints) Churchyard.
15   Croydon (Mitcham Road) Cemetery.
16   Croydon (Queen's Road) Cemetery.
18   Shirley (St John) Churchyard.
27   Godstone (St Nicholas) Churchyard.
29   Limpsfield (St Peter) Churchyard.
32   Tandridge (St Peter) Churchyard.
34   Battersea Cemetery,Morden.
36   Morden (St Laurence) Churchyard.
37   Mitcham Burial Ground.
38   Streatham Park Cemetery.
41   Reigate Cemetery.
43   Buckland (St Mary) Churchyard.
45   Chipstaed (St Margaret) Churchyard.
47   Kingswood (St Andrew) Churchyard.
52   Walton-on-the-Hill (St Peter) Churchyard.
55   Sutton Cemetery.
57   Wimbledon (Gap Road) Cemetery.
58   Wimbledon (St Mary-on-the-Hill) Churchyard.
60   Byfleet (St Mary) Churchyard.
62   Valley End (St Saviour) Churchyard,Chobham.
64   Addlestone Burial Ground.
70   Holmwood (St Mary Magdalene) Churchyard,Capel.
72   Ockley Cemetery.
75   Dorking Cemetery.
76   East Molesey Cemetery.
78   Egham (St Jude's) Cemetery.
80   Ashtead (St Giles) Churchyard.
83   Cobham Cemetery.
84   Ewell (St Mary) Churchyard.
86   Hatchford (St Matthew) Churchyard,Cobham.
88   Little Bookahm Churchyard.
91   Epsom Cemetery.
93   Claygate (Holy Trinity) Churchyard.
94   Esher (Christ Church) Churchyard.
95   Long Ditton (St Mary) Churchyard.
96   Thames Ditton (St Nicholas) Churchyard.
97   Ash Cemetery,Ash and Normandy.
99   Frensham (St Mary) Churchyard.
102 Shottermill (St Stephen) Churchyard.
103 Tilford (All Saints) Churchyard,Farnham Rural.
104 Wyke (St Mark) Churchyard,Ash and Normandy.
106 Farnham Civil Cemetery.
110 Wrecclesham (St Peter) Churchyard Extension.
112 Frimley (St Peter) Churchyard.
113 York Town (St Michael) Churchyard.
114 Busbridge (St John the Baptist) Churchyard.
115 Godalming New Cemetery.
118 Guildford (Stoke) Cemetery.
126 Send (St Mary) Churchyard,Send and Ripley.
128 Shere (St James) Churchyard.
131 Worplesdon (St Mary) Churchyard.
132 Ham (St Andrew) Churchyard.
134 Bramley Cemetery.
135 Chiddingfold (St Mary) Churchyard.
136 Cranleigh Cemetery.
138 Grayswood (All Saints) Churchyard,Witley.
148 Kingston-on-Thames Cemetery.
150 Fulham New Cemetery,North Sheen.
151 Petersham (St Peter) Churchyard.
152 Richmond Cemetery.

153 Surbiton Cemetery.
154 Malden (St John the Baptist) Churchyard.
156 Walton-on-Thames Cemetery.
157 Weybridge Cemetery.
158 Windlesham Additional Burial Ground.
159 Windlesham (Bagshot) Burial Ground.
160 Brookwood Cemetery (The London Necropolis).
161 Horsell (St Mary) churchyard.
162 Woking Crematorium.

SUSSEX.

2   Arundel Roman Catholic Cemetery.
4   Bognor Regis Cemetery.
5   Chichester Cemetery.
9   Lyminster (St Mary Magdalene) Churchyard.
13   Coolhurst Churchyard,Lower Beeding.
15   Crawley Monastery Burial Ground.
19   Nuthurst (St Andrew) Churchyard.
23   Slinfold (St Peter) Churchyard.
24   Warnham (St Margaret) Churchyard.
27   Horsham (Hills) Cemetery.
30   Easebourne (St Mary) Churchyard.
55   Old Shoreham Cemetery.
57   Southwick (St Michael) Churchyard.
58   Henfield Cemetery.
72   West Dean Cemetery.
88   Westhampnett (St Peter) Churchyard.
93   Heene (St Botolph) Churchyard Extension.
95   Worthing (Broadwater) Cemetery.
102 Sedlescombe (St John the Baptist) Churchyard.
107 Bexhill Cemetery.
110 Brighton and Preston Cemetery.
111 Brighton Borough Cemetery.
112 Brighton Extramural Cemetery.
114 Rottingdean (St Margaret) Churchyard.
124 Glynde Churchyard.
125 Hamsey (St Peter) Churchyard.
128 Ringmer (St Mary) Churchyard.
134 Hurstpierpoint (Holy Trinity) Churchyard.
136 Hurstpierpoint Old Cemetery.
138 Lindfield (Walstead) Cemetery.
139 Newtimber (St John) Churchyard.
143 Cuckfield Cemetery.
144 Eastbourne (Ocklynge) Cemetery.
156 Coleman's Hatch (Holy Trinity) Churchyard,Hartfield.
159 Forest Row Cemetery.
165 East Grinstead (Mount Noddy) Cemetery.
176 Fairlight (St Andrew) Churchyard.
177 Guestling (St Lawrence) Churchyard.
178 Hastings Cemetery,Ore.
182 Aldrington (St Leonard) Churchyard.
183 Hove Cemetery.
184 Hove (St Andrew) Churchayrd.
185 Lewes Cemetery.
187 Lewes (St John the Baptist-Subcastro) Churchyard.
189 Southover (St John the Baptist) Churchyard.
190 Kingston-near-Lewes (St Pancras) Churchyard.
197 Rye Cemetery,Rye Foreign.
199 Winchelsea (St Thomas) Churchyard.
200 Seaford Cemetery.
201 Burwash (St Bartholomew) Churchyard.
203 Eridge Green (Holy Trinity) Churchyard,Frant.
204 Frant (St Alban) Churchyard.
216 Framfield (St Thomas Becket) Churchyard.
220 Isfield (St Margaret) Churchyard.
225 Waldron (All Saints) Churchyard.
226 Uckfield Cemetery.

WALES.

1	Aberdare Cemetery,Glamorgan.
3	Barry (Merthyr Dyfan) Cemetery,Glamorgan.
4	Bridgend Cemetery,Glamorgan.
7	Nolton (St Mary) Churchyard,Glamorgan.
12	Llanfabon (St Mabon) Churchyard,Glamorgan.
13	Llanfaban (St Mabon) Churchyard Extension,Glamorgan.
16	Ystrad Mynach (Holy Trinity) Churchyard,Glamorgan.
17	Cardiff Cemetery,Glamorgan.
19	Cardiff (Llandaff) Cemetery,Glamorgan.
20	Llanishen (St Isan) Churchyard,Glamorgan.
26	Radyr (St John the Baptist) Old Churchyard,Glamorgan.
29	St Fagans (St Fagan) Churchyard,Glamorgan.
30	St George-super-Ely (St George) Churchyard,Glamorgan.
31	St Nicholas Churchyard,Glamorgan.
35	Whitchurch (St Mary) Churchyard,Glamorgan.
37	Llanblethian (St John the Baptist) Churchyard,Glamorgan.
54	Reynoldston (St George) Churchyard,Glamorgan.
77	Merthyr Tydfil (Ffrwd) Cemetery,Glamorgan.
78	Merthyr Tydfil (Pant) Cemetery,Glamorgan.
83	Mountain Ash (Maesyrarian) Cemetery,Glamorgan.
85	Neath (Ynysmaerdy) Cemetery,Glamorgan.
86	Aberpergwm (St Cattwg) Churchyard Private Extension, Neath Higher,Glamorgan.
95	Pontrhydyfen (Jerusalem) Calvinistic Methodist Chapelyard, Michaelston Higher,Glamorgan.
107	Penarth Cemetery,Glamorgan.
118	Pyle (St James) Churchyard,Glamorgan.
119	St Bride's Major (St Bridget) churchyard,Glamorgan.
135	Pontypridd (Glyntaff) Cemetery,Glamorgan.
137	Newton Nottage (St John the Baptist) Churchyard,Glamorgan.
149	Rhondda (Treorchy) Cemetery,Glamorgan.
152	Cockett (St Peter) Churchyard,Glamorgan.
163	Morriston (Horeb) Congregational Chapelyard,Glamorgan.
165	Sketty (Bethel) Welsh Congregational Chapelyard,Glamorgan.
166	Sketty (St Paul) Churchyard,Glamorgan.
167	Swansea (Cwmgelly) Cemetery,Glamorgan.
168	Swansea (Danygraig) Cemetery,Glamorgan.
171	Swansea (Oystermouth) Cemetery.Glamorgan.
177	Cwmswyg Congregational Chapelyard,Traianglas,Brecknock.
178	Devynnock (St Cynog) Churchyard,Maescar,Brecknock.
195	Penderyn (St Cynog) Churchyard,Brecknock.
199	Ystradgynlais (St Cynog) Churchyard,Ystradgynlais Lower,Brecknock.
201	Llanfihangel Ystrad (St Michael) Churchyard,Cardigan.
203	Aberystwyth Cemetery,Cardigan.
212	Cardigan Cemetery.
214	Llandygwydd (St Tygwydd) Churchyard,Cardigan.
231	Llangranog (St David) Churchyard,Cardigan.
238	Llangeitho (St Ceitho) Churchyard,Cardigan.
245	Carmarthen Cemetery.
251	Llanllwch (St Luke) Churchyard,Carmarthen.
278	Llanegwad (St Egwad) Churchyard,Carmarthen.
289	Llanelly Church Cemetery,Carmarthen.
306	Llanfihangel Ar Arth (St Michael) Churchyard,Carmarthen.
358	Welshpool (Christ Church) Churchyard,Montgomery.
361	Fishguard Church Cemetery,Pembroke.
367	Haverfordwest St Mary Church Cemetery,Pembroke.
368	Haverfordwest (St Thomas of Canterbury) Churchyard,Pembroke.
372	Herbrandston (St Mary) Churchyard,Pembroke.
383	Treffgarne (St Michael) Churchyard,Pembroke.
389	Milford Haven Cemetery,Pembroke.
393	Llawhaden (St Aidan) Churchyard,Pembroke.
402	Pembroke Dock (Llanion) Cemetery,Pembroke.
416	Stackpole Elidor (SS Elidyr and James) Churchyard,Pembroke.
429	Llandrindod Wells Cemetery,Radnor.
440	Llanyre (St LLyr) Churchyard,Radnor.
447	Llanedwen (St Edwen) Churchyard,Anglesey.
460	Holyhead (St Mary) Roman Catholic Churchyard,Anglesey.
462	Llangefni Cemetery,Anglesey.
491	Bangor (Glanadda) Cemetery,Caernarvon.
497	Llanbeblig (St Peblig) Churchayrd,Caernarvon.

498	Conway (St Agnes) Churchyard,Caernarvon.
518	Clynnog Fawr (St Beuno) Churchyard,Clynnog,Caernarvon.
531	Llanwnda (St Gwyndaf) Churchyard,Caernarvon.
535	Llandudno (Great Orme's Head) Cemetery,Caernarvon.
536	Llandudno (St Tudno) Churchyard,Caernarvon.
537	Llanrhos (SS Eleri and Mary) Churchyard,Caernarvon.
564	Penmaenmawr (Dwygyfylchi) Cemetery,Caernarvon.
568	Abergele Cemetery,Denbigh.
571	Colwyn Bay (Bronynant) Cemetery,Denbigh.
597	Llanbedr Dyffryn Clwyd (St Peter) Churchyard,Denbigh.
609	St George (St George) Churchyard,Denbigh.
613	Wrexham Cemetery,Denbigh.
619	Gresford (All Saints) Churchyard,Denbigh.
629	Ruabon Cemetery,Denbigh.
637	Hawarden (St Deiniol) Churchyard,Flint.
646	Caerfallwch (St Paul) Churchyard,Northop,Flint.
648	Gwernafield (Holy Trinity) Churchyard,Mold Rural,Flint.
658	Pontblyddyn (Christ Church) Churchyard,Mold Rural,Flint.
659	Whitford (SS Beuno and Mary) Churchyard,Flint.
664	Bangor Monachorum (St Dunawd) Churchyard,Flint.
671	Rhyl Church Cemetery,Flint.
672	Rhyl Town Cemetery,Flint.
673	Bodelwyddan (St Margaret) Churchyard,Flint.
677	St Asaph Cathedral Churchyard,Flint.
681	Harlech (St Tanwg) Churchyard,Merioneth.
684	Llanfair (St Mary) Churchyard,Marioneth.
690	Trawsfyndd (Penycefn) Cemetery,Merioneth.
692	Brithdir (St Mark) Churchyard,Brithdir and Islaw'roreth,Merioneth.
693	Llanaber (St Mary) Churchyard,Merioneth.
706	Corwen (SS Mael and Sulien) Churchyard,Merioneth.
713	Festiniog (Llan) Cemetery,Merioneth.
714	Festiniog (Newborough) Burial Ground,Merioneth.
725	Aberdovey Cemetery,Merioneth.

WARWICKSHIRE.

1	Acock's Green (St Mary) Churchyard.
3	Birmingham (Brandwood End) Cemetery.
5	Birmingham General Cemetery.
6	Birmingham (Handsworth) Cemetery.
7	Birmingham (Lodge Hill) Cemetery.
9	Birmingham (Witton) Cemetery.
10	Birmingham (Yardley) Cemetery.
12	Edgbaston (St Bartholomew) Churchyard.
14	Erdington (St Barnabas) Churchyard.
16	Handsworth (St Mary) Churchyard.
19	King's Norton (St Nicholas) Churchyard.
22	Northfield (St Laurence) Churchyard Extension.
23	Perry Barr (St John) Churchyard.
32	Studley (St Mary) Churchyard.
37	Atherstone Cemetery.
47	Long Compton (SS Peter and Paul) Churchyard.
50	Coventry (London Road) Cemetery.
57	Farnborough (St Botolph) Churchyard.
60	Wyken (St Mary Magdalene) Churchyard.
65	Castle Bromwich (SS Mary and Margaret) Churchyard.
66	Coleshill Cemetery.
67	Curdworth (St Peter) Churchyard.
74	Monks Kirby (St Edith) Churchyard.
75	Chilvers Coton (All Saints) Churchyard.
81	Astley (St Mary) Churchyard.
83	Leamington (Milverton) Cemetery.
84	Leamington (Whitnash Road) Cemetery.
88	Brinklow Cemetery.
96	Wolston Cemetery.
97	Rugby (Clifton Road) Cemetery.
98	Rugby (St Marie) Roman Catholic Churchyard.
100	Knowle (SS John the Baptist and Ann) Churchyard.
101	Olton Franciscan Cemetery,Solihull.
102	Salter Street (St Patrick) Churchyard,Tanworth.
115	Southam (St James) Churchyard.

129 Wellesbourne (St Peter) Churchyard,Wellesbourne Hastings.
134 Hill (St James the Great) Churchyard.
135 Sutton Coldfield Cemetery.
143 Budbrooke (St Michael) Churchyard.
151 Warwick Cemetery,Budbrooke.

WILTSHIRE.
1   Amesbury Cemetery.
2   Bulford Church Cemetery.
3   Durrington Cemetery.
4   Figheldean (St Michael) Churchyard.
12   Wilsford (St Michael) Churchyard.
14   Winterbourne Gunner (St Mary) Churchyard.
16   Atworth (St Michael) Churchyard.
18   Holt Cemetery.
25   East Tytherton Moravian Burial Ground,Bremhill.
28   Yatesbury (All Saints) Churchyard.
29   Chippenham Cemetery.
56   Devizes Cemetery,Roundway.
64   Chiseldon Cemetery.
86   Sopworth (St Mary) Churchyard.
100 Melksham Cemetery.
115 Tidworth Military Cemetery,North Tidworth.
116 Upavon Cemetery.
121 Chilton Foliat (St Mary) Churchyard.
128 East Harnham (All Saints) Churchyard.
129 Salisbury (London Road) Cemetery.
142 Swindon (Radnor Street) Cemetery.
145 Chicklade (All Saints) Churchyard.
153 Swallowcliffe (St Peter) Churchyard.
157 Bishopstrow (St Aldhelm) Churchyard.
167 Sutton Veny (St John) Churchyard.
176 Keevil (St Leonard) Churchyard.
179 Wilton Cemetery.
180 Barford St Martin Cemetery.
186 Burcombe (St John the Baptist) Churchyard,Burcombe Without.
194 Salisbury (Devizes Road) Cemetery,Bemerton.

YORKSHIRE.
1   Hull (Hedon Road) Cemetery.
2   Hull Western Cemetery.
3   Hull Northern Cemetery.
5   Hull General Cemetery.
11   Beverley (St Martin's) Cemetery.
12   Beverley (St Mary's) Cemetery.
22   Bridlington Cemetery.
35   Sledmere (St Mary) Churchyard.
38   Fulford Water Burial Ground.
42   Filey (St Oswald) Churchyard.
45   Hessle Cemetery.
46   Hornsea Cemetery.
62   Burstwick (All Saints) Churchyard.
63   Easington Cemetery.
81   Barlby (All Saints) Churchyard.
83   Kirk Ella Church Cemetery.
93   Sigglesthorne (St Laurence) Churchyard.
97   Withernsea (St Nicholas) Churchyard.
98   York Cemetery.
100 Aysgarth (St Andrew) Churchyard,Gould.
106 Thornton Watlass (St Mary) Churchyard.
110 Eryholme (St Mary) Churchyard.
123 Huntington (All Saints) Churchyard.
126 Guisborough Cemetery.
138 Finghall (St Andrew) Churchyard.
159 Northallerton Cemetery.
171 Thornton Dale (All Saints) Churchyard.
172 Coatham (Christ Church) Churchyard.
176 Richmond Cemetery.
178 Catterick Cemetery.
181 Hipswell (St John) Churchyard.

185 Scarborough Cemetery.
186 Brompton (All Saints) Churchyard.
192 Seamer (St Martin) Churchyard.
208 Kirk Leavington (St Martin) Churchyard.
222 Whitby Cemetery.
230 Bishopthorpe (St Andrew) Churchyard.
244 Goole Cemetery.
245 Acomb (St Stephen) Churchyard.
249 Little Ouseburn (Holy Trinity) Churchyard.
250 Moor Monkton (All Saints) Churchyard.
256 Harrowgate (Grove Road) Cemetery.
274 Knaresborough Cemetery.
292 Rawdon (St Peter) Churchyard.
294 Ripon Cemetery.
303 Selby Cemetery.
305 Acaster Selby (St John) Churchyard.
308 Healaugh (St John the Baptist) Churchyard.
311 Kirkby Wharfe (St John the Baptist) Churchyard Extension,Kirkby Wharfe and North Milford.
321 Sandal Magna (St Helen) Churchyard.
323 Wakefield Cemetery.
328 Wath-upon-Dearne Cemetery.
335 Spofforth (All Saints) Churchyard,Spofforth-with-Stockeld.
344 Calverley (St Wilfred) Churchyard.
346 Farsley (St John) Churchyard.
361 Lawnswood Cemetery.
362 Leeds (Burmantofts) Cemetery.
363 Leeds (Gelderd Road) English Hebrew Cemetery.
368 Leeds (Hunslet Old) Cemetery.
372 Meanwood (Holy Trinity) Churchyard.
373 Moor Allerton (St John) Churchyard.
375 Roundhay (St John) Churchyard.
381 Methley (St Oswald) Churchyard.
383 Pudsey Cemetery.
388 Pool (St Wilfrid) Churchyard.
396 Bingley Cemetery.
408 Bradford (Scholemoor) Cemetery.
410 Bradford (Undercliffe) Cemetery.
411 Buttershaw (St Paul) Churchyard.
417 Idle (Holy Trinity) Churchyard.
418 Idle Upper Chapel (Congregational) Cemetery.
425 Wibsey (Holy Trinity) Churchyard.
428 Burley-in-Wharfedale Church Cemetery.
436 Haworth (St Michael) Churchyard.
438 Ilkley Cemetery.
439 Keighley (Utley) Cemetery.
447 Otley,Newall-with-Clifton and Lindley Cemetery.
462 Kirkby Malham (St Michael) Churchyard.
467 Shelf Wesleyan Chapelyard.
468 Shipley (Hirst Wood) Church Burial Ground.
469 Shipley (Nab Wood) Cemetery.
474 Addingham (St Peter) Churchyard.
475 Bolton Abbey (SS Mary and Cuthbert) Churchyard.
481 Gargrave (St Andrew) Churchyard.
482 Kettlewell (St Mary) Churchyard,Kettlewell-with-Starbotton.
483 Kildwick (St Andrew) Churchyard.
485 Rylstone (St Peter) Churchyard.
487 Thornton-in-Craven (St Oswald) Churchyard,Thornton.
500 Doncaster Cemetery.
501 Doncaster (Christ Church) Churchyard.
504 Campsall Old Cemetery.
528 Rotherham (Masbrough) Cemetery.
543 Ecclesall (All Saints) Churchyard.
546 Sheffield (Abbey Lane) Cemetery.
547 Sheffield (Burngreave) Cemetery.
548 Sheffield (City Road) Cemetery.
551 Sheffield General Cemetery.
557 Sheffield (St Michael's) Roman Catholic Cemetery.
561 Wadsley Churchyard.
569 Tickhill (St Mary) Churchyard.

570 Altofts Cemetery.
574 Ardsley (Christ Church) Churchyard.
575 Barnsley Cemetery.
583 Brighouse Cemetery.
588 Dewsbury Cemetery.
590 Dewsbury Moor (St John) Churchyard.
591 Lower Whitley (SS Mary and Michael) Churchyard.
595 Drighlington (St Paul) Churchyard.
597 Elland-cum-Greetland Cemetery.
606 Halifax (Lister Lane) Cemetery.
607 Halifax (Stoney Royd) Cemetery.
619 Salterhebble (All Saints) Churchyard.
635 Brockholes (St George) Churchyard.
639 Armitage Bridge (St Paul) Churchyard.
643 Huddersfield (Edgerton) Cemetery.
644 Huddersfield (Lockwood) Cemetery.
645 Lindley (St Stephen) Churchyard.
652 Salendine Nook Baptist Chapelyard.
677 Ossett (Holy Trinity) Churchyard.
686 Friezland (Christ Church) Churchyard.
705 Cleckheaton (St John) Churchyard.
719 Outwood Cemetery.
730 Shore General Baptist Chapelyard.
737 Heptonstall Slack Baptist Cemetery.
738 Wadsworth (Wainsgate) Baptist Chapelyard.
740 Bradfield (St Nicholas) Churchyard.

——————— APPENDIX 2 ———————

This is a list of abreviations used in the list of officers. Some are not
mentioned as they are self evident. Others are a combination of the
abreviations listed below.

ACapt,ALt,etc	Acting Captain,Acting Lieutenant,etc
AA Bty	Anti Aircraft Battery
AC or Amm Col	Ammunition Column
acc	Accidentally
A Cyc Cps	Army Cyclist Corps
Amb	Ambulance
Amm Pk	Ammunition Park
Art	Artillery
A & SH	Argyl & Sutherland Highlanders
Att	Attached
Aux	Auxilliary
Ayr Yeo	Ayrshire Yeomanry
Bde	Brigade
Beds	Bedfordshire Regiment
BlkW	Black Watch
Bn	Battalion
Bord R	Border Regiment
BRCS	British Red Cross Society
Bty	Battery
Bucks	Buckinghamshire Regiment
Cam H	Cameron Highlanders
Can	Canadian
Capt	Captain
Cav	Cavalry
CCS	Casualty Clearing Station
Ches	Cheshire Regiment
Cld Gds	Coldstream Guards
Cmd & Staff	Command and Staff
Cmdg	Commanding
Cmdt	Commandant

Col	Colonel
Co or Coy	Company
Conn Rgrs	Connaught Rangers
Cps	Corps
CR	Cemetery Register
DAC	Divisional Ammunition Column
DCLI	Duke of Cornwall's Light Infantry
Ded	Died
Derby Yeo	Derbyshire Yeomany
Dev	Devonshire Regiment
Div	Division
DLI	Durham Light Infantry
Dors	Dorset Regiment
Dow	Died of Wounds
Drags	Dragoons
Drags Gds	Dragoon Guards
DubF	Dublin Fusiliers
E Afr or EA	East African
EAUL	East African Unattached List
E Kent	East Kent Regiment
E Lancs	East Lancashire Regiment
E Rid Yeo	East Riding Yeomanry
E Surr	East Surrey Regiment
E Yorks	East Yorkshire Regiment
Emp Coy	Employment Company
Ess	Essex Regiment
Ex	Formerly
FA	Field Artillery (or Field Ambulance if RAMC)
FC	Field Company
Fd Sqd	Field Squadron
Fife & Forfar Yeo	Fife and Forfar Yeomanry
Garr Bn	Garrison Battalion
Gds	Guards
Gds MGC	Guards Machine Gun Regiment
GHQ	General Head Quarters
GL	General List
Glam Yeo	Glamorgan Yeomanry
Glouc	Gloucestershire Regiment
Gord H	Gordon Highlanders
Gren Gds	Grenadier Guards
HAC	Honourable Artillery Company
Hamps	Hampshire Regiment
HB	Heavy Battery
Herts	Hertfordshire Regiment
High Cyc Bn	Highland Cyclists Battalion
HLI	Highland Light Infantry
HQ	Headquarters
HT	Horse Transport
Huss	Hussars
IA	Indian Army
IARO	Indian Army Reserve of Officers
IAUL	Indian Army Unattached List
Imp Cam Cps	Imperial Camel Corps
IMS	Indian Medical Service
Ind	Indian
Inf	Infantry
InniskF	Inniskilling Fusiliers
Intel Cps	Intellegence Corps
Ir Gds	Irish Guards
IWT	Inland Water Transport

KAR	Kings African Rifles		RFA	Royal Field Artillery
KEdw Horse	King Edward Horse		RFC	Royal Flying Corps
KOSB	Kings Own Scottish Borderers		R Fus	Royal Fusiliers
KRRC	Kings Royal Rifle Corps		RGA	Royal Garrison Artillery
KSLI	Kings Shropshire Light Infantry		RHA	Royal Horse Artillery
			RH Gds	Royal Horse Guards
Lab Cps	Labour Corps		RHFA	Royal Horse & Field Artillery
Lanc F	Lancashire Fusiliers		Rif	Rifles
Leic	Leicestershire Regiment		RIM	Royal Indian Marine
Leinst	Leinster Regiment		R Ir Rif	Royal Irish Rifles
Life Gds	Life Guards		R Innisk F	Royal Inniskillin Fusiliers\
Lincs	Lincolnshire Regiment		R Lancs	Royal Lancashire Regiment
LN Lancs	Loyal North Lancashire Regiment		R Munst F	Royal Munster Fusiliers
Lond	London Regiment		RN Dev Yeo	Royal North Devon Yeomanry
Lpool	Liverpool Regiment		RoO	Reserve of Officers
2Lt	Second Lieutenant		RR of Cav	Reserve Regiment of Cavalry
Lt	Lieutenant		R Scots F	Royal Scots Fusiliers
Maj	Major		R Suss	Royal Sussex Regiment
Manch	Manchester Regiment		R War	Royal Warwickshire Regiment
MGC	Machine Gun Corps		R W Kent	Royal West Kent Regiment
MID	Mentioned in Despatches		R W Surr	Royal West Surrey Regiment
Middx	Middlesex Regiment			
Mil Works Serv	Military Works Service		SB	Siege Battery
Min of Muns	Ministry of Munitions		Sfth H	Seaforth Highlanders
Mon	Monmouthshire Regiment		SH	Static Hospital
MR	Memorial Register		SL	Special List
MT	Mechanical Transport		S Lancs	South Lancashire Regiment
Mtd	Mounted		SNurse	Staff Nurse
Mtrs	Moters		Som LI	Somerset Light Infantry
Munst F	Munster Fusiliers		Sp Co	Special Company
			S Staffs	South Staffordshire Regiment
N	North or Northern		S&T	Supply & Transport Corps
N & D	Nottinghamshire & Derbyshire Regiment		St JAB	St John's Ambulance Brigade
N Cyc Bn	Northern Cyclist Battalion		Suff	Suffolk Regiment
Nhampt	Northamptonshire Regiment		Surr Yeo	Surrey Yeomanry
Nig R	Nigerian Regiment		SW Bord	South Wales Borderers
N Ir Horse	North Irish Horse			
N Mid HB	North Midland Heavy Battery		TCapt,TLt,etc	Temporary Captain,Temporary Lieutenant,Etc
Norf	Norfolk Regiment		Tank Cps	Tank Corps
Notts Yeo	Nottinghamshire Yeomanry		TC	Tunnelling Company
N Som Yeo	North Somerset Yeomanry		TFNS	Territorial Force Nursing Service
N Staffs	North Staffordshire Regiment		TMB	Trench Mortar Battery
Numb F	Northumberland Fusiliers		Trn	Train
NZ	New Zealand			
			War Yeo	Warwickshire Yeomanry
O&BLI	Oxfordshire & Buckinghamshire Light Infantry		WGds	Welsh Guards
Obs Grp	Observer Group		Wmoreld&Cumbld Yeo	Westmoreland & Cumberland Yeomanry
OTC	Officer Training Corps		Wilts	Wiltshire Regiment
Oxf Yeo	Oxfordshire Yeomanry		Worc	Worcestershire Regiment
			W Rid	West Riding Regiment
Pnrs	Pioneers		W Som Yeo	West Somerset Yeomanry
Pow	Prisoner of War		W Yorks	West Yorkshire Regiment
QAIMNS	Queen Alexander's Imperial Military Nursing Service		Y & L	Yorkshire & Lancashire Regiment
			Yeo	Yeomanry
RACh Dept	Royal Army Chaplains Department		YLI	Yorkshire Light Infantry
RAF	Royal Air Force		Yorks	Yorkshire Regiment
RAMC	Royal Army Medical Corps			
RAOC	Royal Army Ordance Corps			
RASC	Royal Army Service Corps			
RAVC	Royal Army Vetinary Corps			
RB	Rifle Brigade			
R Berks	Royal Berkshire Regiment			
R Dub F	Royal Dublin Fusiliers			
RE	Royal Engineers			
Res	Reserve